McGraw-Hill's

Taxation of Individuals and Business Entities

Brian C. Spilker
Brigham Young University
Editor

Benjamin C. Ayers
The University of Georgia

Edmund Outslay
Michigan State University

Connie D. Weaver
Texas A&M University

John A. Barrick
Brigham Young University

John R. Robinson
Texas A&M University

Ron G. Worsham
Brigham Young University

Mc Graw Hill Education

McGRAW-HILL'S TAXATION OF INDIVIDUALS AND BUSINESS ENTITIES, 2019 EDITION, TENTH EDITION

Published by McGraw-Hill Education, 2 Penn Plaza, New York, NY 10121. Copyright © 2019 by McGraw-Hill Education. All rights reserved. Printed in the United States of America. Previous editions © 2018, 2017, and 2016. No part of this publication may be reproduced or distributed in any form or by any means, or stored in a database or retrieval system, without the prior written consent of McGraw-Hill Education, including, but not limited to, in any network or other electronic storage or transmission, or broadcast for distance learning.

Some ancillaries, including electronic and print components, may not be available to customers outside the United States.

This book is printed on acid-free paper.

1 2 3 4 5 6 7 8 9 LWI 21 20 19 18

ISBN   978-1-259-91839-1
MHID   1-259-91839-4
ISSN   1946-7745

Executive Portfolio Manager: *Kathleen Klehr*
Product Developers: *Danielle Andries, Erin Quinones*
Marketing Manager: *Zach Rudin*
Content Project Managers: *Lori Koetters, Jill Eccher, Brian Nacik*
Buyer: *Susan K. Culbertson*

Design: *Matt Backhaus*
Content Licensing Specialist: *Lorraine Buczek*
Cover Image: © *Spotmatik/Alamy*
Compositor: *Aptara®, Inc.*
Printer: *LSC Communications*

All credits appearing on page are considered to be an extension of the copyright page.

The Internet addresses listed in the text were accurate at the time of publication. The inclusion of a website does not indicate an endorsement by the authors or McGraw-Hill Education, and McGraw-Hill Education does not guarantee the accuracy of the information presented at these sites.

mheducation.com/highered

Dedications

We dedicate this book to:

My family, whose love and support helped make this book possible, and to Professor Dave Stewart for his great example and friendship over the last three decades.

Brian Spilker

My wife, Marilyn, daughters Margaret Lindley and Georgia, son Benjamin, and parents Bill and Linda.

Ben Ayers

My wife, Jill, and my children Annika, Corinne, Lina, Mitch, and Connor.

John Barrick

My family, Jane, Mark, Sarah, Chloe, Lily, Jeff, and Nicole, and to Professor James E. Wheeler, my mentor and friend.

Ed Outslay

JES, Tommy, and Laura.

John Robinson

My family: Dan, Travis, Alix, and Alan.

Connie Weaver

My wife, Anne, sons Matthew and Daniel, and daughters Whitney and Hayley.

Ron Worsham

About the Authors

Brian Spilker (PhD, University of Texas at Austin, 1993) is the Robert Call/Deloitte Professor in the School of Accountancy at Brigham Young University. He teaches taxation at Brigham Young University. He received both BS (Summa Cum Laude) and MAcc (tax emphasis) degrees from Brigham Young University before working as a tax consultant for Arthur Young & Co. (now Ernst & Young). After his professional work experience, Brian earned his PhD at the University of Texas at Austin. In 1996, he was selected as one of two nationwide recipients of the Price Waterhouse Fellowship in Tax Award. In 1998, he was a winner of the American Taxation Association and Arthur Andersen Teaching Innovation Award for his work in the classroom; he has also been awarded for his use of technology in the classroom at Brigham Young University. Brian researches issues relating to tax information search and professional tax judgment. His research has been published in journals such as *The Accounting Review, Organizational Behavior and Human Decision Processes, Journal of the American Taxation Association, Behavioral Research in Accounting, Journal of Accounting Education, Journal of Corporate Taxation,* and *Journal of Accountancy.*

Courtesy Brian Spilker

Ben Ayers (PhD, University of Texas at Austin, 1996) holds the Earl Davis Chair in Taxation and is the dean of the Terry College of Business at the University of Georgia. He received a PhD from the University of Texas at Austin and an MTA and BS from the University of Alabama. Prior to entering the PhD program at the University of Texas, Ben was a tax manager at KPMG in Tampa, Florida, and a contract manager with Complete Health, Inc., in Birmingham, Alabama. He is the recipient of 11 teaching awards at the school, college, and university levels, including the Richard B. Russell Undergraduate Teaching Award, the highest teaching honor for University of Georgia junior faculty members. His research interests include the effects of taxation on firm structure, mergers and acquisitions, and capital markets and the effects of accounting information on security returns. He has published articles in journals such as *The Accounting Review, Journal of Finance, Journal of Accounting and Economics, Contemporary Accounting Research, Review of Accounting Studies, Journal of Law and Economics, Journal of the American Taxation Association,* and *National Tax Journal.* Ben was the 1997 recipient of the American Accounting Association's Competitive Manuscript Award, the 2003 and 2008 recipient of the American Taxation Association's Outstanding Manuscript Award, and the 2016 recipient of the American Taxation Association's Ray M. Sommerfeld Outstanding Tax Educator Award.

Courtesy Ben Ayers

Courtesy John Barrick

John Barrick (PhD, University of Nebraska at Lincoln, 1998) is currently an associate professor in the Marriott School at Brigham Young University. He served as an accountant at the United States Congress Joint Committee on Taxation during the 110th and 111th Congresses. He teaches taxation in the graduate and undergraduate programs at Brigham Young University. He received both BS and MAcc (tax emphasis) degrees from Brigham Young University before working as a tax consultant for Price Waterhouse (now PricewaterhouseCoopers). After his professional work experience, John earned his PhD at the University of Nebraska at Lincoln. He was the 1998 recipient of the American Accounting Association, Accounting, Behavior, and Organization Section's Outstanding Dissertation Award. John researches issues relating to tax corporate political activity. His research has been published in journals such as *Organizational Behavior and Human Decision Processes, Contemporary Accounting Research,* and *Journal of the American Taxation Association.*

Courtesy Ed Outslay

Ed Outslay (PhD, University of Michigan, 1981) is a professor of accounting and the Deloitte/Michael Licata Endowed Professor of Taxation in the Department of Accounting and Information Systems at Michigan State University, where he has taught since 1981. He received a BA from Furman University in 1974 and an MBA and PhD from the University of Michigan in 1977 and 1981. Ed currently teaches graduate classes in corporate taxation, multiunit enterprises, accounting for income taxes, and international taxation. In February 2003, Ed testified before the Senate Finance Committee on the Joint Committee on Taxation's Report on Enron Corporation. MSU has honored Ed with the Presidential Award for Outstanding Community Service, Distinguished Faculty Award, John D. Withrow Teacher-Scholar Award, Roland H. Salmonson Outstanding Teaching Award, Senior Class Council Distinguished Faculty Award, MSU Teacher-Scholar Award, and MSU's 1st Annual Curricular Service-Learning and Civic Engagement Award in 2008. Ed received the Ray M. Sommerfeld Outstanding Tax Educator Award in 2004 and the Lifetime Service Award in 2013 from the American Taxation Association. He has also received the ATA Outstanding Manuscript Award twice, the ATA/Deloitte Teaching Innovations Award, and the 2004 Distinguished Achievement in Accounting Education Award from the Michigan Association of CPAs. In 2017, Ed received the American Accounting Association / J. Michael and Mary Ann Cook Prize given in "foremost recognition of an individual who consistently demonstrates the attributes of a superior teacher in the discipline of accounting." Ed has been recognized for his community service by the Greater Lansing Chapter of the Association of Government Accountants, the City of East Lansing (Crystal Award), and the East Lansing Education Foundation. He received a National Assistant Coach of the Year Award in 2003 from AFLAC and was named an Assistant High School Baseball Coach of the Year in 2002 by the Michigan High School Baseball Coaches Association.

John Robinson (PhD, University of Michigan, 1981) is the Patricia '77 and Grant E. Sims '77 Eminent Scholar Chair in Business. Prior to joining the faculty at Texas A&M, John was the C. Aubrey Smith Professor of Accounting at the University of Texas at Austin, Texas, and he taught at the University of Kansas where he was the Arthur Young Faculty Scholar. In 2009–2010 John served as the Academic Fellow in the Division of Corporation Finance at the Securities and Exchange Commission. He has been the recipient of the Henry A. Bubb Award for outstanding teaching, the Texas Blazer's Faculty Excellence Award, and the MPA Council Outstanding Professor Award. John also received the 2012 Outstanding Service Award from the American Taxation Association (ATA) and in 2017 was named the Ernst & Young and ATA Ray Sommerfeld Outstanding Educator. John served as the 2014–2015 president (elect) of the ATA and is the ATA's president for 2015–2016. John conducts research in a broad variety of topics involving financial accounting, mergers and acquisitions, and the influence of taxes on financial structures and performance. His scholarly articles have appeared in *The Accounting Review, The Journal of Accounting and Economics, Journal of Finance, National Tax Journal, Journal of Law and Economics, Journal of the American Taxation Association, The Journal of the American Bar Association*, and *The Journal of Taxation*. John's research was honored with the 2003 and 2008 ATA Outstanding Manuscript Awards. In addition, John was the editor of *The Journal of the American Taxation Association* from 2002–2005. Professor Robinson received his J.D. (*Cum Laude*) from the University of Michigan in 1979, and he earned a PhD in accounting from the University of Michigan in 1981. John teaches courses on individual and corporate taxation and advanced accounting.

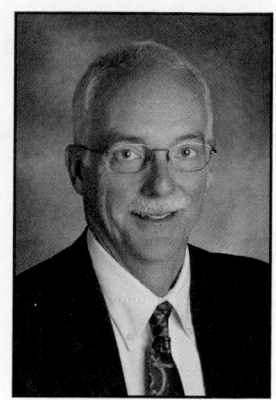

Courtesy John Robinson

Connie Weaver (PhD, Arizona State University, 1997) is the KPMG Professor of Accounting at Texas A&M University. She received a PhD from Arizona State University, an MPA from the University of Texas at Arlington, and a BS (chemical engineering) from the University of Texas at Austin. Prior to entering the PhD Program, Connie was a tax manager at Ernst & Young in Dallas, Texas, where she became licensed to practice as a CPA. She teaches taxation in the Professional Program in Accounting and the Executive MBA program at Texas A&M University. She has also taught undergraduate and graduate students at the University of Wisconsin–Madison and the University of Texas at Austin. She is the recipient of several teaching awards, including the 2006 American Taxation Association/Deloitte Teaching Innovations award, the David and Denise Baggett Teaching award, and the college and university level Association of Former Students Distinguished Achievement award in teaching. Connie's current research interests include the effects of tax and financial incentives on corporate decisions and reporting. She has published articles in journals such as *The Accounting Review, Contemporary Accounting Research, Journal of the American Taxation Association, National Tax Journal, Accounting Horizons, Journal of Corporate Finance,* and *Tax Notes*. Connie is the senior editor of *The Journal of the American Taxation Association* and she serves on the editorial board of *Contemporary Accounting Research*.

Courtesy Connie Weaver

Ron Worsham (PhD, University of Florida, 1994) is an associate professor in the School of Accountancy at Brigham Young University. He teaches taxation in the graduate, undergraduate, MBA, and Executive MBA programs at Brigham Young University. He has also taught as a visiting professor at the University of Chicago. He received both BS and MAcc (tax emphasis) degrees from Brigham Young University before working as a tax consultant for Arthur Young & Co. (now Ernst & Young) in Dallas, Texas. While in Texas, he became licensed to practice as a CPA. After his professional work experience, Ron earned his PhD at the University of Florida. He has been honored for outstanding innovation in the classroom at Brigham Young University. Ron has published academic research in the areas of taxpayer compliance and professional tax judgment. He has also published legal research in a variety of areas. His work has been published in journals such as *Journal of the American Taxation Association, The Journal of International Taxation, The Tax Executive, Tax Notes, The Journal of Accountancy,* and *Practical Tax Strategies*.

Courtesy Ron Worsham

TEACHING THE CODE IN CONTEXT

   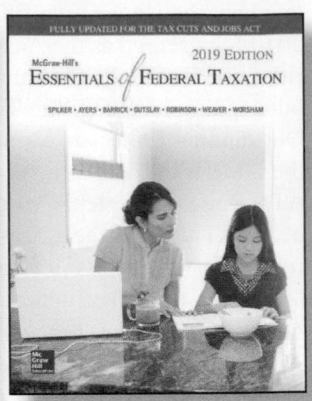

The bold innovative approach used by McGraw-Hill's Taxation series is quickly becoming the most popular choice of course materials among instructors and students. It's apparent why the clear, organized, and engaging delivery of content, paired with the most current and robust tax code updates, has been adopted by more than 600 schools across the country.

McGraw-Hill's Taxation is designed to provide a unique, innovative, and engaging learning experience for students studying taxation. The breadth of the topical coverage, **the storyline approach to presenting the material,** the emphasis on the tax and nontax consequences of multiple parties involved in transactions, and the integration of financial and tax accounting topics make this book ideal for the modern tax curriculum.

"Do you want the best tax text? This is the one to use. It has a storyline in each chapter that can relate to real life issues."

Leslie A. Mostow
– University of Maryland, College Park

"This text provides broad coverage of important topics and does so in a manner that is easy for students to understand. The material is very accessible for students."

Kyle Post
– Tarleton State University

Since the first manuscript was written in 2005, 449 professors have contributed 499 book reviews, in addition to 29 focus groups and symposia. Throughout this preface, their comments on the book's organization, pedagogy, and unique features are a testament to the **market-driven nature of *Taxation's* development.**

"I think this is the best book available for introductory and intermediate courses in taxation."

Shane Stinson
– University of Alabama

A MODERN APPROACH FOR TODAY'S STUDENT

Spilker's taxation series was built around the following five core precepts:

1 **Storyline Approach:** Each chapter begins with a storyline that introduces a set of characters or a business entity facing specific tax-related situations. Each chapter's examples are related to the storyline, providing students with opportunities to **learn the code in context.**

2 **Integrated Examples:** In addition to providing examples in-context, we provide **"What if"** scenarios within many examples to **illustrate how variations in the facts might or might not change the answers.**

3 **Conversational Writing Style:** The authors took special care to write *McGraw-Hill's Taxation* in a way that fosters a friendly dialogue between the content and each individual student. The tone of the presentation is intentionally conversational—creating the impression of *speaking with* **the student,** as opposed to *lecturing to* the student.

4 **Superior Organization of Related Topics:** *McGraw-Hill's Taxation* provides two alternative topic sequences. In the *McGraw-Hill's Taxation of Individuals and Business Entities* volume, the individual topics generally follow the tax form sequence, with an individual overview chapter and then chapters on income, deductions, investment-related issues, and the tax liability computation. The topics then transition into business-related topics that apply to individuals. This volume then provides a group of specialty chapters dealing with topics of particular interest to individuals (including students), including separate chapters on home ownership, compensation, and retirement savings and deferred compensation. This volume concludes with a chapter covering the taxation of business entities. Alternatively, in the *Essentials of Federal Taxation* volume, the topics follow a more traditional sequence, with topics streamlined (no specialty chapters) and presented in more of a life-cycle approach.

5 **Real-World Focus:** Students learn best when they see how concepts are applied in the real world. For that reason, real-world examples and articles are included in **"Taxes in the Real World"** boxes throughout the book. These vignettes demonstrate current issues in taxation and show the relevance of tax issues in all areas of business.

> The in-text examples of how to complete tax returns(is a strength of this text). These help students improve their overall understanding of the material as it moves from something abstract to something tangible the student can produce."
>
> Christine Cheng–Louisiana State University

A STORYLINE APPROACH THAT RESONATES WITH STUDENTS

Each chapter begins with a storyline that introduces a set of characters facing specific tax-related situations. This revolutionary approach to teaching tax emphasizes real people facing real tax dilemmas. Students learn to apply practical tax information to specific business and personal situations. As their situations evolve, the characters are brought further to life.

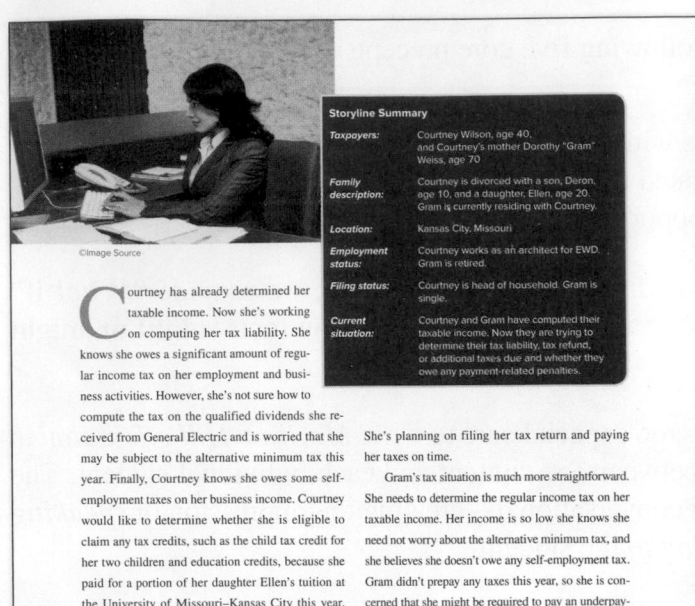

©Image Source

Courtney has already determined her taxable income. Now she's working on computing her tax liability. She knows she owes a significant amount of regular income tax on her employment and business activities. However, she's not sure how to compute the tax on the qualified dividends she received from General Electric and is worried that she may be subject to the alternative minimum tax this year. Finally, Courtney knows she owes some self-employment taxes on her business income. Courtney would like to determine whether she is eligible to claim any tax credits, such as the child tax credit for her two children and education credits, because she paid for a portion of her daughter Ellen's tuition at the University of Missouri–Kansas City this year. Courtney is hoping that she has paid enough in taxes during the year to avoid underpayment penalties.

She's planning on filing her tax return and paying her taxes on time.

Gram's tax situation is much more straightforward. She needs to determine the regular income tax on her taxable income. Her income is so low she knows she need not worry about the alternative minimum tax, and she believes she doesn't owe any self-employment tax. Gram didn't prepay any taxes this year, so she is concerned that she might be required to pay an underpayment penalty. She also expects to file her tax return and pay her taxes by the looming due date.

Storyline Summary

Taxpayers:	Courtney Wilson, age 40, and Courtney's mother Dorothy "Gram" Weiss, age 70
Family description:	Courtney is divorced with a son, Deron, age 10, and a daughter, Ellen, age 20. Gram is currently residing with Courtney.
Location:	Kansas City, Missouri
Employment status:	Courtney works as an architect for EWD. Gram is retired.
Filing status:	Courtney is head of household. Gram is single.
Current situation:	Courtney and Gram have computed their taxable income. Now they are trying to determine their tax liability, tax refund, or additional taxes due and whether they owe any payment-related penalties.

Examples

Examples are the cornerstone of any textbook covering taxation. For this reason, *McGraw-Hill's Taxation* authors took special care to create clear and helpful examples that relate to the storyline of the chapter. Students learn to refer to the facts presented in the storyline and apply them to other scenarios—in this way, they build a greater base of knowledge through application. Many examples also include "What if?" scenarios that add more complexity to the example or explore related tax concepts.

Example 2-1

Bill and Mercedes file their 2014 federal tax return on September 6, 2015, after receiving an automatic extension to file their return by October 15, 2015. In 2018, the IRS selects their 2014 tax return for audit. When does the statute of limitations end for Bill and Mercedes's 2014 tax return?

Answer: Assuming the six-year and "unlimited" statute of limitation rules do not apply, the statute of limitations ends on September 6, 2018 (three years after the later of the actual filing date and the *original* due date).

What if: When would the statute of limitations end for Bill and Mercedes for their 2014 tax return if the couple filed the return on March 22, 2015 (before the original due date of April 15, 2015)?

Answer: In this scenario the statute of limitations would end on April 15, 2018, because the later of the actual filing date and the original due date is April 15, 2015.

THE PEDAGOGY YOUR STUDENTS NEED TO PUT THE CODE IN CONTEXT

Taxes in the Real World

Taxes in the Real World are short boxes used throughout the book to demonstrate the real-world use of tax concepts. Current articles on tax issues, the real-world application of chapter-specific tax rules, and short vignettes on popular news about tax are some of the issues covered in Taxes in the Real World boxes.

> "The Spilker text makes tax easy for students to understand. **It integrates great real-world examples so students can see how topics will be applied in practice.** The integration of the tax form and exhibits of the tax forms in the text are outstanding."
>
> – Kristen Bigbee, Texas Tech University

TAXES IN THE REAL WORLD — Tax Policy: Republicans versus Democrats

Oliver Wendell Holmes said "taxes are the price we pay to live in a civilized society." Both Democrats and Republicans desire the same things: a civilized society and a healthy economy. However, neither party can agree on what defines a civilized society or which path best leads to a healthy economy. The U.S. national debt is $20 trillion dollars and growing, yet the only thing we might agree on is that something has gone wrong. Regardless of which party or candidate you support, each party's agenda will affect your income and taxes in various ways.

To explore the divide, let's examine excerpts from each party's National Platform from our most recent presidential election (2016).

Republicans

"We are the party of a growing economy that gives everyone a chance in life, an opportunity to learn, work, and realize the prosperity freedom makes possible."

"Government cannot create prosperity, though government can limit or destroy it. Prosperity is the product of self-discipline, enterprise, saving and investment by individuals, but it is not an end in itself. Prosperity provides the means by which citizens and their families can maintain their independence from government, raise their children by their own values, practice their faith, and build communities of cooperation and mutual respect."

"Republicans consider the establishment of a pro-growth tax code a moral imperative. More than any other public policy, the way government raises revenue—how much, at what rates, under what circumstances, from whom, and for whom—

of taxes. Democrats will claw back tax breaks for companies that ship jobs overseas, eliminate tax breaks for big oil and gas companies, and crack down on inversions and other methods companies use to dodge their tax responsibilities . . . We will then use the revenue raised from fixing the corporate tax code to reinvest in rebuilding America and ensuring economic growth that will lead to millions of good-paying jobs."

"We will ensure those at the top contribute to our country's future by establishing a multi-millionaire surtax to ensure millionaires and billionaires pay their fair share. In addition, we will shut down the "private tax system" for those at the top, immediately close egregious loopholes like those enjoyed by hedge fund managers, restore fair taxation on multimillion dollar estates, and ensure millionaires can no longer pay a lower rate than their secretaries. At a time of near-record corporate profits, slow wage growth, and rising costs, we need to offer tax relief to middle-class families—not those at the top."

"We will offer tax relief to hard working, middle-class families for the cost squeeze they have faced for years from rising health care, childcare, education, and other expenses." https://www.democrats.org/party-platform#preamble

Conclusion

Each party fundamentally believes the government should create/maintain cities and states that form a civilized society, and that government should foster a healthy economy. However, they choose very different paths to reach this objec-

The Key Facts

The Key Facts provide quick synopses of the critical pieces of information presented throughout each chapter.

The **tax base** defines what is actually taxed and is usually expressed in monetary terms, whereas the **tax rate** determines the level of taxes imposed on the tax base and is usually expressed as a percentage. For example, a sales tax rate of 6 percent on a purchase of $30 yields a tax of $1.80 ($1.80 = $30 × .06).

Federal, state, and local jurisdictions use a large variety of tax bases to collect tax. Some common tax bases (and related taxes) include taxable income (federal and state income taxes), purchases (sales tax), real estate values (real estate tax), and personal property values (personal property tax).

Different portions of a tax base may be taxed at different rates. A single tax applied to an entire base constitutes a **flat tax**. In the case of **graduated taxes**, the base is divided

THE KEY FACTS
How to Calculate a Tax

- Tax = Tax base × Tax rate
- The tax base defines what is actually taxed and is usually expressed in monetary terms.
- The tax rate determines the level of taxes imposed

Exhibits

Today's students are visual learners, and *McGraw-Hill's Taxation* understands this student need by making use of clear and engaging charts, diagrams, and tabular demonstrations of key material.

> "It is easily accessible to students as it is written in easy-to-understand language, and contains sufficient examples to illustrate complicated tax concepts and calculations."
>
> Machiavelli Chao
> – University of California, Irvine: The Paul Merage School of Business

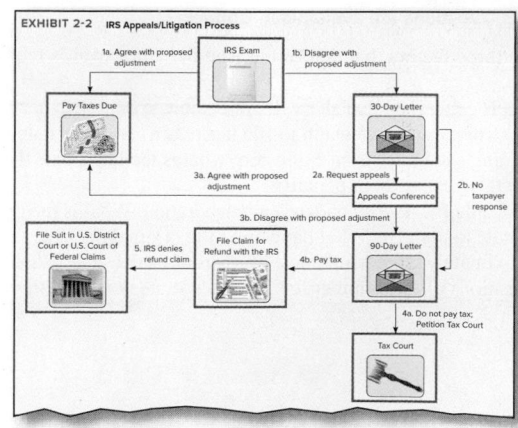

EXHIBIT 2-2   IRS Appeals/Litigation Process

PRACTICE MAKES PERFECT WITH A

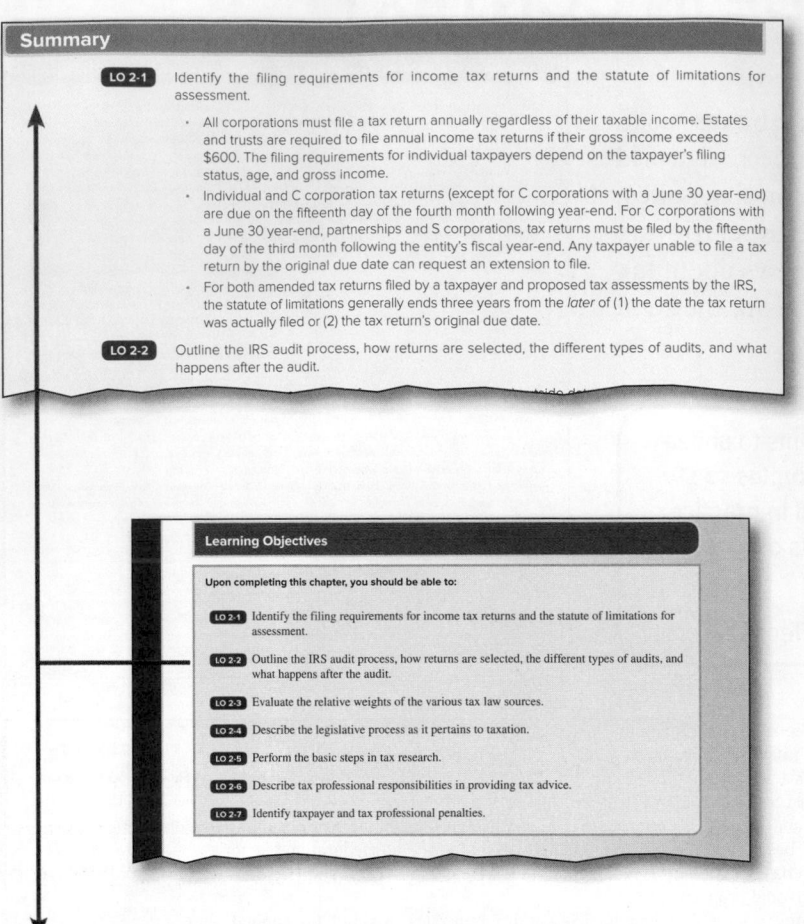

Summary

A unique feature of *McGraw-Hill's Taxation* is the end-of-chapter summary organized around learning objectives. Each objective has a brief, bullet-point summary that covers the major topics and concepts for that chapter, including references to critical exhibits and examples. All end-of-chapter material is tied to learning objectives.

Summary

LO 2-1 Identify the filing requirements for income tax returns and the statute of limitations for assessment.

- All corporations must file a tax return annually regardless of their taxable income. Estates and trusts are required to file annual income tax returns if their gross income exceeds $600. The filing requirements for individual taxpayers depend on the taxpayer's filing status, age, and gross income.
- Individual and C corporation tax returns (except for C corporations with a June 30 year-end) are due on the fifteenth day of the fourth month following year-end. For C corporations with a June 30 year-end, partnerships and S corporations, tax returns must be filed by the fifteenth day of the third month following the entity's fiscal year-end. Any taxpayer unable to file a tax return by the original due date can request an extension to file.
- For both amended tax returns filed by a taxpayer and proposed tax assessments by the IRS, the statute of limitations generally ends three years from the *later* of (1) the date the tax return was actually filed or (2) the tax return's original due date.

LO 2-2 Outline the IRS audit process, how returns are selected, the different types of audits, and what happens after the audit.

Learning Objectives

Upon completing this chapter, you should be able to:

LO 2-1 Identify the filing requirements for income tax returns and the statute of limitations for assessment.

LO 2-2 Outline the IRS audit process, how returns are selected, the different types of audits, and what happens after the audit.

LO 2-3 Evaluate the relative weights of the various tax law sources.

LO 2-4 Describe the legislative process as it pertains to taxation.

LO 2-5 Perform the basic steps in tax research.

LO 2-6 Describe tax professional responsibilities in providing tax advice.

LO 2-7 Identify taxpayer and tax professional penalties.

DISCUSSION QUESTIONS

Discussion Questions are available in Connect®.

Discussion Questions

Discussion questions, now available in *Connect*, are provided for each of the major concepts in each chapter, providing students with an opportunity to review key parts of the chapter and answer evocative questions about what they have learned.

LO 2-1 1. Name three factors that determine whether a taxpayer is required to file a tax return.

LO 2-1 2. Benita is concerned that she will not be able to complete her tax return by April 15. Can she request an extension to file her return? By what date must she do so? Assuming she requests an extension, what is the latest date that she could file her return this year without penalty?

LO 2-1 3. Agua Linda Inc. is a calendar-year corporation. What is the original due date for the corporate tax return? What happens if the original due date falls on a Saturday?

LO 2-2 4. Approximately what percentage of tax returns does the IRS audit? What are the implications of this number for the IRS's strategy in selecting returns for audit?

WIDE VARIETY OF ASSIGNMENT MATERIAL

Problems

Problems are designed to test the comprehension of more complex topics. Each problem at the end of the chapter is tied to one of that chapter's learning objectives, with multiple problems for critical topics.

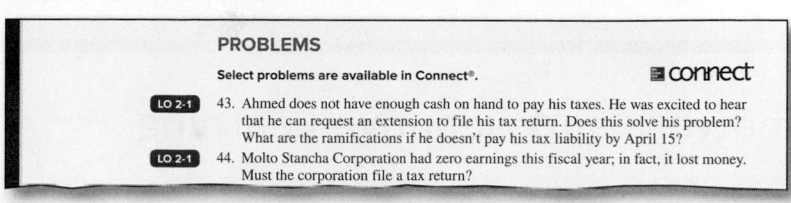

Tax Forms Problems

Tax forms problems are a set of requirements included in the end-of-chapter material of the 2019 edition. These problems require students to complete a tax form (or part of a tax form), provid-

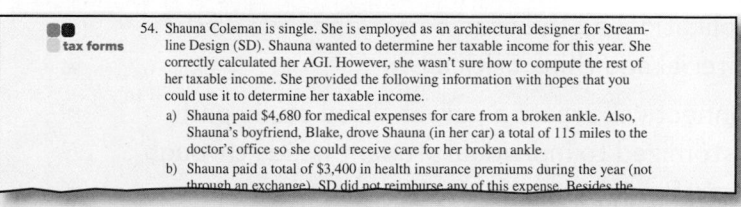

ing students with valuable experience and practice with filling out these forms. These requirements—and their relevant forms—are also included in *Connect*. Each tax form problem includes an icon to differentiate it from regular problems.

Research Problems

Research problems are special problems throughout the end-of-chapter assignment material. These require students to

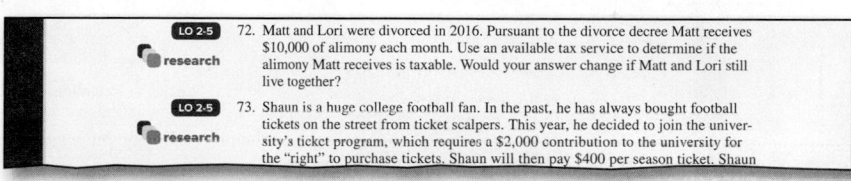

do both basic and more complex research on topics outside of the scope of the book. Each research problem includes an icon to differentiate it from regular problems.

Planning Problems

Planning problems are another unique set of problems included in the end-of-chapter assignment material. These require students to test their tax planning

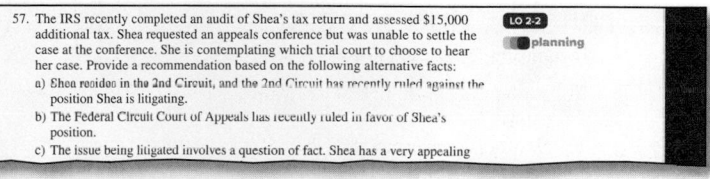

skills after covering the chapter topics. Each planning problem includes an icon to differentiate it from regular problems.

Comprehensive and Tax Return Problems

Comprehensive and tax return problems address multiple concepts in a single problem. Comprehensive problems are ideal for cumulative topics; for this reason, they are located at the end of all

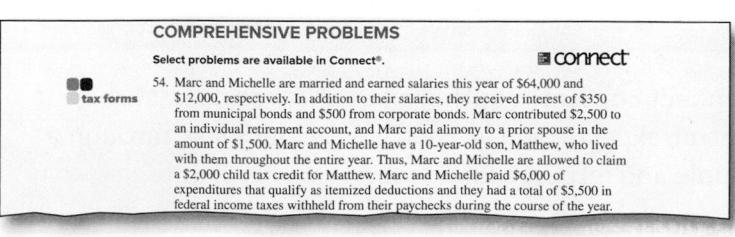

chapters. In the end-of-book Appendix C, we include tax return problems that cover multiple chapters. **Additional tax return problems are also available in *Connect* and *Instructor Resource Center*. These problems range from simple to complex and cover individual taxation, corporate taxation, partnership taxation, and S corporation taxation.**

McGraw-Hill Connect® is a highly reliable, easy-to-use homework and learning management solution that utilizes learning science and award-winning adaptive tools to improve student results.

Homework and Adaptive Learning

- Connect's assignments help students contextualize what they've learned through application, so they can better understand the material and think critically.
- Connect will create a personalized study path customized to individual student needs through SmartBook®.
- SmartBook helps students study more efficiently by delivering an interactive reading experience through adaptive highlighting and review.

Over **7 billion questions** have been answered, making McGraw-Hill Education products more intelligent, reliable, and precise.

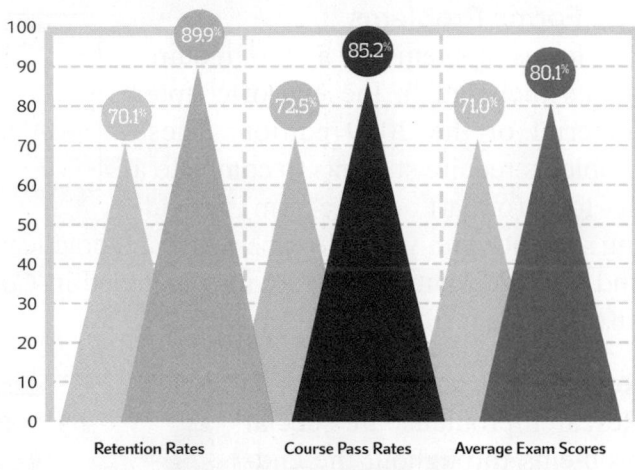

Connect's Impact on Retention Rates, Pass Rates, and Average Exam Scores

70.1% 89.9% 72.5% 85.2% 71.0% 80.1%

Retention Rates   Course Pass Rates   Average Exam Scores

without Connect   with Connect

Using **Connect** improves retention rates by **19.8 percentage points,** passing rates by **12.7 percentage points, and** exam scores by **9.1 percentage points.**

73% of instructors who use **Connect** require it; instructor satisfaction **increases** by 28% when **Connect** is required.

Quality Content and Learning Resources

- Connect content is authored by the world's best subject matter experts, and is available to your class through a simple and intuitive interface.
- The Connect eBook makes it easy for students to access their reading material on smartphones and tablets. They can study on the go and don't need internet access to use the eBook as a reference, with full functionality.
- Multimedia content such as videos, simulations, and games drive student engagement and critical thinking skills.

Robust Analytics and Reporting

©Hero Images/Getty Images

- Connect Insight® generates easy-to-read reports on individual students, the class as a whole, and on specific assignments.

- The Connect Insight dashboard delivers data on performance, study behavior, and effort. Instructors can quickly identify students who struggle and focus on material that the class has yet to master.

- Connect automatically grades assignments and quizzes, providing easy-to-read reports on individual and class performance.

Impact on Final Course Grade Distribution

without Connect		with Connect
22.9%	A	31.0%
27.4%	B	34.3%
22.9%	C	18.7%
11.5%	D	6.1%
15.4%	F	9.9%

More students earn **As** and **Bs** when they use **Connect**.

Trusted Service and Support

- Connect integrates with your LMS to provide single sign-on and automatic syncing of grades. Integration with Blackboard®, D2L®, and Canvas also provides automatic syncing of the course calendar and assignment-level linking.

- Connect offers comprehensive service, support, and training throughout every phase of your implementation.

- If you're looking for some guidance on how to use Connect, or want to learn tips and tricks from super users, you can find tutorials as you work. Our Digital Faculty Consultants and Student Ambassadors offer insight into how to achieve the results you want with Connect.

www.mheducation.com/connect

DIGITAL LEARNING ASSETS TO IMPROVE STUDENT OUTCOMES

"The quality of the online materials in Connect and Learnsmart are market-leading and unmatched in the tax arena."

Jason W. Stanfield
– Ball State University

Connect helps students learn more efficiently by providing feedback and practice material when they need it, where they need it. Connect grades homework automatically and gives immediate feedback on any questions students may have missed. The extensive assignable, gradable end-of-chapter content includes problems, comprehensive problems (available as auto-graded tax forms), and discussion questions. Also, select questions have been redesigned to test students' knowledge more fully. They now include tables for students to work through rather than requiring that all calculations be done offline.

Through November, Tex has received gross income of $120,000. For December, Tex is considering whether to accept one more work engagement for the year. Engagement 1 will generate $7,000 of revenue at a cost of $4,000, which is deductible for AGI. In contrast, engagement 2 will generate $7,000 of revenue at a cost of $3,000, which is deductible as an itemized deduction. Tex files as a single taxpayer. (use the tax rate schedules.)

a. Calculate Tex's taxable income assuming he chooses engagement 1 and assuming he chooses engagement 2. Assume he has no itemized deductions other than those generated by engagement 2.

	Description	Engagement 1	Engagement 2
(1)	Gross income before new work engagement	$ 120,000	$ 120,000
(2)	Income from engagement	7,000	7,000
(3)	Additional for AGI deduction	(4,000)	
(4)	Adjusted gross income	$ 123,000	$ 127,000
(5)	Greater		
(6)	Greater of itemized deductions or standard deduction		

Auto-Graded Tax Forms

The auto-graded **Tax Forms** in Connect provide a much-improved student experience when solving the tax-form based problems. The tax form simulation allows students to apply tax concepts by completing the actual tax forms online with automatic feedback and grading for both students and instructors.

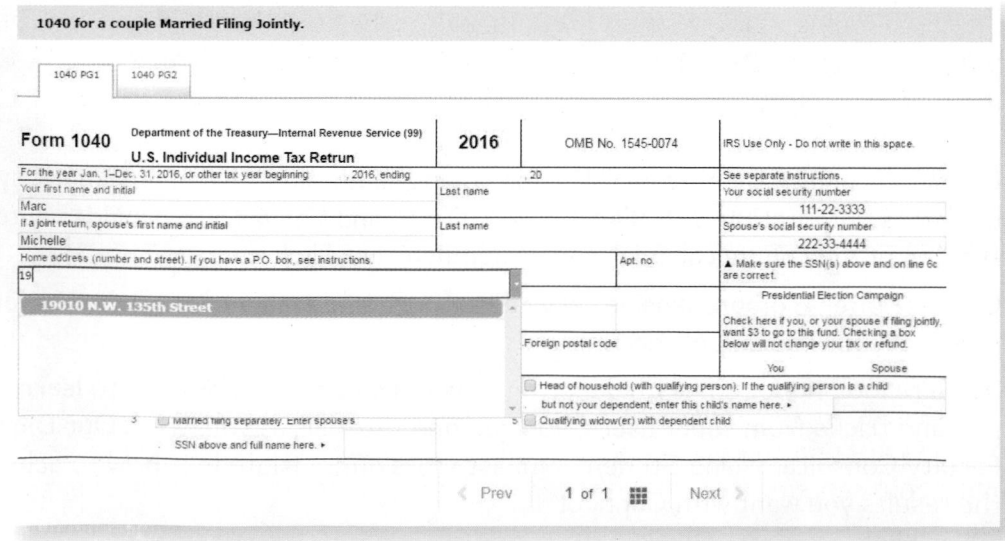

Guided Examples

The **Guided Examples,** or "hint" videos, in Connect provide a narrated, animated, step-by-step walk-through of select problems similar to those assigned. These short presentations can be turned on or off by instructors and provide reinforcement when students need it most.

TaxACT®

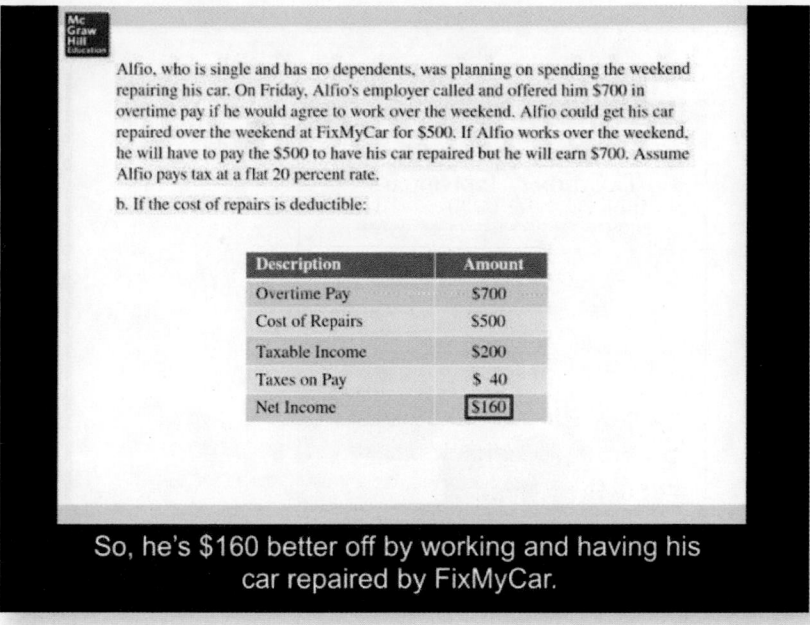

TaxAct *McGraw-Hill's* **Professional** *Taxation* can be packaged with tax software from TaxACT, one of the leading preparation software companies in the market today. The 2017 edition includes availability of both *Individuals* and *Business Entities* software, including the 1040 Forms and TaxACT Preparer's Business 3-Pack (with Forms 1065, 1120, and 1120S).

Please note, TaxACT is only compatible with PCs and not Macs. However, we offer easy-to-complete licensing agreement templates that are accessible within Connect and the Instructor Resources Center to enable school computer labs to download the software onto campus hardware for free.

Roger's CPA

ROGER | *CPA Review* McGraw-Hill Education has partnered with Roger CPA Review, a global leader in CPA Exam preparation, to provide students a smooth transition from the accounting classroom to successful completion of the CPA Exam. While many aspiring accountants wait until they have completed their academic studies to begin preparing for the CPA Exam, research shows that those who become familiar with exam content earlier in the process have a stronger chance of successfully passing the CPA Exam.

Accordingly, students using these McGraw-Hill materials will have access to sample CPA Exam multiple-choice questions and Task-based Simulations from Roger CPA Review, with expert-written explanations and solutions. All questions are either directly from the AICPA or are modeled on AICPA questions that appear in the exam. Task-based Simulations are delivered via the Roger CPA Review platform, which mirrors the look, feel, and functionality of the actual exam.

McGraw-Hill Education and Roger CPA Review are dedicated to supporting every accounting student along their journey, ultimately helping them achieve career success in the accounting profession. For more information about the full Roger CPA Review program, exam requirements, and exam content, visit www.rogercpareview.com.

McGraw-Hill Customer Experience Group Contact Information

At McGraw-Hill, we understand that getting the most from new technology can be challenging. That's why our services don't stop after you purchase our products. You can contact our Product Specialists 24 hours a day to get product training online. Or you can search the knowledge bank of Frequently Asked Questions on our support website. For Customer Support, call **800-331-5094,** or visit www.mhhe.com/support. One of our Technical Support Analysts will be able to assist you in a timely fashion.

Four Volumes to Fit

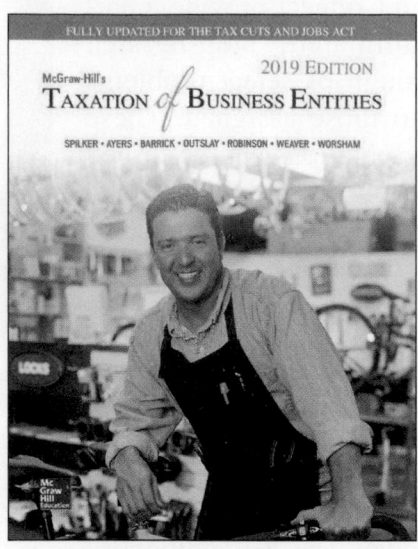

McGraw-Hill's Taxation of Individuals is organized to emphasize topics that are most important to undergraduates taking their first tax course. The first three chapters provide an introduction to taxation and then carefully guide students through tax research and tax planning. Part II discusses the fundamental elements of individual income tax, starting with the tax formula in Chapter 4 and then proceeding to more discussion on income, deductions, investments, and computing tax liabilities in Chapters 5–8. Part III then discusses tax issues associated with business-related activities. Specifically, this part addresses business income and deductions, accounting methods, and tax consequences associated with purchasing assets and property dispositions (sales, trades, or other dispositions). Part IV is unique among tax textbooks; this section combines related tax issues for compensation, retirement savings, and home ownership.

Part I: Introduction to Taxation
  1. An Introduction to Tax
  2. Tax Compliance, the IRS, and Tax Authorities
  3. Tax Planning Strategies and Related Limitations

Part II: Basic Individual Taxation
  4. Individual Income Tax Overview, Dependents, and Filing Status
  5. Gross Income and Exclusions
  6. Individual Deductions
  7. Investments
  8. Individual Income Tax Computation and Tax Credits

Part III: Business-Related Transactions
  9. Business Income, Deductions, and Accounting Methods
  10. Property Acquisition and Cost Recovery
  11. Property Dispositions

Part IV: Specialized Topics
  12. Compensation
  13. Retirement Savings and Deferred Compensation
  14. Tax Consequences of Home Ownership

McGraw-Hill's Taxation of Business Entities begins with the process for determining gross income and deductions for businesses, and the tax consequences associated with purchasing assets and property dispositions (sales, trades, or other dispositions). Part II provides a comprehensive overview of entities and the formation, reorganization, and liquidation of corporations. Unique to this series is a complete chapter on accounting for income taxes, which provides a primer on the basics of calculating the income tax provision. Included in the narrative is a discussion of temporary and permanent differences and their impact on a company's book "effective tax rate." Part III provides a detailed discussion of partnerships and S corporations. The last part of the book covers state and local taxation, multinational taxation, and transfer taxes and wealth planning.

Part I: Business-Related Transactions
  1. Business Income, Deductions, and Accounting Methods
  2. Property Acquisition and Cost Recovery
  3. Property Dispositions

Part II: Entity Overview and Taxation of C Corporations
  4. Entities Overview
  5. Corporate Operations
  6. Accounting for Income Taxes
  7. Corporate Taxation: Nonliquidating Distributions
  8. Corporate Formation, Reorganization, and Liquidation

Part III: Taxation of Flow-Through Entities
  9. Forming and Operating Partnerships
  10. Dispositions of Partnership Interests and Partnership Distributions
  11. S Corporations

Part IV: Multijurisdictional Taxation and Transfer Taxes
  12. State and Local Taxes
  13. The U.S. Taxation of Multinational Transactions
  14. Transfer Taxes and Wealth Planning

Four Course Approaches

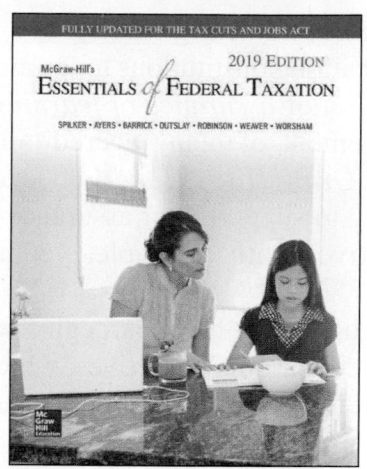

McGraw-Hill's Taxation of Individuals and Business Entities covers all chapters included in the two split volumes in one convenient volume. See Table of Contents.

McGraw-Hill's Essentials of Federal Taxation is designed for a one-semester course, covering the basics of taxation of individuals and business entities. To facilitate a one-semester course, *McGraw-Hill's Essentials of Federal Taxation* folds the key topics from the investments, compensation, retirement savings, and home ownership chapters in *Taxation of Individuals* into three individual taxation chapters that discuss gross income and exclusions, *for* AGI deductions, and *from* AGI deductions, respectively. The essentials volume also includes a two-chapter C corporation sequence that uses a life-cycle approach covering corporate formations and then corporate operations in the first chapter and nonliquidating and liquidating corporate distributions in the second chapter. This volume is perfect for those teaching a one-semester course and for those who struggle to get through the 25-chapter comprehensive volume.

SUPPLEMENTS FOR INSTRUCTORS

Assurance of Learning Ready

Many educational institutions today are focused on the notion of *assurance of learning,* an important element of many accreditation standards. *McGraw-Hill's Taxation* is designed specifically to support your assurance of learning initiatives with a simple, yet powerful, solution.

Each chapter in the book begins with a list of numbered learning objectives, which appear throughout the chapter as well as in the end-of-chapter assignments. Every test bank question for *McGraw-Hill's Taxation* maps to a specific chapter learning objective in the textbook. Each test bank question also identifies topic area, level of difficulty, Bloom's Taxonomy level, and AICPA and AACSB skill area.

AACSB Statement

McGraw-Hill Education is a proud corporate member of AACSB International. Understanding the importance and value of AACSB accreditation, *McGraw-Hill's Taxation* recognizes the curricula guidelines detailed in the AACSB standards for business accreditation by connecting selected questions in the text and the test bank to the general knowledge and skill guidelines in the revised AACSB standards.

The statements contained in *McGraw-Hill's Taxation* are provided only as a guide for the users of this textbook. The AACSB leaves content coverage and assessment within the purview of individual schools, the mission of the school, and the faculty. While *McGraw-Hill's Taxation* and the teaching package make no claim of any specific AACSB qualification or evaluation, we have, within the text and test bank, labeled selected questions according to the eight general knowledge and skill areas.

TestGen

TestGen is a complete, state-of-the-art test generator and editing application software that allows instructors to quickly and easily select test items from McGraw Hill's TestGen testbank content and to organize, edit, and customize the questions and answers to rapidly generate paper tests. Questions can include stylized text, symbols, graphics, and equations that are inserted directly into questions using built-in mathematical templates. With both quick-and-simple test creation and flexible and robust editing tools, TestGen is a test generator system for today's educators.

A HEARTFELT THANKS TO THE MANY COLLEAGUES WHO SHAPED THIS BOOK

The version of the book you are reading would not be the same book without the valuable suggestions, keen insights, and constructive criticisms of the list of reviewers below. Each professor listed here contributed in substantive ways to the organization of chapters, coverage of topics, and use of pedagogy. We are grateful to them for taking the time to read chapters or attend reviewer conferences, focus groups, and symposia in support of the development for the book:

Previous Edition Reviewers

Donna Abelli, *Mount Ida College*
Joseph Assalone, *Rowan College at Gloucester County*
Valeriya Avdeev, *William Paterson University*
Robyn Barrett, *St. Louis Community College*
Kevin Baugess, *ICDC College*
Christopher Becker, *Coastal Carolina University*
Jeanne Bedell, *Keiser University*
Marcia Behrens, *Nichols College*
Michael Belleman, *St. Clair County Community College*
David Berman, *Community College of Philadelphia*
Tim Biggart, *Berry College*

Cynthia Bird, *Tidewater Community College*
Lisa Blum, *University of Louisville*
Rick Blumenfeld, *Sierra College*
Cindy Bortman Boggess, *Babson College*
Cathalene Bowler, *University of Northern Iowa*
Justin Breidenbach, *Ohio Wesleyan University*
Suzon Bridges, *Houston Community College*
Stephen Bukowy, *UNC Pembroke*
Esther Bunn, *Stephen F. Austin State University*
Holly Caldwell, *Bridgewater College*
James Campbell, *Thomas College*
Alisa Carini, *UCSD Extension*

Ronald Carter, *Patrick Henry Community College*
Cynthia Caruso, *Endicott College*
Paul Caselton, *University of Illinois Springfield*
Amy Chataginer, *Mississippi Gulf Coast Community College*
Machiavelli Chao, *University of California, Irvine*
Max Chao, *University of California, Irvine*
Christine Cheng, *Louisiana State University*
Lisa Church, *Rhode Island College*
Marilyn Ciolino, *Delgado Community College*
Wayne Clark, *Southwest Baptist University*
Ann Cohen, *University at Buffalo, SUNY*
Sharon Cox, *University of Illinois–Urbana-Champaign*
Terry Crain, *University of Oklahoma–Norman*
Roger Crane, *Indiana University East*
Brad Cripe, *Northern Illinois University*
Curtis J. Crocker, *Southern Crescent Technical College*
Richard Cummings, *University of Wisconsin–Whitewater*
Joshua Cutler, *University of Houston*
William Dams, *Lenoir Community College*
Nichole Dauenhauer, *Lakeland Community College*
Susan Snow Davis, *Green River College*
Jim Desimpelare, *University of Michigan–Ann Arbor*
Julie Dilling, *Moraine Park Technical College*
Steve Dombrock, *Carroll University*
Dr. Vicky C. Dominguez, *College of Southern Nevada*
Michael P. Donohoe, *University of Illinois-Urbana-Champaign*
John Dorocak, *California State University–San Berdinado*
Amy Dunbar, *University of Connecticut–Storrs*
John Eagan, *Morehouse College*
Reed Easton, *Seton Hall University*
Elizabeth Ekmekjian, *William Paterson University*
Ann Esarco, *Columbia College Columbia*
Frank Faber, *St. Joseph's College*
Michael Fagan, *Raritan Valley Community College*
Frank Farina, *Catawba College*
Andrew Finley, *Claremont McKenna*
Tim Fogarty, *Case Western Reserve University*
Mimi Ford, *Middle Georgia State University*
Wilhelmina Ford, *Middle Georgia State University*
George Frankel, *San Francisco State University*
Lawrence Friedken, *Penn State University*
Stephen Gara, *Drake University*
Robert Gary, *University of New Mexico*
Greg Geisler, *University of Missouri–St. Louis*
Earl Godfrey, *Gardner Webb University*
Thomas Godwin, *Purdue University*
David Golub, *Northeastern University*
Marina Grau, *Houston Community College*
Brian Greenstein, *University of Delaware*
Patrick Griffin, *Lewis University*
Lillian Grose, *University of Holy Cross*
Rosie Hagen, *Virginia Western Community College*
Marcye Hampton, *University of Central Florida*
Cass Hausserman, *Portland State University*
Rebecca Helms, *Ivy Tech Community College*
Melanie Hicks, *Liberty University*
Mary Ann Hofmann, *Appalachian State University*
Robert Joseph Holdren, *Muskingum University*
Bambi Hora, *University of Central Oklahoma*
Carol Hughes, *Asheville Buncombe Technical Community College*

Helen Hurwitz, *Saint Louis University*
Rik Ichiho, *Dixie State University*
Kerry Inger, *Auburn University*
Paul Johnson, *Mississippi Gulf Coast CC–JD Campus*
Athena Jones, *University of Maryland University College*
Andrew Junikiewicz, *Temple University*
Susan Jurney, *University of Arkansas Fayetteville*
Sandra Kemper, *Regis University*
Jon Kerr, *Baruch College–CUNY*
Lara Kessler, *Grand Valley State University*
Janice Klimek, *University of Central Missouri*
Pamela Knight, *Columbus Technical College*
Satoshi Kojima, *East Los Angeles College*
Dawn Konicek, *Idaho State University*
Jack Lachman, *Brooklyn College*
Brandon Lanciloti, *Freed-Hardeman University*
Stacie Laplante, *University of Wisconsin–Madison*
Suzanne Laudadio, *Durham Tech*
Stephanie Lewis, *Ohio State University–Columbus*
Troy Lewis, *Brigham Young University*
Teresa Lightner, *University of North Texas*
Robert Lin, *California State University–East Bay*
Chris Loiselle, *Cornerstone University*
Bruce Lubich, *Penn State–Harrisburg*
Narelle Mackenzie, *San Diego State University, National University*
Michael Malmfeldt, *Shenandoah University*
Kate Mantzke, *Northern Illinois University*
Robert Martin, *Kennesaw State University*
Anthony Masino, *East Tennessee State University*
Paul Mason, *Baylor University*
Lisa McKinney, *University of Alabama at Birmingham*
Allison McLeod, *University of North Texas*
Lois McWhorter, *Somerset Community College*
Janet Meade, *University of Houston*
Michele Meckfessel, *University of Missouri St. Louis*
Frank Messina, *University of Alabama at Birmingham*
R Miedaner, *Lee University*
Ken Milani, *University of Notre Dame*
Karen Morris, *Northeast Iowa Community College*
Stephanie Morris, *Mercer University*
Michelle Moshier, *University at Albany*
Leslie Mostow, *University of Maryland, College Park*
James Motter, *Indiana University-Purdue University Indianapolis*
Jackie Myers, *Sinclair Community College*
Michael Nee, *Cape Cod Community College*
Liz Ott, *Casper College*
Sandra Owen- *Indiana State University–Bloomington*
Edwin Pagan, *Passaic County Community College*
Jeff Paterson, *Florida State University*
Ronald Pearson, *Bay College*
Martina Peng, *Franklin University*
James Pierson, *Franklin University*
Sonja Pippin, *University of Nevada–Reno*
Anthony Pochesci, *Rutgers University*
Kyle Post, *Tarleton State University*
Christopher Proschko, *Texas State University*
Joshua Racca, *University of Alabama*
Francisco Rangel, *Riverside City College*
Pauline Ash Ray, *Thomas University*

Luke Richardson, *University of South Florida*
Rodney Ridenour, *Montana State University Northern*
John Robertson, *Arkansas State University*
Susan Robinson, *Georgia Southwestern State University*
Morgan Rockett, *Moberly Area Community College*
Miles Romney, *Michigan State University*
Ananth Seetharaman, *Saint Louis University*
Alisa Shapiro, *Raritan Valley Community College*
Deanna Sharpe, *University of Missouri*
Wayne Shaw, *Southern Methodist University*
Sonia Singh, *University of Florida*
Georgi Smatrakalev, *Florida Atlantic University*
Lucia Smeal, *Georgia State University*
Pamela Smith, *University of Texas at San Antonio*
Adam Spoolstra, *Johnson County Community College*
Joe Standridge, *Sonoma State*
Jason Stanfield, *Ball State University*
George Starbuck, *McMurry University*
James Stekelberg, *University of Arizona*
Shane Stinson, *University of Alabama*

Terrie Stolte, *Columbus State Community College*
Gloria Jean Stuart, *Georgia Southern University*
Kenton Swift, *University of Montana*
Erin Towery, *The University of Georgia*
Ronald Unger, *Temple University*
Karen Wallace, *Ramapo College*
Natasha Ware, *Southeastern University*
Luke Watson, *University of Florida*
Sarah Webber, *University of Dayton*
Cassandra Weitzenkamp, *Peru State College*
Marvin Williams, *University of Houston—Downtown*
Chris Woehrle, *American College*
Jennifer Wright, *Drexel University*
Massood Yahya-Zadeh, *George Mason University*
James Yang, *Montclair State University*
Scott Yetmar, *Cleveland State University*
Charlie Yuan, *Elizabeth City State University*
Xiaoli Yuan, *Elizabeth City State University*
Mingjun Zhou, *DePaul University*

Acknowledgments

We would like to thank the many talented people who made valuable contributions to the creation of this tenth edition. William A. Padley of Madison Area Technical College, Deanna Sharpe of the University of Missouri–Columbia, and Troy Lewis of Brigham Young University checked the page proofs and solutions manual for accuracy; we greatly appreciate the hours they spent checking tax forms and double-checking our calculations throughout the book. Teressa Farough, Troy Lewis of Brigham Young University, Lara Kessler of Grand Valley State University and Eric McLimore accuracy-checked the test bank. Thank you to Troy Lewis, Monika Turek, and Jason Stanfield for your contributions to the Smartbook revision for this edition. Special thanks to Troy Lewis of Brigham Young University for his sharp eye and valuable feedback throughout the revision process. Thanks as well to Marilyn Isaacks from Agate Publishing for managing the supplement process. Finally, William A. Padley of Madison Area Technical College, Deanna Sharpe of the University of Missouri–Columbia, and Vivian Paige of Old Dominion University greatly contributed to the accuracy of McGraw-Hill's *Connect* for the 2019 edition.

We also appreciate the expert attention given to this project by the staff at McGraw-Hill Education, especially Tim Vertovec, Managing Director; Kathleen Klehr, Executive Portfolio Manager; Danielle Andries, Senior Product Developer; Erin Quinones, Product Developer; Lori Koetters, Brian Nacik, and Jill Eccher, Content Project Managers; Matt Backhaus, Designer; Natalie King, Marketing Director; Zach Rudin, Marketing Manager; and Sue Culbertson, Senior Buyer.

Changes in *Taxation of Individuals and Business Entities*, 2019 Edition

For the 2019 edition of McGraw-Hill's *Taxation of Individuals and Business Entities,* many changes were made in response to feedback from reviewers and focus group participants:

- All **tax forms** have been **updated for the latest available tax form as of March 2018.** In addition, **chapter content** throughout the text has been **updated to reflect tax law changes through March 2018.**

Other notable changes in the 2019 edition include:

Chapter 1

- Updated tax rates for 2018 and Examples 1-3 through 1-7.
- Updated Social Security Wage base for 2018.
- Updated unified Tax Credit for 2018.
- Deleted Taxes in the Real World: Affordable Care Act amount for 2018 which was repealed.
- Updated Taxes in the Real World: National Debt for current debt limit.
- Updated Exhibit 1-4 for 2017 Federal revenues by source from Treasury.
- Updated Exhibit 1-5 for 2017 State revenues by source from U.S. Census.

Chapter 2

- Updated gross income thresholds by filing status for 2018 for new tax law changes.
- Updated discussion of filing requirements for married taxpayers for new tax law changes.
- Revised discussion of Preparer Tax Identification Numbers (PTIN).
- Revised end of chapter problems to reflect tax law changes.

Chapter 3

- Updated tax rates for 2018.
- Added Taxes in the Real World: Tax Reform and Tax Planning.
- Updated Exhibit 3-3 for new tax rates post TCJA.
- Modified Examples 3-7 and 3-8 to reflect changes in tax planning from TCJA.

Chapter 4

- Streamlined Learning Objective 4-1.
- Edited Learning Objective 4-2 to emphasize dependents instead of exemptions.
- Updated Exhibit 4-1 to reflect changes in the Individual Tax Formula

- Updated Exhibit 4-7 to reflect standard deduction amounts for 2018.
- Edited Exhibit 4-5 to remove moving expenses.
- Changed Example 4-2 to replace moving expenses with IRA contribution.
- Updated discussion of child tax credits to reflect new law.
- Updated examples to reflect changes in child tax credit under new tax law.
- Revised section on personal and dependency exemptions to emphasize who qualifies as a dependent of the taxpayer.
- Revised discussion of why determining filing status is important.
- Revised filing status discussion to emphasize claiming a dependent rather than claiming an exemption for a dependent.
- Edited flowcharts in appendices to emphasize claiming a dependent rather than claiming an exemption for a dependent.
- Added two new discussion questions to address questions relating to the new tax law.
- Deleted one problem dealing with dependency exemptions.
- Edited approximately 10 percent of the problems to reflect changes in the tax law allowing the deduction for qualified business income or dependency exemptions.
- Updated tax rates for 2018.
- Updated tax forms from 2016 to 2017 forms.

Chapter 5

- Revised discussion of claim of right doctrine for individuals required to repay compensation for tax law changes.
- Updated discussion of alimony for tax law changes.
- Updated discussion of employee awards for length of service or safety awards for tax law changes.
- Clarified discussion of the deductibility of gambling expenses for tax law changes.
- Updated discussion of discharge of indebtedness for tax law changes.
- Revised discussion of fringe benefits and moving expenses for tax law changes.
- Added a discussion of accountable plan reimbursements.

- Updated for 2018 amounts for Flexible Spending Account contributions.
- Revised discussion of Section 529 plans for tax law changes.
- Added Taxes in the Real World on the taxation of prizes.
- Updated for 2018 foreign income exclusion amounts.
- Updated for annual gift tax exclusion and unified tax credit for 2018.
- Revised discussion of athletic scholarships.
- Updated U.S. Series EE Bond interest income exclusion for 2018.
- Updated tax forms from 2016 to 2017 forms.
- Updated end of chapter problems for tax law changes

Chapter 6

- Revised discussion of deductibility of business versus investment related expenses under for tax law changes.
- Revised Exhibit 6-1: Individual Business and Investment Related Deductions for AGI, from AGI, and Not Deductible.
- Added discussion for new excess business loss limitation.
- Revised discussion of moving expenses for tax law changes.
- Revised discussion of alimony deduction for tax law changes.
- Revised discussion of deduction for interest on qualified education loan for tax law changes.
- Eliminate discussion of expired deduction for qualified education expenses.
- Updated AGI floor for medical expense itemized deduction for tax law change.
- Updated mileage rate for medical expense itemized deduction for 2018.
- Added discussion on new cap on itemized deductions for taxes.
- Revised discussion of mortgage interest deduction to reflect new cap on acquisition indebtedness and non-deductibility of interest on home-equity indebtedness.
- Revised discussion of investment interest expense deduction for tax law change that eliminates the deduction for investment expenses as itemized deductions.
- Revised discussion of charitable contributions for new 60 percent AGI limit for cash contributions to public charities and private operating foundations.
- Revised Exhibit 6-8: Summary of Charitable Contributions Limitation Rules.
- Revised discussion of casualty and theft losses on personal-use assets for tax law changes.
- Revised discussion of miscellaneous itemized deductions to reflect tax law changes that eliminated these

deductions subject to 2 percent AGI floor (employee business expenses, tax preparation fees, hobby expenses, investment expenses)
- Eliminated discussion of itemized deduction and personal exemption phase-outs repealed by tax law changes.
- Updated standard deduction amounts for tax law changes.
- Eliminated discussion of personal and dependency exemptions repealed by tax law changes.
- Added discussion for new deduction for qualified business income.
- Updated tax forms from 2016 to 2017 forms.
- Substantially revised end of chapter problems for tax law changes.

Chapter 7

- Added Taxes in the Real World: So You Want to Invest in Bitcoin.
- Updated tax rates in all examples and problems for 2018.
- Revised discussion about when qualified dividends are taxed at 0, 15, or 20 percent based on TCJA changes.
- Modified definition of capital assets to exclude self-created patents, inventions, models or designs, and secret formulas.
- Updated Exhibit 7-3.
- Revised discussion about how taxpayers determine whether capital gains are taxed at 0, 15, or 20 percent.
- Added new key terms: maximum zero rate amount and maximum 15-percent rate amount.
- Added new Exhibit 7-3 to illustrate maximum zero rate amount and maximum 15-percent rate amounts by filing status and income.
- Updated examples for changes in capital gains rate thresholds.
- Clarified footnote 26 to reflect the requirement to add back seven percent of excluded §1202 gain for AMT purposes.
- Substantially revised the method for calculating tax liability on net capital gains and related example 7-9.
- Revised discussion on investment expenses and investment interest expense.
- Updated note on cost basis required to be reported by brokers.
- Added new discussion question regarding sale of passive activity.
- Updated tax forms from 2016 to 2017 forms.

Chapter 8

- Updated tax rate schedules to reflect tax law changes.
- Updated discussion of marriage penalty or benefit for tax law changes.

- Revised discussion of kiddie tax for tax law changes.
- Revised discussion of the tax calculation for preferentially taxed capital gains and dividends for tax law changes.
- Updated AMT discussion for new tax law changes related to adjustments, exemption amounts, and phase-out of exemptions.
- Updated AMT tax rate schedule for 2018.
- Updated Social Security Tax wage base and Self-Employment Tax base for 2018.
- Revised discussion of Medicare and additional Medicare tax.
- Updated discussion of child tax credit for tax law changes.
- Updated Lifetime Learning Credit phase-out for 2018.
- Updated discussion of education credits for expiration of the deduction for qualified education expenses.
- Updated Earned Income Credit amounts for 2018.
- Updated tax forms from 2016 to 2017 forms.
- Revised end of chapter problems for tax law changes.

Chapter 9

- Introduction was updated and the learning objectives were consolidated.
- Revised descriptions of deductions to reflect changes in the Tax Cuts and Jobs Act.
- Revised descriptions of general limitations on business deductions to reflect changes in the Tax Cuts and Jobs Act.
- Added text description and example of new business interest limitation.
- Revised text discussion of limitations on business deductions for meals and entertainment.
- Revised examples to reflect changes in the Tax Cuts and Jobs Act.
- Revised examples and text discussion for updated 2018 mileage rates.
- Added new TIRW to describe application of substantiation rules and the Cohan rule.
- Deleted discussion and illustration of domestic manufacturing deduction eliminated in the Tax Cuts and Jobs Act.
- Revised text description, examples, and Exhibit 9-2 to reflect changes in casualty loss deductions in the Tax Cuts and Jobs Act.
- Revised footnotes and added example of 52-53 week year.
- Revised text descriptions of cash method, UNICAP, and inventory accounting to reflect changes in the Tax Cuts and Jobs Act.
- Revised accounting for advanced payments of revenue to reflect accounting method changes in the Tax Cuts and Jobs Act.

- Revised accounting method changes to reflect new provisions in the Tax Cuts and Jobs Act updated dates in examples.
- Revised Exhibit 9-6 for changes in solutions due to accounting method changes in the Tax Cuts and Jobs Act.
- Eliminated discussion questions on domestic manufacturing deduction and added new discussion questions about business interest limitation.
- Revised discussion questions to reflect accounting method changes in the Tax Cuts and Jobs Act.
- Eliminated problems on domestic manufacturing deduction and added new problems with business interest limitation.
- Revised problems to reflect accounting method changes in the Tax Cuts and Jobs Act.

Chapter 10

- Modified story line to better apply to changes in tax law.
- Updated all examples for new purchase price on Teton's assets.
- Updated Exhibit 10-2 for Weyerhaueser's 2016 assets.
- Updated tax rates for 2018.
- Updated footnote 2 relating to depreciation allowed or allowable.
- Added new footnote to explain the opportunity to expense new roofs post TCJA.
- Added new preface to the depreciation section to explain impact of TCJA and under what conditions MACRS may be relevant.
- Moved the discussion about mid-quarter convention to new Appendix B.
- Added discussion to explain changes to qualified improvement property.
- Revised Example 10-7 (old 10-12) to include depreciation for two years on real property.
- Revised section on §179 amounts to reflect the larger 2018 amounts post-TCJA.
- Added footnote relating to definition of qualified real property for purposes of §179.
- Updated Examples 10-9 through 10-12 (old Examples 10-14 through 10-17) for 2018 §179 amounts.
- Substantially revised bonus depreciation section to include TCJA changes in percentages and qualified property.
- Added new Exhibit 10-8 to illustrate Bonus Depreciation Percentages.
- Added bonus depreciation Example 10-13.
- Revised listed property discussion to reflect removal of computer equipment as listed property.
- Updated discussion and Exhibit 10-9 (old 10-8) relating to automobile depreciation limits.

- Updated examples in listed property section to reflect TCJA changes.
- Added new discussion about the use of §179 for automobiles.
- Added new discussion and examples about the interaction of bonus depreciation and the automobile depreciation limitations. Includes new discussion of method for calculating depreciation on automobiles after year 1 when 100 percent bonus depreciation is taken.
- Added Taxes in the Real World: Cost Segregation.
- Updated Exhibit 10-10 (old 10-9) to reflect Teton's use of bonus depreciation in addition to §179 and MACRS for two years of asset acquisitions.
- Updated tax forms from 2016 to 2017 forms.
- Added new footnote 64 to describe treatment of R&D costs after 2021.
- Updated and revised end-of-chapter problems for §179 amounts and bonus depreciation rules post-TCJA.

Chapter 11

- Modified story line to better apply to changes in tax law
- Updated examples for new purchase price on Teton's assets.
- Updated Exhibit 11-4 for changes to capital gains threshold amounts.
- Added discussion about how changes to depreciation from TCJA might affect dispositions.
- Updated Exhibit 11-6 for changes to Teton's assets.
- Modified discussion on like-kind exchanges to reflect application to real property only.
- Modified Examples 11-15, 11-16, and 11-17 for like-kind exchanges.
- Updated discussion for involuntary conversion when contrasting qualified property to like-kind exchanges.
- Updated like-kind exchange EOC problems.
- Updated tax rates for 2018.
- Updated tax forms from 2016 to 2017 forms.

Chapter 12

- Updated qualified transportation fringe benefit amounts for 2018.
- Updated Section 163(m) limitation on executive compensation.
- Updated 70 percent of examples for change in corporate tax rates.
- Updated tax forms to 2017.
- Inserted new discussion of qualified equity grants.
- Updated Taxes in the Real World for 2017 proxy statement information.
- Updated nontaxable fringe benefit section for changes in qualified moving expenses.

- Updated 50 percent of end of chapter problems for tax law changes.

Chapter 13

- Streamlined wording in Learning Objectives 13-4 and 13-5.
- Changed marginal tax rates in storyline to reflect tax rate brackets effective for 2018.
- Updated footnote 1 to reflect the 2017 OASDI Trustees report.
- Updated inflation adjusted limits for defined benefit plans, defined contribution plans, and individually managed plans.
- Updated Exhibit 13-6 to reflect the most recent proxy statement for Coca-Cola Company.
- Revised discussion of employer issues for deferred compensation to indicate that employers can no longer use deferred compensation to circumvent the $1,000,000 compensation deduction limitation under §162(m).
- Removed old discussion question 31 dealing with deferred compensation and the §162(m) limitation.
- Revised discussion in IRA section to use modified AGI rather than AGI when describing deduction and contribution limitations.
- Updated flowcharts in appendices to reflect modified AGI rather than AGI when describing IRA deduction and contribution limitations.
- Updated modified AGI phase-out thresholds for deductible contributions to traditional IRAs and contributions to Roth IRAs.
- Added discussion question comparing modified AGI and AGI.
- Edited marginal tax rates in problems to reflect tax rate schedule under new tax law.
- Modified Taxes in the Real World relating to Roth and traditional retirement savings vehicles to ask how new tax laws might affect this choice for taxpayers.
- Updated calculations for limits on self-employed retirement accounts to reflect updated 2018 social security wage base limitation.
- Updated Saver's credit information for 2018.
- Added an explanation requirement to Discussion Question 8.

Chapter 14

- Streamlined Learning Objectives 14-2, 14-5, and 14-6.
- Revised LO 14-3 to emphasize home mortgage interest deduction.
- Revised storyline summary information to reflect higher income for taxpayers and new marginal tax rate consistent with 2018 tax rate brackets.
- Streamlined introductory paragraph to the chapter.

- Revised Exhibit 14-1 to eliminate deduction for home mortgage insurance and to eliminate exclusion for forgiveness of debt on home mortgage foreclosure because these items have not been extended to 2017 or 2018 (as of press time).
- Moved discussion of deduction of home mortgage insurance and exclusion for forgiveness of debt on home mortgage to a footnote.
- Included explanation of leverage in second paragraph in Personal Use of the Home section.
- Retitled section on Interest Expense on Home-Related Debt to Home Mortgage Interest Deduction and revised discussion in first paragraph to reflect recent tax law changes affecting mortgage interest deductions.
- Revised discussion of home mortgage interest to reflect new limitation on acquisition indebtedness and to reflect the fact that interest on home equity indebtedness is no longer deductible.
- Removed detailed discussion of determining limitation on deductibility of interest when qualifying debt exceeds the limitation.
- Revised Taxes in the Real World on home interest deductions to reflect the changes in limits to acquisition indebtedness and the elimination of interest deduction for home equity indebtedness.
- Added explanation of refinancing in Points section.
- Revised discussion on real property taxes to reflect $10,000 limitation on the itemized deduction for taxes, including examples and problems.
- Added new Taxes in the Real World emphasizing Airbnb.
- Revised discussion of the IRS method and the Tax Court method to reflect the circumstances in which each is more favorable given the new tax law.
- Clarified discussion about home office expense requirements.
- Revised discussion about home office expenses to indicate that employees can no longer claim the deduction.
- Revised Appendix B to reflect the $10,000 limit on the itemized deduction for taxes.
- Updated tax forms from 2016 to 2017.
- Updated settlement statement in Appendix A to reflect 2018 information.
- Removed five discussion questions/problems that are no longer relevant given new tax law.
- Revised/added 17 discussion questions/problems to reflect new tax law.

Chapter 15

- Clarified the discussion in "Rights, Responsibilities, and Legal Arrangements among Owners."

- Added mention of Certificate of Organization as a required filing to create a new LLC in certain states.
- Updated notes to Exhibit 15-1 to clarify that certain limited partnerships are eligible for IPOs.
- Moved discussion of deduction in Taxes in the Real World on Comparing Entities Selected with more recent data from the IRS.
- Replaced the entire section on Double Taxation with new section on Taxation of Business Entity Income. This section includes discussion of how flow-through entity income is taxed under new law and includes discussion on deduction for qualified business income and discussion of the self-employment tax for business owners.
- Revised discussion of how C corporations are taxed. This section includes discussion of the new tax rate for C corporations, the revised NOL rules, and the new DRD percentages.
- Added a section on owner compensation.
- Added section on deductibility of entity losses to include revised NOL rules for C corporations and the new excess loss limitation for noncorporate taxpayers.
- Updated Taxes in the Real Word: Best Entity Choice for Small Businesses? to reflect findings from a more recent study. Also, added information about the number of small businesses filing as partnerships and as S corporations.
- Revised discussion of Converting to Other Entity Types to reflect changes in the tax law and reasons why owners may wish to convert, given the new law.
- Revised the final discussion in the storyline. The taxpayer now chooses a C corporation rather than a partnership form for tax purposes.
- Revised Ethics discussion to include a situation where owner is potentially paying himself too little compensation.
- Changed or revised approximately 25 percent of the end of chapter problems.

Chapter 16

- Updated the discussion on stock option compensation.
- Revised Taxes in the Real World for Facebook stock options.
- Updated the compliance section for new year-end filing.

Chapter 17

- Updated the Taxes in the Real World saga of Weatherford.
- Updated the material to incorporate the new FASB rules on disclosures of deferred tax assets and liabilities.

- Updated the Microsoft uncertain tax benefit footnote disclosure.
- Updated the FASB's projects involving accounting for income taxes.

Chapter 18

- Recharacterized stock dividends as distributions (throughout the chapter).
- Simplified and streamline the introduction to dividends and corporate distributions.
- Clarified explanation of deductible expense in the calculation of E&P.
- Clarified the introduction into the ordering of E&P distributions.
- Revised the description of noncash distributions to be consistent throughout the chapter.
- Revised E&P calculations and examples for changes in the Tax Cuts and Jobs Act.
- Explained dividend signaling in simpler terms.
- Revised examples for changes in the Tax Cuts and Jobs Act.
- Revised the description of stock dividends.
- Clarified the explanation of stock distributions.
- Clarified and defined *bright line* (objective) tests.
- Elaborated on the strategic purpose of redemptions.
- Added Time Warner redemption as TIRW.
- Eleven problems modified for changes in the Tax Cuts and Jobs Act.

Chapter 19

- Clarified purpose of Section 351 in introduction.
- Clarified some definitions and terms in the introduction.
- Revised description of contributions to capital for changes in the Tax Cuts and Jobs Act.
- Minor revisions to text under learning objective 3.
- Added two new TIRWs. One illustrates a 338(h)(10) election with a tax receivable and the other is new example of corporate tax-free acquisition.
- Revised Forward Triangular Type A merger description to state rule then example.
- Revised Triangular Type A merger description to state rule then example.
- Revised Type B acquisition description to state rule then example.
- Revised examples for changes in the Tax Cuts and Jobs Act.
- Revised 8 discussion questions.
- Clarified several questions and added two new acquisition research questions.
- Three problems revised to reflect changes in the Tax Cuts and Jobs Act.

Chapter 20

- Updated the discussion of self-employment income from partnerships to include the impact of recent case law.
- Revised the opening storyline of the chapter. The chapter assumes the taxpayer chooses to operate the business as a partnership for tax purposes.
- Added discussion on the new rule dealing with the availability of the cash method of accounting for partnerships.
- Added discussion on the new limitation on business interest deductions in the partnerships setting.
- Added discussion on new deduction for qualified business income.
- Added discussion on new excess business loss limitation and how it interacts with other loss limitation rules.
- Updated tax forms from 2016 to 2017 forms.
- Added material related to how the passive activity loss rules apply to publicly traded partnerships.
- Revised four problems to reflect changes in the Tax Cut and Jobs Act.

Chapter 21

- Clarified the approach for making a §754 election.
- Revised the definition of substantial built-in loss to reflect changes in the Tax Cut and Jobs Act.

Chapter 22

- Revised discussion of debt basis rules.
- Added discussion of 30 percent of taxable income limitation on the deduction for business interest expense under new tax law.
- Added discussion of deduction for qualified business income under new tax law.
- Added discussion of excess business loss limitation under new tax law.
- Added discussion of new PTTP distributions for eligible terminated S corporations under new tax law.
- Updated Social Security Tax wage base for 2018.
- Updated tax forms from 2016 to 2017 forms.
- Revised end of chapter problems for tax law changes.

Chapter 23

- Updated Amazon sales tax collection information.
- Updated federal/state adjustments for income taxes.

Chapter 24

- Updated the discussion on the OECD base erosion and profit-shifting project.
- Updated the proposals for international tax reform.
- Updated the discussion on inversions.

Chapter 25

- Revised Exhibit 25-2 and description of common features of the transfer taxes to reflect changes in the Tax Cuts and Jobs Act.
- Revised calculations, text descriptions, and examples to reflect changes in the Tax Cuts and Jobs Act.
- Replaced Exhibit 25-5 with 2017 Form 709.
- Revised calculations, text descriptions, and examples to reflect changes in the Tax Cuts and Jobs Act.
- Replaced Exhibit 25-8 with 2018 Form 706.
- Revised examples for changes in the Tax Cuts and Jobs Act.
- Revised 4 discussion questions and 23 problems to reflect changes in the Tax Cuts and Jobs Act.

NEW! Resources for 2017 Tax Cuts and Jobs Act—Available in 2018© and 2019©

- Brief Explainer Videos—Offers insights to students into new tax laws by comparing and contrasting with old tax code.
- Chapter Overviews—Identifies the tax law changes for each learning objective.
- Individual Chapter Guides—Provides summary description of new tax laws, expanding on the chapter overview.
- Problem Map—Marks the end-of-chapter content and test bank content affected by new tax laws in an easily navigable spreadsheet.
- Tagged Content in Connect—Added metadata tags to help instructors filter for end-of-chapter/test bank content impacted by 2017 tax reform.
- PowerPoints on Tax Changes—New slides detailing the updated laws on a chapter-by-chapter basis.
- Ongoing Author Webinars and Teaching Tips

As We Go to Press

The 2019 Edition is current through March, 2018. You can visit the *Connect Library* for updates that occur after this date.

Table of Contents

4 Individual Income Tax Overview, Dependents, and Filing Status

5 Gross Income and Exclusions

11   Property Dispositions

12   Compensation

13 Retirement Savings and Deferred Compensation

14 Tax Consequences of Home Ownership

15 Entities Overview

18   Corporate Taxation: Nonliquidating Distributions

19   Corporate Formation, Reorganization, and Liquidation

McGraw-Hill's

Taxation of Individuals and Business Entities

1 An Introduction to Tax

Learning Objectives

Upon completing this chapter, you should be able to:

LO 1-1 Demonstrate how taxes influence basic business, investment, personal, and political decisions.

LO 1-2 Discuss what constitutes a tax and the general objectives of taxes.

LO 1-3 Describe the different tax rate structures and calculate a tax.

LO 1-4 Identify the various federal, state, and local taxes.

LO 1-5 Apply appropriate criteria to evaluate alternative tax systems.

©Andrew Rich/Getty Images

Storyline Summary

Taxpayer: Margaret

Employment status: Margaret is a full-time student at the University of Georgia.

Current situation: She is beginning her first tax class.

Margaret is a junior beginning her first tax course. She is excited about her career prospects as an accounting major but hasn't had much exposure to taxes. On her way to campus she runs into an old friend, Eddy, who is going to Washington, D.C., to protest recent proposed changes to the U.S. tax system. Eddy is convinced the IRS is evil and that the current tax system is blatantly unfair and corrupt. He advocates a simpler, fairer way of taxation. Margaret is intrigued by Eddy's passion but questions whether he has a complete understanding of the U.S. tax system. She decides to withhold all judgments about it (or about pursuing a career in taxation) until the end of her tax course. ∎

LO 1-1   WHO CARES ABOUT TAXES AND WHY?

A clear understanding of the role of taxes in everyday decisions will help you make an informed decision about the value of studying taxation or pursuing a career in taxation. One view of taxation is that it represents an inconvenience every April 15th (the annual due date for filing federal individual tax returns without extensions). However, the role of taxation is much more pervasive than this view suggests. Your study of this subject will provide you a unique opportunity to develop an informed opinion about taxation. As a business student, you can overcome the mystery that encompasses popular impressions of the tax system and perhaps, one day, share your expertise with friends or clients.

What are some common decisions you face that taxes may influence? In this course, we alert you to situations in which you can increase your return on investments by up to one-third! Even the best lessons in finance courses can't approach the increase in risk-adjusted return that smart tax planning provides. Would you like to own your home someday? Tax deductions for home mortgage interest and real estate taxes can reduce the after-tax costs of owning a home relative to renting. Thus, when you face the decision to buy or rent, you can make an informed choice if you understand the relative tax advantages of home ownership. Would you like to retire someday? Understanding the tax-advantaged methods of saving for retirement can increase the after-tax value of your retirement nest egg—and thus increase the likelihood that you can afford to retire, and do so in style. Other common personal financial decisions that taxes influence include: choosing investments, evaluating alternative job offers, saving for education expenses, and doing gift or estate planning. Indeed, taxes are a part of everyday life and have a significant effect on many of the personal financial decisions all of us face.

The role of taxes is not limited to personal finance. Taxes play an equally important role in fundamental business decisions such as the following:

- What organizational form should a business use?
- Where should the business locate?
- How should business acquisitions be structured?
- How should the business compensate employees?
- What is the appropriate mix of debt and equity for the business?
- Should the business rent or own its equipment and property?
- How should the business distribute profits to its owners?

Savvy business decisions require owners and managers to consider all costs and benefits in order to evaluate the merits of a transaction. Although taxes don't necessarily dominate these decisions, they do represent large transaction costs that businesses should factor into the financial decision-making process.

Taxes also play a major part in the political process. U.S. presidential candidates often distinguish themselves from their opponents based upon their tax rhetoric. Indeed, the major political parties generally have very diverse views of the appropriate way to tax the public.[1] Determining who is taxed, what is taxed, and how much is taxed are tough questions with nontrivial answers. Voters must have a basic understanding of taxes to evaluate the merits of alternative tax proposals. Later in this chapter, we'll introduce criteria you can use to evaluate alternative tax proposals.

---

[1]The U.S. Department of the Treasury provides a "history of taxation" on its website (www.treasury.gov/resource-center/faqs/Taxes/Pages/historyrooseveltmessage.aspx). You may find it interesting to read this history in light of the various political parties in office at the time.

TAXES IN THE REAL WORLD　Tax Policy: Republicans versus Democrats

Oliver Wendell Holmes said "taxes are the price we pay to live in a civilized society." Both Democrats and Republicans desire the same things: a civilized society and a healthy economy. However, neither party can agree on what defines a civilized society or which path best leads to a healthy economy. The U.S. national debt is $20 trillion dollars and growing, yet the only thing we might agree on is that something has gone wrong. Regardless of which party or candidate you support, each party's agenda will affect your income and taxes in various ways.

To explore the divide, let's examine excerpts from each party's National Platform from our most recent presidential election (2016).

Republicans

"We are the party of a growing economy that gives everyone a chance in life, an opportunity to learn, work, and realize the prosperity freedom makes possible."

"Government cannot create prosperity, though government can limit or destroy it. Prosperity is the product of self-discipline, enterprise, saving and investment by individuals, but it is not an end in itself. Prosperity provides the means by which citizens and their families can maintain their independence from government, raise their children by their own values, practice their faith, and build communities of cooperation and mutual respect."

"Republicans consider the establishment of a pro growth tax code a moral imperative. More than any other public policy, the way government raises revenue—how much, at what rates, under what circumstances, from whom, and for whom—has the greatest impact on our economy's performance. It powerfully influences the level of economic growth and job creation, which translates into the level of opportunity for those who would otherwise be left behind."

"A strong economy is one key to debt reduction, but spending restraint is a necessary component that must be vigorously pursued." https://www.gop.com/platform/restoring-the-american-dream/

Democrats

"At a time of massive income and wealth inequality, we believe the wealthiest Americans and largest corporations must pay their fair share of taxes. Democrats will claw back tax breaks for companies that ship jobs overseas, eliminate tax breaks for big oil and gas companies, and crack down on inversions and other methods companies use to dodge their tax responsibilities . . . We will then use the revenue raised from fixing the corporate tax code to reinvest in rebuilding America and ensuring economic growth that will lead to millions of good-paying jobs."

"We will ensure those at the top contribute to our country's future by establishing a multimillionaire surtax to ensure millionaires and billionaires pay their fair share. In addition, we will shut down the "private tax system" for those at the top, immediately close egregious loopholes like those enjoyed by hedge fund managers, restore fair taxation on multimillion dollar estates, and ensure millionaires can no longer pay a lower rate than their secretaries. At a time of near-record corporate profits, slow wage growth, and rising costs, we need to offer tax relief to middle-class families—not those at the top."

"We will offer tax relief to hard working, middle-class families for the cost squeeze they have faced for years from rising health care, childcare, education, and other expenses." https://www.democrats.org/party-platform#preamble

Conclusion

Each party fundamentally believes the government should create/maintain cities and states that form a civilized society, and that government should foster a healthy economy. However, they choose very different paths to reach this objective. Democrats want to raise taxes on the wealthy and create government programs which cost more money, while Republicans wish to lower taxes and decrease government size and spending. Both motives are pure; however, current and cumulative deficits indicate that current revenue is insufficient to meet government spending. Solving these problems will require civil discourse, education and research/information in order to find realistic, effective solutions.

Republicans: https://www.gop.com/platform/restoring-the-american-dream/
Democrats: https://www.democrats.org/party-platform#preamble

In summary, taxes affect many aspects of personal, business, and political decisions. Developing a solid understanding of taxation should allow you to make informed decisions in these areas. Thus, Margaret can take comfort that her semester will likely prove useful to her personally. Who knows? Depending on her interest in business, investment, retirement planning, and the like, she may ultimately decide to pursue a career in taxation.

LO 1-2 # WHAT QUALIFIES AS A TAX?

"Taxes are the price we pay for a civilized society." —Oliver Wendell Holmes, Jr.

Taxes have been described in many terms: some positive, some negative, some printable, some not. Let's go directly to a formal definition of a tax, which should prove useful in identifying alternative taxes and discussing alternative tax systems.

A **tax** *is a payment required by a government that is unrelated to any specific benefit or service received from the government.* The general purpose of a tax is to fund the operations of the government (to raise revenue). Taxes differ from fines and penalties in that taxes are not intended to punish or prevent illegal behavior. Nonetheless, by allowing deductions from income, our federal tax system does encourage certain behaviors like charitable contributions, retirement savings, and research and development. Thus, we can view it as discouraging other legal behavior. For example, **sin taxes** impose relatively high surcharges on alcohol and tobacco products.[2] Cigarette taxes include a $1.01 per pack federal tax, a state tax in all 50 states, and also a few municipal taxes as well.[3]

Key components of the definition of a tax are that the payment is:

- Required (it is not voluntary);
- Imposed by a government agency (federal, state, or local); and
- Not tied directly to the benefit received by the taxpayer.

This last point is not to say that taxpayers receive no benefits from the taxes they pay. They benefit from national defense, a judicial system, law enforcement, government-sponsored social programs, an interstate highway system, public schools, and many other government-provided programs and services. The distinction is that taxes paid are not *directly* related to any specific benefit received by the taxpayer. For example, the price of admission to Yellowstone National Park is a fee rather than a tax because a specific benefit is received.

Can taxes be assessed for special purposes, such as a 1 percent sales tax for education? Yes. Why is an **earmarked tax,** a tax that *is* assessed for a specific purpose, still considered a tax? Because the payment made by the taxpayer does not directly relate to the specific benefit *received by the taxpayer.*

Example 1-1

Margaret travels to Birmingham, Alabama, where she rents a hotel room and dines at several restaurants. The price she pays for her hotel room and meals includes an additional 2 percent city surcharge to fund roadway construction in Birmingham. Is this a tax?

Answer: Yes. The payment is required by a local government and does not directly relate to a specific benefit that Margaret receives.

Example 1-2

Margaret's parents, Bill and Mercedes, recently built a house and were assessed $1,000 by their county government to connect to the county sewer system. Is this a tax?

Answer: No. The assessment was mandatory and it was paid to a local government. However, the third criterion was not met since the payment directly relates to a specific benefit (sewer service) received by the payees. For the same reason, tolls, parking meter fees, and annual licensing fees are also not considered taxes.

[2]Sin taxes represent an interesting confluence of incentives. On the one hand, demand for such products as alcohol, tobacco, and gambling is often relatively inelastic because of their addictive quality. Thus, taxing such a product can raise substantial revenues. On the other hand, one of the arguments for sin taxes is frequently the social goal of *reducing* demand for such products.

[3]Federal excise taxes on cigarettes are found in §5701(b). State taxes are as much as $4.35 per pack in New York, Anchorage, New York City, and Chicago impose municipal taxes as well.

HOW TO CALCULATE A TAX

`LO 1-3`

In its simplest form, the amount of tax equals the tax base multiplied by the tax rate:

Eq. 1-1 Tax = Tax Base × Tax Rate

The **tax base** defines what is actually taxed and is usually expressed in monetary terms, whereas the **tax rate** determines the level of taxes imposed on the tax base and is usually expressed as a percentage. For example, a sales tax rate of 6 percent on a purchase of $30 yields a tax of $1.80 ($1.80 = $30 × .06).

Federal, state, and local jurisdictions use a large variety of tax bases to collect tax. Some common tax bases (and related taxes) include taxable income (federal and state income taxes), purchases (sales tax), real estate values (real estate tax), and personal property values (personal property tax).

Different portions of a tax base may be taxed at different rates. A single tax applied to an entire base constitutes a **flat tax.** In the case of **graduated taxes,** the base is divided into a series of monetary amounts, or **brackets,** and each successive bracket is taxed at a different (gradually higher or gradually lower) percentage rate.

Calculating some taxes—income taxes for individuals or corporations, for example—can be quite complex. Advocates of flat taxes argue that the process should be simpler. But as we'll see throughout the text, most of the difficulty in calculating a tax rests in determining the tax *base*, not the tax rate. Indeed, there are only three basic tax rate structures (proportional, progressive, and regressive), and each can be mastered without much difficulty.

> **THE KEY FACTS**
> **How to Calculate a Tax**
> - Tax = Tax base × Tax rate
> - The tax base defines what is actually taxed and is usually expressed in monetary terms.
> - The tax rate determines the level of taxes imposed on the tax base and is usually expressed as a percentage.
> - Different portions of a tax base may be taxed at different rates.

DIFFERENT WAYS TO MEASURE TAX RATES

Before we discuss the alternative tax rate structures, let's first define three different tax rates that will be useful in contrasting the different tax rate structures: the marginal, average, and effective tax rates.

The **marginal tax rate** is the tax rate that applies to the *next additional increment* of a taxpayer's taxable income (or deductions). Specifically,

Eq. 1-2
$$\text{Marginal Tax Rate} = \frac{\Delta \text{Tax*}}{\Delta \text{Taxable Income}} = \frac{(\text{New Total Tax} - \text{Old Total Tax})}{(\text{New Taxable Income} - \text{Old Taxable Income})}$$
*Δ means *change in.*

where "old" refers to the current tax and "new" refers to the revised tax after incorporating the additional income (or deductions) in question. In graduated income tax systems, additional income (deductions) can push a taxpayer into a higher (lower) tax bracket, thus changing the marginal tax rate.

Example 1-3

Margaret's parents, Bill and Mercedes, file a joint tax return. They have $160,000 of taxable income this year (after all tax deductions). Assuming the following federal tax rate schedule applies, how much federal income tax will they owe this year?[4]

(continued on page 1-6)

[4]The tax rate schedules for single, married filing jointly, married filing separately, and head of household are included in Appendix D.

Married Filing Jointly (and Surviving Spouses)

Not over $19,050	10% of taxable income
$19,050 to $77,400	$1,905 + 12% of taxable income in excess of $19,050
$77,400 to $165,000	$8,907 + 22% of taxable income in excess of $77,400
$165,000 to $315,000	$28,179 + 24% of taxable income in excess of $165,000
$315,000 to $400,000	$64,179 + 32% of taxable income in excess of $315,000
$400,000 to $600,000	$91,379 + 35% of taxable income in excess of $400,000
Over $600,000	$161,379 + 37% of taxable income in excess of $600,000

Answer: Bill and Mercedes will owe $27,079 computed as follows:

$$\$27,079 = \$8,907 + 22\%(\$160,000 - \$77,400)$$

Note that in this graduated tax rate structure, the first $19,050 of taxable income is taxed at 10 percent, the next $58,350 of taxable income (between $19,050 and $77,400) is taxed at 12 percent, and Bill and Mercedes's last $82,600 of taxable income (between $77,400 and $160,000) is taxed at 22 percent.

Many taxpayers incorrectly believe that all their income is taxed at their marginal rate. This mistake leads people to say, "I don't want to earn any additional money because it will put me in a higher tax bracket." Bill and Mercedes are currently in the 22 percent marginal tax rate bracket, but notice that not all their income is taxed at this rate. Their *marginal* tax rate is 22 percent. This means that small increases in income will be taxed at 22 percent, and small increases in tax deductions will generate tax *savings* of 22 percent. If Bill and Mercedes receive a large increase in income (or in deductions) such that they change tax rate brackets, we could not identify their marginal tax rate simply by knowing their current tax bracket.

Example 1-4

Bill, a well-known economics professor, signs a publishing contract with an $80,000 royalty advance. Using the rate schedule from Example 1-3, what would Bill and Mercedes's marginal tax rate be on this additional $80,000 of taxable income?

Answer: 23.88 percent, computed as follows:

Description	Amount	Explanation
(1) Taxable income with additional $80,000 of taxable income	$240,000.00	$80,000 plus $160,000 taxable income (Example 1-3)
(2) Tax on $240,000 taxable income	$ 46,179.00	Using the rate schedule in Example 1-3, $46,179 = $28,179 + 24% ($240,000 − $165,000)

Description	Amount	Explanation
(3) Taxable income before additional $80,000 of taxable income	$160,000.00	Example 1-3
(4) Tax on $160,000 taxable income	$ 27,079.00	Example 1-3
Marginal tax rate on additional $80,000 of taxable income	**23.88%**	$\dfrac{\Delta \text{Tax}}{\Delta \text{Taxable income}} = [(2) - (4)]/[(1) - (3)]$

Note that Bill and Mercedes's marginal tax rate on the $80,000 increase in taxable income rests *between* the 22 percent and 24 percent bracket rates because a portion of the additional income ($165,000 − $160,000 = $5,000) is taxed at 22 percent, with the remaining income ($240,000 − $165,000 = $75,000) taxed at 24 percent.

Example 1-5

Assume now that, instead of receiving a book advance, Bill and Mercedes start a new business that *loses* $90,000 this year (it results in $90,000 of additional tax deductions). What would be their marginal tax rate for these deductions?

Answer: 21.18 percent, computed as follows:

Description	Amount	Explanation
(1) Taxable income with additional $90,000 of tax deductions	$70,000	$160,000 taxable income (Example 1-3) less $90,000
(2) Tax on $90,000 taxable income	$ 8,019	Using the rate schedule in Example 1-3, $8,019 = $1,905 + 12% × ($70,000 − $19,050)
(3) Taxable income before additional $90,000 of tax deductions	$70,000	Example 1-3
(4) Tax on $70,000 taxable income	$27,079	Example 1-3
Marginal tax rate on additional $60,000 of tax deductions	**21.18%**	$\dfrac{\Delta \text{Tax}}{\Delta \text{Taxable income}} = [(2)-(4)]/[(1)-(3)]$

Bill and Mercedes's marginal tax rate on $90,000 of additional deductions (21.18 percent) differs from their marginal tax rate on $80,000 of additional taxable income (23.88 percent) in these scenarios because the relatively large increase in deductions in Example 1-5 causes some of their income to be taxed in a lower tax rate bracket, while the relatively large increase in income in Example 1-4 causes some of their income to be taxed in a higher tax rate bracket. Taxpayers often will face the same marginal tax rates for small changes in income and deductions.

The marginal tax rate is particularly useful in tax planning because it represents the rate of taxation or savings that would apply to additional taxable income (or tax deductions). In the Tax Planning Strategies and Related Limitations chapter, we discuss basic tax planning strategies that use the marginal tax rate.

The **average tax rate** represents a taxpayer's average level of taxation on each dollar of taxable income. Specifically,

Eq. 1-3

$$\text{Average Tax Rate} = \frac{\text{Total Tax}}{\text{Taxable Income}}$$

The average tax rate is often used in budgeting tax expense as a portion of income (i.e., determining what percent of taxable income earned is paid in tax).

The **effective tax rate** represents the taxpayer's average rate of taxation on each dollar of total income (sometimes referred to as economic income), including taxable *and* nontaxable income. Specifically,

Eq. 1-4

$$\text{Effective Tax Rate} = \frac{\text{Total Tax}}{\text{Total Income}}$$

Relative to the average tax rate, the effective tax rate provides a better depiction of a taxpayer's tax burden because it gives the taxpayer's total tax paid as a ratio of the sum of both taxable and nontaxable income earned.

THE KEY FACTS

Different Ways to Measure Tax Rates

- Marginal tax rate
  - The tax that applies to the next increment of income or deduction.
  - $= \dfrac{\Delta \text{Tax}}{\Delta \text{Taxable income}}$
  - Useful in tax planning.
- Average tax rate
  - A taxpayer's average level of taxation on each dollar of *taxable* income.
  - $= \dfrac{\text{Total tax}}{\text{Taxable income}}$
  - Useful in budgeting tax expense.
- Effective tax rate
  - A taxpayer's average rate of taxation on each dollar of *total* income (taxable *and* nontaxable income).
  - $= \dfrac{\text{Total tax}}{\text{Total income}}$
  - Useful in comparing the relative tax burdens of taxpayers.

Example 1-6

Assuming Bill and Mercedes have $160,000 of taxable income and $10,000 of nontaxable income, what is their average tax rate?

Answer: 16.92 percent, computed as follows:

Description	Amount	Explanation
(1) Taxable income	$160,000.00	
(2) Tax on $160,000 taxable income	$ 27,079.00	Example 1-3
Average tax rate	**16.92%**	$\dfrac{\text{Total tax}}{\text{Taxable income}} = (2)/(1)$

We should not be surprised that Bill and Mercedes's average tax rate is lower than their marginal tax rate because, although they are currently in the 22 percent tax rate bracket, not all of their taxable income is subject to tax at 22 percent. The first $19,050 of their taxable income is taxed at 10 percent, their next $58,350 is taxed at 12 percent, and only their last $82,000 of taxable income is taxed at 22 percent. Thus, their average tax rate is considerably lower than their marginal tax rate.

Example 1-7

Again, given the same income figures as in Example 1-6 ($160,000 of taxable income and $10,000 of nontaxable income), what is Bill and Mercedes's effective tax rate?

Answer: 15.93 percent, computed as follows:

Description	Amount	Explanation
(1) Total income	$170,000.00	$160,000 taxable income plus $10,000 in nontaxable income (Example 1-6)
(2) Tax on $160,000 taxable income	$ 27,079.00	Example 1-3
Effective tax rate	**15.93%**	$\dfrac{\text{Total tax}}{\text{Total income}} = (2)/(1)$

Should we be surprised that the effective tax rate is lower than the *average* tax rate? No, because except when the taxpayer has more nondeductible expenses (such as fines or penalties) than nontaxable income (such as tax-exempt interest), the effective tax rate will be equal to or less than the average tax rate.

TAX RATE STRUCTURES

There are three basic tax rate structures used to determine a tax: proportional, progressive, and regressive.

Proportional Tax Rate Structure

A **proportional tax rate structure,** also known as a flat tax, imposes a constant tax rate throughout the tax base. As the tax base increases, the taxes paid increase proportionally. Because this rate stays the same throughout all levels of the tax base, the marginal tax rate remains constant and, in fact, equals the average tax rate (see Exhibit 1-1). The new corporate tax rate, which is a constant rate of 21 percent, is an example of flat tax.

To calculate the tax owed for a proportional tax, simply use Equation 1-1 to multiply the tax base by the tax rate.

Eq. 1-5 $\text{Proportional tax} = \text{Tax base} \times \text{Tax rate}$

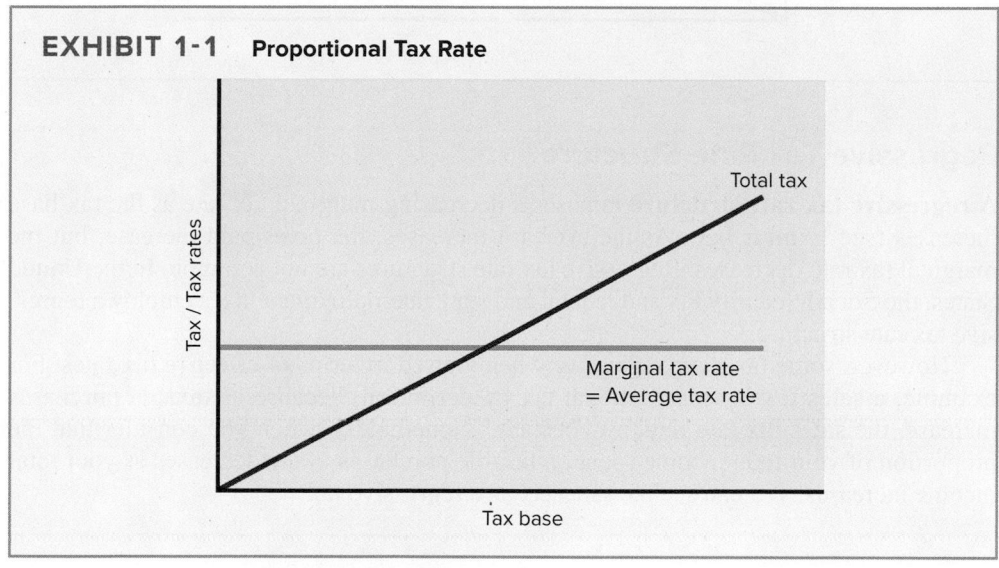

EXHIBIT 1-1 **Proportional Tax Rate**

Example 1-8

Knowing her dad is a serious Bulldog fan, Margaret buys a $100 sweatshirt in downtown Athens. The city of Athens imposes a sales tax rate of 7 percent. How much tax does Margaret pay on the purchase?

Answer: $100 purchase (tax base) × 7% (tax rate) = $7

Progressive Tax Rate Structure

A **progressive tax rate structure** imposes an increasing marginal tax rate as the tax base increases. Thus as the tax base increases, both the marginal tax rate and the taxes paid increase. Common examples of progressive tax rate structures include federal and most state income taxes. The tax rate schedule in Example 1-3 is a progressive tax rate structure. As illustrated in Exhibit 1-2, the average tax rate in a progressive tax rate structure will always be less than or equal to the marginal tax rate.

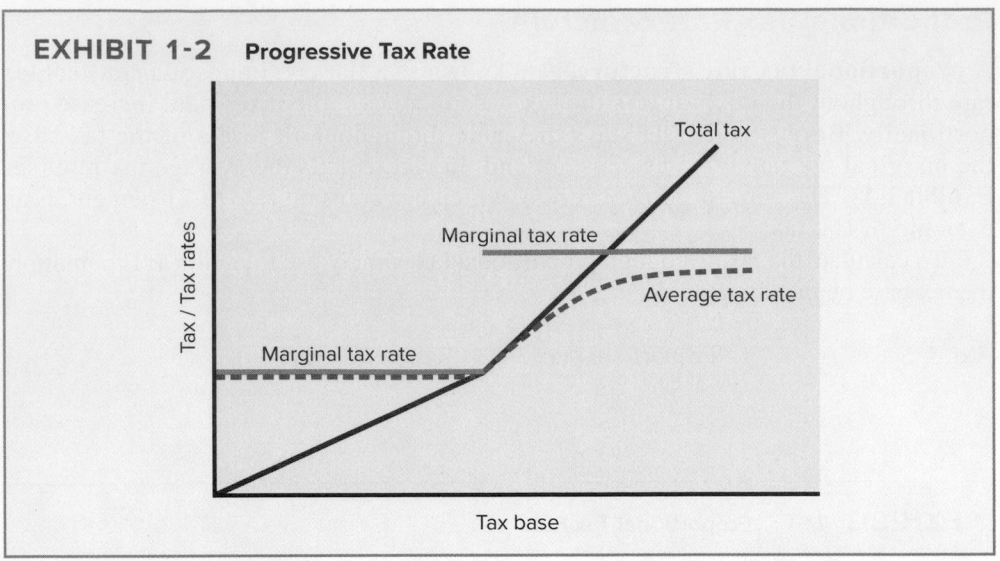

EXHIBIT 1-2   Progressive Tax Rate

Regressive Tax Rate Structure

A **regressive tax rate structure** imposes a decreasing marginal tax rate as the tax base increases (see Exhibit 1-3). As the tax base increases, the taxes paid increase, but the marginal tax rate decreases. Regressive tax rate structures are not common. In the United States, the Social Security tax and federal and state unemployment taxes employ a regressive tax rate structure.[5]

However, some taxes are regressive when viewed in terms of effective tax rates. For example, a sales tax is a proportional tax by definition, because as taxable purchases increase, the sales tax rate remains constant.[6] Nonetheless, when you consider that the proportion of your total income spent on taxable purchases likely decreases as your total income increases, you can see the sales tax as a regressive tax.

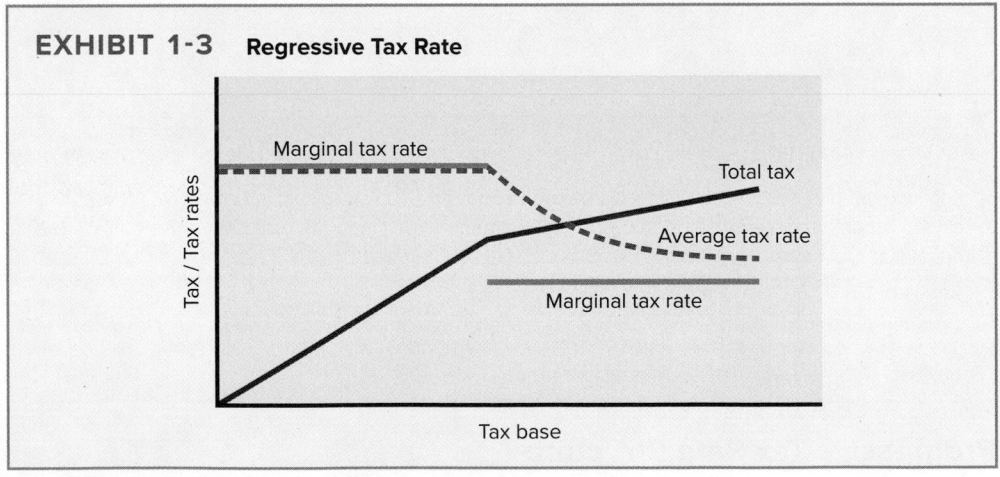

EXHIBIT 1-3   Regressive Tax Rate

[5]Wages subject to the Social Security tax (6.2 percent in 2018) are capped each year ($135,200 in 2018). Wages in excess of the cap are not subject to the tax. As might be expected, the maximum Social Security retirement benefit is capped as a function of the maximum wage base. Likewise, the federal and state unemployment tax bases and related unemployment benefits are capped.

[6]For example, a destitute taxpayer likely spends all he makes on food and other items subject to the sales tax; thus, all of his income is subject to a sales tax. In contrast, a wealthy taxpayer likely spends only a small fraction of his income on items subject to sales tax (while saving the rest). Thus, less of wealthy taxpayers' total income is subject to the sales tax, which ultimately results in a lower effective tax rate.

Example 1-9

Bill and Mercedes have two single friends, Elizabeth and Marc, over for dinner. Elizabeth earns $300,000 as CFO of a company and spends $70,000 on purchases subject to the 7 percent sales tax. Marc, who earns $75,000 as a real estate agent, spends $30,000 of his income on taxable purchases. Let's compare their marginal, average, and effective tax rates for the sales tax with those of Bill and Mercedes, who spend $50,000 of their income on taxable purchases:

	Elizabeth	Bill and Mercedes	Marc
(1) Total income	$300,000	$ 170,000	$ 75,000
(2) Total purchases subject to 7% sales tax	$ 70,000	$ 50,000	$ 30,000
(3) Sales tax paid	$ 4,900	$ 3,500	$ 2,100
Marginal tax rate	7.0%	7.0%	7.0%
Average tax rate (3)/(2)	7%	7%	7%
Effective tax rate (3)/(1)	1.6%	2.1%	2.8%

Is the sales tax regressive?

Answer: Yes. In terms of *effective* tax rates, the sales tax is regressive.

THE KEY FACTS
Tax Rate Structures

- A proportional tax rate structure
  - Imposes a constant tax rate throughout the tax base.
  - As a taxpayer's tax base increases, the taxpayer's taxes increase proportionally.
  - The marginal tax rate remains constant and always equals the average tax rate.
- A progressive tax rate structure
  - Imposes an increasing marginal tax rate as the tax base increases.
  - As a taxpayer's tax base increases, both the marginal tax rate and the taxes paid increase.
- A regressive tax rate structure
  - Imposes a decreasing marginal tax rate as the tax base increases.
  - As a taxpayer's tax base increases, the marginal tax rate decreases while the total taxes paid increases.

When we consider the marginal and average tax rates in Example 1-9, the sales tax has a proportional tax rate structure. But when we look at the *effective* tax rates, the sales tax is a regressive tax. Indeed, Marc, who has the smallest total income, bears the highest effective tax rate, despite all three taxpayers being subject to the same marginal and average tax rates. Why do we see such a different picture when considering the effective tax rate? Because unlike the marginal and average tax rates, the effective tax rate captures the *incidence* of taxation, which relates to the ultimate economic burden of a tax. Thus, a comparison of effective tax rates is more informative about taxpayers' relative tax burdens.

TYPES OF TAXES

LO 1-4

"You can't live with 'em. You can't live without 'em." This statement has often been used in reference to bosses, parents, spouses, and significant others. To some degree, it applies equally as well to taxes. Although we all benefit in multiple ways from tax revenues, and all civilized nations impose them, it would be hard to find someone who *enjoys* paying them. Most people don't object to the idea of paying taxes. Instead, it's the way taxes are levied that many people, like Margaret's friend Eddy, dislike. Hence, the search for the "perfect" tax can be elusive. The following paragraphs describe the major types of taxes currently used by federal, state, and local governments. After this discussion, we describe the criteria for evaluating alternative tax systems.

Federal Taxes

The federal government imposes a variety of taxes to fund federal programs such as national defense, Social Security, an interstate highway system, educational programs, and Medicare. Major federal taxes include the individual and corporate income taxes, employment taxes, estate and gift taxes, and excise taxes (each discussed in detail in the following paragraphs). Notably absent from this list are sales tax (a common tax levied by most state and local governments) and **value-added tax** (a type of sales tax also referred to as a VAT). Value-added taxes are imposed on the producers of goods and services

---

THE KEY FACTS
Federal Taxes

- Income tax
  - The most significant tax assessed by the U.S. government.
  - Represents approximately 60 percent (combined corporate and individual) of all tax revenues collected in the United States.
  - Levied on individuals, corporations, estates, and trusts.
- Employment and unemployment taxes
  - Second-largest group of taxes imposed by the U.S. government.

(continued)

- Employment taxes consist of the Old Age, Survivors, and Disability Insurance (OASDI) tax, commonly called the Social Security tax, and the Medical Health Insurance (MHI) tax, also known as the Medicare tax.
- Unemployment taxes fund temporary unemployment benefits for individuals terminated from their jobs without cause.
- Excise taxes
  - Third-largest group of taxes imposed by the U.S. government.
  - Levied on the *quantity* of products sold.
- Transfer taxes
  - Levied on the fair-market values of wealth transfers upon death or by gift.

based on the value added to the goods and services at each stage of production. They are quite common in Europe.

Income Tax　The most significant tax assessed by the U.S. government is the individual **income tax,** representing approximately 47.3 percent of all tax revenues collected in the United States in 2016. Despite the magnitude and importance of the federal income tax, its history is relatively short. Congress enacted the first U.S. personal income tax in 1861 to help fund the Civil War. This relatively minor tax (with a maximum tax rate of 5 percent) was allowed to expire in 1872. In 1892, Congress resurrected the income tax, but not without dissension among the states. In 1895, the income tax was challenged in *Pollock v. Farmers' Loan and Trust Company,* 157 U.S. 429 (1895). The U.S. Supreme Court ruled that the income tax was unconstitutional because direct taxes were prohibited by the Constitution unless the taxes were apportioned across states based upon their populations. This ruling, however, did not deter Congress. In July 1909, Congress sent a proposed constitutional amendment to the states to remove any doubt as to whether income taxes were allowed by the Constitution—and in February 1913, the 16th Amendment was ratified.

　Congress then enacted the Revenue Act of 1913, which included a graduated income tax structure with a maximum rate of 6 percent. The income tax has been an important source of tax revenues for the U.S. government ever since. Today, income taxes are levied on individuals (maximum rate of 37 percent), corporations (flat rate of 21 percent), estates (maximum rate of 37 percent), and trusts (maximum rate of 37 percent). Higher income taxpayers must also pay a 3.8 percent tax on their net investment income. As Exhibit 1-4 illustrates, the individual income tax and employment taxes represent the largest sources of federal tax revenues. We discuss each of these taxes in greater detail later in the text.

Employment and Unemployment Taxes　Employment and unemployment taxes are the second-largest group of taxes imposed by the U.S. government. **Employment taxes** consist of the Old Age, Survivors, and Disability Insurance (OASDI) tax, commonly called the Social Security tax, and the Medical Health Insurance (MHI) tax, known as the Medicare tax. The **Social Security tax** pays the monthly retirement, survivor, and disability benefits for qualifying individuals, whereas the **Medicare tax** pays for medical insurance for individuals who are elderly or disabled. The tax base for the Social Security

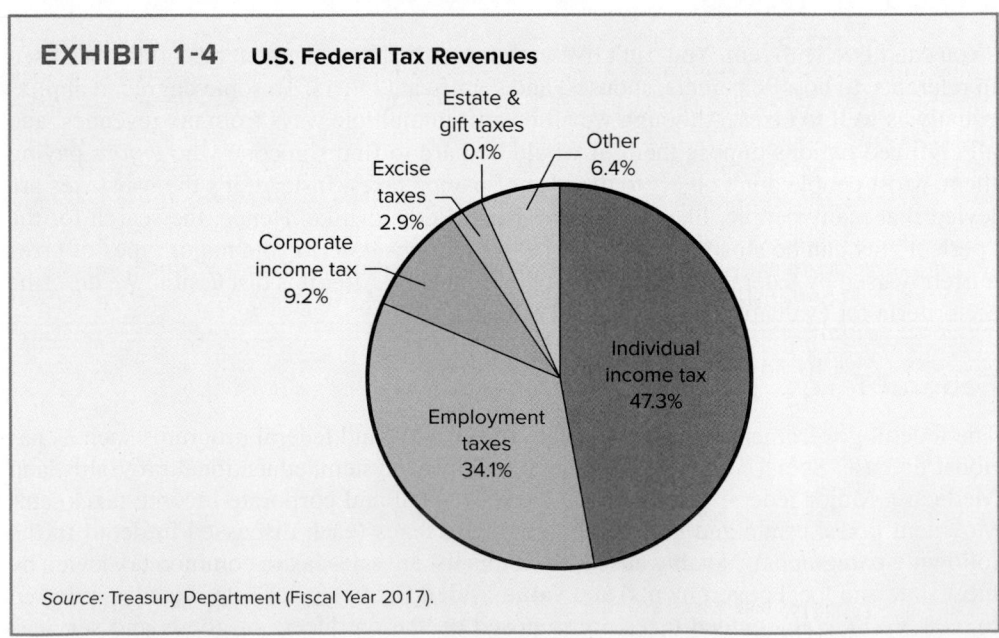

EXHIBIT 1-4　**U.S. Federal Tax Revenues**

Estate & gift taxes 0.1%

Other 6.4%

Excise taxes 2.9%

Corporate income tax 9.2%

Individual income tax 47.3%

Employment taxes 34.1%

Source: Treasury Department (Fiscal Year 2017).

and Medicare taxes is wages or salary, and the rates are 12.4 percent and 2.9 percent, respectively, in 2018. In 2018, the tax base for the Social Security tax is capped at $135,200 (wages over this cap are not subject to the tax). The tax base for the Medicare tax is not capped. Employers and employees split these taxes equally. Self-employed individuals, however, must pay these taxes in their entirety. In this case, the tax is often referred to as the **self-employment tax.** We discuss these taxes in more depth later in the text. There is a .9 percent Additional Medicare Tax levied on income earned by employees (employers are exempt) and self-employed taxpayers on income exceeding a threshold amount (see the Individual Income Tax Computation and Tax Credits chapter for details).

In addition to the Social Security and Medicare taxes, employers are also required to pay federal and state **unemployment taxes,** which fund temporary unemployment benefits for individuals terminated from their jobs without cause. As you might expect, the tax base for the unemployment taxes is also wages or salary. Currently, the federal unemployment tax rate is 6.0 percent. The wage base is the first $7,000 of wages received during the year. The U.S. government allows a credit for state unemployment taxes paid up to 5.4 percent. Thus, the effective federal unemployment tax rate may be as low as .6 percent (6.0% − 5.4% = .6%).[7]

Excise Taxes **Excise taxes** are taxes levied on the retail sale of particular products. They differ from other taxes in that the tax base for an excise tax typically depends on the *quantity* purchased, rather than a monetary amount. The federal government imposes a number of excise taxes on goods such as alcohol, diesel fuel, gasoline, and tobacco products and on services such as telephone use, air transportation, and the use of tanning beds. In addition, states often impose excise taxes on these same items.

Example 1-10

On the drive home from Florida to Athens, Georgia, Margaret stops at Gasup-n-Go. On each gallon of gasoline she buys, Margaret pays 18.4 cents of federal excise tax and 7.5 cents of state excise tax (plus 4 percent sales tax). Could Margaret have avoided paying excise tax had she stopped in Florida instead?

Answer: No. Had she stopped in Florida instead, Margaret would have paid the same federal excise tax. Additionally, Florida imposes higher state taxes on gas.

Because the producer of the product pays the excise tax to the government, many people are not even aware that businesses build these taxes into the prices consumers pay. Nonetheless, consumers bear the burden of the taxes because of the higher price.

Transfer Taxes Although they are a relatively minor tax compared to the income tax in terms of revenues collected, federal **transfer taxes**—estate and gift taxes—can be substantial for certain individual taxpayers and have been the subject of much debate in recent years. The **estate tax** (labeled the "death tax" by its opponents) and **gift taxes** are based on the fair market values of wealth transfers made upon death or by gift, respectively. In 2018, the maximum rate imposed on gifts is 37 percent. Most taxpayers, however, are not subject to estate and gift taxation because of the annual gift exclusion and gift and estate unified tax credits. The annual gift exclusion allows a taxpayer to transfer $15,000 of gifts per donee (gift recipient) each year without gift taxation. In 2018, the unified tax credit exempts from taxation $11,200,000 in bequests (transfers upon death) and gifts. Thus, only large transfers are subject to the gift and estate taxes.

---

[7]Although employers pay both federal and state unemployment taxes, all unemployment benefits actually are administered and paid by state governments.

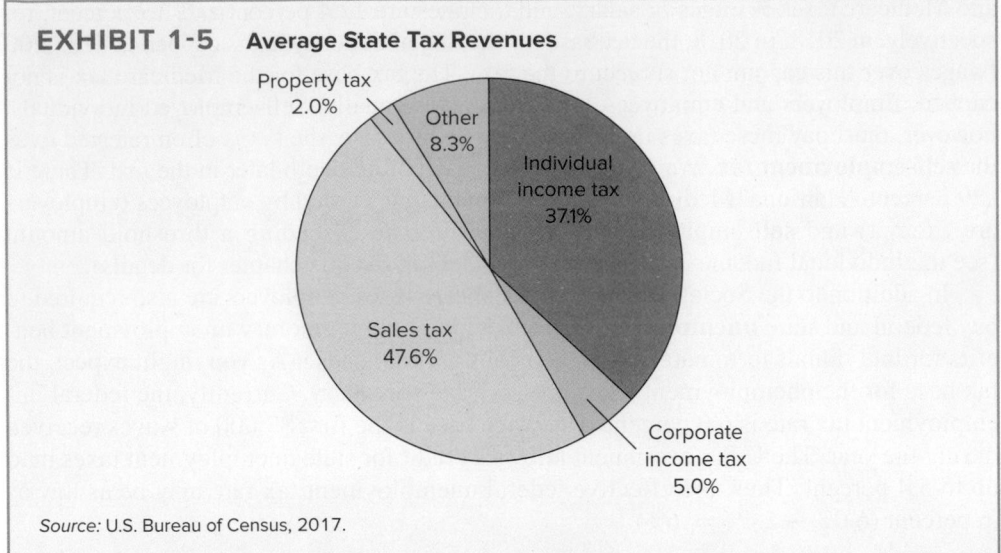

EXHIBIT 1-5   Average State Tax Revenues

- Property tax 2.0%
- Other 8.3%
- Individual income tax 37.1%
- Corporate income tax 5.0%
- Sales tax 47.6%

Source: U.S. Bureau of Census, 2017.

THE KEY FACTS

State and Local Taxes

- Sales and use taxes
  - The tax base for a sales tax is the retail price of goods and some services.
  - The tax base for the use tax is the retail price of goods owned, possessed, or consumed within a state that were *not* purchased within the state.
- Property taxes
  - Property taxes are ad valorem taxes, meaning that the tax base for each property is the fair market value of that property.
  - Real property taxes consist of taxes on land, structures, and improvements permanently attached to land.
  - Personal property taxes include taxes on all other types of property, both tangible and intangible.
- Income taxes
  - Most state taxable income calculations largely conform to the federal taxable income calculations, with a limited number of modifications.
- Excise taxes
  - States typically impose excise taxes on items subject to federal excise tax.

State and Local Taxes

Like the federal government, state and local governments (such as counties, cities, and school districts) use a variety of taxes to generate revenues for their programs (such as education, highways, and police and fire departments). Some of the more common **state and local taxes** include income taxes, sales and use taxes, excise taxes, and property taxes. Typically, as shown in Exhibit 1-5, the largest state tax revenues are generated by individual income taxes and state sales taxes—in contrast to federal revenues, which rely primarily on income and employment taxes. Local tax revenues are predominantly from sales and property taxes.

Income Taxes   Currently, most states and the District of Columbia impose income taxes on individuals and corporations who either reside in or earn income within the state.[8] This requires individuals living in these states to file a state tax return in addition to the federal return they already file. Calculations of individual and corporate taxable income vary with state law. Nonetheless, most state taxable income calculations largely conform to the federal taxable income calculations, with a limited number of modifications, although the tax rates are significantly less than the federal rate. The state of California is a notable exception because it has numerous modifications. Certain local governments such as New York City also impose an income tax and, again, the local calculations generally follow the respective state taxable income calculation.

Sales and Use Taxes   Most states, the District of Columbia, and local governments impose sales and use taxes. The tax base for a **sales tax** is the retail price of goods and some services, and retailers are responsible for collecting and remitting the tax; typically, sales tax is collected at the point of sale. The tax base for the **use tax** is the

---

[8]Currently, Alaska, Florida, Nevada, South Dakota, Texas, Washington, and Wyoming have no personal income tax, and New Hampshire and Tennessee only tax individual dividend and interest income. Nevada and Wyoming do not impose taxes on corporate income, and South Dakota only taxes banks. Washington imposes a gross receipts tax instead of a corporate income tax. Texas and Ohio have an activity-based tax that is based on net income or gross receipts.

retail price of goods owned, possessed, or consumed within a state that were *not* purchased within the state. The purpose of a use tax is to discourage taxpayers from buying goods out of state in order to avoid or minimize the sales tax in their home state. At the same time, by eliminating the incentive to purchase goods out of state, a use tax removes any competitive disadvantage a retailer may incur from operating in a state with a high sales tax. To avoid the potential of double taxing residents on sales taxes, states that impose a sales tax allow residents to take a credit for sales tax paid on goods purchased out of state.

Example 1-11

Margaret buys three new Lands' End shirts for her dad for $100. Because Lands' End does not have a business presence in Florida (Margaret's home state), it does not collect Florida sales tax on the $100 purchase. Does Margaret's purchase escape Florida taxation?

Answer: No. Because Florida has a 6 percent use tax, Margaret is liable for $6 in use tax on the purchase ($6 = $100 × .06).

Despite the potential importance of the use tax as a source of state tax revenue, states have only recently begun to enforce it. Poor compliance is therefore not surprising; indeed, many individuals have never heard of the use tax. While it is relatively easy to enforce it on goods obtained out of state if they are subject to a registration requirement, such as automobiles, it is quite difficult for states to tax most other out-of-state purchases. The state of Florida is not likely to search your closet to look for tax-evaded Lands' End shirts. Note, however, there are several bills before Congress to modernize Internet taxation and to try to subject all Internet sales to sales taxes.

Property Taxes   State and local governments commonly use two types of property taxes as sources of revenue: **real property taxes** and **personal property taxes.** Both are **ad valorem taxes,** meaning that the tax base for each is the fair market value of the property, and both are generally collected annually (if imposed at all).

Real property consists of land, structures, and improvements permanently attached to land, whereas *personal property* includes all other types of property, both tangible and intangible. Common examples of tangible personal property potentially subject to state and local taxation include automobiles, boats, private planes, business inventory, equipment, and furniture. Intangible personal property potentially subject to state and local taxation includes stocks, bonds, and intellectual property.

Of the two types, real property taxes are easier to administer because real property is not movable and purchases often have to be registered with the state, thereby making it easy to identify the tax base and taxpayer. Furthermore, the taxing body can estimate market values for real property without much difficulty. In contrast, personal property is generally mobile (thus easier to hide) and may be more difficult to value; therefore, personal property taxes are difficult to enforce. Accordingly, whereas all states and the District of Columbia provide for a real property tax, only a majority of states currently impose personal property taxes, most of which are assessed at the time of licensing or registration. However, most states do collect personal property taxes on business property.

Excise Taxes   We've said that the tax base for excise taxes is typically the quantity of an item or service purchased. States typically impose excise taxes on items subject to federal excise tax. Transactions subject to state excise tax often include the sale of alcohol, diesel fuel, gasoline, tobacco products, and telephone services.

Implicit Taxes

All the taxes discussed above are **explicit taxes;** that is, they are taxes directly imposed by a government and are easily quantified. **Implicit taxes,** on the other hand, are indirect taxes—not paid directly to the government—that result from a tax advantage the government grants to certain transactions to satisfy social, economic, or other objectives. Implicit taxes are defined as the reduced before-tax return that a tax-favored asset produces because of its tax-advantaged status. Let's examine this concept more closely.

First of all, what does it mean to be *tax-favored*? An asset is said to be tax-favored when the income the asset produces is either excluded from the tax base or subject to a lower (preferential) tax rate, or if the asset generates some other tax benefit such as large tax deductions. These tax benefits, *all other things equal*, result in higher after-tax profits (or lower after-tax costs) from investing in the tax-advantaged assets.

Why do tax-advantaged assets bear an implicit tax, or a reduced before-tax return as a result of the tax advantage? The answer is simple economics. The tax benefits associated with the tax-favored asset increase the demand for the asset. Increased demand drives up the price of the asset, which in turn reduces its before-tax return, which is an implicit tax by definition. Consider Example 1-12.

Example 1-12

Consider two bonds, one issued by the Coca-Cola Co. and the other issued by the State of Georgia. Both bonds have similar nontax characteristics (risk, for example), the same face value of $10,000, and the same market interest rate of 10 percent. The only difference between the two bonds is that the interest income from the Coca-Cola Co. bond is subject to a 20 percent income tax rate, whereas the interest income from the State of Georgia bond is tax-exempt with a 0 percent tax rate. Which of the two bonds is a better investment and should therefore have a higher demand?

	Price	Before-Tax* Return	Interest Income	Income† Tax	After-Tax Income	After-Tax* Return
Coca-Cola Bond	$10,000	10%	$1,000	$200	$ 800	8%
State of GA Bond	$10,000	10%	$1,000	$ 0	$1,000	10%

*Before-tax return is calculated as the before-tax income divided by the price of the bond. Likewise, after-tax return is calculated as the after-tax income divided by the price of the bond.
†Income tax equals the taxable interest income ($1,000) multiplied by the assumed income marginal tax rate (20 percent).

Answer: Compare the after-tax returns of the bonds. Given the difference between the return after taxes (10 percent vs. 8 percent), the better investment—again, all other investment features being equal—is the State of Georgia bond because it provides a higher *after*-tax return. Because all investors in this example should prefer to buy the State of Georgia bond, the demand for the bond will be high, and its price should increase. This increase in price leads to a lower before-tax return due to the bond's tax-favored status (this is an implicit tax).

Example 1-12 is a basic illustration of the need to consider the role of taxes in investment decisions. Without understanding the relative tax effects associated with each bond, we cannot correctly compare their after-tax returns.

At what point in Example 1-12 would you be indifferent between investing in the Coca-Cola Co. bond and the State of Georgia bond? Assuming both bonds have the same nontax characteristics, you would be indifferent between them when they both provide the same after-tax rate of return. This could occur if the State of Georgia raised the price of its bond from $10,000 to $12,500 ($1,000 interest/$12,500 price = 8% return). Or the State of Georgia could lower its bond interest payment from $1,000 to $800 ($800 interest/$10,000 price = 8% return). Either way, the State of Georgia benefits from selling the tax-exempt bonds—either at a higher price or at a lower interest rate relative to other bonds. Let's look more closely at this latter option, because it is, in fact, what many tax-exempt bond issuers choose to do.

	Price	Before-Tax Return	Interest Income	Income Tax	After-Tax Income	After-Tax Return
Coca-Cola Bond	$10,000	10%	$1,000	$200	$800	8%
State of GA Bond	$10,000	8%	$ 800	$ 0	$800	8%

At this point, assuming each bond has the same nontax characteristics, an investor should be indifferent between the Coca-Cola Co. bond and the State of Georgia bond. What is the tax burden on investors choosing the Coca-Cola Co. bond? Coca-Cola Co. bond investors are paying $200 of income taxes (explicit taxes). What is the tax burden on investors choosing the State of Georgia bond? While it is true they are subject to zero income taxes (explicit taxes), they are subject to implicit taxes in the form of the $200 less in interest income they accept. This $200 of reduced interest income (2 percent reduced before-tax rate of return) is an implicit tax. Although the investors in the State of Georgia bond are not paying this tax directly, they are paying it indirectly.

Does this happen in real life? Yes. Municipal bond interest income (interest income paid on bonds issued by state and local governments) generally is not subject to federal income taxation. Because of their tax-advantaged status, municipalities are able to pay a lower interest rate on their bond issuances and investors are willing to accept the lower rate. This type of indirect federal subsidy allows municipalities to raise money at a reduced cost without the need for direct federal subsidy or approval.

Although we were able to quantify the implicit taxes paid in the above example, in reality it is very difficult to estimate the amount of implicit taxes paid. For example, the federal government subsidizes housing by allowing taxpayers to deduct mortgage interest on their principal residence. Does this subsidy result in an implicit tax in the form of higher housing prices? Probably. Nonetheless, it would be difficult to quantify this implicit tax.

Despite the difficulty of quantifying implicit taxes, you should understand the concept of implicit taxes so you can make informed judgments about the attractiveness of alternative investments and the relative total tax burdens of tax-advantaged investments (considering both explicit and implicit taxes).

> **THE KEY FACTS**
>
> **Implicit Taxes**
>
> - Implicit taxes are indirect taxes that result from a tax advantage the government grants to certain transactions to satisfy social, economic, or other objectives.
> - Implicit taxes are defined as the reduced before-tax return that a tax-favored asset produces because of its tax-advantaged status.
> - Implicit taxes are difficult to quantify but important to understand in evaluating the relative tax burdens of tax-advantaged investments.

EVALUATING ALTERNATIVE TAX SYSTEMS

LO 1-5

Although it may appear that tax systems are designed without much forethought, in truth lawmakers engage in continuous debate over the basic questions of whom to tax, what to tax, and how much to tax. Margaret's friend Eddy is obviously upset with what he views as an unfair tax system. But fairness, as we will discuss shortly, is often like beauty—it is in the eye of the beholder. What is fair to one may seem blatantly unfair to others. In the following paragraphs, we offer various criteria (sufficiency, equity, certainty, convenience, and economy) you can use to evaluate alternative tax systems.[9] Satisfying everyone at the same time is difficult. Hence, the spirited debate on tax reform.

[9]Adam Smith identified and described the latter four criteria in *The Wealth of Nations*.

Sufficiency

Judging the **sufficiency** of a tax system means assessing the amount of the tax revenues it must generate and ensuring that it provides them. For a country's tax system to be successful, it must provide sufficient revenues to pay for governmental expenditures for a defense system, social services, and so on. This sounds easy enough: Estimate the amount of government expenditures that will be required, and then design the system to generate enough revenues to pay for these expenses. In reality, however, accurately estimating governmental expenditures and revenues is a rather daunting and imprecise process. Estimating governmental expenditures is difficult because it is impossible to predict the unknown. For example, in recent years governmental expenditures have increased due to the growth of Homeland Security, the Afghanistan and Iraq Wars, natural disasters, economic stimulus, and health care. Likewise, estimating governmental revenues is difficult because tax revenues are the result of transactions influenced by these same national events, the economy, and other factors. Thus, precisely estimating and matching governmental expenditures with tax revenues is nearly impossible.

The task of estimating tax revenues becomes even more daunting when the government attempts to make significant changes to the existing tax system or design a new one. Whenever Congress proposes changing who is taxed, what is taxed, or how much is taxed, its members must consider the taxpayer response to the change. That affects the amount of tax collected, and forecasters' prediction of what taxpayers will do affects the amount of revenue they estimate.

Static versus Dynamic Forecasting   One option in forecasting revenue is to ignore how taxpayers may alter their activities in response to a tax law change and instead base projected tax revenues on the existing state of transactions, a process referred to as **static forecasting.** However, this type of forecasting may result in a large discrepancy in projected versus actual tax revenues if taxpayers do change their behavior.

The other choice is to attempt to account for possible taxpayer responses to the tax law change, a process referred to as **dynamic forecasting.** Dynamic forecasting is ultimately only as good as the assumptions underlying the forecasts and does not guarantee accurate results. Nonetheless, considering how taxpayers may alter their activities in response to a tax law change is a useful exercise to identify the potential ramifications of the change, even if the revenue projections ultimately miss the mark. For more information about the Congressional Revenue Estimating Process, including dynamic scoring, see the Joint Committee on Taxation explanation at https://www.jct.gov/publications. html?func=startdown&id=3720.

Example 1-13

The city of Heflin would like to increase tax revenues by $2,000,000 to pay for needed roadwork. A concerned taxpayer recently proposed increasing the cigarette excise tax from $1.00 per pack of cigarettes to $6.00 per pack to raise the additional needed revenue. Last year, 400,000 packs of cigarettes were sold in the city. Will the tax be successful in raising the $2,000,000 revenue?

Answer: Not likely. The proposed tax increase of $5, and the assumption that 400,000 packs will still be sold, is an example of static forecasting: It ignores that many taxpayers may respond to the tax change by quitting, cutting down, or buying cheaper cigarettes in the next town.

In some cases, static forecasting can lead to a tax consequence that is the opposite of the desired outcome. In Example 1-13, we might estimate that given Heflin's close proximity to other cities with a $1.00 cigarette tax, the number of packs of cigarettes sold within the city would drop significantly to, say, 50,000. In this case, the tax increase would actually *decrease* tax revenues by $100,000 ($400,000 existing tax − $300,000 new tax)—not a good outcome if the goal was to increase tax revenues.

Income versus Substitution Effects   Example 1-13 described proposed changes in an excise tax, which is a proportional tax. In terms of a progressive tax such as an *income* tax, a tax rate increase or an expansion of the tax base can result in one of two taxpayer responses, both of which are important for dynamic forecasting. The **income effect** predicts that when taxpayers are taxed more (when, say, a tax rate increases from 25 to 28 percent), they will work harder to generate the same after-tax dollars. The **substitution effect** predicts that when taxpayers are taxed more, rather than working more they will substitute nontaxable activities like leisure pursuits for taxable ones because the marginal value of taxable activities has decreased. Which view is accurate? The answer depends on the taxpayer. Consider the following examples.

Example 1-14

Margaret's friend George, who earns $40,000 taxable income as a mechanic, is taxed at an average rate of 10 percent (resulting in $4,000 of tax). If Congress increases the income tax rate such that George's average tax rate increases from 10 percent to 25 percent, how much more income tax will he pay?

Answer: It depends on whether the income effect or the substitution effect is operating. Assuming George is single and cannot afford a net decrease in his after-tax income, he will likely work more (the income effect rules). Prior to the tax rate increase, George had $36,000 of after-tax income ($40,000 taxable income less $4,000 tax). With the increased tax rate, George will have to earn $48,000 of taxable income to keep $36,000 after taxes [$48,000 − ($48,000 × .25) = $36,000]. Thus, if the income effect rules, the government will collect $12,000 of federal income tax from George, or $8,000 more than under the previous lower tax rate. In this scenario, the tax change increases government revenues because of the increased tax rate *and* the increased tax base.

Whether the substitution effect or the income effect will describe any individual taxpayer's reaction to a tax increase is something we can only guess. But some factors—such as having higher disposable income—are likely to correlate with the substitution effect.

Example 1-15

What if: Now let's assume that George is married and has two young children. Both he and his wife work, and they file a tax return jointly with a 10 percent average tax rate. Either of their incomes is sufficient to meet necessities, even after the tax rate increase. But fixed child care costs make the marginal wage rate (the after-tax hourly wage less hourly child care cost) more sensitive to tax rate increases. In this case, the lower-earning spouse may choose to work less. Suppose George quits his full-time job and takes a part-time position that pays $10,000 to spend more time with his kids and to pursue his passion, reading sports novels. What are the taxes on George's income?

Answer: In this case, George will owe $2,500 tax ($10,000 × .25 = $2,500). Here, the substitution effect operates and the government collects much less than it would have if George had maintained his full-time position, because the tax rate increase had a negative effect on the tax base.

As Examples 1-14 and 1-15 illustrate, the response to a tax law change can vary by taxpayer and can greatly affect the magnitude of tax revenues generated by the change. Herein lies one of the challenges in significantly changing an existing tax system or designing a new one: If a tax system fails to generate sufficient revenues, the government must seek other sources to pay for governmental expenditures. The most common source of these additional funds for the federal government is the issuance of debt instruments such as Treasury bonds. This, however, is only a short-term solution to a budget deficit. Debt issuances require both interest and principal payments, which require the federal government to identify even more sources of revenue to service the debt issued or to cut governmental spending (both of which may be unpopular choices with voters). A third option is for the government to default on its debt obligations. However, the costs of this option are potentially devastating. If the historical examples of Mexico, Brazil, Argentina, and Greece are any guide, a U.S. government default on its debt obligations would likely devalue the U.S. dollar severely and have extreme negative consequences for the U.S. capital markets.

The best option is for the government to match its revenues with its expenses—that is, not to spend more than it collects. State governments seem to be more successful in this endeavor than the U.S. federal government. Indeed, all states except Vermont require a balanced budget each year, whereas the federal government has had deficit spending for most of the last 40 years.

TAXES IN THE REAL WORLD National Debt

How much debt does the U.S. have today? About $20.2 trillion. Almost $14.7 trillion of the national debt is held by public investors, including individual bondholders, institutional investors, and foreign governments such as China, Japan, the United Kingdom, and Brazil. The $5.5 trillion remaining amount represents intragovernmental holdings—primarily Social Security.

Is $20.2 trillion too much to handle? The key issue is fiscal sustainability: the ability to pay off a debt in the future. Rising debt also has other negative consequences, such as higher interest payments, a need for higher taxes, restrictions on policy makers' fiscal policy choices, and the increased probability of a sudden fiscal crisis. If nothing is done to change the national debt trajectory, the debt will grow faster than the economy.

Is the national debt sustainable? The federal government has recently been recording budget deficits that are a larger share of the economy than any year since the end of World War II. With an aging population, Social Security and other benefits will require larger expenditures. By the end of the current decade, barring any significant policy shifts, the vast majority of federal tax revenue will be consumed by just four expenditures: interest on the debt, Medicare, Medicaid, and Social Security. To finance other government expenditures, including defense and all other discretionary programs, policy makers will have to borrow the money to pay for them.

Equity

We've looked at the challenges of designing a tax system that provides sufficient revenues to pay for governmental expenditures. An equally challenging issue is how the tax burden should be distributed across taxpayers. At the heart of this issue is the concept of **equity,** or fairness. Fairness is inherently subject to personal interpretation, and informed minds often disagree about what is fair. There is no "one-size-fits-all" definition of equity or fairness. Nonetheless, it is informative to consider in broad terms what makes a fair or equitable tax system.

In general terms, a tax system is considered fair or equitable if the tax is based on the taxpayer's ability to pay. Taxpayers with a greater ability to pay tax, pay more tax. In broad terms, each of the federal, state, and local taxes we've discussed satisfies this criterion. For example, those individuals with greater taxable income, purchases, property, and estates (upon death) generally pay higher dollar amounts in federal income tax, sales tax, property tax, and estate tax. If this is the case, why is there so much debate over the fairness of the U.S. income tax system? The answer is that equity is more complex than our first definition suggests. Let's take a closer look.

Horizontal versus Vertical Equity   Two basic types of equity are relevant to tax systems. **Horizontal equity** means that two taxpayers in similar situations pay the same tax. In broad terms, each of the federal, state, and local taxes discussed satisfy this definition. Two individual taxpayers with the same taxable income, same purchases, same value of property, and same estate value pay the same federal income tax, sales tax, property tax, and estate tax. However, on closer inspection we might argue that each of these tax systems is *not* horizontally equitable. Here are some examples:

- Two individual taxpayers with the same income will not pay the same federal income tax if one individual's income was earned as salary and the other individual's income was tax-exempt municipal bond interest income, dividend income, or capital gain(s) income, which can be subject to a lower tax rate.
- Two individuals with the same dollar amount of purchases will not pay the same sales tax if one buys a higher proportion of goods that are subject to a lower sales tax rate, such as groceries.
- Two individuals with real estate of the same value will not pay the same property tax if one individual owns farmland, which is generally subject to a lower property tax rate.
- Finally, two individuals with estates of the same value will not pay the same estate tax if one individual bequeaths more of her property to charity or a spouse, because these transfers are not subject to estate tax.

These failures of horizontal equity are due to what we call *tax preferences*. Governments provide tax preferences for a variety of reasons, such as to encourage investment or to further social objectives. Whether we view these tax preferences as appropriate greatly influences whether we consider a tax system to be fair in general and horizontally equitable in particular.

The second type of equity to consider in evaluating a tax system is **vertical equity.** Vertical equity is achieved when taxpayers with greater ability to pay tax, pay more tax than taxpayers with less ability to pay. We can think of vertical equity in terms of tax dollars paid or in terms of tax rates. Proponents of a flat income tax or of a sales tax—both of which are proportional tax rate structures—are more likely to argue that vertical equity is achieved when taxpayers with a greater ability to pay tax, simply pay more in tax *dollars*. Proponents of a progressive tax system are more likely to argue that taxpayers with a greater ability to pay should be subject to a higher tax *rate*. This view is based upon the argument that the *relative* burden of a flat tax rate decreases as a taxpayer's income increases. Which is the correct answer? There is no correct answer. Nonetheless, many feel very strongly regarding one view or the other.

Our discussion has focused on how we can view alternative tax rate structures in terms of vertical equity, ignoring the role that the tax base plays in determining vertical equity. Indeed, focusing on the tax rate structure in evaluating a tax system is appropriate only if the tax base chosen—whether it's taxable income, purchases, property owned, or something else—accurately portrays a taxpayer's ability to pay. This can be a rather strong assumption. Consider the sales tax in Example 1-9. Although taxable purchases in this example increase as the taxpayers' total incomes increase, total incomes increase at a much faster rate than taxable purchases. Thus, the gap between taxable purchases and total income widens as total income increases. The end result is that the effective tax rates for those with a greater ability to pay are *lower* than for those taxpayers with a lesser ability to pay, making this tax regressive. Regressive tax rate structures are generally considered not to satisfy vertical equity, unless you strongly believe that those with a greater ability to pay do so simply by paying more tax dollars, albeit at a lower tax rate. In sum, evaluating vertical equity in terms of effective tax rates may be much more informative than simply evaluating tax rate structures.

Certainty

Certainty means that taxpayers should be able to determine when to pay the tax, where to pay the tax, and how to determine the tax. Determining when and where to pay each of the taxes previously discussed is relatively easy. For example, individual federal income tax returns and the remaining balance of taxes owed must be filed with the Internal Revenue Service each year on or before April 15th. Likewise, sales taxes, property taxes, and excise taxes are each determined with relative ease: Sales taxes are based on the value of taxable purchases, property taxes are generally based on assessed property values, and excise taxes are based on the number of taxable units purchased. Indeed, these taxes are calculated for the taxpayer and often charged at regular intervals or at the point of purchase; they do not require a tax return.

In contrast, income taxes are often criticized as being too complex. What are taxable versus nontaxable forms of income? What are deductible/nondeductible expenses? When should income or expenses be reported? For wage earners with few investments, the answers to these questions are straightforward. For business owners and individuals with a lot of investments, the answers are nontrivial. Yearly tax law changes enacted by Congress can make it more difficult to determine a taxpayer's current tax liability, much less plan for the future.

Convenience

Convenience suggests that a tax system should be designed to facilitate the collection of tax revenues without undue hardship on the taxpayer or the government. Various tax systems meet this criterion by tying the collection of the tax as closely as possible to the transaction that generates it (when it is most convenient to pay the tax). For example, retailers collect sales taxes when buyers purchase goods. Thus, it is difficult for the buyer to avoid paying sales tax, assuming she is transacting with an ethical retailer. Likewise, employers withhold federal income and Social Security taxes directly from wage earners' paychecks, which speeds the government's collection of the taxes and makes it difficult for taxpayers to evade taxes. If tax withholdings are not sufficient relative to the taxpayer's anticipated income tax liability, or if the taxpayer is self-employed, he or she is required to make quarterly estimated tax installments. Individual quarterly estimated payments are due on April 15, June 15, September 15, and January 15, whereas corporate estimated tax payments are due on the 15th day of the third, sixth, ninth, and twelfth months of the corporation's fiscal year.

Economy

Economy requires that a good tax system should minimize the compliance and administration costs associated with the tax system. We can view economy from both the taxpayer's and the government's perspectives. Believe it or not, most tax systems fare well in terms of economy, at least from the government's perspective. For example, the current IRS budget represents approximately $\frac{1}{2}$ of a percent of every tax dollar collected. Compared to the typical costs of a collection agency, this is quite low.

How about from the taxpayer's perspective? Here the picture is a bit different. The sales tax imposes no administrative burden on the taxpayer and only small administrative costs on the local retailer. However, out-of-state sellers argue that collecting and remitting use taxes for thousands of state and city jurisdictions would be a substantial burden. Other taxes such as excise taxes and property taxes also impose minimal administrative costs on the taxpayer. In contrast, as we've seen, the income tax is often criticized for the compliance costs imposed on the taxpayer. Indeed, for certain taxpayers, record-keeping costs, accountant fees, attorney fees, and so on can be substantial. Advocates of alternative tax systems often challenge the income tax on this criterion.

THE KEY FACTS

Evaluating Alternative Tax Systems—Certainty, Convenience, and Economy

- Certainty
  - Certainty means taxpayers should be able to determine when, where, and how much tax to pay.
  - Determining when and where to pay each of the taxes previously discussed is relatively easy.
  - The income tax has been criticized for the complexity of determining how much to pay.
- Convenience
  - Convenience means a tax system should be designed to facilitate the collection of tax revenues without undue hardship on the taxpayer or the government.
  - Various tax systems meet this criterion by tying the collection of the tax as closely as possible to the transaction that generates it.
- Economy
  - Economy means a tax system should minimize compliance and administration costs.
  - Economy can be viewed from both the taxpayer's and the government's perspectives.

Evaluating Tax Systems—The Trade-Off

At the heart of any debate about tax reform are fundamental decisions and concessions based on the five criteria we've just discussed. Interestingly enough, much of the debate regarding alternative tax systems can be reduced to a choice between simplicity and fairness. Those taxes that generally are simpler and easier to administer, such as the sales tax, are typically viewed as less fair. Those taxes that can be viewed as more fair, such as the federal income tax, often are more complex to administer. Thus, Margaret's friend Eddy faces a difficult choice about which type of tax system to advocate, as do all taxpayers. An understanding of the evaluative criteria should be helpful to anyone trying to reconcile the trade-offs among alternative tax proposals.

CONCLUSION

In almost any society, taxes are a part of life. They influence decisions about personal finance, investment, business, and politics. In this chapter, we introduced the basic concepts of why one should study tax, what a tax is, and how to calculate a tax. We also discussed various tax rates, tax rate structures, and different types of taxes imposed by federal, state, and local governments. Finally, we discussed the criteria that one might use to evaluate alternative tax rate systems. To make informed personal finance, investment, business, and political decisions, one must have a basic understanding of these items. In the following chapters we expand the discussion of how taxes influence these decisions while providing a basic understanding of our federal income tax system. Read on and learn more!

Summary

Demonstrate how taxes influence basic business, investment, personal, and political decisions.   **LO 1-1**

- Taxes are significant costs that influence many basic business, investment, and personal decisions.
  - *Business decisions* include what organizational form to take; where to locate; how to compensate employees; determining the appropriate debt mix; owning versus renting equipment and property; how to distribute profits; and so forth.
  - *Investment decisions* include alternative methods for saving for education or retirement, and so forth.
  - *Personal finance decisions* include evaluating job offers; gift or estate planning; owning a home versus renting; and so forth.
- Taxes also play a major part in the political process. Major parties typically have very diverse views on whom, what, and how much to tax.

Discuss what constitutes a tax and the general objectives of taxes.   **LO 1-2**

- The general purpose of taxes is to fund the government. Unlike fines or penalties, taxes are not meant to punish or prevent illegal behavior; but "sin taxes" (on alcohol, tobacco, tanning beds, etc.) are meant to discourage some behaviors.
- To qualify as a tax, three criteria are necessary: the payment must be (1) required (it is not voluntary), (2) imposed by a government (federal, state, or local), and (3) not tied directly to the benefit received by the taxpayer.

Describe the different tax rate structures and calculate a tax.   **LO 1-3**

- Tax = Tax rate × Tax base, where the tax base is what is taxed and the tax rate is the level of taxes imposed on the base. Different portions of a tax base may be taxed at different rates.

- There are three different tax rates that are useful in contrasting the different tax rate structures, tax planning, and/or assessing the tax burden of a taxpayer: the marginal, average, and effective tax rates.
- The *marginal* tax rate is the tax that applies to the next increment of income or deduction. The *average* tax rate represents a taxpayer's average level of taxation on each dollar of taxable income. The *effective* tax rate represents the taxpayer's average rate of taxation on each dollar of total income (taxable *and* nontaxable income).
- The three basic tax rate structures are proportional, progressive, and regressive.
  - A *proportional* tax rate structure imposes a constant tax rate throughout the tax base. As a taxpayer's tax base increases, the taxpayer's taxes increase proportionally. The marginal tax rate remains constant and always equals the average tax rate. A common example is a sales tax.
  - A *progressive* tax rate imposes an increasing marginal tax rate as the tax base increases. As a taxpayer's tax base increases, both the marginal tax rate and the taxes paid increase. A common example is the U.S. federal income tax.
  - A *regressive* tax rate imposes a decreasing marginal tax rate as the tax base increases. As a taxpayer's tax base increases, the marginal tax rate decreases while the total taxes paid increases.

LO 1-4 Identify the various federal, state, and local taxes.

- Federal taxes include the income tax, employment taxes (Social Security and Medicare taxes), unemployment taxes, excise taxes (levied on quantity purchased), and transfer taxes (estate and gift taxes).
- State and local taxes include the income tax (levied by most states), sales tax (levied on retail sales of goods and some services), use tax (levied on the retail price of goods owned or consumed within a state that were purchased out of state), property taxes (levied on fair market value of real and personal property), and excise taxes.
- Implicit taxes are indirect taxes that result from a tax advantage the government grants to certain transactions to satisfy social, economic, or other objectives. They are defined as the reduced before-tax return that a tax-favored asset produces because of its tax-advantaged status.

LO 1-5 Apply appropriate criteria to evaluate alternative tax systems.

- Sufficiency involves assessing the aggregate size of the tax revenues that must be generated and ensuring that the tax system provides these revenues. Static forecasting ignores how taxpayers may alter their activities in response to a proposed tax law change and bases projected tax revenues on the existing state of transactions. In contrast, dynamic forecasting attempts to account for possible taxpayer responses to a proposed tax law change.
- Equity considers how the tax burden should be distributed across taxpayers. Generally, a tax system is considered fair or equitable if the tax is based on the taxpayer's ability to pay—that is, taxpayers with a greater ability to pay tax, pay more tax. Horizontal equity means that two taxpayers in similar situations pay the same tax. Vertical equity is achieved when taxpayers with greater ability to pay tax, pay more tax relative to taxpayers with a lesser ability to pay tax.
- Certainty means taxpayers should be able to determine when, where, and how much tax to pay.
- Convenience means a tax system should be designed to facilitate the collection of tax revenues without undue hardship on the taxpayer or the government.
- Economy means a tax system should minimize its compliance and administration costs.

KEY TERMS

ad valorem taxes (1-15)
average tax rate (1-7)
bracket (1-5)
certainty (1-22)

convenience (1-22)
dynamic forecasting (1-18)
earmarked tax (1-4)
economy (1-22)

effective tax rate (1-7)
employment taxes (1-12)
equity (1-20)
estate tax (1-13)

excise taxes (1-13)

explicit taxes (1-16)

flat tax (1-5)

gift tax (1-13)

graduated taxes (1-5)

horizontal equity (1-21)

implicit taxes (1-16)

income effect (1-19)

income tax (1-12)

local tax (1-14)

marginal tax rate (1-5)

Medicare tax (1-12)

personal property tax (1-15)

progressive tax rate structure (1-9)

proportional tax rate structure (1-9)

real property tax (1-15)

regressive tax rate structure (1-10)

sales tax (1-14)

self-employment tax (1-13)

sin taxes (1-4)

Social Security tax (1-12)

state tax (1-14)

static forecasting (1-18)

substitution effect (1-19)

sufficiency (1-18)

tax (1-4)

tax base (1-5)

tax rate (1-5)

transfer taxes (1-13)

unemployment tax (1-13)

use tax (1-14)

value-added tax (1-11)

vertical equity (1-21)

DISCUSSION QUESTIONS

Discussion Questions are available in Connect®.   **connect**

1. Jessica's friend Zachary once stated that he couldn't understand why someone would take a tax course. Why is this a rather naïve view? **LO 1-1**

2. What are some aspects of business that require knowledge of taxation? What are some aspects of personal finance that require knowledge of taxation? **LO 1-1**

3. Describe some ways in which taxes affect the political process in the United States. **LO 1-1**

4. Courtney recently received a speeding ticket on her way to the university. Her fine was $200. Is this considered a tax? Why or why not? **LO 1-2**

5. Marlon and Latoya recently started building a house. They had to pay $300 to the county government for a building permit. Is the $300 payment a tax? Why or why not? **LO 1-2**

6. To help pay for the city's new stadium, the city of Birmingham recently enacted a 1 percent surcharge on hotel rooms. Is this a tax? Why or why not? **LO 1-2**

7. As noted in Example 1-2, tolls, parking meter fees, and annual licensing fees are not considered taxes. Can you identify other fees that are similar? **LO 1-2**

8. If the general objective of our tax system is to raise revenue, why does the income tax allow deductions for charitable contributions and retirement plan contributions? **LO 1-2**

9. One common argument for imposing so-called sin taxes is the social goal of *reducing* demand for such products. Using cigarettes as an example, is there a segment of the population that might be sensitive to price and for whom high taxes might discourage purchases? **LO 1-2**

10. Dontae stated that he didn't want to earn any more money because it would "put him in a higher tax bracket." What is wrong with Dontae's reasoning? **LO 1-3**

11. Describe the three different tax rates discussed in the chapter and how taxpayers might use them. **LO 1-3**

12. Which is a more appropriate tax rate to use to compare taxpayers' tax burdens— the average or the effective tax rate? Why? **LO 1-3**

13. Describe the differences between proportional, progressive, and regressive tax rate structures. **LO 1-3**

14. Arnold and Lilly have recently had a heated discussion about whether a sales tax is a proportional tax or a regressive tax. Arnold argues that a sales tax is regressive. Lilly counters that the sales tax is a flat tax. Who is correct? **LO 1-3**

15. Which is the largest tax collected by the U.S. government? What types of taxpayers are subject to this tax? **LO 1-4**

LO 1-4   16. What is the tax base for the Social Security and Medicare taxes for an employee or employer? What is the tax base for Social Security and Medicare taxes for a self-employed individual? Is the self-employment tax in addition to or in lieu of federal income tax?

LO 1-4   17. What are unemployment taxes?

LO 1-4   18. What is the distinguishing feature of an excise tax?

LO 1-4   19. What are some of the taxes that currently are unique to state and local governments? What are some of the taxes that the federal, state, and local governments each utilize?

LO 1-4   20. The state of Georgia recently increased its tax on a pack of cigarettes by $2. What type of tax is this? Why might Georgia choose this type of tax?

LO 1-4   21. What is the difference between a sales tax and a use tax?

LO 1-4   22. What is an ad valorem tax? Name an example of this type of tax.

LO 1-4   23. What are the differences between an explicit and an implicit tax?

LO 1-4   24. When we calculate average and effective tax rates, do we consider implicit taxes? What effect does this have on taxpayers' perception of equity?

LO 1-4   25. Benjamin recently bought a truck in Alabama for his business in Georgia. What different types of federal and state taxes may affect this transaction?

LO 1-5   26. Kobe strongly dislikes SUVs and is appalled that so many are on the road. He proposes to eliminate the federal income tax and replace it with a $50,000 annual tax per SUV. Based on the number of SUVs currently owned in the United States, he estimates the tax will generate exactly the amount of tax revenue currently collected from the income tax. What is wrong with Kobe's proposal? What type of forecasting is Kobe likely using?

LO 1-5   27. What is the difference between the income and substitution effects? For which types of taxpayers is the income effect more likely descriptive? For which types of taxpayers is the substitution effect more likely descriptive?

LO 1-5   28. What is the difference between horizontal and vertical equity? How do tax preferences affect people's view of horizontal equity?

LO 1-3 LO 1-5   29. Montel argues that a flat income tax rate system is vertically equitable. Oprah argues that a progressive tax rate structure is vertically equitable. How do their arguments differ? Who is correct?

LO 1-3 LO 1-5   30. Discuss why evaluating vertical equity simply based on tax rate structure may be less than optimal.

LO 1-4 LO 1-5   31. Compare the federal income tax to sales taxes using the "certainty" criterion.

LO 1-5   32. Many years ago a famous member of Congress proposed eliminating federal income tax withholding. What criterion for evaluating tax systems did this proposal violate? What would likely have been the result of eliminating withholding?

LO 1-5   33. "The federal income tax scores very high on the economy criterion because the current IRS budget is relatively low compared to the costs of a typical collection agency." Explain why this statement may be considered wrong.

PROBLEMS

Select problems are available in Connect®.   **McGraw Hill connect**

LO 1-3   34. Chuck, a single taxpayer, earns $75,000 in taxable income and $10,000 in interest from an investment in City of Heflin bonds. Using the U.S. tax rate schedule, how much federal tax will he owe? What is his average tax rate? What is his effective tax rate? What is his current marginal tax rate?

35. Using the facts in problem 34, if Chuck earns an additional $40,000 of taxable income, what is his marginal tax rate on this income? What is his marginal rate if, instead, he had $40,000 of additional deductions? **LO 1-3**

36. Campbell, a single taxpayer, earns $400,000 in taxable income and $2,000 in interest from an investment in State of New York bonds. Using the U.S. tax rate schedule, how much federal tax will she owe? What is her average tax rate? What is her effective tax rate? What is her current marginal tax rate? **LO 1-3**

37. Using the facts in problem 36, if Campbell earns an additional $15,000 of taxable income, what is her marginal tax rate on this income? What is her marginal rate if, instead, she had $15,000 of additional deductions? **LO 1-3**

38. Jorge and Anita, married taxpayers, earn $150,000 in taxable income and $40,000 in interest from an investment in City of Heflin bonds. Using the U.S. tax rate schedule for married filing jointly (see Example 1-3), how much federal tax will they owe? What is their average tax rate? What is their effective tax rate? What is their current marginal tax rate? **LO 1-3**

39. Using the facts in problem 38, if Jorge and Anita earn an additional $100,000 of taxable income, what is their marginal tax rate on this income? What is their marginal rate if, instead, they report an additional $100,000 in deductions? **LO 1-3**

40. Scot and Vidia, married taxpayers, earn $240,000 in taxable income and $5,000 in interest from an investment in City of Tampa bonds. Using the U.S. tax rate schedule for married filing jointly (see Example 1-3), how much federal tax will they owe? What is their average tax rate? What is their effective tax rate? What is their current marginal tax rate? **LO 1-3**

41. Using the facts in problem 40, if Scot and Vidia earn an additional $80,000 of taxable income, what is their marginal tax rate on this income? How would your answer differ if they, instead, had $80,000 of additional deductions? **LO 1-3**

42. Melinda invests $200,000 in a City of Heflin bond that pays 6 percent interest. Alternatively, Melinda could have invested the $200,000 in a bond recently issued by Surething Inc. that pays 8 percent interest and has risk and other nontax characteristics similar to the City of Heflin bond. Assume Melinda's marginal tax rate is 25 percent. **LO 1-3** **LO 1-4**
    a) What is her after-tax rate of return for the City of Heflin bond?
    b) How much explicit tax does Melinda pay on the City of Heflin bond?
    c) How much implicit tax does she pay on the City of Heflin bond?
    d) How much explicit tax would she have paid on the Surething Inc. bond?
    e) What would have been her after-tax rate of return on the Surething Inc. bond?

43. Hugh has the choice between investing in a City of Heflin bond at 6 percent or investing in a Surething bond at 9 percent. Assuming that both bonds have the same nontax characteristics and that Hugh has a 40 percent marginal tax rate, in which bond should he invest? **LO 1-3** **LO 1-4** **planning**

44. Using the facts in problem 43, what interest rate does Surething Inc. need to offer to make Hugh indifferent between investing in the two bonds? **LO 1-3** **LO 1-4** **planning**

45. Fergie has the choice between investing in a State of New York bond at 5 percent and a Surething bond at 8 percent. Assuming that both bonds have the same nontax characteristics and that Fergie has a 30 percent marginal tax rate, in which bond should she invest? **LO 1-3** **LO 1-4** **planning**

46. Using the facts in problem 45, what interest rate does the State of New York bond need to offer to make Fergie indifferent between investing in the two bonds? **LO 1-3** **LO 1-4** **planning**

LO 1-3   47. Given the following tax structure, what minimum tax would need to be assessed on Shameika to make the tax progressive with respect to average tax rates?

Taxpayer	Salary	Muni-Bond Interest	Total Tax
Mihwah	$10,000	$10,000	$600
Shameika	$50,000	$30,000	$???

LO 1-3   48. Using the facts in problem 47, what minimum tax would need to be assessed on Shameika to make the tax progressive with respect to effective tax rates?

LO 1-3   LO 1-5   49. Song earns $100,000 taxable income as an interior designer and is taxed at an average rate of 20 percent (i.e., $20,000 of tax). If Congress increases the income tax rate such that Song's average tax rate increases from 20 percent to 25 percent, how much more income tax will she pay assuming that the income effect is descriptive? What effect will this tax rate change have on the tax base and tax collected?

LO 1-3   LO 1-5   50. Using the facts from problem 49, what will happen to the government's tax revenues if Song chooses to spend more time pursuing her other passions besides work in response to the tax rate change and earns only $75,000 in taxable income? What is the term that describes this type of reaction to a tax rate increase? What types of taxpayers are likely to respond in this manner?

LO 1-5   51. Given the following tax structure, what tax would need to be assessed on Venita to make the tax horizontally equitable?

Taxpayer	Salary	Total Tax
Mae	$10,000	$ 600
Pedro	$20,000	$ 1,500
Venita	$10,000	$???

LO 1-5   52. Using the facts in problem 51, what is the minimum tax that Pedro should pay to make the tax structure vertically equitable based on the tax rate paid? This would result in what type of tax rate structure?

LO 1-5   53. Using the facts in problem 51, what is the minimum tax that Pedro should pay to make the tax structure vertically equitable with respect to the amount of tax paid? This would result in what type of tax rate structure?

LO 1-5   54. Consider the following tax rate structure. Is it horizontally equitable? Why or why not? Is it vertically equitable? Why or why not?

Taxpayer	Salary	Total Tax
Rajiv	$10,000	$600
LaMarcus	$20,000	$600
Dory	$10,000	$600

LO 1-5   55. Consider the following tax rate structure. Is it horizontally equitable? Why or why not? Is it vertically equitable? Why or why not?

Taxpayer	Salary	Total Tax
Marilyn	$10,000	$ 600
Kobe	$20,000	$3,000
Alfonso	$30,000	$6,000

LO 1-5   56. Consider the following tax rate structure. Is it horizontally equitable? Why or why not? Is it vertically equitable? Why or why not?

Taxpayer	Salary	Total Tax
Rodney	$10,000	$600
Keisha	$10,000	$600

57. Lorenzo is considering starting a trucking company either in Texas or Oklahoma. He will relocate his family, which includes his wife, children, and parents, to reside in the same state as his business. What types of taxes may influence his decision of where to locate his business?

LO 1-1   **LO 1-4**
 planning

58. Congress would like to increase tax revenues by 10 percent. Assume that the average taxpayer in the United States earns $65,000 and pays an average tax rate of 15 percent. If the income effect is in effect for all taxpayers, what average tax rate will result in a 10 percent increase in tax revenues? This is an example of what type of forecasting?

LO 1-3   **LO 1-5**
planning

59. Locate the IRS website at www.irs.gov/. For every $100 the IRS collected, how much was spent on the IRS's collection efforts? What tax system criterion does this information help you to evaluate with respect to the current U.S. tax system?

LO 1-5
research

60. Using the Internet, find a comparison of income tax rates across states. What state currently has the highest income tax rate? In considering individual tax burdens across states, what other taxes should you consider?

LO 1-4
research

ROGER | *CPA Review*

Sample CPA Exam questions from Roger CPA Review are available in Connect as support for the topics in this text. These Multiple Choice Questions and Task-Based Simulations include expert-written explanations and solutions and provide a starting point for students to become familiar with the content and functionality of the actual CPA Exam.

Tax Compliance, the IRS, and Tax Authorities

Learning Objectives

Upon completing this chapter, you should be able to:

LO 2-1 Identify the filing requirements for income tax returns and the statute of limitations for assessment.

LO 2-2 Outline the IRS audit process, how returns are selected, the different types of audits, and what happens after the audit.

LO 2-3 Evaluate the relative weights of the various tax law sources.

LO 2-4 Describe the legislative process as it pertains to taxation.

LO 2-5 Perform the basic steps in tax research.

LO 2-6 Describe tax professional responsibilities in providing tax advice.

LO 2-7 Identify taxpayer and tax professional penalties.

©Robert Nicholas/AGE Fotostock

Storyline Summary

Taxpayers:	Bill and Mercedes
Family description:	Bill and Mercedes are married with one daughter, Margaret, and live in Tampa, Florida.
Employment status:	Bill is an economics professor; Mercedes is a small business owner.
Filing status:	Married, filing jointly
Current situation:	Bill and Mercedes face an IRS audit involving a previous year's interest deductions.

Bill and Mercedes received a notice from the Internal Revenue Service (IRS) that their return is under audit for certain interest deductions. As you might expect, they are quite concerned, especially because it has been several years since they claimed the deductions and they worry that all their supporting documentation may not be in place. Several questions run through their minds. How could the IRS audit a return that was filed so long ago? Why was their tax return selected, and what should they expect during the audit? The interest deductions they reported were based on advice from their CPA. What would cause the IRS and a CPA to interpret the law differently? What is their financial exposure if the deductions are ultimately disallowed? Will they have to pay interest and penalties in addition to the tax they might owe? ■

Even the most conservative taxpayer is likely to feel anxiety after receiving an IRS notice. This chapter will help answer Bill and Mercedes's questions and provide an overview of the audit process and tax research. While all taxpayers should understand these basics of our tax system, aspiring accountants should be especially familiar with them.

LO 2-1 TAXPAYER FILING REQUIREMENTS

To file or not to file? Unlike Hamlet's "to be or not to be," this question has a pretty straightforward answer. Filing requirements are specified by law for each type of taxpayer. All corporations must file a tax return annually regardless of their taxable income. Estates and trusts are required to file annual income tax returns if their gross income exceeds $600.[1]

The filing requirements for individual taxpayers are a little more complex. Specifically, they depend on the taxpayer's filing status (single, married filing jointly, and so on, discussed in more detail in the Individual Income Tax Overview, Dependents, and Filing Status chapter), age, and gross income (income before deductions). Exhibit 2-1 lists the 2018 gross income thresholds for taxpayers based on their filing status, gross income, and age. As detailed in Exhibit 2-1, the gross income thresholds are calculated as the sum of the standard deduction and additional deductions for taxpayers age 65 or older.[2] These amounts are indexed for inflation and thus change each year. For certain taxpayers, such as the self-employed and those claimed as dependents by another taxpayer, lower gross income thresholds apply.

EXHIBIT 2-1   2018 Gross Income Thresholds by Filing Status

Filing Status and Age (in 2018)	2018 Gross Income	Explanation
Single	$12,000	$12,000 standard deduction
Single, 65 or older	$13,600	$12,000 standard deduction + $1,600 additional deduction
Married, filing a joint return	$24,000	$24,000 standard deduction
Married, filing a joint return, one spouse 65 or older	$25,300	$24,000 standard deduction + $1,300 additional deduction
Married, filing a joint return, both spouses 65 or older	$26,600	$24,000 standard deduction + $2,600 additional deductions (2)
Married, filing a separate return	$ 0	
Head of household	$18,000	$18,000 standard deduction
Head of household, 65 or older	$19,600	$18,000 standard deduction + $1,600 additional deduction
Surviving spouse with a dependent child	$24,000	$24,000 standard deduction
Surviving spouse, 65 or older, with a dependent child	$25,300	$24,000 standard deduction + $1,300 additional deduction

Source: www.irs.gov

Whether a taxpayer is due a refund (which occurs when taxes paid exceed tax liability) does *not* determine whether a taxpayer must file a tax return. Gross income determines whether a tax return is required. Further, note that even a taxpayer whose gross income falls below the respective threshold is not precluded from filing a tax return.

[1]Estates file income tax returns during the administration period (i.e., before all of the estate assets are distributed).

[2]IRC §6012. We describe the standard deduction in detail later in the text. A married taxpayer is required to file a tax return (regardless of gross income) if: (i) such individual and his spouse, at the close of the taxable year, did not have the same household as their home; (ii) the individual's spouse files a separate return; or (iii) the individual or his spouse is a dependent of another taxpayer who has income (other than earned income) in excess of $500.

Indeed, taxpayers due a refund *should* file a tax return to receive the refund (or claim a refundable tax credit), even if they are not required to file a tax return.

Tax Return Due Date and Extensions

Like the filing requirements, due dates for tax returns vary based on the type of taxpayer. Individual tax returns are due on the fifteenth day of the fourth month following year-end—that is, April 15 for calendar-year individuals. (Due dates that fall on a Saturday, Sunday, or holidays are automatically extended to the next day that is not a Saturday, Sunday, or holiday.) Similarly, tax returns for taxable corporations ("C" corporations) are generally due on the fifteenth day of the fourth month following the corporation's year-end. The exception is for tax returns for C corporations with a June 30 year-end, which are due on the fifteenth day of the third month (September 15th). For both partnerships and S corporations (generally nontaxable corporations), tax returns must be filed by the fifteenth day of the third month following the entity's year-end (March 15 for calendar-year partnerships or S corporations). Any individual, partnership, or S corporation unable to file a tax return by the original due date can, by that same deadline, request a six-month extension to file, which is granted automatically by the IRS. Similarly, C corporations may request an automatic five-, six-, or seven-month extension to file depending on the corporation's year-end.[3]

An extension allows the taxpayer to delay filing a tax return but does *not* extend the due date for tax payments. Thus, when a taxpayer files an extension, she must estimate how much tax will be owed. If a taxpayer fails to pay the entire balance of tax owed by the original due date of the tax return, the IRS charges the taxpayer interest on the underpayment from the due date of the return until the taxpayer pays the tax.[4] The interest rate charged depends on taxpayer type (individual or corporation) and varies quarterly with the federal short-term interest rate.[5] For example, the interest rate for tax underpayments for individuals equals the federal short-term rate plus three percentage points.[6]

What happens if the taxpayer does not file a tax return by the time required, whether April 15 or an extended deadline? As you might guess, the IRS imposes penalties on taxpayers failing to comply with the tax law. In many cases, the penalties can be quite substantial (see later discussion in this chapter). In the case of failure to file a tax return, the penalty equals 5 percent of the tax due for each month (or partial month) that the return is late. However, the maximum penalty is generally 25 percent of the tax owed, and the failure-to-file penalty does not apply if the taxpayer owes no tax.

Statute of Limitations

Despite the diligent efforts of taxpayers and tax professionals, it is quite common for tax returns to contain mistakes. Some may be to the taxpayer's advantage and others may be to the government's advantage. Regardless of the nature of the mistake, the taxpayer is obligated to file an amended return to correct the error (and request a refund or pay a deficiency) if the statute of limitations has not expired for the tax return. Likewise, the IRS can propose adjustments to the taxpayer's return if the statute of limitations for the return has not expired.

By law, the **statute of limitations** defines the period in which the taxpayer can file an amended tax return or the IRS can assess a tax deficiency for a specific tax year. For both amended tax returns filed by a taxpayer and proposed tax assessments by the IRS, the statute of limitations generally ends three years from the *later* of (1) the date the tax return was actually filed or (2) the tax return's original due date.

> **THE KEY FACTS**
>
> **Filing Requirements and Due Dates**
>
> - Filing requirements
>   - Filing requirements are specified by law for each type of taxpayer.
>   - For individuals, filing requirements vary by filing status, gross income, and age.
>   - Gross income thresholds are indexed each year for inflation.
> - Due dates
>   - The due date for tax returns varies based on the type of taxpayer.
>   - Individual tax returns are due on April 15 for calendar-year individuals.
>   - Due dates that fall on a Saturday, Sunday, or holiday are automatically extended to the next day that is not a Saturday, Sunday, or holiday.
>   - Any taxpayer unable to file a tax return by the original due date can request an extension to file.
>   - An extension allows the taxpayer to delay filing a tax return but does *not* extend the due date for tax payments.

---

[3]June 30 year-end C corporations may request a seven-month extension. All other C corporations may request a six-month extension.

[4]The tax law also imposes a penalty for late payment in addition to the interest charged on the underpayment. We briefly discuss this penalty later in the chapter and in the Individual Income Tax Computation and Tax Credits chapter.

[5]The federal short-term rate is determined from a one-month average of the market yields from marketable obligations of the United States with maturities of three years or less.

[6]This same interest rate applies to individuals who overpay their taxes (i.e., receive a tax refund and interest payment as a result of an IRS audit or from filing an amended tax return).

The statute of limitations for IRS assessment can be extended in certain circumstances. For example, a six-year statute of limitations applies to IRS assessments if the taxpayer omits items of gross income that exceed 25 percent of the gross income reported on the tax return. For fraudulent returns, or if the taxpayer fails to file a tax return, the news is understandably worse. The statute of limitations remains open indefinitely in these cases.

Example 2-1

Bill and Mercedes file their 2014 federal tax return on September 6, 2015, after receiving an automatic extension to file their return by October 15, 2015. In 2018, the IRS selects their 2014 tax return for audit. When does the statute of limitations end for Bill and Mercedes's 2014 tax return?

Answer: Assuming the six-year and "unlimited" statute of limitation rules do not apply, the statute of limitations ends on September 6, 2018 (three years after the later of the actual filing date and the *original* due date).

What if: When would the statute of limitations end for Bill and Mercedes for their 2014 tax return if the couple filed the return on March 22, 2015 (before the original due date of April 15, 2015)?

Answer: In this scenario the statute of limitations would end on April 15, 2018, because the later of the actual filing date and the original due date is April 15, 2015.

Taxpayers should prepare for the possibility of an audit by retaining all supporting documents (receipts, canceled checks, etc.) for a tax return until the statute of limitations expires. After the statute of limitations expires, taxpayers can discard the majority of supporting documents but should still keep a copy of the tax return itself, as well as any documents that may have ongoing significance, such as those establishing the taxpayer's *basis* or original investment in existing assets like personal residences and long-term investments.

LO 2-2   IRS AUDIT SELECTION

Why me? This is a recurring question in life and definitely a common taxpayer question after receiving an IRS audit notice. The answer, in general, is that a taxpayer's return is selected for audit because the IRS has data suggesting the taxpayer's tax return has a high probability of a significant understated tax liability. Budget constraints limit the IRS's ability to audit a majority or even a large minority of tax returns. Currently, fewer than 1 percent of all tax returns are audited. Thus, the IRS must be strategic in selecting returns for audit in an effort to promote the highest level of voluntary taxpayer compliance and increase tax revenues.

Specifically, how does the IRS select tax returns for audit? The IRS uses a number of computer programs and outside data sources (newspapers, financial statement disclosures, informants, and other public and private sources) to identify tax returns that may have an understated tax liability. Common computer initiatives include the **DIF (Discriminant Function) system,** the **document perfection program,** and the **information matching program.** The most important of these initiatives is the DIF system. The DIF system assigns a score to each tax return that represents the probability the tax liability on the return has been underreported (a higher score = a higher likelihood of underreporting). The IRS derives the weights assigned to specific tax return attributes from historical IRS audit adjustment data from the National Research Program.[7] The DIF system then uses these (undisclosed) weights to score each tax return based on the tax return's characteristics. Returns with higher DIF scores are reviewed to determine whether an audit is the best course of action.

---

[7]Similar to its predecessor, the Taxpayer Compliance Measurement Program, the National Research Program (NRP) analyzes a large sample of tax returns that are randomly selected for audit. From these randomly selected returns, the IRS identifies tax return characteristics (e.g., deductions for a home office, unusually high tax deductions relative to a taxpayer's income) associated with underreported liabilities, weights these characteristics, and then incorporates them into the DIF system. The NRP analyzes randomly selected returns to ensure that the DIF scorings are representative of the population of tax returns.

All returns are checked for mathematical and tax calculation errors, a process referred to as the document perfection program. Individual returns are also subject to the information matching program. This program compares the taxpayer's tax return to information submitted to the IRS from other taxpayers like banks, employers, mutual funds, brokerage companies, and mortgage companies. Information matched includes items such as wages (Form W-2 submitted by employers), interest income (Form 1099-INT submitted by banks), and dividend income (Form 1099-DIV submitted by brokerage companies). For tax returns identified as incorrect via the document perfection and information matching programs, the IRS recalculates the taxpayer's tax liability and sends a notice explaining the adjustment. If the taxpayer owes tax, the IRS will request payment of the tax due. If the taxpayer overpaid tax, the IRS will send the taxpayer a refund of the overpayment.

In addition to computer-based methods for identifying tax returns for audit, the IRS may use a number of other audit initiatives that target taxpayers working in certain industries, engaging in certain transactions like the acquisition of other companies, or having specific attributes like home office deductions. Taxpayers of a given size and complexity, such as large publicly traded companies, may be audited every year.

TAXES IN THE REAL WORLD   Turning in Your Neighbor Can Pay Big Bucks

The Wall Street Journal reported that in April 2011 the IRS made its first payment under a new taxpayer whistleblower program that promises large rewards for turning in tax cheats. Under the large-award whistleblower program (where unpaid taxes, interest, and penalties exceed $2 million and the tax cheat, if an individual, has gross income exceeding $200,000 in at least one year), whistleblowers can be paid between 15 and 30 percent of the taxes, interest, and penalties collected by the IRS. Under the small-award whistleblower program (tax, interest, and penalty underpayments of $2 million or less), the IRS may pay whistleblowers up to 15 percent of the unpaid taxes and interest collected. Whistleblowers use IRS Form 211 (www.IRS.gov) to apply for the program, and as you might expect, all whistleblower payments received are fully taxable. In its first payment, the IRS awarded $4.5 million to a former in-house accountant for a large financial services firm. Given the potential windfall to whistleblowers, you might expect a long line of "concerned" citizens applying for the program. You would be correct. As of January 2017, the IRS Commissioner announced that the IRS has paid out more than $465 million in awards since 2007, on collection of $3.4 billion based on whistleblower information.

Source: Based on: "Taxes: How to Turn in Your Neighbor to the IRS," *The Wall Street Journal,* WSJ.com, September 3, 2011.

How was Bill and Mercedes's tax return selected for audit? Given the audit focus on certain deductions, the IRS likely selected their return for audit because the amount or type of the deductions resulted in a high DIF score. IRS personnel then determined that the deductions warranted further review and, thus, selected the tax return for audit.

ETHICS

After Bill and Mercedes's tax return was selected for audit, Bill read on the Internet speculation that filing a paper tax return (instead of filing electronically) and extending a tax return deadline decrease the chance of IRS audit. Bill has convinced Mercedes that they need to use these strategies in the future and look for other ways to avoid audit. Has Bill crossed an ethical boundary?

Types of Audits

The three types of IRS audits are correspondence, office, and field examinations. **Correspondence examinations** are the most common. These audits, as the name suggests, are conducted by mail and generally are limited to one or two items on the taxpayer's return. Of the three types of audits, correspondence audits are generally the narrowest in scope and the least complex. The IRS typically requests supporting documentation for one or more items on the taxpayer's return, like charitable contributions deducted, for example. When appropriate documentation is promptly supplied, these audits typically can be concluded relatively quickly. Of course, they can also be expanded to address other issues that arise as a result of the IRS's inspection of taxpayer documents.

Office examinations are the second most common audit. As the name suggests, the IRS conducts them at its local office. These audits are typically broader in scope and more complex than correspondence examinations. Small businesses, taxpayers operating sole proprietorships, and middle- to high-income individual taxpayers are more likely, if audited, to have office examinations. In these examinations, the taxpayer receives a notice that identifies the items subject to audit, requests substantiation for these items as necessary, and notifies the taxpayer of the date, time, and location of the exam. Taxpayers may attend the examination alone or with representation, such as their tax adviser or attorney, or simply let their tax adviser or attorney attend on their behalf.

Field examinations are the least common audit. The IRS conducts these at the taxpayer's place of business or the location where the taxpayer's books, records, and source documents are maintained. Field examinations are generally the broadest in scope and the most complex of the three audit types. They can last months to years and generally are limited to business returns and the most complex individual returns.

What type of exam do you think Bill and Mercedes will have? Because their return is an individual tax return and the audit is restricted to a relatively narrow set of deductions, their return will likely be subject to a correspondence audit. If the audit were broader in scope, an office examination would be more likely.

After the Audit   After the examination, the IRS agent provides a list of proposed adjustments (if any) to the taxpayer for review. If he or she agrees to the proposed changes, the taxpayer signs an agreement form (Form 870) and pays the additional tax owed or receives the proposed refund. If the taxpayer disputes the proposed changes, the taxpayer will receive a **30-day letter** giving him or her 30 days to either (1) request a conference with an appeals officer, who is independent and resides in a separate IRS division from the examining agent, or (2) agree to the proposed adjustment. An appeals officer would consider the merits of the unresolved issues as well as the "hazards of litigation"—that is, the probability that the IRS will lose if the case is brought to court and the resulting costs of a taxpayer-favorable ruling. If the taxpayer chooses the appeals conference and reaches an agreement with the IRS there, the taxpayer can then sign Form 870. If the taxpayer and IRS still do not agree on the proposed adjustment at the appeals conference, or the taxpayer chooses not to request an appeals conference, the IRS will send the taxpayer a **90-day letter.** See Exhibit 2-2.

Why would a taxpayer prefer one trial court over others? To understand this, we must appreciate the basic distinguishing factors of each. First and foremost, it is relatively common for the U.S. Tax Court, local U.S. District Court, or the U.S. Court of Federal Claims to interpret and rule differently on the same basic tax issue. Given a choice of courts, the taxpayer should prefer the court most likely to rule favorably on his or her particular issues. The courts also differ in other ways. For example, the U.S. District Court is the only court that provides for a jury trial; the U.S. Tax Court is the only court that allows tax cases to be heard *before* the taxpayer pays the disputed liability and the only court with a small claims division (hearing claims involving disputed liabilities of $50,000 or less); and the U.S. Tax Court judges are tax experts, whereas the U.S. District Court and U.S. Court of Federal Claims judges are generalists. The taxpayer should consider each of these factors in choosing a trial court. For example, if the taxpayer feels very confident in her tax return position but does not have sufficient funds to pay the disputed liability, she will prefer the U.S. Tax Court. If, instead, the taxpayer is litigating a tax return position

THE KEY FACTS

IRS Audits

- The three types of IRS audits are correspondence, office, and field examinations.
- After the audit, the IRS will send the taxpayer a 30-day letter, which provides the taxpayer the opportunity to pay the proposed assessment or request an appeals conference.
- If an agreement is not reached at appeals or the taxpayer does not pay the proposed assessment, the IRS will send the taxpayer a 90-day letter.
- After receiving the 90-day letter, the taxpayer may pay the tax or petition the U.S. Tax Court to hear the case.
- If the taxpayer chooses to pay the tax, the taxpayer may then request a refund of the tax and eventually sue the IRS for refund in the U.S. District Court or the U.S. Court of Federal Claims.

EXHIBIT 2-2   IRS Appeals/Litigation Process

IRS Exam: ©Imageroller/Alamy Stock Photo; Supreme Court: ©McGraw-Hill Education/Jill Braaten, photographer (also known as a *statutory notice of deficiency*) explains that the taxpayer has 90 days to either (1) pay the proposed deficiency or (2) file a petition in the U.S. Tax Court to hear the case.[8] The **U.S. Tax Court** is a national court whose judges are tax experts who hear only tax cases. If the taxpayer would like to litigate the case but prefers it to be heard in the local **U.S. District Court** or the **U.S. Court of Federal Claims,** the taxpayer must pay the tax deficiency first, then request a refund from the IRS, and then sue the IRS for refund in the court after the IRS denies the refund claim.

that is low on technical merit but high on emotional appeal, a jury trial in the local U.S. District Court may be the best option.

What happens after the taxpayer's case has been decided in a trial court? The process may not be quite finished. After the trial court's verdict, the losing party has the right to request one of the 13 **U.S. Circuit Courts of Appeals** to hear the case. Exhibit 2-3 depicts the specific appellant courts for each lower-level court. Both the U.S. Tax Court and local U.S. District Court cases are appealed to the specific U.S. Circuit Court of Appeals based on the taxpayer's residence.[9] Cases litigated in Alabama, Florida, and Georgia, for example, appeal to the U.S. Circuit Court of Appeals for the 11th Circuit, whereas those tried in Louisiana, Mississippi, and Texas appeal to the 5th Circuit. In contrast, all U.S. Court of Federal Claims cases appeal to the U.S. Circuit Court of Appeals for the Federal

[8]If the taxpayer lacks the funds to pay the assessed tax, there is legitimate doubt as to whether the taxpayer owes part or all of the assessed tax, or collection of the tax would cause the taxpayer economic hardship or be unfair or inequitable, the taxpayer can request an offer in compromise with the IRS to settle the tax liability for less than the full amount assessed by completing Form 656.

[9]Decisions rendered by the U.S. Tax Court Small Claims Division cannot be appealed by the taxpayer or the IRS.

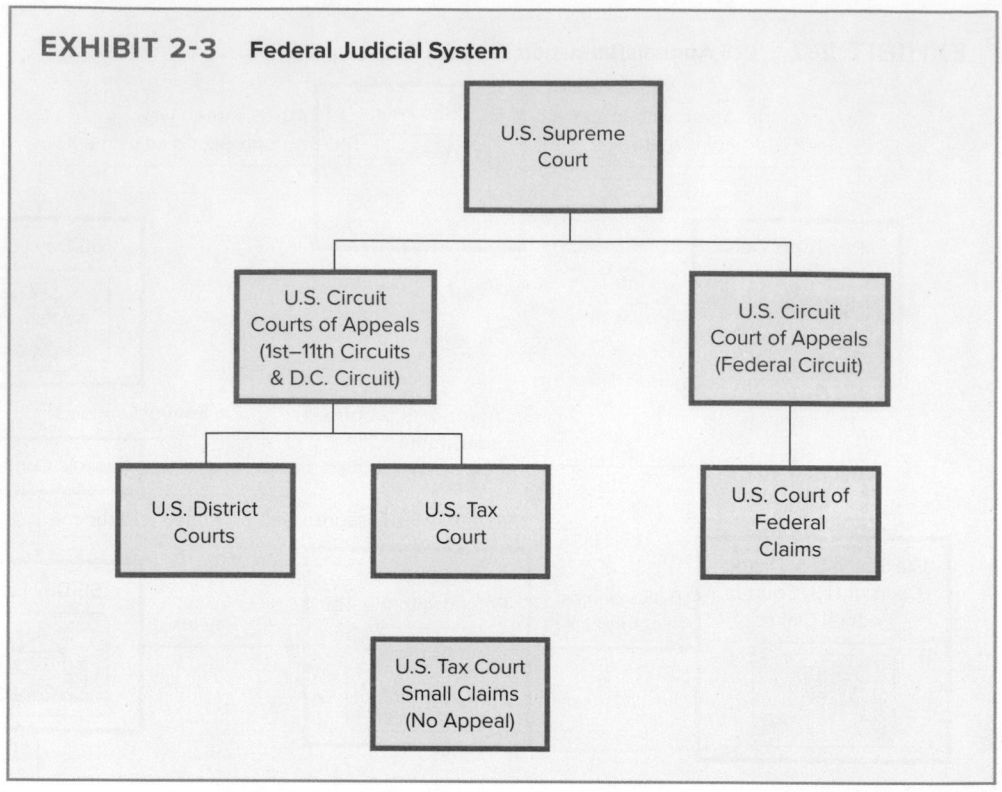

EXHIBIT 2-3 Federal Judicial System

Circuit (located in Washington, D.C.). Exhibit 2-4 depicts the geographic regions for each of the 11 U.S. Circuit Courts of Appeals defined by numerical region. Not depicted are the U.S. Circuit Court of Appeals for the District of Columbia and the U.S. Circuit Court of Appeals for the Federal Circuit.

Through the initial selection of a trial court—U.S. District Court, U.S. Tax Court, or U.S. Court of Federal Claims—the taxpayer has the ability to determine which circuit court would hear an appeal of the case (the U.S. Circuit Court of Appeals based on residence or the U.S. Circuit Court of Appeals for the Federal Circuit). Alternative circuit courts may interpret the law differently, and therefore, in choosing a trial-level court, the taxpayer should consider the relevant circuit courts' judicial histories to determine which circuit court (and thus, which trial court) would be more likely to rule in his or her favor.

After an appeals court hears a case, the losing party has one last option to receive a favorable ruling: a petition to the **U.S. Supreme Court** to hear the case. However, given the quantity of other cases appealed to the U.S. Supreme Court that are of national importance, the Supreme Court agrees to hear only a few tax cases a year—cases with great significance to a broad cross-section of taxpayers or cases litigating issues in which there has been disagreement among the circuit courts. For most tax cases, the Supreme Court refuses to hear the case (denies the *writ of certiorari*) and litigation ends with the circuit court decision.

Although litigation of tax disputes is quite common, taxpayers should carefully consider the pros and cons. Litigation can be very costly financially and emotionally, and thus it is more appropriately used as an option of last resort, after all other appeal efforts have been exhausted.

What is the likely course of action for Bill and Mercedes's audit? It is too soon to tell. Before you can assess the likely outcome of their audit, you need a better understanding of both the audit issue and the relevant tax laws that apply to the issue. The next section explains alternative tax law sources. After we discuss the various sources of our tax laws,

EXHIBIT 2-4 Geographic Boundaries for the U.S. Circuit Courts of Appeals

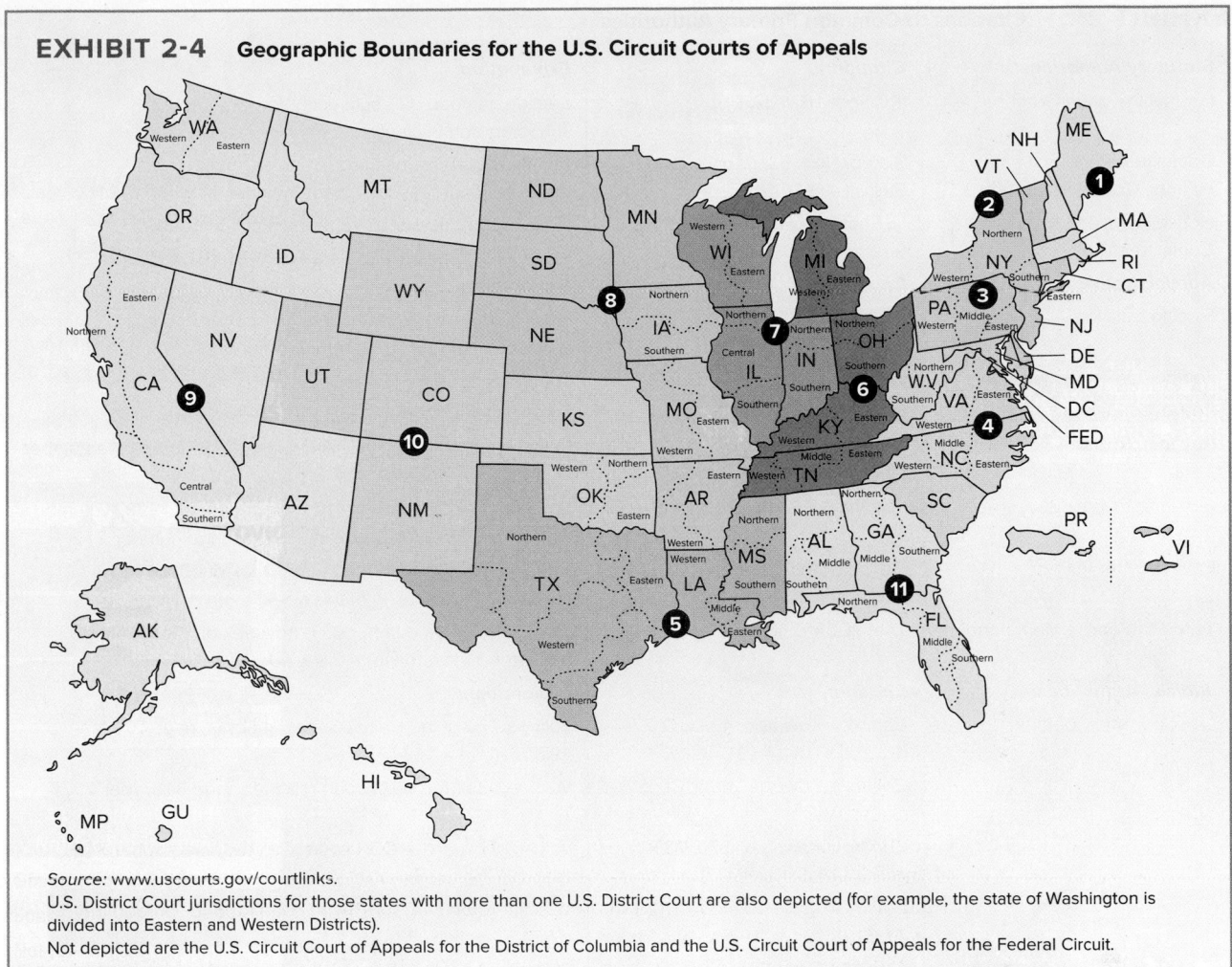

Source: www.uscourts.gov/courtlinks.

U.S. District Court jurisdictions for those states with more than one U.S. District Court are also depicted (for example, the state of Washington is divided into Eastern and Western Districts).

Not depicted are the U.S. Circuit Court of Appeals for the District of Columbia and the U.S. Circuit Court of Appeals for the Federal Circuit.

we'll describe how Bill and Mercedes (or their CPA) can research the sources to identify the best possible course of action.[10]

TAX LAW SOURCES

LO 2-3 LO 2-4

There are two broad categories of tax authorities: primary authorities and secondary authorities. **Primary authorities** are official sources of the tax law generated by the legislative branch (statutory authority issued by Congress), judicial branch (rulings by the U.S. District Courts, U.S. Tax Court, U.S. Court of Federal Claims, U.S. Circuit Courts of Appeals, or U.S. Supreme Court), and executive/administrative branch (Treasury and IRS pronouncements). Exhibit 2-5 displays the most common primary sources, their respective citations, and related explanations. We'll discuss each of these authorities below.

Secondary authorities are unofficial tax authorities that interpret and explain the primary authorities, such as tax research services (discussed below), tax articles from professional journals and law reviews, newsletters, and textbooks. For quick questions, practitioners often use the *CCH Master Tax Guide* or *RIA Federal Tax Handbook*.

---

[10]Accountants should be mindful to not engage in the unauthorized practice of law. In years past, several court cases have addressed this issue without providing a clear understanding between practicing tax accounting and the unauthorized practice of law. At present, tax accountants are not likely to overstep their responsibilities if they limit their advice to tax issues and leave the general legal advice and drafting of legal documents to attorneys.

EXHIBIT 2-5   Citations to Common Primary Authorities

Statutory Authorities:	Citation:	Explanation:
Internal Revenue Code	IRC Sec. 162(e)(2)(B)(i)	Section number 162, subsection e, paragraph 2, subparagraph B, clause i
Committee Reports: Senate Finance Committee Report	S. Rep. No. 353, 82d Cong., 1st Sess. 14 (1951)	Senate report number 353, Congress number 82, Congressional session 1, page number 14, year 1951
House Ways and Means Committee Report	H. Rep. No. 242, 82d Cong., 1st Sess. 40 (1951)	House report number 242, Congress number 82, Congressional session 1, page number 40, year 1951
Administrative Authorities:	**Citation:**	**Explanation:**
Final Regulation	Reg. Sec. 1.217-2(c)(1)	Type of regulation (1 = income tax), code section 217, regulation number 2, paragraph c, subparagraph number 1
Temporary Regulation	Temp. Reg. Sec. 1.217-2(c)(1)	Same as final regulation
Proposed Regulation	Prop. Reg. Sec. 1.217-2(c)(1)	Same as final regulation
Revenue Ruling	Rev. Rul. 77-262, 1977-2 C.B. 41	Ruling number 77-262 (262nd ruling of 1977), volume number of cumulative bulletin 1977-2, page number 41
Revenue Procedure	Rev. Proc. 99-10, 1999-1 C.B. 272	Procedure number 99-10 (10th procedure of 1999), volume number of cumulative bulletin 1999-1, page number 272
Private Letter Ruling	PLR 200601001	Year 2006, week number 01 (1st week of 2006), ruling number 001 (1st ruling of the week)
Technical Advice Memorandum	TAM 200402001	Year 2004, week number 02 (2nd week of 2004), ruling number 001 (1st ruling of the week)
Judicial Authorities:	**Citation:**	**Explanation:**
U.S. Supreme Court	*Comm. v. Kowalski,* 434 U.S. 77 (S. Ct., 1977)	Volume 434 of the United States Reporter, page 77, year 1977
	Comm. v. Kowalski, 98 S. Ct. 315 (S. Ct., 1977)	Volume 98 of the West court reporter, page 315, year 1977
	Comm. v. Kowalski, 77-2 USTC par. 9,748 (S. Ct., 1977)	Volume 77-2 of the CCH court reporter, paragraph 9,748, year 1977
	Comm. v. Kowalski, 40 AFTR2d 77-6128 (S. Ct., 1977)	Volume 40 of the RIA AFTR2d court reporter, paragraph 77-6128, year 1977
U.S. Circuit Court of Appeals	*Azar Nut Co. v. Comm.,* 931 F.2d 314 (5th Cir., 1991)	Volume 931 of the West F.2d court reporter, page 314, circuit 5th, year 1991
	Azar Nut Co. v. Comm., 91-1 USTC par. 50,257 (5th Cir., 1991)	Volume 91-1 of the CCH USTC court reporter, paragraph 50,257, circuit 5th, year 1991
	Azar Nut Co. v. Comm., 67 AFTR2d 91-987 (5th Cir., 1991)	Volume 67 of the RIA AFTR2d court reporter, paragraph 91-987, year 1991
U.S. Tax Court—Regular decision	*L.A. Beeghly,* 36 TC 154 (1962)	Volume 36 of the Tax Court reporter, page 154, year 1962
U.S. Tax Court—Memorandum decision	*Robert Rodriguez,* RIA TC Memo 2005-012	Paragraph number 2005-012 of the RIA Tax Court Memorandum reporter
	Robert Rodriguez, 85 TCM 1162 (2005)	Volume 85 of the CCH Tax Court Memorandum reporter, page 1162, year 2005
U.S. Court of Federal Claims	*J.R. Cohen v. U.S.,* 510 F. Supp. 297 (Fed. Cl., 1993)	Volume 510 of the West F. Supp. court reporter, page 297, year 1993
	J.R. Cohen v. U.S., 72 AFTR2d 93-5124 (Fed. Cl., 1993)	Volume 72 of the RIA AFTR2d court reporter, paragraph 93-5124, year 1993
	J.R. Cohen v. U.S., 93-1 USTC par. 50,354 (Fed. Cl., 1993)	Volume 93-1 of the CCH USTC court reporter, paragraph 50,354, year 1993
U.S. District Court	*Waxler Towing Co., Inc. v. U.S.,* 510 F. Supp. 297 (W.D, TN, 1981)	Volume 510 of the West F. Supp. court reporter, page 297, Western District (W.D.), state Tennessee, year 1981
	Waxler Towing Co., Inc. v. U.S., 81-2 USTC par. 9,541 (W.D., TN, 1981)	Volume 81-2 of the CCH USTC court reporter, paragraph 9,541, Western District (W.D.), state Tennessee, year 1981
	Waxler Towing Co., Inc. v. U.S., 48 AFTR2d 81-5274 (W.D., TN, 1981)	Volume 48 of the RIA AFTR2d court reporter, paragraph 81-5274, Western District (W.D.), state Tennessee, year 1981

EXHIBIT 2-6   Common Secondary Tax Authorities

Tax Research Services:	*Professional Journals:*
BNA Tax Management Portfolios	*Journal of Accountancy*
CCH Standard Federal Tax Reporter	*Journal of Taxation*
CCH Tax Research Consultant	*Practical Tax Strategies*
RIA Federal Tax Coordinator	*Taxes*
RIA United States Tax Reporter	*Tax Adviser*
Newsletters:	*Quick Reference Sources:*
Daily Tax Report	*IRS Publications*
Federal Tax Weekly Alert	*CCH Master Tax Guide*
Tax Notes	*RIA Federal Tax Handbook*
Law Reviews:	*Textbooks:*
Tax Law Review (New York University School of Law)	*McGraw-Hill's Taxation of Individuals and Business Entities*
Virginia Tax Review (University of Virginia School of Law)	*McGraw-Hill's Essentials of Federal Taxation*

Secondary authorities may be very helpful in understanding a tax issue, but they hold little weight in a tax dispute (hence their "unofficial" status). Thus, tax advisers should always be careful to verify their understanding of tax law by examining primary authorities directly and to *never* cite secondary authority in a research memo. Exhibit 2-6 lists some of the common sources of secondary authority.

TAXES IN THE REAL WORLD   Google: Not Authoritative on Tax Matters

While Internet super giant Google may be the king of all cyberspace knowledge, the Tax Court ruled in *Woodard v. Comm.,* TC Summary Opinion 2009 150, that a Google search does not constitute reasonable cause to excuse a Harvard MBA/CPA from taking an incorrect tax return position. The Tax Court noted that although the taxpayer had not worked as an accountant for years before filing his tax return, "his accounting degree, MBA, and CPA training, no matter how stale, undoubtedly taught him what sources could be relied upon as definitive; such as, for example, the Internal Revenue Code and the income tax regulations, both of which are readily available on the Internet."

Legislative Sources: Congress and the Constitution

The three legislative or statutory tax authorities are the U.S. Constitution, the Internal Revenue Code, and tax treaties. The **U.S. Constitution** is the highest authority in the United States, but it provides very little in the way of tax law since it contains no discussion of tax rates, taxable income, or other details. Instead, the 16th Amendment provides Congress the ability to tax income directly, from whatever source derived, without apportionment across the states.

Various attempts to amend the U.S. Constitution with regard to taxation—for example, one effort to repeal the 16th Amendment entirely and one to require a two-thirds majority in both houses to raise taxes—have so far met with failure.

Internal Revenue Code   The second (and main) statutory authority is the **Internal Revenue Code of 1986,** as amended, known as the Code. The Internal Revenue Code has the same authoritative weight as tax treaties and Supreme Court rulings. Thus, a taxpayer should feel very confident in a tax return position, such as taking a deduction, that is specifically allowed by the Code. The Internal Revenue Code is unique in that all federal tax authorities—all administrative and judicial authorities except tax treaties

EXHIBIT 2-7 Tax Legislation Process

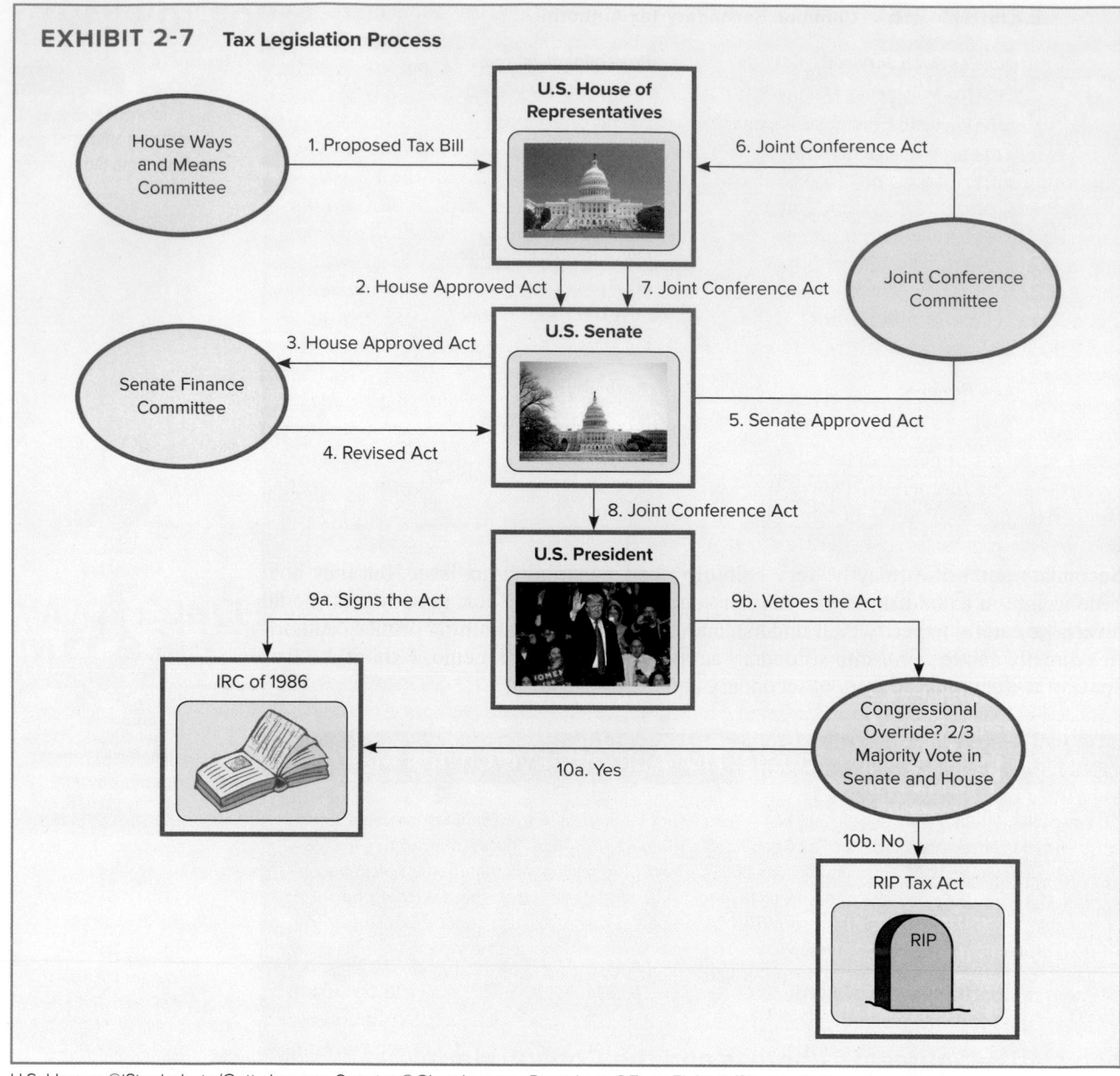

U.S. House: ©iStockphoto/Getty Images; Senate: ©Glow Images; President: ©Evan El-Amin/Shutterstock

and the Constitution—can be seen as an interpretation of it. Hence, understanding the relevant code section(s) is critical to being an efficient and effective tax professional.

Congress enacts tax legislation virtually every year that changes the Code; 1986 was simply the last major overhaul. Prior to 1986, tax law changes were incorporated into the Internal Revenue Code of 1954, the year a new numbering system and other significant changes were introduced. Before that, tax law changes were incorporated into the Internal Revenue Code of 1939, which was the year the tax law was first codified.

The Legislative Process for Tax Laws   Exhibit 2-7 illustrates the legislative process for enacting tax laws. As required by the U.S. Constitution (Article 1, Section 7), "All bills for raising revenue shall originate in the House of Representatives." The Senate may propose tax legislation, but the first to formally consider a bill will be the House, typically within its Ways and Means Committee. After the committee debates the proposed legislation and drafts a bill, the bill goes to the House of Representatives floor for debate and ultimately a vote (either yea or nay without modification). If the bill is approved, it becomes an *act* and is sent to the Senate, which typically refers the act to the Senate Finance Committee. Not to be outdone by the House, the Senate Finance Committee usually amends the act during its deliberations. After the revised act passes the Senate Finance Committee, it goes to the Senate for debate and vote. Unlike representatives, senators may modify the proposed legislation during their debate.

If the Senate passes the act, both the House and Senate versions of the legislation are sent to the Joint Conference Committee, which consists of members of the House Ways and Means Committee and the Senate Finance Committee. During the Joint Conference Committee deliberations, committee members debate the two versions of the proposed legislation. Possible outcomes for any specific provision in the proposed legislation include adoption of the Senate version, the House version, or some compromise version of the two acts. Likewise, the Joint Conference Committee may simply choose to eliminate specific provisions from the proposed legislation or fail to reach a compromise, thereby terminating the legislation.

After the Joint Conference Committee approves the act, the revised legislation is sent to the House and Senate for vote. If both the House and Senate approve it, the act is sent to the president for his or her signature. If the president signs the act, it becomes law and is incorporated into the Internal Revenue Code of 1986 (Title 26 of the U.S. Code, which contains *all* codified laws of the United States). If the president vetoes the legislation, Congress may override the veto with a two-thirds positive vote in both the House and the Senate.

The House Ways and Means Committee, Senate Finance Committee, and Joint Conference Committee each produce a committee report that explains the current tax law, proposed change in the law, and reasons for the change. These committee reports are considered statutory sources of the tax law and may be very useful in interpreting tax law changes and understanding congressional intent. These committee reports are especially important after new legislation has been enacted because, with the exception of the Code, there will be very little authority interpreting the new law (i.e., no judicial or administrative authorities because of the time it takes for the new law to be litigated or for the IRS to issue interpretative guidance).

Basic Organization of the Code The Internal Revenue Code is divided into subtitles, chapters, subchapters, parts, subparts, and sections. All existing and any new tax laws are placed in the Code within a specific subtitle, chapter, subchapter, part, subpart, and section. When referencing a tax law, the researcher generally refers to the law simply by its code section. Code sections are numbered from 1 to 9834, with gaps in the section numbers to allow new code sections to be added to the appropriate parts of the Code as needed. Each code section is further divided into subsections, paragraphs, subparagraphs, and clauses to allow more specific reference or citation. See Exhibit 2-5 for an example code citation and explanation.

Memorizing the various subtitles and chapters of the Code has limited value (except to impress your friends at parties). However, understanding the *organization* of the Code is important, especially for the aspiring tax accountant. (See Exhibit 2-8.) First, you must understand the organization of a code section, its subsections, paragraphs, subparagraphs, and clauses to be able to cite the respective law correctly as, for example, IRC Sec. 162(b)(2). Second, note that many provisions in the Code apply only to specific parts of the Code. For example, it is quite common for a code section to include the phrase "for purposes of this chapter, ..." If you do not understand what laws are encompassed in the chapter, it will be very difficult for you to interpret the code section and determine its applicability to a research question.

Finally, remember that code sections addressing similar transactions, such as deductions, or topics, such as C corporations, are grouped together. Consider a researcher faced with the question of whether an item of income is taxable. If the researcher understands the organization of the Code, she can quickly focus her research on code sections 61–140, which provide a broad definition of gross income, list items specifically included in gross income, and identify items specifically excluded from gross income.

THE KEY FACTS

Statutory Authorities

- U.S. Constitution
  - The 16th Amendment provides Congress the ability to tax income directly, from whatever source derived, without apportionment across the states.
- Internal Revenue Code
  - The main statutory authority is the Internal Revenue Code of 1986.
  - The Internal Revenue Code has the same authoritative weight as tax treaties and Supreme Court rulings.
  - Changes to the Code are passed by the House of Representatives and Senate and signed into law by the president.
  - The House Ways and Means Committee and Senate Finance Committee oversee tax legislation in the House of Representatives and Senate, respectively.
  - When referencing a tax law, the researcher generally refers to the law by its code section.
- Treaties
  - Tax treaties are agreements negotiated between countries that describe the tax treatment of entities subject to tax in both countries.

EXHIBIT 2-8   Example of Code Organization

Subtitle A—Income Taxes

　Chapter 1—Income Taxes

　　Subchapter A—Determination of Tax Liability

　　　Part I—Definition of Gross Income, Adjusted Gross Income, Taxable Income, etc. (Sec. 61–68)

　　　　Sec. 61—Gross Income Defined

　　　　Sec. 62—Adjusted Gross Income Defined

　　　　Sec. 63—Taxable Income Defined

　　　　　Subsection 63(c)—Standard Deduction

　　　　　　Paragraph 63(c)(2)—Basic Standard Deduction

　　　　　　　Subparagraph 63(c)(2)(A)

　　　　　　　Clause 63(c)(2)(A)(i)

　　　Part II—Items Specifically Included in Gross Income (Sec. 71–90)

　　　　Sec. 71—Alimony

　　　　Sec. 72—Annuities

　　　　Sec. 73—Services of Child

　　　　Sec. 74—Prizes & Awards

　　　Part III—Items Specifically Excluded from Gross Income (Sec. 101–140)

　　　　Sec. 101—Certain Death Benefits

　　　　Sec. 102—Gifts and Inheritances

　　　　Sec. 103—Interest on State & Local Bonds

Tax Treaties   **Tax treaties** are negotiated agreements between countries that describe the tax treatment of entities subject to tax in both countries, such as U.S. citizens earning investment income in Spain. The U.S. president has the authority to enter into a tax treaty with another country after receiving the Senate's advice. If you are a U.S. citizen earning income abroad or an accountant with international clients, you need knowledge of U.S. tax laws, the foreign country's tax laws, and the respective tax treaty between the U.S. and the foreign country for efficient tax planning. Because the focus in this text is on U.S. tax laws, we only briefly mention the importance of tax treaties as a statutory authority.

Example 2-2

Bill recently spent a summer in Milan, Italy, teaching a graduate level economics course. While in Italy he earned a $20,000 stipend from Bocconi University and some interest in a temporary banking account that he established for the trip. What tax laws must Bill consider to understand any tax liability from his $20,000 stipend?

Answer: U.S. tax laws, Italian tax laws, and the U.S.–Italy tax treaty will determine the tax consequences of the amounts Bill earned in Italy.

Judicial Sources: The Courts

Our judicial system has the ultimate authority to interpret the Internal Revenue Code and settle disputes between the IRS and taxpayers. As Exhibit 2-3 illustrates, there are five basic sources of judicial authority (three trial-level courts, 13 U.S. Circuit Courts of Appeals, and the Supreme Court). We've noted that the Supreme Court, along with the Code, represents the highest tax-specific authority. An important distinction between the two, however, is that the Supreme Court does not establish law but instead simply interprets and applies the Code (along with other authorities). Thus, the Code and the Supreme Court should never be in conflict.[11]

[11]The Supreme Court does have the authority to declare a Code provision unconstitutional.

THE KEY FACTS

Judicial Authorities

• Our judicial system has the ultimate authority to interpret the Internal Revenue Code and settle disputes between taxpayers and the IRS.

• The Supreme Court is the highest judicial authority.

• Beneath the Supreme Court, the decisions of the 13 Circuit Courts of Appeals represent the next highest judicial authority.

　　　　(continued)

Below the Supreme Court, the decisions of the 13 U.S. Circuit Courts of Appeals represent the next highest judicial authority. The lowest level of judicial authority consists of three different types of trial-level courts (94 U.S. District Courts that hear cases involving taxpayers that reside within their respective district, the U.S. Court of Federal Claims, and the U.S. Tax Court). Given that the U.S. Tax Court hears only tax cases and that its judges are "tax experts," its decisions typically have more weight than those rendered by a district court or the U.S. Court of Federal Claims.[12] Likewise, because the U.S. Court of Federal Claims hears a much narrower set of issues than U.S. District Courts (only monetary claims against the U.S. government), its decisions have more weight than district court decisions.

In rendering court decisions, all courts apply the judicial doctrine of ***stare decisis.*** This doctrine means that a court will rule consistently with (a) its previous rulings (unless, due to evolving interpretations of the tax law over time, the court decides to overturn an earlier decision) and (b) the rulings of higher courts with appellate jurisdiction (the courts its cases are appealed to). The implication of *stare decisis* is that a circuit court will abide by Supreme Court rulings and its own rulings, whereas a trial-level court will abide by Supreme Court rulings, its respective circuit court's rulings, and its own rulings. For example, a district court in California would follow U.S. 9th Circuit and Supreme Court rulings as well as the court's own rulings.

The doctrine of *stare decisis* presents a special problem for the U.S. Tax Court because it appeals to different circuit courts based on the taxpayer's residence. To implement the doctrine of *stare decisis*, the tax court applies the **Golsen rule.**[13] The Golsen rule simply states that the tax court will abide by rulings of the circuit court that has appellate jurisdiction for a case.

> **THE KEY FACTS**
>
> - The lowest level of judicial authority consists of three different types of trial-level courts (U.S. District Courts, U.S. Court of Federal Claims, and the U.S. Tax Court).
> - U.S. Tax Court decisions typically are considered to have more authoritative weight than decisions rendered by a district court or the U.S. Court of Federal Claims.
> - All courts apply the judicial doctrine of *stare decisis*, which means that a court will rule consistently with its previous rulings and the rulings of higher courts with appellate jurisdiction.

Example 2-3

What if: If Bill and Mercedes opt to litigate their case in the U.S. Tax Court, by which circuit court's rulings will the court abide?

Answer: Because Bill and Mercedes live in Florida, the U.S. Tax Court will abide the circuit court with appellate jurisdiction in Florida, which happens to be the U.S. 11th Circuit Court.

Administrative Sources: The U.S. Treasury

Regulations, Revenue Rulings, and Revenue Procedures The Treasury Department, of which the IRS is a bureau, is charged with administering and interpreting the tax laws of the United States, among other duties such as printing money and advising the president on economic issues. **Regulations** are the Treasury Department's official interpretation of the Internal Revenue Code, have the highest authoritative weight, and often contain examples of the application of the Code that may be particularly helpful to the tax researcher. Regulations are issued in three different forms: final, temporary, and proposed. The names are very descriptive. **Final regulations** are regulations that have been issued in final form, and thus, unless or until revoked, they represent the Treasury's interpretation of the Code. **Temporary regulations** have a limited life (three years for regulations issued after November 20, 1988). Nonetheless, during their life, they carry the same authoritative weight as final regulations. Finally, all regulations are issued in the form of **proposed regulations** first, to allow public comment on them. Proposed regulations do not carry the same authoritative weight as temporary or final regulations.

In addition to being issued in three different forms, regulations also serve three basic purposes: interpretative, procedural, and legislative. Most regulations are issued as

> **THE KEY FACTS**
>
> **Administrative Authorities**
>
> - The Treasury Department is charged with administering and interpreting the tax laws.
> - Regulations
>   - Regulations are the Treasury Department's official interpretation of the Internal Revenue Code and have the highest authoritative weight.
>   - Regulations are issued in three different forms (proposed, temporary, and final) and serve three basic purposes (interpretative, procedural, and legislative).

---

[12]The Tax Court renders both "regular" and "memorandum" decisions. Regular decisions involve new or unusual points of law, whereas memorandum decisions involve questions of fact or the application of existing law. Both decisions have similar authoritative weight. Decisions issued by the Tax Court's Small Claims division may not be cited as precedent.

[13]54 TC 742 (1970).

(continued)

- Revenue rulings and revenue procedures
  - Revenue rulings and revenue procedures are second in administrative authoritative weight after regulations.
  - Revenue rulings address the application of the Code and regulations to a specific factual situation.
  - Revenue procedures explain in greater detail IRS practice and procedures in administering the tax law.
- Letter rulings
  - Letter rulings are less authoritative but more specific than revenue rulings and regulations.
  - Private letter rulings represent the IRS's application of the Code and other tax authorities to a specific transaction and taxpayer.

interpretative or procedural regulations. As the names suggest, **interpretative regulations** represent the Treasury's interpretation of the Code. In Bill and Mercedes's case, these might be the regulations issued under IRC Sec. 163, which discuss interest deductions. **Procedural regulations** explain Treasury Department procedures as they relate to administering the Code. Again, for Bill and Mercedes's case, these might be the regulations issued under IRC Sec. 6501 regarding the statute of limitations for IRS assessment and collection. **Legislative regulations,** the rarest type, are issued when Congress specifically directs the Treasury Department to create regulations to address an issue in an area of law. In these instances, the Treasury is actually writing the law instead of interpreting the Code. Because legislative regulations represent tax law instead of an interpretation of tax law, legislative regulations generally have been viewed to have more authoritative weight than interpretative and procedural regulations. However, in *Mayo Foundation for Medical Education & Research v. U.S.,* 131 S.Ct. 704 (2011), the Supreme Court held (subject to specific conditions) that all Treasury regulations warrant deference. It is thus a very difficult process to challenge any regulation, and taxpayers are cautioned not to take tax return positions inconsistent with regulations.

Revenue rulings and revenue procedures are second in administrative authoritative weight after regulations. But unlike regulations, revenue rulings address the application of the Code and regulations to a specific factual situation. Thus, while **revenue rulings** have less authoritative weight, they provide a much more detailed interpretation of the Code as it applies to a specific transaction and fact pattern. For example, Rev. Rul. 87-22 discusses the deductions of prepaid interest (points) a taxpayer may claim when refinancing the mortgage for a principal residence, whereas the Code and regulations do not specifically address this issue. Although revenue rulings are binding on the IRS (until revoked, superseded, or modified), courts may agree or disagree with a revenue ruling. Thus, while revenue rulings should be carefully evaluated because they represent the IRS's interpretation, courts may provide a different interpretation of the tax law that a taxpayer might choose to follow. **Revenue procedures** are also much more detailed than regulations. They explain in greater detail IRS practice and procedures in administering the tax law. For example, Rev. Proc. 87-56 provides the specific depreciation lives for depreciable assets (discussed in the Property Acquisition and Cost Recovery chapter). As with revenue rulings, revenue procedures are binding on the IRS until revoked, modified, or superseded.

Letter Rulings   Below revenue rulings and revenue procedures in authoritative weight rest letter rulings. As you might guess, letter rulings are less authoritative but more specific than revenue rulings and regulations. Letter rulings generally may not be used as precedent by taxpayers. However, they may be cited as authority to avoid the substantial understatement of tax penalty under IRC Sec. 6662 imposed on taxpayers and the related tax practitioner penalty under IRC Sec. 6694 (discussed later in this chapter). **Private letter rulings** represent the IRS's application of the Code and other tax authorities to a specific transaction and taxpayer. Private letter rulings are issued in response to a taxpayer request and are common for proposed transactions with potentially large tax implications. For example, companies commonly request a private letter ruling to ensure that a proposed corporate acquisition meets the definition of a tax-free exchange. However, the IRS also maintains a list of certain issues on which it refuses to rule, such as the tax consequences of proposed federal tax legislation. Each year, the IRS publishes an updated list of these transactions in a revenue procedure.

Other types of letter rulings include determination letters and technical advice memorandums. **Determination letters,** issued by local IRS directors, are generally not controversial. An example of a determination letter is the request by an employer for the IRS to rule that the taxpayer's retirement plan is a "qualified plan." **Technical advice memorandums** differ from private letter rulings in that they are generated for completed transactions and usually are requested by an IRS agent during an IRS audit.

Is this a comprehensive list of IRS pronouncements? No. In addition to the pronouncements listed above, the IRS issues several less common types, which are beyond the scope of this text. A couple of other pronouncements, however, warrant some discussion. As we mentioned above, the IRS and taxpayers litigate tax cases in a number of courts and jurisdictions. Obviously, the IRS wins some of these cases and loses others. Except for Supreme Court cases, whenever the IRS loses, it may issue an **acquiescence** or **nonacquiescence** as guidance for how the IRS intends to respond to the loss. Although an acquiescence indicates that the IRS has decided to *follow* the court's adverse ruling in the future, it does not mean that the IRS *agrees* with it. Instead, it simply means that the IRS will no longer litigate this issue.

A nonacquiescence has the exact opposite implications and alerts taxpayers that the IRS does plan to continue to litigate this issue. Finally, the IRS also issues **actions on decisions,** which explain the background reasoning behind an IRS acquiescence or non-acquiescence.[14] What are noticeably absent from the list of administrative authorities? IRS publications and tax return form instructions. *Neither are considered primary authorities and should not be cited as precedent. Likewise, it is not advisable to rely on either to avoid taxpayer or tax practitioner penalties.*

TAX RESEARCH

LO 2-5

Now that you have a basic understanding of the different types of tax authority, why do you think that the IRS and taxpayers disagree with respect to the tax treatment of a transaction? In other words, why would the IRS and Bill and Mercedes's CPA reach different conclusions regarding the deductibility of certain expenses? The answer is that, because the Code does not specifically address the tax consequences of each transaction type or every possible variation of a particular transaction, the application of the tax law is subject to debate and differing interpretations by the IRS, courts, tax professionals, taxpayers, and so on. Tax research, therefore, plays a vital role in allowing us to identify and understand the varying authorities that provide guidance on an issue; assess the relative weights of differing authorities; understand the risks associated with different tax return positions; and ultimately, draw an appropriate conclusion regarding the application of the tax law to the issue. The following paragraphs describe the basic process of tax research that tax professionals use to identify and analyze tax authorities to answer tax questions. We will then revisit Bill and Mercedes's issue and view the research memo prepared by their CPA.

Step 1: Understand Facts

To answer a tax question, you must understand it. To understand the question, you must know the facts. There are two basic types of facts: open facts and closed facts. *Open facts* have not yet occurred, such as the facts associated with a proposed transaction. *Closed facts* have already occurred. The distinction between open and closed facts is important because, unlike closed facts, open facts can be altered, and different facts may result in very different tax consequences. Open facts allow the taxpayer to arrange a transaction to achieve the most advantageous outcome. Thus, they are especially important in tax planning.

How do you establish the facts for a research question? Interview clients, speak with third parties such as attorneys and brokers, and review client documents such as contracts, prior tax returns, wills, trust documents, deeds, and corporate minutes. When interviewing clients, remember that not many are tax experts. Thus, it is up to the tax professional to ask the correct initial and follow-up questions to obtain all the relevant facts. Also consider nontax factors, such as a client's personal values or objectives, because these often put constraints on tax-planning strategies.

Step 2: Identify Issues

A tax professional's ability to identify issues is largely a function of his or her type of tax expertise. A tax expert in a particular area will typically be able to identify quickly the

---

[14]Actions on decisions have no precedential value but may be cited as authority to avoid the substantial understatement of tax penalty under IRC Sec. 6662 imposed on taxpayers and the related tax practitioner penalty under IRC Sec. 6694 (discussed later in this chapter).

THE KEY FACTS

Tax Research

- The five steps in tax research are (1) understand the facts, (2) identify issues, (3) locate relevant authorities, (4) analyze the tax authorities, and (5) document and communicate research results.
- The two types of tax services that tax professionals use in tax research are annotated tax services, arranged by code section, and topical services, arranged by topic.
- Research questions often consist of questions of fact or questions of law.
  - The answer to a question of fact hinges upon the facts and circumstances of the taxpayer's transaction.
  - The answer to a question of law hinges upon the interpretation of the law, such as interpreting a particular phrase in a code section.
- When the researcher identifies that different authorities have conflicting views, she should evaluate the "hierarchy," jurisdiction, and age of the authorities.
- Once the tax researcher has identified relevant authorities, she must make sure that the authorities are still valid and up to date.

(continued)

- The most common end product of a research question is a research memo, which has five basic parts: (1) facts, (2) issues, (3) authority list, (4) conclusion, and (5) analysis.

specific tax issues that relate to transactions in that area. For example, an expert in corporate acquisitions would quickly identify the tax consequences and specific issues of alternative acquisition types. A novice, on the other hand, would likely identify broader issues first and then more specific issues as he or she researched the relevant tax law.

What's the best method to identify tax issues? First of all, get a good understanding of the client's facts. Then, combine your understanding of the facts with your knowledge of the tax law. Let's consider the example of Bill and Mercedes's interest deduction. For an expert in this particular area, the issues will be immediately evident. For a novice, the initial response may take the form of a series of general questions: (1) Is this item of expense deductible? (2) Is that item of income taxable? (3) In what year should the expense be deducted? (4) In what year should the item of income be taxed? After you identify these types of general issues, your research will enable you to identify the more specific issues that ultimately determine the tax ramifications of the transaction.

Example 2-4

Elizabeth, Bill and Mercedes's friend who is a shareholder and the CFO of a company, loaned money to her company to help it avoid declaring bankruptcy. Despite Elizabeth's loan, the company did file for bankruptcy, and Elizabeth was not repaid the loan. What issues would a researcher consider?

Answer: The first questions to ask are whether Elizabeth can deduct the bad debt expense and, if so, as what type of deduction? As the researcher delves more into the general issue, he would learn that the type of deduction depends on whether Elizabeth's debt is considered a business or nonbusiness bad debt. This more specific issue depends on whether Elizabeth loaned the money to the company to protect her job (business bad debt) or to protect her stock investment in the company (nonbusiness bad debt). Bad-debt expenses incurred for nonbusiness debts (investment-related debts) are deducted as capital losses and thus subject to limitations (discussed in the Investments chapter), whereas bad-debt expenses for business debts (business-related debts) are ordinary deductions and not limited.

Why might this case be a good one to litigate in U.S. District Court?

Answer: Because a jury might be more likely to be convinced to assess Elizabeth's motives favorably.

Step 3: Locate Relevant Authorities

Step three in the research process is to locate the relevant authorities (code sections, regulations, court cases, revenue rulings) that address the tax issue. Luckily, tax services can aid the researcher in identifying relevant authorities. Most, if not all, of these services are available on the Internet (with a subscription) and thus offer the flexibility to conduct research almost anywhere.[15]

There are two basic types of tax services: annotated and topical. **Annotated tax services** are arranged by Internal Revenue Code section. That is, for each code section, an annotated service includes the code section; a listing of the code section history; copies of congressional committee reports that explain changes to the code section; a copy of all the regulations issued for the specific code section; the service's unofficial explanation of the code section; and brief summaries (called annotations) of relevant court cases, revenue rulings, revenue procedures, and letter rulings that address issues specific to the code section. Two examples of annotated tax services are Commerce Clearing House's (CCH) Standard Federal Tax Reporter and Research Institute of America's (RIA) United States Tax Reporter.

---

[15]www.IRS.gov contains a lot of information (tax forms, IRS publications, etc.) that may be especially useful for answering basic tax questions. In addition, tax publishers, such as CCH and RIA, produce quick reference tax guides (e.g., the *CCH Master Tax Guide* or the *RIA Federal Tax Handbook*) that may be used to answer basic tax questions.

Topical tax services are arranged by topic, such as taxable forms of income, tax-exempt income, and trade or business expenses. For each topic, the services identify tax issues that relate to each topic and then explain and cite authorities relevant to the issue (code sections, regulations, court cases, revenue rulings, etc.). Beginning tax researchers often prefer topical services, because they generally are easier to read. Some examples of topical federal tax services include BNA's Tax Management Portfolios, CCH's Tax Research Consultant, and RIA's Federal Tax Coordinator.

How does a researcher use these services? An expert would probably go directly to the relevant portions of an annotated or topical service. A novice may conduct a keyword search in the service, use the tax service's topical index, or browse the tax service to identify the relevant portions. Some suggestions for identifying keywords: Try to describe the transaction in three to five words. An ideal keyword search typically includes (1) the relevant area of law and (2) a fact or two that describes the transaction. Try to avoid keywords that are too broad (income, deduction, taxable) or too narrow.

Example 2-5

Bill and Mercedes refinanced the mortgage on their principal residence a couple of years ago when their original mortgage's four-year balloon payment came due. Their mortgage institution charged Bill and Mercedes $3,000 of points (prepaid interest) upon the refinancing in order to give them a reduced interest rate. On their CPA's advice, Bill and Mercedes deducted the $3,000 in the year they paid it, but upon audit, the IRS disallowed the deduction. What is the research issue?

Answer: The issue is, should Bill and Mercedes have deducted the $3,000 of points in the year they paid it?

What are some keywords that could identify the relevant tax authority?

Answer: Points (area of law), interest (area of law), refinancing (fact that describes the transaction).

Keyword searching is more an art than an exact science. As you gain a better understanding of different areas of the tax law, you'll become much more efficient at using keywords. If keyword searching is not proving beneficial, check your spelling, make sure you're searching within the correct database, rethink your keywords, use another research method, use another tax service, or as a last resort, take a break.

While utilizing keyword searches or other research methods to identify potentially relevant areas of law and tax authorities, constantly ask yourself whether you are indeed in the correct area of law. Once the answer to this question is an authoritative yes, you can delve deeper into the area of law and related authorities to answer the question.

Step 4: Analyze Tax Authorities

Once a researcher identifies relevant authorities, she must read carefully to ensure she fully understands them, as well as their application to the research problem. Two basic types of issues researchers will encounter are questions of fact and questions of law.

The answer to a **question of fact** hinges upon the facts and circumstances of the taxpayer's transaction. For example, whether a trade or business expense is "ordinary," "necessary," "reasonable," and thus deductible, is a question of fact. If you're researching a question of fact, understand *which* facts determine the answer—in this case, which facts make an expense "ordinary," "necessary," and "reasonable" and which do not. In this type of question, the researcher will focus on understanding how various facts affect the research answer and identifying authorities with fact patterns similar to her client's.

The answer to a **question of law** hinges upon the interpretation of the law, such as a particular phrase in a code section (see the sample research memo in Exhibit 2-9 for an example of a question of law). If a researcher is faced with this type of question, she will

EXHIBIT 2-9   Sample Internal Research Memo

Below is the memo Bill and Mercedes's CPA drafted after researching their issue.

Date:	July 8, 2018
Preparer:	Joe Staff
Reviewer:	Sandra Miller
Subject:	Deductibility of Points Paid in Refinancing
Facts:	Four years ago Bill and Mercedes's credit union provided them a $250,000 mortgage loan for their new home. The mortgage loan was a four-year interest-only note with a balloon payment at the end of four years. Bill and Mercedes (Floridians residing in the 11th Circuit) chose this type of loan to allow them to minimize their mortgage payment until their other house was sold. After 18 months, Bill and Mercedes sold their other house and refinanced their original short-term loan with a 15-year conventional mortgage. The credit union charged Bill and Mercedes $3,000 in points (prepaid interest) upon the refinancing.
Issue:	Can Bill and Mercedes deduct the points in the year they paid them?
Authorities:	IRC Sec. 461(g).
	Rev. Rul. 87-22, 1987-1 CB 146.
	J.R. Huntsman v. Comm. (8 Cir., 1990), 90-2 USTC par. 50,340, rev'g 91 TC 917 (1988).
	AOD 1991-002.
	P.G. Cao v. Comm. (9 Cir., 1996), 96-1 USTC par. 50,167, aff'g 67 TCM 2171 (1994).
Conclusion:	Because Bill and Mercedes's refinancing represents an integrated step in securing permanent financing for their home, substantial authority supports their deduction of the $3,000 in points this year.
Analysis:	IRC Sec. 461(g)(1) provides that cash-method taxpayers (Bill and Mercedes) must amortize prepaid interest (points) over the life of the loan instead of receiving a current deduction. IRC Sec. 461(g)(2) provides an exception to the general rule of Sec. 461(g)(1). Specifically, IRC Sec. 461(g)(2) allows cash-method taxpayers to deduct points in the year paid if the related debt was incurred "in connection with the purchase or improvement of," and secured by, the taxpayer's principal residence. The question whether Bill and Mercedes should amortize or currently deduct the points paid to refinance the mortgage on their principal residence depends upon the interpretation of "in connection with the purchase or improvement of" found in IRC Sec. 461(g)(2).
	There are two basic interpretations of "in connection with the purchase or improvement of." In Revenue Ruling 87-22, the IRS rules that points incurred in refinancing a mortgage on a taxpayer's residence are deductible in the year paid to the extent that the taxpayer uses the loan proceeds to improve the taxpayer's residence. Thus, points paid to simply refinance an existing mortgage without improving the residence must be amortized over the life of the loan.
	In contrast, in *J.R. Huntsman v. Comm.*, the 8th Circuit Court interpreted the phrase "in connection with the purchase or improvement of" much more broadly and held that points incurred to refinance a mortgage on the taxpayer's principal residence are currently deductible if the refinancing represents an *integrated step to secure permanent financing* for the taxpayer's residence. The facts in *J.R. Huntsman v. Comm.* are very similar to Bill and Mercedes's facts. Like Bill and Mercedes, the taxpayers in *J.R. Huntsman v. Comm.* also purchased their principal residence using a short-term loan with a "balloon" payment. When the balloon payment came due, the taxpayers obtained a permanent mortgage on their home (a 30-year conventional mortgage). The 8th Circuit Court held that in this case the permanent mortgage was acquired to extinguish the short-term financing and finalize the purchase of the home. "Thus, where taxpayers purchase a principal residence with a short-term three-year loan secured by a mortgage on the residence, and replace the loan with permanent financing . . . , the permanent mortgage obtained is sufficiently in connection with the purchase of the home to fall within the exception provided for by section 461(g)(2)."
	In Action on Decision 1991-002, the IRS has indicated that it will not follow the *J.R. Huntsman v. Comm.* decision outside the 8th Circuit (in the 11th Circuit where Bill and Mercedes live). Nonetheless, other courts (the 9th Circuit in *P.G. Cao v. Comm.*) have indicated a willingness to apply the 8th Circuit's interpretation of IRC Sec. 461(g)(2). That is, they have allowed deductibility of points incurred in refinancing if the refinancing occurred to secure permanent financing, instead of for some other reason such as to secure a lower interest rate.
	Given the similarity in facts between Bill and Mercedes's refinancing and those in *J.R. Huntsman v. Comm.* (refinancing of a short-term note to secure permanent financing), substantial authority supports a current deduction of the points paid.

spend much of her time researching the various interpretations of the code section and take note of which authorities interpret the code differently and why.

For many tax questions, the answer is clear with no opposing interpretations or contrary authorities. For other questions, the researcher may identify that different authorities have conflicting views. In this situation, the tax researcher should evaluate the hierarchical level, jurisdiction, and age of the authorities, placing more weight on higher and newer authorities that have jurisdiction over the taxpayer. A tax researcher will become more adept at this process as she gains experience.

Once the tax researcher has identified relevant authorities, she must make sure the authorities are still valid and up to date. For court cases, a **citator**—a research tool that allows you to check the status of several types of tax authorities—can be used to review the history of a case to find out, for example, whether it was subsequently appealed and overturned and to identify subsequent cases that cite it. Favorable citations (for example, a citation of the case by another authority in support of its ruling) strengthen a case. In contrast, unfavorable ones weaken it (for example, a citation of the case by another authority that questions or limits the case's decision). Citators can also check the status of revenue rulings, revenue procedures, and other IRS pronouncements. Checking the status of the Code is fairly simple: just locate the current version. Checking the status of regulations is a little more complicated. Most tax services alert researchers if a regulation has not been updated for certain changes in the Code. If this is the case, the researcher should evaluate whether the changes in the Code make the regulation obsolete.

As you will see in the analysis section of the sample research memo drafted by Bill and Mercedes's CPA (see Exhibit 2-9), whether they should amortize (deduct over the life of the loan) or currently deduct the points paid to refinance the mortgage on their principal residence is a question of law that ultimately depends upon the interpretation of a particular phrase: "in connection with the purchase or improvement of" found in IRC Sec. 461(g)(2). Is there a correct answer to this question? No. There is no clear-cut answer. Rather, this is a situation where the tax professional must use professional judgment. Because there is substantial authority supporting the current deduction of the points (discussed in detail in the sample memo), Bill and Mercedes should be able to deduct the points currently without risk of penalty. However, they should be aware that the IRS has clearly stated in an action on decision that it will fight this issue outside the 8th Circuit—for example, in the 11th Circuit, where Bill and Mercedes live.

Step 5: Document and Communicate the Results

After a researcher finishes her research, the final step of the process is to document and communicate the results. The most common end product of a research question is the internal research memo the researcher drafts for her supervisor's attention. The memo has five basic parts: (1) facts, (2) issues, (3) authority list, (4) conclusion, and (5) analysis. The purpose of the memo is to inform the reader of the answer to a research question, and thus, it should be written in an objective manner by discussing all relevant authorities to the research question, including those authorities that support, as well as those that conflict with, the answer. Below are some suggestions for each part of the memo. Compare these to the execution within the sample internal research memo presented in Exhibit 2-9.

Facts   Discuss facts relevant to the question presented—that is, facts that provide necessary background of the transaction (generally, who, what, when, where, and how much) and those facts that may influence the research answer. Keeping the fact discussion relatively brief will focus the reader's attention on the relevant characteristics of the transaction.

Issues   State the specific issues that the memo addresses. This section confirms that you understand the research question, reminds the reader of the question being analyzed, and allows future researchers to determine whether the analysis in the memo is relevant. Issues should be written as specifically as possible and limited to one or two sentences per issue.

Authorities In this section, cite the relevant tax authorities that apply to the issue, such as the IRC, court cases, and revenue rulings. How many authorities should you cite? Enough to provide a clear understanding of the issue and interpretation of the law. Remember, in order to reach an accurate assessment of the strength of your conclusion, you should consider authorities that may support your desired conclusion, as well as those that may go against it.

Conclusion There should be one conclusion per issue. Each conclusion should answer the question as briefly as possible and, preferably, indicate why the answer is what it is.

Analysis The goal of the analysis is to provide the reader a clear understanding of the area of law and specific authorities that apply. Typically, you will organize an analysis to discuss first the general area(s) of law (the code section), and then the specific authorities (court cases, revenue rulings) that apply to the research question. How many authorities should you discuss? As many as necessary to provide the reader an understanding of the issue and relevant authorities. After you discuss the relevant authorities, apply the authorities to your client's transaction and explain how the authorities result in your conclusion.

Client Letters In addition to internal research memos, tax professionals often send their clients letters that summarize their research and recommendations. Basic components of the client letter include: (1) research question and limitations, (2) facts, (3) analysis, and (4) closing. Below are some suggestions for each part of the client letter. Compare these to the execution within the sample client letter presented in Exhibit 2-10.

Research Question and Limitations After the salutation (Dear Bill and Mercedes) and social graces (I enjoyed seeing you last week . . .), clearly state the research question addressed and any disclaimers related to the work performed. This portion of the letter ensures that the tax professional and client have a mutual understanding of the question researched and any limitations on the research performed. As in a memo, issues should be written as specifically as possible and be limited to one or two sentences. Most accounting firms have standard boilerplate language regarding the limitations on work performed that is included in every client letter.

Facts Briefly summarize the facts relevant to the question presented—that is, facts that provide necessary background of the transaction and those facts that may influence the research answer. Keeping the fact discussion relatively brief will focus the client's attention on the relevant characteristics of the transaction.

Analysis Summarize the relevant authorities (including citations in most situations) and their implications for the client's research question using precise language appropriate for the client's level of tax expertise. The length of this portion of the letter will vary with the complexity of the research question and the client's interest in understanding the specific research details.

Closing In this section, summarize the key outcome(s) of the research conducted and any recommended client action, thank the client for requesting your service, and remind the client to contact you with additional questions or for further assistance.

In the case of Bill and Mercedes's interest deduction, their CPA recommended a tax return position that the IRS disallowed upon audit. Did their CPA violate her professional responsibilities by recommending a position the IRS disallowed? Good question. Let's take a look at the rules governing tax professional responsibilities.

EXHIBIT 2-10 **Sample Client Letter**

Below is the client letter that Bill and Mercedes's CPA sent to them.

Dear Bill and Mercedes,

I enjoyed seeing you last week at the Tampa Bay Boys and Girls Clubs charity auction. What a great event for such a worthy cause!

Thank you for requesting my advice concerning the tax treatment of the points paid when refinancing your mortgage.

My research is based upon the federal income tax laws that apply as of the date of this letter and the facts that you have provided as follows. Four years ago your credit union provided you a $250,000 interest-only note on your home that required a balloon payment at the end of four years. You chose this type of loan to minimize your mortgage payment until your previous house sold. After 18 months, you sold your previous house and refinanced the original short-term loan with a 15-year conventional mortgage. The credit union charged you $3,000 in points upon the refinancing.

After a thorough review of the applicable tax authority, I found there is substantial authority supporting a current deduction of the $3,000 points paid. IRC Sec. 461(g)(2) allows cash-method taxpayers to deduct points in the year paid if the related debt was incurred "in connection with the purchase or improvement of," and secured by, the taxpayer's principal residence. There are two basic interpretations of "in connection with the purchase or improvement of." The IRS has ruled (Revenue Ruling 87-22) that points paid to simply refinance an existing mortgage without improving the residence must be amortized over the life of the loan. In contrast, in *J.R. Huntsman v. Comm.*, the 8th Circuit Court held that points incurred to refinance a mortgage on the taxpayer's principal residence are currently deductible if the refinancing represents an *integrated step to secure permanent financing* for the taxpayer's residence.

The facts in *J.R. Huntsman v. Comm.* are very similar to your facts. Like you, the taxpayers in *J.R. Huntsman v. Comm.* purchased their principal residence using a short-term loan with a balloon payment. When the balloon payment came due, the taxpayers obtained a permanent mortgage on their home. The 8th Circuit Court held that in this case the permanent mortgage was acquired to finalize the purchase of the home and allowed the current deduction of the points.

J.R. Huntsman v. Comm. provides substantial authority to support a current deduction of the $3,000 points paid to refinance your initial short-term mortgage. In addition, other courts have applied the 8th Circuit's interpretation of IRC Sec. 461(g)(2), which adds "strength" to the 8th Circuit decision. However, the IRS has indicated that it will not follow the *J.R. Huntsman v. Comm.* decision outside the 8th Circuit (in the 11th Circuit where you live). Accordingly, the IRS would likely disallow the $3,000 deduction upon audit, and thus, while you have substantial authority to deduct the points currently, there is risk in doing so.

I would be happy to discuss this issue with you in more depth since these types of issues are always difficult. Likewise, if you have any other questions or issues with which I may assist you, please do not hesitate to contact me. Thank you again for requesting my advice.

Sincerely,

Sandra Miller, CPA

TAX PROFESSIONAL RESPONSIBILITIES

LO 2-6

Tax practitioners are subject to a variety of statutes, rules, and codes of professional conduct. Some examples include the American Institute of CPAs (AICPA) Code of Professional Conduct, the AICPA **Statements on Standards for Tax Services (SSTS),** the IRS's Circular 230, and statutes enacted by a CPA's specific state board of accountancy. Tax practitioners should absolutely have a working knowledge of these statutes, rules, and guidelines because (1) they establish the professional standards for the practitioner and (2) failure to comply with the standards could result in adverse consequences for the tax professional, such as being admonished, suspended, or barred from practicing before the IRS; being admonished, suspended, or expelled from the AICPA; or suffering suspension or revocation of the CPA license. Given the voluminous nature of applicable statutes, rules, and codes, we will simply provide a brief overview of the major common sources of tax professional standards.

CPAs who are members of the AICPA are bound by the AICPA Code of Professional Conduct and Statements on Standards for Tax Services. Other tax professionals use these provisions as guidance of professional standards. The AICPA Code of Professional Conduct is not specific to tax practice and provides broader professional standards that are especially relevant for auditors—that is, for those independent CPAs charged with examining an entity's financial statements. Provisions included in the Code of Professional Conduct address the importance of a CPA maintaining independence from the client and using due professional care in carrying out responsibilities. Additional provisions limit the acceptance of contingent fees, preclude discreditable acts such as signing a false return, and prohibit false advertising and charging commissions. Most of these provisions rightly fall under the heading of common sense. Nonetheless, a regular review should prove useful to the practicing CPA.

The AICPA's Statements on Standards for Tax Services (SSTS) recommend appropriate standards of practice for tax professionals and are intended to complement other provisions that govern tax practice (e.g., Circular 230 discussed below). One objective of these standards is to encourage increased understanding by the Treasury, IRS, and the public of a CPA's professional standards. Many state boards of accountancy have adopted similar standards, thus making the SSTS especially important. Currently, seven SSTS describe the tax professional standards when recommending a tax return position, answering questions on a tax return, preparing a tax return using data supplied by a client, using estimates on a tax return, taking a tax return position inconsistent with a previous year's tax return, discovering a tax return error, and giving tax advice to taxpayers. Exhibit 2-11 provides a brief summary of each SSTS. Most important from a research perspective, SSTS No. 1 provides that a tax professional must comply with the standards imposed by the applicable tax authority when recommending a tax return position or preparing or signing a tax return. IRC Sec. 6694 provides these standards for federal tax purposes.

IRC Sec. 6694 imposes a penalty on a *tax practitioner* for any position that is not supported by **substantial authority.**[16] A good tax professional evaluates whether supporting authority is substantial based upon the supporting and opposing authorities' weight and relevance. Substantial authority suggests the probability that the taxpayer's position will be sustained upon audit or litigation is in the 35 to 40 percent range or above. The tax practitioner can also avoid penalty under IRC Sec. 6694 if the tax return position has at least a reasonable basis (is supported by one or more tax authorities) and the position is disclosed on the taxpayer's return.

Example 2-6

Did Bill and Mercedes's CPA meet her professional standards as provided by SSTS No. 1?

Answer: Yes. Based on *J.R. Huntsman v. Comm.*, it is safe to conclude that there is a 35 to 40 percent or greater probability that the current points deduction will be sustained upon judicial review. Specifically, Bill and Mercedes's facts are very similar to those in *J.R. Huntsman v. Comm.*, and subsequent courts have interpreted the phrase "in connection with" consistently with *J.R. Huntsman v. Comm.*

Circular 230, issued by the IRS, provides regulations governing tax practice and applies to all persons practicing before the IRS. There are five parts of Circular 230. Subpart A describes who may practice before the IRS (CPAs, attorneys, enrolled agents) and

---

[16]The "more likely than not" standard, defined as a greater than 50 percent chance of a position being sustained on its merits, applies to tax shelters and other reportable transactions specified by the IRS.

EXHIBIT 2-11   Summary of the AICPA Statements on Standards for Tax Services

SSTS No 1: Tax Return Positions

A tax professional should comply with the standards, if any, imposed by the applicable tax authority for recommending a tax return position, or preparing or signing a tax return. If the tax authority has no written standards (or if they are lower than the following standard), the tax professional may recommend a tax return position or prepare or sign a return when she has a good-faith belief that the position has a realistic possibility of being sustained if challenged, or if there is a reasonable basis for the position and it is *adequately disclosed* on the tax return.

SSTS No. 2: Answers to Questions on Returns

A tax professional should make a reasonable effort to obtain from the taxpayer the information necessary to answer all questions on a tax return.

SSTS No. 3: Certain Procedural Aspects of Preparing Returns

In preparing or signing a tax return, a tax professional may rely without verification on information that a taxpayer or a third party has provided, unless the information appears to be incorrect, incomplete, or inconsistent.

SSTS No. 4: Use of Estimates

Unless prohibited by statute or rule, a tax professional may use taxpayer estimates in preparing a tax return if it is impractical to obtain exact data and if the estimated amounts appear reasonable based on the facts and circumstances known by the professional.

SSTS No. 5: Departure from a Position Previously Concluded in an Administrative Proceeding or Court Decision

A tax professional may sign a tax return that contains a departure from a position previously concluded in an administrative or court proceeding if the tax professional adheres to the standards of SSTS No. 1. This rule does not apply if the taxpayer is bound to a specific tax treatment in the later year, such as by a formal closing agreement with the IRS.

SSTS No. 6: Knowledge of Error: Return Preparation and Administrative Proceedings

A tax professional must advise the taxpayer promptly of an error and its potential consequences when she learns of an error in a previously filed tax return, an administrative hearing (such as an audit), or the taxpayer's failure to file a required return. The tax professional should include a recommendation for appropriate measures the taxpayer should take. The professional is not obligated to inform the IRS of the error, nor may she do so without the taxpayer's permission, except when required by law. However, in an administrative proceeding only, the tax professional should request the taxpayer's agreement to disclose the error to the IRS. If the taxpayer refuses to disclose the error to the IRS, the professional may consider terminating the professional relationship with the taxpayer.

SSTS No. 7: Form and Content of Advice to Taxpayers

In providing advice to taxpayers, tax professionals must use judgment that reflects professional competence and serves the taxpayer's needs. The professional should ensure that the standards under SSTS No. 1 are satisfied for all advice rendered. The professional is not obligated to communicate with a taxpayer when subsequent events affect advice previously provided except when implementing plans associated with the advice provided or when the professional is obligated to do so by specific agreement.

AICPA Statements

THE KEY FACTS

Tax Professional Responsibilities

- Tax practitioners are subject to a variety of statutes, rules, and codes of professional conduct.
- The AICPA's seven Statements on Standards for Tax Services (SSTS) recommend appropriate standards of practice for tax professionals.
  - Many state boards of accountancy have adopted standards similar to the SSTS standards.
- Circular 230 provides regulations governing tax practice and applies to all persons practicing before the IRS.
  - There is a good bit of overlap between Circular 230 and the AICPA SSTS.

---

what practicing before the IRS means (tax return preparation, representing clients before the IRS, and so on).[17] Subpart B describes the duties and restrictions that apply to individuals governed by Circular 230. Included in Subpart B are provisions discussing the submission of records to the IRS, guidelines when a practitioner discovers a tax return error, restrictions on charging contingency fees, prohibition of sharing employment with someone suspended from practicing before the IRS, stringent rules relating to providing advice for tax shelters, and standards for when a practitioner can recommend a tax return

[17]Similar to attorneys and CPAs, enrolled agents and registered tax return preparers can represent taxpayers before the IRS. To become an enrolled agent, you must have either worked for the IRS for five years or pass a comprehensive examination.

position.[18] Subparts C and D explain sanctions and disciplinary proceedings for practitioners violating the Circular 230 provisions. Subpart E concludes with a few miscellaneous provisions (such as the Circular 230 effective date). There is a good bit of overlap between Circular 230 and the AICPA SSTS.

Although Circular 230 provides many rules governing tax practice, the Internal Revenue Code and other Treasury regulations often contain requirements specific to tax professionals. Thus, it is important for tax professionals to keep abreast of all applicable guidance, regardless of the specific authoritative source. A good example of this is the tax-preparer registration requirement in Reg. §1.6109-2, which requires that all paid tax-return preparers apply for and receive a preparer tax identification number (PTIN). Although not a particularly daunting registration requirement, it is important nonetheless as failure to include the tax-return preparer's PTIN on tax returns is subject to a $50 penalty per violation.

LO 2-7 TAXPAYER AND TAX PRACTITIONER PENALTIES

THE KEY FACTS

Taxpayer and Tax Practitioner Penalties

- The IRS can impose both criminal and civil penalties to encourage tax compliance by both tax professionals and taxpayers.
- The standard of conviction is higher in a criminal trial, but the penalties are also much higher.
- A taxpayer will not be subject to an underpayment penalty if there is substantial authority that supports the tax return position.
- A tax practitioner will also not be subject to penalty for recommending a tax return position if there is substantial authority that supports the position.

In addition to motivating good behavior via tax professional standards, the IRS can impose both criminal and civil penalties to encourage tax compliance by both tax professionals and taxpayers. **Civil penalties** are much more common, generally come in the form of monetary penalties, and may be imposed when tax practitioners or taxpayers violate tax statutes without reasonable cause—say, as the result of negligence, intentional disregard of pertinent rules, willful disobedience, or outright fraud. Some common examples of civil penalties are listed in Exhibit 2-12.

Criminal penalties are much less common than civil penalties, although they have been used to incarcerate some notorious criminals who escaped conviction for other crimes. (Prohibition-era mobster Al Capone was convicted and put in prison for tax evasion.) Criminal penalties are commonly charged in tax evasion cases, which include willful intent to defraud the government, but are imposed only after normal due process, including a trial. Compared to civil cases, the standard of conviction is higher in a criminal trial; guilt must be proven beyond a reasonable doubt (versus the "clear and convincing evidence" standard for civil tax fraud). However, the penalties are also much higher, such as fines up to $100,000 for individuals plus a prison sentence.

Assuming the IRS assesses additional tax upon audit, will the taxpayer always be subject to penalty? No. While the taxpayer will have to pay interest on the underpayment, he or she will *not* be subject to an underpayment penalty *if there is substantial authority that supports the tax return position.*[19] As discussed above, substantial authority suggests that the probability the taxpayer's position will be sustained upon audit or litigation is in the 35 to 40 percent range or higher.

Example 2-7

What is Bill and Mercedes's exposure to penalties in their IRS audit?

Answer: None. Why? Because "substantial tax authority" supports their tax return position and the disputed tax liability is relatively small (the tax savings on a $3,000 tax deduction), Bill and Mercedes have no penalty exposure. Nonetheless, Bill and Mercedes will owe interest on the disputed tax liability unless the IRS recants its position in the audit or appeals process (or if the case is litigated and Bill and Mercedes win).

---

[18]Circular 230 imposes the same tax practitioner standards as in IRC Sec. 6694 for when a tax practitioner generally may recommend a tax return position (substantial authority and no disclosure or reasonable basis with disclosure).

[19]The taxpayer can also avoid penalty if the tax return position has at least a reasonable basis (i.e., supported by one or more tax authorities) and the position is disclosed on the taxpayer's return (IRC Sec. 6662).

EXHIBIT 2-12   **Civil Penalties Imposed for Tax Violations**

Taxpayers		Tax Practitioners	
Failure to file a tax return	5% of tax due per month (or partial month). Maximum penalty is 25% of net tax due. If the tax return is not filed within 60 days of the due date (including extensions), the minimum penalty is the smaller of $210 or 100% of the unpaid tax.	Failure to provide a copy of the tax return to a taxpayer	$50 per violation
Failure to pay tax owed	0.5% of tax due per month (or partial month). Reduces the failure to file a tax return penalty, if applicable. Maximum combined failure to file and failure to pay tax penalty is 5% of net tax due per month not to exceed 25% of net tax due. Minimum combined penalty if the tax return is not filed within 60 days of the due date (including extensions) is the smaller of $210 or 100% of the unpaid tax.	Failure to sign a tax return	$50 per violation
Failure to make estimated payments	Penalty varies with federal short-term interest rate and underpayment.	Failure to include the tax practitioner's ID number on the tax return	$50 per violation
Substantial understatement of tax	20% of understatement	Failure to keep a listing of taxpayers or tax returns	$50 per violation
Underpayment of tax due to transactions lacking economic substance	20% or 40% of understatement		
Providing false withholding information	$500	Failure to keep a listing of employees	$50 per violation
Fraud	75% of liability attributable to fraud	Understatement due to unreasonable position	Greater of $1,000 or 50% of income derived from preparing the taxpayer's tax return.
		Willful understatement of tax	Greater of $5,000 or 75% of income derived from preparing the taxpayer's tax return.
		Organizing, promoting, etc. an abusive tax shelter	Lesser of $1,000 or 100% of gross income derived from tax shelter. If activity is based on fraudulent statements, the penalty equals 50% of gross income derived from tax shelter.
		Aiding and abetting the understatement of a tax liability	$1,000 ($10,000 if related to corporate taxes).

As we explained in Example 2-6, Bill and Mercedes's CPA met her professional standards (as defined currently in SSTS No. 1) by recommending a tax return position that meets the "Substantial Authority" standard. Likewise, because substantial tax authority supports the tax return position, Bill and Mercedes's CPA should also not have penalty exposure under IRC Sec. 6694.

CONCLUSION

Now that we have a full understanding of the issue under audit for Bill and Mercedes, what is their likely outcome? Another good question. The IRS has stated that it will continue to disallow a current deduction for points incurred for refinanced mortgages. Nonetheless, the courts appear to follow *J.R. Huntsman v. Comm.*, and therefore, the IRS stands a strong possibility of losing this case if litigated. In an IRS appeals conference, the appeals officer may consider the hazards of litigation. Accordingly, Bill and Mercedes have a good likelihood of a favorable resolution at the appeals conference.

In this chapter we discussed several of the fundamentals of tax practice and procedure: taxpayer filing requirements, the statute of limitations, the IRS audit process, the primary tax authorities, tax research, tax professional standards, and taxpayer and tax practitioner penalties. For the tax accountant, these fundamentals form the basis for much of her work. Likewise, tax research forms the basis of much of a tax professional's compliance and planning services. Even for the accountant who doesn't specialize in tax accounting, gaining a basic understanding of tax practice and procedure is important. Assisting clients with the IRS audit process is a valued service that accountants provide, and clients expect all accountants to understand basic tax procedure issues and how to research basic tax issues.

Summary

LO 2-1 Identify the filing requirements for income tax returns and the statute of limitations for assessment.

- All corporations must file a tax return annually regardless of their taxable income. Estates and trusts are required to file annual income tax returns if their gross income exceeds $600. The filing requirements for individual taxpayers depend on the taxpayer's filing status, age, and gross income.

- Individual and C corporation tax returns (except for C corporations with a June 30 year-end) are due on the fifteenth day of the fourth month following year-end. For C corporations with a June 30 year-end, partnerships and S corporations, tax returns must be filed by the fifteenth day of the third month following the entity's fiscal year-end. Any taxpayer unable to file a tax return by the original due date can request an extension to file.

- For both amended tax returns filed by a taxpayer and proposed tax assessments by the IRS, the statute of limitations generally ends three years from the *later* of (1) the date the tax return was actually filed or (2) the tax return's original due date.

LO 2-2 Outline the IRS audit process, how returns are selected, the different types of audits, and what happens after the audit.

- The IRS uses a number of computer programs and outside data sources to identify tax returns that may have an understated tax liability. Common computer initiatives include the DIF (Discriminant Function) system, the document perfection program, and the information matching program.

- The three types of IRS audits consist of correspondence, office, and field examinations.

- After the audit, the IRS will send the taxpayer a 30-day letter, which provides the taxpayer the opportunity to pay the proposed assessment or request an appeals conference. If an agreement is not reached at appeals or the taxpayer does not pay the proposed assessment, the IRS will send the taxpayer a 90-day letter. At this time, the taxpayer may pay the tax or petition the U.S. Tax Court to hear the case. If the taxpayer chooses to pay the tax, the taxpayer may then request a refund of the tax and eventually sue the IRS for a refund in the U.S. District Court or the U.S. Court of Federal Claims.

Evaluate the relative weights of the various tax law sources.   `LO 2-3`

- Primary authorities are official sources of the tax law generated by the legislative branch (statutory authority issued by Congress), judicial branch (rulings by the U.S. District Court, U.S. Tax Court, U.S. Court of Federal Claims, U.S. Circuit Courts of Appeals, or U.S. Supreme Court), or executive/administrative branch (Treasury and IRS pronouncements). Secondary authorities are unofficial tax authorities that interpret and explain the primary authorities.

Describe the legislative process as it pertains to taxation.   `LO 2-4`

- Exhibit 2-7 illustrates the legislative process for enacting tax law changes. Bills proceed from the House Ways and Means Committee to the House of Representatives. If approved, the act is sent to the Senate Finance Committee with a revised version then sent to the U.S. Senate. If approved, the Joint Conference Committee considers the acts passed by the House of Representatives and Senate. If a compromise is reached, the revised act is sent to the House of Representatives; if approved, it is then sent to the Senate; and if approved by the Senate, it is then sent to the president. If signed by the president, the act is incorporated into the IRC of 1986. If the president vetoes the legislation, Congress may override the veto with a two-thirds positive vote in both the House of Representatives and Senate.

Perform the basic steps in tax research.   `LO 2-5`

- The five basic steps in tax research are (1) understand the facts, (2) identify issues, (3) locate relevant authorities, (4) analyze the tax authorities, and (5) document and communicate research results.
- When the researcher identifies that different authorities have conflicting views, she should evaluate the "hierarchy," jurisdiction, and age of the authorities, placing more weight on higher and newer authorities that have jurisdiction over the taxpayer.

Describe tax professional responsibilities in providing tax advice.   `LO 2-6`

- Tax practitioners are subject to a variety of statutes, rules, and codes of professional conduct. Some examples include the American Institute of CPAs (AICPA) Code of Professional Conduct, the AICPA Statements on Standards for Tax Services (SSTS), the IRS's Circular 230, and statutes enacted by a CPA's specific state board of accountancy.
- The AICPA's Statements on Standards for Tax Services (SSTS) recommend appropriate standards of practice for tax professionals. Many state boards of accountancy have adopted similar standards, thus making the SSTS especially important. Currently, there are seven SSTS (summarized in Exhibit 2-11) that describe the tax professional standards.
- Circular 230 provides regulations governing tax practice and applies to all persons practicing before the IRS. There is a good bit of overlap between Circular 230 and the AICPA SSTS.

Identify taxpayer and tax professional penalties.   `LO 2-7`

- The IRS can impose both criminal and civil penalties to encourage tax compliance by both tax professionals and taxpayers. Civil penalties are much more common, generally come in the form of monetary penalties, and may be imposed when tax practitioners or taxpayers violate tax statutes without reasonable cause. Some common examples of civil penalties are listed in Exhibit 2-12.
- Criminal penalties are much less common than civil penalties and are commonly charged in tax evasion cases. Compared to civil cases, the standard of conviction is higher in a criminal trial, but the penalties are also much higher.
- A taxpayer will not be subject to an underpayment penalty if there is substantial authority that supports the tax return position.
- A tax practitioner will also not be subject to penalty for recommending a tax return position if there is substantial authority that supports the position.

KEY TERMS

30-day letter (2-6)

90-day letter (2-6)

acquiescence (2-17)

action on decision (2-17)

annotated tax service (2-18)

Circular 230 (2-24)

citator (2-21)

civil penalties (2-26)

correspondence examination (2-5)

criminal penalties (2-26)

determination letters (2-16)

DIF (Discriminant Function) system (2-4)

document perfection program (2-4)

field examination (2-6)

final regulations (2-15)

Golsen rule (2-15)

information matching program (2-4)

Internal Revenue Code of 1986 (2-11)

interpretative regulations (2-16)

legislative regulations (2-16)

nonacquiescence (2-17)

office examination (2-6)

primary authorities (2-9)

private letter rulings (2-16)

procedural regulations (2-16)

proposed regulations (2-15)

question of fact (2-19)

question of law (2-19)

regulations (2-15)

revenue procedures (2-16)

revenue rulings (2-16)

secondary authorities (2-9)

stare decisis (2-15)

Statements on Standards for Tax Services (SSTS) (2-23)

statute of limitations (2-3)

substantial authority (2-24)

tax treaties (2-14)

technical advice memorandum (2-16)

temporary regulations (2-15)

topical tax service (2-19)

U.S. Circuit Courts of Appeals (2-7)

U.S. Constitution (2-11)

U.S. Court of Federal Claims (2-7)

U.S. District Court (2-7)

U.S. Supreme Court (2-8)

U.S. Tax Court (2-7)

writ of certiorari (2-8)

DISCUSSION QUESTIONS

Discussion Questions are available in Connect®.

connect

LO 2-1 1. Name three factors that determine whether a taxpayer is required to file a tax return.

LO 2-1 2. Benita is concerned that she will not be able to complete her tax return by April 15. Can she request an extension to file her return? By what date must she do so? Assuming she requests an extension, what is the latest date that she could file her return this year without penalty?

LO 2-1 3. Agua Linda Inc. is a calendar-year corporation. What is the original due date for the corporate tax return? What happens if the original due date falls on a Saturday?

LO 2-2 4. Approximately what percentage of tax returns does the IRS audit? What are the implications of this number for the IRS's strategy in selecting returns for audit?

LO 2-2 5. Explain the difference between the DIF system and the National Research Program. How do they relate to each other?

LO 2-2 6. Describe the differences between the three types of audits in terms of their scope and taxpayer type.

LO 2-2 7. Simon just received a 30-day letter from the IRS indicating a proposed assessment. Does he have to pay the additional tax? What are his options?

LO 2-2 8. Compare and contrast the three trial-level courts.

LO 2-3 9. Compare and contrast the three types of tax law sources and give examples of each.

LO 2-3 10. The U.S. Constitution is the highest tax authority but provides very little in the way of tax laws. What are the next highest tax authorities beneath the U.S. Constitution?

LO 2-3 11. Jackie has just opened her copy of the Code for the first time. She looks at the table of contents and wonders why it is organized the way it is. She questions whether it makes sense to try and understand the Code's organization. What are some reasons why understanding the organization of the Internal Revenue Code may prove useful?

LO 2-3 12. Laura Li, a U.S. resident, worked for three months this summer in Hong Kong. What type of tax authority may be especially useful in determining the tax consequences of her foreign income?

13. What are the basic differences between regulations, revenue rulings, and private letter rulings? `LO 2-3`

14. Under what circumstance would the IRS issue an acquiescence? A nonacquiescence? An action on decision? `LO 2-3`

15. Carlos has located a regulation that appears to answer his tax research question. He is concerned because the regulation is a temporary regulation. Evaluate the authoritative weight of this type of regulation. Should he feel more or less confident in his answer if the regulation is a proposed regulation? `LO 2-3`

16. Tyrone recently read a regulation that Congress specifically requested the IRS to issue. What type of regulation is this? How does this regulation's authoritative weight compare to other regulations? `LO 2-3`

17. In researching a tax question, you find only one authority (a trial-level court opinion) that is directly on point. Which court would you least prefer to have hear this case and why? `LO 2-3`

18. What is *stare decisis* and how does it relate to the Golsen rule? `LO 2-3`

19. Mason was shocked to learn that the current Code is the Internal Revenue Code of 1986. He thought that U.S. tax laws change more frequently. What is wrong with Mason's perception? `LO 2-4`

20. Describe in general the process by which new tax legislation is enacted. `LO 2-4`

21. What are the three committees that debate proposed tax legislation? What documents do these committees generate, and how might they be used? `LO 2-4`

22. The president recently vetoed a tax act passed by the House and Senate. Is the tax act dead? If not, what will it take for the act to be passed? `LO 2-4`

23. What are the five basic parts of an internal research memo? `LO 2-5`

24. What is the difference between primary and secondary authorities? Explain the role of each authority type in conducting tax research. `LO 2-5`

25. Jorge is puzzled that the IRS and his CPA could legitimately reach different conclusions on a tax issue. Why does this happen? `LO 2-5`

26. What is the difference between open and closed facts? How is this distinction important in conducting tax research? `LO 2-5`

27. In writing a research memo, what types of facts should be included in the memo? `LO 2-5`

28. Amber is a tax expert, whereas Rob is a tax novice. Explain how their process in identifying tax issues may differ. `LO 2-5`

29. Discuss the basic differences between annotated and topical tax services. How are these services used in tax research? `LO 2-5`

30. In constructing a keyword search, what should the keyword search include? `LO 2-5`

31. Lindsey has become very frustrated in researching a tax issue using keyword searches. What suggestions can you give her? `LO 2-5`

32. Nola, a tax novice, has a fairly simple tax question. Besides tax services, what are some sources that she can use to answer her question? `LO 2-5`

33. Armando identifies a tax research question as being a question of fact. What types of authorities should he attempt to locate in his research? `LO 2-5`

34. How are citators used in tax research? `LO 2-5`

35. What is the general rule for how many authorities a research memo should discuss? `LO 2-5`

36. Identify some of the sources for tax professional standards. What are the potential ramifications of failing to comply with these standards? `LO 2-6`

37. Levi is recommending a tax return position to his client. What standard must he meet to satisfy his professional standards? What is the source of this professional standard? `LO 2-6`

38. What is Circular 230? `LO 2-6`

LO 2-7   39. What are the basic differences between civil and criminal tax penalties?

LO 2-7   40. What are some of the most common civil penalties imposed on taxpayers?

LO 2-7   41. What are the taxpayer's standards to avoid the substantial understatement of tax penalty?

LO 2-7   42. What are the tax practitioner's standards to avoid a penalty for recommending a tax return position?

PROBLEMS

Select problems are available in Connect®.

LO 2-1   43. Ahmed does not have enough cash on hand to pay his taxes. He was excited to hear that he can request an extension to file his tax return. Does this solve his problem? What are the ramifications if he doesn't pay his tax liability by April 15?

LO 2-1   44. Molto Stancha Corporation had zero earnings this fiscal year; in fact, it lost money. Must the corporation file a tax return?

LO 2-1   45. The estate of Monique Chablis earned $450 of income this year. Is the estate required to file an income tax return?

LO 2-1   46. Jamarcus, a full-time student, earned $2,500 this year from a summer job. He had no other income this year and will have zero federal income tax liability this year. His employer withheld $300 of federal income tax from his summer pay. Is Jamarcus required to file a tax return? Should Jamarcus file a tax return?

LO 2-1   47. Shane has never filed a tax return despite earning excessive sums of money as a gambler. When does the statute of limitations expire for the years in which Shane has not filed a tax return?

LO 2-1   48. Latoya filed her tax return on February 10 this year. When will the statute of limitations expire for this tax return?

LO 2-1   49. Using the facts from the previous problem, how would your answer change if Latoya understated her income by 40 percent? How would your answer change if Latoya intentionally failed to report as taxable income any cash payments she received from her clients?

LO 2-2   50. Paula could not reach an agreement with the IRS at her appeals conference and has just received a 90-day letter. If she wants to litigate the issue but does not have sufficient cash to pay the proposed deficiency, what is her best court choice?

LO 2-2   51. In choosing a trial-level court, how should a court's previous rulings influence the choice? How should circuit court rulings influence the taxpayer's choice of a trial-level court?

LO 2-2   52. Sophia recently won a tax case litigated in the 7th Circuit. She has just heard that the Supreme Court denied the *writ of certiorari*. Should she be happy or not, and why?

LO 2-2   53. Campbell's tax return was audited because she failed to report interest she earned on her tax return. What IRS audit selection method identified her tax return?

LO 2-2   54. Yong's tax return was audited because he calculated his tax liability incorrectly. What IRS audit procedure identified his tax return for audit?

LO 2-2   55. Randy deducted a high level of itemized deductions two years ago relative to his income level. He recently received an IRS notice requesting documentation for his itemized deductions. What audit procedure likely identified his tax return for audit?

LO 2-2   56. Jackie has a corporate client that has recently received a 30-day notice from the IRS with a $100,000 tax assessment. Her client is considering requesting an appeals conference to contest the assessment. What factors should Jackie advise her client to consider before requesting an appeals conference?

planning

57. The IRS recently completed an audit of Shea's tax return and assessed $15,000 additional tax. Shea requested an appeals conference but was unable to settle the case at the conference. She is contemplating which trial court to choose to hear her case. Provide a recommendation based on the following alternative facts:

    `LO 2-2`

    `planning`

    a) Shea resides in the 2nd Circuit, and the 2nd Circuit has recently ruled against the position Shea is litigating.

    b) The Federal Circuit Court of Appeals has recently ruled in favor of Shea's position.

    c) The issue being litigated involves a question of fact. Shea has a very appealing story to tell but little favorable case law to support her position.

    d) The issue being litigated is highly technical, and Shea believes strongly in her interpretation of the law.

    e) Shea is a local elected official and would prefer to minimize any local publicity regarding the case.

58. Juanita, a Texas resident (5th Circuit), is researching a tax question and finds a 5th Circuit case ruling that is favorable and a 9th Circuit case that is unfavorable. Which circuit case has more "authoritative weight" and why? How would your answer change if Juanita were a Kentucky resident (6th Circuit)?

    `LO 2-3`

59. Faith, a resident of Florida (11th Circuit), recently found a circuit court case that is favorable to her research question. Which two circuits would she prefer to have issued the opinion?

    `LO 2-3`

60. Robert has found a "favorable" authority directly on point for his tax question. If the authority is a court case, which court would he prefer to have issued the opinion? Which court would he least prefer to have issued the opinion?

    `LO 2-3`

61. Jamareo has found a "favorable" authority directly on point for his tax question. If the authority is an administrative authority, which specific type of authority would he prefer to answer his question? Which administrative authority would he least prefer to answer his question?

    `LO 2-3`

62. For each of the following citations, identify the type of authority (statutory, administrative, or judicial) and explain the citation.

    `LO 2-3`

    a) Reg. Sec. 1.111-1(b)

    b) IRC Sec. 469(c)(7)(B)(i)

    c) Rev. Rul. 82-204, 1982-2 C.B. 192

    d) *Amdahl Corp.*, 108 TC 507 (1997)

    e) PLR 9727004

    f) *Hills v. Comm.*, 50 AFTR2d 82-6070 (11th Cir., 1982)

63. For each of the following citations, identify the type of authority (statutory, administrative, or judicial) and explain the citation.

    `LO 2-3`

    a) IRC Sec. 280A(c)(5)

    b) Rev. Proc. 2004-34, 2004-1 C.B. 911

    c) *Lakewood Associates*, RIA TC Memo 95-3566

    d) TAM 200427004

    e) *U.S. v. Muncy*, 2008-2 USTC par. 50,449 (E.D., AR, 2008)

64. Justine would like to clarify her understanding of a code section recently enacted by Congress. What tax law sources are available to assist Justine?

    `LO 2-4`

65. Aldina has identified conflicting authorities that address her research question. How should she evaluate these authorities to make a conclusion?

    `LO 2-5`

66. Georgette has identified a 1983 court case that appears to answer her research question. What must she do to determine if the case still represents "current" law?

    `LO 2-5`

67. Sandy has determined that her research question depends upon the interpretation of the phrase "not compensated by insurance." What type of research question is this?

    `LO 2-5`

LO 2-5

research

68. J. C. has been a professional gambler for many years. He loves this line of work and believes the income is tax-free.

a) Use an available tax research service to determine whether J. C.'s thinking is correct. Is the answer to this question found in the Internal Revenue Code? If not, what type of authority answers this question?

b) Write a memo communicating the results of your research.

LO 2-5

research

69. Katie recently won a ceramic dalmatian valued at $800 on a television game show. She questions whether this prize is taxable since it was a "gift" she won on the show.

a) Use an available tax research service to answer Katie's question.

b) Write a letter to Katie communicating the results of your research.

LO 2-5

research

70. Pierre recently received a tax penalty for failing to file a tax return. He was upset to receive the penalty, but he was comforted by the thought that he will get a tax deduction for paying the penalty.

a) Use an available tax research service to determine if Pierre is correct.

b) Write a memo communicating the results of your research.

LO 2-5

research

71. Paris was happy to provide a contribution to her friend Nicole's campaign for mayor, especially after she learned that charitable contributions are tax deductible.

a) Use an available tax service to determine whether Paris can deduct this contribution.

b) Write a memo communicating the results of your research.

LO 2-5

research

72. Matt and Lori were divorced in 2016. Pursuant to the divorce decree Matt receives $10,000 of alimony each month. Use an available tax service to determine if the alimony Matt receives is taxable. Would your answer change if Matt and Lori still live together?

LO 2-5

research

73. Shaun is a huge college football fan. In the past, he has always bought football tickets on the street from ticket scalpers. This year, he decided to join the university's ticket program, which requires a $2,000 contribution to the university for the "right" to purchase tickets. Shaun will then pay $400 per season ticket. Shaun understands that the price paid for the season tickets is not tax deductible as a charitable contribution. However, contributions to a university are typically tax deductible.

a) Use an available tax service to determine how much, if any, of Shaun's $2,000 contribution for the right to purchase tickets is tax deductible.

b) Write a letter to Shaun communicating the results of your research.

LO 2-5

research

74. Latrell recently used his Delta Skymiles to purchase a free round-trip ticket to Milan, Italy (value $1,200). The frequent flyer miles used to purchase the ticket were generated from Latrell's business travel as a CPA. Latrell's employer paid for his business trips, and he was not taxed on the travel reimbursement.

a) Use an available tax research service to determine how much income, if any, Latrell will have to recognize as a result of purchasing an airline ticket with Skymiles earned from business travel.

b) Write a memo communicating the results of your research.

LO 2-5

research

75. Benjamin, a self-employed bookkeeper, takes a CPA review course ($1,500 cost) to help prepare for the CPA exam.

a) Use an available tax research service to determine if Benjamin may deduct the cost of the CPA exam course.

b) Write a memo communicating the results of your research.

76. Randy has found conflicting authorities that address a research question for one of his clients. The majority of the authorities provide an unfavorable answer for his client. According to Randy's estimates, if the client takes the more favorable position on its tax return then there is approximately a 48 percent chance that the position will be sustained upon audit or judicial proceeding. If the client takes this position on its tax return, will Randy be subject to penalty? Will the client potentially be subject to penalty?   `LO 2-6`

77. Using the same facts from the previous problem, how would your answer change if Randy estimates that there is only a 20 percent chance that the position will be sustained upon audit or judicial proceeding?   `LO 2-6`

78. Sasha owes additional tax imposed in a recent audit. In addition to the tax, will she be assessed other amounts? If so, how will these amounts be determined?   `LO 2-7`

79. Maurice has a client that recently asked him about the odds of the IRS detecting cash transactions not reported on a tax return. What are some of the issues that Maurice should discuss with his client?   `LO 2-7`

ROGER | CPA Review

Sample CPA Exam questions from Roger CPA Review are available in Connect as support for the topics in this text. These Multiple Choice Questions and Task-Based Simulations include expert-written explanations and solutions and provide a starting point for students to become familiar with the content and functionality of the actual CPA Exam.

Tax Planning Strategies and Related Limitations

Learning Objectives

Upon completing this chapter, you should be able to:

LO 3-1 Identify the objectives of basic tax planning strategies.

LO 3-2 Apply the timing strategy.

LO 3-3 Apply the concept of present value to tax planning.

LO 3-4 Apply the income shifting strategy.

LO 3-5 Apply the conversion strategy.

LO 3-6 Describe basic judicial doctrines that limit tax planning strategies.

LO 3-7 Contrast tax avoidance and tax evasion.

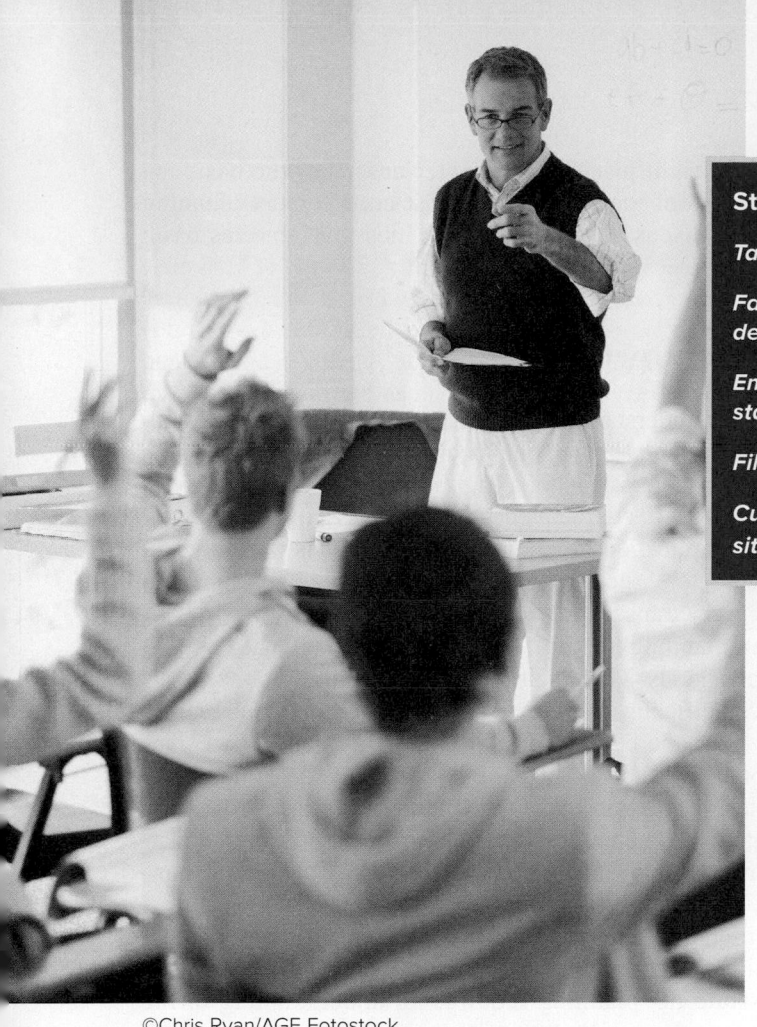

©Chris Ryan/AGE Fotostock

Storyline Summary

Taxpayers:	Bill and Mercedes
Family description:	Bill and Mercedes are married with one daughter, Margaret.
Employment status:	Bill is an economics professor; Mercedes is a small business owner.
Filing status:	Married, filing jointly
Current situation:	Bill and Mercedes want to engage in low risk tax planning strategies.

While working with their CPA during their audit, Bill and Mercedes decide to inquire about low risk tax planning opportunities. Specifically, they would like to gain a better understanding of how to maximize their after-tax income without increasing their potential for another audit. (Although it was fun and educational, one audit is enough!) Mercedes is convinced that, as a small business owner (Lavish Interior Designs Inc.), she pays more than her fair share of taxes. Likewise, Bill, an avid investor, wonders whether he is missing the mark by not considering taxes in his investment decisions. ■

Bill and Mercedes have come to the right place. This chapter describes the basic tax planning concepts that form the basis of the simplest to most complex tax planning transactions. In the process we also discuss the judicial doctrines that serve as basic limits on tax planning.

LO 3-1 BASIC TAX PLANNING OVERVIEW

Effective tax planning requires a basic understanding of the roles that tax and nontax factors play in structuring business, investment, and personal decisions. Although tax factors may not be the sole or even the primary determinant of a transaction or its structure, taxes can significantly affect the costs or benefits associated with business, investment, and personal transactions. Thus, the tax implications of competing transactions warrant careful consideration. Likewise, nontax factors, such as the taxpayer's financial goals or legal constraints, are an integral part of every transaction.

In general terms, effective tax planning maximizes the taxpayer's after-tax wealth while achieving the taxpayer's nontax goals. Maximizing after-tax wealth is not necessarily the same as minimizing taxes. Specifically, maximizing after-tax wealth requires us to consider both the tax and nontax costs and benefits of alternative transactions, whereas tax minimization focuses solely on a single cost—taxes. Indeed, if the goal of tax planning were simply to minimize taxes, the simplest way to achieve it would be to earn no income at all. Obviously, this strategy has potential limitations—most notably, the unattractive nontax consequence of poverty. Thus, it is necessary to consider the nontax ramifications of any planning strategy.

Virtually every transaction includes three parties: the taxpayer, the other transacting party, and the uninvited silent party that specifies the tax consequences of the transaction—the government. Astute tax planning requires an understanding of the tax and nontax costs from the perspectives of both the taxpayer *and* the other parties. For example, as discussed in the Compensation chapter, it would be impossible for an employer to develop an effective compensation plan without considering the tax and nontax costs associated with different compensation arrangements from both the employer's and the employees' perspectives. With sound tax planning, the employer can design a compensation package that generates value for employees while reducing costs for the employer. (One way to achieve this goal is through the use of nontaxable fringe benefits, such as health insurance, which are deductible expenses to the employer but not taxable income to employees.) Throughout the text, we highlight situations where this multilateral approach to tax planning is especially important.

In this chapter we discuss three basic tax planning strategies that represent the building blocks of tax planning:

1. *Timing* (deferring or accelerating taxable income and tax deductions).
2. *Income shifting* (shifting income from high- to low-tax-rate taxpayers).
3. *Conversion* (converting income from high- to low-tax-rate activities).

THE KEY FACTS

The Basics of Tax Planning

- Effective tax planning maximizes the taxpayer's after-tax wealth while achieving the taxpayer's nontax goals.
- Virtually every transaction includes three parties: the taxpayer, the other transacting party, and the uninvited silent party that specifies the tax consequences of the transaction—the government.
- Astute tax planning requires an understanding of the tax and nontax costs from the perspectives of both the taxpayer *and* the other parties.

LO 3-2 LO 3-3 LO 3-6 TIMING STRATEGIES

One of the cornerstones of basic tax planning is the idea of *timing*. *When* income is taxed or an expense is deducted affects the associated "real" tax costs or savings. This is true for two reasons. First, the time when income is taxed or an expense is deducted affects the *present value* of the taxes paid on income or the tax savings on deductions. Second, the tax costs of income and tax savings of deductions vary as *tax rates* change. The tax costs on income are higher when tax rates are higher and lower when tax rates are lower. Likewise, the tax savings on deductions are higher when tax rates are higher and lower when tax rates are lower. Let's look at the effects of present value and tax rates on the timing strategy.

Present Value of Money

The concept of **present value**—also known as the time value of money—basically states that $1 received today is worth *more* than $1 received in the future. Is this true, or is this some type of new math?

It's true. Assuming an investor can earn a positive **after-tax rate of return** such as 5 percent, $1 invested today should be worth $1.05 in one year.[1] Specifically,

Eq. 3-1

$$\text{Future Value} = \text{Present Value} \times (1 + r)^n$$
$$= \$1 \times (1 + .05)^1 = \$1.05$$

where $1 is the present value, r is the after-tax rate of return (5 percent), and n is the investment period (1 year). Hence, $1 today is equivalent to $1.05 in one year. The implication of the time value of money for tax planning is that the timing of a cash inflow or a cash outflow affects the present value of the income or expense.

Example 3-1

Bill is given the choice of receiving a $1,000 nontaxable gift today or a $1,000 nontaxable gift in one year. Which would Bill prefer? Assume Bill could invest $1,000 today and earn an 8 percent return after taxes in one year. If he receives the gift today, how much would the $1,000 be worth in one year?

Answer: The $1,000 gift today would be worth $1,080 in one year, and thus Bill should prefer to receive the gift today. Specifically,

$$\text{Future Value} = \text{Present Value} \times (1 + r)^n$$
$$= \$1,000 \times (1 + .08)^1 = \$1,080$$

In terms of *future value*, the choice in the above example between receiving $1,000 today and $1,000 in one year simplifies to a choice between $1,080 and $1,000. For even the least materialistic individual, choosing $1,080—that is, $1,000 *today*—should be straightforward.

Often tax planners find it useful to consider sums not in terms of future value, but rather in terms of present value. How would we restate the choice in Example 3-1 in terms of present value? Obviously, the present value of receiving $1,000 today is $1,000, but what is the *present value* of $1,000 received in one year? The answer depends on the **discount factor,** which we derive from the taxpayer's expected after-tax rate of return. The discount factor is very useful for calculating the present value of future inflows or outflows of cash. We can derive the discount factor for a given rate of return simply by rearranging the future value equation (Eq. 3-1) from above:

Eq. 3-2

$$\text{Present Value} = \text{Future Value}/(1 + r)^n$$
$$= \$1/(1 + .08)^1 = \$0.926$$
Therefore, the discount factor = 0.926

THE KEY FACTS

Present Value of Money

- The concept of present value—also known as the time value of money—states that $1 received today is worth *more* than $1 received in the future.
- The implication of the time value of money for tax planning is that the timing of a cash inflow or a cash outflow affects the present value of the income or expense.
- Present Value = Future Value/$(1 + r)^n$.
- When we are considering cash inflows, higher present values are preferred; when we are considering cash outflows, lower present values are preferred.

[1]Assuming a constant marginal tax rate (t), after-tax rate of return (r) may be calculated as follows: $r = R \times (1 - t)$, where R is the taxpayer's before-tax rate of return.

EXHIBIT 3-1 **Present Value of a Single Payment at Various Annual Rates of Return**

Year	4%	5%	6%	7%	8%	9%	10%	11%	12%
1	.962	.952	.943	.935	.926	.917	.909	.901	.893
2	.925	.907	.890	.873	.857	.842	.826	.812	.797
3	.889	.864	.840	.816	.794	.772	.751	.731	.712
4	.855	.823	.792	.763	.735	.708	.683	.659	.636
5	.822	.784	.747	.713	.681	.650	.621	.593	.567
6	.790	.746	.705	.666	.630	.596	.564	.535	.507
7	.760	.711	.665	.623	.583	.547	.513	.482	.452
8	.731	.677	.627	.582	.540	.502	.467	.434	.404
9	.703	.645	.592	.544	.500	.460	.424	.391	.361
10	.676	.614	.558	.508	.463	.422	.386	.352	.322
11	.650	.585	.527	.475	.429	.388	.350	.317	.287
12	.625	.557	.497	.444	.397	.356	.319	.286	.257
13	.601	.530	.469	.415	.368	.326	.290	.258	.229
14	.577	.505	.442	.388	.340	.299	.263	.232	.205
15	.555	.481	.417	.362	.315	.275	.239	.209	.183

Applying the discount factor, we can see that $1,000 received in one year is worth $926 in today's dollars. Thus, in terms of present value, Bill's choice in Example 3-1 simplifies to a choice between a cash inflow of $1,000 today and a cash inflow worth $926 today. Again, choosing $1,000 today is pretty straightforward.

Exhibit 3-1 provides the discount factors for a lump sum (single payment) received in *n* periods using various rates of return. Tax planners frequently utilize such tables for quick reference in calculating present value for sums under consideration.

Example 3-2

At a recent holiday sale, Bill and Mercedes purchased $1,000 worth of furniture with "no money down and no payments for one year!" How much money is this deal really worth? (Assume their after-tax rate of return on investments is 10 percent.)

Answer: The discount factor of .909 (Exhibit 3-1, 10% Rate of Return column, Year 1 row) means the present value of $1,000 is $909 ($1,000 × .909 = $909)—so Bill and Mercedes save $91 ($1,000 − $909 = $91).

While Example 3-1 considers a $1,000 cash inflow, Example 3-2 addresses a $1,000 cash *outflow*. In terms of present value, choosing between paying $1,000 today and paying $1,000 in a year simplifies to choosing a cash outflow of either $1,000 (by paying today) or $909 (by paying in one year). Most people would prefer to pay $909. Indeed, financial planners always keep the following general rule of thumb in mind: When considering *cash inflows, prefer higher present values;* when considering *cash outflows, prefer lower present values.*

The Timing Strategy When Tax Rates Are Constant

In terms of tax planning, remember that *taxes paid* represent cash *outflows*, while *tax savings* generated from tax deductions are cash *inflows*. This perspective leads us to two basic tax-related timing strategies when tax rates are constant (not changing):

1. Accelerate tax deductions (deduct in an earlier period).
2. Defer recognizing taxable income (recognize in a later period).

Accelerating tax deductions to an earlier period increases the present value of the tax savings from the deduction. That is, tax savings received now have a higher present value than the same amount received a year from now.

Deferring income to a later period decreases the present value of the tax cost of the income. That is, taxes paid a year from now have a lower present value than taxes paid today. These two strategies are summarized in Exhibit 3-2.

EXHIBIT 3-2   **The Timing Tax Strategy When Tax Rates Are Constant**

Item	Recommendation	Why?
Tax deductions	Accelerate tax deductions into earlier years.	Maximizes the present value of tax savings from deductions.
Taxable income	Defer taxable income into later tax years.	Minimizes the present value of taxes paid.

Example 3-3

Mercedes, a calendar-year taxpayer, uses the cash method of accounting for her small business.[2] On December 28, she receives a $10,000 bill from her accountant for consulting services related to her small business. She can avoid late payment charges by paying the $10,000 bill before January 10 of next year. Let's assume that Mercedes's marginal tax rate is 32 percent *this year and next* and that she can earn an after-tax rate of return of 10 percent on her investments. When should she pay the $10,000 bill—this year or next?

Answer: If Mercedes pays the bill this year, she will receive a tax deduction on this year's tax return.[3] If she pays the bill in January, she will receive a tax deduction on next year's tax return (one year later). She needs to compare the after-tax costs of the accounting service, using the present value of the tax savings for each scenario:

Description	Option 1: Pay $10,000 bill *this year*	Option 2: Pay $10,000 bill *next year*
Tax deduction	$10,000	$10,000
Marginal tax rate	× 32%	× 32%
Tax savings	$ 3,200	$ 3,200
Discount factor	× 1	× .909
Present value tax savings	$ 3,200	$ 2,909
After-tax cost of accounting services:		
Before-tax cost	$10,000	$10,000
Less: Present value tax savings	− 3,200	− 2,909
After-tax cost of accounting services	$6,800	$ 7,091

Since Mercedes would surely rather spend $6,800 than $7,091 for accounting services, paying the bill in December is the clear winner.

[2]In the Business Income, Deductions, and Accounting Methods chapter, we discuss the basic accounting methods (e.g., cash vs. the accrual method), which influence the timing of when income and deductions are recognized for tax purposes.

[3]Accelerating her payment from January 10 to December 31 will increase the present value of the $10,000 cash outflow by 10 days. Thus, there is a minor present value cost associated with accelerating her payment.

In terms of accelerating deductions, the intent of the timing strategy is to accelerate the tax deduction significantly *without* accelerating the actual cash outflow that generates the expense. Indeed, if we assume a marginal rate of 32 percent and an after-tax return of 8 percent, accelerating a $1,000 cash outflow by one year to realize $320 in tax savings actually *increases* the after-tax *cost* of the expense from $629.68 to $680.

Present Value Comparison		
Description	Present value of net cash outflow *today*	Present value of net cash outflow in *one year*
Cash outflow	$1,000	$1,000.00
Less: Tax savings (outflow × 32% tax rate)	− 320	− 320.00
Net cash outflow	$ 680	$ 680.00
Present value factor	× 1	× .926
Present value of net cash outflow today	$ 680	$ 629.68

Generally speaking, whenever a taxpayer can accelerate a deduction without also substantially accelerating the cash outflow, the timing strategy will be more beneficial.

Is the accelerating deductions strategy utilized in the real world? Yes. While it is particularly effective for cash-method taxpayers, who can often control the year in which they pay their expenses, all taxpayers have *some* latitude in timing deductions. Common examples of the timing strategy include accelerating depreciation deductions for depreciable assets, using LIFO instead of FIFO for inventory, and accelerating the deduction of certain prepaid expenses.[4] For large corporations, the benefits associated with this timing strategy can be quite substantial. Thus, tax planners spend considerable time identifying the proper period in which to recognize expenses and evaluating opportunities to accelerate deductions.

Are there certain taxpayer or transaction attributes that enhance the advantages of accelerating deductions? Absolutely. Higher tax rates, higher rates of return, larger transaction amounts, and the ability to accelerate deductions by two or more years all increase the benefits of accelerating deductions. To demonstrate this for yourself, simply rework Example 3-3 and substitute any of the following: 50 percent tax rate, 12 percent after-tax rate of return, $100,000 expense, or a five-year period difference in the timing of the expense deduction. The benefits of accelerating deductions become much more prominent with these changes.

Deferring income recognition is an equally beneficial timing strategy, especially when the taxpayer can defer the recognition of income significantly without deferring the actual receipt of income very much. Consider the following example.

Example 3-4

In early December, Bill decides he would like to sell $100,000 of his Dell Inc. stock, which cost $20,000 10 years ago. Assume Bill's tax rate on the $80,000 gain will be 15 percent and his typical after-tax rate of return on investments is 7 percent. What effect would deferring the sale to January have on Bill's after-tax income on the sale?

[4]See the discussion of accounting methods in the Business Income, Deductions, and Accounting Methods chapter.

Answer:

	Present Value Comparison	
Description	**Option 1: Sell the $100,000 stock in December[5]**	**Option 2: Sell the $100,000 stock in January[5]**
Sales price	$100,000	$100,000
Less: Cost of stock	− 20,000	− 20,000
Gain on sale	$ 80,000	$ 80,000
Marginal tax rate	× 15%	× 15%
Tax on gain	$ 12,000	$ 12,000
Discount factor	× 1	×.935
Present value tax cost	$ 12,000	$ 11,220
After-tax income from sale:		
Before-tax income	$100,000	$100,000
Less: Present value tax cost	− 12,000	− 11,220
After-tax income from sale	**$ 88,000**	**$ 88,780**

Bill would doubtlessly prefer to earn $88,780 to $88,000, so from a tax perspective, selling the Dell Inc. stock in January is preferable. An important nontax issue for Bill to consider is the possibility that the stock price may fluctuate between December and January.

Income deferral represents an important aspect of investment planning (discussed in the Investments chapter), retirement planning (discussed in the Retirement Savings and Deferred Compensation chapter), and certain property transactions (discussed in the Property Dispositions chapter). Income-related timing considerations also affect tax planning for everyday business operations, such as determining the appropriate period in which to recognize income (e.g., cash or accrual accounting method for income and deduction recognition, and depreciation methods).

Do certain taxpayer or transaction attributes enhance the advantages of deferring income? Yes. The list is very similar to that for accelerating deductions: Higher tax rates, higher rates of return, larger transaction amounts, and the ability to defer revenue recognition for longer periods of time increase the benefits of deferral. To demonstrate this for yourself, simply rework Example 3-4 using any of the following: 50 percent tax rate, 12 percent after-tax rate of return on investments, or $200,000 gain.[6]

The Timing Strategy When Tax Rates Change

When tax rates change, the timing strategy requires a little more consideration because the tax costs of income and the tax savings from deductions will now vary. The higher the tax rate, the higher the tax savings for a tax deduction. The lower the tax rate, the lower

THE KEY FACTS

The Timing Strategy

- The time at which income is taxed or an expense is deducted affects the *present value* of the taxes paid on income or tax savings on deductions.
- The tax costs of income and tax savings of deductions vary as *tax rates* change.
- When tax rates are constant, tax planners prefer to defer income and accelerate deductions.
- When tax rates are increasing, the taxpayer must calculate the optimal tax strategies for deductions and income.
- When tax rates are decreasing, taxpayers should accelerate tax deductions into earlier years and defer taxable income to later years.

[5]This will require Bill to pay the tax on the gain no later than April 15 of the following year (i.e., three months after the sale for option 1 and 15 months after the sale for option 2). If Bill and Mercedes's current-year withholding and estimated payments do not equal or exceed 110 percent of their previous year's tax liability, they will have to make an estimated payment by January 15 to avoid the failure to make estimated tax payment penalty (discussed later in the Individual Income Tax Computation and Tax Credits chapter). This example assumes that Bill and Mercedes can avoid the underpayment of estimated tax penalty discussed in the Individual Income Tax Computation and Tax Credits chapter by paying 110 percent of their previous year's tax liability in both options 1 and 2. Thus, they can defer paying the tax on the gain until April 15 of the year following the sale.

[6]In Example 3-4, increasing the deferral period (e.g., from one to five years) also increases the benefits of tax deferral but requires additional assumptions regarding the expected five-year return of the Dell Inc. stock (assuming he does not sell the stock for five years) and his new investment (assuming he sells the Dell Inc. stock and immediately reinvests the after-tax proceeds).

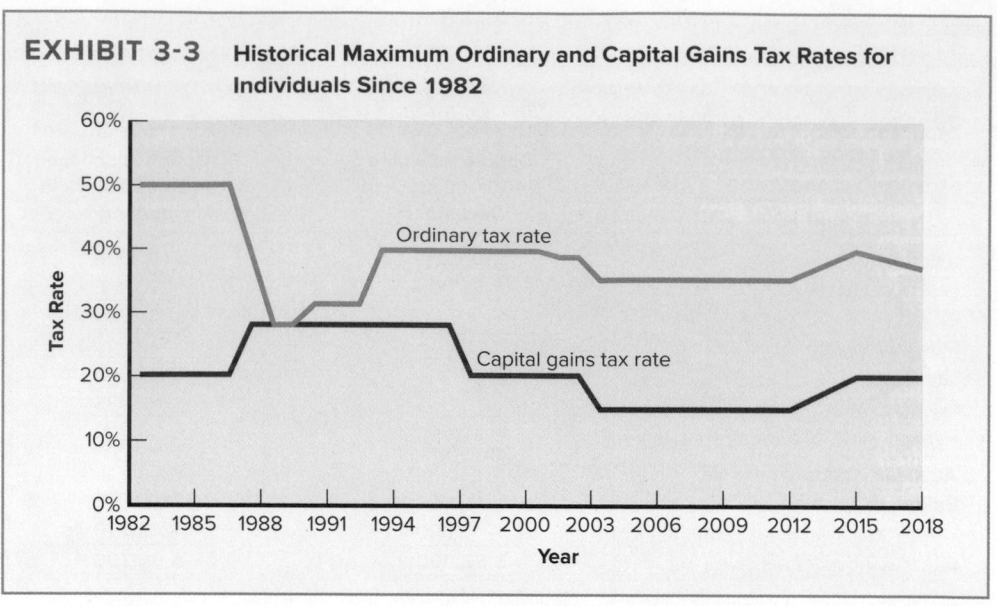

EXHIBIT 3-3   Historical Maximum Ordinary and Capital Gains Tax Rates for Individuals Since 1982

the tax costs for taxable income. *All other things being equal, taxpayers should prefer to recognize deductions during high-tax-rate years and income during low-tax-rate years.* The implication is that before a taxpayer implements the timing strategies suggested above (accelerate deductions, defer income), she should consider whether her tax rates are likely to change. In fact, as we discuss below, increasing tax rates may even suggest the taxpayer should *accelerate* income and *defer* deductions.

What would cause a taxpayer's marginal tax rate to change? The taxpayer's taxable income can change for a variety of reasons, such as changing jobs, retiring, or starting a new business. Indeed, in the Introduction to Tax chapter, we demonstrated how a taxpayer's marginal tax rate changes as income or deductions change. Marginal tax rates can also change because of tax legislation. We discussed the tax legislative process in the Tax Compliance, the IRS, and Tax Authorities chapter and noted that Congress frequently enacts tax legislation because lawmakers use taxes to raise revenue, stimulate the economy, and so on. For example, the Tax Cuts and Jobs Act enacted on December 22, 2017 lowered the top ordinary tax rate from 39.6 percent to 37 percent. In the last 35 years, Congress has changed the maximum statutory tax rates that apply to ordinary income, such as wages and business income, or capital gains, such as gains from the sale of stock, for individual taxpayers no fewer than eleven times (see Exhibit 3-3).

Let's take a look at how changing tax rates affect the timing strategy recommendations. Exhibit 3-4 presents recommendations for when tax rates are increasing. The taxpayer must actually calculate the optimal tax strategies for deductions and income when tax rates are increasing. Specifically, because accelerating deductions causes them to be

EXHIBIT 3-4   The Timing Tax Strategy When Tax Rates Are Increasing

Item	Recommendation	Why?
Tax deductions	Requires calculation to determine optimal strategy.	The taxpayer must calculate whether the benefit of accelerating deductions outweighs the disadvantage of recognizing deductions in a *lower*-tax-rate year.
Taxable income	Requires calculation to determine optimal strategy.	The taxpayer must calculate whether the benefit of deferring income outweighs the disadvantage of recognizing income in a *higher*-tax-rate year.

recognized in a *lower*-tax-rate year, the taxpayer must calculate whether the benefit of accelerating the deduction outweighs the disadvantage. Likewise, because deferring income causes income to be recognized in a *higher*-tax-rate year, the taxpayer must calculate whether the benefit of deferring income outweighs the disadvantage.

Example 3-5

Having decided she needs new equipment for her business, Mercedes is now considering whether to make the purchase and claim a corresponding $10,000 deduction at year-end or next year. Mercedes anticipates that, with the new machinery, her business income will rise such that her marginal rate will increase from 24 percent this year to 32 percent next year. Assuming her after-tax rate of return is 8 percent, what should Mercedes do?

Answer: Given rising tax rates, Mercedes must calculate the after-tax cost of the equipment for *both* options and compare present values.

Present Value Comparison		
Description	Option 1: Pay $10,000 bill *this year*	Option 2: Pay $10,000 bill *next year*
Tax deduction	$10,000	$10,000
Marginal tax rate	× 24%	× 32%
Tax savings	$ 2,400	$ 3,200
Discount factor	× 1	× .926
Present value tax savings	$ 2,400	$ 2,963
After-tax cost of equipment:		
Before-tax cost	$10,000	$10,000
Less: Present value tax savings	− 2,400	− 2,963
After-tax cost of equipment	$ 7,600	$ 7,037

Paying the $10,000 next year is the clear winner.

In the above example, if the choice were either to recognize $10,000 of *income* this year or next, the *amounts* would be exactly the same but the conclusion would be different, and Mercedes would prefer to receive $7,600 of after-tax income this year instead of $7,037. (Remember, when considering cash *inflows*, we prefer the *higher* present value.) Are these always the answers when tax rates are increasing? No, the answer will depend on both the taxpayer's after-tax rate of return and the magnitude of the tax rate increase.

Now let's consider the recommendations when tax rates are *decreasing*—a common scenario when an individual reaches retirement. Exhibit 3-5 presents the timing strategy

EXHIBIT 3-5 **The Timing Tax Strategy When Tax Rates Are Decreasing**

Item	Recommendation	Why?
Tax deductions	Accelerate tax deductions into earlier years.	Maximizes the present value of tax savings from deductions due to the acceleration of the deductions into *earlier* years with a *higher* tax rate.
Taxable income	Defer taxable income into later tax years.	Minimizes the present value of taxes paid due to the deferral of the income to later years with a *lower* tax rate.

How does tax reform affect taxpayers' tax planning? It depends! There is little debate that tax reform affects taxpayers' decisions, but *how* it affects their decisions is a function of the enacted tax laws, and taxpayers' circumstances. Provisions to reduce the tax rate, eliminate the interest deduction on corporate debt, and change the tax treatment of capital expenditures affect the after-tax cost of investments, making them more difficult to appropriately value. As a result, it is more difficult for taxpayers to determine the appropriate tax planning strategy.

For companies in the business of investing, such as private equity firms and real estate investment companies, the various tax provisions can have a big and potentially negative impact. For example, it is fairly common for private equity firms to use leveraged buyouts to acquire portfolio companies. Eliminating interest deductions reduces the value of the portfolio companies and, consequently, reduces the profitability of private equity firms. Therefore, this provision might encourage taxpayers to reduce debt usage on investment purchases (an example of the conversion strategy). Capital intensive businesses will see tax benefits from a tax provision that allows full expensing of capital investments, leading to their use of the timing strategy to purchase assets in the time period when these assets can be immediately expensed rather than depreciated. Similarly, a reduction in tax rates can generate additional tax benefits by encouraging taxpayers to accelerate deductions in a year with higher tax rates or to defer income so it is realized in a year with lower tax rates, a basic tax timing strategy.

With tax reform, it is certain that taxpayers are assessing how their tax strategies might change.

Source: Based on: "Tax reform uncertainty testing alternative investors," http://www.pionline.com/article/20170417/PRINT/304179983/tax-reform-uncertainty-testing-alternative-investors, April 17, 2017.

THE KEY FACTS

Limitations to the Timing Strategy

- Timing strategies contain several inherent limitations.
- Whenever a taxpayer is unable to accelerate a deduction without also accelerating the cash outflow, the timing strategy will be less beneficial.
- Tax law generally requires taxpayers to continue their investment in an asset in order to defer income recognition for tax purposes.
- A deferral strategy may not be optimal if the taxpayer has severe cash flow needs, if continuing the investment would generate a low rate of return compared to other investments, if the current investment would subject the taxpayer to unnecessary risk, and so on.
- The constructive receipt doctrine, which provides that a taxpayer must recognize income when it is actually *or* constructively received, also restricts income deferral for cash-method taxpayers.

recommendations in this case. The recommendations are clear. Taxpayers should accelerate tax deductions into earlier years to reap the tax savings from *accelerating* deductions to *higher*-tax-rate years. Likewise, taxpayers should defer taxable income to later years to enjoy the tax benefits of *deferring* taxable income to *lower*-tax-rate years.

Limitations to Timing Strategies　Timing strategies contain certain inherent limitations. First, tax laws generally require taxpayers to continue their investment in an asset in order to defer income recognition for tax purposes. In other words, deferral is generally not an option if a taxpayer has "cashed out" of an investment.[7] For example, Bill could not sell his Dell stock in December and then choose not to recognize the income until January. A deferral strategy may not be optimal if (1) the taxpayer has severe cash flow needs, (2) continuing the investment would generate a low rate of return compared to other investments, or (3) the current investment would subject the taxpayer to unnecessary risk. For example, the risk that the value of Bill's investment in Dell Inc. will decline from December to January in Example 3-4 may lead Bill to forgo deferring his stock sale until January. Again, the astute taxpayer considers both the tax *and* nontax ramifications of deferring income.

A second limitation results from the **constructive receipt doctrine,** which also restricts income deferral for cash-method taxpayers.[8] Unlike accrual-method taxpayers, cash-method taxpayers report income for tax purposes when the income is *received*, whether it is in the form of cash, property, or services.[9] The cash method affords taxpayers

---

[7]See the discussions of like-kind exchanges in the Property Dispositions chapter, investment planning in the Investments chapter, and retirement planning in the Retirement Savings and Deferred Compensation chapter.

[8]Later in this chapter we discuss other judicial doctrines that apply to all planning strategies.

[9]As we discuss in depth in the Business Income, Deductions, and Accounting Methods chapter, accrual-method taxpayers report income when it is earned. In general, income is deemed earned when all events have occurred that fix the taxpayer's right to the income and the income can be estimated with reasonable accuracy. Thus, income recognition for accrual-method taxpayers generally is not tied to payment. Receipt of prepaid income by accrual-method taxpayers may trigger income recognition in certain circumstances. The constructive receipt doctrine may apply in these situations.

some leeway in determining when to recognize income, because such taxpayers can control when they bill their clients. However, the constructive receipt doctrine provides that a taxpayer must recognize income when it is actually *or* constructively received. Constructive receipt is deemed to have occurred if the income has been credited to the taxpayer's account or if the income is unconditionally available to the taxpayer, the taxpayer is aware of the income's availability, and there are no restrictions on the taxpayer's control over the income.

Example 3-6

Mercedes's brother-in-law, Carlos, works for King Acura, which recently instituted a bonus plan that pays year-end bonuses each December to employees rated above average for their customer service. Carlos is expecting a $10,000 bonus this year that will be paid on December 31. Thinking he'd prefer to defer this income until next year, Carlos plans to take a vacation on December 30 so that he will not receive his bonus check until January. Will Carlos's strategy work?

Answer: No, the constructive receipt doctrine applies here. Because Carlos's check was unconditionally available to him on December 31, he was aware of its availability, and there were no restrictions on his control over the income on that date, Carlos must report the income in the current year.

What could taxpayers do to avoid Carlos's problem in the future? They could request that their employer institute a company policy of paying bonuses on January 1, which would allow all employees to report the bonus income in that year. However, if the employer is a cash-method taxpayer, this creates a potential conflict with its employees.[10] Such an employer would most likely prefer to deduct the bonus in the current year, which requires the bonuses to be paid in December. This conflict would not exist if the employer were an accrual-method taxpayer, because paying the bonuses in January would not affect its ability to deduct the bonuses in the previous year.[11]

INCOME-SHIFTING STRATEGIES

LO 3-4   LO 3-6

We've seen that the value of a tax deduction, or the tax cost of income, varies with the marginal tax rate. We've also seen that tax rates can vary across time, which leads to basic tax planning strategies regarding when to recognize deductions and income. Tax rates can also vary across *taxpayers* or *jurisdictions* (states, countries), which leads to still other tax planning strategies—for example, shifting income from high-tax-rate taxpayers to low-tax-rate taxpayers or shifting deductions from low-tax-rate taxpayers to high-tax-rate taxpayers.

The type of taxpayers who benefit most from this strategy are (1) related parties, such as family members or businesses and their owners, who have varying marginal tax rates and are willing to shift income for the benefit of the group; and (2) taxpayers operating in multiple jurisdictions with different marginal tax rates. In any case, tax planners should seek only legitimate methods of shifting income that will withstand IRS scrutiny. In the following section we discuss transactions between family members, followed by a discussion of transactions between owners and their businesses, and finally a discussion of income shifting across jurisdictions.

---

[10]Because King Acura carries inventory, the cash method is not allowed for transactions related to its inventory (e.g., cost of goods sold, sales, etc.). However, King Acura is permitted to use the cash method for other transactions. This mixed method is referred to as the "hybrid" method of accounting.

[11]§267(a)(2). When an employee/shareholder and an employer/corporation are related (i.e., the employee/shareholder owns more than 50 percent of the value of the employer corporation), the corporation is not allowed to deduct the compensation expense until the employee/shareholder includes the payment in income.

Transactions between Family Members and Limitations

One of the most common examples of income shifting is high-tax-rate parents shifting income to low-tax-rate children. For example, Bill and Mercedes have a 32 percent marginal tax rate, whereas their daughter, Margaret, has a 10 percent marginal tax rate. Assuming their marginal tax rates remain constant with relatively modest changes in income, every $1 of income that Bill and Mercedes shift to Margaret reduces the family's tax liability by 22 cents [$1 × (32% − 10%)]. Thus, if Bill and Mercedes shift $10,000 of taxable income to Margaret, the family's after-tax income will increase by $2,200. Can taxpayers legally do this? Yes and no. As you might expect, there are limitations on this type of income shifting.

The **assignment of income doctrine** requires income to be taxed to the taxpayer who actually earns it.[12] Merely attributing your paycheck or dividend to another taxpayer does not transfer the tax liability associated with the income. The assignment of income doctrine implies that, in order to shift income to a taxpayer, that taxpayer must actually earn the income. For example, if Mercedes would like to shift some of her business income to Margaret, Margaret must actually earn it. One way to accomplish this would be for Mercedes to employ Margaret in her business and pay her a $10,000 salary. The effects of this transaction are to decrease Mercedes's taxable income by $10,000 because of tax-deductible salary expense, and to increase Margaret's income by the $10,000 taxable salary. What if Margaret is paid $10,000 to answer Mercedes's business phone one Saturday afternoon every month? Does this seem reasonable? Not likely. The IRS frowns upon this type of aggressive strategy.

Indeed, the IRS closely scrutinizes such **related-party transactions**—that is, financial activities among family members (also among owners and their businesses, or among businesses owned by the same owners). Unlike **arm's length transactions,** in which each transacting party negotiates for his or her own benefit, related-party transactions are useful for taxpayers who are much more willing to negotiate for their own common good to the detriment of the IRS. For example, would Mercedes pay an unrelated party $10,000 to answer the phone once a month? Doubtful.[13]

Are there other ways to shift income to children? For example, could Bill shift some of his investment income to Margaret? Yes, but there's a catch. The assignment of income applies what is referred to as the "fruit and the tree" analogy [*Lucas v. Earl* (S. Ct., 1930), 8 AFTR 10287]. For the owner to avoid being taxed on the fruit from the tree (the income), the owner must transfer the tree. Thus, to shift investment income, Bill would also have to transfer ownership in the underlying investment assets to Margaret.[14] Is there a problem with this requirement? Not for Margaret. However, Bill would likely prefer to maintain his wealth. The nontax disadvantages of transferring wealth to implement the income-shifting strategy often outweigh the tax benefits of the transfer. For example, most parents either could not afford to or would have serious reservations about transferring significant wealth to their children—a prime example of how nontax costs may override tax considerations.

Transactions between Owners and
Their Businesses and Limitations

Income shifting is not limited to transactions within a family unit. One of the most common examples occurs between owners and their businesses. Let's consider Mercedes's interior design business. Currently, Mercedes operates her business as a sole proprietorship. A sole proprietorship (unlike a C corporation) is not a separate reporting entity, and thus, Mercedes reports her business income and deductions on her individual tax return. Shifting

---

[12]Later in this chapter we discuss other judicial doctrines that apply to all planning strategies.

[13]The Internal Revenue Code also contains specific provisions to curtail benefits from related-party transactions. For example, as we discuss in the Property Dispositions chapter, §267 disallows a tax deduction for losses on sales to related parties (even if the sale was consummated at the asset's fair market value).

[14]Further, as we discuss in the Individual Income Tax Computation and Tax Credits chapter, the "kiddie tax" may apply when parents shift too much investment income to children. The kiddie tax restricts the amount of a child's investment income that can be taxed at the child's (lower) tax rate subjects the rest to trust (higher) tax rates.

income to or from her sole proprietorship offers no benefit because all of her sole proprietorship income is reported on her tax return, regardless of whether it is attributed to her personally or to her business. On the other hand, if Mercedes operated her interior design business as a C corporation, shifting income to or from the C corporation may make good financial sense because the corporation would be a separate entity with tax rates distinct from Mercedes's individual tax rate. Shifting income to herself from the C corporation may allow Mercedes to decrease the tax on her business profits, thereby increasing her after-tax income. This strategy may become more common with the recent significant drop in the corporate tax rates compared to the small decrease in individual tax rates. Example 3-7 illustrates the savings obtainable from this strategy.

Example 3-7

Mercedes is considering incorporating her interior design business. She projects $200,000 of business profit next year. Excluding this profit, Bill and Mercedes expect $70,000 of taxable income next year. If Mercedes would like to minimize her current-year tax liability, should she incorporate her business? (Use the married filing jointly and corporate tax rates in Appendix D to answer this question.)

Answer: If Mercedes does not incorporate her business, the first $7,400 of her business profits will be taxed at 12 percent (from $70,000 to $77,400 of taxable income, the marginal tax rate is 12 percent. The next $87,600 (from $77,400 to $165,000 of taxable income) would be taxed at 22 percent. The remaining $105,000 (from $165,000 to $270,000 of taxable income) would be taxed at 24 percent. Upon reviewing the corporate tax rate schedule, you should note that the corporate tax rate is a flat 21 percent, and is lower than Bill and Mercedes's current marginal tax rate of 24 percent. Thus, there appears to be some opportunity for Mercedes to reduce her current-year tax liability by incorporating her business.[15]

In order to shift income from the corporation to the owner, the corporation must create a tax deduction for itself in the process. Compensation paid to employee–owners is the most common method of shifting income from corporations to their owners. Compensation expense is deductible by the corporation and is generally taxable to the employee. (See the Compensation chapter for a broader discussion of nontaxable compensation benefits.) Having the business owner rent property to the corporation or loan money to the corporation are also effective income-shifting methods, because both transactions generate tax deductions for the corporation and income for the shareholder. Because corporations don't get a tax deduction for dividends paid, paying dividends is *not* an effective way to shift income. Having a corporation pay dividends actually results in "double taxation"—the profits generating the dividends are taxed first at the corporate level, and then at the shareholder level. Depending on the taxpayer's tax rate and their dividend tax rate, this strategy may be a good one though under the new tax law it can be quite complicated, and recommending this tax planning strategy without analyzing the taxpayer's situation may not be a good way to keep your job as a tax consultant.

After a taxpayer identifies the opportunity and appropriate method to shift income (compensation paid to a related party), he or she can easily determine the optimal amount to shift depending on the taxpayers' marginal tax rates.

Example 3-8

Assuming Mercedes's goal is to minimize her current-year federal income tax liability, how much of the $200,000 business income should her corporation report?

Answer: It should report $192,600. Comparing the two tax rate schedules reveals how to calculate this number.

(continued on page 3-14)

---

[15]Note that this is a simplified discussion of one of many tax issues associated with incorporating a business and assumes Mercedes's business does not qualify for the deduction for qualified business income discussed in the Individual Deductions chapter. In addition, as discussed later in this chapter, Mercedes must consider the judicial doctrines (economic substance, business purpose, etc.) in making this decision. She also needs to consider further tax planning opportunities described in the following example.

Step 1: Would Mercedes rather have income taxed at 21 percent (the corporation's tax rate) or 12 percent (Bill and Mercedes's marginal tax rate before recognizing any profit from Mercedes's business)? Twelve percent is the obvious answer. To take advantage of Bill and Mercedes's 12 percent tax bracket, Mercedes should shift $7,400 of the expected $200,000 in profits to herself and Bill—via a salary paid to Mercedes.

Step 2: Assuming Bill and Mercedes report $77,400 of income, their marginal tax rate will now be 22 percent, and thus Mercedes's choice is to have additional income taxed at 22 percent (Bill and Mercedes's marginal tax rate) or at 21 percent (the corporation's tax rate). Twenty-one percent is the clear answer. To take advantage of the 21 percent corporate tax rate, the corporation should retain the remaining $192,600 of the expected $200,000 in profits.

How much current federal income tax does this strategy save Bill and Mercedes? The corporation's and Bill and Mercedes's combined federal income tax liability will be $49,353 ($40,446 for the corporation plus $8,907 for Bill and Mercedes) compared to $53,379 for Bill and Mercedes if the business is operated as a sole proprietorship. Thus, they will save $4,026.[16]

Are there nontax disadvantages of the income-shifting-via-incorporating strategy? Yes. For example, one nontax disadvantage for Mercedes is that her new corporation now has $152,154 of her after-tax profits ($192,600 profits less $40,446 of corporate tax). If Mercedes has personal cash-flow needs that require use of the $152,154, this is not a viable strategy. Indeed, it's advantageous only if the business owner intends to reinvest the business profits into the business. Furthermore, any subsequent transactions between Mercedes and the corporation would clearly be related-party transactions. Thus, Mercedes should be prepared for IRS scrutiny.[17]

As the above example illustrates, tax-avoiding strategies can be quite beneficial and as Bill and Mercedes's personal (nonbusiness) income increases (i.e., their tax bracket increases on personal income), the strategies will produce even greater tax savings. With the decrease in the corporate tax rate from 35 percent to 21 percent, we are likely to see an increasing preference for businesses to operate as corporations. However, tax planning strategies also entail some financial risks if they fail to pass muster with the IRS.

ETHICS

Agnes Meher is the owner of LuPat, a profitable construction company that she operates as a sole proprietorship. As a sole proprietor, Agnes reports the business income from LuPat on her individual tax return. Agnes expects the business to generate $400,000 of taxable income this year. Combined with her other income, this will put her in the top tax bracket (37 percent). Agnes has two children named Ellie Mae and Spencer, ages 9 and 11, respectively, who do not currently have any taxable income. Agnes would like to shift some of her income from LuPat to Ellie Mae and Spencer to reduce the overall tax burden from the business income. To shift the income, Agnes hired Ellie Mae and Spencer to perform some janitorial and clerical services for LuPat, paying each child $20,000. What do you think of Agnes's strategy?

---

[16]This strategy will result in the eventual double taxation of the income retained in Mercedes's corporation. Specifically, Mercedes will eventually have to pay tax on the income retained by the corporation, either in the form of taxable dividends from the corporation or a taxable gain when she sells or liquidates the corporation. The present value of this additional layer of tax reduces the tax savings from this strategy. The longer that the second layer of tax is deferred, the more advantageous this strategy will be. In addition, the example ignores employment-related taxes. These calculations are beyond the scope of this chapter.

[17]The taxpayer should maintain documentation for related-party transactions (e.g., notes for related-party loans and contemporaneous documentation of reasonable compensation paid to related parties).

Income Shifting across Jurisdictions and Limitations

Taxpayers that operate in multiple jurisdictions (states, countries) also apply the income-shifting strategy. Specifically, income earned in different jurisdictions—whether in the United States or abroad, and for state income tax purposes, income earned in different states—is often taxed very differently. With a proper understanding of the differences in tax laws across jurisdictions, taxpayers can use these differences to maximize their after-tax wealth.

Example 3-9

Carlos's employer, King Acura, has two locations. Its main location is in South Dakota (a state with no corporate tax), with a secondary location in North Dakota (maximum corporate state tax rate of 4.31 percent). What tax planning strategy may save money for King Acura?

Answer: The most obvious strategy is to shift income from the North Dakota location to the South Dakota location, thereby reducing King Acura's state income tax liability by about 4.31 cents for every dollar of income shifted.[18]

A number of possibilities exist to execute a strategy such as King Acura's in Example 3-9. Assuming that the North Dakota and South Dakota locations exchange cars, the firm could shift income via *transfer pricing* (using the price the South Dakota location charges the North Dakota location for cars transferred to North Dakota). Likewise, if the South Dakota location (the corporate headquarters) provides a legitimate support function for the North Dakota location, the firm should allocate a portion of the overhead and administrative expenses from the South Dakota location to the North Dakota location.

What are some of the limitations of income shifting across jurisdictions? First, taxing authorities are fully aware of the tax benefits of strategically structuring transactions across tax borders (across countries or states). Thus, the IRS closely examines transfer pricing on international transactions. Similarly, state tax authorities scrutinize interstate transactions between related taxpayers. Second, when taxpayers locate in low-tax-rate jurisdictions to, in effect, shift income to a tax-advantaged jurisdiction, they may bear **implicit taxes** (i.e., additional costs attributable to the jurisdiction's tax advantage). For example, the demand for workers, services, or property in low-tax-rate jurisdictions, whether a foreign country or a low-tax state, may increase the nontax costs associated with operating a business there enough to offset the tax advantages. Finally, negative publicity from moving operations (and jobs) from the United States to a lower-tax jurisdiction may more than offset any tax benefits associated with these strategies.

THE KEY FACTS

The Income-Shifting Strategy

- Income shifting exploits the differences in tax rates across taxpayers or jurisdictions.
- Common examples of income shifting include high-tax-rate parents shifting income to low-tax-rate children, businesses shifting income to their owners, and taxpayers shifting income from high-tax jurisdictions to low-tax jurisdictions. The assignment of income doctrine requires income to be taxed to the taxpayer who actually earns the income.
- The IRS closely monitors income-shifting strategies that involve related-party transactions.

CONVERSION STRATEGIES

LO 3-5

We've now seen how tax rates can vary across time and taxpayers. They can also vary across different *activities*. For example, ordinary income such as salary, interest income, and business income received by individual taxpayers is taxed at their ordinary marginal

---

[18]Because state taxes are deductible for federal tax purposes, every dollar of state taxes reduced with this strategy will increase King Acura's federal income tax liability by its federal marginal tax rate (e.g., 21 percent). Thus, the net tax savings for every dollar of income shifted from North Dakota to South Dakota will be 3.4 percent, which equals the state tax savings (4.31 percent) less the federal tax increase resulting from the lost state tax deduction (4.31% × 21%).

tax rates. Long-term capital gains, which are gains from the sale of investment assets held longer than one year, and dividends are taxed at lower tax rates (currently a maximum of 20 percent), and still other forms of income like nontaxable compensation benefits and municipal bond interest are tax-exempt. Expenses from different types of activities may also be treated very differently for tax purposes. Business expenses are generally fully tax deductible, whereas tax deductions for investments may be limited, and tax deductions for personal expenses may be completely disallowed. In sum, the tax law does not treat all types of income or deductions the same. This understanding forms the basis for the conversion strategy—recasting income and expenses to receive the most favorable tax treatment.

To implement the conversion strategy, the taxpayer must be aware of the underlying differences in tax treatment across various types of income, expenses, and activities and have some ability to alter the nature of the income or expense to receive the more advantageous tax treatment. What are some common examples of the conversion strategy? In the Individual Income Tax Overview, Dependents, and Filing Status chapter, we explain character differences in income and deductions. In the Investments chapter, we consider investment planning and the advantages of investing in assets that generate preferentially taxed income. In the Individual Deductions chapter, we explain the basic differences between business and investment activities and what characteristics result in the more favorable "business" designation for expense deductions. In the Compensation chapter and the Retirement Savings and Deferred Compensation chapter, we discuss compensation planning and the benefits of restructuring employee compensation from currently taxable compensation to nontaxable or tax-deferred forms of compensation, such as employer-provided health insurance and retirement contributions.

To analyze the benefits of the conversion strategy, you often compare the after-tax rates of return of alternative investments rather than the **before-tax rates of return.** Given a stationary marginal tax rate, you can calculate an investment's after-tax rate of return as follows:

Eq. 3-3

$$\text{After-Tax Rate of Return} = \text{Before-Tax Rate of Return} \\ - (\text{Before-Tax Rate of Return} \\ \times \text{Marginal Tax Rate})$$

which simplifies to

Eq. 3-4

$$\text{After-Tax Rate of Return} = \text{Before-Tax Rate of Return} \\ \times (1 - \text{Marginal Tax Rate})$$

Example 3-10

Bill is contemplating three different investments, each with the same amount of risk:

1. A high-dividend stock that pays 8.5 percent dividends annually but has no appreciation potential.
2. Taxable corporate bonds that pay 9 percent interest annually.
3. Tax-exempt municipal bonds that pay 6 percent interest annually.

Assuming that dividends are taxed at 20 percent and that Bill's marginal tax rate on ordinary income is 32 percent, which investment should Bill choose?

Answer: To answer this question, we must compute Bill's after-tax rate of return for each investment. The after-tax rates of return for the three investments are

Investment Choice	Computation	After-Tax Rate of Return
High-dividend stock	8.5% × (1 − 20%) =	6.8%
Corporate bond	9% × (1 − 32%) =	6.1
Municipal bond	6% × (1 − 0%) =	6.0

Accordingly, Bill should choose the dividend-yielding stock.

What marginal tax rate on ordinary income would make Bill indifferent between the dividend-yielding stock and the corporate bond?

Answer: The dividend-yielding stock has an after-tax rate return of 6.8 percent. For Bill to be indifferent between this stock and the corporate bond, the corporate bond would need a 6.8 percent after-tax rate of return. We can use Equation 3-4 to solve for the marginal tax rate.

After-Tax Rate of Return = Before-Tax Rate of Return × (1 − Marginal Tax Rate)

6.8% = 9% × (1 − Marginal Tax Rate)

Marginal Tax Rate = 24.44%

Let's check this answer: After-Tax Rate of Return = 9% × (1 − 24.44%) = 6.8%

Example 3-10 shows how taxpayers may compare investments when the investment period is one year. However, when taxpayers hold investments for more than a year they potentially receive benefits from combining the timing strategy and the conversion strategy. First, they may be able to defer recognizing gains on the assets until they sell them—the longer the deferral period, the lower the present value of the tax when taxpayers ultimately sell the assets. Second, they may pay taxes on the gains at preferential rates. For example, taxpayers who invest in a corporate stock (capital asset) that does not pay dividends will defer gain on any stock appreciation until they sell the stock, and because it is a capital asset held longer than one year, their gains will be taxed at the lower preferential tax rate for long-term capital gains. These tax advantages provide taxpayers with a greater after-tax rate of return on these investments than they would obtain from less tax-favored assets that earn equivalent before-tax rates of return. Investors who quickly sell investments pay taxes on gains at higher, ordinary rates and incur significantly greater transaction costs. Nevertheless, taxpayers should balance the tax benefits available for holding assets with the risk that the asset values will have declined by the time they want to sell the assets.

To compare investments with differing time horizons, taxpayers use the annualized after-tax rate of return. In general, the after-tax rate of return on any investment is $(FV/I)^{1/n} - 1$ where FV is the future value after taxes, I is the investment (in after-tax dollars), and n is the number of investment periods.[19]

Example 3-11

What if: Assume Bill decides to purchase Intel stock for $50,000 and hold the shares for five years. If the Intel stock grows at a constant 8 percent before-tax rate and does not pay any dividends, how much cash will Bill accumulate after taxes after five years, assuming a long-term capital gains tax rate of 20 percent?

Answer: $68,773, computed as follows:

Description	Amount	Explanation
(1) Proceeds from sale	$ 73,466	[$50,000 × (1 + 0.08)^5]
(2) Basis in shares	50,000	This is the investment in the shares.
(3) Gain realized on sale	$ 23,466	(1) − (2)
(4) Tax rate on gain	× 20%	Low rate for long-term capital gain*
(5) Tax on gain	$ 4,693	(3) × (4)
After-tax cash after 5 years	**$68,773**	(1) − (5)

*Assumes Bill doesn't have any capital losses.

(continued on page 3-18)

[19]Financial calculators designate this calculation as the IRR or internal rate of return.

What annual after-tax rate of return will Bill earn on the money invested?

Answer: 6.58 percent [($68,773/$50,000)$^{1/5}$ − 1].

What if: What would be the after-tax rate of return if Bill held the stock for 18 years?

Answer: 7.03 percent, computed as follows:

Description	Amount	Explanation
(1) Proceeds from sale	$199,801	[$50,000 × (1 + 0.08)^{18}]
(2) Basis in shares	50,000	This is the investment in the shares.
(3) Gain realized on sale	$149,801	(1) − (2)
(4) Tax rate on gain	× 20%	Low rate for long-term capital gain*
(5) Tax on gain	$ 29,960	(3) × (4)
After-tax cash after 18 years	$169,841	(1) − (5)
After-tax rate of return after 18 years	**7.03%**	[($169,841/$50,000)$^{1/18}$ − 1]

*Assumes Bill doesn't have any capital losses.

What if: How does Bill's rate of return on the Intel stock held for five years compare to a taxable corporate bond that pays 9 percent interest annually and is held for five years?

Answer: The annualized rate of return on the stock held for five years is 6.58 percent, as shown above. Because the interest on the taxable corporate bond is taxed annually, the annual after-tax rate of return does not change with the investment horizon and will equal 6.1 percent, as shown in Example 3-10 [9% × (1 − 32%)]. In this situation, the combined tax benefits from the timing and conversion strategies cause the stock investment to generate a higher annualized after-tax return than the taxable corporate bond even though its pretax return is lower.

Limitations of Conversion Strategies

Like other tax planning strategies, conversion strategies face potential limitations. The Internal Revenue Code itself also contains several specific provisions that prevent the taxpayer from changing the nature of expenses, income, or activities to a more tax-advantaged status, including (among many others) the depreciation recapture rules discussed in the Property Dispositions chapter and the luxury auto depreciation rules discussed in the Property Acquisition and Cost Recovery chapter. In addition, as discussed in the Introduction to Tax chapter, implicit taxes may reduce or eliminate the advantages of tax-preferred investments (such as municipal bonds or any investment taxed at preferential tax rates) by decreasing their before-tax rate of returns. Thus, implicit taxes may reduce the advantages of the conversion strategy.

 ADDITIONAL LIMITATIONS TO TAX PLANNING STRATEGIES: JUDICIALLY-BASED DOCTRINES

The IRS has several other doctrines at its disposal for situations in which it expects taxpayer abuse. These doctrines have developed from court decisions and apply across a wide variety of transactions and planning strategies (timing, income shifting, and conversion). The **business purpose doctrine,** for instance, allows the IRS to challenge and disallow business expenses for transactions with no underlying business motivation, such as the travel cost of a spouse accompanying a taxpayer on a business trip. The **step-transaction doctrine** allows the IRS to collapse a series of related transactions into one transaction to determine the tax consequences of the transaction. The **substance-over-form doctrine** allows the IRS to consider the transaction's substance regardless of its form and, where appropriate, to reclassify the transaction according to its substance.

Finally, the **economic substance doctrine** requires transactions to meet two criteria to obtain tax benefits. First, a transaction must meaningfully change a taxpayer's economic position (excluding any federal income tax effects). Second, the taxpayer must have a substantial purpose (other than tax avoidance) for the transaction. Economic substance is clearly related to several other doctrines such as the business purpose, step-transaction, and substance-over-form doctrines; however, the economic substance doctrine was incorporated into the Internal Revenue Code in 2010 as §7701(o). This codification standardizes the requirement for transactions to meet both tests. None of the other doctrines have yet been codified.

The courts have been inconsistent with the application of the tests, with some requiring the transaction to meet either the business purpose or economic substance and others requiring that it meet both tests. A key part of the codification of the economic substance doctrine is a stiff penalty of 40 percent of the underpayment for failing to meet the requirements—reduced to 20 percent if the taxpayer makes adequate disclosure. In the Tax Compliance, the IRS, and Tax Authorities chapter, we noted that the Internal Revenue Code is the ultimate tax authority. The business purpose, step-transaction, substance-over-form, and economic substance doctrines allow the IRS to state the tax consequences of transactions that follow only the form of the Internal Revenue Code and not the spirit.

You can often assess whether the business purpose, step-transaction, or substance-over-form doctrines apply by using the "smell test." If the transaction "smells bad," one of these doctrines likely applies. (Transactions usually "smell bad" when the primary purpose is to avoid taxes and not to accomplish an independent business objective.) For example, using the substance-over-form doctrine, the IRS would likely reclassify most of the $10,000 paid to Margaret for answering the phone one Saturday afternoon a month as a gift from Mercedes to Margaret (see the earlier discussion of income shifting and transactions between family members), even though the transaction was structured as compensation and Margaret did do some work for her mother. This recharacterization would unwind the income-shifting benefits for the amount considered to be a gift, because gifts to family members are not tax deductible. In sum, the *substance* of the transaction must be justifiable, not just the form.

TAX AVOIDANCE VERSUS TAX EVASION

Each of the general tax planning strategies discussed in this book falls within the confines of legal **tax avoidance**. Tax avoidance has long been endorsed by the courts and even Congress. Recall, for example, that Congress specifically encourages tax avoidance by excluding municipal bond income from taxation, preferentially taxing dividend and capital gain income, and enacting other provisions. Likewise, the courts have often made it quite clear that taxpayers are under no moral obligation to pay more taxes than required by law. As an example, in *Commissioner v. Newman,* 159 F.2d 848 (2 Cir., 1947), which considered a taxpayer's ability to shift income to his children using trusts, Judge Learned Hand included the following statement in his dissenting opinion:

> Over and over again courts have said that there is nothing sinister in so arranging one's affairs as to keep taxes as low as possible. Everybody does so, rich or poor; and all do right, for nobody owes any public duty to pay more than the law demands: taxes are enforced exactions, not voluntary contributions. To demand more in the name of morals is mere cant.

In contrast to tax avoidance, **tax evasion**—that is, the willful attempt to defraud the government—falls outside the confines of legal tax avoidance and thus may land the perpetrator within the confines of a federal prison. (Recall from the Tax Compliance, the IRS, and Tax Authorities chapter that the rewards of tax evasion include stiff monetary penalties and imprisonment.) When does tax avoidance become tax evasion? Very good question. In many cases a clear distinction exists between avoidance (such as not paying tax on municipal bond interest) and evasion (not paying tax on a $1,000,000 game show

THE KEY FACTS

Additional Limitations to Tax Planning Strategies: Judicial Doctrines

- Certain judicial doctrines restrict the common tax planning strategies (timing, income shifting, and conversion).
  - The business purpose doctrine allows the IRS to challenge and disallow business expenses for transactions with no underlying business motivation.
  - The step-transaction doctrine allows the IRS to collapse a series of related transactions into one transaction to determine the tax consequences of the transaction.
  - The substance-over-form doctrine allows the IRS to reclassify a transaction according to its substance.
  - The economic substance doctrine requires transactions have both an economic effect aside from the tax effect and a substantial purpose aside from reduction of tax liability.

LO 3-7

THE KEY FACTS

Tax Evasion versus Tax Avoidance

- Tax avoidance is the legal act of arranging your transactions to minimize taxes paid.
- Tax evasion is the willful attempt to defraud the government by not paying taxes legally owed.
- Tax evasion falls outside the confines of legal tax avoidance.

prize). In other cases, the line is less clear. In these situations, professional judgment, the use of a smell test, and consideration of the business purpose, step-transaction, substance-over-form, and economic substance doctrines may prove useful.

TAXES IN THE REAL WORLD Cheating the IRS

Few people like to pay taxes, but most of us do so. Some, however, try to cheat the IRS, including the rich and famous (among them, Mike "The Situation" Sorrentino, Chris Tucker, and rapper DMX). Folks who are trying to escape the reach of the IRS may fail to file tax returns, claim deductions to which they're not entitled, make up fake business expenses, or otherwise try to disguise how much money they really made. These tax evaders cost the government a lot of money. The average annual "tax gap" for 2008–2010, the most recent period for which the IRS has estimated the amount of owed taxes that weren't paid on time, is $458 billion (see https://www.irs.gov/newsroom/the-tax-gap).

The main cause of the tax gap is underreporting income, accounting for $376 billion of the IRS's missing money. Not filing returns and underpaying taxes owed were two other causes. Some of that money fails to make it into the hands of the government through innocent accounting

mistakes or the inability of taxpayers to pay even though they want to. But some of it goes missing due to deliberate fraud.

In fiscal year (FY) 2016, the IRS initiated 3,395 criminal investigations related to tax code violations (these aren't the same as audits, which are much more common—1.03 million individuals were audited in FY 2016). The number of criminal investigations is relatively small, especially considering the millions of taxpayers in the United States. But once the IRS starts an investigation, there's a good chance it will lead to a conviction and prison time for the offender. The IRS boasts of a 79.5 percent conviction rate (2,699 sentenced/3,395 investigations) on these criminal tax cases.

Source: "Avoid an Audit: 6 Tax Lessons from Celebrities." http://www.cheatsheet.com/personal-finance/5-lessons-from-celebrity-tax-cheats.html/?a=viewall April 4, 2016 and the IRS Criminal Divisions 2016 Annual Report. https://www.irs.gov/pub/foia/ig/ci/2016_annual_report_02092017.pdf.

As you might expect, tax evasion is a major problem for the IRS that vigorous prosecution alone has not been able to solve. Is tax evasion a victimless crime? No. Because the federal government must replace lost tax revenues by imposing higher taxes on others, honest taxpayers are the true victims of tax evasion. Currently, the most recent federal government estimates indicate that tax evasion costs the federal government more than $450 billion annually in lost tax revenues. As citizens and residents of the United States, each of us must recognize our obligation to support our country. As future accountants and business professionals, we also must recognize the inherent value of high ethical standards, which call for us to do the right thing in *all* situations. Business professionals have learned over and over that the costs of doing otherwise far exceed any short-term gains.

CONCLUSION

In this chapter we discussed three basic tax planning strategies—timing, income shifting, and conversion—and their related limitations. Each of these strategies exploits the variation in taxation across different dimensions. The timing strategy exploits the variation in taxation across time: The real tax costs of income decrease as taxation is deferred; the real tax savings associated with tax deductions increase as tax deductions are accelerated. However, because tax rates may change over time and the tax costs of income and tax savings of deductions vary with tax rates, tax planning should consider the effects of such changes on the timing strategy. The income-shifting strategy exploits the variation in taxation across taxpayers or jurisdictions. The assignment of income doctrine limits aggressive attempts to shift income across taxpayers. In addition, related-party transactions receive close IRS attention given the increased likelihood of taxpayer abuses in these transactions. Finally, the conversion strategy exploits the variation in taxation rates across activities, although implicit taxes may reduce the advantages of this strategy. In addition to limitations specific to each planning strategy, the judicial doctrines of business purpose, step-transaction, and substance-over-form broadly apply to a wide range of transactions and planning strategies.

The timing, income-shifting, and conversion strategies represent the building blocks for the more sophisticated tax strategies that tax professionals employ on a daily basis. Combining an understanding of these basic tax planning strategies with knowledge of our tax law will provide you with the tools necessary to identify, evaluate, and implement tax planning strategies. Throughout the remainder of the text, we will discuss how these strategies can be applied to different transactions.

Summary

Identify the objectives of basic tax planning strategies.   **LO 3-1**

- Effective tax planning maximizes the taxpayer's after-tax wealth while achieving the taxpayer's nontax goals. Maximizing after-tax wealth is not necessarily the same as tax minimization. Maximizing after-tax wealth requires one to consider both the tax and nontax costs and benefits of alternative transactions, whereas tax minimization focuses solely on a single cost (i.e., taxes).

- Virtually every transaction involves three parties: the taxpayer, the other transacting party, and the uninvited silent party that specifies the tax consequences of the transaction (i.e., the government). Astute tax planning requires an understanding of the tax and nontax costs from the taxpayer's *and* the other parties' perspectives.

Apply the timing strategy.   **LO 3-2**

- One of the cornerstones of basic tax planning involves the idea of *timing*—that is, *when* income is taxed or an expense is deducted affects the associated "real" tax costs or savings. This is true for two reasons. First, the timing of when income is taxed or an expense is deducted affects the *present value* of the taxes paid on income or the tax savings on deductions. Second, the tax costs of income and the tax savings from deductions vary as *tax rates* change.

- When tax rates are constant, tax planners prefer to defer income (i.e., to reduce the present value of taxes paid) and accelerate deductions (i.e., to increase the present value of tax savings). Higher tax rates, higher rates of return, larger transaction amounts, and the ability to accelerate deductions or defer income by two or more years increase the benefits of the timing strategy.

- When tax rates change, the timing strategy requires a little more consideration because the tax costs of income and the tax savings from deductions vary as *tax rates* change. When tax rates are increasing, the taxpayer must calculate the optimal tax strategies for deductions and income. When tax rates are decreasing, the recommendations are clear. Taxpayers should accelerate tax deductions into earlier years and defer taxable income to later years.

- Timing strategies contain several inherent limitations. Generally speaking, whenever a taxpayer must accelerate a cash outflow to accelerate a deduction, the timing strategy will be less beneficial. Tax law generally requires taxpayers to continue their investment in an asset in order to defer income recognition for tax purposes. A deferral strategy may not be optimal if the taxpayer has severe cash flow needs, if continuing the investment would generate a low rate of return compared to other investments, if the current investment would subject the taxpayer to unnecessary risk, and so on. The constructive receipt doctrine, which provides that a taxpayer must recognize income when it is actually or constructively received, also restricts income deferral for cash-method taxpayers.

LO 3-3   Apply the concept of present value to tax planning.

- The concept of present value—also known as the time value of money—basically states that $1 today is worth *more* than $1 in the future. For example, assuming an investor can earn a positive return (e.g., 5 percent after taxes), $1 invested today should be worth $1.05 in one year. Hence, $1 today is equivalent to $1.05 in one year.
- The implication of the time value of money for tax planning is that the timing of a cash inflow or a cash outflow affects the present value of the income or expense.

LO 3-4   Apply the income shifting strategy.

- The income-shifting strategy exploits the differences in tax rates across taxpayers or jurisdictions. Three of the most common examples of income shifting are high-tax-rate parents shifting income to low-tax-rate children, businesses shifting income to their owners, and taxpayers shifting income from high-tax jurisdictions to low-tax jurisdictions.
- The assignment of income doctrine requires income to be taxed to the taxpayer who actually earns the income. In addition, the IRS closely monitors such related-party transactions— that is, financial activities among family members, among owners and their businesses, or among businesses owned by the same owners. Implicit taxes may also limit the benefits of income shifting via locating in tax-advantaged jurisdictions.

LO 3-5   Apply the conversion strategy.

- Tax law does not treat all types of income or deductions the same. This understanding forms the basis for the conversion strategy—recasting income and expenses to receive the most favorable tax treatment. To implement the conversion strategy, one must be aware of the underlying differences in tax treatment across various types of income, expenses, and activities and have some ability to alter the nature of the income or expense to receive the more advantageous tax treatment.
- Common examples of the conversion strategy include investment planning to invest in assets that generate preferentially taxed income; compensation planning to restructure employee compensation from currently taxable compensation to nontaxable or tax-deferred forms of compensation; and corporate distribution planning to structure corporate distributions to receive the most advantageous tax treatment.
- The Internal Revenue Code contains specific provisions that prevent the taxpayer from changing the nature of expenses, income, or activities to a more tax-advantaged status. Implicit taxes may also reduce or eliminate the advantages of conversion strategies.

LO 3-6   Describe basic judicial doctrines that limit tax planning strategies.

- The constructive receipt doctrine, which may limit the timing strategy, provides that a taxpayer must recognize income when it is actually *or* constructively received. Constructive receipt is deemed to have occurred if the income has been credited to the taxpayer's account or if the income is unconditionally available to the taxpayer, the taxpayer is aware of the income's availability, and there are no restrictions on the taxpayer's control over the income.
- The assignment of income doctrine requires income to be taxed to the taxpayer who actually earns the income. The assignment of income doctrine implies that, in order to shift income to a taxpayer, that taxpayer must actually earn the income.
- The business purpose, step-transaction, and substance-over-form doctrines apply across a wide variety of transactions and planning strategies (timing, income shifting, and conversion).
- The business purpose doctrine allows the IRS to challenge and disallow business expenses for transactions with no underlying business motivation, such as the travel cost of a spouse accompanying a taxpayer on a business trip.
- The step-transaction doctrine allows the IRS to collapse a series of related transactions into one transaction to determine the tax consequences of the transaction.
- The substance-over-form doctrine allows the IRS to consider the transaction's substance regardless of its form and, where appropriate, reclassify the transaction according to its substance.

- The codified economic substance doctrine requires transactions to have a substantial purpose and to meaningfully change a taxpayer's economic position in order for a taxpayer to obtain tax benefits.

Contrast tax avoidance and tax evasion.

`LO 3-7`

- Tax avoidance is the legal act of arranging one's transactions, and so on, to minimize taxes paid. Tax evasion is the willful attempt to defraud the government (i.e., by not paying taxes legally owed). Tax evasion falls outside the confines of legal tax avoidance.
- In many cases a clear distinction exists between avoidance (e.g., not paying tax on municipal bond interest) and evasion (e.g., not paying tax on a $1,000,000 game show prize). In other cases, the line between tax avoidance and evasion is less clear. In these situations, professional judgment, the use of a "smell test," and consideration of the business purpose, step-transaction, and substance-over-form doctrines may prove useful.

KEY TERMS

after-tax rate of return (3-3)
arm's length transactions (3-12)
assignment of income doctrine (3-12)
before-tax rate of return (3-16)
business purpose doctrine (3-18)

constructive receipt doctrine (3-10)
discount factor (3-3)
economic substance doctrine (3-19)
implicit tax (3-15)
present value (3-3)

related-party transaction (3-12)
step-transaction doctrine (3-18)
substance-over-form doctrine (3-18)
tax avoidance (3-19)
tax evasion (3-19)

DISCUSSION QUESTIONS

Discussion Questions are available in Connect®.

McGraw Hill Education **connect**

1. "The goal of tax planning is to minimize taxes." Explain why this statement is not true. `LO 3-1`
2. Describe the three parties engaged in every business transaction and how understanding taxes may aid in structuring transactions. `LO 3-1`
3. In this chapter we discuss three basic tax planning strategies. What different features of taxation does each of these strategies exploit? `LO 3-1`
4. What are the two basic timing strategies? What is the intent of each? `LO 3-2`
5. Why is the timing strategy particularly effective for cash-method taxpayers? `LO 3-2`
6. What are some common examples of the timing strategy? `LO 3-2`
7. What factors increase the benefits of accelerating deductions or deferring income? `LO 3-2`
8. How do changing tax rates affect the timing strategy? What information do you need to determine the appropriate timing strategy when tax rates change? `LO 3-2` `LO 3-3`
9. Describe the ways in which the timing strategy has limitations. `LO 3-2` `LO 3-6`
10. The concept of the time value of money suggests that $1 today is not equal to $1 in the future. Explain why this is true. `LO 3-3`
11. Why is understanding the time value of money important for tax planning? `LO 3-3`
12. What two factors increase the difference between present and future values? `LO 3-3`
13. What factors have to be present for income shifting to be a viable strategy? `LO 3-4`
14. Name three common types of income shifting. `LO 3-4`
15. What are some ways that a parent could effectively shift income to a child? What are some of the disadvantages of these methods? `LO 3-4`
16. What is the key factor in shifting income from a business to its owners? What are some methods of shifting income in this context? `LO 3-4`

LO 3-4   17. Explain why paying dividends is not an effective way to shift income from a corporation to its owners.

LO 3-5   18. What are some of the common examples of the conversion strategy?

LO 3-5   19. What is needed to implement the conversion strategy?

LO 3-5   20. Explain how implicit taxes may limit the benefits of the conversion strategy.

LO 3-5 **LO 3-6**   21. Clark owns stock in BCS Corporation that he purchased in January of the current year. The stock has appreciated significantly during the year. It is now December of the current year, and Clark is deciding whether or not he should sell the stock. What tax and nontax factors should Clark consider before making the decision on whether to sell the stock now?

planning

LO 3-5   22. Do after-tax rates of return for investments in either interest- or dividend-paying securities increase with the length of the investment? Why or why not?

LO 3-5   23. Cameron purchases stock in both Corporation X and Corporation Y. Neither corporation pays dividends. The stocks both earn an identical before-tax rate of return. Cameron sells stock in Corporation X after three years and he sells the stock in Corporation Y after five years. Which investment likely earned a greater after-tax return? Why?

LO 3-5   24. Under what circumstances would you expect the after-tax return from an investment in a capital asset to approach that of tax-exempt assets (assuming equal before-tax rates of return)?

LO 3-5   25. Laurie is thinking about investing in one or several of the following investment options:

planning

Corporate bonds (ordinary interest paid annually)
Dividend-paying stock (qualified dividends)
Life insurance (tax-exempt)
Savings account
Growth stock

a) Assuming all of the options earn similar returns before taxes, rank Laurie's investment options from highest to lowest according to their after-tax returns.

b) Which of the investments employ the deferral and/or conversion tax planning strategies?

c) How does the time period of the investment affect the returns from these alternatives?

d) How do these alternative investments differ in terms of their nontax characteristics?

LO 3-5   26. What is an "implicit tax" and how does it affect a taxpayer's decision to purchase municipal bonds?

LO 3-6   27. Several judicial doctrines limit basic tax planning strategies. What are they? Which planning strategies do they limit?

LO 3-6   28. What is the constructive receipt doctrine? What types of taxpayers does this doctrine generally affect? For what tax planning strategy is the constructive receipt doctrine a potential limitation?

LO 3-6   29. Explain the assignment of income doctrine. In what situations would this doctrine potentially apply?

LO 3-6   30. Relative to arm's-length transactions, why do related-party transactions receive more IRS scrutiny?

LO 3-6   31. Describe the business purpose, step-transaction, and substance-over-form doctrines. What types of tax planning strategies may these doctrines inhibit?

LO 3-7   32. What is the difference between tax avoidance and tax evasion?

LO 3-7   33. What are the rewards of tax avoidance? What are the rewards of tax evasion?

LO 3-7   34. "Tax avoidance is discouraged by the courts and Congress." Is this statement true or false? Please explain.

PROBLEMS

Select problems are available in Connect®.

connect

35. Yong recently paid his accountant $10,000 for elaborate tax planning strategies that exploit the timing strategy. Assuming this is an election year and there could be a power shift in the White House and Congress, what is a potential risk associated with Yong's strategies?

`LO 3-2`
`planning`

36. Billups, a physician and cash-method taxpayer, is new to the concept of tax planning and recently learned of the timing strategy. To implement the timing strategy, Billups plans to establish a new policy that allows all his clients to wait two years to pay their co-pays. Assume that Billups does not expect his marginal tax rates to change. What is wrong with his strategy?

`LO 3-2` `LO 3-3`
`planning`

37. Tesha works for a company that pays a year-end bonus in January of each year (instead of December of the preceding year) to allow employees to defer the bonus income. Assume Congress recently passed tax legislation that decreases individual tax rates as of next year. Does this increase or decrease the benefits of the bonus deferral this year? What if Congress passed legislation that increased tax rates next year? Should Tesha ask the company to change its policy this year? What additional information do you need to answer this question?

`LO 3-2` `LO 3-3`
`planning`

38. Isabel, a calendar-year taxpayer, uses the cash method of accounting for her sole proprietorship. In late December she received a $20,000 bill from her accountant for consulting services related to her small business. Isabel can pay the $20,000 bill anytime before January 30 of next year without penalty. Assume her marginal tax rate is 40 percent this year and next year, and that she can earn an after-tax rate of return of 12 percent on her investments. When should she pay the $20,000 bill—this year or next?

`LO 3-2` `LO 3-3`
`planning`

39. Using the facts from the previous problem, how would your answer change if Isabel's after-tax rate of return were 8 percent?

`LO 3-2` `LO 3-3`
`planning`

40. Manny, a calendar-year taxpayer, uses the cash method of accounting for his sole proprietorship. In late December he performed $20,000 of legal services for a client. Manny typically requires his clients to pay his bills immediately upon receipt. Assume Manny's marginal tax rate is 37 percent this year and next year, and that he can earn an after-tax rate of return of 12 percent on his investments. Should Manny send his client the bill in December or January?

`LO 3-2` `LO 3-3`
`planning`

41. Using the facts from the previous problem, how would your answer change if Manny's after-tax rate of return were 8 percent?

`LO 3-2` `LO 3-3`
`planning`

42. Reese, a calendar-year taxpayer, uses the cash method of accounting for her sole proprietorship. In late December, she received a $20,000 bill from her accountant for consulting services related to her small business. Reese can pay the $20,000 bill anytime before January 30 of next year without penalty. Assume Reese's marginal tax rate is 32 percent this year and will be 37 percent next year, and that she can earn an after-tax rate of return of 12 percent on her investments. When should she pay the $20,000 bill—this year or next?

`LO 3-2` `LO 3-3`
`planning`

43. Using the facts from the previous problem, when should Reese pay the bill if she expects her marginal tax rate to be 35 percent next year? 24 percent next year?

`LO 3-2` `LO 3-3`
`planning`

44. Hank, a calendar-year taxpayer, uses the cash method of accounting for his sole proprietorship. In late December, he performed $20,000 of legal services for a client. Hank typically requires his clients to pay his bills immediately upon receipt. Assume his marginal tax rate is 32 percent this year and will be 37 percent next year, and that he can earn an after-tax rate of return of 12 percent on his investments. Should Hank send his client the bill in December or January?

`LO 3-2` `LO 3-3`
`planning`

LO 3-2 **LO 3-3**   45. Using the facts from the previous problem, when should Hank send the bill if he
planning   expects his marginal tax rate to be 35 percent next year? 24 percent next year?

LO 3-3   46. Geraldo recently won a lottery and chose to receive $100,000 today instead of an
equivalent amount in 10 years, computed using an 8 percent rate of return. Today,
he learned that interest rates are expected to increase in the future. Is this good news
for Geraldo given his decision?

LO 3-3   47. Assume Rafael can earn an 8 percent after-tax rate of return. Would he prefer
planning $1,000 today or $1,500 in five years?

LO 3-3   48. Assume Ellina earns a 10 percent after-tax rate of return and that she owes a friend
planning $1,200. Would she prefer to pay the friend $1,200 today or $1,750 in four years?

LO 3-3   49. Jonah has the choice of paying Rita $10,000 today or $40,000 in 10 years. Assume
planning   Jonah can earn a 12 percent after-tax rate of return. Which should he choose?

LO 3-3   50. Bob's Lottery Inc. has decided to offer winners a choice of $100,000 in 10 years or
planning   some amount currently. Assume that Bob's Lottery Inc. earns a 10 percent after-tax
rate of return. What amount should Bob offer lottery winners currently, in order for
him to be indifferent between the two choices?

LO 3-4   51. Tawana owns and operates a sole proprietorship and has a 37 percent marginal tax
planning   rate. She provides her son, Jonathon, $8,000 a year for college expenses. Jonathon
works as a pizza delivery person every fall and has a marginal tax rate of 15
percent.

a) What could Tawana do to reduce her family tax burden?

b) How much pretax income does it currently take Tawana to generate the $8,000
(after taxes) given to Jonathon?

c) If Jonathon worked for his mother's sole proprietorship, what salary would she
have to pay him to generate $8,000 after taxes (ignoring any Social Security,
Medicare, or self-employment tax issues)?

d) How much money would the strategy in part (c) save?

LO 3-4   52. Moana is a single taxpayer who operates a sole proprietorship. She expects her
planning   taxable income next year to be $250,000, of which $200,000 is attributed to her
sole proprietorship. Moana is contemplating incorporating her sole proprietorship.
Using the single individual tax brackets and the corporate tax rate, find out how
much current tax this strategy could save Moana (ignore any Social Security,
Medicare, or self-employment tax issues). How much income should be left in the
corporation?

LO 3-4   53. Orie and Jane, husband and wife, operate a sole proprietorship. They expect their
planning   taxable income next year to be $450,000, of which $250,000 is attributed to the sole
proprietorship. Orie and Jane are contemplating incorporating their sole proprietorship. Using the married-joint tax brackets and the corporate tax rate, find out how
much current tax this strategy could save Orie and Jane. How much income should
be left in the corporation?

LO 3-4   54. Hyundai is considering opening a plant in two neighboring states. One state has a
planning   corporate tax rate of 10 percent. If operated in this state, the plant is expected to
generate $1,000,000 pretax profit. The other state has a corporate tax rate of 2 per-
cent. If operated in this state, the plant is expected to generate $930,000 of pretax
profit. Which state should Hyundai choose? Why do you think the plant in the state
with a lower tax rate would produce a lower before-tax income?

LO 3-4 **LO 3-6**   55. Bendetta, a high-tax-rate taxpayer, owns several rental properties and would like to
planning   shift some income to her daughter, Jenine. Bendetta instructs her tenants to send
their rent checks to Jenine so Jenine can report the rental income. Will this shift the
income from Bendetta to Jenine? Why, or why not?

56. Using the facts in the previous problem, what are some ways that Bendetta could shift some of the rental income to Jenine? What are the disadvantages associated with these income-shifting strategies?

    LO 3-4 **LO 3-6**
    planning

57. Daniel is considering selling two stocks that have not fared well over recent years. A friend recently informed Daniel that one of his stocks has a special designation, which allows him to treat a loss up to $50,000 on this stock as an ordinary loss rather than the typical capital loss. Daniel figures that he has a loss of $60,000 on each stock. If Daniel's marginal tax rate is 35 percent and he has $120,000 of other capital gains (taxed at 15 percent), what is the tax savings from the special tax treatment?

    LO 3-5
    planning

58. Dennis is currently considering investing in municipal bonds that earn 6 percent interest, or in taxable bonds issued by the Coca-Cola Company that pay 8 percent. If Dennis's tax rate is 22 percent, which bond should he choose? Which bond should he choose if his tax rate is 32 percent? At what tax rate would he be indifferent between the bonds? What strategy is this decision based upon?

    LO 3-5
    planning

59. Helen holds 1,000 shares of Fizbo Inc. stock that she purchased 11 months ago. The stock has done very well and has appreciated $20/share since Helen bought the stock. When sold, the stock will be taxed at capital gains rates (the long-term rate is 15 percent and the short-term rate is the taxpayer's marginal tax rate). If Helen's marginal tax rate is 35 percent, how much would she save by holding the stock an additional month before selling? What might prevent Helen from waiting to sell?

    LO 3-5
    planning

60. Anne's marginal income tax rate is 32 percent. She purchases a corporate bond for $10,000 and the maturity, or face value, of the bond is $10,000. If the bond pays 5 percent per year before taxes, what is Anne's annual after-tax rate of return from the bond if the bond matures in one year? What is her annual after-tax rate of return if the bond matures in 10 years?

    LO 3-5

61. Irene is saving for a new car she hopes to purchase either four or six years from now. Irene invests $10,000 in a growth stock that does not pay dividends and expects a 6 percent annual before-tax return (the investment is tax deferred). When she cashes in the investment after either four or six years, she expects the applicable marginal tax rate on long-term capital gains to be 25 percent.

    LO 3-5
    planning

    a) What will be the value of this investment four years from now? Six years from now?

    b) When Irene sells the investment, how much cash will she have after taxes to purchase the new car (four and six years from now)?

62. Komiko Tanaka invests $12,000 in LymaBean, Inc. LymaBean does not pay any dividends. Komiko projects that her investment will generate a 10 percent before-tax rate of return. She plans to invest for the long term.

    LO 3-5
    planning

    a) How much cash will Komiko retain, after taxes, if she holds the investment for five years and then sells it when the long-term capital gains rate is 15 percent?

    b) What is Komiko's after-tax rate of return on her investment in part (a)?

    c) How much cash will Komiko retain, after taxes, if she holds the investment for five years and then sells when the long-term capital gains rate is 25 percent?

    d) What is Komiko's after-tax rate of return on her investment in part (c)?

    e) How much cash will Komiko retain, after taxes, if she holds the investment for 15 years and then sells when the long-term capital gains rate is 15 percent?

    f) What is Komiko's after-tax rate of return on her investment in part (e)?

63. Alan inherited $100,000 with the stipulation that he "invest it to financially benefit his family." Alan and his wife Alice decided they would invest the inheritance to help them accomplish two financial goals: purchasing a Park City vacation home and saving for their son Cooper's education.

	Vacation Home	Cooper's Education
Initial investment	$50,000	$50,000
Investment horizon	5 years	18 years

Alan and Alice have a marginal income tax rate of 32 percent (capital gains rate of 15 percent) and have decided to investigate the following investment opportunities.

	5 Years	Annual After-Tax Rate of Return	18 Years	Annual After-Tax Rate of Return
Corporate bonds (ordinary interest taxed annually)	5.75%		4.75%	
Dividend-paying stock (no appreciation and dividends are taxed at 15%)	3.50%		3.50%	
Growth stock	FV = $65,000		FV = $140,000	
Municipal bond (tax-exempt)	3.20%		3.10%	

Complete the two annual after-tax rates of return columns for each investment and provide investment recommendations for Alan and Alice.

64. Duff is really interested in decreasing his tax liability, and by his very nature he is somewhat aggressive. A friend of a friend told him that cash transactions are more difficult for the IRS to identify and, thus, tax. Duff is contemplating using this "strategy" of not reporting cash collected in his business to minimize his tax liability. Is this tax planning? What are the risks with this strategy?

65. Using the facts from the previous problem, how would your answer change if, instead, Duff adopted the cash method of accounting to allow him to better control the timing of his cash receipts and disbursements?

66. Using an available tax service or the Internet, identify three basic tax planning ideas or tax tips suggested for year-end tax planning. Which basic tax strategy from this chapter does each planning idea employ?

67. Jayanna, an advertising consultant, is contemplating instructing some of her clients to pay her in cash so that she does not have to report the income on her tax return. Use an available tax service to identify the three basic elements of tax evasion and penalties associated with tax evasion. Write a memo to Jayanna explaining tax evasion and the risks associated with her actions.

68. Using the IRS website (https://www.irs.gov/uac/The-Tax-Gap), how large is the current estimated "tax gap" (i.e., the amount of tax underpaid by taxpayers annually)? What group of taxpayers represents the largest "contributors" to the tax gap?

 ROGER | *CPA Review*

Sample CPA Exam questions from Roger CPA Review are available in Connect as support for the topics in this text. These Multiple Choice Questions and Task-Based Simulations include expert-written explanations and solutions and provide a starting point for students to become familiar with the content and functionality of the actual CPA Exam.

Individual Income Tax Overview, Dependents, and Filing Status

Learning Objectives

Upon completing this chapter, you should be able to:

LO 4-1 Describe the formula for calculating an individual taxpayer's taxes payable or refund.

LO 4-2 Explain the requirements for determining who qualifies as a taxpayer's dependent.

LO 4-3 Determine a taxpayer's filing status.

Tara Hall just completed a unit on individual taxation in her undergraduate tax class at South Dakota State University. She was excited to share her knowledge with her parents, Rodney and Anita Hall, as they prepared their tax return. Rodney and Anita have been married for over 25 years, and they have filed a joint tax return each year. The Halls' 12-year-old son Braxton lives at home but Tara, who is 21, lives nearby in the university dorms. Further, in January of this year, Rodney's younger brother Shawn moved in with the Halls. The Halls expect Shawn to live with them for at least one year and maybe two. Every year Rodney and Anita use tax-preparation software to complete their tax return, but they are not always sure they understand the final result. This year, with Tara's help, they hope that will change. ■

Storyline Summary	
Taxpayers:	Rodney and Anita Hall
Other household members:	Tara, their 21-year-old daughter, and Braxton, their 12-year-old son. Shawn, Rodney's brother, also lives with the Halls.
Location:	Brookings, South Dakota
Employment status:	Rodney is a manager for a regional grocery chain. His annual salary is $74,000. Anita works as a purchasing-card auditor at South Dakota State University. Her annual salary is $56,000.
Current situation:	Determining their tax liability

This chapter and the next four discuss the fundamental elements of the individual income tax formula. This is the overview chapter; the other chapters provide more depth on individual income tax topics. Here we introduce the individual income tax formula, summarize its components, describe requirements for determining who qualifies as a taxpayer's dependent, and explain how to determine a taxpayer's filing status. The Gross Income and Exclusions chapter explains gross income, the Individual Deductions chapter describes deductible expenses to determine adjusted gross income and taxable income, and the Investments chapter discusses tax issues associated with investments. Finally, the Individual Income Tax Computation and Tax Credits chapter addresses issues associated with calculating a taxpayer's tax liability and discusses tax return filing concerns.

LO 4-1

THE INDIVIDUAL INCOME TAX FORMULA

Each year, individuals file tax returns to report their **taxable income,** the tax base for the individual income tax, to the Internal Revenue Service.[1] Exhibit 4-1 presents a simplified formula for calculating taxable income. As we discuss in more detail below, this formula reflects recent tax law changes.

EXHIBIT 4-1   Individual Tax Formula

	Gross income
Minus:	*For AGI (above the line) deductions*
Equals:	Adjusted gross income (AGI)
Minus:	*From AGI (below the line) deductions:*
	(1) *Greater* of
	(a) Standard deduction or
	(b) Itemized deductions and
	(2) Deduction for qualified business income
Equals:	Taxable income
Times:	Tax rates
Equals:	Income tax liability
Plus:	Other taxes
Equals:	Total tax
Minus:	Credits
Minus:	Prepayments
Equals:	Taxes due or (refund)

Beginning with gross income, this formula is embedded in the first two pages of the individual income tax Form 1040, the form individuals generally use to report their taxable income.[2] Exhibit 4-2 presents the first two pages of the 2017 Form 1040 edited to replace the line on page 2 for personal and dependency exemption deductions with the deduction for qualified business income. The 2018 tax forms, which will reflect recent tax law changes, were unavailable at the time we went to press. The last line on page 1 of Form 1040 is **adjusted gross income (AGI)**, an important reference point in the income tax formula. Let's look at the components of the individual tax formula and provide a brief description of each of the key elements.

Gross Income

The U.S. tax laws are based on the **all-inclusive income concept.** Under this concept, **gross income** generally includes all **realized income** from *whatever source derived.*[3] Realized income is income generated in a transaction with a second party in which there

---

[1]See Exhibit 1 in the Tax Compliance, the IRS, and Tax Authorities chapter for a description of who must file a tax return.

[2]To see the 1913 version of the individual tax form, go to http://www.irs.gov/pub/irs-utl/1913.pdf.

[3]§61(a).

Form **1040**   Department of the Treasury—Internal Revenue Service   (99)
U.S. Individual Income Tax Return   **2017**   OMB No. 1545-0074   IRS Use Only—Do not write or staple in this space.

For the year Jan. 1–Dec. 31, 2017, or other tax year beginning , 2017, ending , 20   See separate instructions.

Your first name and initial	Last name	Your social security number

If a joint return, spouse's first name and initial	Last name	Spouse's social security number

Home address (number and street). If you have a P.O. box, see instructions.   Apt. no.   ▲ Make sure the SSN(s) above and on line 6c are correct.

City, town or post office, state, and ZIP code. If you have a foreign address, also complete spaces below (see instructions).

Presidential Election Campaign
Check here if you, or your spouse if filing jointly, want $3 to go to this fund. Checking a box below will not change your tax or refund.   ☐ You   ☐ Spouse

Foreign country name	Foreign province/state/county	Foreign postal code

Filing Status

Check only one box.

1 ☐ Single
2 ☐ Married filing jointly (even if only one had income)
3 ☐ Married filing separately. Enter spouse's SSN above and full name here. ▶
4 ☐ Head of household (with qualifying person). (See instructions.) If the qualifying person is a child but not your dependent, enter this child's name here. ▶
5 ☐ Qualifying widow(er) (see instructions)

Exemptions

6a ☐ **Yourself.** If someone can claim you as a dependent, **do not** check box 6a . . . . .
b ☐ **Spouse** . . . .

c **Dependents:**	(2) Dependent's social security number	(3) Dependent's relationship to you	(4) ✓ if child under age 17 qualifying for child tax credit (see instructions)
(1) First name Last name			☐
			☐
			☐
			☐

If more than four dependents, see instructions and check here ▶ ☐

d   Total number of exemptions claimed . . . .

Boxes checked on 6a and 6b
No. of children on 6c who:
• lived with you
• did not live with you due to divorce or separation (see instructions)
Dependents on 6c not entered above
Add numbers on lines above ▶

Income

Attach Form(s) W-2 here. Also attach Forms W-2G and 1099-R if tax was withheld.

If you did not get a W-2, see instructions.

7	Wages, salaries, tips, etc. Attach Form(s) W-2	7	
8a	**Taxable** interest. Attach Schedule B if required	8a	
b	**Tax-exempt** interest. **Do not** include on line 8a . . .	8b	
9a	Ordinary dividends. Attach Schedule B if required	9a	
b	Qualified dividends	9b	
10	Taxable refunds, credits, or offsets of state and local income taxes	10	
11	Alimony received	11	
12	Business income or (loss). Attach Schedule C or C-EZ	12	
13	Capital gain or (loss). Attach Schedule D if required. If not required, check here ▶ ☐	13	
14	Other gains or (losses). Attach Form 4797	14	
15a	IRA distributions . 15a	b Taxable amount . . .	15b	
16a	Pensions and annuities 16a	b Taxable amount . . .	16b	
17	Rental real estate, royalties, partnerships, S corporations, trusts, etc. Attach Schedule E	17	
18	Farm income or (loss). Attach Schedule F	18	
19	Unemployment compensation	19	
20a	Social security benefits 20a	b Taxable amount . . .	20b	
21	Other income. List type and amount	21	
22	Combine the amounts in the far right column for lines 7 through 21. This is your **total income** ▶	22	

Adjusted Gross Income

23	Educator expenses	23	
24	Certain business expenses of reservists, performing artists, and fee-basis government officials. Attach Form 2106 or 2106-EZ	24	
25	Health savings account deduction. Attach Form 8889 .	25	
26	Moving expenses. Attach Form 3903	26	
27	Deductible part of self-employment tax. Attach Schedule SE .	27	
28	Self-employed SEP, SIMPLE, and qualified plans . .	28	
29	Self-employed health insurance deduction . . .	29	
30	Penalty on early withdrawal of savings	30	
31a	Alimony paid b Recipient's SSN ▶	31a	
32	IRA deduction	32	
33	Student loan interest deduction	33	
34	Reserved for future use	34	
35	Domestic production activities deduction. Attach Form 8903	35	
36	Add lines 23 through 35	36	
37	Subtract line 36 from line 22. This is your **adjusted gross income** . . . . . ▶	37	

For Disclosure, Privacy Act, and Paperwork Reduction Act Notice, see separate instructions.   Cat. No. 11320B   Form **1040** (2017)

(continued)

EXHIBIT 4-2 Form 1040, pages 1 and 2 (*continued*)

Form 1040 (2017)   Page **2**

Tax and Credits	38	Amount from line 37 (adjusted gross income)	38	
	39a	Check if: ☐ **You** were born before January 2, 1953, ☐ **Spouse** was born before January 2, 1953, ☐ Blind. ☐ Blind. } **Total boxes** checked ▶ 39a		
	b	If your spouse itemizes on a separate return or you were a dual-status alien, check here ▶ 39b ☐		
Standard Deduction for— • People who check any box on line 39a or 39b **or** who can be claimed as a dependent, see instructions. • All others: Single or Married filing separately, $6,350 Married filing jointly or Qualifying widow(er), $12,700 Head of household, $9,350	40	**Itemized deductions** (from Schedule A) **or** your **standard deduction** (see left margin)	40	
	41	Subtract line 40 from line 38	41	
	42	**Exemptions.** If line 38 is $156,900 or less, multiply $4,050 by the number on line 6d. Otherwise, see instructions	42	
	43	**Taxable income.** Subtract line 42 from line 41. If line 42 is more than line 41, enter -0-	43	
	44	**Tax** (see instructions). Check if any from: **a** ☐ Form(s) 8814 **b** ☐ Form 4972 **c** ☐	44	
	45	**Alternative minimum tax** (see instructions). Attach Form 6251	45	
	46	Excess advance premium tax credit repayment. Attach Form 8962	46	
	47	Add lines 44, 45, and 46 ▶	47	
	48	Foreign tax credit. Attach Form 1116 if required	48	
	49	Credit for child and dependent care expenses. Attach Form 2441	49	
	50	Education credits from Form 8863, line 19	50	
	51	Retirement savings contributions credit. Attach Form 8880	51	
	52	Child tax credit. Attach Schedule 8812, if required	52	
	53	Residential energy credit. Attach Form 5695	53	
	54	Other credits from Form: **a** ☐ 3800 **b** ☐ 8801 **c** ☐	54	
	55	Add lines 48 through 54. These are your **total credits**	55	
	56	Subtract line 55 from line 47. If line 55 is more than line 47, enter -0- ▶	56	
Other Taxes	57	Self-employment tax. Attach Schedule SE	57	
	58	Unreported social security and Medicare tax from Form: **a** ☐ 4137 **b** ☐ 8919	58	
	59	Additional tax on IRAs, other qualified retirement plans, etc. Attach Form 5329 if required	59	
	60a	Household employment taxes from Schedule H	60a	
	b	First-time homebuyer credit repayment. Attach Form 5405 if required	60b	
	61	Health care: individual responsibility (see instructions) Full-year coverage ☐	61	
	62	Taxes from: **a** ☐ Form 8959 **b** ☐ Form 8960 **c** ☐ Instructions; enter code(s)	62	
	63	Add lines 56 through 62. This is your **total tax** ▶	63	
Payments If you have a qualifying child, attach Schedule EIC.	64	Federal income tax withheld from Forms W-2 and 1099	64	
	65	2017 estimated tax payments and amount applied from 2016 return	65	
	66a	**Earned income credit (EIC)**	66a	
	b	Nontaxable combat pay election 66b		
	67	Additional child tax credit. Attach Schedule 8812	67	
	68	American opportunity credit from Form 8863, line 8	68	
	69	Net premium tax credit. Attach Form 8962	69	
	70	Amount paid with request for extension to file	70	
	71	Excess social security and tier 1 RRTA tax withheld	71	
	72	Credit for federal tax on fuels. Attach Form 4136	72	
	73	Credits from Form: **a** ☐ 2439 **b** ☐ Reserved **c** ☐ 8885 **d** ☐	73	
	74	Add lines 64, 65, 66a, and 67 through 73. These are your **total payments** ▶	74	
Refund Direct deposit? See instructions.	75	If line 74 is more than line 63, subtract line 63 from line 74. This is the amount you **overpaid**	75	
	76a	Amount of line 75 you want **refunded to you.** If Form 8888 is attached, check here ▶ ☐	76a	
	▶ b	Routing number _____ ▶ c Type: ☐ Checking ☐ Savings		
	▶ d	Account number _____		
	77	Amount of line 75 you want **applied to your 2018 estimated tax** ▶ 77		
Amount You Owe	78	**Amount you owe.** Subtract line 74 from line 63. For details on how to pay, see instructions ▶	78	
	79	Estimated tax penalty (see instructions) 79		

Third Party Designee

Do you want to allow another person to discuss this return with the IRS (see instructions)? ☐ **Yes.** Complete below. ☐ **No**

Designee's name ▶	Phone no. ▶	Personal identification number (PIN) ▶

Sign Here

Joint return? See instructions. Keep a copy for your records.

Under penalties of perjury, I declare that I have examined this return and accompanying schedules and statements, and to the best of my knowledge and belief, they are true, correct, and accurately list all amounts and sources of income I received during the tax year. Declaration of preparer (other than taxpayer) is based on all information of which preparer has any knowledge.

Your signature	Date	Your occupation	Daytime phone number
Spouse's signature. If a joint return, **both** must sign.	Date	Spouse's occupation	If the IRS sent you an Identity Protection PIN, enter it here (see inst.)

Paid Preparer Use Only

Print/Type preparer's name	Preparer's signature	Date	Check ☐ if self-employed	PTIN
Firm's name ▶			Firm's EIN ▶	
Firm's address ▶			Phone no.	

Go to *www.irs.gov/Form1040* for instructions and the latest information.   Form **1040** (2017)

Source: Form 1040, 2017, www.irs.gov/Form1040

is a measurable change in property rights between parties (for example, appreciation in a stock investment would not represent realized income unless the taxpayer sold the stock).

Certain tax provisions allow taxpayers to permanently exclude specific types of realized income from gross income (excluded income items are never taxable) and other provisions allow taxpayers to defer including certain types of realized income items in gross income until a subsequent year (deferred income items are included in gross income in a later year). Realized income items that taxpayers permanently exclude from taxation are referred to as **exclusions.** Realized income items that taxpayers include in gross income in a subsequent year are called **deferrals.** Exhibit 4-3 provides a partial listing of common income items included in gross income, their character (discussed below), and where in the text we provide more detail on each income item. Exhibit 4-4 provides a partial listing of common exclusions and deferrals and indicates where in the text we discuss each in more detail.

EXHIBIT 4-3 **Partial Listing of Common Income Items**

Income Item	Character	Discussed in More Detail in These Chapters
Compensation for services including fringe benefits	Ordinary	Gross Income and Exclusions and Compensation
Business income	Ordinary	Business Income, Deductions, and Accounting Methods
Gains from selling property	Ordinary or capital[4]	Investments and Property Dispositions
Interest and dividends	Ordinary or qualified dividend	Gross Income and Exclusions and Investments
Rents and royalties	Ordinary	Gross Income and Exclusions, Investments, and Tax Consequences of Home Ownership
Alimony (pre-2019 decree) and annuities	Ordinary	Gross Income and Exclusions
Retirement income	Ordinary	Retirement Savings and Deferred Compensation
Income from the discharge of indebtedness	Ordinary	Gross Income and Exclusions

EXHIBIT 4-4 **Partial Listing of Common Exclusions and Deferrals**

Exclusion or Deferral Item	Exclusion or Deferral	Discussed in These Chapters
Interest income from municipal bonds	Exclusion	Gross Income and Exclusions
Gift and inheritance	Exclusion	Gross Income and Exclusions
Gain on sale of personal residence	Exclusion	Gross Income and Exclusions and Tax Consequences of Home Ownership
Life insurance proceeds	Exclusion	Gross Income and Exclusions
Installment sale	Deferral	Property Dispositions
Like-kind exchange	Deferral	Property Dispositions

Character of Income   While gross income increases taxable income dollar for dollar, certain types of gross income are treated differently than other types of gross income for purposes of computing a taxpayer's taxable income and income tax liability. For example, one type of income may be taxed at a different rate than another type of

---

[4]Dispositions of assets used in a trade or business for more than a year generate an intermediate character of income called §1231 gain or loss. Ultimately, §1231 gains and losses are treated as either ordinary or capital on the tax return.

income. The *type* of income is commonly referred to as the **character of income.** The most common characters of income are as follows:

- Ordinary: This is income or loss that is taxed at the ordinary rates provided in the tax rate schedules in Appendix D, or that offsets income taxed at these rates, and is not capital in character.
- Capital: These are gains or losses on the disposition or sale of capital assets. In general, capital assets are all assets *other than*
    1. Accounts receivable from the sale of goods or services.
    2. Inventory and other assets held for sale in the ordinary course of business.
    3. Assets used in a trade or business, including supplies.[5]

Nonbusiness assets such as personal-use automobiles or personal residences and assets held for investment such as stocks and bonds are capital assets.

Capital gains and losses are further characterized as long-term (when the taxpayer owns the capital asset for more than one year before selling it) or short-term (when the taxpayer owns the capital asset for one year or less before selling it). A gain on a sale of a capital asset is generally included in gross income. If the gain is a long-term capital gain, it is generally taxed at a 15 percent tax rate (taxed at 20 percent for high-income taxpayers and 0 percent for low-income taxpayers). If the gain is a short-term capital gain, the gain is taxed at ordinary income rates. Note that even though a short-term capital gain is taxed at ordinary rates, it is still considered to be a capital gain and not ordinary income.

A loss on the sale of a capital asset—no matter how long the taxpayer holds the asset before selling—generates a deduction for the taxpayer in the year of sale (a *for* AGI deduction, as discussed below). However, the deduction for the loss is limited to $3,000 for the year (losses in excess of the limit are carried forward indefinitely). If the taxpayer sells a personal-use asset like a personal automobile or personal residence at a loss, the loss is not deductible.

When a taxpayer sells more than one capital asset during the year, the gains and losses are netted together. A net loss is subject to the $3,000 annual deduction limit. A net gain may be taxed at 15, 20, or 0 percent or at the ordinary rates depending on the outcome of the netting process and the taxpayer's taxable income. We discuss the netting process in detail in the Investments chapter.[6]

- Qualified dividend: Shareholders receiving dividends from corporations include the dividend income in gross income. If the dividend meets the qualified dividend requirements, it is generally taxed at a rate of 15 percent (taxed at 20 percent for high-income taxpayers and 0 percent for low-income taxpayers).[7] If a dividend does not meet the qualified dividend requirement, it is taxed at ordinary rates. Because qualified dividends (and long-term capital gains) are taxed at a **preferential tax rate** (a rate lower than the ordinary income rate), qualified dividends (and long-term capital gains) can be referred to as **preferentially taxed income.** While qualified dividends are taxed at the same rate as long-term capital gains, qualified dividends are not included in the capital gain and loss netting process. Therefore, qualified dividend is a separate and distinct character from capital.

Example 4-1

Rodney earned a salary of $74,000, and Anita earned a salary of $56,000. The Halls also received $600 of interest income from investments in corporate bonds and $300 of interest income from investments in municipal bonds. This was their only realized income during the year. What is the Halls' gross income?

---

[5]See §1221(a) for the definition of a capital asset.

[6]As we discover in the Investments chapter, certain capital gains may be taxed at a maximum rate of 25 percent and others may be taxed at a maximum rate of 28 percent.

[7]A qualified dividend generally includes dividends distributed by a U.S. corporation if the shareholder meets certain holding period requirements for the stock. These requirements are discussed in more detail in the Investments chapter.

Answer: $130,600, computed as follows:

Description	Amount	Explanation
(1) Rodney's salary	$ 74,000	
(2) Anita's salary	56,000	
(3) Interest from corporate bonds	600	
Gross income	**$130,600***	(1) + (2) + (3)

*The $300 of interest income from municipal bonds is excluded from gross income.

What is the character of the salary, the interest income from the corporate bonds, and the interest income from the investments in municipal bonds?

Answer: The salary and interest income from corporate bonds are ordinary income. The interest income from the municipal bonds is excluded from gross income.

What if: Suppose this year the Halls sold shares of stock in XYZ Corporation at a $4,000 gain (their only transaction involving a capital asset). They purchased the stock three years ago. What would be the character of the gain? At what rate would the gain be taxed?

Answer: This is a long-term capital gain because stock is a capital asset and the Halls owned the stock for more than a year before selling. Given their income level, the gain would be taxed at a maximum rate of 15 percent.

What if: Suppose this year the Halls sold stock at a $4,000 loss (their only transaction involving a capital asset). They purchased the stock three years ago. What is the character of the loss? How much of the loss may the Halls deduct this year?

Answer: This is a long-term capital loss, because the stock is a capital asset and the Halls owned the stock for more than a year before selling. The Halls can deduct $3,000 of the loss as a *for* AGI deduction this year. The remaining $1,000 loss is carried over to next year.

What if: Suppose this year the Halls sold a personal automobile at a $4,000 loss. They purchased the automobile three years ago. What is the character of the loss? How much of the loss may the Halls deduct in the current year?

Answer: This is a long-term capital loss, because the automobile is a capital asset and the Halls owned the auto for more than a year before selling. However, the Halls are not allowed to deduct any of the $4,000 loss this year or any year because the automobile is a personal-use asset.

Deductions

Deductions reduce a taxpayer's taxable income. However, they are not necessarily easy to come by because, in contrast to the all-inclusive treatment of income, deductions are *not allowed unless a specific tax law allows them.* Thus, deductions are a matter of **legislative grace.** The tax laws provide for two distinct types of deductions in the individual tax formula: for adjusted gross income (AGI) deductions and from AGI deductions. As indicated in the individual tax formula, gross income minus **for AGI deductions** equals AGI, and AGI minus **from AGI deductions** equals taxable income. Congress identifies whether the deductions are *for* or *from* AGI when it enacts new legislation that grants deductions. The distinction between the deduction types is particularly important because AGI is a reference point often used in determining the extent to which taxpayers are allowed to claim certain tax benefits. For example, taxpayers with AGI in excess of certain thresholds lose tax benefits from items such as the child tax credit and education credits (we discuss credits below).

For AGI Deductions   For AGI deductions tend to be deductions associated with business activities and certain investing activities. Because *for* AGI deductions reduce AGI (deducted on page 1 of Form 1040), they are referred to as **"deductions above the line."** The "line" in this case is AGI, which is the last line on page 1 of Form 1040 (see Exhibit 4-2). Prior to 2018, moving expenses were a common for AGI deduction. However, the recent tax law eliminated moving expenses as a deduction for all taxpayers but members of the armed forces. Exhibit 4-5 provides a partial listing of common *for* AGI deductions under new tax law and indicates where in the text we discuss them.

THE KEY FACTS

For and From AGI Deductions

- *For* AGI deductions
  - Reduce AGI.
  - Are referred to as deductions "above the line."
  - Are generally more valuable than *from* AGI deductions.
- *From* AGI deductions
  - Deduct *from* AGI to determine taxable income.
  - Are referred to as deductions "below the line."

EXHIBIT 4-5 Partial Listing of Common *for* AGI Deductions

For AGI Deduction	Discussed in More Detail in These Chapters
Alimony paid (pre-2019 decree)	Individual Deductions
Health insurance deduction for self-employed taxpayers	Individual Deductions
Rental and royalty expenses	Individual Deductions and Tax Consequences of Home Ownership
Capital losses (*net* losses limited to $3,000 for the year)	Investments
One-half of self-employment taxes paid	Individual Income Tax Computation and Tax Credits
Business expenses	Business Income, Deductions, and Accounting Methods
Losses on dispositions of assets used in a trade or business	Property Dispositions
Contributions to qualified retirement accounts [e.g., 401Ks and individual retirement accounts (IRAs)]	Retirement Savings and Deferred Compensation

Example 4-2

Rodney made a $5,000 deductible (for AGI) contribution to his individual retirement account (IRA). What is the Halls' adjusted gross income?

Answer: $125,600, computed as follows:

Description	Amount	Explanation
(1) Gross income	$ 130,600	Example 4-1
(2) IRA contribution	(5,000)	*For* AGI deduction (see Exhibit 4-5)
Adjusted gross income	**$125,600**	(1) + (2)

From AGI Deductions From AGI deductions are commonly referred to as **"deductions below the line"** because they are deducted after AGI has been determined (deducted on page 2 of Form 1040). For years prior to 2018, from AGI deductions included **itemized deductions,** the **standard deduction,** and personal and dependency exemptions. However, beginning in 2018 the new tax law added a from AGI deduction that is generally equal to 20 percent of a taxpayer's qualified business income (QBI) and it eliminates the deduction for personal and dependency exemptions. While the deduction for QBI is a from AGI deduction, it is not an itemized deduction. Thus, beginning in 2018, individuals can deduct the QBI deduction and *either* their itemized deductions *or* a fixed amount called the standard deduction as from AGI deductions. Taxpayers generally deduct the higher of the standard deduction or itemized deductions. Exhibit 4-6 identifies the primary categories of itemized deductions.

EXHIBIT 4-6 Primary Categories of Itemized Deductions

- *Medical and dental expenses:* Deductible to the extent these expenses exceed 7.5 percent of AGI.
- *Taxes:* State and local income taxes, sales taxes, real estate taxes, personal property taxes, and other taxes (an aggregate $10,000 deduction limitation applies to taxes).
- *Interest expense:* Mortgage and investment interest expense.
- *Gifts to charity (charitable contributions).*
- *Other miscellaneous deductions:* Gambling losses (to the extent of gambling winnings) and certain other deductions.

Note: Itemized deductions are detailed on Schedule A of Form 1040. We discuss itemized deductions in more depth in the Individual Deductions chapter.

The amount of the standard deduction varies by taxpayer filing status (we discuss filing status in more detail later in the chapter); the government indexes this deduction for inflation. Exhibit 4-7 presents the basic standard deduction amounts by filing status for 2017 and 2018. The new tax law significantly increased the standard deduction amounts for 2018. Special rules may alter the allowable standard deduction for certain taxpayers. We discuss these departures from the basic standard deduction amounts in the Individual Deductions chapter.

EXHIBIT 4-7   Standard Deduction Amounts by Filing Status*

	2017	2018
Married filing jointly	$12,700	$24,000
Qualifying widow or widower	12,700	24,000
Married filing separately	6,350	12,000
Head of household	9,350	18,000
Single	6,350	12,000

*Married taxpayers 65 years of age or over and/or blind are entitled to an additional standard deduction of $1,300 ($1,300 for age and another $1,300 for blindness); single and head of household taxpayers 65 years of age or over and/or blind are entitled to an additional standard deduction of $1,600 (one for age and another for blindness). (See the Individual Deductions chapter for more detail.) For individuals claimed as a dependent on another tax return, the 2018 standard deduction is the greater of (1) $1,050 or (2) $350 plus earned income not to exceed the standard deduction amount for those who are not dependents (see the Individual Income Tax Computation and Tax Credits chapter for more detail).

Example 4-3

Rodney and Anita Hall annually file a joint tax return. They paid a total of $11,000 for expenditures that qualified as itemized deductions and they had no qualified business income (QBI). What is the total amount of *from* AGI deductions Rodney and Anita are allowed to deduct on their tax return?

Answer: $24,000, computed as follows:

Description	Amount	Explanation
(1) Standard deduction	$24,000	Married filing joint filing status (see Exhibit 4-7)
(2) Itemized deductions	11,000	
(3) Greater of (1) or (2)	24,000	The standard deduction exceeds itemized deductions.
(4) QBI deduction	0	No qualified business income
Total deductions *from* AGI	**$24,000**	(3) + (4). (Also referred to as deductions "below the line.")

What if: What would be the amount of the Halls' *from* AGI deductions if, instead of the original facts, Rodney and Anita had paid a total of $11,000 in expenditures that qualified as itemized deductions and they were allowed to claim a $1,000 QBI deduction based on $5,000 of qualified business income they reported?

Answer: $25,000, computed as follows:

Description	Amount	Explanation
(1) Standard deduction	$24,000	Married filing joint filing status (see Exhibit 4-7)
(2) Itemized deductions	11,000	
(3) Greater of (1) or (2)	24,000	The standard deduction exceeds itemized deductions.
(4) QBI deduction	1,000	QBI of $5,000 × 20%
Total deductions *from* AGI	**$25,000**	(3) + (4). (Also referred to as deductions "below the line.")

What if: What would be the amount of the Halls' *from* AGI deductions if, instead of the original facts, Rodney and Anita had paid a total of $28,000 in expenditures that qualified as itemized deductions?

(continued on page 4-10)

Answer: $28,000, computed as follows:

Description	Amount	Explanation
(1) Standard deduction	$24,000	Married filing joint filing status (see Exhibit 4-7)
(2) Itemized deductions	28,000	
(3) Greater of (1) or (2)	28,000	The standard deduction exceeds itemized deductions.
(4) QBI deduction	0	No qualified business income
Total deductions *from* AGI	**$28,000**	(3) + (4). (Also referred to as deductions "below the line.")

Income Tax Calculation

After determining taxable income, taxpayers can generally calculate their regular income tax liability using either a **tax table** or a **tax rate schedule,** depending on their filing status and income level (taxpayers with taxable income under $100,000 generally must use the tax tables).[8] See Appendix D for the regular tax rate schedules. However, as we discussed above, certain types of income included in taxable income are taxed at rates different from those in the tables or tax rate schedules. The 2017 tax rate schedules had seven different income tax brackets (10, 15, 25, 28, 33, 35, and 39.6 percent). The 2018 tax rate schedules also have seven different income tax brackets but the rates change for all but the first bracket (10, 12, 22, 24, 32, 35, and 37 percent). Overall, for a given level of taxable income, a taxpayer's tax liability will generally be lower under the 2018 tax rate schedules.

Example 4-4

With Tara's help, the Halls have determined their taxable income to be $101,600, as follows:

Description	Amount	Explanation
(1) Adjusted gross income	$125,600	Example 4-2
(2) *From* AGI deductions	$ (24,000)	Example 4-3
Taxable income	**$101,600**	(1) + (2)

They have also determined that all of their income is ordinary income. What is their tax liability?

Answer: $14,231. See the married filing jointly tax rate schedule in Appendix D. {$8,907 + $5,324 [22% × ($101,600 − $77,400)]}.

What if: Using the tax rate schedules, what would the Halls' tax liability be if their taxable income were $12,000 (all ordinary income)?

Answer: $1,200 ($12,000 × 10%).

What if: Assume that in addition to the $101,600 of ordinary income, the Halls also reported $5,000 of long-term capital gain subject to a 15 percent tax rate. How much tax would they pay on the additional $5,000 gain?

Answer: $750 ($5,000 × 15%). Long-term capital gains (gains on the sale of a capital asset owned for more than a year) are generally taxed at a 15 percent rate. Note that the Halls' taxable income is $106,600. $101,600 of the income is taxed at ordinary rates and $5,000 is taxed at the preferential percent rate.

---

[8]For administrative convenience and to prevent low- and middle-income taxpayers from making mathematical errors using a rate schedule, the IRS provides tax tables that present the gross tax for various amounts of taxable income. For simplicity, we use the tax rate schedule to determine tax liabilities in the examples presented in this text.

Other Taxes

In addition to the individual income tax, individuals may also be required to pay other taxes such as the **alternative minimum tax (AMT)** or **self-employment taxes.** These taxes are imposed on tax bases other than the individual's regular taxable income. Furthermore, taxpayers with relatively high AGI are subject to a 3.8 percent net investment income tax on unearned (investment) income and a .9 percent additional Medicare tax on earned income. We discuss these taxes in more detail in the Individual Income Tax Computation and Tax Credits chapter.

Tax Credits

Individual taxpayers may reduce their tax liabilities by **tax credits** to determine their total taxes payable. Like deductions, tax credits are specifically granted by Congress and are narrowly defined. Unlike deductions, which reduce *taxable income*, tax credits *directly reduce taxes payable*. Thus, a $1 deduction reduces taxes payable by $1 times the marginal tax rate while a $1 credit reduces taxes payable by $1. Common tax credits include the child tax credit [$2,000 per qualifying child (under the age of 17 at year end), up from $1,000 per child under 2017 tax law and a $500 credit for other qualifying dependents], the child and dependent care credit, the earned income credit, the American opportunity credit, and the lifetime learning credit. We discuss credits in more detail in the Individual Income Tax Computation and Tax Credits chapter.

Tax Prepayments

After calculating the total tax and subtracting their available credits, taxpayers determine their taxes due (or tax refund) by subtracting tax prepayments from the total tax remaining after credits. Tax prepayments include: (1) **withholdings,** or income taxes withheld from the taxpayer's salary or wages by her employer, (2) **estimated tax payments** the taxpayer makes for the year (paid directly to the IRS), and (3) tax that the taxpayer overpaid on the prior-year tax return that the taxpayer elects to apply as an estimated payment for the current tax year instead of receiving as a refund.

   If tax prepayments exceed the total tax after subtracting credits, the taxpayer receives a tax refund (or elects to apply the refund as an estimated tax payment) for the difference. If tax prepayments are less than the total tax after credits, the taxpayer owes additional tax and potentially a penalty for the underpayment.

Example 4-5

Based on their calculation in Example 4-4, Rodney and Anita Hall's tax liability is $14,231. The Halls had $12,100 of federal income taxes withheld by their employers from their paychecks and are able to claim a $2,000 child tax credit for their 12-year-old son Braxton and a $500 child tax credit for Tara. What is the Halls' tax due or tax refund?

Answer: $369 tax refund, computed as follows:

Description	Amount	Explanation
(1) Tax liability	$ 14,231	Example 4-4
(2) Tax credits	(2,500)	Child tax credit: $2,000 for Braxton and $500 for Tara.
(3) Tax prepayments	(12,100)	
Tax refund	**$ (369)**	(1) + (2) + (3)

Although it is not explicitly stated in the individual tax formula, a taxpayer's filing status affects many parts of the tax formula, including the standard deduction amount and the applicable income tax rate schedule, among others. In the next section, we describe the rules for determining a taxpayer's filing status. However, because a taxpayer's filing status may depend on whether the taxpayer has dependents for tax purposes, we first discuss how to identify who qualifies as a taxpayer's dependent.

LO 4-2   DEPENDENTS OF THE TAXPAYER

For 2017, taxpayers could claim and deduct a personal exemption for themselves. Married taxpayers filing jointly could claim and deduct two personal exemptions (one for each spouse). Individual taxpayers could generally claim and deduct a personal exemption for themselves (unless they qualified as a dependent of another taxpayer). Further, to provide some tax relief for those supporting others, a taxpayer was allowed to claim and deduct an exemption for each person who qualified as the taxpayer's dependent. For 2017, taxpayers could deduct (from AGI) $4,050 for each exemption they could claim.

However, under new tax law effective in 2018, the deduction for personal and dependency exemptions is reduced to zero. Nevertheless, as mentioned previously, it remains necessary to determine who qualifies as a dependent of the taxpayer for purposes of determining filing status, eligibility for certain tax credits, and other tax-related computations.

Dependency Requirements

To qualify as a dependent of another, an individual:

1. Must be a citizen of the United States or a resident of the United States, Canada, or Mexico.
2. Must *not* file a joint return with his or her spouse unless there is no tax liability on the couple's joint return and there would not have been any tax liability on either spouse's tax return if they had filed separately.[9]
3. Must be considered either a **qualifying child** *or* a **qualifying relative** of the taxpayer.[10]

While the requirements for determining a qualifying child and a qualifying relative have some similarities, the qualifying relative requirements are broader in scope.

Qualifying Child   To be considered a qualifying child of a taxpayer, an individual must satisfy the following four tests: (1) relationship, (2) age, (3) residence, and (4) support.[11]

Relationship test.   A qualifying child must be an eligible relative of the taxpayer. Eligible relatives include the taxpayer's:

- Child or descendant of a child. For this purpose, a child includes a taxpayer's adopted child, stepchild, and eligible foster child.

---

[9]Rev. Rul. 54-567, 1954-2 C.B. 108.

[10]§152.

[11]Technically, an individual is not eligible to be a qualifying child of another if she filed a joint return with her spouse (other than to claim a refund) [see §152(c)(1)(E)]. However, because this is also a requirement to be claimed as a dependent, we do not discuss the requirement separately here.

- Sibling or descendant of sibling. For this purpose, a sibling includes a taxpayer's half-brother, half-sister, stepbrother, or stepsister.

Under this definition, the taxpayer's grandchild would qualify as an eligible relative, as would the taxpayer's sister's grandchild.

Age test. A qualifying child must be younger than the taxpayer and *either* (1) under age 19 at the end of the year or (2) under age 24 at the end of the year *and* a full-time student.[12] A person is a full-time student if she was in school full-time during any part of each of five calendar months during the calendar year.[13] An individual of any age who is permanently and totally disabled is deemed to have met the age test.[14]

Residence test. A qualifying child must have the same principal residence as the taxpayer for *more* than half the year. Time that a child or the taxpayer is *temporarily* away from the taxpayer's home because the child or taxpayer is ill, is pursuing an education, or has other special circumstances is counted as though the child or taxpayer were living in the taxpayer's home.[15]

Support test. A qualifying child must *not* have provided more than half of his or her *own* support (living expenses) for the year. Such support generally includes:

- Food, school lunches, toilet articles, and haircuts.
- Clothing.
- Recreation—including toys, summer camp, horseback riding, entertainment, and vacation expenses.
- Medical and dental care.
- Child care expenses.
- Allowances and gifts.
- Wedding costs.
- Lodging.
- Education—including board, uniforms at military schools, and tuition. When determining who provided the support for a taxpayer's *child* who is a full-time student, scholarships are excluded from the computation.[16]

Example 4-6

Rodney and Anita have two children: Braxton, age 12, who lives at home, and Tara, age 21, who is a full-time student and does not live at home. Tara earned $9,000 from a summer job, but she did *not* provide more than half of her own support during the year. Are Braxton and Tara qualifying dependent children of Rodney and Anita?

(continued on page 4-14)

---

[12]§152(c)(3)(A).

[13]§152(f)(2).

[14]§152(c)(3)(B).

[15] Reg. §1.152-1(b).

[16]§152(f)(5) and §152(f)(1). This provision requires that the student be a son, daughter, stepson, stepdaughter, or an eligible foster child of the taxpayer.

Answer: Yes, see analysis of factors below:

Test	Braxton	Tara
Relationship	Yes, son.	Yes, daughter.
Age	Yes, under age 19 at end of year (and younger than his parents).	Yes, under age 24 at year-end *and* full-time student (and younger than her parents).
Residence	Yes, lived at home entire year.	Yes, time away at college is considered as time at home if Tara plans to live in her parents' home again at some point (it is a temporary absence).
Support	Yes, does not provide more than half of own support.	Yes, does not provide more than half of own support.

Because they both meet all the requirements, Braxton and Tara are qualifying children to the Halls. So, both Braxton and Tara are the Halls' dependents.

What if: Suppose Tara provided more than half of her own support. Would she be considered a qualifying child of her parents?

Answer: No. She would fail the support test.

What if: Assume the original facts apply but now Tara is age 25. Would she be considered a qualifying dependent child of her parents?

Answer: No. She would fail the age test. Note, however, that Tara could still qualify as her parents' dependent as a qualifying relative (see Example 4-8 below).

What if: Assume the original facts, except now suppose that Braxton is Anita's stepbrother's son. Would Braxton be considered a qualifying dependent child of Rodney and Anita?

Answer: Yes. Braxton meets the relationship test because he is the descendant of Anita's stepbrother (sibling).

Tiebreaking rules. The requirements for determining who is a qualifying child leave open the possibility that one person could be a qualifying child to more than one taxpayer. In these circumstances, the taxpayer who has priority for claiming the person as a dependent is based on the following tiebreaking rules:

1. If the person is a qualifying child of a parent, the parent is entitled to claim the person as a dependent. This situation could arise, for example, when a child lives with her mother *and* her grandparents. In this case, the mother has priority for claiming the the child as a dependent over the grandparents.

2. If the individual is a qualifying child to both parents, the parent with whom the child has resided for the longest period of time during the year has priority for claiming the person as a dependent. This situation may arise in a year when the child lives with both parents for more than half of the year, but the parents separate or divorce in the latter part of the year. Note, however, that for a child of divorced parents, the noncustodial parent (the parent the child does not live with) can claim the child as a dependent qualifying child if the custodial parent signs a form indicating that he or she will not claim the child as a dependent and the noncustodial parent attaches the form to his or her tax return.[17]

3. Finally, if the child resides with each parent for equal amounts of time during the year or the qualifying child resides with a taxpayer who is not the child's parent, the taxpayer with the *highest AGI* has priority for claiming the child as a dependent.[18]

---

[17]See §152(e). The custodial signs Form 8332, and the noncustodial parent attaches it to his or her tax return.

[18]However, if the parents may claim the child as a qualifying child but no parent does so, another taxpayer may claim the individual as a qualifying child but only if the other individual's AGI is higher than the AGI of any parent of the child [§152(c)(4)(C)].

Example 4-7

In the previous example, we established that Rodney and Anita's son Braxton is their qualifying dependent child. Braxton's Uncle Shawn—Rodney's brother—lived in the Halls' home (the same home Braxton lived in) for more than 11 months during the year. Does Braxton meet the requirements to be considered Shawn's qualifying child?

Answer: Yes, see analysis of factors below.

Test	Braxton
Relationship	Yes, son of Shawn's brother.
Age	Yes, under age 19 at end of year (and younger than Shawn).
Residence	Yes, lived in same residence as Shawn for more than half the year.
Support	Yes, does not provide more than half of his own support.

Thus, Braxton is considered to be Rodney and Anita's qualifying child *and* he is considered to be Shawn's qualifying child. Under the tiebreaker rules, who is allowed to claim Braxton as a dependent for the year?

Answer: Rodney and Anita. Under the first tiebreaking rule, Rodney and Anita are allowed to claim Braxton as a dependent because they are Braxton's parents.

What if: Suppose Shawn is Rodney's cousin. Would Braxton be considered Shawn's qualifying child?

Answer: No, Braxton does not meet the relationship test for Shawn if he is Rodney's cousin. Braxton is not the descendant of Shawn's sibling.

Qualifying Relative   A qualifying relative is a person who is *not* a qualifying child *and* satisfies (1) a relationship test, (2) a support test, and (3) a gross income test.

Relationship test.   As you might expect, the relationship test for a qualifying relative is more inclusive than the relationship test for a qualifying child. A person meets the qualifying relative relationship test who either (1) has a qualifying family relationship with the taxpayer or (2) meets the qualifying relative "member of the household" test. A qualifying family relationship with the taxpayer includes the following:

- A descendant or ancestor of the taxpayer. For this purpose, a child includes a taxpayer's adopted child, stepchild, and eligible foster child, and a parent includes a stepmother and stepfather.
- A sibling of the taxpayer, including a stepbrother or a stepsister.
- A son or daughter of the brother or sister of the taxpayer (cousins do not qualify).
- A sibling of the taxpayer's mother or father.
- An in-law (mother-in-law, father-in-law, sister-in-law, brother-in-law, son-in-law, or daughter-in-law) of the taxpayer.

A person meets the qualifying relative "member of the household" test if that person has the same principal place of abode as the taxpayer for the entire year (*even if the person does not have a qualifying family relationship with the taxpayer*).[19]

Support test.   The support test generally requires that the taxpayer pay more than half the qualifying relative's support/living expenses (note that this is a different support test than the support test for a qualifying child). As we discussed above, support/

---

[19]A person is considered to live with the taxpayer for the entire year if he or she was either born during the year or died during the year and resided with the taxpayer for the remaining part of the year.

living expenses include rent, food, medicine, and clothes, among other things. Just as with the qualifying child support test, scholarships of children of a taxpayer who are full-time students are excluded from the support test.[20] Under a multiple support agreement, taxpayers who don't pay over half of an individual's support may still be allowed to claim the individual as a dependent under the qualifying relative rules if the following apply:[21]

1. No one taxpayer paid over one-half of the individual's support.
2. The taxpayer and at least one other person provided more than half the support of the individual, and the taxpayer and the other person(s) would have been allowed to claim the individual as a dependent except for the fact that they did not provide over half of the support of the individual.
3. The taxpayer contributed *over* 10 percent of the individual's support for the year.
4. Each other person who provided *over* 10 percent of the individual's support [see requirement (2) above] provides a signed statement to the taxpayer agreeing not to claim the individual as a dependent. The taxpayer includes the names, addresses, and Social Security numbers of each other person on Form 2120, which the taxpayer attaches to her Form 1040.

Multiple support agreements are commonly used in situations when siblings support elderly parents.

Gross income test.   The gross income test requires that a qualifying relative's gross income for the year be *less* than $4,150 in 2018.[22]

Example 4-8

What if: Suppose Tara is age 25, is a full-time student, and does not live with her parents. Tara earned $3,000 from a summer job, and her parents provided more than half her support. Does Tara qualify as her parents' dependent?

Answer: Yes, as their qualifying relative. She is too old to be their qualifying child.

Test	Explanation
Relationship	Yes, Rodney and Anita's daughter.
Support	Yes, the Halls provide more than half of Tara's support.
Gross income	Yes, Tara's gross income for the year is less than $4,150.

Tara's parents may claim her as a dependent. Note that if Tara's gross income were at least $4,150, she would *not* qualify as her parents' dependent.

Example 4-9

In determining who qualified as their dependents, Rodney and Anita evaluated whether Shawn is their *qualifying relative*. Assuming Shawn's gross income for the year is $42,000, the Halls provided food and lodging for Shawn valued at $8,000, and Shawn paid for his other living expenses valued at $14,000, is Shawn a qualifying relative of the Halls?

---

[20]§152(f)(5) and §152(f)(1). Just as with a qualifying child, this provision requires that the student be a son, daughter, stepson, stepdaughter, or an eligible foster child of the taxpayer.

[21]§152(d)(3).

[22]This is the amount that taxpayers could have deducted for each personal or dependency exemption in 2018 before the new tax law eliminated the deduction for exemptions.

Answer: No, as analyzed below.

Test	Explanation
Relationship	Yes, Rodney's brother.
Support	No, the Halls provided $8,000 of support to Shawn, but Shawn provided $14,000 of his own support. Because the Halls provided less than half of Shawn's support, Shawn does not pass the support test.
Gross income	No, Shawn's gross income for the year is $42,000, which exceeds $4,150, so Shawn fails the gross income test.

Because Shawn fails the support test and the gross income test, he is not a qualifying relative of the Halls. Consequently, they cannot claim Shawn as a dependent.

What if: Assume that Shawn received $5,000 of tax-exempt interest during the year and that this is his only source of income. Does he fail the gross income test? (Note, however, that Shawn would still fail the support test so he would not be a qualifying relative of the Halls no matter the outcome of the gross income test.)

Answer: No. Because tax-exempt interest is excluded from gross income, Shawn's gross income is $0, so he passes the gross income test.

What if: Assume the original facts in the example except now suppose that Shawn paid for his $14,000 of living expenses with interest he had received from tax-exempt bonds. Would Shawn pass the support test?

Answer: No. The Halls would not have provided more than half of Shawn's support. The fact that Shawn received the money he spent on his support from tax-exempt income does not matter. All that matters is that he provided more than half of his own support.

What if: Assume that Anita's 92-year-old grandfather Juan lives in an apartment by himself near the Halls' residence. His gross income for the year is $3,000. Assuming the Halls provide more than half of Juan's living expenses for the year, would Juan be a qualifying relative of the Halls?

Answer: Yes, as analyzed below.

Test	Explanation
Relationship	Yes, Anita's grandfather.
Support	Yes, as assumed in the facts, the Halls provide more than half of Juan's support.
Gross income	Yes, Juan's gross income for the year is $3,000, which is less than $4,150, so Juan passes the gross income test.

What if: Assume that Anita's 92-year-old grandfather Juan lives in an apartment by himself and reports gross income for the year of $3,000. Anita provided 40 percent of Juan's support, Juan provided 25 percent of his own support, Anita's brother Carlos provided 30 percent of the support, and Anita's sister Kamella provided 5 percent of Juan's support. Who is eligible to claim Juan as a dependent under a multiple support agreement?

Answer: Anita and Carlos. Anita and Carlos are eligible because (1) no one taxpayer provided more than half of Juan's support, (2) Anita and Carlos together provided more than half of Juan's support and Juan would have been both Anita's and Carlos's qualifying relative except for the fact that neither provided over half of Juan's support, and (3) Anita and Carlos each provided over 10 percent of Juan's support (Kamella provided only 5 percent of Juan's support so she is not eligible). Anita and Carlos will need to agree on who will claim Juan as a dependent. Assuming they agree that Anita will claim Juan as a dependent, she will need to receive a signed statement from Carlos agreeing not to claim Juan as a dependent and she will need to attach Form 2120 to her (and Rodney's) tax return providing Carlos's name, address, and Social Security number.

What if: Assume the facts in the prior what-if scenario in which Anita is allowed to claim Juan as a dependent under a multiple support agreement. If Anita is not allowed to deduct a dependency exemption for Juan, why should Anita care whether Juan is her dependent or not?

Answer: While, under the new tax law, Anita is not entitled to a dependency exemption deduction for Juan, she is eligible to claim a $500 child tax credit for Juan because he is Anita's dependent and he is not a qualifying child.

What if: Assume Juan lives in an apartment by himself and is a friend of the family but is unrelated to either Rodney or Anita. His gross income is $3,000 and the Halls provide over half of his support. Is Juan a qualifying relative of the Halls?

(continued on page 4-18)

Answer: No, as analyzed below.

Test	Explanation
Relationship	No, not related to the Halls and his principal place of abode is not in the Halls' household for the *entire* year. If the Halls' home was his principal place of abode for the entire year, he would have met the relationship test even though he's not actually related to anyone in the Hall family.
Support	Yes, as assumed in the facts, the Halls provide more than half of Juan's support.
Gross income	Yes, Juan's gross income for the year is $3,000, which is less than $4,150, so Juan passes the gross income test.

The Halls would not be able to claim Juan as a dependent because he fails the qualifying relative relationship test under this set of facts.

The rules for determining who is a qualifying child and who is a qualifying relative for tax purposes overlap to some extent. The primary differences between the two sets of rules are:

1. The relationship requirement is more broadly defined for qualifying relatives than for qualifying children.
2. Qualifying children are subject to age restrictions while qualifying relatives are not.
3. Qualifying relatives are subject to a gross income restriction while qualifying children are not.
4. Taxpayers need not provide more than half a qualifying child's support (though the child cannot provide more than half of her own support), but they must provide more than half of the support of a qualifying relative.
5. Qualifying children are subject to a residence test (they must have the same primary residence as the taxpayer for more than half the year), while qualifying relatives are not. Exhibit 4-8 summarizes the dependency requirements.

EXHIBIT 4-8 Summary of Dependency Requirements

Test	Qualifying Child	Qualifying Relative
Relationship	Taxpayer's child, stepchild, foster child, sibling, half-brother or half-sister, stepbrother or stepsister, or a descendant of any of these relatives.	Taxpayer's descendant or ancestor, sibling, stepmother, stepfather, stepbrother or stepsister, son or daughter of taxpayer's sibling, sibling of the taxpayer's mother or father, in-laws, and anyone else who has the same principal place of abode as the taxpayer for the entire year (even if not otherwise related).
Age	Younger than the taxpayer claiming the individual as a qualifying child and under age 19 or a full-time student under age 24. Also anyone totally and permanently disabled.	Not applicable.
Residence	Lives with taxpayer for more than half of the year (includes temporary absences for things such as illness and education).	Not applicable.
Support	The qualifying child must not provide more than half of his or her own support.	Taxpayer must have provided more than half of the support for the qualifying relative.
Gross income	Not applicable.	Gross income less than $4,150 in 2018.
Other	Not applicable.	Not a qualifying child.

Finally, an individual who is a dependent of another is not allowed to claim any dependents.[23] Appendix A at the end of this chapter provides a flowchart for determining whether an individual qualifies as the taxpayer's dependent.

ETHICS

Blake was 21 years of age at the end of the year. During the year, he was a full-time college student. He also worked part-time and earned $8,000, which he used to pay all $6,000 of his living expenses. Blake's parents, Troy and Camille, claimed him as a dependent on their joint tax return. After filing the return, Troy told Blake they owed him $3,001 for his annual living expenses. What do you think of Troy and Camille's strategy to claim Blake as a dependent?

FILING STATUS

LO 4-3

Each year taxpayers determine their **filing status** according to their marital status at year-end and whether they have any dependents. A taxpayer's filing status is important because, as we discussed above, it determines:

- The applicable tax rate schedule for determining the taxpayer's tax liability.
- The taxpayer's standard deduction amount.
- The AGI threshold for reductions in certain tax benefits such as the itemized deduction for medical expenses and certain tax credits, among other benefits.

Each year, all taxpayers filing tax returns file under one of the following five filing statuses:

1. Married filing jointly
2. Married filing separately
3. Qualifying widow or widower (surviving spouse)
4. Single
5. Head of household

Married Filing Jointly and Married Filing Separately

Married couples may file tax returns jointly (**married filing jointly**) or separately (**married filing separately**). To be married for filing status purposes, taxpayers must be married on the last day of the year. When one spouse dies during the year, at the end of the year the surviving spouse is considered to be *married* to the spouse who died unless the surviving spouse has remarried during the year. Married couples filing joint returns combine their income and deductions and agree to share joint and several liability for the tax liability on the return. That is, they are both ultimately responsible for seeing that the tax is paid.

When married couples file separately, each spouse reports the income he or she received during the year and the deductions he or she is claiming on a tax return separate from that of the other spouse.[24] So that married taxpayers can't file separately to gain more combined tax benefits than they would be entitled to if they were to file jointly, tax-related items for married filing separate (MFS) taxpayers—such as tax rate schedules and standard deduction amounts, among others—are generally one-half what they are for married filing joint (MFJ) taxpayers. Also, if one spouse deducts itemized deductions, the other spouse is required to deduct itemized deductions even if his or her standard deduction amount is more than the total itemized deductions. Thus, only in unusual circumstances does it make economic sense for *tax* purposes for married couples to file separately.

THE KEY FACTS

Filing Status for Married Taxpayers

- Married filing jointly
  - Taxpayers are legally married as of the last day of the year.
  - When one spouse dies during the year the surviving spouse is still considered to be married for tax purposes during the year of the spouse's death.
  - Both spouses are ultimately responsible for paying the joint tax.
- Married filing separately
  - Taxpayers are legally married as of the last day of the year.
  - Generally no tax advantage to filing separately (usually a disadvantage).
  - Each spouse is ultimately responsible for paying his or her own tax.
  - Couples may choose to file separately (generally for nontax reasons).
- Qualifying widow or widower
  - When a taxpayer's spouse dies, the surviving spouse can file as a qualifying widow or widower for two years after the year of the spouse's death if the surviving spouse remains unmarried and maintains a household for a dependent child.

---

[23] See §152(b)(1).

[24] As we discuss in the Gross Income and Exclusions chapter, under community property laws of certain states, one spouse may be treated as receiving income earned by the other spouse.

However, it may be wise for married couples to file separately for *nontax* reasons. For example, a spouse who does not want to be liable for the other spouse's income tax liability, or a spouse who is not in contact with the other spouse, may want to file separately (see abandoned spouse discussion below).

Example 4-10

Rodney and Anita Hall are married at the end of the year. What is their filing status?

Answer: Married filing jointly, unless they choose to file separately.

What if: Assume that in 2018 the Halls file a joint return. In 2019, Rodney and Anita divorce and the IRS audits their 2018 tax return and determines that, due to overstating their deductions, the Halls underpaid their taxes by $2,000. Who must pay the tax?

Answer: Both Rodney and Anita are responsible for paying. If the IRS can't locate Rodney, it can require Anita to pay the full $2,000 even though she earned $56,000 and Rodney earned $74,000.

What if: Assume that in 2018 the Halls file separate tax returns. In 2019, Rodney and Anita divorce and the IRS audits the Halls' separate tax returns. It determines that by overstating deductions, Rodney understated his tax liability by $1,500 and Anita understated her tax liability by $500. Further, the IRS cannot locate Rodney. What is the maximum amount of taxes Anita is liable for?

Answer: $500. Because she filed a separate return, she is responsible for the tax liability associated with her separate tax return, and she is not responsible for the taxes associated with Rodney's tax return.

TAXES IN THE REAL WORLD **Tax Status for Same-Sex Married Couples**

In June 2013, the Supreme Court struck down the federal "Defense of Marriage Act" (DOMA) which meant that same-sex couples who were married in a state that authorized and recognized same-sex marriages would now be treated as married for federal income tax purposes. However, couples who were in a registered domestic partnership, civil union, or other similar formal relationship recognized under state law were *not* recognized as married for federal income tax purposes.

In June 2015, the Supreme Court ruled that the 14th Amendment of the Constitution guarantees a right to same-sex marriage. This ruling unifies marital status at the federal and state levels. A taxpayer's marital status is important for determining income tax filing status and has implications for other areas of the tax law (estate and gift tax, for example).

Source: Obergefell vs. Hodges, 576 U.S. _____ (2015).

Qualifying Widow or Widower (Surviving Spouse)

When a taxpayer's spouse dies, the taxpayer is no longer legally married. However, to provide tax relief for widows and widowers *with dependents*, taxpayers who meet certain requirements qualify for **qualifying widow or widower** filing status, also called surviving spouse status, for up to two years *after* the end of the year in which the other spouse died. Recall that for tax purposes, they are still considered to be married at the end of the year of the spouse's death. Taxpayers are eligible for qualifying widow or widower filing status if they (1) remain unmarried and (2) pay over half the cost of maintaining a household where a child who qualifies as the taxpayer's dependent lived for the entire year (except for temporary absences).[25]

[25]§2(a).

The dependent child must be a child or stepchild (including an adopted child but not a foster child) of the taxpayer.

Example 4-11

What if: Assume that last year Rodney passed away, and during the current year Anita did not remarry but maintained a household for Braxton and Tara, her dependent children. Under these circumstances, what is Anita's filing status for the current year?

Answer: Qualifying widow. Last year, the year of Rodney's death, Anita qualified to file a joint return with Rodney. This year, she is a qualifying widow because she has not remarried and she has maintained a household for the entire year for her dependent children. She will qualify as a surviving spouse next year (two years after Rodney's death) if she does not remarry and she continues to maintain a household for Braxton and/or Tara for the entire year.

Single

Unmarried taxpayers who do not qualify for head of household status (discussed below) file as **single** taxpayers. As we discuss below, an unmarried taxpayer generally must have a dependent who is a qualifying person to qualify for head of household filing status.

Example 4-12

Shawn Hall, Rodney's brother, was divorced in January and is unmarried at the end of the year. Shawn does not claim any dependents. What is his filing status?

Answer: Single. Because Shawn is unmarried at the end of the year, and he does not have any dependents, his filing status is single.

Head of Household

In terms of tax rate schedules and standard deduction amounts, the **head of household** filing status is less favorable than the married filing jointly and qualifying widow or widower filing statuses. However, it is more favorable than married filing separately and single filing statuses (see tax rates and standard deduction amounts provided in Appendix D). To qualify for head of household filing status, a taxpayer must:

- Be unmarried (or be considered unmarried under the provisions discussed below) at the end of the year.
- Not be a qualifying widow or widower.
- Pay more than half the costs of keeping up a home for the year.
- Have a "qualifying person" live in the taxpayer's home for more than half the year (except for temporary absences such as military service, illness, or schooling). However, if the qualifying person is the taxpayer's *dependent* parent, the parent is not required to live with the taxpayer. A qualifying person may not qualify more than one person for head of household filing status. Exhibit 4-9 describes who is considered a qualifying person for purposes of head of household filing status.[26]

> **THE KEY FACTS**
>
> **Filing Status for Unmarried Taxpayers**
>
> - Single
>   - Unmarried taxpayers at year-end who do not qualify for head of household.
> - Head of household
>   - Unmarried taxpayers or taxpayers considered to be unmarried at year-end.
>   - Must pay more than half of the costs of maintaining a household in which a qualifying person lives for more than half of the tax year or must pay more than half of the costs of maintaining a separate household for a parent who qualifies as taxpayer's dependent.

---

[26]§2(b). The new tax law imposes due diligence requirements for paid preparers in determining eligibility for a taxpayer to file as head of household and a $500 penalty each time a paid preparer fails to meet these requirements. See §6695(g).

EXHIBIT 4-9 **Who Is a Qualifying Person for Determining Head of Household Filing Status?**
(Adapted from Table 4 in IRS Publication 501)

IF the person is the taxpayer's . . .	And . . .	THEN, the person is . . .
Qualifying child	the person is single,	a qualifying person, whether or not the taxpayer can claim the person as a dependent.**
	the person is married and the taxpayer may claim the person as a dependent,	a qualifying person.**
	the person is married and the taxpayer may not claim the person as a dependent,	not a qualifying person.
Qualifying relative who is the taxpayer's mother or father	the taxpayer may not claim the taxpayer's mother or father as a dependent,	not a qualifying person.
	the taxpayer may claim the taxpayer's mother or father as a dependent,	a qualifying person even if the taxpayer's mother or father did not live with the taxpayer. However, the taxpayer must have paid more than half the costs to maintain the household of the mother or father.
Qualifying relative other than the taxpayer's mother or father	the person did not live with the taxpayer for more than half the year,	not a qualifying person.
	the taxpayer can claim the person as a dependent, the person lived with the taxpayer for more than half the year, and the person is related to the taxpayer through a qualifying family relationship,	a qualifying person.
	the person is the taxpayer's qualifying relative only because the person lived with the taxpayer as a member of the taxpayer's household for the entire year (the person does not have a qualifying family relationship with the taxpayer),	not a qualifying person.
	the taxpayer cannot claim the person as a dependent or the taxpayer can claim the person as a dependent only because of a multiple support agreement,	not a qualifying person.

*Appendix B at the end of this chapter includes a flowchart for determining whether a person is a qualifying person for head of household filing status.
**If a custodial parent allows the noncustodial parent to claim the child as a dependent under a divorce decree, the agreement is ignored for purposes of this test.
Source: Adapted from Table 4 in IRS Publication 501.

Example 4-13

What if: Assume Rodney and Anita divorced last year. During the current year, Braxton lives with Anita for the entire year and Anita pays all the costs of maintaining the household for herself and Braxton. Under these circumstances, what is Anita's filing status for the year?

Answer: Head of household. Anita is unmarried at the end of the year, she provides more than half the costs of maintaining her household, Braxton lives with her for more than half of the year, and Braxton is her qualifying child.

What if: Assume Rodney and Anita divorced last year. During the current year, Braxton lives with Anita for the entire year, and Anita pays all the costs of maintaining the household for herself and Braxton. Assume that Anita allowed Rodney to claim Braxton as a dependent under the divorce decree. Under these circumstances, what is Anita's filing status for the year?

Answer: Head of household. Braxton is a qualifying person for Anita (the custodial parent) even though Anita is not claiming Braxton as a dependent. Braxton is not a qualifying person for Rodney (the noncustodial parent).

What if: Assume that Rodney and Anita divorced last year. If Braxton is Anita's cousin (rather than her son) and he lives with Anita in her home from June 15 through December 31, what is Anita's filing status for the year?

Answer: Single. Anita does not qualify for head of household filing status because Braxton is not her qualifying child (he fails the relationship test) or her qualifying relative (he fails the relationship test because he did not live in Anita's home for the entire year and he does not have a qualifying family relationship with Anita because he is her cousin).

What if: Assume that Rodney and Anita divorced last year, Braxton is Anita's cousin, and Braxton lives with Anita in her home for the entire year. What is Anita's filing status for the year?

Answer: Single. Even though Braxton is Anita's qualifying relative, Braxton meets the qualifying relative relationship test only because he lived with Anita for the entire year (not because he had a qualifying family relationship with her). Therefore, while Anita may claim Braxton as a dependent, she does not qualify for the head of household filing status.

What if: Assume Rodney's brother Shawn lived with the Halls, but Shawn paid more than half the costs of maintaining a separate apartment that is the principal residence of his mother, Sharon. Sharon's gross income is $1,500. Because Shawn provided more than half of Sharon's support during the year, and because Sharon's gross income was only $1,500, she qualifies as Shawn's dependent relative. In these circumstances, what is Shawn's filing status?

Answer: Head of household. Shawn paid more than half the costs of maintaining a separate household where his mother resides, and his mother qualifies as his dependent.

If Sharon's gross income were at least $4,150, she would fail the dependency gross income test and would not qualify as Shawn's dependent. If she did not qualify as his dependent, she would not be a qualifying person, and Shawn would not qualify for the head of household filing status. Also, if Sharon were Shawn's grandmother rather than his mother, she would not be a qualifying person (no matter the amount of her gross income) and Shawn would not qualify for head of household status. Sharon must be Shawn's parent in order for her to qualify Shawn as a head of household.

Married Individuals Treated as Unmarried (Abandoned Spouse)   In certain situations a couple may be legally married at the end of the year but living apart. Although the couple could technically file a joint tax return, this is often not desirable from a nontax perspective, because each spouse would be assuming responsibility for paying tax on income earned by either spouse whether it was reported or not. However, because both spouses are married at the end of the year, their only other option is to file under the tax-unfavorable married filing separately filing status.

To provide tax relief in these situations, the tax laws treat a married taxpayer *as though he or she were unmarried* at the end of the year if the taxpayer meets the following requirements:

- The taxpayer is married at the end of the year (or is not *legally* separated from the other spouse).
- The taxpayer does not file a joint tax return with the other spouse.
- The taxpayer pays *more than half* the costs of maintaining his or her home for the entire year, and this home is the principal residence for a child (who qualifies as the taxpayer's dependent[27]) for *more than half* the year (the child must be a child of the taxpayer, including adopted child, stepchild, or eligible foster child[28]).
- The taxpayer lived apart from the other spouse for the last six months of the year (the other spouse did not live at all in the taxpayer's home during the last six months—temporary absences due to illness, education, business, vacation, or military service count as though the spouse still lived in the taxpayer's home).

If the taxpayer meets these requirements, he or she also meets the head of household filing status requirements and may file as head of household for the year. The primary objective of this tax rule is to provide tax relief to one spouse who has been abandoned by or separated from the other spouse and left to care for a dependent child. Thus, a married taxpayer who qualifies as unmarried under this provision is

[27]A taxpayer meets this test if the taxpayer (custodial parent) cannot claim the child as a dependent only because he or she agreed under a divorce decree to allow the noncustodial to claim the child as a dependent.
[28]§152(f).

frequently referred to as an **abandoned spouse.** Nevertheless, the provision may still apply even when no spouse has been abandoned. For example, a couple may separate by mutual consent. Further, if both spouses meet the requirements, both spouses may qualify as being unmarried in the same year and thus both may qualify for head of household filing status.

Example 4-14

What if: Assume that last year, Rodney and Anita informally separated (they did not *legally* separate). Rodney moved out of the home and into his own apartment. Anita stayed in the Halls' home with Braxton. During the current year, Anita paid more than half the costs of maintaining the home for herself and Braxton. Even though Rodney and Anita were legally married at the end of the year, they filed separate tax returns. Under these circumstances, is Anita considered to be married or unmarried for tax purposes?

Answer: Unmarried. Anita meets the requirements for being treated as unmarried determined as follows (see requirements above):

- Anita is married to Rodney at the end of the year.
- Anita filed a tax return separate from Rodney's.
- Anita paid more than half the costs of maintaining her home, and her home was the principal residence for Braxton, who is her dependent child.
- Rodney did not live in Anita's home for the last six months of the year (in fact, he didn't live there at any time during the entire year).

What if: Given that Anita meets the requirements for being treated as unmarried, what is her filing status?

Answer: Head of household. Since Anita meets the abandoned spouse requirements she also meets the head of household filing status requirements. Without the abandoned spouse rule, Anita would have been required to file as married filing separately. Rodney's filing status, however, is married filing separately. Note, however, that if Rodney's new residence became Tara's principal residence, Rodney would also be treated as unmarried and would be eligible for head of household filing status.

Appendix C at the end of this chapter includes a flowchart for determining a tax-payer's filing status.

SUMMARY OF INCOME TAX FORMULA

Tara crunched some numbers and put together a summary of her parents' taxable income calculation. She determined that her parents will receive a $369 tax refund when they file their tax return. Tara's summary is provided in Exhibit 4-10, and Exhibit 4-11 presents pages 1 and 2 of the Halls' Form 1040.

EXHIBIT 4-10 **Taxable Income and Tax Calculation Summary for Rodney and Anita Hall**

Description	Amount	Explanation
(1) Gross income	130,600.00	Example 4-1
(2) For AGI deductions	(5,000.00)	Example 4-2, line (2)
(3) Adjusted gross income	$ 125,600.00	(1) + (2)
(4) From AGI deductions	$ (24,000.00)	Example 4-3
(5) Taxable income	$101,600.00	(3) + (4)
(6) Income tax liability	$ 14,231.00	Example 4-4
(7) Credits	(2,500.00)	Example 4-5, line (2)
(8) Tax prepayments	(12,100.00)	Example 4-5, line (3)
Tax (refund)	$ (369.00)	(9) + (10) + (11)

EXHIBIT 4-11 Form 1040

Form **1040** Department of the Treasury—Internal Revenue Service (99)
U.S. Individual Income Tax Return 2017 OMB No. 1545-0074 IRS Use Only—Do not write or staple in this space.

For the year Jan. 1–Dec. 31, 2017, or other tax year beginning , 2017, ending , 20 | See separate instructions.

Your first name and initial	Last name	Your social security number
Rodney	Hall	2 2 4 5 6 1 2 4 5

If a joint return, spouse's first name and initial | Last name | Spouse's social security number
Anita | Hall | 3 2 4 4 3 3 4 7 8

Home address (number and street). If you have a P.O. box, see instructions. | Apt. no. | ▲ Make sure the SSN(s) above and on line 6c are correct.
665 Henry Avenue

City, town or post office, state, and ZIP code. If you have a foreign address, also complete spaces below (see instructions).
Brookings, SD, 57007

Presidential Election Campaign
Check here if you, or your spouse if filing jointly, want $3 to go to this fund. Checking a box below will not change your tax or refund. ☐ You ☐ Spouse

Foreign country name | Foreign province/state/county | Foreign postal code

Filing Status

Check only one box.

1. ☐ Single
2. ☑ Married filing jointly (even if only one had income)
3. ☐ Married filing separately. Enter spouse's SSN above and full name here. ▶
4. ☐ Head of household (with qualifying person). (See instructions.) If the qualifying person is a child but not your dependent, enter this child's name here. ▶
5. ☐ Qualifying widow(er) (see instructions)

Exemptions

6a ☑ **Yourself.** If someone can claim you as a dependent, **do not** check box 6a . . . . . .
b ☑ **Spouse** . . . .

c **Dependents:**

If more than four dependents, see instructions and check here ▶ ☐

(1) First name Last name	(2) Dependent's social security number	(3) Dependent's relationship to you	(4) ✓ if child under age 17 qualifying for child tax credit (see instructions)
Tara Hall	2 4 2 6 8 9 9 4 5	Daughter	☐
Braxton Hall	2 4 2 2 3 7 8 4 5	Son	☑
			☐
			☐

Boxes checked on 6a and 6b **2**
No. of children on 6c who:
• lived with you **2**
• did not live with you due to divorce or separation (see instructions)
Dependents on 6c not entered above
Add numbers on lines above ▶ **4**

d Total number of exemptions claimed . . . .

Income

Attach Form(s) W-2 here. Also attach Forms W-2G and 1099-R if tax was withheld.

If you did not get a W-2, see instructions.

7	Wages, salaries, tips, etc. Attach Form(s) W-2	7	130,000
8a	**Taxable** interest. Attach Schedule B if required	8a	600
b	**Tax-exempt** interest. **Do not** include on line 8a . . .	8b	300	
9a	Ordinary dividends. Attach Schedule B if required	9a	
b	Qualified dividends	9b		
10	Taxable refunds, credits, or offsets of state and local income taxes	10	
11	Alimony received	11	
12	Business income or (loss). Attach Schedule C or C-EZ	12	
13	Capital gain or (loss). Attach Schedule D if required. If not required, check here ▶ ☐	13	
14	Other gains or (losses). Attach Form 4797	14	
15a	IRA distributions . 15a	b Taxable amount . . .	15b	
16a	Pensions and annuities 16a	b Taxable amount . . .	16b	
17	Rental real estate, royalties, partnerships, S corporations, trusts, etc. Attach Schedule E	17	
18	Farm income or (loss). Attach Schedule F	18	
19	Unemployment compensation	19	
20a	Social security benefits 20a	b Taxable amount . . .	20b	
21	Other income. List type and amount	21	
22	Combine the amounts in the far right column for lines 7 through 21. This is your **total income** ▶	22	130,600

Adjusted Gross Income

23	Educator expenses	23	
24	Certain business expenses of reservists, performing artists, and fee-basis government officials. Attach Form 2106 or 2106-EZ	24	
25	Health savings account deduction. Attach Form 8889 .	25	
26	Moving expenses. Attach Form 3903	26	
27	Deductible part of self-employment tax. Attach Schedule SE .	27	
28	Self-employed SEP, SIMPLE, and qualified plans . .	28	
29	Self-employed health insurance deduction	29	
30	Penalty on early withdrawal of savings	30	
31a	Alimony paid b Recipient's SSN ▶	31a	
32	IRA deduction	32	5,000
33	Student loan interest deduction	33	
34	Reserved for future use	34	
35	Domestic production activities deduction. Attach Form 8903	35	
36	Add lines 23 through 35 . . . . ▶	36	5,000
37	Subtract line 36 from line 22. This is your **adjusted gross income** . . . . . . ▶	37	125,600

For Disclosure, Privacy Act, and Paperwork Reduction Act Notice, see separate instructions. | Cat. No. 11320B | Form **1040** (2017)

(continued)

EXHIBIT 4-11   *(continued)*

Form 1040 (2017)   Page **2**

Tax and Credits	38	Amount from line 37 (adjusted gross income)	38	125,600
	39a	Check if: ☐ **You** were born before January 2, 1953, ☐ Blind. ☐ **Spouse** was born before January 2, 1953, ☐ Blind. } Total boxes checked ▶ 39a		
	b	If your spouse itemizes on a separate return or you were a dual-status alien, check here ▶ 39b ☐		
Standard Deduction for— • People who check any box on line 39a or 39b **or** who can be claimed as a dependent, see instructions. • All others: Single or Married filing separately, $6,350 Married filing jointly or Qualifying widow(er), $12,700 Head of household, $9,350	40	**Itemized deductions** (from Schedule A) **or** your **standard deduction** (see left margin) . .	40	24,000
	41	Subtract line 40 from line 38	41	101,600
	42	**Exemptions.** If line 38 is $156,900 or less, multiply $4,050 by the number on line 6d. Otherwise, see instructions	42	
	43	**Taxable income.** Subtract line 42 from line 41. If line 42 is more than line 41, enter -0- . .	43	101,600
	44	**Tax** (see instructions). Check if any from: **a** ☐ Form(s) 8814 **b** ☐ Form 4972 **c** ☐ ____	44	14,231
	45	**Alternative minimum tax** (see instructions). Attach Form 6251	45	
	46	Excess advance premium tax credit repayment. Attach Form 8962	46	
	47	Add lines 44, 45, and 46 . . . . ▶	47	14,231
	48	Foreign tax credit. Attach Form 1116 if required	48		
	49	Credit for child and dependent care expenses. Attach Form 2441	49		
	50	Education credits from Form 8863, line 19	50		
	51	Retirement savings contributions credit. Attach Form 8880	51		
	52	Child tax credit. Attach Schedule 8812, if required . . .	52	2,500	
	53	Residential energy credit. Attach Form 5695	53		
	54	Other credits from Form: **a** ☐ 3800 **b** ☐ 8801 **c** ☐	54		
	55	Add lines 48 through 54. These are your **total credits**	55	2,500
	56	Subtract line 55 from line 47. If line 55 is more than line 47, enter -0- . . . . ▶	56	11,731
Other Taxes	57	Self-employment tax. Attach Schedule SE	57	
	58	Unreported social security and Medicare tax from Form: **a** ☐ 4137 **b** ☐ 8919 . .	58	
	59	Additional tax on IRAs, other qualified retirement plans, etc. Attach Form 5329 if required . .	59	
	60a	Household employment taxes from Schedule H	60a	
	b	First-time homebuyer credit repayment. Attach Form 5405 if required	60b	
	61	Health care: individual responsibility (see instructions) Full-year coverage ☐	61	
	62	Taxes from: **a** ☐ Form 8959 **b** ☐ Form 8960 **c** ☐ Instructions; enter code(s) ____	62	
	63	Add lines 56 through 62. This is your **total tax** . . . . ▶	63	11,731
Payments If you have a qualifying child, attach Schedule EIC.	64	Federal income tax withheld from Forms W-2 and 1099 . .	64	12,100	
	65	2017 estimated tax payments and amount applied from 2016 return	65		
	66a	**Earned income credit (EIC)**	66a		
	b	Nontaxable combat pay election 66b ____			
	67	Additional child tax credit. Attach Schedule 8812	67		
	68	American opportunity credit from Form 8863, line 8 . . .	68		
	69	Net premium tax credit. Attach Form 8962	69		
	70	Amount paid with request for extension to file	70		
	71	Excess social security and tier 1 RRTA tax withheld . . .	71		
	72	Credit for federal tax on fuels. Attach Form 4136 . . .	72		
	73	Credits from Form: **a** ☐ 2439 **b** ☐ Reserved **c** ☐ 8885 **d** ☐	73		
	74	Add lines 64, 65, 66a, and 67 through 73. These are your **total payments** . . . . ▶	74	12,100
Refund Direct deposit? See instructions.	75	If line 74 is more than line 63, subtract line 63 from line 74. This is the amount you **overpaid**	75	369
	76a	Amount of line 75 you want **refunded to you.** If Form 8888 is attached, check here . ▶ ☐	76a	369
	b	Routing number ____ ▶ **c** Type: ☐ Checking ☐ Savings		
	d	Account number ____		
	77	Amount of line 75 you want **applied to your 2018 estimated tax** ▶ 77 ____		
Amount You Owe	78	**Amount you owe.** Subtract line 74 from line 63. For details on how to pay, see instructions ▶	78	
	79	Estimated tax penalty (see instructions) . . . . 79 ____		

Third Party Designee   Do you want to allow another person to discuss this return with the IRS (see instructions)? ☐ **Yes.** Complete below.   ☐ No

Designee's name ▶   Phone no. ▶   Personal identification number (PIN) ____

Sign Here   Under penalties of perjury, I declare that I have examined this return and accompanying schedules and statements, and to the best of my knowledge and belief, they are true, correct, and accurately list all amounts and sources of income I received during the tax year. Declaration of preparer (other than taxpayer) is based on all information of which preparer has any knowledge.

Joint return? See instructions. Keep a copy for your records.

Your signature	Date	Your occupation	Daytime phone number
Spouse's signature. If a joint return, **both** must sign.	Date	Spouse's occupation	If the IRS sent you an Identity Protection PIN, enter it here (see inst.) ____

Paid Preparer Use Only

Print/Type preparer's name	Preparer's signature	Date	Check ☐ if self-employed	PTIN
Firm's name ▶			Firm's EIN ▶	
Firm's address ▶			Phone no.	

Go to *www.irs.gov/Form1040* for instructions and the latest information.   Form **1040** (2017)

CONCLUSION

Recently enacted tax law introduced changes to the individual income tax formula. This chapter presents an overview of the individual income tax formula under the new tax law and provides rules for determining who qualifies as a taxpayer's dependents and for determining a taxpayer's filing status. In the Gross Income and Exclusions chapter, we turn our attention to determining gross income. In the Individual Deductions chapter, we describe deductions available to taxpayers when computing their taxable income. In the Individual Income Tax Computation and Tax Credits chapter, we conclude our review of the individual income tax formula by determining how to compute a taxpayer's tax liability and her taxes due or tax refund.

Appendix A   Dependency Exemption Flowchart (Part I)

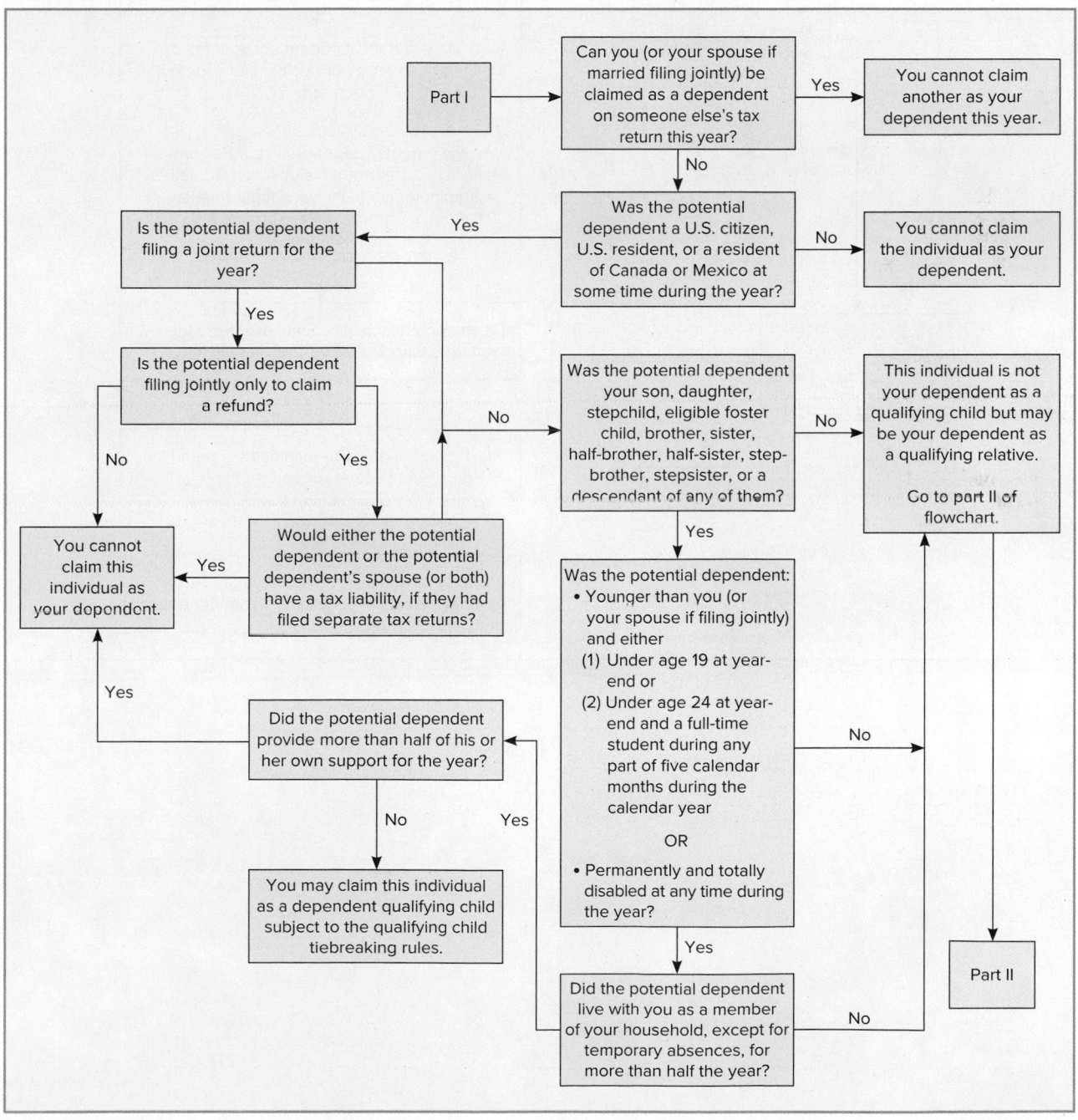

Appendix A (Part II)

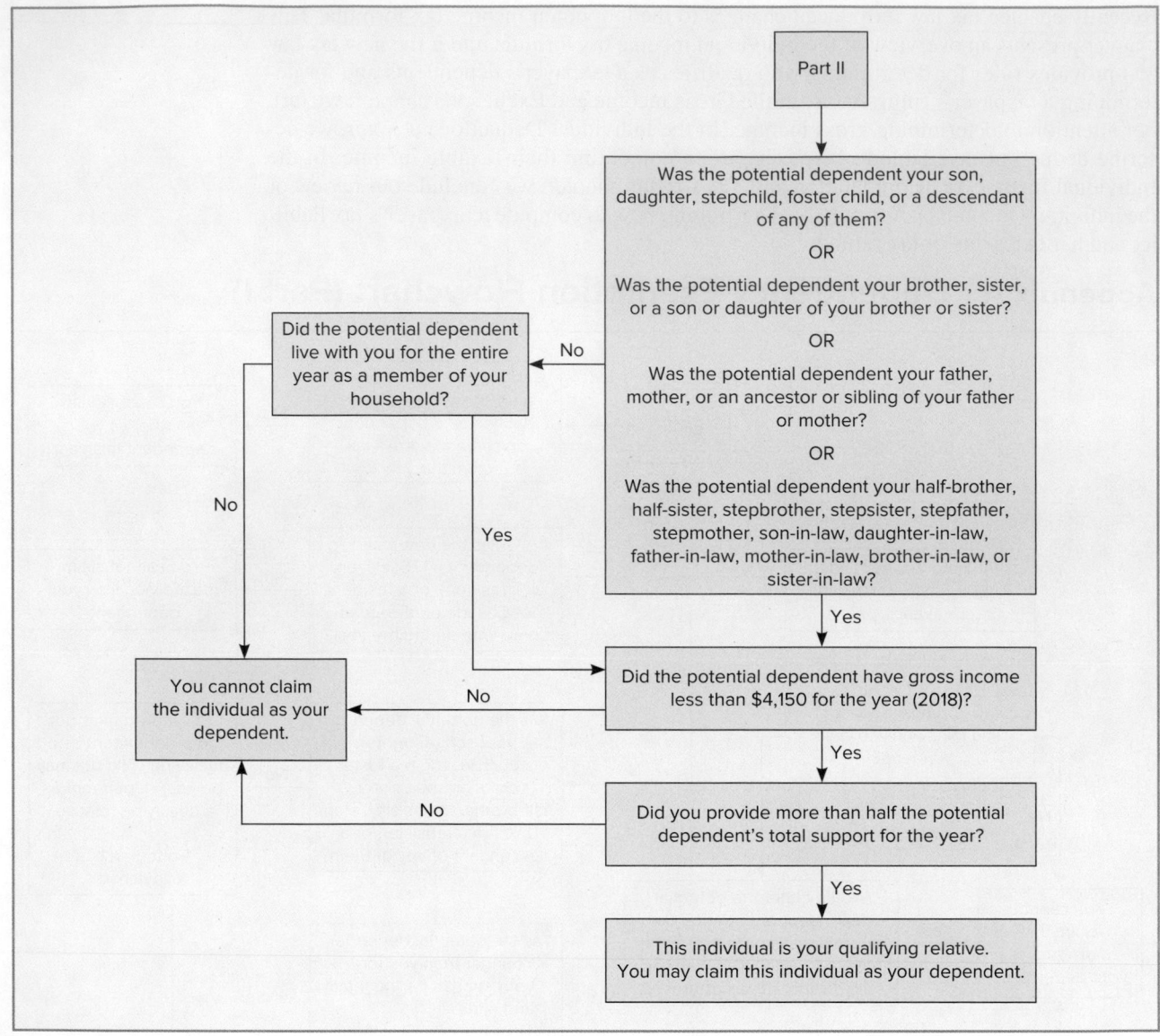

Appendix B   Qualifying Person for Head of Household Filing Status Flowchart

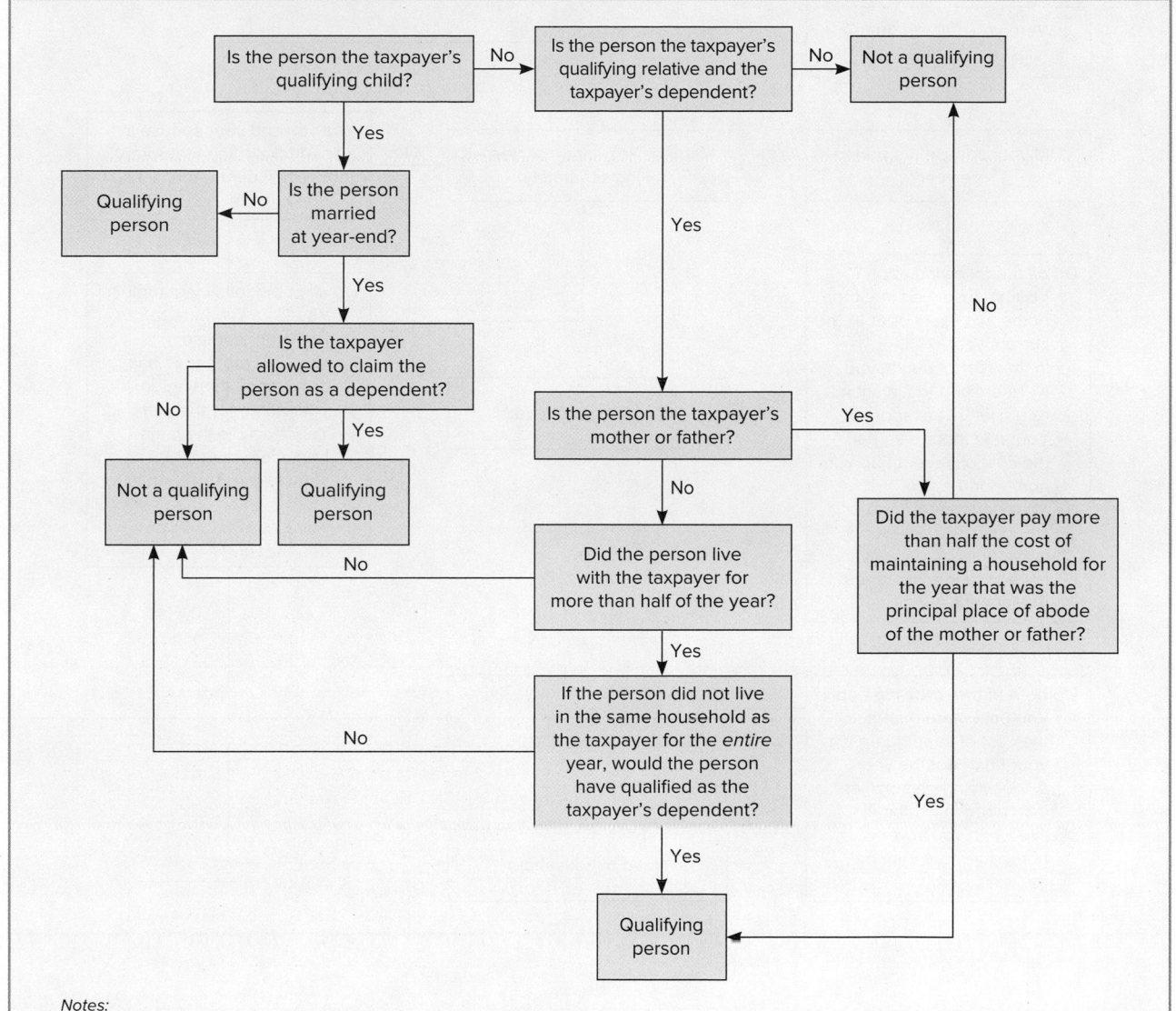

Notes:
- If a custodial parent agrees under a divorce decree to allow the noncustodial parent to claim the person as a dependent, the agreement is ignored for purposes of this test.
- If the taxpayer can claim the person as a dependent only because of a multiple support agreement, that person is not a qualifying person.
- One qualifying person may not qualify more than one person for head of household filing status.

Appendix C Determination of Filing Status Flowchart

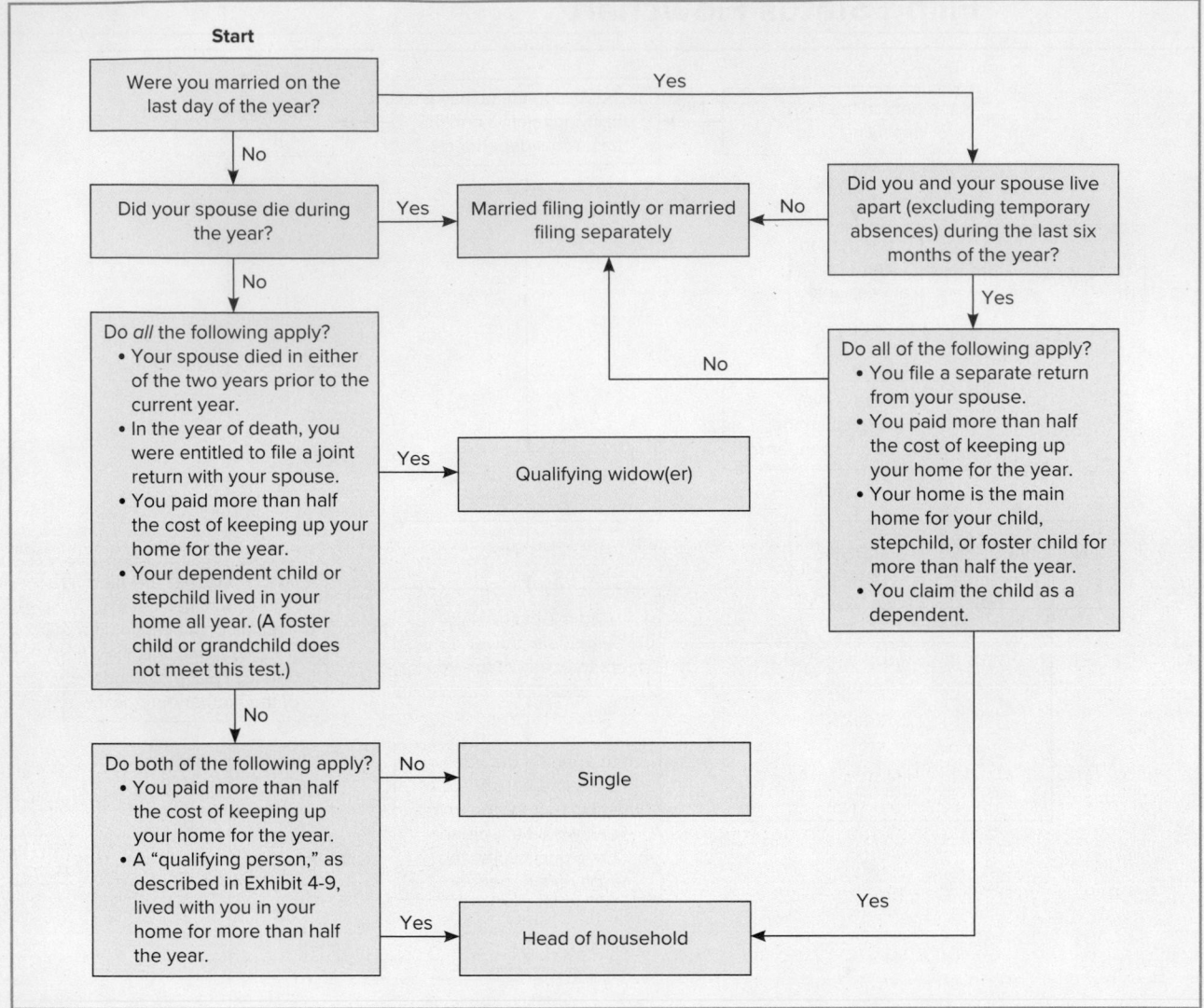

Summary

LO 4-1 Describe the formula for calculating an individual taxpayer's taxes payable or refund.

- Generally, taxpayers are taxed on all income they realize during the year, no matter the source. However, the tax laws allow taxpayers to permanently exclude or to defer to a later year certain types of income they realize during the year.
- Income items that taxpayers are allowed to permanently exclude from income are called *exclusions*. Realized income items that taxpayers are not taxed on until a future period are called *deferrals*.
- Taxpayers include gross income on their tax returns.
- The character of the income determines how the income is treated for tax purposes, including, potentially, the rate at which the income is taxed.

- Ordinary income is taxed at the rates provided in the tax rate schedules; long-term capital gains (after a netting process) and qualified dividends are taxed at a maximum rate of 0, 15, or 20 percent, depending on the taxpayer's taxable income.

- Capital gains and losses arise from the sale or disposition of capital assets. In general a capital asset is any asset other than accounts receivable from the sale of goods or services, inventory, and assets used in a trade or business. If a capital asset is owned for more than a year before it is sold, the capital gain or loss is long-term. Otherwise, it is short-term.

- Taxpayers may deduct up to $3,000 of net capital loss for the year (excess of capital losses over capital gains for the year) against ordinary income. The remainder is suspended and carried over to the next year.

- Even though a personal-use asset meets the capital asset definition, a taxpayer is not allowed to deduct a loss on the sale or disposition of a personal-use asset.

- Deductions reduce a taxpayer's taxable income. The two types of deductions are *for* AGI deductions and *from* AGI deductions.

- Gross income minus *for* AGI deductions equals adjusted gross income (AGI). *For* AGI deductions are deductions "above the line," the last line on the front page of the individual tax form, Form 1040.

- *For* AGI deductions tend to relate to business activities and certain investment activities.

- AGI minus *from* AGI deductions equals taxable income.

- *From* AGI deductions include the deduction for qualified business income and either the standard deduction or itemized deductions. *From* AGI deductions are referred to as "deductions below the line."

- AGI is an important reference point in the individual tax formula because it is often used in other tax-related calculations.

- Taxpayers generally deduct itemized deductions when the amount of the itemized deductions exceeds the standard deduction. The standard deduction varies by filing status and is indexed for inflation. Special rules may alter the standard deduction amount for certain taxpayers.

- Taxpayers are no longer allowed to deduct amounts for personal and dependency exemptions.

- Taxpayers generally calculate the tax on their taxable income by referring to tax tables or tax rate schedules.

- Taxpayers may be required to pay the alternative minimum tax (AMT), self-employment tax, the 3.8 percent net investment income tax on unearned (investment) income, and/or the .9 percent additional Medicare tax on earned income in addition to their regular income tax.

- Tax credits reduce taxpayers' tax liability dollar for dollar, while deductions decrease taxable income dollar for dollar.

- Taxpayers prepay taxes during the year through withholdings by employers, estimated tax payments, or prior-year overpayments applied toward the current-year tax liability.

- If tax prepayments exceed the taxpayer's total tax after credits, the taxpayer receives a refund. If tax prepayments are less than the total tax after credits, the taxpayer owes additional tax with his or her tax return.

Explain the requirements for determining who qualifies as a taxpayer's dependent.   **LO 4-2**

- Individuals who qualify as the dependent of another are not allowed to claim any dependents.

- Taxpayers may claim as dependents those who (1) are citizens of the United States or residents of the United States, Canada, or Mexico and (2) meet the joint tax return test, and are considered either a qualifying child or a qualifying relative of the taxpayer.

- A child must meet a relationship test, an age test, a residence test, and a support test to qualify as a qualifying child.

- A person who is not a qualifying child may be considered a qualifying relative by meeting a relationship test, a support test, and a gross income test.

LO 4-3   Determine a taxpayer's filing status.

- Taxpayers may file their tax returns as married filing jointly, married filing separately, qualifying widow or widower (also referred to as surviving spouse), single, or head of household.

- Married taxpayers may file a joint return or they may file separately. It is generally more advantageous for tax purposes to file jointly, if married. However, for nontax reasons, it may be advantageous to file separately.

- Each spouse is ultimately responsible for paying the tax on a joint return no matter who received the income.

- For two years after the year in which one spouse dies, the surviving spouse may file as a qualifying widow or widower as long as he or she (1) remains unmarried and (2) maintains a household for a dependent child (child, stepchild, or adopted child).

- Unmarried taxpayers who do not qualify for head of household status file as single taxpayers.

- An unmarried taxpayer who is not a qualifying widow or widower may file as head of household if the person pays more than half the costs of maintaining a household that is, for *more* than half the taxable year, the principal place of abode for a qualifying person (if the qualifying person is a parent, the parent need not reside with the taxpayer). In general, for an individual to be a qualifying person, the taxpayer must be able to claim the person as a dependent and the person must be considered to be related to the taxpayer even if the person does not live with the taxpayer for the entire year. That is, the taxpayer and the person must be related through a qualifying family relationship. See Exhibit 4-9 for a flow-chart for determining whether an individual is a qualifying person for purposes of determining head of household filing status.

KEY TERMS

abandoned spouse (4-24)
adjusted gross income (AGI) (4-2)
all-inclusive income concept (4-2)
alternative minimum tax (AMT) (4-11)
character of income (4-6)
deductions (4-7)
deductions above the line (4-7)
deductions below the line (4-8)
deferrals (4-5)
estimated tax payments (4-11)
exclusions (4-5)

filing status (4-19)
for AGI deductions (4-7)
from AGI deductions (4-7)
gross income (4-2)
head of household (4-21)
itemized deductions (4-8)
legislative grace (4-7)
married filing jointly (4-19)
married filing separately (4-19)
preferential tax rate (4-6)
preferentially taxed income (4-6)
qualifying child (4-12)

qualifying relative (4-12)
qualifying widow or widower (4-20)
realized income (4-2)
self-employment taxes (4-11)
single (4-21)
standard deduction (4-8)
tax credits (4-11)
taxable income (4-2)
tax rate schedule (4-10)
tax tables (4-10)
withholdings (4-11)

DISCUSSION QUESTIONS

Discussion Questions are available in Connect®.

LO 4-1   1. How are realized income, gross income, and taxable income similar, and how are they different?

LO 4-1   2. Are taxpayers required to include all realized income in gross income? Explain.

LO 4-1   3. All else being equal, should taxpayers prefer to exclude income or to defer it? Why?

LO 4-1   4. Why should a taxpayer be interested in the character of income received?

LO 4-1   5. Is it easier to describe what a capital asset is or what it is not? Explain.

6. Are all capital gains (gains on the sale or disposition of capital assets) taxed at the same rate? Explain.   `LO 4-1`

7. Are taxpayers allowed to deduct net capital losses (capital losses in excess of capital gains)? Explain.   `LO 4-1`

8. Compare and contrast *for* and *from* AGI deductions. Why are *for* AGI deductions likely more valuable to taxpayers than *from* AGI deductions?   `LO 4-1`

9. What is the difference between gross income and adjusted gross income, and what is the difference between adjusted gross income and taxable income?   `LO 4-1`

10. How do taxpayers determine whether they should deduct their itemized deductions or utilize the standard deduction?   `LO 4-1`

11. How was the income tax formula for individuals changed for 2018 by the new tax law?   `LO 4-1`

12. Why are some deductions called "above the line" deductions and others called "below the line" deductions? What is the "line"?   `LO 4-1`

13. If taxpayers are not allowed to claim deductions for dependency exemptions, is it necessary to determine who qualifies as a taxpayer's dependents? Briefly explain.   `LO 4-1`

14. What is the difference between a tax deduction and a tax credit? Is one more beneficial than the other? Explain.   `LO 4-1`

15. What types of federal income-based taxes, other than the regular income tax, might taxpayers be required to pay? In general terms, what is the tax base for each of these other taxes on income?   `LO 4-1`

16. Identify three ways taxpayers can pay their income taxes to the government.   `LO 4-1`

17. If a person meets the qualifying relative tests for a taxpayer, is that person automatically considered to be a dependent of the taxpayer?   `LO 4-1`

18. Emily and Tony are recently married college students. Can Emily qualify as her parents' dependent? Explain.   `LO 4-2`

19. Compare and contrast the relationship test requirements for a qualifying child with the relationship requirements for a qualifying relative.   `LO 4-2`

20. In general terms, what are the differences in the rules for determining who is a qualifying child and who qualifies as a dependent as a qualifying relative? Is it possible for someone to be a qualifying child and a qualifying relative of the same taxpayer? Why or why not?   `LO 4-2`

21. How do two taxpayers determine who has priority to claim a person as a dependent if the person is a qualifying child of two taxpayers when neither taxpayer is a parent of the child (assume the child does not qualify as a qualifying child for either parent)? How do parents determine who claims the child as a dependent if the child is a qualifying child of both parents when the parents are divorced or file separate tax returns?   `LO 4-2`

22. Isabella provides 30 percent of the support for her father Hastings, who lives in an apartment by himself and has no gross income. Is it possible for Isabella to claim her father as a dependent? Explain.   `LO 4-2`

23. What requirements do an abandoned spouse and a qualifying widow or widower have in common?   `LO 4-3`

24. True or False. For purposes of determining head of household filing status, the taxpayer's mother or father is considered to be a qualifying person of the taxpayer (even if the mother or father does not qualify as the taxpayer's dependent) as long as the taxpayer pays more than half the costs of maintaining the household of the mother or father. Explain.   `LO 4-3`

LO 4-3 25. Is a qualifying relative always a qualifying person for purposes of determining head of household filing status?

LO 4-3 26. For tax purposes, why is the married filing jointly tax status generally preferable to the married filing separately filing status? Why might a married taxpayer prefer *not* to file a joint return with the taxpayer's spouse?

LO 4-3 27. What does it mean to say that a married couple filing a joint tax return has joint and several liability for the taxes associated with the return?

PROBLEMS

Select problems are available in Connect®.

LO 4-1 28. Jeremy earned $100,000 in salary and $6,000 in interest income during the year. Jeremy's employer withheld $11,200 of federal income taxes from Jeremy's paychecks during the year. Jeremy has one qualifying dependent child who lives with him. Jeremy qualifies to file as head of household and has $23,000 in itemized deductions.

a) Determine Jeremy's tax refund or taxes due.

b) Assume that in addition to the original facts, Jeremy has a long-term capital gain of $4,000. What is Jeremy's tax refund or tax due including the tax on the capital gain?

c) Assume the original facts except that Jeremy had only $7,000 in itemized deductions. What is Jeremy's tax refund or tax due?

LO 4-1 29. David and Lilly Fernandez have determined their tax liability on their joint tax return to be $1,700. They have made prepayments of $1,500 and also have a child tax credit of $2,000. What is the amount of their tax refund or taxes due?

LO 4-1
planning 30. Rick, who is single, has been offered a position as a city landscape consultant. The position pays $125,000 in cash wages. Assume Rick has no dependents. Rick deducts the standard deduction instead of itemized deductions.

a) What is the amount of Rick's after-tax compensation (ignore payroll taxes)?

b) Suppose Rick receives a competing job offer of $120,000 in cash compensation and nontaxable (excluded) benefits worth $5,000. What is the amount of Rick's after-tax compensation for the competing offer? Which job should he take if taxes are the only concern?

LO 4-1
planning 31. Through November, Cameron has received gross income of $120,000. For December, Cameron is considering whether to accept one more work engagements for the year. Engagement 1 will generate $7,000 of revenue at a cost to Cameron of $3,000, which is deductible for AGI. In contrast, engagement 2 will generate $5,000 of qualified business income (QBI) which is eligible for the 20% QBI deduction. Cameron files as a single taxpayer.

a) Calculate Cameron's taxable income assuming he chooses engagement 1 and assuming he chooses engagement 2. Assume he has no itemized deductions.

b) Which engagement maximizes Cameron's after-tax cash flow? Explain.

LO 4-1
planning 32. Nitai, who is single and has no dependents, was planning on spending the weekend repairing his car. On Friday, Nitai's employer called and offered him $500 in overtime pay if he would agree to work over the weekend. Nitai could get his car repaired over the weekend at Autofix for $400. If Nitai works over the weekend, he will have to pay the $400 to have his car repaired but he will earn $500. Assume Nitai pays tax at a flat 12 percent rate.

a) Strictly considering tax factors, should Nitai work or repair his car if the $400 he must pay to have his car fixed is not deductible?

b) Strictly considering tax factors, should Nitai work or repair his car if the $400 he must pay to have his car fixed is deductible *for* AGI?

33. Rank the following three single taxpayers in order of the magnitude of taxable income (from lowest to highest) and explain your results.   `LO 4-1` `LO 4-2`

	Ahmed	Baker	Chin
Gross income	$90,000	$90,000	$90,000
Deductions *for* AGI	14,000	7,000	0
Itemized deductions	$0	$7,000	$14,000
Deduction for qualified business income	0	2,000	10,000

34. Aishwarya's husband passed away in 2017. She needs to determine whether Jasmine, her 17-year-old stepdaughter, who is single, qualifies as her dependent in 2018. Jasmine is a resident but not a citizen of the United States. She lived in Aishwarya's home from June 15 through December 31, 2018. Aishwarya provided more than half of Jasmine's support for 2018.   `LO 4-2`

a) Is Aishwarya allowed to claim Jasmine as a dependent for 2018?

b) Would Aishwarya be allowed to claim Jasmine as a dependent for 2018 if Aishwarya provided more than half of Jasmine's support in 2018, Jasmine lived in Aishwarya's home from July 15 through December 31 of 2018, and Jasmine reported gross income of $5,000 for the year?

c) Would Aishwarya be allowed to claim Jasmine as a dependent for 2018 if Aishwarya provided more than half of Jasmine's support in 2018, Jasmine lived in Aishwarya's home from July 15 through December 31 of 2018, and Jasmine reported gross income of $2,500 for the year?

35. The Samsons are trying to determine whether they can claim their 22-year-old adopted son, Jason, as a dependent. Jason is currently a full-time student at an out-of-state university. Jason lived in his parents' home for three months of the year and he was away at school for the rest of the year. He received $9,500 in scholarships this year for his outstanding academic performance and earned $4,800 of income working a part-time job during the year. The Samsons paid a total of $5,000 to support Jason while he was away at college. Jason used the scholarship, the earnings from the part-time job, and the money from the Samsons as his only sources of support.   `LO 4-2`

a) Can the Samsons claim Jason as their dependent?

b) Assume the original facts except that Jason's grandparents, not the Samsons, provided him with the $5,000 worth of support. Can the Samsons (Jason's parents) claim Jason as their dependent? Why or why not?

c) Assume the original facts except substitute Jason's grandparents for his parents. Determine whether Jason's grandparents can claim Jason as a dependent.

d) Assume the original facts except that Jason earned $5,500 while working part-time and used this amount for his support. Can the Samsons claim Jason as their dependent? Why or why not?

36. John and Tara Smith are married and have lived in the same home for over 20 years. John's uncle Tim, who is 64 years old, has lived with the Smiths since March of this year. Tim is searching for employment but has been unable to find any—his gross income for the year is $2,000. Tim used all $2,000 toward his own support. The Smiths provided the rest of Tim's support by providing him with lodging valued at $5,000 and food valued at $2,200.   `LO 4-2`

a) Are the Smiths able to claim Tim as a dependent?

b) Assume the original facts except that Tim earned $10,000 and used all the funds for his own support. Are the Smiths able to claim Tim as a dependent?

     c) Assume the original facts except that Tim is a friend of the family and not John's uncle.

     d) Assume the original facts except that Tim is a friend of the family and not John's uncle and Tim lived with the Smiths for the entire year.

LO 4-2

37. Francine's mother Donna and her father Darren separated and divorced in September of this year. Francine lived with both parents until the separation. Francine does *not* provide more than half of her own support. Francine is 15 years old at the end of the year.

     a) Is Francine a qualifying child to Donna?

     b) Is Francine a qualifying child to Darren?

     c) Assume Francine spends more time living with Darren than Donna after the separation. Who may claim Francine as a dependent?

     d) Assume Francine spends an equal number of days with her mother and her father and that Donna has AGI of $52,000 and Darren has AGI of $50,000. Who may claim Francine as a dependent?

LO 4-2

38. Jamel and Jennifer have been married 30 years and have filed a joint return every year of their marriage. Their three daughters, Jade, Lindsay, and Abbi, are ages 12, 17, and 22, respectively, and all live at home. None of the daughters provides more than half of her own support. Abbi is a full-time student at a local university and does not have any gross income.

     a) Which, if any, of the daughters qualify as dependents of Jamel and Jennifer?

     b) Assume the original facts except that Abbi is married. She and her husband live with Jamel and Jennifer while attending school and they file a joint return. Abbi and her husband reported a $1,000 tax liability on their tax return. If all parties are willing, can Jamel and Jennifer claim Abbi as a dependent on their tax return? Why or why not?

     c) Assume the same facts as part (b), except that Abbi and her husband report a $0 tax liability on their joint tax return. Also, if the couple had filed separately, Abbi would not have had a tax liability on her return but her husband would have had a $250 tax liability on his separate return. Can Jamel and Jennifer claim Abbi as a dependent on their tax return? Why or why not?

     d) Assume the original facts except that Abbi is married. Abbi files a separate tax return. Abbi's husband files a separate tax return and reports a $250 tax liability on the return. Can Jamel and Jennifer claim Abbi as a dependent?

LO 4-2 **LO 4-3**

39. Dean Kastner is 78 years old and lives by himself in an apartment in Chicago. Dean's gross income for the year is $2,500. Dean's support is provided as follows: Himself (5 percent), his daughters Camille (25 percent) and Rachel (30 percent), his son Zander (5 percent), his friend Frankie (15 percent), and his niece Sharon (20 percent).

     a) Absent a multiple support agreement, of the parties mentioned in the problem, who may claim Dean as a dependent?

     b) Under a multiple support agreement, who is eligible to claim Dean as a dependent? Explain.

     c) Assume that Camille is allowed to claim Dean as a dependent under a multiple support agreement. Camille is single, and Dean is her only dependent. What is Camille's filing status?

LO 4-2

research

40. Mel and Cindy Gibson's 12-year-old daughter Rachel was abducted on her way home from school on March 15, 2018. Police reports indicated that a stranger had physically dragged Rachel into a waiting car and sped away. Everyone hoped that the kidnapper and Rachel would be located quickly. However, as of the end of the year, Rachel was still missing. The police were still pursuing several promising

leads and had every reason to believe that Rachel was still alive. In 2019, Rachel was returned safely to her parents.

a) Are the Gibsons allowed to claim Rachel as a dependent for 2018 even though she only lived in the Gibsons' home for two-and-one-half months? Explain and cite your authority.

b) Assume the original facts except that Rachel is unrelated to the Gibsons but she has been living with them since January 2013. The Gibsons have claimed Rachel as a dependent for the years 2013 through 2017. Are the Gibsons allowed to claim Rachel as a dependent for 2018? Explain and cite your authority.

41. Kimberly is divorced and the custodial parent of a three-year-old girl named Bailey. Kimberly and Bailey live with Kimberly's parents, who pay all the costs of maintaining the household (such as mortgage, property taxes, and food). Kimberly pays for Bailey's clothing, entertainment, and health insurance costs. These costs comprised only a small part of the total costs of maintaining the household. Kimberly does not qualify as her parents' dependent.   `LO 4-2` `LO 4-3`

a) Determine the appropriate filing status for Kimberly.

b) What if Kimberly lived in her own home and provided all the costs of maintaining the household?

42. Lee is 30 years old and single. Lee paid all the costs of maintaining his household for the entire year. Determine Lee's filing status in each of the following alternative situations: `LO 4-2` `LO 4-3`

a) Lee is Ashton's uncle. Ashton is 15 years old and has gross income of $5,000. Ashton lived in Lee's home from April 1 through the end of the year.

b) Lee is Ashton's uncle. Ashton is 20 years old, not a full-time student, and has gross income of $7,000. Ashton lived in Lee's home from April 1 through the end of the year.

c) Lee is Ashton's uncle. Ashton is 22 years old and was a full-time student from January through April. Ashton's gross income was $5,000. Ashton lived in Lee's home from April 1 through the end of the year.

d) Lee is Ashton's cousin. Ashton is 18 years old, has gross income of $3,000, and is not a full-time student. Ashton lived in Lee's home from April 1 through the end of the year.

e) Lee and Ashton are cousins. Ashton is 18 years old, has gross income of $3,000, and is not a full-time student. Ashton lived in Lee's home for the entire year.

43. Ray Albertson is 72 years old and lives by himself in an apartment in Salt Lake City. Ray's gross income for the year is $3,000. Ray's support is provided as follows: himself (9 percent), his daughters Diane (20 percent) and Karen (15 percent), his sons Mike (20 percent) and Kenneth (10 percent), his friend Milt (14 percent), and his cousin Henry (12 percent).   `LO 4-2` `LO 4-3`

a) Absent a multiple support agreement, of the parties mentioned in the problem, who may claim Ray as a dependent?

b) Under a multiple support agreement, who is eligible to claim Ray as a dependent? Explain.

c) Assume that under a multiple support agreement, Diane claims Ray as a dependent. Diane is single with no other dependents. What is her filing status?

44. Juan and Bonita are married and have two dependent children living at home. This year, Juan is killed in an avalanche while skiing.   `LO 4-3`

a) What is Bonita's filing status this year?

b) Assuming Bonita doesn't remarry and still has two dependent children living at home, what will her filing status be next year?

c) Assuming Bonita doesn't remarry and doesn't have any dependents next year, what will her filing status be next year?

LO 4-3   45. Gary and Lakesha were married on December 31 last year. They are now preparing their taxes for the April 15 deadline and are unsure of their filing status.

   a) What filing status options do Gary and Lakesha have for last year?

   b) Assume instead that Gary and Lakesha were married on January 1 of this year. What is their filing status for last year (neither has been married before and neither had any dependents last year)?

LO 4-3   46. Elroy, who is single, has taken over the care of his mother Irene in her old age. Elroy pays the bills relating to Irene's home. He also buys all her groceries and provides the rest of her support. Irene has no gross income.

   a) What is Elroy's filing status?

   b) Assume the original facts except that Elroy has taken over the care of his grandmother, Renae, instead of his mother. What is Elroy's filing status?

   c) Assume the original facts except that Elroy's mother, Irene, lives with him and receives an annual $5,700 taxable distribution from her retirement account. Elroy still pays all the costs to maintain the household. What is his filing status?

LO 4-3   47. Kano and his wife, Hoshi, have been married for 10 years and have two children under the age of 12. The couple has been living apart for the last two years and both children live with Kano. Kano has provided all the means necessary to support himself and his children. Kano and Hoshi do not file a joint return.

   a) What is Kano's filing status?

   b) Assume the original facts except that Kano and Hoshi separated in May of the current year. What is Kano's filing status?

   c) Assume the original facts except that Kano and Hoshi separated in November of this year. What is Kano's filing status?

   d) Assume the original facts except that Kano's parents, not Kano, paid more than half of the cost of maintaining the home in which Kano and his children live. What is Kano's filing status?

LO 4-3   48. Horatio and Kelly were divorced at the end of last year. Neither Horatio nor Kelly re-married during the current year and Horatio moved out of state. Determine the filing status of Horatio and Kelly for the current year in the following independent situations:

   a) Horatio and Kelly did not have any children and neither reported any dependents in the current year.

   b) Horatio and Kelly had one child, Amy, who turned 10 years of age in the current year. Amy lived with Kelly for all of the current year and Kelly provided all of her support.

   c) Assume the same facts as in part (b) but Kelly allowed Horatio to claim Amy as a dependent under the divorce decree even though Amy did not reside with Horatio at all during the current year.

   d) Assume the original facts except that during the current year Madison, a 17-year-old friend of the family, lived with Kelly (for the entire year) and was fully supported by Kelly.

   e) Assume the original facts except that during the current year Kelly's mother, Janet, lived with Kelly. For the current year, Kelly was able to claim Janet as a dependent under a multiple support agreement.

LO 4-2 **LO 4-3**   49. In each of the following *independent* situations, determine the taxpayer's filing status and the number of dependents the taxpayer is allowed to claim.

   a) Frank is single and supports his 17-year-old brother, Bill. Bill earned $3,000 and did not live with Frank.

   b) Geneva and her spouse reside with their son, Steve, who is a 20-year-old under-graduate student at State University. Steve earned $13,100 at a part-time summer job, but he deposited this money in a savings account for graduate school. Geneva paid all of the $12,000 cost of supporting Steve.

c) Hamish's spouse died last year and Hamish has not remarried. Hamish supports his father, Reggie, age 78, who lives in a nursing home and had interest income this year of $2,500.

d) Irene is married but has not seen her spouse since February. She supports her spouse's 18-year-old child, Dolores, who lives with Irene. Dolores earned $4,500 this year.

c) Assume the same facts as in part (d). Also, assume that Craig is Irene's husband. Craig supports his 12-year-old son Ethan, who lives with Craig. Ethan did not earn any income.

50. In each of the following *independent* cases, determine the taxpayer's filing status and the number of dependents the taxpayer is allowed to claim.   **LO 4-2**   **LO 4-3**

a) Alexandra is a blind widow (her spouse died five years ago) who provides a home for her 18-year-old nephew, Newt. Newt's parents are dead and so Newt supports himself. Newt's gross income is $5,000.

b) Bharati supports and maintains a home for her daughter, Daru, and son-in-law, Sam. Sam earned $15,000 and filed a joint return with Daru, who had no income.

c) Charlie intended to file a joint return with his spouse, Sally. However, Sally died in December. Charlie has not remarried.

d) Deshi cannot convince his spouse to consent to signing a joint return. The couple has not separated.

e) Edith and her spouse support their 35-year-old son, Slim. Slim is a full-time college student who earned $5,500 over the summer in part-time work.

51. Jasper and Crewella Dahvill were married in year 0. They filed joint tax returns in years 1 and 2. In year 3, their relationship was strained and Jasper insisted on filing a separate tax return. In year 4, the couple divorced. Both Jasper and Crewella filed single tax returns in year 4. In year 5, the IRS audited the couple's joint year 2 tax return and each spouse's separate year 3 tax returns. The IRS determined that the year 2 joint return and Crewella's separate year 3 tax return understated Crewella's self-employment income, causing the joint return year 2 tax liability to be understated by $4,000 and Crewella's year 3 separate return tax liability to be understated by $6,000. The IRS also assessed penalties and interest on both of these tax returns. Try as it might, the IRS has not been able to locate Crewella, but they have been able to find Jasper.   **LO 4-3**

a) What amount of tax can the IRS require Jasper to pay for the Dahvill's year 2 joint return? Explain.

b) What amount of tax can the IRS require Jasper to pay for Crewella's year 3 separate tax return? Explain.

52. Janice Traylor is single. She has an 18-year-old son named Marty. Marty is Janice's only child. Marty has lived with Janice his entire life. However, Marty recently joined the Marines and was sent on a special assignment to Australia. During the current year, Marty spent nine months in Australia. Marty was extremely homesick while in Australia, since he had never lived away from home. However, Marty knew this assignment was only temporary, and he couldn't wait to come home and find his room just the way he left it. Janice has always filed as head of household, and Marty has always been considered a qualifying child (and he continues to meet all the tests with the possible exception of the residence test due to his stay in Australia). However, this year Janice is unsure whether she qualifies as head of household due to Marty's nine-month absence during the year. Janice has come to you for advice on whether she qualifies for head of household filing status. What do you tell her?   **LO 4-3**   **research**

53. Doug Jones submitted his 2018 tax return on time and elected to file a joint tax return with his wife, Darlene. Doug and Darlene did not request an extension for their 2018 tax return. Doug and Darlene owed and paid the IRS $124,000 for their 2018 tax year. Two years later, Doug amended his return and claimed married filing   **LO 4-3**   **research**

separate status. By changing his filing status, Doug sought a refund for an overpayment for the tax year 2018 (he paid more tax in the original joint return than he owed on a separate return). Is Doug allowed to change his filing status for the 2018 tax year and receive a tax refund with his amended return?

COMPREHENSIVE PROBLEMS

Select problems are available in Connect®.

tax forms

54. Marc and Michelle are married and earned salaries this year of $64,000 and $12,000, respectively. In addition to their salaries, they received interest of $350 from municipal bonds and $500 from corporate bonds. Marc contributed $2,500 to an individual retirement account, and Marc paid alimony to a prior spouse in the amount of $1,500. Marc and Michelle have a 10-year-old son, Matthew, who lived with them throughout the entire year. Thus, Marc and Michelle are allowed to claim a $2,000 child tax credit for Matthew. Marc and Michelle paid $6,000 of expenditures that qualify as itemized deductions and they had a total of $5,500 in federal income taxes withheld from their paychecks during the course of the year.

a) What is Marc and Michelle's gross income?

b) What is Marc and Michelle's adjusted gross income?

c) What is the total amount of Marc and Michelle's deductions *from* AGI?

d) What is Marc and Michelle's taxable income?

e) What is Marc and Michelle's taxes payable or refund due for the year? (Use the tax rate schedules.)

f) Complete the first two pages of Marc and Michelle's Form 1040 (use the most recent form available).

tax forms

55. Demarco and Janine Jackson have been married for 20 years and have four children who qualify as their dependents (Damarcus, Janine, Michael, and Candice). The couple received salary income of $100,000, qualified business income of $10,000 from an investment in a partnership, and they sold their home this year. They initially purchased the home three years ago for $200,000 and they sold it for $250,000. The gain on the sale qualified for the exclusion from the sale of a principal residence. The Jacksons incurred $16,500 of itemized deductions, and they had $3,550 withheld from their paychecks for federal taxes. They are also allowed to claim a child tax credit for each of their children. However, because Candice is 18 years of age, the Jacksons may claim a child tax credit for other qualifying dependents for Candice.

a) What is the Jacksons' taxable income, and what is their tax liability or (refund)?

b) Complete the first two pages of the Jacksons' Form 1040 (use the most recent form available).

c) What would their taxable income be if their itemized deductions totaled $28,000 instead of $16,500?

d) What would their taxable income be if they had $0 itemized deductions and $6,000 of *for* AGI deductions?

e) Assume the original facts but now suppose the Jacksons also incurred a loss of $5,000 on the sale of some of their investment assets. What effect does the $5,000 loss have on their *taxable income*?

f) Assume the original facts but now suppose the Jacksons own investments that appreciated by $10,000 during the year. The Jacksons believe the investments will continue to appreciate, so they did not sell the investments during this year. What is the Jacksons' taxable income?

56. Camille Sikorski was divorced last year. She currently provides a home for her 15-year-old daughter Kaly. Kaly lived in Camille's home for the entire year, and Camille paid for all the costs of maintaining the home. She received a salary of $105,000 and contributed $6,000 of it to a qualified retirement account (a *for* AGI deduction). She also received $10,000 of alimony from her former husband. Finally, Camille paid $15,000 of expenditures that qualified as itemized deductions.

   a) What is Camille's taxable income?

   b) What would Camille's taxable income be if she incurred $24,000 of itemized deductions instead of $15,000?

   c) Assume the original facts but now suppose Camille's daughter, Kaly, is 25 years old and a full-time student. Kaly's gross income for the year was $5,000. Kaly provided $3,000 of her own support, and Camille provided $5,000 of support. What is Camille's taxable income?

57. Tiffany is unmarried and has a 15-year-old qualifying child. Tiffany has determined her tax liability to be $3,525, and her employer has withheld $1,500 of federal taxes from her paycheck. Tiffany is allowed to claim a $2,000 child tax credit for her qualifying child. What amount of taxes will Tiffany owe (or what amount will she receive as a refund) when she files her tax return?

ROGER | *CPA Review*

Sample CPA Exam questions from Roger CPA Review are available in Connect as support for the topics in this text. These Multiple Choice Questions and Task-Based Simulations include expert-written explanations and solutions and provide a starting point for students to become familiar with the content and functionality of the actual CPA Exam.

chapter

5

Gross Income and Exclusions

Learning Objectives

Upon completing this chapter, you should be able to:

LO 5-1 Apply the concept of realization.

LO 5-2 Discuss the distinctions between the various sources of income, including income from services and property.

LO 5-3 Apply basic income exclusion provisions to compute gross income.

©Image Source

The past year was a year of change for Courtney Wilson. After her divorce from Al Wilson, Courtney assumed sole custody of their 10-year-old son, Deron, and their 20-year-old daughter, Ellen. Looking for a fresh start in January, Courtney quit her job as an architect in Cincinnati, Ohio, and moved to Kansas City, Missouri. Courtney wanted to pursue several promising job opportunities in Kansas City and be close to Ellen while she attends the University of Missouri–Kansas City. Courtney's 70-year-old mother "Gram" also lives in Kansas City and is in relatively good health. However, Courtney's father, "Gramps," passed away last December from cancer. At Courtney's insistence, Gram moved in with Courtney and Deron in April.

In late April, Courtney broke her wrist in a mountain biking accident and was unable to work for two weeks. Thankfully, Courtney's disability insurance paid her for lost wages during her time away from work.

While her personal life has been in disarray, Courtney's financial prospects have been improving. Shortly after arriving in Kansas City, Courtney was fortunate to land a job as an architect

with Earth Wise Design (EWD). EWD provided Courtney the following compensation and benefits this year:

- Salary $118,000.
- Medical and life insurance premiums.
- Contribution of 10 percent of her base salary to her qualified retirement account.
- No-interest loan with a promise to forgive the loan principal over time if she continues her employment with EWD.
- Performance bonus for her first year on the job.

Courtney also received other payments unrelated to her employment with EWD as follows:

- Alimony from her ex-husband, Al.
- Child support from her ex-husband, Al.
- Consulting income.
- Dividend, interest, and rental income.
- Refund of state taxes she paid last year.

Before Gram moved in with Courtney, she lived alone in an apartment in Kansas City. After Gramps died, Gram was dependent on her Social Security

Storyline Summary

Taxpayers:	Courtney Wilson, age 40 Courtney's mother, Dorothy "Gram" Weiss, age 70
Family description:	Courtney is divorced with a son, Deron, age 10, and a daughter, Ellen, age 20. Gram is currently residing with Courtney.
Location:	Kansas City, Missouri
Employment status:	Courtney works as an architect for EWD. Her salary is $118,000. Gram is unemployed.
Current situation:	Determining what income is taxable.

benefits. In early April, Gram received the proceeds from Gramps's life insurance policy. She invested part of the proceeds in an annuity contract that will pay Gram a fixed amount per year. Gram also invested some of the proceeds in the stock of a local corporation. She used the rest of the life insurance proceeds to purchase a certificate of deposit and start a savings account. Gram also spent some of her spare time completing sweepstakes entries. Her hard work paid off when she won a WaveRunner in a sweepstakes contest.

Until their divorce, Courtney's husband always prepared their income tax return. Since EWD hired her, Courtney has become anxious about her income tax and whether her withholding will be sufficient to cover her tax bill. Courtney is also worried about Gram's tax situation, because Gram did not make any tax payments this year. ■

In the previous chapter, we presented an overview of individual taxation. In this chapter, we begin to dig deeper into the tax formula to determine a taxpayer's gross income. We focus on whether income is included or excluded from a taxpayer's gross income rather than the rate at which the income is taxed. In the next three chapters, we continue to work through the individual tax formula to determine the tax liabilities for Courtney and Gram. The Individual Deductions chapter describes deductible expenses to determine adjusted gross income and taxable income, the Investments chapter discusses the taxation of investments, and the Individual Income Tax Computation and Tax Credits chapter addresses issues associated with calculating the tax liability, tax credits, and tax return filing concerns.

LO 5-1 REALIZATION AND RECOGNITION OF INCOME

As we learned in the previous chapter, **gross income** is income that taxpayers realize, recognize, and report on their tax returns for the year. In the previous chapter, we discussed gross income in general terms. In this chapter we explain the requirements for taxpayers to recognize gross income, and we discuss the most common sources of gross income.

What Is Included in Gross Income?

The definition of gross income for tax purposes is provided in §61(a) as follows:

> GENERAL DEFINITION.—Except as otherwise provided in this subtitle, gross income means all income *from whatever source derived* (emphasis added).

In addition to providing this all-inclusive definition of income, §61 includes a list of examples of gross income such as compensation for services, business income, rents, royalties, interest, and dividends. However, it is clear that unless a tax provision says otherwise, gross income includes *all* income. Thus, gross income is *broadly* defined. Reg. §1.61-(a) provides further insight into the definition of gross income as follows:

> Gross income means all income from whatever source derived, unless excluded by law. Gross income includes income realized in any form, whether in money, property, or services.

Based on §61(a), Reg. §1.61-(a), and various judicial rulings, taxpayers *recognize* gross income when (1) they receive an economic benefit, (2) they realize the income, *and* (3) no tax provision allows them to exclude or defer the income from gross income for that year.[1] Let's address each of these three requirements for recognizing gross income.

Economic Benefit Taxpayers must receive an economic benefit (i.e., receive an item of value) to have gross income. Common examples of economic benefit include compensation for services (compensation in the form of cash, other property, or even services received), proceeds from property sales (typically cash, property, or debt relief), and income from investments or business activities (such as business income, rents, interest, and dividends). How about when a taxpayer borrows money? Is the economic benefit criterion met? No, because when a taxpayer borrows money, the economic benefit received (the cash received) is completely offset by the liability the taxpayer is required to pay in return for borrowing the funds (the debt amount plus interest).

Realization Principle As indicated in Reg. §1.61-(a), the tax definition of income adopts the **realization principle.** Under this principle, income is realized when (1) a taxpayer engages in a transaction with another party, and (2) the transaction results in a measurable change in property rights. In other words, assets or services are exchanged for cash, claims to cash, or other assets with determinable value.

The concept of realization for tax purposes closely parallels the concept of realization for financial accounting purposes. Requiring a transaction to trigger realization reduces the uncertainty associated with determining the *amount* of income, because a change in rights can typically be traced to a specific moment in time and is generally accompanied by legal documentation.

Example 5-1

In April, Gram used part of the life insurance proceeds she received from Gramps's death to purchase 50 shares in Acme Corporation for $30 per share. From April to the end of December, the value of the shares fluctuated between $40 and $25, but on December 31, the shares were worth $35. If Gram does *not* sell the shares, how much income from her stockholdings in Acme Corporation does she *realize* for the year?

Answer: $0. Unless Gram sells the stock, she does not enter into a transaction resulting in a measurable change of property rights with a second party. Thus, she does not realize income even though she experienced an economic benefit from the appreciation of the stock from $30 per share to $35 per share.

Adopting the realization principle for defining gross income provides two major advantages. First, because parties to the transaction must agree to the value of the exchanged property rights, the transaction allows the income to be measured objectively. Second, the transaction often provides the taxpayer with the **wherewithal to pay** taxes (at least when the taxpayer receives cash in the transaction). That is, the transaction itself provides the taxpayer with the funds to pay taxes on income generated by the transaction. Thus, it reduces the possibility that the taxpayer will be required to sell other assets to pay the taxes on the income from the transaction. Note, however, that when taxpayers receive property or services in a transaction (instead of cash), realization has also occurred (despite the absence of wherewithal to pay).

---

[1]For tax purposes it matters not whether income is obtained through legal or illegal activities (e.g., embezzlement). See *Eugene James v. U.S.* (1961, S. Ct.), 7 AFTR 2d 1361.

Recognition   Taxpayers who realize an economic benefit must include the benefit in gross income unless a specific provision of the tax code says otherwise. That is, taxpayers are generally required to *recognize* all realized income by reporting it as gross income on their tax returns. However, as we describe later in this chapter, through exclusions Congress allows taxpayers to permanently exclude certain types of income from gross income and through deferrals it allows taxpayers to defer certain types of income from gross income until a subsequent year. Thus, it is important to distinguish between realized and recognized income.

Other Income Concepts

The tax laws, administrative authority, and judicial rulings have established several other concepts important for determining an individual's gross income.

Form of Receipt   A common misperception is that taxpayers must receive cash to realize and recognize gross income. However, Reg. §1.61-(a) indicates that taxpayers realize income whether they receive money, property, *or* services in a transaction. For example, **barter clubs** facilitate the exchange of rights to goods and services between members, many of whom have the mistaken belief that they need not recognize income on the exchanges. However, when members exchange property, they realize and recognize income at the market price, the amount that outsiders are willing to pay for the goods or services. Also, other taxpayers who exchange or trade goods or services with each other must recognize the value of the goods or services as income, even when they do not receive any cash. Indeed, taxpayers have the legal and ethical responsibility to report realized income (assuming no exclusion provision applies) no matter the form of its receipt or whether the IRS knows the taxpayer received the income.

Example 5-2

What if: Suppose during March, Gram paid no rent to her neighbor (also her landlord). Although the neighbor typically charges $350 per month for rent, he allowed Gram to live rent-free in exchange for babysitting his infant son. What income would Gram and Gram's neighbor realize and recognize on this exchange?

Answer: $350. Gram and the neighbor each would recognize $350 of income for March. The neighbor recognizes $350 of rental receipts because this is the value of the babysitting services the neighbor received in lieu of a cash payment for rent from Gram (an economic benefit the neighbor realized through the exchange). Gram recognizes $350 of babysitting income, because this is the value of the services provided to her neighbor (an economic benefit was realized because Gram was not required to pay rent).

Return of Capital Principle   When taxpayers sell assets, they must determine the extent to which they include the sale proceeds in gross income. Initially, the IRS was convinced that Congress's all-inclusive definition of income required taxpayers to include *all* sale proceeds in gross income. Taxpayers, on the other hand, argued that a portion of proceeds from a sale represented a return of the cost or capital investment in the underlying property, called **tax basis.** The courts determined that when receiving a payment for property, taxpayers are allowed to recover the cost of the property tax-free. Consequently, when taxpayers sell property, they are allowed to reduce the sale proceeds by their unrecovered investment in the property to determine the realized gain from the sale.[2] When

---

[2]§1001(a).

the tax basis exceeds the sale proceeds, the **return of capital** principle generally applies to the extent of the sale proceeds. The excess of basis over sale proceeds is generally not considered to be a return of capital, but rather a loss that is deductible only if specifically authorized by the tax code. Below, we revisit the return of capital principle when we discuss asset dispositions.

The return of capital principle gets complicated when taxpayers sell assets and collect the sale proceeds over several periods. In these cases, the principle is usually modified by law to provide that the return of capital occurs pro rata as the proceeds are collected over time. We discuss this issue in more detail later in this chapter when we discuss the taxation of annuities.

Recovery of Amounts Previously Deducted A refund is not typically included in gross income because it usually represents a return of capital. For example, a refund of $1,000 on an auto purchased for $12,000 simply reduces the net cost of the vehicle to $11,000. Likewise, a $200 refund of a $700 business expense is not included in gross income but instead reduces the net expense to $500. However, if the refund is made for an expenditure deducted in a *previous* year, then under the **tax benefit rule** the refund is included in gross income to the extent that the prior deduction produced a tax benefit.[3] For example, suppose an individual paid a $1,000 business expense claimed as a *for* AGI deduction in 2017, but $250 of the expense was subsequently reimbursed in 2018. Because the $250 business deduction produced a tax benefit in 2017 (reduced taxable income), the $250 refund in 2018 would be included in income.

The application of the tax benefit rule is more complex for individuals who itemize deductions. An itemized deduction produces a tax benefit only to the extent that total itemized deductions exceed the standard deduction. For example, suppose an individual's total itemized deductions exceeded the standard deduction by $100. A refund of $150 of itemized deductions would cause the individual's itemized deductions to fall $50 beneath the standard deduction. If the refund occurred in the same year as the expense, the individual would have elected the standard deduction, and the refund would have caused taxable income to increase by only $100 (because of the difference between claiming the standard deduction and using the total itemized deductions that would have been claimed in the absence of any refund). If the refund occurs the year after the deduction is claimed, then only $100 of the $150 refund would be included in gross income under the tax benefit rule. The $100 is added to taxable income in the year of the refund, because this is the increment in taxable income that would have resulted if the refund had been issued in the year the itemized deduction was claimed.

Example 5-3

In 2017 Courtney paid $3,500 in Ohio state income taxes, and she included this payment with her other itemized deductions when she filed her federal income tax return in March of 2018. Courtney filed her 2017 federal return as a head of household and claimed $15,600 of itemized deductions. She also filed an Ohio state income tax return in March of 2018 and discovered she only owed $3,080 in Ohio income tax for 2017. Hence, Courtney received a $420 refund of her Ohio income tax in June of 2018. How much of the $420 refund, if any, is Courtney required to include in her gross income in 2018? The answer depends upon the standard deduction for 2017. Help Courtney apply the tax benefit rule (the standard deduction for head of household filing status in 2017 was $9,350).

(continued on page 5-6)

[3]§111.

Answer: All $420. Courtney is required to include the entire refund in her 2018 gross income because her itemized deduction for the $420 of state income taxes that she overpaid last year reduced her taxable income by $420. Accordingly, because she received a tax benefit (deduction) for the entire $420 overpayment, she must include it all in gross income in 2018. See the following for the calculation of the amount of tax benefit Courtney received from the $420 overpayment of taxes in 2017.

Deduction	Amount	Explanation
(1) Itemized deductions	$15,600	
(2) 2017 standard deduction	9,350	Head of household filing status
(3) Reduction in taxable income	15,600	Greater of (1) and (2)
(4) Itemized deductions adjusted for the $420 refund	15,180	(1) – $420
(5) Reduction in taxable income after adjustment for the $420 refund	15,180	Greater of (2) and (4)
Tax benefit due to prior deduction or $420 refund	**$ 420**	(3) – (5)

What if: Let's consider *alternative* fact patterns provided in Scenarios A and B to further illustrate the application of the tax benefit rule.

Scenario A: In 2017 Courtney's itemized deductions, including $3,500 in state taxes, were $5,500.

Scenario B: In 2017 Courtney's itemized deductions, including $3,500 in state taxes, were $9,550.

How much of the $420 refund would Courtney include in her 2018 gross income in Scenarios A and B?

Answer Scenario A: $0. As computed below, Courtney received $0 tax benefit from the $420 tax overpayment in 2017, so she need not include any of the refund in her gross income.

Answer Scenario B: $200. As computed below, Courtney received a $200 tax benefit (reduction in taxable income) from the $420 state tax overpayment in 2017, so she must include $200 of the refund in her 2018 gross income.

Deduction	Scenario A Amount	Scenario B Amount	Explanation
(1) Itemized deductions	$5,500	$9,550	
(2) 2017 standard deduction	9,350	9,350	Head of household filing status
(3) Reduction in taxable income	9,350	9,550	Greater of (1) and (2)
(4) Itemized deductions adjusted for the $420 refund	5,080	9,130	(1) – $420
(5) Reduction in taxable income adjusted for the $420 refund	9,350	9,350	Greater of (2) and (4)
Tax benefit due to prior deduction of $420 refund	**$ 0**	**$ 200**	(3) – (5)

When Do Taxpayers Recognize Income?

Individual taxpayers generally file tax returns reporting their taxable income for a calendar-year period, whereas corporations often use a fiscal year-end. In either case, the taxpayer's method of accounting generally determines the year in which realized income is recognized and included in gross income.

Accounting Methods Most large corporations use the accrual method of accounting. Under the **accrual method,** income is generally recognized when earned, and expenses are generally deducted in the period when liabilities are incurred. In contrast, most individuals use the **cash method** as their overall method of accounting.[4] Under the cash method, taxpayers recognize income in the period they receive it (in the form of cash,

---

[4]Taxpayers involved in a business may use the accrual or hybrid overall method of accounting. We discuss these methods in the Business Income, Deductions, and Accounting Methods chapter.

property, or services), rather than when they actually earn it. Likewise, cash-method tax-payers claim deductions when they make expenditures, rather than when they incur liabilities. The cash method greatly simplifies the computation of income for the overwhelming majority of individuals, many of whom have neither the time nor the training to apply the accrual method. Another advantage of the cash method is that taxpayers may have some control over when income is received and expenses are paid. Because of this control, tax-payers can more easily use the timing tax planning strategy (described in the Tax Planning Strategies and Related Limitations chapter) to lower the present value of their tax bill.

Constructive Receipt   Taxpayers using the cash method of accounting may try to shift income from the current year to the next year when they receive payments near year-end. For instance, taxpayers may merely delay cashing a check or avoid picking up a compensation payment until after year-end. The courts responded to this ploy by devising the **constructive receipt doctrine**.[5] The constructive receipt doctrine states that a taxpayer realizes and recognizes income when it is actually or *constructively* received. Constructive receipt is deemed to occur when the income has been credited to the taxpayer's account or when the income is unconditionally available to the taxpayer, the taxpayer is aware of the income's availability, and there are no restrictions on the taxpayer's control over the income.

THE KEY FACTS

Income Recognition

- Cash-method taxpayers recognize income when it is received.
- Income is realized regardless of whether payments are received in money, property, *or* services.
- Income is taxed in the period in which a cash-method taxpayer has a right to receive payment without substantial restrictions.

Example 5-4

Courtney is a cash-method taxpayer. Based on her outstanding performance at work, Courtney earned a $4,800 year-end bonus. On December 28, Courtney's supervisor told her that her bonus was issued as a separate check and that Courtney could pick up the check in the accounting office anytime. Courtney did not pick up the check until January 2 of the next year, and she did not cash it until late January. When does Courtney realize and recognize the $4,800 income?

Answer: On December 28 of the tax year in question. Courtney *constructively* received the check that year because it was unconditionally available to her on December 28, she was aware of the check's availability, and there were no restrictions on her control over the check. Courtney must include the $4,800 bonus in gross income for that year, even though she did not actually receive the funds until late January of the next year.[6]

Claim of Right   The **claim of right doctrine** is another judicial doctrine created to address the timing of income recognition. Specifically, this doctrine addresses when a taxpayer receives income in one period but is required to return the payment in a subsequent period. The claim of right doctrine states that income has been realized if a taxpayer receives income and there are no restrictions on the taxpayer's use of the income (e.g., the taxpayer does not have an obligation to repay the amount). A common example of the claim of right doctrine is a cash bonus paid to employees based on company earnings. Despite *potentially* having to repay the bonuses (for example, in the case of a "claw-back" provision that requires repayment if the company has an earnings restatement), employees would include the bonuses in gross income in the year received because there are no restrictions on their use of the income.[7]

[5]Justice Holmes summarized this doctrine as follows: "The income that is subject to a man's unfettered command and that he is free to enjoy at his own option may be taxed to him as his income, whether he sees fit to enjoy it or not." *Corliss v. Bowers,* 281 US 378 (1930).

[6]Note also that Courtney's employer would include her bonus on Courtney's W-2 for the year in which it issued the check.

[7]§1341 provides relief for a taxpayer who recognizes taxable income because of the claim of right doctrine and in a later year determines that she does not have a claim of right. Specifically, §1341 provides that if a taxpayer recognizes taxable income in an earlier year because she has a "claim of right" (unrestricted right) to the income received, a deduction is then allowable in a later year because she did not have an unrestricted right to the income, and if the related tax deduction exceeds $3,000, then the tax imposed in the later year is the lesser of (1) the tax for the taxable year computed with the deduction or (2) the tax for the taxable year computed without the deduction, less a tax credit for the previous tax paid on the item of income. Beginning in 2018, individuals who are required to repay compensation previously recognized in a prior year under the claim of right doctrine are not allowed a deduction for the repayment if the amount does not exceed $3,000.

Who Recognizes the Income?

In addition to determining when taxpayers realize and recognize income, we must also consider *who* (which taxpayer) recognizes the income. This question often arises when taxpayers attempt to shift income to other related taxpayers through the income-shifting strategy. For example, a father (with a high marginal income tax rate) might wish to assign his paycheck to his baby daughter (with a low marginal income tax rate) to minimize their collective tax burden.

Assignment of Income The courts developed the **assignment of income doctrine** to prevent taxpayers from arbitrarily transferring the taxation on their income to others. In essence, the assignment of income doctrine holds that the taxpayer who earns income from services must recognize the income. Likewise, income from property, such as dividends and interest, is taxable to the person who actually owns the income-producing property.[8] For example, interest income from a bond is taxable to the person who owns the bond during the time the interest income accrues. Thus, to shift income from property to another person, a taxpayer must also transfer the *ownership* in the property to the other person.

Example 5-5

What if: Courtney would like to begin saving for Deron's college tuition. If Courtney were to direct EWD to deposit part of her salary in Deron's bank account, who would pay tax on the salary income?

Answer: Courtney would be taxed on her entire salary as income because she earned the income.[9] The payment to Deron would be treated as a gift and would not be taxable to him (gifts are excluded from the recipient's income, as discussed later in the chapter).

What if: Suppose Courtney wanted to shift her rental income to Deron. What would she need to do to ensure that her rental income is taxed to Deron?

Answer: Courtney would have to transfer her ownership in the rental property to Deron in order for Deron to be taxed on the rental income.[10]

Community Property Systems While most states use a common law system, nine states (Arizona, California, Idaho, Louisiana, Nevada, New Mexico, Texas, Washington, and Wisconsin) implement **community property systems.** Under community property systems, the income earned from services by one spouse is treated as though it were earned equally by both spouses. Also, property acquired by either spouse during the marriage is usually community property and is treated as though it is owned equally by each spouse.[11] Property that a spouse brings into a marriage is treated as that spouse's separate property. For federal income tax purposes, the community property system has the following consequences:

- Half the income earned from the *services* of one spouse is included in the gross income of the other spouse.
- Half the income from property held as *community* property by the married couple is included in the gross income of each spouse.

---

[8]This rule of thumb is also referred to as the "fruit and the tree" doctrine because of the analogy to fruit belonging to the tree upon which it was grown. See *Lucas v. Earl* (1930) 281 US 111 and *Helvering v. Horst* (1940) 311 US 112.

[9]Note also that EWD has the responsibility of issuing a W-2 to the taxpayer who provided the services—Courtney in this case.

[10]As explained in the Individual Income Tax Computation and Tax Credits chapter, the tax savings from such a transfer would be mitigated in the calculation of Deron's tax by the so-called "kiddie" tax. Likewise, Courtney should consider the gift tax implications of this transfer before transferring the property to Deron.

[11]Property acquired during the marriage via gift or inheritance or purchased with a spouse's separate property is considered separate property.

- In five community property states (Arizona, California, Nevada, New Mexico, and Washington), all the income from property owned *separately* by one spouse is included in that spouse's gross income.
- In Texas, Louisiana, Wisconsin, and Idaho, half the income from property owned *separately* by one spouse is included in the gross income of each spouse.

In contrast, for federal income tax purposes, the common law system has the following consequences:

- All the income earned from the *services* of one spouse is included in the gross income of the spouse who earned it.
- For property owned *separately*, all the income from the separately owned property is included in that spouse's gross income.
- For property owned *jointly* (i.e., not separately), each co-owner is taxed on the income attributable to his or her share of the property. For example, suppose that a parcel of property is jointly owned by husband and wife. One-half of income from the property would be included in the gross income of each spouse. Similarly, income from property owned by three or more persons would be included in the gross income of each co-owner based on his or her respective ownership share.

Example 5-6

In the year prior to their divorce, Courtney and Al Wilson lived in Ohio, a common law state and filed married filing separately. That year, Al earned $90,000 of annual salary and Courtney earned $60,000. How much of the income earned by Al and by Courtney in the year prior to the divorce did Al report on his individual tax return? How much income did Courtney report on her individual tax return?

Answer: Because they resided in a common law state, Al reports the $90,000 that he earned on his own tax return, and Courtney reports the entire $60,000 she earned on her own tax return.

What if: How much of this income would Al have been required to include on his individual tax return, and how much of this income would Courtney have been required to report on her individual tax return, if they lived in California, a community property state?

Answer: If they resided in a community property state, both Al and Courtney would have included $75,000 of the $150,000 the couple had jointly earned [(Al's $90,000 + Courtney's $60,000)/2] on their respective individual tax returns.

If a couple files a joint tax return, the community property rules do not affect the aggregate taxes payable by the couple, because the income of both spouses is aggregated on the return. However, when couples file separate tax returns, their combined tax liability may depend on whether they live in a common law state, a community property state that shares income from separate property equally between spouses, or a community property state that does not split income from separate property between spouses.[12]

TYPES OF INCOME

LO 5-2

Now that we have a basic understanding of the general definition of gross income and related concepts, let's turn our attention to specific *types* of income subject to taxation. Our discussion is organized around income from services, income from property, and other sources of income.

---

[12]§66 provides rules that allow spouses living apart in community property states to be taxed on their individual income from services if (1) the taxpayers live apart for the entire year, (2) they do not file a joint tax return with each other, and (3) they do not transfer any of the income from services between each other.

Income from Services

Income from labor is one of the most common sources of gross income, and it is rarely exempt from taxation. Payments for services including salary, wages, and fees that a taxpayer earns through services in a nonemployee capacity are all considered income from services and so is unemployment compensation. Income from services is often referred to as **earned income** because it is generated by the efforts of the taxpayer (this also includes business income earned by a taxpayer even if the taxpayer's business is selling inventory).

Example 5-7

EWD pays Courtney a salary of $118,000. In addition, Courtney earned and received $19,500 in fees from consulting work she did on weekends independent of her employment with EWD. She incurred $1,500 in miscellaneous expenses for supplies and transportation while doing the consulting work. What is Courtney's total *income* from services (earned income), from her employment and from her self-employment activities?

Answer: $136,000, consisting of her $118,000 salary and her $19,500 business income from her consulting activities, less the $1,500 of expenses related to her consulting activities. Note that business deductions are *for* AGI deductions that taxpayers subtract from their gross business income to derive net business income or loss, reported on page 1 of Form 1040. We discuss *for* AGI deductions in greater detail in the Individual Deductions chapter.

Income from Property

Income from property, often referred to as **unearned income,** may take different forms, such as gains or losses from the sale of property, dividends, interest, rents, royalties, and annuities.[13] The tax treatment of unearned income depends upon the type of income and, in some circumstances, the type of transaction generating the income. For example, as discussed in the Individual Income Tax Overview, Dependents, and Filing Status chapter, qualified dividends and long-term capital gains are taxed at preferential tax rates, whereas other unearned income is generally taxed at ordinary tax rates. Likewise, while gains or losses are typically recognized in the current period, certain types of gains and losses are postponed indefinitely. We discuss annuity income and property dispositions briefly in the following paragraphs. We discuss income from property in more detail in subsequent chapters.

Example 5-8

Courtney owns 1,000 shares of GE stock that she registered in a dividend reinvestment plan. Under this plan, all dividends are automatically used to purchase more shares of the stock. This year, GE declared and paid $700 in dividends on Courtney's stock. Must Courtney include the dividend in her gross income for the year?

Answer: Yes. Courtney includes the $700 of dividends (unearned income) in her gross income. The fact that Courtney chose to reinvest the dividends does not affect their taxability, because she received an economic benefit and change in property rights associated with the dividend.

Example 5-9

Gram purchased a $100,000, three-year certificate of deposit (CD) with a portion of the life insurance proceeds she received on Gramps's death. At year-end, her CD account is credited with $4,100 of interest, and her savings account is credited with $650 of interest. Courtney had a total of $271 of interest credited to her savings account and $50 credited to her checking account during the year. How much interest must Gram and Courtney include in their gross income for the year?

---

[13]The tax definition of unearned income is different from the financial accounting definition. Unearned income for financial accounting purposes is a liability that represents advance payments for goods or services.

Answer: Gram must include the $4,100 of interest credited to her CD account and the $650 of interest credited to her savings account this year, regardless of whether she withdraws the interest or not. Courtney must include the $271 of interest credited to her savings account and the $50 credited to her checking account, regardless of whether she withdraws the interest or not.

Example 5-10

Courtney owns a condo in town that she rents to tenants. This year, the condo generated $14,000 of rental revenue. Courtney incurred $4,000 in real estate taxes, $2,500 in utility expenses, $500 in advertising expenses, and $2,000 of depreciation and other expenses associated with the rental. What effect does the rental have on Courtney's *gross income*? What effect does the rental have on Courtney's *taxable income*?

Answer: The rent increases Courtney's *gross income* by $14,000. However, after considering her allowable deductions for the rental, Courtney will report only $5,000 of *taxable income* from rental activities, computed as follows:

Description	Amount
Rental revenue	$14,000
Less allowable deductions:	
Real estate taxes	(4,000)
Utilities	(2,500)
Advertising	(500)
Depreciation and other expenses	(2,000)
Total rental expenses	(9,000)
Net rental income	**$ 5,000**

Annuities An **annuity** is an investment that pays a stream of equal payments over time. Individuals often purchase annuities as a means of generating a fixed income stream during retirement. There are two basic types of annuities: (1) annuities paid over a fixed period and (2) annuities paid over a person's life (for as long as the person lives). The challenge from a tax perspective is to determine how much of each annuity payment represents gross income (income taxed at ordinary tax rates) and how much represents a nontaxable *return of capital* (return of the original investment). For both types of annuities, the tax law deems a *portion* of each annuity payment as a nontaxable return of capital and the remainder as gross income. Taxpayers use the *annuity exclusion ratio* to determine the portion of each payment that is a nontaxable return of capital.

$$\text{Annuity exclusion ratio} = \frac{\text{Original investment}}{\text{Expected value of annuity}} = \text{Return of capital percentage}$$

For fixed annuities, the expected value is the number of payments times the amount of the payment. In other words, for an annuity payable over a fixed term, the return of capital is simply the original investment divided by the number of payments. The number of payments, however, is uncertain for annuities paid over a person's life. For these annuities, taxpayers must use IRS tables to determine the expected value based upon the taxpayer's life expectancy at the start of the annuity.[14]

---

[14]See Reg. §1.72-9. Special rules under §72(d) apply to annuities from qualified retirement plans. These rules only apply when a taxpayer makes an after-tax contribution to a qualified employer retirement plan (which is uncommon). In most cases, taxpayers only make pretax contributions to qualified retirement plans, which results in fully taxable annuity distributions.

To calculate the expected value of the annuity, the number of annual payments from the table (referred to as the expected return multiple) is multiplied by the annual payment amount. Taxpayers with an annuity paid over the life of one person (a single-life annuity) use the expected return multiple from the table, a portion of which is presented in Exhibit 5-1.

EXHIBIT 5-1   Table for Expected Return Multiple for Ordinary Single-Life Annuity

Age at Annuity Starting Date	Expected Return Multiple
68	17.6
69	16.8
70	16.0
71	15.3
72	14.6

Some annuities provide payments over the lives of two people. For example, a taxpayer may purchase an annuity that provides an annual payment each year until both the taxpayer *and* the taxpayer's spouse pass away. This type of annuity is called a joint-life annuity. The IRS provides a separate table for determining the expected number of payments from joint-life annuities.

A taxpayer receiving a life annuity who lives longer than his or her estimated life expectancy will ultimately receive more than the expected number of payments. The entire amount of these "extra" payments is included in the taxpayer's gross income, because the taxpayer has completely recovered her investment in the annuity by the time she receives them. If the taxpayer dies *before* receiving the expected number of payments, the amount of the unrecovered investment (the initial investment less the amounts received, which is treated as a nontaxable return of capital) is deducted on the taxpayer's final income tax return.[15]

Example 5-11

In January of this year, Gram purchased an annuity from UBET Insurance Co. that will pay her $10,000 per year for the next 15 years. Gram received the first $10,000 payment in December. Gram paid $99,000 for the annuity and will receive $150,000 over the life of the annuity (15 years × $10,000 per year). How much of the $10,000 payment received by Gram in December should she include in her gross income?

Answer: $3,400. Because Gram purchased a fixed-payment annuity, the portion of the annuity payment included in gross income is calculated as follows:

Description	Amount	Explanation
(1) Investment in annuity contract	$99,000	
(2) Number of payments	15	
(3) Return of capital per payment	$ 6,600	(1)/(2)
(4) Amount of each payment:	$10,000	
Gross income per payment	**$ 3,400**	(4) − (3)

What if: Assume the annuity Gram purchased pays her $1,000 per month over the remainder of her life. Gram (70 years old) paid $99,000 for the annuity, and she received her first $1,000 payment in December of this year. How much income would she recognize on the $1,000 payment?

---

[15]The unrecovered cost of the annuity is deducted as a miscellaneous itemized deduction. See §72(b)(3) and §67(b)(10).

Answer: $484.40, computed as follows:

Description	Amount	Explanation
(1) Investment in annuity contract	$ 99,000	
(2) Expected return multiple	16	Exhibit 5-1, 70 years old
(3) Amount of each payment	$ 1,000	
(4) Expected return	$192,000	(2) × (3) × 12 months
(5) Return of capital percentage	51.56%	(1)/(4)
(6) Return of capital per payment	$ 515.60	(3) × (5)
Taxable income per payment	**$ 484.40**	(3) − (6)

After Gram receives her entire $99,000 as a return of capital, each subsequent $1,000 annuity payment would be fully taxable.

Property Dispositions Taxpayers can realize a gain or loss when disposing of an asset. Consistent with the return of capital principle we discussed above, taxpayers are allowed to recover their investment in property (tax basis) before they realize any gain. A loss is realized when the proceeds are less than the tax basis in the property. Because the return of capital principle generally applies only to the extent of the sale proceeds, a loss does not necessarily reduce the taxpayer's taxable income. A loss will reduce the taxpayer's taxable income only if the loss is deductible. Exhibit 5-2 presents a general formula for computing the gain or loss from the sale of an asset.

EXHIBIT 5-2 **Formula for Calculating Gain (Loss) from Sale of an Asset**

Sales proceeds
Less: Selling expenses
= Amount realized
Less: Tax basis (investment) in property sold
= Gain (loss) on sale

> **THE KEY FACTS**
>
> **Return of Capital**
>
> • Taxpayers are allowed to recover the capital invested in property tax-free.
> • Payments from purchased annuities are part income and part return of capital.
> • When property is sold or disposed of, the realized gain or loss equals the sale proceeds reduced by the tax basis of the property.

The rate at which taxpayers are taxed on *gains* from property dispositions and the extent to which they can deduct *losses* from property dispositions depends on whether they used the asset for business purposes, investment purposes, or personal purposes. For example, as we discussed in the Individual Income Tax Overview, Dependents, and Filing Status chapter, long-term capital gains realized by individuals are taxed at preferential tax rates, and deductions for net capital losses realized by individuals are limited to $3,000 per year. In contrast, losses realized on assets used for personal purposes are generally not deductible. We discuss specific rules associated with property dispositions in the Investments and Property Dispositions chapters.

Example 5-12

On December 31, Gram sold her 50 shares of Acme Corporation stock for $40 per share. Gram also paid $150 in broker's commissions on the sale. Gram originally purchased the shares in April of this year for $30 per share. How much gross income does Gram recognize from the stock sale?

Answer: Gram recognizes $350 gross income on the sale, computed as follows:

Sale proceeds ($40 × 50 shares)	$2,000
Less: Selling expenses	−150
= Amount realized	$1,850
Less: Tax basis (investment) in property sold ($30 × 50 shares)	−1,500
Gain (loss) on sale	**$ 350**

Other Sources of Gross Income

Taxpayers may receive income from sources other than their efforts (earned income from wages or business) and their property (unearned income such as dividends and interest). In this section we briefly summarize other common types of gross income. If by chance you encounter other types of income that are not specifically discussed here, remember that the tax law is based upon the all-inclusive income concept. That is, unless a specific provision grants exclusion or deferral, economic benefits that are realized generate gross income. This basic understanding of the structure of our tax law (and research skills to investigate the taxability of specific income types) will serve you well as you evaluate whether realized income should be included in gross income.

Income from Flow-Through Entities   Individuals may invest in various business entities. The type of entity for tax purposes for a business affects how the income generated by the business is taxed. For example, income earned by a corporation (other than an S corporation) is taxed at the entity level as opposed to the owner level. In contrast, the income and deductions from a **flow-through entity,** such as a partnership or S corporation (a corporation electing S corporation status), "flow through" to the owners of the entity (partners or shareholders). That is, the owners report income or deductions as though they operated a portion of the business personally. Specifically, each partner or S corporation shareholder reports his or her share of the entity's income and deductions, generally in proportion to his or her ownership percentage, on his or her individual tax return.[16]

Because different types of income and deductions may be treated differently for tax purposes (e.g., qualified dividends are eligible for a special low tax rate), each item the partners or shareholders report on their tax returns retains its underlying tax characteristics. That is, the partners are treated as if they personally received their share of each item of the flow-through entity's income. For example, corporate dividend income paid to a partnership is reported and taxed as dividend income on the partners' individual tax returns. Also, it is important to note that owners of flow-through entities are taxed on their share of the entity's income whether or not cash is distributed to them. When owners receive cash distributions from the entity, the distributions are generally treated as a return of capital to the extent of their investment (tax basis) in the entity and, therefore, are not included in the owner's gross income. Distributions in excess of basis are taxable. Partnerships and S corporations report to each partner or shareholder that partner's or shareholder's share of partnership and S corporation income (or loss) on Schedule K-1, which is filed with the partnership and S corporation's annual information returns (Form 1065 and 1120S, respectively).[17]

Example 5-13

What if: Suppose that Courtney is a 40 percent partner in KJZ partnership. KJZ reported $20,000 of business income and $3,000 of interest income for the year. KJZ also distributed $1,000 of cash to Courtney. What amount of gross income from her ownership in KJZ partnership would Courtney report for the current year?

Answer: $9,200, consisting of $8,000 of business income ($20,000 × 40%) and $1,200 of interest income ($3,000 × 40%). Courtney would not include the $1,000 distribution in her gross income because it was a return of her investment.

Alimony   When couples legally separate or divorce, one spouse may be required to provide financial support to the other in the form of **alimony.** The tax law defines alimony as (1) a transfer of *cash* made under a written separation agreement or divorce decree and stipulates that (2) the separation or divorce decree does not designate the payment as

---

[16]The deduction of losses from partnerships and S corporations are subject to several limitations that we discuss in the Investments chapter.

[17]See Forms 1065 and 1120S on the IRS website, www.irs.gov.

something other than alimony, (3) in the case of legally separated (or divorced) taxpayers under a separation or divorce decree, the spouses do not live together when the payment is made, and (4) the payments cannot continue after the death of the recipient.[18]

For tax purposes, a transfer between former spouses represents alimony only if it meets this definition. For any divorce or separation agreement executed before January 1, 2019, if a payment meets the definition of alimony, then the amount of the payment is included in the gross income of the person receiving it and is deductible *for* AGI by the person paying it. Thus, alimony shifts income from one spouse to the other.[19] In contrast, for any divorce or separation agreement executed after December 31, 2018, alimony payments are not included in the gross income of the person receiving the payments and are not deductible by the person paying alimony.

Example 5-14

In addition to paying child support, under the divorce decree executed in 2017 Al is required to pay Courtney $20,000 cash each year until she dies. The decree does not designate this amount as a payment for something other than alimony, and Al and Courtney do not live together. Does this payment qualify as alimony?

Answer: Yes. These payments qualify as alimony for tax purposes because (1) they are cash payments made under a divorce decree, (2) they are not designated as something other than alimony, (3) Al and Courtney do not live together, and (4) the payments cease on Courtney's death. In the current year, Al made a $20,000 alimony payment to Courtney. Courtney includes all $20,000 in her gross income. To ensure that the income is taxed only once, Al is allowed to treat the entire payment as a deduction *for* AGI.

What if: Suppose that Courtney and Al's divorce agreement was executed in 2019. What amount of the $20,000 payment would Courtney include in her gross income and would Al deduct?

Answer: Because the divorce agreement was executed after December 31, 2018, Courtney would not include the $20,000 payment in gross income, and Al would not treat the payment as a deduction *for* AGI.

There may be other types of payments that *do not qualify as alimony*. These include (1) property divisions (who gets the car, house, or china?) and (2) child support payments fixed by the divorce or separation agreement.[20] In any event, if a transfer of property between spouses does *not* meet the definition of alimony, the *recipient* of the transfer *excludes* the value of the transfer from income, and the person transferring the property is not allowed to deduct the value of the property transferred.

Example 5-15

As required by the divorce decree, Al made $10,000 in child support payments during the year to Courtney to help her support Deron. Al is required to make child support payments until Deron is 18 years old. Is the current-year payment considered alimony?

Answer: No. The $10,000 of child support payments are not income to Courtney. They are not alimony because the divorce decree specifies that they are for child support. Consequently, Courtney does not include these payments in gross income, and Al does not deduct them.

---

[18]§71(b). In addition, certain payments to third parties on behalf of the spouse, such as mortgage payments, can also qualify as payments in cash.

[19]To minimize tax-avoidance income shifting between a higher tax rate payor of alimony and a lower tax rate recipient of alimony pursuant to divorce agreement or separation agreement executed before 2019, Congress enacted a complex set of restrictions called the *anti-front loading* rules that make it difficult for taxpayers to disguise property payments as alimony payments.

[20]§71(c).

Example 5-16

As part of the divorce agreement executed in 2017, Al transferred his interest in their joint residence to Courtney. The couple did not have any outstanding debt on the home. At the time of the divorce, the home was valued at $500,000 and Al's share was valued at $250,000. What were the tax consequences of the home ownership transfer to Courtney?

Answer: Because the transfer was not a cash transfer, it did not qualify as alimony. Consequently, Courtney would not have recognized the $250,000 as income, and Al would not have deducted the $250,000 transfer.

Prizes, Awards, and Gambling Winnings Prizes, awards, and gambling winnings, such as raffle or sweepstakes prizes or lottery winnings, are included in gross income.

Example 5-17

After devoting much of her free time during the year to filling out sweepstakes entries, Gram hit the jackpot. She won a WaveRunner worth $7,500 in a sweepstakes sponsored by *Reader's Digest*. How much of the prize, if any, must Gram include in her gross income?

Answer: Gram must include the full $7,500 value of the WaveRunner in her gross income. Note that because she must pay taxes on the winnings, she is not really getting the WaveRunner for "free."

There are three specific, narrowly defined exceptions to this rule. First, awards for scientific, literary, or charitable achievement such as the Nobel Prize are excluded from gross income, *but only if* (1) the recipient was selected without any action on his part to enter the contest or proceeding, (2) the recipient is not required to render substantial future services as a condition to receive the prize or award, and (3) the payer of the prize or award transfers the prize or award to a federal, state, or local governmental unit or qualified charity such as a church, school, or charitable organization designated by the taxpayer.[21] The obvious downside of this exception is that the award recipient does not actually get to receive or keep the cash from the award. However, for tax purposes it is more beneficial for the recipient to exclude the award from income entirely by immediately transferring it to a charitable organization than it is to receive the award, recognize the income, and then contribute funds to a charity for a charitable deduction.

Designating the award for payment to a federal, state, or local governmental unit or qualified charity has the same effect as claiming the transfer as a deduction *for* AGI. However, by receiving the award, recognizing the income, and then contributing funds to a charity, the taxpayer is deducting the donation as a deduction *from* AGI. As we discussed in the Individual Income Tax Overview, Dependents, and Filing Status chapter, deductions *for* AGI are likely more advantageous than deductions *from* AGI.

The second exception is for employee *awards for length of service or safety achievement*.[22] These nontaxable awards are limited per employee per year to $400 of tangible property other than cash, cash equivalents, gift cards, gift coupons or gift certificates, or vacations, meals, lodging, tickets to theater or sporting events, stocks,

---

[21]§74(b).

[22]Prizes or awards from an employer-sponsored contest are fully taxable.

bonds, other securities, and other similar items.[23] The award is not excluded from the employee's income if circumstances suggest it is disguised compensation.[24]

The third narrowly defined exception is for the value of any awards (medals) and prize money received by Team USA athletes from the U.S. Olympic Committee on account of competition in the Olympic and Paralympic games. While there is no limit on the exclusion amount, the exclusion does *not* apply to a taxpayer for any year in which the taxpayer's AGI (after excluding the award) exceeds $1 million ($500,000 for a married individual filing a separate return).[25]

TAXES IN THE REAL WORLD   You've Won a Brand New Car!

Who hasn't dreamed of hearing that famous phrase on the *Price is Right*? Well, while many have dreamed of winning the Showcase Showdown, those who have had the pleasure of doing so have learned that those fabulous prizes come with substantial extras in the form of federal and state income taxes and even sales taxes. Indeed, winners of those fabulous new model cars get the pleasure of paying sales tax on the cars before they are handed the keys and federal and California income taxes in the year of their big win and 15 minutes of fame. To add a bit of insult to injury, taxes are paid on the value of the MSRP (manufacturer suggested retail price) of the car—not on the value that might be negotiated at the dealer. Nonetheless, a win is a win, even if it is not quite as lucrative as imagined.

Taxpayers must include the *gross* amount of their gambling winnings for the year in gross income.[26] Taxpayers are allowed to deduct their gambling losses and related gambling expenses to the extent of their gambling winnings, but the losses and related expenses are usually deductible as miscellaneous itemized deductions.[27] For professional gamblers, however, the losses and related expenses are deductible (to the extent of gambling winnings) *for* AGI.

ETHICS

While vacationing you find a $100 bill on the beach. Nobody saw you find it. Assuming the find meets the definition of gross income, would you report it as taxable income? Why or why not? Would your answer differ if you found $100,000 instead of $100?

Social Security Benefits   Over the last 40 years, the taxation of Social Security benefits has changed considerably. Forty years ago, Social Security benefits were completely excluded from income. Today, taxpayers may be required to include *up to* 85 percent of the benefits in gross income *depending* on the amount of the taxpayer's filing status, Social Security benefits, and *modified* AGI.[28] Modified AGI is regular AGI

---

[23]§74(c).

[24]The $400 limit is increased to $1,600 for qualified award plans (written plans that do not discriminate in favor of highly compensated employees). However, the *average* cost of all qualified plan awards from an employer is limited to $400. Managers, administrators, clerical employees, or professional employees are not eligible for an exclusion for a safety award.

[25]§74(d).

[26]Subject to *de minimis* rules, payers of gambling winnings report winnings to recipients and the IRS on Form W-2G.

[27]See Rev. Rul. 83-130, 1983-2 CB 148.

[28]§86(d) applies to monthly benefits under title II of the Social Security Act and tier 1 railroad retirement benefits. The Social Security Administration reports Social Security benefits on Form SSA-1099.

(excluding Social Security benefits) plus tax-exempt interest income, excluded foreign income (discussed later in the chapter), and certain other deductions *for* AGI.[29] The calculation of the amount of Social Security benefits to be included in income is depicted on the IRS worksheet in the appendix at the end of this chapter.[30] The calculation is complex, to say the least. However, the taxability of Social Security benefits can be summarized as follows:

Single taxpayers:

1. If modified AGI + 50 percent of Social Security benefits ≤ $25,000, Social Security benefits are not taxable.
2. If $25,000 < modified AGI + 50 percent of Social Security benefits ≤ $34,000, taxable Social Security benefits are the lesser of (a) 50 percent of the Social Security benefits or (b) 50 percent of (modified AGI + 50 percent of Social Security benefits − $25,000).
3. If modified AGI + 50 percent of Social Security benefits > $34,000, taxable Social Security benefits are the lesser of (a) 85 percent of Social Security benefits or (b) 85 percent of (modified AGI + 50 percent of Social Security benefits − $34,000), plus the lesser of (1) $4,500 or (2) 50 percent of Social Security benefits.

Taxpayers filing married separate:

Taxable Social Security benefits are the lesser of (a) 85 percent of the Social Security benefits or (b) 85 percent of the taxpayer's modified AGI + 50 percent of Social Security benefits.

Taxpayers filing married joint:

1. If modified AGI + 50 percent of Social Security benefits ≤ $32,000, Social Security benefits are not taxable.
2. If $32,000 < modified AGI + 50 percent of Social Security benefits ≤ $44,000, taxable Social Security benefits are the lesser of (a) 50 percent of the Social Security benefits or (b) 50 percent of (modified AGI + 50 percent of Social Security benefits − $32,000).
3. If modified AGI + 50 percent of Social Security benefits > $44,000, taxable Social Security benefits are the lesser of (a) 85 percent of Social Security benefits or (b) 85 percent of (modified AGI + 50 percent of Social Security benefits − $44,000), plus the lesser of (1) $6,000 or (2) 50 percent of Social Security benefits.

The implications of the above calculations are that the Social Security benefits of taxpayers with relatively low taxable income are not taxable, and that 85 percent of the Social Security benefits of taxpayers with moderate to high taxable income are taxable.

Example 5-18

Gram received $7,200 of Social Security benefits this year. Suppose that Gram's modified AGI is $16,000. What amount of the Social Security benefits must Gram include in her gross income?

Answer: $0. Gram's modified AGI plus one-half of her Social Security benefits is $19,600 [$16,000 modified AGI + ($7,200 Social Security benefits × 50%)], which is below $25,000. Hence, Gram may *exclude* the entire $7,200 of Social Security income from gross income.

What if: Assume that Gram received $7,200 of Social Security benefits this year and that her modified AGI is $50,000. What amount of benefits must Gram include in her gross income?

Answer: $6,120 ($7,200 × 85%).

What if: Assume that Gram received $7,200 of Social Security benefits this year and that her modified AGI is $26,400. What amount of benefits must Gram include in her gross income?

Answer: $2,500. Gram is single and her modified AGI + 50 percent of Social Security benefits falls between $25,000 and $34,000. Her taxable Social Security benefits are the lesser of (a) 50 percent of the Social Security benefits ($7,200 × 50% = $3,600) or (b) 50 percent of [$26,400 modified

---

[29]See §86(b)(2).

[30]Because the 2018 worksheet was not available at the time the book went to press, we include the 2017 worksheet in the appendix at the end of the chapter. The 2017 worksheet can be used to determine the taxable portion of Social Security benefits received in 2018.

AGI + $3,600 (50 percent of Social Security benefits) − $25,000] = $2,500. Thus, her taxable Social Security benefits are $2,500.

What if: Assume that Gram received $7,200 of Social Security benefits this year and that her modified AGI is $31,400. What amount of benefits must Gram include in her gross income?

Answer: $4,450. Gram is single and her modified AGI + 50 percent of Social Security benefits exceeds $34,000. Her taxable Social Security benefits are the lesser of (a) 85 percent of Social Security benefits ($7,200 × 85% = $6,120) or (b) 85 percent of [$31,400 modified AGI + $3,600 (50 percent of Social Security benefits) − $34,000] = $850, plus the lesser of (1) $4,500 or (2) 50 percent of Social Security benefits (50% × $7,200 − $3,600). This calculation simplifies to the lesser of (a) $6,120 or (b) $4,450 [$850 + lesser of (1) $4,500 or (2) $3,600]. Thus, Gram's taxable Social Security benefits are $4,450.

Imputed Income   Besides realizing *direct* economic benefits like wages and interest, taxpayers sometimes realize *indirect* economic benefits that they must include in gross income as **imputed income.** Bargain purchases (such as goods sold by an employer to an employee at a discount) and below-market loans (such as a loan from an employer to an employee at a zero or unusually low interest rate) are two common examples of taxable indirect economic benefits. Both bargain purchases and below-market loans generally result in tax consequences (such as gross income or taxable gifts) if the purchase or loan transaction is not an "arms-length" transaction (such as transactions between an employer and employee, owner and entity, or among family members).

For bargain purchases, the tax consequences vary based on the relationship of the parties. For example, a bargain purchase by an employee from an employer results in taxable compensation income to the employee, a bargain purchase by a shareholder from a corporation results in a taxable dividend to the shareholder, and a bargain purchase between family members is deemed to be a gift from one family member to the other (as discussed later in the chapter, gifts are nontaxable for income tax purposes but are potentially subject to gift tax, to be paid by the person making the gift).

Although the general rule is that bargain purchases by an employee from an employer create taxable compensation income to the employee, the tax law does provide a limited exclusion for employee bargain purchases. Specifically, employees may exclude (a) a discount on employer-provided goods as long as the discount does not exceed the employer's gross profit percentage on all property offered for sale to customers and (b) up to 20 percent employer-provided discounts on services. Discounts in excess of these amounts are taxable as compensation.[31]

Example 5-19

To create more space for Gram, Courtney received EWD architectural design services as part of her compensation package and at a substantial discount. EWD's services were valued at $35,000, but Courtney was charged only $22,000. How much of the discount must Courtney include in gross income?

Answer: $6,000, computed as follows:

Description	Amount	Explanation
(1) Value of services EWD provided to Courtney	$35,000	
(2) Courtney's cost of the services	22,000	
(3) Discount on services	$13,000	(1) − (2)
(4) Excludable discount	7,000	(1) × 20%
Discount in excess of 20% is included in gross income	**$ 6,000**	(3) − (4)

For below-market loans, the indirect economic benefit conveyed to the borrower (such as an employee, shareholder, or family member) is a function of the amount of the loan and the difference in the market interest rate and the rate actually charged by the lender (such as an employer, corporation, or family member). To eliminate any tax

[31]§132(a)(2).

advantages of below-market loans, the tax law generally requires the lender and borrower to treat the transaction as if:

1. The borrower paid the lender the difference between the applicable federal interest rate (compounded semiannually) and the actual interest paid. This difference is called *imputed interest*.
2. The lender then returned the imputed interest to the borrower.[32]

The deemed "payment" of the imputed interest in these transactions is treated as interest income to the lender and interest expense to the borrower. The deductibility of the interest expense for the borrower depends on how she used the loan proceeds (for business, investment, or personal purposes). As we learn in the next chapter, business interest expense is a deduction *for* AGI, investment interest expense is an itemized deduction subject to limitations, and personal interest is generally not deductible. The tax consequences of the "return" of the imputed interest from the lender to the borrower vary based on the relationship of the parties (similar to the case of a bargain purchase). For example, the return of the imputed interest from an employer lender to an employee borrower is treated by both parties as taxable compensation paid to the employee, the return of the imputed interest from a corporation to a shareholder is considered a dividend, and a return of imputed interest by a family member to another family member is considered a gift. The imputed interest rules generally do not apply to aggregate loans of $10,000 or less between the lender and borrower [§7872(c)].[32]

Example 5-20

At the beginning of January, EWD provides Courtney with a $100,000 zero-interest loan. Assume the applicable federal interest rate (compounded semiannually) is 4 percent. Courtney used the loan proceeds to acquire several personal-use assets (an automobile and other items). What amount is Courtney required to include in gross income in the current year?

Answer: $4,000, computed as follows:

Description	Amount	Explanation
(1) Loan principal	$100,000	
(2) Applicable federal interest rate compounded semiannually	4%	
(3) Interest on loan principal at federal rate	$ 4,000	(1) × (2)
(4) Interest paid by Courtney	0	
Imputed interest included in Courtney's gross income	**$ 4,000**	(3) − (4)

Courtney will include the $4,000 imputed interest in gross income as compensation and will also incur an imputed interest expense of $4,000 for the year. EWD will (a) deduct $4,000 of compensation expense and (b) report $4,000 of interest income. In this example, we assume Courtney used the proceeds for personal purposes so she is not allowed to deduct the interest expense.

What if: Assume the same facts except that EWD had loaned Courtney $10,000 at a zero-interest rate. How much imputed interest income would Courtney be required to include in her gross income for the year?

Answer: $0. The imputed interest rules don't apply because the loan did not exceed $10,000.

Discharge of Indebtedness   In general, when a taxpayer's debt is forgiven by a lender (the debt is discharged), the taxpayer must include the amount of debt relief in gross income.[33]

---

[32]For "gift" loans (loans between individuals), the $10,000 *de minimis* exception is not available for loan proceeds used to purchase or carry income-producing assets. Likewise, the $10,000 *de minimis* exception is not available for compensation-related loans or corporate-shareholder loans where the principal purpose of the loans is to avoid federal tax. For gift loans of $100,000 or less, the imputed interest is limited to the borrower's net investment income (investment income, such as interest income or other investment income not taxed at preferential rates, less related investment expenses). If the borrower's net investment income is $1,000 or less, the imputed interest rules do not apply. §7872(d). The exception for gift loans of $100,000 or less is not available for loans where the principal purpose of the loans is to avoid federal tax.

[33]§61(a)(12). Income from discharge of indebtedness is also realized when debt is forgiven by lenders other than employers, such as banks and credit card companies.

To provide tax relief for insolvent taxpayers—taxpayers with liabilities, including tax liabilities, exceeding their assets—a **discharge of indebtedness** is *not* taxable if the taxpayer is insolvent before *and* after the debt forgiveness.[34] If the discharge of indebtedness makes the taxpayer solvent, the taxpayer recognizes gross income to the extent of his solvency.[35] For example, if a taxpayer is discharged of $30,000 of debt and this causes him to be solvent by $10,000 (after the debt relief, the taxpayer's assets exceed his liabilities by $10,000), the taxpayer must include $10,000 in gross income.[36]

Example 5-21

In the previous example, Courtney borrowed $100,000 from EWD. Because EWD wants to keep Courtney as an employee, it agreed to forgive $10,000 of loan principal at the end of each year that Courtney stays on board. On December 31 of this year, EWD formally cancels $10,000 of Courtney's indebtedness. How much of this debt relief is Courtney required to include in gross income?

Answer: All $10,000 is included in Courtney's gross income.

EXCLUSION PROVISIONS

LO 5-3

So far in this chapter, we've discussed various types of income taxpayers must realize and recognize by reporting it on their tax returns in the current year. However, there are specific types of income that taxpayers realize but are allowed to permanently *exclude* from gross income or temporarily *defer* from gross income until a subsequent period. As we discussed in the previous chapter, exclusions and deferrals are the result of specific congressional action and are narrowly defined. Because taxpayers are not required to recognize income that is excluded or deferred, we refer to tax laws allowing exclusions or deferrals as **nonrecognition provisions.** Nonrecognition provisions result from various policy objectives. In very general terms, Congress allows most exclusions and deferrals for two primary reasons: (1) to subsidize or encourage particular activities or (2) to be fair to taxpayers (such as mitigating the inequity of double taxation). Our discussion in this chapter focuses on exclusions.

Common Exclusions

Because exclusion provisions allow taxpayers to permanently remove certain income items from their tax base, they are particularly taxpayer-friendly. We begin by introducing three common exclusion provisions, the exclusions of municipal bond interest, gain on the sale of a personal residence, and fringe benefits. We continue with a survey of other exclusion provisions based on their underlying purpose: education, double taxation, and sickness and injury.[37]

Municipal Bond Interest   The most common example of an exclusion provision is the exclusion of interest on **municipal bonds.** Municipal bonds include bonds issued by state and local governments located in the United States, and this exclusion is generally recognized as a subsidy to state and local governments (the exclusion allows state and local

---

[34]§108(a)(1)(B).

[35]§108(a)(3).

[36]Other circumstances in which taxpayers may exclude a discharge of indebtedness are beyond the scope of this chapter. See §108(f) for discussion of the limited exclusions of student loan forgiveness for loans requiring students to work for a specified time in certain professions or student loans forgiven on account of death or total and permanent disability of the student. See §108(a)(1)(E) for discussion of the exclusion of up to $2,000,000 of home mortgage forgiveness from 2007 through 2017. See §108(i) for a discussion of the deferral of debt forgiveness income for businesses reacquiring debt at a discounted price in 2009 and 2010. This provision allows taxpayers to recognize the debt forgiveness income ratably over the five-year period 2014 through 2018.

[37]Another common exclusion we discuss in detail in the Retirement Savings and Deferred Compensation chapter is the exclusion of earnings on Roth retirement savings accounts.

governments to offer bonds at a lower before-tax interest rate). In contrast, interest on U.S. government obligations (such as Treasury bills) is taxable for federal tax purposes but is tax-exempt for state and local tax purposes.

Example 5-22

Courtney holds a $10,000 City of Cincinnati municipal bond. The bond pays 5 percent interest annually. Courtney acquired the bond a few years ago. The city used the proceeds from the bond issuance to help pay for renovations on a major league baseball stadium. In late December, Courtney received $500 of interest income from the bond for the year. How much of the $500 interest from the municipal bond may Courtney *exclude* from her gross income?

Answer: All $500 because the interest is from a municipal bond.

Gains on the Sale of Personal Residence   The tax law provides several provisions that encourage or subsidize home ownership, and the exclusion of the gain on the sale of a personal residence is a common example of one such provision. Specifically, taxpayers meeting certain home ownership *and* use requirements can permanently exclude up to $250,000 ($500,000 if married filing jointly) of realized gain on the sale of their principal residence.[38] Gain in excess of the excludable amount generally qualifies as long-term capital gain subject to tax at preferential rates. To satisfy the ownership test, the taxpayer must have owned the residence (house, condominium, trailer, or houseboat) for a total of two or more years during the five-year period ending on the date of the sale. To satisfy the use test, the taxpayer must have used the property as her principal residence for a total of two or more years (noncontiguous use is permissible) during the five-year period ending on the date of the sale. The tax law limits each taxpayer to one exclusion every two years. Married couples filing joint returns are eligible for the full $500,000 exclusion if *either* spouse meets the ownership test and *both* spouses meet the principal-use test. However, if *either* spouse is ineligible for the exclusion because he or she personally used the $250,000 exclusion on another home sale during the two years before the date of the current sale, the couple's available exclusion is reduced to $250,000.[39]

Example 5-23

What if: Assume that in October of this year, Courtney sold her home in Cincinnati. Courtney and her ex-husband purchased the home four years ago for $400,000, and Courtney received the house in the divorce settlement and lived there until she moved to Kansas City in January. She sold the home for $550,000. How much taxable gain does she recognize on the sale of the home?

Answer: $0. Because Courtney satisfies the two-year ownership and two-year use test, she may exclude up to $250,000 of gain from the sale of her home. Thus, Courtney may exclude the entire $150,000 gain that she realized on the sale ($550,000 sales price less $400,000 basis).

What if: Assume the same facts except Courtney sold the home for $700,000. How much taxable gain does she recognize on the sale of the home?

Answer: $50,000. Because Courtney satisfies the two-year ownership and two-year use test, she may exclude $250,000 of the $300,000 gain from the sale of her home ($700,000 sales price less $400,000 basis). Thus, Courtney recognizes a $50,000 taxable gain on the sale.

---

[38]§121.

[39]We discuss the rules for sale of principal residence in more detail in the Tax Consequences of Home Ownership chapter, including relief rules for taxpayers who cannot meet the ownership and use test due to unusual or hardship circumstances and the limitation on the gain exclusion for taxpayers using a home for something other than a principal residence for a period (nonqualified use) before using the home as a principal residence.

Fringe Benefits   In addition to paying salary and wages, many employers provide employees with **fringe benefits.** For example, an employer may provide an employee with an automobile to use for personal purposes, pay for an employee to join a health club, pay for an employee's moving expenses, or pay for an employee's home security. In general, the value of these benefits is *included* in the employee's gross income as compensation for services. However, certain fringe benefits, called "qualified" fringe benefits, are excluded from gross income.[40] Exhibit 5-3 lists some of the most common fringe benefits excluded from an employee's gross income.

In addition to offering excluded fringe benefits, many employers make contributions to retirement plans on behalf of their employees. Subject to specific rules that we discuss in the Retirement Savings and Deferred Compensation chapter, these contributions (as well as employee contributions from salary) are not currently included in the employee's gross income but are deferred until the employee withdraws the contributions and related earnings from the plan. We discuss fringe benefits in more depth in the Compensation chapter.

Example 5-24

EWD paid $6,000 this year for Courtney's health insurance premiums and $150 in premiums for her $40,000 group-term life insurance policy. How much of the $6,150 in benefits can Courtney exclude from her gross income?

Answer: Courtney can exclude all $6,150 in benefits from her gross income. All health insurance premiums paid by an employer on an employee's behalf are excluded from the employee's income. In addition, premiums employers pay on an employee's behalf for group-term life insurance (up to $50,000 of coverage) are also excluded from the employee's gross income.

Example 5-25

In December, Courtney mailed a newsletter to several dozen friends and relatives with a recent picture of her son, daughter, and mother. Courtney printed both the newsletter and the photos on printers at work (with permission of EWD). Courtney would have paid $55 for the duplicate newsletters and photos at a nearby copy center. How much of this $55 benefit that Courtney received from EWD may she *exclude* from her gross income?

Answer: All $55 is excluded. The $55 benefit is considered a nontaxable *de minimis* (so minor to merit disregard) fringe benefit because it is small in amount and infrequent.

Employee expense reimbursements.   As a common fringe benefit, many employees are reimbursed for their employee business expenses by their employers. If an employee is required to submit documentation supporting expenses to receive reimbursement and the employer reimburses only legitimate business expenses, then the employer's reimbursement plan qualifies as an **accountable plan.** Under an accountable plan (which is the most common method for reimbursement), employees *exclude* expense reimbursements from gross income and do *not* deduct the reimbursed expenses. In contrast, if employees receive employer reimbursements for legitimate business expenses but do not have to

[40]Most nontaxable fringe benefits are listed with "items specifically excluded from gross income" in §§101–140 of the Internal Revenue Code. Employers are generally prohibited from discriminating among employees with respect to nontaxable fringe benefits (i.e., they cannot offer them only to executives). Note that §132 provides an exclusion of qualified moving expense reimbursements for members of the Armed Forces of the United States on active duty who move pursuant to a military order. This exclusion is not available to other individuals.

EXHIBIT 5-3   Common Qualified Fringe Benefits (excluded from employee's gross income)

Item	Description
Medical and dental health insurance coverage [§106]	An employee may exclude from income the cost of medical and insurance coverage and dental health insurance premiums the employer pays on an employee's behalf.[41]
Life insurance coverage [§79]	Employees may exclude from income the value of life insurance premiums the employer pays on an employee's behalf for up to $50,000 of group-term life insurance.
De minimis (small) benefits [§132(a)(4)]	As a matter of administrative convenience, Congress allows employees to exclude from income relatively small and infrequent benefits employees receive at work (such as limited use of a business copy machine).
Meals and lodging for the employer's provided convenience [§119]	Employees may exclude employer-provided meals and lodging if they (1) are provided on the employer's business premises to the employee (and spouse and dependents); (2) are provided for the employer's convenience (such as allowing the employee to be on-call 24 hours a day or continue working on-site over lunch); and (3) the employee accepts the lodging as a condition of employment (for lodging only).
Employee educational assistance programs [§127]	Employees may exclude up to $5,250 of employer-provided educational assistance benefits covering tuition, books, and fees for any instruction that improves the taxpayer's capabilities, whether or not job-related or part of a degree program.
No additional cost services [§132(a)(1)]	Employees may exclude the value of services provided by an employer that generate no substantial costs to the employer (such as free flight benefits for airline employees on a space-available basis or free hotel service for hotel employees).
Qualified employee discounts [§132(a)(2)]	Employees may exclude (a) a discount on employer-provided goods as long as the discount does not exceed the employer's gross profit percentage on all property offered for sale to customers and (b) up to 20 percent employer-provided discount on services. Discounts in excess of these amounts are taxable as compensation. See Example 5-19.
Dependent care benefits [§129]	Employees may exclude up to $5,000 for benefits paid or reimbursed by employers for caring for children under age 13 or dependents or spouses who are physically or mentally unable to care for themselves.
Working condition fringe benefits [§132(a)(3)]	Employees may exclude from income any benefit or reimbursement of a benefit provided by an employer that would be deductible as an ordinary and necessary expense by the employee if the employee had paid the expense.
Qualified transportation benefits [§132(a)(5)]	Employees may exclude up to $260 per month of employer-provided parking and up to $260 per month of the combined value of employer-provided mass transit passes and the value of a carpool vehicle for employee use.
Cafeteria plans [§125]	Cafeteria plans allow employees to choose between various nontaxable fringe benefits (such as health insurance and dental insurance) and cash. These benefits are tax-free to the extent the taxpayer chooses nontaxable fringe benefits and taxable to the extent the employee receives cash.
Flexible spending accounts [§125]	Flexible spending accounts (or FSAs) allow employees to set aside a portion of their *before*-tax salary for payment of health and/or dependent-care benefits. These amounts must be used by the end of the year or within the first two and a half months of the next plan year, or employees forfeit the unused balance. In lieu of allowing the two-and-a-half-month grace period at the beginning of each new year, employers can allow employees to carry over up to $500 of unused amounts to be used anytime during the next year (it is the employer's choice). This option does not apply to dependent-care flexible spending accounts. For 2018, the amount of before-tax salary an employee may set aside for medical expenses is limited to $2,650 and the before-tax amount that may be set aside for dependent-care expenses is limited to $5,000.

submit documentation supporting the expenses, the reimbursement is considered taxable compensation, and the employee is *not* allowed to deduct the expenses as employment-related expenses (reimbursed or not). You can imagine that employees really favor accountable plans.

[41]The cost of medical coverage paid by an employer and offered through a health insurance exchange is not an excludable benefit unless the employer is a small employer that elects to make all of its full-time employees eligible for plans offered through the small business health options program (SHOP). For this purpose, a small employer is an employer that employs an average of at least one but 100 or fewer employees during business days in the prior year, and employs at least one employee on the first day of the plan year. In 2015, SHOP is open to employers with 50 or fewer full-time equivalent employees. Beginning in 2016, some states opened SHOPs to employers with up to 100 full-time equivalent employees.

TAXES IN THE REAL WORLD   Have Phone, Will Call Tax-Free

In years past, the IRS classified employee cell phones issued by employers as a taxable benefit (i.e., taxable compensation) and required employees to keep detailed records to substantiate business versus personal use of the phone. As you might expect, the classification and record-keeping requirements were not met with great enthusiasm. In 2011, the IRS reversed its course and now considers an employer-issued cell phone as an excludable fringe benefit (both for business and personal use) when the phone is provided primarily for noncompensatory business reasons. Even better, the IRS no longer requires record keeping for employees to receive the tax-free treatment. See Notice 2011-72.

Education-Related Exclusions

As an incentive for taxpayers to participate in higher education (education beyond high school), Congress excludes certain types of income if the funds are used for higher education. In the following paragraphs, we discuss exclusions for scholarships and exclusions for certain types of investment plans used to save for college.[42]

Scholarships   College students seeking a degree can exclude from gross income scholarships (including Pell grants) that pay for tuition, fees, books, supplies, and other equipment *required* for the student's courses.[43] Any excess scholarship amounts (such as for room or board) are fully taxable. The scholarship exclusion applies only if the recipient is *not* required to perform services in exchange for receiving the scholarship. "Scholarships" that represent compensation for past, current, or future services are fully taxable. However, tuition waivers or reductions provided by an educational institution for undergraduate courses for student employees or for graduate courses for teaching or research assistants are not taxable.

What about athletic scholarships? Good question. The IRS has ruled that the value of athletic scholarships is excludable from gross income if it: (1) is awarded to students by a university that *expects* but *does not require* the students to participate in a particular sport; (2) requires no particular activity in lieu of participation; and (3) is not canceled if the student cannot participate.[44] Like other scholarships, athletic scholarships are only excludable from gross income to the extent they pay for tuition, fees, books, supplies, and other equipment required for the student's courses. Any excess amount (for example, for room and board) is taxable.

THE KEY FACTS

Education Exclusions

- Students seeking a college degree can exclude scholarships that pay for required tuition, fees, books, and supplies.
- Taxpayers can elect to exclude interest earned on Series EE savings bonds when the redemption proceeds are used to pay qualified higher-education expenses.
- The exclusion of interest on Series EE savings bonds is restricted to taxpayers with modified AGI below specific limits.

Example 5-26

Ellen, Courtney's daughter, received a $700 scholarship from the University of Missouri–Kansas City that pays $400 of her tuition and provides $300 cash for books. Ellen spent $350 on books. How much of the scholarship may she exclude from gross income?

Answer: All $700 is excluded. Ellen may exclude all of the scholarship for tuition and she may exclude the $300 cash she received for books because she spent all $300 purchasing her books for school.

What if: How much is Ellen allowed to exclude if she spent only $250 on books?

Answer: $650 is excluded. Ellen excludes all of the scholarship for her tuition and $250 of the $300 in cash payments because she spent $250 on books. She must include the excess cash payment of $50 ($300 − $250) in her gross income.

---

[42]A detailed explanation is available in IRS Publication 970 *Tax Benefits for Education* available on the IRS website at www.irs.gov.
[43]§117(b)(2).
[44]Rev. Rul. 77-263, 1977-2 CB 47.

Other Educational Subsidies Taxpayers are allowed to exclude from gross income earnings on investments in qualified education plans such as 529 plans and Coverdell education savings accounts as long as they use the earnings to pay for qualifying educational expenditures.

With 529 plans, parents, grandparents, and other individuals are allowed to contribute up to the maximum allowed by state-sponsored 529 plans to fund the qualified educational costs of future *college* students and, subject to limitations, educational costs of students at public, private, or religious elementary or secondary schools.[45] Earnings in 529 plans are distributed tax-free provided they are used for qualified higher-education expenses (no annual limit) or tuition expense attributable to public, private, or religious elementary or secondary schools (subject to a $10,000 limit per beneficiary per year). Qualified higher education expenses include tuition, books, supplies, required equipment and supplies, computer equipment and software, and reasonable room and board costs attending a higher education institution. If, on the other hand, distributions are made to the beneficiary for other purposes or exceed the $10,000 limit for tuition expenses attributable to public, private, or religious elementary or secondary schools, the earnings distributed are taxed to the beneficiary at the beneficiary's tax rate and are subject to an additional 10 percent penalty, while distributions of the original investment (contributions) to the beneficiary are treated as gifts.[46] Similarly, distributions to contributors (e.g., parents, grandparents) that represent earnings on their contributions are included in contributors' gross income and are also subject to the 10 percent penalty.

With a Coverdell account, yearly contributions to the account are limited to $2,000 for each beneficiary, and distributions may be used to pay for qualified educational costs of kindergarten through 12th grade and qualified higher-education expenses such as tuition, books, fees, supplies, and reasonable room and board.[47] The $2,000 contribution limit for Coverdell accounts phases out as AGI (modified to include certain types of excluded foreign income) increases from $190,000 to $220,000 for married filing jointly taxpayers, and from $95,000 to $110,000 for all other taxpayers.

U.S. Series EE Bonds The federal government issues bonds that allow taxpayers to acquire the bonds at a discount and redeem the bonds for a fixed amount over stated time intervals. These bonds don't generate any cash in the form of interest until the taxpayer redeems the bond. At redemption, the amount of the redemption price in excess of the acquisition price is interest included in gross income.[48] U.S. Series EE bonds fall into this category. However, an exclusion is available for interest from Series EE bonds. This exclusion requires that the redemption proceeds be used to pay for higher-education expenses of the taxpayer, the taxpayer's spouse, or a dependent of the taxpayer. Qualified higher-education expenses include the tuition and fees required for enrollment or attendance at an eligible educational institution. Taxpayers may also exclude the interest income if they contribute the proceeds to a qualified tuition program.

The exclusion is partially reduced or eliminated for taxpayers exceeding a fixed level of modified adjusted gross income (adjusted gross income before the educational savings bond exclusion, the foreign-earned income exclusion, discussed below, and certain other deductions).[49] If the taxpayer's modified AGI exceeds the thresholds in the redemption

---

[45]Contribution limits vary according to the state administering the 529 plan. In addition, more than half the states offer a state tax deduction or credit to residents contributing to the 529 plan sponsored by the state in which the contributors reside.

[46]Under §529(c)(3), multiple distributions received under these circumstances are treated as annuities. As a result, a portion of each distribution would be treated as a gift with the remainder treated as income.

[47]§530(b). This definition of qualified higher education expenses is consistent with the definition used in §221(d)(2) to determine if interest paid on education-related loans is deductible (see the Individual Deductions chapter).

[48]Alternatively, taxpayers can elect to include the annual increase in the redemption value in gross income rather than waiting to recognize all the income on redemption. See §454(a).

[49]§135(c)(4).

year, the exclusion is phased out (gradually reduced) until all of the interest from the bonds is taxed.[50]

Exclusions That Mitigate Double Taxation

Congress provides certain exclusions that eliminate the potential double tax that may arise for gifts, inheritances, and life insurance proceeds.

Gifts and Inheritances   Individuals may transfer property to other taxpayers without receiving or expecting to receive value in return. If the *transferor* is alive at the time of the transfer, the property transfer is called a **gift.** If the property is transferred from the decedent's estate (the transferor is deceased), it is called an **inheritance.** These transfers are generally subject to a federal transfer tax, *not* the income tax. Gifts are typically subject to the federal gift tax and inheritances are typically subject to a federal estate tax.[51] Thus, gift and estate taxes are imposed on *transfer* of the property and *not included in income by the recipient.* The exclusion of gifts and inheritances from income taxation avoids the potential double taxation (transfer and income taxation) on these transfers.

Example 5-27

Ellen graduated from high school last year. As a graduation present, Gram purchased a $1,500 travel package for Ellen, so that Ellen could go on a Caribbean cruise. Last year, Ellen also received an inheritance of $2,000 from Gramps's estate. How much gross income does Ellen recognize on the $1,500 gift she received from Gram and the $2,000 inheritance she received from Gramps's estate?

Answer: $0. Ellen is allowed to exclude the entire gift and the entire amount of the inheritance from her gross income. Consequently, she does not recognize any gross income from these transactions.

Life Insurance Proceeds   In some ways, life insurance proceeds are similar to inheritances. When the owner of the life insurance policy dies, the beneficiary receives the death benefit proceeds. The decedent (or the decedent's estate) is generally subject to estate taxation on the amount of the insurance proceeds. In order to avoid potential double taxation on the life insurance proceeds, the tax laws allow taxpayers receiving life insurance proceeds to exclude the proceeds from gross income.[52] However, when the insurance proceeds are paid over a period of time rather than in a lump sum, a portion of the payments represents interest and must be included in gross income. In addition, the life insurance proceeds exclusion generally does not apply when a life insurance policy is transferred to another party for valuable consideration. In this case, the eventual life insurance proceeds collected by the purchaser are excluded up to the sum of the purchase price of the policy and any subsequent premiums, with remaining proceeds taxable as ordinary income.[53]

What happens if a taxpayer cashes out a policy before death? The tax treatment varies based on the specific facts. Generally, if a taxpayer simply cancels a life insurance contract and is paid the policy's cash surrender value, she would recognize ordinary income to the extent the proceeds received exceed previous premiums paid. If premiums paid exceed the proceeds received, the loss is not deductible. If, however, the taxpayer is terminally ill (medically certified with an illness expected to cause death within 24 months), early

---

[50]In 2018, the phase-out range begins at $119,300 of modified adjusted gross income for married taxpayers filing joint returns. For all other taxpayers, the phase-out range begins at $79,550.

[51]As a general rule, for 2018, the federal gift tax does not apply to relatively small gifts ($15,000 or less per person per year), and the federal estate tax only applies to transfers from larger estates (over $11,200,0000).

[52]§101. The exclusion does not apply if the insurance policy is sold by the owner.

[53]This exception to the exclusion does not apply if the recipient of the policy is the insured, a partner of the insured, a partnership in which the insured is a partner, or a corporation in which the insured is an officer or shareholder. This exception also does not apply to policies transferred by gift or tax-free exchange. §101(a)(2).

receipt of life insurance proceeds in the form of **accelerated death benefits** is not taxable. If a taxpayer is chronically ill (medically certified to require substantial assistance for daily living activities or due to cognitive impairment), life insurance proceeds are not taxable to the extent they are used to pay for the taxpayer's long-term care.

Example 5-28

What if: Gramps received $200,000 of accelerated death benefits from a life insurance policy last year when he was diagnosed with terminal cancer with an expected life of less than one year. How much gross income would the $200,000 payment generate?

Answer: None, because Gramps was medically certified as terminally ill with an illness expected to cause death within 24 months.

What if: Due to financial issues, several years ago Gramps transferred a $100,000 life insurance policy on his life to a business associate for $5,000. Since that time, the business associate has continued to pay the annual premiums on the policy (totaling $20,000 before Gramps's death). Upon Gramps's death, the life insurance company paid the business associate the policy's $100,000 face value. How much of the $100,000 payment is taxable?

Answer: $75,000. Because the business associate purchased the life insurance policy from Gramps for valuable consideration, she may exclude the $100,000 proceeds up to the sum of the purchase price of the policy ($5,000) and any subsequent premiums ($20,000), with the remaining proceeds ($100,000 − $5,000 − $20,000 = $75,000) taxable as ordinary income.

THE KEY FACTS

Exclusions to Mitigate Double Taxation

- Gifts and inheritances are subject to federal transfer taxes and are, therefore, excluded from the income of the recipient.
- A maximum of $103,900 (2018) of foreign-earned income can be excluded from gross income for qualifying individuals.
- To be eligible for the foreign-earned income exclusion, the taxpayer must live in the foreign country for 330 days in a consecutive 12-month period.

Foreign-Earned Income   U.S. citizens are subject to tax on all income whether it is generated in the United States or in foreign countries. Because most foreign countries also impose tax on income earned within their borders, U.S. citizens could be subject to both U.S. and foreign taxation on income earned abroad. To provide relief from this potential double taxation, Congress allows taxpayers to exclude foreign-earned income (income from foreign sources for personal services performed) up to an annual maximum amount. Income from pensions, annuities, salary paid by the U.S. government, or deferred compensation does not qualify for the exclusion. The maximum exclusion is indexed for inflation, and in 2018 the maximum is $103,900. Rather than claim this exclusion, taxpayers may deduct foreign taxes paid as itemized deductions or they may claim the foreign tax credit for foreign taxes paid on their foreign-earned income.[54]

To determine whether claiming the annual exclusion, the deduction, or the foreign tax credit is most advantageous, taxpayers should compare the tax effects of each option. To claim the annual exclusion instead of the foreign tax deduction or credit, the taxpayer must elect to do so using Form 2555. Taxpayers who elect to use the exclusion may revoke the election for later years and use the foreign tax credit or deduct foreign taxes paid. However, once a taxpayer revokes the exclusion election, she may not reelect to use the exclusion before the sixth tax year after the tax year the revocation was made.

As you might expect, individuals must meet certain requirements to qualify for the foreign-earned income exclusion. To be eligible for the annual exclusion, a taxpayer must have her tax home in a foreign country and (1) be considered a resident of the foreign country by living in the country for the entire year (calendar year) or (2) live in the foreign country for 330 days in a consecutive 12-month period, which might occur over two tax years. The *maximum* exclusion is reduced pro rata for each day during the calendar year that is not part of the qualifying 12-month period.

Taxpayers meeting the requirement for the foreign-earned income exclusion may also exclude from income reasonable housing costs (paid by an employer) that exceed 16 percent of the statutory foreign-earned income exclusion amount for the year (exceed 16 percent × $103,900 = $16,624 in 2018). The exclusion, however, is limited to a maximum of 14 percent of the statutory exclusion amount (14 percent × $103,900 = $14,546 in 2018). Thus, in

---

[54]See §911(b)(2), the Individual Deductions chapter, and the Individual Income Tax Computations and Credits chapter.

2018, if a taxpayer incurs housing costs (provided by an employer) exceeding $16,624, she may exclude such excess costs up to $14,546 (thus, the first $16,624 of employer-provided housing costs are included in gross income).[55] The housing exclusion limit is also subject to daily proration if the taxpayer's qualifying 12-month period occurs over two tax years.

Example 5-29

What if: Assume Courtney is considering a transfer to EWD's overseas affiliate. If she transfers, she anticipates she will earn approximately $120,000 in salary. How much of her expected $120,000 annual salary will Courtney be allowed to exclude from her gross income, assuming she meets the residency requirements?

Answer: She is eligible to exclude $103,900 of her $120,000 of compensation from U.S. taxation in 2018. However, her entire $120,000 salary may be subject to the foreign country's income tax.

What if: Assume Courtney decides to transfer, but she expects her 12-month qualifying period to include only 200 days in the first year and 140 days in the second year. How much of her expected $65,000 salary in the first year will she be allowed to exclude from gross income?

Answer: $56,932 [$103,900 full exclusion × 200/365 (days in foreign country/days in year)].

What if: Assume that Courtney expects her 12-month qualifying period to include 200 days in the first year and that she expects her salary to be $45,000 during this period. How much of her expected $45,000 salary will she be allowed to exclude from gross income?

Answer: All $45,000. She can exclude up to $56,932 of salary from income (see above computation).

What if: Assume that if Courtney transfers, EWD's overseas affiliate will also pay for her housing while overseas ($25,000 per year). How much of the $25,000 housing payments may Courtney exclude assuming she lives in the country for the entire year?

Answer: $8,376. Since Courtney meets the requirements for the foreign-earned income exclusion, she may exclude the employer-provided housing costs that exceed $16,624 (16% × $103,900), up to a maximum exclusion of $14,546 (14% × $103,900). Thus, Courtney may exclude $8,376 [the lesser of (a) $8,376 ($25,000 housing cost less $16,624) or (b) $14,546].

Sickness and Injury-Related Exclusions

The tax laws provide several exclusion provisions for taxpayers who are sick or injured. One explanation for these exclusions is that payments for sickness or injury are considered returns of (human) capital.

Workers' Compensation   The provision for workers' compensation is relatively straightforward. Taxpayers receive workers' compensation benefits when they are unable to work because of a work-related injury. Any payments a taxpayer receives from a state-sponsored workers' compensation plan are excluded from the taxpayer's income.[56] Note that this treatment is *opposite* that of *unemployment* compensation, which is fully taxable.

Payments Associated with Personal Injury   Historically, the question of which payments associated with a personal injury were excludable was controversial. In 1996 Congress settled the matter by deciding that all payments associated with compensating a taxpayer for a *physical* injury (including payments for past, current, and future lost wages) are excluded from gross income. That is, the tax laws specify that any *compensatory damages* on account of a *physical injury* or *physical sickness* are nontaxable. Thus, damages taxpayers receive for emotional distress associated with a physical injury are excluded.

In contrast, *punitive damages* are *fully taxable,* because they are intended to punish the harm-doer rather than to compensate the taxpayer for injuries. Likewise, taxpayers receiving damages for emotional distress that are not associated with a physical injury

---

[55]§911(c).
[56]§104.

must include those payments in income. In general, all other awards (those that do not relate to physical injury or sickness or are payments for the medical costs of treating emotional distress) are included in gross income.

Example 5-30

In February, Courtney's cousin, Kelsey, was struck and injured by a bus while walking in a crosswalk. Because the bus driver was negligent, the bus company settled Kelsey's claim by paying her $1,500 for medical expenses and $500 for emotional distress associated with the accident. How much of the $2,000 Kelsey received from the bus company may she *exclude* from her gross income?

Answer: All $2,000. Kelsey may exclude the $1,500 she received for medical expenses and the $500 payment she received for emotional distress because these damages were associated with Kelsey's physical injury.

What if: Assume Kelsey sued the bus company and was awarded $5,000 in punitive damages. How much of the $5,000 would Kelsey be able to exclude from her gross income?

Answer: $0. Payments for punitive damages are not excludable. Kelsey would be required to include the entire $5,000 in her gross income.

THE KEY FACTS

Exclusions Related to Sickness and Injury

- Payments from workers' compensation plans are excluded from gross income.
- Payments received as compensation for a *physical* injury are excluded from gross income, but punitive damages are included in gross income.
- Reimbursements by health and accident insurance policies for medical expenses paid by the taxpayer are excluded from gross income.
- Disability payments received from an *employee-purchased* policy are excluded from gross income.

Health Care Reimbursement   Any reimbursement a taxpayer receives from a health and accident insurance policy for medical expenses paid by the taxpayer during the current year is excluded from gross income. The exclusion applies regardless of whether the taxpayer, her employer, or someone else purchased the health and accident policy for the taxpayer. Of course, the tax benefit rule may require inclusion of reimbursements of medical expenses that were deducted by the taxpayer in a prior year.

Disability Insurance   The exclusion provisions for **disability insurance** are more restrictive than those for workers' compensation payments or reimbursements from a health and accident insurance plan. Disability insurance, sometimes called *wage replacement insurance*, pays the insured individual for wages lost when the individual misses work due to injury or disability. If an individual purchases disability insurance directly, the cost of the policy is not deductible, but any disability benefits are excluded from gross income.

Disability insurance may also be purchased on an individual's behalf by an employer. The employer may allow employees to choose whether the premiums paid on their behalf are to be considered taxable compensation or a nontaxable fringe benefit. If the premiums are taxable compensation to the employee, the policy is considered to have been purchased by the employee. If the premium paid for by the employer is a nontaxable fringe benefit to the employee, the policy is considered to have been purchased by the employer. This distinction is important because only payments taxpayers receive from an *employee-purchased* policy are excluded from their gross income. If the employer pays the premiums for an employee as a nontaxable fringe benefit, the employee must include all disability benefits in gross income.

Example 5-31

Courtney purchased disability insurance last year. In late April of this year, she broke her wrist in a mountain biking accident and could not work for two weeks. Courtney's doctor bills totaled $2,000, of which $1,600 was reimbursed by her health insurance purchased by EWD. How much of the $1,600 health insurance reimbursement for medical expenses is Courtney allowed to *exclude* from her gross income?

Answer: All $1,600 is excluded. All medical expense reimbursements from health insurance are excluded from a taxpayer's gross income.

Courtney also received $600 for lost wages due to the accident from her disability insurance policy. How much of the $600 is Courtney allowed to exclude from her gross income?

Answer: All $600 is excluded. Courtney can exclude the entire amount because she paid the premiums on the policy.

What if: How much of the $600 payment for lost wages from the disability insurance policy would Courtney exclude if EWD paid the disability insurance premium on her behalf as a nontaxable fringe benefit?

Answer: $0 would be excluded. In this circumstance the policy would be considered to be purchased by the employer, so Courtney would not be allowed to exclude any of the payment from gross income. She would include the payment in gross income and be taxed on the entire $600.

What if: How much of the $600 payment for lost wages from the disability insurance policy would Courtney be allowed to exclude if she paid half the cost of the policy with after-tax dollars and EWD paid the other half as a taxable fringe benefit?

Answer: All $600 would be excluded. Because Courtney paid for the entire cost of the policy with after-tax dollars, she would be allowed to exclude all of the disability insurance benefit. Note that if EWD had paid for half the cost of the policy as a nontaxable fringe benefit, Courtney would have been able to exclude $300, not $600.

Deferral Provisions

We've described exclusion provisions that allow taxpayers to permanently eliminate certain types of income from their tax base. Other code sections, called *deferral provisions,* allow taxpayers to defer (but not permanently exclude) the recognition of certain types of realized income. Transactions generating deferred income include **installment sales,** like-kind exchanges, involuntary conversions, and contributions to non-Roth **qualified retirement accounts.** We "defer" our detailed discussion of these transactions to subsequent chapters.

INCOME SUMMARY

At the end of the year, Courtney calculated her income and Gram's income. Exhibit 5-4 presents Courtney's income calculation, Exhibit 5-5 displays how this income would be reported on the front page of Courtney's tax return, and Exhibit 5-6 presents Gram's income calculation. Note that Courtney's actual *gross* income equals her total income on page 1 of her Form 1040 plus her $1,500 consulting expenses (see Example 5-7) and her $9,000 deductions for rental expenses (see Example 5-10), which are both *for* AGI deductions. Because Gram doesn't have any business, rental, or royalty deductions, her gross income is equal to her total income on line 22 of page 1 of her tax return (not included here).

EXHIBIT 5-4 Courtney's Income

Description	Amount	Reference
(1) Salary (line 7, 1040 page 1)	$ 118,000	Example 5-7
(2) Employment bonus award (line 7, 1040 page 1)	4,800	Example 5-4
(3) Discount architectural design services (line 7, 1040 page 1)	6,000	Example 5-19
(4) Compensation on below-market loan from EWD (line 7, 1040 page 1)	4,000	Example 5-20
(5) Discharge of indebtedness (line 7, 1040 page 1)	10,000	Example 5-21
(6) Interest income (line 8a, 1040 page 1)	321	Example 5-9
(7) Dividends (lines 9a and 9b, 1040 page 1)	700	Example 5-8
(8) State tax refund (line 10, 1040 page 1)	420	Example 5-3
(9) Alimony (line 11, 1040 page 1)	20,000	Example 5-14
(10) Net business income (line 12, 1040 page 1)	18,000	Example 5-7
(11) Net rental income (line 17, 1040 page 1)	5,000	Example 5-10
Total income as presented on line 22 of front page of 1040 (see Exhibit 5-5)	**$187,241**	Sum of (1) through (11)

EXHIBIT 5-5 **Courtney's Tax Return**

(total income as reported on 1040 page 1, lines 7–22)

If more than four dependents, see instructions and check here ▶ ☐					☐ ☐ ☐	(see instructions) Dependents on 6c not entered above
	d Total number of exemptions claimed					Add numbers on lines above ▶ ☐

Income	7	Wages, salaries, tips, etc. Attach Form(s) W-2			7	142,800
	8a	**Taxable** interest. Attach Schedule B if required			8a	321
Attach Form(s)	b	**Tax-exempt** interest. **Do not** include on line 8a . . .	**8b**	500		
W-2 here. Also	9a	Ordinary dividends. Attach Schedule B if required			9a	700
attach Forms	b	Qualified dividends	**9b**	700		
W-2G and	10	Taxable refunds, credits, or offsets of state and local income taxes			10	420
1099-R if tax	11	Alimony received			11	20,000
was withheld.	12	Business income or (loss). Attach Schedule C or C-EZ			12	18,000
	13	Capital gain or (loss). Attach Schedule D if required. If not required, check here ▶ ☐			13	
If you did not	14	Other gains or (losses). Attach Form 4797			14	
get a W-2,	15a	IRA distributions .	15a		**b** Taxable amount . . .	15b	
see instructions.	16a	Pensions and annuities	16a		**b** Taxable amount . . .	16b	
	17	Rental real estate, royalties, partnerships, S corporations, trusts, etc. Attach Schedule E			17	5,000
	18	Farm income or (loss). Attach Schedule F			18	
	19	Unemployment compensation			19	
	20a	Social security benefits	20a		**b** Taxable amount . . .	20b	
	21	Other income. List type and amount _____			21	
	22	Combine the amounts in the far right column for lines 7 through 21. This is your **total income** ▶			22	187,241

Source: Form 1040

EXHIBIT 5-6 **Gram's Income**

Deduction	Amount	Reference
Interest income	$ 4,750	Example 5-9
Annuity income	3,400	Example 5-11
Gain on stock sale	350	Example 5-12
Sweepstakes winnings (WaveRunner)	7,500	Example 5-17
Income for current year	$16,000	

CONCLUSION

In this chapter we explained the basic concepts of income realization and recognition, identified and discussed the major types of income, and described the most common income exclusions. We discovered that many exclusions are related to specific congressional objectives, but that absent a specific exclusion, realized income should be included in gross income. In the next chapter, we turn our attention to the deductions available to taxpayers when computing their taxable income. We will continue to follow Courtney and Gram in their quest to determine their taxable income and corresponding tax liability.

Appendix   2017 Social Security Worksheet from Form 1040

<u>2017 Form 1040—Lines 20a and 20b</u>

Social Security Benefits Worksheet—Lines 20a and 20b   *Keep for Your Records*

Before you begin:	✓ Complete Form 1040, lines 21 and 23 through 32, if they apply to you. ✓ Figure any write-in adjustments to be entered on the dotted line next to line 36 (see the instructions for line 36). ✓ If you are married filing separately and you lived apart from your spouse for all of 2017, enter "D" to the right of the word "benefits" on line 20a. If you don't, you may get a math error notice from the IRS. ✓ Be sure you have read the *Exception* in the line 20a and 20b instructions to see if you can use this worksheet instead of a publication to find out if any of your benefits are taxable.

1. Enter the total amount from **box 5** of **all** your **Forms SSA-1099** and **Forms RRB-1099.** Also, enter this amount on Form 1040, line 20a .... **1.** _____

2. Multiply line 1 by 50% (0.50) .... **2.** _____

3. Combine the amounts from Form 1040, lines 7, 8a, 9a, 10 through 14, 15b, 16b, 17 through 19, and 21 .... **3.** _____

4. Enter the amount, if any, from Form 1040, line 8b .... **4.** _____

5. Combine lines 2, 3, and 4 .... **5.** _____

6. Enter the total of the amounts from Form 1040, lines 23 through 32, plus any write-in adjustments you entered on the dotted line next to line 36 .... **6.** _____

7. Is the amount on line 6 less than the amount on line 5?

   ☐ **No.** (STOP) None of your social security benefits are taxable. Enter -0- on Form 1040, line 20b.

   ☐ **Yes.** Subtract line 6 from line 5 .... **7.** _____

8. If you are:
   • Married filing jointly, enter $32,000
   • Single, head of household, qualifying widow(er), or married filing separately and you **lived apart** from your spouse for all of 2017, enter $25,000

   • Married filing separately and you lived with your spouse at any time in 2017, skip lines 8 through 15; multiply line 7 by 85% (0.85) and enter the result on line 16. Then, go to line 17 .... **8.** _____

9. Is the amount on line 8 less than the amount on line 7?

   ☐ **No.** (STOP) None of your social security benefits are taxable. Enter -0- on Form 1040, line 20b. If you are married filing separately and you **lived apart** from your spouse for all of 2017, be sure you entered "D" to the right of the word "benefits" on line 20a.

   ☐ **Yes.** Subtract line 8 from line 7 .... **9.** _____

10. Enter: $12,000 if married filing jointly; $9,000 if single, head of household, qualifying widow(er), or married filing separately and you **lived apart** from your spouse for all of 2017 .... **10.** _____

11. Subtract line 10 from line 9. If zero or less, enter -0- .... **11.** _____

12. Enter the **smaller** of line 9 or line 10 .... **12.** _____

13. Enter one-half of line 12 .... **13.** _____

14. Enter the **smaller** of line 2 or line 13 .... **14.** _____

15. Multiply line 11 by 85% (0.85). If line 11 is zero, enter -0- .... **15.** _____

16. Add lines 14 and 15 .... **16.** _____

17. Multiply line 1 by 85% (0.85) .... **17.** _____

18. **Taxable social security benefits.** Enter the **smaller** of line 16 or line 17. Also enter this amount on Form 1040, line 20b .... **18.** _____

(TIP) *If any of your benefits are taxable for 2017 **and** they include a lump-sum benefit payment that was for an earlier year, you may be able to reduce the taxable amount. See* Lump-Sum Election *in Pub. 915 for details.*

Summary

LO 5-1   Apply the concept of realization.

- Income is typically realized with a transaction that allows economic benefit to be identified and measured.
- Unless realized income is deferred or excluded, it is included in gross income in the period dictated by the taxpayer's accounting method.
- The accrual method of accounting recognizes income in the period it is earned, and this method is typically used by large corporations.
- The cash method of accounting recognizes income in the period received, and this method offers a simple and flexible method of accounting typically used by individuals.
- The return of capital principle, constructive receipt doctrine, and assignment of income doctrine affect how much income is recognized, when income is recognized, and who recognizes income, respectively.

LO 5-2   Discuss the distinctions between the various sources of income, including income from services and property.

- Income from services is called earned income, whereas income from property is called unearned income.
- A portion of annuity payments and proceeds from sales of property is a nontaxable return of capital.
- Earned and unearned income generated by flow-through business entities is reported by partners and Subchapter S shareholders.
- Other sources of income include alimony payments, unemployment compensation, Social Security benefits, prizes and awards, bargain purchases, imputed interest on below-market loans, and discharge of indebtedness.

LO 5-3   Apply basic income exclusion provisions to compute gross income.

- Interest received from holding state and local indebtedness (municipal interest) is excluded from gross income.
- A taxpayer satisfying certain home ownership and use requirements can permanently exclude up to $250,000 ($500,000 if married filing jointly) of realized gain on the sale of her principal residence.
- Employment-related nonrecognition provisions include a variety of excludable fringe benefits.
- Gifts, inheritances, life insurance proceeds, and foreign-earned income up to $103,900 are excluded from gross income in order to mitigate the effects of double taxation.
- Common injury-related nonrecognition provisions include the exclusions for workers' compensation, personal injury payments and reimbursements from health insurance policies, and certain payments from disability policies.

KEY TERMS

accelerated death benefits (5-28)
accountable plan (5-23)
accrual method (5-6)
alimony (5-14)
annuity (5-11)
assignment of income doctrine (5-8)
barter clubs (5-4)
cash method (5-6)
claim of right doctrine (5-7)
community property systems (5-8)

constructive receipt doctrine (5-7)
disability insurance (5-30)
discharge of indebtedness (5-21)
earned income (5-10)
flow-through entity (5-14)
fringe benefits (5-23)
gift (5-27)
gross income (5-2)
imputed income (5-19)
inheritance (5-27)

installment sale (5-31)
municipal bond (5-21)
nonrecognition provisions (5-21)
qualified retirement accounts (5-31)
realization principle (5-3)
return of capital (5-5)
tax basis (5-4)
tax benefit rule (5-5)
unearned income (5-10)
wherewithal to pay (5-3)

DISCUSSION QUESTIONS

Discussion Questions are available in Connect®.

1. Based on the definition of gross income in §61 and related regulations, what is the general presumption regarding the taxability of income realized? **LO 5-1**

2. Based on the definition of gross income in §61, related regulations, and judicial rulings, what are the three criteria for recognizing taxable income? **LO 5-1**

3. Describe the concept of realization for tax purposes. **LO 5-1**

4. Compare and contrast realization of income with recognition of income. **LO 5-1**

5. Tim is a plumber who joined a barter club. This year Tim exchanges plumbing services for a new roof. The roof is properly valued at $2,500, but Tim would have only billed $2,200 for the plumbing services. What amount of income should Tim recognize on the exchange of his services for a roof? Would your answer change if Tim would have normally billed $3,000 for his services? **LO 5-1**

6. Andre constructs and installs cabinets in homes. Blair sells and installs carpet in apartments. Andre and Blair worked out an arrangement whereby Andre installed cabinets in Blair's home and Blair installed carpet in Andre's home. Neither Andre nor Blair believes they are required to recognize any gross income on this exchange because neither received cash. Do you agree with them? Explain. **LO 5-1**

7. What issue precipitated the return of capital principle? Explain. **LO 5-1**

8. Compare how the return of capital principle applies when: (1) a taxpayer sells an asset and collects the sale proceeds immediately, and (2) a taxpayer sells an asset and collects the sale proceeds over several periods (an installment sale). If Congress wanted to maximize revenue from installment sales, how would it have applied the return of capital principle for installment sales? **LO 5-1**

9. This year Jorge received a refund of property taxes that he deducted on his tax return last year. Jorge is not sure whether he should include the refund in his gross income. What would you tell him? **LO 5-1**

10. Describe in general how the cash method of accounting differs from the accrual method of accounting. **LO 5-1**

11. Janet is a cash-method, calendar-year taxpayer. She received a check for services provided in the mail during the last week of December. However, rather than cash the check, Janet decided to wait until the following January because she believes that her delay will cause the income to be realized and recognized next year. What would you tell her? Would it matter if she didn't open the envelope? Would it matter if she refused to check her mail during the last week of December? Explain. **LO 5-1**

12. The cash method of accounting means that taxpayers don't recognize income unless they receive cash or cash equivalents. True or false? Explain. **LO 5-1**

13. Contrast the constructive receipt doctrine with the claim of right doctrine. **LO 5-1**

14. Dewey is a lawyer who uses the cash method of accounting. Last year Dewey provided a client with legal services worth $55,000, but the client could not pay the fee. This year Dewey requested that in lieu of paying Dewey $55,000 for the services, the client could make a $45,000 gift to Dewey's daughter. Dewey's daughter received the check for $45,000 and deposited it in her bank account. How much of this income is taxed, if any, to Dewey? Explain. **LO 5-1**

15. Clyde and Bonnie were married this year. Clyde has a steady job that will pay him about $37,000, while Bonnie does odd jobs that will produce about $28,000 of income. They also have a joint savings account that will pay about $400 of interest. If Clyde and Bonnie reside in a community property state and file married-separate tax returns, how much gross income will Clyde and Bonnie each report? Is there any difference if they reside in a common law state? Explain. **LO 5-2**

LO 5-2   16. Distinguish earned income from unearned income, and provide an example of each.

LO 5-2   17. Jim purchased 100 shares of stock this year and elected to participate in a dividend reinvestment program. This program automatically uses dividends to purchase additional shares of stock. This year Jim's shares paid $350 of dividends and he used these funds to purchase additional shares of stock. These additional shares are worth $375 at year-end. What amount of dividends, if any, should Jim declare as income this year? Explain.

LO 5-2   18. Jerry has a certificate of deposit at the local bank. The interest on this certificate was credited to his account on December 31 of last year, but he didn't withdraw the interest until January of this year. When is the interest income taxed?

LO 5-2   19. Conceptually, when taxpayers receive annuity payments, how do they determine the amount of the payment they must include in gross income?

LO 5-2   20. George purchased a life annuity to provide him monthly payments for as long as he lives. Based on IRS tables, George's life expectancy is 100 months. Is George able to recover his cost of the annuity if he dies before he receives 100 monthly payments? Explain. What happens for tax purposes if George receives more than 100 payments?

LO 5-2   21. Brad purchased land for $45,000 this year. At year-end Brad sold the land for $51,700 and paid a sales commission of $450. What effect does this transaction have on Brad's gross income? Explain.

LO 5-2   22. Tomiko is a 50 percent owner (partner) in the Tanaka partnership. During the year, the partnership reported $1,000 of interest income and $2,000 of dividends. How much of this income must Tomiko include in her gross income?

LO 5-2   23. Clem and Ida have been married for several years, but in 2018 they finalized their divorce. In the divorce decree, Clem agreed to deed his car to Ida and pay Ida $10,000 per year for four years (but not beyond her death). Will either of these transfers qualify as alimony for tax purposes? Explain.

LO 5-2   24. Larry Bounds has won the Gold Bat Award for hitting the longest home run in Major League Baseball this year. The bat is worth almost $35,000. Under what conditions can Larry exclude the award from his gross income? Explain.

LO 5-2   25. Rory and Nicholi, single taxpayers, each annually receive Social Security benefits of $15,000. Rory's taxable income from sources other than Social Security exceeds $200,000. In contrast, the Social Security benefits are Nicholi's only source of income. What percentage of the Social Security benefits must Rory include in his gross income? What percentage of Social Security benefits is Nicholi required to include in his gross income?

LO 5-2   26. Rolando purchases a golf cart from his employer, E-Z-Go Golf Carts, for a sizable discount. Explain the rules for determining if Rolando's purchase results in taxable income for him.

LO 5-2   27. When an employer makes a below-market loan to an employee, what are the tax consequences to the employer and employee?

LO 5-2   28. Explain why an insolvent taxpayer is allowed to exclude income from the discharge of indebtedness if the taxpayer remains insolvent after receiving the debt relief.

LO 5-3   29. What are the basic requirements to exclude the gain on the sale of a personal residence?

LO 5-3   30. Explain why an employee should be concerned about whether his employer reimburses business expenses using an "accountable" plan.

LO 5-3   31. Cassie works in an office and has access to several professional color printers. Her employer allows Cassie and her fellow employees to use the printers to print color postcards for the holidays. This year Cassie printed out two dozen postcards worth almost $76. Must Cassie include this amount in her gross income this year? Explain your answer.

32. What are some common examples of taxable and tax-free fringe benefits?   `LO 5-3`

33. Explain how state and local governments benefit from the provisions that allow taxpayers to exclude interest on state and local bonds from their gross income.   `LO 5-3`

34. Explain why taxpayers are allowed to exclude gifts and inheritances from gross income even though these payments are realized and clearly provide taxpayers with the wherewithal to pay.   `LO 5-3`

35. Describe the kinds of insurance premiums an employer can pay on behalf of an employee without triggering includible compensation to the employee.   `LO 5-3`

36. How are state-sponsored 529 educational savings plans taxed if investment returns are used for educational purposes? Are the returns taxed differently if they are not ultimately used to pay for education costs?   `LO 5-3`

37. Jim was injured in an accident and his surgeon botched the medical procedure. Jim recovered $5,000 from the doctors for pain and suffering and $2,000 for emotional distress. Determine the taxability of these payments and briefly explain to Jim the apparent rationale for including or excluding these payments from gross income.   `LO 5-3`

38. Tom was just hired by Acme Corporation and has decided to purchase disability insurance. This insurance promises to pay him weekly benefits to replace his salary should he be unable to work because of disability. Disability insurance is also available through Acme as part of its compensation plan. Acme pays these premiums as a nontaxable fringe benefit, but the plan promises to pay about 10 percent less in benefits. If Tom elects to have Acme pay the premiums, then his compensation will be reduced by an equivalent amount. Should tax considerations play a role in Tom's choice to buy disability insurance through Acme or on his own? Explain.   `LO 5-3`

PROBLEMS

Select problems are available in Connect®.   ![connect logo]

39. For the following independent cases, determine whether economic income is present and, if so, whether it must be included in gross income (i.e., is it realized and recognized for tax purposes?).   `LO 5-1`

   a) Asia owns stock that is listed on the New York Stock Exchange, and this year the stock increased in value by $20,000.

   b) Ben sold stock for $10,000 and paid a sales commission of $250. Ben purchased the stock several years ago for $4,000.

   c) Bessie is a partner in SULU Enterprises LLC. This year SULU reported that Bessie's share of rental income was $2,700 and her share of municipal interest was $750.

40. Devon owns 1,000 shares of stock worth $10,000. This year he received 200 additional shares of this stock from a stock dividend. His 1,200 shares are now worth $12,500. Must Devon include the dividend paid in stock in income?   `LO 5-1`   `research`

41. XYZ declared a $1 per share dividend on August 15. The date of record for the dividend was September 1 (the stock began selling *ex-dividend* on September 2). The dividend was paid on September 10. Ellis is a cash-method taxpayer. Determine if he must include the dividends in gross income under the following independent circumstances.   `LO 5-1`   `research`

   a) Ellis bought 100 shares of XYZ stock on August 1 for $21 per share. Ellis received $100 on September 10. Ellis still owns the shares at year-end.

b) Ellis bought 100 shares of XYZ stock on August 1 for $21 per share. Ellis sold his XYZ shares on September 5 for $23 per share. Ellis received the $100 dividend on September 10 (note that even though Ellis didn't own the stock on September 10, he still received the dividend because he was the shareholder on the record date).

c) Ellis bought 100 shares of XYZ stock for $22 per share on August 20. Ellis received the $100 dividend on September 10. Ellis still owns the shares at year-end.

LO 5-1

research

42. For the following independent cases, determine whether economic income is present and, if so, whether it must be included in gross income. Identify a tax authority that supports your analysis.

a) Hermione discovered a gold nugget (valued at $10,000) on her land.

b) Jay embezzled $20,000 from his employer and has not yet been apprehended.

c) Keisha found $1,000 inside an old dresser. She purchased the dresser at a discount furniture store at the end of last year and found the money after the beginning of the new year. No one has claimed the money.

LO 5-1

43. Although Hank is retired, he is an excellent handyman and often works part-time on small projects for neighbors and friends. Last week his neighbor, Mike, offered to pay Hank $500 for minor repairs to his house. Hank completed the repairs in December of this year. Hank uses the cash method of accounting and is a calendar-year taxpayer. Compute Hank's gross income for this year from each of the following alternative transactions:

a) Mike paid Hank $200 in cash in December of this year and promised to pay the remaining $300 with interest in three months.

b) Mike paid Hank $100 in cash in December of this year and gave him a negotiable promissory note for $400 due in three months with interest. Hank sold the note in January for $350.

c) Mike gave Hank tickets to the big game in January. The tickets have a face value of $50 but Hank could sell them for $400. Hank went to the game with his son.

d) Mike bought Hank a new set of snow tires. The tires typically sell for $500, but Mike bought them on sale for $450.

LO 5-1

44. Jim recently joined the Austin Barter Club, an organization that facilitates the exchange of services between its members. This year Jim provided lawn-mowing services to other club members. Jim received the following from the barter club. Determine the amount, if any, Jim should include in his gross income in each of the following situations:

a) Jim received $275 of car repair services from another member of the club.

b) Jim received a $150 credit that gave him the option of receiving a season pass at a local ski resort from another member of the club. However, he forgot to request the pass by the end of the ski season and his credit expired.

c) Jim received a $450 credit that can only be applied for goods or services from club members next year.

LO 5-1

research

45. Last year Acme paid Ralph $15,000 to install a new air-conditioning unit at its headquarters building. The air conditioner did not function properly, and this year Acme requested that Ralph return the payment. Because Ralph could not repair one critical part in the unit, he refunded the cost of the repair, $5,000, to Acme.

a) Is Ralph required to include the $15,000 payment he received last year in his gross income from last year?

b) What are the tax implications of the repayment if Ralph was in the 35 percent tax bracket when he received the $15,000 payment from Acme, but was in the 24 percent tax bracket when he refunded $5,000 to Acme?

46. Louis files as a single taxpayer. In April of this year he received a $900 refund of   **LO 5-1**
    state income taxes that he paid last year. How much of the refund, if any, must
    Louis include in gross income under the following independent scenarios? Assume
    the standard deduction last year was $6,350.

    a) Last year Louis claimed itemized deductions of $6,600. Louis's itemized deduc-
       tions included state income taxes paid of $1,750.

    b) Last year Louis had itemized deductions of $4,800 and he chose to claim the
       standard deduction. Louis's itemized deductions included state income taxes paid
       of $1,750.

    c) Last year Louis claimed itemized deductions of $7,790. Louis's itemized deduc-
       tions included state income taxes paid of $2,750.

47. L. A. and Paula file as married taxpayers. In August of this year, they received a   **LO 5-1**
    $5,200 refund of state income taxes that they paid last year. How much of the
    refund, if any, must L. A. and Paula include in gross income under the following
    independent scenarios? Assume the standard deduction last year was $12,700.

    a) Last year L. A. and Paula had itemized deductions of $10,200, and they chose to
       claim the standard deduction.

    b) Last year L. A. and Paula claimed itemized deductions of $23,300. Their
       itemized deductions included state income taxes paid of $7,500.

    c) Last year L. A. and Paula claimed itemized deductions of $15,500. Their
       itemized deductions included state income taxes paid of $10,500.

48. Clyde is a cash-method taxpayer who reports on a calendar-year basis. This year   **LO 5-1**
    Paylate Corporation has decided to pay Clyde a year-end bonus of $1,000. Determine
    the amount Clyde should include in his gross income this year under the following
    circumstances:

    a) Paylate Corporation wrote the check and put it in his office mail slot on Decem-
       ber 30 of this year, but Clyde did not bother to stop by the office to pick it up
       until after year-end.

    b) Paylate Corporation mistakenly wrote the check for $100. Clyde received the
       remaining $900 after year-end.

    c) Paylate Corporation mailed the check to Clyde before the end of the year (and it
       was delivered before year-end). Although Clyde expected the bonus payment, he
       decided not to collect his mail until after year-end.

    d) Clyde picked up the check in December, but the check could not be cashed im-
       mediately because it was postdated January 10.

49. Identify the amount, if any, that these individuals must include in gross income in   **LO 5-2**
    the following independent cases. Assume that the individuals use the cash method
    of accounting and report income on a calendar-year basis.

    a) Elmer was an extremely diligent employee this year and his employer gave him
       three additional days off with pay (Elmer's gross pay for the three days totaled
       $1,200, but his net pay was only $948).

    b) Amax purchased new office furniture and allowed each employee to take home
       old office furniture valued at $250.

50. Ralph owns a building that he is trying to lease. Ralph is a calendar-year, cash-   **LO 5-2**
    method taxpayer and is trying to evaluate the tax consequences of three different
    lease arrangements. Under lease 1, the building rents for $500 per month, payable   **research**
    on the first of the next month, and the tenant must make a $500 security deposit that
    is refunded at the end of the lease. Under lease 2, the building rents for $5,500 per
    year, payable at the time the lease is signed, but no security deposit is required.
    Under lease 3, the building rents for $500 per month, payable at the beginning of
    each month, and the tenant must pay a security deposit of $1,000 that is to be
    applied toward the rent for the last two months of the lease.

a) What amounts are included in Ralph's gross income this year if a tenant signs lease 1 on December 1 and makes timely payments under that lease?

b) What amounts are included in Ralph's gross income this year if the tenant signs lease 2 on December 31 and makes timely payments under that lease?

c) What amounts are included in Ralph's gross income this year if the tenant signs lease 3 on November 30 and makes timely payments under that lease?

LO 5-2 51. Anne purchased an annuity from an insurance company that promised to pay her $20,000 per year for the next 10 years. Anne paid $145,000 for the annuity, and in exchange she will receive $200,000 over the term of the annuity.

a) How much of the first $20,000 payment should Anne include in gross income?

b) How much income will Anne recognize over the term of the annuity?

LO 5-2 52. Larry purchased an annuity from an insurance company that promises to pay him $1,500 per month for the rest of his life. Larry paid $170,820 for the annuity. Larry is in good health and he is 72 years old. Larry received the first annuity payment of $1,500 this month. Use the expected number of payments in Exhibit 5-1 for this problem.

a) How much of the first payment should Larry include in gross income?

b) If Larry lives more than 15 years after purchasing the annuity, how much of each additional payment should he include in gross income?

c) What are the tax consequences if Larry dies just after he receives the 100th payment?

LO 5-2 53. Gramps purchased a joint survivor annuity that pays $500 monthly over his remaining life and that of his wife, Gram. Gramps is 70 years old and Gram is 65 years old. Gramps paid $97,020 for the contract. How much income will Gramps recognize on the first payment?

research

LO 5-2 54. Lanny and Shirley divorced in 2018 and do not live together. Shirley has custody of their child, Art, and Lanny pays Shirley $22,000 per year. All property was divided equally.

a) How much should Shirley include in income if Lanny's payments are made in cash but will cease if Shirley dies or remarries?

b) How much should Shirley include in income if $12,000 of Lanny's payments is designated as "nonalimony" in the divorce decree?

c) How much should Shirley include in income if Lanny's payments drop to $15,000 once Art reaches the age of 18?

LO 5-2 55. For each of the following independent situations, indicate the amount the taxpayer must include in gross income and explain your answer:

a) Phil won $500 in the scratch-off state lottery. There is no state income tax.

b) Ted won a compact car worth $17,000 in a TV game show. Ted plans to sell the car next year.

c) Al Bore won the Nobel Peace Prize of $500,000 this year. Rather than take the prize, Al designated that the entire award should go to Weatherhead Charity, a tax-exempt organization.

d) Jerry was awarded $2,500 from his employer, Acme Toons, when he was selected most handsome employee for Valentine's Day this year.

e) Ellen won a $1,000 cash prize in a school essay contest. The school is a tax-exempt entity, and Ellen plans to use the funds to pay her college education.

f) Gene won $400 in the office March Madness pool.

LO 5-2 56. Grady received $8,200 of Social Security benefits this year. Grady also reported salary and interest income this year. What amount of the benefits must Grady include in his gross income under the following five independent situations?

a) Grady files single and reports salary of $12,100 and interest income of $250.

b) Grady files single and reports salary of $22,000 and interest income of $600.

c) Grady files married joint and reports salary of $75,000 and interest income of $500.

d) Grady files married joint and reports salary of $44,000 and interest income of $700.

e) Grady files married separate and reports salary of $22,000 and interest income of $600.

57. George and Weezy received $30,200 of Social Security benefits this year ($12,000 for George; $18,200 for Weezy). They also received $5,000 of interest from jointly owned City of Ranburne bonds and dividend income. What amount of the Social Security benefits must George and Weezy include in their gross income under the following independent situations?   `LO 5-2`

a) George and Weezy file married joint and receive $8,000 of dividend income from stocks owned by George.

b) George and Weezy file married separate and receive $8,000 of dividend income from stocks owned by George.

c) George and Weezy file married joint and receive $30,000 of dividend income from stocks owned by George.

d) George and Weezy file married joint and receive $15,000 of dividend income from stocks owned by George.

58. Nikki works for the Shine Company, a retailer of upscale jewelry. How much taxable income does Nikki recognize under the following scenarios?   `LO 5-2`

a) Nikki buys a diamond ring from Shine Company for $10,000 (normal sales price, $14,000; Shine Company's gross profit percentage is 40 percent).

b) Nikki receives a 25 percent discount on jewelry restoration services offered by Shine Company. This year, Nikki had Shine Company repair a set of antique earrings (normal repair cost $500; discounted price $375).

59. Wally is employed as an executive with Pay More Incorporated. To entice Wally to work for Pay More, the corporation loaned him $20,000 at the beginning of the year at a simple interest rate of 1 percent. Wally would have paid interest of $2,400 this year if the interest rate on the loan had been set at the prevailing federal interest rate.   `LO 5-2`

a) Wally used the funds as a down payment on a speedboat and repaid the $20,000 loan (including $200 of interest) at year-end. Does this loan result in any income to either party, and if so, how much?

b) Assume instead that Pay More forgave the loan and interest on December 31. What amount of gross income does Wally recognize this year? Explain.

60. Jimmy has fallen on hard times recently. Last year he borrowed $250,000 and added an additional $50,000 of his own funds to purchase $300,000 of undeveloped real estate. This year the value of the real estate dropped dramatically, and Jimmy's lender agreed to reduce the loan amount to $230,000. For each of the following independent situations, indicate the amount Jimmy must include in gross income and explain your answer: `LO 5-3`

a) The real estate is worth $175,000 and Jimmy has no other assets or liabilities.

b) The real estate is worth $235,000 and Jimmy has no other assets or liabilities.

c) The real estate is worth $200,000 and Jimmy has $45,000 in other assets but no other liabilities.

61. Grady is a 45-year-old employee with AMUCK Garbage Corporation. AMUCK pays group-term life insurance premiums for employees, and Grady chose the maximum face amount of $120,000. What amount, if any, of the premium AMUCK paid on his behalf must Grady include in his gross income for the year? Provide a tax authority to support your answer.   `LO 5-3`
`research`

LO 5-3   62. Fred currently earns $9,000 per month. Fred has been offered the chance to transfer for three to five years to an overseas affiliate. His employer is willing to pay Fred $10,000 per month if he accepts the assignment. Assume that the maximum foreign-earned income exclusion for next year is $103,900.

a) How much U.S. gross income will Fred report if he accepts the assignment abroad on January 1 of next year and works overseas for the entire year? If Fred's employer also provides him free housing (cost of $20,000), how much of the $20,000 is excludable from Fred's income?

b) Suppose that Fred's employer has offered Fred a six-month overseas assignment beginning on January 1 of next year. How much U.S. gross income will Fred report next year if he accepts the six-month assignment abroad and returns home on July 1 of next year?

c) Suppose that Fred's employer offers Fred a permanent overseas assignment beginning on March 1 of next year. How much U.S. gross income will Fred report next year if he accepts the permanent assignment abroad? Assume that Fred will be abroad for 305 days out of 365 next year. If Fred's employer also provides him free housing (cost of $16,000 next year), how much of the $16,000 is excludable from Fred's income?

LO 5-3   63. For each of the following situations, indicate how much the taxpayer is required to include in gross income and explain your answer:

a) Steve was awarded a $5,000 scholarship to attend State Law School. The scholarship pays Steve's tuition and fees.

b) Hal was awarded a $15,000 scholarship to attend State Hotel School. All scholarship students must work 20 hours per week at the school residency during the term.

LO 5-3   64. Cecil cashed in a Series EE savings bond with a redemption value of $14,000 and an original cost of $9,800. For each of the following independent scenarios, calculate the amount of interest Cecil will include in his gross income assuming he files as a single taxpayer:

a) Cecil plans to spend all of the proceeds to pay his son's tuition at State University. Cecil's son is a full-time student, and Cecil claims his son as a dependent. Cecil estimates his modified adjusted gross income at $63,100.

b) Assume the same facts in part (a), except Cecil plans to spend $4,200 of the proceeds to pay his son's tuition at State University, and Cecil estimates his modified adjusted gross income at $60,600.

LO 5-3   65. Grady is a member of a large family and received the following payments this year. For each payment, determine whether the payment constitutes realized income and determine the amount of each payment Grady must include in his gross income.

a) A gift of $20,000 from Grady's grandfather.

b) One thousand shares of GM stock worth $120 per share inherited from Grady's uncle. The uncle purchased the shares for $25 each, and the shares are worth $125 at year-end.

c) A gift of $50,000 of Ford Motor Bonds. Grady received the bonds on October 31, and he received $1,500 of semiannual interest from the bonds on December 31.

d) A loan of $5,000 for school expenses from Grady's aunt.

LO 5-3   66. Bart is the favorite nephew of his aunt Thelma. Thelma transferred several items of value to Bart. For each of the following transactions, determine the effect on Bart's gross income.

a) Thelma gave Bart an auto worth $22,000. Thelma purchased the auto three years ago for $17,000.

b) Thelma elects to cancel her life insurance policy, and she gives the cash surrender value of $15,000 to Bart.

c) Bart is the beneficiary of a $100,000 whole life insurance policy on the life of Thelma. Thelma died this year, and Bart received $100,000 in cash.

d) Bart inherited 500 shares of stock from Thelma's estate. Thelma purchased the shares many years ago for $1,200, and the shares are worth $45,000 at her death.

67. Terry was ill for three months and missed work during this period. During his illness, Terry received $4,500 in sick pay from a disability insurance policy. What amounts are included in Terry's gross income under the following independent circumstances?

a) Terry has disability insurance provided by his employer as a nontaxable fringe benefit. Terry's employer paid $2,800 in disability premiums for Terry this year.

b) Terry paid $2,800 in premiums for his disability insurance this year.

c) Terry's employer paid the $2,800 in premiums for Terry, but Terry elected to have his employer include the $2,800 as compensation on Terry's W-2.

d) Terry has disability insurance whose cost is shared with his employer. Terry's employer paid $1,800 in disability premiums for Terry this year as a nontaxable fringe benefit, and Terry paid the remaining $1,000 of premiums from his after-tax salary.

68. Tim's parents plan to provide him with $50,000 to support him while he establishes a new landscaping business. In exchange for the support, Tim will maintain the landscape at his father's business. Under what conditions will the transfer of $50,000 be included in Tim's gross income? Explain. Do you have a recommendation for Tim and his parents?

69. What amounts are included in gross income for the following taxpayers? Explain your answers.

a) Janus sued Tiny Toys for personal injuries from swallowing a toy. Janus was paid $30,000 for medical costs and $250,000 for punitive damages.

b) Carl was injured in a car accident. Carl's insurance paid him $500 to reimburse his medical expenses and an additional $250 for the emotional distress Carl suffered as a result of the accident.

c) Ajax published a story about Pete and as a result Pete sued Ajax for damage to his reputation. Ajax lost in court and paid Pete an award of $20,000.

d) Bevis was laid off from his job last month. This month he drew $800 in unemployment benefits.

70. This year, Janelle received $200,000 in life insurance proceeds. Under the following scenarios, how much of the $200,000 is taxable?

a) Janelle received the proceeds upon the death of her father, Julio.

b) Janelle received the $200,000 proceeds because she was diagnosed with colon cancer (life expectancy of six months), and she needed the proceeds for her care.

c) The proceeds related to a life insurance policy she purchased for $35,000 from a friend in need. After purchase, Janelle paid annual premiums that total $22,000.

71. This year, Leron and Sheena sold their home for $750,000 after all selling costs. Under the following scenarios, how much taxable gain does the home sale generate for Leron and Sheena?

a) Leron and Sheena bought the home three years ago for $150,000 and lived in the home until it sold.

b) Leron and Sheena bought the home one year ago for $600,000 and lived in the home until it sold.

c) Leron and Sheena bought the home five years ago for $500,000. They lived in the home for three years until they decided to buy a smaller home. Their home has been vacant for the past two years.

LO 5-3

72. Dontae's employer has offered him the following employment package. What is Dontae's gross income from his employment?

Salary	$400,000
Health insurance	10,000
Dental insurance	1,500
Membership to Heflin Country Club	20,000
Season tickets to Atlanta Braves games	5,000
Tuition reimbursement for graduate courses	4,000
Housing allowance (for a McMansion in his neighborhood of choice)	40,000

COMPREHENSIVE PROBLEMS

Select problems are available in Connect®.

73. Charlie was hired by Ajax this year as a corporate executive and a member of the board of directors. During the current year, Charlie received the following payments or benefits paid on his behalf.

Salary payments	$92,000
Contributions to qualified pension plan	10,200
Qualified health insurance premiums	8,400
Year-end bonus	15,000
Annual director's fee	10,000
Group-term life insurance premiums (face = $40,000)	750
Whole life insurance premiums (face = $100,000)	1,420
Disability insurance premiums (no special elections)	4,350

a) Charlie uses the cash method and calendar year for tax purposes. Calculate Charlie's gross income for the current year.

b) Suppose that Ajax agrees to pay Charlie an additional $100,000 once Charlie completes five years of employment. Will this agreement alter Charlie's gross income this year relative to your part (a) answer? Explain.

c) Suppose that in exchange for his promise to remain with the firm for the next four years, Ajax paid Charlie four years of director's fees in advance. Will this arrangement alter Charlie's gross income this year relative to your part (a) answer? Explain.

d) Assume that in lieu of a year-end bonus Ajax transferred 500 shares of Bell stock to Charlie as compensation. Further assume that the stock was listed at $35 per share and Charlie would sell the shares by year-end, at which time he expected the price to be $37 per share. Will this arrangement alter Charlie's gross income this year relative to your part (a) answer? Explain.

e) Suppose that in lieu of a year-end bonus Ajax made Charlie's house payments (a total of $23,000). Will this arrangement alter Charlie's gross income this year relative to your part (a) answer? Explain.

74. Irene is disabled and receives payments from a number of sources. The interest payments are from bonds that Irene purchased over past years and a disability insurance policy that Irene purchased herself. Calculate Irene's gross income.

Interest, bonds issued by City of Austin, Texas	$ 2,000
Social Security benefits	8,200
Interest, U.S. Treasury bills	1,300
Interest, bonds issued by Ford Motor Company	1,500
Interest, bonds issued by City of Quebec, Canada	750
Disability insurance benefits	19,500
Distributions from qualified pension plan	5,400

75. Ken is 63 years old and unmarried. He retired at age 55 when he sold his business, Understock.com. Though Ken is retired, he is still very active. Ken reported the following financial information this year. Assume Ken files as a single taxpayer. Determine Ken's gross income and complete page 1 of Form 1040 for Ken.

   a) Ken won $1,200 in an illegal game of poker (the game was played in Utah, where gambling is illegal).

   b) Ken sold 1,000 shares of stock for $32 a share. He inherited the stock two years ago. His tax basis (or investment) in the stock was $31 per share.

   c) Ken received $25,000 from an annuity he purchased eight years ago. He purchased the annuity, to be paid annually for 20 years, for $210,000.

   d) Ken received $13,000 in disability benefits for the year. He purchased the disability insurance policy last year.

   e) Ken decided to go back to school to learn about European history. He received a $500 cash scholarship to attend. He used $300 to pay for his books and tuition, and he applied the rest toward his new car payment.

   f) Ken's son, Mike, instructed his employer to make half of his final paycheck of the year payable to Ken as a gift from Mike to Ken. Ken received the check on December 30 in the amount of $1,100.

   g) Ken received a $610 refund of the $3,600 in state income taxes his employer withheld from his pay last year. Ken claimed $6,400 in itemized deductions last year (the standard deduction for a single filer was $6,350).

   h) Ken received $30,000 of interest from corporate bonds and money market accounts.

76. Consider the following letter and answer Shady's question.

   To my friendly student tax preparer:

   Hello, my name is Shady Slim. I understand you are going to help me figure out my gross income for the year . . . whatever that means. It's been a busy year and I'm a busy man, so let me give you the lowdown on my life and you can do your thing.

   I was unemployed at the beginning of the year and got $2,000 in unemployment compensation. I later got a job as a manager for Roca Cola. I earned $55,000 in base salary this year. My boss gave me a $5,000 Christmas bonus check on December 22. I decided to hold on to that check and not cash it until next year, so I won't have to pay taxes on it this year. Pretty smart, huh? My job's pretty cool. I get a lot of fringe benefits like a membership to the gym that costs $400 a year and all the Roca Cola I can drink, although I can't really drink a whole lot—I figure $40 worth this year.

   As part of my manager duties, I get to decide on certain things like contracts for the company. My good buddy, Eddie, runs a bottling company. I made sure that he won the bottling contract for Roca Cola for this year (even though his contract wasn't quite the best). Eddie bought me a Corvette this year for being such a good friend. The Corvette cost $50,000 and I'm sure he bought it for me out of the goodness of his heart. What a great guy!

   Here's a bit of good luck for the year. Upon leaving my office one day, I found $8,000 lying in the street! Well, one person's bad luck is my good luck, right?

   I like to gamble a lot. I won a $27,000 poker tournament in Las Vegas this year. I also won about $5,000 over the year playing the guys at our Friday night poker game. Can you believe that I didn't lose anything this year?

   Speaking of the guys, one of them hit me with his car as we were leaving the game one night. He must have been pretty ticked that he lost! I broke my right leg and my left arm. I sued the guy and got $11,000 for my medical expenses, $3,000 to pay my psychotherapist for the emotional problems I had relating to the injuries (I got really depressed!), and I won $12,000 in punitive damages. That'll teach him that he's not so tough without his car!

Another bit of bad luck. My uncle Monty died this year. I really liked the guy, but the $200,000 inheritance I received from him made me feel a little better about the loss. I did the smart thing with the money and invested it in stocks and bonds and socked a little into my savings account. As a result, I received $600 in dividends from the stock, $200 in interest from the municipal bonds, and $300 in interest from my savings account.

My ex-wife, Alice, is still paying me alimony. She's a lawyer who divorced me in 2015 because I was "unethical" or something like that. Since she was making so much money and I was unemployed at the time, the judge ruled that she had to pay ME alimony. Isn't that something? She sent me $3,000 in alimony payments this year. She still kind of likes me, though. She sent me a check for $500 as a Christmas gift this year. I didn't get her anything, though.

So there you go. That's this year in a nutshell. Can you figure out my gross income and complete page 1 of Form 1040 for me? And since you're a student, this is free, right? Thanks, I owe you one! Let me know if I can get you a six-pack of Roca Cola or something.

tax forms

77. Diana and Ryan Workman were married on January 1 of last year. Diana has an eight-year-old son, Jorge, from her previous marriage. Ryan works as a computer programmer at Datafile Inc. (DI) earning a salary of $96,000. Diana is self-employed and runs a day care center. The Workmans reported the following financial information pertaining to their activities during the current year.

a) Ryan earned a $96,000 salary for the year.

b) Ryan borrowed $12,000 from DI to purchase a car. DI charged him 2 percent interest ($240) on the loan, which Ryan paid on December 31. DI would have charged Ryan $720 if interest had been calculated at the applicable federal interest rate.

c) Diana received $2,000 in alimony and $4,500 in child support payments from her former husband. They divorced in 2016.

d) Diana won a $900 cash prize at her church-sponsored Bingo game.

e) The Workmans received $500 of interest from corporate bonds and $250 of interest from a municipal bond. Diana owned these bonds before she married Ryan.

f) The couple bought 50 shares of ABC Inc. stock for $40 per share on July 2. The stock was worth $47 a share on December 31. The stock paid a dividend of $1.00 per share on December 1.

g) Diana's father passed away on April 14. She inherited cash of $50,000 from her father and his baseball card collection, valued at $2,000. As the beneficiary of her father's life insurance policy, Diana also received $150,000.

h) The couple spent a weekend in Atlantic City in November and came home with gross gambling winnings of $1,200.

i) Ryan received $400 cash for reaching 10 years of continuous service at DI.

j) Ryan was hit and injured by a drunk driver while crossing a street at a crosswalk. He was unable to work for a month. He received $6,000 from his disability insurance. DI paid the premiums for Ryan, but it reported the amount of the premiums as compensation to Ryan on his year-end W-2.

k) The drunk driver who hit Ryan in part (j) was required to pay his $2,000 medical costs, $1,500 for the emotional trauma he suffered from the accident, and $5,000 for punitive damages.

l) For meeting his performance goals this year, Ryan was informed on December 27 that he would receive a $5,000 year-end bonus. DI (located in Houston, Texas) mailed Ryan's bonus check from its payroll processing center (Tampa, Florida) on December 28. Ryan didn't receive the check at his home until January 2.

m) Diana is a 10 percent owner of MNO Inc., a Subchapter S corporation. The company reported ordinary business income for the year of $92,000. Diana acquired the MNO stock two years ago.

n) Diana's day care business collected $35,000 in revenues. In addition, customers owed her $3,000 at year-end. During the year, Diana spent $5,500 for supplies, $1,500 for utilities, $15,000 for rent, and $500 for miscellaneous expenses. One customer gave her use of his vacation home for a week (worth $2,500) in exchange for Diana allowing his child to attend the day care center free of charge. Diana accounts for her business activities using the cash method of accounting.

o) Ryan's employer pays the couple's annual health insurance premiums of $5,500 for a qualified plan.

Required:

a) Assuming the Workmans file a joint tax return, determine their gross income.

b) Using your answer in part (a), complete page 1 of Form 1040 through line 22 for the Workmans.

c) Assuming the Workmans live in California, a community property state, and that Diana and Ryan file separately, what is Ryan's gross income?

d) Using your answer in part (c), complete page 1 of Form 1040 through line 22 for Ryan Workman.

ROGER | *CPA Review*

Sample CPA Exam questions from Roger CPA Review are available in Connect as support for the topics in this text. These Multiple Choice Questions and Task-Based Simulations include expert-written explanations and solutions and provide a starting point for students to become familiar with the content and functionality of the actual CPA Exam.

6 Individual Deductions

Taxpayers:	Courtney Wilson, age 40 Courtney's mother, Dorothy "Gram" Weiss, age 70
Family description:	Courtney is divorced with a son, Deron, age 10, and a daughter, Ellen, age 20. Gram is currently residing with Courtney. Ellen is currently a full-time student.
Location:	Kansas City, Missouri
Employment status:	Courtney works as an architect for EWD. Gram is retired.
Filing status:	Courtney files as a head of household. Gram files as a single taxpayer.
Current situation:	Courtney and Gram are trying to determine their allowable deductions and compute taxable income.

Now that Courtney has determined her gross income, she still must determine her deductions to compute taxable income. Fortunately, Courtney keeps detailed records of all the expenditures she believes to be deductible. Besides expenses associated with her weekend consulting work and rental property, Courtney incurred some significant costs moving from Cincinnati to Kansas City. She also paid self-employment taxes on her consulting income. Courtney is confident some of these items are deductible, but she isn't quite sure which items are deductible and how much.

Based on her review of prior-year tax returns, Courtney has a pretty good handle on her itemized deductions. She incurred some extra medical expenses to treat a broken wrist from a mountain biking accident and had additional state income taxes withheld from her paycheck. Courtney paid real estate taxes for her personal residence and investment property and interest expense on loans secured by her new home. She also donated (cash and property) to her favorite charities.

Gram wasn't as busy as Courtney this year. Gram paid a penalty for cashing in her certificate of deposit early. She also paid some medical expenses and donated money to her local church. Gram is a little frustrated because she doesn't incur enough itemized deductions to exceed the standard deduction amount. Gram recently heard that she might be able to save taxes by "bunching" her itemized deductions into one year. She's hoping to learn a little bit more about this technique. In any event, Gram didn't pay any taxes during the year and she wants to learn how much she's going to owe. ∎

In the previous chapter, we determined *gross income* for both Courtney and Gram. To compute their taxable income, however, we need to identify their deductions. As emphasized previously, taxpayers are not allowed to deduct expenditures unless there is a specific tax law authorizing the deductions. And as we learn in this chapter, Congress grants many deductions for taxpayers for a variety of reasons.

As we discussed in the Individual Income Tax Overview, Dependents, and Filing Status chapter, deductions appear in one of two places in the individual income tax formula. Deductions "*for* AGI" (also called deductions "above the line") are subtracted directly from gross income.[1] Next, deductions "*from* AGI" (also called deductions "below the line") are subtracted directly *from* AGI, resulting in taxable income. Deductions *for* AGI are generally preferred over deductions *from* AGI because deductions above the line reduce taxable income dollar for dollar. In contrast, deductions *from* AGI sometimes have no effect on taxable income. Further, because many of the limitations on tax benefits for higher income taxpayers are based upon AGI, deductions *for* AGI often reduce these limitations, thereby increasing potential tax benefits. Thus, it's important to determine both the amount of the deduction and whether it's a deduction *for* AGI or *from* AGI. We begin our discussion of deductions by describing deductions *for* AGI, and we conclude by tackling itemized deductions, the standard deduction, and the deduction for qualified business income.

LO 6-1   DEDUCTIONS *FOR* AGI

Congress allows taxpayers to claim a variety of deductions *for* AGI.[2] To provide an overview, we select a cross-section of deductions *for* AGI and classify them into three categories:

1. Deductions *directly* related to **business activities.**
2. Deductions *indirectly* related to business activities.
3. Deductions subsidizing specific activities.

We've organized our discussion around these categories to illustrate the variety of deductions *for* AGI and explain why Congress provides preferential treatment for certain deductions.

Deductions Directly Related to Business Activities

As a matter of equity, Congress allows taxpayers involved in business activities to deduct expenses incurred to generate business income. That is, because taxpayers include the revenue they receive from doing business in gross income, they should be allowed to deduct against gross income the expenses they incur to generate those revenues.

To begin, we must define "business activities" and, for reasons we discuss below, we must distinguish business activities from **investment activities.** In general, for tax purposes, activities are either *profit-motivated* or motivated by personal objectives. Profit-motivated activities are, in turn, classified as either (1) business activities or (2) investment activities. Business activities are sometimes referred to as a **trade or business,** and these activities require a relatively high level of involvement or effort.

---

[1]Most, but not all, deductions *for* AGI appear on lines 23 through 35 on page 1 of Form 1040. The term "above the line" refers to the placement of deductions *for* AGI before the last line of the first page of Form 1040. This last line is the taxpayer's AGI.

[2]§62 identifies deductions *for* AGI.

For example, if an individual is a full-time employee, the individual is in the business of being an employee. Self-employed individuals are also engaged in business activities.

Unlike business activities, investment activities are profit-motivated activities that *don't* require a high degree of involvement or effort.[3] Instead, investment activities involve investing in property for appreciation or for income payments. An individual who occasionally buys land or stock in anticipation of appreciation or dividend payments is engaged in an investment activity.

Example 6-1

Suppose that Courtney purchased a parcel of land for its appreciation potential. Would her ownership in the land be considered a business or investment activity?

Answer: Courtney's activity would most likely be considered an investment activity, because she acquired the land for its appreciation potential and she does not plan to exercise any special effort to develop the property or to become actively involved in other real estate speculation.

What if: Suppose that Courtney frequently buys and sells land or develops land to sell in small parcels to those wanting to build homes. Would Courtney's activity be considered a business or investment activity?

Answer: Courtney's activity would most likely be considered a business activity because she is actively involved in generating profits from the land by developing it rather than simply holding the land for appreciation.

The distinction between business and investment activities is critical for determining whether a deduction associated with the activity is above or below the line or even deductible. With one exception, business expenses are deducted *for* AGI. The lone exception is unreimbursed employee business expenses, which, unfortunately, are not deductible for years beginning after 2017.[4] In contrast, investment-related expenses, if deductible at all, are deductible as itemized deductions with one exception. Expenses associated with rental and royalty activities are deductible *for* AGI regardless of whether the activity qualifies as an investment or a business. Exhibit 6-1 summarizes the rules for classifying business and investment-related expenses as *for* AGI deductions, *from* AGI deductions, or not deductible.

EXHIBIT 6-1 Individual Business and Investment-Related Expense Deductions *for* AGI, *from* AGI, and Not Deductible

	Deduction Type		
Activity Type	**Deduction *for* AGI**	**Deduction *from* AGI (itemized deduction)**	**Not Deductible**
Business activities	Self-employed business expenses	N/A	Unreimbursed employee business expenses
Investment activities	Rental and royalty expenses	Investment interest expense	Other investment expenses

[3]§162 generally authorizes trade or business expense deductions, while §212 generally authorizes deductions for investment activities. The distinction between these activities is discussed in the Business Income, Deductions, and Accounting Methods chapter.

[4]Prior to 2018, both unreimbursed employee business expenses and other investment expenses were deductible *from* AGI as miscellaneous itemized deductions subject to a 2 percent of AGI floor.

Trade or Business Expenses   Congress limits business deductions to expenses directly related to the business activity and those that are **ordinary and necessary** for the activity.[5] This means that deductible expenses must be appropriate and helpful for generating a profit. Although business deductions are one of the most common deductions *for* AGI, they are not readily visible on the front page of Form 1040. Instead, these deductions are reported with business revenues on Schedule C of Form 1040. Schedule C, presented in Exhibit 6-2, is essentially an income statement for the business that identifies typical ordinary and necessary business expenses. Taxpayers transfer the *net* income or loss from Schedule C to Form 1040 (page 1), line 12.

EXHIBIT 6-2   Parts I and II from Schedule C Profit or Loss from Business

Part I   Income

1	Gross receipts or sales. See instructions for line 1 and check the box if this income was reported to you on Form W-2 and the "Statutory employee" box on that form was checked ▶ ☐	1
2	Returns and allowances	2
3	Subtract line 2 from line 1	3
4	Cost of goods sold (from line 42)	4
5	**Gross profit.** Subtract line 4 from line 3	5
6	Other income, including federal and state gasoline or fuel tax credit or refund (see instructions)	6
7	**Gross income.** Add lines 5 and 6 ▶	7

Part II   Expenses. Enter expenses for business use of your home **only** on line 30.

8	Advertising	8		18	Office expense (see instructions)	18
9	Car and truck expenses (see instructions)	9		19	Pension and profit-sharing plans	19
10	Commissions and fees	10		20	Rent or lease (see instructions):	
11	Contract labor (see instructions)	11		a	Vehicles, machinery, and equipment	20a
12	Depletion	12		b	Other business property	20b
13	Depreciation and section 179 expense deduction (not included in Part III) (see instructions)	13		21	Repairs and maintenance	21
				22	Supplies (not included in Part III)	22
				23	Taxes and licenses	23
				24	Travel, meals, and entertainment:	
14	Employee benefit programs (other than on line 19)	14		a	Travel	24a
15	Insurance (other than health)	15		b	Deductible meals and entertainment (see instructions)	24b
16	Interest:			25	Utilities	25
a	Mortgage (paid to banks, etc.)	16a		26	Wages (less employment credits)	26
b	Other	16b		27a	Other expenses (from line 48)	27a
17	Legal and professional services	17		b	**Reserved for future use**	27b
28	**Total expenses** before expenses for business use of home. Add lines 8 through 27a ▶					28
29	Tentative profit or (loss). Subtract line 28 from line 7					29
30	Expenses for business use of your home. Do not report these expenses elsewhere. Attach Form 8829 unless using the simplified method (see instructions). **Simplified method filers only:** enter the total square footage of: (a) your home: _____ and (b) the part of your home used for business: _____. Use the Simplified Method Worksheet in the instructions to figure the amount to enter on line 30					30
31	**Net profit or (loss).** Subtract line 30 from line 29. • If a profit, enter on both **Form 1040, line 12** (or **Form 1040NR, line 13**) and on **Schedule SE, line 2.** (If you checked the box on line 1, see instructions). Estates and trusts, enter on **Form 1041, line 3.** • If a loss, you **must** go to line 32.					31
32	If you have a loss, check the box that describes your investment in this activity (see instructions). • If you checked 32a, enter the loss on both **Form 1040, line 12,** (or **Form 1040NR, line 13**) and on **Schedule SE, line 2.** (If you checked the box on line 1, see the line 31 instructions). Estates and trusts, enter on **Form 1041, line 3.** • If you checked 32b, you **must** attach Form 6198. Your loss may be limited.					32a ☐ All investment is at risk. 32b ☐ Some investment is not at risk.

For Paperwork Reduction Act Notice, see the separate instructions.   Cat. No. 11334P   Schedule C (Form 1040) 2017

Source: Form1040

Example 6-2

Besides being employed by EWD, Courtney is also a self-employed architectural consultant (a business activity). This year her consulting activity generated $19,500 of revenue and incurred $1,500 in expenses (primarily travel and transportation expenses). How does she report the revenue and deductions from the activity?

Answer: Courtney reports the $19,500 of revenue and deducts the $1,500 of business expenses *for* AGI on her Schedule C. Her net income of $18,000 from her consulting activities is included on the front page (line 12) of her individual tax return.

---

[5]§162. In the Business Income, Deductions, and Accounting Methods chapter, we address the requirements for deductible business expenses in detail.

Rental and Royalty Expenses   Taxpayers are allowed to deduct their expenses associated with generating rental or royalty income *for* AGI.[6] Like business expenses, rental and royalty expenses do not appear directly on the front page of Form 1040. Instead, rental and royalty deductions are reported with rental and royalty revenues on Schedule E of Form 1040.[7] Schedule E, presented in Exhibit 6-3, is essentially an income statement for the taxpayer's rental or royalty activities. Taxpayers transfer the *net* income or loss from Schedule E to Form 1040 (page 1), line 17.

Rental and royalty endeavors are most commonly considered to be investment activities, but like trade or business expenses, rental and royalty deductions are claimed above the line.[8] Perhaps rental and royalty expenses are deductible *for* AGI because Congress believed that these activities usually require more taxpayer involvement than other types of investment activities. Despite this preferential treatment, the deductibility of rental losses (where expenses exceed income) is subject to limitations (basis, at-risk, passive loss, and excess business loss rules). We discuss the excess business loss rules later in this chapter and the basis, at-risk, and passive loss rules in the Investments chapter when we discuss similar limitations that apply to investments in flow-through entities.

EXHIBIT 6-3   **Page 1 of Schedule E Rental or Royalty Income**

Income:	Properties:		A	B	C
3	Rents received	3			
4	Royalties received	4			
Expenses:					
5	Advertising	5			
6	Auto and travel (see instructions)	6			
7	Cleaning and maintenance	7			
8	Commissions	8			
9	Insurance	9			
10	Legal and other professional fees	10			
11	Management fees	11			
12	Mortgage interest paid to banks, etc. (see instructions)	12			
13	Other interest	13			
14	Repairs	14			
15	Supplies	15			
16	Taxes	16			
17	Utilities	17			
18	Depreciation expense or depletion	18			
19	Other (list) ▶	19			
20	Total expenses. Add lines 5 through 19	20			
21	Subtract line 20 from line 3 (rents) and/or 4 (royalties). If result is a (loss), see instructions to find out if you must file **Form 6198**	21			
22	Deductible rental real estate loss after limitation, if any, on **Form 8582** (see instructions)	22	( )(	)(	)
23a	Total of all amounts reported on line 3 for all rental properties	23a			
b	Total of all amounts reported on line 4 for all royalty properties	23b			
c	Total of all amounts reported on line 12 for all properties	23c			
d	Total of all amounts reported on line 18 for all properties	23d			
e	Total of all amounts reported on line 20 for all properties	23e			
24	**Income.** Add positive amounts shown on line 21. **Do not** include any losses		24		
25	**Losses.** Add royalty losses from line 21 and rental real estate losses from line 22. Enter total losses here		25	(	)
26	**Total rental real estate and royalty income or (loss).** Combine lines 24 and 25. Enter the result here. If Parts II, III, IV, and line 40 on page 2 do not apply to you, also enter this amount on Form 1040, line 17, or Form 1040NR, line 18. Otherwise, include this amount in the total on line 41 on page 2		26		

For Paperwork Reduction Act Notice, see the separate instructions.   Cat. No. 11344L   Schedule E (Form 1040) 2017

Source: Form 1040

[6]§212(a)(4).

[7]Rental income and expenses for renting personal property (e.g., equipment, furniture, etc.) instead of real property is generally reported on Schedule C (not Schedule E). If the rental of personal property is not considered a trade or business, the rental income and expenses are reported on lines 21 and 36, respectively, of Form 1040.

[8]Royalties are received for allowing others to use property or rights to property. For example, royalties are paid for allowing others to use or sell copyrighted material, such as books or plays, or to extract natural resources from property. The amount of the royalty is often a percentage of total revenues derived from the property or rights to property.

Example 6-3

> Courtney owns a condominium that she rents to tenants. This year she received $14,000 in rental revenue and incurred $9,000 of expenses associated with the rental, including management fees, maintenance, and depreciation. How does she report the revenue and expenses for tax purposes?
>
> **Answer:** Courtney reports the $14,000 of rental receipts and deducts the $9,000 of rental expenses *for* AGI on Schedule E. The net rental income of $5,000 is reported on the front page (line 17) of her individual tax return.

Losses on Dispositions   As we discuss in more detail in the Property Dispositions chapter, taxpayers disposing of business assets at a loss are allowed to deduct the losses *for* AGI. Also, individual taxpayers selling investment (capital) assets at a loss are allowed to deduct the "capital" losses against other capital gains. If the capital losses exceed the capital gains, they can deduct up to $3,000 as a net capital loss in a particular year. Losses in excess of the $3,000 limit are carried forward indefinitely to subsequent years, in which they are deductible subject to the same limitations.

Flow-Through Entities   Income from flow-through entities such as partnerships, LLCs, and S corporations passes through to the owners of those entities and is reported on Schedule E of the tax returns of the owners. Similarly, any expenses and losses incurred by the entity pass through to the entity owners, who typically treat them as deductions *for* AGI, subject to certain restrictions (basis, at-risk, and passive loss rules) that we discuss in the Investments chapter and the excess business loss limitation that we discuss next.

Excess Business Loss Limitation   For years beginning after 2017, taxpayers are not allowed to deduct an **"excess business loss"** for the year. Rather, excess business losses are carried forward to subsequent years as a net operating loss carryforward. The excess business loss limitation applies to losses that are otherwise deductible under the basis, at-risk, and passive loss rules. An excess business loss for the year is the excess of aggregate business deductions for the year over the sum of aggregate business gross income or gain of the taxpayer plus a threshold amount. The threshold amount for 2018 is $500,000 for married taxpayers filing jointly and $250,000 for other taxpayers. The threshold amounts are indexed for inflation. In the case of partnership or S corporation business losses, the provision applies at the partner or shareholder level.

Example 6-4

> **What if:** Suppose that Courtney invested in a partnership, and that this year her share of business losses from the partnership are $270,000. Assume that the $270,000 loss is deductible under the basis, at-risk, and passive loss rules. How much of the loss would be deductible?
>
> **Answer:** $250,000. Deductible net business losses are limited to $250,000 ($500,000 for taxpayers married filing jointly). The $20,000 excess business loss would be carried forward next year as a net operating loss.

Deductions Indirectly Related to Business Activities

Taxpayers can incur expenses in activities that are not directly related to making money but that they would not have incurred if they were not involved in a business activity. Taxpayers are allowed to deduct some of these expenses that are indirectly related to business activities as deductions *for* AGI. We describe these deductions below.

Moving Expenses   For years prior to 2018, moving expenses associated with changing a taxpayer's principal place of work were deductible subject to a distance test and a time employed test associated with the move. For years after 2017, moving expenses generally are not deductible (and employer reimbursements of moving expenses are taxable). The lone exception is for members of the Armed Forces (or their spouse or dependents) on active duty that move pursuant to a military order and incident to a permanent change of station. Their moving costs are nontaxable if paid by their employer and deductible if the costs are not paid by their employer.[9]

Example 6-5

This year, Courtney moved from Cincinnati to Kansas City, her new place of work with EWD. She incurred considerable expenses associated with the move (none were reimbursed). Can Courtney deduct the expenses of moving her residence to Kansas City?

Answer: No. Because Courtney does not meet the exception for members of the Armed Forces (or their spouse or dependents) on active duty, she cannot deduct the moving costs.

Health Insurance Deduction by Self-Employed Taxpayers   The cost of health insurance is essentially a personal expense. However, *employers* often pay a portion of health insurance premiums for employees as a qualified fringe benefit. Employers are allowed to deduct health insurance premiums as compensation expense, while employees are allowed to *exclude* these premiums from gross income. The health insurance fringe benefit does not apply to self-employed taxpayers because they are not "employees." So to provide equitable treatment, Congress allows self-employed taxpayers to claim personal health insurance premiums for the taxpayer, the taxpayer's spouse, the taxpayer's dependents, and the taxpayer's children under age 27 (regardless of whether the child is a dependent of the taxpayer) as deductions *for* AGI, but only to the extent of the self-employment income derived from the specific trade or business.[10]

This deduction is intended to help self-employed taxpayers who must pay their own insurance premiums. Consequently, self-employed taxpayers are *not* allowed to deduct health care insurance premiums if the taxpayer is eligible to participate in an employer-provided health plan. This restriction applies regardless of whether the health plan is sponsored by either an employer of the taxpayer or an employer of the taxpayer's spouse, and it is irrelevant whether the taxpayer actually participates in the plan.[11]

Self-Employment Tax Deduction   Employees and employers each pay Social Security and Medicare tax on employee salaries. Employers deduct the Social Security and Medicare taxes they pay on employee salaries. In contrast, because self-employed individuals do not have an employer, these individuals are required to pay self-employment tax. This tax represents both the employee's *and* the employer's share of the Social Security and Medicare taxes. Unfortunately for the self-employed, the self-employment tax is

---

[9]§217.

[10]§162(l). As we'll explain shortly, health insurance premiums also qualify as itemized deductions as medical expenses, but itemizing these deductions may not produce any tax benefits. To the extent that self-employed taxpayers do not have sufficient self-employment income to deduct all of their health insurance premiums as a *for* AGI deduction, they may deduct the remaining premiums as an itemized deduction. Finally, subject to certain restrictions, self-employed taxpayers who purchase health insurance through an exchange, have household incomes below 400 percent of the poverty line, and are not eligible for affordable coverage through an employer health plan that provides at least 60 percent of the expected costs for covered services can receive a premium tax credit under §36B. Any premiums offset by the tax credit cannot be deducted as either a *for* AGI or itemized deduction.

[11]§162(l)(2)(B).

not considered a business expense. To put self-employed individuals on somewhat equal footing with other employers who are allowed to deduct the *employer's* share of the Social Security and Medicare taxes, however, self-employed taxpayers are allowed to deduct the employer portion of the self-employment tax they pay.

Example 6-6

As we indicated in Example 6-2, Courtney reported $18,000 of net income from her self-employed consulting activities. She will pay $482 in self-employment taxes on this income, with $241 representing the employer portion of the self-employment tax.[12] What amount of self-employment tax can she deduct this year?

Answer: $241 (the employer portion of the self-employment tax).

Penalty for Early Withdrawal of Savings   Taxpayers are allowed a deduction *for* AGI for any interest income an individual forfeits to a bank as a penalty for prematurely withdrawing a certificate of deposit or similar deposit. This deduction reduces the taxpayer's net interest income to the amount she actually received. Otherwise, taxpayers would be required to report the full amount of interest income as taxable income and unfortunately, the forfeited interest would be a nondeductible investment expense.

Example 6-7

Gram invested $100,000 in a three-year certificate of deposit (CD). On December 31, she decides to cash out the certificate of deposit after holding it for less than a year. She receives the $4,100 of interest income the CD had generated up to the withdrawal date, less a $410 early withdrawal penalty. How will Gram report the interest and early withdrawal for tax purposes?

Answer: Gram reports $4,100 as interest income this year and deducts the $410 early withdrawal penalty as a deduction *for* AGI.

Deductions Subsidizing Specific Activities

To address specific policy objectives, Congress provides that certain expenditures are deductible *for* AGI. For example, alimony payments paid pursuant to divorce or separation agreements executed before 2019 are deductible *for* AGI to maintain equity given that these payments are taxable to the recipient. In contrast, contributions to retirement savings are deductible *for* AGI to encourage savings.[13] Further, Congress created a deduction *for* AGI to encourage and subsidize higher education. Taxpayers are allowed to deduct *for* AGI, subject to certain limitations, interest expense on **qualified educational loans.**[14] As we discuss throughout the text, Congress has also

---

[12]In this case, Courtney uses the following equation to determine her total self-employment tax: $18,000 × .9235 × .029 = $482 (Courtney's business income is subject to the Medicare tax but not the Social Security tax due to the level of her salary). Of the total self-employment tax, the employer portion is calculated as $18,000 × .9235 × .0145 = $241. We discuss how to compute the self-employment tax in detail in the Individual Income Tax Computation and Tax Credits chapter.

[13]See the Gross Income and Exclusions chapter for a detailed discussion of alimony and the Retirement Savings and Deferred Compensation chapter for a detailed discussion of the tax consequences of retirement savings.

[14]See §221. For years prior to 2018, taxpayers could also deduct tuition and fees paid for the taxpayer or dependent at a postsecondary institution of higher education. The deduction was limited (maximum of $4,000) and subject to a phase-out based upon the taxpayer's AGI (with modification). At press time, this deduction has not been extended to years after 2017. See §222.

created a number of related provisions, including education tax credits, to encourage and subsidize higher education.

Deduction for Interest on Qualified Education Loans   Qualified education loans are loans whose proceeds are used to pay qualified education expenses. Qualified education expenses encompass expenses paid for the education of the taxpayer, the taxpayer's spouse, or a taxpayer's dependent to attend a postsecondary institution of higher education.[15] These expenses include tuition and fees, books and expenses required for enrollment, room and board, and other necessary supplies and expenses, including travel.

The deduction for interest expense on qualified education loans is the amount of interest paid up to $2,500. However, the deduction is reduced (phased out) for taxpayers depending on the taxpayer's filing status and modified AGI. Modified AGI for this purpose is AGI *before* deducting interest expense on the qualified education loans. Married individuals who file separately are not allowed to deduct this expense under any circumstance. The deduction limitations for other taxpayers are summarized in Exhibit 6-4.

THE KEY FACTS

Interest on Education Loans

- Up to $2,500 of interest on education loans is deductible *for* AGI.
- A loan qualifies as an education loan if the proceeds are used to fund qualified education.
- The interest deduction is phased out for taxpayers with AGI exceeding $65,000 ($135,000 if married filing jointly).

EXHIBIT 6-4   Summary of Limitations on Deduction of Interest on Education Loans

Panel A: AGI Limitations	
Modified AGI Level	**Deduction**
Not over $65,000 ($135,000 for married filing jointly)	Amount paid up to $2,500
Above $65,000 ($135,000 for married filing jointly) but below $80,000 ($165,000 for married filing jointly)	Amount paid up to $2,500 reduced by the phase-out amount. The phase-out amount is the amount paid up to $2,500 times the phase-out percentage (see Panel B for the phase-out percentage computation).
Equal to or above $80,000 ($165,000 for married filing jointly)	Zero

Panel B: Phase-Out Percentage*	
Filing Status	**Phase-Out Percentage**
Single or head of household	(Modified AGI − $65,000)/$15,000
Married filing jointly	(Modified AGI − $135,000)/$30,000

*Married taxpayers filing separately are ineligible for the deduction.

Example 6-8

What if: Assume that Courtney's brother Jason paid interest on a qualified education loan that he used to pay the tuition and fees for his three daughters to attend State University. In 2018, Jason was married and filed a joint return, paid $2,000 of interest expense on the loan, and reported modified AGI of $147,000. What amount of interest expense on the education loan is Jason allowed to deduct as a *for* AGI deduction?

(continued on page 6-10)

---

[15]Postsecondary education includes courses at a university, college, or vocational school, including internship programs leading to a degree or certificate.

Answer: $1,200, computed as follows:

Description	Amount	Explanation
(1) Modified AGI	$147,000	AGI before higher education deductions
(2) Amount of interest paid up to $2,500	2,000	Lesser of amount paid ($2,000) or $2,500
(3) Phase-out (reduction) percentage	40%	[(1) − $135,000]/$30,000)
(4) Phase-out amount (reduction in maximum)	800	(2) × (3)
Deductible interest expense	**$ 1,200**	(2) − (4)

Summary: Deductions *for* AGI

Business expenses and rental and royalty expenses are two of the most important deductions *for* AGI. There are other important deductions *for* AGI that are indirectly related to business or provided to subsidize certain activities. After we have determined the deductions *for* AGI, we can compute AGI. Exhibits 6-5 and 6-6 summarize the computation of AGI for Courtney and Gram. Exhibit 6-7 shows Courtney's AGI calculation as presented on the front page of her Form 1040.

EXHIBIT 6-5 Courtney's Adjusted Gross Income

Description	Amount	Reference
Gross income for current year	$ 197,741	Exhibit 5-4 and related discussion
Deductions *for* AGI:		
Business expenses	(1,500)	Example 6-2
Rental expenses	(9,000)	Example 6-3
Employer-portion of self-employment taxes	(241)	Example 6-6
Adjusted gross income	**$187,000**	

EXHIBIT 6-6 Gram's Adjusted Gross Income

Description	Amount	Reference
Gross income for current year	$ 16,000	Exhibit 5-6
Deduction *for* AGI:		
Penalty for early withdrawal of savings	(410)	Example 6-7
Adjusted gross income	**$15,590**	

Once we have determined AGI, we calculate taxable income by identifying deductions *from* AGI. These deductions consist of (1) the greater of itemized deductions or the standard deduction and (2) the deduction for qualified business income. We address these deductions next.

LO 6-2 DEDUCTIONS *FROM* AGI: ITEMIZED DEDUCTIONS

There are a variety of itemized deductions. Many itemized deductions are personal in nature but are allowed to subsidize desirable activities such as home ownership and charitable giving. Other itemized deductions, such as medical expenses, provide relief for taxpayers whose ability to pay taxes has been involuntarily reduced. We discuss itemized deductions in the order they appear on the individual tax return, Form 1040, Schedule A.

EXHIBIT 6-7   Courtney's AGI Computation on Form 1040, Page 1

Income	7	Wages, salaries, tips, etc. Attach Form(s) W-2		**7**		142,800
	8a	**Taxable** interest. Attach Schedule B if required		**8a**		321
Attach Form(s)	b	**Tax-exempt** interest. **Do not** include on line 8a . . .	**8b**	500		
W-2 here. Also	9a	Ordinary dividends. Attach Schedule B if required		**9a**		700
attach Forms	b	Qualified dividends	**9b**	700		
W-2G and	10	Taxable refunds, credits, or offsets of state and local income taxes		**10**		420
1099-R if tax	11	Alimony received		**11**		20,000
was withheld.	12	Business income or (loss). Attach Schedule C or C-EZ		**12**		18,000
	13	Capital gain or (loss). Attach Schedule D if required. If not required, check here ▶ ☐		**13**		
If you did not	14	Other gains or (losses). Attach Form 4797		**14**		
get a W-2,	15a	IRA distributions .	**15a**		b Taxable amount . . .	**15b**	
see instructions.	16a	Pensions and annuities	**16a**		b Taxable amount . . .	**16b**	
	17	Rental real estate, royalties, partnerships, S corporations, trusts, etc. Attach Schedule E		**17**		5,000
	18	Farm income or (loss). Attach Schedule F		**18**		
	19	Unemployment compensation		**19**		
	20a	Social security benefits	**20a**		b Taxable amount . . .	**20b**	
	21	Other income. List type and amount _____		**21**		
	22	Combine the amounts in the far right column for lines 7 through 21. This is your **total income** ▶		**22**		187,241
Adjusted Gross Income	23	Educator expenses	**23**			
	24	Certain business expenses of reservists, performing artists, and fee-basis government officials. Attach Form 2106 or 2106-EZ	**24**			
	25	Health savings account deduction. Attach Form 8889 .	**25**			
	26	Moving expenses. Attach Form 3903	**26**			
	27	Deductible part of self-employment tax. Attach Schedule SE .	**27**	241		
	28	Self-employed SEP, SIMPLE, and qualified plans . .	**28**			
	29	Self-employed health insurance deduction	**29**			
	30	Penalty on early withdrawal of savings	**30**			
	31a	Alimony paid b Recipient's SSN ▶	**31a**			
	32	IRA deduction	**32**			
	33	Student loan interest deduction	**33**			
	34	Reserved for future use	**34**			
	35	Domestic production activities deduction. Attach Form 8903	**35**			
	36	Add lines 23 through 35		**36**		241
	37	Subtract line 36 from line 22. This is your **adjusted gross income** . . . . . . ▶		**37**		187,000

For Disclosure, Privacy Act, and Paperwork Reduction Act Notice, see separate instructions.   Cat. No. 11320B   Form **1040** (2017)

Source: Form 1040

Medical Expenses

The medical-expense deduction is designed to provide relief for taxpayers whose ability to pay taxes is seriously hindered by health-related circumstances. Qualified medical expenses include any payments for the care, prevention, diagnosis, or cure of injury, disease, or bodily function that are not reimbursed by health insurance or are not paid for through a "flexible spending account."[16] Taxpayers may also deduct medical expenses incurred to treat their spouses and their dependents.[17] Common medical expenses include:

- Prescription medication, insulin, and medical aids such as eyeglasses, contact lenses, and wheelchairs. Over-the-counter medicines are generally not deductible.
- Payments to medical care *providers* such as doctors, dentists, and nurses and medical care *facilities* such as hospitals.
- Transportation for medical purposes.
- Long-term care facilities.
- Health insurance premiums (if not deducted *for* AGI by self-employed taxpayers) and insurance for long-term care services.[18,19]

---

[16]Taxpayers participating in flexible spending accounts are allowed to direct that a fixed amount of their salary be placed in an account to pay for medical expenses. The salary paid into these accounts is excluded from gross income and used to pay for medical expenses. See the Compensation chapter.

[17]For the purpose of deducting medical expenses, a dependent need not meet the gross income test [§213(a)], and a child of divorced parents is considered a dependent of both parents [§213(d)(5)]. We discuss the general requirements for dependency in the Individual Income Tax Overview, Dependents, and Filing Status chapter.

[18]This includes the annual cost of Medicare and prescription insurance withheld from the Social Security recipient's benefits checks.

[19]The portion of any premiums for health insurance purchased through an exchange and offset by a premium tax credit under §36B is not deductible as an itemized deduction.

Example 6-9

In April, Courtney broke her wrist in a mountain biking accident. She paid $2,000 for a visit to the hospital emergency room and follow-up visits with her doctor. While she recuperated, Courtney paid $300 for prescription medicine and $700 to a therapist for rehabilitation. Courtney's insurance reimbursed her $1,840 for these expenses. What is the amount of Courtney's qualified medical expenses?

Answer: $1,160, computed as follows:

Description	Deduction
Emergency room and doctor visits	$ 2,000
Prescription medication	300
Physical therapy	700
Total qualifying medical expenses	$3,000
Less insurance reimbursement	−1,840
Qualified medical expenses from the accident	**$1,160**

Medical expenses for cosmetic surgery or other similar procedures are not deductible unless the surgery or procedure is necessary to ameliorate a deformity arising from, or directly related to, a congenital abnormality, a personal injury resulting from an accident or trauma, or a disfiguring disease.[20]

TAXES IN THE REAL WORLD   Are Discretionary Medical Expenses Deductible?

While cosmetic surgery is generally not deductible, discretionary medical costs may be deducted where the procedure affects the structure or function of the body. Take, for example, procedures that facilitate pregnancy by overcoming infertility. In IRS Letter Ruling 200318017, the IRS ruled that egg donor fees and expenses related to obtaining a willing donor, paid by a taxpayer who could not conceive using her own eggs, qualified as deductible medical expenses because they were incurred in preparation of the taxpayer's medical procedure (the implantation of a donated egg). Deductible expenses included the donor's fee for her time and expense in following the procedures to ensure successful egg retrieval, the agency's fee for procuring the donor and coordinating the transaction, expenses for medical and psychological testing and assistance of the donor before and after the procedure, and legal fees for preparing a contract between the taxpayer and the donor.

What about the same type of expenses paid by a single male to father a child through a surrogate? Are those expenses deductible? No, because in that situation, the expenses are not related to an underlying medical condition or defect of the taxpayer, nor are they affecting any structure or function of his body. See *William Magdalin,* TC Memo 2008-293.

Source: William Magdalin, TC Memo 2008-293.

Transportation and Travel for Medical Purposes   Taxpayers traveling for the primary purpose of receiving essential and deductible medical care may deduct the cost of lodging while away from home overnight (with certain restrictions) and transportation.[21] Taxpayers using personal automobiles for medical transportation purposes may deduct a standard mileage allowance in lieu of actual costs. For 2018, the mileage rate is 18 cents a mile.

---

[20]§213(d)(9)(A).

[21]The cost of travel for and essential to medical care, including lodging (with certain limitations) is also deductible if the expense is not extravagant and the travel has no significant element of personal pleasure. However, under §213(d)(2) the deduction for the cost of lodging is limited to $50 per night per individual.

Example 6-10

Gram drove Courtney, *in Courtney's car,* 110 miles back and forth from the doctor's office and the physical therapist's facility during the period Courtney was being treated for her broken wrist. What is the amount of Courtney's qualifying medical expense for her trips to the doctor's office?

Answer: $20 (110 × $0.18, rounded).

Hospitals and Long-Term Care Facilities   Taxpayers may deduct the cost of meals and lodging at hospitals. However, the cost of meals and lodging at other types of facilities such as nursing homes are deductible only when the principal purpose for the stay is medical care rather than convenience.[22] Of course, taxpayers may deduct the costs of actual medical care whether the care is provided at hospitals or other long-term care facilities.

Example 6-11

Gram considered moving into a long-term care facility before she decided she would move in with Courtney. The facility was not primarily for medical care and would have cost Gram $36,000 a year. During discussions with facility administrators, Gram learned that typically 20 percent of the total cost for the facility is allocable to medical care. If Gram were to stay in the facility for an entire year, what amount of the long-term care costs would qualify as a medical expense for Gram?

Answer: $7,200 ($36,000 × 20% allocable to medical care).

Medical Expense Deduction Limitation   The deduction for medical expenses is limited to the amount of unreimbursed qualified medical expenses paid during the year (no matter when the services were provided) *reduced* by 7.5 percent of the taxpayer's AGI for 2017 and 2018 (and 10 percent thereafter). This restriction is called a **floor limitation** because it eliminates any deduction for amounts below the floor. The purpose of a floor limitation is to restrict a deduction to taxpayers with substantial qualified expenses. Because this floor limitation is set at a high percentage of AGI, unreimbursed medical expenses rarely produce tax benefits, especially for high-income taxpayers.

Example 6-12

This year Courtney incurred $2,400 in unreimbursed qualified medical expenses (including the $1,160 of qualifying medical expenses associated with the accident [Example 6-9] and the $20 transportation deduction for mileage [Example 6-10]). Given that Courtney's AGI is $187,000, what is the amount of Courtney's itemized medical expense deduction?

Answer: $0, computed as follows:

Description	Expense
Total unreimbursed qualified medical expenses	$ 2,400
Minus: 7.5% of AGI ($187,000 × 7.5%)	(14,025)
Medical expense itemized deduction	**$ 0**

(continued on page 6-14)

[22]Taxpayers may deduct the cost of long-term care facilities if they are chronically ill under a prescribed plan of care. A taxpayer is deemed to be chronically ill, generally, if she or he cannot perform at least two daily living tasks (eating, bathing, dressing, toileting, transferring, continence) for 90 days or more. §7702B. Taxpayers may also deduct long-term care insurance premiums, which are limited annually based on the age of the taxpayer.

What if: What amount of medical expenses would Courtney be allowed to deduct if her AGI was $20,000?

Answer: $900, computed as follows:

Description	Expense
Total unreimbursed qualified medical expenses	$ 2,400
Minus: 7.5% of AGI ($20,000 × 7.5%)	(1,500)
Medical expense itemized deduction	**$ 900**

Taxes

Individuals may deduct as itemized deductions the payments they made during the year for the following taxes:

- State, local, and foreign *income* taxes, including state and local taxes paid during the year through employer withholding, estimated tax payments, and overpayments on the prior-year return that the taxpayer applies to the current year (the taxpayer asks the state to keep the overpayment rather than refund it).
- State and local real estate taxes on property held for personal or investment purposes.
- State and local personal property taxes that are assessed on the *value* of the specific property.[23]

Taxpayers may elect to deduct state and local sales taxes *instead* of deducting state and local income taxes. This election is particularly advantageous for taxpayers in states that don't have an individual state income tax.[24] For years after 2017, the total itemized deduction for taxes is limited to $10,000 ($5,000 for a taxpayer filing married separate).

Example 6-13

During the year, Courtney paid $6,700 of state income taxes through withholding from her paycheck. She also paid $2,700 of real estate taxes on her personal residence and $980 of real estate taxes on an investment property she owns in Oklahoma. Finally, Courtney paid $180 as a registration fee for her automobile (the fee is based on the year the automobile was manufactured, not its value). What amount of these payments can Courtney deduct as itemized deductions?

Answer: $10,000 ($6,700 state taxes + $2,700 real estate taxes on residence + $980 real estate taxes on investment property, limited to $10,000). Courtney is not allowed to deduct the registration fee for her car because the fee is not based on the value of the automobile.

What if: Suppose that on April 1, 2018, Courtney filed her 2017 state tax return and was due a refund from the state in the amount of $420. However, Courtney elected to have the state keep the overpayment and apply it to her 2018 tax payments. Assume that Courtney also had the $6,700 of state income tax withholding but only had $1,500 of real estate taxes in total. What amount of income taxes is Courtney allowed to deduct as an itemized deduction in 2018?

Answer: $8,620 ($6,700 withholding + $420 overpayment applied to 2018 + $1,500 real estate taxes). The treatment of the overpayment is the same as if Courtney had received the refund in 2018 and then remitted it to the state as payment of 2018 taxes. Because she paid the tax in 2018, she is allowed to deduct the tax in 2018. Recall that under the tax benefit rule (see the Gross Income and Exclusions chapter), Courtney was required to include the $420 in her 2018 gross income.

---

[23]§164.

[24]The deduction can be based upon either the amount paid or the amount published in the IRS tables (IRS Publication 600) based upon the state of residence, income, and number of dependents. The states with no income tax are Alaska, Florida, Nevada, South Dakota, Texas, Washington, and Wyoming. Tennessee and New Hampshire have no state income tax on wages but do impose a tax on unearned income.

Interest

There are two itemized deductions for interest expense.[25] First, subject to limitations described in more detail in the Tax Consequences of Home Ownership chapter, individuals can deduct interest paid on acquisition indebtedness secured by a qualified residence (the taxpayer's principal residence and one other residence).[26] Acquisition indebtedness is any debt secured by a qualified residence that is incurred in acquiring, constructing, or substantially improving the residence.[27]

The home mortgage interest deduction is limited by a cap on acquisition indebtedness that varies based upon when the indebtedness originated. For acquisition indebtedness incurred after December 15, 2017, taxpayers may only deduct mortgage interest on up to $750,000 of acquisition indebtedness ($375,000 if married filing separately). For acquisition indebtedness incurred before December 16, 2017, the limitation on acquisition indebtedness is $1,000,000 ($500,000 if filing married separate), even if the debt is refinanced after December 15, 2017. When a taxpayer has both acquisition indebtedness incurred before December 16, 2017, and after December 15, 2017, the $750,000 ($375,000) limit is reduced (not below zero) by the acquisition indebtedness incurred before December 16, 2017.

As we discuss in more detail in the Investments chapter, individuals can also deduct interest paid on loans used to purchase investment assets such as stocks, bonds, or land (investment interest expense). The deduction of investment interest is limited to a taxpayer's net investment income.[28] Any investment interest in excess of the net investment income limitation carries forward to the subsequent year. Taxpayers are not allowed to deduct interest on personal credit card debt or on loans to acquire (and secured by) personal-use automobiles.

> **Example 6-14**
>
> Courtney acquired her home in Kansas City in January of this year for $300,000 (also its value throughout the year). She purchased it by paying $40,000 as a down payment and borrowing $260,000 from a credit union. Her home is the collateral for the loan. During the year, Courtney paid $15,800 in interest on the loan. How much of this interest may Courtney deduct?
>
> **Answer:** $15,800. Because Courtney's home mortgage is secured by her home, she is allowed to deduct the interest expense on the home as an itemized deduction.

Charitable Contributions

Congress encourages donations to charities by allowing taxpayers to deduct contributions of money and other property to *qualified* domestic charitable organizations. Qualified charitable organizations include organizations that engage in educational, religious, scientific, governmental, and other public activities.[29] Political and campaign contributions are not deductible even though they arguably indirectly support the government (contributions to which are generally deductible).

---

[25]Interest paid on loans where the proceeds are used in a trade or business is fully deductible as a business expense deduction *for* AGI.

[26]Prior to 2018, taxpayers could deduct mortgage interest on up to $100,000 of home-equity indebtedness ($50,000 if married filing separately). Prior to 2018, taxpayers could also deduct premiums paid or accrued on mortgage insurance (insurance premiums paid by the borrower to protect the lender against the borrower defaulting on the loan) as qualified residence interest expense. At press time, the deduction for mortgage insurance premiums has not been extended to 2018.

[27]Subject to rules discussed in the Tax Consequences of Home Ownership chapter, points paid on indebtedness incurred in acquiring a home are also generally deductible as mortgage interest expense in the year the loan originates and points to refinance a home mortgage are typically amortized and deducted over the life of the loan (but see research memo in the Tax Compliance, the IRS, and Tax Authorities chapter for an exception).

[28]§163(d). Net investment income is defined as investment income minus investment expenses. Because investment expenses are no longer deductible as itemized deductions, the investment interest expense deduction is effectively limited to the taxpayer's investment income.

[29]§170(c). The IRS Exempt Organizations Select Check (https://www.irs.gov/charities-non-profits/exempt-organizations-select-check) lists the organizations that the IRS has determined to be qualified charities.

Example 6-15

This year Courtney donated $1,700 to the American Red Cross. She also gave $200 in cash to various homeless people she met on the streets during the year. What amount of these donations is Courtney allowed to deduct as a charitable contribution?

Answer: $1,700. Because the American Red Cross is a public charity recognized by the IRS, Courtney may deduct her $1,700 charitable contribution to it as an itemized deduction. However, despite Courtney's charitable intent, her donations to the homeless are not deductible as charitable contributions because individuals do not qualify as charitable organizations.

What if: Suppose that instead of transferring cash to homeless people on the streets, Courtney donated $200 cash to a local food bank that is listed in the IRS Exempt Organizations Select Check as a qualified charity. The food bank provides meals to those in need. Would Courtney be allowed to deduct this contribution?

Answer: Yes, because the food bank is a qualified charity.

The *amount* of the charitable contribution deduction depends on whether the taxpayer contributes money or other property to the charity. Note that in virtually all circumstances, donations are deductible only if the contribution is substantiated by written records.[30]

Contributions of Money Cash contributions are deductible in the year paid, including donations of cash or by check, electronic funds transfers, credit card charges, and payroll deductions.[31] Taxpayers are also considered as making monetary contributions for the cost of transportation and travel for charitable purposes if there is no significant element of pleasure or entertainment in the travel. When taxpayers use their personal vehicles for charitable transportation purposes, they may deduct, as a cash contribution, a standard mileage allowance for each mile driven (14 cents a mile in 2018). While taxpayers are allowed to deduct their transportation costs and other out-of-pocket costs of providing services for charities, they are not allowed to deduct the value of the services they provide for charities.

Example 6-16

Once a month, Courtney does volunteer work at a Goodwill Industries outlet about 20 miles from her home. Altogether, Courtney traveled 500 miles during the year driving to and from the Goodwill outlet. Courtney has determined that the services she provided during the year are reasonably valued at $1,500. What amount is Courtney allowed to deduct for her volunteer work with Goodwill Industries?

Answer: $70. Courtney is *not* allowed to deduct the value of the services she provides to Goodwill. However, she is allowed to deduct the $70 cost of her transportation to and from the Goodwill outlet (500 miles × 14 cents per mile).

[30]For example, to deduct monetary donations, taxpayers must keep a bank record or a written communication from the charity showing the name of the charity and the date and amount of the contribution. In addition, to deduct charitable contributions for cash or noncash contributions of $250 or more, a taxpayer must receive a written acknowledgment from the charity that shows the amount of cash and a description of any property contributed. The acknowledgment must also state whether the donee organization provided any goods or services to the donor for the contribution and if so, either include a description and estimate of the value of the goods or services provided by the donee organization or, if applicable, a statement that the goods or services provided by the donee organization consist entirely of intangible religious benefits. See Publication 526 for more information.

[31]When individual taxpayers mail a contribution, they are allowed to deduct the contribution when they place the payment in the mail. When they pay via credit card, they are allowed to deduct the contribution on the day of the charge. Rev. Rul. 78-38, 1978-1 CB 67.

Taxpayers receiving goods or services from a charity in exchange for a contribution may deduct only the amount of the contribution *in excess of the fair market value of the goods or services they receive* in exchange for their contribution.[32]

Contributions of Property Other Than Money   When a taxpayer donates *property* to a charity, the *amount* the taxpayer is allowed to deduct depends on whether the property is **capital gain property** or **ordinary income property.**

Capital gain property.   In general, taxpayers are allowed to deduct the *fair market value* of capital gain property on the date of the donation. Capital gain property is any appreciated asset that would have generated a *long-term* capital gain if the taxpayer had sold the property for its fair market value instead of contributing the asset to charity. To qualify as long-term, the taxpayer must have held the asset for more than a year. Capital assets include the following assets:

- Investment assets (stocks, bonds, land held for investment, paintings, etc.).
- Business assets (to the extent that gain on the sale of the business asset would *not* have been considered ordinary income).[33]
- Personal-use assets.

Contributing capital gain property is a particularly tax-efficient way to make charitable contributions because taxpayers are allowed to deduct the fair market value of the property and they are *not* required to include the appreciation on the asset in gross income.

Example 6-17

In December of the current year, Courtney donated 100 shares of stock in JBD Corp. to her church, a qualified charity. Courtney purchased the stock several years ago for $2,600, but the shares were worth $10,600 at the time of the donation. What is the amount of Courtney's charitable deduction for donating the stock?

Answer: $10,600. Because the stock is an appreciated investment asset held for more than a year, it qualifies as capital gain property. Hence, Courtney is allowed to deduct the $10,600 fair market value of the stock, and she is *not* required to recognize any of the $8,000 realized gain ($10,600 − $2,600).

Certain contributions of capital gain property do not qualify for a fair market value deduction. The deduction for capital gain property that is *tangible personal property* is limited to the *adjusted basis* of the property if the charity uses the property for a purpose that is *unrelated* to its charitable purpose.[34] That is, this restriction applies to capital gain property that is (1) tangible, (2) personal property (not realty), and (3) unrelated to the charity's operations. The third requirement does not apply if, at the time of the donation, the taxpayer reasonably anticipates that the charity will put the property to a related use.

---

[32]Reg. §1.170A-1(h). To help with this determination, a charity that provides goods or services in return for a contribution of more than $75 must provide contributors with a written statement estimating the value of goods and services that the charity has provided to the donor.

[33]These assets are considered to be §1231(b) assets. We discuss the tax treatment of dispositions of business assets in the Property Dispositions chapter.

[34]Reg. §1.170A-4(b)(2). The taxpayer's deduction for donating capital gain property is also limited to basis if the taxpayer contributes capital gain property other than publicly traded stock to a private nonoperating foundation. There are also other exceptions in which capital gain property might not otherwise qualify for deduction at value, such as the subsequent sales of donated property by the charity. These exceptions are beyond the scope of this text.

Example 6-18

What if: Suppose that Courtney donated a religious-themed painting to her church. Courtney purchased the painting several years ago for $2,600, but the painting was worth $10,600 at the time of the donation. When Courtney contributed the painting, she reasonably expected the church to hang the painting in the chapel. What would be the amount of Courtney's charitable contribution deduction?

Answer: $10,600. Because Courtney reasonably expected the church to use the painting in a manner related to its tax-exempt purpose, Courtney is allowed to deduct the full fair market value of the painting without recognizing the $8,000 realized gain.

What if: Suppose that Courtney was told at the time she donated the painting that the church intended to sell it and use the cash to help fund expansion of the church building. What would be Courtney's charitable contribution deduction?

Answer: $2,600, the adjusted basis of the property. Because the church expects to sell it, the painting is being used for a purpose unrelated to the charitable purpose of the church. Thus, Courtney may deduct only the tax basis of the painting.

What if: Suppose that Courtney donated stock to her church ($10,600 current fair market value, originally purchased several years ago for $2,600) and the church informed her that it intended to immediately sell the stock. What would be the amount of Courtney's charitable contribution deduction?

Answer: $10,600. Stock is intangible property, not tangible personal property. Hence, Courtney would deduct the fair market value of the stock.

Ordinary income property.   Taxpayers contributing ordinary income property can deduct only the *lesser* of (1) the property's fair market value or (2) the property's adjusted basis. Ordinary income property consists of all assets other than capital gain property. That is, ordinary income property is property that if sold would generate income taxed at ordinary rates. This includes the following types of assets:

- Assets the taxpayer has held for a year or less.
- Inventory the taxpayer sells in a trade or business.
- Business assets held for more than a year to the extent the taxpayer would recognize ordinary income under the depreciation recapture rules if the taxpayer had sold the property.[35]
- Assets, including investment assets and personal-use assets, with a value *less than* the taxpayer's basis in the assets (assets that have declined in value).

Example 6-19

Before her move from Cincinnati, Courtney decided to donate her excess possessions to Goodwill Industries. Courtney estimated that she paid over $900 for these items, including clothing, a table, and a couch. However, although the items were in excellent condition, they were worth only $160. What amount can Courtney deduct for her donation of these items?

Answer: $160. Because Courtney's possessions have declined in value, they are considered to be ordinary income property. Consequently, Courtney may deduct the lesser of (1) the fair market value of $160 or (2) her tax basis in the property of $900.

Charitable Contribution Deduction Limitations   The amount of a taxpayer's charitable contribution deduction for the year is limited to a **ceiling** or maximum deduction. The ceiling depends upon the type of property the taxpayer donates and the nature of the charity receiving the donation; donations to public charities (charities

---

[35]We discuss depreciation recapture in the Property Dispositions chapter.

that are publicly supported such as churches and schools) and **private operating foundations** (privately sponsored foundations that actually fund and conduct charitable activities) are subject to less stringent restrictions than other charities. In general, cash donations to public charities and private operating foundations are limited to 60 percent of the taxpayer's AGI, whereas property donations to public charities and private operating foundations are limited to 50 percent of the taxpayer's AGI. Deductions for contributions of capital gain property to public charities and private operating foundations are generally limited to 30 percent of the taxpayer's AGI. Deductions for cash and property contributions to **private nonoperating foundations** (privately sponsored foundations that disburse funds to other charities, such as the Bill and Melinda Gates Foundation) are limited to 30 percent of the taxpayer's AGI. Finally, deductions for contributions of capital gain property to private nonoperating foundations are limited to 20 percent of the taxpayer's AGI. Exhibit 6-8 summarizes the charitable contribution limitations for individual taxpayers.

When taxpayers make contributions that are subject to different percentage limitations, they apply the AGI limitations in the following sequence:

Step 1: Determine the limitation for the 60 percent contributions.

Step 2: Apply the limitations to the 50 percent contributions. The 50 percent contribution limit is AGI × 50% minus the contributions subject to the 60 percent limit.

Step 3: Apply the limitations to the 30 percent contributions. The 30 percent contribution limit is the *lesser* of (a) AGI × 30%, or (b) AGI × 50% minus the contributions subject to the 50 percent limit and the contributions subject to the 60 percent limit.

Step 4: Apply the limitations to the 20 percent contributions. The 20 percent contribution limit is the *lesser* of (a) AGI × 20%, (b) AGI × 30% minus contributions subject to 30 percent limit, or (c) AGI × 50% minus the contributions subject to the 50 percent limit, the contributions subject to the 60 percent limit, and the contributions subject to the 30% limit.

EXHIBIT 6-8   **Summary of Charitable Contribution Limitation Rules**

Contribution Type	Public Charity and Private Operating Foundation	Private Nonoperating Foundation
Cash:		
Amount	Cash amount	Cash amount
AGI limit	60%	30%
Capital gain property:		
Amount	FMV	Basis*
AGI limit	30%	20%
Ordinary income property:		
Amount	Lesser of Basis or FMV	Lesser of Basis or FMV
AGI limit	50%	30%

*FMV if the stock is publicly traded [§170(e)(5)].

When a taxpayer's contributions exceed the AGI ceiling limitation for the year, the excess contribution is treated as though it were made in the subsequent tax year and is subject to the same AGI limitations in the next year. The excess contribution can be carried forward for five years before it expires. If a charitable contribution deduction is carried forward, the current-year contributions must first be used when applying the AGI percentage limitations. However, because the ceiling limitations are fairly generous, taxpayers exceed the ceiling limitations only in unusual circumstances.

Example 6-20

This year Courtney made the following contributions to qualified charities:

Organization	Amount	Type	AGI Limitation	Reference
Red Cross	$ 1,700	Cash	60%	Example 6-15
Goodwill Industries	70	Cash-mileage	60	Example 6-16
Goodwill Industries	160	Ordinary income property	50	Example 6-19
Church	10,600	Capital gain property	30	Example 6-17
Total contributions	**$12,530**			

After applying the AGI limitations, how much of the $12,530 in contributions is Courtney allowed to deduct if she itemizes her deductions?

Answer: 12,530, computed as follows:

Description	Amount	Explanation
(1) AGI	$187,000	Exhibit 6-5
(2) 60% contributions	1,770	($1,700 + 70)
(3) 60% AGI contribution limit	112,200	(1) × 60%
(4) Allowable 60% deductions	**1,770**	Lesser of (2) or (3)
(5) 50% contributions	160	
(6) 50% AGI contribution limit	91,730	[(1) × 50%] − (4)
(7) Allowable 50% deductions	**160**	Least of (5) or (6)
(8) 30% contributions	10,600	
(9) 30% AGI contribution limit	56,100	(1) × 30%
(10) Remaining 50% AGI contribution limit	91,570	(6) − (7)
(11) Allowable 30% deductions	**10,600**	Least of (8), (9), or (10)
Deductible charitable contributions	**$ 12,530**	(4) + (7) + (11)

What if: Suppose that Courtney's AGI was $30,000. After applying the AGI limitations, how much of the $12,530 in contributions would Courtney be allowed to deduct if she itemizes her deductions?

Answer: $10,930, computed as follows:

Description	Amount	Explanation
(1) AGI	$ 30,000	
(2) 60% contributions	1,770	($1,700 + 70)
(3) 60% AGI contribution limit	18,000	(1) × 60%
(4) Allowable 60% deductions	**1,770**	Lesser of (2) or (3)
(5) 50% contributions	160	
(6) 50% AGI contribution limit	13,230	[(1) × 50%] − (4)
(7) Allowable 50% deductions	**160**	Least of (5) or (6)
(8) 30% contributions	10,600	
(9) 30% AGI contribution limit	9,000	(1) × 30%
(10) Remaining 50% AGI contribution limit	13,070	(6) − (7)
(11) Allowable 30% deductions	**9,000**	Least of (8), (9), or (10)
Deductible charitable contributions	**$10,930**	(4) + (7) + (11)

This year, Courtney would not be allowed to deduct $1,600 of her $10,600 capital gain property contribution to her church. However, she would carry forward the $1,600 to next year (and up to four years after that, if necessary) and treat it as though she made a $1,600 contribution next year subject to the 30 percent of AGI limitation.

Sabrina loves the latest fashions, but she is also very charitable. Every year she donates her previous year's clothing to Goodwill to make room in her closet for this year's fashions. Sabrina estimates the value of her donation to be approximately $6,000. Sabrina recently learned that because her donation exceeds $5,000, she must support her donation with an appraisal and a signed statement by the appraiser on Form 8283. Sabrina decides to claim a charitable deduction of $4,900 to avoid the appraisal requirement. What do you think of Sabrina's decision? Do you think that nationally there is an abnormally large number of charitable contributions valued just under $5,000?

Casualty and Theft Losses on Personal-Use Assets

Individuals cannot deduct losses they realize when they sell or dispose of assets used for personal purposes (personal-use assets as opposed to business or investment assets). Prior to 2018, taxpayers could deduct casualty losses (defined as losses arising from a *sudden, unexpected,* or *unusual* event such as a "fire, storm, or shipwreck" or from theft) on personal-use assets subject to a $100 floor each casualty and 10 percent of AGI floor for all casualty losses in the year. After 2017, only casualty losses on personal-use assets attributable to a federally declared disaster are deductible (subject to the $100 floor and 10 percent of AGI floor).[36]

Miscellaneous Itemized Deductions

Prior to 2018, there were a number of expenses including unreimbursed employee business expenses, tax preparation fees, investment expenses (other than real estate tax or investment interest expense), and hobby expenses (limited to hobby income), among others, that were deductible as **miscellaneous itemized deductions** subject to a 2 percent of AGI floor.[37] After 2017, these expenses are no longer deductible. The nondeductibility of these expenses is especially painful for taxpayers with hobbies, as hobby revenues are included in gross income but hobby expenses are no longer deductible (unless they are deductible as real estate taxes or mortgage interest expense).

Despite the nondeductibility of several expenses previously deductible as miscellaneous deductions subject to the 2 percent of AGI floor, there a few expenses that remain deductible as miscellaneous itemized deductions not subject to the 2 percent of AGI floor. Perhaps because gambling includes a significant element of personal enjoyment (losers may think otherwise), individuals include all gambling winnings for the year in gross income, but they may also deduct gambling expenses and gambling losses losses *to the extent of gambling winnings* for the year.[38] The deductible gambling losses are miscellaneous itemized deductions; therefore, *losses don't directly offset winnings.*[39] Casualty

> **THE KEY FACTS**
>
> **Miscellaneous Itemized Deductions**
>
> - Employee business expenses, tax preparation fees, investment expenses (other than real estate tax or investment interest expense), and hobby expenses are no longer deductible.
> - Gambling expenses and gambling losses losses are deductible to the extent of gambling winnings for the year.

[36]§165. As we discuss in more detail in the Business Income, Deductions, and Accounting Methods chapter, businesses may deduct casualty and theft losses of business property as a deduction *for* AGI. Further, casualty or theft losses on investment assets are deductible as a miscellaneous itemized deduction.

[37]Hobbies are revenue-generating activities for primarily personal enjoyment rather than profit. The IRS considers a list of factors (taxpayer's history of income or losses with the activity, taxpayer's expertise or his advisers, taxpayer's time and effort expended in the activity, activity's elements of personal pleasure or recreation, etc.) in determining whether an activity is a hobby or for profit.

[38]§165(d).

[39]If gambling is deemed to be a business activity (see *Linda M. Myers,* TC Summary Opinion 2007-194), then the taxpayer reports gambling winnings, expenses, and losses on Schedule C (not as a miscellaneous itemized deduction). However, gambling expenses and losses remain only deductible to the extent of gambling winnings.

and theft losses on property held for investment (not personal use property) and the uncovered cost of a life annuity (if the taxpayer died before recovering the full cost of the annuity) also are deductible as miscellaneous itemized deductions.

Summary of Itemized Deductions

This part of the chapter examined the various itemized deductions. Some of these deductions are subject to limitations in the form of floor limitations or caps. All require good records and a good understanding to support and maximize your deductions.

Example 6-21

Given Courtney's current year AGI of $187,000, what is the amount of her total itemized deductions she may claim on her tax return?

Answer: Courtney's itemized deductions for the year are $38,330, calculated as follows:

Description	Amount	Reference
Taxes	$10,000	Example 6-13
Home mortgage interest	15,800	Example 6-14
Charitable contributions	12,530	Example 6-20
Total itemized deductions	**$38,330**	

Exhibit 6-9 presents Courtney's itemized deductions on Form 1040, Schedule A. As with other forms, we use the 2017 form since the 2018 form was not available at press time.

LO 6-3 THE STANDARD DEDUCTION

Standard Deduction

The **standard deduction** is a flat amount that most individuals can elect to deduct *instead* of deducting their itemized deductions (if any). That is, taxpayers generally deduct *the greater of their standard deduction or their itemized deductions.*

The amount of the standard deduction varies according to the taxpayer's filing status, age, and eyesight. The basic standard deduction is greater for married taxpayers filing jointly and those supporting a family (head of household) than it is for married taxpayers filing separately and unmarried taxpayers not supporting a family. Taxpayers who are at least 65 years of age on the last day of the year or are blind are entitled to additional standard deduction amounts above and beyond their basic standard deduction.[40] Exhibit 6-10 summarizes the standard deduction amounts.[41] With significantly larger standard deduction amounts in 2018, many more taxpayers are expected now to deduct the standard deduction instead of deducting itemized deductions.

For 2018, the additional standard deduction for either age and/or blindness is $1,300 for married taxpayers and $1,600 for taxpayers who are not married. Thus, a blind individual who is 65 years old and single is entitled to a standard deduction of $15,200 ($12,000 + $1,600 + $1,600). A married couple filing a joint return with one spouse over age 65 and one spouse considered legally blind is entitled to a standard deduction of $26,600 ($24,000 + $1,300 + $1,300). Finally, for an individual who is eligible to be claimed as a dependent on another's return, the standard deduction is the greater of (1) $1,050 or (2) $350 plus the individual's earned income limited to the regular standard deduction. The additional standard deduction amounts for age and blindness, if any, are not impacted by the preceding limitation for eligible dependents.

---

[40]Taxpayers are considered 65 on the day before their 65th birthday. Taxpayers are considered to be blind if they have a certified statement from their eye doctor or registered optometrist that their corrected vision of their better eye is no better than 20/200 or their field of vision is 20 degrees or less.

[41]The standard deduction amount is indexed for inflation.

EXHIBIT 6-9 Courtney's Form 1040, Schedule A

SCHEDULE A (Form 1040)				Itemized Deductions				OMB No. 1545-0074

SCHEDULE A (Form 1040)

Department of the Treasury
Internal Revenue Service (99)

Itemized Deductions

▶ Go to *www.irs.gov/ScheduleA* for instructions and the latest information.
▶ Attach to Form 1040.

Caution: If you are claiming a net qualified disaster loss on Form 4684, see the instructions for line 28.

OMB No. 1545-0074

2017

Attachment
Sequence No. **07**

Name(s) shown on Form 1040	Your social security number
Courtney Wilson	123-45-6789

Medical and Dental Expenses

Caution: Do not include expenses reimbursed or paid by others.

1	Medical and dental expenses (see instructions)	**1**	2,400	
2	Enter amount from Form 1040, line 38 · **2** · 187,000			
3	Multiply line 2 by 7.5% (0.075)	**3**	14,025	
4	Subtract line 3 from line 1. If line 3 is more than line 1, enter -0-		**4**	0

Taxes You Paid

5	State and local (**check only one box**): a ☑ Income taxes, **or** b ☐ General sales taxes	**5**	6,320	
6	Real estate taxes (see instructions)	**6**	3,680	
7	Personal property taxes	**7**		
8	Other taxes. List type and amount ▶ _____	**8**		
9	Add lines 5 through 8		**9**	10,000

Interest You Paid

Note:
Your mortgage interest deduction may be limited (see instructions).

10	Home mortgage interest and points reported to you on Form 1098	**10**	15,800	
11	Home mortgage interest not reported to you on Form 1098. If paid to the person from whom you bought the home, see instructions and show that person's name, identifying no., and address ▶ _____	**11**		
12	Points not reported to you on Form 1098. See instructions for special rules	**12**		
13	Reserved for future use	**13**		
14	Investment interest. Attach Form 4952 if required. See instructions	**14**		
15	Add lines 10 through 14		**15**	15,800

Gifts to Charity

If you made a gift and got a benefit for it, see instructions.

16	Gifts by cash or check. If you made any gift of $250 or more, see instructions	**16**	1,770	
17	Other than by cash or check. If any gift of $250 or more, see instructions. You **must** attach Form 8283 if over $500	**17**	10,760	
18	Carryover from prior year	**18**		
19	Add lines 16 through 18		**19**	12,530

Casualty and Theft Losses

20	Casualty or theft loss(es) other than net qualified disaster losses. Attach Form 4684 and enter the amount from line 18 of that form. See instructions	**20**	

Job Expenses and Certain Miscellaneous Deductions

21	Unreimbursed employee expenses—job travel, union dues, job education, etc. Attach Form 2106 or 2106-EZ if required. See instructions. ▶ _____	**21**	
22	Tax preparation fees	**22**	
23	Other expenses—investment, safe deposit box, etc. List type and amount ▶ _____	**23**	
24	Add lines 21 through 23	**24**	
25	Enter amount from Form 1040, line 38 · **25**		
26	Multiply line 25 by 2% (0.02)	**26**	
27	Subtract line 26 from line 24. If line 26 is more than line 24, enter -0-	**27**	

Other Miscellaneous Deductions

28	Other—from list in instructions. List type and amount ▶ _____	**28**	

Total Itemized Deductions

29	Is Form 1040, line 38, over $156,900? ☐ **No.** Your deduction is not limited. Add the amounts in the far right column for lines 4 through 28. Also, enter this amount on Form 1040, line 40. ☐ **Yes.** Your deduction may be limited. See the Itemized Deductions Worksheet in the instructions to figure the amount to enter.	**29**	38,330
30	If you elect to itemize deductions even though they are less than your standard deduction, check here ▶ ☐		

For Paperwork Reduction Act Notice, see the Instructions for Form 1040.   Cat. No. 17145C   Schedule A (Form 1040) 2017

Source: Form1040

EXHIBIT 6-10   Standard Deduction Amounts*

2017 Amounts		
Filing Status	Basic Standard Deduction	Additional Standard Deduction for Age and/or Blindness at End of Year
Married filing jointly	$12,700	$1,250
Head of household	9,350	1,550
Single	6,350	1,550
Married filing separately	6,350	1,250

2018 Amounts		
Filing Status	Basic Standard Deduction	Additional Standard Deduction for Age and/or Blindness at End of Year
Married filing jointly	$24,000	$1,300
Head of household	18,000	1,600
Single	12,000	1,600
Married filing separately	12,000	1,300

*For individuals claimed as a dependent on another return, the 2018 standard deduction is the greater of (1) $1,050 or (2) $350 plus earned income not to exceed the standard deduction amount of those who are not dependents.

Example 6-22

What is Courtney's standard deduction for the year?

Answer: $18,000. Because Courtney is unmarried at the end of the year and she maintains a household for more than six months for Deron and Ellen, who both qualify as her dependents (as qualifying children), Courtney's filing status is head of household, which allows her to claim a standard deduction of $18,000.

Given that Courtney's itemized deductions are $38,330, will Courtney deduct her itemized deductions or her standard deduction?

Answer: She will deduct her itemized deductions because they exceed her standard deduction.

What if: Suppose that Courtney's 10-year-old son, Deron, earned $600 this summer by mowing lawns for neighbors. If Deron is Courtney's dependent, what amount of standard deduction can Deron claim on his individual return?

Answer: Deron will claim a minimum standard deduction of $1,050 because he is Courtney's dependent. Hence, Deron will not pay any income tax because his taxable income is reduced to zero by the standard deduction.[42]

What if: Would there be any difference in the amount of the standard deduction if Deron earned $2,100?

Answer: Because of the amount of his earnings, Deron would claim a standard deduction in the amount of his earned income plus $350. Hence, Deron would claim a standard deduction of $2,450 and he would not pay any income tax.[43]

What if: Suppose Deron earned $14,000.

Answer: Again, Deron would claim a standard deduction in the amount of his earned income plus $350. However, Deron's standard deduction is limited to $12,000, the maximum allowable standard deduction for a taxpayer filing single.

---

[42]Deron will need to file a tax return because his self-employment income exceeds $400 and, as explained in the Individual Income Tax Computation and Tax Credits chapter, he will likely owe self-employment tax.

[43]As mentioned previously, Deron will need to file a tax return because his self-employment income exceeds $400 and, as explained in the Individual Income Tax Computation and Tax Credits chapter, he will likely owe self-employment taxes.

From the government's standpoint, the standard deduction serves two purposes. First, to help taxpayers with lower income, it automatically provides a minimum amount of income that is not subject to taxation. Second, it eliminates the need for the IRS to verify and audit itemized deductions for those taxpayers who choose to deduct the standard deduction. From the taxpayers' perspective, the standard deduction allows them to avoid taxation on a portion of their income, and for those not planning to itemize deductions, it eliminates the need to substantiate and collect information about them.

The standard deduction, however, is a double-edged sword. While it reduces taxes by offsetting income with an automatic deduction, it eliminates the tax benefits of itemized deductions up to the amount of the standard deduction. This is a very important point to consider when evaluating the tax benefits of itemized deductions.

Example 6-23

In Example 6-21, we determined that Courtney is entitled to deduct $38,330 of itemized deductions this year. How much do Courtney's itemized deductions reduce her taxable income relative to a situation in which she has $0 itemized deductions?

Answer: $20,330. Because Courtney files as a head of household, she would have been able to deduct $18,000 as a standard deduction even if she had not incurred *any* itemized deductions. Consequently, her itemized deductions reduce her taxable income by only $20,330 ($38,330 − $18,000) beyond what her taxable income would have been if she did not itemize deductions.

Bunching Itemized Deductions   Some taxpayers may deduct the standard deduction every year because their itemized deductions always fall just short of the standard deduction amount and thus never produce any tax benefit. They may gain some tax benefit from their itemized deductions by implementing a simple tax planning strategy called **bunching itemized deductions.** The basic strategy consists of shifting itemized deductions into one year such that the amount of itemized deductions exceeds the standard deduction for the year, and then deducting the standard deduction in the next year (or vice versa).

Because individuals are cash-method taxpayers, they may shift certain itemized deductions by accelerating payment into the current year. For example, a taxpayer could make charitable contributions at the end of December rather than at the beginning of January in the following year. Taxpayers' ability to shift itemized deductions is limited because the timing of these payments is not completely discretionary. For example, real estate taxes have due dates, state taxes are generally paid throughout the year via withholding, and employees may incur and be required to pay business expenses throughout the year. However, taxpayers who annually make a certain amount of charitable contributions, for example, may consider lumping contributions for two years into one year and not contributing in the next year.[44]

Example 6-24

What if: Gram is 70 years old and files as a single taxpayer. This year Gram paid deductible medical expenses (after the AGI floor limitation) of $4,000. She also contributed $7,500 to her local church. This year her total itemized deductions were $11,500 ($4,000 medical + $7,500 charitable). Assuming Gram will have similar expenditures next year, what amount of additional deductions would Gram have been able to deduct this year if she had bunched her deductions by making her 2018 and 2019 charitable contributions in 2018? Use the 2018 standard deduction amounts for both 2018 and 2019.

(continued on page 6-26)

---

[44]Of course, as we discussed in the Tax Planning Strategies and Related Limitations chapter, taxpayers adopting this strategy must also consider the time value of money for the contribution amounts they pay in advance to determine whether a tax planning strategy designed to save taxes makes economic sense.

Answer: $5,400, computed as follows:

	No Bunching		Bunching	
	2018	**2019**	**2018**	**2019**
(1) Standard deduction*	$13,600	$13,600	$13,600	$13,600
(2) Itemized deductions	11,500	11,500	19,000	4,000
Greater of (1) and (2)	$13,600	$13,600	$19,000	$13,600
Total deductions (combined years)	$27,200 ($13,600 + $13,600)		$32,600 ($19,000 + $13,600)	
Deductions gained through bunching	**$5,400** ($32,600 bunching deductions − $27,200 nonbunching deductions)			

*For 2018, her standard deduction is the $12,000 standard deduction for single taxpayers plus an additional $1,600 standard deduction amount for age. (See Exhibit 6-10.) For 2019, we assume she has the same standard deduction as 2018.

LO 6-4

DEDUCTION FOR QUALIFIED BUSINESS INCOME

Deduction for Qualified Business Income

The last *from* AGI deduction that we will cover is the **deduction for qualified business income.** If applicable, this deduction is allowed as a *from* AGI deduction in addition to the taxpayer's itemized deductions or standard deduction. The deduction applies to taxpayers with qualified business income from a partnership, S Corporation, or sole proprietorship. Specifically, a taxpayer may deduct the lesser of:

(a) 20 percent of the taxpayer's **qualified business income** from a **qualified trade or business** (after application of the wage limit), plus 20 percent of the taxpayer's qualified real estate investment trust dividends and qualified publicly traded partnership income, if any or

(b) 20 percent of the excess, if any, of taxable income over the taxpayer's net capital gains (including qualified dividends).[45]

A qualified trade or business is any trade or business other than a **specified service trade or business** and other than the trade or business of being an employee. A specified service trade or business is any trade or business involving the performance of services in the fields of health, law, consulting, athletics, financial services, brokerage services, or any trade or business where the principal asset of such trade or business is the reputation or skill of one or more of its employees or owners, or which involves the performance of services that consist of investing and investment management trading, or dealing in securities, partnership interests, or commodities. Architecture and engineering services (their services build things) are specifically excluded from the definition of specified service trade or business.

For any year in which the taxpayer's taxable income (before the deduction for qualified business income) is less than $157,500 ($315,000, if married filing jointly), the exclusion for specified service trades or business will not apply (the business will

---

[45]The rules are a little more complex if the taxpayer receives cooperative dividends (known as patronage dividends) paid from the cooperative's profits to its members. Subject to limitations, cooperative dividends are eligible for the deduction for qualified business income.

be deemed a qualified trade or business). This means that a taxpayer operating a business that is not a qualified trade or business still gets the deduction for qualified business income if his or her taxable income is low enough. For taxpayers with taxable income above $157,500 ($315,000, if married filing jointly), the exclusion from the definition of a qualified business for specified service trades or businesses phases in over a $50,000 range ($100,000, in the case of a joint return). The exclusion from the definition of a qualified business for specified service trades or businesses is fully phased in for taxpayers with taxable income in excess of $207,500 ($415,000 in the case of a joint return).

Example 6-25

As described in Example 5-7, Courtney performs architectural consulting services outside of her employment with EWD. Will her income from the architectural services be considered qualified business income?

Answer: Yes. Architectural services are not a specified service or trade business. Thus, her income from the architectural services would be qualified trade or business income.

What if: Assume Courtney decides to establish a sole proprietorship to perform investment advising services. This year, Courtney reports $250,000 of taxable income before the deduction for qualified business income. Will her income from investment advisory services be considered qualified business income?

Answer: No. Investment advisory services fall within the definition of a specified service or trade business. Because her taxable income exceeds $207,500 ($157,500 + $50,000 phase-in range), the exclusion from the specified service trades or business rules based on taxable income does not apply. Thus, her investment advisory service income would not be considered qualified trade or business income. Consequently, she is not eligible for the deduction for qualified business income on that income.

What if: Assume Courtney decides to establish a sole proprietorship to perform investment advising services. This year, Courtney reports $100,000 of taxable income before the deduction for qualified business income. Will her income from investment advisory services be considered qualified business income?

Answer: Yes. Because her taxable income falls below the $157,500, the exclusion for specified service trades or businesses will not apply (the business will be deemed a qualified trade or business). Consequently, she is eligible for the deduction for qualified business income on that income.

What if: Assume Courtney decides to establish a sole proprietorship to perform investment advising services. This year, Courtney reports $187,500 of taxable income before the deduction for qualified business income. Will her income from advisory services be considered qualified business income?

Answer: If Courtney had $187,500 of taxable income (before the deduction for qualified business income), 60 percent of her investment advising income would not be considered qualified business income [[($187,500 taxable income − $157,500)/($50,000 phase-out range)] = 60%]. The remaining 40 percent of her investment advising income would be considered qualified business income.

Qualified business income is the net amount of qualified items of income, gain, deduction, and loss with respect to the taxpayer's qualified trade or business conducted within the United States. Qualified items do not include specified investment-related income, deductions, or loss (e.g., capital gains or losses, dividends, interest income not allocable to a trade or business, etc.).[46] If the net amount of qualified business income from all qualified trades or businesses during the taxable year is a loss, it is carried forward as a loss from a qualified trade or business in the next taxable year.[47]

---

[46]Qualified business income does not include any amount paid by an S corporation that is treated as reasonable compensation of the taxpayer or any guaranteed payment for services rendered with respect to the trade or business.

[47]Similar to a qualified trade or business that has a qualified business loss for the current taxable year, any deduction allowed in a subsequent year is reduced (but not below zero) by 20 percent of any carryover qualified business loss.

Limitations

The deduction for qualified business income cannot exceed the greater of:

(i) 50 percent of the wages paid with respect to the qualified trade or businesses, or

(ii) the sum of 25 of percent of the wages with respect to the qualified trade or businesses plus 2.5 percent of the unadjusted basis, immediately after acquisition, of all qualified property in the qualified trade or businesses.[48]

For purposes of the wage-based limit, each partner or S corporation shareholder is treated as having wages for the year equal to his or her allocable share from the partnership or S corporation. The wage-based limits only apply to taxpayers with taxable income in excess of $157,500 ($315,000, in the case of a joint return)). The wage limit is phased in ratably over $50,000 ($100,000 for married filing joint returns) so that it fully applies to taxpayers with taxable income in excess of $207,500 ($415,000 for married filing joint return).

Example 6-26

Courtney reports taxable income this year of $148,670 ($187,000 AGI less $38,330 itemized deductions, see Example 6-20) before the deduction for qualified business income, and she has no capital gains and $700 of qualified dividends included in her taxable income (see Exhibit 5-4). Her architectural consulting services generate $18,000 of qualified business income, and she paid no wages in this business. What is Courtney's deduction for qualified business income?

Answer: $3,600. Because her taxable income before the deduction for qualified business income is less than $157,500, the wage limitation does not apply. Likewise, Courtney is not limited by the taxable income limitation because 20 percent of her qualified business income ($18,000 × 20% = $3,600) is less than 20 percent of her taxable income in excess of her qualified dividends and before the deduction [($148,670 taxable income − $700 qualified dividends) × 20% = $29,594]. Thus, Courtney's deduction for qualified business income is $3,600 ($18,000 qualified business income × 20%).

What if: Assume Courtney reports taxable income this year of $300,000 (before the deduction for qualified business income), has no qualified dividends or capital gains, and that her architectural consulting business generates $75,000 of qualified business income, has no qualified property and pays $20,000 of wages. What is Courtney's deduction for qualified business income?

Answer: $10,000. Before limitation, 20 percent of Courtney's qualified business income is $15,000 ($75,000 × 20%), and the greater of:

(a) 50 percent of the wages paid by the qualified business ($20,000 × 50% = $10,000) or

(b) 25 percent of the wages paid by the qualified business ($20,000 × 25% = $5,000) plus 2.5 percent of the unadjusted basis of qualified property ($0 × 2.5% = $0)

is $10,000. Because her taxable income of $300,000 exceeds the $157,500 phase-in threshold by more than $50,000, the wage limit fully applies. Thus, Courtney's deduction for qualified business income is limited to $10,000. Courtney is not limited by the taxable income limitation because 20 percent of her qualified business income after application of the wage limitation ($10,000) is less than 20 percent of her taxable income before the deduction ($300,000 × 20% = $60,000).

What if: Assume that Courtney reports taxable income this year of $177,500 (before the deduction for qualified business income), has no qualified dividends or capital gains, and that her architectural consulting business generates $75,000 of qualified business income, has no qualified property, and has $20,000 of wages. What is Courtney's deduction for qualified business income?

---

[48]Qualified property is tangible, depreciable property held and available for use at the end of the tax year, used in the production of qualified business income during the year, for which the depreciable period has not ended by the end of the tax year. The depreciable period with respect to qualified property of a taxpayer means the period beginning on the date the property is first placed in service by the taxpayer and ending on the later of (a) the date 10 years after that date, or (b) the last day of the last full year in the applicable recovery period that would apply to the property under §168 [without regard to §168(g)].

Answer: $13,000. Before limitation, 20 percent of Courtney's qualified business income is $15,000 ($75,000 × 20 percent), and the greater of:

(a) 50 percent of the wages paid by the qualified business ($20,000 × 50% = $10,000) or

(b) 25 percent of the wages paid by the qualified business ($20,000 × 25% = $5,000) plus 2.5 percent of the unadjusted basis of qualified property ($0 × 2.5% = $0)

is $10,000. Because her taxable income of $177,500 exceeds the $157,500 phase-in threshold by $20,000, the wage limit is phased in by 40 percent [[($177,500 − $157,500)/$50,000} phase-in range = 40 percent]. Courtney's wage limit of $5,000 (the excess of (a) 20 percent of business income of $15,000 over (b) 50 percent of wages, $10,000 ($20,000 × 50%)) is phased in by 40 percent. Thus, her deduction for qualified business income is limited to $13,000 [$15,000 − ($5,000 × 40%)]. Courtney is not limited by the taxable income limitation because 20 percent of her qualified business income after application of the wage limitation ($13,000) is less than 20 percent of her taxable income before the deduction ($177,500 × 20% = $35,500).

Taxable Income Summary

We now have enough information to calculate Courtney's and Gram's taxable income. Exhibit 6-11 shows Courtney's taxable income calculation and Exhibit 6-12 illustrates how this information would be displayed on page 2 of Courtney's Form 1040.

Exhibit 6-13 provides Gram's taxable income calculation.

EXHIBIT 6-11 Courtney's Taxable Income

Description	Amount	Reference
AGI	$187,000	Exhibit 6-5
Less: Greater of (1) itemized deductions ($38,330)		
or (2) standard deduction ($18,000)	(38,330)	Example 6-21
Less: Deduction for qualified business income	(3,600)	Example 6-26
Taxable income	$145,070	

EXHIBIT 6-12 Courtney's Taxable Income Computation as Presented on Form 1040, Page 2

Form 1040 (2017)   Page **2**

Tax and Credits	38	Amount from line 37 (adjusted gross income)	38		187,000
	39a	Check if: ☐ **You** were born before January 2, 1953, ☐ **Spouse** was born before January 2, 1953, ☐ Blind. ☐ Blind. } Total boxes checked ▶ **39a**			
	b	If your spouse itemizes on a separate return or you were a dual-status alien, check here ▶ 39b☐			
Standard Deduction for—	40	**Itemized deductions** (from Schedule A) **or** your **standard deduction** (see left margin) . .	40		38,330
• People who check any box on line	41	Subtract line 40 from line 38	41		148,670
	42	Deduction for qualified business income	42		3,600
	43	**Taxable income.** Subtract line 42 from line 41. If line 42 is more than line 41, enter -0- . .	43		145,070

Source: Form1040

EXHIBIT 6-13 Gram's Taxable Income

Description	Amount	Reference
(1) AGI	$15,590	Exhibit 6-6
(2) Greater of (a) itemized deductions ($11,500)		
or (b) standard deduction ($13,600)	(13,600)	Example 6-24
Taxable income	$ 1,990	(1) + (2)

Note that because Gram's gross income of $16,000 (Exhibit 5-6) is more than her basic standard deduction amount ($13,600), she is required to file a tax return.

CONCLUSION

We started this chapter with Courtney's and Gram's gross incomes. In this chapter, we first identified the duo's separate deductions *for* AGI and computed their AGI. We then determined their *from* AGI deductions. Courtney deducted her itemized deductions because they exceeded her standard deduction. Gram, on the other hand, deducted her standard deduction. Finally, Courtney was able to take advantage of the deduction for qualified business income, while Gram did not have any qualified business income. By subtracting their *from* AGI deductions from their AGI, we determined taxable income for both Courtney and Gram. With this knowledge, we proceed to the next two chapters and address issues relating to investments and determining the amount of tax Courtney and Gram are required to pay on their taxable income.

Summary

LO 6-1 Identify the common deductions necessary for calculating adjusted gross income (AGI).

- Deductions *for* AGI may be categorized into those that are directly or indirectly business-related and those that address specific policy issues.
- The business-related deductions *for* AGI include business expenses, rent and royalty expenses, self-employment taxes, medical and health insurance by self-employed taxpayers, and forfeited interest.
- Other common deductions *for* AGI include the deductions for interest on student loans and early withdrawal penalties.

LO 6-2 Describe the different types of itemized deductions available to individuals.

- The medical expense deduction is designed to provide tax benefits to needy individuals but is subject to significant floor limitation.
- The itemized deduction for interest is limited to home mortgage interest and investment interest, and the latter is limited by net investment income.
- The deduction for charitable contributions extends to contributions of money and property to qualifying charities. The charitable deduction is subject to ceiling limitations, which are more restrictive for donations of property.
- The deduction for taxes is subject to a cap and includes state income and property taxes. Sales taxes can be deducted in lieu of deducting state and local income taxes.

LO 6-3 Determine the standard deduction available to individuals.

- Taxpayers generally deduct the greater of their standard deduction or their itemized deductions.
- The amount of the standard deduction varies according to the taxpayer's filing status, age, and eyesight.

LO 6-4 Calculate the deduction for qualified business income.

- The deduction for qualified business income is a from AGI deduction in addition to the taxpayer's itemized deduction or standard deduction.
- The deduction is limited to qualified trades or businesses and is subject to a number of limitations.

KEY TERMS

bunching itemized deductions (6-25)

business activities (6-2)

capital gain property (6-17)

ceiling (6-18)

deduction for qualified business income (6-26)

excess business loss (6-6)

floor limitation (6-13)

investment activities (6-2)

miscellaneous itemized deductions (6-21)

ordinary and necessary (6-4)

ordinary income property (6-17)

private nonoperating foundations (6-19)

private operating foundations (6-19)

qualified educational loans (6-8)

qualified business income (6-26)

qualified trade or business (6-26)

specified service trade or business (6-26)

standard deduction (6-22)

trade or business (6-2)

DISCUSSION QUESTIONS

Discussion Questions are available in Connect®.

1. It has been suggested that tax policy favors deductions *for* AGI compared to itemized deductions. Describe two ways in which deductions *for* AGI are treated more favorably than itemized deductions.   **LO 6-1**

2. How is a business activity distinguished from an investment activity? Why is this distinction important for the purpose of calculating federal income taxes?   **LO 6-1**

3. Explain why Congress allows self-employed taxpayers to deduct the cost of health insurance above the line (*for* AGI) when employees can only itemize this cost as a medical expense. Would a self-employed taxpayer ever prefer to claim health insurance premiums as an itemized deduction rather than a deduction *for* AGI? Explain.   **LO 6-1**

4. Explain why Congress allows self-employed taxpayers to deduct the employer portion of their self-employment tax.   **LO 6-1**

5. Using the Internal Revenue Code, describe two deductions *for* AGI that are not discussed in this chapter.   **LO 6-1**   **research**

6. Explain why Congress allows taxpayers to deduct interest forfeited as a penalty on the premature withdrawal from a certificate of deposit.   **LO G-1**

7. Describe the mechanical limitation on the deduction for interest on qualified educational loans.   **LO 6-1**

8. Explain why the medical expense provisions are sometimes referred to as "wherewithal" deductions and how this rationale is reflected in the limit on these deductions.   **LO 6-2**

9. Describe the type of medical expenditures that qualify for the medical expense deduction. Does the cost of meals consumed while hospitalized qualify for the deduction? Do over-the-counter drugs and medicines qualify for the deduction?   **LO 6-2**

10. Under what circumstances can a taxpayer deduct medical expenses paid for a member of his family? Does it matter if the family member reports significant amounts of gross income and cannot be claimed as a dependent?   **LO 6-2**

11. What types of taxes qualify to be deducted as itemized deductions? Would a vehicle registration fee qualify as a deductible tax?   **LO 6-2**

12. Explain the argument that the deductions for charitable contributions and home mortgage interest represent indirect subsidies for these activities.   **LO 6-2**

13. Cash donations to charity are subject to a number of very specific substantiation requirements. Describe these requirements and how charitable gifts can be substantiated. Describe the substantiation requirements for property donations.   **LO 6-2**   **research**

LO 6-2 14. Describe the conditions in which a donation of property to a charity will result in a charitable contribution deduction of fair market value and when it will result in a deduction of the tax basis of the property.

LO 6-2 15. Jake is a retired jockey who takes monthly trips to Las Vegas to gamble on horse races. Jake also trains racehorses part time at his Louisville ranch. So far this year, Jake has won almost $47,500 during his trips to Las Vegas while spending $27,250 on travel expenses and incurring $62,400 of gambling losses. Explain how Jake's gambling winnings and related costs will be treated for tax purposes.

LO 6-2
research 16. Frank paid $3,700 in fees for an accountant to tabulate business information (Frank operates as a self-employed contractor and files a Schedule C). The accountant also spent time tabulating Frank's income from his investments and determining Frank's personal itemized deductions. Explain to Frank whether or not he can deduct the $3,700 as a business expense or as an itemized deduction, and provide a citation to an authority that supports your conclusion.

LO 6-2 17. Contrast ceiling and floor limitations, and give an example of each.

LO 6-2 18. Identify which itemized deductions are subject to floor limitations, ceiling limitations, or some combination of these limits.

LO 6-3 19. Describe the tax benefits from "bunching" itemized deductions in one year. Describe the characteristics of the taxpayers who are most likely to benefit from using bunching and explain why this is so.

LO 6-3 20. Explain how the standard deduction is rationalized and why the standard deduction might be viewed as a floor limit on itemized deductions.

LO 6-3
research 21. Determine whether a taxpayer can change his or her election to itemize deductions once a return is filed. (*Hint:* Read about itemization under Reg. §1.63-1.)

LO 6-4 22. Describe what is meant by qualified business income for purposes of the deduction for qualified business income.

LO 6-4 23. Under what circumstances would business income from an accounting practice qualify for the deduction for qualified business income?

PROBLEMS

Select problems are available in Connect®.

LO 6-1 24. Clem is married and is a skilled carpenter. Clem's wife, Wanda, works part-time as a substitute grade school teacher. Determine the amount of Clem's expenses that are deductible *for* AGI this year (if any) under the following independent circumstances:

a) Clem is self-employed and this year he incurred $525 in expenses for tools and supplies related to his job. Since neither were covered by a qualified health plan, Wanda paid health insurance premiums of $3,600 to provide coverage for herself and Clem (not through an exchange).

b) Clem and Wanda own a garage downtown that they rent to a local business for storage. This year they incurred expenses of $1,250 in utilities and $780 in depreciation.

c) Clem paid self-employment tax of $15,300 (the employer portion is $7,650), and Wanda had $3,000 of Social Security taxes withheld from her pay.

d) Clem paid $45 to rent a safe deposit box to store his coin collection. Clem has collected coins intermittently since he was a boy, and he expects to sell his collection when he retires.

LO 6-1 25. Don Juan, a single taxpayer, is the sole owner of DJ's Inc., an S Corporation. This year, DJ's Inc. incurred a massive $600,000 business loss, all of which is allocable to Don Juan as the sole shareholder. Assume that $600,000 loss is not limited by the basis, at-risk, or passive loss rules, and that Don Juan has no other business income or business losses. How much of the $600,000 loss will Don Juan be able to deduct this year? What happens to any loss not deducted this year?

26. Smithers is a self-employed individual who earns $30,000 per year in self-employment income. Smithers pays $2,200 in annual health insurance premiums (not through an exchange) for his own medical care. In each of the following situations, determine the amount of the deductible health insurance premium for Smithers before any AGI limitation.   `LO 6-1`

    a) Smithers is single and the self-employment income is his only source of income.

    b) Smithers is single, but besides being self-employed, Smithers is also employed part-time by SF Power Corporation. This year Smithers elected not to participate in SF's health plan.

    c) Smithers is self-employed and he is also married. Smithers's spouse, Samantha, is employed full-time by SF Power Corporation and is covered by SF's health plan. Smithers is not eligible to participate in SF's health plan.

    d) Smithers is self-employed and he is also married. Smithers's spouse, Samantha, is employed full-time by SF Power Corporation and is covered by SF's health plan. Smithers elected not to participate in SF's health plan.

27. Hardaway earned $100,000 of compensation this year. He also paid (or had paid for him) $3,000 of health insurance (not through an exchange). What is Hardaway's AGI in each of the following situations? (Ignore the effects of Social Security and self-employment taxes.)   `LO 6-1`

    a) Hardaway is an employee and his employer paid Hardaway's $3,000 of health insurance for him as a nontaxable fringe benefit. Consequently, Hardaway received $97,000 of taxable compensation and $3,000 of nontaxable compensation.

    b) Hardaway is a self-employed taxpayer, and he paid $3,000 of health insurance himself. He is not eligible to participate in an employer-sponsored plan.

28. Betty operates a beauty salon as a sole proprietorship. Betty also owns and rents an apartment building. This year Betty had the following income and expenses. Determine Betty's AGI and complete page 1 of Form 1040 for Betty. You may assume that Betty will owe $2,502 in self-employment tax on her salon income, with $1,251 representing the employer portion of the self-employment tax. You may also assume that her divorce from Rocky was finalized in 2016.   `LO 6-1`

    tax forms

Interest income	$11,255
Salon sales and revenue	86,360
Salaries paid to beauticians	45,250
Beauty salon supplies	23,400
Alimony paid to her ex-husband, Rocky	6,000
Rental revenue from apartment building	31,220
Depreciation on apartment building	12,900
Real estate taxes paid on apartment building	11,100
Real estate taxes paid on personal residence	6,241
Contributions to charity	4,237

29. Lionel is an unmarried law student at State University Law School, a qualified educational institution. This year Lionel borrowed $24,000 from County Bank and paid interest of $1,440. Lionel used the loan proceeds to pay his law   `LO 6-1`

school tuition. Calculate the amounts Lionel can deduct for interest on higher-education loans under the following circumstances:

a) Lionel's AGI before deducting interest on higher-education loans is $50,000.

b) Lionel's AGI before deducting interest on higher-education loans is $74,000.

c) Lionel's AGI before deducting interest on higher-education loans is $90,000.

LO 6-1 30. This year Jack intends to file a married-joint return. Jack received $167,500 of salary and paid $5,000 of interest on loans used to pay qualified tuition costs for his dependent daughter, Deb. This year Jack has also paid moving expenses of $4,300 and $28,300 of alimony to his ex-wife, Diane, who divorced him in 2012.

a) What is Jack's adjusted gross income?

b) Suppose that Jack also reported income of $8,800 from a half share of profits from a partnership. Disregard any potential self-employment taxes on this income. What AGI would Jack report under these circumstances?

LO 6-1 **LO 6-2** 31. In each of the following independent cases, indicate the amount (1) deductible *for* AGI, (2) deductible *from* AGI, and (3) deductible neither *for* nor *from* AGI before considering income limitations or the standard deduction.

a) Ted paid $50 rent on a safety deposit box at the bank. In this box he kept the few shares of stock that he owned.

b) Tyler paid $85 for minor repairs to the fence at a rental house he owned.

c) Timmy paid $545 for health insurance premiums this year (not through an exchange and not with pretax dollars). Timmy is employed full-time and his employer paid the remaining premiums as a qualified fringe benefit.

d) Tess paid $1,150 of state income taxes on her consulting income.

LO 6-1 **LO 6-2** 32. In each of the following independent cases, indicate the amount (1) deductible *for* AGI, (2) deductible *from* AGI, and (3) deductible neither *for* nor *from* AGI before considering income limitations or the standard deduction.

a) Fran spent $90 for uniforms for use on her job. Her employer reimbursed her for $75 of this amount under an accountable plan (and did not report the reimbursement as wages).

b) Timothy, a plumber employed by ACE Plumbing, spent $65 for small tools to be used on his job, but he was not reimbursed by ACE.

c) Jake is a perfume salesperson. Because of his high pay, he receives no allowance or reimbursement from his employer for advertising expenses even though his position requires him to advertise frequently. During the year, he spent $2,200 on legitimate business advertisements.

d) Trey is a self-employed, special-duty nurse. He spent $120 for uniforms.

e) Mary, a professor at a community college, spent $340 for magazine subscriptions. The magazines were helpful for her research activities, but she was not reimbursed for the expenditures.

f) Wayne lost $325 on the bets he made at the race track, but he won $57 playing slot machines.

LO 6-2 33. Penny, a full-time biochemist, loves stock car racing. To feed her passion, she bought a used dirt-track car and has started entering some local dirt-track races. The prize money is pretty small ($1,000 for the winner), but she really is not in it for the money. Penny reported the following income and expenses from her nights at the track:

Prize money	$2,500
Expenses:	
Transportation from her home to the races	1,000
Depreciation on the dirt-track car	4,000
Entry fees	3,500
Oil, gas, supplies, repairs for the dirt-track car	2,050

What are the tax effects of Penny's racing income and expenses assuming that the racing activity is a hobby for Penny?

34. Simpson, age 45, is a single individual who is employed full-time by Duff Corporation. This year Simpson reports AGI of $50,000 and has incurred the following medical expenses:

LO 6-2

Dentist charges	$ 900
Physician charges	1,800
Optical charges	500
Cost of eyeglasses	300
Hospital charges	2,100
Prescription drugs	250
Over-the-counter drugs	450
Medical insurance premiums (not through an exchange)	775

a) Calculate the amount of medical expenses that will be included with Simpson's itemized deductions after any applicable limitations.

b) Suppose that Simpson was reimbursed for $250 of the physician's charges and $1,200 for the hospital costs. Calculate the amount of medical expenses that will be included with Simpson's itemized deductions after any applicable limitations.

35. This year Tim is age 45 and is considering enrolling in an insurance program that provides for long-term care insurance. He is curious about whether the insurance premiums are deductible as a medical expense and, if so, what the maximum amount is that can be deducted in any year.

LO 6-2

 research

36. Doctor Bones prescribed physical therapy in a pool to treat Jack's broken back. In response to this advice (and for no other reason), Jack built a swimming pool in his backyard and strictly limited use of the pool to physical therapy. Jack paid $25,000 to build the pool, but he wondered if this amount could be deducted as a medical expense. Determine if a capital expenditure such as the cost of a swimming pool qualifies for the medical expense deduction.

LO 6-2

 research

37. Charles has AGI of $50,000 and has made the following payments related to (1) land he inherited from his deceased aunt and (2) a personal vacation taken last year. Calculate the amount of taxes Charles may include in his itemized deductions for the year under the following circumstances:

LO 6-1   LO 6-2

State inheritance tax on the land	$1,200
County real estate tax on the land	1,500
School district tax on the land	690
City special assessment on the land (replacing curbs and gutters)	700
State tax on airline tickets (paid on vacation)	125
Local hotel tax (paid during vacation)	195

a) Suppose that Charles holds the land for appreciation.

b) Suppose that Charles holds the land for rent.

c) Suppose that Charles holds the land for appreciation and that the vacation was actually a business trip.

LO 6-2   38. Dan has AGI of $50,000 and paid the following taxes during this tax year. Calculate how much Dan can deduct for taxes as an itemized deduction this year.

State income tax withholding	$1,400
State income tax estimated payments	750
Federal income tax withholding	3,000
Social Security tax withheld from wages	2,100
State excise tax on liquor	400
Automobile license (based on the car's weight)	300
State sales tax paid	475

LO 6-1 **LO 6-2**   39. Tim is a single, cash-method taxpayer with an AGI of $50,000. In April of this year, Tim paid $1,020 with his state income tax return for the previous year. During the year, Tim had $5,400 of state income tax and $18,250 of federal income tax withheld from his salary. In addition, Tim made estimated payments of $1,360 and $1,900 of state and federal income taxes, respectively. Finally, Tim expects to receive a refund of $500 for state income taxes when he files his state tax return for this year in April next year. What is the amount of taxes that Tim can deduct as an itemized deduction?

LO 6-2   40. This year Randy paid $28,000 of interest. (Randy borrowed $450,000 to buy his residence, which is currently worth $500,000.) Randy also paid $2,500 of interest on his car loan and $4,200 of margin interest to his stockbroker (investment interest expense). How much of this interest expense can Randy deduct as an itemized deduction under the following circumstances?

a) Randy received $2,200 of interest this year and no other investment income or expenses. His AGI is $75,000.

b) Randy had no investment income this year, and his AGI is $75,000.

LO 6-2   41. This year, Major Healy paid $40,000 of interest on a mortgage on his home (he borrowed $800,000 to buy the residence in 2015; $900,000 original purchase price and value at purchase), $6,000 of interest on a $120,000 home equity loan on his home (loan proceeds were used to buy antique cars), and $10,000 of interest on a mortgage on his vacation home (borrowed $200,000 to purchase the home in 2010; home purchased for $500,000). Major Healy's AGI is $220,000. How much interest expense can Major Healy deduct as an itemized deduction?

LO 6-2   42. Ray Ray made the following contributions this year.

Charity	Property	Cost	FMV
Athens Academy School	Cash	$ 5,000	$ 5,000
United Way	Cash	4,000	4,000
American Heart Association	Antique painting	15,000	75,000
First Methodist Church	Coca-Cola stock	12,000	20,000

Determine the maximum amount of charitable deduction for each of these contributions *ignoring* the AGI ceiling on charitable contributions and assuming that the American Heart Association plans to sell the antique painting to fund its operations. Ray Ray has owned the painting and Coca-Cola stock since 1990.

LO 6-2   43. Calvin reviewed his cancelled checks and receipts this year for charitable contributions, which included a painting and IBM stock. He has owned the IBM stock and painting since 2005.

Donee	Item	Cost	FMV
Hobbs Medical Center	IBM stock	$5,000	$22,000
State Museum	Antique painting	5,000	3,000
A needy family	Food and clothes	400	250
United Way	Cash	8,000	8,000

Calculate Calvin's charitable contribution deduction and carryover (if any) under the following circumstances.

a) Calvin's AGI is $100,000.

b) Calvin's AGI is $100,000 but the State Museum told Calvin that it plans to sell the painting.

c) Calvin's AGI is $50,000.

d) Calvin's AGI is $100,000 and Hobbs is a private nonoperating foundation.

e) Calvin's AGI is $100,000 but the painting is worth $10,000.

44. In addition to cash contributions to charity, Dean decided to donate shares of stock and a portrait painted during the earlier part of the last century. Dean purchased the stock and portrait many years ago as investments. Dean reported the following recipients: **LO 6-2**

Charity	Property	Cost	FMV
State University	Cash	$15,000	$15,000
Red Cross	Cash	14,500	14,500
State History Museum	Painting	5,000	82,000
City Medical Center	Dell stock	28,000	17,000

a) Determine the maximum amount of charitable deduction for each of these contributions *ignoring* the AGI ceiling on charitable contributions.

b) Assume that Dean's AGI this year is $150,000. Determine Dean's itemized deduction for his charitable contributions this year and any carryover.

c) Suppose Dean is a dealer in antique paintings and had held the painting for sale before the contribution. What is Dean's charitable contribution deduction for the painting in this situation (ignoring AGI limitations)?

d) Suppose that Dean's objective with the donation to the museum was to finance expansion of the historical collection. Hence, Dean was not surprised when the museum announced the sale of the painting because of its limited historical value. What is Dean's charitable contribution deduction for the painting in this situation (ignoring AGI limitations)?

45. Trevor is a single individual who is a cash-method, calendar-year taxpayer. For each of the next two years (year 1 and year 2), Trevor expects to report AGI of $80,000, contribute $8,000 to charity, and pay $2,800 in state income taxes.   **LO 6-2** planning

a) Estimate Trevor's taxable income for year 1 and year 2 using the 2018 amounts for the standard deduction for both years.

b) Now assume that Trevor combines his anticipated charitable contributions for the next two years and makes the combined contribution in December of year 1. Estimate Trevor's taxable income for each of the next two years using the 2018 amounts for the standard deduction. Reconcile the total taxable income to your solution to part (a).

c) Trevor plans to purchase a residence next year, and he estimates that additional property taxes and residential interest will cost $2,000 and $10,000, respectively, each year. Estimate Trevor's taxable income for each of the next two years (year 1 and year 2) using the 2018 amounts for the standard deduction and also assuming Trevor makes the charitable contribution of $8,000 and state tax payments of $2,800 in each year.

d) Assume that Trevor makes the charitable contribution for year 2 and pays the real estate taxes for year 2 in December of year 1. Estimate Trevor's taxable income for year 1 and year 2 using the 2018 amounts for the standard deduction. Reconcile the total taxable income to your solution to part (c).

e) Explain the conditions in which the bunching strategy in part (d) will generate tax savings for Trevor.

LO 6-2 46. Simon lost $5,000 gambling this year on a trip to Las Vegas. In addition, he paid $2,000 to his broker for managing his $200,000 portfolio and $1,500 to his accountant for preparing his tax return. In addition, Simon incurred $2,500 in transportation costs commuting back and forth from his home to his employer's office, which were not reimbursed. Calculate the amount of these expenses that Simon is able to deduct (assuming he itemizes his deductions).

LO 6-1 **LO 6-2** 47. Tammy teaches elementary school history for the Metro School District. In 2018 she has incurred the following expenses associated with her job:

Noncredit correspondence course on history	$ 900
Teaching cases for classroom use	1,800

Tammy's employer does not provide any funding for the correspondence course or teaching cases. Identify the amount and type (for AGI or from AGI) of deductible expenses.

LO 6-3 48. Stephanie is 12 years old and often assists neighbors on weekends by babysitting their children. Calculate the 2018 standard deduction Stephanie will claim under the following independent circumstances (assume that Stephanie's parents will claim her as a dependent).

a) Stephanie reported $850 of earnings from her babysitting.

b) Stephanie reported $1,500 of earnings from her babysitting.

c) Stephanie reported $18,000 of earnings from her babysitting.

LO 6-4 49. Roquan, a single taxpayer, is an attorney and practices as a sole proprietor. This year, Roquan had net business income of $90,000 from his law practice. Assume that Roquan pays $40,000 wages to his employees, he has $10,000 of property (unadjusted basis of equipment he purchased last year), has no capital gains or qualified dividends, and his taxable income before the deduction for qualified business income is $100,000.

a) Calculate Roquan's deduction for qualified business income.

b) Assume the same facts as earlier, except Roquan's taxable income before the deduction for qualified business income is $300,000.

LO 6-4 50. Katie is a shareholder in Engineers One, a civil engineering company. This year, Katie's share of net business income from Engineers One is $200,000. Assume that Katie's allocation of wages paid by Engineers One to its employees is $300,000 and her allocation of Engineers One's qualified property is $150,000 (unadjusted basis of equipment, all purchased within the past three years). Assume Katie has no other business income, no capital gains or qualified dividends, and that her taxable income before the deduction for qualified business income is $400,000.

a) Calculate Katie's deduction for qualified business income.

b) Assume the same facts as earlier, except Katie's net business income from Engineers One is $400,000 and taxable income before the deduction for qualified business income is $350,000.

COMPREHENSIVE PROBLEMS

Select problems are available in Connect®.

51. This year Evan graduated from college and took a job as a deliveryman in the city. Evan was paid a salary of $67,300 and he received $700 in hourly pay for part-time work over the weekends. Evan summarized his expenses below:

Cost of moving his possessions to the city (125 miles away)	$1,200
Interest paid on accumulated student loans	2,800
Cost of purchasing a delivery uniform	1,400
Contribution to State University deliveryman program	1,300

Calculate Evan's AGI and taxable income if he files single. Assume that interest payments were initially required on Evan's student loans this year.

52. Read the following letter and help Shady Slim with his tax situation. Please assume that his gross income is $172,900 (which consists only of salary) for purposes of this problem.

tax forms

December 31, 2018

To the friendly student tax preparer:

Hi, it's Shady Slim again. I just got back from my 55th birthday party, and I'm told that you need some more information from me in order to complete my tax return. I'm an open book! I'll tell you whatever I think you need to know.

Let me tell you a few more things about my life. As you may recall, I am divorced from my wife, Alice. I know that it's unusual, but I have custody of my son, Shady, Jr. The judge owed me a few favors and I really love the kid. He lives with me full-time and my wife gets him every other weekend. I pay the vast majority of my son's expenses. I think Alice should have to pay some child support, but she doesn't have to pay a dime. The judge didn't owe me that much, I guess.

I had to move this year after getting my job at Roca Cola. We moved on February 3 of this year, and I worked my job at Roca Cola for the rest of the year. I still live in the same state, but I moved 500 miles away from my old house. I hired a moving company to move our stuff at a cost of $2,300, and I drove Junior in my car. Junior and I got a hotel room along the way that cost us $65 (I love Super 8!).

Can you believe I'm still paying off my student loans, even after 15 years? I paid a total of $900 in interest on my old student loans this year.

Remember when I told you about that guy that hit me with his car? I had a bunch of medical expenses that were not reimbursed by the lawsuit or by my insurance. I incurred a total of $20,000 in medical expenses, and I was only reimbursed for $11,000. Good thing I can write off medical expenses, right?

I contributed a lot of money to charity this year (and have receipt documentation for all contributions). I'm such a nice guy! I gave $1,000 in cash to the March of Dimes. I contributed some of my old furniture to the church. It was some good stuff! I contributed a red velvet couch and my old recliner. The furniture is considered vintage and is worth $5,000 today (the appraiser surprised me!), even though I only paid $1,000 for it back in the day. When I contributed the furniture, the pastor said he didn't like the fabric and was going to sell the furniture to pay for some more pews in the church. Oh well, some people just have no taste, right? Roca Cola had a charity drive for the United Way this year and I contributed $90. Turns out, I don't even miss it, because Roca Cola takes it right off my paycheck every month . . . $15 a month starting in July. My pay stub verifies that I contributed the $90 to the United Way. Oh, one other bit of charity from me this year. An old buddy of mine was down on his luck. He lost his job and his house. I gave him $500 to help him out.

I paid a lot of money in interest this year. I paid a total of $950 in personal credit card interest. I also paid $18,000 in interest on my $500,000 home mortgage that helped me buy my dream home. I also paid $2,000 in real estate taxes for my new house.

A few other things I want to tell you about this year. Someone broke into my house and stole my kid's brand new bicycle and my set of golf clubs. The total loss from theft was $900. I paid $125 in union dues this year. I had to pay $1,200 for new suits for my job. Roca Cola requires its managers to wear suits every day on the job. I spent a total of $1,300 to pay for gas to commute to my job this year.

Oh, this is pretty cool. I've always wanted to be a firefighter. I spent $1,400 in tuition to go to the local firefighter's school. I did this because someone told me that I can deduct the tuition as an itemized deduction, so the money would be coming back to me.

That should be all the information you need right now. Please calculate my taxable income and complete pages 1 and 2 of Form 1040 (through taxable income, line 43) and Schedule A. You're still doing this for free, right?

53. Jeremy and Alyssa Johnson have been married for five years and do not have any children. Jeremy was married previously and has one child from the prior marriage. He is self-employed and operates his own computer repair store. For the first two months of the year, Alyssa worked for Office Depot as an employee. In March, Alyssa accepted a new job with Super Toys Inc. (ST), where she worked for the remainder of the year. This year, the Johnsons received $255,000 of gross income. Determine the Johnsons' AGI given the following information:

a) Expenses associated with Jeremy's store include $40,000 in salary (and employment taxes) to employees, $45,000 of supplies, and $18,000 in rent and other administrative expenses.

b) As a salesperson, Alyssa incurred $2,000 in travel expenses related to her employment that were not reimbursed by her employer.

c) The Johnsons own a piece of raw land held as an investment. They paid $500 of real property taxes on the property and they incurred $200 of expenses in travel costs to see the property and to evaluate other similar potential investment properties.

d) The Johnsons own a rental home. They incurred $8,500 of expenses associated with the property.

e) Jeremy paid $4,500 for health insurance coverage for himself (not through an exchange). Alyssa was covered by health plans provided by her employer, but Jeremy is not eligible for the plan until next year.

f) Jeremy paid $2,500 in self-employment taxes ($1,250 represents the employer portion of the self-employment taxes).

g) Jeremy paid $5,000 in alimony and $3,000 in child support from his prior marriage (divorced in 2010).

h) The Johnsons donated $2,000 to their favorite charity.

tax forms

54. Shauna Coleman is single. She is employed as an architectural designer for Streamline Design (SD). Shauna wanted to determine her taxable income for this year. She correctly calculated her AGI. However, she wasn't sure how to compute the rest of her taxable income. She provided the following information with hopes that you could use it to determine her taxable income.

a) Shauna paid $4,680 for medical expenses for care from a broken ankle. Also, Shauna's boyfriend, Blake, drove Shauna (in her car) a total of 115 miles to the doctor's office so she could receive care for her broken ankle.

b) Shauna paid a total of $3,400 in health insurance premiums during the year (not through an exchange). SD did not reimburse any of this expense. Besides the health insurance premiums and the medical expenses for her broken ankle, Shauna had Lasik eye surgery last year and she paid $3,000 for the surgery (she received no insurance reimbursement). She also incurred $450 of other medical expenses for the year.

c) SD withheld $1,800 of state income tax, $7,495 of Social Security tax, and $14,500 of federal income tax from Shauna's paychecks throughout the year.

d) In 2018, Shauna was due a refund of $250 for overpaying her 2017 state taxes. On her 2017 state tax return that she filed in April 2018, she applied the overpayment toward her 2018 state tax liability. She estimated that her state tax liability for 2018 will be $2,300.

e) Shauna paid $3,200 of property taxes on her personal residence. She also paid $500 to the developer of her subdivision, because he had to replace the sidewalk in certain areas of the subdivision.

f) Shauna paid a $200 property tax based on the state's estimate of the value of her car.

g) Shauna has a home mortgage loan in the amount of $220,000 that she secured when she purchased her home. The home is worth about $400,000. Shauna paid interest of $12,300 on the loan this year.

h) Shauna made several charitable contributions throughout the year. She contributed stock in ZYX Corp. to the Red Cross. On the date of the contribution, the fair market value of the donated shares was $1,000 and her basis in the shares was $400. Shauna originally bought the ZYX Corp. stock in 2008. Shauna also contributed $300 cash to State University and religious artifacts she has held for several years to her church. The artifacts were valued at $500 and Shauna's basis in the items was $300. Shauna had every reason to believe the church would keep them on display indefinitely. Shauna also drove 200 miles doing church-related errands for her minister. Finally, Shauna contributed $1,200 of services to her church last year.

i) Shauna paid $250 in investment advisory fees and another $150 to have her tax return prepared (that is, she paid $150 in 2018 to have her 2017 tax return prepared).

j) Shauna is involved in horse racing as a hobby. During the year, she won $2,500 in prize money and incurred $10,000 in expenses. She has never had a profitable year with her horse-racing activities, so she acknowledges that this is a hobby for federal income tax purposes.

k) Shauna sustained $2,000 in gambling losses over the year (mostly horse-racing bets) and only had $200 in winnings.

Required:

a) Determine Shauna's taxable income and complete page 2 of Form 1040 (through taxable income, line 43) and Schedule A assuming her AGI is $107,000.

b) Determine Shauna's taxable income and complete page 2 of Form 1040 (through taxable income, line 43) and Schedule A assuming her AGI is $207,000.

55. Joe and Jessie are married and have one dependent child, Lizzie. Lizzie is currently in college at State University. Joe works as a design engineer for a manufacturing firm while Jessie runs a craft business from their home. Jessie's craft business consists of making craft items for sale at craft shows that are held periodically at various locations. Jessie spends considerable time and effort on her craft business and it has been consistently profitable over the years. Joe and Jessie own a home and pay interest on their home loan (balance of $220,000) and a personal loan to pay for Lizzie's college expenses (balance of $35,000). Neither Joe nor Jessie is blind or over age 65, and they plan to file as married joint. Based on their estimates, determine Joe and Jessie's AGI and taxable income for the year and complete

pages 1 and 2 of Form 1040 (through taxable income, line 43) and Schedule A. Assume that the employer portion of the self-employment tax on Jessie's income is $831. Joe and Jessie have summarized the income and expenses they expect to report this year as follows:

Income:

Joe's salary	$124,100
Jessie's craft sales	18,400
Interest from certificate of deposit	1,650
Interest from Treasury bond funds	716
Interest from municipal bond funds	920

Expenditures:

Federal income tax withheld from Joe's wages	$13,700
State income tax withheld from Joe's wages	6,400
Social Security tax withheld from Joe's wages	7,482
Real estate taxes on residence	6,200
Automobile licenses (based on weight)	310
State sales tax paid	1,150
Home mortgage interest	14,000
Interest on Masterdebt credit card	2,300
Medical expenses (unreimbursed)	1,690
Joe's employee expenses (unreimbursed)	2,400
Cost of Jessie's craft supplies	4,260
Postage for mailing crafts	145
Travel and lodging for craft shows	2,230
Self-employment tax on Jessie's craft income	1,662
College tuition paid for Lizzie	5,780
Interest on loans to pay Lizzie's tuition	3,200
Lizzie's room and board at college	12,620
Cash contributions to the Red Cross	525

ROGER | *CPA Review*

Sample CPA Exam questions from Roger CPA Review are available in Connect as support for the topics in this text. These Multiple Choice Questions and Task-Based Simulations include expert-written explanations and solutions and provide a starting point for students to become familiar with the content and functionality of the actual CPA Exam.

chapter

7 Investments

Learning Objectives

Upon completing this chapter, you should be able to:

LO 7-1 Explain how interest income and dividend income are taxed.

LO 7-2 Compute the tax consequences associated with the disposition of capital assets, including the netting process for calculating gains and losses.

LO 7-3 Calculate the deduction for investment interest expense.

LO 7-4 Apply tax-basis, at-risk, and passive activity loss limits to losses from passive investments.

©Image Source

Courtney has settled into her new Kansas City location and is now focusing on her investment portfolio. When her father, "Gramps," passed away last December, he left Courtney an inheritance of $100,000 with the stipulation that she "invest it to financially benefit her family." After considerable thought, Courtney decided to invest the inheritance to accomplish two financial goals. First, she wants to save for her son Deron's college education. She figures that if she immediately invests $50,000 of the inheritance for his college education, she should have a significant sum accumulated when Deron starts college in eight years. Second, she decided that she will immediately invest the remaining $50,000 for five years and use the accumulation to make a significant down payment on a vacation home in Park City, Utah, a town she fell in love with during a college ski trip. Courtney is concerned about how different investment choices will be taxed and how this might affect her ability to meet her financial goals.

Courtney's uncle Jeb, who is single, has sold several investments during the year and hopes to use the proceeds to fulfill his lifelong dream of owning a sailboat. He is uncertain about how much tax he will owe after selling the assets. ■

Storyline Summary

Taxpayers:	Courtney Wilson, age 40 Courtney's uncle, Jeb Landers, age 65
Family description:	Courtney is divorced with a son, Deron, age 10, and a daughter, Ellen, age 20. Jeb is single.
Location:	Kansas City, Missouri
Employment status:	Courtney works as an architect for EWD. Her salary is $118,000. Jeb is recently retired.
Current situation:	Courtney is deciding how to invest her inheritance. Jeb is concerned about the tax effects of selling investment assets.

INVESTMENTS OVERVIEW

Investors are attracted to certain investments according to their investment philosophy and their appetite for risk, among other things. Some prefer investments that provide a consistent income stream. Others prefer investments that have significant appreciation potential but provide no current cash flows. These investment attributes affect the before-tax rates of return on investments. However, taxes are levied on **investment income,** and thus, it would be unwise to make an investment without considering the tax cost.

For example, it is possible that two investments with identical before-tax rates of return will generate different after-tax rates of return because the investments are taxed differently. Indeed, it is possible that an investment with a lower before-tax rate of return compared to an alternative investment will have a higher after-tax rate of return because income from the investment is taxed at a later date or at a lower rate than the alternative investment.

Two key tax characteristics that affect after-tax rates of return from investments are (1) the timing of tax payments or tax benefits and (2) the rate at which investment income or gains are taxed or deductible expenses or losses generate tax savings. Not surprisingly, these variables are directly related to the timing and conversion tax planning strategies introduced in the Tax Planning Strategies and Related Limitations chapter.

Income from **portfolio investments,** which are investments producing **dividends,** interest, royalties, annuities, or capital gains, may be taxed at ordinary or preferential rates, or they may be exempt from taxation. Further, depending on the type of investment, tax on income from a portfolio investment may be imposed annually or may be deferred until the taxpayer sells the investment. Losses from portfolio investments are deferred until the investment is sold and are typically subject to limitations.

In contrast to portfolio investments, **passive investments** generate **operating income** and **operating losses.** Operating income is always taxed annually at ordinary rates, while operating losses are either deducted annually at ordinary rates or deferred and deducted later at ordinary rates, depending on the investor's circumstances. Losses from passive investments are also subject to limitations.

This chapter explores several common portfolio and passive investments, discusses important tax and nontax considerations relevant for those investments, and compares investment rates of return on an after-tax basis.

LO 7-1   PORTFOLIO INCOME: INTEREST AND DIVIDENDS

Taxpayers who desire current cash flows from their investments may choose investments that generate interest or regular dividends. Investments generating interest income include **certificates of deposit (CDs),** savings accounts, corporate **bonds,** and governmental bonds. Investments generating dividend income include direct equity investments in corporate stocks and investments in **mutual funds** that invest in corporate stock.[1] Although all these investments generate current cash flows, they differ significantly in terms of their economic and tax consequences.

By lending money to banks, governmental entities, or corporations, investors essentially become debt holders. As such, they are legally entitled to receive periodic interest payments *and* to recover the amount of principal loaned. In the case of bonds, the principal is the **maturity value** or **face value** of the bonds. Interest payments and the time and manner of repayment of the loan principal are defined either contractually for CDs and savings accounts, or by bond covenants for loans made either to governments or corporations.

In contrast, investors who purchase stocks become shareholders (also called equity holders) of a corporation. As shareholders, they are entitled to receive dividends if the

---

[1]Mutual funds are portfolios of investment assets managed by professional money managers. Generally, the income earned by mutual funds flows through to the owners of mutual fund shares who pay the resulting taxes due. The nature of the assets held by the mutual fund determines the character of the income.

company declares dividends and to *indirectly* share in either the future appreciation or depreciation in the value of a corporation through stock ownership. Unlike debt holders, shareholders are not legally entitled to receive dividend payments or to recover their initial investment. Thus, from an investor's perspective, debt tends to be less risky than equity.

For tax purposes, individual investors typically are taxed on both interest and dividend income when they receive it. However, interest income is taxed at ordinary rates, while dividend income is generally taxed at lower capital gains rates.

Interest

In general, taxpayers recognize interest income from investments when they receive the interest payments.[2] Taxpayers investing in savings accounts, money market accounts, CDs, and most bonds receive interest payments based on a stated annual rate of return at yearly or more frequent intervals.

Special rules apply for determining the timing and amount of interest from bonds when there is a **bond discount**—that is, when bonds are issued at an amount below the maturity value—or a **bond premium**—that is, when bonds are issued at an amount above the maturity value. Below we discuss these rules as they apply to corporate, U.S. Treasury bonds, and **U.S. savings bonds.**

Corporate and U.S. Treasury Bonds

Both corporations and the U.S. Treasury raise money from debt markets by issuing bonds.[3] Corporate bonds, **Treasury bonds,** and **Treasury notes** are issued at maturity value, at a discount, or at a premium, depending on prevailing interest rates.[4] Treasury bonds and Treasury notes pay a stated rate of interest semiannually.[5] However, corporate bonds may pay interest at a stated "coupon" rate, or they may not provide any periodic interest payments. Corporate bonds that do not pay periodic interest are called **zero-coupon bonds.** Overall, the consequences of holding corporate or Treasury bonds are very similar. The two primary differences are that (1) interest from Treasury bonds is exempt from *state* taxation while interest from corporate bonds is not, and (2) Treasury bonds always pay interest periodically while corporate bonds may or may not. The tax rules for determining the timing and amount of interest income from corporate and U.S. Treasury bonds are as follows:

- Taxpayers include the actual interest payments they receive in gross income.
- If the bond was issued at a discount, special **original issue discount (OID)** rules apply. Taxpayers are required to amortize the discount and include the amount of the current year **amortization** in gross income in addition to any interest payments the taxpayer actually receives.[6] In the case of corporate zero-coupon bonds, this means taxpayers must report and pay taxes on income related to the bonds even though they did not receive *any* payments from the bonds. Bond issuers or brokers are responsible for calculating the yearly amortization of the original issue discount and providing this information to investors using Form 1099-OID.

---

[2]Interest income is reported on Part I of Schedule B filed with taxpayers' Form 1040.

[3]Investors in corporate bonds assume more risk than investors in Treasury securities because they are relying on the creditworthiness of the corporation issuing the bonds. To compensate bondholders for this additional risk, corporate bonds usually yield higher before-tax rates of return than Treasury securities.

[4]The bonds are issued at a discount (premium) if the market interest rate is higher (lower) than the stated rate on the bonds.

[5]Treasury notes and bonds differ in terms of their maturities. Treasury notes are issued with 2-, 5-, and 10-year maturities. In contrast, Treasury bonds are issued with maturities greater than 10 years. From this point forward, we use the term Treasury bonds to refer to both Treasury notes and Treasury bonds.

[6]§1272. Original issue discount is amortized semiannually under the constant yield method, which is consistent with the approach used to amortize bond discount under GAAP.

- If the bond was issued at a premium, taxpayers may *elect* to amortize the premium.[7] Taxpayers or their advisers are responsible for determining the yearly amortization of bond premium if the election to amortize the premium has been made. The amount of the current year amortization offsets a portion of the actual interest payments that taxpayers must include in gross income. The original tax basis of the bond includes the premium and is reduced by any amortization of bond premium over the life of the bond.

- If the bond is purchased in the secondary bond market at a discount, the taxpayer treats all or some of the **market discount** as interest income *when she sells the bond or the bond matures.*[8] If the bond is sold prior to **maturity,** a ratable amount of the market discount (based on the number of days the bond is held over the number of days until maturity when the bond is purchased), called the **accrued market discount,** is treated as interest income on the date of sale.[9] If the bond is held to maturity, the entire bond discount is treated as interest income at maturity.

- If the bond is purchased in the secondary bond market at a premium, the premium is treated exactly like original issue bond premiums. As a result, the taxpayer may elect to amortize the **market premium** to reduce the annual interest income received from the bond. Otherwise, the premium remains as part of the tax basis of the bond and affects the capital gain or loss the taxpayer recognizes when the taxpayer sells or redeems the bond.

U.S. Savings Bonds   U.S. savings bonds such as Series EE or Series I bonds are issued at either face value or at a discount. These bonds do not pay periodic interest; rather, interest accumulates over the term of the bonds and is paid when investors redeem them at maturity or earlier.[10] That is, the amount of interest income taxpayers recognize *when they redeem* the bonds is the excess of the bond proceeds over the taxpayer's **basis** in the bonds, meaning its purchase price. Taxpayers may elect to include the increase in the bond redemption value in their income each year, but this is generally not advisable because it accelerates the income from the bond without providing any cash to pay the taxes.[11] Finally, interest from Series EE and Series I bonds may be excluded from gross income to the extent the bond proceeds are used to pay qualifying educational expenses. However, this exclusion benefit is subject to phase-out based on the taxpayer's AGI.

Example 7-1

What if: Assume that Courtney was deciding whether to invest the $50,000 earmarked for the Park City vacation home in (1) Series EE savings bonds that mature in exactly five years, (2) original issue AMD Corporation *zero-coupon* bonds that mature in exactly five years, or (3) U.S. Treasury bonds that pay $46,250 at maturity in five years trading in the secondary bond market with a stated annual interest rate of 10 percent. Further, assume that all bonds yield 8 percent annual before-tax rates of return compounded semiannually. At the end of the first year, (1) the redemption value of the EE savings bonds would be $54,080, or (2) Courtney would receive a Form 1099-OID from AMD reporting

---

[7]§171. Like an original issue discount, a bond premium is amortized semiannually under the constant yield method—the same method used to amortize bond premiums under GAAP. Unlike premiums on taxable bonds, premiums on tax-exempt bonds must always be amortized.

[8]§1276(a). Under §1278(b)(1), taxpayers may elect to include the amortization of market discount in their income annually. However, this election accelerates the recognition of income from the market discount and is therefore usually not advisable.

[9]§1276(b).

[10]Series EE savings bonds are issued at a discount and Series I savings bonds are issued at maturity value. EE bonds provide a constant rate of return while Series I bonds provide a return that is indexed for inflation and thus increases over time.

[11]§454(a). Investors that make this election report the annual increase in the redemption value of their savings bonds using savings bond redemption tables published by the Treasury Department.

$4,080 of OID amortization for the year, or (3) she would receive two semiannual interest payments of $2,312.50 from the Treasury bonds. Under the general rules, how much interest income from each bond would Courtney report at the end of the first year?

Answer: $0 from the Series EE savings bonds, $4,080 from the AMD bonds, and $4,625 (two semiannual payments of $2,312.50) from the Treasury bonds. Note, however, that Courtney could *elect* to include the $4,080 increase in redemption value of the Series EE bonds in interest income even though she did not receive any interest payments on the bonds (probably not optimal). She also could *elect* to amortize $637.50 of the $3,750 premium ($50,000 purchase price less the $46,250 maturity value) on the Treasury bonds to offset the $4,625 in actual interest payments she received on the bonds (probably a good idea). The calculations required to amortize the premium on the Treasury bonds for the first year are reflected in the following table:

Semiannual Period	(A) Adjusted Basis of Bonds at Beginning of Semiannual Period	(B) Interest Received and Reported ($46,250 × 10% × .5)	(C) Interest Earned (A) × 8% × .5	Premium Amortization (B) − (C)
1	$50,000.00	$2,312.50	$2,000.00	$312.50
2	49,687.50	2,312.50	1,987.50	325.00
Yearly Total		4,625.00	3,987.50	637.50

Intuitively, would Courtney be better or worse off purchasing the Series EE savings bonds rather than a corporate bond to save for the Park City home?

Answer: Courtney would be better off purchasing the Series EE savings bonds in two respects. First, she wouldn't have to pay state income taxes on the interest earned from the savings bonds. Second, she would be able to defer paying taxes on the accumulated interest from the savings bonds until the savings bonds are cashed in at maturity.

Intuitively, would Courtney be better or worse off purchasing the AMD zero-coupon bonds rather than a corporate bond to save for the Park City home?

Answer: She would be worse off because she would have to pay taxes currently from the OID amortization on the AMD bonds without receiving any cash flow from the bonds to pay the taxes due.

Example 7-2

What If: Assume that on January 1, Courtney used the $50,000 earmarked for the Park City vacation home to purchase AMD zero-coupon bonds in the *secondary bond market* almost immediately after the bonds were originally issued. If they mature in exactly five years and have a maturity value of $74,000, how much interest income will Courtney report at the end of the first year and in the year the bonds mature?

Answer: $0 in the first year and $24,000 in the year the bonds mature. Because the AMD zero-coupon bonds were not purchased at original issue, the entire $24,000 market discount on the bonds will be reported as interest income when the bonds mature. Thus, Courtney will not report any income related to the AMD bonds until the year the bonds mature.

What if: Assume the same facts as above, except Courtney purchased U.S. Series EE bonds instead of AMD zero-coupon bonds to fund the Park City vacation home in five years. How much interest income will she report at the end of the first year and in the year the bonds mature?

Answer: $0 in the first year and $24,000 in the year the EE savings bonds mature. This is exactly the same outcome as the investment in the AMD zero-coupon bonds (ignoring possible state income tax effects).

As our discussion suggests, for certain types of investments such as savings accounts, money market accounts, and CDs, computing the annual taxable interest income is relatively straightforward. However, for investments in bonds, the process is much more involved. Exhibit 7-1 summarizes the general rule and exceptions for the timing of interest payments and related tax payments.

EXHIBIT 7-1 Timing of Interest Payments and Taxes

General Rule	Exception	Exception
Interest Received Annually and Taxed Annually	**Interest Received at Sale or Maturity and Taxed at Sale or Maturity**	**Interest Received at Sale or Maturity but Taxed Annually**
• Savings accounts • CDs • Money market accounts • Bond interest payments actually received in the year	• Accrued market discount on bonds • Interest earned on U.S. savings bonds	• Original issue discount (OID) on corporate and Treasury bonds

Dividends

Historically, dividends received by investors have been taxed at the same rate as interest income; however, in 2003 Congress changed the law for dividends to mitigate the so-called "double tax" on dividend income.[12] Consistent with the general rule for taxing interest income, dividend payments (including reinvested dividends) are taxed annually.[13] However, as we discuss in the Individual Income Tax Computation and Tax Credits chapter, **qualified dividends** are taxed at a preferential rate: 0, 15, or 20 percent, depending on the taxpayer's filing status and amount of taxable income.[14] Qualified dividends are those paid by domestic or certain qualified foreign corporations provided investors hold the dividend-paying stock for *more than* 60 days during the 121-day period that begins 60 days before the **ex-dividend date,** the first day on which purchasers of the stock would not be entitled to receive a declared dividend on the stock.[15] Exhibit 7-2 illustrates the 121-day period surrounding the ex-dividend date.

Nonqualified dividends are not eligible for the reduced rate and are therefore taxed at ordinary rates. Corporations report the amounts of the dividends and indicate whether the dividends are potentially eligible for the preferential rate when they send Form 1099-DIV to shareholders after year-end. However, shareholders ultimately must determine whether they qualify for the preferential rate by confirming they held the stock for the required number of days around the ex-dividend date.

EXHIBIT 7-2 Holding Period for Qualified Dividends

121-day period

Ex-dividend day

60 days   60 days

[12]Because corporations pay income taxes, dividends are taxed once at the corporate level, when the income used to pay dividends is earned by the corporation, and a second time when dividends are received by investors.

[13]Dividends are reported on Part II of Schedule B filed with taxpayers' Form 1040.

[14]The tax rate for qualified dividends follows the capital gains tax rates as discussed later in this chapter.

[15]Qualified foreign corporations are those incorporated in a U.S. possession (e.g., Puerto Rico, U.S. Virgin Islands), those eligible for the benefits of a comprehensive income tax treaty with the United States, or those whose shares are readily traded on an established U.S. securities market.

Example 7-3

What if: Assume Courtney (head of household filing status) decides to purchase dividend-paying stocks to achieve her financial objectives. She invests $50,000 in Xerox stock, which she intends to hold for five years and then sell to fund the Park City home down payment. She invests another $50,000 in Coca-Cola stock, which she intends to hold for eight years and then sell to fund her son's education. How much dividend income will Courtney report at the end of the first year if the dividend payments provide an 8 percent rate of return on her investments?[16]

Answer: At the end of the first year, Courtney will report $4,000 ($50,000 × .08) of dividend income from her investment in the Xerox stock and $4,000 ($50,000 × .08) of dividend income from her investment in the Coca-Cola stock, for a total of $8,000 of dividend income.

What if: Assume Courtney's ordinary marginal tax rate is 32 percent. How much tax will Courtney owe on her dividend income if the dividends are nonqualified?

Answer: Courtney will owe $2,560 ($8,000 × 32%) of tax if the dividends are nonqualified because the income will be taxed at her ordinary income tax rate.

What if: What amount of tax will Courtney owe if the dividends are qualified? Assume Courtney's tax rate on qualified dividends is 15 percent.

Answer: Courtney will owe $1,200 ($8,000 × 15%) of tax if the dividends are qualified because qualified dividends are taxed at preferential rates.

Because dividend income is generally taxed at lower rates than interest income, it appears that taxpayers seeking current cash flows from their investments should favor dividend-paying investments over interest-paying investments. This raises the question why anyone would ever prefer investments paying interest over those paying dividends. Remember, though, that savvy investors also should consider nontax factors, such as before-tax rates of return, risk, and liquidity needs when choosing among investments. These fundamental differences explain why investors may continue to seek out interest income in spite of the associated tax disadvantages.

PORTFOLIO INCOME: CAPITAL GAINS AND LOSSES   LO 7-2

Investors who don't need annual cash flows from their investments may prefer to invest in assets with the expectation that the investments will appreciate in value over time, providing cash at some point in the future when they sell the assets. Investors also may be willing to assume greater risk in exchange for greater returns than those provided by interest or dividend-paying investments. For example, they might purchase raw land, fine art, rare coins, precious gems or metals, growth stocks (stock in corporations that reinvest their earnings to grow the company as opposed to distributing them to shareholders in the form of dividends), mutual fund shares, or even vintage automobiles. Purchasing any such asset is not without risk. Indeed, investments held solely for appreciation potential *may* actually decline in value.

When taxpayers buy and hold assets with appreciation potential, they typically are investing in **capital assets.** As we discuss in the Individual Income Tax Overview, Dependents, and Filing Status chapter, capital assets are typically investment-type assets and personal-use assets.[17] Thus, artwork, corporate stock, bonds, your personal residence, and even your iPhone are capital assets.

---

[16]Annual rates of return from dividend-paying stocks are typically lower than the rates of return from taxable bonds. However, it is assumed here that the rates of return are equal for the sake of comparability.

[17]§1221 defines capital assets in the negative. This code section excludes the following from the definition of a capital asset: inventory, depreciable property or real property used in a trade or business, certain self-created intangibles, accounts or notes receivable, U.S. government publications, certain commodities, derivative financial instruments, certain hedging transactions, and supplies. Self-created patents, inventions, models or designs (whether or not patented), and secret formulas or processes are among the intangibles excluded from the definition of a capital asset.

While it may be enjoyable to view collectible fine art in your home or watch a stock portfolio grow in value on quarterly brokerage statements, from a tax perspective the real advantages of investing in capital assets are that (1) gains are deferred for tax purposes until the taxpayer sells or otherwise disposes of the assets,[18] and (2) gains generally are taxed at preferential rates relative to ordinary income.[19] Why the favorable treatment? One reason is that taxpayers may not have the wherewithal (cash) to pay the tax on their gains until they sell the investment. Another is that the preferential tax rate provides an incentive for taxpayers to invest in assets that may stimulate the economy. Investors can capture these tax benefits when they sell capital assets at a gain. However, when they sell capital assets at a loss, their ability to deduct the loss may be limited.

When a taxpayer sells a capital asset for more than its **tax basis,** he or she recognizes a capital gain; if a taxpayer sells a capital asset for less than its tax basis, he or she recognizes a capital loss (to the extent the loss is deductible).[20] The amount realized or the selling price of a capital asset includes the cash and fair market value of other property received, less broker's fees and other selling costs. The basis of any asset, including a capital asset, is generally the taxpayer's cost of acquiring the asset, including the initial purchase price and other costs incurred to purchase or improve the asset.[21] Thus, the tax basis of corporate stock purchased from a stockbroker includes the cost of the stock and any additional brokerage fees paid by the taxpayer to acquire the stock. Also, the tax basis in a personal residence includes the initial purchase price plus the cost of subsequent improvements to the home.

TAXES IN THE REAL WORLD So You Want to Invest in Bitcoin

Since 2014, bitcoin usage has increased dramatically, averaging over 250,000 transactions per day over the last year (https://blockchain.info/charts/n-transactions?timespan=1year&daysAverageString=7). But, what does it mean to invest in bitcoin and what effect does it have on a taxpayer's income? Although not the only way, the most common way to invest in bitcoin is to use a buy and hold strategy (called "hodling"). This strategy is profitable when the investor buys low and sells high. The appreciation represents the profit from the investment. Bitcoin is a form of virtual currency, which is a "digital representation of value that functions as a medium of exchange, a unit of account, and/or a store of value" (Notice 2014-21). Interestingly, the IRS says virtual currency is "property" and not currency. Therefore, taxpayers follow the tax principles that apply to property transactions when determining the income or loss from bitcoin investments rather than treating such income or loss as currency subject to potential foreign currency gains and losses. For taxpayers holding bitcoin as an investment, any gains or losses are treated as capital.

Keeping in mind that bitcoin is property and not currency for tax purposes is important especially when bitcoin is spent. Bitcoin users have a taxable event each time they purchase goods or services with bitcoin. Each transaction requires the investor to calculate the gain or loss on the disposition of the bitcoin investment, report these gains and losses on Form 8949 and Schedule D (for capital asset transactions), and apply the appropriate tax rate depending on the holding period and the investor's tax bracket. If the transaction results in a loss from the bitcoin, the loss will be subject to the capital loss limitations discussed later in the chapter. And remember . . . taxes are paid in dollars, not bitcoin!

Source: IRS Notice 2014-21. https://www.irs.gov/pub/irs-drop/n-14-21.pdf

---

[18]Similarly, interest related to the market discount on bonds and the original issue discount on U.S. EE savings bonds accumulates free of tax until the bonds mature or are sold. However, ordinary rather than capital gains rates apply when the tax must finally be paid.

[19]Mutual funds that generate current income by regularly selling capital assets or by holding income-producing securities are an exception to this general rule. However, tax-efficient mutual funds that only buy and hold growth stocks are treated more like other capital assets for tax purposes (capital gains are deferred until mutual fund shares are sold).

[20]As discussed below, losses on personal assets are not deductible for tax purposes.

[21]Brokers are required to report to the IRS the cost basis of securities their customers sell if the securities were purchased on or after January 1, 2013.

Because taxpayers cannot accurately compute the gain or loss on the sale of a capital asset without knowing its basis, it is important for them to maintain accurate records to track their basis in capital assets. This process is relatively straightforward for unique assets such as a personal residence or individual jewels in a taxpayer's jewelry collection. However, capital assets such as shares of stock are much more homogeneous and difficult to track.

For example, a taxpayer may purchase blocks of stock in a given corporation at different times over a period of several years, paying a different price per share for each block of stock acquired. When the taxpayer sells shares of this stock in subsequent years, what basis does she use to compute gain or loss? By default, taxpayers are required to use the **first-in, first-out (FIFO) method** of determining the basis of the shares they sell.[22] However, if they (or their broker) track the basis of their stock, taxpayers can sell (or instruct their broker to sell) specific shares using the **specific identification method** to determine the basis of the shares they sell.[23] Taxpayers using the specific identification method can choose to sell their high-basis stock first, minimizing their gains or increasing their losses on stock dispositions.

Example 7-4

After Courtney's car broke down, she decided to buy a new one. To fund the down payment, she sold 200 shares of Cisco stock at the current market price of $40 per share for a total amount realized of $8,000. Courtney held the following blocks of Cisco stock at the time of the sale:

Cisco Corporation Stock Ownership					
Holding Period	(1) Cost per Share	(2) Shares	(1) × (2) Basis	Basis of 200 Shares Sold	Explanation
5 years	$25	250	$6,250	$5,000	FIFO basis ($25 × 200)
2 years	$32	250	$8,000	$6,400	Specific ID basis ($32 × 200)

How much capital gain will Courtney recognize if she uses the FIFO method of computing the basis in the Cisco shares sold?

Answer: $3,000. $8,000 amount realized ($40 × 200) minus $5,000 FIFO basis ($25 × 200). As indicated in the table above, under the FIFO (oldest first) method, the shares sold have a holding period of five years.

What if: How much capital gain will Courtney recognize if she uses the specific identification method of computing the basis in the shares sold to minimize the taxable gain on the sale?

Answer: $1,600. $8,000 amount realized ($40 × 200) minus $6,400 ($32 × 200). To minimize her gain on the sale under the specific identification method, Courtney would choose to sell the 200 shares with the highest basis. As indicated in the table above, the shares with the higher basis are those acquired and held two years for $32 per share.

Note in the above example that Courtney receives $8,000 from the stock sale ($40 per share × 200 shares sold) regardless of the method she uses to compute the basis of the shares she sells. The difference between the FIFO and specific identification methods lies in the amount of taxable gain on the *current* sale. Over time, as taxpayers sell all their stock, both methods will ultimately allow them to fully recover their cost in the investments. However, applying the specific identification method will result in lower capital gains taxes currently and thereby minimize the present value of the taxes paid on stock sales.

---

[22]Reg. §1.1012-1(c)(1).

[23]Beginning in 2011, brokerage firms are required to report cost basis and type of capital gain (short-term or long-term) on form 1099-B provided to investors. These requirements have phased in over several years and as of 2017, brokerage firms and other financial institutions are required to provide this information for equity securities (including ETFs and RICs) as well as for debt securities.

Types of Capital Gains and Losses

Taxpayers selling capital assets they have held for a year or less recognize **short-term capital gains or losses.**[24] Taxpayers selling capital assets they have held for more than a year recognize **long-term capital gains or losses.** Short-term capital gains are taxed at ordinary rather than preferential rates. In contrast, long-term capital gains are taxed at preferential rates. However, not all long-term capital gains are created equal. Just like dividends, most long-term capital gains are taxed at either 0 percent, 15 percent, or 20 percent, depending on the taxpayer's filing status and taxable income as shown in Exhibit 7-3. The **maximum zero rate amount** defines the threshold for the zero percent rate to apply to capital gains. When taxable income is between the maximum zero percent and the **maximum 15 percent rate amount** capital gains are taxed at 15 percent. These maximum rate amounts are often referred to as breakpoints. When taxable income is above the 15 percent rate amount, capital gains are taxed at 20 percent. However, certain long-term capital gains are taxed at a maximum rate of 25 percent, also known as **unrecaptured §1250 gain,** while others are taxed at a maximum rate of 28 percent, specifically gain from **collectibles** and gain from **qualified small business stock,** for tax policy reasons.

EXHIBIT 7-3

Preferential Tax Rates	Taxable Income by Filing Status[†]			
	Married Filing Joint	**Married Filing Separate**	**Single**	**Head of Household**
0%*	0 – $77,200	0 – $38,600	0 – $38,600	0 – $51,700
15%**	$77,201 – $479,000	$38,601 – $239,500	$38,601 – $425,800	$51,701 – $452,400
20%	$479,000+	$239,500+	$425,801+	$452,401+

[†]When determining which capital gains tax rate applies, capital gains and qualified dividends that fall within the range of taxable income specified in the table are included in taxable income last.
*The highest income amount in this range for each filing status is referred to as the maximum zero rate amount.
**The highest income amount in this range for each filing status is referred to as the maximum 15 percent amount.

25 Percent Gains   When individuals sell depreciable real property held more than one year at a gain, a portion (or even all) of the gain may be taxed at a maximum rate of 25 percent (the unrecaptured §1250 gain portion), and a portion may be taxed as a 0/15/20 percent gain. In the Property Dispositions chapter, we discuss the details of how to compute the amount of 25 percent gain and the amount of 0/15/20 percent gain when an individual sells depreciable real property; however, we include a brief discussion in this chapter because the amount of 25 percent gain affects the capital gain and loss netting process we discuss in this chapter.

Example 7-5

What if: Assume Jeb Landers (single), Courtney's uncle, recently sold a rental home for $160,000. He originally acquired the home many years ago for $100,000, and he has fully depreciated it for tax purposes. Assume that $100,000 of the gain (the unrecaptured §1250 gain portion) is taxed at a maximum rate of 25 percent. If Jeb's taxable income (before considering this gain) is $210,000, what tax does he owe on the gain if he did not sell any other property during the year?

Answer: $34,000. Because Jeb's tax basis in the home is $0 (he has fully depreciated it), his gain on the sale is $160,000. Jeb first determines the tax on the portion of the gain taxed at a maximum of 25 percent. Jeb owes 25 percent tax on the $100,000, resulting in $25,000 of tax on this portion of the gain ($100,000 × 25%) because his marginal tax rate on $210,000 is 35 percent, which is higher than the maximum tax rate of 25 percent for this type of gain. Jeb's taxable income after including the 25 percent gain is now

---

[24]Nonbusiness bad debt is treated as a short-term capital loss no matter how long the debt was outstanding before it became worthless. Whether a bad debt is considered to be a business or nonbusiness bad debt for individuals depends on the facts and circumstances. In general, if the taxpayer experiencing the loss is in the business of loaning money, the bad debt should be considered to be business bad debt; otherwise, the bad debt will likely be considered nonbusiness bad debt.

$310,000 ($210,000 + $100,000). To determine the capital gains tax rate for the remaining $60,000 gain, Jeb must determine how much of the gain falls within the 15 percent range. Jeb's 15 percent range is $38,600 to $425,800. With a starting point of $310,000, adding the $60,000 gain makes his taxable income $370,000. Because the entire $60,000 gain is within the 15 percent range, Jeb owes $9,000 of tax on this portion ($60,000 × 15%). In total, he owes $34,000 of tax on the gain ($25,000 + $9,000).

What if: Suppose Jeb's taxable income is $475,000 rather than $210,000 before considering the gain on the sale of the rental home. What tax does he owe on the gain?

Answer: $37,000. The $100,000 is taxed at 25 percent for a tax of $25,000. The remaining $60,000 of gain is taxed at 20 percent because Jeb's taxable income including the 25 percent gain ($575,000) places him in the 20 percent rate for long-term capital gains ($425,801+). Consequently, he owes $12,000 of tax on this portion ($60,000 × 20%). In total, Jeb owes $37,000 of tax on the gain ($25,000 + $12,000).

28 Percent Gains   Gains from two types of capital assets are taxable at a maximum 28 percent rate. The first type, collectibles, consists of works of art, rugs or antiques, metals or gems, stamps or coins, alcoholic beverages, or other similar items held for more than one year.[25] The second type is qualified small business stock held for *more than five years*.[26] In general, §1202 defines qualified small business stock as stock received at *original issue* from a C corporation with a gross tax basis in its assets both before and after the issuance of no more than $50,000,000 and with at least 80 percent of the value of its assets used in the active conduct of certain qualified trades or businesses. Under this definition, many investors and employees who hold stock in closely held corporations are likely to hold qualified small business stock. When taxpayers sell qualified small business stock after holding it for more than five years, they may exclude a portion of the gain on the sale from regular taxation. Exhibit 7-4 shows the excluded portion of the gain based on the date the taxpayer acquired the stock.

EXHIBIT 7-4   Exclusion for §1202 Stock Held More Than Five Years

Acquisition Date	Exclusion	Effective Capital Gains Tax Rate
After September 27, 2010	100%	0%
After February 17, 2009, and before September 28, 2010	75	7
After August 10, 1993, and before February 18, 2009	50	14

The capital gain not excluded from income is taxed at 28 percent. For example, using the minimum exclusion percentage of 50 percent, the effective capital gains tax rate is 14 percent.[27]

Example 7-6

What if: Assume that Jeb (single) sold his stock in Gangbusters Inc., a qualified small business stock, for $200,000 on December 12, 2018. He acquired the stock on November 8, 2010, and his basis in the stock is $50,000. How much tax will he owe on the sale if his ordinary marginal rate is 32 percent?

Answer: $0. Because Jeb held the qualified small business stock for more than five years and because he acquired the stock when the exclusion percentage was 100 percent, he will exclude the entire $150,000 gain from income.

(continued on page 7-12)

[25]§408(m).

[26]§1(h)(7).

[27]The maximum exclusion is the greater of $10,000,000 ($5,000,000 for married taxpayers filing separately) or 10 times the adjusted basis of the stock [see §1202(b)(1)]. The Protecting Americans from Tax Hikes Act of 2015 (PATH Act) made permanent the exclusion of 100 percent of the gain on the sale or exchange of qualified small business stock acquired after September 27, 2010, and held for more than five years. However, for AMT purposes, taxpayer must add back 7 percent of the excluded gain as a tax preference. Lastly, the excluded gain is not subject to the net investment income tax of 3.8 percent imposed on capital gains (and other investment income) on high-income taxpayers.

> **What if:** Assume instead that Jeb sold his Gangbusters stock on December 12, 2018, but had acquired it on February 17, 2015. How much tax will he owe on the sale?
>
> **Answer:** $22,500. Because Jeb didn't hold the stock for more than five years, he must recognize all $150,000 of long-term capital gain. This gain is taxed at 15 percent, yielding a total tax due of $22,500.

Exhibit 7-5 presents the maximum tax rates applicable to capital gains.

EXHIBIT 7-5 **Classification of Capital Gains by Maximum Applicable Tax Rates**

Short-Term or Long-Term	Type	Maximum Rate
Short-term	All	37%*
Long-term	Collectibles	28*
Held > 5 years	Qualified small business stock	14%**
Long-term	Unrecaptured §1250 gain from depreciable realty	25*
Long-term	All remaining capital gains (and §1231 gains) not included elsewhere	20†, ‡

*Lower rates will apply when the taxpayer's ordinary rate is less than the rates reflected in this exhibit.
**The maximum rate of 15 percent applies when the lowest exclusion percentage of 50 percent is in effect.
†This gain is taxed at 0 percent to the extent the taxpayer's income is below the maximum zero rate amount, taxed at 20 percent to the extent the taxpayer's income is above the maximum 15 percent rate amount, and taxed at 15 percent otherwise. When determining which capital gains tax rate applies, capital gains and qualified dividends that fall within the range of taxable income specified in the table are included in taxable income last. For the maximum zero and 15 percent rate amounts see Exhibit 7-3.
‡High-income taxpayers may also be subject to an additional 3.8 percent net investment income tax on capital gains.

Netting Process for Gains and Losses To this point, our discussion of applicable tax rates for capital gains hasn't considered situations in which taxpayers recognize both capital gains and capital losses in the same year. To determine the appropriate tax treatment for the capital gains and losses recognized during the year, the taxpayer must complete a netting process. This netting process can be complex when taxpayers recognize capital losses and long-term capital gains subject to different maximum tax rates. In essence, the netting process separates capital gains and losses into short-term and three different long-term categories (based on the maximum rate applicable to the long-term gains). Although the process is complex, the underlying intuition is to have taxpayers net all long-term capital gains and losses together allowing long-term losses to offset the highest rate long-term gains first. Then, taxpayers use **net long-term capital losses** to offset net short-term gains or **net short-term capital losses** to offset net long-term gains.

After completing the netting process, taxpayers must calculate the tax consequences of the resulting outcomes. Net short-term capital gains are taxed at the same rate as ordinary income. **Net long-term capital gains** are taxed at a maximum of 28 percent if from the collectible and §1202 category, a maximum of 25 percent if from the unrecaptured §1250 gain category, or 0/15/20 percent for all other long-term capital gains. In the 0/15/20 percent category, net long-term gains are taxed at 20 percent to the extent the taxpayer's taxable income exceeds the maximum 15 percent rate amount based on filing status; at 0 percent to the extent taxable income is below the maximum zero rate amount based on filing status; and at 15 percent otherwise.[28] We discuss the taxation of capital gains in more detail later in the chapter.

Taxpayers can deduct up to $3,000 ($1,500 if married filing separately) of net capital losses against ordinary income. Net capital losses in excess of $3,000 ($1,500 if married filing separately) retain their short- or long-term character and are carried forward and treated as though they were incurred in the subsequent year. Short-term losses are applied first to reduce ordinary income when the taxpayer recognizes both short- and long-term net capital losses. Capital loss carryovers for individuals never expire.

[28]Note that the maximum zero rate amount does not coincide directly with the end of a tax bracket amount for any filing status. Similarly, the maximum 15 percent rate amount does not match up with the end of a tax bracket. Both thresholds are either $100 or $200 below the tax brackets depending on filing status.

The following is a step-by-step guide to the capital gains and losses netting process.

Step 1: Net all short-term capital gains and short-term capital losses, including any short-term capital loss carried forward from the prior year. A net positive amount is a **net short-term capital gain.** A net negative amount is a **net short-term capital loss.** If there are no long-term capital gains or losses, the netting process is complete. Otherwise, continue to Step 2.

Step 2: Separate long-term capital gains and losses into three rate groups (28 percent, 25 percent, and 0/15/20 percent). Place any net long-term capital loss carried over from the prior year into the 28 percent rate group. Sum the gains and losses within each group. The outcome will be a net 28 percent gain or loss, a 25 percent gain (there are no 25 percent losses), and/or a net 0/15/20 percent gain or loss. Proceed to Step 3.

Step 3: (a) If neither the 0/15/20 percent nor the 28 percent rate groups from Step 2 nets to a gain, transfer the net loss (if any) in the 0/15/20 percent rate group to the 28 percent rate group, combine it with the loss in that group (if any), and proceed to Step 4.

(b) If none of the long-term rate groups from Step 2 nets to a loss, proceed to Step 6.

(c) Combining net gains and losses in long-term rate groups:

1. If Step 2 results in net losses in both the 28 percent and 0/15/20 percent rate groups, combine the net losses and then apply them to offset gains in the 25 percent rate group. If the losses exceed the gain, the result is a net long-term capital loss. Proceed to Step 4. If the gain exceeds the losses, the result is a net long-term capital gain. Proceed to Step 6.

2. If the Step 2 outcomes include a net loss in the 28 percent rate group and net gains in the other rate groups, apply the net loss from the 28 percent rate group to the gain in the 25 percent rate group until the 25 percent rate group gain is reduced to zero. Then offset any remaining 28 percent rate group loss against the net gain in the 0/15/20 percent rate group. If the net loss from the 28 percent rate group exceeds the net gains from the other rate groups, the net loss is a net long-term capital loss. Proceed to Step 4. If gain remains in the 25 percent and/or 0/15/20 percent rate groups after applying the loss, the result is a net long-term capital gain. Proceed to Step 6.

3. If the amounts from Step 2 include a net loss in the 0/15/20 percent rate group and net gains in the 28 percent and/or the 25 percent rate groups, apply the net loss from the 0/15/20 percent rate group to the net gain in the 28 percent rate group until the net gain is reduced to zero. Then offset any remaining loss against the gain in the 25 percent rate group. If the net loss from the 0/15/20 percent rate group exceeds the net gains from the other rate groups, the net loss is a net long-term capital loss. Proceed to Step 4. If gain remains in the 28 percent and/or 25 percent rate groups after applying the loss, the result is a net long-term capital gain. Proceed to Step 6.

Step 4: If there is no net short-term capital gain or loss from Step 1, the netting process is complete; apply the net capital loss deduction limitation ($3,000 or $1,500 if married filing separately) and ignore the remaining steps. If the result from Step 1 is a net short-term capital loss *and* the result from Step 3 is a net long-term capital loss, the netting process is complete: Apply the net capital loss deduction limitation and ignore the remaining steps. Otherwise, continue on to Step 5.

Step 5: If Step 1 produces a net short-term capital gain *and* Step 3 produces a net long-term capital loss, combine the net short-term capital gain and the net long-term capital loss.

(a) If the outcome is a net loss, the netting process is complete. Apply the net capital loss deduction limitation described previously.

(b) If the outcome is a net gain, the net gain is treated the same as a net short-term capital gain and is taxed at ordinary rates. The netting process is complete.

Step 6: If there is no net short-term capital gain or loss from Step 1, the netting process is complete. The tax on the net long-term capital gain (also called a net capital gain) remaining in each long-term group is determined as described in the next section. If the Step 1 outcome is a net short-term capital gain, skip to Step 7. If the Step 1 outcome is a net short-term capital loss *and* Step 3 results in a net gain in any (or all) of the long-term rate groups, first use the short-term capital loss to offset the gain in the 28 percent rate group (if any), then the gain in the 25 percent rate group (if any), and finally the gain in 0/15/20 percent rate group (if any).

(a) If the net short-term capital loss exceeds all gains in the long-term rate groups, the netting process is complete. Apply the net capital loss deduction limitation described previously.

(b) If the net short-term capital loss does not offset all of the gain in any (or all) of the long-term rate groups, the netting process is complete. The result is a **net capital gain** (net long-term capital gains in excess of net short-term capital losses). The tax on the gain remaining in each long-term group is determined as described in the next section.

Step 7: If Step 1 produces a net short-term capital gain *and* Step 3 produces a net long-term capital gain(s), the netting process is complete. The tax on the remaining gains is determined as described in the next section.

Example 7-7

Jeb Landers has recently retired and now wants to pursue his lifelong dream of owning a sailboat. To come up with the necessary cash, he sells the following investments:

Stock	Market Value	Basis	Capital Gain/Loss	Scenario 1 Type	Scenario 2 Type
A	$40,000	$ 5,000	$ 35,000	Long	Short
B	20,000	30,000	(10,000)	Long	Short
C	20,000	12,000	8,000	Short	Long
D	17,000	28,000	(11,000)	Short	Long

Based on the information in Scenario 1, what is the amount and nature of Jeb's capital gains and losses?

Answer: $22,000 net capital gain (treated as long-term capital gain), computed as follows:

Step 1: Net short-term gains and short-term losses. The $8,000 short-term gain on stock C is netted against the $11,000 short-term loss on stock D, yielding a net short-term capital loss of $3,000.

Step 2: Separate long-term gains and losses into rate groups and sum within the groups. Both long-term transactions are 0/15/20 percent types. The $35,000 long-term gain on stock A is netted against the $10,000 long-term loss on stock B, producing a net long-term capital gain of $25,000.

Step 3: 3(a) does not apply. 3(b) applies and requires skipping to Step 6.

Step 4: Not required.

Step 5: Not required.

Step 6: Combine the net long-term capital gain of $25,000 with the net short-term capital loss of $3,000. This step results in a net capital gain of $22,000. The netting process is complete.

What if: Consider the original facts, except that Scenario 2 dictates the long- and short-term capital gains. What is the amount and character of Jeb's net gain (or loss) on the sale of the shares in this situation?

Answer: $22,000 net short-term capital gain, computed as follows:

Step 1: The gain from stock A would first be netted with the loss from stock B to produce a $25,000 net short-term capital gain [$35,000 + ($10,000)].

Step 2: The loss from stock D and the gain from stock C are both 0/15/20 percent types and are combined to provide a net long-term capital loss of $3,000 [($11,000) + $8,000].

Step 3: 3(a) applies because the loss from Step 2 is the only long-term amount and we proceed to Step 4.

Step 4: Continue to Step 5.

Step 5: 5(b) applies. The results from Step 1 and Step 2 are netted to reach a $22,000 net short-term capital gain [$25,000 + ($3,000)].

Example 7-7 included long-term capital gains and losses only in the 0/15/20 percent group. Example 7-8 shows the netting process when taxpayers also sell long-term capital assets and recognize gains subject to the 25 percent and/or 28 percent capital gains rates.

Example 7-8

What if: Assume that in addition to selling stocks, Jeb sold gold coins and a rental home as follows:

Capital Asset	Market Value	Tax Basis	Capital Gain/Loss	Scenario 1 Type
A stock	$ 40,000	$ 5,000	$ 35,000	Long 0/15/20%
B stock	20,000	30,000	(10,000)	Long 0/15/20%
C stock	20,000	12,000	8,000	Short
D stock	17,000	28,000	(11,000)	Short
Gold coins	4,000	3,000	1,000	Long 28%
Rental home	200,000	80,000	120,000	Long 25% and 0/15/20%*
Overall gain			$143,000	

*$50,000 of the gain is 25 percent gain and the remaining $70,000 is 0/15/20 percent gain.

Assuming Jeb did not sell any other capital assets during the year, he recognizes an overall capital gain of $143,000. What is (are) the maximum tax rate(s) applicable to this gain?

Answer: $95,000 of gain is subject to a 0/15/20 percent maximum rate and $48,000 of gain is subject to a 25 percent maximum rate, computed as follows:

Step 1: $3,000 net short-term capital loss [$8,000 + ($11,000)].

Step 2: Stock A and Stock B are placed in the 0/15/20 percent group, the gold coins are placed in the 28 percent group, $50,000 of the gain from the sale of the rental home is placed in the 25 percent group, and the remaining $70,000 gain from the rental home is placed in the 0/15/20 percent group. The sum of the gains and losses in each group results in a 28 percent net gain of $1,000, a 25 percent gain of $50,000, and a net $95,000 gain in the 0/15/20 percent group.

Step 3: 3(a) does not apply. 3(b) applies because all of the long-term rate groups have a net gain from Step 2. We proceed to Step 6.

Step 4: Not required.

Step 5: Not required.

Step 6: Move the $3,000 loss from Step 1 into the 28 percent group to offset the $1,000 gain. Next, move the remaining $2,000 loss [$1,000 gain on gold + ($3,000) short-term loss from Step 1] into the 25 percent group to offset against the $50,000 gain. The netting process is complete at this point because the net short-term capital loss does not offset all of the gains in the long-term rate groups (Step 6[b]) and only gains remain in the long-term rate groups.

Step 7: Not required.

(continued on page 7-16)

THE KEY FACTS

25 Percent and 28 Percent Rate Capital Gains

- Certain gains from the sale of depreciable real property held long-term are taxed at a maximum rate of 25 percent (unrecaptured §1250 gain).
- Gains from collectibles and from qualified small business stock not held for five years are taxed at a maximum rate of 28 percent.
- When taxpayers have 25 percent or 28 percent rate capital gains, the netting process requires that losses be applied to higher rate groups before lower rate groups.
- When taxable income without long-term capital gains exceeds the maximum 15-percent rate amount, 25 and 28 percent capital gains are taxed at their maximum rate. Otherwise applicable capital gains rates must be adjusted to reflect their inclusion in lower ordinary income rate brackets.

Jeb's netting process is reflected in the following table:

Description	Short-Term	Long-Term 28%	Long-Term 25%	Long-Term 0/15/20%
Stock C	$8,000			
Stock D	(11,000)			
Step 1:	(3,000)			
Coins		$1,000		
Unrecaptured §1250 Gain			$50,000	
Remaining Gain from Rental Property				$70,000
Stock A				35,000
Stock B				(10,000)
Step 2:		$1,000	$50,000	$95,000
Step 6:	(3,000) ⟶	(3,000)		
		(2,000) ⟶	(2,000)	
			$48,000	
Summary			$48,000	$95,000
Maximum Rate			25%	0/15/20%

Reporting capital gains and losses   When taxpayers sell capital assets, they report the details of their sales on Form 8949 (dates of sale and purchase are additional items provided on Form 8949). After listing their sales on Form 8949, taxpayers then use Schedule D to summarize the sales and apply the basic capital gains netting process. Exhibits 7-6 and 7-7 illustrate how Jeb would report his stock sales in Example 7-7, Scenario 1.

Calculating Tax Liability on Net Capital Gains   So, we've learned how to determine the *maximum* tax rates applicable to different types of capital gains. How do we go about actually calculating the effect these gains have on the taxpayer's tax liability? Follow these basic guidelines:

- If the taxpayer's ordinary income (total taxable income excluding long-term capital gains and qualified dividends) is above the maximum 15 percent rate amount, the capital gains for each of the 0/15/20 percent, 25 percent, and 28 percent groups are taxed at their maximum rates.
- If the taxpayer's taxable income (including capital gains and qualified dividends) is below the maximum zero rate amount, the capital gains for the 0/15/20 percent group are taxed at 0 percent, and the 25 percent and 28 percent gains are taxed at the taxpayer's ordinary rate. Thus, the taxpayer's tax is calculated using the ordinary tax rates on the taxpayer's taxable income including the 25 percent and 28 percent gains and excluding the 0/15/20 percent gains, which are taxed at 0 percent.
- For other situations, use the following steps to determine the tax on the gains:[29]

    Step 1:   Fill up the 10, 12, 22, 24, 32, 35, and 37 percent tax rate brackets with taxable income, exclusive of long-term capital gains (and qualified dividends) subject to preferential rates.

    Step 2:   Next, if there is any remaining space below the beginning of the 32 percent bracket after step 1, add any 25 percent rate capital gains to the amount from step 1 until reaching the end of the 24 percent bracket. This 25 percent rate capital gain is taxed at the ordinary rates provided in the tax rate schedule.

[29]§1(h).

EXHIBIT 7-6 Jeb's Form 8949

Form **8949**

Department of the Treasury
Internal Revenue Service

Sales and Other Dispositions of Capital Assets

▶ Go to *www.irs.gov/Form8949* for instructions and the latest information.

▶ File with your Schedule D to list your transactions for lines 1b, 2, 3, 8b, 9, and 10 of Schedule D.

OMB No. 1545-0074

20**17**

Attachment
Sequence No. **12A**

Name(s) shown on return

Jeb Landers

Social security number or taxpayer identification number

Before you check Box A, B, or C below, see whether you received any Form(s) 1099-B or substitute statement(s) from your broker. A substitute statement will have the same information as Form 1099-B. Either will show whether your basis (usually your cost) was reported to the IRS by your broker and may even tell you which box to check.

Part I **Short-Term.** Transactions involving capital assets you held 1 year or less are short term. For long-term transactions, see page 2.

Note: You may aggregate all short-term transactions reported on Form(s) 1099-B showing basis was reported to the IRS and for which no adjustments or codes are required. Enter the totals directly on Schedule D, line 1a; you aren't required to report these transactions on Form 8949 (see instructions).

You *must* check Box A, B, *or* C below. Check only one box. If more than one box applies for your short-term transactions, complete a separate Form 8949, page 1, for each applicable box. If you have more short-term transactions than will fit on this page for one or more of the boxes, complete as many forms with the same box checked as you need.

- ☑ **(A)** Short-term transactions reported on Form(s) 1099-B showing basis was reported to the IRS (see **Note** above)
- ☐ **(B)** Short-term transactions reported on Form(s) 1099-B showing basis **wasn't** reported to the IRS
- ☐ **(C)** Short-term transactions not reported to you on Form 1099-B

1 (a) Description of property (Example: 100 sh. XYZ Co.)	(b) Date acquired (Mo., day, yr.)	(c) Date sold or disposed of (Mo., day, yr.)	(d) Proceeds (sales price) (see instructions)	(e) Cost or other basis. See the **Note** below and see *Column (e)* in the separate instructions	(f) Code(s) from instructions	(g) Amount of adjustment	(h) Gain or (loss). Subtract column (e) from column (d) and combine the result with column (g)
Stock C	3/01/18	11/15/18	20,000	12,000			8,000
Stock D	2/02/18	6/09/18	17,000	28,000			(11,000)
2 Totals. Add the amounts in columns (d), (e), (g), and (h) (subtract negative amounts). Enter each total here and include on your Schedule D, **line 1b** (if **Box A** above is checked), **line 2** (if **Box B** above is checked), or **line 3** (if **Box C** above is checked) ▶			37,000	40,000			(3,000)

Note: If you checked Box A above but the basis reported to the IRS was incorrect, enter in column (e) the basis as reported to the IRS, and enter an adjustment in column (g) to correct the basis. See *Column (g)* in the separate instructions for how to figure the amount of the adjustment.

For Paperwork Reduction Act Notice, see your tax return instructions.   Cat. No. 37768Z   Form **8949** (2017)

EXHIBIT 7-6   Jeb's Form 8949 (*continued*)

Form 8949 (2017)   Attachment Sequence No. **12A**   Page **2**

Name(s) shown on return. Name and SSN or taxpayer identification no. not required if shown on other side	Social security number or taxpayer identification number
Jeb Landers	

Before you check Box D, E, or F below, see whether you received any Form(s) 1099-B or substitute statement(s) from your broker. A substitute statement will have the same information as Form 1099-B. Either will show whether your basis (usually your cost) was reported to the IRS by your broker and may even tell you which box to check.

Part II   **Long-Term.** Transactions involving capital assets you held more than 1 year are long term. For short-term transactions, see page 1.

Note: You may aggregate all long-term transactions reported on Form(s) 1099-B showing basis was reported to the IRS and for which no adjustments or codes are required. Enter the totals directly on Schedule D, line 8a; you aren't required to report these transactions on Form 8949 (see instructions).

You *must* check Box D, E, *or* F below. Check only one box. If more than one box applies for your long-term transactions, complete a separate Form 8949, page 2, for each applicable box. If you have more long-term transactions than will fit on this page for one or more of the boxes, complete as many forms with the same box checked as you need.

☑ **(D)** Long-term transactions reported on Form(s) 1099-B showing basis was reported to the IRS (see **Note** above)

☐ **(E)** Long-term transactions reported on Form(s) 1099-B showing basis **wasn't** reported to the IRS

☐ **(F)** Long-term transactions not reported to you on Form 1099-B

1 (a) Description of property (Example: 100 sh. XYZ Co.)	(b) Date acquired (Mo., day, yr.)	(c) Date sold or disposed of (Mo., day, yr.)	(d) Proceeds (sales price) (see instructions)	(e) Cost or other basis. See the **Note** below and see *Column (e)* in the separate instructions	(f) Code(s) from instructions	(g) Amount of adjustment	(h) Gain or (loss). Subtract column (e) from column (d) and combine the result with column (g)
Stock A	11/07/15	3/06/18	40,000	5,000			35,000
Stock B	7/09/14	9/01/18	20,000	30,000			(10,000)
2 Totals. Add the amounts in columns (d), (e), (g), and (h) (subtract negative amounts). Enter each total here and include on your Schedule D, **line 8b** (if **Box D** above is checked), **line 9** (if **Box E** above is checked), or **line 10** (if **Box F** above is checked) ▶			60,000	35,000			25,000

Note: If you checked Box D above but the basis reported to the IRS was incorrect, enter in column (e) the basis as reported to the IRS, and enter an adjustment in column (g) to correct the basis. See *Column (g)* in the separate instructions for how to figure the amount of the adjustment.

Form **8949** (2017)

Source: IRS Form 8949, 2017

EXHIBIT 7-7   Jeb's Schedule D

SCHEDULE D (Form 1040) Department of the Treasury Internal Revenue Service (99)	**Capital Gains and Losses** ▶ Attach to Form 1040 or Form 1040NR. ▶ Go to *www.irs.gov/ScheduleD* for instructions and the latest information. ▶ Use Form 8949 to list your transactions for lines 1b, 2, 3, 8b, 9, and 10.	OMB No. 1545-0074 2017 Attachment Sequence No. **12**

Name(s) shown on return	Your social security number
Jeb Landers	

Part I   Short-Term Capital Gains and Losses—Assets Held One Year or Less

See instructions for how to figure the amounts to enter on the lines below. This form may be easier to complete if you round off cents to whole dollars.	**(d)** Proceeds (sales price)	**(e)** Cost (or other basis)	**(g)** Adjustments to gain or loss from Form(s) 8949, Part I, line 2, column (g)	**(h) Gain or (loss)** Subtract column (e) from column (d) and combine the result with column (g)
1a Totals for all short-term transactions reported on Form 1099-B for which basis was reported to the IRS and for which you have no adjustments (see instructions). However, if you choose to report all these transactions on Form 8949, leave this line blank and go to line 1b .				
1b Totals for all transactions reported on Form(s) 8949 with **Box A** checked	37,000	40,000		(3,000)
2 Totals for all transactions reported on Form(s) 8949 with **Box B** checked				
3 Totals for all transactions reported on Form(s) 8949 with **Box C** checked				

4 Short-term gain from Form 6252 and short-term gain or (loss) from Forms 4684, 6781, and 8824 .	**4**	
5 Net short-term gain or (loss) from partnerships, S corporations, estates, and trusts from Schedule(s) K-1	**5**	
6 Short-term capital loss carryover. Enter the amount, if any, from line 8 of your **Capital Loss Carryover Worksheet** in the instructions	**6** (	)
7 **Net short-term capital gain or (loss).** Combine lines 1a through 6 in column (h). If you have any long-term capital gains or losses, go to Part II below. Otherwise, go to Part III on the back	**7**	(3,000)

Part II   Long-Term Capital Gains and Losses—Assets Held More Than One Year

See instructions for how to figure the amounts to enter on the lines below. This form may be easier to complete if you round off cents to whole dollars.	**(d)** Proceeds (sales price)	**(e)** Cost (or other basis)	**(g)** Adjustments to gain or loss from Form(s) 8949, Part II, line 2, column (g)	**(h) Gain or (loss)** Subtract column (e) from column (d) and combine the result with column (g)
8a Totals for all long-term transactions reported on Form 1099-B for which basis was reported to the IRS and for which you have no adjustments (see instructions). However, if you choose to report all these transactions on Form 8949, leave this line blank and go to line 8b .				
8b Totals for all transactions reported on Form(s) 8949 with **Box D** checked	60,000	35,000		25,000
9 Totals for all transactions reported on Form(s) 8949 with **Box E** checked				
10 Totals for all transactions reported on Form(s) 8949 with **Box F** checked.				

11 Gain from Form 4797, Part I; long-term gain from Forms 2439 and 6252; and long-term gain or (loss) from Forms 4684, 6781, and 8824	**11**	
12 Net long-term gain or (loss) from partnerships, S corporations, estates, and trusts from Schedule(s) K-1	**12**	
13 Capital gain distributions. See the instructions	**13**	
14 Long-term capital loss carryover. Enter the amount, if any, from line 13 of your **Capital Loss Carryover Worksheet** in the instructions	**14** (	)
15 **Net long-term capital gain or (loss).** Combine lines 8a through 14 in column (h). Then go to Part III on the back	**15**	25,000

For Paperwork Reduction Act Notice, see your tax return instructions.   Cat. No. 11338H   Schedule D (Form 1040) 2017

Source: IRS Schedule D Form 1040, 2017

Step 3: Next, if, after including all of the 25 percent gain (step 2), there is still space remaining below the beginning of the 32 percent bracket, add any 28 percent rate capital gain until reaching the end of the 24 percent bracket. This 28 percent rate capital gain is taxed at the ordinary rates provided in the tax rate schedule.

Step 4: Next, if there is room below the maximum zero rate amount after applying step 3, add any 0/15/20 percent rate capital gain until reaching the maximum zero rate amount. This 0/15/20 percent rate capital gain is taxed at 0 percent. If there is additional 0/15/20 percent capital that increases taxable income above the maximum zero rate amount, add the 0/15/20 percent capital gain until reaching the maximum 15 percent rate amount. This 0/15/20 percent capital gain is taxed at 15 percent. If there is additional 0/15/20 percent capital gain that increases taxable income above the maximum 15 percent rate amount, this 0/15/20 percent capital gain is taxed at 20 percent.

Step 5: Finally, any remaining 25 percent rate capital gain (not taxed in step 2) is taxed at 25 percent. Any remaining 28 percent rate capital gain (not taxed in step 3) is taxed at 28 percent. If, however, a taxpayer's tax liability would be lower using the ordinary tax rates for all ordinary income and capital gains [which is possible but not typical], the taxpayer would simply owe tax based on the ordinary tax rates.

Example 7-9

What if: Let's return to the facts of the previous example in which Jeb recognized a $48,000 25 percent net capital gain and a $95,000 0/15/20 percent net capital gain. Also, assume that Jeb's taxable income before considering the net capital gains is $10,000. His filing status is single. What is Jeb's gross tax liability for the year?

Answer: $22,949.50, computed as follows:

Amount and Type of Income	Applicable Rate	Tax	Explanation
$9,525; ordinary	10%	$ 952.50	$9,525 × 10%. The first $9,525 of Jeb's $10,000 of ordinary income is taxed at 10 percent (see single tax rate schedule for this and other computations).
$475; ordinary	12%	57.00	$475 × 12%. Jeb's remaining $475 of ordinary income ($10,000 − $9,525) is taxed at 12 percent.
$28,700; 25 percent rate capital gains	12%	3,444.00	$28,700 × 12%. The end of Jeb's 12 percent bracket is $38,700 minus $10,000 ($9,525 + $475) already taxed. Jeb's ordinary tax rate of 12 percent is lower than the maximum 25 percent rate for these gains, so it is taxed at the lower ordinary rate.
$19,300; 25 percent rate capital gains	22%	4,246.00	$19,300 × 22%. $48,000 total 25% gain minus $28,700 percent gain already taxed at 12 percent. Jeb's ordinary tax rate of 22 percent is lower than the maximum 25 percent rate for these gains, so it is taxed at the lower ordinary rate.
$95,000; 15 percent rate capital gains	15%	14,250.00	$95,000 × 15%. All of the 15 percent gain is between Jeb's maximum zero rate amount ($38,600) and maximum 15 percent rate amount ($425,800), so it is all taxed at 15 percent.
Gross tax liability		$22,949.50	

What if: Suppose Jeb's 0/15/20 percent capital gain was $400,000 rather than $95,000. What is Jeb's gross tax liability for the year?

Answer: $70,309.50, computed as follows:

Amount and Type of Income	Applicable Rate	Tax	Explanation
$9,525; ordinary	10%	$ 952.50	$9,525 × 10%. The first $9,525 of Jeb's $10,000 of ordinary income is taxed at 10 percent (see single tax rate schedule for this and other computations).
$475; ordinary	12%	57.00	$475 × 12%. Jeb's remaining $475 of ordinary income ($10,000 − $9,525) is taxed at 12 percent.
$28,700; 25 percent rate capital gains	12%	3,444.00	$28,700 × 12%. The end of Jeb's 12 percent bracket is $38,700 minus $10,000 ($9,525 + $475) already taxed. Jeb's ordinary tax rate of 12 percent is lower than the maximum 25 percent rate for these gains, so it is taxed at the lower ordinary rate.
$19,300; 25 percent rate capital gains	22%	4,246.00	$19,300 × 22%. $48,000 total 25% gain minus $28,700 percent gain already taxed at 12 percent. Jeb's ordinary tax rate of 22 percent is lower than the maximum 25 percent rate for these gains, so it is taxed at the lower ordinary rate.
$367,800; 0/15/20 percent rate capital gains	15%	55,170.00	$367,800 × 15%. $367,800 represents the 0/15/20 percent gain that is below the maximum 15 percent rate amount ($425,800) after including the other taxable amounts. ($425,800 − $19,300 − $28,700 − $475 − $9,525). This gain is taxed at 15 percent.
$32,200; 0/15/20 percent rate capital gains	20%	6,440.00	$32,200 × 20%. The remaining 0/15/20 percent gain ($400,000 − $367,800) that is above the maximum 15 percent rate amount ($425,800). This gain is taxed at the maximum 20 percent.
Gross tax liability		**$70,309.50**	

Limits for Capital Loss Deductions

We've discussed the general rule that taxpayers may deduct capital losses against capital gains in the netting process, and that individual taxpayers may deduct up to $3,000 ($1,500 if married filing separately) of net capital losses against ordinary income in a given year. This general rule is subject to certain exceptions, however, as described below.

Losses on the Sale of Personal-Use Assets   We've seen that personal-use assets fall within the category of capital assets. When taxpayers sell personal-use assets, what are the tax consequences? Consider an engaged taxpayer who calls off the wedding plans. After getting the ring back from his former fiancée, the taxpayer sells the engagement ring for more than its purchase price. Does he recognize a taxable gain? Absolutely—the gain from the sale of a personal-use asset is taxable even though it was not purchased for its appreciation potential. The tax rate on the gain depends on the amount of time between the date the taxpayer purchased the ring and the date he sold it, and on the netting process involving the seller's other capital gains and losses during the year. What if a taxpayer sold her car for less than she paid for it? Does she get to deduct the capital loss? Unfortunately, no—losses on the sale of personal-use assets are *not* deductible and therefore never become part of the netting process.

Capital Losses on Sales to Related Parties   When taxpayers sell capital assets at a loss to related parties, they are not able to deduct the loss.[30] As we described in detail in the Property Dispositions chapter, the related party acquiring the asset may eventually be allowed to deduct all, a portion, or none of the disallowed loss on a subsequent sale.

Wash Sales   Consider the case of a taxpayer attempting to do some tax planning near the end of the year: She has invested in the stock of several corporations; some of these investments have appreciated while others have declined in value. The taxpayer wants to capture the tax benefit of the stock losses in the current year to offset ordinary income (up to $3,000) or to offset other capital gains she has already recognized during the year. However, she can't deduct the losses until she sells the stock. Why might this be a problem? If the taxpayer believes that the stocks with unrealized losses are likely to appreciate in the near future, she may prefer *not* to sell those stocks but rather to keep them in her investment portfolio. What might this taxpayer do to deduct the losses while continuing to hold the investment in the stocks? For one, she might be tempted to sell the stocks and then immediately buy them back. Or, she might buy more of the same stock and then sell the stock she originally held to recognize the losses. With this strategy, she hopes to realize (and then recognize or deduct) the losses and, at the end of the day, still hold the stocks in her investment portfolio.

Although that might sound like a great plan, certain **wash sale** tax rules prevent this strategy from accomplishing the taxpayer's objective. A wash sale occurs when an investor sells or trades stock or securities at a loss *and* within 30 days *either before or after* the day of sale buys substantially identical stocks or securities.[31] Because the day of sale is included, the 30 days before and after period creates a 61-day window during which the wash sale provisions may apply.[32] When the wash sale provisions apply to a sale of stock, realized losses are not recognized; instead, the amount of *the unrecognized loss is added to the basis of the newly acquired stock.* Congress created this rule to prevent taxpayers from accelerating losses on securities that have declined in value without actually altering their investment in the securities. The 61-day period ensures that taxpayers cannot deduct losses from stock sales without exposing themselves to the risk that the stock they sold will subsequently increase in value.

Example 7-10

What if: Suppose Courtney owns 100 shares of Cisco stock that she purchased in June 2016 for $50 a share. On December 21, 2018, Courtney sells the shares for $40 a share to generate cash for the holidays. This sale generates a capital loss of $1,000 [$4,000 sale proceeds (100 × $40) − $5,000 tax basis ($50 × 100)]. Later, however, Courtney decides that Cisco might be a good long-term investment. On January 3, 2019 (13 days later), Courtney purchases 100 shares of Cisco stock for $41 a share ($4,100). Does Courtney realize a short-term or a long-term capital loss on the December 21 sale?

Answer: Long-term capital loss. She held the stock for more than one year (June 2016 to December 2018) before selling.

---

[30]§267(a).

[31]Substantially identical stocks or securities include contracts or options to buy substantially identical securities. However, corporate bonds and preferred stock are not generally considered substantially identical to common stock of the same corporation.

[32]§1091.

How much of the realized $1,000 long-term capital loss can Courtney recognize or deduct on her 2018 tax return?

Answer: Zero. Because Courtney sold the stock at a loss and purchased the same stock within the 61-day period centered on the date of sale (30 days before December 21, and 30 days after December 21), the wash sale rules disallow the loss in 2018. Had Courtney waited another 18 days to repurchase the Cisco shares, she could have avoided the wash sale rules. In that case, under the general rules for capital loss deductibility, Courtney *would* be able to deduct the $1,000 capital loss from the sale against her ordinary income on her 2018 income tax return.

What tax basis will Courtney have in the Cisco stock she purchased (or repurchased) on January 3, 2019?

Answer: $5,100. Under the wash sale rules, Courtney adds the $1,000 disallowed loss to the basis of the stock she purchased on January 3. Thus, she now owns 100 shares of Cisco stock with a $5,100 basis in the shares, which is $1,000 more than she paid for it.

What if: How much of the $1,000 realized loss would Courtney have recognized if she had only purchased 40 shares of Cisco stock instead of 100 shares on January 3, 2019?

Answer: $600. The wash sale rules disallow the loss to the extent taxpayers acquire other shares in the 61-day window. In this situation, Courtney only acquired 40 percent (40 of 100) of the shares she sold at a loss within the window. Consequently, she must disallow 40 percent, or $400, of the loss, and she is allowed to deduct the remaining $600 loss.

ETHICS

In December, T. D. Weber evaluated his stock portfolio and found that his DLW Inc. common stock had declined in value since he purchased it. He decides to sell the DLW stock on December 15. However, he would like to retain an interest in the company. So, knowing that he needs to avoid the wash sale rules, when he sells the common stock on December 15 and deducts the loss on his return for the year. T.D. simultaneously purchases an equivalent amount of preferred stock in DLW Inc. On January 17 of the next year, he sells the preferred stock and repurchases DLW common stock. What do you think of his strategy from an ethical perspective?

Balancing Tax Planning Strategies for Capital Assets with Other Goals

When taxpayers invest in capital assets and hold the assets for more than a year, they receive at least two benefits. First, they are able to defer recognizing gains on the assets until they sell them—the longer the deferral period, the lower the present value of the capital gains tax when taxpayers ultimately sell the assets. Second, they pay taxes on the gains at preferential rates. These tax advantages provide taxpayers with a greater after-tax rate of return on these investments than they would obtain from less tax-favored assets that earn equivalent before-tax rates of return. Investors who quickly sell investments pay taxes on gains at higher, ordinary rates and incur significantly greater transaction costs than those who hold for a longer period. Nevertheless, taxpayers should balance the tax benefits available for holding assets with the risk that the asset values will have declined by the time they want to sell the assets.

THE KEY FACTS

Capital Gains and Losses

- Tax on the appreciation of capital assets is deferred until the asset is sold.
  - The longer the holding period, the greater the after-tax rate of return for a given before-tax rate of return.
- Tracking the basis of stock sold
  - FIFO method is the default.
  - Specific identification is allowed.
- Capital gains and losses
  - Long-term capital gain if the asset is held more than a year before sold; short-term otherwise.
  - Net long-term capital gains are taxed at the maximum 0/15/20 percent rate.
  - ($3,000) net capital loss is deductible annually against ordinary income.
  - Losses on personal-use assets are not deductible.
  - Losses on wash sales are not deductible but are added to the basis of new shares acquired.
- Basic tax planning strategies
  - Hold capital assets for more than a year before selling.
  - Sell loss capital assets to offset gains.

Example 7-11

What if: Assume Courtney decides to purchase Intel stock for $100,000. She plans to hold half the shares for five years to purchase the Park City home and hold the other half for 8 years to pay for Deron's education. If the Intel stock grows at a constant 8 percent before-tax rate and does not pay any dividends, how much cash will Courtney accumulate after taxes for the Park City home?

(*continued on page 7-24*)

Answer: $69,946, computed as follows:

Description	Amount	Explanation
1. Proceeds from sale	$73,466	$[\$50,000 \times (1 + .08)^5]$
2. Basis in fund shares	50,000	This is the nondeductible investment in the shares.
3. Gain realized on sale	$23,466	(1) − (2)
4. Tax rate on gain	× 15%	Low rate for long-term capital gain.*
5. Tax on gain	$ 3,520	(3) × (4)
After-tax cash for Park City home	**$69,946**	(1) − (5)

*Assumes Courtney doesn't have any capital losses.

How much cash will Courtney accumulate after taxes for Deron's education?

Answer: $86,165, computed as follows:

Description	Amount	Explanation
1. Proceeds from sale	$92,547	$[\$50,000 \times (1 + .08)^8]$
2. Basis in fund shares	50,000	This is the nondeductible investment in the shares.
3. Gain realized on sale	$42,547	(1) − (2)
4. Tax rate on gain	× 15%	Low rate for long-term capital gain.*
5. Tax on gain	$ 6,382	(3) × (4)
After-tax cash for education goal	**$86,165**	(1) − (5)

*Assumes Courtney doesn't have capital losses.

When investing in capital assets, taxpayers run the risk that some of their investments may decline in value. Thus, a productive strategy for managing investments in capital assets is to sell investments with built-in losses. This strategy is commonly referred to as "loss harvesting." By selectively selling loss assets, taxpayers can reduce their taxes by deducting up to $3,000 against their ordinary income and by reducing the amount of capital gains that would otherwise be subject to tax during the year. This is particularly beneficial for taxpayers who have short-term capital gains that will be taxed at higher ordinary rates absent off-setting capital losses. Note, however, that taxpayers should not sell investments to gain tax benefits if they believe the potential economic benefit of holding the investment outweighs the tax benefits of selling the stock. Also, keep in mind that capital losses on stock sales may not be deductible due to the wash sale rules discussed above.

PORTFOLIO INCOME SUMMARY

As we've discussed the tax consequences of various investments up to this point in the chapter, we have proceeded from the least tax-advantaged (taxed annually at ordinary rates) to the most tax-advantaged (tax deferred at capital gains rates). By moving along this continuum from investments taxed annually at ordinary rates (corporate bonds[33]) to investments taxed annually at capital gains rates (dividend-paying stock), investors are in essence employing the conversion planning strategy referred to repeatedly throughout this text. As they move from dividend-paying stock to growth stock, which provides tax deferral in addition to preferential tax rates, taxpayers combine the conversion strategy with the basic strategy of shifting income from one time period to another.

In this chapter and elsewhere in this text, we emphasize that tax planning must not be done in a vacuum or without considering all relevant parties and taxpayers' economic and

---

[33]We refer here to corporate bonds issued or acquired at face value.

personal objectives. Because investments typically are not designed to accommodate the specific needs of each individual investor, considering the other party in the deal is not as relevant when investing as it is in other transactions. However, it is vital that investors carefully balance the tax characteristics of their investment options with the other attributes of their investment options, such as risk and liquidity.

INVESTMENT INTEREST EXPENSE

LO 7-3

Now that we've discussed how *income* from various forms of investments is taxed, let's explore the deductibility of expenses taxpayers incur to acquire or maintain their investments. Beginning in 2018, the only expense associated with investments that remains deductible is **investment interest expense.**[34]

When taxpayers borrow money to acquire investments, the interest expense they pay on the loan is investment interest expense. For example, if you borrow funds to buy stock, any interest you pay on the loan would be considered investment interest expense. However, to the extent taxpayers borrow to purchase investments that produce tax-exempt income, such as municipal bonds, they are not allowed to deduct the related interest expense.[35] Although the TCJA eliminated the deduction for investment expenses, it did not eliminate the deduction for investment interest expense. Investment interest expense may be deductible as an itemized deduction.[36] It is, however, subject to a limitation. Technically, a taxpayer's investment interest expense deduction for the year is limited to the taxpayer's **net investment income** for the year.[37]

To avoid confusion, we use the term investment income rather than the term net investment income to discuss the investment interest expense limitation. Because the TCJA eliminated the deduction for investment expenses, net investment income is simply gross investment income. Gross investment income includes interest, annuity, and royalty income not derived in the ordinary course of a trade or business. It also includes net *short*-term capital gains, and nonqualified dividends. However, investment income generally does not include capital gains taxed at a preferential rate and qualified dividends because of the preferential rate.

Example 7-12

What if: Suppose that during the year, Courtney recognized the following income from investments: $3,000 of qualified dividends and $500 of taxable interest. What is Courtney's investment income?

Answer: $500. The taxable interest is included, and the qualified dividends are excluded because they are taxed at a preferential rate.

---

[34]Prior to 2018, investment expenses (including expenses for investment management fees, fees to collect interest and dividends, safe deposit box rental fees, attorney and accounting fees that are necessary to produce investment income, and investment advisor fees) were deductible as an itemized deduction but subject to limitations. These expenses are no longer deductible after the TCJA. However, rental expenses are deductible under §212 as we discuss in the Individual Deductions chapter. Investment expenses from rental and royalty-related activities are deductible as *for* AGI and not as itemized deductions and thus remain deductible after the TCJA.

[35]§163.

[36]§265.

[37]The investment interest expense limitation is calculated on Form 4952.

Taxpayers may deduct their investment interest expense up to the amount of their investment income. Any investment interest expense in excess of investment income is carried over and treated as though it was incurred in the next year when it is subject to the same limitations. The carryover amount never expires. That is, taxpayers can carry over the excess investment interest expense until they generate sufficient investment income to deduct it.

Example 7-13

What if: Continuing with Example 7-12, suppose that in July of this year, Courtney purchased a parcel of undeveloped land as an investment for $120,000. She made a $20,000 down payment and financed the remaining $100,000 with a loan from her local credit union. The interest rate on the loan was 9 percent, payable annually. During the year, Courtney paid $4,500 in interest expense on the loan. Because the loan was used to purchase an investment, the interest expense is investment interest expense. What amount of this investment interest expense is Courtney allowed to deduct this year?

Answer: $500. Although she incurred $4,500 of investment interest expense, her deduction for the current year is limited to her $500 investment income (see Example 7-12). The $4,000 of investment interest expense that is not deductible this year is carried forward until Courtney generates enough investment income to deduct it.

Congress allows taxpayers to *elect to include* preferentially taxed income in investment income if they are willing to subject this income to tax at the ordinary (not preferential) tax rates. Taxpayers who make this election benefit from increasing their investment income and thus increasing their current year investment interest expense deduction. However, this additional deduction comes at a price because they must subject their capital gains and qualified dividends included in investment income (that would have been taxed at preferential rates if not for the election) to ordinary tax rates.[38]

Example 7-14

In Examples 7-12 and 7-13, we discovered that Courtney paid $4,500 of investment interest expense during the year but was only able to deduct $500 of the interest expense because her net investment income was only $500. However, as indicated in Example 7-12, Courtney also received $3,000 of qualified dividends that were *excluded* from the net investment income computation. Courtney may elect to increase her investment income by the amount of the qualified dividends (and increase her investment interest expense deduction), but by doing so, she must subject the qualified dividends to her ordinary tax rate (32 percent) instead of the preferential rate (15 percent). Thus, Courtney is faced with a choice of whether to include the $3,000 dividend in investment income and tax it at ordinary rates (Alternative 1) or exclude it from investment income and tax it at preferential rates (Alternative 2). How much more investment interest expense is she allowed to deduct under Alternative 1 than Alternative 2?

---

[38]Note that the election is not an all-or-nothing proposition. Taxpayers can elect to include all or only a portion of their preferentially-taxed capital gains and qualified dividends in investment income. However, the amount they include in investment income is subject to tax at ordinary tax rates.

Answer: $3,000 more under Alternative 1, computed as follows:

Alternative 1: *Include the $3,000 dividends in investment income.*

Description	Amount	Explanation
1. Increase in investment income	$3,000	Elect to include dividends in investment income.
2. Increase in investment interest expense deduction	**3,000**	Investment interest expense deduction increased from $500 to $3,500.
3. Tax benefit from additional deduction	960	(2) × 32%
4. Tax cost of taxing dividends at ordinary rate	510	(1) × (32% − 15%)
5. Current savings from election to include dividends in net investment income	450	(3) − (4)
Investment interest expense carryforward	$1,000	$4,500 total − $3,500 deducted

Alternative 2: *Exclude the $3,000 dividends from investment income.*

Description	Amount	Explanation
Forgone tax benefit available *this year* under Alternative 1	$ 450	Under Alternative 2, Courtney doesn't receive the tax savings available under Alternative 1.
1. Increase in investment interest expense carryforward	3,000	Investment interest expense not deducted under Alternative 2.
Total investment interest expense carryforward	$4,000	(1) + $1,000 investment interest expense carryforward under Alternative 1.

Whether it makes sense to elect to include capital gains and qualified dividends in investment income depends on the taxpayer's circumstances and personal preferences. As we see in Example 7-14, Courtney could save $450 this year by electing to include this income in investment income. However, by doing so, she is forgoing $3,000 of investment interest expense carryforward ($4,000 − $1,000) that would be available to offset ordinary income in future years.

Net Investment Income Tax

A net investment income tax is imposed on net investment income.[39] The tax imposed is 3.8 percent of the lesser of (a) net investment income or (b) the excess of modified adjusted gross income over $250,000 for married-joint filers and surviving spouses, $125,000 for married separate filers, and $200,000 for other taxpayers. Modified adjusted gross income equals adjusted gross income increased by income excluded under the foreign-earned income exclusion less any disallowed deductions associated with the

[39]§1411. For purposes of the net investment income tax (NIIT), the definition of net investment income differs from that of investment income in the previous section. Net investment income for purposes of the NIIT includes interest, dividends, annuities, royalties, rents, income from passive activities, and gains from the disposition of assets generating these types of income. Allowable related deductions (including rental property taxes and related state income taxes) reduce income to obtain net investment income.

foreign-earned income exclusion. The tax is calculated and reported on Form 8960. Additional details and examples of the tax are provided in the Individual Income Tax Computation and Tax Credits chapter.

LO 7-4   PASSIVE ACTIVITY INCOME AND LOSSES

Thus far we have discussed how taxpayers may invest in business- and income-producing activities and earn various forms of income that are taxed as *portfolio income*. For example, taxpayers acquiring stock in a **C corporation** that files tax returns and pays taxes or taxpayers purchasing bonds issued by a corporation are taxed on the portfolio income these investments generate in the form of dividends and interest. On the other hand, a taxpayer may passively invest directly in an income-producing enterprise by purchasing rental property. Similarly, a taxpayer could passively invest in a partial interest in a trade or business or rental activity by acquiring an ownership interest in a **flow-through entity** that doesn't pay taxes, such as a partnership, limited liability company (taxed as a partnership), or an S corporation (taxed similar to a partnership by shareholders' election). This section addresses the taxation of these passive activities.

Whether an investor makes a direct investment in rental property or makes an indirect investment in a business or rental activity through a partnership, limited liability company, or S corporation, the *actual operating income or loss* from these investments flows through to the taxpayer as it is earned and is treated as ordinary income or ordinary loss. If trade or business or rental activities (held either directly or indirectly through flow-through entities) generate ordinary operating income, taxpayers report it on their tax returns and it is taxed at ordinary rates. However, if these activities generate operating losses, the operating losses must clear three hurdles to be deductible currently. The three loss limits are the tax-basis, at-risk, and passive loss limits.

The tax-basis hurdle limits a taxpayer's deductible operating losses to the taxpayer's tax basis in the business or rental activity. This limitation is very similar to loss limitations that apply when a taxpayer sells an investment asset such as corporate stock or another similar capital asset. Recall that the formula for determining gain or loss on an exchange is the amount realized less the taxpayer's adjusted basis in the property. If a taxpayer were to sell an asset for nothing, the loss would be the amount of her tax basis in the property, but no more.

Obviously, in order to apply the tax-basis loss limitation, we must first determine the taxpayer's tax basis in the activity. Very generally speaking, the tax basis is the taxpayer's investment in the activity adjusted for certain items (namely, income, debt, and investments). The adjustments are beyond the scope of this chapter; however, tax basis is discussed in chapters relating to flow-through entities.

When a loss from a business or business-related activity clears the tax-basis hurdle, it next must clear an **at-risk** hurdle on its journey toward deductibility.[40] The at-risk rules are meant to limit the ability of investors to deduct "artificial" ordinary losses produced with certain types of debt. These rules serve to limit ordinary losses to a taxpayer's economic risk in an activity. Generally, a taxpayer is considered to be "at risk" in an activity to the extent of any cash personally contributed to the activity and certain other adjustments similar (but not identical) to those for tax basis.[41] Because the computation of the tax basis and the at-risk amount are so similar, a taxpayer's tax basis and her at-risk amount in the activity are frequently the same, so that when she clears the tax-basis hurdle for deducting a loss, she also clears the at-risk hurdle. If the at-risk amount does differ from the tax basis, the at-risk amount will be less than the tax basis. Losses that do not clear the at-risk hurdle are suspended until the taxpayer generates more at-risk amounts to absorb the loss or until the activity is sold, when they may offset the seller's gain from the disposition of the activity.

---

[40]§465.

[41]A detailed discussion of these adjustments is beyond the scope of this chapter.

Example 7-15

What if: Assume that instead of investing solely in assets that generate portfolio income, Courtney used $10,000 of the inheritance from "Gramps" to acquire a 5 percent interest in a limited partnership (a flow-through entity) called Color Comfort Sheets (CCS). Courtney's share of CCS's loss for the year is $15,000. What amount of this loss is Courtney allowed to deduct after applying the tax basis and at-risk limitations?

Answer: $10,000. Since Courtney's tax basis and at-risk amount in her CCS interest are both $10,000 (the amount of cash invested), the tax-basis and at-risk amount limitations result in the same limitation. Thus, Courtney may deduct $10,000 of the $15,000 loss before considering the passive activity loss limits discussed below.

Even when a taxpayer has sufficient tax basis and sufficient amounts at risk to absorb a loss from a business-related activity, the loss may still be limited by the passive activity loss rules. Prior to 1986, investors were able to use ordinary losses from certain passive activities to offset portfolio income (interest, dividends, and capital gains), salary income, and self-employment income, including income from other trades or businesses they were actively involved in managing. During this time, a **tax shelter** industry thrived by marketing investments to wealthy investors designed primarily to generate ordinary losses that could be used to shield other income from tax. To combat this practice, Congress introduced the passive activity loss rules.[42] Specifically, these rules limit the ability of investors in certain passive activities involving interests in trades or businesses and in rental property, including real estate, to use their ordinary losses from these activities currently to reduce taxable income from other sources.[43] The passive activity loss rules are applied to any losses remaining *after* applying the tax-basis and at-risk loss limits.

Passive Activity Definition

The **passive activity loss (PAL) rules** define a passive activity as "any activity which involves the conduct of a trade or business, and in which the taxpayer does not materially participate." According to the tax code, participants in rental activities, including rental real estate, and limited partners in partnerships are generally deemed to be passive participants, and participants in all other trade or business activities are passive unless their involvement in an activity is "regular, continuous, and substantial." Clearly, these terms are quite subjective and difficult to apply. Fortunately, regulations provide more certainty in this area by listing seven separate tests for material participation.[44] An individual, other than a limited partner, can be classified as a material participant in an activity by meeting any one of the seven tests in Exhibit 7-8. Therefore, investors who purchase rental property or an interest in a trade or business without intending to be involved in the management of the trade or business are classified as passive participants, and these activities are classified as passive activities with respect to them.

Income and Loss Categories

Under the passive activity loss rules, each item of a taxpayer's income or loss for the year is placed in one of three categories. Losses from the *passive* category cannot

---

[42]§469.

[43]Before passage of the passive activity loss rules, the "at-risk rules" in §465 were adopted in an attempt to limit the ability of investors to deduct "artificial" ordinary losses. Given the similarity of the at-risk and tax-basis computations, especially for real estate investments, the at-risk rules were not entirely successful at accomplishing this objective. The passive activity loss rules were adopted as a backstop to the at-risk rules and both sets of rules may potentially apply to a given activity.

[44]§1.469-5T.

EXHIBIT 7-8   Tests for Material Participation

Individuals are generally considered material participants for the activity if they meet any *one* of these tests:

1. The individual participates in the activity more than 500 hours during the year.

2. The individual's activity constitutes substantially all of the participation in such activity by all individuals, including nonowners.

3. The individual participates more than 100 hours during the year, and the individual's participation is not less than any other individual's participation in the activity.

4. The activity qualifies as a "significant participation activity" (more than 100 hours spent during the year) and the aggregate of all "significant participation activities" is greater than 500 hours for the year.

5. The individual materially participated in the activity for any 5 of the preceding 10 taxable years.

6. The individual materially participated for any three preceding years in any personal service activity (personal services in health, law, accounting, architecture, etc.).

7. Taking into account all the facts and circumstances, the individual participates on a regular, continuous, and substantial basis during the year.

offset income from other categories. The three different categories are as follows (see Exhibit 7-9):

1. *Passive activity income or loss*—income or loss from an activity in which the taxpayer is not a material participant.

2. *Portfolio income*—income from investments including capital gains and losses, dividends, interest, annuities, and royalties.

3. *Active business income*—income from sources in which the taxpayer is a material participant. For individuals, this includes salary and self-employment income. Thus, an individual with income in this category is no longer an investor with respect to this source of income given that we define investors in this chapter as individuals with portfolio and/or passive income and losses.

The impact of segregating taxpayers' income in these categories is to limit their ability to apply passive activity losses against income in the other two categories. In effect, passive activity losses are suspended and remain in the passive income or loss category until the taxpayer generates passive income, either from the passive activity producing the loss or from some other passive activity, or until the taxpayer sells the entire activity that gener-

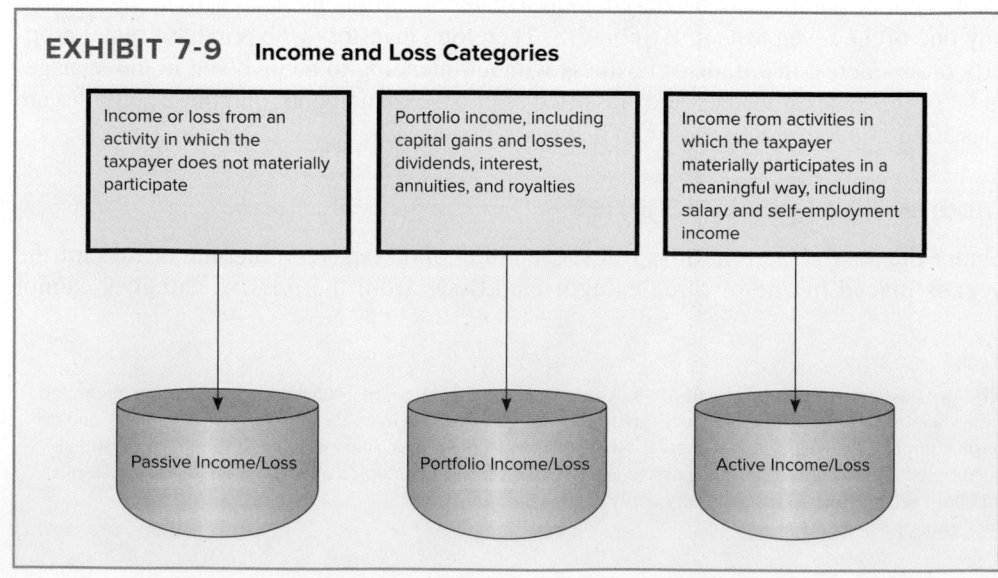

EXHIBIT 7-9   Income and Loss Categories

Income or loss from an activity in which the taxpayer does not materially participate	Portfolio income, including capital gains and losses, dividends, interest, annuities, and royalties	Income from activities in which the taxpayer materially participates in a meaningful way, including salary and self-employment income
Passive Income/Loss	Portfolio Income/Loss	Active Income/Loss

ated the passive loss in a taxable transaction. On the sale, current and suspended passive losses from the activity are first applied to reduce gain from the sale of the activity, then to reduce net passive income from other passive activities, and then to reduce nonpassive income.[45] However, these passive losses that are allowed when the activity is sold may be limited by the excess business loss rules discussed in the Individual Deductions chapter.[46]

Example 7-16

What if: Let's return to the facts in the previous example, in which Courtney's share of CCS loss is $15,000, her tax basis in her CCS interest is $10,000, and her at-risk amount in the activity is also $10,000. Further assume that Courtney received $170,000 in combined salary, $4,000 of taxable interest income from corporate bonds, $3,000 of dividends, and $5,000 of long-term capital gains. Finally, assume that Courtney also owns a rental condominium that generated $8,000 of net income. How would each of these income or loss items be allocated among the passive, portfolio, and active income and loss categories?

Answer: Courtney's $10,000 loss from CCS remaining after applying the tax-basis and at-risk loss limits is placed in the passive category because, as a limited partner, Courtney did not materially participate in the activity. Further, her $8,000 of net income from her rental property is included in the passive category because rental activities are generally considered to be passive. The $4,000 of taxable interest income, $3,000 of dividends, and $5,000 of long-term capital gains are all included in the portfolio income category. Finally, the $170,000 of salary is included in the active income category.

What if: What is Courtney's AGI for the year assuming, other than the items described above, no other items affect her AGI?

Answer: $182,000, computed as follows:

Description	Amount	Explanation
1. Active income	$170,000	Salary
2. Portfolio income	12,000	Interest of $4,000; dividends of $3,000; $5,000 of long-term capital gains.
3. Passive income	0	$10,000 passive loss that clears tax-basis and at-risk hurdles and $8,000 of passive income. However, the passive loss clearing the basis and at-risk hurdles is deductible only to the extent of passive income. The suspended passive loss is ($2,000).
AGI	**$182,000**	(1) + (2) + (3)

What if: In addition to the facts above, assume that at the beginning of next year Courtney sells her limited partnership interest for $12,000. If Courtney's tax basis on the date of sale is $0, what effect does the sale have on her AGI?

Answer: $10,000 increase in AGI, computed as follows:

Description	Amount	Explanation
1. Capital gain	$12,000	Gain recognized = $12,000 − $0 tax basis
2. Ordinary loss	0	The ($5,000) loss that was suspended at the basis level is not deductible on the sale. This loss expires unused. There was no loss suspended at the at-risk level or it would have been deductible on the sale.
3. Ordinary loss	(2,000)	This is the loss that was suspended at the passive loss level last year.
Increase in AGI	**$10,000**	(1) + (2) + (3)

THE KEY FACTS

Passive Activities

- Ordinary losses from flow-though entities and other enterprises will be classified as passive if the taxpayer is not a material participant.
- Losses from limited partnerships and from rental activities, including rental real estate, are generally deemed to be passive losses.
- Passive loss rules limit losses from passive activities to passive income from other sources.
  - Active business income such as salary and self-employment income is not passive income.
  - Investment-type income such as interest and dividends is portfolio income, not passive income.
  - Passive losses in excess of passive income are suspended and deductible against passive income in the future or when the taxpayer sells the passive activity generating the loss.
  - Income from passive activities is subject to the net investment income tax.

---

[45]§469(g).

[46]The excess business loss rules limit these losses to $250,000 or $500,000 depending on filing status.

THE KEY FACTS

Rental Real Estate Losses

- Rental real estate exception to passive loss rules
  - Applies to active participants in rental property.
  - Deduct up to $25,000 of rental real estate loss against ordinary income.
  - $25,000 maximum deduction phased out by 50 cents for every dollar of AGI over $100,000 (excluding the rental loss deduction).
  - Fully phased out at $150,000 of AGI.

Rental Real Estate Exception to the Passive Activity Loss Rules

Tax laws are renowned for exceptions to rules and, not surprisingly, the general rule that passive activity losses cannot be used to offset nonpassive types of income is subject to a few important exceptions. The one we choose to discuss here applies to lower-to-middle income individuals with rental real estate.[47] A taxpayer who is an **active participant in a rental activity** may be allowed to deduct up to $25,000 of the rental loss against other types of income. To be considered an active participant, the taxpayer must (1) own at least 10 percent of the rental property and (2) participate in the process of making management decisions such as approving new tenants, deciding on rental terms, and approving repairs and capital expenditures.

Consistent with a number of tax benefits, the exception amount for active owners is phased out as adjusted gross income increases. The $25,000 maximum exception amount is phased out by 50 cents for every dollar the taxpayer's adjusted gross income (before considering the rental loss) exceeds $100,000. Consequently, the entire $25,000 deduction is phased out when the taxpayer's adjusted gross income reaches $150,000.

Example 7-17

What if: Assume that Jeb Landers, Courtney's uncle, owns and rents a condominium. Jeb is involved in approving new tenants for the rental home and in managing its maintenance. During the year, he reported a net loss of $5,000 from the rental activity, and he had sufficient tax-basis and at-risk amounts to absorb the loss. Further, his only sources of income during the year were $126,000 of salary and $22,000 of long-term capital gains. Given Jeb's $5,000 loss from his rental home, how much of the loss can he deduct currently and what is his passive loss carryforward?

Answer: Jeb's rental loss deductible in the current year is $1,000, and his passive loss carryforward is $4,000. Because Jeb meets the definition of an "active participant" and has adjusted gross income of less than $150,000, before considering his rental loss, he may deduct a portion of the loss against his other income. His $1,000 deduction is computed as follows:

Description	Amount	Explanation
1. Maximum deduction available before phase-out	$25,000	
2. Phase-out of maximum deduction	24,000	[($148,000 − 100,000) × .5]
3. Maximum deduction in current year	$ 1,000	(1) − (2)
4. Rental loss in current year	5,000	
5. Rental loss deductible in current year	**1,000**	Lesser of (3) or (4)
Passive loss carryforward	$ 4,000	(4) − (3)

What if: Assume that Jeb's salary for the year had been $50,000 and he reported $22,000 from the sale of his stock. How much of his rental loss could he deduct currently?

Answer: Because Jeb's adjusted gross income would be only $72,000 under this scenario, he could deduct his entire $5,000 rental loss during the year.

Net Investment Income Tax on Net Passive Income

Earlier in this chapter we noted that taxpayers with modified AGI over certain thresholds are required to pay a 3.8 percent tax on their net investment income (in addition to the income tax). In calculating net investment income for this tax, taxpayers must include their net passive income.

---

[47]§469(b)(7) provides another important exception to the general rule that all real estate activities are passive. To overcome this presumption, taxpayers must spend more than half their time working in real estate trades or businesses and for more than 750 hours during the year. This exception benefits individuals who spend a substantial amount of time in activities like real estate development and construction.

Example 7-18

What if: Suppose Courtney has income from her salary of $170,000. Assume that in addition to this income, Courtney also owns 50 percent of an S corporation in which she does not materially partici-pate. The S corporation is profitable and generates $105,000 of flow-through income to her this year. Courtney paid $5,000 of state income taxes related to the S corporation income. Thus her net invest-ment income from the activity is $100,000. How much net investment income tax will Courtney owe?

Answer: $2,660, calculated as follows:

Description	Amount	Explanation
1. Net investment income	$100,000	Income from passive investment
2. Modified AGI	270,000	$170,000 salary + $100,000 S corporation income
3. Modified AGI threshold	200,000	
4. Excess modified AGI above threshold	70,000	(2) − (3)
5. Net investment income tax base	70,000	Lesser of (1) or (4)
Net investment income tax	**2,660**	(5) × 3.8%

What if: Assume that Courtney spends 525 hours participating in the activity during the year. How much net investment income tax will she owe?

Answer: $0. Because Courtney materially participates in the S corporation, the flow-through income is no longer passive income and she will not be subject to the net investment income tax.

CONCLUSION

Investors and their advisers face numerous tax rules that apply to investment income. Understanding these rules is important, not only to comply with the tax law, but also to make wise investment choices. Investments differ in terms of their potential for implement-ing the conversion and shifting tax planning strategies. Failing to consider these strategies when investing will lead to less than optimal results. By carefully weighing nontax invest-ment objectives along with the tax characteristics of different investment options, informed investors will be better equipped to select investments appropriate for them.

Summary

Explain how interest income and dividend income are taxed.   **LO 7-1**

- Investors seeking current income invest in interest-bearing securities or dividend-paying stocks.
- Interest income received from certificates of deposit, U.S. Treasury securities, corporate bonds, and other similar investments is typically taxed annually at ordinary rates.
- Accrued market discount on bonds and interest earned on U.S. savings bonds is taxed at sale or maturity, while original issue discount on bonds is taxed annually.
- Bond premiums increase the tax basis of bonds and affect the amount of capital gains or losses investors report.
- Taxpayers may elect to amortize bond premiums to reduce the amount of annual interest reported on bonds purchased at a premium.
- Dividend income, like interest income, is taxed when it is received. However, most dividend income currently is taxed at preferential capital gains rates.

Compute the tax consequences associated with the disposition of capital assets, including the netting process for calculating gains and losses.   **LO 7-2**

- When taxpayers sell stock, they may determine the basis of the stock using the specific identification method or the FIFO method.

- Capital assets held for more than one year generate long-term capital gains or losses on sale or disposition. Other capital assets generate short-term capital gains or losses on sale or disposition.
- Generally, net long-term capital gains in excess of net short-term losses are taxed at either a 0, 15, or 20 percent tax rate, depending on the taxpayers' income.
- Unrecaptured §1250 gain is taxed at a maximum 25 percent rate, and gains from collectibles and §1202 stock are taxed at a maximum 28 percent rate.
- Up to $3,000 of net capital losses are deductible against ordinary income for the year.
- A taxpayer's capital gains and losses for the year are reported on Form 8949 and Schedule D of Form 1040.
- Wash sale provisions prevent taxpayers from selling stock at a loss, deducting the loss, and replacing the stock sold with the same stock or substantially identical securities within 30 days either before or after the day of sale.
- Losses on the disposition of property held for personal use are not deductible.
- Because of the deferral of the capital gains tax, after-tax rates of return from capital assets will increase as an investor's investment horizon increases.

LO 7-3   Calculate the deduction for investment interest expense.

- Investment expenses are not deductible.
- Investment interest expense is deductible to the extent of net investment income.
- Because investment expenses are not deductible after 2017, net investment income is equivalent to gross investment income.
- Preferentially-taxed capital gains and qualified dividends are not included in investment income unless the taxpayer elects to tax them as ordinary income.

LO 7-4   Apply tax-basis, at-risk, and passive activity loss limits to losses from passive investments.

- A taxpayer's share of operating losses from passive flow-through entities and other trade or business activities are deductible to the extent they clear the tax-basis, at-risk, and passive activity loss hurdles.
- A taxpayer's ordinary losses from flow-through entities and other trade or business activities may be classified as passive if the taxpayer's involvement is not regular, continuous, and substantial.
- A taxpayer's operating losses from rental activities are, with limited exceptions, deemed to be passive regardless of the taxpayer's activity level.
- A taxpayer's passive losses from an activity are limited to passive income from all other sources until disposition of the activity. On disposition, current and prior passive losses from an activity can be used but may be subject to the excess business loss limitations.
- A rental real estate exception allows taxpayers to deduct up to $25,000 of operating losses from rental real estate annually provided they are actively involved in managing the rental real estate and have adjusted gross income of less than $150,000.

KEY TERMS

accrued market discount (7-4)
active participant in a rental activity (7-32)
amortization (7-3)
at-risk amount (7-28)
basis (7-4)
bonds (7-2)
bond discount (7-3)
bond premium (7-3)
C corporation (7-28)
capital asset (7-7)
certificate of deposit (CD) (7-2)
collectibles (7-10)

dividends (7-2)
ex-dividend date (7-6)
face value (7-2)
first-in, first-out (FIFO) method (7-9)
flow-through entities (7-28)
investment income (7-2)
investment interest expense (7-25)
long-term capital gains or losses (7-10)
market discount (7-4)
market premium (7-4)
maturity (7-4)
maturity value (7-2)

maximum 15 percent rate amount (7-10)
maximum zero rate amount (7-10)
mutual funds (7-2)
net capital gain (7-14)
net investment income (7-25)
net long-term capital gain (7-12)
net long-term capital loss (7-12)
net short-term capital gain (7-13)
net short-term capital loss (7-12)
operating income (7-2)
operating loss (7-2)
original issue discount (OID) (7-3)

passive activity loss (PAL) rules (7-29)	short-term capital gains or losses (7-10)	Treasury notes (7-3)
passive investments (7-2)	specific identification method (7-9)	unrecaptured §1250 gain (7-10)
portfolio investments (7-2)	tax basis (7-8)	U.S. savings bonds (7-3)
qualified dividends (7-6)	tax shelter (7-29)	wash sale (7-22)
qualified small business stock (7-10)	Treasury bonds (7-3)	zero-coupon bonds (7-3)

DISCUSSION QUESTIONS

Discussion Questions are available in Connect®.   Mc Graw Hill **connect**

1. Describe how interest income and dividend income are taxed. What are the similarities and differences in their tax treatment?   `LO 7-1`

2. What is the underlying policy rationale for the current tax rules applicable to interest income and dividend income?   `LO 7-1`

3. Compare and contrast the tax treatment of interest from a Treasury bond and qualified dividends from corporate stock.   `LO 7-1`

4. How are Treasury notes and Treasury bonds treated for federal and state income tax purposes?   `LO 7-1`

5. Why would taxpayers generally prefer the tax treatment of market discount to the treatment of original issue discount on corporate bonds?   `LO 7-1`

6. In what ways are U.S. savings bonds treated more favorably for tax purposes than corporate bonds?   `LO 7-1`

7. When should investors consider making an election to amortize the market discount on a bond into income annually? [*Hint:* See §1278(b).]   `LO 7-1` planning

8. Why might investors purchase interest-paying securities rather than dividend-paying stocks?   `LO 7-1`

9. Compare and contrast the tax treatment of dividend-paying stocks and growth stocks.   `LO 7-1`

10. What is the definition of a capital asset? Give three examples of capital assets.   `LO 7-2`

11. Why does the tax law allow a taxpayer to defer gains accrued on a capital asset until the taxpayer actually sells the asset?   `LO 7-2`

12. Why does the tax law provide preferential rates on certain capital gains?   `LO 7-2`

13. What is the deciding factor in determining whether a capital gain is a short-term or long-term capital gain?   `LO 7-2`

14. What methods may taxpayers use to determine the adjusted basis of stock they have sold?   `LO 7-2`

15. What tax rate applies to net short-term capital gains?   `LO 7-2`

16. What limitations are placed on the deductibility of capital losses for individual taxpayers?   `LO 7-2`

17. What happens to capital losses that are not deductible in the current year?   `LO 7-2`

18. Are all long-term capital gains taxable at the same maximum rate? If not, what rates may apply to long-term capital gains?   `LO 7-2`

19. This year, David, a taxpayer in the highest tax rate bracket, has the option to purchase either stock in a Fortune 500 company or qualified small business stock in his friend's corporation. All else being equal, which of the two will he prefer from a tax perspective if he intends to hold the stock for six years? Which would he prefer if he only plans to hold the stock for two years?   `LO 7-2` planning

20. What is a "wash sale"? What is the purpose of the wash sale tax rules?   `LO 7-2`

21. Nick does not use his car for business purposes. If he sells his car for less than he paid for it, does he get to deduct the loss for tax purposes? Why or why not?   `LO 7-2`

22. Describe three basic tax planning strategies available to taxpayers investing in capital assets.   `LO 7-2` planning

23. Clark owns stock in BCS Corporation that he purchased in January of the current year. The stock has appreciated significantly during the year. It is now December of the current year, and Clark is deciding whether or not he should sell the stock. What   `LO 7-2` planning

tax and nontax factors should Clark consider before making the decision on whether to sell the stock now?

LO 7-3 24. Are dividends and capital gains considered to be investment income for purposes of determining the amount of a taxpayer's deductible investment interest expense for the year?

LO 7-3 25. How is the amount of net investment income determined for a taxpayer?

LO 7-3 26. What limitations are placed on the deductibility of investment interest expense? What happens to investment interest expense that is not deductible because of the limitations?

LO 7-3 27. When taxpayers borrow money to buy municipal bonds, are they allowed to deduct interest expense on the loan? Why or why not?

LO 7-3 28. What types of losses may potentially be characterized as passive losses?

LO 7-4 29. What are the implications of treating losses as passive?

LO 7-4 30. Discuss the treatment of suspended passive losses upon the sale of a passive activity.

LO 7-4 31. What tests are applied to determine if losses should be characterized as passive?

LO 7-4 32. All else being equal, would a taxpayer with passive losses prefer to have wage income or passive income?

planning

PROBLEMS

Select problems are available in Connect®.

LO 7-1 33. Matt recently deposited $20,000 in a savings account paying a guaranteed interest rate of 4 percent for the next 10 years. If Matt expects his marginal tax rate to be 22 percent for the next 10 years, how much interest will he earn after-tax for the first year of his investment? How much interest will he earn after-tax for the second year of his investment if he withdraws enough cash every year to pay the tax on the interest he earns? How much will he have in the account after four years? How much will he have in the account after seven years?

LO 7-1 34. Dana intends to invest $30,000 in either a Treasury bond or a corporate bond. The Treasury bond yields 5 percent before tax and the corporate bond yields 6 percent before tax. Assuming Dana's federal marginal rate is 24 percent and her marginal state rate is 5 percent, which of the two options should she choose? If she were to move to another state where her marginal state rate would be 10 percent, would her choice be any different? Assume that Dana itemizes deductions.

LO 7-1 35. At the beginning of his current tax year, David invests $12,000 in original issue U.S. Treasury bonds with a $10,000 face value that mature in exactly 10 years. David receives $700 in interest ($350 every six months) from the Treasury bonds during the current year, and the yield to maturity on the bonds is 5 percent.

a) How much interest income will he report this year if he elects to amortize the bond premium?

b) How much interest will he report this year if he does not elect to amortize the bond premium?

LO 7-1 36. Seth invested $20,000 in Series EE savings bonds on April 1. By December 31, the published redemption value of the bonds had increased to $20,700. How much interest income will Seth report from the savings bonds in the current year absent any special election?

LO 7-1 37. At the beginning of her current tax year, Angela purchased a zero-coupon corporate bond at original issue for $30,000 with a yield to maturity of 6 percent. Given that she will not actually receive any interest payments until the bond matures in 10 years, how much interest income will she report this year assuming semiannual compounding of interest?

LO 7-1 38. At the beginning of his current tax year, Eric bought a corporate bond with a maturity value of $50,000 from the secondary market for $45,000. The bond has a stated annual interest rate of 5 percent payable on June 30 and December 31, and it matures in five years on December 31. Absent any special tax elections, how much interest income will Eric report from the bond this year and in the year the bond matures?

39. Hayley recently invested $50,000 in a public utility stock paying a 3 percent annual dividend. If Hayley reinvests the annual dividend she receives net of any taxes owed on the dividend, how much will her investment be worth in four years if the dividends paid are qualified dividends? (Hayley's marginal income tax rate is 32 percent.) What will her investment be worth in four years if the dividends are nonqualified?   LO 7-1

40. Five years ago, Kate purchased a dividend-paying stock for $10,000. For all five years, the stock paid an annual dividend of 4 percent before tax and Kate's marginal tax rate was 24 percent. Every year Kate reinvested her after-tax dividends in the same stock. For the first two years of her investment, the dividends qualified for the 15 percent capital gains rate; however, for the last three years the 15 percent dividend rate was repealed and dividends were taxed at ordinary rates.   LO 7-1   planning

    a) What is the current value (at the beginning of year 6) of Kate's investment assuming the stock has not appreciated in value?

    b) What will Kate's investment be worth three years from now (at the beginning of year 9) assuming her marginal tax rate increases to 35 percent for the next three years?

41. John bought 1,000 shares of Intel stock on October 18, 2014, for $30 per share plus a $750 commission he paid to his broker. On December 12, 2018, he sells the shares for $42.50 per share. He also incurs a $1,000 fee for this transaction.   LO 7-2

    a) What is John's adjusted basis in the 1,000 shares of Intel stock?

    b) What amount does John realize when he sells the 1,000 shares?

    c) What is the gain/loss for John on the sale of his Intel stock? What is the character of the gain/loss?

42. Dahlia is in the 32 percent tax rate bracket and has purchased the following shares of Microsoft common stock over the years: LO 7-2

Date Purchased	Shares	Basis
7/10/2008	400	$12,000
4/20/2009	300	10,750
1/29/2010	500	12,230
11/02/2012	250	7,300

    If Dahlia sells 800 shares of Microsoft for $40,000 on December 20, 2018, what is her capital gain or loss in each of the following assumptions?

    a) She uses the FIFO method.

    b) She uses the specific identification method and she wants to minimize her current year capital gain.

43. Karyn loaned $20,000 to her co-worker to begin a new business several years ago. If her co-worker declares bankruptcy on June 22 of the current year, is Karyn allowed to deduct the bad debt loss this year? If she can deduct the loss, what is the character of the loss?   LO 7-2   research

44. Sue has 5,000 shares of Sony stock that have an adjusted basis of $27,500. She sold the 5,000 shares of stock for cash of $10,000, and she also received a piece of land as part of the proceeds. The land was valued at $20,000 and had an adjusted basis to the buyer of $12,000. What is Sue's gain or loss on the sale of 5,000 shares of Sony stock?   LO 7-2

45. Matt and Meg Comer are married and file a joint tax return. They do not have any children. Matt works as a history professor at a local university and earns a salary of $64,000. Meg works part-time at the same university. She earns $31,000 a year. The couple does not itemize deductions. Other than salary, the Comers' only other source of income is from the disposition of various capital assets (mostly stocks).   LO 7-2

    a) What is the Comers' tax liability for 2018 if they report the following capital gains and losses for the year?

Short-term capital gains	$ 9,000
Short-term capital losses	(2,000)
Long-term capital gains	15,000
Long-term capital losses	(6,000)

b) What is the Comers' tax liability for 2018 if they report the following capital gains and losses for the year?

Short-term capital gains	$ 1,500
Short-term capital losses	0
Long-term capital gains	13,000
Long-term capital losses	(10,000)

LO 7-2 46. Grayson is in the 24 percent tax rate bracket and has sold the following stocks in 2018:

	Date Purchased	Basis	Date Sold	Amount Realized
Stock A	1/23/1994	$ 7,250	7/22/2018	$ 4,500
Stock B	4/10/2018	14,000	9/13/2018	17,500
Stock C	8/23/2016	10,750	10/12/2018	15,300
Stock D	5/19/2008	5,230	10/12/2018	12,400
Stock E	8/20/2018	7,300	11/14/2018	3,500

a) What is Grayson's net short-term capital gain or loss from these transactions?

b) What is Grayson's net long-term gain or loss from these transactions?

c) What is Grayson's overall net gain or loss from these transactions?

d) What amount of the gain, if any, is subject to the preferential rate for certain capital gains?

LO 7-2 47. George bought the following amounts of Stock A over the years:

	Date Purchased	Number of Shares	Adjusted Basis
Stock A	11/21/1992	1,000	$24,000
Stock A	3/18/1998	500	9,000
Stock A	5/22/2007	750	27,000

On October 12, 2018, he sold 1,200 of his shares of Stock A for $38 per share.

a) How much gain/loss will George have to recognize if he uses the FIFO method of accounting for the shares sold?

b) How much gain/loss will George have to recognize if he specifically identifies the shares to be sold by telling his broker to sell all 750 shares from the 5/22/2007 purchase and 450 shares from the 11/21/1992 purchase?

LO 7-2 48. During the current year, Ron and Anne sold the following assets:

Capital Asset	Market Value	Tax Basis	Holding Period
L stock	$ 50,000	$41,000	> 1 year
M stock	28,000	39,000	> 1 year
N stock	30,000	22,000	< 1 year
O stock	26,000	33,000	< 1 year
Antiques	7,000	4,000	> 1 year
Rental home	300,000*	90,000	> 1 year

*$30,000 of the gain is 25 percent gain (from accumulated depreciation on the property).

a) Given that Ron and Anne have taxable income of only $20,000 (all ordinary) before considering the tax effect of their asset sales, what is their gross tax liability for 2018 assuming they file a joint return?

b) Given that Ron and Anne have taxable income of $400,000 (all ordinary) before considering the tax effect of their asset sales, what is their gross tax liability for 2018 assuming they file a joint return?

LO 7-2 49. In 2018, Tom and Amanda Jackson (married filing jointly) have $200,000 of taxable income before considering the following events:

a) On May 12, 2018, they sold a painting (art) for $110,000 that was inherited from Grandma on July 23, 2016. The fair market value on the date of Grandma's death was $90,000 and Grandma's adjusted basis of the painting was $25,000.

b) They applied a long-term capital loss carryover from 2017 of $10,000.

c) They recognized a $12,000 loss on the 11/1/2018 sale of bonds (acquired on 5/12/2008).

d) They recognized a $4,000 gain on the 12/12/2018 sale of IBM stock (acquired on 2/5/2018).

e) They recognized a $17,000 gain on the 10/17/2018 sale of rental property (the only §1231 transaction) of which $8,000 is reportable as gain subject to the 25 percent maximum rate and the remaining $9,000 is subject to the 0/15/20 percent maximum rates (the property was acquired on 8/2/2012).

f) They recognized a $12,000 loss on the 12/20/2018 sale of bonds (acquired on 1/18/2018).

g) They recognized a $7,000 gain on the 6/27/2018 sale of BH stock (acquired on 7/30/2009).

h) They recognized an $11,000 loss on the 6/13/2018 sale of QuikCo stock (acquired on 3/20/2011).

i) They received $500 of qualified dividends on 7/15/2018.

Complete the required capital gains netting procedures and calculate the Jacksons' 2018 tax liability.

50. For 2018, Sherri has a short-term loss of $2,500 and a long-term loss of $4,750.   **LO 7-2**

a) How much loss can Sherri deduct in 2018?

b) How much loss will Sherri carry over to 2019, and what is the character of the loss carryover?

51. Three years ago, Adrian purchased 100 shares of stock in X Corp. for $10,000. On   **LO 7-2**
December 30 of year 4, Adrian sells the 100 shares for $6,000.

a) Assuming Adrian has no other capital gains or losses, how much of the loss is Adrian able to deduct on her year 4 tax return?

b) Assume the same facts as in part (a), except that on January 20 of year 5, Adrian purchases 100 shares of X Corp. stock for $6,000. How much loss from the sale on December 30 of year 4 is deductible on Adrian's year 4 tax return? What basis does Adrian take in the stock purchased on January 20 of year 5?

52. Christopher sold 100 shares of Cisco stock for $5,500 in the current year. He purchased   **LO 7-2**
the shares several years ago for $2,200. Assuming his ordinary income tax rate is 24 percent, and he has no other capital gains or losses, how much tax will he pay on this gain?

53. Christina, who is single, purchased 100 shares of Apple Inc. stock several years ago   **LO 7-2**
for $3,500. During her year-end tax planning, she decided to sell 50 shares of Apple for $1,500 on December 30. However, two weeks later, Apple introduced its latest iPhone, and she decided that she should buy the 50 shares (cost of $1,600) of Apple back before prices skyrocket.

a) What is Christina's deductible loss on the sale of 50 shares? What is her basis in the 50 new shares?

b) Assume the same facts, except that Christina repurchased only 25 shares for $800. What is Christina's deductible loss on the sale of 50 shares? What is her basis in the 25 new shares?

54. Arden purchased 300 shares of AMC common stock several years ago for $1,500.   **LO 7-2**
On April 30, Arden sold the shares of AMC common for $500 and then purchased 250 shares of AMC preferred stock two days later for $700. The AMC preferred stock is not convertible into AMC common stock. What is Arden's deductible loss from the sale of the 300 shares of AMC common stock?   **research**

55. Shaun bought 300 shares of Dental Equipment Inc. several years ago for $10,000.   **LO 7-2**
Currently the stock is worth $8,000. Shaun's marginal tax rate this year is 24 percent, and he has no other capital gains or losses. Shaun expects to have a marginal rate of 32 percent next year, but he also expects to have a long-term capital gain of $10,000. To minimize taxes, should Shaun sell the stock on December 31 of this year or January 1 of next year (ignore the time value of money)?   **planning**

LO 7-3

56. Mickey and Jenny Porter file a joint tax return, and they itemize deductions. The Porters incur $2,000 in investment expenses. They also incur $3,000 of investment interest expense during the year. The Porters' income for the year consists of $150,000 in salary and $2,500 of interest income.

a) What is the amount of the Porters' investment interest expense deduction for the year?

b) What would their investment interest expense deduction be if they also had a ($2,000) long-term capital loss?

LO 7-3
planning

57. On January 1 of year 1, Nick and Rachel Sutton purchased a parcel of undeveloped land as an investment. The purchase price of the land was $150,000. They paid for the property by making a down payment of $50,000 and borrowing $100,000 from the bank at an interest rate of 6 percent per year. At the end of the first year, the Suttons paid $6,000 of interest to the bank. During year 1, the Suttons' only source of income was salary. On December 31 of year 2, the Suttons paid $6,000 of interest to the bank and sold the land for $210,000. They used $100,000 of the sale proceeds to pay off the $100,000 loan. The Suttons itemize deductions and are subject to a marginal ordinary income tax rate of 32 percent.

a) Should the Suttons treat the capital gain from the land sale as investment income in year 2 in order to minimize their year 2 tax bill? If so, how much could the Suttons save?

b) How much does this cost or save them in year 2?

LO 7-3
research

58. George recently received a great stock tip from his friend, Mason. George didn't have any cash on hand to invest, so he decided to take out a $20,000 loan to facilitate the stock acquisition. The loan terms are 8 percent interest with interest-only payments due each year for five years. At the end of the five-year period the entire loan principal is due. When George closed on the loan on April 1, 2018, he decided to invest $16,000 in stock and to use the remaining $4,000 to purchase a four-wheel recreation vehicle. George is unsure how he will treat the interest paid on the $20,000 loan. In 2018, George paid $1,200 interest expense on the loan. For tax purposes, how should he treat the 2018 interest expense? (*Hint:* Visit www.irs.gov and consider IRS Publication 550.)

LO 7-4

59. Larry recently invested $20,000 (tax basis) in purchasing a limited partnership interest. His at-risk amount is also $20,000. In addition, Larry's share of the limited partnership loss for the year is $2,000, his share of income from a different limited partnership is $1,000, and he has $3,000 of dividend income from the stock he owns. How much of Larry's $2,000 loss from the limited partnership can he deduct in the current year?

LO 7-4

60. Rubio recently invested $20,000 (tax basis) in purchasing a limited partnership interest. His at-risk amount is $15,000. In addition, Rubio's share of the limited partnership loss for the year is $22,000, his share of income from a different limited partnership is $5,000, and he has $40,000 in wage income and $10,000 in long-term capital gains.

a) How much of Rubio's $22,000 loss is allowed considering only the tax-basis loss limitations?

b) How much of the loss from part (a) is allowed under the at-risk limitations?

c) How much of Rubio's $22,000 loss from the limited partnership can he deduct in the current year considering all limitations?

LO 7-4

61. Molly Grey (single) acquired a 30 percent limited partnership interest in Beau Geste LLP several years ago for $48,000. At the beginning of year 1, Molly has tax basis and an at-risk amount of $20,000. In year 1, Beau Geste incurs a loss of $180,000 and does not make any distributions to the partners.

• In year 1, Molly's AGI (excluding any income or loss from Beau Geste) is $60,000. This includes $10,000 of passive income from other passive activities.

• In year 2, Beau Geste earns income of $30,000. In addition, Molly contributes an additional $30,000 to Beau Geste during year 2. Molly's AGI in year 2 is $63,000 (excluding any income or loss from Beau Geste). This amount includes $8,000 in income from her other passive investments.

a) Based on the above information, determine the following amounts:

- At-risk amount at the end of year 1.
- At-risk amount at the end of year 2.
- Losses allowed under the at-risk rules in year 2.
- Total suspended passive losses at the end of year 1.
- Total suspended at-risk losses at the end of year 2.
- Deductible losses in year 1.
- Year 2 AGI after considering Beau Geste events.

b) Briefly describe actions Molly Grey could undertake in year 2 to utilize any suspended passive losses from year 1.

62. Anwer owns a rental home and is involved in maintaining it and approving renters. During the year he has a net loss of $8,000 from renting the home. His other sources of income during the year are a salary of $111,000 and $34,000 of long-term capital gains. How much of Anwer's $8,000 rental loss can he deduct currently if he has no sources of passive income?

LO 7-4

COMPREHENSIVE PROBLEM

Select problems are available in Connect®.

63. During 2018, your clients, Mr. and Mrs. Howell, owned the following investment assets:

tax forms

Investment Assets	Date Acquired	Purchase Price	Broker's Commission Paid at Time of Purchase
300 shares of IBM common	11/22/2015	$ 10,350	$ 100
200 shares of IBM common	4/3/2016	43,250	300
3,000 shares of Apple preferred	12/12/2016	147,000	1,300
2,100 shares of Cisco common	8/14/2017	52,500	550
420 shares of Vanguard mutual fund	3/2/2018	14,700	No-load fund*

*No commissions are charged when no-load mutual funds are bought and sold.

Because of the downturn in the stock market, Mr. and Mrs. Howell decided to sell most of their stocks and the mutual fund in 2018 and to reinvest in municipal bonds. The following investment assets were sold in 2018:

Investment Assets	Date Sold	Sale Price	Broker's Commission Paid at Time of Sale
300 shares of IBM common	5/6	$ 13,700	$ 100
3,000 shares of Apple preferred	10/5	221,400	2,000
2,100 shares of Cisco common	8/15	63,250	650
451 shares of Vanguard mutual fund	12/21	15,700	No-load fund*

*No commissions are charged when no-load mutual funds are bought and sold.

The Howells' broker issued them a Form 1099-B showing the sales proceeds net of the commissions paid. For example, the IBM sales proceeds were reported as $13,600 on the Form 1099-B they received.

In addition to the sales reflected in the table above, the Howells provided you with the following additional information concerning 2018:

- The Howells received a Form 1099-B from the Vanguard mutual fund reporting a $900 long-term capital gain distribution. This distribution was reinvested in 31 additional Vanguard mutual fund shares on 6/30/2018.

- In 2013, Mrs. Howell loaned $6,000 to a friend who was starting a new multilevel marketing company called LD3. The friend declared bankruptcy in 2018, and Mrs. Howell has been notified she will not be receiving any repayment of the loan.
- The Howells have a $2,300 short-term capital loss carryover and a $4,800 long-term capital loss carryover from prior years.
- The Howells did not instruct their broker to sell any particular lot of IBM stock.
- The Howells earned $3,000 in municipal bond interest, $3,000 in interest from corporate bonds, and $4,000 in qualified dividends.
- Assume the Howells have $130,000 of wage income during the year.

a) Go to the IRS website (www.irs.gov) and download the most current version of Form 8949 and Schedule D. Use Form 8949 and page 1 of Schedule D to compute net long-term and short-term capital gains. Then, compute the Howells' tax liability for the year (ignoring the alternative minimum tax and any phase-out provisions) assuming they file a joint return, they have no dependents, they don't make any special tax elections, and their itemized deductions total $25,000. Assume that asset bases are reported to the IRS.

b) Are there any tax planning recommendations related to the stock sales that you should have shared with the Howells before their decision to sell?

c) Assume the Howells' short-term capital loss carryover from prior years is $82,300 rather than $2,300 as indicated above. If this is the case, how much short-term and long-term capital loss carryover remains to be carried beyond 2018 to future tax years?

R ROGER | CPA Review

Sample CPA Exam questions from Roger CPA Review are available in Connect as support for the topics in this text. These Multiple Choice Questions and Task-Based Simulations include expert-written explanations and solutions and provide a starting point for students to become familiar with the content and functionality of the actual CPA Exam.

Individual Income Tax Computation and Tax Credits

Upon completing this chapter, you should be able to:

LO 8-1 Determine a taxpayer's regular tax liability.

LO 8-2 Compute a taxpayer's alternative minimum tax liability.

LO 8-3 Calculate a taxpayer's employment and self-employment taxes payable.

LO 8-4 Compute a taxpayer's allowable child tax credit, child and dependent care credit, American opportunity credit, lifetime learning credit, and earned income credit.

LO 8-5 Explain how to compute a taxpayer's underpayment, late filing, and late payment penalties.

©Image Source

Storyline Summary

Taxpayers:	Courtney Wilson, age 40, and Courtney's mother Dorothy "Gram" Weiss, age 70
Family description:	Courtney is divorced with a son, Deron, age 10, and a daughter, Ellen, age 20. Gram is currently residing with Courtney.
Location:	Kansas City, Missouri
Employment status:	Courtney works as an architect for EWD. Gram is retired.
Filing status:	Courtney is head of household. Gram is single.
Current situation:	Courtney and Gram have computed their taxable income. Now they are trying to determine their tax liability, tax refund, or additional taxes due and whether they owe any payment-related penalties.

Courtney has already determined her taxable income. Now she's working on computing her tax liability. She knows she owes a significant amount of regular income tax on her employment and business activities. However, she's not sure how to compute the tax on the qualified dividends she received from General Electric and is worried that she may be subject to the alternative minimum tax this year. Finally, Courtney knows she owes some self-employment taxes on her business income. Courtney would like to determine whether she is eligible to claim any tax credits, such as the child tax credit for her two children and education credits, because she paid for a portion of her daughter Ellen's tuition at the University of Missouri–Kansas City this year. Courtney is hoping that she has paid enough in taxes during the year to avoid underpayment penalties.

She's planning on filing her tax return and paying her taxes on time.

Gram's tax situation is much more straightforward. She needs to determine the regular income tax on her taxable income. Her income is so low she knows she need not worry about the alternative minimum tax, and she believes she doesn't owe any self-employment tax. Gram didn't prepay any taxes this year, so she is concerned that she might be required to pay an underpayment penalty. She also expects to file her tax return and pay her taxes by the looming due date.

to be continued . . .

In earlier chapters we've learned how to compute taxable income for taxpayers such as Courtney and Gram. This chapter describes how to determine a taxpayer's tax liability for the year. We discover that the process is not as easy as simply applying taxable income to the applicable tax rate schedule or tax table. Taxpayers may generate taxable income that is taxed at rates not provided in the tax rate schedules or tax tables. We will learn that they may also be required to pay taxes in addition to the regular income tax. We also describe tax credits taxpayers may use to reduce their gross taxes payable. We conclude the chapter by describing taxpayer filing requirements and identifying certain penalties taxpayers may be required to pay when they underpay or are late paying their taxes. We start our coverage by explaining how to compute one's regular tax liability.

LO 8-1 REGULAR FEDERAL INCOME TAX COMPUTATION

Once taxpayers have determined their taxable income, they are ready to compute their gross tax from a series of progressive tax rates called a **tax rate schedule.**

Tax Rate Schedules

Congress has constructed four different tax rate schedules for individuals. The applicable tax rate schedule is determined by the taxpayer's filing status, which we discussed in depth in the Individual Income Tax Overview, Dependents, and Filing Status chapter. Recall that a taxpayer's filing status is one of the following:

1. Married filing jointly.
2. Qualifying widow or widower, also referred to as surviving spouse.
3. Married filing separately.
4. Head of household.
5. Single.

As we described in the Introduction to Tax chapter, a tax rate schedule is composed of several ranges of income taxed at different (increasing) rates. Each separate range of income subject to a different tax rate is referred to as a **tax bracket.** While each filing status has its own tax rate schedule (married filing jointly and qualifying widow or widower use the same rate schedule), all tax rate schedules consist of tax brackets taxed at 10 percent, 12 percent, 22 percent, 24 percent, 32 percent, 35 percent, and 37 percent. However, the width or range of income within each bracket varies by filing status. In general, the tax brackets are widest and higher levels of income are taxed at the lowest rates for the married filing jointly filing status, followed by the head of household filing status, single filing status, and finally, the married filing separately filing status.

The tax rate schedule for each filing status is provided in Appendix D. Notice that the married filing separately schedule is the same as the married filing jointly schedule except that the taxable income levels listed in the schedule are exactly one-half the taxable income levels for married filing jointly.

Example 8-1

As we determined in the Individual Deductions chapter, Courtney files under the head of household filing status and her 2018 taxable income is $145,070 (see Exhibit 6-11).

What if: For now, let's *assume* that all of Courtney's income is taxed as ordinary income. That is, assume that none of her income is taxed at a preferential rate (some is, but we'll address this in a bit). What is the tax on her taxable income?

Answer: $27,715. Using the head of household tax rate schedule, her taxable income falls in the 24 percent marginal tax rate bracket, in between $82,500 and $157,500, so her tax is computed as follows:

Description	Amount	Explanation
(1) Base tax	$ 12,698	From head of household tax rate schedule for taxpayer with taxable income in 24% bracket.
(2) Income taxed at marginal tax rate	62,570	$145,070 − $82,500 from head of household tax rate schedule.
(3) Marginal tax rate	24%	From head of household tax rate schedule.
(4) Tax on income at marginal tax rate	15,017	(2) × (3)
Tax on taxable income	**$27,715**	(1) + (4), rounded

Example 8-2

As we determined in the Individual Deductions chapter, Gram files under the single filing status. In the Individual Deductions chapter we calculated her 2018 taxable income to be $1,990 (see Exhibit 6-13). None of her income is taxed at a preferential rate. What is the tax on her taxable income using the tax rate schedules?

Answer: $199 ($1,990 × 10%)

For administrative convenience and to prevent low- and middle-income taxpayers from making mathematical errors using a tax rate schedule, the IRS provides **tax tables** that present the gross tax for various amounts of taxable income under $100,000 and filing status (it's impractical to provide a table for essentially unlimited amounts of income). Taxpayers with taxable income less than $100,000 generally must use the tax tables to determine their tax liability.[1]

Because the tax tables generate nearly the same tax as calculated from the tax rate schedule, we use the tax rate schedules throughout this chapter.

Marriage Penalty or Benefit

An interesting artifact of the tax rate schedules is that they can impose what some refer to as a **marriage penalty,** but they may actually produce a **marriage benefit.** A marriage penalty (benefit) occurs when, for a given level of income, a married couple incurs a greater (lesser) tax liability by using the married filing jointly tax rate schedule to determine the tax on their joint income than they would have owed (in total) if each spouse had used the single tax rate schedule to compute the tax on their individual incomes. Exhibit 8-1 explores the marriage penalty in a scenario in which both spouses earn income and another in which only one spouse earns income. As the exhibit illustrates, the marriage penalty applies to couples with two wage earners with high incomes, but a marriage benefit applies to couples with single breadwinners. For couples with two wage earners with moderate to low incomes, there is typically not a marriage penalty.

Exceptions to the Basic Tax Computation

In certain circumstances, taxpayers cannot completely determine their final tax liability from their tax rate schedule or tax table. Taxpayers must perform additional computations to determine their tax liability (1) when they recognize long-term capital gains or receive dividends that are taxed at preferential (lower) rates, (2) when they receive investment income subject to the net investment income tax, or (3) when the taxpayer is a child and the child's unearned income is taxed using the trusts and estates tax rates. We describe these additional computations in detail below.

[1]Exceptions to this requirement include taxpayers subject to the kiddie tax, with qualified dividends or capital gains, or claiming the foreign-earned income exclusion. You may view the tax tables in the instructions for Form 1040 located at www.irs.gov/.

EXHIBIT 8-1   **2018 Marriage Penalty (Benefit): Two-Income vs. Single-Income Married Couple***

Married Couple	Taxable Income	Tax If Filing Jointly (1)	Tax If Filing Single† (2)	Marriage Penalty (Benefit) (1) − (2)
Scenario 1: *Two wage earners*				
Wife	$350,000		$ 98,189.50	
Husband	350,000		$ 98,189.50	
Combined	$700,000	$198,379	$196,379	$2,000
Scenario 2: *One wage earner*				
Wife	$700,000		$224,689.50	
Husband	0		0	
Combined	$700,000	$198,379	$224,689.50	$(26,310.50)

*This analysis assumes the taxpayers do not owe any alternative minimum tax (discussed below).
†Married couples do not actually have the option of filing as single. If they choose not to file jointly they must file as married filing separately.

Preferential Tax Rates for Capital Gains and Dividends   As we described in detail in the Investments chapter, certain capital gains and certain dividends are taxed at a lower or **preferential tax rate** relative to other types of income. In general, the preferential tax rate is 0 percent, 15 percent, or 20 percent.[2] The preferential tax rates vary with the taxpayer's taxable income. See Appendix D for the tax brackets by filing status that apply to preferentially taxed capital gains and dividends. Taxpayers with income subject to the preferential rate (long-term capital gains and qualified dividends) can use the following three-step process to determine their tax liability.

Step 1: Split taxable income into the portion that is subject to the preferential rate and the portion taxed at the ordinary rates.

Step 2: Compute the tax separately on each type of income. Note that the income that is not taxed at the preferential rate is taxed at the ordinary tax rates using the tax rate schedule for the taxpayer's filing status.

Step 3: Add the tax on the income subject to the preferential tax rates and the tax on the income subject to the ordinary rates. This is the taxpayer's regular tax liability.

Example 8-3

Courtney's taxable income of $145,070 includes $700 of qualified dividends from GE (Example 5-8). What is her tax liability on her taxable income?

Answer: $27,652, computed at head of household rates as follows:

Description	Amount	Explanation
(1) Taxable income	$145,070	Exhibit 6-11
(2) Preferentially taxed income	700	Exhibit 5-4
(3) Income taxed at ordinary rates	$144,370	(1) − (2)

[2]As we discovered in the Investments chapter, some types of income may be taxed at a preferential rate of 28 percent or 25 percent. In addition, as we discuss later in this chapter, dividends and capital gains for higher income taxpayers are subject to the 3.8 percent net investment income tax.

Description	Amount	Explanation
(4) Tax on income taxed at ordinary rates	$ 27,546.80	[$12,698 + ($144,370 − $82,500) × 24%]
(5) Tax on preferentially taxed income	105	(2) × 15% [Preferential tax rate for taxpayer filing head of household with income between $51,701 and $452,400]
Tax on taxable income	**$27,652**	(4) + (5), rounded

In this example, what is Courtney's tax savings from having the dividends taxed at the preferential rate rather than the ordinary rate?

Answer: $63. $700 × (24% − 15%). This is the amount of the dividend times the difference in the ordinary and preferential tax rates.

What if: Assume that Courtney's taxable income is $462,400, including $15,000 of qualified dividends taxed at the preferential rate. What would be Courtney's tax liability under these circumstances?

Answer: $133,638, computed using the head of household tax rate schedule as follows:

Description	Amount	Explanation
(1) Taxable income	$ 462,400	
(2) Preferentially taxed income	15,000	
(3) Income taxed at ordinary rates	447,400	(1) − (2)
(4) Tax on income at ordinary tax rates	$ 130,888	$44,298 + [($447,400 − $200,000) × 35%] (See tax rate schedule for head of household.)
(5) Tax on preferentially taxed income	2,750	[($5,000 × 15%) + ($10,000 × 20%)]*
Tax	**$133,638**	(4) + (5)

*Courtney had $15,000 of preferentially taxed income. $10,000 of her dividends fall in the 20 percent preferential tax bracket ($462,400 taxable income − $452,400 end of 20 percent preferential tax bracket; see preferential tax rate schedule for head of household). The remaining $5,000 is taxed at 15 percent (15 percent bracket for preferentially taxed income extends from $51,701 to $452,400 for head of household)

Net Investment Income Tax   Higher-income taxpayers are required to pay a 3.8 percent tax on net investment income. For purposes of the **net investment income tax,** net investment income equals the sum of:

1. Gross income from interest, dividends, annuities, royalties, and rents (unless these items are derived in a trade or business to which the net investment income tax does not apply).
2. Income from a trade or business that is a passive activity or a trade or business of trading financial instruments or commodities.
3. Net gain from disposing of property (other than property held in a trade or business in which the net investment income tax does not apply).[3]
4. Less the allowable deductions that are allocable to items 1, 2, and 3.

Tax-exempt interest, veterans' benefits, excluded gain from the sale of a principal residence, distributions from qualified retirement plans, and any amounts subject to self-employment tax are not subject to the net investment income tax.

The tax imposed is 3.8 percent of the lesser of (1) net investment income or (2) the excess of modified adjusted gross income over $250,000 for married joint filers and surviving spouses, $125,000 for married separate filers, and $200,000 for other taxpayers.

---

[3]However, the income, gain, or loss attributable to invested working capital of a trade or business is subject to the net investment income tax. §1411(c)(3).

Modified adjusted gross income equals adjusted gross income increased by income excluded under the foreign-earned income exclusion less any disallowed deductions associated with the foreign-earned income exclusion.[4]

Example 8-4

Courtney's AGI (and modified AGI) is $187,000, and her investment income consists of $321 of taxable interest, $700 of dividends, and $5,000 of rental income. How much net investment income tax will Courtney owe?

Answer: $0. Because Courtney's modified AGI ($187,000) is less than the $200,000 threshold for the net investment income tax for a taxpayer filing as head of household, she will not be subject to the tax.

What if: Assume that Courtney's AGI (and modified AGI) is $225,000. How much net investment income tax will Courtney owe?

Answer: $229, calculated as follows:

Description	Amount	Explanation
(1) Net investment income	$ 6,021	$321 interest + $700 dividends + $5,000 rental income
(2) Modified AGI	225,000	
(3) Modified AGI threshold	200,000	
(4) Excess modified AGI above threshold	25,000	(2) − (3)
(5) Net investment income tax base	6,021	Lesser of (1) or (4)
Net investment income tax	**$ 229**	(5) × 3.8%

Kiddie Tax   Parents can reduce their family's income tax bill by shifting income that would otherwise be taxed at their higher tax rates to their children whose income is taxed at lower rates. However, as we described in the Gross Income and Exclusions chapter, under the assignment of income doctrine, taxpayers cannot simply assign or transfer income to other parties. Earned income, or income from services or labor, is taxed to the person who earns it. Thus, it's difficult for a parent to shift *earned* income to a child. However, unearned income or income from property such as dividends from stocks or interest from bonds is taxed to the *owner* of the property. Thus, a parent can shift unearned income to a child by transferring actual ownership of the income-producing property to the child. By transferring ownership, the parent runs the risk that the child will sell the asset or use it in a way unintended by the parent. However, this risk is relatively small for parents transferring property ownership to younger children.

The tax laws reduce parents' ability to shift unearned income to children through the so-called **kiddie tax.** The kiddie tax provisions apply (or potentially apply) to a child if (1) the child is under 18 years old at year-end, (2) the child is 18 at year-end but her earned income does *not* exceed half of her support, or (3) the child is over age 18 but under age 24 at year-end and is a full-time student during the year, and her earned income does not exceed half of her support (excluding scholarships).[5] The kiddie tax does not apply to a married child filing a joint tax return or to a child without living parents. In general terms, if the kiddie tax applies, children must pay tax on a

---

[4]Taxpayers compute the net investment income tax using Form 8960.

[5]§1(g)(2)(A).

certain amount of their **net unearned income** (discussed below) at tax rates that apply to trusts and estates (see Appendix D) rather than at their own marginal tax rate.[6]

The kiddie tax base is the child's net unearned income. Net unearned income is the *lesser* of (1) the child's gross *unearned income* minus $2,100[7] or (2) the child's taxable income (the child is not taxed on more than her taxable income).[8] Consequently, the kiddie tax does not apply unless the child has *unearned* income in *excess* of $2,100. Thus the kiddie tax limits, but does not eliminate, the tax benefit gained by a family unit when parents transfer income-producing assets to children.

Example 8-5

What if: Suppose that during 2018, Deron received $5,100 in interest from the IBM bond, and he received another $2,200 in interest income from a money market account that his parents have been contributing to over the years. Is Deron potentially subject to the kiddie tax?

Answer: Yes, Deron is younger than 18 years old at the end of the year and his net unearned income exceeds $2,100.

What is Deron's taxable income and corresponding tax liability?

Answer: $6,250 taxable income and $996 tax liability, calculated as follows:

Description	Amount	Explanation
(1) Gross income/AGI	$ 7,300	$5,100 interest from IBM bond + $2,200 interest. All unearned income.
(2) Standard deduction	1,050	Minimum for taxpayer claimed as a dependent on another return (no earned income, so must use minimum). See the Individual Deductions chapter.
(3) Taxable income	**$6,250**	(1) − (2)
(4) Gross unearned income minus $2,100	5,200	(1) − 2,100
(5) Net unearned income	$ 5,200	Lesser of (3) or (4)
(6) Kiddie tax	$ 891	[[$255 + ([((5) − $2,550) × 24%])]], see trust and estate tax rate schedule in Appendix D.
(7) Taxable income taxed at Deron's rate	1,050	(3) − (5)
(8) Tax on taxable income using Deron's tax rates	$ 105	(7) × 10% (See single filing status, $1,050 taxable income.)
Deron's total tax liability	**$ 996**	(6) + (8)

(continued on page 8-8)

---

[6]§1(g). Both the ordinary tax rates and preferential tax rates for trusts and estates apply to taxpayers subject to the kiddie tax. Consequently, for preferentially taxed capital gains and dividends, the 0 percent rate applies to taxable income between $0 and $2,600, the 15 percent rate applies to taxable income between $2,601 and $12,700, and the 20 percent rate applies to taxable income over $12,700.

[7]The $2,100 consists of $1,050 of the child's standard deduction (even if the child is entitled to a larger standard deduction) plus an extra $1,050. See the Individual Deductions chapter for a discussion of the standard deduction for the dependent of another taxpayer. If the child itemizes deductions, then the calculation becomes more complex and is beyond the scope of this text.

[8]§1(g)(4).

> **What if:** Assume Deron's only source of income is qualified dividends of $5,200 (unearned income). What is his taxable income and tax liability?
>
> **Answer:** Taxable income is $4,150; tax liability is $75, computed as follows:
>
> | Description | Amount | Explanation |
> |---|---|---|
> | (1) Gross income/(AGI) | $ 5,200 | Qualified dividends, all unearned income. |
> | (2) Minimum standard | 1,050 | Minimum for taxpayer claimed as a dependent deduction on another return (all unearned income, so must use minimum). See the Individual Deductions chapter. |
> | **(3) Taxable income** | **$4,150** | (1) − (2) |
> | (4) Gross unearned income minus $2,100 | 3,100 | (1) − $2,100 |
> | (5) Net unearned income | $ 3,100 | Lesser of (3) or (4) |
> | (6) Kiddie tax | $ 75 | [($2,600 × 0%) + ((5) − $2,600) × 15%)], see trust and estate tax rate schedule for preferentially taxed dividends. |
> | (7) Taxable income taxed at Deron's rate | 1,050 | (3) − (5) |
> | (8) Tax on taxable income using Deron's tax rates | $ 0 | (8) × 0%, see single tax rate schedule for preferentially taxed dividends. |
> | **Deron's total tax liability** | **$ 75** | (6) + (8) |

As we've just described, all individual taxpayers must pay federal income taxes on their federal taxable income. However, taxpayers may be liable for other federal taxes in addition to the regular tax liability. Many taxpayers are also required to pay the alternative minimum tax, and some working taxpayers are required to pay employment or self-employment taxes. We delve into these additional taxes below.

LO 8-2 ALTERNATIVE MINIMUM TAX

Each year, a number of taxpayers are required to pay the **alternative minimum tax (AMT)** in addition to their regular tax liability. The **alternative minimum tax system** was implemented in 1986 (earlier variations date back to the late 1960s) to ensure that taxpayers generating income pay some *minimum* amount of income tax each year. After several years in which a large number of taxpayers were subject to AMT, 2017 tax law changes were designed to reduce the number of taxpayers subject to AMT. The tax is targeted at higher-income taxpayers who are benefiting from or are perceived by the public to be benefiting from the excessive use (more than Congress intended) of tax preference items such as exclusions, deferrals, and deductions to reduce or even eliminate their tax liabilities.

In general terms, the alternative minimum tax is a tax on an *alternative* tax base meant to more closely reflect economic income than the regular income tax base. Thus the **alternative minimum tax (AMT) base** is more inclusive (or more broadly defined) than is the regular income tax base. To compute their AMT, taxpayers first compute their regular income tax liability. Then they compute the AMT base and multiply the base by the applicable alternative tax rate.[9] They must pay the AMT only when the tax on the AMT base exceeds their regular tax liability.

---

[9]The rate of the alternative minimum tax (AMT) is set below that of the income tax with the objective of avoiding the perception that the AMT is an additional assessment.

Alternative Minimum Tax Formula

Regular taxable income is the starting point for determining the alternative minimum tax. As the AMT formula in Exhibit 8-2 illustrates, taxpayers make several "plus" and "minus" adjustments to regular taxable income to compute alternative minimum taxable income (AMTI). They then arrive at the AMT base by subtracting an AMT exemption from AMTI. Taxpayers multiply the AMT base by the AMT rate to determine their **tentative minimum tax.** Finally, to determine their alternative minimum tax, taxpayers subtract their regular tax liability from the tentative minimum tax. The alternative minimum tax is the *excess* of the tentative minimum tax over the regular tax. If the regular tax liability equals or exceeds the tentative minimum tax, taxpayers need not pay any AMT. Individual taxpayers compute their AMT on Form 6251 (see Exhibit 8-4).

Alternative Minimum Taxable Income (AMTI)   In order to compute alternative minimum taxable income (AMTI), taxpayers make several **alternative minimum tax adjustments** to regular taxable income. Many of these are plus adjustments that are added to regular taxable income to reach AMTI and some are minus adjustments that are subtracted from regular taxable income to determine AMTI. Consequently, these adjustments tend to expand the regular income tax base to more closely reflect economic income.

EXHIBIT 8-2   **Formula for Computing the Alternative Minimum Tax**

	Regular Taxable Income
Plus:	Standard deduction if taxpayer deducted the standard deduction in computing regular taxable income
Plus or *Minus:*	Other adjustments*
	Alternative minimum taxable income
Minus:	AMT exemption amount (if any)
Equals:	Tax base for AMT
Times:	AMT rate
Equals:	Tentative minimum tax
Minus:	Regular tax
Equals:	Alternative minimum tax

*Technically, some of these adjustments are referred to as preference items and some are referred to as adjustments. We refer to all of these items as *adjustments* for simplicity's sake.

Adjustments.   Taxpayers first add back to regular taxable income the standard deduction amount, but only if they deducted it in determining taxable income. Taxpayers add back the standard deduction because it is a deduction that does not reflect an actual economic outflow from the taxpayer.[10] Taxpayers are then required to make several adjustments to compute AMTI. Exhibit 8-3 describes the most common of these adjustments, and Exhibit 8-4 presents Form 6251, which taxpayers use to calculate the AMT. Because 2018 forms were not available at press time, we present the 2017 form as an example of the form.

The major itemized deductions that are deductible for both regular tax and AMT purposes using the *same limitations* are:

- Charitable contributions.
- Home mortgage interest expenses.
- Gambling losses.

Some deductions are deductible for regular tax and AMT purposes but have different limitations. For example, interest income that is tax exempt for regular tax purposes but included in the AMT base is included in investment income for determining the AMT investment interest expense deduction.

---

[10]The standard deduction is accomplished on Form 6251 by beginning with taxable income before the standard deduction if the taxpayer does not itemize.

EXHIBIT 8-3 Common AMT Adjustments

Adjustment	Description
Plus adjustments: Tax-exempt interest from private activity bonds	Taxpayers must add back interest income that was excluded for regular tax purposes if the bonds were used to fund private activities (privately owned baseball stadium or private business subsidies) and not for the public good (build or repair public roads). However, taxpayers do not add back interest income from private activity bonds if the bonds were issued in either 2009 or 2010. Taxpayers do not personally make the determination of whether a bond is a private activity bond. Instead, interest from private activity bonds is denoted as such on Form 1099 that taxpayers receive.
Real property and personal property taxes deducted as itemized deductions	Deductible for regular tax purposes (subject to $10,000 limitation for itemized tax deduction), but not for AMT purposes.
State income or sales taxes	Deductible for regular tax purposes (subject to $10,000 limitation for itemized tax deduction), but not for AMT purposes.
Plus or Minus adjustment: Depreciation	Taxpayers must compute their depreciation expense for AMT purposes. For certain types of assets, the regular tax method is more accelerated than the AMT method. In any event, if the regular tax depreciation exceeds the AMT depreciation, this is a plus adjustment. If the AMT depreciation exceeds the regular tax depreciation, this is a minus adjustment.
Minus adjustments: State income tax refunds included in regular taxable income	Because state income taxes paid are not deductible for AMT purposes, refunds are not taxable (they do not increase the AMT base).
Gain or loss on sale of depreciable assets	Due to differences in regular tax and AMT depreciation methods, taxpayers may have a different adjusted basis (cost minus accumulated depreciation) for regular tax and for AMT purposes. Thus, they may have a different gain or loss for regular tax purposes than they do for AMT purposes. If regular tax gain exceeds AMT gain, this is a minus adjustment. Because AMT accumulated depreciation will never exceed regular tax accumulated depreciation, this would never be a plus adjustment.

Example 8-6

Courtney continued to work on her AMT computation by determining the other adjustments she needs to make to determine her alternative minimum taxable income (AMTI). What is Courtney's AMTI?

Answer: $155,150, computed as follows:

Description	Amount	Explanation
(1) Taxable income	$ 145,070	Exhibit 6-11
Plus adjustments:		
(2) Tax-exempt interest on Cincinnati bond used to pay for renovations to major league baseball stadium (Private activity bond: issued in 2005)	500	Example 5-22
(3) Itemized deduction for taxes	10,000	Example 6-13
Minus adjustments:		
(4) State income tax refund	(420)	Example 5-3
Alternative minimum taxable income	**$155,150**	Sum of (1) through (4)

EXHIBIT 8-4   2017 Form 6251 (Page 1 of 2)

Form **6251**

Department of the Treasury
Internal Revenue Service (99)

Alternative Minimum Tax—Individuals

▶ Go to *www.irs.gov/Form6251* for instructions and the latest information.
▶ **Attach to Form 1040 or Form 1040NR.**

OMB No. 1545-0074

2017

Attachment
Sequence No. **32**

Name(s) shown on Form 1040 or Form 1040NR

Your social security number

Part I   Alternative Minimum Taxable Income (See instructions for how to complete each line.)

1	If filing Schedule A (Form 1040), enter the amount from Form 1040, line 41, and go to line 2. Otherwise, enter the amount from Form 1040, line 38, and go to line 7. (If less than zero, enter as a negative amount.)	1	
2	Reserved for future use	2	
3	Taxes from Schedule A (Form 1040), line 9	3	
4	Enter the home mortgage interest adjustment, if any, from line 6 of the worksheet in the instructions for this line	4	
5	Miscellaneous deductions from Schedule A (Form 1040), line 27.	5	
6	If Form 1040, line 38, is $156,900 or less, enter -0-. Otherwise, see instructions	6	( )
7	Tax refund from Form 1040, line 10 or line 21	7	( )
8	Investment interest expense (difference between regular tax and AMT).	8	
9	Depletion (difference between regular tax and AMT)	9	
10	Net operating loss deduction from Form 1040, line 21. Enter as a positive amount	10	
11	Alternative tax net operating loss deduction	11	( )
12	Interest from specified private activity bonds exempt from the regular tax	12	
13	Qualified small business stock, see instructions	13	
14	Exercise of incentive stock options (excess of AMT income over regular tax income)	14	
15	Estates and trusts (amount from Schedule K-1 (Form 1041), box 12, code A)	15	
16	Electing large partnerships (amount from Schedule K-1 (Form 1065-B), box 6)	16	
17	Disposition of property (difference between AMT and regular tax gain or loss)	17	
18	Depreciation on assets placed in service after 1986 (difference between regular tax and AMT)	18	
19	Passive activities (difference between AMT and regular tax income or loss)	19	
20	Loss limitations (difference between AMT and regular tax income or loss)	20	
21	Circulation costs (difference between regular tax and AMT)	21	
22	Long-term contracts (difference between AMT and regular tax income)	22	
23	Mining costs (difference between regular tax and AMT)	23	
24	Research and experimental costs (difference between regular tax and AMT)	24	
25	Income from certain installment sales before January 1, 1987	25	( )
26	Intangible drilling costs preference	26	
27	Other adjustments, including income-based related adjustments	27	
28	**Alternative minimum taxable income.** Combine lines 1 through 27. (If married filing separately and line 28 is more than $249,450, see instructions.)	28	

Part II   Alternative Minimum Tax (AMT)

29	Exemption. (If you were under age 24 at the end of 2017, see instructions.)		

IF your filing status is . . .	AND line 28 is not over . . .	THEN enter on line 29 . . .	
Single or head of household	$120,700	$54,300	
Married filing jointly or qualifying widow(er)	160,900	84,500	
Married filing separately	80,450	42,250	

} 29

If line 28 is **over** the amount shown above for your filing status, see instructions.

30	Subtract line 29 from line 28. If more than zero, go to line 31. If zero or less, enter -0- here and on lines 31, 33, and 35, and go to line 34	30	
31	• If you are filing Form 2555 or 2555-EZ, see instructions for the amount to enter. • If you reported capital gain distributions directly on Form 1040, line 13; you reported qualified dividends on Form 1040, line 9b; **or** you had a gain on both lines 15 and 16 of Schedule D (Form 1040) (as refigured for the AMT, if necessary), complete Part III on the back and enter the amount from line 64 here. • **All others:** If line 30 is $187,800 or less ($93,900 or less if married filing separately), multiply line 30 by 26% (0.26). Otherwise, multiply line 30 by 28% (0.28) and subtract $3,756 ($1,878 if married filing separately) from the result.	31	
32	Alternative minimum tax foreign tax credit (see instructions)	32	
33	Tentative minimum tax. Subtract line 32 from line 31	33	
34	Add Form 1040, line 44 (minus any tax from Form 4972), and Form 1040, line 46. Subtract from the result any foreign tax credit from Form 1040, line 48. If you used Schedule J to figure your tax on Form 1040, line 44, refigure that tax without using Schedule J before completing this line (see instructions)	34	
35	**AMT.** Subtract line 34 from line 33. If zero or less, enter -0-. Enter here and on Form 1040, line 45	35	

For Paperwork Reduction Act Notice, see your tax return instructions.   Cat. No. 13600G   Form **6251** (2017)

Source: Form 6251

AMT Exemption   To help ensure that most taxpayers aren't required to pay the alternative minimum tax, Congress allows taxpayers to deduct an **alternative minimum tax (AMT) exemption** amount to determine their alternative minimum tax base.[11] The amount of the exemption depends on the taxpayer's filing status. The exemption is phased out (reduced) by 25 cents for every dollar the AMTI exceeds the threshold amount. Exhibit 8-5 identifies, by filing status, the base exemption amount, the phase-out threshold, and the range of AMTI over which the exemption is phased out for 2018. The exemption amounts and phase-out thresholds are considerably higher in 2018 than in prior years due to tax law changes enacted in 2017.

EXHIBIT 8-5   2018 AMT Exemptions

Filing Status	Exemption	Phase-Out Begins at This Level of AMTI	Phase-Out Complete for This Level of AMTI
Married filing jointly	$109,400	$1,000,000	$1,437,600
Married filing separately	54,700	500,000	718,800
Head of household and single	70,300	500,000	781,200

Example 8-7

THE KEY FACTS

Alternative Minimum Tax (AMT)

- Implemented to ensure taxpayers pay some minimum level of income tax.
- AMT base
  - More broad than regular income tax base.
  - No deductions for standard deduction, state income taxes, and property taxes in addition to other adjustments.
- AMT exemption amounts for 2018
  - $109,400 married filing jointly.
  - $54,700 married filing separately.
  - $70,300 single or head of household.
  - Phased out by 25 cents for each dollar of AMTI over threshold.
- AMT rates
  - 26 percent on first $191,100 of AMT base.
  - 28 percent on AMT base in excess of $191,100.
  - Net long-term capital gains and qualified dividends taxed at same preferential rates used for regular tax purposes.
- AMT is the excess of tentative minimum tax (tax on AMT base) over regular tax liability.

What is Courtney's AMT base?

Answer: $84,850, computed by subtracting her allowable exemption amount from her AMTI as follows:

Description	Amount	Explanation
(1) AMTI	$155,150	Example 8-6
(2) Full AMT exemption (head of household)	70,300	Exhibit 8-5
(3) Exemption phase-out threshold	500,000	
(4) AMTI in excess of exemption phase-out threshold	0	(1) − (3)
(5) Exemption phase-out percentage	25%	
(6) Exemption phase-out amount	0	(4) × (5), rounded
(7) Deductible exemption amount	70,300	(2) − (6)
AMT base	**$ 84,850**	(1) − (7)

What if: Suppose Courtney's AMTI is $700,000. What is Courtney's AMT base?

Answer: $679,700, computed as follows:

Description	Amount	Explanation
(1) AMTI	$ 700,000	
(2) Full AMT exemption (head of household	70,300	Exhibit 8-5
(3) Exemption phase-out threshold	500,000	
(4) AMTI in excess of exemption phase-out	200,000	(1) − (3)
(5) Exemption phase-out percentage	25%	
(6) Exemption phase-out amount	50,000	(4) × (5)
(7) Deductible exemption amount	20,300	(2) − (6)
AMT base	**$679,700**	(1) − (7)

Tentative Minimum Tax and AMT Computation   Taxpayers compute the tentative minimum tax by multiplying the AMT base by the applicable AMT rates. The 2018 AMT tax rate schedule consists of the following two brackets:

- 26 percent on the first $191,100 (indexed for inflation annually) of AMT base for all taxpayers other than married taxpayers filing separately ($95,550, indexed for inflation annually, for married taxpayers filing separately).

[11]Similar to standard deduction amounts, the AMT exemption is indexed for inflation. The phase-out threshold amounts are also indexed annually for inflation.

- 28 percent on AMT base in excess of $191,100 (indexed for inflation annually) for all taxpayers other than married taxpayers filing separately ($95,550, indexed for inflation annually, for married taxpayers filing separately).

However, for AMT purposes long-term capital gains and dividends are taxed at the same preferential rate as they were taxed for regular tax purposes (generally 0 percent, 15 percent, or 20 percent).

Example 8-8

Courtney's AMT base is $84,850. However, Courtney also received $700 in dividends that are included in the base but are subject to a tax rate of 15 percent even under the AMT system. The remaining $84,150 ($84,850 − $700) is taxed at the normal AMT rates. What is Courtney's tentative minimum tax?

Answer: $21,984, computed as follows:

Description	Amount	Explanation
(1) AMT base	$ 84,850	Example 8-7
(2) Dividends taxed at preferential rate	700	Example 8-3
(3) Tax rate applicable to dividends	15%	
(4) Tax on dividends	105	(2) × (3)
(5) AMT base taxed at regular AMT rates	84,150	(1) − (2)
(6) Regular AMT tax rate	26%	For AMT base below $191,100.
(7) Tax on AMT base taxed at regular AMT rates	21,879	(5) × (6), rounded
Tentative minimum tax	**$21,984**	(4) + (7)

Taxpayers subtract their regular tax liability from their tentative minimum tax to determine their AMT.[12] If the taxpayer's regular tax liability is equal to or exceeds the tentative minimum tax liability, the taxpayer does not owe any AMT.

Example 8-9

What is Courtney's alternative minimum tax liability?

Answer: $0, computed as follows:

Description	Amount	Reference
(1) Tentative minimum tax	$21,984	Example 8-8
(2) Regular tax liability	27,652	Example 8-3
Alternative minimum tax	**$ 0**	(1) − (2) ($0 if negative)

Courtney owes alternative minimum tax in addition to her regular tax liability.

In some situations, taxpayers who pay the AMT are entitled to a **minimum tax credit** to use when the regular tax exceeds the tentative minimum tax. They can use the credit to offset regular tax but not below the tentative minimum tax for that year.[13]

---

[12]As might be expected, self-employment taxes and the net investment income tax are not considered as part of a taxpayer's regular tax liability in determining whether a taxpayer owes AMT.

[13]The credit applies only when the taxpayer has positive adjustments that will reverse and become negative adjustments in the future. For example, depreciation, gain or loss on asset sales, and incentive stock option bargain element adjustments (see the Compensation chapter) fall into this category. Due to the nature of her adjustments, Courtney does not qualify for the minimum tax credit.

LO 8-3   EMPLOYMENT AND SELF-EMPLOYMENT TAXES

As we discussed in the Introduction to Tax chapter, employees and self-employed tax-payers must pay employment (or self-employment) taxes known as FICA taxes.[14] The FICA tax consists of a Social Security and a Medicare component that are payable by both employees and employers. The **Social Security tax** is intended to provide basic pension coverage for the retired and disabled. The **Medicare tax** helps pay medical costs for qualified individuals. Because Social Security and Medicare taxes are paid by working taxpayers but received by retired taxpayers, Social Security and Medicare taxes represent intergenerational transfers. The Social Security tax rate is 12.4 percent on the tax base (limited to $128,400 in 2018), and the Medicare tax rate is 2.9 percent on the tax base. An **additional Medicare tax** of .9 percent applies on the tax base in excess of $200,000 ($125,000 for married filing separately; $250,000 for married filing jointly). Below we discuss these taxes apply for employees, employers, and self-employed taxpayers.

Employee FICA Taxes Payable

THE KEY FACTS

Employee FICA Tax

- Social Security tax
  - 6.2 percent rate on wage base.
  - 2018 wage base limit is $128,400.
- Medicare tax
  - 1.45 percent rate on wage base.
  - Wage base unlimited.
- Additional Medicare tax
  - .9 percent rate on wage base in excess of $200,000 ($125,000 for married filing separately; $250,000 married filing jointly).

Both employees and employers have to pay **FICA taxes** on employee salary, wages, and other compensation paid by employers. The Social Security tax rate for employees is 6.2 percent of their salary or wages (wage base limited to $128,400 in 2018), the Medicare tax rate for employees is 1.45 percent of their salary or wages, and the additional Medicare tax rate is .9 percent on salary or wages in excess of $200,000 ($125,000 for married filing separate; $250,000 of combined salary or wages for married filing joint).

Employers withhold the employees' FICA tax liabilities from the employees' pay-checks for both the Social Security tax and the Medicare tax. For the additional Medicare tax, employers are required to withhold the tax at a rate of .9 percent for any salary or wages above $200,000, irrespective of the taxpayer's filing status (e.g., single, married filing separate, married filing joint, or head of household).[15] Taxpayers use Form 8959 to determine their liability for the additional Medicare tax and report all of the additional Medicare tax withheld as a tax payment on Form 1040.

Employers must also pay their portion of the Social Security tax (6.2 percent of employee salary or wages) and Medicare tax (1.45 percent of employee salary or wages, regardless of the amount of salary or wages). In contrast to employees, employers are not subject to the additional Medicare tax on employee salary or wages.

Example 8-10

While she was attending school full-time, Ellen received $15,000 in wages working part-time for an off-campus employer during the year. How much in FICA taxes should Ellen's employer have withheld from her paychecks during the year?

Answer: $1,148, computed as follows:

Description	Amount	Reference
(1) Wages	$15,000	
(2) Social Security tax rate	6.2%	
(3) Social Security tax	930	(1) × (2)
(4) Medicare tax rate	1.45%	
(5) Medicare tax	218	(1) × (4)
FICA taxes withheld	**$ 1,148**	(3) + (5)

---

[14]FICA stands for Federal Insurance Contributions Act.

[15]To avoid potential underpayment penalty, taxpayers can request additional income tax withholding or make estimated tax payments to pay any Medicare tax that otherwise would have been owed upon filing their tax return.

Example 8-11

During 2018, Courtney received a total of $142,800 in employee compensation from EWD. Recall that the compensation consisted of $118,000 in wages, $4,800 performance bonus, $6,000 discount for architectural design services, $4,000 compensation for a below-market loan, and $10,000 forgiveness of debt (see Exhibit 5-4). What is her FICA tax liability on this income?

Answer: $10,032, computed as follows:

Description	Amount	Reference
(1) Compensation subject to FICA tax	$142,800	
(2) Social Security tax base limit for 2018	128,400	
(3) Compensation subject to Social Security tax	128,400	Lesser of (1) or (2)
(4) Social Security tax rate	6.2%	
(5) Social Security tax	7,961	(3) × (4), rounded
(6) Medicare tax rate	1.45%	
(7) Medicare tax	2,071	(1) × (6), rounded
FICA taxes	**$ 10,032**	(5) + (7)

What amount of FICA taxes for the year must EWD pay on Courtney's behalf?

Answer: $10,032, which includes $7,961 of Social Security tax ($128,400 × 6.2%) and $2,071 of Medicare tax ($142,800 × 1.45%).

What if: Suppose Courtney received a total of $220,000 in employee compensation. What would be her FICA tax liability on this income?

Answer: $11,331, computed as follows:

Description	Amount	Reference
(1) Compensation subject to FICA tax	$220,000	
(2) Social Security tax base limit for 2018	128,400	
(3) Compensation subject to Social Security tax	128,400	Lesser of (1) or (2)
(4) Social Security tax rate	6.2%	
(5) Social Security tax	7,961	(3) × (4), rounded
(6) Medicare tax rate	1.45%	
(7) Compensation subject to Medicare tax	220,000	(1)
(8) Additional Medicare tax rate on compensation in excess of $200,000	.9%	
(9) Compensation subject to additional Medicare tax	20,000	Greater of [(1) − $200,000] or $0
(10) Medicare tax and additional Medicare tax	3,370	[(6) × (7)] + [(8) × (9)]
FICA taxes	**$ 11,331**	(5) + (10)

What amount of FICA taxes for the year must EWD pay on Courtney's behalf?

Answer: $11,151, which includes $7,961 of Social Security tax ($128,400 × 6.2%) and $3,190 of Medicare tax ($220,000 × 1.45%).

Employees who work for multiple employers within a calendar year may receive aggregate compensation that exceeds the Social Security wage base. Because each employer is required to withhold Social Security taxes on the employee's wages until the employee has reached the wage base limit *with that employer,* the employee may end up paying Social Security tax in excess of the required maximum. As it does in situations in which excess Medicare tax has been withheld, the IRS treats the excess Social Security tax paid through withholding as an additional federal income tax payment (or credit) on Page 2 of

Form 1040. The government refunds the excess withholding to the employee through either lower taxes payable with the tax return or a larger tax refund. Employers, on the other hand, are not able to recover excess Social Security taxes paid on behalf of their employees.

Example 8-12

What if: Suppose Courtney worked for her former employer Landmark Architects Inc. (LA), in Cincinnati for two weeks in January 2018 before moving to Kansas City. During those two weeks, Courtney would have earned $4,000 in salary. LA would have withheld $306 in FICA taxes from her final paycheck consisting of $248 of Social Security taxes ($4,000 × 6.2%) and $58 of Medicare taxes ($4,000 × 1.45%). How much excess Social Security tax would have been withheld from Courtney's combined salaries from LA and EWD during 2018?

Answer: $248 ($4,000 wages earned with LA × 6.2% Social Security rate). Due to the $128,400 Social Security tax wage base for the year, Courtney's Social Security tax liability is limited to $7,961 ($128,400 × 6.2%). However, through employer withholding, she would have paid a total of $8,209 in Social Security taxes, consisting of $248 withheld by LA ($4,000 × 6.2%) and $7,961 withheld by EWD ($128,400 × 6.2%). Thus, given these facts, Courtney's *excess* Social Security tax withheld was $248 ($8,209 − $7,961). Courtney would get this amount back from the government through either lower taxes payable with her tax return or a larger tax refund.

Self-Employment Taxes

While employees share their FICA (Social Security and Medicare) tax burden with employers, self-employed taxpayers must pay the *entire* FICA tax burden on their self-employment earnings.[16] Like FICA taxes for employees, self-employment taxes consist of both Social Security and Medicare taxes. Because their FICA taxes are based on their self-employment earnings, FICA taxes for self-employed taxpayers are referred to as **self-employment taxes.** The base for the Social Security component of the self-employment tax is limited to $128,400. The base for the Medicare portion of the self-employment tax is unlimited. Taxpayers use Schedule SE to determine their Social Security tax and 2.9 percent Medicare tax on self-employment earnings, and they use Form 8959 to determine the additional Medicare tax on self-employment earnings. Although applied to self-employment earnings, the additional Medicare tax is not considered technically a part of the self-employment tax. The process for determining the taxpayer's self-employment taxes (and additional Medicare tax) payable requires the following steps:

Step 1: Compute the amount of the taxpayer's net income from self-employment activities that is subject to self-employment taxes. This is generally the taxpayer's net income from **Schedule C** of Form 1040. Schedule C reports the taxpayers self-employment–related income and expenses.

Step 2: Multiply the amount from Step 1 by 92.35 percent. The product is called **net earnings from self-employment.** Because self-employed taxpayers are responsible for paying the entire amount of their FICA taxes, they are allowed an implicit deduction for the 7.65 percent "employer's portion" of the taxes,

---

[16]As we discussed in the Gross Income and Exclusions and Individual Deductions chapters, self-employed taxpayers report their self-employment earnings on Schedule C of Form 1040. Individuals who are partners in partnerships and who are actively involved in the partnerships' business activities may be required to pay self-employment taxes on the income they are allocated from the partnerships. They would report these earnings on Schedule E of Form 1040.

leaving 92.35 percent (100% − 7.65%) of the full amount subject to self-employment taxes. Note that the 7.65 percent consists of the 6.2 percent Social Security tax and 1.45 percent Medicare tax. Net earnings from self-employment is the base for the self-employment tax. If net earnings from self-employment is less than $400, the taxpayer is not subject to self-employment tax (but is still subject to income tax on the earnings).

Step 3: Compute the Social Security tax. The Social Security tax component of the self-employment tax equals 12.4 percent [the combined Social Security tax rate for employer and employee (6.2% + 6.2% = 12.4%)] multiplied by the lesser of (a) the taxpayer's net earnings from self-employment (from Step 2) or (b) $128,400 (the maximum tax base for the Social Security tax).

Step 4: Compute the Medicare tax. The Medicare tax component of the self-employment tax equals 2.9 percent [the combined Medicare tax rate for employer and employee (1.45% + 1.45% = 2.9%)] multiplied by the net earnings from self-employment (from Step 2).

Step 5: Compute the additional Medicare tax. The additional Medicare tax due on net self-employment earnings equals .9 percent multiplied by the greater of (1) zero or (2) net earnings from self-employment (from Step 2) less $200,000 ($125,000 for married filing separately; $250,000 for married filing jointly). The additional Medicare tax is considered an "employee" tax (and not a "self-employment" tax).

Note that, as we discussed in the Individual Deductions chapter, taxpayers are allowed to deduct the employer portion of their self-employment taxes as a *for* AGI deduction.

Example 8-13

What if: Assume that Courtney's only income for the year is her $18,000 in net self-employment income from her weekend consulting business. What amount of self-employment taxes and additional Medicare tax would Courtney be required to pay on this income?

Answer: $2,543 self-employment taxes and $0 of additional Medicare tax, computed as follows:

Step 1: $18,000 of net self-employment income subject to self-employment taxes.

Step 2: $18,000 × .9235 = $16,623. This is net earnings from self-employment.

Step 3: $16,623 × 12.4% = $2,061. This is Courtney's Social Security tax payable for her self-employment income.

Step 4: $16,623 × 2.9% = $482. This is Courtney's Medicare tax payable for her self-employment income.

Step 5: $0. Since Courtney's net earnings from self-employment do not exceed $200,000, she is not subject to the additional Medicare tax.

Total $2,543 self-employment taxes [sum of Steps (3) and (4)] and **$0** of additional Medicare tax [Step (5)].

Under these circumstances, Courtney would be able to deduct $1,272 as a *for* AGI deduction for the employer portion of self-employment taxes she paid [i.e., $16,623 × (6.2% + 1.45%)].

When a taxpayer receives both employee compensation and self-employment earnings in the same year, the calculation of Social Security and additional Medicare taxes is a bit more complicated. For the Social Security tax component, the taxpayer's total earnings subject to the Social Security tax are capped at $128,400. In these situations, the taxpayer's Social Security tax liability on the employee compensation is determined as if the employee had no self-employment income. The taxpayer then computes her Social Security tax on her net self-employment earnings. This ordering is favorable for taxpayers because it allows them to use up all or a portion of the Social Security wage base limit with their employee income (taxed at 6.2 percent) before they determine the Social Security tax on their net earnings from self-employment (taxed at 12.4 percent). Consequently, if an employee's wages exceed the Social Security tax wage base limitation, she is not required to pay any Social Security tax on her self-employment earnings.

Likewise, the additional Medicare tax calculation is more complicated when (1) the taxpayer receives both employee compensation and self-employment earnings or (2) the taxpayer files married jointly with a spouse receiving employee compensation or net self-employment earnings. For taxpayers not filing married jointly, the additional Medicare tax equals .9 percent of the taxpayer's salary or wages and net self-employment earnings in excess of $200,000 ($125,000 for married filing separately). For married filing jointly taxpayers, the additional Medicare tax equals .9 percent of the taxpayer's and his or her spouse's salary or wages and net self-employment earnings in excess of $250,000.

The calculation of the taxpayer's Social Security and Medicare taxes on self-employment earnings in these settings can be determined as follows:[17]

Social Security Tax:

Step 1: Determine the limit on the Social Security portion of the self-employment tax base by subtracting the employee compensation from the Social Security wage base ($128,400 in 2018) (not below $0).

Step 2: Determine the net earnings from self-employment (self-employment earnings times 92.35 percent).

Step 3: Multiply the lesser of Steps 1 and 2 by 12.4 percent. This is the amount of Social Security taxes due on the self-employment income.

Medicare Tax:

Step 4: Multiply the amount from Step 2 by 2.9 percent, the combined Medicare tax rate for employer and employee.

Additional Medicare Tax:

Step 5: Add the amount from Step 2 and the taxpayer's compensation. If married filing jointly, also add the spouse's compensation and net earnings from self-employment (spouse's self-employment earnings times 92.35 percent).

Step 6: Multiply the greater of [(a) zero or (b) the amount from Step 5 minus $200,000 ($125,000 for married filing separately; $250,000 for married filing jointly)] by .9 percent.

Step 7: Take the amount from Step 6 and subtract the amount of the .9 percent additional Medicare tax withheld by the taxpayer's employer (and his or her spouse's employer if married filing jointly). This is the .9 percent additional Medicare tax due on the self-employment income.

---

[17]If net earnings from self-employment is less than $400, the taxpayer is *not* subject to self-employment tax (but the taxpayer is still subject to income tax on the earnings).

Example 8-14

In 2018, Courtney received $142,800 in taxable compensation from EWD (see Example 8-11) and $18,000 in self-employment income from her weekend consulting activities (see Example 6-2). What are Courtney's *self-employment taxes* and additional Medicare tax payable on her $18,000 of income from self-employment? Assume that Courtney's employer correctly withheld $7,961 of Social Security tax and $2,071 of Medicare tax.

Answer: $482 of self-employment taxes and $0 of additional Medicare tax, computed as follows:

Description	Amount	Explanation
(1) Social Security wage base limit less employee compensation subject to Social Security tax	$ 0	$128,400 − $128,400, limited to $0
(2) Net earnings from self-employment	16,623	$18,000 × 92.35%
(3) Social Security portion of self-employment tax	0	[Lesser of Step (1) or (2)] × 12.4%
(4) Medicare tax	482	Step (2) × 2.9%
(5) Sum of taxpayer's compensation and net earnings from self-employment	159,423	$142,800 + Step (2)
(6) [Greater of (a) zero or (b) the amount from Step (5) minus $200,000] × 0.9%	0	0 × 0.9%
(7) Step (6) less any additional Medicare tax withheld by Courtney's employer	0	0 − 0
Steps (3) + (4) + (7)	$ 482	$0 + $482 + $0. [**$482** of self-employment taxes (3) + (4) and **$0** of additional Medicare tax]

As we reported in Example 6-6, Courtney is entitled to a $241 *for* AGI deduction for the employer portion of the $482 self-employment taxes she incurred during the year ($16,623 × 1.45% employer portion of the Medicare tax rate = $241)

Example 8-15

What if: Let's change the facts and assume that Courtney received $100,000 of taxable compensation from EWD in 2018, and she received $180,000 in self-employment income from her consulting activities. What amount of self-employment taxes and additional Medicare tax is Courtney required to pay on her $180,000 of business income? Assume that Courtney's employer correctly withheld $6,200 of Social Security tax, $1,450 of Medicare tax, and $0 of additional Medicare tax.

Answer: $8,343 of self-employment taxes and $596 of additional Medicare tax, computed as follows:

Description	Amount	Explanation
(1) Social Security wage base limit less employee compensation subject to Social Security tax	$ 28,400	$128,400 − $100,000, limited to $0
(2) Net earnings from self-employment	166,230	$180,000 × 92.35%
(3) Social Security portion of self-employment tax	3,522	[Lesser of Step (1) or (2)] × 12.4%, rounded
(4) Medicare tax	4,821	Step (2) × 2.9%, rounded

(*continued on page 8-20*)

Description	Amount	Explanation
(5) Sum of taxpayer's compensation and net earnings from self-employment	266,230	$100,000 + Step (2)
(6) [Greater of (a) zero or (b) the amount from Step (5) minus $200,000] × 0.9%	596	$66,230 × 0.9%, rounded
(7) Step (6) less any additional Medicare tax withheld by Courtney's employer	596	$596 − $0
Steps (3) + (4) + (7)	$ 8,939	$3,522 + $4,821 + $596. [**$8,343** of self-employment taxes (3) + (4) and **$596** of additional Medicare tax]

What if: Now let's assume that Courtney is married and files jointly. Assume that Courtney received $100,000 of taxable compensation from EWD in 2018 and $180,000 in self-employment income from her weekend consulting activities. In addition, her husband received $75,000 of taxable compensation from his employer. What amount of self-employment taxes and additional Medicare tax is Courtney required to pay on her $180,000 of business income? Assume that Courtney's employer correctly withheld $6,200 of Social Security tax, $1,450 of Medicare tax, and $0 of additional Medicare tax, and that her husband's employer correctly withheld $4,650 of Social Security tax, $1,088 of Medicare tax, and $0 of additional Medicare tax.

Answer: $8,343 of self-employment taxes and $821 of additional Medicare tax, computed as follows:

Description	Amount	Explanation
(1) Social Security wage base limit less employee compensation subject to Social Security tax	$ 28,400	$128,400 − $100,000, limited to $0
(2) Net earnings from self-employment	166,230	$180,000 × 92.35%
(3) Social Security portion of self-employment tax	3,522	[Lesser of Step (1) or (2)] × 12.4%, rounded
(4) Medicare tax	4,821	Step (2) × 2.9%, rounded
(5) Sum of taxpayer's and spouse's compensation and net earnings from self-employment	341,230	$100,000 + $75,000 + Step (2)
(6) [Greater of (a) zero or (b) the amount from Step (5) minus $250,000] × 0.9%	821	$91,230 × 0.9%, rounded
(7) Step (6) less any additional Medicare tax withheld by Courtney's employer and her husband's employer	821	$821 − $0
Steps (3) + (4) + (7)	$ 9,164	$3,522 + $4,821 + $821. [**$8,343** of self-employment taxes (3) + (4) and **$821** of additional Medicare tax]

Unlike employees, whose employers withhold tax throughout the year on their behalf, self-employed taxpayers must satisfy their self-employment tax obligations through periodic, usually quarterly, estimated tax payments. Taxpayers who are employed and self-employed (an employee with a business on the side, like Courtney) may have their employers withhold enough taxes to cover both their income, self-employment, and additional Medicare tax obligations. Any self-employment or additional Medicare taxes not paid through these mechanisms must be paid with the self-employed taxpayer's individual tax return.

continued from page 8-1 . . .

Courtney was enjoying her work with EWD, but she also really liked her weekend consulting work. A couple of months ago, after she had played an integral part in completing a successful project, her boss jokingly mentioned that, if Courtney ever decided to leave EWD to work for herself as a full-time consultant, EWD would love to hire her back for contract work. This caused Courtney to start thinking about the possibilities of starting her own consulting business. She always had some interest in working for herself, but she is not at a point in her life where she can take significant financial risks even if it might mean a more satisfying career. Courtney knows that before making such a move she would need to seriously consider the nontax issues associated with self-employment and learn more about the tax consequences of working as an independent contractor. She is particularly interested in the tax consequences of working for EWD as an independent contractor (contract worker) relative to working for EWD as an employee. ■

Employee vs. Self-Employed (Independent Contractor)

Determining whether an individual should be taxed as an **employee** or as an **independent contractor** can be straightforward or quite complex, depending on the specific arrangement between the parties. In its published guidance, the IRS stipulates that an employer/employee relationship exists when the party for whom services are performed has the right to direct or control the individual performing services.[18] To assist taxpayers in deciding whether the party receiving services has the requisite amount of control over the individual providing services, the IRS has published a list of 20 factors to consider.[19] A few of the factors suggesting independent contractor rather than employee status include the contractor's ability to:

1. Set her own working hours.
2. Work part-time.
3. Work for more than one firm.
4. Realize either a profit or a loss from the activities.
5. Perform work somewhere other than on an employer's premises.
6. Work without frequent oversight.

When these factors are absent, individuals are more likely to be classified as employees. Rather than simply summing the number of factors in favor of independent contractor status and those in favor of employee status, however, taxpayers and their advisers should use the factors as guides in determining the overall substance of the contractual relationship.

Whether a taxpayer is classified as an employee or as an independent contractor (self-employed) has both tax and nontax consequences to the employer and the taxpayer. The best classification for the taxpayer is situation-specific.

Employee vs. Independent Contractor Comparison   The two primary *tax* differences between independent contractors and employees relate to (1) the amount of FICA taxes payable and (2) the deductibility of business expenses.[20] However, there are several nontax factors to consider as well. In the previous section, we detailed how

---

[18]IRS Publication 1779. Independent Contractor or Employee brochure.

[19]Rev. Rul. 87-41, 1987-1 CB 296.

[20]Also, independent contractors generally receive a Form 1099 from each client reporting the gross income they received from the client during the year. Employees receive Form W-2 reporting the compensation the employee received from the employer during the year.

THE KEY FACTS

Employee vs. Independent Contractor

- Employees
  - Less control over how, when, and where to perform duties.
  - Pay 6.2 percent Social Security tax subject to limit.
  - Pay 1.45 percent Medicare tax.
  - Pay additional Medicare tax of .9 percent on salary or wages above $200,000 ($125,000 for married filing separate; $250,000 of combined salary or wages for married filing joint).
- Independent contractors
  - More control over how, when, and where to perform duties.
  - Report income and expenses on Form 1040, Schedule C.
  - Pay 12.4 percent Social Security tax subject to limit.
  - Pay Medicare tax of 2.9 percent.

(continued)

- Pay additional Medicare tax of .9 percent on net self-employment earnings above $200,000 ($125,000 for married filing separate; $250,000 of combined salary or wages for married filing joint).

- Self-employment tax base is 92.35 percent of net self-employment income.

- Deduct the employer portion of self-employment taxes paid *for* AGI.

to determine the FICA taxes payable for employees and independent contractors (self-employed taxpayers). In terms of the deductibility of business expenses, as we discussed in the Individual Deductions chapter, *employees* who incur unreimbursed business expenses relating to their employment cannot deduct these expenses. In contrast, as we also described in the Individual Deductions chapter, self-employed independent contractors are able to deduct expenses relating to their business activities as *for* AGI deductions, which they can deduct without restriction. While these factors appear to favor independent contractor status over employee status, note that employees generally don't incur many unreimbursed expenses relating to their employment. Thus, even though independent contractors may be able to deduct more expenses than employees, they typically incur more costs in doing business.

When taxpayers are classified as independent contractors rather than employees, they are not eligible for nontaxable fringe benefits available to employees, such as health care insurance, retirement plan benefits, and others. Further, independent contractors are responsible for paying their estimated tax liability throughout the year because the employer does not withhold taxes from an independent contractor's pay. However, as we mentioned above, taxpayers are allowed to deduct the employer portion of the self-employment taxes they pay.

From the employer's perspective, it is generally less costly to hire an independent contractor than an employee, because the employer need not provide these benefits or withhold or pay any FICA taxes on behalf of an independent contractor. As a result, an employer may be willing to offer an apparently higher level of taxable compensation to an independent contractor than to a similarly situated employee. However, after considering all relevant factors, the taxpayer may do better receiving less compensation as an employee than slightly higher compensation as an independent contractor.

ETHICS

Sudipta is an accounting major who works during the day and takes classes in the evening. He was excited to finally land his first accounting job doing the books for a local dry cleaners. In his new job, Sudipta works 30 hours a week at the dry cleaners' main office. His excitement quickly dampened when he realized that his new employer was not withholding any income taxes or FICA taxes from his paycheck. Apparently, Sudipta's employer is treating him as an independent contractor. Sudipta likes his job, appreciates the money he is earning, but recognizes that he should be treated as an employee instead of an independent contractor. What would you do if you were Sudipta?

Example 8-16

What if: Let's compare Courtney's compensation as an employee with EWD to her compensation if she were to work for EWD as an independent contractor. Assume Courtney works an average of 40 hours per week for 50 weeks per year to earn a salary of $100,000; in addition she receives fringe benefits including a 5 percent contribution to her retirement plan, life insurance coverage, and health insurance coverage. Would Courtney be "made whole" in terms of her hourly rate if EWD agreed to pay her $55 an hour for her contract work (10 percent more than her hourly rate as an employee)?

Answer: Not very likely. As an independent contractor, Courtney must pay more costly self-employment taxes (at nearly twice the rate of employment taxes) under the new arrangement. In addition, she will be ineligible for the nontaxable fringe benefits (retirement plan contributions, life insurance, and health coverage) she was receiving as an employee and will not receive as a contractor.

We've described how to calculate a taxpayer's regular tax liability, alternative minimum tax liability, Social Security and Medicare tax liability, additional Medicare tax liability, and self-employment tax liability. These tax liabilities sum to a taxpayer's gross tax liability. While Gram's gross tax is simply her regular income tax liability of $199 (see Example 8-2), Courtney's gross tax includes other taxes. Courtney's gross tax liability is calculated in Exhibit 8-6.

EXHIBIT 8-6 Courtney's Gross Tax

Description	Amount	Explanation
(1) Regular federal income tax	$ 27,652	Example 8-3
(2) Alternative minimum tax	0	Example 8-9
(3) Self-employment tax	482	Example 8-14
Gross tax	$ 28,134	(1) + (2) + (3)

Taxpayers reduce their gross tax by tax credits and tax prepayments (withholding and estimated tax payments) for the year. As indicated in Exhibit 8-7, if the gross tax exceeds the tax credits and prepayments, the taxpayer owes additional taxes when she files her tax

EXHIBIT 8-7 Formula for Computing Net Tax Due or Refund

Gross tax
Minus: Tax credits
Minus: Prepayments
Net tax due (refund)

return. In contrast, if the prepayments exceed the gross tax after applying tax credits, the taxpayer is entitled to a tax refund. We next explore available tax credits and conclude the chapter by dealing with taxpayer prepayments.

TAX CREDITS

Congress provides a considerable number of credits for taxpayers. **Tax credits** reduce a taxpayer's *tax liability* dollar for dollar. In contrast, deductions reduce *taxable income* dollar for dollar, but the tax savings deductions generated depend on the taxpayer's marginal tax rate. Because tax credits generate tax savings independent of a taxpayer's marginal tax rate, they are a popular tax policy tool for avoiding the perception that tax benefits for certain tax policies are distributed disproportionately to taxpayers with higher incomes and corresponding higher marginal tax rates. Further, tax credits are powerful tax policy tools because they directly affect taxes due. By using tax credits, policy makers can adjust the magnitude of the tax effects of tax policy without changing tax rates.

LO 8-4

Tax credits can be either nonrefundable or refundable. A **nonrefundable credit** may reduce a taxpayer's gross tax liability to zero, but if the amount of the credit exceeds the amount of the taxpayer's gross tax liability, the credit in excess of the gross tax liability is not refunded to the taxpayer. It expires without ever providing tax benefits, unless it can be carried over to a different year. Refundable credits in excess of a taxpayer's gross tax liability are refunded to the taxpayer.

Tax credits are generally classified into one of three categories: nonrefundable personal, refundable personal, or business credits, depending on the nature of the credit. The primary exception to this general rule is the foreign tax credit. The foreign tax credit is a hybrid between personal and business credits because, like nonrefundable personal credits, it reduces the taxpayer's liability before business credits but, like business credits, unused foreign tax credits can be carried over to use in other years.

Nonrefundable Personal Credits

Congress provides many nonrefundable personal tax credits to generate tax relief for certain groups of individuals. For example, the child tax credit (partially refundable) provides tax relief for taxpayers who provide a home for dependent children, and the child and dependent care credit provides tax relief for taxpayers who incur expenses to care for their children and other dependents in order to work. The American opportunity credit (partially refundable) and the lifetime learning credit help taxpayers pay for the cost of higher education. Because the child tax credit, the child and dependent care credit, and the American opportunity and lifetime learning credits are some of the most common nonrefundable personal credits, we discuss them in detail.

Child Tax Credit   Taxpayers may claim a $2,000 **child tax credit** for *each qualifying child* [same definition for dependency purposes—see §152(c) and the Individual Income Tax Overview, Dependents, and Filing Status chapter] who is under age 17 at the end of the year and who is claimed as their dependent.[21] To claim the credit for a qualifying child, the taxpayers must provide the qualifying child's Social Security number on the tax return. Taxpayers may also claim a $500 credit for qualifying dependents other than qualifying children for which the $2,000 credit is claimed. Social Security numbers are not required to be reported to claim the $500 child tax credit for these dependents. The credit is subject to phase-out based on the taxpayer's AGI. The phase-out threshold depends on the taxpayer's filing status and is provided in Exhibit 8-8.

> **THE KEY FACTS**
>
> **Child Tax Credit**
>
> - Taxpayers may claim a $2,000 credit for each qualifying child under age 17 or $500 credit for other qualifying dependents.
> - Credit is phased out for taxpayers with AGI above threshold.
>   - Lose $50 for every $1,000 or portion thereof that AGI exceeds threshold.

EXHIBIT 8-8   Child Tax Credit Phase-Out Threshold

Filing Status	Phase-Out Threshold
Married filing jointly	$400,000
Married filing separately	200,000
Head of household and single	200,000

The total amount of the credit is phased out, but not below zero, by $50 for each $1,000 *or portion thereof* by which the taxpayer's AGI exceeds the applicable threshold. Taxpayers can determine their allowable child tax credit after the phase-out by using the following four steps:

Step 1: Determine the excess AGI by subtracting the threshold amount (see Exhibit 8-8) from the taxpayer's AGI.

Step 2: Divide the excess AGI from Step 1 by 1,000 and round up to the next whole number.

Step 3: Multiply the amount from Step 2 by $50. This is the amount of the total credit that is phased out or disallowed.

Step 4: Subtract the amount from Step 3 from the total credit before phase-out (limited to $0) to determine the allowable child tax credit.

Because the phase-out is based upon a fixed amount ($50) rather than a percentage, the phase-out range varies according to the amount of credit claimed.[22]

---

[21]§24(a).

[22]The child tax credit is partially refundable. The $500 child tax credit is nonrefundable. The refundable portion of the credit is the lesser of (1) $1,400 per each qualifying child for which the $2,000 credit is claimed, (2) the taxpayer's earned income in excess of $2,500 times 15 percent, or (3) the amount of the unclaimed portion of the otherwise nonrefundable credit. Thus, if a taxpayer has enough tax liability to absorb the nonrefundable portion of the credit, the refundable portion is reduced to zero. The computation is modified for taxpayers with three or more qualifying children. See IRS Publication 972 for more information relating to the child tax credit.

Example 8-17

Both Ellen and Deron are Courtney's qualifying children. Courtney may claim a $2,000 child tax credit for Deron because he is under age 17 at the end of the year. Courtney cannot claim the $2,000 child tax credit for Ellen because she is not under age 17 at the end of the year, but Courtney may claim the $500 credit for Ellen because she is a qualified dependent. What amount of child tax credit is Courtney allowed to claim for Deron and Ellen after accounting for the credit phase-out?

Answer: $2,500. Because Courtney's AGI of $187,000 (Exhibit 6-5) does not exceed the $200,000 phase-out threshold (Exhibit 8-8), she may claim full credit of $2,000 for Deron and $500 for Ellen.

What if: Suppose Courtney's AGI is $230,000. How much child tax credit may she claim for Deron and Ellen?

Answer: $1,000, computed as follows:

Description	Amount	Explanation
(1) AGI	$230,000	
(2) Phase-out threshold	200,000	Exhibit 8-8
(3) AGI in excess of threshold	30,000	(1) − (2)
(4) Credit phase-out increment	30	(3)/1,000)
(5) Credit phase-out	1,500	(4) × 50
(6) Credit before phase-out	2,500	$2,000 for Deron; $500 for Ellen
Credit after phase-out	**$ 1,000**	(6) − (5)

Child and Dependent Care Credit   The child and dependent care credit is a tax subsidy to help taxpayers pay the cost of providing care for their dependents to allow taxpayers to work or look for work. The amount of the credit is based on the amount of the taxpayer's expenditures to provide care for one or more qualifying persons. A qualifying person includes (1) a dependent under the age of 13, and (2) a dependent or spouse who is physically or mentally incapable of caring for herself or himself and who lives in the taxpayer's home for more than half the year.

The amount of expenditures eligible for the credit is the *least* of the following three amounts:

1. The total amount of dependent care expenditures for the year.
2. $3,000 for one qualifying person or $6,000 for two or more qualifying persons.
3. The taxpayer's earned income including wage, salary, or other taxable employee compensation, or net earnings from self-employment. Married taxpayers must file a joint tax return and the amount of earned income for purposes of the dependent care credit limitation is the earned income of the lesser-earning spouse.[23]

Expenditures for care qualify whether the care is provided outside or within the home. But they do *not* qualify if the caregiver is a dependent relative or child of the taxpayer.[24] The amount of the credit is calculated by multiplying qualifying expenditures by the appropriate credit percentage. The credit percentage is based upon the taxpayer's AGI level and begins at 35 percent for taxpayers with AGI of $15,000 or less. The maximum dependent care credit is 20 percent for taxpayers with AGI over $43,000. Exhibit 8-9 provides the dependent care credit percentage for different levels of AGI.

THE KEY FACTS

Child and Dependent Care Credit

- Designed to help taxpayers who work or seek work when they must provide care for dependents.
- Nonrefundable.
- Based on maximum qualifying expenditures multiplied by the rate based on AGI.
  - Maximum expenditures are $3,000 for one qualifying person or $6,000 for two or more qualifying persons.
  - Rate is 35 percent for the lowest AGI taxpayers and 20 percent for the highest.

[23]If the lesser-earning spouse cannot work due to a disability or is a full-time student, the lesser-earning spouse is *deemed* to have earned $250 a month if the couple is computing the credit for one qualifying person or $500 a month if the couple is computing the credit for more than one qualifying person.

[24]§21(e)(6). Also, the regulations indicate that the costs of summer school and tutoring programs are indistinguishable from general education and, therefore, do not qualify for the credit [see Reg. §1.21-1(b)].

EXHIBIT 8-9   Child and Dependent Care Credit Percentage

If AGI is over	but not over	then the percentage is
$ 0	15,000	35%
15,000	17,000	34
17,000	19,000	33
19,000	21,000	32
21,000	23,000	31
23,000	25,000	30
25,000	27,000	29
27,000	29,000	28
29,000	31,000	27
31,000	33,000	26
33,000	35,000	25
35,000	37,000	24
37,000	39,000	23
39,000	41,000	22
41,000	43,000	21
43,000	No limit	20

Example 8-18

What if: Suppose that this year, Courtney paid a neighbor $3,200 to care for her 10-year-old son, Deron, so Courtney could work. Would Courtney be allowed to claim the child and dependent care credit for the expenditures she made for Deron's care?

Answer: Yes. (1) Courtney paid for Deron's care to allow her to work, and (2) Deron is a qualifying person for purposes of the credit because (a) he is Courtney's dependent and (b) he is under 13 years of age at the end of the year.

What amount of child and dependent care credit, if any, would Courtney be allowed to claim for the $3,200 she spent to provide Deron's care given her AGI is $187,000?

Answer: $600, computed as follows:

Description	Amount	Explanation
(1) Dependent care expenditures	$ 3,200	
(2) Limit on qualifying expenditures for one dependent	3,000	
(3) Courtney's earned income	160,800	$142,800 compensation from EWD + $18,000 business income (see Example 8-14)
(4) Expenditures eligible for credit	3,000	Least of (1), (2), and (3)
(5) Credit percentage rate	20%	AGI over $43,000 (see Exhibit 8-9)
Dependent care credit	**$ 600**	(4) × (5)

What if: If Courtney's AGI (and her earned income) were only $31,500, what would be her child and dependent care credit?

Answer: $780, computed as follows:

Description	Amount	Explanation
(1) Dependent care expenditures	$ 3,200	
(2) Limit on qualifying expenditures for one dependent	3,000	
(3) Courtney's earned income	31,500	
(4) Expenditures eligible for credit	3,000	Least of (1), (2), and (3)
(5) Credit percentage rate	26%	AGI between $31,000 and $33,000 (see Exhibit 8-9)
Dependent care credit	**$ 780**	(4) × (5)

Education Credits Congress provides the American opportunity credit (AOC) and the lifetime learning credit to encourage taxpayers and their dependents to obtain higher education by reducing the costs of the education. Taxpayers may claim credits for eligible expenditures made for themselves, their dependents, and third parties on behalf of the taxpayers' dependents.[25] If a student is claimed as a dependent of another taxpayer, only that taxpayer may claim the education credits (even if the dependent or another third party actually pays the education expenses).[26] Married taxpayers filing separate returns are not eligible for the AOC or the lifetime learning credit.

The AOC is available for students in their first four years of postsecondary (post high school) education. To qualify, students must be enrolled in a qualified postsecondary educational institution at least half-time.[27] The amount of the credit is 100 percent of the first $2,000 of eligible expenses paid by the taxpayer (or another person) plus 25 percent of the next $2,000 of eligible expenses paid by the taxpayer (or another person). Thus, the maximum AOC for eligible expenses paid for any one person is $2,500 [$2,000 + (25% × $2,000)]. To be eligible for the 2018 credit, taxpayers must pay the eligible expenses in 2018 for any academic period beginning in 2018 or in the first three months of 2019.[28]

Eligible expenses for the AOC include tuition, fees, and course materials (cost of books and other materials) needed for courses of instruction at an eligible educational institution.[29] The AOC is applied on a *per student* basis. Consequently, a taxpayer with three eligible dependents can claim a maximum AOC of $2,500 for *each* dependent. The AOC is subject to phase-out based on the taxpayer's AGI. The credit is phased out pro rata for taxpayers with AGI between $80,000 and $90,000 ($160,000 – $180,000 for married taxpayers filing jointly).[30] Forty percent of a taxpayer's allowable AOC is refundable.[31]

Example 8-19

Courtney paid $2,000 of tuition and $300 for books for Ellen to attend the University of Missouri–Kansas City during the summer following the end of her first year. What is the maximum American opportunity credit (AOC) (before phase-out) Courtney may claim for these expenses?

Answer: $2,075. Because the cost of tuition and books is an eligible expense, Courtney may claim a maximum AOC before phase-out of $2,075 [($2,000 × 100%) + ($2,300 – $2,000) × 25%].

How much AOC is Courtney allowed to claim on her 2018 tax return (how much can she claim after applying the phase-out)?

Answer: $0. Because Courtney's AGI exceeds the head of household limit of $90,000, she is not allowed to claim any AOC.

THE KEY FACTS

Education Credits

- American opportunity credit
  - Qualifying expenses include tuition for a qualifying student incurred during the first four years at a qualifying institution of higher education.
  - Maximum credit of $2,500 per student calculated as percentage of maximum of $4,000 qualifying expenses.

(continued)

[25]§25A(g)(3).

[26]If a third party pays the education expenses of a student claimed as a dependent by another taxpayer, the dependent is deemed to have paid the education expenses and the taxpayer claiming the student as a dependent is allowed to claim the credit for the expenses.

[27]§25A(b). Generally, eligible institutions are those eligible to participate in the federal student loan program [§25A(f)(2)].

[28]Reg. §1.25A-3(e).

[29]§25A(i)(3). Eligible expenses for both the AOC and the lifetime learning credit must be reduced by scholarships received to pay for these expenses or other amounts received as reimbursements for the expenses (Pell grants, employer-sponsored reimbursement plans, Educational IRAs, 529 plans, and the like). The cost of room and board or other personal expenses do not qualify as eligible expenses for either the AOC or the lifetime learning credit.

[30]§25A(i)(4).

[31]§25A(i)(5). The refundability of the tax credit is not applicable to a taxpayer that is a child subject to the "kiddie tax" rules —i.e., a child (a) who does not file a joint return, (b) has at least one living parent, and who is either (1) under 18 years old at year-end, (2) 18 at year-end with earned income that does not exceed half of her support, or (3) over age 18 but under age 24 at year-end, is a full-time student during the year, and has earned income that does not exceed half of her support.

- Subject to phase-out for taxpayers with AGI in excess of $80,000 ($160,000 married filing jointly).
- Lifetime learning credit
  - Qualifying expenses include costs at a qualifying institution associated with acquiring or improving job skills.
  - Maximum credit of $2,000 per taxpayer calculated as percentage of maximum of $10,000 in annual expenses.
  - Subject to phase-out for taxpayers with AGI in excess of $57,000 ($114,000 married filing jointly).

What if: How much AOC would Courtney have been allowed to claim on her 2018 tax return if she were married and filed a joint return with her husband (assuming the couple's AGI is $162,000)?

Answer: $1,867, computed as follows:

Description	Amount	Explanation
(1) AOC before phase-out	$ 2,075	
(2) AGI	162,000	
(3) Phase-out threshold	160,000	
(4) Excess AGI	2,000	(2) − (3)
(5) Phase-out range for taxpayer filing for married filing jointly	20,000	$180,000 − $160,000
(6) Phase-out percentage	10%	(4)/(5)
(7) Phase-out amount	208	(1) × (6)
AOC after phase-out	**$ 1,867**	(1) − (7)

What if: Suppose Courtney could claim a $1,867 AOC in 2018 (after phase-out). How much of this credit would be refundable?

Answer: $747 ($1,867 × 40%).

The lifetime learning credit is a nonrefundable credit that applies to the cost of tuition and fees (but generally not books) for any course of instruction to acquire or improve a taxpayer's job skills.[32] This includes the cost of professional or graduate school tuition (expenses are not limited to those incurred in the first four years of postsecondary education). The credit is equal to 20 percent of eligible expenses up to an annual maximum of $10,000 of eligible expenses (maximum of $2,000). The credit for a year is based on the amount paid during that year for an academic period beginning in that year or the first three months of the following year.

In contrast to the American opportunity credit, the lifetime learning credit limit applies to the taxpayer (a married couple filing a joint return may claim only $2,000 of lifetime learning credit). Thus, a taxpayer with multiple eligible dependents can claim a maximum lifetime learning credit of only $2,000. Finally, the credit is phased out pro rata for taxpayers with AGI between $57,000 and $67,000 ($114,000 and $134,000 for married taxpayers filing jointly).[33]

Example 8-20

Courtney paid $1,550 to attend a class at the local university to help her improve her job skills. How much lifetime learning credit can Courtney claim before applying the phase-out?

Answer: $310 ($1,550 × 20%)

How much lifetime learning credit is Courtney allowed to claim on her 2018 tax return (how much can she claim after applying the phase-out)?

Answer: $0. Because Courtney's AGI exceeds the head of household limit of $67,000, she is not allowed to claim any lifetime learning credit.

[32] §25A(f)(1).
[33] §25A(d).

For expenses that qualify for both the AOC and lifetime learning credit (tuition and fees during the first four years of postsecondary education), taxpayers may choose which credit to use, but they may not claim both credits for the same student in the same year.

Example 8-21

What if: Suppose Courtney paid $5,000 of tuition for Ellen to attend the University of Missouri–Kansas City during the summer following the end of her first year. Further assume that Courtney's AGI is $45,000, so her education credits are not subject to phase-out. Courtney would be allowed to claim the maximum AOC of $2,500 on the first $4,000 of the qualifying educational expenditures. Assuming Courtney used $4,000 of the educational expenses to claim the maximum AOC, would she be allowed to claim the lifetime credit on the remaining $1,000 of tuition costs ($5,000 total expenses − $4,000 maximum AOC expenses)?

Answer: No. If Courtney claims any AOC for Ellen's expenditures, she is not allowed to claim a lifetime learning credit for Ellen's expenditures (even for the expenses not used in computing the AOC).

Refundable Personal Credits

Several personal credits are refundable, the most common of which is the earned income credit, which we discuss below.

Earned Income Credit The **earned income credit** is a refundable credit that is designed to help offset the effect of employment taxes on compensation paid to low-income taxpayers and to encourage lower-income taxpayers to seek employment. Because it is refundable (if the credit exceeds the tax after considering nonrefundable credits, the taxpayer receives a refund for the excess), it is sometimes referred to as a *negative income tax*. The credit is available for qualified individuals who have earned income for the year.[34] Qualified individuals generally include (1) those who have at least one qualifying child (same definition of qualifying child for dependent purposes—see the Individual Income Tax Overview, Dependents, and Filing Status chapter) and (2) those who do not have a qualifying child for the taxable year but who live in the United States for more than half the year, are at least 25 years old but younger than 65 years old at the end of the year, and are not a dependent of another taxpayer. Earned income includes wages, salaries, tips, and other employee compensation included in gross income and net earnings from self-employment. Taxpayers with investment income such as interest, dividends, and capital gains in excess of $3,500 are ineligible for the credit.[35]

The amount of the credit depends on the taxpayer's filing status, the number of the taxpayer's qualifying children who live in the home for more than half of the year, and the amount of the taxpayer's earned income. To be eligible for the credit, married taxpayers must file a joint tax return. The credit is computed by multiplying the appropriate credit percentage times the taxpayer's earned income up to a maximum amount. The credit percentage depends upon the number of qualifying children in the home and is subject to a phase-out based upon AGI (or earned income if greater). As summarized in Exhibit 8-10, the earned income credit increases as taxpayers receive earned income up to the maximum amount of earned income eligible for the credit. However, as taxpayers earn more income, the credit begins to phase out and is completely eliminated once taxpayers' earned income reaches established levels.

---

[34]§32.
[35]§32(i).

EXHIBIT 8-10   2018 Earned Income Credit Table

Qualifying Children	(1) Maximum Earned Income Eligible for Credit	(2) Credit %	(3) Maximum Credit (1) × (2)	(4) Credit Phase-Out for AGI (or earned income if greater) Over This Amount	(5) Phase-Out Percentage	No Credit When AGI (or earned income if greater) Equals or Exceeds This Amount (4) + [(3)/(5)]
Married taxpayers filing joint returns						
0	$ 6,780	7.65%	$ 519	$14,170	7.65%	$20,950
1	10,180	34	3,461	24,350	15.98	46,010
2	14,290	40	5,716	24,350	21.06	51,492
3+	14,290	45	6,431	24,350	21.06	54,884
All taxpayers *except* married taxpayers filing joint returns						
0	$ 6,780	7.65%	$ 519	$ 8,490	7.65%	$15,270
1	10,180	34	3,461	18,660	15.98	40,320
2	14,290	40	5,716	18,660	21.06	45,802
3+	14,290	45	6,431	18,660	21.06	49,194

Example 8-22

Courtney's earned income for the year is $160,800 (Example 8-18) and her AGI is $187,000 (Exhibit 6-5). Deron and Ellen both qualify as Courtney's qualifying children. What amount of earned income credit is Courtney entitled to claim on her 2018 tax return?

Answer: $0. Courtney's AGI (which is greater than her earned income) exceeds the $45,802 limit for unmarried taxpayers with two qualifying children. Consequently, Courtney is not allowed to claim any earned income credit.

What if: Assume Courtney's only source of income for the year was $30,000 in salary. Also assume Courtney's AGI for the year was $30,000. What would be Courtney's earned income credit in these circumstances?

Answer: $3,328, computed as follows:

Description	Amount	Explanation
(1) Earned income	$30,000	
(2) Maximum earned income eligible for earned income credit for taxpayers filing as head of household with two qualifying children	14,290	Exhibit 8-10
(3) Earned income eligible for credit	14,290	Lesser of (1) and (2)
(4) Earned income credit percentage for taxpayer with two qualifying children	40%	
(5) Earned income credit before phase-out	5,716	(3) × (4)
(6) Phase-out threshold begins at this level of AGI (or earned income if greater)	18,660	See Exhibit 8-10 for head of household filing status and two qualifying children.
(7) Greater of (a) AGI or (b) earned income, less the phase-out threshold	11,340	(1) − (6) In this example, AGI equals earned income.
(8) Phase-out percentage	21.06%	See Exhibit 8-10.
(9) Credit phase-out amount	2,388	(7) × (8), rounded
Earned income credit after phase-out	**$ 3,328**	(5) − (9)

TAXES IN THE REAL WORLD Taking a Bite Out of Earned Income Tax Credit Abuse

The IRS has special reporting requirements (Form 8867) for tax professionals filing tax returns that include an earned income tax credit. Form 8867, the Paid Preparer's Earned Income Credit Checklist, is intended to ensure that tax professionals use appropriate due diligence in determining the amount of, and a taxpayer's eligibility for, the earned income tax credit.

Why the extra concern with the earned income tax credit? Because the earned income tax credit is a refundable tax credit, the potential for abuse (fraudulent claim) is quite high. Only paid tax preparers are required to complete the form, and failure to do so can result in a $500 penalty for each failure. See Form 8867 and IRC Sec. 6695(g).

Source: See Form 8867 and IRC Sec. 6695(g).

Other Refundable Personal Credits Other refundable personal tax credits include a portion of the child tax credit (discussed above), excess FICA withholdings (see discussion above under FICA taxes), and taxes withheld on wages and estimated tax payments. We address withholdings and estimated taxes below when we discuss tax prepayments.

Business Tax Credits

Business tax credits are designed to provide incentives for taxpayers to hire certain types of individuals or to participate in certain business activities. For example, Congress provides the employment tax credit to encourage businesses to hire certain unemployed individuals, and it provides the research and development credit to encourage businesses to expend funds to develop new technology. Business tax credits are *nonrefundable* credits. However, when business credits other than the foreign tax credit (discussed below) exceed the taxpayer's gross tax for the year, the credits are carried back one year and forward 20 years to use in years when the taxpayer has sufficient gross tax liability to use them.

Why discuss business credits in an individual tax chapter? We discuss business credits here because self-employed individuals may qualify for them. Also, individuals may be allocated business credits from flow-through entities (partnerships, LLCs, and S corporations). Finally, individuals working as employees overseas or receiving dividends from investments in foreign securities may qualify for the foreign tax credit.

Foreign Tax Credit U.S. citizens must pay U.S. tax on their worldwide income. However, when they generate some or all of their income in other countries, they generally are required to pay income taxes to the foreign country where they earned their income. Without some form of tax relief, taxpayers earning income overseas would be double-taxed on this income. When taxpayers pay income taxes to foreign countries, for U.S. tax purposes they may treat the payment in one of three ways: (1) as we discussed in the Gross Income and Exclusions chapter when we introduced the foreign-earned income exclusion, taxpayers may exclude the foreign-earned income from U.S. taxation (in which case they would not deduct or receive a credit for any foreign taxes paid); (2) they may include the foreign income in their gross income and deduct the foreign taxes paid as itemized deductions (subject to $10,000 limitation on itemized tax deductions); or (3) they may include foreign income in gross income and claim a foreign tax credit for the foreign taxes paid. Here, we discuss the foreign tax credit.

The foreign tax credit helps reduce the double tax taxpayers may face when they pay income taxes on foreign-earned income to the United States and to foreign countries. Taxpayers are allowed to claim a foreign tax credit, against their U.S. tax liability, for the income taxes they pay to foreign countries.[36] In certain situations, taxpayers may not be able to claim the full amount of foreign tax paid as a credit. This restriction may apply when the taxpayer's foreign tax rate is higher than the U.S. tax rate on the foreign earnings. Taxpayers generally benefit from claiming credits rather than deductions for foreign taxes paid because credits reduce their liabilities dollar for dollar. However, when the foreign tax credit is restricted (see above), taxpayers may benefit by claiming deductions for the taxes paid (subject to $10,000 limitation on itemized tax deductions) instead of credits.

As we discussed above, the foreign tax credit may be limited in circumstances in which a taxpayer's effective foreign tax rate exceeds her U.S. tax rate. In addition, as a nonrefundable credit, it can reduce the taxpayer's tax liability only to zero (but not create a refund). When the use of a foreign tax credit is limited, taxpayers may carry back unused credits one year and carry forward the credits up to 10 years.[37]

Tax Credit Summary

Exhibit 8-11 identifies several tax credits and for each credit identifies the credit type, notes the IRC section allowing the credit, and describes the credit.

Credit Application Sequence

As we've discussed, credits are applied against a taxpayer's gross tax. However, we still must describe what happens when the taxpayer's allowable credits exceed the taxpayer's gross tax. Keep in mind that nonrefundable personal credits and business credits may be used to reduce a taxpayer's gross tax to zero, but not below zero.[38] In contrast, by definition, a refundable credit may reduce a taxpayer's gross tax below zero. This excess refundable credit generates a tax refund for the taxpayer.

When a nonrefundable personal credit exceeds the taxpayer's gross tax, it reduces the gross tax to zero, but the excess credit (credit in excess of the taxpayer's gross tax) disappears. That is, the taxpayer may not carry over any excess nonrefundable personal credits to use in other years. However, when a business credit or foreign tax credit exceeds the gross tax, it reduces the taxpayer's gross tax to zero, but the excess credit may be carried forward or back to be used in other years when the taxpayer has sufficient gross tax to use the credit (subject to certain time restrictions discussed above).

Because the tax treatment of excess credits depends on the type of credit, it is important to identify the sequence in which taxpayers apply the credits when they have more than one type of credit for the year. In this case, they apply the credits against their gross tax in the following order: (1) nonrefundable personal credits, (2) business credits, and (3) refundable credits. This sequence maximizes the chances that taxpayers will receive full benefit for their tax credits.

Because, as we discuss above, the foreign tax credit is a hybrid credit subject to a unique set of application rules, we exclude it from our general discussion on applying credits. Exhibit 8-12 summarizes the order in which the credits are applied against gross tax and indicates the tax treatment of any excess credits.

---

[36]§904.

[37]See IRS Publication 514, "Foreign Tax Credit for Individuals," for more information about the foreign tax credit.

[38]In general, nonrefundable personal credits can offset a taxpayer's regular tax and AMT (§26) but not self-employment tax. The limitation on business credits is more complex. We limit our discussion here to basic concepts. See §38(c) for the detailed limitations.

EXHIBIT 8-11   Summary of Selected Tax Credits

Credit	Type of Credit	IRC	Description
Child and dependent care credit	Nonrefundable personal	§21	Credit for taxpayers who pay dependent care expenses due to their employment activities.
Credit for elderly and disabled	Nonrefundable personal	§22	Credit for elderly low-income taxpayers who retire because of a disability.
Adoption expense credit	Nonrefundable personal	§23	Credit for qualified adoption-related expenses.
Child tax credit	Nonrefundable and refundable personal	§24	Credit for providing home for dependent children under the age of 17.
American opportunity credit	Nonrefundable and refundable personal	§25A	Credit for higher education expenses for the first four years of postsecondary education.
Lifetime learning credit	Nonrefundable personal	§25A	Credit for higher education expenses.
Saver's credit	Nonrefundable personal	§25B	Credit for contributing to qualified retirement plans.
Residential energy	Nonrefundable personal	§25D	Credit for qualified expenditures for solar electric property, solar water heating property, fuel cell property, wind energy property, and qualified geothermal heat pump property.
Earned income credit	Refundable personal	§32	Credit to encourage low-income taxpayers to work.
Premium tax credit	Refundable personal	§36B	Credit for health insurance purchased through an exchange for individuals and families with household incomes between 100% and 400% of the poverty line.
Credit for increasing research activities	Business	§41	Credit to encourage research and development.
Employer-provided child care credit	Business	§45F	Credit for providing child care for employees.
Small employer health insurance credit	Business	§45R	Credit to encourage employer-provided health insurance.
Rehabilitation credit	Business	§47	Credit for expenditures to renovate or restore older business buildings.
Energy credit	Business	§48	Credit for businesses that invest in energy conservation measures.
Work opportunity credit	Business	§51	Credit for hiring certain qualified veterans.
Foreign tax credit	Hybrid business and personal	§904	Credit to reduce effects of double taxation of foreign income.

EXHIBIT 8-12   Credit Application

Credit Type	Order Applied	Excess Credit
Nonrefundable personal	First	Lost
Business	Second	Carryback and carryover
Refundable personal	Last	Refunded

Example 8-23

What if: As we describe in Example 8-2, Gram's gross tax liability is $199. For illustrative purposes, let's assume Gram is entitled to an $800 nonrefundable personal tax credit, a $700 business tax credit, and a $600 refundable personal tax credit. What is the amount of Gram's refund or taxes due?

Answer: $600 refund. Gram would apply these credits as follows:

Description	Amount	Treatment of Excess Credit
Gross tax liability	$ 199	Example 8-2
Nonrefundable personal credits	(199)	$601 ($800 – $199) excess credit expires unused
Business credits	0	$700 carried back one year or forward 20 years (10 years for foreign tax credit)
Refundable personal credits	**(600)**	Generates $600 tax refund to Gram

LO 8-5 TAXPAYER PREPAYMENTS AND FILING REQUIREMENTS

After determining their tax liabilities, taxpayers must file a tax return and pay any additional tax due or receive a refund. When they don't pay enough taxes during the year or are late filing their tax return or paying their taxes due, they may be subject to certain penalties.

Prepayments

The income tax must be paid on a *pay-as-you-go* basis. This means it must be prepaid via **withholding** from salary or through periodic **estimated tax payments** during the tax year. Employees pay tax through withholding, and self-employed taxpayers generally pay taxes through estimated tax payments. Employers are required to withhold taxes from an employee's wages based upon the employee's marital status, exemptions, and estimated annual pay. Wages include both cash and noncash remuneration for services, and employers remit withholdings to the government on behalf of employees. At the end of the year, employers report the amounts withheld to each employee via Form W-2. Estimated tax payments are required of employees only if withholdings are insufficient to meet the taxpayer's tax liability. For calendar-year taxpayers, estimated tax payments are due on April 15, June 15, and September 15 of the current year and January 15 of the following year. If the due date falls on a Saturday, Sunday, or holiday, it is automatically extended to the next day that is not a Saturday, Sunday, or holiday.

Example 8-24

Courtney's gross tax liability for the year, including federal income tax, alternative minimum tax, and self-employment taxes is $28,134 (see Exhibit 8-6), and her net tax liability is $25,634 after the $2,500 child tax credit (see Example 8-17). However, because she had only $21,634 withheld from her paycheck by EWD (per her Form W-2 received from her employer), she underpaid $4,000 for the year ($25,634 – $21,634). Because Courtney did not pay her full tax liability, she may be subject to underpayment penalties discussed below. If she had been aware that her withholding would be insufficient, she could have increased her withholding at any time during the year (even in her December paycheck) or made estimated tax payments of $1,000 on April 17, June 15, and September 17 in 2018 and January 15, 2019 ($4,000/4).

What if: If Courtney were self-employed (instead of employed by EWD) and thus had no tax withholdings by an employer, she would be required to pay quarterly estimated tax payments. In this scenario, she would need to pay $6,408.50 ($25,634/4 = $6,408.50) by April 17, June 15, and September 17 of 2018 and $6,408.50 by January 15, 2019, to cover her gross tax liability of $25,634.

Underpayment Penalties When taxpayers like Courtney fall behind on their tax prepayments, they may be subject to an **underpayment penalty.**[39] Taxpayers with unpredictable income streams may be particularly susceptible to this penalty because it is difficult for them to accurately estimate their tax liability for the year. To help taxpayers who may not be able to predict their earnings for the year and to provide some margin of error for those who can, the tax laws provide some **safe-harbor provisions.** Under these provisions taxpayers can avoid underpayment penalties if their withholdings and estimated tax payments equal or exceed one of the following two safe harbors: (1) 90 percent of their *current tax liability* or (2) 100 percent of their *previous-year tax liability* (110 percent for individuals with AGI greater than $150,000).

These two safe harbors determine on a quarterly basis the minimum tax prepayments that a taxpayer must have made to avoid the underpayment penalty. The first safe harbor requires that a taxpayer must have paid at least 22.5 percent (90 percent/4 = 22.5 percent) of the *current*-year liability via withholdings or estimated tax payments by April 15 to avoid the underpayment penalty for the first quarter. Similarly by June 15, September 15, and January 15, the taxpayer must have paid 45 percent (22.5 percent × 2), 67.5 percent (22.5 percent × 3), and 90 percent (22.5 percent × 4), respectively, of the current-year liability via withholding or estimated tax payments to avoid the underpayment penalty in the second, third, and fourth quarters.[40] In determining taxpayers' prepayments for a quarter, tax withholdings are generally treated as though they are withheld evenly throughout the year. In contrast, estimated tax payments are credited to the taxpayer's account when they are remitted.

Example 8-25

Because all Courtney's prepayments were made through withholding by EWD, the payments are treated as though they were made evenly throughout the year. What are Courtney's actual and required withholdings under the 90 percent safe-harbor provision throughout the year?

Answer: See the following table:

Dates	(1) Actual Withholding	(2) Required Withholding	(1) – (2) Over- (Under-) Withheld
April 17, 2018	$5,409	$5,768	$(359)
	($21,634 × .25)	($25,634 × .9 × .25)	
June 15, 2018	$10,817	$11,535	(718)
	($21,634 × .50)	($25,634 × .9 × .50)	
September 17, 2018	$16,226	$17,303	(1,077)
	($21,634 × .75)	($25,634 × .9 × .75)	
January 15, 2019	$21,634	$23,071	(1,437)
		($25,634 × .9 × 1)	

It looks like Courtney is underwithheld in each quarter.

The second safe harbor requires that by April 15, June 15, September 15, and January 15, the taxpayer must have paid 25 percent, 50 percent (25 percent × 2), 75 percent (25 percent × 3), and 100 percent (25 percent × 4), respectively, of the *previous*-year tax liability (110 percent of the previous-year tax liability for individuals with AGI greater than $150,000), via withholding or estimated tax payments, to avoid the underpayment penalty in the first, second, third, and fourth quarters.

---

[39]§6654.

[40]As an alternative method of estimating safe harbor, (1) taxpayers can compute 90 percent of the current liability using the seasonal method. This method allows taxpayers to estimate 90 percent of their current tax liability by annualizing their taxable income earned through the month prior to the payment date (e.g., through March for April 15, May for June 15, and August for September 15). Taxpayers with uneven taxable income throughout the year with smaller taxable income earlier in the year benefit from this method.

A taxpayer who does not satisfy either of the safe-harbor provisions can compute the underpayment penalty owed using Form 2210. The underpayment penalty is determined by multiplying the **federal short-term interest rate** plus 3 percentage points by the amount of tax underpayment per quarter. For purposes of this computation, the quarterly tax underpayment is the difference between the taxpayer's quarterly withholding and estimated tax payments and the required minimum tax payment under the first or second safe harbor (whichever is less). If the taxpayer does not complete Form 2210 and remit the underpayment penalty with the taxpayer's tax return, the IRS will compute and assess the penalty for the taxpayer.

Example 8-26

In the previous example, we discovered that Courtney was underwithheld in each quarter based on the first (90 percent of current year) safe-harbor provision. Assuming Courtney was underwithheld by even more under the second (100 percent of prior year) safe-harbor provision, she is required to pay an underpayment penalty based on the underpayments determined using the first safe-harbor provision. Assuming the federal short-term rate is 5 percent, what is Courtney's underpayment penalty for 2018?

Answer: $72, computed as follows:

Description	First Quarter	Second Quarter	Third Quarter	Fourth Quarter
Underpayment	$359	$718	$1,077	$1,437
Times: Federal rate + 3% (5% + 3%)	× 8%	× 8%	× 8%	× 8%
	$ 29	$ 57	$ 86	$ 115
Times one quarter of a year[41]	× 25%	× 25%	× 25%	× 25%
Underpayment penalty per quarter	$ 7	$ 14	$ 22	$ 29

That's a lot of work to figure out a $72 penalty: (7 + 14 + 22 + 29)

As a matter of administrative convenience, taxpayers are not subject to underpayment penalties if they had no tax liability in the previous year, or if their tax payable is less than $1,000 after subtracting their withholding amounts (but not estimated payments).

Example 8-27

Gram's tax liability for the year is $199 (Example 8-2), but she did not have any taxes withheld during the year, and she did not make any estimated tax payments. What is Gram's underpayment penalty?

Answer: $0. Because Gram's $199 tax payable after subtracting her withholding amounts ($199 tax – $0 withholding) is less than $1,000, she is not subject to an underpayment penalty.

Filing Requirements

Individual taxpayers are required to file a tax return only if their gross income exceeds certain thresholds, which vary based on the taxpayer's filing status and age. However, a taxpayer may prefer to file a tax return even when she is not required to do so. For example, a taxpayer with gross income less than the threshold may want to file a tax

---

[41]Form 2210 actually computes the penalty per quarter based on the number of days in the quarter divided by the number of days in the year. For simplicity, we assume this ratio is per quarter.

return to receive a refund of income taxes withheld. In general, the thresholds are simply the applicable standard deduction amount for the different filing statuses.[42] With the increased standard deduction amounts in 2018, fewer taxpayers are now required to file.

Individual tax returns are due on April 15 for calendar-year individuals (the fifteenth day of the fourth month following year-end). If the due date falls on a Saturday, Sunday, or holiday, it is automatically extended to the next day that is not a Saturday, Sunday, or holiday. Taxpayers unable to file a tax return by the original due date can request (by that same deadline) a six-month extension to file, which is granted automatically by the IRS. The extension gives the taxpayer additional time to file the tax return, but it does *not* extend the due date for paying the tax.

Late Filing Penalty The tax law imposes a **late filing penalty** on taxpayers who do not file a tax return by the required date (the original due date plus extension).[43] The penalty equals 5 percent of the amount of tax owed for each month (or fraction of a month) that the tax return is late, with a maximum penalty of 25 percent. For fraudulent failure to file, the penalty is 15 percent of the amount of tax owed per month with a maximum penalty of 75 percent. If the taxpayer owes no tax as of the due date of the tax return (plus extension), the tax law does not impose a late filing penalty.

Late Payment Penalty An extension allows the taxpayer to delay filing a tax return but does not extend the due date for tax payments. If a taxpayer fails to pay the entire balance of tax owed by the original due date of the tax return, the tax law imposes a **late payment penalty** from the due date of the return until the taxpayer pays the tax.[44] The late payment penalty equals .5 percent of the amount of tax owed for each month (or fraction of a month) that the tax is not paid.

The combined maximum penalty that may be imposed for late payment and late filing (nonfraudulent) is 5 percent per month (25 percent in total). For late payment and filing due to fraud, the combined maximum penalty for late payment and late filing is 15 percent per month (75 percent in total).

THE KEY FACTS

Taxpayer Prepayments and Underpayment Penalties

- Taxpayers prepay their tax via withholding from salary or through periodic estimated tax payments during the tax year.
- Estimated tax payments are required only if withholdings are insufficient to meet the taxpayer's tax liability.
- For calendar-year taxpayers, estimated tax payments are due on April 15, June 15, and September 15 of the current year and January 15 of the following year.
- Taxpayers can avoid an underpayment penalty if their withholdings and estimated tax payments equal or exceed one of two safe harbors.
- The underpayment penalty is determined by multiplying the federal short-term interest rate plus 3 percentage points by the amount of tax underpayment per quarter.

Example 8-28

Courtney filed her tax return on April 10 and included a check with the return for $4,072 made payable to the United States Treasury. The $4,072 consisted of her underpaid tax liability of $4,000 (Example 8-24) and her $72 underpayment penalty (Example 8-26).

What if: If Courtney had waited until May 1 to file her return and pay her taxes, what late filing and late payment penalties would she owe?

Answer: Her combined late filing penalty and late payment penalty would be $200 ($4,000 late payment × 5 percent × 1 month or portion thereof—the combined penalty is limited to 5 percent per month).

THE KEY FACTS

Filing Requirements and Filing-Related Penalties

- Filing requirements vary based on the taxpayer's filing status, age, and gross income.
- Individual tax returns are due on April 15 for calendar-year individuals.
- Taxpayers unable to file a tax return by the original due date can request a six-month extension to file.
- The tax law imposes penalties on taxpayers who do not file a tax return (by the original due date plus extension) or pay the tax owed (by the original due date).

TAX SUMMARY

Courtney's and Gram's net taxes due, including an underpayment penalty for Courtney, are provided in Exhibits 8-13 and 8-15, respectively. Exhibit 8-14 illustrates how this information would be presented on Courtney's tax return by providing Courtney's Form 1040, page 2. We use 2017 forms as 2018 forms were not available at press time.

[42]§6012. Filing requirements for individuals who are dependents of other taxpayers are subject to special rules that consider the individual's unearned income, earned income, and gross income. See IRS Publication 17, "Your Federal Income Tax."

[43]§6651.

[44]§6651. As we discussed in the Tax Compliance, the IRS, and Tax Authorities chapter, the tax law also assesses interest on any tax underpayments until the tax is paid (§6601).

EXHIBIT 8-13   Courtney's Net Tax Payable

Description	Amount	Reference
(1) Regular federal income tax	$ 27,652	Example 8-3
(2) Alternative minimum tax	0	Example 8-9
(3) Self-employment tax	482	Example 8-14
(4) Gross tax	$ 28,134	(1) + (2) + (3)
(5) Tax credits	$ (2,500)	Examples 8-17, 8-19, 8-20, and 8-22
(6) Prepayments	$(21,634)	Example 8-24
(7) Underpayment penalties	72	Example 8-26
Tax and penalties due with tax return	$ 4,072	

EXHIBIT 8-14   Courtney's Net Tax Payable (as presented on her Form 1040, page 2)

Form 1040 (2017)   Page **2**

				Amount
Tax and Credits	38	Amount from line 37 (adjusted gross income)	38	187,000
	39a	Check if: ☐ **You** were born before January 2, 1953, ☐ Blind. ☐ **Spouse** was born before January 2, 1953, ☐ Blind. **Total boxes checked ▶** 39a		
	b	If your spouse itemizes on a separate return or you were a dual-status alien, check here ▶ ☐ 39b		
Standard Deduction for— • People who check any box on line 39a or 39b **or** who can be claimed as a dependent, see instructions. • All others: Single or Married filing separately, $6,350 Married filing jointly or Qualifying widow(er), $12,700 Head of household, $9,350	40	**Itemized deductions** (from Schedule A) or your **standard deduction** (see left margin)	40	38,330
	41	Subtract line 40 from line 38	41	148,670
	42	Deduction for qualified business income	42	3,600
	43	**Taxable income.** Subtract line 42 from line 41. If line 42 is more than line 41, enter -0-	43	145,070
	44	**Tax** (see instructions). Check if any from: **a** ☐ Form(s) 8814 **b** ☐ Form 4972 **c** ☐	44	27,652
	45	**Alternative minimum tax** (see instructions). Attach Form 6251	45	
	46	Excess advance premium tax credit repayment. Attach Form 8962	46	
	47	Add lines 44, 45, and 46 ▶	47	27,652
	48	Foreign tax credit. Attach Form 1116 if required ... 48		
	49	Credit for child and dependent care expenses. Attach Form 2441 ... 49		
	50	Education credits from Form 8863, line 19 ... 50		
	51	Retirement savings contributions credit. Attach Form 8880 ... 51		
	52	Child tax credit. Attach Schedule 8812, if required ... 52	2,500	
	53	Residential energy credit. Attach Form 5695 ... 53		
	54	Other credits from Form: **a** ☐ 3800 **b** ☐ 8801 **c** ☐ ... 54		
	55	Add lines 48 through 54. These are your **total credits**	55	2,500
	56	Subtract line 55 from line 47. If line 55 is more than line 47, enter -0- ▶	56	25,152
Other Taxes	57	Self-employment tax. Attach Schedule SE	57	482
	58	Unreported social security and Medicare tax from Form: **a** ☐ 4137 **b** ☐ 8919	58	
	59	Additional tax on IRAs, other qualified retirement plans, etc. Attach Form 5329 if required	59	
	60a	Household employment taxes from Schedule H	60a	
	b	First-time homebuyer credit repayment. Attach Form 5405 if required	60b	
	61	Health care: individual responsibility (see instructions) Full-year coverage ☐	61	
	62	Taxes from: **a** ☐ Form 8959 **b** ☐ Form 8960 **c** ☐ Instructions; enter code(s)	62	
	63	Add lines 56 through 62. This is your **total tax** ▶	63	25,634
Payments If you have a qualifying child, attach Schedule EIC.	64	Federal income tax withheld from Forms W-2 and 1099 ... 64	21,634	
	65	2017 estimated tax payments and amount applied from 2016 return ... 65		
	66a	**Earned income credit (EIC)** ... 66a		
	b	Nontaxable combat pay election ... 66b		
	67	Additional child tax credit. Attach Schedule 8812 ... 67		
	68	American opportunity credit from Form 8863, line 8 ... 68		
	69	Net premium tax credit. Attach Form 8962 ... 69		
	70	Amount paid with request for extension to file ... 70		
	71	Excess social security and tier 1 RRTA tax withheld ... 71		
	72	Credit for federal tax on fuels. Attach Form 4136 ... 72		
	73	Credits from Form: **a** ☐ 2439 **b** ☐ Reserved **c** ☐ 8885 **d** ☐ ... 73		
	74	Add lines 64, 65, 66a, and 67 through 73. These are your **total payments** ▶	74	21,634
Refund Direct deposit? See instructions.	75	If line 74 is more than line 63, subtract line 63 from line 74. This is the amount you **overpaid**	75	
	76a	Amount of line 75 you want refunded to you. If Form 8888 is attached, check here ▶ ☐	76a	
	b	Routing number _____ ▶ **c** Type: ☐ Checking ☐ Savings		
	d	Account number _____		
	77	Amount of line 75 you want **applied to your 2018 estimated tax** ▶ 77		
Amount You Owe	78	**Amount you owe.** Subtract line 74 from line 63. For details on how to pay, see instructions ▶	78	4,072
	79	Estimated tax penalty (see instructions) ... 79	72	

Third Party Designee   Do you want to allow another person to discuss this return with the IRS (see instructions)? ☐ **Yes.** Complete below. ☐ **No**
Designee's name ▶   Phone no. ▶   Personal identification number (PIN) ▶

Sign Here   Under penalties of perjury, I declare that I have examined this return and accompanying schedules and statements, and to the best of my knowledge and belief, they are true, correct, and accurately list all amounts and sources of income I received during the tax year. Declaration of preparer (other than taxpayer) is based on all information of which preparer has any knowledge.
Joint return? See instructions. Keep a copy for your records.
Your signature | Date | Your occupation | Daytime phone number
Spouse's signature. If a joint return, **both** must sign. | Date | Spouse's occupation | If the IRS sent you an Identity Protection PIN, enter it here (see inst.)

Paid Preparer Use Only
Print/Type preparer's name | Preparer's signature | Date | Check ☐ if self-employed | PTIN
Firm's name ▶ | | Firm's EIN ▶
Firm's address ▶ | | Phone no.

Go to *www.irs.gov/Form1040* for instructions and the latest information.   Form **1040** (2017)

Source: www.irs.gov/Form1040

EXHIBIT 8-15   Gram's Tax Payable

Description	Amount	Reference
(1) Gross tax	$199	Example 8-2
(2) Alternative minimum tax	0	
(3) Self-employment tax	0	
(4) Gross tax	$199	(1) + (2) + (3)
(5) Tax credits	0	
(6) Prepayments	0	
(7) Penalties	0	
Tax due with return	$199	(4) − (5) − (6) − (7)

CONCLUSION

This chapter reviewed the process for determining an individual's gross and net tax liability. We discovered that taxpayers may be required to pay regular federal income tax, alternative minimum tax, and employment-related tax. Taxpayers are able to offset their gross tax liability dollar for dollar with various types of tax credits and by the amount of tax they prepay during the year. Taxpayers must pay additional taxes with their tax return or they may receive a refund when they file their tax return depending on their gross tax liability and their available tax credits and tax prepayments. The previous chapters have covered the basic individual tax formula. The next three chapters address issues relevant for taxpayers involved in business activities.

Summary

Determine a taxpayer's regular tax liability.   **LO 8-1**

- Individual income is taxed using progressive tax rate schedules with rates ranging from 10 percent to 37 percent.
- Marginal tax rates depend on filing status and amount of taxable income.
- Progressive tax rate schedules may lead to either a marriage penalty or a marriage benefit for married taxpayers.
- Long-term capital gains and qualified dividends are taxed at either 0 percent, 15 percent, or 20 percent, depending on the amount of taxable income.
- A 3.8 percent tax is levied on net investment income for higher-income taxpayers.
- Strategies to shift investment income from parents to children are limited by the "kiddie tax" whereby children's investment income is taxed using the trust and estate tax rate schedule.

Compute a taxpayer's alternative minimum tax liability.   **LO 8-2**

- The AMT was designed to ensure that higher-income taxpayers pay some minimum level of income tax.
- The AMT base is broader than the regular income tax base. The AMT base is designed to more closely reflect economic income, as opposed to regular taxable income.
- The starting point for calculating AMT is regular taxable income. To compute AMTI, taxpayers add back items that are not deductible for AMT purposes (but were deducted for regular tax purposes) and items taxable for AMT purposes (but tax exempt or deferred for regular tax purposes). Taxpayers then subtract the allowable AMT exemption to generate the AMT base. They then apply the AMT rates and compare the product (the tentative minimum tax) to their regular tax liability. They owe AMT if the tentative minimum tax exceeds the regular tax liability.
- The AMT exemption depends on the taxpayer's filing status and is subject to phase-out of 25 cents for each dollar of AMTI over the specific thresholds based on filing status.

- The 2018 AMT tax rates are 26 percent up to $191,100 of AMT base ($95,550 of AMT base for married taxpayers filing separately) and 28 percent thereafter. However, long-term capital gains and qualified dividends are subject to the same preferential rate at which they are taxed for regular tax purposes.
- The amount of the AMT is the excess of the tentative minimum tax over the taxpayer's regular tax liability.

LO 8-3 Calculate a taxpayer's employment and self-employment taxes payable.

- Employees' wages are subject to FICA tax. For employees, the Social Security component is 6.2 percent, the Medicare component 1.45 percent, and the additional Medicare tax is .9 percent. For employers, the Social Security component is 6.2 percent and the Medicare component is 1.45 percent. The Social Security tax applies to the first $128,400 of salary or wages in 2018. The wage base on the Medicare tax is unlimited. The additional Medicare tax applies to employees (not employers) on salary or wages above $200,000 ($125,000 for married filing separate; $250,000 of combined salary or wages for married filing joint).
- Self-employed taxpayers pay self-employment tax on their net self-employment income (92.35 percent of their net Schedule C income). They pay Social Security tax of 12.4 percent and Medicare tax of 2.9 percent on their net self-employment income. The Social Security tax applies to the first $128,400 of net Schedule C income in 2018. The base for the Medicare tax is unlimited. Self-employed taxpayers are also subject to the additional Medicare tax of .9 percent on net self-employment earnings in excess of $200,000 ($200,000 ($125,000 for married filing separate; $250,000 of combined salary or wages for married filing joint).
- The determination as to whether to treat a worker as an independent contractor or as an employee for tax purposes is a subjective test based in large part on the extent of control the worker has over things such as the nature, timing, and location of work performed.
- Independent contractors are able to deduct ordinary and necessary business expenses as *for* AGI deductions. Employees cannot deduct unreimbursed employee business expenses.
- Independent contractors may deduct the employer portion of their self-employment taxes paid during the year. Employees may not deduct their FICA taxes.
- Independent contractors are required to pay self-employment tax, which represents the employer and employee portions of FICA taxes. Further, independent contractors must pay estimated taxes on their income because the employer does not withhold taxes from the independent contractor's paychecks.
- Hiring independent contractors is generally less costly for employers than is hiring employees. Employers do not pay FICA taxes, withhold taxes, or provide fringe benefits for independent contractors.

LO 8-4 Compute a taxpayer's allowable child tax credit, child and dependent care credit, American opportunity credit, lifetime learning credit, and earned income credit.

- Tax credits are generally classified into one of three categories: business, nonrefundable personal, or refundable personal credits.
- Nonrefundable personal tax credits provide tax relief to specified groups of individuals.
- The child tax credit is $2,000 for a qualifying child under the age of 17 and $500 for other qualified dependents.
- The child and dependent care credit is provided to help taxpayers pay the cost of providing care for their dependents and allow taxpayers to work or to look for work.
- The American opportunity credit provides a credit for a percentage of the costs of the first four years of a student's college education. Forty percent of the credit is refundable.
- The lifetime learning credit provides a credit for a percentage of the costs for instruction in a postsecondary degree program or the costs to acquire or improve a taxpayer's job skills.
- Nonrefundable credits are first used to reduce a taxpayer's gross tax but cannot reduce the gross tax below zero. Any excess credit is lost unless it is allowed to be carried to a different tax year.
- The earned income credit is refundable but subject to a very complex calculation.
- Business credits reduce the tax after applying nonrefundable credits. Any credit in excess of the remaining tax is generally allowed to be carried over or back to be used in other years.
- Refundable credits are the last credit applied to the tax after applying nonrefundable and business credits. Any refundable credit in excess of the remaining tax is treated as an overpayment and refunded to the taxpayer.

Explain how to compute a taxpayer's underpayment, late filing, and late payment penalties.   `LO 8-5`

- The income tax must be prepaid via withholding from salary or through periodic estimated tax payments during the tax year. Estimated tax payments are required only if withholdings are insufficient to meet the taxpayer's tax liability. For calendar-year taxpayers, estimated tax payments are due on April 15, June 15, and September 15 of the current year and January 15 of the following year.

- Taxpayers can avoid an underpayment penalty if their withholdings and estimated tax payments equal or exceed one of two safe harbors: (1) 90 percent of current-year tax or (2) 100 percent of previous-year tax (110 percent if AGI exceeds $150,000). If the taxpayer does not satisfy either of the safe-harbor provisions, the underpayment penalty is determined by multiplying the federal short-term interest rate plus 3 percentage points by the amount of tax underpayment per quarter.

- Individual taxpayers are required to file a tax return only if their *gross income* exceeds certain thresholds, which vary based on the taxpayer's filing status, age, and gross income.

- Individual tax returns are due on April 15 for calendar-year individuals. Taxpayers unable to file a tax return by the original due date can request a six-month extension to file.

- The tax law imposes penalties on taxpayers who do not file a tax return (by the original due date plus extension) or pay the tax owed (by the original due date). The failure-to-file penalty equals 5 percent of the amount of tax owed for each month (or fraction thereof) that the tax return is late with a maximum penalty of 25 percent. The late payment penalty equals .5 percent of the amount of tax owed for each month (or fraction thereof) that the tax is not paid. The combined maximum penalty that may be imposed for late filing and late payment is 5 percent per month (25 percent in total). The late filing and late payment penalties are higher if fraud is involved.

KEY TERMS

additional Medicare tax (8-14)	federal short-term interest rate (8-36)	nonrefundable credit (8-23)
alternative minimum tax (AMT) (8-8)	FICA taxes (8-14)	preferential tax rate (8-4)
alternative minimum tax adjustments (8-9)	independent contractor (8-21)	safe-harbor provisions (8-35)
	kiddie tax (8-6)	Schedule C (8-16)
alternative minimum tax (AMT) base (8-8)	late filing penalty (8-37)	self-employment taxes (8-16)
	late payment penalty (8-37)	Social Security tax (8-14)
alternative minimum tax (AMT) exemption (8-12)	marriage benefit (8-3)	tax bracket (8-2)
	marriage penalty (8-3)	tax credits (8-23)
alternative minimum tax system (8-8)	Medicare tax (8-14)	tax rate schedule (8-2)
business tax credits (8-31)	minimum tax credit (8-13)	tax tables (8-3)
child tax credits (8-24)	net earnings from self-employment (8-16)	tentative minimum tax (8-9)
earned income credit (8-29)		underpayment penalty (8-35)
employee (8-21)	net investment income tax (8-5)	withholding (8-34)
estimated tax payments (8-34)	net unearned income (8-7)	

DISCUSSION QUESTIONS

Discussion Questions are available in Connect®.   connect

1. What is a tax bracket? What is the relationship between filing status and the width of the tax brackets in the tax rate schedule?   `LO 8-1`

2. In 2018, for a taxpayer with $50,000 of taxable income, without doing any actual computations, which filing status do you expect to provide the lowest tax liability? Which filing status provides the highest tax liability?   `LO 8-1`

3. What is the tax marriage penalty and when does it apply? Under what circumstances would a couple experience a tax marriage benefit?   `LO 8-1`

LO 8-1 4. Once they've computed their taxable income, how do taxpayers determine their regular tax liability? What additional steps must taxpayers take to compute their tax liability when they have preferentially taxed income?

LO 8-1 5. Are there circumstances in which preferentially taxed income (long-term capital gains and qualified dividends) is taxed at the same rate as ordinary income? Explain.

research

LO 8-1 6. Augustana received $10,000 of qualified dividends this year. Under what circumstances might the entire $10,000 of income not be taxed at the same rate?

LO 8-1 7. What is the difference between earned and unearned income?

LO 8-1 8. Does the kiddie tax eliminate the tax benefits gained by a family when parents transfer income-producing assets to children? Explain.

LO 8-1 9. Does the kiddie tax apply to all children no matter their age? Explain.

LO 8-1 10. What is the kiddie tax? Explain.

LO 8-1 11. Lauren is 17 years old. She reports earned income of $3,000 and unearned income of $6,200. Is it likely that she is subject to the kiddie tax? Explain.

LO 8-2 12. In very general terms, how is the alternative minimum tax system different from the regular income tax system? How is it similar?

LO 8-2 13. Describe, in general terms, why Congress implemented the AMT.

LO 8-2 14. Do taxpayers always add back the standard deduction when computing alternative minimum taxable income? Explain.

LO 8-2 15. The starting point for computing alternative minimum taxable income is regular taxable income. What are some of the plus adjustments, plus or minus adjustments, and minus adjustments to regular taxable income to compute alternative minimum taxable income?

LO 8-2 16. Describe what the AMT exemption is and who is and isn't allowed to deduct the exemption. How is it similar to the standard deduction and how is it dissimilar?

LO 8-1 **LO 8-2** 17. How do the AMT tax rates compare to the regular income tax rates?

LO 8-2 18. Is it possible for a taxpayer who pays AMT to have a marginal tax rate higher than the stated AMT rate? Explain.

LO 8-2 19. What is the difference between the tentative minimum tax (TMT) and the AMT?

LO 8-3 20. Are an employee's entire wages subject to the FICA tax? Explain.

LO 8-3 21. Bobbie works as an employee for Altron Corp. for the first half of the year and for Betel Inc. for the rest of the year. She is relatively well paid. What FICA tax issues is she likely to encounter? What FICA tax issues do Altron Corp. and Betel Inc. need to consider?

LO 8-3 22. Compare and contrast an employee's FICA tax payment responsibilities with those of a self-employed taxpayer.

LO 8-3 23. When a taxpayer works as an employee and as a self-employed independent contractor during the year, how does the taxpayer determine her employment and self-employment taxes payable?

LO 8-3 24. What are the primary factors to consider when deciding whether a worker should be considered an employee or a self-employed taxpayer for tax purposes?

LO 8-3 25. How do the tax consequences of being an employee differ from those of being self-employed?

LO 8-3 26. Mike wanted to work for a CPA firm but he also wanted to work on his father's farm in Montana. Because the CPA firm wanted Mike to be happy, they offered to let him work for them as an independent contractor during the fall and winter and let him return to Montana to work for his father during the spring and summer. He was very excited to hear that they were also going to give him a 5 percent

planning

higher "salary" for the six months he would be working for the firm over what he would have made over the same six-month period if he worked full-time as an employee (i.e., an increase from $30,000 to $31,500). Should Mike be excited about his 5 percent raise? Why or why not? What counteroffer could Mike reasonably suggest?

27. How are tax credits and tax deductions similar? How are they dissimilar?   LO 8-4

28. What are the three types of tax credits? Explain why it is important to distinguish between the different types of tax credits.   LO 8-4

29. Explain why there is such a large number and variety of tax credits.   LO 8-4

30. What is the difference between a refundable and nonrefundable tax credit?   LO 8-4

31. Is the child tax credit a refundable or nonrefundable credit? Explain.   LO 8-4

32. Diane has a job working three-quarter time. She hired her mother to take care of her two small children so Diane could work. Do Diane's child care payments to her mother qualify for the child and dependent care credit? Explain.   LO 8-4

33. The amount of the child and dependent care credit is based on the amount of the taxpayer's expenditures to provide care for one or more qualifying persons. Who is considered to be a qualifying person for this purpose?   LO 8-4

34. Compare and contrast the lifetime learning credit with the American opportunity credit.   LO 8-4

35. Jennie's grandfather paid her tuition this fall to State University (an eligible educational institution). Jennie is claimed as a dependent by her parents, but she also files her own tax return. Can Jennie claim an education credit for the tuition paid by her grandfather? What difference would it make, if any, if Jennie did not qualify as a dependent of her parents (or anyone else)?   LO 8-4

   research

36. Why is the earned income credit referred to as a negative income tax?   LO 8-4

37. Under what circumstances can a college student qualify for the earned income credit?   LO 0-4

38. How are business credits similar to personal credits? How are they dissimilar?   LO 8-4

39. When a U.S. taxpayer pays income taxes to a foreign government, what options does the taxpayer have when determining how to treat the expenditure on her U.S. individual income tax return?   LO 8-4

40. Describe the order in which different types of tax credits are applied to reduce a taxpayer's tax liability.   LO 8-4

41. Describe the two methods that taxpayers use to prepay their taxes.   LO 8-5

42. What are the consequences of a taxpayer underpaying his or her tax liability throughout the year? Explain the safe-harbor provisions that may apply in this situation.   LO 8-5

43. Describe how the underpayment penalty is calculated.   LO 8-5

44. What determines if a taxpayer is required to file a tax return? If a taxpayer is not required to file a tax return, does this mean that the taxpayer should not file a tax return?   LO 8-5

45. What is the due date for individual tax returns? What extensions are available?   LO 8-5

46. Describe the consequences for failure to file a tax return and late payment of taxes owed.   LO 8-5

PROBLEMS

Select problems are available in Connect®.

■ connect

LO 8-1 47. Whitney received $75,000 of taxable income in 2018. All of the income was salary from her employer. What is her income tax liability in each of the following alternative situations?

a) She files under the single filing status.

b) She files a joint tax return with her spouse. Together their taxable income is $75,000.

c) She is married but files a separate tax return. Her taxable income is $75,000.

d) She files as a head of household.

LO 8-1 48. In 2018, Lisa and Fred, a married couple, had taxable income of $300,000. If they were to file separate tax returns, Lisa would have reported taxable income of $125,000 and Fred would have reported taxable income of $175,000. What is the couple's marriage penalty or benefit?

LO 8-1 49. In 2018, Jasmine and Thomas, a married couple, had taxable income of $150,000. If they were to file separate tax returns, Jasmine would have reported taxable income of $140,000 and Thomas would have reported taxable income of $10,000. What is the couple's marriage penalty or benefit?

LO 8-1 50. Lacy is a single taxpayer. In 2018, her taxable income is $40,000. What is her tax liability in each of the following alternative situations?

a) All of her income is salary from her employer.

b) Her $40,000 of taxable income includes $1,000 of qualified dividends.

c) Her $40,000 of taxable income includes $5,000 of qualified dividends.

LO 8-1 51. Henrich is a single taxpayer. In 2018, his taxable income is $450,000. What is his income tax and net investment income tax liability in each of the following alternative scenarios?

a) All of his income is salary from his employer.

b) His $450,000 of taxable income includes $2,000 of long-term capital gain that is taxed at preferential rates.

c) His $450,000 of taxable income includes $55,000 of long-term capital gain that is taxed at preferential rates.

d) Henrich has $195,000 of taxable income, which includes $50,000 of long-term capital gain that is taxed at preferential rates. Assume his modified AGI is $210,000.

LO 8-1 52. In 2018, Sheryl is claimed as a dependent on her parents' tax return. Sheryl did not provide more than half her own support. What is Sheryl's tax liability for the year in each of the following alternative circumstances?

a) She received $7,000 from a part-time job. This was her only source of income. She is 16 years old at year-end.

b) She received $7,000 of interest income from corporate bonds she received several years ago. This is her only source of income. She is 16 years old at year-end.

c) She received $7,000 of interest income from corporate bonds she received several years ago. This is her only source of income. She is 20 years old at year-end and is a full-time student.

d) She received $7,000 of qualified dividend income. This is her only source of income. She is 16 years old at year-end.

53. In 2018, Carson is claimed as a dependent on his parents' tax return. Carson's parents provided most of his support. What is Carson's tax liability for the year in each of the following alternative circumstances?

    a) Carson is 17 years old at year-end and earned $14,000 from his summer job and part-time job after school. This was his only source of income.

    b) Carson is 23 years old at year-end. He is a full-time student and earned $14,000 from his summer internship and part-time job. He also received $5,000 of qualified dividend income.

    LO 8-1

54. Brooklyn files as a head of household for 2018. She claimed the standard deduction of $18,000 for regular tax purposes. Her regular taxable income was $80,000. What is Brooklyn's AMTI?

    LO 8-2

55. Sylvester files as a single taxpayer during 2018. He itemizes deductions for regular tax purposes. He paid charitable contributions of $7,000, real estate taxes of $1,000, state income taxes of $4,000, and mortgage interest of $2,000 on $30,000 of acquisition indebtedness on his home. Sylvester's regular taxable income is $100,000. What is Sylvester's AMTI?

    LO 8-2

56. In 2018, Nadia has $100,000 of regular taxable income. She itemizes her deductions as follows: real property taxes of $1,500, state income taxes of $2,000, and mortgage interest expense of $10,000 (acquisition indebtedness of $200,000). In addition, she receives tax-exempt interest of $1,000 from a municipal bond (issued in 2006) that was used to fund a new business building for a (formerly) out-of-state employer. Finally, she received a state tax refund of $300 from the prior year.

    a) What is Nadia's AMTI this year if she deducted $15,000 of itemized deductions last year and did not owe any AMT last year? Complete Form 6251 (through line 28) for Nadia.

    b) What is Nadia's AMTI this year if she deducted the standard deduction last year and did not owe any AMT last year? Complete Form 6251 (through line 28) for Nadia.

    LO 8-2

    tax forms

57. In 2018, Sven is single and has $120,000 of regular taxable income. He itemizes his deductions as follows: real property tax of $2,000, state income tax of $4,000, and mortgage interest expense of $15,000 (acquisition debt of $300,000). He also has a positive AMT depreciation adjustment of $500. What is Sven's alternative minimum taxable income (AMTI)? Complete Form 6251 (through line 28) for Sven.

    LO 8-2

    tax forms

58. Olga is married and files a joint tax return with her husband. What amount of AMT exemption may she deduct under each of the following alternative circumstances?

    a) Her AMTI is $390,000.

    b) Her AMTI is $1,080,000.

    c) Her AMTI is $1,500,000.

    LO 8-2

59. Corbett's AMTI is $600,000. What is his AMT exemption under the following alternative circumstances?

    a) He is married and files a joint return.

    b) He is married and files a separate return.

    c) His filing status is single.

    d) His filing status is head of household.

    LO 8-2

60. In 2018, Juanita is married and files a joint tax return with her husband. What is her tentative minimum tax in each of the following alternative circumstances?

    a) Her AMT base is $100,000, all ordinary income.

    b) Her AMT base is $250,000, all ordinary income.

    LO 8-2

c) Her AMT base is $100,000, which includes $10,000 of qualified dividends.

d) Her AMT base is $250,000, which includes $10,000 of qualified dividends.

LO 8-2 61. Steve's tentative minimum tax for 2018 is $245,000. What is his AMT if
a) His regular tax is $230,000?
b) His regular tax is $250,000?

LO 8-2

tax forms 62. In 2018, Janet and Ray are married filing jointly. They have five dependent children under 18 years of age. Janet and Ray's taxable income is $2,400,000 and they itemize their deductions as follows: state income taxes of $10,000, and mortgage interest expense of $25,000 (acquisition debt of $300,000). What is Janet and Ray's AMT? Complete Form 6251 for Janet and Ray.

LO 8-2

tax forms 63. In 2018, Deon and NeNe are married filing jointly. Deon and NeNe's taxable income is $1,090,000, and they itemize their deductions as follows: real property taxes of $10,000, charitable contributions of $30,000, and mortgage interest expense of $40,000 ($700,000 acquisition debt for home). What is Deon and NeNe's AMT? Complete Form 6251 for Deon and NeNe.

LO 8-3 64. Brooke, a single taxpayer, works for Company A for all of 2018, earning a salary of $50,000.
a) What is her FICA tax obligation for the year?
b) Assume Brooke works for Company A for half of 2018, earning $50,000 in salary, and she works for Company B for the second half of 2018, earning $90,000 in salary. What is Brooke's FICA tax obligation for the year?

LO 8-3 65. Rasheed works for Company A, earning $350,000 in salary during 2018. Assuming he is single and has no other sources of income, what amount of FICA tax will Rasheed pay for the year?

LO 8-3 66. Alice is single and self-employed in 2018. Her net business profit on her Schedule C for the year is $140,000. What is her self-employment tax liability and additional Medicare tax liability for 2018?

LO 8-3 67. Kyle, a single taxpayer, worked as a free-lance software engineer for the first three months of 2018. During that time, he earned $44,000 of self-employment income. On April 1, 2018, Kyle took a job as a full-time software engineer with one of his former clients, Hoogle Inc. From April through the end of the year, Kyle earned $178,000 in salary. What amount of FICA taxes (self-employment and employment related) does Kyle owe for the year?

LO 8-3 68. Eva received $60,000 in compensation payments from JAZZ Corp. during 2018. Eva incurred $5,000 in business expenses relating to her work for JAZZ Corp. JAZZ did not reimburse Eva for any of these expenses. Eva is single and she deducts a standard deduction of $12,000. Based on these facts answer the following questions:
a) Assume that Eva is considered to be an *employee*. What amount of FICA taxes is she required to pay for the year?
b) Assume that Eva is considered to be an *employee*. What is her regular income tax liability for the year?
c) Assume that Eva is considered to be a *self-employed contractor*. What is her self-employment tax liability and additional Medicare tax liability for the year?
d) Assume that Eva is considered to be a *self-employed contractor*. What is her regular tax liability for the year?

69. Terry Hutchison worked as a self-employed lawyer until two years ago when he retired. He used the cash method of accounting in his business for tax purposes. Five years ago, Terry represented his client ABC Corporation in an antitrust lawsuit against XYZ Corporation. During that year, Terry paid self-employment taxes on all of his income. ABC won the lawsuit but Terry and ABC could not agree on the amount of his earnings. Finally, this year, the issue got resolved and ABC paid Terry $90,000 for the services he provided five years ago. Terry plans to include the payment in his gross income, but because he spends most of his time playing golf and absolutely no time working on legal matters, he does not intend to pay self-employment taxes on the income. Is Terry subject to self-employment taxes on this income?

LO 8-3

research

70. Trey has two dependents, his daughters, ages 14 and 17, at year-end. Trey files a joint return with his wife. What amount of child credit will Trey be able to claim for his daughters under each of the following alternative situations?

LO 8-4

   a) His AGI is $100,000.
   b) His AGI is $420,000.
   c) His AGI is $420,100, and his daughters are ages 10 and 12.

71. Julie paid a day care center to watch her two-year-old son while she worked as a computer programmer for a local start-up company. What amount of child and dependent care credit can Julie claim in each of the following alternative scenarios?

LO 8-4

   a) Julie paid $2,000 to the day care center and her AGI is $50,000 (all salary).
   b) Julie paid $5,000 to the day care center and her AGI is $50,000 (all salary).
   c) Julie paid $4,000 to the day care center and her AGI is $25,000 (all salary).
   d) Julie paid $2,000 to the day care center and her AGI is $14,000 (all salary).
   e) Julie paid $4,000 to the day care center and her AGI is $14,000 ($2,000 salary and $12,000 unearned income).

72. In 2018, Elaine paid $2,800 of tuition and $600 for books for her dependent son to attend State University this past fall as a freshman. Elaine files a joint return with her husband. What is the maximum American opportunity credit that Elaine can claim for the tuition payment and books in each of the following alternative situations?

LO 8-4

   a) Elaine's AGI is $80,000.
   b) Elaine's AGI is $168,000.
   c) Elaine's AGI is $184,000.

73. In 2018, Laureen is currently single. She paid $2,800 of qualified tuition and related expenses for each of her twin daughters Sheri and Meri to attend State University as freshmen ($2,800 each for a total of $5,600). Sheri and Meri qualify as Laureen's dependents. Laureen also paid $1,900 for her son Ryan's (also Laureen's dependent) tuition and related expenses to attend his junior year at State University. Finally, Laureen paid $1,200 for herself to attend seminars at a community college to help her improve her job skills. What is the maximum amount of education credits Laureen can claim for these expenditures in each of the following alternative scenarios?

LO 8-4

planning

   a) Laureen's AGI is $45,000.
   b) Laureen's AGI is $95,000.
   c) Laureen's AGI is $45,000 and Laureen paid $12,000 (not $1,900) for Ryan to attend graduate school (i.e., his fifth year, not his junior year).

LO 8-4   74. In 2018, Amanda and Jaxon Stuart have a daughter who is 1 year old. The Stuarts are full-time students and they are both 23 years old. Their only sources of income are gains from stock they held for three years before selling and wages from part-time jobs. What is their earned income credit in the following alternative scenarios if they file jointly?

a) Their AGI is $15,000, consisting of $5,000 of capital gains and $10,000 of wages.

b) Their AGI is $15,000, consisting of $10,000 of lottery winnings (unearned income) and $5,000 of wages.

c) Their AGI is $25,000, consisting of $20,000 of wages and $5,000 of lottery winnings (unearned income).

d) Their AGI is $25,000, consisting of $5,000 of wages and $20,000 of lottery winnings (unearned income).

e) Their AGI is $10,000, consisting of $10,000 of lottery winnings (unearned income).

LO 8-4   75. In 2018, Zach is single with no dependents. He is not claimed as a dependent on another's return. All of his income is from salary and he does not have any *for* AGI deductions. What is his earned income credit in the following alternative scenarios?

a) Zach is 29 years old and his AGI is $5,000.

b) Zach is 29 years old and his AGI is $10,000.

c) Zach is 29 years old and his AGI is $19,000.

d) Zach is 24 years old and his AGI is $5,000.

LO 8-4   76. This year Luke has calculated his gross tax liability at $1,800. Luke is entitled to a $2,400 nonrefundable personal tax credit, a $1,500 business tax credit, and a $600 refundable personal tax credit. In addition, Luke has had $2,300 of income taxes withheld from his salary. What is Luke's net tax due or refund?

LO 8-5
planning   77. This year Lloyd, a single taxpayer, estimates that his tax liability will be $10,000. Last year, his total tax liability was $15,000. He estimates that his tax withholding from his employer will be $7,800.

a) Is Lloyd required to increase his withholding or make estimated tax payments this year to avoid the underpayment penalty? If so, how much?

b) Assuming Lloyd does not make any additional payments, what is the amount of his underpayment penalty? Assume the federal short-term rate is 5 percent.

LO 8-5
planning   78. This year, Paula and Simon (married filing jointly) estimate that their tax liability will be $200,000. Last year, their total tax liability was $170,000. They estimate that their tax withholding from their employers will be $175,000. Are Paula and Simon required to increase their withholdings or make estimated tax payments this year to avoid the underpayment penalty? If so, how much?

LO 8-5
planning   79. This year, Santhosh, a single taxpayer, estimates that his tax liability will be $100,000. Last year, his total tax liability was $15,000. He estimates that his tax withholding from his employer will be $35,000. Is Santhosh required to increase his withholding or make estimated tax payments this year to avoid the underpayment penalty? If so, how much?

LO 8-5   80. For the following taxpayers, determine if they are required to file a tax return in 2018.

a) Ricko, single taxpayer, with gross income of $15,000.

b) Fantasia, head of household, with gross income of $17,500.

   c) Ken and Barbie, married taxpayers with no dependents, with gross income of $20,000.

   d) Dorothy and Rudolf, married taxpayers, both age 68, with gross income of $25,500.

   e) Janyce, single taxpayer, age 73, with gross income of $13,500.

81. For the following taxpayers, determine the due date of their tax returns.

   a) Jerome, a single taxpayer, is not requesting an extension this year. Assume the due date falls on a Tuesday.

   b) Lashaunda, a single taxpayer, requests an extension this year. Assume the extended due date falls on a Wednesday.

   c) Barney and Betty, married taxpayers, do not request an extension this year. Assume the due date falls on a Sunday.

   d) Fred and Wilma, married taxpayers, request an extension this year. Assume the extended date falls on a Saturday.

82. Determine the amount of the late filing and late payment penalties that apply for the following taxpayers.

   a) Jolene filed her tax return by its original due date but did not pay the $2,000 in taxes she owed with the return until one and a half months later.

   b) Oscar filed his tax return and paid his $3,000 tax liability seven months late.

   c) Wilfred, attempting to evade his taxes, did not file a tax return or pay his $10,000 in taxes for several years.

COMPREHENSIVE PROBLEMS

Select problems are available in Connect®.

83. In 2018, Jack is single and has two children, ages 10 and 12. Jack works full-time and earns an annual salary of $195,000 as a consultant. Jack files as a head of household and does not itemize his deductions. In the fall of this year, he was recently offered a position with another firm that would pay him an additional $35,000.

   a) Calculate the marginal tax rate on the additional income, *excluding employment taxes,* to help Jack evaluate the offer.

   b) Calculate the marginal tax rate on the additional income, *including employment taxes,* to help Jack evaluate the offer.

84. Reba Dixon is a fifth-grade schoolteacher who earned a salary of $38,000 in 2018. She is 45 years old and has been divorced for four years. She receives $1,200 of alimony payments each month from her former husband (divorced in 2016). Reba also rents out a small apartment building. This year Reba received $50,000 of rental payments from tenants and she incurred $19,500 of expenses associated with the rental.

    Reba and her daughter Heather (20 years old at the end of the year) moved to Georgia in January of this year. Reba provides more than one-half of Heather's support. They had been living in Colorado for the past 15 years, but ever since her divorce, Reba has been wanting to move back to Georgia to be closer to her family. Luckily, last December, a teaching position opened up and Reba and Heather decided to make the move. Reba paid a moving company $2,010 to move their personal belongings, and she and Heather spent two days driving the 1,426 miles to Georgia.

Reba rented a home in Georgia. Heather decided to continue living at home with her mom, but she started attending school full-time in January at a nearby university. She was awarded a $3,000 partial tuition scholarship this year, and Reba helped out by paying the remaining $500 tuition cost. If possible, Reba thought it would be best to claim the education credit for these expenses.

Reba wasn't sure if she would have enough items to help her benefit from itemizing on her tax return. However, she kept track of several expenses this year that she thought might qualify if she was able to itemize. Reba paid $5,800 in state income taxes and $12,500 in charitable contributions during the year. She also paid the following medical-related expenses for herself and Heather:

Insurance premiums	$5,795
Medical care expenses	1,100
Prescription medicine	350
Nonprescription medicine	100
New contact lenses for Heather	200

Shortly after the move, Reba got distracted while driving and she ran into a street sign. The accident caused $900 in damage to the car and gave her whiplash. Because the repairs were less than her insurance deductible, she paid the entire cost of the repairs. Reba wasn't able to work for two months after the accident. Fortunately, she received $2,000 from her disability insurance. Her employer, the Central Georgia School District, paid 60 percent of the premiums on the policy as a nontaxable fringe benefit and Reba paid the remaining 40 percent portion.

A few years ago, Reba acquired several investments with her portion of the divorce settlement. This year she reported the following income from her investments: $2,200 of interest income from corporate bonds and $1,500 interest income from City of Denver municipal bonds. Overall, Reba's stock portfolio appreciated by $12,000 but she did not sell any of her stocks.

Heather reported $6,200 of interest income from corporate bonds she received as gifts from her father over the last several years. This was Heather's only source of income for the year.

Reba had $10,000 of federal income taxes withheld by her employer. Heather made $1,000 of estimated tax payments during the year. Reba did not make any estimated payments. Reba had qualifying insurance for purposes of the Affordable Care Act (ACA).

Required:

a) Determine Reba's federal income taxes due or taxes payable for the current year. Complete pages 1 and 2 of Form 1040 for Reba.

b) Is Reba allowed to file as a head of household or single?

c) Determine the amount of FICA taxes Reba was required to pay on her salary.

d) Determine Heather's federal income taxes due or payable.

85. John and Sandy Ferguson got married eight years ago and have a seven-year-old daughter, Samantha. In 2018, John worked as a computer technician at a local university earning a salary of $152,000, and Sandy worked part-time as a receptionist for a law firm earning a salary of $29,000. John also does some Web design work on the side and reported revenues of $4,000 and associated expenses of $750. The Fergusons received $800 in qualified dividends and a $200 refund of their state income taxes. The Fergusons always itemize their deductions and their itemized deductions were well over the standard deduction amount last year. The Fergusons had qualifying insurance for purposes of the Affordable Care Act (ACA).

The Fergusons reported making the following payments during the year:

- State income taxes of $4,400. Federal tax withholding of $21,000
- Alimony payments to John's former wife of $10,000 (divorced in 2014).
- Child support payments for John's child with his former wife of $4,100.
- $12,200 of real property taxes.
- Sandy was reimbursed $600 for employee business expenses she incurred. She was required to provide documentation for her expenses to her employer.
- $3,600 to Kid Care day care center for Samantha's care while John and Sandy worked.
- $14,000 interest on their home mortgage ($400,000 acquisition debt).
- $3,000 interest on a $40,000 home-equity loan. They used the loan to pay for a family vacation and new car.
- $15,000 cash charitable contributions to qualified charities.
- Donation of used furniture to Goodwill. The furniture had a fair market value of $400 and cost $2,000.

Required:

What is the Fergusons' 2018 federal income taxes payable or refund, including any self-employment tax and AMT, if applicable? Complete pages 1 and 2 of Form 1040 and Form 6251 for John and Sandy.

 ROGER | CPA Review

Sample CPA Exam questions from Roger CPA Review are available in Connect as support for the topics in this text. These Multiple Choice Questions and Task-Based Simulations include expert-written explanations and solutions and provide a starting point for students to become familiar with the content and functionality of the actual CPA Exam.

Business Income, Deductions, and Accounting Methods

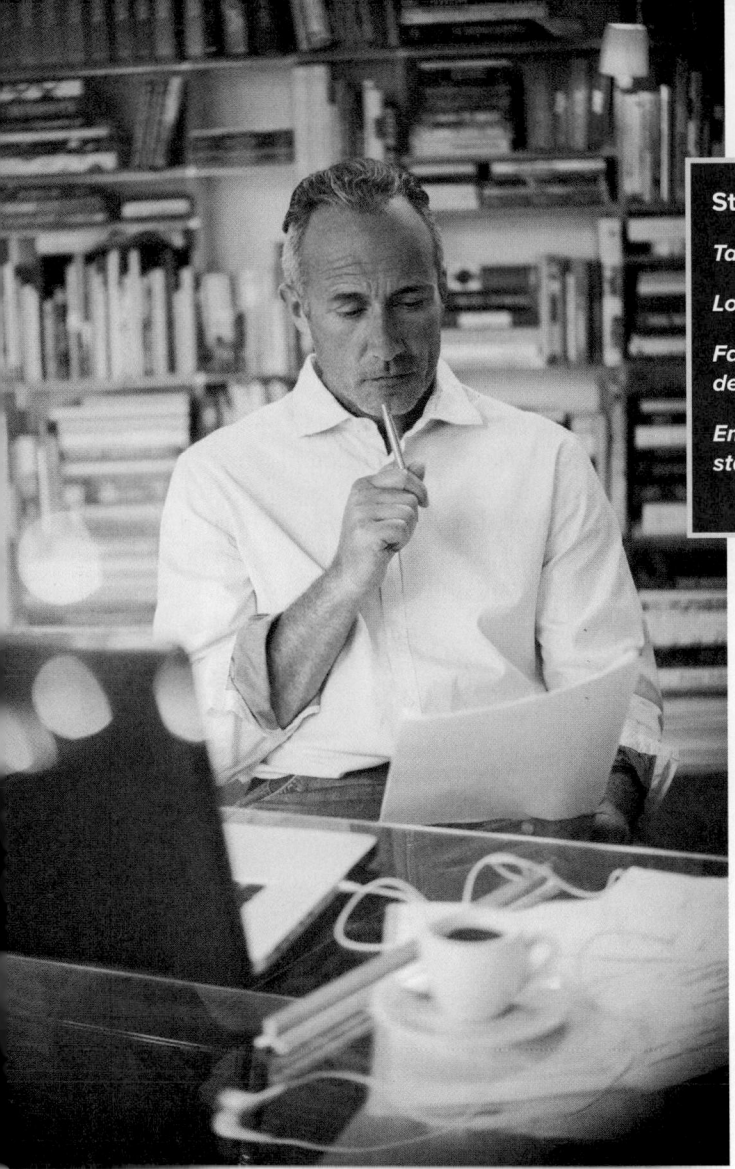

©Tom Merton/Caiaimage/Getty Images

Rick Grime graduated from Texas A&M University with a degree in agronomy, and for the past few years he has been employed by a landscape architect in Dallas. Nearly every day that Rick went to work, he shared ideas with his employer about improving the business. Rick finally decided to take his ideas and start his own landscaping business in his hometown of San Antonio, Texas. In mid-April, Rick left his job and moved his belongings to San Antonio. Once in town, Rick discovered he had to do a lot of things to start his business. First, he registered his new business name (Green Acres Landscaping, LLC) and established a bank account for the business. Next, he rented a used sport utility vehicle (SUV) and a shop for his place of business. Rick didn't know much about accounting for business activities, so he hired a CPA, Jane Bronson, to help him. Jane and Rick decided that Green Acres would operate as a sole proprietorship, but Jane suggested that as the business grew, he might want to consider organizing it as a different type of legal entity. Operating as a corporation, for instance, would allow him to invite new investors or business partners to help fund future expansion. Rick formally started his business on May 1. He spent a lot of time attracting new customers, and he figured he would hire employees as he needed them.

to be continued . . .

In previous chapters, we've emphasized the process of determining gross income and deductions for *individuals*. This chapter describes the process for determining income for *businesses*. Keep in mind that the concepts we discuss in this chapter generally apply to all types of tax entities, including sole proprietorships (such as Rick's company, Green Acres), partnerships, entities tax as partnerships (such as LLCs), S corporations, and C corporations.[1] Because Rick is a sole proprietor, our examples emphasize business income and deductions from his personal perspective. Proprietors report business income on Schedule C of their individual income tax returns. However, the choice of the organizational form is a complex decision that is described in the Entities Overview chapter.

Schedule C income is subject to both individual income and self-employment taxes. Entities other than sole proprietorships report income on tax forms separate from the owners' tax returns. For example, partnerships report taxable income on Form 1065, S corporations report taxable income on Form 1120S, and C corporations report taxable income on Form 1120. Of all these entity types, generally only C corporations pay taxes on their income.

BUSINESS GROSS INCOME

In most respects, the rules for determining business gross income are the same as for determining gross income for individuals. Gross income includes "all income from whatever source derived."[2] The tax laws specifically indicate that this definition includes gross income from "business." Generally speaking, income from business includes gross profit from inventory sales (sales minus cost of goods sold), income from services provided to customers, and income from renting property to customers. Just like individuals, businesses are allowed to exclude certain types of realized income from gross income, such as municipal bond interest.

BUSINESS DEDUCTIONS

> **THE KEY FACTS**
>
> **Business Expenses**
>
> - Business expenses must be incurred in pursuit of profits, not personal goals.
> - A deduction must be ordinary and necessary (appropriate and helpful).
> - Only reasonable amounts are allowed as deductions.

Because Congress intended for taxable income to reflect the *net* increase in wealth from a business, it is only fair that businesses be allowed to deduct expenses incurred to generate business income. Typically, Congress provides *specific* statutory rules authorizing deductions. However, as you can see from the following excerpt from IRC §162, the provision authorizing business deductions is relatively broad and ambiguous:

> There shall be allowed as a deduction all the ordinary and necessary expenses paid or incurred during the taxable year in carrying on any trade or business . . .

This provision authorizes taxpayers to deduct expenses for "trade or business" activities.[3] The tax code does not define the phrase "trade or business," but it's clear that the objective of business activities is to make a profit. Thus, the law requires that a business expense be made in the pursuit of profits rather than the pursuit of other, presumably personal, motives.

When a taxpayer's activity does not meet the "for profit" requirement, it is treated as a hobby, an activity motivated by personal objectives. A taxpayer engaged in a hobby cannot deduct expenses associated with that activity (commencing in 2018).

---

[1]S corporations are treated as flow-through entities (S corporation income is taxed to its owners) while C corporations are taxed as separate taxable entities.

[2]§61(a).

[3]§212 contains a sister provision to §162 allowing deductions for ordinary and necessary expenses incurred for the production of income ("investment expenses") and for the management and maintenance of property (including expenses incurred in renting property in situations when the rental activity is not considered to be a trade or business). A business activity, sometimes referred to as a trade or business, requires a relatively high level of involvement or effort from the taxpayer. Unlike business activities, investments are profit-motivated activities that don't require a high degree of taxpayer involvement or effort.

Ordinary and Necessary

Business expenditures must be both **ordinary and necessary** to be deductible. An *ordinary* expense is an expense that is normal or appropriate for the business under the circumstances.[4] An expense is *not* necessarily required to be typical or repetitive in nature to be considered ordinary. For example, a business could deduct the legal fees it expends to defend itself in an antitrust suit. Although an antitrust suit would be atypical and unusual for most businesses, defending the suit would probably be deemed ordinary because it would be expected under the circumstances. A *necessary* expense is an expense that is helpful or conducive to the business activity, but the expenditure need not be essential or indispensable. For example, a deduction for metric tools would qualify as ordinary and necessary even if there was only a small chance that a repairman might need these tools. The "ordinary and necessary" requirements are applied on a case-by-case basis, and while the deduction depends on individual circumstances, the IRS is often reluctant to second-guess business decisions. Exhibit 9-1 presents examples of expenditures that are ordinary and necessary for typical businesses.

EXHIBIT 9-1   **Examples of Typical Ordinary and Necessary Business Expenses**

• Advertising	• Office expenses
• Car and truck expenses	• Rent
• Depreciation	• Repairs
• Employee compensation and benefits	• Supplies
• Insurance	• Travel
• Interest	• Utilities
• Legal fees	• Wages

Example 9-1

Outside Rick's office is a small waiting room for clients. Rick paid $50 for several books to occupy clients while waiting for appointments. These are hardcover books with photographs and illustrations of landscape designs. Rick believes that the books will inspire new designs and alleviate boredom for potential clients, and he deducted the $50 cost as a business expense. Is he correct?

Answer: Under the law, expenses directly connected to a business are deductible if the expenditure is ordinary and necessary. The phrase *ordinary and necessary* is interpreted as *helpful or conducive to business activity.* In Rick's situation, it seems highly unlikely that the IRS or a court would conclude that the cost of these books is not ordinary and necessary. What do you think?

What if: Suppose that Rick's hobby was pre-Columbian Maya civilization. Do you think Rick would be able to deduct the cost of a new treatise on translating Maya script if he placed the book in his waiting room? Why or why not?

ETHICS

Sheri is an attorney who operates as a sole practitioner. Despite her busy schedule, in the past Sheri found time for her family. This year Sheri took on two new important clients, and she hired a personal assistant to help her manage her schedule and make timely court filings. Occasionally, Sheri asked her assistant to assist her with personal tasks such as having her car serviced or buying groceries. Do you think that Sheri should treat her assistant's entire salary as a business expense? Would your answer be any different if personal assistants were to commonly perform these tasks for other busy professionals, such as corporate executives and accountants?

[4]*Welch v. Helvering* (1933), 290 US 111.

Reasonable in Amount

Ordinary and necessary business expenses are deductible only *to the extent* they are also **reasonable in amount.** The courts have interpreted this requirement to mean that an expenditure is not reasonable when it is extravagant or exorbitant.[5] If the expenditure is extravagant in amount, the courts presume the excess amount is spent for personal rather than business reasons and is not deductible.

Determining whether an expenditure is reasonable is not an exact science, and not surprisingly, taxpayers and the IRS may have different opinions. Generally, the courts and the IRS test for extravagance by comparing the amount of the expense to a market price or an **arm's length amount.** If the amount of the expense is within the range of amounts typically charged in the market by unrelated persons, the amount is considered to be reasonable. The underlying issue is *why* a profit-motivated taxpayer would pay an extravagant amount. Hence, reasonableness is most likely to be an issue when a payment is made to an individual related to the taxpayer or when the taxpayer enjoys some incidental benefit from the expenditure.

Example 9-2

During the busy part of the year, Rick could not keep up with all the work. Therefore, he hired four part-time employees and paid them $10 an hour to mow lawns and pull weeds for an average of 20 hours a week. When things finally slowed down in late fall, Rick released his four part-time employees. Rick paid a total of $22,000 in compensation to the four employees. He still needed some extra help now and then, so he hired his brother, Tom, on a part-time basis. Tom performed the same duties as the prior part-time employees (his quality of work was about the same). However, Rick paid Tom $25 per hour because Tom is a college student and Rick wanted to provide some additional support for Tom's education. At year-end, Tom had worked a total of 100 hours and received $2,500 from Rick. What amount can Rick deduct for the compensation he paid to his employees?

Answer: $23,000. Rick can deduct the entire $22,000 paid to the four part-time employees. However, he can only deduct $10 an hour for Tom's compensation because the extra $15 per hour Rick paid Tom is unreasonable in amount.[6] The remaining $15 per hour is considered a personal (nondeductible) gift from Rick to Tom. Hence, Rick can deduct a total of $23,000 for compensation expense this year [$22,000 + ($10 × 100)].

LO 9-2 LIMITATIONS ON BUSINESS DEDUCTIONS

For a variety of reasons, Congress specifically prohibits or limits a business's ability to deduct certain expenditures that appear to otherwise meet the general business expense deductibility requirements.

Expenditures against Public Policy

Businesses occasionally incur fines and penalties and may even pay illegal bribes and kickbacks. However, these payments are not deductible for tax purposes.[7] Congress disallows these expenditures under the rationale that allowing them would subsidize illegal activities and frustrate public policy. Interestingly enough, businesses conducting an illegal activity (selling stolen goods or conducting illegal gambling) are allowed

---

THE KEY FACTS

Limitations on Business Deductions

- No business deductions are allowable for expenditures that are against public policy (bribes) or are political contributions.
- Expenditures that benefit a period longer than 12 months generally must be capitalized.
- No deductions are allowable for expenditures associated with the production of tax-exempt income.
- Personal expenditures are not deductible.

---

[5]§162(a) and *Comm. v. Lincoln Electric Co.* (CA-6, 1949), 176 F.2d 815.

[6]In practice, this distinction is rarely cut and dried. Rick may be able to argue for various reasons that Tom's work is worth more than $10 an hour but perhaps not as much as $25 per hour. We use this example to illustrate the issue of reasonable expenses and not to discuss the merits of what actually is reasonable compensation to Tom.

[7]§162(c) and Reg. §1.162-21. This prohibition applies to fines and penalties imposed by a government or governmental unit unless the taxpayer establishes that the payment is either restitution, remediation, or required to come into compliance with the law. Fines and penalties imposed by other organizations, such as a fine levied by NASCAR or the NFL, would be fully deductible if the payment otherwise qualified as an ordinary and necessary business expense.

to offset gross income with the cost of the illegal goods (the cost of goods sold) and deduct other ordinary and necessary business expenses incurred in conducting the illegal business activity. However, they are not allowed to deduct fines, penalties, bribes, or illegal kickbacks.[8] Of course, the IRS is probably more concerned that many illegal businesses fail to report *any* income than that illegal businesses overstate deductions.[9]

Political Contributions and Lobbying Costs

Perhaps to avoid the perception that the federal government subsidizes taxpayer efforts to influence politics, the tax laws prohibit deductions for political contributions and most lobbying expenses.[10]

Example 9-3

In July, the city fined Rick $200 for violating the city's watering ban when he watered a newly installed landscape. Later, Rick donated $250 to the mayor's campaign for reelection. Can Rick deduct these expenditures?

Answer: No. Rick cannot deduct either the fine or the political contribution as a business expense because the tax laws specifically prohibit deductions for these expenditures.

Capital Expenditures

Whether a business uses the cash or the accrual method of accounting, it must capitalize expenditures for *tangible* assets such as buildings, machinery and equipment, furniture and fixtures, and similar property that have useful lives of more than one year (12 months).[11] For tax purposes, businesses recover the cost of capitalized tangible assets (other than land) through depreciation.

Businesses also capitalize the cost to create or acquire *intangible* assets such as patents, goodwill, start-up costs, and organizational expenditures.[12] They recover the costs of capitalized intangible assets either through amortization (when the tax laws allow them to do so) or upon disposition of the assets. Prepaid expenses are also subject to capitalization, but there is a special exception that we discuss under accounting methods later in this chapter.[13]

Expenses Associated with the Production of Tax-Exempt Income

Expenses that do not help businesses generate *taxable* income are not allowed to offset taxable income. For example, this restriction disallows interest expense deductions for businesses that borrow money and invest the loan proceeds in municipal (tax-exempt)

---

[8]*Comm. v. Sullivan* (1958), 356 US 27. In addition, beginning after December 22, 2017, no deduction is allowed for any settlement, payout, or attorney fees related to sexual harassment or abuse if the payments are subject to a nondisclosure agreement.

[9]§280E explicitly prohibits drug dealers from deducting any business expenses associated with this "business" activity. However, drug dealers are able to deduct cost of goods sold because cost of goods sold is technically a reduction in gross income and not a business expense. See Reg. §1.61-3(a).

[10]§162(e).

[11]Reg. §1.263(a)-2(d)(4). The act of recording the asset is sometimes referred to as *capitalizing* the expenditure.

[12]Reg. §1.263(a)-4(b). The extent to which expenditures for intangible assets must be capitalized is explored in *Indopco v. Comm.* (1992), 503 US 79.

[13]See §195, §197, and §248 for provisions that allow taxpayers to amortize the cost of certain intangible assets.

bonds. It also disallows deductions for life insurance premiums businesses pay on policies that cover the lives of officers or other key employees and compensate the business for the disruption and lost income they may experience due to a key employee's death. Because the death benefit from the life insurance policy is not taxable, the business is not allowed to deduct the insurance premium expense associated with this nontaxable income.

Example 9-4

Rick employs Joan, an arborist who specializes in trimming trees and treating local tree ailments. Joan generates a great deal of revenue for Rick's business, but she is in her mid-60s and suffers from diabetes. In November, Rick purchased a "key employee" term life-insurance policy on Joan's life. The policy cost Rick $720 and will pay Rick (Green Acres) a $20,000 death benefit if Joan passes away during the next 12 months. What amount of life insurance policy premium can Rick deduct?

Answer: $0. Rick cannot deduct the $720 premium on the life insurance policy because the life insurance proceeds from the policy are tax-exempt.

What if: Suppose Rick purchased the life insurance policy on Joan's life and allowed Joan to name the beneficiary. The policy cost Rick $720 and will pay the beneficiary a $20,000 death benefit if Joan passes away during the next 12 months. What amount of life insurance policy premium can Rick deduct?

Answer: $720. In this scenario, Rick can deduct the entire premium of $720 as a *compensation* expense because the benefit of the policy inures to Joan and not to Rick's business.

Personal Expenditures

Taxpayers are not allowed to deduct **personal expenses** unless the expenses are "expressly" authorized by a provision in the law.[14] While the tax laws do not define personal expenses, they imply the scope of personal expenses by stating that "personal, living, or family expenses" are not deductible. Therefore, at a minimum, the costs of food, clothing, and shelter are assumed to be personal and nondeductible. Of course, there are the inevitable exceptions when otherwise personal items are specially adapted to business use. For example, taxpayers may deduct the cost of uniforms or special clothing they purchase for use in their business, if the clothing is not appropriate to wear as ordinary clothing outside the place of business. However, when the clothing is adaptable as ordinary clothing, the cost of the clothing is a nondeductible personal expenditure.

Example 9-5

Rick spent $500 to purchase special coveralls that identify his landscaping service and provide a professional appearance. How much of the cost for the clothing can Rick deduct as a business expense?

Answer: All $500. While the cost of clothing is inherently personal, Rick can deduct the $500 cost of the coveralls because, due to the design and labeling on the coveralls, they are not suitable for ordinary use.

---

[14]§262(a).

Many business owners, particularly small business owners such as sole proprietors, may be in a position to use business funds to pay for items that are entirely personal in nature. For example, a sole proprietor could use the business checking account to pay for family groceries. These expenditures, even though funded by the business, are not deductible.

Expenditures made by a taxpayer for education, such as tuition and books, are often related to a taxpayer's business aspirations. However, educational expenditures are not deductible as business expenses unless the taxpayer is self employed and the education maintains or improves skills required by the individual in his existing trade or business. Education expenses necessary to meet minimum requirements for an occupation are not deductible. For example, tuition payments for courses to satisfy the education requirement to sit for the CPA exam are not deductible. This is an example of education that qualifies the taxpayer for a new trade or business rather than improving his skills in an existing trade or business. However, education expense necessary to maintain the skill of a self employed taxpayer would be a deductible business expense.

TAXES IN THE REAL WORLD Web Sales and the Cohan Rule

Thomas began collecting coins in 1958 and later inherited his father's coin collection. He wasn't employed during 2013, so he actively engaged in buying and selling coins and related items (such as silver ingots and items issued by the Franklin Mint) on eBay using PayPal. At year end, PayPal filed a Form 1099-K reporting sales of $37,013 by Thomas during 2013. However, Thomas failed to report these sales on his return, and because he didn't report these sales, Thomas also didn't claim the costs he incurred in making his eBay sales. The IRS subsequently assessed a tax deficiency of $12,905 based on unreported income of $37,013.

The law generally requires the Tax Court to presume that the deficiency determined by the IRS is correct, and hence, Thomas had the burden of proving them wrong. At trial the IRS conceded that Thomas was engaged in a "trade or business" with the intent to earn a profit. However, Thomas was still required to substantiate expenses for any deductions by producing records sufficient to enable the court to determine the correct tax liability. Unfortunately, Thomas maintained no records of any kind to establish his cost or other bases in the coins and related items that he sold on eBay.

Despite a continuance at trial, Thomas was unable to present any documentation to establish his cost of goods. Rather, he submitted eBay records of his sales and coin catalogs tracking the market prices during 2010–2013. Thomas

testified that he turned over his inventory fairly quickly and the sales records provided some support for this contention. On the other hand, Thomas also sold some of the coins he had previously collected or inherited.

If a taxpayer with inadequate business records testifies credibly that he incurred certain expenses, under the Cohan rule the Court can estimate the amount of deductions. This rule originated with George M. Cohan who was a Broadway star in the early 1900s. He was audited by the IRS which disallowed many of his business- and entertainment-related expenses. The IRS argued that without receipts, the expenses were nondeductible despite Cohan's credible testimony in court. The 2nd Circuit Court of appeals agreed with Cohan and forced the IRS to accept estimates of his expenses. *Cohan v. Commissioner*, 39 F. 2d 540 (2d Cir. 1930)

Under the Cohan rule, the Court is not required to guess at a number but must have some basis for an estimate. In Thomas's case, the Tax Court evaluated his testimony and decided that Thomas substantiated a cost of goods sold of $12,000 (a nice round number) and expense deductions of $4,430 for PayPal fees, Internet charges, and postage. As a side note, Thomas was also assessed an accuracy-related penalty because he did not make a good-faith effort to determine his tax correctly.

Source: Thomas R. Huzella, TC Memo 2017-20.

Mixed-Motive Expenditures

Business owners in general, and owners of small or closely held businesses in particular, often make expenditures that are motivated by *both* business and personal concerns. These **mixed-motive expenditures** are of particular concern to lawmakers and the IRS because of the tax incentive to disguise nondeductible personal expenses as deductible business expenses. Thus, deductions for business expenditures with potentially personal motives are closely monitored and restricted. The rules for determining the amount of *deductible* mixed-motive expenditures depend on the type of expenditure. Here we review the rules for determining the deductible portion of mixed-motive expenditures for meals, travel and transportation, and the use of property for both business and personal purposes.

Meals   Because everyone needs to eat, even business meals contain a significant personal element. To allow for this personal element, taxpayers may deduct only 50 percent of actual business meals.[15] In addition, to deduct any portion of the cost of a meal as a business expense, (1) the amount must be reasonable under the circumstances, (2) the taxpayer (or an employee) must be present when the meal is furnished, and (3) the meal must be directly associated with the active conduct of the taxpayer's business.[16]

Example 9-6

Rick went out to dinner with prospective clients to discuss Rick's ideas for landscaping several business properties. After dinner, Rick and the prospective clients attended the theater. Rick paid $540 for the meal and $850 for the tickets, amounts that were reasonable under the circumstances. What amount of these expenditures can Rick deduct as a business expense?

Answer: Rick can deduct $270 [$540 × 50%], representing half the cost of the meal, as a business expense, as long as he can substantiate the business purpose and substantial nature of the dinner discussion. The cost of the tickets to the theater is a nondeductible entertainment expense.

What if: Suppose that Rick did not discuss business with the clients either before, during, or after the meal. What amount of the expenditures can Rick deduct as a business expense?

Answer: $0. In this scenario, Rick cannot deduct the cost of the meal because the activity was not directly related to or associated with a substantial business discussion.

Travel and Transportation   Under certain conditions, sole proprietors and self-employed taxpayers may deduct the cost of travel and transportation for business purposes. Transportation expenses include the direct cost of transporting the taxpayer to and from business sites. However, the cost of commuting between the taxpayer's home and regular place of business is personal and, therefore, not deductible. If the taxpayer uses a vehicle for business, the taxpayer can deduct the costs of operating the vehicle plus depreciation on the vehicle's tax basis. Alternatively, in lieu of deducting these costs, the taxpayer may simply deduct a standard amount for each business mile driven. The standard mileage rate represents the per-mile cost of operating an automobile (including depreciation or lease payments).[17] For 2018, the standard mileage rate has been set at 54.5 cents per mile. To be deductible, the transportation must be for business reasons. If the transportation is primarily for personal purposes, the cost is not deductible.

---

[15]§274 also provides some exceptions to the 50 percent reduction for meals, such as meals provided as employee compensation. Taxpayers can also use a *per diem* rate (an automatic, flat amount per meal) in lieu of actual expenditures to determine the amount of the deduction.

[16]Under §274, there are special limits placed on certain expenditures, such as those related to expenditures associated with conventions and travel.

[17]This mileage rate is updated periodically (sometimes two or three times within a year) to reflect changes in the cost of operating a vehicle.

Example 9-7

Rick decided to lease an SUV to drive between his shop and various work sites. Rick carefully documents the business use of the SUV (8,100 miles this year) and his operating expenses ($5,335 this year, including $3,935 for gas, oil, and repairs and $1,400 for lease payments). At no time does Rick use the SUV for personal purposes. What amount of these expenses may Rick deduct as business expenses?

Answer: $5,335. Since Rick uses the SUV in his business activities, he can deduct (1) the $5,335 cost of operating and leasing the SUV or (2) $4,414.50 for the 8,100 business miles driven this year (54.5 cents per mile × 8,100 miles). Assuming Rick chooses to deduct operating expenses and lease payments in lieu of using the mileage rate, he can deduct $5,335.

In contrast to transportation expenses, travel expenses are only deductible if the taxpayer is *away from home* overnight while traveling. This distinction is important because, besides the cost of transportation, the deduction for **travel expenses** includes meals (50 percent), lodging, and incidental expenses. A taxpayer is considered to be away from home overnight if the travel is away from the primary place of business and of sufficient duration to require sleep or rest (typically this will be overnight). When a taxpayer travels solely for business purposes, *all* of the costs of travel are deductible (but only 50 percent of meals). When the travel has both business and personal aspects, the deductibility of the transportation costs depends upon whether business is the *primary* purpose for the trip. If the primary purpose of a trip is business, the transportation costs are fully deductible, but meals (50 percent), lodging, and incidental expenditures are limited to those incurred during the business portion of the travel.[18] If the taxpayer's primary purpose for the trip is personal, the taxpayer may not deduct *any* transportation costs to arrive at the location but may deduct meals (50 percent), lodging, transportation, and incidental expenditures for the *business* portion of the trip. The primary purpose of a trip depends upon facts and circumstances and is often the subject of dispute.

The rule for business travel is modified somewhat if a trip abroad includes both business and personal activities. Like the rule for domestic travel, if foreign travel is primarily for personal purposes, then only those expenses directly associated with business activities are deductible. However, unlike the rule for domestic travel, when foreign travel is primarily for business purposes, a portion of the round-trip transportation costs is not deductible. The nondeductible portion is typically computed based on a time ratio such as the proportion of personal days to total days (travel days count as business days).[19]

Example 9-8

Rick paid a $300 registration fee for a three-day course in landscape design. The course was held in upstate New York (Rick paid $700 for airfare to attend) and he spent four days away from home. He spent the last day sightseeing. During the trip, Rick paid $150 a night for three nights' lodging, $50 a day for meals, and $70 a day for a rental car. What amount of these travel-related expenditures may Rick deduct as business expenses?

(continued on page 9-10)

---

[18]Note that travel days are considered business days. Also, special limitations apply to a number of travel expenses that are potentially abusive, such as luxury water travel, foreign conventions, conventions on cruise ships, and travel expenses associated with taking a companion.

[19]Foreign transportation expense is deductible without prorating under special circumstances authorized in §274(c). For example, the cost of getting abroad is fully deductible if the travel is for one week or less or if the personal activity constitutes less than one-fourth of the travel time.

Answer: $1,435 for business travel and $300 for business education. The primary purpose for the trip appears to be business because Rick spent three days on business activities versus one day on personal activities. He can deduct travel costs, computed as follows:

Deductible Travel Costs		
Description	**Amount**	**Explanation**
Airfare	$ 700	Primary purpose is business
Lodging	450	3 business days × $150 a day
Meals	75	3 business days × $50 a day × 50% limit
Rental car	210	3 business days × $70 a day
Total business travel expenses	**$1,435**	

What if: Assume Rick stayed in New York for 10 days, spending 3 days at the seminar and 7 days sightseeing. What amount could he deduct?

Answer: In this scenario Rick can deduct $735 for business travel and $300 for business education. Rick would not be able to deduct the $700 cost of airfare because the trip is primarily personal, as evidenced by the seven days of personal activities compared to only three days of business activities.

Deductible Travel Costs		
Description	**Amount**	**Explanation**
Airfare	$ 0	Primary purpose is personal
Lodging	450	3 business days × $150 a day
Meals	75	3 business days × $50 a day × 50% limit
Rental car	210	3 business days × $70 a day
Total business travel expenses	**$735**	

What if: Assume the original facts in the example except Rick traveled to London (rather than upstate New York) for 10 days, spending 6 days at the seminar and 4 days sightseeing. What amount could he deduct?

Answer: In this scenario Rick can deduct $1,890 for travel (computed below) and $300 for business education.

Deductible Travel Costs		
Description	**Amount**	**Explanation**
Airfare to London	$ 420	6 business days/10 total days × $700
Lodging in London	900	6 business days × $150 a day
Meals	150	6 business days × $50 a day × 50% limit
Rental car	420	6 business days × $70 a day
Total business travel expenses	**$1,890**	

Rick is allowed to deduct $420 of the $700 airfare (60 percent) because he spent 6 of the 10 days on the trip conducting business activities.

Property Use Several types of property may be used for both business and personal purposes. For example, business owners often use automobiles, computers, or cell phones for both business and personal purposes.[20] However, because expenses relating to these assets

---

[20]These types of assets are referred to as "listed property." Note that cell phones and computers are specifically exempted from the definition of listed property [§280F(d)(4)(A)], as amended by the 2010 Small Business Act §2043(a).

are deductible only to the extent the assets are used for business purposes, taxpayers must allocate the expenses between the business and personal use portions. For example, if a full year's expense for a business asset is $1,000, but the asset is only used for business purposes 90 percent of the time, then only $900 of expense can be deducted ($1,000 × 90%). The calculation of depreciation on mixed-use assets is discussed in the Property Acquisition and Cost Recovery chapter.

Example 9-9

Rick occasionally uses his personal auto (a BMW) to drive to interviews with prospective clients and to drive back and forth between his shop and various work sites. This year Rick carefully recorded that the BMW was driven 562 miles for business activities and 10,500 miles in total. What expenses associated with the BMW may Rick deduct?

Answer: $306. Based on the standard mileage rate of 54.5 cents per mile, Rick can deduct $306 (562 × 54.5 cents) for business use of his BMW. Alternatively, Rick can track the operating expenses of the BMW (including depreciation) and deduct the business portion [based upon the percentage of business miles driven to total miles driven (562 business miles/10,500 total miles)]. Once Rick chooses his method of accounting for the business use of the BMW, he must use this same method in future periods.

Record Keeping and Other Requirements Because distinguishing business purposes from personal purposes is a difficult and subjective task, the tax laws include provisions designed to help the courts and the IRS determine the business element of mixed-motive transactions. Under these provisions, taxpayers must maintain specific, written, contemporaneous records (of time, amount, and business purpose) for mixed-motive expenses. For example, as we discussed above, the tax laws prohibit any deductions for business meals unless substantial business discussions accompany the meal. Consequently, when taxpayers incur meal expenses, they must document the business purpose and the extent of the business discussion to deduct any of the expenditures.[21]

Limitation on Business Interest Deductions

The deduction for business interest expense is limited to the sum of (1) business interest income and (2) 30 percent of the adjusted taxable income of the taxpayer for the taxable year. Adjusted taxable income is taxable income of the taxpayer computed without regard to (1) any item of income, gain, deduction, or loss which is not properly allocable to a trade or business; (2) any business interest expense or business interest income; (3) the amount of any net operating loss deduction; and (4) deductions allowable for depreciation, amortization, or depletion.[22] Business interest expense is defined as interest paid or accrued on indebtedness allocable to a trade or business. Business interest income means the amount of interest includible in gross income which is also properly allocable to a trade or business. However, business interest expense does not include investment interest expense, and business interest income does not include investment income. For example, business interest expense would include interest paid on a loan used to purchase business equipment, but would not include interest paid on a loan to purchase stock for investment purposes. The amount of any business interest expense not allowed as a deduction for any taxable year is carried forward indefinitely. The limitation does not apply to any taxpayer with average annual gross receipts of $25 million or less for the prior three taxable years.

THE KEY FACTS

Business Interest Limitation

- The deduction of business interest expense is limited to business interest income plus 30 percent of the business's adjusted taxable income.
- Adjusted taxable income is taxable income allocable to the business computed without interest income and before depreciation and interest expense deductions.
- Disallowed business interest expense can be carried forward indefinitely.

---

[21]§274 requires substantiation of all elements of travel, including sufficient corroborating evidence. Although there are a few exceptions to this rule, approximations and estimates are generally not sufficient. Also, taxpayers must maintain records to deduct the business portion of mixed-use assets such as cars used for both business and personal purposes. Note that when the taxpayer is unable to substantiate other deductions, the court may estimate the deductible amount under the Cohan rule (*George Cohan v. Com.,* (1930, CA2), 39 F2d 540).

[22]Adjusted taxable income of the taxpayer cannot be less than zero. Under §163(j) the interest expense disallowance is determined at the filer level but special rules apply to pass-through entities. For years after 2021, adjusted taxable income is not reduced for depreciation, amortization, and depletion.

Example 9-10

What if: Suppose that at the beginning of the year Rick borrowed $300,000 to provide liquidity for starting up Green Acres. Suppose further that at year-end Rick had paid $9,000 in interest and that Green Acres reported $70,000 of revenue from services and incurred $47,000 of deductible expenses. The deductible expenses included $5,000 of depreciation but did not include the interest expense. What amount of interest can Rick deduct as a business expense for Green Acres?

Answer: $9,000. Green Acres is not subject to the business interest expense limitation because Rick's gross receipts do not exceed the $25 million average receipts test.

What if: Suppose the interest expense limitation applies to Green Acres. What amount of business interest expense could Rick deduct for Green Acres?

Answer: $8,400. Green Acres generated $28,000 of adjusted taxable income. Adjusted taxable income is the amount of revenue less expense before interest and depreciation ($70,000 – $42,000). The 2018 business interest limitation is 30 percent of the adjusted taxable income or $8,400. The $600 of disallowed interest from 2018 is carried over into 2019.

LO 9-3   SPECIFIC BUSINESS DEDUCTIONS

As we discussed above, the tax code provides general guidelines for determining whether business expenditures are deductible. We learned that to be deductible, business expenditures must be ordinary, necessary, and reasonable in amount. In some cases, however, the tax laws identify specific items businesses are allowed to deduct. We discuss several of these deductions below.

Losses on Dispositions of Business Property

Businesses are generally allowed to deduct losses incurred when selling or disposing of business assets.[23] The calculation of losses from business property dispositions can be complex, but the main idea is that businesses realize and recognize a loss when the asset's tax basis exceeds the sale proceeds. We will discuss the rules governing the tax treatment of gains and losses on asset disposition in more detail in the Property Dispositions chapter.

Example 9-11

What if: Assume that in late October, Rick purchased a used trailer to transport equipment to work sites. Rick bought the trailer for what he thought was a bargain price of $1,000. However, shortly after Rick acquired it, the axle snapped and was not repairable. Rick was forced to sell the trailer to a parts shop for $325. What amount can Rick deduct as a loss from the trailer sale?

Answer: $675, because the trailer was a business asset (amount realized of $325 minus adjusted basis of $1,000). (Note that Rick is not allowed to deduct depreciation on the trailer because he disposed of it in the same year he acquired it.)

Business Casualty Losses

Businesses can incur losses when their assets are stolen, damaged, or completely destroyed by a force outside the control of the business. These events are called casualties.[24] Businesses may deduct **casualty losses** in the year the casualty occurs or in the year the theft of an asset is discovered. The amount of the loss deduction depends on whether the asset is (1) completely destroyed or stolen or (2) only partially destroyed. When its asset

---

[23]In most circumstances businesses may *not* deduct losses on assets sold to related persons. We describe who qualifies as a related person later in this chapter.

[24]Casualties are unexpected events driven by forces outside the control of the taxpayer that damage or destroy a taxpayer's property. §165 lists "fire, storm, and shipwreck" as examples of casualties.

is *completely* destroyed or stolen, the business calculates the amount of the loss as though it sold the asset for the insurance proceeds, if any. That is, the loss is the amount of insurance proceeds minus the adjusted tax basis of the asset. If the asset is damaged but not completely destroyed, the amount of the loss is the amount of the insurance proceeds minus the *lesser* of (1) the asset's adjusted tax basis or (2) the decline in the value of the asset due to the casualty. For individuals, business casualty losses and casualty losses associated with rentals and royalties are deducted *for* AGI.

Example 9-12

What if: Suppose Rick acquired business equipment several years ago for $9,000 and had deducted $4,000 of depreciation expense against the asset. Hence, the equipment's adjusted tax basis was $5,000 ($9,000 − $4,000). Suppose further that a fire destroyed the asset, and at that time the asset was worth $1,000 and insured for $250. What would be the amount of his business casualty loss?

Answer: $4,750, computed as follows:

Insurance proceeds	$ 250
Minus adjusted tax basis	−5,000
Casualty loss deduction	**$(4,750)**

ACCOUNTING PERIODS

LO 9-4

So far we've discussed how to determine a business's income and how to determine its deductible business expenses. In this section, we discuss accounting periods, which affect when taxpayers determine their income and deductions. Businesses must report their income and deductions over a fixed **accounting period** or **tax year.** A full tax year consists of 12 full months. A tax year can consist of a period less than 12 months (a short tax year) in certain circumstances. For instance, a business may report income for such a short year in its first year of existence (for example, it reports income on a calendar year-end and starts business after January 1) or in its final year of existence (for example, a calendar-year business ends its business before December 31). Short tax years in a business's initial or final year are treated the same as full years. A business also may have a short year when it changes its tax year, and this can occur when the business is acquired by new owners. In these situations, special rules may apply for computing the tax liability of the business.[25]

There are three types of tax years, each with different year-ends:

1. A calendar year ends on December 31.
2. A **fiscal year** ends on the last day of a month other than December.
3. A 52/53-week year. This is a fiscal year that ends on the same day of the week that is the last such day in the month or on the same day of the week nearest the end of the month. For example, a business could adopt a 52/53-week fiscal year that (1) ends on the last Saturday in July each year or (2) ends on the Saturday closest to the end of July (although this Saturday might be in August rather than July).[26]

THE KEY FACTS

Accounting Periods

- Individuals and proprietorships generally account for income using a calendar year-end.
- Corporations are allowed to choose a fiscal year.
- Partnerships and other flow-through entities generally use a tax year consistent with their owners' tax years.

---

[25]§443. Discussion of tax consequences associated with these short years is beyond the scope of this text.

[26]Businesses with inventories, such as retailers, can benefit from 52/53-week year-ends. These year-ends can facilitate inventory counts (e.g., the store is closed, such as over a weekend) and financial reporting.

Not all types of tax years are available to all types of businesses. The rules for determining the tax years available to the business depend on whether the business is a sole proprietorship, a **flow-through entity,** or a C corporation. These rules are summarized as follows:

- *Sole proprietorships*: Because individual proprietors must report their business income on their individual returns, proprietorships use a calendar year-end to report their business income.[27]
- *Flow-through entities*: Partnerships and S corporations are flow-through entities (partners and S corporation owners report the entity's income directly on their own tax returns), and these entities generally must adopt tax years consistent with the owners' tax years.[28] Because owners are allocated income from flow-through entities on the last day of the entity's taxable year, the tax laws impose the tax year consistency requirement to minimize income tax deferral opportunities for the owners.
- *C corporations*: C corporations are generally allowed to select a calendar, fiscal, or 52/53-week year-end.

A business adopts a calendar year-end or fiscal year-end by filing its initial tax return. In contrast, a business adopts a 52/53-week year-end by filing a special election with the IRS. Once a business establishes its tax year, it generally must receive permission from the IRS to change.

Example 9-13

Rick is a calendar-year taxpayer. What tax year must Rick use to report income from Green Acres?

Answer: Calendar year. This is true even though Rick began his business in May of this year. He will calculate income and expense for his landscaping business over the calendar year and include business income and deductions from May through December of this year on Schedule C of his individual tax return.

What if: Suppose that Rick incorporated Green Acres at the time he began his business. What tax year could Green Acres adopt?

Answer: If Green Acres was operated as a C corporation, it could elect a calendar year-end, a fiscal year-end, or a 52/53-week year-end. If it were an S corporation, it likely would use a calendar year-end.

LO 9-5

ACCOUNTING METHODS

Once a business adopts a tax year, it must determine which items of income and deduction to recognize during a particular year. Generally speaking, the taxpayer's **accounting methods** determine the tax year in which a business recognizes a particular item of income or deduction. Because accounting methods affect the *timing* of when a taxpayer reports income and deductions, these methods are very important for taxpayers using a timing tax strategy to defer income or accelerate deductions.[29]

---

[27]Virtually all individual taxpayers use a calendar-year tax year.

[28]See §706 for the specific restrictions on year-ends for partnerships and §1378 for restrictions on S corporations. If they can show a business purpose (a difficult task), both partnerships and S corporations can adopt year-ends other than those used by their owners.

[29]Accounting methods do not determine whether an item of income is taxable or an expense is deductible. Accordingly, accounting methods generally do not affect the total income or deductions recognized over the lifetime of the business.

Financial and Tax Accounting Methods

Many businesses are required to generate financial statements for nontax reasons. For example, publicly traded corporations must file financial statements with the Securities and Exchange Commission (SEC) based on generally accepted accounting principles (GAAP). Also, privately owned businesses borrowing money from banks are often required to generate financial statements under GAAP, so that the lender can evaluate the business's creditworthiness. In reporting financial statement income, businesses have incentives to select accounting methods permissible under GAAP that *accelerate income* and *defer deductions*. In contrast, for tax planning purposes, businesses have incentives to choose accounting methods that *defer income* and *accelerate deductions*. This natural tension between financial reporting incentives and tax reporting incentives may be the reason the tax laws sometimes require businesses to use the same accounting methods for tax purposes that they use for financial accounting purposes. In other words, in many circumstances, if businesses want to defer taxable income, they must also defer book income.[30]

Sometimes the tax laws require businesses to use different, presumably more appropriate, accounting methods for tax purposes. Consequently, for policy and administrative reasons, the tax laws also identify several circumstances when businesses must use specific tax accounting methods to determine taxable income no matter what accounting method they use for financial reporting purposes. We will now turn our attention to accounting methods prescribed by the tax laws. With certain restrictions, businesses are able to select their *overall* accounting method and accounting methods for *specific* items or transactions. We will cover each of these in turn.

Overall Accounting Method

Businesses must choose an overall method of accounting to track and report their business activities for tax purposes. The overriding requirement for any tax accounting method is that the method must "clearly reflect income" and be applied consistently.[31] The two primary overall methods are the cash method and the accrual method. Businesses also may choose a hybrid method (some accounts on the cash method and others on the accrual method).

Cash Method A taxpayer (or business) using the cash method of accounting recognizes revenue when property or services are actually or constructively received. This is generally true no matter when the business sells the goods or performs the service that generates the revenue. Likewise, a business adopting the cash method generally recognizes deductions when the expense is paid. Thus, the timing of the liability giving rise to the expense is usually irrelevant.

Keep in mind that a cash-method business receiving payments in *noncash* form (as property or services) must recognize the noncash payments as gross income when the goods or services are received. Also, in certain circumstances, a business expending cash on ordinary and necessary business expenses may not be allowed to *currently* deduct the expense at the time of the payment. For example, cash-method taxpayers (and accrual-method taxpayers) are not allowed to deduct prepaid interest expense and cannot usually deduct prepaid expenses or payments that create a tangible or intangible asset.[32] However, the regulations provide a **12-month rule** for prepaid business expenses to simplify the process of determining whether to capitalize or immediately expense payments that create benefits for a relatively brief period of time, such as insurance,

---

[30]§446(a). Businesses that use different accounting methods for book and tax income must typically file a Schedule M-1 or Schedule M-3 that reconciles the results from the two accounting methods.

[31]§446(b).

[32]263(a).

security, rent, and warranty service contracts. When a business prepays business expenses, it may *immediately* deduct the prepayment if (1) the contract period does not last more than a year *and* (2) the contract period does not extend beyond the end of the taxable year following the tax year in which the taxpayer makes the payment.[33] If the prepaid expense does not meet both these criteria, the business must capitalize the prepaid amount and amortize it over the length of the contract whether the business uses the cash or accrual method of accounting.[34]

Example 9-14

On July 1 of this year, Rick paid $1,200 for a 12-month insurance policy that covers his business property from accidents and casualties from July 1 of this year through June 30 of next year. How much of the $1,200 expenditure may Rick deduct this year if he uses the cash method of accounting for his business activities?

Answer: $1,200. Because the insurance coverage does not exceed 12 months and does not extend beyond the end of next year, Rick is allowed to deduct the entire premium payment under the 12-month rule.

What if: Suppose the insurance policy was for 12 months but the policy ran from February 1 of next year, through January 31 of the following year. How much of the expenditure may Rick deduct this year if he uses the cash method of accounting for his business activities?

Answer: $0. Even though the contract period is 12 months or less, Rick is required to capitalize the cost of the prepayment for the insurance policy because the contract period extends beyond the end of next year.

What if: Suppose Rick had paid $1,200 for an *18-month* policy beginning July 1 of this year and ending December 31 of next year. How much may he deduct this year if he uses the cash method of accounting for his business activities?

Answer: $400. In this scenario, because the policy exceeds 12 months, Rick is allowed to deduct the portion of the premium pertaining to this year. Hence, this year, he would deduct $400 [(6 months/18 months) × $1,200]. He would deduct the remaining $800 in the next year.

Accrual Method   Businesses using the accrual method to determine taxable income follow rules similar to GAAP with two basic differences.[35] First, as we discuss below, requirements for recognizing taxable income tend to be structured to recognize income earlier than the recognition rules for financial accounting. Second, requirements for accruing tax deductions tend to be structured to recognize less accrued expenses than the recognition rules for financial reporting purposes. These differences reflect the underlying objectives of financial accounting income and taxable income. The objective of financial accounting is to provide useful information to stakeholders such as creditors, prospective investors, and shareholders. Because financial accounting methods are designed to guard against businesses overstating their profitability to these users, financial accounting tends to bias against *overstating* income. In contrast, the government's main objective for writing tax laws is to collect revenues. Thus, tax accounting rules for accrual-method businesses tend to bias against *understating* income. These differences will become apparent as we describe tax accounting rules for businesses.

---

[33]This 12-month rule applies to both cash-method and accrual-method taxpayers. However, for accrual-method taxpayers to deduct prepaid expenses, they must meet both the 12-month rule requirements and the economic performance requirements that we discuss in the next section.

[34]Reg. §1.263(a)-4(f).

[35]Prior to 2018, C corporations and partnerships with C corporation partners were generally required to use the accrual method. However, beginning in 2018, unless they are tax shelters, these entities can use the cash method if they report average gross receipts of $25 million or less for the three-tax-year period ending with the prior tax year.

continued from page 9-1...

Rick's CPA, Jane, informed him that he needs to select an overall method of accounting for Green Acres to compute its taxable income. Jane advised Rick to use the cash method. However, Rick wanted to prepare GAAP financial statements and use the accrual method of accounting. He decided that if Green Acres was going to become a big business, it needed to act like a big business. Finally, after much discussion, Rick and Jane reached a compromise. For the first year, they decided they would track Green Acres's business activities using both the cash *and* the accrual methods. In addition, they would also keep GAAP-based books for financial purposes. When filing time comes, Rick will need to decide which method to use in reporting taxable income. Jane told Rick that he could wait until he filed his tax return to select the overall accounting method for tax purposes. ■

Accrual Income

Businesses using the accrual method of accounting generally recognize income when they meet the all-events test.

All-Events Test for Income

The all-events test requires that businesses recognize income when (1) all events have occurred that determine or fix their right to receive the income and (2) the amount of the income can be determined with reasonable accuracy.[36] Assuming the amount of income can be determined with reasonable accuracy, businesses meet the all-events requirement on the *earliest* of the following three dates:

1. When they complete the task required to earn the income. Businesses earn income for services as they provide the services, and they generally earn income from selling property when the title of the property passes to the buyer.
2. When the payment for the task is due from the customer.
3. When the business receives payment for the task.

Generally, beginning in 2018, the all-events test is satisfied no later than the tax year in which such income is recognized on their financial statements.

Example 9-15

In early fall, Rick contracted with a dozen homeowners to landscape their yards. Rick agreed to do the work for an aggregate of $11,000. Rick and his crew started in the fall and completed the jobs in December of this year. However, he didn't mail the bills until after the holidays and didn't receive any payments until the following January. When must Rick recognize the income from this work?

Answer: Under the accrual method, Rick would recognize the entire $11,000 as income this year because his right to the income is fixed at year-end, when Rick and his crew complete the work. Under the cash method, however, Rick would not recognize the $11,000 as income until next year, when he receives it.

Taxation of Advance Payments of Income (Unearned Income)

In some cases, businesses receive income payments *before* they actually earn the income (they receive a prepayment). When the business must recognize a prepayment as income depends on the type of income. The rule for interest and rental income is relatively strict. Businesses must recognize unearned rental and unearned interest income *immediately* upon receipt (the income is recognized before it is earned). However, businesses are not required to recognize security deposits received from rental customers because they incur

[36]Reg. §1.451-1(a).

a liability to return the deposits when they receive the payments.[37] The income recognition rules are less strict when businesses receive advance payments for services or goods.

Advance Payments for Goods and Services   For financial reporting purposes, a business does not immediately recognize income on payments it receives for services to be provided in the future. For financial reporting purposes, an advance payment for goods and services is recorded as a debit for cash received and a credit to a liability account (unearned income). The business then recognizes the *financial* income from the services or sales as it performs the services or provides the goods. In contrast, for tax purposes, the all-events test generally requires businesses receiving advance payments for goods and services to recognize the income when they receive the payment, rather than when they deliver the goods or perform the services. This rule is called the full inclusion method.

The law provides an exception to immediate recognition. Specifically, businesses receiving advance payments for goods and services may elect to defer recognizing the advance as income until the tax year following the year they receive the payment.[38] This one-year deferral method does *not* apply (1) if (or to the extent to which) the income is actually earned by the end of the year of receipt, (2) to the extent that the advance was included in financial reporting income, or (3) if the advance was for interest or rent (taxpayers must recognize unearned interest and rental income on receipt).

Example 9-16

In late November 2018, Rick received a $7,200 payment in advance from a client for monthly landscaping services from December 1, 2018, through November 30, 2020 ($300 a month for 24 months). When must Rick recognize the income from the advance payment for services?

Answer: Under the accrual method, if Rick elects the deferral method to account for advance payments, he would initially recognize the $300 income he earned in December 2018. In 2019, he would recognize the remaining $6,900 (rather than only the $3,600 related to 2019) because he is not allowed to defer the prepayments for more than a year. If Rick does not elect the deferral method, he would recognize the entire prepayment of $7,200 as income upon receipt in 2018. Under the cash method, Rick would recognize the entire prepayment, $7,200, as income upon receipt in 2018.

What if: Suppose that rather than receiving payment in advance for services, Rick's client paid $7,200 in 2018 for landscape supplies that Rick purchased and provided in 2019. When must Rick recognize the income from the advance payment for goods?

Answer: Using the accrual method, if Rick elects the deferral method to account for advance payments, he would not recognize any income in 2018 because none of the income had been earned in 2018. Rick would then recognize the entire $7,200 in 2019. If Rick did not elect the deferral method, he would recognize the entire $7,200 in 2018. Under the cash method, Rick would recognize the entire $7,200 in 2018.

Inventories

Many businesses generate income by selling products they acquire for resale or products they manufacture. When selling inventory is a material income-producing factor, larger businesses generally must account for gross profit (sales minus cost of goods sold) using the accrual method, even if the business is a cash-method taxpayer. However, beginning in 2018, taxpayers need not use the accrual method to account for inventory if they report average gross receipts of $25 million or less or less for the three-tax year period ending with the prior tax year. Instead, these taxpayers can generally treat purchases of goods for sale as either non-incidental materials or use an accounting method that conforms to the taxpayer's financial accounting treatment of inventory.

---

[37]*Comm. v. Indianapolis Power & Light Co.* (1990), 493 US 203. In this case, it was determined that customer deposits required by a public utility weren't taxable income because the right to keep the deposits depended on events outside of the taxpayer's control, such as the decision to have the deposit applied to future bills.

[38]IRC §451(c). Prior to 2018, this exception was provided under Rev. Proc. 2004-34, 2004-1 CB 991.

Businesses that account for inventory must determine their inventory costs to accurately compute taxable income. This requires businesses to maintain records of balances for finished goods inventory and, if applicable, for partially finished goods and raw materials. Inventory costs include the purchase price of raw materials (minus any discounts), shipping costs, and any indirect costs it allocates to the inventory under the **uniform cost capitalization (UNICAP) rules.**[39]

Uniform Capitalization   The tax laws require businesses that account for inventories to capitalize certain direct and indirect costs associated with inventories.[40] Congress enacted these rules primarily for two reasons. First, the rules accelerate tax revenues for the government by deferring deductions for the capitalized costs until the business sells the associated inventory. Thus, there is generally a one-year lag between when businesses initially capitalize the costs and when they deduct them. Second, Congress designed the "uniform" rules to reduce variation in the costs businesses include in inventory and Congress intended these provisions to apply to large manufacturers and resalers.[41]

Under these uniform cost capitalization rules, large businesses are generally required to capitalize more costs to inventory for tax purposes than they capitalize under financial accounting rules. Under GAAP, businesses generally include in inventory only those costs incurred within their production facility. In contrast, the UNICAP rules require businesses to allocate to inventory the costs they incur inside the production facility and the costs they incur outside the facility to support production (or inventory acquisition) activities. For example, under the UNICAP provisions, a business must capitalize at least a portion of the compensation paid to employees in its purchasing department, general and administrative department, and even its information technology department, to the extent these groups provide support for the production process. In contrast, businesses immediately expense these items as period costs for financial accounting purposes. The regulations provide guidance on the costs that must be allocated to inventory. Selling, advertising, and research are specifically identified as costs that do not have to be allocated to inventory under the UNICAP provisions.[42]

Example 9-17

What if: Green Acres sells trees but Rick anticipates selling flowers, shrubs, and other plants in future years. Ken is Rick's employee in charge of purchasing inventory. Ken's compensation this year is $30,000, and Rick estimates that Ken spends about 5 percent of his time acquiring inventory and the remaining time working on landscaping projects. Assuming Rick was required to apply the UNICAP rules, how would he allocate Ken's compensation under the UNICAP rules?

Answer: If the UNICAP rules applied to Green Acres, Rick would allocate $1,500 ($30,000 × 5%) of Ken's compensation to the cost of the inventory Green Acres acquired this year. In contrast, Ken's entire salary would be expensed as a period cost for financial accounting purposes. (Note, however, because Green Acres's gross receipts for the year are under $25 million, it is not *required* to apply the UNICAP rules.)

Inventory Cost-Flow Methods   Once a business determines the cost of its inventory, it must use an inventory cost-flow method to determine its cost of goods sold. Three primary cost-flow methods are (1) the **first-in, first-out (FIFO) method,** (2) the **last-in, first-out (LIFO) method,** and (3) the **specific identification method.** Businesses might

---

[39]Inventory valuation allowances are generally not allowed, but taxpayers can adopt the lower of cost or market method of inventory valuation. In addition, under certain conditions specific goods not salable at normal prices can be valued at bona fide selling prices less direct cost of disposition.

[40]§263A(a).

[41]Beginning in 2018, taxpayers need not employ UNICAP to adjust inventory costs if they report average gross receipts of $25 million or less or less for the three-tax year period ending with the prior tax year.

[42]Reg. §1.263A–1(e)(3)(iii).

be inclined to use FIFO or LIFO methods when they sell similar, relatively low-cost, high-volume products such as cans of soup or barrels of oil. These methods simplify inventory accounting because the business need not track the individual cost of each item it sells. In contrast, businesses that sell distinct, relatively high-cost, low-volume products might be more likely to adopt the specific identification method. For example, jewelry and used-car businesses would likely use the specific identification method to account for their cost of sales. In general terms, when costs are increasing, a business using the FIFO method will report a higher gross margin than if it used the LIFO method. The opposite is true if costs are decreasing.

Example 9-18

In late August, Rick purchased 10 oak saplings (immature trees) for a total purchase price of $3,000. In September, he purchased 12 more for a total price of $3,900, and in late October, he purchased 15 more for $5,000. The total cost of each lot of trees was determined as follows:

Purchase Date	Trees	Direct Cost	Other Costs	Total Cost
August 20	10	$ 3,000	$200	$ 3,200
September 15	12	3,900	300	4,200
October 22	15	5,000	400	5,400
Totals	37	$11,900	$900	$12,800

Before the end of the year, Green Acres sold 20 of the oak saplings (5 from the August lot, 5 from the September lot, and 10 from the October lot) for cash. To illustrate the effects of inventory accounting, assume that Rick prefers to keep inventory records (recall that taxpayers are not required to keep inventories for tax purposes if their average annual gross receipts are under $25 million). What is Green Acres's gross profit from sales of oak saplings if the sales revenue totaled $14,000 (all collected by year-end), and what is its ending oak sapling inventory under the accrual and cash methods of accounting?

Answer: Under the accrual method, Green Acres's gross profit from sapling sales and its ending inventory balance for the remaining oak saplings under the FIFO, LIFO, and specific identification cost-flow methods is as follows:

	FIFO	LIFO	Specific ID
Sales	$14,000	$14,000	$14,000
Cost of goods sold	−6,700	−7,150	−6,950
Gross profit	$ 7,300	$ 6,850	$ 7,050
Ending inventory:			
August 20 trees	$ 0	$ 3,200	$ 1,600
September 15 trees	700	2,450	2,450
October 22 trees	5,400	0	1,800
Total ending inventory	**$ 6,100**	**$ 5,650**	**$ 5,850**

Under both the accrual and cash methods, Rick is allowed to elect to deduct the cost of purchases as non-incidental materials and supplies. Hence, Rick could deduct the $12,800 currently. However, if Rick elects to keep an inventory of his trees, he would be entitled to choose his inventory method (LIFO, FIFO, or specific identification) and deduct the cost of goods sold under that method.

When costs are subject to inflation over time, a business would get the best of both worlds if it adopted the FIFO method for financial reporting purposes and the LIFO method for tax purposes. Not surprisingly, the tax laws require that a business can use

LIFO for tax purposes only if it also uses LIFO for financial reporting purposes.[43] While this "conformity" requirement may not matter to entities not required to generate financial reports, it can be very restrictive to publicly traded corporations.

Accrual Deductions

Generally, when accrual-method businesses incur a liability relating to a business expense, they account for it by crediting a liability account (or by crediting cash if they pay the liability at the time they incur it) and debiting an expense account. However, to claim a tax deduction for the expense, the expense must meet (1) an **all-events test** *and* (2) an **economic performance test.**[44] While the all-events test for recognizing deductions is similar to the all-events test for recognizing income, the additional economic performance requirement makes the deduction recognition rules more stringent than the income recognition rules. The deduction rules generally preclude businesses from deducting estimated expenses or reserves.

All-Events Test for Deductions   For a business to recognize a deduction, the events that establish the liability giving rise to the deduction must have occurred, and the amount of the liability must be determinable with reasonable accuracy.[45]

Example 9-19

On November of this year, Rick agreed to a one-year $6,000 contract with Ace Advertising to produce a radio ad campaign. Ace agreed that Rick would owe nothing under the contract unless his sales increase a minimum of 25 percent over the next six months. What amount, if any, may Rick deduct this year for this contract under the accrual and cash methods?

Answer: Under the accrual method, Green Acres is not allowed to recognize *any* deduction this year for the liability. Even though Ace will have completed two months of advertising for Green Acres by the end of the year, its guarantee means that Rick's liability is not fixed until and unless his sales increase by 25 percent. Under the cash method, Rick would not deduct any of the cost of the campaign this year because he has not paid anything to Ace.

Economic Performance   Even when businesses meet the all-events test, they still must clear the economic performance hurdle to recognize the tax deduction. Congress added the economic performance requirement because in some situations taxpayers claimed current deductions and delayed paying the associated cash expenditures for years. Thus, the delayed payment reduced the real (present value) cost of the deduction. This requirement specifies that businesses may not recognize a deduction for an expense until the underlying activity generating the associated liability has occurred. Thus, an accrual-method business is not allowed to deduct a prepaid business expense even if it qualifies to do so under the 12-month rule (discussed above) unless it also has met the economic performance test with respect to the liability associated with the expense.

The specific requirements for the economic performance test differ based on whether the liability has arisen from:

- Receiving goods or services *from* another person.
- Use of property.
- Providing goods or services *to* another person.
- Certain activities creating **payment liabilities.**

> **THE KEY FACTS**
>
> **Accrual of Business-Expense Deductions**
>
> - Both all-events and economic performance are required for deducting accrued business expenses.
> - The all-events test requires that the business be liable for the payment.
> - Economic performance generally requires that the underlying activity generating the liability has occurred in order for the associated expense to be deductible.

[43]§472(c).
[44]§461(h).
[45]§461.

Receiving goods and (or) services from another person. When a business agrees to pay another person for goods or services, the business deducts the expense associated with the liability only when the other person provides the goods or services (assuming the all-events test is met for the liability). An exception to this general rule occurs when a business hires another person to provide goods or services and the business actually pays the liability before the other person provides the goods or services. In this circumstance, the business may treat the actual payment as economic performance as long as it reasonably expects the other person to provide the goods or all of the services within three and one-half months after the payment.[46]

Example 9-20

On December 15, 2018, Rick hires Your New Fence LLC (YNF) to install a concrete wall for one of his clients by paying $1,000 of the cost as a down payment and agreeing to pay the remaining $7,000 when YNF finishes the wall. YNF was not going to start building the wall until early 2019, so as of the end of the year Rick has not billed his client for the wall. Rick expects YNF to finish the wall by the end of April. What amount associated with his liability to YNF is Rick allowed to deduct in 2018 and 2019?

Answer: Under the accrual method, Rick is not entitled to a deduction in 2018. Rick will deduct his full $8,000 cost of the wall in 2019 when YNF builds the wall, because economic performance occurs as YNF provides the services, even though Rick paid for part of the goods and services in 2018. Under the cash method, Rick would deduct $1,000 (his down payment) in 2018 and the remainder in 2019 when he pays the remainder on the contract.

What if: Assume that Rick expected YNF to finish building the wall by the end of January 2019. What amount associated with this liability to YNF is Rick allowed to deduct in 2018 and 2019?

Answer: Under the accrual method, Rick is allowed to deduct $1,000 in 2018 because Rick actually paid this amount in 2018 and he reasonably expected YNF to finish its work on the wall within 3½ months after he made the payment to YNF on December 15. Rick would deduct the remaining $7,000 cost of the wall in 2019 when YNF builds the wall. Under the cash method, Rick deducts the $1,000 down payment in 2018 and the remaining $7,000 when he makes the payment in 2019.

Renting or leasing property from another person. When a business enters into an agreement to rent or lease property from another person, economic performance occurs over the rental period. Thus, the business is allowed to deduct the rental expense over the lease.

Example 9-21

On May 1, 2018, Rick paid $7,200 in advance to rent his shop for 12 months ($600 per month). What amount may Rick deduct for rent in 2018 if he accounts for his business activities using the accrual method?

Answer: $4,800 ($600 × 8 months use). Even though the rent is a prepaid business expense under the 12-month rule (the contract period is for 12 months and the contract period does not extend beyond 2019), he must deduct the rent expense over the term of the lease because that is when economic performance occurs.

What if: Assuming the original facts, what amount of the $7,200 rental payment may Rick deduct in 2018 if he is using the cash method of accounting for his business?

Answer: $7,200. In this case, Rick may deduct the expense under the 12-month rule. He does not have to meet the economic performance requirement to deduct the expense because the economic performance requirements apply to accrual-method taxpayers, but not cash-method taxpayers.

---

[46]Reg. §1.461-4(d)(6).

Example 9-22

On November 1, 2018, Rick paid $2,400 to rent a trailer for 24 months. What amount of this payment may Rick deduct and when may he deduct it?

Answer: Under the accrual method, even though Rick paid the entire rental fee in advance, economic performance occurs over the 24-month rental period. Thus, Green Acres deducts $200 for the trailer rental in 2018, $1,200 in 2019, and $1,000 in 2020. Because the rental period exceeds 12 months, the amount and timing of the deductions are the same under the cash method.

Providing goods and services to another person. Businesses liable for providing goods and services to other persons meet the economic performance test as they provide the goods or services that satisfy the liability.

Example 9-23

In the summer, Rick landscaped a city park. As part of this service, Rick agreed to remove a fountain from the park at the option of the city parks committee. In December 2018, the committee decided to have Rick remove the fountain. Rick began the removal in December and paid an employee $850 on December 31. Rick completed the removal work in the spring of 2019 and paid an employee $685 on March 31. What amounts will Rick deduct for the removal project and when may he deduct them?

Answer: Under the accrual method, Rick is allowed to deduct his costs as he provides the services. Consequently, in 2018 Rick can deduct $850 for the cost of the services provided by his employee in 2018. In 2019, Rick can deduct the remaining $685 cost of the services provided by his employee in 2019. Under the cash method, the amount and timing of his deductions would be the same as under the accrual method.

Payment liabilities. Economic performance occurs for certain liabilities only when the business actually pays the liability. Thus, accrual-method businesses incurring payment liabilities are essentially on the cash method for deducting the associated expenses. Exhibit 9-2 describes different categories of these payment liabilities.

EXHIBIT 9-2 **Categories of Payment Liabilities**

Economic performance occurs when the taxpayer pays liabilities associated with:

- Workers' compensation, tort, breach of contract, or violation of law.
- Rebates and refunds.
- Awards, prizes, and jackpots.
- Insurance, warranties, and service contracts provided *to* the business. (*Note:* This relates to insurance, warranties, and product service contracts that cover the taxpayer and *not* a warranty that the taxpayer provides to others.)
- Taxes.[47]
- Other liabilities not provided for elsewhere.

Recurring item exception. One of the most common exceptions to economic performance is the **recurring item** exception. This exception is designed to minimize the cost of applying economic performance to expenses that occur on a regular basis. Under this exception, accrual method taxpayers can deduct certain accrued expenses even if economic performance has not occurred by year-end.[48] A recurring item is a liability

---

[47]While taxes are generally not deducted until they are paid, §461(c) allows businesses to elect to accrue the deduction for real property taxes ratably over the tax period instead of deducting them when they actually pay them.

[48]§461(h)(3).

that is expected to recur in future years and is either not material in amount or deducting the expense currently matches with revenue. Payment liabilities, such as insurance, rebates and refunds, are deemed to meet the matching requirement.[49] In addition, the all-events test must be satisfied at year-end and actual economic performance of the item must occur within a reasonable time after year-end (but prior to the filing of the tax return, which could be up to 8½ months with an extension). As a final note, the recurring item exception does not apply to workers' compensation or tort liabilities.

Example 9-24

If clients are not completely satisfied with Green Acres's landscaping work, Rick offers a $200 refund with no questions asked. Near the end of 2018, Rick had four clients request refunds. Rick incurred the liability for the refunds this year. However, Rick was busy during the holiday season, so he didn't pay the refunds until January 2019. When should Rick deduct the customer refunds?

Answer: Because refunds are payment liabilities, economic performance does not occur until Rick actually pays the refunds. Consequently, Rick deducts the $800 of refunds in 2019 even though the liability for the refunds met the all-events test in 2018. Under the cash method, Rick would not deduct the refunds until he paid them in 2019.

What if: Suppose that Rick expected that $800 of refunds would typically be accrued at year-end. Under what conditions could Rick deduct the refunds in 2018 if he elects to use accrual accounting?

Answer: To claim $800 of deductions for the refunds in 2018, either the accrued refunds must not be material in amount or a 2018 deduction must better match 2018 revenue than 2019 revenue. Fortunately, Rick doesn't need to worry about the matching requirement. Under the regulations refunds are deemed to meet the matching requirement for purposes of the recurring item exception. Rick must also expect actual economic performance (payment) within a reasonable time after year-end (but not longer than 8½ months or the filing of the tax return). Note also that Rick must elect to deduct the refunds in 2018 using the recurring item exception and then must follow this method in future periods.

Accrual-method taxpayers that prepay business expenses for payment liabilities (insurance contracts, warranties, and product service contracts provided to the taxpayer) that qualify as recurring items are allowed to immediately deduct the prepayments subject to the 12-month rule for prepaid expenses. Thus, the deductible amounts for Rick's prepaid insurance contracts in Example 9-14 are the same for both the cash method and accrual method of accounting. Exhibit 9-3 describes the requirements for economic performance for the different types of liabilities.

EXHIBIT 9-3   Economic Performance

Taxpayer incurs liability from	Economic performance occurs
Receiving goods and services *from* another person.	When the goods or services are provided to the taxpayer or with payment if the taxpayer reasonably expects actual performance within 3½ months.
Renting or leasing property *from* another person.	Ratably over the time period during which the taxpayer is entitled to use the property or money.
Providing goods and services *to* another person.	When the taxpayer incurs costs to satisfy the liability or provide the goods and services.
Activities creating "payment" liabilities.	When the business actually makes payment.
Interest expense.	As accrued. This technically does not fall within the economic performance rules but it is a similar concept.

Bad Debt Expense   When accrual method businesses sell a product or a service on credit, they debit accounts receivable and credit sales revenue for both financial and tax purposes. However, because businesses usually are unable to collect the full amount of their accounts receivable, they incur bad debt expense (a customer owes them a debt that the

[49]Reg §1.461-5(b)(5)(ii).

customer will not pay). For financial reporting purposes, the business estimates the amount of the bad debt, debits bad debt expense, and credits an allowance for doubtful accounts. However, for tax purposes, businesses are allowed to deduct bad debt expense only when the debt actually becomes worthless within the taxable year.[50] Consequently, for tax purposes, businesses determine which debts are uncollectible and write them off by debiting bad debt expense and directly crediting the actual account receivable account that is uncollectible. This required method of determining bad debt expense for tax purposes is called the **direct write-off method.** In contrast, the method used for financial reporting purposes is called the **allowance method.** Businesses reporting taxable income on the cash method of accounting are *not* allowed to deduct bad debt expenses, because they do not include receivables in taxable income (they do not credit revenue until they actually receive payment).

Example 9-25

At year-end, Rick estimates that about $900 of the receivables from his landscaping services will be uncollectible, but he has identified only one client, Jared, who will definitely not pay his bill. Jared, who has skipped town, owes Rick $280 for landscaping this fall. What amount of bad debt expense may Rick deduct for the year?

Answer: For financial reporting purposes, Rick recognizes a $900 bad debt expense. However, for tax purposes, under the accrual method, Rick can deduct only $280—the amount associated with specifically writing off Jared's receivable. Under the cash method, Rick would not be able to claim any deduction, because he did not receive a payment from Jared and thus did not recognize income on the amount Jared owed him.

Limitations on Accruals to Related Persons   To prevent businesses and related persons from working together to defer taxes, the tax laws prevent an accrual-method business from accruing (and deducting) an expense for a liability owed to a related person using the cash method until the related person recognizes the income associated with the payment.[51] For this purpose, related persons include:

- Family members, including parents, siblings, and spouses.
- Shareholders and C corporations when the shareholder owns more than 50 percent of the corporation's stock.[52]
- Owners of partnerships and S corporations no matter the ownership percentage.[53]

This issue frequently arises in situations in which a business employs the owner or a relative of an owner. The business is not allowed to deduct compensation expense owed to the related party until the year in which the related person includes the compensation in income. However, this related-person limit extends beyond compensation to any accrued expense the business owes to a related cash-method taxpayer.

Example 9-26

In December, Rick asked his retired father, Lee, to help him finish a landscaping job. By the end of 2018, Rick owed Lee $2,000 of (reasonable) compensation for his efforts, which he paid in January 2019. What amount of this compensation may Rick deduct and when may he deduct it?

Answer: If Rick uses the accrual method and Lee the cash method, Rick will not be able to deduct the $2,000 compensation expense until 2019. Rick is Lee's son, so Rick and Lee are "related" persons for tax purposes. Consequently, Rick can deduct the compensation only when Lee includes the payment in his taxable income in 2019. If Rick uses the cash method, he will deduct the expense when he pays it in January 2019.

[50]§166(a).
[51]§267(a).
[52]Certain constructive ownership rules apply in determining ownership percentages for this purpose. See §267(c).
[53]See §267(b) for related-person definitions.

Comparison of Accrual and Cash Methods

From a business perspective, the two primary advantages of adopting the cash method over the accrual method are that (1) the cash method provides the business with more flexibility to time income and deductions by accelerating or deferring payments (timing tax planning strategy) and (2) bookkeeping for the cash method is easier. For example, a cash-method taxpayer could defer revenue by waiting to bill clients for goods or services until after year-end, thereby increasing the likelihood that customers would send payment after year-end. There are some concerns with this tax strategy. For example, delaying the bills might increase the likelihood that the customers will not pay their bills at all.

The primary advantage of the accrual method over the cash method is that it better matches revenues and expenses. For that reason, external financial statement users who want to evaluate a business's financial performance prefer the accrual method. Consistent with this idea, the cash method is not allowed for financial reporting under GAAP.

Although the cash method is by far the predominate accounting method among sole proprietors, it is less common in other types of businesses. As we noted previously, tax laws generally prohibit large C corporations and partnerships with corporate partners from using the cash method of accounting.[54] Exhibit 9-4 details the basic differences in accounting for income and deductions under the accrual and cash methods of accounting.

EXHIBIT 9-4 Comparison of Cash and Accrual Methods

Income or Expense Item	Cash Method	Accrual Method
Income recognition.	Actually or constructively received.	Taxable once the all-events test is satisfied.
Unearned rent and interest income.	Taxable on receipt.	Taxable on receipt.
Advance payment for goods and services.	Taxable on receipt.	Taxed when received or taxpayers can elect to be taxed in the following year of receipt if not earned by end of year of receipt.
General deduction recognition.	Deduct when paid; economic performance does not apply.	Deduct once all-events test and economic performance test are both satisfied.
Expenditures for tangible assets with a useful life of more than one year.	Capitalize and apply cost recovery.	Same as the cash method.
Expenditures for intangible assets other than prepaid business expenses.	Capitalize and amortize if provision in code allows it.	Same as the cash method.
Prepaid business expenses.	Immediately deductible. However, amortize if contract period exceeds 12 months or extends beyond the end of the next taxable year.	Same as cash method for payment liabilities; otherwise, apply all-events and economic performance tests to ascertain when to capitalize and amortize.
Prepaid interest expense.	Not deductible until interest accrues.	Same as the cash method.
Bad debt expense.	Not deductible because sales on account not included in income.	Deduct under direct write-off method.

[54]Recall that these entities are able to adopt the cash method if their average annual gross receipts for the three tax years ending with the prior tax year do not exceed $25 million (see §448).

At year-end, Rick determined that Green Acres had collected a total of $78,000 of service revenue and $12,575 in other expenses (not described elsewhere in examples but listed in Exhibit 9-5). Rick is debating whether to adopt the cash or accrual method. To help him resolve his dilemma, Jane calculates Green Acres's taxable income under the cash and accrual methods assuming that Rick elects not to maintain an inventory (summarized in Exhibit 9-5). What are the differences between the two calculations?

Answer: Jane provided the following summary of the differences between taxable income under the cash method and taxable income under the accrual method:

Description	(1) Accrual	(2) Cash	(1)–(2) Difference	Example
Revenue:				
Credit sales	11,000	0	+11,000	9-15
Prepaid revenue	300	7,200	−6,900	9-16
Expenses:				
Prepaid services	0	−1,000	+1,000	9-20
Prepaid rent expense	−4,800	−7,200	+2,400	9-21
Bad debts	−280	0	−280	9-25
Total difference (accrual income > cash income)			**+ 7,220**	

After comparing the revenue and expenses recognized under the two accounting methods, Jane explains that the selection of the accrual method for Green Acres means that Rick will be taxed on an additional $7,220 of income this year.

The business income for Green Acres under the accrual and cash methods is summarized in Exhibit 9-5. After reflecting on these numbers and realizing that he would recognize $7,220 more taxable income (and self-employment income subject to self-employment tax) this year under the accrual method, Rick determined that it made sense to instead adopt the cash method of accounting for Green Acres's first tax return. Meanwhile, he knew he had to include Green Acres's business income on Schedule C of his individual tax return. Exhibit 9-6 presents Rick's Schedule C for Green Acres using the cash method of accounting.

Adopting an Accounting Method

We've seen that businesses use overall accounting methods (cash, accrual, or hybrid) and many specific accounting methods (inventory cost-flow assumption, methods of accounting for prepaid income for goods and services, and methods for accounting for prepaid expenses, among other methods) to account for their business activities. For tax purposes, it's important to understand how and when a business technically adopts an accounting method, because once it does so, it must get the IRS's permission to change the method.

Businesses generally elect their accounting methods by using them on their tax returns. However, when the business technically adopts a method depends on whether it is a **permissible accounting method** or an **impermissible accounting method.** So far, our discussion has emphasized accounting methods permissible under the tax laws. A business adopts a permissible accounting method by using and reporting the tax results of the method for at least one year. However, businesses may unwittingly (or intentionally) use impermissible accounting methods. For example, a business using the allowance method for determining bad debt expense for tax purposes is using an impermissible accounting method because the tax laws prescribe the use of the direct write-off method for determining bad debt expense. A business adopts an impermissible method by using and reporting the results of the method for two consecutive years.

EXHIBIT 9-5   Green Acres's Net Business Income

Description	Cash	Accrual	Example
Income			
Service revenue:			
Landscaping revenue	$ 78,000	$ 78,000	9-27
December landscape service	0	11,000	9-15
Prepaid landscape services	7,200	300	9-16
Sales of inventory:			
Tree sales	14,000	14,000	9-18
Gross Profit	**$99,200**	**$103,300**	
Nonincidental materials and supplies	$ 12,800	$ 12,800	9-18
Car and truck expense:			
SUV operating expense	5,335	5,335	9-7
BMW operating expense	306	306	9-9
Insurance	1,200	1,200	9-14
Rent:			
Shop	7,200	4,800	9-21
Trailer	200	200	9-22
Travel and business meals:			
Travel to NY seminar	1,435	1,435	9-8
Business dinner with clients	270	270	9-6
Wages and subcontractor fees:			
Part-time employees	23,000	23,000	9-2
Full-time employee (Ken)	30,000	30,000	9-17
Fountain removal (part-time employee)	850	850	9-23
Fence installation (prepaid subcontractor)	1,000	0	9-20
Other expenses:			
Books for waiting room	50	50	9-1
Education—seminar	300	300	9-8
Uniforms	500	500	9-5
Bad debts	0	280	9-25
Other expenses not in examples:			
Advertising	1,160	1,160	
Depreciation	4,000	4,000	
Interest	300	300	
Legal and professional services	1,040	1,040	
Office expense	1,500	1,500	
Repairs and maintenance	1,975	1,975	
Taxes and licenses	400	400	
Utilities	2,200	2,200	
Total deductions	**$97,021**	**$ 93,901**	
Net Business Income	**$ 2,179**	**$ 9,399**	

Changing Accounting Methods

Once a business has adopted an accounting method, it must generally receive permission to change the method, regardless of whether it is a permissible or an impermissible method.[55] A taxpayer requests permission to change accounting methods by

[55]For tax years beginning after 2017, there is a special exception for taxpayers who change accounting methods under the $25 million gross receipts test either by switching to the cash method or who opt to treat purchases of goods for sale as noninventory. These changes in accounting method are treated as initiated by the taxpayer and no longer need the consent of the Secretary.

EXHIBIT 9-6 **Green Acres Schedule C**

SCHEDULE C (Form 1040)	**Profit or Loss From Business** (Sole Proprietorship)	OMB No. 1545-0074
Department of the Treasury Internal Revenue Service (99)	▶ Go to *www.irs.gov/ScheduleC* for instructions and the latest information. ▶ **Attach to Form 1040, 1040NR, or 1041; partnerships generally must file Form 1065.**	2017 Attachment Sequence No. 09

Name of proprietor	Social security number (SSN)
RICK GRIME	000-00-0000

A Principal business or profession, including product or service (see instructions)
LANDSCAPING

B Enter code from instructions ▶ 5 7 1 6 3 0

C Business name. If no separate business name, leave blank.
GREEN ACRES LANDSCAPING

D Employer ID number (EIN) (see instr.)
0 0 0 0 0 0 0 0 0

E Business address (including suite or room no.) ▶ **BUCKSNORT STREET**
City, town or post office, state, and ZIP code **SAN ANTONIO, TX 78208**

F Accounting method: **(1)** ☑ Cash **(2)** ☐ Accrual **(3)** ☐ Other (specify) ▶ _____

G Did you "materially participate" in the operation of this business during 2017? If "No," see instructions for limit on losses . ☑ Yes ☐ No

H If you started or acquired this business during 2017, check here . . . . ▶ ☑

I Did you make any payments in 2017 that would require you to file Form(s) 1099? (see instructions) . . . . ☐ Yes ☑ No

J If "Yes," did you or will you file required Forms 1099? . . . . ☐ Yes ☐ No

Part I **Income**

1	Gross receipts or sales. See instructions for line 1 and check the box if this income was reported to you on Form W-2 and the "Statutory employee" box on that form was checked . . . . ▶ ☐	1	99,200
2	Returns and allowances	2	
3	Subtract line 2 from line 1	3	99,200
4	Cost of goods sold (from line 42)	4	
5	**Gross profit.** Subtract line 4 from line 3	5	99,200
6	Other income, including federal and state gasoline or fuel tax credit or refund (see instructions)	6	
7	**Gross income.** Add lines 5 and 6 . . . . ▶	7	99,200

Part II **Expenses.** Enter expenses for business use of your home **only** on line 30.

8	Advertising	8	1,160	18	Office expense (see instructions)	18	1,500
9	Car and truck expenses (see instructions)	9	5,641	19	Pension and profit-sharing plans .	19	
				20	Rent or lease (see instructions):		
10	Commissions and fees .	10		a	Vehicles, machinery, and equipment	20a	7,400
11	Contract labor (see instructions)	11	1,000	b	Other business property . . .	20b	
12	Depletion	12		21	Repairs and maintenance . . .	21	1,975
13	Depreciation and section 179 expense deduction (not included in Part III) (see instructions)	13	4,000	22	Supplies (not included in Part III) .	22	12,800
				23	Taxes and licenses	23	400
				24	Travel, meals, and entertainment:		
14	Employee benefit programs (other than on line 19) . .	14		a	Travel	24a	1,435
15	Insurance (other than health)	15	1,200	b	Deductible meals and entertainment (see instructions) .	24b	270
16	Interest:			25	Utilities	25	2,200
a	Mortgage (paid to banks, etc.)	16a	300	26	Wages (less employment credits) .	26	53,850
b	Other	16b		27a	Other expenses (from line 48) . .	27a	850
17	Legal and professional services	17	1,040	b	**Reserved for future use** . . .	27b	

28	**Total expenses** before expenses for business use of home. Add lines 8 through 27a . . . . . ▶	28	97,021
29	Tentative profit or (loss). Subtract line 28 from line 7	29	2,179

30 Expenses for business use of your home. Do not report these expenses elsewhere. Attach Form 8829 unless using the simplified method (see instructions).

Simplified method filers only: enter the total square footage of: (a) your home: _____

and (b) the part of your home used for business: _____ . Use the Simplified

Method Worksheet in the instructions to figure the amount to enter on line 30 . . . .

30	

31 **Net profit or (loss).** Subtract line 30 from line 29.

- If a profit, enter on both **Form 1040, line 12** (or **Form 1040NR, line 13**) and on **Schedule SE, line 2.** (If you checked the box on line 1, see instructions). Estates and trusts, enter on **Form 1041, line 3.**

- If a loss, you **must** go to line 32.

31	2,179

32 If you have a loss, check the box that describes your investment in this activity (see instructions).

- If you checked 32a, enter the loss on both **Form 1040, line 12,** (or **Form 1040NR, line 13**) and on **Schedule SE, line 2.** (If you checked the box on line 1, see the line 31 instructions). Estates and trusts, enter on **Form 1041, line 3.**

- If you checked 32b, you **must** attach **Form 6198.** Your loss may be limited.

32a ☑ All investment is at risk.
32b ☐ Some investment is not at risk.

For Paperwork Reduction Act Notice, see the separate instructions. Cat. No. 11334P Schedule C (Form 1040) 2017

Source: Form 1040

filing Form 3115 with the IRS. The IRS automatically approves certain types of accounting method changes, but for others the business must provide a good business purpose for the change and pay a fee. The IRS also requires permission when a business must change from using an impermissible method; this requirement helps the IRS to certify that the business properly makes the transition to a permissible method. In essence, the IRS requires the business to report its own noncompliance. Why would a business do so? Besides complying with the tax laws, a business might report its own noncompliance to receive leniency from the IRS. Without getting into the details, the IRS is likely to assess fewer penalties and less interest expense for noncompliance when the business reports the noncompliance before the IRS discovers it on its own.

Tax Consequences of Changing Accounting Methods When a business changes from one accounting method to another, the business determines its taxable income for the year of change using the new method. Furthermore, the business must make an adjustment to taxable income that effectively represents the cumulative difference, as of the beginning of the tax year, between the amount of income (or deductions) recognized under the old accounting method and the amount that would have been recognized for all prior years if the new method had been applied. This adjustment is called a **§481 adjustment.** The §481 adjustment prevents the duplication or omission of items of income or deduction due to a change in accounting method. If the §481 adjustment increases taxable income, the taxpayer recognizes the total adjustment spread evenly over four years beginning with the year of the change (25 percent of the full adjustment each year).[56] If the adjustment decreases taxable income, the taxpayer recognizes it entirely in the year of change.[57]

Example 9-28

What if: Suppose that at the end of 2018, Green Acres has $24,000 of accounts receivable. Assuming Green Acres uses the cash method of accounting in 2018, it would not include the $24,000 of receivables in income in determining its 2018 taxable income. Suppose further that Rick decides to switch Green Acres to the accrual method of accounting in 2019 by filing a Form 3115 and receiving permission from the IRS. What is Rick's §481 adjustment for his change in accounting method from the cash to the accrual method?

Answer: $24,000 increase to income and because this adjustment is income-increasing, the total is spread evenly over four years ($6,000 in 2019 and each of the subsequent three years). Since Rick would use the accrual method in 2019, he would *not* include payments he receives for the $24,000 receivables as income because he earned this income in 2018 (not 2019). Instead, Rick would be required to make a §481 adjustment to ensure that he does not *omit* these items from taxable income. His total §481 adjustment is to increase income by $24,000. Because this is an income-increasing adjustment, Rick includes $6,000 of the adjustment (25 percent) in Green Acres's taxable income in 2019. He would likewise include a $6,000 income-increasing §481 adjustment in each of the subsequent three years.

What if: Suppose that at the end of 2018, Green Acres has $4,000 of accounts payable instead of $24,000 of accounts receivable. What is Rick's §481 adjustment for his change in accounting method from the cash to the accrual method in 2019?

Answer: In this instance Green Acres would have a negative (income-decreasing) §481 adjustment of $4,000 because the $4,000 of expenses would have accrued in 2018 but would not have been deducted. Hence, Green Acres would be entitled to deduct the full $4,000 as a negative §481 adjustment amount in 2019.

---

[56]Taxpayers with positive §481 adjustments less than $25,000 can elect to recognize the entire amount in the year of change. Rev. Proc. 2002-19, 2002 IRB 696.

[57]Taxpayers changing accounting methods under the Tax Cuts and Jobs Act will need to make § 481 adjustments for those changes.

CONCLUSION

This chapter discusses issues relating to business income and deductions. We learned that the income rules for businesses are very similar to those for individuals and that businesses may deduct only ordinary and necessary business expenses and other business expenses specifically authorized by law. We also described several business expense limitations and discussed the accounting periods and methods businesses may use in reporting taxable income to the IRS. The issues described in this chapter are widely applicable to all types of business entities, including sole proprietorships, partnerships, S corporations, and C corporations.

Summary

Identify common business deductions.   **LO 9-1**

- Ordinary and necessary business expenses are allowed as deductions to calculate net income from activities entered into with a profit motive.
- Only reasonable amounts are allowed as business expense deductions. Extravagant or excessive amounts are likely to be characterized by personal motives and are disallowed.

Determine the limits on deducting business expenses.   **LO 9-2**

- The law specifically prohibits deducting expenses that are against public policy (such as fines or bribes) and expenses that produce tax-exempt income.
- Expenses benefiting more than 12 months must be capitalized and special limits and record-keeping requirements are applied to business expenses that may have personal benefits, such as meals.
- The deduction of business interest expense is limited to business interest income plus 30 percent of the business's adjusted taxable income. Adjusted taxable income is taxable income before depreciation and interest deductions allocable to the business activity. Disallowed business interest expense can be carried forward indefinitely.

Identify special business deductions specifically permitted under the tax laws.   **LO 9-3**

- Special calculations are necessary for deductions such as the deduction for casualty losses. The deduction when an asset is damaged (not destroyed) is limited to the lesser of the reduction in value or the adjusted tax basis of the asset.

Describe accounting periods available to businesses.   **LO 9-4**

- Accounting periods and methods are chosen at the time of filing the first tax return.
- There are three types of tax years—calendar year, fiscal year, and 52/53-week year—and each tax year is distinguished by year-end.

Apply cash and accrual methods to determine business income and expense deductions.   **LO 9-5**

- Under the cash method, taxpayers recognize revenue when they actually or constructively receive property or services and they recognize deductions when they actually pay the expense. Taxpayers, including C corporations and partnerships with C corporation partners but not tax shelters, can elect to use the cash method if their average annual gross receipts is $25 million or less. Under this rule, C corporations and partnerships with C corporation partners can elect to use the cash method.
- Under the accrual method, the all-events test requires that income be recognized when all the events have occurred that are necessary to fix the right to receive payments and the amount of the payments can be determined with reasonable accuracy.
- Except for taxpayers who meet the $25 million gross receipts test, the accrual method must be used to account for sales and purchases for businesses where inventories are an income-producing factor.

- Under the accrual method, accrued expenses can be deducted only when the all-events test and the economic performance test both have been met. The application of the economic performance test depends, in part, on the type of business expense.
- Changes in accounting method or accounting period typically require the consent of the IRS and a §481 adjustment to taxable income. A negative adjustment is included in income for the year of change, whereas a positive adjustment is spread over four years.

KEY TERMS

12-month rule (9-15)
accounting methods (9-14)
accounting period (9-13)
all-events test (9-21)
allowance method (9-25)
arm's length amount (9-4)
casualty losses (9-12)
direct write-off method (9-25)
economic performance
    test (9-21)

first-in, first-out (FIFO)
    method (9-19)
fiscal year (9-13)
flow-through entities (9-14)
impermissible accounting
    method (9-27)
last-in, first-out (LIFO) method (9-19)
mixed-motive expenditures (9-8)
ordinary and necessary (9-3)
payment liabilities (9-21)

permissible accounting method (9-27)
personal expenses (9-6)
reasonable in amount (9-4)
recurring item (9-23)
§481 adjustment (9-30)
specific identification method (9-19)
tax year (9-13)
travel expenses (9-9)
uniform cost capitalization
    (UNICAP) rules (9-19)

DISCUSSION QUESTIONS

Discussion Questions are available in Connect®.

connect

LO 9-1 1. What is an "ordinary and necessary" business expenditure?

LO 9-1 2. Explain how cost of goods is treated when a business sells inventory.

LO 9-1 3. Whether a business expense is "reasonable in amount" is often a difficult question. Explain why determining reasonableness is difficult, and describe a circumstance where reasonableness is likely to be questioned by the IRS.

LO 9-1 4. Jake is a professional dog trainer who purchases and trains dogs for use by law enforcement agencies. Last year Jake purchased 500 bags of dog food from a large pet food company at an average cost of $30 per bag. This year, however, Jake purchased 500 bags of dog food from a local pet food company at an average cost of $45 per bag. Under what circumstances would the IRS likely challenge the cost of Jake's dog food as unreasonable?

LO 9-2 5. What kinds of deductions are prohibited as a matter of public policy? Why might Congress deem it important to disallow deductions for expenditures that are against public policy?

LO 9-2 6. Provide an example of an expense associated with the production of tax-exempt income, and explain what might happen if Congress repealed the prohibition against deducting expenses incurred to produce tax-exempt income.

LO 9-2 7. Peggy is a rodeo clown, and this year she expended $1,000 on special "funny" clothes and outfits. Peggy would like to deduct the cost of these clothes as work-related because she refuses to wear the clothes unless she is working. Under what circumstances can Peggy deduct the cost of her clown clothes?

research

LO 9-2 8. Jimmy is a sole proprietor of a small dry-cleaning business. This month Jimmy paid for his groceries by writing checks from the checking account dedicated to the dry-cleaning business. Why do you suppose Jimmy is using his business checking account rather than his personal checking account to pay for personal expenditures?

LO 9-2 9. Troy operates an editorial service that employs two editors. These editors often entertain authors to encourage them to use Troy's service. This year Troy reimbursed the editors $3,000 for the cost of meals and $6,200 for the cost of entertaining authors. Describe whether Troy can deduct the cost of the meals and entertainment.

10. Jenny uses her car for both business and personal purposes. She purchased the auto this year and drove 11,000 miles on business trips and 9,000 miles for personal transportation. Describe how Jenny will determine the amount of deductible expenses associated with the auto. `LO 9-2`

11. What expenses are deductible when a taxpayer combines both business and personal activities on a trip? How do the rules for international travel differ from the rules for domestic travel? `LO 9-1` `LO 9-2`

12. Clyde lives and operates a sole proprietorship in Dallas, Texas. This year Clyde found it necessary to travel to Fort Worth (about 25 miles away) for legitimate business reasons. Is Clyde's trip likely to qualify as "away from home"? Why would this designation matter? `LO 9-2`

13. Describe the record-keeping requirements for deducting business expenses, including mixed-motive expenditures. `LO 9-2`

14. Describe the computation of the limit placed on the business interest deduction. Is the disallowed interest ever deductible? `LO 9-2`

15. Explain the difference between calculating a loss deduction for a business asset that was partially damaged in an accident and calculating a loss deduction for a business asset that was stolen or completely destroyed in an accident. `LO 9-3`

16. How do casualty loss deductions differ when a business asset, as opposed to a personal-use asset, is completely destroyed? `LO 9-3`

17. What is the difference between a full tax year and a short tax year? Describe circumstances in which a business may have a short tax year. `LO 9-4`

18. Explain why a taxpayer might choose one tax year-end over another if given a choice. `LO 9-4`

19. Compare and contrast the different year-ends available to sole proprietorships, flow-through entities, and C corporations. `LO 9-4`

20. Why does the law generally require partnerships to adopt a tax year consistent with the year used by the partners? `LO 9-4`

21. How does an entity choose its tax year? Is it the same process no matter the type of tax year-end the taxpayer adopts? `LO 9-4`

22. Explain when an expenditure should be "capitalized" based upon accounting principles. From time to time, it is suggested that all business expenditures should be deducted when incurred for tax purposes. Do you agree with this proposition, and if so, why? `LO 9-5`

23. Describe the 12-month rule for determining whether and to what extent businesses should capitalize or immediately deduct prepaid expenses such as insurance or security contracts. Explain the apparent rationale for this rule. `LO 9-5`

24. Explain why Congress sometimes mandates that businesses use particular accounting methods while other times Congress is content to require businesses to use the same accounting methods for tax purposes that they use for financial accounting purposes. `LO 9-5`

25. Why is it not surprising that specific rules differ between tax accounting and financial accounting? `LO 9-5`

26. Fred is considering using the accrual method for his next business venture. Explain to Fred the conditions for recognizing income for tax purposes under the accrual method. `LO 9-5`

27. Describe the all-events test for determining income and describe how to determine the date on which the all-events test has been met. `LO 9-5`

LO 9-5 28. Compare and contrast the tax treatment for rental income received in advance and advance payments for goods and services.

LO 9-5 29. Compare and contrast the rules for determining the tax treatment of advance payments for services versus advance payments for goods.

LO 9-5 30. Jack operates a plumbing business as a sole proprietorship and uses the cash method. Besides providing plumbing services, Jack also sells plumbing supplies to homeowners and other plumbers. The sales of plumbing supplies constitute less than $20,000 per year, and this is such a small portion of Jack's income that he does not keep physical inventories for the supplies. Describe how Jack would account for sales and purchases of plumbing supplies using the accrual method.

LO 9-5 31. Explain why Congress enacted the UNICAP rules and describe the burdens these rules place on taxpayers.

LO 9-5 32. Compare and contrast financial accounting rules with the tax rules under UNICAP (§263A). Explain whether the UNICAP rules tend to accelerate or defer income relative to the financial accounting rules.

LO 9-5 33. Compare and contrast the tests for accruing income and those for accruing deductions for tax purposes.

LO 9-5 34. Compare and contrast when taxpayers are allowed to deduct the cost of warranties provided by others to the taxpayer (i.e., purchased by the taxpayer) and when taxpayers are allowed to deduct the costs associated with warranties they provide (sell) to others.

LO 9-5 35. Describe when economic performance occurs for the following expenses:
   a) Workers' compensation
   b) Rebates and refunds
   c) Insurance, warranties, and service contracts provided *to* the business
   d) Taxes

LO 9-5 36. On December 31 of the current year, a taxpayer prepays an advertising company to provide advertising services for the next 10 months. Using the 12-month rule and the economic performance rules, contrast when the taxpayer would be able to deduct the expenditure if the taxpayer uses the cash method of accounting versus if the taxpayer uses the accrual method of accounting.

LO 9-5 37. Compare and contrast how bad debt expense is determined for financial accounting purposes and how the deduction for bad debts is determined for accrual-method taxpayers. How do cash-method taxpayers determine their bad debt expense for accounts receivable?

LO 9-5 38. Describe the related-person limitation on accrued deductions. What tax savings strategy is this limitation designed to thwart?

LO 9-5 39. What are the relative advantages of the cash and accrual methods of accounting?

LO 9-5 40. Describe how a business adopts a permissible accounting method. Explain whether a taxpayer can adopt an impermissible accounting method.

LO 9-5 41. Describe why the IRS might be skeptical of permitting requests for changes in accounting method without a good business purpose.

LO 9-5 42. What is a §481 adjustment, and what is the purpose of this adjustment?

PROBLEMS

Select problems are available in Connect®.   connect

LO 9-1 43. Manny hired his brother's firm to provide accounting services to his business. During the current year, Manny paid his brother's firm $82,000 for services even though other firms were willing to provide the same services for $40,000. How much of this expenditure, if any, is deductible as an ordinary and necessary business expenditure?

44. Michelle operates a food truck. Indicate the amount (if any) that she can deduct as an ordinary and necessary business deduction in each of the following situations and explain your solution.   `LO 9-1` `LO 9-2`

    a) Michelle moves her food truck between various locations on a daily rotation. Last week, Michelle was stopped for speeding. She paid a fine of $125 for speeding, including $80 for legal advice in connection with the ticket.

    b) Michelle paid $750 to reserve a parking place for her food truck for the fall football season outside the local football arena. Michelle also paid $95 for tickets to a game for her children.

    c) Michelle provided a candidate with free advertising painted on her truck during the candidate's campaign for city council. Michelle paid $500 to have the ad prepared and an additional $200 to have the ad removed from the truck after the candidate lost the election.

45. Indicate the amount (if any) that Josh can deduct as an ordinary and necessary business deduction in each of the following situations and explain your solution.   `LO 9-1` `LO 9-2`

    a) Josh borrowed $50,000 from First State Bank using his business assets as collateral. He used the money to buy City of Blanksville bonds. Over the course of a year, Josh paid interest of $4,200 on the borrowed funds, but he received $3,500 of interest on the bonds.

    b) Josh purchased a piece of land for $45,000 in order to get a location to expand his business. He also paid $3,200 to construct a new driveway for access to the property.

    c) This year Josh paid $15,000 to employ the mayor's son in the business. Josh would typically pay an employee with these responsibilities about $10,000 but the mayor assured Josh that after his son was hired, some city business would be coming his way.

    d) Josh paid his brother, a mechanic, $3,000 to install a robotic machine for Josh's business. The amount he paid to his brother is comparable to what he would have paid to an unrelated person to do the same work. Once the installation was completed by his brother, Josh began calibrating the machine for operation. However, by the end of the year, he had not started using the machine in his business.

46. Ralph operates a business that acts as a sales representative for a large firm that produces and sells precious metals to electronic manufacturers. Ralph contacts manufacturers and convinces them to sign contracts for delivery of metals. Ralph's company earns a commission on the sales. This year, Ralph contacted a jeweler to engrave small lapel buttons for each of his clients. Ralph paid $20 each for the lapel buttons and the jeweler charged Ralph an additional $12 for engraving. The electronic manufacturers, however, prohibit their employees from accepting gifts related to sales contracts. Can Ralph deduct the cost of the lapel buttons as business gifts?   `LO 9-2` `research`

47. Melissa recently paid $400 for round-trip airfare to San Francisco to attend a business conference for three days. Melissa also paid the following expenses: $250 fee to register for the conference, $300 per night for three nights lodging, $200 for meals, and $150 for cab fare.   `LO 9-2`

    a) What amount of the travel costs can Melissa deduct as business expenses?

    b) Suppose that while Melissa was on the coast, she also spent two days sightseeing the national parks in the area. To do the sightseeing, she paid $1,000 for transportation, $800 for lodging, and $450 for meals during this part of her trip, which she considers personal in nature. What amount of the travel costs can Melissa deduct as business expenses?

c) Suppose that Melissa made the trip to San Francisco primarily to visit the national parks and only attended the business conference as an incidental benefit of being present on the coast at that time. What amount of the airfare can Melissa deduct as a business expense?

d) Suppose that Melissa's permanent residence and business was located in San Francisco. She attended the conference in San Francisco and paid $250 for the registration fee. She drove 100 miles over the course of three days and paid $90 for parking at the conference hotel. In addition, she spent $150 for breakfast and dinner over the three days of the conference. She bought breakfast on the way to the conference hotel and she bought dinner on her way home each night from the conference. What amount of the travel costs can Melissa deduct as business expenses?

LO 9-2   48. Kimberly is a self-employed taxpayer. She recently spent $1,000 for airfare to travel to Italy. What amount of the airfare is deductible in each of the following alternative scenarios?

a) Her trip was entirely for personal purposes.

b) On the trip, she spent eight days on personal activities and two days on business activities.

c) On the trip, she spent seven days on business activities and three days on personal activities.

d) Her trip was entirely for business purposes.

LO 9-2   49. Ryan is self-employed. This year Ryan used his personal auto for several long business trips. Ryan paid $1,500 for gasoline on these trips. His depreciation on the car if he was using it fully for business purposes would be $3,000. During the year, he drove his car a total of 12,000 miles (a combination of business and personal travel).

a) Ryan can provide written documentation of the business purpose for trips totaling 3,000 miles. What business expense amount can Ryan deduct (if any) for these trips?

b) Ryan estimates that he drove approximately 1,300 miles on business trips, but he can only provide written documentation of the business purpose for trips totaling 820 miles. What business expense amount can Ryan deduct (if any) for these trips?

LO 9-1   **LO 9-2**   50. Christopher is a cash-method, calendar-year taxpayer, and he made the following cash payments related to his business this year. Calculate the after-tax cost of each payment assuming Christopher has a 37 percent marginal tax rate.

a) $500 fine for speeding while traveling to a client meeting.

b) $800 of interest on a short-term loan incurred in September and repaid in November. Half of the loan proceeds were used immediately to pay salaries and the other half was invested in municipal bonds until November.

c) $600 for office supplies in May of this year. He used half of the supplies this year and he will use the remaining half by February of next year.

d) $450 for several pairs of work boots. Christopher expects to use the boots about 80 percent of the time in his business and the remainder of the time for hiking. Consider the boots to be a form of clothing.

LO 9-2   51. Heather paid $15,000 to join a country club in order to meet potential clients. This year she paid $4,300 in greens fees when golfing with clients and paid an additional $5,700 for meals when Heather business meetings with clients in the clubhouse conference rooms. Under what circumstances, if any, can Heather deduct the $25,000 paid to the country club this year?

52. Assume Sarah is a cash-method, calendar-year taxpayer, and she is considering making the following cash payments related to her business. Calculate the after-tax cost of each payment assuming she is subject to 37 percent marginal tax rate.   **LO 9-1** **LO 9-2**

    a) $2,000 payment for next year's property taxes on her place of business.

    b) $800 to reimburse the cost of meals incurred by employees while traveling for the business.

    c) $1,200 for football tickets to entertain out-of-town clients during contract negotiations.

    d) $500 contribution to the mayor's reelection campaign.

53. Renee operates a proprietorship selling collectibles over the web, and last year she purchased a building for $24 million for her business. This year, Renee's proprietorship reported revenue of $85 million and incurred total expenses of $78.1 million. Her expenses included cost of goods sold of $48.5 million, sales commissions paid of $16.9 million, $10.5 million of interest paid on the building mortgage, and $12.7 million of depreciation.   **LO 9-2**

    a. What is Renee's adjusted taxable income for purposes of calculating the limitation on business interest expense?

    b. What is the maximum amount of business interest expense that Renee can deduct this year, and how is the disallowed interest expense (if any) treated?

    c. Suppose that Renee's revenue includes $5 million of business interest income. What is the maximum amount of business interest expense that Renee can deduct this year?

54. This year Amy purchased $2,000 of equipment for use in her business. However, the machine was damaged in a traffic accident while Amy was transporting the equipment to her business. Note that because Amy did not place the equipment into service during the year, she does not claim any depreciation expense for the equipment.   **LO 9-3**

    a) After the accident, Amy had the choice of repairing the equipment for $1,800 or selling the equipment to a junk shop for $300. Amy sold the equipment. What amount can Amy deduct for the loss of the equipment?

    b) After the accident, Amy repaired the equipment for $800. What amount can Amy deduct for the loss of the equipment?

    c) After the accident, Amy could not replace the equipment so she had the equipment repaired for $2,300. What amount can Amy deduct for the loss of the equipment?

55. In July of this year, Stephen started a proprietorship called ECR (which stands for electric car repair). ECR uses the cash method of accounting and Stephen has produced the following financial information for this year: **LO 9-3**

    tax forms

    - ECR collected $81,000 in cash for repairs completed during the year and an additional $3,200 in cash for repairs that will commence after year-end.

    - Customers owe ECR $14,300 for repairs completed this year, and while Stephen isn't sure which bills will eventually be paid, he expects to collect all but about $1,900 of these revenues next year.

    ECR has made the following expenditures:

Interest expense	$ 1,250
Shop rent ($1,500 per month)	27,000
Utilities	1,075
Contract labor	8,250
Compensation	21,100
Liability insurance premiums ($350 per month)	4,200
Term life insurance premiums ($150 per month)	1,800

The interest paid relates to interest accrued on a $54,000 loan made to Stephen in July of this year. Stephen used half of the loan to pay for 18 months of shop rent, and the remainder he used to upgrade his personal wardrobe. In July, Stephen purchased 12 months of liability insurance to protect against liability should anyone be injured in the shop. ECR has only one employee (the remaining workers are contract labor), and this employee thoroughly understands how to repair an electric propulsion system. On November 1 of this year, Stephen purchased a 12-month term-life policy that insures the life of this "key" employee. Stephen paid Gecko Insurance Company $1,800; in return, Gecko promises to pay Stephen a $40,000 death benefit if this employee dies any time during the next 12 months.

Fill out a draft of the front page of Stephen's Schedule C.

LO 9-5

planning

56. Nicole is a calendar-year taxpayer who accounts for her business using the cash method. On average, Nicole sends out bills for about $12,000 of her services at the first of each month. The bills are due by the end of the month, and typically 70 percent of the bills are paid on time and 98 percent are paid within 60 days.

a) Suppose that Nicole is expecting a 2 percent reduction in her marginal tax rate next year. Ignoring the time value of money, estimate the tax savings for Nicole if she postpones mailing the December bills until January 1 of next year.

b) Describe how the time value of money affects your calculations.

c) Would this tax savings strategy create any additional business risks? Explain.

LO 9-5

57. Jeremy is a calendar-year taxpayer who sometimes leases his business equipment to local organizations. He recorded the following receipts this year. Indicate the extent to which these payments are taxable income to Jeremy this year if Jeremy is (1) a cash-method taxpayer and (2) an accrual-method taxpayer.

a) $1,000 deposit from the Ladies' Club, which wants to lease a trailer. The club will receive the entire deposit back when the trailer is returned undamaged.

b) $800 from the Ladies' Club for leasing the trailer from December of this year through March of next year ($200 per month).

c) $300 lease payment received from the Men's Club this year for renting Jeremy's trailer last year. Jeremy billed the club last year but recently he determined that the Men's Club would never pay him, so he was surprised when he received the check.

LO 9-5

58. Brown Thumb Landscaping is a calendar-year, accrual-method taxpayer. In September, Brown Thumb negotiated a $14,000 contract for services it would provide to the city in November of the current year. The contract specifies that Brown Thumb will receive $4,000 in October as a down payment for these services and it will receive the remaining $10,000 in January of next year.

a) How much income from this $14,000 contract will Brown Thumb recognize in the current year? Explain.

b) How much income from this $14,000 contract will Brown Thumb recognize in the current year if it uses the cash method of accounting?

c) Suppose that the total amount to be paid under the contract with the city is estimated at $14,000 but may be adjusted to $12,000 next year during the review of the city budget. What amount from the contract, if any, should Brown Thumb recognize as income this year? Explain.

d) Suppose that in addition to the basic contract, Brown Thumb will be paid an additional $3,000 if its city landscape design wins the annual design competition next year. Should Brown Thumb accrue $3,000 revenue this year? Why or why not?

LO 9-5

59. In January of year 0, Justin paid $4,800 for an insurance policy that covers his business property for accidents and casualties. Justin is a calendar-year taxpayer who

uses the cash method of accounting. What amount of the insurance premium may Justin deduct in year 0 in each of the following alternative scenarios?

a) The policy covers the business property from April 1 of year 0 through March 31 of year 1.

b) The policy begins on February 1 of year 1 and extends through January 31 of year 2.

c) Justin pays $6,000 for a 24-month policy that covers the business from April 1, year 0, through March 31, year 2.

d) Instead of paying an insurance premium, Justin pays $4,800 to rent his business property from April 1 of year 0 through March 31 of year 1.

60. Ben teaches golf lessons at a country club under a business called Ben's Pure Swings (BPS). He operates this business as a sole proprietorship on the accrual basis of accounting. Use the following accounting information for BPS to complete the firm's Schedule C:

LO 9-5

tax forms

This year BPS billed clients for $86,700 and collected $61,000 in cash for golf lessons completed during the year. In addition, BPS collected an additional $14,500 in cash for lessons that will commence after year-end. Ben hopes to collect about half of the outstanding billings next year but the rest will likely be written off.

Besides providing private golf lessons, BPS also contracted with the country club to staff the driving range. This year, BPS billed the country club $27,200 for the service. The club paid $17,000 of the amount but disputed the remainder. By year-end, the dispute had not been resolved, and while Ben believes he is entitled to the money, he has still not collected the remaining $10,200.

BPS has accrued the following expenses (explained below):

Advertising (in the clubhouse)	$13,150
Pro golf teachers' membership fees	860
Supplies (golf tees, balls, etc.)	4,720
Club rental	6,800
Malpractice insurance	2,400
Accounting fees	8,820

The expenditures were all paid for this calendar year with several exceptions. First, Ben initiated his golfer's malpractice insurance on June 1 of this year. The $2,400 insurance bill covers the last six months of this calendar year and the first six months of next year. At year-end, Ben had only paid $600, but he has assured the insurance agent he will pay the remaining $1,800 early next year. Second, the amount paid for club rental ($100 per week) represents rental charges for the last 6 weeks of the previous year, the 52 weeks in this calendar year, and the first 10 weeks of next year. Ben has also mentioned that BPS only pays for supplies that are used at the club. Although BPS could buy the supplies for half the cost elsewhere, Ben likes to "throw some business" to the golf pro shop because it is operated by his brother.

Fill out a draft of Parts I and II on the front page of a Schedule C for BPS.

61. On April 1 of year 0 Stephanie received a $9,000 payment for full payment on a three-year service contract (under the contract Stephanie is obligated to provide advisory services for the next three years).

LO 9-5

a) What amount of income should Stephanie recognize in year 0 if she uses the accrual method of accounting (she recognized $2,250 for financial accounting purposes)?

b) What amount of income will Stephanie recognize in year 1 if she uses the accrual method of accounting?

c) What amount of income will Stephanie recognize in year 2 if she uses the accrual method of accounting?

d) What amount of income will Stephanie recognize in year 0 if she recognizes $5,000 of income from the contract for financial statement purposes?

LO 9-5 62. In October of year 0, Janine received a $6,000 payment from a client for 25 months of security services she will provide starting on November 1 of year 0. This amounts to $240 per month.

a) When must Janine recognize the income from the $6,000 advance payment for services if she uses the cash method of accounting?

b) When must Janine recognize the income from the $6,000 advance payment for services if she uses the accrual method of accounting?

c) Suppose that instead of services, Janine received the payment for a security system (inventory) that she will deliver and install in year 2. When would Janine recognize the income from the advance payment for inventory sale if she uses the accrual method of accounting and she elects to use the deferral method for reporting income from advance payments? For financial accounting purposes, she reports the income when the inventory is delivered.

d) Suppose that instead of services, Janine received the payment for inventory to be delivered next year. When would Janine recognize the income from the advance payment for sale of goods if she uses the accrual method of accounting and she does not elect to use the deferral method for advance payments?

LO 9-5 63. Nicole's business uses the accrual method of accounting and accounts for inventory with specific identification. In year 0, Nicole received a $4,500 payment with an order for inventory to be delivered to the client early next year. Nicole has the inventory ready for delivery at the end of year 0 (she purchased the inventory in year 0 for $2,300).

a) When does Nicole recognize the $2,200 of gross profit ($4,500 revenue minus $2,300 cost of the inventory) if she does not elect to use the deferral method?

b) When does Nicole recognize the $2,200 of gross profit from the inventory sale if she elects to use the deferral method?

c) How would Nicole account for the inventory-related transactions if she uses the cash method of accounting and her annual sales are usually less than $100,000?

d) How would Nicole account for the inventory-related transactions if she uses the cash method of accounting and her annual sales are usually over 50 million per year?

LO 9-5 64. This year Amber purchased a factory to process and package landscape mulch. Approximately 20 percent of management time, space, and expenses are spent on this manufacturing process.

		Costs (in thousands)	Tax Inventory
Material:	Mulch and packaging	$ 5,000	?
	Administrative supplies	250	?
Salaries:	Factory labor	12,000	?
	Sales & advertising	3,500	?
	Administration	5,200	?
Property taxes:	Factory	4,600	?
	Offices	2,700	?
Depreciation:	Factory	8,000	?
	Offices	1,500	?

a) At the end of the year, Amber's accountant indicated that the business had processed 10 million bags of mulch but only 1 million bags remained in the ending inventory. What is Amber's tax basis in her ending inventory if the UNICAP rules are used to allocate indirect costs to inventory? (Assume direct costs are allocated to inventory according to the level of ending inventory. In contrast, indirect costs are first allocated by time spent and then according to level of ending inventory.)

b) Under what conditions could Amber's business avoid having to apply UNICAP rules to allocate indirect costs to inventory for tax purposes?

65. Suppose that David has elected to account for inventories and has adopted the last-in, first-out (LIFO) inventory-flow method for his business inventory of widgets (purchase prices below).

LO 9-5

Widget	Purchase Date	Direct Cost	Other Costs	Total Cost
#1	August 15	$2,100	$100	$2,200
#2	October 30	2,200	150	2,350
#3	November 10	2,300	100	2,400

In late December, David sold widget #2 and next year David expects to purchase three more widgets at the following estimated prices:

Widget	Purchase Date	Estimated Cost
#4	Early spring	$2,600
#5	Summer	2,260
#6	Fall	2,400

a) What cost of goods sold and ending inventory would David record if he elects to use the LIFO method this year?

b) If David sells two widgets next year, what will be his cost of goods sold and ending inventory next year under the LIFO method?

c) How would you answer (a) and (b) if David had initially selected the first-in, first-out (FIFO) method instead of LIFO?

d) Suppose that David initially adopted the LIFO method, but wants to apply for a change to FIFO next year. What would be his §481 adjustment for this change, and in what year(s) would he make the adjustment?

66. On November 1 of year 0, Jaxon borrowed $50,000 from Bucksnort Savings and Loan for use in his business. In December, Jaxon paid interest of $4,500 relating to the 12-month period from November of year 0 through October of year 1.

LO 9-5

a) How much interest, if any, can Jaxon deduct in year 0 if his business uses the cash method of accounting for tax purposes?

b) How much interest, if any, can Jaxon deduct in year 0 if his business uses the accrual method of accounting for tax purposes?

67. Matt hired Apex Services to repair his business equipment. On November 1 of year 0, Matt paid $2,000 for the repairs that he expects to begin in early March of year 1.

LO 9-5

a) What amount of the cost of the repairs can Matt deduct in year 0 if he uses the cash method of accounting for his business?

b) What amount of the cost of the repairs can Matt deduct in year 0 if he uses the accrual method of accounting for his business?

c) What amount of the cost of the repairs can Matt deduct in year 0 if he uses the accrual method and he expects the repairs to be done by early February?

d) What amount of the cost of the repairs can Matt deduct in year 0 if he uses the cash method of accounting and he expects the repairs to be done by early February?

LO 9-5 68. Circuit Corporation (CC) is a calendar-year, accrual-method taxpayer. CC manufactures and sells electronic circuitry. On November 15, year 0, CC enters into a contract with Equip Corp (EC) that provides CC with exclusive use of EC's specialized manufacturing equipment for the five-year period beginning on January 1 of year 1. Pursuant to the contract, CC pays EC $100,000 on December 30, year 0. How much of this expenditure is CC allowed to deduct in year 0 and in year 1?

LO 9-5 69. This year (year 0) Elizabeth agreed to a three-year service contract with an engineering consulting firm to improve efficiency in her factory. The contract requires Elizabeth to pay the consulting firm $1,500 for each instance that Elizabeth requests its assistance. The contract also provides that Elizabeth only pays the consultants if their advice increases efficiency as measured 12 months from the date of service. This year Elizabeth requested advice on three occasions and she has not yet made any payments to the consultants.

a) How much should Elizabeth deduct in year 0 under this service contract if she uses the accrual method of accounting?

b) How much should Elizabeth deduct in year 0 under this service contract if she uses the cash method of accounting?

LO 9-5 70. Travis is a professional landscaper. He provides his clients with a one-year (12-month) warranty for retaining walls he installs. In June of year 1, Travis installed a wall for an important client, Sheila. In early November, Sheila informed Travis that the retaining wall had failed. To repair the wall, Travis paid $700 cash for additional stone that he delivered to Sheila's location. Travis also offered to pay a mason $800 to repair the wall on November 20 of year 1. Due to some bad weather and the mason's work backlog, the mason agreed to finish the work by the end of January of year 2. Even though Travis expected the mason to finish the project by the end of February, Travis informed the mason that he would pay the mason the $800 when he completed the job.

a) Assuming Travis is an accrual-method taxpayer, how much can he deduct in year 1 from these activities?

b) Assuming Travis is a cash-method taxpayer, how much can he deduct in year 1 from these activities?

LO 9-5
research

71. Adam elects the accrual method of accounting for his business. What amount of deductions does Adam recognize in year 0 for the following transactions?

a) Adam guarantees that he will refund the cost of any goods sold to a client if the goods fail within a year of delivery. In December of year 0, Adam agreed to refund $2,400 to clients, and he expects to make payment in January of year 1.

b) On December 1 of year 0, Adam paid $480 for a one-year contract with CleanUP Services to clean his store. The agreement calls for services to be provided on a weekly basis.

c) Adam was billed $240 for annual personal property taxes on his delivery van. Because this was the first time Adam was billed for these taxes, he did not make payment until January. However, he considers the amounts immaterial.

LO 9-5 72. Rebecca is a calendar-year taxpayer who operates a business. She made the following business-related expenditures in December of year 0. Indicate the amount of these payments that she may deduct in year 0 under both the cash method of accounting and the accrual method of accounting.

a) $2,000 for an accountant to evaluate the accounting system of Rebecca's business. The accountant spent three weeks in January of year 1 working on the evaluation.

b) $2,500 for new office furniture. The furniture was delivered on January 15, year 1.

c) $3,000 for property taxes payable on her factory.

d) $1,500 for interest on a short-term bank loan relating to the period from November 1, year 0, through March 31, year 1.

73. BCS Corporation is a calendar-year, accrual-method taxpayer. BCS was formed and   **LO 9-5**
    started its business activities on January 1, year 0. It reported the following informa-
    tion for year 0. Indicate BCS's deductible amount for year 0 in each of the following
    alternative scenarios.

    a) BCS provides two-year warranties on products it sells to customers. For its year
       0 sales, BCS estimated and accrued $200,000 in warranty expense for financial
       accounting purposes. During year 0, BCS actually spent $30,000 repairing its
       product under the warranty.

    b) BCS accrued an expense for $50,000 for amounts it anticipated it would be re-
       quired to pay under the workers' compensation act. During year 0, BCS actually
       paid $10,000 for workers' compensation–related liabilities.

    c) In June of year 0, a display of BCS's product located in its showroom fell and
       injured a customer. The customer sued BCS for $500,000. The case is scheduled
       to go to trial next year. BCS anticipates that it will lose the case and accrued a
       $500,000 expense on its financial statements.

    d) Assume the same facts as in (c) except that BCS was required to pay $500,000
       to a court-appointed escrow fund in year 0. If BCS loses the case in year 1, the
       money from the escrow fund will be transferred to the customer suing BCS.

    e) On December 1 of year 0, BCS acquired equipment from Equip Company. As
       part of the purchase, BCS signed a warranty agreement with Equip so that Equip
       would warranty the equipment for two years (from December 1 of year 0 through
       November 30 of year 2). The cost of the warranty was $12,000. BCS paid Equip
       for the warranty in January of year 1.

74. This year William provided $4,200 of services to a large client on credit. Unfortu-   **LO 9-5**
    nately, this client has recently encountered financial difficulties and has been unable
    to pay William for the services. Moreover, William does not expect to collect for his
    services. William has "written off" the account and would like to claim a deduction
    for tax purposes.

    a) What amount of deduction for bad debt expense can William claim this year if he
       uses the accrual method?

    b) What amount of deduction for bad debt expense can William claim this year if he
       uses the cash method?

75. Dustin has a contract to provide services to Dado Enterprises. In November of   **LO 9-5**
    year 0, Dustin billed Dado $10,000 for the services he rendered during the year.
    Dado is an accrual-method proprietorship that is owned and operated by
    Dustin's father.

    a) What amount of revenue must Dustin recognize in year 0 if Dustin uses the cash
       method and Dado remits payment for the services in December of year 0? What
       amount can Dado deduct in year 0?

    b) What amount of revenue must Dustin recognize in year 0 if Dustin uses the
       accrual method and Dado remits payment for the services in December of year
       0? What amount can Dado deduct in year 0?

    c) What amount of revenue must Dustin recognize in year 0 if Dustin uses the cash
       method and Dado remits payment for the services in January of year 1? What
       amount can Dado deduct in year 0?

d) What amount of revenue must Dustin recognize in year 0 if Dustin uses the accrual method and Dado remits payment for the services in January of year 1? What amount can Dado deduct in year 0?

LO 9-5 76. Nancy operates a business that uses the accrual method of accounting. In December, Nancy asked her brother, Hank, to provide her business with consulting advice. Hank billed Nancy for $5,000 of consulting services in year 0 (a reasonable amount), but Nancy was only able to pay $3,000 of the bill by the end of year 0. However, Nancy paid the remainder of the bill in year 1.

a) How much of the $5,000 consulting services will Hank include in his income in year 0 if he uses the cash method of accounting? What amount can Nancy deduct in year 0 for the consulting services?

b) How much of the $5,000 consulting services will Hank include in his income in year 0 if he uses the accrual method of accounting? What amount can Nancy deduct in year 0 for the consulting services?

LO 9-5 77. Erin is considering switching her business from the cash method to the accrual method at the beginning of next year (year 1). Determine the amount and timing of her §481 adjustment assuming the IRS grants Erin's request in the following alternative scenarios.

a) At the end of year 0/beginning of year 1, Erin's business has $15,000 of accounts receivable and $18,000 of accounts payable that have not been recorded for tax purposes.

b) At the end of year 0/beginning of year 1, Erin's business reports $25,000 of accounts receivable and $9,000 of accounts payable that have not been recorded for tax purposes.

COMPREHENSIVE PROBLEMS

Select problems are available in Connect®.

78. Joe operates a business that locates and purchases specialized assets for clients, among other activities. Joe uses the accrual method of accounting but he doesn't keep any significant inventories of the specialized assets that he sells. Joe reported the following financial information for his business activities during year 0. Determine the effect of each of the following transactions on the taxable business income.

a) Joe has signed a contract to sell gadgets to the city. The contract provides that sales of gadgets are dependent upon a test sample of gadgets operating successfully. In December, Joe delivers $12,000 worth of gadgets to the city that will be tested in March. Joe purchased the gadgets especially for this contract and paid $8,500.

b) Joe paid $180 for entertaining a visiting out-of-town client. The client didn't discuss business with Joe during this visit, but Joe wants to maintain good relations to encourage additional business next year.

c) On November 1, Joe paid $600 for premiums providing for $40,000 of "key man" insurance on the life of Joe's accountant over the next 12 months.

d) At the end of year 0, Joe's business reports $9,000 of accounts receivable. Based upon past experience, Joe believes that at least $2,000 of his new receivables will be uncollectible.

e) In December of year 0, Joe rented equipment to complete a large job. Joe paid $3,000 in December because the rental agency required a minimum rental of three months ($1,000 per month). Joe completed the job before year-end, but he returned the equipment at the end of the lease.

f) Joe hired a new sales representative as an employee and sent her to Dallas for a week to contact prospective out-of-state clients. Joe ended up reimbursing his employee $300 for airfare, $350 for lodging, and $250 for meals (Joe provided adequate documentation to substantiate the business purpose for the meals). Joe requires the employee to account for all expenditures in order to be reimbursed.

g) Joe uses his BMW (a personal auto) to travel to and from his residence to his factory. However, he switches to a business vehicle if he needs to travel after he reaches the factory. Last month, the business vehicle broke down and he was forced to use the BMW both to travel to and from the factory and to visit work sites. He drove 120 miles visiting work sites and 46 miles driving to and from the factory from his home. Joe uses the standard mileage rate to determine his auto-related business expenses.

h) Joe paid a visit to his parents in Dallas over the Christmas holidays. While he was in the city, Joe spent $50 to attend a half-day business symposium. Joe paid $200 for airfare, $50 for meals during the symposium, and $20 on cab fare to the symposium.

79. Jack, a geologist, had been debating for years whether or not to venture out on his own and operate his own business. He had developed a lot of solid relationships with clients and he believed that many of them would follow him if he were to leave his current employer. As part of a New Year's resolution, Jack decided he would finally do it. Jack put his business plan together and, on January 1 of this year, Jack opened his doors for business as a C corporation called Geo-Jack (GJ). Jack is the sole shareholder. Jack reported the following financial information for the year (assume GJ reports on a calendar year, uses the accrual method of accounting and elects to account for inventory).

a) In January, GJ rented a small business office about 12 miles from Jack's home. GJ paid $10,000, which represented a damage deposit of $4,000 and rent for two years ($3,000 annually).

b) GJ earned and collected $290,000 performing geological-related services and selling its specialized digging tool [see part (i)].

c) GJ received $50 interest from municipal bonds and $2,100 interest from other investments.

d) GJ purchased some new equipment in February for $42,500. It claimed depreciation on these assets during the year in the amount of $6,540.

e) GJ paid $7,000 to buy luxury season tickets for Jack's parents for State U football games.

f) GJ paid Jack's father $10,000 for services that would have cost no more than $6,000 if Jack had hired any other local business to perform the services. While Jack's dad was competent, he does not command such a premium from his other clients.

g) In an attempt to get his name and new business recognized, GJ paid $7,000 for a one-page ad in the *Geologic Survey*. It also paid $15,000 in radio ads to be run through the end of December.

h) GJ leased additional office space in a building downtown. GJ paid rent of $27,000 for the year.

i) In November, Jack's office was broken into and equipment valued at $5,000 was stolen. The tax basis of the equipment was $5,500. Jack received $2,000 of insurance proceeds from the theft.

j) GJ incurred a $4,000 fine from the state government for digging in an unauthorized digging zone.

k) GJ contributed $3,000 to lobbyists for their help in persuading the state government to authorize certain unauthorized digging zones.

l) On July 1, GJ paid $1,800 for an 18-month insurance policy for its business equipment. The policy covers the period July 1 of this year through December 31 of next year.

m) GJ borrowed $20,000 to help with the company's initial funding needs. GJ used $2,000 of funds to invest in municipal bonds. At the end of the year, GJ paid the $1,200 of interest expense that accrued on the loan during the year.

n) Jack lives 12 miles from the office. He carefully tracked his mileage and drove his truck 6,280 miles between the office and his home. He also drove an additional 7,200 miles between the office and traveling to client sites. Jack did not use the truck for any other purposes. He did not keep track of the specific expenses associated with the truck. However, while traveling to a client site, Jack received a $150 speeding ticket. GJ reimbursed Jack for business mileage and for the speeding ticket.

o) GJ purchased two season tickets (20 games) to attend State U baseball games for a total of $1,100. Jack took existing and prospective clients to the games to maintain contact and find further work. This was very successful for Jack as GJ gained many new projects through substantial discussions with the clients following the games.

p) GJ reimbursed employee-salespersons $3,500 for meals involving substantial business discussion.

q) GJ had a client who needed Jack to perform work in Florida. Because Jack had never been to Florida before, he booked an extra day and night for sightseeing. Jack spent $400 for airfare and booked a hotel for three nights ($120/night). (Jack stayed two days for business purposes and one day for personal purposes.) He also rented a car for $45 per day. The client arranged for Jack's meals while Jack was doing business. GJ reimbursed Jack for all expenses.

r) GJ paid a total of $10,000 of wages to employees during the year and cost of goods sold was $15,000.

Required:

a) What is GJ's net business income for tax purposes for the year?

b) As a C corporation, does GJ have a required tax year? If so, what would it be?

c) If GJ were a sole proprietorship, would it have a required tax year-end? If so, what would it be?

d) If GJ were an S corporation, would it have a required tax year-end? If so, what would it be?

80. Rex loves to work with his hands and is very good at making small figurines. Three years ago, Rex opened Bronze Age Miniatures (BAM) for business as a sole proprietorship. BAM produces miniature characters ranging from sci-fi characters (his favorite) to historical characters like George Washington (the most popular). Business has been going very well for him, and he has provided the following information relating to his business. Calculate the business taxable income for BAM assuming that BAM elects to account for their inventory of miniatures.

a) Rex received approval from the IRS to switch from the cash method of accounting to the accrual method of accounting effective January 1 of this year. At the end of last year, BAM reported accounts receivable that had not been included in income under the accrual method of $14,000 and accounts payable that had not been deducted under the accrual method of $5,000.

b) In March, BAM sold 5,000 miniature historical figures to History R Us Inc. (HRU), a retailer of historical artifacts and figurines, for $75,000.

c) HRU was so impressed with the figurines that it purchased in March that it wanted to contract with BAM to continue to produce the figurines for it for the next three years. HRU paid BAM $216,000 ($12 per figurine) on October 30 of this year, to produce 500 figurines per month for 36 months beginning on November 1 of this year. BAM delivered 500 figurines on November 30 and again on December 30. Rex elects to use the deferral method to account for the transaction.

d) Though the sci-fi figurines were not quite as popular, BAM sold 400 figurines at a sci-fi convention in April. Rex accepted cash only and received $11,000 for these sales.

e) In January, BAM determined that it would not be able to collect on $2,000 of its beginning-of-the-year receivables, so it wrote off $2,000 of specific receivables. BAM sold 100,000 other figurines on credit for $120,000. BAM estimates that it will be unable to collect 5 percent of the sales revenue from these sales but it has not been able to specifically identify any accounts to write off.

f) Assume that BAM correctly determined that its cost of goods sold using an appropriate inventory method is $54,000 this year.

g) The sci-fi convention in April was held in Chicago, Illinois. Rex attended the convention because he felt it was a good opportunity to gain new customers and to get new ideas for figurines. He paid $350 round-trip airfare, $100 for entrance to the convention, $210 for lodging, $65 for cab fare, and $110 for meals during the trip. He was busy with business activities the entire trip.

h) On August 1, BAM purchased a 12-month insurance policy that covers its business property for accidents and casualties through July 31 of next year. The policy cost BAM $3,600.

i) BAM reported depreciation expense of $8,200 for this year.

j) Rex had previously operated his business out of his garage, but in January he decided to rent a larger space. He entered into a lease agreement on February 1 and paid $14,400 ($1,200 per month) to possess the space for the next 12 months (February of this year through January of next year).

k) Before he opened his doors for business, Rex spent $30,000 investigating and otherwise getting ready to do business. He expensed $5,000 immediately and is amortizing the remainder using the straight-line method over 180 months.

l) In December, BAM agreed to a 12-month, $8,000 contract with Advertise-With-Us (AWU) to produce a radio ad campaign. BAM paid $3,000 up front (in December of this year) and AWU agreed that BAM would owe the remaining $5,000 only if BAM's sales increased by 15 percent over the 9-month period after the contract was signed.

m) In November of this year, BAM paid $2,500 in business property taxes (based on asset values) covering the period December 1 of this year through November 30 of next year. In November of last year, BAM paid $1,500 for business property taxes (based on asset values) covering the period December 1 of last year through November 30 of this year.

81. Bryan followed in his father's footsteps and entered into the carpet business. He owns and operates I Do Carpet (IDC). Bryan prefers to install carpet only, but in order to earn additional revenue, he also cleans carpets and sells carpet-cleaning supplies. Compute his taxable income for the current year considering the following items:

a) IDC contracted with a homebuilder in December of last year to install carpet in 10 new homes being built. The contract price of $80,000 includes $50,000 for materials (carpet). The remaining $30,000 is for IDC's service of installing the carpet. The contract also stated that all money was to be paid up front. The homebuilder paid IDC in full on December 28 of last year. The contract required IDC to complete the work by January 31 of this year. Bryan purchased the necessary carpet on January 2 and began working on the first home January 4. He completed the last home on January 27 of this year.

b) IDC entered into several other contracts this year and completed the work before year-end. The work cost $130,000 in materials and IDC elects to immediately deduct supplies. Bryan billed out $240,000 but only collected $220,000 by year-end. Of the $20,000 still owed to him, Bryan wrote off $3,000 he didn't expect to collect as a bad debt from a customer experiencing extreme financial difficulties.

c) IDC entered into a three-year contract to clean the carpets of an office building. The contract specified that IDC would clean the carpets monthly from July 1 of this year through June 30 three years hence. IDC received payment in full of $8,640 ($240 a month for 36 months) on June 30 of this year.

d) IDC sold 100 bottles of carpet stain remover this year for $5 per bottle (it collected $500). Rex sold 40 bottles on June 1 and 60 bottles on November 2. IDC had the following carpet-cleaning supplies on hand for this year, and IDC has elected to use the LIFO method of accounting for inventory under a perpetual inventory system:

Purchase Date	Bottles	Total Cost
November last year	40	$120
February this year	35	112
July this year	25	85
August this year	40	140
Totals	140	$457

e) On August 1 of this year, IDC needed more room for storage and paid $900 to rent a garage for 12 months.

f) On November 30 of this year, Bryan decided it was time to get his logo on the sides of his work van. IDC hired We Paint Anything Inc. (WPA) to do the job. It paid $500 down and agreed to pay the remaining $1,500 upon completion of the job. WPA indicated it wouldn't be able to begin the job until January 15 of next year, but the job would only take one week to complete. Due to circumstances beyond its control, WPA wasn't able to complete the job until April 1 of next year, at which time IDC paid the remaining $1,500.

g) In December, Bryan's son, Aiden, helped him finish some carpeting jobs. IDC owed Aiden $600 (reasonable) compensation for his work. However, Aiden did not receive the payment until January of next year.

h) IDC also paid $1,000 for interest on a short-term bank loan relating to the period from November 1 of this year through March 31 of next year.

82. Hank started a new business, Hank's Donut World (HW for short), in June of last year. He has requested your advice on the following specific tax matters associated with HW's first year of operations. Hank has estimated HW's income for the first year as follows:

Revenue:		
Donut sales	$252,000	
Catering revenues	71,550	$323,550
Expenditures:		
Donut supplies	$124,240	
Catering expense	27,910	
Salaries to shop employees	52,500	
Rent expense	40,050	
Accident insurance premiums	8,400	
Other business expenditures	6,850	−259,950
Net income		$ 63,600

HW operates as a sole proprietorship and Hank reports on a calendar year. Hank uses the cash method of accounting and plans to do the same with HW (HW has no inventory of donuts because unsold donuts are not salable). HW does not purchase donut supplies on credit nor does it generally make sales on credit. Hank has provided the following details for specific first-year transactions.

- A small minority of HW clients complained about the catering service. To mitigate these complaints, Hank's policy is to refund dissatisfied clients 50 percent of the catering fee. By the end of the first year, only two HW clients had complained but had not yet been paid refunds. The expected refunds amount to $1,700, and Hank reduced the reported catering fees for the first year to reflect the expected refund.

- In the first year, HW received a $6,750 payment from a client for catering a monthly breakfast for 30 consecutive months beginning in December. Because the payment didn't relate to last year, Hank excluded the entire amount when he calculated catering revenues.

- In July, HW paid $1,500 to ADMAN Co. for an advertising campaign to distribute fliers advertising HW's catering service. Unfortunately, this campaign violated a city code restricting advertising by fliers, and the city fined HW $250 for the violation. HW paid the fine, and Hank included the fine and the cost of the campaign in "other business" expenditures.

- In July, HW also paid $8,400 for a 24-month insurance policy that covers HW for accidents and casualties beginning on August 1 of the first year. Hank deducted the entire $8,400 as accident insurance premiums.

- In May of the first year, Hank signed a contract to lease the HW donut shop for 10 months. In conjunction with the contract, Hank paid $2,000 as a damage deposit and $8,050 for rent ($805 per month). Hank explained that the damage deposit was refundable at the end of the lease. At this time, Hank also paid $30,000 to lease kitchen equipment for 24 months ($1,250 per month). Both leases began on June 1 of the first year. In his estimate, Hank deducted these amounts ($40,050 in total) as rent expense.

- Hank signed a contract hiring WEGO Catering to help cater breakfasts. At year-end, WEGO asked Hank to hold the last catering payment for the year, $9,250, until after January 1 (apparently because WEGO didn't want to report the income on its tax return). The last check was delivered to WEGO in January after the end of the first year. However, because the payment related to the first year of operations, Hank included the $9,250 in last year's catering expense.

- Hank believes that the key to the success of HW has been hiring Jimbo Jones to supervise the donut production and manage the shop. Because Jimbo is such an important employee, HW purchased a "key-employee" term-life insurance policy on his life. HW paid a $5,100 premium for this policy and it will pay HW a $40,000 death benefit if Jimbo passes away any time during the next 12 months. The term of the policy began on September 1 of last year and this payment was included in "other business" expenditures.

- In the first year, HW catered a large breakfast event to celebrate the city's anniversary. The city agreed to pay $7,100 for the event, but Hank forgot to notify the city of the outstanding bill until January of this year. When he mailed the bill in January, Hank decided to discount the charge to $5,500. On the bill, Hank thanked the mayor and the city council for their patronage and asked them to "send a little more business our way." This bill is not reflected in Hank's estimate of HW's income for the first year of operations.

Required:

a) Hank files his personal tax return on a calendar year, but he has not yet filed last year's personal tax return nor has he filed a tax return reporting HW's results for the first year of operations. Explain when Hank should file the tax return for HW and calculate the amount of taxable income generated by HW last year.

b) Determine the taxable income that HW will generate if Hank chooses to account for the business under the accrual method.

c) Describe how your solution might change if Hank incorporated HW before he commenced business last year.

research

83. R.E.M., a calendar-year corporation and Athens, Georgia, band, recently sold tickets ($20,000,000) for concerts scheduled in the United States for next year and the following two years. For financial statement purposes, R.E.M. will recognize the income from the ticket sales when it performs the concerts, and R.E.M is obligated to return the ticket payments should a concert be cancelled. For tax purposes, R.E.M. uses the accrual method and would prefer to defer the income from the ticket sales until after the concerts are performed. This is the first time that it has sold tickets one or two years in advance. Michael Stipe has asked your advice. Write a memo to Michael explaining your findings.

ROGER | *CPA Review*

Sample CPA Exam questions from Roger CPA Review are available in Connect as support for the topics in this text. These Multiple Choice Questions and Task-Based Simulations include expert-written explanations and solutions and provide a starting point for students to become familiar with the content and functionality of the actual CPA Exam.

Property Acquisition and Cost Recovery

Learning Objectives

Upon completing this chapter, you should be able to:

LO 10-1 Describe the cost recovery methods for recovering the cost of personal property, real property, intangible assets, and natural resources.

LO 10-2 Determine the applicable cost recovery (depreciation) life, method, and convention for tangible personal and real property and the deduction allowable under basic MACRS.

LO 10-3 Calculate the deduction allowable under the additional special cost recovery rules (§179, bonus, and listed property).

LO 10-4 Calculate the deduction for amortization.

LO 10-5 Explain cost recovery of natural resources and the allowable depletion methods.

©Brand X Pictures/Superstock

Storyline Summary

Taxpayer: Teton Mountaineering Technology, LLC (Teton)—a calendar-year single-member LLC (treated as a sole proprietorship for tax purposes)

Location: Cody, Wyoming

President/ Founder: Steve Dallimore

Current situation: Teton has acquired property for its manufacturing operations and wants to understand the tax consequences of property acquisitions.

Several years ago while climbing the Black Ice Couloir (pronounced "cool-wahr") in Grand Teton National Park, Steve Dallimore and his buddy got into a desperate situation. The climbers planned to move fast and light and to be home before an approaching storm reached the Teton. But just shy of the summit, climbing conditions forced them to turn back. Huddled in a wet sleeping bag in a dark snow cave waiting for the tempest to pass, Steve had an epiphany—he conceived of a design for a better ice-climbing tool. Since that moment, Steve has been working toward making his dream—designing and selling his own line of climbing equipment—a reality. Steve spent the next few years planning his business while continuing his current sales career. In December 2016, Steve decided to exercise his stock options, leave his sales position, and start Teton Mountaineering Technology (Teton). At the beginning of 2017, Steve identified a location for his business in Cody, Wyoming, and purchased a building and some equipment to begin his business. He soon discovered the he needed help dealing with the tax issues related to his business assets.

to be continued . . .

Steve obviously has many issues to resolve and decisions to make. In this chapter, we focus on the tax issues relating to the assets Steve acquires for use in his new business. In particular, we explain how Teton determines its cost recovery (depreciation, amortization, and depletion) deductions for the assets in the year the business begins and in subsequent years.[1] These deductions can generate significant tax savings for companies in capital-intensive industries.

This chapter explores the tax consequences of acquiring new or used property, depreciation methods businesses may use to recover the cost of their assets, and other special cost recovery incentives. The Tax Cuts and Jobs Act made many changes to the way taxpayers will determine their depreciation deductions. Although these changes dramatically accelerate the depreciation deductions for many assets, they do not apply to all assets. Therefore, it is still important to understand the basic depreciation rules as we discuss in more detail later in the chapter. To begin, we discuss the amount that is subject to cost recovery. We then discuss the basic depreciation rules, followed by the special incentives. We also address the tax consequences of using intangible assets and natural resources in business activities.

LO 10-1 COST RECOVERY AND TAX BASIS FOR COST RECOVERY

Most businesses make a significant investment in property, plant, and equipment that is expected to provide benefits over a number of years. For both financial accounting and generally for tax accounting purposes, businesses must capitalize the cost of assets with a useful life of more than one year (on the balance sheet) rather than expense the cost immediately. Businesses are allowed to use various methods to allocate the cost of these assets over time because the assets are subject to wear, tear, and obsolescence.

The method of **cost recovery** depends on the nature of the underlying asset. **Depreciation** is the method of deducting the cost of *tangible* personal and real property (other than land) over time. **Amortization** is the method of deducting the cost of **intangible assets** over time. Finally, **depletion** is the method of deducting the cost of natural resources over time. Exhibit 10-1 summarizes these concepts.

Generally, a significant portion of a firm's assets consists of property, plant, equipment, intangibles, or even natural resources. In most cases, this holds true for small businesses like Teton and also for large publicly traded companies. For example, Exhibit 10-2 describes the assets held by Weyerhaeuser, a publicly traded timber company. As indicated in Exhibit 10-2, Weyerhaeuser has over $1.5 billion in property and equipment (net of depreciation) and $14.3 billion in timber (net of depletion), together comprising roughly 80 percent of its assets.

Businesses must choose accounting methods for the assets acquired during the year. Attention to detail is important because the **tax basis** of an asset must be reduced by the cost recovery deductions allowed or *allowable*.[2] This means that if a business fails to deduct (by mistake or error) the allowable amount of depreciation for the year, the business still must reduce the asset's tax basis by the depreciation the taxpayer could have deducted under the method the business is using to depreciate the asset. This means that the business will never receive a tax benefit for the amount of depreciation it failed to deduct.

EXHIBIT 10-1 Assets and Cost Recovery

Asset Type	Cost Recovery Method
Personal property comprises tangible assets such as automobiles, equipment, and machinery.	Depreciation
Real property comprises buildings and land (although land is nondepreciable).	Depreciation
Intangible assets are nonphysical assets such as goodwill and patents.	Amortization
Natural resources are commodities that are considered valuable in their natural form such as oil, coal, timber, and gold.	Depletion

[1]Cost recovery is the common term used to describe the process by which businesses allocate the cost of their fixed assets over the time period in which the assets are used.

[2]If a business discovers that it failed to claim allowable depreciation in a previous year, it can deduct the depreciation it failed to claim in prior years in the current year by filing an automatic consent to a change in accounting method using Form 3115 (Rev. Procs. 2002-9, 2004-11, and 2015-14).

EXHIBIT 10-2   **Weyerhaeuser Assets**

Assets (in millions) per 2016 10-K Statement	2016	2015
Total current assets	$ 1,622	$ 3,639
Property and equipment, net (Note 7)	1,562	1,233
Construction in progress	213	144
Timber and timberlands at cost, less depletion charged to disposals	14,299	6,552
Minerals and mineral rights, less depletion	319	14
Investments in and advances to equity affiliates (Note 8)	56	—
Goodwill	40	40
Deferred tax assets (Note 19)	293	254
Restricted assets held by special purpose entities (Note 8)	615	615
Other	224	229
Total assets	$19,243	$12,720

Basis for Cost Recovery

Businesses may begin recouping the cost of purchased business assets once they begin using the asset in their business (place it in service).[3] Once the business establishes its cost in an asset, the business recovers the cost of the asset through cost recovery deductions such as depreciation, amortization, or depletion. The amount of an asset's cost that has yet to be recovered through cost recovery deductions is called the asset's **adjusted basis** or **tax basis**.[4] An asset's adjusted basis can be computed by subtracting the accumulated depreciation (or amortization or depletion) from the asset's initial cost or historical basis.[5]

For most assets, the initial basis is the cost plus all the expenses to purchase, prepare for use, and begin using the asset. These expenses include sales tax, shipping costs, and installation costs. The financial accounting and tax rules for computing an asset's basis are very similar. Thus, a purchased asset's initial basis is generally the same for both tax and book purposes.[6] So how do taxpayers know whether they should immediately deduct the cost of an asset or capitalize and depreciate it? Taxpayers generally capitalize assets with useful lives over one year, but there are exceptions to this rule. The Treasury has issued regulations that are quite lengthy (over 200 pages) and complex to guide taxpayers in answering this question.[7] The regulations provide a *de minimis* safe harbor that allows taxpayers to

> **THE KEY FACTS**
>
> **Cost Basis**
>
> - An asset's cost basis includes all costs needed to purchase the asset, prepare it for use, and begin using it.
> - Cost basis is usually the same for book and tax purposes.
> - Special basis rules apply when personal-use assets are converted to business use and when assets are acquired through nontaxable transactions, gifts, or inheritances.

[3]Basis is defined under §1012. The mere purchase of an asset does not trigger cost recovery deductions. A business must begin using the asset for business purposes (place it in service) in order to depreciate the asset. However, because businesses generally acquire and place assets in service at the same time, we refer to these terms interchangeably throughout the chapter.

[4]Throughout the chapter we use several different terms to refer to an asset's tax basis. The differences in these terms are somewhat subtle but can often be important. For example, an asset's initial basis refers to the tax basis of an asset at the time the taxpayer initially acquires the asset. If a taxpayer purchases the asset, the initial basis is the same as its cost. However, if a taxpayer acquires the asset through means other than purchase (e.g., gift, inheritance, nontaxable transaction, or conversion from personal use), the initial basis will typically differ from the asset's cost. We discuss some of these differences in the Property Dispositions chapter. The broad term, tax basis, refers to an asset's carrying value for tax purposes at a given point in time. When an asset's initial basis is recovered through depreciation, amortization, or depletion, the asset's tax basis is often referred to as the adjusted tax basis or sometimes simply the adjusted basis. It is not common to use the term adjusted tax basis for assets that are not subject to cost recovery. For example, the tax basis for a common stock investment would typically be referred to simply as its tax basis rather than its adjusted tax basis. Finally, the depreciable basis of an asset refers to the amount of the initial basis that can be depreciated over time using the regular depreciation rules. In many cases, the depreciable basis and the initial basis are the same—for example in the case of real property (i.e., buildings). However, the depreciable basis may differ from the initial basis when taxpayers take advantage of special incentives such as §179 expensing or bonus depreciation that accelerate an asset's cost recovery in the year it is placed in service.

[5]§1011.

[6]However, special basis rules apply when an asset is acquired through a nontaxable transaction. See discussion in the Property Dispositions chapter.

[7]Reg. §1.263(a)-1, -2, and -3.

immediately deduct low cost personal property items used in their business. The definition of low-cost depends on whether the taxpayer has an applicable financial statement, which generally means a certified, audited financial statement. If taxpayers have an applicable financial statement, they may use the *de minimis* safe harbor to immediately deduct amounts paid for tangible property up to $5,000 per invoice or item.[8] If taxpayers don't have an applicable financial statement, they may use the safe harbor to deduct amounts up to $2,500 per invoice or item. Taxpayers generally use the invoice amount to determine whether they meet the safe harbor; however, if the total invoice amount exceeds the $5,000/$2,500 threshold and the invoice provides detailed cost information about each item, taxpayers may immediately deduct individual items that are less than the threshold amount. Taxpayers must capitalize the cost of personal property that does not fall under the *de minimis* safe harbor provision.[9]

When a business acquires multiple assets for one purchase price, the tax laws require the business to determine a cost basis for each separate asset. For example, for Teton's building purchase, Teton must treat the building and land as separate assets. In these types of acquisitions, businesses determine the cost basis of each asset by allocating a portion of the purchase price to each asset based on that asset's value relative to the total value of all the assets the business acquired in the same purchase. The asset values are generally determined by an appraisal.[10]

Example 10-1

Steve determined that he needed machinery and office furniture for a manufacturing facility and a design studio (located in Cody, Wyoming). During 2017, Steve purchased the following assets and incurred the following costs to prepare the assets for business use. His cost basis in each asset is determined as follows:

Asset	Date Acquired	(1) Purchase Price	(2) Business Preparation Costs	(1) + (2) Cost Basis
Office furniture	2/3/17	$ 20,000		$ 20,000
Warehouse	5/1/17	270,000*	$ 5,000 (minor modifications)	275,000
Land (10 acres)	5/1/17	75,000*		75,000
Machinery	7/22/17	600,000	$ 10,000 (delivery and setup)	610,000
Delivery truck (used)	8/17/17	25,000		25,000

*Note that the warehouse and the land were purchased together for $345,000. Steve and the seller determined that the value (and cost) of the warehouse was $270,000 and the value (and cost) of the land was $75,000.

What if: Assume Steve acquired a printer for $800 on July 9. Would he immediately deduct the cost of the printer or capitalize it?

Answer: Assuming that Steve has a policy to expense items costing $2,500 or less for nontax purposes, he would be able to immediately deduct the cost of the printer under the *de minimis* safe harbor.[11]

When a business incurs additional costs associated with an asset after the asset has been placed in service, are these costs immediately deducted or are they capitalized? In general, the answer depends on whether the expenditure constitutes routine maintenance on the asset or whether it results in a "betterment, restoration, or new or different

[8]Taxpayers must have accounting procedures in place at the beginning of the year treating items costing less than a specified dollar figure as an expense for nontax purposes.

[9]Separate rules apply when taxpayers purchase materials and supplies to be used in their business (Reg. §1.162-3).

[10]Reg. §1.167(a)-5.

[11] Later in this chapter, we discuss alternative ways to immediately deduct the cost of certain assets (§179 expensing and bonus depreciation). The first step however is to determine if it must be capitalized or immediately deducted under the Treasury regulations for §263.

use for the property."[12] Taxpayers can immediately deduct the costs if they meet the routine maintenance safe harbor rules provided in the Treasury regulations.[13] Routine maintenance is defined as preventative or cyclical maintenance that is an essential part of the ongoing care and upkeep of a building or building system. Costs related to the replacement of damaged or worn parts with comparable and commercially available replacement parts arising from inspecting, cleaning, and testing of the property are immediately deductible if two conditions are met. First, the taxpayer must fully expect to perform the activity more than once during a 10-year period (for buildings and structures related to buildings), or more than once during the property's class life (for property other than buildings). Second, the safe harbor cannot be used to deduct expenses incurred from major renovations, restorations, or improvements.

Example 10-2

What if: Suppose that Steve's business requires an annual safety certification on all its equipment and machinery. As a result of a required inspection of the machinery, Steve finds a defect in the engine of one of his machines and must replace the engine at a cost of $3,000. Can Steve immediately deduct the cost of the new engine?

Answer: Steve's business requires an annual safety certification inspection; thus Steve meets the requirement of reasonably expecting to perform the activity more than once during the machinery's class life. Assuming that Steve replaces the engine with a comparable, commercially available engine, he may immediately deduct the $3,000 cost of the new engine.

If the routine maintenance safe harbor rules do not apply, then taxpayers must determine whether the costs result in a betterment, restoration, or adaptation for a new or different use for the property.[14] If so, they must capitalize the costs; if not, they may immediately deduct the costs.[15] For example, if the roof of Teton's warehouse was completely replaced because it was leaking, Steve would be required to capitalize the costs to replace the roof as a restoration because a significant portion (100 percent) of a major component was replaced. If Teton needed to replace only 10 percent of the roof, Steve would most likely be able to immediately deduct the costs.[16]

Special rules apply when determining the tax basis of assets converted from personal to business use or assets acquired through a nontaxable exchange, gift, or inheritance. If an asset is used for personal purposes and is later converted to business (or rental) use, the basis for cost recovery purposes is the *lesser* of (1) the cost basis of the asset or (2) the fair market value of the asset on the date of conversion to business use.[17] This rule prevents taxpayers from converting a nondeductible personal loss into a deductible business loss. For example, if Steve had purchased a truck for $20,000 several years ago for personal use but decided to use it as a delivery truck when its value had declined to $15,000, his basis in the

---

[12]Reg. §1.263(a)-3.

[13]The routine maintenance safe harbor is discussed in Reg. §1.263(a)-3(i). In addition to the routine maintenance safe harbor, the regulations provide an additional safe harbor for small taxpayers. This safe harbor allows taxpayers with average annual gross receipts over the last three years of $10 million or less to immediately deduct amounts paid for maintenance and improvement on buildings with an unadjusted basis of $1 million or less if the amounts expended are less than the lesser of 2 percent of the building's unadjusted basis or $10,000 [Reg. §1.263(a)-3(h)].

[14]Reg. §1.263(a)-3.

[15]The regulations provide detailed guidelines for taxpayers to use to establish when they have expenditures related to these three distinct concepts. Coverage of these concepts is beyond the scope of this chapter. See Reg. §1.263(a)-3 for details.

[16]After 2017, Steve may have an opportunity to expense the cost of the roof under §179 (discussed later in the chapter) as the TCJA modified the definition of real property for purposes of the expensing provision.

[17]Reg. §§1.167(g)-1 and 1.168(i)-4(b). However, this rule creates an interesting situation when selling converted assets. The taxpayer uses the lower of the adjusted basis or the fair market value at the time of the conversion for computing loss but uses the adjusted basis to compute a gain when selling converted assets.

truck for cost recovery purposes would be $15,000. The $5,000 decline in the truck's value from $20,000 to $15,000 would be a nondeductible personal loss to Steve, and the reduction in basis ensures that he will not be allowed to deduct the loss as a business loss.

Assets acquired through a nontaxable exchange, such as a like-kind exchange (like-kind exchanges are discussed later in the Property Dispositions chapter), generally take the same basis the taxpayer had in the property that the taxpayer transferred in the transaction. Assets acquired by gift have a carryover basis. This means that the taxpayer's basis in property received through a gift is generally the same basis the transferor had in the property.[18] For example, if Steve's parents gave him equipment worth $45,000 to help him start his business and his parents had purchased the equipment 10 years earlier for $25,000, Steve's basis in the equipment would be $25,000 (the same basis his parents had in the equipment). Assets acquired through inheritance generally receive a basis equal to the fair market value on the transferor's date of death.[19] For example, if Steve inherited a building worth $90,000 from his grandfather who originally paid $35,000 for it, Steve's basis would be $90,000 (its fair market value at date of death) because Steve acquired it through an inheritance.

ETHICS

Catherine Travis is starting a new business. She has several assets that she wants to use in her business that she has been using personally. Since she plans to convert several assets from personal to business use, she will need to find out how much each asset is worth so she can determine her basis for depreciating the assets. Catherine has decided that getting an appraisal would be too costly so she simply uses her cost basis for the assets. What do you think of Catherine's strategy for determining her business asset bases?

LO 10-2 DEPRECIATION

THE KEY FACTS

Tax Depreciation
- To depreciate an asset, a business must determine:
  - Original basis
  - Depreciation method
  - Recovery period
  - Depreciation convention

As a preface to this section, the TCJA made many changes to how taxpayers will recover the cost of their assets for the next several years. In this chapter, we discuss the depreciation provisions both before and after the TCJA effective dates for several reasons. First, existing assets continue to follow the rules in place before the tax law change; therefore, for assets placed in service before the effective dates of the TCJA, taxpayers will need to understand the rules in effect at the time the assets were placed in service. Second, the new provisions provide very generous deductions for personal property; however, taxpayers may opt out of these provisions and instead can follow the pre-TCJA ruless. Taxpayers with large losses may opt to forgo the large depreciation deductions provided under the TCJA to reduce their losses, which may be subject to limitations (e.g., NOL limitations and excess business loss limitations). These taxpayers would then use the standard depreciation methods used prior to the TCJA. Third, for assets that do not qualify for the special provisions in the TCJA, taxpayers must fall back to the standard depreciation methods used under prior law. Finally, the TCJA expanded §179 expensing and extended bonus depreciation; however, bonus depreciation is temporary and is scheduled to begin phasing out for assets placed in service after December 31, 2022. Therefore, it is important to include discussions for the rules in effect before and after the TCJA.

With that in mind, we proceed by discussing the basic rules in effect prior to the enactment of the TCJA. These rules continue to apply to assets placed in service before the TCJA effective date. In this section, we consider how Steve could have depreciated the assets he acquired in 2017. We will then discuss the special rules (§179, bonus depreciation, and listed property), which were modified and expanded by the TCJA.

Since 1986, businesses calculate their tax depreciation using the **Modified Accelerated Cost Recovery System (MACRS)**—which is pronounced "makers" by tax accountants.[20] Compared to financial (book) depreciation, MACRS tax depreciation is quite simple. To

[18]§1015. The basis may be increased if the transferor is required to pay gift tax on the transfer [see §1015(d)]. In addition, special dual basis rules apply if the basis in the gifted property at the gift date is greater than its fair market value.

[19]§1014. In certain circumstances, the estate can elect an alternative valuation date six months after death.

[20]IRS Publication 946 provides a useful summary of MACRS depreciation.

compute MACRS depreciation for an asset, the business need only know the asset's *initial basis,* date placed in service, the applicable *depreciation method*, the asset's **recovery period** (or depreciable "life"), and the applicable depreciation *convention* (the amount of depreciation deductible in the year of acquisition and the year of disposition). The method, recovery period, and convention vary based on whether the asset is **personal property** or **real property.** Before we turn our attention to the determination of the depreciation deduction for personal property, it is important to emphasize that there may be a difference in when an asset is acquired and when it is placed in service. Being placed in service requires that the property is in a condition or state of readiness and availability for a specifically assigned function. This requirement is often met when an asset is acquired but may not be when additional installation is required or modifications must be made to ready the asset for its intended use.[21]

TAXES IN THE REAL WORLD What a Difference a Day (or two) Makes

Taxpayers may begin taking depreciation deductions on their tax returns for business assets "placed in service" during the taxable year. As one taxpayer recently found out, determining when an asset is placed in service is not as simple as purchasing and using an asset. Michael Brown, a wealthy insurance salesman, purchased a $22 million Bombardier Challenger 604 airplane for use in his business. He took possession of the plane on December 30, 2003, and flew the plane across the country on business trips before the end of the year. Accordingly, Brown claimed about $11 million of bonus depreciation on his 2003 tax return. In January 2004, the plane was grounded for a period of time while a conference table and a display screen were added at an additional cost of $500,000. These improvements were "needed" and "required" for his insurance business, according to Brown.

The IRS challenged Brown's bonus depreciation deduction claiming that the plane was not "placed in service" in 2003. The issue is when the plane was regularly available for use in its specifically intended function. Per Brown's testimony, he insisted on having the conference table and display screen so he could conduct business on the plane. Because of this testimony that determined the plane's specifically intended function, the Tax Court denied the bonus depreciation deduction for 2003.

The outcome of this case illustrates the importance of determining the specific function for an asset and whether seemingly minor (2 percent) upgrades can make the asset substantially unavailable for its specifically intended function. It seems the taxpayer's own testimony of the plane's specifically intended function drove the Tax Court's decision to disallow the bonus depreciation deduction.

Source: Brown, T. C. Memo. 2013-275.

Personal Property Depreciation

Personal property includes all tangible property, such as computers, automobiles, furniture, machinery, and equipment, other than real property. Note that *personal* property and *personal-use* property are not the same thing. Personal property denotes any property that is not real property (e.g., building and land) while personal-use property is any property used for personal purposes (e.g., a personal residence is personal-use property even though it is real property). Personal property is relatively short-lived and subject to obsolescence as compared to real property.

Depreciation Method   MACRS provides three acceptable methods for depreciating personal property: 200 percent (double) declining balance (DB), 150 percent declining balance, and straight-line.[22] The 200 percent declining balance method is the default method. This method takes twice the straight-line amount of depreciation in the first year and continues to take twice the straight-line percentage on the asset's declining basis until switching to the straight-line method in the year that the straight-line method over the

---

[21]§1.167(a)-11(e)(1)(1) and Brown v Commissioner, TC Memo 2013-275.

[22]MACRS includes two depreciation systems: the general depreciation system (GDS) and the alternative depreciation system (ADS). MACRS provides three methods under GDS (200 percent DB, 150 percent DB, and straight-line) and one method under ADS (straight-line).

remaining life provides a greater depreciation expense. Fortunately, as we describe below, the IRS provides depreciation tables to simplify the calculations.

Profitable businesses with relatively high marginal tax rates generally choose to use the 200 percent declining balance method because it generates the largest depreciation deduction in the early years of the assets' lives and, thus, the highest current-year after-tax cash flows. For tax planning purposes, companies that currently have lower marginal tax rates but expect their marginal tax rates to increase in the near future may elect the straight-line method because that method generates less depreciation in the early years of the asset's life, relatively, and more depreciation in the later years when their marginal tax rates may increase.

Example 10-3

If Teton wants to accelerate its current depreciation deductions to the extent possible, what method should it use to depreciate its office furniture, machinery, and delivery truck?

Answer: The 200 percent declining balance method (default). Teton could elect to use either the 150 percent declining balance or the straight-line method, if it wants a less accelerated method for determining its depreciation deductions.

Each year, businesses elect the depreciation method for the assets placed in service during *that year*. Specifically, businesses elect one depreciation method for all similar assets they acquired that year.[23] Thus, if a business acquires several different machines during the year, it must use the same method to depreciate all of the machines. However, the methods may differ for machines acquired in different tax years.

Depreciation Recovery Period   For financial accounting purposes, an asset's recovery period (depreciable life) is based on its taxpayer-determined estimated useful life. In contrast, for tax purposes an asset's recovery period is predetermined by the IRS in Rev. Proc. 87-56. This revenue procedure helps taxpayers categorize each of their assets based upon the property's description. Once the business has determined the appropriate categories for its assets, it can use the revenue procedure to identify the recovery period for all assets in a particular category. For example, Teton placed office furniture in service during the year. By examining the excerpt from Rev. Proc. 87-56 provided in Exhibit 10-3, you can see that Category or Asset Class 00.11 includes office furniture and that assets in this category, including Teton's office furniture, have a recovery period of seven years (emphasis in excerpt added through bold text).[24]

While even this small excerpt from Rev. Proc. 87-56 may seem a bit intimidating, you can classify the vast majority of business assets acquired by knowing a few common recovery periods. Exhibit 10-4 lists the most commonly purchased assets and their recovery periods.

To this point, our discussion has emphasized computing regular MACRS depreciation for new assets. Does the process change when businesses acquire used assets? No, it is exactly the same. For example, Teton purchased a *used* delivery truck. The fact that the truck is used does not change its MACRS recovery period. No matter how long the previous owner used the truck, Teton will restart the five-year recovery period for light general-purpose trucks to depreciate the delivery truck (see Exhibit 10-4).

Under MACRS, the tax recovery period for machinery and equipment is seven years. Using Rev. Proc. 87-56, Teton has determined the cost recovery periods for the personal property it purchased and placed in service during 2017. Exhibit 10-5 summarizes this information.

[23]Technically, similar assets are assets in the same property class.

[24]The "alternative" recovery period in Rev. Proc. 87-56 refers to an asset's life under the alternative depreciation system referred to as ADS (which we discuss later in this chapter). The class life referred to in Rev. Proc. 87-56 refers to the midpoint of asset depreciation range (ADR) applicable under pre-ACRS and has little or no meaning under MACRS.

EXHIBIT 10-3   Excerpt from Revenue Procedure 87-56

Description of Assets Included		Years	
Specific depreciable assets used in all business activities, except as noted:	Class Life	General Recovery Period	Alternative Recovery Period
00.11 Office Furniture, Fixtures, and Equipment: Includes furniture and fixtures that are not a structural component of a building. Includes such assets as desks, files, safes, and communications equipment. Does not include communications equipment that is included in other classes.	10	7	10
00.12 Information Systems: Includes computers and their peripheral equipment used in administering normal business transactions and the maintenance of business records.	6	5	5
00.241 Light General Purpose Trucks: Includes trucks for use over the road (actual unloaded weight less than 13,000 pounds) . . .	4	5	5
34.0 Manufacture of Fabricated Metal Products Special Tools: Includes assets used in the production of metal cans, tinware . . .	12	7	12

EXHIBIT 10-4   Recovery Period for Most Common Business Assets

Asset Description (Summary of Rev. Proc. 87-56)	Recovery Period
Cars, light general-purpose trucks, and computers and peripheral equipment	5 years
Office furniture, fixtures, and equipment	7 years

EXHIBIT 10-5   Teton Personal Property Summary (Base Scenario)

Asset	Date Acquired	Quarter Acquired	Cost Basis	Recovery Period	Reference
Office furniture	2/3/17	1st	$ 20,000	7	Example 10-1; Exhibit 10-3
Machinery	7/22/17	3rd	610,000	7	Example 10-1; Exhibit 10-3
Delivery truck	8/17/17	3rd	25,000	5	Example 10-1; Exhibit 10-3
Total personal property			$655,000		

Depreciation Conventions   Once a business has determined the depreciation methods and recovery periods for the assets it placed in service during the year, it then must determine the applicable depreciation conventions. The depreciation convention specifies the portion of a full year's depreciation the business can deduct for an asset in the year the asset is first placed in service *and* in the year the asset is sold. For *personal property*, taxpayers must use either the **half-year convention** or the **mid-quarter convention.** But, taxpayers are *not* free to choose between the two conventions. The half-year convention applies most of the time, particularly after the TCJA. However, under certain conditions taxpayers are required to use the mid-quarter convention (discussed below). The depreciation convention is determined annually. Once the convention is determined for the assets acquired during the year, the convention remains the same for the entire recovery period for those assets.

Before MACRS, taxpayers were required the use of the half-year convention for all personal property placed in service during the year. However, Congress believed that many businesses took unfair advantage of the half-year convention by purposely acquiring assets at the end of the year that they otherwise would have acquired at the beginning of the next taxable year. Thus, businesses received one-half of a year's worth of depreciation for assets that they used for only a small portion of the year. Even though the half-year convention is the default convention, policy makers introduced the *mid-quarter convention* under MACRS to limit or prevent this type of opportunistic behavior. Nevertheless, as we discuss below, the new tax laws allow taxpayers to accelerate their cost recovery deductions no matter when during the year the assets are placed in service. Consequently, the mid-quarter convention will likely have limited application to assets placed in service after December 31, 2017.

Half-year convention.   The half-year convention allows one-half of a full year's depreciation in the year the asset is placed in service (and in the year in which it is disposed), regardless of when it was actually placed in service. For example, when the half-year convention applies to a calendar-year business, an asset placed in service on either February 3 or August 17 is treated as though it was placed in service on July 1, which is the middle of the calendar year. Thus, under this convention, Teton would deduct one-half of a year's worth of depreciation for the machinery, office furniture, and delivery truck even though it acquired the machinery, delivery truck, and office furniture at various times during the year (see Exhibit 10-5). The half-year convention is built into the depreciation tables provided by the IRS, which simplifies the depreciation calculation for the year the asset is placed into service.

Mid-quarter convention.   Businesses must use the mid-quarter convention when *more than 40 percent* of their total *tangible personal property* that they place in service during the year is placed in service during the *fourth* quarter. Under the mid-quarter convention, businesses treat assets *as though* they were placed in service during the middle of the *quarter* in which the business actually placed the assets into service. For example, when the mid-quarter convention applies, if a business places an asset in service on December 1 (in the fourth quarter) it must treat the asset as though it was placed in service on November 15, which is the middle of the fourth quarter. Consequently, the business deducts only one-half of a quarter's worth of depreciation in the year the asset is placed in service (depreciation for the second half of November and the entire month of December). In addition, if the mid-quarter convention applies, businesses must use the convention for all tangible personal property placed in service during the year. The mid-quarter test is applied after the §179 expense but before bonus depreciation (discussed later in the chapter), meaning that any property expensed under §179 is not included in the mid-quarter test. The IRS depreciation tables have built in the mid-quarter convention to simplify the calculations.

For assets placed in service under the TCJA regime (effective for assets acquired after September 27, 2017), the mid-quarter convention will be largely irrelevant as businesses can use either §179 or 100 percent bonus depreciation to recover the cost in full in the year of acquisition. However, for assets placed in service before TCJA and assets that fail to qualify for §179 and bonus depreciation, the mid-quarter convention may apply.

Calculating Depreciation for Personal Property   Once a business has identified the applicable method, recovery period, and convention for personal property, tax depreciation is relatively easy to calculate because the Internal Revenue Service provides depreciation percentage tables in Rev. Proc. 87-57. The percentages in the depreciation tables for tangible personal property incorporate the method and convention. Accordingly, there are separate tables for each combination of depreciation method (200 percent declining balance, 150 percent declining balance, and straight-line) and convention (half-year and mid-quarter; each quarter has its own table). To determine the depreciation for an asset for the year, use the following steps:

Step 1: Determine the appropriate convention (half-year or mid-quarter) by determining whether more than 40 percent of qualified property was placed in service in the last quarter of the tax year.

Step 2: Locate the applicable table provided in Rev. Proc. 87-57 also reproduced in Appendix A of this chapter.

Step 3: Select the column that corresponds with the asset's recovery period.

Step 4: Find the row identifying the year of the asset's recovery period.

The tables are constructed so that the intersection of the row and column provides the percentage of the asset's *initial basis* that is deductible as depreciation expense for the particular year. Thus, depreciation expense for a particular asset is the product of the percentage from the table and the asset's *initial basis*.

Applying the Half-Year Convention   Consider Table 1 in Appendix A at the end of the chapter that shows the depreciation percentages for MACRS 200 percent declining balance using the half-year convention. If a seven-year asset is placed into service during the current year, the depreciation percentage is 14.29 percent (the intersection of row 1 [year 1] and the seven-year property column).

Notice from Table 1 that the depreciation percentages for five-year property extend for six years and the percentages for seven-year property extend for eight years. Why does it take six years to fully depreciate an asset with a five-year recovery period and eight years for a seven-year asset? Because the business does not deduct a full year's depreciation in the first year, an entire year of depreciation is effectively split between the first and last year. For example, when the half-year convention applies to a five-year asset, the taxpayer deducts one-half of a year's depreciation in year 1 and one-half of a year's depreciation in year 6.

Example 10-4

Teton is using the 200 percent declining balance method and half-year convention to compute depreciation expense on its 2017 personal property additions. What is Teton's 2017 depreciation expense for these assets?

Answer: $95,027, computed as follows:

Asset	Date Placed in Service	(1) Original Basis	(2) Rate	(1) × (2) Depreciation
Office furniture	February 3	$ 20,000	14.29%	$ 2,858
Machinery	July 22	610,000	14.29	87,169
Used delivery truck	August 17	25,000	20.00	5,000
Total				**$95,027**

Because the office furniture and machinery have a seven-year recovery period and it is the first year for depreciation, the depreciation rate is 14.29 percent (see Table 1). The depreciation rate for the used delivery truck (five-year property) is 20 percent and is determined in a similar manner.

Calculating depreciation for assets in years after the year of acquisition is also relatively simple. Again, using Table 1 to compute depreciation for the second year, the taxpayer would multiply the asset's initial basis by the percentage in the *year 2* row; in the following year, the taxpayer would use the percentage in the *year 3* row; and so on.

Example 10-5

What if: Assume that Teton holds the tangible personal property it acquired and placed in service in 2017 until the assets are fully depreciated. Using the IRS provided tables (see Table 1), how would Teton determine its depreciation expense for 2017 through 2024?

Answer: See the following table:

(continued on page 10-12)

		Depreciation Over Asset Recovery Period			
Recovery Period	**Year**	**7-Year Office Furniture**	**7-Year Machinery**	**5-Year Delivery Truck**	**Yearly Total**
1	2017	$ 2,858	$ 87,169	$ 5,000	$ 95,027
2	2018	4,898	149,389	8,000	162,287
3	2019	3,498	106,689	4,800	114,987
4	2020	2,498	76,189	2,880	81,567
5	2021	1,786	54,473	2,880	59,139
6	2022	1,784	54,412	1,440	57,636
7	2023	1,786	54,473	N/A	56,259
8	2024	892	27,206	N/A	28,098
Accumulated Depreciation		$20,000	$610,000	$25,000	$655,000

Half-year convention for year of disposition. Businesses often sell or dispose of assets before they fully depreciate them. Recall that the half-year convention applies in both the year of acquisition and the year of disposition. Note, however, that the tables can't anticipate when a business may dispose of an asset. Accordingly, the tables only provide depreciation percentages for assets assuming the asset won't be disposed of before it is fully depreciated. That is, for each year in the asset's recovery period, the tables provide a percentage for an entire year's worth of depreciation. So, to calculate the depreciation for the year of disposition, the business first calculates depreciation for the *entire year* as if the property had not been disposed of. Then the business applies the half-year convention by multiplying the full year's depreciation by 50 percent (one-half of a year's depreciation).[25] Note, however, that if a business acquires and disposes of an asset in the same tax year, it is not allowed to claim any depreciation on the asset.

Example 10-6

What if: Assume that Teton sells all of its office furniture in 2018 (the year after it buys it). What is Teton's depreciation for the office furniture in the year of disposition (2018)?

Answer: $2,449, calculated using the MACRS Half-Year Convention Table (Table 1) as follows:

Asset	Amount	Explanation
(1) Office furniture	$20,000	Original basis
(2) Depreciation percentage	24.49%	Seven-year property, year 2
(3) Full year of depreciation	$ 4,898	(1) × (2)
(4) Half-year convention percentage	50%	Depreciation limit in year of disposal
Depreciation in year of disposal	**$ 2,449**	(3) × (4)

What if: Assume that Teton sold all of its office furniture in year 1 (the year it bought it and placed it in service). How much depreciation expense can Teton deduct for the office furniture in year 1?

Answer: $0. A business is not allowed to claim any depreciation expense for assets it acquires and disposes of in the same tax year.

[25]Suppose Teton sells the 5-year delivery truck in year 6 on January 5. What depreciation percentage should Teton use for purposes of determining year 6 depreciation? Teton should take one-half year's depreciation on the truck. The percentage shown in Table 1 for the year of an asset's recovery period (in this case, year 6) already reflects the half-year convention, so Teton would take $1,440 of depreciation regardless of when during year 6 the truck was sold.

Applying the Mid-Quarter Convention   When the mid-quarter convention applies, the process for computing depreciation is the same as it is when the half-year convention applies, except that businesses use a different set of depreciation tables (a separate table for each quarter). After categorizing the assets by recovery period and grouping them into quarters, businesses consult the Mid-Quarter Convention Tables (Tables 2a–d in Appendix A to this chapter) to determine the depreciation rate for each asset group.

The depreciation deduction for an asset is the product of the asset's original basis and the percentage from the table.

Example 10-7

What if: For this example, assume the machinery Teton placed in service in Exhibit 10-5 was placed in service on November 1, 2017 rather than July 22 (see table below). What is Teton's 2017 depreciation for its personal property additions?

Answer: $30,527, computed as follows:

Asset	Purchase Date	Quarter	Original Basis	Rate	Depreciation
Office furniture (7-year)	February 3	1st	$ 20,000	25.00%	$ 5,000
Delivery truck (5-year)	August 17	3rd	25,000	15.00%	3,750
Machinery (7-year)	November 1	4th	610,000	3.57%	21,777
					$30,527

The mid-quarter convention applies because more than 40 percent of the assets were placed in service during the last quarter of the year ($610,000/$655,000 = 93%). The office furniture rate of 25 percent is located in Table 2a. See the columns for property placed into service during the first quarter (first two columns); select the seven-year recovery period column (last column), and the year 1 row. The process for determining the rate for the delivery truck and machinery follows the same method using Tables 2c and 2d, respectively.

THE KEY FACTS

Mid Quarter Convention

- The mid-quarter convention is required when more than 40 percent of personal property is placed in service during the fourth quarter of the tax year.

- Each quarter has its own depreciation table. Once the mid-quarter convention applies, the taxpayer must continue to use it over the assets' entire recovery period.

- If an asset is disposed of before it is fully depreciated, use the formula given to determine the allowable depreciation in the year of disposition.

The process for calculating depreciation for assets in years after acquisition is the same as the process we described for the half-year convention except the taxpayer uses the MACRS Mid-Quarter Convention Tables (Table 2 in Appendix A) for the appropriate quarter rather than the MACRS Half-Year Convention Table (Table 1).

Mid-quarter convention for year of disposition.   Calculating depreciation expense in the year of sale or disposition is a bit more involved when the mid-quarter convention applies than when it does not. When the mid-quarter convention applies, the asset is treated as though it is sold in the middle of the quarter of which it was actually sold. The process for calculating mid-quarter convention depreciation for the year of sale is exactly the same as the process for using the half-year convention, except that instead of multiplying the full year's depreciation by 50 percent, the business multiplies the amount of depreciation it would have been able to claim on the asset if it had not sold the asset (a full year's depreciation) by the applicable percentage in Exhibit 10-6.

EXHIBIT 10-6   **Mid-Quarter Convention Percentage of Full Year's Depreciation in Year of Disposition**

Quarter of Disposition	Percentage	Calculation*
1st	12.5%	1.5/12
2nd	37.5	4.5/12
3rd	62.5	7.5/12
4th	87.5	10.5/12

*The calculation is the number of months the taxpayer held or is deemed to have held the asset in the year of disposition divided by 12 months in the year.

Example 10-8

What if: Assume that Teton depreciates its personal property under the mid-quarter convention (Example 10-7), and that it sells its office furniture in the third quarter of 2018. The office furniture ($20,000 original basis) was placed into service during the first quarter of 2017 and has a seven-year recovery period. What is Teton's 2018 depreciation for the office furniture?

Answer: $30,527, computed as follows:

Description	Amount	Explanation
(1) Original basis	$20,000	Example 10-7
(2) 2018 depreciation percentage	21.43%	Table 2a, mid-quarter, first quarter table, 7-year property, year 2
(3) Full year depreciation	$4,286	(1) × (2)
(4) Percentage of full year's depreciation in year of disposition if mid-quarter convention applies	62.5%	From Exhibit 10-6; asset disposed of in third quarter
Depreciation in year of disposition	**$2,679**	(3) × (4)

THE KEY FACTS

Real Property Depreciation

- Real property is depreciated using the straight-line method.
- Real property uses the mid-month convention.
- Residential property has a recovery period of 27.5 years.
- Nonresidential property placed in service on or after May 13, 1993, has a life of 39 years.
- Nonresidential property placed in service after December 31, 1986, and before May 13, 1993, has a recovery period of 31.5 years.

Real Property

The TCJA made no changes to the depreciation of real property except to reclassify certain improvements to be eligible for §179.[26] Therefore, for real property placed in service after TCJA, businesses will calculate their depreciation on real property as described below.

For depreciation purposes, real property is classified as land, *residential rental* property, or *nonresidential property*. Land is nondepreciable. Residential rental property consists of dwelling units such as houses, condominiums, and apartment complexes. Residential rental property has a 27.5-year recovery period. Nonresidential property consists of all other buildings (office buildings, manufacturing facilities, shopping malls, and the like). Nonresidential property placed in service on or after May 13, 1993, has a 39-year recovery period, and nonresidential property placed in service after December 31, 1986, and before May 13, 1993, has a 31.5-year recovery period. Exhibit 10-7 summarizes the recovery periods for real property.

If a building is substantially improved (i.e., expanded) at some point after the initial purchase, the building addition is treated as a new asset with the same recovery period of the original building. For example, if Teton expanded its warehouse 10 years after the building was placed in service, the expansion or building addition would be depreciated as a *new, separate* asset over 39 years because it is nonresidential property.

An important area of tax practice related to real property is cost segregation. This practice attempts to partition or divide the costs of a building into two or more categories. The first category is the building itself, which has a recovery period as noted in Exhibit 10-7. The second category is building components (tangible personal property

EXHIBIT 10-7   Recovery Period for Real Property

Asset Description (Summary from Rev. Proc. 87-57)	Recovery Period
Residential	27.5 years
Nonresidential property placed in service on or after May 13, 1993	39 years
Nonresidential property placed in service before May 13, 1993	31.5 years

[26]Section 179(f)(2) now classifies the following improvements to nonresidential real property as eligible for immediate expensing: roofs; heating, ventilation and air-conditioning systems; fire protection and alarm systems; and security systems. In addition, §179(f)(1) allows qualified improvements (any improvement to an interior portion of a nonresidential building placed in service after the date the building was placed in service) to be eligible for §179. Qualified improvements do not include expansions, additions of elevators/escalators, or improvements to the internal structural framework of the building; therefore, these items are not eligible to be immediately deducted under §179 [§168(e)(6)(B)].

associated with the building such as electrical and plumbing fixtures that have a shorter recovery period and accelerated depreciation method). Cost segregation utilizes engineers and construction experts who divide the costs between real and tangible personal property. This can generate significant tax savings due to the difference in the present value of the tax savings from the accelerated depreciation deductions associated with personal property relative to real property.

Applicable Method   All depreciable real property is depreciated for tax purposes using the straight-line method. This is generally consistent with depreciation methods used for financial accounting purposes.

Applicable Convention   All real property is depreciated using the mid-month convention. The **mid-month convention** allows the owner of real property to expense one-half of a month's depreciation for the month in which the property was placed in service (and in the month of the year it is sold as well). This is true regardless of whether the asset was placed in service at the beginning or at the end of the month. For example, if Teton placed its warehouse into service on May 1 (or on *any* other day in May), it would deduct *one-half* of a month's depreciation for May and then full depreciation for the months June through December.

Depreciation Tables   Just as it does for personal property, the IRS provides depreciation tables for real property. The depreciation tables for 27.5 years, 31.5 years, and 39 years real property are reproduced as Tables 3, 4, and 5, respectively, in Appendix A. The percentage of the asset's original basis that is depreciated in a particular year is located at the intersection of the month the asset was placed in service (column) and the year of depreciation (row).

Example 10-9

As indicated in Example 10-1, Teton's initial basis in the warehouse it purchased on May 1, 2017, is $275,000. What is Teton's 2017 and 2018 depreciation on its warehouse?

Answer: $4,414 in 2017 and $7,051 in 2018, calculated as follows:

Warehouse	Method	Recovery Period	Date Placed in Service	(1) Basis	(2) Rate	(1) × (2) Depreciation
2017	SL	39	5/1/2017	$275,000	1.605%	$4,414
2018	SL	39	5/1/2017	275,000	2.564%	7,051

What if: What would be Teton's 2017 and 2018 depreciation expense if, instead of a warehouse, the building was an apartment building that it rented to Teton's employees?

Answer: $6,251 in 2017 and $9,999 in 2018, calculated as follows:

Apartment Bldg	Method	Recovery Period	Date Placed in Service	(1) Basis	(2) Rate	(1) × (2) Depreciation
2017	SL	27.5	5/1/2017	$275,000	2.273%	$6,251
2018	SL	27.5	5/1/2017	275,000	3.636%	9,999

*The 1.605 percent for the year is found in the 39-year table (Table 5, in Appendix A) in the fifth column (fifth month) and first row (first year).

†The 2.273 percent for the year is found in the 27.5-year table (Table 3, in Appendix A) in the fifth column (fifth month) and first row (first year).

When using depreciation tables for real property, it is important to stay in the month column corresponding with the month the property was originally placed in service.[27] Thus, to calculate depreciation for real property placed in service in May (the fifth month), businesses will *always* (for each year of depreciation) find the current-year rate factor in the fifth column for that asset. This is true even if the asset is sold in a subsequent year in July (it's easy to make the mistake of using the seventh column to calculate the depreciation for the year of disposition in this situation).

[27]Failure to do so will result in the wrong depreciation expense and is technically a change in accounting method (which requires filing of Form 3115 with the IRS).

Mid-month convention for year of disposition. Businesses deduct one-half of a month's depreciation in the month they sell or otherwise dispose of real property. For example, if Teton sold its warehouse on March 5 of year 2, it would deduct two and one-half months of depreciation in that year for the warehouse (depreciation for January, February, and one-half of March). Calculating depreciation expense in the year of sale or disposition for mid-month convention assets is similar to the calculation under the mid-quarter convention. When the mid-month convention applies, the asset is treated as though it is sold in the *middle of the month* of which it was actually sold. The simplest process for calculating mid-month convention depreciation for the year of sale consists of the following four steps:

Step 1: Determine the amount of depreciation deduction for the asset as if the asset was held for the entire year.

Step 2: Subtract one-half of a month from the month in which the asset was sold (if sold in third month, subtract .5 from 3 to get 2.5). (Subtract half of a month because the business is treated as though the asset was disposed of in the middle of the third month—not the end.)

Step 3: Divide the amount determined in Step 2 by 12 months (2.5/12). This is the fraction of the full year's depreciation the business is eligible to deduct.

Step 4: Multiply the Step 3 outcome by the full depreciation determined in Step 1.

These steps are summarized in the following formula:

Mid-month depreciation for year of disposition

$$= \text{Full year's depreciation} \times \frac{(\text{Month in which asset was disposed of} - .5)}{12}$$

Example 10-10

What if: Assume that Teton sells its warehouse on March 5, 2018 (the year after Teton buys it). What is Teton's depreciation for the warehouse in the year of disposition?

Answer: $1,469, computed using the four-step procedure outlined above as follows.

Step 1: Determine full year's depreciation: $275,000 × 2.564%* = $7,051

Step 2: 3 (month sold) − .5 = 2.5

Step 3: 2.5/12

Step 4: $7,051 × 2.5/12 = $1,469 (see formula above)

*The 2.564 percent (full-year percentage) in Step 1 is obtained from the MACRS Mid-Month Table for 39-year property (Table 5) placed in service during the fifth month (year 2 row).

Storyline Summary

Taxpayer:	Teton Mountaineering Technology, LLC (Teton)—a calendar-year single-member LLC (treated as a sole proprietorship for tax purposes)
Location:	Cody, Wyoming
President/Founder	Steve Dallimore

continued from page 10-2 . . .

During 2017, Teton had huge success, generating a large profit. To continue to grow the business and increase Teton's production capacity, Steve acquired more assets in 2018. He has heard about ways to "write off" the costs of business assets and wants to learn more.

to be continued . . .

SPECIAL RULES RELATING TO COST RECOVERY   `LO 10-3`

In addition to the basic MACRS rules, several additional provisions affect the depreciation of personal property. Congress often uses these special rules for economic stimulus or to curb perceived taxpayer abuses. The TCJA substantially modifies and extends these special rules (§179, bonus depreciation, and listed property). For many businesses, the calculation of MACRS depreciation for its personal property will become a thing of the past because of the expansion of these special rules. It is worth noting, however, that Congress did not make all of the changes permanent. For example, the changes to bonus depreciation are effective for property placed in service before January 1, 2023 with a subsequent four-year phase-out. We discuss these rules below.

Immediate Expensing (§179)   Policy makers created §179 as an incentive to help small businesses purchasing new or used tangible personal property. This incentive is commonly referred to as the **§179 expense** or *immediate expensing* election.[28] This provision will have limited application under TCJA because bonus depreciation discussed below allows taxpayers to immediately deduct assets' initial basis. As discussed earlier in the chapter, businesses must generally depreciate assets over the assets' recovery periods. However, under §179, businesses may elect to immediately expense up to $1,000,000 of tangible personal property placed in service during 2018.[29,30] Businesses can also use immediate expensing for off-the-shelf computer software and qualified real property.[31] They may also elect to deduct less than the maximum. When businesses elect to deduct a certain amount of §179 expense, they immediately expense all or a portion of an asset's basis or several assets' bases. To reflect this immediate depreciation, they must reduce the basis of the asset or assets (to which they applied the §179 amount) *before* they compute MACRS depreciation (from the tables).

Exhibit 10-8 shows the assets Teton acquires in 2018.

EXHIBIT 10-8   Teton's 2018 Asset Acquisitions

Asset	Cost	Date Placed in Service
Computers & information systems	$ 920,000	March 3
Delivery truck*	80,000	May 26
Machinery	1,200,000	August 15
Total	$2,200,000	

*Steve had used this truck personally and converted it to business use in May.

Example 10-11

What if: Assume Teton is eligible for and elects to immediately deduct $800,000 of §179 expense against the basis of the machinery acquired in 2018 (see Exhibit 10-8). (Note that Teton could have elected to deduct up to $1,000,000.) What is the amount of Teton's current-year depreciation deduction, including regular MACRS depreciation and the §179 expense on its machinery (assuming the half-year convention applies)?

(continued on page 10-18)

---

[28]Intangibles and tangible personal property that are used less than 50 percent for business and most real property are not eligible for immediate expensing.

[29]The maximum allowable expense under §179 is indexed for inflation beginning with years after 2018.

[30]These maximum amounts are per tax return. Thus, if an individual has multiple businesses with asset acquisitions, the taxpayer may only deduct up to these maximum amounts for the combined businesses.

[31]Qualified real property means improvements to nonresidential real property placed in service after the date the building was placed in service including roofs; heating, ventilation, and air-conditioning; fire protection and alarm systems; and security systems.

Answer: $857,160, computed as follows:

Description	Amount	Explanation
(1) Machinery	$1,200,000	Exhibit 10-8
(2) §179 expense	800,000	
(3) Remaining basis in machinery	$ 400,000	(1) − (2)
(4) MACRS depreciation rate for 7-year machinery	14.29%	Rate from Table 1
(5) MACRS depreciation expense on machinery	$ 57,160	(3) × (4)
Total depreciation on machinery	**$ 857,160**	(2) + (5)

What if: Assume that Teton was eligible for and elected to claim the maximum amount of §179 expense. What would be its total current-year depreciation deduction, including MACRS depreciation and §179 expense (assuming the half-year convention applies)?

Answer: $1,028,580, computed as follows:

Description	Amount	Explanation
(1) Machinery	$ 1,200,000	Exhibit 10-8
(2) §179 expense	1,000,000	Maximum expense in 2018
(3) Remaining basis in machinery	$ 200,000	(1) − (2)
(4) MACRS depreciation rate for 7-year machinery	14.29%	Rate from Table 1
(5) MACRS depreciation expense on machinery	$ 28,580	(3) × (4)
Total depreciation on machinery	**$1,028,580**	(2) + (5)

Limits on immediate expensing. The maximum amount of §179 expense a business may elect to claim for the year is subject to a phase-out limitation. Under the phase-out limitation, businesses must reduce the $1,000,000 maximum available expense dollar for dollar for the amount of *tangible personal property* purchased and placed in service during 2018 over a $2,500,000 threshold.[32] Thus if a business places $3,500,000 ($2,500,000 threshold plus $1,000,000) or more of tangible personal property into service during 2018, its maximum available §179 expense for the year is $0. The phased-out portion of the maximum expense disappears and does *not* carry over to another year.

Example 10-12

What if: Let's assume that during 2018, Teton placed into service $2,400,000 of machinery (up from the Exhibit 10-8 amount of $1,200,000), $920,000 of computers, and an $80,000 delivery truck for a total of $3,400,000 tangible *personal* property placed in service for the year. What is Teton's maximum §179 expense after applying the phase-out limitation?

Answer: $100,000, computed as follows:

Description	Amount	Explanation
(1) Property placed in service in 2018	$3,400,000	Exhibit 10-8
(2) Threshold for §179 phase-out	2,500,000	2018 amount [§179(b)(2)]
(3) Phase-out of maximum §179 expense	900,000	(1) − (2)
(4) Maximum §179 expense before phase-out	1,000,000	§179(b)(1)
(5) Phase-out of maximum §179 expense	900,000	From (3)
Maximum §179 expense after phase-out*	**$ 100,000**	(4) − (5)

*Note that this is the maximum expense after phase-out but *before* the taxable income limitation we discuss next.

---

[32]The threshold under §179 is indexed for inflation beginning with years after 2018.

What if: Assume further that on November 13, Teton acquired and placed in service a storage building costing $400,000. Taking the building into account, what is Teton's maximum §179 amount after the phase-out?

Answer: $100,000, the same answer as above. The phase-out is based on the amount of tangible personal property placed in service during the year. Because the warehouse is *real property* (not qualified), its acquisition has no effect on Teton's maximum §179 expense.

Businesses may elect to claim the §179 expense for the year up to the maximum amount available (after computing the phase-out—see the previous example). When a business elects to claim a certain amount of §179 expense, it must reduce the basis of the asset(s) to which the expense is applied. It then computes regular depreciation on the remaining basis after reducing the basis of the asset(s) for the §179 expense.

A business's *deductible* §179 expense is limited to the taxpayer's business income after deducting all expenses (including regular and bonus depreciation) except the §179 expense. Consequently, the §179 expense cannot create or extend a business's net operating loss. Taxpayers' business income includes income from all businesses. For example, a sole-proprietor's business income for purposes of §179 would include the income not only from all Schedules C but also from regular wages. If a business claims more §179 expense than it is allowed to deduct due to the taxable income limitation, it carries the excess forward (indefinitely) and deducts it in a subsequent year, subject to the taxable income limitation (but not the phase-out limitation) in the subsequent year.[33]

Example 10-13

What if: Let's assume the facts of the previous example, where Teton's maximum §179 expense after applying the phase-out limitation is $100,000. Also assume that Teton elects to claim the entire $100,000 expense and it chooses to apply it against the machinery. Further assume that Teton reports $400,000 of taxable income before deducting any §179 expense and depreciation. What amount of total depreciation (including §179 expense) is Teton able to deduct on the machinery for the year?

Answer: $400,000, computed as follows:

Description	Amount	Explanation
(1) Machinery	$2,400,000	Example 10-11
(2) Elected §179 expense	100,000	
(3) Remaining basis	$2,300,000	(1) − (2)
(4) MACRS depreciation rate for 7-year machinery, year 1	14.29%	See Table 1
(5) MACRS depreciation expense on machinery	$ 328,670	(3) × (4)
(6) Deductible §179 expense	71,330	Taxable income limitation ($400,000 − $328,670)
(7) Total depreciation expense on machinery for the year	**$ 400,000**	(5) + (6)
(8) Excess §179 expense	$ 28,670	(2) − (6)

THE KEY FACTS

§179 Expenses

- $1,000,000 of tangible personal property can be immediately expensed in 2018.
- Businesses are eligible for the full amount of this expense when tangible personal property placed in service is less than $2,500,000. Beginning at $2,500,000, the §179 expense is phased out, dollar-for-dollar. When assets placed in service reach $3,500,000, no §179 expense can be taken.
- §179 expenses are also limited to a business's taxable income before the §179 expense. §179 expenses cannot create losses.

[33]Businesses typically elect only to expense the currently deductible amount since the taxable income limitation may also limit their §179 expense in future years just as it does for the current year. Electing the amount deductible after the taxable income limitation also maximizes the current year depreciation deduction.

What is the amount of Teton's excess §179 expense (elected expense in excess of the deductible amount due to the taxable income limitation), and what does Teton do with it for tax purposes?

Answer: $28,670. See the above table for the computation (line 8). Teton carries this $28,670 excess §179 expense forward to future years and may deduct it subject to the taxable income limitation. Note that the depreciable basis of the machinery remaining after the §179 expense is $2,300,000 because the depreciable basis is reduced by the full $100,000 of §179 expense elected even though the deductible §179 expense was limited to $71,330 in the current year.

Choosing the assets to immediately expense. Businesses qualifying for immediate expensing are allowed to choose the asset or assets (from tangible personal property placed in service during the year) they immediately expense under §179. If a business's objective is to maximize its current depreciation deduction, it should immediately expense the asset

Example 10-14

What if: Let's assume that on June 1, Teton placed into service five-year property costing $1,400,000 and seven-year property costing $1,400,000 and had no other fixed asset additions during the year. Further assume that Teton is not subject to the taxable income limitation for the §179 expense. What is Teton's depreciation deduction (including §179 expense) if it elects to apply the full §179 expense against the five-year property (Scenario A)? What is its depreciation deduction if it applies the full §179 expense against its seven-year property (Scenario B)?

Answer: $1,280,060 if it applies the full §179 expense to the five-year property (Scenario A) and $1,337,160 if it applies it to the seven-year property (Scenario B). See the computations below:

Description	(Scenario A) §179 Expense on 5-Year Property	(Scenario B) §179 Expense on 7-Year Property	Explanation
(1) Original basis	$1,400,000	$1,400,000	
(2) Elected §179 expense	1,000,000	1,000,000	Maximum expense
(3) Remaining basis	400,000	400,000	(1) − (2)
(4) MACRS depreciation rate	20%	14.29%	See Table 1
(5) MACRS depreciation expense	$ 80,000	$ 57,160	(3) × (4)
(6) Deductible §179 expense	1,000,000	1,000,000	Maximum §179 expense allowed this year.
(7) MACRS depreciation on other property	200,060	280,000	This is the depreciation on the $1,400,000 7-year property in the 5-year column ($1,400,000 × 14.29% = $200,060 and on the $1,400,000 5-year property in the 7-year column ($1,400,000 × 20% = $280,000).
Total depreciation expense	**$1,280,060**	**$1,337,160**	(5) + (6) + (7)

Note that Teton deducts $57,100 more in depreciation expense if it applies the §179 expense to the seven-year property.

with the lowest first-year cost recovery percentage including bonus depreciation (discussed in the next section).[34, 35]

Bonus Depreciation   Since 2001, businesses have had the ability to immediately deduct a percentage of the acquisition cost of qualifying assets under rules known as **bonus depreciation.**[36] The percentage allowable for each tax year during this period has changed many times ranging from 30 percent to 100 percent. Just prior to the TCJA, the bonus percentage was 50 percent. However, the TCJA increased the percentage to 100 percent for qualified property acquired after September 27, 2017. This provision (and the enhancement of §179) simplifies the depreciation calculation for many businesses because they can deduct the full amount of certain assets placed in service during the year.[37] There are several nuances of this provision that businesses need to consider. We discuss them in this section.

Bonus depreciation is mandatory for all taxpayers that qualify. However, taxpayers may elect out of bonus depreciation (on a property class basis) by attaching a statement to their tax return indicating they are electing not to claim bonus depreciation.[38] That is, taxpayers can elect out of bonus depreciation for all of their 5-year class property but still claim bonus for all of their 7-year property acquisitions. The election to opt out of bonus depreciation is made annually. Businesses in a loss position may want to elect out of bonus depreciation to reduce these losses, which may be limited under the NOL rules. In addition, businesses may want to elect out of bonus and use §179 instead because §179 allows taxpayers to pick and choose carefully which assets to expense whereas bonus is all-or-nothing based on property class. For taxpayers claiming the deduction, bonus depreciation is calculated after the §179 expense but before regular MACRS depreciation.[39] Bonus depreciation is a temporary provision and the percentage phases down after five years.[40] The bonus depreciation percentages by year are provided in Exhibit 10-9.

EXHIBIT 10-9   **Bonus Depreciation Percentages**[41]

Placed in Service	Bonus Depreciation Percentage
September 28, 2017 – December 31, 2022	100 percent
2023	80 porcent
2024	60 percent
2025	40 percent
2026	20 percent
2027 and after	None

[34]Treasury Regulation §1.168(d)-1(b)(4)(i).

[35]Looking at Tables 2a and 2c in Appendix A, if a business has to choose between immediately expensing seven-year property placed in service in the first quarter or five-year property placed in service in the third quarter, which asset should it elect to expense under §179 if it wants to maximize its current-year depreciation expense? The answer is the five-year asset because its first-year depreciation percentage is 15 percent, while the seven-year asset's first-year depreciation percentage is 25 percent. Finally, note that businesses reduce the basis of the assets for the §179 expense before computing whether the mid-quarter convention applies.

[36]§168(k)(1).

[37]Many states do not allow bonus depreciation, so businesses will be required to calculate their depreciation using basic MACRS for those state tax returns.

[38]§168(k)(7). Property classes are broader categories of the asset classes discussed in Rev. Proc. 87-56. There are nine property classes of assets: 3-year, 5-year, 7-year, 10-year, 15-year, 20-year, 25-year, residential rental property, and nonresidential real property.

[39]Reg. §1.168(k)-1(a)(2)(iii) and Reg. §1.168(k)-1(d)(3) Example (2).

[40]§168(k)(6).

[41]A transition rule allows taxpayers to use a 50 percent bonus percentage for their first taxable year ending after September 27, 2017 [§168(k)(10)(A)].

Qualified property.   Taxpayers must first determine whether the assets acquired during the year are eligible for bonus depreciation. To qualify, property must meet the following requirements:[42]

(1) New or used property (as long as the property had not previously been used by the taxpayer),[43]

(2) Have a regular depreciation life of 20 years or less,

(3) Computer software,[44]

(4) Water utility property, or

(5) Qualified film, television, and live theatrical productions.[45]

Example 10-15

What if: Assume that Teton claims bonus depreciation for the eligible personal property acquired in Exhibit 10-8.

Asset	Date acquired	Cost Basis	Recovery Period
Computers & information systems	3/3/2018	$ 920,000	5
Delivery truck*	5/26/2018	80,000	5
Machinery	8/15/2018	1,200,000	7
Total		$2,200,000	

*Steve had used this truck personally and converted it to business use in May.

Assuming Teton elects no §179 expense, what is Teton's bonus depreciation?

Answer: $2,120,000, computed as follows:

Description	Amount	Explanation
(1) Qualified property	$ 2,120,000	All but the delivery truck
(2) Bonus depreciation rate	100%	§168(k)(1)(A) and §168(k)(6)(i)
Bonus depreciation	**$2,120,000**	(1) × (2)

Note that the delivery truck is not eligible for bonus depreciation. Although used property usually qualifies, the truck is ineligible because Steve used the truck before converting it to business property. The delivery truck's cost will be recovered using basic MACRS rules.

---

[42]Under prior law, qualified improvements were considered eligible for bonus depreciation, and Congress likely intended for this property to be eligible. However, due to a technical error in the TCJA, qualified improvement property is currently considered 39-year property and is not eligible for bonus depreciation (although it is eligible for §179).

[43]§168(k)(2)((E)(ii). Taxpayers may not use bonus depreciation for assets received as a gift or inheritance, for like-kind property (unless the taxpayer pays money in addition to the exchanged property), for property received in nontaxable exchanges (reorganizations), or for property acquired from a related entity.

[44]For this purpose, computer software means any program designed to cause a computer to perform a desired function. This software has a basic MACRS cost recovery period of five years.

[45]Qualified film, television, and live theatrical productions are defined in §181.

What if: Assuming Teton elects the maximum §179 expense, what is Teton's bonus depreciation?

Answer: $1,200,000, computed as follows:

Description	Amount	Explanation
(1) §179 qualified property	$ 2,200,000	
(2) §179 expense	1,000,000	Maximum expense
(3) Remaining basis	$ 1,200,000	(1) – (2)
(4) Remaining amount eligible for bonus depreciation	1,200,000	Remaining amount relates to the computers and the machinery. Because the truck is not eligible for bonus depreciation, we apply the §179 expense first to the truck to maximize the current-year depreciation deduction. We next apply the §179 expense to the machinery (7-year), which reduces its basis to $280,000.
(5) Bonus depreciation rate	100%	§168(k)(1)(A) and §168(k)(6)(A)(i)
(6) Bonus depreciation	**$1,200,000**	(4) × (5)

What if: Assuming Teton elects the maximum §179 and bonus depreciation, what is Teton's total depreciation on its personal property?

Answer: $2,200,000. Teton is able to fully depreciate its tangible personal property placed in service in 2018 due to a combination of §179 ($1,000,000) and bonus depreciation ($1,200,000). Teton does not need to calculate regular MACRS depreciation on any of its tangible personal property. Alternatively, Teton could elect to take §179 on the delivery truck only and use bonus depreciation on the remaining assets. This option would produce $80,000 of §179 expense and $2,120,000 of bonus depreciation, for a total of $2,200,000.

Listed Property   Most business-owned assets are used for business rather than personal purposes. For example, Weyerhaeuser employees probably have little or no personal interest in using Weyerhaeuser's timber-harvesting equipment during their free time. In contrast, business owners and employees may find some business assets, such as company automobiles or laptop computers, conducive to personal use.

Business assets that tend to be used for both business and personal purposes are referred to as **listed property.** For example, automobiles, other means of transportation (planes, boats, and recreation vehicles), and even digital cameras are considered to be listed property. The tax law limits the allowable depreciation on listed property to the portion of the asset used for business purposes.

How do taxpayers compute depreciation for listed property? First, they must determine the percentage of business versus personal use of the asset for the year. If the business-use percentage for the year exceeds 50 percent, the deductible depreciation is limited to the full annual depreciation multiplied by the business-use percentage for the year. Listed property used in trade or business more than 50 percent of the time is eligible for the §179 expensing election and bonus depreciation (limited to the business-use percentage).

THE KEY FACTS

Listed Property

- When an asset is used for both personal and business use, calculate the business-use percentage.
- If the business-use percentage is above 50 percent, the allowable depreciation is limited to the business-use percentage.
- If a listed property's business-use percentage ever falls to or below 50 percent, depreciation for all previous years is retroactively restated using MACRS straight-line method.

Example 10-16

What if: Assume that, in addition to the assets Teton purchased in 2018 presented in Exhibit 10-8, it also purchased a new digital camera for $2,000 that its employees use for business on weekdays. On weekends, Steve uses the camera for his photography hobby. Since the camera is listed property, Teton must assess the business-use percentage to properly calculate its deductible depreciation for the camera. Assuming that Teton determines the business-use percentage to be 75 percent, what is Teton's depreciation deduction on the camera for the year (ignoring bonus depreciation and §179 expensing)?

Answer: $300, computed as follows:

Description	Amount	Explanation
(1) Original basis of camera	$2,000	
(2) MACRS depreciation rate	20%	5-year property, year 1, half-year convention
(3) Full MACRS depreciation expense	$ 400	(1) × (2)
(4) Business-use percentage	75%	
Depreciation deduction for year	**$ 300**	(3) × (4)

When the business-use percentage of an asset is 50 percent or less, the business must compute depreciation for the asset using the MACRS *straight-line* method over the MACRS ADS (alternative depreciation system) recovery period.[46] For five-year assets such as automobiles, the assets on which the personal-use limitation is most common, the MACRS ADS recovery period is also five years. However, for seven-year assets, the ADS recovery period is generally 10 years.[47]

If a business initially uses an asset more than 50 percent of the time for business (and appropriately adopts the 200 percent declining balance method, §179, or bonus depreciation) but subsequently its business use drops to 50 percent or below, the depreciation expense for all prior years must be recomputed as if the business had been using the straight-line depreciation over the ADS recovery period the entire time. The firm must then recapture any excess accelerated depreciation (including §179 and bonus depreciation) it deducted over the straight-line depreciation that it should have deducted by adjusting the current-year depreciation. In practical terms, the business can use the following five steps to determine its current depreciation expense for the asset:

Step 1: Compute depreciation for the year it drops to 50 percent or below using the straight-line method (this method also applies to all subsequent years).

Step 2: Compute the amount of depreciation the taxpayer would have deducted if the taxpayer had used the straight-line method over the ADS recovery period for all prior years (recall that depreciation is limited to the business-use percentage in those years).

Step 3: Compute the amount of depreciation (including §179 and bonus depreciation) the taxpayer actually deducted on the asset for all prior years.

Step 4: Subtract the amount from Step 2 from the amount in Step 3. The difference is the prior-year accelerated depreciation in excess of straight-line depreciation.

Step 5: Subtract the excess accelerated depreciation determined in Step 4 from the current-year straight-line depreciation in Step 1. This is the business's allowable depreciation expense on the asset for the year. If the prior-year excess depreciation from Step 4 exceeds the current-year straight-line depreciation in Step 1, the business is not allowed to deduct any depreciation on the asset for the year and must recognize additional ordinary income for the amount of the excess.

This five-step process is designed to place the business in the same position it would have been in if it had used straight-line depreciation during all years of the asset's life.

---

[46]This is the alternative recovery period listed in Rev. Proc. 87-56. See §168(g)(3)(C) and Reg. §1.280F-3T(d)(1).

[47]However, there are exceptions to this general rule. For example, the ADS recovery period for certain machinery for food and beverages is 12 years and the ADS recovery period for machinery for tobacco products is 15 years. Thus, it is important to check Rev. Proc. 87-56 to verify the ADS recovery period in these situations.

Example 10-17

What if: Assume that, consistent with the previous example, in 2018 Teton used the camera 75 percent of the time for business purposes and deducted $1,500 depreciation expense on the camera. However, in year 2, Teton's business-use percentage falls to 40 percent. What is Teton's depreciation deduction for the camera in year 2?

Answer: $10, computed using the five-step process described above as follows:

Description	Amount	Explanation*
(1) Straight-line depreciation in current year	$160	$2,000/5 years × 40 percent business-use percentage (Step 1)
(2) Prior-year straight-line depreciation	150	$2,000/5 × 50 percent (half-year convention) × 75 percent business-use percentage (Step 2)
(3) Prior-year accelerated depreciation	300	Example 10-14 (prior example) (Step 3)
(4) Excess accelerated depreciation	150	(3) – (2) (Step 4)
Allowable current-year depreciation	**$ 10**	(1) – (4) (Step 5)

*Note that the MACRS ADS recovery period (five years) for digital cameras (qualified technological equipment) is the same as the standard MACRS recovery period (five years).

What if: Now assume that, in 2018, Teton took bonus depreciation and deducted $1,500 depreciation expense ($2,000 × 100% × 75%) on the camera. However, in year 2, Teton's business-use percentage falls to 40 percent. What is Teton's depreciation deduction for the camera in year 2?

Answer: $0 depreciation deduction and $1,190 of ordinary income because excess accelerated depreciation exceeds current-year straight-line depreciation, computed as follows:

Description	Amount	Explanation
(1) Straight-line depreciation in current year	$160	$2,000/5 years × 40 percent business use
(2) Prior-year straight-line depreciation	150	$2,000/5 × 50 percent (half-year convention) × 75 percent business-use percentage from year 1
(3) Prior-year accelerated depreciation	1,500	Bonus depreciation
(4) Excess accelerated depreciation	1,350	(3) – (2)
Allowable current-year depreciation (income)	**($1,190)**	(1) – (4)

TAXES IN THE REAL WORLD   Cost Segregation

Consider a taxpayer that purchases a strip mall for $1 million, excluding land, in July. Typically, the taxpayer records the purchase as a 39-year asset and depreciates it using a straight-line method according to the MACRS rules for depreciating real property. After five years, the taxpayer would have claimed $114,330 of depreciation deductions on the property. Is it possible for the taxpayer to accelerate the depreciation deductions on the property to take advantage of the timing tax planning strategy? Yes, with the help of a cost segregation study! Cost segregation is the process of identifying personal property assets that are included in the purchase price of real property such as a strip mall. Cost segregation separates out the personal property from the real property for tax reporting purposes. Personal property includes a building's nonstructural elements, exterior land improvements, and indirect construction costs. Now suppose a cost segregation study on the strip mall identifies five-year property of $200,000, 15-year property of $250,000, and 39-year property of $550,000. The taxpayer would claim $345,562 of depreciation expense over the five-year period, even without considering bonus depreciation on the identified personal property. Taking bonus depreciation into consideration, the total depreciation over the five years would be $512,882, an increase of almost $398,552 in deductions over the five-year period!

Luxury Automobiles　As we discussed in the Business Income, Deductions, and Accounting Methods chapter, §162 limits business deductions to those considered to be "ordinary, necessary, and reasonable" to prevent subsidizing (giving a tax deduction for) unwarranted business expenses. Although these terms are subject to interpretation, most taxpayers agree that for purposes of simply transporting passengers for business-related purposes, the cost of acquiring and using a Ford Focus is more likely to be ordinary, necessary, and reasonable than the cost of acquiring and using a Ferrari California—although perhaps not as exhilarating. Since either vehicle should be able to transport an employee or business owner from the office to a business meeting, the Ford Focus should be just as effective at accomplishing the business purpose as the Ferrari.

If this is true, why should the government help taxpayers pay for expensive cars with tax savings from large depreciation deductions associated with automobiles? Congress decided it shouldn't. Therefore, with certain exceptions we discuss below, the tax laws generally limit the annual depreciation expense for automobiles. Each year, the IRS provides a maximum depreciation schedule for automobiles placed in service during that particular year.[48] In 2018, taxpayers are allowed to expense $8,000 of bonus depreciation above the otherwise allowable maximum depreciation (maximum depreciation of $18,000).[49] Exhibit 10-10 summarizes these schedules for automobiles placed in service for each year from 2018 back to 2015. The TCJA substantially increased the limitations in 2018 perhaps because the limitations had become severe relative to automobile prices. That is, a limit of $3,160 would apply for an automobile costing more than $15,800, which most would not consider a "luxury" car.

EXHIBIT 10-10　**Automobile Depreciation Limits**

Recovery Year	Year Placed in Service			
	2018	**2017**	**2016**	**2015**
1	10,000*	3,160*	3,160*	3,160*
2	16,000	5,100	5,100	5,100
3	9,600	3,050	3,050	3,050
4 and after	5,760	1,875	1,875	1,875

*$8,000 additional depreciation is allowed when bonus depreciation is claimed (§168(k)(2)(F)).

Ignoring bonus depreciation for a moment, businesses placing automobiles into service during the year determine depreciation for the automobiles by first computing regular MACRS depreciation (using the appropriate convention). They then compare it to the maximum depreciation amount for the first year of the recovery period based on the IRS-provided tables. Businesses are allowed to deduct the lesser of the two. Each subsequent year, businesses should compare the regular MACRS amount with the limitation amount and deduct the lesser of the basic MACRS depreciation or the limitation. In 2018, if the half-year convention applies, the table limits the depreciation on automobiles placed in service during the year costing more than $50,000.[50] Automobiles to which the depreciation limits apply are commonly referred to as **luxury automobiles.**[51] Comparing the lifetime depreciation for two cars—say, a 2019 Honda Civic and a 2019 Porsche 911—we can see that the annual depreciation deduction is lower and the recovery period much shorter for the Civic than for the Porsche. In fact, the Porsche will take 17 years to fully depreciate!

[48]These limitations are indexed for inflation and change annually. §280F(a)(1)(A) provides the 2018 limitations for automobiles.

[49]§168(k)(2)(F)(i).

[50]In 2018, the full first-year depreciation on an automobile costing $50,000 is $10,000 ($50,000 × 20 percent). This is the amount of the first-year limit for automobiles placed in service in 2018.

[51]Correspondingly, the depreciation limits on automobiles are commonly referred to as the *luxury auto depreciation limits.*

Example 10-18

What is the maximum annual depreciation deduction available for 2018 (year 1) on a 2019 Honda Civic costing $19,150 and a 2019 Porsche 911 costing $112,000 (ignoring bonus depreciation)?

Answer: $3,830 for the Honda and $10,000 for the Porsche. See the following depreciation schedules for each automobile.

Luxury Auto Depreciation		
Year/Make	**2019 Honda Civic**	**2019 Porsche 911**
Model	DX 2dr Coupe	Carrera 4S
Price	$19,150	$112,000
Depreciation		
Year 1	$ 3,830	$ 10,000
Year 2	6,128	16,000
Year 3	3,677	9,600
Year 4	2,206	5,760
Year 5	2,206	5,760
Year 6	1,103	5,760
Year 7		5,760
Year 8		5,760
Years 9-16		5,760
Year 17		1,520

The depreciation schedule for the Honda Civic follows the standard depreciation amounts calculated under MACRS because these annual amounts are lower than the limitations. The Honda is fully depreciated in year 6. The MACRS depreciation amounts for the Porsche, however, exceed the limitations so the schedule shows the limited amount of depreciation each year. The limitations extend the recovery period for the Porsche to 17 years—however, it is unlikely the business will actually hold the Porsche through year 17.

The luxury automobile limitations don't apply to vehicles weighing more than 6,000 pounds (for example, large SUVs) and those that charge for transportation such as taxi cabs, limousines, and hearses. It also excludes delivery trucks and vans. Thus, businesses owning these vehicles are allowed to claim §179, bonus, and regular MACRS depreciation expense for these vehicles.[52]

Just like businesses using other types of listed property, businesses using automobiles exceeding the automobile limitation for business and personal purposes may deduct depreciation on the asset only to the extent of business use. Business use is determined by miles driven for business purposes relative to total miles driven for the year.[53] Consequently, if a business places a luxury automobile into service in 2018 and uses the automobile 90 percent of the time for business purposes during the year (9,000 miles for business and 1,000 miles of personal use), the owner's depreciation (ignoring bonus depreciation) on the auto for the year is limited to $9,000 (year 1 full depreciation of $10,000 × 90 percent business use—see Exhibit 10-10).[54] Further, if the business use falls to 50 percent or less in any subsequent year, just as with other listed property, the taxpayer must use the straight-line method of depreciation and reduce depreciation expense by the amount of excess accelerated depreciation (see Example 10-17). However, because straight-line depreciation is also limited by the luxury auto depreciation limits, it may turn out that the business doesn't have any excess accelerated depreciation.

[52]§280F(d)(5)(A).

[53]As an alternative to deducting depreciation expense and other costs of operating an automobile, taxpayers using automobiles for both personal and business purposes may deduct a standard mileage rate for each mile of business use. In 2018 the business mileage rate is 54.5 cents per mile.

[54]Even if the business-use percentage multiplied by the MACRS depreciation is greater than the $10,000 maximum, the depreciation amount is limited to the maximum depreciation amount times the business-use percentage.

Automobiles and §179. Are businesses allowed to deduct §179 expensing on luxury automobiles? The answer is yes, but . . . the luxury car limitation in 2018 is $10,000 and this limit applies regardless of whether the taxpayer claims regular MACRS depreciation or §179 expensing on the car. So, for cars that cost more than $50,000, the taxpayer doesn't benefit by electing §179 because the regular MACRS depreciation deduction would be greater than $10,000 but would be limited to $10,000 anyway. For cars that cost less than $50,000, taxpayers could benefit by electing to take $10,000 of §179 expense on the car to boost the depreciation deduction in first year. For instance, in Example 10-18, the regular MACRS depreciation amount for the Honda Civic was only $3,830. By electing §179, a taxpayer could increase the first-year depreciation deduction to $10,000.

Recall that large SUVs (those weighing more than 6,000 pounds) are not subject to the luxury car limitations. Therefore a business will calculate its regular MACRS depreciation each year without the limitations for passenger cars. For these vehicles, businesses may take a §179 expense amount of $25,000 in 2018 in the acquisition year in addition to their MACRS depreciation (calculated after the §179 expense).[55]

Automobiles and bonus depreciation. But wait! Why don't businesses simply use bonus depreciation to fully recover the cost of their automobiles in the year they buy the vehicle? For passenger cars (automobiles weighing 6,000 pounds or less), the luxury car limitations still apply. With bonus depreciation taxpayers are allowed to increase the limitation in the first year by $8,000 making the first-year limit $18,000 in 2018.

Example 10-19

What if: Suppose Teton purchases a $62,000 car, which is used 100 percent of the time for business purposes. Teton would like to claim bonus depreciation. What is Teton's depreciation deduction for the car in 2018?

Answer: $18,000, calculated as follows:

Description	Amount	Explanation
(1) Automobile	$ 62,000	
(2) Bonus percentage	100%	§168(k)(1) and §168(k)(6)(A)(i)
(3) MACRS depreciation	$ 62,000	(1) × (2)
(4) Luxury car limitation	18,000	Luxury car limitation [[$10,000 [§280F(a) (1)] + $8,000 [§168(k)(2)(F)]]]
Year 1 depreciation	**$18,000**	Lesser of (3) or (4)

In year 1, Teton's regular depreciation on the car would have been $12,400 ($62,000 × 20 percent MACRS percentage). This amount is greater than the $10,000 automobile limitation, so without taking bonus Teton would be limited to $10,000 of depreciation on the car. By taking bonus depreciation, Teton is able to increase 2018 depreciation by $8,000.

However, in years 2–6 (recovery period for passenger cars), taxpayers must again compare the regular MACRS amount in each year to the car limitation in Exhibit 10-10 for the year. If the taxpayer claims bonus depreciation, then technically, all of the allowable depreciation was taken in year 1 (100 percent bonus depreciation) even though the taxpayer was limited by the automobile limitations. This means that there is no regular depreciation remaining for years 2–6. So, absent a special rule, taxpayers would not be allowed to take ANY depreciation for those years. The remaining cost to be recovered would occur beginning in year 7 using the limitation for year 4 and after. Fortunately the IRS provides a way for taxpayers to continue to take depreciation in years 2–6 when they claim bonus depreciation.[56] The entire calculation involves a 6-step process as follows:

---

[55]This amount is indexed for inflation beginning with years after 2018 (§179(b)(6)).
[56]Rev. Proc. 2011-26.

Year 1:

Step 1: Deduct the lower of the cost of the automobile or the first year limitation from Exhibit 10-10 plus the additional $8,000 bonus amount, which is $18,000 for 2018.

Step 2: Calculate depreciation "as if" the bonus amount in year 1 were 50 percent rather than 100 percent. This step requires taxpayers to take 50 percent of the basis as bonus then reduce the original basis by the 50 percent bonus amount to calculate the regular MACRS depreciation on the remaining basis.

Step 3: Subtract the actual depreciation taken in year 1 from Step 1 from the "as if" year 1 depreciation amount determined in Step 2. If positive, this unrecovered basis is not deductible until after the MACRS recovery period expires (year 7).

Step 4: Determine the "as if" remaining depreciable basis amount. The remaining basis for calculating years 2–6 depreciation is the original cost less the 50 percent bonus.

Years 2–6:

Step 5: The remaining depreciable basis calculated in Step 4 is depreciated by taking the lesser of 1) the MACRS depreciation on the remaining basis or 2) the automobile limitation from Exhibit 10-10 for each recovery year.

Years 7 and after:

Step 6: If any basis remains undepreciated after the end of year 6 (the end of the MACRS recovery period) because of the automobile limitations, it is recovered beginning in year 7 but is limited to the amount provided in Exhibit 10-10 for periods 4 and after.

Example 10-20

What if: Same facts as in Example 10-19. What is Teton's depreciation on the car in year 2?

Answer: $9,920, calculated as follows:

Step	Amount	Description
Step 1: Year 1 depreciation	$18,000	Calculated in Example 10-19
Step 2: "As if" year 1 depreciation	37,200	"As if" year 1 depreciation is 50% bonus depreciation of $31,000 ($62,000 × 50%) plus MACRS depreciation on the remaining $31,000 basis of $6,200 ($31,000 × 20%).
Step 3: Unrecovered basis	19,200	Step 2 - Step 1; This is the unrecovered basis, which will be deductible beginning in year 7.
Step 4: Remaining "as if" depreciable basis	31,000	Cost of $62,000 × 50%. This is the remaining depreciable basis.
Step 5: Year 2 depreciation	$ 9,920	Lesser of $9,920 [$31,000 (Step 4) x 32% (5-year property, year 2 MACRS percentage)] or $16,000 (Year 2 limitation)
Step 6: Recovery of Step 3 amount	N/A	The unrecovered basis from step 3 will be recovered beginning in year 7 and has no impact on the year 2 depreciation amount.

Can taxpayers avoid this calculation? Yes! There are at least two ways to avoid having to calculate depreciation on cars in this way. First, taxpayers can elect out of bonus depreciation. By electing out of bonus, taxpayers would calculate the depreciation on automobiles as the lesser of the regular MACRS depreciation or the limitation amount for each year. The downside of electing out of bonus for automobiles is that the election must be done on a property class basis. Automobiles are in the 5-year property class, but so are computers and office machinery (calculators and copiers). So, if taxpayers elect out of bonus for automobiles, they also elect out for other assets included in the 5-year property class. The second way to avoid this calculation is to purchase SUVs that weigh more than

6,000 pounds instead of passenger cars. These large SUVs are not subject to the listed property automobile limitations. Taxpayers can deduct the full cost of these vehicles in the first year under the bonus depreciation rules.

Depreciation for the Alternative Minimum Tax

Individuals are subject to tax under the alternative minimum tax (AMT) system.[57] In determining their alternative minimum taxable income, individuals may be required to recalculate their depreciation expense. For AMT purposes, the allowable recovery period and conventions are the same for all depreciable assets as they are for regular tax purposes.[58] However, for AMT purposes, businesses are not allowed to use the 200 percent declining balance method to depreciate tangible personal property. Rather, they must choose from the 150 percent declining balance method or the straight-line method to depreciate the property for AMT purposes. The difference between regular tax depreciation and AMT depreciation is an adjustment that is either added to or subtracted from regular taxable income in computing the alternative minimum tax base.[59] In contrast, the §179 expense and bonus depreciation are equally deductible for both regular tax and AMT purposes. Depreciation of real property is the same for both regular tax and AMT purposes.

Depreciation Summary

Teton's depreciation for 2018 on all its assets is summarized in Exhibit 10-11 and Exhibit 10-12 presents Teton's depreciation as it would be reported on its tax return on Form 4562 (assuming Teton does not elect §179 and elects out of bonus depreciation for assets acquired in 2017).

EXHIBIT 10-11   **Teton's 2018 Depreciation Expense**

	Date Acquired	Original Basis	§179 Expense	Remaining Basis*	Bonus Depreciation	Remaining basis	Depreciation Expense	Reference
2017 Assets								
Machinery	7/22/2017	$ 610,000	—	$610,000	—	$ 610,000	$ 149,389	Example 10-5
Office furniture	2/3/2017	20,000	—	20,000	—	20,000	4,898	Example 10-5
Delivery truck	8/17/2017	25,000	—	25,000	—	25,000	8,000	Example 10-5
Warehouse	5/1/2017	275,000	—	275,000	—	275,000	7,051	Example 10-9
Land	5/1/2017	75,000	—	75,000	—	75,000	—	N/A
2018 Assets								
Computers & info systems	3/3/2018	920,000	—	920,000	920,000	—	—	Example 10-15 *What if* scenario
Delivery truck	5/26/2018	80,000	80,000	—	—	—	—	Example 10-15 *What if* scenario
Machinery	8/15/2018	1,200,000	920,000	280,000	280,000	—	—	Example 10-15 *What if* scenario
§179 expense							1,000,000	Example 10-15 *What if* scenario
Bonus depreciation							1,200,000	Example 10-15 *What if* scenario
Total 2018 Depreciation Expense							**$2,369,338**	

[57]Corporations are no longer subject to the alternative minimum tax for tax years after December 31, 2017.

[58]This is true for assets placed in service after 1998.

[59]If the taxpayer elected either the 150 percent declining balance or the straight-line method for regular tax depreciation of tangible personal property, then there is no AMT adjustment with respect to that property.

EXHIBIT 10-12   Teton's Form 4562 Parts I–IV for Depreciation (Assumes $1,500,000 of taxable income before the §179 expense)

Form **4562**

Department of the Treasury
Internal Revenue Service   (99)

Depreciation and Amortization
(Including Information on Listed Property)
▶ Attach to your tax return.
▶ Go to *www.irs.gov/Form4562* for instructions and the latest information.

OMB No. 1545-0172

2017

Attachment
Sequence No. **179**

Name(s) shown on return	Business or activity to which this form relates	Identifying number
Steve Dallimore	**Teton Mountaineering Technologies, LLC**	

Part I   **Election To Expense Certain Property Under Section 179**
Note: If you have any listed property, complete Part V before you complete Part I.

1 Maximum amount (see instructions)	**1**	1,000,000
2 Total cost of section 179 property placed in service (see instructions)	**2**	1,200,000
3 Threshold cost of section 179 property before reduction in limitation (see instructions)	**3**	2,500,000
4 Reduction in limitation. Subtract line 3 from line 2. If zero or less, enter -0-	**4**	0
5 Dollar limitation for tax year. Subtract line 4 from line 1. If zero or less, enter -0-. If married filing separately, see instructions	**5**	1,000,000

6 **(a)** Description of property	**(b)** Cost (business use only)	**(c)** Elected cost	
Machinery	1,200,000	920,000	
Delivery Truck	80,000	80,000	

7 Listed property. Enter the amount from line 29	**7**	
8 Total elected cost of section 179 property. Add amounts in column (c), lines 6 and 7	**8**	1,000,000
9 Tentative deduction. Enter the **smaller** of line 5 or line 8	**9**	1,000,000
10 Carryover of disallowed deduction from line 13 of your 2016 Form 4562	**10**	
11 Business income limitation. Enter the smaller of business income (not less than zero) or line 5 (see instructions)	**11**	1,000,000
12 Section 179 expense deduction. Add lines 9 and 10, but don't enter more than line 11	**12**	1,000,000
13 Carryover of disallowed deduction to 2018. Add lines 9 and 10, less line 12 ▶ **13**		

Note: Don't use Part II or Part III below for listed property. Instead, use Part V.

Part II   **Special Depreciation Allowance and Other Depreciation (Don't** include listed property.**)** (See instructions.)

14 Special depreciation allowance for qualified property (other than listed property) placed in service during the tax year (see instructions)	**14**	1,200,000
15 Property subject to section 168(f)(1) election	**15**	
16 Other depreciation (including ACRS)	**16**	

Part III   **MACRS Depreciation (Don't** include listed property.**)** (See instructions.)

Section A

17 MACRS deductions for assets placed in service in tax years beginning before 2017	**17**	169,338
18 If you are electing to group any assets placed in service during the tax year into one or more general asset accounts, check here . . . . ▶ ☐		

Section B—Assets Placed in Service During 2017 Tax Year Using the General Depreciation System

(a) Classification of property	**(b)** Month and year placed in service	**(c)** Basis for depreciation (business/investment use only—see instructions)	**(d)** Recovery period	**(e)** Convention	**(f)** Method	**(g)** Depreciation deduction
19a 3-year property						
b 5-year property						
c 7-year property						
d 10-year property						
e 15-year property						
f 20-year property						
g 25-year property			25 yrs.		S/L	
h Residential rental property			27.5 yrs.	MM	S/L	
			27.5 yrs.	MM	S/L	
i Nonresidential real property			39 yrs.	MM	S/L	
				MM	S/L	

Section C—Assets Placed in Service During 2017 Tax Year Using the Alternative Depreciation System

20a Class life					S/L	
b 12-year			12 yrs.		S/L	
c 40-year			40 yrs.	MM	S/L	

Part IV   **Summary** (See instructions.)

21 Listed property. Enter amount from line 28	**21**	
22 **Total.** Add amounts from line 12, lines 14 through 17, lines 19 and 20 in column (g), and line 21. Enter here and on the appropriate lines of your return. Partnerships and S corporations—see instructions .	**22**	2,369,338
23 For assets shown above and placed in service during the current year, enter the portion of the basis attributable to section 263A costs **23**		

For Paperwork Reduction Act Notice, see separate instructions.   Cat. No. 12906N   Form **4562** (2017)

Source: IRS Form 4562, 2017

AMORTIZATION

Businesses recover the cost of intangible assets through amortization rather than depreciation. Intangible assets in the form of capitalized expenditures, such as capitalized **research and experimentation (R&E) costs** or **covenants not to compete,** do not have physical characteristics. Nonetheless, they may have determinable lives. While research and experimentation costs may have an indeterminate life, a covenant not to compete, for example, would have a life equal to the stated term of the contractual agreement. When the life of intangible assets cannot be determined, taxpayers recover the cost of the assets when they dispose of them—unless they are assigned a specific tax recovery period.

For tax purposes, an intangible asset can be placed into one of the following four general categories:

1. §197 purchased intangibles.
2. Start-up expenditures and organizational costs.
3. Research and experimentation costs.
4. Patents and copyrights.

Businesses amortize all intangible assets in these categories using the straight-line method for both financial accounting and tax purposes.

Section 197 Intangibles

> **THE KEY FACTS**
>
> **§197 Intangible Assets**
>
> • Purchased intangibles are amortized over a period of 180 months, regardless of their explicitly stated lives.
>
> • The full-month convention applies to amortizable assets.

When a business purchases the *assets* of another business for a single purchase price, the business must determine the initial basis of each of the assets it acquired in the transaction. To determine basis, the business must allocate a portion of the purchase price to each of the individual assets acquired in the transaction. Generally, under this approach, each asset acquired (cash, machinery, and real property, for example) takes a basis equal to its fair market value. However, some of the assets acquired in the transaction may not appear on the seller's balance sheet. In fact, a substantial portion of a business's value may exist in the form of intangible assets such as customer lists, patents, trademarks, trade names, goodwill, going-concern value, covenants not to compete, and so forth. Nearly all these assets are amortized according to §197 of the Internal Revenue Code—hence, they are often referred to as **§197 intangibles.**

According to §197, these assets have a recovery period of 180 months (15 years), *regardless of their actual life.*[60] For example, when a business buys an existing business, the owner selling the business often signs a covenant not to compete for a specified period such as five years.[61] Even though a five-year covenant not to compete clearly has a fixed and determinable life, it must be amortized over 180 months (15 years). The **full-month convention** applies to the amortization of purchased intangibles. This convention allows taxpayers to deduct an entire month's worth of amortization for the month of purchase and all subsequent months in the year. The full-month convention also applies in the month of sale or disposition.[62]

---

[60]§197 was Congress's response to taxpayers manipulating the valuation and recovery periods assigned to these purchased intangibles.

[61]A covenant not to compete is a contract between the seller of a business and its buyer that the seller will not operate a similar business that would compete with the previous business for a specified period of time.

[62]Reg. §1.197-2(g)(l)(i) illustrates the special rules that apply when a taxpayer sells a §197 intangible or the intangible becomes worthless and the taxpayer's basis in the asset exceeds the sale proceeds (if any). A business may recognize a loss on the sale or disposition only when the business does not hold any other §197 assets that the business acquired in the *same initial transaction.* Otherwise, the taxpayer may not deduct the loss on the sale or disposition until the business sells or disposes of *all* of the other §197 intangibles that it purchased in the same initial transaction. The same loss disallowance rule applies if a §197 intangible expires before it is fully amortized.

What if: Assume that on January 30, 2017, Teton acquires a competitor's assets for $350,000.[63] Of the $350,000 purchase price, $125,000 is allocated to tangible assets and $225,000 is allocated to §197 intangible assets (patent, goodwill, and a customer list with a three-year life).[64] For each of the first three years, Teton would deduct one-fifteenth of the basis of each asset as amortization expense. What is Teton's accumulated amortization and remaining basis in each of these §197 intangibles after three years?

Answer: See the table below:

Description	Patent	Goodwill	Customer List
Basis	$25,000	$150,000	$50,000
Accumulated amortization (3/15 of original basis)	(5,000)	(30,000)	(10,000)
Remaining basis	$20,000	$120,000	$40,000

When a taxpayer sells a §197 intangible for more than its basis, the taxpayer recognizes gain. We describe how to characterize this type of gain in the next chapter.

Organizational Expenditures and Start-Up Costs

Organizational expenditures include expenditures to form and organize a business in the form of a corporation or a partnership.[65] Organizational expenditures typically include costs of organizational meetings, state fees, accounting service costs incident to organization, and legal service expenditures such as document drafting, taking minutes of organizational meetings, and creating terms of the original stock certificates. These costs are generally incurred prior to the starting of business (or shortly thereafter) but relate to creating the business entity. The costs of selling or marketing stock do *not* qualify as organizational expenditures and cannot be amortized.[66]

What if: Suppose Teton was organized as a corporation rather than a sole proprietorship (sole proprietorships cannot expense organizational expenditures). Steve paid $35,000 of legal costs to Scott, Tang, and Malan to draft the corporate charter and articles of incorporation, $10,000 to Harvey and Stratford for accounting fees related to the organization; and $7,000 for organizational meetings, $5,000 for stock issuance costs, and $1,000 for state fees related to the incorporation. What amounts of these expenditures qualify as organizational costs?

Answer: $53,000, computed as follows (with the exception of the stock issuance costs, each of Teton's expenses qualify as amortizable organizational expenditures):

Description	Qualifying Organizational Expenditures
Legal drafting of corporate charter and articles of incorporation	$ 35,000
Accounting fees related to organization	10,000
Organizational meetings	7,000
Stock issuance costs	0
State incorporation fees	1,000
Total	**$53,000**

THE KEY FACTS

Organizational Expenditures and Start-Up Costs

- Taxpayers may immediately expense up to $5,000 of organizational expenditures and $5,000 of start-up costs.
- The immediate expense rule has a dollar-for-dollar phase-out that begins at $50,000 for organizational expenditures and for start-up costs. Thus, when organizational expenditures or start-up costs exceed $55,000 there is no immediate expensing.

[63]If a business acquires a corporation's stock (rather than assets) there is no goodwill assigned for tax purposes, and the purchase price simply becomes the basis of the stock purchased.

[64]A customer base is the value assigned to current customers (i.e., the lists that will allow the new owner to capture future benefits from the current customers).

[65]§248 for corporations and §709 for partnerships. Sole proprietorships cannot deduct organizational expenditures.

[66]These syndication costs are capitalized and deducted on the final tax return.

Businesses may *immediately expense* up to $5,000 of organizational expenditures.[67] However, corporations and partnerships incurring more than $50,000 in organizational expenditures must phase out (reduce) the $5,000 immediate expense amount dollar for dollar for expenditures exceeding $50,000. Thus, businesses incurring at least $55,000 of organizational expenditures are not allowed to immediately expense any of the expenditures.

Example 10-23

What if: Suppose Teton is a corporation and it wants to maximize its first-year organizational expenditure deduction. As described in Example 10-22, Teton incurred $53,000 of organizational expenditures in year 1. How much of the organizational expenditures can Teton immediately deduct in year 1?

Answer: $2,000, computed as follows:

Description	Amount	Explanation
(1) Maximum immediate expense	$ 5,000	§248(a)(1)
(2) Total organizational expenditures	53,000	Example 10-22
(3) Phase-out threshold	50,000	§248(a)(1)(B)
(4) Immediate expense phase-out	3,000	(2) − (3)
(5) Allowable immediate expense	**2,000**	(1) − (4), but not below zero
Remaining organizational expenditures	$51,000*	(2) − (5)

What if: Assuming that Teton is a corporation and that it incurred $41,000 of organizational expenditures in year 1, how much of the organizational expenditures could Teton immediately expense in year 1?

Answer: $5,000, computed as follows:

Description	Amount	Explanation
(1) Maximum immediate expense	$ 5,000	§248(a)(1)
(2) Total organizational expenditures	41,000	
(3) Phase-out threshold	50,000	§248(a)(1)(B)
(4) Immediate expense phase-out	0	(2) − (3), limit to zero
(5) Allowable immediate expense	**5,000**	(1) − (4)
Remaining organizational expenditures	$36,000*	(2) − (5)

What if: Assuming that Teton is a corporation and it incurred $60,000 of organizational expenditures in year 1, how much of the organizational expenditures could Teton immediately expense in year 1?

Answer: $0, computed as follows:

Description	Amount	Explanation
(1) Maximum immediate expense	$ 5,000	§248(a)(1)
(2) Total organizational expenditures	60,000	
(3) Phase-out threshold	50,000	§248(a)(1)(B)
(4) Immediate expense phase-out	10,000	(2) − (3)
(5) Allowable immediate expense	**0**	(1) − (4)
Remaining organizational expenditures	$60,000*	(2) − (5)

*As we discuss below, Teton amortizes the remaining organizational costs.

Businesses amortize organizational expenditures that they do not immediately expense using the straight-line method over a recovery period of 15 years (180 months).

[67]§248(a)(1) for corporations or §709 for partnerships.

Example 10-24

What if: Assume Teton is a corporation and it amortizes the $51,000 of organizational expenditures remaining after it immediately expenses $2,000 of the costs (see the first *what-if* scenario in Example 10-23). If Teton began business on February 1 of year 1, how much total cost recovery expense for the organizational expenditures is Teton able to deduct in year 1? How much cost recovery expense will Teton be able to deduct in year 2?

Answer: $5,117 in year 1 and $3,400 in year 2, computed as follows:

Description	Amount	Explanation
(1) Total organizational expenditures	$53,000	Example 10-22
(2) Amount immediately expensed	2,000	Example 10-23
(3) Expenditures subject to straight-line amortization	$51,000	(1) − (2)
(4) Recovery period in months	180	15 years §248(a)(2)
(5) Monthly straight-line amortization	283.33	(3)/(4)
(6) Teton business months during year 1	× 11	February through December
(7) Year 1 straight-line amortization	3,117	(5) × (6)
Total year 1 cost recovery expense for organizational expenditures	**$ 5,117**	(2) + (7)
Total year 2 cost recovery expense	**3,400**	(3)/15 years

Start-up costs are costs businesses incur to, not surprisingly, start up a business.[68] Start-up costs apply to all types of business forms.[69] These costs include costs associated with investigating the possibilities of and actually creating or acquiring a trade or business. For example, costs Teton incurs in deciding whether to locate the business in Cody, Wyoming, or Bozeman, Montana, are start-up costs. Start-up costs also include costs that would normally be deductible as ordinary business expenses except that they don't qualify as business expenses because they are incurred before the trade or business activity actually begins. For example, costs Teton incurs to train its employees before the business begins are start-up costs.

The rules for immediately expensing and amortizing start-up costs are the same as those for immediately expensing and amortizing organizational expenditures. Consequently, businesses incurring at least $55,000 of start-up costs are not allowed to immediately expense any of the costs. The limitations are computed separately for organizational expenditures and for start-up costs. Thus, a business could immediately expense $5,000 of organizational expenditures and $5,000 of start-up costs in its first year of business in addition to the 15-year amortization amount.

Example 10-25

What if: Assume that in January of year 1 (before it began business on February 1) Teton spent $4,500 investigating the climbing hardware market, creating company logos, and determining the locations for both the office and manufacturing facility. The $4,500 of expenditures qualify as start-up costs. How much of the $4,500 of start-up costs is Teton allowed to immediately expense?

Answer: All $4,500. Teton is allowed to immediately expense the entire $4,500 because its total start-up costs do not exceed $50,000. Teton could have immediately expensed up to $5,000 of start-up costs as long as its total start-up costs did not exceed $50,000.

[68]§195.

[69]Recall that rules for amortizing organizational expenditures apply only to corporations and partnerships.

Exhibit 10-13 illustrates the timing of organizational expenditures, start-up costs, and normal trade or business expenses.

EXHIBIT 10-13   Summary of Timing for Organizational Expenditures, Start-Up Costs, and Normal Trade or Business Expenses

Research and Experimentation Expenditures

To stay competitive, businesses often invest in activities they believe will generate innovative products or significantly improve their current products or processes. These research and experimentation costs include expenditures for research laboratories, including salaries, materials, and other related expenses. Businesses may immediately expense these costs or they may *elect* to capitalize these costs and amortize them using the straight-line method over the determinable useful life or, if there is no determinable useful life, over a period of not less than 60 months, beginning in the month benefits are first derived from the research.[70] However, if a business elects to capitalize and amortize the costs, it must stop amortizing the costs if and when the business receives a patent relating to the expenditures. When the business obtains a patent, it adds any remaining basis in the costs to the basis of the patent and it amortizes the basis of the patent over the patent's life (see discussion below).

Patents and Copyrights

The manner in which a business amortizes a patent or copyright depends on whether the business directly purchases the patent or copyright or whether it self-creates the intangibles. Businesses directly purchasing patents or copyrights (not in an asset acquisition to which §197 applies) amortize the cost over the remaining life of the patents or copyrights.[71] Businesses receiving "self-created" patents or copyrights amortize the cost or basis of the self-created intangible assets over their legal lives. The costs included in the basis of a self-created patent or copyright include legal costs, fees, and, as we discussed above, unamortized research and experimentation expenditures associated with the creation of the patent or copyright. However, because the patent approval process is slow, the unamortized research and experimentation costs included in the patent's basis are likely to be relatively small because, with a five-year recovery period, the research and experimentation costs would likely be mostly or even fully amortized by the time the patent is approved.

---

[70]See §174. High-tax-rate taxpayers may choose to deduct these costs while low-tax-rate taxpayers may prefer to capitalize and amortize them so that they will have more future deductions when they generate more income. The research and experimentation credit is also available to some businesses. Beginning in tax years after December 31, 2021, taxpayers will no longer have the option of immediately expensing these costs. Rather, these costs will be capitalized and amortized ratably over five years beginning with the midpoint of the year in which the costs were incurred.

[71]§167(f).

Example 10-26

In September of year 1, Teton purchased a patent with a remaining life of 10 years from Chouinard Equipment for $60,000. What amount of amortization expense is Teton allowed to deduct for the patent in year 1?

Answer: $2,000, computed as follows:

Description	Amount	Explanation
(1) Cost of patent	$60,000	
(2) Remaining life of patent in months	120	10 years
(3) Monthly amortization	$ 500	(1)/(2)
(4) Months in year 1 Teton held patent	× 4	September through December
(5) Monthly straight-line amortization	**$ 2,000**	(3) × (4)
Unamortized cost of patent at end of year 1	$58,000	(1) − (5)

Amortizable Intangible Asset Summary

Exhibit 10-14 summarizes the different types of amortizable intangible assets, identifies the recovery period of these assets, and describes the applicable amortization method for each asset. Exhibit 10-14 also identifies the applicable convention for each type of amortizable intangible asset and identifies the financial accounting treatment for recovering the cost of the intangible assets under GAAP.

EXHIBIT 10-14   Summary of Amortizable Assets

Asset Description	Recovery Period (months)	Applicable Method	Applicable Convention	Financial Accounting Treatment
§197 purchased intangibles, including goodwill, trademarks, patents, and covenants not to compete[72]	180	Straight-line	Full-month beginning with month of purchase	ASC 350 tests for annual impairment
Organizational expenditures and start-up costs that are required to be capitalized	180	Straight-line	Full-month in month business begins	AICPA SOP 98-5
Research and experimentation costs that are capitalized	Determinable useful life, or (not less than) 60; ceases when patent is issued.	Straight-line	Full-month in first month that benefits from research are obtained	Expensed
Self-created patents and copyrights	Actual life	Straight-line	Full-month in month intangible is obtained	Expensed
Purchased patents and copyrights	Remaining life	Straight-line	Full-month in month intangible is obtained	Expensed

[72]A patent or copyright that is part of a basket purchase (several assets together) is treated as a §197 intangible. A patent or copyright that is purchased separately is simply amortized over its remaining life (§167[f]).

Exhibit 10-15 presents Teton's amortization expense as it would be reported on its tax return on Form 4562 (the exhibit assumes that Teton is a corporation so it can amortize organizational expenditures). The amortization is reported on line 43 because it is Teton's second year in business. The amortization would be reported on line 42 (with more detail) had this been Teton's first year in business.

EXHIBIT 10-15   Teton Form 4562, Part VI Amortization of Organizational Expenditures and Patent

Part VI Amortization

(a) Description of costs	(b) Date amortization begins	(c) Amortizable amount	(d) Code section	(e) Amortization period or percentage	(f) Amortization for this year
42 Amortization of costs that begins during your 2017 tax year (see instructions):					
43 Amortization of costs that began before your 2017 tax year				**43**	9,400
44 Total. Add amounts in column (f). See the instructions for where to report				**44**	9,400

Form **4562** (2017)

Source: IRS Form 4562, 2017

---

continued from page 10-16...

Teton was developing some additional employee parking on a lot adjacent to the warehouse when the excavation crew discovered a small gold deposit. Steve called his friend Ken, who had some experience in mining precious metals, to see what Ken thought of the find. Ken was impressed and offered Steve $150,000 for the rights to the gold. Steve accepted the offer on Teton's behalf. ∎

LO 10-5   # DEPLETION

Depletion is the method taxpayers use to recover their capital investment in natural resources. Depletion is a particularly significant deduction for businesses in the mining, oil and gas, and forestry industries. These businesses generally incur depletion expense as they use the natural resource. Specifically, businesses compute annual depletion expense under both the cost and percentage depletion methods and deduct the larger of the two.[73]

Under **cost depletion,** taxpayers must estimate or determine the number of recoverable units or reserves (tons of coal, barrels of oil, or board feet of timber, for example) that remain at the beginning of the year and allocate a pro rata share of the property's adjusted basis to each unit. To determine the cost depletion amount, taxpayers then multiply the per-unit basis amount by the number of units sold during the year.[74]

---

[73]Depletion of timber and major integrated oil companies must be calculated using only the cost depletion method (no percentage depletion is available).

[74]§612.

Example 10-27

Ken's cost basis in the gold is the $150,000 he paid for it. Based on a mining engineer's estimate that the gold deposit probably holds 1,000 ounces of gold, Ken can determine his cost depletion. What is Ken's cost depletion for year 1 and year 2, assuming he extracts and sells 300 and 700 ounces of gold in year 1 and year 2, respectively?

Answer: $45,000 in year 1 and $105,000 in year 2, computed as follows:

Description	Amount	Explanation
(1) Cost basis in gold	$ 150,000	
(2) Estimated ounces of gold	1,000	
(3) Per-ounce cost depletion rate	150	(1)/(2)
(4) Year 1 ounces sold	300	
(5) Year 1 cost depletion	**$ 45,000**	(3) × (4)
(6) Basis remaining after year 1 depletion	105,000	(1) − (5)
(7) Year 2 ounces sold	700	
(8) Year 2 cost depletion	**$105,000**	(7) × (3)
Basis remaining after year 2 depletion	$ 0	(6) − (8)

Ken is not eligible for cost depletion after year 2 because as of the end of year 2, his cost basis has been reduced to $0.

THE KEY FACTS

Depletion

- Cost depletion involves estimating resource reserves and allocating a pro-rata share of basis based on the number of units extracted.
- Percentage depletion is determined by a statutory percentage of gross income that is permitted to be expensed each year. Different resources have different statutory percentages (i.e., gold, tin, coal).
- Taxpayers may expense the larger of cost or percentage depletion.

Because the cost depletion method requires businesses to estimate the number of units of the resource they will actually extract, it is possible that their estimate will prove to be inaccurate. If they underestimate the number of units, they will fully deplete the cost basis of the resource before they have fully extracted the resource. Once they have recovered the entire cost basis of the resource, businesses are not allowed to use cost depletion to determine depletion expense. They may, however, continue to use percentage depletion (see discussion below). If a business overestimates the number of units to be extracted, it will still have basis remaining after the resource has been fully extracted. In these situations, the business deducts the unrecovered basis once it has sold all the remaining units.

The amount of **percentage depletion** for a natural resource business activity is determined by multiplying the *gross income* from the resource extraction activity by a fixed percentage based on the type of natural resource, as indicated in Exhibit 10-16.[75]

EXHIBIT 10-16   **Applicable Percentage Depletion Rates**

Statutory Percentage	Natural Resources (partial list)
5 percent [§613(b)(6)]	Gravel, pumice, and stone
14 percent [§613(b)(3)]	Asphalt rock, clay, and other metals
15 percent [§613(b)(2)]	Gold, copper, oil shale, and silver
15 percent [§613A(c)(1)]	Domestic oil and gas
22 percent [§613(b)(1)]	Platinum, sulfur, uranium, and titanium

Source: §613.

In many cases, percentage depletion may generate *larger* depletion deductions than cost depletion. Recall that taxpayers are allowed to deduct the greater of cost or percentage depletion. Businesses reduce their initial basis in the resource when they deduct

[75]§613.

percentage depletion. However, once the initial basis is exhausted, they are allowed to continue to deduct percentage (but not cost) depletion. This provides a potentially significant governmental subsidy to extraction businesses that have completely recovered their costs in a natural resource.[76]

Note that businesses deduct percentage depletion when they *sell* the natural resource, and they deduct cost depletion in the year they *produce* or *extract* the natural resource. Also, percentage depletion cannot exceed 50 percent (100 percent in the case of oil and gas properties) of the taxable income from the natural resource business activity before considering the depletion expense, while cost depletion has no such limitation.

Example 10-28

In Example 10-27, Ken determined his cost depletion expense for the gold. However, because he is allowed to deduct the greater of cost or percentage depletion each year, he set out to determine his percentage depletion for year 2. Assuming that Ken has gross (taxable) income from the gold mining activity before depletion expense of $200,000 ($50,000), $600,000 ($450,000), and $600,000 ($500,000) in year 1, year 2, and year 3, respectively, what is his percentage depletion expense for each of these three years?

Answer: $25,000, $90,000, and $90,000 for years 1, 2, and 3, respectively, computed as follows:

	Year 1	Year 2	Year 3	Explanation
(1) Taxable income from activity (before depletion expense)	$ 50,000	$450,000	$500,000	
(2) Gross income	$200,000	$600,000	$600,000	
(3) Percentage	× 15%	× 15%	× 15%	Exhibit 10-16
(4) Percentage depletion expense before limit	$ 30,000	$ 90,000	$ 90,000	(2) × (3)
(5) 50 percent of taxable income limitation	$ 25,000	$225,000	$250,000	(1) × 50%
Allowable percentage depletion	**$ 25,000**	**$ 90,000**	**$ 90,000**	Lesser of (4) or (5)

Finally, as we discussed above, a business's depletion deduction is the greater of either the annual cost or percentage depletion.

Example 10-29

Based on his computations of cost depletion and percentage depletion, Ken was able to determine his deductible depletion expense. Using the cost and percentage depletion computations from Examples 10-27 and 10-28, what is Ken's deductible depletion expense for years 1, 2, and 3?

Answer: $45,000 for year 1, $105,000 for year 2, and $90,000 for year 3, computed as follows:

Tax Depletion Expense	Year 1	Year 2	Year 3	Explanation
(1) Cost depletion	$ 45,000	$ 105,000	$ 0	Example 10-27
(2) Percentage depletion	25,000	90,000	90,000	Example 10-28
Allowable expense	**$45,000**	**$105,000**	**$90,000**	Greater of (1) or (2)

---

[76]Percentage depletion in excess of basis is an AMT preference item.

CONCLUSION

This chapter describes and discusses how businesses recover the costs of their tangible and intangible assets. Cost recovery is important because it represents a significant tax deduction for many businesses. Businesses must routinely make choices that affect the amount and timing of these deductions. Further understanding cost recovery basics helps businesses determine how to compute and characterize the gain and loss they recognize when they sell or otherwise dispose of business assets. We address the interaction between cost recovery deductions and gain and loss on property dispositions in the next chapter.

Appendix A   MACRS Tables

TABLE 1   MACRS Half-Year Convention

	Depreciation Rate for Recovery Period					
Year	3-Year	5-Year	7-Year	10-Year	15-Year	20-Year
1	33.33%	20.00%	14.29%	10.00%	5.00%	3.750%
2	44.45	32.00	24.49	18.00	9.50	7.219
3	14.81	19.20	17.49	14.40	8.55	6.677
4	7.41	11.52	12.49	11.52	7.70	6.177
5		11.52	8.93	9.22	6.93	5.713
6		5.76	8.92	7.37	6.23	5.285
7			8.93	6.55	5.90	4.888
8			4.46	6.55	5.90	4.522
9				6.56	5.91	4.462
10				6.55	5.90	4.461
11				3.28	5.91	4.462
12					5.90	4.461
13					5.91	4.462
14					5.90	4.461
15					5.91	4.462
16					2.95	4.461
17						4.462
18						4.461
19						4.462
20						4.461
21						2.231

TABLE 2a   MACRS Mid-Quarter Convention: *For property placed in service during the first quarter*

	Depreciation Rate for Recovery Period	
Year	5-Year	7-Year
1	35.00%	25.00%
2	26.00	21.43
3	15.60	15.31
4	11.01	10.93
5	11.01	8.75
6	1.38	8.74
7		8.75
8		1.09

TABLE 2b   **MACRS Mid-Quarter Convention:** *For property placed in service during the second quarter*

Depreciation Rate for Recovery Period		
Year	5-Year	7-Year
1	25.00%	17.85%
2	30.00	23.47
3	18.00	16.76
4	11.37	11.97
5	11.37	8.87
6	4.26	8.87
7		8.87
8		3.34

TABLE 2c   **MACRS Mid-Quarter Convention:** *For property placed in service during the third quarter*

Depreciation Rate for Recovery Period		
Year	5-Year	7-Year
1	15.00%	10.71%
2	34.00	25.51
3	20.40	18.22
4	12.24	13.02
5	11.30	9.30
6	7.06	8.85
7		8.86
8		5.53

TABLE 2d   **MACRS-Mid Quarter Convention:** *For property placed in service during the fourth quarter*

Depreciation Rate for Recovery Period		
Year	5-Year	7-Year
1	5.00%	3.57%
2	38.00	27.55
3	22.80	19.68
4	13.68	14.06
5	10.94	10.04
6	9.58	8.73
7		8.73
8		7.64

TABLE 3 Residential Rental Property Mid-Month Convention Straight Line—27.5 Years

Year	Month Property Placed in Service											
	1	2	3	4	5	6	7	8	9	10	11	12
1	3.485%	3.182%	2.879%	2.576%	2.273%	1.970%	1.667%	1.364%	1.061%	0.758%	0.455%	0.152%
2–9	3.636	3.636	3.636	3.636	3.636	3.636	3.636	3.636	3.636	3.636	3.636	3.636
10	3.637	3.637	3.637	3.636	3.636	3.637	3.636	3.636	3.636	3.636	3.636	3.636
11	3.636	3.636	3.636	3.637	3.637	3.636	3.637	3.636	3.637	3.637	3.637	3.637
12	3.637	3.637	3.637	3.636	3.636	3.637	3.636	3.637	3.636	3.636	3.636	3.636
13	3.636	3.636	3.636	3.637	3.637	3.636	3.637	3.636	3.637	3.637	3.637	3.637
14	3.637	3.637	3.637	3.636	3.636	3.637	3.636	3.637	3.636	3.636	3.636	3.636
15	3.636	3.636	3.636	3.637	3.637	3.636	3.637	3.636	3.637	3.637	3.637	3.637
16	3.637	3.637	3.637	3.636	3.636	3.637	3.636	3.637	3.636	3.636	3.636	3.636
17	3.636	3.636	3.636	3.637	3.637	3.636	3.636	3.636	3.637	3.637	3.637	3.637
18	3.637	3.637	3.637	3.636	3.636	3.637	3.636	3.637	3.636	3.636	3.636	3.636
19	3.636	3.636	3.636	3.637	3.637	3.636	3.636	3.636	3.637	3.637	3.637	3.637
20	3.637	3.637	3.637	3.636	3.636	3.637	3.637	3.637	3.636	3.636	3.636	3.636
21	3.636	3.636	3.636	3.637	3.637	3.636	3.636	3.636	3.637	3.637	3.637	3.637
22	3.637	3.637	3.637	3.636	3.636	3.637	3.637	3.637	3.636	3.636	3.636	3.636
23	3.636	3.636	3.636	3.637	3.637	3.636	3.636	3.636	3.637	3.637	3.637	3.637
24	3.637	3.637	3.637	3.636	3.636	3.637	3.637	3.637	3.636	3.636	3.636	3.636
25	3.636	3.636	3.636	3.637	3.637	3.636	3.636	3.636	3.637	3.637	3.637	3.637
26	3.637	3.637	3.637	3.636	3.636	3.637	3.637	3.637	3.636	3.636	3.636	3.636
27	3.636	3.636	3.636	3.636	3.636	3.636	3.636	3.636	3.636	3.636	3.636	3.636
28	1.97	2.273	2.576	2.879	3.182	3.485	3.636	3.636	3.636	3.636	3.636	3.636
29							0.152	0.455	0.758	1.061	1.364	1.667

TABLE 4 Nonresidential Real Property Mid-Month Convention Straight Line—31.5 Years (for assets placed in service before May 13, 1993)

Year	Month Property Placed in Service											
	1	2	3	4	5	6	7	8	9	10	11	12
1	3.042%	2.778%	2.513%	2.249%	1.984%	1.720%	1.455%	1.190%	0.926%	0.661%	0.397%	0.132%
2–7	3.175	3.175	3.175	3.175	3.175	3.175	3.175	3.175	3.175	3.175	3.175	3.175
8	3.175	3.174	3.175	3.174	3.175	3.174	3.175	3.175	3.175	3.175	3.175	3.175
9	3.174	3.175	3.174	3.175	3.174	3.175	3.174	3.175	3.174	3.174	3.174	3.175
10	3.175	3.174	3.175	3.174	3.175	3.174	3.175	3.174	3.175	3.175	3.175	3.174
11	3.174	3.175	3.174	3.175	3.174	3.175	3.174	3.175	3.174	3.174	3.174	3.175
12	3.175	3.174	3.175	3.174	3.175	3.174	3.175	3.174	3.175	3.175	3.175	3.174
13	3.174	3.175	3.174	3.175	3.174	3.175	3.174	3.175	3.174	3.174	3.174	3.175
14	3.175	3.175	3.175	3.174	3.175	3.174	3.175	3.174	3.175	3.175	3.175	3.174
15	3.174	3.175	3.175	3.175	3.174	3.175	3.174	3.175	3.174	3.174	3.174	3.175
16	3.175	3.174	3.174	3.174	3.175	3.174	3.175	3.174	3.175	3.175	3.175	3.174
17	3.174	3.175	3.175	3.175	3.174	3.175	3.174	3.175	3.174	3.174	3.174	3.175
18	3.175	3.174	3.174	3.174	3.175	3.174	3.175	3.174	3.175	3.175	3.175	3.174
19	3.174	3.175	3.175	3.175	3.174	3.175	3.174	3.175	3.174	3.174	3.174	3.175
20	3.175	3.174	3.174	3.174	3.175	3.174	3.175	3.174	3.175	3.175	3.175	3.174
21	3.174	3.175	3.175	3.175	3.174	3.175	3.174	3.175	3.174	3.174	3.174	3.175
22	3.175	3.174	3.174	3.174	3.175	3.174	3.175	3.174	3.175	3.175	3.175	3.174
23	3.174	3.175	3.175	3.175	3.174	3.175	3.174	3.115	3.174	3.174	3.174	3.175
24	3.175	3.174	3.174	3.174	3.175	3.174	3.175	3.175	3.175	3.175	3.175	3.174
25	3.174	3.175	3.175	3.175	3.174	3.175	3.174	3.174	3.174	3.174	3.174	3.175
26	3.175	3.174	3.174	3.174	3.175	3.174	3.175	3.175	3.175	3.175	3.175	3.174
27	3.174	3.175	3.175	3.175	3.174	3.175	3.174	3.174	3.174	3.174	3.174	3.175
28	3.175	3.174	3.174	3.174	3.175	3.174	3.175	3.175	3.175	3.175	3.175	3.174
29	3.174	3.175	3.175	3.175	3.174	3.175	3.174	3.174	3.174	3.174	3.174	3.175
30	3.175	3.174	3.174	3.174	3.175	3.174	3.175	3.175	3.175	3.175	3.175	3.174
31	3.174	3.175	3.175	3.175	3.174	3.175	3.174	3.174	3.174	3.174	3.174	3.175
32	1.720	1.984	2.249	2.513	2.778	3.042	3.175	3.175	3.175	3.174	3.175	3.174
33							0.132	0.397	0.661	0.926	1.190	1.455

TABLE 5 Nonresidential Real Property Mid-Month Convention Straight Line—39 Years (for assets placed in service on or after May 13, 1993)

Year	Month Property Placed in Service											
	1	2	3	4	5	6	7	8	9	10	11	12
1	2.461%	2.247%	2.033%	1.819%	1.605%	1.391%	1.177%	0.963%	0.749%	0.535%	0.321%	0.107%
2–39	2.564	2.564	2.564	2.564	2.564	2.564	2.564	2.564	2.564	2.564	2.564	2.564
40	0.107	0.321	0.535	0.749	0.963	1.177	1.391	1.605	1.819	2.033	2.247	2.461

Summary

Describe the cost recovery methods for recovering the cost of personal property, real property, intangible assets, and natural resources.   LO 10-1

- Tangible personal and real property (depreciation), intangibles (amortization), and natural resources (depletion) are all subject to cost recovery.
- An asset's initial basis is the amount that is subject to cost recovery. Generally, an asset's initial basis is its purchase price, plus the cost of any other expenses incurred to get the asset in working condition.
- The taxpayer's basis of assets acquired in a nontaxable exchange is the same basis the taxpayer transferred to acquire the property received.
- Expenditures on an asset are either expensed currently or capitalized as a new asset. Expenditures for routine or general maintenance of the asset are expensed currently. Expenditures that better, restore, or adapt an asset to a new use are capitalized.
- When acquiring a business and purchasing a bundle of property, the basis of each asset is determined as the fair market value of the asset.

Determine the applicable cost recovery (depreciation) life, method, and convention for tangible personal and real property and the deduction allowable under basic MACRS.   LO 10-2

- Tax depreciation is calculated under the Modified Accelerated Cost Recovery System (MACRS).
- MACRS for tangible personal property is based upon recovery period (Rev. Proc. 87-56), method (200 percent declining balance, 150 percent declining balance, and straight-line), and convention (half-year or mid-quarter).
- Real property is divided into two groups for tax purposes: residential rental and nonresidential. The recovery period is 27.5 years for residential property and 31.5 years or 39 years for nonresidential property, depending on when the property was placed in service. The depreciation method is straight-line and the convention is mid-month.

Calculate the deduction allowable under the additional special cost recovery rules (§179, bonus, and listed property).   LO 10-3

- §179 allows taxpayers to expense tangible personal property. The deduction is limited by the amount of property placed in service and taxable income.
- Bonus depreciation allows taxpayers to immediately deduct 100 percent of qualified property in the year of acquisition.
- Listed property includes automobiles, other means of transportation, and assets that tend to be used for both business and personal purposes. Depreciation is limited to the expense multiplied by business-use percentage. Special rules apply if business use is less than or equal to 50 percent.
- Additional limitations apply to luxury automobiles.

Calculate the deduction for amortization.   LO 10-4

- Intangible assets (such as patents, goodwill, and trademarks) have their costs recovered through amortization.
- Intangible assets are amortized (straight-line method) using the full-month convention.
- Intangibles are divided into four types (§197 purchased intangibles, start-up costs and organizational expenditures, research and experimentation, and self-created intangibles).

Explain cost recovery of natural resources and the allowable depletion methods.   LO 10-5

- Depletion allows a taxpayer to recover his or her capital investment in natural resources.
- Two methods of depletion are available, and the taxpayer must calculate both and take the one that results in the larger depletion deduction each year.
- Cost depletion allows taxpayers to estimate number of units and then allocate a pro rata share of the basis to each unit extracted during the year.
- Percentage depletion allows the taxpayer to take a statutory determined percentage of gross income as an expense. Deductions are not limited to basis.

KEY TERMS

adjusted basis (10-3)

amortization (10-2)

bonus depreciation (10-21)

cost depletion (10-38)

cost recovery (10-2)

covenant not to compete (10-32)

depletion (10-2)

depreciation (10-2)

full-month convention (10-32)

half-year convention (10-9)

intangible assets (10-2)

listed property (10-23)

luxury automobile (10-26)

mid-month convention (10-15)

mid-quarter convention (10-9)

Modified Accelerated Cost Recovery
  System (MACRS) (10-6)

organizational expenditures (10-33)

percentage depletion (10-39)

personal property (10-7)

real property (10-7)

recovery period (10-7)

research and experimentation (R&E)
  costs (10-32)

§179 expense (10-17)

§197 intangibles (10-32)

start-up costs (10-35)

tax basis (10-2)

DISCUSSION QUESTIONS

Discussion Questions are available in Connect®.

LO 10-1   1. Explain why certain long-lived assets are capitalized and recovered over time rather than immediately expensed.

LO 10-1   2. Explain the differences and similarities between personal property, real property, intangible property, and natural resources. Also, provide an example of each type of asset.

LO 10-1   3. Explain the similarities and dissimilarities between depreciation, amortization, and depletion. Describe the cost recovery method used for each of the four asset types (personal property, real property, intangible property, and natural resources).

LO 10-1   4. Is an asset's initial or cost basis simply its purchase price? Explain.

LO 10-1   5. Compare and contrast the basis of property acquired via purchase, conversion from personal use to business or rental use, nontaxable exchange, gift, and inheritance.

LO 10-1   6. Explain why the expenses incurred to get an asset in place and operable should be included in the asset's basis.

LO 10-1   7. Graber Corporation runs a long-haul trucking business. Graber incurs the following expenses: replacement tires, oil changes, and a transmission overhaul. Which of these expenditures may be deducted currently and which must be capitalized? Explain.

LO 10-2   8. MACRS depreciation requires the use of a recovery period, method, and convention to depreciate tangible personal property assets. Briefly explain why each is important to the calculation.

LO 10-2   9. Can a taxpayer with very little current-year income choose to not claim any depreciation deduction for the current year and thus save depreciation deductions for the future when the taxpayer expects to be more profitable?

planning **LO 10-2**   10. What depreciation methods are available for tangible personal property? Explain the characteristics of a business likely to adopt each method.

LO 10-2   11. If a business places several different assets in service during the year, must it use the same depreciation method for all assets? If not, what restrictions apply to the business's choices of depreciation methods?

LO 10-2   12. Describe how you would determine the MACRS recovery period for an asset if you did not already know it.

13. Compare and contrast the recovery periods used by MACRS and those used under generally accepted accounting principles (GAAP). `LO 10-2` research

14. What are the two depreciation conventions that apply to tangible personal property under MACRS? Explain why Congress provides two methods. `LO 10-2`

15. A business buys two identical tangible personal property assets for the same price. It buys one at the beginning of the year and one at the end of the year. Under what conditions would the taxpayer's depreciation on each asset be exactly the same? Under what conditions would it be different? `LO 10-2`

16. AAA Inc. acquired a machine in year 1. In May of year 3, it sold the asset. Can AAA find its year 3 depreciation percentage for the machine on the MACRS table? If not, what adjustment must AAA make to its full-year depreciation percentage to determine its year 3 depreciation? `LO 10-2`

17. There are two recovery period classifications for real property. What reasons might Congress have to allow residential real estate a shorter recovery period than nonresidential real property? `LO 10-2`

18. Discuss why Congress has instructed taxpayers to depreciate real property using the mid-month convention as opposed to the half-year convention used for tangible personal property. `LO 10-2`

19. If a taxpayer has owned a building for 10 years and decides that it should make significant improvements to the building, what is the recovery period for the improvements? `LO 10-2` research

20. Compare and contrast the differences between computing depreciation deduction for tangible personal property and computing depreciation deduction for real property under both the regular tax and alternative tax systems. `LO 10-2`

21. Discuss how the property limitation restricts large businesses from taking the §179 expense. `LO 10-3`

22. Explain the two limitations placed on the §179 deduction. How are they similar? How are they different? `LO 10-3`

23. Compare and contrast the types of businesses that would and would not benefit from the §179 expense. `LO 10-3`

24. What strategies will help a business maximize its current depreciation deductions (including §179)? Why might a taxpayer choose *not* to maximize its current depreciation deductions? `LO 10-3`

25. Why might a business claim a reduced §179 expense amount in the current year rather than claiming the maximum amount available? `LO 10-3`

26. Describe assets that are considered to be listed property. Why do you think Congress requires them to be "listed"? `LO 10-3`

27. Are taxpayers allowed to claim depreciation deduction on assets they use for both business and personal purposes? What are the tax consequences if the business use drops from above 50 percent in one year to below 50 percent in the next? `LO 10-3`

28. Discuss why Congress limits the amount of depreciation deduction businesses may claim on certain automobiles. `LO 10-3`

29. Compare and contrast how a Land Rover SUV and a Mercedes Benz sedan are treated under the luxury auto rules. Also include a discussion of the similarities and differences in available §179 expense. `LO 10-3`

30. What is a §197 intangible? How do taxpayers recover the costs of these intangibles? How do taxpayers recover the cost of a §197 intangible that expires (such as a covenant not to compete)? `LO 10-4`

LO 10-4   31. Compare and contrast the tax and financial accounting treatment of goodwill. Are taxpayers allowed to deduct amounts associated with self-created goodwill?

LO 10-4   32. Compare and contrast the similarities and differences between organizational expenditures and start-up costs for tax purposes.

LO 10-4   33. Discuss the method used to determine the amount of organizational expenditures or start-up costs that may be immediately expensed in the year a taxpayer begins business.

LO 10-4   34. Explain the amortization convention applicable to intangible assets.

LO 10-4   35. Compare and contrast the recovery periods of §197 intangibles, organizational expenditures, start-up costs, and research and experimentation expenses.

LO 10-5   36. Compare and contrast the cost and percentage depletion methods for recovering the costs of natural resources. What are the similarities and differences between the two methods?

LO 10-5   37. Explain why percentage depletion has been referred to as a government subsidy.

PROBLEMS

Select problems are available in Connect®.

LO 10-1   38. Jose purchased a delivery van for his business through an online auction. His winning bid for the van was $24,500. In addition, Jose incurred the following expenses before using the van: shipping costs of $650; paint to match the other fleet vehicles at a cost of $1,000; registration costs of $3,200, which included $3,000 of sales tax and a registration fee of $200; wash and detailing for $50; and an engine tune-up for $250. What is Jose's cost basis for the delivery van?

LO 10-1

research

39. Emily purchased a building to store inventory for her business. The purchase price was $760,000. Emily also paid legal fees of $300 to acquire the building. In March, Emily incurred $2,000 to repair minor leaks in the roof (from storm damage earlier in the month) and $5,000 to make the interior suitable for her finished goods. What is Emily's cost basis in the new building?

LO 10-1

research

40. In January, Prahbu purchases a new machine for use in an existing production line of his manufacturing business for $90,000. Assume that the machine is a unit of property and is not a material or supply. Prahbu pays $2,500 to install the machine, and after the machine is installed, he pays $1,300 to perform a critical test on the machine to ensure that it will operate in accordance with quality standards. On November 1, the critical test is complete, and Prahbu places the machine in service on the production line. On December 3, Prahbu pays another $3,300 to perform periodic quality control testing after the machine is placed in service. How much will Prahbu be required to capitalize as the cost of the machine?

LO 10-1   41. Dennis contributed business assets to a new business in exchange for stock in the company. The exchange did not qualify as a nontaxable exchange. The fair market value of these assets was $287,000 on the contribution date. Dennis's original basis in the assets he contributed was $143,000, and the accumulated depreciation on the assets was $78,000.

a) What is the business's basis in the assets it received from Dennis?

b) What would be the business's basis if the transaction qualified as a nontaxable exchange?

LO 10-1   42. Brittany started a law practice as a sole proprietor. She owned a computer, printer, desk, and file cabinet she purchased during law school (several years ago) that she is planning to use in her business. What is the depreciable basis that Brittany should use in her business for each asset, given the following information?

Asset	Purchase Price	FMV at Time Converted to Business Use
Computer	$5,500	$3,800
Printer	3,300	3,150
Desk	4,200	4,000
File cabinet	3,200	3,225

43. Meg O'Brien received a gift of some small-scale jewelry manufacturing equipment **LO 10-1** that her father had used for personal purposes for many years. Her father originally purchased the equipment for $1,500. Because the equipment is out of production and no longer available, the property is currently worth $4,000. Meg has decided to begin a new jewelry manufacturing trade or business. What is her depreciable basis for depreciating the equipment?

44. Gary inherited a Maine summer cabin on 10 acres from his grandmother. His grand- **LO 10-1** parents originally purchased the property for $500 in 1950 and built the cabin at a cost of $10,000 in 1965. His grandfather died in 1980 and when his grandmother recently passed away, the property was appraised at $500,000 for the land and $700,000 for the cabin. Since Gary doesn't currently live in New England, he decided that it would be best to put the property to use as a rental. What is Gary's basis in the land and in the cabin?

45. Wanting to finalize a sale before year-end, on December 29, WR Outfitters sold to **LO 10-1** Bob a warehouse and the land for $125,000. The appraised fair market value of the warehouse was $75,000, and the appraised value of the land was $100,000.

a) What is Bob's basis in the warehouse and in the land?

b) What would be Bob's basis in the warehouse and in the land if the appraised value of the warehouse was $50,000 and the appraised value of the land was $125,000?

c) Which appraisal would Bob likely prefer?

46. At the beginning of the year, Poplock began a calendar-year dog boarding business **LO 10-2** called Griff's Palace. Poplock bought and placed in service the following assets during the year:

Asset	Date Acquired	Cost Basis
Computer equipment	3/23	$ 5,000
Dog-grooming furniture	5/12	7,000
Pickup truck	9/17	10,000
Commercial building	10/11	270,000
Land (one acre)	10/11	80,000

Assuming Poplock does not elect §179 expensing and elects not to use bonus depreciation, answer the following questions:

a) What is Poplock's year 1 depreciation deduction for each asset?

b) What is Poplock's year 2 depreciation deduction for each asset?

47. DLW Corporation acquired and placed in service the following assets during the year: **LO 10-2**

Asset	Date Acquired	Cost Basis
Computer equipment	2/17	$ 10,000
Furniture	5/12	17,000
Commercial building	11/1	270,000

Assuming DLW does not elect §179 expensing and elects not to use bonus depreciation, answer the following questions:

a) What is DLW's year 1 cost recovery for each asset?

b) What is DLW's year 3 cost recovery for each asset if DLW sells all of these assets on 1/23 of year 3?

 48. At the beginning of the year, Dee began a calendar-year business and placed in service the following assets during the year:

Asset	Date Acquired	Cost Basis
Computer equipment	3/23	$ 5,000
Furniture	5/12	7,000
Pickup truck	9/15	10,000
Commercial building	10/11	270,000

Assuming Dee does not elect §179 expensing and elects not to use bonus depreciation, answer the following questions:

a) What is Dee's year 1 cost recovery for each asset?

b) What is Dee's year 2 cost recovery for each asset?

 49. Parley needs a new truck to help him expand Parley's Plumbing Palace. Business has been booming and Parley would like to accelerate his tax deductions as much as possible (ignore §179 expense and bonus depreciation for this problem). On April 1, Parley purchased a new delivery van for $25,000. It is now September 26 and Parley, already in need of another vehicle, has found a deal on buying a truck for $22,000 (all fees included). The dealer tells him if he doesn't buy the truck (Option 1), it will be gone tomorrow. There is an auction (Option 2) scheduled for October 5 where Parley believes he can get a similar truck for $21,500, but there is also a $500 auction fee. Parley makes no other asset acquisitions during the year.

a) Which option allows Parley to generate more depreciation deductions this year (the vehicles are not considered to be luxury autos)?

b) Assume the original facts, except that the delivery van was placed in service one day earlier on March 31 rather than April 1. Which option generates more depreciation deduction?

LO 10-2 50. Way Corporation disposed of the following tangible personal property assets in the current year. Assume that the delivery truck is not a luxury auto. Calculate Way Corporation's 2018 depreciation deduction (ignore §179 expense and bonus depreciation for this problem).

Asset	Date Acquired	Date Sold	Convention	Original Basis
Furniture (7-year)	5/12/14	7/15/18	HY	$ 55,000
Machinery (7-year)	3/23/15	3/15/18	MQ	72,000
Delivery truck* (5-year)	9/17/16	3/13/18	HY	20,000
Machinery (7-year)	10/11/17	8/11/18	MQ	270,000
Computer (5-year)	10/11/18	12/15/18	HY	80,000

*Used 100 percent for business.

LO 10-2 51. On November 10 of year 1 Javier purchased a building, including the land it was on, to assemble his new equipment. The total cost of the purchase was $1,200,000; $300,000 was allocated to the basis of the land and the remaining $900,000 was allocated to the basis of the building.

a) Using MACRS, what is Javier's depreciation deduction on the building for years 1 through 3?

b) What would be the year 3 depreciation deduction if the building was sold on August 1 of year 3?

c) Answer the question in part (a), except assume the building was purchased and placed in service on March 3 instead of November 10.

d) Answer the question in part (a), except assume that the building is residential property.

e) What would be the depreciation for 2018, 2019, and 2020 if the property were nonresidential property purchased and placed in service November 10, 2001 (assume the same original basis)?

52. Carl purchased an apartment complex for $1.1 million on March 17 of year 1. Of the purchase price, $300,000 was attributable to the land the complex sits on. He also installed new furniture into half of the units at a cost of $60,000.

a) What is Carl's allowable depreciation deduction for his real property for years 1 and 2?

b) What is Carl's allowable depreciation deduction for year 3 if the real property is sold on January 2 of year 3?

53. Evergreen Corporation (calendar-year-end) acquired the following assets during the current year:

Asset	Date Placed in Service	Original Basis
Machinery	October 25	$ 70,000
Computer equipment	February 3	10,000
Used delivery truck*	August 17	23,000
Furniture	April 22	150,000

*The delivery truck is not a luxury automobile.

a) What is the allowable MACRS depreciation on Evergreen's property in the current year assuming Evergreen does not elect §179 expense and elects out of bonus depreciation?

b) What would be the allowable MACRS depreciation on Evergreen's property in the current year if Evergreen does not elect out of bonus depreciation?

54. Convers Corporation (calendar-year-end) acquired the following assets during the current tax year:

Asset	Date Placed in Service	Original Basis
Machinery	October 25	$ 70,000
Computer equipment	February 3	10,000
Delivery truck*	March 17	23,000
Furniture	April 22	150,000
Total		$253,000

*The delivery truck is not a luxury automobile.

In addition to these assets, Convers installed new flooring (qualified improvement property) to its office building on May 12 at a cost of $300,000.

a) What is the allowable MACRS depreciation on Convers's property in the current year assuming Convers does not elect §179 expense and elects out of bonus depreciation?

b) What is the allowable MACRS depreciation on Convers's property in the current year assuming Convers does not elect out of bonus depreciation (but does not take §179 expense)

LO 10-2 **LO 10-3** 55. Harris Corp. is a technology start-up and is in its second year of operations. The company didn't purchase any assets this year but purchased the following assets in the prior year:

Asset	Placed in Service	Basis
Office equipment	August 14	$10,000
Manufacturing equipment	April 15	68,000
Computer system	June 1	16,000
Total		$94,000

Harris did not know depreciation was tax deductible until it hired an accountant this year and didn't claim any depreciation deduction in its first year of operation.

a) What is the maximum amount of depreciation deduction Harris Corp. can deduct in its second year of operation?

b) What is the basis of the office equipment at the end of the second year?

LO 10-2 **LO 10-3** 56. AMP Corporation (calendar-year-end) has 2018 taxable income of $900,000 for purposes of computing the §179 expense. During 2018, AMP acquired the following assets:

Asset	Placed in Service	Basis
Machinery	September 12	$1,550,000
Computer equipment	February 10	365,000
Office building	April 2	480,000
Total		$2,395,000

a) What is the maximum amount of §179 expense AMP may deduct for 2018?

b) What is the maximum total depreciation including §179 expense, that AMP may deduct in 2018 on the assets it placed in service in 2018 assuming no bonus depreciation?

LO 10-2 **LO 10-3** 57. Assume that TDW Corporation (calendar-year-end) has 2018 taxable income of $650,000 for purposes of computing the §179 expense. The company acquired the following assets during 2018:

Asset	Placed in Service	Basis
Machinery	September 12	$1,270,000
Computer equipment	February 10	263,000
Furniture	April 2	880,000
Total		$2,413,000

a) What is the maximum amount of §179 expense TDW may deduct for 2018?

b) What is the maximum total depreciation including §179 expense, that TDW may deduct in 2018 on the assets it placed in service in 2018 assuming no bonus depreciation?

LO 10-2 **LO 10-3** 58. Assume that Timberline Corporation has 2018 taxable income of $240,000 for purposes of computing the §179 expense. It acquired the following assets in 2018:

Asset	Purchase Date	Basis
Furniture (7-year)	December 1	$ 450,000
Computer equipment (5-year)	February 28	90,000
Copier (5-year)	July 15	30,000
Machinery (7-year)	May 22	480,000
Total		$1,050,000

a) What is the maximum amount of §179 expense Timberline may deduct for 2018? What is Timberline's §179 carryforward to 2019, if any?

b) What would Timberline's maximum depreciation deduction be for 2018 assuming no bonus depreciation?

c) What would Timberline's maximum depreciation deduction be for 2018 if the machinery cost $3,000,000 instead of $480,000 and assuming no bonus depreciation?

59. Dain's Diamond Bit Drilling purchased the following assets this year. Assume its taxable income for the year was $53,000 for purposes of computing the §179 expense (assume no bonus depreciation).

Asset	Purchase Date	Original Basis
Drill bits (5-year)	January 25	$ 90,000
Drill bits (5-year)	July 25	95,000
Commercial building	April 22	220,000

a) What is the maximum amount of §179 expense Dain may deduct for the year?

b) What is Dain's maximum depreciation deduction for the year (including §179 expense)?

c) If the January drill bits' original basis was $2,875,000, what is the maximum amount of §179 expense Dain may deduct for the year?

d) If the January drill bits' original basis was $3,875,000, what is the maximum amount of §179 expense Dain may deduct for the year?

60. Assume that ACW Corporation has 2018 taxable income of $1,000,000 for purposes of computing the §179 expense. The company acquired the following assets during 2018 (assume no bonus depreciation):

Asset	Placed in Service	Basis
Machinery	September 12	$ 470,000
Computer equipment	February 10	70,000
Delivery truck	August 21	93,000
Qualified improvement property	April 2	$1,380,000
Total		$2,013,000

a) What is the maximum amount of §179 expense ACW may deduct for 2018?

b) What is the maximum *total* depreciation that ACW may deduct in 2018 on the assets it placed in service in 2018?

61. Chaz Corporation has taxable income in 2018 of $312,000 for purposes of computing the §179 expense and acquired the following assets during the year:

Asset	Placed in Service	Basis
Office furniture	September 12	$1,280,000
Computer equipment	February 10	930,000
Delivery truck	August 21	68,000
Total		$2,278,000

What is the maximum *total* depreciation deduction that Chaz may deduct in 2018?

62. Woolard Supplies (a sole proprietorship) has taxable income in 2018 of $240,000 before any depreciation deductions (§179, bonus, or MACRS) and placed some office furniture into service during the year. The furniture had been used previously by Liz Woolard (the owner of the business) before it was placed in service by the business.

Asset	Placed in Service	Basis
Office furniture (used)	March 20	$1,200,000

a) If Woolard elects $50,000 of §179, what is Woolard's total depreciation deduction for the year?

b) If Woolard elects the maximum amount of §179 for the year, what is the amount of deductible §179 expense for the year? What is the *total* depreciation that Woolard may deduct in 2018? What is Woolard's §179 carryforward amount to next year, if any?

c) Woolard is concerned about future limitations on its §179 expense. How much §179 expense should Woolard expense this year if it wants to maximize its depreciation this year and avoid any carryover to future years?

63. Assume that Sivart Corporation has 2018 taxable income of $1,750,000 for purposes of computing the §179 expense and acquired several assets during the year. The delivery truck was acquired in a nontaxable transaction.

Asset	Placed in Service	Basis
Machinery	June 12	$1,440,000
Computer equipment	February 10	70,000
Delivery truck—used	August 21	93,000
Furniture	April 2	310,000
Total		$1,913,000

a) What is the maximum amount of §179 expense Sivart may deduct for 2018?

b) What is the maximum *total* depreciation (§179, bonus, MACRS) that Sivart may deduct in 2018 on the assets it placed in service in 2018?

64. Acorn Construction (calendar-year-end C corporation) has had rapid expansion during the last half of the current year due to the housing market's recovery. The company has record income and would like to maximize its cost recovery deduction for the current year. Acorn provided you with the following information:

Asset	Placed in Service	Basis
New equipment and tools	August 20	$1,800,000
Used light duty trucks	October 17	1,500,000
Used machinery	November 6	525,000
Total		$3,825,000

The used assets had been contributed to the business by its owner in a nontaxable transaction.

a) What is Acorn's maximum cost recovery deduction in the current year?

b) What planning strategies would you advise Acorn to consider?

LO 10-3   65. Phil owns a ranch business and uses four-wheelers to do much of his work. Occasionally, though, he and his boys will go for a ride together as a family activity. During year 1, Phil put 765 miles on the four-wheeler that he bought on January 15 for $6,500. Of the miles driven, only 175 miles were for personal use. Assume four-wheelers qualify to be depreciated according to the five-year MACRS schedule and the four-wheeler was the only asset Phil purchased this year.

a) Calculate the allowable depreciation for year 1 (ignore the §179 expense and bonus depreciation).

b) Calculate the allowable depreciation for year 2 if total miles were 930 and personal use miles were 400 (ignore the §179 expense and bonus depreciation).

66. Assume that Ernesto purchased a digital camera on July 10 of year 1 for $3,000. In year 1, 80 percent of his computer usage was for his business and 20 percent was for personal photography activities. This was the only asset he placed in service during year 1. Ignoring any potential §179 expense and bonus depreciation, answer the questions for each of the following alternative scenarios:

    a) What is Ernesto's depreciation deduction for the camera in year 1?

    b) What would be Ernesto's depreciation deduction for the camera in year 2 if his year 2 usage was 75 percent business and 25 percent for personal use?

    c) What would be Ernesto's depreciation deduction for the camera in year 2 if his year 2 usage was 45 percent business and 55 percent for personal use?

    d) What would be Ernesto's depreciation deduction for the camera in year 2 if his year 2 usage was 30 percent business and 70 percent for personal use?

67. Lina purchased a new car for use in her business during 2018. The auto was the only business asset she purchased during the year and her business was extremely profitable. Calculate her maximum depreciation deductions (including §179 expense unless stated otherwise) for the automobile in 2018 and 2019 (Lina doesn't want to take bonus depreciation for 2018 or 2019) in the following alternative scenarios (assuming half-year convention for all):

    a) The vehicle cost $35,000 and business use is 100 percent (ignore §179 expense).

    b) The vehicle cost $80,000, and business use is 100 percent.

    c) The vehicle cost $80,000, and she used it 80 percent for business.

    d) The vehicle cost $80,000, and she used it 80 percent for business. She sold it on March 1 of year 2.

    e) The vehicle cost $80,000, and she used it 20 percent for business.

    f) The vehicle cost $80,000 and is an SUV that weighs 6,500 pounds. Business use was 100 percent.

68. Tater Meer purchased a new car for use in her business during 2018 for $75,000. The auto was the only business asset she purchased during the year and her business was very profitable. Calculate Tater's maximum depreciation deductions for the automobile in 2018 and 2019 under the following scenarios:

    a) Tater does not want to take §179 expense and she elects out of bonus depreciation.

    b) Tater wants to maximize her 2018 depreciation using bonus depreciation.

69. Burbank Corporation (calendar-year-end) acquired the following property this year:

Asset	Placed in Service	Basis
Used copier	November 12	$ 7,800
New computer equipment	June 6	14,000
Furniture	July 15	32,000
New delivery truck	October 28	19,000
Luxury auto	January 31	70,000
Total		$142,800

Burbank acquired the copier in a nontaxable transaction when the shareholder contributed the copier to the business in exchange for stock.

    a) Assuming no bonus or §179 expense, what is Burbank's maximum cost recovery deduction for this year?

    b) Assuming Burbank would like to maximize its cost recovery deductions by claiming bonus and §179 expense, which assets should Burbank immediately expense?

c) What is Burbank's maximum cost recovery deduction this year assuming it elects §179 expense and claims bonus depreciation?

LO 10-3

 research

70. Paul Vote purchased the following assets this year (ignore §179 expensing and bonus depreciation when answering the questions below):

Asset	Purchase Date	Basis
Machinery	May 12	$ 23,500
Computers	August 13	20,000
Warehouse	December 13	180,000

a) What is Paul's allowable MACRS depreciation for the property?

b) What is Paul's allowable alternative minimum tax (AMT) depreciation for the property? You will need to find the AMT depreciation tables to compute the depreciation.

LO 10-4

research

71. After several profitable years running her business, Ingrid decided to acquire the assets of a small competing business. On May 1 of year 1, Ingrid acquired the competing business for $300,000. Ingrid allocated $50,000 of the purchase price to goodwill. Ingrid's business reports its taxable income on a calendar-year basis.

a) How much amortization expense on the goodwill can Ingrid deduct in year 1, year 2, and year 3?

b) In lieu of the original facts, assume that Ingrid purchased only a phone list with a useful life of 5 years for $10,000. How much amortization expense on the phone list can Ingrid deduct in year 1, year 2, and year 3?

LO 10-4

72. Juliette formed a new business to sell sporting goods this year. The business opened its doors to customers on June 1. Determine the amount of start-up costs Juliette can immediately expense (not including the portion of the expenditures that are amortized over 180 months) this year in the following alternative scenarios:

a) She incurred start-up costs of $2,000.

b) She incurred start-up costs of $45,000.

c) She incurred start-up costs of $53,500.

d) She incurred start-up costs of $63,000.

e) How would you answer parts (a) through (d) if she formed a partnership or a corporation and she incurred the same amount of organizational expenditures rather than start-up costs (how much of the organizational expenditures would be immediately deductible)?

LO 10-4

73. Nicole organized a new corporation. The corporation began business on April 1 of year 1. She made the following expenditures associated with getting the corporation started:

Expense	Date	Amount
Attorney fees for articles of incorporation	February 10	$32,000
March 1–March 30 wages	March 30	4,500
March 1–March 30 rent	March 30	2,000
Stock issuance costs	April 1	20,000
April 1–May 30 wages	May 30	12,000

a) What is the total amount of the start-up costs and organizational expenditures for Nicole's corporation?

b) What amount of the start-up costs and organizational expenditures may the corporation immediately expense in year 1 (excluding the portion of the expenditures that are amortized over 180 months)?

c) What amount can the corporation deduct as amortization expense for the organizational expenditures and for the start-up costs for year 1 [not including the amount determined in part (b)]?

d) What would be the total allowable organizational expenditures if Nicole started a sole proprietorship instead of a corporation?

74. Bethany incurred $20,000 in research and experimental costs for developing a specialized product during July of year 1. Bethany went through a lot of trouble and spent $10,000 in legal fees to receive a patent for the product in August of year 3. Bethany expects the patent to have a remaining useful life of 10 years.

a) What amount of research and experimental expenses for year 1, year 2, and year 3 may Bethany deduct if she elects to amortize the expenses over 60 months?

b) How much *patent* amortization expense would Bethany deduct in year 3, assuming she elected to amortize the research and experimental costs over 60 months?

c) If Bethany chose to capitalize but *not* amortize the research and experimental expenses she incurred in year 1, how much patent amortization expense would Bethany deduct in year 3?

75. Last Chance Mine (LC) purchased a coal deposit for $750,000. It estimated it would extract 12,000 tons of coal from the deposit. LC mined the coal and sold it, reporting gross receipts of $1 million, $3 million, and $2 million for years 1 through 3, respectively. During years 1–3, LC reported net income (loss) from the coal deposit activity in the amount of ($20,000), $500,000, and $450,000, respectively. In years 1–3, LC actually extracted 13,000 tons of coal as follows:

(1) Tons of Coal	(2) Basis	Depletion (2)/(1) Rate	Tons Extracted per Year		
			Year 1	Year 2	Year 3
12,000	$750,000	$62.50	2,000	7,200	3,800

a) What is Last Chance's cost depletion for years 1, 2, and 3?

b) What is Last Chance's percentage depletion for each year (the applicable percentage for coal is 10 percent)?

c) Using the cost and percentage depletion computations from parts (a) and (b), what is Last Chance's actual depletion expense for each year?

COMPREHENSIVE PROBLEMS

Select problems are available with Connect®.

76. Karane Enterprises, a calendar-year manufacturer based in College Station, Texas, began business in 2017. In the process of setting up the business, Karane has acquired various types of assets. Below is a list of assets acquired during 2017:

tax forms

Asset	Cost	Date Placed in Service
Office furniture	$ 150,000	02/03/2017
Machinery	1,560,000	07/22/2017
Used delivery truck*	40,000	08/17/2017

*Not considered a luxury automobile.

During 2017, Karane was very successful (and had no §179 limitations) and decided to acquire more assets this next year to increase its production capacity. These are the assets acquired during 2018:

Asset	Cost	Date Placed in Service
Computers & info. system	$ 400,000	03/31/2018
Luxury auto[†]	80,000	05/26/2018
Assembly equipment	1,200,000	08/15/2018
Storage building	700,000	11/13/2018

[†]Used 100% for business purposes.

Karane generated taxable income in 2018 of $1,732,500 for purposes of computing the §179 expense.

Required:

a) Compute the maximum 2017 depreciation deductions including §179 expense (ignoring bonus depreciation).

b) Compute the maximum 2018 depreciation deductions including §179 expense (ignoring bonus depreciation).

c) Compute the maximum 2018 depreciation deductions including §179 expense, but now assume that Karane would like to take bonus depreciation.

d) Now assume that during 2018, Karane decides to buy a competitor's assets for a purchase price of $1,350,000. Compute the maximum 2018 cost recovery including §179 expense and bonus depreciation. Karane purchased the following assets for the lump-sum purchase price.

Asset	Cost	Date Placed in Service
Inventory	$220,000	09/15/2018
Office furniture	230,000	09/15/2018
Machinery	250,000	09/15/2018
Patent	198,000	09/15/2018
Goodwill	2,000	09/15/2018
Building	430,000	09/15/2018
Land	20,000	09/15/2018

e) Complete Part I of Form 4562 for part (b) (use the most current form available).

tax forms

77. While completing undergraduate school work in information systems, Dallin Bourne and Michael Banks decided to start a technology support company called eSys Answers. During year 1, they bought the following assets and incurred the following start-up fees:

Year 1 Assets	Purchase Date	Basis
Computers (5-year)	October 30, Y1	$15,000
Office equipment (7-year)	October 30, Y1	10,000
Furniture (7-year)	October 30, Y1	3,000
Start-up costs	October 30, Y1	17,000

In April of year 2, they decided to purchase a customer list from a company providing virtually the same services, started by fellow information systems students preparing to graduate. The customer list cost $10,000 and the sale was completed on April 30. During their summer break, Dallin and Michael passed on internship opportunities in an attempt to really grow their business into something they could do full-time after graduation. In the summer, they purchased a small van (for transportation, not considered a luxury auto) and a pinball machine (to help attract new employees). They bought the van on June 15, Y2, for $15,000 and spent $3,000 getting it ready to put into service. The pinball machine cost $4,000 and was placed in service on July 1, Y2.

Year 2 Assets	Purchase Date	Basis
Van	June 15, Y2	$18,000
Pinball machine (7-year)	July 1, Y2	4,000
Customer list	April 30, Y2	10,000

Assume that eSys Answers does not claim any §179 expense or bonus depreciation.

a) What are the maximum cost recovery deductions for eSys Answers for Y1 and Y2?

b) Complete eSys Answers's Form 4562 for Y1 (use the most current form available).

c) What is eSys Answers's basis in each of its assets at the end of Y2?

78. Diamond Mountain was originally thought to be one of the few places in North America to contain diamonds, so Diamond Mountain Inc. (DM) purchased the land for $1,000,000. Later, DM discovered that the only diamonds on the mountain had been planted there and the land was worthless for mining. DM engineers discovered a new survey technology and discovered a silver deposit estimated at 5,000 pounds on Diamond Mountain. DM immediately bought new drilling equipment and began mining the silver.

In years 1–3 following the opening of the mine, DM had net (gross) income of $200,000 ($700,000), $400,000 ($1,100,000), and $600,000 ($1,450,000), respectively. Mining amounts for each year were as follows: 750 pounds (year 1), 1,450 pounds (year 2), and 1,800 pounds (year 3). At the end of year 2, engineers used the new technology (which had been improving over time) and estimated there was still an estimated 6,000 pounds of silver deposits.

DM also began a research and experimentation project with the hopes of gaining a patent for its new survey technology. Diamond Mountain Inc. chose to capitalize research and experimentation expenditures and to amortize the costs over 60 months or until it obtained a patent on its technology. In March of year 1, DM spent $95,000 on research and experimentation. DM spent another $75,000 in February of year 2 for research and experimentation. In September of year 2, DM paid $20,000 of legal fees and was granted the patent in October of year 2 (the entire process of obtaining a patent was unusually fast).

Answer the following questions regarding DM's activities (assume that DM tries to maximize its deductions if given a choice).

a) What is DM's depletion expense for years 1–3?

b) What is DM's research and experimentation amortization for years 1 and 2?

c) What is DM's basis in its patent and what is its amortization for the patent in year 2?

11 Property Dispositions

Learning Objectives

Upon completing this chapter, you should be able to:

LO 11-1 Calculate the amount of gain or loss recognized on the disposition of assets used in a trade or business.

LO 11-2 Describe the general character types of gain or loss recognized on property dispositions.

LO 11-3 Calculate depreciation recapture.

LO 11-4 Describe the tax treatment of unrecaptured §1250 gains.

LO 11-5 Describe the tax treatment of §1231 gains or losses, including the §1231 netting process.

LO 11-6 Explain common exceptions to the general rule that realized gains and losses are recognized currently.

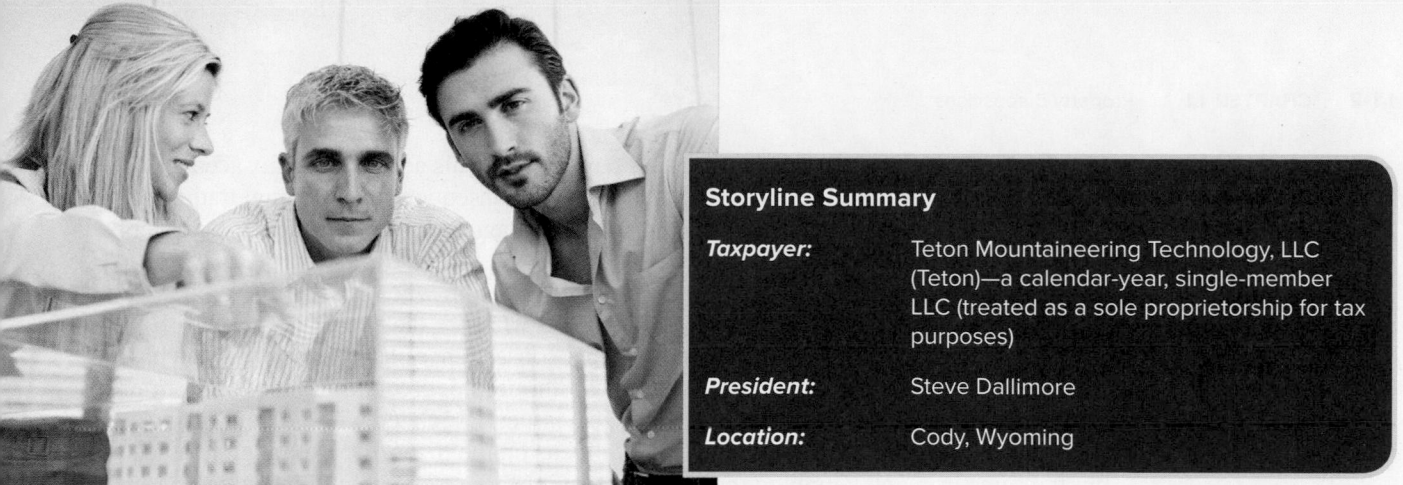

©Frank and Helena/Getty Images

Storyline Summary

Taxpayer:	Teton Mountaineering Technology, LLC (Teton)—a calendar-year, single-member LLC (treated as a sole proprietorship for tax purposes)
President:	Steve Dallimore
Location:	Cody, Wyoming

By most measures, Teton Mountaineering Technology, LLC (Teton), has become a success, with sponsored climbers summiting the world's highest peaks, satisfied customers creating brand loyalty, and profitability improving steadily. However, after several years of operation, some of Teton's machinery is wearing out and must be replaced. Further, because Teton has outgrown its manufacturing capacity, Steve is considering whether to expand the company's current facility or sell it and build a new one in a different location. Steve would like to know how any asset dispositions will affect Steve's tax bill.

Steve has found a willing buyer for some of Teton's land, and he has options for trading the land. For tax purposes, does it matter whether he sells or trades the land? Steve also has questions about how to best manage Teton's acquisitions and dispositions of real property. It all seems a bit overwhelming. . . . He picks up the phone and dials his tax accountant's number. ■

You can imagine why Steve might be eager to reach out to his accountant. Tax accounting widely impacts business decisions: What are the tax consequences of selling, trading, or even abandoning business assets? Are the tax consequences the same whether taxpayers sell machinery, inventory, or investment assets? Does it matter for tax purposes whether Teton is structured as a sole proprietorship or a corporation when it sells its warehouse? If Steve sells his personal sailboat, car, or furniture, what are the tax consequences?

In the previous chapter we explained the tax consequences associated with purchasing assets and recovering the cost of the assets through depreciation, amortization, or depletion. This chapter explores fundamental tax issues associated with property dispositions (sales, trades, or other dispositions). We focus on the disposition of tangible assets, but the same principles apply to the sale of intangible assets and natural resources.

LO 11-1 DISPOSITIONS

Taxpayers can dispose of assets in many ways. For example, a taxpayer could sell an asset, donate it to charity, trade it for a similar asset, take it to the landfill, or have it destroyed in a natural disaster. No matter how it is accomplished, every asset disposition triggers a realization event for tax purposes. To calculate the amount of gain or loss taxpayers realize when they sell assets, they must determine the amount realized on the sale and the *adjusted basis* of each asset they are selling.

Amount Realized

Simply put, the **amount realized** by a taxpayer from the sale or other disposition of an asset is everything of *value* received from the buyer *less* any selling costs.[1] Although taxpayers typically receive cash when they sell property, they may also accept marketable securities, notes receivable, similar assets, or any combination of these items as payment. Additionally, taxpayers selling assets such as real property subject to loans or mortgages may receive some debt relief. In this case, they would increase their amount realized by the amount of debt relief (the buyer's assumption of the seller's liability increases the seller's amount realized). The amount realized computation is captured in the following formula:

$$\text{Amount realized} = \text{Cash received} + \text{Fair market value of other property} + \text{Buyer's assumption of liabilities} - \text{Seller's expenses}$$

Example 11-1

Teton wants to upgrade its old manufacturing machinery that is wearing out. On November 1 of the current year, Teton sells the machinery for $230,000 cash and marketable securities valued at $70,500. Teton paid a broker $500 to find a buyer. What is Teton's amount realized on the sale of the machinery?

Answer: $300,000, computed as follows:

Description	Amount	Explanation
(1) Cash received	$230,000	
(2) Marketable securities received	70,500	
(3) Broker commission paid	(500)	
Amount realized	**$300,000**	(1) + (2) + (3)

Determination of Adjusted Basis

In the previous chapter, we discussed the basis for cost recovery and focused on purchased assets in which the initial basis is the asset's cost. However, taxpayers may acquire assets

[1]*S.C. Chapin,* CA-8, 50-1 USTC ¶9171.

without purchasing them. For example, a taxpayer may acquire an asset as a gift or as an inheritance. In either case, the taxpayer does not purchase the asset, so the taxpayer's initial basis in the asset must be computed as something other than purchase price. Although there are many situations when an asset's initial basis is not the asset's cost, we focus on three cases: gifts, inherited assets, and property converted from personal use to business use.

Gifts A gift is defined as a transfer of property proceeding from a detached and disinterested generosity, out of affection, respect, admiration, charity, or like impulses.[2] The initial basis of gift property to a recipient (donee) depends on whether the value of the asset exceeds the donor's basis on the date of the gift. If the fair market value of the asset on the date of the gift is greater than the donor's basis, then the asset's initial basis to the recipient of the gift will be the same as the donor's basis.[3] That is, the donor's basis carries over to the donee.

If the asset has declined in value since the donor acquired it (fair market value at the date of the gift is less than the donor's basis), then special dual basis rules apply. A dual basis means that the gift property has one basis to the donee if the donee sells the property at a price above the donor's basis and a different basis if the donee sells the property at a price below the fair market value at the date of the gift. Interestingly, the donee will not know the basis for calculating gain or loss until the donee sells the property. Thus, the basis of gifted property that has declined in value depends on the sales price of the asset subsequent to the gift. The donee uses the carryover basis if the asset is sold for a gain (sales price > donor's basis), whereas the donee uses the fair market value at the date of the gift if the asset is sold for a loss (sales price < FMV at date of gift). If the asset sells at a price between the donor's basis and the fair market value at the date of the gift, then the donee's basis at the time of the sale is set equal to the selling price and the donee does not recognize gain or loss on the sale. The dual basis rule prevents the transfer of unrealized losses from one taxpayer to another by gift.

When the dual basis rules apply, the donee's holding period of the asset depends on whether the gift property subsequently sells for a gain or loss. If the donor's basis is used to determine the gain, the holding period includes that of the donor. If the fair market value at the date of the gift is used to figure the loss, the holding period starts on the date of the gift. If the asset subsequently sells at a price between the donor's basis and the fair market value at the date of the gift, the holding period is irrelevant because there is no recognized gain or loss.

Inherited Property For inherited property, the general rule is that the heir's basis in property passing from a decedent to the heir is the fair market value on the date of the decedent's death.[4] The holding period of inherited property is deemed to be long-term regardless of how long the heir owns the property.[5]

Property Converted from Personal Use to Business Use The basis for determining the gain or loss on the sale of converted property depends on whether the property appreciated or declined in value during the time the property was used personally. For appreciated property (the fair market value at the date of the conversion is greater than the taxpayer's basis in the property), the taxpayer will use the taxpayer basis to calculate depreciation and gain or loss at disposition.

For property that has declined in value, taxpayers may try to convert nondeductible personal losses to business losses by converting the property into business property and then selling it. In order to prevent this from occurring, the dual basis rules apply. If the fair market value at the date of conversion is below the taxpayer's basis, the taxpayer will use the fair market value at the date of conversion as the basis for calculating loss and will use the basis at date of conversion to calculate gain. The fair market value at the date of conversion is also the basis used to calculate depreciation on property that has declined in

[2]*Comr. v. Duberstein,* 363 U.S. 278 (1960), rev'g 265 F.2d 28 (6th Cir. 1959), rev'g T. C. Memo 1958–4.
[3]§1015(a). The basis to the donee may be increased if the donor is required to pay gift tax on the gift.
[4]§1014(a)(1). An alternate valuation date may be used to determine the basis to the heirs if elected by the estate.
[5]§1223(9).

value prior to the conversion regardless of whether the taxpayer subsequently sells the property for a gain or a loss. After conversion, the taxpayer adjusts the basis (whether gain or loss) for depreciation deductions from the date of conversion to the date of disposition. If the property later sells for an amount that falls between the adjusted basis for gain and the adjusted basis for loss, the basis for the sale is treated as the sales price so that the taxpayer does not recognize gain or loss on the sale.[6]

Example 11-2

Assume that Steve received 100 shares of FZL stock from his grandfather on January 8. On the date of the gift, the stock was worth $15,000. Steve's grandfather originally purchased the stock 10 years earlier for $10,000. What is Steve's initial basis in the stock?

Answer: Since the stock had appreciated in value while Steve's grandfather owned it, Steve's initial basis is a carryover basis of $10,000.

What if: Assume that on the date of the gift, the fair market value of the stock was $8,000. What is Steve's initial basis in the stock?

Answer: Steve's initial basis depends on the price for which he later sells the stock. If Steve sells the stock six months later at a price greater than $10,000, his basis is the $10,000 carryover basis. He will recognize a long-term capital gain because his holding period is 10½ years (i.e., it includes the time his grandfather owned the stock). If he sells the stock six months later at a price less than $8,000, his basis is $8,000, the fair market value at the date of the gift. He will recognize a short-term capital loss because his holding period is only six months (i.e., it begins on the date of the gift). If he sells the stock for a price that is between $10,000 and $8,000, his basis is the sales price and he recognizes no gain or loss (his holding period does not matter).

What if: Assume that Steve inherited the stock from his grandfather on January 8. What is Steve's initial basis if the fair market value is (a) $15,000 and (b) $8,000 at the time of his grandfather's death?

Answer: Steve's initial basis is the fair market value at the date of his grandfather's death regardless of whether the value is greater or less than his grandfather's original cost. If the fair market value is $15,000, Steve's initial basis is $15,000. If the fair market value is $8,000, Steve's initial basis is $8,000. Steve's holding period is long-term regardless of how long he actually holds the stock because it is inherited property.

What if: Assume Steve owns some mountaineering equipment that he uses personally and purchased two years ago for $4,000. On March 20, he converts the equipment into business-use property when the fair market value of the equipment is $5,000. What is Steve's initial basis in the equipment for business purposes?

Answer: Because the equipment appreciated in value before Steve converted it to business use, his basis is his original cost of $4,000. Steve will use the $4,000 as his initial basis for calculating cost recovery and determining his adjusted basis when he sells or otherwise disposes of the equipment.

What if: Assume that the equipment that Steve converts from personal to business use has a fair market value of $3,000 at the date of conversion. What is Steve's initial basis in the equipment for business purposes?

Answer: The equipment declined in value before Steve converted it to business use. In order to prevent Steve from converting his $1,000 personal loss into a business loss, his initial basis for business purposes will depend on whether he subsequently sells the equipment at a gain or loss. His initial basis for loss (and cost recovery) is the $3,000 fair market value at the conversion date. His initial basis for gain is his $4,000 original cost.

What if: Assume that the equipment that Steve converts from personal to business use has a fair market value of $3,000 at the date of conversion. Two years later, after taking $500 of depreciation deductions, he sells the equipment for $3,300. What is Steve's adjusted basis in the equipment for purposes of determining the gain or loss on the disposition?

Answer: Steve's initial basis for loss was the $3,000 fair market value at the conversion date, and his initial basis for gain was the $4,000 original cost. At the time of the sale, the adjusted basis for loss is $2,500, and the adjusted basis for gain is $3,500. Because the sales price falls between the adjusted basis for gain and the adjusted basis for loss, the adjusted basis is assumed to be equal to the sales price of $3,300.

---

[6]Reg. §1.165-9(b)(2) and Reg. §1.167(g)-1.

The **adjusted basis** for determining the gain or loss on the sale of an asset is the initial basis (however determined) reduced by depreciation or other types of cost recovery deductions allowed (or allowable) on the property. The adjusted basis of an asset can be determined using the following formula:

$$\text{Adjusted basis} = \text{Initial basis} - \text{Cost recovery allowed (or allowable)}$$

Example 11-3

To determine its realized gain or loss on the sale, Teton must calculate the adjusted basis of the machinery it sold in Example 11-1 for $300,000. Teton originally purchased the machinery for $610,000 three years ago. For tax purposes, Teton depreciated the machinery using MACRS (seven-year recovery period, 200 percent declining balance method, and half-year convention).

The machinery's adjusted basis at the time of the sale is $228,658, computed as follows:

Description	Tax	Explanation
(1) Initial basis	$ 610,000	Example 10-1
(2) Year 1	(87,169)	Example 10-5
(3) Year 2	(149,389)	Example 10-5
(4) Year 3	(106,689)	Example 10-5
(5) Year 4	(38,095)	$76,189 (Example 10-5) × 50% (half-year convention)
(6) Accumulated depreciation	(381,342)	(2) + (3) + (4) + (5)
Adjusted basis	**$228,658**	(1) + (6)

Because businesses generally use more highly accelerated depreciation methods for tax purposes than they do for book purposes, the tax-adjusted basis of a particular asset is likely to be lower than the book-adjusted basis.

Realized Gain or Loss on Disposition

The amount of gain or loss taxpayers realize on a sale or other disposition of assets is simply the amount they realize minus their adjusted basis in the disposed assets.[7] The formula for computing **realized gain or loss** is as follows:

$$\text{Gain or (loss) realized} = \text{Amount realized} - \text{Adjusted basis}$$

Example 11-4

In Example 11-1 we learned that Teton sold machinery for a total amount realized of $300,000, and in Example 11-3 we learned that its basis in the machinery was $228,658. What is Teton's realized gain or loss on the sale of the machinery?

Answer: $71,342, computed as follows:

Description	Amount	Explanation
(1) Amount realized	$300,000	Example 11-1
(2) Adjusted basis	(228,658)	Example 11-3
Gain realized	**$ 71,342**	(1) + (2)

Exhibit 11-1 details the important formulas necessary to determine realized tax gains and losses.

[7]§1001(a).

EXHIBIT 11-1   **Summary of Formulas for Computing Gain or Loss Realized on an Asset Disposition**

- Gain (loss) realized = Amount realized − Adjusted basis; where
  - Amount realized = Cash received + Fair market value of other property + Buyer's assumption of seller's liabilities − Seller's expenses
- Adjusted basis = Initial basis − Cost recovery deductions

So far, our examples have used one of Teton's asset sales to demonstrate how to compute gain or loss realized when property is sold. However, as we describe in Exhibit 11-2, Teton disposed of several assets during the year. We refer to this exhibit throughout the chapter as a reference point for discussing the tax issues associated with property dispositions.

EXHIBIT 11-2   **Teton's Asset Dispositions:* Realized Gain (Loss) for Tax Purposes**

Asset	(1) Amount Realized	(2) Initial Basis	(3) Accumulated Depreciation	(4) [(2) − (3)] Adjusted Basis	(5) [(1) − (4)] Gain (Loss) Realized
Machinery	$300,000	$610,000	$381,342	$228,658	$ 71,342
Office furniture	23,000	20,000	14,000	6,000	17,000
Delivery truck	2,000	25,000	17,500	7,500	(5,500)
Warehouse	350,000	275,000	15,000	260,000	90,000
Land	175,000	75,000	0	75,000	100,000
Total gain realized					$272,842

*These are the assets initially purchased by Teton in Example 10-1. This chapter generally assumes that Teton has been in business for four years. For simplicity, this chapter assumes Teton did not previously elect any §179 immediate expensing and opted out of bonus depreciation.

Recognized Gain or Loss on Disposition

As a general rule, taxpayers realizing gains and losses during a year must recognize the gains or losses. **Recognized gains or losses** are gains (losses) that increase (decrease) taxpayers' gross income.[8] Thus, taxpayers must report recognized gains and losses on their tax returns. Although taxpayers must immediately recognize the vast majority of realized gains and losses, in certain circumstances they may be allowed to defer recognizing gains to subsequent periods, or they may be allowed to permanently exclude the gains from taxable income. However, taxpayers may also be required to defer losses to later periods and, in more extreme cases, they may have their realized losses permanently disallowed. We address certain nonrecognition provisions later in the chapter.

LO 11-2   ## CHARACTER OF GAIN OR LOSS

In order to determine how a recognized gain or loss affects a taxpayer's income tax liability, the taxpayer must determine the *character* or type of gain or loss recognized. Ultimately, every gain or loss is characterized as either ordinary or capital (long-term or short-term). As described below, businesses may recognize certain gains or losses (known as §1231) on property dispositions that require some intermediary steps, but even the §1231 gains or losses are eventually characterized as ordinary or capital (long-term).

---

[8]Recall under the return of capital principle we discussed in the Gross Income and Exclusions chapter, when a taxpayer sells an asset, the taxpayer's adjusted basis is a return of capital and not a deductible expense.

The character of a gain or loss is important because gains and losses of different characters are treated differently for tax purposes. For example, ordinary income (loss) is generally taxed at ordinary rates (fully deductible against ordinary income). However, capital gains may be taxed at preferential (lower) rates, while deductions for capital losses are subject to certain restrictions. The character of the gains or losses taxpayers recognize when they sell assets depend on the character of the assets they are selling. The character of an asset depends on how the taxpayer used the asset and how long the taxpayer owned the asset (the holding period) before selling it.

In general terms, property can be used in a trade or business, treated as inventory or accounts receivable of a business, held for investment, or used for personal purposes. The holding period may be short-term (one year or less) or long-term (more than a year). Exhibit 11-3 provides a table showing the character of assets (ordinary, capital, or §1231) depending on how taxpayers used the assets and the length of time they held the property before selling it.

EXHIBIT 11-3   **Character of Assets Depending on Property Use and Holding Period**

| Holding Period | Property Use | | |
	Trade or Business	Investment or Personal-Use Assets*	Inventory and Accounts Receivable
Short-term (one year or less)	Ordinary	Short-term capital	Ordinary
Long-term (more than one year)	§1231†	Long-term capital	Ordinary

*Gains on the sale of personal-use assets are taxable, but losses on the sale of personal-use assets are not deductible.
†As we describe later in the chapter, gain or loss is eventually characterized as ordinary or capital (long-term).

Ordinary Assets

Ordinary assets are generally assets created or used in a taxpayer's trade or business. For example, inventory is an **ordinary asset** because it is held for sale to customers in the ordinary course of business. Accounts receivable are ordinary assets because receivables are generated from the sale of inventory or business services. Other assets used in a trade or business such as machinery and equipment are also considered to be ordinary assets if they have been used in a business for *one year or less*. For example, if Teton purchased a forklift for the warehouse but sold it six months later, the gain or loss would be ordinary. When taxpayers sell ordinary assets at a gain, they recognize an ordinary gain that is taxed at ordinary rates. When taxpayers sell ordinary assets at a loss, they deduct the loss against other ordinary income.

Capital Assets

A **capital asset** is generally something held for investment (stocks and bonds) for the **production of income** (a for-profit activity that doesn't rise to the level of a trade or business) or for personal use (your car, house, or personal computer).[9] Whether an asset qualifies as a capital asset depends on the purpose for which the taxpayer uses the asset. Thus, the same asset may be considered a capital asset to one taxpayer and an ordinary asset to another taxpayer. For example, a piece of land held as an investment because it is expected to appreciate in value over time is a capital asset to that taxpayer. However, the same piece of land held as inventory by a real estate developer would be an ordinary asset. Finally, the same piece of land would be a §1231 asset if the taxpayer held it for more than one year and used it in a trade or business (e.g., as a parking lot).

[9]§1221 defines what is not a capital asset. Broadly speaking, a *capital asset* is any property *other than* property used in a trade or business (e.g., inventory, manufacturing equipment) or accounts (or notes) receivable acquired in a business from the sale of services or property.

Individual taxpayers generally prefer capital gains to ordinary income because certain capital gains are taxed at lower rates and capital gains may offset capital losses that cannot be deducted against ordinary income. Individuals also prefer ordinary losses to capital losses because ordinary losses are deductible without limit, while individuals may deduct only $3,000 of net capital losses against ordinary income each year. Corporate taxpayers may prefer capital gains to ordinary income because capital gains may offset capital losses that they would not be allowed to offset otherwise. Corporations are not allowed to deduct net capital losses, but they are allowed to carry net capital losses back three years and forward five years to offset net capital gains in those years. Exhibit 11-4 reviews the treatment of capital gains and losses for individuals and corporations.

EXHIBIT 11-4   **Review of Capital Gains and Losses**

Taxpayer Type	Preferential Rates	Loss Limitations
Individuals	• Net capital gains on assets held more than one year are taxed at 15 percent (0 percent to the extent taxable income including the gain is below the maximum zero percent threshold and 20 percent to the extent taxable income including capital gains is above the maximum 15 percent threshold). When determining which capital gains tax rate applies, capital gains that fall within the range of taxable income specified in Appendix D are included in taxable income last. • Unrecaptured §1250 gains on real property held more than one year remaining after the netting process are taxed at a maximum rate of 25 percent. • Net gains on collectibles held for more than a year are taxed at a maximum rate of 28 percent. • Net capital gains on assets held one year or less are taxed at ordinary rates.	• Individuals may annually deduct up to $3,000 of net capital losses against ordinary income. • Losses can be carried forward indefinitely but not carried back.
Corporations	• No preferential rates; taxed at ordinary rates	• No offset against ordinary income. • Net capital losses can generally be carried back three years and forward five years to offset net capital gains in those years.

Section 1231 Assets

Section 1231 assets are depreciable assets and land used in a trade or business (including rental property) held by taxpayers for *more* than one year.[10] At a general level, when a taxpayer sells a §1231 asset, the taxpayer recognizes a §1231 gain or loss. As discussed above, however, ultimately §1231 gains or losses are characterized as ordinary or capital on a taxpayer's return. When taxpayers sell multiple §1231 assets during the year, they combine or "net" their §1231 gains and §1231 losses together. If the netting results in a net §1231 gain, the net gain is treated as a long-term capital gain. If the netting results in a net §1231 loss, the net loss is treated as an ordinary loss. Because net §1231 gains are treated as capital gains and §1231 losses are treated as ordinary losses, §1231 assets are tax favored relative to other types of assets.

---

[10]As noted above, property used in a trade or business and held for *one year or less* is ordinary income property.

As we discuss below, §1231 gains on individual depreciable assets may be recharacterized as ordinary income under the depreciation recapture rules. However, because land is not depreciable, when taxpayers sell or otherwise dispose of land that qualifies as §1231 property, the gain or loss from the sale is always characterized as a §1231 gain or loss. Thus, we refer to land as a pure §1231 asset.

In order to acquire another parcel of land to expand its manufacturing capabilities, Teton sold five acres of land that it had been using in its trade or business for $175,000. Teton purchased the land several years ago for $75,000. What is the amount and character of Teton's gain recognized on the land?

Answer: $100,000 §1231 gain, calculated as follows:

Description	Amount	Explanation
(1) Amount realized	$ 175,000	
(2) Original basis and current adjusted basis	75,000	
Gain (loss) realized and recognized	**$100,000**	(1) − (2) §1231 gain

What if: Assume that Teton sold the land for $50,000. What would be the character of the ($25,000) loss it would recognize?

Answer: §1231 loss.

What if: Assume that the land was the only asset Teton sold during the year. How would the §1231 gain or §1231 loss on the sale ultimately be characterized on its tax return?

Answer: If Teton recognized a §1231 gain on the sale, it would be characterized as a long-term capital gain on its return. If Teton recognized a §1231 loss on the sale, it would be characterized as an ordinary loss.

DEPRECIATION RECAPTURE

LO 11-3

Although Congress intended for businesses to receive favorable treatment on economic gains from the economic *appreciation* of §1231 assets, it did not intend for this favorable treatment to apply to gains that were created artificially through depreciation deductions that offset ordinary income. For example, if a taxpayer purchases an asset for $100 and sells it three years later for the same amount, we would generally agree that there is no economic gain on the disposition of the asset. However, if the taxpayer claimed depreciation deductions of $70 during the three years of ownership, the taxpayer would recognize a $70 gain on the disposition simply because the depreciation deductions reduced the asset's adjusted basis. Depreciation is an ordinary deduction that offsets income that would otherwise be taxed at ordinary rates.

Absent tax rules to the contrary, the gain recognized by the taxpayer upon the sale of the asset would be treated as long-term capital gain and would be taxed at a preferential rate (for individuals). Thus, depreciation deductions save taxes at the ordinary rate but the gains created by depreciation generate income taxed at a preferential rate. This potential asymmetrical treatment led Congress to implement the concept of **depreciation recapture.** Depreciation recapture potentially applies to gains (but not losses) on the sale of depreciable or amortizable business property. When depreciation recapture applies, it changes the character of the gain on the sale of a §1231 asset (all or a portion of the gain) from §1231 gain into ordinary income. Note, however, that depreciation recapture does not affect losses recognized on the disposition of §1231 assets.

The method for computing the amount of depreciation recapture depends on the type of §1231 asset the taxpayer is selling (personal property or real property). As presented in

Exhibit 11-5, §1231 assets can be categorized as pure §1231 assets (land), §1245 assets (personal property), or §1250 assets (real property). Whether personal or real property is sold, it is important to understand that depreciation recapture changes only the *character* but not the *amount* of gain recognized.

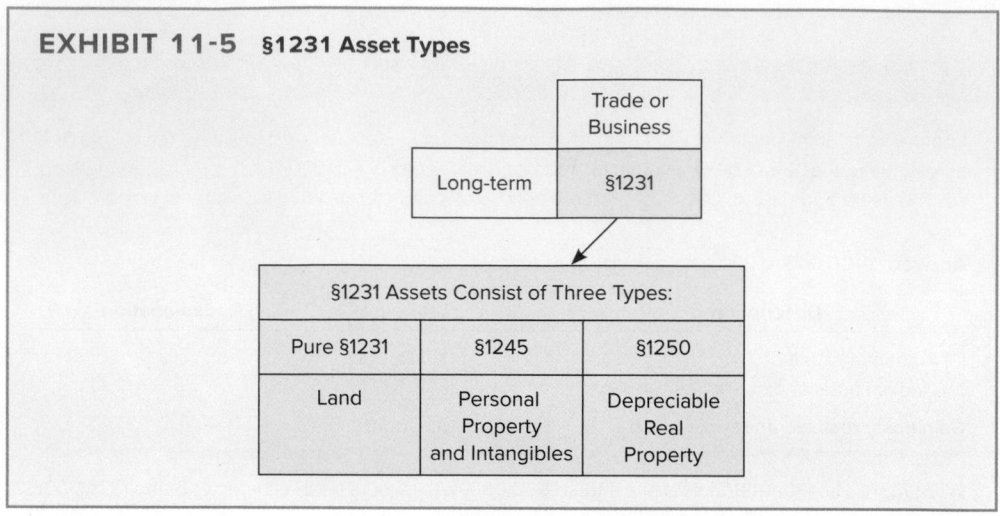

EXHIBIT 11-5   **§1231 Asset Types**

§1245 Property

Tangible personal property (machinery, equipment, and automobiles) and amortizable intangible property (patents, copyrights, and purchased goodwill) are a subset of §1231 property known as **§1245 property.**[11] The gain from the sale of §1245 property is characterized as ordinary income to the extent the gain was created by depreciation or amortization deductions. The amount of *ordinary income* (§1245 depreciation recapture) taxpayers recognize when they sell §1245 property is the lesser of (1) recognized gain on the sale *or* (2) total accumulated depreciation (or amortization) on the asset.[12] The remainder of any recognized gain is characterized as §1231 gain.[13] The sum of the ordinary income (due to depreciation recapture) and the §1231 gain on the sale equals the *total* gain recognized because depreciation recapture changes only the character of the gain, not the amount.

When taxpayers sell or dispose of §1245 property, they encounter one of the following three scenarios involving gain or loss:

Scenario 1:   They recognize a gain created solely through depreciation deductions.

Scenario 2:   They recognize a gain created through both depreciation deductions and actual asset appreciation.

Scenario 3:   They recognize a loss.

The following discussion considers each of these scenarios.

---

[11]An exception in the law is that §1245 property also includes nonresidential real property placed in service between 1981 and 1986 (ACRS) for which the taxpayer elected accelerated depreciation.

[12]§1245 recapture is commonly referred to as "full" depreciation recapture because it may cause a taxpayer to recapture the entire accumulated depreciation amount as ordinary income. §1245 recapture applies notwithstanding any other provision of the Internal Revenue Code (depreciation recapture trumps all other tax rules (e.g., installment sales)).

[13]As a practical matter, taxpayers are unlikely to recognize any §1231 gain on the disposition of personal property because the real economic value of most tangible personal property does not increase over time as the property is used.

Scenario 1: Gain Created Solely through Cost Recovery Deductions   Most §1231 assets that experience wear and tear or obsolescence generally do not appreciate in value. Thus, when a taxpayer sells these types of assets at a gain, the gain is usually created because the taxpayer's depreciation deductions associated with the asset reduced the asset's adjusted basis faster than the real decline in the asset's economic value. That is, the entire gain is artificially generated through depreciation and absent these deductions, the taxpayer would recognize a loss on the sale of the asset. Therefore, the entire gain on the disposition is recaptured (or characterized) as ordinary income under §1245 (recall that without depreciation recapture the gain would be §1231 gain, which can generate long-term capital gain and could create a double benefit for the taxpayer: ordinary depreciation deductions and preferentially-taxed capital gain upon disposition).

Example 11-6

As indicated in Exhibit 11-2, Teton sold machinery for $300,000. What is the amount and character of the gain Teton recognizes on the sale?

Answer: $71,342 of ordinary income under the §1245 depreciation recapture rules and $0 of §1231 gain, computed as follows:

Machinery Sale: Scenario 1 (Original scenario sales price = $300,000)		
Description	**Amount**	**Explanation**
(1) Amount realized	$300,000	Exhibit 11-2
(2) Original basis	610,000	Exhibit 11-2
(3) Accumulated depreciation	381,342	Exhibit 11-2
(4) Adjusted basis	228,658	(2) − (3)
(5) Gain (loss) recognized	71,342	(1) − (4)
(6) Ordinary income (§1245 depreciation recapture)	**$ 71,342**	Lesser of (3) or (5)
§1231 gain	0	(5) − (6)

Note that in this situation, because Teton's entire gain is created through depreciation deductions reducing the basis, the entire gain is treated as ordinary income under §1245.

What if: What would be the amount and character of Teton's gain without the depreciation recapture rules?

Answer: $71,342 of §1231 gain. Note that the recapture rules change the character of the gain but not the amount of the gain.

Both §179 expensing and bonus depreciation allow taxpayers to accelerate the depreciation taken on assets in the year of acquisition. After the Tax Jobs and Cuts Act (TCJA), many taxpayers will fully deduct the cost of acquired assets. These provisions, however, require that taxpayers reduce the basis of the assets by the amount of depreciation taken. When taxpayers deduct the full cost of an asset under these rules, the asset's basis is reduced to zero. As a result, taxpayers will have larger gains post-TCJA and the gains will typically be ordinary in character.

Scenario 2: Gain Due to Both Cost Recovery Deductions and Asset Appreciation   Assets subject to cost recovery deductions may actually *appreciate* in value over time. When these assets are sold, the recognized gain must be divided into ordinary gain from depreciation recapture and §1231 gain. The portion of the gain created through cost recovery deductions is recaptured as ordinary income. The remaining gain (the gain due to economic appreciation) is §1231 gain.

Example 11-7

What if: Let's assume the same facts as in Example 11-6 and Exhibit 11-2, except that Teton sells the machinery for $620,000. What is the amount and character of the gain Teton would recognize on this sale?

Answer: $381,342 of ordinary income under the §1245 depreciation recapture rules and $10,000 of §1231 gain due to the asset's economic appreciation, computed as follows:

Machinery Sale: Scenario 2 (Assumed sales price = $620,000)		
Description	**Amount**	**Explanation**
(1) Amount realized	$ 620,000	
(2) Original basis	610,000	Exhibit 11-2
(3) Accumulated depreciation	$ 381,342	Exhibit 11-2
(4) Adjusted basis	228,658	(2) − (3)
(5) Gain (loss) recognized	391,342	(1) − (4)
(6) Ordinary income	**$381,342**	Lesser of (3) or (5)
(§1245 depreciation recapture)		
§1231 gain	**$ 10,000**	(5) − (6)

Note that taxpayers can quickly determine their §1231 gain (if any) when they sell §1245 property by subtracting the asset's *initial* basis from the amount realized. For example, in Example 11-7, the §1231 gain is $10,000 ($620,000 amount realized less the $610,000 original basis).

Scenario 3: Asset Sold at a Loss   Many §1231 assets, such as computer equipment or automobiles, tend to decline in value faster than the corresponding depreciation deductions reduce the asset's adjusted basis. When taxpayers sell or dispose of these assets before the assets are fully depreciated, they recognize a loss on the disposition. Because the depreciation recapture rules don't apply to losses, taxpayers selling §1245 property at a loss recognize a §1231 loss.

Example 11-8

What if: Let's assume the same facts as in Example 11-6 and Exhibit 11-2, except that Teton sells the machinery for $180,000. What is the amount and character of the gain or loss Teton would recognize on this sale?

Answer: A $48,658 §1231 loss, computed as follows:

Machinery Sale: Scenario 3 (Assumed sales price = $180,000)		
Description	**Amount**	**Explanation**
(1) Amount realized	$180,000	
(2) Original basis	610,000	Exhibit 11-2
(3) Accumulated depreciation	381,342	Exhibit 11-2
(4) Adjusted basis	228,658	(2) − (3)
(5) Gain (loss) recognized	(48,658)	(1) − (4)
(6) Ordinary income	$ 0	Lesser of (3) or (5)
(§1245 depreciation recapture)		(limited to $0)
§1231 (loss)	**$(48,658)**	(5) − (6)

Exhibit 11-6 graphically illustrates the §1245 depreciation recapture computations for the machinery sold in Scenarios 1, 2, and 3, presented in Examples 11-6, 11-7, and 11-8, respectively.[14]

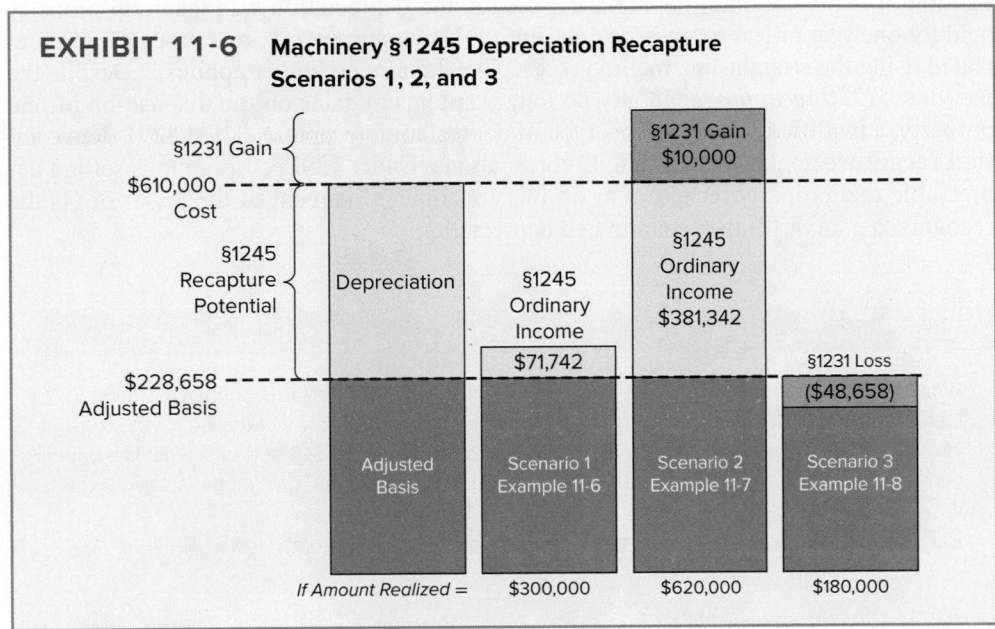

EXHIBIT 11-6   Machinery §1245 Depreciation Recapture Scenarios 1, 2, and 3

Example 11-9

In Example 11-6 (Scenario 1), we characterized the gain Teton recognized when it sold its machinery. For completeness, let's characterize the gain or loss Teton recognized on the other two §1245 assets it sold during the year (see Exhibit 11-2). Teton sold its office furniture for $23,000 and its delivery truck for $2,000. What is the amount and character of gain or loss Teton recognizes on the sale of the office furniture and the delivery truck?

Answer: Office furniture: $14,000 ordinary income and $3,000 §1231 gain. Delivery truck: $5,500 §1231 loss. The computations supporting the answers are as follows:

Description	Office Furniture	Delivery Truck	Explanation
(1) Amount realized	$ 23,000	$ 2,000	Exhibit 11-2
(2) Initial basis	20,000	25,000	Exhibit 11-2
(3) Accumulated depreciation	14,000	17,500	Exhibit 11-2
(4) Adjusted basis	6,000	7,500	(2) − (3)
(5) Gain (loss) recognized	17,000	(5,500)	(1) − (4)
(6) Ordinary income (§1245 depreciation recapture)	**$14,000**	**$ 0**	Lesser of (3) or (5), limited to $0
§1231 gain (loss)	**$ 3,000**	**$(5,500)**	(5) − (6)

§1250 Depreciation Recapture for Real Property

Depreciable real property, such as an office building or a warehouse, sold at a gain is *not* subject to §1245 depreciation recapture. Rather, it is subject to a different type of recapture called §1250 depreciation recapture. Thus, depreciable real property is frequently

---

[14]The authors thank PwC for allowing us to use this exhibit.

referred to as **§1250 property.** Under §1250, when depreciable real property is sold at a gain, the amount of gain recaptured as ordinary income is limited to *additional* depreciation, defined as the excess of *accelerated* depreciation deductions on the property over the amount that would have been deducted if the taxpayer had used the straight-line method of depreciation to depreciate the asset and depreciation was taken on property held for one year or less (even if straight-line).[15] Under current law, real property is depreciated using the straight-line method so §1250 recapture no longer applies.[16] Despite the fact that *§1250 recapture* generally no longer applies to gains on the disposition of real property, a modified version of this type of depreciation recapture called **§291 depreciation recapture** applies, but only to C corporations. Under §291, corporations selling depreciable real property recapture as ordinary income 20 percent of the lesser of (1) the recognized gain or (2) the accumulated depreciation.

Example 11-10

What if: Suppose that Teton was organized as a C corporation and that, as described in Exhibit 11-2, it sold its existing warehouse. Let's assume the same facts: Teton sold the warehouse for $350,000, it initially purchased the warehouse for $275,000, and it has deducted $15,000 of straight-line depreciation deductions as of the date of the sale. What is Teton's recognized gain on the sale and what is the character of its gain on the sale?

Answer: $90,000 gain recognized; $3,000 ordinary income and $87,000 §1231 gain, computed as follows:

Description	Amount	Explanation
(1) Amount realized	$350,000	Exhibit 11-2
(2) Initial basis	275,000	Exhibit 11-2
(3) Accumulated depreciation	15,000	Exhibit 11-2
(4) Adjusted basis	260,000	(2) − (3)
(5) Gain (loss) recognized	90,000	(1) − (4)
(6) Lesser of accumulated depreciation or recognized gain	15,000	Lesser of (3) or (5)
(7) §291 recapture (ordinary income)	**$ 3,000**	20% × (6)
§1231 gain	**$ 87,000**	(5) − (7)

LO 11-4

OTHER PROVISIONS AFFECTING THE RATE AT WHICH GAINS ARE TAXED

Other provisions, other than depreciation recapture, may affect the rate at which gains are taxed. The first potentially applies when individuals sell §1250 property at a gain, and the second potentially applies when taxpayers sell property to related persons at a gain.

Unrecaptured §1250 Gain for Individuals

Except for assets held 12 months or less, neither corporations nor individuals recognize §1250 recapture on the sale of §1250 property when it is sold at a gain. Instead, corporations recognize §291 recapture as ordinary income on the sale of these assets. Individuals,

---

[15]§1250 recapture is commonly referred to as *partial depreciation recapture.*

[16]Accelerated depreciation was allowed for real property placed in service before 1987. Such property had a maximum recovery period of 19 years, which means that as of 2005 all of this property is now fully depreciated under both the accelerated and straight-line depreciation methods.

however, do not recognize ordinary income from the sale of §1250 property when it is held long term. Rather, individual taxpayers treat a gain resulting from the disposition of §1250 property as a §1231 gain and combine it with other §1231 gains and losses to determine whether a net §1231 gain or a net §1231 loss results for the year.

After the §1231 netting process (described below), if the gain on the sale of the §1250 property is ultimately determined to be a long-term capital gain, the taxpayer must determine the rate at which the gain will be taxed. Tax policy makers have determined that the portion of the gain caused by depreciation deductions reducing the basis, called **unrecaptured §1250 gain,** should be taxed at a maximum rate of 25 percent (taxed at the ordinary rate if the ordinary rate is lower than 25 percent) and not the 0/15/20 percent rate generally applicable to other types of long-term capital gains. Consequently, when an individual sells §1250 property at a gain, the amount of the gain taxed at a maximum rate of 25 percent is the *lesser* of (1) the recognized gain or (2) the accumulated depreciation on the asset.[17] The remainder of the gain is taxed at a maximum rate of 0/15/20 percent.[18]

Example 11-11

Teton bought its warehouse for $275,000, depreciated it $15,000, and sold it for $350,000. What is the amount and character of the gain Teton (and thus Steve) reports on the sale? (Recall that income of sole proprietorships is taxed directly to the owner of the business.)

Answer: $90,000 of §1231 gain, which includes $15,000 of unrecaptured §1250 gain, computed as follows:

Description	Amount	Explanation
(1) Amount realized	$350,000	Exhibit 11-2
(2) Original basis	275,000	Exhibit 11-2
(3) Accumulated depreciation	15,000	Exhibit 11-2
(4) Adjusted basis	260,000	(2) − (3)
(5) Gain (loss) recognized	90,000	(1) − (4)
(6) Unrecaptured §1250 gain	$ 15,000	Lesser of (3) or (5)
(7) Remaining §1231 gain	$ 75,000	(5) − (6)
Total §1231 gain	**$ 90,000**	(6) + (7)

What if: Suppose Steve's marginal ordinary tax rate is 32 percent. What amount of tax will he pay on the gain (assuming no other asset dispositions)?

Answer: $15,000, computed as follows:

Description	(1) Gain	(2) Rate	(1) × (2) Tax	Explanation
Long-term capital gain (unrecaptured §1250 gain portion)	$15,000	25%	$ 3,750	This is the gain due to depreciation deductions.
Long-term capital gain (15 percent portion)	75,000	15%	11,250	Taxed at 15 percent because Steve's taxable income including the capital gain is below the maximum 15 percent rate threshold.
Totals	$90,000		$15,000	

Because Steve did not sell any other §1231 assets during the year, the entire §1231 gain is treated as a long-term capital gain that is split into a portion taxed at 25 percent and a portion taxed at 15 percent.

THE KEY FACTS

Unrecaptured §1250 Gains

- Depreciable real property sold at a gain is §1250 property but is no longer subject to §1250 recapture unless it is held 12 months or less.
- The lesser of the (1) recognized gain or (2) accumulated depreciation on the assets is called *unrecaptured* §1250 gain.
- Unrecaptured §1250 gain is §1231 gain that, if ultimately characterized as a long-term capital gain, is taxed at a maximum rate of 25 percent.

---

[17]The amount taxed at a maximum rate of 25 percent cannot exceed the amount of the taxpayer's net §1231 gain.

[18]These rates (25 or 0/15/20 percent) apply to net §1231 gains after a netting process for capital gains, which we discuss in the Investments chapter.

Characterizing Gains on the Sale of Depreciable Property to Related Persons

Under §1239, when a taxpayer sells property to a *related person* and the property is depreciable property to the *buyer*, the entire gain on the sale is characterized as ordinary income to the *seller*.[19] Without this provision, related taxpayers could create tax savings by currently generating capital or §1231 gains through selling appreciated assets to related persons who would receive future ordinary deductions through depreciation expense on the basis of the property (stepped up to fair market value through the sale) acquired in the transaction.

The §1239 recapture provision is different from depreciation recapture in the sense that the seller is required to recognize ordinary income for depreciation deductions the buyer will receive *in the future*, while depreciation recapture requires taxpayers to recognize ordinary income for depreciation deductions they have received *in the past*. In both cases, however, the tax laws are designed to provide symmetry between the character of deductions an asset generates and the character of income the asset generates when it is sold. When depreciation recapture and the §1239 recapture provision apply to the same gain, the depreciation recapture rule applies first.

For purposes of §1239, a related person includes an individual and his or her controlled (more than 50 percent owned) corporation or partnership or a taxpayer and any trust in which the taxpayer (or spouse) is a beneficiary.[20]

Example 11-12

What if: Suppose that Teton is organized as a C corporation and Steve is the sole shareholder. Steve sells equipment that he was using for personal purposes to Teton for $90,000 (he originally purchased the equipment for $80,000). The equipment was a capital asset to Steve because he had been using it for personal purposes (he did not depreciate it). What is the amount and character of the gain Steve would recognize on the sale?

Answer: $10,000 of ordinary income (amount realized $90,000 − $80,000 adjusted basis). Even though Steve is selling what is a capital asset to him, because it is a depreciable asset to Teton and because Steve and Teton are considered to be related persons, Steve is required to characterize the entire amount of gain as ordinary under §1239. Without the §1239 provision, Steve would have recognized a capital gain.

Exhibit 11-7 provides a flowchart for determining the character of gains and losses on the taxable sale of assets used in a trade or business.

LO 11-5 CALCULATING NET §1231 GAINS OR LOSSES

Once taxpayers determine the amount and character of gain or loss they recognize on *each* §1231 asset they sell during the year, they still have work to do to determine whether the gains or losses will be treated as ordinary or capital. After recharacterizing §1231 gain as ordinary income under the §1245 and §291 (if applicable) depreciation recapture rules and the §1239 related-person rules, the remaining §1231 gains and losses are netted together.[21] Recall that a portion of the §1231 gains may include unrecaptured §1250 gains that are taxed at a maximum of 25 percent. When netting the §1231 losses against §1231 gains,

---

[19]§1239. §707(b)(2) contains a similar provision for partnerships.

[20]Additional related persons for purposes of §1239 include two corporations that are members of the same controlled group, a corporation and a partnership if the same person owns more than 50 percent of both entities, two S corporations controlled by the same person, and an S corporation and a C corporation controlled by the same person.

[21]If any of the §1231 gains and losses result from casualty or theft, these gains and losses are netted together first. If a net loss results, the net loss from §1231 casualty and theft events are treated as ordinary loss. Net gains from casualty and theft are treated as other §1231 gains and continue through the normal §1231 netting process.

EXHIBIT 11-7

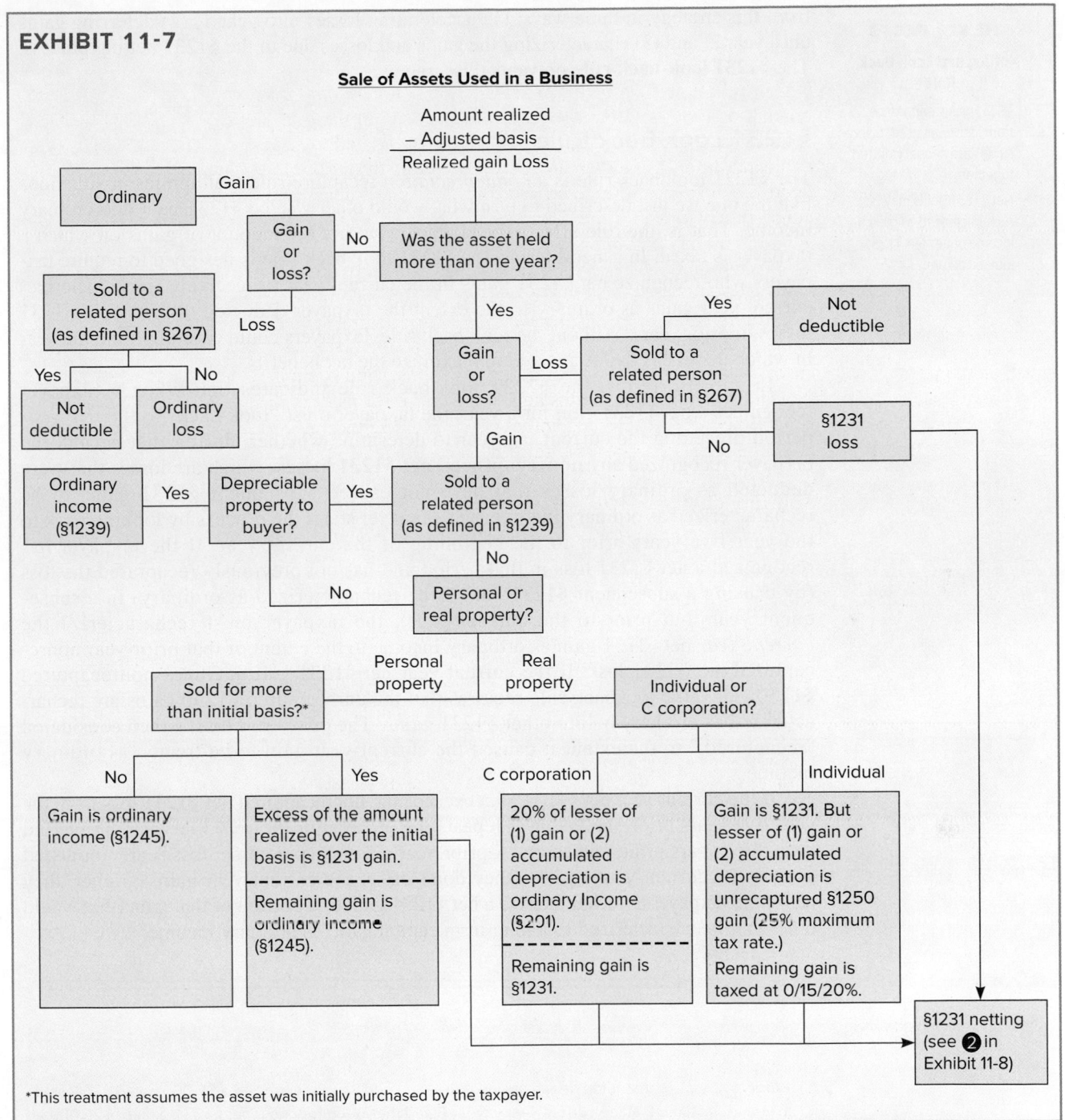

Sale of Assets Used in a Business

*This treatment assumes the asset was initially purchased by the taxpayer.

the losses first offset regular §1231 gains before offsetting unrecaptured §1250 gains. If the gains exceed the losses, the net gain becomes a long-term capital gain (a portion of which may be taxed at the maximum rate of 25 percent). If the losses exceed the gains, the net loss is treated as an ordinary loss.

A taxpayer could obtain significant tax benefits by discovering a way to have all §1231 gains treated as long-term capital gains and all §1231 losses treated as ordinary losses. The *annual* netting process makes this task impossible for a *particular* year. However, a taxpayer who owns multiple §1231 assets could sell the §1231 loss assets at the end of year 1 and the §1231 gain assets at the beginning of year 2. The taxpayer could benefit from this strategy in three ways: (1) accelerating losses into year 1, (2) deferring gains until year 2, and (3) characterizing the gains and losses due to the §1231 netting process. The **§1231 look-back rule** prevents this strategy.

§1231 Look-Back Rule

The §1231 look-back rule is a *nondepreciation* recapture rule that applies in situations like the one we just described to turn what would otherwise be §1231 gain into ordinary income. That is, the rule affects the character but not the amount of gains on which a taxpayer is taxed. In general terms, the §1231 look-back rule is designed to require taxpayers who recognize net §1231 gains in the current year to recapture (recharacterize) current-year gains as ordinary to the extent the taxpayer deducted ordinary net §1231 losses in prior years. Without the look-back rule, taxpayers could carefully time the year in which the §1231 assets are sold to maximize the tax benefits.

In specific terms, the §1231 look-back rule indicates that when a taxpayer recognizes a net §1231 gain for a year, the taxpayer must "look-back" to the *five-year* period preceding the current tax year to determine whether, during that period, the taxpayer recognized any **nonrecaptured net §1231 losses,** which are losses that were deducted as ordinary losses that have not caused subsequent §1231 gains to be recharacterized as ordinary income. The taxpayer starts the process by looking back to the year five years prior to the beginning of the current year. If the taxpayer has recognized a net §1231 loss in that period and has not previously recaptured the loss (by causing a subsequent §1231 gain to be recharacterized as ordinary) in a subsequent year (but prior to the current year), the taxpayer must recharacterize the *current-year* net §1231 gain as ordinary income to the extent of that prior-year nonrecaptured net §1231 loss. If the current year net §1231 gain includes nonrecaptured §1250 gains, the lookback rule requires that the unrecaptured §1250 gains are recharacterized as ordinary before other §1231 gains. The prior-year loss is then considered "recaptured," to the extent it caused the current-year gain to be treated as ordinary income.

If the current-year net §1231 gain exceeds the nonrecaptured net §1231 loss from the year five years prior, the taxpayer repeats the process for the year four years prior, and then three years prior, and so on. A prior year's nonrecaptured net losses are not netted against the current year's gains (they don't offset the current-year gains); rather, they cause the taxpayer to recharacterize a net §1231 gain or a portion of that gain (that would otherwise be characterized as a long-term capital gain) as ordinary income.

Example 11-13

What if: Suppose that Teton began business in year 1 and that it recognized a $7,000 net §1231 loss in year 1. Assume that the current year is year 6 and that Teton reports a *net* §1231 gain of $25,000 for the year. Teton did not recognize any §1231 gains or losses in years 2–5. For year 6, what would be the ultimate character of the $25,000 net §1231 gain?

Answer: $7,000 ordinary income and $18,000 long-term capital gain. Because it recognized a net §1231 loss in year 1, it must recharacterize $7,000 of its net §1231 gain in year 6 as ordinary income. The remaining $18,000 §1231 gain is taxed as long-term capital gain.

What if: Assume the same facts as above, except that Teton also recognized a $2,000 net §1231 loss in year 5. For year 6, what would be the ultimate character of the $25,000 net §1231 gain?

Answer: $9,000 ordinary income and $16,000 long-term capital gain. Note that the overall gain is still $25,000, but to the extent of the $7,000 loss in year 1 and the $2,000 loss in year 5, the §1231 gain is recharacterized as ordinary income under the §1231 look-back rule.

ETHICS

Emma Bean operates a yoga studio and wants to sell some of her business equipment and a piece of land that is used as a parking lot. She expects to realize a $10,000 loss on the equipment and a $15,000 gain on the land. Emma has talked to her accountant and has learned about the look-back rule for §1231 property. To avoid any negative effects, she has decided to game the system and sell the land this year and then sell the equipment early next year. What do you think about her strategy to avoid the look-back rule?

As we've mentioned before, ultimately, all of a taxpayer's §1231 gains and losses must be characterized as ordinary or capital for purposes of determining the taxpayer's tax liability. Exhibit 11-8 summarizes the process of characterizing §1231 gains and losses as ordinary or capital.

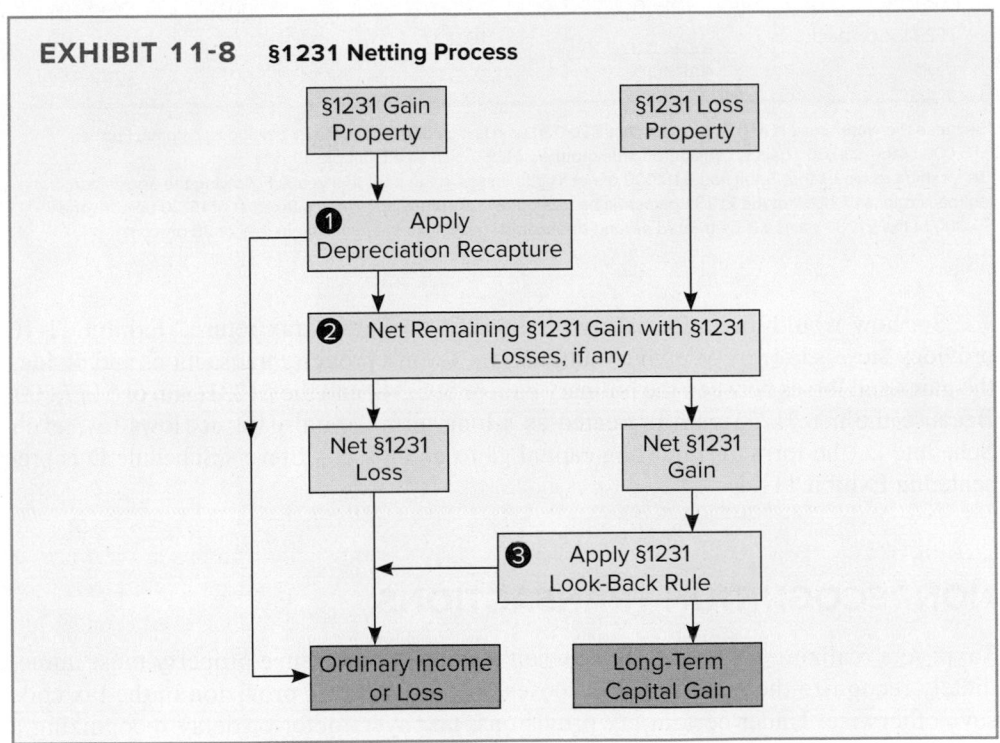

EXHIBIT 11-8   §1231 Netting Process

The following provides details on Steps 1–3 from Exhibit 11-8:

Step 1:   Apply the *depreciation* recapture rules (and the §1239 recapture rules) to §1231 assets sold at a gain (any recaptured amounts become ordinary).

Step 2:   Net the remaining §1231 gains with the §1231 losses. The §1231 losses offset regular §1231 gains before the unrecaptured §1250 gains. If the netting process yields a §1231 loss, the net §1231 loss becomes an ordinary loss.

Step 3:   If the netting process produces a net §1231 gain, the taxpayer applies the §1231 look-back rule to determine if any of the remaining §1231 gain should be recharacterized as ordinary gain. Under the lookback rule, the unrecaptured §1250 gains will be recharacterized before the regular §1231 gains. Any gain remaining after applying the look-back rule is treated as long-term capital gain (including unrecaptured §1250 gain). This gain is included in the capital gains netting process, which is discussed in the Investments chapter.

GAIN OR LOSS SUMMARY

As indicated in Exhibit 11-2, Teton sold several assets during the year. Exhibit 11-9 summarizes the character of the gain or loss Teton (and thus Steve) recognized on each asset sale.

EXHIBIT 11-9 Summary of Teton Gains and Losses on Property Dispositions

Asset	(1) §1245 Ordinary Gain	(2) Total Ordinary Gain	(3) §1231 Gain (Loss)	(2) + (3) Total Gain
Machinery	$71,342	$71,342	$ 0	$ 71,342
Office furniture	14,000	14,000	3,000	17,000
Delivery truck	0	0	(5,500)	(5,500)
Warehouse	0	0	90,000*	90,000
Land	0	0	100,000	100,000
§1231 look-back		10,000	(10,000)†	0
Totals	$85,342	$95,342	$177,500*	$272,842

*Because the warehouse is §1231 property, the $90,000 gain is included in the §1231 gain (loss) column. Further, $15,000 of the $90,000 gain is considered unrecaptured §1250 gain (see Example 11-11).
†This exhibit assumes that Teton had $10,000 of net §1231 losses in the prior five years. Following the application of the lookback rule, $172,500 of the §1231 gains will be treated as long-term capital gains taxed at 0/15/20 percent and $5,000 of the §1231 gains will be treated as long-term capital gains taxed at a maximum rate of 25 percent.

So, how would this information be reported on Steve's tax return? Exhibit 11-10 provides Steve's Form 4797, which summarizes Teton's property transactions and divides the gains and losses between the ordinary gain of $95,342 and the §1231 gain of $177,500. Because the net §1231 gain is treated as a long-term capital gain, it flows to Steve's Schedule D (the form for reporting capital gains and losses). Steve's Schedule D is presented in Exhibit 11-11.

LO 11-6

NONRECOGNITION TRANSACTIONS

Taxpayers realizing gains and losses when they sell or exchange property must immediately recognize the gain for tax purposes unless a specific provision in the tax code says otherwise. Under certain tax provisions, taxpayers defer or delay recognizing a gain or loss until a subsequent period. We first explore tax provisions that allow taxpayers to defer recognizing realized gains. Congress allows taxpayers to defer recognizing gains in certain types of exchanges because the exchange itself does not provide the taxpayers with the wherewithal (cash) to pay taxes on the realized gain if the taxpayers were required to immediately recognize the gain. In particular, we discuss common **nonrecognition transactions** such as like-kind exchanges, involuntary conversions, installment sales, and other business-related transactions such as business formations and reorganizations.

Like-Kind Exchanges

Taxpayers involved in a business may have valid reasons to trade business assets to others for similar business assets. For example, a taxpayer may want to trade land used in its business for a different parcel of land in a better location. As we discussed earlier in this chapter, taxpayers exchanging property *realize* gains (or losses) on exchanges just as

EXHIBIT 11-10   Teton's (on Steve's return) Form 4797

Form **4797**	**Sales of Business Property** (Also Involuntary Conversions and Recapture Amounts Under Sections 179 and 280F(b)(2)) ▶ Attach to your tax return. ▶ Go to *www.irs.gov/Form4797* for instructions and the latest information.	OMB No. 1545-0184 **20**17
Department of the Treasury Internal Revenue Service		Attachment Sequence No. **27**

Name(s) shown on return	Identifying number
Steve Dallimore (Teton Mountaineering Technology, LLC)	

1 Enter the gross proceeds from sales or exchanges reported to you for 2017 on Form(s) 1099-B or 1099-S (or substitute statement) that you are including on line 2, 10, or 20. See instructions **1**

Part I **Sales or Exchanges of Property Used in a Trade or Business and Involuntary Conversions From Other Than Casualty or Theft—Most Property Held More Than 1 Year** (see instructions)

2	**(a)** Description of property	**(b)** Date acquired (mo., day, yr.)	**(c)** Date sold (mo., day, yr.)	**(d)** Gross sales price	**(e)** Depreciation allowed or allowable since acquisition	**(f)** Cost or other basis, plus improvements and expense of sale	**(g) Gain or (loss)** Subtract (f) from the sum of (d) and (e)
	Delivery truck	Yr0	Yr4	2,000	17,500	25,000	(5,500)
	Land	Yr0	Yr4	175,000	0	75,000	100,000

3	Gain, if any, from Form 4684, line 39	**3**	
4	Section 1231 gain from installment sales from Form 6252, line 26 or 37	**4**	
5	Section 1231 gain or (loss) from like-kind exchanges from Form 8824	**5**	
6	Gain, if any, from line 32, from other than casualty or theft	**6**	93,000
7	Combine lines 2 through 6. Enter the gain or (loss) here and on the appropriate line as follows:	**7**	187,500

Partnerships (except electing large partnerships) and S corporations. Report the gain or (loss) following the instructions for Form 1065, Schedule K, line 10, or Form 1120S, Schedule K, line 9. Skip lines 8, 9, 11, and 12 below.

Individuals, partners, S corporation shareholders, and all others. If line 7 is zero or a loss, enter the amount from line 7 on line 11 below and skip lines 8 and 9. If line 7 is a gain and you didn't have any prior year section 1231 losses, or they were recaptured in an earlier year, enter the gain from line 7 as a long-term capital gain on the Schedule D filed with your return and skip lines 8, 9, 11, and 12 below.

8	Nonrecaptured net section 1231 losses from prior years. See instructions	**8**	10,000
9	Subtract line 8 from line 7. If zero or less, enter -0-. If line 9 is zero, enter the gain from line 7 on line 12 below. If line 9 is more than zero, enter the amount from line 8 on line 12 below and enter the gain from line 9 as a long-term capital gain on the Schedule D filed with your return. See instructions	**9**	177,500

Part II **Ordinary Gains and Losses** (see instructions)

10 Ordinary gains and losses not included on lines 11 through 16 (include property held 1 year or less):

11	Loss, if any, from line 7	**11** (	)
12	Gain, if any, from line 7 or amount from line 8, if applicable	**12**	10,000
13	Gain, if any, from line 31	**13**	85,342
14	Net gain or (loss) from Form 4684, lines 31 and 38a	**14**	
15	Ordinary gain from installment sales from Form 6252, line 25 or 36	**15**	
16	Ordinary gain or (loss) from like-kind exchanges from Form 8824.	**16**	
17	Combine lines 10 through 16	**17**	95,342

18 For all except individual returns, enter the amount from line 17 on the appropriate line of your return and skip lines a and b below. For individual returns, complete lines a and b below:

a If the loss on line 11 includes a loss from Form 4684, line 35, column (b)(ii), enter that part of the loss here. Enter the part of the loss from income-producing property on Schedule A (Form 1040), line 28, and the part of the loss from property used as an employee on Schedule A (Form 1040), line 23. Identify as from "Form 4797, line 18a." See instructions . . | **18a** | |

b Redetermine the gain or (loss) on line 17 excluding the loss, if any, on line 18a. Enter here and on Form 1040, line 14 | **18b** | 95,342 |

For Paperwork Reduction Act Notice, see separate instructions.	Cat. No. 13086I	Form **4797** (2017)

EXHIBIT 11-10   Teton's (On Steve's return) Form 4797 (*continued*)

Form 4797 (2017)   Page **2**

Part III   **Gain From Disposition of Property Under Sections 1245, 1250, 1252, 1254, and 1255** (see instructions)

19	(a) Description of section 1245, 1250, 1252, 1254, or 1255 property:			(b) Date acquired (mo., day, yr.)	(c) Date sold (mo., day, yr.)
A	Machinery			Yr0	Yr4
B	Office furniture			Yr0	Yr4
C	Warehouse			Yr0	Yr4
D					

	These columns relate to the properties on lines 19A through 19D. ▶		Property A	Property B	Property C	Property D
20	Gross sales price (**Note:** *See line 1 before completing.*) .	20	300,000	23,000	350,000	
21	Cost or other basis plus expense of sale	21	610,000	20,000	275,000	
22	Depreciation (or depletion) allowed or allowable. . .	22	381,342	14,000	15,000	
23	Adjusted basis. Subtract line 22 from line 21. . . .	23	228,658	6,000	260,000	
24	Total gain. Subtract line 23 from line 20	24	71,342	17,000	90,000	
25	**If section 1245 property:**					
a	Depreciation allowed or allowable from line 22 . . .	25a	381,342	14,000		
b	Enter the **smaller** of line 24 or 25a	25b	71,342	14,000		
26	**If section 1250 property:** If straight line depreciation was used, enter -0- on line 26g, except for a corporation subject to section 291.					
a	Additional depreciation after 1975. See instructions .	26a				
b	Applicable percentage multiplied by the **smaller** of line 24 or line 26a. See instructions	26b				
c	Subtract line 26a from line 24. If residential rental property or line 24 isn't more than line 26a, skip lines 26d and 26e	26c				
d	Additional depreciation after 1969 and before 1976. .	26d				
e	Enter the **smaller** of line 26c or 26d	26e				
f	Section 291 amount (corporations only)	26f				
g	Add lines 26b, 26e, and 26f.	26g			0	
27	**If section 1252 property:** Skip this section if you didn't dispose of farmland or if this form is being completed for a partnership (other than an electing large partnership).					
a	Soil, water, and land clearing expenses	27a				
b	Line 27a multiplied by applicable percentage. See instructions	27b				
c	Enter the **smaller** of line 24 or 27b	27c				
28	**If section 1254 property:**					
a	Intangible drilling and development costs, expenditures for development of mines and other natural deposits, mining exploration costs, and depletion. See instructions	28a				
b	Enter the **smaller** of line 24 or 28a	28b				
29	**If section 1255 property:**					
a	Applicable percentage of payments excluded from income under section 126. See instructions	29a				
b	Enter the **smaller** of line 24 or 29a. See instructions .	29b				

Summary of Part III Gains.   Complete property columns A through D through line 29b before going to line 30.

30	Total gains for all properties. Add property columns A through D, line 24	30	178,342
31	Add property columns A through D, lines 25b, 26g, 27c, 28b, and 29b. Enter here and on line 13	31	85,342
32	Subtract line 31 from line 30. Enter the portion from casualty or theft on Form 4684, line 33. Enter the portion from other than casualty or theft on Form 4797, line 6	32	93,000

Part IV   **Recapture Amounts Under Sections 179 and 280F(b)(2) When Business Use Drops to 50% or Less** (see instructions)

			(a) Section 179	(b) Section 280F(b)(2)
33	Section 179 expense deduction or depreciation allowable in prior years.	33		
34	Recomputed depreciation. See instructions	34		
35	Recapture amount. Subtract line 34 from line 33. See the instructions for where to report . .	35		

Form **4797** (2017)

EXHIBIT 11-11 Steve's Schedule D (Assumes Steve had no other capital gains and losses other than those incurred by Teton)

SCHEDULE D (Form 1040)	Capital Gains and Losses	OMB No. 1545-0074
Department of the Treasury Internal Revenue Service (99)	▶ Attach to Form 1040 or Form 1040NR. ▶ Go to *www.irs.gov/ScheduleD* for instructions and the latest information. ▶ Use Form 8949 to list your transactions for lines 1b, 2, 3, 8b, 9, and 10.	20**17** Attachment Sequence No. **12**

Name(s) shown on return	Your social security number
Steve Dallimore	

Part I Short-Term Capital Gains and Losses—Assets Held One Year or Less

See instructions for how to figure the amounts to enter on the lines below. This form may be easier to complete if you round off cents to whole dollars.	**(d)** Proceeds (sales price)	**(e)** Cost (or other basis)	**(g)** Adjustments to gain or loss from Form(s) 8949, Part I, line 2, column (g)	**(h) Gain or (loss)** Subtract column (e) from column (d) and combine the result with column (g)
1a Totals for all short-term transactions reported on Form 1099-B for which basis was reported to the IRS and for which you have no adjustments (see instructions). However, if you choose to report all these transactions on Form 8949, leave this line blank and go to line 1b .				
1b Totals for all transactions reported on Form(s) 8949 with **Box A** checked				
2 Totals for all transactions reported on Form(s) 8949 with **Box B** checked				
3 Totals for all transactions reported on Form(s) 8949 with **Box C** checked				

4 Short-term gain from Form 6252 and short-term gain or (loss) from Forms 4684, 6781, and 8824 .	**4**	
5 Net short-term gain or (loss) from partnerships, S corporations, estates, and trusts from Schedule(s) K-1	**5**	
6 Short-term capital loss carryover. Enter the amount, if any, from line 8 of your **Capital Loss Carryover Worksheet** in the instructions	**6** ( )	
7 **Net short-term capital gain or (loss).** Combine lines 1a through 6 in column (h). If you have any long-term capital gains or losses, go to Part II below. Otherwise, go to Part III on the back	**7**	

Part II Long-Term Capital Gains and Losses—Assets Held More Than One Year

See instructions for how to figure the amounts to enter on the lines below. This form may be easier to complete if you round off cents to whole dollars.	**(d)** Proceeds (sales price)	**(e)** Cost (or other basis)	**(g)** Adjustments to gain or loss from Form(s) 8949, Part II, line 2, column (g)	**(h) Gain or (loss)** Subtract column (e) from column (d) and combine the result with column (g)
8a Totals for all long-term transactions reported on Form 1099-B for which basis was reported to the IRS and for which you have no adjustments (see instructions). However, if you choose to report all these transactions on Form 8949, leave this line blank and go to line 8b .				
8b Totals for all transactions reported on Form(s) 8949 with **Box D** checked				
9 Totals for all transactions reported on Form(s) 8949 with **Box E** checked				
10 Totals for all transactions reported on Form(s) 8949 with **Box F** checked.				

11 Gain from Form 4797, Part I; long-term gain from Forms 2439 and 6252; and long-term gain or (loss) from Forms 4684, 6781, and 8824	**11**	177,500
12 Net long-term gain or (loss) from partnerships, S corporations, estates, and trusts from Schedule(s) K-1	**12**	
13 Capital gain distributions. See the instructions	**13**	
14 Long-term capital loss carryover. Enter the amount, if any, from line 13 of your **Capital Loss Carryover Worksheet** in the instructions	**14** ( )	
15 **Net long-term capital gain or (loss).** Combine lines 8a through 14 in column (h). Then go to Part III on the back	**15**	177,500

For Paperwork Reduction Act Notice, see your tax return instructions. Cat. No. 11338H **Schedule D (Form 1040) 2017**

taxpayers do by selling property for cash. However, taxpayers exchanging property for property are in a different situation than taxpayers selling the same property for cash. Taxpayers exchanging one piece of business property for another haven't changed their relative economic position, since both before and after the exchange they hold similar assets for use in their business. Further, exchanges of property do not generate the wherewithal (cash) for the taxpayers to pay taxes on the gain they realize and recognize on the exchanges. While taxpayers selling property for cash must immediately recognize gain on the sale, taxpayers exchanging property for assets other than cash must defer recognizing gain (or loss) realized on the exchange if they meet certain requirements. This type of deferred gain (or loss) transaction is commonly referred to as a **like-kind exchange** or §1031 exchange.[22]

Like-kind exchange treatment can provide taxpayers with significant tax advantages by allowing them to defer gain (and current taxes payable) that would otherwise be recognized immediately.[23] For an exchange to qualify as a like-kind exchange for tax purposes, the transaction must meet the following three criteria:

1. Real property is exchanged "solely for like-kind" property.
2. Both the real property given up and the real property received in the exchange by the taxpayer are either "used in a trade or business" or "held for investment" by the taxpayer.
3. The "exchange" must meet certain time restrictions.

Below, we discuss each of these requirements in detail.

Definition of Like-Kind Property

> ## THE KEY FACTS
>
> **Like-Kind Property**
> - Real property
>   - All real property used in a trade or business or held for investment is considered "like kind" with other real property used in a trade or business or held for investment.
> - Ineligible property
>   - Domestic property exchanged for property used in a foreign country and all property used in a foreign country.
>   - Real property held for sale.

Real property is eligible for like-kind treatment while personal property is not.[24] Real property is considered to be "like-kind" with any other type of real property as long as the real property is used in a trade or business or held for investment. For example, from Teton's perspective, its warehouse on 10 acres is considered to be like-kind with a nearby condominium, a 20-acre parcel of raw land across town, or even a Manhattan skyscraper. Real property held for sale is not eligible for like-kind treatment, so taxpayers whose business is to buy and sell real property cannot do so using the like-kind exchange rules.[25] In addition, real property located in the United States and real property located outside the United States are not like-kind.

Property Use

Even when property meets the definition of like-kind property, taxpayers can exchange the property in a qualifying like-kind exchange only if they used the transferred property in a trade or business or for investment *and* they will use the property received in the exchange in a trade or business or for investment. For example, Teton could exchange its warehouse on 10 acres for a 200-acre parcel of land it intends to hold as an investment in a qualifying like-kind exchange, because Teton was using the warehouse in its business and it will hold the land as an investment. However, if Steve exchanged his cabin in Maine for a personal residence in Wyoming, the exchange would not qualify because Steve used the Maine residence for personal purposes, and he would be using the Wyoming property for personal rather than business or investment purposes. In fact, even if Steve were renting his Maine cabin (meaning it qualifies as investment property) when he exchanged it for his principal residence in Wyoming, the exchange

---

[22]Prior to the TCJA, personal property could be exchanged under the like-kind exchange rules. The TCJA eliminated this benefit for property other than real property.

[23]Like-kind exchanges are defined in §1031 of the Internal Revenue Code.

[24]In contrast, financial accounting rules require businesses to recognize (for financial accounting purposes) any gain they realize in a like-kind exchange transaction.

[25]§1031(a)(2).

would not qualify for like-kind exchange treatment because *both* properties must meet the use test for Steve (the personal residence does not qualify as business or investment property).

Timing Requirements for a Like-Kind Exchange

The like-kind rules require an exchange of real property for real property; however, a simultaneous exhange may not be practical or possible. For example, taxpayers may not always be able to immediately (or even eventually) find another party who is willing to exchange properties with them. In these situations taxpayers often use **third-party intermediaries** to facilitate like-kind exchanges.

When a third party is involved, the taxpayer transfers the like-kind property to the intermediary, who then sells the property and uses the proceeds to acquire the new property for the taxpayer.[26] Because the third party must sell the taxpayer's old property and locate and purchase suitable replacement property, this process is subject to delay. Does a delay in the completion of the exchange disqualify an otherwise allowable like-kind exchange? Not necessarily. The tax laws do not require a simultaneous exchange of assets, but they do impose some timing requirements to ensure that a transaction is completed within a reasonable time in order to qualify as a **deferred like-kind exchange** (not simultaneous)—often referred to as a *Starker exchange*.[27]

The two timing rules applicable to like-kind exchanges are that (1) the taxpayer must *identify* the like-kind replacement property within 45 days after transferring the property given up in the exchange, and (2) the taxpayer must receive the replacement like-kind property within 180 days (or the due date of the tax return including extensions) after the taxpayer initially transfers property in the exchange.[28] The time limits force the taxpayer to close the transaction within a specified time period in order to be able to report the tax consequences of the transaction. Exhibit 11-12 provides a diagram of a like-kind exchange involving a third-party intermediary.

> **THE KEY FACTS**
>
> **Timing Requirements**
> - Like-kind property exchanges may involve intermediaries.
> - Taxpayers must identify replacement like-kind property within 45 days of giving up their real property.
> - Like-kind property must be received within 180 days of when the taxpayer transfers real property in a like-kind exchange.

EXHIBIT 11-12   Diagram of Deferred or Starker Exchange

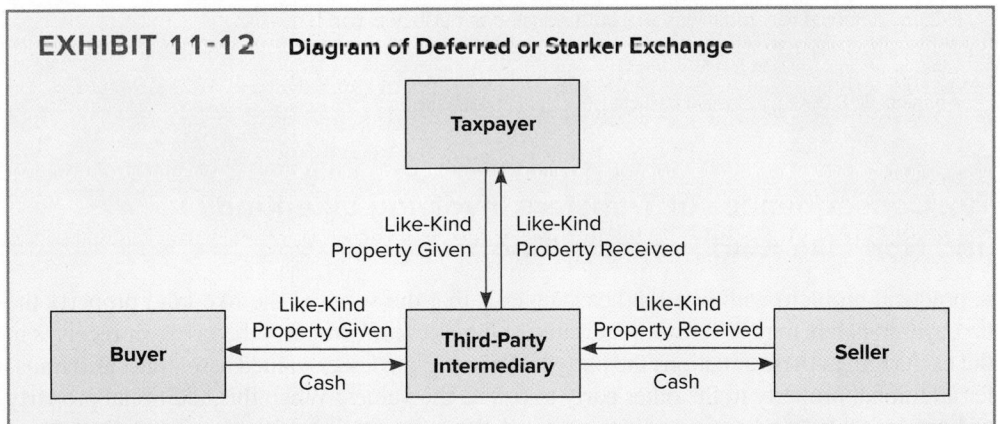

---

[26]Exchanges involving third-party intermediaries are very common with real estate exchanges. For real estate, taxpayers must use a "qualified exchange intermediary," such as a title company, and cannot use a personal attorney (because attorneys are considered to be the taxpayer's agent).

[27]The term *Starker exchange* refers to a landmark court case that first allowed deferred exchanges (*T.J. Starker, Appellant v. United States of America*, 79-2 USTC ¶9541). The rules for deferred exchanges are found in §1031(a)(3). The tax laws also allow for reverse like-kind exchanges where replacement property is acquired before the taxpayer transfers the like-kind property.

[28]The taxpayer must identify at least one like-kind asset; however, since failure to obtain the asset disqualifies the transaction from having deferred like-kind exchange status, the taxpayer may identify up to three alternatives to hedge against the inability to obtain the first identified asset. Generally, a taxpayer must obtain only one to facilitate the exchange [see Reg. §1.1031(k)-1(c)(4)].

When a taxpayer fails to meet the timing requirements, the exchange fails to qualify for like-kind treatment and is fully taxable.

Example 11-14

What if: Suppose that on November 16 of year 1 Steve transferred a parcel of real property that he was holding as an investment to a third-party intermediary with the intention of exchanging the property for another suitable investment property. By what date does Steve need to identify the replacement property?

Answer: December 31 of year 1, which is 45 days after Steve transferred the property to the intermediary.[29]

Assuming Steve identifies the replacement property within the 45-day time period, by what date does he need to receive the replacement property in order to qualify for like-kind exchange treatment?

Answer: May 15 of year 2, which is 180 days from November 16, the date he transferred the property to the intermediary (assuming Steve extends his tax return and that it is not a leap year).

Tax Consequences When Like-Kind Property Is Exchanged Solely for Like-Kind Property

As we've discussed, when taxpayers exchanging property meet the like-kind exchange requirements, they do not recognize gain or loss on the exchange. They also establish or receive an **exchanged basis** in the like-kind property they receive. That is, they exchange the basis they had in the property given up and transfer it to the basis of the property received.[30]

Example 11-15

Teton would like to trade land worth $29,500 (adjusted basis of $18,000) for land in a different location that is also worth $29,500. How much gain does Teton recognize on this exchange?

Answer: $0. Teton's exchange qualifies as a like-kind exchange and the $11,500 realized gain ($29,500 amount realized minus $18,000) adjusted basis) is deferred.

What is Teton's basis in the new land?

Answer: $18,000, the basis it had in the old land it exchanged.

THE KEY FACTS

Like-Kind Exchanges Involving Boot

- Non-like-kind property is known as *boot*.
- When boot is given as part of a like-kind transaction:
  - The asset received is recorded in two parts: (1) property received in exchange for like-kind property and (2) property received in a sale (bought by the boot).
- When boot is received:
  - Boot received usually creates recognized gain.
  - Gain recognized is lesser of gain realized or boot received.

Tax Consequences of Transfers Involving Like-Kind and Non-Like-Kind Property (Boot)

A practical problem with like-kind exchanges is that the value of the like-kind property the taxpayer transfers may differ from the value of the like-kind property the taxpayer receives in the exchange. In these situations the party transferring the lesser-valued asset must also transfer additional property to the other party to equate the values. When this additional property or **boot** (non-like-kind property) is transferred, the party receiving it apparently fails the first like-kind exchange requirement that like-kind property be exchanged solely for like-kind property. Nevertheless, if a taxpayer receives boot in addition to like-kind property, the transaction can still qualify for like-kind exchange treatment, but the taxpayer is required to recognize realized gain *to the extent of the boot received*.[31] As a practical matter, this means the taxpayer's recognized gain is the *lesser of* (1) gain realized or (2) boot received.

---

[29]The identification period begins on the date the taxpayer transfers the property and ends at midnight on the 45th day after the transfer. Similarly, the exchange period begins on the date of the transfer and ends at midnight on the earlier of the 180th day after the transfer or the due date (including extensions) for the taxpayer's return. Reg. §1.1031(k)-1(b)(2).

[30]If the asset is a depreciable asset, the taxpayer continues to depreciate the new asset as if it were the old asset.

[31]§1031(b).

The reason a taxpayer must recognize gain is that the taxpayer is essentially selling a portion of the like-kind property for the boot in a taxable exchange. The receipt of boot triggers taxable gain (but not a taxable loss) in an otherwise qualifying like-kind exchange. If the taxpayer transfers loss property (adjusted basis is greater than fair market value) in a qualifying like-kind exchange, the taxpayer defers recognition of the loss until the taxpayer sells or disposes of the loss property in a taxable transaction—so it may be important for tax planning purposes to avoid the like-kind exchange rules if the taxpayer wishes to currently recognize the loss.[32] When a taxpayer recognizes gain in a like-kind exchange, the character of the gain depends on the character of the asset transferred by the taxpayer (the depreciation recapture rules apply when characterizing gains).

Example 11-16

What if: Suppose that Teton trades land with a value of $29,500 and an adjusted basis of $18,000 for land in a different location valued at $27,500. To equate the value of the property exchanged, the other party also pays Teton $2,000. What gain or loss does Teton realize on the exchange and what gain or loss does Teton recognize on the exchange?

Answer: $11,500 realized gain and $2,000 recognized gain, calculated as follows:

Description	Amount	Explanation
(1) Amount realized from machine	$ 27,500	
(2) Amount realized from boot (cash)	2,000	
(3) Total amount realized	29,500	(1) + (2)
(4) Adjusted basis	18,000	
(5) Gain realized	**$11,500**	(3) − (4)
Gain recognized	$ 2,000	Lesser of (2) or (5)

What is the character of Teton's $2,000 gain?

Answer: §1231 gain. Teton will include the gain in its §1231 netting process when it eventually recognizes the gain in a taxable transaction.

What if: Suppose the same facts as above, except that Teton's adjusted basis in the land was $29,000. What amount of gain would Teton recognize on the exchange?

Answer: $500. Teton recognizes the lesser of (1) $500 gain realized ($29,500 minus $29,000) or (2) $2,000 boot received.

When taxpayers receive like-kind property and boot in a like-kind exchange, their basis in the like-kind property can be computed in two ways as shown in Exhibit 11-13:

EXHIBIT 11-13   Like-kind Basis Calculation

Simplified Method	Method under §1031(d)
Fair market value of like-kind property received	Adjusted basis of like-kind property surrendered
− Deferred gain, or	+ Adjusted basis of boot given
+ Deferred loss	+ Gain recognized
= Basis of like-kind property received	− Fair market value of boot received
	− Loss recognized
	= Basis of like-kind property received

---

[32]§1031(a) states that no gain or loss is recognized in a qualifying like-kind exchange.

The basis of boot received in the exchange is always the boot's fair market value. The formula for computing basis ensures that the taxpayer's deferred gain or loss on the exchange (the gain or loss realized that is not recognized) is captured in the difference between the value and the basis of the new property received. Consequently, taxpayers defer realized gains or losses on qualifying like-kind exchanges; they do not exclude them. Taxpayers will ultimately recognize the gain or loss when they dispose of the new asset in a taxable transaction.[33]

Example 11-17

What if: Assume the facts in Example 11-16, where Teton exchanged land with a value of $29,500 and an adjusted basis of $18,000 for land valued at $27,500 and $2,000 cash. Teton recognized $2,000 on the exchange. What is Teton's basis in the new land it received from the dealer?

Answer: $18,000, computed using the simplified method, as follows:

Description	Amount	Explanation
(1) Amount realized from land	$ 27,500	Fair market value of new land
(2) Amount realized from boot (cash)	2,000	
(3) Total amount realized	29,500	(1) + (2)
(4) Adjusted basis of land	18,000	
(5) Gain realized	11,500	(3) − (4)
(6) Gain recognized	$ 2,000	Lesser of (2) or (5)
(7) Deferred gain	9,500	(5) − (6)
Adjusted basis in new land	**$18,000**	(1) − (7)

Anything a taxpayer receives in an exchange other than like-kind property is considered boot. This includes cash, other property, or even the amount of a taxpayer's liability transferred to (assumed by) the other party in the exchange. Let's return to the previous example. If, instead of paying Teton $2,000 of cash, the buyer had assumed Teton's $2,000 liability secured by Teton's old land, the tax consequences would have been identical. The buyer relieved Teton of $2,000 of debt, and the debt relief is treated the same as if the buyer had paid Teton cash and Teton had paid off its $2,000 liability. Generally, when a taxpayer both transfers and receives boot in an otherwise qualifying like-kind exchange, the taxpayer must recognize any realized gain to the extent of the boot received. That is, the taxpayer is not allowed to offset boot received with boot paid.[34] However, when the taxpayer receives boot in the form of liabilities, the taxpayer is allowed to net any boot paid against the (liability) boot received.[35]

Reporting Like-Kind Exchanges

Like-kind exchange transactions are reported on Form 8824. Exhibit 11-14 presents the computations from Form 8824 reflecting the like-kind exchange of the land in Example 11-15.

---

[33]Additionally, the deferred gain is subject to depreciation recapture when the asset is eventually disposed of in a taxable disposition.

[34]However, Reg. §1.1031(j)-1 provides an exception where multiple like-kind exchanges are made in a single exchange.

[35]Further details of this important exception are beyond the scope of our discussion. See the examples provided in Reg. §1.1031(d)-2 for further guidance.

EXHIBIT 11-14 Form 8824, Part III (From exchange in Example 11-15)

Form 8824 (2017)   Page **2**

Name(s) shown on tax return. Do not enter name and social security number if shown on other side.   Your social security number

Steve Dallimore (Teton Mountaineering Technology LLC)

Part III Realized Gain or (Loss), Recognized Gain, and Basis of Like-Kind Property Received

Caution: *If you transferred **and** received **(a)** more than one group of like-kind properties or **(b)** cash or other (not like-kind) property, see **Reporting of multi-asset exchanges** in the instructions.*

Note: *Complete lines 12 through 14 **only** if you gave up property that was not like-kind. Otherwise, go to line 15.*

12	Fair market value (FMV) of other property given up	**12**	
13	Adjusted basis of other property given up	**13**	
14	Gain or (loss) recognized on other property given up. Subtract line 13 from line 12. Report the gain or (loss) in the same manner as if the exchange had been a sale	**14**	
	Caution: *If the property given up was used previously or partly as a home, see **Property used as home** in the instructions.*		
15	Cash received, FMV of other property received, plus net liabilities assumed by other party, reduced (but not below zero) by any exchange expenses you incurred. See instructions . . .	**15**	0
16	FMV of like-kind property you received	**16**	29,500
17	Add lines 15 and 16	**17**	29,500
18	Adjusted basis of like-kind property you gave up, net amounts paid to other party, plus any exchange expenses **not** used on line 15. See instructions	**18**	18,000
19	**Realized gain or (loss).** Subtract line 18 from line 17	**19**	11,500
20	Enter the smaller of line 15 or line 19, but not less than zero	**20**	0
21	Ordinary income under recapture rules. Enter here and on Form 4797, line 16. See instructions	**21**	
22	Subtract line 21 from line 20. If zero or less, enter -0-. If more than zero, enter here and on Schedule D or Form 4797, unless the installment method applies. See instructions	**22**	0
23	**Recognized gain.** Add lines 21 and 22	**23**	0
24	Deferred gain or (loss). Subtract line 23 from line 19. If a related party exchange, see instructions	**24**	11,500
25	**Basis of like-kind property received.** Subtract line 15 from the sum of lines 18 and 23 . .	**25**	18,000

Involuntary Conversions

Usually, when taxpayers sell, exchange, or abandon property they intend to do so. However, sometimes taxpayers may involuntarily dispose of property due to circumstances beyond their control. The tax law refers to these types of property dispositions as **involuntary conversions.**[36] Involuntary conversions occur when property is partially or wholly destroyed by a natural disaster or accident, stolen, condemned, or seized via eminent domain by a governmental agency. Tragic examples of this include the results of Hurricanes Harvey, Irma, and Maria in 2017. Even in situations when taxpayers experience a loss of property due to theft, disaster, or other circumstances, they might realize a gain for tax purposes if they receive replacement property or insurance proceeds in excess of their basis in the property that was stolen or destroyed.

Taxpayers may experience a tremendous financial hardship if they are required to recognize the realized gain in these circumstances. For example, let's consider a business that acquired a building for $100,000. The building appreciates in value, and when it is worth $150,000 it is destroyed by fire. The building is fully insured at its replacement cost, so the business receives a check from the insurance company for $150,000. The problem for the business is that it realizes a $50,000 gain on this involuntary conversion ($150,000 insurance proceeds minus $100,000 basis in property without considering depreciation). Assuming the business's income is taxed at a 32 percent marginal rate, it must pay $16,000 of tax on the insurance money it receives. That leaves it with only $134,000 to replace property worth $150,000. This hardly seems equitable. Congress provides special tax laws to allow taxpayers to defer the gains on such *involuntary* conversions.

Taxpayers may defer realized gains on both direct and indirect involuntary conversions. **Direct conversions** occur when taxpayers receive a direct property replacement for the involuntarily converted property. For example, a municipality that is widening its

THE KEY FACTS

Involuntary Conversions

- Gain is deferred when appreciated property is involuntarily converted in an accident or natural disaster.
- Basis of property directly converted is carried over from the old property to the new property.
- In an indirect conversion, gain recognized is the lesser of:
  - Gain realized, or
  - Amount of reimbursement the taxpayer does not reinvest in qualified property.
- Qualified replacement property must be of a similar or related use to the original property.

[36]§1033.

streets may seize land from a taxpayer through its eminent domain and compensate the taxpayer with another parcel of similar value. In this case, the taxpayer would not recognize gain on the exchange of property and would take an adjusted basis in the new parcel of land equal to the taxpayer's basis in the land that was claimed by the municipality. Just as with like-kind exchanges, an exchanged basis (basis of old property exchanged for basis of new property) ensures that the gain built into the new property (fair market value minus adjusted basis) includes the same gain that was built into the old property.

Indirect conversions occur when taxpayers receive money for the involuntarily converted property through insurance reimbursement or some other type of settlement. Taxpayers meeting the involuntary conversion requirements may *elect* to either recognize or defer realized gain on the conversions. Indirect conversions are more common than direct conversions. Taxpayers can defer realized gains on indirect conversions *if* they acquire **qualified replacement property** within a prescribed time limit, which is generally two years (three years in case of condemnation) after the close of the tax year in which they receive the proceeds.[37]

In contrast to the like-kind exchange rules, both personal and real property can qualify for the tax treatment under the involuntary conversion rules. Qualified replacement property is defined somewhat narrowly to be similar *and* related in service or use to qualify.[38] For example, a bowling alley is not qualified replacement property for a pool hall, even though both are real properties used for entertainment purposes. This definition is stricter than the like-kind exchange rules that would allow the bowling alley to be exchanged for any other real property, including a pool hall. In addition, the involuntary conversion rules allow a taxpayer's personal residence (personal-use property) to qualify for gain deferral; however, qualified replacement property of a personal residence is restricted to another residence. Taxpayers recognize realized gain to the extent that they do not reinvest the reimbursement proceeds in qualified property. However, just as in like-kind exchanges, taxpayers do not recognize more gain than they realize on involuntary conversions. That is, a taxpayer's recognized gain on an involuntary conversion can be determined by the following formula: Recognized gain on involuntary conversion is equal to the *lesser of* (1) the gain realized on the conversion or (2) the amount of reimbursement the taxpayer does *not reinvest* in qualified property.

The character of any gain recognized in an involuntary conversion depends on the nature of the asset that was converted—including depreciation recapture, if applicable. The basis of the replacement property in an involuntary conversion is calculated in the same way it is for like-kind exchange property (see Exhibit 11-13 Simplified Method). That is, the basis of the replacement property is the fair market value of the new property minus the deferred gain on the conversion.

Example 11-18

What if: Assume that one of Teton's employees was in a traffic accident while driving a delivery van. The employee escaped without serious injury but the van was totally destroyed. Before the accident, Teton's delivery van had a fair market value of $15,000 and an adjusted basis of $11,000 (the cost basis was $15,000 and accumulated depreciation on the van was $4,000). Teton received $15,000 of insurance proceeds to cover the loss. Teton was considering two alternatives for replacing the van: Alternative 1 was to purchase a new delivery van for $20,000 and Alternative 2 was to purchase a used delivery van for $14,000. What gain or loss does Teton recognize under Alternative 1 and Alternative 2?

Answer: $0 gain recognized under Alternative 1 and $1,000 gain recognized under Alternative 2 (see computations below). Teton qualifies for a deferral because the new property (delivery van) has a similar and related use to the old property (delivery van). But it must recognize gain under Alternative 2 because it did not reinvest all of the insurance proceeds in a replacement van.

What is Teton's basis in the replacement property it acquired under Alternative 1 and Alternative 2?

---

[37]§1033(a)(2)(B). The time period varies depending on the type of property converted. Additionally, the IRS may consent to an extension of the time period for replacement.

[38]The similar and related-use test has been developed through a variety of administrative pronouncements and judicial law.

Answer: $16,000 in Alternative 1 and $11,000 in Alternative 2, computed as follows:

Description	Alternative 1 Amount	Alternative 2 Amount	Explanation
(1) Amount realized	$15,000	$15,000	
(2) Adjusted basis	11,000	11,000	
(3) Gain realized	4,000	4,000	(1) – (2)
(4) Insurance proceeds	15,000	15,000	
(5) Proceeds reinvested	15,000	14,000	
(6) Amount not reinvested	0	1,000	(4) – (5)
(7) Gain recognized	**0**	**1,000**	Lesser of (3) or (6)*
(8) Deferred gain	4,000	3,000	(3) – (7)
(9) Value of replacement property	20,000	14,000	
Basis of replacement property	**16,000**	**11,000**	(9) – (8)

*The character of the $1,000 recognized gain is ordinary income under §1245 (lesser of gain recognized or accumulated depreciation).

Involuntary conversions share several characteristics with like-kind exchanges, such as the concept of qualified property, time period restrictions, the method of computing gain recognized (lesser of realized gain or cash received in addition to qualifying property), and basis calculation (gain or loss from old property remains built into new property). However, there are two important differences between like-kind exchanges and involuntary conversions. First, involuntary conversion rules allow taxpayers to defer gains on both personal and real property (business, investment, or personal-use property); whereas, the like-kind exchange rules limit the deferral treatment to only real property (business or investment use). Second, taxpayers experiencing a loss from involuntary conversion may immediately deduct the loss as a casualty loss either as a business loss or as a personal loss, if qualified (federally-declared disaster area), depending on the nature of the loss.

TAXES IN THE REAL WORLD   Weather Break

Weather conditions across the country have caused hardship to many cattle farmers. Drought in the Southwest or floods in the Plains could cause cattle farmers to sell more of their herds than normal because they may not have enough crops to feed the livestock. To aid these farmers, the IRS offers relief in the form of an election to postpone recognizing gain from the sale of livestock sold due to weather-related conditions. What's the catch? The livestock must be replaced within a two-year period. In essence, the IRS allows cattle farmers to take advantage of the §1033 (involuntary conversion) rules.

As an alternative, if a taxpayer sells livestock because of weather-related conditions, he or she may be able to defer reporting the sale of the livestock for a one-year period. As a result of these two possibilities, cattle farmers may need to consider whether they will replace the livestock to take advantage of the involuntary conversion provision or whether the one-year deferral will better suit their plans.

Installment Sales

In general, when taxpayers sell property for cash and collect the entire sale proceeds in one lump-sum payment, they immediately recognize gain or loss for tax purposes. However, taxpayers selling property don't always collect the sale proceeds in one lump sum from the buyer. For example, the buyer may make a down payment in the year of sale and then agree to pay the remainder of the sale proceeds over a period of time. This type of arrangement is termed an **installment sale.** Technically, an installment sale is any sale of property where the seller receives at least one payment in a taxable year subsequent to the year of disposition of the property.[39]

Taxpayers selling property via an installment sale realize gains to the extent the selling price (the amount realized) exceeds their adjusted basis in the property sold. The

[39]§453(b)(1).

THE KEY FACTS

Installment Sales

- Sale of property where the seller receives at least one payment in a taxable year subsequent to the year of disposition of the property.
- Must recognize a portion of gain on each installment payment received.
- Gains from installment sales are calculated as follows:

  Gross profit percentage = Gross profit/Contract price

  Gain recognized = Gross profit percentage × Principal payment received in the year
- Inventory, marketable securities, and depreciation recapture cannot be accounted for under installment sale rules.
- Installment sale rules do not apply to losses.

installment sale rules stay true to the wherewithal-to-pay concept and allow taxpayers selling property in this manner to use the installment method of recognizing *gain* on the sale over time.[40] The installment method does not apply to property sold at a loss. Under the installment method, taxpayers determine the amount of realized gain on the transaction, and they recognize the gain pro rata as they receive the installment payments. So, by the time they have received all the installment payments, they will have recognized all the initial realized gain.[41] For financial accounting purposes, businesses selling property on an installment basis generally immediately recognize the realized gain on their financial statements.[42]

To calculate the amount of gain the taxpayer (seller) must recognize on each installment payment received, the seller must compute the gross profit percentage on the transaction. The gross profit percentage is calculated as follows:

$$\text{Gross profit percentage} = \frac{\text{Gross profit}}{\text{Contract price}}$$

The gross profit percentage indicates the percentage of the contract price that will ultimately be recognized as gain. Gross profit is calculated as the sales price minus the adjusted basis of the property being sold. The contract price is the sales price less the seller's liabilities that are assumed by the buyer. To calculate the portion of a particular payment that is currently recognized as gain, the seller multiplies the amount of the payments received during the year (including the year of sale) by the gross profit percentage (note that once established, the gross profit percentage does not change). As in fully taxable transactions, the character of gain taxpayers recognize using the installment method is determined by the character of the asset sold.

Example 11-19

What if: Suppose Teton decides to sell five acres of land adjacent to the warehouse for $100,000. The basis for the land is $37,500. Teton agrees to sell the property for four equal payments of $25,000—one now (in year 1) and the other three on January 1 of the next three years—plus interest. What amount of gain does Teton realize on the sale and what amount of gain does it recognize in year 1?

Answer: The realized gain on the transaction is $62,500 ($100,000 amount realized less $37,500 adjusted basis), and the year 1 recognized gain is $15,625, computed as follows:

Description	Amount	Explanation
(1) Sales price	$100,000	
(2) Adjusted basis	37,500	
(3) Gross profit	$ 62,500	(1) − (2)
(4) Contract price	$100,000	(1) − assumed liabilities (-0-)
(5) Gross profit percentage	62.5%	(3)/(4)
(6) Payment received in year 1	$ 25,000	
Gain recognized in year 1	**$ 15,625**	(5) × (4)

Because Teton used the land in its trade or business and it held the land for more than a year, the character of the gain is §1231 gain.

[40]Technically, a taxpayer selling property on an installment basis at a gain is required to use the installment method of reporting the recognized gain from the transaction. However, taxpayers are allowed to *elect* out of using the installment method §453(d).

[41]Because the seller in an installment sale is essentially lending money to the buyer, the buyer makes the required installment payments to the seller and the buyer pays interest to the seller for the money the buyer is borrowing. Any interest income received by the seller is immediately taxable as ordinary income. Special rules apply regarding interest for installment sales of more than $150,000 (see §453A).

[42]One exception is that the installment sale method, similar to the tax installment method, is used for financial accounting purposes when there is doubt that the business will collect the receivable.

The formula for determining the basis of an installment note receivable is (1 − gross profit percentage) × remaining payments on note. Because the gross profit percentage reflects the percentage of the installment payments that will be recognized as gain, (1 − gross profit percentage) is the percentage that is not recognized as gain because it reflects a return of capital (basis).

Gains Ineligible for Installment Reporting

Not all gains are eligible for installment sale reporting. Taxpayers selling marketable securities or inventory on an installment basis may not use the installment method to report gain on the sales. Similarly, any depreciation recapture (including §1245, §1250, and §291 depreciation recapture) is not eligible for installment reporting and must be recognized in the year of sale.[43] However, the §1231 gain remaining after the depreciation recapture can be recognized using the installment method. To ensure that any depreciation recapture is not taxed twice (once immediately and then a second time as payments are received), immediately taxable recapture-related gains are *added to* the adjusted basis of the property sold to determine the gross profit percentage. The increase in basis reduces the gain realized, which also reduces the gross profit percentage and the amount of future gain that will ultimately be recognized as the taxpayer receives the installment payments.

Example 11-20

What if: Assume that Teton agrees to sell some of its machinery for $90,000 for two equal payments of $45,000 plus interest. Teton's original basis was $80,000 and accumulated depreciation on the machinery was $30,000. Teton will receive one payment in year 1 (the current year) and the other payment in year 2. What is the amount and character of the gain Teton recognizes on the sale in year 1?

Answer: $30,000 ordinary income and $5,000 of §1231 gain, computed as follows:

Description	Amount	Explanation
(1) Sales price	$ 90,000	
(2) Initial basis	80,000	
(3) Accumulated depreciation	(30,000)	
(4) Adjusted basis	50,000	(2) + (3)
(5) Realized gain (loss)	$ 40,000	(1) − (4)
(6) Ordinary income from depreciation recapture (not eligible for installment reporting)	**$30,000**	Ordinary income; lesser of (3) or (5)
(7) Gain eligible for installment reporting	$ 10,000	(5) − (6)
(8) Contract price	$ 90,000	(1) − assumed liabilities (-0-)
(9) Gross profit percentage	11.11%	(7)/(8)
(10) Payment received in year 1	$ 45,000	
Installment gain recognized in year 1	**$ 5,000**	(10) × (9) §1231 gain

What is the amount and character of the gain Teton recognized upon receipt of the payment in year 2?

Answer: $5,000 of §1231 gain ($45,000 payment received times the gross profit percentage of 11.11 percent).

Other Nonrecognition Provisions

Several tax law provisions allow businesses to change the form or organization of their business while deferring the realized gains for tax purposes. For example, a sole

---

[43]§453(i).

proprietor can form his business as a corporation or contribute assets to an existing corporation and defer the gain realized on the exchange of assets for an ownership interest in the business entity.[44] Without the nonrecognition provision, the tax cost of forming a corporation may be large enough to deter taxpayers from doing so. Nonrecognition rules also apply to taxpayers forming partnerships or contributing assets to partnerships.[45] In still other corporate transactions, such as mergers, divisions (spin-offs or split-offs), or reorganizations, corporations can often do so in tax-deferred transactions.[46] While these transactions generally result in deferred gain or loss for the involved parties, the specific details of these topics can easily fill entire chapters. Further coverage is beyond the scope of this text.

Related-Person Loss Disallowance Rules

Taxpayers selling business or investment property at a loss to unrelated persons are generally able to deduct the loss.[47] This makes sense in most situations because taxpayers are selling the property for less than their remaining investment (adjusted basis) in the property, and after the sale, the taxpayer's investment in the property is completely terminated. In contrast, when a taxpayer sells property at a loss to a related person, she effectively retains some element of control over the property through the related person. Consistent with this idea, §267(a) disallows recognition of losses on sales to related persons. Under §267, related persons include individuals with family relationships, including siblings, spouses, ancestors, and lineal descendants. Related persons also include an individual and a corporation if the individual owns more than 50 percent of the value of the stock of the corporation.[48]

Example 11-21

What if: Suppose Teton is formed as a corporation and Steve is its sole shareholder. Teton is looking to make some long-term investments to fund its anticipated purchase of a new manufacturing facility. Steve currently owns 1,000 shares of stock in his previous company, Northeastern Corp., which he intends to sell in the near future. Steve initially paid $40 a share for the stock but the stock is currently valued at $30 a share. While Steve believes the stock has good long-term potential, he needs cash now to purchase a personal residence in Cody, Wyoming. Steve believes selling the shares to Teton makes good sense because he can deduct the loss and save taxes now and Teton can benefit from the expected long-term appreciation of the stock. If Steve sells 1,000 shares of Northeastern Corp. stock to Teton for $30 per share, what amount of loss will he realize and what amount of loss will he recognize for tax purposes?

Answer: $10,000 loss realized and $0 loss recognized, determined as follows:

Description	Amount	Explanation
(1) Amount realized on sale	$30,000	(1,000 × $30)
(2) Adjusted basis in stock	40,000	(1,000 × $40)
(3) Loss realized on sale	**(10,000)**	(1) – (2)
Loss recognized on sale	**$ 0**	Losses on sales to related persons are disallowed.

Because Steve owns more than 50 percent of Teton (he owns 100 percent), Steve and Teton are considered to be related persons. Consequently, Steve is not allowed to recognize any loss on the sale.

---

[44]§351.

[45]§721.

[46]§368(a) contains the numerous variations and requirements of these tax-deferred reorganizations.

[47]Capital losses are subject to certain limitations for individuals and corporate taxpayers (§1211).

[48]§267(a). The related-person rules include both direct ownership as well as indirect ownership (ownership attributed to the taxpayer from related persons). See §267(c) for a description of the indirect ownership rules.

Although taxpayers are not allowed to immediately deduct losses when they sell property to the related person, the related-person buyer may be able to subsequently deduct the disallowed loss by selling the property to an *unrelated* third party at a gain. The rules follow:

- If the related buyer sells the property at a gain (the related-person buyer sells it for more than she purchased it for) greater than the disallowed loss, the entire loss that was disallowed for the related-person seller is deductible by the buyer.
- If the related-person buyer subsequently sells the property and the related-person seller's disallowed loss exceeds the related person's gain on the subsequent sale, the related-person buyer may only deduct or offset the previously disallowed loss *to the extent of the gain* on the sale to the unrelated third party—the remaining disallowed loss expires unused.
- If the related-person buyer sells the property for less than her purchase price from the related seller, the disallowed loss expires unused.
- The holding period for the related-person buyer begins on the date of the sale between the related persons.[49]

Example 11-22

What if: Let's return to Example 11-21, where Steve sold 1,000 shares of Northeastern Corp. stock to Teton (a corporation) for $30,000. As we discovered in that example, Steve realized a $10,000 loss on the sale, but he was not allowed to deduct it because Steve and Teton are related persons. Let's assume that a few years after Teton purchased the stock from Steve, Teton sells the Northeastern Corp. stock to an unrelated third party. What gain or loss does *Teton* recognize when it sells the stock in each of three scenarios, assuming it sells the stock for $37,000 in Scenario 1, $55,000 in Scenario 2, and $25,000 in Scenario 3?

Answer: $0 gain or loss in Scenario 1, $15,000 gain in Scenario 2, and $5,000 loss in Scenario 3, computed as follows:

Description	Scenario 1	Scenario 2	Scenario 3	Explanation
(1) Amount realized	$ 37,000	$ 55,000	$25,000	
(2) Adjusted basis	30,000	30,000	30,000	Example 11-21 (Teton's purchase price)
(3) Realized gain (loss)	7,000	25,000	(5,000)	(1) − (2)
(4) Benefit of Steve's ($10,000) disallowed loss	(7,000)	(10,000)	0	Loss benefit limited to realized gain.
Recognized gain (loss)	**$ 0**	**$ 15,000**	**$(5,000)**	(3) + (4)

In Scenario 1, $3,000 of Steve's $10,000 remaining disallowed loss expires unused. In Scenario 3, Steve's entire $10,000 disallowed loss expires unused.

CONCLUSION

This chapter describes and discusses the tax consequences associated with sales and other types of property dispositions. We've learned how to determine the amount of gain or loss taxpayers recognize when they sell or otherwise dispose of property, and we've learned how to determine the character of these gains and losses. Tax accountants who understand the rules and concepts of property dispositions are able to comply with the tax law and advise clients of potential tax planning opportunities and avoid pitfalls associated with various nonrecognition provisions.

[49]Reg. §1.267(d)-1(c)(3).

Summary

LO 11-1 Calculate the amount of gain or loss recognized on the disposition of assets used in a trade or business.

- Dispositions occur in the form of sales, trades, or other realization events.
- Gain realized is the amount realized less the adjusted basis of an asset.
- Amount realized is everything of value received in the transaction less any selling costs.
- Adjusted basis is the historical cost or initial basis of an asset less any cost recovery deductions applied against the asset.
- Gain realized on asset dispositions is not always recognized.

LO 11-2 Describe the general character types of gain or loss recognized on property dispositions.

- Recognized gains must be characterized as ordinary, capital, or §1231. An asset's character is a function of the asset's use and holding period.
- Ordinary assets are derived from normal transactions of the business (revenues and accounts receivable), the sale of short-term trade or business assets, and depreciation recapture.
- Capital assets are assets that are held either for investment or for personal use (a taxpayer's principal residence).
- §1231 assets consist of property used in a taxpayer's trade or business that has been held for more than one year.
- Net §1231 gains are treated as long-term capital gains and net §1231 losses are treated as ordinary losses.

LO 11-3 Calculate depreciation recapture.

- §1231 assets, other than land, are subject to cost recovery deductions (depreciation), which generate ordinary deductions.
- Gains that are created through depreciation deductions are subject to depreciation recapture. Any remaining gain is §1231 gain.
- Depreciation recapture does not change the amount of the gain but simply converts or recharacterizes the gain from §1231 to ordinary.
- Different recapture rules apply to tangible personal property (§1245) and real property (§291 for C corporations only and §1250).

LO 11-4 Describe the tax treatment of unrecaptured §1250 gains.

- When individuals sell §1250 property at a gain, the portion of the gain generated by depreciation deductions is called unrecaptured §1250 gain.
- This gain is a §1231 gain that, when treated as a capital gain after the §1231 netting process, flows into the capital gain/loss process (see the Investments chapter) and is taxed at a maximum rate of 25 percent.
- If a taxpayer sells an asset at a gain to a related person and the asset is a depreciable asset to the related person, the seller must characterize the entire gain as ordinary income.

LO 11-5 Describe the tax treatment of §1231 gains or losses, including the §1231 netting process.

- After applying the depreciation recapture rules, taxpayers calculate the net §1231 gain or loss.
- If a net §1231 loss results, the loss will become ordinary and offset ordinary income.
- If a net §1231 gain results, the §1231 look-back rule must be applied.
- After applying the look-back rule, any remaining net §1231 gain is a long-term capital gain.

LO 11-6 Explain common exceptions to the general rule that realized gains and losses are recognized currently.

- Like-kind exchanges involve trading or exchanging real property used in a business or held for investment for similar real property. The gain is deferred unless boot or non-like-kind property is received.

- Involuntary conversions are the losses on property through circumstances beyond taxpayers' control. Reasons include natural disasters, accidents, theft, or condemnation.

- Installment sales occur when any portion of the amount realized is received in a year subsequent to the disposition. A portion of the gain is initially deferred, but then recognized over time as payments are received.

- §267 related-person losses are disallowed but the related-person buyer may be able to deduct the disallowed loss if she subsequently sells the property at a gain.

KEY TERMS

adjusted basis (11-5)	installment sale (11-31)	recognized gain or loss (11-6)
amount realized (11-2)	involuntary conversion (11-29)	§291 depreciation recapture (11-14)
boot (11-26)	like-kind exchange (11-24)	§1231 assets (11-8)
capital asset (11-7)	nonrecaptured net §1231 losses (11-18)	§1231 look-back rule (11-18)
deferred like-kind exchange (11-25)	nonrecognition transaction (11-20)	§1245 property (11-10)
depreciation recapture (11-9)	ordinary asset (11-7)	§1250 property (11-14)
direct conversion (11-29)	production of income (11-7)	third-party intermediaries (11-25)
exchanged basis (11-26)	qualified replacement property (11-30)	unrecaptured §1250 gain (11-15)
indirect conversion (11-30)	realized gain or loss (11-5)	

DISCUSSION QUESTIONS

Discussion Questions are available in Connect®.

1. Compare and contrast different ways in which a taxpayer triggers a realization event by disposing of an asset.   `LO 11-1`

2. Potomac Corporation wants to sell a warehouse that it has used in its business for 10 years. Potomac is asking $450,000 for the property. The warehouse is subject to a mortgage of $125,000. If Potomac accepts Wyden Inc.'s offer to give Potomac $325,000 in cash and assume full responsibility for the mortgage on the property, what amount does Potomac realize on the sale?   `LO 11-1`

3. Montana Max sells a 2,500-acre ranch for $1,000,000 in cash, a note receivable of $1,000,000, and debt relief of $2,400,000. He also pays selling commissions of $60,000. In addition, Max agrees to build a new barn on the property (cost $250,000) and spend $100,000 upgrading the fence on the property before the sale. What is Max's amount realized on the sale?   `LO 11-1`

4. Hawkeye sold farming equipment for $55,000. It bought the equipment four years ago for $75,000, and it has since claimed a total of $42,000 in depreciation deductions against the asset. Explain how to calculate Hawkeye's adjusted basis in the farming equipment.   `LO 11-1`

5. When a taxpayer sells an asset, what is the difference between realized and recognized gain or loss on the sale?   `LO 11-1`

6. What does it mean to characterize a gain or loss? Why is characterizing a gain or loss important?   `LO 11-2`

7. Explain the difference between ordinary, capital, and §1231 assets.   `LO 11-2`

8. Discuss the reasons why individuals generally prefer capital gains over ordinary gains. Explain why corporate taxpayers might prefer capital gains over ordinary gains.   `LO 11-2`

9. Dakota Conrad owns a parcel of land he would like to sell. Describe the circumstances in which the sale of the land would generate §1231 gain or loss, ordinary gain or loss, or capital gain or loss. Also, describe the circumstances under which Dakota would not be allowed to deduct a loss on the sale.   `LO 11-2`

LO 11-2   10. Lincoln has used a piece of land in her business for the past five years. The land qualifies as §1231 property. It is unclear whether Lincoln will have to recognize a gain or loss when she eventually sells the asset. She asks her accountant how the gain or loss would be characterized if she decides to sell. Her accountant says that selling §1231 assets gives sellers "the best of both worlds." Explain what her accountant means by this.

LO 11-3   11. Explain Congress's rationale for depreciation recapture.

LO 11-3   12. Compare and contrast §1245 recapture and §1250 recapture.

LO 11-3   13. Why is depreciation recapture not required when assets are sold at a loss?

LO 11-3   14. What are the similarities and differences between the tax benefit rule and depreciation recapture?

LO 11-3 **LO 11-4**   15. Are both corporations and individuals subject to depreciation recapture when they sell depreciable real property at a gain? Explain.

LO 11-4   16. How is unrecaptured §1250 gain for individuals similar to depreciation recapture? How is it different?

LO 11-4   17. Explain why gains from depreciable property sold to a related taxpayer are treated as ordinary income under §1239.

LO 11-5   18. Bingaman Resources sold two depreciable §1231 assets during the year. One asset resulted in a large gain (the asset was sold for more than it was purchased for) and the other in a small loss. Describe the §1231 netting process for Bingaman.

LO 11-5   19. Jeraldine believes that when the §1231 look-back rule applies, the taxpayer deducts a §1231 loss in a previous year against §1231 gains in the current year. Explain whether Jeraldine's description is correct.

LO 11-5   20. Explain the purpose behind the §1231 look-back rule.

LO 11-5   21. Does a taxpayer apply the §1231 look-back rule in a year when the taxpayer recognizes a net §1231 loss? Explain.

LO 11-4 **LO 11-5**   22. Describe the circumstances in which an individual taxpayer with a net §1231 gain will have different portions of the gain taxed at different rates.

LO 11-6   23. Rocky and Bullwinkle Partnership sold a parcel of land during the current year and realized a gain of $250,000. Rocky and Bullwinkle did not recognize gain related to the sale of the land on its tax return. Is this possible? Explain how a taxpayer could realize a gain but not recognize it.

LO 11-6   24. Why does the tax code allow taxpayers to defer gains on like-kind exchanges? How do the tax laws ensure that the gains (or losses) are deferred and not permanently excluded from a taxpayer's income?

LO 11-6   25. Describe the like-kind property requirements for real property for purposes of qualifying for a like-kind exchange. Explain whether land held for investment by a corporation will qualify as like-kind property with land held by an individual for personal use.

LO 11-6   26. Salazar Inc., a Colorado company, is relocating to a nearby town. It would like to trade its real property for some real property in the new location. While Salazar has found several prospective buyers for its real property and has also located several properties that are acceptable in the new location, it cannot find anyone willing to trade Salazar Inc. for its property in a like-kind exchange. Explain how a third-party intermediary could facilitate Salazar's like-kind exchange.

LO 11-6   27. Minuteman wants to enter into a like-kind exchange by exchanging its old New England manufacturing facility for a ranch in Wyoming. Minuteman is using a third-party intermediary to facilitate the exchange. The purchaser of the manufacturing facility wants to complete the transaction immediately but, for various reasons, the ranch transaction will not be completed for three to four months. Will this delay cause a problem for Minuteman's desire to accomplish this through a like-kind exchange? Explain.

28. Olympia Corporation, of Kittery, Maine, wants to exchange its manufacturing facility for Bangor Company's warehouse. Both parties agree that that Olympia's building is worth $100,000 and that Bangor's building is worth $95,000. Olympia would like the transaction to qualify as a like-kind exchange. What could the parties do to equalize the value exchanged but still allow the exchange to qualify as a like-kind exchange? How would the necessary change affect the tax consequences of the transaction? `LO 11-6`

29. Compare and contrast the similarities and differences between like-kind exchanges and involuntary conversions for tax purposes. `LO 11-6`

30. What is an installment sale? How do the tax laws ensure that taxpayers recognize all the gain they realize on an installment sale? How is depreciation recapture treated in an installment sale? Explain the gross profit ratio and how it relates to gains recognized under installment method sales. `LO 11-6`

31. Mr. Kyle owns stock in a local publicly traded company. Although the stock price has declined since he purchased it two years ago, he likes the long-term prospects for the company. If Kyle sells the stock to his sister because he needs some cash for a down payment on a new home, is the loss deductible? If Kyle is right and the stock price increases in the future, how is his sister's gain computed if she sells the stock? `LO 11-6`

PROBLEMS

Select problems are available in Connect®.   ▤ connect

32. Rafael sold an asset to Jamal. What is Rafael's amount realized on the sale in each of the following alternative scenarios? `LO 11-1`
    a) Rafael received $80,000 cash and a vehicle worth $10,000. Rafael also paid $5,000 in selling expenses.
    b) Rafael received $80,000 cash and was relieved of a $30,000 mortgage on the asset he sold to Jamal. Rafael also paid a commission of $5,000 on the transaction.
    c) Rafael received $20,000 cash, a parcel of land worth $50,000, and marketable securities of $10,000. Rafael also paid a commission of $8,000 on the transaction.

33. Alan Meer inherits a hotel from his grandmother, Mary, on February 11 of the current year. Mary bought the hotel for $730,000 three years ago. Mary deducted $27,000 of cost recovery on the hotel before her death. The fair market value of the hotel in February is $725,000. (Assume that the alternative valuation date is not used.) `LO 11-1`
    a) What is Alan's adjusted basis in the hotel?
    b) If the fair market value of the hotel at the time of Mary's death was $500,000, what is Alan's basis?

34. Shasta Corporation sold a piece of land to Bill for $45,000. Shasta bought the land two years ago for $30,600. What gain or loss does Shasta realize on the transaction? `LO 11-1`

35. Lassen Corporation sold a machine to a machine dealer for $25,000. Lassen bought the machine for $55,000 and has claimed $15,000 of depreciation expense on the machine. What gain or loss does Lassen realize on the transaction? `LO 11-1`

36. Hannah Tywin owns 100 shares of MM Inc. stock. She sells the stock on December 11 for $25 per share. She received the stock as a gift from her Aunt Pam on March 20 of this year when the fair market value of the stock was $18 per share. Aunt Pam originally purchased the stock seven years ago at a price of $12 per share. What is the amount and character of Hannah's recognized gain on the stock? `LO 11-1` `LO 11-2`

LO 11-1 **LO 11-2** 37. On September 30 of last year, Rex received some investment land from Holly as a gift. Holly's adjusted basis was $50,000 and the land was valued at $40,000 at the time of the gift. Holly acquired the land five years ago. What is the amount and character of Rex's recognized gain (loss) if he sells the land on May 12 this year at the following prices?

a) $32,000

b) $70,000

c) $45,000

LO 11-1 **LO 11-2** 38. Franco converted a building from personal to business use in May 2016 when the fair market value was $55,000. He purchased the building in July 2013 for $80,000. On December 15 of this year, Franco sells the building for $40,000. On the date of sale, the accumulated depreciation on the building is $5,565. What is Franco's recognized gain or loss on the sale?

LO 11-2 39. Identify each of White Corporation's following assets as an ordinary, capital, or §1231 asset.

a) Two years ago, White used its excess cash to purchase a piece of land as an investment.

b) Two years ago, White purchased land and a warehouse. It uses these assets in its business.

c) Manufacturing machinery White purchased earlier this year.

d) Inventory White purchased 13 months ago that is ready to be shipped to a customer.

e) Office equipment White has used in its business for the past three years.

f) 1,000 shares of stock in Black Corporation that White purchased two years ago because it was a good investment.

g) Account receivable from a customer with terms 2/10, net 30.

h) Machinery White held for three years and then sold at a loss of $10,000.

LO 11-3 **LO 11-4** 40. In year 0, Canon purchased a machine to use in its business for $56,000. In year 3, Canon sold the machine for $42,000. Between the date of the purchase and the date of the sale, Canon depreciated the machine by $32,000.

a) What is the amount and character of the gain Canon will recognize on the sale, assuming that it is a partnership?

b) What is the amount and character of the gain Canon will recognize on the sale, assuming that it is a corporation?

c) What is the amount and character of the gain Canon will recognize on the sale, assuming that it is a corporation and the sale proceeds were increased to $60,000?

d) What is the amount and character of the gain Canon will recognize on the sale, assuming that it is a corporation and the sale proceeds were decreased to $20,000?

LO 11-3 **LO 11-4** 41. In year 0, Longworth Partnership purchased a machine for $40,000 to use in its business. In year 3, Longworth sold the machine for $35,000. Between the date of the purchase and the date of the sale, Longworth depreciated the machine by $22,000.

a) What is the amount and character of the gain (loss) Longworth will recognize on the sale?

b) What is the amount and character of the gain (loss) Longworth will recognize on the sale if the sale proceeds are increased to $45,000?

c) What is the amount and character of the gain (loss) Longworth will recognize on the sale if the sale proceeds are decreased to $15,000?

42. On August 1 of year 0, Dirksen purchased a machine for $20,000 to use in its business. On December 4 of year 0, Dirksen sold the machine for $18,000.

    a) What is the amount and character of the gain or loss Dirksen will recognize on the sale?

    b) What is the amount and character of the gain or loss Dirksen will recognize on the sale if the machine is sold on January 15 of year 1 instead?

43. Rayburn Corporation has a building that it bought during year 0 for $850,000. It sold the building in year 5. During the time it held the building Rayburn depreciated it by $100,000. What is the amount and character of the gain or loss Rayburn will recognize on the sale in each of the following alternative situations?

    a) Rayburn receives $840,000.

    b) Rayburn receives $900,000.

    c) Rayburn receives $700,000.

44. Moran owns a building he bought during year 0 for $150,000. He sold the building in year 6. During the time he held the building he depreciated it by $32,000. What is the amount and character of the gain or loss Moran will recognize on the sale in each of the following alternative situations?

    a) Moran received $145,000.

    b) Moran received $170,000.

    c) Moran received $110,000.

45. Hart, an individual, bought an asset for $500,000 and has claimed $100,000 of depreciation deductions against the asset. Hart has a marginal tax rate of 32 percent. Answer the questions presented in the following alternative scenarios (assume Hart had no property transactions other than those described in the problem):

    a) What is the amount and character of Hart's recognized gain if the asset is tangible personal property sold for $450,000? What effect does the sale have on Hart's tax liability for the year?

    b) What is the amount and character of Hart's recognized gain if the asset is tangible personal property sold for $550,000? What effect does the sale have on Hart's tax liability for the year?

    c) What is the amount and character of Hart's recognized gain if the asset is tangible personal property sold for $350,000? What effect does the sale have on Hart's tax liability for the year?

    d) What is the amount and character of Hart's recognized gain if the asset is a nonresidential building sold for $450,000? What effect does the sale have on Hart's tax liability for the year?

    e) Now assume that Hart is a C corporation. What is the amount and character of its recognized gain if the asset is a nonresidential building sold for $450,000? What effect does the sale have on Hart's tax liability for the year (assume a 21 percent tax rate)?

    f) Assuming that the asset is real property, which entity type should be used to minimize the taxes paid on real estate gains?

46. Luke sold a building and the land on which the building sits to his wholly owned corporation, Studemont Corp., at fair market value. The fair market value of the building was determined to be $325,000; Luke built the building several years ago at a cost of $200,000. Luke had claimed $45,000 of depreciation expense on the building. The fair market value of the land was determined to be $210,000 at the time of the sale; Luke purchased the land many years ago for $130,000.

    a) What is the amount and character of Luke's recognized gain or loss on the building?

    b) What is the amount and character of Luke's recognized gain or loss on the land?

LO 11-5   47. Buckley, an individual, began business two years ago and has never sold a §1231 asset. Buckley has owned each of the assets since he began the business. In the current year, Buckley sold the following business assets:

Asset	Original Cost	Accumulated Depreciation	Gain/Loss
Computers	$ 6,000	$ 2,000	$(3,000)
Machinery	10,000	4,000	(2,000)
Furniture	20,000	12,000	7,000
Building	100,000	10,000	(1,000)

Assuming Buckley's marginal ordinary income tax rate is 32 percent, answer the questions for the following alternative scenarios:

a) What is the character of Buckley's gains or losses for the current year? What effect do the gains and losses have on Buckley's tax liability?

b) Assume that the amount realized increased so that the building was sold at a $6,000 gain instead. What is the character of Buckley's gains or losses for the current year? What effect do the gains and losses have on Buckley's tax liability?

c) Assume that the amount realized increased so that the building was sold at a $15,000 gain instead. What is the character of Buckley's gains or losses for the current year? What effect do the gains and losses have on Buckley's tax liability?

LO 11-3   LO 11-4   48. Lily Tucker (single) owns and operates a bike shop as a sole proprietorship. In 2018, she sells the following long-term assets used in her business:

LO 11-5

Asset	Sales Price	Cost	Accumulated Depreciation
Building	$230,000	$200,000	$52,000
Equipment	80,000	148,000	23,000

Lily's taxable income before these transactions is $160,500. What are Lily's taxable income and tax liability for the year?

LO 11-3   LO 11-4   49. Shimmer Inc. is a calendar-year-end, accrual-method corporation. This year, it sells the following long-term assets:

LO 11-5

Asset	Sales Price	Cost	Accumulated Depreciation
Building	$650,000	$642,000	$37,000
Sparkle Corporation stock	130,000	175,000	n/a

Shimmer does not sell any other assets during the year, and its taxable income before these transactions is $800,000. What are Shimmer's taxable income and tax liability for the year?

LO 11-5   50. Aruna, a sole proprietor, wants to sell two assets that she no longer needs for her business. Both assets qualify as §1231 assets. The first is machinery and will generate a $10,000 §1231 loss on the sale. The second is land that will generate a $7,000 §1231 gain on the sale. Aruna's ordinary marginal tax rate is 32 percent.

planning

a) Assuming she sells both assets in December of year 1 (the current year), what effect will the sales have on Aruna's tax liability?

b) Assuming that Aruna sells the land in December of year 1 and the machinery in January of year 2, what effect will the sales have on Aruna's tax liability for each year?

c) Explain why selling the assets in separate years will result in greater tax savings for Aruna.

51. Bourne Guitars, a corporation, reported a $157,000 net §1231 gain for year 6. LO 11-5

    a) Assuming Bourne reported $50,000 of nonrecaptured net §1231 losses during years 1–5, what amount of Bourne's net §1231 gain for year 6, if any, is treated as ordinary income?

    b) Assuming Bourne's nonrecaptured net §1231 losses from years 1–5 were $200,000, what amount of Bourne's net §1231 gain for year 6, if any, is treated as ordinary income?

52. Tonya Jefferson (single), a sole proprietor, runs a successful lobbying business in Washington, DC. She doesn't sell many business assets, but she is planning on retiring and selling her historic townhouse, from which she runs her business, to buy a place somewhere sunny and warm. Tonya's townhouse is worth $1,000,000 and the land is worth another $1,000,000. The original basis in the townhouse was $600,000, and she has claimed $250,000 of depreciation deductions against the asset over the years. The original basis in the land was $500,000. Tonya has located a buyer that would like to finalize the transaction in December of the current year. Tonya's marginal ordinary income tax rate is 35 percent and her capital gains tax rate is 20 percent. LO 11-5 planning

    a) What amount of gain or loss does Tonya recognize on the sale? What is the character of the gain or loss? What effect does the gain or loss have on her tax liability?

    b) In addition to the original facts, assume that Tonya reports the following nonrecaptured net §1231 loss:

Year	Net §1231 Gains/(Losses)
Year 1	$(200,000)
Year 2	0
Year 3	0
Year 4	0
Year 5	0
Year 6 (current year)	?

    What amount of gain or loss does Tonya recognize on the sale? What is the character of the gain or loss? What effect does the gain or loss have on her year 6 (the current year) tax liability?

    c) As Tonya's tax adviser, you suggest that Tonya sell the townhouse in year 7 in order to reduce her taxes. What amount of gain or loss does Tonya recognize on the sale in year 7?

53. Morgan's Water World (MWW), an LLC, opened several years ago. MWW has reported the following net §1231 gains and losses since it began business. Net §1231 gains shown are before the lookback rule. LO 11-5

Year	Net §1231 Gains/(Losses)
Year 1	$ (11,000)
Year 2	5,000
Year 3	(21,000)
Year 4	(4,000)
Year 5	17,000
Year 6	(43,000)
Year 7 (current year)	113,000

    What amount, if any, of the current year (year 7) $113,000 net §1231 gain is treated as ordinary income?

LO 11-5   54. Hans runs a sole proprietorship. Hans has reported the following net §1231 gains and losses since he began business. Net §1231 gains shown are before the lookback rule.

Year	Net §1231 Gains/(Losses)
Year 1	$(65,000)
Year 2	15,000
Year 3	0
Year 4	0
Year 5	10,000
Year 6	0
Year 7 (current year)	50,000

a) What amount, if any, of the year 7 (current year) $50,000 net §1231 gain is treated as ordinary income?

b) Assume that the $50,000 net §1231 gain occurs in year 6 instead of year 7. What amount of the gain would be treated as ordinary income in year 6?

LO 11-6   55. Independence Corporation needs to replace some of the assets used in its trade or business and is contemplating the following exchanges:

Exchange	Asset Given Up by Independence	Asset Received by Independence
A	Office building in Chicago, IL	Piece of land in Toronto, Canada
B	Large warehouse on two acres	Small warehouse on 22 acres
C	Office building in Green Bay, WI, used in the business	Apartment complex in Newport Beach, CA, that will be held as an investment

Determine whether each exchange qualifies as a like-kind exchange. Also, explain the rationale for why each qualifies or does not qualify as a like-kind exchange.

LO 11-6   56. Kase, an individual, purchased some property in Potomac, Maryland, for $150,000 approximately 10 years ago. Kase is approached by a real estate agent representing a client who would like to exchange a parcel of land in North Carolina for Kase's Maryland property. Kase agrees to the exchange. What is Kase's realized gain or loss, recognized gain or loss, and basis in the North Carolina property in each of the following alternative scenarios?

a) The transaction qualifies as a like-kind exchange and the fair market value of each property is $675,000.

b) The transaction qualifies as a like-kind exchange and the fair market value of each property is $100,000.

LO 11-6   57. Longhaul Real Estate exchanged a parcel of land it held for sale in Bryan, Texas, for a warehouse in College Station, Texas. Will the exchange qualify for like-kind treatment?

 research

LO 11-6   58. Twinbrook Corporation needed to upgrade to a larger manufacturing facility. Twinbrook first acquired a new manufacturing facility for $2,100,000 cash and then transferred the facility it was using (building and land) to White Flint Corporation for $2,000,000 three months later. Does the exchange qualify for like-kind exchange treatment? (*Hint:* Examine Revenue Procedures 2000-37 and 2004-51.) If not, can you propose a change in the transaction that will allow it to qualify?

research

LO 11-6   59. Woodley Park Corporation currently owns two parcels of land (parcel 1 and parcel 2). It owns a warehouse facility on parcel 1. Woodley needs to acquire a new and larger manufacturing facility. Woodley was approached by Blazing Fast Construction (which specializes in prefabricated warehouses) about acquiring Woodley's existing warehouse on parcel 1. Woodley indicated that it would prefer to exchange its

research

existing facility for a new and larger facility in a qualifying like-kind exchange. Blazing Fast indicated that it could construct a new manufacturing facility on parcel 2 to Woodley's specification within four months. Woodley and Blazing Fast agreed to the following arrangement. First, Blazing Fast would construct the new warehouse on parcel 2 and then relinquish the property to Woodley within four months. Woodley would then transfer the warehouse facility and land parcel 1 to Blazing Fast. All of the property exchanged in the deal was identified immediately and the construction was completed within 180 days. Does the exchange of the new building for the old building and parcel 1 qualify as a like-kind exchange? (*Hint*: See *DeCleene v. Commissioner,* 115 TC 457.)

60. Metro Corp. traded Land A for Land B. Metro originally purchased Land A for $50,000 and Land A's adjusted basis was $25,000 at the time of the exchange. What is Metro's realized gain or loss, recognized gain or loss, and adjusted basis in Land B in each of the following alternative scenarios?   `LO 11-6`

   a) The fair market value of Land A and of Land B is $40,000 at the time of the exchange. The exchange does not qualify as a like-kind exchange.

   b) The fair market value of Land A and of Land B is $40,000. The exchange qualifies as a like-kind exchange.

   c) The fair market value of Land A is $35,000 and Land B is valued at $40,000. Metro exchanges Land A and $5,000 cash for Land B. Land A and Land B are like-kind property.

   d) The fair market value of Land A is $45,000 and Metro trades Land A for Land B valued at $40,000 and $5,000 cash. Land A and Land B are like-kind property.

61. Prater Inc. enters into an exchange in which it gives up its warehouse on 10 acres of land and receives a tract of land. A summary of the exchange is as follows: `LO 11-6`

Transferred	FMV	Original Basis	Accumulated Depreciation
Warehouse	$300,000	$225,000	$45,000
Land	50,000	50,000	
Mortgage on warehouse	30,000		
Cash	20,000	20,000	

Assets received	FMV
Land	$340,000

   What is Prater's realized and recognized gain on the exchange and its basis in the assets it received in the exchange?

62. Baker Corporation owned a building located in Kansas. Baker used the building for its business operations. Last year a tornado hit the property and completely destroyed it. This year, Baker received an insurance settlement. Baker had originally purchased the building for $350,000 and had claimed a total of $100,000 of depreciation deductions against the property. What is Baker's realized and recognized gain or (loss) on this transaction and what is its basis in the new building in the following alternative scenarios?   `LO 11-6`

   a) Baker received $450,000 in insurance proceeds and spent $450,000 rebuilding the building during the current year.

   b) Baker received $450,000 in insurance proceeds and spent $500,000 rebuilding the building during the current year.

   c) Baker received $450,000 in insurance proceeds and spent $400,000 rebuilding the building during the current year.

   d) Baker received $450,000 in insurance proceeds and spent $450,000 rebuilding the building during the next three years.

LO 11-6   63. Russell Corporation sold a parcel of land valued at $400,000. Its basis in the land was $275,000. For the land, Russell received $50,000 in cash in year 0 and a note providing that Russell will receive $175,000 in year 1 and $175,000 in year 2 from the buyer.

    a) What is Russell's realized gain on the transaction?

    b) What is Russell's recognized gain in year 0, year 1, and year 2?

LO 11-6   64. In year 0, Javens Inc. sold machinery with a fair market value of $400,000 to Chris. The machinery's original basis was $317,000 and Javens's accumulated depreciation on the machinery was $50,000, so its adjusted basis to Javens was $267,000. Chris paid Javens $40,000 immediately (in year 0) and provided a note to Javens indicating that Chris would pay Javens $60,000 a year for six years beginning in year 1. What is the amount and character of the gain that Javens will recognize in year 0? What amount and character of the gain will Javens recognize in years 1 through 6?

LO 11-6

research   65. Ken sold a rental property for $500,000. He received $100,000 in the current year and $100,000 each year for the next four years. Of the sales price, $400,000 was allocated to the building and the remaining $100,000 was allocated to the land. Ken purchased the property several years ago for $300,000. When he initially purchased the property, he allocated $225,000 of the purchase price to the building and $75,000 to the land. Ken has claimed $25,000 of depreciation deductions over the years against the building. Ken had no other sales of §1231 or capital assets in the current year. For the year of the sale, determine Ken's recognized gain or loss and the character of Ken's gain, and calculate Ken's tax due because of the sale (assuming his marginal ordinary tax rate is 32 percent). (*Hint:* See the examples in Reg. §1.453-12.)

LO 11-6

planning   66. Hill Corporation is in the leasing business and faces a marginal tax rate of 21 percent. It has leased a building to Whitewater Corporation for several years. Hill bought the building for $150,000 and claimed $20,000 of depreciation deductions against the asset. The lease term is about to expire and Whitewater would like to acquire the building. Hill has been offered two options to choose from:

Option	Details
Like-kind exchange	Whitewater would provide Hill with a like-kind building. The like-kind building has a fair market value of $135,000.
Installment sale	Whitewater would provide Hill with two payments of $69,000. It would use the proceeds to purchase another building that it could also lease.

    Ignoring time value of money, which option provides the greatest after-tax value for Hill, assuming it is indifferent between the proposals based on nontax factors?

LO 11-6   67. Deirdre sold 100 shares of stock to her brother, James, for $2,400. Deirdre purchased the stock several years ago for $3,000.

    a) What gain or loss does Deirdre recognize on the sale?

    b) What amount of gain or loss does James recognize if he sells the stock for $3,200?

    c) What amount of gain or loss does James recognize if he sells the stock for $2,600?

    d) What amount of gain or loss does James recognize if he sells the stock for $2,000?

COMPREHENSIVE PROBLEMS

Select problems are available in Connect®.   connect

68. Two years ago, Bethesda Corporation bought a delivery truck for $30,000 (not subject to the luxury auto depreciation limits). Bethesda used MACRS 200 percent declining balance and the half-year convention to recover the cost of the truck, but it did not elect §179 expensing and opted out of bonus depreciation. Answer the questions for the following alternative scenarios.

   a) Assuming Bethesda used the truck until it sold it in March of year 3, what depreciation expense can it claim on the truck for years 1 through 3?

   b) Assume that Bethesda claimed $18,500 of depreciation expense on the truck before it sold it in year 3. What is the amount and character of the gain or loss if Bethesda sold the truck in year 3 for $17,000 and incurred $2,000 of selling expenses on the sale?

   c) Assume that Bethesda claimed $18,500 of depreciation expense on the truck before it sold it in year 3. What is the amount and character of the gain or loss if Bethesda sold the truck in year 3 for $35,000 and incurred $3,000 of selling expenses on the sale?

69. Hauswirth Corporation sold (or exchanged) a warehouse in year 0. Hauswirth bought the warehouse several years ago for $65,000 and it has claimed $23,000 of depreciation expense against the building.

   a) Assuming that Hauswirth receives $50,000 in cash for the warehouse, compute the amount and character of Hauswirth's recognized gain or loss on the sale.

   b) Assuming that Hauswirth exchanges the warehouse in a like-kind exchange for some land with a fair market value of $50,000, compute Hauswirth's gain realized, gain recognized, deferred gain, and basis in the new land.

   c) Assuming that Hauswirth receives $20,000 in cash in year 0 and a $50,000 note receivable that is payable in year 1, compute the amount and character of Hauswirth's gain in year 0 and in year 1.

 research

70. Fontenot Corporation sold some machinery to its majority owner Gray (an individual who owns 60 percent of Fontenot). Fontenot purchased the machinery for $100,000 and has claimed a total of $40,000 of depreciation expense deductions against the property. Gray will provide Fontenot with $10,000 cash today and provide a $100,000 note that will pay Fontenot $50,000 one year from now and $50,000 two years from now.

   a) What gain does Fontenot realize on the sale?

   b) What is the amount and character of the gain that Fontenot must recognize in the year of sale (if any) and each of the two subsequent years? (*Hint:* Use the Internal Revenue Code and start with §453; please give appropriate citations.)

71. Moab Inc. manufactures and distributes high-tech biking gadgets. It has decided to streamline some of its operations so that it will be able to be more productive and efficient. Because of this decision it has entered into several transactions during the year.

 tax forms

   Part (1): Determine the gain/loss realized and recognized in the current year for each of these events. Also determine whether the gain/loss recognized will be §1231, capital, or ordinary.

   a) Moab Inc. sold a machine that it used to make computerized gadgets for $27,300 cash. It originally bought the machine for $19,200 three years ago and has taken $8,000 depreciation.

   b) Moab Inc. held stock in ABC Corp., which had a value of $12,000 at the beginning of the year. That same stock had a value of $15,230 at the end of the year.

   c) Moab Inc. sold some of its inventory for $7,000 cash. This inventory had a basis of $5,000.

d) Moab Inc. disposed of an office building with a fair market value of $75,000 for another office building with a fair market value of $55,000 and $20,000 in cash. It originally bought the office building seven years ago for $62,000 and has taken $15,000 in depreciation.

e) Moab Inc. sold some land held for investment for $28,000. It originally bought the land for $32,000 two years ago.

f) Moab Inc. sold another machine for a note payable in four annual installments of $12,000. The first payment was received in the current year. It originally bought the machine two years ago for $32,000 and has claimed $9,000 in depreciation expense against the machine.

g) Moab Inc. sold stock it held for eight years for $2,750. It originally purchased the stock for $2,100.

h) Moab Inc. sold another machine for $7,300. It originally purchased this machine six months ago for $9,000 and has claimed $830 in depreciation expense against the asset.

Part (2): From the recognized gains/losses determined in part (1), determine the net §1231 gain/loss and the net ordinary gain/loss Moab will recognize on its tax return. Moab Inc. also has $2,000 of nonrecaptured net §1231 losses from previous years.

Part (3): Complete Moab Inc.'s Form 4797 for the year. Use the most current form available.

research

72. Vertovec Inc., a large local consulting firm in Utah, hired several new consultants from out of state last year to help service its expanding list of clients. To aid in relocating the consultants, Vertovec Inc. purchased the consultants' homes in their prior location if the consultants were unable to sell their homes within 30 days of listing them for sale. Vertovec Inc. bought the homes from the consultants for 5 percent less than the list price and then continued to list the homes for sale. Each home Vertovec Inc. purchased was sold at a loss. By the end of last year, Vertovec had suffered a loss totaling $250,000 from the homes. How should Vertovec treat the loss for tax purposes? Write a memo to Vertovec Inc. explaining your findings and any planning suggestions that you may have if Vertovec Inc. continues to offer this type of relocation benefit to newly hired consultants.

tax forms

73. WAR (We Are Rich) has been in business since 1985. WAR is an accrual method sole proprietorship that deals in the manufacturing and wholesaling of various types of golf equipment. Hack & Hack CPAs has filed accurate tax returns for WAR's owner since WAR opened its doors. The managing partner of Hack & Hack (Jack) has gotten along very well with the owner of WAR—Mr. Someday Woods (single). However, in early 2018, Jack Hack and Someday Woods played a round of golf and Jack, for the first time ever, actually beat Mr. Woods. Mr. Woods was so upset that he fired Hack & Hack and has hired you to compute his 2018 taxable income. Mr. Woods was able to provide you with the following information from prior tax returns. The taxable income numbers reflect the results from all of Mr. Wood's activities *except for the items separately stated*. You will need to consider how to handle the separately stated items for tax purposes. Also, note that the 2013–2017 numbers do not reflect capital loss carryovers.

	2013	2014	2015	2016	2017
Ordinary taxable income	$ 4,000	$ 2,000	$94,000	$170,000	$250,000
Other items not included in ordinary taxable income					
Net gain (loss) on disposition of §1231 assets	3,000	10,000		(6,000)	
Net long-term capital gain (loss) on disposition of capital assets	(15,000)	1,000	(7,000)		(7,000)

In 2018, Mr. Woods had taxable income in the amount of $480,000 before considering the following events and transactions that transpired in 2018:

a) On January 1, 2018, WAR purchased a plot of land for $100,000 with the intention of creating a driving range where patrons could test their new golf equipment. WAR never got around to building the driving range; instead, WAR sold the land on October 1, 2018, for $40,000.

b) On August 17, 2018, WAR sold its golf testing machine, "Iron Byron" and replaced it with a new machine "Iron Tiger." "Iron Byron" was purchased and installed for a total cost of $22,000 on February 5, 2014. At the time of sale, "Iron Byron" had an adjusted tax basis of $4,000. WAR sold "Iron Byron" for $25,000.

c) In the months October through December 2018, WAR sold various assets to come up with the funds necessary to invest in WAR's latest and greatest invention—the three-dimple golf ball. Data on these assets are provided below:

Asset	Placed in Service (or Purchased)	Sold	Initial Basis	Accumulated Depreciation	Selling Price
Someday's black leather sofa (used in office)	4/4/17	10/16/18	$ 3,000	$ 540	$ 2,900
Someday's office chair	3/1/16	11/8/18	8,000	3,000	4,000
Marketable securities	2/1/15	12/1/18	12,000	0	20,000
Land held for investment	7/1/17	11/29/18	45,000	0	48,000
Other investment property	11/30/16	10/15/18	10,000	0	8,000

d) Finally, on May 7, 2018, WAR decided to sell the building where it tested its plutonium shaft, lignite head drivers. WAR purchased the building on January 5, 2006, for $190,000 ($170,000 for the building, $20,000 for the land). At the time of the sale, the accumulated depreciation on the building was $50,000. WAR sold the building (with the land) for $300,000. The fair market value of the land at the time of sale was $45,000.

Part (1): Compute Mr. Woods's taxable income *after* taking into account the transactions described above.

Part (2): Compute Mr. Woods's tax liability for the year. (Ignore any net investment income tax for the year and assume the 20 percent qualified business income deduction is included in taxable income before these transactions.)

Part (3): Complete Mr. Woods's Form 8949, Schedule D, and Form 4797 (use the most current version of these schedules) to be attached to his Form 1040. Assume that asset bases are not reported to the IRS.

74. Fizbo Corporation is in the business of breeding and racing horses. Fizbo has taxable income of $5,000,000 other than from these transactions. It has nonrecaptured §1231 losses of $10,000 from 2014 and $13,000 from 2012.

Consider the following transactions that occur during 2018:

a) A building with an adjusted basis of $300,000 is totally destroyed by fire. Fizbo receives insurance proceeds of $400,000, but does not plan to replace the building. The building was built 12 years ago at a cost of $420,000 and was used to provide lodging for employees.

b) Fizbo sells four acres of undeveloped farmland (used for grazing) for $50,000. Fizbo purchased the land 15 years ago for $15,000.

c) Fizbo sells a racehorse for $250,000. The racehorse was purchased four years ago for $200,000. Total depreciation taken on the racehorse was $160,000.

d) Fizbo exchanges equipment that was purchased three years ago for $300,000 for $100,000 of IBM common stock. The adjusted basis of the equipment is $220,000. If straight-line depreciation had been used, the adjusted basis would be $252,000.

e) On November 1, Fizbo sold XCON stock for $50,000. Fizbo had purchased the stock on December 12, 2017, for $112,000.

Part (1): After *all* netting is complete, what is Fizbo's total amount of income from these transactions to be treated as ordinary income or loss? What is its capital gain or loss?

Part (2): What is Fizbo's taxable income for the year after including the effects of these transactions?

R **ROGER** | *CPA Review*

Sample CPA Exam questions from Roger CPA Review are available in Connect as support for the topics in this text. These Multiple Choice Questions and Task-Based Simulations include expert-written explanations and solutions and provide a starting point for students to become familiar with the content and functionality of the actual CPA Exam.

12 Compensation

Learning Objectives

Upon completing this chapter, you should be able to:

LO 12-1 Explain the tax implications of compensation in the form of salary and wages from the perspective of the employee and the employer.

LO 12-2 Describe the tax implications of various forms of equity-based compensation from the perspective of the employee and the employer.

LO 12-3 Compare and contrast taxable and nontaxable fringe benefits and explain their tax consequences for the employee and the employer.

©Alija/Getty Images

Storyline Summary

Taxpayers:	Julie and Ethan Clark
Location:	San Diego, California
Employment status:	Julie—mid-level executive for Premier Computer Corporation (PCC); current salary $240,000 Ethan—mechanical engineer; current salary $70,000
Filing status:	Married filing jointly
Dependents:	Two children
Marginal ordinary tax rate:	24 percent
Long-term capital gain rate:	15 percent
Current situation:	Julie is considering an offer for the vice president of marketing position with Technology Products Inc (TPI).
Taxpayer:	TPI Corporation (a C corporation)
Location:	San Diego, California
Ownership:	Publicly traded corporation
Industry:	Manufacturer of high-technology products
CEO:	Daniella Hewitt
Tax rate:	21 percent
Current situation:	Recruiting Julie Clark for VP of marketing position

Julie and Ethan Clark and their two children have lived in San Diego, California, for some time. Julie has decided her career is at a crossroads. On the one hand, her employment as a mid-level executive for Premier Computer Corporation (PCC) is going well, but the work is not as challenging as it used to be. She suspects that, given her skills and abilities, she could put her career on the fast track with the right opportunity, engaging in more fulfilling work and gaining a significant increase in compensation.

Julie was sitting at her desk contemplating her career when she received yet another call from a corporate headhunter. While she usually quickly dismissed such calls, this time her interest and curiosity were piqued and she gave her full attention. He asked if she had any interest in a vice president of marketing position with a publicly traded company located nearby. After the headhunter answered a few of her questions, Julie gave him the go-ahead to set up an interview.

A couple of weeks later, Julie had been through two rounds of interviews for the marketing VP position when she received a call informing her that she was the one Technology Products Inc. (TPI) wanted for the job, and that an offer letter with the details was on its way. The letter indicated TPI was offering a $280,000 salary (a significant increase from her current salary). TPI was also offering her several types of equity-based compensation and some attractive fringe benefits. While excited by the letter, Julie knew she needed to learn more about the equity-based compensation alternatives and the other forms of compensation TPI was offering before she could adequately evaluate the offer and reach her decision.

to be continued . . .

As TPI's letter to Julie illustrates, employers are able to offer many different forms of compensation to employees. They can also pay some compensation now and defer some to the future. Each type of compensation has unique tax and nontax consequences.

This chapter addresses the tax and nontax consequences of *current* compensation packages from both the employee's and the employer's perspectives. For deferred compensation see the Retirement Savings and Deferred Compensation chapter.

LO 12-1 SALARY AND WAGES

Current compensation paid to **employees** in the form of **salary** and **wages,** usually in cash, has tax consequences to both employees and employers. Below, we address the tax (and nontax) considerations of salary and wages from the employee's perspective, followed by the employer's perspective.

Employee Considerations for Salary and Wages

Employees receiving salary generally earn a fixed amount of compensation for the year no matter how many hours they work. In addition, salaried employees may be eligible for bonuses if they satisfy certain criteria. In contrast, employees receiving wages generally get paid on an hourly, daily, or piecework basis. Salary, bonus, and wages are all taxed to employees as ordinary income. Employees generally recognize income from salary and wages as they receive it.[1] As we discussed in detail in the Individual Income Tax Computation and Tax Credits chapter, employees must pay **FICA taxes** on their wages.[2] FICA taxes consist of both a Social Security and a Medicare component.

At the end of each year, employees receive a **Form W-2** (see Exhibit 12-1) from their employers, summarizing their salary or wage compensation and the various amounts withheld from their paychecks during the year.[3] Employees simply report their wages on Page 1, line 7, of the 2017 federal Form 1040 and report their federal income taxes withheld on line 64 of Page 2 (the line number references may be different on the 2018 federal Form 1040). Self-employed taxpayers receive a Form 1099-MISC indicating the compensation they received, which they report on Schedule C.

Tax Withholding   When employees begin employment with a company, they complete a **Form W-4** to supply the information the company needs in order to withhold the correct amount of tax from each paycheck. Specifically, employees use Form W-4 to indicate (1) whether to withhold at the single rate or at the lower married rate, (2) the number of withholding allowances the employee chooses to claim (the more withholding allowances claimed, the less the withholding amount), and (3) whether the employee wants an additional amount of tax withheld each period above the amount based on the number of allowances claimed.

Employer Considerations for Salary and Wages

Deductibility of Salary and Wage Payments   Employers receive a deduction for reasonable salaries, wages, and other compensation.[4] Determining whether compensation is reasonable in amount is a **facts and circumstances test** that requires considering the

---

> **THE KEY FACTS**
>
> **Employment-Related Forms**
>
> - **Form W-2**
>   - Summarizes an employee's taxable salary and wages.
>   - Provides annual federal and state withholding information.
>   - Generated by employer on an annual basis.
> - **Form W-4**
>   - Supplies an employee's withholding information to employer.
>   - Generated by employee.
>   - Numbers reported on form remain constant unless employee makes changes.
> - **Form 1099-MISC**
>   - Summarizes an independent contractor's or non-employee's taxable compensation.
>   - Generated by person or entity paying the compensation.

---

[1]Reg. §1.451-1(a).

[2]FICA stands for Federal Insurance Contributions Act.

[3]Compensation received by taxpayers who are self-employed is not considered to be salary and wages.

[4]§162(a)(1). As we discuss in the Business Income, Deductions, and Accounting Methods chapter, all business expenses (not just compensation) must be reasonable in amount to be fully deductible.

EXHIBIT 12-1 Form W-2*

a Employee's social security number		Safe, accurate, FAST! Use IRS e-file	Visit the IRS website at www.irs.gov/efile

OMB No. 1545-0008

b Employer identification number (EIN)	1 Wages, tips, other compensation	2 Federal income tax withheld
c Employer's name, address, and ZIP code	3 Social security wages	4 Social security tax withheld
	5 Medicare wages and tips	6 Medicare tax withheld
	7 Social security tips	8 Allocated tips
d Control number	9 Verification code	10 Dependent care benefits
e Employee's first name and initial Last name Suff.	11 Nonqualified plans	12a See instructions for box 12
	13 Statutory employee Retirement plan Third-party sick pay	12b
	14 Other	12c
		12d
f Employee's address and ZIP code		

15 State Employer's state ID number	16 State wages, tips, etc.	17 State income tax	18 Local wages, tips, etc.	19 Local income tax	20 Locality name

Form **W-2** Wage and Tax Statement **2017** Department of the Treasury—Internal Revenue Service

Copy B—To Be Filed With Employee's FEDERAL Tax Return.
This information is being furnished to the Internal Revenue Service.

Source: The 2018 Form W-2 was unavailable at press time. Please visit the IRS website (www.irs.gov) for the final 2018 form.

duties of the employee, the complexities of the business, and the amount of salary compared with the income of the business, prevailing rates of compensation and external comparison to other businesses among other things. The amount of salary paid in excess of the amount considered reasonable is not deductible. The reasonable compensation limit typically applies to closely held businesses where either the employee is an owner of the business or the employee is a relative of the business owner. If the IRS determines that the shareholder/employee compensation is unreasonable, the nondeductible portion of the compensation may be recharacterized as a dividend to the shareholder.[5] For a discussion of tax planning opportunities between shareholders/employees, see the Entities Overview chapter. Currently there are incentives for corporations to pay lower salaries to shareholders/employees in order to have more of their income taxed at the lower corporate rate rather than the higher individual rate.

The timing of the compensation deduction depends on the employer's method of accounting. Cash method employers generally deduct the salary and wages when they pay employees.[6] Accrual-method employers deduct salary and wages payable to employees as the compensation becomes fixed and determinable.[7] This general rule for accrual-method employers holds even in situations when the employer accrues compensation expense in one year but actually pays the employee in the subsequent year, as long as the employer

[5]Reg. §1.162-8.
[6]Reg. §1.461-1(a)(1).
[7]Reg. §1.461-1(a)(2). See the Business Income, Deductions, and Accounting Methods chapter for a detailed discussion of the cash and accrual accounting methods.

THE KEY FACTS

Compensation Deductibility for Accrual-Basis Taxpayers

- Compensation expense accrued at end of year *is* deductible in year accrued if
  - Paid to an *unrelated* party within 2½ months of year-end.
- Compensation expense accrued at end of year *is not* deductible when paid if
  - Paid to *related* person owning more than 50 percent of the employer corporation.

makes the payment within 2½ months after the employer's year-end. If the employer pays the employee more than 2½ months after the employer's year-end, the wages are considered deferred compensation and are not deductible by the employer until the employee receives the payment and recognizes the salary as income.[8] Because most employers pay regular salary and wages to employees each month (or more frequently), the 2½-month rule is likely to be more of an issue for accrued compensation—such as one-time year-end bonuses or vacation pay—than it is for normal wages.

Example 12-1

When does PCC deduct the $240,000 salary it paid to Julie in the current year?

Answer: All $240,000 in the current year.

What if: Suppose that PCC paid Julie $240,000 of salary during the current year and it paid her a bonus of $20,000 that was approved before year end and paid on February 1 of the subsequent year. When would PCC deduct the compensation paid to Julie?

Answer: All $260,000 in the current year because the salary and bonus were fixed in the current year and the bonus was paid within 2½ months after the employer's year end.

What if: Assume the same facts as in the previous what if except that the bonus was paid on April 1 of the subsequent year. When would PCC deduct the compensation paid to Julie?

Answer: $240,000 in the current year and $20,000 in the subsequent year. The bonus will be deductible in the subsequent year because it was not paid within 2½ months after the PCC's year-end.

The after-tax cost of providing this salary is generally much less than the before-tax cost.[9] While profitable corporations now have a 21 percent tax rate, the marginal tax rate for other businesses could be as high as 37 percent for sole proprietorships and flow-through entities. The formula for computing the after-tax cost of the salary (the cost after subtracting the tax savings from the deduction), or any deductible expense, for that matter, is as follows:

Formula: Deductible expenditure × (1 − Marginal tax rate)

Example 12-2

What are PCC's before-tax and after-tax cost of paying Julie a $240,000 salary (ignoring FICA taxes)?

Answer: $240,000 before-tax cost and $189,600 after-tax cost, computed as follows:

Description	Amount	Explanation
Before-tax cost of salary		
(1) **Salary**	**$240,000**	
(2) 1 − Marginal tax rate	× 79%	(1 − 21%). Corporate tax rate is 21%.
After-tax cost of salary	**$189,600**	(1) × (2)

> **THE KEY FACTS**
>
> **Compensation Deductibility for Accrual-Method Taxpayers**
>
> - Compensation expense accrued at end of year *is generally* deductible if paid within 2½ months of year-end.
> - Compensation expense accrued at end of year *is not* deductible until paid, even if within 2½ months of year end, if employer and employee are related persons.

Compensation deduction restrictions. Special compensation deduction rules may apply when the employer and employee are considered to be related persons and when an employee is considered to be a "covered employee." We discuss each of these situations below.

[8] Reg. §1.404(b)-1T(A-2). We discuss tax issues and consequences relating to deferred compensation in the Retirement Savings and Deferred Compensation chapter.

[9] As discussed in the Individual Income Tax Computation and Tax Credits chapter, employers are required to pay FICA taxes on employees' compensation. Employers may also be required to pay other expenses based on employee wages such as workers' compensation insurance.

When an accrual method employer and a cash method employee are considered to be "related persons" the employer is not allowed to deduct compensation accrued at year end until it actually pays the employee, even if the payment is within 2½ months of year end.[10] This rule prevents an employers and employees with close relationships from accelerating the deduction for the employer while deferring the income to the employee. For this purpose, corporate employers are considered to be related persons if the employee owns directly or indirectly more than 50 percent of the value of the corporation's stock.[11] Employees are treated as owning indirectly any stock owned by family members. For this purpose, family members include the employee's spouse, siblings, ancestors (parents, grandparents, etc.) and lineal descendants (children, grandchildren, etc).

Example 12-3

What if: Suppose that PCC paid Julie $240,000 of salary during the current year and it paid her a bonus of $20,000 that was approved before year end and paid on February 1 of the subsequent year. Further, assume that Julie owns 10 percent of the PCC stock and her father owns 45 percent of the PCC stock. When would PCC deduct the compensation paid to Julie?

Answer: $240,000 of salary is deductible in the current year and the $20,000 bonus is deductible in the subsequent year. The bonus is not deductible to PCC (an accrual-method employer) until the year that Julie (the cash method, related person) receives and recognizes the bonus as income. Julie is a related person to PCC because her direct ownership (10 percent of PCC stock) plus her indirect ownership (45 percent of PCC stock attributed to her from her father) in PCC stock is greater than 50 percent.

THE KEY FACTS

Limits on Salary Deductibility of Publicly Traded Corporations

- $1 million maximum annual compensation deduction per covered employee.
  - Covered employees are the CEO, CFO, and the three other highest compen¬sated officers.
  - A covered employee for any year after 2016 will be considered a covered employee for all future years.
  - Limit does not apply to performance-based compensation contract in existence on November 2, 2017 that is not materially modified.

For taxable years beginning on or after January 1, 2018, the deduction for compensation with respect to a covered employee of a publicly held corporation is limited to $1 million per year per covered employee.[12] For this purpose, compensation includes all amounts paid to the employee and amounts excludable as nontaxable fringe benefits. Covered employees include the principal executive officer (CEO), principal financial officer (CFO), and the three highest paid officers other than the CEO and CFO. If an employee was a covered employee for any year beginning after December 31, 2016, that employee will be considered a covered employee for all subsequent years. That is, once an employee is a covered employee with respect to a particular employer, that employee will be considered to be a covered employee with respect to that employer for purposes of the deduction limitation for all future years.[13] The covered employee deduction limitation applies to all publicly-traded corporations and certain other corporations.[14]

Example 12-4

Assume that TPI, Julie's potential employer has been actively searching for a new CEO. The board of directors eventually chose Daniella Hewitt. During negotiations, Daniella indicated she wanted a $1.5 million salary and a performance-based bonus of $1 million upon reaching certain performance objectives. If the board of directors agrees to her request, and the performance objectives are met, what are TPI's before-tax and after-tax costs of paying Daniella (a covered employee) a $1.5 million salary and a $1 million bonus during the current year?

(continued on page 12-6)

[10]§267(a)(2).

[11]See §267(b) for the complete definition of "related" persons.

[12]§162(m).

[13] A covered employee is still considered a covered employee even after the employment relationship ends due to death or a change in employment. For example, compensation paid to a beneficiary after the employee's death or to a former spouse under a domestic relations order would be non-deductible to the extent the compensation exceed the $1 million limit.

[14]The limit applies to foreign private issuers that meet the definition of a publicly held corporation (even if not subject to the Securities Exchange Act), and possibly large private C or S corporations (as of press date this was not clear in the tax law).

Answer: $2,500,000 before-tax cost and $2,290,000 after-tax cost: computed as follows:

Description	Amount	Explanation
Before-tax cost of salary		
(1) **Salary**	$1,500,000	
(2) **Bonus**	$1,000,000	
(3) Deductible amount	$ 1,000,000	Limited to $1,000,000 because Daniella is a covered employee. Corporate tax rate is 21%.
(4) Marginal tax rate	× 21%	
(5) Tax savings from compensation deduction	$ 210,000	(3) × (4)
After-tax cost of salary	**$2,290,000**	(1) + (2) − (5)

Note that the after-tax cost of the salary is significantly higher for covered employees than non-covered employees (compare with Example 12-2) due to the $1,000,000 compensation deduction limitation.

For taxable years beginning prior to January 1, 2018, and for compensation paid under a binding contract in existence on November 2, 2017 (that has not been materially modified after that date) the $1 million per year deduction limitation does not apply to performance-based compensation (e.g., stock option compensation, performance-based bonuses, and commissions).

Example 12-5

Assume that TPI, Julie's potential employer was still paying compensation to its former CEO during 2018. Under the compensation contract in existence before November 2, 2017, TPI paid the former CEO a salary of $1.5 million and $1 million for a performance-based bonus. What are TPI's before-tax and after-tax costs of paying the former CEO (a covered employee) a $1.5 million salary and $1 million in performance-based bonus during 2018 under an agreement in existence before November 2, 2017?

Answer: $2,500,000 before-tax cost and $2,080,000 after-tax cost: computed as follows:

Description	Amount	Explanation
Before-tax cost of salary		
(1) **Salary**	$1,500,000	
(2) **Bonus**	$1,000,000	
(3) Deductible amount	$ 2,000,000	$1,000,000 limitation on (1) + performance-based bonus (2) Corporate tax rate is 21%.
(4) Marginal tax rate	× 21%	
(5) Tax savings from compensation deduction	$ 420,000	(3) × (4)
After-tax cost of salary	**$2,080,000**	(1) + (2) − (5)

Note that the after-tax cost of the salary is lower than the after-tax cost of salary in Example 12-4 because performance-based compensation is deductible for contracts in existence before November 2, 2017. This provides an incentive to keep pre-existing contracts in place for covered employees.

What if: What are TPI's before-tax and after-tax costs of paying a non-covered employee a $1.5 million salary and $1 million performance-based bonus during 2018?

(continued on page 12-7)

Answer: $2,500,000 before-tax cost and $1,975,000 after-tax cost: computed as follows:

Description	Amount	Explanation
Before-tax cost of salary		
(1) **Salary**	**$1,500,000**	
(2) **Commissions**	**$1,000,000**	
(3) Deductible amount	$ 2,500,000	No limitation to compensation for a non-covered employee.
(4) Marginal tax rate	× 21%	Corporate tax rate is 21%.
(5) Tax savings from compensation deduction	$ 525,000	(3) × (4)
After-tax cost of salary	**$1,975,000**	(1) + (2) − (5)

The after-tax cost of the compensation for a non-covered employee is lower than the after-tax cost of equal salary paid to covered employees because there are no limitations on deductibility for non-covered employees.

TAXES IN THE REAL WORLD   Are CEOs Rewarded for Tax Dodging?

In 2011, the Institute for Policy Studies reported that 25 U.S. companies paid their CEOs more than they paid the U.S. government in taxes. The list of companies included: International Paper, General Electric, Verizon, Boeing, and Ford Motor Company. On average, the companies reported $1.6 billion in profits and $16.7 million in executive compensation. In total, the companies also reported 556 subsidiaries located in tax havens, $12.6 million in campaign contributions, and $129 million in lobbying expenditures (campaign contributions and lobbying expenditures are nondeductible for tax). On average, these CEOs were paid $5.9 million more than the average of CEOs comprising the S&P 500. It appears that employers reward CEOs for investing in corporate political activity.

As this example illustrates, the $1 million deduction limitation can have a considerable impact on the after-tax cost of providing compensation to covered employees.

EQUITY-BASED COMPENSATION

LO 12-2

continued from page 12-1 . . .

As she read TPI's offer letter more carefully, Julie discovered that on the first day of January following her acceptance of the offer, she would be granted 200 nonqualified stock options (NQOs), 50 incentive stock options (ISOs), and 10,000 shares of restricted stock. Each stock option would give her the right to purchase 100 shares of stock (50 ISOs allow up to 5,000 shares and 200 NQOs allow up to 20,000 shares) at a fixed price equal to the market value of TPI stock on the date of grant. As she read on, Julie noticed that she would not be able to exercise either type of stock option (purchase TPI stock for the exercise price stated in the options) until the options vest (the options become hers when they vest), which would be two years from the grant date. Further, Julie understood that, after the restricted stock vests (one year from the grant date on January 1), she would be free to do what she wanted with it. The last detail Julie noticed when reading this part of the offer letter was that both types of options expire 10 years from the grant date. She understood this to mean that if she did not exercise her options sometime before their expiration date, she would lose them. Julie also remembered that the HR director mentioned that TPI was considering granting restricted stock units (RSUs) in the future. Julie wondered if restricted stock and RSUs were the same thing?

Although it is obvious to Julie that the value of the options and restricted stock will increase as the share price of TPI increases from the current share price of $5 per share, she remains unsure about the terminology used in this section of the letter. She realizes she needs to know more about the economic and tax implications of stock options restricted stock, and maybe RSUs before making her decision.

to be continued . . .

THE KEY FACTS

Equity-Based Compensation

- Stock options
  - Allow employees to purchase stock at a definitive price.
- Restricted stock
  - Form of compensation that provides actual stock ownership to employees after restrictions lapse.
- Restricted stock units
  - Grant valued in terms of company stock, but company stock is not issued at the time of the grant. After vesting, the company distributes shares or the cash equivalent of the number of shares used to value the unit.

Equity-based compensation such as stock options and restricted stock provides risks and potential rewards not available with other forms of compensation.[15] If the employer's stock price increases after it grants options and restricted stock, employees can be rewarded handsomely. On the other hand, if the employer's stock price doesn't increase, the stock options will expire worthless, and the value of the restricted stock will be limited.

Employers use equity-based compensation, in part, to motivate their employees to take a share of ownership in their companies. When employees hold employer options and stock, their compensation is more directly tied to the fortunes of their employer and its shareholders—that is, employees' compensation increases in tandem with their employer's stock price. This philosophy is reflected in an excerpt from Adobe's 2017 proxy statement, presented in Exhibit 12-2.

EXHIBIT 12-2   **Excerpt from Adobe's 2017 Proxy Statement**

Goals of Equity Compensation

We use equity compensation to motivate and reward strong corporate performance and to retain valued executive officers. We also use equity incentive awards as a means to attract and recruit qualified executives. We believe that equity awards serve to align the interests of our Named Executive Officers (NEOs) with those of our stockholders by rewarding them for stock price growth. By having a significant percentage of our NEOs' target tax deductible compensation payable in the form of multi-year equity and, thus, subject to higher risk and longer vesting than cash compensation, our NEOs are motivated to take actions that will benefit Adobe and its stockholders in the long term.

THE KEY FACTS

Stock Option Terminology

- *Incentive stock options* (ISOs) satisfy certain tax code requirements to provide favorable tax treatment to employees.
- *Nonqualified stock options* (NQOs) are any options that don't meet the requirements for being classified as incentive stock options.
- The *grant date* is the date employees are initially allocated stock options.
- The *exercise date* is the date that employees purchase stock using their options.

(continued)

In addition to its motivational effects, equity-based compensation has traditionally brought employers cash flow benefits as well. How? Unless employers purchase their own stock in a market transaction to satisfy option exercises and stock grants, there are no cash outflows associated with this form of compensation. In fact, employers actually *receive* cash from their employees in the amount of the exercise price on the options exercised. There are a couple of downsides to this benefit, however.

First, employers experience the opportunity cost of selling shares at a discounted price to employees rather than selling them at fair market value on the open market. Second, when employers issue new shares to satisfy option exercises and stock grants, the total number of shares outstanding increases, and therefore, earnings per share are diluted, which is a detriment to existing shareholders. Employers can avoid diluting earnings per share if they use their cash reserves to buy back shares before issuing shares as equity based compensation.[16] However, from a cash-flow perspective, this is no different from paying cash compensation.

---

[15]As with other forms of compensation, equity-based compensation is subject to FICA.

[16]Because earnings per share is calculated by dividing earnings by the number of shares of stock outstanding, for a given level of earnings, earnings per share could even increase when new shares are issued to satisfy option exercises if earnings increase by an amount that more than offsets the effect of issuing new shares into the market.

Stock Options

Stock options are a form of equity-based compensation that gives the employee the legal right to buy employer stock at a set price between the date the stock options **vest** and the expiration date of the options.[17] The stipulated price at which employees can purchase the employer stock is referred to as the **exercise price** or **strike price.** At any point between vesting and expiration, the employee may exercise the option by paying the employer the exercise price. Stock options have several important characteristics: (1) employees have no incentive to exercise options when the employer's share price is depressed, (2) once the option vests the employee must use cash to purchase the employer's stock, and (3) once purchased the employer stock is subject to investment risk. As suggested in Exhibit 12-3, the value of stock option awards depends on the exercise price, the company's future share price, the exercise date of the options, and the timing for selling the shares received from the **option exercise.**

- The *exercise price* (or *strike price*) is the amount paid to acquire shares with stock options.
- The *bargain element* is the difference between the fair market value of stock and the exercise price on the exercise date.
- The *vesting date* is the time when stock options granted can be exercised.

Example 12-6

What if: Given the assumptions in the stock option timeline shown in Exhibit 12-3, what is Julie's economic loss from her stock options if the value of TPI shares fall to $3 per share and remains there after the options are granted?

Answer: Zero. If TPI's stock price never increases above the $5 per share exercise price before the expiration date of the options, Julie will not exercise her options to purchase TPI shares, and those options will expire worthless.

If the employer's stock appreciates so that the market value exceeds the exercise price, the options are valuable and the employee will almost certainly exercise the options. The exercise of the option to purchase the employer's stock requires the payment of cash equal to the exercise price. Additionally, once the employee owns the shares the employee is subject to investment risk on those shares (the risk that the value of the stock will go down). Employees who exercise options to purchase employer stock experience an increase in before-tax net worth equal to the difference between the market value of the acquired shares and the exercise price on the date of exercise. This difference is called the **bargain element.**

Example 12-7

Given the assumptions in the stock option timeline shown in Exhibit 12-3, how much will it cost Julie to exercise all her options at the end of year 3 (before taxes), and what would Julie's economic gain be if she were to immediately exercise the options and sell the shares (before taxes)?[18]

Answer: $125,000 cost to exercise; $375,000 economic gain before taxes, calculated as follows:

Description	Amount	Explanation
(1) Shares acquired	25,000	(20,000 NQOs and 5,000 ISOs)
(2) Exercise price	$ 5	Exhibit 12-3
(3) **Cash needed to exercise**	**$125,000**	(1) × (2)
(4) Market price	$ 20	Exhibit 12-3
(5) Market value of shares	$ 500,000	(1) × (4)
Economic gain before taxes (bargain element)	**$375,000**	(5) − (3)

[17]Vesting dates are frequently specified as future calendar dates or they may be triggered when certain events occur (i.e., predefined performance objectives are met, or the company has been sold).

[18]According to the facts presented in Exhibit 12-3, Julie could have exercised her options as early as the vesting date for her options at the end of year 2. We assume she waits one year to exercise her options to better illustrate the implications of deferring the option exercise beyond the vesting date. In reality, it is quite common for employees to exercise at least a portion of their stock options on the vesting date.

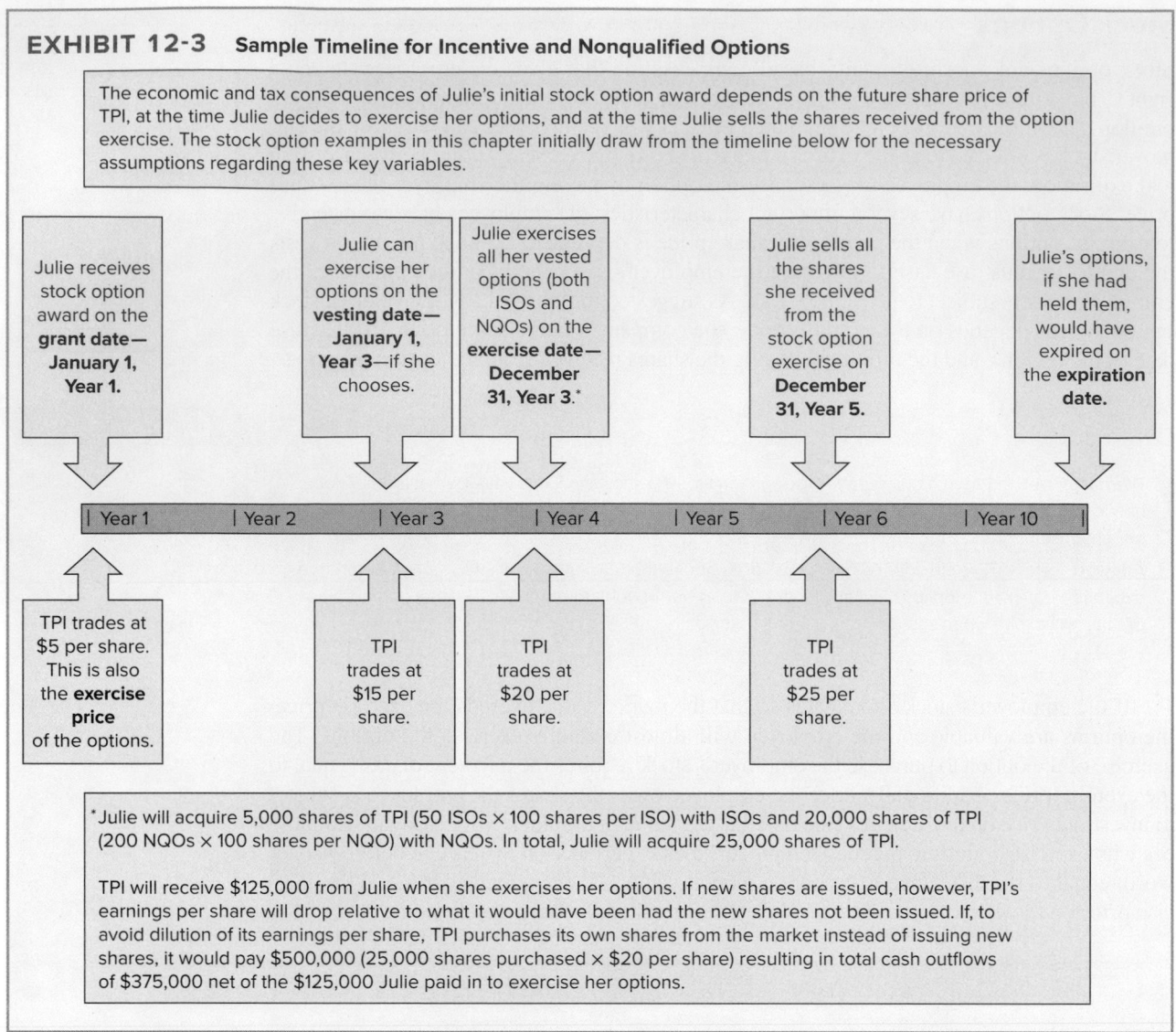

EXHIBIT 12-3 Sample Timeline for Incentive and Nonqualified Options

The economic and tax consequences of Julie's initial stock option award depends on the future share price of TPI, at the time Julie decides to exercise her options, and at the time Julie sells the shares received from the option exercise. The stock option examples in this chapter initially draw from the timeline below for the necessary assumptions regarding these key variables.

Julie receives stock option award on the **grant date—January 1, Year 1.**

Julie can exercise her options on the **vesting date—January 1, Year 3**—if she chooses.

Julie exercises all her vested options (both ISOs and NQOs) on the **exercise date—December 31, Year 3.***

Julie sells all the shares she received from the stock option exercise on **December 31, Year 5.**

Julie's options, if she had held them, would have expired on the **expiration date.**

| Year 1 | Year 2 | Year 3 | Year 4 | Year 5 | Year 6 | Year 10 |

TPI trades at $5 per share. This is also the **exercise price** of the options.

TPI trades at $15 per share.

TPI trades at $20 per share.

TPI trades at $25 per share.

*Julie will acquire 5,000 shares of TPI (50 ISOs × 100 shares per ISO) with ISOs and 20,000 shares of TPI (200 NQOs × 100 shares per NQO) with NQOs. In total, Julie will acquire 25,000 shares of TPI.

TPI will receive $125,000 from Julie when she exercises her options. If new shares are issued, however, TPI's earnings per share will drop relative to what it would have been had the new shares not been issued. If, to avoid dilution of its earnings per share, TPI purchases its own shares from the market instead of issuing new shares, it would pay $500,000 (25,000 shares purchased × $20 per share) resulting in total cash outflows of $375,000 net of the $125,000 Julie paid in to exercise her options.

There are three reasons why an employee might want to exercise options to purchase employer stock and then immediately sell at least a portion of the stock. First, the employee may not have enough cash on hand to cover the cost of exercising the options. Second, the employee may not have enough cash on hand to cover the tax liability from exercising the options. Third, the employee bears investment risk with respect to the employer stock and would like to diversify their investment portfolio by investing in other stocks. For these reasons, employees may also engage in a **same-day sale** or **cashless exercise.** An employer-provided stockbroker typically facilitates a same-day sale.

Employee Tax Considerations for Stock Options   Stock options are classified for tax purposes as either **nonqualified stock options (NQOs)** or **incentive stock options (ISOs).** These classifications differ in terms of when and how the bargain element is taxed. To appreciate the differences, it's important to understand what happens on the **grant date,** the **vesting date,** the **exercise date,** and the date the shares are ultimately sold.

For both types of options, employees experience no tax consequences on the grant date and vesting date. However, when they exercise *nonqualified* stock options, employees report ordinary income equal to the total bargain element on the shares of stock acquired (as if they were sold)—whether they hold the shares or sell them immediately.[19] A taxpayer's basis in the shares acquired with the NQOs is the fair market value of the shares on the date of exercise. Thus the basis includes the exercise price plus the ordinary income the taxpayer recognizes on the exercise (the bargain element). In contrast, when *incentive* stock options are exercised, employees don't report any income for regular tax purposes (as long as they don't immediately sell their shares). Their basis in shares acquired with ISOs is the exercise price. The holding period for stock shares acquired with NQOs and ISOs begins on the exercise date.

When taxpayers exercise incentive stock options, the bargain element is added to their alternative minimum taxable income, and increases the likelihood that the employee will have an alternative minimum tax liability. We discuss the alternative minimum tax in the Individual Income Tax Computation and Tax Credits chapter.

Example 12-8

On the date Julie exercises her options (Exhibit 12-3 at a price of $5 per share), she acquires 20,000 shares of TPI with NQOs (200 NQOs × 100 shares per NQO) and 5,000 shares with ISOs (50 ISOs × 100 shares per ISO). Given that the bargain element for each share she purchased is $15, how much income will Julie report on the day she exercises the options?

Answer: $300,000 ordinary income from the NQOs, calculated below, and $0 for the ISOs (she must include the bargain element of $75,000 on the 5,000 ISOs in her AMT calculation).

Description	Amount	Explanation
(1) Shares acquired with NQOs	20,000	
(2) Market price per share	$ 20	Exhibit 12-3
(3) Exercise price	5	Exhibit 12-3
(4) Bargain element per share	$ 15	(2) − (3)
Bargain element (ordinary income)	**$300,000**	(1) × (4)

What is Julie's basis in the 20,000 shares she acquired with NQOs?

Answer: $400,000. [$100,000 (20,000 shares × $5 per share exercise price) + $300,000 (bargain element taxed as ordinary income).]

What is Julie's basis in the 5,000 shares she acquired through ISOs?

Answer: $25,000 is the regular tax basis (5,000 shares acquired × $5 per share exercise price). $100,000 is the AMT basis ($25,000 regular tax basis + the $75,000 bargain element).

What if: What will Julie's tax liability be from exercising the NQOs, assuming that her income was $610,000 before the exercise?

Answer: $111,000 ($300,000 bargain element × 37%). The tax liability may cause her to sell shares in order to pay her tax liability.

What will Julie's tax liability be if she acquired 5,000 shares from exercising the ISOs?

Answer: $0 regular tax liability but the $75,000 bargain element included in her AMT income will increase the likelihood that she will have an AMT liability.

Once they've exercised their stock options, employees face different tax consequences depending on the type of option. Employees who purchase stock with NQOs and retain the stock are in the same position for tax purposes as any other investor: Their basis in the stock is the fair market value on the date they exercised the options (this is the exercise price of the stock plus the bargain element), and any *future* appreciation or depreciation of the stock will be treated for tax purposes as either short-term or long-term capital gain(s) or loss(es) depending on the holding period, which begins on the date of exercise.

---

[19]The bargain element income is reflected on an employee's Form W-2 and the applicable income and payroll taxes are withheld.

Example 12-9

What if: Suppose that five years after Julie exercised her NQOs and acquired 20,000 TPI shares with a basis of $20 per share, she sold all of the shares for $25 per share. What is the amount and character of the gain she will recognize on the sale?

Answer: $100,000 long-term capital gain, calculated as follows:

Description	Amount	Explanation
(1) Amount realized (sale proceeds)	$500,000	(20,000 × $25)
(2) Tax basis	400,000	Example 12-8
Long-term capital gain recognized	**$100,000**	(1) − (2)

What if: Suppose Julie sold the shares for $25 per share six months after she exercised them. What is the character of the $100,000 gain she recognized on the sale?

Answer: Short-term capital gain because she held the shares for one year or less before selling.

Employees who acquire shares through the exercise of ISOs also have a potential tax benefit: If they hold such shares *for at least two years after the grant date and one year after the exercise date,* they will not be taxed until they sell the stock.[20] When they sell, employees will treat the difference between the sale proceeds and the tax basis (the exercise price) as a long-term capital gain in the year of disposition. Thus, employees generally prefer ISOs to NQOs.

Example 12-10

What if: Suppose that five years after Julie exercised her ISOs and acquired 5,000 TPI shares with a basis of $5 per share, she sold all of the shares for $25 per share. What is the amount and character of the gain she will recognize on the sale?

Answer: Julie will recognize a $100,000 long-term capital gain, calculated as follows:

Description	Amount	Explanation
(1) Amount realized	$ 125,000	(5,000 × $25)
(2) Tax basis	25,000	Example 12-8
Long-term capital gain recognized	**$100,000**	(1) − (2)

If the two-year and one-year requirements are not met, the premature sale of stock is classified as a **disqualifying disposition,** and the bargain element is taxed at the time of sale ordinary income.[21] Thus, when holders of ISOs execute same-day sales, they forgo the potential benefit of deferring the gain and having the bargain element taxed at lower capital gains rates—but they also eliminate the investment risk they would otherwise have to bear if they attempted to satisfy the two-year-from-grant-date and one-year-from-exercise holding period requirements.

Example 12-11

What if: Assume that Julie exercised her ISOs and executed a same-day sale of the 5,000 shares on the vesting date (January 1, year 3) when the share price was $15. What is the amount and character of income she will recognize on these transactions?

Answer: $50,000 ordinary income, as calculated below. Because Julie's sale is a disqualifying disposition, the transactions are recast as though she exercised nonqualified options.

---

[20]§422(a)(1).
[21]Reg. § 1.421-2(b)(1)(i) .

Description	Amount	Explanation
(1) Shares acquired with ISOs that were disqualified (became NQOs)	5,000	
(2) Market price per share	$ 15	
(3) Exercise price	5	Exhibit 12-3
(4) Bargain element per share	$ 10	(2) − (3)
Bargain element (ordinary income)	**$50,000**	(1) × (4)

What if: Assume that Julie exercised her ISOs and had a disqualifying disposition of the 5,000 shares nine months after exercise (September 1, year 4) when the share price was $13. What is the amount and character of income she will recognize on these transactions?

Answer: $40,000 ordinary income, as calculated below. Because Julie's sale is a disqualifying disposition and the market price of the employer's stock has declined since the exercise date, the bargain element is the difference between the fair market value on the date of the disqualifying disposition and the exercise price.

Description	Amount	Explanation
(1) Shares acquired with ISOs that were disqualified 9 months later	5,000	
(2) Market price on date of disqualifying disposition	$ 13	
(3) Exercise price	5	Exhibit 12-3
(4) Bargain element per share	$ 8	(2) − (3)
Ordinary income	**$40,000**	(1) × (4)

TAXES IN THE REAL WORLD Stock Options

Sometimes, stock option compensation is the icing on the cake. Other times, options are the entire cake. According to Oracle Corporation's 2017 proxy statement, it paid founder and CEO Larry Ellison an annual salary of $1 in cash ($1 is not a misprint) and stock options worth over $22 million and option awards worth over $18 million.

No need to pay taxes on the compensation now; once the shares vest, Ellison can choose when to exercise the shares and, consequently, time his tax payments as well.

Source: Oracle Corporation 2016 Proxy Statement.

Employer Tax Considerations for Stock Options   As is true for employees, an employer's tax treatment of stock options depends on whether the options are NQOs or ISOs.

Nonqualified options.   With NQOs, employers deduct the bargain element that employees recognize as income when the employees exercise the NQOs. From the employer's perspective, no other date is relevant for tax purposes.

Example 12-12

What if: Suppose that in year 3, Julie exercises NQOs to acquire 20,000 shares of TPI, and she reports $300,000 of ordinary income for the bargain element of the exercise (see Example 12-8). How much compensation expense for Julie's stock option exercise can TPI deduct in year 3?

Answer: $300,000. TPI can deduct the bargain element of Julie's exercise.

Note that this tax deduction is not tied to a cash payment. Thus, unless employers purchase their own shares to satisfy their employees' stock option exercises, they'll be entitled to a tax deduction without incurring any cash outflow.

Incentive stock options. Employers typically don't view incentive stock options as favorably as NQOs, because (1) ISOs don't provide them with the same tax benefits (no tax deduction) and (2) the IRS regulatory requirements for ISOs can be cumbersome. That is, as long as the employee doesn't sell the stock in a disqualifying disposition, the employer does not get a tax deduction for ISOs. For this reason, employers lose potential tax benefits by issuing ISOs rather than NQOs. On the other hand, start-up companies or employers with net operating losses may actually benefit by issuing ISOs instead of NQOs. Due to their zero percent tax rate, companies in this position don't lose tax benefits by granting ISOs; however, because of the potential tax benefits ISOs provide to their employees relative to NQOs, they may be able to persuade their employees to accept relatively fewer ISOs than NQOs.

ETHICS

Many companies use stock options as a form of equity compensation—to motivate executives and key employees. Some stock option issuers have either backdated and/or repriced stock options. Backdating is an illegal practice by which a company chooses a date in the past when the stock price was at its lowest point in order to maximize executive compensation. Stock option repricing is used when stock options are underwater (the market price is below the strike price). Repricing simply resets the strike price to a price below the current market price. While backdating options is illegal and obviously unethical, what do you think about the practice of repricing stock options?

Accounting issues. The Financial Accounting Standards Board (FASB) mandated the expensing of stock options (both NQOs and ISOs) for financial accounting purposes for years beginning on or after January 1, 2006.[22] Companies must measure the economic value of options on the grant date and then amortize this cost on a straight-line basis over the vesting period of the options.[23]

Example 12-13

THE KEY FACTS

Stock Option Expense: GAAP vs. Tax

- For tax purposes, employers deduct the bargain element of NQOs on the exercise date but receive no tax deduction for ISOs unless they become disqualified.

- For GAAP purposes, employers expense the estimated value of the option pro rata over the vesting period.

What if: Assume that an accounting employee benefits specialist calculated the economic value of Julie's stock option grant (NQOs and ISOs) to be $32,000. Also assume that Julie's options vest 50 percent in year 1 (the year of the grant) and 50 percent in year 2. What compensation expense for book purposes would TPI report for Julie's stock options in year 1 and year 2?

Answer: $16,000 ($32,000 × 50%) in year 1 and $16,000 in year 2.

As you probably realize by now, the tax rules governing the treatment of stock options differ markedly from generally accepted accounting principles in terms of both the amount and the timing of the stock option expense. To compare the tax and book treatment, we present TPI's book expense and tax deduction resulting from its stock option grant to Julie (given prior assumptions) in Exhibit 12-4.

The tremendous difference between the book and tax numbers presented in Exhibit 12-4 is driven by the increase in TPI's share price, from $5 on the date of grant to $20 on the date of exercise. The economic valuation of the stock options used to determine the book expense did not anticipate the extent of the stock appreciation before exercise.

[22]Accounting Standards Codification (ASC) 718, Stock Compensation.

[23]Although the exercise price of compensatory stock options typically equals the stock price on the date of grant, compensatory options are, nevertheless, economically valuable on the grant date. They have economic value because the stock price may eventually exceed the exercise price before the options expire. To determine economic value, companies typically use either the Black-Scholes option pricing model or the binomial option pricing model.

EXHIBIT 12-4 TPI's Tax Deductions and Book Expense from Stock Option Grant to Julie

	Tax Deduction if Stock Price Increases	Tax Deduction if Stock Price Decreases	Book Expense
Year 1	$ 0	$0	$16,000
Year 2	0	0	16,000
Year 3	300,000	0*	0

*There would be no exercise because the exercise price exceeds the stock price.

Restricted Stock

Like stock options described above, **restricted stock** can't be sold or otherwise treated as owned by employees until they legally have the right to sell the shares on the vesting date. However, unlike the stock acquired through options exercises, employees receive employer stock that is restricted (cannot be sold) until the vesting date lapses *without having to pay for it,* after which they can either sell it immediately or retain it. Restricted stock awards come with voting rights immediately because the employee actually owns the stock from the moment the award is granted.

Exhibit 12-5, provides a timeline of an employee's restricted stock award.

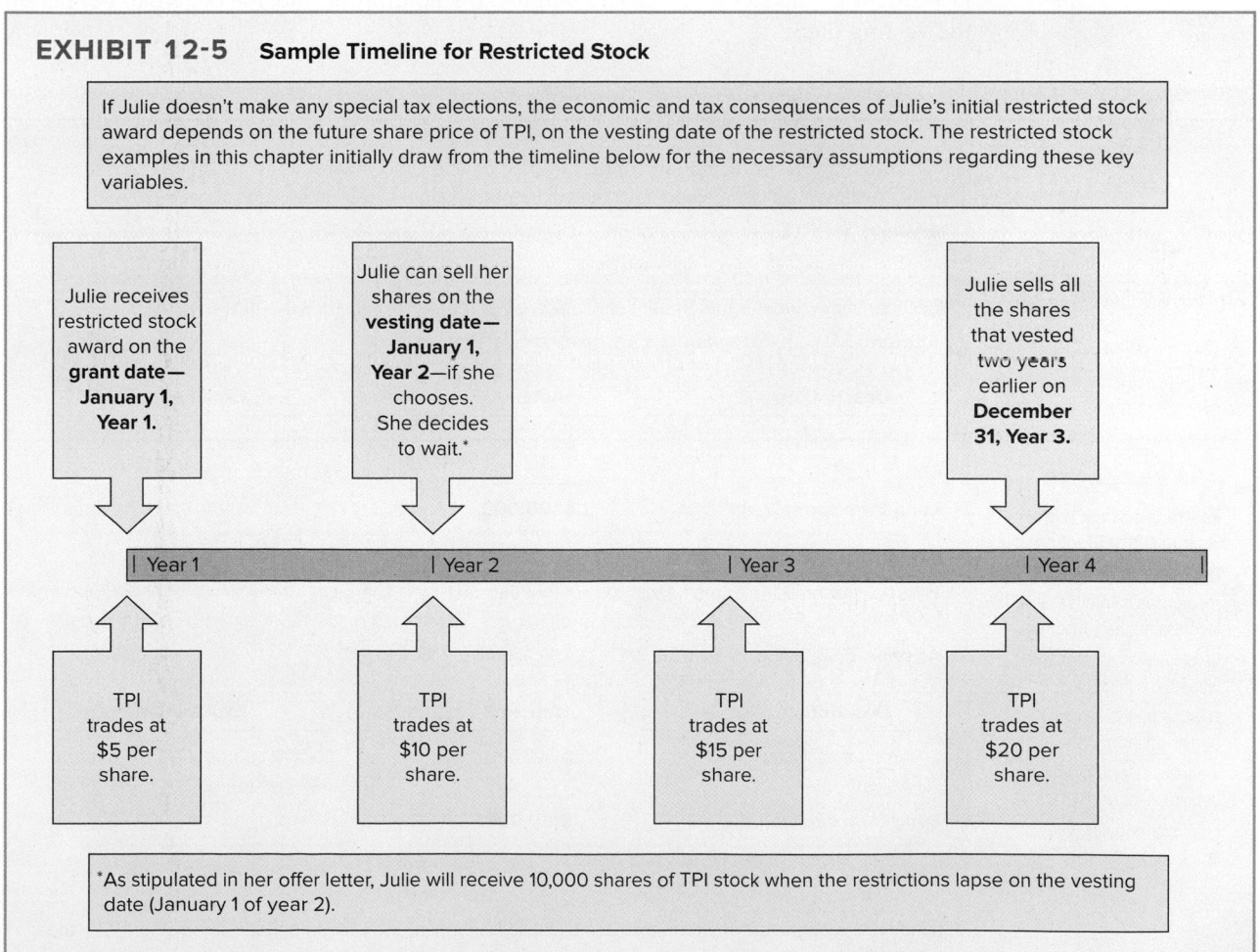

EXHIBIT 12-5 Sample Timeline for Restricted Stock

If Julie doesn't make any special tax elections, the economic and tax consequences of Julie's initial restricted stock award depends on the future share price of TPI, on the vesting date of the restricted stock. The restricted stock examples in this chapter initially draw from the timeline below for the necessary assumptions regarding these key variables.

Julie receives restricted stock award on the **grant date— January 1, Year 1.**

Julie can sell her shares on the **vesting date— January 1, Year 2**—if she chooses. She decides to wait.*

Julie sells all the shares that vested two years earlier on **December 31, Year 3.**

| Year 1 | Year 2 | Year 3 | Year 4 |

TPI trades at $5 per share.

TPI trades at $10 per share.

TPI trades at $15 per share.

TPI trades at $20 per share.

*As stipulated in her offer letter, Julie will receive 10,000 shares of TPI stock when the restrictions lapse on the vesting date (January 1 of year 2).

Example 12-14

Given the assumptions regarding the 10,000 shares of restricted stock that will vest on January 1, Year 2 in Exhibit 12-5, how much would Julie's wealth increase (before taxes) on the vesting date if the employer's stock is trading at $10 on January 1, Year 2?

Answer: Julie's wealth would increase by $100,000 (10,000 shares × $10 per share) (before taxes).

What if: Assuming that the stock decreased to $3 per share on the vesting date, by how much would Julie's wealth increase or decrease on the vesting date?

Answer: $30,000 increase ($3 × 10,000). Until the vesting date, Julie was not entitled to any economic benefit from the restricted stock. On the vesting date, however, she is entitled to stock valued at $30,000. Thus, the vesting of Julie's restricted stock increases her wealth even if the stock price decreases between the grant date and vesting date (unlike options, which would be worthless).

THE KEY FACTS

Restricted Stock *without* 83(b) Election

- No tax consequences on grant date.
- Employee recognizes ordinary income on fair market value of stock on vesting date.
- Holding period for stock begins on vesting date.
- Employer deducts fair market value of stock on vesting date.

Employee Tax Considerations for Restricted Stock Restricted stock is taxed like NQOs with two important distinctions: While employees receiving NQOs are taxed on the bargain element of the shares when they exercise their options, employees receiving restricted stock are taxed on the *full fair market value* of the shares *on the date the restrictions lapse*. They are taxed on the fair market value of the stock because they are entitled to receive the stock without any payment requirements (contrast this with the exercise price paid for stock options).[24] Any subsequent appreciation in the value of the stock is taxed as either long-term or short-term capital gain(s) or loss(es) when the taxpayer sells the stock, depending on the holding period and future movement of the stock price. The employee's holding period for the stock begins on the vesting date.

Example 12-15

Assume that the restricted stock vests in year 2 when the market price is $10 per share (see Exhibit 12-5). What is the amount and character of the income Julie recognizes in year 2?

Answer: $100,000 ordinary income (10,000 shares × $10 per share).

Assume the same facts as above and that Julie sells the shares in year 4 when the market price is $20 per share. What is the amount and character of the income she will recognize on the sale?

Answer: $100,000 long-term capital gain, calculated as follows:

Description	Amount	Explanation
(1) Amount realized	$ 200,000	10,000 shares × $20 per share
(2) Tax basis	100,000	Gain recognized on vesting date
Long-term capital gain	**$100,000**	(1) − (2)

THE KEY FACTS

Restricted Stock *with* Section 83(b) Election

- On grant date, employee recognizes market value of stock as ordinary income.
- Employee takes fair market value basis in stock.
- Holding period for stock begins on grant date.
- If employee never vests, no deduction for basis in stock.
- Employer deducts value of stock on grant date.

What if: Assume the original facts except that Julie sells the shares in year 4 and the market price is now $4 per share. What is the amount and character of the gain or loss she recognizes on the sale?

Answer: $60,000 long-term capital loss, calculated as follows:

Description	Amount	Explanation
(1) Amount realized	$ 40,000	10,000 shares × $4 per share
(2) Adjusted basis	100,000	Gain recognized on vesting date
Long-term capital loss	**$(60,000)**	(1) − (2)

[24]The income recognized when the restrictions lapse is compensation income that is subject to FICA and other payroll taxes.

83(b) Election. An **83(b) election** accelerates the ordinary income recognition on the fair market value of a restricted stock award from the vesting date (when the restrictions lapse) to the grant date. Simply put, the 83(b) election allows the taxpayer to treat the restricted stock award as if there were no restrictions. Employees may make the election no later than 30 days after the grant date. The election is irrevocable. Accelerating income is generally undesirable from a tax planning perspective (see the Tax Planning Strategies and Related Limitations chapter); however, if an employee receives restricted stock worth a nominal amount it almost always makes sense to make the election. If the employee believes the employer's stock value will increase between the grant date and the date the restrictions lapse, the election converts appreciation that would have been taxed as compensation income at ordinary rates into capital gain that is taxed at long-term capital gain rates (assuming the shares are held for more than one year after the grant date).

Example 12-16

What if: How much tax on the restricted stock will Julie pay in year 1 if she does not make a 83(b) election?

Answer: $0. The stock has not vested yet so she has no income.

What if: How much tax on the restricted stock will Julie pay in year 1 if she makes an 83(b) election?

Answer: $12,000 [$50,000 ordinary income (10,000 shares × $5 per share) × 24 percent marginal ordinary tax rate].

What if: How much tax will Julie pay in year 2 on the restricted stock (the year the restricted stock vests) if she does not make an 83(b) election in year 1 (the stock is trading at $10 a share on the vest date)?

Answer: $24,000 [$100,000 ordinary income (10,000 shares × $10 per share) × 24 percent marginal ordinary tax rate].

What if: How much tax will Julie pay in year 2 on the restricted stock if she makes the 83(b) election in year 1?

Answer: $0. With the 83(b) election, Julie treated the stock as though it vested in year 1, not year 2, so she does not have a taxable event in year 2 when the stock actually vests.

What if: How much tax will Julie pay in year 4 on the restricted stock when she sells the stock for $20 a share (on December 31) if she *does not* make the 83(b) election in year 1?

Answer: $15,000 [[$200,000 (10,000 × $20) − $100,000 tax basis (fair market value on vesting date in year 2)] × 15 percent long-term capital gains rate].

What if: How much tax would Julie pay in year 4 on the restricted stock when she sells the stock for $20 a share (on December 31) if she made the 83(b) election in year 1?

Answer: $22,500 [[$200,000 (10,000 × $20) − $50,000 tax basis (fair market value in year 1 when she made the 83(b) election)] × 15 percent long-term capital gains rate].

Given the analyses above, what amount of taxes would Julie save by making the 83(b) election (ignoring the time value of money)?

Answer: $10,000 ($50,000 with election; $60,000 without), computed as follows:

Taxes Payable		
Description	**With Election**	**Without Election**
Year 1 taxes on ordinary income	$ 12,000	$ 0
Year 2 taxes on ordinary income	0	24,000
Year 4 taxes on long-term capital gains	22,500	15,000
Total taxes	**$34,500**	**$39,000**

(continued on page 12-18)

Note that Julie reduces her tax because the election allowed her to convert $50,000 of income from ordinary income taxed at 24 percent into long-term capital gain taxed at 15 percent.

Also note that this computation overstates to some degree the benefits of making the 83(b) election because it ignores the time value of money. In order to have a greater portion of her gains taxed at the preferential capital gain rates, Julie gave up some tax deferral when she accelerated $50,000 of income from year 4 into year 1.

Employees making the 83(b) election essentially trade off some additional current tax now in order to convert ordinary income into a long-term capital gain later. Accordingly, the 83(b) election is advisable when the potential for growth in the stock value is high and the amount of additional current tax is manageable. If an employee makes an 83(b) election and then forfeits the stock for any reason, the employee cannot deduct the loss on the forfeiture.[25] Thus, the risk of making the election is that if the employee forfeits the stock, tax would have been paid on value never received.

Employer Tax Considerations for Restricted Stock Like the tax treatment of NQOs, the employer's deduction for restricted stock equals the amount of ordinary income reported by its employees. The timing of the deduction is determined by the employee's decision regarding the 83(b) election. If the employee makes an 83(b) election, the employer claims the deduction in the year the restricted stock is granted. Otherwise, the employer claims a deduction when the restrictions lapse.

The accounting treatment for restricted stock is similar to the accounting treatment for stock options.[26] If restricted stock grants vest over time, the market value of restricted stock on the *date of grant* is expensed pro rata over the vesting period.

Example 12-17

What if: Given the assumptions in Exhibit 12-5, what amount can TPI deduct for tax purposes in year 1 and in year 2 assuming Julie *does not* make an 83(b) election?

Answer: $0 in year 1 and $100,000 in year 2 (10,000 shares of restricted stock vested × $10 per share market price at vesting date).

What if: What amount can TPI deduct in year 1 and in year 2 if Julie *does* make an 83(b) election?

Answer: $50,000 in year 1 (10,000 shares of restricted stock awarded × $5 per share market price on the grant date) and $0 in year 2.

What is TPI's compensation expense for financial accounting purposes for Julie's restricted stock in year 1 and in year 2?

Answer: $50,000 book expense in year 1. Because the value of Julie's restricted stock award on the date of grant is $50,000, TPI expenses the award on its books over the vesting period, which in this case is just one year (it has a one-year vesting period).

THE KEY FACTS

Restricted Stock Expense: GAAP vs. Tax

- For tax purposes, employers deduct the market value of stock when the employee recognizes income.
- For GAAP purposes, employers deduct the market value at grant date value over the vesting period.

Restricted Stock Units (RSUs) RSUs are units that are valued in employer stock at the time of grant. However, unlike restricted stock, upon settlement RSUs can be exchanged for employer stock, cash, or some combination of cash and stock depending upon the terms of the RSU agreement. RSUs do not provide dividend income, as the actual shares are not owned by the employee; however, some employers contractually pay a dividend equivalent to the employee. RSUs are growing in popularity and are used by companies like Apple (see Exhibit 12-6) and Amazon. The value of the RSUs are taxed to the employee as ordinary income when the restrictions lapse. Unlike restricted stock, employees with RSUs cannot make an 83(b) election. Employers receive a deduction equal to the fair market value of the RSUs when the vesting restrictions lapse.

[25]Reg. §1.83-2(a).
[26]ASC 718.

EXHIBIT 12-6   **Excerpt from Apple Inc.'s 2017 Proxy Statement**

Long-Term Equity Elements and Awards

Our executive compensation program emphasizes long-term shareholder value creation through the use of equity awards in the form of (restricted stock units) RSUs to deliver long-term compensation incentives. The Compensation Committee has discretion to approve awards with different vesting conditions as it deems necessary to meet the objectives of our executive compensation program.

Performance-Based RSUs. The number of performance-based RSUs granted to our named executive officers that vest depends on Apple's total shareholder return relative to the other companies in the S&P 500 for the performance period ("Relative TSR"). The Compensation Committee chose Relative TSR as a straightforward and objective metric for Apple's shareholders to evaluate our performance against the performance of other companies and to align the interests of our named executive officers with the interests of shareholders.

Time-Based RSUs. Equity awards with time-based vesting align the interests of our executives with the interests of our shareholders and promote the stability and retention of a strong executive team over the longer term. Vesting schedules for time-based awards generally require continuous service over multiple years. . .

Employees of publicly traded companies have access to an efficient market to liquidate equity-based compensation when liquidity needs arise. In contrast, employees of private companies do not have an efficient market to help them alleviate liquidity constraints created through purchasing and/or paying tax liabilities on equity-based compensation. To alleviate this liquidity inequity, the tax laws allow employees of private company to elect to defer the income tax liability for equity based compensation in the form of **qualified equity grant** for up to five years.[27]

A qualified equity grant is qualified stock, received by a qualified employee, of an eligible corporation. Qualified stock is either an NQO or RSU issued as compensation to a qualified employee.[28] A qualified employee is not an excluded employee of an eligible corporation, where excluded employees include a one percent (or greater) owner at any time in the prior 10 years or a covered employee of the employer at any time.[29] An eligible corporation is a non-publicly traded corporation that grants NQOs or RSUs to at least 80 percent of their domestic employees.[30] Qualified equity grants are designed specifically to help the rank-and-file employees of these private companies. Qualified employees must make an 83(i) election (similar to an 83(b) election) no later than 30 days after 1) the first date the employee's right to the RSU is substantially vested or is transferable, whichever occurs earlier, or 2) the date the employee exercises a NQO.[31] Instead of including income at the exercise of a NQO or vesting of an RSU, the employee's qualified equity grant will be subject to income tax at the earliest of the following dates: 1) the date the qualified stock is transferrable, 2) the date the employee becomes an "excluded employee," 3) the date on which any stock of the employer becomes publicly traded, 4) the date that is five years after the rights of the employee in such qualified stock are transferable or are not subject to a substantial risk of forfeiture, or 5) the date the employee revokes the 83(i) election.[32]

Equity-Based Compensation Summary

To summarize our discussion of the tax treatment of equity-based compensation, Exhibit 12-7 highlights the general tax treatment of NQOs, ISOs, and restricted stock on a per share basis from both employee and employer perspectives given an arbitrary time

---

[27]§83(i) applies to qualified equity grants sold after December 31, 2017.

[28]§83(i)(2).

[29]§83(i)(3).

[30]§83(i)(2).

[31]§83(i)(4).

[32]§83(i)(2). Additional details of qualified equity grants were unknown at printing or beyond the scope of this text.

series of share prices. In addition to showing future share prices, the exhibit assumes options are exercisable for the share price on the grant date.

EXHIBIT 12-7 Reportable Income and Deductions from Equity-Based Compensation (for given time frame and stock prices)

	Party Affected	NQOs	ISOs	Restricted Stock
Grant date–year 1	Employee	No effect	No effect	No effect
Stock (exercise) price = $1/share	Employer	No effect	No effect	No effect
Vesting date–year 4 Stock price = $6/share	Employee	No effect	No effect	$6/share ordinary income
	Employer	No effect	No effect	$6/share ordinary deduction
Exercise date for options–year 6	Employee	$10/share ordinary income	No effect*	N/A
Stock price = $11/share	Employer	$10/share ordinary deduction	No effect	N/A
Sale date–year 8	Employee	$5/share	$15/share	$10/share
Stock price = $16/share	Employee	LT capital gain	LT capital gain	Capital gain
	Employer	No effect	No effect	No effect

*$10 per share is included in alternative minimum taxable income.

LO 12-3 # FRINGE BENEFITS

continued from page 12-8...
The final section of TPI's offer letter indicated Julie would receive fringe benefits in the form of health and dental insurance (value of $18,000), $750,000 of group-term life insurance, a biennial $30,000 automobile allowance, employer educational assistance, and a flexible spending account for medical expenses. ■

Employees generally receive most of their compensation in the form of cash salary or wages. However, employers often provide noncash benefits to employees in addition to their cash compensation. These **fringe benefits** range from the common (health insurance) to the exotic (use of a corporate aircraft). As a general rule, because fringe benefits are employee compensation, they are taxable to the employee on receipt. In fact, fringe benefits are specifically mentioned in the definition of gross income. As we indicated in the Gross Income and Exclusions chapter, IRC §61(a) indicates that, "gross income means all income from whatever source derived, including . . . (1) Compensation for services, including fees, commissions, *fringe benefits,* and similar items" (emphasis added). This definition of income notwithstanding, the tax laws specifically *exclude* certain fringe benefits from an employee's gross income. Thus, some fringe benefits are taxable and others are not.

Taxable Fringe Benefits

Taxable fringe benefits are fringe benefits not specifically excluded from gross income. Congress views many of the taxable fringe benefits as luxuries and chooses not to subsidize them. Taxable fringe benefits include such things as below-market interest

---

THE KEY FACTS

Taxable Fringe Benefits

- Employees recognize compensation income on all benefits received unless specifically excluded by tax laws.
- Employees treat benefits received like taxable cash compensation, which are subject to FICA.
- Employer deducts cost and pays employer's share of FICA taxes on benefit.

rate loans (see discussion in the Gross Income and Exclusions chapter), gym memberships, season tickets to the local NBA team, an automobile allowance for a personal automobile, moving expense reimbursements, and anything else not specifically excluded by the tax laws. Employers generally provide taxable fringe benefits to executives and higher-salaried employees rather than to the rank-and-file employees.

Employee Considerations for Taxable Fringe Benefits   From an employee's perspective, taxable fringe benefits are treated just like cash. Employees recognize ordinary compensation income when they receive taxable benefits and, just as they do with salary, pay FICA taxes on the value of the benefit. As a result, taxable fringe benefits cost employees the amount of tax they must pay on the benefits.

Example 12-18

Julie's offer includes a biennial auto allowance of up to $30,000. That is, every other year, TPI will reimburse Julie for an automobile purchase up to $30,000. TPI provides this benefit to executives that interact with the public on a regular basis. Julie purchases a Toyota 4Runner with a retail price of $35,000. What income tax is Julie required to pay if she applies the auto allowance toward the purchase? What is Julie's after-tax cost of the automobile if her marginal tax rate is 24 percent (ignoring FICA taxes)?

Answer: $7,200 in income taxes and $12,200 of after-tax cost, computed as follows:

Description	Amount	Explanation
(1) Fair market value of Toyota	$ 35,000	
(2) Automobile allowance	30,000	Taxable fringe benefit
(3) Julie's additional cost	5,000	(1) − (2)
(4) **Income tax on allowance**	**7,200**	(2) × 24%
Total after-tax cost	**$12,200**	(3) + (4)

From Julie's perspective, this is a pretty good deal—particularly if she was willing to pay the market price for the car.

Employees may prefer a taxable benefit to an equivalent amount of cash when they benefit from employer-provided quantity or group discounts associated with the benefit. For example, many companies pay employees' premiums for **group-term life insurance** as a fringe benefit, in part, because they can purchase the insurance at a lower rate than employees could individually. However, employees must recognize a certain amount of gross income when employers pay life insurance premiums for employee policies with a death benefit in excess of $50,000.[33] Consequently, a portion of the group-term life insurance benefit is taxable and a portion is nontaxable. In these circumstances, the employer determines the employee's taxable amount using a table provided in the Treasury Regulations. An excerpt of this table is provided in Exhibit 12-18.[34] To compute the annual taxable benefit, taxpayers use the following steps:

Step 1:   Subtract $50,000 from the death benefit of their employer-provided group-term life insurance policy.

Step 2:   Divide the Step 1 result by $1,000.

[33]§79.

[34]Reg. §1.79-3(d)(2) provides an age-based table and instructions to calculate the employee's includable amount.

Step 3: Multiply the result from Step 2 by the cost per $1,000 of protection for one month from the table (Exhibit 12-8) based on the taxpayer's age.

Step 4: Multiply the outcome of Step 3 by the number of months the benefit was received during the taxable year.

EXHIBIT 12-8   Uniform Premiums for $1,000 of Group-Term Life Insurance Protection

5-Year Age Bracket	Cost per $1,000 of Protection for One Month
Under 25	$0.05
25 to 29	.06
30 to 34	.08
35 to 39	.09
40 to 44	.10
45 to 49	.15
50 to 54	.23
55 to 59	.43
60 to 64	.66
65 to 69	1.27
70 and above	2.06

Source: Reg. §1.79-3(d)(2) provides an age-based table and instructions to calculate the employee's includable amount.

Example 12-19

Julie's offer from TPI includes $750,000 of group-term life insurance. TPI's cost to provide Julie the insurance is $500 per year. If Julie were to purchase the insurance herself she would pay $2,000 per year. Assume that Julie is 37 years old. Based on the Treasury's table (see Exhibit 12-10), the monthly premium per $1,000 of insurance is $.09. What is Julie's taxable compensation from receiving the group-term life insurance benefit? What does this benefit cost Julie (ignoring FICA taxes)?

Answer: $756 of taxable compensation and $181 cost to Julie (all taxes), calculated as follows. Julie's cost is the income and Medicare taxes she must pay on the compensation.

Group-Term Life Insurance Description	Amount	Explanation
(1) Insurance coverage	$750,000	Provided by employer
(2) Excluded coverage	(50,000)	Nontaxable portion
(3) Taxable benefit	$700,000	(1) + (2) (Step 1)
(4) Divide by 1,000	1,000	Divide by 1,000 (Step 2)
(5) Result of Step 2	700	(3)/(4)
(6) Monthly cost per $1,000	× 0.09	Taxable portion per $1,000 (from Exhibit 12-10)
(7) Monthly benefit	$ 63	(5) × (6), (Step 3)
(8) Months	× 12	Annualize monthly taxable amount
(9) Annual taxable benefit	**$ 756**	(7) × (8) (Step 4)
Income taxes paid	$ 181	(9) × 24%

Note that Julie's income tax cost is not based on TPI's actual cost ($500) of providing the policy.

Taxpayers receiving taxable fringe benefits may experience some financial strain because they must pay the tax on the benefits. Frequently, when corporations provide taxable fringe benefits to senior executives, they also provide the executives enough cash to cover the taxes so the benefit(s) costs the executive nothing.[35] This is commonly referred to as a *gross-up*. For

[36]Companies generally choose a formula to determine how much cash (gross-up) they need to pay the employee in addition to the taxable benefit to ensure the benefit costs the employee nothing.

example, ConocoPhillips's 2017 proxy statement reveals that it made payments of $22 million to R.M. Lance, its chairman, and that the additional cash is for "Expatriate Tax Benefits" in 2014.[36] Employees can choose to forgo a benefit if they prefer not to pay taxes on it.

Employer Considerations for Taxable Fringe Benefits   Like employees, employers treat taxable fringe benefits just like cash compensation. That is, the employer has an outlay for the cost of the benefit and deducts its *cost* of the benefit, not the *value* of the benefit to the employee.[37] As we mention above, employers are often able to purchase fringe benefits at a lower cost than individual employees can. For example, employers may receive a group discount for purchasing life insurance, automobiles, financial or tax planning services, or accident insurance.

Example 12-20

In Example 12-16, TPI provided Julie with $750,000 of group-term life insurance. Its cost of providing the entire $750,000 of coverage is $500 per year. If Julie were to purchase the policy herself, it would cost her $2,000 per year. What is TPI's after-tax cost of the partially taxable group-term life insurance benefit it provided to Julie?

Answer: TPI's after-tax cost of the benefit provided is $395, calculated as follows:

Description	Amount	Explanation
(1) Cost of policy	$ 500	
(2) Income tax benefit	(105)	(1) × 21%
Total after-tax cost	**$395**	(1) + (2)

Finally, employers may discriminate between employees when providing taxable benefits. That is, they can select which employees receive the taxable benefits and which do not. Not surprisingly, the more highly compensated employees tend to receive these benefits. For example, as described in an excerpt from Walmart's 2017 proxy statement in Exhibit 12-9, Walmart's perquisite and supplemental benefits provide certain officers with use of the company aircraft and home security systems. Walmart is unlikely to offer these same benefits to its hourly sales associates.

EXHIBIT 12-9   **Excerpt from Walmart's 2017 Proxy Statement**

What perquisites and other benefits do our NEOs receive?

Our named executive officers (NEOs) receive a limited number of perquisites and supplemental benefits. We cover the cost of annual physical examinations for our NEOs and provide each NEO with personal use of our aircraft for a limited number of hours each year. Our NEOs also receive company-paid life and accidental death and dismemberment insurance. Additionally, our NEOs are entitled to benefits available to officers generally, such as participation in the Deferred Compensation Matching Plan, and benefits available to Associates generally, including a Walmart discount card, a limited 15 percent match of purchases of Shares through our Associate Stock Purchase Plan, participation in our 401(k) Plan, medical benefits, and foreign business travel insurance. We provide these perquisites and supplemental benefits to attract talented executives to our company and to retain our current executives, and we believe their limited cost is outweighed by the benefits to our company.

---

[36]This amount represents the tax gross-up payments made on behalf of Mr. Lance in connection with his nonpermanent relocation, at the company's request, to Singapore, consistent with the company's policy for all employees.

[37]The employer also has an outlay for the cost of the employer's share of FICA taxes on the taxable portion of benefits it provides to employees and receives a deduction for the FICA taxes paid.

TAXES IN THE REAL WORLD Fringe Benefits

Google Takes Off

At Alphabet (Google's parent), the company's stock price isn't the only thing that has taken off; its executive usage of aircraft paid for by the company has as well. According to two excerpts from Alphabet's 2017 Proxy Statement, this amount exceeds $1 million:

In 2015, we paid for personal security for Eric, Sundar, Ruth, and David. Pursuant to our Non-Commercial Aircraft Policy, which sets forth guidelines and procedures for the personal use of non-commercial aircraft, named executive officers and their guests may use company aircraft with appropriate approvals and pay tax on any associated imputed income.

Corporate Use of Personal Aircraft

Eric E. Schmidt beneficially owns 100% of one aircraft and 33% of another aircraft, both of which are used by Eric and our other executive officers from time to time for business trips. The reimbursement rate for use of these aircraft is $7,500 per hour. Our Board of Directors approved this hourly reimbursement rate based upon a competitive analysis of comparable chartered aircraft rates that showed that the reimbursement rate is at or below market rates for the charter of similar aircraft. In 2016, we used these aircraft for business-related travel services for certain of our executive officers, including Eric, and we reimbursed Eric approximately $1,908,750. Due to the fact that the $7,500 hourly rate paid for the use of these aircraft is less than the actual operational costs incurred by Eric as owner of these aircraft, Eric does not profit from the use of these aircraft.

Google will receive a deduction for the amount paid to Eric for use of the aircraft. Both the personal security expenses and personal use of the corporate aircraft are taxable fringe benefits to the executives.

Nontaxable Fringe Benefits

For policy reasons, Congress specifically excludes certain fringe benefits, such as health insurance, from employees' gross income to encourage employers to provide the benefits.[38] We refer to excluded benefits as **nontaxable fringe benefits.** Other nontaxable fringe benefits enable taxpayers to become or stay employed, including meals or lodging for the convenience of the employer, educational assistance, dependent-care benefits, and transportation-related benefits. Finally, some benefits are excluded for simplicity's sake, such as no-additional-cost services, qualified employee discounts, and *de minimis* (small) fringe benefits. Exhibit 12-10 provides a partial list of nontaxable fringe benefits, and in the text that follows, we discuss these benefits in more detail.

Group-Term Life Insurance As we mentioned in the taxable benefits section, employees may exclude from income the employer-provided benefit for the first $50,000 of group-term life insurance.[39] Any remaining group-term life insurance benefit is taxable (see Example 12-19). An employer may not discriminate between employees in providing nontaxable group-term life insurance benefits.

Health and Accident Insurance and Benefits When employers pay for **health and accident insurance** for an employee and the employee's spouse and dependents, the employee excludes the benefit from her gross income.[40] For example, if TPI pays health premiums of $18,000 for Julie and her family, Julie is not required to include this $18,000 fringe benefit in her gross income.[41] Further, when employees receive cash reimbursements

---

[38]The nontaxable fringe benefits are listed with "items specifically excluded from gross income" in §§101–140 of the Internal Revenue Code. Employers are generally prohibited from discriminating among employees with respect to nontaxable fringe benefits (they cannot offer them only to executives). This chapter indicates whether or not discrimination for a particular benefit is allowed. However, the discrimination rules are complex and vary from benefit to benefit in ways too numerous to explain in detail in this text.

[39]§79.

[40]§106.

[41]If Julie were to purchase the health insurance with after-tax dollars the equivalent would be $23,684 [$18,000 / (1 − .24 marginal tax rate)].

EXHIBIT 12-10 Common Forms of Nontaxable Fringe Benefits

Benefit	Description
Group-term life insurance (§79)	Employer-paid premiums on up to $50,000 group-term life insurance policy are excluded from employees' income.
Health benefits (§§105–106)	Employer-paid premiums covering health, medical, and dental insurance and the benefits provided through the insurance.
Meals or lodging for the convenience of the employer (§119)*	Meals provided on employer's premises and lodging provided by the employer as a condition of employment are excluded from an employee's income. Meals are 50% deductible by the employer.
Employee educational assistance (§127)	Up to $5,250 exclusion for tuition, books, and fees. See IRS Publication 970, *Tax Benefits for Education*.
Dependent care benefits (§129)	Up to $5,000 exclusion for cost of providing care for a dependent who is under 13 years old or a dependent who is disabled.
No-additional-cost services [§132(a)(1)]	Benefits that don't cost the employer a material amount.
Qualified employee discounts [§132(a)(2)]	Reduced prices on employer's product within certain limits.
Working condition fringe benefits [§132(a)(3)]*	A benefit provided by an employer that would be deductible as an ordinary and necessary business expense by the employee if the employee rather than the employer paid the expense.
De minimis fringe benefits [§132(a)(4)]*	Relatively small and infrequently provided benefits.
Qualified transportation fringe benefits [§132(a)(5)]*	Mass transit passes up to monthly limit of $260, qualified parking up to monthly limit of $260, or use of company owned carpool vehicles (vans).
Cafeteria plans (§125)	A plan where employees can choose from among various nontaxable fringe benefits or cash. Taxable to the extent employees receive cash.

*Employer may discriminate in providing this benefit.

for medical care, they can exclude the reimbursement from gross income.[42] For example, if TPI reimburses Julie for $450 of medical co-payments she makes during the year, Julie excludes the $450 from gross income. Generally, employers may not discriminate between employees when providing health and accident insurance benefits.[43]

TAXES IN THE REAL WORLD Free Lunch

Apple, Google, and Facebook are famous for their cafeterias, which have been chronicled in *Bon Appetit* and other foodie magazines. These cafeterias are light years ahead of the dorm cafeteria you ate in as a college freshman. And better yet, meals are either free or almost free for employees. However, the secret is out—and now the IRS is questioning whether these benefits are taxable or nontaxable. To be considered nontax-able, the benefit has to be provided "for the convenience of the employer" rather than as a way to attract and compensate employees. These companies are arguing that without these cafeterias employees will be away from the company premises more and lose the opportunity to talk together, both of which are detrimental to the employer. Employers can deduct only 50 percent of these expenses.

[42]§105(b). However, reimbursement in excess of costs is included in income.

[43]However, employers may exclude part-time employees from participation.

Meals and Lodging for the Convenience of the Employer The value of certain meals and lodging the employer provides to an employee may be excluded from an employee's gross income if the benefit meets two criteria: (1) the meals and lodging are provided on the employer's business premises to the employee (and the employee's spouse and dependents, if any) and (2) the meals and lodging are provided for the convenience of the employer.[44] For example, employers may provide meals at their place of business so employees can continue working efficiently without taking time off to go out to eat. Accounting firms frequently provide meals to tax professionals working late during tax season. Employers are allowed to deduct the 50 percent of meals provided to employees for the convenience of the employer. That is, the cost is not subject to the 50 percent deductibility limitation on meals we discussed in the Business Income, Deductions, and Accounting Methods chapter.[45] Employers may generally discriminate between employees in providing **for the convenience of the employer benefits.**

Example 12-21

What if: Assume that last year Julie purchased 25 meals, at a cost of $500, on evenings when she worked late. Julie turned in expense reports and receipts for the meals totaling $500, which PCC reimbursed. What is the amount Julie must include in income?

Answer: Julie will not include the value of any of the overtime meals in income because they were provided for PCC's convenience.

In some situations, employers may provide lodging for employees and require employees to live on the business premises as a condition of their employment. In these cases, employees may exclude the value of the lodging from gross income.[46] For example, an employer may require an apartment complex manager to live in an apartment in the complex (free of charge) so the employee can respond to tenant needs, provide security, and handle emergencies. The apartment manager can exclude the value of the lodging from gross income.

Employee Educational Assistance Employees can exclude from income up to $5,250 of employee **educational assistance benefits** covering tuition, books, and fees.[47] Amounts received in excess of this limit are taxed as compensation to the employee. (See IRS Publication 970 for details related to education benefits.) This includes amounts employers provide for employee undergraduate- or graduate-level courses or for courses that lead to a professional degree. Amounts excluded from income cannot qualify for educational credits (such as the American opportunity and lifetime learning credits).

Dependent Care Benefits Employees can exclude up to $5,000 for benefits paid or reimbursed by employers for caring for children under age 13 or dependents or spouses who are physically or mentally unable to care for themselves.[48] Excluded amounts do not qualify for the child and dependent care credit (see the Individual Income Tax Computation and Tax Credits chapter).

No-Additional-Cost Services Employees can exclude the value of **no-additional-cost services.** These are any services employers provide to employees in the ordinary course of business that generate no substantial costs to the employer (including

---

[44]§119(a)(1).
[45]§274(n).
[46]§119(a)(2).
[47]§127(a)(2). The discrimination and eligibility rules are provided in §127(b)(2).
[48]§129.

opportunity costs).[49] For example, airline companies can provide employees with free flight benefits on a space-available basis, hoteliers can allow employees to use vacant hotel rooms, and telephone companies can provide free basic phone service to their employees—all without the employees recognizing gross income. Exhibit 12-11 describes no-cost benefits that airline companies like JetBlue provide to their employees.[50]

EXHIBIT 12-11   Flight Benefits

JetBlue, like most other airlines, offers the following flight benefits to employees:

- It's our favorite perk! JetBlue crewmembers enjoy the benefit of free standby travel on JetBlue, as well as reduced-rate standby travel on some other airlines.

Source: See http://www.jetblue.com/work-here/benefits.aspx

Example 12-22

What if: Assume that Julie's current employer, PCC, has a division that provides wireless Internet service and virus protection software. Because PCC has such a large contract with a national provider, its contract has sufficient bandwidth to allow employees to use the service without incurring additional cost. The market value of the services is $1,080 per year. What amount of this benefit must Julie include in her gross income?

Answer: $0. Julie may exclude the value of the wireless Internet service from her income because it qualifies as a no-additional-cost service under §132.

Qualified Employee Discounts   Employers frequently allow employees to purchase the employer's goods and services at a discount. Employees may exclude **qualified employee discounts** from income as long as they don't acquire *goods* at a discount greater than the average gross profit percentage for the employer's goods.[51] This can be a fairly significant nontaxable benefit to employees, particularly for higher-priced products. For example, Ford Motor Company allows employees a substantial discount on its Ford and Lincoln brand cars. Exhibit 12-12 presents an excerpt from the IBM website describing the IBM employee product purchase plan, which allows employees to acquire home appliances at a significant discount. Employees may also exclude qualified employee discounts on *services* as long as the discount is not more than 20 percent of the price offered to customers.

EXHIBIT 12-12   Excerpt from IBM's Website

Employee Purchase Program

Up to 25% off PCs for IBMers, friends & family. Free extended warranties & ground shipping!

See https://www-store.shop.ibm.com/shop/used/us-en/icpeusepp/login

---

From a nontax perspective, employers can use this qualified fringe benefit to entice and retain employees.

---

[49]§132(a)(1).

[50]See http://www.jetblue.com/work-here/benefits.aspx

[51]§132(a)(2).

Example 12-23

What if: Assume that Julie's current employer, PCC, allows all employees to purchase computers (both laptops and desktops) from its retail stores at a discount. Julie purchased two computers during the current year: a laptop for $1,600 (retails for $2,100, with a cost to PCC of $1,500) and a desktop for $1,300 (retails for $1,800, with a cost of $1,250). Julie saved $500 ($2,100 − $1,600) on the laptop and $500 ($1,800 − $1,300) on the desktop. Assume that PCC's average gross profit percentage is 25 percent. What amount of the discount must Julie include in her gross income?

Answer: Julie must include $50 in her gross income. The $50 of income is from the desktop because the employee discount of $500 ($1,800 retail price less the $1,300 purchase price) exceeds the $450 discount allowed ($1,800 retail price × 25% average gross profit percentage). The $500 savings on the laptop may be excluded from her income because the savings are less than the $525 ($2,100 × 25%) allowable qualified employee discount.

What if: Suppose that the laptop Julie purchased for $1,600 has a cost of $1,700 (instead of $1,500 as stated above). What amount of the tax savings on the laptop must Julie include in her gross income?

Answer: Zero for the laptop, because Julie's employee discount of $500 is still less than the allowable qualified employee discount of $525 ($2,100 × 25%). The qualified discount is tied to PCC's gross profit percentage, not the purchase price of a specific item.

What if: Assume that Julie's current employer, PCC, allows all employees to receive one free computer each year. Julie selected the laptop (retails for $2,100, with a cost to PCC of $1,500) as her free computer. What amount must PCC include in Julie's gross income?

Answer: $1,575. Julie's cost of the computer ($0) is $1,575 less than PCC's sales price ($2,100) less its gross profit percentage, $525 ($2,100 × 25%). Therefore, she must include $1,575 in income. Employee discounts only qualify as a allowable qualified employee discount to the extent they don't exceed the employer's gross profit percentage.

Working Condition Fringe Benefits   Employees may exclude from income any benefit or reimbursement of a benefit provided by an employer. For example, if a company or firm reimburses its employees for professional licensing costs or dues (e.g., CPA or bar fees or AICPA dues), the reimbursement may be excluded from an employee's income.[52] Additionally, telephones or computers provided to employees for business use may be excluded. Employers may discriminate between employees with respect to **working condition fringe benefits.**

Example 12-24

What if: Assume that Julie's employer reimburses executives for business-related continuing education courses as well as travel costs related to such education. Julie attended a certificate (nondegree program) course at the University of Chicago this year. Her costs were as follows: $2,500 for the course, $600 for airfare, $800 for hotels, and $200 for books and course materials. PCC reimbursed Julie for the entire $4,100 ($2,500 + $600 + $800 + $200). What amount of the reimbursement must Julie include in her gross income?

Answer: $0. The reimbursement qualifies as a working condition fringe benefit.

What if: Assume that Ethan's employer allows all of its engineers to take home products for consumer testing and evaluation. For example, Ethan is currently designing a new disc brake system for mountain bikes. So Ethan is allowed to check out up to three mountain bikes at a time to see how various brake systems work. The annual rental value of products Ethan uses is $2,500. What amount of the annual rental value must Ethan include in his gross income?

Answer: $0. The value of the consumer testing products is an excludable working condition fringe benefit.

---

[52]Employees can exclude reimbursements from their income if they properly document their expenses through expense reports, mileage logs, and receipts.

De Minimis **Fringe Benefits**   Employees can also exclude from income occasional or incidental *de minimis* **fringe benefits.**[53] These typically include occasional personal use of a copy machine, company-sponsored picnics, noncash traditional holiday gifts (Thanksgiving turkey or Christmas ham), and occasional tickets to sporting or theatrical events. Employers are allowed to discriminate between employees when providing *de minimis* fringe benefits. Who do you think gets to use a company's NBA tickets—the new employee or the boss?

Qualified Transportation Fringe Benefits   Employees may exclude from income the value of certain transportation benefits they receive from employers, whether employers pay for these benefits directly or reimburse employees for the transportation costs.[54] These **qualified transportation fringe benefits** eligible for exclusion include the value of company-owned carpool vehicles for commuting to and from work, the cost of mass transit passes, and the cost of qualified parking near the workplace. In 2018, the maximum exclusion for the carpool vehicle and mass transit pass is $260 per month and the maximum exclusion for the qualified parking benefit is also up to $260 per month. Employers may discriminate with respect to these benefits.

Cafeteria Plans and Flexible Spending Accounts (FSAs)   Employers choose the benefits they make available to employees. Some employers offer a standard package of benefits that employees can either take or leave. Standard benefits typically include health and dental insurance for the employee and family, dependent care benefits, and group-term life insurance for the employee. However, a standard benefit plan is not optimal for all employees because each employee has individual needs. So how can employers tailor their benefits to the needs of employees? The answer is cafeteria plans and flexible spending accounts.

Under a **cafeteria plan,** employers determine the total cost of benefits they are willing to provide for each employee. Each employee then either chooses (or buys) benefits up to the determined amount from a menu of nontaxable fringe benefits or may receive a cash equivalent in lieu of forgone benefits.[55] However, cash received from a cafeteria plan is taxable compensation to employees. Cafeteria plans are popular because each employee may desire different types of nontaxable fringe benefits. For example, if an employer provides $3,000 of dependent care benefits to every employee, the benefits would be worthless to employees without dependents. Through a cafeteria plan, employees can select the benefits best suited to their needs. For example, instead of selecting dependent care benefits, an employee with no dependents could choose any combination of nontaxable benefits such as dental insurance, educational benefits, or cash if none of the benefits are desirable.

Employers can also offer **flexible spending accounts (FSAs),** which allow employees to set aside a portion of their before-tax salary for payment of either health and/or dependent-care benefits. These plans allow employees to set aside either employee contributions (on a before-tax basis) or employer contributions (a leftover cafeteria plan amount) to pay for medical-related expenses (such as co-payments and prescriptions) or dependent care. The Patient Protection and Affordable Care Act reduces the limit for medical-related expenses to $2,650 in 2018. Generally, amounts placed in flexible spending accounts must be used for qualifying benefits during the FSA plan year (which is often the calendar year). Employers may no longer allow employees to use the remaining balance from one year within the first two and a half months of the next FSA plan year. Up to $500 of the prior year remaining balance

---

[53]§132(a)(4).

[54]§132(a)(5) which is defined in §132(f).

[55]§125.

may be carried forward to the subsequent plan year, but excess amounts are forfeited by the employee.

Employee and Employer Considerations for Nontaxable Fringe Benefits

Nontaxable fringe benefits are very attractive to employees because their after-tax cost of these benefits is zero.[56] Employees do not pay for the benefits and they are not taxed on the value of the benefits they receive. In contrast to taxable fringe benefits, nontaxable fringe benefits cannot, with a few exceptions noted above, be provided on a discriminatory basis (that is, they cannot be given to some employees and not others). Employers deduct the cost of providing the benefits, which, thanks to group or quantity discounts, can be considerably lower than the cost to the employee of purchasing the benefit(s) separately. Employers may deduct the cost of providing nontaxable fringe benefits except for qualified parking, qualified transportation fringe benefits, and 50 percent of the meals provided for the convenience of the employer on the employer's premises. IRS publication 15-B "Employer's Tax Guide to Fringe Benefits" (available at www.IRS.gov) provides tax guidance for employers providing fringe benefits.

Tax Planning with Fringe Benefits

The fact that employees can exclude nontaxable fringe benefits from gross income, while employers can deduct the cost of providing them (just as they deduct the cost of taxable fringe benefits), gives rise to compensation-related tax-planning opportunities that may benefit both the employee and the employer.

Example 12-25

TPI proposed to reimburse Julie $5,000 a year for her educational expenses. What amount of this employee educational assistance reimbursement would be a nontaxable fringe benefit to Julie?

Answer: All $5,000. Julie can exclude up to $5,250 per year as an employee educational assistance fringe benefit.

What if: Assume that TPI will not reimburse Julie's educational expenses unless Julie is willing to accept a reduction in salary. Assuming Julie is subject to a 24 percent marginal tax rate, how much salary should Julie be willing to forgo to receive the $5,000 of nontaxable employee educational assistance fringe benefit (ignoring FICA taxes)?

Answer: $6,579, computed as follows:

Description	Amount	Explanation
(1) Annual fringe benefit	$ 5,000	
(2) Marginal ordinary tax rate	24%	
Before-tax compensation required to pay for annual fringe benefit	**$6,579**	(1)/[1 − (2)]

---

[56]Furthermore, there are nontax reasons for employees to value nontaxable benefits, such as the fact that many employer-provided group health insurance plans allow for preexisting health conditions, whereas employees may not be able to obtain health insurance plans that cover preexisting health conditions on their own.

Example 12-26

What if: Assume that instead of an educational benefit, TPI will pay Julie $6,579 of salary that she can then use to pay for her educational expenses. What is TPI's after-tax cost of paying $6,579 of salary to Julie assuming its marginal tax rate is 21 percent?

Answer: $5,197, calculated as follows:

Description	Amount	Explanation
(1) Taxable salary paid	$ 6,579	
(2) Income tax benefit	(1,382)	(1) × 21%
Total after-tax cost of salary	**$5,197**	(1) + (2)

What if: Assume that TPI will provide Julie $5,000 of employee educational assistance qualified fringe benefits. What will be its after-tax cost of paying the $5,000 nontaxable fringe benefit to Julie?

Answer: $3,950 calculated as follows:

Description	Amount	Explanation
(1) Nontaxable fringe benefit paid	$ 5,000	
(2) Income tax benefit	(1,050)	(1) × 21%
Total after-tax cost of nontaxable benefit	**$3,950**	(1) + (2)

Can an employer and an employee work together to implement the conversion tax planning strategy to make both the employee and the employer better off by substituting desired nontaxable fringe benefits for taxable salary in the compensation package? The answer is yes!

Example 12-27

What if: As shown in Example 12-25, Julie is indifferent between receiving (1) $6,579 in salary or (2) $5,000 in nontaxable employee educational assistance benefits. Consequently, if TPI paid Julie $5,000 in nontaxable benefits and any amount of additional salary, she would be better off than she would be by receiving no educational assistance and $6,579 in salary. As shown in Example 12-26, TPI would be better off after taxes by providing Julie with (1) $5,000 in nontaxable benefits (cost of $3,950) rather than (2) salary of $6,579 (after-tax cost of $5,197). What amount of salary could TPI provide in addition to the $5,000 of nontaxable benefits to make it indifferent between providing the educational assistance and the additional salary or providing salary of $6,579?

Answer: $1,578 additional salary, calculated as follows:

Description	Amount	Explanation
(1) After-tax cost of salary	$ 5,197	Example 12-26
(2) After-tax cost of fringe benefit	3,950	Example 12-26
(3) After-tax cost of additional salary	$ 1,247	(1) − (2)
(4) After-tax cost percentage	79%	(1 − .21)
Additional before-tax salary	**$1,578**	(3)/(4)

To summarize, if TPI reimburses Julie's educational expenses and provides her with additional salary of any amount below $1,578, it will be better off than it would be by not providing the educational expenses and paying her $6,579 in salary. Julie is better off if TPI reimburses her educational expenses and gives her any additional salary than she is if it doesn't reimburse her educational expenses but pays her $6,579 of salary.

Fringe Benefits Summary

Fringe benefits, both taxable and nontaxable, can make up a significant portion of an employee's compensation. Fringe benefits are taxable unless the tax laws specifically exclude them from gross income. Taxable fringe benefits usually represent a luxury perk, while nontaxable fringe benefits are generally excluded for public policy reasons. At this point, you should be able to distinguish between taxable and nontaxable fringe benefits. Exhibit 12-13 presents an excerpt from Disney Company's 2017 proxy statement. Read through the excerpt and see whether you can identify which of the benefits received by CEO Robert Iger are taxable and which are nontaxable.

Iger's taxable benefits include the personal air travel, security, wellness-related purposes, reimbursement for financial consulting, and perhaps part of the group-term life insurance. His nontaxable benefits include theme park access (a no-additional-cost service), merchandise discounts (qualified employee discount), occasional sporting events (*de minimis* fringe benefit), educational expense reimbursements, health insurance, and group-term life insurance (some of this coverage may be taxable).

Recall the fringe benefits included in Julie's offer letter: health and dental insurance (valued at $18,000), $750,000 of group-term life insurance, a biennial $30,000 automobile allowance, and a flexible spending account for medical expenses (no amounts given—assume she elects $1,500). She also received a reimbursement of $5,000 of

EXHIBIT 12-13   **Excerpt from Disney Company's 2017 Proxy Statement Dealing with Fringe Benefits**

The following table identifies the incremental cost of each perquisite or personal benefit that exceeded the greater of $25,000 or 10% of the total amount of perquisites and personal benefits for a named executive officer in fiscal 2016.

Fiscal 2016 Perquisites and Personal Benefits					
Executive	**Year**	**Personal Air Travel**	**Security**	**Other**	**Total**
Robert A. Iger	2016	$282,831	$869,476	$32,350	$1,184,657

The incremental cost to the Company of the items specified above was determined as follows:

- Personal air travel: the actual catering costs, landing and ramp fees, fuel costs and lodging costs incurred by flight crew plus a per hour charge based on the average hourly maintenance costs for the aircraft during the year for flights that were purely personal in nature, and a pro rata portion of catering costs where personal guests accompanied a named executive officer on flights that were business in nature. Where a personal flight coincided with the repositioning of an aircraft following a business flight, only the incremental costs of the flight compared to an immediate repositioning of the aircraft are included. As noted on pages 23 to 24, above, Mr. Iger is required for security reasons to use corporate aircraft for all of his personal travel.

- Security: the actual costs incurred by the Company for providing security equipment and services.

The "Other" column in the table above includes, to the extent a named executive officer elected to receive any of these benefits, the incremental cost to the Company of the vehicle benefit, personal air travel or security services where the cost to the Company was less than $25,000, reimbursement of up to $1,000 per calendar year for wellness-related purposes such as fitness, nutrition and stress management, and reimbursement of expenses for financial consulting. With respect to Mr. Iger, the "Other" column also includes legal fees incurred in connection with the renegotiation of his employment agreement.

The named executive officers also were eligible to receive the other benefits described in the Compensation Discussion and Analysis under the discussion of "Benefits and Perquisites" in the "Compensation Program Elements" section, which involved no incremental cost to the Company or are offered through group life, health or medical reimbursement plans that are available generally to all of the Company's salaried employees.

EXHIBIT 12-14 Summary of Julie's Nonsalary Benefits from TPI

Benefit	Nontaxable Fringe	Taxable Fringe	Employee After-Tax Benefit	Employer After-Tax Cost
Auto allowance		X	**$22,800** ($30,000 − $7,200) Example 12-18	**$23,700** [$30,000 × (1 − .21)]
Health and dental insurance	X		**$18,000** [($18,000 × (1 − .0)]	**$14,220** [$18,000 × (1 − .21)]
Flexible spending account	X		**$1,500** [($1,500 × (1 − .0)]	**$1,185** [$1,500 × (1 − .21)]
Parking reimbursement	X		**$2,400** [($2,400 × (1 − .0)]	**$2,400** [$2,400 × (1 − .0)]
Group-term life insurance	X	X	**$1,605** ($2,000 − $395) (Examples 12-19, 20)	**$395** [$500 × (1 − .21)] (Examples 12-20)
Education assistance benefits	X		**$5,000** [($5,000 × (1 − .0)] (Examples 12-25)	**$3,950** [$5,000 × (1 − .21)] (Examples 12-26)
Total			**$51,305**	**$45,850**

educational expenses (see Example 12-25). Which of these benefits are taxable and which are nontaxable? Exhibit 12-14 summarizes how each of these benefits is classified for tax purposes, Julie's after-tax benefit, and TPI's after-tax cost.

CONCLUSION

Individuals and employers routinely make choices involving compensation issues. As they do so, they must understand how alternative forms of compensation are taxed. In this chapter, we have discussed the tax compliance and planning implications associated with common types of payment including salary and wages, equity-based compensation (such as stock options and restricted stock), and taxable and nontaxable fringe benefits from both employee and employer perspectives. Throughout, we have emphasized that both tax and nontax issues must be considered in the broader context of compensation planning. Armed with the information provided in this chapter, future employees and employers can approach the compensation decisions they will undoubtedly face with more confidence and insight.

Summary

Explain the tax implications of compensation in the form of salary and wages from the perspective of the employee and the employer.

LO 12-1

- Employees are taxed on salary at ordinary income rates.
- Employees use Form W-4 to supply their employer with withholding information. Employees can use the W-4 to manage withholding throughout the year because withholding is treated as though it is withheld evenly throughout the year for estimated tax purposes.
- Cash-method employers deduct wages when paid. Accrual-method employers deduct wages when accrued as long as the wages are paid within 2½ months of year-end. If paid after 2½ months of year-end, wages are deductible when the employee recognizes the income (when paid). When an employer accrues wages to a related-person employee (more than 50 percent ownership), the wages are not deductible until the employee recognizes the income (when paid).
- Employers' after-tax cost of wages is the cost of the wages minus the tax benefit of the deduction for the wages.

- For publicly traded corporations, the tax deduction for compensation paid to covered employees, CEO, CFO, and the three other most highly compensated officers, is limited to $1,000,000 per year per individual.

LO 12-2 Describe the tax implications of various forms of equity-based compensation from the perspective of the employee and the employer.

- Stock options and restricted stock are common forms of equity-based compensation. Although both reward employees for increases in the stock price of their employers, there are fundamental economic differences between them.
- Stock options are either nonqualified stock options (NQOs) or incentive stock options (ISOs) for tax purposes.
- Employees recognize ordinary income equal to the bargain element on NQOs when they are exercised. Employers are able to deduct the bargain element when NQOs are exercised. Any appreciation in the value of shares subsequent to the exercise of NQOs is treated as capital gain by employees when the shares are sold.
- If certain holding period requirements are met, employees exercising ISOs don't recognize any income until the shares received from the exercised options are sold. When the shares are sold, the difference between the exercise price and the share price is long-term capital gain (assuming appreciation). Employers are not permitted a deduction for ISOs.
- Generally, employees prefer ISOs and employers prefer NQOs because of differences in the way the two types of options are taxed.
- Employers treat stock options differently for book and tax purposes.
- Employees recognize ordinary income from restricted stock equal to the fair market value of the stock on the vesting date. Employers receive a corresponding tax deduction.
- Employees may elect to recognize taxable income from restricted stock on the date it is received rather than on the vesting date if they make a §83(b) election. Although this election accelerates the recognition of income, it gives the employee the ability to convert ordinary income from further appreciation into a capital gain.
- RSUs are units valued in employer stock at the time of grant, but unlike restricted stock, upon settlement RSUs can be exchanged for employer stock, cash, or some combination of cash and stock depending upon the terms of the RSU agreement.
- Qualified employees may elect to defer recognition of taxable income from a Qualified Equity Grant if they make a 83(i) election. A Qualified Equity Grant is qualified stock, received by a qualified employee, of an eligible corporation.

LO 12-3 Compare and contrast taxable and nontaxable fringe benefits and explain their tax consequences for the employee and the employer.

- Fringe benefits are taxable to the employee unless the Code specifically excludes the benefit from gross income. Taxable fringe benefits are generally luxury perks, such as corporate air travel and security.
- Nontaxable fringe benefits include up to $50,000 of group-term life insurance, health benefits, meals and lodging for the convenience of the employer, educational assistance, dependent care benefits, qualified employee discounts, and qualified transportation benefits (among others).

KEY TERMS

83(b) election (12-17)
bargain element (12-9)
cafeteria plan (12-29)
cashless exercise (12-10)
de minimis fringe benefit (12-29)
disqualifying disposition (12-12)
educational assistance benefit (12-26)
employee (12-2)
exercise date (12-10)

exercise price (12-9)
facts and circumstances test (12-2)
FICA taxes (12-2)
flexible spending account (FSA) (12-29)
for the convenience of the employer benefits (12-26)
Form W-2 (12-2)
Form W-4 (12-2)

fringe benefits (12-20)
grant date (12-10)
group-term life insurance (12-21)
health and accident insurance (12-24)
incentive stock option (ISO) (12-10)
no-additional-cost services (12-26)
nonqualified stock option (NQO) (12-10)
nontaxable fringe benefit (12-24)

option exercise (12-9)	restricted stock (12-15)	vest (12-9)
qualified employee discount (12-27)	salary (12-2)	vesting date (12-10)
qualified equity grant (12-19)	same-day sale (12-10)	wages (12-2)
qualified transportation fringe benefit (12-29)	strike price (12-9)	working condition fringe benefit (12-28)
	taxable fringe benefit (12-20)	

DISCUSSION QUESTIONS

Discussion Questions are available in Connect®.

1. Nicole and Braxton are each 50 percent shareholders of NB Corporation. Nicole is also an employee of the corporation. NB is a calendar-year taxpayer and uses the accrual method of accounting. The corporation pays its employees monthly on the first day of the month after the salary is earned by the employees. What issues must NB consider with respect to the deductibility of the wages it pays to Nicole if Nicole is Braxton's sister? What issues arise if Nicole and Braxton are unrelated? **LO 12-1**

2. Holding all else equal, does an employer with a higher marginal tax rate or lower marginal tax rate have a lower after-tax cost of paying a particular employee's salary? Explain. **LO 12-1**

3. What nontax reasons explain why a corporation may choose to cap its executives' salaries at $1 million? **LO 12-1**

4. What tax reasons explain why a corporation may choose to cap its executives' salaries at $1 million? **LO 12-1**

5. From an *employee* perspective, how are ISOs treated differently from NQOs for tax purposes? In general, for a given number of options, which type of stock option should employees prefer? **LO 12-2**

6. From an *employer* perspective, how are ISOs treated differently from NQOs for tax purposes? In general, for a given number of options, which type of stock option should employers prefer? **LO 12-2**

7. Why do employers use stock options in addition to salary to compensate their employees? For employers, are stock options treated more favorably than salary for tax purposes? Explain. **LO 12-2**

8. What is a "disqualifying disposition" of ISOs, and how does it affect employees who have exercised ISOs? **LO 12-2**

9. Compare and contrast how employers record book and tax expense for stock options. **LO 12-2**

10. How is the tax treatment of restricted stock different from that of NQOs? How is it similar? **LO 12-2**

11. Matt just started work with Boom Zoom Inc., a manufacturer of credit-card-sized devices for storing and playing back music. Due to the popularity of its devices, analysts expect Boom Zoom's stock price to increase dramatically. In addition to his salary, Matt received Boom Zoom restricted stock. How will Matt's restricted stock be treated for tax purposes? Should Matt consider making the 83(b) election? What are the factors he should consider in making this decision? From a tax perspective, would this election help or hurt Boom Zoom? **LO 12-2**

12. What risks are assumed by employees making a 83(b) election on a restricted stock grant? **LO 12-2**

13. Explain the differences and similarities between fringe benefits and salary as forms of compensation. **LO 12-3**

14. When an employer provides group-term life insurance to an employee, what are the tax consequences for the employee? What are the tax consequences for the employer? **LO 12-3**

15. Compare and contrast the employer's tax consequences of providing taxable versus nontaxable fringe benefits. **LO 12-3**

LO 12-3   16. Mike is working his way through college and trying to make ends meet. Tara, a friend, is graduating soon and tells Mike about a really great job opportunity. She is the onsite manager for an apartment complex catering to students. The job entails working in the office for about 10 hours a week, collecting rent each month, and answering after-hours emergency calls. The owner of the apartment complex requires the manager to live onsite as a condition of employment. The pay is $10 per hour, plus a rent-free apartment (worth about $500 per month). Tara then tells him the best part: the rent-free apartment is tax-free. Knowing that you are a tax student, Mike asks you if the rent-free apartment is really tax-free or if Tara is mistaken. Explain to Mike whether the compensation for the apartment is really a nontaxable fringe benefit.

LO 12-3   17. Assume that your friend has accepted a position working as an accountant for a large automaker. As a signing bonus, the employer provides the traditional cash incentive but also provides the employee with a vehicle not to exceed a retail price of $25,000. Explain to your friend whether the value of the vehicle is included, excluded, or partially included in the employee's gross income.

LO 12-3   18. Explain why an employee might accept a lower salary to receive a nontaxable fringe benefit. Why might an employee *not* accept a lower salary to receive a nontaxable fringe benefit?

LO 12-3   19. Describe a cafeteria plan and discuss why an employer would provide a cafeteria plan for its employees.

LO 12-3   20. Explain why Congress allows employees to receive certain fringe benefits tax-free but others are taxable.

LO 12-3   21. Explain the policy reason for including the value of a country club membership provided to an executive as a taxable fringe benefit.

LO 12-3   22. Describe the circumstances in which an employee may not value a nontaxable fringe benefit.

PROBLEMS

Select problems are available in Connect®.   **connect**

LO 12-1   23. North Inc. is a calendar-year C corporation, accrual-basis taxpayer. At the end of year 1, North accrued and deducted the following bonuses for certain employees for financial accounting purposes.

- $7,500 for Lisa Tanaka, a 30 percent shareholder.
- $10,000 for Jared Zabaski, a 35 percent shareholder.
- $12,500 for Helen Talanian, a 20 percent shareholder.
- $5,000 for Steve Nielson, a 0 percent shareholder.

Unless stated otherwise, assume these shareholders are unrelated.

How much of the accrued bonuses can North Inc. deduct in year 1 under the following alternative scenarios?

a) North paid the bonuses to the employees on March 1 of year 2.

b) North paid the bonuses to the employees on April 1 of year 2.

c) North paid the bonuses to employees on March 1 of year 2 and Lisa and Jared are related to each other, so they are treated as owning each other's stock in North.

d) North paid the bonuses to employees on March 1 of year 2 and Lisa and Helen are related to each other, so they are treated as owning each other's stock in North.

24. Jorgensen High Tech Inc. is a calendar-year, accrual-method taxpayer. At the end of year 1, Jorgensen accrued and deducted the following bonuses for certain employees for financial accounting purposes.   LO 12-1

    - $40,000 for Ken.
    - $30,000 for Jayne.
    - $20,000 for Jill.
    - $10,000 for Justin.

    How much of the accrued bonuses can Jorgensen deduct in year 1 under the following alternative scenarios?

    a) Jorgensen paid the bonuses to the employees on March 1 of year 2.

    b) Jorgensen paid the bonuses to the employees on April 1 of year 2.

    c) Jorgensen paid the bonuses to employees on March 1 of year 2, and there is a requirement that the employee remain employed with Jorgensen on the payment date to receive the bonus.

    d) Jorgensen paid the bonuses to employees on March 1 of year 2, and there is a requirement that the employee remain employed with Jorgensen on the payment date to receive the bonus; if not, the forfeited bonus is reallocated to the other employees.

25. Lynette is the CEO of publicly traded TTT Corporation and earns a salary of $200,000 in the current year. Assume TTT is profitable. What is TTT Corporation's after-tax cost of paying Lynette's salary?   LO 12-1

26. Marcus is the CEO of publicly traded ABC Corporation and earns a salary of $1,500,000. Assume ABC has a 21 percent marginal tax rate. What is ABC's after-tax cost of paying Marcus's salary?   LO 12-1

27. Cammie received 100 NQOs (each option provides a right to purchase 10 shares of MNL stock for $10 per share) at the time she started working for MNL Corporation (5/1/Y1) four years ago when MNL's stock price was $8 per share. Now that MNL's stock price is $40 per share (8/15/Y5), she intends to exercise all of her options. After acquiring the 1,000 MNL shares with her options, she held the shares for over one year (10/1/Y6) and sold them at $60 per share.   LO 12-2
tax forms

    a) What are Cammie's taxes due on the grant date (5/1/Y1), exercise date (8/15/Y5), and sale date (10/1/Y6), assuming her ordinary marginal rate is 32 percent and her long-term capital gains rate is 15 percent?

    b) What are MNL Corporation's tax savings on the grant date (5/1/Y1), exercise date (8/15/Y5), and sale date (10/1/Y6), assuming its marginal tax rate is 21 percent?

    c) Complete Cammie's Form 8949 and Schedule D for the year of sale. Also assume that the sale transaction of the MNL Corporation stock was not reported to Cammie on a Form 1099-B.

28. Yost received 300 NQOs (each option gives Yost the right to purchase 10 shares of Cutter Corporation stock for $15 per share) at the time he started working for Cutter Corporation three years ago. Cutter's stock price was $15 per share. Yost exercises all of his options when the share price is $26 per share. Two years after acquiring the shares, he sold them at $47 per share.   LO 12-2
planning

    a) What are Yost's taxes due on the grant date, exercise date, and sale date, assuming his ordinary marginal rate is 35 percent and his long-term capital gains rate is 15 percent?

    b) What are Cutter Corporation's tax consequences (amount of deduction and tax savings from deduction) on the grant date, the exercise date, and the date Yost sells the shares, assuming its marginal tax rate is 21 percent?

    c) Assume that Yost is "cash poor" and needs to engage in a same-day sale in order to buy his shares. Due to his belief that the stock price is going to increase significantly, he wants to maintain as many shares as possible.

How many shares must he sell in order to cover his purchase price and taxes payable on the exercise?

d) Assume that Yost's options were exercisable at $20 and expired after five years. If the stock only reached $18 dollars during its high point during the five-year period, what are Yost's tax consequences on the grant date, the exercise date, and the date the shares are sold, assuming his ordinary marginal rate is 35 percent and his long-term capital gains rate is 15 percent?

LO 12-2   29. Haven received 200 NQOs (each option gives him the right to purchase 20 shares of Barlow Corporation stock for $7 per share) at the time he started working for Barlow Corporation three years ago when its stock price was $7 per share. Now that Barlow's share price is $50 per share, he intends to exercise all of his options. After acquiring the 4,000 Barlow shares with his options, he intends to hold the shares for more than one year and then sell the shares when the price reaches $75 per share.

a) What are Haven's taxes due on the grant date, exercise date, and sale date, assuming his ordinary marginal rate is 32 percent and his long-term capital gains rate is 15 percent?

b) What are the cash flow effects for Barlow Corporation resulting from Haven's option exercise if Barlow's marginal tax rate is 21 percent? How would it change if Barlow's marginal rate were 0 percent?

LO 12-2   30. Mark received 10 ISOs (each option gives him the right to purchase 10 shares of Hendricks Corporation stock for $5 per share) at the time he started working for Hendricks Corporation five years ago when Hendricks's stock price was $5 per share. Now that Hendricks's share price is $35 per share, Mark intends to exercise all of his options and hold all of his shares for more than one year. Assume that more than a year after exercise, Mark sells the stock for $35 a share.

a) What are Mark's taxes due on the grant date, the exercise date, and the date he sells the shares, assuming his ordinary marginal rate is 32 percent and his long-term capital gains rate is 15 percent?

b) What are Hendricks's tax consequences on the grant date, the exercise date, and the date Mark sells the shares, assuming its marginal tax rate is 21 percent?

LO 12-2   31. Antonio received 40 ISOs (each option gives him the right to purchase 20 shares of Zorro stock for $3 per share) at the time he started working for Zorro Corporation six years ago. Zorro's stock price was $3 per share at the time. Now that Zorro's stock price is $50 per share, Antonio intends to exercise all of his options and immediately sell all the shares he receives from the options exercise.

a) What are Antonio's taxes due on the grant date, the exercise date, and the date the shares are sold, assuming his ordinary marginal rate is 32 percent and his long-term capital gains rate is 15 percent?

b) What are Zorro's tax consequences on the grant date, the exercise date, and the date Antonio sells the shares, assuming its marginal tax rate is 21 percent?

c) What are the cash flow effects of these transactions to Antonio, assuming his ordinary marginal rate is 24 percent and his long-term capital gains rate is 15 percent?

d) What are the cash flow effects to Zorro Corporation resulting from Antonio's option exercise if Zorro's marginal tax rate is 21 percent?

LO 12-2   32. Harmer Inc. is now a successful company. In the early days (before it became
planning   profitable), it issued ISOs to its employees. Now Harmer is trying to decide whether to issue NQOs or ISOs to its employees. Initially, Harmer would like to give each employee 20 options (each option allows the employee to acquire one share of Harmer stock). For purposes of this problem, assume that the options are exercised in three years (*three years from now*) and that the underlying stock is sold in five years (*five years from now*). Assume that taxes are paid at the

same time the income generating the tax is recognized. Also assume the following facts:

- The after-tax discount rate for both Harmer Inc. and its employees is 10 percent.
- The corporate tax rate is 21 percent.
- The personal (employee) ordinary income rate is 37 percent.
- The personal (employee) long-term capital gains rate is 20 percent.
- The exercise price of the options is $7.
- The market price of Harmer at date of grant is $5.
- The market price of Harmer at date of exercise is $25.
- The market price of Harmer at date of sale is $35.

Answer the following questions:

a) Considering these facts, which type of option plan, NQO or ISO, should Harmer Inc. prefer? Explain.

b) Assuming Harmer issues NQOs, what is Harmer's tax benefit from the options for each employee in the year each employee exercises the NQOs?

c) Assuming Harmer issues ISOs, what is the tax benefit to Harmer in the year the ISOs are exercised?

d) Which type of option plan should Harmer's employees prefer?

e) What is the present value of each employee's after-tax cash flows from year 1 through year 5 if the employees receive ISOs?

f) What is the present value of each employee's after-tax cash flows from year 1 through year 5 if the employees receive NQOs?

g) How many NQOs would Harmer have to grant to keep its employees indifferent between NQOs and 20 ISOs?

33. On January 1, year 1, Dave received 1,000 shares of restricted stock from his employer, RRK Corporation. On that date, the stock price was $7 per share. Dave's restricted shares will vest at the end of year 2. He intends to hold the shares until the end of year 4 when he intends to sell them to help fund the purchase of a new home. Dave predicts the share price of RRK will be $30 per share when his shares vest and will be $40 per share when he sells them.   `LO 12-2`

a) If Dave's stock price predictions are correct, what are the taxes due on these transactions to Dave if his ordinary marginal rate is 32 percent and his long-term capital gains rate is 15 percent?

b) If Dave's stock price predictions are correct, what are the tax consequences of these transactions to RRK if its marginal rate is 21 percent?

34. On January 1, year 1, Dave received 1,000 shares of restricted stock from his employer, RRK Corporation. On that date, the stock price was $7 per share. On receiving the restricted stock, Dave made the 83(b) election. Dave's restricted shares will vest at the end of year 2. He intends to hold the shares until the end of year 4 when he intends to sell them to help fund the purchase of a new home. Dave predicts the share price of RRK will be $30 per share when his shares vest and will be $40 per share when he sells them. Assume that Dave's price predictions are correct and answer the following questions: `LO 12-2`

a) What are Dave's taxes due if his ordinary marginal rate is 32 percent and his long-term capital gains rate is 15 percent?

b) What are the tax consequences of these transactions to RRK if its marginal rate is 21 percent?

35. On January 1, year 1, Jessica received 10,000 shares of restricted stock from her employer, Rocket Corporation. On that date, the stock price was $10 per share. On   `LO 12-2`

receiving the restricted stock, Jessica made the 83(b) election. Jessica's restricted shares will all vest at the end of year 4. After the shares vest, she intends to sell them immediately to fund an around-the-world cruise. Unfortunately, Jessica decided that she couldn't wait four years and she quit her job to start her cruise on January 1, year 3.

a) What are Jessica's taxes due in year 1 assuming her marginal tax rate is 35 percent and her long-term capital gains rate is 15 percent?

b) What are Jessica's taxes due in year 3 assuming her marginal tax rate is 35 percent and her long-term capital gains rate is 15 percent?

LO 12-2   36. On May 1, year 1, Anna received 5,000 shares of restricted stock from her employer, Jarbal Corporation. On that date, the stock price was $5 per share. On receiving the restricted stock, Anna made the 83(b) election. Anna's restricted shares will all vest on May 1, year 3. After the shares vest, she intends to sell them immediately to purchase a condo. True to her plan, Anna sold the shares immediately after they were vested.

a) What is Anna's ordinary income in year 1?

b) What is Anna's gain or loss in year 3 if the stock is valued at $1 per share on the day the shares vest?

c) What is Anna's gain or loss in year 3 if the stock is valued at $9 per share on the day the shares vest?

d) What is Anna's gain or loss in year 3 if the stock is valued at $5 per share on the day the shares vest?

LO 12-2
planning   37. On January 1, year 1, Tyra started working for Hatch Corporation. New employees must choose immediately between receiving 7 NQOs (each NQO provides the right to purchase for $5 per share 10 shares of Hatch stock) or 50 restricted shares. Hatch's stock price is $5 on Tyra's start date. Either form of equity-based compensation will vest in two years. Tyra believes that the stock will be worth $15 per share in two years and $25 in four years when she will sell the stock. Tyra's marginal tax rate is 32 percent and her long-term capital gains rate is 15 percent. Assuming that Tyra's price predictions are correct, answer the following questions (ignore present value, and use nominal dollars):

a) What are the cash-flow effects to Tyra in the year she receives the options, in the year the options vest and she exercises the options, and in the year she sells the stock if she chooses the NQOs?

b) What are the cash-flow effects to Tyra in the year she receives the restricted stock, in the year the stock vests, and in the year she sells the stock if Tyra chooses the restricted stock?

c) What are the cash-flow effects to Tyra in the year she receives the restricted stock, in the year the stock vests, and in the year she sells the stock if she makes an 83(b) election?

d) What recommendation would you give Tyra? Explain.

LO 12-3   38. Nicole's employer, Poe Corporation, provides her with an automobile allowance of $20,000 every other year. Her marginal tax rate is 32 percent. Poe Corporation has a marginal tax rate of 21 percent. Answer the following questions relating to this fringe benefit.

a) What is Nicole's after-tax benefit if she receives the allowance this year?

b) What is Poe's after-tax cost of providing the auto allowance?

LO 12-3
research   39. Bills Corporation runs a defense contracting business that requires security clearance. To prevent unauthorized access to its materials, Bills requires its security personnel to be on duty except for a 15-minute break every two hours. Since the nearest restaurants are a 25-minute round trip, Bills provides free lunches to its security personnel. Bills has never included the value of these meals in its employees' compensation. Bills is currently under audit, and the IRS agent wants to deny Bills a deduction for past meals. The agent also wants Bills to begin including the value of

the meals in employee compensation starting with the current year. As Bills's tax adviser, provide a recommendation on whether to appeal the agent's decision. (*Hint:* See *Boyd Gaming Corp.*, CA-9, 99-1 USTC ¶50,530 (Acq.), 177 F3d 1096.)

40. Lars Osberg, a single taxpayer with a 35 percent marginal tax rate, desires health insurance. The health insurance will cost Lars $8,500 to purchase if he pays for it himself through the health exchange (Lars's AGI is too high to receive any tax deduction for the insurance as a medical expense). Volvo, Lars's employer, has a 21 percent marginal tax rate. Answer the following questions about this benefit.

a) What is the maximum amount of before-tax salary Lars would give up to receive health insurance from Volvo?

b) What would be the after-tax cost to Volvo to provide Lars with health insurance if it could purchase the insurance through its group plan for $5,000?

c) Assume that Volvo could purchase the insurance for $5,000. Lars is interested in getting health insurance and he is willing to receive a lower salary in exchange for the health insurance. What is the least amount by which Volvo would be willing to reduce Lars's salary while agreeing to pay his health insurance?

d) Will Volvo and Lars be able to reach an agreement by which Volvo will provide Lars with health insurance?

41. Seiko's current salary is $85,000. Her marginal tax rate is 32 percent and she fancies European sports cars. She purchases a new auto each year. Seiko is currently a manager for an Idaho Office Supply. Her friend, knowing of her interest in sports cars, tells her about a manager position at the local BMW and Porsche dealer. The new position pays only $75,000 per year, but it allows employees to purchase one new car per year at a discount of $15,000. This discount qualifies as a nontaxable fringe benefit. In an effort to keep Seiko as an employee, Idaho Office Supply offers her a $10,000 raise. Answer the following questions about this analysis.

a) Assuming it has a 21 percent marginal tax rate, what is the annual after-tax cost to her Idaho Office Supply (the office equipment company) if it provides Seiko with the $10,000 increase in salary?

b) Financially, which offer is better for Seiko on an after-tax basis and by how much? (Assume that Seiko is going to purchase the new car whether she switches jobs or not.)

c) What salary would Seiko need to receive from her Idaho Office Supply to make her financially indifferent (after taxes) between receiving additional salary from Idaho Office Supply and accepting a position at the auto dealership?

42. JDD Corporation provides the following to its employee, Ahmed (age 47):

Salary	$300,000
Health insurance	10,000
Dental insurance	2,000
Life insurance	3,000
Dependent care	5,000
Professional dues	500
Personal use of company jet	200,000

The life insurance is a group-term life insurance policy that provides $200,000 of coverage for Ahmed. Assuming Ahmed is subject to a marginal tax rate of 32 percent, what is his after-tax benefit of receiving each of these benefits?

43. Gray's employer is now offering group-term life insurance. The company will provide each employee with $100,000 of group-term life insurance. It costs Gray's employer $300 to provide this amount of insurance to Gray each year. Assuming

that Gray is 52 years old, determine the monthly premium that Gray must include in gross income as a result of receiving the group-term life benefit.

LO 12-3 44. Brady graduated from SUNY—New Paltz with his bachelor's degree recently. He works for Makarov & Company CPAs. The firm pays his tuition ($10,000 per year) for him so that he can receive his Master of Science in Taxation, which will qualify him to sit for the CPA exam. How much of the $10,000 tuition benefit does Brady need to include in gross income?

LO 12-3 45. Meg works for Freedom Airlines in the accounts payable department. Meg and all other employees receive free flight benefits (for the employee, family, and 10 free buddy passes for friends per year) as part of its employee benefits package. If Meg uses 30 flights with a value of $12,350 this year, how much must she include in her compensation this year?

LO 12-3 46. Sharmilla works for Shasta Lumber, a local lumber supplier. The company annually provides each employee with a Shasta Lumber shirt so that employees look branded **research** and advertise for the business while wearing the shirts. Are Shasta's employees required to include the value of the shirts in income?

LO 12-3 47. LaMont works for a company in downtown Chicago. The company encourages employees to use public transportation (to save the environment) by providing them **research** with transit passes at a cost of $265 per month.

a) If LaMont receives one pass (worth $265) each month, how much of this benefit must he include in his gross income each year?

b) If the company provides each employee with $265 per month in parking benefits, how much of the parking benefit must LaMont include in his gross income each year?

LO 12-3 48. Jarvie loves to bike. In fact, he has always turned down better-paying jobs to work in bicycle shops where he gets an employee discount. At Jarvie's current shop, Bad Dog Cycles, each employee is allowed to purchase four bicycles a year at a discount. Bad Dog has an average gross profit percentage on bicycles of 25 percent. During the current year, Jarvie bought the following bikes:

Description	Retail Price	Cost	Employee Price
Specialized road bike	$3,200	$2,000	$2,240
Rocky Mountain mountain bike	3,800	3,200	3,040
Trek road bike	2,700	2,000	1,890
Yeti mountain bike	3,500	2,500	2,800

a) What amount is Jarvie required to include in taxable income from these purchases?

b) What amount of deductions is Bad Dog allowed to claim from these transactions?

LO 12-1 **LO 12-3** 49. Matt works for Fresh Corporation. Fresh offers a cafeteria plan that allows each employee to receive $15,000 worth of benefits each year. The menu of benefits is as follows:

Benefit	Cost
Health insurance—single	$ 5,000
Health insurance—with spouse	$ 8,000
Health insurance—with spouse and dependents	$11,000
Dental and vision	$ 1,500
Dependent care—any specified amount up to $5,000	Variable
Adoption benefits—any specified amount up to $5,000	Variable
Educational benefits—any specified amount (no limit)	Variable
Cash—any specified amount up to $15,000 plan benefit	Variable
401(k)—any specified amount up to $10,000	Variable

For each of the following independent circumstances, determine the amount of income Matt must recognize and the amount of deduction Fresh may claim:

a) Matt selects the single health insurance and places $10,000 in his 401(k).

b) Matt selects the single health insurance, is reimbursed $5,000 for MBA tuition, and takes the remainder in cash.

c) Matt selects the single health insurance and is reimbursed for MBA tuition of $10,000.

d) Matt gets married and selects the health insurance with spouse and takes the rest in cash to help pay for the wedding.

e) Matt elects to take all cash.

COMPREHENSIVE PROBLEMS

Select problems are available with Connect®.

tax forms

50. Pratt is ready to graduate and leave College Park. His future employer (Ferndale Corp.) offers the following four compensation packages from which Pratt may choose. Pratt will start working for Ferndale on January 1, year 1.

Benefit Description	Option 1	Option 2	Option 3	Option 4
Salary	$60,000	$50,000	$45,000	$45,000
Health insurance	No coverage	5,000	5,000	5,000
Restricted stock	0	0	1,000 shares	0
NQOs	0	0	0	100 options

Assume that the restricted stock is 1,000 shares that trade at $5 per share on the grant date (January 1, year 1) and are expected to be worth $10 per share on the vesting date at the end of year 1 and that no 83(b) election is made. Assume that the NQOs (100 options that each allow the employee to purchase 10 shares at $5 exercise price). The stock trades at $5 per share on the grant date (January 1, year 1) and is expected to be worth $10 per share on the vesting date at the end of year 1 and that the options are exercised and sold at the end of the year. Also assume that Pratt spends on average $3,000 on health-related costs that would be covered by insurance if he has coverage. Assume that Pratt's marginal tax rate is 35 percent. Assume that Pratt spends $3,000 in after-tax dollars for health expenses when he doesn't have health insurance coverage (treat this as an outflow), and that there is no effect when he has health insurance coverage. (Ignore FICA taxes and time value of money considerations).

a) What is the after-tax value of each compensation package for year 1?

b) If Pratt's sole consideration is maximizing after-tax value for year 1, which scheme should he select?

c) Assuming Pratt chooses Option 3 and sells the stock on the vesting date (on the last day of year 1), complete Pratt's Schedule D for the sale of the restricted stock.

51. Santini's new contract for 2018 indicates the following compensation and benefits:

Benefit Description	Amount
Salary	$130,000
Health insurance	9,000
Restricted stock grant	2,500
Bonus	5,000
Hawaii trip	4,000
Group-term life insurance	1,600
Parking ($290 per month)	3,480

Santini is 54 years old at the end of 2018. He is single and has no dependents. Assume that the employer matches $1 for $1 for the first $6,000 that the employee contributes to his 401(k) during the year. The restricted stock grant is 500 shares granted when the market price was $5 per share. Assume that the stock vests on December 31, 2018, and that the market price on that date is $7.50 per share. Also assume that Santini is willing to make any elections to reduce equity-based compensation taxes. The Hawaii trip was given to him as the outstanding salesperson for 2017. The group-term life policy gives him $150,000 of coverage. Assume that Santini does not itemize deductions for the year. Determine Santini's taxable income and income tax liability for 2018.

planning   52. Sylvana is given a job offer with two alternative compensation packages to choose from. The first package offers her $250,000 annual salary with no qualified fringe benefits. The second package offers $235,000 annual salary plus health and life insurance benefits. If Sylvana were required to purchase the health and life insurance benefits herself, she would need to pay $10,000 annually after taxes. Assume her marginal tax rate is 35 percent.

a) Which compensation package should she choose and by how much would she benefit in after-tax dollars by choosing this package?

b) Assume the second package offers $230,000 plus benefits instead of $235,000 plus benefits. Which compensation package should she choose and by how much would she benefit in after-tax dollars by choosing this package?

planning   53. In the current year, Jill, age 35, received a job offer with two alternative compensation packages to choose from. The first package offers her $90,000 annual salary with no qualified fringe benefits and requires her to pay $3,500 a year for parking and to purchase life insurance at a cost of $1,000. The second package offers $80,000 annual salary, employer-provided health insurance, annual free parking (worth $315 per month), $200,000 of life insurance (purchasing on her own would have been $1,000 annually), and free flight benefits (she estimates that it will save her $5,000 per year). If Jill chooses the first package, she will purchase the health and life insurance benefits herself at a cost of $1,000 annually after taxes and spend another $5,000 in flights while traveling. Assume her marginal tax rate is 32 percent.

a) Which compensation package should she choose, and by how much would she benefit in after-tax dollars by choosing this compensation package instead of the alternative package?

b) Assume the first package offers $100,000 salary instead of $90,000 salary and the other benefits and costs are the same. Which compensation package should she choose, and by how much would she benefit in after-tax dollars by choosing this package?

ROGER | *CPA Review*

Sample CPA Exam questions from Roger CPA Review are available in Connect as support for the topics in this text. These Multiple Choice Questions and Task-Based Simulations include expert-written explanations and solutions and provide a starting point for students to become familiar with the content and functionality of the actual CPA Exam.

chapter 13
Retirement Savings and Deferred Compensation

Learning Objectives

Upon completing this chapter, you should be able to:

LO 13-1 Describe the tax and nontax aspects of employer-provided defined benefit plans from both the employer's and the employee's perspective.

LO 13-2 Explain and determine the tax consequences associated with employer-provided defined contribution plans, including traditional 401(k) and Roth 401(k) plans.

LO 13-3 Describe the tax implications of deferred compensation from both the employer's and the employee's perspective.

LO 13-4 Compare and determine the tax consequences of traditional and Roth IRAs (individual retirement accounts).

LO 13-5 Describe retirement savings options for self-employed taxpayers and compute the limitations for deductible contributions to these accounts.

LO 13-6 Compute the saver's credit.

©Paul Bradbury/AGE Fotostock

Tina Hillman

Tina Hillman has just completed her last exam, finally fulfilling the requirements for a bachelor's degree in accounting. It is the end of June and she will finally have some time to vacation and see her family before September, when she will start her professional career working in the tax department of Corporate Business Associates (CBA). While Tina is looking forward to the time off, she is also eager to start making money instead of just spending it. She had a great experience during her internship at CBA last year. She had some challenging but enjoyable work assignments, and she got along very well with the staff. Overall, she is excited about the work opportunities she will get at CBA.

Storyline Summary

Taxpayer:	Tina Hillman
Location:	Chicago, Illinois
Employment status:	Graduating student about to begin career in the tax department of Corporate Business Associates
Starting salary:	$60,000 per year
Filing status:	Single
Dependents:	None
Marginal tax rate:	Current year 12 percent, next year 22 percent
Taxpayer:	Lisa Whitlark
Location:	Chicago, Illinois
Employment status:	Recently promoted to chief financial officer (CFO) for Corporate Business Associates
Salary:	$400,000
Filing status:	Married, filing jointly
Marginal tax rate:	32 percent
Dependents:	Spouse and three children
Taxpayer:	Dave Allan
Location:	Chicago, Illinois
Employment status:	Recently retired as CFO for Corporate Business Associates after 20 years of employment with the company
Salary at retirement:	$490,000
Retirement benefits:	Participant in Corporate Business Associates's defined benefit plan, 401(k) plan, and nonqualified deferred compensation plan
Filing status:	Married filing jointly
Dependents:	Spouse
Marginal tax rate:	35 percent for current year
Taxpayer:	Corporate Business Associates (CBA)
Location:	Chicago, Illinois
Marginal tax rate:	21 percent
Status:	Publicly traded corporation

Tina recently received an information packet about the benefits available to her as a CBA employee. The information indicated that Tina would be eligible to participate in CBA's 401(k) retirement plan on January 1 of next year. Tina plans on contributing to the plan as soon as she is eligible, because CBA matches every dollar contributed by the employee with $2 contributed by the company. In the meantime, Tina wonders whether she has any retirement savings options during the current year while she waits to become eligible to participate in CBA's retirement plan.

Lisa Whitlark

Lisa Whitlark is finally getting used to her new responsibilities. She was recently promoted to the position of chief financial officer (CFO) for CBA. Lisa applied for the position a few months ago when CBA announced that Dave Allan, the former CFO, would be retiring. Lisa had been working as CBA's tax director for the last 10 years. As a top executive of the company, Lisa is now eligible to participate in CBA's nonqualified deferred compensation program. She didn't have this option as a tax director. Lisa knows she should consider both tax and nontax factors when deciding whether and to what extent she will participate in the plan.

Dave Allan

Dave Allan couldn't believe that he was actually going to retire at the end of the year. Looking back, his successful career had passed so quickly. At age 72, he is now ready to move on and spend time seeing the world with his wife. Dave's retirement plans are going to be quite expensive. Fortunately, he has accumulated substantial retirement benefits during his CBA career. Dave will be receiving retirement benefits from CBA's defined benefit plan, 401(k) plan, and nonqualified deferred compensation plan. He knows he has some choices about the timing and amounts of his distributions from these plans. Dave wants to be sure to evaluate both the tax and the nontax considerations before making these decisions. ∎

At different stages in their careers, taxpayers are likely to face issues similar to those confronting Tina, Lisa, and Dave. Saving for retirement is not always easy, because it requires forgoing cash now in order to receive benefits at some point in the future. However, not saving for retirement can be a costly mistake, because it's not likely that government-promised Social Security benefits alone will satisfy most taxpayers' retirement needs.[1]

Many employers help employees save for retirement by sponsoring retirement plans on their behalf. These plans may be "qualified" retirement plans or "nonqualified" deferred compensation plans. Qualified plans are subject to certain restrictions not applicable to nonqualified plans. Both qualified and nonqualified plans are useful tools

[1]Under current law, the projected cost of Social Security generally increases faster than projected income because of the aging of the baby-boom generation, continuing low fertility since the baby-boom period, and increasing life expectancy. Social Security's total expenditures have exceeded noninterest income of its combined trust funds since 2010. The 2017 Social Security Trustees report projects that the Social Security Trust fund reserves will be depleted in 2034. See https://www.ssa.gov/oact/tr/2017/tr2017.pdf.

through which employers can achieve various compensation-related goals. In this chapter, we discuss the tax and nontax consequences for both employers and employees of qualified retirement plans and nonqualified plans, including issues relating to contributions to and distributions from these plans. We also discuss individually managed retirement savings plans available to certain individual taxpayers and qualified retirement plans available to self-employed taxpayers.

EMPLOYER-PROVIDED QUALIFIED PLANS

Traditional **qualified retirement plans** grew from a congressional concern that, if unregulated, employers might not adequately fund and protect employee pension benefits and might be tempted to provide lavish retirement plans to highly compensated employees such as executives and business owners to the detriment of rank-and-file employees. To address these concerns, Congress mandated that employer-provided plans receive tax-favored qualified plan status only if they meet certain requirements, thus ensuring that the plan does not discriminate against rank-and-file employees, and promised benefits are secure. Over the years, the rules addressing these issues have evolved, but the concept of a qualified plan eligible for favorable tax treatment remains the same.

Employer-provided qualified plans can be generally classified as **defined benefit plans** or **defined contribution plans.** As the name suggests, defined benefit plans spell out the specific benefit the employee will receive on retirement. In contrast, defined contribution plans specify the maximum annual contributions that employers and employees may contribute to the plan. While we explore both basic plan types below, we emphasize defined contribution plans because they are much more common than defined benefit plans.

DEFINED BENEFIT PLANS

`LO 13-1`

Defined benefit plans are traditional pension plans used by many older and more established companies and tax-exempt organizations. These plans provide standard retirement benefits to employees based on a fixed formula. The formula to determine the standard retirement benefit is usually a function of years of service and employees' compensation levels as they near retirement. For employees who retire in 2018, the maximum annual benefit they can receive is the *lesser* of (1) 100 percent of the average of the employee's three highest years of compensation or (2) $220,000.[2]

Example 13-1

CBA provides a defined benefit plan for its employees. The plan uses a fixed formula to determine employee benefits. The formula specifies a benefit of 2 percent for each year of service, up to a maximum of 50 percent (25 years of service), of the average of the employee's three highest years of salary. In 2018, Dave retires from CBA. On the date of retirement, Dave had been a CBA employee for 20 years. The average of his three highest years of salary was $450,000. What is Dave's annual benefit from the defined benefit plan?

Answer: $180,000 a year. The benefit is calculated by multiplying 40 percent (2 percent for each of his 20 years of service) by $450,000 (the average of his highest three years of salary).

What if: Assume the same facts except that the average of Dave's three highest years of salary was $600,000. What is the annual benefit he will receive from the plan?

Answer: $220,000. The lesser of (1) $240,000 ($600,000 × 40%) or (2) $220,000.

---

[2]§415(b)(1). The maximum benefit is adjusted annually for inflation.

Vesting

We've discussed the idea that an employee's benefit is based on the number of years she works for an employer. When an employee works for an employer for only a short time before leaving, her benefit depends on her salary, the number of full years she worked for the employer, and the employer's vesting schedule. **Vesting** is the process of becoming legally entitled to a certain right or property. Thus, a taxpayer vests in retirement benefits (becomes legally entitled to the retirement benefits) once she has met certain requirements set forth by the employer. The most restrictive vesting requirements an employer can impose on a qualified defined benefit plan is a five-year "cliff" or a seven-year graded vesting schedule.[3] Under the **cliff vesting** option, after a certain period of time, benefits vest all at once. With a **graded vesting** schedule, the employee's vested benefit increases each full year she works for the employer. Exhibit 13-1 features the five-year cliff and seven-year graded minimum vesting schedules for defined benefit plans.

EXHIBIT 13-1   **Defined Benefit Plans Minimum Vesting Schedules***

Full Years of Service	5-Year Cliff	7-Year Graded
1	0%	0%
2	0	0
3	0	20
4	0	40
5	100	60
6	N/A	80
7	N/A	100

*Percent of employee benefit no longer subject to forfeiture.

Example 13-2

What if: CBA provides a defined benefit plan to its employees. Under the plan, employees earn a benefit equal to 2 percent of their average salary for every year of service, using their three highest years of compensation. CBA implements a seven-year graded vesting schedule as part of the plan. If Tina works for CBA for four years, earning annual salaries of $60,000, $65,000, $70,000, and $75,000, and then leaves to work for another employer, what annual benefit will she be entitled to receive (i.e., what is her vested benefit)?

Answer: $2,240, computed as follows:

Description	Amount	Explanation
(1) Average of three highest years of salary	$70,000	($65,000 + 70,000 + 75,000)/3
(2) Benefit percentage	× 8%	Four years of service × 2 percent per year
(3) Full annual benefit	$ 5,600	(1) × (2)
(4) Vesting percentage	× 40%	Four years of service on 7-year graded vesting schedule (see Exhibit 13-1)
Vested benefit	**$ 2,240**	(3) × (4) = Amount that she is allowed to keep

Tina would forfeit her unvested benefit of $3,360 ($5,600 − $2,240 vested benefit).

What if: Assume the same facts except that CBA uses a five-year cliff schedule. What would be Tina's vested benefit?

Answer: $0. She did not work for CBA for five years, so her benefits in CBA's defined benefit plan do not vest.

---

[3]§411(a) specifies maximum vesting periods for employer contributions to qualified plans. Employers are allowed to adopt more generous vesting requirements such as immediate vesting if they choose.

Distributions

When their benefits have vested, employees are entitled to receive future distributions according to the provisions of the plan. These distributions are taxable as ordinary income in the year received.[4] Distributions from defined benefit plans (and defined contribution plans) are subject to early distribution requirements and to minimum distribution requirements. Distributions violating these requirements are penalized. However, because defined benefit plans typically don't permit payout arrangements that would trigger the early distribution or minimum distribution penalties, these penalties are of greater concern to participants in defined contribution plans. Consequently, we address these penalties in more detail when we discuss distributions from defined contribution plans.

Nontax Considerations

From a nontax perspective, a defined benefit plan imposes administrative burdens and risks on the employer sponsoring the plan. A significant amount of work is required to track employee benefits and to compute required contributions to the plan. Because defined benefit plans require employers to provide particular benefits to employees on retirement, the employer bears the investment risk associated with investments within the plan. Beyond the additional administrative costs and risk, defined benefit plans impose significant funding costs on employers relative to alternative retirement plans. Consequently, in recent years, many employers have begun replacing defined benefit plans with defined contribution plans.

> **THE KEY FACTS**
>
> **Defined Benefit Plans**
>
> - Employer, not employee, bears investment risk of plan.
> - Early and minimum distribution rules apply but are usually not restrictive.

TAXES IN THE REAL WORLD   Define Your Benefit and Deduct It While You're at It

Because defined benefit plans create significantly more administrative burdens and economic risks for employers than defined contribution plans, they are losing popularity with employers. However, self-employed taxpayers and taxpayers running family businesses may be able to use defined benefit plans to contribute significantly more to qualified retirement plans on behalf of themselves and working family members than they would otherwise be able to. Former Florida governor (and presidential candidate at the time he released his tax returns) Jeb Bush provides Exhibit A for this strategy.

Bush released his tax returns in July 2015. His tax returns reported that he claimed deductions for payments to "pension and profit-sharing plans" that averaged $350,000 a year for the previous five years. Bush's (completely legal) defined benefit plan was set up for two people working for his consulting firm, Jeb Bush & Associates LLC. Those in the know believe the plan likely covered him and his son, Jeb Bush Jr. The $350,000 annual contribution average is more than three times the contribution limit otherwise allowable for a defined contribution plan. Why was Bush able to contribute so much more to a defined benefit plan than he could have contributed to a defined contribution plan?

Under a defined benefit plan, the business is allowed to contribute as much as required to fund the expected benefit it must pay to the recipient. Because Bush started the plan when he was nearing retirement age, the business was allowed to contribute (and deduct) significantly more to fund his retirement than if he had started the plan when he had a longer time to work before retirement. In contrast, contributions to defined contribution plans are limited to $61,000 per year (in 2018) for taxpayers who are at least 50 years of age (and $55,000 per year for those who are not), no matter when they are planning to retire.

Source: Based on: Mark Maremont, "Pension Plan Cut Jeb Bush's Taxes," *The Wall Street Journal*, updated July 2, 2015, http://www.wsj.com/articles/jeb-bushs-pension-cut-his-taxes-1435858574.

---

[4]Distributions of both defined benefit plans and defined contribution plans are reported to taxpayers on Form 1099-R.

LO 13-2 DEFINED CONTRIBUTION PLANS

Defined contribution plans provide an alternate way for employers to help employees save for retirement. While defined contribution plans and defined benefit plans have similar overall objectives, they are different in important ways. First, in a defined contribution plan, employers maintain a separate account for *each* participating employee. Second, defined contribution plans specify the up-front contributions the employer will make to the employee's separate account, rather than specifying the ultimate benefit the employee will receive from the plan. Third, employees are often allowed to contribute to their own defined contribution plans, and in many instances they contribute more than their employers do. Finally, employees are generally free to choose how amounts in their retirement accounts are invested. If investments in the plan perform well, employees benefit; if they perform poorly, employees suffer the financial consequences. Thus, defined contribution plans shift funding responsibility and investment risk from the employer to the employee.

Employers may provide different types of defined contribution plans, such as 401(k) plans (used by for-profit companies), 403(b) plans (used by nonprofit organizations, including educational institutions), 457 plans (used by government agencies), profit sharing plans, and money purchase pension plans.[5] They may even offer multiple defined contribution plans. Because of their popularity, we use 401(k) plans here to represent the general category of defined contribution plans. However, no matter what defined contribution plan(s) employers provide, employers must ensure that their plans meet certain requirements relating to annual contribution limits and vesting requirements. Also, to a greater extent than with defined benefit plans, participants in defined contribution plans should be careful to avoid the penalties associated with either early distributions or insufficient minimum distributions from these plans (discussed later in the chapter).

Employer Matching

Employers, but not employees, typically contribute to certain defined contribution plan types such as profit-sharing plans (contributions may be made based on a fixed formula based on profits or may be at the employer's discretion) and money-purchase plans (contributions are a fixed percentage of the employee's compensation). In contrast, employees contribute to 401(k) type plans. Many employers also "match" employee contributions to these plans.

When deciding whether to contribute to a 401(k) plan, employees should take into account the matching policies of their employers. The match can range from a small percentage (25 cents on the dollar) to a multiple of the employee's contribution. A dollar-for-dollar match gives employees a 100 percent immediate, no-risk return on their contributions. Thus, whenever possible, employees should contribute enough to receive the full match from the employer.

Example 13-3

Tina's offer from CBA includes participation in its 401(k) plan effective the beginning of next year. The plan's formula provides that CBA will match employee contributions on a two-for-one basis up to employee contributions of 4 percent of the employee's annual salary. Next year when she's eligible, Tina will contribute 4 percent of her salary to the plan. Assuming a $60,000 salary for next year, how much will Tina contribute and how much will CBA contribute to Tina's 401(k) account?

Answer: Tina will contribute $2,400 ($60,000 × 4%) to her 401(k) account and CBA will contribute $4,800 ($2,400 × 2).

---

[5]401(k), 403(b), and 457 plans reflect the Code sections describing the plans.

Contribution Limits

For 2018, the sum of employer *and* employee contributions to an employee's defined contribution account(s) is limited to the *lesser* of (1) $55,000 ($61,000 for employees who are at least 50 years of age by the end of the year) or (2) 100 percent of the employee's compensation for the year.[6] *Employee* contributions to an employee's 401(k) account are limited to $18,500 (or $24,500 for employees who reach age 50 by the end of the year).[7] While this limit applies only to employee contributions, the $55,000 (or $61,000) limit still applies to the sum of employer and employee contributions. For example, if an employee under age 50 contributes the maximum $18,500 to her employer-sponsored 401(k) plan in 2018, the employer's contribution would be limited to $36,500 ($55,000 − $18,500).[8] Because of this limit on employer contributions, highly compensated employees may not be able to receive the full employer match available to other employees.

Example 13-4

Before Dave retires at the end of 2018, he continues to contribute to his CBA-sponsored 401(k) account. CBA matches employee contributions on a two-for-one basis up to 4 percent of the employee's salary. Dave is 72 years old at the end of the year; he earned a salary of $490,000 during the year and contributed $24,500 to his 401(k) account. How much will CBA contribute to Dave's 401(k) account?

Answer: $36,500 [$61,000 (Dave is 50+ years old) minus $24,500 (Dave's contribution)]. Without the limitation, CBA would have contributed $39,200 ($490,000 × 4% × 2) to Dave's account.

What if: Assume Dave contributed $23,500 to his 401(k) account. How much would CBA contribute to his account?

Answer: $37,500. Note that this is a better deal for Dave because $61,000 ends up in his account either way, but he funded $23,500 of the contribution instead of $24,500.

Vesting

When employees contribute to a defined contribution plan, they are fully vested in the accrued benefit from those contributions (employee contributions plus earnings on their contributions). However, employees vest in the accrued benefit from employer contributions (employer contributions plus earnings on the contributions) based on the plan's vesting schedule. When they do not maintain separate employee accounts, companies calculate the accrued benefit from employee contributions by multiplying the total accrued benefit in the account by the ratio of employee contributions to total contributions (employee plus employer) to the account.[9] The accrued benefit from employer contributions is the difference between the total accrued benefit and the accrued benefit from employee contributions.

The minimum vesting requirements for defined contribution plans are a bit more accelerated than the five-year cliff and seven-year graded vesting schedules applicable to defined benefit plans. For defined contribution plans, employers have the option of

---

[6]§415(c)(1). The amount is indexed for inflation under §415(d)(1)(C). Note that the increase in the limit for taxpayers age 50 and older increases the amount the employee can contribute but does not affect the limit the employer can contribute.

[7]§402(g)(1). The amount is indexed for inflation under §402(g)(4).

[8]If an employee participates in more than one defined contribution plan, these limits apply to the total employee and employer contributions to all defined contribution plans. Thus, in a situation where the employee participates in more than one defined contribution plan, the contribution limits for any one defined contribution plan may be less than the overall contribution limits described here.

[9]§411(c).

providing three-year cliff or six-year graded vesting. These minimum vesting schedules are presented in Exhibit 13-2.

EXHIBIT 13-2 Defined Contribution Plans Minimum Vesting Schedules*

Full Years of Service with Employer	3-Year Cliff	6-Year Graded
1	0%	0%
2	0	20
3	100	40
4	N/A	60
5	N/A	80
6	N/A	100

*Percent of employer contributions no longer subject to forfeiture.

Example 13-5

THE KEY FACTS

Traditional Defined Contribution Plans: Vesting and After-Tax Cost

- Employee must vest to be entitled to employer contributions (and earnings on those contributions) using:
  - 3-year cliff vesting schedule.
  - 6-year graded vesting schedule.
- Employee contributes before-tax amounts (contributions are deductible).
- After-tax cost is before-tax contribution minus tax savings from contribution.

What if: Suppose that in three and one-half years the balance in Tina's 401(k) account is $33,000. In total, Tina has contributed $9,000 to the account and CBA has contributed $18,000. Also assume that Tina is 40 percent vested in her accrued benefit from CBA contributions. What is Tina's vested benefit?

Answer: $19,800 [$11,000 accrued benefit from her contributions + $8,800, which is 40 percent of the $22,000 accrued benefit from CBA contributions]. Tina is fully vested in the $11,000 accrued benefit from her contributions ($33,000 total accrued benefit in account × $9,000 employee contributions/$27,000 total contributions to her account) and 40 percent vested in the $22,000 accrued benefit from CBA contributions ($33,000 total accrued benefit in account minus $11,000 accrued benefit from her contributions).

After-Tax Cost of Contributions to Traditional (non-Roth) Defined Contribution Plans

Employer-sponsored traditional defined contribution plans include all plans except Roth 401(k) plans (discussed below). Employees effectively deduct their contributions to traditional defined contribution plans, because contributions are removed from their taxable salary (they are, however, still subject to FICA taxes on funds contributed to defined contribution plans).[10] Consequently, the after-tax cost of a contribution to a traditional defined contribution plan is the contribution amount minus the tax savings generated by the deduction from the contribution.

Example 13-6

Tina contributed $2,400 to her CBA-sponsored traditional 401(k) account in her first full calendar year with CBA. Given Tina's marginal tax rate of 22 percent, what is the after-tax cost of her $2,400 contribution?

Answer: $1,872 computed as follows:

Description	Amount	Explanation
(1) Contribution amount	$ 2,400	Cost of contribution before tax savings
(2) Tax savings from contribution	(528)	$2,400 deduction × 22 percent marginal tax rate
After-tax cost of contribution	**$1,872**	(1) + (2)

[10]Employees pay the same FICA taxes no matter how much they contribute to defined contribution plans.

Distributions from Traditional Defined Contribution Plans

When employees receive distributions (that is, take withdrawals) from traditional defined contribution plans, the distributions are taxed as ordinary income. However, when employees receive distributions from these plans either too early or too late, they must pay a penalty in addition to the income taxes they owe on the distributions. Generally, employees who receive distributions before they reach

- 59½ years of age or
- 55 years of age *and* have separated from service (retired or let go by employer)

are subject to a 10 percent nondeductible penalty on the amount of the early distributions.

Example 13-7

What if: Assume that when she reaches 60 years of age, Lisa Whitlark retires from CBA and receives a $60,000 distribution from her traditional 401(k) account in the year she retires. Assuming her marginal ordinary tax rate is 32 percent, what amount of tax and penalty will Lisa pay on the distribution?

Answer: $19,200 taxes ($60,000 × 32%) + $0 penalty (she is over 59½ years of age on date of distribution).

What if: Assume that when Lisa is 57 years of age and still employed by CBA, she requests and receives a $60,000 distribution from her traditional 401(k) account. What amount of tax and penalty is Lisa required to pay on the distribution?

Answer: $19,200 taxes ($60,000 × 32%) + $6,000 penalty ($60,000 × 10%).

What if: Assume that Lisa's employment is terminated by CBA when she is 57 years old. In that same year, she requests and receives a $60,000 distribution from her traditional 401(k) account. What amount of tax and penalty is Lisa required to pay on the distribution?

Answer: $19,200 taxes ($60,000 × 32%) + $0 penalty (she is over 55 years of age and has separated from service with CBA).

Taxpayers who fail to receive a minimum distribution for (pertaining to) a particular year are also penalized. The year for which taxpayers must receive their *first* minimum distribution is the *later* of:

- The year in which the employee reaches 70½ years of age.
- The year in which the employee retires.

Taxpayers must receive their first required minimum distribution no later than April 1 of the year after the year to which the distribution pertains.[11] Taxpayers generally must receive minimum distributions for subsequent years by the end of the years to which they pertain. Thus, a retired taxpayer who turns 70½ years of age in 2017 must receive a minimum distribution for 2018 by April 1, 2019. The same taxpayer must also receive a minimum distribution for 2019 by December 31, 2019.

The amount of the minimum required distribution for a particular year is the taxpayer's account balance at the end of the year *prior to* the year to which the distribution pertains, multiplied by a percentage from an IRS Uniform Lifetime Table. The percentage

> **THE KEY FACTS**
>
> **Traditional Defined Contribution Plans: Distributions**
>
> - Taxed at ordinary rates.
> - 10 percent penalty on early distributions:
>   - Before 59½ years of age if not retired or
>   - Before 55 years of age if retired or let go.
> - Minimum distribution requirements:
>   - Must receive by April 1 of the later of (1) the year after the year in which taxpayer reaches 70½ years of age or (2) the year after the year in which the employee retires.
>   - Retired employee who waits until year after 70½ to begin receiving distributions must receive two distributions in year of first distribution.
>   - 50 percent penalty to the extent required minimimum distributions are not made.

---

[11]The amount of the required minimum distribution *for the year* in which a retired employee turns 70½ is the same whether the employee receives the distribution in the year she turns 70½ or whether she defers receiving the distribution until the next year (no later than April 1).

is based on the distribution period (in years), which depends on the taxpayer's age at the end of the year to which the distribution pertains. An abbreviated version of the table is presented in Exhibit 13-3.[12]

EXHIBIT 13-3 **Abbreviated Uniform Lifetime Table**

Age of Participant	Distribution Period	Applicable Percentage*
70	27.4	3.65%
71	26.5	3.77
72	25.6	3.91
73	24.7	4.05
74	23.8	4.20
75	22.9	4.37
76	22.0	4.54
77	21.2	4.72

*The applicable percentage is calculated by dividing 1 by the relevant distribution period.

Example 13-8

What if: Suppose that Dave retires from CBA in 2018 at age 72 (and he is still 72 at year-end). When must he receive his minimum distribution for 2018 from his traditional 401(k) account?

Answer: By April 1, 2019.

What if: Assuming Dave retires in 2018 and that his traditional 401(k) account balance on December 31, 2017, is $3,500,000, what is the amount of the minimum distribution Dave must receive by April 1, 2019?

Answer: $136,850 ($3,500,000 × 3.91%). The percentage from the IRS table for determining this minimum distribution is based on Dave's age at the end of 2018, which is 72 years old.

What if: Assuming Dave's traditional 401(k) account balance on December 31, 2018, is $3,700,000, what is the minimum distribution for 2019 Dave must receive sometime during 2019 (in addition to the $136,850 distribution by April 1)?

Answer: $149,850 ($3,700,000 × 4.05%) must be received by Dave during 2019.

The consequences for failing to receive timely minimum distributions from defined contribution plans are even more severe than for receiving distributions too early. Taxpayers incur a 50 percent nondeductible penalty on the amount of a minimum distribution they should have received but did not (the penalty is payable as an additional tax for the calendar year containing the last day by which the amount is required to be distributed). It is vital that payouts from defined contribution plans be monitored, to avoid not only the 10 percent premature distribution penalty but also the 50 percent penalty for failing to receive timely required minimum distributions.

Example 13-9

What if: In the previous example, we determined that Dave must receive a minimum distribution of $136,850 from his traditional 401(k) account by April 1, 2019. If Dave does not receive any distribution before April 1, 2019, what penalty will he be required to pay?

Answer: $68,425 ($136,850 × 50%). Dave will pay this penalty as an other tax on his 2019 tax return. This nondeductible penalty is a strong incentive to take the required minimum distributions or at least to take the penalty into consideration when developing a distribution plan.

[12]See Reg. §1.401(a)(9)-9 Q&A 2 to reference the full version of the table. The table provided in this exhibit applies in most circumstances.

What if: Assume that Dave received his first distribution from his traditional 401(k) account on March 1, 2019, in the amount of $100,000 but he did not receive any other distributions before April 1, 2019. What penalty is Dave required to pay?

Answer: $18,425 [($136,850 − $100,000) × 50%]

In contrast to defined benefit plans, defined contribution plans often provide distribution options that could trigger the penalty for premature distributions for the uninformed or unwary. For example, an employee who retires (or is fired) and takes a lump-sum distribution from her defined contribution account in a year before the year in which she turns 55 will be subject to a 10 percent early-distribution penalty on the entire amount of the distribution. Employees who receive such lump-sum distributions may avoid the 10 percent penalty by electing to "roll over" (deposit) the distributions into one of the individually managed retirement plans we discuss later in this chapter.

After-Tax Rates of Return for Traditional Defined Contribution Plans

For a given before-tax rate of return and a constant tax rate, the longer the taxpayer defers distributions from a traditional defined contribution plan, the greater the taxpayer's after-tax rate of return on the retirement account, because deferring the distribution reduces the present value of the taxes paid on the distribution. A taxpayer's after-tax rate of return also depends on the taxpayer's marginal tax rate at the time she contributes to the plan and at the time she receives distributions from the plan. All else being equal, the higher her marginal tax rate at the time she contributes to the plan, the higher the after-tax rate of return (the higher tax rate increases the tax savings from the deduction); likewise, the lower her marginal tax rate at the time she receives distributions from the plan, the higher the after-tax rate of return (the lower rate reduces the taxes from the distribution).

Of course, any employer contributions to an employee's account, such as CBA's two-for-one matching contributions to Tina's account, significantly increase the after-tax rate of return (and after-tax accumulation) because the contributions increase the employee's after-tax proceeds, but the employee's cost of these contributions is zero.

Exhibit 13-4 summarizes the tax aspects of defined benefit and defined contribution plans.

Roth 401(k) Plans

Employers that provide **traditional 401(k)** plans to employees may also provide **Roth 401(k)** plans. As we discuss below, employee tax consequences for Roth 401(k) plans differ from tax consequences of other traditional defined contribution plans.

When employers provide a Roth 401(k) plan, employees may elect to contribute to the plan instead of or in addition to contributing to a traditional 401(k) plan. However, *employer* contributions to an employee's 401(k) account must go to the employee's traditional 401(k) account rather than to the employee's Roth 401(k) account. Consequently, the balance in an employee's Roth 401(k) account must consist only of the employee's contributions and the earnings on those contributions. Because employers providing Roth 401(k) plans to employees are not allowed to contribute to the Roth plans, these employers are required to maintain traditional 401(k) accounts for each employee participating in the Roth 401(k) plan.

In contrast to contributions to traditional 401(k) plans, employee contributions to Roth 401(k) accounts are *not* deductible and, therefore, do not produce any immediate tax

THE KEY FACTS

Roth 401(k) Defined Contribution Plans

- Employees but not employers may contribute.
  - Employers contribute only to traditional 401(k) plans.
- Contributions are not deductible.
- Same contribution limits as for traditional 401(k) plans.

EXHIBIT 13-4   Defined Benefit Plan versus Defined Contribution Plan Summary

	Defined Benefit Plan	Defined Contribution Plan
Benefits	• Specifies benefit employee receives on retirement. • Maximum benefit in 2018 is the lesser of (1) 100 percent of average of highest three years' compensation or (2) $220,000.	• Specifies the amounts employer and employee contribute to the account. • Ultimate benefit depends on earnings on contributions.
Payout type	• Life annuity. • Lump-sum distribution of the present value of standard benefit.	• Life annuity. • Lump sum. • Fixed number of years.
Funding requirements	• Employers fund increase in expected future liability each year.	• No funding requirement other than to make required contributions to employee accounts.
Employer's contributions tax deductible?	• Yes.	• Yes, but limited to 25 percent of aggregate employee annual compensation.
Employee's contributions tax deductible?	• No employee contributions.	• Yes, subject to limitations on the amount that can be contributed [$18,500 ($24,500 if 50 or older) maximum contribution to 401(k) plan in 2018].
Contribution limits	• Not applicable.	• In 2018, lesser of (1) $55,000 ($61,000 for taxpayers at least 50 years of age at end of year) and (2) 100 percent of the employee's compensation for year.
Other factors	• All employees paid from same account. • Heavy administrative burden. • Employers make investment choices and assume investment risk.	• Separate accounts for each employee. • Employees assume investment risk.
Vesting requirements	• 5-year cliff or • 7-year graded	• 3-year cliff or • 6-year graded • Employee contributions vest immediately.
Distributions	• Taxed as ordinary income. • No 10 percent penalty if either 59½ years of age or 55 years of age and retired. • Minimum distributions required by April 1 of year after the later of (1) year employee reaches 70½ or (2) year employee retires.	• Taxed as ordinary income (except Roth-type accounts). • No 10 percent penalty if either 59½ years of age or 55 years of age and retired. • Minimum distributions requirements same as for defined benefit plan.

savings for employees. Therefore, employees wanting to contribute a certain amount to a Roth 401(k) plan must earn more than that specified amount in order to have the desired contribution amount remaining *after* paying taxes on the amount they earn. For example, assume an employee with a 22 percent marginal tax rate wants to contribute $2,000 to a Roth 401(k) account. To earn the funds to make this contribution, the employee must earn $2,564 before taxes. The tax on the $2,564 of income is $564 ($2,564 × 22%). This leaves the taxpayer with $2,000 after taxes ($2,564 before taxes minus $564 in taxes) to contribute to the Roth 401(k) account.

Example 13-10

What if: Let's assume that CBA offers a Roth 401(k) plan in addition to its traditional 401(k) plan. In her first full calendar year of employment with CBA, Tina elects to contribute 4 percent of her $60,000 salary to CBA's Roth 401(k) plan instead of CBA's traditional 401(k) plan. What is Tina's after-tax cost of this $2,400 contribution (her marginal tax rate is 22 percent)?

Answer: $2,400. Her after-tax cost is her $2,400 contribution because the contribution does not generate any tax savings.

What is Tina's before-tax cost of the contribution? That is, how much did Tina need to earn before taxes to fund the $2,400 after-tax contribution?

Answer: $3,077. Because her marginal tax rate is 22 percent, she needs to earn $3,077 before taxes [$2,400/(1 − .22)] to have $2,400 to contribute to the Roth 401(k) after taxes [$3,077 × (1 − .22)]. When she contributes $2,400 *after taxes* to the Roth 401(k), she is contributing $3,077 *before taxes.*

While contributions to Roth 401(k) accounts are not deductible and, as a result, do not generate any current tax savings, *qualified* distributions from Roth 401(k) accounts are excluded from gross income. Because contributions to Roth 401(k) accounts are not deductible and qualified distributions from Roth 401(k) accounts are not taxable, the before-tax rate of return equals the after-tax rate of return on Roth 401(k) accounts. Note also that because qualified Roth 401(k) distributions are excluded from income, in contrast to traditional 401(k) distributions, they do not increase AGI and thus do not cause AGI-based tax benefit phase-outs (e.g., certain itemized deductions and tax credits), and they do not cause an increase in the taxation of the recipient's Social Security benefits (see the Gross Income and Exclusions chapter for a discussion of the taxation of Social Security benefits).

> **THE KEY FACTS**
>
> **Roth 401(k) Defined Contribution Plans**
>
> - Qualified distributions are not taxable.
>   - Account must be open for five years before distribution.
>   - Employee must be at least 59½ at time of distribution.
> - Nonqualified distributions
>   - Distributions of account earnings are taxable and subject to 10 percent penalty if taxpayer is not either 59½ years of age or 55 and retired.
>   - Distributions of contributions are not taxed or penalized.
>   - Distribution × Ratio of contributions to account balance is nontaxable. The remainder of distribution is from account earnings.
> - After-tax return equals before-tax return.

Example 13-11

What if: In the previous example, Tina contributed $2,400 to her Roth 401(k) account in her first calendar year on the job with CBA. Let's assume that Tina leaves this contribution in the account until she retires in 40 years at the age of 63, that her contribution earns an annual 8 percent before-tax rate of return, and that her marginal tax rate will be 30 percent when she receives the distribution. How much will Tina have accumulated after taxes if she withdraws the initial contribution and all the earnings on the contribution when she retires?

Answer: $52,139 ($2,400 × 1.08^{40}). Tina's after-tax rate of return on her $2,400 after-tax contribution is exactly 8 percent, the same as the before-tax rate of return. With a Roth 401(k), the after-tax rate of return should always equal the before-tax rate of return because the contributions are not deductible and distributions are not taxable.

Qualified distributions from Roth 401(k) accounts are those made after the employee's account has been open for five taxable years *and* the employee is at least 59½ years of age. All other distributions are nonqualified distributions. When a taxpayer receives a *nonqualified* distribution from a Roth 401(k) account, the tax consequences of the distribution depend on the extent to which the distribution is from the account earnings and the extent to which it is from the employee's contributions to the account. Nonqualified distributions of account *earnings* are fully taxable. Nonqualified distributions of account earnings are also subject to a 10 percent early distribution penalty unless the taxpayer is either 59½ years of age at the time of the distribution or at least 55 years of age and retired at the time of the distribution.

Nonqualified distributions of the taxpayer's account *contributions* are not subject to tax because the taxpayer did not deduct these amounts. If less than the entire balance in the plan is distributed, the nontaxable portion of the distribution is calculated by multiplying the amount of the distribution by the ratio of account contributions to the total account balance. This formula is very similar to the formula described in the Gross Income and Exclusions chapter for determining the nontaxable portion of an annuity payment.

Example 13-12

What if: In the previous example, Tina contributed $2,400 to CBA's Roth 401(k) plan, her account generated an 8 percent before-tax rate of return, and she withdrew the entire balance 40 years after the contribution. Let's assume that at the end of year 6 Tina needs cash, so she withdraws $1,000 from the account when the account balance is $3,808 and her marginal tax rate is 24 percent. How much tax and penalty, if any, is Tina required to pay on this nonqualified distribution?

Answer: $89 tax and $37 penalty, computed as follows:

Description	Amount	Explanation
(1) Contribution to Roth 401(k) (nondeductible)	$2,400	Beginning of year 1
(2) Account balance end of year 6	3,808	$2,400 × 1.08^6
(3) Nonqualified distribution end of year 6	1,000	
(4) Percentage of distribution that is not taxable	63.03%	(1)/(2)
(5) Nontaxable portion of distribution	630	(3) × (4)
(6) Taxable portion of distribution	370	(3) − (5)
(7) Marginal tax rate in year 6	24%	
(8) Regular income tax on distribution	**89**	**(6) × (7)**
(9) Penalty tax percentage for early distributions	10%	
(10) Penalty tax on early distribution	**37**	**(6) × (9)**
Total tax and penalty on early distribution	$ 126	(8) + (10)

Finally, note that the minimum distribution requirements applicable to traditional 401(k) accounts also apply to Roth 401(k) accounts.

Comparing Traditional Defined Contribution Plans and Roth 401(k) Plans

We've described and discussed the tax consequences associated with participating in traditional and Roth 401(k) plans. So which is better for employees? If given a choice, which type of 401(k) plan should you contribute to? While many factors should be considered in making this decision, perhaps the most important is the taxpayer's current marginal tax rate (the rate in the year of contributions) compared to the taxpayer's expected future marginal tax rate (the expected rate in the year of distributions). Taxpayers generally should prefer traditional 401(k) plans when their current marginal rate is higher (greater tax savings derived from deductions) than their expected future marginal rate (lower tax cost on income from distributions), and they should prefer Roth 401(k) plans when their current marginal rate is lower than their expected future tax rate.

When future rates are higher than current rates, taxpayers should generally prefer Roth 401(k) plans, because the forgone tax savings from a nondeductible contribution is smaller when the marginal tax rate is lower and the tax savings from excluding the distribution from income is greater when the marginal tax rate is higher. While current and expected future marginal tax rates are important to consider, other factors relevant to this decision include the uncertainty of future tax rates and the taxpayer's risk tolerance for this uncertainty, and the way a taxpayer reinvests the tax savings from contributions to traditional 401(k) plans. A detailed discussion of all factors relevant to this decision is beyond the scope of this text. Exhibit 13-5 summarizes and compares the tax consequences of traditional 401(k) plans and Roth 401(k) plans.

EXHIBIT 13-5 Traditional 401(k) Plan versus Roth 401(k) Plan Summary

	Traditional 401(k) Plans	Roth 401(k) Plans
Employer contributions allowed	• Yes.	• No.
Tax consequences to employer	• Contributions deductible when paid.	• Not applicable.
Tax consequences to employee	• Contributions are deductible.	• Contributions are not deductible.
Distributions	• Taxed as ordinary income. • No 10 percent penalty if the taxpayer is at least 59½ years of age or at least 55 years of age and retired at time of distribution. • If life annuity or joint and survivor annuity, no penalty even if not 55 years of age. • Minimum distributions required by April 1 of the later of (1) the year after the year in which the employee reaches 70½ or (2) the year after the year in which the employee retires. • Failure to meet minimum distribution timing and amount requirements triggers 50 percent penalty.	• Qualified distributions not taxed. • Qualified distributions when account is open for at least 5 years and employee has reached age 59½. • No 10 percent penalty on taxable part of nonqualified distribution if the taxpayer is at least 59½ years of age or at least 55 years of age and retired at time of distribution. • If life annuity or joint and survivor annuity, no penalty even if not 55 years of age. • Minimum distribution requirements and penalties are the same as for traditional 401(k) plans. • If nonqualified distribution, nontaxable percentage of distribution is the ratio of contributions to total account value.

NONQUALIFIED DEFERRED COMPENSATION PLANS

LO 13-3

So far, our discussion has emphasized the tax and nontax aspects of employer-provided *qualified* defined benefit and defined contribution plans. In addition to or perhaps in lieu of these types of qualified plans, employers may offer **nonqualified deferred compensation** plans to certain employees.

Nonqualified Plans versus Qualified Defined Contribution Plans

Deferred compensation plans permit employees to defer (or contribute) current salary in exchange for a future payment from the employer. From an employee's perspective, the tax consequences of contributions to and distributions from nonqualified plans are similar to those for qualified defined contribution plans. For example, just as with defined contribution plans, employee contributions to nonqualified deferred compensation (NQDC) plans reduce the employee's taxable income in the year of contribution.[13] Also, just as with qualified plans, employees are not taxed on the balance in their accounts until they receive distributions. Finally, like distributions from qualified plans, distributions from NQDC plans are taxed as ordinary income.

---

[13]Technically, employees participating in NQDC plans defer the receipt of current salary and employers credit the employee's account for the amount of the deferral. This has the same effect as if the employee had actually made a deductible contribution (*for* AGI) to her account, as an employee participating in a defined contribution plan would do.

Example 13-13

CBA provides a nonqualified deferred compensation plan under which executives may elect to defer up to 10 percent of their salary. Dave Allan has been participating in the plan by deferring a portion of his salary each year for the last 15 years. The balance in his deferred compensation account is currently $2,000,000. In keeping with a fixed payment schedule Dave elected under the plan, he receives a $50,000 distribution. What amount of tax must Dave pay on the distribution (recall that his marginal tax rate is 35 percent)?

Answer: $17,500 ($50,000 × .35).

For employers, NQDC plans are treated differently than qualified plans. For example, because nonqualified plans are not subject to the same restrictions that govern qualified plans, employers may discriminate in terms of who they allow to participate in the plan. In fact, employers generally restrict participation in nonqualified plans to more highly compensated employees. Employers are also not required to fund nonqualified plans. That is, they do not have to formally set aside and accumulate funds specifically to pay the deferred compensation obligation when it comes due. Rather, they typically retain funds deferred by employees under the plan, use the funds for business operations, and pay the deferred compensation out of their general funds when it becomes payable.

Because employers retain, control, and generate income on funds deferred by employees under nonqualified plans, employers are allowed to deduct only *actual payments* of deferred compensation to employees. That is, employers cannot deduct the amount of deferred compensation they accrue each year. Thus, for tax purposes, an employer may not deduct the deferred compensation when an employee initially earns it, even though the company becomes liable for the deferred compensation payment. In contrast, for financial accounting purposes, companies generally expense deferred compensation in the year employees earn it and record a corresponding deferred compensation liability.[14]

Employee Considerations

Should employees participate in nonqualified plans when given the chance? The decision obviously involves several considerations. First, employees must decide whether the benefits they expect to receive from qualified retirement plans (or other sources) will be adequate to provide for their expected costs during retirement. Next, they should consider whether they can afford to defer current salary. This may not be a significant concern for most eligible participants, however, because nonqualified plans are generally available only to highly compensated employees who may not have the liquidity concerns that lower-compensated employees may face. Also, employees should consider the expected after-tax rate of return on the deferred salary relative to what they could earn by receiving that salary currently and personally investing it.

Generally, larger employers allow employees participating in nonqualified plans to choose how their deferred compensation will be invested from among alternative investments provided under the plan (money market, various bond funds, and stock funds, among others). However, because employers do not actually invest compensation deferred under the plan on the employee's behalf, the employer credits the employee's account *as if* the employee's contributions had been invested in the employee's

---

THE KEY FACTS

Nonqualified Deferred Compensation Plans

- Employee defers current income in exchange for future payment.
  - Employee is taxed when payment is received.
  - Employee generally selects investment choices up front to determine return on deferral.
  - Just as for traditional deferred compensation plans, after-tax rate of return depends on before-tax rate of return, marginal tax rate at time of deferral, and marginal tax rate at time of distribution.
  - Payment is not guaranteed. If employer doesn't pay, employee becomes unsecured creditor.

---

[14]Employers record additional expense and liability as earnings on the deferred compensation accumulate.

deemed investment choices. The description of Coca-Cola Company's nonqualified retirement plan, presented in Exhibit 13-6, illustrates this concept.

EXHIBIT 13-6   **Description of Nonqualified Retirement Plan**
Excerpt from Coca-Cola Company's proxy statement

Deferred Compensation Plan. The Deferred Compensation Plan is a nonqualified and unfunded deferred compensation program offered to approximately 1,000 U.S. based Company employees in 2016. International service associates do not participate in the Deferred Compensation Plan. Eligible participants may defer up to 80% of base salary and up to 95% of their annual incentive. The Company has the benefit of full unrestricted use of all amounts deferred under the Deferred Compensation Plan until such amounts are required to be distributed to the plan participants. Gains and losses are credited based on the participant's election of a variety of deemed investment choices. The Company does not match any employee deferral or guarantee a return. Participants' accounts may or may not appreciate and may depreciate depending on the performance of their deemed investment choices. None of the deemed investment choices provide returns at above-market or preferential rates. All deferrals are paid out in cash upon distribution. Participants may schedule a distribution during employment or may opt to receive their balance after separation from service.

Source: Excerpt from Coca-Cola Company's proxy statement.

Just as with qualified defined contribution plans, other than Roth 401(k) plans, an employee's after-tax rate of return on deferred compensation depends on the employee's investment choices *and* on the employee's marginal tax rates at the time of the contribution and at the time of the distribution.

Example 13-14

As a new executive with CBA, Lisa Whitlark is eligible to participate in the company's nonqualified deferred compensation (NQDC) plan. Recall that CBA provides a plan under which executives may elect to defer up to 10 percent of their salary. In her first year with CBA, Lisa elects to defer $40,000 of salary ($400,000 × 10%) under the plan. Because her current marginal income tax rate is 32 percent, she saves $12,800 in taxes by deferring the salary ($40,000 × 32%). Consequently, her after-tax cost of deferring the compensation is $27,200 ($40,000 − $12,800). Lisa plans to receive a distribution from the nonqualified plan in 20 years when she expects her marginal tax rate to be 32 percent. She selects a stock index fund as her deemed investment choice. She expects the fund to provide an 8 percent before-tax rate of return on her $40,000 deferral. What will Lisa receive after taxes from her $40,000 deferral?

Answer: $126,778 after-tax accumulation, computed as follows:

Description	Amount	Explanation
Contribution to plan	$ 40,000	Deferral of 10 percent of her current salary
Times future value factor	× 1.08^{20}	8 percent annual rate of return for 20 years
Future value of deferred compensation	186,438	Value of deferral/distribution 20 years after deferral
Minus: taxes payable on distribution	(59,660)	$186,438 value of account × 32 percent marginal tax rate
After-tax proceeds from distributions	**$126,778**	Value of account minus taxes payable on distribution

Deferring salary to a future period can be an effective tax planning technique, particularly when the employee anticipates her marginal tax rate will be lower in the year she will receive the deferred compensation than it is in the year she defers the salary. In fact, if employees had complete flexibility as to when they could receive distributions from deferred compensation plans, they would likely accelerate distributions from deferred compensation plans into years they knew with certainty would have relatively low marginal tax rates. This strategy is limited, however, by rules requiring employees to specify the timing of the future payments when they decide to participate in deferred compensation plans.[15]

Employees considering participating in nonqualified deferred compensation plans should also consider the potential financial risks of doing so. Recall that employers are not required to fund nonqualified plans. So there's always the possibility that the employer may become bankrupt and not have the funds to pay the employee on the scheduled distribution dates. If the employer is not able to make the payments, the employee becomes an unsecured creditor of the company and may never receive the full compensation owed to her. Consequently, the employee should evaluate the financial stability of the company when deciding whether to defer compensation under the employer's plan.

Employer Considerations

It's pretty clear that nonqualified plans can provide significant benefits to employees. How might employers benefit from providing nonqualified plans? First, employers may benefit if they are able to earn a better rate of return on the deferred compensation than the rate of return they are required to pay employees participating in the plan. In addition, employers can use nonqualified plans to achieve certain hiring objectives. For example, nonqualified plans could be a component of a compensation package a company may use to attract prospective executives. Deferred compensation can also be used to compensate an employee when the employer's percentage contribution to the employee's qualified retirement account is limited by the annual contribution limit. Deferred compensation is not subject to the qualified retirement account contribution limits.

Likewise, deferring compensation may be an important tax planning tool for employers when their current marginal tax rates are low (they are experiencing net operating losses so their current marginal tax rate is 0 percent) and they expect their future marginal tax rates when deferred compensation is paid to be significantly higher because they expect to return to profitability (unless tax rates increase, the marginal rate would be 21 percent). In effect, deferring compensation into a year with a higher marginal tax rate increases the after-tax benefit of the compensation deduction, which reduces the after-tax cost of the compensation to the employer. Recent tax legislation has dramatically reduced corporate tax rates and thus increased the after-tax cost of paying current compensation. The extent to which the corporate rate reduction affects the popularity of nonqualified deferred compensation plans remains to be seen.

Exhibit 13-7 summarizes and compares qualified retirement plans and nonqualified deferred compensation plans.

INDIVIDUALLY MANAGED QUALIFIED RETIREMENT PLANS

We've covered tax and nontax issues relating to both qualified and nonqualified employer-sponsored retirement savings plans. However, not all employers provide retirement savings plans, and when they do, some employees may not be eligible to participate, while others who are eligible may elect not to participate in these plans. The tax

---

THE KEY FACTS

Nonqualified Deferred Compensation Plans

- Employer promises to pay deferred compensation at some point in future.
  - Deduct when paid to employee.
  - Not required to fund obligation.
  - Use to accomplish compensation objectives such as providing more deferred compensation to employees who are over contribution limits on qualified plans.
  - Employer's marginal tax rates at time of deferral relative to those at time of payment affect after-tax cost of providing deferred compensation relative to current compensation.

---

[15]§409A. These rules do provide, however, that specified payments from deferred compensation plans may commence while employees are still employed.

EXHIBIT 13-7   **Qualified Plans versus Nonqualified Plans Summary**

	Qualified Plans	Nonqualified Plans
Types	• Defined benefit (Pension). • Defined contribution [401(k)].	• Deferred compensation.
Requirements	• May not discriminate against "rank and file" employees of the company. • Funding or contribution requirements. • Vesting requirements.	• May discriminate. • Generally provided to executives and highly compensated employees. • No formal funding requirements (employee is essentially an unsecured creditor). • No formal vesting requirements.
Tax consequences to employers	• Immediately deduct contributions to plan (amount funded).	• No deduction until paid to employee.
Tax consequences to employees	• Employee contributions deductible unless to Roth-type account. • Earnings deferred until distributed to employee. • Employer contributions not immediately taxed. • Distributions from non-Roth accounts treated as ordinary income.	• Employee contributions (or deferrals) are deductible. • Taxed as ordinary income when received. • Earnings deferred until distributed to employee.

laws provide opportunities for these taxpayers to provide for their own retirement security through individually managed retirement plans. The **individual retirement account (IRA)** is the most common of the individually managed retirement plans. Other types of individually managed plans are available to self-employed taxpayers.

INDIVIDUAL RETIREMENT ACCOUNTS

LO 13-4

Taxpayers who meet certain eligibility requirements can contribute to **traditional IRAs,** to **Roth IRAs,** or to both. Just like traditional and Roth 401(k) plans, traditional IRAs and Roth IRAs have different tax characteristics. In fact, in most respects, the tax characteristics of traditional 401(k) plans mirror those of traditional IRAs, and the tax characteristics of Roth 401(k) plans mirror those of Roth IRA accounts. To minimize redundancy, we focus on the tax characteristics that differ between employer-sponsored 401(k) plans and self-managed IRAs.

Traditional IRAs

Contributions   Deductible contributions to IRAs are *for* AGI deductions. The maximum deductible contribution for a taxpayer in 2018 depends on the taxpayer's age as follows:

- $5,500 deduction limit if the taxpayer is less than 50 years of age at year-end.[16,17]
- $6,500 deduction limit if the taxpayer is at least 50 years of age at year-end.[18]
- $0 deduction if the taxpayer is at least 70½ years of age at year-end.

---

[16]Lump-sum distributions from qualified plans other than Roth 401(k)s received prior to retirement are frequently rolled over into traditional IRA accounts to avoid the 10 percent premature distribution penalty and current taxation. Rollover contributions are not subject to normal contribution limits for traditional IRAs.

[17]The IRA contribution limit is indexed for inflation.

[18]The $1,000 increase in the deduction limit for older taxpayers is granted to allow taxpayers nearing retirement age to "catch up" on contributions they may have not made in previous years.

THE KEY FACTS

Traditional IRAs

- 2018 deductible contribution limit:
  - Lesser of $5,500 or earned income.
  - For taxpayers over 50, lesser of $6,500 or earned income.
- If taxpayers participate in employer-provided plan:
  - For 2018, deduction limit phased out for single taxpayers with MAGI between $63,000 and $73,000, and for married filing jointly taxpayers with MAGI between $101,000 and $121,000.
  - Special rules if one spouse is covered by plan and the other is not.

The deductible contribution limit may be further restricted depending on the following factors:

- The taxpayer's participation in an employer-sponsored retirement plan.
- The taxpayer's filing status.
- The amount of the taxpayer's earned income.
- The taxpayer's modified AGI (MAGI). For purposes of determining the deductible amount of traditional IRA contributions, MAGI is the taxpayer's AGI disregarding the IRA deduction itself and certain other items.[19]

Unmarried taxpayers not participating in an employer-sponsored retirement plan may deduct IRA contributions up to the *lesser* of

- $5,500 ($6,500 for taxpayers 50+ years of age).
- Earned income.

As we discuss in the Gross Income and Exclusions chapter, earned income generally includes income actually earned through the taxpayer's efforts, such as wages, salaries, tips, and other employee compensation, plus the amount of the taxpayer's net earnings from self-employment. Alimony income is also considered earned income for this purpose.

Example 13-15

In the year she graduated from college, Tina earned $25,000. She earned $5,000 in salary working part-time while she was in school and she earned $20,000 in salary working for CBA from September through December. To get an early start saving for retirement, she contributed $5,000 to a *traditional* IRA (recall that Tina is not eligible to participate in CBA's 401(k) retirement plan until January of next year). How much of this contribution may Tina deduct?

Answer: $5,000. Because Tina is not participating in an employer-sponsored retirement plan during the current year, she may deduct the full $5,000 contribution as a *for* AGI deduction, reducing her AGI from $25,000 to $20,000.

For *unmarried taxpayers* who actively participate in an employer-sponsored retirement plan, the deduction limits are the same as for those who do not participate, except that the maximum deduction is phased out based on the taxpayer's MAGI as follows:

- No phase-out if MAGI is equal to or less than $63,000.
- Proportional phase-out of full limit for MAGI between $63,000 and $73,000 [The phase-out percentage is computed as follows: (MAGI minus $63,000) divided by ($73,000 − $63,000). For example, if the MAGI is $65,000, the taxpayer loses 20 percent of contribution limit].
- Full phase-out (no deduction) if MAGI is equal to or greater than $73,000.

Married taxpayers can make deductible contributions to separate IRAs (i.e., an IRA for each spouse) subject to limitations. If the married couple files jointly, before any AGI-based phase-out amounts (discussed below), the maximum deduction for the spouse with the *higher* amount of earned income is the same as it is for unmarried taxpayers [$5,500

[19]§219(g)(3).

($6,500 if at least 50 years of age at year-end) or earned income if it is less]. However, the maximum deduction for the spouse with the *lower* amount of earned income is limited to the lesser of

- $5,500 ($6,500 if this spouse is age 50+).
- Total earned income of both spouses reduced by deductible and nondeductible contributions to the higher-earning spouse's traditional IRA and by contributions to the higher-earning spouse's Roth IRA.[20]

The contribution to the lesser-earning spouse's IRA is called a **spousal IRA.** The money in the account belongs to the lower-earning spouse no matter where the funds for the contribution came from.

If a spouse is an active participant in an employer's retirement plan and the couple files jointly, the maximum deduction for that spouse's contribution is phased out based on the *couple's* MAGI as follows:

- No phase-out if the couple's MAGI is equal to or less than $101,000.
- Proportional phase-out of full limit for MAGI between $101,000 and $121,000 (for example, if the couple's MAGI is $113,000, the couple loses 60 percent of deductible contribution limit).
- Full phase-out (no deduction) if MAGI is equal to or greater than $121,000.

If one spouse is an active participant in an employer's retirement plan and the other is not and the couple files jointly, the deduction for the spouse who is not an active participant is phased out based on the couple's MAGI as follows (the phase-out applies whether the spouse is the higher- or lower-earning spouse):

- No phase-out if the couple's MAGI is equal to or less than $189,000.
- Proportional phase-out of full limit for MAGI between $189,000 and $199,000.
- Full phase out (no deduction) if MAGI is equal to or greater than $199,000.

Married taxpayers who file separately may also make deductible contributions to an IRA. The maximum deduction is the lesser of

- $5,500 ($6,500 if taxpayer is 50+).
- The taxpayer's earned income.

However, if either spouse is an active participant in an employer's retirement plan and they file separately, then each spouse's deductible contribution (including the non-active participant spouse's contribution) is phased out over that spouse's MAGI as follows:

- No phase-out if the taxpayer's MAGI is $0 (also no tax benefit of deducting).
- Proportional phase-out of full limit for MAGI between $0 and $10,000.
- Full phase-out (no deduction) if MAGI is equal to or greater than $10,000.

If the couple files separate tax returns and did not live with each other at any time during the year, they will be treated as unmarried taxpayers for purposes of the IRA deduction limitations. Appendix A at the end of this chapter provides a flowchart for identifying traditional IRA deduction limitations.

> **THE KEY FACTS**
>
> **Traditional IRAs**
> - If taxpayer does not participate in employer-provided plan but spouse does
>   - Deduction limit phased out for MAGI between $189,000 and $199,000.
> - Distribution taxed as ordinary income
>   - If distribution before taxpayer is 59½, 10 percent penalty generally applies.

[20]§219(c).

Example 13-16

In her first full calendar year working for CBA, Tina earns $60,000. Because she contributes $2,400 of her salary to CBA's 401(k) plan, her AGI is $57,600 ($60,000 − $2,400). Tina would like to make the maximum deductible contribution to her IRA. Assuming the 2018 limitations apply, how much is she allowed to deduct?

Answer: $5,500. Because Tina is a participant in CBA's retirement plan, the $5,500 deduction limit is subject to phase-out. However, because Tina's MAGI is less than the beginning of the phase-out threshold ($63,000), she is allowed to deduct the maximum contribution.

What if: Assume that in her first full calendar year working for CBA, Tina earns $67,000. Because she contributes $2,400 of her salary to CBA's 401(k) plan, her MAGI is $64,600 ($67,000 − $2,400). Tina would like to make the maximum deductible contribution to her IRA. How much is she allowed to deduct?

Answer: $4,620. The deductible amount before considering MAGI limitations is $5,500. However, because Tina is a participant in CBA's retirement plan, the $5,500 deduction limit is subject to phase-out. Because Tina's MAGI is 16 percent of the way through the $63,000 − $73,000 phase-out range for a single taxpayer [($64,600 − $63,000)/($73,000 − $63,000)], the $5,500 deductible contribution limit is reduced by 16 percent, to $4,620 [$5,500 × (1 − .16)]. So, $4,620 is the maximum deductible contribution she can make to her traditional IRA.

What if: Assume that Tina is married and files a joint return with her spouse Steve. Tina participates in CBA's 401(k) plan and she receives $60,000 in salary from CBA for the year. Steve is a full-time student and is unemployed. The couple's MAGI before considering IRA contributions is $60,000. What is Tina's maximum deductible IRA contribution for the year? What is Steve's maximum deductible IRA contribution for the year?

Answer: Tina's maximum deductible contribution for the year is $5,500. Because Tina is married, files a joint return, and reports MAGI under $101,000 with her husband, her contribution is not phased out at all even though she is an active participant in CBA's retirement plan.

Steve's maximum deductible contribution for the year is also $5,500. Because Steve reports less earned income than Tina (in fact he doesn't report any earned income for the year), his deductible IRA contribution is limited to the lesser of (1) $5,500 or (2) $54,500 ($60,000 − $5,500), which is the couple's earned income minus Tina's deductible IRA contribution.

What if: Assume the same facts as the preceding what-if example except that Tina and Steve file separately. What is each spouse's maximum deductible IRA contribution for the year?

Answer: $0 for Tina and $0 for Steve. Tina is ineligible to make a deductible IRA contribution because her MAGI of $60,000 exceeds the $10,000 phase-out limit, and Steve may not make a deductible contribution to the IRA because he does not report any earned income.

Nondeductible Contributions   For all taxpayers, to the extent the maximum deductible contribution is phased out based on MAGI, taxpayers can still make *nondeductible* contributions of up to $5,500 per year ($6,500 for taxpayers who are at least 55 years of age at year-end). Taxpayers who have reached age 70½ by year-end are not allowed to contribute at all to an IRA. Earned income limitations (including the spousal IRA limits) that apply to deductible IRA contributions also apply to nondeductible contributions. That is, a taxpayer must have earned income in order to make nondeductible contributions to a traditional IRA (with the exception of a spouse who is contributing to a spousal IRA). The earnings on nondeductible contributions grow tax-deferred until the taxpayer receives distributions from the IRA. On distribution, the taxpayer is taxed on the earnings generated by the nondeductible contributions but not on the actual nondeductible contributions. When taxpayers take partial distributions from an IRA to which they have made deductible and nondeductible contributions, each distribution consists of a taxable and nontaxable component. The portion of the distribution that is nontaxable is the ratio of the nondeductible contributions to the total account balance at the time of the distribution.

This is exactly the same formula used in Example 13-12 to determine the nontaxable portion of nonqualified distributions from Roth 401(k) accounts and is similar to the formula described in the Gross Income and Exclusions chapter for determining the nontaxable portion of an annuity payment. Most taxpayers exceeding the deductibility limits on traditional IRAs would likely do better by contributing to a Roth IRA, if eligible, instead of making nondeductible contributions to traditional IRAs.

Taxpayers who are eligible to contribute to an IRA may contribute to the IRA up to the unextended tax return due date (generally, April 15 of the subsequent year). That is, as long as the taxpayer makes a contribution to the IRA by April 15 of year 2, the contribution counts as though it were made during year 1 (the prior calendar year).

Distributions   Just like distributions from traditional 401(k) plans, distributions from traditional IRAs are taxed as ordinary income to the taxpayer. Taxpayers withdrawing funds from traditional IRAs before reaching the age of 59½ are also subject to a 10 percent early-distribution penalty on the amount of the withdrawal. Distributions exempt from the early distribution penalties include account proceeds distributed in the form of a life annuity (fixed payment each month or year over the taxpayer's life) and account proceeds used for qualifying medical expenses, health insurance premiums for the owner, qualified higher education expenses, or first-time home purchases (proceeds for first time home purchases are limited to $10,000).[21] Taxpayers must receive their first required minimum distribution by April 1 of the year following the year in which they reach 70½ years of age. Because the distribution rules for traditional IRAs are so similar to the rules for traditional 401(k) accounts, taxpayers with traditional IRAs face virtually the same issues as participants in traditional 401(k) plans when planning for distributions. Thus, they should be careful to avoid the 10 percent penalty while taking similar steps to maximize the tax deferral on their traditional IRA account balances.

Roth IRAs

As an alternative to traditional IRAs, taxpayers meeting certain requirements can contribute to Roth IRAs. Contributions to Roth IRAs are *not* deductible, and *qualifying* distributions from Roth IRAs are *not* taxable.

Contributions   Roth IRAs are subject to the same annual contribution limits as traditional IRAs [the lesser of $5,500 ($6,500 if at least age 50 at year-end) or earned income]. Further, the same spousal IRA rules that apply to traditional IRAs apply to Roth IRA contributions. These limits apply to the sum of a taxpayer's contributions to deductible IRAs, nondeductible IRAs, and Roth IRAs.

Whether taxpayers participate in an employer-sponsored retirement plan or not, the Roth IRA contribution limitation phases out based on modified AGI (MAGI) as follows:[22]

Unmarried taxpayers
- No phase-out if the taxpayer's MAGI is $120,000 or below.
- Proportional phase-out of full limit for MAGI between $120,000 and $135,000.
- Full phase-out (no contribution) if MAGI is $135,000 or higher.

Married taxpayers filing jointly
- No phase-out if the taxpayer's MAGI is $189,000 or below.
- Proportional phase-out of full limit for MAGI between $189,000 and $199,000.
- Full phase-out (no contribution) if MAGI is $199,000 or higher.

Married taxpayers filing separately
- No phase-out if the taxpayer's MAGI is $0.
- Proportional phase-out of full limit if taxpayer's MAGI is between $0 and $10,000.
- Full phase-out (no contribution) if taxpayer's MAGI is equal to or greater than $10,000.

Appendix B at the end of this chapter provides a flowchart for determining Roth IRA contribution limits.

THE KEY FACTS

Roth IRAs

- Contributions are not deductible.
- Same contribution limits as traditional IRAs but
  - For 2018, contribution phases out for MAGI between $120,000 and $135,000 for unmarried taxpayers and between $189,000 and $199,000 for married taxpayers filing jointly.
- Qualified distributions are not taxable.
  - To qualify, account must be open for at least five years before distribution and distribution must be made after taxpayer reaches 59½ years of age (among others).
- Nonqualified distributions of account earnings
  - Taxed at ordinary rates and subject to 10 percent penalty if the taxpayer is not at least 59½ years of age at the time of the distribution.
- Distributions come first from contributions and then from account earnings.

---

[21]§72(t). A first-time homebuyer is someone who did not own a principal residence in the two years before acquiring the new home [see §72(t)(8)(D)].

[22]Modified AGI (MAGI) for this purpose is the same as it is for traditional IRA contributions but it excludes income from rolling over a traditional IRA to a Roth IRA. See §408A(c)(3)(B)(i).

Distributions *Qualified* distributions from Roth IRAs are not taxable. A qualified distribution is a distribution from funds or earnings from funds in a Roth IRA if the distribution occurs at least five years after the taxpayer opened the Roth IRA[23] and meets one of the following requirements:

- Distribution is made on or after the date the taxpayer reaches 59½ years of age,
- Distribution is made to a beneficiary (or to the estate of the taxpayer) on or after the death of the taxpayer,
- Distribution is attributable to the taxpayer being disabled, or
- Distribution is used to pay qualified acquisition costs for first-time homebuyers (limited to $10,000).[24]

All other distributions are considered to be *nonqualified* distributions.

Nonqualified distributions are not necessarily taxable, however. Because taxpayers do not deduct Roth IRA contributions, they are able to withdraw the contributions tax-free at any time. However, *nonqualified* distributions of the *earnings* of a Roth IRA are taxable as ordinary income. The distributed earnings are also subject to a 10 percent penalty unless the taxpayer is 59½ years of age at the time of the distribution.[25] Nonqualified distributions are deemed to come

- First from the taxpayer's contributions (nontaxable),
- Then from account earnings after the total contributions have been distributed [note that this is different from the equivalent rule for Roth 401(k) plans].

Thus, taxpayers can treat the Roth IRA as an emergency savings account to the extent of their contributions without incurring any penalties.

ETHICS

Ryan had just finished a finance class and had learned about the importance of the time value of money. With this knowledge, he wanted to start saving for retirement. Last year Ryan had a job and earned $2,000. After paying his expenses, he placed the remaining $500 in a savings account in the bank. This year, however, Ryan decided to focus on his studies so he did not earn any income. He paid his living expenses through student loans. At the end of the current year, Ryan contributed $400 to a Roth IRA. On his tax return for the year, Ryan reported $400 of self-employment income (even though he didn't earn any). Why did Ryan report this "phantom" income? What do you think of his strategy?

Example 13-17

What if: Assume that when Tina started working for CBA, she made a one-time contribution of $4,000 to a Roth IRA. Years later, she retired at the age of 65 when the value of her Roth account was $60,000. If Tina receives a $10,000 distribution from her Roth IRA, what amount of taxes (and penalty, if applicable) must she pay on the distribution (assume her ordinary marginal rate is 30 percent)?

Answer: $0 taxes and $0 penalty. Qualified Roth IRA distributions are not taxable.

What if: Assume the same facts as above, except that Tina received a $10,000 distribution when she was 57 years of age. What amount of taxes (and penalty, if applicable) is she required to pay on the distribution (assume a 30 percent ordinary marginal rate)?

Answer: $2,400 in total consisting of $1,800 in taxes ($6,000 earnings distributed × 30 percent marginal tax rate) and $600 penalty ($6,000 earnings × 10 percent penalty rate). Because Tina has not reached age 59½ at the time of the distribution, this is a nonqualified distribution. Consequently, she is

---

[23]The five-year period starts on January 1 of the year in which the contribution was made and ends on the last day of the fifth taxable year. See Reg §1.408A-6, Q&A2 and Q&A-5(b).

[24]§408A(d)(2).

[25]See §72(t)(2) for other exceptions to the penalty.

taxed on the $6,000 distribution of earnings ($10,000 distribution minus $4,000 contribution). She is penalized on the distribution of earnings because she is not 59½ years of age at the time of the distribution.

What if: Assume that when Tina was 62 years old, she opened a Roth IRA, contributing $4,000. Three years later, Tina withdrew the entire account balance of $5,000. What amount of taxes (and penalty, if applicable) must Tina pay on the distribution (assume her marginal tax rate is 30 percent)?

Answer: $300 of taxes ($1,000 earnings × 30 percent marginal tax rate) but $0 penalty. The distribution is a nonqualified distribution because Tina did not have the Roth IRA open for five years before receiving the distribution. Consequently, she must pay tax on the $1,000 earnings portion of the distribution ($5,000 − $4,000) but she is not penalized on the distribution because she was over 59½ years of age at the time of the distribution.

In contrast to taxpayers with traditional IRAs, taxpayers are *not* required to take minimum distributions from Roth IRAs. Thus, taxpayers can minimize distributions from Roth IRAs to maintain a source of tax-free income during their lifetime.

Rollover from Traditional to Roth IRA

Many taxpayers made contributions to traditional IRAs before Roth IRAs were available. Some taxpayers may have contributed to traditional IRAs and then later decided they should have contributed to Roth IRAs. The tax laws accommodate these taxpayers by allowing them to transfer funds from a traditional IRA (and other qualified defined contribution plans) to a Roth IRA.[26] This transfer of funds is called a **rollover.** When taxpayers do this, however, the entire amount taken out of the traditional IRA is taxed at ordinary rates but is not subject to the 10 percent penalty tax as long as the taxpayer contributes the *full amount* (before-tax) to a Roth IRA within 60 days of the withdrawal from the traditional IRA.[27]

Example 13-18

What if: Let's assume that in the year she graduated from college and began working for CBA, Tina made a fully deductible $4,000 contribution to a *traditional* IRA. Three years later, when her marginal tax rate is 22 percent, she rolls over the entire $5,000 account balance into a Roth IRA. What amount of taxes is she required to pay on the rollover?

Answer: $1,100 ($5,000 × 22%). The entire $5,000 transferred from the IRA to the Roth IRA is taxed at 22 percent but is not subject to the 10 percent early withdrawal penalty. Even though Tina pays $1,100 in taxes on the transfer, she is required to contribute $5,000 to the Roth IRA within 60 days from the time she withdraws the money from the traditional IRA.

What if: What are the tax consequences if Tina pays the $1,100 tax bill and contributes only $3,900 to the Roth IRA?

Answer: She must pay a $110 penalty. The penalty is 10 percent of the $1,100 that she withdrew from the IRA and did not contribute to the Roth IRA ($5,000 − $3,900).

THE KEY FACTS

Roth IRAs

- Rollovers from traditional IRAs to Roth IRAs.
  - Amount withdrawn from traditional IRA is fully taxable but not penalized.
  - Taxpayer must contribute full amount withdrawn to Roth IRA account within 60 days of withdrawal.
  - Amounts withdrawn but not contributed are subject to tax and 10 percent penalty.

Why would anyone be willing to pay taxes currently in order to avoid paying taxes later? Typically, a rollover from a traditional to a Roth IRA makes sense when a taxpayer's marginal tax rate is currently low (when the tax cost of the rollover is low) and expected to be significantly higher in the future (when the expected benefit of the rollover is high). Note that high-income taxpayers may not be allowed to contribute to Roth IRAs due to the AGI restrictions on contribution limits. However, because currently there is no AGI restriction on who may roll over funds from a traditional IRA (or other qualified

[26]See Notice 2009-75, 2009-39 IRB.

[27]§408(d)(3). Taxpayers who roll over funds from a traditional IRA (or other traditional retirement account) to a Roth IRA must wait at least five years from the date of the rollover to withdraw the funds from the rollover in order to avoid a 10 percent penalty on the distribution [§408(d)(3)(F)].

defined contribution plan) into a Roth IRA, high-income taxpayers who would like to fund a Roth IRA may do so through a rollover.[28]

Comparing Traditional and Roth IRAs

So, which type of IRA is better for taxpayers? The tax considerations are very similar to those we already discussed when we compared traditional and Roth 401(k) plans. In general, after-tax rates of return from traditional IRAs will exceed those from Roth IRAs when marginal tax rates decline. However, after-tax rates of return from Roth IRAs will exceed those from traditional IRAs when tax rates increase.

Unrelated to marginal tax rates, Roth IRAs have other advantages relative to traditional IRAs, as follows:

- Taxpayers can contribute to Roth IRAs at any age. In contrast, taxpayers are not allowed to make deductible contributions to traditional IRAs once they have reached 70½ years of age.
- The minimum distribution requirements for traditional IRAs do not apply to Roth IRAs. This provision permits owners of Roth IRAs to use their accounts to generate tax-free returns long after retirement.
- Taxpayers can withdraw their Roth contributions tax-free at any time without paying tax or paying a penalty. Taxpayers who withdraw their traditional IRA contributions are taxed on the distribution and potentially penalized.

Exhibit 13-8 summarizes tax-related requirements for traditional and Roth IRAs.

EXHIBIT 13-8   **Traditional IRA versus Roth IRA Summary**

	Traditional IRA	Roth IRA
Contributions requirements	• Taxpayer must not be a participant in an employer-sponsored plan or, if participating in an employer-provided plan, must meet certain income thresholds. Those above the threshold will have deductible portion of contribution phased out.	• No deduction allowed for contributions. Must meet certain income requirements to be able to contribute to a Roth IRA.
Contributions	• Deductible unless taxpayer is a participant in an employer plan and has high AGI. • Nondeductible contributions allowed.	• Not deductible. • May not contribute if high AGI.
Maximum contribution	• Lesser of $5,500 per taxpayer ($6,500 for taxpayers over 50 years old) or earned income.	• Same as traditional IRA.
	• The contribution limits apply to the sum of contributions to traditional deductible IRAs, nondeductible IRAs, and Roth IRAs for the year. • For married couples filing jointly, contributions for the lesser earning spouse may not exceed the total earned income of both spouses reduced by deductible and nondeductible contributions to the other spouse's traditional IRA and by contributions to the other spouse's Roth IRA.	
Contribution dates	• Can contribute up to unextended tax return due date, generally April 15.	• Same as traditional IRA.
Distributions	• Generally taxed as ordinary income. • If made before 59½, generally subject to 10 percent penalty. • If nondeductible contribution made, allocate distribution between taxable and nontaxable amounts similar to annuity rules. • Minimum distributions required by April 1 of the year after the year in which the taxpayer reaches 70½. • Failure to meet minimum distribution timing and amount requirements triggers 50 percent penalty.	• Qualified distributions are not taxed. • Generally, distributions are qualified after account has been open for five years and employee has reached the age of 59½. • Nonqualified distributions are not taxed to the extent of prior contributions. • Nonqualified distributions of earnings are subject to tax at ordinary rates and are also subject to a 10 percent penalty if the taxpayer is not at least 59½ years of age at the time of the distribution. • No minimum distribution requirements.

[28]§408A(c)(3).

TAXES IN THE REAL WORLD   Roth or Traditional Retirement Savings Vehicle?

With increasing budgetary deficits and the government's increasing need for revenues, one can reasonably anticipate that future tax rates will exceed current tax rates. With increasing tax rates, taxpayers should favor Roth 401(k) plans and Roth IRAs over traditional retirement savings vehicles. Yet, less than 10 percent of employees who could contribute to Roth 401(k) plans choose to do so and more than 15 times more taxpayers use traditional IRAs than use Roth IRAs. Why are so many more taxpayers choosing traditional retirement savings options when Roth accounts may theoretically provide a greater after-tax sum at retirement? It could be that there are not a lot of taxpayers who expect their marginal tax rates to be higher at retirement than they are now, it could

be that taxpayers prefer deductible retirement savings contributions for the current tax savings, or it could be that taxpayers believe that in the future Congress may change the tax laws so that distributions from Roth accounts will become taxable. A sound response to the tax law uncertainty would be to hedge your bets and include some retirement savings in traditional accounts and some in Roth accounts so that you can adapt to changing tax laws over time.

It remains to be seen what effect recent tax rate cuts have on taxpayers' choice to invest in traditional versus Roth-type retirement plans.

Source: Carolyn T. Geer, "Bad Math: Taxes Rise as Savings Fall," *The Wall Street Journal*, January 20, 2013.

SELF-EMPLOYED RETIREMENT ACCOUNTS

LO 13-5

We've discussed retirement savings opportunities available to employees. However, many taxpayers are self-employed small business owners who do not have access to employer-sponsored plans.[29] Moreover, individually managed retirement plans such as traditional and Roth IRAs are not particularly attractive to self-employed taxpayers due to the relatively low contribution limits on these plans. What retirement savings options, then, are available to the self-employed?

Congress has created a number of retirement savings plans for self-employed taxpayers. Two of the more popular are simplified employee pension (SEP) IRAs and individual (or "self employed") 401(k) plans. These are defined contribution plans that generally work the same way as employer-provided plans. That is, amounts set aside in these plans are deducted from income, earnings are free of tax until distributed, and distributions from the plans are fully taxable.[30] As we discuss below, these plans differ in terms of their annual contribution limits. They also have different nontax characteristics, including their suitability for businesses with employees other than the owner and their administration costs. As you might expect, these factors should be considered when self-employed small business owners choose a retirement plan.[31] We describe SEP IRAs and individual 401(k) plans below.[32]

Simplified Employee Pension (SEP) IRA

A simplified employee pension (SEP) can be administered through an individual retirement account (IRA) called a **SEP IRA**.[33] The owner of a sole proprietorship can make

> **THE KEY FACTS**
>
> **Self-Employed Retirement Accounts**
> - Popular plans include SEP IRAs and individual 401(k)s.
> - Similar to (non-Roth) qualified defined contribution plans.
>   - Contributions are deductible and distributions are taxable.

---

[29]Because sole proprietorships with self-employment income are very common, we assume in our examples and explanations here that any self-employment income originates from a sole proprietorship. In some cases, however, partners and LLC members may also have self-employment income from a partnership or LLC.

[30]"Keogh" self-employed defined benefit plans are also an option. Generally, defined benefit plans are attractive to older, self-employed individuals with profitable businesses because they allow for greater deductible contributions. However, they are usually more costly to maintain than the defined contribution plans we mention here.

[31]Many investment firms provide comparisons to help taxpayers select self-employed retirement plans. One particularly good comparison is provided by Fidelity Investments at www.fidelity.com/retirement/small-business/compare-plans-chart.

[32]A Savings Incentive Match Plans for Employees (SIMPLE) IRA is another popular form of retirement plan for the self-employed. For those earning lower amounts of self-employment income, the contribution limits for a SIMPLE IRA are generally higher than contribution limits for SEP IRAs.

[33]§408(k).

annual contributions directly to her SEP IRA. For 2018, the annual contribution is limited to the *lesser* of:

- $55,000 or
- 20 percent of Schedule C net income, after reducing Schedule C net income by the deduction for the employer's portion of self-employment taxes paid (50 percent of the self-employment taxes paid).[34]

Contributions can be made up to the extended due date of the tax return.[35]

Example 13-19

THE KEY FACTS

Self-Employed Retirement Accounts

- SEP IRA 2018 contribution limit.
  - Lesser of (1) $55,000 or (2) 20 percent of Schedule C net income (after reducing Schedule C net income by the deduction for the employer's portion of self-employment taxes paid).

What if: Dave (assume age 64) reports Schedule C net income of $40,000 during the current year. If he sets up a SEP IRA for himself, what is the maximum contribution he may make to the plan (assuming he has no other source of employee or self-employment income)?

Answer: $7,435, computed as follows:

Description	Amount	Explanation
(1) First limit on contribution	$55,000	
(2) Schedule C net income minus the self-employment tax deduction	37,174	$40,000 − ($40,000 × .9235 × 15.3% × 50%)
(3) Percentage for limitation based on (2)	20%	
(4) Second limit on contribution	7,435	(2) × (3)
Maximum contribution	**$ 7,435**	Lesser of (1) or (4)

What if: Assume Dave is 48 years old at the end of the year. What is his maximum deductible contribution?

Answer: $7,435. Dave's maximum deductible contribution for a SEP IRA does not depend on his age.

What if: Suppose Dave reports $310,000 of Schedule C net income rather than $40,000. What is his maximum deductible contribution to his SEP IRA account?

Answer: $55,000, the lesser of (1) $55,000 or (2) $59,578 {20% × [$310,000 − ((($310,000 × .9235 − $128,400} × 2.9% × 50%) + ($128,400 × 15.3% × 50%))]}.

Nontax Considerations   If a sole proprietor has hired employees, the sole proprietor *must* contribute to the employees' respective SEP IRAs based on their compensation. Because owners may view this requirement as being too favorable to employees, the SEP IRA is best suited for sole proprietors who do not have employees or who are willing to provide generous benefits to their employees. From an administrative perspective, SEP IRAs are easy to set up and have relatively low administrative costs from year to year.

Individual 401(k) Plans

Individual 401(k) plans are strictly for sole proprietors (and their spouses) who do not have employees. Under this type of plan, for 2018 the sole proprietor can contribute the lesser of:

- $55,000 or
- 20 percent of Schedule C net income, after reducing Schedule C net income by the deduction for the employer's portion of self-employment taxes paid (50 percent of self-employment taxes paid) (employer's contribution) plus an additional $18,500 (employee's contribution).

[34]The Individual Income Tax Computation and Tax Credits chapter addresses self-employment taxes in more detail. Also note that for SEP IRAs no catch-up contributions are allowed for taxpayers 50 years and older.
[35]§404(h). This is October 15 for a calendar-year taxpayer.

Further, if the sole proprietor is at least 50 years of age by the end of the tax year, she may contribute an *additional* $6,000 as a catch-up contribution. Thus, a self-employed taxpayer with sufficient self-employment earnings who is at least 50 years of age at year-end could contribute up to $61,000 to an individual 401(k) for 2018 ($55,000 + $6,000).

Finally, even though the individual 401(k) contribution limits provide for taxpayers to contribute an additional $18,500 or $24,500 (this includes the additional $6,000 for taxpayers at least 50 years of age at year-end) relative to a SEP IRA, a taxpayer's individual 401(k) contributions for the year are not allowed to exceed the taxpayer's Schedule C net income minus the self-employment tax deduction. Consequently, a taxpayer with limited self-employment income may not be able to take advantage of the additional $18,500 ($24,500) of contributions that individual 401(k)s allow relative to SEP IRAs.

Example 13-20

What if: Suppose that Dave is 64 years old at the end of the year, reports $40,000 of Schedule C net income, and has no other sources of income. What is the maximum amount he can contribute to an individual 401(k) account?

Answer: $31,935, computed as follows:

Description	Amount	Explanation
(1) First limit on contribution	$ 55,000	
(2) Schedule C net income minus the self-employment tax deduction	37,174	$40,000 − ($40,000 × .9235 × 15.3% × 50%)
(3) Percentage for limitation based on (2)	20%	
(4) Limit on employer's contribution	7,435	(2) × (3)
(5) Limit on employee's contribution	18,500	
(6) Second limitation	25,935	(4) + (5)
(7) Maximum contribution before catch-up contribution	25,935	Lesser of (1) or (6)
(8) Catch-up contribution	6,000	Dave is 64 years old at year-end
Maximum contribution	**$31,935**	(7) + (8), not to exceed (2)

THE KEY FACTS

Self-Employed Retirement Accounts

- Individual 401(k) 2018 contribution limit.
  - Lesser of (1) $55,000 or (2) 20 percent of Schedule C net income (after reducing Schedule C net income by the deduction for the employer's portion of self-employment taxes paid) plus $18,500.
  - Taxpayers who are at least 50 years old at the end of the year may contribute an additional $6,000 per year (maximum of $61,000, if self-employment earnings are sufficient).
  - Contribution cannot exceed Schedule C net income minus self-employment tax deduction.

Example 13-21

What if: Assume Dave is 48 years old at the end of the year, reports $40,000 of Schedule C net income, and has no other sources of income. What is his maximum deductible contribution to his individual 401(k) account?

Answer: $25,935. This is the same as the amount he could contribute as a 64-year-old (see prior example), minus the $6,000 catch-up adjustment ($31,935 − $6,000).

What if: Assume the same facts as above except that Dave (age 64) earned $10,000 of Schedule C net income rather than $40,000. What is his maximum deductible contribution to his individual 401(k)?

(continued on page 13-30)

Answer: $9,294, computed as follows (Dave's contribution is limited to his Schedule C net income minus self-employment tax deduction):

Description	Amount	Explanation
(1) First limit on contribution	$55,000	
(2) Schedule C net income minus self-employment tax deduction	9,294	$10,000 − ($10,000 × .9235 × 15.3% × 50%)
(3) Percentage for limitation based on (2)	20%	
(4) Limit on employer's contribution	1,859	(2) × (3)
(5) Limit on employee's contribution	18,500	
(6) Second limitation	20,359	(4) + (5)
(7) Maximum contribution before catch-up contribution	20,359	Lesser of (1) or (6)
(8) Catch-up contribution	6,000	Dave is 72 years old at year-end.
Maximum contribution	**$ 9,294**	(7) + (8), not to exceed (2)

Example 13-22

What if: Assume Dave (age 64) earned $400,000 of Schedule C net income. What is his maximum deductible contribution to his individual 401(k)?

Answer: $61,000, computed as follows:

Description	Amount	Explanation
(1) First limit on contribution	$ 55,000	
(2) Schedule C net income minus self-employment tax deduction	$386,683	$400,000 − {[(400,000 × .9235 − 128,400) × 2.9% × 50%] + [128,400 × 15.3% × 50%]}
(3) Percentage for limitation based on (2)	20%	
(4) Limit on employer's contribution	77,337	(2) × (3)
(5) Limit on employee's contribution	18,500	
(6) Second limitation	95,837	(4) + (5)
(7) Maximum contribution before catch-up contribution	55,000	Lesser of (1) or (6)
(8) Catch-up contribution	6,000	Dave is 64 years old at year-end.
Maximum contribution	**$ 61,000**	(7) + (8), not to exceed (2)

Nontax Considerations   As we mentioned above, the individual 401(k) plan is not available for sole proprietors with employees, so providing benefits to employees under the plan is not a concern. However, the administrative burden of establishing, operating, and maintaining a 401(k) plan is potentially higher than it is for the other self-employed plans.

LO 13-6

SAVER'S CREDIT

To encourage middle- and low-income taxpayers to take advantage of the retirement savings opportunities discussed in this chapter, Congress provides an additional saver's credit for an individual's elective contribution of up to $2,000 to any of the qualified retirement plans discussed in this chapter, including employer-sponsored qualified plans, traditional and Roth IRA plans, and self-employed qualified plans. The credit is provided *in addition to* any deduction the taxpayer is allowed for contributing to a retirement account. It is calculated by multiplying the taxpayer's contribution, up to a maximum of $2,000, by the applicable percentage depending on the taxpayer's filing status and AGI. The credit is nonrefundable. Exhibit 13-9 provides the applicable percentages for 2018 according to a taxpayer's filing status and AGI.[36]

EXHIBIT 13-9   2018 Applicable Percentages for Saver's Credit by Filing Status and AGI

Applicable Percentage	Joint Filers AGI	Heads of Household AGI	All Other Filers AGI
50%	0 to $38,000	0 to $28,500	0 to $19,000
20	$38,001 to $41,000	$28,501 to $30,750	$19,001 to $20,500
10	$41,001 to $63,000	$30,751 to $47,250	$20,501 to $31,500
No credit available	Above $63,000	Above $47,250	Above $31,500

In addition to restricting the credit to taxpayers with AGI below a certain threshold, the credit is also restricted to individuals who are 18 years of age or older, are not claimed as dependents by another taxpayer, and are not full-time students at a qualified educational organization during each of five calendar months of the taxpayer's tax year.[37] Although limited in scope, the saver's credit provides some tax benefits for those taxpayers who qualify.

Example 13-23

What if: Tina earned $24,000 during the year she began working for CBA. She earned $4,000 in salary working part-time while she was in school and $20,000 in salary working for CBA from September through December. To get an early start saving for retirement, assume she contributed $4,000 to a traditional IRA. Because Tina did not participate in an employer-sponsored retirement plan during the current year she may deduct the full $4,000 contribution as a *for* AGI deduction, reducing her AGI from $24,000 to $20,000. What amount of saver's credit, if any, is Tina allowed to claim, assuming she was a full-time student during four months of the year?

Answer: $400 ($2,000 × 20 percent applicable credit).

What if: What saver's credit may Tina claim if her AGI is $15,000?

Answer: $1,000 ($2,000 × 50 percent applicable credit).

CONCLUSION

The decisions that employees like Tina, Lisa, and Dave must deal with highlight the role that tax issues play in this important area. Employers, like their employees, must also pay careful attention to tax considerations when deciding on retirement savings vehicles to offer their employees. Further, as has been a recurring theme throughout this book, nontax issues play an equal, if not more important, role in the retirement savings decisions of both employees and employers.

---

[36]For this purpose, AGI is determined without considering the foreign-earned income exclusion provided for U.S. residents living abroad under §911.

[37]§152(f)(2).

Appendix A (Page 1) Traditional IRA Deduction Limitations

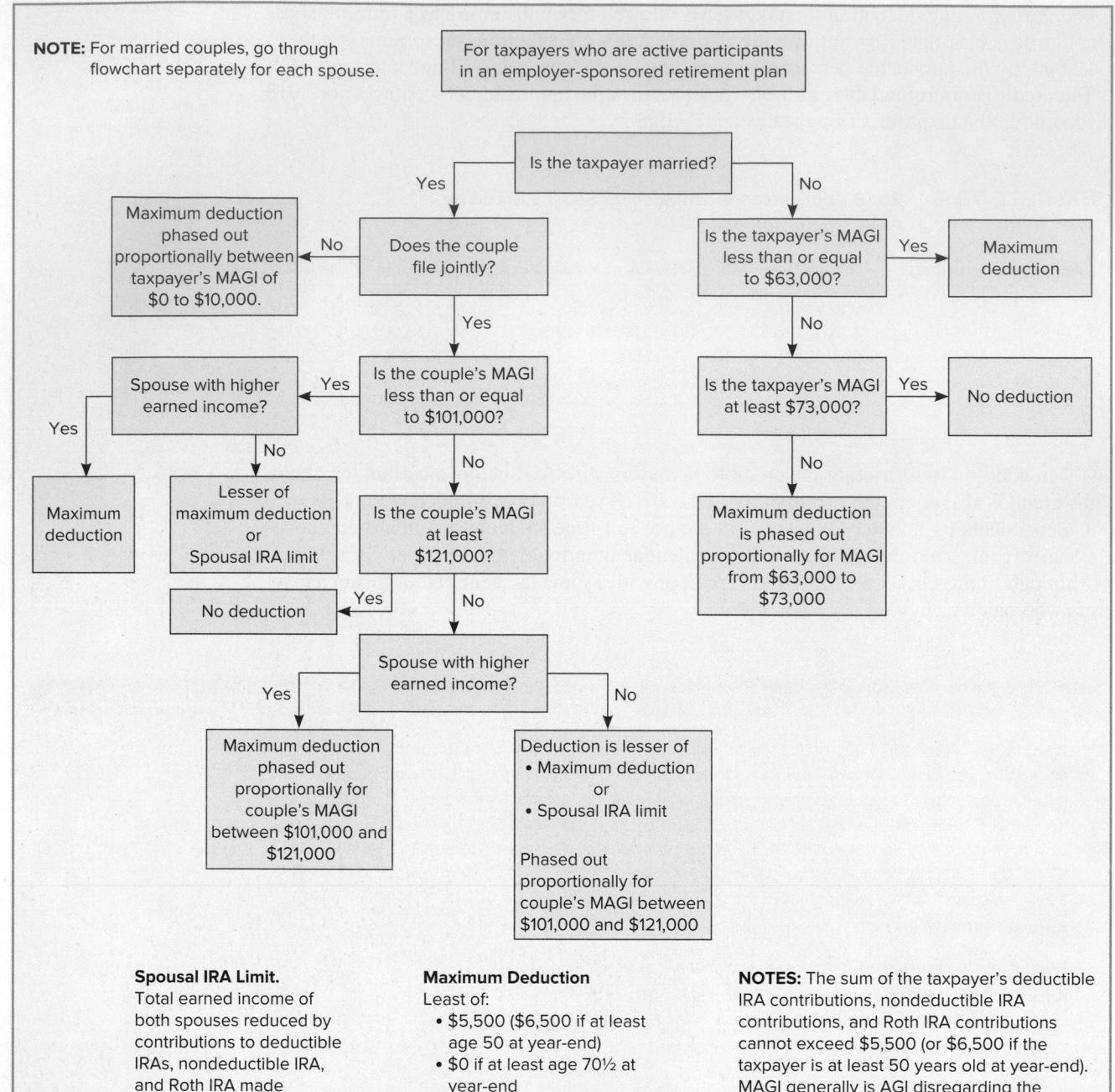

NOTE: For married couples, go through flowchart separately for each spouse.

For taxpayers who are active participants in an employer-sponsored retirement plan

Is the taxpayer married?

Yes → Does the couple file jointly?

No → Maximum deduction phased out proportionally between taxpayer's MAGI of $0 to $10,000.

Does the couple file jointly? **Yes** → Is the couple's MAGI less than or equal to $101,000?

Is the couple's MAGI less than or equal to $101,000? **Yes** → Spouse with higher earned income?

Spouse with higher earned income? **Yes** → Maximum deduction

Spouse with higher earned income? **No** → Lesser of maximum deduction or Spousal IRA limit

Is the couple's MAGI less than or equal to $101,000? **No** → Is the couple's MAGI at least $121,000?

Is the couple's MAGI at least $121,000? **Yes** → No deduction

Is the couple's MAGI at least $121,000? **No** → Spouse with higher earned income?

Spouse with higher earned income? **Yes** → Maximum deduction phased out proportionally for couple's MAGI between $101,000 and $121,000

Spouse with higher earned income? **No** → Deduction is lesser of
• Maximum deduction
or
• Spousal IRA limit

Phased out proportionally for couple's MAGI between $101,000 and $121,000

Is the taxpayer married? **No** → Is the taxpayer's MAGI less than or equal to $63,000?

Is the taxpayer's MAGI less than or equal to $63,000? **Yes** → Maximum deduction

Is the taxpayer's MAGI less than or equal to $63,000? **No** → Is the taxpayer's MAGI at least $73,000?

Is the taxpayer's MAGI at least $73,000? **Yes** → No deduction

Is the taxpayer's MAGI at least $73,000? **No** → Maximum deduction is phased out proportionally for MAGI from $63,000 to $73,000

Spousal IRA Limit.
Total earned income of both spouses reduced by contributions to deductible IRAs, nondeductible IRA, and Roth IRA made by higher-earning spouse.

Maximum Deduction
Least of:
• $5,500 ($6,500 if at least age 50 at year-end)
• $0 if at least age 70½ at year-end
• Taxpayer's earned income for year

NOTES: The sum of the taxpayer's deductible IRA contributions, nondeductible IRA contributions, and Roth IRA contributions cannot exceed $5,500 (or $6,500 if the taxpayer is at least 50 years old at year-end). MAGI generally is AGI disregarding the deduction for the IRA contribution itself.

(Page 2) Traditional IRA Deduction Limitations

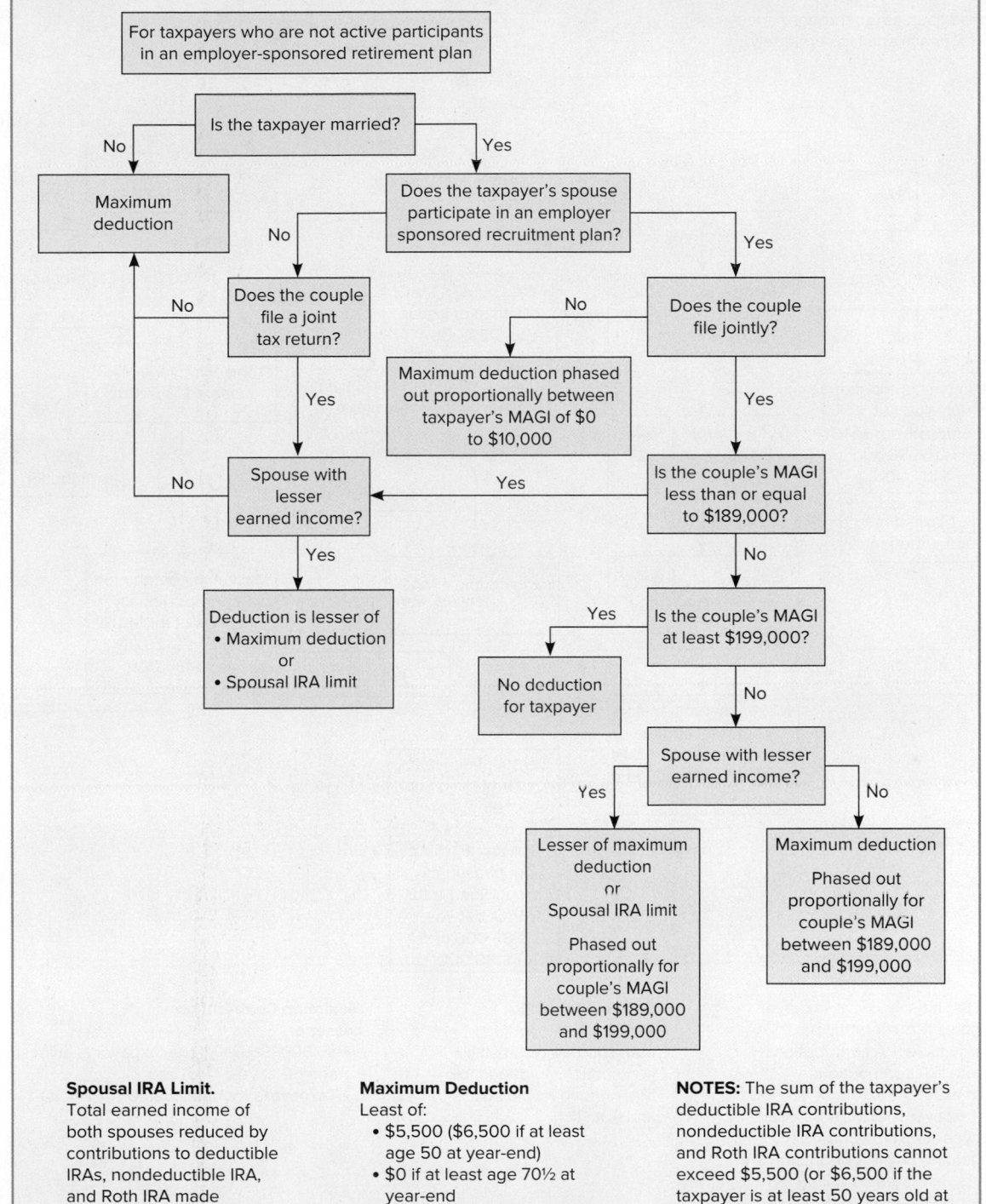

For taxpayers who are not active participants in an employer-sponsored retirement plan

Is the taxpayer married?

No → Maximum deduction

Yes → Does the taxpayer's spouse participate in an employer sponsored recruitment plan?

No → Does the couple file a joint tax return?

No → (to Maximum deduction)

Yes → Spouse with lesser earned income?

No → (to Maximum deduction)

Yes → Deduction is lesser of
• Maximum deduction
  or
• Spousal IRA limit

Does the couple file a joint tax return? No → Maximum deduction phased out proportionally between taxpayer's MAGI of $0 to $10,000

Does the taxpayer's spouse participate... Yes → Does the couple file jointly?

No → Maximum deduction phased out proportionally between taxpayer's MAGI of $0 to $10,000

Yes → Is the couple's MAGI less than or equal to $189,000?

Yes → Spouse with lesser earned income?

No → Is the couple's MAGI at least $199,000?

Yes → No deduction for taxpayer

No → Spouse with lesser earned income?

Yes → Lesser of maximum deduction
or
Spousal IRA limit

Phased out proportionally for couple's MAGI between $189,000 and $199,000

No → Maximum deduction

Phased out proportionally for couple's MAGI between $189,000 and $199,000

Spousal IRA Limit.
Total earned income of both spouses reduced by contributions to deductible IRAs, nondeductible IRA, and Roth IRA made by higher-earning spouse.

Maximum Deduction
Least of:
• $5,500 ($6,500 if at least age 50 at year-end)
• $0 if at least age 70½ at year-end
• Taxpayer's earned income for year

NOTES: The sum of the taxpayer's deductible IRA contributions, nondeductible IRA contributions, and Roth IRA contributions cannot exceed $5,500 (or $6,500 if the taxpayer is at least 50 years old at year-end). MAGI generally is AGI disregarding the deduction for the IRA contribution itself.

Appendix B Roth IRA Contribution Limits

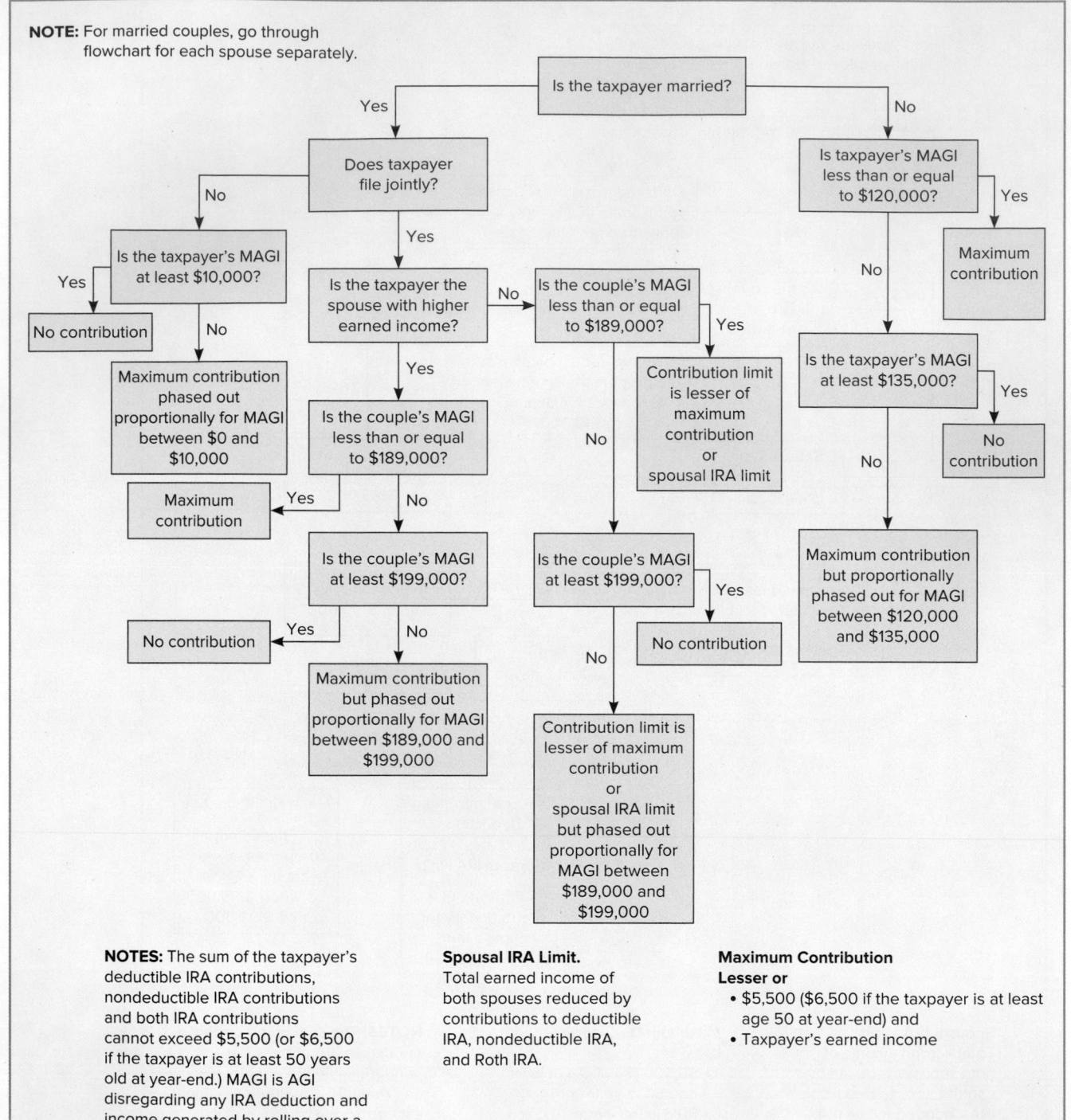

NOTE: For married couples, go through flowchart for each spouse separately.

NOTES: The sum of the taxpayer's deductible IRA contributions, nondeductible IRA contributions and both IRA contributions cannot exceed $5,500 (or $6,500 if the taxpayer is at least 50 years old at year-end.) MAGI is AGI disregarding any IRA deduction and income generated by rolling over a traditional IRA into a Roth IRA.

Spousal IRA Limit.
Total earned income of both spouses reduced by contributions to deductible IRA, nondeductible IRA, and Roth IRA.

Maximum Contribution
Lesser or
- $5,500 ($6,500 if the taxpayer is at least age 50 at year-end) and
- Taxpayer's earned income

Summary

Describe the tax and nontax aspects of employer-provided defined benefit plans from both the employer's and the employee's perspective.   **LO 13-1**

- Benefits are determined based on years of service and salary. The maximum annual benefit is capped and adjusted upward annually for inflation.
- Benefits vest over time using (at a minimum) either a five-year cliff or seven-year graded vesting schedule.
- Employers deduct cash contributions to fund the plan and employees treat cash distributions as ordinary income in the year received.
- Employers bear investment risk with defined benefit plans.
- Premature distribution and minimum distribution penalties don't typically apply to defined benefit distributions.
- Because of the high cost of funding and maintaining defined benefit plans, they are waning in popularity.

Explain and determine the tax consequences associated with employer-provided defined contribution plans, including traditional 401(k) and Roth 401(k) plans.   **LO 13-2**

- Employers specify the amount they will contribute to defined contribution plans instead of the annual benefit. However, employers are not permitted to contribute to Roth 401(k) plans.
- Employees may contribute to either a traditional 401(k) or a Roth 401(k) account, and they determine how employer and employee contributions are invested. Employees bear investment risk with defined contribution plans.
- Annual employer and employee contributions are limited and maximum contribution amounts are adjusted annually for inflation.
- Employer contributions to traditional plans vest over time using (at a minimum) either a three-year cliff or six-year graded vesting schedule.
- Employers deduct their contributions to traditional defined contribution plans.
- Employee contributions to traditional defined contribution plans are excluded from their taxable wages on Form W-2. Employee contributions to Roth 401(k) plans are not excluded.
- Distributions from traditional 401(k) plans are taxable at ordinary rates and qualified distributions from Roth 401(k) plans are not taxable.
- Distributions from both traditional 401(k) and Roth 401(k) plans are subject to premature and minimum distribution penalties.
- After-tax rates of return from Roth 401(k) plans are generally superior to those from traditional 401(k) plans when marginal tax rates are increasing.

Describe the tax implications of deferred compensation from both the employer's and the employee's perspective.   **LO 13-3**

- Employees elect to defer current salary in exchange for promised future payments from the employer.
- Because the employer's promise of future payment is unsecured, employees recognize ordinary income when future payments are received. Employers wait to deduct payments until cash is actually paid.
- The after-tax rate of return and costs from deferred compensation arrangements to employees and employers depend on the current and future marginal tax rates of both the employee and the employer.
- Deferred compensation can be used to overcome constraints imposed on employer contributions to an employee's qualified retirement account.
- Employees bear more risk with deferred compensation relative to other forms of retirement savings because employees are unsecured creditors of their employers and because the investments upon which their compensation is based have risk.

LO 13-4 Compare and determine the tax consequences of traditional and Roth IRAs (individual retirement accounts).

- The same inflation-adjusted annual contribution limits apply to both traditional IRAs and Roth IRAs.
- The deduction for traditional IRA contributions is phased out for taxpayers covered by a retirement plan at work and with AGI above certain inflation-adjusted amounts. Special rules pertain for spouses not covered by an employer plan.
- The ability to contribute to a Roth IRA is phased out for individuals with AGI above certain inflation-adjusted amounts.
- Distributions from traditional IRAs are taxed at ordinary rates. A 10 percent premature distribution penalty generally applies to distributions from traditional IRAs received before age 59½.
- Distributions from Roth IRAs received after a Roth IRA account has been open for at least five years and after the recipient reaches age 59½ are not taxable. The earnings component of any distributions not meeting these requirements is generally taxable and subject to the 10 percent premature distribution penalty.
- Taxpayers generally prefer Roth IRAs to traditional IRAs when they expect their marginal tax rates to increase.

LO 13-5 Describe retirement savings options for self-employed taxpayers and compute the limitations for deductible contributions to these accounts.

- Self-employed individuals may set up their own qualified pension plans such as SEP IRAs and individual 401(k) plans.
- Contribution limits generally parallel those for employer-sponsored plans, allowing self-employed individuals to have the same access to qualified plans that employees have.
- Self-employed individuals with employees may have to incur the cost of covering their employees when they establish a qualified retirement plan.

LO 13-6 Compute the saver's credit.

- Individuals may receive up to a $1,000 tax credit for contributions they make to IRAs and employer-sponsored qualified plans.
- The amount of the credit is a function of the taxpayer's filing status and AGI.

KEY TERMS

cliff vesting (13-4)
defined benefit plans (13-3)
defined contribution plans (13-3)
graded vesting (13-4)
individual retirement account (IRA) (13-19)

nonqualified deferred compensation (13-15)
qualified retirement plans (13-3)
rollover (13-25)
Roth 401(k) (13-11)
Roth IRA (13-19)

SEP IRA (13-27)
spousal IRA (13-21)
traditional 401(k) (13-11)
traditional IRA (13-19)
vesting (13-4)

DISCUSSION QUESTIONS

Discussion Questions are available in Connect®.

LO 13-1 **LO 13-2** 1. How are defined benefit plans different from defined contribution plans? How are they similar?

LO 13-1 2. Describe how an employee's benefit under a defined benefit plan is computed.

LO 13-1 **LO 13-2** 3. What does it mean to vest in a defined benefit or defined contribution plan?

LO 13-1 **LO 13-2** 4. Compare and contrast the minimum vesting requirements for defined benefit plans and defined contribution plans.

LO 13-1 **LO 13-2** 5. What are the nontax advantages and disadvantages of defined benefit plans relative to defined contribution plans?

6. Describe the maximum annual benefit that taxpayers may receive under defined benefit plans.   `LO 13-1`

7. Describe the distribution or payout options available to taxpayers participating in qualified defined benefit plans. How are defined benefit plan distributions to recipients taxed?   `LO 13-1`

8. Describe the minimum distribution requirements for defined benefit plans. Are these requirements typically an item of concern for taxpayers? Explain.   `LO 13-1` `LO 13-2`

9. Compare and contrast the employer's responsibilities for providing a defined benefit plan to employees relative to providing a defined contribution plan.   `LO 13-1` `LO 13-2`

10. Describe how an employee's benefit under a defined contribution plan is determined.   `LO 13-2`

11. Is there a limit to how much an employer and/or employee may contribute to an employee's defined contribution account(s) for the year? If so, describe the limit.   `LO 13-2`

12. Cami (age 52 and married) was recently laid off as part of her employer's reduction in workforce program. Cami's annual AGI was usually around $50,000. Shortly after Cami's employment was terminated, her employer distributed the balance of her employer-sponsored 401(k) account to her. What could Cami do to avoid being assessed the 10 percent early distribution penalty?   `LO 13-2`

13. When may employees begin to receive defined contribution plan distributions without penalty?   `LO 13-2`

14. Describe the circumstances under which distributions from defined contribution plans are penalized. What are the penalties?   `LO 13-2`

15. Brady Corporation has a profit-sharing plan that allocates 10 percent of all after-tax income to employees. The profit sharing is allocated to individual employees based on relative employee compensation. The profit-sharing contributions vest to employees under a six-year graded plan. If an employee terminates his or her employment before fully vesting, the plan allocates the forfeited amounts among the remaining participants according to their account balances. Is this forfeiture allocation policy discriminatory, and will it cause the plan to lose its qualified status? Use Rev. Rul. 81-10 to help formulate your answer.   `LO 13-2` **research**

16. What does it mean if an employer "matches" employee contributions to 401(k) plans?   `LO 13-2`

17. What nontax factor(s) should an employee consider when deciding whether and to what extent to participate in an employer's 401(k) plan?   `LO 13-2` **planning**

18. What are the differences between a traditional 401(k) and a Roth 401(k) plan?   `LO 13-2`

19. Can employers match employee contributions to Roth 401(k) plans? Explain.   `LO 13-2`

20. Describe the annual limitation on employer and employee contributions to traditional 401(k) and Roth 401(k) plans.   `LO 13-2`

21. When a company is limited by the tax laws in the amount it can contribute to an employee's 401(k) plan, what will it generally do to make the employee whole? Is this likely an issue for rank-and-file employees? Why or why not?   `LO 13-2` `LO 13-3`

22. From a tax perspective, how would taxpayers determine whether they should contribute to a traditional 401(k) or a Roth 401(k)?   `LO 13-2` **planning**

23. Could a taxpayer contributing to a traditional 401(k) plan earn an after-tax return *greater* than the before-tax return? Explain.   `LO 13-2`

24. Explain the *tax* similarities and differences between qualified defined contribution plans and nonqualified deferred compensation plans from an *employer's* perspective.   `LO 13-2` `LO 13-3`

25. Explain the *tax* similarities and differences between qualified defined contribution plans and nonqualified deferred compensation plans from an *employee's* perspective.   `LO 13-2` `LO 13-3`

LO 13-2 **LO 13-3** 26. Explain the *nontax* similarities and differences between qualified defined contribution plans and nonqualified deferred compensation plans from an *employer's* perspective.

LO 13-2 **LO 13-3** 27. Explain the *nontax* similarities and differences between qualified defined contribution plans and nonqualified deferred compensation plans from an *employee's* perspective.

LO 13-3 **planning** 28. From a *tax* perspective, what issues does an employee need to consider in deciding whether to defer compensation under a nonqualified deferred compensation plan or to receive it immediately?

LO 13-3 **planning** 29. From a *nontax* perspective, what issues does an employee need to consider in deciding whether to defer compensation under a nonqualified deferred compensation plan or to receive it immediately?

LO 13-3 30. What are reasons why companies provide nonqualified deferred compensation plans for certain employees?

LO 13-3 31. Are companies allowed to decide who can and cannot participate in nonqualified deferred compensation plans? Briefly explain.

LO 13-1 **LO 13-2** **LO 13-3** 32. How might the ultimate benefits to an employee who participates in a qualified retirement plan of a company differ from the ultimate benefits to an employee who participates in a nonqualified deferred compensation plan of the company if the company experiences bankruptcy before the employee is scheduled to receive the benefits?

LO 13-4 33. Deductions for traditional IRAs and contributions to Roth IRAs are phased out based on modified AGI (MAGI). In general terms, how does MAGI for purposes of determining the traditional IRA deduction differ from AGI and how does it differ from MAGI for purposes of determining whether a taxpayer can contribute to a Roth IRA?

LO 13-4 34. What are the primary tax differences between traditional IRAs and Roth IRAs?

planning **LO 13-4** 35. Describe the circumstances in which it would be more favorable for a taxpayer to contribute to a traditional IRA rather than a Roth IRA and vice versa.

LO 13-4 36. What are the requirements for a taxpayer to make a deductible contribution to a traditional IRA? Why do the tax laws impose these restrictions?

LO 13-4 37. What is the limitation on a deductible IRA contribution for 2018?

LO 13-4 38. Compare the minimum distribution requirements for traditional IRAs to those of Roth IRAs.

LO 13-4 39. How are qualified distributions from Roth IRAs taxed? How are nonqualified distributions taxed?

LO 13-4 40. Explain when a taxpayer will be subject to the 10 percent penalty when receiving distributions from a Roth IRA.

LO 13-4 41. Is a taxpayer who contributed to a traditional IRA able to transfer or "roll over" the money into a Roth IRA? If yes, explain the tax consequences of the transfer.

LO 13-4 42. Assume a taxpayer makes a nondeductible contribution to a traditional IRA. How does the taxpayer determine the taxability of distributions from the IRA on reaching retirement?

LO 13-4 43. When a taxpayer receives a nonqualified distribution from a Roth IRA, is the entire amount of the distribution treated as taxable income?

LO 13-5 44. What types of retirement plans are available to self-employed taxpayers?

LO 13-5 45. Compare and contrast the annual limitations on deductible contributions to SEP IRAs and individual 401(k) accounts for self-employed taxpayers.

planning **LO 13-5** 46. What are the nontax considerations for self-employed taxpayers deciding whether to set up a SEP IRA or an individual 401(k)?

LO 13-6 47. What is the saver's credit and who is eligible to receive it?

LO 13-6 48. What is the maximum saver's credit available to taxpayers? What taxpayer characteristics are relevant to the determination?

LO 13-6 49. How is the saver's credit computed?

PROBLEMS

Select problems are available in Connect®.

50. Javier recently graduated and started his career with DNL Inc. DNL provides a defined benefit plan to all employees. According to the terms of the plan, for each full year of service working for the employer, employees receive a benefit of 1.5 percent of their average salary over their highest three years of compensation from the company. Employees may accrue only 30 years of benefit under the plan (45 percent). Determine Javier's annual benefit on retirement, before taxes, under each of the following scenarios:

    a) Javier works for DNL for three years and three months before he leaves for another job. Javier's annual salary was $55,000, $65,000, $70,000, and $72,000 for years 1, 2, 3, and 4, respectively. DNL uses a five-year cliff vesting schedule.

    b) Javier works for DNL for three years and three months before he leaves for another job. Javier's annual salary was $55,000, $65,000, $70,000, and $72,000 for years 1, 2, 3, and 4, respectively. DNL uses a seven-year graded vesting schedule.

    c) Javier works for DNL for six years and three months before he leaves for another job. Javier's annual salary was $75,000, $85,000, $90,000, and $95,000 for years 4, 5, 6, and 7, respectively. DNL uses a five-year cliff vesting schedule.

    d) Javier works for DNL for six years and three months before he leaves for another job. Javier's annual salary was $75,000, $85,000, $90,000, and $95,000 for years 4, 5, 6, and 7, respectively. DNL uses a seven-year graded vesting schedule.

    e) Javier works for DNL for 32 years and three months before retiring. Javier's annual salary was $175,000, $185,000, $190,000, and $195,000 (note that he didn't work for the entire year in the year he retired so he received only a portion of the annual salary in the year he retired) for his final four years of employment.

51. Alicia has been working for JMM Corp. for 32 years. Alicia participates in JMM's defined benefit plan. Under the plan, for every year of service for JMM she is to receive 2 percent of the average salary of her three highest years of compensation from JMM. She retired on January 1, 2018. Before retirement, her annual salary was $570,000, $600,000, and $630,000 for 2015, 2016, and 2017. What is the maximum benefit Alicia can receive in 2018?

52. Tim has worked for one employer his entire career. While he was working, he participated in the employer's defined contribution plan [traditional 401(k)]. At the end of 2018, Tim retires. The balance in his defined contribution plan is $2,000,000 at the end of 2017.

 tax forms

    a) What is Tim's minimum required distribution for 2018 in 2019 if he is 68 years old at the end of 2018?

    b) What is Tim's minimum required distribution for 2018 if he turns 70½ during 2018 and he has not turned 71 years old by the end of 2018? When must he receive this distribution?

    c) What is Tim's minimum required distribution for 2018 in 2019 if he is 73 years old at the end of 2018?

    d) Assuming that Tim is 75 years old at the end of 2018 and his marginal tax rate is 32 percent, what amount of his distribution will he have remaining after taxes if he receives only a distribution of $50,000 for 2018?

    e) Complete Form 5329, page 2, to report the minimum distribution penalty in part (d). Use the most recent form available.

53. Matthew (48 at year-end) develops cutting-edge technology for SV Inc., located in Silicon Valley. In 2018, Matthew participates in SV's money purchase pension plan

LO 13-1

LO 13-1

LO 13-2

LO 13-2

(a defined contribution plan) and in his company's 401(k) plan. Under the money purchase pension plan, SV contributes 15 percent of an employee's salary to a retirement account for the employee up to the amount limited by the tax code. Because it provides the money purchase pension plan, SV does not contribute to the employee's 401(k) plan. Matthew would like to maximize his contribution to his 401(k) account after SV's contribution to the money purchase plan.

a) Assuming Matthew's annual salary is $400,000, what amount will SV contribute to Matthew's money purchase plan? What can Matthew contribute to his 401(k) account in 2018?

b) Assuming Matthew's annual salary is $240,000, what amount will SV contribute to Matthew's money purchase plan? What can Matthew contribute to his 401(k) account in 2018?

c) Assuming Matthew's annual salary is $60,000, what amount will SV contribute to Matthew's money purchase plan? What amount can Matthew contribute to his 401(k) account in 2018?

d) Assume the same facts as part (c), except that Matthew is 54 years old at the end of 2018. What amount can Matthew contribute to his 401(k) account in 2018?

LO 13-2

54. In 2018, Maggy (34 years old) is an employee of YBU Corp. YBU provides a 401(k) plan for all its employees. According to the terms of the plan, YBU contributes 50 cents for every dollar the employee contributes. The maximum employer contribution under the plan is 15 percent of the employee's salary (if allowed, YBU contributes until the employee has contributed 30 percent of her salary).

a) Maggy worked for YBU Corporation for 3½ years before deciding to leave effective July 1, 2018. Maggy's annual salary during this time was $45,000, $52,000, $55,000, and $60,000 (she only received half of her $60,000 2018 salary). Assuming Maggy contributed 8 percent of her salary (including her 2018 salary) to her 401(k) account, what is Maggy's vested account balance when she leaves YBU (exclusive of account earnings)? Assume YBU uses three-year cliff vesting.

b) Same question as part (a), except YBU uses six-year graded vesting.

c) Maggy wants to maximize YBU's contribution to her 401(k) account in 2018. How much should Maggy contribute to her 401(k) account assuming her annual salary is $100,000 (she works for YBU for the entire year)?

d) Same question as part (c), except Maggy is 55 years old rather than 34 years old at the end of the year.

LO 13-2

55. In 2018, Nina contributes 10 percent of her $100,000 annual salary to her 401(k) account. She expects to earn a 7 percent before-tax rate of return. Assuming she leaves this (and any employer contributions) in the account until she retires in 25 years, what is Nina's after-tax accumulation from her 2018 contributions to her 401(k) account?

a) Assume Nina's marginal tax rate at retirement is 30 percent.

b) Assume Nina's marginal tax rate at retirement is 20 percent.

c) Assume Nina's marginal tax rate at retirement is 40 percent.

LO 13-2

56. Kathleen, age 56, works for MH, Inc., in Dallas, Texas. Kathleen contributes to a Roth 401(k) and MH contributes to a traditional 401(k) on her behalf. Kathleen has contributed $30,000 to her Roth 401(k) over the past six years. The current balance in her Roth 401(k) account is $50,000 and the balance in her traditional 401(k) is $40,000. Kathleen needs cash because she is taking a month of vacation to travel the world. Answer the following questions relating to distributions from

Kathleen's retirement accounts assuming her marginal tax rate for ordinary income is 24 percent.

a) If Kathleen receives a $10,000 distribution from her traditional 401(k) account, how much will she be able to keep after paying taxes and penalties, if any, on the distribution?

b) If Kathleen receives a $10,000 distribution from her Roth 401(k) account, how much will she be able to keep after paying taxes and penalties, if any, on the distribution?

c) If Kathleen retires from MH and then she receives a $10,000 distribution from her traditional 401(k), how much will she be able to keep after paying taxes and penalties, if any, on the distribution?

d) If Kathleen retires from MH and then she receives a $10,000 distribution from her Roth 401(k), how much will she be able to keep after paying taxes and penalties, if any, on the distribution?

e) Assume the original facts except that Kathleen is 60 years of age, not 56. If Kathleen receives a $10,000 distribution from her Roth 401(k) (without retiring), how much will she be able to keep after paying taxes and penalties, if any, on the distribution?

57. In 2018, Nitai (age 40) contributes 10 percent of his $100,000 annual salary to a Roth 401(k) account sponsored by his employer, AY Inc. AY Inc. matches employee contributions to the employee's traditional 401(k) account dollar-for-dollar up to 10 percent of the employee's salary. Nitai expects to earn a 7 percent before-tax rate of return. Assume he leaves the contributions in the Roth 401(k) and traditional 401(k) accounts until he retires in 25 years and that he makes no additional contributions to either account. What are Nitai's after-tax proceeds from the Roth 401(k) and traditional 401(k) accounts after he receives the distributions, assuming his marginal tax rate at retirement is 30 percent? `LO 13-2`

58. Marissa participates in her employer's nonqualified deferred compensation plan. For 2018, she is deferring 10 percent of her $320,000 annual salary. Assuming this is her only source of income and her marginal income tax rate is 32 percent, how much *tax* does Marissa save in 2018 by deferring this income (ignore payroll taxes)? `LO 13-3` `planning`

59. Paris participates in her employer's nonqualified deferred compensation plan. For 2018, she is deferring 10 percent of her $320,000 annual salary. Assuming this is her only source of income and her marginal income tax rate is 32 percent, how much does deferring Paris's income save her employer (after taxes) in 2018? The marginal tax rate of her employer is 21 percent (ignore payroll taxes). `LO 13-3`

60. Leslie participates in IBO's nonqualified deferred compensation plan. For 2018, she is deferring 10 percent of her $300,000 annual salary. Based on her deemed investment choice, Leslie expects to earn a 7 percent before-tax rate of return on her deferred compensation, which she plans to receive in 10 years. Leslie's marginal tax rate in 2018 is 32 percent. IBO's marginal tax rate is 21 percent (ignore payroll taxes in your analysis). `LO 13-3` `planning`

a) Assuming Leslie's marginal tax rate in 10 years (when she receives the distribution) is 33 percent, what is Leslie's after-tax accumulation on the deferred compensation?

b) Assuming Leslie's marginal tax rate in 10 years (when she receives the distribution) is 20 percent, what is Leslie's after-tax accumulation on the deferred compensation?

c) Assuming IBO's cost of capital is 8 percent after taxes, how much deferred compensation should IBO be willing to pay Leslie that would make it indifferent between paying 10 percent of Leslie's current salary or deferring it for 10 years?

LO 13-3

planning

61. XYZ Corporation has a deferred compensation plan under which it allows certain employees to defer up to 40 percent of their salary for five years. For purposes of this problem, ignore payroll taxes in your computations.

   a) Assume XYZ has a marginal tax rate of 21 percent for the foreseeable future and earns an after-tax rate of return of 8 percent on its assets. Joel Johnson, XYZ's VP of finance, is attempting to determine what amount of deferred compensation XYZ should be willing to pay in five years that would make XYZ indifferent between paying the current salary of $10,000 and paying the deferred compensation. What amount of deferred compensation would accomplish this objective?

   b) Assume Julie, an XYZ employee, has the option of participating in XYZ's deferred compensation plan. Julie's marginal tax rate is 37 percent and she expects the rate to remain constant over the next five years. Julie is trying to decide how much deferred compensation she will need to receive from XYZ in five years to make her indifferent between receiving the current salary of $10,000 and receiving the deferred compensation payment. If Julie takes the salary, she will invest it in a taxable corporate bond paying interest at 5 percent annually (after taxes). What amount of deferred compensation would accomplish this objective?

LO 13-4

62. John (age 51 and single) has earned income of $3,000. He has $30,000 of unearned (capital gain) income.

   a) If he does not participate in an employer-sponsored plan, what is the maximum deductible IRA contribution John can make in 2018?

   b) If he does participate in an employer-sponsored plan, what is the maximum deductible IRA contribution John can make in 2018?

   c) If he does not participate in an employer-sponsored plan, what is the maximum deductible IRA contribution John can make in 2018 if he has earned income of $10,000?

LO 13-4

63. William is a single writer (age 35) who recently decided that he needs to save more for retirement. His 2018 AGI before the IRA contribution deduction is $66,000 (all earned income).

   a) If he does not participate in an employer-sponsored plan, what is the maximum deductible IRA contribution William can make in 2018?

   b) If he does participate in an employer-sponsored plan, what is the maximum deductible IRA contribution William can make in 2018?

   c) Assuming the same facts as in part (b), except his AGI before the IRA contribution deduction is $76,000, what is the maximum deductible IRA contribution William can make in 2018?

LO 13-4

64. In 2018, Susan (44 years old) is a highly successful architect and is covered by an employee-sponsored plan. Her husband, Dan (47 years old), however, is a Ph.D. student and unemployed. Compute the maximum deductible IRA contribution for each spouse in the following alternative situations.

   a) Susan's salary and the couple's AGI before any IRA contribution deductions is $193,000. The couple files a joint tax return.

   b) Susan's salary and the couple's AGI before any IRA contribution deductions is $123,000. The couple files a joint tax return.

   c) Susan's salary and the couple's AGI before any IRA contribution deductions is $83,000. The couple files a joint tax return.

   d) Susan's salary and her AGI before the IRA contribution deduction is $83,000. Dan reports $5,000 of AGI before the IRA contribution deduction (earned income). The couple files separate tax returns.

LO 13-4

tax forms

65. In 2018, Rashaun (62 years old) retired and planned on immediately receiving distributions (making withdrawals) from his traditional IRA account. The balance of his IRA account is $160,000 (before reducing it for withdrawals/distributions

described below). Over the years, Rashaun has contributed $40,000 to the IRA. Of his $40,000 contributions, $30,000 was *nondeductible* and $10,000 was *deductible*. Assume Rashaun did not make any contributions to the account during 2018.

a) If Rashaun currently withdraws $20,000 from the IRA, how much tax will he be required to pay on the withdrawal if his marginal tax rate is 24 percent?

b) If Rashaun currently withdraws $70,000 from the IRA, how much tax will he be required to pay on the withdrawal if his marginal tax rate is 28 percent?

c) Using the information provided in part (b), complete Form 8606, Part I, to report the taxable portion of the $70,000 distribution (withdrawal). Use the most current form available.

66. Brooklyn has been contributing to a traditional IRA for seven years (all deductible contributions) and has a total of $30,000 in the account. In 2018, she is 39 years old and has decided that she wants to get a new car. She withdraws $20,000 from the IRA to help pay for the car. She is currently in the 24 percent marginal tax bracket. What amount of the withdrawal, after tax considerations, will Brooklyn have available to purchase the car? `LO 13-4`

67. Jackson and Ashley Turner (both 45 years old) are married and want to contribute to a Roth IRA for Ashley. In 2018, their AGI is $191,000. Jackson and Ashley each earned half of the income. `LO 13-4`

a) How much can Ashley contribute to her Roth IRA if they file a joint return?

b) How much can Ashley contribute if she files a separate return?

c) Assume that Ashley earned all of the couple's income and that she contributed the maximum amount she is allowed to contribute to a Roth IRA. What amount can be contributed to Jackson's Roth IRA?

68. Harriet and Harry Combs (both 37 years old) are married and both want to contribute to a Roth IRA. In 2018, their AGI before any IRA contribution deductions is $50,000. Harriet earned $46,000 and Harry earned $4,000. `LO 13-4`

a) How much can Harriet contribute to her Roth IRA if they file a joint return?

b) How much can Harriet contribute if she files a separate return?

c) How much can Harry contribute to his Roth IRA if they file separately?

69. Michael is single and 35 years old. He is a participant in his employer's sponsored retirement plan. How much can Michael contribute to a Roth IRA in each of the following alternative situations? `LO 13-4`

a) Michael's AGI before the IRA contribution deduction is $50,000. Michael contributed $3,000 to a traditional IRA.

b) Michael's AGI is $80,000 before any IRA contributions.

c) Michael's AGI is $135,000 before any IRA contributions.

70. George (age 42 at year-end) has been contributing to a traditional IRA for years (all deductible contributions) and his IRA is now worth $25,000. He is planning on transferring (or rolling over) the entire balance into a Roth IRA account. George's marginal tax rate is 24 percent. `LO 13-4`

a) What are the tax consequences to George if he takes $25,000 out of the traditional IRA and puts the entire amount into a Roth IRA?

b) What are the tax consequences to George if he takes $25,000 out of the traditional IRA, pays the taxes due from the IRA distribution, and contributes the remaining distribution to the Roth IRA?

c) What are the tax consequences to George if he takes $25,000 out of the traditional IRA, keeps $10,000 to pay taxes and to make a down payment on a new car, and contributes the remaining distribution to the Roth IRA?

71. Jimmer has contributed $15,000 to his Roth IRA and the balance in the account is $18,000. In the current year, Jimmer withdrew $17,000 from the Roth IRA to pay `LO 13-4`

for a new car. If Jimmer's marginal ordinary income tax rate is 24 percent, what amount of tax and penalty, if any, is Jimmer required to pay on the withdrawal in each of the following alternative situations?

a) Jimmer opened the Roth account 44 months before he withdrew the $17,000 and Jimmer is 62 years of age.

b) Jimmer opened the Roth account 44 months before he withdrew the $17,000 and Jimmer is age 53.

c) Jimmer opened the Roth account 76 months before he withdrew the $17,000 and Jimmer is age 62.

d) Jimmer opened the Roth account 76 months before he withdrew the $17,000 and Jimmer is age 53.

LO 13-4

planning

72. John is trying to decide whether to contribute to a Roth IRA or a traditional IRA. He plans on making a $5,000 contribution to whichever plan he decides to fund. He currently pays tax at a 32 percent marginal income tax rate but he believes that his marginal tax rate in the future will be 28 percent. He intends to leave the money in the Roth IRA or traditional IRA accounts for 30 years and he expects to earn a 6 percent before-tax rate of return on the account.

a) How much will John accumulate after taxes if he contributes to a Roth IRA (consider only the funds contributed to the Roth IRA)?

b) How much will John accumulate after taxes if he contributes to a traditional IRA (consider only the funds contributed to the Roth IRA)?

c) Without doing any computations, explain whether the traditional IRA or the Roth IRA will generate a greater after-tax rate of return.

LO 13-4

73. Sherry, who is 52 years of age, opened a Roth IRA three years ago. She has contributed a total of $12,000 to the Roth IRA ($4,000 a year). The current value of the Roth IRA is $16,300. In the current year, Sherry withdraws $14,000 of the account balance to purchase a car. Assuming Sherry's marginal tax rate is 24 percent, how much of the $14,000 withdrawal will she retain after taxes to fund her car purchase?

LO 13-4

74. Seven years ago, Halle (currently age 41) contributed $4,000 to a Roth IRA account. The current value of the Roth IRA is $9,000. In the current year Halle withdraws $8,000 of the account balance to use as a down payment on her first home. Assuming Halle's marginal tax rate is 24 percent, how much of the $8,000 withdrawal will she retain after taxes to fund her house down payment?

LO 13-4

research

planning

75. Yuki (age 45 at year-end) has been contributing to a traditional IRA for years (all deductible contributions), and her IRA is now worth $50,000. She is trying to decide whether she should roll over her traditional IRA into a Roth IRA. Her current marginal tax rate is 24 percent. She plans to withdraw the entire balance of the account in 20 years and she expects to earn a before-tax rate of return of 5 percent on her retirement accounts and a 4 percent after-tax rate of return on all investments outside of her retirement accounts. For each of the following alternative scenarios, indicate how much more or less Yuki will accumulate after taxes in 20 years if she rolls over her traditional IRA into a Roth IRA. Be sure to include the opportunity cost of having to pay taxes on the rollover.

a) When she withdraws the retirement funds in 20 years, she expects her marginal tax rate to be 35 percent.

b) When she withdraws the retirement funds in 20 years, she expects her marginal tax rate to be 18 percent.

c) Assume the same facts as in part (b), except that she earns a 3 percent after-tax rate of return on investments outside of the retirement accounts.

d) In general terms, reconcile your answer from part (b) with your answer to part (c) (no numbers required).

76. Sarah was contemplating making a contribution to her traditional individual retirement account for 2018. She determined that she would contribute $5,500 to her IRA and she deducted $5,500 for the contribution when she completed and filed her 2018 tax return on February 15, 2019. Two months later, on April 15, Sarah realized that she had not yet actually contributed the funds to her IRA. On April 15, she went to the post office and mailed a $5,500 (for all) check to the bank holding her IRA. The bank received the payment on April 18. In which year is Sarah's $5,500 contribution deductible?   `LO 13-4` `research`

77. Elvira is a self-employed taxpayer who turns 42 years old at the end of the year (2018). In 2018, her net Schedule C income was $130,000. This was her only source of income. This year, Elvira is considering setting up a retirement plan. What is the maximum amount Elvira may contribute to the self-employed plan in each of the following situations?   `LO 13-5` `planning`

     a) She sets up a SEP IRA.

     b) She sets up an individual 401(k).

78. Hope is a self-employed taxpayer who turns 54 years old at the end of the year (2018). In 2018, her net Schedule C income was $130,000. This was her only source of income. This year, Hope is considering setting up a retirement plan. What is the maximum amount Hope may contribute to the self-employed plan in each of the following situations?   `LO 13-5` `planning`

     a) She sets up a SEP IRA.

     b) She sets up an individual 401(k).

79. Rita is a self-employed taxpayer who turns 39 years old at the end of the year (2018). In 2018, her net Schedule C income was $300,000. This was her only source of income. This year, Rita is considering setting up a retirement plan. What is the maximum amount Rita may contribute to the self-employed plan in each of the following situations?   `LO 13-5`

     a) She sets up a SEP IRA.

     b) She sets up an individual 401(k).

80. Reggie is a self-employed taxpayer who turns 59 years old at the end of the year (2018). In 2018, his net Schedule C income was $300,000. This was his only source of income. This year, Reggie is considering setting up a retirement plan. What is the maximum amount he may contribute to the self-employed plan in each of the following situations?   `LO 13-5`

     a) He sets up a SEP IRA.

     b) He sets up an individual 401(k).

81. Desmond is 25 years old and he participates in his employer's 401(k) plan. During the year, he contributed $3,000 to his 401(k) account. What is Desmond's saver's credit in each of the following alternative scenarios?   `LO 13-6`

     a) Desmond is not married and has no dependents. His AGI after deducting his 401(k) contribution is $34,000.

     b) Desmond is not married and has no dependents. His AGI after deducting his 401(k) contribution is $17,500.

     c) Desmond files as a head of household and has an AGI of $44,000.

     d) Desmond and his wife file jointly and report an AGI of $30,000 for the year.

82. Penny is 57 years old and she participates in her employer's 401(k) plan. During the year, she contributed $2,000 to her 401(k) account. Penny's AGI is $29,000 after deducting her 401(k) contribution. What is Penny's saver's credit in each of the following alternative scenarios?   `LO 13-6`

     a) Penny is not married and has no dependents.

     b) Penny files as a head of household and she has three dependents.

c) Penny files as a head of household and she has one dependent.

d) Penny is married and files a joint return with her husband. They have three dependents.

e) Penny files a separate tax return from her husband. She claims two dependent children on her return.

COMPREHENSIVE PROBLEMS

Select problems are available in Connect®.

83. Jacquiline is unmarried and age 32. Even though she participates in an employer-sponsored retirement plan, Jacquiline contributed $3,000 to a traditional IRA during the year. Jacquiline files as a head of household, her AGI before the contribution is $43,000, and her marginal tax rate is 12 percent. What is the after-tax cost of her $3,000 traditional IRA contribution?

84. Ian retired in June 2017 at the age of 69 (he turned 70 in August 2017). Ian's retirement account was valued at $490,000 at the end of 2016 and $500,000 at the end of 2017. He has had all of his retirement accounts open for 15 years. What is Ian's required minimum distribution for 2018 under each of the following alternative scenarios?

a) Ian's retirement account is a traditional 401(k) account.

b) Ian's retirement account is a Roth 401(k) account.

c) Ian's retirement account is a traditional IRA.

d) Ian's retirement account is a Roth IRA.

85. Alex is 31 years old and has lived in Los Alamos, New Mexico, for the last four years where he works at the Los Alamos National Laboratory (LANL). LANL provides employees with a 401(k) plan and for every $1 an employee contributes (up to 9 percent of the employee's salary) LANL contributes $3 (a 3-to-1 match). The plan provides a six-year graded vesting schedule. Alex is now in his fifth year working for LANL, and his current year salary is $170,000. Alex's marginal tax rate is 24 percent in 2018. Answer the following questions relating to Alex's retirement savings in 2018.

a) Assume that over the past four years, Alex has contributed $45,000 to his 401(k) and his employer has contributed $115,000 to the plan. The plan has an account balance of $175,000. What is Alex's vested account balance in his 401(k)?

b) Because Alex considers his employer's matching contributions "free money," he wants to maximize the amount of LANL's contributions. What is the least amount Alex can contribute and still maximize LANL's contribution?

c) In need of cash to build a home theater, Alex withdrew $30,000 from his traditional 401(k) account. What amount of the withdrawal, after taxes and penalties, will Alex have available to complete his project?

d) Assume that Alex contributes $10,000 to his traditional 401(k) account this year. Also assume that in 30 years, Alex retires (at age 61) and withdraws the $10,000 contribution made this year *and* all the earnings generated by the contribution. Also assume that his marginal tax rate at the time he retires is 25 percent. Ignore any prior or subsequent contributions to his plan. If Alex earns a 6 percent annual before-tax rate of return, what are his after-tax proceeds from the distribution?

e) Assume that Alex is 74 years old at the end of the year, retired, and that his marginal tax rate is 25 percent. His account balance in his traditional 401(k) was $1,250,000 at the end of last year. What is the minimum distribution Alex must receive from his 401(k) account for this year? If Alex receives a $43,000 distribution from his 401(k) account (his only distribution during the year), what amount will he be able to keep after taxes and penalties (if any)?

86. Tommy (age 47) and his wife, Michelle (age 49), live in Columbus, Ohio, where Tommy works for Callahan Auto Parts (CAP) as the vice president of the brakes division. Tommy's 2018 salary is $360,000. CAP allows Tommy to participate in its nonqualified deferred compensation plan in which participants can defer 15 percent of their salary for five years. Tommy also participates in CAP's qualified 401(k) plan. Tommy's current marginal tax rate is 24 percent and CAP's current marginal tax rate is 21 percent.

a) Assuming Tommy earns a 6 percent *after-tax* rate of return and he expects his marginal tax rate to be 30 percent in five years, what before-tax deferred compensation payment in five years would make him indifferent between receiving the deferred compensation payment or 15 percent of his salary now (ignore payroll taxes)?

b) Assuming CAP has an 8 percent *after-tax* rate of return and expects its marginal tax rate to be 35 percent in five years, how much would it be willing to pay in five years to be indifferent between paying the deferred compensation or paying 15 percent of Tommy's salary now (ignore payroll taxes)?

c) Will Tommy and CAP be able to come to an agreement on deferring Tommy's salary?

d) Assume that Tommy and Michelle have an AGI of $105,000 before IRA deductions by either spouse. The AGI includes $10,000 that Michelle earned working part-time (but she does not participate in an employer-sponsored retirement plan). Tommy and Michelle file a joint return. What is the maximum deductible contribution Tommy and Michelle may make to a traditional IRA?

c) Tommy has a balance of $55,000 in his traditional IRA. Due to some recent tax cuts, his marginal tax rate is 22 percent, so he would like to roll his traditional IRA into a Roth IRA. What are the tax consequences to Tommy if he takes $55,000 out of the IRA, pays the taxes due from the traditional IRA distribution, and contributes the remaining distribution to the Roth IRA?

87. Gerry (age 56) and Elaine (age 54) have been married for 12 years and file a joint tax return. The couple lives in an apartment in downtown Manhattan. Gerry's father, Mortey, recently retired from Del Boca Vista Corporation (DBVC), where he worked for many years. Mortey participated in DBVC's defined benefit plan. Elaine is an editor and works for Pendent Publishing earning an annual $150,000 salary in 2018. Gerry is a self-employed stand-up comedian and had net business income of $46,000 in 2018. At the advice of their neighbor, Gerry and Elaine have come to you for help in answering several retirement savings-related questions.

a) The DBVC defined benefit plan specifies a benefit of 1.5 percent for each year of service, up to a maximum of 30 percent (20 years of service), of the average of the employee's three highest years of salary. Mortey worked for the company for 25 years and earned $75,000, $78,000, and $84,000 over his final three years of service. What is Mortey's annual benefit from DBVC's defined benefit plan?

b) Elaine has worked at Pendent Publishing since January 1, 2013. The company offers a defined contribution plan. It matches 100 percent of employee contributions to the plan up to 6 percent of her salary. Prior to 2018, Elaine had contributed $40,000 to the plan and her employer had contributed $28,000 to the plan. In 2018, Elaine contributed $17,000 to her traditional 401(k). What is the amount of her employer's matching contribution for 2018? Assuming the company uses a six-year graded vesting schedule, what is Elaine's vested balance in the plan at the end of 2018? (For simplicity, disregard the plan's earnings.)

c) Elaine tells you that her employer has offered her $30,000 in 10 years to defer 10 percent of her current salary (defer $15,000). Assuming that the couple's marginal tax rate is currently 32 percent, they earn an after-tax rate of return of 8 percent, and they expect their marginal tax rate to be 28 percent in 10 years, should Elaine accept her company's offer? What is the minimum amount she should be willing to accept (ignoring nontax factors and payroll taxes)?

d) Gerry has a SEP IRA and would like to contribute as much as possible to this account. What is the maximum contribution Gerry can make to his SEP IRA in 2018?

e) Assuming Gerry had an individual 401(k), what is the maximum amount he could contribute to the plan in 2018?

f) Gerry also has a traditional IRA with an account balance of $42,000. He would like to convert the traditional IRA to a Roth IRA. Gerry would like to pay the least amount of tax possible in rolling the account over. Assume the couple's marginal tax rate is 32 percent. What is the least amount of tax Gerry will be required to pay on the rollover?

g) Assume that Gerry rolled over his traditional IRA into a Roth IRA six years ago (rather than in 2018) and that the account now has a balance of $78,000. The couple is considering buying their first home and would like to pay as much down as possible. They have heard from their friends that they can take the funds from their Roth IRA and use it to buy their first home. Are their friends correct? What would you advise them to do?

h) Assume that Gerry and Elaine made total contributions of $20,000 to their qualified retirement accounts in 2018. Also assume that their AGI is $40,500. What would be the amount of their saver's credit for 2018?

ROGER | *CPA Review*

Sample CPA Exam questions from Roger CPA Review are available in Connect as support for the topics in this text. These Multiple Choice Questions and Task-Based Simulations include expert-written explanations and solutions and provide a starting point for students to become familiar with the content and functionality of the actual CPA Exam.

chapter
14
Tax Consequences of Home Ownership

Learning Objectives

Upon completing this chapter, you should be able to:

LO 14-1 Determine whether a home is considered a principal residence, a residence (not principal), or a nonresidence for tax purposes.

LO 14-2 Compute the taxable gain on the sale of a residence.

LO 14-3 Determine the amount of the home mortgage interest deduction.

LO 14-4 Discuss the deductibility of real property taxes.

LO 14-5 Explain the tax issues and consequences associated with rental use of the home.

LO 14-6 Compute the limitations on home office deductions.

©Spotmatik/Alamy Stock Photo

Storyline Summary

Taxpayers:	Tyler and Jasmine Jefferson
Location:	Chicago, Illinois
Employment status:	Tyler—Newly hired VP of Sales for GLO Corporation earning an annual salary of $320,000 per year. Jasmine—graphic designer, earning an annual salary of $37,000 per year.
Filing status:	Married filing jointly
Dependents:	Two children
Marginal tax rate:	32 percent

With the extra income Tyler Jefferson is earning in his new position as VP of Sales for GLO Corporation, his family now has greater financial flexibility, but with the money come new possibilities. For one, Tyler and Jasmine Jefferson would like to sell their current home and purchase a larger one closer to Tyler's work. Fortunately, the value of their home has increased considerably since they purchased it, which should allow them to make a substantial down payment on a new home. Still, they would need to acquire financing to make the purchase. Jasmine likes the idea of buying a vacation home in Scottsdale, Arizona. Besides the great weather (she and Tyler both love golf), Scottsdale has the added benefit of being near Jasmine's family. Jasmine is trying to sell the second-home idea to Tyler by suggesting that, to help defray the costs, they could rent the house when they're not there. Finally, Jasmine is seriously considering a transition to self-employment as a graphic designer. She believes that, with her experience and contacts, she can find enough clients to keep busy most of the time—and she very much likes the idea of setting aside a room in their primary home as her workplace. ∎

When making these decisions, the Jeffersons should consider the tax consequences of their actions. For example, will the gain on the sale of their current home be taxable? Will the interest expense on the new home be fully deductible? Should they pay points to obtain a lower interest rate on the home loan? If they rent out the vacation home for part of the year, how do they account for the related income and expenses for tax purposes? If Jasmine sets up a home office, will the Jeffersons be allowed any tax deductions for expenses relating to their home? This chapter answers these and other relevant questions for the Jeffersons and for others interested in the tax consequences of home ownership.

LO 14-1

The starting point for identifying the tax consequences of home ownership is first determining whether the taxpayer owns a **dwelling unit.** A dwelling unit is property that provides a place suitable for people to occupy (live and sleep). For tax purposes, a dwelling unit includes the following:

- House
- Condominium
- Mobile home
- Boat
- Other similar property[1]

A taxpayer may acquire a dwelling unit solely for personal use, for some mixture of personal and rental use, or solely for rental use. Each year, the dwelling unit is classified as either a residence or a nonresidence (rental property) based on how the taxpayer used the unit. The dwelling unit (we refer to a dwelling unit and a "home" interchangebly) is considered to be a residence if the taxpayer's number of personal-use days of the home is more than the greater of

1. 14 days or
2. 10 percent of the number of rental days during the year.[2]

Thus, to determine whether a dwelling unit is a residence or not, the taxpayer needs to calculate the number of days the home (dwelling unit) was used for personal use during the year and the number of days the home was rented out during the year. So what counts as a day of personal use and what counts as a day of rental use? A day of personal use includes any day for which

- The taxpayer (owner) or any other owner of the home stays in the home.
- A relative of an owner stays in the home, even if the relative pays full fair market value rent, unless the home is the relative's principal residence (discussed below).
- A nonowner stays in the home under a vacation home exchange or swap arrangement.
- The taxpayer rents out the property for less than fair market value.[3]

A day of rental use includes any day for which

- The taxpayer rents out the property at fair market value.
- The home is being repaired or maintained for rental use.

Days when the home is available for rent, but not actually rented out, *do not count* as either personal or rental days.

When a dwelling unit is determined to be a residence, the taxpayer must determine whether the residence is the taxpayer's **principal residence** in order to determine certain

---

[1]§280A(f)(1). A dwelling unit does not include a hotel, motel, inn, or similar establishment.
[2]§280A(d)(1).
[3]§280A(d)(2).

tax consequences associated with the property (for certain purposes, the taxpayer need only determine whether the property is a residence). What makes a residence a "principal" residence? When a taxpayer lives in more than one residence during the year, the determination of which residence is the principal residence depends on the facts and circumstances, such as

- The amount of time the taxpayer spends at each residence during the year.
- The proximity of each residence to the taxpayer's place of employment.
- The principal place of abode (living and sleeping) of the taxpayer's immediate family.
- The taxpayer's mailing address for bills and correspondence.

To summarize, with respect to a particular taxpayer for a particular year, a dwelling unit or home can be classified as either a

- Principal residence,
- Residence (not principal), or a
- Nonresidence (rental property).

We refer to these property classifications throughout the chapter as we describe the tax consequences of home ownership. Exhibit 14-1 lists deductions and other tax provisions available for each property type. We discuss each of these tax provisions, including limitations, throughout the chapter. Also, Appendix B at the end of this chapter provides a flowchart for determining the tax status of a home used for rental purposes.

EXHIBIT 14-1   **Tax Provisions by Property Type**

Tax Provision	Property Type		
	Principal Residence	Residence (not principal)	Nonresidence
Home mortgage interest deductions (*from* AGI)	X	X	
Real property taxes (*from* AGI deduction)	X	X	X
Deductions associated with rental use, if any (*for* AGI)	X	X	X
Exclusion of gain on sale of home	X	X*	X*

*Must have previously been a principal residence to qualify.

We begin our discussion by considering the tax consequences associated with personal use of the home. We then discuss the tax consequences of rental use of the home, and we conclude the chapter by discussing the tax consequences of business use of the home.

PERSONAL USE OF THE HOME

To buy or to rent? This is a difficult question with no single answer. The decision to purchase a home is a significant one that includes both nontax and tax considerations. Primary nontax factors favoring home ownership include the home's potential to appreciate as an investment. As the value of the home increases, so does the homeowner's net worth.

A home is frequently an individual's most significant investment. Therefore, home ownership also carries significant potential risk. When real estate values decline, the

THE KEY FACTS

Tax and Nontax Consequences of Home Ownership

- Nontax consequences
  - Large investment.
  - Potential for big return (or loss) on investment with use of leverage.
  - Risk of default on home loan.
  - Time and costs of maintenance.
  - Limited mobility.
- Tax consequences
  - Deductible interest expense.
  - Excludable gain on sale.
  - Deductible real property taxes on home.
  - Rental and business-use possibilities.

owner's net worth also declines. Homeowners borrowing funds to purchase their home have the potential to achieve high returns on their cash investment due to the power of leverage (the homeowner provides the down payment and the bank provides the rest of the cash to purchase the home), but a home is by no means a liquid asset. Furthermore, homeowners must assume the risk associated with the possible default on the loan. If the owner does not make the mortgage payments required by the terms of the loan, the lender may repossess the home. Homeowners also are responsible for the cost or effort required to repair, maintain, and landscape the home. Finally, because building, buying, selling, and moving in or out of a home are expensive and time-consuming tasks, home ownership reduces the ability to relocate to take advantage of new opportunities.

On the tax side, the government clearly smiles on home ownership, given the deductions available to homeowners that are unavailable to renters. In fact, the deductibility of mortgage interest on owner-occupied homes has historically been ranked in the top ten on the government's list of projected "tax expenditures" (tax breaks provided to taxpayers). Besides the deduction for interest payments made on home mortgages, other tax benefits of home ownership include the deduction of real estate taxes paid on the home, the exclusion of gain on the sale of the home, and the deduction of expenses relating to business offices in the home. Homeowners also may gain tax benefits associated with owning and renting a vacation home. We address the tax consequences of home ownership throughout this chapter.

LO 14-2 Exclusion of Gain on Sale of Personal Residence

When a taxpayer sells a personal residence, she *realizes* a gain or a loss calculated by subtracting the basis of the home from the amount she receives from the buyer (minus selling costs). The basis of the residence depends on how the taxpayer acquired the home. The general rules for determining the basis of the home are as follows:

- Purchase: the cost of the home.
- Inheritance: the fair market value of the home on the date of the decedent's death.
- Gift: the donor's basis.
- Conversion of rental home to residence: the taxpayer's basis in the rental home at the time of the conversion.

Because a personal residence is a capital asset, the gain a taxpayer recognizes by selling the residence is a capital gain. However, because a personal residence is also a personal-use asset, the loss on the sale of a personal residence is a nondeductible personal loss.[4] This is an important limitation for many taxpayers when the housing market is depressed. When a taxpayer sells a personal residence at a gain, the tax consequences are generally more favorable. In fact, taxpayers meeting certain requirements are allowed to exclude a certain amount of realized gain on the sale.[5] The maximum exclusion depends on filing status as follows:

- $500,000 for married filing jointly taxpayers.
- $250,000 for other taxpayers.

Gain in excess of the excludable amount generally qualifies as long-term capital gain subject to tax at preferential rates. Further, gain in excess of the exclusion amount is considered to be investment income for purposes of determining the 3.8 percent net investment income tax discussed in the Individual Income Tax Computation and Tax Credits chapter.

---

[4]§165(c).

[5]Prior to 2018, taxpayers were allowed to exclude gain they realized on debt forgiveness when a lender foreclosed on their home. This provision had not been extended to 2018 as of the time we went to press.

Requirements   To qualify for the exclusion, the taxpayer must meet both ownership and use tests for the residence:

Ownership test: The taxpayer must have owned the property for a total of two or more years during the five-year period ending on the date of the sale. The ownership test prevents a taxpayer from purchasing a home, fixing it up, and soon thereafter selling it and excluding the gain—a real estate investment practice termed **flipping.** In these circumstances, the gain is primarily due to the taxpayer's efforts in remodeling the home, not to general appreciation in the value of the property.

Use test: The taxpayer must have *used* the property as her principal residence (see earlier discussion) for a total of two or more years during the five-year period ending on the date of the sale. The exclusion provision was designed to provide tax benefits to homeowners rather than investors or landlords. The use test helps ensure that taxpayers using the exclusion have realized gains from selling the home they actually lived in as opposed to selling an investment or rental property.

Note that the periods of ownership and use need not be continuous, nor do they need to cover the same two-year period. In fact, a taxpayer could rent a home and live in it as her principal residence during 2013 and then again during 2015, purchase the home and rent it to someone else during 2016 and 2017, and then sell the home at the beginning of 2018—and *still* meet the ownership and use tests!

> **THE KEY FACTS**
>
> **Exclusion of Gain on Sale of Personal Residence**
>
> - Must meet ownership and use tests.
>   - Must own home for at least two of five years before sale.
>   - Must use home as principal residence for at least two of five years before sale.
>   - For married couples to qualify for maximum exclusion on a joint return, one spouse must meet the ownership test and both spouses must meet the use test.

Example 14-1

The Jeffersons sold their home in Denver, Colorado, before moving to Chicago. They sold the Denver home for $450,000. The Jeffersons initially purchased the home for $350,000. They owned and lived in the home (as their principal residence) for four years before selling. How much of the $100,000 gain realized on the sale ($450,000 − $350,000) are they allowed to exclude?

Answer: All $100,000. The Jeffersons qualified for the full exclusion available to married couples filing jointly because they met the ownership and use tests. Consequently, they are allowed to exclude the entire $100,000 of gain and could have excluded up to $500,000 of gain on the sale.

How do the ownership and use tests apply to married couples filing joint returns? Married couples filing joint returns are eligible for the full $500,000 exclusion if *either* spouse meets the ownership test and *both* spouses meet the principal-use test. However, if either spouse meets the ownership test but only one spouse meets the principal-use test, the couple's exclusion is limited to $250,000 on the couple's joint tax return.

Example 14-2

What if: Suppose that when Tyler and Jasmine were married, Jasmine moved into Tyler's home located in Denver, Colorado. Tyler had purchased the home two years before the marriage. After the marriage, the couple lived in the home together as their principal residence for four years before selling the home and moving to Chicago. Tyler was the sole owner of the home for the entire six years he resided in the home. Would gain on the sale of the home qualify for the $500,000 exclusion available to married couples filing jointly even though Jasmine was never an owner of the home?

Answer: Yes. Gain on the sale qualifies for the full $500,000 exclusion available to married couples filing jointly because Tyler has met the ownership test, and both Tyler and Jasmine have met the use test.

What if: Suppose that Tyler and Jasmine lived in the home together for only one year before selling it. Would the couple be allowed to exclude any gain on the sale?

Answer: Yes, however, because Jasmine does not meet the use test, they would qualify only for the $250,000 exclusion even if they were to file a joint return.

If a widow or widower sells a home that he or she owned and occupied with the decedent spouse (the spouse who died), the surviving spouse is entitled to the full $500,000 exclusion provided he or she sells the home within two years after the date of death of the spouse. Finally, once a taxpayer claims a home sale exclusion, she is not eligible to claim another exclusion until at least two years pass from the time of the first sale (see the unforeseen circumstances discussion for an exception to this general rule).

General rule exceptions for nonqualified use, unforeseen circumstances and depreciation. In certain circumstances, taxpayers who otherwise meet the ownership and use requirements may have their exclusion limited under a "nonqualified use" provision. In other circumstances, taxpayers who fail the ownership and/or use tests are allowed to exclude gain on the sale of their residence under an "unforeseen" circumstances provision. Finally, taxpayers who have claimed depreciation deductions on their home for rental or business use (see discussion later in the chapter) may be required to recognize gain on the sale of their residence that otherwise would have been excluded. Let's first discuss the nonqualified use provision.

Under the general rules for the home sale exclusion, taxpayers could exclude gain on the sale of a vacation home or rental property (including gain accrued while it was not a principal residence) simply by moving into the property and using it as their principal residence for two years before selling it. To limit a taxpayer's ability to benefit from this strategy, the nonqualified use provision reduces the taxpayer's otherwise excludable gain on the home sale if, on or after January 1, 2009, the taxpayer used or uses the home for something other than a principal residence (termed *nonqualified use*).[6] The period of nonqualified use does not include any portion of the five-year period ending on the date of the sale that is after the last date that such property is used as the principal residence of the taxpayer or the taxpayer's spouse. This exception allows the taxpayer time to sell the principal residence after moving out of it without having to count the time the house is available for sale as nonqualified use (if it were considered to be nonqualified use, the amount of gain the taxpayer would be eligible to exclude would be reduced).

If the nonqualified use limitation applies, the percentage of the realized gain that must be recognized is the ratio of the period of nonqualified use divided by the period of time the taxpayer owned the home (acquisition date through date of sale). Note that this provision does not reduce the maximum exclusion; it reduces the amount of realized gain eligible for exclusion.

Example 14-3

What if: Suppose the Jeffersons purchased home 1 on January 1, 2015, for $350,000. They lived in home 1 as their principal residence until January 1, 2018, when they moved into a new principal residence (home 2). They finally sold home 1 on January 1, 2020, for $450,000. What amount of the $100,000 gain on the sale of home 1 ($450,000 amount realized minus $350,000 basis) may the Jeffersons exclude from gross income?

Answer: All $100,000. The Jeffersons meet the ownership and use tests (they owned and used home 1 as their principal residence for at least two of the five years prior to January 1, 2020), so they qualify for a maximum exclusion of $500,000. Further, the gain eligible for the exclusion is *not* reduced because the Jeffersons stopped using home 1 as a principal residence after January 1, 2018, and they sold the home within five years of this date.

What if: Assume the same facts as above, except that on January 1, 2019, the Jeffersons moved back into home 1 and used it as their principal residence until they sold it for $450,000 on January 1, 2020. What amount of the $100,000 gain on the sale of home 1 may the Jeffersons exclude from income?

Answer: $80,000. The Jeffersons meet the ownership and use tests for home 1 and therefore qualify for the maximum potential $500,000 exclusion. However, because they stopped using the home as their principal residence for a period on or after January 1, 2009 (nonqualified use from January 1, 2018–January 1, 2019), and they used the home as their principal residence immediately before selling (January 1, 2019–January 1, 2020), the gain eligible for exclusion must be reduced. The percentage of the gain that is not eligible for exclusion is 20 percent, which is the period of nonqualified use (one year: January 1, 2019–January 1, 2020) divided by the total period of time the Jeffersons owned the home (five years: January 1, 2015–January 1, 2020). Therefore, the Jeffersons must reduce their gain eligible for exclusion by $20,000 ($100,000 gain × 20% reduction percentage), allowing them to exclude $80,000 of the $100,000 gain from gross income.

---

[6]§121(b)(5).

Sometimes taxpayers are unable to meet the two-year requirements for the ownership and use tests due to unforeseen circumstances. For example, a taxpayer may be forced to sell his home before he meets the ownership and use requirements due to a change in employment, significant health issues, or other unforeseen financial difficulties.[7] In such cases, the *maximum* exclusion amount ($500,000 for married filing jointly, $250,000 otherwise) is reduced based on the amount of time the taxpayer owned and used the home as a principal residence before selling. For example, if a single taxpayer owned and used a home as a principal residence for six months before selling due to unforeseen circumstances, the maximum exclusion would be $62,500, which is one-fourth of what it would be otherwise (6 months of ownership and use divided by 24 months required under the general rule, multiplied by the full $250,000 exclusion for single taxpayers). The maximum exclusion available to a taxpayer selling under these circumstances is expressed in the formula presented in Exhibit 14-2.

EXHIBIT 14-2   **Formula for Determining Maximum Home Sale Exclusion in Unforeseen Circumstances**

Maximum exclusion in unforeseen circumstances =
Full exclusion × Qualifying months/24 months, where

Full exclusion = $250,000 for single taxpayers or $500,000 for taxpayers filing a joint return.

Qualifying months = the number of months the taxpayer met the ownership and use requirements for the home before *selling* it.

24 months = the number of months the taxpayer must own and use the home as a principal residence to qualify for the full exclusion.[8]

Source: See Reg §1.121-3(g).

Example 14-4

What if: Let's assume that when the Jeffersons moved from Denver, they purchased a home in Chicago for $375,000 and moved into the home on July 1, 2017. In January of 2018, Tyler accepted a work opportunity with a different employer located in Miami, Florida. On February 1, 2018, the Jeffersons sold their home for $395,000 and permanently relocated to Miami. How much of the $20,000 realized gain ($395,000 − $375,000) on their Chicago home sale can the Jeffersons exclude from taxable income?

Answer: All $20,000. The Jeffersons lived in the home for only seven months (July 1, 2017, to February 1, 2018), so they do not meet either the ownership or the use test to qualify for the maximum exclusion. However, under the unforeseen circumstances provision, they are eligible for a reduced maximum exclusion computed as follows: $500,000 (maximum exclusion) × 7 (qualifying months)/24 = $145,833. Because the amount they are able to exclude ($145,833) exceeds the $20,000 gain they realized on the sale, they are able to exclude all $20,000.

What if: Assume the same facts, except that the Jeffersons realized a $150,000 gain on the sale of their home. How much of the realized gain would they recognize and at what rate would this gain be taxed?

Answer: $150,000 gain realized minus $145,833 exclusion = $4,167 short-term capital gain (the home is a capital asset that the Jeffersons owned for one year or less). Assuming the Jeffersons did not recognize any other capital gains during the year, the $4,167 would be taxed at the Jeffersons' 32 percent marginal tax rate (see storyline summary at beginning of chapter).

Note, as the previous example illustrates, that under the so-called unforeseen circumstances provision, it is the *full exclusion* that is reduced, not necessarily the excludable gain. Consequently, if a taxpayer's gain on the sale of a residence is less than the maximum

[7]The IRS recently ruled that a couple's need to move because of a birth of a second child was an unforeseen circumstance (LTR 201628002).

[8]Taxpayers may choose to use the number of days the taxpayer fully qualified for the exclusion divided by 730 days. See Reg §1.121-3(g).

exclusion (after the unforseen circumstances adjustment), the taxpayer may exclude the entire amount of the gain.

Finally, taxpayers who used their home for business purposes (home office expense) or rental purposes are not allowed to exclude gain attributable to depreciation deductions incurred after May 6, 1997. Rather, this gain is treated as unrecaptured §1250 gain and is subject to a maximum 25 percent tax rate (see the Investments chapter for a detailed discussion of unrecaptured §1250 gain).

LO 14-3   Home Mortgage Interest Deduction

A primary tax benefit of owning a home is that taxpayers are generally allowed to deduct the interest they pay on their home mortgage loans as an itemized deduction. Taxpayers generate tax savings and reduce the after-tax cost of their mortgage payments to the extent of their deductible interest payments. However, because the recently enacted tax law nearly doubled the standard deduction for years after 2017, fewer taxpayers are likely to itemize deductions and benefit from deducting home mortgage interest and those that do benefit only to the extent that mortgage interest exceeds the standard deduction (when added to other itemized deductions). Nevertheless, taxpayers with significant nonmortgage interest itemized deductions (e.g., charitable contributions, state income taxes, and real property taxes) can generate substantial tax savings from the home mortgage interest deduction.

Example 14-5

During the current year, Tyler and Jasmine own a home with an average mortgage balance of $400,000. They pay interest at 5 percent annually on the loan, and they qualify to deduct the interest expense as an itemized deduction. The Jeffersons' marginal income tax rate is 32 percent, and before counting mortgage interest, their itemized deductions exceed the standard deduction. What is the before- and after-tax cost of their mortgage interest expense for the year?

Answer: $20,000 before-tax cost and $13,600 after-tax cost, computed as follows:

Description	Amount	Explanation
(1) Before-tax interest expense	$ 20,000	$400,000 × 5% (all deductible)
(2) Marginal tax rate	× 32%	
(3) Tax savings from interest expense	6,400	(1) × (2)
After-tax cost of interest expense	**$13,600**	(1) − (3)

Note that the $6,400 tax savings generated by the mortgage interest expense deduction reduces the after-tax cost of their monthly mortgage payment by $533 ($6,400/12).

What if: Assume the original facts except that before counting the mortgage interest expense, the Jeffersons' itemized deductions were $6,000 below the standard deduction. How much tax savings would the $20,000 mortgage interest expense generate for the Jeffersons?

Answer: $4,480. ($14,000 × 32%). The first $6,000 of mortgage interest expense increases the Jeffersons' itemized deductions to equal the standard deduction but does not affect their taxable income. The remaining $14,000 increases itemized deductions above the standard deduction and thus reduces taxable income, producing tax savings.

What if: Assume that instead of buying a home, the Jeffersons rented a home and paid $1,667 a month for rent expense. What would be the before- and after-tax cost of the $20,000 annual rental payments?

Answer: $20,000 before-tax cost and $20,000 after-tax cost. Because rental payments are not deductible, they do not generate tax savings, so the before- and after-tax cost of the rental payments is the same.

Despite the apparent tax savings from buying versus renting a home, it is important to consider that nontax factors could favor renting over purchasing a home.

Taxpayers are allowed to deduct interest paid on the principal amount of **acquisition indebtedness** (subject to a limitation discussed below) as an itemized deduction.[9] Acquisition indebtedness is any debt secured by a **qualified residence** that is incurred in acquiring, constructing, or substantially improving the residence. To understand what this means exactly, let's define a couple of terms.

Debt secured by residence: A debt is secured by a residence when the residence is the collateral for the loan. If the owner does not make the payments on the loan, the lender may take possession of the home to satisfy the owner's responsibility for the debt.

Qualified residence: A qualified residence is the taxpayer's principal residence *and* one other residence (see previous discussion for definition of principal residence and of residence). For a taxpayer with *more* than two residences, the property to be treated as the second qualified residence is an annual election— that is, the taxpayer can choose to deduct interest related to a particular second home one year and a different second home the next. The second residence is often a vacation home where the taxpayer resides part time.

Limitation on Acquisition Indebtedness For purposes of determining the deductible amount of mortgage interest expense, the amount of acquisition indebtedness is limited to a fixed amount based on when the indebtedness originated. For acquisition indebtedness incurred after December 15, 2017, the amount of acquisition indebtedness is limited to $750,000 ($375,000 for married taxpayers filing separately). For acquisition indebtedness incurred before December 16, 2017, the amount of acquisition indebtedness is limited to $1,000,000 ($500,000 for married taxpayers filing separately), even if the debt is **refinanced** after December 15, 2017.[10] When a taxpayer has both acquisition indebtedness incurred before December 16, 2017 and acquisition indebtedness incurred after December 15, 2017, the $750,000 ($375,000) limit is reduced (not below zero) by the acquisition indebtedness incurred before December 16, 2017.

Example 14-6

What if: Assume that in January of 2018, the Jeffersons purchased a home in Chicago costing $900,000 by making a down payment of $100,000 and taking out an $800,000 loan secured by the home. During the year, the Jeffersons paid $35,000 of interest on the mortgage. How much of the interest are the Jeffersons allowed to deduct?

Answer: $32,813 ($35,000 × $750,000/$800,000). Interest on $750,000 of $800,000 is deductible because the acquisition indebtedness was incurred after December 15, 2017, so the acquisition indebtedness is limited to $750,000 for purposes of determining their deductible mortgage interest.

What if: Assume that on December 1, 2017, the Jeffersons purchased a home in Chicago costing $900,000 by making a down payment of $100,000 and taking out an $800,000 loan secured by the home. During 2018, the Jeffersons paid $39,000 of interest on the mortgage. How much of the interest are the Jeffersons allowed to deduct?

Answer: $39,000. All of the interest is deductible because the acquisition indebtedness was incurred before December 16, 2017, and it is under the $1,000,000 limit.

(continued on page 14-10)

THE KEY FACTS

Home Mortgage Interest Deduction

- Deduction allowed for home mortgage interest on acquisition indebtedness.
  - Principal residence and one other residence.
- Acquisition Indebtedness
  - Proceeds used to acquire or substantially improve home.
  - Limited to $1,000,000 if incurred prior to 12/16/2017.
  - Limited to $750,000 if incurred after 12/15/2017.

---

[9] §163(h)(3). Prior to 2018, taxpayers could also deduct interest paid on up to $100,000 of home-equity indebtedness ($50,000 if married filing separately) as an itemized deduction. For tax years prior to 2018, taxpayers could deduct mortgage insurance as a home interest itemized deduction. However, this deduction had not yet been extended 2018 as of press time.

[10] §163(h)(3)(F). For tax years prior to 2018, taxpayers could deduct interest paid on up to $100,000 of home-equity indebtedness ($50,000 if married filing separately) as an itemized deduction. They could also deduct home mortgage insurance as a home mortgage interest itemized deduction. However, for tax years after 2017, interest on home equity indebtedness is no longer deductible and the provision allowing an itemized deduction for home mortgage insurance had not been extended to 2018 as of press time.

What if: Assume that on December 1, 2017, the Jeffersons purchased a home in Chicago costing $900,000 by making a down payment of $100,000 and taking out an $800,000 loan secured by the home. In June of 2019, the Jeffersons refinanced the remaining $770,000 balance of the loan to get a lower interest rate. Are the Jeffersons allowed to deduct all the interest on the refinanced loan?

Answer: Yes. The Jeffersons can deduct all of the interest on the refinanced loan even though the balance exceeds $750,000, because the original acquisition indebtedness occurred before December 16, 2017, when the acquisition debt limit was $1,000,000.

Once acquisition indebtedness is established for a qualifying residence (or for the sum of two qualifying residences), principal payments reduce it and only additional indebtedness secured by the residence(s) *and* incurred to substantially improve the residence(s) increase acquisition indebtedness. Does refinancing affect the amount of indebtedness? Unless the taxpayer uses proceeds from the refinance to substantially improve her residence, the refinanced loan is treated as acquisition debt only to the extent that the principal amount of the refinancing does not exceed the amount of the acquisition debt immediately before the refinancing. Consequently, the amount borrowed in excess of the remaining principal on the original loan that is not used to substantially improve the residence does not qualify as acquisition indebtedness. Interest on the "excess" part of this loan is not deductible.[11]

Example 14-7

What if: Assume the Jeffersons purchased a home in Chicago costing $430,000 by making a down payment of $30,000 and taking out a $400,000 loan secured by the home. What is the Jeffersons' acquisition indebtedness?

Answer: $400,000. This is debt secured by a qualified residence that is incurred in acquiring, constructing, or substantially improving the residence.

What if: Now assume that when they moved to Chicago, the Jeffersons purchased a home costing $430,000 by making a down payment of $400,000, and taking out a $30,000 loan secured by the home. During the next few years, the Jeffersons paid $10,000 of principal on the loan, thereby reducing the loan balance to $20,000. Subsequently, needing cash, the Jeffersons refinanced their mortgage by taking out a loan, secured by their residence, for $150,000. With the $150,000 they paid off the $20,000 balance on the original loan and used the $130,000 of extra cash for purposes unrelated to the home. After the refinance, what is the Jeffersons' acquisition indebtedness?

Answer: $20,000, the same amount as before the refinance. The only way to increase acquisition indebtedness once it is established is to borrow money to substantially improve the home. Thus, the Jeffersons' interest deductions on the home will be limited to the interest expense on the $20,000 acquisition indebtedness.

What if: Assume the same facts as the previous what-if example except that the Jeffersons used $40,000 of the cash from the loan to build a new garage on their property. After the refinance, what is the Jeffersons' acquisition indebtedness?

Answer: $60,000 ($20,000 original loan principal + $40,000 used to substantially improve the home).

---

[11]When taxpayers have multiple acquisition debt loans that combined exceed the acquisition debt limit, they can determine the deductible interest expense using either the simplified or the exact method described in Treas. Reg. §1.163-10T(d) and (e), respectively.

Taxpayers (other than married taxpayers filing separately) are allowed to deduct interest paid on up to either $1,000,000 or $750,000 of aquisition indebtedness (depending on when the debt occurred) on their principal residence (and one other residence). In 2012, the Tax Court concluded that the indebtedness limit for interest deductions is a per-residence(s) limit and not a per-taxpayer limit. For example, if two unmarried taxpayers jointly acquire (in 2018) and reside in a home, the qualifying debt limit for both taxpayers combined would be $750,000. However, in 2015, the 9th Circuit Court of Appeals overruled the 2012 Tax Court decision and concluded that the qualifying debt limit applies on a per-taxpayer basis and not a per-residence(s) basis. In 2016, the IRS acquiesced to this decision (2016-31 IRB 193). Consequently, two unmarried taxpayers who jointly acquire a home in 2018 can each deduct interest on up to $750,000 of acquisition debt ($1,500,000 of acquisition debt in total). If the two taxpayers were married, together they would be able to deduct interest on up to only $750,000 of acquisition debt. Now, that's a marriage penalty!

Source: Voss v. Comm. 2015-2 USTC par. 50427 (9 Cir. 8/27/2015), rev'g Sophy, 138 TC 204, (2012).

Points A home buyer arranging financing for a home typically incurs several loan-related fees or expenses, including "points." A **point** is 1 percent of the principal amount of the loan. In general, borrowers pay points to lenders in exchange for reduced interest rates on loans. However, borrowers may also pay lenders for other purposes (e.g., to compensate lenders for the service of providing the loan). In order for taxpayers to deduct points, the points must be paid for a reduced interest rate (rather than for the service of providing the loan).[12] However, to minimize possible disputes regarding the deductibility of points and as a matter of administrative convenience, the IRS will treat points as deductible **qualified residence interest** if the following requirements are met:[13]

1. The **settlement statement**—a document that details the monies paid out and received by the buyer and seller as part of the loan transaction—must clearly designate the amounts as points payable in connection with the loan, for example as "loan origination fees," "loan discount," or "discount points." These amounts are typically provided on lines 801 and 802 of the settlement statement. (See Appendix A at the end of this chapter for a sample settlement statement for the Jeffersons.)

2. The amounts must be computed as a percentage of the stated principal amount of the loan.

3. The amounts paid must conform to an established business general practice of charging points for loans in the area in which the residence is located, and the amount of the points paid must not exceed the amount generally charged in that area.

4. The amounts must be paid in connection with the acquisition of the taxpayer's *principal residence* and the loan *must be secured by that residence* (the deduction for points is not available for points paid in connection with a loan for a second home). Points paid on a home acquisition loan in excess of the acquisition debt limit are not deductible.

5. The buyer must provide enough funds in the down payment on the home to at least equal the cost of the points (the buyer is not allowed to borrow from the lender to pay the points). However, points paid by the *seller* to the lender in connection with the taxpayer's loan are treated as paid directly by the taxpayer. Consequently, such points are generally deductible by the buyer.

[12]§461(g)(2).
[13]Rev. Proc. 94-27 1994-1 C.B. 613.

Note that points paid in *refinancing* a home loan (financing the home again with a new loan, typically at a lower interest rate) are not immediately deductible by the home-owner. These points must be amortized and deducted on a straight-line basis over the life of the loan.[14]

Now that we understand how points are treated for tax purposes, let's consider the home buyer's decision whether to pay points to obtain a lower interest rate on a home loan. From an economic standpoint, the buyer must choose between (1) paying extra money up front and having lower monthly mortgage payments or (2) paying less initially and having larger monthly payments.

When the taxpayer can afford to pay points, deciding whether to do so generally requires a "break-even" analysis. Essentially, the taxpayer determines how long it will take to recoup the after-tax cost of the point(s) through the after-tax interest savings on the loan. Generally speaking, the longer the taxpayer plans on staying in the home and maintaining the loan (not refinancing it), the more likely it is financially beneficial to pay points to obtain a lower interest rate. However, paying points can be costly if, after too short a time, the taxpayer sells the home or refinances the home loan. In these situations, the taxpayer may not reach the break-even point. Further, because the deduction for points is an itemized deduction, paying points only generates tax savings to the extent the points paid exceed the standard deduction when combined with other itemized deductions.

Example 14-8

Tyler and Jasmine are seeking financing for their new $800,000 home. They are paying $500,000 down and borrowing the remaining $300,000 to be paid back over 30 years. They have the choice of paying 2 discount points ($6,000) and getting a fixed interest rate of 4 percent or paying no discount points and getting a fixed interest rate of 5 percent. Assume the points meet the immediate deductibility requirements, the Jeffersons' marginal tax rate is 32 percent, they pay interest only (no principal) for the first three years of the loan, and their other itemized deductions exceed the standard deduction. What is the Jeffersons' break-even point for paying the points?

Answer: Two years, calculated as follows:

Loan summary: $300,000; 5 percent rate with no points or 4 percent rate with 2 points ($6,000). Assume the Jeffersons pay interest only (no principal) for the first three years.

Description	Amounts	Calculation
(1) Initial cash outflow from paying points	$(6,000)	$300,000 × 2%
(2) Tax benefit from deducting points	1,920	(1) × 32%
(3) After-tax cost of points	(4,080)	(1) + (2)
(4) Before-tax *savings per year* from 4% vs. 5% interest rate	3,000	$300,000 × (5% − 4%)
(5) *Forgone tax benefit per year* of higher interest rate	(960)	(4) × 32%
(6) After-tax savings per year of 4% vs. 5% interest rate	$ 2,040	(4) + (5)
Break-even point in years	**2 years**	(3)/(6)

The break-even analysis in Example 14-8, while a useful exercise, oversimplifies the calculations a bit. Why? Because it doesn't take into account the present value of the tax savings, nor the increasing principal that would be paid on a traditional principal-and-interest-type loan. In reality the cost of the points is immediate, while the savings

---

[14]See the Tax Compliance, the IRS, and Tax Authorities chapter research memo and *J.R. Huntsman v. Comm.* (8 Cir., 1990), 90-2 USTC par. 50,340, rev'g 91 TC 917 (1988) for a limited exception to this rule.

comes later—so the break-even point on a present value basis is likely a little longer than two years. Also, the more principal paid on the loan, the lower the amount of interest paid each month—so savings from the lower interest rate declines over time, which would also extend the break-even point.

Because points paid on a refinancing are deducted over the life of the loan, the break-even point for paying points on a refinanced mortgage is longer than the break-even point for an original mortgage of the same amount.

Example 14-9

What if: Assume that the Jeffersons have a $300,000 mortgage on their home. They have decided to refinance with a new 30-year mortgage in order to get a lower interest rate. The Jeffersons have the option of paying 2 discount points ($6,000) and obtaining a 4 percent interest rate or obtaining a 5 percent with no discount points. Assuming the Jeffersons' marginal tax rate is 32 percent, they pay interest only on the loan for the first three years (no principal), and the Jeffersons' other itemized deductions exceed the standard deduction amount. What is the Jeffersons' approximate break-even point for paying the points on the refinance?

Answer: 2.85 years, calculated as follows:

Loan summary: $300,000; 5 percent rate with no points or 4 percent rate with 2 points ($6,000). Assume the Jeffersons pay interest only (no principal) for the first three years.

Description	Points	Notes
(1) Initial cash outflow from paying points	$(6,000)	$300,000 × 2%
(2) Tax benefit from deducting points	0	
(3) After-tax cost of points	(6,000)	(1) + (2)
(4) Before-tax savings per year from 4% vs. 5% interest rate	3,000	$300,000 × (5% − 4%)
(5) Forgone tax benefit per year of higher interest payments	(960)	(4) × 32%
(6) After-tax savings per year of 4% vs. 5% interest rate	2,040	(4) + (5)
(7) Annual tax savings from amortizing points	64	(1)/30 years × 32%
(8) Annual after-tax cash flow benefit of paying points	$ 2,104	(6) + (7)
Break-even point in years	**2.85 years**	(3)/(0)

The reason for the longer break-even point is that the points effectively cost more because they are not immediately deductible on a refinance.

Real Property Taxes

LO 14-4

Owners of personal residences and other types of real estate such as land, rental properties, business buildings, and other types of real property are generally required to pay **real property taxes.** These taxes are assessed by local governments and are based on the fair market value of the property.[15] Real property taxes support general public welfare by providing funding for local public needs such as schools and roads.

Local governments set the tax rates applied to the value of the property annually based on their financial needs for the year. The applicable rates may depend on the type of real estate. For example, the tax rate for real estate used in a business may be higher than the rates for residential real property. Taxpayers conducting self-employment activities can deduct real property tax payments from business income as *for* AGI deductions. For landlords such payments are *for* AGI deductions from rental income. For other

---

[15]Local governments tend to understate the fair market value of property when appraising it to minimize the chances that the taxpayer will contest the appraisal.

individuals, real property taxes are deductible as itemized deductions. However, beginning in 2018, the itemized deduction for all taxes combined [state and local income (or sales), real property, and personal property tax] is limited to $10,000 ($5,000 for married taxpayers filing separately).

Taxpayers are not allowed to deduct fees paid for setting up water and sewer services or for assessments for local benefits such as streets and sidewalks.[16] They generally add these expenditures to the basis of their property.

Frequently, homeowners pay their real estate taxes through an **escrow** (holding) **account** with their mortgage lender. Each monthly payment to the lender includes an amount that represents roughly one-twelfth of the anticipated real property taxes for the year. The actual tax payment (or payments if the taxes are due more than once a year) is made by the mortgage company with funds accumulated in the escrow account. The homeowner gets to deduct the property taxes when they are paid to the taxing jurisdiction, not when the homeowner makes payments for these taxes to the escrow account.

Who is responsible for paying the taxes when an owner sells a personal residence or other type of real estate during the year? Is it the owner at the time the taxes are due? Who receives the corresponding tax deduction? In most situations, the buyer and seller divide the responsibility for the tax payments based on the portion of the property tax year that each party held the property. This allocation of taxes between buyer and seller is generally spelled out in the settlement statement when the sale becomes final (see Appendix A to this chapter for a sample settlement statement for the Jeffersons). For tax purposes, it doesn't matter who actually pays the tax, although generally the current owner has the responsibility to do so. As long as the taxes are paid, the tax deduction is based on the relative amount of time each party owned the property during the year (or the period over which the property taxes are payable).[17]

Example 14-10

On February 1, Tyler and Jasmine purchased a new home for $800,000. At the time of the purchase, it was estimated that the property tax bill on the home for the year would be $8,000 ($800,000 × 1%). Assume that the tax bill is paid and that the property tax bill is based on a calendar year. During the year, the Jeffersons paid $15,000 in state income taxes and they did not pay any taxes other than state income taxes and real property taxes during the year. What is their itemized deduction for taxes for the year?

Answer: $10,000. Before even considering real property taxes, the Jeffersons reached the $10,000 itemized deduction limit for taxes. Consequently, the real property taxes do not increase their itemized deductions.

What if: Assume the same facts except that the Jeffersons did not pay any taxes other than real property taxes during the year. What would be their itemized deduction for taxes for the year?

Answer: $7,333. Because the seller lived in the home for one-twelfth of the year (January) and the Jeffersons lived in the home for eleven-twelfths of the year (February through December), the seller will deduct $667 of the property taxes (one-twelfth) and the Jeffersons will deduct $7,333. The Jeffersons could have deducted up to $2,667 ($10,000 minus $7,333) of other taxes for the year.

---

[16]Reg. §1.164-4(a).

[17]The seller gets a deduction (subject to the $10,000 limit) for the taxes allocable for the period of time up to and including the day *before* the date of the sale. The taxes allocable to the day of the sale through the end of the property tax year are deductible by the buyer. See §164(d).

RENTAL USE OF THE HOME

A taxpayer with the financial means to do so may purchase a second home as a vacation home, a rental property, or a combination of the two. A taxpayer may own a second home outright or may share ownership with others through a timeshare or fractional ownership arrangement. Or a taxpayer may rent out their home or part of their home using an online service such as Airbnb. The nontax benefits of owning a second home include a fixed vacation destination, the ability to trade the use of the home with an owner of a home in a different location, the opportunity to generate income through rentals, and the potential appreciation of the second home as an investment. The nontax costs of owning a second home include the initial purchase cost, maintenance costs, the hassle of dealing with renters or property managers, and the downside risk associated with holding the second home as an investment.

The tax consequences of owning a second home depend on whether the home qualifies as a residence (see discussion at the beginning of the chapter) and on the number of days the taxpayer rents out the home. The home is categorized in one of three ways:

1. Residence with minimal rental use (rented for 14 or fewer days).
2. Residence with significant rental use (rented for 15 or more days).
3. Nonresidence.

Recall that, as we discussed earlier in the chapter, a property is considered a "residence" for tax purposes if the taxpayer uses the home for personal purposes for *more than* the greater of 14 days or 10 percent of the number of rental days during the year. For example, if a taxpayer rents her home for 200 days and uses it for personal purposes for 21 days or more, the home is considered to be a residence for tax purposes. If the same taxpayer used the home for personal purposes for 20 days, the home would be considered a nonresidence for tax purposes.

Residence with Minimal Rental Use

The law is simple for taxpayers who rent out a residence for a minimal amount of time during the year (i.e., they live in it for at least 15 days and they rent it for 14 or fewer days). These taxpayers are not required to include the gross receipts in rental income and they are not allowed to deduct any expenses related to the rental.[18] They are, however, allowed to claim as itemized deductions any home mortgage interest and real property taxes on the second home (subject to limits discussed above).

Example 14-11

The Jeffersons purchased a vacation home in a golf community in Scottsdale, Arizona, in January. They spent 10 days vacationing in the home in early March and another 15 days vacationing in the home in mid-December. In early February, they rented the home for 14 days to a group of golfers who were in town to attend a PGA Tour golf tournament and play golf. The Jeffersons received $6,000 in rent from the group, and the Jeffersons incurred $1,000 of expenses relating to the rental home (other than mortgage interest and real property taxes). The Jeffersons did not rent out the property again for the rest of the year. How much will the $5,000 net income from the rental increase their taxable income?

Answer: Zero! Because the Jeffersons lived in the home for at least 15 days and rented out the home for 14 or fewer days during the year, they do not report the rental income to the IRS, and they do not deduct expenses associated with the rental. The Jeffersons saved $1,600 in taxes by excluding the $5,000 of net rental income ($5,000 net income × 32 percent marginal tax rate). Note that they can also claim the home the mortgage interest and real property taxes (subject to the $10,000 itemized deduction limit for taxes) on the property for the *full year* as itemized deductions.

[18]§280A(g).

ETHICS

Carey and Pat were good friends and neighbors in an upscale neighborhood near several highly rated golf courses in Arizona. During the winter, both Carey and Pat decided to rent their homes (at a premium) to groups of golfers from the New York area who wanted to get out of the snow and enjoy sunshine and golf for a couple of weeks during the winter. While their homes were rented, Carey and Pat vacationed together in Cancun. In January 2018, Carey rented his home for 14 days and received $14,000 in rent. Pat also rented his home for the same 14 days and received $16,000 in rent. Near the end of the 14-day rental period, Pat got a call from the renters, who wanted to extend their stay for one day. Pat agreed to the extension and charged the group $2,000 for the extra day. When preparing his 2018 tax return, Pat discovered that taxpayers who rent their home for more than 14 days are required to report all their rental income on their tax returns. Pat didn't think it was fair that he had to pay taxes on the rental income while Carey did not just because Pat rented his home for one more day than Carey in 2018. Consequently, Pat decided that he had rented his property for 14 days and given the renters the last day for free. What do you think about Pat's approach to solving his tax problem?

A taxpayer with a strategically located second (or even first) home can take advantage of this favorable tax rule by renting the property to those in town to attend high-profile events such as the Olympics, the Masters golf tournament, the Super Bowl, and Mardi Gras—and excluding potentially large rental payments from taxable income.

Residence with Significant Rental Use (Vacation Home)

When a home qualifies as a residence and the taxpayer rents out the home for 15 days or more, the rental revenue is included in gross income, expenses to obtain tenants (advertising and realtor commissions) are fully deductible as direct rental expenses, and expenses relating to the home are allocated between personal and rental use. The expenses allocated to personal use are not deductible except under nonrental tax provisions as itemized deductions. (These deductions include mortgage interest, real property taxes, and certain casualty losses on the home.)

When the gross rental revenue exceeds the sum of the direct rental expenses and the expenses allocated to the rental use of the home, the taxpayer is allowed to deduct the expenses in full. However, when these expenses exceed the rental revenue, the deductibility of the expenses is limited. In these situations, taxpayers divide each of the rental expenses into one of three categories or "tiers." The tier 1, 2, and 3 expenses for rental property are described in Exhibit 14-3.

The taxpayer first deducts tier 1 expenses (expenses to obtain tenants and the mortgage interest and real property taxes that are allocated to rental use[19]) in full. This is true even when tier 1 expenses exceed the gross rental revenue.[20] Second, the taxpayer deducts tier 2 expenses.[21] However, the tier 2 expense deductions are limited to the gross rental revenue in excess of tier 1 expenses. Any tier 2 expenses not deducted in the current year due to the income limitation are suspended and carried forward to the next year.

Finally, the taxpayer deducts tier 3 expense (depreciation calculated using the straight-line method over 27.5 years). The tier 3 expense deduction is limited to the gross rental revenue in excess of tier 1 and tier 2 expenses. Any tier 3 expenses not deductible because of the income limitation are suspended and carried forward to the subsequent year. The nondeductible tier 3 expense does not reduce the basis in the home. The three

[19]Technically, expenses to obtain tenants (advertising and realtor commissions) are a reduction in gross rental income for tax purposes. However, we classify them as tier 1 expenses to simplify the discussion.

[20]The rental activity associated with a home that falls into the residence-with-significant-rental-use category is not considered to be a passive activity, so income or loss generated from the activity is not considered to be passive income or passive loss [§469(j)]. See discussion of passive loss rules below.

[21]§280A(c)(5). Also see IRS Publication 527, "Residential Rental Property (Including Rental of Vacation Homes)."

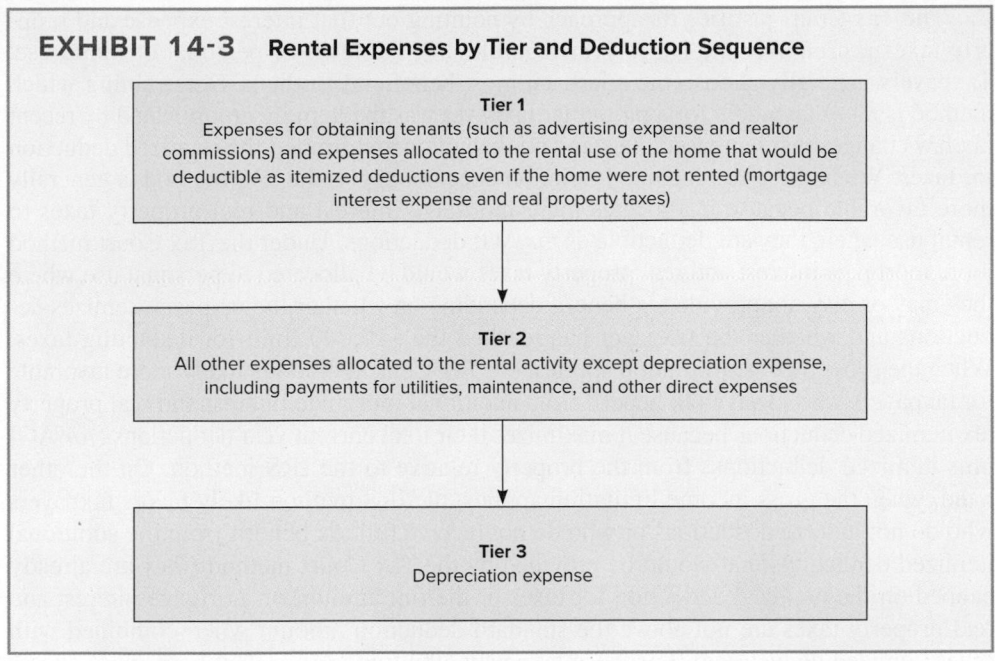

EXHIBIT 14-3   Rental Expenses by Tier and Deduction Sequence

Tier 1
Expenses for obtaining tenants (such as advertising expense and realtor commissions) and expenses allocated to the rental use of the home that would be deductible as itemized deductions even if the home were not rented (mortgage interest expense and real property taxes)

Tier 2
All other expenses allocated to the rental activity except depreciation expense, including payments for utilities, maintenance, and other direct expenses

Tier 3
Depreciation expense

tier deduction sequence is designed to maximize taxpayer deductions for expenses that would be deductible even without any rental use of the home (most commonly, mortgage interest and real property taxes) and to minimize the allowable depreciation deductions for the home. This sequence is more favorable for taxpayers who do not itemize deductions or whose potential mortgage interest and/or real property tax deductions are limited (e.g., limit on itemized deduction for taxes) and it is less favorable to other taxpayers.

As we mentioned above, expenses associated with the rental use of the home must be allocated between rental use and personal use of the home. These expenses are *generally* allocated to rental use based on the ratio of the number of days of rental use to the total number of days the property was used for rental and personal purposes (see Exhibit 14-4). All expenses not allocated to rental use are allocated to personal use.

The only potential exception to the general allocation rule is the allocation of mortgage interest expense and real property taxes (both tier 1 expenses). The IRS and the Tax Court disagree on how to allocate these particular expenses. The IRS allocates these expenses the same way as all other expenses. However, the Tax Court allocates interest and taxes to rental use based on the ratio of days the property was rented over the number of days in the year, rather than the number of days the property was used for any purpose during the year.[22] The **IRS** and **Tax Court allocation methods** are described in Exhibit 14-4.

EXHIBIT 14-4   Tax Court versus IRS Method of Allocating Expenses

Rental Allocation	IRS Method	Tax Court Method
Mortgage interest and property taxes (tier 1 expenses)	$\text{Expense} \times \dfrac{\text{Total rental days}}{\text{Total days used}}$	$\text{Expense} \times \dfrac{\text{Total rental days}}{\text{Days in year}}$
All other expenses	$\text{Expense} \times \dfrac{\text{Total rental days}}{\text{Total days used}}$	$\text{Expense} \times \dfrac{\text{Total rental days}}{\text{Total days used}}$

[22]The Tax Court method of allocating these expenses is also referred to as the Bolton method after the taxpayer in the court case in which the Tax Court approved this method of allocating deductions. While the court case initially was tried in the Tax Court, the decision in favor of the taxpayer was appealed to the Ninth Circuit Court that also ruled in favor of the taxpayer and sanctioned the use of the Tax Court or Bolton method of allocating interest expense. *Bolton v. Commissioner,* 82-2 USTC par. 9699 (CA 9), Affirming Tax Court, 77 TC 104.

The Tax Court justifies its approach by pointing out that interest expense and property taxes accrue over the entire year regardless of the level of personal or rental use. Taxpayers generally choose the approach most beneficial to them. Determining which method is more favorable for a particular taxpayer was made more complicated by recent tax law changes that increased the standard deduction and limited the itemized deduction for taxes. When the gross income limitation does not apply, the IRS method is generally more favorable because it allocates more mortgage interest and real property taxes to rental use where they are deductible as *for* AGI deductions. Under the Tax Court method more mortgage interest and real property taxes would be allocated to personal use where they may or may not provide tax benefit depending on whether the taxpayer itemizes deductions and whether the taxpayer has reached the $10,000 limit for deducting taxes. When the gross income limitation applies, the Tax Court method is likely more favorable for taxpayers who receive tax benefit from additional mortgage interest and real property tax itemized deductions because it maximizes their total current year deductions (*for* AGI plus itemized deductions) from the property relative to the IRS method. On the other hand, when the gross income limitation applies, the IRS method likely favors taxpayers who do not itemize deductions or who do not receive full tax benefit from the additional itemized deductions that would be provided by the Tax Court method (they are already capped on the itemized deduction for taxes or the full amount of mortgage interest and real property taxes are not above the standard deduction amount when combined with other itemized deductions). For these taxpayers, the trade-off is they have more excess tier 2 and tier 3 deductions that they carry over and deduct in a subsequent year instead of having more itemized deductions that provide little to no tax benefit. In any event, use of the Tax Court method likely involves more risk of IRS scrutiny than the IRS method.

Example 14-12

At the beginning of the year, the Jeffersons purchased a vacation home in Scottsdale, Arizona, for $500,000 ($400,000 for the building and $100,000 for the land). They paid $200,000 down and financed the remaining $300,000 with a 6 percent mortgage secured by the home. During the year, the Jeffersons used the home for personal purposes for 30 days and rented it out for 200 days. Thus, the home falls in the residence-with-significant-rental-use category. They received $37,500 of rental revenue and incurred $500 of rental advertising expenses. How are their expenses allocated to the rental use under the IRS and Tax Court methods?

Answer: See the following summary of allocation of expenses associated with the home:

Allocation Method to Rental Use					
Expense	Amount	Tier	IRS Method (200/230)	Tax Court Method (200/365 Tier 1 200/230 other)	
Advertising*	$ 500	1	$ 500	$ 500	
Interest	18,000	1	15,652	9,863	
Real estate taxes	5,000	1	4,348	2,740	
Total tier 1 expenses	**$23,500**	1	**$20,500**	**$13,103**	
Utilities	4,500	2	3,913	3,913	
Repairs	1,800	2	1,565	1,565	
Insurance	3,500	2	3,043	3,043	
Maintenance	3,200	2	2,783	2,783	
Total tier 2 expenses	**$13,000**	2	**$11,304**	**$11,304**	
Tier 3: Depreciation	**$13,939**	3	**$12,121**	**$12,121**	
Total expenses	$ 50,439				

*Advertising is a direct expense of the rental so it is fully deductible against rental revenue.

Net Income from Rental	IRS Method	Tax Court Method
Rental receipts	$ 37,500	$ 37,500
Less tier 1 expenses	(20,500)	(13,103)
Income after tier 1 expenses	17,000	24,397
Less tier 2 expenses	(11,304)	(11,304)
Income after tier 2 expenses	5,696	13,093
Less tier 3 expenses	(5,696)	(12,121)
Taxable rental income	**$ 0**	**$ 972**
Interest itemized deduction	$ 2,348	$ 8,137
(Real property tax itemized deduction)	652	2,260
Deductible rental expenses	37,500	36,528
(sum of tier 1, 2, and 3 expenses)		
Total itemized and rental expenses	**$40,500**	**$46,925**

At first glance, it appears that the Tax Court method is more favorable for the Jeffersons. After all, the Jeffersons are able to claim $6,425 more total deductions under the Tax Court method compared to the IRS method ($46,925 − $40,500). While the IRS method allows the Jefferson to deduct $972 more *for* AGI (rental) deductions than the Tax Court method ($37,500 − $36,528), the Tax Court method allows the Jeffersons to potentially deduct $5,789 more in mortgage interest expense ($8,137 − $2,348) and $1,608 more in real property taxes ($2,260 − $652) as itemized deductions. However, on closer inspection, it is not clear whether the Tax Court or the IRS method is more favorable for two reasons. First, the Jeffersons are allowed to carry forward to next year the $6,425 of depreciation expense that they did not deduct this year under the IRS method. That is, they were not able to deduct the $6,425 this year but they will be able to deduct it in a subsequent year if they generate enough income. Second, the Jeffersons report $1,608 more in real property taxes under the Tax Court method than under the IRS method. However, as indicated in Example 14-10, the Jeffersons exceed the $10,000 limit on the itemized deduction for taxes so the additional $1,608 of real property taxes does not increase their itemized deductions and it provides no tax benefit. The Tax Court gives the Jeffersons more deductions in the current year but the IRS method gives them more deductions in the current plus future years (assuming they generate enough income).

Taxpayers report their rental activities on Schedule E of Form 1040. The deductible tier 1, tier 2, and tier 3 expenses are *for* AGI deductions. Exhibit 14-5 displays the completed Schedule E for the Jeffersons' Scottsdale vacation home using the Tax Court method. Note that net rental income is considered to be investment income for purposes of determining the 3.8 percent net investment income tax (discussed in the Individual Income Tax Computation and Tax Credits chapter).

THE KEY FACTS

Rental Use of the Home

- Nonresidence
  - Rental use is at least 1 day and personal use is no more than the *greater* of (1) 14 days or (2) 10 percent of rental days.
  - Allocate expenses to rental and personal use.
  - Rental deductions in excess of rental income are deductible subject to passive loss limitation rules.
  - Interest expense allocated to personal use is not deductible.

TAXES IN THE REAL WORLD   Airbnb Anyone?

Online home rental communities such as Airbnb, HomeAway, and VRBO provide a marketplace that connects travelers looking for lodging with taxpayers seeking rental income from renting all (or part) of their homes. Online rental communities continue to grow as travelers increasingly seek lodging bargains. For example, reportedly, Airbnb recognized $1.7 billion in revenue in 2016 and is projecting revenue of $2.8 billion in 2017 and as much as $8.5 billion in revenue in 2020 (see http://fortune.com/2017/02/15/airbnb-profits/).

Taxpayers renting entire homes or even just a bedroom on Airbnb must deal with the tax consequences discussed in the Rental Use of the Home section of this chapter. See https://www.forbes.com/sites/anthonynitti/2015/11/09/renting-your-home-on-airbnb-be-aware-of-the-tax-consequences/#31e78cbfc518 for a discussion of the tax consequences of those renting their homes (consistent with the discussion in this chapter) and the tax consequences of renting out part of the home (beyond the scope of this chapter).

EXHIBIT 14-5   Jeffersons' Schedule E for Vacation Home Rental

SCHEDULE E (Form 1040)	**Supplemental Income and Loss**	OMB No. 1545-0074
Department of the Treasury Internal Revenue Service (99)	(From rental real estate, royalties, partnerships, S corporations, estates, trusts, REMICs, etc.) ▶ Attach to Form 1040, 1040NR, or Form 1041. ▶ Go to *www.irs.gov/ScheduleE* for instructions and the latest information.	**20 17** Attachment Sequence No. **13**

Name(s) shown on return	Your social security number
Tyler and Jasmine Jefferson	321-54-9876

Part I   Income or Loss From Rental Real Estate and Royalties   Note: If you are in the business of renting personal property, use **Schedule C** or **C-EZ** (see instructions). If you are an individual, report farm rental income or loss from **Form 4835** on page 2, line 40.

A Did you make any payments in 2017 that would require you to file Form(s) 1099? (see instructions) . . . . . ☐ Yes ☑ No
B If "Yes," did you or will you file required Forms 1099? . . . . ☐ Yes ☐ No

1a Physical address of each property (street, city, state, ZIP code)

A   Hole-in-One Blvd. Scottsdale, Arizona, 85262
B
C

1b	Type of Property (from list below)	2 For each rental real estate property listed above, report the number of fair rental and personal use days. Check the **QJV** box only if you meet the requirements to file as a qualified joint venture. See instructions.		Fair Rental Days	Personal Use Days	QJV
A	1		A	200	30	☐
B			B			☐
C			C			☐

Type of Property:
1 Single Family Residence   3 Vacation/Short-Term Rental 5 Land   7 Self-Rental
2 Multi-Family Residence   4 Commercial   6 Royalties   8 Other (describe)

Income:	Properties:		A	B	C
3	Rents received	3	37,500		
4	Royalties received	4			
Expenses:					
5	Advertising	5	500		
6	Auto and travel (see instructions)	6			
7	Cleaning and maintenance	7	2,783		
8	Commissions.	8			
9	Insurance	9	3,043		
10	Legal and other professional fees	10			
11	Management fees	11			
12	Mortgage interest paid to banks, etc. (see instructions)	12	9,863		
13	Other interest.	13			
14	Repairs.	14	1,565		
15	Supplies	15			
16	Taxes	16	2,740		
17	Utilities	17	3,913		
18	Depreciation expense or depletion	18	12,121		
19	Other (list) ▶	19			
20	Total expenses. Add lines 5 through 19	20	36,528		
21	Subtract line 20 from line 3 (rents) and/or 4 (royalties). If result is a (loss), see instructions to find out if you must file **Form 6198**	21	972		
22	Deductible rental real estate loss after limitation, if any, on **Form 8582** (see instructions)	22	( )	( )	( )

23a	Total of all amounts reported on line 3 for all rental properties	23a	37,500	
b	Total of all amounts reported on line 4 for all royalty properties	23b		
c	Total of all amounts reported on line 12 for all properties	23c	9,863	
d	Total of all amounts reported on line 18 for all properties	23d	12,121	
e	Total of all amounts reported on line 20 for all properties	23e	36,528	

24	**Income.** Add positive amounts shown on line 21. **Do not** include any losses	24	972
25	**Losses.** Add royalty losses from line 21 and rental real estate losses from line 22. Enter total losses here .	25	( )
26	**Total rental real estate and royalty income or (loss).** Combine lines 24 and 25. Enter the result here. If Parts II, III, IV, and line 40 on page 2 do not apply to you, also enter this amount on Form 1040, line 17, or Form 1040NR, line 18. Otherwise, include this amount in the total on line 41 on page 2 . . .	26	972

For Paperwork Reduction Act Notice, see the separate instructions.   Cat. No. 11344L   Schedule E (Form 1040) 2017

Source: Schedule E (Form 1040) 2017

Nonresidence (Rental Property)

For property in this category, the taxpayer includes the rental revenue in gross income and deducts all rental expenses *allocated to the rental use* of the property as *for* AGI deductions (all on Schedule E). When the property is used for even a day for personal purposes, the expenses must be allocated between the rental usage and the personal usage.[23] In this situation, however, the law does *not* allow the taxpayer to deduct mortgage interest that is not allocated to rental use, because the taxpayer does not meet the minimum personal use required for the deduction (the home is not a qualified residence—see earlier discussion). However, the taxpayer is still allowed to deduct, as an itemized deduction, real property taxes that are not allocated to the rental property (subject to the $10,000 deduction limitation for taxes). In contrast to the case for a residence with significant rental use, the rental expenses deduction for a nonresidence is not limited to gross income. However, a rental loss from a nonresidence is considered a passive loss and thus is subject to the passive activity loss limitations discussed below.[24]

	Example 14-13

What if: Suppose that at the beginning of the year, the Jeffersons purchased a vacation home in Scottsdale, Arizona, for $400,000. They paid $100,000 down and financed the remaining $300,000 with a 6 percent mortgage secured by the home. During the year, the Jeffersons *did not use the home for personal purposes* and they rented the home for 200 days. They received $37,500 in gross rental revenue for the year and incurred $50,439 of expenses relating to the rental property. How much can the Jeffersons deduct in this situation?

Answer: The good news is that the deductions are not limited to gross income from the rental so they can tentatively deduct all $50,439, generating a $12,939 loss on the property ($37,500 − $50,439). The bad news is that, as we discuss below, the loss may not be immediately deductible due to the passive activity loss limitations.

Exhibit 14-6 summarizes the tax rules relating to a home used for rental purposes depending on the extent of rental (and personal use). Appendix B to this chapter provides a flowchart summarizing the implementation of these rules.

Losses on Rental Property   A rental property can be a great investment that gets the best of all worlds. It could (1) appreciate in value, (2) produce annual positive cash flow (rental receipts exceed expenses other than depreciation), and (3) generate tax losses that reduce the taxes the owner is required to pay on other sources of income. Consider the Jeffersons' second-home property, purchased for $400,000 and used primarily as a rental home (see Example 14-15), which we'll assume has appreciated to $440,000 by the end of 2018. The property has appreciated by $40,000, produced a positive cash flow of $1,000 ($37,500 rental income minus expenses other than depreciation of $36,500 [$50,439 total expenses minus depreciation expense of $13,939]), and generated a net tax loss of $12,939. This loss apparently saves the Jeffersons $4,140 in taxes ($12,939 × 32% marginal tax rate).

Thus, the increase in the Jeffersons' wealth from their second-home investment for the year appears to be $45,140 ($40,000 appreciation + $1,000 rental cash flow + $4,140 tax savings). But as noted elsewhere in this text, when a tax outcome seems too good to be true, it usually is. Read on.

Passive activity loss rules.   In the Investments chapter, we introduced the passive activity loss rules that indicate taxpayers may only deduct passive losses for a year to the extent of their passive income. We also learned that, by definition, a rental activity (including a second-home rental that falls in the nonresidence category) is considered to

[23]§280A(e).

[24]If the home rental is deemed to be a not-for-profit activity, deductions allocated to the rental are nondeductible.

EXHIBIT 14-6   **Summary of Tax Rules Relating to Home Used for Rental Purposes**

	Residence with Minimal Rental Use	Residence with Significant Rental Use	Nonresidence
Classification test	Reside in home for at least 15 days and rent home for 14 or fewer days during the year.	Rent home for 15 days or more and use home for personal purposes for more than the greater of (1) 14 days or (2) 10 percent of the total rental days.	Rent home for at least 1 day, and personal use does not exceed the greater of (1) 14 days or (2) 10 percent of the rental days.
Rental revenue	Exclude from gross income.	Include in gross income.	Include in gross income.
Direct rental expenses unrelated to home use	Not deductible.	Fully deductible *for* AGI (loss not subject to passive activity loss rules).	Deductible *for* AGI but subject to passive activity loss rules.
Treatment of mortgage interest and real property taxes	Deductible as itemized deductions.	Allocate between personal-use days and rental days; interest and taxes allocated to rental days are deductible as rental expenses; interest and taxes allocated to personal-use days are deductible as itemized deductions subject to the limitations on home mortgage interest and taxes.	Allocated between personal-use days and rental days; interest and taxes allocated to rental days are deductible as rental expenses; taxes allocated to personal-use days are deductible as itemized deductions (subject to the $10,000 deduction limit for taxes); interest allocated to personal-use days is not deductible.
Treatment of all other expenses	Not deductible.	Allocate between personal-use days and rental days; expenses allocated to personal-use days are not deductible; expenses allocated to rental days are deductible as rental expenses to the extent of rental revenue minus the sum of direct rental expenses, rental mortgage interest, and real property taxes when expenses allocated to rental days exceed the rental income.	Allocated between personal-use days and rental days; expenses allocated to personal-use days are not deductible; expenses allocated to rental days are deductible and can generate a loss but the loss is subject to passive activity loss rules.
Excess expenses	Not applicable.	Rental expenses in excess of rental income minus the sum of direct rental expenses, rental mortgage interest, and real property taxes are carried forward to the next year.	Not applicable; rental expenses are deductible, even if they create a rental loss.

be a passive activity.[25] Because they are passive losses, losses from rental properties are generally not allowed to offset other ordinary or investment type income. However, as we also discussed the Investments chapter, a taxpayer who is an **active participant in a rental activity** may be allowed to deduct up to $25,000 of the rental loss against nonpassive income.[26] Consistent with a number of tax benefits, the exception amount for active owners is phased out as adjusted gross income increases: The $25,000 maximum exception amount is phased out by 50 cents for every dollar the taxpayer's adjusted gross income (before considering the rental loss) exceeds $100,000. Consequently, the entire $25,000 is phased out when the taxpayer's adjusted gross income reaches $150,000.

Example 14-14

Suppose the Jeffersons incurred a $12,939 passive loss from their Scottsdale rental home (as described in Example 14-13), and they did not receive any passive income during the year. Assuming that their current-year AGI is $250,000 and they are considered to be active participants in the rental activity, how much of the rental loss are the Jeffersons allowed to deduct this year under the rental real estate exception to the passive activity loss rules?

Answer: $0. Because their adjusted gross income exceeds $150,000, the $25,000 deduction exception to the passive activity loss rules is completely phased out. Consequently, the Jeffersons are not allowed to deduct any of the $12,939 rental loss for the year.

What if: How much of the $12,939 loss could the Jeffersons deduct for the year if their adjusted gross income (before considering the rental loss) were $120,000?

Answer: In this case, they could deduct the entire $12,939 loss. The $25,000 exception amount would be reduced by a $10,000 phase-out [50 cents × ($120,000 − $100,000)]. The maximum amount of the rental loss that can offset ordinary income would therefore be reduced from $25,000 to $15,000 ($25,000 − $10,000 phased out). However, because their loss is less than $15,000, they may deduct the entire $12,939 rental loss against their other sources of income for the year.

Are passive losses from rental real estate activities that taxpayers are not allowed to deduct in the current year permanently disallowed? No, these losses are suspended until the taxpayer generates passive income or sells the property that generated the passive loss. On the sale, in addition to reporting gain or loss from the sale of the property, the taxpayer is allowed to deduct suspended passive losses against ordinary income.

BUSINESS USE OF THE HOME   `LO 14-6`

Because a personal residence is a personal use asset, utility payments and depreciation due to wear and tear are not deductible expenses. However, self-employed taxpayers (not employees) who use their home—or at least part of their home—for business purposes may be able to deduct expenses associated with their home use if they meet certain stringent requirements.[27]

To qualify for **home office deductions,** a taxpayer must use her home—or part of her home—*exclusively and regularly* as either

1. The principal place of business for any of the taxpayer's trade or businesses, or
2. As a place to meet with patients, clients, or customers in the normal course of business.

---

[25]Recall that second homes falling into the significant-personal-and-rental-use category are not passive activities. See §469(j).

[26]§469(i).

[27]§280A. If taxpayers rent the home they occupy and they meet the requirements for business use of the home, they can deduct part of the rent they pay. To determine the amount of the deduction, multiply the rental payment by the percentage of the home used for business purposes.

Taxpayers fail the exclusive use test if they use the area of the home in question for any personal purpose.

What if: Jasmine recently quit her job as an employee for an advertising firm because, with the move to the new home, the commute was too long. She has decided to go it alone as a self-employed graphic designer. She uses a large room in the basement of the Jeffersons' new home as her office. The room has been wired for all her office needs. Once or twice a week, Tyler sits at the desk in the room and surfs the Web to read up on his favorite sports teams. Is the office space eligible for a home office deduction?

Answer: No. The office is not used exclusively for Jasmine's business. Tyler's personal use of the office disqualifies the office for the home office deduction.

The taxpayer is not required to meet the exclusive use test in order to claim the home office deduction if the taxpayer either

- Uses part of the home for the storage of inventory or product samples.
- Uses part of the home as a day care facility.

When a taxpayer has more than one business location, including the home, which is the taxpayer's principal place of business? This is a facts-and-circumstances determination based upon

- The relative importance of the activities performed at each place where the taxpayer conducts business (more income from an activity generally means it is a more important activity) and
- The total time spent doing work at each location.

However, by definition, a taxpayer's principal place of business also includes the place of business used by the taxpayer for the administrative or management activities of the taxpayer's trade or business, if there is no other fixed location of the trade or business where the taxpayer conducts substantial administrative or management activities of the trade or business.[28]

If a taxpayer meets with clients or patients in her home during the normal course of business, she qualifies for the home office deduction even if the home is not her principal place of business. However, the clients or patients must visit the taxpayer's home *in person*. Communication through telephone calls or other types of communication technology does not qualify.

What if: Jasmine recently quit her job as an employee for an advertising firm because, with the move to the new home, the commute was too long. She has decided to go it alone as a self-employed graphic designer. She uses a large room in the basement of the Jeffersons' new home as her office. The room has been wired for all her office needs. The Jeffersons use the room exclusively for Jasmine's graphic design business use. Does this space qualify for the home office deduction?

Answer: Yes. While Jasmine will spend a good deal of time meeting with clients outside her home office, she has no other fixed location for her trade or business. Further, the office is used exclusively for business purposes. Consequently, the office qualifies for the home office deduction subject to certain limitations described below.

[28]§280A(c)(1).

TAXES IN THE REAL WORLD If You Want The Bathroom to Qualify as a Part of a Home Office, You Better Lock It and Keep the Key

The IRS and a taxpayer with seven years of IRS work experience have battled over home office expenses in the Tax Court. The taxpayer operated an accounting business, and he used a bedroom in his residence exclusively for his accounting business. The taxpayer included the bathroom adjacent to the bedroom in his home office square footage. However, because the taxpayer testified that his children and personal guests occasionally used the bathroom, the Tax Court determined that the bathroom was not used exclusively for business purposes (the children and personal guests may beg to differ), and it disallowed the expenses associated with the bathroom square footage. See *Luis Bulas*, T.C. Memo. 2011-201 (2011).

Source: Luis Bulas, T.C. Memo. 2011-201 (2011).

Direct versus Indirect Expenses

When taxpayers qualify for home office deductions, they are allowed to deduct only actual expenses that are related—either directly or indirectly—to their business. Direct expenses are expenses incurred in maintaining the room or part of the home that is set aside for business use. They include painting or costs of other repairs to the area.[29] These expenses are deductible in full as home office expenses. Indirect expenses are expenses incurred in maintaining and using the entire home. Indirect expenses include insurance, utilities, interest, real property taxes, general repairs, and depreciation on the home as if it were used entirely for business purposes. Depreciation on the home is calculated using nonresidential real property depreciation tables (straight-line depreciation over 39 years). In contrast to direct expenses that are fully deductible, only indirect expenses *allocated* to the home office space are deductible.

How do taxpayers allocate indirect expenses to the home office space? If the rooms in the home are roughly of equal size, the taxpayer may allocate the indirect expenses to the business portion of the home based on the number of rooms. In a 10-room home, a taxpayer using one room for qualifying business use is allowed to deduct 10 percent of the indirect expenses. Or the taxpayer may allocate indirect expenses based on the square footage of the business-use room relative to the total square footage in the home. If the home is 5,000 square feet and the home office is 250 square feet, the taxpayer may deduct 5 percent of the indirect expenses. Unrelated expenses such as painting a room not used for business purposes are not deductible.

In lieu of allocating actual expenses to home office use, the IRS allows taxpayers to use an optional simplified method for computing home office expenses.[30] Under the simplified method, taxpayers are not allowed to deduct any *actual* expenses relating to qualified business use of the home (including depreciation). Instead, taxpayers electing the simplified method deduct, subject to limitations described below, the allowable business use square footage of the office (not to exceed 300 square feet) multiplied by $5 per square foot. Thus, this method generates a maximum deduction of $1,500 (300 square feet × $5 per square foot). In addition, taxpayers using this method are allowed to deduct all of their home mortgage interest and real property taxes as itemized deductions on Schedule A. Taxpayers may choose from year to year whether to use the simplified method or the actual expense method.

---

[29]The basic local telephone service charge, including taxes, for the first telephone line into a home is a nondeductible personal expense. However, charges for business long-distance phone calls on that line, as well as the cost of a second line into the home used exclusively for business, are deductible business expenses. However, these expenses are not deducted as home office expenses. Rather, these expenses are deducted separately on the appropriate form or schedule. Taxpayers filing Schedule C (Form 1040) would deduct these expenses as utilities.

[30]Rev. Proc. 2013-13.

Example 14-17

The Jeffersons moved into their new $800,000, 6,000-square-foot home on February 1 (the home building was valued at $600,000, and the land was valued at $200,000.) Jasmine quit her job and set up a 420-square-foot home office in the basement on that same date. Through the end of the calendar year, the Jeffersons incurred several expenses relating to their home (see table below). Assuming they qualify for the home office deduction, they would sum the direct expenses and the indirect expenses allocated to the office. They would allocate the indirect expenses based on the square footage of the office compared to the rest of the home. Using the actual expense method, what amount of home-related expenses would qualify as home office expenses?

Answer: $4,575. See allocation below. All direct expenses and 7 percent of the indirect expenses would be allocated to the home office (420 office square footage/6,000 home square footage). The Jeffersons would allocate the expenses as follows:

Total Expense	Type	(A) Amount	(B) Office %	(A) × (B) Home Office Expense
Painting office	Direct	$ 200	100%	$ 200
Real property taxes	Indirect	11,000	7	770
Home interest expense	Indirect	27,917	7	1,954
Electricity	Indirect	2,600	7	182
Gas and other utilities	Indirect	2,500	7	175
Homeowner's insurance	Indirect	5,000	7	350
Depreciation	Indirect	13,482	7	944
Total expenses		$62,699		**$4,575**

The expenses attributable to the home office are deductible subject to the limitations discussed below. Also, as discussed below, the Jeffersons are able to deduct the home interest expense not allocated to the home office as an itemized deduction.

What if: Suppose Jasmine elects to use the simplified method for determining home office expenses. What would be the amount of their home office expenses?

Answer: $1,500 (300 square feet × $5 per square foot). Even though the Jeffersons' home office is 420 square feet, for purposes of the home office expense under the simplified method, the square footage is limited to 300 square feet.

What if: Suppose the Jeffersons elect to use the simplified method for home office expenses. What amount of home mortgage interest expenses and real property taxes would they be able to deduct on Schedule A as itemized deductions?

Answer: Home mortgage interest expense, $27,917; $11,000 of real property taxes before considering the $10,000 itemized deduction limit on taxes. The Jeffersons also paid $15,000 in state income taxes. Consequently, of the total $26,000 they paid in taxes, they can deduct $10,000 as an itemized deduction.

Limitations on Deductibility of Expenses

The process for determining the home office expense deduction using the actual expense method is similar to the process used to determine deductions for vacation homes. When net business income (net Schedule C income) before the home office deduction exceeds total home office expenses (before applying any limitations), the full amount of the expenses is deductible. However, when home office expenses exceed net Schedule C income (before the home office deduction), the deduction is potentially limited.

In these situations, taxpayers first divide home office expenses into one of three categories or tiers. Tier 1 expenses consist of mortgage interest and real property taxes allocated to the business use of the home. Tier 2 expenses consist of all other expenses allocated to the business use of the home except depreciation. Tier 3 expense consists of depreciation.

Taxpayers first deduct tier 1 expenses in full, even when they exceed net Schedule C income before the home office deduction.[31] Second, taxpayers deduct tier 2 expenses.

[31]§280A(c)(5).

However, deductible tier 2 expenses are limited to net Schedule C income before home office deductions minus tier 1 expenses (that is, deducting tier 2 expenses cannot create a net Schedule C loss). Any tier 2 expenses not deductible due to the income limitation are suspended and carried forward to the next year, subject to the same limitations. Finally, taxpayers deduct tier 3 expenses. The deductible tier 3 expense is limited to net Schedule C income before the home office deduction minus tier 1 and deductible tier 2 expenses (tier 3 expense cannot create a net Schedule C loss). The nondeductible portion of tier 3 expense is carried forward to the next year, subject to the same limitations.

Under the simplified method, the expense, as calculated by multiplying the square footage by the $5 application rate, is limited to net Schedule C income before home office deductions. Further, taxpayers using the simplified method in a particular year may not carry over expenses disallowed by the income limitation and they may not deduct expenses carried over to that year under the actual expense method. However, disallowed expenses under the actual expense method can be carried over to a subsequent year in which the taxpayer uses the actual expense method for determining the home office expense deduction.

Example 14-18

For the year, Jasmine generated $4,000 of net business income before the home office deduction from her graphic design business. Her home office expenses before limitation total $4,575 (see Example 14-17). The expenses consist of painting the office $200, real property taxes $770, home interest expense $1,954, electricity $182, gas and other utilities $175, homeowner's insurance $350, and depreciation $944. What is the total amount of tier 1, tier 2, and tier 3 expenses?

Answer: Tier 1 expenses are $2,724 (real property taxes $770 and home interest expense of $1,954); tier 2 expenses are $907 (painting office $200, electricity $182, gas and other utilities $175, and homeowner's insurance $350); and tier 3 expense is $944 (depreciation).

What is Jasmine's net income from the business after claiming the home office deduction and what expenses, if any, will she carry over to next year?

Answer: $0 net income, as shown in the table below. She will carry over $575 of depreciation expense.

	Net Income from Business
Gross business receipts	$4,000
Less tier 1 expenses	(2,724)
Income after tier 1 expenses	1,276
Less tier 2 expenses	(907)
Income after tier 2 expenses	369
Less tier 3 expenses	(369)
Taxable business income	**$ 0**

Due to the income limitation, Jasmine is allowed to deduct only $369 of the $944 depreciation expense. She will carry over the remaining $575 ($944 minus $369) to next year to deduct as a home office expense (tier 3) subject to the same limitations.

What if: Suppose Jasmine uses the simplified method of determining home office expenses. What amount of the $1,500 expense (300 square feet × $5 application rate) will she be allowed to deduct?

Answer: She can deduct all $1,500, because the home office expense is less than the $4,000 net business income before the home office deduction.

What if: Assume the same facts as in the previous what-if scenario except that net business income before the home office deduction is now $1,200. What amount of the $1,500 home office expense will Jasmine be allowed to deduct?

Answer: $1,200. The home office expense deduction under the simplified method is limited to net business income before the home office deduction. Jasmine is not allowed to carry over the $300 nondeductible portion of the expense to a subsequent year ($1,500 total expense minus $1,200 deductible expense).

When a taxpayer deducts depreciation as a home office expense, the depreciation expense reduces the basis of the taxpayer's home. Consequently, when the taxpayer sells the home, the gain on the sale will be greater than it would have been had the taxpayer not deducted depreciation expense. Further, the gain on the sale of the home attributable to depreciation deductions (incurred after 5/6/1997) is not eligible to be excluded under the home sale exclusion provision. Rather, the gain is treated as unrecaptured §1250 gain and is subject to a maximum 25 percent tax rate (see the Property Dispositions chapter for a detailed discussion of unrecaptured §1250 gain).

Example 14-19

At the beginning of the year, the Jeffersons' basis in their home was $800,000. Jasmine's first-year home office deductions included $369 in depreciation expense. What is the Jeffersons' adjusted basis in the home at the end of the year?

Answer: $799,631 ($800,000 minus $369 deductible depreciation expense).

What if: Now suppose that the Jeffersons meet the ownership and use tests for the home sale exclusion and they sell the home for $900,000. Assume the only depreciation expense the Jeffersons have deducted is the $369 they deducted in the year they bought the home. Consequently, their adjusted basis in the home on the date of sale is $799,631 and they realize a gain of $100,369 on the sale. How much of the gain, if any, must they recognize on the sale?

Answer: $369. They can exclude $100,000 of gain. However, they are not allowed to exclude the remaining $369 gain caused by the depreciation expense for the home office. The Jeffersons must pay $92 of tax on the gain ($369 × 25% unrecaptured §1250 gain).

Taxpayers using the simplified method for deducting home office expenses are not allowed to deduct depreciation expense. Consequently, the simplified method does not affect the taxpayer's adjusted basis in the home. However, if a taxpayer switches from the simplified method in one year to the actual expense method in a subsequent year, the taxpayer is required to use modified depreciation tables to compute depreciation expense under the actual expense method.

Allowing taxpayers to deduct part of their home-related expenses as business expenses creates temptations for taxpayers to deduct home-related expenses that don't meet the deduction requirements. Not surprisingly, the IRS is very concerned about taxpayers inappropriately deducting expenses relating to their home. Consequently, expenses for business use of the home are some of the most highly scrutinized deductions available to taxpayers. Self-employed taxpayers claiming home office deductions must file a Form 8829 "Expenses for Business Use of Your Home" when deducting home office expenses on a tax return. With the high level of scrutiny applied to home office expenses, taxpayers should be sure to have documentation available to support their deductions. Exhibit 14-7 includes Form 8829 for Jasmine based on the information in Examples 14-17 and 14-18.

CONCLUSION

When deciding whether to invest in a home as a primary residence, a vacation home, or even a rental home, prospective owners should consider both nontax and tax factors relating to the ownership of the property. The tax code includes several provisions favorable to homeowners. This chapter is intended to provide current and prospective homeowners with enough insight on tax and nontax consequences of home ownership to allow them to make informed investment and compliance decisions when applicable.

EXHIBIT 14-7

Form **8829**

Department of the Treasury
Internal Revenue Service (99)

Expenses for Business Use of Your Home

▶ File only with Schedule C (Form 1040). Use a separate Form 8829 for each
home you used for business during the year.
▶ Go to *www.irs.gov/Form8829* for instructions and the latest information.

OMB No. 1545-0074

2017

Attachment
Sequence No. **176**

Name(s) of proprietor(s)	Your social security number
Jasmine Jefferson	**674-65-6564**

Part I   Part of Your Home Used for Business

1	Area used regularly and exclusively for business, regularly for daycare, or for storage of inventory or product samples (see instructions)	**1**	420
2	Total area of home	**2**	6,000
3	Divide line 1 by line 2. Enter the result as a percentage	**3**	7 %

For daycare facilities not used exclusively for business, go to line 4. All others, go to line 7.

4	Multiply days used for daycare during year by hours used per day	**4**		hr.
5	Total hours available for use during the year (365 days x 24 hours) (see instructions)	**5**	8,760	hr.
6	Divide line 4 by line 5. Enter the result as a decimal amount . . .	**6**	.	

7	Business percentage. For daycare facilities not used exclusively for business, multiply line 6 by line 3 (enter the result as a percentage). All others, enter the amount from line 3 . . . . . ▶	**7**	7 %

Part II   Figure Your Allowable Deduction

8	Enter the amount from Schedule C, line 29, **plus** any gain derived from the business use of your home, **minus** any loss from the trade or business not derived from the business use of your home (see instructions)			**8**	4,000

See instructions for columns **(a)** and **(b)** before completing lines 9–21.

		(a) Direct expenses	**(b)** Indirect expenses		
9	Casualty losses (see instructions).	**9**			
10	Deductible mortgage interest (see instructions)	**10**		27,917	
11	Real estate taxes (see instructions)	**11**		11,000	
12	Add lines 9, 10, and 11	**12**		38,917	
13	Multiply line 12, column (b), by line 7. . . .		**13**	2,724	
14	Add line 12, column (a), and line 13				**14** 2,724
15	Subtract line 14 from line 8. If zero or less, enter -0-				**15** 1,276
16	Excess mortgage interest (see instructions) .	**16**			
17	Insurance	**17**		5,000	
18	Rent	**18**			
19	Repairs and maintenance	**19**	200		
20	Utilities	**20**		5,100	
21	Other expenses (see instructions).	**21**			
22	Add lines 16 through 21	**22**	200	10,100	
23	Multiply line 22, column (b), by line 7.		**23**	707	
24	Carryover of prior year operating expenses (see instructions) . .		**24**		
25	Add line 22, column (a), line 23, and line 24				**25** 907
26	Allowable operating expenses. Enter the **smaller** of line 15 or line 25				**26** 907
27	Limit on excess casualty losses and depreciation. Subtract line 26 from line 15				**27** 369
28	Excess casualty losses (see instructions)	**28**			
29	Depreciation of your home from line 41 below	**29**	944		
30	Carryover of prior year excess casualty losses and depreciation (see instructions)	**30**			
31	Add lines 28 through 30				**31** 944
32	Allowable excess casualty losses and depreciation. Enter the **smaller** of line 27 or line 31 . .				**32** 369
33	Add lines 14, 26, and 32.				**33** 4,000
34	Casualty loss portion, if any, from lines 14 and 32. Carry amount to **Form 4684** (see instructions)				**34**
35	**Allowable expenses for business use of your home.** Subtract line 34 from line 33. Enter here and on Schedule C, line 30. If your home was used for more than one business, see instructions ▶				**35** 4,000

Part III   Depreciation of Your Home

36	Enter the **smaller** of your home's adjusted basis or its fair market value (see instructions) . .	**36**	800,000
37	Value of land included on line 36	**37**	200,000
38	Basis of building. Subtract line 37 from line 36	**38**	600,000
39	Business basis of building. Multiply line 38 by line 7.	**39**	42,000
40	Depreciation percentage (see instructions).	**40**	2.247 %
41	Depreciation allowable (see instructions). Multiply line 39 by line 40. Enter here and on line 29 above	**41**	944

Part IV   Carryover of Unallowed Expenses to 2018

42	Operating expenses. Subtract line 26 from line 25. If less than zero, enter -0-	**42**	
43	Excess casualty losses and depreciation. Subtract line 32 from line 31. If less than zero, enter -0-	**43**	575

For Paperwork Reduction Act Notice, see your tax return instructions.   Cat. No. 13232M   Form **8829** (2017)

Source: Form 8829 (2017)

Appendix A   Sample Settlement Statement for the Jeffersons (page 1)

OMB Approval No. 2502-0265

A. Settlement Statement (HUD-1)

B. Type of Loan

1. ☐ FHA	2. ☐ RHS	3. ☒ Conv. Unins.	6. File Number:	7. Loan Number:	8. Mortgage Insurance Case Number:
4. ☐ VA	5. ☐ Conv. Ins.		1355	6788	

C. Note: This form is furnished to give you a statement of actual settlement costs. Amounts paid to and by the settlement agent are shown. Items marked "(p.o.c.)" were paid outside the closing; they are shown here for informational purposes and are not included in the totals.

D. Name & Address of Borrower:	E. Name & Address of Seller:	F. Name & Address of Lender:
Tyler Jefferson Jasmine Jefferson 225 El Tejon Dr. Chicago, IL 60612	Ian Sabin 525 Roberts Ln. Glencoe, IL 60022	125 Decatur St. Chicago, IL 60612

G. Property Location:	H. Settlement Agent:	I. Settlement Date:
225 El Tejon Dr. Chicago, IL 60612 Lot 1, Block 2, Dozier Estates Cook County, Illinois	Beardsley Settlement Group	1/31/2018
	Place of Settlement: 425 McCray St., Chicago, IL 60612	

J. Summary of Borrower's Transaction

100. Gross Amount Due from Borrower	
101. Contract sales price	$800,000.00
102. Personal property	
103. Settlement charges to borrower (line 1400)	$28,116.00
104.	
105.	
Adjustment for items paid by seller in advance	
106. City/town taxes to	
107. County taxes to	
108. Assessments to	
109.	
110.	
111.	
112.	
120. Gross Amount Due from Borrower	**$828,116.00**
200. Amount Paid by or in Behalf of Borrower	
201. Deposit or earnest money	$20,000.00
202. Principal amount of new loan(s)	$300,000.00
203. Existing loan(s) taken subject to	
204.	
205.	
206.	
207.	
208.	
209.	
Adjustments for items unpaid by seller	
210. City/town taxes to	
211. County taxes 1/1/2018 to 1/31/2018	$1,000.00
212. Assessments to	
213.	
214.	
215.	
216.	
217.	
218.	
219.	
220. Total Paid by/for Borrower	**$321,000.00**
300. Cash at Settlement from/to Borrower	
301. Gross amount due from borrower (line 120)	$828,116.00
302. Less amounts paid by/for borrower (line 220)	($321,000.00)
303. Cash ☒ From ☐ To Borrower	**$507,116.00**

K. Summary of Seller's Transaction

400. Gross Amount Due to Seller	
401. Contract sales price	$800,000.00
402. Personal property	
403.	
404.	
405.	
Adjustment for items paid by seller in advance	
406. City/town taxes to	
407. County taxes to	
408. Assessments to	
409.	
410.	
411.	
412.	
420. Gross Amount Due to Seller	**$800,000.00**
500. Reductions In Amount Due to seller	
501. Excess deposit (see instructions)	
502. Settlement charges to seller (line 1400)	$51,700.00
503. Existing loan(s) taken subject to	
504. Payoff of first mortgage loan	
505. Payoff of second mortgage loan	
506.	
507.	
508.	
509.	
Adjustments for items unpaid by seller	
510. City/town taxes to	
511. County taxes 1/1/2018 to 1/31/2018	$1,000.00
512. Assessments to	
513.	
514.	
515.	
516.	
517.	
518.	
519.	
520. Total Reduction Amount Due Seller	**$52,700.00**
600. Cash at Settlement to/from Seller	
601. Gross amount due to seller (line 420)	$800,000.00
602. Less reductions in amounts due seller (line 520)	($52,700.00)
603. Cash ☒ To ☐ From Seller	**$747,300.00**

The Public Reporting Burden for this collection of information is estimated at 35 minutes per response for collecting, reviewing, and reporting the data. This agency may not collect this information, and you are not required to complete this form, unless it displays a currently valid OMB control number. No confidentiality is assured; this disclosure is mandatory. This is designed to provide the parties to a RESPA covered transaction with information during the settlement process.

(page 2)

L. Settlement Charges					Paid From Borrower's Funds at Settlement	Paid From Seller's Funds at Settlement
700. Total Real Estate Broker Fees		based on price $800,000 @ 6.0% = $48,000				
Division of commission (line 700) as follows :						
701. $ 24,000.00	to	Selling Agent Co.				
702. $ 24,000.00	to	Listing Agent Co.				
703. Commission paid at settlement						$48,000.00
704.						

800. Items Payable in Connection with Loan						
801. Our origination charge 1.0%			$ 3,000.00	(from GFE #1)		
802. Your credit or charge (points) for the specific interest rate chosen		2.0%	$ 6,000.00	(from GFE #2)		
803. Your adjusted origination charges				(from GFE #A)	$9,000.00	
804. Appraisal fee to	Drumqoole Appraisal Co.			(from GFE #3)	$400.00	
805. Credit report to	O'Brien Credit Check Inc.			(from GFE #3)	$40.00	
806. Tax service to				(from GFE #3)		
807. Flood certification to				(from GFE #3)		
808.						
809.						
810.						
811.						

900. Items Required by Lender to be Paid in Advance						
901. Daily interest charges from 1/31/2018 to 2/10/2018 @ $ 41.10		/day		(from GFE #10)	$411.00	
902. Mortgage insurance premium for	months to			(from GFE #3)		
903. Homeowner's insurance for	years to			(from GFE #11)		
904.						

1000. Reserves Deposited with Lender						
1001. Initial deposit for your escrow account				(from GFE #9)		
1002. Homeowner's insurance	2	months @ $ 100.00	per month	$ 200.00		
1003. Mortgage insurance		months @ $	per month	$		
1004. Property Taxes	11	months @ $ 1,000.00	per month	$ 11,000.00		
1005.		months @ $	per month	$		
1006.		months @ $	per month	$		
1007. Aggregate Adjustment				-$		

1100. Title Charges						
1101. Title services and lender's title insurance				(from GFE #4)	$250.00	
1102. Settlement or closing fee	Beardsley Settlement Group		$			$300.00
1103. Owner's title insurance	Title Insurance Co.			(from GFE #5)	$3,250.00	
1104. Lender's title insurance			$			
1105. Lender's title policy limit $						
1106. Owner's title policy limit $						
1107. Agent's portion of the total title insurance premium to			$			
1108. Underwriter's portion of the total title insurance premium to			$			
1109. Document Preparation to Buckles & Pitts, L.L.P						$200.00
1110.						
1111.						

1200. Government Recording and Transfer Charges						
1201. Government recording charges				(from GFE #7)		
1202. Deed $ 40.00	Mortgage $ 50.00		Release $			$90.00
1203. Transfer taxes				(from GFE #8)		
1204. City/County tax/stamps	Deed $ 450.00	Mortgage $ 350.00				$800.00
1205. State tax/stamps	Deed $ 1,250.00	Mortgage $ 1,000.00				$2,250.00
1206.						

1300. Additional Settlement Charges						
1301. Required services that you can shop for				(from GFE #6)		
1302. Survey to Beardsley Settlement Group			$		$125.00	
1303. Pest Inspection to Clark's Pest Control			$			$60.00
1304.						
1305.						

1400. Total Settlement Charges (enter on lines 103, Section J and 502, Section K)	$28,116.00	$51,700.00

Appendix B Flowchart of Tax Rules Relating to Home Used for Rental Purposes (page 1)

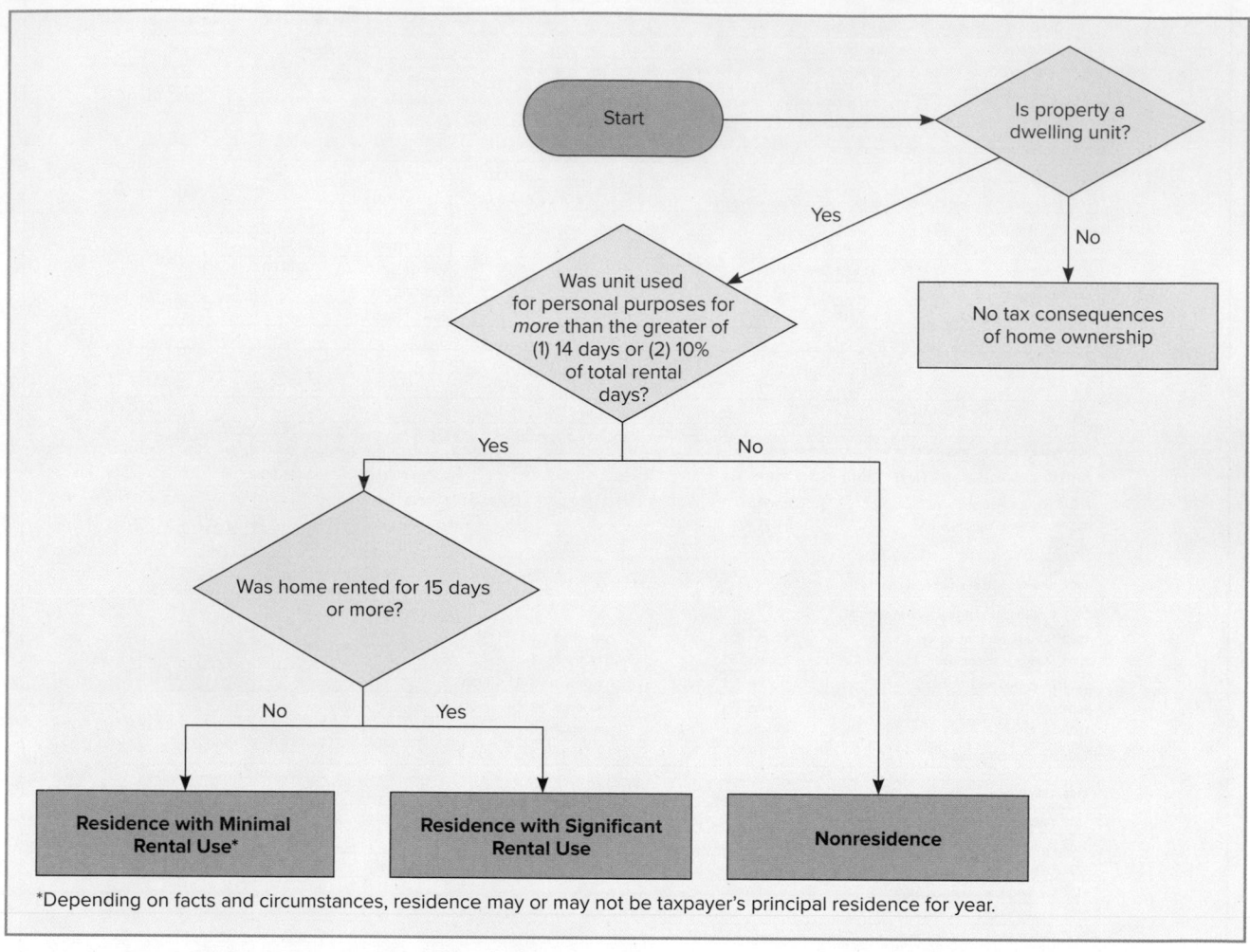

*Depending on facts and circumstances, residence may or may not be taxpayer's principal residence for year.

(page 2)

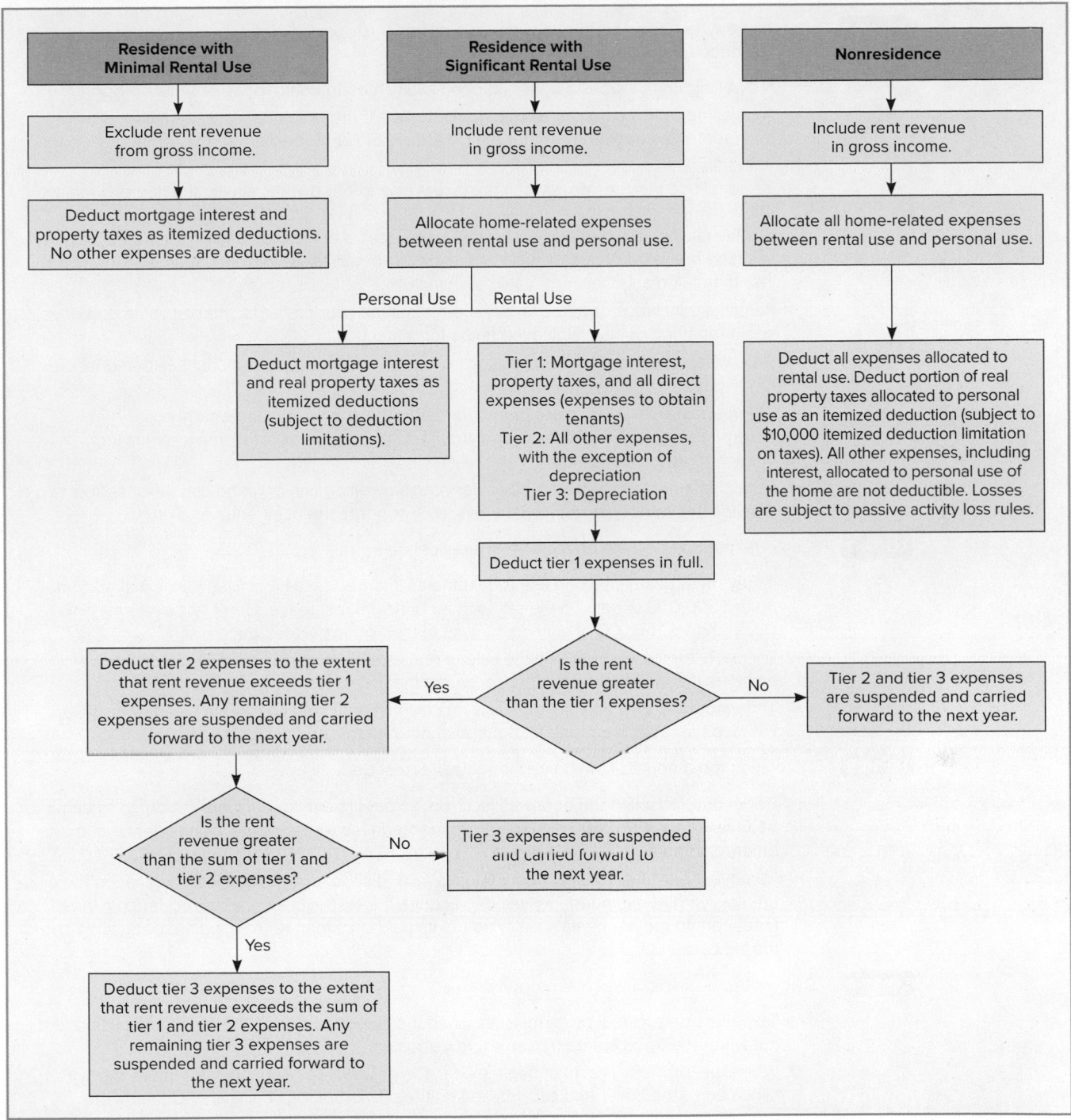

Summary

LO 14-1 Determine whether a home is considered a principal residence, a residence (not principal), or a nonresidence for tax purposes.

- A dwelling unit includes a house, condominium, mobile home, boat, or similar property.
- A dwelling unit is considered to be a residence if the taxpayer's personal use of the unit (home) exceeds the greater of (1) 14 days or (2) 10 percent of the rental days during the year.
- Personal use includes days when the taxpayer or other owners stay in the home; a relative of the owner stays in the home (even if the relative pays full fair market value, unless the relative is using the home as a principal residence); a nonowner stays in the home under a vacation home exchange or swap arrangement; or the taxpayer rents out the property for less than fair market value.
- Rental use includes days the taxpayer rents out the property at fair market value and days spent repairing or maintaining the home for rental use.
- Days when the home is available for rent but not rented out do not count as personal or rental days.
- When a taxpayer owns more than one residence, the principal residence is determined based on the facts and circumstances, such as total time spent living in each residence.
- For a particular taxpayer for a particular year, a dwelling unit or home can be classified as a principal residence, residence (not principal), or nonresidence (rental property).

LO 14-2 Compute the taxable gain on the sale of a residence.

- If they meet ownership and use requirements, married taxpayers filing jointly may exclude up to $500,000 of gain on the sale of their principal residence. Other taxpayers may exclude up to $250,000 of gain on the sale of their principal residence.
- To qualify for the exclusion on the sale of real estate, taxpayers must own and use the home as their principal residence for two of the five years preceding the sale.
- The amount of gain eligible for exclusion may be reduced if on or after January 1, 2009, the taxpayer uses the home for a purpose other than as a principal residence.

LO 14-3 Determine the amount of the home mortgage interest deduction.

- Depending on when the debt was incurred, taxpayers may deduct interest on up to either $1,000,000 or $750,000 of acquisition indebtedness for their principal residence and one other residence.
- Taxpayers may immediately deduct points paid (discount points and loan origination fees) on qualifying home mortgages used to acquire the taxpayer's principal residence if they meet certain requirements. Qualifying points paid on a loan refinancing are deductible over the life of the loan.

LO 14-4 Discuss the deductibility of real property taxes.

- Taxpayers deduct real property taxes when the taxes are paid to the taxing jurisdiction and not when the taxes are paid to an escrow account.
- When real property is sold during the year, the property tax deduction for the property is allocated to the buyer and seller based on the portion of the year that each holds the property, no matter which party pays the taxes.
- The itemized deduction for all taxes combined (state income, real property, and personal property tax) is limited to $10,000 ($5,000 for married taxpayers filing separately).

LO 14-5 Explain the tax issues and consequences associated with rental use of the home.

- Taxpayers who live in a home for 15 days or more and rent the home out for 14 days or less (a residence with minimal rental use) do not include gross rental receipts in taxable income and do not deduct rental expenses.
- Taxpayers who both reside in and rent out a home for a significant portion of the year (a residence with significant rental use) include rental revenue in gross income, deduct direct rental expenses not relating to the home (expenses to obtain tenants), and allocate

home-related expenses between personal use and rental use of the home. They deduct mortgage interest expense and real property taxes allocated to the rental use of the home as *for* AGI deductions and the mortgage interest expense and real property taxes allocated to the personal use of the home as itemized deductions (subject to limitations). The remaining deductions allocated to the rental use of the home are deductible in a particular sequence and the amount of these deductions cannot exceed rental revenue in excess of direct rental expenses and rental mortgage interest and real property taxes.

- Net rental income reported on Schedule E is potentially subject to the net investment income tax discussed in the Individual Income Tax Computation and Tax Credits chapter. This tax applies to net investment income for high-income taxpayers.

- Taxpayers who rent out a home with minimal or no personal use (nonresidence) include rental receipts in income and deduct all rental expenses. In this situation expenses exceeding income are subject to the passive activity loss rules.

- Taxpayers may be able to deduct up to $25,000 of passive loss on their rental home if they are active participants with respect to the property. This deduction is phased out for taxpayers with adjusted gross income between $100,000 and $150,000.

Compute the limitations on home office deductions.

LO 14-6

- To deduct expenses relating to a home office, the taxpayer must be self-employed and use the home office exclusively and regularly for business purposes.

- Home-related expenses are allocated between business expenses and personal expenses based on the size of the office relative to the size of the home.

- Mortgage interest and real property taxes allocated to business use of the home are deductible in full without regard to the income of the business.

- Other expenses allocated to the business use of the home are deducted in a particular sequence. The deduction for these expenses cannot exceed the taxpayer's net Schedule C income (before home office expenses) minus the mortgage interest and real property taxes allocated to business use of the home.

- Taxpayers electing the simplified method for claiming home office expenses may deduct $5 per square foot up to 300 square feet.

KEY TERMS

acquisition indebtedness (14-9)

active participant in a rental activity (14-23)

dwelling unit (14-2)

escrow account (14-14)

flipping (14-5)

home office deductions (14-23)

IRS allocation method (14-27)

point (14-11)

principal residence (14-2)

qualified residence (14-9)

real property taxes (14-13)

refinance (14-9)

settlement statement (14-11)

Tax Court allocation method (14-17)

DISCUSSION QUESTIONS

Discussion Questions are available in Connect®.

Mc Graw Hill Education **connect**

1. How does a taxpayer determine whether a dwelling unit is treated as a residence or nonresidence for tax purposes?

LO 14-1

2. For tax purposes, does a residence need to be situated at a fixed location? Explain.

LO 14-1

3. When determining whether a dwelling unit is treated as a residence or a nonresidence for tax purposes, what constitutes a day of personal use and what constitutes a day of rental use?

LO 14-1

4. A taxpayer owns a home in Salt Lake City, Utah, and a second home in St. George, Utah. How does the taxpayer determine which home is her principal residence for tax purposes?

LO 14-1

LO 14-2   5. What are the ownership and use requirements a taxpayer must meet to qualify for the exclusion of gain on the sale of a residence?

LO 14-2   6. Under what circumstances, if any, can a taxpayer fail to meet the ownership and use requirements but still be able to exclude all of the gain on the sale of a principal residence?

LO 14-2   7. Under what circumstances can a taxpayer meet the ownership and use requirements for a residence but still not be allowed to exclude all realized gain on the sale of the residence?

LO 14-2   8. A taxpayer purchases and lives in a home for a year. The home appreciates in value by $50,000. The taxpayer sells the home and purchases a new home. What information do you need to obtain to determine whether the taxpayer is allowed to exclude the gain on the sale of the first home?

LO 14-3   9. Juanita owns a principal residence in New Jersey, a cabin in Montana, and a houseboat in Hawaii. All of these properties have mortgages incurred before 2017 on which Juanita pays interest. What limits, if any, apply to Juanita's home mortgage interest deductions? Explain whether deductible interest is deductible *for* AGI or *from* AGI.

LO 14-3   10. For purposes of determining a taxpayer's deductible home mortgage interest, does it matter when the taxpayer incurred the debt to acquire the home? Explain.

LO 14-3   11. Lars and Leigha saved up for years before they purchased their dream home. They were considering (1) using all of their savings to make a large down payment on the home (90 percent of the value of the home) and barely scraping by without backup savings, or (2) making a more modest down payment (50 percent of the value of the loan) and holding some of the savings in reserve as needed if funds got tight. They decided to make a large down payment because they figured they could always refinance the home to pull some equity out of it if they needed cash. What advice would you give them about the tax consequences of their decision?

LO 14-3   12. Is it possible for a taxpayer to have more than one loan that is treated as acquisition indebtedness for tax purposes? Explain.

LO 14-3   13. Why might it be good advice from a tax perspective to think hard before deciding to quickly pay down mortgage debt?

LO 14-3   14. With recent tax law changes, are taxpayers likely to receive more or less tax savings from home mortgage interest deductions?

LO 14-3   15. Compare and contrast the characteristics of a deductible point from a nondeductible point on a first home mortgage.

LO 14-3   16. Is the break-even period generally longer for points paid to reduce the interest rate on initial home loans or points paid for the same purpose on a refinance? Explain.

planning   **LO 14-3**   17. Under what circumstances is it likely to be economically beneficial to pay points to reduce the interest rate on a home loan?

LO 14-3   18. Harry decides to finance his new home with a 30-year fixed mortgage. Because he figures he will be in this home for a long time, he decides to pay a fully deductible discount point on his mortgage to reduce the interest rate. Assume that Harry itemizes deductions and has a constant marginal tax rate over time. Will the time required to recover the cost of the discount point be shorter or longer if Harry makes extra principal payments starting in the first year (as opposed to not making any extra principal payments)? Explain.

LO 14-3 **LO 14-4**   19. Consider the settlement statement in Appendix A to this chapter. What amounts on the statement are the Jeffersons allowed to deduct on their 2018 tax return? Indicate the settlement statement line number for each deductible amount (discuss any issues that must be addressed to determine deductibility) and label each deduction as a *for* AGI deduction or a *from* AGI deduction.

20. A taxpayer sells a piece of real property in year 1. The amount of year 1 real property taxes is estimated at the closing of the sale and the amounts are allocated between the buyer and the taxpayer. At the end of year 1, the buyer receives a property tax bill that is higher than the estimate. After paying the tax bill, the buyer contacts the taxpayer at the beginning of year 2 and asks the taxpayer to pay the taxpayer's share of the shortfall. The taxpayer sends a check to the buyer. Should the taxpayer be concerned that she won't get to deduct the extra tax payment because it was paid to the buyer and not to the taxing jurisdiction? Explain.   `LO 14-4`

21. Are real property taxes subject to any deduction limitations? Explain.

22. Is a homeowner allowed a property tax deduction for amounts included in the monthly mortgage payment that are earmarked for property taxes? Explain.   `LO 14-4`

23. Is it possible for a taxpayer to receive rental income that is not subject to taxation? Explain.   `LO 14-5` ▪ planning

24. Halle just acquired a vacation home. She plans on spending several months each year vacationing in the home and renting out the property for the rest of the year. She is projecting tax losses on the rental portion of the property for the year. She is not too concerned about the losses because she is confident she will be able to use the losses to offset her income from other sources. Is her confidence misplaced? Explain.   `LO 14-5`

25. A taxpayer stays in a second home for the entire month of September. He would like the home to fall into the residence-with-significant-rental-use category for tax purposes. What is the maximum number of days he can rent out the home and have it qualify?   `LO 14-5` ▪ planning

26. Compare and contrast the IRS method and the Tax Court method for allocating expenses between personal use and rental use for vacation homes. Include the Tax Court's justification for departing from the IRS method in your answer.   `LO 14-5`

27. In what circumstances is the IRS method for allocating expenses between personal use and rental use for second homes more beneficial to a taxpayer than the Tax Court method?   `LO 14-5`

28. Under what circumstances would a taxpayer who generates a loss from renting a home that is not a residence be able to fully deduct the loss? What potential limitations apply?   `LO 14-5`

29. Describe the circumstances in which a taxpayer acquires a home and rents it out and is not allowed to deduct a portion of the interest expense on the loan the taxpayer used to acquire the home.   `LO 14-5`

30. Is it possible for a rental property to generate a positive annual cash flow and at the same time produce a loss for tax purposes? Explain.   `LO 14-5`

31. How are the tax issues associated with home offices and vacation homes used as rentals similar? How are the tax issues or requirements dissimilar?   `LO 14-5` `LO 14-6`

32. Are employees or self-employed taxpayers more likely to qualify for and benefit from the home office deduction? Explain.   `LO 14-6`

33. Compare and contrast the manner in which employees and employers report home office deductions on their tax returns.   `LO 14-6`

34. For taxpayers qualifying for home office deductions, what are considered to be indirect expenses of maintaining the home? How are these expenses allocated to personal and home office use? Can taxpayers choose to calculate home office expenses without regard to actual expenses allocated to the home office? Explain.   `LO 14-6`

35. What limitations exist for self-employed taxpayers in deducting home office expenses, and how does the taxpayer determine which expenses are deductible and which are not in situations when the overall amount of the home office deduction is limited?   `LO 14-6`

LO 14-2 LO 14-6 36. A self-employed taxpayer deducts home office expenses including depreciation expense. The taxpayer then sells the home at a $100,000 gain. Assuming the taxpayer meets the ownership and use tests, does the full gain qualify for exclusion? Explain.

PROBLEMS

Select problems are available in Connect®.

LO 14-1 37. Several years ago, Junior acquired a home that he vacationed in part of the time and rented out part of the time. During the current year Junior:

- Personally stayed in the home for 22 days.
- Rented it to his favorite brother at a discount for 10 days.
- Rented it to his least favorite brother for 8 days at the full market rate.
- Rented it to his friend at a discounted rate for 4 days.
- Rented the home to third parties for 58 days at the market rate.
- Did repair and maintenance work on the home for 2 days.
- Marketed the property and made it available for rent for 150 days during the year (but did not rent it out).

How many days of personal use and how many days of rental use did Junior experience on the property during the year?

LO 14-1 38. Lauren owns a condominium. In each of the following alternative situations, determine whether the condominium should be treated as a residence or a nonresidence for tax purposes.

a) Lauren lives in the condo for 19 days and rents it out for 22 days.

b) Lauren lives in the condo for 8 days and rents it out for 9 days.

c) Lauren lives in the condo for 80 days and rents it out for 120 days.

d) Lauren lives in the condo for 30 days and rents it out for 320 days.

LO 14-2 39. Steve and Stephanie Pratt purchased a home in Spokane, Washington, for $400,000. They moved into the home on February 1 of year 1. They lived in the home as their primary residence until June 30 of year 5, when they sold the home for $700,000.

a) What amount of gain on the sale of the home are the Pratts required to include in taxable income?

b) Assume the original facts, except that Steve and Stephanie live in the home until January 1 of year 3, when they purchase a new home and rent out the original home. They finally sell the original home on June 30 of year 5 for $700,000. Ignoring any issues relating to depreciation taken on the home while it is being rented, what amount of realized gain on the sale of the home are the Pratts required to include in taxable income?

c) Assume the same facts as in part (b), except that the Pratts live in the home until January of year 4 ,when they purchase a new home and rent out the first home. What amount of realized gain on the sale of the home will the Pratts include in taxable income if they sell the first home on June 30 of year 5 for $700,000?

d) Assume the original facts, except that Stephanie moves in with Steve on March 1 of year 3 and the couple is married on March 1 of year 4. Under state law, the couple jointly owns Steve's home beginning on the date they are married. On December 1 of year 3, Stephanie sells her home that she lived in before she moved in with Steve. She excludes the entire $50,000 gain on the sale on her individual year 3 tax return. What amount of gain must the couple recognize on the sale in June of year 5?

40. Steve and Stephanie Pratt purchased a home in Spokane, Washington, for $400,000. **LO 14-2** They moved into the home on February 1 of year 1. They lived in the home as their primary residence until November 1 of year 1, when they sold the home for $500,000. The Pratts' marginal ordinary tax rate is 35 percent.

   a) Assume that the Pratts sold their home and moved because they didn't like their neighbors. How much gain will the Pratts recognize on their home sale? At what rate, if any, will the gain be taxed?

   b) Assume the Pratts sell the home because Stephanie's employer transfers her to an office in Utah. How much gain will the Pratts recognize on their home sale?

   c) Assume the same facts as in part (b), except that the Pratts sell their home for $700,000. How much gain will the Pratts recognize on the home sale?

   d) Assume the same facts as part (b), except that on December 1 of year 0 the Pratts sold their home in Seattle and excluded the $300,000 gain from income on their year 0 tax return. How much gain will the Pratts recognize on the sale of their Spokane home?

41. Steve Pratt, who is single, purchased a home in Spokane, Washington, for $400,000. **LO 14-2** He moved into the home on February 1 of year 1. He lived in the home as his primary residence until June 30 of year 5, when he sold the home for $700,000.

   a) What amount of gain will Steve be required to recognize on the sale of the home?

   b) Assume the original facts, except that the home is Steve's vacation home and he vacations there four months each year. Steve does not ever rent the home to others. What gain must Steve recognize on the home sale?

   c) Assume the original facts, except that Steve married Stephanie on February 1 of year 3 and the couple lived in the home until they sold it in June of year 5. Under state law, Steve owned the home by himself. How much gain must Steve and Stephanie recognize on the sale (assume they file a joint return in year 5).

42. Celia has been married to Daryl for 52 years. The couple has lived in their current **LO 14-2** home for the last 20 years. In October of year 0, Daryl passed away. Celia sold their home and moved into a condominium. What is the maximum exclusion Celia is entitled to if she sells the home on December 15 of year 1?

43. Sarah (single) purchased a home on January 1, 2008, for $600,000. She eventually **LO 14-2** sold the home for $800,000. What amount of the $200,000 gain on the sale does Sarah recognize in each of the following alternative situations? (Assume accumulated depreciation on the home is $0.)

   a) Sarah used the home as her principal residence through December 31, 2016. She used the home as a vacation home from January 1, 2017, until she sold it on January 1, 2019.

   b) Sarah used the property as a vacation home through December 31, 2016. She then used the home as her principal residence from January 1, 2017, until she sold it on January 1, 2019.

   c) Sarah used the home as a vacation home from January 1, 2008, until January 1, 2018. She used the home as her principal residence from January 1, 2018, until she sold it on January 1, 2019.

   d) Sarah used the home as a vacation home from January 1, 2008, through December 31, 2012. She used the home as her principal residence from January 1, 2013, until she sold it on January 1, 2018.

44. Troy (single) purchased a home in Hopkinton, Massachusetts, on January 1, 2007, **LO 14-2** for $300,000. He sold the home on January 1, 2018, for $320,000. How much gain must Troy recognize on his home sale in each of the following alternative situations?

a) Troy rented out the home from January 1, 2007, through November 30, 2008. He lived in the home as his principal residence from December 1, 2008, through the date of sale. Assume accumulated depreciation on the home at the time of sale was $7,000.

b) Troy lived in the home as his principal residence from January 1, 2007, through December 31, 2013. He rented out the home from January 1, 2014, through the date of the sale. Assume accumulated depreciation on the home at the time of sale was $2,000.

c) Troy lived in the home as his principal residence from January 1, 2007, through December 31, 2015. He rented out the home from January 1, 2016, through the date of the sale. Assume accumulated depreciation on the home at the time of sale was $0.

d) Troy rented out the home from January 1, 2007, through December 31, 2013. He lived in the home as his principal residence from January 1, 2014, through December 31, 2014. He rented out the home from January 1, 2015, through December 31, 2015, and lived in the home as his principal residence from January 1, 2016, through the date of the sale. Assume accumulated depreciation on the home at the time of sale was $0.

LO 14-3   45. Javier and Anita Sanchez purchased a home on January 1, 2018, for $600,000 by paying $200,000 down and borrowing the remaining $400,000 with a 7 percent loan secured by the home. The loan requires interest-only payments for the first five years. The Sanchezes would itemize deductions even if they did not have any deductible interest. The Sanchezes' marginal tax rate is 32 percent.

a) What is the after-tax cost of the interest expense to the Sanchezes in 2018?

b) Assume the original facts, except that the Sanchezes rent a home and pay $21,000 in rent during the year. What is the after-tax cost of their rental payments in 2018?

c) Assuming the interest expense is their only itemized deduction for the year and that Javier and Anita file a joint return, have great eyesight, and are under 60 years of age, what is the after-tax cost of their 2018 interest expense?

LO 14-3   46. Javier and Anita Sanchez purchased a home on January 1 of year 1 for $1,000,000 by paying $200,000 down and borrowing the remaining $800,000 with a 6 percent loan secured by the home. The Sanchezes made interest only payments on the loan in years 1 and 2.

a) Assuming year 1 is 2017, how much interest would the Sanchezes deduct in year 2?

b) Assuming year 1 is 2018, how much interest would the Sanchezes deduct in year 2?

c) Assume year 1 is 2018 and by the beginning of year 4, the Sanchezes have paid down the principal amount of the loan to $500,000. They borrow $100,000 using a loan secured by the home in order to finish their basement. The new loan carries a 7 percent interest rate. What amount of interest can the Sanchezes deduct on the $100,000 loan?

d) Assume year 1 is 2018 and by the beginning of year 4, the Sanchezes have paid down the principal amount of the loan to $500,000. They borrow $100,000 using a loan secured by the home in order to purchase a new car. The new loan carries a 7 percent interest rate. What amount of interest can the Sanchezes deduct on the $100,000 loan?

LO 14-3   47. Lewis and Laurie are married and jointly own a home valued at $240,000. They recently paid off the mortgage on their home. The couple borrowed money from the local credit union in January of 2018. How much interest may the couple deduct in each of the following alternative situations? (Assume they itemize deductions no matter the amount of interest.)

a) The couple borrows $40,000, and the loan is secured by their home. The couple pays $1,600 interest on the loan during the year, and the couple files a joint return.

b) The couple borrows $110,000, and the loan is secured by their home. They use the loan proceeds to add a room to their home. The couple pays $5,200 interest on the loan during the year, and the couple files a joint return.

48. On January 1 of year 1, Arthur and Aretha Franklin purchased a home for $1.5 million by paying $200,000 down and borrowing the remaining $1.3 million with a 7 percent loan secured by the home. The Franklins paid interest only on the loan for year 1 and year 2 (unless stated otherwise).   **LO 14-3**

    a) What is the amount of interest expense the Franklins may deduct in year 2 assuming year 1 is 2017?

    b) What is the amount of interest expense the Franklins may deduct in year 2 assuming year 1 is 2018?

    c) Assume that year 1 is 2018 and that in year 2, the Franklins pay off the entire loan but at the beginning of year 3, they borrow $300,000 secured by the home at a 7 percent rate. They make interest-only payments on the loan during the year. What amount of interest expense may the Franklins deduct in year 3 on this loan? (Assume the Franklins do not use the loan proceeds to improve the home.)

49. On January 1 of 2018, Jason and Jill Marsh acquired a home for $500,000 by paying $400,000 down and borrowing $100,000 with a 7 percent loan secured by the home. On January 1 of 2019, the Marshes needed cash so they refinanced the original loan by taking out a new $250,000, 7 percent loan. With the $250,000 proceeds from the new loan, the Marshes paid off the original $100,000 loan and used the remaining $150,000 to fund their son's college education.   **LO 14-3**

    a) What amount of interest expense on the refinanced loan may the Marshes deduct in 2019?

    b) Assume the original facts, except that the Marshes use the $150,000 cash from the refinancing to add two rooms and a garage to their home. What amount of interest expense on the refinanced loan may the Marshes deduct in 2019?

50. Jennifer has been living in her current principal residence for three years. Six months ago Jennifer decided that she would like to purchase a second home near a beach so she can vacation there for part of the year. Despite her best efforts, Jennifer has been unable to find what she is looking for. Consequently, Jennifer recently decided to change plans. She purchased a parcel of land for $200,000 with the intention of building her second home on the property. To acquire the land, she borrowed $200,000 secured by the land. Jennifer would like to know whether the interest she pays on the loan before construction on the house is completed is deductible as mortgage interest.   **LO 14-3**

    a) How should Jennifer treat the interest if she has begun construction on the home and plans to live in the home in 12 months from the time construction began?

    b) How should Jennifer treat the interest if she hasn't begun construction on the home but plans to live in the home in 15 months?

    c) How should Jennifer treat the interest if she has begun construction on the home but doesn't plan to live in the home for 37 months from the time construction began?

LO 14-3

planning

51. Rajiv and Laurie Amin are recent college graduates looking to purchase a new home. They are purchasing a $200,000 home by paying $20,000 down and borrowing the other $180,000 with a 30-year loan secured by the home. The Amins have the option of (1) paying no discount points on the loan and paying interest at 8 percent or (2) paying 1 discount point on the loan and paying interest of 7.5 percent. Both loans require the Amins to make interest-only payments for the first five years. Unless otherwise stated, the Amins itemize deductions irrespective of the amount of interest expense. The Amins are in the 24 percent marginal ordinary income tax bracket.

   a) Assuming the Amins *do not itemize deductions*, what is the break-even point for paying the point to get a lower interest rate?

   b) Assuming the Amins do itemize deductions, what is the break-even point for paying the point to get a lower interest rate?

   c) Assume the original facts, except that the amount of the loan is $300,000. What is the break-even point for the Amins for paying the point to get a lower interest rate?

   d) Assume the original facts, except that the $180,000 loan is a refinance instead of an original loan. What is the break-even point for paying the point to get a lower interest rate?

   e) Assume the original facts, except that the amount of the loan is $300,000 and the loan is a refinance and not an original loan. What is the break-even point for paying the point to get a lower interest rate?

LO 14-4

52. Peter and Shaline Johnsen moved into a home in a new subdivision. Theirs was one of the first homes in the subdivision. During the year, they paid $1,500 in real property taxes to the state government, $500 to the developer of the subdivision for an assessment to pay for the sidewalks, and $900 for real property taxes on land they hold as an investment. What amount of property taxes are the Johnsens allowed to deduct assuming their itemized deductions exceed the standard deduction amount before considering any property tax deductions and they pay $5,000 of state income taxes for the year and no other deductible taxes?

LO 14-4

53. Jesse Brimhall is single. In 2018, his itemized deductions were $9,000 before considering any real property taxes he paid during the year. Jesse's adjusted gross income was $70,000 (also before considering any property tax deductions). In 2018, he paid real property taxes of $3,000 on property 1 and $1,200 of real property taxes on property 2. He did not pay any other deductible taxes during the year.

   a) If property 1 is Jesse's primary residence and property 2 is his vacation home (he does not rent it out at all), what is his taxable income after taking property taxes into account?

   b) If property 1 is Jesse's business building (he owns the property) and property 2 is his primary residence, what is his taxable income after taking property taxes into account (ignore the deduction for qualified business income)?

   c) If property 1 is Jesse's primary residence and property 2 is a parcel of land he holds for investment, what is his taxable income after taking property taxes into account?

LO 14-4

54. Craig and Karen Conder purchased a new home on May 1 of year 1 for $200,000. At the time of the purchase, it was estimated that the real property tax rate for the year would be 1 percent of the property's value. How much in property taxes on the new home are the Conders allowed to deduct under each of the following circumstances? Assume the Conders' itemized deductions exceed the standard deduction before considering property taxes and the property tax is the only deductible tax they pay during the year.

   a) The property tax estimate proves to be accurate. The seller and the Conders paid their share of the tax. The full property tax bill is paid to the taxing jurisdiction by the end of the year.

b) The actual property tax bill was 1.05 percent of the property's value. The Conders paid their share of the estimated tax bill and the entire difference between the 1 percent estimate and the 1.05 percent actual tax bill and the seller paid the rest. The full property tax bill is paid to the taxing jurisdiction by the end of the year.

c) The actual property tax bill was .95 percent of the property's value. The seller paid their share of taxes based on the 1 percent estimate and the Conders paid the difference between what the seller paid and the amount of the final tax bill. The full property tax bill is paid to the taxing jurisdiction by the end of the year.

55. Kirk and Lorna Newbold purchased a new home on August 1 of year 1 for $300,000. At the time of the purchase, it was estimated that the real property tax rate for the year would be .5 percent of the property's value. Because the taxing jurisdiction collects taxes on a July 1 year-end, it was estimated that the Newbolds would be required to pay $1,375 in property taxes for the property tax year relating to August through June of year 2 ($300,000 × .005 × 11/12). The seller would be required to pay the $125 for July of year 1. Along with their monthly payment of principal and interest, the Newbolds paid $125 to the mortgage company to cover the property taxes. The mortgage company placed the money in escrow and used the funds in the escrow account to pay the property tax bill in July of year 2. The Newbolds' itemized deductions exceed the standard deduction before considering real property and they don't pay any other deductible taxes during the year.   `LO 14-4`

a) How much in real property taxes can the Newbolds deduct for year 1?

b) How much in real property taxes can the Newbolds deduct for year 2?

c) Assume the original facts, except that the Newbolds were not able to collect $125 from the seller for the property taxes for July of year 1. How much in real property taxes can the Newbolds deduct for year 1 and year 2?

d) Assume the original facts, except that the tax bill for July 1 of year 1 through June 30 of year 2 turned out to be $1,200 instead of $1,500. How much in real property taxes can the Newbolds deduct in year 1 and year 2?

56. Jenae and Terry Hutchings own a parcel of land as tenants by entirety. That is, they both own the property but when one of them dies the other becomes the sole owner of the property. For nontax reasons, Jenae and Terry decide to file separate tax returns for the current year. Jenae paid the entire $3,000 property tax bill for the land. How much of the $3,000 property tax payment is each spouse entitled to deduct in the current year assuming they pay no other deductible taxes during the year?   `LO 14-4`

`research`

57. Dillon rented his personal residence at Lake Tahoe for 14 days while he was vacationing in Ireland. He resided in the home for the remainder of the year. Rental income from the property was $6,500. Expenses associated with use of the home for the entire year were as follows: `LO 14-5`

Real property taxes	$ 3,100
Mortgage interest	12,000
Repairs	1,500
Insurance	1,500
Utilities	3,900
Depreciation	13,000

a) What effect does the rental have on Dillon's AGI?

b) What effect does the rental have on Dillon's itemized deductions (assuming he itemizes deductions before considering deductions associated with the home)?

Use the following facts to answer problems 58 and 59.

Natalie owns a condominium near Cocoa Beach in Florida. This year, she incurs the following expenses in connection with her condo:

Insurance	$1,000
Advertising expense	500
Mortgage interest	3,500
Property taxes	900
Repairs & maintenance	650
Utilities	950
Depreciation	8,500

During the year, Natalie rented out the condo for 75 days, receiving $10,000 of gross income. She personally used the condo for 35 days during her vacation.

tax forms

58. Assume Natalie uses the IRS method of allocating expenses to rental use of the property.

a) What is the total amount of *for* AGI (rental) deductions Natalie may deduct in the current year related to the condo?

b) What is the total amount of itemized deductions Natalie may deduct in the current year related to the condo?

c) If Natalie's basis in the condo at the beginning of the year was $150,000, what is her basis in the condo at the end of the year?

d) Assume that gross rental revenue was $2,000 (rather than $10,000). What amount of *for* AGI deductions may Natalie deduct in the current year related to the condo (assuming she itemizes deductions before considering deductions associated with the condo)?

e) Using the original facts, complete Natalie's Form 1040, Schedule E, for this property. Also, partially complete Natalie's 1040, Schedule A, to include her *from* AGI deductions related to the condo.

59. Assume Natalie uses the Tax Court method of allocating expenses to rental use of the property.

a) What is the total amount of *for* AGI (rental) deductions Natalie may deduct in the current year related to the condo (assuming she itemizes deductions before considering deductions associated with the condo)?

b) What is the total amount of itemized deductions Natalie may deduct in the current year related to the condo?

c) If Natalie's basis in the condo at the beginning of the year was $150,000, what is her basis in the condo at the end of the year?

d) Assume that gross rental revenue was $2,000 (rather than $10,000). What amount of *for* AGI deductions may Natalie deduct in the current year related to the condo?

Use the following facts to answer problems 60, 61, and 62.

Alexa owns a condominium near Cocoa Beach in Florida. This year, she incurs the following expenses in connection with her condo:

Insurance	$ 2,000
Mortgage interest	6,500
Property taxes	2,000
Repairs & maintenance	1,400
Utilities	2,500
Depreciation	14,500

During the year, Alexa rented out the condo for 100 days. She did not use the condo at all for personal purposes during the year. Alexa's AGI from all sources other than the rental property is $200,000. Unless otherwise specified, Alexa has no sources of passive income.

60. Assume Alexa receives $30,000 in gross rental receipts.   `LO 14-5`

    a) What effect do the expenses associated with the property have on her AGI?

    b) What effect do the expenses associated with the property have on her itemized deductions?

61. Assuming Alexa receives $20,000 in gross rental receipts, answer the following questions: `LO 14-5`

    a) What effect does the rental activity have on her AGI for the year?

    b) Assuming that Alexa's AGI from other sources is $90,000, what effect does the rental activity have on Alexa's AGI? Alexa makes all decisions with respect to the property.

    c) Assuming that Alexa's AGI from other sources is $120,000, what effect does the rental activity have on Alexa's AGI? Alexa makes all decisions with respect to the property.

    d) Assume that Alexa's AGI from other sources is $200,000. This consists of $150,000 salary, $10,000 of dividends, $25,000 of long-term capital gain, and net rental income from another rental property in the amount of $15,000. What effect does the Cocoa Beach Condo rental activity have on Alexa's AGI?

62. Assume that in addition to renting the condo for 100 days, Alexa uses the condo for 8 days of personal use. Also assume that Alexa receives $30,000 of gross rental receipts and her itemized deductions exceed the standard deduction before considering expenses associated with the condo. Answer the following questions: `LO 14-5`   planning

    a) What is the total amount of *for* AGI deductions relating to the condo that Alexa may deduct in the current year? Assume she uses the IRS method of allocating expenses between rental and personal days.

    b) What is the total amount of *from* AGI deductions relating to the condo that Alexa may deduct in the current year? Assume she uses the IRS method of allocating expenses between rental and personal days.

    c) Would Alexa be better or worse off after taxes in the current year if she uses the Tax Court method of allocating expenses?

63. Brooke owns a sole proprietorship in which she works as a management consultant. She maintains an office in her home where she meets with clients, prepares bills, and performs other work-related tasks. The home office is 300 square feet and the entire house is 4,500 square feet. Brooke incurred the following home-related expenses during the year. Unless indicated otherwise, assume Brooke uses the actual expense method to compute home office expenses.   `LO 14-6`

tax forms

Real property taxes	$ 3,600
Interest on home mortgage	14,000
Operating expenses of home	5,000
Depreciation	12,000
Repairs to home theater room	1,000

    a) What amount of each of these expenses is allocated to the home office?

    b) What are the total amounts of tier 1, tier 2, and tier 3 expenses, respectively, allocated to the home office?

    c) If Brooke reported $2,000 of Schedule C net income before the home office expense deduction, what is the amount of her home office expense deduction and what home office expenses, if any, would she carry over to next year?

d) Assuming Brooke reported $2,000 of Schedule C income before the home office expense deduction, complete Form 8829 for Brooke's home office expense deduction. Also assume the value of the home is $500,000 and the adjusted basis of the home (exclusive of land) is $468,019.

e) Assume that Brooke uses the simplified method for computing home office expenses. If Brooke reported $2,000 of Schedule C net income before the home office expense deduction, what is the amount of her home office expense deduction and what home office expenses, if any, would she carry over to next year?

Use the following facts to answer problems 64 and 65.

Rita owns a sole proprietorship in which she works as a management consultant. She maintains an office in her home (500 square feet) where she meets with clients, prepares bills, and performs other work-related tasks. Her business expenses, other than home office expenses, total $5,600. The following home-related expenses have been allocated to her home office under the actual expense method for calculating home office expenses.

Real property taxes	$1,600
Interest on home mortgage	5,100
Operating expenses of home	800
Depreciation	1,600

Also, assume that, not counting the sole proprietorship, Rita's AGI is $60,000.

LO 14-6

64. Assume Rita's consulting business generated $15,000 in gross income.

a) What is Rita's home office deduction for the current year?

b) What would Rita's home office deduction be if her business generated $10,000 of gross income instead of $15,000? (Answer for both the actual expense method and the simplified method.)

c) Given the original facts, what is Rita's AGI for the year?

d) Given the original facts, what types and amounts of expenses will she carry over to next year?

LO 14-6

65. Assume Rita's consulting business generated $13,000 in gross income for the current year. Further, assume Rita uses the actual expense method for computing her home office expense deduction.

a) What is Rita's home office deduction for the current year?

b) What is Rita's AGI for the year?

c) Assuming the original facts, what types and amounts of expenses will she carry over to next year?

LO 14-2 **LO 14-6**

66. Alisha, who is single, owns a sole proprietorship in which she works as a management consultant. She maintains an office in her home where she meets with clients, prepares bills, and performs other work-related tasks. She purchased the home at the beginning of year 1 for $400,000. Since she purchased the home and moved into it she has been able to deduct $10,000 of depreciation expenses to offset her consulting income. At the end of year 3, Alisha sold the home for $500,000. What is the amount of taxes Alisha will be required to pay on the gain from the sale of the home? Alisha's ordinary marginal tax rate is 30 percent. (Ignore the net investment income tax.)

COMPREHENSIVE PROBLEMS

Select problems are available in Connect®.   ▪️connect

planning

67. Derek and Meagan Jacoby recently graduated from State University and Derek accepted a job in business consulting while Meagan accepted a job in computer programming. Meagan inherited $75,000 from her grandfather who recently passed away. The couple is debating whether they should buy or rent a home. They located a rental home that meets their needs. The monthly rent is $2,250. They also found a three-bedroom home that would cost $475,000 to purchase. The Jacobys could use Meagan's inheritance for a down payment on the home. Thus, they would need to borrow $400,000 to acquire the home. They have the option of paying 2 discount points to receive a fixed interest rate of 4.5 percent on the loan or paying no points and receiving a fixed interest rate of 5.75 percent for a 30-year fixed loan.

    Though anything could happen, the couple expects to live in the home for no more than five years before relocating to a different region of the country. Derek and Meagan don't have any school-related debt, so they will save the $75,000 if they don't purchase a home. Also, consider the following information:

- The couple's marginal tax rate is 24 percent.
- Regardless of whether they buy or rent, the couple will itemize their deductions.
- If they buy, the Jacobys would purchase and move into the home on January 1, 2018.
- If they buy the home, the property taxes for the year are $3,600.
- Disregard loan-related fees not mentioned above.
- If the couple does not buy a home, they will put their money into their savings account where they earn 5 percent annual interest.
- Assume that all unstated costs are equal between the buy and rent option.

Required:

Help the Jacobys with their decisions by answering the following questions:

a) If the Jacobys decide to rent the home, what is their after-tax cost of the rental for the first year? (Include income from the savings account in your analysis.)

b) What is the approximate break-even point in years (or months) for paying the points to receive a reduced interest rate? (To simplify this computation, assume the Jacobys will make interest-only payments, and ignore the time value of money.)

c) What is the after-tax cost (in interest and property taxes) of living in the home for 2018? Assume that the Jacobys' interest rate is 5.75 percent, they do not pay discount points, they make interest-only payments for the first year, and the value of the home does not change during the year.

d) Assume that on March 1, 2018, the Jacobys sold their home for $525,000, so that Derek and Meagan could accept job opportunities in a different state. The Jacobys used the sale proceeds to (1) pay off the $400,000 principal of the mortgage, (2) pay a $10,000 commission to their real estate broker, and (3) make a down payment on a new home in the different state. However, the new home cost only $300,000. What gain or loss do the Jacobys realize and recognize on the sale of their home and what amount of taxes must they pay on the gain, if any? (Assume they make interest-only payments on the loan.)

e) Assume the same facts as in part (d), except that the Jacobys sell their home for $450,000 and they pay a $7,500 commission. What effect does the sale have on their 2018 income tax liability? Recall that the Jacobys are subject to an ordinary marginal tax rate of 24 percent and assume that they do not have any other transactions involving capital assets in 2018.

68. James and Kate Sawyer were married on New Year's Eve of 2017. Before their marriage, Kate lived in New York and worked as a hair stylist for one of the city's top salons. James lives in Atlanta where he works for a public accounting firm earning an annual salary of $100,000. After their marriage, Kate left her job in New York and moved into the couple's newly purchased 3,200-square-foot home in Atlanta. Kate incurred $2,200 of moving expenses. The couple purchased the home on January 3, 2018, by paying $100,000 down and obtaining a $400,000 mortgage for the remainder. The interest rate on this loan was 7 percent and the Sawyers made interest-only payments on the loan through June 30, 2018 (assume they paid exactly one-half of a year's worth of interest on this loan by June 30). On July 1, 2018, the Sawyers borrowed an additional $50,000, secured by the home, in order to make home improvements. The interest rate on the loan was 7 percent (assume they paid exactly one-half of a year's worth of interest on this loan by year-end).

    Shortly after moving into the new home, Kate started a new business called Kate's Beauty Cuts LLC. She set up shop in a 384-square-foot corner room of the couple's home and began to get it ready for business. The room conveniently had a door to the outside providing customers direct access to the shop. Kate paid $2,100 to have the carpet replaced with a tile floor. She also paid $1,200 to have the room painted with vibrant colors and $650 to have the room rewired for appropriate lighting. Kate ran an ad in the local newspaper and officially opened her shop on January 24, 2018. By the end of the year, Kate's Beauty Cuts LLC generated $40,000 of *net* income before considering the home office deduction. The Sawyers incurred the following home-related expenditures during 2018:

    - $4,200 of real property taxes.
    - $2,000 for homeowner's insurance.
    - $2,400 for electricity.
    - $1,500 for gas and other utilities.

    They determined depreciation expense for their entire house was $17,424.

    Also, on March 2, Kate was able to finally sell her one-bedroom Manhattan condominium for $478,000. She purchased the condo, which she had lived in for six years prior to her marriage, for $205,000.

    Kate owns a vacation home in Myrtle Beach, South Carolina. She purchased the home several years ago, largely as an investment. To help cover the expenses of maintaining the home, James and Kate decided to rent the home out. They rented the home for a total of 106 days at fair market value (this included 8 days that they rented the home to James's brother Jack). In addition to the 106 days, Kate allowed a good friend and customer, Clair, to stay in the home for half-price for 2 days. James and Kate stayed in the home for 6 days for a romantic getaway and another 3 days in order to do some repair and maintenance work on the home. The rental revenues from the home in 2018 were $18,400. The Sawyers incurred the following expenses associated with the home:

    - $9,100 of interest (assume not limited by acquisition debt limit).
    - $3,400 of real property taxes.
    - $1,900 for homeowner's insurance.
    - $1,200 for electricity.
    - $1,600 for gas, other utilities, and landscaping.
    - $5,200 for depreciation.

Required:

Determine the Sawyers' taxable income for 2018. Disregard self-employment taxes and the deduction for qualified business income. Assume the couple paid $4,400 in state income taxes and files a joint return. For determining deductible home office expenses and allocating expenses to the rental, the Sawyers would like to use the methods that minimize their overall taxable income for the year.

 ROGER | CPA Review

Sample CPA Exam questions from Roger CPA Review are available in Connect as support for the topics in this text. These Multiple Choice Questions and Task-Based Simulations include expert-written explanations and solutions and provide a starting point for students to become familiar with the content and functionality of the actual CPA Exam.

15 Entities Overview

Upon completing this chapter, you should be able to:

LO 15-1 Discuss the legal and nontax characteristics of different types of legal entities.

LO 15-2 Describe the different types of entities for tax purposes.

LO 15-3 Identify fundamental differences in tax characteristics across entity types.

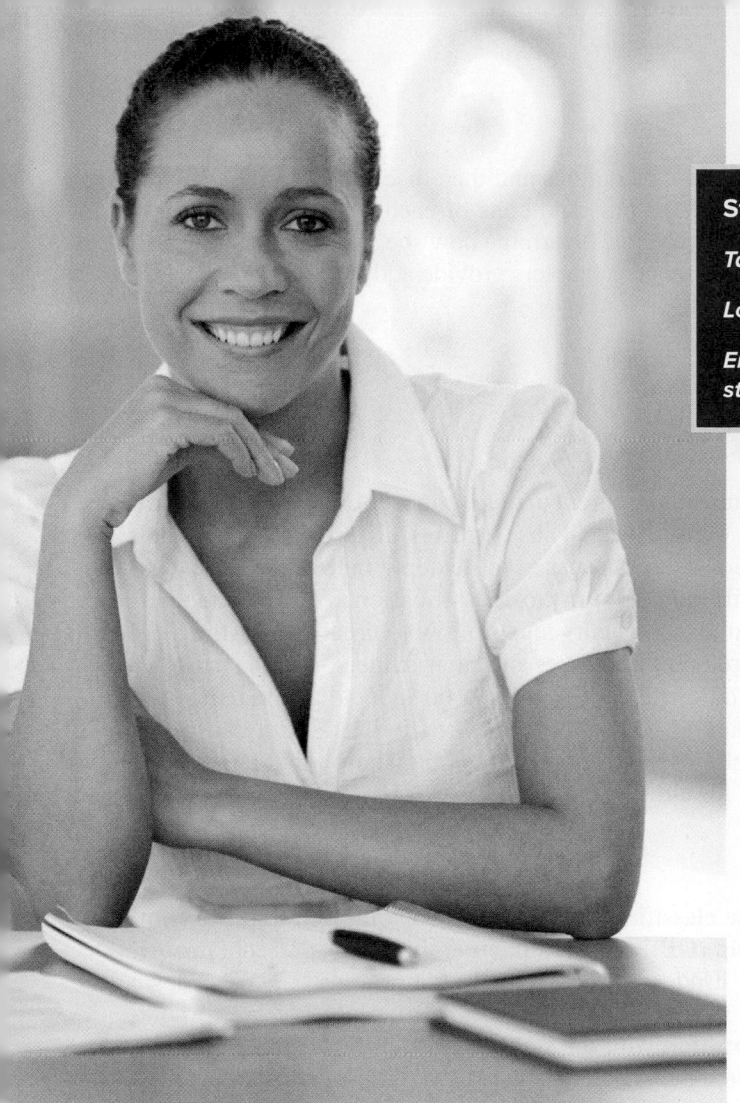

©PhotoAlto/MediaBakery

Storyline Summary

Taxpayer: Nicole Johnson

Location: Salt Lake City, Utah

Employment status: State government employee with entrepreneurial ambitions

Nicole Johnson is currently employed by the Utah Chamber of Commerce in Salt Lake City, Utah. While she enjoys the relatively short workweeks, she eventually would like to work for herself. In her current position, she deals with a lot of successful entrepreneurs who have become role models for her. Nicole has also developed an extensive list of contacts that should serve her well when she starts her own business. It has taken a while, but Nicole believes she has finally developed a viable new business idea. Her idea is to design and manufacture bed sheets that have various colored patterns and are made of unique fabric blends. The sheets look great and are extremely comfortable whether the bedroom is warm or cool. She has had several friends try out her prototype sheets and they have consistently given the sheets rave reviews. With this encouragement, Nicole started giving serious thought to making "Color Comfort Sheets" a money-making enterprise.

Nicole has enough business background to realize that she is embarking on a risky path, but one, she hopes, with significant potential rewards. After creating some initial income projections, Nicole realized that it will take a few years for the business to become profitable.

While Nicole's original plan was to start the business by herself, she is considering seeking out another equity owner so that she can add financial resources and business experience to the venture. Nicole feels like she has a grasp on her business plan, but she still needs to determine how to organize the business for tax purposes. After doing some research, Nicole learned that she should consider many factors in order to determine the "best" entity type for her business. Each type of entity has advantages and disadvantages from both tax and nontax perspectives, and the best entity for a business depends on the goals, outlook, and strategy for that particular business and its owners. She understands that she has more work to do to make an informed decision.

to be continued . . .

This chapter explores various types of legal entities and then discusses entities available for tax purposes. We outline some of the pros and cons of each entity type from both nontax and tax perspectives, as we help Nicole determine how she will organize her business to best accomplish her goals. Subsequent chapters provide additional detail concerning the tax characteristics of each entity type.

LO 15-1 ENTITY LEGAL CLASSIFICATION AND NONTAX CHARACTERISTICS

When forming new business ventures, entrepreneurs can choose to house their operations under one of several basic entity types. These entities differ in terms of their legal and tax considerations. In fact, as we discuss in more depth below, the legal classification of a business may be different from its tax classification. These entities differ in terms of the formalities that entrepreneurs must follow to create them, the legal rights and responsibilities conferred on the entities and their owners, and the tax rules that determine how the entities and owners will be taxed on income generated by the entities. CPAs are frequently asked to help clients choose the best entity choice for their businesses. CPAs can help clients navigate recent tax legislation that has significantly changed the tax landscape for entity choice.

Legal Classification

Generally, a business entity may be classified as a **corporation,** a **limited liability company (LLC),** a **general partnership (GP),** a **limited partnership (LP),** or a **sole proprietorship** (not formed as an LLC).[1] Under state law, corporations are recognized as legal entities separate from their owners (shareholders). Business owners legally form corporations by filing **articles of incorporation** with the state in which they organize the business. State laws also recognize limited liability companies (LLCs) as legal entities separate from their owners (members). Business owners create limited liability companies by filing either a **certificate of organization** or **articles of organization** with the state in which they are organizing the business (depending on the state).

Partnerships are formed under state partnership statutes and the degree of formality required depends on the type of partnership being formed. General partnerships may be formed by written agreement among the partners, called a **partnership agreement,** or they may be formed informally without a written agreement when two or more owners join together in an activity to generate profits. Although general partners are not required to file partnership agreements with the state, general partnerships are still considered to be legal entities separate from their owners under state laws. Unlike general partnerships, limited partnerships are usually organized by written agreement and typically must file a **certificate of limited partnership** to be recognized by the state.[2]

Finally, for state law purposes, sole proprietorships are *not* treated as legal entities separate from their individual owners. As a result, sole proprietors are not required to formally organize their businesses with the state, and they hold title to business assets in their own names rather than in the name of their businesses.

Nontax Characteristics

Rather than identify and discuss all possible nontax entity characteristics, we compare and contrast several prominent characteristics across the different legal entity types.

---

[1]Variations of these entities include limited liability partnerships (LLPs), limited liability limited partnerships (LLLPs), professional limited liability companies (PLLCs), and professional corporations (PCs).

[2]Similar to limited partnerships, LLPs, LLLPs, PLLCs, and PCs must register with the state to receive formal recognition.

Responsibility for Liabilities   Whether the entity or the owner(s) is ultimately responsible for paying the liabilities of the business depends on the type of entity. Under state law, a corporation is solely responsible for its liabilities.[3] Similarly, LLCs and not their members are responsible for the liabilities of the business.[4] For entities formed as partnerships, all general partners are ultimately responsible for the liabilities of the partnership. In contrast, limited partners are not responsible for the partnership's liabilities.[5] However, limited partners are not allowed to actively participate in the activities of the business.

Finally, if a business is conducted as a sole proprietorship, the individual owner is responsible for the liabilities of the business. However, individual business owners may organize their businesses as single-member LLCs. In exchange for observing the formalities of organizing as an LLC, they receive the liability protection afforded LLC members.[6]

Rights, Responsibilities, and Legal Arrangements among Owners   State corporation laws specify the rights and responsibilities of corporations and their shareholders. For example, to retain limited liability protection for shareholders, corporations must create, regularly update, and comply with a set of bylaws (internal rules governing how the corporation is run). They must have a board of directors. They must have regular board meetings and regular (at least annual) shareholder meetings, and they must keep minutes of these meetings. They must also issue shares of stock to owners (shareholders) and maintain a stock ledger reflecting stock ownership. They must comply with annual filing requirements specified by the state of incorporation, pay required filing fees, and pay required corporate taxes, if any. Consequently, shareholders have no flexibility to alter their legal treatment with respect to one another (rights are determined solely by stock ownership not by agreements), with respect to the corporation, or with respect to outsiders. In contrast, while state laws provide default provisions specifying rights and responsibilities of LLCs and their members, members have the flexibility to alter their arrangement by spelling out, through an operating agreement, the management practices of the entity and the rights and responsibilities of the members consistent with their wishes. Thus, LLCs allow more flexible business arrangements than do corporations.

Like LLC statutes, state partnership laws provide default provisions specifying the partners' legal rights and responsibilities for dealing with each other absent an agreement to the contrary. Because partners have the flexibility to depart from the default provisions, they frequently craft partnership agreements that are consistent with their preferences.

Although in many instances having the flexibility to customize business arrangements is desirable, sometimes inflexible governance rules mandated by state statute are needed to limit the participation of owners in management when their participation becomes impractical. For example, when businesses decide to "go public" with an **initial public offering (IPO)** on one of the public securities exchanges, they usually solicit a

> **THE KEY FACTS**
>
> **Legal Classification and Nontax Characteristics of Entities**
>
> - State law generally classifies entities as either corporations, limited liability companies, general partnerships, limited partnerships, or sole proprietorships.
> - Corporations and limited liability companies shield all their owners against the entity's liabilities.
> - Corporations are less flexible than other entities but are generally better suited to going public.

---

[3]Payroll tax liabilities are an important exception to this general rule. Shareholders of closely held corporations may be held responsible for these liabilities.

[4]When closely held corporations and LLCs borrow from banks or other lenders, shareholders or members are commonly asked to personally guarantee the debt. To the extent they do this, they become personally liable to repay the loan in the event the corporation or LLC is unable to repay it.

[5]Limited liability limited partnerships (LLLPs) are limited partnerships in which general and limited partners are protected from the liabilities of the entity. Also, professional service businesses such as accounting firms and law firms are generally not allowed to operate as corporations, LLCs, or limited partnerships. These businesses are frequently organized as limited liability partnerships (LLPs), professional limited liability companies (PLLCs), or professional corporations (PCs). Owners of a PLLC or a PC are protected from liabilities of the entity other than liabilities stemming from their own negligence. LLPs do not provide protection against liabilities stemming from a partner's own negligence or from the LLP's contractual liabilities.

[6]Shareholders of corporations and LLC members are responsible for liabilities stemming from their own negligence.

vast pool of potential investors to become corporate shareholders.[7] State corporation laws prohibit shareholders from directly amending corporate governance rules and from directly participating in management—they have only the right to vote for corporate directors or officers. In comparison, LLC members generally have the right to amend the LLC operating agreement, provide input, and manage LLCs. Obviously, managing a publicly traded business would be next to impossible if thousands of owners had the legal right to change operating rules and directly participate in managing the enterprise.

Exhibit 15-1 summarizes several nontax characteristics of different types of legal entities.

EXHIBIT 15-1   Business Types: Legal Entities and Nontax Characteristics

Nontax Characteristics	Corporation	LLC	General Partnership	Limited Partnership	Sole Proprietorship
Must formally organize with state	Yes	Yes	No	Yes	No*
Responsibility for liabilities of business	Entity	Entity	General partner(s)	General partner(s)	Owner†
Legal arrangement among owners	Not flexible	Flexible	Flexible	Flexible	Not applicable
Suitable for initial public offering	Yes	No	No	No^	No

*A sole proprietor must organize with the state if she forms a single-member LLC.
†The owner is not responsible for the liabilities of the business if the sole proprietorship is organized as an LLC. However, the owner is responsible for liabilities stemming from her own negligence and for any liabilities the owner personally guarantees.
^While it is uncommon, certain limited partnerships are eligible for IPOs.

As summarized in Exhibit 15-1, corporations and LLCs have the advantage in liability protection, LLCs and partnerships have an advantage over other entities in terms of legal flexibility, and corporations have the advantage when owners want to take a business public.

continued from page 15-1 . . .

As an initial step in the process of selecting the type of legal entity to house Color Comfort Sheets (CCS), Nicole began to research nontax issues that might be relevant to her decision. Early in her research she realized that the nontax benefits unique to traditional corporations were relevant primarily to large, publicly traded corporations. Although Nicole was very optimistic about CCS's prospects, she knew it would likely be a long time, if ever, before it went public. However, she remained interested in limiting her own and other potential investors' liability in the new venture, so she began to dig a little deeper. As she perused the Utah state website, she learned that corporations and LLCs are the only legal entities that can completely shield investors from liabilities. Although Nicole doesn't anticipate any trouble from her future creditors, she decides to limit her choice of legal entity to either a corporation or LLC.

At this point in her information-gathering process, Nicole is leaning toward the LLC option because she is not sure she wants to deal with board meetings and all the other formalities of operating a corporation; however, she decides to assemble a five-year forecast of CCS's expected operating results and to learn a little more about the way corporations and LLCs are taxed before making a final decision.

to be continued . . .

[7]The vast majority of IPOs involve corporate shares; however, limited partnership interests are occasionally sold in IPOs. Like shareholders, limited partners are typically not allowed to participate in management. Limited partnerships are used for public offerings in lieu of corporations when they qualify for favorable partnership tax treatment available to some publicly traded partnerships.

ENTITY TAX CLASSIFICATION

A business's legal form may be different from its tax form. We discussed the legal form of business entities above. We now discuss the tax form of business entities. In general terms, for tax purposes business entities can be classified as either separate taxpaying entities or **flow-through entities.** Separate taxpaying entities pay tax on their own income. In contrast, flow-through entities generally don't pay taxes because income from these entities flows through to their business owners, who are responsible for paying tax on the income.

How do we determine whether a particular business entity is treated as a separate tax-paying entity or as a flow-through entity for tax purposes? According to Treasury Regulations, commonly referred to as the "check-the-box" regulations, entities that are legal corporations under state law are, by default, treated as **C corporations** for tax purposes. These corporations and their shareholders are subject to tax provisions in Subchapter C (and not Subchapter S) of the Internal Revenue Code.[8] C corporations report their taxable income to the IRS on Form 1120. However, shareholders of *legal* corporations may qualify to make a special tax election known as an "S" election, thus permitting the corporation to be taxed as a flow-through entity called an **S corporation.**[9] S corporations and their shareholders are subject to tax provisions in Subchapter S of the Internal Revenue Code. S corporations report the results of their operations to the IRS on Form 1120S.

Also under the check-the-box regulations, unincorporated entities are, by default, treated as flow-through entities.[10] However, owners of an unincorporated entity can still elect to have their business taxed as a C corporation instead of as the default flow-through entity.[11] In fact, the owner(s) of an unincorporated entity could elect to have the business taxed as a C corporation and then make a second election to have the "C corporation" taxed as an S corporation (provided that it meets the S corporation eligibility requirements).[12] Before making such elections, however, the business owner(s) would need to be convinced that the move makes sense from a tax perspective.[13] The nontax considerations do not change because these elections do not affect the legal classification of the entity.

Finally, unincorporated flow-through entities (all flow-through entities except S corporations) are treated for tax purposes as either partnerships, sole proprietorships, or **disregarded entities** (considered to be the same entity as the owner).[14] Unincorporated entities (including LLCs) with more than one owner are treated as partnerships.[15] Partnerships report their operating results to the IRS on Form 1065. Unincorporated entities (including LLCs) with only one *individual* owner such as sole proprietorships and **single-member LLCs** are treated as sole proprietorships.[16] Income from businesses taxed as sole proprietorships is reported on Schedule C of Form 1040. Similarly, unincorporated entities with only one *corporate* owner, typically a single-member LLC, are disregarded for tax purposes. Thus, income and losses from this single, corporate-member LLC is reported as if it had originated from a division of the corporation and is reported directly on the single-member corporation's return. Exhibit 15-2 provides a flowchart for determining the tax form of a business entity under the check-the-box regulations. Taxpayers check the box by filing Form 8832.

> ### THE KEY FACTS
>
> **Tax Classification of Legal Entities**
>
> - Corporations are C corporations unless they make a valid S election.
> - Unincorporated entities are taxed as partnerships if they have more than one owner.
> - Unincorporated entities are taxed as sole proprietorships if held by a single individual or as disregarded entities if held by a single entity.
> - Unincorporated entities may elect to be treated as C corporations. They then may make an S election if eligible.

---

[8]Reg. §301.7701-3(a).

[9]§1362(a). Because §1361 limits the number and type of shareholders of corporations qualifying to make an S election, some corporations are ineligible to become S corporations.

[10]Reg. §301.7701-3(b). However, §7704 mandates that unincorporated publicly traded entities be taxed as corporations unless their income predominately consists of certain types of passive income.

[11]Reg. §301.7701-3(a).

[12]In general, a noncorporate entity that is eligible to elect to be treated as a corporation can elect to be treated as a corporation for tax purposes and as an S corporation in one step by filing a timely S corporation election.

[13]As presented in Exhibit 15-3, compared to corporations, unincorporated entities taxed as partnerships have more favorable ownership requirements and more favorable tax treatment on nonliquidating and liquidating distributions of noncash property.

[14]Reg. §301.7701-3(a).

[15]Reg. §301.7701-3(b)(i).

[16]Reg. §301.7701-3(b)(ii).

EXHIBIT 15-2 **Determining the tax form of a business entity under check-the-box regulations**

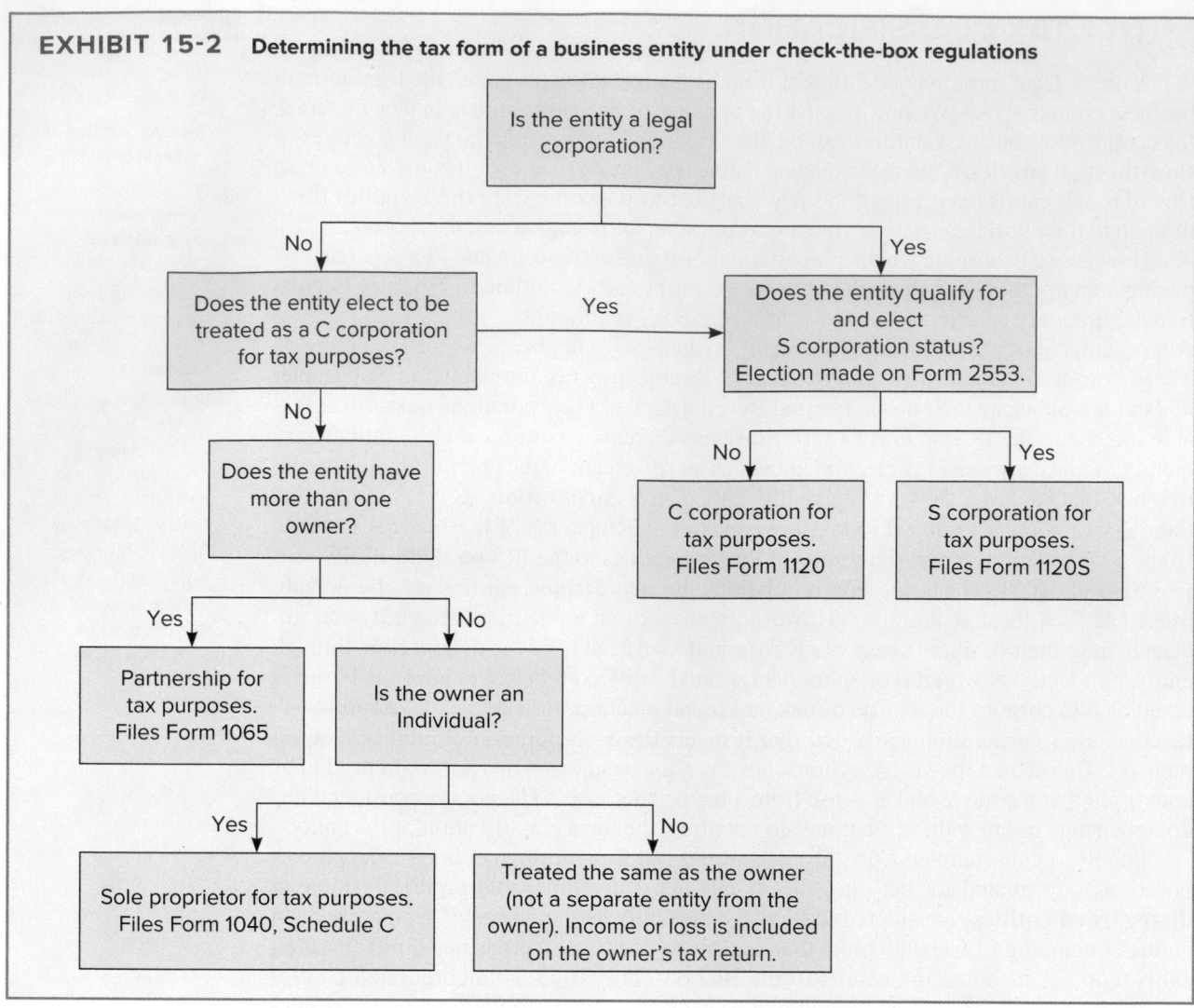

To summarize, although there are other types of legal entities, there are really only four categories of business entities recognized by the U.S. tax system, as follows:

1. C corporation (separate taxpaying entity; income reported on Form 1120).
2. S corporation (flow-through entity; income reported on Form 1120S).
3. Partnership (flow-through entity; income reported on Form 1065).
4. Sole proprietorship (flow-through entity; income reported on Form 1040, Schedule C).

Example 15-1

What if: Assume Nicole legally forms CCS as a corporation (with only common stock) by filing articles of incorporation with the state. What are her options for classifying CCS for tax purposes if she is the only shareholder of CCS?

Answer: Nicole may treat CCS as either a C corporation or an S corporation. The default tax classification is a C corporation for tax purposes. However, given the facts provided, CCS is eligible to make an election to be taxed as an S corporation.[17]

[17]§1361(b).

What if: Assume Nicole legally forms CCS as an LLC (with only one class of ownership rights) by filing articles of organization with the state. What are her options for classifying CCS for tax purposes if she is the only member of CCS?

Answer: The default classification for CCS is a sole proprietorship because CCS is unincorporated with one individual member. However, Nicole may elect to have CCS taxed as a C corporation or as an S corporation. CCS can be treated as a C corporation because unincorporated entities may elect to be taxed as corporations. Further, eligible entities taxed as corporations can elect to be treated as S corporations. Given the facts provided, CCS is eligible to elect to be treated as a corporation and to be treated as an S corporation.

What if: Assume Nicole legally forms CCS as an LLC and allows other individuals or business entities to become members in return for contributing their cash, property, or services to CCS. What is the default tax classification of CCS under these assumptions?

Answer: Partnership. The default tax classification for unincorporated entities with more than one owner is a partnership.

It might seem at this point that owners of businesses classified as flow-through entities would be treated the same for tax purposes; however, that is true only in a general sense. We see in this and other chapters that there are subtle and not-so-subtle differences in ways the owners of ventures classified as S corporations, partnerships, and sole proprietorships are taxed.[18]

ENTITY TAX CHARACTERISTICS

LO 15-3

In choosing among the available options for the tax form of business entities, owners and their advisers must carefully consider whether tax rules that apply to a particular tax classification would be either more or less favorable than tax rules under other alternative tax classifications. The specific tax rules they must compare and contrast are unique to their situations; however, certain key differences in the tax rules tend to be relevant in many scenarios. We turn our attention to the taxation of business entity income, owner compensation, and the tax treatment of entity losses, because these are a few of the most important tax characteristics to consider when selecting the tax form of the entity. Later in the chapter we preview other tax factors that differ between entities, and we identify the chapter where each factor is discussed in detail.

Taxation of Business Entity Income

The taxation of a business entity's income depends on whether the entity is a flow-through entity or a C corporation. Flow-through entity income is taxed once to the owner when the income "flows through" or is allocated (on paper) to entity owners at the end of the year, whether or not the income is distributed to them. The income is included on the owners' tax returns as if they had earned the income themselves. Flow-through entity owners are not, however, taxed when the income is actually distributed to them. C corporation income is taxed twice. The income is first taxed to the corporation at the corporate tax rate. A C corporation's income is taxed again to the shareholders when the corporation distributes the income as a dividend or when the shareholders sell their stock.[19]

The Taxation of Flow-Through Entity Business Income The tax that flow-through entity owners pay on the entity's business income depends in large part on the owner's marginal income tax rate. For 2017, the maximum marginal tax rate was 39.6 percent.

---

[18]The Business Income, Deductions, and Accounting Methods chapter explains how sole proprietors are taxed, and the Forming and Operating Partnerships, Dispositions of Partnership Interests and Partnership Distributions, and the S Corporations chapters explain how partners and S corporation shareholders are taxed.

[19]Distributions to C corporation shareholders are taxed as dividends to the extent they come from the "earnings and profits" (similar to economic income) of corporations.

For 2018, the top rate declined to 37 percent. Nevertheless, flow-through entity owners' tax burden on the flow through income also depends on whether the income is eligible for the qualified business income deduction, whether it is subject to the net investment income tax, and whether it is subject to self-employment tax and the additional Medicare tax. Below, we discuss the deduction for qualified business income, the net investment income tax, the self-employment tax, the additional Medicare tax, and the overall tax rate on flow-through entity income (assuming the owners are individuals).

Deduction for qualified business income.   This deduction applies to individuals with **qualified business income (QBI)** from flow-through entities, including partnerships, S corporations, or sole proprietorships.[20] That is, this is a deduction for individuals not for business entities. In general, a taxpayer can deduct 20 percent of the amount of qualified business income allocated to them from the entity, subject to certain limitations.[21] Qualified business income is the net business income from a qualified trade or business conducted in the United States. To qualify, the business income must be from a business other than a **specified service trade or business.** In general, a specified service trade or business includes all service businesses other than architecture and engineering.[22] Business income does not include income earned as an employee or investment type income such as capital gains, dividends, and investment interest income. The deduction is a *from* AGI deduction but is not an itemized deduction. Therefore, individuals can claim the deduction even though they claim the standard deduction instead of itemized deductions.

Net investment income tax.   When an owner of an entity taxed as a partnership or a shareholder of an S corporation does not work for the entity (that is, the owner is a passive owner or investor in the entity), the business income allocated to the taxpayer is considered to be "passive" income.[23] Because passive income is considered to be investment income for purposes of the net investment income tax, passive owners of flow-through entities may be required to pay net investment income tax on income allocated to them from the business. The net investment income tax rate is 3.8 percent and it applies only when a taxpayer's (modified) AGI exceeds certain thresholds. The threshold amount is $250,000 for married taxpayers filing jointly and surviving spouses, $125,000 for married taxpayers filing separately, and $200,000 for all other taxpayers.[24]

Self-employment tax and the additional Medicare tax.   Self-employment income is subject to self-employment tax and the additional Medicare tax. Whether a flow-through entity's business income is considered to be self-employment income to an owner depends on the type of entity and the owner's involvement in the entity's business activities.

---

[20]§199A.

[21]Under §199A(b)(2)(B), the deduction cannot exceed the greater of 50 percent of the wages paid with respect to the qualified trade or business, or the sum of 25 percent of the wages with respect to the qualified trade or business plus 2.5 percent of the unadjusted basis, immediately after acquisition, of all qualified property in the qualified trade or business. This limit does not apply to taxpayers with taxable income (before the deduction) below a certain threshold and the limitation phases in over a range of taxable income above the threshold [see §199A(b)(3)]. The limit is applied at the individual owner level and is beyond the scope of this chapter.

[22]§199A(d)(2) defines specified service trade or businesses as any trade or business involving the performance of services in the fields of health, law, accounting, actuarial science, performing arts, consulting, athletics, financial services, brokerage services, or any trade or business where the principal asset of such trade or business is the reputation or skill of one or more of its employees or which involves the performance of services that consist of investing and investment management trading, or dealing in securities, partnership interests, or commodities. The specified service trade or business requirement does not apply to taxpayers with taxable income (before the deduction) below a certain threshold and the requirement phases in over a range of taxable income above the threshold [see §199A(d)(3)].

[23]See §469. We discuss specific tests for determining when an owner is a passive investor in the Forming and Operating Partnerships chapter.

[24]See §1411.

An S corporation's business income allocated to a shareholder is not self-employment income to the shareholder. In contrast, a sole proprietorship's income is self-employment income to the sole proprietor. The determination isn't as clear for the business income allocated to owners of entities taxed as a partnership. For these entities, whether business income is self-employment income to an owner depends on the owner's involvement in the entity's business activities.[25]

When an owner's allocation of business income is determined to be self-employment income, the owner must pay self-employment tax and potentially the additional Medicare tax on the income. Both the self-employment tax and additional Medicare tax are based on the taxpayer's **net earnings from self-employment.** Net earnings from self-employment is 92.35 percent of a taxpayer's self-employment income.[26] For 2018, the self-employment tax is 15.3 percent of the first $128,400 (reduced by compensation received as an employee) of net earnings from self-employment plus 2.9 percent of net earnings from self-employment above $128,400 (reduced by compensation received as an employee). Taxpayers can deduct 50 percent of the self-employment taxes they pay as a *for* AGI deduction. The additional Medicare tax is .9 percent of the earned income (employee compensation plus net earnings from self-employment) in excess of a threshold amount. The threshold amount is $250,000 for married taxpayers filing jointly and surviving spouses, $125,000 for married taxpayers filing separately, and $200,000 for all other taxpayers.[27] Taxpayers are not allowed to deduct any of the additional Medicare tax they pay.

EXAMPLE 15-2

What if: Assume that Nicole chooses to form CCS as an S corporation. She makes the following assumptions:

- CCS's taxable income is $500,000 and all of the income is business income.
- Her marginal ordinary tax rate is 37 percent.
- Nicole is eligible for the full deduction for qualified business income on the flow-through income from CCS.
- The income is not passive income and is therefore not subject to the net investment income tax.
- Because CCS is an S corporation, the flow-through business income from CCS is not self-employment income to Nicole.

What is the overall tax rate on CCS's business income?

Answer: 29.6 percent, computed as follows:

Description	Amount	Explanation
(1) Business income allocated to Nicole	$500,000	
(2) Deduction for qualified business income	(100,000)	(1) × 20 percent
(3) Net taxable income to Nicole from CCS	400,000	(1) + (2)
(4) Earnings after-entity-level tax	37%	Marginal tax rate
(5) Owner-level income tax	148,000	(3) × (4)
Overall tax rate on business income allocation	29.6%	(5)/(1)

(continued on page 15-10)

---

[25]We discuss more details of determining whether business income allocated to partners is self-employment income in the Forming and Operating Partnerships chapter.

[26]See §1402. Taxing 92.35 percent of self-employment income for self-employment tax and additional Medicare tax purposes provides the taxpayer with an implicit 7.65 percent deduction for the employer's portion of the 15.3 percent self-employment tax.

[27]The self-employment tax is assessed on an individual by individual basis. The additional Medicare tax applies to combined earned income of both spouses if married filing jointly.

What if: Assume the original facts except that the income from CCS is not eligible for the deduction for qualified business income. What is the overall tax rate on CCS's business income?

Answer: 37 percent. The entire $500,000 business income is taxed to Nicole at her marginal ordinary tax rate of 37%.

What if: Assume the original facts except the income from CCS is not eligible for the deduction for qualified business income and that Nicole is a passive investor in CCS and Nicole must pay the 3.8 percent net investment income tax on the income. What is the overall tax rate on the income of CCS?

Answer: 40.8 percent. The full $500,000 of business income is taxed to Nicole at her marginal ordinary tax rate of 37 percent plus the net investment income tax rate of 3.8 percent.

EXAMPLE 15-3

What if: Assume that Nicole forms CCS as an LLC with another investor so that CCS is taxed as a partnership. Nicole makes the following assumptions:
- CCS earns business income of $1,000,000 and her share of the business income is $500,000.
- Her marginal ordinary tax rate is 37 percent.
- Nicole is entitled to the full deduction for qualified business income on the flow-through income from CCS.
- Because Nicole works full-time for the entity, the business income allocated to her is self-employment income.
- Nicole's marginal self-employment tax rate is 2.9 percent (other sources of income put her over the $128,400 threshold).
- The income allocation is subject to the additional Medicare tax.

What is the overall tax rate on the CCS business income allocated to Nicole?

Answer: 32.61 percent, computed as follows:

Description	Amount	Explanation
(1) Business income allocated to Nicole	$500,000	
(2) Deduction for qualified business income	(100,000)	(1) × 20 percent
(3) Deduction for 50 percent of self-employment tax	(6,695)	(1) × .9235 × .029 × .5
(4) Income net of Nicole's deductions	393,305	
(5) Owner-level income tax	145,523	(4) × 37 percent
(6) Self-employment tax	13,391	(1) × .9235 × .029
(7) Additional Medicare tax	4,156	(1) × .9235 × .009
(8) Total tax paid on CCS business income allocations	$163,070	(6) + (7) + (8)
Overall tax rate on business income allocation	32.61%	(9)/(1)

What if: Assume the original facts except that the business income allocation is not qualified business income (QBI). What is the overall tax rate on the CCS business income allocated to Nicole?

Answer: 40.01 percent. The only difference between the original and the new facts in this what-if example is that Nicole would pay an additional $37,000 in income tax ($100,000 QBI deduction × 37 percent tax rate). Consequently, the overall taxes due on the business income allocation would be $200,070 ($163,070 + $37,000) and the overall tax rate would be 40.01 percent ($200,070/$500,000).

What if: Assume the original facts except the income from CCS is not eligible for the QBI deduction and that Nicole is a passive investor in CCS so that Nicole must pay the net investment income tax on the income but not the self-employment tax or the additional Medicare tax. What is the overall tax rate on the CCS business income allocated to Nicole?

Answer: 40.8 percent. The entire $500,000 business income allocation is taxed to Nicole at her marginal ordinary tax rate of 37 percent plus the percent net investment income tax rate of 3.8 percent.

In summary, while income from a flow-through entity is taxed only once, the overall tax rate on the entity's business income depends on whether the income (and the owner) qualifies for the deduction for qualified business income and whether the income is subject to the net investment tax or is considered to be self-employment income.

Overall Tax Rate of C Corporation Income   C corporations are taxed on their taxable income at corporate rates. For tax years beginning before 2018, the tax rate depended on where the corporation's taxable income fell in the corporate tax rate schedule. The lowest marginal tax rate for corporations was 15 percent and the top marginal rate was 39 percent. The most profitable corporations were taxed at a flat 35 percent rate. For tax years beginning after 2017, the corporate tax rate has been cut to a flat 21 percent. Thus, for most corporations, corporate tax rates have decreased significantly. The tax rate on the second level of tax on a C corporation's income depends on whether the shareholder is an individual, a C corporation, an **institutional shareholder,** a tax exempt entity, or a foreign entity.

Individual shareholders.   The tax rate on dividends to individual taxpayers depends on the individual's taxable income. High-income taxpayers are taxed on dividends at a 20 percent rate, low-income taxpayers are taxed at a 0 percent rate, and others are taxed on dividends at a 15 percent rate.[28] Also, as discussed above, taxpayers with (modified) AGI in excess of a threshold amount pay an additional 3.8 percent net investment income tax on dividends.

Example 15-4

What if: Assume that Nicole forms CCS as a C corporation and she makes the following assumptions:
- CCS earns taxable income of $500,000.
- CCS will distribute all of its after-tax earnings annually as a dividend.
- Nicole's marginal ordinary tax rate is 37 percent and her dividend tax rate is 23.8 percent (including the net investment income tax).

What is the overall tax rate on CCS's taxable income??

Answer: 39.8 percent, computed as follows:

Description	Amount	Explanation
(1) Taxable income	$ 500,000	
(2) Corporate tax rate	21%	Flat corporate tax rate
(3) Corporate-level tax	**$105,000**	(1) × (2) [first level of tax]
(4) Income remaining after taxes and amount distributed as a dividend	$ 395,000	(1) − (3)
(5) Dividend tax rate	23.8%	20% dividend rate + 3.8% net investment income tax rate
(6) Shareholder-level tax on dividend	$ 94,010	(4) × (5) [second level of tax]
(7) Total tax paid on corporate taxable income	**$199,010**	(3) + (6)
Overall tax rate on corporate taxable income	**39.8%**	(7)/(1)

Note that the overall rate is not 44.8 percent (21 percent corporate rate + 23.8 percent shareholder rate) because the amount of corporate-level tax ($105,000) is income that is not taxed twice (it is paid to the government, not to the shareholders).

(*continued on page 15-12*)

[28]To the extent the dividend income increases a taxpayer's taxable income beyond specific "breakpoints" the dividend is taxed at a higher rate. For 2018, the breakpoint between the 0 and 15 percent rate is $77,200 for married taxpayers filing jointly, $51,700 for head of household filers, and $38,600 for all other taxpayers. The breakpoint between the 15 percent and 20 percent rate is $479,000 for married taxpayers filing jointly, $239,500 for married taxpayers filing separately, $425,800 for single taxpayers, and $452,400 for head of household filers.

What if: Assume that Nicole forms CCS as a C corporation and she makes the following assumptions:
- CCS earns taxable income of $500,000.
- CCS distributes 25 percent of its after-tax earnings as a dividend and retains the rest to grow the business.
- Nicole's marginal ordinary tax rate is 37 percent and her dividend tax rate is 23.8 percent (including the net investment income tax).

Answer: 25.7 percent, computed as follows:

Description	Amount	Explanation
(1) Taxable income	$ 500,000	
(2) Corporate tax rate	21%	Flat corporate tax rate
(3) Corporate-level tax	**$105,000**	(1) × (2) [first level of tax]
(4) Income remaining after taxes and amount distributed as a dividend	$ 395,000	(1) − (3)
(5) Dividend	$98,750	(4) × 25% distributed
(6) Dividend tax rate	23.8%	20% dividend rate + 3.8% net investment income tax rate
(7) Shareholder-level tax on dividend	**$ 23,503**	(5) × (6) [second level of tax]
(8) Total tax paid on corporate taxable income	**$128,503**	(3) + (7)
Overall tax rate on corporate taxable income	**25.7%**	(8)/(1)

The overall tax rate is lower in this situation because CCS retains most of its after-tax income and thus protects that portion of its income from immediate double taxation. If CCS retained all of its after-tax earnings, the current overall tax rate on its income would have been 21 percent (the corporate tax rate). Also, while the overall tax rate is lower when CCS distributes less of its income, Nicole also receives less cash from the business ends up with less cash from the business.

Shareholders that are C corporations. Shareholders that are C corporations are taxed on dividends at 21 percent, the same rate as they are taxed on ordinary income. In addition, dividends received by a corporation are potentially subject to another (third) level of tax when the corporation receiving the dividend distributes its earnings as dividends to its shareholders. This potential for more than two levels of tax on the same before-tax earnings prompted Congress to allow corporations to claim the **dividends received deduction** (DRD). In the next chapter, we discuss the DRD in detail, but the underlying concept is that a corporation *receiving* a dividend is allowed to deduct a certain percentage of the dividend from its taxable income to offset the potential for additional layers of taxation on the dividend when it distributes the dividend to its shareholders. For tax years beginning before 2018, the dividends received deduction percentage was 70, 80, or 100 percent of the dividend received, depending on the level of the recipient corporation's ownership in the dividend-paying corporation's stock. For tax years beginning after 2017, the dividends received deduction is reduced to 50, 65, or 100 percent. Thus, for tax years beginning after 2017, a corporation's net tax rate on a dividend received is 10.5 percent if it claims a 50 percent DRD [.21 tax rate × (1 minus .5 DRD)], 7.35 percent if it claims a 65 percent DRD [.21 tax rate × (1 minus .65 DRD)], and 0 percent if it claims a 100 percent DRD [.21 × (1 minus 1.0 DRD)].

Example 15-5

What if: Assume that Nicole invites a corporation to invest in CCS in exchange for a 10 percent share in the company. Nicole makes the following assumptions as part of her calculations:
- CCS is a C corporation.
- CCS earns taxable income of $500,000.
- CCS will pay out all of its after-tax earnings annually as a dividend.

Given these assumptions, what would be the overall tax rate on the corporate investor's share of CCS's income given that the corporation would be eligible for the 50 percent dividends received deduction?

Answer: 29.3 percent, computed as follows:

Description	Amount	Explanation
(1) Taxable income	$500,000	
(2) Corporate tax rate	21%	
(3) Entity-level tax	$105,000	(1) × (2) [first level of tax]
(4) After-tax income	$395,000	(1) – (3)
(5) Corporate investor's dividend	$39,500	(4) × 10%
(6) Taxable dividend	$19,750	(5) × (1 – 50% DRD)
(7) Corporate investor's share of entity-level tax	$10,500	(3) × 10% investor's share
(8) Corporate investor's tax on dividend	$4,148	(6) × 21% corporate tax rate
(9) Total tax paid on corporate taxable income	$14,648	(7) + (8)
Overall tax rate on corporate taxable income	**29.3%**	(9)/[(1) × 10% investor's share]

Note: The income of the corporate shareholder will be taxed again when the corporate shareholder distributes it to its own shareholders.

Institutional shareholders.   Pension and retirement funds are some of the largest institutional shareholders of corporations. However, these entities do not pay shareholder-level tax on the dividends they receive. Ultimately, retirees pay the second tax on this income when they receive retirement distributions from these funds. While retirees pay the second tax at ordinary rates, not the reduced dividend rates, they are able to defer the tax until they receive fund distributions.

Tax-exempt and foreign shareholders.   Tax-exempt organizations such as churches and universities are exempt from tax on their investment income, including dividend income from investments in corporate stock. Similarly, foreign investors may be eligible for reduced rates on dividend income depending on the tax treaty, if any, their country of residence has signed with the United States.

As we discuss and illustrate above, C corporation income is subject to **double taxation.** The first tax is paid by the corporation when it earns the income and the second tax is paid by the shareholder when the corporation distributes its earnings as dividends to shareholders. Can C corporations avoid the second level of tax entirely by not paying dividends? The answer is generally no because even when corporations retain after-tax income, their shareholders pay the second level of tax at capital gains rates on the undistributed income when they sell their stock because the undistributed income indirectly increases the value of their stock and thus increases their gain when they sell the stock. Assuming the shareholder is an individual and the shareholder owns stock in a corporation for more than a year, the gain is taxed at the same rates as the tax rates on qualified dividends we discussed above (0, 15, or 20 plus 3.8 percent net investment income tax for higher income taxpayers). Because this second level of tax is deferred until taxpayers sell their stock, the longer they hold the stock, the less the tax cost on a present value basis. In the extreme, taxpayers can avoid the second level of income tax completely on their stock appreciation by holding the stock until death. At death, gain built into the stock is eliminated because the stock takes basis equal to the value of the stock on the date of death.[29] Shareholders other than individuals will face different tax consequences when they sell their shares. When shareholders that

[29]See §1014.

are C corporations eventually sell the stock they are taxed on capital gains at a flat 21 percent tax rate. Consequently, income from stock appreciation may expose income to *more* than two levels of taxation because capital gains from selling stock doesn't qualify for the dividends received deduction. Also, institutional shareholders don't pay tax when they sell their stock and recognize capital gains. However, retirees generally pay tax on the gains at ordinary rates when they receive distributions from their retirement accounts. Finally, tax-exempt shareholders do not pay tax on capital gains from selling stock, and foreign investors are generally not subject to U.S. tax on their capital gains from selling corporate stock.

Finally, the tax law provides incentives for C corporations to distribute income rather than to retain it for the purpose of avoiding the second level of tax. First, **personal holding companies** (closely held corporations generating primarily investment income) are subject to a 20 percent **personal holding company tax** on their undistributed income.[30] Second, corporations that retain earnings for the purpose of avoiding the second level of tax are subject to a 20 percent **accumulated earnings tax** on the retained earnings.[31] Corporations are not considered to be retaining earnings for tax avoidance purposes, and are not subject to the accumulated earnings tax to the extent they reinvest the earnings in assets necessary for their business or to the extent they retain liquid assets for reasonable planned needs of the business.

Under the tax rate system prior to 2018, flow-through entities were generally considered to be superior to corporations for tax purposes because they generated income that was taxed only once while corporations produced income that was taxed twice, with the first level of tax imposed at a rate comparable to the individual tax rate. However, for years after 2017, under new tax law, the corporate tax rate is significantly lower than the maximum individual tax rate. Further, new tax law provides a deduction for qualified business income (QBI) for individuals who are owners of flow-through entities. This tax legislation makes the optimal choice of entity based on overall tax rates of the entity's business income less clear than it was under prior law. It is important to note, however, that the corporate tax rate reduction is a permanent change while the QBI deduction is scheduled to expire in 2026. The overall tax rate on a flow-through entity's business income depends on whether the flow-through entity's business income is eligible for the QBI deduction and whether the income is subject to the net investment income tax or the self-employment tax and the additional Medicare tax. For C corporations, the overall tax rate depends in large part on the extent to which the corporation distributes its after-tax earnings as a dividend to its shareholders. As we saw in Example 15-2, the overall tax rate on CCS's taxable income as a flow-through entity ranged from 29.6 percent to 40.8 percent depending on whether the QBI deduction and the net investment income tax applied. In Example 15-4, the overall tax rate on CCS's taxable income as a C corporation ranged from 21 percent when CCS retained all of its after-tax income to 39.8 percent when it distributed all of its after-tax income.

Owner Compensation   Entity owners who work for the entity are compensated in different ways, depending on the entity type. Owners of S corporations and C corporations receive compensation as employees. Owners of flow-through entities taxed as partnerships receive compensation in the form of guaranteed payments. Sole proprietors don't receive a separate compensation payment because a sole proprietorship is the same entity as the individual sole proprietor.

S corporations and C corporations deduct the wages paid to shareholders/employees to calculate the entity's business income. They also pay (and deduct) the employer's portion of the FICA tax (social security tax plus Medicare tax) on the employee's behalf. The employer's portion of the tax is 7.65 percent of the employee's first $128,400 of

[30]§541.

[31]See §§531–533.

employee compensation and 1.45 percent of employee compensation above $128,400. The shareholder/employee is taxed on the wages received at ordinary rates and is required to pay the employee's portion of the FICA tax, which is generally the same as the employer's portion. When considering both the employer's and employee's portions of the FICA tax, the overall FICA rate is 15.3 percent of the first $128,400 of wages and 2.9 percent of the rest. This is the same rate as the self-employment tax rate. Also, similar to self-employment income, employee compensation is subject to the additional Medicare tax when the taxpayer's AGI is over the threshold amount (discussed above).

Entities taxed as partnerships deduct guaranteed payments made to owners working for the entity. However, the entity is not required to pay FICA tax on the owner-worker's behalf because guaranteed payments are self-employment income and self-employment taxes are the sole responsibility of the owner-worker.[32] The owner-worker is taxed on the amount of the guaranteed payment at ordinary rates and is required to pay self-employment tax and potentially additional Medicare tax on the income, depending on their income level (see prior discussion on computing the self-employment tax). A sole proprietorship does not pay deductible compensation to the sole proprietor. All of the income of a sole proprietorship is self-employment income and, consequently, is subject to self-employment tax and the additional Medicare tax.

Owner compensation provides potential tax planning opportunities, depending on the type of entity. For S corporations, business income allocations to owners are not subject to FICA or self-employment tax. However, wages paid to owner/employees are subject to FICA tax. (Recall that the combined employer/employee FICA rate is the same as the self-employment tax rate.) Consequently, as we discuss in the S corporations chapter, S corporations have a tax incentive to pay lower salary/wages to shareholders/employees that is subject to FICA tax so there is more business income to allocate to shareholders/employees that is not subject to FICA or self-employment tax (lower deductible wages means higher business income allocations). Further, S corporations have an incentive to reduce wages to shareholder/employees in order to increase business income because employee compensation is not eligible for the deduction for qualified business income, but business income allocations to shareholders are eligible. In the extreme, S corporations may prefer to pay zero wages to shareholders/employees in order to maximize business income allocations to them. However, to the extent an S corporation shareholder receives an unreasonably low salary for the services provided, the IRS may reclassify some of the shareholder's business income allocation as salary.

In contrast to S corporations, entities taxed as partnerships don't have an incentive to decrease guaranteed payments in order to increase business income allocations in an attempt to save self-employment taxes to owners. This is because both guaranteed payments and business income allocations are self-employment income to the owner-worker. However, similar to S corporations, entities taxed as partnerships have an incentive to reduce guaranteed payments to owner-workers in order to increase business income allocations to them because guaranteed payments are not eligible for the qualified business income but allocations of business income are eligible. Finally, relative to both S corporations and entities taxed as partnerships, sole proprietorships may be the most advantageous for purposes of maximizing the qualified business income deduction in certain situations. This is because the sole proprietorship's qualifying business income is not reduced by a deduction for compensation paid to the owner/ sole proprietor.

For C corporations, tax planning opportunities have potentially shifted with the steep reduction in the corporate tax rate relative to individual rates. Prior to the rate reduction, corporations could avoid double taxation of their income by paying deductible salaries to shareholders/employees. This income would be taxed once to the employee at ordinary

---

[32]Taxpayers pay self-employment tax on self-employment income and FICA taxes on employee compensation.

rates that are similar to the corporate rate. The IRS could evaluate compensation to employee/shareholders to determine if the compensation was unreasonably high for the work the employee/shareholder was doing and, to the extent it was, reclassify the excess compensation as nondeductible dividends. Currently, however, with the corporate rate significantly lower than the maximum individual rate, corporations have an incentive to pay lower salaries to shareholders/employees in order to have more of their income taxed at the lower corporate rate. By reducing deductible salaries, more of the corporate income is subject to tax at the lower 21 percent tax rate. If the income is paid as salaries, it will be subject to the individual rate (top rate is 37 percent) and subject to both the employer and employee's portion of the FICA tax. This type of strategy is more likely to be useful for closely held corporations where all of the owners work for the corporation. It remains to be seen how the IRS will respond to such strategies.

While the overall tax rate of an entity's income and the tax treatment of owner compensation are important entity choice factors, it is important to consider the tax treatment of the entity's losses and other tax characteristics when choosing a tax entity for a new business.

Deductibility of Entity Losses

When a C corporation's tax deductions exceed its income for the year, the excess is called a **net operating loss (NOL).** While NOLs provide no tax benefit to C corporations for the year they incur them, corporations may use NOLs to offset corporate taxable income and reduce corporate taxes in other years. The specific tax treatment for a NOL depends on when the NOL was generated. For NOLs generated in tax years ending before 2018, corporations could carry the NOLs back and offset up to 100 percent of taxable income (before the NOL deduction) reported in the two preceding years and carry it forward to offset up to 100 percent of taxable income for up to 20 years. Under new tax law, corporations can carry NOLs generated in tax years ending after 2017 forward indefinitely but they are not allowed to carry them back. Further, the deduction for post 2017 NOLs is limited to 80 percent of taxable income (before the NOL deduction) for a given year.[33] In any event, losses from C corporations are *not* available to offset shareholders' personal income.

In contrast to losses generated by C corporations, losses generated by sole proprietorships and other flow-through entities are generally available to offset the owners' personal income, subject to certain restrictions. For example, the owner of an entity taxed as a partnership or an S corporation shareholder may deduct losses from the entity only to the extent of the owner's basis in her ownership interest in the flow-through entity. In addition, deductibility of losses from flow-through entities may be further limited by the at-risk and passive activity loss limitation. The at-risk limitation is similar to the basis limitation but slightly more restrictive. The passive activity loss limitation typically applies to individual investors who are passive investors in the flow-through entity. For passive investors, the business activities of the entity are called passive activities. In these circumstances, taxpayers can deduct losses from passive activities only to the extent they have income from other passive activities. Due to the complex nature of these limitations, we defer a detailed discussion of these limitations until the Forming and Operating Partnerships chapter.

For tax years beginning after 2017, individual taxpayers are not allowed to deduct an **"excess business loss"** for the year. An excess business loss is the excess of aggregate business deductions for the year over the sum of aggregate business gross income or gain of the taxpayer plus a threshold amount. The threshold amount for a tax year is $500,000 for married taxpayers filing jointly and $250,000 for other taxpayers. The amounts are indexed for inflation. Excess business losses include business losses from sole proprietorships, entities taxed as partnerships, and S corporations. In the case of an S corporation or of an entity

---

[33]We discuss the net operating loss deduction in more detail in the Corporate Operations chapter.

taxed as a partnership, the provision applies at the owner level. Excess business losses are carried forward and used in subsequent years. The excess business loss limitation applies to losses that are otherwise deductible after applying the basis, at-risk, and passive loss rules. See the Forming and Operating Partnerships chapter for more details.

The ability to deduct flow-through losses against other sources of income can be a significant issue for owners of new businesses because new businesses tend to report losses early on as the businesses get established. If owners form a new business as a C corporation, the corporate-level losses provide no current tax benefit to the shareholders. The fact that C corporation losses are trapped at the corporate level can impose a higher tax cost for shareholders initially doing business as a C corporation relative to a flow-through entity such as an S corporation or an entity taxed as a partnership.

TAXES IN THE REAL WORLD Will Entity Selection Be Affected by the New Tax Law?

In its Statistics of Income Tax Report, the Internal Revenue Service reported the following information relating to tax entity selection by business owners as of 2013 (the most recent year reported). Sole proprietorships were the most common followed by S corporations, entities taxed as partnerships, and then C corporations. Nevertheless, C corporations by far generated the most business entity receipts and net income. Under recent tax legislation, the C corporation tax rate was reduced from 35 percent to 21 percent and owners of flow-through entities are allowed a new deduction for qualified business income generated by the entity. Going forward, how do you expect the percentage of each entity type to change, if at all, under the new tax system? It is likely we will see a shift toward C corporations as the entity of choice?

	Number of Entities	Business Receipts	Net Income (Including deficits)
Totals for all entities	33,423,187	$33,260,092,484	$3,065,208,464
Entity Type	**Percentage**	**Percentage**	**Percentage**
C corporations	4.82	61.24	46.64
S corporations	12.74	20.55	17.93
General partnerships	1.69	1.22	3.56
Limited partnerships	1.25	3.89	10.00
LLCs (taxed as partnerships)	6.84	9.02	9.72
Sole proprietorships (nonfarm)	72.03	4.09	12.15
Other*	.63	0	0

*Other includes Real Estate Investment Trusts (REITs) and Regulated Investment Companies (RICs). Neither type of entity has business receipts or net income.

Source: https://www.irs.gov/statistics/soi-tax-stats-integrated-business-data Tax Year 2013.

ETHICS

Troy is the sole shareholder and CEO of BQT. BQT is a very profitable S corporation. Until recently, Troy's salary was in line with the salaries of comparable CEOs. However, Troy recently learned that he could reduce his tax burden if he were to reduce his salary. In particular, by lowering his salary Troy would receive less employee compensation that is subject to FICA tax and is not eligible for the qualified business income deduction, and he would be allocated more business income that is not subject to FICA tax and qualifies for the qualified business income deduction. After considering the potential benefits, Troy decided to cut his salary in half. Do you think Troy's decision is ethical? Why or why not?

THE KEY FACTS

Taxation of Entity Income

- Flow-through entity income is taxed at the owner's tax rate. Individuals are taxed at a top marginal income rate of 37 percent on business income allocated to them from a flow-through entity.
- Flow-through entity owners who receive qualified business income from a flow-through entity are allowed to claim a qualified business income deduction equal to 20 percent of the qualified business income allocated to them (subject to certain limitations).
- Business income allocations to passive owners of flow-through entities may be subject to the 3.8 percent net investment income tax.
- Business income allocated to S corporation shareholders is not subject to self-employment tax.
- Owners of entities taxed as a partnership may be subject to self-employment tax on business income allocations, depending on the owner's involvement in the business activities.
- Sole proprietors are subject to self-employment tax on the sole proprietorship's income.
- C corporation taxable income is subject to a flat 21 percent tax rate.
- Individuals who are C corporation shareholders are generally taxed at a maximum rate of 20 percent on dividends received. Further, certain taxpayers may be charged a 3.8 percent net investment income tax on dividends and capital gains.
- C corporation shareholders that are themselves C corporations are generally eligible to receive a 50 percent or greater dividends received deduction (DRD).

(continued)

Example 15-6

- C corporation shareholders who are individuals generally pay capital gains taxes when shares are sold at a gain.
- S corporation and C corporation shareholders receive employee compensation for work they do for the entity.
- Owner-workers for entities taxed as a partnership receive compensation in the form of guaranteed payments. Guaranteed payments are self-employment income.

What if: Assume that Nicole organizes CCS as a C corporation and that, in spite of her best efforts as CEO of the company, CCS reports a tax loss of $50,000 in its first year of operation (year 1). Also assume that Nicole's marginal tax rate is 37 percent and her husband's salary for year 1 is $200,000. Nicole files a joint tax return with her husband. How much tax will CCS pay in year 1 and how much tax will Nicole (and her husband) pay on the $200,000 of other taxable income if CCS is organized as a C corporation?

Answer: CCS will pay $0 in taxes because it reports a loss for tax purposes. However, CCS can carry the loss forward to future years and can use the loss to offset up to 80 percent of its taxable income in a given year. Because Nicole may not use the CCS loss to offset her husband's salary, she (and her husband) must pay $74,000 in taxes. See the computations in the table below.

What if: Suppose CCS is organized as an S corporation and Nicole's stock basis in CCS before the year 1 loss is $100,000. How much tax will CCS pay in year 1, and how much tax will Nicole (and her husband) pay on the $200,000 salary?

Answer: CCS will pay $0 taxes (S corporations are not taxpaying entities) and Nicole will pay $55,500 in taxes. See the computations in the table below.

Description	C Corporation	S Corporation (flow-through)	Explanation
(1) Taxable income (loss)	$ (50,000)	$ (50,000)	
(2) CCS corporate-level tax	**$ 0**	**$ 0**	No taxable income
(3) Nicole's other income	$200,000	$200,000	
(4) CCS loss available to offset Nicole's other income	$ 0	$ (50,000)	$0 if C corp. (1) if S corporation (flow-through entity)
(5) Nicole's other income reduced by entity loss	$200,000	$150,000	(3) + (4)
(6) Nicole's marginal ordinary tax rate	37%	37%	
Nicole's tax on other income	**$ 74,000**	**$ 55,500**	(5) × (6)

What if: Suppose CCS is organized as an S corporation and Nicole's stock basis before the $50,000 year 1 loss is $100,000. Further, assume that Nicole does not participate in CCS's business activities; that is, assume she is a passive investor in the business entity. How much tax will Nicole (and her husband) pay on the $200,000 of other income?

Answer: $74,000. Because Nicole is a passive investor, she is not allowed to deduct the loss allocated to her this year. She must carry it over and use it in future years (this assumes neither Nicole nor her husband have income from other investments in which they are passive investors).

As the example above illustrates, owners' ability to immediately use start-up losses from flow-through entities to offset income from other sources is a tax advantage of flow-through entities over C corporations.

OTHER TAX CHARACTERISTICS

There are many tax factors that differ across entities and can influence the entity selection decision. Exhibit 15-3 provides an overview of these tax characteristics. The exhibit describes the general rules for each tax characteristic as it relates to C corporations, S corporations, entities taxed as partnerships, and sole proprietorships, and it ranks the entities on each characteristic (1 is most tax favorable). Finally, it identifies the chapters where detail on these tax characteristics can be found.

EXHIBIT 15-3 Comparison of Tax Characteristics across Entities

Tax Characteristic	C Corporation	Entity Taxed as Partnership	S Corporation	Sole Proprietorship	Summary
Owner limits	At least one shareholder.	At least two owners.	Not more than 100; no corporations, partnerships, nonresident aliens, or certain trusts.	N/A	Limitations are least strict for C corporations and most strict for S corporations. S corporations are the only entity with significant owner limitations. More detail for this factor is discussed in the S Corporations chapter.
Rank[1]	1	2	3	N/A	
Owner contributions of appreciated property to entity	Tax deferred to shareholder if certain requirements are met.	Tax deferred to owner.	Tax deferred to shareholder if certain requirements are met.	N/A	This factor favors entities taxed as partnerships because partners are not required to meet special requirements in order to avoid recognizing gain on the contribution of appreciated property to the partnership, but shareholders of both C and S corporations are required to meet certain requirements to avoid recognizing gain on such contributions to the corporation. More detail for this factor is provided in the Corporate Formation, Reorganization, and Liquidation, the Forming and Operating Partnerships, and the S Corporations chapters.
Rank	2	1	2	N/A	
Accounting periods	Generally, any tax year that ends on the last day of any month.[2]	Generally, must use tax year that matches tax year of owners (special rules when not all owners have same tax year-end).	Calendar year.	Generally a calendar year.	C corporations generally have the most flexibility to select their year-end. But because C corporations are not flow-through entities, this is not a real advantage or disadvantage from a tax perspective. Partnerships generally are not free to choose their year-end but they can have a year-end that is a different year-end from some of the owners. Because this allows some partners to defer reporting income, this factor favors partnerships over S corporations. S corporations generally have the same calendar year-end as their shareholders. More detail for this factor is provided in the Business Income, Deductions, and Accounting Methods, the Forming and Operating Partnerships, and the S Corporations chapters.
Rank	2	1	2	N/A	
Overall accounting method	Generally, must use accrual method unless smaller corporation.[3]	Generally, allowed to use cash or accrual method.	Generally, allowed to use cash or accrual method.	Cash or accrual method.	Entities taxed as partnerships, S corporations, and sole proprietorships generally have more flexibility to choose their overall accounting method than do C corporations. The cash method makes it easier for these entities to plan the timing of income and expenses than does the accrual method. More detail for this factor is provided in the Business Income, Deductions, and Accounting Methods, the Corporate Operations, the Forming and Operating Partnerships, and the S Corporations chapters.
Rank	4	1	2	1	
Allocation of income or loss items to owners	N/A	Allocations based on partnership agreement (can differ from ownership percentages).	Allocations based on stock ownership percentages.	N/A	This factor applies to partnerships and S corporations only. Partnerships have more flexibility than S corporations to determine how to allocate income and loss items to entity owners. More detail for this factor is provided in the Forming and Operating Partnerships and the S Corporations chapters.
Rank	N/A	1	2	N/A	

(continued on page 15-20)

Tax Characteristic	C Corporation	Entity Taxed as Partnership	S Corporation	Sole Proprietorship	Summary
Share of flow-through entity debt included in basis of owner's equity interest	N/A	Increase basis in ownership interest by owner's share of entity's debt.	No increase in stock basis for debt of entity (special rules if shareholder lends money to S corporation).	N/A	Partners are allowed to increase the basis in their ownership interest by their share of the partnership's debt; S corporation shareholders generally are not. This factor favors partnerships over S corporations. More detail for this factor is provided in the the Forming and Operating Partnerships and the S Corporations chapters.
Rank	N/A	1	2	N/A	
Nonliquidating distributions of noncash property	Gains recognized on distributions of appreciated property and losses disallowed on distributions of appreciated property.	Generally no gain or loss recognized on noncash property distributions.	Same as C corporation.	N/A	This factor favors partnerships for distributions of appreciated and depreciated property. More detail for this factor is provided in the Corporate Taxation: Nonliquidating Distributions, the Dispositions of Partnership Interests and Partnership Distributions, and the S Corporations chapters.
Rank	2	1	1		
Liquidating distributions	Gain and loss (certain losses disallowed).	Generally no gain or loss.	Gain and loss (certain losses disallowed).	N/A	This factor tends to favor partnerships if the liquidating entities have gain assets, and it tends to favor corporations if the entities have loss assets. More detail for this factor is provided in the Corporate Formation, Reorganization, and Liquidation, the Dispositions of Partnership Interests and Partnership Distributions, and the S Corporations chapters.
Rank	1	1	1	N/A	

---

[1]"Rank" orders the entities based on the particular characteristic (1 is most favorable).

[2]C corporations that qualify as personal service corporations (PSCs) are generally required to use a calendar year. In general, a personal service corporation is a corporation whose shareholders perform professional services such as law, engineering, and accounting. See §448(d)(2) for more detail.

[3]For tax years before 2018, corporations with average gross receipts in excess of $5 million over the three prior years could not use the cash method. For tax years beginning after 2017, the gross receipts test limit for the cash method was increased to $25 million.

[4]C corporations that are qualified personal service corporations are required to use the cash method.

Converting to Other Entity Types

With the significant reduction in corporate tax rates for tax years beginning after 2017, owners of existing flow-through entities may reevaluate their entity status and determine whether they prefer to have their entity taxed as a C corporation rather than as a flow-through entity. Fortunately for flow-through entity owners wanting to change entity type, it is easy and inexpensive to convert flow-through entities, including sole proprietorships, into C corporations. Owners of S corporations can revoke their election to be taxed as an S corporation and be taxed as a C corporation (see the S Corporations chapter for details on this process). As we discussed in the Entity Tax Classification section of this chapter, owners of entities taxed as partnerships and sole proprietors doing business as an LLC can retain the same legal entity type but make a check-the-box election to be taxed as a C corporation. Alternatively, owners of partnerships and sole proprietors can contribute the assets of the business entity to a newly formed corporation in a tax-deferred transaction without any special tax elections.[34] However, because this alternative involves creating a new legal entity, nontax factors (e.g., cost of creating a new entity, changing asset title to new entity, etc.) may make this option less desirable than the check-the-box election to be taxed as a C corporation.

Conversely, with the new tax law providing a deduction for qualified business income and slightly lower individual tax rates, C corporation shareholders may prefer to have their business taxed as a flow-through entity rather than as a C corporation. Shareholders of existing corporations really have only two options for converting into flow-through entities. First, shareholders of C corporations could make an election to treat the corporation as an S corporation (flow-through entity), if they are eligible to do so. This option is not available for many corporations due to the tax rule restrictions prohibiting certain corporations from operating as S corporations.[35] The only other option is for the shareholders to liquidate the corporation and form the business as an entity taxed as a partnership or sole proprietorship for tax purposes. This may not be a viable option, however, because the taxes imposed on liquidating corporations with appreciated assets can be punitive, even with the significantly lower corporate tax rate under the new law. As described in Exhibit 15-3, liquidating corporations are taxed on the appreciation in the assets they distribute to their shareholders in liquidation. Further, shareholders of liquidating corporations are also taxed on the difference between the fair market value of the assets they receive from the liquidating corporation and the tax basis in their stock. Effectively, the total double-tax cost of liquidating a corporation can swamp expected tax savings from operating as a flow-through entity. The tax cost of liquidating an entity is a factor to consider when making the tax entity choice for a business.

Example 15-7

What if: Assume we are years down the road and that Nicole is the sole shareholder of CCS (a C corporation). CCS's assets have a fair market value of $10 million and adjusted tax basis of $6 million ($4 million built-in gain). Further assume that the corporate tax rate is 21 percent, Nicole's stock basis in CCS is $2 million, and her marginal tax rate on long-term capital gains is 23.8 percent (20 percent capital gains rate + 3.8 percent net investment income tax). How much tax would CCS and Nicole be required to pay if CCS were to liquidate in order to form an LLC?

Answer: $2,544,080. This would be a steep tax price to pay for changing from a C corporation to an LLC.

Description	Amount	Explanation
(1) FMV of CCS assets	$10,000,000	
(2) Adjusted basis of CCS assets	6,000,000	
(3) CCS taxable income on liquidation	4,000,000	(1) − (2)
(4) Corporate tax rate	21%	
(5) Entity-level tax	840,000	(3) × (4)

(*continued on page 15-22*)

---

[34]§351 and Rev. Rul. 84-111 1984-2 CB 88.

[35]See the S Corporations chapter for details on making the S corporation election.

Description	Amount	Explanation
(6) After-tax assets distributed to Nicole	$ 9,160,000	(1) − (5)
(7) Nicole's stock basis	2,000,000	
(8) Nicole's long-term capital gain on distribution	7,160,000	(6) − (7)
(9) Nicole's marginal tax rate on gain	23.8%	
(10) Shareholder-level tax	1,704,080	(8) × (9)
Total entity and shareholder-level tax on liquidation	**$ 2,544,080**	(5) + (10)

continued from page 15-4...

Nicole quickly determined she would legally form CCS as an LLC in Utah. This would provide her with limited liability and allow her complete flexibility for determining the tax entity type of CCS. If at some point she wanted to convert CCS into a corporation in Utah, she was advised that she could make the conversion simply by filing some paperwork. Nicole's five-year forecast of CCS's expected operating results showed that CCS would generate losses for the first three years and then become very profitable thereafter. With these projections in hand, Nicole first considered forming CCS as a partnership for tax purposes (she was planning on bringing in another investor) or electing to become an S corporation. Nicole determined that income allocated to her from CCS would be eligible for the deduction for qualified business income whether she operated CCS as a partnership or an S corporation. She then compared the specific tax rules applicable to partnerships and S corporations before deciding her preference between the two tax entity types. She identified some differences that could sway her decision one way or the other. Supporting a decision to select a partnership, Nicole learned she would likely be able to deduct the projected start-up losses from CCS more quickly with a partnership compared with an S corporation because she could include a share of the partnership's debt in her tax basis in her ownership interest (whereas she would not be able to include a share of the S corporation's debt in the tax basis of her ownership interest). Nicole also hoped to attract corporate investors, and she discovered that a partnership can have corporate partners but that S corporations are not permitted to have corporate shareholders. Supporting a decision to select an S corporation, Nicole learned that S corporations appear to have a compelling advantage over partnerships in reducing the self-employment tax of owners active in managing their businesses. Nicole decided that she preferred a partnership over an S corporation because she would be willing to potentially incur additional self-employment taxes with a partnership in exchange for the ability to deduct her losses sooner and for the freedom to solicit corporate investors. Nicole then turned her attention to whether she preferred to operate CCS as a C corporation rather than a partnership. Favoring the partnership tax entity choice was the fact that Nicole would be able to immediately deduct initial losses of the business against her personal income. Favoring the C corporation choice was the overall tax rate on the CCS income when it becomes profitable. She reasoned that the corporate tax rate is significantly lower than her marginal individual tax rate and she planned to grow CCS by having CCS retain rather than distribute its income and subject it to a second level of tax. Consequently, Nicole determined that the overall tax rate to CCS income would be significantly lower if she operated CCS as a C corporation. Further, as a C corporation she would be able to solicit corporate owners and eventually take CCS public if her projections went as planned. After much thought and analysis, Nicole chose to make the election necessary to have CCS taxed as a C corporation. With this big decision out of the way, Nicole could focus on applying for a small business loan from her local bank and on having her attorney take the necessary steps to formally organize CCS as a limited liability company. ■

CONCLUSION

Any time a new business is formed, and periodically thereafter as circumstances change (such as relevant tax law), business owners must carefully evaluate what type of business entity will maximize the after-tax profits from their business ventures. Many of the key factors to consider in the entity selection decision-making process are outlined in this chapter. When making the entity selection decision, owners must carefully balance the tax and nontax characteristics unique to the entities available to them. This chapter explains how various legal entities are treated for tax purposes and how certain tax characteristics differ between entity types. Moreover, it also identifies some of the more important nontax issues that come to bear on the choice of entity decision. With this understanding, taxpayers and their advisers will be better prepared to face this frequently encountered business decision. In the Forming and Operating Partnerships chapter, we return to Nicole and Color Comfort Sheets LLC to examine the tax rules that apply to Nicole and other members in CCS as they form the entity for tax purposes and begin business operations.

Summary

Discuss the legal and nontax characteristics of different types of legal entities.   **LO 15-1**

- Entities that differ in terms of their legal characteristics include corporations, limited liability companies, general partnerships, limited partnerships, and sole proprietorships.
- Corporations are formally organized by filing articles of incorporation with the state. They are legally separate entities and protect their shareholders from the liabilities of the corporation. State corporation laws dictate interactions between corporations and shareholders. As a result, shareholders have limited flexibility to customize their business arrangements with the corporation and other shareholders. State corporate governance rules do, however, facilitate initial public offerings.
- Limited liability companies are formally organized by filing articles of organization with the state. Like corporations, they are separate legal entities that shield their members from liabilities. In contrast to corporations, state LLC statutes give members a great deal of latitude in customizing their business arrangements with the LLC and other members.
- General partnerships may be organized informally without state approval, but limited partnerships must file a certificate of limited partnership with the state to organize. Although they are considered to be legally separate entities, they provide either limited or no liability protection for partners. While limited partners in limited partnerships have liability protection, general partners are fully exposed to the liabilities of the partnership. General and limited partnerships are given a great deal of latitude in customizing their partnership agreements.
- Sole proprietorships are businesses legally indistinguishable from their sole individual owners. As such, they are very flexible but provide no liability protection. Sole proprietors can obtain liability protection by converting to a single-member LLC.

Describe the different types of entities for tax purposes.   **LO 15-2**

- The four categories of business entities recognized by our tax system include: C corporations, S corporations, partnerships, and sole proprietorships.
- Legal corporations that don't make the S election are treated as C corporations and therefore pay taxes. All other entities recognized for tax purposes are flow-through entities.
- Legal corporations that qualify for and make the S election are treated as S corporations.
- Unincorporated entities with more than one owner are treated as partnerships.
- Unincorporated entities with one owner are treated as sole proprietorships, where the sole owner is an individual, or as disregarded entities otherwise.

LO 15-3   Identify fundamental differences in tax characteristics across entity types.

- Flow-through entity income is taxed once at the owner level. For individual owners, the top rate is 37 percent. Flow-through income may also be subject to the net investment income tax for passive investors or the self-employment tax for those involved in the business activities of a partnership or sole proprietorship.

- Flow-through business owners are eligible to deduct 20 percent of their qualified business income as a *from* AGI deduction that is not an itemized deduction. The deduction is subject to certain limitations determined at the individual level.

- Qualified business income is generally nonservice business income generated in the United States.

- Flow-through entity business income allocated to passive owners is subject to the 3.8 percent net investment income tax for taxpayers with AGI over a threshold dependent on filing status.

- Self-employment income is subject to self-employment tax and additional Medicare tax.

- S corporation business income allocated to shareholders is not self-employment income.

- Sole proprietorship income is self-employment income to the sole proprietor.

- Whether business income of entities taxed as a partnership is self-employment income to an owner depends on the owner's involvement in the entity's business activities.

- Corporate taxable income is taxed at the corporate level and again at the shareholder level. For tax years beginning after 2017, the corporate tax rate is reduced to 21 percent. This significantly reduces the first level of tax on corporate income. The second level of tax is paid at the shareholder level when the corporation distributes after-tax earnings as a dividend or when the shareholder sells the stock. The tax rate for the second level of tax depends on the type of shareholder.

- Dividends and long-term capital gains are taxed at a top rate of 23.8 percent (20 percent dividend plus 3.8 percent net investment income tax). Corporate shareholders are taxed on dividends and capital gains at the corporate tax rate. However, corporations are entitled to deduct 50, 65, or 100 percent of dividends received based on the extent of their ownership in the distributing corporation.

- Corporations can defer the second level of tax by not distributing their after-tax income. However, corporations that retain earnings for tax avoidance rather than business purposes may be subject to the accumulated earnings tax or the personal holding company tax. These taxes reduce the incentive for corporations to retain earnings in order to avoid the second level of tax. Corporations are allowed to retain earnings to invest in their business.

- Business entity owners who work for the entity are compensated in different ways, depending on the type of entity.

- S corporation and C corporation shareholders who work for the entity receive employee compensation.

- Owners who work for entities taxed as partnerships receive guaranteed payments that are self-employment income to the owner-worker.

- Sole proprietors don't receive compensation from the business because the sole proprietorship and the sole proprietor are the same entity for tax purposes.

- Operating losses from S corporations and entities taxed as partnerships flow through to the owners. Owners may deduct these losses only to the extent of the basis in their ownership interest. The losses must also clear "at-risk" limitations and passive activity loss limitations in order for the owners to deduct the loss.

- The at-risk limitation is similar to the basis limitation. The passive activity loss limitations typically apply to individual investors who do little, if any, work relating to the business activities of the flow-through entity (referred to as passive activities to the individual investors). In these circumstances, taxpayers can deduct such losses only to the extent they have income from other passive activities.

- Flow-through entity individual owners are not allowed to deduct an excess business loss for the year. This provision potentially limits losses that would otherwise be deductible after applying the at-risk and passive activity loss limitations.

- Shareholders can mitigate the double tax by increasing the time they hold shares before selling.

- C corporation losses are referred to as net operating losses (NOLs).

- C corporations incurring NOLs before 2018 can carry the losses back two years and forward up to 20 years to offset up to 100 percent of taxable income in those years. C corporations incurring losses after 2017 can carry the losses forward indefinitely but may not carry the losses back. Further, the NOL deduction is limited to 80 percent of taxable income without the deduction in those years.

- C corporations may have one or many shareholders. S corporations may have one shareholder and as many as 100 unrelated shareholders; but corporations, nonresident aliens, partnerships, and certain trusts may not be S corporation shareholders. Partnerships must have at least two partners but are not restricted to a maximum number of partners. Sole proprietorships may have only one owner.

- Gains and income from contributing appreciated property to business entities are more easily deferred with partnerships compared to C and S corporations.

- S corporations, partnerships, and sole proprietorships are generally required to use tax year-ends conforming to the tax year-ends of their owners. C corporations may use any tax year-end.

- C corporations generally must use the accrual method unless they are a smaller corporation (average gross receipts of $25 million or less in the prior three years). S corporations may use either the cash or accrual method of accounting. Partnerships generally may use either the cash or accrual method. Sole proprietorships may use either the cash or accrual method.

- Income and losses may be specially allocated to partners based on the partnership agreement. This gives partnerships a great deal of flexibility in determining how the risks and rewards of the enterprise are shared among partners. In contrast, income and losses must be allocated pro rata to S corporation shareholders consistent with their ownership percentages.

- Partners, but not S corporation shareholders, may add their share of entity debt to the basis in their ownership interest.

- Generally, distributions of appreciated property trigger gain at both the corporate and shareholder level when made to shareholders of C corporations; trigger gain at the corporate level when made to S corporation shareholders; and don't trigger any gain at all when made to partners.

- On liquidation, C and S corporations will generally recognize gains and losses on distributed assets. In contrast, partnerships and their partners generally do not recognize gains or losses on liquidating distributions.

- Converting a flow-through entity into a C corporation for tax purposes is generally fairly easy and inexpensive to do. S corporation shareholders can revoke the S corporation election and partnerships (and sole proprietorships formed as LLCs) can check the box to be taxed as a corporation or partnerships, and sole proprietors can contribute assets to a corporate entity in tax-deferred transactions.

- C corporations wanting to convert to a flow-through entity have two options. They may elect to become an S corporation if eligible, or they may liquidate the corporation and organize as a new entity. Taxes from liquidating C corporations can be significant when C corporations have appreciated assets.

KEY TERMS

accumulated earnings tax (15-14)

articles of incorporation (15-2)

articles of organization (15-2)

C corporation (15-5)

certificate of limited partnership (15-2)

certificate of organization (15-2)

corporation (15-2)

disregarded entities (15-5)

dividends received deduction (15-12)

double taxation (15-13)

excess business loss (15-16)

flow-through entities (15-5)

general partnership (GP) (15-2)

initial public offering (IPO) (15-3)

institutional shareholders (15-11)

limited liability company (LLC) (15-2)

limited partnership (LP) (15-2)

net earnings from
   self-employment (15-9)

net operating loss (NOL) (15-16)

partnership agreement (15-2)

personal holding companies (15-14)

personal holding company tax (15-14)

qualified business income (QBI) (15-8)

S corporation (15-5)

single-member LLCs (15-5)

sole proprietorship (15-2)

specified service trade or
   business (15-8)

DISCUSSION QUESTIONS

Discussion Questions are available in Connect®.   ▣ connect·

LO 15-1   1. What are the most common legal entities used for operating a business? How are these entities treated similarly and differently for state law purposes?

LO 15-1   2. How do business owners create legal entities? Is the process the same for all entities? If not, what are the differences?

LO 15-1   3. What is an operating agreement for an LLC? Are operating agreements required for limited liability companies? If not, why might it be important to have one?

LO 15-1   4. Explain how legal entities differ in terms of the liability protection they afford their owners.

LO 15-1   5. Why are C corporations still popular despite the double tax on their income?

LO 15-1   6. Why is it a nontax advantage for corporations to be able to trade their stock on the stock market?

LO 15-1   7. How do corporations protect shareholders from liability? If you formed a small corporation, would you be able to avoid repaying a bank loan from your community bank if the corporation went bankrupt? Explain.

LO 15-1 **LO 15-2**   8. Other than corporations, are there other legal entities that offer liability protection? Are any of them taxed as flow-through entities? Explain.

LO 15-2   9. In general, how are unincorporated entities classified for tax purposes?

LO 15-2   10. Can unincorporated legal entities ever be treated as corporations for tax purposes? Can corporations ever be treated as flow-through entities for tax purposes? Explain.

LO 15-2   11. What are the differences, if any, between the legal and tax classifications of business entities?

LO 15-2   12. What types of business entities does the U.S. tax system recognize?

LO 15-3   13. For flow-through entities with individual owners, how many times is flow-through entity income taxed, who pays the tax, and what is the tax rate?

LO 15-3   14. What is the qualified business income deduction and how does it affect the tax rate on flow-through entity income?

LO 15-3   15. Doug is considering investing in one of two partnerships that will build, own, and operate a hotel. One is located in Canada and one is located in Arizona. Assuming both investments will generate the same before-tax rate of return, which entity should Doug invest in when considering the after-tax consequences of the investment? Assume Doug's marginal rate is 37 percent, he will be a passive investor in the business, and he will report the flow-through income from either entity on his tax return. Explain (ignore any foreign tax credit issues).

LO 15-3   16. Is business income allocated from a flow-through entity to its owner's self-employment income? Explain.

LO 15-3   17. Who pays the first level of tax on a C corporation's income? What is the tax rate applicable to the first level of tax? Did recent tax law changes increase or decrease the corporate tax rate?

LO 15-3   18. Who pays the second level of tax on a C corporation's income? What is the tax rate applicable to the second level of tax and when is it levied?

LO 15-3   19. Is it possible for shareholders to defer or avoid the second level of tax on corporate income? Briefly explain.

LO 15-3   20. How does a corporation's decision to pay dividends affect its overall tax rate?

21. Is it possible for the overall tax rate on corporate taxable income to be lower than the tax rate on flow-through entity taxable income? If so, under what conditions would you expect the overall corporate tax rate to be lower? `LO 15-3`

22. Assume Congress increases individual tax rates on ordinary income while leaving all other tax rates unchanged. How would this change affect the overall tax rate on corporate taxable income? How would this change affect overall tax rates for owners of flow-through entities? `LO 15-3`

23. Assume Congress increases the dividend tax rate to the ordinary tax rate while leaving all other tax rates unchanged. How would this change affect the overall tax rate on corporate taxable income? `LO 15-3`

24. Evaluate the following statement: "When dividends and long-term capital gains are taxed at the same rate, the present value of the taxes paid on corporate income is the same whether the corporation distributes its after-tax earnings as a dividend or whether it reinvests the after-tax earnings to increase the value of the corporation." `LO 15-3`

25. If XYZ Corporation is a shareholder of BCD Corporation, how many levels of tax is BCD's before-tax income potentially subject to? Has Congress provided any tax relief for this result? Explain. `LO 15-3`

26. How many times is income from a C corporation taxed if a retirement fund is the owner of the corporation's stock? Explain. `LO 15-3`

27. For tax purposes, how is the compensation paid to an S corporation shareholder similar to compensation paid to an owner of an entity taxed as a partnership? How is it different? `LO 15-3`

28. Why might it be a good tax planning strategy for an S corporation with one shareholder to pay a salary to the shareholder on the low end of what the services are potentially worth? `LO 15-3`

29. When a C corporation reports a loss for the year, can shareholders use the loss to offset their personal income? Why or why not? `LO 15-3`

30. Is a current-year net operating loss of a C corporation available to offset income from the corporation in other years? Explain. `LO 15-3`

31. Would a corporation with a small amount of current-year taxable income (before the net operating loss deduction) and a large net operating loss carryover have a tax liability for the current year? Explain. `LO 15-3`

32. In its first year of existence, SMS, an S corporation, reported a business loss of $10,000. Michelle, SMS's sole shareholder, reports $50,000 of taxable income from sources other than SMS. What must you know to determine whether she can deduct the $10,000 loss against her other income? Explain. `LO 15-3`

33. ELS, an S corporation, reported a business loss of $1,000,000. Ethan, ELS's sole shareholder, is involved in ELS's daily business activities and he reports $1,200,000 of taxable income from sources other than ELS. What must you know in order to determine how much, if any, of the $1,000,000 loss Ethan may deduct in the current year? Explain. `LO 15-3`

34. Why are S corporations less favorable than C corporations and entities taxed as partnerships in terms of owner-related limitations? `LO 15-3`

35. Are C corporations or flow-through entities (S corporations and entities taxed as partnerships) more flexible in terms of selecting a tax year-end? Why are the tax rules in this area different for C corporations and flow-through entities? `LO 15-3`

36. Which entity types are generally allowed to use the cash method of accounting? `LO 15-3`

37. According to the tax rules, how are profits and losses allocated to owners of entities taxed as partnerships (partners or LLC members)? How are they allocated to S corporation shareholders? Which entity permits greater flexibility in allocating profits and losses? `LO 15-3`

LO 15-3 38. Compare and contrast the FICA tax burden of S corporation shareholder-employees and LLC members (assume an LLC taxed as a partnership) receiving compensation for working for the entity (guaranteed payments) and business income allocations to S corporation shareholders and LLC members assuming the owners are actively involved in the entity's business activities. How does your analysis change if the owners are not actively involved in the entity's business activities?

LO 15-3 39. Explain how liabilities of an LLC (taxed as a partnership) or an S corporation affect the amount of tax losses from the entity that limited liability company members and S corporation shareholders may deduct. Do the tax rules favor LLCs or S corporations?

LO 15-3 40. Compare the entity-level tax consequences for C corporations, S corporations, and entities taxed as partnerships for both nonliquidating and liquidating distributions of noncash property. Do the tax rules tend to favor one entity type more than the others? Explain.

LO 15-3 41. If entities taxed as partnerships and S corporations are both flow-through entities for tax purposes, why might an owner prefer one form over the other for tax purposes? List separately the tax factors supporting the decision to operate as either an entity taxed as a partnership or as an S corporation.

LO 15-3 42. What are the tax advantages and disadvantages of converting a C corporation into an (taxed as a partnership)?

PROBLEMS

Select problems are available in Connect®.

LO 15-1 43. Visit your state's official website and review the information there related to forming and operating business entities in your state. Write a short report explaining the steps for organizing a business in your state and summarizing any tax-related information you found.

  research

LO 15-3 44. Andrea would like to organize SHO as either an LLC (taxed as a sole proprietorship) or a C corporation. In either form, the entity is expected to generate an 11 percent annual before-tax return on a $200,000 investment. Andrea's marginal income tax rate is 35 percent and her tax rate on dividends and capital gains is 15 percent. Andrea will also pay a 3.8 percent net investment income tax on dividends and capital gains she recognizes. If Andrea organizes SHO as an LLC, Andrea will be required to pay an additional 2.9 percent for self-employment tax and an additional .9 percent for the additional Medicare tax. Further, she is eligible to claim the full deduction for qualified business income. Assume that SHO will pay out all of its after-tax earnings every year as a dividend if it is formed as a C corporation.

   a) How much cash after taxes would Andrea receive from her investment in the first year if SHO is organized as either an LLC or a C corporation?

   b) What is the overall tax rate on SHO's income in the first year if SHO is organized as an LLC or as a C corporation?

LO 15-3 45. Jacob is a member of WCC (an LLC taxed as a partnership). Jacob was allocated $100,000 of business income from WCC for the year. Jacob's marginal income tax rate is 37 percent. The business allocation is subject to 2.9 percent of self-employment tax and .9 percent additional Medicare tax.

   a) What is the amount of tax Jacob will owe on the income allocation if the income is not qualified business income?

   b) What is the amount of tax Jacob will owe on the income allocation if the income is qualified business income (QBI) and Jacob qualifies for the full QBI deduction?

46. Amanda would like to organize BAL as either an LLC (taxed as a sole proprietorship) or a C corporation. In either form, the entity is expected to generate an 8 percent annual before-tax return on a $500,000 investment. Amanda's marginal income tax rate is 37 percent and her tax rate on dividends and capital gains is 23.8 percent (including the 3.8 percent net investment income tax). If Amanda organizes BAL as an LLC, she will be required to pay an additional 2.9 percent for self-employment tax and an additional .9 percent for the additional Medicare tax. Also, she is eligible to claim a full deduction for qualified business income on BAL's income. Assume that BAL will distribute half of its after-tax earnings every year as a dividend if it is formed as a C corporation.

     LO 15-3

    a) How much cash after taxes would Amanda receive from her investment in the first year if BAL is organized as either an LLC or a C corporation?

    b) What is the overall tax rate on BAL's income in the first year if BAL is organized as an LLC or as a C corporation?

47. Sandra would like to organize BAL as either an LLC (taxed as a sole proprietorship) or a C corporation. In either form, the entity is expected to generate an 8 percent annual before-tax return on a $500,000 investment. Sandra's marginal income tax rate is 37 percent and her tax rate on dividends and capital gains is 23.8 percent (including the 3.8 percent net investment income tax). If Sandra organizes BAL as an LLC, she will be required to pay an additional 2.9 percent for self-employment tax and an additional .9 percent for the additional Medicare tax. BAL's income is not qualified business income (QBI) so Sandra is not allowed to claim the QBI deduction. Assume that BAL will distribute all of its after-tax earnings every year as a dividend if it is formed as a C corporation.

    LO 15-3

    a) How much cash after taxes would Sandra receive from her investment in the first year if BAL is organized as either an LLC or a C corporation?

    b) What is the overall tax rate on BAL's income in the first year if BAL is organized as an LLC or as a C corporation?

48. Tremaine would like to organize UTA as either an S Corporation or a C corporation. In either form, the entity will generate a 9 percent annual before-tax return on a $1,000,000 investment. Tremaine's marginal income tax rate is 37 percent and his tax rate on dividends and capital gains is 23.8 percent (including the net investment income tax). If Tremaine organizes UTA as an S corporation he will be allowed to claim the deduction for qualified business income. Also, because Tremaine will participate in UTA's business activities, the income from UTA will not be subject to the net investment income tax. Assume that UTA will pay out 25 percent of its after-tax earnings every year as a dividend if it is formed as a C corporation.

    LO 15-3

    research

    a) How much cash after taxes would Tremaine receive from his investment in the first year if UTA is organized as either an S corporation or a C corporation?

    b) What is the overall tax rate on UTA's income in the first year if UTA is organized as an S corporation or as a C corporation?

    c) What is the overall tax rate on UTA's income in the first year if it is organized as an S corporation but UTA's income is not qualified business income?

    d) What is the overall tax rate on UTA's income if UTA's income is not qualified business income and Tremaine is a passive investor in UTA?

49. Marathon Inc. (a C corporation) reported $1,000,000 of taxable income in the current year. During the year, it distributed $100,000 as dividends to its shareholders as follows:

     LO 15-3

    tax forms

    • $5,000 to Guy, a 5 percent individual shareholder.
    • $15,000 to Little Rock Corp., a 15 percent shareholder (C corporation).
    • $80,000 to other shareholders.

a) How much of the dividend payment did Marathon deduct in determining its taxable income?

b) Assuming Guy's marginal ordinary tax rate is 37 percent, how much tax will he pay on the $5,000 dividend he received from Marathon Inc. (including the net investment income tax)?

c) What amount of tax will Little Rock Corp. pay on the $15,000 dividend it received from Marathon Inc. (50 percent dividends received deduction)?

d) Complete Form 1120 Schedule C for Little Rock Corp. to reflect its dividends received deduction. (Note that the 2017 form is not updated for DRD percentages effective in 2018. If using 2017 form, report the DRD on line 1).

e) On what line on page 1 of Little Rock Corp.'s Form 1120 is the dividend from Marathon Inc. reported, and on what line of Little Rock Corp.'s Form 1120 is its dividends received deduction reported?

LO 15-3

research

50. After several years of profitable operations, Javell, the sole shareholder of JBD Inc., a C corporation, sold 22 percent of her JBD stock to ZNO Inc., a C corporation in a similar industry. During the current year JBD reports $1,000,000 of after-tax income. JBD distributes all of its after-tax earnings to its two shareholders in proportion to their shareholdings. How much tax will ZNO pay on the dividend it receives from JBD? What is ZNO's tax rate on the dividend income (after considering the DRD)? [*Hint:* See IRC §243.]

LO 15-3

51. Mackenzie is considering conducting her business, Mac561, as either a single-member LLC or as an S corporation. Determine Mackenzie's after-tax cash flow from the entity's business income and any compensation she receives from the business assuming her marginal ordinary income tax rate is 37 percent, her marginal FICA rate on employee compensation is 1.45 percent, her marginal self-employment tax rate is 2.9 percent, and any employee compensation or self-employment income she receives is subject to the .9 percent additional Medicare tax. Finally, Mac561 generated $200,000 of business income before considering the deduction for compensation Mac561 pays to Mackenzie and Mackenzie can claim the full qualified business income deduction on Mac561's business income.

a) Mackenzie conducted Mac561 as a single-member LLC.

b) Mackenzie conducted Mac561 as an S corporation and she received a salary of $100,000. All business income allocated to her is also distributed to her.

c) Mackenzie conducted Mac561 as an S corporation and she received a salary of $20,000. All business income allocated to her is also distributed to her.

d) Which entity/compensation combination generated the most after-cash flow for Mackenzie? What are the primary contributing factors favoring this combination?

LO 15-3

52. In its first year of existence (year 1), SCC corporation (a C corporation) reported a loss for tax purposes of $30,000. How much tax will SCC pay in year 2 if it reports taxable income from operations of $20,000 before considering loss carryovers under the following assumptions?

a) Year 1 is 2017.

b) Year 1 is 2018.

LO 15-3

53. In its first year of existence (year 1), Willow Corp. (a C corporation) reports a loss for tax purposes of $50,000. In year 2 it reports a $40,000 loss. For year 3, it reports taxable income from operations of $100,000 before any loss carryovers. How much tax will Willow Corp. pay in year 3, what is its NOL carryover to year 4, and when will the NOL expire under the following assumptions?

a) Year 1 is 2017.

b) Year 1 is 2018.

54. Damarcus is a 50 percent owner of Hoop (a business entity). In the current year, Hoop reported a $100,000 business loss. Answer the following questions associated with each of the following alternative scenarios.

    LO 15-3

    a) Hoop is organized as a C corporation and Damarcus works full-time as an employee for Hoop. Damarcus has a $20,000 basis in his Hoop stock. How much of Hoop's loss is Damarcus allowed to deduct against his other income?

    b) Hoop is organized as an LLC taxed as a partnership. Fifty percent of Hoop's loss is allocated to Damarcus. Damarcus works full-time for Hoop (he is not considered to be a passive investor in Hoop). Damarcus has a $20,000 basis in his Hoop ownership interest and he also has a $20,000 at-risk amount in his investment in Hoop. Damarcus does not report income or loss from any other business activity investments. How much of the $50,000 loss allocated to him by Hoop is Damarcus allowed to deduct this year?

    c) Hoop is organized as an LLC taxed as a partnership. Fifty percent of Hoop's loss is allocated to Damarcus. Damarcus does not work for Hoop at all (he is a passive investor in Hoop). Damarcus has a $20,000 basis in his Hoop ownership interest and he also has a $20,000 at-risk amount in his investment in Hoop. Damarcus does not report income or loss from any other business activity investments. How much of the $50,000 loss allocated to him by Hoop is Damarcus allowed to deduct this year?

    d) Hoop is organized as an LLC taxed as a partnership. Fifty percent of Hoop's loss is allocated to Damarcus. Damarcus works full-time for Hoop (he is not considered to be a passive investor in Hoop). Damarcus has a $70,000 basis in his Hoop ownership interest and he also has a $70,000 at-risk amount in his investment in Hoop. Damarcus does not report income or loss from any other business activity investments. How much of the $50,000 loss allocated to him by Hoop is Damarcus allowed to deduct this year?

    e) Hoop is organized as an LLC taxed as a partnership. Fifty percent of Hoop's loss is allocated to Damarcus. Damarcus does not work for Hoop at all (he is a passive investor in Hoop). Damarcus has a $20,000 basis in his Hoop ownership interest and he also has a $20,000 at-risk amount in his investment in Hoop. Damarcus reports $10,000 of income from a business activity in which he is a passive investor. How much of the $50,000 loss allocated to him by Hoop is Damarcus allowed to deduct this year?

55. Danni is a single 30 percent owner of Kolt (a business entity). In the current year, Kolt reported a $1,000,000 business loss. Answer the following questions associated with each of the following alternative scenarios:

    LO 15-3

    a) Kolt is organized as a C corporation and Danni works 20 hours a week as an employee for Kolt. Danni has a $200,000 basis in her Kolt stock. How much of Kolt's loss is Danni allowed to deduct this year against her other income?

    b) Kolt is organized as an LLC taxed as a partnership. Thirty percent of Kolt's loss is allocated to Danni. Danni works 20 hours a week on Kolt business activities (she is not considered to be a passive investor in Kolt). Danni has a $400,000 basis in her Kolt ownership interest and she also has a $400,000 at-risk amount in her investment in Kolt. Danni does not report income or loss from any other business activity investments. How much of the $300,000 loss allocated to her from Kolt is Danni allowed to deduct this year?

    c) Kolt is organized as an LLC taxed as a partnership. Thirty percent of Kolt's loss is allocated to Danni. Danni is not involved in Kolt business activities. Consequently, she is considered to be a passive investor in Kolt. Danni has a $400,000 basis in her Kolt ownership interest and she also has a $400,000 at-risk amount in her investment in Kolt. Danni does not report income or loss from any other business activity investments. How much of the $300,000 loss allocated to her from Kolt is Danni allowed to deduct this year?

LO 15-3

research

56. Mickey, Mickayla, and Taylor are starting a new business (MMT). To get the business started, Mickey is contributing $200,000 for a 40 percent ownership interest, Mickayla is contributing a building with a value of $200,000 and a tax basis of $150,000 for a 40 percent ownership interest, and Taylor is contributing legal services for a 20 percent ownership interest. What amount of gain is each owner required to recognize under each of the following alternative situations?
[*Hint:* Look at §351 and §721.]
a) MMT is formed as a C corporation.
b) MMT is formed as an S corporation.
c) MMT is formed as an LLC.

LO 15-3

research

57. Dave and his friend Stewart each own 50 percent of KBS. During the year, Dave receives $75,000 compensation for services he performs for KBS during the year. He performed a significant amount of work for the entity and he was heavily involved in management decisions (he was not a passive investor in KBS). After deducting Dave's compensation, KBS reports taxable income of $30,000. How much FICA and/or self-employment tax is Dave required to pay on his compensation and his share of the KBS income if KBS is formed as a C corporation, an S corporation, or a limited liability company (ignore the .9 percent additional Medicare tax)?

LO 15-3

research

58. Rondo and his business associate, Larry, are considering forming a business entity called R&L but they are unsure about whether to form it as a C corporation, an S corporation, or an LLC taxed as a partnership. Rondo and Larry would each invest $50,000 in the business. Thus, each owner would take an initial basis in his ownership interest of $50,000 no matter which entity type is formed. Shortly after the formation of the entity, the business borrowed $30,000 from the bank. If applicable, this debt will be shared equally between the two owners.
a) After taking the loan into account, what is Rondo's tax basis in his R&L stock if R&L is formed as a C corporation?
b) After taking the loan into account, what is Rondo's tax basis in his R&L stock if R&L is formed as an S corporation?
c) After taking the loan into account, what is Rondo's tax basis in his R&L ownership interest if R&L is formed and taxed as a partnership?

LO 15-3

research

59. Kevin and Bob have owned and operated SOA as a C corporation for a number of years. When they formed the entity, Kevin and Bob each contributed $100,000 to SOA. They each have a current basis of $100,000 in their SOA ownership interest. Information on SOA's assets at the end of year 5 is as follows (SOA does not have any liabilities):

Assets	FMV	Adjusted Basis	Built-in Gain
Cash	$200,000	$200,000	$ 0
Inventory	80,000	40,000	40,000
Land and building	220,000	170,000	50,000
Total	$500,000		

At the end of year 5, SOA liquidated and distributed half of the land, half of the inventory, and half of the cash remaining after paying taxes (if any) to each owner.

Assume that, excluding the effects of the liquidating distribution, SOA's taxable income for year 5 is $0.

a) What is the amount and character of gain or loss SOA will recognize on the liquidating distribution?

b) What is the amount and character of gain or loss Kevin will recognize when he receives the liquidating distribution of cash and property? Recall that his stock basis is $100,000 and he is treated as having sold his stock for the liquidation proceeds.

COMPREHENSIVE PROBLEMS

Select problems are available with Connect®.

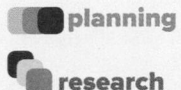

planning

research

60. Daisy Taylor has developed a viable new business idea. Her idea is to design and manufacture cookware that remains cool to the touch when in use. She has had several friends try out her prototype cookware and they have consistently given the cookware rave reviews. With this encouragement, Daisy started giving serious thought to starting up a business called "Cool Touch Cookware" (CTC).

Daisy understands that it will take a few years for the business to become profitable. She would like to grow her business and perhaps at some point "go public" or sell the business to a large retailer.

Daisy, who is single, decided to quit her full-time job so that she could focus all of her efforts on the new business. Daisy had some savings to support her for a while but she did not have any other source of income. She was able to recruit Kesha and Aryan to join her as initial equity investors in CTC. Kesha has an MBA and a law degree. Kesha was employed as a business consultant when she decided to leave that job and work with Daisy and Aryan. Kesha's husband earns close to $300,000 a year as an engineer (employee). Aryan owns a *very* profitable used car business. Because buying and selling used cars takes all his time, he is interested in becoming only a passive investor in CTC. He wanted to get in on the ground floor because he really likes the product and believes CTC will be wildly successful. While CTC originally has three investors, Daisy and Kesha have plans to grow the business and seek more owners and capital in the future.

The three owners agreed that Daisy would contribute land and cash for a 30 percent interest in CTC, Kesha would contribute services (legal and business advisory) for the first two years for a 30 percent interest, and Aryan would contribute cash for a 40 percent interest. The plan called for Daisy and Kesha to be actively involved in managing the business while Aryan would not be. The three equity owners' contributions are summarized as follows:

Daisy Contributed	FMV	Adjusted Basis	Ownership Interest
Land (held as investment)	$120,000	$70,000	30%
Cash	30,000		
Kesha Contributed			
Services	150,000		30
Aryan Contributed			
Cash	200,000		40

Working together, Daisy and Kesha made the following five-year income and loss projections for CTC. They anticipate the business will be profitable and that it will continue to grow after the first five years.

Cool Touch Cookware 5-Year Income and Loss Projections	
Year	**Income (Loss)**
1	$(200,000)
2	(80,000)
3	(20,000)
4	60,000
5	180,000

With plans for Daisy and Kesha to spend a considerable amount of their time working for and managing CTC, the owners would like to develop a compensation plan that works for all parties. Down the road, they plan to have two business locations (in different cities). Daisy would take responsibility for the activities of one location and Kesha would take responsibility for the other. Finally, they would like to arrange for some performance-based financial incentives for each location.

To get the business activities started, Daisy and Kesha determined CTC would need to borrow $800,000 to purchase a building to house its manufacturing facilities and its administrative offices (at least for now). Also, in need of additional cash, Daisy and Kesha arranged to have CTC borrow $300,000 from a local bank and to borrow $200,000 cash from Aryan. CTC would pay Aryan a market rate of interest on the loan but there was no fixed date for principal repayment.

Required:

Identify significant tax and nontax issues or concerns that may differ across entity types and discuss how they are relevant to the choice of entity decision for CTC.

 research

61. Cool Touch Cookware (CTC) has been in business for about 10 years now. Daisy and Kesha are each 50 percent owners of the business. They initially established the business with cash contributions. CTC manufactures unique cookware that remains cool to the touch when in use. CTC has been fairly profitable over the years. Daisy and Kesha have both been actively involved in managing the business. They have developed very good personal relationships with many customers (both wholesale and retail) that, Daisy and Kesha believe, keep the customers coming back.

On September 30 of the current year, CTC had all of its assets appraised. Below is CTC's balance sheet, as of September 30, with the corresponding appraisals of the fair market value of all of its assets. Note that CTC has several depreciated assets. CTC uses the hybrid method of accounting. It accounts for its gross margin-related items under the accrual method and it accounts for everything else using the cash method of accounting.

Assets	Adjusted Tax Basis	FMV
Cash	$150,000	$150,000
Accounts receivable	20,000	15,000
Inventory*	90,000	300,000
Equipment	120,000	100,000
Investment in XYZ stock	40,000	120,000
Land (used in the business)	80,000	70,000
Building	200,000	180,000
Total assets	$700,000	$935,000

Liabilities	
Accounts payable	$ 40,000
Bank loan	60,000
Mortgage on building	100,000
Equity	500,000
Total liabilities and equity	$700,000

*CTC uses the LIFO method for determining the adjusted basis of its inventory. Its basis in the inventory under the FIFO method would have been $110,000.

'In addition, Daisy and Kesha had the entire business appraised at $1,135,000, which is $200,000 more than the value of the identifiable assets.

From January 1 of the current year through September 30, CTC reported the following income:

Ordinary business income	$530,000
Dividends from XYZ stock	12,000
Long-term capital losses	15,000
Interest income	3,000

Daisy and Kesha are considering changing the business form of CTC.

Required:

a) Assume CTC is organized as a C corporation. Identify significant tax and nontax issues associated with converting CTC from a C corporation to an S corporation. [*Hint:* See IRC §1374 and §1363(d).]

b) Assume CTC is organized as a C corporation. Identify significant tax and nontax issues associated with converting CTC from a C corporation to an LLC. Assume CTC converts to an LLC (taxed as a partnership) by distributing its assets to its shareholders, who then contribute the assets to a new LLC. [*Hint:* See IRC §§331, 336, and 721(a).]

c) Assume that CTC is a C corporation with a net operating loss carryforward as of the beginning of the year in the amount of $2,000,000. Identify significant tax and nontax issues associated with converting CTC from a C corporation to an LLC (taxed as a partnership). Assume CTC converts to an LLC by distributing its assets to its shareholders, who then contribute the assets to a new LLC. [*Hint:* See IRC §§172(a), 331, 336, and 721(a).]

ROGER | *CPA Review*

Sample CPA Exam questions from Roger CPA Review are available in Connect as support for the topics in this text. These Multiple Choice Questions and Task-Based Simulations include expert-written explanations and solutions and provide a starting point for students to become familiar with the content and functionality of the actual CPA Exam.

chapter

16 Corporate Operations

Learning Objectives

Upon completing this chapter, you should be able to:

LO 16-1 Identify those income and expense items that cause a corporation's financial accounting net income to differ from its taxable income.

LO 16-2 Compute a corporation's taxable income and associated income tax liability using financial statement information.

LO 16-3 Describe a corporation's tax return reporting and estimated tax payment obligations.

LO 16-4 Calculate a corporation's alternative minimum tax credit carryforward.

©Sam Edwards/age fotostock

Storyline Summary

Premiere Computer Corporation (PCC)
Medium-sized publicly traded company
Manufactures and sells computers and computer-related equipment
Calendar-year taxpayer

Elise Brandon
Newly hired tax associate for a large public accounting firm
Currently assigned to review the federal income tax return for PCC

Today was Elise's first day on the job as a tax associate for a public accounting firm. Shortly after she arrived, Rachel, a tax manager, introduced herself and took Elise around the office to meet some of the people with whom she would be working. After the introductions, Rachel told Elise she would like her to review the federal tax return for Premiere Computer Corporation (PCC).

PCC is a medium-sized publicly traded C corporation that manufactures computers and computer-related equipment. PCC has been a client of the firm for several years. Overall, PCC has been a fairly profitable company, but last year the company experienced a bit of a setback, incurring its first tax loss in many years.

Elise was excited about her opportunity, and she was confident her accounting education had adequately prepared her to successfully complete the assignment. She also knew that tax reform enacted in 2017 made significant changes to corporate taxation. When Rachel spoke with Elise about the assignment, she advised her to first review PCC's tax return and tax return workpapers from last year to get an idea how to review the return. Next, she should start with the audited numbers on the income statement and examine the book-to-tax adjustments that caused taxable income to differ from PCC's net income before income taxes. Rachel counselled Elise to identify those book and tax differences as being "temporary" or "permanent" because she was eventually going to compute the company's accounting "income tax provision" from this information. Rachel encouraged Elise to keep her posted on her progress and ask questions when necessary to keep the project on budget.

to be continued . . .

In this chapter we explore the process of computing and reporting taxable income for C corporations. As we discussed in the Entities Overview chapter, C corporations are legal and taxpaying entities separate from their shareholders. Each year, C corporations are required to compute their taxable income and pay tax on the income. In contrast to individuals, C corporations often compute taxable income by starting with their book (financial accounting) income and making adjustments for book–tax differences.

LO 16-1   # CORPORATE TAXABLE INCOME FORMULA

The formula for computing corporate taxable income and individual taxable income is similar in some respects and different in others. Exhibit 16-1 compares the corporate income tax formula with the individual tax formula.

EXHIBIT 16-1   **Corporate and Individual Tax Formulas**

	Corporate Tax Formula	Individual Tax Formula
	Gross income	Gross income
Minus:	Deductions	*For* AGI deductions
Equals		Adjusted gross income
Minus:		*From* AGI deductions
		(1) Deduction for qualified business income, and
		(2) *Greater* of: (a) Standard deduction or (b) Itemized deductions
Equals	Taxable income	Taxable income
Times	Tax rates	Tax rates
Equals	Regular income tax liability	Regular income tax liability
Add	Other taxes	Other taxes
Equals	Total tax	Total tax
Minus	Credits	Credits
Minus	Prepayments	Prepayments
Equals	Taxes due (or refund)	Taxes due (or refund)

Corporations compute gross income as do other types of business entities and individual taxpayers. In contrast to individual taxpayers, corporations do not calculate adjusted gross income (AGI). Like other businesses, corporations are allowed to deduct ordinary and necessary business expenditures (see discussion in the Business Income, Deductions, and Accounting Methods chapter). Unlike individual taxpayers, corporations treat all deductions as related to a trade or business. Corporations also do not receive a standard deduction. Consequently, the formula for computing a corporation's taxable income is relatively straightforward.

Accounting Periods and Methods

In the Business Income, Deductions, and Accounting Methods chapter, we discussed accounting periods and methods for all types of business entities. We learned that corporations measure their taxable income over a tax year and that their tax year must be the same as their financial accounting year. A corporation must elect its tax year (which it can subsequently change) when it files its first income tax return.

A corporation's choice of accounting methods will determine when income and deductions are recognized. As we discuss in the Business Income, Deductions, and Accounting Methods chapter, accounting methods include overall methods of accounting (accrual method, cash method, or hybrid method) and accounting methods for individual items such as inventory (for example, LIFO or FIFO) or depreciation (accelerated or straight line). For tax purposes, corporations have some flexibility in choosing methods of accounting for individual

THE KEY FACTS

Corporate Taxable Income Formula and Accounting Periods and Methods

- The corporate tax formula is similar to the individual tax formula, but corporations don't itemize deductions.
- Corporations with annual average gross receipts of $25 million or less over the three prior tax years (or a shorter period for new corporations) may use the cash method.

items or transactions. However, corporations generally are required to use the accrual overall method of accounting.[1] For tax purposes, corporations with annual average gross receipts of $25 million or less for the three years prior to the current tax year can elect to use the cash method of accounting.[2] Corporations that have not been in existence for at least three years compute their annual average gross receipts over the prior periods they have been in existence to determine if they are permitted to use the cash method of accounting. For tax years beginning after December 31, 2107, accrual method taxpayers must include in gross income an item of income no later than the taxable year in which such income is taken into account as revenue in an "applicable financial statement" (generally a Form 10-K filed with the SEC or an audited financial statement prepared in accordance with GAAP). This exception does not apply to the installment method or the percentage-of-completion method.

TAXES IN THE REAL WORLD Choosing Tax Accounting Methods

For certain transaction types, corporations face an interesting choice between permissible accounting methods. A corporation could select an accounting method that tends to defer income or accelerate deductions from certain types of transactions, or it could choose a method that tends to accelerate income or defer deductions. A research study by accounting professors provides evidence that when faced with this decision, publicly traded corporations tend to select income *accelerating* methods, while privately held corporations tend to select income *deferring* methods.[3] Why the difference?

Recall that generally speaking, the tax treatment of a transaction follows the book treatment. Publicly traded corporations are generally more concerned with increasing financial statement income to satisfy stockholders and potential investors. If corporations have to report higher levels of taxable income and pay more taxes as a result, that's OK. Privately held corporations are just the opposite. They don't need to impress shareholders with accelerated earnings. They would rather reap the benefits of paying lower current taxes even if it means reporting lower book income. This research illustrates the fact that nontax considerations may be more important than tax factors in the decision-making process. After all, a business's objective should not be to minimize taxes but rather to maximize after-tax cash flows.

COMPUTING CORPORATE TAXABLE INCOME

LO 16-2

To compute taxable income, most corporations begin with **book (financial reporting) income** and then make adjustments for **book–tax differences** to reconcile to the tax numbers.[4]

Book–Tax Differences

Many items of income and expense are accounted for differently for book and tax purposes. The following discussion describes several common book–tax differences applicable to corporations. Each book–tax difference can be considered "unfavorable" or "favorable" depending on its effect on taxable income relative to book income. Any book–tax difference that requires an add-back to book income to compute taxable income is an **unfavorable book–tax difference** because it increases taxable income (and taxes payable) relative to book income. Any book–tax difference that requires corporations to subtract the difference from book income in computing taxable income is a **favorable book–tax difference** because it decreases taxable income (and taxes payable) relative to book income.

---

[1]See the Business Income, Deductions, and Accounting Methods chapter for a detailed discussion of determining the timing of taxable income and tax deductions under the accrual method.

[2]§448. Other special types of corporations such as qualified family farming corporations and qualified personal service corporations may use the cash method of accounting. A C corporation that fails the $25 million gross receipts test is precluded from using the cash method for the year in which the test is not satisfied but can resume using the cash method in future years in which the test is satisfied. The $25 million annual average gross receipts test is indexed for inflation for taxable years beginning after 2018.

[3]See C. B. Cloyd, J. Pratt, and T. Stock, "The Use of Financial Accounting Choice to Support Aggressive Tax Positions: Public and Private Firms," *Journal of Accounting Research* 34 (Spring 1996), pp. 23–43.

[4]This chapter generally assumes that GAAP is used to determine book income numbers.

In addition to the favorable/unfavorable distinction, book–tax differences can be categorized as permanent or temporary. **Permanent book–tax differences** arise from items that are income or deductions during the year for either book or tax purposes but not both. Permanent differences *do not reverse* over time, so over the long-term, the *total* amount of income or deductions for the items is different for book and tax purposes. In contrast, **temporary book–tax differences** reverse over time such that, over the long-term, corporations recognize the same amount of income or deductions for the items on their income statements as they recognize on their tax returns. Temporary book–tax differences arise because the income or deduction items are included in financial accounting income in one year and in taxable income in a different year. Temporary book–tax differences that are *initially* favorable (unfavorable) become unfavorable (favorable) in future years when they reverse.

Distinguishing between permanent and temporary book–tax differences is important for at least two reasons. First, as we discuss later in the chapter, large corporations are *required to disclose* their permanent and temporary book–tax differences on a schedule attached to their tax returns. Second, the distinction is useful for those responsible for computing and tracking book–tax differences. For temporary book–tax differences, it is important to understand how the items were accounted for in previous years to appropriately account for current year reversals. In contrast, for permanent book–tax differences, corporations need only consider current year amounts to determine book–tax differences. Below we describe some of the most common book–tax differences.

Common Permanent Book–Tax Differences

As we describe in the Business Income, Deductions, and Accounting Methods chapter, businesses, including corporations, are allowed to exclude certain income items from gross income, and they are not allowed to deduct certain expenditures for tax purposes. Because these income items are included in book income, and the expenditures are deducted for financial reporting purposes, they generate permanent book–tax differences. Exhibit 16-2 identifies several permanent book–tax differences associated with items we discuss in the Business Income, Deductions, and Accounting Methods chapter, explains their tax treatment, and identifies whether the items create favorable or unfavorable book–tax differences.

> **THE KEY FACTS**
>
> **Computing Corporate Regular Taxable Income**
>
> - Corporations reconcile from book income to taxable income.
>   - Favorable (unfavorable) book–tax differences decrease (increase) taxable income relative to book income.
>   - Permanent book–tax differences arise in one year and never reverse.
>   - Temporary book–tax differences arise in one year and reverse in a subsequent year.

Example 16-1

Elise reviewed PCC's prior-year tax return and its current-year trial balance. She discovered that PCC earned $12,000 of interest income from City of San Diego municipal bonds issued in 2016; expensed $34,000 for premiums on key employee life insurance policies; and expensed $28,000 in business-related meal expenses for the year. What amount of permanent book–tax differences does PCC report from these transactions? Are the differences favorable or unfavorable?

Answer: See Elise's summary of these items below:

Item	Adjustment (Favorable) Unfavorable	Notes
Interest income from City of San Diego municipal bonds issued in 2016	$ (12,000)	Income excluded from gross income.
Premiums paid for key employee life insurance policies	34,000	Premiums paid to insure lives of key company executives are not deductible for tax purposes.
Business-related meals	14,000	$28,000 expense for book purposes, but only 50 percent deductible for tax purposes.

EXHIBIT 16-2 Common Permanent Book–Tax Differences Associated with Items Discussed in the Business Income, Deductions, and Accounting Methods Chapter

Description	Explanation	Difference
Interest income from municipal bonds	Income included in book income, excluded from taxable income for regular tax purposes	Favorable
Death benefit from life insurance on key employees	Income included in book income, excluded from taxable income	Favorable
Interest expense on loans to acquire investments generating tax-exempt income	Deductible for books, but expenses incurred to generate tax-exempt income are not deductible for tax	Unfavorable
Life insurance premiums for which corporation is beneficiary	Deductible for books, but expenses incurred to generate tax-exempt income (life insurance death benefit) are not deductible for tax	Unfavorable
Business-related meal expenses	Fully deductible for books but only 50 percent deductible for tax	Unfavorable
Fines and penalties and political contributions	Deductible for books but not for tax	Unfavorable
Business-related entertainment expenses	Deductible for books, but not deductible for tax	Unfavorable

Federal income tax expense. Corporations deduct federal income tax expense (called a "provision for income taxes") in determining their book income [determined under ASC (Accounting Standards Codification) 740]. However, they are not allowed to deduct federal income tax expense for tax purposes.[5] The book–tax provision acts as a permanent difference if the corporation is reconciling after-tax book income with taxable income.

Example 16-2

What if: Assume that PCC's audited financial reporting income statement indicates that its federal income tax provision (expense) is $2,000,000.[6] What is PCC's book–tax difference for the year associated with this expense? Is the difference favorable or unfavorable? Is it permanent or temporary?

Answer: $2,000,000 unfavorable, permanent book–tax difference because PCC is not allowed to deduct federal income tax expense for tax purposes.

---

[5]§275(a)(1).

[6]Note that this example is presented in *what-if* form because this is not the income tax expense PCC will report in its financial statements. We compute PCC's actual income tax expense in the Accounting for Income Taxes chapter.

Common Temporary Book–Tax Differences   Corporations experience temporary book–tax differences because the accounting methods they apply to determine certain items of income and expense for financial reporting purposes differ from those they use for tax purposes. Unlike permanent book–tax differences, temporary book–tax differences balance out over time, so corporations eventually recognize the same amount of income or deduction for the particular item. Exhibit 16-3 identifies common book–tax differences associated with items we discuss in other chapters. Exhibit 16-4 summarizes PCC's temporary book–tax differences described in Exhibit 16-3.

EXHIBIT 16-3   Common Temporary Book–Tax Differences Associated with Items Discussed in Other Chapters

Description	Explanation	Initial Difference*
Depreciation expense (Property Acquisition and Cost Recovery chapter)	Difference between depreciation expense for tax purposes and depreciation expense for book purposes.	Favorable
Gain or loss on disposition of depreciable assets (Property Dispositions chapter)	Difference between gain or loss for tax and book purposes when corporation sells or disposes of depreciable property. Difference generally arises because depreciation expense, and thus the adjusted basis of the asset, is different for tax and book purposes. This difference is essentially the reversal of the book–tax difference for the depreciation expense on the asset sold or disposed of.	Unfavorable
Bad debt expense (Business Income, Deductions, and Accounting Methods chapter)	Direct write-off method for tax purposes; allowance method for book purposes.	Unfavorable
Unearned rent revenue (Business Income, Deductions, and Accounting Methods chapter)	Taxable on receipt but recognized when earned for book purposes.	Unfavorable
Deferred compensation (Business Income, Deductions, and Accounting Methods chapter)	Deductible when accrued for book purposes, but deductible when paid for tax purposes if accrued but not paid within 2.5 months after year-end. Also, accrued compensation to shareholders owning more than 50 percent of the corporation is not deductible until paid.	Unfavorable
Organizational expenses and start-up costs (Property Acquisition and Cost Recovery chapter)	Immediately deducted for book purposes but capitalized and amortized for tax purposes (limited immediate expensing allowed for tax).	Unfavorable
Warranty expense and other estimated expenses (Business Income, Deductions, and Accounting Methods chapter)	Estimated expenses deducted for book purposes, but actual expenses deducted for tax purposes.	Unfavorable
UNICAP (§263A) (Business Income, Deductions, and Accounting Methods chapter)	Certain expenditures deducted for book purposes, but capitalized to inventory for tax purposes. Difference reverses when inventory is sold. There is an exception for taxpayers with an annual average of $25 million or less in gross receipts over the three prior years.	Unfavorable
Interest expense [§163(j)] (Business Income, Deductions, and Accounting Methods chapter)	The deduction for interest expense is disallowed to the extent it exceeds the sum of business interest income and 30% of adjusted taxable income (ATI). There is an exception for taxpayers with an annual average of $25 million or less in gross receipts over the three prior years. Unused amounts can be carried forward indefinitely. ATI is defined as taxable income computed without regard to any business interest expense or business interest income. It also excludes depreciation and amortization.	Unfavorable

*Note that each of the initial book–tax differences will reverse over time [the initially favorable (unfavorable) book–tax differences will reverse to become unfavorable (favorable) book–tax differences in the future].

EXHIBIT 16-4   PCC's Temporary Book–Tax Differences Associated with Items Discussed in Other Chapters

Item	(1) Books (Dr) Cr	(2) Tax (Dr) Cr	(2) − (1) Difference (Favorable) Unfavorable
Depreciation expense	$(2,400,000)	$(3,100,000)	$(700,000)
Gain on fixed asset disposition	54,000	70,000	16,000
Bad debt expense	(165,000)	(95,000)	70,000
Warranty expense	(580,000)	(410,000)	170,000
Deferred compensation	(300,000)	(450,000)	(150,000)

Dividends.   Corporations receiving dividends from other corporations may account for the dividends in different ways for book and tax purposes. For tax purposes, corporations receiving dividends include the dividends in gross income.[7] For financial reporting purposes, accounting for the dividend depends on the level of stock ownership in the distributing corporation. The *general* rules for such investments are summarized as follows:

- If the receiving corporation owns less than 20 percent of the stock of the distributing corporation, the receiving corporation includes the dividend in income (same as tax; no book–tax difference).

- If the receiving corporation owns at least 20 percent but not more than 50 percent of the distributing corporation's stock, the receiving corporation usually includes a pro rata portion of the distributing corporation's earnings in its book income under the "equity method of accounting" (ASC 323) and does not include the dividend in its income, resulting in a temporary favorable or unfavorable book–tax difference for the difference between the pro rata share of equity income reported on the books and the dividend amount reported on the tax return.

- If the receiving corporation owns more than 50 percent of the distributing corporation's stock, the receiving corporation and the distributing corporation usually consolidate their financial reporting books (ASC 810) and the intercompany dividend is eliminated (book–tax difference beyond the scope of this text).[8]

Example 16-3

What if: Assume that PCC owns 30 percent of the stock of BCS, a U.S. corporation, and applies the equity method of accounting for book purposes. During 2018, BCS distributed a $40,000 dividend to PCC. BCS reported $100,000 of net income for 2018. Based on this information, what is PCC's 2018 book–tax difference relating to the dividend and its investment in BCS (ignore the dividends received deduction)? Is the difference favorable or unfavorable?

(continued on page 16-8)

---

[7]As we discuss later in the chapter, corporations are entitled to deduct a certain percentage of the dividends received based on the level of the receiving corporation's ownership in the distributing corporation.

[8]Note that 80 percent ownership is required to file a consolidated tax return.

Answer: $10,000 unfavorable book–tax difference, computed as follows:

Description	Amount	Explanation
(1) Dividend received in 2018 (included in 2018 taxable income but not in book income)	$ 40,000	
(2) BCS 2018 net income	$100,000	
(3) PCC's ownership in BCS stock	30%	
(4) PCC's book income from BCS investment	$ 30,000	(2) × (3)
Unfavorable book–tax difference associated with dividend	**$ 10,000**	(1) − (4)

What if: Assume the same facts as above, except that PCC owns 10 percent of BCS rather than 30 percent. What would be PCC's 2018 book–tax difference relating to the dividend and its investment in BCS (ignore the dividends received deduction)?

Answer: $0. PCC includes the $40,000 dividend in income for both book and tax purposes.

when written off as impaired creates permanent unfavorable

Goodwill acquired in an acquisition.   When a corporation acquires the stock of another corporation in a cash (taxable) transaction, the tax basis of the assets of the target corporation generally carry over. As a result, the tax basis of self-created assets such as goodwill carries over unchanged (usually close to zero). The accounting rules (ASC Topic 805) require the target corporation's identifiable assets to be reported at fair value, with any residual amount allocated to book goodwill. Such book goodwill generally is subject to impairment testing (private companies can elect to amortize the book goodwill over 10 years). A book/tax difference does not arise until the goodwill is written off as impaired, at which time the book expense creates a (permanent) unfavorable difference.

In less frequent acquisitions, the acquiring corporation may acquire the assets of another business directly in a taxable transaction. When this occurs, the assets acquired will get a "new" tax basis equal to fair market value. Any residual will be allocated to tax goodwill, which is amortizable over 15 years (180 months).[9] In this case, the goodwill will have both a tax and book basis, which may be the same or different because of differences in the purchase price computation. As the corporation amortizes the goodwill for tax purposes, the resulting book–tax difference is treated as a favorable temporary difference (if book and tax goodwill are different, the accounting becomes more complex and is beyond the scope of this book). If the corporation writes the goodwill off as impaired in a future period, the excess of book goodwill impaired over the amortized goodwill for tax purposes is treated as an unfavorable book–tax difference.[10]

Example 16-4

What if: Suppose that on July 1, 2018, PCC acquired the assets of another business in a taxable acquisition. As part of the transaction, PCC recognized $180,000 of goodwill for both financial accounting and tax purposes. During 2018, PCC amortized $6,000 of the goodwill for tax purposes ($180,000/180 months × 6 months during year) and did not impair any of the goodwill for financial accounting purposes. What was PCC's book–tax difference associated with this goodwill in 2018? Is it a favorable or unfavorable difference? Is the difference permanent or temporary?

Answer: $6,000 favorable, temporary book–tax difference. The amount of capitalized goodwill is the same for book and tax purposes, and PCC deducted $6,000 of the goodwill for tax purposes and none for book purposes.

[9]§197. Self-created goodwill is not amortizable for tax purposes.

[10]When corporations acquire the stock of another corporation, they often recognize book goodwill but do not recognize any tax goodwill. When this book goodwill is written off as impaired, it generates a permanent unfavorable book–tax difference. Private companies can elect to amortize book goodwill over 10 years or less.

What if: Assume that at the end of 2019, PCC recorded a $30,000 goodwill impairment expense on its income statement. What is PCC's book–tax difference associated with its goodwill during 2019? Is the difference favorable or unfavorable? Is the difference permanent or temporary?

Answer: $18,000 unfavorable, temporary book–tax difference, computed as follows:

Description	Amount	Explanation
(1) Goodwill initially recorded on 7/1/18 acquisition	$180,000	
(2) Goodwill impairment recorded in 2019	$ 30,000	This write-down is expensed for book purposes.
(3) Months over which goodwill amortized for tax purposes.	180	15 years × 12 months = 180 months
(4) Tax goodwill amortization expense for 2019	$ 12,000	[(1)/(3)] × 12 months
Unfavorable book–tax temporary difference associated with goodwill in 2019	**$ 18,000**	(2) − (4)

Corporate-Specific Deductions and Associated Book–Tax Differences

Certain deductions and corresponding limitations apply specifically to corporations. In this section, we introduce these deductions and identify book–tax differences associated with the deductions.

Stock Options Corporations often compensate executives and other employees with stock options. Stock options allow recipients to acquire stock in the corporation issuing the options at a predetermined price over a specified period of time. To acquire the stock, employees exercise the options and pay the **exercise price.** The exercise price is usually at or above the stock price on the day the options are issued to the employee. For example, when a corporation's stock is trading for $10 per share, a corporation might issue (or grant) 100 stock options to an employee that allow the employee to purchase up to 100 shares of the corporation's stock for $10 a share. In most cases, after receiving the options, employees must wait a certain amount of time, the **requisite service period,** before they are able to exercise them (they must wait until the options **vest** before they can exercise them). If employees quit working for the corporation before the options vest, they forfeit the options.

Stock options are valuable to employees when the stock price appreciates above the exercise price because, when the options vest, employees can use them to purchase the stock at a below-market price. Stock options are a popular form of compensation because they provide incentives for employees receiving the options to work to increase the value of the corporation's stock and thereby benefit themselves and other stockholders.

For tax purposes, the tax treatment to the corporation (and the employee[11]) depends on whether the options are **incentive stock options (ISOs)** (less common, more administrative requirements for the corporation to qualify) or **nonqualified stock options (NQOs)** (more common, options that don't qualify as ISOs).[12] Corporations issuing ISOs generally do not deduct compensation expense associated with the options for tax purposes. In contrast, for NQOs, corporations deduct the difference

---

[11]Employees do not recognize any compensation income when they exercise incentive stock options. However, for nonqualified options, they recognize compensation (ordinary) income for the difference between the value of the stock and the exercise price on the date of exercise. This chapter emphasizes the tax treatment of the options from the corporation's perspective.

[12]Requirements for options to qualify as incentive stock options are more restrictive than the requirements for nonqualified stock options. The formal requirements for incentive stock options are beyond the scope of this text.

between the fair market value of the stock and the exercise price of the option—the **bargain element**—as compensation expense in the year in which employees exercise the stock options.

For book purposes (ASC Topic 718), corporations are required to recognize a *book expense* for stock options they grant.[13] Corporations granting stock options after 2005 are required to estimate the fair value of the options at the time they issue them—that is, on the **grant date.** They deduct the estimated fair value of the options when the employee services are received—during the requisite service period, which is presumed to be the **vesting period.** Book–tax differences for options granted after 2005 may be permanent, temporary, or a combination of both. For ISOs, the book compensation expense is an unfavorable permanent difference.

Example 16-5

What if: Assume that on January 1, 2018, PCC issued 10,000 incentive stock options (ISOs) with an estimated fair value of $6 per option. The options vest at the end of four years. For 2018, PCC records a $15,000 compensation expense related to the ISOs (10,000 options × $6 / 4 years). What is PCC's 2018 book–tax difference associated with the incentive stock options? Would the difference be favorable or unfavorable? Would the difference be permanent or temporary?

Answer: $15,000 unfavorable, permanent difference. PCC does not deduct compensation expense relating to the ISOs for tax purposes.

Nonqualified options (NQOs) generate temporary book–tax differences. Corporations initially recognize temporary book–tax differences associated with stock options for the fair value of options spread over the employee's requisite service period. This initial temporary difference is always unfavorable because the corporation deducts the fair value of the options over the requisite service period for book purposes but does not deduct compensation expense for tax purposes until the employee exercises the stock options. This initial unfavorable temporary book–tax difference generally becomes a favorable temporary book–tax difference when the employee actually exercises the stock options (assuming the amount of the tax deduction at the exercise date exceeds the estimated fair value of the NQOs at the grant date).

When an employee exercises the NQO, the tax deduction, which is the difference between the fair market value of the stock purchased less the option price, likely will differ from the compensation expense recorded on the income statement over the requisite service period.

Example 16-6

On January 1, 2018, PCC granted 20,000 NQOs with an estimated $10 fair value per option ($200,000 total fair value). Each option entitled the recipient to purchase one share of PCC stock for $10 a share (the per-share price of PCC stock on January 1, 2018, when the options were granted). The options vested at the end of the day on December 31, 2019. No options were exercised in 2018 or 2019. For 2018 and 2019, PCC deducted compensation expense of $100,000 for book purposes. What is PCC's book–tax difference associated with the nonqualified options in 2018? in 2019? Is the difference favorable or unfavorable? Is it permanent or temporary?

Answer: $100,000 unfavorable, temporary book–tax difference in both 2018 and 2019. PCC reports $100,000 of compensation expense for book purposes in 2018 and 2019 and $0 for tax purposes (the options were not exercised in 2018 or 2019).

---

[13]ASC 718 is effective for years beginning after June 15, 2005, for large publicly traded corporations and for years beginning after December 15, 2005, for small publicly traded corporations and nonpublicly traded entities. Corporations could have elected to expense stock options for book purposes before the effective date of ASC 718.

What if: Assume the same facts as above and that on March 1, 2020, employees exercised all 20,000 options at a time when the PCC stock was trading at $25 per share. What is PCC's book–tax difference associated with the stock options in 2020? Is it a permanent difference or a temporary difference? Is it favorable or unfavorable?

Answer: $200,000 favorable, temporary book–tax difference in 2020 and a $100,000 favorable permanent book–tax difference. PCC gets a $300,000 tax deduction in 2020, equal to the number of shares exercised times the bargain element of $15 per option exercised ($25 − $10). $200,000 of the tax deduction is a reversal of the 2018–2019 unfavorable, temporary book–tax difference. The excess $100,000 tax deduction is a favorable permanent difference.

Exhibit 16-5 summarizes the book and tax treatment of stock options.

EXHIBIT 16-5   **Book and Tax Treatment of Stock Options**

Description	Book Deduction	Tax Deduction	Book–Tax Difference
Incentive stock option	Initial estimated fair value of stock options / requisite service period	No deduction	Unfavorable, permanent
Nonqualified stock option (in years before exercise)	Initial estimated fair value of stock options / requisite service period	No deduction until exercise	Unfavorable, temporary
Nonqualified stock option (in year of exercise)	Initial estimated fair value of stock options / requisite service period	Bargain element*	Favorable, temporary (reversing unfavorable, temporary difference in prior years)
			Favorable, permanent difference if the bargain element exceeds the initial estimated value of stock options; unfavorable permanent difference otherwise

*The bargain element is the difference between the fair market value of the stock and the exercise price on the date the employee exercises the stock options.

TAXES IN THE REAL WORLD   Facebook's Billion Dollar NQO Tax Benefit

When Facebook filed its Registration Statement for its Initial Public Offering in February 2012, it was revealed that CEO Mark Zuckerberg had been granted nonqualifying stock options (NQOs) to purchase 120 million additional shares of the company for 6 cents per share. The company also informed potential investors that Zuckerberg intended to exercise these options when the company became a publicly traded company. Zuckerberg subsequently exercised his option to purchase 60 million additional Facebook shares prior to the IPO at a time when the value of the shares was $2,276,677,500. This transaction (fair value of the Facebook stock on the exercise date less the exercise price) simultaneously created a tax deduction for Facebook and compensation income to Zuckerberg of approximately $2,273 million! The company's tax benefit of $800 million also created an $800 million tax bill for Zuckerberg. In total, employees of Facebook exercised 135.5 million NQOs in 2012, resulting in a tax benefit to the company of more than $1 billion, of which $451 million was recovered as a refund for taxes paid in 2010–2011. The cash proceeds received by the company from the employees' exercise of the NQOs was only $17 million.

(*continued on page 16-12*)

The publicity surrounding the stock option exercise by Zuckerberg and the subsequent deduction granted to Facebook did not go unnoticed in Congress. Then-Senator Carl Levin of Michigan expressed outrage that a "profitable" U.S. company could eliminate its tax liability because of the tax deduction granted (legally) by U.S. tax laws. Senator Levin emphasized that Facebook's actions were within the tax law but exclaimed that, "As with so much of our tax code, it's not the law-breaking that shocks the conscience, it's the stuff that's perfectly legal." Senator Levin neglected to mention that the income taxes saved by Facebook were offset by the income taxes paid by Zuckerberg.

In 2014, 2015, 2016, and 2017 executives from Facebook continued to exercise their stock options and provided the company with excess tax benefits of more than $1.8 billion, $1.7 billion, $875 million, and $1.2 billion, respectively.

Source: All of the information is publicly available on Facebook's Form 10-K and Proxy Statement for 2012, 2014, 2015, 2016, and 2017.

Net Capital Losses   For corporations, all net capital gains (long- and short-term) are taxed at the ordinary income tax rate of 21 percent. Corporations will generally prefer capital gains to ordinary income when they have incurred net capital losses because only capital gains can be netted against capital losses in a particular year.[14] Unlike individuals, corporations cannot deduct net capital losses against ordinary income (individuals can deduct up to $3,000 of net capital losses in a year against ordinary income).[15]

When corporations recognize net capital losses for a year, they are permitted to carry the capital losses back three years, called a **net capital loss carryback,** and forward five years, called a **net capital loss carryover,** to offset net capital gains in the three years before the current tax year and then to offset net capital gains in the five years after the current tax year.[16] The capital loss carrybacks and carryovers must be applied in a particular order. If a corporation reports a net capital loss in year 4, it must first carry back the loss to year 1, then year 2, and then year 3. If the net capital loss remains after the carryback period, the corporation carries the loss forward to year 5 first, then year 6, then year 7, then year 8, and finally year 9. If the capital loss carryover has not been fully absorbed by the end of the fifth year after it was incurred (year 9), the carryover expires unused.

Although corporations may carry back net capital losses, they may not carry back a capital loss if doing so creates or increases the net operating loss of the corporation (excess of deductions over income) in the year to which it is carried back (see discussion of net operating losses in the next section).[17]

For financial reporting purposes, corporations deduct net capital losses in the year they are incurred. Thus, corporations recognizing net capital losses report unfavorable book–tax differences in the year they incur the losses and favorable book–tax differences in the year they use capital loss carrybacks or carryovers.

Example 16-7

During 2018, PCC sold Intel stock at a $12,000 gain and also reported a $40,000 capital loss on the disposition of land held for investment. PCC has not recognized a net capital gain or loss since 2013. PCC has a net operating loss carryover from 2017. What is PCC's net capital loss for the year?

Answer: $28,000 loss; [$12,000 + ($40,000)]. Because PCC did not recognize any net capital gains in 2015, 2016, or 2017, it may not carry back the loss (note that PCC could not carry back the loss to 2017 in any event because it recognized a net operating loss in that year as evidenced by its net operating loss carryover from 2017).

---

[14]§1211(a).

[15]§1211(b). Individuals are also allowed to carry net capital losses forward indefinitely.

[16]§1212(a).

[17]§1212(a)(1)(A)(ii). To allow a corporation to carry back a net capital loss to absorb capital gains in a net operating loss year would increase the NOL carryforward by the amount of the net capital loss used to offset the capital gain. This freed-up NOL would have a 20-year or indefinite carryover (depending on the year incurred) rather than the 5-year carryover of the net capital loss.

What amount of book–tax difference does this loss trigger? Is the difference favorable or unfavorable? Is it temporary or permanent?

Answer: $28,000 unfavorable, temporary book–tax difference.

What if: Assume that in 2018, PCC reported a net capital loss of $28,000 and that it reported a $7,000 net capital gain in 2015, no net capital gain or loss in 2016, and a $4,000 net capital gain in 2017. What is the amount of its net capital loss carryover to 2019? PCC reported a net operating loss in 2017 but did not report a net operating loss in either 2015 or 2016.

Answer: $21,000. PCC first carries back the $28,000 loss to 2015, offsetting the $7,000 net capital gain in that year. PCC then carries the remaining $21,000 loss [($28,000) + $7,000] back to 2017. However, because PCC reported a net operating loss in 2017, it is not allowed to offset the $4,000 net capital gain with the capital loss carryback. Consequently, the $21,000 unused capital loss carryover is carried forward to 2019.

What if: Suppose PCC did not recognize any net capital gains in prior years but that next year (2019) it recognizes a net capital gain of $5,000 (before considering any capital loss carryovers). What will be its book–tax difference associated with capital gains and losses next year? Is it favorable or unfavorable? Is it temporary or permanent?

Answer: Next year, PCC would report a $5,000 favorable, temporary book–tax difference because it would be allowed to deduct $5,000 of its $28,000 capital loss carryover for tax purposes. This is a reversal of $5,000 of the unfavorable temporary $28,000 book–tax difference from the prior year.

Net Operating Losses   Compare the tax burdens of Corporation A and Corporation B. Corporation A reports $1,000,000 of taxable income and pays $210,000 of tax in year 1 and again in year 2. In contrast, Corporation B reports $4,000,000 of taxable income in year 1 and a $2,000,000 loss in year 2. Absent any special tax provisions, Corporation B would pay $840,000 of tax in year 1 and no tax in year 2. Over the same two-year period both Corporation A and Corporation B reported $2,000,000 of (net) taxable income, yet Corporation B paid twice the tax Corporation A paid ($840,000 vs. $420,000).

The inequity for Corporation B is that, because it is required to report taxable income on an annual basis, it receives no tax benefit for its $2,000,000 loss (deductions in excess of gross income) in year 2. To ease the tax burden on corporations that aren't consistently profitable (for tax purposes), the tax laws allow those that report deductions in excess of gross income in a particular year to carry over the excess deductions to reduce taxable income and taxes payable in years when gross income exceeds deductions. This excess of deductions over gross income is referred to as a **net operating loss (NOL).** A corporation's net operating loss for the current year is the excess of its deductions over its gross income with the following adjustments:

- A corporation does not deduct an NOL generated in another year in calculating its current year NOL.
- A corporation may deduct a capital loss carryover against a net capital gain arising in the current year in calculating its NOL, but it may not deduct a capital loss carryback against a net capital gain in calculating its NOL.

Corporations can carry a net operating loss arising in tax years beginning after December 31, 2017, forward indefinitely, referred to as a **net operating loss carryover,** and offset up to 80 percent of taxable income in those future years. Net operating losses arising in prior years could be carried back 2-years, referred to as a **net operating loss carryback,** and forward 20 years. NOLs subject to the 20-year carryover rule can offset 100 percent of taxable income in those future years. NOL carryovers are deducted on a FIFO basis.

Example 16-8

What if: Assume that in 2018 PCC reported a $300,000 net operating loss. In 2019, PCC reported taxable income of $300,000 before any NOL carryovers. What is PCC's 2019 taxable income and NOL carryover to 2020?

Answer: $240,000, with a $60,000 NOL carryover to 2020. PCC can deduct the 2018 NOL carryover against 80 percent of 2019 taxable income.

What if: Assume that in 2018 PCC reported $120,000 of deductions and $90,000 of gross income (including $6,000 of net capital gain). PCC also has a $15,000 NOL carryover from 2017 and an $8,000 net capital loss carryover from 2017. What are PCC's net operating loss and capital loss carryovers to 2019 and when do they expire?

Answer: $15,000 net operating loss carryover from 2017 that expires at the end of 2037 if unused; a $36,000 net operating loss carryover from 2018 that can be carried forward indefinitely, and a $2,000 net capital loss carryover from 2017 that expires at the end of 2022 if unused. PCC's 2017 NOL is unused in 2018 because PCC reports an NOL in 2018 and it does not deduct NOL carryovers in determining its 2018 NOL. In 2018, PCC is able to offset the $6,000 net capital gain included in gross income with $6,000 of the $8,000 net capital loss carryover from 2017. This reduces PCC's gross income to $84,000 ($90,000 − $6,000) and increases its deductions in excess of gross income (its current year NOL) to $36,000 ($120,000 − $84,000). Finally, PCC's 2017 capital loss carryover is reduced by the $6,000 absorbed portion to $2,000 ($8,000 minus $6,000 used in 2018).

For financial reporting purposes, corporations report losses in the year they incur them. Consequently corporations report unfavorable temporary book–tax differences in the year they generate NOLs. Because corporations do not deduct NOL carryovers in determining book income, they report favorable *temporary* book–tax differences in the year they deduct the NOL carryovers for tax purposes. A corporation reports its NOL carryforward amounts on Schedule K to Form 1120.

Example 16-9

What if: Assume that last year PCC incurred a $24,000 net operating loss. Last year's NOL becomes an NOL carryover to this year that is available to reduce its current-year taxable income of $100,000. What is PCC's current-year book–tax difference associated with its NOL carryover? Is the difference favorable or unfavorable? Is it permanent or temporary?

Answer: $24,000 favorable, temporary book–tax difference. The net operating loss carryover from the prior year is deductible for tax purposes but not for book purposes. The NOL carryover is fully deductible because it is less than 80 percent of current-year taxable income.

Charitable Contributions   Like individuals, corporations are allowed to deduct charitable contributions to qualified charitable organizations.[18] However, the deduction and timing limitations are a little different for corporations than for individual taxpayers. Generally, corporations are allowed to deduct the amount of money they contribute, the fair market value of **capital gain property** they donate—that is, property that would generate long-term capital gain if sold—and the adjusted basis of **ordinary income property** they donate—that is, property that if sold would generate income taxed at ordinary rates. This chapter emphasizes the tax consequences of cash donations by corporations to qualified charities.[19] Generally, corporations are allowed to deduct charitable

---

[18]The IRS has a database of qualifying charities on its website (http://www.irs.gov/Charities-&-Non-Profits/Organizations-Eligible-to-Receive-Tax-Deductible-Charitable-Contributions). Qualifying organizations tend to be those engaging in educational, scientific, governmental, and other public activities.

[19]For more details on the tax consequences of charitable contributions, see §170.

contributions at the time they make payment to charitable organizations (subject to an overall taxable income limitation we discuss below). However, corporations using the accrual method of accounting can deduct contributions in the year *before* they actually pay the contribution when (1) their board of directors approves the payment and (2) they actually pay the contributions within three and one-half months of their tax year.[20]

Example 16-10

On December 1, 2018, the PCC board of directors approved a $110,000 cash contribution to the American Red Cross (ARC). For financial reporting purposes, PCC accrued and expensed the donation in 2018. PCC transferred the cash to the ARC on March 1, 2019. Does PCC report a book–tax difference associated with the charitable contribution (assume the taxable income limitation does not apply)?

Answer: No book–tax difference. For tax purposes, as an accrual-method taxpayer PCC may deduct the $110,000 contribution in 2018 because it paid the donation to the ARC within three and one-half months after year-end.

What if: Assume the same facts as above, except that PCC transferred the cash to the ARC on April 30, 2019. Does PCC report a book–tax difference associated with the charitable contribution (assume the taxable income limitation does not apply)?

Answer: Yes, PCC reports a $110,000 unfavorable, temporary book–tax difference in 2018. A calendar-year-end corporation such as PCC must pay the charitable contribution by the 15th day of the fourth month after its year-end (April 15). This book–tax difference will reverse and become a $110,000 favorable, temporary book–tax difference in 2019 when PCC deducts the contribution for tax purposes.

A corporation's deductible charitable contributions for the year may not exceed 10 percent of its **charitable contribution limit modified taxable income.** A corporation's charitable contribution limit modified taxable income is its taxable income *before* deducting the following:

1. *Any* charitable contributions.
2. The dividends received deduction (DRD) (discussed below).
3. Capital loss *carrybacks.*

Note that capital loss and NOL *carryovers are deductible* in determining charitable contribution limit modified taxable income. Capital loss *carrybacks* are *not deductible* for charitable contribution limitation purposes because they are unknown when corporations must determine the limitation (they arise in a future year).

Due to the 10 percent limitation, a corporation's charitable contribution deduction for the year is the *lower* of (1) the amount of charitable contributions to qualifying charities (including charitable contribution carryovers—discussed below) or (2) 10 percent of charitable contribution limit modified taxable income.

> **THE KEY FACTS**
>
> **Charitable Contributions**
>
> - Charitable contribution deductions
>   - Deductible when they accrue if approved by board of directors and paid within 3.5 months of year-end (2.5 months for corporations with a June 30 year-end).
>   - Deductions limited to 10 percent of charitable contribution deduction modified taxable income.
>   - Contributions in excess of 10 percent limit carried forward up to five years.

Example 16-11

What if: Assume that PCC's 2018 taxable income before considering the charitable contribution limitation was $100,000. The taxable income computation includes an $18,000 charitable contribution deduction, a $20,000 DRD, a $24,000 NOL carryover, a $4,000 capital loss carryover (offsets $4,000 of capital gain), and $25,000 of depreciation expense. Under these circumstances, what would be PCC's 2018 deductible charitable contribution?

(continued on page 16-16)

---

[20]§170(a)(2). For corporations with tax years with a June 30 year-end from 2016–2025, the charitable contribution must be paid within two and one-half months after the year-end to be deductible in the year authorized.

Answer: $13,800 deductible charitable contribution, computed as follows:

Description	Amount	Explanation
(1) Taxable income before charitable contribution limitation	$100,000	
(2) Charitable contribution deduction before limitation	$ 18,000	Not deductible in computing limitation
(3) Dividends received deduction	$ 20,000	Not deductible in computing limitation
(4) Charitable contribution limit modified taxable income*	$138,000	Sum of (1) through (3)
(5) Tax deduction limitation percentage	10%	§170(b)(2)(A)
(6) Charitable contribution deduction limitation	$ 13,800	(4) × (5)
(7) Charitable contribution deduction for year	**$ 13,800**	Lesser of (2) or (6)
Charitable contribution carryover	$ 4,200	(2) − (7)

*Note that the NOL and capital loss carryover are not added back to compute line (4) because they are deductible in determining the charitable contribution limit modified taxable income.

Corporations making current-year charitable contributions in excess of the 10 percent modified taxable limitation may carry forward the excess for up to five years after the year in which the carryover arises. Carryforwards are absorbed on a first-in, first-out (FIFO) basis and are applied after the current year contribution deduction. Corporations can deduct the carryover in future years to the extent the 10 percent limitation does not restrict deductions for charitable contributions corporations actually make in those years. Unused carryovers expire after five years.

Example 16-12

What if: Under the assumptions provided in the previous example, we determined that PCC had a $4,200 charitable contribution carryover (it was not able to deduct $4,200 of its $18,000 contribution from 2018). Assume that in 2019, PCC contributed $10,000 to charity, and its charitable contribution limit modified taxable income was $110,000. What would be PCC's deductible charitable contribution in 2019? What would its charitable contribution carryover be at the end of 2019? When would it expire?

Answer: $11,000 charitable contribution deduction. This is the lesser of the charitable contribution limit of $11,000 ($110,000 × 10%) or $14,200 ($10,000 current year contribution plus $4,200 carryover from prior year). The carryover is $3,200 ($14,200 − $11,000). Because the current-year contribution uses the limit first, the $3,200 carryover is from the excess contribution in 2018 and it will expire if it has not been used by the end of 2023.

Corporations report _unfavorable, temporary_ book–tax differences to the extent the 10 percent modified taxable income limitation restricts the amount of their charitable contribution tax deduction. That is, they recognize unfavorable, temporary book–tax differences in the amount of the charitable contribution carryover they generate for the year. Conversely, corporations report _favorable, temporary_ book–tax differences when they deduct charitable contribution carryovers because they deduct the carryovers for tax purposes, but not book purposes.

Example 16-13

In 2018, PCC donated a total of $700,000 of cash to the American Red Cross. Elise knew she had to apply the 10 percent taxable income limitation to verify the amount PCC deducted for tax purposes. For 2018, PCC's taxable income before any charitable contribution, NOL carryovers from prior years, and dividends received deduction was $6,287,000 (see Exhibit 16-7 later in the text for the computation). What is PCC's charitable contribution deduction for the year? What is its charitable contribution carryover to next year, if any?

Answer: $626,300 charitable contribution deduction and $73,700 charitable contribution carryover, computed as follows:

Description	Amount	Explanation
(1) Taxable income before *any* charitable contribution, NOL carryover from previous year, and DRD	$6,287,000	Exhibit 16-7
(2) NOL *carryover* from previous year	(24,000)	Deductible in determining taxable income limit
(3) Charitable contribution limit modified taxable income	$6,263,000	(1) + (2)
(4) Total charitable contributions for year	$ 700,000	
(5) Tax deduction limitation percentage	10%	§170(b)(2)(A)
(6) Charitable contribution deduction limitation	$ 626,300	(3) × (5)
(7) Charitable contribution deduction for year	**$ 626,300**	Lesser of (4) or (6)
Charitable contribution carryover*	**$ 73,700**	(4) − (7)

*As we discuss above, the carryover expires if it has not been used during the five-year period after the current year.

What is PCC's book–tax difference associated with its charitable contribution? Is the difference favorable or unfavorable? Is it permanent or temporary?

Answer: $73,700 unfavorable, temporary book–tax difference.

Dividends Received Deduction   When corporations receive dividends from other corporations, they are taxed on the dividends at their ordinary tax rate, not the preferential tax rates available to individual taxpayers. Unlike individuals, corporations are allowed a dividends received deduction (DRD) that reduces the actual tax they pay on the dividends.[21] The DRD is designed to mitigate the extent to which corporate earnings are subject to three (or perhaps even more) levels of taxation. Corporate taxable income is subject to triple taxation when a corporation pays tax on its income and then distributes its after-tax income to shareholders that are corporations. Corporate shareholders are taxed on the dividends, creating the second tax. When corporate shareholders distribute their after-tax earnings as dividends to their shareholders the income is taxed for a third time. The dividends received deduction reduces the amount of the second-level tax and thus mitigates the impact of triple taxation (or more) of earnings that corporations distribute as dividends.

For tax years beginning after December 31, 2017, corporations generally compute their dividends received deduction by multiplying the dividend amount by 50 percent, 65 percent, or 100 percent, depending on their level of ownership in the distributing corporation's stock. For tax years ending in 2018 or before, the DRD percentages were 70 percent,

THE KEY FACTS

Dividends Received Deduction

- Dividends received deduction
  - Generally lesser of deduction percentage (50 percent, 65 percent, or 100 percent) based on ownership × DRD modified taxable income.
  - Limitation doesn't apply if full DRD creates or increases a corporation's NOL.
  - Generates favorable, permanent difference.

[21]§243. Also, §246(c) describes certain dividends that are ineligible for the dividends received deduction.

80 percent, and 100 percent, respectively. Congress reduced the DRD when the corporate tax rate was reduced to 21 percent to keep the effective tax rate on dividends equivalent to the rate when the corporate tax rate was 35 percent. Exhibit 16-6 summarizes the stock ownership thresholds and the corresponding dividends received deduction percentage. Only dividends received from domestic corporations are eligible for this DRD. For tax years beginning after December 31, 2017, certain dividends from 10 percent-or-more owned foreign corporations are eligible for a 100 percent DRD, which is discussed in the U.S. Taxation of Multinational Transactions chapter.

EXHIBIT 16-6   **Stock Ownership and Dividends Received Deduction Percentage**

Receiving Corporation's Stock Ownership in Distributing Corporation's Stock	Dividends Received Deduction Percentage
Less than 20 percent	50%
At least 20 percent but less than 80 percent	65%
80 percent or more[22]	100

Example 16-14

During 2018, PCC received a $30,000 dividend from Apple Inc. PCC owns less than 1 percent of the Apple Inc. stock. What is PCC's DRD associated with the dividend?

Answer: $15,000 ($30,000 × 50%).

What if: PCC's marginal tax rate on the dividend *before* considering the effect of the dividends received deduction is 21 percent. What is PCC's marginal tax rate on the Apple Inc. dividend income *after* considering the dividends received deduction?

Answer: 10.5 percent marginal tax rate on dividend income, computed as follows:

Description	Amount	Explanation
(1) Dividend from Apple	$ 30,000	
(2) The percentage DRD	50%	Less than 20 percent ownership in Apple
(3) Dividends received deduction	**$15,000**	(1) × (2)
(4) Dividend subject to taxation after DRD	$ 15,000	(1) − (3)
(5) Marginal ordinary tax rate	21%	
(6) Taxes payable on dividend *after* DRD	$ 3,150	(4) × (5)
Marginal tax rate on dividend *after* DRD	**10.5%**	(6)/(1)

Deduction limitation.   The dividends received deduction is limited to the product of the applicable dividends received deduction percentage (see Exhibit 16-6) and **DRD modified taxable income.**[23] DRD modified taxable income is the dividend-receiving corporation's taxable income *before* deducting the following:

- DRD.
- NOL carryover.
- Capital loss *carrybacks.*[24]

[22]To qualify for the 100 percent dividends received deduction, the receiving and distributing corporations must be in the same affiliated group as described in §1504. The 80 percent ownership requirement is the minimum ownership level required for inclusion in the same affiliated group.

[23]When corporations receive dividends from multiple corporations with different deduction percentages, according to §246(b)(3), the limitations first apply to the 65% dividends received deduction and then the 50% dividends received deduction.

[24]§246(b)(1).

Example 16-15

What if: Suppose that during 2018, PCC received a $30,000 dividend from Apple Inc. and that PCC owns less than 1 percent of the Apple Inc. stock. Further assume that PCC's taxable income before the dividends received deduction was $50,000 in Scenario A and $25,000 in Scenario B. To arrive at the taxable income under both scenarios (before the DRD), PCC deducted a $3,000 NOL carryover, and a $4,000 capital loss carryover. What is PCC's dividends received deduction associated with the dividend in Scenario A and in Scenario B?

Answer: $15,000 in Scenario A and $13,500 in Scenario B, computed as follows:

Description	Scenario A	Scenario B	Explanation
(1) Taxable income before the dividends received deduction (includes dividend income)	$ 50,000	$ 25,000	
(2) NOL carryover	3,000	3,000	
(3) DRD modified taxable income	$ 53,000	$ 28,000	(1) + (2)
(4) Dividend income	$ 30,000	$ 30,000	
(5) Dividends received deduction percentage based on ownership	50%	50%	§243(a)
(6) Dividends received deduction before limitation	$ 15,000	$ 15,000	(4) × (5)
(7) Dividends received deduction limitation	$ 26,500	$ 13,500	(3) × (5)
DRD deductible	**$15,000**	**$13,500**	Lesser of (6) or (7)

Note that the capital loss carryover is deductible in determining the DRD modified taxable income so it is not added back to taxable income to arrive at DRD modified taxable income.

The modified taxable income limitation *does not apply* if, after deducting the *full* dividends received deduction (dividend × DRD percentage), a corporation reports a current-year net operating loss. That is, if after deducting the full dividends received deduction, the corporation has a net operating loss, the corporation is allowed to deduct the *full* dividends received deduction no matter what the modified taxable income limitation is.[25] As the following example illustrates, this rule can cause some unusual results.

Example 16-16

What if: Let's assume that PCC reports gross income of $80,000, *including* $40,000 of dividend income from TOU Corp. PCC owns 25 percent of TOU Corp. stock so its applicable DRD percentage is 65 percent (see Exhibit 16-6). Finally, let's consider two alternative scenarios. In Scenario A, PCC reports $54,000 of business expenses deductible in determining its DRD modified taxable income. In Scenario B, PCC reports $55,000 of business expenses deductible in determining its DRD modified taxable income. For each scenario, what is PCC's DRD modified taxable income? For each scenario, what is PCC's dividends received deduction?

(continued on page 16-20)

[25]§246(b)(2).

Scenario A Answer: $26,000 DRD modified taxable income; $16,900 dividends received deduction (see computation below).

Scenario B Answer: $25,000 DRD modified taxable income; $26,000 dividends received deduction, computed as follows:

Description	Scenario A	Scenario B	Explanation
(1) Gross income other than dividends	$ 40,000	$ 40,000	
(2) Dividend income	40,000	40,000	
(3) Gross income	$ 80,000	$ 80,000	(1) + (2)
(4) Business expenses deductible in determining the DRD modified taxable income	54,000	55,000	
(5) DRD modified taxable income (note this is taxable income before the DRD)	**$26,000**	**$25,000**	(3) − (4)
(6) Full dividends received deduction	$ 26,000	$ 26,000	(2) × 65%
(7) DRD modified taxable income limitation	16,900	16,250	(5) × 65%
(8) Taxable income (loss) after deducting full DRD	0	(1,000)	(5) − (6)
DRD deductible	**16,900**	**26,000**	Lesser of (6) or (7) unless (8) is negative, then (6)

Compare the results in Scenario A and Scenario B in the previous example. In Scenario B, PCC's DRD is $9,100 larger than it is in Scenario A ($26,000 − $16,900), despite the fact that the only difference in the two scenarios is that PCC reports $54,000 of business expenses in Scenario A and $55,000 of business expenses in Scenario B. Interestingly, the tax laws allow a corporation to increase its DRD by $9,100 for a $40,000 dividend simply by incurring $1,000 more in expenses (or potentially even $1 more).

Because the dividends received deduction is strictly a tax deduction and not a book deduction, *any* dividends received deduction creates a *favorable, permanent* book–tax difference.

Example 16-17

From her review of PCC's dividend income computations, Elise determined that the only dividend PCC received during the year was a $30,000 dividend from Apple Inc., a U.S. corporation. Because PCC owns a very small percentage of Apple Inc. stock (less than 1 percent) Elise determined that PCC was entitled to a 50 percent dividends received deduction. PCC's "modified taxable income" before any NOL and DRD is $5,660,700. What is PCC's book–tax difference associated with its dividends received deduction? Is the difference favorable or unfavorable? Is it permanent or temporary?

Answer: $15,000 favorable, permanent book–tax difference, computed as follows:

Description	Amount	Explanation
(1) Taxable income before NOL and DRD (DRD modified taxable income)	$5,660,700	Exhibit 16-7 ($5,636,700 + 24,000 NOL)
(2) Dividend income	$ 30,000	Exhibit 16-7
(3) Applicable DRD percentage	50%	Own less than 20 percent of Apple
(4) Full dividends received deduction	$ 15,000	(2) × (3)
(5) Dividends received deduction taxable income limitation	$2,830,350	(1) × (3)
(6) Book deductible dividends received deduction	0	No book DRD
(7) Tax deductible dividends received deduction	$ 15,000	Lesser of (4) or (5)
(Favorable) permanent book–tax difference	**$ (15,000)**	(6) – (7)

Taxable Income Summary

Exhibit 16-7 presents Elise's template for reconciling PCC's book and taxable income. Note that the template does not follow the typical financial accounting format because it organizes the information to facilitate the taxable income computation. In particular, it puts the deductions in the sequence in which they are deducted for tax purposes.

Corporate Income Tax Liability

When corporations calculate their taxable income, they compute their tax liability using a flat rate of 21 percent. Blended tax rates apply to fiscal year corporations for years beginning in 2017 and ending in 2018.

Example 16-18

Elise determined that PCC's taxable income is $5,621.700. What is its income tax liability?

Answer: $1,180,557, computed using a flat tax rate of 21 percent.

COMPLIANCE

LO 16-3

Corporations report their taxable income on Form 1120. Exhibit 16-8 presents the front page of PCC's current year Form 1120 through the tax liability.

Form 1120 includes a schedule for corporations to report their book–tax differences and reconcile their book and taxable income. Corporations with total assets of less than $10,000,000 report their book–tax differences on Schedule M-1. Corporations with total assets of $10,000,000 or more are required to report their book–tax differences on

EXHIBIT 16-7 PCC Book–Tax Reconciliation Template

Description	Book Income (Dr) Cr	Book–Tax Adjustments (Dr)†		Taxable Income (Dr) Cr
Revenue from sales	$60,000,000			$60,000,000
Cost of goods sold	(38,000,000)			(38,000,000)
Gross profit	$22,000,000			$22,000,000
Other income:				
Dividend income	30,000			30,000
Interest income	120,000	(12,000)Ex. 1		108,000
Capital gains (losses)	(28,000)		28,000Ex. 7	0
Gain on fixed asset dispositions	54,000		16,000 Exh. 4	70,000
Gross income	$22,176,000			$22,208,000
Expenses:				
Compensation	(9,868,000)			(9,868,000)
Deferred compensation	(300,000)	(150,000) Exh. 4		(450,000)
Stock option compensation	(100,000)		100,000Ex. 6	0
Bad debt expense	(165,000)		70,000 Exh. 4	(95,000)
Charitable contributions	Moved below			
Depreciation	(2,400,000)	(700,000) Exh. 4		(3,100,000)
Advertising	(1,920,000)			(1,920,000)
Warranty expenses	(580,000)		170,000 Exh. 4	(410,000)
Meals	(28,000)		14,000Ex. 1	(14,000)
Life insurance premiums	(34,000)		34,000Ex. 1	0
Other expenses	(64,000)			(64,000)
Federal income tax expense	(2,000,000)*		2,000,000Ex. 2	0
Total expenses *before* charitable contribution, NOL, and DRD	(17,459,000)			(15,921,000)
Income *before* charitable contribution, NOL, and DRD	4,717,000			$ 6,287,000
NOL carryover from prior year		(24,000)Ex. 9		(24,000)
Taxable income for charitable contribution limitation purposes				6,263,000
Charitable contributions	(700,000)		73,700Ex. 13	(626,300)
Taxable income before DRD				5,636,700
Dividends received deduction (DRD)		(15,000)Ex. 17		(15,000)
Book/taxable income	**$ 4,017,000**			**$ 5,621,700**

*This number is used only for illustrative purposes. In the Accounting for Income Taxes chapter, we compute the correct federal income tax expense (also referred to as the federal income tax provision).

†Note that the superscript by each book–tax difference identifies the example (Ex.) or exhibit (Exh.) where the adjustment is calculated. Also note that the numbers in the debit column are favorable book–tax adjustments while numbers in the credit column are unfavorable book–tax adjustments.

Schedule M-3.[26] Because corporations report book–tax differences as adjustments to book income to compute taxable income on either Schedule M-1 or M-3, these book-to-tax adjustments are often referred to as **Schedule M adjustments, M adjustments,** and even "Ms" (plural version of M).

[26]Corporations with at least $10 million but less than $50 million in total assets at tax year-end are permitted to file Schedule M-1 in place of Schedule M-3, Parts II and III. Schedule M-3, Part I, lines 1–12 continue to be required for these taxpayers. Corporations with $10 million to $50 million in total assets may voluntarily file Schedule M-3 Parts II and III rather than Schedule M-1.

EXHIBIT 16-8   PCC Form 1120 page 1, through tax refund

Form **1120**	**U.S. Corporation Income Tax Return**	OMB No. 1545-0123
Department of the Treasury Internal Revenue Service	For calendar year 2017 or tax year beginning _____, 2017, ending _____, 20 ____ ▶ Go to *www.irs.gov/Form1120* for instructions and the latest information.	**2017**

A Check if:
1a Consolidated return (attach Form 851) . ☐
  b Life/nonlife consolidated return . . . ☐
2 Personal holding co. (attach Sch. PH) . ☐
3 Personal service corp. (see instructions) . ☐
4 Schedule M-3 attached ☐

TYPE OR PRINT	Name **Premier Computer Corporation**	**B** Employer identification number **12-3456789**
	Number, street, and room or suite no. If a P.O. box, see instructions. **1533 East Crown Drive**	**C** Date incorporated **01/01/2000**
	City or town, state, or province, country, and ZIP or foreign postal code **Denver, CO 80239**	**D** Total assets (see instructions) $ **9,500,000**

E Check if: (1) ☐ Initial return **(2)** ☐ Final return **(3)** ☐ Name change **(4)** ☐ Address change

Income

1a	Gross receipts or sales	1a	60,000,000		
b	Returns and allowances	1b			
c	Balance. Subtract line 1b from line 1a			1c	60,000,000
2	Cost of goods sold (attach Form 1125-A)			2	38,000,000
3	Gross profit. Subtract line 2 from line 1c			3	22,000,000
4	Dividends (Schedule C, line 19)			4	30,000
5	Interest			5	108,000
6	Gross rents			6	
7	Gross royalties			7	
8	Capital gain net income (attach Schedule D (Form 1120))			8	
9	Net gain or (loss) from Form 4797, Part II, line 17 (attach Form 4797) . .			9	70,000
10	Other income (see instructions—attach statement)			10	
11	**Total income.** Add lines 3 through 10 . . . . ▶			11	22,208,000

Deductions (See instructions for limitations on deductions.)

12	Compensation of officers (see instructions—attach Form 1125-E) . . . ▶			12	1,500,000
13	Salaries and wages (less employment credits)			13	8,818,000
14	Repairs and maintenance			14	
15	Bad debts			15	95,000
16	Rents			16	
17	Taxes and licenses			17	
18	Interest			18	
19	Charitable contributions			19	626,300
20	Depreciation from Form 4562 not claimed on Form 1125-A or elsewhere on return (attach Form 4562) . .			20	3,100,000
21	Depletion			21	
22	Advertising			22	1,920,000
23	Pension, profit-sharing, etc., plans			23	
24	Employee benefit programs			24	
25	Domestic production activities deduction (attach Form 8903)			25	
26	Other deductions (attach statement)			26	488,000
27	**Total deductions.** Add lines 12 through 26 . . . . ▶			27	16,547,300
28	Taxable income before net operating loss deduction and special deductions. Subtract line 27 from line 11.			28	5,660,700
29a	Net operating loss deduction (see instructions)	29a	24,000		
b	Special deductions (Schedule C, line 20)	29b	15,000		
c	Add lines 29a and 29b			29c	39,000

Tax, Refundable Credits, and Payments

30	**Taxable income.** Subtract line 29c from line 28. See instructions	30	5,621,700
31	Total tax (Schedule J, Part I, line 11)	31	1,180,557
32	Total payments and refundable credits (Schedule J, Part II, line 21) . . .	32	1,328,000
33	Estimated tax penalty. See instructions. Check if Form 2220 is attached . . ▶ ☐	33	
34	**Amount owed.** If line 32 is smaller than the total of lines 31 and 33, enter amount owed	34	
35	**Overpayment.** If line 32 is larger than the total of lines 31 and 33, enter amount overpaid	35	147,443
36	Enter amount from line 35 you want: **Credited to 2018 estimated tax** ▶ _____ Refunded ▶	36	147,443

Sign Here

Under penalties of perjury, I declare that I have examined this return, including accompanying schedules and statements, and to the best of my knowledge and belief, it is true, correct, and complete. Declaration of preparer (other than taxpayer) is based on all information of which preparer has any knowledge.

▶ _____ _____ ▶ _____
Signature of officer   Date   Title

May the IRS discuss this return with the preparer shown below? See instructions. ☐ Yes ☐ No

Paid Preparer Use Only

Print/Type preparer's name	Preparer's signature	Date	Check ☐ if self-employed	PTIN
Firm's name ▶			Firm's EIN ▶	
Firm's address ▶			Phone no. ▶	

For Paperwork Reduction Act Notice, see separate instructions.   Cat. No. 11450Q   Form **1120** (2017)

Source: Form 1120

EXHIBIT 16-9   Form 1120, Schedule M-1

Schedule M-1   Reconciliation of Income (Loss) per Books With Income per Return

Note: The corporation may be required to file Schedule M-3. See instructions.

1	Net income (loss) per books	4,017,000	7	Income recorded on books this year not included on this return (itemize):	
2	Federal income tax per books	2,000,000			
3	Excess of capital losses over capital gains .	28,000		Tax-exempt interest $ 12,000	
4	Income subject to tax not recorded on books this year (itemize): _____gain on disposition_____ _____of fixed asset				12,000
		16,000	8	Deductions on this return not charged against book income this year (itemize):	
5	Expenses recorded on books this year not deducted on this return (itemize):		a	Depreciation . . $ 700,000	
a	Depreciation . . . . $ _____		b	Charitable contributions $ _____	
b	Charitable contributions . $ 73,700			_____deferred comp 150,000_____	
c	Travel and entertainment . $ 14,000				850,000
	Other $374,000, see Statement 1	461,700	9	Add lines 7 and 8	862,000
6	Add lines 1 through 5	6,522,700	10	Income (page 1, line 28)—line 6 less line 9	5,660,700

Schedule M-1
Statement 1
Other expenses recorded on books this year not deducted on this return

Compensation expense (stock options)	$100,000
Bad debt expense	70,000
Warranty expense	170,000
Life insurance premiums	34,000
Total other expenses	$374,000

Source: Form 1120, Schedule M-1

Because PCC's total assets are $9,500,000 (see Exhibit 16-8, line D), it may complete a Schedule M-1 rather than a Schedule M-3. Exhibit 16-9 presents PCC's completed Schedule M-1 based on the information provided in Exhibit 16-7 (the 2017 form is used because the 2018 form was unavailable at the time the book went to press). Schedule M-1 is a relatively short schedule, and it does not require corporations to provide much detail about the nature of their book–tax differences.

The schedule begins on line 1 with book income after taxes. The left-hand column includes all unfavorable book–tax differences (add-backs to book income to arrive at taxable income). In general, the top part of the left column is for income items and the bottom part is for expense items. The right-hand column consists of all favorable book–tax differences. The top part of the right column is for income items and the bottom part includes expense items.

Finally, note that Schedule M-1 (and Schedule M-3) reconciles to taxable income *before* the net operating loss deduction and the dividends received deduction.[27] Consequently, to fully reconcile book and taxable income, corporations must deduct net operating loss carryovers and dividends received deductions from line 10 on Schedule M-1 (or the amount on line 30d on Schedule M-3).

Example 16-19

In reviewing her work on PCC's tax return, Elise wanted to check to make sure that she could reconcile from the bottom line of the Schedule M-1 to PCC's taxable income. She noted that line 10 of PCC's Schedule M-1 was $5,660,700. How should Elise reconcile from this number to PCC's taxable income?

[27]Schedule M-1 (and the Schedule M-3) reconciles to line 28 on Form 1120. Line 28 is taxable income before the net operating loss and special deductions (the dividends received deduction).

Answer: Start with the amount on line 10 and subtract PCC's NOL carryover and its DRD, as illustrated below:

Description	Amount	Explanation
(1) Schedule M-1 taxable income reconciliation total	$ 5,660,700	Form 1120, Schedule M-1, line 10
(2) Net operating loss deduction	(24,000)	Exhibit 16-7
(3) Dividends received deduction	(15,000)	Exhibit 16-7
Taxable income	**$5,621,700**	(1) + (2) + (3)

Schedule M-3 requires corporations to report significantly more information than Schedule M-1 does. For example, Schedule M-3 includes more than 60 specific types of book–tax differences, while Schedule M-1 includes only 10 summary lines. Furthermore, Schedule M-3 requires corporations to identify each book–tax difference as either temporary or permanent. The IRS created Schedule M-3 in hopes of providing a better and more efficient starting point for agents to identify and scrutinize large dollar compliance issues.

Form 1120 also requires corporations to complete Schedule M-2, which provides a reconciliation of the corporation's beginning and ending balance in its unappropriated retained earnings from its financial accounting balance sheet (reported on Schedule L). Corporations with total receipts and total assets of less than $250,000 are not required to complete Schedules L, M-1, and M-2.

ETHICS

Elizabeth (Liz) Young, senior manager in the tax group in the Cleveland office of Tics & Tax, an international professional services firm, was reviewing the work papers related to the 2017 tax return to be filed by her biggest client, General Inertia. She was intrigued by one of the items listed under "other deductions" (line 26 of Form 1120), which was described as a "settlement amount" of $100 million. After consulting with the director of taxes at General Inertia, Dee Ductit, Liz discovered the amount related to a settlement with the Department of Justice (DOJ) for violation of the False Claims Act. Dee described the settlement as a "penalty" (her words) the firm had to pay to the federal government because one of its divisions billed the Department of Defense (DOD) for work that was not performed in relation to a contract to provide helicopters to the DOD.

Dee's use of the term "penalty" caused Liz to wonder whether such a payment was deductible for tax purposes (the company also deducted the payment on its financial statements). In particular, she remembered that Code §162(f) specifically prohibits the deduction of "any fine or similar penalty paid to a government for the violation of any law." When Liz asked to see the settlement letter from the DOJ, she was told that the client's legal department considered the terms of the letter to be confidential, but that the company's reason for deducting the amount was that the letter did not describe the settlement as a "penalty" and specifically stated that "nothing in the agreement characterizes the payments for federal income tax purposes."

General Inertia is a long-term client that provides the firm with $10 million in audit and tax fees annually. Dee informed Liz that the company was willing to take the "risk" in deducting the full amount of the settlement payment because its IRS auditors were unlikely to question the item, and the "tax refund" from deducting the settlement ($35 million) would help alleviate some short-term cash flow problems the company was having. In fact, the company hoped to use the "refund" to pay off parts suppliers that were threatening to take the company to court over nonpayment. The company also preferred not to provide any further disclosure or description of the deduction in the tax return so as not to alert the IRS to a potential tax audit issue.

What do you think of the tax director's approach to filing the company's tax return? What would you do if you were in Liz's position?[28]

---

[28]See S. Convery and E. Outslay, "Assessing Professional Ethics in Tax: A Case on Uncertain Tax Positions," *Journal of Accounting Education* 30, March 2012, 80–99. Congress enacted section 162(f) in the Tax Cuts and Jobs Act to deny deductions for these types of payments for tax years beginning after December 31, 2017.

Consolidated Tax Returns   An affiliated group of corporations may elect to file a **consolidated tax return**—that is, the group files a tax return as if it were one entity for tax purposes. An **affiliated group** exists when one corporation owns at least 80 percent of (1) the total voting power and (2) the total stock value of another corporation.[29] Filing a consolidated tax return allows the losses of one group member to offset the income of other members. Further, income from certain intercompany transactions is deferred until realized through a transaction outside of the affiliated group. However, losses from certain intercompany transactions are deferred until realized through a transaction outside of the affiliated group.

Affiliated groups cannot file a consolidated tax return unless they elect to do so. Because the election is binding on subsequent years, it should be made with care. Consolidated tax returns may impose additional administrative and compliance costs on the taxpayers. The consolidated tax return laws are very complex and beyond the scope of this text. Further, the rules for consolidated reporting for financial statement purposes are different from the tax rules.

Corporate Tax Return Due Dates and Estimated Taxes

The tax return due date for most C corporations (those with a tax year-end other than June 30) is three and one-half months after the corporation's year-end. Thus, a calendar-year corporation's unextended tax return due date is April 15. Corporations requesting an extension can extend the due date for filing their tax returns (not for paying the taxes) for six months (October 15 for calendar-year corporations). Corporations with a June 30 year-end will have a September 15 due date (the 15th day of the third month following the end of the fiscal year), and the extended due date will continue to be seven months after the regular due date (April 15) through the fiscal year ending June 30, 2026.

Corporations with a federal income tax liability of $500 or more (including the alternative minimum tax—discussed below) are required to pay their tax liability for the year in quarterly estimated installments.[30] The installments are due on the 15th day of the 4th, 6th, 9th, and 12th months of their tax year.[31] When corporations file their tax returns, they determine whether they must pay estimated tax underpayment penalties. Generally, corporations are subject to underpayment penalties if they did not pay 25 percent, 50 percent, 75 percent, and 100 percent of their required annual payment with their first, second, third, and fourth installment payments, respectively.[32] The required annual payment is the *least* of:

1. 100 percent of the tax liability on the prior year's return, but only if there was a positive tax liability on the return and the prior-year return covered a 12-month period (however, see discussion of the exception that applies to corporations with taxable income above $1 million).
2. 100 percent of the current-year tax liability (corporations usually don't rely on this method to compute the required payment because they won't know what their current-year liability is until they complete their tax returns—after the estimated tax due dates).
3. 100 percent of the estimated current-year tax liability using the annualized income method (discussed below).[33]

From a cash management perspective (considering the time value of money), it generally makes sense for corporations to make the *minimum* required estimated payment installments for each quarter. Thus, as each estimated tax due date approaches, corporations will generally compute the required estimated payment under the prior-year tax method (if available) and under the annualized method and pay the lesser of the two.

---

[29]§1504(a).

[30]§6655; §6655(e).

[31]§6655(c).

[32]§6665(d).

[33]§6655(e). Corporations may also use the adjusted seasonal income method of determining their required estimated tax payments. This method is similar in concept to the annualized method but is less common and beyond the scope of this text.

The **annualized income method** is perhaps the most popular method of determining estimated tax payments (particularly for corporations that can't use the prior-year tax liability to compute their current-year estimated tax payment obligations), because corporations can use this method as a safe harbor to avoid estimated payment penalties. Under this method, corporations measure their taxable income as of the end of each quarter and then annualize (project) the amount to calculate their estimated taxable income and tax liability for the year. They use estimated annual tax liability at the end of each quarter to calculate the minimum required estimated payment for that quarter. Corporations use the first-quarter taxable income to project their annual tax liability for the *first and second quarter* estimated tax payments. They use taxable income at the end of the second quarter to calculate the third quarter estimated tax payment requirement, and taxable income at the end of the third quarter to calculate their fourth quarter payment requirement. Exhibit 16-10 shows the formula for computing estimated taxable income under the annualized income method.

EXHIBIT 16-10   Estimated Taxable Income Computation under Annualized Income Method

Installment	(1) Taxable Income (first __ months of year)	(2) Annualization Factor	(1) × (2) Annual Estimated Taxable Income
First quarter	3	12/3 = 4	
Second quarter	3	12/3 = 4	
Third quarter	6	12/6 = 2	
Fourth quarter	9	12/9 = 1.3333	

Example 16-20

PCC determined its taxable income at the close of the first, second, and third quarters as follows:

Quarter-End	Cumulative Taxable Income
First	$1,000,000
Second	3,200,000
Third	4,000,000

What is its annual estimated taxable income for estimated tax purposes as of the end of the first, second, third, and fourth quarters, respectively?

Answer: $4,000,000 for the first and second quarters, $6,400,000 for the third quarter, and $6,666,667 for the fourth quarter, computed as follows:

Installment	(1) Taxable Income	(2) Annualization Factor	(1) × (2) Annual Estimated Taxable Income
First quarter	$1,000,000	12/3 = 4	**$4,000,000**
Second quarter	1,000,000	12/3 = 4	**4,000,000**
Third quarter	3,200,000	12/6 = 2	**6,400,000**
Fourth quarter	5,000,000	12/9 = 1.333	**6,666,667**

Once corporations have determined their annual estimated taxable income for each quarter, they can use the formulas in Exhibit 16-10 to compute the required estimated tax installments for each quarter under the annualized income method.

EXHIBIT 16-11 Estimated Taxable Income Computation under Annualized Income Method

Installment	(1) Annual Estimated Taxable Income	(2) Tax on Estimated Taxable Income	(3) Percentage of Tax Required to Be Paid	(4) (2) × (3) Required Cumulative Payment	(5) Prior Cumulative Payment	(4) − (5) Required Estimated Tax Payment
First quarter			25%			
Second quarter			50			
Third quarter			75			
Fourth quarter			100			

Example 16-21

Based on the estimated taxable income in Example 16-20, what are PCC's required estimated tax payments for the year under the annualized income method?

Answer: $210,000 for the first and second quarters, $588,000 for the third quarter, and $392,000 for the fourth quarter, computed as follows:

Installment	(1) Annual Estimated Taxable Income	(2) Tax on Estimated Taxable Income (flat 21%)	(3) Percentage of Tax Required to Be Paid	(4) (2) × (3) Required Cumulative Payment	(5) Prior Cumulative Payments	(4) − (5) Required Estimated Tax Payment
First quarter	$4,000,000	$ 840,000	25%	$ 210,000	$ 0	**$210,000**
Second quarter	4,000,000	840,000	50	420,000	210,000	**210,000**
Third quarter	6,400,000	1,344,000	75	1,008,000	420,000	**588,000**
Fourth quarter	6,666,667	1,400,000	100	1,400,000	$1,008,000	**392,000**

Can PCC use its prior-year tax liability to determine its current-year estimated tax payments?

Answer: No. PCC reported a net operating loss last year and did not pay taxes so it may not use its prior-year tax liability to determine its current-year estimated tax payments.

Can PCC use its current-year tax liability to determine its current-year estimated tax payments?

Answer: Yes. As we determined in Example 16-18, PCC's actual tax liability for the year is $1,180,557. So, PCC could have avoided estimated tax penalties by paying in $295,139 each quarter ($1,180,557 × 25%). However, it did not know this amount when it was required to make its estimated tax payments so it would likely have used the annualized income method of determining its estimated tax payments to protect itself from penalties.

"Large" corporations, defined as corporations with over $1,000,000 of taxable income in *any* of the three years prior to the current year,[34] may use the prior-year tax liability to determine their first quarter estimated tax payments only. If they use the prior-year tax liability to determine their first quarter payment, their second quarter payment must catch up their estimated payments. That is, the second quarter payment must be large enough for the sum of the first and second quarter payments to equal or exceed 50 percent of the corporation's projected current-year tax liability.[35]

[34]§6655(g)(2).
[35]§6655(d).

Example 16-22

What if: Assume that in 2017 PCC reported taxable income of $2,000,000 and a tax liability of $680,000. Further, PCC determined its required estimated tax payments under the annualized method as described in the previous example. What would be PCC's required minimum estimated tax payments for each quarter for the current year? (Ignore the current-year tax requirement because PCC is unsure what its current-year tax will be.)

Answer: $170,000 for the first quarter, $250,000 for the second quarter, $588,000 for the third quarter, and $392,000 for the fourth quarter, computed as follows:

Installment	(1) Estimated Tax Payment under Prior Year Tax Exception	(2) Estimated Tax Payment under Annualized Method	(3) Required Cumulative Payment for Quarter × [sum of the lesser of (1) or (2) through quarter]	(4) Prior Cumulative Payments	(5) (3) − (4) Required Estimated Tax Payment
First quarter	$170,000*	$210,000	$ 170,000	$ 0	**$170,000**
Second quarter	Not applicable*	210,000	420,000	170,000	**250,000**
Third quarter	Not applicable*	588,000	1,008,000	420,000	**588,000**
Fourth quarter	Not applicable*	320,000	1,400,000	1,008,000	**392,000**

*Because PCC is a large corporation, it may determine its first quarter estimated tax payment using its prior-year liability ($680,000 × 25% = $170,000). However, it must use the annualized method to determine its second, third, and fourth quarter required payments.

With its second installment, PCC must have paid in $420,000. Because it only paid in $170,000 with the first quarter installment, it must pay $250,000 with its second quarter payment.

What if: Assume the same facts as above, except that last year PCC paid $200,000 in tax and PCC is not a large corporation. What would be PCC's required minimum estimated tax payments for each quarter (ignore the current year tax requirement)?

Answer: $50,000 for the first quarter, $50,000 for the second quarter, $50,000 for the third quarter, and $50,000 for the fourth quarter, computed as follows:

Installment	(1) Estimated Tax Payment under Prior Year Tax Exception ($200,000/4)	(2) Estimated Tax Payment under Annualized Method	(3) Required Cumulative Payment for Quarter × [sum of the lesser of (1) or (2) through quarter ×]	(4) Prior Cumulative Payments	(5) (3) − (4) Required Estimated Tax Payment
First quarter	$50,000	$210,000	$ 50,000	$ 0	**$50,000**
Second quarter	50,000	210,000	100,000	50,000	**50,000**
Third quarter	50,000	588,000	150,000	100,000	**50,000**
Fourth quarter	50,000	320,000	200,000	150,000	**50,000**

PCC can use the prior-year tax to determine its minimum required estimated tax payments.

Corporations that have underpaid their estimated taxes for any quarter must pay an underpayment penalty calculated on Form 2220. The amount of the penalty is based on the underpayment rate (or interest rate), the amount of the underpayment, and the period of the underpayment. The interest rate is generally the federal short-term interest rate plus 3 percent. The period of the underpayment is the due date for the installment through the earlier of (1) the date the payment is made or (2) the due date of the tax return without extensions. The penalties are not deductible.[36]

[36]§6655(b)(2).

continued from page 16-1 . . .

Elise figured she was done when she sat down to discuss her review of PCC's tax return with Rachel. Rachel had only a few review comments. One sounded pretty important, though. Rachel asked Elise whether PCC paid any alternative minimum tax in prior years that had created a minimum tax credit carryforward. Elise told Rachel she would get back to her on that one. She left Rachel's office and immediately started researching the alternative minimum tax.

LO 16-4 CORPORATE ALTERNATIVE MINIMUM TAX CREDIT CARRYFORWARDS

In the early 1980s Congress became concerned that many large corporations were reporting positive financial income to shareholders but reporting tax losses or minimal taxable income to the IRS and, as a result, not paying what the voting public perceived to be their fair share of taxes. A common perception was that big businesses (and wealthy individuals) had the ability and sophistication to avoid paying taxes while middle-class taxpayers were carrying a disproportionate amount of the country's tax burden. Congress addressed this perceived inequity by enacting the corporate (and individual) **alternative minimum tax (AMT)** as part of the Tax Reform Act of 1986. The alternative minimum tax was a tax on a base broader than the regular tax base. It was designed to require corporations to pay some minimum level of tax even when they had low or no regular taxable income due to certain tax breaks they gained from the tax code.

Corporations computed their alternative minimum tax by multiplying their AMT base by the 20 percent AMT rate and then subtracting their regular tax liability from the product of the base and rate.[37] To compute their AMT base, corporations started with regular taxable income, added preference items, added or subtracted certain adjustments, and then subtracted an exemption amount. Exhibit 16-12 presents the corporate AMT formula.

In the Tax Cuts and Jobs Act, Congress repealed the AMT for taxable years beginning after December 31, 2017. Corporations that paid the AMT received a minimum tax credit that could be carried forward indefinitely to offset the excess of regular tax over the AMT in future years. In essence, the AMT acted as a prepayment of the regular tax. Under the TCJA, minimum tax credits existing after the repeal can offset a corporation's

EXHIBIT 16-12 Corporate AMT Formula

Taxable income or loss before NOL deduction
Add: Preference items
Add or subtract: Adjustments
Preadjustment AMT income
Add or subtract: Adjusted current earnings (ACE) adjustment
Subtract: AMT NOL deduction
Alternative minimum taxable income (AMTI)
Subtract: Exemption
AMT base
× 20%
Gross AMT
− AMT foreign tax credit
Tentative minimum tax
Subtract: Regular income tax
Alternative minimum tax if positive

---

[37]§55(a).

regular tax liability for any taxable year to which the AMT no longer applies. For tax years beginning in 2018, 2019, and 2020, 50 percent of the minimum tax credit in excess of the regular tax liability is refundable. Any remaining credit is fully refundable in 2021.

Example 16-23

Elise reviewed PCC's prior-year tax returns to determine if the company had an MTC carryforward to 2018. She was relieved to discover that PCC had not been subject to the AMT in prior years.

What if: Assume PCC had a $200,000 MTC carryforward to 2018. What would be PCC's tax liability in 2018 after applying the MTC carryforward? Assume the precredit income tax liability for 2018 was $1,180,557.

Answer: $980,557. The MTC is less than the regular tax in 2018, so the entire MTC can be taken.

CONCLUSION

A C corporation is a separate legal and taxpaying entity from its stockholders. Consequently, it must compute and report its own taxable income to the IRS. This chapter described the process of computing a corporation's taxable income and the associated tax liability for C corporations. We learned that book income is the starting point for calculating taxable income. Corporations adjust their book income for book–tax differences that arise because they account for many items of income and deduction differently for book purposes than they do for tax purposes. Some of these book–tax differences are temporary (the differences balance out over time) and some are permanent in nature (they don't balance out over the long term). As we discover in the next chapter, the distinction between temporary and permanent book–tax differences is critical for corporations computing their income tax expense or benefit for financial accounting purposes.

Summary

Identify those income and expense items that cause a corporation's financial accounting net income to differ from its taxable income. **LO 16-1**

- A corporation's taxable income is gross income minus deductions.
- The corporate tax formula is similar to the individual formula except that corporations don't itemize deductions or deduct standard deductions.
- Corporations may generally elect any tax year for reporting their taxable income, but the year must coincide with their financial accounting year.
- The timing of a corporation's income and deductions depends on the corporation's overall accounting method and its methods for specific transactions.
- Corporations are generally required to use the accrual overall method of accounting. However, smaller corporations may be allowed to use the cash method.

Compute a corporation's taxable income and associated income tax liability using financial statement information. **LO 16-2**

- Corporations typically compute taxable income by starting with book income and adjusting for book–tax differences.
- Book–tax differences are favorable when they reduce taxable income relative to book income and unfavorable when they increase it.
- Book–tax differences are permanent when the amount of income or deduction items is different for book and tax purposes and the amount will not reverse in the future.
- Book–tax differences are temporary when the amount of income or deduction items is different for book and tax purposes in the current year but the same for book and tax purposes over the long term. That is, temporary book–tax differences reverse over time.

- Common permanent book–tax differences include interest from municipal bonds (favorable), life insurance premiums on policies covering key employees (unfavorable), and one-half of meals expense, among others.

- Common temporary book–tax differences include depreciation expense, gain or loss on sale of depreciable assets, bad-debt expense, purchased goodwill amortization, and warranty expense, among others.

- Stock options granted when ASC 718 applies can generate temporary and permanent book–tax differences.

- Corporations may not deduct net capital losses for tax purposes. However, they may carry them back three years and forward five years to offset capital gains in those other years.

- When computing their net operating losses for the year, corporations may not deduct net operating losses from other years or net capital losses from other years.

- Subject to limitation, corporations can deduct the amount of money, the fair market value of capital gain property, and the adjusted basis of ordinary income property they donate to charity.

- The charitable contribution deduction for the year is limited to 10 percent of taxable income before deducting the charitable contribution, the dividends received deduction, and capital loss carrybacks. Amounts in excess of the limitation can be carried forward for up to five years.

- Corporations are allowed a deduction for dividends received to help mitigate potential triple taxation of the income distributed as a dividend. The amount of the deduction depends on the corporation's ownership in the distributing corporation. The deduction is 50 percent if the ownership is less than 20 percent; the deduction is 65 percent if the ownership is at least 20 percent but less than 80 percent; and finally, the deduction is 100 percent if the ownership is 80 percent or more.

- The dividends received deduction (DRD) is subject to a taxable income limitation. This limitation does not apply if the full DRD extends or creates a net operating loss for the corporation in the current year.

- A corporation's tax rate is a flat 21 percent unless blended rates apply to a fiscal year corporation with years beginning in 2017 and ending in 2018.

LO 16-3 Describe a corporation's tax return reporting and estimated tax payment obligations.

- Corporations file their tax returns on Form 1120, which is due three and one-half months after the corporation's year-end beginning in 2016 (two and one-half months for years prior to 2016 and for corporations with a June 30 year-end through 2025). Corporations can apply for an extension of the due date for filing the return for six months.

- Small corporations report their book–tax differences on Schedule M-1 of Form 1120. Large corporations (assets of $10 million or more) report them on Schedule M-3. Schedule M-3 requires much more detail than Schedule M-1.

- Corporations pay income taxes through estimated tax payments. Each payment should be 25 percent of their required annual payment. The installments are due on the 15th day of the 4th, 6th, 9th, and 12th months of the corporation's taxable year.

- Corporations' required annual payment is the least of (1) 100 percent of their current-year tax liability, (2) 100 percent of their prior-year tax liability (but only if they had a positive tax liability in the prior year), or (3) 100 percent of the estimated current-year tax liability using the annualized income method. Large corporations may rely on (2) only to compute their first quarter estimated payment requirement.

LO 16-4 Calculate a corporation's alternative minimum tax credit carryforward.

- The alternative minimum tax was a tax on a broader base than the regular tax. It ensured that corporations were not able to avoid taxes entirely by receiving tax-advantaged treatment for regular income tax items. The alternative minimum tax rate was repealed for tax years beginning after December 31, 2017.

- Existing minimum tax credits (MTC) can offset the regular tax liability for any taxable year following 2017, after deducting certain credits. For tax years beginning in 2018, 2019, and 2020, 50 percent of the MTC in excess of the regular tax liability is refundable. Any remaining MTC is fully refundable in 2021.

KEY TERMS

affiliated group (16-26)

alternative minimum tax
  (AMT) (16-30)

annualized income method (16-27)

bargain element (16-10)

book (financial reporting)
  income (16-3)

book–tax differences (16-3)

capital gain property (16-14)

charitable contribution limit
  modified taxable income (16-15)

consolidated tax return (16-26)

DRD modified taxable income (16-18)

exercise price (16-9)

favorable book–tax difference (16-3)

grant date (16-10)

incentive stock option (ISO) (16-9)

M adjustments (16-22)

net capital loss carryback (16-12)

net capital loss carryover (16-12)

net operating loss (NOL) (16-13)

net operating loss carryback (16-13)

net operating loss carryover (16-13)

nonqualified stock option
  (NQO) (16-9)

ordinary income property (16-14)

permanent book–tax
  differences (16-4)

requisite service period (16-9)

Schedule M adjustments (16-22)

temporary book–tax differences (16-4)

unfavorable book–tax difference (16-3)

vest (16-9)

vesting period (16-10)

DISCUSSION QUESTIONS

Discussion Questions are available in Connect®.

1. In general terms, identify the similarities and differences between the corporate taxable income formula and the individual taxable income formula. `LO 16-1`

2. Is a corporation's choice of its tax year independent from its year-end for financial accounting purposes? `LO 16-1`

3. Can C corporations use the cash method of accounting? Explain. `LO 16-1`

4. Briefly describe the process of computing a corporation's taxable income assuming the corporation must use GAAP to determine its book income. How might the process differ for corporations not required to use GAAP for book purposes? `LO 16-2`

5. What role does a corporation's audited financial statements play in determining its taxable income? `LO 16-2`

6. What is the difference between favorable and unfavorable book–tax differences? `LO 16-2`

7. What is the difference between permanent and temporary book–tax differences? `LO 16-2`

8. Why is it important to be able to determine whether a particular book–tax difference is permanent or temporary? `LO 16-2`

9. Describe the relation between the book–tax differences associated with depreciation expense and the book–tax differences associated with gain or loss on disposition of depreciable assets. `LO 16-2`

10. When a corporation receives a dividend from another corporation, does the dividend generate a book–tax difference to the dividend-receiving corporation (ignore the dividends received deduction)? Explain. `LO 16-2`

11. Describe how goodwill with a zero basis for tax purposes but not for book purposes leads to a permanent book–tax difference when the book goodwill is written off as impaired. `LO 16-2`

12. Describe how goodwill amortized for tax purposes but not for book purposes (i.e., no impairment) leads to temporary book–tax differences. `LO 16-2`

13. Describe the book–tax differences that arise from incentive stock options granted after ASC 718 became effective. `LO 16-2`

14. Describe the book–tax differences that arise from nonqualified stock options granted after ASC 718 became effective. `LO 16-2`

LO 16-2 15. How do corporations account for capital gains and losses for tax purposes? How is this different from the way individuals account for capital gains and losses?

LO 16-2 16. What are the common book–tax differences relating to accounting for capital gains and losses? Do these differences create favorable or unfavorable book-to-tax adjustments?

LO 16-2 17. What is the carryover period for a net operating loss? Does it depend on the year in which the NOL arose? Explain.

LO 16-2 18. Compare and contrast the general rule for determining the amount of the charitable contribution if the corporation contributes capital gain property versus ordinary income property.

LO 16-2 19. Which limitations might restrict a corporation's deduction for a cash charitable contribution? Explain how to determine the amount of the limitation.

LO 16-2 20. For tax purposes, what happens to a corporation's charitable contributions that are not deducted in the current year because of the taxable income limitation?

LO 16-2 21. What are common book–tax differences relating to corporate charitable contributions? Are these differences favorable or unfavorable?

LO 16-2 22. Why does Congress provide the dividends received deduction for corporations receiving dividends?

LO 16-2 23. How does a corporation determine the percentage for its dividends received deduction? Explain.

LO 16-2 24. What limitations apply to the amount of the allowable dividends received deduction?

LO 16-3 25. How is the Schedule M-1 similar to and different from a Schedule M-3? How does a corporation determine whether it must complete Schedule M-1 or Schedule M-3 when it completes its tax return?

LO 16-3 26. What is the due date for a calendar-year corporation tax return Form 1120 for 2018? Is it possible to extend the due date? Explain.

LO 16-3 27. How does a corporation determine the minimum amount of estimated tax payments it must make to avoid underpayment penalties? How do these rules differ for large corporations?

LO 16-3 28. Describe the annualized income method for determining a corporation's required estimated tax payments. What advantages does this method have over other methods?

LO 16-4 29. Briefly describe the process of computing a corporation's minimum tax credit carryover.

PROBLEMS

Select problems are available in Connect®.

LO 16-1 30. LNS corporation reports book income of $2,000,000. Included in the $2,000,000 is $15,000 of tax-exempt interest income. LNS reports $1,345,000 in ordinary and necessary business expenses. What is LNS corporation's taxable income for the year?

LO 16-1 31. ATW corporation currently uses the FIFO method of accounting for its inventory for book and tax purposes. Its beginning inventory for the current year was $8,000,000. Its ending inventory for the current year was $7,000,000. If ATW had been using the LIFO method of accounting for its inventory, its beginning inventory would have been $7,000,000 and its ending inventory would have been $5,500,000. ATW corporation's tax rate is 21 percent.

   a) How much more in taxes did ATW corporation pay for the current year because it used the FIFO method of accounting for inventory rather than the LIFO method?

   b) Why would ATW use the FIFO method of accounting if doing so causes it to pay more taxes on a present value basis? (Note that the tax laws don't allow corporations to use the LIFO method of accounting for inventory unless they also use the LIFO method of accounting for inventory for book purposes.)

32. ELS corporation is about to begin its sixth year of existence. Assume that ELS reported gross receipts for each of its first five years of existence for Scenarios A, B, and C as follows: LO 16-1

Year of Existence	Scenario A	Scenario B	Scenario C
1	$ 20,000,000	$15,000,000	$24,500,000
2	25,000,000	25,000,000	25,000,000
3	60,000,000	35,000,000	30,000,000
4	80,000,000	35,000,000	40,000,000
5	100,000,000	40,000,000	55,000,000

   a) In what years is ELS allowed to use the cash method of accounting under Scenario A?

   b) In what years is ELS allowed to use the cash method of accounting under Scenario B?

   c) In what years is ELS allowed to use the cash method of accounting under Scenario C?

33. On its year 1 financial statements, Seatax Corporation, an accrual-method taxpayer, reported federal income tax expense of $570,000. On its year 1 tax return, it reported a tax liability of $650,000. During year 1, Seatax made estimated tax payments of $700,000. What book–tax difference, if any, associated with its federal income tax expense should Seatax have reported when computing its year 1 taxable income? Is the difference favorable or unfavorable? Is it temporary or permanent?   LO 16-2

34. Assume Maple Corp. has just completed the third year of its existence (year 3). The table below indicates Maple's ending book inventory for each year and the additional §263A costs it was required to include in its ending inventory. Maple immediately expensed these costs for book purposes. In year 2, Maple sold all of its year 1 ending inventory, and in year 3 it sold all of its year 2 ending inventory.   LO 16-2

	Year 1	Year 2	Year 3
Ending book inventory	$2,400,000	$2,700,000	$2,040,000
Additional §263A costs	60,000	70,000	40,000
Ending tax inventory	$2,460,000	$2,770,000	$2,080,000

   a) What book–tax difference associated with its inventory did Maple report in year 1? Was the difference favorable or unfavorable? Was it permanent or temporary?

   b) What book–tax difference associated with its inventory did Maple report in year 2? Was the difference favorable or unfavorable? Was it permanent or temporary?

   c) What book–tax difference associated with its inventory did Maple report in year 3? Was the difference favorable or unfavorable? Was it permanent or temporary?

35. JDog corporation owns stock in Oscar Inc. JDog received a $10,000 dividend from Oscar Inc. What temporary book–tax difference associated with the dividend will JDog report for the year in the following alternative scenarios (income difference only—ignore the dividends received deduction)?   LO 16-2

   a) JDog owns 5 percent of the Oscar Inc. stock. Oscar's income for the year was $500,000.

   b) JDog owns 40 percent of the Oscar Inc. stock. Oscar's income for the year was $500,000.

36. On July 1 of year 1, Riverside Corp. (RC), a calendar-year taxpayer, acquired the assets of another business in a taxable acquisition. When the purchase price was allocated to the assets purchased, RC determined it had purchased $1,200,000 of   LO 16-2

goodwill for both book and tax purposes. At the end of year 1, RC determined that the goodwill had not been impaired during the year. In year 2, however, RC concluded that $200,000 of the goodwill had been impaired and wrote down the goodwill by $200,000 for book purposes.

a) What book–tax difference associated with its goodwill should RC report in year 1? Is it favorable or unfavorable? Is it permanent or temporary?

b) What book–tax difference associated with its goodwill should RC report in year 2? Is it favorable or unfavorable? Is it permanent or temporary?

LO 16-2 37. Assume that on January 1, year 1, ABC Inc. issued 5,000 stock options with an estimated value of $10 per option. Each option entitles the owner to purchase one share of ABC stock for $25 a share (the per share price of ABC stock on January 1, year 1, when the options were granted). The options vest at the end of the day on December 31, year 2. All 5,000 stock options were exercised in year 3 when the ABC stock was valued at $31 per share. Identify ABC's year 1, 2, and 3 tax deductions and book–tax differences (indicate whether permanent and/or temporary) associated with the stock options under the following alternative scenarios:

a) The stock options are incentive stock options and ASC 718 applies to the options.

b) The stock options are nonqualified stock options and ASC 718 applies to the options.

LO 16-2 38. Assume that on January 1, year 1, XYZ Corp. issued 1,000 nonqualified stock options with an estimated value of $4 per option. Each option entitles the owner to purchase one share of XYZ stock for $14 a share (the per share price of XYZ stock on January 1, year 1, when the options were granted). The options vest 25 percent a year (on December 31) for four years (beginning with year 1). All 500 stock options that had vested to that point were exercised in year 3 when the XYZ stock was valued at $20 per share. No other options were exercised in year 3 or year 4. Identify XYZ's year 1, 2, 3, and 4 tax deductions and book–tax difference (identify as permanent and/or temporary) associated with the stock options.

LO 16-2 39. What book–tax differences in year 1 and year 2 associated with its capital gains and losses would ABD Inc. report in the following alternative scenarios? Identify each book–tax difference as favorable or unfavorable and as permanent or temporary.

a)

	Year 1	Year 2
Capital gains	$20,000	$ 5,000
Capital losses	8,000	0

b)

	Year 1	Year 2
Capital gains	$ 8,000	$ 5,000
Capital losses	20,000	0

c)

	Year 1	Year 2
Capital gains	$ 0	$50,000
Capital losses	25,000	30,000

d)

	Year 1	Year 2
Capital gains	$ 0	$40,000
Capital losses	25,000	0

e) Answer for year 6 only.

	Year 1	Years 2–5	Year 6
Capital gains	$ 0	$ 0	$15,000
Capital losses	10,000	0	0

f) Answer for year 7 only.

	Year 1	Years 2–6	Year 7
Capital gains	$ 0	$ 0	$15,000
Capital losses	10,000	0	0

40. What book–tax differences in year 1 and year 2 associated with its capital gains and losses would DEF Inc. report in the following alternative scenarios? Identify each book–tax difference as favorable or unfavorable and as permanent or temporary.   **LO 16-2**

a) In year 1, DEF recognized a loss of $15,000 on land that it had held for investment. In year 1, it also recognized a $30,000 gain on equipment it had purchased a few years ago. The equipment sold for $50,000 and had an adjusted basis of $20,000. DEF had deducted $40,000 of depreciation on the equipment. In year 2, DEF recognized a capital loss of $2,000.

b) In year 1, DEF recognized a loss of $15,000 on land that it had held for investment. It also recognized a $20,000 gain on equipment it had purchased a few years ago. The equipment sold for $50,000 and had an adjusted basis of $30,000. DEF had deducted $15,000 of tax depreciation on the equipment.

41. MWC Corp. is currently in the sixth year of its existence (2018). In 2013–2017, it reported the following income and (losses) (before net operating loss carryovers or carrybacks).   **LO 16-2**

2013	$(70,000)
2014	(30,000)
2015	60,000
2016	140,000
2017	(25,000)
2018	300,000

If MWC elected to carry over the 2017 NOL, what is its 2018 taxable income after the NOL deduction? What is its 2018 book–tax difference associated with its NOL? Is it favorable or unfavorable? Is it permanent or temporary?

42. Assume that in 2018 Hill Corporation reported a net operating loss of $10,000 that it carried forward to 2019. In 2018 Hill also reported a net capital loss of $3,000 that it carried forward to 2019. In 2019, ignoring any carryovers from other years, Hill reported a loss for tax purposes of $50,000. The current-year loss includes a $12,000 net capital gain. What is Hill's 2019 net operating loss?   **LO 16-2**

43. Cedar Corporation reported a net operating loss in 2018 of $25,000,000. In 2019, Cedar reported taxable income before any NOL carryovers of $20,000,000. What is Cedar's taxable income in 2019 and any NOL carryover to 2020?

44. Golf Corp. (GC), a calendar-year accrual-method corporation, held its directors' meeting on December 15 of year 1. During the meeting the board of directors authorized GC to pay a $75,000 charitable contribution to the World Golf Foundation, a qualifying charity.   **LO 16-2**

a) If GC actually pays $50,000 of this contribution on January 15 of year 2 and the remaining $25,000 on or before April 15 of year 2, what book–tax difference will it report associated with the contribution in year 1 (assume the 10 percent limitation does not apply)? Is it favorable or unfavorable? Is it permanent or temporary?

b) Assuming the same facts as in part (a), what book–tax difference will GC report in year 2 (assuming the 10 percent limitation does not apply)? Is it favorable or unfavorable?

c) If GC actually pays $50,000 of this contribution on January 15 of year 2 and the remaining $25,000 on May 15 of year 2, what book–tax difference will it report associated with the contribution in year 1 (assume the 10 percent limitation does not apply)? Is it favorable or unfavorable? Is it permanent or temporary?

d) Assuming the same facts as in part (c), what book–tax difference will GC report in year 2 (assuming the 10 percent limitation does not apply)? Is it favorable or unfavorable?

LO 16-2 45. In year 1 (the current year), OCC Corp. made a charitable donation of $200,000 to the Jordan Spieth Family Foundation (a qualifying charity). For the year, OCC reported taxable income of $1,500,000 before deducting any charitable contributions, before deducting its $20,000 dividends received deduction, and before deducting its $40,000 NOL carryover from last year.

a) What amount of the $200,000 donation is OCC allowed to deduct for tax purposes in year 1?

b) In year 2, OCC did not make any charitable contributions. It reported taxable income of $300,000 before any charitable contribution deductions and before a $15,000 dividends received deduction. What book–tax difference associated with the charitable contributions will OCC report in year 2? Is the difference favorable or unfavorable? Is it permanent or temporary?

c) Assume the original facts and those provided in part (b). In years 3, 4, and 5, OCC reported taxable losses of $50,000. Finally, in year 6 it reported $1,000,000 in taxable income before any charitable contribution deductions. It did not have any dividends received deduction. OCC did not actually make any charitable donations in year 6. What book–tax difference associated with charitable contributions will OCC report in year 6?

LO 16-2 46. In year 1 (the current year), LAA Inc. made a charitable donation of $100,000 to the American Red Cross (a qualifying charity). For the year, LAA reported taxable income of $550,000, which included a $100,000 charitable contribution deduction (before limitation), a $50,000 dividends received deduction, and a $10,000 net operating loss carryover from year 0. What is LAA Inc.'s charitable contribution deduction for year 1?

LO 16-2
research 47. Coattail Corporation (CC) manufactures and sells women's and children's coats. This year, CC donated 1,000 coats to a qualified public charity. The charity distributed the coats to needy women and children throughout the region. At the time of the contribution, the fair market value of each coat was $80. Determine the amount of CC's charitable contribution (the taxable income limitation does not apply) for the coats assuming the following:

a) CC's adjusted basis in each coat was $30.

b) CC's adjusted basis in each coat was $10.

LO 16-2
research 48. Maple Corp. owns several pieces of highly valued paintings that are on display in the corporation's headquarters. This year, it donated one of the paintings valued at $100,000 (adjusted basis of $25,000) to a local museum for the museum to display. What is the amount of Maple Corp.'s charitable contribution deduction for the painting (assuming income limitations do not apply)? What would be Maple's deduction if the museum sold the painting one month after it received it from Maple?

LO 16-2 49. Riverbend Inc. received a $200,000 dividend from stock it held in Hobble Corporation. Riverbend's taxable income is $2,100,000 before deducting the dividends received deduction (DRD), a $40,000 NOL carryover, and a $100,000 charitable contribution.

a) What is Riverbend's deductible DRD assuming it owns 10 percent of Hobble Corporation?

b) Assuming the facts in part (a), what is Riverbend's marginal tax rate on the dividend?

c) What is Riverbend's DRD assuming it owns 60 percent of Hobble Corporation?

d) Assuming the facts in part (c), what is Riverbend's marginal tax rate on the dividend?

e) What is Riverbend's DRD assuming it owns 85 percent of Hobble Corporation (and is part of the same affiliated group)?

f) Assuming the facts in part (e), what is Riverbend's marginal tax rate on the dividend?

50. Wasatch Corp. (WC) received a $200,000 dividend from Tager Corporation (TC). WC owns 15 percent of the TC stock. Compute WC's deductible DRD in each of the following situations: **LO 16-2**

a) WC's taxable income (loss) without the dividend income or the DRD is $10,000.

b) WC's taxable income (loss) without the dividend income or the DRD is $(10,000).

c) WC's taxable income (loss) without the dividend income or the DRD is $(99,000).

d) WC's taxable income (loss) without the dividend income or the DRD is $(101,000).

e) WC's taxable income (loss) without the dividend income or the DRD is $(500,000).

f) What is WC's book–tax difference associated with its DRD in part (a)? Is the difference favorable or unfavorable? Is it permanent or temporary?

51. Last year, TBA Corporation, a calendar-year taxpayer, reported a tax liability of $100,000. TBA confidently anticipates a current-year tax liability of $240,000. What minimum estimated tax payments should TBA make for the first, second, third, and fourth quarters, respectively (ignore the annualized income method), assuming the following: **LO 16-3**

a) TBA is not considered to be a large corporation for estimated tax purposes.

b) TBA is considered to be a large corporation for estimated tax purposes.

52. Last year, BTA Corporation, a calendar-year taxpayer, reported a net operating loss of $10,000 and a $0 tax liability. BTA confidently anticipates a current-year tax liability of $240,000. What minimum estimated tax payments should BTA make for the first, second, third, and fourth quarters, respectively (ignore the annualized income method), assuming the following: **LO 16-3**

a) BTA is not considered to be a large corporation for estimated tax purposes.

b) BTA is considered to be a large corporation for estimated tax purposes.

53. For the current year, LNS corporation reported the following taxable income at the end of its first, second, and third quarters. What are LNS's minimum first, second, third, and fourth quarter estimated tax payments determined using the annualized income method?   **LO 16-3**

Quarter-End	Cumulative Taxable Income
First	$1,000,000
Second	1,600,000
Third	2,400,000

LO 16-3

planning

54. Last year, JL Corporation's tax liability was $900,000. For the current year, JL Corporation reported the following taxable income at the end of its first, second, and third quarters (see table below). What are JL's minimum required first, second, third, and fourth quarter estimated tax payments (ignore the actual current-year tax safe harbor)?

Quarter-End	Cumulative Taxable Income
First	$ 500,000
Second	1,250,000
Third	2,250,000

LO 16-3

55. Last year, Cougar Corp. (CC) reported a net operating loss of $25,000. In the current year, CC expected its current-year tax liability to be $260,000 so it made four equal estimated tax payments of $65,000 each. Cougar closed its books at the end of each quarter. The following schedule reports CC's taxable income at the end of each quarter:

Quarter-End	Cumulative Taxable Income
First	$ 300,000
Second	700,000
Third	1,000,000
Fourth	1,500,000

CC's current-year tax liability on $1,500,000 of taxable income is $315,000. Does CC owe underpayment penalties on its estimated tax payments? If so, for which quarters does it owe the penalty?

COMPREHENSIVE PROBLEMS

Select problems are available in Connect®.

56. Compute MV Corp.'s 2018 taxable income given the following information relating to its year 1 activities. Also, compute MV's Schedule M-1 assuming that MV's federal income tax expense for book purposes is $100,000.

   • Gross profit from inventory sales of $500,000 (no book–tax differences).

   • Dividends MV received from 25 percent-owned corporation of $100,000 (assume this is also MV's pro rata share of the distributing corporation's earnings).

   • Expenses *other than* DRD, charitable contribution (CC), and net operating loss (NOL) are $350,000 (no book–tax differences).

   • NOL carryover from prior year of $10,000.

   • Cash charitable contribution of $120,000.

57. Compute HC Inc.'s current year taxable income given the following information relating to its 2018 activities. Also, compute HC's Schedule M-1 assuming that HC's federal income tax expense for book purposes is $30,000.

   • Gross profit from inventory sales of $310,000 (no book–tax differences).

   • Dividends HC received from 28 percent-owned corporation of $120,000 (this is also HC's pro rata share of the corporation's earnings).

- Expenses *other than* DRD, charitable contribution (CC), and net operating loss (NOL) are $300,000 (no book–tax differences).
- NOL carryover from prior year of $12,000.
- Cash charitable contribution of $50,000.

58. Timpanogos Inc. is an accrual-method calendar-year corporation. For 2018, it reported financial statement income after taxes of $1,152,000. Timpanogos provided the following information relating to its 2018 activities:

tax forms

Life insurance proceeds as a result of CEO's death	$ 200,000
Revenue from sales (for both book and tax purposes)	2,000,000
Premiums paid on the key-person life insurance policies. The policies have no cash surrender value.	21,000
Charitable contributions	180,000
Cost of goods sold for book and tax purposes	300,000
Interest income on tax-exempt bonds issued in 2017	40,000
Interest paid on loan obtained to purchase tax-exempt bonds	45,000
Rental income payments received and earned in 2018	15,000
Rental income payments received in 2017 but earned in 2018	10,000
Rental income payments received in 2018 but not earned by year-end	30,000
MACRS depreciation	55,000
Book depreciation	25,000
Net capital loss	42,000
Federal income tax expense for books in 2018	500,000

Required:

a) Reconcile book income to taxable income for Timpanogos Inc. Be sure to start with book income and identify all of the adjustments necessary to arrive at taxable income.

b) Identify each book–tax difference as either permanent or temporary.

c) Complete Schedule M-1 for Timpanogos.

d) Compute Timpanogos Inc.'s tax liability for 2018.

59. XYZ is a calendar-year corporation that began business on January 1, 2017. For 2018, it reported the following information in its current-year audited income statement. Notes with important tax information are provided below.

tax forms

Required:

Identify the book-to-tax adjustments for XYZ.

a) Reconcile book income to taxable income and identify each book–tax difference as temporary or permanent.

b) Compute XYZ's income tax liability.

c) Complete XYZ's Schedule M-1.

d) Complete XYZ's Form 1120, page 1 (use the most current form available). Ignore estimated tax penalties when completing this form.

e) Determine the quarters for which XYZ is subject to underpayment of estimated tax penalties (see estimated tax information below).

XYZ Corp. Income Statement for Current Year	Book Income	Book to Tax Adjustments (Dr.)	Cr.	Taxable Income
Revenue from sales	$ 40,000,000			
Cost of goods sold	(27,000,000)			
Gross profit	$ 13,000,000			
Other income:				
Income from investment in corporate stock	300,000[1]			
Interest income	20,000[2]			
Capital gains (losses)	(4,000)			
Gain or loss from disposition of fixed assets	3,000[3]			
Miscellaneous income	50,000			
Gross income	$ 13,369,000			
Expenses:				
Compensation	(7,500,000)[4]			
Stock option compensation	(200,000)[5]			
Advertising	(1,350,000)			
Repairs and maintenance	(75,000)			
Rent	(22,000)			
Bad debt expense	(41,000)[6]			
Depreciation	(1,400,000)[7]			
Warranty expenses	(70,000)[8]			
Charitable donations	(500,000)[9]			
Meals	(18,000)			
Goodwill impairment	(30,000)[10]			
Organizational expenditures	(44,000)[11]			
Other expenses	140,000[12]			
Total expenses	$(11,390,000)			
Income before taxes	$ 1,979,000			
Provision for income taxes	(720,000)[13]			
Net Income after taxes	$ 1,259,000[14]			

Notes

1. XYZ owns 30 percent of the outstanding Hobble Corp. (HC) stock. Hobble Corp. reported $1,000,000 of income for the year. XYZ accounted for its investment in HC under the equity method and it recorded its pro rata share of HC's earnings for the year. HC also distributed a $200,000 dividend to XYZ.
2. Of the $20,000 interest income, $5,000 was from a City of Seattle bond issued in 2017 that was used to fund public activities, $7,000 was from a Tacoma City bond issued in 2015, $6,000 was from a fully taxable corporate bond, and the remaining $2,000 was from a money market account.
3. This gain is from equipment that XYZ purchased in February and sold in December (i.e., it does not qualify as §1231 gain).
4. This includes total officer compensation of $2,500,000 (no one officer received more than $1,000,000 compensation).
5. This amount is the portion of incentive stock option compensation that was expensed during the year (recipients are officers).
6. XYZ actually wrote off $27,000 of its accounts receivable as uncollectible.
7. Tax depreciation was $1,900,000.
8. In the current year, XYZ did not make any actual payments on warranties it provided to customers.
9. XYZ made $500,000 of cash contributions to qualified charities during the year.
10. On July 1 of this year XYZ acquired the assets of another business. In the process it acquired $300,000 of goodwill. At the end of the year, XYZ wrote off $30,000 of the goodwill as impaired.
11. XYZ expensed all of its organizational expenditures for book purposes. XYZ expensed the maximum amount of organizational expenditures allowed for tax purposes.
12. The other expenses do not contain any items with book–tax differences.
13. This is an estimated tax provision (federal tax expense) for the year. (In a subsequent chapter, we will learn how to compute the correct tax provision.) Assume that XYZ is not subject to state income taxes.

Estimated Tax Information

XYZ made four equal estimated tax payments totaling $480,000. For purposes of estimated tax liabilities, assume XYZ reported a tax liability of $800,000 in 2017. During 2018, XYZ determined its taxable income at the end of each of the four quarters as follows:

Quarter-End	Cumulative Taxable Income (Loss)
First	$ 350,000
Second	800,000
Third	1,000,000

Finally, assume that XYZ is not a large corporation for purposes of estimated tax calculations.

 ROGER | *CPA Review*

Sample CPA Exam questions from Roger CPA Review are available in Connect as support for the topics in this text. These Multiple Choice Questions and Task-Based Simulations include expert-written explanations and solutions and provide a starting point for students to become familiar with the content and functionality of the actual CPA Exam.

chapter

17 Accounting for Income Taxes

Learning Objectives

Upon completing this chapter, you should be able to:

LO 17-1 Describe the objectives behind FASB ASC Topic 740, *Income Taxes*, and the income tax provision process.

LO 17-2 Calculate the current and deferred income tax expense or benefit components of a company's income tax provision.

LO 17-3 Determine how to calculate a valuation allowance.

LO 17-4 Explain how a company accounts for its uncertain income tax positions under FASB ASC Topic 740.

LO 17-5 Describe how a company computes and discloses the components of its effective tax rate.

Storyline Summary

Elise Brandon

Employment status: Tax associate for a large public accounting firm.

Assigned to prepare the federal income tax provision and income-tax-related balance sheet accounts and footnote disclosures for Premiere Computer Corporation, a nonaudit client.

Premiere Computer Corporation
Medium-sized publicly traded company. Manufactures and sells computers and computer-related equipment. Calendar-year taxpayer.

Tax rate: 21 percent.

Elise felt a great sense of accomplishment when she completed her review of the federal income tax return for Premiere Computer Corporation (PCC). She was glad the return was filed on time and did not need to be extended. With the tax return filed, Elise was assigned to help the PCC tax department compute the federal income tax provision for the company's soon-to-be-published income statement and to determine the correct amounts in the company's income-tax-related balance sheet accounts. She also was given responsibility for helping prepare the income tax note to the financial statements.[1]

Elise was aware that, as a result of more stringent independence requirements imposed by the Sarbanes Oxley Act, her colleagues in the tax group were getting a lot of engagements to help prepare the income tax provision for nonaudit clients. In fact, her firm now considered accounting for income taxes to be a "core competency" for all tax staff and prepared a training course for everyone. Having recently attended the firm's training on the subject, Elise was eager to apply her new knowledge to an actual client situation. She knew that developing her skill set in this complex topic would make her more valuable to her firm and her clients.[2]

to be continued . . .

---

[1]Publicly traded companies usually file their financial statements (Form 10-K) with the Securities and Exchange Commission well before they file their income tax returns with the Internal Revenue Service, often by as much as six months. The company must estimate its current-year income tax liability when it files its financial statements and then adjust for any "provision to return" differences in the quarter (Form 10-Q) in which the tax return is filed. In today's post–Sarbanes-Oxley environment, staff from public accounting firms that are not a company's auditors often are hired to help prepare the company's income tax provision under ASC 740 because many companies do not have staff with the expertise to make this calculation.

[2]An international tax services partner at a major public accounting firm testified before members of Congress that her firm spent more than 7,000 hours auditing a client's accounting for income taxes for its 2011 Form 10-K. See Beth Carr, "Written Testimony for Senate Permanent Subcommittee on Investigations," September 20, 2012, available at www.hsgac.senate.gov/download/?id=47a0da59-0d31-4b64-ad0a-47cca27d0e46.

Most of the items of income (revenue) and deductions (expenses) that are included in a company's taxable income also are included in the company's net (book) income before taxes. Not all these items are included in the computations in the same accounting period, however, which creates a "temporary" mismatch of the amounts of these items included in taxable income and pretax book income in a given year. Other items are included in only one of the computations, which creates a "permanent" mismatch of the amount of these items included in taxable income and pretax book income. A company must take these temporary and permanent differences into account in computing its income tax provision on the income statement and its deferred income taxes payable (liabilities) or refundable (assets) on the balance sheet.

FASB Accounting Standards Codification Topic 740, *Income Taxes* (hereafter, ASC 740), governs the computation and disclosure of a company's income tax provision (expense or benefit) and its expected future income tax liabilities or benefits related to "events" that have been recorded on either the financial statement or the tax return. ASC 740 codifies the majority of accounting and reporting guidance related to income taxes, primarily FAS 109. Accounting for income taxes guidance related to accounting for investments under the equity method, stock compensation, business combinations, foreign currency translation, and industry subtopics such as real estate, entertainment, and oil and gas is embedded within the ASC topic that deals with that issue. The Emerging Issues Task Force (EITF)[3] and the Securities and Exchange Commission continue to provide guidance on issues related to accounting for income taxes.

A company's failure to accurately compute the income tax provision and related balance sheet accounts can lead to the issuance of a material weakness statement by the auditor and, in some cases, a restatement of the financial statements. Not surprisingly, individuals who understand these complex and sometimes counterintuitive rules are in great demand by public accounting firms and industry.

This chapter discusses the basic rules for how a company computes and discloses its current-year income tax provision and its future income taxes payable or refundable, using the facts related to Premiere Computer Corporation in the Corporate Operations chapter. We focus on the portion of the provision that relates to federal income taxes.

LO 17-1   OBJECTIVES OF ACCOUNTING FOR INCOME TAXES AND THE INCOME TAX PROVISION PROCESS

In addition to filing its federal, state and local, and non-U.S. income tax returns, Premiere Computer Corporation, along with all other U.S. publicly traded corporations and many privately held corporations, must prepare financial statements in accordance with generally accepted accounting principles (GAAP) issued by the FASB (Financial Accounting Standards Board). Under GAAP, a company includes as part of its income statement a "provision" for the income tax expense or benefit that is associated with the pretax net income or loss reported on the income statement. The income tax provision includes not only current-year taxes payable or refundable, but also any changes to future income taxes payable or refundable that result from differences in the timing of when an item is reported on the tax return compared to the financial statement. The company records the amount of future income taxes payable as a **deferred tax liability** and future income taxes refundable as a **deferred tax asset** on its balance sheet.

---

[3]The Emerging Issues Task Force is a committee of accounting practitioners who assist the FASB in providing timely guidance on emerging issues and the implementation of existing standards.

TAXES IN THE REAL WORLD What A Tangled Web We Weave . . .

On March 1, 2011, Weatherford International informed its shareholders that it would be late in issuing its Form 10-K because of a material weakness in internal control over the company's financial reporting for income taxes. As a result, management cautioned its investors not to rely on any of its financial statements issued for the years 2007–2010. Management estimated the total financial reporting error to be around $500 million. At a press conference the next day, the CEO made the following statement:

> To a degree, the discipline of tax within our Company is a two-headed animal—one, planning, and two, process. Both pieces must work well in order for us to be able to maximize the value of our multinational status. This mistake, the embarrassment of which is difficult, if not impossible to quantify, highlights that we have work to do on strengthening the process piece. We will work hard to make sure this happens with all appropriate speed and effectiveness.*

Weatherford remedied the deficiencies during 2013 and restated its 2009–2011 financial statements in December 2012. During 2012, the company hired a new vice president of taxes and 25 additional "qualified tax professionals." In addition, it spent considerable resources engaging third-party tax advisers and consultants to assist with enhancing internal controls over financial reporting for income taxes and developing and implementing a remediation plan; revising the process for the quarterly and annual tax provisions; recruiting positions within the tax and financial reporting departments; and providing income tax accounting training to tax and financial staff. These expenditures were disclosed in the company's Proxy Statement in June 2013. Outside advisers had provided more than 272,000 hours of time to the restatement and remediation at a cost of over $100 million.

The remediation was completed by the end of December 2013, to management's great relief. However, the company announced that the SEC and the Department of Justice were investigating the circumstances surrounding the material weakness and the weaknesses in the company's internal controls that led to restatement. In addition, shareholders filed a lawsuit charging that Weatherford provided misleading financial statements. In September 2016, the SEC announced that its investigation had uncovered fraudulent accounting for income taxes committed by two company employees that understated (overstated) the company's income tax provision (profit after tax) by $461 million from 2007 to 2010.

The SEC fined Weatherford $140 million for violating the Securities Act of 1933 and the Securities Exchange Act of 1934. The company's outside auditors also were fined $11.8 million for failing to comply with Public Company Accounting Oversight Board (PCAOB) auditing standards, and for not exhibiting professional skepticism and "fortitude" in their audit of Weatherford's tax accounting procedures.

*Final transcript of Weatherford International to adjust 2007–2010 results due to "material weakness" in its income tax reporting—Conference Call. Available at http://www.sec.gov.

Source: Available at http://www.sec.gov.

Why Is Accounting for Income Taxes So Complex?

ASC 740 provides the general rules that apply to the computation of a company's income tax provision. The basic principles that underlie these rules are fairly straightforward, but the application of the rules themselves can be very complex. Much of the complexity is due to the fact that the U.S. tax laws are complex and often ambiguous. In addition, companies frequently prepare their financial statements (Form 10-K) much earlier than their corresponding tax returns. For example, a calendar-year corporation generally files its Form 10-K with the SEC in February or early March, but it might not file its federal income tax return (Form 1120) with the Internal Revenue Service (IRS) until September or October.[4] As a result, management often must exercise a high degree of judgment in estimating the income tax return positions currently and in future years when a tax return position might be challenged by the tax authorities.

---

[4]The due date for a federal income tax return filed by a calendar-year corporation is April 15, but corporations can request a five-month extension to October 15 by filing Form 7004 and paying any remaining tax liability.

After the tax return has been filed, it may take five years or more before it is audited by the IRS and the final tax liability is determined.[5] For example, General Electric Company (GE) mentioned in its Form 10-K for 2017 that the IRS was auditing its tax returns for 2012 and 2013 and had begun the audit for 2014 and 2015. GE also noted that it files more than 5,000 income tax returns in over 290 global taxing jurisdictions!

Objectives of ASC 740

ASC 740 applies only to *income* taxes levied by the U.S. federal government, U.S. state and local governments, and non-U.S. ("foreign") governments. The FASB defines an *income tax* as a tax *based on income*. This definition excludes property taxes, excise taxes, sales taxes, and value-added taxes. Companies report nonincome taxes as expenses in the computation of their net income before taxes.

ASC 740 has two primary objectives. One is to "recognize the amount of taxes payable or refundable in the current year," referred to as the **current tax liability or asset**.[6] A second objective is to "recognize deferred tax liabilities and assets for the future tax consequences of events that have been recognized in an entity's financial statements or tax returns."[7] Both objectives relate to reporting a company's income tax amounts on the balance sheet, not on the income statement. The FASB refers to this method as the "asset and liability approach" to accounting for income taxes.[8] The FASB chose this approach because it is the most consistent with the definitions in FASB Concepts Statement No. 6, *Elements of Financial Statements*, and produces the most useful and understandable information.[9]

To compute the deferred tax liability or asset, a company calculates the future tax effects attributable to temporary book and tax differences and **tax carryforwards**.[10] As you learned in the Corporate Operations chapter, temporary differences generally can be thought of as revenue (income) or expenses (deductions) that will appear on both the income statement and the tax return but in different periods. Temporary differences that are cumulatively favorable (that is, cause cumulative taxable income to be less than cumulative pretax book income) create deferred tax liabilities, while temporary differences that are cumulatively unfavorable (cause cumulative taxable income to exceed cumulative pretax book income) create deferred tax assets.

Example 17-1

Before she began the income tax provision process, Elise knew she needed to get the ending balances in PCC's deferred tax accounts from the prior year. Accordingly, she retrieved PCC's prior year balance sheet (Exhibit 17-1) and the deferred tax component of the company's income tax note (Exhibit 17-2).

Looking at Exhibit 17-2, what income tax accounts appear on PCC's balance sheet from the prior year?

Answer: PCC has a net deferred tax liability of $1,680,210.

Since its inception, has PCC had net favorable or unfavorable temporary differences (i.e., has PCC's cumulative pretax net income been greater or less than its taxable income)?

Answer: PCC's net deferred tax liability indicates that the company has had net cumulative favorable temporary differences, which indicates its cumulative pretax net income has exceeded its cumulative taxable income.

---

[5]Although the statute of limitations for a filed income tax return is three years, large corporations often agree to extend the statute for a longer period of time to allow the IRS to audit the return. As a result, a corporation's tax return may not be audited for five or more years from the date it is filed.

[6]ASC 740-10-10-1(a).

[7]ASC 740-10-10-1(b).

[8]FAS 109, ¶63. (This paragraph was not codified in ASC 740.)

[9]FAS 109, ¶63.

[10]ASC 740-10-25-2(b).

EXHIBIT 17-1   PCC Balance Sheet at 12/31/2017

Assets	
Current Assets	
Cash	$10,722,380
Municipal bonds	300,000
Accounts receivable	17,250,000
Less: Allowance for bad debts	(345,000)
Accounts receivable (net)	16,905,000
Inventory	4,312,500
Total current assets	$32,239,880
Noncurrent Assets	
Fixed assets	$60,000,000
Less: Accumulated depreciation	(12,000,000)
Fixed assets (net)	48,000,000
Life insurance (cash surrender value)	1,100,000
Investments	497,960
Goodwill	180,000
Total noncurrent assets	49,777,960
Total assets	$82,017,840
Liabilities and Shareholders' Equity	
Current Liabilities	
Accounts payable	$20,013,000
Reserve for warranties	430,000
Total current liabilities	$20,443,000
Noncurrent Liabilities	
Long-term debt	$40,000,000
Deferred compensation	1,200,000
Deferred tax liabilities	1,680,210
Total noncurrent liabilities	$42,880,210
Total liabilities	$63,323,210
Shareholders' Equity	
Common stock (par value = $1)	$ 500,000
Additional paid-in capital	5,000,000
Retained earnings	13,194,630
Total shareholders' equity	$18,694,630
Total liabilities and shareholders' equity	$82,017,840

EXHIBIT 17-2   PCC Deferred Tax Accounts at 12/31/2017

Deferred Tax Assets	
Allowance for bad debts	$ 72,450
Reserve for warranties	90,300
Net operating loss carryforward	5,040
Deferred compensation	252,000
Capital loss carryforward	—
Contribution carryforward	—
Total deferred tax assets	$ 419,790
Valuation allowance for deferred tax assets	—
Deferred tax assets, net of valuation allowance	$ 419,790
Deferred Tax Liabilities	
Depreciation	(2,100,000)
Total deferred tax liabilities	$(2,100,000)
Net deferred tax liabilities	$(1,680,210)

The Income Tax Provision Process

A company computes the two components of its income tax provision (current and deferred) separately (independently) for each category of income tax (U.S. federal, U.S. state and local, and international) and then combines the components to produce the total income tax provision. We can summarize the formula to compute a company's total income tax provision as:

> Total income tax provision = Current income tax expense (benefit)
> + Deferred income tax expense (benefit)

A company computes its federal income tax provision using a six-step process. These steps are:

1. Adjust pretax net income or loss for all permanent differences.
2. Identify all temporary differences and tax carryforward amounts.
3. Calculate the current income tax expense or benefit (refund).
4. Determine the ending balances in the balance sheet deferred tax asset and liability accounts.
5. Evaluate the need for a valuation allowance for gross deferred tax assets.
6. Calculate the deferred income tax expense or benefit.

LO 17-2 CALCULATING THE CURRENT AND DEFERRED INCOME TAX EXPENSE OR BENEFIT COMPONENTS OF A COMPANY'S INCOME TAX PROVISION

continued from page 17-1 . . .

Elise gathered the financial statement and tax return data she needed to get started, beginning with the workpaper template she reviewed to verify PCC's taxable income. (Exhibit 17-3 reproduces the book–tax reconciliation template from Exhibit 16-7, excluding the estimated book federal income tax expense of $2,000,000. Elise identified each of the book–tax adjustments as being either permanent (P) or temporary (T). She was ready to begin the process of computing PCC's federal income tax provision using the six-step method she had learned at firm training.

to be continued . . .

Step 1: Adjust Pretax Net Income for All Permanent Differences

As you learned in the Corporate Operations chapter, not all book–tax differences meet the definition of a temporary difference. Some differences will appear only on the income statement or the tax return but not on both. Examples of items that affect only the income statement are tax-exempt interest income and nondeductible fines. Items that appear only on the tax return include the dividends received deduction and the excess tax over book benefit from the exercise of nonqualified stock options. Although they are not defined as such in ASC 740, most accounting professionals refer to these types of book–tax differences as **permanent book-tax differences.**

A company does not take permanent differences into account in computing its balance sheet deferred tax assets and liabilities. Permanent differences enter into the company's computation of taxable income and thus affect the current tax expense or

EXHIBIT 17-3 PCC Book–Tax Reconciliation Template for 2018

Premiere Computer Corporation				
Income Statement for Current Year	Book Income	Book–Tax Adjustments (Dr)	Cr	Taxable Income
Revenue from sales	$ 60,000,000			$60,000,000
Cost of goods sold	(38,000,000)			(38,000,000)
Gross profit	$ 22,000,000			$22,000,000
Other income:				
Dividend income	30,000			30,000
Interest income (P)	120,000	(12,000)		108,000
Capital gains (losses) (T)	(28,000)		28,000	0
Gain on fixed asset dispositions (T)	54,000		16,000	70,000
Gross income	$ 22,176,000			$22,208,000
Expenses:				
Compensation	(9,868,000)			(9,868,000)
Deferred compensation (T)	(300,000)	(150,000)		(450,000)
Stock option compensation (T)	(100,000)		100,000	0
Bad debt expense (T)	(165,000)		70,000	(95,000)
Charitable contributions (T)	(700,000)		73,700	(626,300)
Depreciation (T)	(2,400,000)	(700,000)		(3,100,000)
Advertising	(1,920,000)			(1,920,000)
Warranty expenses (T)	(580,000)		170,000	(410,000)
Meals (P)	(28,000)		14,000	(14,000)
Life insurance premiums (P)	(34,000)		34,000	0
Other expenses	(64,000)			(64,000)
Total expenses *before* NOL, DRD	$(16,159,000)			$16,547,300
Income *before* NOL, DRD	$ 6,017,000			$ 5,660,700
NOL carryforward from prior year (T)	0	(24,000)		(24,000)
Dividends received deduction (P)	0	(15,000)		(15,000)
Book/taxable income	$ 6,017,000	(901,000)	505,700	$ 5,621,700

benefit, either increasing or decreasing it. As a result, permanent differences usually affect a company's **effective tax rate**—or its income tax provision/pretax net income—and appear as part of the company's reconciliation of its effective tax rate with its statutory U.S. tax rate (21 percent in PCC's case).[11] We discuss ASC 740 disclosure requirements in a later section of this chapter.

Exhibit 17-4 provides a list of common permanent differences you will encounter in practice.

EXHIBIT 17-4 Common Permanent Differences

Life insurance proceeds	Disallowed premiums on officers' life insurance
Tax-exempt interest income	Dividends received deduction
Nondeductible tax penalties and fines	The windfall tax benefit from exercise of
Tax credits	nonqualified stock options
Political contributions	Entertainment expenses
Disallowed business-related meals	

[11]Prior to 2017, the windfall tax benefit from a nonqualified stock option deduction that was not treated as a temporary difference was recorded in additional paid-in capital in years prior to 2017 (public) or 2018 (private) (refer back to the previous discussion of stock option deductions in the Corporate Operations chapter).

Example 17-2

Elise went back to the template she used to review PCC's taxable income and identified the book–tax adjustments that were considered permanent in nature. What are PCC's permanent differences and are they favorable or unfavorable?

Answer: A net unfavorable permanent difference of $21,000, computed as follows:

Permanent Differences	(Favorable) Unfavorable
Tax-exempt interest income	$ (12,000)
Meals	14,000
Life insurance premiums	34,000
Dividends received deduction	(15,000)
Net unfavorable permanent difference	**$ 21,000**

Example 17-3

Elise used the net unfavorable permanent difference of $21,000 to adjust PCC's pretax net income. What is PCC's pretax net income adjusted for permanent differences?

Answer: $6,038,000, computed as follows:

PCC pretax net income	$ 6,017,000
Net unfavorable permanent difference	21,000
PCC pretax net income adjusted for permanent differences	**$6,038,000**

Elise remembered that her instructor at ASC 740 training referred to this intermediate computation as a company's **book equivalent of taxable income.** That is, this amount represents the book income that ultimately will be taxable, either currently or in the future.

Step 2: Identify All Temporary Differences and Tax Carryforward Amounts

ASC 740 formally defines a *temporary difference* as

> A difference between the tax basis of an asset or liability . . . and its reported amount in the financial statements that will result in taxable or deductible amounts in future years when the reported amount of the asset or liability is recovered or settled, respectively.[12]

As you learned in the Corporate Operations chapter, temporary differences commonly arise in four instances, as discussed below.

Revenues or Gains That Are Taxable after They Are Recognized in Financial Income An example of this type of favorable book–tax adjustment is gain from an installment sale that is recognized for financial accounting purposes in the year of sale but recognized over the collection period for tax purposes.[13]

Expenses or Losses That Are Deductible after They Are Recognized in Financial Income Examples of this type of unfavorable book–tax adjustment include bad debt expenses, warranty expenses, and accrued compensation and vacation pay that are recorded using the reserve method for financial accounting purposes but can be

---

[12]ASC 740-10-20 Glossary.

[13]Consistent with the terminology introduced in the Corporate Operations chapter, a "favorable" book–tax adjustment is one that reduces current-year taxable income compared to current-year net income.

deducted only when paid on the tax return.[14] Capitalized inventory costs under §263A also fall into this category, as do nonqualified stock option compensation expenses that are recorded at the grant date for financial reporting purposes but do not become tax deductible until the exercise date.

Revenues or Gains That Are Taxable before They Are Recognized in Financial Income An example of such an unfavorable book–tax adjustment is a prepayment of income that is recognized in the year received for tax purposes but not recognized for financial accounting purposes until the revenue is earned.

Expenses or Losses That Are Deductible before They Are Recognized in Financial Income A common example of such a favorable book–tax adjustment is the excess of tax depreciation over financial reporting depreciation.

Temporary differences also can arise from items that cannot be associated with a particular asset or liability for financial accounting purposes but produce revenue (income) or expense (deduction) that has been recognized in the financial statement and will result in taxable or deductible amounts in future years. For example, a net operating loss carryover and a net capital loss carryover create unfavorable temporary differences in the year they arise without being associated with a specific asset or liability.

Exhibit 17-5 lists common temporary differences.

EXHIBIT 17-5 Common Temporary Differences

Depreciation	Reserves for bad debts (uncollectible accounts)
Accrued vacation pay	Inventory costs capitalized under §263A
Prepayments of income	Warranty reserves
Installment sale income	Stock option expense under ASC 718
Pension plan deductions	Accrued bonuses and other compensation
Accrued contingency losses	Net operating loss and net capital loss carryovers

Identifying Taxable and Deductible Temporary Differences

Taxable Temporary Difference From a balance sheet perspective, a **taxable temporary difference**[15] generally arises when the financial reporting (book) basis of an asset exceeds its corresponding tax basis or when the financial reporting (book) basis of a liability is less than its corresponding tax basis. Subsequent recovery of the financial statement balance sheet basis of the asset or payment of the balance sheet liability will cause taxable income to exceed book income, by either creating a tax gain or reducing a tax deduction. The future tax cost associated with a taxable temporary difference is recorded on the balance sheet as a deferred tax liability. Taxable temporary differences generally arise when (1) revenues or gains are taxable *after* they are recognized in net income (e.g., gross profit from an installment sale) and (2) expenses or losses are deductible on the tax return *before* they reduce net income (e.g., excess tax depreciation over financial accounting depreciation).

Deductible Temporary Difference **Deductible temporary differences**[16] generally arise when (1) revenues or gains are taxable *before* they are recognized in net income (e.g., prepayments of subscriptions) and (2) expenses or losses are deductible on

---

[14]Consistent with the terminology introduced in the Corporate Operations chapter, an "unfavorable" book–tax adjustment is one that increases current-year taxable income compared to current-year net income.

[15]ASC 740-10-25-23.

[16]ASC 740-10-25-23.

THE KEY FACTS

Identifying Taxable and Deductible Temporary Differences

- ASC 740 defines a temporary difference as a difference between the financial reporting and tax basis of an asset or liability that will create a future tax liability or benefit when the difference reverses.
- A cumulative excess of book over tax basis gives rise to a taxable temporary difference.
- The future tax cost associated with a taxable temporary difference is recorded on the balance sheet as a deferred tax liability.
- A cumulative excess of tax over book basis gives rise to a deductible temporary difference.
- The future tax benefit associated with a deductible temporary difference is recorded on the balance sheet as a deferred tax asset.

the tax return *after* they reduce net income (e.g., reserves for product warranty or uncollectible accounts). From a balance sheet perspective, a deductible temporary difference generally arises when the financial reporting (book) basis of an asset is less than its corresponding tax basis or the financial reporting (book) basis of a liability exceeds its corresponding tax basis. Subsequent recovery of the financial reporting balance sheet basis of the asset or payment of the balance sheet liability will cause taxable income to be less than book income, by either creating a tax loss or increasing a tax deduction. The future tax benefit associated with a deductible temporary difference is recorded on the balance sheet as a deferred tax asset.

Unfavorable temporary differences that do not have balance sheet accounts, such as net operating loss carryovers, net capital loss carryovers, and charitable contribution carryovers, must be tracked to ensure that the appropriate adjustment is made to a company's deferred tax asset accounts when the carryover is used on a future tax return.

Example 17-4

Elise decided to separate PCC's temporary differences as being cumulatively favorable or cumulatively unfavorable (see Exhibit 17-3). What are PCC's taxable (cumulatively favorable) temporary differences?[17]

Answer: PCC has one taxable temporary difference that arises in the current year—the excess of current-year tax depreciation over book depreciation in the amount of $684,000. The gain on the sale of the fixed asset appears as an unfavorable difference, but it actually represents the reversal of a previously recorded favorable difference, the excess of tax over book depreciation. This "drawdown" of a previously recorded taxable temporary difference reduces the cumulatively favorable temporary differences arising in the current year. Elise summarized the taxable temporary differences as follows:

Taxable Temporary Differences	Amount
Excess of tax over book depreciation	$ (700,000)
Gain on fixed asset dispositions	16,000
Total taxable temporary differences	**$(684,000)**

What are PCC's deductible (cumulatively unfavorable) temporary differences?

Answer: The deduction of previously accrued deferred compensation and PCC's use of its net operating loss carryover appear as favorable temporary differences in 2018, but they are actually reversals of prior-year unfavorable temporary differences and reduce the cumulatively unfavorable temporary differences. PCC has net deductible temporary differences of $267,700, computed as follows:

Deductible Temporary Differences	Amount
Net capital loss carryforward	$ 28,000
Deferred compensation	(150,000)
Stock option compensation	100,000
Bad debt expense	70,000
Charitable contribution carryforward	73,700
Warranty expense	170,000
NOL carryforward from prior year	(24,000)
Total deductible temporary differences	**$ 267,700**

For the year, PCC has a net taxable (favorable) temporary difference of $(416,300) [$(684,000) + $267,700].

---

[17]The correct way to make this calculation is to compare book and tax balance sheet basis differences. As we mentioned earlier, PCC does not keep a tax balance sheet, which means the provision work requires "rolling forward" cumulative book and tax differences from prior years.

Step 3: Compute the Current Income Tax Expense or Benefit

In many respects, the computation of the current portion of a company's tax provision appears to be straightforward. ASC 740 defines the **current income tax expense or benefit** as

> The amount of income taxes paid or payable (or refundable) for a year as determined by applying the provisions of the enacted tax law to the taxable income or excess of deductions over revenues for that year.[18]

In most cases, the major component of a company's current income tax expense or benefit is the income tax liability or refund from its current-year operations. However, there are other items that enter into the computation that do not appear on the company's income tax return (Form 1120), which adds to the complexity of the computation.

In practice, the computation of a company's current income tax expense or benefit rarely equals the actual taxes paid on the company's current-year tax returns. In particular, the current component of PCC's income tax provision also can be impacted by prior-year income tax refunds from current-year carrybacks of a net capital loss,[19] IRS audit adjustments from prior-year tax returns,[20] and changes in the company's **uncertain tax positions**—a company's reserve for taxes it has not paid but could pay in the future for positions taken on the current- and prior-year income tax returns.[21]

Example 17-5

Elise used her summary of permanent and temporary differences to verify her earlier computation of PCC's taxable income. Does using her summary of PCC's permanent and temporary differences verify her earlier computation?

Answer: Yes!

PCC pretax net income	$ 6,017,000
Net unfavorable permanent difference (from Example 17-2)	21,000
Net favorable temporary differences (from Example 17-4)	(416,300)
PCC taxable income	**$5,621,700**

What is PCC's current income tax expense, assuming a tax rate of 21 percent?

Answer: $1,180,557, computed as follows:

PCC taxable income	$ 5,621,700
	× 21%
PCC federal income tax payable	**$1,180,557**

What tax accounting journal entry does PCC make to record its current tax expense?

Answer:

Current income tax expense	1,180,557	
Current income taxes payable (or cash)		1,180,557

THE KEY FACTS

Computing the Deferred Income Tax Expense or Benefits

- Identify current-year changes in taxable and deductible temporary differences.
- Determine ending balances in each deferred tax asset and liability balance sheet account.
- Identify carryovers (net operating loss, capital loss, charitable contributions) not on the balance sheet.
- The current-year deferred income tax expense or benefit is the difference between the deferred tax asset and liability balances at the beginning of the year and the end of the year, as well as changes in tax carryovers.

---

[18]ASC 740-10-20 Glossary.

[19]Requested on Form 1139 or Form 1120X.

[20]Agreed to on Form 5701.

[21]Calculated in the uncertain tax position workpapers.

Step 4: Determine the Ending Balances in the Balance Sheet Deferred Tax Asset and Liability Accounts

continued from page 17-6...

Having calculated the current portion of PCC's income tax provision, Elise turned her attention to computing the deferred component of PCC's income tax provision. She knew from training that the technically correct method to compute PCC's deferred tax provision is to compare the financial accounting (book) basis of each asset and liability with its corresponding tax basis. Elise had the financial accounting basis of each account from the balance sheet, but like many companies, PCC did not keep a formal **tax accounting balance sheet.**[22] Elise would need to use an alternate method to calculate the change in the adjusted book–tax basis differences for each account she identified as being a temporary difference.

The FASB could have decided that a company should report only the "as paid" income taxes on its income statement. Investors and policy makers might favor this approach because it would disclose the actual income taxes paid or refunded (cash outflow or inflow) in the current year. However, reporting only income taxes currently payable ignores one of the basic premises underlying financial accounting, which is that the accrual method of accounting provides more relevant information to investors and creditors than the cash method of accounting.[23]

The deferred income tax expense or benefit portion of a company's income tax provision reflects the change during the year in a company's balance sheet deferred tax liabilities or assets.[24] This information provides investors and other interested parties with a measure of a company's expected future income-tax-related cash inflows or outflows resulting from book–tax differences that are temporary in nature or from tax carryovers.

ASC 740 takes an asset and liability or balance sheet approach to the computation of the deferred tax expense or benefit. The computations are based on the change in the differences between the financial accounting (book) adjusted basis of an asset or liability and its corresponding adjusted tax basis from the beginning of the year to the end of the year. Under GAAP, the company is presumed to recover these basis differences over time, resulting in future sacrifices of a company's resources (in the case of liabilities) or future recoveries of a company's resources (in the case of assets). These expected future recoveries of assets or future sacrifices of assets to settle liabilities give rise to future (deferred) tax payments or refunds that are recorded in the income tax provision in the year the differences arise rather than in the year in which the future taxes are paid or recovered.

The future tax cost of a taxable (cumulatively favorable) temporary difference is recorded on the balance sheet as a deferred tax liability. The company computes the deferred tax liability using the **enacted tax rate** that is expected to apply to taxable income in the period(s) in which the deferred tax liability is expected to be settled.[25]

---

[22]Schedule L to Form 1120 requests that the taxpayer report its financial statement balance sheet. An increasing number of corporations are finding that a "best practice" is to maintain a tax basis balance sheet separate from the financial accounting balance sheet.

[23]ASC 230, Statement of *Cash Flows,* requires an enterprise to separately disclose income taxes paid as part of the statement itself or in a note to the financial statements (usually the income taxes note or a supplemental cash flow note).

[24]ASC 740-10-20 Glossary.

[25]ASC 740-10-30-2. For federal income tax provision purposes, a corporation applies the regular tax rate in computing its deferred tax assets and liabilities. The alternative minimum tax credit carryforward is treated as a prepaid income tax and is reported as a deferred tax asset on the balance sheet.

Example 17-6

Lacking a formal tax-basis balance sheet, Elise identified the current-year temporary differences and adjusted ("rolled forward") the cumulative differences at the beginning of the year to get the end-of-the-year adjusted book–tax basis differences. She used this change in the adjusted book–tax basis difference to compute the deferred tax expense or benefit for the current year. Elise reviewed her schedules of favorable and unfavorable temporary differences (from Example 17-4). She identified one favorable temporary difference related to an asset recorded on the balance sheet—the excess of tax depreciation over book depreciation. Elise retrieved the fixed asset workpapers and recorded the changes in the financial accounting and tax accumulated depreciation balances of PCC's fixed assets from the beginning of the year to the end of the year related to current-year depreciation.

*Financial accounting change in accumulated depreciation**	
Beginning of the year	$12,000,000
End of the year	14,400,000
Net change	$ 2,400,000

*Tax accounting change in accumulated depreciation**	
Beginning of the year	$22,000,000
End of the year	25,100,000
Net change	$ 3,100,000

*Not given in the original facts; assumed for purposes of this example.

The net increase in tax accounting accumulated depreciation over the corresponding financial accounting depreciation created a current-year $700,000 favorable (taxable) temporary difference (i.e., the cumulative difference between the financial accounting basis of the fixed assets increased by $700,000 over its corresponding tax basis). This increase in the cumulative favorable temporary difference requires an *increase* in PCC's deferred tax liabilities.

By what amount will PCC increase its deferred tax liabilities as a result of the increase in the adjusted book basis over the adjusted tax basis in these assets from the beginning of the year to the end of the year?

Answer: $147,000, computed as $700,000 × 21 percent.

What tax accounting journal entry does PCC record related to this transaction?
Answer:

Deferred income tax expense	147,000	
Deferred income tax liability		147,000

What if: Assume current-year book depreciation exceeded current-year tax depreciation by $700,000. What adjustment to the balance sheet would PCC be required to make?
Answer: PCC would *decrease* its deferred tax liability on the balance sheet by $147,000.

Example 17-7

Elise also saw that accumulated depreciation decreased as a result of PCC's sale of a fixed asset during the year (see Exhibit 17-3). She observed from the workpapers that PCC sold the fixed asset for $100,000, its original cost (not given in the original facts, assumed for purposes of this example). The book basis of the asset was $46,000, resulting in a book gain of $54,000. The tax gain on the sale was $70,000, which corresponds to a decrease in accumulated tax depreciation of $70,000 (i.e., the tax basis of the asset was $30,000). The excess of the reduction in accumulated tax depreciation over

(continued on page 17-14)

accumulated book depreciation of $16,000 corresponds to the excess of the tax gain over the book gain on the sale.

Financial accounting change in accumulated depreciation on the fixed asset sold	
Beginning of the year	$54,000
End of the year	0
Net change	$54,000
Tax accounting change in accumulated depreciation on the fixed asset sold	
Beginning of the year	$70,000
End of the year	0
Net change	$70,000

By what amount will PCC *decrease* its deferred tax liabilities as a result of the decrease in the tax-over-book basis in this asset from the beginning of the year to the end of the year?

Answer: $3,360, computed as $16,000 × 21 percent.

What tax accounting journal entry does PCC record *related to this transaction*?

Answer:

Deferred income tax liability	3,360	
Deferred income tax benefit		3,360

This drawdown of the excess of tax accumulated depreciation over book accumulated depreciation requires a reduction in the previously recorded deferred tax liability that resulted from the book–tax difference created by the excess of tax depreciation over book depreciation in prior periods.

By what amount will PCC increase its current income tax expense as a result of this transaction (the tax gain was $70,000)?

Answer: $14,700, computed as $70,000 × 21 percent.

What tax accounting journal entry does PCC record *related to this transaction*?

Answer:

Current income tax expense	14,700	
Income taxes payable		14,700

What is the net impact of this transaction on PCC's income tax provision?

Answer: A net increase of $11,340, computed as:

Current income tax expense	$ 14,700
Deferred income tax benefit	(3,360)
Net increase in PCC's income tax provision	**$11,340**

What do these journal entries accomplish?

Answer: The $11,340 provision reflects the tax expense related to the book gain of $54,000, computed as follows:

Book gain on sale of the fixed asset	$ 54,000
	× 21%
Net increase in PCC's income tax provision	**$11,340**

The recording of a deferred tax liability for years in which tax depreciation exceeds book depreciation anticipates the difference in the book and tax gain that will result when the fixed asset eventually is recovered, either through sale or depreciation of the entire basis.

Example 17-8

Using her cumulative temporary differences template, Elise recorded the cumulative taxable temporary differences and the corresponding deferred tax liability at the beginning of the year (BOY) and the end of the year (EOY) to determine the change in the deferred tax liability related to accumulated depreciation.

		Premiere Computer Corporation Temporary Difference Scheduling Template				
Taxable Temporary Differences	BOY Cumulative T/D	Beginning Deferred Taxes (@ 21%)	Current-Year Change	EOY Cumulative T/D	Ending Deferred Taxes (@ 21%)
Accumulated depreciation	(10,000,000)*	**(2,100,000)**	(684,000)	(10,684,000)	**(2,243,640)**

*$22,000,000 − $12,000,000, from Example 17-6.

What is the net increase in PCC's deferred tax liability related to fixed assets for 2018?

Answer: $143,640, the change in the cumulative deferred tax liability from the beginning of the year ($2,100,000) to the end of the year ($2,243,640).

This amount corresponds to the increase in the deferred tax liability due to the current-year change in the book–tax difference related to depreciation ($700,000) less the reduction in the deferred tax liability due to the change in the book–tax difference related to accumulated depreciation written off on the sale of the fixed asset ($16,000).

What tax accounting journal entry does PCC record related to the change in total deferred tax liabilities from the beginning of the year to the end of the year?

Answer:

Deferred income tax expense	143,640	
Deferred income tax liability		143,640

Using a template that tracks the cumulative changes in the book–tax differences related to balance sheet accounts becomes especially important when a company's enacted tax rate changes. For example, the Tax Cuts and Jobs Act reduced the corporate tax rate to 21 percent for tax years beginning after December 31, 2017. The bill was signed by the president on December 22, 2017. As a result, corporations were required to revalue their U.S. deferred tax assets and liabilities existing on December 22, 2017, to reflect the lower tax rate. This discussion points to the fact that the focus of ASC 740 is to have the balance sheet deferred tax accounts reflect the tax that will be due or refunded when the underlying temporary differences reverse in a future period.

Example 17-9

What if: Assume PCC's tax rate decreased from 34 percent in 2017 to 21 percent in 2018. By what amount would PCC increase or decrease its balance sheet deferred tax liability related to the fixed asset account?

(continued on page 17-16)

Answer: PCC would *decrease* its deferred tax liability related to fixed assets by $1,300,000, calculated as follows:

Premiere Computer Corporation Temporary Difference Scheduling Template			
Taxable Temporary Differences	Cumulative T/D as of December 22, 2017	Deferred Taxes (@ 34%)	Revalued Cumulative T/D (@21%)
Accumulated depreciation	(10,000,000)	(3,400,000)	(2,100,000)

PCC would use a tax rate of 21 percent to compute the ending balance in its deferred tax liability related to fixed assets as of December 22, 2017. The net decrease in the deferred tax liability related to accumulated depreciation is $1,300,000 ($3,400,000 − $2,100,000).

What tax accounting journal entry did PCC record on December 22, 2017, *related to fixed assets*?

Answer:

Deferred income tax liability	1,300,000	
Deferred income tax expense		1,300,000

This "prior period adjustment" to the deferred tax liability balance would reduce PCC's income tax provision in the fourth quarter of 2017 and be treated as a "discrete item" in the company's effective tax rate reconciliation for 2017 (discussed later in the chapter).

Example 17-10

Returning to her temporary differences template, Elise recorded the deductible (cumulatively unfavorable) temporary differences and the corresponding deferred tax assets at the beginning of the year (BOY) and the end of the year (EOY) to determine the change in PCC's deferred tax assets during the current year.

Premiere Computer Corporation Temporary Difference Scheduling Template					
Deductible Temporary Differences	BOY Cumulative T/D	Beginning Deferred Taxes (@ 21%)	Current-Year Change	EOY Cumulative T/D	Ending Deferred Taxes (@ 21%)
Allowance for bad debts	$ 345,000	$ 72,450	$ 70,000	$ 415,000	$ 87,150
Reserve for warranties	430,000	90,300	170,000	600,000	126,000
Net operating loss	24,000	5,040	(24,000)	0	0
Deferred compensation	$ 1,200,000	252,000	(150,000)	1,050,000	220,500
Stock option compensation	0	0	100,000	100,000	21,000
Net capital loss carryover	0	0	28,000	28,000	5,880
Contribution carryover	0	0	73,700	73,700	15,477
Total	$1,999,000	$419,790	$ 267,700	$2,266,700	$476,007

What is the net increase in PCC's total deferred income tax assets for 2018?

Answer: $56,217, the change in the cumulative deferred tax asset from the beginning of the year balance of $419,790 to the end of the year balance of $476,007.

What tax accounting journal entry does PCC record *related to deferred tax assets*?

Answer:

Deferred income tax assets	56,217	
Deferred income tax benefit		56,217

DETERMINING WHETHER A VALUATION ALLOWANCE IS NEEDED

`LO 17-3`

Step 5: Evaluate the Need for a Valuation Allowance for Gross Deferred Tax Assets

ASC 740 specifically precludes PCC or any company from discounting (recording the present value of) the deferred income tax liability or asset related to a temporary difference based on when the asset is expected to be recovered or the liability settled. The FASB debated whether discounting deferred income tax assets and liabilities would provide more relevant information to investors, but ultimately it decided that the complexity and cost of making the computation outweighed any benefits investors and creditors might receive.[26]

In lieu of discounting, ASC 740 requires that a company evaluate each of its gross deferred income tax assets on the balance sheet and assess the likelihood the expected tax benefit will be *realized* in a future period. The income tax benefits reflected in the deferred tax assets can be realized (converted into cash) only if the company expects to have sufficient taxable income or tax liability in the future or carryback period to absorb the unused tax deductions or credits before they expire.

Determining the Need for a Valuation Allowance

Under ASC 740, if a company determines that it is more likely than not (with a likelihood greater than 50 percent) that some portion or all of the deferred tax assets will not be realized in a future period, it must offset the deferred tax assets with a **valuation allowance** to reflect the amount the company does not expect to realize in the future.[27] Valuation allowances operate as *contra accounts* to the deferred income tax assets on the balance sheet, much like the allowance for bad debts a company must estimate for its accounts receivable. Companies usually disclose the amount of the valuation allowance in the income tax footnote to the financial statements.

Management must assess whether it is more likely than not that a deferred income tax asset will *not* be realized in the future based on all available evidence, both positive and negative. ASC 740 identifies four sources of potential future taxable income, two of which are objective and two of which are subjective and determined by management judgment.[28] The objective sources are (1) future reversals of existing taxable temporary differences and (2) taxable income in prior carryback year(s). The subjective sources are (1) expected future taxable income exclusive of reversing temporary differences and carryforwards and (2) tax planning strategies.

Future Reversals of Existing Taxable Temporary Differences   Existing taxable (cumulatively favorable) temporary differences provide taxable income when they are recovered in a future period. For example, the recovery of the excess of an asset's financial accounting (book) basis over its tax basis, whether through sale or depreciation, will cause taxable income to be higher than pretax net income in the periods in which the excess financial accounting basis is recovered. If the reversing taxable temporary differences provide sufficient future taxable income to absorb the reversing deductible temporary differences, the company does not record a valuation allowance against the deferred tax asset.

---

[26]FAS 109, ¶¶198–199. (These paragraphs were not codified in ASC 740.)

[27]ASC 740-10-30-5(e).

[28]ASC 740-10-30-18.

THE KEY FACTS

Determining whether a Valuation Allowance is Needed

- A valuation allowance is required if it is more likely than not that some or all of the deferred tax asset will not be realized in the future.
- To make this determination, a company must determine its sources of future (or past) taxable income.
  - Taxable income in carryback years.
  - Reversing taxable temporary differences in future years.
  - Expected taxable income in future years from other than reversing taxable temporary differences.
  - Expected taxable income in future taxable years from implementing tax planning strategies.
- A company must evaluate positive and negative evidence in deciding whether a valuation allowance is needed.
- A company must monitor whether increases or decreases should be made to the valuation allowance account every quarter.

Taxable Income in Prior Carryback Year(s) The company does not record a valuation allowance if the tax benefit from the realization of a deferred income tax asset can be carried back to a prior year that has sufficient taxable income (or capital gain net income in the case of a net capital loss carryback) to absorb the realized tax benefit.

Expected Future Taxable Income Exclusive of Reversing Temporary Differences and Carryforwards ASC 740 allows a company to consider taxable income it expects to earn in future periods in determining whether a valuation allowance is necessary. The company might support its predictions of future taxable income with evidence of existing contracts or a sales backlog that will produce enough taxable income to realize the deferred tax asset when it reverses. In addition, the company could demonstrate that it has a strong earnings history if a deferred tax asset arises from a loss that could be considered out of the ordinary and not from a continuing condition. Firms in cyclical industries, such as automobile manufacturers, builders, and airlines, traditionally have cited a history of past income as evidence of expected future income.

Tax Planning Strategies The most subjective source of future taxable income to support the realization of a deferred income tax asset is the company's ability and willingness to employ tax strategies in those future periods to create the taxable income needed to absorb the deferred tax asset. ASC 740 allows a company to consider actions it might take to create sufficient taxable income to absorb a deferred income tax asset, provided such actions (1) are prudent and feasible; (2) are actions an enterprise would take only to prevent an operating loss or tax credit carryforward from expiring unused; and (3) would result in realization of the deferred tax assets.

The company does not have to implement the strategy to avoid recording a valuation allowance, but management must be willing and able to execute the strategy if the need arises. Tax planning strategies could include (1) selling and leasing back operating assets, (2) changing inventory accounting methods (e.g., from LIFO to FIFO), (3) refraining from making voluntary contributions to the company pension plan, (4) electing to capitalize certain expenditures (e.g., research and development costs) rather than deduct them currently, (5) selling noncore assets, (6) converting tax-exempt investments into taxable investments, and (7) electing the alternative depreciation system (straight line instead of declining balance).

Negative Evidence That a Valuation Allowance Is Needed ASC 740 requires that a company consider negative evidence as well as positive evidence in determining whether it is more likely than not that a deferred income tax asset will not be realized in the future. Negative evidence includes (1) cumulative (book) losses in recent years, (2) a history of net operating (capital) losses and credits expiring unused, (3) an expectation of losses in the near future, and (4) unsettled circumstances that, if resolved unfavorably, will result in losses from continuing operations in future years (e.g., the loss of a patent on a highly profitable drug).[29] As a general rule, public accounting firms interpret "recent years" with regard to cumulative book losses as a rolling 12 quarters (i.e., 36 months). As with all general rules, there are exceptions depending on the industry.

---

[29]ASC 740-10-30-21.

TAXES IN THE REAL WORLD Berkshire Hathaway's $29 Billion Gift From Congress

When Berkshire Hathaway released its highly anticipated Form 10-K for 2017, the company announced that its gain in net worth for the year was $65.3 billion, but as CEO Warren Buffett noted, "A large portion of our gain did not come from anything we accomplished at Berkshire. The $65 billion gain is nonetheless real – rest assured of that. But only $36 billion came from Berkshire's operations. The remaining $29 billion was delivered to us in December when Congress rewrote the U.S. Tax Code."[30] What was the source of this $29 billion? Deferred tax accounting! At September 30, 2017, Berkshire Hathaway had a net deferred tax liability on its balance sheet of $85 billion, most of which was tax-effected at 35% (the statutory tax rate). When Congress reduced the corporate tax rate to 21%, Berkshire Hathaway was required to revalue this liability at 21% to the extent the associated taxable temporary differences were associated with U.S. book-tax differences. Using a back-of-the-envelope calculation, the $85 billion deferred tax liability translates to approximately $240 billion of book-tax differences ($85 / .35). Valued at 21%, this net book-tax difference would translate to a deferred tax liability of $51 billion. Berkshire Hathaway would reduce its net deferred tax liability from $85 billion to $51 billion. The $34 billion reduction in the balance sheet basis would be accompanied by a decrease in deferred tax expense of $34 billion, thus increasing net income after tax and, ultimately, retained earnings (net worth), by $34 billion. The company stated in its Form 10-K that the benefit from revaluing its deferred tax accounts was approximately $30 billion.

Example 17-11

Elise created a workpaper that listed PCC's ending balances in its deferred tax assets and liabilities at December 31, 2018 (from Examples 17-8 and 17-10), as follows:

PCC Deferred Tax Accounts at 12/31/2018

Deferred Tax Assets	
Allowance for bad debts	$ 87,150
Reserve for warranties	126,000
Net operating loss carryforward	0
Deferred compensation	220,500
Stock option compensation	21,000
Net capital loss carryforward	5,880
Charitable contribution carryforward	15,477
Total deferred tax assets	**$ 476,007**
Deferred tax liabilities	
Depreciation	(2,243,640)
Total deferred tax liabilities	$ (2,243,640)
Net deferred tax liabilities	**$(1,767,633)**

[30]Warren Buffett's Letter to the Shareholders of Berkshire Hathaway, Inc., February 24, 2018, page 3.

What *positive* evidence should Elise consider in her evaluation as to whether PCC should record a valuation allowance against some or all of the deferred tax assets?

Answer: PCC has an excess of deferred tax liabilities over deferred tax assets of $1,767,633. When the book–tax depreciation difference reverses in the future, this will provide PCC with enough taxable income to absorb the reversing deferred tax assets.

What *negative* evidence should Elise consider in her evaluation as to whether PCC should record a valuation allowance against some or all of the deferred tax assets?

Answer: The deferred tax asset related to the charitable contribution carryover has a short carryover expiration date (five years). Elise may need to schedule out when the depreciation differences will reverse to determine if the reversals alone will provide PCC with enough taxable income to absorb the contribution carryover within the next five years.

More problematic, the net capital loss carryover has both a short carryover expiration date (five years) and requires PCC to recognize net capital gains in future periods to absorb the net capital loss. A reversal of the book–tax depreciation temporary difference will not provide PCC with net capital gain to absorb the net capital loss carryover.

What other sources of *positive* evidence should Elise consider in her evaluation as to whether PCC should record a valuation allowance against the deferred tax asset related to the net capital loss carryover?

Answer: Two additional sources of positive evidence are management's projections of future taxable income from sources other than reversing taxable temporary differences and future taxable income from tax planning strategies. Because PCC is in the business of manufacturing and selling computer-related equipment, any additional taxable income it generates from selling additional equipment will produce ordinary income. The company likely will have to rely on an assertion that management has a "prudent" *tax planning strategy* it would be willing to use to generate net capital gain in the future. An example of such a strategy might be management's willingness to sell a parcel of land held for investment to generate a capital gain sufficient to absorb the net capital loss.

Example 17-12

What if: Assume PCC has had net book losses of $5,000,000 and $2,500,000 in 2016 and 2017, respectively. How might this additional fact influence Elise's assessment about the need for a valuation allowance?

Answer: PCC would have a cumulative book loss of $1,483,000 over the past 36 months at December 31, 2018 (combined book losses of $7,500,00 in excess of 2017 book income of $6,017,000 from Exhibit 17-3). ASC 740 states that a cumulative loss "in recent years" is considered objective negative evidence that may be hard to overcome. Elise would have to consider other sources of positive evidence that will outweigh the "significant" negative evidence in this situation. Often, the national office of the firm will make the determination as to whether a valuation allowance is required when a client experiences a 36-month cumulative loss.

Example 17-13

What if: Assume PCC just lost a big account to its competitor but the company reported cumulative net income in the current and prior two years. How might this additional fact influence Elise's assessment about the need for a valuation allowance?

Answer: Expectations of future events can outweigh historic results. In this case, Elise would have to seriously consider whether a valuation allowance would be required to the extent that reversing taxable temporary differences would not absorb expected future losses.

Step 6: Calculate the Deferred Income Tax Expense or Benefit

Example 17-14

After discussing with management its assessment of the company's sources of future taxable income, Elise concurred with management that the company did not need to record a valuation allowance for 2018. Elise now had the pieces to determine PCC's deferred income tax expense or benefit for 2018. Using the solutions from Examples 17-8 and 17-10, what is PCC's deferred income tax provision for 2018?

Answer: $87,423 net deferred tax expense, computed as follows:

Gross deferred tax expense	$143,640	(Example 17-8)
Gross deferred tax benefit	(56,217)	(Example 17-10)
Net deferred tax expense	**$ 87,423**	

What is PCC's total income tax provision for 2018 (also use the solution from Example 17-5)?

Answer: $1,267,980 income tax expense, computed as follows:

Current tax expense	$ 1,180,557	(Example 17-5)
Gross deferred tax expense	143,640	
Gross deferred tax benefit	(56,217)	
Income tax expense	**$1,267,980**	

There is a straightforward back-of-the-envelope method of verifying the ASC 740 approach to calculating PCC's total tax provision. Under the assumption that all temporary differences will appear on a tax return in a current or future period, the total tax provision should reflect the tax that ultimately will be paid on pretax net income adjusted for permanent differences. Remember from Example 17-3 that this amount is sometimes referred to as a company's _book equivalent of taxable income_. The total income tax provision should equal the company's tax rate times its book equivalent of taxable income. We emphasize that this approach to computing a company's income tax provision is not in accordance with GAAP and will not provide the correct answer when there are changes in a company's income tax rate.

Example 17-15

Elise retrieved her computation of PCC's book equivalent of taxable income (from Example 17-3), as follows:

PCC pretax net income	$6,017,000
Net unfavorable permanent difference	21,000
PCC book equivalent of taxable income	$6,038,000

What is PCC's total tax provision using book equivalent of taxable income as a base?

Answer: $1,267,980, computed as follows:

PCC's book equivalent of taxable income	$ 6,038,000
	× 21%
PCC's total tax provision	**$1,267,980**

This computation confirms the computation made under ASC 740 from Example 17-15.

LO 17-4 # ACCOUNTING FOR UNCERTAINTY IN INCOME TAX POSITIONS

As you have learned in your study of the U.S. income tax laws, the answer to every tax question is not always certain. Taxpayers and the IRS can differ in their opinions as to whether an expenditure is deductible or must be capitalized, or whether income is taxable or is deferred or exempt from taxation. When irresolvable disputes arise, the taxpayer can petition the courts to resolve the tax treatment of a transaction. Taxpayers and the IRS can appeal decisions of the lower courts to the appellate courts and ultimately to the U.S. Supreme Court.

Taxpayers also take tax positions that can be disputed by state and local taxing authorities and international tax authorities. For example, the taxpayer and a state (international) tax authority may differ on whether the taxpayer has earned income in that jurisdiction and should pay tax on such income. The courts may not resolve this issue for many years after the original transaction takes place. If the courts do not resolve the issue in the taxpayer's favor, the taxpayer will be subject to interest and possible penalties on the tax owed.

For financial accounting purposes, a company must determine whether it can record the current or future tax benefits from an uncertain tax position in its financial statement for the period in which the transaction takes place, knowing that the ultimate resolution of the tax position may not be known until some time in the future.

FAS 109 as originally written provided no specific guidance on how to deal with uncertain tax positions. As a result, companies generally applied the principles of FAS 5, *Accounting for Contingencies* (codified as ASC 450), to uncertain tax positions. The FASB became concerned that companies were not applying FAS 5 uniformly, leading to diversity in practice and financial statements that were not comparable. After much debate, the FASB issued FASB Interpretation (FIN) No. 48, *Accounting for Uncertainty in Income Taxes—An Interpretation of FASB Statement No. 109*, in July 2006, effective for years beginning after December 15, 2006. FIN 48 has been codified in ASC 740. The objective of FIN 48 is to provide a uniform approach to recording and disclosing tax benefits resulting from tax positions that are considered to be uncertain.

ASC 740 (FIN 48) applies a two-step process to evaluating tax positions. ASC 740 refers to the first step as *recognition*.[31] A company must determine whether it is *more likely than not* (a greater than 50 percent probability) that a tax position will be sustained on examination by the IRS or other taxing authority, including resolution of any appeals within the court system, based on the technical merits of the position. In making this determination, the company must presume that the taxing authority (IRS) will examine the tax position with full knowledge of all relevant information. In other words, the company cannot take into account the possibility that the taxing authority will not audit the uncertain tax position (playing the "audit lottery").

The second step is referred to as *measurement*.[32] If the tax position meets the more-likely-than-not threshold (a subjective determination), the company must determine the amount of the benefit to record in the financial statements or, from an ASC 740 perspective, how much of its claimed tax benefit the company is not allowed to recognize. (ASC 740 refers to this unclaimed amount as "unrecognized tax benefits.") Under ASC 740, the company records the largest amount of the benefit, as calculated on a cumulative probability basis, which is more likely than not to be realized on the ultimate settlement of the tax position.

Application of ASC 740 to Uncertain Tax Positions

ASC 740 applies to all *tax positions* dealing with income taxes. As a result, it pertains to a tax position taken on a current or previously filed tax return and a tax position that will

---

[31]ASC 740-10-25-5 through 25-7.
[32]ASC 740-10-30-7.

be taken on a future tax return that is reflected in the financial statements as a deferred tax asset or liability. ASC 740 also applies to tax positions that result in permanent differences (e.g., the domestic production activities deduction and credits) and to decisions not to file a tax return in a particular jurisdiction. For example, assume a company deducts an expenditure on its current tax return, which the IRS may challenge on audit in a future period. The deduction produces a net operating loss that will be carried forward and offset against future taxable income. ASC 740 addresses whether the company can *recognize* the deferred tax asset related to the NOL carryforward on its balance sheet. Once the recognition hurdle has been overcome, the company must then evaluate whether it is more likely than not that the deferred tax asset will be *realized* in the future period (i.e., whether a valuation allowance should be recorded).

Step 1: Recognition   A company first must determine whether it is more likely than not that its tax position on a particular account will be sustained on IRS examination based on its technical merits. If the company believes this threshold has been met, it can record (recognize) the tax benefit of the tax position on its financial statements as a reduction in its current tax expense or an increase in its deferred tax benefit. The company must presume the IRS will examine this tax position with full knowledge of all relevant information. However, in deciding whether the more-likely-than-not threshold has been met, the company can take into account how the tax position might be resolved if litigated. This requires the company to evaluate the sources of authority that address this issue (i.e., the tax law, regulations, legislative history, IRS rulings, and court opinions).

Step 2: Measurement   After the company determines that the more-likely-than-not recognition threshold has been met, it must compute the amount of the tax benefit to recognize in its financial statements. ASC 740 states that the tax position is to be measured as

> the largest amount of tax benefit that is greater than 50 percent likely of being realized upon ultimate settlement with a taxing authority that has full knowledge of all relevant information.[33]

This measurement process requires the company to make a cumulative probability assessment of all likely outcomes of the audit and litigation process. The company then recognizes the amount that has a greater than 50 percent probability of being sustained on examination and subsequent litigation.

The amount of the tax benefit that is not recognized ("unrecognized tax benefit") is recorded as a liability on the balance sheet (usually labeled as "Income Taxes Payable"). The corresponding "debit" to record the balance sheet liability is to *current* income tax expense (or a decrease in income tax benefit). If the company expects the uncertain tax position to be resolved in the next 12 months, the balance sheet payable is characterized as current. Otherwise, the payable is characterized as being noncurrent. The increase in tax expense is added to the current portion of the provision under the theory that this is an on-demand liability.

Example 17-16

Assume PCC had taken a research credit of $500,000 on its 2018 tax return. There was some discussion about whether all of the company's activities qualified for the credit.

What threshold must be met before PCC can *recognize* any of the tax benefit from the "uncertain" portion of the research credit on its financial statements?

Answer: PCC must determine that it is more likely than not that its tax position on the research credit will be sustained by the IRS on examination based on its technical merits.

[33]Ibid.

Example 17-17

PCC determined that it was more likely than not that the tax position would be sustained on audit and litigation. The tax department calculated the probability of receiving a full or partial benefit after resolution of the issue as follows:

Potential Estimated Tax Benefit	Individual Probability of Being Realized (%)	Cumulative Probability of Being Realized (%)
$500,000	60	60
$300,000	25	85
$200,000	10	95
$0	5	100

Based on these probabilities, how much of the uncertain tax benefit of $500,000 can PCC recognize?

Answer: $500,000. PCC can recognize all $500,000 of the research credit tax benefit because this amount is the largest amount that has a greater than 50 percent cumulative probability of being realized on the ultimate settlement of the tax position.

Example 17-18

What if: Assume PCC's tax department had assessed the cumulative probabilities of sustaining the research credit tax benefit as follows:

Potential Estimated Tax Benefit	Individual Probability of Being Realized (%)	Cumulative Probability of Being Realized (%)
$500,000	40	40
$300,000	30	70
$200,000	20	90
0	10	100

Based on these probabilities, how much of the uncertain tax benefit of $500,000 can PCC recognize?

Answer: $300,000. PCC can recognize $300,000 of the research credit tax benefit because this amount is the largest amount that has a greater than 50 percent cumulative probability of being realized on the ultimate settlement of the tax position. This translates into management believing that $300,000 of the uncertain research credit will be sustained on audit.

What would be PCC's journal entry to record the portion of the tax benefit that cannot be recognized?

Answer: PCC would establish a liability for the $200,000 difference between the amount of the benefit received on the current-year tax return ($500,000) and the amount the company ultimately expects to receive ($300,000). PCC would record the following journal entry:

Current income tax expense	200,000	
Income taxes payable		200,000

The income taxes payable account is characterized as noncurrent on the balance sheet if PCC does not expect the "uncertain tax position" (UTP) to be resolved within the next 12 months. The uncertain tax benefit is recorded as a current tax expense because this is the additional amount of taxes PCC would pay if it prepared its tax return by deducting only $300,000 of the uncertain research credit instead of $500,000.

Subsequent Events

ASC 740 requires a company to monitor subsequent events (e.g., the issuance of new regulations, rulings, court opinions) that might change the company's assessment that a tax position will be sustained on audit and litigation. As facts and circumstances change, a company must reevaluate the tax benefit amount it expects to realize in the future. For example, the Treasury might issue a regulation or ruling that clarifies its tax position on a particular item. This regulation could change a company's assessment that its tax position meets the more-likely-than-not threshold required for recognition.

In July 2015, the U.S. Tax Court held in favor of Altera, Inc. that the IRS's challenge to its transfer pricing methodology (inter-company cost sharing for the development of intangibles) was invalid. After the decision, the IRS filed an appeal with the U.S. Court of Appeals for the Ninth Circuit, which is still pending in 2018. Microsoft Corp., which had a similar tax-related uncertain tax position, concluded that no adjustment should be made to the company's uncertain tax benefit balance because of their was still uncertainty as to the ultimate outcome of the case. On the other hand, Jupiter Networks viewed the *Altera* decision as new information that allowed the company to reduce its uncertain tax benefit related to its cost sharing arrangements. The different reactions of these two companies to the same court case decision illustrates that the application of this accounting pronouncement is subject to management judgement.

Interest and Penalties

ASC 740 requires a company to accrue interest and any applicable penalties on liabilities it establishes for potential future tax obligations. The interest (net of the tax benefit from deducting it on a future tax return when paid) and penalties (which are not tax deductible) can be treated as part of the company's UTP-related income tax expense and income tax payable or can be recognized as interest or penalties separate from the UTP-related income tax expense. ASC 740 only requires that the company apply its election consistently from period to period. This election creates the potential for diversity in practice. For example, General Motors Corporation treats accrued interest and penalties on its uncertain tax positions as part of its selling, general, and administrative expenses, while Ford Motor Company treats accrued interest and penalties on its uncertain tax positions as part of its income tax provision.

Disclosures of Uncertain Tax Positions

One of the most controversial aspects of ASC 740 is its expansion of the disclosure requirements related to liabilities recorded due to uncertain tax positions (UTPs). ASC 740 requires the company to roll forward all unrecognized tax benefits (UTBs) on a worldwide aggregated basis. Specific line items must disclose (1) the gross amounts of increases and decreases in liabilities related to uncertain tax positions as a result of tax positions taken during a prior period, (2) the gross amounts of increases and decreases in liabilities related to uncertain tax positions as a result of tax positions taken during the current period, (3) the amounts of decreases in liabilities related to uncertain tax positions relating to settlements with taxing authorities, and (4) reductions in liabilities related to uncertain tax positions as a result of a lapse of the applicable statute of limitations (the taxing authority can no longer audit the tax return on which the tax position was taken). The UTP disclosure by Microsoft Corporation is illustrated in Exhibit 17-6.

EXHIBIT 17-6   **The UTP Disclosure of Microsoft Corporation**

The aggregate changes in the balance of unrecognized tax benefits were as follows:

Year Ended June 30	(In millions)		
	2017	**2016**	**2015**
Balance, beginning of year	**$10,104**	$ 9,599	$8,714
Decreases related to settlements	**(4)**	(201)	(50)
Increases for tax positions related to the current year	**1,277**	1,086	1,091
Increases for tax positions related to prior years	**397**	115	94
Decreases for tax positions related to prior years	**(49)**	(377)	(144)
Decreases due to lapsed statutes of limitations	**(48)**	(118)	(106)
Balance, end of year	**$11,677**	$10,104	$9,599

Opponents of FIN 48 worried that the UTB disclosures would provide the IRS with a "roadmap" to a company's uncertain tax positions.[34] The FIN 48 disclosures have not provided the IRS with the hoped-for details because the UTP disclosure does not identify the tax jurisdictions to which the uncertain tax positions relate.

Schedule UTP (Uncertain Tax Position) Statement

IRS Commissioner Shulman announced that the IRS would begin asking large corporations to report their financial statement uncertain tax positions on new Schedule UTP beginning in tax year 2010. The commissioner stated that the goals of the new schedule would be to increase transparency and efficiency in identifying audit issues and help the IRS prioritize the selection of issues and taxpayers for audit. Schedule UTP requires corporations to report any federal income tax position for which an unrecognized tax benefit has been recorded in an audited financial statement. A corporation must identify the IRC section or sections relating to the position, indicate whether the position involves a temporary or permanent difference, identify whether the tax position is a major tax position (10 percent or more of the total), rank the tax position by size, and provide a "concise" description of the UTP. Corporations with assets of $10 million or more must file Schedule UTP.

ETHICS

Pete Campbell, senior manager in the tax group in the Boston office of Bean Counters LLP, an international professional services firm, was reviewing the workpapers related to the uncertain tax positions prepared by his biggest client, Pro Vision Inc. Pete noticed that the client took the position that it did not need to record an uncertain tax benefit for a significant transaction because it had a "should level" opinion from its law firm. (A "should level" tax opinion means that the law firm believes there is a 70 to 90 percent probability that the tax benefit from the transaction will be allowed if litigated.) When Pete asked to see the tax opinion, he was told by the firm's tax director that the company did not want to disclose the item for fear the IRS also would ask to see the opinion. Pete has always had a good working relationship with the tax staff at Pro Vision and trusts their integrity.

Should Pete take the tax director's word when auditing the company's reserve for uncertain tax positions? What would you do if you were in Pete's position?

---

[34]Jesse Drucker, "Lifting the Veil on Tax Risk—New Accounting Rule Lays Bare a Firm's Liability If Transaction Is Later Disallowed by the IRS," *The Wall Street Journal,* May 25, 2007.

FINANCIAL STATEMENT DISCLOSURE AND THE COMPUTATION OF A CORPORATION'S EFFECTIVE TAX RATE

LO 17-5

Balance Sheet Classification

For the years beginning after December 15, 2016 (December 15, 2017, for all business entities other than public companies), ASC 740 requires publicly traded and privately held companies to disclose all deferred tax assets and liabilities on their balance sheets as noncurrent. Prior to the change, a business entity classified its deferred tax assets and liabilities based on the classification of the asset or liability to which the deferred tax account related. For example, a deferred tax liability related to a long-term asset (e.g., depreciation of a fixed asset) was classified as noncurrent because the related asset was classified as noncurrent on the balance sheet. Deferred tax liabilities and assets not related to a specific asset (e.g., a net operating loss carryover or organizational expenditures capitalized for tax purposes) were classified based on the expected reversal date of the temporary difference.

Income Tax Footnote Disclosure

In addition to the above balance sheet disclosure requirements, ASC 740 mandates that a company disclose the components of the net deferred tax assets and liabilities reported on its balance sheet and the total valuation allowance recognized for deferred tax assets.[35] Most companies provide this information in a footnote to the financial statements (often referred to as the *income tax footnote*). Publicly traded companies must disclose the approximate "tax effect" of each type of temporary difference and carryforward that gives rise to a *significant* portion of the net deferred tax liabilities and deferred tax assets.[36] Privately held (nonpublic) companies only need to disclose the types of significant temporary differences without disclosing the tax effects of each type. ASC 740 does not define the term *significant*, although the SEC requires a publicly traded company to disclose separately the components of its total deferred tax assets and liabilities that are 5 percent or more of the total balance.[37] Exhibit 17-7 provides the disclosure of PCC's deferred tax accounts in its income tax footnote.

ASC 740 also requires publicly traded companies to disclose the significant components of their income tax provision (expense or benefit) attributable to continuing operations in either the financial statements or a note thereto.[38] These components include the (1) current tax expense or benefit, (2) deferred tax expense or benefit, (3) the benefits of operating loss carryforwards, (4) adjustments of a deferred tax liability or asset for enacted changes in tax laws or rates, and (5) adjustments of the beginning-of-the-year balance of a valuation allowance because of a change in circumstances that causes a change in management's judgment about the realizability of the recognized deferred tax assets.

Computation and Reconciliation of the Income Tax Provision with a Company's *Hypothetical* Tax Provision
ASC 740 requires a company to reconcile its (a) reported income tax provision attributable to continuing operations with (b) the amount of income tax expense that would result from applying its U.S. statutory tax rate

---

[35] ASC 740-10-50-2.
[36] ASC 740-10-50-6.
[37] ASC 740-10-50-8 and SEC Regulation S-X, §210.4-08(h).
[38] ASC 740-10-50-9.

EXHIBIT 17-7   **PCC's Income Tax Note to Its Financial Statements**

NOTE 5 INCOME TAXES

The Company's income (loss) from continuing operations before the income tax provision by taxing jurisdiction is as follows:

	2018
United States	$6,017,000

The provision (benefit) for income taxes is as follows:

	2018
Current tax provision (benefit)	
Federal (U.S.)	$1,180,557
Deferred tax expense (benefit)	
Federal (U.S.)	87,423
Income tax provision	$1,267,980

The significant components of the Company's deferred tax assets and liabilities as of December 31, 2018, are as follows:

	2018
Deferred tax *assets*	
Allowance for bad debts	$ 87,150
Reserve for warranties	126,000
Deferred compensation	220,500
Stock option compensation	21,000
Capital loss carryover	5,880
Contribution carryover	15,477
Total deferred tax assets	$ 476,007
Valuation allowance	0
Deferred tax assets net of valuation allowance	$ 473,007
Deferred tax *liabilities*	
Depreciation	$(2,243,640)
Total deferred tax liabilities	(2,243,640)
Net deferred tax liabilities	$(1,767,633)

The capital loss carryover and the contribution carryover expire in 2023 if unused.

A reconciliation of income taxes computed by applying the statutory U.S. income tax rate to the Company's income before income taxes to the income tax provision is as follows:

	2018
Amount computed at the statutory U.S. tax rate (21%)	$1,263,570
Tax-exempt income	(2,520)
Nondeductible meals	2,940
Nondeductible life insurance premiums	7,140
Dividends received deduction	(3,150)
Income tax provision	$1,267,980

The cash amount paid during 2018 for income taxes, net of refunds, was $1,180,557.

to its pretax net income or loss from continuing operations.[39] Alternately, a company can present the reconciliation in terms of tax rates, comparing its statutory tax rate with its effective tax rate (income tax provision/pretax income from continuing operations).

Differences between a company's income tax provision and its hypothetical tax provision can arise from several sources. Income taxes paid to a state or municipality increase a company's total income tax provision over its hypothetical income tax expense. Income taxes paid to a jurisdiction outside the United States can increase or decrease a company's

---

[39]ASC 740-10-50-12. The income tax provision computed using the statutory tax rate is often referred to as the hypothetical income tax expense.

total income tax provision over its hypothetical income tax expense, depending on whether the jurisdiction taxes the company's income at more or less than the U.S. statutory rate. Permanent differences also affect the computation of a company's income tax provision. Favorable permanent differences (e.g., tax-exempt income) decrease the income tax provision relative to the hypothetical income tax provision. Unfavorable permanent differences (e.g., nondeductible fines and penalties) increase the income tax provision relative to the hypothetical income tax provision.

ASC 740 requires a publicly traded company to disclose the estimated amount and nature of each significant reconciling item, which the SEC defines as an amount equal to or greater than 5 percent of the hypothetical provision. The SEC requires nonpublicly traded companies to disclose the nature of significant reconciling items but not the reconciling amount.

Example 17-19

Elise used her schedule of permanent differences (from Example 17-2) to reconcile PCC's income tax provision ($1,267,980, from Example 17-15) with the company's hypothetical income tax provision. The permanent differences from Example 17-2 are reproduced below:

Permanent Differences	(Favorable) Unfavorable
Tax-exempt interest income	$ (12,000)
Meals	14,000
Life insurance premiums	34,000
Dividends received deduction	(15,000)

PCC's pretax net income from continuing operations in 2018 is $6,017,000 (from Exhibit 17-7).

What is PCC's *hypothetical* income tax provision for 2018?

Answer: $1,263,570, computed as $6,017,000 × 21 percent.

What is PCC's *effective tax rate* for 2018?

Answer: 21.1 percent, computed as $1,267,980/$6,017,000.

PCC's reconciliation of its hypothetical income tax provision with its actual income tax provision in 2018 was presented in Exhibit 17-7. The tax cost or benefit from each permanent difference is computed by multiplying the permanent difference (from above) times 21 percent.

Answer:

	2018
Amount computed at statutory U.S. tax rate (21%)	$1,263,570
Tax-exempt income	(2,520)
Nondeductible meals	2,940
Nondeductible life insurance premiums	7,140
Dividends received deduction	(3,150)
Income tax provision	$1,267,980

The SEC requires its registrants to separately disclose only those components of their effective tax rate reconciliations that equal or exceed 5 percent of the "hypothetical" tax expense. In the above reconciliation, PCC would only be required to separately disclose the items that equal or exceed $63,178 ($1,263,570 × 5%). None of the reconciling items exceed this amount. All of the reconciling items could be netted in the reconciliation.

Provide a reconciliation of PCC's statutory income tax rate (21 percent) with its actual effective tax rate (21.1 percent) in 2018. The percentage effect of each permanent difference is computed by dividing the tax cost or benefit from the item (from above) by PCC's pretax net income ($6,017,000).

(*continued on page 17-30*)

Answer:

	2018
Statutory U.S. tax rate	21.0%
Tax-exempt income	(0.0)
Nondeductible meals	(0.0)
Nondeductible life insurance premiums	0.1%
Dividends received deduction	(0.0)
Effective tax rate	21.1%

PCC's income tax note to its financial statements (Exhibit 17-7) provides the disclosure of PCC's reconciliation of its effective tax rate.

Importance of a Corporation's Effective Tax Rate   The effective tax rate often serves as a benchmark for companies in the same industry. However, nonrecurring events can sometimes have a significant impact on the effective tax rate. To mitigate the impact of such aberrational events, companies and their investors may use (at least for internal purposes) a different measure of effective tax rate that backs out one-time and nonrecurring events. This effective tax rate is referred to as the company's **structural tax rate.** The structural effective tax rate often is viewed as more representative of the company's effective tax rate from its normal (recurring) operations. In our example, PCC does not appear to have any nonrecurring reconciling items, which would make its effective tax rate and its structural tax rate the same.

Analysts often compute a company's **cash tax rate,** the cash taxes paid divided by pretax book income, in their evaluation of the company's tax status. As the name implies, the cash tax rate excludes deferred taxes. PCC's cash tax rate in 2018 is 19.6 percent ($1,180,557/$6,017,000). Companies that have significant favorable temporary differences can have a cash tax rate that is much lower than their accounting effective tax rate. For example, Amazon.com, Inc., reported an accounting effective tax rate of 36.6 percent and a cash tax rate of 10.6 percent in 2016!

Interim Period Effective Tax Rates

In addition to annual reports (Form 10-K), PCC also must report earnings on a quarterly basis (Form 10-Q). ASC 740-270, *Interim Reporting*, governs the preparation of these quarterly statements. ASC 740-270-30-6, states that "at the end of each interim period the entity should make its best estimate of the effective tax rate expected to be applicable for the full fiscal year" and apply this rate to the income reported in the quarterly statement. A company must reconsider its estimate of the annual rate each quarter. When the estimate changes, the company must adjust the cumulative tax provision for the year-to-date earnings to reflect the new expected annual rate. The adjusting amount becomes the company's income tax provision for the quarter.

Accounting for the Tax Cuts and Jobs Act

The changes made to the tax law by the Tax Cuts and Jobs Act, especially the reduction of the corporate tax rate to 21 percent, required companies to make significant remeasurements of their deferred tax accounts. Because the bill was signed into law on

December 22, 2017, companies were required to remeasure their deferred tax accounts as of the enactment date and include any changes in the financial statement (either the Form 10-K or Form 10-Q) that included the enactment date. The SEC recognized that the closeness of the enactment date to either the year-end or the quarter-end would make it onerous for companies to comply with ASC 740 in such a short period of time. As a result, the SEC issued Staff Accounting Bulletin (SAB) 118 to alleviate this potentially burdensome task. According to SAB 118, companies can have up to 12 months ("measurement period") from the enactment date to complete their remeasurement of their deferred tax accounts. Companies are permitted to record a provisional amount for adjustments required by the tax act for which the accounting is incomplete provided the company can make a "reasonable estimate" of the adjustment. The SEC expects enhanced disclosure of the adjustments that are provisional or incomplete and cannot be reasonably estimated.

Microsoft's disclosure of the impact of the tax act in its Form 10-Q for December 31, 2017 exemplifies the disclosure required by the SEC:

> The TCJA is effective in the second quarter of fiscal year 2018. As of December 31, 2017, we have not completed our accounting for the tax effects of the TCJA. During the quarter, we recorded a provisional net charge based on reasonable estimates for those tax effects. The provisional net charge is subject to revisions as we complete our analysis of the TCJA, collect and prepare necessary data, and interpret any additional guidance issued by the U.S. Treasury Department, Internal Revenue Service ("IRS"), FASB, and other standard-setting and regulatory bodies. Adjustments may materially impact our provision for income taxes and effective tax rate in the period in which the adjustments are made. Our accounting for the tax effects of the TCJA will be completed during the measurement period, which should not extend beyond one year from the enactment date.

FASB PROJECTS RELATED TO ACCOUNTING FOR INCOME TAXES

As part of its Disclosure Framework project, the FASB has proposed expanding the information to be provided in the income tax footnote. In particular, the FASB is considering whether to require companies to report pretax income from continuing operations, the associated income tax provision, and cash taxes paid as either U.S. or non-U.S. The FASB also wants increased disclosure regarding the nature and amounts of the valuation allowance recorded and released during the reporting period. The FASB issued a proposed Accounting Statement Update in July 2016 on this topic but has yet to formalize the disclosure requirements.

CONCLUSION

In this chapter we discussed the basic rules that govern the computation of a company's U.S. income tax provision. As a result of increased SEC and PCAOB scrutiny, the need for individuals who understand these rules has increased dramatically. The FASB requires a company to take a balance sheet approach to computing its current and future (deferred) tax liabilities or benefits (assets). The income tax provision that appears on a company's income statement becomes the amount necessary to adjust the beginning balances of these accounts to their appropriate ending balances. The FASB and SEC also impose disclosure requirements for how a company reports its tax accounts in the financial statement amounts and notes to the financial statements.

Summary

LO 17-1 Describe the objectives behind FASB ASC Topic 740, *Income Taxes*, and the income tax provision process.

- Objectives of ASC 740:
  - To recognize a current income tax liability or asset for the company's taxes payable or refundable in the current year.
  - To recognize a deferred income tax liability or asset for the income tax effects of the company's temporary differences and carryovers.
- The income tax provision process consists of six steps:
  - Adjust net income before income taxes for all permanent differences.
  - Identify all temporary differences and tax carryforward amounts.
  - Calculate the current income tax expense or benefit (refund).
  - Determine the ending balances in the balance sheet deferred tax asset and liability accounts.
  - Evaluate the need for a valuation allowance for gross deferred tax assets.
  - Calculate the deferred income tax expense or benefit.

LO 17-2 Calculate the current and deferred income tax expense or benefit components of a company's income tax provision.

- The company first adjusts its pretax net income or loss for permanent and temporary book–tax differences to compute taxable income or loss. The company then applies the appropriate tax rate to taxable income (loss) to compute the tax return current tax expense or benefit.
- The company adjusts its tax return income tax liability or benefit for audit refunds or deficiencies from prior-year tax returns and for income tax benefits from stock option exercises treated as permanent differences.
- A company computes its deferred income tax expense or benefit by applying the applicable tax rate to the change in the cumulative balance sheet temporary differences between the financial accounting basis of an asset or liability and its corresponding tax basis from the beginning of the year to the end of the year.
- The future tax benefits from deductible (cumulatively unfavorable) temporary differences are recorded as deferred tax assets.
- The future tax costs of favorable taxable (cumulatively favorable) temporary differences are recorded as deferred tax liabilities.

LO 17-3 Determine how to calculate a valuation allowance.

- If a company determines that it is more likely than not (a greater than 50 percent probability) that some portion or all of the deferred tax assets will not be realized in a future period, it must offset the deferred tax assets with a valuation allowance to reflect the amount the company does not expect to realize in the future.
- The determination as to whether it is more likely than not that a deferred tax asset will not be realized in the future must be based on all available evidence, both positive and negative.
- ASC 740 identifies four sources of prior and future taxable income to consider: (1) future reversals of existing taxable temporary differences, (2) taxable income in prior carryback year(s), (3) expected future taxable income exclusive of reversing temporary differences and carryforwards, and (4) expected income from tax strategies.

LO 17-4 Explain how a company accounts for its uncertain income tax positions under FASB ASC Topic 740.

- A company must determine whether it can record the tax benefits from an "uncertain" tax position in its financial statement for the period in which the transaction takes place, knowing that the ultimate resolution of the tax position may not be known until some future period.

- ASC 740 applies a two-step process to evaluating uncertain tax positions:
  - Recognition: A company must determine whether it is more likely than not (a greater than 50 percent probability) that a tax position will be sustained upon examination by the IRS or other taxing authority, including resolution of any appeals within the court system, based on the technical merits of the position.
  - Measurement: If the tax position meets the more-likely-than-not threshold (a subjective determination), the company must determine the amount of the benefit to record in the financial statements.
- Under ASC 740, the amount to be recorded is the largest amount of the benefit, as calculated on a cumulative probability basis, which is more likely than not to be realized on the ultimate settlement of the tax position.

Describe how a company computes and discloses the components of its effective tax rate. **LO 17-5**

- For annual periods beginning after December 15, 2016, ASC 740 requires a business entity to disclose all of its deferred tax liabilities and assets as noncurrent on its balance sheet.
- A company also is required to present the "significant" components of the income tax provision (expense or benefit) attributable to continuing operations.
- ASC 740 requires publicly traded companies to reconcile their reported income tax expense (benefit) from continuing operations with the *hypothetical* tax expense that would have resulted from applying the domestic federal statutory rate to pretax income from continuing operations. Alternatively, the company can compute an *effective tax rate* from its continuing operations and reconcile it with the domestic federal statutory rate (21 percent).
- A company computes its effective tax rate by dividing its income tax provision (benefit) from continuing operations by its pretax net income from continuing operations.
- Items that cause the effective tax rate to differ from the statutory tax rate include permanent differences, audit adjustments, state and local taxes, and international taxes.

KEY TERMS

book equivalent of taxable
  income (17-8)
cash tax rate (17-30)
current income tax expense
  (benefit) (17-11)
current tax liability (asset) (17-4)
deductible temporary
  difference (17-9)

deferred tax asset (17-2)
deferred tax liability (17-2)
effective tax rate (17-7)
enacted tax rate (17-12)
permanent book-tax
  differences (17-6)
structural tax rate (17-30)

tax accounting balance
  sheet (17-12)
tax carryforwards (17-4)
taxable temporary
  difference (17-9)
uncertain tax positions (17-11)
valuation allowance (17-17)

DISCUSSION QUESTIONS

Discussion Questions are available in Connect®.   Mc Graw Hill **connect**

1. Identify some of the reasons why accounting for income taxes is complex. **LO 17-1**
2. True or False: ASC 740 applies to all taxes paid by a corporation. Explain. **LO 17-1**
3. True or False: ASC 740 is the sole source for the rules that apply to accounting for income taxes. Explain. **LO 17-1**
4. How does the fact that most corporations file their financial statements several months before they file their income tax returns complicate the income tax provision process? **LO 17-1**
5. What distinguishes an *income tax* from other taxes? **LO 17-1**
6. Briefly describe the six-step process by which a company computes its income tax provision. **LO 17-1**

LO 17-2   7. What are the two components of a company's income tax provision? What does each component represent about a company's income tax provision?

LO 17-2   8. True or False: All differences between book and taxable income, both permanent and temporary, affect a company's effective tax rate. Explain.

LO 17-2   9. When does a temporary difference resulting from an expense (deduction) create a taxable temporary difference? A deductible temporary difference?

LO 17-2   10. When does a temporary difference resulting from income create a taxable temporary difference? A deductible temporary difference?

LO 17-2   11. Briefly describe what is meant by the *asset and liability* or *balance sheet* approach taken by ASC 740 with respect to computing a corporation's deferred tax provision.

LO 17-2   12. Why are cumulatively favorable temporary differences referred to as taxable temporary differences?

LO 17-2   13. Why are cumulatively unfavorable temporary differences referred to as deductible temporary differences?

LO 17-2   14. In addition to the current-year tax return taxes payable or refundable, what other transactions can affect a company's current income tax provision?

LO 17-2 LO 17-4   15. What is an unrecognized tax benefit and how does it affect a company's current income tax expense?

LO 17-2   16. True or False: When Congress changes the corporate tax rates, only the current-year book–tax temporary differences are measured using the new rates. Explain.

LO 17-2   17. True or False: All temporary differences have a financial accounting basis. Explain.

LO 17-3   18. What is the purpose behind a valuation allowance as it applies to deferred tax assets?

LO 17-3   19. What is the difference between *recognition* and *realization* in the recording of a deferred tax asset on a balance sheet?

LO 17-3   20. Briefly describe the four sources of taxable income a company evaluates in determining if a valuation allowance is necessary.

LO 17-3   21. Which of the four sources of taxable income are considered objective and which are considered subjective? Which of these sources generally receives the most weight in analyzing whether a valuation allowance is necessary?

LO 17-3   22. What are the elements that define a tax planning strategy as it applies to determining if a valuation allowance is necessary? Provide an example where a tax planning strategy may be necessary to avoid recording a valuation allowance.

LO 17-3   23. When does a company remove a valuation allowance from its balance sheet?

LO 17-3   24. What is a company's *book equivalent of taxable income* and how does this computation enter into the income tax provision process?

LO 17-4   25. What motivated the FASB to issue FIN 48?

LO 17-4   26. Briefly describe the two-step process a company must undertake when it evaluates whether it can record the tax benefit from an uncertain tax position under ASC 740.

LO 17-4   27. Distinguish between *recognition* and *measurement* as they relate to the computation of unrecognized tax benefits under ASC 740.

LO 17-4   28. What is a *tax position* as it relates to the application of ASC 740 to uncertain tax positions?

LO 17-4   29. True or False: A company determines its unrecognized tax benefits with respect to a transaction only at the time the transaction takes place; subsequent events are ignored. Explain.

LO 17-4   30. True or False: ASC 740 requires that a company treat potential interest and penalties related to an unrecognized tax benefit as part of its income tax provision. Explain.

31. Where on the balance sheet does a company report its unrecognized tax benefits? `LO 17-4`

32. Why did many companies oppose FIN 48 when it was first proposed? `LO 17-4`

33. How does a company disclose deferred tax assets and liabilities on its balance sheet? `LO 17-5`

34. Under what conditions can a company net its current deferred tax assets with its current deferred tax liabilities on the balance sheet? `LO 17-5`

35. True or False: A publicly traded company must disclose all of the components of its deferred tax assets and liabilities in a footnote to the financial statements. Explain. `LO 17-5`

36. What is a company's *hypothetical* income tax provision and what is its importance in a company's disclosure of its income tax provision in the tax footnote? `LO 17-5`

37. Briefly describe the difference between a company's effective tax rate, cash tax rate, and structural tax rate. `LO 17-5`

PROBLEMS

Select problems are available in Connect®.   connect

38. Which of the following taxes is *not* accounted for under ASC 740? `LO 17-1`
    a) Income taxes paid to the U.S. government.
    b) Income taxes paid to the French government.
    c) Income taxes paid to the city of Detroit.
    d) Property taxes paid to the city of Detroit.
    e) All of the above taxes are accounted for under ASC 740.

39. Which of the following organizations can issue rules that govern accounting for income taxes? `LO 17-1`
    a) FASB.
    b) SEC.
    c) IRS.
    d) (a) and (b) above.
    e) All of the above organizations.

40. Find the paragraph(s) in ASC 740 that deals with the following items (access ASC 740 on the FASB website, http://www.fasb.org, and then click on "Standards"). You will need a Username and Password from your instructor. `LO 17-1` research
    a) The objectives and basic principles that underlie ASC 740.
    b) Examples of book–tax differences that create temporary differences.
    c) The definition of a *tax planning strategy*.
    d) Examples of positive evidence in the valuation allowance process.
    e) Rules relating to financial statement disclosure.

41. Woodward Corporation reported pretax book income of $1,000,000. Included in the computation were favorable temporary differences of $200,000, unfavorable temporary differences of $50,000, and favorable permanent differences of $100,000. Compute the company's current income tax expense or benefit. `LO 17-2`

42. Cass Corporation reported pretax book income of $10,000,000. During the current year, the reserve for bad debts increased by $100,000. In addition, tax depreciation exceeded book depreciation by $200,000. Cass Corporation sold a fixed asset and reported book gain of $50,000 and tax gain of $75,000. Finally, the company received $250,000 of tax-exempt life insurance proceeds from the death of one of its officers. Compute the company's current income tax expense or benefit. `LO 17-2`

LO 17-2   43. Grand Corporation reported pretax book income of $600,000. Tax depreciation exceeded book depreciation by $400,000. In addition, the company received $300,000 of tax-exempt municipal bond interest. The company's prior-year tax return showed taxable income of $50,000. Compute the company's current income tax expense or benefit.

LO 17-2   44. Chandler Corporation reported pretax book income of $2,000,000. Tax depreciation exceeded book depreciation by $500,000. During the year the company capitalized $250,000 into ending inventory under §263A. Capitalized inventory costs of $150,000 in beginning inventory were deducted as part of cost of goods sold on the tax return. Compute the company's taxes payable or refundable.

LO 17-2   45. Davison Company determined that the book basis of its office building exceeded the tax basis by $800,000. This basis difference is properly characterized as

   a) A permanent difference.

   b) A taxable temporary difference.

   c) A deductible temporary difference.

   d) A favorable book–tax difference.

   e) Both (b) and (d) above are correct.

LO 17-2   46. Abbot Company determined that the book basis of its allowance for bad debts is $100,000. There is no corresponding tax basis in this account. The basis difference is properly characterized as

   a) A permanent difference.

   b) A taxable temporary difference.

   c) A deductible temporary difference.

   d) A favorable book–tax difference.

   e) Both (b) and (d) above are correct.

LO 17-2   47. Which of the following items is *not* a temporary book–tax basis difference?

   a) Warranty reserve accruals.

   b) Accelerated depreciation.

   c) Capitalized inventory costs under §263A.

   d) Nondeductible stock option compensation from exercising an ISO.

   e) All of the above are temporary differences.

LO 17-2   48. Which of the following book–tax differences does *not* create a favorable temporary book–tax basis difference?

   a) Tax depreciation for the period exceeds book depreciation.

   b) Bad debts charged off in the current period exceed the bad debts accrued in the current period.

   c) Inventory costs capitalized under §263A deducted as part of current-year tax cost of goods sold are less than the inventory costs capitalized in ending inventory.

   d) Vacation pay accrued for tax purposes in a prior period is deducted in the current period.

   e) All of the above create a favorable temporary book–tax difference.

LO 17-2   49. Lodge Inc. reported pretax book income of $5,000,000. During the year, the company increased its reserve for warranties by $200,000. The company deducted $50,000 on its tax return related to warranty payments made during the year. What is the impact on taxable income compared to pretax book income of the book–tax difference that results from these two events?

   a) Favorable (decreases taxable income).

   b) Unfavorable (increases taxable income).

   c) Neutral (no impact on taxable income).

50. Which of the following book–tax basis differences results in a deductible temporary difference?   **LO 17-2**

   a) Book basis of a fixed asset exceeds its tax basis.

   b) Book basis of a pension-related liability exceeds its tax basis.

   c) Prepayment of income included on the tax return but not on the income statement (the transaction is recorded as a liability on the balance sheet).

   d) All of the above result in a deductible temporary difference.

   e) Both (b) and (c) result in a deductible temporary difference.

51. Shaw Corporation reported pretax book income of $1,000,000. Included in the computation were favorable temporary differences of $200,000, unfavorable temporary differences of $50,000, and favorable permanent differences of $100,000. Compute the company's deferred income tax expense or benefit.   **LO 17-2**

52. Shaw Inc. reported pretax book income of $10,000,000. During the current year, the reserve for bad debts increased by $100,000. In addition, tax depreciation exceeded book depreciation by $200,000. Shaw Inc. sold a fixed asset and reported book gain of $50,000 and tax gain of $75,000. Finally, the company received $250,000 of tax-exempt life insurance proceeds from the death of one of its officers. Compute the company's deferred income tax expense or benefit.   **LO 17-2**

53. Harrison Corporation reported pretax book income of $600,000. Tax depreciation exceeded book depreciation by $400,000. In addition, the company received $300,000 of tax-exempt municipal bond interest. The company's prior-year tax return showed taxable income of $50,000. Compute the company's deferred income tax expense or benefit.   **LO 17-2**

54. Identify the following items as creating a temporary book–tax difference, permanent book–tax difference, or no book–tax difference.   **LO 17-2**

Item	Temporary Difference	Permanent Difference	No Difference
Reserve for warranties			
Accrued pension liability			
Goodwill not amortized for tax purposes but subject to impairment under ASC 350			
Meal expenses			
Life insurance proceeds			
Net capital loss carryover			
Nondeductible fines and penalties			
Accrued vacation pay liability paid within the first two and one-half months of the next tax year			

55. Which of the following items is *not* a permanent book–tax difference?   **LO 17-2**

   a) Tax-exempt interest income.

   b) Tax-exempt insurance proceeds.

   c) Windfall tax benefits from the exercise of an NQO

   d) Meal expenses.

   e) First-year expensing under §179.

56. Ann Corporation reported pretax book income of $1,000,000. Included in the computation were favorable temporary differences of $200,000, unfavorable temporary differences of $50,000, and favorable permanent differences of $100,000. Compute the company's book equivalent of taxable income. Use this number to compute the company's total income tax provision or benefit.   **LO 17-2**

LO 17-2   57. Burcham Corporation reported pretax book income of $600,000. Tax depreciation exceeded book depreciation by $400,000. In addition, the company received $300,000 of tax-exempt municipal bond interest. The company's prior-year tax return showed taxable income of $50,000. Compute the company's book equivalent of taxable income. Use this number to compute the company's total income tax provision or benefit.

LO 17-3   58. Adams Corporation has total deferred tax assets of $3,000,000 at year-end. Management is assessing whether a valuation allowance must be recorded against some or all of the deferred tax assets. What level of assurance must management have, based on the weight of available evidence, that some or all of the deferred tax assets will not be realized before a valuation allowance is required?

a) Probable.

b) More likely than not.

c) Realistic possibility.

d) Reasonable.

e) More than remote.

LO 17-3   59. Which of the following evidence would *not* be considered positive in determining whether Adams Corporation needs to record a valuation allowance for some or all of its deferred tax assets?

a) The company forecasts future taxable income because of its backlog of orders.

b) The company has unfavorable temporary differences that will create future taxable income when they reverse.

c) The company has tax-planning strategies that it can implement to create future taxable income.

d) The company has cumulative net income over the current and prior two years.

e) The company had a net operating loss carryover expire in the current year.

LO 17-3   60. As of the beginning of the year, Gratiot Company recorded a valuation allowance of $200,000 against its deferred tax assets of $1,000,000. The valuation allowance relates to a net operating loss carryover from the prior year. During the year, management concludes that the valuation allowance is no longer necessary because it forecasts sufficient taxable income to absorb the NOL carryover. What is the impact of management's reversal of the valuation allowance on the company's effective tax rate?

a) Increases the effective tax rate.

b) Decreases the effective tax rate.

c) No impact on the effective tax rate.

LO 17-3   61. Which of the following evidence would be considered negative in determining whether Gratiot Corporation needs to record a valuation allowance for some or all of its deferred tax assets?

a) The company forecasts future taxable income because of its backlog of orders.

b) The company has a cumulative net loss over the current and prior two years.

c) The company has unfavorable temporary differences that will create future taxable income when they reverse.

d) The company had a net operating loss carryover expire in the current year.

e) Both (b) and (d) constitute negative evidence in assessing the need for a valuation allowance.

LO 17-3   62. Saginaw Inc. completed its first year of operations with a pretax loss of $500,000. The tax return showed a net operating loss of $600,000, which the company will carry forward. The $100,000 book–tax difference results from excess tax depreciation over book depreciation. Management has determined that it should record a valuation allowance equal to the net deferred tax asset. Assuming the current tax expense is zero, prepare the journal entries to record the deferred tax provision and the valuation allowance.

63. Access the 2017 Form 10-Ks for General Motors, Inc. and Berkshire Hathaway. What was the impact of the Tax Cuts and Jobs Act on their income tax provision for 2017? Why was the impact in opposite directions (i.e., in one case the provision increased and in the other it decreased)?

LO 17-3

research

64. Montcalm Corporation has total deferred tax assets of $3,000,000 at year-end. Of that amount, $1,000,000 results from the current expensing of an expenditure that the IRS might assert must be capitalized on audit. Management is trying to determine if it should not recognize the deferred tax asset related to this item under ASC 740. What confidence level must management have that the item will be sustained on audit before it can recognize any portion of the deferred tax asset under ASC 740?

LO 17-4

   a) Probable.
   b) More likely than not.
   c) Realistic possibility.
   d) Reasonable.
   e) More than remote.

65. Which of the following statements about uncertain tax positions (UTP) is correct?

LO 17-4

   a) UTP applies only to tax positions accounted for under ASC 740 taken on a filed tax return.
   b) UTP applies to all tax positions accounted for under ASC 740, regardless of whether the item is taken on a filed tax return.
   c) UTP deals with both the recognition and realization of deferred tax assets.
   d) If a tax position meets the more-likely-than-not standard, the entire amount of the deferred tax asset or current tax benefit related to the tax position can be recognized under ASC 740.
   e) Statements (b), (c), and (d) are correct.

66. Cadillac Square Corporation determined that $1,000,000 of its research tax credit on its current-year tax return was uncertain, but that it was more likely than not to be sustained on audit. Management made the following assessment of the company's potential tax benefit from the deduction and its probability of occurring.

LO 17-4

Potential Estimated Benefit (000s)	Individual Probability of Occurring (%)	Cumulative Probability of Occurring (%)
$1,000,000	40	40
$750,000	25	65
$500,000	20	85
0	15	100

What amount of the tax benefit related to the uncertain tax position from the research tax credit can Cadillac Square Corporation recognize in calculating its income tax provision in the current year?

67. How would your answer to problem 66 change if management determined that there was only a 50/50 chance any portion of the $1,000,000 research tax credit would be sustained on audit?

LO 17-4

LO 17-4 68. As part of its UTP assessment, Penobscot Company records interest and penalties related to its unrecognized tax benefit of $500,000. Which of the following statements about recording this amount is most correct?

a) Penobscot must include the amount in its income tax provision.

b) Penobscot must record the amount separate from its income tax provision.

c) Penobscot can elect to allocate a portion of the amount to both its income tax provision and its general and administrative expenses provided the company discloses which option it has chosen.

d) Penobscot can elect to record the entire amount as part of its income tax provision or separate from its income tax provision, provided the company discloses which option it has chosen.

e) Statements (c) and (d) are both correct.

LO 17-5 69. What was Alphabet, Inc.'s (Google) accounting effective tax rate for 2017? What items caused the company's accounting effective tax rate to differ from the "hypothetical" tax rate of 35 percent? What was the company's cash effective tax rate for 2017? What factors cause a company's cash tax rate to differ from its accounting effective tax rate? You can access Alphabet Inc.'s Form 10-K for 2017 at the company's website or the SEC EDGAR website.

research

LO 17-5 70. Beacon Corporation recorded the following deferred tax assets and liabilities:

Current deferred tax assets	$ 650,000
Current deferred tax liabilities	(400,000)
Noncurrent deferred tax assets	1,000,000
Noncurrent deferred tax liabilities	(2,500,000)
Net deferred tax liabilities	$ 1,250,000)

All of the deferred tax accounts relate to temporary differences that arose as a result of the company's U.S. operations. Which of the following statements describes how Beacon should disclose these accounts on its balance sheet?

a) Beacon reports a net deferred tax liability of $1,250,000 on its balance sheet as noncurrent.

b) Beacon nets the deferred tax assets and the deferred tax liabilities and reports a net deferred tax asset of $1,650,000 and a net deferred tax liability of $2,900,000 on its balance sheet.

c) Beacon can elect to net the current deferred tax accounts and the noncurrent tax accounts and report a net current deferred tax asset of $250,000 and a net deferred tax liability of $1,500,000 on its balance sheet.

d) Beacon is required to net the current deferred tax accounts and the noncurrent deferred tax accounts and report a net current deferred tax asset of $250,000 and a net deferred tax liability of $1,500,000 on its balance sheet.

LO 17-5 71. ASC 740 requires a company to disclose those components of its deferred tax assets and liabilities that are considered

a) Relevant.

b) Significant.

c) Important.

d) Major.

LO 17-5 72. Which of the following temporary differences creates a deferred tax asset?

a) Allowance for bad debts.

b) Goodwill amortization for tax, but not book, purposes.

c) Cumulative excess of tax over book depreciation.

d) Inventory capitalization under §263A.

e) Both (a) and (d) above create a deferred tax asset.

73. Which formula represents the calculation of a company's effective tax rate? `LO 17-5`
    a) Income taxes paid/Taxable income.
    b) Income taxes paid/Pretax income from continuing operations.
    c) Income tax provision/Taxable income.
    d) Income tax provision/Pretax income from continuing operations.

74. Which of the following items is *not* a reconciling item in the income tax footnote? `LO 17-5`
    a) State income taxes.
    b) Foreign income taxes.
    c) Accrued pension liabilities.
    d) Dividends received deduction.
    e) Tax-exempt municipal bond interest.

75. Randolph Company reported pretax net income from continuing operations of `LO 17-5`
    $800,000 and taxable income of $500,000. The book–tax difference of $300,000
    was due to a $200,000 favorable temporary difference relating to depreciation, an
    unfavorable temporary difference of $80,000 due to an increase in the reserve for
    bad debts, and a $180,000 favorable permanent difference from the receipt of life
    insurance proceeds.
    a) Compute Randolph Company's current income tax expense.
    b) Compute Randolph Company's deferred income tax expense or benefit.
    c) Compute Randolph Company's effective tax rate.
    d) Provide a reconciliation of Randolph Company's effective tax rate with its hypo-
       thetical tax rate of 21 percent.

76. Which of the following pronouncements should a company consult in computing its `LO 17-5`
    quarterly income tax provision?
    a) ASC 740.
    b) ASC 230.
    c) ASC 718.
    d) ASC 810.
    e) SarbOX 404.

COMPREHENSIVE PROBLEMS

Select problems are available with Connect®. connect

77. You have been assigned to compute the income tax provision for Motown Memories
    Inc. (MM) as of December 31, 2018. The company's income statement for 2018 is
    provided below:

Motown Memories Inc. Statement of Operations at December 31, 2018	
Net sales	$50,000,000
Cost of sales	28,000,000
Gross profit	$22,000,000
Compensation	$ 2,000,000
Selling expenses	1,500,000
Depreciation and amortization	4,000,000
Other expenses	500,000
Total operating expenses	$ 8,000,000
Income from operations	$14,000,000
Interest and other income	1,000,000
Income before income taxes	$15,000,000

You identified the following permanent differences:

Interest income from municipal bonds	$ 50,000
Nondeductible meals	20,000
Nondeductible fines	5,000

MM prepared the following schedule of temporary differences from the beginning of the year to the end of the year:

Motown Memories Inc. Temporary Difference Scheduling Template					
Taxable Temporary Differences	BOY Cumulative T/D	Beginning Deferred Taxes (@ 21%)	Current Year Change	EOY Cumulative T/D	Ending Deferred Taxes (@ 21%)
Accumulated depreciation	(8,000,000)	(1,680,000)	(1,000,000)	(9,000,000)	**(1,890,000)**
Deductible Temporary Differences	BOY Cumulative T/D	Beginning Deferred Taxes (@ 21%)	Current Year Change	EOY Cumulative T/D	Ending Deferred Taxes (@ 21%)
Allowance for bad debts	200,000	42,000	50,000	250,000	52,500
Reserve for warranties	100,000	21,000	20,000	120,000	25,200
Inventory §263A adjustment	240,000	50,400	60,000	300,000	63,000
Deferred compensation	50,000	10,500	10,000	60,000	12,600
Accrued pension liabilities	3,000,000	630,000	250,000	3,250,000	682,500
Total	**3,590,000**	**753,900**	**390,000**	**3,980,000**	**835,800**

Required:

a) Compute MM's current income tax expense or benefit for 2018.

b) Compute MM's deferred income tax expense or benefit for 2018.

c) Prepare a reconciliation of MM's total income tax provision with its hypothetical income tax expense of 21% in both dollars and rates.

78. You have been assigned to compute the income tax provision for Tulip City Flowers Inc. (TCF) as of December 31, 2018. The company's income statement for 2018 is provided below:

Tulip City Flowers Inc. Statement of Operations at December 31, 2018	
Net sales	$20,000,000
Cost of sales	12,000,000
Gross profit	$ 8,000,000
Compensation	$ 500,000
Selling expenses	750,000
Depreciation and amortization	1,250,000
Other expenses	1,000,000
Total operating expenses	$ 3,500,000
Income from operations	$ 4,500,000
Interest and other income	25,000
Income before income taxes	$ 4,525,000

You identified the following permanent differences:

Interest income from municipal bonds	$10,000
Nondeductible stock compensation	5,000
Nondeductible fines	1,000

TCF prepared the following schedule of temporary differences from the beginning of the year to the end of the year:

Tulip City Flowers Inc. Temporary Difference Scheduling Template					
Taxable Temporary Differences	BOY Cumulative T/D	Beginning Deferred Taxes (@ 21%)	Current Year Change	EOY Cumulative T/D	Ending Deferred Taxes (@ 21%)
Accumulated depreciation	(5,000,000)	(1,050,000)	(500,000)	(5,500,000)	(1,155,000)
Deductible Temporary Differences	**BOY Cumulative T/D**	**Beginning Deferred Taxes (@ 21%)**	**Current Year Change**	**EOY Cumulative T/D**	**Ending Deferred Taxes (@ 21%)**
Allowance for bad debts	100,000	21,000	10,000	110,000	23,100
Prepaid income	0	0	20,000	20,000	4,200
Deferred compensation	50,000	10,500	10,000	60,000	12,600
Accrued pension liabilities	500,000	105,000	100,000	600,000	126,000
Total	650,000	136,500	140,000	790,000	165,900

Required:

a) Compute TCF's current income tax expense or benefit for 2018.

b) Compute TCF's deferred income tax expense or benefit for 2018.

c) Prepare a reconciliation of TCF's total income tax provision with its hypothetical income tax expense of 21% in both dollars and rates.

79. Access the 2017 Form 10-K for Facebook, Inc., and answer the following questions.

research

Required:

a) Using information from the company's Income Statement and Income Taxes footnote, what was the company's effective tax rate for 2017? Show how the rate is calculated.

b) Using information from the Statement of Cash Flows, calculate the company's cash tax rate.

c) What does the company's Income Taxes note tell you about where the company earns its international income? Why does earning income in these countries cause the effective tax rate to decrease?

d) What item creates the company's largest deferred tax asset? Explain why this item creates a deductible temporary difference.

e) What item creates the company's largest deferred tax liability? Explain why this item creates a taxable temporary difference.

f) How does the company classify its income taxes payable related to its unrecognized tax benefits on the balance sheet?

g) How does the company treat interest and penalties related to its unrecognized tax benefits?

80. Spartan Builders Corporation is a builder of high-end housing with locations in major metropolitan areas throughout the Midwest. At June 30, 2018, the company has deferred tax assets totaling $10 million and deferred tax liabilities of $5 million, all of which relate to U.S. temporary differences. Reversing taxable temporary differences and taxable income in the carryback period can be used to support approximately $2 million of the $10 million gross deferred tax asset. The remaining $8 million of gross deferred tax assets will have to come from future taxable income.

   The company has historically been profitable. However, significant losses were incurred in fiscal years 2016 and 2017. These two years reflect a cumulative loss of $10 million ($7 million of which was due to a write-down of inventory), with losses of $3 million expected in 2018. Beginning in fiscal 2019, management decided to get out of the metropolitan Chicago market, which had become oversaturated with new houses.

   Evaluate the company's need to record a valuation allowance for the $10 million of gross deferred tax assets. What positive and negative evidence would you weigh?

ROGER | *CPA Review*

Sample CPA Exam questions from Roger CPA Review are available in Connect as support for the topics in this text. These Multiple Choice Questions and Task-Based Simulations include expert-written explanations and solutions and provide a starting point for students to become familiar with the content and functionality of the actual CPA Exam.

Corporate Taxation: Nonliquidating Distributions

Learning Objectives

Upon completing this chapter, you should be able to:

LO 18-1 Explain the framework that applies to the taxation of property distributions from a corporation to a shareholder.

LO 18-2 Compute a corporation's earnings and profits and a shareholder's dividend income.

LO 18-3 Explain the taxation of stock distributions.

LO 18-4 Comprehend the tax consequences of stock redemptions.

LO 18-5 Describe the tax consequences of a partial liquidation to the corporation and its shareholders.

©Javier Perini CM/Image Source

Storyline Summary

Taxpayer:	Jim Wheeler
Location:	East Lansing, Michigan
Employment status:	Co-owner of Spartan Cycle and Repair (75 percent)
Taxpayer:	Ginny Gears
Location:	East Lansing, Michigan
Employment status:	Co-owner of Spartan Cycle and Repair (25 percent)

Jim Wheeler and Ginny Gears are old friends who met at the Mid-Michigan Cycling Club. They often discussed their shared dream of owning and operating a high-end bicycle shop in East Lansing, Michigan. Many of their friends in the club often remarked how difficult it was to get parts and have their bicycles repaired locally. Jim found himself repairing his friends' bicycles using the knowledge he gained while working at a bicycle shop during his undergraduate days at the University of Colorado. Ginny majored in marketing at Michigan State University (MSU) and was eager to put her marketing and management skills to work in her own business.

A few years ago, Jim and Ginny fulfilled their dream by launching Spartan Cycle and Repair (SCR). Their business had humble beginnings, as most start-up companies do. By borrowing from Jim's father Walt, they raised the $50,000 capital they needed to purchase inventory and the necessary repair tools. They also leased a vacant building on Grand River Avenue. On the advice of their accountant and their lawyer, Jim and Ginny organized their company as a C corporation, with Jim owning 75 percent of the corporation's stock and Ginny owning the remaining 25 percent. Jim's responsibilities include doing the bicycle repairs and deciding which bicycle brands to carry, while Ginny is responsible for managing and marketing the business. Jim works approximately 10 hours per week at the store, and he currently receives a modest salary of $15,000 per year. Ginny works half-time at the store and currently receives a salary of $25,000 per year.

Since the company's inception, Jim and Ginny have used most of the company's profits to pay back the loan to Jim's father and expand the store's inventory and marketing activities. By the end of this year, SCR had become very successful, as evidenced by the significant amount of cash ($300,000) in the company's bank accounts. Jim and Ginny made many sacrifices, both financially and socially, to make the business successful. Over a café latte at the local gourmet coffee shop, Jim and Ginny decided it was time to think about distributing some of the company's profits to reward their hard work. Jim admitted he had his eye on a dark green BMW sedan, which retailed for approximately $48,000, fully loaded. Ginny was a bit more restrained, hoping she could put a down payment on a condominium in the newly developed Evergreen Commons being constructed near their store. She estimated she would need approximately $16,000 for the down payment.

Jim and Ginny are also considering distributing cash from SCR. The latest proposal is for SCR to distribute $64,000 at year-end ($48,000 to Jim and $16,000 to Ginny).

to be continued . . .

At some point during the life of a company, especially in the case of a closely held business, the shareholders will likely want to distribute some of the company's accumulated profits. If the business is operated as a C corporation, the company can distribute its *after-tax* profits to its shareholders in the form of a **dividend, stock redemption,** or, in rare cases, a **partial liquidation.** This chapter addresses the tax consequences to the corporation and its shareholders when a C corporation makes distributions to its shareholders.[1] If Jim and Ginny had elected to operate their business through an S corporation or partnership, the entity-level taxation of the company's earnings would be eliminated. The tax consequences of these two flow-through entity choices are discussed in more detail in later chapters.

LO 18-1 TAXATION OF PROPERTY DISTRIBUTIONS

The characterization of a distribution from a corporation to a shareholder has important tax consequences to both the shareholders and the corporation. If the tax law characterizes the distribution as a dividend, the corporation may not deduct the amount paid in computing its taxable income. In addition, the shareholder must include the gross amount of the dividend received in gross income. The nondeductibility of the distribution by the corporation, coupled with the taxation of the distribution to the shareholder, creates *double taxation* of the corporation's income, first at the corporate level and then at the shareholder level. The double taxation of distributed corporate income has been a fundamental principle of the U.S. income tax since 1913.

Historically, tax planning focused on eliminating or mitigating the second level of taxation on C corporation earnings. For example, if the distribution can instead be characterized as salary, bonus, interest, or rent, the corporation can deduct the amount paid in computing its taxable income. Currently, the corporate tax rate (21 percent) is significantly lower than the maximum individual tax rate (37 percent). Hence, it is conceivable that some taxpayers may save taxes by choosing to have a business entity taxed as a C corporation. In other words, depending on the timing and form of distributions of profits, subjecting a business to double taxation may be preferable to operating the business as a flow-through entity and subjecting the income to a single tax, albeit at a higher rate.

The Internal Revenue Code, Subchapter C (§§301-385) provides guidelines and rules for determining the tax status of distributions from a C corporation to its shareholders. The recipient of a distribution or payment in exchange for stock (stock redemption) generally receives preferential tax treatment on the distribution in the form of a reduced tax rate or as a nontaxable return of capital or both.

---

[1]Corporations subject to the corporate tax are referred to as *C corporations* because Subchapter C (§§301–385) governs the tax consequences of distributions between a corporation and its shareholders.

DETERMINING THE DIVIDEND AMOUNT FROM EARNINGS AND PROFITS

LO 18-2

Overview

When a corporation distributes property to shareholders in their capacity as shareholders, the shareholders will characterize the distribution as either dividend income or a return of capital. They include the portion characterized as dividend income in their gross income. In contrast, a return of capital is considered not income, but rather a reduction in the shareholder's tax basis in the stock. If the return of capital exceeds the tax basis of the stock, then the excess distribution (above basis) is taxed as a capital gain from the sale of the shares.[2]

Corporate distributions of "property" usually take the form of cash, but distributions can also consist of other tangible or intangible property. Special rules apply when a corporation distributes its own stock, in the form of **stock dividends,** to its shareholders.[3]

Dividends Defined

A dividend is any distribution of property made by a corporation to its shareholders out of its earnings and profits (E&P) account. Congress intended earnings and profits to be a measure of the corporation's *economic earnings* available for distribution to its shareholders. Hence, earnings and profits is similar in concept to financial accounting retained earnings, but the computation of E&P can be very different.

Corporations must keep two separate E&P accounts: one for the current year, called **current earnings and profits,** and one for undistributed earnings and profits accumulated in all prior years, called **accumulated earnings and profits.**

Each year corporations compute their *current* E&P by making specific adjustments to taxable income (discussed below). When E&P is positive, income distributions can be deemed to be dividends. Any current E&P that is not distributed to shareholders is then added to *accumulated* E&P at the beginning of the next taxable year. Distributions reduce E&P but cannot produce (or increase) a deficit (a negative balance) in E&P. That is, dividend treatment requires positive E&P, but E&P can have a deficit balance if losses exceed income. In other words, a corporation cannot distribute E&P if there is a deficit in E&P, and only losses can create a deficit in E&P. A corporation that makes a distribution in excess of its total E&P (i.e., a return of capital) must report the distribution on Form 5452 and include a calculation of its E&P balance to support the tax treatment.

> **THE KEY FACTS**
>
> **Adjustments to Taxable Income (Loss) to Compute Current E&P**
>
> - A corporation makes the following adjustments to taxable income to compute current E&P:
>   - Include certain income that is excluded from taxable income.
>   - Disallow certain expenses that are deducted in computing taxable income.
>   - Deduct certain expenses that are excluded from the computation of taxable income.
>   - Defer deductions or accelerate income due to separate accounting methods required for E&P purposes.

Example 18-1

Jim owns 75 percent of the SCR stock, while Ginny owns the remaining 25 percent. Jim has a tax basis in his Spartan Cycle and Repair (SCR) stock of $24,000. Ginny's tax basis in her SCR stock is $10,000.

What if: Assume SCR has current earnings and profits (E&P) of $30,000 and no accumulated earnings and profits. At year-end, SCR makes a $64,000 distribution—a $48,000 distribution to Jim and a $16,000 distribution to Ginny.

What is the tax treatment of the distribution to Jim and Ginny?

(continued on page 18-4)

---

[2]§301(c).
[3]§317.

Answer: Only $30,000 of the $64,000 distribution is treated as a dividend. The distribution in excess of E&P is treated as a return of capital.

Jim treats the $48,000 distribution for tax purposes as follows:

- $22,500 is treated as a dividend (46.875 percent ($30,000/$64,000) of the $48,000 is current E&P).
- $24,000 is a nontaxable reduction in his stock tax basis (return of capital).
- $1,500 is treated as gain from the deemed sale of his stock (capital gain).

Note that a distribution cannot reduce a shareholder's stock basis below zero.

Ginny treats the $16,000 distribution for tax purposes as follows:

- $7,500 is treated as a dividend (46.875 percent of $16,000 is current E&P).
- $8,500 is a nontaxable reduction in her stock tax basis (return of capital).

What is Jim and Ginny's tax basis in their SCR stock after the distribution?

Answer: Jim has a zero basis in his SCR stock, while Ginny has a remaining tax basis of $1,500 ($10,000 − $8,500) in her SCR stock.

Computing Earnings and Profits

The concept of earnings and profits (E&P) has been part of the tax laws since 1916. Although Congress has never provided a precise definition of E&P, it is generally accepted that E&P is supposed to represent the economic income eligible for distribution to shareholders. For example, E&P includes both taxable and nontaxable income, indicating that Congress intended E&P to represent a corporation's economic income. As a result, shareholders may be taxed on distributions of income that is not taxable income to the corporation. Hence, the effects of E&P can be somewhat counterintuitive.

A corporation begins the computation of current E&P with taxable income or loss. It then makes adjustments required by the Internal Revenue Code (IRC) or the accompanying regulations and IRS rulings. These adjustments fall into four broad categories:

1. Certain nontaxable income is included in E&P.
2. Certain deductions do not reduce E&P.
3. Certain nondeductible expenses reduce E&P.
4. The timing of certain items of income and deduction is modified for E&P calculations because separate accounting methods are required for E&P purposes.[4]

Nontaxable Income Included in Current E&P   Tax-exempt income represents economic income and can be distributed to shareholders. Thus, tax-exempt income increases E&P. Common examples of tax-exempt income included in E&P are tax-exempt municipal interest and tax-exempt life insurance proceeds.

Example 18-2

SCR reported taxable income of $100,000 and $5,000 of tax-exempt interest from its investment in City of East Lansing municipal bonds. What amount will SCR report as current earnings and profits?

Answer: SCR will report current earnings and profits of $105,000. SCR must include the $5,000 of tax-exempt interest in the computation of current E&P.

[4]§312.

Deductible Expenses That Do Not Reduce Current E&P Deductions that require no cash outlay by the corporation or are carryovers from another tax year do not represent current economic outflows and cannot be used to reduce E&P. Examples include the dividends received deduction, net capital loss carryovers from a different tax year, net operating loss carryovers from a different tax year, and charitable contribution carryovers from a prior tax year.[5]

Nondeductible Expenses That Reduce Current E&P A corporation reduces its current E&P for certain items that are not deductible in computing its taxable income but require a cash outflow. Examples of such expenses include:

- Federal income taxes paid or accrued (depending on the corporation's method of accounting).
- Expenses incurred in earning tax-exempt income (such income is included in E&P).
- Current-year charitable contributions in excess of 10 percent of taxable income (there is no 10 percent limitation for E&P purposes).
- Premiums on life insurance contracts in excess of the increase in the policy's cash surrender value.
- Current-year net capital loss (there is no limit on capital losses for E&P purposes).
- Meals expenses disallowed (only 50 percent of the meals is generally deductible).
- Entertainment expenses are nondeductible.
- Nondeductible lobbying expenses and political contributions.
- Penalties and fines.

Items Requiring Separate Accounting Methods for E&P Purposes A corporation must generally use the same accounting method for computing E&P and taxable income. For example, a gain or loss deferred for tax purposes under the like-kind exchange rules (§1031) or the involuntary conversion rules is also deferred for E&P purposes. A corporation using the accrual method for regular income tax purposes generally must use the accrual method for E&P purposes. However, there are some important differences between the accounting methods used to compute taxable income and current E&P. Hence, the adjustments to taxable income reflect differences in both the recognition and the timing of certain items of income and expense. There is a relatively long list of adjustments in deriving current E&P from taxable income; some are positive and others are negative.

Some types of income deferred or excluded from current-year taxable income must be included in the computation of current E&P in the year in which the transaction occurs. For example, if a corporation uses the installment sales method for tax purposes, the deferred gain from current-year sales must be included in current E&P. This difference reverses in future years when the installment payments are received and increase taxable income but not current E&P in the year of receipt. In other cases, gain deferred from taxation is not added back in the E&P computation.

Certain expenses currently deducted in the computation of taxable income are deferred in computing E&P.[6] For example, organizational expenditures, which can be deducted currently or amortized for income tax purposes, must be capitalized for E&P

---

[5]The deduction allowed for employee exercises of nonqualified stock options reduces current E&P because the bargain element of the option reflects an economic cost to the corporation (even though it does not require a cash outflow from the corporation).

[6]§312(n). Section 312(n) was added in 1984 to "ensure that a corporation's earnings and profits more closely conform to its economic income."

purposes. Depreciation must be computed using the prescribed E&P method. For property acquired after 1986, the alternative depreciation system must be used. This system requires that assets be depreciated using a straight-line method over the asset's "midpoint class life" (40 years in the case of realty).[7] This generally results in more accelerated depreciation for taxable income purposes than for E&P purposes (bonus depreciation is not allowed for E&P purposes). Further, amounts expensed under §179 (first year expensing) must be amortized over five years for E&P purposes.

For any given year, adjustments in this category may increase or decrease current E&P because these adjustments are timing differences that reverse over time.

Example 18-3

This year, SCR reported taxable income of $500,000 and paid federal income tax of $105,000. SCR reported the following items of income and expense:

- $50,000 of depreciation.
- $7,000 dividends received deduction.
- $10,000 net operating loss from the prior year.
- $5,000 of tax-exempt interest.
- $6,000 of nondeductible meals and entertainment expense.
- $4,000 net capital loss from the current year.

For E&P purposes, depreciation computed under the alternative depreciation method is $30,000.

What is SCR's current E&P?

Answer: $427,000, computed as follows:

Taxable income	$ 500,000
Add:	
Tax-exempt interest	5,000
Dividends received deduction	7,000
NOL carryover	10,000
Excess of regular tax depreciation over E&P depreciation	20,000
Subtract:	
Federal income taxes	(105,000)
Nondeductible meals and entertainment	(6,000)
Net capital loss for the current year	(4,000)
Current E&P	**$427,000**

What if: Assume SCR also reported a tax-deferred gain of $100,000 as the result of a §1031 exchange and deferred $75,000 of gain from an installment sale during the year. What is SCR's current E&P under these circumstances?

Answer: Current E&P would equal $502,000 ($427,000 + $75,000). Deferred gains from §1031 (like-kind) exchanges are not included in the computation of current E&P, but all gain from current-year installment sales is included in current E&P. In future years, SCR would back out any deferred gain recognized in taxable income from the installment sale in its computation of current E&P.

What if: Assume SCR did not report any gains from the sale of property and instead reported a $450,000 loss from a sale of property. What is SCR's current E&P under these circumstances?

Answer: Current E&P would be a deficit balance of $23,000 ($427,000 − $450,000). The balance of E&P can be negative, but E&P cannot be driven below zero by distributions.

[7]§168(g)(2).

Exhibit 18-1 provides a summary of common adjustments made to compute current E&P. The IRC does not impose a statute of limitations on the computation of E&P. Hence, many corporations (public and private) make the initial computation of accumulated E&P only after years of operations. This computation often requires significant resources because the annual adjustments necessary to derive the current E&P from taxable income have not been well documented in the past, and it is necessary to derive the current E&P for each year to calculate accumulated E&P.

EXHIBIT 18-1 Template for Computing Current Earnings and Profits

---

Taxable Income (Net Operating Loss)

Add: **Exclusions from Taxable Income**
- Tax-exempt bond interest.
- Life insurance proceeds.
- Federal tax refunds (if a cash-basis taxpayer).
- Increase in cash surrender value of corporate-owned life insurance policy.

Add: **Deductions Allowed for Tax Purposes but Not for E&P**
- Dividends received deduction.
- NOL deduction carrybacks and carryforwards.
- Net capital loss carryforwards.
- Contribution carryforwards.

Subtract: **Deductions Allowed for E&P Purposes but Not for Tax Purposes**
- Federal income taxes paid or accrued.
- Expenses of earning tax-exempt income.
- Current-year charitable contributions in excess of the 10 percent limitation.
- Nondeductible premiums on life insurance policies.
- Current-year net capital loss.
- Penalties and fines.
- Nondeductible portion of meal expense.
- Entertainment expenses.
- Disallowed lobbying expenses, dues, and political contributions.
- Decrease in cash surrender value of corporate-owned life insurance policy.

Add or Subtract: **Timing Differences Due to Separate Accounting Methods for Taxable Income and E&P**
- Installment method. Add deferred gain under installment method in year of sale and subtract recognized gain in subsequent years.
- Depreciation. Compare depreciation (other than §179 expense) under regular tax rules to E&P depreciation (bonus depreciation is not allowed). Add back difference if taxable income depreciation exceeds E&P depreciation. Subtract difference if E&P depreciation exceeds taxable income depreciation for the year.
- Section 179 expense. Immediately deductible for taxable income purposes. Deductible over five years for E&P purposes. Add back in year of §179 expense but subtract in subsequent years.
- Inventory. If LIFO is used for tax purposes, FIFO must be used for E&P calculations.
- Gain or loss on sale of depreciable assets. Subtract greater taxable gain (lesser taxable loss) due to lower asset basis for taxable income purposes than for E&P purposes. This is a reversal of the depreciation deduction adjustment.
- Long-term contracts. Percentage completion method is required for E&P. Compare the income recognized under both methods. Add back if more income under the completed contract method and subtract if more income under the percentage completion method year.
- Depletion. Must use the cost depletion method for E&P purposes. If using percentage depletion for taxable income, add back the difference if percentage depletion exceeds cost depletion for the year. Otherwise, subtract the excess of cost depletion over percentage depletion for the year.

Equals: **Current Earnings and Profits**

Ordering of E&P Distributions

Corporations use current and accumulated E&P accounts in determining the amount of distributions that are deemed to be dividends. Distributions are designated as dividends in the following order:

1. Distributions are dividends up to the balance of current E&P.
2. Distributions in excess of current E&P are dividends up to the balance in accumulated E&P.

Under these ordering rules, whether a distribution is characterized as a dividend depends on whether the balances in these two accounts are positive or negative. As a result, there are only four possible scenarios:

1. Positive current E&P, positive accumulated E&P.
2. Positive current E&P, negative accumulated E&P.
3. Negative current E&P, positive accumulated E&P.
4. Negative current E&P, negative accumulated E&P.

Positive Current E&P and Positive Accumulated E&P   Corporate distributions are deemed to be paid out of current E&P first. If distributions exceed current E&P, the amount distributed from current E&P is allocated pro rata to all the distributions made during the year. Any distribution out of accumulated E&P is allocated to the recipients in the chronological order in which the distributions were made.[8] This ordering of distributions is particularly important when distributions exceed current E&P and either the identity of the shareholders receiving the distributions changes or a shareholder's percentage ownership changes during the year. Current E&P is determined on the last day of the tax year before reduction for current-year distributions.

Example 18-4

What if: Assume SCR reported current E&P of $40,000, and the balance in accumulated E&P was $16,000. On December 31, SCR distributed $48,000 to Jim and $16,000 to Ginny. What amount of dividend income do Jim and Ginny report, and what is the balance of E&P for SCR at the beginning of next year?

Answer: Jim and Ginny report $42,000 and $14,000 of dividend income, respectively. The distribution is first deemed to be paid from current E&P to each shareholder in proportion to their ownership interests on the date of the distribution: $30,000 to Jim (equal to $40,000 × 75%) and $10,000 to Ginny (equal to $40,000 × 25%). The $24,000 distribution in excess of current E&P ($64,000 − $40,000) is then deemed to be paid from accumulated E&P ($16,000) in proportion to ownership interests ($12,000 to Jim and $4,000 to Ginny). The remaining distribution of $8,000 ($64,000 total minus $40,000 current E&P and $16,000 accumulated E&P) is a return of capital. Hence, Jim will reduce his stock basis by $6,000 and Ginny will reduce her stock basis by $2,000.

SCR has a zero balance in accumulated E&P at the beginning of the next year because all current and accumulated E&P was distributed during the year.

What if: Assume that SCR's current E&P is $40,000 and its accumulated E&P is $15,000. Also, assume that Jim is the sole shareholder of SCR and that he received a $45,000 distribution on June 1. Assume that after the June distribution Jim sold all his SCR shares to Ginny, who received a $15,000 dividend on December 31. What is the amount and the character of each distribution?

Answer: Jim has a $45,000 dividend. Ginny has a $10,000 dividend and a $5,000 return of capital. Of the $40,000 of current E&P, $30,000 is allocated to Jim's distribution and $10,000 is allocated to Ginny's distribution. Current E&P is allocated between the two distributions in proportion to the total distributions (the calculation for June 1 is $40,000 × [$45,000/$60,000]). However, because Jim's distribution took place before Ginny's distribution, the accumulated E&P is allocated to Jim's distribution ($15,000), leaving $0 in remaining accumulated E&P to be allocated to Ginny's distribution. Ginny is allocated only $10,000 of E&P, leaving her with an excess distribution of $5,000 ($15,000 − $10,000). This excess distribution is treated as a nontaxable reduction of her basis in the SCR stock.

---

[8]Reg. §1.316-2(b) and Rev. Rul. 74-164, 1974-1 C.B. 74.

Positive Current E&P and Negative Accumulated E&P   Distributions deemed paid out of current E&P are taxable as dividends. Distributions in excess of current E&P in this scenario will first be treated as nontaxable reductions in the shareholders' tax basis in their stock. Any excess received over their stock basis will be treated as a (capital) gain from sale of the stock.

What if: Assume SCR reported current E&P of $60,000. The balance in accumulated E&P at the beginning of the year was negative $20,000. On December 31, SCR distributed $48,000 to Jim and $16,000 to Ginny. Jim has a tax basis in his SCR stock of $24,000. Ginny's tax basis in her SCR stock is $10,000. What amount of income will Jim and Ginny report?

Answer: Jim and Ginny will report $45,000 and $15,000 of dividend income, respectively. The distribution is first deemed to be paid from current E&P ($45,000 to Jim and $15,000 to Ginny). No additional amount is treated as a dividend because SCR has negative accumulated E&P.

What tax basis will Jim and Ginny have in their SCR stock after the distribution?

Answer: The amount in excess of current E&P ($3,000 to Jim, $1,000 to Ginny) would be treated as a nontaxable return of capital because Jim and Ginny have enough tax basis in their SCR stock to absorb the amount paid in excess of E&P. Jim's tax basis in his SCR stock after the distribution would be $21,000 ($24,000 − $3,000), and Ginny's tax basis in her SCR stock after the distribution would be $9,000 ($10,000 − $1,000).

What is SCR's remaining balance in accumulated E&P at the end of the year?

Answer: SCR has a $20,000 deficit (negative) balance in accumulated E&P.

Negative Current E&P and Positive Accumulated E&P   When current E&P is negative, the tax status of a dividend is determined by total E&P on the date of the distribution. This requires the corporation to prorate the negative current E&P to the distribution date and add it to accumulated E&P at the beginning of the year to determine total E&P at the distribution date. Distributions in excess of accumulated E&P in this scenario are treated as reductions in the shareholders' tax basis in their stock. Any excess over their stock basis will be treated as a capital gain.

What if: Assume SCR reported current E&P of negative $20,000. The balance in accumulated E&P at the beginning of the year was $60,000. On June 30, SCR distributed $48,000 to Jim and $16,000 to Ginny. Jim has a tax basis in his SCR stock of $24,000. Ginny's tax basis in her SCR stock is $10,000. What amount of dividend income do Jim and Ginny report?

Answer: Jim and Ginny report $37,500 and $12,500 of dividend income, respectively. Because current E&P is negative, SCR must determine its total E&P on the distribution date. SCR prorates the full-year negative current E&P to June 30 [6 months/12 months × ($20,000) = ($10,000)]. The negative current E&P of $10,000 is added to the beginning balance in accumulated E&P of $60,000 to get total E&P as of July 1 of $50,000. Because their distributions were made at the same time, Jim is allocated 75 percent of the total E&P and Ginny is allocated the remaining 25 percent.

What tax basis do Jim and Ginny have in their SCR stock after the distribution?

Answer: $13,500 for Jim and $6,500 for Ginny. The amount in excess of total E&P ($10,500 to Jim, $3,500 to Ginny) is treated first as a nontaxable return of capital. Jim reduces the basis in his SCR stock to $13,500 ($24,000 − $10,500). Ginny reduces the basis in her SCR stock to $6,500 ($10,000 − $3,500).

What is SCR's remaining balance in accumulated E&P at the end of the year?

Answer: Negative $10,000, computed as follows:

Beginning balance	$ 60,000
Prorated negative current E&P, 1/1–6/30	(10,000)
Dividends	(50,000)
Prorated negative current E&P, 7/1–12/31	(10,000)
Ending balance (deficit)	**$(10,000)**

THE KEY FACTS

Dividend Distributions

- The amount distributed as a dividend equals:
  - Cash distributed.
  - Fair market value of noncash property distributed.
  - Reduced by any liabilities assumed by the shareholder on property received.
  - Limited to available E&P (see Exhibit 18-2).

Negative Current E&P and Negative Accumulated E&P When current E&P and accumulated E&P are both negative, none of the distribution is treated as a dividend. Distributions in this scenario will be a return of capital treated as a reduction in the shareholders' tax basis in their stock. Any excess over their stock basis will be treated as a capital gain.

Example 18-7

What if: Assume SCR reported current E&P of negative $50,000. The balance in accumulated E&P at the beginning of the year was negative $60,000. Jim has a tax basis in his SCR stock of $24,000. Ginny's tax basis in her SCR stock is $10,000. On December 31 of this year, SCR distributed $48,000 to Jim and $16,000 to Ginny. What amount of dividend income do Jim and Ginny report this year?

Answer: $0 to Jim and $0 to Ginny. Because current E&P and accumulated E&P are negative, the entire distribution would be treated as either a return of capital or a capital gain.

What is the tax basis in the SCR stock for Jim and Ginny?

Answer: The amount in excess of total E&P ($48,000 to Jim, $16,000 to Ginny) is treated first as a nontaxable return of capital. Jim reduces the basis in his SCR stock to $0 ($24,000 − $48,000, limited to $0). Ginny reduces the basis in her SCR stock to $0 ($10,000 − $16,000, limited to $0).

What amount of capital gain do Jim and Ginny report as a result of the distribution?

Answer: Jim has a capital gain of $24,000, the amount by which the distribution exceeds the tax basis in his SCR stock ($48,000 − $24,000). Ginny has a capital gain of $6,000, the amount by which the distribution exceeds the tax basis in her SCR stock ($16,000 − $10,000).

What is SCR's remaining balance in accumulated E&P at the end of the year?

Answer: A deficit (negative) balance of $110,000, the sum of the accumulated E&P deficit of $60,000 plus the current E&P deficit of $50,000.

Exhibit 18-2 summarizes the rules for determining whether a distribution represents dividend income. When both balances are negative, the distribution is treated as a return of capital (tax-free to the extent of the shareholder's tax basis in his or her stock and capital gain in excess of this amount), and the deficits in E&P are unaffected. When both balances are positive, the distribution is treated as a dividend to the extent of current E&P at year-end and then to the extent of the balance of accumulated E&P. A distribution in excess of current and accumulated E&P is treated as a return of capital. When current E&P is negative and accumulated E&P is positive, distributions are dividend income to the extent of accumulated E&P after netting against the deficit in current E&P (up to the date of the distribution). The distribution reduces accumulated E&P but not below zero. Finally, when accumulated E&P is negative and current E&P is positive, distributions are dividend income to the extent of current E&P.

EXHIBIT 18-2 **Summary of E&P Status and Taxability of Cash Distributions**

Balance in Current E&P at the Time of the Distribution	Balance in Accumulated E&P at the Time of the Distribution	
	Negative	**Positive**
Negative	Distributions are a return of capital.	Distributions are dividend income to extent of accumulated E&P after netting against deficit in current E&P.
Positive	Distributions are dividend income to extent of current E&P.	Distributions are dividend income to extent of current E&P and the balance of accumulated E&P.

Distributions of Noncash Property to Shareholders

On occasion, a shareholder will receive a distribution of property other than cash. These distributions are more complex because the liability affects the amount distributed and any difference between the value and the tax basis of the property can affect the calculation of E&P. To begin, when noncash property is received, the shareholder determines the amount distributed as follows:

> Money received
> + Fair market value of other property received
> − Liabilities assumed by the shareholder on property received
> _____
> Amount distributed[9]

Example 18-8

What if: Assume Ginny elected to receive $15,000 in cash and a Fuji custom touring bike that had a fair market value of $1,000. Suppose that SCR has current E&P of $100,000 and no accumulated E&P. What amount of dividend income will Ginny report this year?

Answer: $16,000. Ginny would include the $15,000 plus the $1,000 fair market value of the bicycle in her gross income as a dividend.

As a general rule, a shareholder's tax basis in noncash property received as a dividend equals the property's fair market value.[10] No downward adjustment is made for liabilities assumed by the shareholder (these are considered part of the property's cost). The shareholder determines fair market value as of the date of the distribution.

Example 18-9

What is Ginny's tax basis in the bicycle she received as a dividend in the previous example?

Answer: $1,000. Ginny has a tax basis in the bicycle of $1,000, the bicycle's fair market value. Ginny would pay an income tax of $150 on receipt of the bicycle (assuming the dividend qualifies for the preferential 15 percent tax rate).

Example 18-10

What if: Assume that, instead of $48,000 in cash, Jim elected to receive a parcel of land SCR had previously purchased for $60,000 for possible expansion. The land has a fair market value of $60,000 and a remaining mortgage of $12,000 attached to it. Jim will assume the mortgage on the land. Suppose that SCR has current E&P of $100,000 and no accumulated E&P. How much dividend income does Jim recognize on the distribution?

Answer: $48,000. Jim recognizes dividend income in an amount equal to the land's fair market value of $60,000 less the mortgage he assumes on the land in the amount of $12,000.

What is Jim's tax basis in the land he receives?

Answer: $60,000. Jim receives a tax basis equal to the land's fair market value. Jim has a $60,000 basis in the land because he recognized $48,000 of income and assumed $12,000 of debt.

---

[9]§301(b).
[10]§301(d).

The Tax Consequences to a Corporation Paying Noncash Property as a Dividend   Besides affecting the amount received by the shareholder, the distribution of noncash property can also affect corporate taxable income and E&P. Taxable income can be affected because gains (but not losses) are recognized by a corporation on the distribution of noncash property.[11] Specifically, the corporation recognizes a taxable gain on the distribution to the extent that the fair market value of property distributed exceeds the corporation's tax basis in the property. Current E&P is increased by the gain calculated using the E&P basis of the property. In contrast, if the fair market value of the property distributed is less than the corporation's tax basis in the property, the corporation does not recognize a deductible loss for either computing taxable income or current E&P.

Example 18-11

What if: Assume SCR had a tax basis of $650 in the Fuji custom touring bike (for both income tax and E&P purposes) that it distributed to Ginny (see the facts in Example 18-8). How much gain, if any, does SCR recognize when it distributes the bicycle to Ginny?

Answer: $350. SCR recognizes a taxable gain of $350 on the distribution of the bicycle to Ginny ($1,000 − $650). Because the bike is considered inventory, SCR would characterize the gain as ordinary income. SCR would pay a corporate level tax of $73.50 on the distribution (21% × $350). The total tax paid by SCR and Ginny (Example 18-9) would be $223.50 ($150 + $73.50). This is a high tax cost to pay to transfer the $1,000 bicycle to Ginny in the form of a dividend. Current E&P for SCR is increased by the gain and reduced by the tax liability.

What if: Assume SCR had a tax basis of $1,200 in the Fuji custom touring bike that it distributed to Ginny. The bicycle's fair market value declined to $1,000 because it was an outdated model. How much loss, if any, does SCR recognize when it distributes the bicycle to Ginny as a dividend?

Answer: $0. SCR is not permitted to recognize a loss on the distribution of the bicycle to Ginny.

What if: Suppose SCR *sold* the bicycle to Ginny for $1,000. How much loss, if any, could SCR recognize if it sold the bicycle to Ginny?

Answer: $200. SCR is permitted to recognize a loss on the sale of property to a shareholder provided it does not run afoul of the related-person loss rules found in §267. To be a related person, Ginny must own *more than* 50 percent of SCR, which she does not in this scenario.

Liabilities   The amount of any liability assumed by the shareholder can also affect the recognized gain. When a liability assumed by the shareholder is greater than the distributed property's fair market value, the property's fair market value is deemed to be the amount of the liability assumed by the shareholder.[12] If the liability assumed is less than the property's fair market value, the gain recognized on the distribution is still the excess of the property's fair market value over its tax basis (i.e., the liability is ignored by the distributing corporation).

Example 18-12

What if: Assume Jim received a parcel of land the company had previously purchased for possible expansion. The land has a fair market value of $60,000 and a remaining mortgage of $12,000 attached to it. SCR has a tax basis in the land of $20,000. Jim will assume the mortgage on the land. SCR has current E&P of $100,000 and no accumulated E&P. How much gain, if any, does SCR recognize when it distributes the land to Jim?

Answer: $40,000 ($60,000 − $20,000). Because the mortgage assumed by Jim is less than the land's fair market value, SCR recognizes gain in an amount equal to the excess of the land's fair market value over its tax basis ($60,000 − $20,000).

[11]§311.

[12]§311(b)(2) refers to §336(b).

> **What if:** Assume the mortgage assumed by Jim was $75,000 instead of $12,000. The land has a fair market value of $60,000, and SCR has a tax basis in the land of $20,000. Jim will assume the mortgage on the land. SCR has current E&P of $100,000. How much gain, if any, does SCR recognize when it distributes the land to Jim?
>
> **Answer:** $55,000 ($75,000 − $20,000). Because the mortgage assumed by Jim exceeds the land's fair market value, SCR treats the land's fair market value as $75,000 and recognizes gain in an amount equal to the excess of the mortgage assumed over its tax basis ($75,000 − $20,000).

Effect of Noncash Property Distributions on E&P

Current E&P. As explained above, the distribution of *appreciated* noncash property (fair market value in excess of income tax basis), results in recognition of a taxable gain by the corporation. If the E&P basis of the property is the same as the income tax basis of the property, the gain recognized increases current E&P and the taxes paid (or payable) on the gain reduce current E&P. If, however, the property's regular income tax basis is different from its E&P basis (e.g., LIFO regular tax basis vs. FIFO E&P basis), or the accumulated depreciation for regular tax is different from accumulated depreciation for E&P purposes, current E&P is increased by the E&P gain (fair market value in excess of E&P basis) and reduced by the income taxes paid (or payable) on the income tax gain.

When a corporation distributes *depreciated* noncash property (regular income tax basis in excess of fair market value of property), it is not allowed to deduct the loss for taxable income purposes. If the E&P basis exceeds the fair market value of the property, the corporation is not allowed to deduct the loss in determining current E&P. Consequently, the distribution of depreciated property (income tax and E&P basis in excess of fair market value) does not affect current E&P.[13]

Accumulated E&P. When a corporation distributes *appreciated* property (fair market value in excess of E&P basis), it reduces accumulated E&P by the fair market value of the property distributed at the end of the year. When it distributes *depreciated* property (E&P basis in excess of fair market value of the property), it reduces accumulated E&P by the E&P basis of the property. When a corporation distributes property subject to a liability at the end of the year, it increases accumulated E&P by the amount of the liability assumed by the shareholder(s) on distribution. Downward adjustments for distributions cannot cause accumulated E&P to drop below zero. Finally, if accumulated E&P is negative, downward adjustments are not allowed.

THE KEY FACTS

Effect of Distributions on E&P

E&P is reduced by distributions as follows:

- Cash distributed.
- E&P basis of noncash *depreciated* property (fair market value less than or equal to its E&P basis).
- Fair market value of noncash *appreciated* property.
- Noncash property distributions are reduced by any liabilities assumed by the shareholder on property received.
- E&P reductions for distributions cannot cause E&P to drop below zero.

Example 18-13

> **What if:** Assume the same facts as in Example 18-12. SCR distributed land to Jim that has a fair market value of $60,000 and a remaining mortgage of $12,000 attached to it. SCR has a tax and E&P basis in the land of $20,000. Jim has assumed the mortgage on the land. SCR has current E&P of $100,000, which includes the net gain of $31,600 from distribution of the land ($40,000 gain less a related tax liability of $8,400) and accumulated E&P at the beginning of the year of $500,000. What is SCR's beginning balance in accumulated E&P at January 1 of next year, as a result of the distribution of the land to Jim?
>
> **Answer:** $552,000, computed as follows:

Accumulated E&P, this year	$500,000
Current E&P	100,000
Fair market value of land distributed	(60,000)
Liability assumed by Jim	12,000
Beginning balance, accumulated E&P, next year	**$552,000**

(continued on page 18-14)

[13]§312(a) and (b).

What if: Assume SCR has current E&P of $40,000, which includes the net gain of $31,600 from distribution of the land ($40,000 gain less a related tax liability of $8,400) and accumulated E&P of $500,000. What is SCR's beginning balance in accumulated E&P at January 1 of next year, as a result of the distribution of the land to Jim?

Answer: $492,000, computed as follows:

Accumulated E&P, this year	$500,000
Current E&P	40,000
Fair market value of land distributed	(60,000)
Liability assumed by Jim	12,000
Beginning balance, accumulated E&P, next year	**$492,000**

What if: Assume the land distributed to Jim has a tax and E&P basis to SCR of $75,000 instead of $20,000. SCR has current E&P of $100,000, which does not include the disallowed loss of $15,000 on the distribution ($60,000 fair market value less $75,000 tax basis). SCR has accumulated E&P at the beginning of the year of $500,000. What is SCR's beginning balance in accumulated E&P at January 1 of next year, after taking the distribution of the land into account?

Answer: $537,000, computed as follows:

Accumulated E&P, this year	$500,000
Current E&P	100,000
E&P basis of land distributed	(75,000)
Liability assumed by Jim	12,000
Beginning balance, accumulated E&P, next year	**$537,000**

TAXES IN THE REAL WORLD   Visteon's Special Distribution

Visteon Corporation is a global automotive supplier that manufactures vehicle information and controls. During 2008 and 2009, weakened economic conditions triggered a global economic recession that severely impacted the automotive sector. Visteon filed voluntary petitions for reorganization relief in 2009, and the company has been profitable since it emerged from bankruptcy in 2010.

Visteon currently has two technology-focused core businesses: vehicle cockpit electronics and thermal energy management. The company's vehicle cockpit electronics product line includes audio systems, infotainment systems, driver information systems, and electronic control modules. In order to focus its operations on automotive cockpit electronics, Visteon sold a subsidiary that generated a pretax gain of approximately $2.3 billion. The sale was completed on June 9, 2015, and Visteon received net cash proceeds of approximately $2.7 billion. The company then announced a plan to return $2.5 billion–$2.75 billion of cash to shareholders through a series of actions including a special distribution.

Based on the tax disclosures in Visteon's annual report, it appears that the company had about a $1 billion deficit in accumulated E&P entering 2015. If Visteon's operations and gain on the sale of the subsidiary generates current E&P of $1.5 billion, then a distribution of $2.5 billion by year-end will generate a taxable dividend of $1.5 billion. Despite the deficit in accumulated E&P, the distribution would come from current E&P. The distribution in excess of current E&P ($1 billion) would be a return of capital to shareholders.

In contrast, if Visteon waits until 2016 to distribute the $2.5 billion, the distribution would generate a dividend of only $500 million. Assuming Visteon doesn't generate any additional E&P in 2016, the current E&P from 2015 would be offset by the deficit in accumulated E&P ($1.5 billion minus $1 billion equals $500 million).

Epilog: Visteon distributed approximately $1.75 billion on January 22, 2016, and authorized a share repurchase program to repurchase up to $500 million of its shares of common stock through December 31, 2016.

Sources: Visteon Corporation 2014 and 2015 Forms 10-K and Form 8-K September 11, 2015.

STOCK DISTRIBUTIONS

Rather than distribute cash to its shareholders, a corporation may instead distribute additional shares of its own stock (or rights to acquire additional shares) to shareholders. A publicly held corporation is likely to distribute additional shares of stock to promote shareholder goodwill (it allows the corporation to retain cash and still provide shareholders with tangible evidence of their interest in corporate earnings), or to reduce the market price of its outstanding shares (the stock distribution reduces the price of shares by increasing their number, making the stock more accessible to a wider range of shareholders). For example, a 5 percent stock distribution will increase the number of shares outstanding by 5 percent. Hence, a shareholder holding 100 shares will own 105 shares after a 5 percent stock distribution. Corporations may also declare a **stock split,** in which the number of shares outstanding is increased by the ratio of the split. For example, a 2-for-1 stock split would double the number of shares outstanding. Hence, a shareholder holding 100 shares will own 200 shares after a 2-for-1 stock split. Stock splits are sometimes used by public corporations to keep stock prices accessible to a diverse group of investors.

Tax Consequences to Shareholders Receiving a Stock Distribution

Nontaxable Stock Distributions   In theory, stock splits and pro rata stock distributions do not provide shareholders with any increase in value. This is because these distributions do not change a shareholders' interest in the corporation except that the shareholder now owns more pieces of paper (shares of stock). As a result, these distributions are generally not included in the shareholders' gross income.[14]

In a nontaxable stock distribution, each shareholder allocates a portion of their tax basis from the stock on which the distribution was issued to the newly issued stock based on the relative fair market value (FMV) of the stock.[15] In the case of a simple distribution of common stock or a stock split where the stock distributed is identical to the stock from which the distribution is made (same class and same fair market value), the new per-share tax basis is the original tax basis divided by the total number of shares held (including the new shares).

For example, assume a shareholder owns 100 shares of Acme Corporation stock, for which she paid $3,000. Acme declares a 100 percent stock distribution and sends the shareholder an additional 100 shares of stock. The shareholder will now own 200 shares of stock with the same tax basis of $3,000. The basis of each share of stock decreases from its original $30 per share ($3,000/100) to $15 per share ($3,000/200). The holding period of the new stock includes the holding period for which the shareholder held the old stock.[16]

Example 18-14

Jim has a tax basis in his SCR stock of $24,000. Ginny's tax basis in her SCR stock is $10,000. Jim owns 75 of the 100 shares of outstanding SCR stock, while Ginny owns the remaining 25 shares.

What if: Assume that for estate and gift tax purposes, SCR declare a 100 percent stock distribution. As a result, Jim will own 150 shares of SCR stock and Ginny will own the remaining 50 shares.

(continued on page 18-16)

---

[14]§305(a). To be nontaxable, a stock distribution must meet two conditions: (1) it must be made with respect to the corporation's common stock, and (2) it must be pro rata with respect to all shareholders (i.e., the shareholders' relative equity positions do not change as a result of the distribution).

[15]§307. Technically, the shares received in the distribution are allocated a portion of the original basis determined by the ratio of FMVs. This computation is necessary when the stock distribution includes a different class of shares (e.g., preferred stock).

[16]§1223(4).

Is the stock distribution taxable to Jim and Ginny?

Answer: No. The stock distribution to Jim and Ginny is nontaxable because it is made pro rata to the shareholders (that is, the distribution did not change their proportional ownership of SCR).

What is the tax basis of each share of SCR stock now held by Jim and Ginny?

Answer: Jim's original tax basis of $24,000 is divided among 150 shares. Hence, each one of Jim's shares has a basis of $160. Ginny's original tax basis of $10,000 is divided among 50 shares. Hence, each one of Ginny's shares has a basis of $200.

THE KEY FACTS

Tax Consequences of Stock Distributions

- Pro rata stock distributions generally are nontaxable.
- Shareholders allocate basis from the "old" stock to the "new" stock based on relative fair market value.
- Non-pro rata stock distributions usually are taxable as dividends.

Taxable Stock Distributions Non-pro rata stock distributions usually are included in the shareholder's gross income as taxable dividends to the extent of the distributing corporation's E&P.[17] This makes sense because the recipient has now received something of value: an increase in the shareholder's claim on the corporation's income and assets. For example, a corporation may give its shareholders the choice between a cash or a stock distribution. In this case, shareholders who elect to receive stock in lieu of money will have a taxable dividend equal to the fair market value of the stock received. When a stock distribution is taxable, the shareholder will have a tax basis in the new stock equal to its fair market value.

LO 18-4 STOCK REDEMPTIONS

continued from page 18-2...

In the original storyline, Jim and Ginny raised some of the initial capital they needed to start SCR by borrowing $50,000 from Jim's father, Walt. An alternate strategy would have been to issue 25 additional shares of SCR stock to Walt in return for $50,000. This change in facts would reduce Jim's ownership percentage in SCR to 60 percent (75 shares/125 shares). Ginny's ownership percentage would decrease to 20 percent (25 shares/125 shares). Walt would own the remaining 20 percent. We will assume this change in facts to continue the storyline.

Walt does not participate in the management of the company. In fact, he was hoping to cash out of SCR when it became profitable and use the money to put a down payment on a condominium in The Villages, a retirement community near Orlando, Florida. With the SCR stock valued at $5,000 per share ($125,000 in total), Walt saw an opportunity to realize his retirement dream. Jim and Ginny saw it as a chance to own all the company's stock, eliminating a potential source of discord should Jim's father disapprove of the way they are managing the company.

By the end of this year, the company expects to have sufficient cash to buy back some or all of Walt's shares of SCR stock. Jim and Ginny were wondering about the potential tax consequences to SCR and Walt under various redemption plans. In particular, Jim and Ginny wanted to know whether there was a tax difference between (1) buying back 5 of Walt's shares this year and the remaining 20 shares equally over the next four years (at 5 shares per year), and (2) buying back all 25 shares this year using an installment note that would pay Walt 20 percent of the purchase price in each of the next five years plus interest. ■

---

[17]§305(b). A technical discussion of all the rules that apply to determining whether a stock distribution is taxable is beyond the scope of this text.

Publicly held corporations buy back (redeem) their stock from existing shareholders for many and varied reasons. For example, a corporation may have excess cash and limited investment opportunities, or management may feel the stock is undervalued. Management may see a large redemption as a way to get analysts to reconsider their valuation of the company or to selectively buy out dissenting shareholders who have become disruptive. Reducing the number of outstanding shares also increases earnings per share (by reducing the number of shares in the denominator of the calculation) and potentially increases the stock's market price.[18]

Privately held corporations often use stock redemptions for other reasons, such as to shift ownership control from older to younger family members who do not have the resources to purchase shares directly or to buy out dissatisfied, disinterested, or deceased shareholders. In addition, redemptions of an ex-spouse's stock can provide liquidity in a divorce agreement and eliminate the individual from management or ownership in the company. Finally, redemptions can provide cash to satisfy estate taxes imposed on the estate of a deceased shareholder of the company.

The Form of a Stock Redemption

A stock redemption is an acquisition by a corporation of its stock from a shareholder in exchange for property, whether the stock so acquired is cancelled, retired, or held as treasury stock.[19] The term *property* in this context has the same meaning as it does for distributions (i.e., cash and noncash property).

Stock redemptions take the form of an exchange in which the shareholders give up their stock in the corporation for property, usually cash. If the form of the transaction is respected, shareholders compute gain or loss (usually capital) by comparing the amount realized (money and the fair market value of other property received) with their tax basis in the stock exchanged.

Without any tax law restrictions, a sole shareholder of a corporation could circumvent the dividend rules by structuring distributions to have the form of an exchange (i.e., a stock redemption). For example, rather than have the corporation make a $100,000 dividend distribution, the shareholder could have the corporation buy back $100,000 of stock from the shareholder. If the shareholder had a tax basis of $60,000 in the stock redeemed, the amount of income reported on the shareholder's tax return would decrease from $100,000 (dividend) to $40,000 (capital gain). At present, both amounts would be taxed at the same preferential tax rate (generally 15 percent), assuming the shareholder held the stock for more than a year. Similar to a dividend, however, the sole shareholder would continue to own 100 percent of the corporation before and after the stock redemption.

Form is not always respected in a redemption, however. The tax law may determine (or the IRS may argue that) the transaction is, in substance, a property distribution, the tax consequences of which should be determined under the dividend rules we discussed above.

The IRC provides both objective (mechanical or **"bright line"**) tests and subjective (judgmental) tests to distinguish when a redemption should be treated as an exchange or a potential dividend.[20] The result is an intricate set of rules that the corporation and its shareholders must navigate carefully to ensure that the shareholders receive the tax treatment they desire. This is especially true in closely held family corporations, where the majority of stock is held by people related to each other through birth or marriage.

While individual shareholders prefer sale treatment, corporate shareholders generally have more incentive for dividend treatment. Dividends from domestic corporations are

---

[18]It is also important to note that corporations are not taxed on gains or losses resulting from transactions in their own stock. §1032.

[19]§317(b).

[20]§302. The IRC also defines when sale treatment is appropriate in some special circumstances. For example, §303 defines when sale treatment is allowed for redemptions of stock to pay death taxes.

eligible for the dividends received deduction (usually 50 or 65 percent), whereas a capital gain is taxed at the corporation's tax rate. A corporation might prefer exchange treatment if the redemption results in a loss, if the corporation has capital loss carryovers, or its stock tax basis as a percentage of the redemption price exceeds the dividends received deduction ratio.

Redemptions That Reduce a Shareholder's Ownership Interest

The IRC allows a shareholder to treat a redemption as an exchange if the transaction meets one of three change-in-stock-ownership tests.[21] These stock ownership tests look at the redemption from the shareholder's perspective.

Redemptions That Are Substantially Disproportionate

The IRC states in §302(b)(2) that a redemption will be treated as an exchange if the redemption is "substantially disproportionate with respect to the shareholder." A shareholder meets this requirement by satisfying all three objective ("bright line") *stock ownership tests*:

1. Immediately after the exchange, the shareholder owns less than 50 percent of the total combined voting power of all classes of stock entitled to vote.
2. The shareholder's percentage ownership of voting stock after the redemption is less than 80 percent of his or her percentage ownership before the redemption.
3. The shareholder's percentage ownership of the aggregate fair market value of the corporation's common stock (voting and nonvoting) after the redemption is less than 80 percent of his or her percentage ownership before the redemption.

For example, suppose a shareholder owns 60 of 100 shares (60 percent) of a corporation's stock prior to a redemption. He must own less than 48 shares of the stock after a redemption to have the redemption treated as an exchange (60% × 80% = 48% and 48 percent is less than 50 percent). In contrast, suppose the same shareholder owns 70 shares of stock before a redemption (70 percent). In this case, a redemption must reduce his ownership below 50 percent to qualify as an exchange. In this example an 80 percent reduction in the percentage owned (70% × 80% = 56%) will not satisfy the 50 percent test.

The determination as to whether a shareholder meets both the 50 percent and 80 percent tests is made on a shareholder-by-shareholder basis. As a result, some shareholders can satisfy the test while others do not. If a shareholder owns multiple classes of common stock (voting and nonvoting), the less-than-80-percent of fair market value test is applied to the shareholder's aggregate ownership of the common stock rather than on a class-by-class basis.

Example 18-15

What if: Assume Walt is not related to either Jim or Ginny. This year, SCR redeemed five shares of his stock in exchange for $25,000. Walt has a tax basis in the five shares of SCR stock of $10,000 ($2,000 per share). What is the tax treatment of the stock redemption to Walt under §302(b)(2)?

Answer: $25,000 dividend. Prior to the redemption, Walt owned 20 percent of SCR (25/125 shares). After the redemption, his ownership percentage in SCR dropped to 16.67 percent (20/120 shares). This redemption does not satisfy the substantially disproportionate test. After the redemption, Walt owns less than 50 percent of SCR stock, but his ownership percentage after the redemption (16.67 percent) does not fall below 80 percent of his ownership percentage prior to the redemption (80% × 20% = 16%). Walt will not be able to treat the redemption as an exchange under this change-in-ownership test. Unless he can satisfy one of the other change-in-ownership tests, Walt will have a $25,000 dividend, assuming SCR has sufficient E&P, rather than a $15,000 capital gain ($25,000 − $10,000).

---

[21]§302(b)(1), (b)(2), and (b)(3).

How many shares of stock would SCR have to redeem from Walt to guarantee exchange treatment under the substantially disproportionate test?

Answer: Six shares. For Walt to meet the 80 percent test, SCR must redeem six shares of stock. The computation is made as follows:

$$\frac{25 - x}{125 - x} < 16\%, \text{ where } x \text{ is the number of shares to be redeemed}$$

Using some algebra, we can compute x to be 5.95, rounded up to six shares.[22] If SCR redeems six shares from Walt, his ownership percentage after the redemption will be 15.97 percent (19/119 shares), which now meets the 80 percent test. The redemption of this one additional share transforms the transaction from a $30,000 dividend (6 shares × $5,000) to an $18,000 capital gain ($30,000 − $12,000).

In determining whether he meets the 50 percent and 80 percent tests, Walt must take into account the **constructive ownership** or stock attribution rules found in §318. Under certain circumstances, these tax rules treat stock owned by other persons (individuals and entities) that are related to the redeeming shareholder as being owned by the redeeming shareholder for purposes of determining whether the shareholder has met the change-in-stock-ownership tests. The purpose of the attribution rules is to prevent shareholders from dispersing stock ownership to either family members who have similar economic interests or entities controlled by the shareholder to avoid having a stock redemption characterized as a dividend.

Family attribution. Individuals are treated as owning the shares of stock owned by their spouse, children, grandchildren, and parents. Stock owned constructively through the family attribution rule cannot be reattributed to another family member through the family attribution rule (this rule is sometimes referred to as *reattribution* or *double attribution*).

Example 18-16

Return to the amended storyline in which Walt is Jim's father and, in exchange for $50,000, he receives 25 shares of SCR stock and 20 percent ownership of the company. This year, SCR redeems six shares of stock from Walt in exchange for $30,000. Walt has a tax basis in the six shares of stock redeemed of $12,000 ($2,000 per share). What is the tax treatment of the stock redemption to Walt under §302(b)(2)?

Answer: $30,000 dividend.

Prior to the redemption, Walt owned 20 percent of SCR (25/125 shares) directly. Under the family attribution rules, he is treated as constructively owning the shares of SCR stock owned by his son Jim (75 shares). In applying the substantially disproportionate change-in-stock-ownership tests, Walt is treated as owning 100 shares of SCR stock (25 + 75), or 80 percent of the SCR stock (100/125 shares). After the redemption, his ownership percentage in SCR drops to 79 percent (94/119 shares). This redemption does not satisfy the substantially disproportionate test because Walt is deemed to own more than 50 percent of the SCR stock after the redemption. As a result, he will have a $30,000 dividend, assuming SCR has sufficient E&P, rather than an $18,000 capital gain ($30,000 − $12,000).

An interesting question arises as to what happens to the tax basis of stock redeemed that is not used in determining the shareholder's tax consequences. This occurs in a redemption treated as a dividend, where the tax basis of the stock redeemed is not subtracted from the amount received from the corporation. Under the current rules, the tax

---

[22]Multiplying both sides by $(125 - x)$, we get $25 - x = 20 - .16x$. Moving x to the right side of the equation and the integers to the left side of the equation, we get $5 = .84x$. Solving for x, we get $x = 5.95$.

basis of the stock redeemed is added back to the tax basis of any shares still held by the shareholder.[23] If the shareholder no longer holds any shares, the tax basis transfers to the stock held by those persons who caused the shareholder to have dividend treatment under the attribution rules.

Example 18-17

In the preceding example, SCR redeemed six shares of stock from Walt for $30,000, and the transaction was treated as a dividend because of the application of the family attribution rules. Walt had a tax basis in the six shares of stock redeemed of $12,000 ($2,000 per share), but this tax basis was not used in determining their taxable income from the transaction.

What is Walt's tax basis in the remaining 19 shares of SCR stock?

Answer: $50,000. Walt adds back the unused $12,000 tax basis in the six shares redeemed to the tax basis of the remaining 19 shares. The tax basis in these remaining shares increases to $50,000, the original tax basis of the 25 shares.

Attribution from entities to owners or beneficiaries.   Owners or beneficiaries of entities can be deemed to own shares of stock owned by the entity itself. Under these rules, partners are deemed to own a pro rata share of their partnership's stock holdings (i.e., a partner who has a 10 percent interest in a partnership is deemed to own 10 percent of any stock owned by the partnership). Beneficiaries are deemed to own a pro rata share of the stock owned by the trust or estate of which they are a beneficiary. Shareholders are deemed to own a pro rata share of their corporation's stock holdings, but only if they own at least 50 percent of the value of the corporation's stock. Other attribution rules, such as family attribution, apply in determining if this 50 percent test is met.

Example 18-18

What if: Assume that Walt is not Jim's father, and besides the 25 shares of SCR that he owns directly, he is a 40 percent partner in a partnership that also owns 25 shares in SCR. The other 60 percent of the partnership is owned by his neighbors, Fred and Ethel, who are unrelated to Walt. How many shares of SCR is Walt treated as owning directly and indirectly through the partnership?

Answer: 35 shares. Walt owns 25 shares directly and another 10 shares indirectly because he is treated as owning a pro rata share of SCR stock owned by the partnership; in this example, 40 percent times 25 shares.

What if: Assume now that Walt is a 40 percent shareholder in Acme Corporation that owns 25 shares in SCR. The other 60 percent of Acme shares is owned by his neighbors, Fred and Ethel, who are unrelated to Walt. How many shares of SCR is Walt treated as owning indirectly through Acme Corporation?

Answer: 0 shares. None of the shares owned by Acme Corporation are attributed to Walt under the constructive ownership rules because Walt does not own at least 50 percent of the stock of Acme Corporation. Stock owned by a corporation (Acme in this example) is attributed to a shareholder only if the shareholder owns at least 50 percent of the corporation's stock. In this case, Walt only owns 40 percent of Acme and therefore SCR shares owned by Acme are not attributed to Walt.

What if: Assume now that Walt is a 60 percent shareholder in Acme Corporation that owns 25 shares in SCR. The other 40 percent of Acme shares is owned by his neighbors, Fred and Ethel, who are unrelated to Walt. How many shares of SCR is Walt treated as owning indirectly through Acme Corporation?

Answer: 15 shares. Walt owns 15 shares indirectly because he is treated as owning a pro rata share of SCR stock owned by Acme; in this example, 60 percent times 25 shares. A portion of Acme's stock in SCR is attributed to Walt because he owns at least 50 percent of the stock of Acme Corporation.

---

[23]Reg. §1.302-2.

Attribution from owners or beneficiaries to entities. Entities can be deemed to own other stock owned by their owners or beneficiaries. Under these rules, a partnership is deemed to own 100 percent of the shares owned by its partners. A trust or estate is deemed to own 100 percent of the shares owned by its beneficiaries. A corporation is deemed to own 100 percent of the shares owned by its shareholders, but only if the shareholder owns at least 50 percent of the value of the corporation's stock (direct plus constructive ownership). Stock that is deemed owned by an entity cannot be reattributed to the other owners in the entity under the entity-to-owner rules previously discussed (this is known as *sideways attribution*).

Example 18-19

What if: Assume that Walt owns 25 shares of SCR and he is a 40 percent partner in a partnership. The other 60 percent of the partnership is owned by Walt's neighbors, Fred and Ethel, who are unrelated to Walt. How many shares of SCR is the partnership treated as owning indirectly through Walt?

Answer: 25 shares. Stock in a corporation (SCR) is attributed from an owner in an entity (Walt) to the entity (the partnership) in full. Under the owner to entity attribution rule, all of Walt's 25 shares would be attributed to the partnership as long as Walt had any ownership interest in the partnership.

What if: Assume the same facts as in the previous what-if example except that the partnership was now Acme Corporation. How many shares of SCR is Acme treated as owning indirectly through Walt?

Answer: 0 shares. Because the entity (Acme) is a corporation, the owner in the entity (Walt) must own at least 50 percent of the stock of the entity (Acme) in order for there to be any attribution from the owner (Walt) to the entity (Acme).

What if: Assume the same facts as in the previous what-if example except that Walt owns 60 percent of Acme Corporation. How many shares of SCR is Acme Corporation treated as owning indirectly through Walt?

Answer: 25 shares. Because the entity (Acme) is a corporation and the owner (Walt) owns at least 50 percent in the entity (Acme) all of Walt's 25 shares in SCR is attributed to Acme Corporation.

Option attribution. A person having an option to purchase stock is deemed to own the stock that the option entitles the person to purchase.

Complete Redemption of the Stock Owned by a Shareholder

The IRC holds that a redemption will be treated as an exchange if it is in "complete redemption of all of the stock of the corporation owned by the shareholder."[24] This test seems redundant with the substantially disproportionate test discussed above; after all, a complete redemption automatically satisfies the 50 percent and 80 percent tests. The difference is in the application of the family attribution rules discussed above.

The stock attribution rules also apply to a complete redemption. This presents a potential problem in family-owned corporations in which the only (or majority) shareholders are parents, children, and grandchildren. Parents who have all their stock redeemed will be treated as having received a dividend if their children or grandchildren continue to own the remaining stock in the corporation because of the operation of the family attribution rules. To provide family members with relief in these situations, the IRC allows shareholders to waive (ignore) the family attribution rules in a complete redemption of their stock.[25] As usual, there are some strings attached.

The first requirement is that the shareholder has no interest in the corporation immediately after the exchange as a "shareholder, employee, director, officer or consultant."[26] These relations to the corporation are referred to as prohibited interests. The second requirement is that the shareholder does not acquire a prohibited interest within 10 years

[24]§302(b)(3).
[25]§302(c)(2).
[26]§302(c).

after the redemption, unless by inheritance (this is known as the *10-year look-forward rule*). Finally, the shareholder must agree to notify the IRS district director within 30 days if he or she acquires a prohibited interest within 10 years after the redemption. These agreements are referred to as **triple i agreements.**[27] The shareholder can still be a creditor of the corporation (i.e., the parents can receive a corporate note in return for their stock if the corporation does not have the cash on hand to finance the redemption).

Example 18-20

Return to the amended storyline in which Walt is Jim's father and he owns 25 shares of SCR stock. Assume SCR redeemed all 25 of his shares this year for $125,000, and for the year SCR has current E&P of $500,000. Walt's tax basis in the SCR shares is $50,000 (25 × $2,000). Under the family attribution rules, Walt would still be treated as constructively owning 75 percent of the SCR stock (Jim would own 75 of the remaining 100 shares in SCR). The $125,000 payment would be treated as a taxable dividend.

What happens to the unused $50,000 tax basis in the SCR stock redeemed?

Answer: The tax basis transfers to Jim's stock, giving him a new tax basis in his SCR stock of $74,000 ($24,000 + $50,000).

How can Walt change the tax treatment of the complete redemption?

Answer: Because Walt has redeemed all his shares, he can waive the family attribution rules, provided he files a triple i agreement with the IRS and does not retain a prohibited interest in SCR (e.g., as an employee or consultant). By waiving the family attribution rules, Walt will be able to treat the redemption as an exchange and report a capital gain of $75,000 ($125,000 − $50,000).

Redemptions That Are Not Essentially Equivalent to a Dividend   The IRC provides that a redemption will be treated as an exchange if it is "not essentially equivalent to a dividend."[28] This is a subjective determination that turns on the facts and circumstances of each case. To satisfy this requirement, there must be a "meaningful" reduction in the shareholder's ownership interest in the corporation as a result of the redemption. Neither the IRS nor the courts provide any mechanical tests to make this determination. As a result of the potential for litigation, shareholder reliance on this test is typically a last resort.[29]

Although the courts have held that a shareholder's interest can include the right to vote and exercise control, participate in current and accumulated earnings, or share in net assets on liquidation, the IRS generally looks at the change in voting power as the key factor. The shareholder's voting power must decrease and be below 50 percent as a result of the exchange before this test can be considered.[30] As before, the stock attribution rules apply to these types of redemptions. Shareholders generally turn to this test to provide exchange treatment for redemptions when they cannot meet the "bright line" tests discussed previously.

---

[27]The agreement gets its name from the clause in which it is described [§302(c)(2)(A)(iii)].

[28]§302(b)(1).

[29]The Supreme Court has held in *United States v. Davis,* 397 U.S. 301, at 313 (1970), that the only way for a shareholder to qualify under this test is for the redemption to "result in a meaningful reduction of the shareholder's proportionate interest in the corporation."

[30]In Rev. Rul. 76-385, 1976-2 C.B. 92, the IRS held that in the case of a "small, minority shareholder, whose relative stock interest is minimal and who exercises no control over the affairs of the corporation," any reduction in proportionate interest is "meaningful." In this ruling, the shareholder's ownership percentage decreased from .0001118% to .0001081%, which would not be considered a "meaningful" reduction by most standards. Because the reduction in stock ownership did not meet the substantially disproportionate tests of §302(b)(2), the shareholder's only hope for exchange treatment was to qualify under §302(b)(1).

Example 18-21

What if: Assume Walt is not related to Jim or Ginny. This year, SCR redeemed five shares of his stock in exchange for $25,000. Walt has a tax basis in the five shares of SCR stock of $10,000 ($2,000 per share). Assume that SCR has sufficient E&P to cover any distribution. What is the tax treatment of the stock redemption to Walt under the *not essentially equivalent to a dividend* test?

Answer: $15,000 capital gain.

Prior to the redemption, Walt owned 20 percent of SCR (25/125 shares). After the redemption, his ownership percentage in SCR drops to 16.67 percent (20/120 shares). This redemption does not satisfy the substantially disproportionate test, which would treat the redemption as an exchange. Walt likely has a case that the redemption should be treated as an exchange because it was *not essentially equal to a dividend*. After all, his ownership percentage decreased (20 percent to 16.67 percent) and is below 50 percent after the redemption. However, the result Walt seeks (exchange treatment) is not guaranteed. For peace of mind, he might prefer having SCR redeem one additional share and have the certainty that the redemption will be treated as an exchange.

Example 18-22

What if: Assume Walt is Jim's father, and SCR redeemed five shares of his stock in exchange for $25,000. Walt has a tax basis in the five shares of SCR stock of $10,000 ($2,000 per share), and SCR has sufficient E&P to cover any distribution. What is the tax treatment of the stock redemption to Walt under the *not essentially equivalent to a dividend* test?

Answer: $25,000 dividend.

Prior to the redemption, Walt is treated as owning 80 percent of SCR (25 shares directly and 75 shares through Jim). After the redemption, his ownership percentage in SCR drops to 79 percent (95/120 shares). This redemption does not satisfy the *not essentially equal to a dividend* test because Walt is treated as owning more than 50 percent of the SCR stock.

TAXES IN THE REAL WORLD   What's Worse than Two Cable Companies?

There are many reasons that companies choose to redeem stock, but a common reason is to reduce the number of shares outstanding. That was the apparent purpose in a 2016 merger of two cable TV companies, Time Warner Cable (NYSE: TWC) and Charter Communications (Nasdaq: CHTR).

Charter proposed a merger with Time Warner where each share of Time Warner would be exchanged for $115 plus shares of Charter that would be equivalent to 0.4562 shares of the combined company (called New Charter). As an alternative, each shareholder of Time Warner could choose to receive $100 plus shares of Charter that would be equivalent to 0.5409 shares of New Charter. The effect of the cash payment was to limit the ownership percentage of the Time Warner stockholders to between approximately 40 percent and 44 percent of the outstanding shares of New Charter Class A common stock immediately following completion of the merger.

Consumers might disagree with the contention of the Time Warner board that this merger would increase the operating efficiency of the cable company but, according to the company's proxy statement, the tax treatment of the redemption was less certain.

Time Warner recommended that Time Warner shareholders treat the cash as a redemption of the portion of their Time Warner shares represented by the cash payment. According to Time Warner, it is likely that the redemption should be treated as a sale by shareholders under §302(a). Time Warner suggested that shareholders would either meet the substantially disproportionate test, the "not essentially equivalent to a dividend" test, or if they sold their shares in New Charter contemporaneously with the merger, as a complete termination of interest.

Source: Time Warner Proxy (DEF14A), August 20, 2015.

Tax Consequences to the Distributing Corporation

The corporation distributing property to shareholders in a redemption generally recognizes gain on the distribution of appreciated property but is not permitted to recognize loss on the distribution of property with a fair market value less than its tax basis.[31]

If the shareholder treats the redemption as a *dividend*, the corporation reduces its E&P by the cash distributed and greater of the fair market value or adjusted basis of other property distributed.[32] If the shareholder treats the redemption as an *exchange*, the corporation reduces E&P at the date of distribution by the percentage of stock redeemed (i.e., if 60 percent of the stock is redeemed, E&P is reduced by 60 percent), not to exceed the fair market value of the property distributed.[33] The distributing corporation reduces its current E&P by any dividend distributions made during the year before reducing its E&P for redemptions treated as exchanges.[34]

The distributing corporation cannot deduct expenses incurred in a stock redemption.[35] The corporation can deduct interest on debt incurred to finance a redemption, however.

Example 18-23

What if: Assume SCR redeemed all of the 25 shares owned by Walt in exchange for $125,000. The stock redeemed represents 20 percent of the total stock outstanding. Walt has a tax basis in his SCR shares of $50,000. Further assume that Walt treated the redemption as an exchange because he waived the family attribution rules and filed a triple i agreement with the IRS.[36] As a result, Walt recognized a capital gain of $75,000 ($125,000 − $50,000). The redemption took place on December 31, on which date SCR had E&P of $500,000. SCR did not make any distributions during the year.

By what amount does SCR reduce its E&P as a result of this redemption?

Answer: $100,000. SCR reduces E&P by the lesser of (1) $100,000 (20% × $500,000) or (2) $125,000, the amount paid to Walt in the redemption.

What if: Assume E&P was $1,000,000 at the end of the year. By what amount does SCR reduce its E&P as a result of this redemption?

Answer: $125,000. SCR reduces E&P by the lesser of (1) $200,000 (20% × $1,000,000) or (2) $125,000, the amount paid to Walt in the redemption.

What if: Assume SCR distributed $100,000 to its shareholders on June 1. E&P was $500,000 at the end of the year, before taking into account the distribution and redemption. By what amount does SCR reduce its E&P as a result of this redemption?

Answer: $80,000. SCR first reduces E&P by the dividend paid during the year to $400,000 ($500,000 − $100,000). SCR then reduces its E&P for the redemption by the lesser of (1) $80,000 (20% × $400,000) or (2) $125,000, the amount paid to Walt in the redemption.

Trends in Stock Redemptions by Publicly Traded Corporations

Traditionally, publicly traded corporations viewed stock redemptions as a tax-efficient means to return cash to their shareholders. Redemptions allow shareholders to "declare their own dividends" by voluntarily selling shares back to the corporation. Many companies increased their dividends after Congress decreased the dividend tax rate to 15 percent or 5 percent (now 0 percent) for individuals in 2003. On the other hand, the impending dividend tax increase at the end of 2012 motivated other companies, such as Costco, to declare special dividends to avoid the anticipated higher shareholder tax. See the Taxes in the Real World relating to Costco for more details.

[31]§311(a) and (b).

[32]§312(a) and §312(b).

[33]§312(n)(7).

[34]Rev. Rul. 74-338, 1974-2 C.B. 101 and Rev. Rul. 74-339, 1974-2 C.B. 103.

[35]§162(k).

[36]The requirements for filing the triple i agreement are found in Reg. §1.302-4T.

TAXES IN THE REAL WORLD Changing Distribution Strategies in Light of Tax Law Changes

Costco Board of Directors Declares Special Cash Dividend

November 29, 2012—Costco (NASDAQ: COST) announced today that its Board of Directors has declared a special $7.00 per share cash dividend, payable on December 18, 2012, to stockholders of record as of the close of business on December 10, 2012. The total dividend payout is expected to be approximately $3 billion, based on the current shares outstanding. When paid, these dividends could be taxed at the top rate of 15%. However, had the dividend been paid two weeks later, the top tax rate would have been 20%.

Richard Galanti, Executive VP and CFO, stated that the special dividend is "our latest effort in returning capital to our shareholders while maintaining our conservative capital structure." Maybe the CFO should have added that Costco was returning capital in a tax-efficient manner?

Source: Costco Form 8-K filed November 29, 2012.

Individuals have a tax incentive to participate in a redemption because gain recognized as a result of the redemption is usually capital gain (which is reduced by the basis of the stock redeemed and can absorb capital losses from other investments). Losses produced by the buyback generally can be deducted against capital gains.

PARTIAL LIQUIDATIONS

LO 18-5

Corporations can contract their operations either by distributing the stock of a subsidiary to their shareholders or by selling the business. In the case of a sale, the corporation may distribute the proceeds from the sale to its shareholders in partial liquidation of the corporation. The distribution may require the shareholders to tender shares of stock back to the corporation or may be pro rata to all the shareholders without an actual exchange of stock.

The tax treatment of a distribution received in a partial liquidation depends on the identity of the shareholder receiving the distribution.[37] All *noncorporate* shareholders receive exchange treatment. This entitles the individual to sale or exchange treatment with respect to the gain or loss recognized on the actual or deemed exchange. If the shareholder is not required to tender stock to the corporation in return for the property received, the shareholder computes gain or loss recognized on the exchange by calculating the tax basis of the shares that would have been transferred to the corporation had the transaction been a stock redemption.

All *corporate* shareholders are subject to the change-in-stock-ownership rules that apply to stock redemptions. This usually results in dividend treatment because partial liquidations almost always involve pro rata distributions. Corporate shareholders generally prefer dividend treatment because of the availability of the dividends received deduction although the benefit of the dividends received deduction could be mitigated if the distribution qualifies as an extraordinary distribution.

For a distribution to be in partial liquidation of the corporation, it must either be "not essentially equivalent to a dividend" (as determined at the corporate level) or the result of the termination of a "qualified trade or business."[38] The technical requirements to meet these requirements are beyond the scope of this text.

> **THE KEY FACTS**
>
> **Tax Consequences to Shareholders in a Partial Liquidation of a Corporation**
>
> - Noncorporate shareholders receive exchange treatment.
> - Corporate shareholders determine their tax consequences using the change-in-stock-ownership rules that apply to stock redemptions.

---

[37]§302(b)(4).

[38]§302(e).

CONCLUSION

In this chapter we learned that a corporation can distribute cash and other property to its shareholders in alternative ways. The most common forms are dividend distributions and stock buybacks (redemptions). The form chosen to make such a distribution affects the tax consequences to the recipients (shareholders) as well as the corporation itself. In some cases, the tax laws or the tax administrators can ignore the form of the transaction and assess tax based on the substance of the transaction. This is common in the case of stock redemptions that can be taxed as dividend payments. The tax rules that apply to these types of distinctions often are complex, and taxpayers and their tax advisers must evaluate them carefully before making a decision.

Summary

 Explain the framework that applies to the taxation of property distributions from a corporation to a shareholder.

- Subchapter C of the Internal Revenue Code (IRC) provides guidelines and rules for determining the tax status of distributions from a taxable ("C") corporation to its shareholders.
- When a corporation distributes property to persons in their capacity as shareholders, the shareholder must determine if the amount received is a dividend.
- If the distribution is of property other than cash, the distributing corporation recognizes gain but not loss on the distribution.

 Compute a corporation's earnings and profits and a shareholder's dividend income.

- The IRC defines a dividend as any distribution of property made by a corporation to its shareholders out of its current or accumulated earnings and profits (E&P).
- Earnings and profits (E&P) is the tax equivalent of financial accounting retained earnings, although the computations can be significantly different.
- A corporation must keep two E&P accounts: current E&P and accumulated E&P.
- The IRC and the related regulations list four basic types of adjustments that a corporation must make to its taxable income to compute current E&P.
  - Inclusion of income that is excluded from taxable income.
  - Disallowance of certain expenses that are deducted in computing taxable income.
  - Deduction of certain expenses that are excluded from the computation of taxable income.
  - Separate accounting methods required for E&P purposes results in both positive and negative adjustments to taxable income.
- The shareholder recognizes a corporate distribution as dividend income up to the amount of E&P. The distribution is the sum of cash received plus the fair market value of property received less any liabilities assumed.
- The distributing corporation recognizes gain, but not loss, on the distribution of noncash property.
- A corporation reduces E&P by the amount of cash distributed, the E&P basis of depreciated (loss) property distributed, and the fair market value of appreciated property distributed, net of any liability assumed by the shareholders.

 Explain the taxation of stock distributions.
- The general rule is that a stock distribution (stock dividend or split) is not taxable.
- The basis of the "new" stock received is computed by allocating basis from the existing stock based on relative fair market value.
- The holding period of the new stock includes the holding period of the existing stock on which the new stock was distributed.
- Non-pro rata stock distributions usually are treated as taxable dividends to the recipients.

Comprehend the tax consequences of stock redemptions.

- If a redemption is treated as an exchange, the shareholder computes gain or loss by comparing the amount realized (money and property received) with the tax-adjusted basis of the stock surrendered.
  - The character of the gain or loss is capital.
  - The basis of noncash property received is its fair market value.
  - The holding period of the property received begins at the date of receipt.
- If the redemption is treated as a dividend, the shareholder will recognize dividend income (to the extent of corporate E&P) equal to the cash and fair market value of other property received.
  - The basis of the property received is its fair market value.
- The IRC treats redemptions as exchanges in transactions in which the shareholder's ownership interest in the corporation has been "meaningfully" reduced relative to other shareholders as a result of the redemption.
- There are three change-in-stock-ownership tests that entitle the shareholder to exchange treatment in a redemption.
- The IRC states that a redemption will be treated as an exchange if the redemption is "not essentially equivalent to a dividend."
  - This is a facts and circumstances determination (subjective).
  - To satisfy this requirement, the courts or IRS must conclude that there has been a "meaningful" reduction in the shareholder's ownership interest in the corporation as a result of the redemption (usually below 50 percent stock ownership).
- The IRC states that a redemption will be treated as an exchange if the redemption is "substantially disproportionate with respect to the shareholder," defined as follows:
  - Immediately after the exchange the shareholder owns less than 50 percent of the total combined voting power of all classes of stock entitled to vote.
  - The shareholder's percentage ownership of voting stock after the redemption is less than 80 percent of his or her percentage ownership before the redemption.
  - The shareholder's percentage ownership of the aggregate fair market value of the corporation's common stock (voting and nonvoting) after the redemption is less than 80 percent of his or her percentage ownership before the redemption.
- The IRC holds that a redemption will be treated as an exchange if the redemption is in "complete redemption of all of the stock of the corporation owned by the shareholder."
- In determining whether the change-in-stock-ownership tests are met, each shareholder's percentage change in ownership in the corporation before and after a redemption must take into account constructive ownership (attribution) rules.
- The attribution rules cause stock owned by other persons to be treated as owned by (attributed to) the shareholder for purposes of determining whether the shareholder has met any of the change-in-stock-ownership tests to receive exchange treatment.
  - Family attribution. Individuals are treated as owning the shares of stock owned by their spouse, children, grandchildren, and parents.
  - Attribution from entities to owners or beneficiaries.
    - Partners are deemed to own a pro rata share of their partnership's stock holdings (i.e., a partner who has a 10 percent interest in a partnership is deemed to own 10 percent of any stock owned by the partnership).
    - Shareholders are deemed to own a pro rata share of their corporation's stock holdings, but only if they own at least 50 percent of the value of the corporation's stock.
  - Attribution from owners or beneficiaries to entities.
    - Partnerships are deemed to own 100 percent of stock owned by partners (i.e., a partnership is deemed to own 100 percent of stock owned by a 10 percent partner).
    - Attribution to a corporation only applies to shareholders owning 50 percent or more of the value of the corporation's stock.
  - Option attribution. A person having an option to purchase stock is deemed to own the stock that the option entitles the person to purchase.

- Shareholders can waive the family attribution rules in a complete redemption of their stock if certain conditions are met.
  - The shareholder has not retained a prohibited interest in the corporation immediately after the exchange (e.g., as a shareholder, employee, director, officer, or consultant).
  - The shareholder does not acquire a prohibited interest within 10 years after the redemption, unless by inheritance (the 10-year look-forward rule).
  - The shareholder agrees to notify the IRS district director within 30 days if she acquires a prohibited interest within 10 years (filing a triple i agreement).
- If the redemption is treated as a dividend by the shareholder, the corporation generally reduces its E&P by the cash distributed and the fair market value of other property distributed.
- If the redemption is treated as an exchange by the shareholder, the corporation reduces E&P at the date of distribution by the percentage of stock redeemed (i.e., if 50 percent of the stock is redeemed, E&P is reduced by 50 percent), not to exceed the fair market value of the property distributed.

LO 18-5   Describe the tax consequences of a partial liquidation to the corporation and its shareholders.

- For a distribution to be a partial liquidation, it must be "not essentially equivalent to a dividend" (as determined at the corporate level, not the shareholder level). The distribution automatically meets this test if the distribution is the result of the termination of a "qualified trade or business."
- The tax treatment of a distribution received in partial liquidation of a corporation depends on the identity of the shareholder receiving it.
  - All noncorporate shareholders get exchange treatment.
  - All corporate shareholders are subject to the stock redemption change-in-ownership rules, which usually result in dividend treatment because partial liquidations are almost always pro rata distributions.

KEY TERMS

accumulated earnings and
    profits (18-3)
bright line tests (18-17)
constructive ownership (18-19)

current earnings and profits (18-3)
dividend (18-2)
partial liquidation (18-2)
stock dividend (18-3)

stock redemption (18-2)
stock split (18-15)
triple i agreement (18-22)

DISCUSSION QUESTIONS

Discussion Questions are available in Connect®.

LO 18-1   1. What is meant by the term *double taxation* of corporate income?

LO 18-1   2. How does the double taxation of corporate distributions affect whether an individual chooses to operate a business as a C corporation or a flow-through entity?

LO 18-1   3. Why might a shareholder who is also an employee prefer receiving a dividend instead of compensation from a corporation?

LO 18-2   4. What are the three potential tax treatments of a cash distribution to a shareholder? Are these potential tax treatments elective by the shareholder?

LO 18-2   5. In general, what is the concept of earnings and profits (E&P) designed to represent?

LO 18-2   6. How does the *current earnings and profits* account differ from the *accumulated earnings and profits* account? Is there any congressional logic for keeping the two accounts separate?

LO 18-2   7. Assume a calendar-year corporation has positive current E&P of $100 and an accumulated deficit (negative) E&P of $200. Under this circumstance, a cash distribution of $100 to the corporation's sole shareholder at year-end will not be treated as a dividend because total E&P is negative $100. True or false? Explain.

8. Assume a calendar-year corporation has a deficit (negative) current E&P of $100 and accumulated E&P of $100. Under this circumstance, a cash distribution of $100 to the corporation's sole shareholder on June 30 will not be treated as a dividend because total E&P at December 31 is $0. True or false? Explain. `LO 18-2`

9. List the four basic adjustments that a corporation makes to taxable income or net loss to compute current E&P. What is the rationale for making these adjustments? `LO 18-2`

10. Assuming adequate amounts of corporate E&P, what is the formula for determining the amount of a noncash distribution a shareholder must include in gross income? `LO 18-2`

11. What income tax issues must a corporation consider before it makes a noncash distribution a shareholder? `LO 18-2`

12. Will the shareholder's tax basis in noncash property received equal the amount included in gross income as a dividend? Under what circumstances will the amounts be different, if any? `LO 18-2`

13. A shareholder receives appreciated noncash property in a corporate distribution and assumes a liability attached to the property. How does the assumption of a liability affect the amount of dividend reported in gross income? `LO 18-2`

14. A shareholder receives appreciated noncash property in a corporate distribution and assumes a liability attached to the property. How does this assumption affect the amount of gain the corporation recognizes? From the corporation's perspective, does it matter if the liability assumed by the shareholder exceeds the property's gross fair market value? `LO 18-2`

15. A corporation distributes *depreciated* noncash property to a shareholder. What impact does the distribution have on the corporation's earnings and profits? `LO 18-2`

16. Why might a corporation issue a stock distribution to its shareholders? `LO 18-3`

17. What tax issue arises when a shareholder receives a nontaxable stock distribution? `LO 18-3`

18. In general, what causes a stock distribution to be taxable to the recipient? `LO 18-3`

19. What are the potential tax consequences to a shareholder who participates in a stock redemption? `LO 18-4`

20. What stock ownership tests must be met before a shareholder receives exchange treatment under the substantially disproportionate change-in-stock-ownership test in a stock redemption? Why is a change-in-stock-ownership test used to determine the tax status of a stock redemption? `LO 18-4`

21. What are the criteria necessary to meet the "not essentially equivalent to a dividend" change in stock ownership test in a stock redemption? `LO 18-4`

22. When might a shareholder have to rely on the "not essentially equivalent to a dividend" test in arguing that a stock redemption should be treated as an exchange for tax purposes? `LO 18-4`

23. Explain why the tax law imposes constructive stock ownership rules on stock redemptions. `LO 18-4`

24. Which members of a family are included in the family attribution rules? Is there any rationale for the family members included in the test? `LO 18-4`

25. Ilya and Olga are brother and sister. Ilya owns 200 shares of stock in Parker Corporation. Is Olga deemed to own Ilya's 200 shares under the family attribution rules that apply to stock redemptions? `LO 18-4`

26. Maria has all of her stock in Mayan Corporation redeemed. Under what conditions will Maria treat the redemption as an exchange and recognize capital gain or loss?

27. What must a shareholder do to waive the family attribution rules in a complete redemption of stock? `LO 18-4`

28. How does a corporation's computation of earnings and profits differ based on the tax treatment of a stock redemption to the shareholder (i.e., as either a dividend or exchange)? `LO 18-4`

LO 18-5 29. How does the tax treatment of a partial liquidation differ from a stock redemption?

LO 18-5 30. Reveille Corporation experienced a complete loss of its lumber mill as the result of a fire. The company received $2 million from the insurance company. Rather than rebuild, Reveille decided to distribute the $2 million to its two shareholders. No stock was exchanged in return. Under what conditions will the distribution meet the requirements necessary to be treated as a partial liquidation and not a dividend? Why does it matter to the shareholders?

PROBLEMS

Select problems are available in Connect®.

LO 18-1 31. Gopher Corporation reported taxable income of $500,000 this year. Gopher paid a dividend of $100,000 to its sole shareholder, Sven Anderson. The dividend meets the requirements to be a qualified dividend, and Sven is subject to a tax rate of 15 percent on the dividend. What is the income tax imposed on the corporate income earned by Gopher and the income tax on the dividend distributed to Sven?

LO 18-1 32. Bulldog Corporation reported taxable income of $500,000 this year, before any deduction for any payment to its sole shareholder and employee, Georgia Brown. Bulldog chose to pay a bonus of $100,000 to Georgia at year-end. The bonus meets the requirements to be "reasonable" and is therefore deductible by Bulldog. Georgia is subject to a marginal tax rate of 35 percent on the bonus. What is the income tax imposed on the corporate income earned by Bulldog and the income tax on the bonus paid to Georgia?

LO 18-2 33. Hawkeye Company reports current E&P of $300,000 this year and accumulated E&P at the beginning of the year of $200,000. Hawkeye distributed $400,000 to its sole shareholder, Ray Kinsella, on December 31 of this year. Ray's tax basis in his Hawkeye stock is $75,000.

a) How much of the $400,000 distribution is treated as a dividend to Ray?

b) What is Ray's tax basis in his Hawkeye stock after the distribution?

c) What is Hawkeye's balance in accumulated E&P as of January 1 of next year?

LO 18-2 34. Jayhawk Company reports current E&P of $300,000 and accumulated E&P of negative $200,000. Jayhawk distributed $400,000 to its sole shareholder, Christine Rock, on the last day of the year. Christine's tax basis in her Jayhawk stock is $75,000.

a) How much of the $400,000 distribution is treated as a dividend to Christine?

b) What is Christine's tax basis in her Jayhawk stock after the distribution?

c) What is Jayhawk's balance in accumulated E&P on the first day of next year?

LO 18-2 35. This year, Sooner Company reports current E&P of negative $300,000. Its accumulated E&P at the beginning of the year was $200,000. Sooner distributed $400,000 to its sole shareholder, Boomer Wells, on June 30 of this year. Boomer's tax basis in his Sooner stock is $75,000.

a) How much of the $400,000 distribution is treated as a dividend to Boomer?

b) What is Boomer's tax basis in his Sooner stock after the distribution?

c) What is Sooner's balance in accumulated E&P on the first day of next year?

LO 18-2 36. This year Bobcat Company reports current E&P of negative $300,000 that accrued evenly throughout the year. At the beginning of the year, Bobcat's accumulated E&P was $200,000. Bobcat distributed $200,000 to its sole shareholder, Melanie Rushmore, on June 30 of this year. Melanie's tax basis in her Bobcat stock was $75,000.

a) How much of the $200,000 distribution is treated as a dividend to Melanie?

b) What is Melanie's tax basis in her Bobcat stock after the distribution?

c) What is Bobcat's balance in accumulated E&P on the first day of next year?

37. This year, Jolt Inc. reported $40,000 of taxable income before any charitable contribution deduction. Jolt contributed $10,000 this year to Goodwill Industries, a public charity. Compute the company's current E&P.   `LO 18-2`

38. Boilermaker Inc. reported taxable income of $500,000 this year and paid federal income taxes of $105,000. Not included in the company's computation of taxable income is tax-exempt income of $20,000, disallowed meals and entertainment expenses of $30,000, and disallowed expenses related to the tax-exempt income of $1,000. Boilermaker deducted depreciation of $100,000 on its tax return. Under the alternative (E&P) depreciation method, the deduction would have been $60,000. Compute the company's current E&P.   `LO 18-2`

39. Gator Inc. reported taxable income of $1,000,000 this year and paid federal income taxes of $210,000. Included in the company's computation of taxable income is gain from the sale of a depreciable asset of $50,000. The income tax basis of the asset was $100,000. The E&P basis of the asset using the alternative depreciation system was $175,000. Compute the company's current E&P.   `LO 18-2`

40. Paladin Inc. reported taxable income of $1,000,000 this year and paid federal income taxes of $210,000. The company reported a capital gain from sale of investments of $150,000, which was partially offset by a $100,000 net capital loss carryover from last year, resulting in a net capital gain of $50,000 included in taxable income. Compute the company's current E&P.   `LO 18-2`

41. Volunteer Corporation reported taxable income of $500,000 from operations this year. During the year, the company made a distribution of land to its sole shareholder, Rocky Topp. The land's fair market value was $75,000 and its tax and E&P basis to Volunteer was $25,000. Rocky assumed a mortgage attached to the land of $15,000. Any gain from the distribution will be taxed at 21 percent. The company had accumulated E&P of $750,000 at the beginning of the year.   `LO 18-2`

    a) Compute Volunteer's total taxable income and federal income tax.

    b) Compute Volunteer's current E&P.

    c) Compute Volunteer's accumulated E&P at the beginning of next year.

    d) What amount of dividend income does Rocky report as a result of the distribution?

    e) What is Rocky's income tax basis in the land received from Volunteer?

42. Tiger Corporation reported taxable income of $500,000 from operations this year. During the year, the company made a distribution of land to its sole shareholder, Mike Fairway. The land's fair market value was $75,000 and its tax and E&P basis to Tiger was $125,000. Mike assumed a mortgage attached to the land of $15,000. Any gain from the distribution will be taxed at 21 percent. The company had accumulated E&P of $750,000 at the beginning of the year.   `LO 18-2`

    a) Compute Tiger's total taxable income and federal income tax.

    b) Compute Tiger's current E&P.

    c) Compute Tiger's accumulated E&P at the beginning of next year.

    d) What amount of dividend income does Mike report as a result of the distribution?

    e) What is Mike's tax basis in the land he received from Tiger?

43. Illini Corporation reported taxable income of $500,000 from operations for this year. During the year, the company made a distribution of an automobile to its sole shareholder, Carly Urbana. The auto's fair market value was $30,000 and its tax basis to Illini was $0. The auto's E&P basis was $15,000. Any gain from the distribution will be taxed at 21 percent. Illini had accumulated E&P of $1,500,000.   `LO 18-2`

    a) Compute Illini's total taxable income and federal income tax.

    b) Compute Illini's current E&P.

c) Compute Illini's accumulated E&P at the beginning of next year.

d) What amount of dividend income does Carly report as a result of the distribution?

e) What is Carly's tax basis in the auto she received from Illini?

LO 18-2 44. Beaver Corporation reported taxable income of $500,000 from operations this year. During the year, the company made a distribution of land to its sole shareholder, Eugenia VanDam. The land's fair market value was $20,000 and its tax and E&P basis to Beaver was $50,000. Eugenia assumed a mortgage on the land of $25,000. Any gain from the distribution will be taxed at 21 percent. Beaver Corporation had accumulated E&P of $1,500,000.

a) Compute Beaver's total taxable income and federal income tax.

b) Compute Beaver's current E&P.

c) Compute Beaver's accumulated E&P at the beginning of next year.

d) What amount of dividend income does Eugenia report as a result of the distribution?

LO 18-2
tax forms
research
45. Tiny and Tim each own half of the 100 outstanding shares of Flower Corporation. This year, Flower reported taxable income of $6,000 and was subject to a 21 percent tax rate. In addition, Flower received $20,000 of life insurance proceeds due to the death of an employee (Flower paid $500 in life insurance premiums this year). Flower had $5,000 of accumulated E&P at the beginning of the year.

a) What is Flower's current E&P?

b) Flower distributed $6,000 on February 15 and $30,000 on August 1. What total amount of dividends will Tiny and Tim report?

c) What amount of capital gain (if any) would Tiny and Tim report on the distributions in part (b) if their stock basis is $2,000 and $10,000, respectively?

d) What form would Flower use to report nondividend distributions?

e) On what form (line) would Tiny and Tim report nondividend distributions?

LO 18-3 46. Hoosier Corporation declared a 2-for-1 stock split to all shareholders of record on March 25 of this year. Hoosier reported current E&P of $600,000 and accumulated E&P of $3,000,000. The total fair market value of the stock distributed was $1,500,000. Barbara Bloomington owned 1,000 shares of Hoosier stock with a tax basis of $100 per share.

a) What amount of taxable dividend income, if any, does Barbara recognize this year? Assume the fair market value of the stock was $150 per share on March 25 of this year.

b) What is Barbara's income tax basis in the new and existing stock she owns in Hoosier Corporation, assuming the distribution is tax-free?

c) How does the stock distribution affect Hoosier's accumulated E&P at the beginning of next year?

LO 18-3 47. Badger Corporation declared a stock distribution to all shareholders of record on March 25 of this year. Shareholders will receive one share of Badger stock for each 10 shares of stock they already own. Madison Cheesehead owns 1,000 shares of Badger stock with a tax basis of $100 per share. The fair market value of the Badger stock was $110 per share on March 25 of this year.

a) What amount of taxable dividend income, if any, does Madison recognize this year?

b) What is Madison's income tax basis in her new and existing stock in Badger Corporation, assuming the distribution is nontaxable?

c) How would you answer parts (a) and (b) if Badger offered shareholders a choice between receiving one additional share of Badger stock for each 10 Badger shares held or receiving $120 cash in lieu of an additional share of stock?

48. Wildcat Company is owned equally by Evan Stone and his sister Sara, each of whom hold 1,000 shares in the company. Sara wants to reduce her ownership in the company, and it was decided that the company will redeem 500 of her shares for $25,000 per share on December 31 of this year. Sara's income tax basis in each share is $5,000. Wildcat has current E&P of $10,000,000 and accumulated E&P of $50,000,000.   **LO 18-4**

   a) What is the amount and character (capital gain or dividend) recognized by Sara as a result of the stock redemption?

   b) What is Sara's income tax basis in the remaining 500 shares she owns in the company?

   c) Assuming the company did not make any dividend distributions during this year, by what amount does Wildcat reduce its E&P as a result of the redemption?

49. Flintstone Company is owned equally by Fred Stone and his sister Wilma, each of whom hold 1,000 shares in the company. Wilma wants to reduce her ownership in the company, and it was decided that the company will redeem 250 of her shares for $25,000 per share on December 31 of this year. Wilma's income tax basis in each share is $5,000. Flintstone has current E&P of $10,000,000 and accumulated E&P of $50,000,000.   **LO 18-4**

   a) What is the amount and character (capital gain or dividend) recognized by Wilma as a result of the stock redemption, assuming only the "substantially disproportionate with respect to the shareholder" test is applied?

   b) Given your answer to part (a), what is Wilma's income tax basis in the remaining 750 shares she owns in the company?

   c) Assuming the company did not make any dividend distributions this year, by what amount does Flintstone reduce its E&P as a result of the redemption?

   d) What other argument might Wilma make to treat the redemption as an exchange?

50. Acme Corporation has 1,000 shares outstanding. Joan and Bill are married, and they each own 20 shares of Acme. Joan's daughter, Shirley, also owns 20 shares of Acme. Joan is an equal partner with Jeri in the J&J partnership, and this partnership owns 60 shares of Acme. Jeri is not related to Joan or Bill. How many shares of Acme is Shirley deemed to own under the stock attribution rules?   **LO 18-4**

51. Bedrock Inc. is owned equally by Barney Rubble and his wife Betty, each of whom hold 1,000 shares in the company. Betty wants to reduce her ownership in the company, and it was decided that the company will redeem 500 of her shares for $25,000 per share on December 31 of this year. Betty's income tax basis in each share is $5,000. Bedrock has current E&P of $10,000,000 and accumulated E&P of $50,000,000.   **LO 18-4**

   a) What is the amount and character (capital gain or dividend) recognized by Betty as a result of the stock redemption, assuming only the "substantially disproportionate with respect to the shareholder" test is applied?

   b) Given your answer to part (a), what is Betty's income tax basis in the remaining 500 shares she owns in the company?

   c) Assuming the company did not make any dividend distributions this year, by what amount does Bedrock reduce its E&P as a result of the redemption?

   d) Can Betty argue that the redemption is "not essentially equivalent to a dividend" and should be treated as an exchange?

52. Assume in problem 51 that Betty and Barney are not getting along and have separated due to marital discord (although they are not legally separated). In fact, they cannot even stand to talk to each other anymore and communicate only through their accountant. Betty wants to argue that she should not be treated as owning any of Barney's stock in Bedrock because of their hostility toward each other. Can   **LO 18-4**

 research

family hostility be used as an argument to void the family attribution rules? Consult Rev. Rul. 80-26, 1980-1 C.B. 66, *Robin Haft Trust v. Comm.*, 510 F.2d 43 (CA-1 1975), *Metzger Trust v. Comm.*, 693 F.2d 459 (CA-5 1982), and *Cerone v. Comm.*, 87 TC 1 (1986).

LO 18-4

53. Boots Inc. is owned equally by Frank Albert and his daughter Nancy, each of whom hold 1,000 shares in the company. Frank wants to retire from the company, and it was decided that the company will redeem all 1,000 of his shares for $25,000 per share on December 31 of this year. Frank's income tax basis in each share is $500. Boots Inc. has current E&P of $1,000,000 and accumulated E&P of $5,000,000.

    a) What must Frank do to ensure that the redemption will be treated as an exchange?

    b) If Frank remained as the chairman of the board after the redemption, what is the amount and character of income (capital gain or dividend) that Frank will recognize this year?

    c) If Frank treats the redemption as a dividend, what happens to his stock basis in the 1,000 shares redeemed?

LO 18-4

research

54. In problem 53, Nancy would like to have Frank stay on as a consultant after all of his shares are redeemed. She would pay him a modest amount of $500 per month. Nancy wants to know if there is any *de minimus* rule such that Frank would not be treated as having retained a prohibited interest in the company because he is receiving such a small amount of money. Consult *Lynch v. Comm.*, 801 F.2d 1176 (CA-9 1986), *reversing* 83 T.C. 597 (1984), *Seda*, 82 T.C. 484 (1984), and *Cerone*, 87 T.C. 1 (1986).

LO 18-4

planning

55. Limited Brands recently repurchased 68,965,000 of its shares, paying $29 per share. The total number of shares outstanding before the redemption was 473,223,066. The total number of shares outstanding after the redemption was 404,258,066. Assume your client owned 20,000 shares of stock in The Limited. What is the minimum number of shares she must tender to receive exchange treatment under the "substantially disproportionate with respect to the shareholder" change-in-ownership rules?

LO 18-4

56. Cougar Company is owned equally by Cat Stevens and a partnership that is owned equally by his father and two unrelated individuals. Cat and the partnership each own 3,000 shares in the company. Cat wants to reduce his ownership in the company, and it is decided that the company will redeem 1,500 of his shares for $25,000 per share. Cat's income tax basis in each share is $5,000. What are the income tax consequences to Cat as a result of the stock redemption, assuming the company has earnings and profits of $10 million?

LO 18-4

planning

57. Oriole Corporation, a privately held company, has one class of voting common stock, of which 1,000 shares are issued and outstanding. The shares are owned as follows:

Larry Byrd	400
Paul Byrd (Larry's son)	200
Lady Byrd (Larry's daughter)	200
Cal Rifkin (unrelated)	200
Total	1,000

Larry is considering retirement and would like to have the corporation redeem all of his shares for $400,000.

    a) What must Larry do or consider if he wants to guarantee that the redemption will be treated as an exchange?

    b) Could Larry act as a consultant to the company and still have the redemption treated as an exchange?

58. Using the facts from problem 57, Oriole Corporation proposes to pay Larry $100,000 and give him an installment note that will pay him $30,000 per year for the next 10 years plus a market rate of interest. Will this arrangement allow Larry to treat the redemption as an exchange? Consult §453(k)(2)(A).

`LO 18-4`
`research`

59. EG Corporation redeemed 200 shares of stock from one of its shareholders in exchange for $200,000. The redemption represented 20 percent of the corporation's outstanding stock. The redemption was treated as an exchange by the shareholder. By what amount does EG reduce its total E&P as a result of the redemption under the following E&P assumptions?

`LO 18-4`

a) EG's total E&P at the time of the distribution was $2,000,000.

b) EG's total E&P at the time of the distribution was $500,000.

60. Spartan Corporation redeemed 25 percent of its shares for $2,000 on July 1 of this year, in a transaction that qualified as an exchange under §302(a). Spartan's accumulated E&P at the beginning of the year was $2,000. Its current E&P is $12,000. Spartan made dividend distributions of $1,000 on June 1 and $4,000 on August 31. Determine the beginning balance in Spartan's accumulated E&P at the beginning of the next year. See Rev. Rul. 74-338, 1974-2 C.B. 101, and Rev. Rul. 74-339, 1974-2 C.B. 103, for help in making this calculation.

`LO 18-4`
`planning`

61. Bonnie and Clyde are the only two shareholders in Getaway Corporation. Bonnie owns 60 shares with a basis of $3,000, and Clyde owns the remaining 40 shares with a basis of $12,000. At year-end, Getaway is considering different alternatives for redeeming some shares of stock. Evaluate whether each of the following stock redemption transactions will qualify for sale and exchange treatment.

`LO 18-4`

a) Getaway redeems 10 of Bonnie's shares for $2,000. Getaway has $20,000 of E&P at year-end and Bonnie is unrelated to Clyde.

b) Getaway redeems 25 of Bonnie's shares for $4,000. Getaway has $20,000 of E&P at year-end and Bonnie is unrelated to Clyde.

c) Getaway redeems 10 of Clyde's shares for $2,500. Getaway has $20,000 of E&P at year-end and Clyde is unrelated to Bonnie.

62. Aggie Corporation made a distribution of $500,000 to Rusty Cedar in partial liquidation of the company on December 31 of this year. Rusty, an individual, owns 100 percent of Aggie Corporation. The distribution was in exchange for 50 percent of Rusty's stock in the company. At the time of the distribution, the shares had a fair market value of $200 per share. Rusty's income tax basis in the shares was $50 per share. Aggie had total E&P of $8,000,000 at the time of the distribution.

`LO 18-5`

a) What is the amount and character (capital gain or dividend) of any income or gain recognized by Rusty as a result of the partial liquidation?

b) Assuming Aggie made no other distributions to Rusty during the year, by what amount does Aggie reduce its total E&P as a result of the partial liquidation?

63. Wolverine Corporation made a distribution of $500,000 to Jim Har Inc. in partial liquidation of the company on December 31 of this year. Jim Har Inc. owns 100 percent of Wolverine Corporation. The distribution was in exchange for 50 percent of Jim Har Inc.'s stock in the company. At the time of the distribution, the shares had a fair market value of $200 per share. Jim Har Inc.'s income tax basis in the shares was $50 per share. Wolverine had total E&P of $8,000,000 at the time of the distribution.

`LO 18-5`

a) What is the amount and character (capital gain or dividend) of any income or gain recognized by Jim Har Inc. as a result of the partial liquidation?

b) Assuming Wolverine made no other distributions to Jim Har Inc. during the year, by what amount does Wolverine reduce its total E&P as a result of the partial liquidation?

COMPREHENSIVE PROBLEMS

Select problems are available in Connect®.

64. Lanco Corporation, an accrual-method corporation, reported taxable income of $1,460,000 this year. Included in the computation of taxable income were the following items:

- MACRS depreciation of $200,000. Straight-line depreciation would have been $120,000.
- A net capital loss carryover of $10,000 from last year.
- A net operating loss carryover of $25,000 from last year.
- $65,000 capital gain from the distribution of land to the company's sole shareholder (see below).

Not included in the computation of taxable income were the following items:

- Tax-exempt income of $5,000.
- Life insurance proceeds of $250,000.
- Excess current-year charitable contribution of $2,500 (to be carried over to next year).
- Tax-deferred gain of $20,000 on a like-kind exchange.
- Federal income tax refund from last year of $35,000.
- Nondeductible life insurance premium of $3,500.
- Nondeductible interest expense of $1,000 on a loan used to buy tax-exempt bonds.

Lanco's accumulated E&P at the beginning of the year was $2,400,000. During the year, Lanco made the following distributions to its sole shareholder, Luigi (Lug) Nutt:

- June 30: $50,000.
- September 30: Parcel of land with a fair market value of $75,000. Lanco's tax basis in the land was $10,000. Lug assumed an existing mortgage on the property of $15,000.

Required:

a) Compute Lanco's current E&P.

b) Compute the amount of dividend income reported by Lug Nutt this year as a result of the distributions.

c) Compute Lanco's accumulated E&P at the beginning of next year.

65. Petoskey Stone Quarry Inc. (PSQ), a calendar-year, accrual-method C corporation, provides landscaping supplies to local builders in northern Michigan. PSQ has always been a family-owned business and has a single class of voting common stock outstanding. The 500 outstanding shares are owned as follows:

Nick Adams	150
Amy Adams (Nick's sister)	150
Abigail Adams (Nick's daughter)	50
Charlie Adams (Nick's son)	50
Sandler Adams (Nick's father)	100
Total shares	500

Nick Adams serves as president of PSQ, and his father Sandler serves as chairman of the board. Amy is the company's CFO, and Abigail and Charlie work as employees of the company. Sandler would like to retire and sell his shares back to the company. The fair market value of the shares is $500,000. Sandler's tax basis is $10,000. The redemption is tentatively scheduled to take place on December 31 of this year. At the beginning of the year, PSQ had accumulated earnings and profits of $2,500,000. The company projects current E&P of $200,000. The company intends to pay pro rata cash dividends of $300 per share to its shareholders on December 1 of this year.

Required:

a) Assume the redemption takes place as planned on December 31 and no elections are made by the shareholders.

   1. What amount of dividend or capital gain will Sandler recognize as a result of the stock redemption?

   2. How will the tax basis of Sandler's stock be allocated to the remaining shareholders?

b) What must Sandler and the other shareholders do to change the tax results you calculated in part (a)?

c) Compute PSQ's accumulated earnings and profits on January 1 of next year, assuming the redemption is treated as an exchange.

66. Thriller Corporation has one class of voting common stock, of which 1,000 shares are issued and outstanding. The shares are owned as follows:

Joe Jackson	400
Mike Jackson (Joe's son)	200
Jane Jackson (Joe's daughter)	200
Vinnie Price (unrelated)	200
Total	1,000

Thriller Corporation has current E&P of $300,000 for this year and accumulated E&P at January 1 of this year of $500,000. During this year, the corporation made the following distributions to its shareholders:

03/31: Distributed $10 per share to each shareholder ($10,000 in total).

06/30: Redeemed 200 shares of Joe's stock for $200,000. Joe's basis in the 200 shares redeemed was $100,000.

09/30: Redeemed 60 shares of Vinnie's stock for $60,000. His basis in the 60 shares was $36,000.

12/31: Distributed $10/share to each shareholder ($7,400 in total).

Required:

a) Determine the tax status of each distribution made this year. (*Hint:* First, consider if the redemptions are treated as dividend distributions or exchanges.)

b) Compute the corporation's accumulated E&P at January 1 of next year.

c) Joe is considering retirement and would like to have the corporation redeem all of his shares for $100,000 plus a 10-year note with a fair market value of $300,000.

   1. What must Joe do or consider if he wants to ensure that the redemption will be treated as an exchange?

   2. Could Joe still act as a consultant to the company?

d) Thriller Corporation must pay attorney's fees of $5,000 to facilitate the stock redemptions. Is this fee deductible?

 ROGER | CPA Review

Corporate Formation, Reorganization, and Liquidation

Learning Objectives

Upon completing this chapter, you should be able to:

LO 19-1 Review the taxation of property dispositions.

LO 19-2 Compute the tax consequences to the parties to a tax-deferred corporate formation.

LO 19-3 Identify the different forms of taxable and tax-deferred acquisitions.

LO 19-4 Determine the tax consequences to the parties to a corporate acquisition.

LO 19-5 Calculate the tax consequences that apply to the parties to a complete liquidation of a corporation.

©DreamPictures/Blend Images LLC

Jim Wheeler and Ginny Gears are excited about the growth of their business, Spartan Cycle and Repair (SCR). The business has a solid base of loyal customers and is showing a healthy profit. Jim and Ginny are ready for some new challenges. They have considered expanding the bicycle business to a new geographic region and branching out into a new line of business. Given the seasonal nature of the demand for bicycle products and repair in Michigan, Jim and Ginny favor a complementary line of business that would provide them with a source of income during the winter months. Ginny is impressed with the growing popularity of snowboarding, especially among young people. Factors that have contributed to this growth include low equipment costs (especially compared to skiing), easily attained skills, a "coolness" attractive to young people, and the sport's inclusion in the Olympic games.

Jim and Ginny are aware of a small snowboarding store in East Lansing called 360 Air, which is also the name of a daring snowboarding maneuver. The business is owned and operated by Al Pine, a rather free-spirited individual whose enthusiasm for the sport is not matched by his business acumen.

Jim and Ginny feel that with some additional capital investment and marketing effort, they could turn Al's snowboarding business into a profitable operation. They set up a meeting with Al to discuss how they could become partners in his business enterprise.

After some negotiation, Jim, Ginny, and Al agree to jointly operate the snowboarding business through a C corporation. Al had been operating his business as a sole proprietorship. As part of the incorporation process, each of the three individuals will make a contribution of property or services to the corporation in return for stock. Al will contribute his existing inventory as well as the building and land on which the building is situated in return for 50 percent of the stock in 360 Air. The corporation will assume the existing mortgage on the property. Jim will contribute cash in exchange for 40 percent of the stock, and Ginny will contribute her marketing services in return for 10 percent of the stock.

Each of the parties wants to know the income tax implications of incorporating Al's ongoing business. In addition, Jim is wondering whether the manner in which they are intending to create the corporation is tax efficient and whether there are other issues they should consider that would lessen the tax burdens of both the corporation and its new shareholders.

to be continued . . .

When creating a business, the owners must choose an organizational form for operating it. The choice of legal entity affects whether and how the income or loss generated by the business is taxed at the entity level and the owner level. At some point during the life of a business, the owners may decide to change its tax status. In the case of an ongoing business, such as 360 Air, changing to corporate tax status will require the transfer of assets and liabilities by one or more of the owners in return for stock in the corporation. These property transfers raise several tax questions. A transfer of assets or liabilities to a corporation in exchange for stock triggers realization of gains and losses and may cause shareholders to recognize gains in the year of the transfer. In addition, shareholders will need to calculate the tax basis of their stock, and the corporation will need to calculate the basis of the assets and liabilities received in the transfer.

LO 19-1 REVIEW THE TAXATION OF PROPERTY DISPOSITIONS

This section provides a brief review of tax rules that apply to transfers of property to a corporation in the incorporation process. Before gain or loss is recognized (included in taxable income), it must first be realized. **Realization** generally occurs when a transaction takes place (that is, when there is an exchange of property rights between two persons).

Exhibit 19-1 provides a template for computing gain or loss realized by a party to a property transaction.

EXHIBIT 19-1   **Computing Gain or Loss Realized in a Property Transaction**[1]

	Amount realized (received)
−	Adjusted tax basis of the property transferred
	Gain (+) or loss (−) realized

THE KEY FACTS

Overview of the Taxation of Property Transactions

- Gain or loss is realized when a person engages in a transaction (an exchange of property rights with another person).
- Gain or loss realized is computed by subtracting the transferor's tax-adjusted basis in the property exchanged from the amount realized in the exchange.
- Gain or loss realized is recognized (included in the computation of taxable income) unless exempted or deferred by a provision of the tax laws.

The **amount realized** is computed using the template in Exhibit 19-2.

EXHIBIT 19-2   **Computing the Amount Realized in a Property Transaction**[2]

	Cash received
+	Fair market value of other property received
+	Liabilities assumed by the transferee on the transferred property
−	Selling expenses incurred in the transaction
−	Liabilities assumed by the transferor on any property received in the exchange
	Amount realized

A property's **adjusted tax basis** is calculated using the template in Exhibit 19-3.

EXHIBIT 19-3   **Computing a Property's Adjusted Tax Basis in a Property Transaction**[3]

	Acquisition basis
+	Capital improvements
−	Depreciation
	Adjusted tax basis

The entire amount of gain or deductible loss realized is recognized unless otherwise provided by the Internal Revenue Code.[4] Gain or loss is not recognized if (1) it is excluded from gross income (the gain or loss will never be recognized) or (2) the gain or deductible loss is deferred from gross income (recognition is postponed to a future period). Transfers of property to a corporation are transactions in which realized gain or loss may be deferred if certain requirements are met.[5] Recognition of a deferred gain or loss is postponed until the property received in the exchange is subsequently disposed of (e.g., recognition of Al's realized gain will be postponed until he sells his stock in 360 Air).

---

[1]§1001(a).

[2]§1001(b).

[3]§1011.

[4]§1001(c). Realized losses must be deductible to be recognized. Nondeductible losses are never recognized.

[5]§351.

LO 19-2   TAX-DEFERRED TRANSFERS OF PROPERTY TO A CORPORATION

A realization event occurs when shareholders transfer cash and noncash property to the corporation in return for stock in the corporation. This transfer typically occurs in the formation of a corporation but it can also happen in subsequent transactions with an existing corporation. The stock can be common or preferred, voting or nonvoting.[6]

Example 19-1

As part of the incorporation of 360 Air, Al Pine will transfer inventory, a building, and land to the corporation in return for 50 percent of the corporation's stock (50 shares). The property has the following fair market values and adjusted bases:

	FMV	Adjusted Basis
Inventory	$ 25,000	$ 15,000
Building	150,000	60,000
Land	200,000	100,000
Total	$375,000	$175,000

The corporation will assume a mortgage of $75,000 attached to the building and land. The fair market value of the 360 Air stock Al will receive in the exchange is $300,000. How much net gain or loss does Al *realize* in the exchange?

Answer: Al realizes a net gain of $200,000 on this transfer, computed as follows:

	Fair market value of 360 Air stock received	$ 300,000
+	Mortgage assumed by 360 Air	75,000
	Amount realized	$ 375,000
−	Adjusted tax basis of the property transferred	175,000
	Gain realized	**$200,000**

Congress provides for the deferral of gain or loss on qualifying transfers of property to a corporation in exchange for stock in order to remove tax consequences as an impediment to forming a corporation. Congress justifies tax deferral because shareholders maintain an interest in the property transferred through a different form of ownership (from direct ownership to indirect ownership through stock). In other words, the shareholders making the transfer have not substantively disposed of their ownership of the property.

Gain or loss deferred in the transfer of property to a corporation in return for stock is reflected in the shareholder's tax basis in the stock received in exchange for the transferred property.[7] A deferred gain *decreases* the shareholder's tax basis in the stock to an amount equal to the stock's fair market value less the gain deferred. A deferred loss *increases* the shareholder's tax basis in the stock to an amount equal to the stock's fair market value plus the loss deferred. In essence, the shareholder's tax basis in the stock received reflects the deferred gain or loss.

---

[6]A category of stock with different rights (e.g., voting rights, dividend rights, liquidation rights) is referred to as a *class* of stock.

[7]§358.

Example 19-2

Assume Al meets the tax law requirements to defer recognizing the $200,000 gain realized in the property transfer to 360 Air. The fair market value of the 360 Air stock he receives in the exchange is $300,000. What is Al's tax basis in the stock received?

Answer: $100,000. To reflect the deferral of the gain in his tax basis in the stock, Al's tax basis must be $100,000 ($300,000 − $200,000 gain deferred). If he subsequently sells the stock for $300,000, Al will recognize the $200,000 gain deferred previously ($300,000 − $100,000).

What if: Assume Al realized a $100,000 loss on the exchange of his property for stock in 360 Air. What would be his tax basis in the stock received?

Answer: $400,000. To reflect the deferral of the loss in his tax basis in the stock, Al's tax basis must be $400,000 ($300,000 + $100,000 loss deferred). If he subsequently sells the stock for $300,000, Al will recognize the $100,000 loss deferred previously ($300,000 − $400,000).

Transactions Subject to Tax Deferral

For shareholders to receive tax deferral in a transfer of property to a corporation, the transferors must meet the requirements of IRC §351. Section 351 applies to those transactions in which one or more shareholders transfer property to a corporation in return for stock and, immediately after the transfer, these same shareholders together control the corporation to which they transferred the property. When the requirements are met, deferral of gain or loss in a §351 transaction is mandatory. Section 351 applies to transfers of property to both C corporations and S corporations.

Section 351 applies only to those **persons** who transfer property to the corporation in exchange for stock (i.e., shareholders). The IRC defines a person for tax purposes as including individuals, corporations, partnerships, and fiduciaries (estates and trusts).[8] Thus, §351 allows individuals like Al to form a corporation and also allows existing corporations such as General Electric to create a subsidiary. The corporation receiving the property in exchange for its own stock is not subject to tax when it receives property.[9]

Meeting the Section 351 Tax Deferral Requirements

The shareholders transferring property to a corporation must meet several requirements for the transfer to be tax-deferred. Some of these requirements are not precisely defined in either the IRC or the regulations. As a result, much of what we understand about the parameters of §351 has developed over time as the IRS and the courts interpreted the law. This incremental approach to understanding the meaning of the law is common throughout Subchapter C of the Internal Revenue Code.[10]

Section 351 Applies Only to the Transfer of Property to the Corporation

Most assets (tangible and intangible) meet the definition of property for purposes of §351. Property includes money, tangible assets, and intangible assets (e.g., company

---

[8] §7701(a)(1).

[9] §1032. Note, however, that under GAAP a corporation will record contributed property at fair value for book purposes. Hence, a contribution of property under §351 will give rise to book–tax differences because different amounts of depreciation will be recorded for book and tax purposes.

[10] Subchapter C encompasses IRC §§301–385 and provides the tax rules for the corporate transactions discussed in this chapter. Tax advisers who specialize in structuring corporate transactions often are referred to as "Subchapter C experts."

name, patents, customer lists, trademarks, and logos). Services are excluded from the definition of property. Thus, a person who receives stock in return for services generally has compensation equal to the fair market value of the stock received.[11]

Example 19-3

As part of the incorporation, Ginny received 10 percent of the stock in 360 Air valued at $60,000 in exchange for her services in setting up the corporation. Will Ginny defer recognition of the $60,000 "gain" she realizes on the transaction?

Answer: No. Ginny must report compensation income of $60,000 as a result of this exchange because services are not considered property under §351.

What if: Suppose Ginny received 10 percent of the stock in 360 Air valued at $60,000 in exchange for a catchphrase she created to provide the company with a distinctive logo. Assume her tax basis in the catchphrase is zero because she created it. Will Ginny defer recognition of the $60,000 gain she realizes on the transfer of the catchphrase?

Answer: Yes. Ginny defers recognition of the $60,000 gain realized because intangibles are considered property under §351.

The Property Transferred to the Corporation Must Be Exchanged for Stock of the Corporation   When property is transferred to a corporation in exchange for stock and other property, only the portion of the property exchanged for stock will qualify for tax deferral. Property (other than stock) received by shareholders is referred to as **boot.** The receipt of boot will cause the shareholder (transferor) to recognize gain, but not loss, realized on the exchange. We will discuss the details of this computation later in the chapter.

The type of stock a shareholder can receive in a §351 exchange is quite flexible and includes voting or nonvoting and common or preferred stock. Stock for purposes of §351 does not include stock warrants, rights, or options.[12] Property transferred in exchange for debt of the corporation is not eligible for deferral under §351.

Example 19-4

What if: Suppose Ginny received a five-year note (debt) in 360 Air valued at $60,000 in exchange for machinery. The original cost of the machinery was $70,000 and Ginny has depreciated it to a basis of zero. Will Ginny defer recognition of the $60,000 gain she realizes on the transfer of the machinery?

Answer: No. Section 351 provides for deferral only when the transferor of property receives stock in return. Ginny must recognize the entire $60,000 gain.

The Transferor(s) of Property to the Corporation Must Be in Control of the Corporation, in the Aggregate, Immediately after the Transfer   Control for purposes of §351 is defined as the ownership of 80 percent or more of the total combined voting power of all voting stock that is issued and outstanding, and 80 percent or more of the total number of shares of each class of nonvoting stock.[13]

---

[11]An individual who receives stock subject to "restrictions" (e.g., she must remain with the company for a certain number of years) does not report compensation income until the restrictions attached to the stock are lifted (§83) unless she elects to value the stock at the date received and report that amount as income (called a "§83(b) election").

[12]§351 precludes nonqualified preferred stock from qualifying as equity eligible for deferral. Nonqualified preferred stock generally has characteristics that cause it to more resemble debt than equity.

[13]§368(c). Voting power is generally defined as the ability of the shareholders to elect members of the corporation's board of directors.

Whether the control test is met is based on the collective ownership of the shareholders transferring property to the corporation immediately after the transfer. Keep in mind that this group of shareholders (sometimes called the *control club*) is composed only of those who have transferred property (not services) in exchange for stock. In addition, the aggregate ownership (not the change in ownership) of these shareholders immediately after the transfer must meet the 80 percent threshold.

ETHICS

Michelle owns appreciated property and she wants to use this property to start a business with her son, Lance. Michelle is considering making a contribution of the property to a newly organized corporation in exchange for 100 percent of the corporate stock. She then contemplates giving half of the stock to Lance in exchange for his promise to manage the business. Do you think this transaction will qualify for §351 treatment? Suppose Michelle promises that she won't transfer the stock for a month after making the contribution of property. Does this make any difference? Compare Rev. Rul. 54-96, 1954-1 CB 111 with *Intermountain Lumber Co.*, 65 TC 1025 (1976).

Example 19-5

What if: Assume Ginny was hesitant to join with Jim and Al in the incorporation of 360 Air. After six months, she changed her mind and received a 10 percent interest in 360 Air stock in exchange for intangibles that qualified as property under §351. The stock was valued at $60,000, and Ginny's tax basis in the intangibles was zero. Will Ginny defer recognition of the $60,000 gain she realized on the exchange under §351?

Answer: No. Ginny is the only transferor and does not control (80 percent or more of) 360 Air immediately after the transfer. As a result, she must recognize the $60,000 gain.

Example 19-6

What if: Suppose Ginny joined with Jim and Al in the incorporation of 360 Air and received 25 percent of the corporation's stock in exchange for services. The stock was valued at $150,000. Al and Jim received the remaining 75 percent of the stock in the company in exchange for appreciated property. Will Al and Jim defer recognition of gain they realize on the exchange of the appreciated property under §351?

Answer: No. Taking into account only the stock received in exchange for property, Al and Jim do not collectively control 360 Air immediately after the transaction. Al and Jim own only 75 percent, not 80 percent. Consequently, the transaction is not eligible for deferral under §351, and all gain realized is recognized.

Generally when a shareholder transfers services and property to the corporation in exchange for stock, that shareholder is considered to be a transferor of property for purposes of the control test. However, if the primary purpose for the shareholder's transfer of property to the corporation is to qualify the exchange of another person under §351, that shareholder would be considered to be a transferor of property only if the value of the stock received for property is not of "relatively small value" compared to the value of the stock received for services.[14] The IRS has stated that, for ruling purposes, property will not be of "relatively small value" if it equals at least 10 percent of the value of the stock received for the services provided.[15]

---

[14]Reg. §1.351-1(a)(1)(ii). Note that this is a factual issue.
[15]Rev. Proc. 77-37, 1977-2 C.B. 568.

Example 19-7

What if: Let's say Ginny joined with Jim and Al in the incorporation of 360 Air primarily to qualify Jim and Al for §351 treatment. Ginny received 25 percent of the corporation's stock in exchange for services and intangibles treated as property. The stock was valued at $150,000. The services were valued at $125,000 and the intangibles were valued at $25,000. Al and Jim received the remaining 75 percent of the stock in the company in exchange for appreciated property. Will Al and Jim defer recognition of gain they realize on the exchange of the appreciated property under §351?

Answer: Yes. The stock Ginny received in exchange for the intangibles exceeds 10 percent of the value of the stock received for the services ($25,000/$125,000 = 20%). For purposes of determining control, Ginny will treat all of the stock she received in 360 Air as having been received for property. Al, Jim, and Ginny will be treated as collectively receiving 100 percent of the 360 Air stock in exchange for property. Hence, Al and Jim will defer gain realized on their exchanges of property for stock. Ginny will recognize compensation of $125,000 on the exchange, but she will defer recognizing any gain realized on the transfer of the intangibles.

What if: Assume Ginny's services were valued at $140,000 and the intangibles were valued at $10,000. Will Al and Jim defer recognition of gain they realize on the exchange of the appreciated property under §351?

Answer: No. Because Ginny's primary purpose in transferring the intangible property was to qualify the transfer for deferral. The fair market value of the stock received for the intangibles is less than 10 percent of the stock received for services ($10,000/$140,000 = 7.14%). As a result, none of the stock Ginny receives in the exchange is counted in the control test. Al, Jim, and Ginny are treated as having received collectively only 75 percent of 360 Air stock in exchange for property. Consequently, §351 does not apply to any of the transferors of the property to 360 Air.

This same rule applies to subsequent transfers of property by an existing shareholder to accommodate a new shareholder's transfer of property to an established corporation. The regulations state that stock received for property that is of "relatively small value" in comparison to the value of the stock already owned will not be considered issued in return for property (i.e., the shareholder making the contribution will not be included in the control test) if the "primary purpose" of the transfer is to qualify the exchanges of another person under §351. The IRS has stated that, for ruling purposes, an existing shareholder must contribute property that has a fair market value of at least 10 percent of the value of the stock already owned to be included in the control test.[16]

Example 19-8

What if: Assume Jim and Ginny were 100 percent shareholders of SCR and wanted to bring Al on board as a 20 percent shareholder. Al will transfer appreciated property to SCR in return for stock in SCR valued at $100,000. Will Al defer recognizing any gain realized on the transfer under §351?

Answer: No. Al does not control SCR "immediately after" the exchange, taking into account only the stock he owns in SCR.

What if: Suppose Jim agreed to make an additional property contribution to SCR at the same time as Al's transfer in order to help Al qualify his transfer under §351. Jim's 75 percent ownership interest in SCR was valued at $300,000 at the time of Al's transfer. How much property (fair market value) must Jim contribute to SCR to have his ownership of stock in SCR counted in determining if Al qualifies for deferral under §351?

Answer: $30,000. For Jim's "accommodation transfer" to be respected by the IRS, he must contribute property with a fair market value of 10 percent or more of the fair market value of his existing stock in SCR (10% × $300,000).

[16]Rev. Proc. 77-37, 1977-2 C.B. 568.

Tax Consequences to Shareholders

The tax basis of stock received in a tax-deferred §351 exchange equals the tax basis of the property transferred less any liabilities assumed by the corporation.[17] The stock is said to have a **substituted basis,** that is, the basis of the property transferred is substituted for the basis of the property received.[18] Exhibit 19-4 provides a template for computing the tax basis of stock received in a tax-deferred §351 transaction.

EXHIBIT 19-4   **Computing the Tax Basis of Stock Received in a Tax-Deferred Section 351 Transaction**

	Cash contributed
+	Tax basis of other property contributed
−	Liabilities assumed by the corporation on property contributed
	Tax basis of stock received

Example 19-9

As part of the incorporation of 360 Air, Al transferred inventory, a building, and land to the corporation in return for 50 percent of the corporation's stock (50 shares). The property transferred to the corporation had the following fair market values and adjusted bases:

	FMV	Adjusted Basis
Inventory	$ 25,000	$ 15,000
Building	150,000	60,000
Land	200,000	100,000
Total	$375,000	$175,000

In addition, the corporation assumed a mortgage of $75,000 attached to the building and land. The fair market value of the 360 Air stock Al received in the exchange was $300,000. As we computed in Example 19-1, Al realizes a gain of $200,000 on the transfer, computed as follows:

	Fair market value of 360 Air stock received	$300,000
+	Mortgage assumed by 360 Air	75,000
	Amount realized	$375,000
−	Adjusted tax basis of the property transferred	175,000
	Gain realized	$200,000

Assuming Al meets the requirements under §351 to defer recognizing the $200,000 gain realized, what is his tax basis in the 50 shares of 360 Air stock he receives in the exchange?

Answer: $100,000. Al's tax basis in his stock must reflect the gain he defers in the exchange. He computes his tax basis in his 360 Air stock as follows:

	Adjusted basis of property contributed	$ 175,000
−	Mortgage assumed by 360 Air	75,000
	Tax basis of 360 Air stock received	**$100,000**

(continued on page 19-10)

---

[17]§358(a).

[18]§7701(a)(44) uses the term *exchanged basis property* for this type of property.

If Al subsequently were to sell his 360 Air stock for its fair market value of $300,000, he would recognize a capital gain of $200,000 ($300,000 − $100,000), an amount equal to the gain he deferred previously.

Example 19-10

What if: Assume Al did not meet the requirements under §351 and was required to recognize the $200,000 gain realized. What is his tax basis in the 50 shares of 360 Air stock he received in the exchange?

Answer: $300,000. Al's tax basis in his stock equals its fair market value. If Al subsequently sells his 360 Air stock for $300,000, he will not recognize any further gain.

Tax Consequences When a Shareholder Receives Boot

A shareholder who receives property other than stock (boot) recognizes gains (but not losses) in an amount not to exceed the lesser of (1) gain realized or (2) the fair market value of the boot received. We calculate the amount of gain recognized when boot is received in a §351 transaction by allocating the boot received to each contributed property using the relative fair market values of the properties.[19] The character of gain recognized (capital gain, §1231 gain, ordinary income) is determined by the type of property to which the gain is allocated.

Example 19-11

What if: Suppose Al received 40 shares of 360 Air stock with a fair market value of $315,000 plus $60,000 in return for his transfer of inventory, a building, and land to the corporation. The property transferred to the corporation had the following fair market values and adjusted bases:

	FMV	Adjusted Basis	Gain Realized
Inventory	$ 25,000	$ 15,000	$ 10,000
Building	150,000	60,000	90,000
Land	200,000	100,000	100,000
Total	$375,000	$175,000	$200,000

What amount of gain does Al recognize on his receipt of the $60,000 boot and what is its character (ordinary or §1231)?

Answer: The $60,000 received by Al constitutes boot received and causes him to recognize some or all of the gain realized on the transfer. He apportions the $60,000 to each of the properties transferred to the corporation based on their relative fair market values. Al recognizes gain on each property transferred in an amount equal to the lesser of the gain realized or the fair market

---

[19]Rev. Rul. 68-55, 1968-1 C.B. 140 and Rev. Rul. 85-164, 1985-2 C.B. 117.

value of the boot apportioned to the property. The computation is made for each property separately as follows:

Inventory	
Fair market value of 360 Air stock and cash received	$ 25,000
Less adjusted basis of the inventory transferred	−15,000
(1) Gain realized	$ 10,000
(2) Boot apportioned (25/375 × $60,000)	4,000
Gain recognized: lesser of (1) or (2)	**$ 4,000**
Character of gain recognized: ordinary	

Building	
Fair market value of 360 Air stock and cash received	$150,000
Less adjusted basis of the building transferred	− 60,000
(1) Gain realized	$ 90,000
(2) Boot apportioned (150/375 × $60,000)	24,000
Gain recognized: lesser of (1) or (2)	**$ 24,000**
Character of gain recognized: §1231[20]	

Land	
Fair market value of 360 Air stock and cash received	$200,000
Less adjusted basis of the building transferred	−100,000
(1) Gain realized	$100,000
(2) Boot apportioned (200/375 × $60,000)	32,000
Gain recognized: lesser of (1) or (2)	**$ 32,000**
Character of gain recognized: §1231	

Al recognizes total gain of $60,000 on this transfer ($4,000 + $24,000 + $32,000) and defers recognition of $140,000 of the $200,000 gain realized ($200,000 − $60,000).

What if: Let's say the land has an adjusted basis of $250,000. What amount of gain or loss does Al now recognize?

Answer: The $60,000 of boot received by Al still must be apportioned among the assets based on relative fair market values. However, Al cannot recognize any of the realized loss on the land because boot only causes gain realized to be recognized. The recomputation for the land is as follows:

Land	
Fair market value of 360 Air stock and cash received	$ 200,000
Less adjusted basis of the building transferred	−250,000
(1) Loss realized	$ (50,000)
(2) Boot apportioned (200/375 × $60,000)	32,000
No loss is recognized	

Al recognizes total gain of $28,000 from receipt of the building and inventory ($24,000 + $4,000). Al defers recognition of $72,000 of gain realized ($6,000 + $66,000) from receipt of the building and inventory and all of the $50,000 loss realized from receipt of the land.

Boot received in a §351 transaction receives a tax basis equal to its fair market value.[21] Al must adjust the tax basis in his 360 Air stock to take into account the boot received and the gain recognized. Exhibit 19-5 provides a template for computing stock basis when boot is received in a §351 transaction.

---

[20]If Al owned more than 50 percent of 360 Air after the transfer, the gain would be treated as ordinary income under §1239(a). Section 1239 converts §1231 gain to ordinary income if the transferor of the property owns more than 50 percent of the corporation and the property is depreciable in the hands of the transferee. The gain also could be unrecaptured §1250 gain subject to a maximum tax rate of 25 percent.

[21]§358(a)(2).

EXHIBIT 19-5 Computing the Tax Basis of Stock in a Section 351 Transaction When Boot Is Received

	Cash contributed
+	Tax basis of other property contributed
+	Gain recognized on the transfer
−	Fair market value of boot received
−	Liabilities assumed by the corporation on property contributed
	Tax basis of stock received

Example 19-12

Return to the original facts in Example 19-11, in which Al received $60,000 and recognized $60,000 gain in the exchange. What is Al's tax basis in his 360 Air stock?

Answer: $175,000. Al computes his tax basis in the 360 Air stock as follows:

	Adjusted basis of property contributed	$ 175,000
+	Gain recognized on the exchange	60,000
−	Fair market value of boot (cash) received	60,000
	Tax basis of stock received	**$175,000**

If Al subsequently sells his 360 Air stock for its current fair market value of $315,000, he would recognize a gain of $140,000 ($315,000 − $175,000), an amount equal to the gain he deferred in the exchange.

Assumption of Shareholder Liabilities by the Corporation

When an unincorporated business (such as Al's sole proprietorship) is incorporated, the newly created corporation frequently assumes the outstanding liabilities of the business, say, accounts payable or mortgages. An important tax issue is whether the assumption of these liabilities by the newly created corporation constitutes boot received by the shareholder transferring the liabilities to the corporation. After all, the shareholder does receive something other than stock in the transaction—that is, relief from debt.

Under the general rule, the corporation's assumption of a shareholder's liability attached to property transferred (e.g., the mortgage attached to the building and land transferred by Al to 360 Air) is *not* treated as boot received by the shareholder.[22] However, there are two important exceptions to this rule.

Tax-Avoidance Transactions If *any* of the liabilities assumed by the corporation are contributed with the purpose of avoiding the federal income tax or if there is no corporate business purpose for the assumption, *all* liabilities assumed are treated as boot to the shareholder.[23] The "avoidance" motive may be present where the corporation assumes debt created by the shareholders immediately prior to the contribution of the encumbered assets. Completing this transaction is essentially equivalent to having the corporation pay the shareholder cash in exchange for the property. The "no business purpose" motive can also be present when shareholders have the corporation assume their personal liabilities (such as grocery bills or alimony).

Liabilities in Excess of Basis Even when liabilities are not treated as boot, the taxpayer is required to recognize gain to the extent the liabilities assumed by the corporation exceed the aggregate tax basis of the properties transferred by the shareholder.[24] The character of §357(c) gain recognized should be based on the character of the transferred assets, but this rule is inadequate if the transfer includes two or more assets of differing character. The regulations indicate that the character of the gain in this situation should be determined by allocating the gain according to the relative fair market value of the transferred assets. Some tax commentators argue that allocating the gain to assets based on their relative built-in gains is an acceptable alternative method of allocating gain across the transferred assets.

[22]§357(a).

[23]§357(b).

[24]§357(c). A liability assumed by the corporation cannot reduce stock basis below zero.

Lisa is the sole proprietor of a business that manufactures solar panels. This week Lisa was approached to exchange her business assets for shares in Burns Power. As part of the exchange, Lisa is requiring Burns Power to assume the home equity loan on her home. Do you think that Lisa should argue that there is no tax-avoidance motive in this arrangement? Suppose that Lisa established her business five years ago by investing funds from a home equity loan. Does this make any difference?

Example 19-13

What if: Assume Al transferred inventory, a building, and land to 360 Air in return for 50 percent of the corporation's stock (50 shares) with a fair market value of $175,000. The corporation will assume a mortgage of $200,000 attached to the land and building. The properties transferred have fair market values and tax bases as follows:

	FMV	Adjusted Basis
Inventory	$ 25,000	$ 15,000
Building	150,000	60,000
Land	200,000	100,000
Total	$375,000	$175,000

Al realizes a gain of $200,000 on the transfer, computed as follows:

	Fair market value of 360 Air stock received	$ 175,000
+	Mortgage assumed by 360 Air	200,000
	Amount realized	$ 375,000
−	Adjusted tax basis of the property transferred	175,000
	Gain realized	**$200,000**

What amount of gain, if any, does Al recognize on the transfer, assuming all of the other requirements of §351 are met?

Answer: $25,000, the excess of the mortgage assumed by 360 Air ($200,000) over the total tax-adjusted basis of the property Al transferred to the corporation ($175,000). Al defers gain of $175,000. The character of the $25,000 gain is determined by allocating the gain to the contributed assets and treating the gain in accordance with the character of each asset. For example, in this case 6.67 percent of the $25,000 gain ($25/$375) would be allocated to the inventory and taxed as ordinary income.

What is Al's tax basis in the 360 Air stock?

Answer: $0, computed as follows:

	Adjusted basis of property contributed	$175,000
+	Gain recognized on the exchange	25,000
−	Mortgage assumed by 360 Air	200,000
	Tax basis of stock received	**$ 0**

If Al sold his 360 Air stock for $175,000 (its current fair market value), he would recognize a gain of $175,000 ($175,000 − $0), an amount equal to the gain he deferred in the exchange.

There is a special exception for the assumption of liabilities the payment of which would give rise to a deduction. The assumption of such liabilities is disregarded in determining whether the liabilities assumed exceed basis.[25] Examples are a corporation assuming the accounts payable of a cash-method sole proprietorship and a subsidiary assuming "payment liabilities" (e.g., accrued vacation pay) of an accrual-method corporation.

[25]357(c)(3). Note that this exception is not available when the liabilities are used to create basis in assets, such as payables related to the purchase of tools.

Example 19-14

What if: Suppose Al transferred inventory, a building, and land to 360 Air in return for 50 percent of the corporation's stock (50 shares) with a fair market value of $175,000. The corporation will assume cash-method accounts payable of $200,000. The properties transferred have fair market values and tax bases as follows:

	FMV	Adjusted Basis
Inventory	$ 25,000	$ 15,000
Building	150,000	60,000
Land	200,000	100,000
Total	$375,000	$175,000

Al realizes a gain of $200,000 on the transfer, computed as follows:

	Fair market value of 360 Air stock received	$ 175,000
+	Payables assumed by 360 Air	200,000
	Amount realized	$ 375,000
−	Adjusted tax basis of the property transferred	175,000
	Gain realized	**$200,000**

What amount of gain, if any, does Al recognize in the transfer, assuming all of the other requirements of §351 are met?

Answer: $0. Al defers recognition of the entire gain of $200,000. The assumption of the cash-method payables is disregarded in computing whether the liabilities assumed exceed the aggregate tax basis of the property transferred.

What is Al's tax basis in the 360 Air stock?

Answer: $175,000, computed as follows:

	Adjusted basis of property contributed	$ 175,000
+	Gain recognized on the exchange	0
−	Payables assumed by 360 Air	0
	Tax basis of stock received	**$175,000**

If Al subsequently sells his 360 Air stock for $175,000 (its current fair market value), he will recognize a gain of $0 ($175,000 − $175,000). This result seems odd at first glance because the gain deferred before was $200,000. However, by transferring the payables to 360 Air, Al is forgoing a $200,000 deduction that he would have received if he paid off the liabilities while operating as a sole proprietorship. This $200,000 "loss" exactly offsets the $200,000 gain he realized when 360 Air assumed the payables, resulting in a net gain of $0.

Tax Consequences to the Transferee Corporation

The corporation receiving property in exchange for its stock does not recognize gain or loss realized on the transfer.[26] In transactions that do not qualify for §351, the corporation will have a fair market value tax basis in the property. In a §351 transaction the corporation will have a tax basis in the property that equals the property's tax basis in the transferor's hands.[27] The transferred property is said to have a **carryover basis** (i.e., the corporation "carries over" the shareholder's basis and holding period in the transferred property).[28] To the extent the shareholder's tax basis carries over to the corporation and

---

[26]§1032.

[27]§362(a).

[28]See §1223(2) and note that §7701(a)(43) refers to this type of property as *transferred basis property.*

the property is §1231 property or a capital asset, the shareholder's holding period also carries over (it *tacks* to the property).[29] This could be important in determining if subsequent gain or loss recognized on the disposition of the property qualifies as a §1231 gain or loss or a long-term capital gain or loss.

If the shareholder recognizes gain as a result of the property transfer, either because the shareholder received boot or the liabilities assumed by the corporation in the exchange exceeded the tax basis of the property contributed by the shareholder, the corporation increases its tax basis in each asset by the gain recognized on that asset. Exhibit 19-6 provides a template for computing the tax basis of each asset received by the corporation in a §351 transaction.

EXHIBIT 19-6 Computing the Tax Basis of Each Asset Received by the Corporation in a Section 351 Transaction

+	Tax basis of the asset contributed by the shareholder
+	Gain recognized by the shareholder on the transfer of the asset to the corporation
	Tax basis of the asset received

Example 19-15

Let's return to the facts in Example 19-11 in which Al received 40 shares of 360 Air stock with a fair market value of $315,000 and $60,000 in return for his transfer of inventory, a building, and land to the corporation. The $60,000 received by Al constituted boot received and caused him to recognize gain on the transfer. The $60,000 was allocated to each of the properties transferred to the corporation based on their relative fair market values. Al recognized gain on each property transferred in an amount equal to the lesser of the gain realized or the fair market value of the boot allocated to the property. Al's tax results from this transaction can be summarized as follows:

	Tax Basis	Gain Recognized
Inventory	$ 15,000	$ 4,000
Building	60,000	24,000
Land	100,000	32,000
Total	$175,000	$60,000

What tax basis does 360 Air get in each of the properties it receives from Al in the exchange?

Answer: 360 Air will carry over Al's tax basis in the property transferred and will increase the tax basis by gain recognized by Al on the transfer. The corporation's tax basis in each of the three properties is as follows:

	Tax Basis	Gain Recognized	360 Air Tax Basis
Inventory	$ 15,000	$ 4,000	$ 19,000
Building	60,000	24,000	84,000
Land	100,000	32,000	132,000
Total	$175,000	$60,000	$235,000

360 Air also will carry over Al's holding period in the building and land transferred because they are §1231 assets.

Tax law limits the ability of a shareholder to transfer a built-in loss to a corporation in a §351 transaction. In particular, if the aggregate adjusted tax basis of property transferred to a corporation by a shareholder in a §351 transfer exceeds the aggregate fair market value of the assets, the aggregate tax basis of the assets in the

[29]§1223(1).

hands of the transferee corporation cannot exceed their aggregate fair market value.[30] The aggregate reduction in tax basis is allocated among the assets transferred in proportion to their respective built-in losses immediately before the transfer. As an alternative, the transferor and transferee can elect under §362(e)(2) to have the transferor reduce her stock basis to fair market value (the duplicate loss is eliminated at either the corporate or shareholder level).

Example 19-16

What if: Assume Al transferred a building and land to the corporation in return for 50 percent of the corporation's stock (50 shares). The property transferred to the corporation had the following fair market values and adjusted bases:

	FMV	Adjusted Basis
Building	$ 75,000	$100,000
Land	200,000	100,000
Total	$275,000	$200,000

The fair market value of the 360 Air stock Al received in the exchange was $275,000.

Assuming the transfer meets the requirements under §351 to defer recognizing the $75,000 net gain realized, what is Al's tax basis in the 50 shares of 360 Air stock he receives in the exchange?

Answer: $200,000. In this case, the aggregate fair market value of the property transferred to the corporation exceeds the aggregate adjusted basis of the property. As a result, Al's tax basis in the stock he receives equals the aggregate adjusted bases of the property transferred.

What is the adjusted basis of the building and land held by 360 Air?

Answer: The building has a carryover basis of $100,000, and the land has a carryover basis of $100,000. Because the aggregate fair market value of the assets transferred to the corporation exceeds the aggregate adjusted basis of the property, 360 Air applies the general basis carryover rules. The building retains its built-in loss of $25,000 at the corporate level.

Example 19-17

What if: Suppose Al transferred a building and land to the corporation in return for 50 percent of the corporation's stock (50 shares). The property transferred to the corporation had the following fair market values and adjusted bases:

	FMV	Adjusted Basis
Building	$ 75,000	$200,000
Land	200,000	100,000
Total	$275,000	$300,000

The fair market value of the 360 Air stock Al received in the exchange was $275,000.

Assuming the transfer meets the requirements under §351 to defer recognizing the $25,000 net loss realized, what is Al's tax basis in the 50 shares of 360 Air stock he receives in the exchange?

Answer: $300,000. In this case, the aggregate adjusted basis of the property transferred to the corporation exceeds the aggregate fair market value of the property. Assuming he doesn't elect to reduce his stock basis to fair market value, Al's tax basis in the stock he receives will equal the adjusted basis of the assets transferred.

[30]§362(e)(2).

What is the adjusted basis of the building and land held by 360 Air?

Answer: An aggregate adjusted basis of $275,000. Because the aggregate fair market value of the property transferred to the corporation is less than the aggregate adjusted bases of the property, 360 Air must reduce the aggregate adjusted bases of the property to their aggregate fair market value. The allocation is made to those assets that have a built-in loss; in this example, this includes only the building. The adjusted basis of the building will be reduced to $175,000 ($200,000 − $25,000 net built-in loss). The adjusted basis of the land will retain its carryover basis of $100,000. This adjustment eliminates the net $25,000 built-in loss at the corporate level.

What alternative election can Al and 360 Air make with respect to these basis reduction rules?

Answer: Al and the corporation can jointly elect to have Al reduce his stock basis to its fair market value of $275,000. The corporation would take a carryover basis of $200,000 in the building and a carryover basis of $100,000 in the land.

Other Issues Related to Incorporating an Ongoing Business

Depreciable Assets Transferred to a Corporation   To the extent a property's tax-adjusted basis carries over from the shareholder, the corporation in effect steps into the shoes of the shareholder and continues to depreciate the carryover basis portion of the property's tax basis using the shareholder's depreciation schedule.[31] Any additional basis (from recognition of gain due to boot received) is treated as a separate asset and is subject to a separate depreciation election (i.e., this one physical asset is treated as two tax assets for depreciation purposes).

Example 19-18

Let's return to the facts in Example 19-11. Recall that Al received 40 shares of 360 Air stock with a fair market value of $315,000 and $60,000 in return for his transfer of inventory, a building, and land to the corporation. The cash received by Al constituted boot received and caused him to recognize $60,000 of gain on the transfer. 360 Air takes Al's tax basis in the property and increases it by the gain recognized by Al on the transfer. The corporation's tax basis in each of the three properties is as follows.

	Tax Basis	Gain Recognized	360 Air Tax Basis
Inventory	$ 15,000	$ 4,000	$ 19,000
Building	60,000	24,000	84,000
Land	100,000	32,000	132,000
Total	$175,000	$60,000	$235,000

360 Air also will carry over Al's holding period in the building and land transferred because they are §1231 assets. How will 360 Air compute the depreciation deduction on the building for the year of the transfer? For this problem, let's assume that the transfer occurs on January 1. Furthermore, let's assume that Al originally purchased the building for $67,400 in September five years ago and has claimed $7,400 of depreciation using straight-line and mid-month conventions over a 39-year recovery period.

(continued on page 19-18)

[31]§168(i)(7)(B)(ii).

> **Answer:** 360 Air carries over Al's depreciation schedule for the building with respect to the $60,000 original basis, but 360 Air depreciates the additional $24,000 as a new asset. With respect to the carryover basis portion of the building, 360 Air uses Al's original cost of $67,400 in the building to calculate the depreciation computation. Al is entitled to .5 month of depreciation on the building in the year of transfer ($67,400 × .02564 × .5/12 = $72), and the corporation is entitled to the remaining 11.5 months of depreciation of $1,656 ($67,400 × .02564 × 11.5/12 = $1,656). The corporation treats the additional $24,000 of basis as a new asset and applies the proper depreciation rate to calculate the additional depreciation. Because the transfer took place in January, 360 Air would be entitled to 11.5 months of depreciation (recall the mid-month convention). Hence, 360 Air would claim additional depreciation of $591 ($24,000 × .02461 = $591) for a total depreciation deduction of $2,247. This bifurcated computation is often ignored or overlooked in practice.

Practitioners often advise against transferring appreciated property (especially real estate) into a closely held corporation. By doing so the shareholder creates two assets with the same built-in gain as the original property (the stock received in the hands of the shareholder and the building owned by the corporation). The federal government can now collect taxes twice on the same gain, once when the corporation sells the property received and a second time when the shareholder sells the stock. You will notice that Congress is not concerned by a duplication of gain result, only a duplication of loss result. By retaining the property outside the corporation, the shareholder can lease the property to the corporation, thereby reducing the corporation's taxable income through rent deductions. Note, however, that there may be valid state tax reasons to own the property inside a corporation, such as lower property taxes.

Contributions to Capital

A **contribution to capital** is a transfer of property to a corporation by a shareholder or nonshareholder for which no stock or other property is received in return. The corporation receiving the property is not taxed on the receipt of the property if the property is contributed by a shareholder.[32] If the property is contributed by a shareholder, the corporation takes a carryover tax basis in the property.[33] If the property is contributed by a nonshareholder (e.g., a city contributes land to induce a corporation to locate its operations there), the corporation recognizes income in the amount of the value of the contributed property.

A capital contribution generally is not a taxable event to the shareholder because the shareholder does not receive any additional consideration in return for the transfer. A shareholder making a capital contribution gets to increase the tax basis in her existing stock in an amount equal to the tax basis of the property contributed.

Section 1244 Stock

Stock is generally a capital asset in the hands of the shareholders, and gains or losses from sale or exchange are capital in nature. For individuals, long-term capital gains are taxed at a maximum tax rate of 20 percent. Losses can only offset capital gains plus $3,000 of ordinary income per year. Section 1244 allows a shareholder to treat a loss on the sale or exchange of stock that qualifies as §1244 stock as an ordinary loss.

Section 1244 applies only to individual shareholders who are the original recipients of the stock. The maximum amount of loss that can be treated as an ordinary loss under

[32]§118.
[33]§362(a)(2).

§1244 is $50,000 per year ($100,000 in the case of married, filing jointly shareholders). For shareholders to qualify for this tax benefit, the corporation from which they received stock must have been a small business corporation when the stock was issued. The IRC defines a small business corporation as one in which the aggregate amount of money and other property received in return for the stock or as a contribution to capital did not exceed $1 million. In our story line, 360 Air qualifies as a small business corporation.

There is an additional requirement that for the five taxable years preceding the year in which the stock is sold, the corporation must have derived more than 50 percent of its aggregate gross receipts from an *active* trade or business. 360 Air meets this test as well. Section 1244 provides a tax benefit to entrepreneurs who create a risky start-up company that ultimately fails.

Example 19-19

What if: Assume Al received 50 shares of 360 Air stock (50 percent of the outstanding stock) with a fair market value of $300,000 in return for his transfer of a building and land to the corporation in a transaction that qualified under §351. As a result of the transfer, Al received a tax basis in the 50 shares of $200,000 ($4,000 per share). Suppose that over time the snowboarding business declined due to a change in weather patterns in Michigan. As a result, Al's 50 shares were worth $50,000 ($1,000 per share). Needing some cash, Al sold all 50 of his shares to Jim for $50,000 and recognized a $150,000 loss [$50,000 − ($4,000 × 50 shares)]. 360 Air qualifies as a small business corporation under §1244. Al has no capital gains in the year of the sale. How much of the loss can Al deduct if he held his stock at least five years, assuming current tax rules, and he is married, filing a joint tax return? What is the character of the loss (capital or ordinary)?

Answer: $103,000, $100,000 of which is ordinary loss and $3,000 of which is capital loss that can reduce up to $3,000 of ordinary income. The remaining $47,000 loss is carried forward as a capital loss.

What tax planning advice would you give Al to maximize the tax treatment of his loss from sale of the stock?

Answer: §1244 imposes an annual limit on the amount of the loss that can be treated as ordinary. To maximize the tax value of his loss, Al should sell enough shares of 360 Air stock to generate a $100,000 loss this year and sell the remaining amount to generate a $50,000 loss next year. In that way, the entire $150,000 loss will be treated as ordinary loss. Of course, delaying the sale of shares is risky because the stock could continue to lose value. Al would need to weigh the tax benefits of the delay against the risk of additional loss.

A special rule applies when §1244 stock is issued by a corporation in a §351 transaction in which the property contributed by the taxpayer (transferor) has an adjusted basis in excess of its fair market value (i.e., a built-in loss). As discussed above, the law limits tax basis of contributed property with built-in losses (basis in excess of value) to the value of the property. However, the shareholder can preserve the basis of the contributed property by electing under §362(e)(2) to reduce the basis of the stock by the built-in loss. If §1244 stock is issued in exchange for such property and the taxpayer has elected to reduce the stock's basis by the built-in loss, then for purposes of §1244 only, the basis of the stock is reduced by an amount equal to the built-in loss at the time of the exchange.

For example, assume a taxpayer transfers property with an adjusted basis of $1,000 and a fair market value of $250 in exchange for 10 shares of §1244 stock in a §351 transaction. The total basis of the stock is $1,000, but solely for purposes of §1244, the total basis of the stock must be reduced by $750, the excess of the adjusted basis of the property exchanged over its fair market value. The total basis of such stock for purposes of §1244 is $250. If the taxpayer sells her 10 shares for $250, she will recognize a loss of $750, all of which must be treated as a capital loss. If she sells the 10 shares for $200, then $50 of her total loss of $800 will be treated as an ordinary loss under §1244 and the remaining $750 will be a capital loss.

LO 19-3 **TAXABLE AND TAX-DEFERRED CORPORATE ACQUISITIONS**

continued from page 19-2...

Jim Wheeler and Ginny Gears are excited about their new business venture with Al Pine. It seems to solve their need to find a source of revenues during the winter months, when the demand for bicycles declines significantly. With that challenge met, Jim and Ginny have turned their attention to expanding their bicycle business to a new geographic region. At the recent Tour de Gaslight race sponsored by the Michigan Bicycle Racing Association, Jim struck up a conversation with Pam Peloton, owner of Wolverine Cycles and Repair (WCR) in Ann Arbor, Michigan. Pam mentioned she is planning to move to Colorado and is looking to sell her business. Jim can see lots of synergies in buying WCR. He and Ginny are familiar with the biking community in Ann Arbor, and they understand the economics of operating a business in a college town. Ginny is also excited about the possibility of expanding their company to Ann Arbor.

A meeting has been set up with Pam to explore the possible acquisition of her business. Pam operates Wolverine Cycles and Repair through a C corporation, which gives Jim and Ginny the opportunity to consider buying the assets of the business directly or buying Pam's stock in the corporation. If they take the stock acquisition route, Jim and Ginny need to consider whether they want to operate their new company as a subsidiary of Spartan Cycle and Repair or in a lateral ownership arrangement (in which their two companies would be "brother-sister" corporations). Operating WCR as a subsidiary of SCR would allow Jim and Ginny to file a consolidated tax return with SCR. Pam is concerned about the tax consequences of each of these options, as are Jim and Ginny.

to be continued...

THE KEY FACTS

Tax Model for Corporate Acquisitions

- The acquiring corporation can acquire the target corporation through either a stock or asset acquisition.
- The acquisition can be structured as either taxable or tax-deferred.
- Taxable asset acquisitions allow the acquiring corporation to step up the tax basis of the assets acquired to fair value.
- In stock acquisitions and tax-deferred asset acquisitions, the tax basis of the target corporation's assets remains at the assets' carryover basis (generally, cost less accumulated depreciation).

At some point in the life of a successful business, its owners likely will consider expanding its scope or geographic location. Businesses can grow internally through expansion or externally by acquiring an existing business. Jim and Ginny prefer to buy Pam's existing business to expand to a new geographic location. Because Pam operates the business through a C corporation, Jim and Ginny have multiple options. Jim and Ginny first need to consider whether they will personally make the acquisition or whether SCR will make the acquisition. Second, they must determine whether this will be an asset or a stock acquisition. Finally, they need to determine the type of consideration to use in the acquisition (SCR stock or cash). Each of these options can result in different tax consequences for the buyer and the seller. Thus, Jim and Ginny will also need to negotiate the form of the transaction with Pam.

In this section of the chapter, we consider the basic ways in which a corporation or its shareholders can acquire the stock or assets of another corporation and the tax consequences that follow the form of the acquisition. This is an extremely complicated and technical area of the tax law. A thorough discussion of all the ways in which an acquisition can take place likely would take up most or all of a semester. As a result, our discussion is limited to the basic types of corporate acquisitions.

The Acquisition Tax Model

When negotiating an acquisition, management of the acquiring corporation must decide whether to acquire the target corporation's assets or stock and what consideration to use (equity, debt, and/or cash). The form of the transaction and the consideration paid will jointly determine the tax status of the transaction.[34] Nontax considerations, such as the ease of transferring stock or the existence of contingent liabilities, often dictate the form of an acquisition by a publicly traded corporation. In contrast, privately held corporations are more likely to make tax considerations a priority.

The shareholders of the target corporation also must decide what consideration to accept in return for their stock or assets in the corporation. Cash provides liquidity and does not decline in value after the acquisition is announced, but it also causes the transaction to be fully or partially taxable to the seller. Receiving equity in the acquiring corporation may allow shareholders to defer paying tax on gain realized on the exchange, but the sellers must accept the risk that the acquiring corporation's stock will decline in value after the deal is announced or consummated.

The technical tax (and accounting) rules that apply to corporate acquisitions are extremely complex. Because the statutory language governing reorganizations is sparse, the IRS and courts often must decide whether the form of a reorganization transaction meets both the literal language of the statute and the substance of the judicial principles that underlie the reorganization provisions. As a result, the reorganization area is heavily laden with administrative and judicial pronouncements. Our goal is to provide you with a basic overview of the most common types of corporate acquisitions that you will see discussed in the business press.

Exhibit 19-7 summarizes the four basic types of transactions that can effect an acquisition of another company. The buyer can purchase either stock or assets in a transaction that is either taxable or tax-deferred (in whole or in part) to the seller. Both sides to the transaction must decide which category they desire to be in after the transaction.

EXHIBIT 19-7   **Types of Corporate Acquisitions**

	Asset Purchase from WCR	Stock Purchase from Pam
Taxable	Cash or debt generally (Cell 1)	Cash or debt generally (Cell 2)
Tax Deferred Reorganization	Type A or Type C reorganization using SCR equity (Cell 3)	Type B reorganization using SCR voting equity (Cell 4)

Often the buyer and seller have different tax incentives (they want to be in different cells), and this requires both sides to negotiate a compromise arrangement that satisfies both parties. For example, the buyer likely prefers to acquire the target corporation's assets in a taxable transaction (cell 1). By purchasing the target corporation's assets in a taxable acquisition, the acquiring corporation gets a stepped-up tax basis in the assets equal to fair market value (cost). To the extent the acquiring corporation can allocate the purchase price to depreciable or amortizable assets, this increases future depreciation or amortization deductions on the acquiring corporation's tax return. It is not uncommon in an acquisition involving publicly traded corporations for goodwill to comprise

---

[34]The form of the transaction and the consideration paid to shareholders does not affect the financial accounting treatment of the acquisition—ASC 805-10-25-1 requires that all business combinations be accounted for using the purchase method.

over 70 percent of the purchase price. If the acquiring corporation can achieve a tax basis in the goodwill, the basis can be amortized over 15 years.[35] If the acquiring corporation makes the acquisition using a tax-deferred technique, then the tax basis of the acquired assets will not be stepped up to fair value and goodwill will have a zero tax basis. Hence, the acquiring company will be ineligible for increased depreciation and amortization deductions.

The seller likely prefers to sell stock in a tax-deferred transaction (cell 3 or cell 4) because any tax on the appreciation in the stock will be postponed. Alternatively, the seller would prefer to sell the stock in a taxable transaction (cell 2) because any gain on the stock will be taxed as capital gains. However, neither of these options provides the acquiring corporation with a stepped-up tax basis in the assets, greatly reducing the future value of the acquisition to the buyer. The seller would likely be reluctant to sell the assets of the corporation in a taxable transaction (cell 1) because the seller would be required to pay both the corporate tax on appreciation of the assets and the individual capital gains tax on the appreciation of the stock. Of course, the buyer might be able to overcome the seller's reluctance by offering a sufficiently high purchase price.

LO 19-4 TAX CONSEQUENCES TO A CORPORATE ACQUISITION

continued from page 19-20...

As part of their negotiations with Pam, Jim and Ginny look over WCR's **tax accounting balance sheet** along with a recent valuation of the assets' fair market values. Pam has held the WCR stock for 10 years and her tax basis in the stock is $50,000. WCR is an accrual-method taxpayer, and as a result, the payables have a tax basis. That is, the corporation deducted the expenses related to the payables when the expenses were accrued. These facts are summarized as follows:

	FMV	Adjusted Basis	Appreciation
Cash	$ 10,000	$ 10,000	
Receivables	5,000	5,000	
Inventory	20,000	10,000	$ 10,000
Building	80,000	50,000	30,000
Land	120,000	60,000	60,000
Total	$235,000	$135,000	$100,000
Payables	4,000	4,000	
Mortgage*	31,000	31,000	
Total	$ 35,000	$ 35,000	

*The mortgage was attached to the building and land.

Jim and Ginny agree to pay Pam $300,000 for her business, an amount that is $100,000 more than the net fair market value of the assets less the liabilities listed on the balance sheet ($235,000 − $35,000). The additional $100,000 reflects an amount to be

[35]§197.

paid for the company's customer list valued at $25,000, with the remaining $75,000 allocated to goodwill.

With the price settled, Jim, Ginny, and Pam now must agree on the form the transaction will take.

to be continued . . .

Taxable Acquisitions

A corporation can acquire an ongoing business through the purchase of its stock or assets in return for cash, debt, or equity or a combination thereof. Cash purchases of stock are the most common form of acquisition of publicly held corporations. Using cash to acquire another company has several nontax advantages; most notably, the acquiring corporation does not "acquire" the target corporation's shareholders in the transaction and does not increase the denominator in its calculation of earnings per share. There are disadvantages to using cash, particularly if the acquiring corporation incurs additional debt to fund the purchase.

If SCR purchases the assets directly from WCR in return for cash (cell 1 in Exhibit 19-7), WCR will recognize gain or loss on the sale of each asset individually. WCR may cease to exist as a separate corporation and might completely liquidate by transferring the net after-tax proceeds received from SCR to its shareholder. If WCR liquidates, Pam recognizes gain or loss on the exchange of her WCR stock for the cash received.

Example 19-20

What if: Assume SCR will purchase WCR's assets for $300,000 and assume the company's liabilities of $35,000. WCR will realize $335,000 ($300,000 + $35,000), which it will allocate to each of the assets sold, as follows:

	Allocation	Adjusted Basis	Gain Realized
Cash	$ 10,000	$ 10,000	$ 0
Receivables	5,000	5,000	0
Inventory	20,000	10,000	10,000
Building	80,000	50,000	30,000
Land	120,000	60,000	60,000
Customer list	25,000	0	25,000
Goodwill	75,000	0	75,000
Total	$335,000	$135,000	$200,000

What amount of gain or loss does WCR recognize on the sale of its assets, and what is the character of the gain or loss (ordinary, §1231, or capital)?

(continued on page 19-24)

Answer: WCR recognizes total gain of $200,000, and WCR pays a corporate-level tax of $42,000 (assuming a tax rate of 21 percent). The character of the gain will be as follows:

	Gain Recognized	Character
Inventory	$ 10,000	Ordinary
Building	30,000	Ordinary (§291) and §1231
Land	60,000	§1231
Customer list	25,000	§1231
Goodwill	75,000	§1231
Total	**$200,000**	

What if: Suppose that WCR opts to go out of existence (liquidate) by exchanging the $258,000 net amount realized after taxes ($300,000 − $42,000) for Pam's WCR stock.

What amount of gain or loss will Pam recognize on the exchange of her WCR stock for the after-tax proceeds from the sale ($258,000)?

Answer: Pam recognizes a long-term capital gain of $208,000 ($258,000 − $50,000 stock basis) and pays a shareholder-level tax of $31,200 ($208,000 × 15% assuming Pam's total taxable income is not above the breakpoint for the 20% capital gains tax rate). The total tax paid using this form of acquisition is $73,200 ($42,000 + $31,200). Pam is left with $226,800 after taxes ($300,000 − $42,000 − $31,200).

Although unattractive to Pam, this deal provides SCR (Jim and Ginny) with the maximum tax benefits. The building will have an increased tax basis of $30,000, which SCR can depreciate over 39 years. The customer list and goodwill will have a tax basis of $25,000 and $75,000, respectively, which SCR can amortize over 15 years on a straight-line basis.[36]

If SCR acquires WCR by acquiring Pam's stock for cash (cell 2 in Exhibit 19-7), WCR retains its tax and legal identity (unless SCR liquidates WCR into itself or merges it into an existing subsidiary). The tax basis of WCR's assets, which will remain unchanged, will not reflect SCR's tax basis (purchase price) in WCR's stock.

Example 19-21

What if: Suppose instead that SCR purchases the WCR stock from Pam for $300,000. What amount of gain or loss does WCR recognize in this transaction?

Answer: WCR will not recognize gain on this form of acquisition because it has not sold any assets directly to SCR.

What amount and character of gain or loss does Pam recognize in this transaction?

Answer: Pam recognizes long-term capital gain of $250,000 ($300,000 − $50,000 stock basis) and pays a shareholder-level tax of $37,500 ($250,000 × 15%). Pam will be left with $262,500 after taxes ($300,000 − $37,500), which is $57,800 more than a direct asset sale ($262,500 − $204,700).

Although attractive to Pam, this deal will not be as attractive a direct asset sale to SCR (Jim and Ginny). The building will retain its same tax basis of $50,000, and the customer list and goodwill will have a tax basis of zero. The customer list and goodwill have a zero tax basis to WCR because they are self-created assets. The tax basis of WCR's assets remain at $135,000. SCR has a tax basis in the WCR stock equal to the purchase price of $300,000.

---

[36]§197. Note that goodwill is not amortized for financial accounting purposes, and the determination of goodwill for accounting purposes under ASC 805-30-30-1 differs from the determination of goodwill for tax purposes under §1060. Hence, even a taxable acquisition can give rise to a book–tax difference because different amounts of goodwill exist for tax and book purposes.

Tax nirvana will be achieved if Pam can treat the transaction as a stock sale and pay a single level of capital gains tax on the gain recognized from the sale, and if SCR can treat the transaction as an asset purchase and receive a step-up in basis of the assets to fair market value. This best of both tax worlds is sometimes available in transactions where a corporate taxpayer purchases 80 percent or more of another corporation's stock within a 12-month period. In such cases, SCR can make a **§338 election** to treat the stock purchase as a deemed asset purchase.

Like most things that appear too good to be true, this election does not come without some cost. The calculation of these tax costs is extremely technical and beyond the scope of this text. In big-picture terms, WCR is treated as if it is selling its assets prior to the transaction and then repurchasing them at fair market value. This deemed sale of assets causes WCR to recognize gain on assets that have appreciated in value. SCR, as the buyer, bears this tax cost because the fair market value of WCR will be reduced by the tax paid. In almost all cases, this tax cost negates the tax benefits of getting a step-up in basis in WCR's assets and is rarely ever elected. For example, it rarely makes economic sense to pay income taxes on a $100 gain just to increase the basis of an asset by $100. The additional tax on the $100 gain would very likely outweigh the present value of the savings from an additional $100 of future depreciation deductions. However, this election might be tax-efficient if WCR has net operating losses or net capital losses that can be used to offset gain from the deemed sale of its assets.

If the target corporation is a subsidiary of the seller, the acquiring corporation and seller can make a joint **§338(h)(10) election** and have the seller report the gain from the deemed sale of the target corporation's assets on its tax return in lieu of reporting the actual gain from the sale of the target corporation stock. The technical rules that apply to §338(h)(10) elections are beyond the scope of this text. These elections, which are more common than a regular §338 election, often achieve tax savings to both parties to the transaction. For example, Dow Chemical sold its AgroFresh subsidiary to a group of investors in 2015. The buyer and seller made a joint §338(h)(10) election, which allowed AgroFresh to record a stepped-up tax basis for its asset. As you can see from the announcement reproduced in the nearby box, this provided almost $400 million in cash tax benefits from amortizing or depreciating the step-up in basis.

TAXES IN THE REAL WORLD Dow Chemical's Tax Receivable from a §338(h)(10)

On July 31, 2015, Dow Chemical sold its AgroFresh business to investors organized as Boulevard Acquisition Corporation. Under the agreement, Dow was to receive cash plus Boulevard common stock valued $1.056 billion. The assets of AgroFresh were stepped up under a Section 338(h)(10) election, and under a *tax receivable* agreement, Dow was entitled to future payments from AgroFresh in the amount of 85 percent of the tax savings resulting from the increased tax basis. AgroFresh estimated that the total undiscounted tax payments to Dow would amount to $337 million over the term of the agreement, implying that the total tax savings from the step-up would amount to around $400 million ($337 million/85 percent). In addition, as a result of the transaction, Dow also reported a $618 million gain from the sale in its financial results for 2015.

Source: Boulevard Acquisition Corp Proxy dated July 16, 2015 and AgroFresh Solutions 10-K dated March 11, 2016.

Tax-Deferred Acquisitions

As you learned previously in this chapter, the tax law allows taxpayers to organize a corporation in a tax-deferred manner under §351. The tax laws also allow taxpayers to *reorganize* their corporate structure in a tax-deferred manner. For tax purposes, **reorganizations** encompass acquisitions and dispositions of corporate assets (including the stock of subsidiaries) and a corporation's restructuring of its capital structure, place of incorporation, or company name. The IRC provides tax deferral to the corporation(s) involved in the reorganization (the parties to the reorganization) and the shareholders if the transaction meets one of seven statutory definitions[37] and satisfies the judicial principles that underlie the reorganization statutes. As before, tax deferral in corporate reorganizations is predicated on the seller's receiving a continuing ownership interest in the assets transferred, in the form of equity in the acquiring corporation.

The statutory language governing corporate reorganizations is rather sparse. It should not be surprising, then, that the IRS and the courts frequently must interpret how changes in the facts related to a transaction's form affect its tax status. The end result has been the development of a complex and confusing legacy of IRS rulings and court decisions that dictate how a reorganization transaction will be taxed. Corporate reorganizations are best left to the tax experts who have devoted much of their professional lives to understanding their intricacies. Our goal is to acquaint you with the basic principles that underlie all corporate reorganizations and provide you with an understanding of the most common forms of corporate acquisitions that are tax-deferred.

Judicial Principles That Underlie All Tax-Deferred Reorganizations

Continuity of Interest (COI)   Tax deferral in a reorganization is based on the presumption that the shareholders of the acquired (target) corporation retain a continuing ownership (equity) interest in the target corporation's assets or historic business through their ownership of stock in the acquiring corporation. The IRC does not provide a **bright line test** to establish that **continuity of interest (COI)** has been met, although the regulations provide an example that says COI has been satisfied when the shareholders of the target corporation, in the aggregate, receive equity equal to 40 percent or more of the total value of the consideration received.[38]

Continuity of Business Enterprise (COBE)   For a transaction to qualify as a tax-deferred reorganization, the acquiring corporation must continue the target corporation's historic business or continue to use a *significant* portion of the target corporation's historic business assets. Whether the historic business assets retained are "significant" is a facts and circumstances test, which adds to the administrative and judicial rulings that are part and parcel of the reorganization landscape. **Continuity of business enterprise (COBE)** does not apply to the historic business or assets of the acquiring corporation; the acquiring corporation can sell off its assets after the reorganization without violating the COBE requirement.

Business Purpose Test   As early as 1935, the Supreme Court stated that transactions with "no business or corporate purpose" should not receive tax deferral even if they

---

[37]The "forms" of corporate reorganizations are defined in §368(a)(1).
[38]Reg. §1.368-1T(e)(2)(v), Example 10.

comply with the statutory requirements.[39] To meet the business purpose test, the acquiring corporation must be able to show a significant business purpose for engaging in the transaction (other than tax avoidance).

Type A Asset Acquisitions

Type A reorganizations (cell 3 in Exhibit 19-7) are statutory **mergers** or **consolidations.**[40] In a merger, either the acquired (target) corporation or the acquiring corporation will cease to exist. For example, SCR could acquire the assets and liabilities of WCR by transferring SCR shares to Pam in exchange for her WCR stock, and WCR would no longer exist. This type of merger is an *upstream* or *forward* acquisition because the target is merged into the acquiring corporation. Alternatively, the target corporation could be the surviving entity, and this type of acquisition is a *downstream* or *reverse* acquisition. In a consolidation, SCR and WCR will transfer their assets and liabilities to a newly formed corporation in return for stock in the new corporation, after which SCR and WCR will both cease to exist.

In a Type A reorganization, the target corporation shareholders defer recognition of gain or loss realized on the receipt of stock of the acquiring corporation. Similar to a §351 transaction, if a target corporation shareholder receives money or other property (boot) from the acquiring corporation or its acquisition subsidiary, the shareholder recognizes *gain* to the extent of the money and fair market value of other property received (not to exceed the gain realized). The shareholder's tax basis in the stock received is a *substituted basis* of the stock transferred plus any gain recognized less any money and the fair market value of other property received. The target corporation's assets remain the same at their (historic) tax basis in a Type A merger.

Exhibit 19-8 provides an illustration of a Type A merger. The consideration that can be paid to Pam is relatively flexible in a Type A merger; the only limitation is that the transaction must satisfy the COI requirement (at least 40 percent of the consideration must be SCR stock). The stock used to satisfy the COI test can be voting or nonvoting, common or preferred.

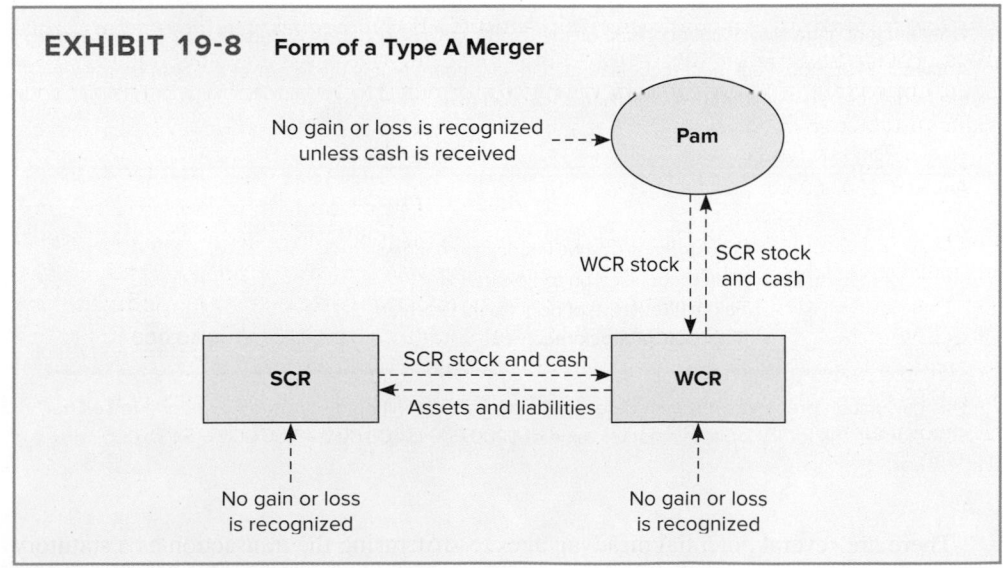

EXHIBIT 19-8   Form of a Type A Merger

No gain or loss is recognized unless cash is received → Pam

WCR stock ↓   SCR stock and cash ↑

SCR ← SCR stock and cash ─ ─ ─ ─ WCR
Assets and liabilities →

No gain or loss is recognized   No gain or loss is recognized

---

[39]*Gregory v. Helvering,* 293 U.S. 465 (1935).

[40]"Type A reorganizations" are so named because they are described in §368(a)(1)(A). Likewise, Type B and Type C reorganizations are described in subparagraphs (B) and (C), respectively.

Example 19-22

What if: Assume WCR will merge into SCR in a Type A reorganization. Under the terms of the deal, SCR will pay Pam $300,000 in SCR stock, after which WCR will merge into SCR. Pam's tax basis in her WCR stock is $50,000. What amount of gain will Pam realize on the exchange of her WCR stock for SCR stock?

Answer: $250,000 ($300,000 − $50,000)

What amount of gain will Pam recognize on the exchange of her WCR stock for SCR stock?

Answer: $0. Because Pam receives only SCR stock, she defers the entire $250,000 gain realized.

What is Pam's tax basis in her SCR stock?

Answer: $50,000. Because Pam defers the entire gain, her tax basis in the SCR stock is a substituted basis from her WCR stock. This preserves the gain deferred for future recognition if Pam should choose to sell her SCR stock in the future for its fair market value of $300,000.

What are SCR's tax bases in the assets it receives from WCR in the merger?

Answer: SCR receives a carryover tax basis in each of the assets received (e.g., the tax basis of the goodwill and customer list will be zero).

Example 19-23

What if: Suppose instead Pam wants some cash as well as SCR stock in the transaction. What is the maximum amount of cash Pam can receive from SCR and not violate the COI rule as illustrated in the regulations?

Answer: $180,000 ($300,000 × 60%). Pam can receive a maximum of 60 percent of the consideration in cash and not violate the COI rule under the regulations.

What if: Assume Pam receives $100,000 plus $200,000 in SCR stock in exchange for all of her WCR stock in a Type A merger. What amount of gain will Pam *realize* on the exchange?

Answer: $250,000 ($300,000 − $50,000)

What amount of gain will Pam *recognize* on the exchange?

Answer: $100,000. Pam must recognize gain in an amount that is the lesser of the gain realized or the boot received. Pam defers recognizing $150,000 gain.

What is Pam's tax basis in her SCR stock?

Answer: $50,000, computed as follows:

	Adjusted basis of WCR stock exchanged	$ 50,000
+	Gain recognized on the exchange	100,000
−	Fair market value of boot (cash) received	100,000
	Tax basis of stock received	**$ 50,000**

This calculation preserves the gain deferred for future recognition if Pam should choose to sell her SCR stock in the future for its fair market value of $200,000 ($200,000 − $50,000 = $150,000).

There are several potential disadvantages to structuring the transaction as a statutory merger. Pam will become a shareholder of SCR, and the historic tax basis of WCR's assets and liabilities will carry over to SCR. Going back to the original set of facts in the above example, Pam will not owe any tax on the transaction but she will not receive any cash. Finally, WCR will cease to exist as a separate corporation. Jim and Ginny expressed a desire to operate WCR as an independent corporation. To accomplish this, SCR will have

EXHIBIT 19-9   Form of a Type A Forward Triangular Merger

to transfer the WCR assets and liabilities to a newly created subsidiary under §351. SCR will incur the additional cost to retitle the assets a second time and pay any state transfer tax on the transfer of the assets. Jim and Ginny can avoid this latter cost by employing a variation of a Type A reorganization called a *forward (upstream) triangular merger.*

Forward Triangular Type A Merger   In a forward triangular merger, the acquiring corporation creates a subsidiary corporation (called, perhaps, SCR Acquisition Subsidiary in our example) that holds stock of the acquiring corporation. The target corporation then merges into this subsidiary with its shareholders (Pam in this case) receiving stock of the acquiring corporation (SCR) in exchange for the stock of the target corporation (WCR). In our example, when the dust clears, WCR assets and liabilities are isolated in a wholly owned subsidiary of SCR. Exhibit 19-9 provides an illustration of a forward triangular Type A merger for determining the tax consequences to the parties in our fictional transaction.

This type of merger is a common vehicle for effecting mergers when the parent corporation stock is publicly traded or the parent corporation is a holding company. For a forward triangular merger to be effective, the transaction must satisfy the requirements to be a straight Type A merger and one additional requirement: The acquisition subsidiary must acquire "substantially all" of the target corporation's properties in the exchange. The IRS interprets "substantially all" to mean 90 percent of the fair market value of the target corporation's net properties ($300,000 × 90% = $270,000) and 70 percent of the fair market value of the target corporation's gross properties ($335,000 × 90% = $301,500). The technical tax rules that apply to determine the tax basis of the acquired assets after the merger are complex and beyond the scope of this text.

Reverse Triangular Type A Merger   Another variation of a Type A reorganization is the *reverse (downstream) triangular merger.* Suppose that WCR holds valuable assets that cannot be easily transferred to another corporation (perhaps employment contracts or licenses). In this scenario, it would not be prudent to dissolve WCR because these valuable assets would be lost. In a reverse triangular merger, the acquiring corporation still creates a subsidiary corporation that holds stock of the acquiring corporation. However, it is the acquisition subsidiary that merges into the acquiring corporation. Again, the shareholders of the target corporation (Pam) receive stock of the acquiring corporation (SCR) in exchange for the stock of the target corporation (WCR). When the dust clears, however, the target corporation (WCR) is still intact, albeit as a wholly owned subsidiary of the acquiring corporation. Reverse triangular Type A mergers are desirable because the transaction preserves the target corporation's existence. Exhibit 19-10 provides an illustration of a reverse triangular Type A merger for determining the tax consequences to the parties in our fictional transaction.

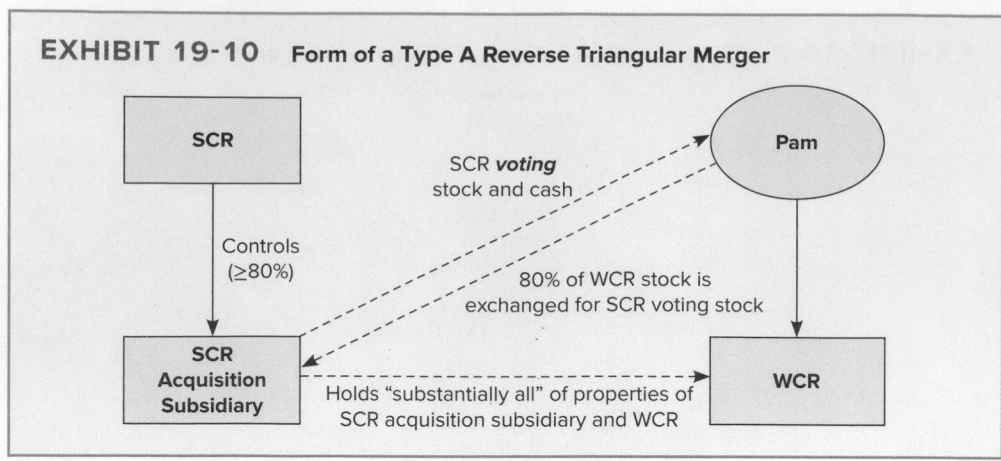

EXHIBIT 19-10 Form of a Type A Reverse Triangular Merger

Three additional requirements must be met to satisfy the requirements for tax deferral in a reverse triangular merger. First, the acquiring corporations must hold "substantially all" of the properties of both the target corporation and the Acquisition Subsidiary. Second, in the exchange, the target corporation's shareholders must transfer an amount of stock in the target corporation that constitutes control of the target corporation (80 percent or more of the target stock). Finally, the target corporation's shareholders must receive *voting stock* of the acquiring corporation in return for target stock that constitutes control of the target corporation. For example, if the SCR Acquisition Subsidiary acquires 100 percent of WCR's stock in the exchange, at least 80 percent of the consideration the SCR Acquisition Subsidiary pays Pam must be in the form of SCR voting stock.

This last requirement often presents too high a hurdle in acquisitions in which the acquiring corporation wants to use a combination of cash and stock to acquire the target corporation. Publicly traded corporations are very sensitive to the amount of stock they use in an acquisition because of the negative effect it can have on the company's earnings per share (issuing additional stock increases the denominator in the earnings per share computation). The technical tax rules that apply to determining the tax basis of WCR's assets after the merger are complex and beyond the scope of this text.

The Walt Disney Company acquired Pixar in a reverse triangular merger. Disney's acquisition subsidiary merged into Pixar, after which the former shareholders of Pixar received Disney stock in exchange for their Pixar stock.

Type B Stock-for-Stock Reorganizations

Type B reorganizations (cell 4 in Exhibit 19-7) are often referred to as **stock-for-stock acquisitions.** The requirements for a tax-deferred Type B reorganization are very restrictive. In particular, the acquiring corporation (SCR) must acquire control (80 percent or more ownership) of the target corporation (WCR) using solely the voting stock of the acquiring corporation. Additional consideration of as little as $1 can taint the transaction and cause it to be fully taxable to the shareholders of the target corporation (Pam). Not surprisingly, Type B reorganizations are rare among publicly traded corporations. Exhibit 19-11 provides an illustration of the form of a Type B merger using our fictional example.

In a Type B reorganization, Pam will defer recognition of any gain or loss realized and take a substituted basis in the SCR stock she receives. SCR takes a carryover basis (from Pam) in the WCR stock received. In the case of publicly traded corporations, this requires the acquiring corporation to determine the tax basis of each share of stock it receives from thousands or even millions of shareholders of the target corporation. In such cases, the IRS allows the acquiring corporation to determine its stock basis using statistical sampling.

EXHIBIT 19-11 Form of a Type B Reorganization

SCR

Solely SCR voting stock

WCR stock

Pam

SCR "controls" WCR
immediately after the exchange

WCR

Example 19-24

What if: Let's say SCR will exchange SCR voting stock for all of Pam's WCR stock in a Type B stock-for-stock reorganization. Pam's tax basis in her WCR stock is $50,000. The fair market value of the SCR stock is $300,000. What amount of gain will Pam *realize* on the exchange of her WCR stock for SCR stock?

Answer: $250,000 ($300,000 − $50,000)

What amount of gain will Pam *recognize* on the exchange of her WCR stock for SCR stock?

Answer: $0. Because Pam receives only SCR stock, she defers the entire $250,000 gain realized.

What is Pam's tax basis in her SCR stock?

Answer: $50,000. Because Pam defers the entire gain, her tax basis in the SCR stock is a substituted basis from her WCR stock. This preserves the gain deferred for future recognition if Pam should choose to sell her SCR stock in the future for its fair market value of $300,000.

What is SCR's tax basis in the WCR stock received in the exchange?

Answer: $50,000. SCR receives a substituted tax basis equal to Pam's basis in her WCR stock.

What is WCR's tax basis in the assets after the exchange?

Answer: The tax basis of WCR's assets remains the same (e.g., the tax basis of the goodwill and customer list will be zero).

What if: Suppose Pam received $10,000 plus $290,000 of SCR stock in the transaction. How does this change in facts affect Pam's tax consequences?

Answer: This transaction will not qualify as a Type B reorganization and the entire realized gain of $250,000 is recognized. For a Type B reorganization to be tax-deferred, Pam cannot receive any cash. Given her desire to move to Colorado, this limitation likely will be a deal breaker.

There are many variations of Type A and Type B acquisitions and other tax-deferred asset-type acquisitions that we do not discuss in this chapter because of complexity. Suffice it to say that tax experts in mergers and acquisitions have a toolbox of ideas and alternatives that allow for countless ways to structure a transaction and achieve tax deferral for the parties to the reorganization. For the novice entering this field of taxation, such variety can be both exhilarating and exasperating. Our goal in this section is to provide you with a glimpse of this intricate area of taxation. A summary of the tax-deferred reorganizations discussed in this section, along with the other forms of tax-deferred reorganizations, is provided in Exhibit 19-12.

EXHIBIT 19-12 Summary of Tax-Deferred Corporate Reorganizations

Form of Reorganization	Description
Statutory Merger Type A	One corporation acquires the assets and liabilities of another corporation in return for stock or a combination of stock and cash. The acquisition is tax-deferred if the transaction satisfies the continuity of interest, continuity of business enterprise, and business purpose test requirements.
Forward Triangular Type A	The acquiring corporation uses stock of its *parent* corporation to acquire the target corporation's stock, after which the target corporation merges into the acquiring corporation. To be tax-deferred, the transaction must meet the requirements to be a Type A merger. In addition, the acquiring corporation must use *solely* the stock of its parent corporation and acquire "substantially all" of the target corporation's property in the transaction.
Reverse Triangular Type A	The acquiring corporation uses stock of its parent corporation to acquire the target corporation's stock, after which the acquiring corporation merges into the target corporation (which becomes a subsidiary of the parent corporation). To be tax-deferred, the transaction must satisfy three requirements: (1) the surviving corporation must hold "substantially all" of the properties of both the surviving and the merged corporations; (2) the target shareholders must transfer in the exchange an amount of stock in the target that constitutes control of the target (80 percent or more of the target's stock); and (3) the target shareholders must receive parent corporation voting stock in return.
Type B	The acquiring corporation uses its voting stock (or the voting stock of its parent corporation) to acquire control (80 percent voting power and 80 percent of nonvoting stock) of the target corporation. To be tax-deferred, the target shareholders must receive *solely* voting stock of the acquiring corporation.
Type C	The acquiring corporation uses its voting stock (or the voting stock of its parent corporation) to acquire "substantially all" of the target corporation's assets. The end result of a Type C reorganization resembles a Type A reorganization. The major difference between a Type C reorganization and a Type A reorganization is that state law governs the form of the Type A merger, while the Internal Revenue Code governs the form of the Type C reorganization.
Type D	Nondivisive Type D: A corporation transfers all or part of its assets to another corporation, and immediately after the transfer the shareholders of the transferor corporation own at least 50 percent of the voting power or value of the transferee corporation. Divisive Type D: A corporation transfers all or part of its assets to another corporation, and immediately after the transfer the shareholders of the transferor corporation own at least 80 percent of the transferee corporation.
Type E	Type E reorganizations are often referred to as recapitalizations. Stock in the corporation (e.g., common) is exchanged for a different class of stock (e.g., preferred) or securities (debt). Recapitalizations can range from an amendment in the corporate charter to a change in the redemption price or liquidating value of stock to an actual exchange of stock between the corporation and its shareholder(s).
Type F	Type F reorganizations are described as a "mere change in identity, form, or place of organization" of a single corporation. A corporation uses a Type F reorganization to change its corporate name or its state (country) of incorporation.
Type G	Type G reorganizations are often referred to as bankruptcy reorganizations. In a Type G reorganization, the corporation transfers all or a part of its assets to another corporation in a Title 11 case, and the stock of the corporation receiving the assets is distributed in a transaction that is tax-deferred.

Tax law also allows corporations to divide by transferring stock of a subsidiary to shareholders in a pro rata distribution (spin-off) or a non-pro rata distribution (split-off).[41] The technical details of these transactions are beyond the scope of this text.

TAXES IN THE REAL WORLD A Big Oil Deal

In 2017 Noble Energy (NYSE: NBL) agreed to exchange stock and cash for Clayton Williams Energy (NYSE: CWEI). Under the agreement, CWEI shareholders would receive cash of $34.75 and approximately 3.722 NBL shares for each CWEI share. The ratio of cash and stock was to be adjusted so that the total value of the NBL stock issued would not be less than 75 percent of the total merger consideration. According to SEC filings, the qualification of the transaction as a "reorganization" within the meaning of Section 368(a) of the Internal Revenue Code of 1986 is a condition to the deal.

COMPLETE LIQUIDATION OF A CORPORATION

LO 19-5

continued from page 19-23 . . .

After several years of trying to get 360 Air off the ground, Jim, Ginny, and even Al realize that there is not enough demand for snowboarding products in East Lansing to make their business venture profitable. Reluctantly, the three owners decide to liquidate the corporation and have constructed the company's tax accounting balance sheet, which is reproduced below.

	FMV	Adjusted Basis	Difference
Cash	$138,000	$138,000	
Receivables	2,000	2,000	
Inventory	10,000	12,000	$ (2,000)
Building	150,000	48,000	102,000
Land	200,000	100,000	100,000
Total	$500,000	$300,000	$200,000

The parties agree that 360 Air will sell off the inventory, land, and building and collect the remaining receivables. After the sale, 360 Air will pay taxes of $42,000 (21 percent times $200,000) on the gains and divide the remaining $558,000 in cash pro rata between the three shareholders (50 percent to Al, 40 percent to Jim, and 10 percent to Ginny). ■

The owners of a corporation may decide at some point to discontinue the corporation's business activities. They may make this decision because the corporation is not profitable, the officers and shareholders wish to change the organizational form of the business (e.g., to a flow-through entity), or the owners want to consolidate operations (e.g., a subsidiary is liquidated into the parent corporation).

A complete liquidation occurs when a corporation acquires all its stock from all its shareholders in exchange for all its net assets, after which the corporation ceases to do business. For tax purposes, a corporation files Form 966 to inform the IRS of its intention to liquidate its tax existence. The form should be filed within 30 days after the board of directors resolve to liquidate the corporation.

---

[41] §355.

Tax Consequences to the Shareholders in a Complete Liquidation

The tax consequences to a shareholder in a complete liquidation depend on (1) whether the shareholder is incorporated and (2) what percentage of the corporation the shareholder owns. In general, all *noncorporate* shareholders receiving liquidating distributions have a fully taxable transaction.[42] The shareholders treat the property received as full payment in exchange for the stock transferred. They compute capital gain or loss by subtracting the stock's tax basis from the money and fair market value of property received in return. If a shareholder assumes the corporation's liabilities on property received as a liquidating distribution, he or she reduces by the amount of the liabilities assumed the amount he or she realized in the computation of gain or loss. The shareholder's tax basis in the property received equals the property's fair market value.

Example 19-25

Ginny received cash of $55,800 (representing her 10 percent ownership in the company's assets of $558,000 after all debts were paid). Ginny's tax basis in the 360 Air stock is $60,000.

What amount of gain or loss will Ginny *realize* on the exchange of her 360 Air stock for 360 Air assets?

Answer: $4,200 capital loss ($55,800 − $60,000).

What amount of loss will Ginny *recognize* on the exchange?

Answer: $4,200. The loss is deductible to the extent of Ginny's capital gains plus an additional $3,000.

Example 19-26

What if: Suppose that rather than sell the land, 360 Air distributed the land with $79,000 cash to Al, representing his 50 percent interest in the net fair market value of the company. Al's tax basis in the 360 Air stock is $100,000.

What amount of gain or loss will Al *realize* on the exchange of his 360 Air stock for 360 Air assets?

Answer: 179,000 capital gain [($200,000 + $79,000) − $100,000].

What amount of gain will Al *recognize* on the exchange?

Answer: $179,000. The entire amount is taxable.

What is Al's tax basis in the cash and land he receives in the liquidation?

Answer: $79,000 and $200,000, respectively. Al receives a tax basis in the assets he receives equal to their fair market values.

Example 19-27

As a result of the complete liquidation of 360 Air, Jim received $223,200 cash (representing his 40 percent ownership in the company's assets of $558,000). His tax basis in 360 Air is $240,000, an amount equal to the cash he contributed when the corporation was formed.

[42]§331.

What amount of gain or loss will Jim *realize* on the exchange of his 360 Air stock for 360 Air assets?

Answer: $16,800 capital loss ($223,200 − $240,000).

What amount of loss will Jim *recognize* on the exchange?

Answer: $16,800. The entire amount could be deductible to the extent of Jim's capital gains. Otherwise, Jim can offset this loss against capital gains and deduct an additional $3,000 of net capital loss. Jim would carry any unused capital loss forward.

Corporate shareholders are also taxed on liquidating distributions unless the corporation owns 80 percent or more of the stock (voting power and value). Corporate shareholders owning 80 percent or more of the stock of the liquidating corporation do not recognize gain or loss on the receipt of liquidating distributions.[43] This nonrecognition treatment is mandatory. The tax basis in the property transferred carries over to the recipient.[44] This deferral provision allows a group of corporations under common control to reorganize their organizational structure without tax consequences.

Example 19-28

What if: Suppose 360 Air was a 100 percent-owned subsidiary of SCR, and SCR liquidated or 360 Air is liquidated into SCR. SCR has a tax basis in its 360 Air stock of $300,000.

What amount of gain or loss will SCR *realize* on the complete liquidation of 360 Air stock for 360 Air assets?

Answer: $200,000 capital gain ($500,000 − $300,000).

What amount of gain will SCR *recognize* on the exchange?

Answer: $0. The gain is not recognized because SCR owns 80 percent or more of 360 Air.

What is SCR's tax basis in the assets and liabilities it receives in the liquidation?

Answer: 360 Air's tax basis in the assets and liabilities will not change. SCR will inherit a carryover tax basis in 360 Air's assets and liabilities.

Tax Consequences to the Liquidating Corporation in a Complete Liquidation

The tax consequences to the liquidating corporation depend on the tax treatment applied to the shareholder to whom the property was distributed.

Taxable Liquidating Distributions Typically, a liquidating corporation recognizes all gains and certain losses on taxable distributions of property to shareholders.[45] The liquidating corporation does not recognize loss if the property is distributed to a related party and either (1) the distribution is non-pro rata, or (2) the asset distributed is disqualified property.[46] A pro rata distribution is one where each of the corporation's assets are distributed to each shareholder in proportion to their ownership interest. A *related*

> **THE KEY FACTS**
>
> **Tax Consequences of a Complete Liquidation**
>
> - Shareholders other than corporations that own 80 percent or more of the liquidating corporation's stock recognize gain and usually loss in a complete liquidation of the corporation.
> - Corporations that own 80 percent or more of the liquidating corporation's stock (vote and value) do not recognize gain or loss in a complete liquidation of the corporation.
> - Shareholders recognizing gain or loss take a tax basis in property received in the complete liquidation equal to its fair market value.
> - Corporate shareholders that defer recognizing gain or loss take a tax basis in property received in the complete liquidation equal to its carryover basis.

[43]§332(a). Shareholders must meet the 80 percent ownership from the time the plan is adopted until the plan is complete.
[44]§334(b)(1).
[45]§336(a).
[46]§336(d)(1).

person generally is defined as a shareholder who owns more than 50 percent of the stock of the liquidating corporation. *Disqualified property* is property acquired within five years of the date of distribution in a tax-deferred §351 transaction or as a nontaxable contribution to capital.

Example 19-29

360 Air made taxable liquidating distributions to Jim, Ginny, and Al during the current year. Al owns 50 percent of the stock, Ginny owns 10 percent, and Jim owns 40 percent. Assume for purposes of this example that 360 Air made a pro rata distribution of all the assets to its three shareholders. The company's tax accounting balance sheet at the time of the distribution is shown below:

	FMV	Adjusted Basis	Difference
Cash	$138,000	$138,000	
Receivables	2,000	2,000	
Inventory	10,000	12,000	$ (2,000)
Building	150,000	48,000	102,000
Land	200,000	100,000	100,000
Total	$500,000	$300,000	$200,000

What amount of gain or loss does 360 Air recognize as a result of the distribution?

Answer: $200,000. 360 Air recognizes all gains and losses on the distribution of its assets in the following amounts and character:

	Gain (Loss) Recognized	Character
Inventory	$ (2,000)	Ordinary
Building	102,000	Ordinary (§291) and §1231
Land	100,000	§1231
Net gain	**$200,000**	

Note that the gain or loss on the complete liquidation is identical to gains and losses that would result if 360 Air had sold all of its assets at fair market value.

Example 19-30

What if: Assume Jim owned 60 percent of the stock, and 360 Air distributed all of the assets except the land to Jim in a non-pro rata distribution. The company's tax accounting balance sheet at the time of the distribution is shown below:

	FMV	Adjusted Basis	Difference
Cash	$138,000	$138,000	
Receivables	2,000	2,000	
Inventory	10,000	12,000	$ (2,000)
Building	150,000	48,000	102,000
Land	200,000	100,000	100,000
Total	$500,000	$300,000	$200,000

What amount of gain or loss does 360 Air recognize as a result of the distribution?

Answer: $202,000 gain, as calculated below. 360 Air recognizes all gains but cannot recognize the $2,000 inventory loss because the distribution is non-pro rata and the loss property is distributed to a related person (Jim owns more than 50 percent of the stock).

	Gain (Loss) Recognized	Character
Inventory	$ 0	
Building	102,000	Ordinary (§291) and §1231
Land	100,000	§1231
Net gain	**$202,000**	

What if: Assume 360 Air distributed all of the inventory, the building, and $90,000 of cash to Ginny in a non-pro rata distribution. What amount of gain or loss does 360 Air recognize as a result of the distribution?

Answer: $200,000. 360 Air can now recognize the $2,000 loss on the distribution of the inventory because the property was not distributed to a related person.

A second loss disallowance rule applies to built-in loss that arises with respect to property acquired in a §351 transaction or as a contribution to capital. A loss on the complete liquidation of such property is not recognized if the property distributed was acquired in a §351 transaction or as a contribution to capital, and a *principal purpose* of the contribution was to recognize a loss by the liquidating corporation.[47] This rule prevents a built-in loss existing at the time of the distribution (basis in excess of fair market value) from being recognized by treating the basis of the property distributed as its fair market value at the time it was contributed to the corporation. This prohibited tax-avoidance purpose is presumed if the property transfer occurs within two years of the liquidation. The presumption can be overcome if the corporation can show that there was a corporate business purpose for contributing the property to the corporation.

This provision is designed as an *anti-stuffing* provision to prevent shareholders from contributing property with built-in losses to a corporation shortly before a liquidation to offset gain property distributed in the liquidation. Earlier in this chapter you learned that Congress added a similar built-in loss disallowance rule that applies to §351 transfers.[48] Under this provision, if the aggregate adjusted tax basis of property transferred to a corporation by a shareholder in a §351 transfer exceeds the aggregate fair market value of the assets, the aggregate tax basis of the assets in the hands of the transferee corporation cannot exceed their aggregate fair market value. The loss disallowance rule that relates to liquidating distributions of built-in loss property received in a §351 transaction applies on an asset-by-asset basis to those assets that retained their built-in loss when contributed to the corporation.

Example 19-31

What if: Suppose Al transferred a building and land to 360 Air in return for 50 percent of the corporation's stock (50 shares) in a transaction that qualified under §351. The property transferred to the corporation had the following fair market values and adjusted bases:

	FMV	Adjusted Basis
Building	$ 75,000	$100,000
Land	200,000	100,000
Total	$275,000	$200,000

(continued on page 19-38)

[47]§336(d)(2).
[48]§362(e)(2).

In this case, the aggregate fair market value of the property transferred to the corporation exceeds the aggregate adjusted basis of the property. As a result, the building will retain its carryover basis of $100,000 and subsequent built-in loss of $25,000.

What if: If the building and land are distributed to Al in complete liquidation of his ownership of 360 Air stock within two years of the §351 transaction, will 360 Air be able to deduct the $25,000 loss on the distribution of the building?

Answer: It depends. Because the liquidating distribution is made within two years of the §351 transaction, the presumption is that Al contributed the property to 360 Air for tax avoidance purposes (i.e., to allow the corporation to deduct the loss). The corporation can rebut this presumption by demonstrating that the contribution of the property by Al had a corporate business purpose at the time of the §351 transaction.

Nontaxable Liquidating Distributions   The liquidating corporation does not recognize gain or loss on distributions of property to an 80 percent corporate shareholder.[49] If any one of the shareholders receives tax deferral in the liquidation, the liquidating corporation cannot recognize any loss, even on distributions to shareholders who receive taxable distributions.[50]

Example 19-32

What if: Assume 360 Air was a 100-percent-owned subsidiary of SCR, and SCR liquidated the company into SCR. SCR has a tax basis in its 360 Air stock of $300,000. The company's tax accounting balance sheet at the time of the distribution is shown below:

	FMV	Adjusted Basis	Difference
Cash	$138,000	$138,000	
Receivables	2,000	2,000	
Inventory	10,000	12,000	$ (2,000)
Building	150,000	48,000	102,000
Land	200,000	100,000	100,000
Total	$500,000	$300,000	$200,000

What amount of gain or loss does 360 Air *recognize* as a result of the liquidation?

Answer: $0. 360 Air does not recognize any gain or loss on the liquidation.

What if: Suppose 360 Air was 80 percent owned by SCR and 20 percent owned by Jim. 360 Air distributed the inventory plus $90,000 to Jim in complete liquidation of his stock. Can 360 Air recognize the $2,000 inventory loss?

Answer: No. 360 Air cannot recognize the loss even though Jim is not a related party and has a taxable distribution. When one shareholder is not taxable on a liquidating distribution (SCR), the liquidating corporation cannot recognize any losses on the distribution of property to any shareholder.

Liquidation-related expenses, including the cost of preparing and effectuating a plan of complete liquidation, are deductible by the liquidating corporation on its final Form 1120. Deferred or capitalized expenditures such as organizational expenditures also are deductible on the final tax return.

[49]§337(a).
[50]§336(d)(3).

CONCLUSION

In this chapter we discussed some of the important tax rules that apply during the life cycle of a C corporation. As the storyline indicates, forming a corporation generally does not create any tax to any of the parties to the transaction. Gain or loss realized by the shareholders on the transfer of property to the corporation is deferred until a later date, either when the shareholder sells his ownership interest or the corporation liquidates. Subsequent acquisitions of new businesses or dispositions of existing businesses also can be achieved in a tax-deferred manner. However, failure to meet all the requirements can convert a tax-deferred transaction into a taxable transaction. A complete liquidation of a corporation generally is a fully taxable transaction to the shareholders and the liquidating corporation, except in the case where a subsidiary is liquidated into its parent corporation.

Summary

Review the taxation of property dispositions.

LO 19-1

- A person realizes gain or loss as a result of engaging in a transaction, which is defined as an exchange of property rights with another person.
- Gain or loss realized is computed by subtracting the adjusted basis of property transferred in the exchange from the amount realized in the exchange.
- The amount realized is computed as cash received plus the fair market value of other property received plus any liabilities assumed by the transferee on the property transferred, reduced by selling expenses and any liabilities assumed by the transferor on property received in the exchange.
- The general tax rule is that gain or loss realized is recognized (included in the computation of taxable income) unless a specific tax rule exempts the gain or loss from being recognized (permanently) or defers such recognition until a future date.

Compute the tax consequences to the parties to a tax-deferred corporate formation.

LO 19-2

- Section 351 applies to transactions in which one or more persons transfer property to a corporation in return for stock, and immediately after the transfer, these same persons control the corporation to which they transferred the property.
- If a transaction meets these requirements, the transferors of property (shareholders) do not recognize (defer) gain or loss realized on the transfer of the property to the corporation.
  - Shareholders contributing property to a corporation in a §351 transaction compute gain or loss realized by subtracting the adjusted basis of the property they contribute to the corporation from the fair market value of the consideration they receive in return (amount realized).
  - Gain, but not loss, is recognized when property other than the corporation's stock (boot) is received in the exchange.
  - Gain is recognized in an amount equal to the *lesser of* the gain realized or the fair market value of boot received.
  - The tax basis of stock received in the exchange equals the tax basis of the property transferred, less any liabilities assumed by the corporation on the property contributed (substituted basis).
  - The shareholder's stock basis is increased by any gain recognized and reduced by the fair market value of any boot received.
- The corporation receiving property for its stock in a §351 exchange does not recognize (excludes) gain or loss realized on the transfer.
  - The tax basis of the property received by the corporation equals the property's tax basis in the transferor's hands (carryover basis).
  - The asset's tax basis is increased by any gain recognized by the shareholder on the transfer of the property to the corporation.

LO 19-3   Identify the different forms of taxable and tax-deferred acquisitions.

- Corporations can be acquired in taxable asset or stock purchases.
- Corporations can be acquired in tax-deferred asset or stock purchases.
- To be tax-deferred, an acquisition must meet certain IRC and judicial requirements to be a reorganization.
  - The judicial requirements, now summarized in the regulations, require continuity of interest, continuity of business enterprise, and business purpose.
- In a Type A tax-deferred acquisition, the target corporation's assets and liabilities are merged into the acquiring corporation (stock-for-assets exchange).
  - Type A acquisitions involving publicly traded corporations often use an acquisition subsidiary (triangular merger) to acquire the target corporation's assets and liabilities.
- In a Type B tax-deferred acquisition, the shareholders of the target corporation exchange their stock for stock of the acquiring corporation (stock-for-stock exchange).
  - Type B acquisitions prohibit the use of cash in the exchange.

LO 19-4   Determine the tax consequences to the parties to a corporate acquisition.

- Shareholders participating in a taxable asset or stock transaction compute gain or loss realized by subtracting the adjusted basis of the stock they surrender to the acquiring corporation from the fair market value of the consideration they receive in the exchange.
- Shareholders participating in a tax-deferred reorganization defer gain and loss realized in the exchange unless cash (boot) is received.
  - Shareholders receiving boot recognize gain, but not loss, in an amount equal to the lesser of the gain realized or the fair market value of the boot received.
- The corporation does not recognize gain on the distribution of its own stock in exchange for property in a reorganization.
- The stock received in return for stock in a tax-deferred reorganization has a tax basis equal to the tax basis of the stock surrendered in the exchange (substituted basis).
- The shareholder's stock basis is increased by any gain recognized and reduced by cash or other boot received.
- The assets transferred to the corporation in a tax-deferred reorganization carry over the tax basis of the shareholders contributing the property (carryover basis).

LO 19-5   Calculate the tax consequences that apply to the parties to a complete liquidation of a corporation.

- Noncorporate shareholders receiving a distribution in complete liquidation of their corporation recognize gain and (usually) loss in the exchange.
- Tax deferral is extended to corporate shareholders owning 80 percent or more of the liquidating corporation.
- The liquidating corporation recognizes gain and (usually) loss on the distribution of property to those shareholders who are taxable on the distribution.
- The liquidating corporation cannot deduct losses on property distributed in the following three situations:
  - The loss property is distributed to a related person and is non-pro rata.
  - The loss property is contributed to the corporation in a §351 transaction and the principal purpose of the contribution is tax avoidance.
  - One of the persons receiving a liquidating distribution is not taxable on the distribution (an 80-percent-or-more corporate shareholder).
- The liquidating corporation does not recognize gain or loss on the distribution of property to a 80 percent or more corporate shareholder.
- The tax basis of each asset received by the shareholder in a taxable complete liquidation equals the asset's fair market value on the date of the distribution.
- The tax basis of each asset received by an 80-percent-or-more corporate shareholder in a tax-deferred complete liquidation carries over from the liquidating corporation.

KEY TERMS

boot (19-6)	continuity of interest (COI) (19-26)	§338 election (19-25)
bright line tests (19-26)	contribution to capital (19-18)	§338(h)(10) election (19-25)
carryover basis (19-14)	merger (19-27)	stock-for-stock acquisition (19-30)
consolidation (19-27)	person (19-5)	substituted basis (19-9)
continuity of business enterprise (COBE) (19-26)	realization (19-2)	tax accounting balance sheet (19-22)
	reorganization (19-26)	

DISCUSSION QUESTIONS

Discussion Questions are available in Connect®.   ≡ connect

1. Discuss the difference between gain realization and gain recognition in a property transaction.   `LO 19-1`
2. What information must a taxpayer gather to determine the *amount realized* in a property transaction?   `LO 19-1`
3. Distinguish between exclusion and deferral in a property transaction.   `LO 19-1`
4. Contrast how a taxpayer's tax basis in property received in a property transaction will be affected if the transaction results in gain exclusion versus gain deferral.   `LO 19-1`
5. What information must a taxpayer gather to determine the *adjusted basis* of property exchanged in a property transaction?   `LO 19-1`
6. Why does Congress allow tax deferral on the formation of a corporation?   `LO 19-2`
7. List the key statutory requirements that must be met before a corporate formation is tax-deferred under §351.   `LO 19-2`
8. What is the definition of *control* for purposes of §351? Why does Congress require the shareholders to control a corporation to receive tax deferral?   `LO 19-2`
9. What is a *substituted basis* as it relates to stock received in exchange for property in a §351 transaction? What is the purpose of attaching a substituted basis to stock received in a §351 transaction?   `LO 19-2`
10. Explain whether the receipt of boot by a shareholder in a §351 transaction causes the transaction to be fully taxable.   `LO 19-2`
11. Explain whether a corporation's assumption of shareholder liabilities will always constitute boot in a §351 transaction.   `LO 19-2`
12. How does the tax treatment differ in cases where liabilities are assumed with a tax avoidance purpose versus where liabilities assumed exceed basis? When would this distinction cause a difference in the tax consequences of the transactions?   `LO 19-2`
13. What is a *carryover basis* as it relates to property received by a corporation in a §351 transaction? What is the purpose of attaching a carryover basis to property received in a §351 transaction?   `LO 19-2`
14. Under what circumstances does property received by a corporation in a §351 transaction not receive a carryover basis? What is the reason for this rule?   `LO 19-2`
15. How does a corporation depreciate an asset received in a §351 transaction in which no gain or loss is recognized by the transferor of the property?   `LO 19-2`
16. Are the tax consequences the same whether a shareholder contributes property to a corporation in a §351 transaction or as a capital contribution? Explain.   `LO 19-2`
17. Why might a corporation prefer to characterize an instrument as debt rather than equity for tax purposes? Are the holders of the instrument indifferent as to its characterization for tax purposes?   `LO 19-2`
18. Under what conditions is it advantageous for a shareholder to hold §1244 stock? Why did Congress bestow these tax benefits on holders of such stock?   `LO 19-2`

LO 19-3 19. Explain when an acquiring corporation would prefer to buy the target corporation's assets directly in an acquisition.

LO 19-3 20. Do the shareholders of the target corporation usually prefer to sell the stock or the assets of the target corporation? Explain.

LO 19-3 21. What is the congressional purpose for allowing tax deferral on transactions that meet the definition of a corporate reorganization?

LO 19-3 22. Describe the advantages (if any) of using a reverse triangular form of Type A reorganization in acquiring other corporations.

LO 19-3 23. What are the key differences in the tax law requirements that apply to forward versus reverse triangular mergers?

LO 19-3 24. What are the key differences in the tax law requirements that apply to a Type A stock-for-assets acquisition versus a Type B stock-for-stock acquisition?

LO 19-4 25. How does the form of a regular §338 election compare and contrast to a §338(h)(10) election?

LO 19-4 26. What tax benefits does the buyer hope to obtain by making a §338 or §338(h)(10) election? Describe how this election might affect the value offered for the target corporation.

LO 19-4 27. In a stock acquisition, describe the difference (if any) between the *tax basis of assets* held by an acquired corporation and the *tax basis of the shares* held by a corporate acquirer.

LO 19-4 28. What is the presumption behind the continuity of ownership interest (COI) requirement in a tax-deferred acquisition? How do the target shareholders determine if COI is met in a Type A reorganization?

LO 19-4 29. W Corporation will acquire all of the assets and liabilities of Z Corporation in a Type A merger, after which W Corporation will sell off all of its assets and liabilities and focus solely on Z Corporation's business. Explain whether the transaction will be taxable because W Corporation fails the *continuity of business enterprise test*.

LO 19-4 30. Compare how a shareholder computes her tax basis in stock received from the acquiring corporation in a forward triangular Type A merger versus a Type B merger.

LO 19-5 31. Do all shareholders receive the same tax treatment in a complete liquidation of a corporation? Explain.

LO 19-5 32. Describe when a corporate shareholder must defer gains on the receipt of distributions of property from the complete liquidation of a subsidiary corporation.

LO 19-5 33. Under what circumstances must a corporate shareholder recognize gains in a complete liquidation?

LO 19-5 34. Under what circumstances will a liquidating corporation be allowed to recognize loss in a non-pro rata distribution?

LO 19-5 35. Compare and contrast the built-in loss duplication rule as it relates to §351 with the built-in loss disallowance rule as it applies to a complete liquidation.

PROBLEMS

Select problems are available in Connect®.

LO 19-2 36. Ramon incorporated his sole proprietorship by transferring inventory, a building, and land to the corporation in return for 100 percent of the corporation's stock. The property transferred to the corporation had the following fair market values and adjusted bases:

	FMV	Adjusted Basis
Inventory	$ 10,000	$ 4,000
Building	50,000	30,000
Land	100,000	50,000
Total	$160,000	$84,000

The fair market value of the corporation's stock received in the exchange equaled the fair market value of the assets transferred to the corporation by Ramon.

a) What amount of gain or loss does Ramon *realize* on the transfer of the property to his corporation?

b) What amount of gain or loss does Ramon *recognize* on the transfer of the property to his corporation?

c) What is Ramon's basis in the stock he receives in his corporation?

37. Carla incorporated her sole proprietorship by transferring inventory, a building, and land to the corporation in return for 100 percent of the corporation's stock. The property transferred to the corporation had the following fair market values and adjusted bases:

LO 19-2

planning

	FMV	Adjusted Basis
Inventory	$ 20,000	$ 10,000
Building	150,000	100,000
Land	250,000	300,000
Total	$420,000	$410,000

The corporation also assumed a mortgage of $120,000 attached to the building and land. The fair market value of the corporation's stock received in the exchange was $300,000.

a) What amount of gain or loss does Carla *realize* on the transfer of the property to the corporation?

b) What amount of gain or loss does Carla *recognize* on the transfer of the property to her corporation?

c) What is Carla's basis in the stock she receives in her corporation?

d) Would you advise Carla to transfer the building and land to the corporation? What tax benefits might she and the corporation receive if she kept the building and land and leased it to the corporation?

38. Ivan incorporated his sole proprietorship by transferring inventory, a building, and land to the corporation in return for 100 percent of the corporation's stock. The property transferred to the corporation had the following fair market values and adjusted bases:

LO 19-2

	FMV	Adjusted Basis
Inventory	$ 10,000	$15,000
Building	50,000	40,000
Land	60,000	30,000
Total	$120,000	$85,000

The fair market value of the corporation's stock received in the exchange equaled the fair market value of the assets transferred to the corporation by Ivan. The transaction met the requirements to be tax-deferred under §351.

a) What amount of gain or loss does Ivan *realize* on the transfer of the property to his corporation?

b) What amount of gain or loss does Ivan *recognize* on the transfer of the property to his corporation?

c) What is Ivan's basis in the stock he receives in his corporation?

d) What is the corporation's adjusted basis in each of the assets received in the exchange?

e) Would the stock held by Ivan qualify as §1244 stock? Why is this determination important for Ivan?

LO 19-2   39. Zhang incorporated her sole proprietorship by transferring inventory, a building, and land to the corporation in return for 100 percent of the corporation's stock. The property transferred to the corporation had the following fair market values and adjusted bases:

	FMV	Adjusted Basis
Inventory	$ 20,000	$ 10,000
Building	150,000	100,000
Land	230,000	300,000
Total	$400,000	$410,000

The corporation also assumed a mortgage of $100,000 attached to the building and land. The fair market value of the corporation's stock received in the exchange was $300,000. The transaction met the requirements to be tax-deferred under §351.

a) What amount of gain or loss does Zhang *realize* on the transfer of the property to her corporation?

b) What amount of gain or loss does Zhang *recognize* on the transfer of the property to her corporation?

c) What is Zhang's tax basis in the stock she receives in the exchange?

d) What is the corporation's adjusted basis in each of the assets received in the exchange?

Assume the corporation assumed a mortgage of $500,000 attached to the building and land. Assume the fair market value of the building is now $250,000 and the fair market value of the land is $530,000. The fair market value of the stock remains $300,000.

e) How much, if any, gain or loss does Zhang recognize on the exchange assuming the revised facts?

f) What is Zhang's tax basis in the stock she receives in the exchange?

g) What is the corporation's adjusted basis in each of the assets received in the exchange?

LO 19-2   40. Sam and Devon agree to go into business together selling college-licensed clothing.

planning   According to the agreement, Sam will contribute inventory valued at $100,000 in return for 80 percent of the stock in the corporation. Sam's tax basis in the inventory is $60,000. Devon will receive 20 percent of the stock in return for providing accounting services to the corporation (these qualify as organizational expenditures). The accounting services are valued at $25,000.

a) What amount of income gain or loss does Sam *realize* on the formation of the corporation? What amount, if any, does he *recognize*?

b) What is Sam's tax basis in the stock he receives in return for his contribution of property to the corporation?

c) What amount of income gain or loss does Devon *realize* on the formation of the corporation? What amount, if any, does he *recognize*?

d) What is Devon's tax basis in the stock he receives in return for his contribution of services to the corporation?

Assume Devon received 25 percent of the stock in the corporation in return for his services.

e) What amount of gain or loss does Sam *recognize* on the formation of the corporation?

f) What is Sam's tax basis in the stock he receives in return for his contribution of property to the corporation?

g) What amount of income, gain, or loss does Devon *recognize* on the formation of the corporation?

h) What is Devon's tax basis in the stock he receives in return for his contribution of services to the corporation?

i) What tax advice could you give Sam and Devon to change the tax consequences?

41. Jekyll and Hyde formed a corporation (Halloween Inc.) on October 31 to develop a drug to address split personalities. Jekyll will contribute a patented formula valued at $200,000 in return for 50 percent of the stock in the corporation. Hyde will contribute an experimental formula worth $120,000 and medical services in exchange for the remaining stock. Jekyll's tax basis in the patented formula is $125,000, whereas Hyde has a basis of $15,000 in his experimental formula.

LO 19-2

tax forms

research

a) Describe the tax consequences of the transaction.

b) Prepare the §351 statement that must be included with the return.

42. Ron and Hermione formed Wizard Corporation on January 2. Ron contributed cash of $200,000 in return for 50 percent of the corporation's stock. Hermione contributed a building and land with the following fair market values and adjusted bases in return for 50 percent of the corporation's stock:

LO 19-2

	FMV	Tax-Adjusted Basis
Building	$ 75,000	$ 20,000
Land	175,000	80,000
Total	$250,000	$100,000

To equalize the exchange, Wizard Corporation paid Hermione $50,000 in addition to her stock.

a) What amount of gain or loss does Ron *realize* on the formation of the corporation? What amount, if any, does he *recognize*?

b) What is Ron's tax basis in the stock he receives in return for his contribution of property to the corporation?

c) What amount of gain or loss does Hermione *realize* on the formation of the corporation? What amount, if any, does she *recognize*?

d) What is Hermione's tax basis in the stock she receives in return for her contribution of property to the corporation?

e) What adjusted basis does Wizard Corporation take in the land and building received from Hermione?

Assume Hermione's adjusted basis in the land was $200,000.

f) What amount of gain or loss does Hermione *realize* on the formation of the corporation? What amount, if any, does she *recognize*?

g) What adjusted basis does Wizard Corporation take in the land and building received from Hermione?

Assume Hermione's adjusted basis in the land was $250,000.

h) What amount of gain or loss does Hermione *realize* on the formation of the corporation? What amount, if any, does she *recognize*?

i) What adjusted basis does Wizard Corporation take in the land and building received from Hermione?

j) What election can Hermione and Wizard Corporation make to allow Wizard Corporation to take a carryover basis in the land?

LO 19-2
planning

43. This year, Jack O. Lantern incurred a $60,000 loss on the worthlessness of his stock in the Creepy Corporation (CC). The stock, which Jack purchased in 2005, met all of the §1244 stock requirements at the time of issue. In December of this year, Jack's wife, Jill, also incurred a $75,000 loss on the sale of Eerie Corporation (EC) stock that she purchased in July 2005 and which also satisfied all of the §1244 stock requirements at the time of issue. Both corporations are operating companies.

   a) How much of the losses incurred on the two stock sales can Jack and Jill deduct this year, assuming they do not have capital gains in the current or prior years?

   b) Assuming they did not engage in any other property transactions this year, how much of a net capital loss will carry over to next year for Jack and Jill?

   c) What would be the tax treatment for the losses if Jack and Jill reported only $60,000 of taxable income this year, excluding the securities transactions?

   d) What tax planning suggestions can you offer the Lanterns to increase the tax benefits of these losses?

LO 19-2

44. Breslin Inc. made a capital contribution of investment property to its 100 percent owned subsidiary, Crisler Company. The investment property had a fair market value of $3,000,000 and a tax basis to Breslin of $2,225,000.

   a) What are the tax consequences to Breslin Inc. on the contribution of the investment property to Crisler Company?

   b) What is the tax basis of the investment property to Crisler Company after the contribution to capital?

LO 19-3
research

45. On September 12, 2017, Inotek Pharmaceuticals agreed to acquire Rocket Pharmaceuticals, Ltd., a privately held biopharmaceutical company in a tax-deferred acquisition. The Form 8-K for Inotek (NASDAQ ticker ITEK, cik 0001281895) describes the transaction and was filed with the SEC on August 13, 2012. You can access the Form 8-K at the SEC's Investor website: (https://www.sec.gov/Archives/edgar/data/1281895/000119312517283239/d421363d8k.htm). Read "Item 1.01, Entry into a Material Definitive Agreement" and determine which form of merger was used to effect the acquisition.

LO 19-3
research

46. On August 28, 2017, Mirna Therapeutics, Inc. (renamed "Synlogic" after the deal), completed its business combination with Synlogic, Inc. The Form 8-K for Synlogic (NASDAQ ticker SYBX, cik 0001667986) describes the transaction and was filed with the SEC on August 28, 2017. You can access the Form 8-K at the SEC's Investor website: (https://www.sec.gov/Archives/edgar/data/1281895/000119312517283239/d421363d8k.htm). Read "Item 1.01, Entry into a Material Definitive Agreement," and determine which form of merger was used to effect the acquisition.

LO 19-4

47. Amy and Brian were investigating the acquisition of a tax accounting business, Bottom Line Inc. (BLI). As part of their discussions with the sole shareholder of the corporation, Ernesto Young, they examined the company's tax accounting balance sheet. The relevant information is summarized as follows:

	FMV	Adjusted Basis	Appreciation
Cash	$ 10,000	$ 10,000	
Receivables	15,000	15,000	
Building	100,000	50,000	$ 50,000
Land	225,000	75,000	150,000
Total	$350,000	$150,000	$200,000
Payables	$ 18,000	$ 18,000	
Mortgage*	112,000	112,000	
Total	$ 130,000	$ 130,000	

*The mortgage is attached to the building and land.

Ernesto was asking for $400,000 for the company. His tax basis in the BLI stock was $100,000. Included in the sales price was an unrecognized customer list valued at $100,000. The unallocated portion of the purchase price ($80,000) will be recorded as goodwill.

a) What amount of gain or loss does BLI recognize if the transaction is structured as a direct asset sale to Amy and Brian? What amount of corporate-level tax does BLI pay as a result of the transaction?

b) What amount of gain or loss does Ernesto recognize if the transaction is structured as a direct asset sale to Amy and Brian and BLI distributes the after-tax proceeds [computed in part (a)] to Ernesto in liquidation of his stock?

c) What are the tax benefits, if any, to Amy and Brian as a result of structuring the acquisition as a direct asset purchase?

48. Using the same facts in problem 47, assume Ernesto agrees to sell his stock in BLI to Amy and Brian for $400,000.   `LO 19-4`

a) What amount of gain or loss does BLI recognize if the transaction is structured as a stock sale to Amy and Brian? What amount of corporate-level tax does BLI pay as a result of the transaction, assuming a tax rate of 21 percent?

b) What amount of gain or loss does Ernesto recognize if the transaction is structured as a stock sale to Amy and Brian?

c) What are the tax benefits, if any, to Amy and Brian as a result of structuring the acquisition as a stock sale?

49. Rather than purchase BLI directly (as in problems 47 and 48), Amy and Brian will have their corporation, Spartan Tax Services (STS), acquire the business from Ernesto in a tax-deferred Type A merger. Amy and Brian would like Ernesto to continue to run BLI, which he agreed to do if he could obtain an equity interest in STS. As part of the agreement, Amy and Brian propose to pay Ernesto $200,000 plus voting stock in STS worth $200,000. Ernesto will become a 10 percent shareholder in STS after the transaction.   `LO 19-4`

a) Will the continuity of ownership interest (COI) requirements for a straight Type A merger be met? Explain.

b) What amount of gain or loss does BLI recognize if the transaction is structured as a Type A merger? What amount of corporate-level tax does BLI pay as a result of the transaction, assuming a tax rate of 21 percent?

c) What amount of gain or loss does Ernesto recognize if the transaction is structured as a Type A merger?

d) What is Ernesto's tax basis in the STS stock he receives in the exchange?

e) What are the tax bases of the BLI assets held by STS after the merger?

50. Robert and Sylvia propose to have their corporation, Wolverine Universal (WU), acquire another corporation, EMU Inc., in a tax-deferred triangular Type A merger using an acquisition subsidiary of WU. The sole shareholder of EMU, Edie Eagle, will receive $250,000 plus $150,000 of WU voting stock in the transaction.   `LO 19-4`

a) Can the transaction be structured as a forward triangular Type A merger? Explain why or why not.

b) Can the transaction be structured as a reverse triangular Type A merger? Explain why or why not.

51. Robert and Sylvia propose to have their corporation, Wolverine Universal (WU), acquire another corporation, EMU Inc., in a stock-for-stock Type B acquisition.   `LO 19-4`

The sole shareholder of EMU, Edie Eagle, will receive $400,000 of WU voting stock in the transaction. Edie's tax basis in her EMU stock is $100,000.

a) What amount of gain or loss does Edie recognize if the transaction is structured as a stock-for-stock Type B acquisition?

b) What is Edie's tax basis in the WU stock she receives in the exchange?

c) What is the tax basis of the EMU stock held by WU after the exchange?

LO 19-5   52. Shauna and Danielle decided to liquidate their jointly owned corporation, Woodward Fashions Inc. (WFI). After liquidating its remaining inventory and paying off its remaining liabilities, WFI had the following tax accounting balance sheet:

	FMV	Adjusted Basis	Appreciation
Cash	$200,000	$200,000	
Building	50,000	10,000	$ 40,000
Land	150,000	90,000	60,000
Total	$400,000	$300,000	$100,000

Under the terms of the agreement, Shauna will receive the $200,000 cash in exchange for her 50 percent interest in WFI. Shauna's tax basis in her WFI stock is $50,000. Danielle will receive the building and land in exchange for her 50 percent interest in WFI. Danielle's tax basis in her WFI stock is $100,000. Assume for purposes of this problem that the cash available to distribute to the shareholders has been reduced by any tax paid by the corporation on gain recognized as a result of the liquidation.

a) What amount of gain or loss does WFI recognize in the complete liquidation?

b) What amount of gain or loss does Shauna recognize in the complete liquidation?

c) What amount of gain or loss does Danielle recognize in the complete liquidation?

d) What is Danielle's tax basis in the building and land after the complete liquidation?

LO 19-5   53. Tiffany and Carlos decided to liquidate their jointly owned corporation, Royal Oak Furniture (ROF). After liquidating its remaining inventory and paying off its remaining liabilities, ROF had the following tax accounting balance sheet:

	FMV	Adjusted Basis	Appreciation (Depreciation)
Cash	$200,000	$200,000	
Building	50,000	10,000	$ 40,000
Land	150,000	200,000	(50,000)
Total	$400,000	$410,000	$(10,000)

Under the terms of the agreement, Tiffany will receive the $200,000 cash in exchange for her 50 percent interest in ROF. Tiffany's tax basis in her ROF stock is $50,000. Carlos will receive the building and land in exchange for his 50 percent interest in ROF. His tax basis in the ROF stock is $100,000. Assume for purposes of this problem that the cash available to distribute to the shareholders has been reduced by any tax paid by the corporation on gain recognized as a result of the liquidation.

a) What amount of gain or loss does ROF recognize in the complete liquidation?

b) What amount of gain or loss does Tiffany recognize in the complete liquidation?

c) What amount of gain or loss does Carlos recognize in the complete liquidation?

d) What is Carlos's tax basis in the building and land after the complete liquidation?

Assume Tiffany owns 40 percent of the ROF stock and Carlos owns 60 percent. Tiffany will receive $160,000 in the liquidation and Carlos will receive the land and building plus $40,000.

e) What amount of gain or loss does ROF recognize in the complete liquidation?

f) What amount of gain or loss does Tiffany recognize in the complete liquidation?

g) What amount of gain or loss does Carlos recognize in the complete liquidation?

h) What is Carlos's tax basis in the building and land after the complete liquidation?

54. Jefferson Millinery Inc. (JMI) decided to liquidate its wholly owned subsidiary, 8 Miles High Inc. (8MH). 8MH had the following tax accounting balance sheet:

  LO 19-5

	FMV	Adjusted Basis	Appreciation
Cash	$200,000	$200,000	
Building	50,000	10,000	$ 40,000
Land	150,000	90,000	60,000
Total	$400,000	$300,000	$100,000

a) What amount of gain or loss does 8MH recognize in the complete liquidation?

b) What amount of gain or loss does JMI recognize in the complete liquidation?

c) What is JMI's tax basis in the building and land after the complete liquidation?

55. Jones Mills Inc. (JMI) decided to liquidate its wholly owned subsidiary, Most Help, Inc. (MH). MH had the following tax accounting balance sheet:

LO 19-5

	FMV	Adjusted Basis	Appreciation
Cash	$200,000	$200,000	
Building	50,000	10,000	40,000
Land	150,000	200,000	(50,000)
Total	$400,000	$410,000	$(10,000)

a) What amount of gain or loss does MH recognize in the complete liquidation?

b) What amount of gain or loss does JMI recognize in the complete liquidation?

c) What is JMI's tax basis in the building and land after the complete liquidation?

COMPREHENSIVE PROBLEMS

Select problems are available in Connect®. connect

56. Several years ago, your client, Brooks Robinson, started an office cleaning service. His business was very successful, owing much to his legacy as the greatest defensive third baseman in major league history and his nickname, "The Human Vacuum Cleaner." Brooks operated his business as a sole proprietorship and used the cash method of accounting. Brooks was advised by his attorney that it is too risky to operate his business as a sole proprietorship and that he should incorporate to limit his liability. Brooks has come to you for advice on the tax implications of incorporation. His balance sheet is presented below. Under the terms of the incorporation, Brooks would transfer the assets to the corporation in return for 100 percent of the company's common stock. The corporation would also assume the company's liabilities (payables and mortgage).

Balance Sheet		
	Adjusted Basis	**FMV**
Assets		
Accounts receivable	$ 0	$ 5,000
Cleaning equipment (net)	25,000	20,000
Building	50,000	75,000
Land	25,000	50,000
Total assets	$100,000	$150,000
Liabilities		
Accounts payable	$ 0	$ 10,000
Salaries payable	0	5,000
Mortgage on land and building	35,000	35,000
Total liabilities	$ 35,000	$ 50,000

a) How much gain or loss does Brooks *realize* on the transfer of each asset to the corporation?

b) How much, if any, gain or loss (on a per asset basis) does Brooks *recognize*?

c) How much gain or loss, if any, must the corporation recognize on the receipt of the assets of the sole proprietorship in exchange for the corporation's stock?

d) What tax basis does Brooks have in the corporation's stock?

e) What is the corporation's tax basis in each asset it receives from Brooks?

f) How would you answer the question in part (b) if Brooks had taken back a 10-year note worth $25,000 plus stock worth $75,000 plus the liability assumption?

g) Will Brooks be able to transfer the accounts receivable to the corporation and have the corporation recognize the income when the receivable is collected?

h) Brooks was depreciating the equipment (200 percent declining balance) and building (straight-line) using MACRS when it was held inside the proprietorship. How will the corporation depreciate the equipment and building? Assume Brooks owned the equipment for four years (seven-year property) and the building for six years.

i) Will the corporation be able to deduct the liabilities when paid? Will it matter which accounting method (cash or accrual) the corporation uses?

j) Would you advise Brooks to transfer the land and building to the corporation? What other tax strategy might you suggest to Brooks with respect to the realty?

57. Your client, Midwest Products Inc. (MPI), is a closely held, calendar-year, accrual-method corporation located in Fowlerville, Michigan. MPI has two operating divisions. One division manufactures lawn and garden furniture and decorative objects (furniture division), while the other division manufactures garden tools and hardware (tool division). MPI's single class of voting common stock is owned as follows:

	Shares	Adjusted Basis	FMV
Iris Green	300	$2,000,000	$3,000,000
Rose Ruby	100	1,200,000	1,000,000
Lily White	100	800,000	1,000,000
Totals	500	$4,000,000	$5,000,000

The three shareholders are unrelated.

Outdoor Living Company (OLC), a publicly held, calendar-year corporation doing business in several midwestern states, has approached MPI about acquiring its furniture division. OLC has no interest in acquiring the tool division, however. OLC's management has several strong business reasons for the acquisition, the most important of which is to expand the company's market into Michigan. Iris, Rose, and Lily are amenable to the acquisition provided it can be accomplished in a tax-deferred manner.

OLC has proposed the following transaction for acquiring MPI's furniture division. On April 30 of this year, OLC will create a 100-percent owned subsidiary, OLC Acquisition Inc. (OLC-A). OLC will transfer to the subsidiary 60,000 shares of OLC voting common stock and $2,000,000. The current fair market value of the OLC voting stock is $50 per share ($3,000,000 in total). Each of the three MPI shareholders will receive a pro rata amount of OLC stock and cash.

As part of the agreement, MPI will sell the tool division before the acquisition, after which MPI will merge into OLC-A under Michigan and Ohio state laws (a forward triangular Type A merger). Pursuant to the merger agreement, OLC-A will acquire all of MPI's assets, including 100 percent of the cash received from the sale of the tool division ($2,000,000), and will assume all of MPI's liabilities. The cash from the sale of the tool division will be used to modernize and upgrade much of the furniture division's production facilities. OLC's management is convinced that the cash infusion, coupled with new management, will make MPI's furniture business profitable. OLC management has no plans to liquidate OLC-A into OLC at any time subsequent to the merger. After the merger, OLC-A will be renamed Michigan Garden Furniture Inc.

a) Determine whether the proposed transaction meets the requirements to qualify as a tax-deferred forward triangular Type A merger. Consult Rev. Rul. 88-48 and Rev. Rul. 2001-25 in thinking about the premerger sale of the tool division assets.

b) Could the proposed transaction qualify as a reverse triangular Type A merger if OLC-A merged into MPI? If not, how would the transaction have to be restructured to meet the requirements to be a reverse triangular merger?

58. Rex and Felix are the sole shareholders of Dogs and Cats Corporation (DCC). After several years of operations using the accrual method, they decided to liquidate the corporation and operate the business as a partnership. Rex and Felix hired a lawyer to draw up the legal papers to dissolve the corporation, but they need some tax advice from you, their trusted accountant. They are hoping you will find a way for them to liquidate the corporation while minimizing their total income tax liability.

Rex has a tax basis in his shares of $60,000 and Felix has a tax basis in his shares of $30,000. DCC's tax accounting balance sheet at the date of liquidation is as follows:

	Adjusted Basis	FMV
Assets		
Cash	$ 30,000	$ 30,000
Accounts receivable	10,000	10,000
Inventory	10,000	20,000
Equipment	30,000	20,000
Building	15,000	30,000
Land	5,000	40,000
Total assets	$100,000	$150,000
Liabilities		
Accounts payable		$ 5,000
Mortgage payable—Building		10,000
Mortgage payable—Land		10,000
Total liabilities		$ 25,000
Shareholders' Equity		
Common stock—Rex (80%)		$100,000
Common stock—Felix (20%)		25,000
Total shareholders' equity		$125,000

a) Compute the gain or loss recognized by Rex, Felix, and DCC on a complete liquidation of the corporation assuming each shareholder receives a pro rata distribution of the corporation's assets and assumes a pro rata amount of the liabilities.

b) Compute the gain or loss recognized by Rex, Felix, and DCC on a complete liquidation of the corporation assuming Felix receives $25,000 in cash and Rex receives the remainder of the assets and assumes all of the liabilities.

Assume Felix received the accounts receivable and equipment and assumed the accounts payable.

c) Will Felix recognize any income when he collects the accounts receivable?

d) Will Felix be able to take a deduction when he pays the accounts payable?

Assume Rex is a corporate shareholder of DCC.

e) Compute the gain or loss recognized by Rex, Felix, and DCC on a complete liquidation of the corporation assuming each shareholder receives a pro rata distribution of the corporation's assets and assumes a pro rata amount of the liabilities.

f) Compute the gain or loss recognized by Rex, Felix, and DCC on a complete liquidation of the corporation assuming Felix receives $25,000 in cash and Rex receives the remainder of the assets and assumes all of the liabilities.

Assume the equipment was contributed by Rex to DCC in a §351 transaction two months prior to the liquidation. At the time of the contribution, the property's fair market value was $25,000.

g) Would the tax result change if the property was contributed one year ago? Two years ago? Three years ago?

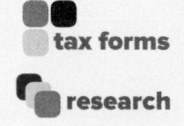
tax forms

research

59. Cartman Corporation owns 90 shares of SP Corporation. The remaining 10 shares are owned by Kenny (an individual). After several years of operations, Cartman decided to liquidate SP Corporation by distributing the assets to Cartman and Kenny. The tax basis of Cartman's shares is $10,000, and the tax basis of Kenny's shares is $7,000. SP reported the following balance sheet at the date of liquidation:

	Adjusted Basis	FMV
Cash	$12,000	$ 12,000
Accounts receivable	8,000	8,000
Stock investment	2,000	10,000
Land	40,000	70,000
Total assets	$62,000	$100,000
Common stock—Cartman (90%)		$ 90,000
Common stock—Kenny (10%)		10,000
Total shareholder equity		$100,000

a) Compute the gain or loss recognized by SP, Cartman, and Kenny on a complete liquidation of the corporation, where SP distributes $10,000 of cash to Kenny and the remaining assets to Cartman.

b) Compute the gain or loss recognized by SP and Kenny on a complete liquidation of the corporation, where SP distributes the stock investment to Kenny and the remaining assets to Cartman. Assume that SP's tax rate is zero.

c) What form needs to be filed with the liquidation of SP?

ROGER | CPA Review

Sample CPA Exam questions from Roger CPA Review are available in Connect as support for the topics in this text. These Multiple Choice Questions and Task-Based Simulations include expert-written explanations and solutions and provide a starting point for students to become familiar with the content and functionality of the actual CPA Exam.

Forming and Operating Partnerships

Learning Objectives

Upon completing this chapter, you should be able to:

LO 20-1 Determine whether a flow-through entity is taxed as a partnership or S corporation.

LO 20-2 Resolve tax issues applicable to partnership formations and other acquisitions of partnership interests, including gain recognition to partners and tax basis for partners and partnerships.

LO 20-3 Determine the appropriate accounting periods and methods for partnerships.

LO 20-4 Calculate and characterize a partnership's ordinary business income or loss and its separately stated items, and demonstrate how to report these items to partners.

LO 20-5 Explain the importance of a partner's tax basis in their partnership interest and the adjustments that affect it.

LO 20-6 Apply the basis, at-risk, and passive activity loss limits to losses from partnerships.

©PhotoAlto/MediaBakery

Storyline Summary

Nicole Johnson

Location:	Salt Lake City, Utah
Status:	Managing member of Color Comfort Sheets LLC
Filing status:	Married to Tom Johnson
Marginal tax rate:	35 percent unless otherwise stated

Sarah Walker

Location:	Salt Lake City, Utah
Status:	Managing member of Color Comfort Sheets LLC
Filing status:	Married to Blaine Walker
Marginal tax rate:	24 percent unless otherwise stated

Chanzz Inc.

Location:	Salt Lake City, Utah
Business:	Managing sports franchises
Status:	Nonmanaging member of Color Comfort Sheets LLC
Filing status:	C Corporation with a June 30 year-end
Marginal tax rate:	28 (blended rate) percent

In the Entities Overview chapter, we introduced you to Nicole Johnson, who decided to turn her sheet-making hobby into a full-time business called Color Comfort Sheets (CCS). Early in 2017, after deciding to organize her new enterprise as a limited liability company (LLC), Nicole turned her attention to raising capital for the business from other investors and a bank loan. Although her limited savings would clearly not be enough to get CCS started, she was willing to contribute a parcel of land in the industrial section of town that she had inherited five years ago from her grandfather. Her friend and mentor, Sarah Walker, offered to contribute time and money to help CCS get off the ground.

With Sarah on board, things seemed to be coming together nicely for Nicole. However, the amount her bank was willing to loan was not enough to fully capitalize CCS, and Nicole and Sarah were unable to invest any more cash into the business to make up the shortfall. Hoping to obtain the additional funding they needed, Nicole and Sarah visited Chance Armstrong, a successful local sports-team owner who had a reputation for being willing to take a chance on new ventures. After listening to Nicole and Sarah's proposal, Chance agreed to invest the additional cash needed to fully fund CCS. Rather than use his personal funds, however, Chance planned to have his closely held corporation, Chanzz Inc., invest in CCS. Unlike Nicole and Sarah, who would take an active role in managing CCS, Chanzz Inc., with everyone's agreement, would not play a part in running the company. By the end of March, CCS had cash, land on which to build its manufacturing facility and offices, and owners who were excited and willing to work hard to make it a successful company.

to be continued . . .

In this chapter, we review the options for operating a business with multiple owners as a **flow-through entity.** In addition, we explain the basic tax consequences of forming and operating business entities taxed as partnerships by examining the specific tax consequences of forming and operating Color Comfort Sheets as a limited liability company (LLC) taxed as a partnership. In the Entities Overview chapter, we learn that Color Comfort Sheets, LLC actually elected to be treated as a C corporation. In this chapter, we assume it did not make this election leaving it to be treated as a partnership for tax purposes.

LO 20-1

FLOW-THROUGH ENTITIES OVERVIEW

Income earned by flow-through entities is usually not taxed at the entity level. Instead, the *owners* of flow-through entities are taxed on the share of entity-level income allocated to them. Thus, unlike income earned by **C corporations,** income from flow-through entities is taxed only once—when it "flows through" to owners of these entities.[1]

Flow-through entities with multiple owners are governed by two somewhat different sets of rules in our tax system.[2] Unincorporated business entities such as **general partnerships, limited partnerships,** and **limited liability companies (LLCs)** are generally treated as partnerships under the rules provided in **Subchapter K** of the Internal Revenue Code.[3] In contrast, corporations whose owners elect to treat them as flow-through entities are classified as such under the rules in **Subchapter S.** These corporations are called **S corporations.** See the Entities Overview chapter for further detail regarding the tax treatment of different entity types.

There are many similarities and a few important differences between the tax rules for partnerships and S corporations. Our focus in this chapter and the next is on the tax rules for partnerships. Then, in the S Corporations chapter, we turn our attention to the tax treatment of S corporations and their shareholders.

TAXES IN THE REAL WORLD Hedge Funds

We can scarcely read the financial press these days without encountering some reference to hedge funds. Hedge funds are private investment funds that have grown in popularity in recent years; they were estimated to have over $7 trillion in assets under management at the end of 2016.[4] According to a study by the Joint Committee on Taxation, most hedge funds are organized as partnerships and their investors are taxed as limited partners.[5]

Aggregate and Entity Concepts

When Congress adopted Subchapter K in 1954, it had to decide whether to follow an **entity approach** and treat tax partnerships as entities separate from their partners or to apply an **aggregate approach** and treat partnerships simply as an aggregation of the partners' separate interests in the assets and liabilities of the partnership. In the end, Congress decided to apply both concepts in formulating partnership tax law. For instance, one of

---

[1]The "check the box" rules determine how various legal entities should be classified for tax purposes. See the discussion in the Entities Overview chapter for a more detailed explanation of these rules.

[2]Unincorporated entities with one individual owner are taxed as *sole proprietorships*. The tax rules relevant to sole proprietorships are discussed in the Business Income, Deductions, and Accounting Methods chapter. In addition to sole proprietorships, other specialized forms of flow-through entities such as real estate investment trusts and regulated investment companies are authorized by the Code. A discussion of these entities is beyond the scope of this chapter.

[3]Publicly traded partnerships may be taxed as corporations. The tax treatment of publicly traded partnerships is more fully developed in the Entities Overview chapter.

[4]*"Private Fund Statistics, Fourth Calendar Quarter 2016,"* SEC Division of Investment Management (sec.gov), July 7, 2017.

[5]*"Present Law and Analysis Relating to Tax Treatment of Partnership Carried Interests and Related Issues, Part I"* (JCX-62-07), September 4, 2007.

the most basic tenets of partnership tax law—that partnerships don't pay taxes—reflects the aggregate approach. However, Congress also adopted other partnership tax rules that fall more squarely on the side of the entity approach. For example, the requirement that partnerships, rather than partners, make most tax elections represents the entity concept. Throughout this and the following chapter, we highlight examples where one or the other basic approach underlies a specific partnership tax rule.

PARTNERSHIP FORMATIONS AND ACQUISITIONS OF PARTNERSHIP INTERESTS

LO 20-2

Acquiring Partnership Interests When Partnerships Are Formed

When a partnership is formed, and afterwards, partners may transfer cash, other tangible or intangible property, and services to the partnership in exchange for an equity interest called a **partnership interest.** Partnership interests represent the bundle of economic rights granted to partners under the partnership agreement (or operating agreement for an LLC).[6] These rights include the right to receive a share of the partnership net assets if the partnership is liquidated, called a **capital interest,** and the right or obligation to receive a share of *future* profits or *future* losses, called a **profits interest.**[7] It is quite common for partners contributing property to receive both capital and profits interests in the exchange. Partners who contribute services instead of property frequently receive only profits interests. The distinction between capital and profits interests is important because the tax rules for partnerships are sometimes applied to them differently.

Contributions of Property Partnership formations are similar to other tax-deferred transactions, such as like-kind exchanges and corporate formations, because realized gains and losses from the exchange of contributed property for partnership interests are either fully or partially deferred for tax purposes, depending on the specifics of the transaction. The rationale for permitting taxpayers to defer realized gains or losses on property contributed to partnerships is identical to the rationale for permitting tax deferral when corporations are formed.[8] From a practical perspective, the tax rules in this area allow entrepreneurs to organize their businesses without having to pay taxes. In addition, these rules follow the aggregate theory of partnership taxation because they recognize that partners contributing property to a partnership still own the contributed property, albeit a smaller percentage, since other partners will also indirectly own the contributed property through their partnership interests.

Gain and loss recognition. As a general rule, neither partnerships nor partners recognize gain or loss when they contribute property to partnerships.[9] This applies to property contributions when a partnership is initially formed and to subsequent property contributions. In this context, the term *property* is defined broadly to include a wide variety of both tangible and intangible assets but not services. The general rule facilitates contributions of property with **built-in gains,** meaning the fair market value is greater than the tax basis, but it discourages contributions of property with **built-in losses,** meaning the fair market value is less than the tax basis. In fact, partners holding property with built-in losses are usually better off selling the property, recognizing the related tax loss, and contributing the cash from the sale to the partnership so it can acquire property elsewhere.

> ### THE KEY FACTS
> **Property Contributions**
> - Partners don't generally recognize gain or loss when they contribute property to partnerships.
> - Initial tax basis for partners contributing property = Basis of contributed property − Debt securing contributed property + Partnership debt allocated to contributing partner + Gain recognized.
> - Contributing partner's holding period in a partnership interest depends on the type of property contributed.

---

[6]The partnership books reflect partners' shares of the partnership's net assets in their individual capital accounts.

[7]An interest in the future profits or losses of a partnership is customarily referred to as a profits interest rather than a profits/loss interest.

[8]The Corporate Formation, Reorganization, and Liquidation chapter discusses the tax rules related to corporate formations.

[9]§721.

Example 20-1

What if: Assume Nicole contributes land to CCS with a fair market value of $120,000 and an adjusted basis of $20,000. What amount of gain or loss would she recognize on the contribution?

Answer: None. Under the general rule for contributions of appreciated property, Nicole will not recognize any of the $100,000 built-in gain from her land.

What if: Suppose Chanzz Inc. contributed equipment with a fair market value of $120,000 and a tax basis of $220,000 to CCS. What amount of the gain or loss would Chanzz Inc. recognize on the contribution?

Answer: None. Chanzz Inc. would not recognize any of the $100,000 built-in loss on the equipment. However, if Chanzz Inc. sold the property to an unrelated party and contributed $120,000 in cash instead of the equipment, it could recognize the $100,000 built-in tax loss. If, for some reason, the equipment Chanzz planned to contribute was uniquely suited to CCS's operations, Chanzz could obtain the same result by selling the equipment to Sarah, who would then contribute the equipment to CCS.

Partner's initial tax basis. Among other things, partners need to determine the tax basis in their partnership interest to properly compute their taxable gains and losses when they sell their partnership interest. A partner's tax basis in her partnership interest is called her **outside basis.** In contrast, the partnership's basis in its assets is its **inside basis.** As we progress through this and the next chapter, you'll see other important reasons for calculating a partner's outside tax basis.

Calculating a partner's initial tax basis in a partnership interest acquired by contributing property and/or cash is relatively straightforward if the partnership doesn't have any debt. The partner will simply have a basis in her partnership interest equivalent to the tax basis of the property and cash she contributed.[10] This rule ensures that realized gains and losses on contributed property are merely deferred until either the contributing partner sells her partnership interest or the partnership sells the contributed property.

Example 20-2

What if: Assume that Sarah contributed $120,000 in cash to CCS in exchange for her partnership interest and that CCS had no liabilities. What is Sarah's outside basis in her partnership interest after the contribution?

Answer: Sarah's basis is $120,000, the amount of cash she contributed to CCS.

What if: Assume Nicole contributed land with a fair market value of $120,000 and an adjusted basis of $20,000 and CCS had no liabilities. What is Nicole's initial tax basis in CCS?

Answer: Nicole's outside basis in CCS is $20,000, the basis of the property she contributed to CCS. If Nicole immediately sold her interest in CCS for $120,000 (the value of the land she contributed), she would recognize gain of $100,000—exactly the amount she would have recognized if she had sold the land instead of contributing it to CCS.

When partnerships have debt, a few additional steps are required to determine a partner's tax basis in her partnership interest. First, each partner must include her share of the partnership's debt in calculating the tax basis in her partnership interest, because partnership tax law treats each partner as borrowing her proportionate share of the partnership's debt and then contributing the borrowed cash to acquire her partnership interest.[11] You can understand the necessity for this basis increase by recalling that the basis of any purchased asset increases by the amount of any borrowed funds used to purchase it.

[10]§722.

[11]§752(a).

Partnerships may have either **recourse debt** or **nonrecourse debt** or both, and the specific approach to allocating partnership debt to individual partners differs for each. The fundamental difference between the two types of debt lies in the legal responsibility partners assume for ultimately paying the debt. Recourse debts are those for which at least one partner has economic risk of loss—that is, they may have to legally satisfy the debt with their own funds. For example, the unsecured debts of general partnerships, such as payables, are recourse debt because general partners are legally responsible for the debts of the partnership. Recourse debt is usually allocated to the partners who will ultimately be responsible for paying it.[12] The partners must consider their partner guarantees, other agreements, and state partnership or LLC statutes in making this determination.

Nonrecourse debts, in contrast, don't provide creditors the same level of legal recourse against partners. Nonrecourse debts such as mortgages are typically secured by real property and only give lenders the right to obtain the secured property in the event the partnership defaults on the debt. Because partners are responsible for paying nonrecourse debts only to the extent the partnership generates sufficient profits, such debts are generally allocated according to partners' profit-sharing ratios. (We discuss an exception to this general rule later in the chapter.[13]) The basic rules for allocating recourse and nonrecourse debt are summarized in Exhibit 20-1.

EXHIBIT 20-1 Basic Rules for Allocating Partnership Debt to Partners

Type of Debt	Allocation Method
Recourse	Allocated to partners with ultimate responsibility for paying debt
Nonrecourse	Allocated according to partners' profit-sharing ratios

The legal structure of entities taxed as partnerships also influences the way partners characterize and allocate partnership debt. Recourse debts in limited partnerships are typically allocated only to general partners, because, as we discuss in the Entities Overview chapter, limited partners are legally protected from a limited partnership's recourse debt holders.[14] Limited partners, however, may be allocated recourse debt if they forgo their legal protection by guaranteeing some or all of the recourse debt. Similarly, LLC members generally treat LLC debt as nonrecourse debt because they, like corporate shareholders, are shielded from the LLC's creditors. However, like limited partners, LLC members may treat debt as recourse debt to the extent they contractually assume risk of loss by agreeing to be legally responsible for paying the debt.[15]

Example 20-3

Sarah and Chanzz Inc. initially each contributed $120,000 and CCS borrowed $60,000 from a bank when CCS was formed. The bank required Nicole, Sarah, and Chanzz Inc. to personally guarantee the bank loan. The terms were structured so each of the members would (1) be responsible for a portion of the debt equal to the percentage of CCS losses allocated to each member (one-third each) and

(continued on page 20-6)

---

[12]Reg. §1.752-2. Under the regulations, partners' obligations for paying recourse debt are determined by assuming a hypothetical, worst-case scenario where partnership assets (including cash) become worthless, and the resulting losses are then allocated to partners. The partners who legally would be responsible for partnership recourse debts under this scenario must be allocated the recourse debt. A detailed description of this approach for allocating recourse debt is beyond the scope of this book.

[13]Reg. §1.752-3 provides the rules for allocating nonrecourse debt, some of which are beyond the scope of this text.

[14]Recall from the Entities Overview chapter that, in limited partnerships, general partners' liability is unlimited, whereas limited partners' liability is usually limited to the amount they have invested.

[15]It's actually quite common for banks and other lenders to require LLC members to personally guarantee loans made to LLCs.

(2) have no right of reimbursement from either CCS or the other members of CCS. How much of the $60,000 bank debt was allocated to each member?

Answer: Each member was allocated $20,000. The debt is treated as recourse debt because the members are personally guaranteeing it. Because each guarantees one-third of the debt, the $60,000 debt is allocated equally among them.

What if: Assuming the $60,000 bank loan is CCS's only debt, what is Sarah's initial basis in her CCS interest after taking her share of CCS's bank debt into account?

Answer: Sarah's basis is $140,000 ($120,000 + $20,000) and consists of her cash contribution plus her share of CCS's $60,000 bank loan.

Another step is needed to determine a partner's outside basis when the partnership assumes *debt of the partner* secured by property the partner contributes to the partnership. Essentially, the contributing partner must treat her debt relief as a deemed cash distribution from the partnership that reduces her outside basis.[16] If the debt securing the contributed property is *nonrecourse debt*, the amount of the debt in excess of the basis of the contributed property is allocated solely to the contributing partner, and the remaining debt is allocated to all partners according to their profit-sharing ratios.[17]

Example 20-4

What if: Nicole contributed $10,000 of cash and land with a fair market value of $150,000 and adjusted basis of $20,000 to CCS when it was formed. The land was encumbered by a $40,000 nonrecourse mortgage executed three years before. Recalling that CCS already had $60,000 in bank debt before Nicole's contribution, what tax bases do Nicole, Sarah, and Chanzz Inc. *initially* have in their CCS interests?

Answer: Their bases are $36,666, $146,666, and $146,666, respectively. Nicole, Sarah, and Chanzz Inc. would determine their initial tax bases as illustrated in the table below:

Description	Nicole	Sarah	Chanzz Inc.	Explanation
(1) Basis in contributed land	$ 20,000			
(2) Cash contributed	10,000	$ 120,000	$ 120,000	Example 20-3
(3) Members' share of $60,000 recourse bank loan	20,000	20,000	20,000	Example 20-3
(4) Nonrecourse mortgage in excess of basis in contributed land	20,000			Nonrecourse debt > basis is allocated only to Nicole
(5) Remaining nonrecourse mortgage	6,666	6,666	6,666	33.33% × [$40,000 – (4)]
(6) Relief from mortgage debt	(40,000)			
Members' initial tax basis in CCS	**$36,666**	**$146,666**	**$146,666**	Sum of (1) through (6)

Although in many instances partners don't recognize gains on property contributions, there is an important exception to the general rule that may apply when property secured by debt is contributed to a partnership. In these situations, the contributing partner recognizes gain *only if* the cash deemed to have been received from a partnership distribution

---

[16]§752(b).

[17]Reg. §1.752-3(a)(2).

exceeds the contributing partner's tax basis in her partnership interest prior to the deemed distribution.[18] Any gain recognized is generally treated as capital gain.[19]

What if: Assume Sarah and Chanzz Inc., but *not* Nicole, personally guarantee all $100,000 of CCS's debt ($60,000 bank loan + $40,000 mortgage on land). How much gain, if any, would Nicole recognize on her contribution to CCS and what would be the basis in her CCS interest?

Answer: Nicole would recognize $10,000 gain and have a $0 basis, computed as follows:

Description	Amount	Explanation
(1) Basis in contributed land	$20,000	Example 20-4
(2) Cash contributed	10,000	Example 20-4
(3) Nicole's share of debt	0	Sarah and Chanzz guaranteed all of CCS's liabilities, including the mortgage on land, thereby turning them into recourse liabilities that should only be allocated to Sarah and Chanzz.
(4) Debt relief	(40,000)	Nicole was relieved of mortgage on land.
(5) Debt relief in excess of basis in contributed land and cash	(10,000)	Sum of (1) through (4)
(6) Capital gain recognized	**10,000**	(5) with opposite sign
Nicole's initial tax basis in CCS	**0**	(5) + (6)

Partner's holding period in partnership interest. Because a partnership interest is a capital asset, its holding period determines whether gains or losses from the disposition of the partnership interest are short-term or long-term capital gains or losses. The length of a partner's holding period for a partnership interest acquired by contributing property depends on the nature of the assets the partner contributed. When partners contribute capital assets or §1231 assets (assets used in a trade or business and held for more than one year), the holding period of the contributed property "tacks on" to the holding period of the partnership interest.[20] Otherwise, it begins on the day the partnership interest is acquired.

What if: Assume Nicole contributed land held for investment (no cash) that she had held for five years in exchange for her partnership interest. One month after contributing the property, she sold her partnership interest and recognized a capital gain. Is the gain long-term or short-term?

Answer: The gain is long-term because the five-year holding period of the land is tacked on to Nicole's holding period for her partnership interest. She is treated as though she held the partnership interest for five years and one month at the time she sold it.

Partnership's tax basis and holding period in contributed property. Just as partners must determine their initial basis in their partnership interests after contributing property,

---

[18] §731(a). However, §707(a)(2)(B) provides that deemed cash received from the relief of debt should be considered as sale proceeds rather than a distribution when circumstances indicate the relief of debt constitutes a disguised sale. Further discussion of disguised sale transactions is beyond the scope of this book.

[19] §731(a). This is equivalent to increasing what would have been a negative basis by the recognized gain to arrive at a zero basis. This mechanism ensures that partners will be left with an initial tax basis of zero any time they recognize gain from a property contribution.

[20] Reg. §1.1223-1(a).

partnerships must establish their inside basis in the contributed property. Measuring both the partner's outside basis and the partnership's inside basis is consistent with the entity theory of partnership taxation. To ensure built-in gains and losses on contributed property are ultimately recognized if partnerships sell contributed property, partnerships generally take a basis in the property equal to the contributing partner's basis in the property at the time of the contribution.[21] Like the adjusted basis of contributed property, the holding period of contributed assets also carries over to the partnership.[22] In fact, the only tax attribute of contributed property that *doesn't* carry over to the partnership is the character of contributed property. Whether gains or losses on dispositions of contributed property are capital or ordinary usually depends on the manner in which the partnership uses contributed property.[23]

Example 20-7

What if: Assume CCS used the land Nicole contributed in its business for one month and then sold it for its fair market value of $150,000. What is the amount and character of the gain CCS would recognize on the sale? (See Example 20-4.)

Answer: CCS recognizes $130,000 of §1231 gain. Nicole's basis in the land prior to the formation of CCS was $20,000. Because CCS receives a carryover basis in the land of $20,000, it recognizes $130,000 of gain when the land is sold for $150,000 ($110,000 in cash and $40,000 of debt relief minus $20,000 basis in land). Also, because CCS used the land in its business and because Nicole's five-year holding period carries over to CCS, the land qualifies as a §1231 asset to CCS, and CCS recognizes §1231 gain when the land is sold. Note that $130,000 of gain is recognized regardless of whether Nicole sells the land, recognizes the gain, and contributes cash to CCS, or CCS sells the land shortly after it is contributed and recognizes the gain.

Unlike corporations, entities taxed as partnerships track the equity of their owners using a capital account for each owner. The methodology for maintaining owners' **capital accounts** depends on the approach these entities use to prepare their financial statements. For example, an entity preparing GAAP financial statements would track each owner's share of the equity using **GAAP capital accounts** maintained using generally accepted accounting principles.

In addition to tracking the inside basis of its assets for tax purposes, partnerships not required to produce GAAP financial statements may decide to use inside tax basis, as well as tax income and expense recognition rules, to maintain their books. Under this approach, a new partnership would prepare its initial balance sheet using the tax basis for its assets. In addition, it would create a **tax capital account** for each new partner, reflecting the tax basis of any property contributed (net of any debt securing the property) and cash contributions. Because each new partner's tax capital account measures that partner's equity in the partnership using tax accounting rules, it will later be adjusted to include the partner's share of earnings and losses, contributions, and distributions.

Besides satisfying bookkeeping requirements, a partnership's tax basis balance sheet can provide useful tax-related information. For example, we can calculate each partner's share of the inside basis of partnership assets by adding the partner's share of debt to her **tax capital account.** Interestingly, partners who acquire their interests by contributing property (without having to recognize any gain) will have an *outside basis* equal to their share of the partnership's total inside basis. However, as we discuss more fully in the next chapter, partners' inside and outside bases will likely be different when they purchase existing partnership interests.

As another alternative to maintaining GAAP capital accounts, partnerships may also maintain their partners' capital accounts using accounting rules prescribed in the §704(b) tax regulations.[24] In fact, many partnership agreements require the partnership to maintain **§704(b) capital accounts** for the partners in addition to tax basis capital accounts. Partnerships set up §704(b) capital accounts in much the same way as tax capital accounts, except that §704(b) capital accounts reflect the fair market value rather

---

[21]§723.
[22]§1223(2).
[23]§702(b). However, §724 provides some important exceptions to this general rule for certain receivables, inventory, and capital loss property.
[24]Reg. §1.704-1(b)(2)(iv).

than the tax basis of contributed assets. Once a partnership begins operations, it can adjust §704(b) capital accounts so they continue to reflect the fair market value of partners' capital interests as accurately as possible. Partnerships may prefer this approach over simply maintaining tax capital accounts because §704(b) capital accounts may be a better measure of the true value of partners' capital interests.

continued from page 20-1...

Before forming CCS, its members agreed to keep its books using the tax basis of contributed assets and tax income and expense recognition rules. After receiving the cash and property contributions from its members and borrowing $60,000 from Nicole's bank, CCS prepared the tax basis balance sheet in Exhibit 20-2.

to be continued . . .

EXHIBIT 20-2   **Color Comfort Sheets LLC**

	Balance Sheet March 31, 2017	
	Tax Basis	**§704(b)/FMV***
Assets:		
Cash	$310,000	$310,000
Land	20,000	150,000
Totals	$330,000	$460,000
Liabilities and Capital:		
Long-term debt	$100,000	$100,000
Capital—Nicole	(10,000)	120,000
Capital—Sarah	120,000	120,000
Capital—Chanzz Inc.	120,000	120,000
Totals	$330,000	$460,000

*The §704(b)/FMV balance sheet is also provided to illustrate the difference in the two approaches to maintaining partners' capital accounts.

Contribution of Services   So far we've assumed partners receive their partnership interests in exchange for contributed property. They may also receive partnership interests in exchange for services they provide to the partnership. For example, an attorney or other service provider might accept a partnership interest in lieu of cash payment for services provided as part of a partnership formation. Similarly, ongoing partnerships may compensate their employees with partnership interests to reduce compensation-related cash payments and motivate employees to behave more like owners. Unlike property contributions, services contributed in exchange for partnership interests may create immediate tax consequences to both the contributing partner *and* the partnership, depending on the nature of the partnership interest received.[25]

Capital interests.   Partners who receive unrestricted capital interests in exchange for services have the right to receive a share of the partnership's capital if it liquidates.[26] Because capital interests represent a current economic entitlement amenable to measurement, partners receiving capital interests for services must treat the amount they would receive if the partnership were to liquidate, or the **liquidation value**[27] of the capital interest, as ordinary

[25]Rev. Proc. 93-27, 1993-2 CB 343 and Rev. Proc. 2001-43, 2001-2 CB 191. In 2005, the IRS issued Prop. Reg. §1.704-1, which will change certain elements of current tax law when it is adopted as a final regulation. The concepts and examples discussed here are consistent with both current law and the proposed regulation.

[26]Certain restrictions, such as vesting requirements, may be placed on partnership interests received for services. We limit our discussion here to unrestricted partnership interests.

[27]Proposed regulations in this area also allow the parties in this transaction to use the fair market value of partnership interests as a measure of value rather than liquidation value.

continued from page 20-9 . . .

Once CCS was organized in March 2017, it built a small production facility on the commercial land Nicole had contributed, purchased and installed the equipment needed to produce sheets, and hired and trained workers—all before the actual production and marketing of the sheets. After production began on July 1, 2017, CCS started selling its sheets to local specialty bedding stores, but this local market was limited. To create additional demand for their product, the members of CCS decided to draw on Sarah's marketing expertise to develop an advertising campaign targeted at home and garden magazines. All members of CCS agreed Sarah would receive, on December 31, 2017, an additional *capital interest* in CCS with a liquidation value of $20,000 *and* an increase in her profit-and-loss-sharing ratio from 33.33 percent to 40 percent (leaving the other members each with a 30 percent share of profits and losses), to compensate her for the time she would spend on this additional project. At this point, CCS's debt remained at $100,000.

to be continued . . .

income.[28] In addition, the tax basis in the capital interest received by the **service partner** will equal the amount of ordinary income he recognizes, and his holding period will begin on the date he receives the capital interest. The partnership either deducts or capitalizes the value of the capital interest, depending on the nature of the services the partner provides. For example, a real estate partnership would capitalize the value of a capital interest compensating a partner for architectural drawings used for a real estate development project.[29] Conversely, the same partnership would deduct the value of a capital interest compensating a partner for providing property management services. When the partnership deducts the value of capital interests used to compensate partners for services provided, it allocates the deduction only to the partners *not* providing services, or **nonservice partners,** because the deduction is related to the segment of the partnership tax year ending immediately before the admission of the new service partner.[30]

Example 20-8

What if: What are the tax consequences to Sarah and CCS if Sarah receives a capital interest (no profits interest) with a $20,000 liquidation value for her marketing services?

Answer: As summarized below, Sarah has $20,000 of ordinary income, and CCS receives a $20,000 ordinary deduction. However, this deduction must be split equally between Nicole and Chanzz Inc. because, in effect, they transferred a portion of their capital to Sarah.

Description	Sarah	Nicole	Chanzz Inc.	Explanation
(1) Ordinary income	$20,000			Liquidation value of capital interest
Ordinary deduction		$(10,000)	$(10,000)	Capital shift from nonservice partners (1) × .5

---

[28]The ordinary income recognized by the service partner is treated as a "guaranteed payment" by the service partner. Guaranteed payments are discussed more fully later in this chapter.

[29]§263(a).

[30]The preamble to Prop. Reg. §1.721-1(b) applies the varying interest rule of §706(d)(1) to the admission of a service partner.

Profits interests.   It's fairly common for partnerships to compensate service partners with profits rather than capital interests. Profits interests are fundamentally different from capital interests, because the only economic benefit they provide is the right to share in the future profits of the partnership. Unlike capital interests, profits interests have no liquidation value at the time they are received. Nonservice partners generally prefer to compensate service partners with profits interests because they don't have to forgo their current share of capital in the partnership and may not ever have to give up anything if the partnership is ultimately unprofitable. Thus, a profits interest is more risky than a capital interest from the perspective of the service partner.

The tax rules applicable to profits interests differ from those pertaining to capital interests due to the fundamental economic differences between them. Because there is no immediate liquidation value associated with a profits interest, the service partner typically will not recognize income and the nonservice partners will not receive deductions.[31] However, future profits and losses attributable to the profits interest are allocated to the service partner (and away from the nonservice partners) as they are generated. In addition, the partnership must adjust debt allocations based on profit-and-loss-sharing ratios to reflect the service partner's new or increased share of profits and losses.

Example 20-9

What if: Assuming Sarah received only a profits interest for her marketing services instead of the capital interest she received in Example 20-8, what are the tax consequences to Sarah, Nicole, Chanzz Inc., and CCS?[32]

Answer: Sarah would not be required to recognize any income, and CCS would not deduct or capitalize any costs. As CCS generates future profits, Sarah will receive a greater share of the profits than she would have otherwise received, and the other two members will receive a correspondingly smaller share. In addition, with the increase in Sarah's profit-and-loss-sharing ratios from 33.33 percent to 40 percent, debt allocations among the partners will change to reflect Sarah's additional entitlement. Note that the debt allocations affect each partner's outside basis. The change in debt allocations is reflected in the table below:

Description	Sarah	Nicole	Chanzz Inc.	Explanation
(1) Increase in debt allocation	$5,334			Loss-sharing ratio increases from 33.33 percent to 40 percent or 6.67 percent ($60,000 recourse bank loan × 6.67% increase in loss-sharing ratio) + ($20,000 nonrecourse mortgage not allocated solely to Nicole × 6.67% increase in profit-sharing ratio).
Decrease in debt allocation		$(2,666)	$(2,666)	(1) × .5

---

[31]Rev. Proc. 93-27 indicates that income is recognized by the service partner "if the profits interest relates to a substantially certain and predictable stream of income," if the partner disposes of the profits interest within two years, or "the profits interest is a limited partnership interest in a publicly traded partnership."

[32]It is common for partnerships to grant a profits interest without an accompanying capital interest.

Example 20-10

What are the tax consequences to Sarah, Nicole, and Chanzz Inc. associated with the capital interest (liquidation value of $20,000) and profits interest Sarah receives for her marketing services?

Answer: The tax consequences associated with giving Sarah *both* a capital and profits interest are summarized in the table below:

Description	Sarah	Nicole	Chanzz Inc.	Explanation
(1) Ordinary income	$20,000			Liquidation value of capital interest
Ordinary deduction		$(10,000)	$(10,000)	Capital shift from nonservice partners, (1) × .5
(2) Increase in debt allocation	5,334			Loss-sharing ratio increases from 33.33 percent to 40 percent or 6.67 percent ($60,000 recourse bank loan × 6.67% increase in loss-sharing ratio) + ($20,000 nonrecourse mortgage not allocated solely to Nicole × 6.67% increase in profit-sharing ratio).
Decrease in debt allocation		$(2,666)	$(2,666)	(2) × .5

TAXES IN THE REAL WORLD Carried Interests

In debates over tax policy, politicians in the news have frequently discussed carried interests as if everyone within earshot understands the term. However, judging from the public's confusion over the issue, not everyone does.

Carried interests are nothing more than profits interests granted to managing partners and key employees of private equity and other similar investment partnerships. Industry norms suggest that typical carried interests provide managing partners with a 20 percent (and sometimes greater) share of profits when partnership investments are eventually sold. Because these investments are typically corporate shares that have been held more than one year,

any income from their sale is treated as long-term capital gain.

The benefits of these types of carried interest arrangements are twofold: Any income managing partners receive is deferred until partnership investments are sold, and, when the income is finally recognized, it is taxed at favorable, long-term capital gains rates. To some politicians and their supporters, this result seems unfair given that carried interests are economically equivalent to deferred salary that is taxed at higher ordinary rates.

Source: For a more detailed description of carried interests, see: "Business Taxation: What Is Carried Interest and How Should It Be Taxed?" in *The Tax Policy Briefing Book* at www.taxpolicycenter.org.

Organizational, Start-Up, and Syndication Costs When partnerships are formed, they typically incur some costs that must be capitalized rather than expensed for tax purposes because they will benefit the partnership over its entire lifespan. This category of expenses includes **organization expenses** associated with legally forming a partnership (such as attorneys' and accountants' fees), **syndication costs** to promote and sell partnership interests, and **start-up costs** that would normally be deducted as operating expenses except that they are incurred before the start of active trade or business. However, with the exception of syndication costs,[33] which are not deductible, the partnership may elect to amortize these

---

[33]Syndication costs are typically incurred by partnerships whose interests are marketed to the public. Thus, syndication expenses are unusual in closely held partnerships.

costs. The Property Acquisition and Cost Recovery chapter provides additional detail about immediately expensing or amortizing business organizational expenses and start-up costs.

Acquisitions of Partnership Interests

After a partnership has been formed and begins operating, new or existing partners can acquire partnership interests in exchange for contributing property and/or services, in which case the tax rules discussed above in the context of forming a partnership still apply. Or new partners may purchase partnership interests from existing partners. Partners who purchase their partnership interests don't have to be concerned with recognizing taxable income when they receive their interests. However, in each of these scenarios they must still determine the initial tax basis and holding period in their partnership interests. Exhibit 20-3 summarizes the rules for determining the tax basis of partnership interests when they are received in exchange for contributed property or services or when they are purchased.

EXHIBIT 20-3   **Summary of Partner's Outside Basis and Holding Period by Acquisition Method**

Acquisition Method	Outside Basis	Holding Period
Contribute Property	Equals basis of contributed property − debt relief + debt allocation + gain recognized.	If property contributed is a capital or §1231 asset, holding period includes holding period of contributed property; otherwise begins on date interest received.
Contribute Services	Equals liquidation value of capital interest + debt allocation. Equals debt allocation if only profits interest received.	Begins on date interest received.
Purchase	Equals cost basis[34] + debt allocation.	Begins on date interest purchased.

THE KEY FACTS

Other Acquisitions of Partnership Interests

- Contributing partner's tax basis and holding period in contributed property carries over to the partnership.
- If service partners report ordinary income, the partnership either expenses or capitalizes the amount depending on the nature of the services provided.
- The tax basis of a purchased partnership interest = Purchase price + Partnership debt allocated to partner, and the holding period begins on the purchase date.

Example 20-11

CCS had overall operating losses from July 1, 2017 (when it began operating), through June 30, 2018. Because of the losses, Chanzz Inc. decided to sell its 30 percent interest in CCS (Chanzz Inc.'s original 33.33 percent interest in CCS was reduced to 30 percent at the end of 2017 when Sarah's interest was increased to compensate her for services provided) on June 30, 2018, to Greg Randall. Like Chanzz Inc., Greg will be a nonmanaging member and guarantee a portion of CCS debt. Greg paid Chanzz Inc. $100,000 for his interest in CCS and was allocated a 30 percent share of CCS debt (CCS's debt remained at $100,000 on June 30, 2018). What is Greg's basis and holding period in CCS?

Answer: Greg's basis of $124,000 in CCS includes the $100,000 amount he paid to purchase the interest plus his $24,000 share of CCS's total $80,000 debt available to be allocated to all members ($60,000 recourse bank loan and $20,000 of nonrecourse mortgage remaining after allocating the first $20,000 to Nicole). Greg's holding period in his CCS interest begins on June 30, 2018.

PARTNERSHIP ACCOUNTING: TAX ELECTIONS, ACCOUNTING PERIODS, AND ACCOUNTING METHODS

LO 20-3

A newly formed partnership must adopt its required tax year-end and decide whether it intends to use either the cash or accrual method as its overall method of accounting. As discussed in the Business Income, Deductions, and Accounting Methods chapter, an entity's tax

---

[34] §742.

year-end determines the cutoff date for including income and deductions in a particular return, and its overall accounting method determines when income and deductions are recognized for tax purposes. Partnerships must frequently make other tax-related elections as well.

Tax Elections

New partnerships determine their accounting periods and make tax elections, including the election of overall accounting method, the election to expense a portion of organizational expenses and start-up costs, and the election to expense tangible personal property. Who formally makes all these elections? In theory, either the partnership or the partners themselves could do so. With just a few exceptions, the partnership tax rules rely on the entity theory of partnership taxation and make the partnership responsible for tax elections.[35] In many instances, the partnership does so in conjunction with filing its annual tax return. For example, it selects an accounting method and determines whether to elect to amortize organizational expenses or start-up costs by simply applying its elections in calculating ordinary business income on its first return. The partnership makes other tax elections by filing a separate document with the IRS, such as Form 3115 when it elects to change an accounting method.

Example 20-12

How will CCS elect its overall accounting method after it begins operations?

Answer: Nicole, Sarah, and Chanzz Inc. may jointly decide on an overall accounting method or, in their LLC operating agreement, they may appoint one of the members to be responsible for making this and other tax elections. Once they have made this decision, CCS makes the election by simply using the chosen accounting method when preparing its first return.

THE KEY FACTS

Partnership Accounting: Tax Elections, Accounting Periods, and Methods

- Partnerships are responsible for making most tax elections.
- A partnership's taxable year is the majority interest taxable year, the common taxable year of the principal partners, or the taxable year providing the least aggregate deferral to the partners.
- Partnerships are generally eligible to use the cash method unless they have average gross receipts over the three prior years of greater than $25 million and have corporate partners.

Accounting Periods

Required Year-Ends Because partners include their share of partnership income or loss in their taxable year ending with the partnership taxable year, or within which the partnership taxable year falls, any partnership tax year other than that of the partners will result in some degree of tax deferral for some or all of the partners.[36] Exhibit 20-4 reflects the tax deferral a partner with a calendar year-end would receive if the corresponding partnership had a January 31 year-end.

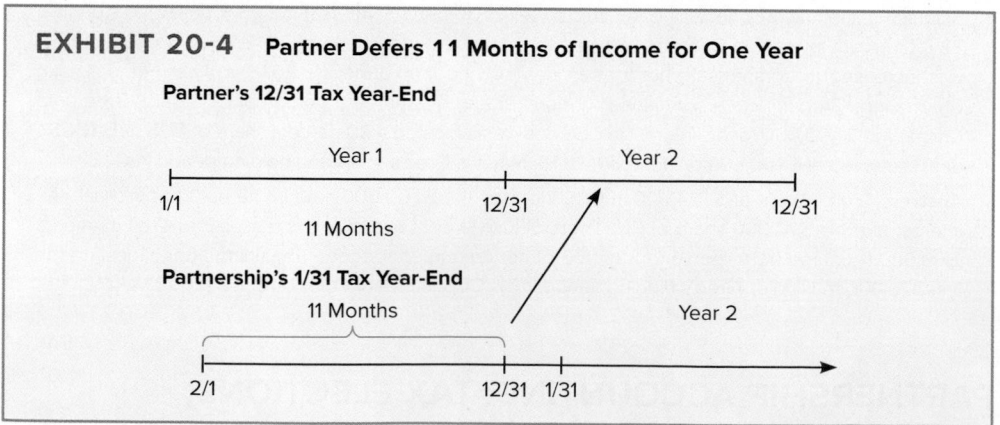

EXHIBIT 20-4 **Partner Defers 11 Months of Income for One Year**

Partner's 12/31 Tax Year-End

Partnership's 1/31 Tax Year-End

Because the partner reports the partnership's year 1 income earned from February 1 until January 31 in the partner's second calendar year (the year within which the partnership's January 31 year-end falls), the partner defers reporting for one year the

---

[35]§703(b). Certain elections are made at the partner level.
[36]§706(a).

11 months of income she was allocated from February 1 through December 31 of her first calendar year.

The government's desire to reduce the aggregate tax deferral of partners (the sum of the deferrals for each individual partner) provides the underlying rationale behind the rules requiring certain partnership taxable year-ends. Partnerships are generally required to use one of three possible tax year-ends.[37] As illustrated in Exhibit 20-5, they must follow a series of steps to determine the appropriate year-end.

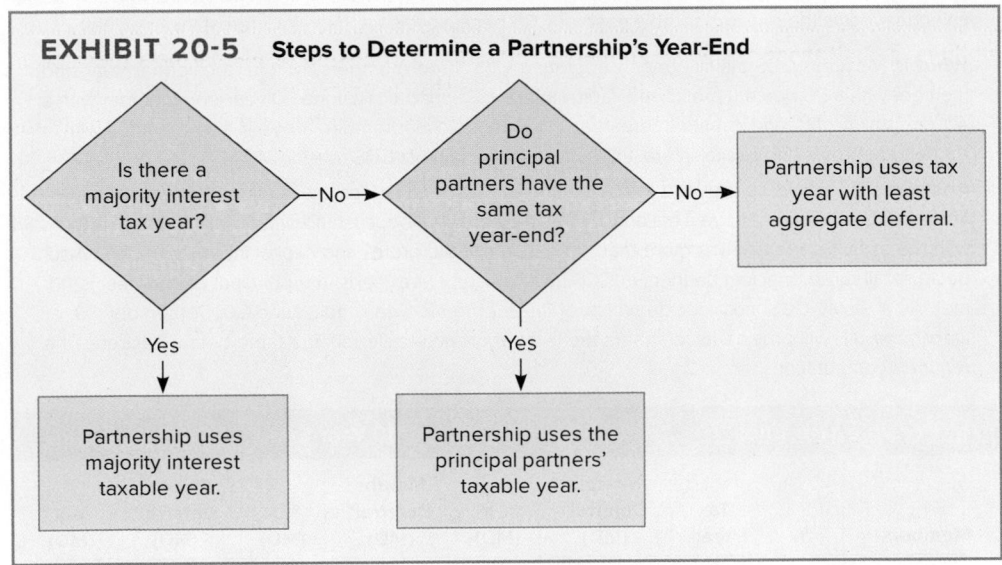

EXHIBIT 20-5   Steps to Determine a Partnership's Year-End

The first potential required tax year is the **majority interest taxable year,** the taxable year of one or more partners who together own more than 50 percent of the capital and profits interests in the partnership.[38] However, there may not be a majority interest taxable year when several partners have different year-ends. For example, if a partnership has two partners with 50 percent capital and profits interests and each has a different tax year, there will be no majority interest taxable year. In that case, the partnership next applies the principal partners test to determine its year-end.

Under the **principal partners** test, the required tax year is the taxable year the principal partners *all* have in common. For this purpose, principal partners are those who have 5 percent or more interest in the partnership profits and capital.[39] Consider a partnership with two calendar-year partners, each with a 20 percent capital and profits interest, and 30 additional fiscal year-end partners, each with less than a 5 percent capital and profits interest. In this scenario, the required taxable year of the partnership is a calendar year corresponding with the taxable year of the partnership's only two principal partners. If, as in the earlier example, the partnership had two 50 percent capital and profits partners with different tax years, it would then use the tax year providing the "least aggregate deferral" to the partners, unless it is eligible to elect an alternative year-end.[40]

The tax year with the **least aggregate deferral** is the one among the tax years of the partners that provides the partner group as a whole with the smallest amount of aggregate tax deferral. Under this approach, the total tax deferral is measured under each potential tax year mathematically by weighting each partner's months of deferral under the potential tax year by each partner's *profits* percentage and then summing the weighted months of deferral for all the partners.

---

[37]Under certain circumstances, other alternative taxable years may be available to partnerships. See Rev. Proc. 2002-38, 2002-1 CB 1037 and §444 for additional information concerning these options.

[38]§706(b)(1)(B)(i).

[39]§706(b)(3).

[40]Reg. §1.706-1(b)(3).

Example 20-13

When CCS began operating in 2017, it had two calendar year-end members, Nicole and Sarah, and one member with a June 30 year-end, Chanzz Inc. What tax year-end must CCS use for 2017?

Answer: CCS was required to use the calendar year as its taxable year unless it was eligible for an alternative year-end. Although Chanzz Inc. had a June 30 taxable year, Nicole and Sarah both had calendar year-ends. Because Nicole and Sarah each initially own 33.33 percent of the capital and profits of CCS, and together they own greater than 50 percent of the profits and capital of CCS, the calendar year is the required taxable year for CCS because it is the majority interest taxable year.

What if: Assume CCS initially began operating with three members: Nicole, a calendar year-end member with a 20 percent profits and capital interest; Chanzz Inc., a June 30 year-end member with a 40 percent profits and capital interest; and Telle Inc., a September 30 year-end member with a 40 percent profits and capital interest. What tax year-end must CCS use for 2017?

Answer: CCS would be required to use a June 30 year-end unless it was eligible for an alternative year-end. CCS does not have a majority interest taxable year because no partner or group of partners with the same year-end owns more than 50 percent of the profits and capital interests in CCS. Also, because all three principal partners in CCS have different year-ends, the principal partner test is not met. As a result, CCS must decide which of three potential year-ends, June 30, September 30, or December 31, will provide its members the least aggregate deferral. The table below illustrates the required computations:

Possible Year-Ends			12/31 Year-End		6/30 Year-End		9/30 Year-End	
Members	%	Tax Year	Months Deferral* (MD)	% × (MD)	Months Deferral* (MD)	% × (MD)	Months Deferral* (MD)	% × (MD)
Nicole	20	12/31	0	0	6	1.2	3	.6
Chanzz Inc.	40	6/30	6	2.4	0	0	9	3.6
Telle Inc.	40	9/30	9	3.6	3	1.2	0	0
Total aggregate deferral				6		**2.4**		4.2

*Months deferral equals number of months between the proposed year-end and partner's year-end.

June 30 is the required taxable year-end because it provides members with the least aggregate tax deferral (2.4 is less than 6 and 4.2).

Accounting Methods

Although partnerships may use the accrual method freely, they may not use the cash method under certain conditions because it facilitates the deferral of income and acceleration of deductions. For example, partnerships with C corporation partners are generally not eligible to use the cash method[41] unless their average annual gross receipts for the three prior taxable years do not exceed $25 million and they otherwise qualify.[42] Entities generally eligible to use the overall cash method of accounting must nevertheless use the accrual method to account for the purchase and sale of inventory unless they unless they have average annual gross receipts over the prior three years of $25 million or less.

---

[41]§448(a)(2). In addition, §448(a)(3) prohibits partnerships classified as "tax shelters" from electing the cash method.

[42]§448(b)(3). If a partnership has not been in existence for at least three years, this test is applied based on the number of years it has been in existence.

Example 20-14

When CCS began operations, its members decided it should elect the cash method of accounting if eligible to do so. Would having a corporate member—Chanzz Inc.—prevent it from electing the cash method?

Answer: No. Although Chanzz Inc. was a founding member of CCS, its ownership share didn't affect the partnership's eligibility to use the cash method since CCS's average annual gross receipts were less than $25 million. If Chanzz Inc. had remained a member of CCS, the cash method might have been unavailable in future years if average annual gross receipts for a three year period exceeded $25 million.

REPORTING THE RESULTS OF PARTNERSHIP OPERATIONS `LO 20-4`

The first section in the Internal Revenue Code dealing with partnerships states emphatically that partnerships are flow-through entities: "A partnership as such shall not be subject to the income tax imposed by this chapter. Persons carrying on business as partners shall be liable for income tax only in their separate or individual capacities."[43] This feature of partnership taxation explains why partnerships are sometimes favored over corporations, whose shareholders are subject to a double tax—once when the income is earned and again when it is distributed to shareholders as a dividend or when the shares are sold.

TAXES IN THE REAL WORLD Publicly Traded Partnerships

Would it surprise you to know that many private equity firms are organized as partnerships for tax purposes? Even more surprising may be the fact that several well-known private equity funds—including Fortress, KKR, and Blackstone—are publicly traded. Publicly traded firms are typically taxed as corporations even if they are legally structured as partnerships or, in the case of these private equity firms, as limited partnerships. However, relying on a provision in the tax code, these private equity funds were able to maintain their tax status as partnerships after their public offerings.[44] Thus, investors purchasing shares in these funds are buying investments that are subject to only one level of taxation but, like shares in a corporation, can be readily traded in a public securities market.

Ordinary Business Income (Loss) and Separately Stated Items

Although partnerships are not taxpaying entities, they are required to file information returns annually. They also distribute information to each partner detailing the amount *and* character of items of income and loss flowing through the partnership.[45] Partners must report these income and loss items on their tax returns even if they don't receive cash distributions from the partnership during the year.

When gathering this information for their partners, partnerships must determine each partner's share of **ordinary business income (loss)** and **separately stated items.** Partnership ordinary business income (loss) is all partnership income (loss) exclusive of any separately stated items of income (loss). Separately stated items share one common characteristic—they are treated differently from a partner's share of ordinary business income (loss) for tax purposes. To better understand why certain items must be separately disclosed to partners, consider how two particular separately stated items, dividend income and capital losses, might affect an individual partner's tax liability. Qualified dividend income allocated to individual partners is taxed at either a 0 percent, 15 percent, or 20 percent rate, depending on individual partners' tax brackets.[46] In a similar vein, individual partners

> **THE KEY FACTS**
>
> **Reporting the Results of Partnership Operations**
>
> - Partnerships file annual information returns reporting their ordinary business income (loss) and separately stated items.
> - Ordinary business income (loss) = Partnership overall income or loss exclusive of separately stated items.
> - Separately stated items change partners' tax liabilities when they are separately stated.

---

[43]§701.

[44]§7704.

[45]Other items, such as tax credits, may also flow through the partnership to partners.

[46]§1(h).

without capital gains during the year may deduct up to $3,000 in capital losses against their ordinary income, while other individual partners with capital gains may deduct more.[47] If a partnership's dividends and capital losses were simply buried in the computation of its overall income or loss for the year, the partner would be unable to apply these specific tax rules to her unique situation and determine her correct tax liability.

The tax code specifically enumerates several common separately stated items, including short-term capital gains and losses, long-term capital gains and losses, §1231 gains and losses, charitable contributions, and dividends.[48] Many more items are considered under regulations issued by the IRS.[49] Exhibit 20-6 lists several other common separately stated items.

EXHIBIT 20-6   Common Separately Stated Items

- Interest income
- Guaranteed payments
- Net earnings (loss) from self-employment
- Tax-exempt income

- Net rental real estate income
- Investment interest expense
- Royalties
- §179 deduction

Example 20-15

After constructing a building and purchasing equipment in its first year of operations ending on December 31, 2017, CCS invested $15,000 of its remaining idle cash in stocks and bonds. CCS's books reflected an overall loss for the year of $80,000. Included in the $80,000 loss were $2,100 of dividend income, $1,200 of short-term capital gains, and a $20,000 deduction for the capital interest transferred to Sarah at the end of 2017 (see Example 20-10). How much ordinary business loss and what separately stated items are allocated to the CCS members for the taxable year ended December 31, 2017?

Answer: As reflected in the table below, CCS has $63,300 of ordinary business loss. In addition, it has $2,100 of dividend income, $1,200 in short-term capital gains, and $20,000 of ordinary deduction (related to the capital interest Sarah received) that are separately stated items. To Nicole, Sarah, and Chanzz Inc., CCS would report $21,100 of ordinary business loss, $700 of dividend income, and $400 of short-term capital gain. In addition, CCS would report $20,000 of ordinary income to Sarah for the capital interest she received, and a $10,000 deduction to Nicole and Chanzz Inc. reflecting the amount of partnership capital they relinquished.

Description	CCS	Nicole $\left(\frac{1}{3}\right)$	Sarah $\left(\frac{1}{3}\right)$	Chanzz Inc. $\left(\frac{1}{3}\right)$
2017 overall net loss	$(80,000)			
Less:				
Dividends	2,100			
Short-term capital gains	1,200			
Ordinary deduction for Sarah's capital interest	(20,000)			
Ordinary business loss	(63,300)	$(21,100)	$(21,100)	$(21,100)
Separately stated Items:				
Dividends	2,100	700	700	700
Short-term capital gains	1,200	400	400	400
Ordinary income for capital interest to Sarah	20,000		20,000	
Ordinary deduction for capital interest to Sarah	(20,000)	(10,000)		(10,000)

---

[47]§1211.

[48]§702.

[49]Reg. §1.702-1(a).

Nicole and Sarah will treat their shares of CCS's ordinary business loss as an *ordinary* loss and include it along with their shares of dividend income and short-term capital gain in their individual tax returns for the year.[50] Chanzz Inc. will also include its share of these items in its annual tax return. But because Chanzz is a corporation, different tax rules apply to its share of dividend income and short-term capital gains. For example, Chanzz will be entitled to the dividends received deduction, while Nicole and Sarah will pay tax on their share of dividend income at individual capital gains rates.

Notice that the character of separately stated items is determined at the partnership level rather than at the partner level.[51] This treatment reflects the entity theory.

Example 20-16

What if: Assume Chanzz Inc. is an investments dealer rather than a sports franchise operator. How would Chanzz Inc. classify its share of the $1,200 gain from the securities sold by CCS during 2017?

Answer: Chanzz Inc. would classify the $1,200 as short-term capital gains. Because the securities CCS sold were capital assets to it, the gain on the sale is a capital gain even though the securities are inventory (an ordinary asset) to Chanzz Inc. That is, we determine the character of the income at the partnership level, not the partner level.

Guaranteed Payments   In addition to dividends, capital gains, and other routine separately stated items, **guaranteed payments** are also a very common separately stated item for partners who receive them. As their name suggests, guaranteed payments are fixed amounts paid to partners regardless of whether the partnership shows a profit or loss for the year.[52] We can think of them—and some partnerships treat them—as economically equivalent to cash salary payments made to partners for services provided.[53] Specifically, they are typically deducted in computing a partnership's ordinary income or loss for the year. Though included in a partnership's ordinary business income (loss) computation, guaranteed payments must, nevertheless, be separately stated to the partners who receive them. This separate reporting serves the same purpose as providing W-2 forms to employees. Because guaranteed payments are similar to salary payments, partners treat them as ordinary income.

continued from page 20-10. . .
Because Sarah received an additional capital interest for marketing services she provided at the end of 2017, she held a 40 percent capital and profits interest, and Nicole and Chanzz Inc. each held a 30 percent capital and profits interest at the beginning of 2018. After Sarah's initial work in formulating a marketing strategy in 2017, Nicole suggested they hire a permanent employee to oversee product marketing. However, because they were unable to find a suitable candidate, Sarah continued to shoulder the product marketing responsibilities in addition to her normal role as a managing member of CCS. To compensate Sarah for her additional workload, all members of CCS agreed to give Sarah a $10,000 guaranteed payment for her marketing efforts in 2018. Exhibit 20-7 provides CCS's income statement for 2018. ■

---

[50]Nicole and Sarah would report their share of ordinary business loss on Schedule E, their share of dividend income on Schedule B, and their share of short-term capital gain on Schedule D of Form 1040.

[51]§702(b).

[52]§707(c).

[53]Fringe benefits that partners receive for services provided such as medical insurance and group-term life insurance are also treated as guaranteed payments. In addition to compensating partners for services provided, guaranteed payments are also made to partners for the use of capital.

EXHIBIT 20-7   Color Comfort Sheets LLC

Income Statement December 31, 2018	
Sales revenue	$ 40,000
Cost of goods sold	(20,000)
Employee wages	(50,000)
Depreciation expense	(18,000)
Guaranteed payments	(10,000)
Miscellaneous expenses	(2,800)
Dividend income	500
Long-term capital gains	300
Overall net loss	$(60,000)

Example 20-17

Given CCS's operating results for 2018 presented in Exhibit 20-7, how much ordinary business loss and what separately stated items will it report on its return for the year? How will it allocate these amounts to its members?

Answer: The table below displays CCS's ordinary business loss and separately stated items and the allocation of these amounts to CCS's members:

Description	CCS	Nicole 30%	Sarah 40%	Chanzz Inc. 30% × 6/12*	Greg 30% × 6/12*
Sales revenue	$40,000				
Cost of goods sold	(20,000)				
Employee wages	(50,000)				
Depreciation expense	(18,000)				
Guaranteed payment to Sarah	(10,000)				
Miscellaneous expenses	(2,800)				
Ordinary business loss	(60,800)	$(18,240)	$(24,320)	$(9,120)	$(9,120)
Separately stated to partners					
Dividends	500	150	200	75	75
Long-term capital gains	300	90	120	45	45
Guaranteed payment			10,000		

*As we noted in Example 20-11, Chanzz Inc. sold out to Greg Randall on June 30, 2018. Therefore, the items related to Chanzz Inc.'s original 30 percent interest must be allocated between Chanzz Inc. and Greg Randall.[54]

THE KEY FACTS

Guaranteed Payments and Self-Employment Income

- Guaranteed payments are separately stated items, are treated as ordinary income by partners receiving them, and are either capitalized or expensed by partnerships.
- Guaranteed payments for services are always treated as self-employment income.
- Shares of ordinary business income (loss) are always treated as self-employment income (loss) by general partners and never treated as self-employment income (loss) by limited partners.
- Shares of ordinary business income (loss) may or may not be treated by LLC members as self-employment income (loss), depending on the extent of their involvement with the LLC.

Self-Employment Tax   Individual partners, like sole proprietors, may be responsible for paying **self-employment taxes** in addition to income taxes on their share of earned income from partnerships.[55] The degree to which partners are responsible for self-employment taxes depends on their legal status as general partners, limited partners, or LLC members and their business activities. General partners report guaranteed payments for services they provide and their share of ordinary business income (loss) as self-employment income (loss) because they are actively involved in managing the partnership. Limited partners, on the other hand, are generally not allowed under state law to participate in the management of limited partnerships. Therefore, their share of ordinary business income (loss) is conceptually more like investment income than trade or business income. As a result, ordinary business income (loss) allocated to limited partners is not subject to self-employment tax. However, if limited partners receive guaranteed payments for services provided to the partnership, they treat those payments as self-employment income.

[54]We assume here that the items are allocated based on the number of months the interest was held. See the Dispositions of Partnership Interests and Partnership Distributions chapter for additional detail regarding methods to account for partners' varying interests in a partnership when a partnership interest is sold.

[55]The Individual Income Tax Computation and Tax Credits chapter and the Entities Overview chapter more fully discuss earned income and related self-employment taxes.

Because LLC members may be either managing or nonmanaging members, the approach to taxing their share of ordinary business income (loss) for self-employment tax purposes does depend to some degree on their level of involvement in the LLC.[56] Tax rules in this area were developed before LLCs became popular, however, so the IRS has not issued any authoritative rules to help LLCs decide whether to characterize their members' shares of ordinary business income (loss) as self-employment income (loss). However, a proposed regulation issued by the IRS and later withdrawn can assist partnerships in drawing the line between aggressive and conservative positions in this area.[57] It provides that LLC members who have personal liability for the debts of the LLC by reason of being an LLC member, who have authority to contract on behalf of the LLC, *or* who participate more than 500 hours in the LLC's trade or business during the taxable year should be classified as general partners when applying the self-employment tax rules.

Historically, the lack of authoritative guidance from the IRS in this area has resulted in a predictable diversity of practice. Indeed, some aggressive taxpayers and their advisers have ignored the proposed regulation entirely and claimed that managing members of LLCs or members providing significant services to their LLCs are similar to limited partners and shouldn't have to pay self-employment taxes at all. This approach has been invalidated by a string of recent court decisions.[58] These decisions follow the spirit of the proposed regulation in that they provide that LLC members with either management control or that actively participate in the trade or business of an LLC should be treated as general partners for self-employment tax purposes and be subject to self-employment tax on their share of ordinary business income (loss).[59]

Example 20-18

For *2018*, should CCS classify Sarah's $10,000 guaranteed payment as self-employment income?

Answer: Yes. The law is clear with respect to guaranteed payments to LLC members—they are always treated as self-employment income.

Using the proposed regulation, will CCS classify Sarah's $24,320 (see Example 20-17) share of ordinary business loss for *2018* as a self-employment loss?

Answer: Yes. Under the proposed regulations, an LLC member who has personal liability for LLC debts or the ability to contract on behalf of the LLC, or who spends more than 500 hours participating in the business of the LLC, is classified as a general partner when applying the self-employment tax rules. Given Sarah's status as a managing member of CCS, at least one but probably all three criteria for classifying her share of CCS's ordinary business loss as self-employment loss will apply. Although these rules have not been finalized and are therefore not authoritative, the IRS would likely follow them because they represent its current thinking on the matter. Applying the law this way, CCS will report a $14,320 self-employment loss ($24,320 share of ordinary business loss + $10,000 guaranteed payment) as a separately stated item to Sarah so she can properly compute her self-employment tax liability on her individual return.

Example 20-19

Using the proposed regulation, will CCS classify Nicole's $18,240 (see Example 20-17) share of ordinary business loss for *2018* as self-employment loss?

Answer: Yes. Because Nicole, like Sarah, is involved in the day-to-day management of CCS, it will classify her entire share of ordinary business loss as self-employment loss, consistent with its classification of Sarah's share of ordinary business loss, and report the amount as a separately stated item to Nicole.

(continued on page 20-22)

---

[56]Guaranteed payments to LLC members are clearly subject to self-employment tax because they are similar to salary payments.

[57]Proposed Reg. §1.1402(a)-2.

[58]See *Renkemeyer, Campbell & Weaver, LLP, et al. v. Commissioner,* 136 TC 137 (2011), Riether, 919 F. Supp.2d 1140 (D. N.M. 2012), and *Castigliola* T.C. Memo. 2017-62.

[59]Of course, these cases also suggest that the opposite should also be true: LLC members without management control or that don't provide significant services should be treated as limited partners for self-employment tax purposes.

> Under the proposed regulation, will CCS treat Greg's $9,120 share of ordinary business loss for *2018* as self-employment loss?
>
> **Answer:** Yes. CCS will treat Greg's share of ordinary business loss as self-employment loss because he has guaranteed a portion of CCS's debt. CCS's total self-employment loss is $41,680, consisting of Sarah's $14,320 self-employment loss (an amount that includes Sarah's share of ordinary business loss offset by her guaranteed payment), Nicole's $18,240 self-employment loss, and Greg's $9,120 self-employment loss.

Limitation on Business Interest Expense As explained in the Business Income, Deductions, and Accounting Methods chapter, the deduction for business interest expense is limited to the sum of (1) business interest income and (2) 30 percent of the adjusted taxable income of the taxpayer for the taxable year.[60] For entities taxed as partnerships, this limitation is applied at the partnership level first. Under this approach, any business interest expense of a partnership that is not disallowed due to the limitation is taken into account in determining the partnership's ordinary business income or loss for the year.

In contrast, disallowed business interest expense is allocated and separately stated to partners, reducing the basis in their partnership interests.[61] Subsequently, the disallowed business interest expense is carried forward indefinitely at the partner level until the partnership has excess business interest expense limitation to allocate to the partners. This will occur whenever the partnership's business interest expense limitation (partnership business interest income plus 30 percent of adjusted taxable income) exceeds the partnership's business interest expense in a given year. Partners may deduct their carried forward disallowed interest expense from a given partnership in any future year to the extent they are allocated excess business interest expense limitation (the adjusted taxable income equivalent is separately stated to partners[62]) from the same partnership.

The limitation on business interest expense does not apply to partnerships with average annual gross receipts for the prior three years that do not exceed $25 million. As a result, the limitation on business interest expense will only apply to a relatively small number of partnerships.

Deduction for Qualified Business Income As we more fully discuss in the Entities Overview chapter, noncorporate owners of flow-through entities, including partnerships, may generally deduct 20 percent of the qualified business income allocated to them from the entity. Qualified business income is the net business income from a qualified trade or business conducted in the United States. In a partnership setting, qualified business income would typically not include a partnership's ordinary business income from most service-related businesses and would also not include a partnership's investment income such as capital gains, dividends, and investment interest income.[63] Further,

[60]§163(j).

[61]§163(j)(4).

[62]Under §163(j)(4)(A)(ii), a partner's share of adjusted taxable income is increased by their distributive share of the partnership's "excess taxable income." Per §163(j)(4)(C), excess taxable income is mathematically equivalent to the amount of a partnership's excess business interest expense limitation divided by 30 percent.

[63]§199A(d)(2) excludes income from certain specified service trade or businesses from the definition of qualified business income. Specified service trade or businesses are defined as any trade or business involving the performance of services in the fields of health, law, accounting, actuarial science, performing arts, consulting, athletics, financial services, brokerage services, or any trade or business where the principal asset of such trade or business is the reputation or skill of one or more of its employees or which involves the performance of services that consist of investing and investment management trading, or dealing in securities, partnership interests, or commodities. The definition specifically excludes architecture and engineering from the definition. The specified service trade or business requirement does not apply to taxpayers with taxable income (before the deduction) below a certain threshold and the requirement phases in over a range of taxable income above the threshold [see §199A(d)(3)].

guaranteed payments received by partners for services provided to the partnership are, by definition, not considered be qualified business income.

To facilitate the partner's calculation of the 20 percent deduction, partnerships must separately state certain items to the partners. First, the partnership must separately state the partners' share of qualified business income for each separate qualified trade or business within the partnership. Further, the partnership must also separately state for each qualified trade or business within the partnership any additional information required for the partners to calculate the limitations on the deduction applied at the partner level.[64]

Net Investment Income Tax

An individual partner's share of gross income from interest, dividends, annuities, royalties, or rents is included in the partner's net investment income when calculating the net investment income tax.[65] In addition, the partner's share of income from a trade or business that is a passive activity, income from a trade or business of trading financial instruments or commodities, and any net gain from disposing of property (other than property used in a trade or business that is not a passive activity) is also included in the partner's net investment income.[66]

Allocating Partners' Shares of Income and Loss

Partnership tax rules provide partners with tremendous flexibility in allocating overall profit and loss as well as specific items of profit and loss to partners, as long as partners agree to the allocations and they have "substantial economic effect." Partnership allocations designed to accomplish business objectives other than reducing taxes will generally have substantial economic effect.[67] If they are not defined in the partnership agreement or do not have substantial economic effect, allocations to partners must be made in accordance with the "partners' interests in the partnership."[68] According to tax regulations, the partners' interests in the partnership are a measure of the partners' economic arrangement and should be determined by considering factors such as their capital contributions, distribution rights, and interests in economic profits and losses (if different from their interests in taxable income and loss). Partnership allocations inconsistent with partners' capital interests or overall profit-and-loss-sharing ratios are called **special allocations.**

Although special allocations are made largely at the discretion of partners, certain special allocations of gains and losses from the sale of partnership property are mandatory. Specifically, when property contributed to a partnership with built-in gains (fair market value greater than tax basis) or built-in losses (tax basis greater than fair market value) is subsequently sold, the partnership must allocate, to the extent possible, the built-in gain or built-in loss (at the time of the contribution) solely to the contributing partner and then allocate any remaining gain or loss to all the partners in accordance with their

---

[64]Under §199A(b)(2)(B), the deduction cannot exceed the greater of 50 percent of the wages paid with respect to the qualified trade or business, or the sum of 25 percent of the wages with respect to the qualified trade or business plus 2.5 percent of the unadjusted basis, immediately after acquisition, of all qualified property in the qualified trade or business. These limitations do not apply to taxpayers with taxable income (before the deduction) below a certain threshold and the limitations phase in over a range of taxable income above the threshold [see §199A(b)(3)].

[65]§1411. The tax imposed is 3.8 percent of the lesser of (a) net investment income or (b) the excess of modified adjusted gross income over $250,000 for married-joint filers and surviving spouses, $125,000 for married separate filers, and $200,000 for other taxpayers. Modified adjusted gross income equals adjusted gross income increased by income excluded under the foreign-earned income exclusion less any disallowed deductions associated with the foreign-earned income exclusion.

[66]§1411(c)(2)(A). For purposes of computing the net investment income tax, a partner's status as either active or passive with respect to an activity is determined according to the §469 passive activity loss rules explained later in this chapter.

[67]Reg. §1.704-1 defines the requirements allocations must satisfy to have substantial economic effect.

[68]§704(b).

profit-and-loss-sharing ratios.[69] This rule prevents contributing partners from shifting their built-in gains and built-in losses to other partners.

Example 20-20

What if: Assume that at the beginning of 2018, Nicole and Sarah decide to organize CCS's marketing efforts by region. Nicole will take responsibility for marketing in the western United States, and Sarah will take responsibility for marketing in the eastern United States. All members agree that CCS's provision for allocating profits and losses in the operating agreement should be amended to provide Nicole and Sarah with better incentives. Specifically, CCS would like to allocate the first 20 percent of profits or losses from each region to Nicole and Sarah. Then, it will allocate any remaining profits or losses from each region among the members in proportion to their capital and profits interests at the end of 2018—40 percent to Sarah and 30 percent each to Nicole and Greg. Will CCS's proposed special allocation of profits and losses be accepted by the IRS?

Answer: Yes. Since CCS is a partnership for federal income tax purposes, it can make special allocations to members, and because the allocations are designed to accomplish a business objective other than tax reduction, the IRS will accept them.[70]

What if: Assume that the land Nicole contributed to CCS had a fair market value of $150,000 and tax basis of $20,000 (see original facts in Example 20-1) and was sold by CCS for $150,000 of consideration almost immediately after it was contributed. How would the resulting $130,000 gain be allocated among the members of CCS?

Answer: Nicole's built-in gain of $130,000 at the time of contribution must be allocated exclusively to her to prevent it from being shifted to other CCS members. Shifting the gain to other members could lower the overall tax liability of the CCS members if Sarah and Greg's marginal tax rates are lower than Nicole's marginal tax rate or it could increase it if their marginal rates are higher.

What if: Suppose CCS held the land Nicole contributed for one year and then sold it on March 31, 2018, for $180,000 instead of $150,000. How should the resulting $160,000 gain be allocated to Nicole, Sarah, and Chanzz Inc.?

Answer: The allocations are $139,000 to Nicole, $12,000 to Sarah, and $9,000 to Chanzz Inc., as reflected in the table below:

Description	CCS	Nicole 30%	Sarah 40%	Chanzz Inc. 30%
Total gain from sale of land	$160,000			
Less:				
Special allocation to Nicole of built-in gain	(130,000)	$ 130,000		
Post-contribution appreciation in land	30,000	9,000	$ 12,000	$ 9,000
Total gain allocations		**$139,000**	**$12,000**	**$9,000**

Partnership Compliance Issues

Although partnerships don't pay taxes, they are required to file **Form 1065,** U.S. Return of Partnership Income (shown in Exhibit 20-8), with the IRS by the 15th day of the 3rd month after their year-end (March 15th for a calendar year-end partnership). Partnerships may receive an automatic six-month extension to file by filing **Form 7004** with the IRS before the original due date of the return.[71] Page 1 of Form 1065

---

[69]§704(c). In addition to requiring built-in gains and losses to be specially allocated to contributing partners, §704(c) also requires depreciation to be specially allocated to noncontributing partners. Tax regulations permit partners to choose among several methods for making these required special allocations. Further discussion of these methods is beyond the scope of this book.

[70]Reg. §1.704-1(b)(5), Example 10, suggests that this type of special allocation would not violate the substantial economic effect rules.

[71]Under §6698, late filing penalties apply if the partnership fails to file by the normal or extended due date for the return. The penalty is $195 times the number of partners in the partnership times the number of months (or fraction thereof) the return is late up to a maximum of 12 months.

details the calculation of the partnership's ordinary business income (loss) for the year, and page 3, **Schedule K,** lists the partnership's ordinary business income (loss) and separately stated items. In addition to preparing Form 1065, the partnership is also responsible for preparing a Schedule K-1 for each partner detailing her individual share of the partnership's ordinary business income (loss) and separately stated items for the year. Once prepared, Schedule K-1s are included with Form 1065 when it is filed, and they are also separately provided to all partners (each partner receives a

---

EXHIBIT 20-8 (PART I)   Page 1 Form 1065
CCS's 2018 Ordinary Business Loss (on 2017 forms)

Form 1065
Department of the Treasury
Internal Revenue Service

U.S. Return of Partnership Income

For calendar year 2017, or tax year beginning _____ , 2017, ending _____ , 20 _____ .
▶ Go to *www.irs.gov/Form1065* for instructions and the latest information.

OMB No. 1545-0123

2017

A Principal business activity **Manufacturing**	Name of partnership **Color Comfort Sheets**	**D** Employer identification number **00072359**
B Principal product or service **Textile Products**	Type or Print — Number, street, and room or suite no. If a P.O. box, see the instructions. **375 East 450 South**	**E** Date business started **April 1, 2017**
C Business code number **31400**	City or town, state or province, country, and ZIP or foreign postal code **Salt Lake City, UT 84608**	**F** Total assets (see the instructions) $ **370,000**

G Check applicable boxes: **(1)** ☐ Initial return **(2)** ☐ Final return **(3)** ☐ Name change **(4)** ☐ Address change **(5)** ☐ Amended return
           (6) ☐ Technical termination - also check (1) or (2)
H Check accounting method: **(1)** ☑ Cash   **(2)** ☐ Accrual   **(3)** ☐ Other (specify) ▶ _____
I Number of Schedules K-1. Attach one for each person who was a partner at any time during the tax year ▶ **4**
J Check if Schedules C and M-3 are attached . . . . ☐

Caution. *Include only trade or business income and expenses on lines 1a through 22 below. See the instructions for more information.*

Income

1a	Gross receipts or sales	**1a**	40,000
b	Returns and allowances	**1b**	
c	Balance. Subtract line 1b from line 1a	**1c**	40,000
2	Cost of goods sold (attach Form 1125-A)	**2**	20,000
3	Gross profit. Subtract line 2 from line 1c	**3**	20,000
4	Ordinary income (loss) from other partnerships, estates, and trusts (attach statement) . .	**4**	
5	Net farm profit (loss) (attach Schedule F (Form 1040))	**5**	
6	Net gain (loss) from Form 4797, Part II, line 17 (attach Form 4797)	**6**	
7	Other income (loss) (attach statement)	**7**	
8	**Total income (loss).** Combine lines 3 through 7	**8**	20,000

Deductions (see the instructions for limitations)

9	Salaries and wages (other than to partners) (less employment credits) . . .	**9**	50,000
10	Guaranteed payments to partners	**10**	10,000
11	Repairs and maintenance	**11**	
12	Bad debts	**12**	
13	Rent	**13**	
14	Taxes and licenses	**14**	
15	Interest	**15**	
16a	Depreciation (if required, attach Form 4562)	**16a**	18,000
b	Less depreciation reported on Form 1125-A and elsewhere on return	**16b**	
		16c	18,000
17	Depletion **(Do not deduct oil and gas depletion.)**	**17**	
18	Retirement plans, etc.	**18**	
19	Employee benefit programs	**19**	
20	Other deductions (attach statement)	**20**	2,800
21	**Total deductions.** Add the amounts shown in the far right column for lines 9 through 20 .	**21**	80,000
22	**Ordinary business income (loss).** Subtract line 21 from line 8	**22**	(60,800)

Sign Here

Under penalties of perjury, I declare that I have examined this return, including accompanying schedules and statements, and to the best of my knowledge and belief, it is true, correct, and complete. Declaration of preparer (other than partner or limited liability company member) is based on all information of which preparer has any knowledge.

▶ _____   ▶ _____
Signature of partner or limited liability company member   Date

May the IRS discuss this return with the preparer shown below (see instructions)? ☐ Yes ☐ No

Paid Preparer Use Only

Print/Type preparer's name	Preparer's signature	Date	Check ☐ if self-employed	PTIN
Firm's name ▶			Firm's EIN ▶	
Firm's address ▶			Phone no.	

For Paperwork Reduction Act Notice, see separate instructions.   Cat. No. 11390Z   Form **1065** (2017)

Source: Form 1065 Department of the Treasury, Internal Revenue Service

EXHIBIT 20-8 (PART II)   Page 3 Form 1065
CCS's 2018 Schedule K (on 2017 forms

Form 1065 (2017)   Page **4**

		Schedule K — Partners' Distributive Share Items			Total amount
Income (Loss)	1	Ordinary business income (loss) (page 1, line 22)	1		60,800
	2	Net rental real estate income (loss) (attach Form 8825)	2		
	3a	Other gross rental income (loss)	3a		
	b	Expenses from other rental activities (attach statement)	3b		
	c	Other net rental income (loss). Subtract line 3b from line 3a	3c		
	4	Guaranteed payments	4		10,000
	5	Interest income	5		
	6	Dividends: a Ordinary dividends	6a		500
		b Qualified dividends	6b	500	
	7	Royalties	7		
	8	Net short-term capital gain (loss) (attach Schedule D (Form 1065)) . . .	8		
	9a	Net long-term capital gain (loss) (attach Schedule D (Form 1065))	9a		300
	b	Collectibles (28%) gain (loss)	9b		
	c	Unrecaptured section 1250 gain (attach statement) . .	9c		
	10	Net section 1231 gain (loss) (attach Form 4797)	10		
	11	Other income (loss) (see instructions) Type ▶	11		
Deductions	12	Section 179 deduction (attach Form 4562)	12		
	13a	Contributions	13a		
	b	Investment interest expense	13b		
	c	Section 59(e)(2) expenditures: **(1)** Type ▶ _____ **(2)** Amount ▶	13c(2)		
	d	Other deductions (see instructions) Type ▶	13d		
Self-Employment	14a	Net earnings (loss) from self-employment	14a		41,680
	b	Gross farming or fishing income	14b		
	c	Gross nonfarm income	14c		20,000
Credits	15a	Low-income housing credit (section 42(j)(5))	15a		
	b	Low-income housing credit (other)	15b		
	c	Qualified rehabilitation expenditures (rental real estate) (attach Form 3468, if applicable)	15c		
	d	Other rental real estate credits (see instructions) Type ▶ _____	15d		
	e	Other rental credits (see instructions) Type ▶ _____	15e		
	f	Other credits (see instructions) Type ▶ _____	15f		
Foreign Transactions	16a	Name of country or U.S. possession ▶ _____			
	b	Gross income from all sources	16b		
	c	Gross income sourced at partner level	16c		
		Foreign gross income sourced at partnership level			
	d	Passive category ▶ _____ e General category ▶ _____ f Other ▶	16f		
		Deductions allocated and apportioned at partner level			
	g	Interest expense ▶ _____ h Other . . . . ▶	16h		
		Deductions allocated and apportioned at partnership level to foreign source income			
	i	Passive category ▶ _____ j General category ▶ _____ k Other ▶	16k		
	l	Total foreign taxes (check one): ▶ Paid ☐ Accrued ☐	16l		
	m	Reduction in taxes available for credit (attach statement)	16m		
	n	Other foreign tax information (attach statement)			
Alternative Minimum Tax (AMT) Items	17a	Post-1986 depreciation adjustment	17a		
	b	Adjusted gain or loss	17b		
	c	Depletion (other than oil and gas)	17c		
	d	Oil, gas, and geothermal properties—gross income	17d		
	e	Oil, gas, and geothermal properties—deductions	17e		
	f	Other AMT items (attach statement)	17f		
Other Information	18a	Tax-exempt interest income	18a		
	b	Other tax-exempt income	18b		
	c	Nondeductible expenses	18c		
	19a	Distributions of cash and marketable securities	19a		
	b	Distributions of other property	19b		
	20a	Investment income	20a		500
	b	Investment expenses	20b		
	c	Other items and amounts (attach statement)			

Form **1065** (2017)

EXHIBIT 20-8 (PART III)   **2018 Schedule K-1 for Sarah Walker (on 2017 forms)**
CCS Operates as an LLC

651117

☒ Final K-1   ☐ Amended K-1   OMB No. 1545-0123

Schedule K-1 (Form 1065)	2017	**Part III** Partner's Share of Current Year Income, Deductions, Credits, and Other Items		

Schedule K-1
(Form 1065)
Department of the Treasury
Internal Revenue Service

2017

For calendar year 2017, or tax year

beginning __ / __ / 2017   ending __ / __ / __

Partner's Share of Income, Deductions, Credits, etc.   ▶ See back of form and separate instructions.

	Part I Information About the Partnership
A	Partnership's employer identification number
	00072359
B	Partnership's name, address, city, state, and ZIP code

Color Comfort Sheets
375 East 450 South
Salt Lake City UT 84608

C	IRS Center where partnership filed return
D	☐ Check if this is a publicly traded partnership (PTP)

	Part II Information About the Partner
E	Partner's identifying number
	429-88-3426
F	Partner's name, address, city, state, and ZIP code

Sarah Walker
549 Laurel Lane
Holladay, UT 84609

G	☒ General partner or LLC member-manager	☐ Limited partner or other LLC member
H	☒ Domestic partner	☐ Foreign partner
I1	What type of entity is this partner? Individual	
I2	If this partner is a retirement plan (IRA/SEP/Keogh/etc.), check here ☐	

J	Partner's share of profit, loss, and capital (see instructions):	
	Beginning	**Ending**
Profit	40 %	40 %
Loss	40 %	40 %
Capital	40 %	40 %

K	Partner's share of liabilities at year end:	
Nonrecourse	$	12,000
Qualified nonrecourse financing	$	8,000
Recourse	$	24,000

L	Partner's capital account analysis:	
Beginning capital account	$	100,000
Capital contributed during the year	$	20,000
Current year increase (decrease)	$	(24,000)
Withdrawals & distributions	$ (	)
Ending capital account	$	96,000

☒ Tax basis   ☐ GAAP   ☐ Section 704(b) book
☐ Other (explain)

M	Did the partner contribute property with a built-in gain or loss?
	☐ Yes ☐ No
	If "Yes," attach statement (see instructions)

Part III — Partner's Share of Current Year Income, Deductions, Credits, and Other Items

1	Ordinary business income (loss)		15	Credits
	(24,320)			
2	Net rental real estate income (loss)			
3	Other net rental income (loss)		16	Foreign transactions
4	Guaranteed payments			
	10,000			
5	Interest income			
6a	Ordinary dividends			
	200			
6b	Qualified dividends			
	200			
7	Royalties			
8	Net short-term capital gain (loss)			
9a	Net long-term capital gain (loss)		17	Alternative minimum tax (AMT) items
	120			
9b	Collectibles (28%) gain (loss)			
9c	Unrecaptured section 1250 gain			
10	Net section 1231 gain (loss)		18	Tax-exempt income and nondeductible expenses
11	Other income (loss)			
			19	Distributions
12	Section 179 deduction			
13	Other deductions			
			20	Other information
			A	200
14	Self-employment earnings (loss)			
A	(14,320)			
C	8,000			

*See attached statement for additional information.

For IRS Use Only

Source: Form 1065 Department of the Treasury, Internal Revenue Service

Schedule K-1 with her income and loss allocations). Exhibit 20-8, parts I through III, displays CCS's return, showing the operating results we summarized in Example 20-17 and Sarah's actual Schedule K-1, reflecting the facts and conclusions in Examples 20-17 and 20-18.[72]

LO 20-5

PARTNER'S ADJUSTED TAX BASIS IN PARTNERSHIP INTEREST

Earlier in this chapter, we discussed how partners measure their initial tax basis in their partnership interests when they contribute property or services to partnerships in exchange for their partnership interests, or when they purchase partnership interests from an existing partner. Unlike the basis in a stock or other similar investment, which is usually fixed, the basis in a partnership interest is dynamic and must be *adjusted* as the partnership generates income and losses, changes its debt levels, and makes distributions to partners. These annual adjustments to a partner's tax basis are required to ensure partners don't double-count taxable income/gains and deductible expenses/losses, either when they sell their partnership interests or when they receive partnership distributions. They also ensure tax-exempt income and nondeductible expenses are not ultimately taxed or deducted.

Partners make the following adjustments to the basis in their partnership interests, annually:

- Increase for actual and deemed cash contributions to the partnership during the year.[73]
- Increase for partner's share of ordinary business income and separately stated income/gain items.
- Increase for partner's share of tax-exempt income.
- Decrease for actual and deemed[74] cash distributions[75] during the year.
- Decrease for partner's share of nondeductible expenses (fines, penalties, etc.).
- Decrease for partner's share of disallowed business interest expense.[76]
- Decrease for partner's share of ordinary business loss and separately stated expense/loss items.

Partners first adjust their bases for items that increase basis, then for distributions, then by nondeductible expenses, and then by deductible expenses and losses to the extent any basis remains after prior adjustments.[77] Basis adjustments that decrease basis may never reduce a partner's tax basis below zero.[78]

Example 20-21

> Given the events that affected CCS and its members during *2017*, what tax basis did Nicole, Sarah, and Chanzz Inc. have in their ownership interests at the end of 2017?

---

[72]We use 2017 forms because 2018 forms were unavailable at the time the book was published.

[73]Recall that partners are deemed to have made a cash contribution to the partnership when they are allocated an additional share of partnership debt.

[74]Recall that partners are deemed to have received a cash distribution from the partnership when they are relieved of partnership debt.

[75]Property distributions to partners are also treated as basis reductions. We discuss property distributions at length in the Dispositions of Partnership Interests and Partnership Distributions chapter.

[76]§163(j)(4)(B)(iii).

[77]Reg. §1.704-1(d)(2).

[78]§705(a)(2).

Answer: Their bases in CCS were $4,000, $152,000, and $114,000, respectively. Their individual tax basis calculations at the end of 2017 are illustrated in the table below:

Description	Nicole	Sarah	Chanzz Inc.	Explanation
(1) Initial tax basis (including debt)	$36,666	$146,666	$146,666	Example 20-4
(2) Dividends	700	700	700	Example 20-15
(3) Short-term capital gains	400	400	400	Example 20-15
(4) Debt reallocation (deemed cash contribution/distribution)	(2,666)	5,334	(2,666)	Example 20-10
(5) Sarah's capital interest	(10,000)	20,000	(10,000)	Examples 20-10, 20-15
(6) CCS's ordinary business loss	(21,100)	(21,100)	(21,100)	Example 20-15
Tax basis on 12/31/17	**$ 4,000**	**$152,000**	**$114,000**	Sum of (1) through (6)

What if: Suppose Sarah sold her LLC interest but forgot to include her share of short-term capital gains when computing her basis to determine her gain on the sale. What are the tax consequences of Sarah's mistake?

Answer: Sarah would be double-taxed on the amount of the short-term capital gain. She was initially taxed on her share of the short-term capital gain allocation, and she will be taxed a second time when she recognizes $400 more gain on the sale than she would have had she included her share of the gain in her basis.

What if: Assume Sarah was allocated $700 of tax-exempt municipal bond income instead of dividend income. What will happen if she neglects to increase her basis in CCS by the $700 tax-exempt income?

Answer: If Sarah were to sell her interest in CCS for a price reflecting the tax-exempt income received, she would, in effect, be converting tax-exempt income into taxable income.

Example 20-22

In addition to the other events of *2018*, CCS increased its debt from $100,000 to $130,000 in the second half of the year. The $30,000 increase was attributable to accounts payable owed to suppliers. Unlike the case of the $60,000 bank loan, the members did not guarantee any of the accounts payable. Therefore, the accounts payable are considered nonrecourse debt because CCS is an LLC. Given this information, what are Nicole's, Sarah's, and Greg's tax bases in CCS at the end of *2018*?

Answer: Their bases are $0, $140,000, and $124,000, respectively. Nicole, Sarah, and Greg would determine their tax basis in CCS at the end of *2018* as illustrated in the table below:

Description	Nicole 30%	Sarah[79] 40%	Greg 30%	Explanation
(1) Tax basis on 1/1/18	$ 4,000	$152,000		Example 20-21
(1) Greg's purchase of Chanzz Inc.'s interest			$124,000	Example 20-11
(2) Dividends	150	200	75	Example 20-17
(3) Long-term capital gains	90	120	45	Example 20-17
(4) Increase in nonrecourse debt from accounts payable (deemed cash contribution)	9,000	12,000	9,000	$30,000 × member's profit-sharing ratio
(5) CCS's ordinary business loss	(18,240)	(24,320)	(9,120)	Example 20-17
Preliminary tax basis	(5,000)	140,000	124,000	Sum of (1) through (5)
Tax basis on 12/31/18	**$ 0***	**$140,000**	**$124,000**	*Nicole's basis can't go below zero.

---

[79]Recall that Sarah received a $10,000 cash guaranteed payment for services she performed in 2018. Cash guaranteed payments generally don't have a direct impact on the recipient partner's tax basis because they are similar to salary payments.

Cash Distributions in Operating Partnerships

Even after a partnership has been formed, partners are likely to continue to receive actual and deemed cash distributions. For example, excess cash may be distributed to partners to provide them with cash flow to pay their taxes or simply for consumption, and deemed cash distributions occur as partnerships pay down their debts. The principles underlying the calculation of a partner's tax basis in her partnership interest highlight the fact that partners are taxed on income as the partnership earns it instead of when it distributes it. If cash is distributed when partners have a positive tax basis in their partnership interests, the distribution effectively represents a distribution of profits that have been previously taxed, a return of capital previously contributed by the partner to the partnership, a distribution of cash the partnership has borrowed, or some combination of the three. Thus, as long as a cash distribution does not exceed a partner's outside basis basis before the distribution, it reduces the partner's tax basis but is not taxed. However, as we highlighted in our discussion of property contributions earlier in this chapter, cash distributions (deemed or actual) in excess of a partner's basis are taxable gains and are generally treated as capital gains.[80]

Example 20-23

What if: In Example 20-22, we determined that Sarah's basis in her partnership interest was $140,000. Assume that in addition to the facts provided in that example, Sarah received a $10,000 distribution in *2018*. What will her basis in CCS or her outside basis be at the end of the year?

Answer: Sarah's tax basis will be $130,000. After making only her positive adjustments for the year (positive adjustments come before negative adjustments such as distributions), she has a basis of $164,320, which is greater than the $10,000 distribution. Thus, the distribution is not taxable because it does not exceed her basis. Sarah will also reduce her basis by the $10,000 distribution in addition to the $24,320 reduction for her share of the ordinary business loss, leaving her with an ending basis of $130,000 ($164,320 − $10,000 − $24,320).

What problem will be created if Sarah does not reduce her basis by the $10,000 distribution?

Answer: After she receives the $10,000 distribution, the value of Sarah's interest will decrease by $10,000. If she doesn't reduce her tax basis by the distribution, selling her interest will produce a $10,000 artificial tax loss.

LO 20-6

LOSS LIMITATIONS

While partners generally prefer not to invest in partnerships with operating losses, these losses generate current tax benefits when partners can deduct them against other sources of taxable income. Unlike capital losses, which are of limited usefulness if taxpayers don't also have capital gains, ordinary losses from partnerships are deductible against any type of taxable income. However, they are deductible on the partner's tax return only when they clear three separate hurdles: (1) tax-basis, (2) at-risk, (3) passive activity, and (4) excess business loss limitations. We discuss each of these hurdles below.

Tax-Basis Limitation

A partner's basis limits the amount of partnership losses the partner can use to offset other sources of income. In theory, a partner's basis represents the amount a partner has invested in a partnership (or may have to invest to satisfy her debt obligations). As a result, partners may not utilize partnership losses in excess of their investment or outside basis in their partnership interests. Any losses allocated in excess of their basis must be suspended and carried forward indefinitely until they have sufficient basis to utilize the losses.[81] Any suspended losses remaining when partners sell or otherwise dispose of their

---

[80]§731.

[81]§704(d).

interests are lost forever. Among other things, partners may create additional tax basis in the future by making capital contributions, by guaranteeing more partnership debt, and by helping their partnership to become profitable.

Example 20-24

In Example 20-22 we discovered Nicole was allocated $5,000 of ordinary loss in excess of her tax basis for 2018, leaving her with a basis of $0 at the end of 2018. What does Nicole do with this loss?

Answer: Nicole will carry forward all $5,000 of ordinary loss in excess of her tax basis indefinitely until her tax basis in CCS becomes positive. To the extent her tax basis increases in the future, the tax-basis limitation will no longer apply to her ordinary loss. Even then, however, the at-risk and/or passive activity loss hurdles may ultimately apply to constrain her ability to deduct the loss on her future tax returns.

What if: Assuming Nicole is allocated $4,000 of income from CCS in 2019, how much of her $5,000 suspended loss will clear the tax basis hurdle in *2019*?

Answer: Nicole's basis will initially increase by $4,000. Then she can apply $4,000 of her suspended loss against this basis increase, leaving her tax basis at $0 and holding a remaining suspended loss of $1,000. The $4,000 loss clearing the tax-basis hurdle must still clear the at-risk and passive activity loss hurdles before Nicole can deduct it on her return.

At-Risk Limitation

The at-risk hurdle or limitation is more restrictive than the tax-basis limitation, because it excludes a type of debt normally included in a partner's tax basis. We have already highlighted the distinction between recourse and nonrecourse debt and noted that partners allocated recourse debt have economic risk of loss, while partners allocated nonrecourse debt have no risk of loss. Instead, the risk of loss on nonrecourse debt is borne by lenders. The **at-risk rules** in §465 were adopted to limit the ability of partners to use nonrecourse debt as a means of creating tax basis to use losses from tax shelter partnerships expressly designed to generate losses for the partners. The at-risk rules limit partners' losses to their amount "at risk" in the partnership—their **at-risk amount.** Generally, a partner's at-risk amount is the same as her tax basis except that, with one exception, the partner's share of certain nonrecourse debts is not included in the at-risk amount. Specifically, the only nonrecourse debts considered to be at risk are nonrecourse real estate mortgages from commercial lenders that are unrelated to borrowers. This type of debt is called **qualified nonrecourse financing.**[82] In addition to qualified nonrecourse financing, partners are considered to be at risk to the extent of cash and the tax basis of property contributed to the partnership. Further, partners are at risk for any partnership recourse debt allocated to them.

Partners apply the at-risk limitation after the tax-basis limitation. Any partnership losses that would otherwise have been allowed under the tax-basis limitation are further limited to the extent they exceed a partner's at-risk amount. Losses limited under the at-risk rules are carried forward indefinitely until the partner generates additional at-risk amounts to utilize the losses, or until they are applied to reduce any gain from selling the partnership interest.

> **THE KEY FACTS**
>
> **Loss Limitations**
>
> - Partnership losses in excess of a partner's tax basis are suspended and carried forward until additional basis is created.
> - Remaining partnership losses are further suspended by the at-risk rules to the extent a partner is allocated nonrecourse debt not secured by real property.
> - If a partner is not a material participant or the partnership is involved in rental activities, losses remaining after application of the tax-basis and at-risk limitations may be used only against other passive income or when the partnership interest is sold.
> - Losses remaining after applying the tax basis, at-risk, and passive active loss limitations are only deductible to the extent they do not add to or create an excess business loss at the partner level.

Example 20-25

In Example 20-22, we discovered Nicole was allocated an ordinary business loss of $18,240. There we also learned that of this loss, $13,240 cleared the tax basis hurdle and $5,000 did not. How much of the $13,240 ordinary business loss that clears the tax basis hurdle will clear the at-risk hurdle?

(continued on page 20-32)

---

[82]§465(b)(6).

Answer: $4,240. The table below summarizes and compares Nicole's calculations to determine her tax basis and at-risk limitations for *2018*:

Example	Description	Tax Basis	At-Risk Amount	Explanation
20-22	(1) Nicole's tax basis on 1/1/18	$ 4,000	$ 4,000	Nicole's tax basis and at-risk amount are the same because she was only allocated recourse debt and qualified nonrecourse financing.
20-22	(2) Dividends	150	150	
20-22	(3) Long-term capital gains	90	90	
20-22	(4) Nonrecourse accounts payable	9,000	0	
	(5) Tax basis and at-risk amount before ordinary business loss	13,240	4,240	Sum of (1) through (4)
20-22	(6) Ordinary business loss	(18,240)		
	(7) Loss clearing the tax-basis hurdle	(13,240)		Loss limited to (5)
	Loss suspended by tax-basis hurdle	(5,000)		(6) – (7)
	(8) Loss clearing tax-basis hurdle		(13,240)	(7)
	(9) Loss clearing at-risk hurdle		**(4,240)**	Loss limited to (5)
	Loss suspended by at-risk hurdle		$(9,000)	(8) – (9)

Although Nicole's $9,000 share of the nonrecourse accounts payable added in *2018* and her investment income of $240 allow her to create enough tax basis in *2018* to get $13,240 of her $18,240 ordinary business loss past the tax-basis limitation, she is not at risk with respect to her $9,000 share of accounts payable because LLC's accounts payable are general nonrecourse debt. Therefore, $9,000 of the $13,240 ordinary business loss clearing the tax-basis hurdle is suspended under the at-risk limitation. As a result, Nicole has two separate losses to carry forward: a $5,000 ordinary loss limited by her tax basis and a $9,000 ordinary loss limited by the at-risk rules, leaving $4,240 of ordinary loss that may be deducted on her *2018* return.

Passive Activity Loss Limitation

Prior to 1986, partners with sufficient tax basis and at-risk amounts were able to utilize ordinary losses from their partnerships to offset portfolio income (i.e., interest, dividends, and capital gains), salary income, and self-employment income from partnerships and other trades or businesses. During this time, a partnership tax shelter industry thrived by marketing to wealthy investors partnership interests designed primarily to generate ordinary losses they could use to shield other income from tax. To combat this practice, Congress introduced the **passive activity loss (PAL) rules**.[83] These rules were enacted as a backstop to the at-risk rules and are applied after the tax-basis and at-risk limitations. Thus, depending on their situation, partners may have to overcome *three separate hurdles* before finally reporting partnership ordinary losses on their returns. In a nutshell, the passive activity loss rules limit the ability of partners in rental real estate partnerships and other partnerships they don't actively manage (passive activities) from using their ordinary losses from these activities (remaining after the application of the tax-basis and at-risk limitations) to reduce other sources of taxable income.

[83]§469. The passive activity loss rules apply primarily to individuals but also to estates, trusts, closely held C corporations, and personal service corporations.

Passive Activity Defined   The passive activity rules define a passive activity as "any activity which involves the conduct of a trade or business,[84] and in which the taxpayer does not materially participate." According to the Code and Treasury regulations, participants in rental activities, including rental real estate,[85] and limited partners without management rights are automatically deemed to be passive participants. In addition, participants in all other activities are passive unless their involvement in an activity is "regular, continuous, and substantial." Clearly, these terms are quite subjective and difficult to apply. Fortunately, regulations provide more certainty in this area by enumerating seven separate tests for material participation.[86] An individual, other than a limited partner, can be classified as a material participant in activities, other than rental activities, by meeting any *one* of the seven tests in Exhibit 20-9.

EXHIBIT 20-9   Tests for Material Participation

1. The individual participates in the activity more than 500 hours during the year.
2. The individual's activity constitutes substantially all the participation in such activity by individuals.
3. The individual participates more than 100 hours during the year and the individual's participation is not less than any other individual's participation in the activity.
4. The activity qualifies as a "significant participation activity" (individual participates for more than 100 hours during the year) and the aggregate of all other "significant participation activities" is greater than 500 hours for the year.
5. The individual materially participated in the activity for any 5 of the preceding 10 taxable years.
6. The activity involves personal services in health, law, accounting, architecture, and so on, and the individual materially participated for any three preceding years.
7. Taking into account all the facts and circumstances, the individual participates on a regular, continuous, and substantial basis during the year.

TAXES IN THE REAL WORLD   Donald Trump's Tax Losses

During his run for the presidency in the fall of 2016, the first page of Donald Trump's New York State resident tax return for 1995 was mailed anonymously to the *New York Times*. When the *Times* subsequently published the first page of President Trump's New York State return, it showed that he reported a loss for the year of nearly $16 million from rental real estate, royalties, partnerships, S corporations, trusts, etc." Given President Trump's status as a real estate developer and owner, it is likely that a significant portion of this loss originated from rental real estate activities held in partnership form. These partnerships frequently generate losses because they are able to deduct depreciation, interest, and other operating costs in determining their taxable income.

President Trump's return also showed that he used the $16 million loss to offset business income of $3.4 million, $6,000 in wages, and $7.4 million in interest he reported earning the same year. For many taxpayers, losses from rental real estate are presumed to be passive losses and therefore may not be used to offset active and portfolio income. So, how was Donald Trump able to use the portion of his $16 million loss attributable to rental real estate to legally shelter his other sources of income? President Trump was likely able to take advantage of the "real estate professional" exception found in §469(c)(6) of the Code. This exception permits individuals that are heavily involved in real property trades or businesses to overcome the presumption that their losses from rental real estate are passive and then go on to establish that their losses are active under one of the material participation tests found in the tax regulations.

---

[84]The term *trade or business* is also deemed to include property held for the production of income, such as rental property.

[85]§469(b)(7) provides an important exception to the general rule that all real estate activities are passive. To overcome this presumption, taxpayers must spend more than half their time working in trades or businesses materially participating in real estate activities and more than 750 hours materially participating in real estate activities during the year. This exception benefits partners that spend a substantial amount of time in partnership activities like real estate development and construction. Moreover, §469(i) permits individual taxpayers to treat up to $25,000 of losses from rental real estate as active losses each year.

[86]26 CFR 1.469-5T.

Income and Loss Baskets Under the passive activity loss rules, each item of a partner's income or loss from all sources for the year is placed in one of three categories or "baskets." Losses from the *passive basket* are not allowed to offset income from other baskets. The three baskets are (see Exhibit 20-10):

1. *Passive activity income or loss*—income or loss from an activity, including partnerships, in which the taxpayer is not a material participant.
2. *Portfolio income*—income from investments, including capital gains and losses, dividends, interest, annuities, and royalties.
3. *Active business income*—income from sources, including partnerships, in which the taxpayer is a material participant. For individuals, this includes salary and self-employment income.

EXHIBIT 20-10 **Income and Loss Baskets**

Income or loss from an activity in which the taxpayer does not materially participate.

Portfolio income, including capital gains and losses, dividends, interest, annuities, and royalties.

Income from activities in which the taxpayer materially participates in a meaningful way, including salary and self-employment income.

Passive Income/Loss

Portfolio Income/Loss

Active Income/Loss

The impact of segregating a partner's income in these baskets is to limit her ability to apply passive activity losses against income in the other two baskets. In effect, passive activity losses are suspended and remain in the passive income or loss basket until the taxpayer generates current-year passive income, either from the passive activity producing the loss or from some other passive activity, or until the taxpayer sells the activity that generated the passive loss.[87] On the sale, in addition to reporting gain or loss from the sale of the property, the taxpayer will be allowed to deduct suspended passive losses as ordinary losses.

ETHICS

Several years ago, Lou, together with his friend Carlo, opened an Italian restaurant in their neighborhood. The venture was formed as an LLC, with Lou receiving a 75 percent ownership interest and Carlo receiving the remaining 25 percent ownership interest. While Lou was primarily responsible for operating the restaurant, Carlo came in only on weekends because he held a full-time job elsewhere. To document the time he spent in the restaurant, Carlo recorded the number of hours he had worked in a logbook at the end of every shift. This year, because of a downturn in the local economy, the restaurant showed a loss for the first time. To be able to deduct his share of this loss when he files his tax return, Carlo would like to establish that he worked more than 500 hours during the year and is therefore a material participant in the restaurant. His logbook shows that he worked for 502 hours during the year; however, he rounded up to the nearest hour at the end of every shift to simplify his record keeping. For example, if he worked 4 hours and 25 minutes during a shift, he wrote 5 hours in the logbook. Should Carlo claim that he is a material participant on the basis of the hours recorded in his logbook and deduct his share of the loss? What would you do?

---

[87]Under §469(k), this rule is even more restrictive for publicly traded partnerships. Passive activity losses from these partnerships may only be utilized to offset future passive income from the same partnership generating the passive activity loss.

Example 20-26

As indicated in Example 20-22, Greg was allocated a $9,120 ordinary loss for *2018* and had a $124,000 tax basis at year-end *after* adjusting his tax basis in his CCS interest for the loss. Given that Greg was allocated $9,000 of nonrecourse debt from accounts payable during *2018*, what is Greg's at-risk amount at the end of the year?

Answer: $115,000. Greg's at-risk amount is calculated by subtracting his $9,000 share of nonrecourse debt from his $124,000 tax basis.

Given Greg's status as a silent or nonmanaging member of CCS, how much of his $9,120 ordinary loss can he deduct in *2018* if he has no other sources of passive income?

Answer: None. Because Greg's tax basis and at-risk amount are large relative to his $9,120 ordinary loss, the tax basis and at-risk hurdles don't limit his loss. However, Greg's $9,120 loss would be classified as a passive loss and suspended until Greg receives passive income from another source—hopefully CCS—or until he disposes of his interest in CCS.

What could Greg do to deduct any losses from CCS in the future?

Answer: He could satisfy one of the seven tests in Exhibit 20-9 to be classified as a material participant in CCS, thereby converting his future CCS losses from passive to active losses. Or he could become a passive participant in some other activity, producing trade or business income that could be offset by any future passive losses from CCS.

Excess Business Loss Limitation

For years beginning after 2017, noncorporate taxpayers are not allowed to deduct an "**excess business loss**" for the year including business losses from entities taxed as partnerships.[88] Rather, excess business losses are carried forward and used in subsequent years. The excess business loss limitation applies to losses that are otherwise deductible under the basis, at-risk, and passive loss rules. An excess business loss for the year is the excess of aggregate business deductions for the year over the sum of aggregate business gross income or gain of the taxpayer plus a threshold amount. The threshold amount for a tax year is $500,000 for married taxpayers filing jointly and $250,000 for other taxpayers. The amounts are indexed for inflation. In the case of partnership business losses, the provision applies at the partner level.

Example 20-27

From Example 20-25 we learned that Nicole would report $150 of dividend income and $90 of long-term capital gains from CCS on her *2018* tax return. Further, we learned that $4,240 of her $18,240 *2018* ordinary loss allocation from CCS cleared both the tax-basis and at-risk hurdles, leaving a total of $14,000 ordinary loss suspended and carried forward. How much of the $4,240 of ordinary loss can Nicole actually deduct on her tax return, given her status as a managing member of CCS?

Answer: Because Nicole is a managing member of CCS, it is likely she will satisfy at least one of the seven tests for material participation in Exhibit 20-9. As a result, she will treat the $4,240 ordinary loss clearing the tax-basis and at-risk hurdles as an active loss. Because Nicole's $4,240 active business loss is less than the $500,000 threshold amount for married taxpayers filing jointly, she does not have an excess business loss and may fully deduct this loss on her tax return.

What if: Suppose that Nicole's share of the 2018 ordinary loss from CCS remaining after applying the tax basis, and at-risk limitation had been $510,000 rather than $4,240. How much of the loss would be deductible on her return?

Answer: $500,000. Deductible net business losses are limited to $500,000 for taxpayers married filing jointly. The $10,000 excess business loss would be carried forward and used in subsequent years.

What if: Assume Nicole was not a managing member of CCS during *2018* and could not satisfy one of the seven material participation tests in Exhibit 20-9. How much of the $4,240 ordinary loss could she deduct on her tax return, assuming she has no other sources of passive income?

Answer: None. Under this assumption, the $4,240 is a passive activity loss and suspended until Nicole either receives some passive income from CCS (or some other source) or sells her interest in CCS. In the end, her entire $18,240 loss from *2018* would be suspended: $5,000 due to the tax-basis limitation, $9,000 due to the at-risk limitation, and $4,240 due to the passive activity loss limitation.

CONCLUSION

This chapter explained the relevant tax rules pertaining to forming and operating partnerships. Specifically, we introduced important tax issues arising from partnership formations, including partner gain or loss recognition and the calculation of inside and outside basis. In addition, we explained accounting periods and methods, allocations of partners' ordinary income (loss) and separately stated items, basis adjustments, and loss limitation rules in the context of an operating partnership. Although it would seem that partnership tax law should be relatively straightforward given that partnerships don't pay taxes, by now you may have come to realize quite the opposite is true. The next chapter continues our discussion of partnership tax law with a focus on dispositions of partnership interests and partnership distributions.

Summary

LO 20-1 Determine whether a flow-through entity is taxed as a partnership or S corporation.

- Unincorporated business entities with more than one owner are taxed as partnerships.
- Shareholders of certain corporations may elect to have them treated as flow-through entities by filing an S election with the IRS.
- Though partnerships and S corporations are both flow-through entities, the tax rules that apply to them differ.
- Partnership tax rules reflect both the aggregate and entity concepts.

LO 20-2 Resolve tax issues applicable to partnership formations and other acquisitions of partnership interests, including gain recognition to partners and tax basis for partners and partnerships.

- As a general rule, partners don't recognize gain or loss when they contribute property to partnerships in exchange for a partnership interest.
- Partnership recourse debt is allocated to partners with ultimate responsibility for paying the debt, and nonrecourse debt is allocated to partners using profit-sharing ratios.
- Partners contributing property encumbered by debt may have to recognize gain, depending on the basis of the property and the amount of the debt.
- Partners contributing property to a partnership will have an initial tax basis in their partnership interest equal to the basis of contributed property less any debt relief plus their share of any partnership debt and any gain they recognize.
- Partners receiving partnership interests by contributing capital assets or §1231 assets have a holding period in their partnership interest that includes the holding period of the contributed property. If they contribute any other type of property instead, their holding period begins on the date the partnership interest is received.
- Partnerships with contributed property have a tax basis and holding period in the property equal to the contributing partner's tax basis and holding period.
- Partners who receive capital interests in exchange for services must report the liquidation value of the capital interest as ordinary income, and the partnership either deducts or capitalizes an equivalent amount depending on the nature of the services provided.
- Partners who receive profits interest in exchange for services don't report any income. However, they share in any subsequent partnership profits and losses.
- Partners who purchase partnership interests have a tax basis in their interests equal to the purchase price plus their shares of partnership debt, and their holding periods begin on the date of purchase.

LO 20-3 Determine the appropriate accounting periods and methods for partnerships.

- Partnerships, rather than individual partners, are responsible for making most tax elections.
- The Code mandates that partners include their share of income (loss) or other partnership items for "any taxable year of the partnership ending within or with the taxable year of the partner."
- Partnerships must use a tax year-end consistent with the majority interest taxable year, the taxable year of the principal partners, or the year-end providing the least aggregate deferral for the partners.

- Partnerships with average annual gross receipts over $25 million that have corporate partners may not use the cash method of accounting. Partnerships eligible to use the overall cash method of accounting must still use the accrual method to account for the purchase and sale of inventory unless they have average annual gross receipts over the prior three years of $25 million or less. Otherwise, partnerships may use either the cash or accrual method of accounting.

Calculate and characterize a partnership's ordinary business income or loss and its separately stated items, and demonstrate how to report these items to partners. **LO 20-4**

- Partnerships must file Form 1065, U.S. Return of Partnership Income, with the IRS annually and must provide each partner with a Schedule K-1 detailing the partner's share of ordinary business income (loss) and separately stated items.

- Separately stated items include short-term and long-term capital gains and losses, dividends, §1231 gains and losses, and other partnership items that may be treated differently at the partner level.

- The character of separately stated items is determined at the partnership rather than at the partner level.

- Guaranteed payments are typically fixed payments made to partners for services provided to the partnership. They are treated as ordinary income by partners who receive them and are either deducted or capitalized by the partnership depending on the nature of services provided.

- Guaranteed payments to any type of partner (or LLC member) and general partners' shares of ordinary business income (loss) are treated as self-employment income (loss).

- Limited partners' shares of ordinary business income (loss) are not treated as self-employment income (loss).

- Though the tax law is uncertain in this area, all or a portion of LLC members' shares of ordinary business income (loss) should be classified as self-employment income (loss) if members are significantly involved in managing the LLC.

- Partnerships provide a great deal of flexibility because they may specially allocate their income, gains, expenses, losses, and other partnership items, as long as the allocations have "substantial economic effect" or are consistent with partners' interests in the partnership. Special allocations of built-in gain or loss on contributed property to contributing partners are mandatory.

Explain the importance of a partner's tax basis in her partnership interest and the adjustments that affect it. **LO 20-5**

- Partners must make specified annual adjustments to the tax basis in their partnership interests to ensure that partnership taxable income/gain or deductible expense/loss items are not double taxed or deducted twice and to ensure that partnership tax-exempt income or nondeductible expense is not taxed or deducted.

- Partners increase the tax basis in their interests by their actual or deemed cash contributions, shares of ordinary business income, separately stated income/gain items, and shares of tax-exempt income.

- Partners decrease the tax basis in their interests by their actual or deemed cash distributions, shares of ordinary business loss, separately stated expense/loss items, and shares of nondeductible expenses.

- A partner's tax basis in their partnership interest may never be reduced below zero.

- Cash distributions that are less than a partner's tax basis in their partnership interest immediately before the distribution are not taxable. However, cash distributions in excess of a partner's tax basis in their partnership interest immediately before the distribution are generally taxable as capital gain.

Apply the basis, at-risk, and passive activity loss limits to losses from partnerships. **LO 20-6**

- In order for losses to provide tax benefits to partners, partnership losses must clear the tax-basis, at-risk, and passive activity loss hurdles (in that order).

- Partnership losses in excess of a partner's tax basis are suspended and may be utilized only when additional tax basis is created.

- Losses clearing the tax-basis hurdle may be utilized only to the extent of the partner's at-risk amount. A partner's at-risk amount generally equals her tax basis (before any reduction for current year losses) less her share of nonrecourse debt that is not secured by real estate.

- If a partner is not a material participant in the partnership or if the partnership is involved in rental activities, losses clearing the tax-basis and at-risk hurdles may be reported on the partner's tax return only when she has passive income from the partnership (or other sources) or when she sells her partnership interest.

- If an individual partner is a material participant in the partnership, losses clearing the tax-basis and at-risk hurdles may be reported on the partner's tax return to the extent she has business income from other sources plus a threshold amount of $500,000 for married taxpayers filing jointly and $250,000 for other taxpayers.

KEY TERMS

aggregate approach (20-2)

at-risk amount (20-31)

at-risk rules (20-31)

built-in gain (20-3)

built-in loss (20-3)

C corporation (20-2)

capital account (20-8)

capital interest (20-3)

entity approach (20-2)

excess business loss (20-35)

flow-through entities (20-2)

Form 1065 (20-24)

Form 7004 (20-24)

GAAP capital accounts (20-8)

general partnership (GP) (20-2)

guaranteed payments (20-19)

inside basis (20-4)

least aggregate deferral (20-15)

limited liability company (LLC) (20-2)

limited partnership (20-2)

liquidation value (20-10)

majority interest taxable year (20-15)

nonrecourse debt (20-5)

nonservice partner (20-10)

ordinary business income (loss) (20-17)

organization costs (20-12)

outside basis (20-4)

partnership interest (20-3)

passive activity loss (PAL) rules (20-32)

principal partner (20-15)

profits interest (20-3)

qualified nonrecourse financing (20-31)

recourse debt (20-5)

S corporation (20-2)

Schedule K (20-25)

§704(b) capital accounts (20-8)

self-employment taxes (20-20)

separately stated items (20-17)

service partner (20-10)

special allocations (20-23)

start-up costs (20-12)

Subchapter K (20-2)

Subchapter S (20-2)

syndication costs (20-12)

tax capital accounts (20-8)

DISCUSSION QUESTIONS

Discussion Questions are available in Connect®.

LO 20-1   1. What is a *flow-through entity*, and what effect does this designation have on how business entities and their owners are taxed?

LO 20-1   2. What types of business entities are taxed as flow-through entities?

LO 20-1   3. Compare and contrast the aggregate and entity concepts for taxing partnerships and their partners.

LO 20-2   4. What is a partnership interest, and what specific economic rights or entitlements are included with it?

LO 20-2   5. What is the rationale for requiring partners to defer most gains and all losses when they contribute property to a partnership?

LO 20-2   6. Under what circumstances is it possible for partners to recognize gain when contributing property to partnerships?

LO 20-2   7. What is *inside basis* and *outside basis*, and why are they relevant for taxing partnerships and partners?

LO 20-2   8. What is *recourse* and *nonrecourse debt*, and how is each generally allocated to partners?

LO 20-2   9. How does the amount of debt allocated to a partner affect the amount of gain a partner recognizes when contributing property secured by debt?

10. What is a tax basis capital account, and what type of tax-related information does it provide?   `LO 20-2`

11. Distinguish between a capital interest and a profits interest, and explain how partners and partnerships treat each when exchanging them for services provided.   `LO 20-2`

12. How do partners who purchase a partnership interest determine the tax basis and holding period of their partnership interests?   `LO 20-2`

13. Why do you think partnerships, rather than the individual partners, are responsible for making most of the tax elections related to the operation of the partnership?   `LO 20-3`

14. If a partner with a taxable year-end of December 31 is in a partnership with a March 31 taxable year-end, how many months of deferral will the partner receive? Why?   `LO 20-3`

15. In what situation will there be a common year-end for the principal partners when there is no majority interest taxable year?   `LO 20-3`

16. Explain the least aggregate deferral test for determining a partnership's year-end and discuss when it applies.   `LO 20-3`

17. When are partnerships eligible to use the cash method of accounting?   `LO 20-3`

18. What is a partnership's ordinary business income (loss) and how is it calculated?   `LO 20-4`

19. What are some common separately stated items, and why must they be separately stated to the partners?   `LO 20-4`

20. Is the character of partnership income/gains and expenses/losses determined at the partnership or partner level? Why?   `LO 20-4`

21. What are guaranteed payments and how do partnerships and partners treat them for income and self-employment tax purposes?   `LO 20-4`

22. How do general and limited partners treat their share of ordinary business income for self-employment tax purposes?   `LO 20-4`

23. What challenges do LLCs face when deciding whether to treat their members' shares of ordinary business income as self-employment income?   `LO 20-4`

24. How much flexibility do partnerships have in allocating partnership items to partners?   `LO 20-4`

25. What are the basic tax-filing requirements imposed on partnerships?   `LO 20-4`

26. In what situations do partners need to know the tax basis in their partnership interests?   `LO 20-5`

27. Why does a partner's tax basis in her partnership interest need to be adjusted annually?   `LO 20-5`

28. What items will increase a partner's basis in her partnership interest?   `LO 20-5`

29. What items will decrease a partner's basis in her partnership interest?   `LO 20-5`

30. What hurdles (or limitations) must partners overcome before they can ultimately deduct partnership losses on their tax returns?   `LO 20-6`

31. What happens to partnership losses allocated to partners in excess of the tax basis in their partnership interests?   `LO 20-6`

32. In what sense is the at-risk loss limitation rule more restrictive than the tax-basis loss limitation rule?   `LO 20-6`

33. How do partners measure the amount they have at risk in the partnership?   `LO 20-6`

34. In what order are the loss limitation rules applied to limit partners' losses from partnerships?   `LO 20-6`

35. How do partners determine whether they are passive participants in partnerships when applying the passive activity loss limitation rules?   `LO 20-6`

36. Under what circumstances can partners with passive losses from partnerships deduct their passive losses?   `LO 20-6`

PROBLEMS

Select problems are available in Connect®.   **■ connect**

LO 20-2

37. Joseph contributed $22,000 in cash and equipment with a tax basis of $5,000 and a fair market value of $11,000 to Berry Hill Partnership in exchange for a partnership interest.
    a) What is Joseph's tax basis in his partnership interest?
    b) What is Berry Hill's basis in the equipment?

LO 20-2

38. Lance contributed investment property worth $500,000, purchased three years ago for $200,000 cash, to Cloud Peak LLC in exchange for an 85 percent profits and capital interest in the LLC. Cloud Peak owes $300,000 to its suppliers but has no other debts.
    a) What is Lance's tax basis in his LLC interest?
    b) What is Lance's holding period in his interest?
    c) What is Cloud Peak's basis in the contributed property?
    d) What is Cloud Peak's holding period in the contributed property?

LO 20-2

39. Laurel contributed equipment worth $200,000, purchased 10 months ago for $250,000 cash and used in her sole proprietorship, to Sand Creek LLC in exchange for a 15 percent profits and capital interest in the LLC. Laurel agreed to guarantee all $15,000 of Sand Creek's accounts payable, but she did not guarantee any portion of the $100,000 nonrecourse mortgage securing Sand Creek's office building. Other than the accounts payable and mortgage, Sand Creek does not owe any debts to other creditors.
    a) What is Laurel's initial tax basis in her LLC interest?
    b) What is Laurel's holding period in her interest?
    c) What is Sand Creek's initial basis in the contributed property?
    d) What is Sand Creek's holding period in the contributed property?

LO 20-2

■ planning

40. Harry and Sally formed the Evergreen Partnership by contributing the following assets in exchange for a 50 percent capital and profits interest in the partnership:

	Basis	Fair Market Value
Harry:		
Cash	$ 30,000	$ 30,000
Land	100,000	120,000
Totals	$130,000	$150,000
Sally:		
Equipment used in a business	200,000	150,000
Totals	$200,000	$150,000

    a) How much gain or loss will Harry recognize on the contribution?
    b) How much gain or loss will Sally recognize on the contribution?
    c) How could the transaction be structured in a different way to get a better result for Sally?
    d) What is Harry's tax basis in his partnership interest?
    e) What is Sally's tax basis in her partnership interest?
    f) What is Evergreen's tax basis in its assets?
    g) Following the format in Exhibit 20-2, prepare a tax basis balance sheet for the Evergreen partnership showing the tax capital accounts for the partners.

LO 20-2

41. Cosmo contributed land with a fair market value of $400,000 and a tax basis of $90,000 to the Y Mountain Partnership in exchange for a 25 percent profits and capital interest in the partnership. The land is secured by $120,000 of nonrecourse debt. Other than this nonrecourse debt, Y Mountain Partnership does not have any debt.
    a) How much gain will Cosmo recognize from the contribution?
    b) What is Cosmo's tax basis in his partnership interest?

42. When High Horizon LLC was formed, Maude contributed the following assets in exchange for a 25 percent capital and profits interest in the LLC: LO 20-2

	Basis	Fair Market Value
Maude:		
Cash	$ 20,000	$ 20,000
Land*	100,000	360,000
Totals	$ 120,000	$380,000

*Nonrecourse debt secured by the land equals $160,000.

James, Harold, and Jenny each contributed $220,000 in cash for a 25 percent profits and capital interest.

a) How much gain or loss will Maude and the other members recognize?

b) What is Maude's tax basis in her LLC interest?

c) What tax basis do James, Harold, and Jenny have in their LLC interests?

d) What is High Horizon's tax basis in its assets?

e) Following the format in Exhibit 20-2, prepare a tax basis balance sheet for High Horizon LLC showing the tax capital accounts for the members.

43. Kevan, Jerry, and Dave formed Albee LLC. Jerry and Dave each contributed $245,000 in cash. Kevan contributed the following assets: LO 20-2

	Basis	Fair Market Value
Kevan:		
Cash	$ 15,000	$ 15,000
Land*	120,000	440,000
Totals	$135,000	$455,000

*Nonrecourse debt secured by the land equals $210,000.

Each member received a one-third capital and profits interest in the LLC.

a) How much gain or loss will Jerry, Dave, and Kevan recognize on the contributions?

b) What is Kevan's tax basis in his LLC interest?

c) What tax basis do Jerry and Dave have in their LLC interests?

d) What is Albee LLC's tax basis in its assets?

e) Following the format in Exhibit 20-2, prepare a tax basis balance sheet for Albee LLC showing the tax capital accounts for the members. What is Kevan's share of the LLC's inside basis?

f) If the lender holding the nonrecourse debt secured by Kevan's land required Kevan to guarantee 33.33 percent of the debt and Jerry to guarantee the remaining 66.67 percent of the debt when Albee LLC was formed, how much gain or loss will Kevan recognize?

g) If the lender holding the nonrecourse debt secured by Kevan's land required Kevan to guarantee 33.33 percent of the debt and Jerry to guarantee the remaining 66.67 percent of the debt when Albee LLC was formed, what are the members' tax bases in their LLC interests?

44. Jim has decided to contribute some equipment he previously used in his sole proprietorship in exchange for a 10 percent profits and capital interest in Fast Choppers LLC. Jim originally paid $200,000 cash for the equipment. Since then, the tax basis in the equipment has been reduced to $100,000 because of tax depreciation, and the fair market value of the equipment is now $150,000.   LO 20-2 research

a) Must Jim recognize any of the potential §1245 recapture when he contributes the machinery to Fast Choppers? [*Hint:* See §1245(b)(3).]

b) What cost recovery method will Fast Choppers use to depreciate the machinery? [*Hint:* See §168(i)(7).]

c) If Fast Choppers were to immediately sell the equipment Jim contributed for $150,000, how much gain would Jim recognize and what is its character? [*Hint:* See §1245 and 704(c).]

LO 20-2

research

45. Ansel purchased raw land three years ago for $200,000 to hold as an investment. After watching the value of the land drop to $150,000, he decided to contribute it to Mountainside Developers LLC in exchange for a 5 percent capital and profits interest. Mountainside plans to develop the property and will treat it as inventory, like all the other real estate it holds.

a) If Mountainside sells the property for $150,000 after holding it for one year, how much gain or loss does it recognize and what is the character of the gain or loss? [*Hint:* See §724.]

b) If Mountainside sells the property for $125,000 after holding it for two years, how much gain or loss does it recognize and what is the character of the gain or loss?

c) If Mountainside sells the property for $150,000 after holding it for six years, how much gain or loss does it recognize and what is the character of the gain or loss?

LO 20-2

research

46. Claude purchased raw land three years ago for $1,500,000 to develop into lots and sell to individuals planning to build their dream homes. Claude intended to treat this property as inventory, like his other development properties. Before completing the development of the property, however, he decided to contribute it to South Peak Investors LLC when it was worth $2,500,000, in exchange for a 10 percent capital and profits interest. South Peak's strategy is to hold land for investment purposes only and then sell it later at a gain.

a) If South Peak sells the property for $3,000,000 four years after Claude's contribution, how much gain or loss is recognized and what is its character? [*Hint:* See §724.]

b) If South Peak sells the property for $3,000,000 five and one-half years after Claude's contribution, how much gain or loss is recognized and what is its character?

LO 20-2

research

47. Reggie contributed $10,000 in cash and a capital asset he had held for three years with a fair market value of $20,000 and tax basis of $10,000 for a 5 percent capital and profits interest in Green Valley LLC.

a) If Reggie sells his LLC interest 13 months later for $30,000 when the tax basis in his partnership interest is still $20,000, how much gain does he report and what is its character?

b) If Reggie sells his LLC interest two months later for $30,000 when the tax basis in his partnership interest is still $20,000, how much gain does he report and what is its character? [*Hint:* See Reg. §1.1223-3.]

LO 20-2

48. Connie recently provided legal services to the Winterhaven LLC and received a 5 percent interest in the LLC as compensation. Winterhaven currently has $50,000 of accounts payable and no other debt. The current fair market value of Winterhaven's capital is $200,000.

a) If Connie receives a 5 percent capital interest only, how much income must she report and what is her tax basis in the LLC interest?

b) If Connie receives a 5 percent profits interest only, how much income must she report and what is her tax basis in the LLC interest?

c) If Connie receives a 5 percent capital and profits interest, how much income must she report and what is her tax basis in the LLC interest?

49. Mary and Scott formed a partnership that maintains its records on a calendar-year basis. The balance sheet of the MS Partnership at year-end is as follows:

	Basis	Fair Market Value
Cash	$ 60	$ 60
Land	60	180
Inventory	72	60
	$192	$300
Mary	$ 96	$150
Scott	96	150
	$192	$300

At the end of the current year, Kari will receive a one-third capital interest only in exchange for services rendered. Kari's interest will not be subject to a substantial risk of forfeiture and the costs for the type of services she provided are typically not capitalized by the partnership. For the current year, the income and expenses from operations are equal. Consequently, the only tax consequences for the year are those relating to the admission of Kari to the partnership.

a) Compute and characterize any gain or loss Kari may have to recognize as a result of her admission to the partnership.

b) Compute Kari's basis in her partnership interest.

c) Prepare a balance sheet of the partnership immediately after Kari's admission showing the partners' tax capital accounts and capital accounts stated at fair market value.

d) Calculate how much gain or loss Kari would have to recognize if, instead of a capital interest, she received a profits interest.

50. Dave LaCroix recently received a 10 percent capital and profits interest in Cirque Capital LLC in exchange for consulting services he provided. If Cirque Capital had paid an outsider to provide the advice, it would have deducted the payment as compensation expense. Cirque Capital's balance sheet on the day Dave received his capital interest appears below:

	Basis	Fair Market Value
Assets:		
Cash	$150,000	$ 150,000
Investments	200,000	700,000
Land	150,000	250,000
Totals	$500,000	$1,100,000
Liabilities and capital:		
Nonrecourse debt	$100,000	$ 100,000
Lance*	200,000	500,000
Robert*	200,000	500,000
Totals	$500,000	$1,100,000

*Assume that Lance's basis and Robert's basis in their LLC interests equal their tax basis capital accounts plus their respective shares of nonrecourse debt.

a) Compute and characterize any gain or loss Dave may have to recognize as a result of his admission to Cirque Capital.

b) Compute each member's tax basis in his LLC interest immediately after Dave's receipt of his interest.

c) Prepare a balance sheet for Cirque Capital immediately after Dave's admission showing the members' tax capital accounts and their capital accounts stated at fair market value.

d) Compute and characterize any gain or loss Dave may have to recognize as a result of his admission to Cirque Capital if he receives only a profits interest.

e) Compute each member's tax basis in his LLC interest immediately after Dave's receipt of his interest if Dave receives only a profits interest.

LO 20-2 51. Last December 31, Ramon sold the 10 percent interest in the Del Sol Partnership that he had held for two years to Garrett for $400,000. Prior to selling his interest, Ramon's basis in Del Sol was $200,000, which included a $100,000 share of nonrecourse debt allocated to him.

a) What is Garrett's tax basis in his partnership interest?

b) If Garrett sells his partnership interest three months after receiving it and recognizes a gain, what is the character of his gain?

LO 20-3 52. Broken Rock LLC was recently formed with the following members:

Name	Tax Year-End	Capital/Profits %
George Allen	December 31	33.33%
Elanax Corp.	June 30	33.33
Ray Kirk	December 31	33.34

What is the required taxable year-end for Broken Rock LLC?

LO 20-3 53. Granite Slab LLC was recently formed with the following members:

Name	Tax Year-End	Capital/Profits %
Nelson Black	December 31	22.0%
Brittany Jones	December 31	24.0
Lone Pine LLC	June 30	4.5
Red Spot Inc.	October 31	4.5
Pale Rock Inc.	September 30	4.5
Thunder Ridge LLC	July 31	4.5
Alpensee LLC	March 31	4.5
Lakewood Inc.	June 30	4.5
Streamside LLC	October 31	4.5
Burnt Fork Inc.	October 31	4.5
Snowy Ridge LP	June 30	4.5
Whitewater LP	October 31	4.5
Straw Hat LLC	January 31	4.5
Wildfire Inc.	September 30	4.5

What is the required taxable year-end for Granite Slab LLC?

LO 20-3 54. Tall Tree LLC was recently formed with the following members:

Name	Tax Year-End	Capital/Profits %
Eddie Robinson	December 31	40%
Pitcher Lenders LLC	June 30	25
Perry Homes Inc.	October 31	35

What is the required taxable year-end for Tall Tree LLC?

LO 20-3 55. Rock Creek LLC was recently formed with the following members:

Name	Tax Year-End	Capital/Profits %
Mark Banks	December 31	35%
Highball Properties LLC	March 31	25
Chavez Builders Inc.	November 30	40

What is the required taxable year-end for Rock Creek LLC?

56. Ryan, Dahir, and Bill have operated Broken Feather LLC for the last four years using a calendar year-end. Each has a one-third interest. Since they began operating, their busy season has run from June through August, with 35 percent of their gross receipts coming in July and August. The members would like to change their tax year-end and have asked you to address the following questions:

    a) Can they change to an August 31 year-end and, if so, how do they make the change? [*Hint:* See Rev. Proc. 2002-38, 2002-1 CB 1037.]

    b) Can they change to a September 30 year-end and, if so, how do they make the change? [*Hint:* See §444.]

57. Ashlee, Hiroki, Kate, and Albee LLC each own a 25 percent interest in Tally Industries LLC, which generates annual gross receipts of over $10 million. Ashlee, Hiroki, and Kate manage the business, but Albee LLC is a nonmanaging member. Although Tally Industries has historically been profitable, for the last three years losses have been allocated to the members. Given these facts, the members want to know whether Tally Industries can use the cash method of accounting. Why or why not? [*Hint:* See §448(b)(3).]

58. Turtle Creek Partnership had the following revenues, expenses, gains, losses, and distributions:

Sales revenue	$ 40,000
Long-term capital gains	2,000
Cost of goods sold	(13,000)
Depreciation—MACRS	(3,000)
Amortization of organization costs	(1,000)
Guaranteed payments to partners for general management	(10,000)
Cash distributions to partners	(2,000)

    a) Given these items, what is Turtle Creek's ordinary business income (loss) for the year?

    b) What are Turtle Creek's separately stated items for the year?

59. Georgio owns a 20 percent profits and capital interest in Rain Tree LLC. For the current year, Rain Tree had the following revenues, expenses, gains, and losses:

Sales revenue	$ 70,000
Gain on sale of land (§1231)	11,000
Cost of goods sold	(26,000)
Depreciation—MACRS	(3,000)
§179 deduction*	(10,000)
Employee wages	(11,000)
Fines and penalties	(3,000)
Municipal bond interest	6,000
Short-term capital gains	4,000
Guaranteed payment to Sandra	(3,000)

    *Assume the §179 property placed in service limitation does not apply.

    a) How much ordinary business income (loss) is allocated to Georgio for the year?

    b) What are Georgio's separately stated items for the year?

60. Richard Meyer and two friends from law school recently formed Meyer and Associates as a limited liability partnership (LLP). Income from the partnership will be split equally among the partners. The partnership will generate fee income primarily from representing clients in bankruptcy and foreclosure matters. While some attorney friends have suggested that partners' earnings will be self-employment income, other attorneys they know from their local bar association meetings claim just the opposite. After examining relevant authority, explain how you would advise Meyer and Associates on this matter. [*Hint:* See §1402(a)(13) and *Renkemeyer, Campbell & Weaver LLP v. Commissioner,* 136 T.C. 137 (2011).]

LO 20-4

61. The partnership agreement of the G&P general partnership states that Gary will receive a guaranteed payment of $13,000, and that Gary and Prudence will share the remaining profits or losses in a 45/55 ratio. For year 1, the G&P partnership reports the following results:

Sales revenue	$ 70,000
Gain on sale of land (§1231)	8,000
Cost of goods sold	(38,000)
Depreciation—MACRS	(9,000)
Employee wages	(14,000)
Cash charitable contributions	(3,000)
Municipal bond interest	2,000
Other expenses	(2,000)

a) Compute Gary's share of ordinary income (loss) and separately stated items to be reported on his year 1 Schedule K-1, including his self-employment income (loss).

b) Compute Gary's share of self-employment income (loss) to be reported on his year 1 Schedule K-1, assuming G&P is a limited partnership and Gary is a limited partner.

c) What do you believe Gary's share of self-employment income (loss) to be reported on his year 1 Schedule K-1 should be, assuming G&P is an LLC and Gary spends 2,000 hours per year working there full time?

LO 20-4

research

62. Hoki Poki, a cash-method general partnership, recorded the following items for its current tax year:

Rental real estate income	$ 2,000
Sales revenue	70,000
§1245 recapture income	8,000
Interest income	2,000
Cost of goods sold	(38,000)
Depreciation—MACRS	(9,000)
Supplies expense	(1,000)
Employee wages	(14,000)
Investment interest expense	(1,000)
Partner's medical insurance premiums paid by Hoki Poki	(3,000)

As part of preparing Hoki Poki's current year return, identify the items that should be included in computing its ordinary business income (loss) and those that should be separately stated. [*Hint:* See Schedule K-1 and related preparer's instructions at www.irs.gov.]

LO 20-4

research

63. On the last day of its current tax year, Buy Rite LLC received $300,000 when it sold a machine it had purchased for $200,000 three years ago to use in its business. At the time of the sale, the basis in the equipment had been reduced to $100,000 due to tax depreciation taken. How much did the members' self-employment earnings from Buy Rite increase when the equipment was sold? [*Hint:* See §1402(a)(3).]

LO 20-4

64. Jhumpa, Stewart, and Kelly are all one-third partners in the capital and profits of Firewalker General Partnership. In addition to their normal share of the partnership's annual income, Jhumpa and Stewart receive an annual guaranteed payment of $10,000 to compensate them for additional services they provide. Firewalker's income statement for the current year reflects the following revenues and expenses:

Sales revenue	$ 340,000
Interest income	3,300
Long-term capital gains	1,200
Cost of goods sold	(120,000)
Employee wages	(75,000)
Depreciation expense	(28,000)
Guaranteed payments	(20,000)
Miscellaneous expenses	(4,500)
Overall net income	$ 97,000

a) Given Firewalker's operating results, how much ordinary business income (loss) and what separately stated items (including the partners' self-employment earnings [loss]) will it report on its return for the year?

b) How will it allocate these amounts to its partners?

c) How much self-employment tax will each partner pay assuming none has any other source of income or loss?

65. This year, Darrel's distributive share from Alcove Partnership includes $6,000 of interest income, $3,000 of dividend income, and $70,000 ordinary business income.   `LO 20-4`

a) Assume that Darrel materially participates in the partnership. How much of his distributive share from Alcove Partnership is potentially subject to the net investment income tax?

b) Assume that Darrel does not materially participate in the partnership. How much of his distributive share from Alcove Partnership is potentially subject to the net investment income tax?

66. This year, Alex's distributive share from Eden Lakes Partnership includes $8,000 of interest income, $4,000 of net long-term capital gains, $2,000 net §1231 gain from the sale of property used in the partnership's trade or business, and $83,000 of ordinary business income.   `LO 20-4`

a) Assume that Alex materially participates in the partnership. How much of his distributive share from Eden Lakes Partnership is potentially subject to the net investment income tax?

b) Assume that Alex does not materially participate in the partnership. How much of his distributive share from Eden Lakes Partnership is potentially subject to the net investment income tax?

67. Lane and Cal each own 50 percent of the profits and capital of HighYield LLC. HighYield owns a portfolio of taxable bonds and municipal bonds, and each year the portfolio generates approximately $10,000 of taxable interest and $10,000 of tax-exempt interest. Lane's marginal tax rate is 35 percent while Cal's marginal tax rate is 12 percent. To take advantage of the difference in their marginal tax rates, Lane and Cal want to modify their operating agreement to specially allocate all of the taxable interest to Cal and all of the tax-exempt interest to Lane. Until now, Lane and Cal had been allocated 50 percent of each type of interest income.   `LO 20-4`   **research**

a) Is HighYield's proposed special allocation acceptable under current tax rules? Why or why not? [*Hint:* See Reg. §1.704-1(b)(2)(iii)(b) and §1.704-1(b)(5) Example (5).]

b) If the IRS ultimately disagrees with HighYield's special allocation, how will it likely reallocate the taxable and tax-exempt interest among the members? [*Hint:* See Reg. §1.704-1(b)(5) Example (5)(ii).]

68. Larry's tax basis in his partnership interest at the beginning of the year was $10,000. If his share of the partnership debt increased by $10,000 during the year and his share of partnership income for the year is $3,000, what is his tax basis in his partnership interest at the end of the year?   `LO 20-5`

69. Carmine was allocated the following items from Piccolo LLC for last year: `LO 20-5`

> Ordinary business loss
> Nondeductible penalties
> Tax-exempt interest income
> Short-term capital gain
> Cash distributions

Rank these items in terms of the order they should be applied to adjust Carmine's tax basis in Piccolo for the year (some items may be of equal rank).

LO 20-5

70. Oscar, Felix, and Marv are all one-third partners in the capital and profits of Eastside General Partnership. In addition to their normal share of the partnership's annual income, Oscar and Felix receive annual guaranteed payments of $7,000 to compensate them for additional services they provide. Eastside's income statement for the current year reflects the following revenues and expenses:

Sales revenue	$ 420,000
Dividend income	5,700
Short-term capital gains	2,800
Cost of goods sold	(210,000)
Employee wages	(115,000)
Depreciation expense	(28,000)
Guaranteed payments	(14,000)
Miscellaneous expenses	(9,500)
Overall net income	$ 52,000

In addition, Eastside owed creditors $120,000 at the beginning of the year but managed to pay down its debts to $90,000 by the end of the year. All partnership debt is allocated equally among the partners. Finally, Oscar, Felix, and Marv had a tax basis of $80,000 in their interests at the beginning of the year.

a) What tax basis do the partners have in their partnership interests at the end of the year?

b) Assume the partners began the year with a tax basis of $10,000 and all the debt was paid off on the last day of the year. How much gain will the partners recognize when the debt is paid off? What tax basis do the partners have in their partnership interests at the end of the year?

LO 20-5

71. Pam, Sergei, and Mercedes are all one-third partners in the capital and profits of Oak Grove General Partnership. Partnership debt is allocated among the partners in accordance with their capital and profits interests. In addition to their normal share of the partnership's annual income, Pam and Sergei receive annual guaranteed payments of $20,000 to compensate them for additional services they provide. Oak Grove's income statement for the current year reflects the following revenues and expenses:

Sales revenue	$ 476,700
Dividend income	6,600
§1231 losses	(3,800)
Cost of goods sold	(245,000)
Employee wages	(92,000)
Depreciation expense	(31,000)
Guaranteed payments	(40,000)
Miscellaneous expenses	(11,500)
Overall net income	$ 60,000

In addition, Oak Grove owed creditors $90,000 at the beginning of the year and $150,000 at the end, and Pam, Sergei, and Mercedes had a tax basis of $50,000 in their interests at the beginning of the year. Also, on December 31 of the current year, Sergei and Mercedes agreed to increase Pam's capital and profits interests from 33.33 percent to 40 percent in exchange for additional services she provided to the partnership. The current liquidation value of the additional capital interest Pam received is $40,000.

a) What tax basis do the partners have in their partnership interests at the end of the year?

b) If, in addition to the expenses listed above, the partnership donated $12,000 to a political campaign, what tax basis do the partners have in their partnership interests at the end of the year assuming the liquidation value of the additional capital interest Pam received at the end of the year remains at $40,000?

72. Laura Davis is a member in a limited liability company that has historically been profitable but is expecting to generate losses in the near future because of a weak local economy. In addition to the hours she works as an employee of a local business, she currently spends approximately 150 hours per year helping to manage the LLC. Other LLC members each work approximately 175 hours per year in the LLC, and the time Laura and other members spend managing the LLC has remained constant since she joined the company three years ago. Laura's tax basis and amount at-risk are large compared to her share of projected losses; however, she is concerned that her ability to deduct her share of the projected losses will be limited by the passive activity loss rules.

    `LO 20-6`

    `research`

    a) As an LLC member, will Laura's share of losses be presumed to be passive as they are for limited partners? Why or why not? [*Hint:* See §469(h)(2), *Garnett v. Commissioner,* 132 T.C. 368 (2009), and Prop. Reg. § 1.469-5(e)(3)(i).]

    b) Assuming Laura's losses are not presumed to be passive, is she devoting sufficient time to the LLC to be considered a material participant? Why or why not?

    c) What would you recommend to Laura to help her achieve a more favorable tax outcome?

73. Alfonso began the year with a tax basis in his partnership interest of $30,000. His share of partnership debt at the beginning and end of the year consists of $4,000 of recourse debt and $6,000 of nonrecourse debt. During the year, he was allocated $40,000 of partnership ordinary business loss. Alfonso does not materially participate in this partnership and he has $1,000 of passive income from other sources.

    `LO 20-6`

    a) How much of Alfonso's loss is limited by his tax basis?

    b) How much of Alfonso's loss is limited by his at-risk amount?

    c) How much of Alfonso's loss is limited by the passive activity loss rules?

74. Jenna began the year with a tax basis of $45,000 in her partnership interest. Her share of partnership debt consists of $6,000 of recourse debt and $10,000 of nonrecourse debt at the beginning of the year and $6,000 of recourse debt and $13,000 of nonrecourse debt at the end of the year. During the year, she was allocated $65,000 of partnership ordinary business loss. Jenna does not materially participate in this partnership and she has $4,000 of passive income from other sources.

    `LO 20-6`

    a) How much of Jenna's loss is limited by her tax basis?

    b) How much of Jenna's loss is limited by her at-risk amount?

    c) How much of Jenna's loss is limited by the passive activity loss rules?

75. Juan Diego began the year with a tax basis in his partnership interest of $50,000. During the year, he was allocated $20,000 of partnership ordinary business income, $70,000 of §1231 losses, and $30,000 of short-term capital losses and received a cash distribution of $50,000.

    `LO 20-5` `LO 20-6`

    `research`

    a) What items related to these allocations does Juan Diego actually report on his tax return for the year? [*Hint:* See Reg. §1.704-1(d)(2) and Rev. Rul. 66-94.]

    b) If any deductions or losses are limited, what are the carryover amounts and what is their character? [*Hint:* See Reg. §1.704-1(d).]

76. Farell is a member of Sierra Vista LLC. Although Sierra Vista is involved in a number of different business ventures, it is not currently involved in real estate either as an investor or as a developer. On January 1, year 1, Farell has a $100,000 tax basis in his LLC interest that includes his $90,000 share of Sierra Vista's general debt obligations. By the end of the year, Farell's share of Sierra Vista's general debt obligations has increased to $100,000. Because of the time he spends in other endeavors, Farell does not materially participate in Sierra Vista. His share

    `LO 20-6`

of the Sierra Vista losses for year 1 is $120,000. As a partner in the Riverwoods Partnership, he also has year 1, Schedule K-1 passive income of $5,000. Farrell is single and has no other sources of business income or loss.

a) Determine how much of the Sierra Vista loss Farell will currently be able to deduct on his tax return for year 1, and list the losses suspended due to tax-basis, at-risk, and passive activity loss limitations.

b) Assuming Farell's Riverwoods K-1 indicates passive income of $30,000, determine how much of the Sierra Vista loss he will ultimately be able to deduct on his tax return for year 1, and list the losses suspended due to tax-basis, at-risk, and passive activity loss limitations.

c) Assuming Farell is deemed to be an active participant in Sierra Vista, determine how much of the Sierra Vista loss he will ultimately be able to deduct on his tax return for year 1, and list the losses suspended due to tax-basis, at-risk, and passive activity loss limitations.

LO 20-6

research

77. Jenkins has a one-third capital and profits interest in the Maverick General Partnership. On January 1, year 1, Maverick has $120,000 of general debt obligations and Jenkins has a $50,000 tax basis (including his share of Maverick's debt) in his partnership interest. During the year, Maverick incurred a $30,000 nonrecourse debt that is not secured by real estate. Because Maverick is a rental real estate partnership, Jenkins is deemed to be a passive participant in Maverick. His share of the Maverick losses for year 1 is $75,000. Jenkins is not involved in any other passive activities, and this is the first year he has been allocated losses from Maverick.

a) Determine how much of the Maverick loss Jenkins will currently be able to deduct on his tax return for year 1, and list the losses suspended due to tax-basis, at-risk, and passive activity loss limitations.

b) If Jenkins sells his interest on January 1, year 2, what happens to his suspended losses from year 1? [*Hint:* See §706(c)(2)(A), Reg. §1.704-1(d)(1), Prop. Reg. §1.465-66(a), and *Sennett v. Commissioner* 80 TC 825 (1983).]

LO 20-6

research

78. Suki and Steve own 50 percent capital and profits interests in Lorinda LLC. Lorinda operates the local minor league baseball team and owns the stadium where the team plays. Although the debt incurred to build the stadium was paid off several years ago, Lorinda owes its general creditors $300,000 (at the beginning of the year) that is not secured by firm property or guaranteed by any of the members. At the beginning of the current year, Suki and Steve had a tax basis of $170,000 in their LLC interests, including their share of debt owed to the general creditors. Shortly before the end of the year they each received a $10,000 cash distribution, even though Lorinda's ordinary business loss for the year was $400,000. Because of the time commitment to operate a baseball team, both Suki and Steve spent more than 1,500 hours during the year operating Lorinda. Both Suki and Steve are single and neither of them have any business income or losses from other sources.

a) Determine how much of the Lorinda loss Suki and Steve will each be able to deduct on their current tax returns, and list their losses suspended by the tax-basis, at-risk, and passive activity loss limitations.

b) Assume that some time before receiving the $10,000 cash distribution, Steve is advised by his tax adviser that his marginal tax rate will be abnormally high during the current year because of an unexpected windfall. To help Steve utilize more of the losses allocated from Lorinda in the current year, his adviser recommends refusing the cash distribution and personally guaranteeing $100,000 of Lorinda's debt, without the right to be reimbursed by Suki. If Steve follows his adviser's recommmendations, how much additional Lorinda loss can he deduct on his current tax return? How does Steve's decision affect the amount of loss Suki can deduct on her current return and the amount and type of her suspended losses?

79. Ray and Chuck own 50 percent capital and profits interests in Alpine Properties LLC. Alpine builds and manages rental real estate, and Ray and Chuck each work full time (over 1,000 hours per year) managing Alpine. Alpine's debt (both at the beginning and end of the year) consists of $1,500,000 in nonrecourse mortgages obtained from an unrelated bank and secured by various rental properties. At the beginning of the current year, Ray and Chuck each had a tax basis of $250,000 in their respective LLC interest, including their share of the nonrecourse mortgage debt. Alpine's ordinary business losses for the current year totaled $600,000, and neither member is involved in other activities that generate passive income.

a) How much of each member's loss is suspended because of the tax-basis limitation?

b) How much of each member's loss is suspended because of the at-risk limitation?

c) How much of each member's loss is suspended because of the passive activity loss limitation? [*Hint:* See §469(b)(7).]

d) If both Ray and Chuck are single and Ray has a current-year loss of $50,000 from a sole proprietorship, how much trade or business loss can each deduct on their tax returns?

COMPREHENSIVE PROBLEMS

Select problems are available in Connect®.

✳ 80. Aaron, Deanne, and Keon formed the Blue Bell General Partnership at the beginning of the current year. Aaron and Deanne each contributed $110,000 and Keon transferred an acre of undeveloped land to the partnership. The land had a tax basis of $70,000 and was appraised at $180,000. The land was also encumbered with a $70,000 nonrecourse mortgage for which no one was personally liable. All three partners agreed to split profits and losses equally. At the end of the first year, Blue Bell made a $7,000 principal payment on the mortgage. For the first year of operations, the partnership records disclosed the following information:

Sales revenue	$470,000
Cost of goods sold	410,000
Operating expenses	70,000
Long-term capital gains	2,400
§1231 gains	900
Charitable contributions	300
Municipal bond interest	300
Salary paid as a guaranteed payment to Deanne (not included in expenses)	3,000

a) Compute the adjusted basis of each partner's interest in the partnership immediately after the formation of the partnership.

b) List the separate items of partnership income, gains, losses, and deductions that the partners must show on their individual income tax returns that include the results of the partnership's first year of operations.

c) Using the information generated in answering parts (a) and (b), prepare Blue Bell's page 1 and Schedule K to be included with its Form 1065 for its first year of operations, along with Schedule K-1 for Deanne.

d) What are the partners' adjusted bases in their partnership interests at the end of the first year of operations?

tax forms

81. The TimpRiders LP has operated a motorcycle dealership for a number of years. Lance is the limited partner, Francesca is the general partner, and they share capital and profits equally. Francesca works full-time managing the partnership. Both the partnership and the partners report on a calendar-year basis. At the start of the current year, Lance and Francesca had bases of $10,000 and $3,000, respectively, and the partnership did not carry any debt. During the current year, the partnership reported the following results from operations:

Net sales	$650,000
Cost of goods sold	500,000
Operating expenses	160,000
Short-term capital loss	2,000
Tax-exempt interest	2,000
§1231 gain	6,000

On the last day of the year, the partnership distributed $3,000 each to Lance and Francesca.

a) What outside basis do Lance and Francesca have in their partnership interests at the end of the year?

b) How much of their losses are currently not deductible by Lance and Francesca because of the tax-basis limitation?

c) To what extent does the passive activity loss limitation apply in restricting their deductible losses for the year?

d) Using the information provided, prepare TimpRiders's page 1 and Schedule K to be included with its Form 1065 for the current year. Also, prepare a Schedule K-1 for Lance and Francesca.

82. LeBron, Dennis, and Susan formed the Bar T LLC at the beginning of the current year. LeBron and Dennis each contributed $200,000 and Susan transferred several acres of agricultural land she had purchased two years earlier to the LLC. The land had a tax basis of $50,000 and was appraised at $300,000. The land was also encumbered with a $100,000 nonrecourse mortgage (i.e., qualified nonrecourse financing) for which no one was personally liable. The members plan to use the land and cash to begin a cattle-feeding operation. Susan will work full time operating the business, but LeBron and Dennis will devote less than two days per year to the operation.

All three members agree to split profits and losses equally. At the end of the first year, Bar T had accumulated $40,000 of accounts payable jointly guaranteed by LeBron and Dennis and had made a $9,000 principal payment on the mortgage. None of the members have passive income from other sources or business income from other sources. LeBron and Dennis are married, while Susan is single.

For the first year of operations, the partnership records disclosed the following information:

Sales revenue	$620,000
Cost of goods sold	380,000
Operating expenses	670,000
Dividends	1,200
Municipal bond interest	300
Salary paid as a guaranteed payment to Susan (not included in expenses)	10,000
Cash distributions split equally among the members at year-end	3,000

a) Compute the adjusted basis of each member's interest immediately after the formation of the LLC.

b) When does each member's holding period for his or her LLC interest begin?

c) What is Bar T's tax basis and holding period in its land?

d) What is Bar T's required tax year-end?

e) What overall methods of accounting were initially available to Bar T?

f) List the separate items of partnership income, gains, losses, deductions, and other items that will be included in each member's Schedule K-1 for the first year of operations. Use the proposed self-employment tax regulations to determine each member's self-employment income or loss.

g) What are the members' adjusted bases in their LLC interests at the end of the first year of operations?

h) What are the members' at-risk amounts in their LLC interests at the end of the first year of operations?

i) How much loss from Bar T, if any, will the members be able to deduct on their individual returns from the first year of operations?

ROGER | *CPA Review*

Sample CPA Exam questions from Roger CPA Review are available in Connect as support for the topics in this text. These Multiple Choice Questions and Task-Based Simulations include expert-written explanations and solutions and provide a starting point for students to become familiar with the content and functionality of the actual CPA Exam.

chapter
21
Dispositions of Partnership Interests and Partnership Distributions

Learning Objectives

Upon completing this chapter, you should be able to:

LO 21-1 Determine the tax consequences to the buyer and seller of the disposition of a partnership interest, including the amount and character of gain or loss recognized.

LO 21-2 Compare operating and liquidating distributions.

LO 21-3 Determine the tax consequences of proportionate operating distributions.

LO 21-4 Determine the tax consequences of proportionate liquidating distributions.

LO 21-5 Explain the significance of disproportionate distributions.

LO 21-6 Explain the rationale for special basis adjustments and the method for calculating them.

©John Lund/Marc Romanelli/Getty Images

In January 2019,* Nicole and Sarah sit in the Color Comfort Sheets (CCS) LLC office discussing the current state of business affairs over a cup of coffee. They both agree they are not doing as well as they had hoped after two years of running the business. Their main topic of discussion this morning is how to turn the business around. Both women know the viability of the business is at stake if they can't figure out how to make it profitable . . . and soon.

As Nicole and Sarah brainstorm various ideas, Nicole's administrative assistant interrupts to announce a phone call from Oscar Winsted, the media mogul. Nicole takes the call. On his top-rated television talk show, Oscar occasionally promotes a product to his viewers based on his own successful experience using it. Apparently, one of Oscar's viewers sent him a set of Color Comfort sheets, and Oscar is so happy with the product that he wants to promote them on his show in about two weeks. Nicole and Sarah are, of course, thrilled with this news. Products Oscar has endorsed in the past have become wildly successful. The focus of Nicole and Sarah's meeting changes dramatically. Now they have to figure out how they can gear up for an immediate increase in production. Nicole and Sarah's analysis of the accounting records reveals that CCS is in a precarious cash position—the business is down to its last $10,000.

Nicole and Sarah immediately call Greg to fill him in on the news. Greg is as thrilled as they are to hear that Oscar will promote their sheets and agrees to kick in an additional $30,000. Nicole

---

*To allow the storyline to continue from the previous example, this chapter begins in 2019. We assume the 2018 tax laws apply for 2019 and subsequent years.

says she will contribute $30,000 and Sarah antes up another $40,000.

The following couple of weeks fly by in a whirlwind of work—phone calls, meetings with bankers, and production scheduling. Oscar's special guest for the show is the popular film star Tom Hughes, promoting his soon-to-be-released movie *Global Warfare*. Tom is good-natured and expresses interest in the sheets. During the show, he announces he will order a set as soon as the broadcast is over. Nicole and Sarah anticipate orders will roll in. Sure enough, before Oscar has even said goodbye to his studio audience, CCS's website traffic has picked up and the phone lines are hopping with new orders.

By the end of 2019, CCS's financial situation has completely turned around; business is booming, the accounting records show a healthy profit, and the partners feel comfortable the trend will continue. Greg decides it is time to talk to Nicole and Sarah about cashing out his investment.

to be continued . . .

This chapter explores the tax consequences associated with selling partnership interests and distributing partnership assets to partners. In the Entities Overview chapter, we learned that Color Comfort Sheets, LLC actually elected to be taxed as a C corporation. In this chapter, we assume it did not make this election leaving it to be treated as a partnership for tax purposes.

LO 21-1   BASICS OF SALES OF PARTNERSHIP INTERESTS

As we've seen in preceding chapters, owners of various business entities receive returns on their investments, either when the business makes distributions or upon the sale of their business interest. Corporate shareholders may sell their stock to other investors or back to the corporation. Likewise, partners may dispose of their interest in several ways: sell to a third party, sell to another partner, or transfer the interest back to the partnership. The payments in a disposition (sale) can come from either another owner of the partnership or a new investor; in either case, the sale proceeds come from outside the partnership.

Selling a **partnership interest** raises unique issues because of the flow-through nature of the entity. For example, is the interest a separate asset, or does the disposition represent the sale of the partner's share of each of the partnership's assets? (See the Forming and Operating Partnerships chapter for a discussion of the entity and aggregate approaches to taxation of flow-through entities.) To the extent the tax rules follow an entity approach, the interest is considered a separate asset and a sale of the partnership interest is very similar to the sale of corporate stock. That is, the partner simply recognizes capital gain or loss on the sale, based on the difference between the sales price and the partner's tax basis in the partnership interest.

Alternately, to the extent the tax rules use the aggregate approach, the disposition represents a sale of the partner's share of each of the partnership's assets. This approach adds some complexity because of the differing character and holding periods of the partnership assets—ordinary, capital, and §1231. The selling partner also has the additional task of allocating the sales proceeds among the underlying assets in order to determine the gain or loss on each.

Rather than strictly following one approach, the tax rules end up being a mixture of the two approaches. When feasible, the entity approach controls; however, if the result distorts the amount or character of income, then the aggregate approach dominates. We discuss the tax consequences of sales of partnership interests by first taking the perspective of the seller (partner), followed by a discussion from the perspective of the buyer (new investor).

Seller Issues

The seller's primary tax concern in a partnership interest sale is calculating the amount and character of gain or loss on the sale. The selling partner calculates the gain or loss as the difference between the amount realized and her **outside basis** in the partnership.[1] Because the selling partner is no longer responsible for her share of the partnership liabilities, any debt relief increases the amount the partner *realizes* from the sale under general tax principles.

Example 21-1

Last year, Chanzz Inc. sold its 30 percent interest in CCS on June 30 to Greg Randall, a wealthy local businessman, to limit its exposure to any further losses. Greg anticipated that CCS would become profitable in the near future and paid Chanzz Inc. $100,000 for its interest in CCS. Chanzz's share of CCS liabilities as of June 30 was $24,000. Chanzz Inc.'s basis in its CCS interest at the sale date was $105,000 (including its share of CCS's liabilities). What amount of gain did Chanzz recognize on the sale?

Answer: $19,000 gain, computed as follows:

Description	Amount	Explanation
(1) Cash and fair market value of property received	$100,000	
(2) Debt relief	24,000	
(3) Amount realized	$124,000	(1) + (2)
(4) Basis in CCS interest	105,000	
Recognized gain	**$ 19,000**	(3) − (4)

THE KEY FACTS

Sale of Partnership Interest

- Seller issues:
  - Gain or loss calculation
    Amount realized:
    Cash and fair market value of property received plus
    Debt relief
    Less: Basis in partnership interest
    Equals: Realized gain or loss
  - Tax year closes with respect to selling partner.
- Buyer issues:
  - Outside basis—cost of the partnership interest plus share of partnership's liabilities.
  - Inside basis—selling partner's inside basis at sale date.
  - No changes to partnership asset bases (unless §754 election is in effect).

The character of the gain or loss from a sale of a partnership interest is generally capital, because partnership interests are capital assets.[2] However, a portion of the gain or loss will be ordinary if a seller realizes any gain or loss attributable to **unrealized receivables** or **inventory items**.[3] Practitioners often refer to these assets that give rise to ordinary gains and losses as **hot assets**.[4] Let's discuss that term further, because these assets are central to determining the tax treatment of many transactions in this chapter.

Hot Assets   As you might expect, unrealized receivables include the right to receive payment for (1) "goods delivered, or to be delivered"[5] or (2) "services rendered, or to be rendered."[6] For cash-method taxpayers, unrealized receivables include amounts earned but not yet received (accounts receivable). Accrual-method taxpayers, however, do not

---

[1]Partners determine their outside basis as discussed in the previous chapter. Importantly, the outside basis includes the selling partner's share of distributive income for the year to the date of the sale.

[2]§731 and §741.

[3]§751(a). Partnerships are required to provide Form 8308 to all the parties to the sale as well as to the IRS. Selling partners include with their tax returns this form as well as a statement detailing the calculation of any ordinary gain from the sale of their interest.

[4]There are actually two definitions of *inventory items* in §751. Section 751(a) inventory items are defined in §751(d) to include *all* inventory items. However, under §751(b), the definition includes only *substantially appreciated* inventory. For purposes of determining the character of gain or loss from the sale of partnership interests, the term *inventory items* includes all inventory as in §751(a). However, these two definitions have created some confusion when using the term *hot assets*. In this chapter, we use the term *hot assets* to refer to unrealized receivables and all inventory items as in §751(a). The definition under §751(b) becomes more relevant when determining the tax treatment in a disproportionate distribution (discussed only briefly later in the chapter).

[5]§751(c)(1).

[6]§751(c)(2).

consider accounts receivable as unrealized receivables because they have already realized and recognized these items as ordinary income. Unrealized receivables also include items the partnership would treat as ordinary income if it sold the asset for its fair market value, such as depreciation recapture under §1245.[7]

Inventory items include classic inventory, defined as property held for sale to customers in the ordinary course of business, but also, more broadly, any assets that are *not* capital assets or §1231 assets.[8] Under this definition, assets such as equipment or real estate used in the business but not held for more than a year and all accounts receivable are considered inventory. This broad definition means cash, capital assets, and §1231 assets are the only properties not considered inventory.[9]

Example 21-2

CCS's balance sheet as of the date of Chanzz's sale of its CCS interest to Greg follows:

Color Comfort Sheets LLC June 30, 2018		
	Tax Basis	**FMV**
Assets		
Cash	$ 27,000	$ 27,000
Accounts receivable	0	13,000
Investments	15,000	12,000
Inventory	1,000	1,000
Equipment (acc. depr. = $20,000)	80,000	86,000
Building	97,000	97,000
Land	20,000	150,000
Totals	$240,000	$386,000
Liabilities and capital		
Long-term debt	$100,000*	
Capital—Nicole	(49,000)	
—Sarah	108,000	
—Chanzz	81,000	
Totals	$240,000	

*Of the $100,000 of long-term debt, $20,000 is allocated solely to Nicole. The remaining $80,000 is allocated to all three owners according to their profit-sharing ratios.

Which of CCS's assets are considered hot assets under §751(a)?

Answer: The hot assets are accounts receivable of $13,000 and $6,000 depreciation recapture (§1245) potential ($86,000 − $80,000) in the equipment. The accounts receivable is an unrealized receivable because CCS has not included it in income for tax purposes under CCS's cash accounting method. The depreciation recapture is also considered an unrealized receivable under §751(a). Inventory would be considered a hot asset; however, because the tax basis and fair market value are equal, it will not affect the character of any gain recognized on the sale.

---

[7]§751(c).

[8]§751(d)(1).

[9]This broad definition of inventory includes all unrealized receivables except for recapture. Recapture items are excluded from the definition of inventory items simply because recapture is not technically an asset; rather, it is merely a portion of gain that results from the sale of property. Recapture is, however, considered an unrealized receivable (i.e., hot asset) under §751(a). This idea is important in determining whether inventory is substantially appreciated for purposes of determining the §751 assets for distributions, as we discuss later in the chapter.

Example 21-3

Review CCS's balance sheet as of the end of 2019.

Color Comfort Sheets LLC December 31, 2019		
	Tax Basis	**FMV**
Assets		
Cash	$390,000	$ 390,000
Accounts receivable	0	40,000
Inventory	90,000	200,000
Investments	60,000	105,000
Equipment (acc. depr. = $50,000)	150,000	200,000
Building (acc. depr. = $10,000)	90,000	100,000
Land—original	20,000	160,000
Land—investment	140,000	270,000
Totals	$940,000	$1,465,000
Liabilities and capital		
Accounts payable	$ 80,000	
Long-term debt		
Mortgage on original land	40,000	
Mortgage on investment land	120,000	
Capital—Nicole	119,000	
—Sarah	332,000	
—Greg	249,000	
Totals	$940,000	

What amount of CCS's assets are considered to be hot assets as of December 31, 2019?

Answer: The hot assets include inventory with a fair market value of $200,000, and unrealized receivables consisting of $50,000 of depreciation recapture potential on the equipment, and $40,000 of accounts receivable.

When a partner sells her interest in a partnership that holds hot assets, she modifies her calculation of the gain or loss to ensure the portion that relates to hot assets is properly characterized as ordinary income. The process for determining the gain or loss follows:

Step 1: Calculate the total gain or loss recognized by subtracting outside basis from the amount realized.

Step 2: Calculate the partner's share of gain or loss from hot assets as if the partnership sold these assets at their fair market value. This represents the ordinary portion of the gain or loss.

Step 3: Finally, subtract the ordinary portion of the gain or loss obtained in Step 2 from the total gain or loss from Step 1. This remaining amount is the capital gain or loss from the sale.[10,11]

[10]The partner must also determine if any portion of the capital gain or loss relates to collectibles (28 percent capital gain property) or to unrecaptured §1250 gains. This is typically referred to as the *look-through rule.*

[11]Any capital gain from the sale of a partnership interest is potentially subject to the 3.8 percent net investment income tax unless the gain is allocable to trade or business assets held by the partnership that generate trade or business income not subject to the tax. See Prop. Reg. §1.1411-7 for a detailed discussion of this concept.

Example 21-4

In Example 21-1, we are reminded that Chanzz Inc. sold its interest in CCS to Greg Randall for $100,000 cash on June 30, 2018. As a result, Chanzz recognized a gain of $19,000 on the sale. What was the character of Chanzz's gain?

Answer: $5,700 of ordinary income and $13,300 of capital gain, determined as follows:

Step 1: Determine the total gain or loss: $19,000 gain (from Example 21-1).

Step 2: Determine the ordinary gain or loss recognized from hot assets:

Asset	(1) Basis	(2) FMV	(3) Gain/Loss (2) − (1)	Chanzz's Share 30% × (3)
Accounts receivable	$ 0	$13,000	$13,000	$ 3,900
Equipment	80,000	86,000	6,000	1,800
Total ordinary income				**$5,700**

Step 3: Determine the capital gain or loss:

Description	Amount	Explanation
(1) Total gain	$ 19,000	From Step 1
(2) Ordinary income from §751(a)	5,700	From Step 2
Capital gain	**$13,300**	(1) − (2)

Example 21-5

What if: Assume the same facts as in Example 21-1, except Greg only paid Chanzz $82,800 cash for its interest in CCS. What would be the amount and character of Chanzz's gain or loss?

Answer: $5,700 of ordinary income and capital loss of $3,900, determined as follows:

Step 1: Determine the total gain or loss recognized:

Description	Amount	Explanation
(1) Cash and fair market value of property received	$ 82,800	
(2) Debt relief	24,000	Chanzz's share of CCS's allocable debt (30% × $80,000)
(3) Amount realized	$106,800	(1) + (2)
(4) Basis in CCS interest	105,000	
Gain recognized	$ 1,800	(3) − (4)

Step 2: Determine the ordinary gain or loss from hot assets:

Asset	(1) Basis	(2) FMV	(3) Gain/Loss (2) − (1)	Chanzz's Share 30% × (3)
Accounts receivable	$ 0	$13,000	$13,000	$ 3,900
Equipment	80,000	86,000	6,000	1,800
Total ordinary income				**$5,700**

Step 3: Determine the capital gain or loss:

Description	Amount	Explanation
(1) Total gain	$ 1,800	From Step 1
(2) Ordinary income from §751(a)	5,700	From Step 2
Capital loss	**$(3,900)**	(1) − (2)

ETHICS

Sarah recently sold her partnership interest for significantly more than her outside basis in the interest. Two separate appraisals were commissioned at the time of the sale to estimate the value of the partnership's hot assets and other assets. The first appraisal estimates the value of the hot assets at approximately $750,000, while the second appraisal estimates the value of these assets at approximately $500,000. Given that the partnership's inside basis for its hot assets is $455,000, Sarah intends to use the second appraisal to determine the character of the gain from the sale of her partnership interest. Is it appropriate for Sarah to ignore the first appraisal when determining her tax liability from the sale of her partnership interest?

Buyer and Partnership Issues

A new investor in a partnership is of course concerned with determining how much to pay for the partnership interest. However, his primary tax concerns are about his outside basis and his share of the inside basis of the partnerships assets. In general, for a sale transaction, the new investor's outside basis will be equal to his cost of the partnership interest.[12] To the extent that the new investor shares in the partnership liabilities, his share of partnership liabilities increases his outside basis.

Example 21-6

When Greg Randall acquired Chanzz's 30 percent interest in CCS for $100,000 on June 30, 2018 (see Example 21-1), he guaranteed his share of CCS's debts just as Chanzz had done. As a result, Greg will be allocated his share of CCS's allocable debt in accordance with his 30 percent profit-sharing ratio. What is the outside basis of Greg's acquired interest?

Answer: $124,000, determined as follows:

Description	Amount	Explanation
(1) Initial tax basis	$ 100,000	Cash paid to Chanzz Inc.
(2) Share of CCS's liabilities	24,000	30% × CCS's allocable debt of $80,000
Outside basis	**$124,000**	(1) + (2)

The partnership experiences very few tax consequences when a partner sells her interest.[13] The sale does not generally affect a partnership's **inside basis** in its assets.[14] The new investor typically "steps into the shoes" of the selling partner to determine her share of the partnership's inside basis of the partnership assets. Consequently, the new investor's

[12]§1012. The outside basis will depend, in part, on how the new investor obtains the interest. For example, a gift generally results in a carryover basis whereas an inherited interest typically results in a basis equal to the fair market value as of the date of the decedent's death.

[13]Later in the chapter, we discuss situations in which the new investor's share of the partnership's asset bases is adjusted after a sale of a partnership interest under §754. Throughout this section, we assume that the partnership does not have a §754 election in effect.

[14]§743.

share of inside basis is equal to the selling partner's share of inside basis at the sale date. Recall from the preceding chapter that each partner has a tax capital account that reflects the tax basis of property and cash contributed by the partner, the partner's share of profits and losses, and distributions to the partner. In a sale of a partnership interest, the selling partner's tax capital account carries over to the new investor.[15]

Example 21-7

Refer to Example 21-2 for CCS's balance sheet as of June 30, 2018. What is Greg's share of CCS's inside basis in its assets immediately after purchasing Chanzz's 30 percent interest in CCS?

Answer: Greg's share is $105,000: the sum of Chanzz's tax capital account of $81,000 and its share of CCS's liabilities of $24,000. Greg simply steps into Chanzz's place after the acquisition. In Example 21-6, we determined Greg's outside basis to be $124,000. A sale of a partnership interest often results in a difference between the new investor's inside and outside bases because the outside basis is the price paid based on fair market value and the inside basis is the seller's share of tax basis in the partnership assets.

Varying Interest Rule If a partner's interest in a partnership increases or decreases during the partnership's tax year, the partnership income or loss allocated to the partner for the year must be adjusted to reflect her *varying interest* in the partnership.[16] Partners' interests increase when they contribute property or cash to a partnership[17] or purchase a partnership interest. Conversely, partners' interests decrease when they receive partnership distributions[18] or sell all or a portion of their partnership interests. Upon the sale of a partnership interest, the partnership tax year closes for the *selling* partner only. Regulations allow partners to choose between two possible methods for allocating income or loss to partners when their interests change during the year.[19] The first method allows the partnership to prorate income or loss to partners with varying interests, while the second method sanctions an interim closing of the partnership's books.

Example 21-8

CCS had a $60,000 overall operating loss for the 2018 calendar year. The issue of how to allocate the 2018 loss between Chanzz Inc. and Greg was easily resolved because CCS's operating agreement specifies the proration method to allocate income or loss when members' interests in CCS change during the year. How much of CCS's 2018 loss will Chanzz be allocated under the proration method?

Answer: Chanzz is allocated a loss of $9,000, which includes its share of CCS's loss but for only one-half the year ($60,000 × 30% share × 6/12 months).[20] On the sale date, Chanzz decreases its outside basis in CCS by the $9,000 loss to determine its adjusted basis to use in calculating its gain or loss on the sale of its interest.

---

[15]An exception occurs when the selling partner contributes property with a built-in loss to the partnership. Only the contributing partner is entitled to that loss [see the Forming and Operating Partnerships chapter and §704(c)(1)(C)]. Therefore, when a new investor buys a partnership interest from a partner that contributed built-in loss property, the new investor reduces his inside basis by the amount of the built-in loss at the contribution date.

[16]§706(d)(1).

[17]If all partners simultaneously contribute property or cash with a value proportionate to their interests, their relative interests will not change.

[18]If all partners receive distributions with a value proportionate to their interests, their relative interests will not change.

[19]Reg. §1.706-1(c).

[20]Reg. §1.706-4(c)(3) requires the calendar-day convention when using the proration method. For the sake of mathematical simplicity, we use number of months here and elsewhere in the chapter when applying the proration method.

Example 21-9

What if: If CCS's overall loss through June 30 was $20,000, how much of the $60,000 overall loss for 2018 will Chanzz and Greg Randall be allocated under an interim closing of the books?

Answer: CCS will allocate $6,000 of loss (30% × $20,000) to Chanzz and $12,000 of loss (30% × $40,000) to Greg.

TAXES IN THE REAL WORLD   Changing the Way Companies Dispose of a Business

Corporate takeovers seemed to be the transaction du jour during the 1990s, but many practitioners are predicting joint ventures will be the defining deal for the current decade. We regularly see articles in *The Wall Street Journal* describing how firms are starting up joint ventures or strategic alliances—or exiting them. For example, McGraw-Hill and the CME Group recently brought the S&P 500 index and the Dow Jones Industrial Average under the same roof by forming a new LLC called S&P/Dow Jones Indices. To form the new joint venture, McGraw-Hill contributed its Standard & Poor's index business and

CME Group contributed its Dow Jones index business. In the end, McGraw-Hill owned 73 percent and the CME Group owned 27 percent of the new venture.

The increase in the number of joint ventures and their possible dissolution or disposition brings an increasing need to understand the partnership tax rules and regulations. More than ever before, corporate tax executives find they must advise senior management on the opportunities and pitfalls of structuring joint ventures and investments as partnerships or LLCs under Subchapter K of the Internal Revenue Code.

BASICS OF PARTNERSHIP DISTRIBUTIONS

LO 21-2

Like shareholders receiving corporate dividend distributions, partners often receive distributions of the partnership profits, known as **operating distributions.** Recall that owners of flow-through entities are taxed currently on their business income regardless of whether the business distributes it. As a result, partners may require cash distributions in order to make quarterly estimated tax payments on their shares of business income. Usually, the general partners (or managing members of LLCs) determine the amount and timing of distributions; however, the partnership (operating) agreement may stipulate some distributions.

Partners may also receive **liquidating distributions.** Because the market for partnership interests is much smaller than for publicly traded stock, partners may have a difficult time finding buyers for their interests. Partnership agreements also often limit purchasers of an interest to the current partner group, to avoid adding an unwanted partner. If the current partner group either cannot or does not want to purchase the interest, the partnership can instead distribute assets to terminate a partner's interest. These liquidating distributions are similar to corporate redemptions of a shareholder's stock. They can also terminate the partnership. We first explore the tax consequences of operating distributions, and then examine the tax treatment for liquidating distributions.

LO 21-3

Operating Distributions

A distribution from a partnership is an operating distribution when the partners continue their interests afterwards. Operating distributions are usually made to distribute the business profits to the partners but can also reduce a partner's ownership. The partnership may distribute money or other assets. Let's look at the tax consequences of distributions of money, and then at the tax consequences of distributing property other than money.

Operating Distributions of Money Only   The general rule for operating distributions states that the partnership does not recognize gain or loss on the distribution of

THE KEY FACTS

Operating Distributions

- **Gain or loss recognition:** Partners generally do not recognize gain or loss. One exception occurs when the partnership distributes money only and the amount is greater than the partner's outside basis.

(continued)

property or money.[21,22] Nor do the general tax rules require a partner to recognize gain or loss when she receives distributed property or money.[23] The partner simply reduces her (outside) basis in the partnership interest by the amount of cash distributed and the inside basis of any property distributed. In general, the partnership's basis in its remaining assets remains unchanged.[24]

Example 21-10

- **Basis of distributed assets:** Partners generally take a carryover basis in the distributed assets. If the partnership distribution includes other property and the combined inside basis is greater than the partner's outside basis, the bases of the other property distributed will be reduced.

- **Remaining outside basis:** In general, partners reduce outside basis by money and other property distributed.

What if: Suppose CCS makes its first distribution to the owners on December 31, 2019: $250,000 each to Nicole and Greg and $333,333 to Sarah. After taking into account their distributive share of CCS's income for the year, the owners have the following predistribution bases in their CCS interests:

Owner	Outside Basis
Nicole	$205,000
Sarah	420,000
Greg	334,000

What are the tax consequences (gain or loss and basis in CCS interest) of the distribution to Sarah?

Answer: Sarah does not recognize any gain or loss on the distribution. She reduces her outside basis from $420,000 to $86,667 ($420,000 − $333,333) after the distribution.

The general rule of no gain is impractical when the partner receives a greater amount of money than her outside basis. She cannot defer gain to the extent of the excess amount because the outside basis is insufficient for a full reduction. Therefore, the partner reduces her outside basis to zero[25] and recognizes gain (generally capital) to the extent the amount of money distributed is greater than her outside basis.[26] A partner *never* recognizes a loss from an *operating* distribution.

Example 21-11

What if: Suppose that in the December 31, 2019, distribution Nicole's distribution consists of $250,000 cash. Her outside basis is $205,000 before the distribution. What are Nicole's gain or loss and basis in her CCS interest after the distribution?

Answer: Nicole has $45,000 capital gain and $0 basis in CCS. Because she receives only money in the distribution, she decreases her outside basis to $0 and must recognize a $45,000 capital gain ($250,000 distribution less $205,000 basis). She recognizes gain because she receives a cash distribution in excess of her outside basis.

Operating Distributions That Include Property Other Than Money   If a partnership makes a distribution that includes property *other than money*, the partners face the problem of determining how much outside basis to allocate to the distributed

---

[21]For distribution purposes, money includes cash, deemed cash from reductions in a partner's share of liabilities, and the fair market value of marketable securities.

[22]§731(b).

[23]§731.

[24]However, if the partnership has a §754 election in effect or if there is a substantial basis reduction, the partnership basis of its remaining assets must be adjusted following a distribution according to §734(b) and §755.

[25]§733.

[26]§731(a)(1).

property.[27] Under the general rule, the partner takes a basis in the distributed property equal to the partnership's basis in the property. This is called a **carryover basis.**[28] The tax rules define the order in which to allocate outside basis to the bases of distributed assets. First, the partner allocates the outside basis to any money received and then to other property as a carryover basis. The remainder is the partner's outside basis after the distribution.

Example 21-12

What if: Suppose CCS's December 31, 2019, distribution to Sarah consists of $133,333 cash and investments (other than marketable securities), with a fair market value of $200,000 and an adjusted basis of $115,000. Sarah has a predistribution outside basis of $420,000. What are the tax consequences (Sarah's gain or loss, basis of distributed assets, outside basis of CCS interest, and CCS's gain or loss) of the distribution?

Answer: Sarah recognizes no gain or loss on the distribution. To determine her bases in the distributed assets, she first allocates $133,333 to the cash and then takes a carryover basis in the investments so her basis in the investments is $115,000. Sarah reduces her outside basis by $248,333 ($133,333 cash + $115,000 basis of investments). Her outside basis after the distribution is $171,667 ($420,000 − $248,333). CCS does not recognize any gain or loss on the distribution.

When the partnership distributes property (other than money) with a basis that exceeds the remaining outside basis (after the allocation to any money distributed), the partner assigns the remaining outside basis to the distributed assets,[29] and the partner's outside basis is reduced to zero.[30] The first allocation of outside basis goes to money, then to hot assets, and finally to other property.[31] In this case, the partner's basis in the property received in the distribution will be less than the property's basis in the hands of the partnership.

Example 21-13

What if: Suppose Nicole's December 31, 2019, distribution consists of $150,000 cash and investments (other than marketable securities) with a fair market value of $100,000 and an adjusted basis of $90,000 to CCS. Her outside basis is $205,000 before the distribution. What are Nicole's tax consequences (gain or loss, basis of distributed assets, and outside basis in CCS interest) of the distribution?

Answer: Nicole recognizes no gain or loss and takes a basis of $55,000 in the investments. Her outside basis in CCS is $0, computed as follows.

Description	Amount	Explanation
(1) Nicole's outside basis	$205,000	
(2) Cash distribution	150,000	
(3) Remaining basis	55,000	(1) − (2); remaining outside basis to be allocated to the distributed investments
(4) Inside basis of investments	90,000	
(5) Basis in investments	55,000	Lesser of (3) or (4)
Nicole's outside basis in CCS	$ 0	(3) − (5)

---

[27]In this context, money includes marketable securities [§731(c)(1)(A)]. The special rules in §731(c) for the treatment of distributed marketable securities are beyond the scope of this book.

[28]§732(a).

[29]§732(a)(2).

[30]§733.

[31]If multiple assets are distributed, then the outside basis will be allocated in accordance with §732(c). We discuss these rules later in conjunction with liquidating distributions.

Because a partner's outside basis includes her share of the partnership liabilities, the outside basis must reflect any changes in a partner's share of partnership debt resulting from a distribution. In essence, a partner treats a reduction of her share of debt as a distribution of cash.[32] If the partner increases her share of debt, the increase is treated as a cash contribution to the partnership.

Example 21-14

What if: Suppose Greg receives land held for investment with a fair market value of $250,000 (adjusted inside basis is $140,000) as his distribution from CCS on December 31, 2019. He agrees to assume the $120,000 mortgage on the land after the distribution. His outside basis is $334,000 before considering the distribution. What are the tax consequences (gain or loss, basis of distributed assets, and outside basis in his CCS interest) of the distribution to Greg?

Answer: Greg does not recognize any gain or loss on the distribution. His basis in the land is $140,000 and his outside basis in CCS is $278,000, determined as follows:

Description	Amount	Explanation
(1) Greg's predistribution outside basis	$ 334,000	
(2) Mortgage assumed by Greg	120,000	
(3) Greg's predistribution share of mortgage	36,000	(2) × 30% ownership
(4) Deemed cash contribution from debt assumption	84,000	(2) − (3)
(5) Greg's outside basis after debt changes	418,000	(1) + (4)
(6) Greg's basis in distributed land	**140,000**	Carryover basis from CCS
Greg's post-distribution outside basis	**$278,000**	(5) − (6)

Greg must first consider the effects of changes in debt before determining the effects of the distribution. The tax rules treat him as making a net contribution of $84,000 cash to the partnership, the difference between the full mortgage he assumes and his predistribution share of the debt. Greg then allocates $140,000 of his outside basis to the land and reduces his outside basis accordingly.

LO 21-4 ## Liquidating Distributions

In contrast to operating distributions in which the partners retain a continuing interest in the partnership, liquidating distributions terminate a partner's interest in the partnership. If the current partners do not have sufficient cash or inclination to buy out the terminating partner, the partnership agreement usually allows the partnership to close out the partner's interest. At some point, all the partners may agree to terminate the partnership, either because they have lost interest in continuing it or because it has not been profitable. In such cases, the partnership may distribute all its assets to the partners in complete partnership liquidation. This latter process is analogous to a complete corporate liquidation (discussed in the Corporate Formation, Reorganization, and Liquidation chapter).

The tax issues in liquidating distributions for partnerships are basically twofold: (1) to determine whether the terminating partner recognizes gain or loss and (2) to allocate his or her outside basis to the distributed assets. The rationale behind the rules for liquidating distributions is simply to replace the partner's outside basis with the underlying partnership assets distributed to the terminating partner. Ideally, there will be no gain or loss on the distribution, and the asset bases will be the same in the partner's hands as they were inside the partnership. Of course, this case rarely occurs. The rules therefore are designed to determine when gain or loss must be recognized and to allocate the partner's outside basis to the distributed assets.

---

[32]§752(b).

Gain or Loss Recognition in Liquidating Distributions   In general, neither partnerships nor partners recognize gain or loss from liquidating distributions. However, there are exceptions. For example, when a terminating partner receives more money in the distribution than her outside basis, she will recognize gain.[33] See Example 21-11 for an illustration in the context of operating distributions.

In contrast to operating distributions, a partner may recognize a *loss* from a liquidating distribution, but only when two conditions are met. These conditions are (1) the distribution includes only cash, unrealized receivables, and/or inventory; *and* (2) the partner's outside basis is greater than the sum of the *inside bases* of the distributed assets.[34] The loss on the distribution is a capital loss to the partner.

Commonly, the terminating partner's share of partnership debt decreases after a liquidating distribution. Any reduction in the partner's share of liabilities is considered a distribution of money to the partner and reduces the outside basis available for allocation of basis to other assets, including inventory and unrealized receivables.

Example 21-15

What if: Suppose on January 1, 2020, CCS liquidates Greg's interest in the LLC by distributing to him cash of $206,000 and inventory with a fair market value of $103,000 (adjusted basis is $43,000). Greg's share of CCS's liabilities as of the liquidation is $66,000. On January 1, 2020, Greg's outside basis in CCS is $334,000, including his share of CCS's liabilities. What is Greg's gain or loss on the liquidation of his CCS interest?

Answer: Greg recognizes a capital loss of $19,000 from the liquidating distribution, computed as follows:

Description	Amount	Explanation
(1) Outside basis before distribution	$334,000	
(2) Debt relief	66,000	Deemed cash distribution
(3) Outside basis after considering debt relief	$268,000	(1) – (2)
(4) Basis of property distributed (cash + inventory)	249,000	
Gain (loss) on distribution	**$(19,000)**	(4) – (3)

Greg recognizes a loss because he meets the two necessary conditions: (1) he receives only cash and inventory in the distribution *and* (2) the sum of the adjusted inside bases of the distributed assets is less than his basis in his CCS interest ($249,000 inside basis in assets versus $268,000 CCS outside basis).

THE KEY FACTS

Gain or Loss Recognition in Liquidating Distributions

- **Generally:** Partners and partnerships do not recognize gain or loss.
- **Exceptions:**
  - **Gain:** Partner recognizes gain when partnership distributes money and the amount exceeds the partner's outside basis in the partnership interest.
  - **Loss:** Partner recognizes loss when two conditions are met: (1) Distribution consists of only cash and hot assets, and (2) the partner's outside basis exceeds the sum of the bases of the distributed assets.

Basis in Distributed Property   A key theme of the partnership tax rules is the idea that the partnership acts merely as a conduit for the partners' business activities. Thus, the rules attempt to keep the basis of the assets the same regardless of whether the partner or the partnership has possession of them. Moving assets in and out of the partnership should therefore have few tax consequences. The primary objective of the basis rules in liquidating distributions is to allocate the partner's entire outside basis in the partnership to the assets the partner receives in the liquidating distribution. The allocation essentially depends on two things: (1) the partnership's bases in distributed assets relative to the partner's outside basis and (2) the type of property distributed—whether it is money, hot assets, or other property. For purposes of distributions, hot assets include unrealized receivables and inventory, as we've defined above. We discuss each of the possible scenarios in Exhibit 21-1 in turn.

---

[33]These rules are very similar to those for operating distributions. When a partner receives money only in complete termination of the partnership interest, any gain on distribution cannot be deferred through a basis adjustment. Therefore, the partner recognizes the gain.

[34]§731(a)(2).

EXHIBIT 21-1 **Alternative Scenarios for Determining Basis in Distributed Property**

Type of Property Distributed	Partner's outside basis is *greater* than inside bases of distributed assets	Partner's outside basis is *less* than inside bases of distributed assets
Money only	Scenario 1	Scenario 3
Money and hot assets	Scenario 1	Scenario 4
Other property included in distribution[35]	Scenario 2	Scenario 5

Partner's Outside Basis Is Greater Than Inside Bases of Distributed Assets

Scenario 1: Distributions of money, inventory, and/or unrealized receivables. If the partnership distributes only money, inventory, and/or unrealized receivables (ordinary income property) and the partner's outside basis is greater than the sum of the inside bases of the distributed assets, the partner recognizes a capital loss.[36] The partner assigns a basis to the distributed assets equal to the partnership's inside basis in the assets and the remaining outside basis is equal to the recognized loss. To prevent a partner from converting a capital loss from her investment into an ordinary loss, the tax law prohibits increasing her basis in unrealized receivables and inventory and requires the partner to recognize a capital loss.[37]

Example 21-16

What if: Suppose Greg has an outside basis in CCS of $334,000, including his share of liabilities of $66,000. In a liquidating distribution, he receives $159,000 cash and inventory with a fair market value and basis of $49,000. Will Greg recognize a gain or loss? Why or why not?

Answer: Greg will recognize a capital loss of $60,000 on the liquidation, computed as follows:

Description	Amount	Explanation
(1) Outside basis before distribution	$334,000	
(2) Debt relief	66,000	Deemed cash distribution
(3) Outside basis after considering debt relief	$268,000	(1) − (2)
(4) Basis of property distributed (cash + inventory)	208,000	
Gain (loss) on distribution	**$(60,000)**	(4) − (3)

In this case, Greg is unable to defer his loss without changing its character. Greg clearly cannot adjust the basis in the cash to defer the loss. *If* he were able to increase his basis in the distributed inventory, he could defer the loss. However, this would produce an ordinary loss of $60,000 when Greg sells the inventory.[38] To prevent the conversion of a capital loss to an ordinary loss, Greg must recognize a $60,000 capital loss.

Scenario 2: Other property included in distributions. Recall that in this scenario the liquidating partner must allocate all her outside basis to the distributed assets. We determined in Scenario 1 that when the partnership distributes only money and/or hot assets

---

[35]This category includes distributions that include other property in addition to or instead of either money or unrealized receivables or inventory. For example, the distributions in this category can include any combination of money, unrealized receivables, and inventory as long as other property is also distributed.

[36]§731(a)(2).

[37]§732(c)(1) and §731(a)(2).

[38]If the inventory distributed to Greg is also considered inventory in his hands, the eventual sale of the inventory will generate ordinary income. If the inventory is a capital asset to Greg, a sale of the asset within five years of the distribution will generate ordinary income. After five years, the gain or loss will be capital.

and the total inside basis of the distributed assets is less than the partner's outside basis, it is impossible to allocate the entire outside basis to the distributed assets without changing the character of a resulting loss. Thus, a partner never increases the bases of hot assets. However, when the partnership distributes other property, in addition to money and/or hot assets, the partner can adjust the basis of the *other* property without converting ordinary gains and losses to capital, and the liquidating partner will not recognize any gain or loss from the distribution.

Example 21-17

What if: Suppose CCS has no liabilities or hot assets and distributes $50,000 in cash and land with a fair market value of $160,000 and an adjusted basis of $20,000 to Greg in complete liquidation of his CCS interest. Greg has an outside basis of $268,000 prior to the distribution. What is Greg's recognized gain or loss on the distribution?

Answer: Greg does not recognize any gain or loss. He receives money and other property with a total basis of $70,000, which is less than his outside basis of $268,000. Greg first reduces his outside basis by the amount of money he receives, and he assigns his remaining outside basis to the land as follows:

Description	Amount	Explanation
(1) Outside basis before distribution	$268,000	
(2) Basis allocated to money distributed	50,000	
Remaining outside basis assigned to land	$218,000	(1) − (2)

Note that Greg increases the basis of the other property received in liquidation (land) from $20,000 to $218,000 in order to allocate his entire outside basis to the distributed assets. In some cases, "other" property might include personal use assets for which the partner may never be able to recover the basis increase.

Example 21-17 illustrates the required basis increase in a very simple situation. In reality, liquidating distributions may include several types of assets. In these situations, to allocate the outside basis to the distributed assets, the partner completes the following, more detailed process:[39]

Step 1: The partner first determines their outside basis net of any debt relief, and then allocates that amount to any money, inventory, and unrealized receivables equal to the partnership's basis in these assets. The partner also assigns a basis to the other distributed property in an amount equal to the partnership's basis in those assets.

Step 2: The partner then allocates the remaining outside basis (full outside basis less the amounts assigned in Step (1) to the other distributed property that has unrealized appreciation to the extent of that appreciation. Thus, if an asset has an adjusted basis to the partnership of $500 and a fair market value of $700, the partner will allocate the first $200 of remaining basis to that asset.[40]

Step 3: The partner allocates any remaining basis to all other property in proportion to the relative *fair market values* of the other property.

$$\text{Basis allocation} = \text{Remaining basis} \times \frac{\text{FMV}_{\text{asset}}}{\text{Sum of FMV}_{\text{distributed other property}}}$$

[39]§732(c)(2).

[40]If the remaining outside basis is insufficient to allocate the full amount of appreciation to the distributed assets in this step, then the partner will allocate the remaining basis in this step to the appreciated assets based on their relative appreciation.

Example 21-18

What if: Suppose CCS makes the following distribution to Greg in liquidation of his CCS interest:

Asset	CCS Tax Basis	Fair Market Value
Cash	$181,000	$181,000
Investment A	5,000	12,000
Investment B	10,000	13,000
Inventory	43,000	103,000

Greg's basis in his CCS interest as of the liquidation is $334,000, including his $66,000 share of CCS's liabilities. What is Greg's recognized gain or loss on the distribution? What are Greg's bases in the distributed assets following the liquidation?

Answer: Greg recognizes no gain or loss on the distribution. Greg's bases in the distributed assets are:

Cash	$181,000
Investment A*	21,120
Investment B*	22,880
Inventory	43,000
Total	$268,000

Because Greg receives other property in the distribution and the distributed asset bases are less than Greg's outside basis (Scenario 2), he will allocate his outside basis as follows:

First, Greg determines his allocable basis:

Description	Amount	Explanation
(1) Basis in CCS before distribution	$334,000	
(2) Debt relief	66,000	Greg's 30 percent share of CCS's debt
Allocable basis	$268,000	(1) − (2)

Next, Greg allocates his remaining outside basis in CCS of $268,000 to the distributed assets by following the allocation process.

Description	Amount	Explanation
Step 1:		
(1) Allocable basis	$268,000	See above
(2) Basis assigned to cash	181,000	
(3) Basis assigned to inventory	43,000	
(4) Initial basis assigned to Investment A	5,000	
(5) Initial basis assigned to Investment B	10,000	
(6) Remaining allocable CCS basis	$ 29,000	(1) − (2) − (3) − (4) − (5)
Step 2:		
(7) Additional basis assigned to Investment A	$ 7,000	Unrealized appreciation on Investment A (FMV of $12,000 less basis of $5,000)
(8) Additional basis assigned to Investment B	3,000	Unrealized appreciation on Investment B (FMV of $13,000 less basis of $10,000)
(9) Remaining allocable CCS basis after Step 2	$ 19,000	(6) − (7) − (8)

Step 3:

(10) Additional basis allocated to other property: Investment A	$ 9,120	Basis allocation = $19,000 × ($12,000/$25,000) = $9,120
(11) Additional basis allocated to other property: Investment B	$ 9,880	Basis allocation = $19,000 × ($13,000/$25,000) = $9,880

In Step 3, Greg allocates the remaining basis to the distributed investments based on their relative fair market values using:

$$\text{Basis allocation} = \text{Remaining basis} \times \frac{\text{FMV}_{asset}}{\text{Sum of FMV}_{distributed\ other\ property}}$$

Thus, Greg's bases in the investments are $21,120 (Investment A) and $22,880 (Investment B):

Description	Inv. A	Explanation	Inv. B	Explanation
(12) Initial basis assignment	$ 5,000	From (4) above	$ 10,000	From (5) above
(13) Basis assigned in Step 2	7,000	From (7) above	3,000	From (8) above
(14) Basis assigned in Step 3	9,120	From (10) above	9,880	From (11) above
Greg's bases in investments	**$21,120**	(12) + (13) + (14)	**$22,880**	(12) + (13) + (14)

Partner's Outside Basis Is Less Than Inside Bases of Distributed Assets

Scenario 3: Distributions of money only.   A partner recognizes a gain (generally capital) if the partnership distributes money (only) that exceeds the partner's outside basis. The gain equals the excess amount received over the outside basis. Example 21-11 illustrates the tax consequences for this scenario in the context of an operating distribution.

Scenario 4: Distributions of money, inventory, and/or unrealized receivables.   In liquidating distributions when the partner's outside basis is less than the inside bases of the distributed assets and the partnership distributes money and any property other than money, the partner reduces the basis in the distributed assets other than money but does not recognize gain or loss. Because the tax law does not restrict *reducing* bases of ordinary income assets, distributions of hot assets and other property will cause reductions in basis. However, the tax law does prescribe a particular sequence for the required reductions.

   If the partnership distributes only money, inventory, and unrealized receivables, the partner reduces the basis of the hot assets distributed (assuming money doesn't exceed basis). The required decrease in the basis of the distributed assets is equal to the difference between the partner's outside basis and the partnership's inside basis in the distributed assets. The partner first assigns her outside basis to the assets received in an amount equal to the assets' inside bases (allocating to money first). Then the partner allocates the required *decrease* to the assets with unrealized depreciation, to eliminate any existing losses built into the distributed assets.[41] Finally, the partner allocates any remaining required decrease to the distributed assets in proportion to their *adjusted bases* (AB), after considering the preceding steps and using the following equation:

$$\text{Basis allocation} = \text{Required decrease} \times \frac{\text{AB}_{asset}}{\text{Sum of AB}_{distributed\ assets}}$$

[41]If the required decrease is insufficient to allocate the full amount of depreciation to the distributed assets in this step, then the partner will allocate the remaining required decrease in this step to the depreciated assets based on their relative unrealized depreciation.

Example 21-19

What if: Suppose CCS makes the following distribution to Greg in liquidation of his CCS interest:

Asset	CCS Tax Basis	Fair Market Value
Cash	$256,000	$256,000
Inventory A	50,000	129,000
Inventory B	25,000	6,000
Total	$331,000	

Greg's basis in his CCS interest as of the liquidation is $334,000, including his $66,000 share of CCS's liabilities. What is Greg's recognized gain or loss on the distribution? What is Greg's basis in the distributed assets following the liquidation?

Answer: Greg does not recognize any gain or loss. His basis in the cash is $256,000; his basis in Inventory A is $10,714; and his basis in Inventory B is $1,286, computed as follows:

First, Greg reduces his outside basis in CCS by his $66,000 debt relief, such that his outside basis allocable to distributed assets is $268,000 ($334,000 − $66,000). He must allocate this remaining basis to the distributed assets using the following steps:

Description	Amount	Explanation
Step 1:		
(1) Allocable basis	$268,000	Basis in CCS of $334,000 − debt relief of $66,000
(2) **Basis assigned to cash**	**256,000**	
(3) Initial basis assigned to Inventory A	50,000	
(4) Initial basis assigned to Inventory B	25,000	
(5) Required decrease	63,000	(2) + (3) + (4) − (1): Initial assignment of basis exceeds Greg's allocable CCS basis
Step 2:		
(6) Required decrease to Inventory B	19,000	Unrealized depreciation on Inventory B (FMV of $6,000 less basis of $25,000)
(7) Remaining required decrease	44,000	(5) − (6)
(8) Interim adjusted basis of Inventory B	6,000	(4) − (6)

Step 3: In Step 3, Greg decreases the basis of the inventory in proportion to its relative adjusted bases determined in Step 2 using the following allocation:

$$\text{Basis allocation} = \text{Required decrease} \times \frac{AB_{asset}}{\text{Sum of } AB_{distributed\ assets}}$$

(9) Required decrease to Inventory A	39,286	Basis reduction = $44,000 × ($50,000/$56,000)
(10) Required decrease to Inventory B	4,714	Basis reduction = $44,000 × ($6,000/$56,000)
Final basis of Inventory A	**10,714**	(3) − (9)
Final basis of Inventory B	**1,286**	(8) − (10)

Example 21-20

What if: Suppose CCS makes the following distribution to Greg in liquidation of his CCS interest:

Asset	CCS Tax Basis	Fair Market Value
Cash	$242,000	$242,000
Accounts receivable	0	12,000
Inventory	72,000	120,000
Total	$314,000	

Greg's basis in his CCS interest as of the liquidation is $334,000, including his share ($66,000) of CCS's liabilities. What is Greg's recognized gain or loss on the distribution? What is Greg's basis in the assets he receives in the liquidating distribution?

Answer: Greg does not recognize any gain or loss on the liquidation. His asset bases are:

Cash	$242,000
Accounts receivable	0
Inventory*	26,000
Total	$268,000

Greg computes the basis as follows:

As a preliminary step to the allocation, he reduces his outside basis in CCS by his $66,000 debt relief, leaving an allocable outside basis of $268,000 ($334,000 − $66,000). He allocates this basis to the distributed assets using the following steps:

Description	Amount	Explanation
Step 1:		
(1) Allocable basis	$268,000	Basis in CCS of $334,000 − debt relief of $66,000
(2) Basis assigned to cash	242,000	
(3) Initial basis assigned to accounts receivable	0	
(4) Initial basis assigned to inventory	72,000	
(5) Required decrease	46,000	(2) + (3) + (4) − (1): Initial assignment of basis exceeds Greg's allocable CCS basis

Step 2: N/A because no assets have unrealized depreciation.

Step 3: In Step 3, Greg decreases the basis of the accounts receivable and inventory in proportion to their relative adjusted bases using the following reduction:

$$\text{Basis allocation} = \text{Required decrease} \times \frac{AB_{asset}}{\text{Sum of } AB_{distributed\ assets}}$$

(6) Required decrease to accounts receivable	0	Basis reduction = $46,000 × ($−0−/$72,000)
(7) Required decrease to inventory	46,000	Basis reduction = $46,000 × ($72,000/$72,000)
Final basis of accounts receivable	0	(3) − (6)
Final basis of inventory	26,000	(4) − (7)

Note that in this scenario, the tax rules recharacterize a portion ($46,000) of Greg's ultimate gain from capital gain to ordinary income. The sum of the bases of the distributed assets ($314,000) exceeds Greg's allocable outside basis ($268,000) by $46,000. Absent the allocation rules illustrated in Example 21-20, this would have been a capital gain to Greg. Instead, as we discuss below, the basis decrease to the hot assets will cause Greg to recognize any gain as ordinary upon sale of these assets.

Scenario 5: Other property included in distributions. In our final scenario, the partnership distributes other property in addition to or instead of money and/or inventory and unrealized receivables, and the partner's outside basis is less than the combined inside bases of the distributed property. The terminating partner does not recognize gain or loss; rather, he decreases the basis in the other property distributed. The process for assigning basis to the distributed assets is similar to the method we described above, although the required basis decrease is focused on the other property rather than the hot assets.[42] The procedure is as follows:

Step 1: The partner first determines their outside basis net of any debt relief, and then allocates that amount to any money, inventory, and unrealized receivables equal to the partnership's basis in these assets. The partner also assigns a basis to any other property equal to the partnership's basis in the other property distributed.

Step 2: The partner then allocates the required decrease (outside basis less partnership adjusted basis in distributed assets) to the other property that has unrealized depreciation to the extent of that depreciation to eliminate inherent losses. Thus, if an asset has an adjusted basis to the partnership of $700 and a fair market value of $600, the asset's basis is first reduced by $100 (unrealized depreciation).

Step 3: If any required decrease remains after accounting for the inherent losses in the distributed assets, the partner then allocates it to all other property in proportion to their adjusted bases. The *adjusted bases* used in this step are the bases from Step 2. We can determine the allocation as follows:

$$\text{Basis reduction} = \text{Required decrease} \times \frac{AB_{asset}}{\text{Sum of } AB_{\text{all distributed other property}}}$$

Example 21-21

What if: Suppose CCS makes the following distribution to Greg in liquidation of his CCS interest:

Asset	CCS Tax Basis	Fair Market Value
Cash	$187,000	$187,000
Investment A	10,000	7,000
Investment B	10,000	18,000
Inventory	70,000	162,000
Total	$277,000	

Greg's basis in his CCS interest as of the liquidation is $334,000, including his $66,000 share of CCS's liabilities. What is Greg's recognized gain or loss on the distribution? What is Greg's basis in the distributed assets following the liquidation?

[42]§732(c)(3).

Answer: Greg does not recognize any gain or loss. His asset bases are as follows:

Cash	$187,000
Investment A	4,530
Investment B	6,470
Inventory	70,000
Total	$268,000

Greg's basis in these assets is determined as follows:

Greg first determines his allocable basis of $268,000 by reducing his CCS basis ($334,000) for the deemed cash distribution relating to his $66,000 share of the reduction in CCS's debt.

Description	Amount	Explanation
Step 1:		
(1) Allocable basis	$268,000	Basis in CCS of $334,000 − debt relief of $66,000
(2) Basis assigned to cash	187,000	
(3) Initial basis assigned to Investment A	10,000	
(4) Initial basis assigned to Investment B	10,000	
(5) Initial basis assigned to inventory	70,000	
(6) Required decrease	9,000	(2) + (3) + (4) + (5) − (1): Initial assignment of basis exceeds Greg's allocable CCS basis
Step 2:		
(7) Required decrease to Investment A	3,000	Unrealized depreciation on Investment A (FMV of $7,000 less basis of $10,000)
(8) Remaining required decrease	6,000	(6) − (7)
(9) Interim basis of Investment A	7,000	(3) − (7)

Step 3: In Step 3, Greg decreases the basis of the other property (Investments A and B) in proportion to their relative adjusted bases using the following allocation:

$$\text{Basis reduction} = \text{Required decrease} \times \frac{AB_{asset}}{\text{Sum of } AB_{\text{all distributed other property}}}$$

(10) Required decrease to Investment A	2,470	Basis reduction = $6,000 × ($7,000/$17,000)
(11) Required decrease to Investment B	3,530	Basis reduction = $6,000 × ($10,000/$17,000)
Final basis of Investment A	4,530	(9) − (10)
Final basis of Investment B	6,470	(4) − (11)

Character and Holding Period of Distributed Assets   For both operating and liquidating distributions, the character of the distributed assets usually stays the same for the partner as it was in the partnership, in order to prevent conversion of ordinary income to capital gain for both operating and liquidating distributions. Thus, if a partner sells certain assets with ordinary character after the distribution, the partner will recognize ordinary income from the sale.[43] These assets include inventory [§751(d)] and unrealized receivables [§751(c)]. For inventory items, the ordinary income "taint" will remain for five years after the distribution. For unrealized receivables, a subsequent sale at any time after the distribution will result in ordinary income. The reverse is not true, however. If a partnership distributes a capital asset that will be inventory to a terminating partner, the partner will have ordinary income from an eventual sale, not capital gain or loss. To ensure the character of any distributed long-term capital gain property retains its character to the partner, the partner's holding period generally includes the partnership's holding period.[44]

Example 21-22

Greg has decided to cash out his investment in CCS in order to invest in another project in which he can more actively participate. After he speaks to Nicole and Sarah about the options, the three owners decide Greg can cash out using one of two options.

Option 1: CCS will liquidate Greg's interest by distributing cash of $242,000; accounts receivable worth $12,000 (adjusted basis is $0); and inventory worth $120,000 (adjusted basis is $72,000).

Option 2: Nicole and Sarah will purchase Greg's interest in CCS. Nicole agrees to purchase two-thirds of Greg's interest for $249,333 cash and Sarah agrees to purchase the remaining one-third for $124,667 cash.

Greg's basis in his 30 percent CCS interest is $334,000, including his share of CCS's liabilities of $66,000. Either event would occur on January 1, 2020, when CCS's balance sheet is as follows:

Color Comfort Sheets LLC January 1, 2020		
	Tax Basis	**FMV**
Assets		
Cash	$390,000	$ 390,000
Accounts receivable	0	40,000
Inventory	90,000	200,000
Investments	60,000	105,000
Equipment (cost = $200,000)	150,000	200,000
Building (cost = $100,000)	90,000	100,000
Land—original	20,000	160,000
Land—investment	140,000	270,000
Totals	$940,000	$1,465,000
Liabilities and capital		
Accounts payable	$ 80,000	
Long-term debt	0	
Mortgage on original land	40,000	
Mortgage on investment land	120,000	
Capital—Nicole	119,000	
—Sarah	332,000	
—Greg	249,000	
Totals	$940,000	

---

[43]§735(a).
[44]§735(b).

What are the tax consequences (amount and character of recognized gain or loss, basis in assets) for Greg under each option?

Answer: *Option 1:* Greg recognizes no gain or loss on the liquidating distribution. His bases in the distributed assets are:

Cash	$242,000
Accounts receivable	0
Inventory	26,000
Total	$268,000

Option 2: Greg recognizes ordinary income of $60,000 and a capital gain of $46,000.

The tax consequences of both options are determined as follows:

Option 1: The distribution allows Greg to defer recognizing any gain or loss on the liquidation. Example 21-20 provides the details of the analysis. Greg has debt relief in an amount equal to his share of CCS's liabilities ($66,000). The debt relief is treated as a distribution of cash, so Greg reduces his outside basis by this amount from $334,000 to $268,000. The difference between the sum of the inside bases of the distributed property and his outside basis is $46,000 ($314,000 − $268,000) and represents a required *decrease* to the bases of assets distributed in liquidation. Greg follows the prescribed method illustrated in Example 21-20 to compute his asset bases.

The basis reduction for these assets allows Greg to defer recognizing a $46,000 gain on the liquidation. The cost to accomplish the deferral is that if Greg sells the inventory and the accounts receivable immediately after the distribution, he will recognize ordinary income of $106,000 as follows:

Amount realized:		
Cash (equal to FMV of accounts receivable	$ 12,000	
and inventory)	120,000	$132,000
Less: Adjusted basis		
Accounts receivable	0	
Inventory	26,000	26,000
Ordinary income		$106,000

The $106,000 ordinary income is $46,000 greater than the inherent gain on these assets of $60,000 ($132,000 − $72,000) had the partnership sold the assets. If Greg selects Option 1, he will not recognize income on the liquidation until he sells the inventory and collects (or sells) the accounts receivable, thereby leaving himself flexibility on the timing of gain recognition.

Option 2: In this option, Greg sells his CCS interest to Nicole and Sarah and receives cash of $374,000 ($249,333 from Nicole and $124,667 from Sarah). Greg computes his total gain or loss as follows:

Amount realized:		
Cash	$374,000	
Debt relief	66,000	$440,000
Less: Basis in CCS interest		334,000
Realized and recognized gain		$106,000

Next, Greg determines the character of the gain from the sale by first identifying the gain related to hot assets.

Hot Asset — CCS	(1) Basis	(2) FMV	(3) Gain/Loss (2) − (1)	Greg's Share 30% × (3)
Accounts receivable	$ 0	$ 40,000	$ 40,000	$12,000
Inventory	90,000	200,000	110,000	33,000
Equipment	150,000	200,000	50,000	15,000
Total ordinary income				$60,000

(continued on page 21-24)

The final step for Greg is to determine the capital gain or loss by subtracting the ordinary portion from the total gain.

Total gain	$106,000
Less: ordinary income from §751(a)	(60,000)
Capital gain	$ 46,000

If he chooses Option 2, Greg will recognize $60,000 of ordinary income and $46,000 of capital gain in 2020.

Example 21-23

Given the tax consequences to Greg in the previous example, should he have CCS liquidate his interest (Option 1) or sell his interest (Option 2)?

Answer: Under Option 1 (the liquidation), Greg is able to defer all recognition of gain until he later sells the distributed assets. This provides him flexibility in when he pays tax on the liquidating distribution. However, when he recognizes any income upon subsequent sales, the character of the income will be ordinary and taxed at ordinary rates. Under Option 2, Greg must recognize income immediately upon the sale: $60,000 of ordinary income and $46,000 of capital gain. He has no future tax liability related to the liquidating distribution. The capital gain could be taxed at a rate as high as 23.8 percent (including the net investment income tax). An additional consideration is that under Option 2 Greg receives cash, rather than a mix of cash and other assets. If he wants to immediately invest the proceeds in another venture, he may prefer a pure cash payment.

continued from page 21-2...

Greg takes the liquidating distribution option (Option 1) offered by CCS to avoid recognizing a gain currently. Although this option doesn't give him as much cash as a sale would have, Greg figures it is enough for another investment and he can avoid paying tax on the distribution this year.

For the first time, CCS has only two owners—Nicole and Sarah. After liquidating Greg's interest, Nicole's interest has increased to 43 percent and Sarah's to 57 percent. Both women are happy with that outcome, although they are sorry to lose Greg's investment in the business. ■

LO 21-5 DISPROPORTIONATE DISTRIBUTIONS

Up to this point in the chapter, our distribution examples have either assumed or represented that each partner received a pro rata share of the partnership's unrealized appreciation in its ordinary assets, as specified in the partnership agreement based on the partner's capital interests. In practice, distributions may not always reflect each partner's proportionate share.[45] Both operating and liquidating distributions can be **disproportionate distributions.** Without going into all the details of these complex rules, let's briefly discuss the implications of distributions in which partners receive either more or less of their share of the unrealized appreciation or losses in so-called hot assets [assets defined in IRC §751(b)

---

[45]A thorough discussion of these issues is beyond the scope of this chapter. Therefore, we will abbreviate our discussion just to give a flavor for the issues and consequences of these disproportionate distributions.

as **substantially appreciated inventory** and unrealized receivables].[46] Note that the definition of hot assets for purposes of disproportionate distributions includes only *substantially appreciated* inventory, not *all* inventory [as is the case under §751(a), the definition we used to characterize the gain in dispositions of partnership interests]. Inventory is considered substantially appreciated if its fair market value is more than 120 percent of its basis.

Suppose a partner receives less than her share of the appreciation in hot assets in a liquidating distribution. This may occur, for example, if a partner receives only cash in a liquidating distribution from a partnership with hot assets. Rather than only applying the rules we discussed above, the partner must treat part of the distribution as a sale or exchange.[47] Basically, the disproportionate distribution rules treat the partner as having sold her share of hot assets to the partnership in exchange for "cold" [non-§751(b)] assets. This deemed sale generates an ordinary gain or loss to the partner on the deemed sale, essentially equal to her share of the appreciation or depreciation in the portion of hot assets not distributed to her. From the partnership's perspective, the partnership is deemed to have purchased the hot assets from the partner in exchange for cold assets. Therefore, the *partnership* recognizes a capital or §1231 gain or loss equal to the remaining partners' inherent gain or loss in the distributed cold assets. The effects are reversed if a partner receives more than her share of the appreciation in a partnership's hot assets.[48] The rules are meant to ensure that partners cannot convert ordinary income into capital gain through distributions. Thus, they require that partners will ultimately recognize their share of the partnership ordinary income regardless of the form of their distributions.

THE KEY FACTS

Disproportionate Distributions

- **When?**

  When a distribution changes a partner's relative share of unrealized appreciation or losses in a partnership's hot assets.

- **Why?**

  To prevent partners from converting ordinary income into capital gains through distributions.

- **How?**

  Partner and partnership must treat part of the distribution as a sale or exchange, which may change the character and timing of income or losses that are recognized.

Example 21-24

What if: Suppose CCS distributes $328,000 in cash to Greg Randall on January 1, 2020, in complete liquidation of Greg's 30 percent interest in CCS. Greg's basis in his CCS interest before the distribution is $334,000. Assume CCS's balance sheet is as follows:

Color Comfort Sheets LLC December 31, 2019		
	Tax Basis	**FMV**
Assets		
Cash	$700,000	$ 700,000
Inventory	240,000	440,000
Totals	$940,000	$1,140,000
Liabilities and capital		
Liabilities	$240,000	
Capital—Nicole	119,000	
—Sarah	332,000	
—Greg	249,000	
Totals	$940,000	

(continued on page 21-26)

[46]Unrealized receivables include the accounts receivable of a cash-method taxpayer, the excess of the fair market value over basis of accounts receivable for accrual-method taxpayers, and depreciation recapture under §1245. The definition of substantially appreciated inventory is broader than simply goods primarily held for sale to customers. It also includes property that would not be classified as capital assets or §1231 assets if sold by the partnership. As a result, receivables are included as "inventory."

[47]§751(b).

[48]The partner would generally recognize capital gain on the deemed sale and the partnership would recognize ordinary income.

Is this distribution disproportionate? What are the implications of the distribution?

Answer: The CCS balance sheet as of December 31, 2019 indicates that CCS's inventory is a hot asset given that its fair market value is more than 120 percent of its basis. Further, the CCS balance sheet indicates that the fair market value of Greg's share of the unrealized appreciation in CCS's hot assets for purposes of disproportionate distributions [§751(b)] is $60,000, or 30 percent of the $200,000 unrealized appreciation in inventory ($440,000 FMV less $240,000 adjusted basis). Since Greg receives only cash in the distribution, he has not received a proportionate share of the unrealized appreciation in CCS's hot assets. Thus, the distribution will be disproportionate.

The tax law treats Greg as having sold his share of the hot assets for cold assets, and he will recognize ordinary income equal to his share of the appreciation on the hot assets not distributed, or $60,000. Absent this provision in the tax law, all of Greg's gains from the distribution would have been treated as capital gains. CCS does not recognize any gain or loss because it has no appreciation in the assets (cash) used to "purchase" the hot assets.

LO 21-6 SPECIAL BASIS ADJUSTMENTS

Recall that when a partner sells her partnership interest, the partnership's inside basis is generally unaffected by the sale. This creates a discrepancy between the new investor's outside basis (cost) and her share of the partnership's inside basis, which artificially changes the potential income or loss at the partnership level. For example, earlier in the chapter Greg Randall purchased Chanzz's 30 percent interest in CCS for $82,800 (see the *what-if* scenario in Example 21-5). Greg's outside basis after the acquisition is $106,800, reflecting the cash payment of $82,800 and his share of CCS's debt at the time of the acquisition, $24,000. However, Greg's share of CCS's inside basis in its assets is $105,000 (see Example 21-7). This is the outcome because the sale does not affect CCS's inside basis and Greg simply steps into Chanzz's shoes for determining his share of the inside basis. The discrepancy reflects Chanzz's unrecognized share of appreciation of CCS's assets (which Greg paid full value for) as of the sale date and causes Greg to be temporarily overtaxed when CCS sells these appreciated assets.

Example 21-25

What if: Assume that Greg acquires his 30% interest in CCS for $82,800 (see Example 21-5). If under this assumption, CCS sells its accounts receivable for their fair market value of $13,000 (adjusted basis is $0) (see Example 21-2 for CCS's balance sheet as of June 30, 2018, the acquisition date), what is the amount and character of gain that Greg recognizes on the sale?

Answer: When CCS sells the accounts receivable, it recognizes $13,000 of ordinary income, of which $3,900 (30 percent) is allocated to Greg. However, when Chanzz sold its interest to Greg, Chanzz was already taxed on the $3,900 allocated portion of that ordinary income under §751(a), and Greg paid full value for his interest in the receivables when he acquired his 30 percent interest in CCS. This means Greg will be taxed on the $3,900 again in 2018, and his outside basis increases by $3,900. Because Greg paid fair market value for his share of the receivables, he should not have any income when they are sold at fair market value. Eventually, when Greg disposes of his CCS interest, his ultimate gain (or loss) on the disposition will be $3,900 less, because of the increase to his outside basis from this additional income; meanwhile, he is overtaxed on the receivables. Greg must report ordinary income today for an offsetting capital loss (or reduced capital gain) in the future when he disposes of his interest.

The tax rules allow the partnership to make an election for a **special basis adjustment** to eliminate discrepancies between the inside and outside bases and to correct the artificial income or loss at the partnership level.[49] For the most part, basis discrepancies arise in two situations: following *sales* of partnership interests, and following *distributions* when a partner receives an asset that takes more or less basis outside the partnership

---

[49]§754. The election is made by including a written statement declaring that the partnership is making the §754 election with the partnership return when filed for the year the election is to take effect.

than it had on the inside and when the partner recognizes a gain or loss on the distribution. Once a partnership makes a §754 election, the partnership is required to make the special basis adjustment for all subsequent sales of partnership interests and partnership distributions. The election can be revoked only with permission from the IRS.

Even without a §754 election in effect, the partnership must adjust its bases if the partnership has a **substantial built-in loss** at the time a partner sells her partnership interest. A substantial built-in loss exists if the partnership's aggregate inside basis in its property exceeds the property's fair market value by more than $250,000 when a transfer of an interest occurs or when the purchasing partner would be allocated a loss of more than $250,000 if the partnership assets were sold for fair market value immediately after the sale.[50] An analogous event—a **substantial basis reduction**—may occur for distributions, which also triggers a mandatory basis adjustment.

Although the election is made under §754, the actual authorization of the special basis adjustment is governed by two separate code sections, depending on which situation gives rise to the adjustment: (1) sale of partnership interest [§743(b)], or (2) distributions [§734(b)]. These two sections determine how much of an adjustment will be made, and §755 then stipulates how the adjustment is allocated among the partnership assets. The relationships among these code sections are depicted in Exhibit 21-2 below.

EXHIBIT 21-2   Special Basis Adjustments

Special Basis Adjustments for Dispositions

The special basis adjustment the partnership makes when a partner sells his partnership interest is designed to give the new investor an inside basis in the partnership assets equal to his outside basis. The basis adjustment in these cases applies *only* to the new investor. The inside bases of the continuing partners remain unchanged, so their income and losses will continue to be accurately allocated. The adjustment is equal to the difference between the new investor's outside basis and his share of inside basis.[51] The new investor's outside basis is generally equal to the cost of his partnership interest plus his share of partnership liabilities.[52] The

[50]§743(d). In this context, a transfer generally refers to sales, exchanges, or transfers at death, not gift transfers.

[51]§743(b).

[52]A partner's share of inside basis is also labeled *previously taxed capital* [§1.743-1(d)]. The technical calculation is determined as follows (but generally equals the partner's tax capital account):

(1) the amount of cash the partner would receive on liquidation after a hypothetical sale of all the partnership assets for their fair market value after the sale of the partnership interest, plus

(2) the amount of taxable loss allocated to the partner from the hypothetical sale, less

(3) the amount of taxable gain allocated to the partner from the hypothetical sale.

special basis adjustment must then be allocated to the assets under allocation rules in §755, which are beyond the scope of this text.

Example 21-26

What if: Suppose Greg acquired Chanzz's 30 percent interest in CCS on June 30, 2018, for $82,800. CCS's balance sheet as of the sale date is assumed to be as follows:

Color Comfort Sheets LLC June 30, 2018		
	Tax Basis	**FMV**
Assets		
Cash	$ 27,000	$ 27,000
Accounts receivable	0	13,000
Investments	15,000	12,000
Inventory	1,000	1,000
Equipment (cost = $100,000)	80,000	86,000
Building	97,000	97,000
Land	20,000	150,000
Totals	$240,000	$386,000
Liabilities and capital		
Long-term debt	$100,000	
Capital—Nicole	(49,000)	
—Sarah	108,000	
—Chanzz	81,000	
Totals	$240,000	

What is the special basis adjustment for Greg's purchase, assuming CCS has a §754 election in effect at the sale date?

Answer: $1,800, the difference between Greg's outside basis and inside basis, calculated as follows:

Description	Amount	Explanation
(1) Cash purchase price	$ 82,800	
(2) Greg's share of CCS debt	24,000	$80,000 × 30%
(3) Initial basis in CCS	$106,800	(1) + (2)
(4) Greg's inside basis	105,000	Chanzz's tax capital ($81,000) plus share of CCS debt ($24,000) (See Example 21-7)
Special basis adjustment	**$ 1,800**	(3) − (4)

When a new investor's special basis adjustment is allocated to depreciable or amortizable assets, the new investor will benefit from additional depreciation or amortization. In some cases, the amounts can be quite substantial, and a new investor may be willing to pay more for a partnership interest with a §754 election in place than he would for a partnership interest without it.

Special Basis Adjustments for Distributions

A similar potential problem exists when the partnership distributes assets to the partners that represent more (or, in some cases, less) than their share of the inside basis in the partnership assets. This usually occurs when a partner recognizes a gain or loss on a distribution or when a partner's basis in the distributed property is different from the partnership's basis in the property. In contrast to the special basis adjustment for sales of partnership interests, the special basis adjustment for distributions affects the common basis of *partnership* property and not merely one partner's basis.

The special basis adjustment can either increase or decrease the basis in the partnership assets. A **positive basis adjustment** will *increase* the basis in the partnership assets (1) when a partner receiving distributed property recognizes a gain on the distribution (for instance, in operating distributions where the partner receives money in excess of her outside basis), and (2) when a partner receiving distributed property takes a basis in the property less than the partnership's basis in the property. The positive adjustment will equal the sum of the gain recognized by the partners receiving distributed property and the amount of the basis reduction.

In Example 21-11, CCS distributed $250,000 cash to Nicole on December 31, 2019, as part of an operating distribution. Because Nicole's outside basis before the distribution was $205,000 and she received only money in the distribution, Nicole was required to recognize a $45,000 gain on the distribution. If CCS had a §754 election in effect, it would have a positive special basis adjustment from the distribution of $45,000.

A **negative basis adjustment** will *decrease* the basis in partnership assets (1) when a partner receiving distributed property in a liquidating distribution recognizes a loss on the distribution, and (2) when a partner receiving distributed property takes a basis in the property greater than the partnership's basis in the property.

The negative adjustment will equal the sum of the recognized loss and the amount of the basis increase made by the partners receiving the distribution. Recall from our previous discussion of distributions that negative adjustments can occur only in liquidating distributions. Only then does a partner recognize a loss or increase the distributed property's basis over its basis prior to the distribution.

In Example 21-15, CCS liquidated Greg's 30 percent interest by distributing cash of $206,000 and inventory with a fair market value of $103,000 (adjusted basis is $43,000). Because Greg's outside basis after considering his debt relief ($268,000) was greater than the sum of the bases of the property distributed ($249,000), Greg recognized a loss of $19,000 on the liquidation. If CCS had a §754 election in effect at the time of this liquidation, CCS would have a negative basis adjustment of $19,000.

As in the case of partnership dispositions, the allocation of the special basis adjustment among the partnership's remaining assets after a distribution is intended to offset any gain or loss the partners would have recognized twice absent the adjustment. The process of allocating the adjustment for distributions is prescribed in §755, and these procedures are beyond the scope of this text.

CONCLUSION

The tax rules for partnership dispositions and distributions are among the most complex in the Internal Revenue Code. This chapter provided an overview of these rules and in some cases plunged into the complexity. We discussed the calculation of gains and losses from the sale of a partnership interest, as well as the basis implications of the purchase to a new investor. In doing so, we discussed how *hot assets* might affect the gain or loss. The chapter also explained the basic rules for determining the tax treatment of partnership distributions.

We illustrated how partnership elections might affect the partnership's basis in assets following partnership interest dispositions or distributions. In general, the tax rules are designed to avoid having business owners make decisions based on tax rules rather than on business principles; however, making this goal a reality provides for some challenging applications.

Summary

LO 21-1 Determine the tax consequences to the buyer and seller of the disposition of a partnership interest, including the amount and character of gain or loss recognized.

- Sellers are primarily concerned about their realized and recognized gain or loss on the sale of their partnership interest.
- Sellers' debt relief is included in the amount realized from the sale.
- Buyers' main tax concerns are determining their basis in the partnership interest they acquire and their inside bases of the partnership assets.
- A buyer's outside basis after an acquisition is generally his cost plus his share of partnership liabilities. A buyer's inside basis is generally the same as the seller's inside basis at the sale date.
- The sale of a partnership interest does not generally affect a partnership's inside basis in its assets.
- A partnership's tax year closes for the selling partner upon the sale of a partnership interest.
- Hot assets include unrealized receivables and inventory items.
- Unrealized receivables include the rights to receive payment for goods delivered or to be delivered, or services rendered or to be rendered, as well as items that would generate ordinary income if the partnership sold the asset for its fair market value, such as depreciation recapture.
- There are actually two definitions of inventory items. The first under §751(a) applies to sales of partnership interests and includes all classic inventory items and assets that are *not* capital or §1231 assets. The second definition of inventory [§751(b)] applies primarily to distributions and includes only substantially appreciated inventory.
- Sellers classify gains and losses from the sale of partnership interests as ordinary to the extent the gain relates to hot assets.
- Hot assets are also important to determine whether a distribution is proportionate or disproportionate.

LO 21-2 Compare operating and liquidating distributions.

- Distributions from a flow-through entity are one mechanism to return business profits or capital to the owners of the entity.
- Distributions may also be used to liquidate an owner's interest in the business or to completely terminate the business.
- Operating distributions include distributions in which the owner retains an interest in the business.

LO 21-3 Determine the tax consequences of proportionate operating distributions.

- Partnerships do not generally recognize gain or loss on the distribution of property.
- Most operating distributions do not result in gain or loss to the partner receiving the distribution. Gains and losses are deferred through basis adjustments to the distributed assets and basis of the partnership interest.
- A partner recognizes a gain from an operating distribution if she receives a distribution of money that exceeds the basis in her partnership interest.
- Partners never recognize losses from operating distributions.

LO 21-4 Determine the tax consequences of proportionate liquidating distributions.

- The tax issues in liquidating distributions are primarily twofold: (1) determining whether the liquidating partner recognizes a gain or loss, and (2) allocating the liquidating partner's basis in her partnership interest to the distributed assets.
- A partner recognizes a gain only when the partner receives more money than her basis in the partnership interest.
- A partner recognizes a loss only when the partnership distributes cash and hot assets and the partner's basis in the partnership interest is greater than the sum of the bases of the assets the partner received in the distribution.

- In all other cases, a partner does not recognize gains or losses from a liquidating distribution; rather, she will simply allocate her basis in the partnership interest to the distributed assets.
- The key to the allocation process is to focus on two factors: (1) the type of property distributed, and (2) whether the total basis in distributed assets is larger or smaller than the partner's basis in the partnership interest.
- The character of the distributed assets usually stays the same to the partner as in the partnership.

Explain the significance of disproportionate distributions.   **LO 21-5**

- Disproportionate distributions occur when the assets distributed in either operating or liquidating distributions do not represent the partner's proportionate share of the partnership's unrealized appreciation in its hot and cold assets.
- A disproportionate distribution causes a shift in the proportion of ordinary income and capital gain income from the partnership. Therefore, the rules require the partner to treat the disproportionate portion of a distribution as a sale or exchange.
- If a partner receives more cold assets than her proportionate share in a distribution, she will generally recognize ordinary income in an amount equal to her share of the appreciation of hot assets not distributed to her. If a partner receives more hot assets than her proportionate share, she will recognize capital gain equal to her share of the appreciation in cold assets not distributed to her.
- The disproportionate distribution rules ensure that partners cannot convert ordinary income into capital gain through distributions.

Explain the rationale for special basis adjustments and the method for calculating them.   **LO 21-6**

- Discrepancies between a partner's inside and outside basis may cause a partner to be overtaxed or undertaxed, at least temporarily. Special basis adjustment rules allow the partnership to eliminate discrepancies between inside and outside bases to correct any artificial income or loss at the partnership level.
- Basis discrepancies may occur following the acquisition of a partnership interest and following distributions where a partner receives more or less than her share of the inside basis in the partnership property.
- When a new investor purchases a partnership interest, she may receive a special basis adjustment equal to the difference between her outside basis and her share of inside basis if the partnership has a §754 election in effect.
- A special basis adjustment is mandatory even without a §754 election in effect when a partnership has a substantial built-in loss at the time a partnership interest is transferred.
- When a partner recognizes a gain from a distribution or takes a basis in distributed property less than the partnership's basis in the property, the partnership will have a positive special basis adjustment to increase the basis in the partnership's assets.
- When a partner recognizes a loss from a liquidating distribution or takes a basis in distributed property greater than the partnership's basis in the property, the partnership will have a negative special basis adjustment to decrease the basis in partnership assets.

KEY TERMS

carryover basis (21-11)
disproportionate distributions (21-24)
hot assets (21-3)
inside basis (21-7)
inventory items (21-3)
liquidating distributions (21-9)

negative basis adjustment (21-29)
operating distributions (21-9)
outside basis (21-3)
partnership interest (21-2)
positive basis adjustment (21-29)
special basis adjustment (21-26)

substantial basis reduction (21-27)
substantial built-in loss (21-27)
substantially appreciated
    inventory (21-25)
unrealized receivables (21-3)

DISCUSSION QUESTIONS

Discussion Questions are available in Connect®.

LO 21-1   1. Joey is a 25 percent owner of Loopy LLC. He no longer wants to be involved in the business. What options does Joey have to exit the business?

LO 21-1   2. Compare and contrast the aggregate and entity approaches for a sale of a partnership interest.

LO 21-1   3. What restrictions might prevent a partner from selling his partnership interest to a third party?

LO 21-1   4. Explain how a partner's debt relief affects his amount realized in a sale of partnership interest.

LO 21-1   5. Under what circumstances will the gain or loss on the sale of a partnership interest be characterized as ordinary rather than capital?

LO 21-1   6. What are *hot assets* and why are they important in the sale of a partnership interest?

LO 21-1   7. For an accrual-method partnership, are accounts receivable considered unrealized receivables? Explain.

LO 21-1   8. Can a partnership have unrealized receivables if it has no accounts receivable?

LO 21-1   9. How do hot assets affect the character of gain or loss on the sale of a partnership interest?

LO 21-1   10. Under what circumstances can a partner recognize both gain and loss on the sale of a partnership interest?

LO 21-1   11. Absent any special elections, what effect does a sale of partnership interest have on the partnership?

 LO 21-1   12. Generally, a selling partner's capital account carries over to the purchaser of the partnership interest. Under what circumstances will this not be the case?

LO 21-2   13. What distinguishes operating from liquidating distributions?

LO 21-3   14. Under what circumstances will a partner recognize a gain from an operating distribution?

LO 21-3   15. Under what circumstances will a partner recognize a loss from an operating distribution?

LO 21-3   16. In general, what effect does an operating distribution have on the partnership?

LO 21-3   17. If a partner's outside basis is less than the partnership's inside basis in distributed assets, how does the partner determine his basis of the distributed assets in an operating distribution?

LO 21-4   18. Under what conditions will a partner recognize gain in a liquidating distribution?

LO 21-4   19. Under what conditions will a partner recognize loss in a liquidating distribution?

LO 21-4   20. Describe how a partner determines his basis in distributed assets in cases in which a partnership distributes only money, inventory, and/or unrealized receivables in a liquidating distribution.

LO 21-4   21. How does a partner determine his basis in distributed assets when the partnership distributes other property in addition to money and hot assets?

LO 21-5   22. SBT partnership distributes $5,000 cash and a parcel of land with a fair market value of $40,000 and a $25,000 basis to the partnership to Sam (30 percent partner). What factors must Sam and SBT consider in determining the tax treatment of this distribution?

LO 21-5   23. Discuss the underlying concern to tax policy makers in distributions in which a partner receives more or less than his share of the partnership's hot assets.

LO 21-5   24. In general, how do the disproportionate distribution rules ensure that partners recognize their share of partnership ordinary income?

LO 21-6   25. Why would a new partner who pays more for a partnership interest than the selling partner's outside basis want the partnership to elect a special basis adjustment?

26. List two common situations that will cause a partner's inside and outside basis to differ. `LO 21-6`

27. Explain why a partnership might not want to make a §754 election to allow special basis adjustments. `LO 21-6`

28. When might a new partner have an upward basis adjustment following the acquisition of a partnership interest? `LO 21-6`

29. When are partnerships mandated to adjust the basis of their assets (inside basis) when a partner sells a partnership interest or receives a partnership distribution? `LO 21-6`

PROBLEMS

Select problems are available in Connect®.

30. Jerry is a 30 percent partner in the JJM Partnership when he sells his entire interest to Lucia for $56,000 cash. At the time of the sale, Jerry's basis in JJM is $32,000. JJM does not have any debt or hot assets. What is Jerry's gain or loss on the sale of his interest? `LO 21-1`

31. Joy is a 30 percent partner in the JOM Partnership when she sells her entire interest to Hope for $72,000 cash. At the time of the sale, Joy's basis in JOM is $44,000 (which includes her $6,000 share of JOM liabilities). JOM does not have any hot assets. What is Joy's gain or loss on the sale of her interest? `LO 21-1`

32. Allison, Keesha, and Steven each own equal interests in KAS Partnership, a calendar year-end, cash-method entity. On January 1 of the current year, Steven's basis in his partnership interest is $27,000. During January and February, the partnership generates $30,000 of ordinary income and $4,500 of tax-exempt income. On March 1, Steven sells his partnership interest to Juan for a cash payment of $45,000. The partnership has the following assets and no liabilities at the sale date: `LO 21-1`

	Tax Basis	FMV
Cash	$30,000	$30,000
Land held for investment	30,000	60,000
Totals	$60,000	$90,000

a) Assuming KAS's operating agreement provides for an interim closing of the books when partners' interests change during the year, what is Steven's basis in his partnership interest on March 1 just prior to the sale?

b) What is the amount and character of Steven's recognized gain or loss on the sale?

c) What is Juan's initial basis in the partnership interest?

d) What is the partnership's basis in the assets following the sale?

33. Grace, James, Helen, and Charles each own equal interests in GJHC Partnership, a calendar year-end, cash-method entity. On January 1 of the current year, James's basis in his partnership interest is $62,000. For the taxable year, the partnership generates $80,000 of ordinary income and $30,000 of dividend income. For the first five months of the year, GJHC generates $25,000 of ordinary income and no dividend income. On June 1, James sells his partnership interest to Robert for a cash payment of $70,000. The partnership has the following assets and no liabilities at the sale date: `LO 21-1`

	Tax Basis	FMV
Cash	$ 27,000	$ 27,000
Land held for investment	80,000	100,000
Totals	$107,000	$127,000

a) Assuming GJHC's operating agreement provides that the proration method will be used to allocate income or loss when partners' interests change during the year, what is James's basis in his partnership interest on June 1 just prior to the sale?

b) What is the amount and character of James's recognized gain or loss on the sale?

c) If GJHC uses an interim closing of the books, what is the amount and character of James's recognized gain or loss on the sale?

LO 21-1 34. At the end of last year, Lisa, a 35 percent partner in the five-person LAMEC Partnership, has an outside basis of $60,000, including her $30,000 share of LAMEC debt. On January 1 of the current year, Lisa sells her partnership interest to MaryLynn for a cash payment of $45,000 and the assumption of her share of LAMEC's debt.

a) What is the amount and character of Lisa's recognized gain or loss on the sale?

b) If LAMEC has $100,000 of unrealized receivables as of the sale date, what is the amount and character of Lisa's recognized gain or loss?

c) What is MaryLynn's initial basis in the partnership interest?

LO 21-1 35. Marco, Jaclyn, and Carrie formed Daxing Partnership (a calendar year-end entity) by contributing cash 10 years ago. Each partner owns an equal interest in the partnership and has an outside basis in his/her partnership interest of $104,000. On January 1 of the current year, Marco sells his partnership interest to Ryan for a cash payment of $137,000. The partnership has the following assets and no liabilities as of the sale date:

	Tax Basis	FMV
Cash	$ 18,000	$ 18,000
Accounts receivable	0	12,000
Inventory	69,000	81,000
Equipment	180,000	225,000
Stock investment	45,000	75,000
Totals	$312,000	$411,000

The equipment was purchased for $240,000, and the partnership has taken $60,000 of depreciation. The stock was purchased seven years ago.

a) What are the *hot assets* [§751(a)] for this sale?

b) What is Marco's gain or loss on the sale of his partnership interest?

c) What is the character of Marco's gain or loss?

d) What are Ryan's inside and outside bases in the partnership on the date of the sale?

LO 21-1 36. Franklin, Jefferson, and Washington formed the Independence Partnership (a calendar year-end entity) by contributing cash 10 years ago. Each partner owns an equal interest in the partnership and has an outside basis in his partnership interest of $104,000. On January 1 of the current year, Franklin sells his partnership interest to Adams for a cash payment of $122,000. The partnership has the following assets and no liabilities as of the sale date:

	Tax Basis	FMV
Cash	$ 18,000	$ 18,000
Accounts receivable	0	12,000
Inventory	69,000	81,000
Equipment	180,000	225,000
Stock investment	45,000	30,000
Totals	$312,000	$366,000

The equipment was purchased for $240,000, and the partnership has taken $60,000 of depreciation. The stock was purchased seven years ago.

a) What is Franklin's overall gain or loss on the sale of his partnership interest?

b) What is the character of Franklin's gain or loss?

37. Travis and Alix Weber are equal partners in the Tralix Partnership, which does not have a §754 election in place. Alix sells one-half of her interest (25 percent) to Michael Tomei for $30,000 cash. Just before the sale, Alix's basis in her entire partnership interest is $75,000, including her $30,000 share of the partnership liabilities. Tralix's assets on the sale date are as follows:

LO 21-1

	Tax Basis	FMV
Cash	$ 40,000	$ 40,000
Inventory	30,000	90,000
Land held for investment	80,000	50,000
Totals	$150,000	$180,000

a) What is the amount and character of Alix's recognized gain or loss on the sale?

b) What is Alix's basis in her remaining partnership interest?

c) What is Michael's basis in his partnership interest?

d) What is the effect of the sale on the partnership's basis in the assets?

38. Newton is a one-third owner of ProRite Partnership. Newton has decided to sell his interest in the business to Betty for $50,000 cash plus the assumption of his share of ProRite's liabilities. Assume Newton's inside and outside bases in ProRite are equal. ProRite shows the following balance sheet as of the sale date:

LO 21-1

	Tax Basis	FMV
Assets		
Cash	$ 80,000	$ 80,000
Receivables	25,000	25,000
Inventory	40,000	85,000
Land	30,000	20,000
Totals	$175,000	$210,000
Liabilities and capital		
Liabilities	$ 60,000	
Capital—Newton	38,333	
—Barbara	38,334	
—Liz	38,333	
Totals	$175,000	

What is the amount and character of Newton's recognized gain or loss?

39. Coy and Matt are equal partners in the Matcoy Partnership. Each partner has a basis in his partnership interest of $28,000 at the end of the current year, prior to any distribution. On December 31 they each receive an operating distribution. Coy receives $10,000 cash. Matt receives $3,000 cash and a parcel of land with a $7,000 fair market value and a $4,000 basis to the partnership. Matcoy has no debt or hot assets.

LO 21-3

a) What is Coy's recognized gain or loss? What is the character of any gain or loss?

b) What is Coy's ending basis in his partnership interest?

c) What is Matt's recognized gain or loss? What is the character of any gain or loss?

d) What is Matt's basis in the distributed property?

e) What is Matt's ending basis in his partnership interest?

LO 21-3   40. Justin and Lauren are equal partners in the PJenn Partnership. The partners formed the partnership seven years ago by contributing cash. Prior to any distributions, the partners have the following bases in their partnership interests:

Partner	Outside Basis
Justin	$22,000
Lauren	22,000

On December 31 of the current year, the partnership makes a pro rata operating distribution of:

Partner	Distribution
Justin	Cash $25,000
Lauren	Cash $18,000
	Property $7,000 (FMV)
	($2,000 basis to partnership)

a) What is the amount and character of Justin's recognized gain or loss?
b) What is Justin's remaining basis in his partnership interest?
c) What is the amount and character of Lauren's recognized gain or loss?
d) What is Lauren's basis in the distributed assets?
e) What is Lauren's remaining basis in her partnership interest?

LO 21-3   41. Adam and Alyssa are equal partners in the PartiPilo Partnership. The partners formed the partnership three years ago by contributing cash. Prior to any distributions, the partners have the following bases in their partnership interests:

Partner	Outside Basis
Adam	$12,000
Alyssa	12,000

On December 31 of the current year, the partnership makes a pro rata operating distribution of:

Partner	Distribution
Adam	Cash $16,000
Alyssa	Cash $8,000
	Property $8,000 (FMV)
	($6,000 basis to partnership)

a) What is the amount and character of Adam's recognized gain or loss?
b) What is Adam's remaining basis in his partnership interest?
c) What is the amount and character of Alyssa's recognized gain or loss?
d) What is Alyssa's basis in the distributed assets?
e) What is Alyssa's remaining basis in her partnership interest?

LO 21-3   42. Karen has a $68,000 basis in her 50 percent partnership interest in the KD Partnership before receiving a current distribution of $6,000 cash and land with a fair market value of $35,000 and a basis to the partnership of $18,000.
a) What is the amount and character of Karen's recognized gain or loss?
b) What is Karen's basis in the land?
c) What is Karen's remaining basis in her partnership interest?

LO 21-3   43. Pam has a $27,000 basis (including her share of debt) in her 50 percent partnership interest in the Meddoc Partnership before receiving any distributions. This year Meddoc makes a current distribution to Pam of a parcel of land with a $40,000 fair market value and a $32,000 basis to the partnership. The land is encumbered with a $15,000 mortgage (the partnership's only liability).

a) What is the amount and character of Pam's recognized gain or loss?

b) What is Pam's basis in the land?

c) What is Pam's remaining basis in her partnership interest?

44. Two years ago, Kimberly became a 30 percent partner in the KST Partnership with a contribution of investment land with a $10,000 basis and a $16,000 fair market value. On January 2 of this year, Kimberly has a $15,000 basis in her partnership interest and none of her pre-contribution gain has been recognized. On January 2 Kimberly receives an operating distribution of a tract of land (not the contributed land) with a $12,000 basis and an $18,000 fair market value.   **LO 21-3**   **research**

a) What is the amount and character of Kimberly's recognized gain or loss on the distribution?

b) What is Kimberly's remaining basis in KST after the distribution?

c) What is KST's basis in the land Kimberly contributed after Kimberly receives this distribution?

45. Rufus is a one-quarter partner in the Adventure Partnership. On January 1 of the current year, Adventure distributes $13,000 cash to Rufus in complete liquidation of his interest. Adventure has only capital assets and no liabilities at the date of the distribution. Rufus's basis in his partnership interest is $18,500.   **LO 21-4**

a) What is the amount and character of Rufus's recognized gain or loss?

b) What is the amount and character of Adventure's recognized gain or loss?

c) If Rufus's basis is $10,000 at the distribution date rather than $18,500, what is the amount and character of Rufus's recognized gain or loss?

46. The Taurin Partnership (calendar year-end) has the following assets as of December 31 of the current year: **LO 21-4**

	Tax Basis	FMV
Cash	$ 45,000	$ 45,000
Accounts receivable	15,000	30,000
Inventory	81,000	120,000
Totals	$141,000	$195,000

On December 31, Taurin distributes $15,000 of cash, $10,000 (FMV) of accounts receivable, and $40,000 (FMV) of inventory to Emma (a one-third partner) in termination of her partnership interest. Emma's basis in her partnership interest immediately prior to the distribution is $40,000.

a) What is the amount and character of Emma's recognized gain or loss on the distribution?

b) What is Emma's basis in the distributed assets?

c) If Emma's basis before the distribution was $55,000 rather than $40,000, what is Emma's recognized gain or loss and what is her basis in the distributed assets?

47. Melissa, Nicole, and Ben are equal partners in the Opto Partnership (calendar year-end). Melissa decides she wants to exit the partnership and receives a proportionate distribution to liquidate her partnership interest on January 1. The partnership has no liabilities and holds the following assets as of January 1:   **LO 21-4**

	Tax Basis	FMV
Cash	$18,000	$18,000
Accounts receivable	0	24,000
Stock investment	7,500	12,000
Land	30,000	36,000
Totals	$55,500	$90,000

Melissa receives one-third of each of the partnership assets. She has a basis in her partnership interest of $25,000.

a) What is the amount and character of any recognized gain or loss to Melissa?

b) What is Melissa's basis in the distributed assets?

c) What are the tax implications (amount and character of gain or loss and basis of assets) to Melissa if her outside basis is $11,000 rather than $25,000?

d) What is the amount and character of any recognized gain or loss from the distribution to Opto?

48. Lonnie Davis has been a general partner in the Highland Partnership for many years and is also a sole proprietor in a separate business. To spend more time focusing on his sole proprietorship, he plans to leave Highland and will receive a liquidating distribution of $50,000 in cash and land with a fair market value of $100,000 (tax basis of $120,000). Immediately before the distribution, Lonnie's basis in his partnership interest is $350,000, which includes his $50,000 share of partnership debt. The Highland Partnership does not hold any hot assets.

a) What is the amount and character of any gain or loss to Lonnie?

b) What is Lonnie's basis in the land?

c) What is the amount and character of Lonnie's gain or loss if he holds the land for 13 months as investment property and then sells it for $100,000?

d) What is the amount and character of Lonnie's gain or loss if he places the land into service in his sole proprietorship and then sells it 13 months later for $100,000?

e) Do your answers to parts (c) and (d) suggest a course of action that would help Lonnie to achieve a more favorable tax outcome?

49. AJ is a 30 percent partner in the Trane Partnership, a calendar year-end entity. On January 1, AJ has an outside basis in his interest in Trane of $73,000, which includes his share of the $50,000 of partnership liabilities. Trane generates $42,000 of income during the year and does not make any changes to its liabilities. On December 31, Trane makes a proportionate distribution of the following assets to AJ to terminate his partnership interest:

	Tax Basis	FMV
Inventory	$55,000	$65,000
Land	30,000	25,000
Totals	$85,000	$90,000

a) What are the tax consequences (gain or loss, basis adjustments) of the distribution to Trane?

b) What is the amount and character of any recognized gain or loss to AJ?

c) What is AJ's basis in the distributed assets?

d) If AJ sells the inventory four years after the distribution for $70,000, what is the amount and character of his recognized gain or loss?

50. David's basis in the Jimsoo Partnership is $53,000. In a proportionate liquidating distribution, David receives cash of $7,000 and two capital assets: (1) land 1 with a fair market value of $20,000 and a basis to Jimsoo of $16,000, and (2) land 2 with a fair market value of $10,000 and a basis to Jimsoo of $16,000. Jimsoo has no liabilities.

a) How much gain or loss will David recognize on the distribution? What is the character of any recognized gain or loss?

b) What is David's basis in the distributed assets?

c) If the two parcels of land had been inventory to Jimsoo, what are the tax consequences to David (amount and character of gain or loss and basis in distributed assets)?

51. Megan and Matthew are equal partners in the J & J Partnership (calendar year-end entity). On January 1 of the current year, they decide to liquidate the partnership. Megan's basis in her partnership interest is $100,000 and Matthew's is $35,000. The two partners receive identical distributions, with each receiving the following assets:

LO 21-4

	Tax Basis	FMV
Cash	$30,000	$30,000
Inventory	5,000	6,000
Land	500	1,000
Totals	$35,500	$37,000

a) What is the amount and character of Megan's recognized gain or loss?

b) What is Megan's basis in the distributed assets?

c) What is the amount and character of Matthew's recognized gain or loss?

d) What is Matthew's basis in the distributed assets?

52. Bryce's basis in the Markit Partnership is $58,000. In a proportionate liquidating distribution, Bryce receives the following assets:

LO 21-4

	Tax Basis	FMV
Cash	$ 8,000	$ 8,000
Land A	20,000	45,000
Land B	20,000	25,000

a) How much gain or loss will Bryce recognize on the distribution? What is the character of any recognized gain or loss?

b) What is Bryce's basis in the distributed assets?

53. Danner Inc. has a $395,000 capital loss carryover that will expire at the end of the current tax year if it is not used. Also, Danner Inc. has been a general partner in the Talisman Partnership for three years and plans to end its involvement with the partnership by receiving a liquidating distribution. Initially, all parties agreed that Danner Inc.'s liquidating distribution would include $50,000 in cash and land with a fair market value of $400,000 (tax basis of $120,000). Immediately before the distribution, Danner's basis in its partnership interest is $150,000, which includes its $100,000 share of partnership debt. The Talisman Partnership does not hold any hot assets.

LO 21-4

a) What is the amount and character of any gain or loss to Danner Inc.?

b) What is Danner Inc.'s basis in the land?

c) Can you suggest a course of action that would help Danner Inc. avoid the expiration of its capital loss carryover?

54. Bella Partnership is an equal partnership in which each of the partners has a basis in his partnership interest of $10,000. Bella reports the following balance sheet:

LO 21-1   LO 21-5
planning

	Tax Basis	FMV
Assets		
Inventory	$20,000	$30,000
Land	10,000	15,000
Totals	$30,000	$45,000
Liabilities and capital		
Capital—Toby	$10,000	
—Kaelin	10,000	
—Andrew	10,000	
Totals	$30,000	

a) Identify the *hot assets* if Toby decides to sell his partnership interest. Are these assets "hot" for purposes of distributions?

b) If Bella distributes the land to Toby in complete liquidation of his partnership interest, what tax issues should be considered?

LO 21-1 LO 21-6 55. Michelle pays $120,000 cash for Brittany's one-third interest in the Westlake Partnership. Just prior to the sale, Brittany's basis in Westlake is $96,000. Westlake reports the following balance sheet:

	Tax Basis	FMV
Assets		
Cash	$ 96,000	$ 96,000
Land	192,000	264,000
Totals	$288,000	$360,000
Liabilities and capital		
Capital—Amy	$ 96,000	
—Brittany	96,000	
—Ben	96,000	
Totals	$288,000	

a) What is the amount and character of Brittany's recognized gain or loss on the sale?

b) What is Michelle's basis in her partnership interest? What is Michelle's inside basis?

c) If Westlake were to sell the land for $264,000 shortly after the sale of Brittany's partnership interest, how much gain or loss would the partnership recognize?

d) How much gain or loss would Michelle recognize?

e) Suppose Westlake has a §754 election in place. What is Michelle's special basis adjustment? How much gain or loss would Michelle recognize on a subsequent sale of the land in this situation?

LO 21-4 LO 21-6 56. Cliff's basis in his Aero Partnership interest is $11,000. Cliff receives a distribution of $22,000 cash from Aero in complete liquidation of his interest. Aero is an equal partnership with the following balance sheet:

	Tax Basis	FMV
Assets		
Cash	$22,000	$22,000
Investment	8,800	8,800
Land	2,200	35,200
Totals	$33,000	$66,000
Liabilities and capital		
Capital—Chris	$11,000	
—Cliff	11,000	
—Cooper	11,000	
Totals	$33,000	

a) What is the amount and character of Cliff's recognized gain or loss? What is the effect on the partnership assets?

b) If Aero has a §754 election in place, what is the amount of the special basis adjustment?

57. Erin's basis in her Kiybron Partnership interest is $3,300. Erin receives a distribution of $2,200 cash from Kiybron in complete liquidation of her interest. Kiybron is an equal partnership with the following balance sheet: **LO 21-4**   **LO 21-6**

	Tax Basis	FMV
Assets		
Cash	$2,200	$2,200
Stock (investment)	1,100	2,200
Land	6,600	2,200
Totals	$9,900	$6,600
Liabilities and capital		
Capital—Erin	$3,300	
—Carl	3,300	
—Grace	3,300	
Totals	$9,900	

a) What is the amount and character of Erin's recognized gain or loss? What is the effect on the partnership assets?

b) If Kiybron has a §754 election in place, what is the amount of the special basis adjustment?

58. Helen's basis in Haywood Partnership is $270,000. Haywood distributes all the land to Helen in complete liquidation of her partnership interest. The partnership reports the following balance sheet just before the distribution: **LO 21-4**   **LO 21-6**

	Tax Basis	FMV
Assets		
Cash	$220,000	$220,000
Stock (investment)	480,000	220,000
Land	110,000	220,000
Totals	$810,000	$660,000
Liabilities and capital		
Capital—Charles	$270,000	
—Esther	270,000	
—Helen	270,000	
Totals	$810,000	

a) What is the amount and character of Helen's recognized gain or loss? What is the effect on the partnership assets?

b) If Haywood has a §754 election in place, what is the amount of the special basis adjustment?

COMPREHENSIVE PROBLEMS

Select problems are available in Connect®.

59. Simon is a 30 percent partner in the SBD Partnership, a calendar year-end entity. As of the end of this year, Simon has an outside basis in his interest in SBD of $188,000, which includes his share of the $60,000 of partnership liabilities. On December 31, SBD makes a proportionate distribution of the following assets to Simon:

	Tax Basis	FMV
Cash	$ 40,000	$ 40,000
Inventory	55,000	65,000
Land	30,000	45,000
Totals	$125,000	$150,000

a) What are the tax consequences (amount and character of recognized gain or loss, basis in distributed assets) of the distribution to Simon if the distribution is an operating distribution?

b) What are the tax consequences (amount and character of recognized gain or loss, basis in distributed assets) of the distribution to Simon if the distribution is a liquidating distribution?

c) Compare and contrast the results from parts (a) and (b).

planning   60. Paolo is a 50 percent partner in the Capri Partnership and has decided to terminate his partnership interest. Paolo is considering two options as potential exit strategies. The first is to sell his partnership interest to the two remaining 25 percent partners, Giuseppe and Isabella, for $105,000 cash and the assumption of Paolo's share of Capri's liabilities. Under this option, Giuseppe and Isabella would each pay $52,500 for half of Paolo's interest. The second option is to have Capri liquidate Paolo's partnership interest with a proportionate distribution of the partnership assets. Paolo's basis in his partnership interest is $110,000, including Paolo's share of Capri's liabilities. Capri reports the following balance sheet as of the termination date:

	Tax Basis	FMV
Assets		
Cash	$ 80,000	$ 80,000
Receivables	40,000	40,000
Inventory	50,000	80,000
Land	50,000	60,000
Totals	$220,000	$260,000
Liabilities and capital		
Liabilities	$ 50,000	
Capital—Paolo	85,000	
—Giuseppe	42,500	
—Isabella	42,500	
Totals	$220,000	

a) If Paolo sells his partnership interest to Giuseppe and Isabella for $105,000, what is the amount and character of Paolo's recognized gain or loss?

b) Giuseppe and Isabella each have a basis in Capri of $55,000 before any purchase of Paolo's interest. What are Giuseppe's and Isabella's bases in their partnership interests following the purchase of Paolo's interest?

c) If Capri liquidates Paolo's partnership interest with a proportionate distribution of the partnership assets ($25,000 deemed cash from debt relief, $15,000 of actual cash, and half of the remaining assets), what is the amount and character of Paolo's recognized gain or loss?

d) If Capri liquidates Paolo's interest, what is Paolo's basis in the distributed assets?

e) Compare and contrast Paolo's options for terminating his partnership interest. Assume Paolo's marginal tax rate is 35 percent and his capital gains rate is 15 percent.

tax forms   61. Carrie D'Lake, Reed A. Green, and Doug A. Divot share a passion for golf and decide to go into the golf club manufacturing business together. On January 2, 2018, D'Lake, Green, and Divot form the Slicenhook Partnership, a general partnership. Slicenhook's main product will be a perimeter-weighted titanium driver with a patented graphite shaft. All three partners plan to actively participate in the business. The partners contribute the following property to form Slicenhook:

Partner	Contribution
Carrie D'Lake	Land, FMV $460,000
	Basis $460,000, Mortgage $60,000
Reed A. Green	$400,000
Doug A. Divot	$400,000

Carrie had recently acquired the land with the idea that she would contribute it to the newly formed partnership. The partners agree to share in profits and losses equally. Slicenhook elects a calendar year-end and the accrual method of accounting.

In addition, Slicenhook received a $1,500,000 recourse loan from Big Bank at the time the contributions were made. Slicenhook uses the proceeds from the loan and the cash contributions to build a state-of-the-art manufacturing facility ($1,200,000), purchase equipment ($600,000), and produce inventory ($400,000). With the remaining cash, Slicenhook invests $45,000 in the stock of a privately owned graphite research company and retains $55,000 as working cash.

Slicenhook operates on a just-in-time inventory system so it sells all inventory and collects all sales immediately. That means that at the end of the year, Slicenhook does not carry any inventory or accounts receivable balances. During 2018, Slicenhook has the following operating results:

Sales		$1,126,000
Cost of goods sold		400,000
Interest income from tax-exempt bonds		900
Qualified dividend income from stock		1,500
Operating expenses		126,000
Depreciation (tax)		
§179 on equipment	$39,000	
Equipment	81,000	
Building	24,000	144,000
Interest expense on debt		120,000

The partnership is very successful in its first year. The success allows Slicenhook to use excess cash from operations to purchase $15,000 of tax-exempt bonds (you can see the interest income already reflected in the operating results). The partnership also makes a principal payment on its loan from Big Bank in the amount of $300,000 and a distribution of $100,000 to each of the partners on December 31, 2018.

The partnership continues its success in 2019 with the following operating results:

Sales		$1,200,000
Cost of goods sold		420,000
Interest income from tax-exempt bonds		900
Qualified dividend income from stock		1,500
Operating expenses		132,000
Depreciation (tax)		
Equipment	$147,000	
Building	30,000	177,000
Interest expense on debt		96,000

The operating expenses include a $1,800 trucking fine that one of its drivers incurred for reckless driving and speeding and meals expense of $6,000.

By the end of 2019, Reed has had a falling out with Carrie and Doug and has decided to leave the partnership. He has located a potential buyer for his partnership interest, Indie Ruff. Indie has agreed to purchase Reed's interest in Slicenhook for $730,000 in cash and the assumption of Reed's share of Slicenhook's debt. Carrie and Doug, however, are not certain that admitting Indie to the partnership is such a good idea. They want to consider having Slicenhook liquidate Reed's interest on January 1, 2020. As of January 1, 2020, Slicenhook has the following assets:

	Tax Basis	FMV
Cash	$ 876,800	$ 876,800
Investment—tax exempts	15,000	18,000
Investment stock	45,000	45,000
Equipment—net of dep.	333,000	600,000
Building—net of dep.	1,146,000	1,440,000
Land	460,000	510,000
Total	$2,875,800	$3,489,800

Carrie and Doug propose that Slicenhook distribute the following to Reed in complete liquidation of his partnership interest:

	Tax Basis	FMV
Cash	$485,000	$485,000
Investment stock	45,000	45,000
Equipment—$200,000 cost, net of dep.	111,000	200,000
Total	$641,000	$730,000

Slicenhook has not purchased or sold any equipment since its original purchase just after formation.

a) Determine each partner's recognized gain or loss upon formation of Slicenhook.

b) What is each partner's initial tax basis in Slicenhook on January 2, 2018?

c) Prepare Slicenhook's opening tax basis balance sheet as of January 2, 2018.

d) Using the operating results, what are Slicenhook's ordinary income and separately stated items for 2018 and 2019? What amount of Slicenhook's income for each period would each of the partners receive?

e) Using the information provided, prepare Slicenhook's page 1 and Schedule K to be included with its Form 1065 for 2018. Also, prepare a Schedule K-1 for Carrie.

f) What are Carrie's, Reed's, and Doug's bases in their partnership interest at the end of 2018 and 2019?

g) If Reed sells his interest in Slicenhook to Indie Ruff, what is the amount and character of his recognized gain or loss? What is Indie's basis in the partnership interest?

h) What is Indie's inside basis in Slicenhook? What effect would a §754 election have on Indie's inside basis?

i) If Slicenhook distributes the assets proposed by Carrie and Doug in complete liquidation of Reed's partnership interest, what is the amount and character of Reed's recognized gain or loss? What is Reed's basis in the distributed assets?

j) Compare and contrast Reed's options for terminating his partnership interest. Assume Reed's marginal ordinary rate is 35 percent and his capital gains rate is 15 percent.

22 S Corporations

Learning Objectives

Upon completing this chapter, you should be able to:

LO 22-1 Describe the requirements and process to elect S corporation status.

LO 22-2 Explain the events that terminate the S corporation election.

LO 22-3 Describe operating issues relating to S corporation accounting periods and methods, and explain income and loss allocations and separately stated items.

LO 22-4 Explain stock-basis calculations, loss limitations, determination of self-employment income, and fringe benefit rules that apply to S corporation shareholders.

LO 22-5 Apply the tax rules for S corporation operating distributions and liquidating distributions.

LO 22-6 Describe the taxes that apply to S corporations, estimated tax requirements, and tax return filing requirements.

©PhotoAlto/MediaBakery

Storyline Summary

Taxpayers: Nicole Johnson, Sarah Walker, and Chance Armstrong

Location: Salt Lake City, Utah

Status: Shareholders of newly formed Color Comfort Sheets Inc. (CCS)

Situation: Formed CCS as a corporation and have elected to have the entity taxed as an S corporation.

I n the Entities Overview chapter, we met Nicole Johnson, who turned her sheet-making hobby into a full-time business called Color Comfort Sheets (CCS). In this chapter, we assume Nicole formed CCS as a corporation, intending to elect S corporation tax status.

When starting the business, Nicole had cash to contribute to CCS but not enough to meet initial needs. She convinced her friend Sarah Walker to invest in CCS and fortunately, after listening to Nicole and Sarah's proposal, local sports team owner Chance Armstrong also agreed to invest.

Nicole and Sarah would take an active role in managing CCS; Chance would not. Nicole contributed a parcel of land and cash in exchange for one-third of CCS's stock. Sarah and Chance each contributed cash for one-third of the stock. With funding in place, CCS began operating on January 1, 2017. However, with the excitement (and turmoil) of starting the new business, it took Nicole, Sarah, and Chance a while to talk with their accountant about electing S corporation status. After several discussions, they filed their S election on May 1, 2017. ■

In this chapter, we discuss the tax and nontax characteristics of an **S corporation,** a hybrid entity that shares some characteristics with C corporations and some with partnerships.[1] S corporations are incorporated under state law and thus have the same legal protections as C corporations. They are governed by the same corporate tax rules that apply in the organization, liquidation, and reorganization of C corporations. However, unlike a C corporation, an S corporation is a flow-through entity and shares many tax similarities with partnerships. For example, basis calculations for S corporation shareholders and partners are similar, the income or loss of an S corporation flows through to its owners, and distributions are generally not taxed to the extent of the owner's basis.

Throughout this chapter, we highlight the tax similarities between S corporations and C corporations and between S corporations and partnerships, while focusing on the unique rules that apply to S corporations. These rules are more complex for S corporations that were once C corporations with previously undistributed **earnings and profits (E&P).**

LO 22-1 S CORPORATION ELECTIONS

Formations

The same rules for forming and contributing property govern S and C corporations. As discussed in the Corporate Formation, Reorganization, and Liquidation chapter, §351 and related provisions apply when one or more persons transfer property to a corporation (C or S) in return for stock, and immediately after the transfer, these persons control the corporation. These rules allow shareholders meeting the requirements to defer gains they realize when they transfer appreciated property to the corporation in exchange for stock. Note that similar rules apply to formations and property contributions to partnerships under §721. One important difference, however, is that partnership tax rules do not impose a control requirement to defer gains (see the Forming and Operating Partnerships chapter for partnership contributions).

S Corporation Qualification Requirements

Unlike C corporations and partnerships, S corporations are limited as to type and number of owners (shareholders).[2] Only U.S. citizens or residents, estates, certain trusts, and certain tax-exempt organizations may be shareholders. No corporations or partnerships can be shareholders.[3] S corporations may have no more than 100 shareholders; family members and their estates count as one shareholder. Family members include a common ancestor (not more than six generations removed) and her lineal descendants and their spouses (or former spouses).[4] Under this broad definition, great-grandparents, grandparents, parents, children, brothers and sisters, grandchildren, great-grandchildren, aunts, uncles, cousins, and the respective spouses are family members for this purpose. A practical implication of these limits is that large, publicly traded corporations cannot elect to be treated as S corporations.

---

[1]S Corporations get their name from Subchapter S of the Internal Revenue Code, which includes code sections 1361–1379.

[2]§1361.

[3]Grantor trusts, qualified Subchapter S trusts, electing small business trusts, certain testamentary trusts, and voting trusts can own S corporation stock. A discussion of these trusts is beyond the scope of this chapter. Eligible tax-exempt shareholders include qualified retirement plan trusts or charitable, religious, educational, etc., organizations that are tax-exempt under §501.

[4]The common ancestor (living or not, owning shares or not) must not be more than six generations removed from the youngest generation of shareholder family members determined at the later of the S corporation election date or the date the first member of the respective family holds the S corporation's stock.

Example 22-1

What if: Suppose CCS was formed with Nicole Johnson, Sarah Walker, and Chanzz Inc., a corporation owned by Chance Armstrong, as shareholders. Would CCS be eligible to elect S corporation status?

Answer: No. Because one of its shareholders is a corporation (Chanzz Inc.), CCS would not be eligible to elect S corporation status.

What if: Suppose Nicole, Sarah, and Chance recruited 97 U.S. residents to become shareholders of CCS. Meanwhile, Nicole gave several of her CCS shares to her grandfather and his bride as a wedding gift and to her first cousin as an MBA graduation gift. After the transfer, CCS had 103 shareholders. Can CCS elect S corporation status?

Answer: Yes. Nicole (descendant of common ancestor), her first cousin (descendant of common ancestor), her grandfather (common ancestor), and her grandfather's wife (spouse of common ancestor) are treated as *one* shareholder for purposes of the 100-shareholder limit.

S Corporation Election

An eligible corporation must make an affirmative election to be treated as an S corporation.[5] In addition to meeting the shareholder requirements above, it must:

- Be a domestic corporation (created or organized in the United States or under U.S. law or the law of any state in the United States).
- Not be a specifically identified ineligible corporation.[6]
- Have only one class of stock.

A corporation is considered to have only one class of stock if all its outstanding shares provide identical distribution and liquidation rights. Differences in voting powers are permissible. In general, debt instruments do not violate the single class of stock requirement unless they are treated as equity elsewhere under the tax law.[7] In addition, §1361 provides safe-harbor rules to ensure that debt obligations are not recharacterized as a second class of stock.[8]

> **THE KEY FACTS**
>
> **S Corporation Election**
>
> - An eligible corporation must make an affirmative election to be treated as an S corporation.
> - Eligible corporations meet the type and number of shareholder requirements, are domestic corporations, are not specifically identified as ineligible corporations, and have only one class of stock.
> - To elect S corporation status, the corporation makes a formal election using Form 2553.

Example 22-2

What if: Suppose Nicole were a resident of Toronto, Canada, and while she formed CCS in Canada under Canadian law, she still planned to do business in the United States. Is CCS eligible to elect S corporation status in the United States?

Answer: No. CCS would not be eligible for S corporation treatment because it was neither organized in the United States nor formed under U.S. laws.

What if: Suppose Nicole resided in Seattle and formed CCS under the state laws of Washington but planned to do a significant amount of business in Canada. Would CCS be eligible to elect S corporation status?

Answer: Yes, because CCS was formed under the laws of a U.S. state.

---

[5]§1362(a).

[6]Ineligible corporations include financial institutions using the reserve method of accounting under §585, insurance companies, corporations allowed a tax credit for income from Puerto Rico and from U.S. possessions under §936, corporations previously electing Domestic International Sales Corporation status, and corporations treated as a taxable mortgage pool.

[7]See §385 for factors considered in determining whether debt should be considered as equity for tax purposes.

[8]§1361(c)(5)(A) provides that straight debt issued during an S corporation year (i.e., not during a C corporation year) will not be treated as a second class of stock. §1361(c)(5)(A) defines straight debt as debt characterized by a written unconditional promise to pay on demand or on a specified date a sum certain in money if (1) the interest rate and interest payment dates are not contingent on profits, the borrower's discretion, or similar factors; (2) the debt is not convertible into stock; and (3) the creditor is an individual (other than a nonresident alien), an estate, a qualified trust, or a person who is actively and regularly engaged in the business of lending money.

To formally elect S corporation status effective as of the beginning of the current tax year, the corporation uses **Form 2553,** either in the prior tax year or on or before the 15th day of the third month of the current tax year.[9] Elections made after the 15th day of the third month of a year are effective at the beginning of the following year. All shareholders on the date of the election must consent to the election.

Example 22-3

What if: Suppose Nicole formed CCS as a C corporation in 2017 with a calendar tax year and finally got around to electing S corporation status on February 20, 2018. What is the earliest effective date of the S election?

Answer: January 1, 2018.

What if: Suppose Nicole formed CCS as a C corporation in 2017 with a calendar tax year and made the S election on March 20, 2018. When is the S election effective?

Answer: It is effective January 1, 2019, because Nicole made the election after March 15, 2018.

Even when the corporation makes the election on or before the 15th day of the third month of its tax year, the election will not be effective until the subsequent year if (1) the corporation did not meet the S corporation requirements for each day of the current tax year before it made the S election, or (2) one or more shareholders who held the stock in the corporation during the current year and before the S corporation election was made did not consent to the election (e.g., a shareholder disposes of his stock in the corporation in the election year before the election is made and fails to consent to the S election).[10]

Example 22-4

What if: Suppose in 2017 Nicole formed CCS as a C corporation (calendar tax year) with Nicole, Sarah, and Chanzz Inc. (a corporation) as shareholders. On January 2, 2018, Chanzz Inc. sold all its shares to Chance Armstrong. On January 31, 2018, CCS filed an S corporation election, with Nicole, Sarah, and Chance all consenting to the election. What is the earliest effective date of the S election?

Answer: January 1, 2019. Because CCS had an ineligible shareholder (Chanzz Inc.) during 2018, the election is not effective until the beginning of 2019.

What if: Suppose in 2017 Nicole formed CCS as a C corporation (calendar tax year) with Nicole, Sarah, and Chance as shareholders. On January 30, 2018, Chance sold his shares to Nicole. On February 15, 2018, CCS filed an S election, with Nicole and Sarah consenting to the election. Chance, however, did not consent to the election. What is the earliest effective date of the S election?

Answer: January 1, 2019. Because Chance was a shareholder until January 30, 2018, and he did not consent to the S election in 2018, the S election is not effective until the beginning of 2019, the year after the election.

The timing of the election may be especially important for C corporations with net operating losses. The reason: Net operating losses attributable to C corporation years generally cannot be carried over to the S corporation. Thus, it may be beneficial to delay the S election until the corporation has utilized its net operating losses.[11]

---

[9]§1362(b). When the IRS determines that taxpayers have reasonable cause for making late elections, it has the authority to treat late elections as timely [§1362(b)(5)]. Rev. Proc. 2013-30 provides a simplified method to provide relief for late elections by submitting Form 2553 to the IRS with a statement that explains (a) that there was either reasonable cause for the late election or the late election was inadvertent and (b) that the taxpayer acted diligently to correct the mistake upon discovery.

[10]Source: §1362(b)(2). Requiring all shareholders who own stock in an S corporation during the year to consent to the election ensures that shareholders who dispose of their stock before the election do not suffer adverse tax consequences from an election to which they did not consent.

[11]Later in this chapter we discuss one exception to the rule that disallows net operating loss carryovers from C corporation to S corporation years. See the discussion of the S corporation built-in gains tax.

S CORPORATION TERMINATIONS

LO 22-2

Once the S election becomes effective, the corporation remains an S corporation until the election is terminated. The termination may be voluntary or involuntary.

Voluntary Terminations

The corporation can make a *voluntary revocation* of the S election if shareholders holding more than 50 percent of the S corporation stock (including nonvoting shares) agree.[12] The corporation files a statement with the IRS revoking the election made under §1362(a) and stating the effective date of the revocation and the number of shares issued and outstanding. In general, voluntary revocations made on or before the 15th day of the third month of the year are effective as of the beginning of the year. A revocation after this period is effective the first day of the following tax year. Alternatively, a corporation may specify the termination date as long as the date specified is on or after the date the revocation is made.[13]

> **THE KEY FACTS**
>
> **S Corporation Qualification Requirements**
>
> - Only U.S. citizens or residents, estates, certain trusts, and certain tax-exempt organizations may be S corporation shareholders.
> - S corporations may have no more than 100 shareholders.
> - For purposes of the 100-shareholder limit, family members and their estates count as only one shareholder.

Example 22-5

What if: Suppose CCS had been initially formed as an S corporation with a calendar year-end. After a couple of years, things were going so well that Nicole and Sarah (each one-third shareholders) wanted to terminate the S election and take CCS public. However, Chance (also a one-third shareholder) was opposed to the S election termination. Can Nicole and Sarah terminate the S election without Chance's consent?

Answer: Yes. To revoke the election, Nicole and Sarah need to own more than 50 percent of the shares, and together they own 66.7 percent.

What if: If Nicole and Sarah file the revocation on February 15, 2019, what is the effective date of the S corporation termination (assuming they do not specify one)?

Answer: January 1, 2019. If they file the S corporation revocation after March 15, 2019, it becomes effective January 1, 2020. Alternatively, CCS could have specified an effective date of the S corporation's termination (in 2019 or after) as long as it was on or after the date the revocation was made.

ETHICS

Suppose Chance Armstrong is a U.S. resident but a French citizen. His mother has recently been diagnosed with a terminal illness, and Chance has decided to move back to France to take care of his mother and her affairs. He anticipates that he will live in France for several years and that he will no longer be considered a U.S. resident. If you were Sarah or Nicole, how would you react to Chance's decision to move? Would you ignore the impact it may have on CCS's S corporation status? Would you pressure Chance to sell his CCS stock to you?

Involuntary Terminations

Involuntary terminations can result from failure to meet requirements (by far the most common reason) or from an excess of passive investment income.

Failure to Meet Requirements   A corporation's S election is automatically terminated if the corporation fails to meet the requirements. The termination is effective on the date it fails the S corporation requirements. If the IRS deems the termination inadvertent, it may allow the corporation to continue to be treated as an S corporation if, within a reasonable period after the inadvertent termination, the corporation takes the necessary steps to meet the S corporation requirements.[14]

---

[12]§1362(d)(1)(B).

[13]§1362(d)(1)(D).

[14]§1362(f). Because the restrictions on S corporation ownership are so specific and exact, many S corporations require their shareholders, as a condition of stock ownership, to enter into a shareholder's agreement. These agreements generally restrict the ability of a shareholder to transfer her stock ownership to any disqualified shareholder.

What if: Suppose CCS was formed as a calendar-year S corporation with Nicole Johnson, Sarah Walker, and Chance Armstrong as equal shareholders. On June 15, 2018, Chance sold his CCS shares to his solely owned C corporation, Chanzz Inc. Is CCS's S election still in effect at the beginning of 2019? If not, when was it terminated?

Answer: No, the election was automatically terminated on June 15, 2018, when Chanzz Inc. became a shareholder because S corporations may not have corporate shareholders.

Excess of Passive Investment Income   If an S corporation has *earnings and profits* from a previous C corporation year (or through a reorganization with a corporation that has earnings and profits), its election is terminated if the S corporation has passive investment income in excess of 25 percent of gross receipts for three consecutive years. If the S corporation never operated as a C corporation or does not have C corporation earnings and profits (either by prior distribution of C corporation earnings and profits, or simply by not having earnings and profits at the effective date of the S election), this provision does not apply.

For purposes of the passive investment income test, **gross receipts** is the total amount of revenues received [including net capital gains from the sale of capital assets and gain (not offset by losses) from the sale of stock and securities] or accrued under the corporation's accounting method, *not* reduced by returns, allowances, cost of goods sold, or deductions. **Passive investment income (PII)** includes gross receipts from royalties, rents, dividends, interest (including tax-exempt interest), and annuities.[15] While net capital gain income is included in gross receipts, it is *not* considered passive investment income. S corporation election terminations due to excess passive investment income are effective on the first day of the year following the third consecutive tax year with excess passive investment income.

What if: Suppose CCS was initially formed as an S corporation with a calendar year-end. During its first three years, it reported passive investment income in excess of 25 percent of its gross receipts. Is CCS's S election terminated under the excess passive investment income test? If so, what is the effective date of the termination?

Answer: No, the excess passive investment income test does not apply to CCS in this situation because CCS has never operated as a C corporation; consequently, it does not have C corporation earnings and profits.

What if: Suppose CCS was initially formed as a C corporation with a calendar year-end. After its first year of operations (very profitable), CCS elected S corporation status, effective January 1, 2018. During 2019, 2020, and 2021, it reported passive investment income in excess of 25 percent of its gross receipts and had undistributed earnings and profits from its C corporation year. Is CCS's S election terminated under the excess passive investment income test? If so, what is the effective date of the termination?

Answer: Yes, it is terminated. Because CCS has C corporation earnings and profits from 2017 and excess passive investment income for three consecutive years as an S corporation, its S election is terminated, effective January 1, 2022.

Short Tax Years

S corporation election terminations frequently create an S corporation *short tax year* (a reporting year less than 12 months) and a C corporation short tax year. The corporation must then allocate its income for the full year between the S and the C corporation years, using the number of days in each short year (the daily method). Or it may use the

---

[15]PII excludes certain rents (e.g., rents derived from the active trade or business of renting property, produced film rents, income from leasing self-produced tangible property, temporary parking fees, etc.).

corporation's normal accounting rules to allocate income to the actual period in which it was earned (the specific identification method).[16] Both short tax year returns are due on the corporation's customary tax return due date (with normal extensions available).

Example 22-8

What if: Suppose CCS was formed as a calendar-year S corporation with Nicole Johnson, Sarah Walker, and Chance Armstrong as equal shareholders. On June 15, 2018, Chance sold his CCS shares (one-third of all shares) to his solely owned C corporation, Chanzz Inc.; terminating CCS's S election on June 15, 2018. Assume CCS reported the following business income for 2018:

Period	Income
January 1 through June 14 (165 days)	$100,000
June 15 through December 31 (200 days)	265,000
January 1 through December 31, 2018 (365 days)	$365,000

If CCS uses the daily method of allocating income between the S corporation short tax year (January 1–June 14) and the C corporation short tax year (June 15–December 31), how much income will it report on its S corporation short tax year return and its C corporation short tax year return for 2018?

Answer: S corporation short tax year = $165,000 ($365,000/365 days × 165 days); C corporation short tax year = $200,000 ($365,000/365 days × 200 days).

What if: If CCS uses the specific identification method to allocate income, how much will it allocate to the S corporation short tax year and how much will it allocate to the C corporation short tax year?

Answer: S corporation short tax year, $100,000; C corporation short tax year, $265,000.

Note that if the entity wanted to minimize the income subject to taxation as a C corporation, it would use the daily method of allocating income.

S Corporation Reelections

After terminating or voluntarily revoking S corporation status, the corporation may elect it again, but it generally must wait until the beginning of the fifth tax year *after* the tax year in which it terminated the election.[17] Thus, if the election was terminated effective the first day of the tax year, the corporation must wait five full years to again become an S corporation.

Example 22-9

What if: Let's return to the facts of the previous example. CCS was formed as a calendar-year S corporation with Nicole Johnson, Sarah Walker, and Chance Armstrong as equal shareholders. On June 15, 2018, Chance sold his CCS shares (one-third of all shares) to his solely owned C corporation, Chanzz Inc., terminating CCS's S election on June 15, 2018. Absent permission from the IRS (see text below), what is the earliest date CCS may again elect to be taxed as an S corporation?

Answer: January 1, 2023. This is the fifth tax year after the year in which the termination became effective.

What if: Assume on February 1, 2018, CCS voluntarily elected to revoke its S corporation status effective January 1, 2019. Absent IRS permission, what is the earliest CCS may again elect to be taxed as an S corporation?

Answer: January 1, 2024. This is the fifth year after the year in which the termination became effective.

THE KEY FACTS

S Corporation Terminations and Reelections

- The S election may be revoked by shareholders holding more than 50 percent of the S corporation's stock (including nonvoting shares).
- A corporation's S election is automatically terminated if (1) the S corporation fails to meet the S corporation requirements, or (2) the S corporation has earnings and profits from a previous C corporation year and has passive investment income in excess of 25 percent of gross receipts for three consecutive years.
- A corporation losing its S corporation status must wait until the beginning of the fifth year after the election is terminated to elect S corporation status again.

---

[16]Use of the specific identification method requires that all shareholders at any time during the S corporation short year and the shareholders on the first day of the C corporation short year consent to the election using the specific identification method [§1362(e)(3)(A)]. However, an S corporation must use the specific identification method to allocate income between the short years (the per day allocation method is not allowed) if there is a sale or exchange of 50 percent or more of the corporation's stock during the year [§1362(e)(6)(D)].

[17]§1362(g).

The IRS may consent to an earlier election under a couple of conditions: (1) if the corporation is now more than 50 percent owned by shareholders who were not owners at the time of termination, or (2) if the termination was not reasonably within the control of the corporation or shareholders with a substantial interest in the corporation and was not part of a planned termination by the corporation or shareholders. Given the potential adverse consequences of an S election termination, the corporation should carefully monitor compliance with the S corporation requirements.

LO 22-3

OPERATING ISSUES

Accounting Methods and Periods

Like partnerships, S corporations determine their accounting periods and make accounting method elections at the entity level. An S corporation makes most of its elections (like electing out of bonus depreciation) in conjunction with the filing of its annual tax return and some by filing a separate request with the IRS. (For example, an application to change accounting methods is filed on Form 3115, separate from the S corporation's tax return.) For an S corporation previously operating as a C corporation, all prior accounting methods carry over to the S corporation.

Recall that both C corporations and partnerships face restrictions on using the cash method. S corporations do not. They may choose the cash, accrual, or hybrid method unless selling inventory is a material income-producing factor for them. In that case they must account for gross profit (sales minus cost of goods sold) using the accrual method, even if they are otherwise cash-method taxpayers. Hence, they would use the hybrid method.

Tax laws also specify permissible tax years for S corporations, but they are a little less cumbersome than for partnerships. S corporations must use a calendar year-end unless they can establish a business purpose for an alternative year-end or a natural business year-end. (For example, a business that receives 25 percent or more of gross receipts for the previous three years in the last two months of the year-end requested would qualify for a noncalendar year-end.)[18]

Income and Loss Allocations

S corporations, like partnerships, are flow-through entities, and thus their profits and losses flow through to their shareholders annually for tax purposes. As we discussed in the Forming and Operating Partnerships chapter, partnerships have considerable flexibility in making special profit and loss allocations to their partners. In contrast, S corporations must allocate profits and losses pro rata, based on the number of outstanding shares each shareholder owns on each day of the tax year.[19]

An S corporation generally allocates income or loss items to shareholders on the last day of its tax year.[20] If a shareholder sells her shares during the year, she will report her share of S corporation income and loss allocated to the days she owned the stock (including the day of sale) using a pro rata allocation. If *all shareholders with changing ownership percentages* during the year agree, the S corporation can instead use its normal accounting rules to allocate income and loss (and other separately stated items, discussed below) to the specific periods in which it realized income and losses.

THE KEY FACTS

Operating Issues

- S corporations are generally required to adopt a calendar tax year.
- S corporations allocate profits and losses to shareholders pro rata, based on the number of outstanding shares each shareholder owns on each day of the tax year.
- S corporations determine each shareholder's share of ordinary business income (loss) and separately stated items.
- Ordinary business income (loss) is all income (loss) exclusive of any separately stated items of income (loss). Separately stated items are tax items that are treated differently than a shareholder's share of ordinary business income (loss) for tax purposes.

Example 22-10

What if: Assume CCS was formed as a calendar-year S corporation with Nicole Johnson, Sarah Walker, and Chance Armstrong as equal (one-third) shareholders. On June 14, 2018, Chance sold his CCS shares to Nicole. CCS reported the following business income for 2018:

---

[18]§1378(b). In addition, S corporations, like partnerships, have the option of electing an alternative taxable year under §444.

[19]§1366(a), §1377(a).

[20]§1366(a).

Period	Income
January 1 through June 14 (165 days)	$100,000
June 15 through December 31 (200 days)	265,000
January 1 through December 31, 2018 (365 days)	$365,000

How much 2018 income is allocated to each shareholder if CCS uses the daily method of allocating income?

Answer: Nicole's allocation is $188,333; Sarah's is $121,667; and Chance's is $55,000, calculated as follows.

	(1) January 1–June 14	(2) June 15–December 31	(1) + (2) Total 2018 Allocation
Nicole	$55,000 ($365,000/365 × 165 × 1/3)	$133,333 ($365,000/365 × 200 × 2/3)	$188,333
Sarah	$55,000 ($365,000/365 × 165 × 1/3)	$66,667 ($365,000/365 × 200 × 1/3)	121,667
Chance	$55,000 ($365,000/365 × 165 × 1/3)	$0	55,000
Totals	$165,000	$200,000	$365,000

How much 2018 income is allocated to each shareholder if CCS uses its normal accounting rules to allocate income to the specific periods in which it was actually earned?

Answer: Nicole's allocation is $210,000 ($100,000 × 1/3 + $265,000 × 2/3); Sarah's is $121,667 ($365,000 × 1/3); and Chance's is $33,333 ($100,000 × 1/3).

Separately Stated Items

Like partnerships, S corporations are required to file tax returns (Form 1120S) annually. In addition, on Form 1120S, Schedule K-1, they supply information to each shareholder detailing the amount *and* character of items of income and loss flowing through the S corporation.[21] Shareholders must report these income and loss items on their tax returns even if they do not receive cash distributions during the year.

S corporations determine each shareholder's share of ordinary business income (loss) and separately stated items. Like partnerships, **ordinary business income (loss)** (also referred to as *nonseparately stated income or loss*) is all income (loss) exclusive of any separately stated items of income (loss). **Separately stated items** are tax items that are treated differently from a shareholder's share of ordinary business income (loss) for tax purposes. The character of each separately stated item is determined at the S corporation level rather than at the shareholder level. The list of common separately stated items for S corporations is similar to that for partnerships, with a couple of exceptions. (For example, S corporations do not report self-employment income and do not have guaranteed payments.) Exhibit 22-1 lists several common separately stated items. See Form 1120S, Schedule K-1 (and related instructions) for a comprehensive list of separately stated items.[22] Similar to partners in a partnership, S corporation shareholders are allowed a 20 percent deduction for qualified business income, calculated and subject to limitations at the shareholder level. See the Entities Overview chapter for a discussion of the deduction. Informational items related

---

[21]Other items, such as tax credits and informational items such as AMT adjustments, also flow through from the S corporation to its shareholders and are reported to shareholders on Form 1120S, Schedule K-1.

[22]Similar to partnerships, S corporations with average annual gross receipts for the prior three years that exceed $25 million are subject to the 30 percent of taxable income limitation on the deduction for business interest expense. The limitation applies at the S corporation level. In years where the adjusted taxable income limitation is binding, the S corporation's excess business interest is allocated to its shareholders as a separately stated item. Shareholders then carry forward their share of excess business interest expense and deduct it when they are allocated a share of the S corportion's excess adjusted taxable income limitation in later years when the adjusted taxable income imitation is not binding.

EXHIBIT 22-1 **Common Separately Stated Items**

- Short-term capital gains and losses
- Long-term capital gains and losses
- Section 1231 gains and losses
- Dividends
- Interest income
- Charitable contributions
- Tax-exempt income
- Net rental real estate income
- Investment interest expense
- Section 179 deduction
- Foreign taxes
- Qualified business income, allocated wages, and unadjusted basis of qualified property

to the deduction calculation [e.g., qualified business income, W-2 wages paid by the S corporation (including owner's compensation), and unadjusted basis of qualified property] are reported to shareholders on Form 1120S, Schedule K-1.

S corporations may hold stock in C corporations, and any dividends S corporations receive will flow through to their shareholders. However, S corporations are not entitled to claim the dividends received deduction (see the Corporate Operations chapter for a discussion of the dividends received deduction).

Assuming CCS operated as a C corporation in 2017 and an S corporation in 2018, Exhibit 22-2 presents the results of operations. CCS's S election was not effective until January 1, 2018, because the shareholders filed the S election after the required date for it to be effective in 2017.

EXHIBIT 22-2

Color Comfort Sheets Income Statement December 31, 2017 and 2018		
	2017, C Corporation	**2018, S Corporation**
Sales revenue	$220,000	$ 520,000
Cost of goods sold	(50,000)	(115,000)
Salary to owners Nicole and Sarah	(70,000)	(90,000)
Employee wages	(45,000)	(50,000)
Depreciation expense	(15,000)	(20,000)
Miscellaneous expenses	(4,000)	(5,000)
Interest income (from investments)	3,000	6,000
Dividend income	1,000	3,000
Overall net income	$ 40,000	$ 249,000

Example 22-11

Assume CCS was a C corporation for tax purposes in 2017 and an S corporation in 2018. Based on its operating results in Exhibit 22-2, what amounts of ordinary business income and separately stated items are allocated to CCS's shareholders for 2017?

Answer: $0 ordinary business income and $0 separately stated items. Because CCS is a C corporation in 2017, its income does *not* flow through to its shareholders.

Based on the information in Exhibit 22-2, what amounts of ordinary business income and separately stated items are allocated to CCS's shareholders for 2018? Assume CCS has qualified property with an unadjusted basis of $300,000 for purposes of the deduction for qualified business income.

Answer: See the following table for the allocations:

Description	CCS	Nicole 1/3	Sarah 1/3	Chance 1/3
		Allocations		
2018 overall net income Less:	$249,000			
Dividends	3,000			
Interest income	6,000			
Ordinary business income	240,000	**$80,000**	**$80,000**	**$80,000**
Separately Stated Items:				
Interest income	6,000	**2,000**	**2,000**	**2,000**
Dividends	3,000	**1,000**	**1,000**	**1,000**
Qualified Business Income				
Informational Items:				
Qualified business income	240,000	80,000	80,000	80,000
Allocated wages	140,000	46,667	46,667	46,666
Unadjusted basis of qualified property	300,000	100,000	100,000	100,000

Nicole, Sarah, and Chance will treat their shares of CCS's ordinary business income as *ordinary* income and include it, along with their shares of interest and dividend income, in their individual tax returns for the year.[23] Qualified business income does not include interest income because it was not allocable to the trade or business. Allocated wages include the $50,000 wages paid to employees and $90,000 wages paid to owners.

SHAREHOLDER'S BASIS

LO 22-4

Just as partners must determine their bases in their partnership interests, S corporation shareholders must determine their bases in the S corporation stock to determine the gain or loss they recognize when they sell the stock, the taxability of distributions, and the deductibility of losses.

Initial Basis   An S corporation shareholder calculates his or her *initial basis* upon formation of the corporation, like a C corporation shareholder. (See the Corporate Formation, Reorganization, and Liquidation chapter for a review.) Specifically, the shareholder's basis in stock received in the exchange equals the tax basis of the property transferred, less any liabilities assumed by the corporation on the property contributed (*substituted basis*). The shareholder's stock basis is increased by any gain recognized; it is reduced by the fair market value of any property received other than stock.[24] If, on the other hand, the shareholder purchased the S corporation stock from another shareholder or the corporation, the new shareholder's basis is simply the purchase price of the stock.[25]

Example 22-12

At the beginning of 2017, Nicole contributed $30,000 of cash and land with a fair market value of $130,000 and an adjusted basis of $125,000 to CCS. The land was encumbered by a $40,000 mortgage executed three years before. Sarah and Chance each contributed $120,000 of cash to CCS. What tax bases do Nicole, Sarah, and Chance have in their CCS stock at the beginning of 2017?

Answer: Nicole's basis is $115,000 ($30,000 cash + $125,000 adjusted basis of land − $40,000 mortgage assumed); Sarah's basis is $120,000; and Chance's basis is $120,000.

[23]Nicole, Sarah, and Chance would report their share of ordinary business income on Schedule E and their share of interest and dividend income on Schedule B of Form 1040.

[24]§358. This assumes the shareholder meets the §351 requirements. If the shareholder's exchange with the corporation does not meet these requirements, the shareholder's basis in the stock is its fair market value.

[25]If the shareholder acquires the stock by gift, her basis in the stock is the lesser of the donor's basis (increased for any gift taxes paid on the stock's appreciation) or the fair market value of the stock. In contrast, if the shareholder acquires the stock by bequest, her basis in the stock is the stock's fair market value on the date of the decedent's death adjusted to reflect any income in respect of the decedent.

Annual Basis Adjustments   While C corporation rules govern the initial stock basis of an S corporation shareholder, subsequent calculations more closely resemble the partnership rules. Specifically, an S corporation shareholder's stock basis is dynamic and must be *adjusted* annually to ensure that (1) taxable income/gains and deductible expenses/losses are *not* double-counted by shareholders either when they sell their shares or when they receive S corporation distributions (for example, because shareholders are taxed on the S corporation's income annually, they should not be taxed again when they receive distributions of the income) and (2) tax-exempt income and nondeductible expenses are not ultimately taxed or deducted.

S corporation shareholders make the following adjustments to their stock basis annually, in the order listed:

- Increase for any contributions to the S corporation during the year.
- Increase for shareholder's share of ordinary business income and separately stated income/gain items (including tax-exempt income).
- Decrease for distributions during the year.
- Decrease for shareholder's share of nondeductible expenses (fines, penalties).
- Decrease for shareholder's share of ordinary business loss and separately stated expense/loss items.[26]

As with a partnership, adjustments that decrease basis may never reduce an S corporation shareholder's tax basis below zero.[27]

S corporation shareholders are not allowed to include any S corporation debt in their stock basis. Recall that partners *are* allowed to include their share of partnership debt in their basis. One implication of this difference is that, everything else equal, an S corporation shareholder's basis will be lower than a partner's basis, due to the exclusion of debt (however, see the discussion of *debt basis* for S corporation shareholders below).

THE KEY FACTS

S Corporation Shareholder's Basis Adjustments

- A shareholder will *increase* the tax basis in his or her stock for:
  - Contributions.
  - Share of ordinary business income.
  - Separately stated income/gain items.
  - Tax-exempt income.
- A shareholder will *decrease* the tax basis in his or her stock for:
  - Cash distributions.
  - Share of nondeductible expenses.
  - Share of ordinary business loss.
  - Separately stated expense/loss items.
  - A shareholder's tax basis may not be negative.

Example 22-13

Given the shareholders' 2017 bases in their CCS stock from the previous example (Nicole, $115,000; Sarah, $120,000; and Chance, $120,000), what basis does each have at the end of 2018, after taking into account the information in Exhibit 22-2 (but before taking into account any distributions, which are discussed below)?

Answer: Nicole, $198,000; Sarah, $203,000; and Chance, $203,000, computed as follows:

Description	Nicole	Sarah	Chance	Explanation
(1) Initial tax basis	$115,000	$120,000	$120,000	Example 22-12
(2) Ordinary business income	80,000	80,000	80,000	Example 22-11
(3) Interest income	2,000	2,000	2,000	Example 22-11
(4) Dividends	1,000	1,000	1,000	Example 22-11
Tax basis in stock at end of 2018	**$198,000**	**$203,000**	**$203,000**	(1) + (2) + (3) + (4)

Note the shareholders do not include any portion of CCS's debt in their stock basis.

What if: Suppose that, in addition to the amounts in Exhibit 22-2, CCS also recognized $1,200 of tax-exempt interest income in 2018. Nicole's share of this separately stated item is $400. Taking this allocation into account, what is Nicole's stock basis at the end of 2018?

Answer: It is $198,400 ($198,000 + $400). The tax-exempt income allocated to Nicole as a separately stated item increases her tax basis to ensure that she is never taxed on her share of the tax-exempt income.

---

[26]Reg. §1.1367-1(g) allows a shareholder to elect to decrease basis by ordinary business losses and separately stated expense/loss items before decreasing basis by nondeductible expenses by attaching a statement to the shareholder's tax return. This election is advantageous because loss/expense deductions are limited to a shareholder's basis, and this election results in a higher basis limitation for deductible loss/expense items.

[27]§1367(a)(2).

Loss Limitations

S corporations have loss-limitation rules similar to those for partnerships. For an S corporation shareholder to deduct it, a loss must clear three separate hurdles: (1) tax-basis, (2) at-risk amount, and (3) passive activity.[28] In addition, for losses that clear each of the three hurdles, S corporation shareholders are not allowed to deduct excess business losses as described below.

Tax-Basis Limitation   S corporation shareholders may not deduct losses in excess of their stock basis. Recall they are not allowed to include debt in their basis; partners are. This restriction makes it more likely that the tax-basis limitation will apply to S corporation shareholders than to similarly situated partners. Losses not deductible due to the tax-basis limitation are not necessarily lost. Rather, they are suspended until the shareholder generates additional basis. The carryover period for the suspended loss is indefinite. However, if the shareholder sells the stock before creating additional basis, the suspended loss disappears unused.

Example 22-14

What if: Suppose at the beginning of 2019, Nicole's basis in her CCS stock was $14,000. During 2019, CCS reported a $60,000 ordinary business loss and no separately stated items. How much of the ordinary loss is allocated to Nicole?

Answer: The loss allocation is $20,000 ($60,000 × 1/3).

How much of the $20,000 loss clears the tax-basis hurdle for deductibility in 2019?

Answer: The amount of Nicole's basis in her CCS stock, or $14,000. The remaining $6,000 of loss does not clear the tax-basis hurdle; it is suspended until Nicole generates additional basis.

Shareholders can mitigate the disadvantage of not including S corporation debt in their stock basis by loaning money directly to their S corporations. These loans create **debt basis,** separate from the stock basis. Losses are limited first to the shareholders' tax bases in their shares and *then* to their bases in any direct loans made to their S corporations.[29] Specifically, if the total amount of items (besides distributions) that decrease the shareholder's basis for the year exceeds the shareholder's stock basis, the excess amount decreases the shareholder's debt basis. Like stock basis, debt basis cannot be decreased below zero. In subsequent years, any net increase in basis for the year restores first the shareholder's debt basis (up to the outstanding debt amount) and then the shareholder's stock basis. If the S corporation repays the debt owed to the shareholder before the shareholder's debt basis is restored, any loan repayment in excess of the shareholder's debt basis will trigger a taxable gain to the shareholder.

Example 22-15

What if: Suppose at the beginning of 2019, Nicole's basis in her CCS stock was $14,000. During 2019, Nicole loaned $8,000 to CCS, and CCS reported a $60,000 ordinary business loss and no separately stated items. How much of the $20,000 ordinary loss allocated to Nicole clears the tax-basis hurdle for deductibility in 2019?

Answer: All $20,000. The first $14,000 of the loss reduces her stock basis to $0, and the remaining $6,000 reduces her debt basis to $2,000 ($8,000 − $6,000).

What if: Suppose in 2020, CCS allocated $9,000 of ordinary business income to Nicole and no separately stated items. What are Nicole's CCS stock basis and debt basis at the end of 2020?

Answer: Her stock basis is $3,000; her debt basis is $8,000. The income first restores debt basis to the outstanding debt amount and then increases her stock basis.

---

[28]S corporations are also subject to the hobby loss rules in §183 that limit loss deductions for activities not engaged in for profit.

[29]§1366(d)(1)(B). These must be direct loans to the corporation. Thus, shareholders do not get debt basis when they guarantee a loan of the S corporation, although they would to the extent they had to "make good" on their guarantee obligation.

At-Risk Limitation   Like partners in partnerships, S corporation shareholders are subject to the *at-risk* rules. They may deduct S corporation losses only to the extent of their **at-risk amount** in the S corporation, as defined in §465. With one notable exception, an S corporation shareholder's at-risk amount is the sum of her stock and debt basis. The primary exception relates to nonrecourse loans and is designed to ensure that shareholders are deemed at risk only when they have an actual risk of loss. Specifically, an S corporation shareholder taking out a nonrecourse loan to make a capital contribution (either cash or other property) to the S corporation generally creates stock basis (equal to the basis of property contributed) in the S corporation but increases her amount at risk by only the net fair market value of her property, if any, used as collateral to secure the nonrecourse loan.[30] The collateral's net fair market value is determined at the loan date.

Likewise, if the shareholder takes out a nonrecourse loan to make a direct loan to the S corporation, the loan creates debt basis but increases her amount at risk only by the net fair market value of her property, if any, used as collateral to secure the nonrecourse loan. When the stock basis plus debt basis is different from the at-risk amount, S corporation shareholders apply the tax-basis loss limitation first, and then the at-risk limitation. Losses limited under the at-risk rules are carried forward indefinitely until the shareholder generates additional at-risk amounts to utilize them or sells the S corporation stock.

Post-Termination Transition Period Loss Limitation   The voluntary or involuntary termination of a corporation's S election creates a problem for shareholders with suspended losses due to the basis and at-risk rules. The reason: These losses are generally not deductible after the S termination date. Shareholders can obtain some relief provided by §1366(d)(3), which allows them to treat any suspended losses existing at the S termination date as occurring on the last day of the **post-termination transition period (PTTP).** In general, the PTTP begins on the day after the last day of the corporation's last taxable year as an S corporation and ends on the later of (a) one year after the last S corporation day or (b) the due date for filing the return for the last year as an S corporation (including extensions).[31]

This rule allows the shareholder to create additional stock basis (by making additional capital contributions) during the PTTP and to utilize suspended losses based on his or her *stock* basis (not debt basis) at the end of the period. Any suspended losses utilized at the end of the PTTP reduce the shareholder's basis in the stock. Any losses not utilized at the end of the period are lost forever.

Example 22-16

What if: Suppose CCS terminated its S election on July 17, 2019. At the end of the S corporation's short tax year ending on July 17, Nicole's stock basis and at-risk amounts were both zero (she has never had debt basis), and she had a suspended loss of $15,000. In 2020, Nicole made additional capital contributions of $10,000 on February 20, 2020, and $7,000 on September 6, 2020. When does the PTTP end for CCS? How much loss may Nicole deduct, and what is her basis in the CCS stock at the end of the PTTP?

Answer: For loss deduction purposes, CCS's PTTP ends on September 15, 2020. That date represents (b) in the "later of (a) or (b)" alternative—(a) one year after the last S corporation day, which would be July 17, 2020, or (b) the due date for filing the return for the last year as an S corporation, including extensions, which would be September 15, 2020, assuming CCS extends its tax return. (Note the short tax year S corporation return is due the same time as the short tax year C corporation return.) Nicole may deduct the entire $15,000 suspended loss because her basis at the end of the PTTP and before the loss deduction is $17,000. (That amount is calculated as a carryover basis of $0 on the last S corporation day plus $17,000 capital contributions during the PTTP.) Nicole's basis in CCS stock after the loss deduction is $2,000 ($17,000 basis at the end of the PTTP less the $15,000 loss deduction).

What if: Suppose Nicole made her second capital contribution on October 22, 2020, instead of September 6, 2020. How much loss can Nicole deduct, and what is her basis in CCS stock at the end of the PTTP?

---

[30]§465(b)(2)(B). In some circumstances (beyond the scope of this text), shareholders do not create stock basis (or debt basis) for contributions (or shareholder loans to the S corporation) that are funded by nonrecourse loans.

[31]§1377(b)(1)(A). §1377(b) indicates that the PTTP also includes the 120-day period beginning on the date of a determination (not the date of the actual termination) that the corporation's S election had terminated for a previous taxable year.

Answer: The loss deduction is $10,000: Nicole's stock basis at the end of the PTTP and before her loss deduction is only $10,000 because the $7,000 contribution occurred after the end of the PTTP. Nicole's basis in the CCS stock at the end of the PTTP and after the loss deduction is zero ($10,000 basis less $10,000 loss deduction). Her basis then increases to $7,000 on October 22, but the $5,000 suspended loss is lost forever.

Passive Activity Loss Limitation   S corporation shareholders, just like partners, are subject to the **passive activity loss rules.** There are no differences in the application of these rules for S corporations; the definition of a passive activity, the tests for material participation, the income and loss baskets, and the passive activity loss carryover rules described in the Forming and Operating Partnerships chapter are exactly the same. Thus, as in partnerships, the passive activity loss rules limit the ability of S corporation shareholders to deduct losses unless they are involved in actively managing the business.[32]

Example 22-17

What if: Suppose in 2020, CCS incurred an ordinary business loss and allocated the loss equally to its shareholders. Assuming Nicole, Sarah, and Chance all had adequate stock basis and at-risk amounts to absorb the losses, which of the three shareholders would be least likely to deduct the loss due to the passive activity limitation rules?

Answer: Chance. Because he is not actively involved in managing CCS's business activities, any loss allocated to him is a passive activity loss.

Excess Business Loss Limitation   For years beginning after 2017, taxpayers are not allowed to deduct an **"excess business loss"** for the year. Rather, excess business losses are carried forward to subsequent years as a net operating loss carryforward. The excess business loss limitation applies to losses that are otherwise deductible under the basis, at-risk, and passive loss rules. An excess business loss for the year is the excess of aggregate business deductions for the year over the sum of aggregate business gross income or gain of the taxpayer plus a threshold amount. The threshold amount for a tax year is $500,000 for married taxpayers filing jointly and $250,000 for other taxpayers. The amounts are indexed for inflation. In the case of partnership or S corporation business losses, the provision applies at the shareholder level.

Self-Employment Income

You might wonder whether an S corporation shareholder's allocable share of ordinary business income (loss) is classified as self-employment income for tax purposes. The answer is no, even when the shareholder actively works for the S corporation.[33]

When a shareholder does work as an employee of and receives a salary from an S corporation, the S corporation treats this salary payment like that made to any other employee: For Social Security taxes, it withholds 6.2 percent of the shareholder's salary or wages subject to the wage limitation ($128,400 in 2018), for Medicare taxes, it withholds 1.45 percent of the shareholder's salary or wages, and for the additional Medicare tax, it withholds .9 percent on any shareholder salary or wages above $200,000.[34] In addition, the S corporation must pay its portion of the Social Security tax (6.2 percent of the shareholder's salary or wages subject to the $128,400 wage limitation in 2018) and Medicare tax (1.45 percent of the shareholder's salary or wages, regardless of the amount of salary or wages). In contrast to shareholder-employees, S corporations are not subject to the additional Medicare tax on employee salary or wages.

[32]§469.

[33]Rev. Rul. 59-221, 1955-1 CB 225.

[34]Although employee liability for the additional Medicare tax varies based on filing status ($250,000 combined salary or wages for married filing jointly; $125,000 salary or wages for married filing separate; $200,000 salary or wages for all other taxpayers), employers are required to withhold the additional Medicare tax on salary or wages above $200,000 irrespective of the taxpayer's filing status.

Because of this stark contrast between the treatment of ordinary business income and that of shareholder salaries, S corporation shareholders may desire to avoid payroll taxes by limiting or even eliminating their salary payments. However, if they work as employees, they are required to pay themselves a reasonable salary for the services they perform. If they pay themselves an unreasonably low salary, the IRS may attempt to reclassify some or all of the S corporation's ordinary business income as shareholder salary!

TAXES IN THE REAL WORLD S Corporation Salary in Question

In 2011, *The Wall Street Journal* reported that over the past 15 years when executive pay skyrocketed, the salaries of S corporation owners declined from 52 percent of the corporation's income in 1995 to 39 percent of the corporation's income in 2007. Over the same period, S corporation income doubled, while S corporation owner salary increased only 26 percent to an average salary of $38,400. Why the low pay? To avoid payroll taxes on salary, of course. The IRS, however, is wise to this strategy and has made this issue a top priority in auditing S corporations. In a recent 8th Circuit Court case, *Watson, P.C. v. U.S.*, the IRS argued that the $24,000 salary to a 20-year CPA/S corporation owner was far too low. In this case, Mr. Watson received a $24,000 salary for his work for his CPA firm while receiving profit distributions of $203,651 and $175,470 from his

S corporation in 2003 and 2004, respectively. The IRS contended that Mr. Watson's true pay was $91,044 for each year—and the 8th Circuit Court agreed with the IRS and district court, ruling that Mr. Watson owed extra tax plus interest and penalties. Factors indicating that Mr. Watson's salary was too low included the following: He was an exceedingly qualified accountant with an advanced degree and 20 years of experience; he worked 35 to 45 hours per week as a primary earner in a reputable firm, which had earnings much greater than comparable firms; the firm had significant gross earnings; and his salary was unreasonably low compared to those of other accountants and to the distributions he received.

Source: Watson, P.C. v. U.S. (8 Cir., 2012) 109 AFTR 2d 2012–1059; Laura Saunders, "The IRS Targets Income Tricks," WSJ.com, January 22, 2011.

Net Investment Income Tax

Just like partners in a partnership, S corporation shareholders are subject to a 3.8 percent net investment income tax on their share of an S corporation's gross income from interest, dividends, annuities, royalties, rents, a trade or business that is a passive activity or a trade or business of trading financial instruments or commodities, and any net gain from disposing of property (other than property held in a trade or business in which the net investment income tax does not apply), less any allowable deductions from these items.[35,36] Likewise, any gain from the sale of S corporation stock (or distributions in excess of basis) is subject to the net investment income tax to the extent it is allocable to assets held by the S corporation that would have generated a net gain subject to the net investment income tax if all S corporation assets were sold at fair market value.[37]

Fringe Benefits

True to their hybrid status, S corporations are treated in part like C corporations and in part like partnerships with respect to tax deductions for qualifying employee fringe benefits.[38] For shareholder-employees who own 2 percent or less of the entity, the S corporation receives C corporation tax treatment. That is, it gets a tax deduction for qualifying fringe benefits, and the benefits are nontaxable to *all* employees. For shareholder-employees who

---

[35]Interest, dividend, annuity, royalty, and rent income derived in the *ordinary* course of a trade or business that is not passive and does not involve financial instrument or commodity trading is exempt from the net investment income tax.

[36]The tax imposed is 3.8 percent of the lesser of (a) net investment income or (b) the excess of modified adjusted gross income over $250,000 for married-joint filers and surviving spouses, $125,000 for married separate filers, and $200,000 for other taxpayers. Modified adjusted gross income equals adjusted gross income increased by income excluded under the foreign earned income exclusion less any disallowed deductions associated with the foreign earned income exclusion.

[37]See Prop. Reg. §1.1411-7.

[38]Qualifying fringe benefits are nontaxable to the employee. Other fringe benefits (nonqualifying) are taxed as compensation to employees.

own more than 2 percent of the S corporation, it receives partnership treatment.[39] That is, it gets a tax deduction, but the otherwise qualifying fringe benefits are taxable to the shareholder-employees who own more than 2 percent.[40]

Fringe benefits taxable to this group include employer-provided health insurance[41] (§106), group-term life insurance (§79), meals and lodging provided for the convenience of the employer (§119), and benefits provided under a cafeteria plan (§125). Examples of benefits that are nontaxable to more than 2 percent shareholder-employees (and partners in a partnership) include employee achievement awards (§74), qualified group legal services plans (§120), educational assistance programs (§127), dependent care assistance programs (§129), no-additional-cost services (§132), qualified employee discounts (§132), working condition fringe benefits (§132), *de minimis* fringe benefits (§132), on-premises athletic facilities (§132), and medical savings accounts (§220).

DISTRIBUTIONS

LO 22-5

S corporations face special rules when accounting for distributions (operating distributions of cash or other property and liquidating distributions).[42]

Operating Distributions

The rules for determining the shareholder-level tax consequences of operating distributions depend on the S corporation's history; specifically whether, at the time of the distribution, it has accumulated *earnings and profits* from a previous year as a C corporation. (See the Corporate Taxation: Nonliquidating Distributions chapter for a discussion of C corporation earnings and profits.) We consider both situations—with and without accumulated earnings and profits.

S Corporation with No C Corporation Accumulated Earnings and Profits

Two sets of historical circumstances could apply here: (1) An entity may have been an S corporation since inception, or (2) it may have been converted from a C corporation but not have C corporation accumulated earnings and profits at the time of the distribution. In both cases, as long as there are no C corporation accumulated earnings and profits, the rules for accounting for the distribution are very similar to those applicable to distributions to partners. That is, shareholder distributions are tax-free to the extent of the shareholders' stock basis (determined after increasing the stock basis for income allocations for the year[43]). If a distribution exceeds the shareholder's stock basis, the shareholder has a capital gain equal to the excess distribution amount.

Example 22-18

What if: Suppose CCS has been an S corporation since its inception. On June 1, 2020, CCS distributed $30,000 to Nicole. Her basis in her CCS stock on January 1, 2020, was $20,000. For 2020, Nicole was allocated $15,000 of ordinary income from CCS and no separately stated items. What is the amount and character of income Nicole recognizes on the distribution, and what is her basis in her CCS stock after the distribution?

Answer: Nicole has $0 income from the distribution and $5,000 basis in stock after the distribution ($35,000 − $30,000). Her stock basis for determining the taxability of the distribution is $35,000, or her beginning basis of $20,000 plus the $15,000 income allocation for the year (which is taxable to Nicole).

(continued on page 22-18)

---

[39]§1372(a).

[40]The §318 attribution rules apply (see the Corporate Taxation: Nonliquidating Distributions chapter) for purposes of determining which shareholders own more than 2 percent.

[41]Note, however, that shareholders who own more than 2 percent are allowed to deduct their insurance costs as *for* AGI deductions [§162(l)].

[42]The §302 stock redemption rules that determine whether a distribution in redemption of a shareholder's stock should be treated as a distribution or a sale or exchange apply to both C corporations and S corporations. See discussion on redemptions in the Corporate Taxation: Nonliquidating Distributions chapter.

[43]§1368(d).

What if: Assume the same facts except that CCS distributed $40,000 to Nicole rather than $30,000. What is the amount and character of income Nicole recognizes on the distribution, and what is her basis in her CCS stock after the distribution?

Answer: Nicole has a $5,000 long-term capital gain (she has held her CCS stock more than one year) and $0 basis in her stock (the distribution reduced her stock basis to $0).

What if: Suppose CCS began in 2017 as a C corporation and elected to be taxed as an S corporation in its second year of operations. In 2017, it distributed all its earnings and profits as a dividend, so it did not have any earnings and profits at the end of 2017. In 2018, it distributed $30,000 to Nicole when her basis in her stock was $35,000. What is the amount and character of income she recognizes on the distribution, and what is her basis in her CCS stock after the distribution?

Answer: Nicole has $0 income on the distribution and $5,000 basis in stock after the distribution ($35,000 − $30,000). Because CCS did not have C corporation earnings and profits at the time of the distribution, her outcome is the same as if CCS had been taxed as an S corporation since inception.

S Corporation with C Corporation Accumulated Earnings and Profits

When an S corporation has accumulated earnings and profits (E&P) from prior C corporation years, the distribution rules are a bit more complex. These rules are designed to ensure that shareholders cannot avoid the dividend tax on dividend distributions out of C corporation accumulated E&P by simply electing S corporation status and then distributing the accumulated E&P. For S corporations in this situation, the tax laws require the corporation to maintain an **accumulated adjustments account (AAA)** to determine the taxability of S corporate distributions. The AAA represents the cumulative income or losses for the period the corporation has been an S corporation. It is calculated as:

The beginning of year AAA balance

\+ Separately stated income/gain items (excluding tax-exempt income)

\+ Ordinary income

\− Separately stated losses and deductions

\− Ordinary losses

\− Nondeductible expenses that are not capital expenditures (except deductions related to generating tax-exempt income)

\− Distributions out of AAA[44]

\= End of year AAA balance

Unlike a shareholder's stock basis, the AAA may have a negative balance. However, the reduction for distributions may not cause the AAA to go negative or to become more negative. Also, unlike stock basis, the AAA is a corporate-level account rather than a shareholder-specific account.

Example 22-19

CCS was originally formed as a C corporation and reported 2017 taxable income (and earnings and profits) of $40,000 (see Exhibit 22-2). Effective the beginning of 2018, it elected to be taxed as an S corporation. In 2018, CCS reported $249,000 of overall income (including separately stated items—see Exhibit 22-2). What is the amount of CCS's AAA for 2018 before considering the effects of distributions?

---

[44]§1368(e)(1)(C). If the current-year income and loss items net to make a negative adjustment to the AAA, the net negative adjustment from these items is made to the AAA *after* any AAA reductions for distributions (i.e., the reduction in AAA for distributions is made before the net negative adjustment for current-year income and loss items).

Answer: $249,000, computed as follows:

Description	Amount	Explanation
(1) Separately stated income	$ 9,000	$6,000 interest income + $3,000 dividend income (see Exhibit 22-2)
(2) Ordinary business income	240,000	Example 22-11
AAA before distributions	**$249,000**	(1) + (2)

What if: Assume that during 2018, CCS distributed $300,000 to its shareholders. What is CCS's AAA at the end of 2018?

Answer: AAA is $0, because the distribution cannot cause AAA to be negative.

What if: Instead of reporting $249,000 of income during 2018, assume that during 2018 CCS reported an ordinary business loss of $45,000, a separately stated charitable contribution of $5,000, and a $6,000 distribution to its shareholders. What is CCS's AAA at the end of 2018?

Answer: AAA is −$50,000. CCS decreases its AAA by the $45,000 business loss and the $5,000 charitable contribution. AAA before distributions is −$50,000. CCS does not decrease AAA by the $6,000 distribution because the distribution cannot cause AAA to be negative or make it more negative.

S corporation distributions are deemed to be paid from the following sources in the order listed:[45]

1. The AAA account (to the extent it has a positive balance).[46]
2. Existing accumulated earnings and profits from years when the corporation operated as a C corporation.
3. The shareholder's stock basis.[47]

S corporation distributions from the AAA (the most common distributions) are treated the same as distributions when the S corporation does not have E&P. They are nontaxable to the extent of the shareholder's basis, and they create capital gains if they exceed the shareholder's stock basis. If an S corporation makes a distribution from accumulated E&P, the distribution is taxable to shareholders as a dividend. (See the Corporate Taxation: Nonliquidating Distributions chapter for the calculation of corporate E&P.) Once an S corporation's accumulated E&P is fully distributed, the remaining distributions reduce the shareholder's remaining basis in the S corporation stock (if any) and are nontaxable. Any excess distributions are treated as capital gain.

---

[45]S corporations may elect to have distributions treated as being first paid out of existing accumulated earnings and profits from C corporation years to avoid the excess net passive income tax. We discuss the excess net passive income tax later in the chapter.

[46]Prior to 1983, S corporations' shareholders were taxed on undistributed taxable income as a deemed distribution. This undistributed income is referred to as *previously taxable income (PTI)*. For S corporations with PTI, distributions are considered to be paid out of PTI (if there is any remaining that has not been distributed) after any distributions out of their AAA. These distributions are also nontaxable to the extent of basis and reduce both the shareholder's basis and PTI.

[47]Technically, the distributions come from the Other Adjustments Account (OAA) and then any remaining shareholder equity accounts (e.g., common stock, paid-in capital). The OAA starts at zero at the S corporation's inception; is increased for tax-exempt income; and is decreased by expenses related to tax-exempt income, any federal taxes paid that are attributable to a C corporation tax year, and any S corporate distributions after the AAA and accumulated E&P have been reduced to zero. As with the AAA, the reduction for distributions may not cause the OAA to go negative or to increase a negative balance. Because from the shareholder's perspective distributions out of the OAA and equity accounts both reduce the shareholder's stock basis, we do not discuss the OAA or other equity accounts in detail.

Example 22-20

What if: Assume at the end of 2018, before considering distributions, CCS's AAA was $24,000 and its accumulated E&P from 2017 was $40,000. Also assume Nicole's basis in her CCS stock is $80,000. If CCS distributes $60,000 on July 1 ($20,000 to each shareholder), what is the amount and character of income Nicole must recognize on her $20,000 distribution, and what is her stock basis in CCS after the distribution?

Answer: $12,000 dividend income and $72,000 stock basis after the distribution, computed as follows:

Description	Amount	Explanation
(1) Total distribution	$60,000	
(2) CCS's AAA beginning balance	24,000	
(3) Distribution from AAA	24,000	Lesser of (1) or (2)
(4) Distribution in excess of AAA	36,000	(1) − (3)
(5) Nicole's share of AAA distribution	8,000	(3) × 1/3 (nontaxable reduction of stock basis)
(6) Nicole's beginning stock basis	80,000	
(7) Nicole's ending stock basis	**72,000**	(6) − (5)
(8) CCS's E&P balance	40,000	
(9) Dividend distribution (from E&P)	36,000	Lesser of (4) or (8)
Nicole's share of dividend	**12,000**	(9) × 1/3

Property Distributions At times, S corporations distribute appreciated property to their shareholders. When they do so, S corporations recognize gain as though they had sold the appreciated property for its fair market value just prior to the distribution.[48] (This rule contrasts with the partnership provisions for property distributions but is consistent with the C corporation rules.) Shareholders who receive the distributed property recognize their distributive share of the deemed gain and increase their stock basis accordingly. On the other hand, S corporations do not recognize losses on distributions of property whose value has declined.

For the shareholder, the amount of a property distribution is the fair market value of the property received (minus any liabilities the shareholder assumes on the distribution). The rules we described above apply in determining the extent to which the amount of the distribution is a tax-free reduction of basis, a capital gain for a distribution in excess of basis, or a taxable dividend to the shareholder.[49] (See the rules for the taxability of distributions for S corporations with and without C corporation accumulated earnings and profits.) Shareholders take a fair market value basis in the property received in the distribution.

Example 22-21

What if: Assume that at the end of 2019, CCS distributes long-term capital gain property (fair market value of $24,000, basis of $15,000) to each shareholder (aggregate property distribution of $72,000 with an aggregate basis of $45,000). At the time of the distribution, CCS has no corporate E&P and Nicole has a basis of $10,000 in her CCS stock. How much gain, if any, does CCS recognize on the distribution? How much income does Nicole recognize as a result of the distribution?

---

[48]§311(b). In addition, the S corporation may incur entity-level tax if the distributed property had built-in gains related to when the corporation converted to an S corporation. We discuss the built-in gains tax later in the chapter.

[49]Note that while S corporation shareholders reduce their stock basis by the fair market value of the property received, partners receiving property distributions from partnerships generally reduce the basis in their partnership interests by the adjusted basis of the distributed property.

Answer: CCS recognizes $27,000 of long-term capital gain and Nicole recognizes $14,000 of long-term capital gain, computed as follows:

Description	Amount	Explanation
(1) FMV of distributed property	$72,000	
(2) CCS's basis in distributed property	45,000	
(3) CCS's LTCG gain on distribution	**27,000**	(1) − (2)
(4) Nicole's share of LTCG from CCS	9,000	(3) × 1/3
(5) Nicole's stock basis after gain allocation	19,000	$10,000 beginning basis + (4)
(6) Distribution to Nicole	24,000	(1) × 1/3
(7) Nicole's stock basis after distribution	0	(5) − (6) limited to $0
(8) LTCG to Nicole on distribution in excess of stock basis	5,000	(6) in excess of (5)
Nicole's total LTCG on distribution	**14,000**	(4) + (8)

Post-Termination Transition Period Distributions   Recall the special tax rules relating to suspended losses at the S corporation termination date. Similarly, §1371(e) provides for special treatment of any S corporation distribution *in cash* after an S election termination and during the post-termination transition period (PTTP). Such cash distributions are tax-free to the extent they do not exceed the corporation's AAA balance and the individual shareholder's basis in the stock.

The PTTP for post-termination distributions is generally the same as the PTTP for deducting suspended losses, discussed above. For determining the taxability of distributions, the PTTP generally begins on the day after the last day of the corporation's last taxable year as an S corporation; it ends on the later of (a) one year after the last S corporation day or (b) the due date for filing the return for the last year as an S corporation (including extensions).[50,51]

Liquidating Distributions

Liquidating distributions of a shareholder interest in an S corporation follow corporate tax rules rather than partnership rules. For a complete liquidation of the S corporation, the rules under §§331 and 336 (discussed in the Corporate Formation, Reorganization, and Liquidation chapter) govern the tax consequences. S corporations generally recognize gain *or* loss on each asset they distribute in liquidation (recall that S corporations recognize gain but not loss on operating distributions of noncash property). These gains and losses are allocated to the S corporation shareholders, increasing or decreasing their stock basis. In general, shareholders recognize gain on the distribution if the value of the property exceeds their stock basis; they recognize loss if their stock basis exceeds the value of the property.

THE KEY FACTS

Property Distributions

- S corporations recognize gains but not losses when they distribute property to their shareholders.
- For shareholders, the amount of the distribution is the fair market value of the property received (minus any liabilities the shareholder assumes on the distribution).
- The rules for determining the taxability of property distributions at the shareholder level are the same as those for cash distributions.
- Shareholders take a fair market value basis in the property received in the distribution.

Example 22-22

What if: Assume that at the end of 2020, CCS liquidates by distributing long-term capital gain property (fair market value of $20,000, basis of $12,000) to each shareholder (aggregate property distribution of $60,000 with an aggregate basis of $36,000). At the time of the distribution, CCS has no corporate E&P

(continued on page 22-22)

---

[50]§1377(b)(1)(A). For purposes of the taxability of distributions, the PTTP also includes: (1) the 120-day period that begins on the date of any determination (court decision, closing agreement, and so on) from an IRS audit that occurs after the S election has been terminated and adjusts the corporation's income, loss, or deduction during the S period; and (2) the 120-day period beginning on the date of a determination (not the date of the actual termination) that the corporation's S election had terminated for a previous taxable year [§1377(b)(1)(B) and (C)].

[51]In addition to the general rules that apply to PTTP distributions, there is a special rule that applies to distributions from an "eligible terminated S corporation" that occur *after* the PTTP. Specifically, distributions from an eligible terminated S corporation that occur after the PTTP are treated as paid *pro rata* from its accumulated adjustments account and from its earnings and profits. An eligible terminated S corporation is any C corporation which (i) was an S corporation on December 21, 2017, (ii) revoked its S corporation election during the two-year period beginning on December 22, 2017, and (iii) had the same owners on December 22, 2017, and on the revocation date (in identical proportions).

and Nicole has a basis of $25,000 in her CCS stock. How much gain or loss, if any, does CCS recognize on the distribution? How much gain or loss does Nicole recognize as a result of the distribution?

Answer: CCS recognizes $24,000 of long-term capital gain and Nicole recognizes $5,000 of net long-term capital loss, computed as follows:

Description	Amount	Explanation
(1) FMV of distributed property	$60,000	
(2) CCS's basis in distributed property	36,000	
(3) **CCS's LTCG gain on distribution**	**24,000**	(1) − (2)
(4) Nicole's share of LTCG from CCS	8,000	(3) × 1/3
(5) Nicole's stock basis after gain allocation	33,000	$25,000 beginning basis + (4)
(6) Distribution to Nicole	20,000	(1) × 1/3
(7) Nicole's LTCL on liquidating distribution	(13,000)	(6) − (5)
Nicole's net LTCL on distribution	**(5,000)**	(4) + (7)

LO 22-6

THE KEY FACTS

Built-in Gains Tax

- The built-in gains tax applies only to S corporations that have a net unrealized built-in gain at the time they convert from C corporations and that recognize net built-in gains during the built-in gains tax recognition period.

- The net unrealized built-in gain represents the net gain (if any) that the corporation would recognize if it sold each asset at its fair market value.

- Recognized built-in gains (losses) include the gain (loss) for any asset sold during the year [limited to the unrealized gain (loss) for the specific asset at the S conversion date].

- The net recognized built-in gain is limited to the lowest of (a) the net recognized built-in gain less any net operating loss (NOL) and capital loss carryovers, (b) the net unrealized built-in gain not yet recognized, and (c) the corporation's taxable income for the year using the C corporation tax rules.

S CORPORATION TAXES AND FILING REQUIREMENTS

Although S corporations are flow-through entities generally not subject to tax, three potential taxes apply to S corporations that previously operated as C corporations: the **built-in gains tax, excess net passive income tax,** and **LIFO recapture tax.** The built-in gains tax is the most common of the three and will be our starting point.

Built-in Gains Tax

Congress enacted the built-in gains tax to prevent C corporations from avoiding corporate taxes on sales of appreciated property by electing S corporation status. The built-in gains tax applies only to an S corporation that has a *net unrealized built-in gain* at the time it converts from a C corporation. Further, for the built-in gains tax to apply, the S corporation must subsequently recognize net built-in gains during the **built-in gains tax recognition period.**[52] The built-in gains tax recognition period is the first five years a corporation operates as an S corporation.

What exactly is a **net unrealized built-in gain?** Measured on the first day of the corporation's first year as an S corporation, it represents the net gain (if any) the corporation would recognize if it sold each asset at its fair market value. For this purpose, we net gains and losses to determine whether indeed there is a net unrealized gain at the conversion date. The corporation's accounts receivable and accounts payable are also part of the computation: Under the cash method, accounts receivable are gain items and accounts payable are loss items. If the S corporation has a net unrealized gain at conversion, it must compute its net recognized built-in gains for each tax year during the applicable built-in gain recognition period to determine whether it is liable for the built-in gains tax.

Example 22-23

CCS uses the accrual method of accounting. At the beginning of 2018, it owned the following assets (but leased its manufacturing facility and its equipment):

Asset	Fair Market Value (FMV)	Adjusted Basis (AB)	Built-in Gain (Loss)
Cash	$ 80,000	$ 80,000	$ 0
Accounts receivable	20,000	20,000	0
Inventory (FIFO)	130,000	110,000	20,000
Land	100,000	125,000	(25,000)
Totals	$330,000	$335,000	$ (5,000)

[52]§1374.

What is CCS's net unrealized built-in gain when it converts to an S corporation on January 1, 2018?

Answer: CCS has $0 net unrealized built-in gain. It has a net unrealized built-in loss, so it is not subject to the built-in gains tax.

What if: Suppose CCS's inventory is valued at $155,000 instead of $130,000. What is its net unrealized built-in gain?

Answer: $20,000. The $45,000 built-in gain on the inventory is netted against the $25,000 built-in loss on the land.

Recognized built-in gains for an S corporation year include (1) the gain for any asset sold during the year (limited to the unrealized gain for the specific asset at the S conversion date) and (2) any income received during the current year attributable to pre-S corporation years (such as collection on accounts receivable for cash-method S corporations). Likewise, recognized built-in losses for a year include (1) the loss for any asset sold during the year (limited to the unrealized loss for the specific asset at the S conversion date) and (2) any deduction during the current year attributable to pre-S corporation years (such as deductions for accounts payable for cash-method S corporations). The net recognized built-in gain for any year is limited to *the least of:*

1. The net of the recognized built-in gains and losses for the year.
2. The net unrealized built-in gains as of the S election date less the net recognized built-in gains in previous years. (This restriction ensures the net recognized built-in gains during the recognition period do not exceed the net unrealized gain at the S conversion date.)
3. The corporation's taxable income for the year, using the C corporation tax rules exclusive of the dividends received deduction and net operating loss deduction.

If taxable income limits the net recognized built-in gain for any year [item (3) above], we treat the excess gain as a recognized built-in gain in the next tax year, *but only if* the next tax year is in the built-in gains tax recognition period. After the net recognized built-in gain to be taxed has been determined using the limitations above, it should be reduced by any net operating loss (NOL) or capital loss carryovers from prior C corporation years.[53] This base is then multiplied by the highest corporate tax rate (currently 21 percent) to determine the built-in gains tax. The built-in gains tax paid by the S corporation is allocated to the shareholders as a loss. The character of the allocated loss (ordinary, capital, §1231) depends on the nature of assets that give rise to the built-in gains tax. Specifically, the loss is allocated proportionately among the character of the recognized built-in gains resulting in the tax.[54] For planning purposes, the S corporation should consider when to recognize built-in losses to reduce its exposure to the built-in gains tax. That is, the company could seek to recognize built-in losses in years with recognized built-in gains, in order to avoid the built-in gains tax.

Example 22-24

What if: Suppose CCS had a net unrealized built-in gain of $20,000. In addition to other transactions in 2018, CCS sold inventory it owned at the beginning of the year; that inventory had built-in gain at the beginning of the year of $40,000 (FMV $150,000; cost basis $110,000). If CCS had been a C corporation in 2018, its taxable income would have been $200,000. How much built-in gains tax must CCS pay in 2018?

Answer: It must pay $4,200 ($20,000 × 21%) in built-in gains tax. CCS must pay a 21 percent tax on the least of (a) $40,000 (recognized built-in gain on inventory), (b) $20,000 (initial net unrealized gain), and (c) $200,000 (taxable income computed as if CCS were a C corporation for 2017). It will reduce the amount of ordinary business income it would otherwise allocate to its shareholders by $4,200— the amount of the built-in gains tax—because the entire amount of the tax is due to inventory sales.

What if: Assume the same facts as above (an initial net unrealized gain of $20,000) except CCS sold two assets that had built-in gains at the time CCS became an S corporation. CCS sold a capital asset

(continued on page 22-24)

---

[53]Capital loss carryovers only reduce built-in gains that are capital gains.
[54]§1366(f)(2).

with a built-in gain of $10,000 and inventory with a built-in gain of $40,000. CCS will still pay a $4,200 built-in gains tax. This tax will be allocated as a loss to its shareholders. What is the character of the $4,200 loss?

Answer: It is an $840 capital loss [$4,200 × (10,000 capital gain/$50,000 total recognized built-in gain)] and a $3,360 ordinary loss [$4,200 × ($40,000 ordinary income from inventory sale/$50,000 total recognized built-in gain)].

What if: Assume that in addition to the initial facts in the example, CCS also had a net operating loss from 2017 (the year it operated as a C corporation) of $15,000. How much built-in gains tax will CCS have to pay in 2018?

Answer: It will pay $1,050 ($5,000 × 21%). CCS is allowed to offset $15,000 of the $20,000 recognized portion of the initial net unrealized gain by its $15,000 net operating loss carryover from 2017.

What if: Suppose CCS had a net unrealized built-in gain of $20,000. In addition to other transactions in 2018, CCS sold inventory it owned at the beginning of the year; that inventory had built-in gain at the beginning of the year of $40,000 (FMV $150,000; AB $110,000). If CCS had been a C corporation in 2018, its taxable income would have been $4,000. How much built-in gains tax would CCS have to pay in 2018?

Answer: $840 ($4,000 × 21%). CCS must pay a 21 percent tax on the least of (a) $40,000 (recognized built-in gain on inventory), (b) $20,000 (initial net unrealized gain), and (c) $4,000 (taxable income computed as if CCS were a C corporation for 2018). Because the tax was limited due to the taxable income limitation, the excess gain of $16,000 ($20,000 recognized built-in gain minus $4,000 gain on which CCS paid tax) is treated as a recognized built-in gain in 2019.

Excess Net Passive Income Tax

If an S corporation previously operated as a C corporation *and* has accumulated earnings and profits at the end of the year from a prior C corporation year, it may be subject to the *excess net passive income tax.*[55] Congress created this tax to encourage S corporations to distribute their accumulated earnings and profits from prior C corporation years. It does not apply to S corporations that never operated as a C corporation, or to S corporations without earnings and profits from prior C corporation years.

The tax is levied on the S corporation's **excess net passive income,** computed as follows:

$$\text{Excess net passive income} = \text{Net passive investment income} \times \frac{\text{Passive investment income} - (25\% \times \text{Gross receipts})}{\text{Passive investment income}}$$

Note that an S corporation has excess net passive income only when (1) it has net passive investment income and (2) its passive investment income exceeds 25 percent of its gross receipts. For purposes of determining excess net passive income, *gross receipts* is the total amount of revenues (including passive investment income) received or accrued under the corporation's accounting method, and not reduced by returns, allowances, cost of goods sold, or deductions. Gross receipts include net capital gains from the sales or exchanges of capital assets and gains from the sales or exchanges of stock or securities (losses do not offset gains). As defined previously in the chapter, passive investment income includes gross receipts from royalties, rents, dividends, interest (including tax-exempt interest), and annuities. **Net passive investment income** is passive investment income decreased by any expenses connected with producing that income.

The excess net passive income tax is imposed on excess net passive income at the highest corporate tax rate (currently 21 percent). For purposes of computing the tax, excess net passive income is limited to taxable income computed as if the corporation were a C corporation (excluding net operating losses). The formula for determining the tax is:

$$\text{Excess net passive income tax} = 21\% \times \text{Excess net passive income}$$

[55]§1375.

Each item of passive investment income that flows through to shareholders is reduced by an allocable share of the excess net passive income tax. The portion of the tax allocated to each item of passive investment income is the amount of the item divided by the total amount of passive investment income.

The IRS may waive the excess net passive income tax in some circumstances—for example, if the S corporation determined in good faith it did not have accumulated earnings and profits at the end of the tax year and within a reasonable period distributed earnings and profits it identified later.[56]

Example 22-25

During 2018 CCS reported the following income (see Exhibit 22-2):

	2018 (S Corporation)
Sales revenue	$520,000
Cost of goods sold	(115,000)
Salary to owners Nicole and Sarah	(90,000)
Employee wages	(50,000)
Depreciation expense	(20,000)
Miscellaneous expenses	(5,000)
Interest income	6,000
Dividend income	3,000
Overall net income	$249,000

What are CCS's passive investment income, net passive investment income, and gross receipts for 2018?

Answer: The amounts are $9,000 passive income ($6,000 interest income + $3,000 dividends); $9,000 net passive investment income (because CCS has $0 expenses in producing passive investment income); and $529,000 gross receipts ($520,000 sales revenue + $3,000 dividends + $6,000 interest income).

What is CCS's excess net passive income tax in 2018, if any?

Answer: Zero. CCS has accumulated earnings and profits from 2017 (see Exhibit 22-2), but it owes zero excess net passive income tax because its passive investment income is less than 25 percent of its gross receipts [$9,000 < $132,250 ($529,000 × 25%)].

What if. Suppose CCS has passive investment income of $180,000 ($120,000 interest + $60,000 dividends), expenses associated with the passive investment income of $20,000, and gross receipts of $700,000 ($520,000 + $180,000). Also, if CCS were a C corporation, its taxable income would have been $249,000; assume it had accumulated earnings and profits of $40,000. What is CCS's excess net passive income tax, if any? What effect, if any, would the excess net passive income tax have on interest and dividends allocated to the shareholders?

Answer: The base for the tax is limited to the lesser of (a) excess net passive income of $4,444 [($180,000 passive investment income minus $20,000 expenses associated with passive investment income) × ($180,000 − 25% × $700,000)/$180,000] or $249,000 (CCS's taxable income if it had been a C corporation). Thus, the base for the tax is limited to $4,444, and the tax is $933 (21% × $4,444).

Interest and dividends allocated to the shareholders will be reduced by the excess net passive income tax. The interest income allocated to shareholders will be reduced by $622 [$933 tax × ($120,000 interest/$180,000 total passive investment income)], and dividend income will be reduced by $311 [$933 × ($60,000 dividend/$180,000)].

What if: Suppose CCS has passive investment income of $180,000, expenses associated with the passive investment income of $20,000, and gross receipts of $700,000 ($520,000 + $180,000). Also, if CCS were a C corporation, its taxable income would have been $2,000; assume it had accumulated earnings and profits of $40,000. What is CCS's excess net passive income tax, if any?

(continued on page 22-26)

---

[56]§1375(d).

> **Answer:** The base for the tax is limited to the lesser of (a) excess net passive investment income of $4,444 [$160,000 × ($180,000 − 25% × $700,000)/$180,000] or (b) $2,000 (taxable income if CCS had been a C corporation). So the tax is $420 (21% × $2,000).

Remember, if an S corporation pays the net excess passive income tax for three years in a row, its S election will be terminated by the excess passive income test.

LIFO Recapture Tax

C corporations that elect S corporation status and use the LIFO inventory method are subject to the *LIFO recapture tax*. The purpose of this tax is to prevent former C corporations from avoiding built-in gains tax by using the LIFO method of accounting for their inventories. Specifically, a LIFO method corporation would not recognize built-in gains unless the corporation invaded its LIFO layers during the built-in gains tax recognition period.

The LIFO recapture tax requires the C corporation to include the **LIFO recapture amount** in its gross income in the last year it operates as a C corporation.[57] That amount equals the excess of the inventory basis computed using the FIFO method over the inventory basis computed using the LIFO method at the end of the corporation's last tax year as a C corporation. In addition to being included in gross income (and taxed at the C corporation's marginal tax rate), the LIFO recapture amount also increases the corporation's adjusted basis in its inventory at the time it converts to an S corporation. The basis increase reduces the amount of net unrealized gain subject to the built-in gains tax.

The corporation pays the LIFO recapture tax (technically a C corporation tax) in four annual installments. The first installment is due on or before the due date (not including extensions) of the corporation's last *C corporation* tax return. The final three annual installments are due each year on or before the due date (not including extensions) of the *S corporation*'s tax return.

The LIFO recapture tax does not preclude the S corporation from using the LIFO method, but it obviously does accelerate the gain attributable to differences between LIFO and FIFO for inventory existing at the time of the S corporation election.

Example 22-26

What if: Suppose CCS uses the LIFO method of accounting for its inventory and elected S corporation status effective January 1, 2019. Assume that at the end of 2018, the basis of the inventory under the LIFO method was $90,000. Under the FIFO method, the basis of the inventory would have been $100,000. Finally, regular taxable income in 2018 was $40,000. What amount of LIFO recapture tax must CCS pay?

Answer: CCS must pay $2,100 [($100,000 FIFO inventory basis − $90,000 LIFO inventory basis) × 21 percent]. The 21 percent tax rate is the marginal rate at which the additional $10,000 of income would have been taxed in 2018 under the corporate tax rate schedule. CCS would increase its basis in its inventory by $10,000 to $100,000 as of the end of 2018, its last year as a C corporation. This would reduce the unrealized net built-in gain on the inventory.

When is CCS required to pay the tax?

Answer: CCS must pay $525 by April 15, 2019 (the unextended due date of the C corporation tax return); March 16, 2020 (March 15 falls on a Sunday); March 15, 2021 ; and March 15, 2022. March 15 is the annual tax return due date for calendar year-end S corporation returns without extensions (see discussion below).

---

[57]§1363(d).

EXHIBIT 22-3, PART I CCS's Form 1120S, page 1

Form **1120S**		**U.S. Income Tax Return for an S Corporation**			OMB No. 1545-0123
Department of the Treasury Internal Revenue Service		▶ Do not file this form unless the corporation has filed or is attaching Form 2553 to elect to be an S corporation. ▶ Go to *www.irs.gov/Form1120S* for instructions and the latest information.			20**17**

For calendar year 2017 or tax year beginning _____ , 2017, ending _____ , 20___

A S election effective date **January 1, 2018**	TYPE OR PRINT	Name **Color Comfort Sheets**	**D** Employer identification number **24-4681012**
B Business activity code number (see instructions) **314000**		Number, street, and room or suite no. If a P.O. box, see instructions. **375 East 459 South**	**E** Date incorporated **January 1, 2017**
C Check if Sch. M-3 attached ☐		City or town, state or province, country, and ZIP or foreign postal code **Salt Lake City, UT 84103**	**F** Total assets (see instructions) $ **370,000**

G Is the corporation electing to be an S corporation beginning with this tax year? ☑ Yes ☐ No If "Yes," attach Form 2553 if not already filed
H Check if: **(1)** ☐ Final return **(2)** ☐ Name change **(3)** ☐ Address change **(4)** ☐ Amended return **(5)** ☐ S election termination or revocation
I Enter the number of shareholders who were shareholders during any part of the tax year . . . . ▶

Caution: Include **only** trade or business income and expenses on lines 1a through 21. See the instructions for more information.

Income

1a	Gross receipts or sales	1a	520,000	
b	Returns and allowances	1b		
c	Balance. Subtract line 1b from line 1a			1c 520,000
2	Cost of goods sold (attach Form 1125-A)			2 115,000
3	Gross profit. Subtract line 2 from line 1c			3 405,000
4	Net gain (loss) from Form 4797, line 17 (attach Form 4797) . . .			4
5	Other income (loss) (see instructions—attach statement) . . .			5
6	**Total income (loss).** Add lines 3 through 5 . . . . ▶			6 405,000

Deductions (see instructions for limitations)

7	Compensation of officers (see instructions—attach Form 1125-E)	7 90,000
8	Salaries and wages (less employment credits)	8 50,000
9	Repairs and maintenance	9
10	Bad debts	10
11	Rents	11
12	Taxes and licenses	12
13	Interest	13
14	Depreciation not claimed on Form 1125-A or elsewhere on return (attach Form 4562)	14 20,000
15	Depletion **(Do not deduct oil and gas depletion.)**	15
16	Advertising	16
17	Pension, profit-sharing, etc., plans	17
18	Employee benefit programs	18
19	Other deductions (attach statement)	19 5,000
20	**Total deductions.** Add lines 7 through 19 . . . . ▶	20 165,000
21	**Ordinary business income (loss).** Subtract line 20 from line 6	21 240,000

Tax and Payments

22a	Excess net passive income or LIFO recapture tax (see instructions) . .	22a	
b	Tax from Schedule D (Form 1120S)	22b	
c	Add lines 22a and 22b (see instructions for additional taxes) . . .		22c
23a	2017 estimated tax payments and 2016 overpayment credited to 2017	23a	
b	Tax deposited with Form 7004	23b	
c	Credit for federal tax paid on fuels (attach Form 4136)	23c	
d	Add lines 23a through 23c		23d
24	Estimated tax penalty (see instructions). Check if Form 2220 is attached . . . . ▶ ☐		24
25	**Amount owed.** If line 23d is smaller than the total of lines 22c and 24, enter amount owed . .		25
26	**Overpayment.** If line 23d is larger than the total of lines 22c and 24, enter amount overpaid . .		26
27	Enter amount from line 26 **Credited to 2018 estimated tax** ▶ _____ **Refunded** ▶		27

Sign Here

Under penalties of perjury, I declare that I have examined this return, including accompanying schedules and statements, and to the best of my knowledge and belief, it is true, correct, and complete. Declaration of preparer (other than taxpayer) is based on all information of which preparer has any knowledge.

▶ _____ _____ ▶ _____
Signature of officer   Date   Title

May the IRS discuss this return with the preparer shown below (see instructions)? ☐ Yes ☐ No

Paid Preparer Use Only

Print/Type preparer's name	Preparer's signature	Date	Check ☐ if self-employed	PTIN
Firm's name ▶			Firm's EIN ▶	
Firm's address ▶			Phone no.	

For Paperwork Reduction Act Notice, see separate instructions. Cat. No. 11510H Form **1120S** (2017)

Source: Form 1120S Department of the Treasury, Internal Revenue Service

EXHIBIT 22-3, PART II CCS's 2018 partial Schedule K (on 2017 forms)

Schedule K		Shareholders' Pro Rata Share Items			Total amount	
Income (Loss)	1	Ordinary business income (loss) (page 1, line 21)		1	240,000	
	2	Net rental real estate income (loss) (attach Form 8825)		2		
	3a	Other gross rental income (loss)	3a			
	b	Expenses from other rental activities (attach statement) . .	3b			
	c	Other net rental income (loss). Subtract line 3b from line 3a		3c		
	4	Interest income		4	6,000	
	5	Dividends: **a** Ordinary dividends		5a	3,000	
		b Qualified dividends	5b	3,000		
	6	Royalties		6		
	7	Net short-term capital gain (loss) (attach Schedule D (Form 1120S))		7		
	8a	Net long-term capital gain (loss) (attach Schedule D (Form 1120S))		8a		
	b	Collectibles (28%) gain (loss)	8b			
	c	Unrecaptured section 1250 gain (attach statement)	8c			
	9	Net section 1231 gain (loss) (attach Form 4797)		9		
	10	Other income (loss) (see instructions) . . Type ▶		10		

Source: Form 1120S Department of the Treasury, Internal Revenue Service
Note: In the revised 2018 Form 1120S, Schedule K, Color Comfort Sheets would also report qualified business income ($240,000), allocable S corporation wages paid to employees ($140,000), and the unadjusted basis of qualified property ($300,000) for purposes of the deduction for qualified business income (as detailed in Example 22-11).

Estimated Taxes

The estimated tax rules for S corporations generally follow the rules for C corporations: S corporations with a federal income tax liability of $500 or more due to the built-in gains tax or excess net passive income tax must estimate their tax liability for the year and pay it in four quarterly estimated installments. However, an S corporation is not required to make estimated tax payments for the LIFO recapture tax.[58]

Filing Requirements

S corporations are required to file **Form 1120S,** U.S. Income Tax Return for an S Corporation, with the IRS by the 15th day of the third month after the S corporation's year-end (e.g., March 15 for a calendar-year-end S corporation). S corporations may receive an automatic, six-month extension by filing **Form 7004** with the IRS prior to the original due date of the return.[59] Thus, the extended due date of an S corporation tax return is generally September 15.

Exhibit 22-3 presents page 1 of CCS's Form 1120S (for its 2018 activities), CCS's partial Schedule K, and Nicole's K-1 (we use 2017 forms because 2018 forms were unavailable at the time this book went to press). Note the K-1 of the 1120S is different from the K-1 of the 1065. In contrast to the 1065 Schedule K-1, the 1120S Schedule K-1 does not report self-employment income, does not allocate entity-level debt to shareholders, and does not allow for shareholders to have profit-and-loss-sharing ratios that are different from shareholders' percentage of stock ownership.

---

[58]Rev. Proc. 94-61, IRB 1994-38,56.

[59]Under §6698, late-filing penalties apply if the S corporation fails to file by the normal or extended due date for the return.

EXHIBIT 22-3, PART III   Nicole's 2018 Schedule K-1 (on 2017 forms)

671117

Schedule K-1 (Form 1120S)	2017		Part III	Shareholder's Share of Current Year Income, Deductions, Credits, and Other Items

☐ Final K-1   ☐ Amended K-1   OMB No. 1545-0123

Schedule K-1
(Form 1120S)
Department of the Treasury
Internal Revenue Service

2017

For calendar year 2017, or tax year

beginning / / 2017   ending / /

Shareholder's Share of Income, Deductions, Credits, etc.   ▶ See back of form and separate instructions.

	Part I Information About the Corporation
A	Corporation's employer identification number
	24-4681012
B	Corporation's name, address, city, state, and ZIP code

Color Comfort Sheets
375 East 450 South
Salt Lake City, UT 84103

C	IRS Center where corporation filed return
Ogden, UT

	Part II Information About the Shareholder
D	Shareholder's identifying number
	123-45-8976
E	Shareholder's name, address, city, state, and ZIP code

Nicole Johnson
811 East 8320 South
Sandy, UT 84094

| **F** | Shareholder's percentage of stock ownership for tax year . . . . | 33.333333 % |

For IRS Use Only

Part III — Shareholder's Share of Current Year Income, Deductions, Credits, and Other Items

1	Ordinary business income (loss)	80,000
2	Net rental real estate income (loss)	
3	Other net rental income (loss)	
4	Interest income	2,000
5a	Ordinary dividends	1,000
5b	Qualified dividends	1,000
6	Royalties	
7	Net short-term capital gain (loss)	
8a	Net long-term capital gain (loss)	
8b	Collectibles (28%) gain (loss)	
8c	Unrecaptured section 1250 gain	
9	Net section 1231 gain (loss)	
10	Other income (loss)	
11	Section 179 deduction	
12	Other deductions	
13	Credits	
14	Foreign transactions	
15	Alternative minimum tax (AMT) items	
16	Items affecting shareholder basis	
17	Other information	
	A	3,000

* See attached statement for additional information.

For Paperwork Reduction Act Notice, see the Instructions for Form 1120S.   www.irs.gov/Form1120S   Cat. No. 11520D   **Schedule K-1 (Form 1120S) 2017**

Source: Form 1120S Department of the Treasury, Internal Revenue Service
Note: In the revised 2018 Form 1120S, Schedule K-1, Color Comfort Sheets would also report Nicole's share of qualified business income ($80,000), allocable S corporation wages paid to employees ($46,667), and the unadjusted basis of qualified property ($100,000) for purposes of the deduction for qualified business income (as detailed in Example 22-11).

COMPARING C AND S CORPORATIONS AND PARTNERSHIPS

Exhibit 22-4 compares tax consequences for C corporations, S corporations, and partnerships discussed in this chapter.

EXHIBIT 22-4   Comparison of Tax Consequences for C and S Corporations and Partnerships

Tax Characteristic	C Corporation	S Corporation	Partnership/LLC
Forming or contributing property to an entity	No gain or loss on contribution of appreciated or depreciated property if transferors of property have control (as defined in §351) after transfer.	Same as C corporation.	Same as C and S corporations except no control requirement (§721 applies to partnerships).
Type of owner restrictions	No restrictions	Only individuals who are U.S. citizens or residents, certain trusts, and tax-exempt organizations.	No restrictions
Number of owner restrictions	No restrictions	Limited to 100 shareholders. (Family members and their estates count as one shareholder.)	Must have more than one owner.
Election	Default status if corporation under state law.	Must formally elect to have corporation taxed as S corporation.	Default status if unincorporated and have more than one owner.
Income and loss allocations	Not allocated to shareholders.	Income and loss flow through to owners based on ownership percentages.	Income and loss flow through to owners but may be allocated based on something other than ownership percentages (special allocations).
Entity debt included in stock (or partnership interest) basis	No	Generally no. However, loans made from shareholder to corporation create debt basis. Losses may be deducted to extent of stock basis and then debt basis.	Yes. All entity liabilities are allocated to basis of partners.
Loss limitations	Losses remain at corporate level.	Losses flow through but subject to basis limitation, at-risk limitation, passive activity limitations, and excess business loss limitation.	Same as S corporations.
Self-employment income status of ordinary income allocations	Not applicable	Not self-employment income.	May be self-employment income depending on partner's status.

EXHIBIT 22-4   *(concluded)*

Tax Characteristic	C Corporation	S Corporation	Partnership/LLC
Salary to owners permitted	Yes	Yes	Generally no. Salary-type payments are guaranteed payments subject to self-employment tax.
Fringe benefits	Can pay nontaxable fringe benefits to owners.	Can pay nontaxable fringe benefits to owners who own 2 percent or less of stock.	May not pay nontaxable fringe benefits to owners.
Operating distributions: Owner tax consequences	Taxable as dividends to extent of earnings and profits.	Generally not taxable to extent of owner's basis.	Same as S corporations.
Operating distributions: Entity tax consequences	Gain on distribution of appreciated property; no loss on distribution of depreciated property.	Same as C corporations.	Generally no gain or loss on distribution of property.
Liquidating distributions	Corporation and shareholders generally recognize gain or loss on distributions.	Same as C corporations.	Partnership and partners generally do not recognize gain or loss on liquidating distributions.
Entity-level taxes	Yes, based on corporate tax rate schedule.	Generally no, but may be required to pay built-in gains tax, excess passive investment income tax, or LIFO recapture tax if converting from C to S corporation.	No
Tax year	Last day of any month or 52/53-week year.	Generally calendar year.	Based on tax year of owners

CONCLUSION

This chapter highlighted the rules specific to S corporations and compared S corporations to C corporations and partnerships. S corporations are a true hybrid entity: They share characteristics with C corporations (the legal protection of a corporation and the tax rules that apply in organizing and liquidating a corporation). They also share characteristics with partnerships (the flow through of the entity's income and loss to its owners, ability to make tax-free distributions to the extent of the owner's basis, and basis calculations for owners).

Although many S corporation attributes follow from the C corporation or partnership rules, several specific attributes unique to S corporations may be particularly important in choosing an entity form or operating an S corporation in a tax-efficient manner. These attributes include unique S corporation taxes, the rules for how debt enters into the basis calculations and loss limitation rules for S corporations, and the rules for how distributions are taxed for S corporations previously operating as C corporations.

Summary

LO 22-1 Describe the requirements and process to elect S corporation status.

- Shareholders of S corporations are able to defer realized gains when they contribute property to the corporation if they have control of the corporation after the contribution.

- S corporations are limited in the type of owners they may have. Only individuals who are U.S. citizens or residents, certain trusts, and certain tax-exempt organizations may be shareholders of S corporations.

- S corporations may have no more than 100 shareholders. For this purpose, family members and their estates count as one shareholder. Family members include a common ancestor and her lineal descendants and their spouses (or former spouses).

- S corporations may have only one class of stock. The stock may have differences in voting rights between shares, but all stock must have identical rights with respect to corporate distribution and liquidation proceeds.

- The S corporation election is made on Form 2553. All shareholders on the date of the election must consent to the election.

- To be effective for the current year, the election must be filed in the prior tax year or on or before the 15th day of the third month of the year. Even then, the election may not be effective in certain circumstances.

LO 22-2 Explain the events that terminate the S corporation election.

- The S corporation election may be voluntarily revoked by shareholders owning more than 50 percent of the S corporation stock. In general, revocations made on or before the 15th day of the third month of the year are effective as of the beginning of the year and revocations after that date are effective on the first day of the next year. Alternatively, the shareholders may choose an alternate date that is not before the revocation election is filed.

- An S corporation's election is automatically terminated on the date it fails to meet the S corporation requirements.

- If an S corporation has earnings and profits from a previous C corporation year, its S election is terminated if it has passive investment income in excess of 25 percent of gross receipts for three consecutive years.

- When an S corporation election is terminated mid-year, the corporation files a short-year tax return for the period it was an S corporation and a short-year tax return for the portion of the year it was a C corporation. It can allocate the income on a per-day basis or it may specifically identify the income to each period.

- When an S corporation's S election is terminated, it may not reelect S status until the beginning of the fifth tax year after the tax year in which the election was terminated.

LO 22-3 Describe operating issues relating to S corporation accounting periods and methods, and explain income and loss allocations and separately stated items.

- When C corporations elect to become S corporations, all prior accounting methods carry over to the S corporation.

- S corporations are generally required to use a calendar tax year.

- Income and losses are allocated to S corporation shareholders pro rata based on the number of outstanding shares each shareholder owns on each day of the tax year or, with shareholder consent, it may use its normal accounting rules to allocate income and loss to the shareholders.

- S corporations determine their ordinary business income and separately stated items for the year and allocate these to the shareholders during the year.

- Separately stated items are tax items treated differently at the shareholder level than a shareholder's share of ordinary business income.

Explain stock-basis calculations, loss limitations, determination of self-employment income, and fringe benefit rules that apply to S corporation shareholders. **LO 22-4**

- An S corporation's shareholder's initial basis in her stock is generally the basis of the property contributed to the corporation minus liabilities assumed by the corporation on the contribution.
- S corporation shareholders adjust their stock basis annually. They increase it for (in this order) contributions to the S corporation during the year, the shareholder's share of ordinary business income, and separately stated income/gain items. They decrease it for distributions during the year, the shareholder's share of nondeductible expenses, and the shareholder's share of ordinary business loss and separately stated expense/loss items. The basis may not be reduced below zero.
- S corporation shareholders are not allowed to include the S corporation's debt in their stock basis. However, they are allowed to create *debt basis* for the amount of loans they make directly to the S corporation. Debt basis can absorb S corporation losses (see below).
- For an S corporation shareholder to deduct them, S corporation losses must clear three separate hurdles: (1) tax-basis limitation in stock (and debt), (2) at-risk amount limitation, and (3) passive activity loss limitation. In addition, for losses that clear each of the three separate hurdles, S corporation shareholders are not allowed to deduct excess business losses.
- Losses suspended at a particular level remain suspended until the shareholder creates additional tax-basis or at-risk amounts, clears the passive loss hurdle, or sells her stock in the S corporation.
- If a shareholder's stock and debt basis is reduced by loss allocations and then increased by subsequent income allocations, the income allocation first increases the debt basis to the debt's outstanding amount before increasing the stock basis.
- When an S corporation's S election is terminated, S corporation shareholders can deduct their share of S corporation losses on the last day of the post-termination transition period as long as the losses are able to clear the three loss limitation hurdles.
- Allocation of ordinary business income is not self-employment income to S corporation shareholders.
- If S corporation shareholders are employees of the corporation, their wages are subject to employment taxes.
- S corporation shareholders are subject to the net investment income tax on their share of an S corporation's gross income from interest, dividends, annuities, royalties, rents, a trade or business that is a passive activity or a trade or business of trading financial instruments or commodities, and generally any net gain from disposing of property, less any allowable deductions from these items.
- Many fringe benefits that are nontaxable to other S corporation employees are taxable to employees who own more than 2 percent of the S corporation.

Apply the tax rules for S corporation operating distributions and liquidating distributions. **LO 22-5**

- Operating distributions from S corporations without accumulated earnings and profits from C corporation years are nontaxable to the extent of the shareholder's basis and then taxable as capital gain to the extent they exceed the shareholder's stock basis.
- Operating distributions from S corporations with accumulated earnings and profits from C corporation years are a nontaxable reduction in stock basis to the extent of the S corporation's accumulated adjustments account, a dividend to the extent of the corporation's earnings and profits, and then a nontaxable return of capital to the extent of the stock basis. Amounts in excess of the stock basis are capital gain.
- The accumulated adjustments account represents the cumulative income or losses for the period the corporation has been an S corporation.
- When S corporations distribute appreciated property to shareholders they must recognize gain on the distribution (the gain is allocated to the shareholders). When they distribute loss property, they are not allowed to deduct the losses. In either case, the fair market value of the property (reduced by liabilities) is the amount of the distribution to the shareholders.

- When an S election is terminated, cash distributions during the post-termination transition period are tax-free to the shareholder to the extent of the S corporation's accumulated adjustments account and the shareholder's stock basis.

- S corporations making liquidating distributions recognize gain or loss on the distributions. The gains or losses are allocated to the shareholders. The shareholders compare the amount received in the liquidating distribution to their stock basis to determine if they recognize gain or loss on the distributions.

LO 22-6   Describe the taxes that apply to S corporations, estimated tax requirements, and tax return filing requirements.

- S corporations that were formerly C corporations may be required to pay the built-in gains tax. The tax applies if the S corporation had a net unrealized built-in gain at the time it converted to an S corporation. It must pay the tax when it recognizes these net built-in gains during its first five years operating as an S corporation.

- The base for the tax is limited to the least of (1) the net of the recognized built-in gains and losses for the year, (2) the net unrealized built-in gains as of the date of the S election date less the net recognized built-in gains in previous years, and (3) the corporation's taxable income for the year using the C corporation tax rules (excluding the dividends received deduction and NOL deduction). The base is then reduced by any net operating loss (NOL) or capital loss carryovers from prior C corporation years.

- S corporations that were formerly C corporations and have C corporation earnings and profits must pay the excess net passive income tax when their passive investment income exceeds 25 percent of their gross receipts.

- The formula for the tax is 21 percent (the highest corporate tax rate) × {net passive investment income × [passive investment income − (25% × gross receipts)]/passive investment income}.

- C corporations that elect to be taxed as S corporations and that use the LIFO method of accounting for inventories must pay the LIFO recapture tax. The tax is the C corporation's marginal tax rate times the excess of the inventory valued under the LIFO method over the inventory valued under the FIFO method at the time the S election became effective. The corporation pays one-quarter of the tax on its final C corporation tax return and the final three installments on its S corporation tax return for the first three years it is an S corporation.

- S corporations that must pay the built-in gains tax or the excess passive income tax generally must pay estimated taxes in four quarterly installments. They are not required to make estimated tax payments for the LIFO recapture tax.

- S corporations file Form 1120S by the 15th day of the third month after the tax year-end (generally March 15).

- S corporations may receive a six-month extension by filing Form 7004.

- On Form 1120S, S corporations report ordinary business income and separately stated items on Schedule K. Each shareholder's portion of items on the Schedule K is reported to the shareholder on her Schedule K-1.

KEY TERMS

accumulated adjustments account (AAA) (22-18)
at-risk amount (22-14)
built-in gains tax (22-22)
built-in gains tax recognition period (22-22)
debt basis (22-13)
earnings and profits (E&P) (22-2)
excess business loss (22-15)

excess net passive income (22-24)
excess net passive income tax (22-22)
Form 1120S (22-28)
Form 2553 (22-4)
Form 7004 (22-28)
gross receipts (22-6)
LIFO recapture amount (22-26)
LIFO recapture tax (22-22)

net passive investment income (22-24)
net unrealized built-in gain (22-22)
ordinary business income (loss) (22-9)
passive activity loss rules (22-15)
passive investment income (PII) (22-6)
post-termination transition period (PTTP) (22-14)
S corporation (22-2)
separately stated items (22-9)

DISCUSSION QUESTIONS

Discussion Questions are available in Connect®.   **connect**

1. In general terms, how are C corporations different from and similar to S corporations?   **LO 22-1**

2. What are the limitations on the number and type of shareholders an S corporation may have? How are these limitations different from restrictions on the number and type of shareholders C corporations or partnerships may have?   **LO 22-1**

3. Why can't large, publicly traded corporations be treated as S corporations?   **LO 22-1**

4. How do the tax laws treat family members for purposes of limiting the number of owners an S corporation may have?   **LO 22-1**

5. Super Corp. was organized under the laws of the state of Montana. It issued common voting stock and common nonvoting stock to its two shareholders. Is Super Corp. eligible to elect S corporation status? Why or why not?   **LO 22-1**

6. Karen is the sole shareholder of a calendar-year-end C corporation she formed last year. If she elects S corporation status this year on February 20, when will the election become effective and why? What if she had made the election on March 20?   **LO 22-1**

7. JB Corporation is a C corporation owned 80 percent by Jacob and 20 percent by Bauer. Jacob would like JB to make an S election but Bauer is opposed to the idea. Can JB elect to be taxed as an S corporation without Bauer's consent? Explain.   **LO 22-1**

8. In what circumstances could a calendar-year C corporation make an election on February 1, year 1, to be taxed as an S corporation in year 1 but not have the election effective until year 2?   **LO 22-1**

9. Theodore, Alvin, and Simon are equal shareholders of Timeless Corp. (an S corporation). Simon wants to terminate the S election, but Theodore and Alvin disagree. Can Simon unilaterally elect to have the S election terminated? If not, what would Simon need to do to have the S election terminated?   **LO 22-2**

10. Juanita is the sole shareholder of Belize Corporation (a calendar-year S corporation). She is considering revoking the S election. It is February 1, year 1. What options does Juanita have for timing the effective date of the S election revocation?   **LO 22-2**

11. Describe the circumstances in which an S election may be involuntarily terminated.   **LO 22-2**

12. Describe a situation in which a former C corporation that elected to be taxed as an S corporation may have its S election automatically terminated, but a similarly situated corporation that has always been taxed as an S corporation would not.   **LO 22-2**

13. When a corporation's S election is terminated mid-year, what options does the corporation have for allocating the annual income between the S corporation short year and the C corporation short year?   **LO 22-2**

14. On June 1, year 1, Jasper Corporation's S election was involuntarily terminated. What is the earliest Jasper may be taxed as an S corporation again? Are there any exceptions to the general rule? Explain.   **LO 22-2**

15. Apple Union (AU), a C corporation with a March 31 year-end, uses the accrual method of accounting. If AU elects to be taxed as an S corporation, what will its year-end and method of accounting be (assuming no special elections)?   **LO 22-3**

16. Compare and contrast the method of allocating income or loss to owners for partnerships and for S corporations.   **LO 22-3**

17. Why must an S corporation report separately stated items to its shareholders? How is the character of a separately stated item determined? How does the S corporation report this information to each shareholder?   **LO 22-3**

18. How do S corporations report dividends they receive? Are they entitled to a dividends received deduction? Why or why not?   **LO 22-3**

LO 22-4   19. Shawn receives stock in an S corporation when it is formed in a tax-deferred transaction by contributing land with a tax basis of $50,000 and encumbered by a $20,000 mortgage. What is Shawn's initial basis in his S corporation stock?

LO 22-4   20. Why is a shareholder's basis in an S corporate stock adjusted annually?

LO 22-4   21. What adjustments are made annually to a shareholder's basis in S corporation stock and in what order? What impact do these adjustments have on a subsequent sale of stock?

LO 22-4   22. Can a shareholder's basis in S corporation stock ever be adjusted to a negative number? Why or why not?

LO 22-4   23. Describe the three hurdles a taxpayer must pass if he wants to deduct a loss from his share in an S corporation. What other loss limitation rule may impact the deductibility of losses from an S corporation?

LO 22-4   24. Is a shareholder allowed to increase her basis in her S corporation stock by her share of the corporation's liabilities, as partners are able to increase the basis of their ownership interest by their share of partnership liabilities? Explain.

LO 22-4   25. How does a shareholder create *debt basis* in an S corporation? How is debt basis similar and dissimilar to stock basis?

LO 22-4   26. When an S corporation shareholder has suspended losses due to the tax-basis or at-risk amount limitation, is he allowed to deduct the losses if the S corporation status is terminated? Why or why not?

LO 22-4   27. When considering C corporations, the IRS checks to see whether salaries paid are too large. In S corporations, however, it usually must verify that salaries are large enough. Account for this difference.

LO 22-4   28. How does the tax treatment of employee fringe benefits reflect the hybrid nature of the S corporation?

LO 22-4   29. If a corporation has been an S corporation since inception, describe how its operating distributions to its shareholders are taxed to the shareholders.

LO 22-4   30. How are the tax consequences of a cash distribution different from those of a noncash property distribution to both the corporation and the shareholders?

LO 22-5   31. What role does debt basis play in determining the taxability of operating distributions to shareholders?

LO 22-5   32. What does the accumulated adjustments account represent? How is it adjusted year by year? Can it have a negative balance?

LO 22-5   33. If an S corporation with accumulated E&P makes a distribution, from what accounts (and in what order) is the distribution deemed to be paid from?

LO 22-5   34. Under what circumstances could a corporation with earnings and profits make a tax-free distribution to its shareholders after the S election termination?

LO 22-5   35. How do the tax consequences of S corporation liquidating distributions differ from the tax consequences of S corporation operating distributions at both the corporate and shareholder levels?

LO 22-6   36. When is an S corporation required to pay a built-in gains tax?

LO 22-6   37. When is an S corporation required to pay the excess net passive income tax?

LO 22-6   38. Is the LIFO recapture tax a C corporation tax or an S corporation tax? Explain.

LO 22-6   39. When must an S corporation make estimated tax payments?

LO 22-6   40. On what form does an S corporation report its income to the IRS? When is the tax return due? What information does the S corporation provide to shareholders to allow them to complete their tax returns?

LO 22-6   41. Compare and contrast S corporations, C corporations, and partnerships in terms of tax consequences at formation, shareholder restrictions, income allocation, basis calculations, compensation to owners, taxation of distributions, and accounting periods.

PROBLEMS

Select problems are available in Connect®.   📘 connect

42. Julie wants to create an S corporation called J's Dance Shoes (JDS). Describe how the items below affect her eligibility for an S election. **LO 22-1**

   a) Because Julie wants all her shareholders to have an equal say in the future of JDS, she gives them equal voting rights and decides shareholders who take a more active role in the firm will have priority in terms of distribution and liquidation rights.

   b) Julie decides to incorporate under the state laws of Utah, since that is where she lives. Once she gets her business up and running, however, she plans on doing extensive business in Mexico.

43. Lucy and Ricky Ricardo live in Los Angeles, California. After they were married, they started a business named ILL Corporation (a C corporation). For state law purposes, the shares of stock in ILL Corp. are listed under Ricky's name only. Ricky signed the Form 2553 electing to have ILL taxed as an S corporation for federal income tax purposes, but Lucy did not sign. Given that California is a community property state, is the S election for ILL Corp. valid? **LO 22-1** **research**

44. Jane has been operating Mansfield Park as a C corporation and decides she would like to make an S election. What is the earliest the election will become effective under each of these alternative scenarios? **LO 22-1**

   a) Jane is on top of things and makes the election on January 1, 2018.

   b) Jane is mostly on top of things and makes the election on January 15, 2018.

   c) Jane makes the election on February 10, 2018. She needed a little time to convince a C corporation shareholder to sell its stock to a qualifying shareholder. That process took all of January, and she was glad to have it over with.

   d) Jane makes the election on March 14, 2018.

   e) Jane makes the election on February 5, 2018. One of the shareholders refused to consent to the S election. He has since sold his shares (on January 15, 2018) to another shareholder who consented to the election.

45. Missy is one of 100 unrelated shareholders of Dalmatian, an S corporation. She is considering selling her shares. Under the following alternative scenarios, would the S election be terminated? Why or why not? **LO 22-2**

   a) Missy wants to sell half her shares to a friend, a U.S. citizen, so they can rename their corporation 101 Dalmatians.

   b) Missy's mother's family wants to be involved with the corporation. Missy splits half her shares evenly among her aunt, uncle, grandfather, and two cousins.

   c) Missy sells half her Dalmatian stock to her husband's corporation.

46. Cathy, Heathcliff, and Isabelle are equal shareholders in Wuthering Heights (WH), an S corporation. Heathcliff has decided he would like to terminate the S election. In the following alternative scenarios, indicate whether the termination will occur and indicate the date if applicable (assume no alternative termination dates are selected). **LO 22-2**

   a) Cathy and Isabelle both decline to agree to the termination. Heathcliff files the termination election anyway on March 14, 2018.

   b) Isabelle agrees with the termination, but Cathy strongly disagrees. The termination is filed on February 16, 2018.

c) The termination seems to be the first thing all three could agree on. They file the election to terminate on March 28, 2018.

d) The termination seems to be the first thing all three could agree on. They file the election to terminate on February 28, 2018.

e) Knowing the other two disagree with the termination, on March 16, 2018, Heathcliff sells one of his 50 shares to his maid, who recently moved back to Bulgaria, her home country.

LO 22-2   47. Assume the following S corporations and gross receipts, passive investment income, and corporate E&P. Will any of these corporations have its S election terminated due to excessive passive income? If so, in what year? All became S corporations at the beginning of year 1.

a) Clarion Corp.

Year	Gross Receipts	Passive Investment Income	Corporate Earnings and Profits
1	$1,353,458	$250,000	$321,300
2	1,230,389	100,000	321,300
3	1,139,394	300,000	230,000
4	1,347,039	350,000	100,000
5	1,500,340	400,000	0

b) Hanson Corp.

Year	Gross Receipts	Passive Investment Income	Corporate Earnings and Profits
1	$1,430,000	$247,000	$138,039
2	700,380	200,000	100,000
3	849,000	190,000	100,000
4	830,000	210,000	80,000
5	1,000,385	257,390	80,000

c) Tiffany Corp.

Year	Gross Receipts	Passive Investment Income	Corporate Earnings and Profits
1	$1,000,458	$250,000	$0
2	703,000	300,480	0
3	800,375	400,370	0
4	900,370	350,470	0
5	670,000	290,377	0

d) Jonas Corp.

Year	Gross Receipts	Passive Investment Income	Corporate Earnings and Profits
1	$1,100,370	$250,000	$500
2	998,000	240,000	400
3	800,350	230,000	300
4	803,000	214,570	200
5	750,000	200,000	100

48. Hughie, Dewey, and Louie are equal shareholders in HDL, an S corporation. HDL's S election terminates under each of the following alternative scenarios. When is the earliest it can again operate as an S corporation?

    a) The S election terminates on August 1, year 2, because Louie sells half his shares to his uncle Walt, a citizen and resident of Scotland.

    b) The S election terminates effective January 1, year 3, because on August 1, year 2, Hughie and Dewey vote (2 to 1) to terminate the election.

49. Winkin, Blinkin, and Nod are equal shareholders in SleepEZ, an S corporation. In the conditions listed below, how much income should each report from SleepEZ for 2018 under both the daily allocation and the specific identification allocation method? Refer to the following table for the timing of SleepEZ's income.

Period	Income
January 1 through March 15 (74 days)	$125,000
March 16 through December 31 (291 days)	345,500
January 1 through December 31, 2018 (365 days)	$470,500

    a) There are no sales of SleepEZ stock during the year.

    b) On March 15, 2018, Blinkin sells his shares to Nod.

    c) On March 15, 2018, Winkin and Nod each sell their shares to Blinkin.

Use the following information to complete problems 50 and 51:

UpAHill Corporation (an S Corporation) Income Statement December 31, Year 1 and Year 2		
	Year 1	**Year 2**
Sales revenue	$175,000	$310,000
Cost of goods sold	(60,000)	(85,000)
Salary to owners Jack and Jill	(40,000)	(50,000)
Employee wages	(15,000)	(20,000)
Depreciation expense	(10,000)	(15,000)
Miscellaneous expenses	(7,500)	(9,000)
Interest income (related to business)	2,000	2,500
Qualified dividend income	500	1,000
Overall net income	$ 45,000	$134,500

50. Jack and Jill are owners of UpAHill, an S corporation. They own 25 and 75 percent, respectively.

    a) What amount of ordinary income and separately stated items are allocated to them for years 1 and 2 based on the information above? Assume that UpAHill Corporation has $100,000 of qualified property (unadjusted basis) in both years.

    b) Complete UpAHill's Form 1120S, Schedule K, for year 1.

    c) Complete Jill's 1120S, Schedule K-1, for year 1.

51. Assume Jack and Jill, 25 and 75 percent shareholders, respectively, in UpAHill Corporation, have tax bases in their shares at the beginning of year 1 of $24,000 and $56,000, respectively. Also assume no distributions were made. Given the income statement above, what are their tax bases in their shares at the end of year 1?

Use the following information to complete problems 52 and 53:

Falcons Corporation (an S Corporation) Income Statement December 31, Year 1 and Year 2		
	Year 1	Year 2
Sales revenue	$300,000	$430,000
Cost of goods sold	(40,000)	(60,000)
Salary to owners Julio and Milania	(40,000)	(80,000)
Employee wages	(25,000)	(50,000)
Depreciation expense	(20,000)	(40,000)
Section 179 expense	(30,000)	(50,000)
Interest income (related to business)	12,000	22,500
Municipal bond income	1,500	4,000
Government fines	0	(2,000)
Overall net income	$158,500	$174,500
Distributions	$ 30,000	$ 50,000

LO 22-3

tax forms

52. Julio and Milania are owners of Falcons Corporation, an S corporation. They each own 50 percent of Falcons Corporation. In year 1, Julio and Milania each received distributions of $15,000 from Falcons Corporation.

a) What amount of ordinary income and separately stated items are allocated to them for year 1 based on the information above? Assume that Falcons Corporation has $200,000 of qualified property (unadjusted basis).

b) Complete Falcons's Form 1120S, Schedule K for year 1.

c) Complete Julio's 1120S, Schedule K-1 for year 1.

LO 22-3

tax forms

53. In year 2, Julio and Milania each received distributions of $25,000 from Falcons Corporation.

a) What amount of ordinary income and separately stated items are allocated to them for year 2 based on the information above? Assume that Falcons Corporation has $200,000 of qualified property (unadjusted basis).

b) Complete Falcons's Form 1120S, Schedule K for year 2.

c) Complete Milania's 1120S, Schedule K-1 for year 2.

LO 22-4

54. Harry, Hermione, and Ron formed an S corporation called Bumblebore. Harry and Hermione both contributed cash of $25,000 to get things started. Ron was a bit short on cash but had a parcel of land valued at $60,000 (basis of $50,000) that he decided to contribute. The land was encumbered by a $35,000 mortgage. What tax bases will each of the three have in his or her stock of Bumblebore?

LO 22-4

55. Jessica is a one-third owner in Bikes-R-Us, an S corporation that experienced a $45,000 loss this year (year 1). If her stock basis is $10,000 at the beginning of the year, how much of this loss clears the hurdle for deductibility (assume the at-risk limitation equals the tax-basis limitation)? If she cannot deduct the whole loss, what happens to the remainder? Is she able to deduct her entire loss if she sells her stock at year-end?

LO 22-4

56. Assume the same facts as in the previous problem, except that at the beginning of year 1 Jessica loaned Bikes-R-Us $3,000. In year 2, Bikes-R-Us reported ordinary income of $12,000. What amount is Jessica allowed to deduct in year 1? What are her stock and debt bases in the corporation at the end of year 1? What are her stock and debt bases in the corporation at the end of year 2?

57. Birch Corp., a calendar-year corporation, was formed three years ago by its sole shareholder, James, who has operated it as an S corporation since its inception. Last year, James made a direct loan to Birch Corp. in the amount of $5,000. Birch Corp. has paid the interest on the loan but has not yet paid any principal. (Assume the loan qualifies as debt for tax purposes.) For the year, Birch experienced a $25,000 business loss. What amount of the loss clears the tax-basis limitation, and what is James's basis in his Birch Corp. stock and Birch Corp. debt in each of the following alternative scenarios?

    `LO 22-4`

    a) At the beginning of the year, James's basis in his Birch Corp. stock was $45,000 and his basis in his Birch Corp. debt was $5,000.

    b) At the beginning of the year, James's basis in his Birch Corp. stock was $8,000 and his basis in his Birch Corp. debt was $5,000.

    c) At the beginning of the year, James's basis in his Birch Corp. stock was $0 and his basis in his Birch Corp. debt was $5,000.

58. Timo is the sole owner of Jazz Inc., an S corporation. On October 31, 2018, Timo executed an unsecured demand promissory note of $15,000 and transferred the note to Jazz (Jazz could require Timo to pay it $15,000 on demand). When Timo transferred the note to Jazz, his tax basis in his Jazz stock was $0. On January 31, 2019, Timo paid the $15,000 to Jazz as required by the promissory note. For the taxable year ending December 31, 2018, Jazz incurred a business loss of $12,000. How much of the loss clears the stock and debt basis hurdles for deductibility?

    `LO 22-4`

    `research`

59. Chandra was the sole shareholder of Pet Emporium that was originally formed as an S corporation. When Pet Emporium terminated its S election on August 31, 2017, Chandra had a stock basis and an at-risk amount of $0. Chandra also had a suspended loss from Pet Emporium of $9,000. What amount of the suspended loss is Chandra allowed to deduct, and what is her basis in her Pet Emporium stock at the end of the post-termination transition period under the following alternative scenarios (assume Pet Emporium files for an extension to file its tax returns)?

    `LO 22-4`

    a) Chandra makes capital contributions of $7,000 on August 30, 2018, and $4,000 on September 14, 2018.

    b) Chandra makes capital contributions of $5,000 on September 1, 2018, and $5,000 on September 30, 2018.

    c) Chandra makes a capital contribution of $10,000 on August 31, 2018.

    d) Chandra makes a capital contribution of $10,000 on October 1, 2018.

60. Neil owns stock in two S corporations, Blue and Green. He actively participates in the management of Blue but maintains ownership in Green only as a passive investor. Neil has no other business investments. Both Blue and Green anticipate a loss this year, and Neil's basis in his stock of both corporations is $0. All else equal, if Neil plans on making a capital contribution to at least one of the corporations this year, to which firm should he contribute in order to increase his chances of deducting the loss allocated to him from the entity? Why?

    `LO 22-4`

    `planning`

61. In the past several years, Shakira had loaned money to Shakira Inc. (an S corporation) to help the corporation keep afloat in a downturn. Her stock basis in the S corporation is now $0, and she had deducted $40,000 in losses that reduced her debt basis from $100,000 to $60,000. Things appear to be turning around this year, and Shakira Inc. repaid Shakira $20,000 of the $100,000 outstanding loan. What is Shakira's income, if any, on the partial loan repayment?

    `LO 22-4`

    `planning`

LO 22-4 62. Adam Fleeman, a skilled carpenter, started a home improvement business with Tom Collins, a master plumber. Adam and Tom are concerned about the payroll taxes they will have to pay. Assume they form an S corporation and each earns a salary of $80,000 from the corporation; in addition, they expect their share of business profits to be $60,000 each. How much Social Security tax and Medicare tax (or self-employment tax) will Adam, Tom, and their corporation have to pay on their salary and profits?

planning **LO 22-4** 63. Using the facts in problem 62, could Adam and Tom lower their payroll tax exposure if they operated their business as a partnership? Why or why not?

LO 22-4 64. This year, Justin B.'s share of S corporation income includes $4,000 of interest income, $5,000 of dividend income, and $40,000 of net income from the corporation's professional service business activity.

a) Assume that Justin B. materially participates in the S corporation. How much of his S corporation income is potentially subject to the net investment income tax?

b) Assume that Justin B. does not materially participate in the S corporation. How much of his S corporation income is potentially subject to the net investment income tax?

LO 22-4 65. Friends Jackie (0.5 percent owner), Jermaine (1 percent owner), Marlon (2 percent owner), Janet (86 percent owner), and Tito (10.5 percent owner) are shareholders in Jackson 5 Inc. (an S corporation). As employees of the company, they each receive health insurance ($10,000 per year benefit), dental insurance ($2,000 per year benefit), and free access to a workout facility located at company headquarters ($500 per year benefit). What are the tax consequences of these benefits for each shareholder and for Jackson 5 Inc.?

LO 22-5 66. Maple Corp., a calendar-year corporation, was formed three years ago by its sole shareholder, Brady, who immediately elected S corporation status. On December 31 of the current year, Maple distributed $30,000 cash to Brady. What is the amount and character of gain Brady must recognize on the distribution in each of the following alternative scenarios?

a) At the time of the distribution, Brady's basis in his Maple Corp. stock was $35,000.

b) At the time of the distribution, Brady's basis in his Maple Corp. stock was $8,000.

c) At the time of the distribution, Brady's basis in his Maple Corp. stock was $0.

LO 22-5 67. Oak Corp., a calendar-year corporation, was formed three years ago by its sole shareholder, Glover, and has always operated as a C corporation. However, at the beginning of this year, Glover made a qualifying S election for Oak Corp., effective January 1. Oak Corp. did not have any C corporation earnings and profits on that date. On June 1, Oak Corp. distributed $15,000 to Glover. What is the amount and character of gain Glover must recognize on the distribution, and what is his basis in his Oak Corp. stock in each of the following alternative scenarios?

a) At the time of the distribution, Glover's basis in his Oak Corp. stock was $35,000.

b) At the time of the distribution, Glover's basis in his Oak Corp. stock was $8,000.

c) At the time of the distribution, Glover's basis in his Oak Corp. stock was $0.

68. Janna has a tax basis of $15,000 in her Mimikaki stock (Mimikaki has been an S corporation since inception). In 2018, Janna was allocated $20,000 of ordinary income from Mimikaki. What is the amount and character of gain she recognizes from end-of-the-year distributions in each of the following alternative scenarios, and what is her stock basis following each distribution?   `LO 22-5`

    a) Mimikaki distributes $10,000 to Janna.

    b) Mimikaki distributes $20,000 to Janna.

    c) Mimikaki distributes $30,000 to Janna.

    d) Mimikaki distributes $40,000 to Janna.

69. Assume the following year 2 income statement for Johnstone Corporation, which was a C corporation in year 1 and elected to be taxed as an S corporation beginning in year 2. Johnstone's earnings and profits at the end of year 1 were $10,000. Marcus is Johnstone's sole shareholder, and he has a stock basis of $40,000 at the end of year 1. What is Johnstone's accumulated adjustments account at the end of year 2, and what amount of dividend income does Marcus recognize on the year 2 distribution in each of the following alternative scenarios?   `LO 22-5`

Johnstone Corporation Income Statement December 31, Year 2	
	Year 2 (S Corporation)
Sales revenue	$150,000
Cost of goods sold	(35,000)
Salary to owners	(60,000)
Employee wages	(50,000)
Depreciation expense	(4,000)
Miscellaneous expenses	(4,000)
Interest income	10,000
Overall net income	$ 7,000

    a) Johnstone distributed $6,000 to Marcus in year 2.

    b) Johnstone distributed $10,000 to Marcus in year 2.

    c) Johnstone distributed $16,000 to Marcus in year 2.

    d) Johnstone distributed $26,000 to Marcus in year 2.

70. At the end of the year, before distributions, Bombay (an S corporation) has an accumulated adjustments account balance of $15,000 and accumulated E&P of $20,000 from a previous year as a C corporation. During the year, Nicolette (a 40 percent shareholder) received a $20,000 distribution (the remaining shareholders received $30,000 in distributions). What is the amount and character of gain Nicolette must recognize from the distribution? What is her basis in her Bombay stock at the end of the year? (Assume her stock basis is $40,000 after considering her share of Bombay's income for the year but before considering the effects of the distribution.)   `LO 22-5`

71. Pine Corp., a calendar-year corporation, was formed three years ago by its sole shareholder, Connor, who has always operated it as a C corporation. However, at the beginning of this year, Connor made a qualifying S election for Pine Corp., effective January 1. Pine Corp. reported $70,000 of C corporation earnings and profits on the effective date of the S election. This year (its first S corporation year), Pine   `LO 22-5`

Corp. reported business income of $50,000. Connor's basis in his Pine Corp. stock at the beginning of the year was $15,000. What is the amount and character of gain Connor must recognize on the following alternative distributions, and what is his basis in his Pine Corp. stock at the end of the year?

a) Connor received a $40,000 distribution from Pine Corp. at the end of the year.

b) Connor received a $60,000 distribution from Pine Corp. at the end of the year.

c) Connor received a $130,000 distribution from Pine Corp. at the end of the year.

d) Connor received a $150,000 distribution from Pine Corp. at the end of the year.

LO 22-5 72. Carolina Corporation, an S corporation, has no corporate E&P from its years as a C corporation. At the end of the year, it distributes a small parcel of land to its sole shareholder, Shadiya. The fair market value of the parcel is $70,000 and its tax basis is $40,000. Shadiya's basis in her stock is $14,000. Assume Carolina Corporation reported $0 taxable income before considering the tax consequences of the distribution.

a) What amount of gain or loss, if any, does Carolina Corporation recognize on the distribution?

b) How much gain must Shadiya recognize (if any) as a result of the distribution, what is her basis in her Carolina Corporation stock after the distribution, and what is her basis in the land?

c) What is your answer to part (a) if the fair market value of the land is $25,000 rather than $70,000?

d) What is your answer to part (b) if the fair market value of the land is $25,000 rather than $70,000?

LO 22-5 73. Last year, Miley decided to terminate the S corporation election of her solely owned corporation on October 17, 2017 (effective immediately), in preparation for taking it public. At the time of the election, the corporation had an accumulated adjustments account balance of $150,000 and $450,000 of accumulated E&P from prior C corporation years, and Miley had a basis in her S corporation stock of $135,000. During 2018, Miley's corporation reported $0 taxable income or loss. Also, during 2018 the corporation made distributions to Miley of $80,000 and $60,000. How are these distributions taxed to Miley assuming the following?

a) Both distributions are in cash, and the first was paid on June 15, 2018, and the second on November 15, 2018.

b) Both distributions are in cash, and the first was paid on June 15, 2018, and the second on September 30, 2018.

c) Assume the same facts as in part (b), except the June 15 distribution was a property (noncash) distribution (fair market value of distributed property equal to basis).

LO 22-6 74. Alabama Corporation, an S corporation, liquidates this year by distributing a parcel of land to its sole shareholder, Mark Ingram. The fair market value of the parcel is $50,000 and its tax basis is $30,000. Mark's basis in his stock is $25,000.

a) What amount of gain or loss, if any, does Alabama Corporation recognize on the distribution?

b) How much gain must Mark recognize (if any) as a result of the distribution and what is his basis in the land?

c) What is your answer to part (a) if the fair market value of the land is $20,000 rather than $50,000?

d) What is your answer to part (b) if the fair market value of the land is $20,000 rather than $50,000?

75. Rivendell Corporation uses the accrual method of accounting and has the following assets as of the end of 2017. Rivendell converted to an S corporation on January 1, 2018.

LO 22-6

Asset	Adjusted Basis	FMV
Cash	$ 40,000	$ 40,000
Accounts receivable	30,000	30,000
Inventory	130,000	60,000
Land	100,000	125,000
Totals	$300,000	$255,000

a) What is Rivendell's net unrealized built-in gain at the time it converted to an S corporation?

b) Assuming the land was valued at $200,000, what would be Rivendell's net unrealized gain at the time it converted to an S corporation?

c) Assuming the land was valued at $125,000 but that the inventory was valued at $85,000, what would be Rivendell's net unrealized gain at the time it converted to an S corporation?

76. Virginia Corporation is a calendar-year corporation. At the beginning of 2018, its election to be taxed as an S corporation became effective. Virginia Corp.'s balance sheet at the end of 2017 reflected the following assets (it did not have any earnings and profits from its prior years as a C corporation).

LO 22-6

Asset	Adjusted Basis	FMV
Cash	$ 20,000	$ 20,000
Accounts receivable	40,000	40,000
Inventory	90,000	200,000
Land	150,000	175,000
Totals	$300,000	$435,000

In 2018, Virginia reported business income of $50,000 (this would have been its taxable income if it were still a C corporation). What is Virginia's built-in gains tax in each of the following alternative scenarios?

a) During 2018, Virginia sold inventory it owned at the beginning of the year for $100,000. The basis of the inventory sold was $55,000.

b) Assume the same facts as part (a), except Virginia had a net operating loss carryover of $24,000 from its time as a C corporation.

c) Assume the same facts as part (a), except that if Virginia were a C corporation, its taxable income would have been $1,500.

77. Tempe Corporation is a calendar-year corporation. At the beginning of 2018, its election to be taxed as an S corporation became effective. Tempe Corp.'s balance sheet at the end of 2017 reflected the following assets (it did not have any earnings and profits from its prior years as a C corporation):

LO 22-6

Asset	Adjusted Basis	FMV
Cash	$ 20,000	$ 20,000
Accounts receivable	40,000	40,000
Inventory	160,000	200,000
Land	150,000	120,000
Totals	$370,000	$380,000

Tempe's business income for the year was $40,000 (this would have been its taxable income if it were a C corporation).

a) During 2018, Tempe sold all of the inventory it owned at the beginning of the year for $210,000. What is its built-in gains tax in 2018?

b) Assume the same facts as in part (a), except that if Tempe were a C corporation, its taxable income would have been $7,000. What is its built-in gains tax in 2018?

c) Assume the original facts except the land was valued at $140,000 instead of $120,000. What is Tempe's built-in gains tax in 2018?

LO 22-6 78. Wood Corporation was a C corporation in 2017 but elected to be taxed as an S corporation in 2018. At the end of 2017, its earnings and profits were $15,500. The following table reports Wood's (taxable) income for 2018 (its first year as an S corporation).

Wood Corporation	
Income Statement	
December 31, 2018	
Sales revenue	$150,000
Cost of goods sold	(35,000)
Salary to owners	(60,000)
Employee wages	(50,000)
Depreciation expense	(4,000)
Miscellaneous expenses	(4,000)
Interest income	8,000
Qualified dividend income	2,000
Overall net income	$ 7,000

What is Wood Corporation's excess net passive income tax for 2018?

LO 22-6 79. Calculate Anaheim Corporation's excess net passive income tax in each of the following alternative scenarios:

a) Passive investment income, $100,000; expenses associated with passive investment income, $40,000; gross receipts, $120,000; taxable income if C corporation, $40,000; corporate E&P, $30,000.

b) Passive investment income, $100,000; expenses associated with passive investment income, $70,000; gross receipts, $120,000; taxable income if C corporation, $1,200; corporate E&P, $30,000.

c) Passive investment income, $100,000; expenses associated with passive investment income, $40,000; gross receipts, $120,000; taxable income if C corporation, $40,000; corporate E&P, $0.

LO 22-5 **LO 22-6** 80. Mark is the sole shareholder of Tex Corporation. Mark first formed Tex as a C corporation. However, in an attempt to avoid having Tex's income double taxed, Mark
planning elected S corporation status for Tex several years ago. On December 31, 2018, Tex reports $5,000 of earnings and profits from its years as a C corporation and $50,000 in its accumulated adjustments account from its activities as an S corporation (including its 2018 activities). Mark discovered that for the first time Tex was going to have to pay the excess net passive income tax. Mark wanted to avoid having to pay the tax but he determined the only way to avoid the tax was to eliminate Tex's E&P by the end of 2018. He determined that, because of the distribution ordering rules (AAA first), he would need to have Tex immediately (in 2018) distribute $55,000 to

him. This would clear out Tex's accumulated adjustments account first and then eliminate Tex's C corporation earnings and profits in time to avoid the excess net passive income tax. Mark was not sure Tex could come up with $55,000 of cash or property in time to accomplish his objective. Does Mark have any other options to eliminate Tex's earnings and profits without first distributing the balance in Tex's accumulated adjustments account?

81. Farve Inc. recently elected S corporation status. At the time of the election, the company had $10,000 of accumulated earnings and profits and a net unrealized gain of $1,000,000 associated with land it had invested in (although some parcels had an unrealized loss). In the next couple of years, most of the income the company expects to generate will be in the form of interest and dividends (approximately $200,000 per year). However, in the future, the company will want to liquidate some of its current holdings in land and possibly reinvest in other parcels. What strategies can you recommend for Farve Inc. to help reduce its potential tax liability as an S corporation?

`LO 22-6`
`planning`

82. Until the end of year 0, Magic Carpets (MC) was a C corporation with a calendar year. At the beginning of year 1 it elected to be taxed as an S corporation. MC uses the LIFO method to value its inventory. At the end of year 0, under the LIFO method, its inventory of rugs was valued at $150,000. Under the FIFO method, the rugs would have been valued at $170,000. How much LIFO recapture tax must MC pay, and what is the due date of the first payment under the following alternative scenarios?

`LO 22-6`

a) Magic Carpets's regular taxable income in year 0 was $65,000.

b) Magic Carpets's regular taxable income in year 0 was $200,000.

COMPREHENSIVE PROBLEMS

Select problems are available in Connect®.   connect

83. Knowshon, sole owner of Moreno Inc., is contemplating electing S status for the corporation (Moreno Inc. is currently taxed as a C corporation). Provide recommendations related to Knowshon's election under the following alternative scenarios:

`planning`

a) At the end of the current year, Moreno Inc. has a net operating loss of $800,000 carryover. Beginning next year, the company expects to return to profitability. Knowshon projects that Moreno will report profits of $400,000, $500,000, and $600,000 over the next three years. What suggestions do you have regarding the timing of the S election? Explain.

b) How would you answer part (a) if Moreno Inc. had been operating profitably for several years and thus had no net operating loss?

c) While several of Moreno Inc.'s assets have appreciated in value (to the tune of $2,000,000), the corporation has one property—some land in a newly identified flood zone—that has declined in value by $1,500,000. Knowshon plans on selling the loss property in the next year or two. Assume that Moreno does not have a net operating loss. What suggestions do you have for timing the sale of the flood zone property and why?

84. Barry Potter and Winnie Weasley are considering making an S election on March 1, 2019, for their C corporation, Omniocular. However, first they want to consider the implications of the following information:

`planning`

- Winnie is a U.S. citizen and resident.
- Barry is a citizen of the United Kingdom, but a resident of the United States.

- Barry and Winnie each own 50 percent of the voting power in Omniocular. However, Barry's stock provides him with a claim on 60 percent of the Omniocular assets in liquidation.
- Omniocular was formed under Arizona state law, but it plans on eventually conducting some business in Mexico.

  a) Is Omniocular eligible to elect S corporation status? If so, when is the election effective?

For the remainder of the problem, assume Omniocular made a valid S election effective January 1, 2019. Barry and Winnie each own 50 percent of the voting power and have equal claim on Omniocular's assets in liquidation. In addition, consider the following information:

- Omniocular reports on a calendar tax year.
- Omniocular's earnings and profits as of December 31, 2018, were $55,000.
- Omniocular's 2018 taxable income was $15,000.
- Omniocular's assets at the end of 2018 are as follows:

Omniocular Assets December 31, 2018		
Asset	**Adjusted Basis**	**FMV**
Cash	$ 50,000	$ 50,000
Accounts receivable	20,000	20,000
Investments in stocks and bonds	700,000	700,000
Investment in land	90,000	100,000
Inventory (LIFO)	80,000*	125,000
Equipment	40,000	35,000
Totals	$980,000	$1,030,000

*$110,000 under FIFO accounting.

- On March 31, 2019, Omniocular sold the land for $42,000.
- In 2019, Omniocular sold all the inventory it had on hand at the beginning of the year. This was the only inventory it sold during the year.

Other Income/Expense Items for 2019	
Sales revenue	$155,000
Salary to owners	(50,000)
Employee wages	(10,000)
Depreciation expense	(5,000)
Miscellaneous expenses	(1,000)
Interest income	40,000
Qualified dividend income	65,000

- Assume that if Omniocular were a C corporation for 2019, its taxable income would have been $88,500.

  b) How much LIFO recapture tax is Omniocular required to pay and when is it due?

  c) How much built-in gains tax, if any, is Omniocular required to pay?

  d) How much excess net passive income tax, if any, is Omniocular required to pay?

  e) Assume Barry's basis in his Omniocular stock was $40,000 on January 1, 2019. What is his stock basis on December 31, 2019?

For the following questions, assume that after electing S corporation status Barry and Winnie had a change of heart and filed an election to terminate Omniocular's S election, effective August 1, 2020.

- In 2020, Omniocular reported the following income/expense items:

	January 1—July 31, 2020 (213 days)	August 1—December 31, 2020 (153 days)	January 1—December 31, 2020
Sales revenue	$ 80,000	$185,000	$ 265,000
Cost of goods sold	(40,000)	(20,000)	(60,000)
Salaries to Barry and Winnie	(60,000)	(40,000)	(100,000)
Depreciation expense	(7,000)	(2,000)	(9,000)
Miscellaneous expenses	(4,000)	(3,000)	(7,000)
Interest income	6,000	5,250	11,250
Overall net income (loss)	$(25,000)	$125,250	$ 100,250

f) For tax purposes, how would you recommend Barry and Winnie allocate income between the short S corporation year and the short C corporation year if they would like to minimize double taxation of Omniocular's income?

g) Assume in part (f) that Omniocular allocates income between the short S and C corporation years in a way that minimizes the double taxation of its income. If Barry's stock basis in his Omniocular stock on January 1, 2020, is $50,000, what is his stock basis on December 31, 2020?

h) When is the earliest tax year in which Omniocular can be taxed as an S corporation again?

85. Abigail, Bobby, and Claudia are equal owners in Lafter, an S corporation that was a C corporation several years ago. While Abigail and Bobby actively participate in running the company, Claudia has a separate day job and is a passive owner. Consider the following information for 2018:

- As of January 1, 2018, Abigail, Bobby, and Claudia each have a basis in Lafter stock of $15,000 and a debt basis of $0. On January 1, the stock basis is also the at-risk amount for each shareholder.

- Bobby and Claudia also are passive owners in Aggressive LLC, which allocated business income of $14,000 to each of them in 2018. Neither has any other source of passive income (besides Lafter, for Claudia).

- On March 31, 2018, Abigail lends $5,000 of her own money to Lafter.

- Anticipating the need for basis to deduct a loss, on April 4, 2018, Bobby takes out a $10,000 loan to make a $10,000 contribution to Lafter. Bobby uses his automobile ($12,000 fair market value) as the sole collateral for his loan (nonrecourse).

- Lafter has an accumulated adjustments account balance of $45,000 as of January 1, 2018.

- Lafter has C corporation earnings and profits of $15,000 as of January 1, 2018.

- During 2018, Lafter reports a business loss of $75,000, computed as follows:

Sales revenue	$ 90,000
Cost of goods sold	(85,000)
Salary to Abigail	(40,000)
Salary to Bobby	(40,000)
Business (loss)	$(75,000)

- Lafter also reported $12,000 of tax-exempt interest income.
  a) What amount of Lafter's 2018 business loss of $75,000 are Abigail, Bobby, and Claudia allowed to deduct on their individual tax returns? What are each owner's stock basis and debt basis (if applicable) and each owner's at-risk amount with respect to the investment in Lafter at the end of 2018?
- During 2019, Lafter made several changes to its business approach and reported $18,000 of business income, computed as follows:

Sales revenue	$208,000
Cost of goods sold	(90,000)
Salary to Abigail	(45,000)
Salary to Bobby	(45,000)
Marketing expense	(10,000)
Business income	$ 18,000

- Lafter also reported a long-term capital gain of $24,000 in 2019.
- Lafter made a cash distribution on July 1, 2019, of $20,000 to each shareholder.
  b) What amount of gain/income does each shareholder recognize from the cash distribution on July 1, 2019?

tax forms

86. While James Craig and his former classmate Paul Dolittle both studied accounting at school, they ended up pursuing careers in professional cake decorating. Their company, Good to Eat (GTE), specializes in custom-sculpted cakes for weddings, birthdays, and other celebrations. James and Paul formed the business at the beginning of 2018, and each contributed $50,000 in exchange for a 50 percent ownership interest. GTE also borrowed $200,000 from a local bank. Both James and Paul had to personally guarantee the loan. Both owners provide significant services for the business. The following information pertains to GTE's 2018 activities:

- GTE uses the cash method of accounting (for both book and tax purposes) and reports income on a calendar-year basis.
- GTE received $450,000 of sales revenue and reported $210,000 of cost of goods sold (it did not have any ending inventory).
- GTE paid $30,000 compensation to James, $30,000 compensation to Paul, and $40,000 of compensation to other employees (assume these amounts include applicable payroll taxes if any).
- GTE paid $15,000 of rent for a building and equipment, $20,000 for advertising, $14,000 in interest expense, $4,000 for utilities, and $2,000 for supplies.
- GTE contributed $5,000 to charity.
- GTE received a $1,000 qualified dividend from a great stock investment (it owned 2 percent of the corporation distributing the dividend), and it recognized $1,500 in short-term capital gain when it sold some of the stock.
- On December 1, 2018, GTE distributed $20,000 to James and $20,000 to Paul.
- GTE has qualified property of $300,000 (unadjusted basis).

Required:

a) Assume James and Paul formed GTE as an S corporation.
- Complete GTE's Form 1120S, page 1; Form 1120 S, Schedule K; and Paul's Form 1120S, Schedule K-1 (note that you should use 2017 tax forms).
- Compute the tax basis of Paul's stock in GTE at the end of 2018.
- What amount of Paul's income from GTE is subject to FICA or self-employment taxes?

- What amount of income, including its character, will Paul recognize on the $20,000 distribution he receives on December 1?
- What amount of tax does GTE pay on the $1,000 qualified dividend it received?

b) Assume James and Paul formed GTE as an LLC.

- Complete GTE's Form 1065, page 1; Form 1065, Schedule K; and Paul's Form 1065, Schedule K-1 (note that you should use 2017 tax forms).
- Compute the tax basis of Paul's ownership interest in GTE at the end of 2018.
- What amount of Paul's income from GTE is subject to FICA or self-employment taxes?
- What amount of income, including its character, will Paul recognize on the $20,000 distribution he receives on December 1?
- What amount of tax does GTE pay on the $1,000 qualified dividend it received?

c) Assume James and Paul formed GTE as a C corporation.

- Complete GTE's Form 1120, page 1 (note that you should use the 2017 tax form).
- Compute the tax basis of Paul's stock in GTE at the end of 2018.
- What amount of Paul's income from GTE is subject to FICA or self-employment taxes?
- What amount of income, including its character, will Paul recognize on the $20,000 distribution he receives on December 1?
- What amount of tax does GTE pay on the $1,000 qualified dividend it received?

ROGER | *CPA Review*

Sample CPA Exam questions from Roger CPA Review are available in Connect as support for the topics in this text. These Multiple Choice Questions and Task-Based Simulations include expert-written explanations and solutions and provide a starting point for students to become familiar with the content and functionality of the actual CPA Exam.

23 State and Local Taxes

Learning Objectives

Upon completing this chapter, you should be able to:

LO 23-1 Describe the primary types of state and local taxes.

LO 23-2 Determine whether a business has sales tax nexus and calculate its sales tax withholding responsibilities.

LO 23-3 Identify whether a business has income tax nexus and determine its state income tax liabilities.

©Jupiterimages/Stockbyte/Getty Images

Storyline Summary

Taxpayer: Ken Brody

Location: Idaho

Status: Sole owner of Wild West River Runners Inc.

Situation: Ken owns retail stores in Idaho and Wyoming that sell merchandise locally; a Wyoming-based Internet store; and provides services in Idaho, Tennessee, Washington, and Wyoming. He must determine the company's state and local tax liabilities.

Ken Brody owns Wild West River Runners Incorporated (Wild West), an Idaho C corporation. Wild West offers both guided white-water rafting adventures and retail sales of related equipment. It provides white-water rafting adventures in Idaho, Tennessee, Washington, and Wyoming and includes retail stores in Idaho and Wyoming and an Internet-based retail store based in Wyoming. Wild West's retail stores sell only locally (they never ship merchandise), but the salesclerks often refer customers to the Internet store (www. wildwestriverrunners.com). Most employees are seasonal (i.e., teachers or college students). During the off-season, a few guides make sales visits with Ken and operate the retail stores. Also during the off-season, Ken attends the annual 10-day Raft and River Show in Phoenix, Arizona, and travels the country promoting Wild West's guided river adventures.

Wild West's Form 1120 shows federal taxable income for the current year of $60,593, and it must calculate its state and local tax liabilities. Because Wild West operates a multistate business, it must identify the states in which it must withhold sales tax, determine the states in which it must file income tax returns, and file income tax returns reflecting its taxable income for each state in which it must file. ■

Like a lot of other businesses, Wild West is a multistate operation. From a business perspective, multistate businesses generally have access to a larger economic base than those operating in a single state. However, with this economic opportunity comes complexity and additional tax burdens.

STATE AND LOCAL TAXES

LO 23-1

The primary purpose of state and local taxes is to raise revenue to finance state governments. All 50 states and the District of Columbia have some combination of three primary revenue sources: sales and use tax, income or franchise tax, and property tax.[1]

This chapter focuses on sales and use taxes (excise taxes levied on the sale or use of tangible personal property within a state) and taxes based on *net* income (income taxes).[2]

Like federal tax law, state tax law includes the following:

- Legislative law (state constitution and tax code).
- Administrative law (regulations and rulings).
- Judicial law (state and federal tax cases).

While businesses deal with a single federal tax code, there are different tax codes for each state in which they are required to pay taxes. This makes state tax research particularly challenging. State tax agencies (such as the California Franchise Tax Board and the New York Department of Finance and Taxation) administer the law and promulgate regulations for their particular states.[3] State and federal courts interpret the law when a state's tax authority and businesses cannot agree on its interpretation or constitutionality. Because of constitutionality questions, judicial law plays a significantly more important role in state tax law than in federal tax law.

It is impractical, if not impossible, to study each individual state statute in one text. Instead, this chapter addresses the most important state and local tax principles at a conceptual level.

The most important question Wild West, or any other business, must answer is whether it is subject to a state's taxing regime. The answer depends on the business's state of **commercial domicile** and whether the business has **nexus** in that state. Commercial domicile is the state where a business is headquartered and directs its operations; this location may be different from the place of incorporation.[4] A business must always collect and remit sales tax from its customers and pay income tax in the state where it is domiciled. **Nondomiciliary businesses**—businesses not domiciled or headquartered in a state—are subject to taxing authorities only where they have nexus. Nexus is the sufficient (or minimum) connection between a business and a state that subjects the business to the state's tax system. As we discuss below, the standard for **sales tax nexus** is different than the standard for **income tax nexus.** The nexus standard varies because the financial and administrative burdens vary across taxes. Sellers collect and remit sales tax for administrative convenience, but the sales tax burden belongs to the buyer in most states. In contrast, income tax is both owed and paid by the business earning the income.

[1]State and local jurisdictions may also tax or levy the following: personal property, capital stock, business licensing, transfer taxes, incorporation, excise, severance, payroll, disability, unemployment, fuel, and telecommunication.

[2]This chapter discusses income and franchise taxes interchangeably. Franchise taxes are imposed for the right to conduct business within a state. Most franchise taxes (such as the California Franchise Tax) are net income based.

[3]A great resource for guidance and forms from specific states can be found on the Federation of Tax Administrator's website, http://www.taxadmin.org/state-tax-forms.

[4]Some companies (e.g., Hewlett-Packard) are incorporated in one state (e.g., Delaware) but domiciled or headquartered in another (e.g., California). These companies pay taxes in both states (although sometimes just a capital stock tax applies in the state of incorporation if there are no activities other than incorporation within a state).

Wild West's commercial domicile is Idaho because it is headquartered there. Consequently, it must collect and remit Idaho sales tax and pay Idaho income tax. Yet, as detailed in Exhibit 23-1, it has activities and sales in other states, and therefore it must collect sales tax and pay income tax in the states in which it has relevant nexus.

EXHIBIT 23-1 Wild West's Activities and Sales by State

Wild West In-State Activities					
State	Sale of Goods	Sale of Services	Employees	Property	Commercial Domicile
Arizona	✓				
California	✓				
Colorado	✓				
Idaho	✓	✓	✓	✓	✓
Tennessee	✓	✓	✓	✓	
Washington	✓	✓	✓	✓	
Wyoming	✓	✓	✓	✓	

Wild West Sales			
State	Goods	Services	Total
Arizona	$ 89,242	$ 0	$ 89,242
California	132,045	0	132,045
Colorado	75,002	0	75,002
Idaho	167,921	625,003	792,924
Tennessee	45,331	357,061	402,392
Washington	41,982	377,441	419,423
Wyoming	185,249	437,755	623,004
Totals	$736,772	$1,797,260	$2,534,032

When a business sells tangible personal property that is included in a state's sales tax base, it must collect and remit the **sales tax** on a periodic basis if it has sales tax nexus in that state.[5] Exhibit 23-2 provides an overview of who bears the burden of sales taxes

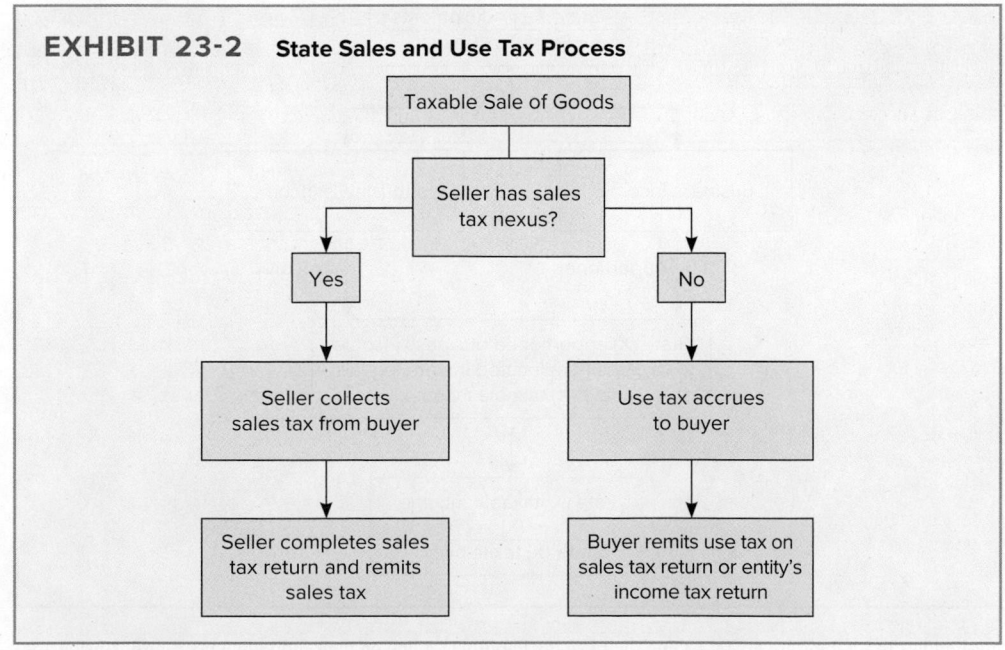

EXHIBIT 23-2 State Sales and Use Tax Process

[5]Businesses remit the sales taxes collected from customers on a sales tax return on a monthly, quarterly, or annual basis depending on the size of the liability and the state law thresholds.

(who must pay and who must collect and remit the tax). Sales tax liability accrues on certain sales of tangible personal property within the state. For example, Wild West's Idaho retail store collects sales tax on goods sold in Idaho stores and remits the tax to the Idaho Department of Revenue. **Use tax** liability accrues in the state where purchased property will be used when no sales tax was paid at the time of purchase. The use tax occurs only when a seller in one state ships goods to a customer in a different state and the seller is not required to collect the sales tax (the seller does not have sales tax nexus in the state to which the goods are shipped). For example, Colorado customers ordering through Wild West's Wyoming-based Internet store (which has no Colorado sales tax nexus) are required to accrue and remit the Colorado use tax (usually through their personal income tax returns).[6] Businesses with sales tax nexus in a state are responsible for remitting the sales tax even when they fail to collect it.

Businesses engaged in **interstate commerce** must also deal with income-tax related issues. If a business meets certain requirements creating income tax nexus, it may be required to remit income tax to that state. The general process of determining a business's state income tax liability is highlighted in Exhibit 23-3. We compute the **state tax base** by making adjustments to federal taxable income. The adjustments are necessary to account for differences between federal income tax laws and state income tax laws. Then we divide the state tax base into **business income** and **nonbusiness income.** Business income (income from business activities) is subject to **apportionment** among states where income tax nexus exists, based on the extent of the business's activities and property in various states. Nonbusiness income (all income except business income—generally investment income) is subject to **allocation** or assignment directly to the business's state of commercial domicile. For states in which the business has income tax nexus, state taxable income is the sum of the business income apportioned to that state plus the nonbusiness income allocated to that state. The business computes its state tax liability for that particular state by multiplying state taxable income by the state's tax rate.

Let's now look in more depth at sales tax and net income-based taxes, the relevant nexus requirements, and the calculation of each tax.

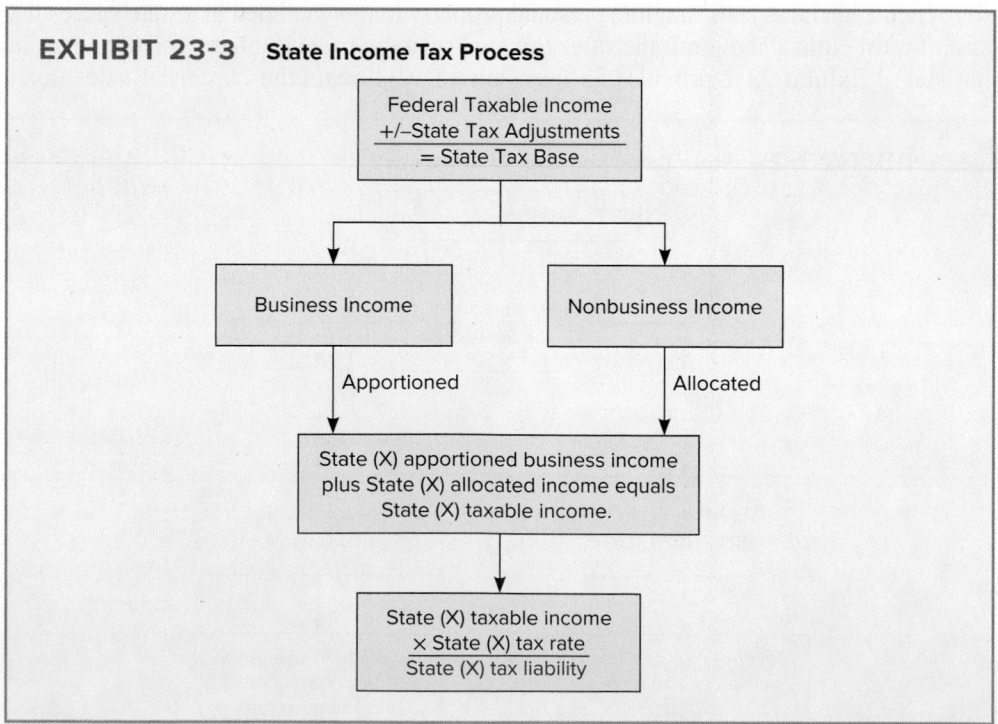

EXHIBIT 23-3 **State Income Tax Process**

Federal Taxable Income
+/−State Tax Adjustments
= State Tax Base

Business Income — Nonbusiness Income

Apportioned — Allocated

State (X) apportioned business income plus State (X) allocated income equals State (X) taxable income.

State (X) taxable income
× State (X) tax rate
State (X) tax liability

[6]Individuals remit their use tax by adding their use tax liability to a line on their individual tax return. Businesses remit their use tax by adding it to any sales tax collected from customers on their sales and use tax return.

SALES AND USE TAXES

LO 23-2

Forty-five states and the District of Columbia impose sales taxes; Alaska, Delaware, Montana, New Hampshire, and Oregon do not. Sales tax must be collected on the state's sales tax base. Generally, sales of tangible personal property are subject to the tax. Most states also tax restaurant meals, rental car usage, hotel room rentals (often at higher tax rates than general sales), and some services (which vary by state). Purchases of inventory for resale are exempt from the sales tax.[7] For example, Wild West's rafting equipment purchases for resale are exempt from sales tax because inventory is taxed when sold, but its office furniture purchased for use in the business are taxable because they represent final sales. Taxable items that are included in the sales tax base vary from state to state. Many states exempt food (except prepared restaurant food) because taxing food is considered to be regressive; that is, it imposes a proportionally higher tax burden on lower-income taxpayers, who spend a greater proportion of their income on food and other necessities. Most states also exempt sales of real property, intangible property, and services. However, many states are expanding the types of services subject to sales tax in order to increase their sales tax revenue.[8]

> **THE KEY FACTS**
>
> **Sales Tax Nexus**
>
> - Nexus is the sufficient connection between a business and a state that allows a state to levy a tax on the business.
> - Sales tax nexus is established through the physical presence of salespeople or property within a state.

TAXES IN THE REAL WORLD Is It Candy or Is It Food?

Items subject to the sales tax vary from state to state. Historically, New York taxed the sale of large marshmallows but exempted the sale of small marshmallows. Large and small marshmallows were treated differently because large marshmallows were considered to be candy, which was included in the sales tax base, while small marshmallows were considered to be a food ingredient and therefore excluded from the sales tax base. Currently, all marshmallows are taxed as a food ingredient.

The Washington state legislature passed a law subjecting candy to sales taxes a few years ago. Any item containing flour was considered a food item, not candy. As a result, Twix bars were exempt while Starburst candy was subject to sales tax. Within a year, Washington voters repealed the tax on candy through a ballot initiative.

Sales Tax Nexus

Have you ever wondered why sometimes you pay sales tax on goods purchased over the Internet and sometimes you don't? The answer is it depends on whether the seller has sales tax nexus. A business is required to collect sales tax from customers in a state only if it has sales tax nexus in that state. For example, if you purchase a book from a local bookstore you paid sales tax, but if you purchased the book from an online seller you didn't pay sales tax (unless you live in a state where the seller has sales tax nexus). While Amazon now collects sales taxes in all states having sales taxes, Exhibit 23-4 explains how Amazon's prior position on sales tax collection could result in a substantial sales tax liability if a state successfully asserts that Amazon's position was wrong.

Businesses that establish sales tax nexus with a state but fail to properly collect sales tax can create significant liabilities that may need to be disclosed for financial reporting purposes.[9] As a result, understanding when a business has sales tax nexus can be extremely important for profitability, business modeling, and compliance.

Businesses create sales tax nexus (the sufficient connection with a state that requires them to collect sales tax) when they have a *physical presence* in the state. Businesses have a physical presence in the state if (1) salespeople (or independent contractors representing a business)

---

[7]Most states grant a reseller's certificate, which exempts purchases of inventory for resale from sales tax.

[8]For example, Connecticut taxes services such as tax preparation.

[9]Sales tax liabilities are ASC 450 contingencies.

EXHIBIT 23-4   **Excerpt from Amazon's 2016 Annual Report**

From the Form 10-K

We Could Be Subject to Additional Sales Tax or Other Indirect Tax Liabilities

An increasing number of states and foreign jurisdictions have considered or adopted laws or administrative practices, with or without notice, that impose additional obligations on remote sellers and online marketplaces to collect transaction taxes such as sales, consumption, value added, or similar taxes. We may not have sufficient lead time to build systems and processes to collect these taxes. Failure to comply with such laws or administrative practices, or a successful assertion by such states or foreign jurisdictions requiring us to collect taxes where we do not, could result in substantial tax liabilities, including for past sales, as well as penalties and interest. In addition, if the tax authorities in jurisdictions where we are already subject to sales tax or other indirect tax obligations were successfully to challenge our positions, our tax liability could increase substantially. In the U.S., Supreme Court decisions restrict states' rights to require remote sellers to collect state and local sales taxes (although some states are seeking to have the Supreme Court revisit these decisions). We support a federal law that would allow states to require sales tax collection by remote sellers under a nationwide system.

We are also subject to U.S. (federal and state) and foreign laws, regulations, and administrative practices that require us to collect information from our customers, vendors, merchants, and other third parties for tax reporting purposes and report such information to various government agencies. The scope of such requirements continues to expand, requiring us to develop and implement new compliance systems. Failure to comply with such laws and regulations could result in significant penalties.

enter a state to obtain sales or (2) tangible property (such as a company-owned truck making deliveries) is located within a state.[10]

The physical presence requirement is a judicial interpretation of the Commerce Clause of the U.S. Constitution. Designed to encourage interstate commerce, this clause gives Congress power "to regulate Commerce with foreign Nations, and among the several States, and with the Indian Tribes." Because Congress has never exercised its right, the courts have determined the sales tax nexus threshold. In *National Bellas Hess,* the U.S. Supreme Court held that an out-of-state mail-order company did not have a sales tax collection responsibility because it lacked physical presence (even though it mailed catalogs and advertised in the state).[11] The mail-order industry used this decision as a competitive advantage for several decades. In *Quill,* the U.S. Supreme Court reaffirmed that out-of-state (nondomiciliary) businesses must have a physical presence in the state before the state may require a business to collect sales tax from in-state customers.[12]

Example 23-1

Wild West sends promotional brochures from Idaho to its Colorado clients. Wild West generated current year sales of $75,002 to Colorado customers, but it has never collected Colorado sales tax or filed a Colorado sales tax return. Wild West has neither employees nor property in Colorado. Does it have sales tax nexus in Colorado?

Answer: No. Wild West lacks the physical presence required for Colorado sales tax nexus and therefore doesn't have Colorado sales tax collection responsibility.

[10]*Scripto, Inc. v. Carson, Sherriff, et al.,* 362 U.S. 207 (1960). Scripto hired independent salespeople to represent the company in Florida. The Supreme Court held that these salespeople were agents of Scripto, who established the physical presence necessary to create sales tax nexus.

[11]*National Bellas Hess, Inc. v. Department of Revenue of the State of Illinois,* 386 U.S. 753 (1967).

[12]*Quill Corporation, Petitioner v. North Dakota,* 504 U.S. 298 (1992).

What if: Assume that in addition to mailing promotional brochures, Ken visits Colorado on promotional trips. Does Wild West have sales tax nexus in Colorado under these circumstances?

Answer: Yes. The physical presence of Wild West's representatives, even for promotional trips, creates Colorado sales tax nexus.

What if: Assume Wild West's representatives (independent contractors), rather than employees, visit Colorado retail stores to solicit additional sales orders. Does Wild West have sales tax nexus in Colorado under these circumstances?

Answer: Yes. The physical presence of Wild West's representatives creates Colorado sales tax nexus. Thus, the result is the same for employees or independent contractors.

TAXES IN THE REAL WORLD Sales Tax Nexus

On January 12, 2018, the United States Supreme Court agreed to hear the case of *South Dakota v. Wayfair Inc.* This sets the stage for possible changes to the physical presence requirement for sales tax nexus. The Court's decision likely will address whether the state can impose a sales tax collection and remittance obligation on sellers that do not have a physical presence in the state, effectively either reaffirming or overturning the long-standing precedent established in *National Bellas Hess v. Illinois* and reaffirmed in *Quill Corp. v. North Dakota*.

A few states have recently passed legislation creating economic sales tax nexus (imposing sales tax nexus on businesses without physical presence), which contradicts current law but is done in anticipation of a successful challenge of *Quill Corp. v. North Dakota*.

The Supreme Court will hear oral arguments in *South Dakota v. Wayfair Inc.* during April of 2018 and issue an opinion in the months following. Businesses should stay current with this ruling and other economic sales tax nexus issues.

Sales Tax Liability

Typically, sellers with sales tax nexus collect customers' sales tax liabilities. For example, Wild West collects sales tax on river rafting equipment it sells from its retail store but not on river guiding *services* it provides. If the seller doesn't have sales tax nexus, then the customer is responsible for remitting a use tax (at the same tax rate as sales tax) to the state in which the property is used. If the buyer is charged a sales tax in another state, the buyer will have a use tax liability for an incremental amount if the state where the property is used has a higher sales tax rate.

Example 23-2

Wild West received $3,500 from a customer named Casey Jarvie residing in Sacramento, California. Of this amount, $500 was for personal rafting equipment shipped to Sacramento, where the sales tax rate is 8.25 percent. The remaining $3,000 was payment for a four-day river raft adventure on the Salmon River in Idaho. Wild West has neither salespeople nor property in California. Does Wild West have a responsibility to collect sales tax from Casey?

Answer: No. Wild West lacks physical presence and does not have sales tax nexus in California; therefore, it has no California sales tax collection requirement.

Because Wild West has no sales tax collection responsibility, does Casey have a use tax liability to the state of California? If so, in what amount?

Answer: Yes. Casey is responsible for remitting $41.25 of use tax ($500 × 8.25%) on his personal California state income tax return for the purchase and use of the personal rafting equipment in California. He is not required to pay California use tax on the river raft adventure purchase because Wild West provided an out of state service (no sales tax is due on the services in Idaho either).

(continued on page 23-8)

What if: If Casey had Wild West hold the goods until he arrived in Burley, Idaho, to pick them up at the time of the trip (assume the sales tax rate in Burley, Idaho, is 6 percent), would Wild West have sales tax collection responsibility? If so, what is the sales tax amount?

Answer: Yes. Because Wild West has physical presence in Idaho, it is required to collect $30 ($500 × 6%) of sales tax and remit it to Idaho. Casey would also have an $11.25 California use tax liability ($41.25 reduced by the $30 remitted to Idaho) in this scenario.

ETHICS

Jill is a Virginia resident who purchased $1,500 of personal use items from Overstock.com and other Internet retailers during the year. While completing her personal tax return using a popular software package, Jill was asked to report her online purchases. After entering these purchases, she noticed that $75 of "use tax" was added to her state tax liability. Jill has never paid this in the past. She decided to delete the online purchase information she had previously entered. What do you think of Jill's failure to report her Virginia use tax?

Large companies often must file sales tax returns in all 45 states that have sales taxes and the District of Columbia.[13] This administrative burden is further complicated by the fact that more than 7,500 tax jurisdictions (including counties, cities, school districts, and other divisions) impose sales taxes, and several hundred rates change annually at various times during the year.[14] The sales tax administrative burden can also be large for small businesses. For example, a local pizzeria that delivers can sometimes be subject to a half-dozen sales tax rates if its delivery services cross city, county, or school district boundaries.

ETHICS

In 2010, Colorado became the first state to require nondomiciliary businesses without sales tax nexus to report all the necessary information to the Colorado Department of Revenue so that Colorado could collect its use tax from its resident individuals and domiciliary businesses. Assume you are responsible for resolving sales tax issues for an online retailer from another state. You believe the Colorado tax is unconstitutional based on a seminar you attended and the advice of your accounting firm. Would you recommend that your company comply with the Colorado law? Would your opinion change if the court issued an injunction prohibiting the state from enforcing the new law?

Example 23-3

Recall from Exhibit 23-1 that Wild West has sales in Arizona, California, Colorado, Idaho, Tennessee, Washington, and Wyoming. Also recall that it has property and employees in Idaho, Tennessee, Washington, and Wyoming. In which states does Wild West have sales tax nexus and, therefore, sales tax collection responsibility?

---

[13]Some counties or political subdivisions of states without state sales taxes (such as Kenal Peninsula Borough in Alaska) impose a county or local sales tax.

[14]Software companies provide sales tax solutions that help companies with the administrative burden. However, they generally fail to indemnify or compensate businesses against errors in their software that result in uncollected sales taxes, which creates a liability for the business.

Answer: Wild West's physical presence of employees and real and personal property create sales tax nexus in Idaho, Tennessee, Washington, and Wyoming.

Using the sales data provided in Exhibit 23-1, how much sales tax must Wild West remit? Assume the following (hypothetical) sales tax rates: Idaho (6 percent); Tennessee (9.25 percent); Washington (7.70 percent); and Wyoming (6 percent).

Answer: It must remit $28,616, computed as follows:

State	(1) Taxable Sales	(2) Rate	(1) × (2) Sales Tax Due
Idaho	$167,921	6.00%	$10,075
Tennessee	45,331	9.25%	4,193
Washington	41,982	7.70%	3,233
Wyoming	185,249	6.00%	11,115
Totals	$440,483		$28,616

Remember, services are not generally subject to sales tax.

TAXES IN THE REAL WORLD Groupon

Have you ever bought a restaurant meal from Groupon? Did you know there is a tax issue complicating these types of purchases? Suppose you pay $25 for a $50 voucher good at your favorite restaurant. You just scored a great deal. Groupon collects the $25 and pays the restaurant $12.50. You show up and order $50 worth of food, and the server brings you the bill. How much sales tax should the restaurant collect from you on the prepared food (which is a taxable item)? You received $50 worth of prepared food (one possible tax base), but you paid only $25 (another possible tax base), and the restaurant received only $12.50 (a third possible tax base). What is the nature of the $12.50 retained by Groupon? Did it provide a good (taxable) or a service (not taxable)? Most restaurants currently collect tax on the entire $50 benefit you received. They probably collect too much tax, but the question remains unanswered for now.

INCOME TAXES

LO 23-3

Forty-six states impose an income tax on corporations; only Nevada, South Dakota, Washington, and Wyoming do not.[15] Forty-three states tax income from partnerships and S corporations. This chapter focuses on C corporations, but the same principles apply to flow-through entities.[16] Most states imposing income-based taxes conform to an entity's federal tax status. For example, an S corporation is treated by the state as a flow-through entity. However, a few states impose minimum taxes on these entities. For example, California imposes a minimum tax of $800 or 1.5 percent tax on the income of all flow-through entities: S corporations and LLCs taxed as partnerships.

Businesses must pay income tax in their state of commercial domicile (where they are headquartered). For example, Wild West is both incorporated and domiciled in Idaho and is therefore subject to Idaho's income tax regime. Until a few decades ago, many businesses believed they were virtually exempt from state income taxes in states other than their state of commercial domicile. However, in *Complete Auto Transit*, the U.S. Supreme Court spelled out four criteria for determining whether states can tax nondomiciliary

[15]Several states (such as California and New York) impose a franchise tax rather than an income tax. Since franchise taxes are generally based upon net income, they are essentially the same as income taxes.

[16]Actually, these states tax individuals, including the income that flows through from partnerships and S corporations (although New Hampshire and Tennessee tax only dividends and interest); Alaska, Florida, Nevada, South Dakota, Texas, Washington, and Wyoming do not.

companies and whether the tax imposed is discriminatory against nondomiciliary (domiciled in another state) businesses.[17] First, a sufficient connection or income tax nexus must exist between the state and the business. Second, a state may tax only a fair portion of a business's income. Businesses must be able to divide or apportion income among the states where income tax nexus exists. Third, the tax cannot be constructed to discriminate against nonresident businesses. For example, states cannot impose a higher tax rate on nondomiciliary businesses than domiciliary businesses. Fourth, the taxes paid must be fairly related to the services the state provides. For example, states provide businesses access to a state's courts, economic base, infrastructure, and so forth.

To determine their state income tax liabilities, businesses must answer the following questions:

- In which states is the business required to file tax returns (in which states does it have income tax nexus)?
- If the business is related to other entities, should it file separate state income tax returns, or should it include the activities of the related entities on its state income tax returns?
- What adjustments to federal taxable income must the business make to calculate state taxable income for each state in which it is required to file?
- If it has income tax nexus in more than one state, how is income divided among the various states in which the business is required to file tax returns?

Income Tax Nexus

Businesses must file income tax returns in states where they have income tax nexus. However, the determination of whether the business has established income tax nexus within a state depends on the nature of its activities in the state. Thus, the rules for determining income tax nexus are not necessarily the same as those for determining sales tax nexus. Physical presence creates income tax nexus for service providers, sellers of real property, and businesses licensing intangibles. However, physical presence does not necessarily create income tax nexus for sellers of tangible personal property if their activities within a state are limited to certain "protected" activities as described by **Public Law 86-272.**

Public Law 86-272 In *Northwestern States Portland Cement*, the U.S. Supreme Court allowed Minnesota to tax an Iowa-based business.[18] By passing Public Law 86-272, Congress placed limits on states' power to impose income taxes on nondomiciliary businesses. Businesses are protected from income tax nexus in a particular state if (and only if) *all* the following apply:

- The tax is based on net income (not gross receipts or revenue).
- The taxpayer sells only tangible personal property in that state.
- The taxpayer's in-state activities are limited to solicitation of sales (see the discussion below for the definition of *solicitation*).
- The taxpayer participates in interstate commerce.
- The taxpayer is nondomiciliary.
- The taxpayer approves orders outside the state.
- The taxpayer delivers goods from outside the state through a common carrier.[19]

---

[17]*Complete Auto Transit, Inc. v. Brady*, 430 U.S. 274 (1977).

[18]*Northwestern States Portland Cement Co. v. Minnesota*, 358 U.S. 450 (1959). Until 1959, there was a common and persistent belief among businesses that state tax accrued only in the business' state of commercial domicile. The *Northwestern States v. Minnesota* decision led to widespread alarm from the business community. This alarm led to an intense lobbying effort that resulted in Congress passing Public Law 86-272 within seven months.

[19]*Common carrier* is a general term referring to delivery businesses (such as FedEx, UPS, DHL, or USPS).

Businesses wishing to avoid income tax nexus based on net income must sell only tangible personal property within the state.[20] Providing services along with property violates the criteria and creates income tax nexus. For example, providing installation services with tangible personal property exceeds solicitation and creates income tax nexus. Businesses selling services, real property, or licensing intangibles are not protected by Public Law 86-272. Income tax nexus for these nonprotected activities simply requires a physical presence similar to establishing sales tax nexus. Only nondomiciliary companies engaging in interstate commerce are protected. Orders taken or received in-state must be sent out of state—say to regional sales offices or headquarters—for approval. The acceptance of orders in the state, or even the power to accept orders, exceeds the protection of Public Law 86-272 and results in the business being subject to an income tax. Accepted orders must be delivered by common carrier. Delivery using the seller's truck violates the criteria and creates income tax nexus, except as permitted by state law (New Jersey, Rhode Island, and South Carolina are among the states that list delivery by private vehicles as a protected activity).

Example 23-4

What if: Assume that Wild West sends employees to Oregon to visit retail stores and solicit orders of rafting equipment only. Does the presence of Wild West's employees in Oregon create income tax nexus in Oregon?

Answer: No. The physical presence of representatives soliciting sales of tangible personal property is a protected activity under Public Law 86-272. Thus, no income tax nexus is created for Wild West in Oregon. Note, however, that this physical presence *would* create sales tax nexus for any sales generated by Wild West in Oregon, unless it has a valid reseller's certificate.

What if: Assume that Ken or other Wild West sales representatives enter Oregon to solicit customers for both rafting equipment and white-water adventures. Does the presence of Wild West's employees create income tax nexus in Oregon?

Answer: Yes. Solicitation of *services* is not a protected activity under Public Law 86-272. Thus, soliciting services creates income tax nexus for Wild West in Oregon and thus creates an income tax filing requirement.

Solicitation.   Public Law 86-272 protects **solicitation** of tangible personal property but doesn't clearly define the term *solicitation*. In *Wisconsin v. Wrigley*, however, the U.S. Supreme Court addressed the definition.[21] Wrigley, based in Illinois, had sales representatives and a regional manager in Wisconsin. Sales meetings were held both in the manager's basement and in a rented hotel space. The sales reps had company cars, a stock of gum, display racks, and promotional literature. The sales activities included handing out promotional materials, free samples, and free display racks; replacing stale gum; handling billing disputes; and occasionally filling orders from their stock of gum and issuing an agency stock check (a bill) to customers. All other orders were sent to Illinois for acceptance and were filled by a common carrier from outside of Wisconsin. In *Wrigley*, the U.S. Supreme Court determined the following activities performed within Wisconsin met the definition of solicitation:

- Soliciting by any form of advertising.
- Carrying samples and promotional materials for display or distribution without charge.
- Passing inquiries or complaints to the home office.
- Checking a customer's inventory for reorder.

---

[20]Taxes calculated based on gross receipts or other bases are not protected by Public Law 86-272.

[21]*Wisconsin Department of Revenue v. William Wrigley, Jr. Co.*, 505 US 214 (1992).

- Maintaining a sample room for two weeks or less; this is known as the **trade show rule.**
- Recruiting, training, and evaluating sales reps using homes or hotels.
- Owning or furnishing personal property and autos used in sales activities.

The U.S. Supreme Court held the following activities do *not* meet the definition of solicitation and, therefore, create income tax nexus with the state in which they take place:

- Making repairs.
- Collecting delinquent accounts.
- Investigating creditworthiness.
- Installing or supervising the installation of property.
- Providing training for employees other than sales reps.
- Approving or accepting orders.
- Repossessing property.
- Securing deposits.
- Maintaining an office (other than an in-home office).

If sales reps know and understand these solicitation rules, they can help businesses avoid income tax nexus in states where they want to avoid it.

TAXES IN THE REAL WORLD Warranty

One of the biggest current issues for out-of-state retailers is the manner in which warranty work is performed. For example, assume you buy a new laptop for school from an online retailer because the price is unbeatable. Two months later you are told by customer support that the hard drive needs to be replaced and you need to ship the computer to Austin, Texas, for repair. You respond that you cannot go a week without your computer, so the retailer agrees to have a local shop do the repair for you. Many companies wrongly assume that hiring an independent representative to do in-state warranty work does not create income tax nexus. The hiring of the independent contractor is an agency relationship that creates income tax nexus for the out-of-state retailer. The Multistate Tax Commission (MTC) is an intergovernmental state tax agency created by the Multistate Tax Compact. The Multistate Tax Compact is a model law passed by the legislature of virtually every state. The MTC issued guidance (MTC Nexus Bulletin 95-1) on this issue more than a decade ago—and taxpayers challenging the ruling have lost time and time again. Retailers with these issues quickly find themselves liable for both current and past income as well as for sales taxes.

Example 23-5

Assume Wild West's Oregon sales reps give store employees free white-water gloves and pass on complaints to the home office. Do these activities create income tax nexus for Wild West in Oregon?

Answer: No. Giving samples (without charge) and passing on complaints, suggestions, and customer inquiries are protected sales activities under Public Law 86-272. Therefore, Wild West is protected from Oregon income tax nexus.

What if: While in Oregon, several sales reps accept checks for down payments on merchandise, repair faulty merchandise, and perform credit checks. Do these activities create income tax nexus in Oregon for Wild West?

Answer: Yes. Each of these activities is an unprotected sales activity, and any or all will create Oregon income tax nexus for Wild West.

Example 23-6

What if: Assume that Ken and other Wild West employees visit Colorado retail stores and hold slide-shows about summer rafting trips. After the slideshows, Ken and the other guides interact with and gather information from potential white-water rafting customers. Do these solicitation activities create income tax nexus?

Answer: Yes. Because white-water rafting trips are services rather than tangible personal property, the physical presence of Wild West employees creates income tax nexus in Colorado.

Does a one-time sales activity violation create income tax nexus? Technically, yes. However, the *Wrigley* decision indicates that *de minimis* (immaterial) activities may be excluded. The decision whether an activity is *de minimis* is a subjective one, however, based on relevant facts and circumstances.

Example 23-7

Assume that Wild West's sales reps occasionally investigate creditworthiness and occasionally repossess property in Oregon. Can Wild West avoid income tax nexus?

Answer: Possibly. Even though the sales reps performed unprotected activities, Wild West can argue that these unprotected activities are *de minimis* because they are not material to its overall operations within Oregon.

Nexus for Nonincome-Based Taxes   Public Law 86-272 only protects businesses from nexus for income-based taxes. Two common nonincome-based taxes are the Texas Margin Tax and the Washington Business and Occupation (B&O) tax. Nexus for nonincome-based taxes simply requires physical presence. While nonincome-based taxes are beyond the scope of this text, recognizing that a different nexus standard exists is vitally important.

Example 23-8

What if: The Texas Margin Tax is calculated on the lesser: 1) gross margin 2) 70 percent of sales revenue, 3) revenue minus compensation, or 4) revenue minus $1 million dollars. Assume that Wild West sends employees into Texas to visit retail stores and solicit orders of rafting equipment. Would the presence of Wild West employees create nonincome-based tax nexus for the Texas Margin Tax?

Answer: Yes. Because the tax is nonincome-based (it is not based on *net* income), Wild West is not protected by Public Law 86-272. Therefore, the physical presence of salespeople soliciting sales of tangible personal property creates nonincome-based tax nexus (but it would *not* have created income tax nexus if the tax were based on net income).

Economic Income Tax Nexus   As we have discussed, businesses must have a physical presence in a state to establish income tax nexus with that state (Public Law 86-272 is the exception). However, many states currently assert economic income tax nexus, without physical presence, on businesses that have an economic presence in the state.[22] South Carolina was the first state to pursue economic income tax nexus. South Carolina disallowed the royalty expenses of Toys 'R' Us South Carolina to Geoffrey (a related Delaware holding company) rather than subject Geoffrey to the South Carolina income tax. States asserting

[22]The Supreme Court's *Quill* decision created doubt on the standard for income tax nexus because in defining sales tax nexus it said that "nexus for other taxes may be different," which the states have interpreted as meaning that physical presence may not be required for other types of taxes. Several recent cases have given de facto income tax nexus to businesses without the requisite physical presence [*Geoffrey, Inc. v. South Carolina Tax Commission,* S.C. Sup. Ct., 313 S.C. (1992); *Lanco, Inc. v. Director, Division of Taxation,* NJ Sup. Ct., Dkt. No.A-89-05 (2006); and *Tax Commissioner of West Virginia v. MBNA America Bank,* N.A., 640 SE 2d 226 (WV 2006)].

economic income tax nexus claim they provide an infrastructure of phone and Internet connections to consumers (an economic base) that nonresident companies use to solicit business (in the same way states provide roads for salespeople to visit the state's customers). For example, West Virginia asserted an income tax liability on a business (MBNA Bank) that merely solicited credit card customers through advertising and phone calls without having physical presence (employees or property) in the state. The West Virginia Supreme Court upheld the assertion, and the U.S. Supreme Court denied MBNA's *writ of certiorari*. However, most experts believe West Virginia's law to be unconstitutional, and that the U.S. Supreme Court's refusal to hear the case was designed to urge Congress to resolve the uncertainty surrounding income tax nexus issues.

Example 23-9

What if: Assume Wild West's Internet store receives and fills an order from a West Virginia customer. Wild West has no physical presence in West Virginia. Does Wild West have economic income tax nexus in West Virginia?

Answer: Perhaps. West Virginia's assertion of economic income tax nexus does not require physical presence. Therefore, Wild West could have economic income tax nexus, which would require it to file an income tax return in West Virginia.

TAXES IN THE REAL WORLD Factor Presence

While several states have asserted economic income tax nexus through state courts, the MTC adopted the Factor Presence Nexus Standard in 2002 (MTC Policy Statement 02-02). This policy asserts that if any business exceeds any of the following criteria for a given state, it is deemed to have economic income tax nexus:

- $50,000 of property
- $50,000 of payroll
- $500,000 of sales, or
- 25 percent of total property, payroll, or sales

A number of states (California, Colorado, Ohio, Oklahoma, and Washington) have recently asserted this standard (or a variation) through either legislation or regulation. If upheld, this standard will change the game by making Public Law 86-272 irrelevant, and it should make all companies not filing income tax returns in a state nervous.

Now that we've explored income tax nexus, let's determine Wild West's income tax nexus and filing requirements.

Example 23-10

Wild West is domiciled in Idaho and has physical presence through property and employees whose activities exceed protected solicitation in Idaho, Tennessee, Washington, and Wyoming. Recall from Exhibit 23-1 that Wild West has sales in the following states: Arizona, California, Colorado, Idaho, Tennessee, Washington, and Wyoming. Where does Wild West have income tax nexus?

Answer: Wild West has income tax nexus in Idaho, Tennessee, Washington, and Wyoming. It has income tax nexus in Idaho because of commercial domicile, physical presence of retail stores (where orders are accepted), and provision of services; it has income tax nexus in Tennessee, Washington, and Wyoming because of physical presence of retail stores (where orders are accepted) or provision of services. Where does Wild West have an income tax filing requirement?

Answer: Wild West will be required to file income tax returns in Idaho and Tennessee. Washington and Wyoming do not have a corporate income tax. Instead, Washington has a gross receipts tax (Business & Occupation tax). Wyoming does not tax corporations. As a result, Wild West will also file a Washington gross receipts return, as we discuss in Example 23-21.

Entities Included on Income Tax Return

When a business operates as more than one legal entity, the way it files its tax return(s) becomes an issue. Some states require a **separate tax return** for each entity with income tax nexus in the state, and others require a **unitary tax return** (one return) for a group of related entities.[23]

Separate Tax Returns   A separate return state requires only those businesses with income tax nexus in the state to file an income tax return. This is generally true even when a group of companies file a federal consolidated tax return with other companies.[24] Most states east of the Mississippi River (except Illinois) are separate-return states; however, states have begun shifting away from separate return requirements over the last decade.

Example 23-11

Wild West has income tax nexus in Tennessee (a separate-return state) because its employees provide services within the state and it owns property there. Must Wild West file a separate Tennessee income tax return?

Answer: Yes. Wild West must file a separate Tennessee income tax return because it has income tax nexus in Tennessee.

What if: Assume Wild West splits into two separate corporations: one that runs retail stores (Wild West Retail) and one that provides the guided rafting services (Wild West Services). How would the split affect Wild West's Tennessee income tax filing requirements?

Answer: Wild West would file two separate income tax returns: one for Wild West Retail and one for Wild West Services. Both companies would have income tax nexus in Tennessee because Wild West Retail's stores do more than solicit sales of tangible personal property and Wild West Service's activities are not protected activities under Public Law 86-272.

THE KEY FACTS

Entities Included on a Tax Return

- Separate-return states require a separate return for each entity that has income tax nexus in the state.
- Unitary states require members of a unitary group to file a single tax return reflecting the combined income of the unitary group if any member of the unitary group has income income tax nexus.
  - Any of three factors characterizes a unitary group: functional integration, centralization of management, and economies of scale.

While separate tax returns are simple, the income reported on separate tax returns can be manipulated through related-entity transactions (through transfer pricing, for example). Another important planning technique is the use of *passive investment companies* (PICs), in which a company simply creates a subsidiary and transfers ownership of its trademarks and patents to an entity within a state that does not tax royalties, interest, and other similar types of intangible income (such as Delaware or Nevada). The new PIC then charges a royalty for use of the intangible, which generates a deductible business expense in the state used and creates income in a little- or no-tax state like Delaware or Nevada. States have implemented laws to fight this type of planning, and ten states have responded by adopting unitary filing requirements. Such "tax planning" opportunities are not available if the related entities are required to file a unitary tax return.

Unitary Tax Returns   States west of the Mississippi River (and Illinois) are unitary-return states. However, since 2004, Georgia, Illinois, Maine, Massachusetts, New Hampshire, New Jersey, New York, Ohio, Rhode Island, and Wisconsin have adopted unitary return filing requirements. Whether a business must file one tax return with other businesses or entities depends on whether these businesses are considered to be a "unitary" group of entities.

---

[23]The separate versus unitary discussion is a complex and controversial discussion even at the graduate tax level. However, a basic understanding of the terminology and concepts can be useful for all accounting professionals.

[24]Some states allow combined reporting, a setting where more than one corporation files together on the same income tax return. However, the tax is calculated as if each corporation filed a separate return and was taxed separately.

In *Mobil,* the U.S. Supreme Court identified the following three factors that can be used to establish whether a group of businesses is unitary:

- Functional integration (vertical or horizontal integration or knowledge transfer).
- Centralization of management (interlocking directors, common officers, or rotation of management between companies).
- Economies of scale (group discounts or other efficiencies due to size).[25]

The unitary concept considers the integration and flow of value, rather than the business's legal form and ownership structure, in establishing which companies file a tax return together. Taxpayers must consider each of the three factors to determine whether two (or more) businesses will be treated as one for state tax purposes.

The important concept here is that companies filing a federal consolidated tax return can be separated, and companies not filing a federal consolidated tax return can become a unitary group.[26] A unitary tax return group includes all members meeting the unitary criteria—whether they have income tax nexus or not.[27] Unitary businesses usually have a flow of value between the various businesses. For example, raw materials or components can flow between businesses or one entity may borrow funds from another. The unitary concept pervades activities in the entire income tax system, including computing taxable income, computing apportionment percentages (discussed later in the chapter), and identifying income tax return filing requirements. The primary difference between separate and unitary states is that separate-return states tax the entire apportioned income of each separate business unit with income tax nexus while unitary-return states tax the entire unitary group using a smaller apportioned percentage.

Example 23-12

What if: As in the previous example, assume Wild West is divided into two separate corporations: Wild West Retail (WWR) and Wild West Services (WWS). Ken owns and manages both companies. The rafting services company purchases all its rafting equipment from the retail stores company. Guides for the rafting company stop at the retail store before trips so customers can purchase any necessary gear, and the store refers customers looking for guided rafting to the rafting services company. Assume the two companies use the same marketing and accounting firms and receive discounts for having multiple bank accounts and insurance policies. Using the *Mobil* factors (functional integration, centralization of management, and economies of scale), are WWR and WWS part of a unitary group?

Answer: Yes. WWR and WWS would likely be considered a unitary group and thus would combine income and file a single tax return. The two companies likely share some integration in that their customer bases have significant overlap, and WWS purchases its equipment from WWR. They share centralization of management in that both are owned and operated by the same individual (Ken). The two companies have some economies of scale because they receive discounts for using the same accounting, banking, insurance, and marketing vendors. Businesses do not have to meet all three factors to be considered a unitary group, but WWR and WWS probably do. As a result, WWR and WWS would likely file a unitary (single) Idaho income tax return.

State Taxable Income

Companies doing business in multiple states must identify the tax return due dates, procedures for filing tax return extensions, and other administrative requirements specific to

---

[25]In *Mobil Oil Corp. v. Vermont Tax Commissioner,* 445 U.S. 425 (1980), the U.S. Supreme Court held that the income of a multistate business can be apportioned if its intrastate and out-of-state activities form a part of a unitary business.

[26]In some cases, different divisions of a single corporation can be separated and in others a partnership and corporation can be joined.

[27]Entities without income tax nexus usually have apportionment factors that are zero. While their incomes increase the unitary group's income, their zero apportionment factors decrease the apportionment factors to the state. Therefore, the inclusion of entities without income tax nexus is usually considered to be nondiscriminatory.

each state. Businesses must also calculate state taxable income for each state in which they must file tax returns. Federal taxable income is generally the starting point for computing state taxable income. Just as corporations reconcile from book income to taxable income (see the Corporate Operations chapter), businesses must reconcile from federal taxable income to state taxable income. This requires them to identify **federal/state adjustments** or differences for *each specific state* before apportioning the income to a particular state in which they have income tax nexus.

Rather than starting from scratch, many states conform to the federal tax law in some way. Most "piggyback" their state tax laws on the federal tax laws (state tax codes generally follow the Internal Revenue Code).[28] Idaho generally conforms to the current Code. Consequently, Wild West will not report many federal/state adjustments. Other states adopt a specific version of the Code (the Code as of a specific date). For example, California adopted the Code as of January 1, 2015 (before that it used the Code as of January 1, 2009). This method requires more federal/state adjustments, because every subsequent change to the Internal Revenue Code results in less conformity between the state law and the federal tax law. Corporations should carefully examine federal/state adjustments for 2018 because states may not fully conform with many of the new federal provisions including bonus depreciation, deemed repatriation, interest deductions, and international provisions including the participation exemption, global intangible low-taxed income, and foreign-derived intangible income.

Because states cannot tax federal interest income (interest from Treasury notes, for example), all states require a negative adjustment (reduction in federal taxable income in adjusting to state taxable income) for federal interest income. Most states require a positive adjustment for state income tax deductions, because they *do not* allow businesses to deduct state income taxes, and they require a positive adjustment for state and local bond interest income if the bond is from another state (i.e., they tax out-of-state bond interest income).[29]

States' tax instruction booklets generally describe common federal/state tax adjustments applicable for that state, but these descriptions are often incomplete and particularly problematic for states with low federal tax conformity. While it is impractical to identify all potential federal/state adjustments, Exhibit 23-5 provides a list of common federal/state adjustments and identifies each as a positive adjustment (state income increasing) or a negative adjustment (state income decreasing).

EXHIBIT 23-5 **Common Federal/State Adjustments**

Positive Adjustments (Increasing Taxable Income)

State and local income taxes

State and local bond interest income from bonds in other states

Federal dividends received deduction

Federal income tax refunds (only in states where federal tax is allowed as a deduction)

Intercompany expenses associated with related persons (for separate-return states)*

MACRS depreciation over state depreciation

Federal bonus depreciation

Negative Adjustments (Decreasing Taxable Income)

U.S. obligation interest income (T-bills, notes, and bonds)

State dividends received deduction

Foreign dividend gross-up

State income tax refunds included on federal return

State depreciation over federal depreciation

*Approximately 20 separate-return states require a positive adjustment of intercompany royalties, interest, and other expenses between related persons. The disallowance prevents companies from extracting profits from high-tax states and placing them in low- or no-tax states.

[28]Also, states may conform or not conform to administrative authority such as Treasury Regulations, Revenue Procedures, and Revenue Rulings.

[29]Thirty-three of the 46 states with an income tax require a positive adjustment for state and local expenses deducted on the federal return.

Example 23-13

Wild West properly included, deducted, or excluded the following items on its federal tax return in the current year:

Item	Amount	Federal Treatment
Idaho income tax	$27,744	Deducted on federal return
Tennessee income tax	18,152	Deducted on federal return
Washington gross receipts tax	6,201	Deducted on federal return
Idaho bond interest income	5,000	Excluded from federal return
Federal T-note interest income	1,500	Included on federal return

Given federal taxable income of $60,593, what is Wild West's state tax base for Idaho and for Tennessee?

Answer: The Idaho state tax base is $102,685; for Tennessee it is $102,685. Bases are calculated as follows:

Federal Taxable Income	Idaho	Tennessee	Source
Wild West	$ 60,593	$ 60,593	Storyline
Positive Adjustments			
Idaho income tax	$ 27,744	$ 27,744	Idaho tax is not deducted.
Tennessee income tax	18,152	18,152	Tennessee tax is not deducted.
Washington gross receipts tax	0	0	Washington tax is not a positive adjustment because it is not an income-based tax.
State bond interest	0	5,000	States exempt their own interest only.
Total positive adjustments	$ 45,896	$ 50,896	
Negative Adjustments			
Federal interest	$ 1,500	$ 1,500	Federal interest is not taxable for state purposes.
Total negative adjustments	$ 1,500	$ 1,500	
State tax base	**$97,685**	**$102,685**	Federal + Positive − Negative

Dividing State Tax Base among States

All state taxable income is taxed in the state of commercial domicile unless the business is taxable in more than one state. An interstate business must separate its business income (earned from business operations) from nonbusiness income (primarily from investments, including rents and royalties). The business must fairly *apportion* its business income among the states in which it conducts business in a manner that creates income tax nexus, whereas it *allocates* or assigns nonbusiness income to a specific state (usually the state of commercial domicile).[30]

Business Income   Business income includes all revenues earned in the ordinary course of business—sales less cost of goods sold and other expenses. Business income is

---

[30]The Multistate Tax Commission has provided guidance on the division of income between states in Article IV of its Compact. The Compact can be found at www.mtc.gov. Also, see the Uniform Division of Income Tax Purposes Act that many states have adopted.

fairly apportioned or divided across the states with income tax nexus.[31] If a business has income tax nexus with a state, it may apportion income to that state—even if the state does not actually impose a tax.[32]

Example 23-14

Recall from the preceding example that Wild West's Idaho and Tennessee state tax bases were $97,685 and $102,685, respectively. Wild West's federal tax return shows the following items of investment income: dividends of $6,000, interest income of $16,005 (which includes $14,505 of bank interest and $1,500 of federal government interest but excludes $5,000 from Idaho bond interest), and rental income of $18,000. What is Wild West's business income for Idaho and Tennessee?

Answer: Idaho and Tennessee business income amounts are $59,180 and $59,180, respectively, calculated as follows:

	Idaho	Tennessee	Explanation
(1) State tax base	$ 97,685	$102,685	Example 23-13
(2) Dividends	6,000	6,000	Federal tax return
(3) Interest income	14,505	19,505	$14,505 (bank interest) + $5,000 of Idaho bond interest (for Tennessee only)
(4) Rental income	18,000	18,000	Federal tax return
(5) Nonbusiness income	$ 38,505	$ 43,505	(2) + (3) + (4)
Business income	**$59,180**	**$ 59,180**	(1) − (5)

Apportionment formula. States set the apportionment formula for income based on some combination of the following factors: sales, payroll, and property. For each state in which it establishes income tax nexus, the business calculates the factors as the ratio of (1) total sales, payroll, or property in a specific state to (2) total sales, payroll, or property everywhere. The sales factor is calculated as follows:

$$\text{Sales factor in state } X = \frac{\text{Total sales in state } X}{\text{Total sales in all states}}$$

The sales factor includes all gross business receipts net of returns, allowances, and discounts.[33] The general rules for determining the amount of sales to include in the sales factor calculation are:

- Sales of tangible personal property are sourced (included) to the destination state (the location where the property is delivered to and used in).
- If the business does not have income tax nexus in the destination state, sales are generally "thrown back" to the state from which the property is shipped; this is called the **throwback rule.**[34] For example, if Wild West ships goods from Idaho to

[31]*Complete Auto Transit, Inc. v. Brady*, 430 U.S. 274 (1977).

[32]Creating income tax nexus in states without an income tax creates "nowhere income"—income that is not taxed anywhere.

[33]There is substantial variation in the apportionment factor across states.

[34]Some states don't have a throwback rule and some states such as California have a double-throwback rule. This rule applies to drop shipments from a state without income tax nexus. For example, if a California company ships goods from Arizona into Colorado and has income tax nexus in neither Arizona nor Colorado, the sales are thrown back from Colorado into Arizona and then thrown back again from Arizona to California.

Montana, where it does not have income tax nexus, the sales are treated as if they are Idaho sales.

- Dock sales should be sourced to the good's ultimate destination (sales picked up by an out-of-state buyer at the seller's in-state dock rather than being shipped to the buyer's out-of-state location).
- Sales of services are generally apportioned to the state in which the services are performed (California and Illinois are exceptions to this general rule, but the list of states that apportion services to the state in which the services are consumed is growing).
- Government sales are sourced in the state from which they were shipped.

TAXES IN THE REAL WORLD The Complexities in Sourcing Receipts from the Sale of Other-Than-Tangible Personal Property

The last 20 years have seen a shift from the use of the equally weighted three-factor formula to the adoption of a single sales-factor formula for apportionment purposes. This shift has made the method of calculating the sales factor more important for both taxpayers and tax administrators. Additionally, over the same period, there has been a significant shift from a goods-based economy to an intangibles- and service-based economy. Consequently, many states have changed their apportionment method for services. While sales of services were traditionally sourced to the state where the services were provided from, many states have now shifted the sourcing to the market where the services are consumed—a destination approach. This means that, in many cases, two states are trying to tax the same services. For example, if an Idaho-based marketing firm creates a campaign for a California-based retailer, both states may assert the right to tax the transaction. Idaho will source the sale to the state in which the marketing campaign was created (Idaho) and California will source the sale to the state where the services will be used (California). Alternatively, if the facts were reversed neither state would assert the right to tax the sale.

Example 23-15

Recall from Exhibit 23-1 that Wild West reported sales of $2,534,032. The sales are split between goods and services and sourced by state as follows:

Wild West Sales			
State	**Goods**	**Services**	**Total**
AZ	$ 89,242	$ 0	$ 89,242
CA	132,045	0	132,045
CO	75,002	0	75,002
ID	167,921	625,003	792,924
TN	45,331	357,061	402,392
WA	41,982	377,441	419,423
WY	185,249	437,755	623,004
Totals	$736,772	$1,797,260	$2,534,032

Recall from Example 23-10 that Wild West has income tax nexus in Idaho, Tennessee, Washington, and Wyoming. Washington has a gross receipts tax and Wyoming does not tax corporations. What are the sales apportionment factors for Idaho and Tennessee?

Answer: The apportionment factors for Idaho and Tennessee are 31.29 percent and 15.88 percent, respectively, calculated from figures in the Total column in the sales table above:

$$\text{Idaho} \qquad \frac{\$792,924}{\$2,534,032} = 31.29\%$$

$$\text{Tennessee} \qquad \frac{\$402,392}{\$2,534,032} = 15.88\%$$

Note the Arizona, California, and Colorado sales are thrown back to Wyoming because the sales were made through the Internet store.

Payroll is generally defined as total compensation paid to employees.[35] The payroll factor is calculated as follows:

- Payroll includes salaries, commissions, bonuses, and other forms of compensation.
- Payroll does not include amounts paid to independent contractors.
- Payroll for each employee is apportioned to a single state (payroll for employees who work in more than one state is sourced to the state where they perform the majority of services).

Example 23-16

Wild West's payments for wages are $737,021, sourced to the states as follows:

Payroll State	Wild West Wages
Idaho	$201,032
Tennessee	148,202
Washington	115,021
Wyoming	272,766
Total	$737,021

What are the payroll apportionment factors for Idaho and Tennessee?

Answer: The payroll apportionment factors for Idaho and Tennessee are 27.28 percent and 20.11 percent, respectively, calculated from the payroll table above:

$$\text{Idaho} \qquad \frac{\$201,032}{\$737,021} = 27.28\%$$

$$\text{Tennessee} \qquad \frac{\$148,202}{\$737,021} = 20.11\%$$

Property generally includes both real and tangible personal property, but not intangible property.[36] The general rules for determining the property factors are:

- Use the average property values for the year [(beginning + ending)/2].
- Value property at historical cost rather than adjusted basis (do not subtract accumulated depreciation in determining value).

[35]The payroll definition varies by state.
[36]Property definitions may vary slightly by state.

- Include property in transit (such as inventory) in the state of destination.
- Include only business property (values of rented investment properties are excluded).
- Include rented or leased property by multiplying the annual rent by 8 and adding this value to the average owned-property factor.[37]

Example 23-17

The historical cost of Wild West's property (before subtracting accumulated depreciation) owned at the beginning and end of the year and rented during the year, by state, is as follows:

	Property		
State	**Beginning**	**Ending**	**Rented**
Idaho	$1,042,023	$1,203,814	$36,000
Tennessee	502,424	531,984	0
Washington	52,327	65,829	60,000
Wyoming	1,420,387	1,692,373	0
Total	$3,017,161	$3,494,000	$96,000

What are the property apportionment factors for Idaho and Tennessee?

Answer: The property apportionment factors for Idaho and Tennessee are 35.07 percent and 12.85 percent, respectively, computed as follows:

	Property and Rents Total				
	Owned Property			**Rented**	
State	**Beginning**	**Ending**	**Average**	**Rents × 8**	**Total**
Idaho	$1,042,023	$1,203,814	$1,122,919	$288,000	$1,410,919
Tennessee	502,424	531,984	517,204		517,204
Washington	52,327	65,829	59,078	$480,000	539,078
Wyoming	1,420,387	1,692,373	1,556,380		1,556,380
Total	$3,017,161	$3,494,000	$3,255,581		$4,023,581

Idaho $\dfrac{\$1,410,919}{\$4,023,581} = 35.07\%$

Tennessee $\dfrac{\$517,204}{\$4,023,581} = 12.85\%$

The average amount for each state from the subtotal property table is added to the inclusion amount from the subtotal rent table to reach the total property numerator for each state.

Historically, most states used an equally weighted three-factor apportionment formula, which was required by the Model Tax Compact. This method adds together the sales, payroll, and property factors and divides the total by 3 to arrive at the apportionment factor (percentages) for each state. Over time most states began shifting to a double-weighted sales factor (doubling the sales factor and then adding the payroll and property factors, and dividing the total by 4). Currently, approximately half the states have moved to a single-weighted sales factor that eliminates the payroll and property factors altogether. California is an example of a state that requires corporations to use a single-weighted sales factor. All else equal, increasing the weight of the sales factor in the apportionment formula

[37]The annual rent is multiplied by 8 to approximate the value of the rental property.

tends to decrease taxes paid by in-state businesses and increase the taxes paid by out-of-state businesses. The reason is that in-state businesses tend to have higher payroll and property factors relative to their sales factor in the state, and out-of-state businesses tend to have higher sales factors than payroll and property factors in other states.

TAXES IN THE REAL WORLD Apportionment: The Gillette Decision

On December 31, 2015, the California Supreme Court reversed the California Court of Appeals decision in *Gillette Co. v. Franchise Tax Board* [196 Cal. Rptr. 3d 486, 363 P.3d 94 (2015)].

The California Court of Appeals had held that a taxpayer could apportion its income to California using the Multistate Tax Compact's evenly weighted three-factor formula, despite statutory language mandating the use of a three-factor, double-weighted sales formula for most corporations for the years at issue.

The California Supreme Court concluded the California Legislature may properly preclude a taxpayer from relying on the Multistate Tax Compact's election provision. On October 12, 2016, the U.S. Supreme Court denied the *Gillette* appeal.

Similarly, the Michigan Appellate Court reversed a 2015 decision favoring IBM this summer and the Michigan Supreme Court denied the consolidate appeal of IBM and 50 other companies.

Similar cases are progressing in Minnesota, Oregon, and Texas. However, it is unclear whether taxpayers can ultimately win this argument.

Example 23-18

Wild West must apportion its business income to Idaho and Tennessee. Its Idaho sales, payroll, and property factors are 31.29 percent, 27.28 percent, and 35.07 percent, respectively. Its Tennessee sales, payroll, and property factors are 15.88 percent, 20.11 percent, and 12.85 percent, respectively. These factors are aggregated from Examples 23-15 through 23-17. What are Wild West's apportionment factors in both states if they use a double-weighted sales factor?

Answer: The apportionment factors for Idaho and Tennessee are 31.23 percent and 16.18 percent, respectively.

Factor	Idaho	Tennessee	Explanation
(1) Sales	31.29%	15.88%	Exhibit 23-15
(2) Sales	31.29	15.88	Exhibit 23-15
(3) Payroll	27.28	20.11	Exhibit 23-16
(4) Property	35.07	12.85	Exhibit 23-17
Apportionment factor	**31.23%**	**16.18%**	[(1) + (2) + (3) + (4)]/4

What if: Assume Tennessee uses an equally weighted three-factor apportionment formula. What are Wild West's apportionment factors?

Answer: The apportionment factor for Tennessee is 16.28 percent. Tennessee's apportionment factor would now be calculated as follows:

Factor	Tennessee	Explanation
(1) Sales	15.88%	
(2) Payroll	20.11	
(3) Property	12.85	
Apportionment factor	**16.28%**	[(1) + (2) + (3)]/3

What if: Assume Idaho uses a single-weighted sales factor apportionment formula. What would Wild West's apportionment factor be?

Answer: The apportionment factor for Idaho would be 31.29 percent. Idaho's apportionment factor would now simply be Wild West's Idaho sales factor. No payroll or property factor would be needed for Idaho.

Nonbusiness Income We've said nonbusiness income includes all income except business income. Here are common types of nonbusiness income and the rules for allocating each type to specific states:[38]

- Allocate interest and dividends to the state of commercial domicile (except interest on working capital, which is business income).
- Allocate rental income to the state where the property generating the rental income is located.
- Allocate royalties to the state where the property is used (if the business has income tax nexus in that state; if not, allocate royalties to the state of commercial domicile).
- Allocate capital gains from investment property to the state of commercial domicile.
- Allocate capital gains from selling rental property to the state where the rental property is located.

Example 23-19

Wild West reports nonbusiness income as follows:

Wild West			
	Idaho	**Tennessee**	
Dividends	$ 6,000	$ 6,000	From Example 23-14
Interest	14,505	19,505	From Example 23-14
Rental income	18,000	18,000	From Example 23-14
Allocable total	$38,505	$43,505	

Wild West's commercial domicile is in Idaho. Its rental income is for real property located in Wyoming. To which state(s) should the firm allocate its nonbusiness income?

Answer: $20,505 to Idaho, and $18,000 to Wyoming, calculated as follows:

Wild West		
Idaho	**$20,505**	$6,000 dividends + $14,505 interest income
Nevada	0	
Tennessee	0	
Washington	0	
Wyoming	**18,000**	Rental income
Total	$ 38,505	

State Income Tax Liability

It is relatively easy to calculate a business's state taxable income and state tax after separating business and nonbusiness income, apportioning business income, and allocating nonbusiness income. Specifically, state taxable income is calculated by multiplying business income by the apportionment factor and then adding any nonbusiness income allocated to the state.

---

[38]Multistate Tax Compact, Article IV, Division of Income, Paragraph 4. Although a few states treat all income as business income.

Example 23-20

What if: Assume Idaho and Tennessee have a hypothetical flat income tax rate of 7.6 percent and 6.5 percent, respectively. What is Wild West's income tax liability for Idaho and Tennessee?

Answer: Its liabilities are $2,963 and $622 in Idaho and Tennessee, respectively, computed as follows:

Description	Idaho	Tennessee	Explanation
(1) State tax base	$ 97,685	$102,685	Example 23-14
(2) Allocable income	$(38,505)	$ (43,505)	Example 23-19
(3) Business income	$ 59,180	$ 59,180	(1) − (2)
(4) Apportionment factor	31.23%	16.18%	Example 23-18
(5) Apportioned income	$ 18,482	$ 9,575	(3) × (4)
(6) Allocable income	$ 20,505	$ 0	Example 23-19
(7) State taxable income	$ 38,987	$ 9,575	(5) + (6)
(8) Tax rate	7.6%	6.5%	
Tax liability	**$ 2,963**	**$ 622**	(7) × (8)

Nonincome-Based Taxes

Several states have nonincome-based taxes. Washington has the Business & Occupation Tax, which is a gross receipts tax. Texas has the Margin Tax, the lesser of a gross margin tax or gross receipts tax (many states are treating the Texas Margin Tax as a tax based on net income). Some states imposing nonincome-based taxes treat all businesses as taxable entities. For example, Texas imposes the Margin Tax on C corporations, S corporations, partnerships, and sole proprietorships that have limited liability. As we discussed earlier, Public Law 86-272 doesn't apply to nexus for nonincome-based taxes such as gross receipts taxes or property taxes; these are deductible for calculating taxable income for net income-based taxes.

Example 23-21

Wild West has nexus in Washington and is subject to that state's business and occupation (B&O) tax. The tax is .471 percent of gross receipts for retailers and 1.5 percent of gross receipts on services. Wild West's gross receipts from retail sales and services in Washington are $41,982 and $377,441, respectively (from Exhibit 23-1). Calculate Wild West's B&O tax.

Answer: Wild West's B&O tax is $5,860, calculated as follows:

Activity	(1) Receipts	(2) Rate	(1) × (2) Tax
Retailing	$ 41,982	0.471%	$ 198
Services	377,441	1.500	5,662
B&O tax			**$5,860**

CONCLUSION

In this chapter, we discussed the fundamentals of state and local taxation with an emphasis on sales and income tax nexus, sales tax, and net income-based corporate taxes. State and local taxes currently make up a significant portion of many businesses' total tax burden and also consume a significant portion of the tax department's time.

Sales tax nexus is established through physical presence. Companies selling tangible personal property must collect sales tax from their customers (where sales tax nexus exists) and remit it to the various states. Income tax nexus requirements vary based on the type of goods or services provided by a business. Tangible personal property sales are protected from income tax nexus by Public Law 86-272 if certain criteria are met. For all other sales, income tax nexus is created by physical presence, although some states are defining the concept of income tax nexus based on economic rather than physical presence.

Businesses subject to multijurisdictional taxation—taxation by more than one government—have many issues in common. A business located in San Diego, California, but also doing business in Tucson, Arizona, will be subject to California and Arizona tax. If it also does business in Rosarito, Mexico, it will be subject to both U.S. and Mexico taxes. State and local taxation and international taxation bring up many of the same issues. For both, businesses must determine which jurisdiction has the right to tax a transaction (nexus) and how to divide income among different jurisdictions. The next chapter examines multinational taxation.

Summary

LO 23-1 Describe the primary types of state and local taxes.

- The primary purpose of state and local taxes is to raise revenue.
- Like federal tax law, state tax law is composed of legislative, administrative, and judicial law.
- Judicial law plays a more important role in state tax law than federal tax law because constitutionality is a primary concern for state tax laws.
- The most important question any taxpayer must answer is whether it is subject to a state's taxing regime.
- Nexus is the connection between a business and a state sufficient to subject the business to the state's tax system.
- When a business sells tangible personal property, either sales or use tax is due. If the seller has sales tax nexus, the seller must collect and remit the tax to the state. Otherwise, the buyer is responsible for paying the use tax.
- Businesses engaged in interstate commerce that have income tax nexus must pay income tax.

LO 23-2 Determine whether a business has sales tax nexus and calculate its sales tax withholding responsibilities.

- Forty-five states and the District of Columbia impose sales taxes.
- The items subject to sales tax vary from state to state.
- Businesses are required to collect sales tax on sales only if they have sales tax nexus with that state.
- For nondomiciliary businesses, sales tax nexus is created through a physical presence (having salespeople or tangible property within the state, for example).

LO 23-3 Identify whether a business has income tax nexus and determine its state income tax liabilities.

- Forty-six states impose an income tax on corporations, and 43 states tax the owners of partnerships and S corporations.
- Businesses must pay income tax in their state of commercial domicile, and nondomiciliary firms are subject to tax if they have income tax nexus in the state.
- Businesses divide or apportion their income among the states where they have established income tax nexus.
- Nexus requirements vary based on the nature of the business's activities: physical presence creates income tax nexus for service providers, sellers of real property, and businesses licensing intangibles; Public Law 86-272 protects solicitation of tangible personal property from income tax nexus.
- Some states require a separate income tax return for each entity with income tax nexus, and others require a unitary (a single) tax return for a group of related entities as long as one of the entities has established income tax nexus in the state.

- Businesses must calculate state taxable income for each state in which they must file a tax return—this requires businesses to identify federal/state adjustments.
- Firms adjust federal taxable income to arrive at their state taxable base.
- The state taxable base of an interstate business is separated into business and nonbusiness income: Business income is apportioned across states using a general formula, and nonbusiness income is allocated to specific states using specific rules.
- Business income is apportioned using some combination of sales, payroll, and property factors.

KEY TERMS

allocation (23-4)

apportionment (23-4)

business income (23-4)

commercial domicile (23-2)

economic income tax nexus (23-14)

federal/state adjustments (23-17)

income tax nexus (23-2)

interstate commerce (23-4)

nexus (23-2)

nonbusiness income (23-4)

nondomiciliary business (23-2)

Public Law 86-272 (23-10)

sales tax (23-3)

sales tax nexus (23-2)

separate tax return (23-15)

solicitation (23-11)

state tax base (23-4)

throwback rule (23-19)

trade show rule (23-12)

unitary tax return (23-15)

use tax (23-4)

DISCUSSION QUESTIONS

Discussion Questions are available in Connect®.

1. Why do states and local jurisdictions assess taxes? `LO 23-1`
2. Compare and contrast the relative importance of judicial law to state and local and federal tax law. `LO 23-1`
3. Describe briefly the nexus concept and explain its importance to state and local taxation. `LO 23-1`
4. What is the difference, if any, between the state of a business's commercial domicile and its state of incorporation? `LO 23-1`
5. What types of property sales are subject to sales tax and why might a state choose to exclude the sales of certain types of property? `LO 23-1`
6. In what circumstances would a business be subject to income taxes in more than one state? `LO 23-1`
7. Describe how the failure to collect sales tax can result in a larger tax liability for a business than failing to pay income taxes. `LO 23-1`
8. Discuss why restaurant meals, rental cars, and hotel receipts are often taxed at a higher-than-average sales tax rate. `LO 23-2`
9. Compare and contrast general sales tax nexus and the "Amazon" rule creating sales tax nexus in New York. `LO 23-2`
10. What is the difference between a sales tax and a use tax? `LO 23-2`
11. Renée operates Scandinavian Imports, a furniture shop in Olney, Maryland, that ships goods to customers in all 50 states. Scandinavian Imports also appraises antique furniture and has recently conducted in-home appraisals in the District of Columbia, Maryland, Pennsylvania, and Virginia. Online appraisals have been done for customers in California, Minnesota, New Mexico, and Texas. Determine where Scandinavian Imports has sales tax nexus. `LO 23-2`
12. Web Music, located in Gardnerville, Nevada, is a new online music service that allows inexpensive legal music downloads. Web Music prides itself on having the fastest download times in the industry. It achieved this speed by leasing server space from 10 regional servers dispersed across the country. Discuss where Web Music has sales tax nexus. `LO 23-2`
13. Discuss possible reasons why the Commerce Clause was included in the U.S. Constitution. `LO 23-2`

LO 23-2 14. Describe the administrative burden businesses face in collecting sales taxes.

LO 23-3 15. Compare and contrast the rules determining where domiciliary and nondomiciliary businesses must file state income tax returns.

LO 23-3 16. Lars operates Keep Flying Incorporated, a used airplane parts business, in Laramie, Wyoming. Lars employs sales agents that visit mechanics in all 50 states to solicit orders. All orders are sent to Wyoming for approval, and all parts are shipped via common carrier. The sales agents are always on the lookout for wrecked, abandoned, or salvage aircraft with rare parts because they receive substantial bonuses for purchasing and salvaging these parts and shipping them to Wyoming. Discuss the states where Keep Flying has income tax nexus.

LO 23-3 17. Explain changes in the U.S. economy that have made Public Law 86-272 partially obsolete. Provide an example of a company for which Public Law 86-272 works well and one for which it does not.

LO 23-3 18. Climb Higher is a distributor of high-end climbing gear located in Paradise, Washington. Its sales personnel regularly perform the following activities in an effort to maximize sales:
- Carry swag (free samples) for distribution to climbing shop employees.
- Perform credit checks of new customers to reduce delivery time of first order of merchandise.
- Check customer inventory for proper display and proper quantities.
- Accept returns of defective goods.

Identify which of Climb Higher's sales activities are protected and unprotected activities under the *Wrigley* Supreme Court decision.

LO 23-3 19. Describe a situation in which it would be advantageous for a business to establish income tax nexus in a state.

LO 23-3 20. States are arguing for economic income tax nexus; provide at least one reason for and one reason against the validity of economic income tax nexus.

LO 23-3 21. Explain the difference between separate-return states and unitary-return states.

LO 23-3 22. Explain the rationale for the factors (functional integration, centralization of management, and economies of scale) that determine whether two or more businesses form a unitary group under the *Mobil* decision.

LO 23-3 23. Compare and contrast the reasons why book/tax and federal/state adjustments are necessary for interest income.

LO 23-3 24. Compare and contrast the ways a multistate business divides business and nonbusiness income among states.

LO 23-3 25. Contrast the treatment of government sales and dock sales for the sales apportionment factor.

LO 23-3 26. Most states have increased the weight of the sales factor for the apportionment of business income. What are some possible reasons?

LO 23-3 27. Compare and contrast federal/state tax differences and book/federal tax differences.

PROBLEMS

Select problems are available in Connect®.

LO 23-2 28. Crazy Eddie Incorporated manufactures baseball caps and distributes them across the northeastern United States. The firm is incorporated and headquartered in New York and sells to customers in Connecticut, Delaware, Massachusetts, New Jersey, New York, Ohio, and Pennsylvania. It has sales reps only where discussed in the scenarios below. Determine the states in which Crazy Eddie has sales tax nexus given the following:

a) Crazy Eddie is incorporated and headquartered in New York. It also has property, employees, salespeople, and intangibles in New York.

b) Crazy Eddie has a warehouse, personal property, and employees in Connecticut.

c) Crazy Eddie has two customers in Delaware. Crazy Eddie receives orders over the phone and ships goods to its Delaware customers using FedEx.

d) Crazy Eddie has independent sales representatives in Massachusetts who distribute baseball-related items for over a dozen companies.

e) Crazy Eddie has salespeople who visit New Jersey. They follow procedures that comply with Public Law 86-272 by sending orders to New York for acceptance. The goods are shipped to New Jersey by FedEx.

f) Crazy Eddie provides graphic design services to another manufacturer located in Ohio. While the services are performed in New York, Crazy Eddie's designers visit Ohio at least quarterly to deliver the new designs and receive feedback.

g) Crazy Eddie receives online orders from its Pennsylvania clients. Because the orders are so large, the goods are delivered weekly on Crazy Eddie's trucks.

29. Brad Carlton operates Carlton Collectibles, a rare-coin shop in Washington, D.C., that ships coins to collectors in all 50 states. Carlton also provides appraisal service upon request. During the last several years the appraisal work has been done either in the D.C. shop or at the homes of private collectors in Maryland and Virginia. Determine the jurisdictions in which Carlton Collectibles has sales tax nexus.   **LO 23-2**

30. Melanie operates Mel's Bakery in Foxboro, Massachusetts, with retail stores in Connecticut, Maine, Massachusetts, New Hampshire, and Rhode Island. Mel's also ships specialty breads nationwide upon request. Determine Mel's sales tax collection responsibility and calculate the sales tax liability for Massachusetts, Connecticut, Maine, New Hampshire, Rhode Island, and Texas, based on the following information: **LO 23-2**

a) The Massachusetts stores earn $500,000 in sales. Massachusetts's sales tax rate is 5 percent; assume it exempts food items.

b) The Connecticut retail stores have $400,000 in sales ($300,000 from in store sales and $100,000 from catering) and $10,000 in delivery charges for catering activities. Connecticut sales tax is 6 percent and excludes food products but taxes prepared meals (catering). Connecticut also imposes sales tax on delivery charges on taxable sales.

c) Mel's Maine retail store has $250,000 of sales ($200,000 for take-out and $50,000 of in-store sales). Maine has a 5 percent sales tax rate and a 7 percent sales tax rate on prepared food; it exempts other food purchases.

d) The New Hampshire retail stores have $250,000 in sales. New Hampshire is one of five states with no sales tax. However, it has a room and meals tax rate of 8 percent. New Hampshire considers any food or beverage served by a restaurant for consumption on or off the premises to be a meal.

e) Mel's Rhode Island stores earn $300,000 in sales. The Rhode Island sales tax rate is 7 percent and its restaurant surtax is 1 percent. Rhode Island considers Mel's a restaurant because its retail store has seating.

f) One of Mel's best customers relocated to Texas, which imposes an 8.25 percent state and local sales tax rate but exempts bakery products. This customer entertains guests regularly and ordered $5,000 of food items this year.

31. Cuyahoga County, Ohio, has a sales tax rate of 8 percent. Determine the state, local, and transit (a local transportation district) portions of the rate. You can find resources on the State of Ohio website, including the following link: http://www.tax.ohio.gov/portals/0/tax_analysis/tax_data_series/sales_and_use/salestaxmapcolor.pdf   **LO 23-2**

 research

LO 23-2   32. Kai operates the Surf Shop in Laie, Hawaii, which designs, manufacturers, and customizes surfboards. Hawaii has a hypothetical 4 percent excise tax rate, technically paid by the seller. However, the state also allows "tax on tax" to be charged, which effectively means a customer is billed 4.166 percent of the sales price. Determine the sales tax the Surf Shop must collect and remit—or the use tax liability the customer must pay—for each of the following orders:

a) Kalani, a Utah customer, places an Internet order for a $1,000 board that will be shipped to Provo, Utah, where the local sales tax rate is 6.85 percent.

b) Scott, an Alabama resident, comes to the retail shop on vacation and has a $2,000 custom board made. Nick uses the board on vacation and then has the Surf Shop ship it to Tuscaloosa, Alabama, where the sales tax rate is 9 percent.

c) Jim, a Michigan resident, places an order for a $2,000 custom board at the end of his vacation. Upon completion, the board will be shipped to Ann Arbor, Michigan, where the sales tax rate is 6 percent.

d) Scott, a Nebraska resident, sends his current surfboard to the Surf Shop for a custom paint job. The customization services come to $800. The board is shipped to Lincoln, Nebraska, where the sales tax rate is 7.25 percent.

LO 23-2   33. Last year, Reggie, a Los Angeles, California, resident, began selling autographed footballs through Trojan Victory (TV) Incorporated, a California corporation. TV has never collected sales tax. Last year it had sales as follows: California ($100,000), Arizona ($10,000), Oregon ($15,000), New York ($50,000), and Wyoming ($1,000). Most sales are made over the Internet and shipped by common carrier. Determine how much sales tax TV should have collected in each of the following situations:

planning

a) California treats the autographed football as tangible personal property subject to an 8.25 percent sales tax rate. Answer for California.

b) California treats the autographed football as part tangible personal property ($50,000) and part services ($50,000), and tangible personal property is subject to an 8.25 percent sales tax rate. Answer for California.

c) TV has no property or other physical presence in New York (10.25 percent) or Wyoming (5 percent). Answer for New York and Wyoming.

d) TV has Reggie deliver a few balls to fans in Arizona (5.6 percent sales tax rate) and Oregon (no sales tax) while attending football games there. Answer for Arizona and Oregon.

e) Related to part (d), can you make any suggestions that would decrease TV's Arizona sales tax liability?

LO 23-2   34. LeMond Incorporated, a Wisconsin corporation, runs bicycle tours in several states. LeMond also has a Wisconsin retail store and an Internet store that ships to out-of-state customers. The bicycle tours operate in Colorado, North Carolina, and Wisconsin, where LeMond has employees and owns and uses tangible personal property. LeMond has real property only in Wisconsin and logs the following sales:

LeMond Sales			
State	Goods	Services	Total
Arizona	$ 34,194	$ 0	$ 34,194
California	110,612	0	110,612
Colorado	25,913	356,084	381,997
North Carolina	16,721	225,327	242,048
Oregon	15,431	0	15,431
Wisconsin	241,982	877,441	1,119,423
Totals	$444,853	$1,458,852	$1,903,705

Assume the following hypothetical tax rates: Arizona (5.6 percent), California (7.75 percent), Colorado (8 percent), North Carolina (6.75 percent), Oregon (8 percent), and Wisconsin (5 percent). How much sales tax must LeMond collect and remit?

35. Kashi Corporation is the U.S. distributor of fencing (sword fighting) equipment imported from Europe. It is incorporated in Virginia and headquartered in Arlington, Virginia; it ships goods to all 50 states. Kashi's employees attend regional and national fencing competitions where they maintain temporary booths to market their goods. Determine whether Kashi has income tax nexus in the following situations:

    LO 23-3

    planning

    a) Kashi is incorporated and headquartered in Virginia. It also has property, employees, salespeople, and intangibles in Virginia. Determine whether Kashi has income tax nexus in Virginia.

    b) Kashi has employees who live in Washington, D.C., and Maryland but perform all their employment-related activities in Virginia. Does Kashi have income tax nexus in Washington, D.C., and Maryland?

    c) Kashi has two customers in North Dakota. It receives their orders over the phone and ships goods to them using FedEx. Determine whether Kashi has income tax nexus in North Dakota.

    d) Kashi has independent sales representatives in Illinois who distribute fencing and other sports-related items for many companies. Does Kashi have income tax nexus in Illinois?

    e) Kashi has salespeople who visit South Carolina for a regional fencing competition for a total of three days during the year. They send all orders to Virginia for credit approval and acceptance, and Kashi ships the goods into South Carolina by FedEx. Determine whether Kashi has income tax nexus in South Carolina.

    f) Kashi has sales reps who visit California for a national fencing competition and several regional competitions for a total of 17 days during the year. They send all orders to Virginia for credit approval and acceptance. The goods are shipped by FedEx into California. Does Kashi have income tax nexus in California?

    g) Kashi receives online orders from its Pennsylvania client. Because the orders are so large, the goods are delivered weekly on Kashi's trucks. Does Kashi have income tax nexus in Pennsylvania?

    h) In addition to shipping goods, Kashi provides fencing lessons in Virginia and Maryland locations. Determine whether Kashi has income tax nexus in Virginia and Maryland.

    i) Given that Kashi ships to all 50 states, are there locations that would decrease Kashi's overall state income tax burden if income tax nexus were created there?

36. Gary Holt LLP provides tax and legal services regarding the tax-exempt bond issues of state and local jurisdictions. Gary typically provides the services from his New York offices. However, for large issuances he and his staff occasionally travel to another state to complete the work. Determine whether the firm has income tax nexus in the following situations:

    LO 23-3

    a) Gary Holt LLP is a New York partnership and headquartered in New York. It also has property and employees in New York. Does it have income tax nexus in New York?

    b) Gary Holt LLP has employees who live in New Jersey and Connecticut and perform all their employment-related activities in New York. Does it have income tax nexus in New Jersey and/or Connecticut?

    c) Gary Holt LLP has two customers in California. Gary personally travels there to finalize the Alameda County bond issuance. Does it have income tax nexus in California?

LO 23-3   37. Root Beer Inc. (RBI) is incorporated and headquartered in Seattle, Washington. RBI runs an Internet business, makerootbeer.com, and sells bottling equipment and other supplies for making homemade root beer. It also has an Oregon warehouse from which it ships goods. Determine whether RBI has income tax nexus in the following situations:

a) Root Beer is incorporated and headquartered in Washington and has property and employees in Oregon and Washington. Determine whether RBI has income tax nexus in Oregon and Washington.

b) Root Beer has hundreds of customers in California but no physical presence (no employees or property). Does it have income tax nexus in California?

c) Root Beer has 500 New York customers but no physical presence (no employees or property). Remember New York has the new Amazon rule. Determine whether RBI has income tax nexus in New York.

LO 23-3   38. Rockville Enterprises manufactures woodworking equipment and is incorporated and based in Evansville, Indiana. All of its real property is in Indiana. Rockville employs a large sales force that travels throughout the United States. Determine whether each of the following is a protected activity in nondomiciliary states under Public Law 86-272:

a) Rockville advertises in Wisconsin using television, radio, and newspapers.

b) Rockville's employees in Illinois check the credit of potential customers.

c) Rockville maintains a booth at an industry trade show in Arizona for 10 days.

d) Sales representatives check the inventory of a Tennessee customer to make sure it has enough stock and that the stock is properly displayed.

e) Rockville holds a management seminar executive retreat for corporate executives over four days in Florida.

f) Sales representatives supervise the repossession of inventory from a customer in Maine that is not making payments on time.

g) Rockville provides automobiles to Idaho and Montana sales representatives.

h) An Alabama sales representative accepts a customer deposit on a large order.

i) Colorado sales reps carry display racks and promotional materials that they place in customers' retail stores without charge.

LO 23-3
research   39. Software Incorporated is a sales and use tax software vendor that provides customers with a license to download and use its software on their machines. Software retains ownership of the software. It has customers in New Jersey and West Virginia. Determine whether Software has economic income tax nexus in these states based on the following decisions: *Lanco, Inc. v. Director, Division of Taxation,* 188 N.J. 380, 908 A. 2nd 176 (2006) and *Tax Commissioner of West Virginia v. MBNA America Bank, N.A.,* 640 SE 2d 226 (WV 2006).

LO 23-3
research   40. Peter Inc., a Kentucky corporation, owns 100 percent of Suvi Inc., a Mississippi corporation. Peter and Suvi file a consolidated federal tax return. Peter has income tax nexus in Kentucky and South Carolina; Suvi has income tax nexus in Mississippi and South Carolina. Kentucky, Mississippi, and South Carolina are separate-return states. In which states must Pete and Suvi file tax returns? Can they file a consolidated return in any states? Explain. (*Hint:* Use South Carolina Form SC 1120 and the related instructions.)

LO 23-3
research   41. Use California Publication 1061 (2016) to identify the various tests California uses to determine whether two or more entities are part of a unitary group.

42. Bulldog Incorporated is a Georgia corporation. It properly included, deducted, or excluded the following items on its federal tax return in the current year:

Item	Amount	Federal Treatment
Georgia income taxes	$25,496	Deducted on federal return
Tennessee income taxes	13,653	Deducted on federal return
Washington gross receipts tax	3,105	Deducted on federal return
Georgia bond interest income	10,000	Excluded from federal return
Federal T-note interest income	4,500	Included on federal return
Bonus Depreciation	15,096	Deducted on federal return

LO 23-3

tax forms

research

Use Georgia's Corporate Income Tax Form 600 and Instructions to determine what federal/state adjustments Bulldog needs to make for Georgia. Bulldog's federal taxable income was $194,302. Calculate its Georgia state tax base and complete Schedule 1, Page 1, of Form 600 for Bulldog.

43. Herger Corporation does business in California, Nevada, and Oregon and has income tax nexus in these states as well. Herger's California state tax base was $921,023 after making the required federal/state adjustments. Herger's federal tax return contains the following items:

LO 23-3

Item	Amount
Federal T-note interest income	$ 5,000
Nevada municipal bond interest income	3,400
California municipal bond interest income	6,000
Interest expense related to T-note interest income	1,400
Royalty income	100,000
Travel expenses	9,025

Determine Herger's business income.

44. Bad Brad sells used semi-trucks and tractor trailers in the Texas panhandle. Bad Brad has sales as follows:

LO 23-3

Bad Brad	
State	**Sales**
Colorado	$ 234,992
Oklahoma	102,150
New Mexico	675,204
Texas	1,085,249
Totals	$2,397,895

Bad Brad is a Texas corporation. Answer the questions in each of the following alternative scenarios.

a) Bad Brad has income tax nexus in Colorado, Oklahoma, New Mexico, and Texas. What are the Colorado, Oklahoma, New Mexico, and Texas sales apportionment factors?

b) Bad Brad has income tax nexus in Colorado and Texas. Oklahoma and New Mexico sales are shipped from Texas (a throwback state). What are the Colorado and Texas sales apportionment factors?

c) Bad Brad has income tax nexus in Colorado and Texas. Oklahoma and New Mexico sales are shipped from Texas (a throwback state); $200,000 of Oklahoma sales were to the federal government. What are the Colorado and Texas sales apportionment factors?

d) Bad Brad has income tax nexus in Colorado and Texas. Oklahoma and New Mexico sales are shipped from Texas (assume Texas is a nonthrowback state). What are the Colorado and Texas sales apportionment factors?

LO 23-3   45. Nicole's Salon, a Louisiana corporation, operates beauty salons in Arkansas, Louisiana, and Tennessee. These salons' payrolls by state are as follows:

Nicole's Salon	
State	**Payroll**
Arkansas	$ 130,239
Louisiana	309,192
Tennessee	723,010
Total	$1,162,441

What are the payroll apportionment factors for Arkansas, Louisiana, and Tennessee in each of the following alternative scenarios?

a) Nicole's Salon has income tax nexus in Arkansas, Louisiana, and Tennessee.

b) Nicole's Salon has income tax nexus in Arkansas, Louisiana, and Tennessee, but $50,000 of the Arkansas amount is paid to independent contractors.

LO 23-3   46. Delicious Dave's Maple Syrup, a Vermont corporation, has property in the following states:

Property		
State	**Beginning**	**Ending**
Maine	$ 923,032	$ 994,221
Massachusetts	103,311	203,109
New Hampshire	381,983	283,021
Vermont	873,132	891,976
Total	$2,281,458	$2,372,327

What are the property apportionment factors for Maine, Massachusetts, New Hampshire, and Vermont in each of the following alternative scenarios?

a) Delicious Dave's has income tax nexus in each of the states.

b) Delicious Dave's has income tax nexus in each of the states, but the Maine total includes $400,000 of investment property that Delicious rents out (unrelated to its business).

c) Delicious Dave's has income tax nexus in each of the states, but it also pays $50,000 to rent property in Massachusetts.

LO 23-3   47. Susie's Sweet Shop has the following sales, payroll, and property factors:

	Iowa	Missouri
Sales	69.20%	32.01%
Payroll	88.00	3.50
Property	72.42	24.04

What are Susie's Sweet Shop's Iowa and Missouri apportionment factors under each of the following alternative scenarios?

a) Iowa and Missouri both use a three-factor apportionment formula.

b) Iowa and Missouri both use a four-factor apportionment formula that double-weights sales.

c) Iowa uses a three-factor formula and Missouri uses a single-factor apportionment formula (based solely on sales).

48. Brady Corporation is a Nebraska corporation, but it owns business and investment property in surrounding states as well. Determine the state where each item of income is allocated. **LO 23-3**

   a) $15,000 of dividend income.

   b) $10,000 of interest income.

   c) $15,000 of rental income for South Dakota property.

   d) $20,000 of royalty income for intangibles used in South Dakota (where income tax nexus exists).

   e) $24,000 of royalty income from Kansas (where income tax nexus does not exist).

   f) $15,000 of capital gain from securities held for investment.

   g) $30,000 of capital gain on real property located in South Dakota.

49. Ashton Corporation is headquartered in Pennsylvania and has a state income tax base there of $500,000. Of this amount, $50,000 was nonbusiness income. Ashton's Pennsylvania apportionment factor is 42.35 percent. The nonbusiness income allocated to Pennsylvania was $32,000. Assuming a Pennsylvania corporate tax rate of 8.25 percent, what is Ashton's Pennsylvania state tax liability? **LO 23-3**

COMPREHENSIVE PROBLEMS

Select problems are available in Connect®.

50. Cloud computing is the use of hosted computer facilities through the Internet. Gmail, RIA Checkpoint, and even your iPhone are some applications of cloud computing.

   a) If HP provides a customized bundle of servers, storage, network and security software, and business application software to a customer in Washington State, how is it taxed?

   b) Is HP leasing tangible personal property, which is taxable, or providing a nontaxable service?

   c) Is the buyer of HP's product subject to Washington sales tax?

   d) Is HP subject to Washington's B&O tax?

51. Sharon Inc. is headquartered in State X and owns 100 percent of Carol Corp., Josey Corp., and Janice Corp., which form a single unitary group. Assume sales operations are within the solicitation bounds of Public Law 86-272. Each of the corporations has operations in the following states:

Domicile State	Sharon Inc. State X (throwback)	Carol Corp. State Y (throwback)	Josey Corp. State Z (nonthrowback)	Janice Corp. State Z (nonthrowback)
Dividend income	$ 1,000	$ 200	$ 300	$ 500
Business income	50,000	30,000	10,000	10,000
Sales: State X	70,000	10,000	10,000	10,000
State Y		40,000	5,000	
State Z		20,000	20,000	10,000
State A	20,000			
State B	10,000			10,000
Property: State X	50,000	20,000		10,000
State Y		80,000		
State Z			25,000	20,000
State A	50,000			
Payroll: State X	10,000	10,000		
State Y		40,000		
State Z			3,000	10,000
State A				10,000

Compute the following for State X assuming a tax rate of 15 percent.

a) Calculate the State X apportionment factor for Sharon Inc., Carol Corp., Josey Corp., and Janice Corp.

b) Calculate the business income apportioned to State X.

c) Calculate the taxable income for State X for each company.

d) Determine the tax liability for State X for the entire group.

52. Happy Hippos (HH) is a manufacturer and retailer of New England crafts headquartered in Camden, Maine. HH provides services and has sales, employees, property, and commercial domicile as follows:

| | | | | | Commercial |
State	Sales	Employees	Property	Services	Domicile
Connecticut	✓	✓		✓	
Maine	✓	✓	✓	✓	✓
Massachusetts	✓	✓			
New York	✓				
Rhode Island	✓	✓			
Vermont	✓	✓	✓	✓	

Happy Hippos In-State Activities

HH's sales of goods and services by state are as follows:

Happy Hippos Sales

State	Goods	Services	Total
Connecticut	$ 78,231	$ 52,321	$130,552
Maine	292,813	81,313	374,126
Massachusetts	90,238		90,238
New York	129,322		129,322
Rhode Island	98,313		98,313
Vermont	123,914	23,942	147,856
Totals	$812,831	$157,576	$970,407

HH has federal taxable income of $282,487 for the current year. Included in federal taxable income are the following income and deductions:

- $12,000 of Vermont rental income.
- City of Orono, Maine, bond interest of $10,000.
- $10,000 of dividends.
- $2,498 of state tax refund included in income.
- $32,084 of state net income tax expense.
- $59,234 of federal depreciation.

Other relevant facts include:

- Maine state depreciation for the year was $47,923, and Maine doesn't allow deductions for state income taxes.
- The employees present in Connecticut, Massachusetts, and Rhode Island are salespeople who perform only activities protected by Public Law 86-272.
- Assume that each of the states is a separate-return state.

HH's payroll is as follows:

Payroll	
State	**Wages**
Connecticut	$ 94,231
Maine	392,195
Massachusetts	167,265
Rhode Island	92,391
Vermont	193,923
Total	$940,005

HH's property is as follows:

Property			
State	**Beginning**	**Ending**	**Rented**
Maine	$ 938,234	$ 937,652	
Vermont	329,134	428,142	$12,000
Total	$1,267,368	$1,365,794	$12,000

a) Determine the states in which HH has sales tax nexus.

b) Calculate the sales tax HH must remit assuming the following (hypothetical) sales tax rates:

- Connecticut (6 percent)
- Maine (8 percent)
- Massachusetts (7 percent)
- New York (8.875 percent)
- Rhode Island (5 percent)
- Vermont (9 percent)

c) Determine the states in which HH has income tax nexus.

d) Determine HH's state tax base for Maine, assuming federal taxable income of $282,487.

e) Calculate business and nonbusiness income.

f) Determine HH's Maine apportionment factors using the three-factor method (assume that Maine is a throwback state).

g) Calculate HH's business income apportioned to Maine.

h) Determine HH's allocation of nonbusiness income to Maine.

i) Determine HH's Maine taxable income.

j) Calculate HH's Maine income tax liability, assuming a Maine income tax rate of 5 percent.

ROGER | *CPA Review*

Sample CPA Exam questions from Roger CPA Review are available in Connect as support for the topics in this text. These Multiple Choice Questions and Task-Based Simulations include expert-written explanations and solutions and provide a starting point for students to become familiar with the content and functionality of the actual CPA Exam.

chapter

24

The U.S. Taxation of Multinational Transactions

Learning Objectives

Upon completing this chapter, you should be able to:

LO 24-1 Describe the basic U.S. framework for taxing multinational transactions and the role of the foreign tax credit limitation.

LO 24-2 Apply the U.S. source rules for common items of gross income and deductions.

LO 24-3 Explain the role of income tax treaties in international tax planning.

LO 24-4 Identify creditable foreign taxes and compute the foreign tax credit limitation.

LO 24-5 Compare the advantages and disadvantages of the different forms of doing business outside the United States.

LO 24-6 Explain the basic U.S. anti-deferral tax regime and identify common sources of subpart F income.

©Ariel Skelley/Blend Images LLC

Storyline Summary

Detroit Doughnut Depot

Privately held company located in Detroit, Michigan. Operated as a C corporation for U.S. tax purposes. Makes and sells fresh baked goods, homemade sandwiches, and premium coffee and tea drinks.

Lily Green

Owner of Detroit Doughnut Depot (3D)

Filing status:	Married filing jointly
Dependents:	Two children
Marginal tax rate:	24 percent

L
ily Green was excited about the growth of her coffee and baked goods business since she opened her store in downtown Detroit in 2008. From its humble beginnings, the Detroit Doughnut Depot (3D) had attracted a solid base of loyal customers who appreciated the freshness and organic ingredients that set the company's products apart from its competitors. Many of Lily's customers were commuters from nearby Windsor, Canada. They often asked Lily whether she ever considered opening a store in Windsor, where they thought she would find a receptive customer base. Lily was intrigued by the idea of "going global" with her business, but she knew she needed to find someone to help her understand the U.S. and Canadian income tax implications of expanding her business to Windsor. Her first questions dealt with how and when she would be subject to Canadian tax and whether her Canadian activities also would be subject to U.S. tax.

Lily Green is about to take part in a growing trend of expansion by U.S. businesses into international markets. In 1983, gross receipts of non-U.S. subsidiaries of U.S. multinational corporations totaled approximately $720 billion; by 2014, that number exceeded $7.5 trillion, a more than tenfold increase.[1] Before-tax profits increased from $57 billion in 1983 to more than $1 trillion in 2013. Companies such as Google Inc. and Apple, Inc., report a significant amount of revenue from international operations. For example, Alphabet Inc. (Google) reported revenue from its international operations of $58.3 billion in 2017, approximately 53 percent of its total revenue.[2] Apple, Inc., reported net sales of $215.6 billion in 2017, approximately 63 percent of which came from outside the United States.

As dramatic as the outflow of investment from the United States has been, the inflow of investment by non-U.S. businesses and individuals into the United States has been just as impressive. According to the U.S. Bureau of Economic Analysis, the total amount of foreign-owned assets in the United States increased by more than 1,000 percent between 1989 and 2016, to $23.9 trillion.[3] U.S. subsidiaries of non-U.S. companies currently employ 6.8 million Americans.[4] Familiar non-U.S. headquartered companies with large U.S. operations include BP Global (United Kingdom), Toyota Motor Corporation (Japan), Honda Motor Corporation (Japan), Nissan Group (Japan), Nestle S.A. (Switzerland), Sony Corporation (Japan), GlaxoSmithKline PLC (United Kingdom), Volkswagen AG (Germany), Samsung Group (South Korea), BMW AG (Germany), Bridgestone Corporation (Japan), Bayer AG (Germany), and Philips Electronics N.V. (Netherlands).

This chapter provides a basic overview of the U.S. tax consequences related to transactions that span more than one national tax jurisdiction (in our storyline, the United States and Canada). We focus primarily on the U.S. tax rules that apply to **outbound transactions,** where a U.S. person engages in a transaction that occurs outside the United States or involves a non-U.S. person.[5] We also discuss briefly the U.S. tax rules that apply to **inbound transactions,** where a non-U.S. person engages in a transaction that occurs within the United States or involves a U.S. person. Most of the U.S. income tax rules that apply to multinational transactions are found in subchapter N of the Internal Revenue Code (IRC) (§861–§999).

LO 24-1

THE U.S. FRAMEWORK FOR TAXING MULTINATIONAL TRANSACTIONS

THE KEY FACTS

Basic Framework for U.S. Taxation of Multinational Transactions

- The United States taxes citizens and residents on their worldwide income and nonresidents on their U.S. source income.

- U.S. corporations owning 10 percent or more of a foreign corporation receive a 100 percent dividends received deduction for dividends received from these corporations.

- A noncitizen is treated as a U.S. resident for income tax purposes if the individual is a permanent resident (has a green card) or meets a substantial presence test.

(continued)

When a U.S. person engages in a transaction that involves a country outside the United States, there arises the issue as to which tax authority or authorities have jurisdiction (i.e., the legal right) to tax that transaction. All governments (national, state, and local) must adopt a basis on which to claim the right to tax income. The criteria they choose to assert their right to tax a person or transaction is called **nexus.** At the national level, governments most often determine nexus by either the geographic source of the income, called **source-based jurisdiction,** or by the taxpayer's citizenship or residence, called **residence-based jurisdiction.**

Once nexus has been established, a government must decide how to allocate and apportion a person's income and expenses to its tax jurisdiction. Under a residence-based approach, a country taxes the worldwide income of the person earning the income. Under a source-based approach, a country taxes only the income earned within its boundaries. When applying a source-based approach, a government must develop source rules to allocate and apportion income and expenses to its jurisdiction. Within the United States, states use

---

[1]Bureau of Economic Analysis, *U.S. Direct Investment Abroad: Financial and Operating Data for U.S. Multinational Companies,* available at www.bea.gov.

[2]As a reference point, Google Inc. reported a loss of $42.3 million in 2005 from international operations.

[3]Bureau of Economic Analysis, *U.S. Net International Investment Position: End of Fourth Quarter and Year 2016.* Available at www.bea.gov.

[4]Organization for International Investment, data available at www.ofii.org.

[5]As used in this chapter, a "person" includes an individual, corporation, partnership, trust, estate, or association. Section 7701(a)(1). The "United States," as used in this context, includes only the 50 states and the District of Columbia. §7701(a)(9).

apportionment formulas that take into account sales, property, and payroll, or some combination of these factors, to apportion income and expenses to their tax jurisdiction.[6]

Income earned by a citizen or resident of one country that has its source in another country can be taxed by both countries. The country where the taxpayer resides can assert residence-based jurisdiction, whereas the country where the income is earned can apply geographic source-based jurisdiction. To mitigate such double taxation and to promote international commerce, governments often allow their residents a tax credit for foreign income taxes paid on *foreign source* income. National governments also enter into income tax treaties with other national governments to mitigate the double taxation of income earned by residents of one country in the other country. Under a treaty, both countries may agree not to tax income earned within their boundaries by a resident of the other country.

The United States applies both residence-based jurisdiction and source-based jurisdiction in asserting its right to tax income. The U.S. government taxes *citizens* and *residents* on their worldwide income, regardless of source (residence-based jurisdiction).[7] In the Tax Cuts and Jobs Act, enacted on December 22, 2017, Congress replaced the worldwide approach with a territorial approach for certain U.S. corporations earning foreign-source income through specified 10 percent-or-more owned foreign corporations. The Act establishes a participation exemption system for foreign income, under which there is allowed a 100 percent deduction for the foreign-source portion of dividends received by domestic corporations that are U.S. shareholders of those foreign corporations. In contrast, the U.S. government only taxes *nonresidents* on income that is "U.S. source" or is connected with the operation of a U.S. trade or business (source-based jurisdiction).

- Nonresident income is characterized as either ECI or FDAP income.
  - ECI income is taxed on a net basis using the U.S. graduated tax rates.
  - FDAP income is taxed on a gross basis through a flat withholding tax.
- The U.S. allows citizens and residents a tax credit for foreign income taxes paid on foreign source income.
- U.S. corporations do not receive a foreign tax credit on dividend income eligible for the 100 percent dividends received deduction.
- The foreign tax credit is limited to the percentage of foreign source taxable income to taxable income times the precredit income tax on total taxable income.

U.S. Taxation of a Nonresident

U.S. source income earned by a nonresident is classified into two categories for U.S. tax purposes: (1) **effectively connected income (ECI)** and (2) **fixed and determinable, annual or periodic income (FDAP).** Income that is effectively connected with a U.S. trade or business is subject to *net taxation* (i.e., gross income minus deductions) at the U.S. tax rate. A nonresident reports such income and related deductions on a U.S. tax return, either a Form 1120F for a nonresident corporation or a Form 1040NR for a nonresident individual. FDAP income, which generally is passive income such as dividends, interest, rents, or royalties, is subject to a *withholding tax* regime applied to gross income. The payor of the FDAP income withholds the tax at the statutory rate (30 percent under U.S. tax law) or less under a treaty arrangement and remits it to the government. The recipient of the FDAP income usually does not have to file a tax return and does not reduce the FDAP income by any deductions. Most countries, including Canada, apply a similar tax regime to U.S. persons earning income within their jurisdiction.[8]

Example 24-1

Lily has decided to open a store in Windsor, Canada, from which she will sell baked goods and sandwiches made in her U.S. store and transported daily across the border. She has elected to operate the store as an unincorporated division, or **branch,** of Detroit Doughnut Depot (3D) for Canadian tax purposes. Will 3D be subject to tax in Canada on any taxable income it earns through its Windsor store?

Answer: Yes. 3D will have nexus in Canada because it operates a business there (residence-based jurisdiction). As a result, Canada and the Province of Ontario will tax the branch's Canadian-source taxable income.

(continued on page 24-4)

---

[6]See the State and Local Taxes chapter for a more thorough discussion of how states apportion income.

[7]The United States is one of two countries, the other being Eritrea, that applies full worldwide taxation based on citizenship as well as residency.

[8]Canada applies a 25 percent withholding tax rate on dividends, rents, and royalties unless reduced under a treaty. Canada does not impose a withholding tax on interest paid to a nonresident dealing at arm's length with the lender.

How will Canada tax 3D's Canadian-source taxable income?

Answer: Canada will apply the appropriate corporate tax rate(s) to the branch's taxable income (gross income less deductions). For 2018, the general Canadian corporate net tax rate is a flat 15 percent after abatements. The province of Ontario also will impose an income tax between 3.5 and 11.5 percent on the branch's taxable income.

What if: Assume 3D does not operate a business in Canada but owns 5 percent of the stock in a Canadian corporation that pays 3D a C$100 dividend each year.[9] How will Canada tax 3D on the dividend income it receives from its investment in the stock of the Canadian company?

Answer: Canada will apply a flat withholding tax of 15 percent on the gross amount of the dividend.[10]

Definition of a Resident for U.S. Tax Purposes

An individual who is not a U.S. citizen is characterized for U.S. tax purposes as either a **resident alien** or a **nonresident alien.** An individual becomes a U.S. resident by satisfying one of two tests found in the IRC.[11] Under the first test, sometimes referred to as the *green card test,* an individual is treated as a resident if he or she possesses a permanent resident visa ("green card") at any time during the calendar year. Under the second test, sometimes referred to as the *substantial presence test,* an individual becomes a U.S. resident when he or she is *physically present* in the United States for 31 days or more during the current calendar year *and* the number of days of physical presence during the current calendar year, plus one-third times the number of days of physical presence during the first preceding year, plus one-sixth times the number of days of physical presence during the second preceding year, equals or exceeds 183 days.[12] As we will discuss later in the chapter, these rules often are modified by treaties between the United States and other countries to limit instances in which an individual might be taxed as a resident by more than one country.

As always, there are a number of exceptions. For example, international students and teachers generally are exempt from the physical presence test for five and two years, respectively. Individuals who are present in the United States during the current year for less than 183 days and who establish that they have a "closer connection" to another country can elect to be exempt from the physical presence test.[13] Other exemptions apply to individuals who experience unexpected medical conditions while in the United States and to commuters from Canada and Mexico who have a U.S. employer.

The residence of a corporation for U.S. tax purposes generally is determined by the entity's country of incorporation. For example, the parent company of Tyco International Plc is incorporated in Ireland, although it is managed in the United States. For U.S. tax purposes, the parent company of Tyco is treated as a nonresident corporation, although its U.S. subsidiaries and U.S. branches are treated as U.S. residents. Some countries, such as the United Kingdom and Ireland, determine a corporation's residence based on where central management of the company is located. The Irish government would treat the parent company of Tyco as a nonresident Irish company because the company is managed in the United States.

---

[9]The national currency of Canada is the Canadian dollar, abbreviated C$.

[10]Under the U.S.–Canada income tax treaty, the withholding tax on this dividend is 15 percent.

[11]§7701(b).

[12]For purposes of this test, a full day is considered any part of a day.

[13]An individual usually satisfies the closer connection test by demonstrating that he or she has a "tax home" in another country. A "tax home" is defined as the taxpayer's regular place of business or *regular place of abode.*

Example 24-2

What if: Assume that for quality-control purposes Lily has decided to do all the baking for her Windsor store in Detroit. Every morning a Windsor employee drives a van to Detroit and picks up the baked goods for sale in Windsor. One of her Windsor employees, Stan Lee Cupp, made the two-hour trip on 132 different days during 2018. He was not physically present in the United States prior to 2018. Will Stan be considered a U.S. resident in 2018 applying only the substantial presence test? Stan is a Canadian citizen and resident.

Answer: No. Although he is physically present in the United States for more than 30 days in 2018, Stan does not satisfy the 183-day test when applying the formula $[132 + (1/3 \times 0) + (1/6 \times 0) = 132]$.

What if: Assume Stan continues to be physically present in the United States for 132 days in 2019 and 2020. Will Stan be considered a U.S. resident in 2019 or 2020 applying only the substantial presence test?

Answer:

2019: No. He does not satisfy the 183-day test when applying the formula $[132 + (1/3 \times 132) + (1/6 \times 0) = 176]$.

2020: Yes. He now satisfies the 183-day test when applying the formula $[132 + (1/3 \times 132) + (1/6 \times 132) = 198]$.

Does Stan qualify for any exceptions that allow him to avoid being treated as a U.S. resident in 2020?

Answer: Yes. Stan can avoid being treated as a U.S. resident under the closer connection test because he was physically present in the United States for less than 183 days in 2020 and his tax home is in Canada. If Stan is in the United States for 183 days or more, he will have to rely on the U.S.–Canada income tax treaty to avoid being considered a U.S. resident for income tax purposes (to be discussed in more detail later in the chapter).

Overview of the U.S. Foreign Tax Credit System

For U.S. taxpayers subject to worldwide taxation of their income, the United States mitigates the double taxation of foreign source income by allowing U.S. taxpayers to claim a **foreign tax credit (FTC)** for foreign income taxes paid on *foreign source* income not eligible for exemption. The United States taxes foreign source income to the extent the foreign taxing jurisdiction did not tax the income at a rate equal to or greater than the U.S. tax rate of 21 percent. The United States does not allow a current year credit for taxes paid in excess of the U.S. tax rate, however. The United States attempts to achieve this residual tax approach through the **foreign tax credit limitation,** which is computed as follows:

$$\frac{\text{Foreign source taxable income}}{\text{Total taxable income}} \times \text{Precredit U.S. tax on total taxable income}$$

For tax years beginning after December 31, 2017, the foreign tax credit limitation is computed separately for four categories of foreign source income—global intangible low-taxed income (GILTI), foreign branch income, passive category income, and general category income. (Special rules apply to income resourced by treaty and income earned in designated countries.) We discuss the type of income placed in each category in more detail later in this chapter. A taxpayer can carry any unused (excess) FTC for the current year back to the previous tax year and then forward to the next 10 future tax years. Foreign taxes paid on income in the GILTI basket cannot be carried back or forward.

Example 24-3

Lily's store in Windsor is an immediate success and reports taxable income on its Canadian operations of C$50,000 for 2018. 3D paid a combined national and provincial income tax of C$9,250 on its taxable income. Because 3D operates the Windsor store as a branch, it also must report the income on its U.S. corporate income tax return along with taxable income from its Detroit operations.[14]

Assuming a translation rate of C$1:US $0.80, 3D reports the Canadian taxable income on its U.S. tax return as $40,000 and reports the Canadian income taxes as $7,400. 3D also reported taxable income from its U.S. operations of $160,000. The company's U.S. income tax on $200,000 of total taxable income is $42,000 before any credit for the income taxes paid to Canada. 3D's income from its Windsor operations is classified as "foreign branch income" for foreign tax credit purposes.

Using the above facts, what is the foreign tax credit limitation that applies to 3D's Canadian income taxes for 2018?

Answer: $8,400, computed as $40,000/$200,000 × $42,000.

where:

$40,000 = Foreign source taxable income

$200,000 = Total taxable income

$42,000 = Precredit U.S. tax on total taxable income

What is 3D's net U.S. tax after subtracting the available foreign tax credit?

Answer: $34,600, computed as $42,000 − $7,400. 3D has an "excess foreign tax credit limitation" of $1,000 (that is, 3D could have incurred an additional $1,000 of foreign taxes and received a full-year credit for them).

What is 3D's effective tax rate on its total taxable income for 2018?

Answer: 21 percent, computed as ($7,400 + $34,600)/$200,000.

What if: Assume 3D pays Canadian income taxes of C$12,800 ($10,240) for 2018 (a tax rate of 26.5 percent). What is its net U.S. tax after subtracting the available foreign tax credit?

Answer: $33,600, computed as $42,000 − $8,400.

The foreign tax credit limitation limits the foreign tax credit to $8,400. 3D now has an "excess foreign tax credit" of $1,840, which 3D can carry forward 10 years. Given the above scenario, what is 3D's effective tax rate on its total taxable income for 2018?

Answer: 21.92% percent, computed as ($10,240 + $33,600)/$200,000. The FTC limitation prevents 3D from getting a current year tax credit on income taxes paid in excess of the U.S. rate of 21 percent.

LO 24-2 ## U.S. SOURCE RULES FOR GROSS INCOME AND DEDUCTIONS

Many of the U.S. tax rules that apply to multinational transactions require taxpayers to determine the jurisdictional (geographic) source (U.S. or foreign) of their gross income.[15] The source rules determine whether income and related deductions are from sources within or without the United States. All developed countries have source-of-income rules, although most practitioners consider the U.S. rules to be the most complex in the world.

The U.S. source-of-income rules are important to *non-U.S. persons* because they limit the scope of U.S. taxation to only their U.S. source income. For *U.S. persons*, the primary purpose of the U.S. source-of-income rules is to calculate *foreign source taxable income* in the numerator of the foreign tax credit limitation. Except in the case of dividends eligible for the 100 percent dividends received deduction, the United States imposes a tax on the worldwide income of U.S. persons, regardless of its source or the U.S. person's residence. The United States cedes *primary jurisdiction* to foreign governments

---

[14]Because 3D is a "small company," the Ontario tax rate is 3.5 percent, which, added to the federal tax rate of 15 percent, creates a combined tax rate of 18.5 percent. Large corporations are subject to a combined tax rate of 26.5 percent if operating in Ontario.

[15]The U.S. federal income tax source rules are found in §861–§865 and the accompanying regulations.

to tax U.S. persons on income earned outside the United States while retaining the *residual* right to tax foreign source income to the extent it has not been "fully taxed" by the foreign government. The net result is that the United States taxes foreign source income earned by U.S. persons at a rate that theoretically reflects the difference between the U.S. tax rate and the foreign tax rate imposed on the income.

U.S. persons must understand the source-of-income rules in other situations. For example, U.S. citizens and residents employed outside the United States may be eligible to exclude a portion of their *foreign source earned income* from U.S. taxation under §911.[16] In addition, U.S. persons who pay U.S.-source FDAP income to foreign payees (e.g., interest or dividends) usually are required to withhold U.S. taxes on such payments.[17] U.S. corporations earning "foreign-derived intangible income" (FDII) receive a 37.5 percent deduction on such income that reduces the effective tax rate on such income to 13.125 percent. U.S. corporations receive a 100 percent DRD on the "foreign-source portion" of dividends received from 10 percent-or-more owned foreign corporations. (These later two situations were added by the Tax Cuts and Jobs Acts and will be discussed later in the chapter.)

The source-of-income rules are definitional in nature; they do not impose a tax liability, create income, or allow a deduction. Although the primary focus of the source rules is on where the economic activity that generates income takes place, the U.S. government also uses the source rules to advance a variety of international tax policy objectives.

Source of Income Rules

The Internal Revenue Code defines nine classes of gross income from sources within the United States[18] and nine classes of gross income from sources outside the United States.[19] A summary of the general rules that apply to common sources of income follows. A detailed discussion of all the exceptions to these rules is beyond the scope of this text.

Interest   As a general rule, the taxpayer looks to the residence of the party *paying* the interest (the borrower) to determine the geographic source of interest received. A borrower's residence is established at the time the interest is paid. Factors that determine an individual's residence include the location of the individual's family; whether the person buys a home, pays foreign taxes, and engages in social and community affairs; and the length of time spent in a country. Under these general rules, interest income is U.S. source if it is paid by the United States or the District of Columbia, a noncorporate U.S. resident, or a U.S. corporation. Although interest income paid by a U.S. bank to a nonresident (e.g., an international student attending a U.S. university) is U.S.-source income, such interest is exempt from U.S. withholding or other income taxation.[20] This exception is designed to attract foreign capital to U.S. banks.

> **THE KEY FACTS**
> **Source Rules**
> - The source rules determine whether income and deductions are treated as U.S. source or foreign source.
> - For a U.S. taxpayer, the source rules primarily determine foreign taxable income in the calculation of the foreign tax credit limitation.
> - For a non-U.S. taxpayer, the source rules determine what income is subject to U.S. taxation.

Example 24-4

3D was dissatisfied with the 1 percent interest rate it received on its checking account at Bank of America in Detroit. Lily's investment adviser suggested the company invest $50,000 in five-year bonds issued by the Canadian government with an interest rate of 3 percent. During 2018, 3D received C$1,500 in interest from the bonds. Per the U.S.–Canada treaty, the Canadian government did not withhold taxes on the payment. Assume the translation rate is C$1:US$1.

What is the source, U.S. or foreign, of the interest Lily receives on the bonds?

Answer: Foreign source. The source of interest income depends on the residence of the borrower at the time the interest is paid. The Canadian government is considered a resident of Canada for U.S. source rule purposes.

---

[16]If certain conditions are met, a U.S. individual can exclude up to $104,100 of earned income from U.S. taxation in 2018 plus additional earnings equal to excess "foreign housing expenses" under §911.

[17]§1441.

[18]§861(a).

[19]§862(a).

[20]§871(i)(2)(A) and §881(d).

Dividends In general, the source of dividend income is determined by the residence of the corporation paying the dividend. Residence usually is determined by the corporation's country of incorporation or organization (in some countries, such as the United Kingdom, a corporation's residence is determined by where its central management is located).

Example 24-5

As part of diversifying its investment portfolio, 3D purchased 200 shares of Scotiabank (Bank of Nova Scotia, Canada). In 2018, Scotiabank paid 3D dividends of C$400. Scotiabank withheld C$60 in taxes (15 percent) on the payment.

What is the source, U.S. or foreign, of the dividend 3D receives on the stock?

Answer: Foreign source. The source of dividend income depends on the residence of the payor of the dividend. Scotiabank is headquartered in Toronto, Canada, and is a resident of Canada for U.S. source rule purposes.

Compensation for Services The source of compensation received for "labor or personal services" is determined by the location where the service is performed. The IRS and the courts have held that the term includes activities of employees, independent contractors, artists, entertainers, athletes, and even corporations offering "personal services" (e.g., accounting). The Code provides a limited **commercial traveler exception,** in which personal service compensation earned by nonresidents within the U.S. is *not* treated as U.S. source if the individual meets the following criteria:

- The individual was present in the United States for not more than 90 days during the current taxable year;[21]
- Compensation for the services does not exceed $3,000; and
- The services are performed for a nonresident alien, foreign corporation, or foreign partnership or for the foreign office of a domestic corporation.[22]

The United States frequently alters the limitations on length of stay and compensation through treaty agreements. In most cases, the 90-day limit is extended to 183 days, and no dollar limit is put on the amount of compensation received.

Compensation for services performed within and outside of the United States must be allocated between U.S. and foreign sources. An individual who receives compensation, other than compensation in the form of fringe benefits, as an employee for labor or personal services performed partly within and partly outside the United States is required to source such compensation on a *time basis*. An individual who receives compensation as an employee for labor or personal services performed partly within and partly outside the United States in the form of fringe benefits (e.g., additional amounts paid for housing or education) is required to source such compensation on a *geographic basis;* that is, determined by the employee's principal place of work.

Example 24-6

What if: Assume that for quality-control purposes Lily has decided to do all the baking for her Windsor store in Detroit. Every morning a Windsor employee drives a truck to Detroit and picks up the baked goods for sale in Windsor. One of her Windsor employees, Stan Lee Cupp, made the 2-hour trip on 120 different days during 2018 (240 hours spent in the United States). 3D paid Stan a salary of C$50,000 during 2018. He worked a total of 1,920 hours during 2018. Assume the translation rate is C$1:US$0.80. How much U.S. source compensation does Stan have in 2018? Base your computation on hours worked.

---

[21]For purposes of this test, a full day is considered to be any part of a day.
[22]§861(a)(3)(A)–(C).

Answer: $5,000 (C$50,000 × 240/1,920 × $0.80). Stan sources his salary for U.S. tax purposes based on where he performed the services. Using hours worked, Stan spent 12.5 percent of his time performing services in the United States (240/1,920).

Using only the exception found in the IRC, will Stan be subject to U.S. tax on his U.S.-source wages in 2018?

Answer: Yes. Stan fails the commercial traveler exception. He is in the United States for more than 90 days during 2018.

What if: Assume Stan limits his trips to 90 days during 2018 (180 hours spent in the United States). Using only the IRC exception, will Stan be subject to U.S. tax on his U.S.-source salary in 2018?

Answer: Yes. Stan still fails the commercial traveler exception. Although he is in the United States for not more than 90 days, his U.S.-source salary is $3,750 (C$50,000 × 180/1,920 × $0.80), which exceeds $3,000.

As we discuss later in the chapter, the U.S.–Canada income tax treaty significantly liberalizes the commercial traveler exception, thus allowing Stan to spend more time in the United States without being taxed by the U.S. government on his U.S.-source wages.

TAXES IN THE REAL WORLD Taxing Professional Golfers

One of the issues that the IRS has struggled with is whether to characterize fees paid to foreign professional golf and tennis players pursuant to on-course/on-court endorsement contracts (e.g., contracts that require wearing a company's logo or using its equipment) as income from royalties or income from personal services, or both. Two recent Tax Court cases with well-known professional golfers illustrate the complexities of this issue.

The first case involved Retief Goosen, a PGA tour member and winner of the 2001 U.S. Open Championship.* Mr. Goosen was a citizen of South Africa and a resident of the United Kingdom, but he spent most of his time competing in the United States and Europe.

Mr. Goosen entered into several endorsement and appearance agreements with sponsors that allowed the sponsor to use his name and likeness to advertise and promote the sponsor's products or in connection with advertising and promoting a specific tournament or event. The "on-course" endorsement agreements required him to wear or use the sponsor's products during golf tournaments, whereas the "off-course" endorsement agreements did not have this requirement.

Mr. Goosen reported all his prize money from golf tournaments and appearance fees in the United States as "effectively connected" income taxable in the United States. He characterized his endorsement fees from on-course endorsements as 50 percent royalty income and 50 percent personal services income. He sourced the personal services income from the on-course endorsement fees to the United States based on the number of days he played within the United States over the total number of days he played golf for the year. Mr. Goosen characterized his endorsement fees from the off-course endorsement agreements as 100 percent royalty income. The IRS argued that the sponsors primarily paid Mr. Goosen to perform personal services, which included playing golf and carrying or wearing the sponsors' products.

The Tax Court awarded a partial victory to both parties. The Court found that Mr. Goosen's name had a value beyond his golf skills and abilities for which his sponsors paid a substantial amount of money for the right to use his name and likeness. The sponsors also valued Goosen's play at tournaments, as evidenced by the fact that the sponsors conditioned the full endorsement fee on his playing in 36 tournaments a year. The Court thus held that his performance of services and the use of his name and likeness were equally important and characterized 50 percent of the endorsement fees from the on-course endorsement agreements as royalty income and 50 percent of the fees as personal services income.

The Court held that Mr. Goosen's earnings from playing golf in the United States was effectively

*Retief Goosen v. Commissioner, 136 T.C. No. 27 (June 9, 2011).

(continued on page 24-10)

connected U.S.-source income. The on-course endorsement and appearance fees and his on-course royalty income also were held to be U.S.-source effectively connected income to the extent they were sourced as U.S.-source income because payment depended on whether he played a specified number of tournaments. Both categories of income were taxed at the regular U.S. graduated tax rates.

The Court held that income Mr. Goosen received from off-course endorsement agreements did not depend on whether he played in golf tournaments. Thus, the income was not effectively connected with a U.S. trade or business and was thus subject to a 30 percent withholding tax to the extent it was treated as U.S.-source income.

The second case involved Sergio Garcia, a Spanish citizen but a resident of Switzerland.[†] The IRS again argued that the "vast majority" of the golfer's endorsement income should be treated as personal services income and subject to U.S. taxation at the regular tax rates. Mr. Garcia characterized 85 percent of his endorsement income as royalty income, which was not subject to U.S. taxation under the U.S.–Swiss income tax treaty. The Tax Court judge held that 65 percent of the endorsement income should be characterized as royalty income. It is interesting to note that the Tax Court apportioned a higher percentage of Mr. Garcia's income as royalties because he was designated as a "global icon" by the golf company that paid him the endorsement fees. The same company regarded Mr. Goosen as a "brand ambassador" and paid him less than Mr. Garcia because the company valued Mr. Garcia's "flash, looks and maverick personality" more than Mr. Goosen's "cool 'Iceman' demeanor."

[†]*Sergio Garcia v. Commissioner,* 140 T.C. No 6 (March 14, 2013).

Rents and Royalties   Rent has its source where the property generating the rent is located. Royalty income has its source where the intangible property or rights generating the royalty are used. Royalties include payments related to intangibles such as patents, copyrights, secret processes and formulas, goodwill, trademarks, trade brands, and franchises. An intangible is "used" in the country that protects the owner against its unauthorized use.

Example 24-7

In 2018, 3D rented its Windsor store for C$2,500 per month, for a total of C$30,000. Under the U.S.–Canada income tax treaty, 3D must withhold U.S. taxes at a 30 percent rate on rent payments that flow from the United States to Canada if the rent is U.S.-source income. Will 3D have to withhold taxes on the rent payments it makes in 2018?

Answer: No. The rent is considered foreign source income because the store that is rented is located in Canada.

Gain or Loss from Sale of Real Property   In general, gain or loss from the sale of realty has its source where the property is located.

Gain or Loss from Sale of Purchased Personal Property   Under the general rule, gain or loss from the sale of purchased personal (nonrealty) property has its source based on the seller's residence.[23] There are many exceptions to this general rule. In particular, gross income (sales minus cost of goods sold) from the sale of purchased inventory is sourced where title passes. Title is deemed to pass at the time when, and the place where, the seller's rights, title, and interest in the property are transferred to the buyer.

[23]Personal property under the source rules includes stock of a corporation. Sales of intangible property such as a patent, copyright, secret process, goodwill, trademark, trade brand, or franchise are subject to different source rules.

Source of Deduction Rules

After determining the source of gross income as being from U.S. or foreign sources, a taxpayer may be required to **allocate** and **apportion** allowable deductions to gross income from each geographical source to compute taxable income from U.S. and foreign sources. For a U.S. taxpayer, this allocation and apportionment process identifies the foreign source deductions that are subtracted from foreign source gross income in computing foreign source taxable income in the numerator of the FTC limitation computation. A non-U.S. taxpayer with gross income that is effectively connected with a U.S. trade or business must identify the U.S. source deductions that are subtracted from U.S. gross income to compute U.S. taxable income.

U.S. and non-U.S. taxpayers can have different motivations in seeking to deduct (or not deduct) expenses from either foreign source or U.S. source gross income. A U.S. taxpayer seeking to maximize the foreign tax credit limitation will want to allocate as few deductions to foreign source gross income as possible, the goal being to make the ratio of foreign source taxable income to total taxable income as close to 100 percent as possible (or whatever ratio is needed to absorb any excess credits). Non-U.S. taxpayers operating in a low-tax-rate country (a tax rate less than the U.S. rate) have a tax incentive to allocate as many deductions to U.S. source income as possible to minimize their U.S. tax liability. Non-U.S. taxpayers operating in a high-tax-rate country (a tax rate greater than the U.S. rate) have a worldwide tax incentive to allocate as many deductions to foreign source income as possible to minimize their worldwide tax liability.

ETHICS

International Contractors, Inc., has been hired by the U.S. government to build roads and bridges in Spartania, a country with which the United States recently signed a treaty. To facilitate the issuance of visas and licenses to begin construction, an official from the Spartanian government asked for 100 "facilitating payments" (also known as "grease payments") of $5,000 each from the company. These payments were customary in Spartania and did not violate Spartanian law. The company intended to deduct the $500,000 payment in its financial statements. It was not clear if these payments violated the Foreign Corrupt Practices Act. To avoid IRS and possible Department of Justice scrutiny, the company's tax director suggested that the payment be described as "taxes and licenses" on the tax return (line 17 of Form 1120) without further details. What do you think of the tax director's advice? What tax and other consequences might result from taking this advice?

General Principles of Allocation and Apportionment   The IRC provides very broad language in describing how to allocate deductions to U.S. and foreign source gross income. The regulations attempt to match deductions with the gross income such deductions were incurred to produce.[24] Matching usually is done based on the "factual relationship" of the deduction to gross income. Deductions that can be directly associated with a particular item of income (e.g., machine depreciation with manufacturing gross profit) are referred to as **definitely related deductions.** Deductions not directly associated with a particular item of gross income (e.g., medical expenses, property taxes, standard deduction) are referred to as **not definitely related deductions** and are allocated to all gross income.

---

[24]Reg. §1.861-8 provides the general rules for allocating and apportioning deductions to U.S. and foreign source gross income.

The regulations require the taxpayer to first allocate (associate) deductions to the class or classes of gross income such deductions were incurred to produce. The taxpayer then apportions the deduction between, in most cases, foreign source and U.S. source gross income. The regulations allow the taxpayer to apportion deductions using a method that reflects the factual relationship between the deduction and the grouping of gross income. Examples include units sold, gross sales or receipts, and gross income.

Example 24-8

Return to the facts in Example 24-3. Lily's store in Windsor reported taxable income on its Canadian operations of C$50,000 for 2018. For U.S. tax purposes, foreign source taxable income was $40,000 (C$50,000 × 0.80). 3D paid a combined national and provincial income tax of C$9,250 ($7,400) on its taxable income (at a tax rate of 18.5 percent). The company reported the $40,000 taxable income on its U.S. corporate income tax return along with $160,000 of taxable income from its Detroit operations. 3D's U.S. income tax on $200,000 of taxable income is $42,000 before any credit for the income taxes paid to Canada. Included in the computation of taxable income was a deduction of $50,000 for advertising that 3D incurred to promote its stores in Detroit and Windsor. 3D elected to apportion the advertising deduction based on sales. For 2018, Detroit sales were $400,000 and Windsor sales were C$125,000 ($100,000). How much of the $50,000 advertising deduction does 3D apportion to its foreign source taxable income for FTC purposes?

Answer: $10,000, computed as $100,000/$500,000 × $50,000,

where:

    $100,000 = Canadian sales

    $500,000 = Total sales

    $50,000   = Advertising deduction

Using the above facts, what is the foreign tax credit limitation that applies to 3D's Canadian income taxes for 2018?

Answer: $6,300, computed as ($40,000 − $10,000)/$200,000 × $42,000,

where:

    $40,000   = Foreign source taxable income before apportionment of any advertising expense

    $10,000   = Apportioned advertising deduction

    $200,000 = Total taxable income

    $42,000   = Precredit U.S. tax on total taxable income

Apportioning some of the advertising deduction to the numerator of 3D's FTC limitation ratio reduces the amount of foreign income taxes that are creditable in 2018. 3D gets a foreign tax credit of $6,300 because the FTC limitation is less than the foreign taxes paid. 3D now has a FTC carryforward of $1,100 ($7,400 − $6,300).

Special Apportionment Rules Special apportionment rules apply to nine categories of deductions, most notably interest, research and experimentation, state and local income taxes, losses on property disposition, and charitable contributions.[25] These special apportionment rules are very complicated, and the details are beyond the scope of this text. The basic rules for interest expense and research and experimentation are discussed below.

Interest expense is allocated to all gross income using as a basis the assets that generated such income. Interest is apportioned based on average tax book value for the year. Assets are attributed to income based on the source and type of income they generate, have generated, or may reasonably be expected to generate. A taxpayer using the tax book value method can elect to use the alternative depreciation system on U.S. assets solely for purposes of apportioning interest expense.

---

[25]The other deductions are stewardship expenses attributable to dividends received, supportive expenses, net operating losses, and legal and accounting fees.

Example 24-9

Expanding on the facts in Example 24-8, 3D borrowed $100,000 from Bank of America in Detroit and paid interest expense of $6,000 in 2018. 3D apportions this interest expense between U.S. and foreign source income using average tax book value. 3D's U.S. assets had an average tax book value of $250,000 and its foreign assets had an average tax book value of $50,000 in 2018. How much of the $6,000 interest deduction does 3D apportion to its foreign source taxable income for FTC purposes? Assume the limitation on business interest does not apply.

Answer: $1,000, computed as $50,000/$300,000 × $6,000,

where:

$50,000   = Average tax book value of Canadian assets

$300,000 = Total average tax book value of all of 3D's assets

$6,000   = Interest expense

Taking into account the apportioned advertising deduction and interest deduction, what is the foreign tax credit limitation that applies to 3D's Canadian income taxes for 2018?

Answer: $6,090, computed as ($40,000 − $10,000 − $1,000)/$200,000 × $42,000,

where:

$40,000   = Foreign source taxable income before apportioned advertising and interest

$10,000   = Apportioned advertising expense

$1,000   = Apportioned interest expense

$200,000 = Total taxable income

$42,000   = Precredit U.S. tax on total taxable income

Allocation of a portion of the interest expense to the numerator of 3D's FTC limitation ratio further reduces the amount of foreign taxes that are creditable in 2018. 3D now has an excess foreign tax credit of $1,310 ($7,400 − $6,090).

Research and experimentation (R&E) expenditures must be apportioned between U.S. and foreign source income using either a sales method or a gross income method. Taxpayers can apportion a percentage of R&E expenditures based on where the research is conducted. The amount that can be sourced under this exclusive apportionment method is 50 percent if the sales method is elected and 25 percent if the gross income method is elected. State and local income taxes are allocated to the gross income with respect to which such state income taxes are imposed. Charitable contributions and the dividends received deductions generally are allocated to U.S. source income. The allocation and apportionment rules of these deductions are complex and beyond the scope of this text.

The foreign tax credit limitation is computed on Form 1118 (corporations) or Form 1116 (individuals). Exhibit 24-1 presents a completed Form 1118 for the cumulative facts in Examples 24-8 and 24-9. Note that the Form 1118 is for tax year 2017 because the revised form for the Tax Cuts and Jobs Act changes was not available when this chapter went to press. The 2017 form does not include the new FTC basket for foreign branch income. The branch income was put in the general limitation basket for this exhibit.

OPERATING ABROAD THROUGH A FOREIGN CORPORATION

The Tax Cuts and Jobs Act made significant changes to the taxation of foreign source income earned through foreign corporations owned 10 percent or more by domestic corporations that meet the definition of a **U.S. shareholder.** U.S. shareholders for this purpose are U.S. corporations owning 10 percent or more of the voting power and value of the foreign corporation. Such foreign source income, to the extent it is not subject to the deemed dividend rules of subpart F (to be discussed later), is eligible for a 100 percent dividends received deduction (**participation exemption**) when distributed to a domestic

THE KEY FACTS

Treaties

- Treaties are designed to encourage cross-border trade by reducing or eliminating the double taxation of such income by the countries that are party to the treaty.

- Treaties define whether and when a resident of one country has nexus in the other country.

- Treaties reduce or eliminate the withholding tax imposed on cross-border payments such as interest, dividends, and royalties.

EXHIBIT 24-1   Form 1118: Foreign Tax Credit Corporations, Schedules A, B, F, and H for 3D Corporation (cumulative facts from Examples 24-9, 24-10, and 24-11)

Form **1118**
(Rev. December 2015)
Department of the Treasury
Internal Revenue Service

Foreign Tax Credit—Corporations

▶ Information about Form 1118 and its separate instructions is at *www.irs.gov/form1118.*
▶ Attach to the corporation's tax return.

For calendar year 20____ , or other tax year beginning _____ , 20____ , and ending _____ , 20____

OMB No. 1545-0123

Name of corporation   **Detroit Doughnut Depot**

Employer identification number

Use a **separate** Form 1118 for each applicable category of income listed below. See **Categories of Income** in the instructions. Also, see **Specific Instructions.** Check only one box on each form.

☐ Passive Category Income
☑ General Category Income
☐ Section 901(j) Income: Name of Sanctioned Country ▶ _____
☐ Income Re-sourced by Treaty: Name of Country ▶ _____

Schedule A   Income or (Loss) Before Adjustments *(Report all amounts in U.S. dollars. See **Specific Instructions**.)*

1. Foreign Country or U.S. Possession (Enter two-letter code; see instructions. Use a separate line for each.) *	Gross Income or (Loss) From Sources Outside the United States (*INCLUDE* Foreign Branch Gross Income here *and* on Schedule F)							
	2. Deemed Dividends (see instructions)		3. Other Dividends		4. Interest	5. Gross Rents, Royalties, and License Fees	6. Gross Income From Performance of Services	7. Other (attach schedule)	8. Total (add columns 2(a) through 7)
	(a) Exclude gross-up	(b) Gross-up (sec. 78)	(a) Exclude gross-up	(b) Gross-up (sec. 78)					
A	CN								40,000	40,000
B										
C										
D										
E										
F										

Totals (add lines A through F)

* For section 863(b) income, NOLs, income from RICs, and high-taxed income, use a single line (see instructions).

Deductions (*INCLUDE* Foreign Branch Deductions here *and* on Schedule F)

	9. Definitely Allocable Deductions				10. Apportioned Share of Deductions Not Definitely Allocable (enter amount from applicable line of Schedule H, Part II, column (d))	11. Net Operating Loss Deduction	12. Total Deductions (add columns 9(e) through 11)	13. Total Income or (Loss) Before Adjustments (subtract column 12 from column 8)
	Rental, Royalty, and Licensing Expenses		(c) Expenses Related to Gross Income From Performance of Services	(d) Other Definitely Allocable Deductions	(e) Total Definitely Allocable Deductions (add columns 9(a) through 9(d))				
	(a) Depreciation, Depletion, and Amortization	(b) Other Expenses							
A				10,000	10,000	1,000		11,000	29,000
B									
C									
D									
E									
F									
Totals				10,000	10,000	1,000		11,000	29,000

For Paperwork Reduction Act Notice, see separate instructions.   Cat. No. 10900F   Form **1118** (Rev. 12-2015)

Form 1118 (Rev. 12-2015)   Page **2**

Schedule B   Foreign Tax Credit *(Report all foreign tax amounts in U.S. dollars.)*

Part I—Foreign Taxes Paid, Accrued, and Deemed Paid *(see instructions)*

	1. Credit is Claimed for Taxes (check one):	2. Foreign Taxes Paid or Accrued (attach schedule showing amounts in foreign currency and conversion rate(s) used)								3. Tax Deemed Paid (from Schedule C—Part I, column 12, Part II, column 8(b), and Part III, column 8)
	☐ Paid ☐ Accrued	Tax Withheld at Source on:			Other Foreign Taxes Paid or Accrued on:				(h) Total Foreign Taxes Paid or Accrued (add columns 2(a) through 2(g))	
	Date Paid Date Accrued	(a) Dividends	(b) Interest	(c) Rents, Royalties, and License Fees	(d) Section 863(b) Income	(e) Foreign Branch Income	(f) Services Income	(g) Other		
A	various					7,400			7,400	
B										
C										
D										
E										
F										
Totals (add lines A through F)						7,400			7,400	

Part II—Separate Foreign Tax Credit *(Complete a **separate** Part II for **each** applicable category of income.)*

1a	Total foreign taxes paid or accrued (total from Part I, column 2(h))	7,400
b	Foreign taxes paid or accrued by the corporation during prior tax years that were suspended due to the rules of section 909 and for which the related income is taken into account by the corporation during the current tax year (see instructions)	
2	Total taxes deemed paid (total from Part I, column 3)	
3	Reductions of taxes paid, accrued, or deemed paid (enter total from Schedule G)	( )
4	Taxes reclassified under high-tax kickout	
5	Enter the sum of any carryover of foreign taxes (from Schedule K, line 3, column (xiv) and from Schedule I, Part III, line 3) plus any carrybacks to the current tax year	7,400
6	Total foreign taxes (combine lines 1a through 5)	7,400
7	Enter the amount from the applicable column of Schedule J, Part I, line 11 (see instructions). If Schedule J is **not** required to be completed, enter the result from the "Totals" line of column 13 of the applicable Schedule A	29,000
8a	Total taxable income from all sources (enter taxable income from the corporation's tax return)	200,000
b	Adjustments to line 8a (see instructions)	
c	Subtract line 8b from line 8a	200,000
9	Divide line 7 by line 8c. Enter the resulting fraction as a decimal (see instructions). If line 7 is greater than line 8c, enter 1	0.145
10	Total U.S. income tax against which credit is allowed (regular tax liability (see section 26(b)) minus American Samoa economic development credit)	42,000
11	Credit limitation (multiply line 9 by line 10) (see instructions)	6,090
12	**Separate foreign tax credit** (enter the smaller of line 6 or line 11 here and on the appropriate line of Part III)	6,090

Part III—Summary of Separate Credits *(Enter amounts from Part II, line 12 for **each** applicable category of income. **Do not** include taxes paid to sanctioned countries.)*

1	Credit for taxes on passive category income	
2	Credit for taxes on general category income	6,090
3	Credit for taxes on income re-sourced by treaty (combine all such credits on this line)	
4	Total (add lines 1 through 3)	6,090
5	Reduction in credit for international boycott operations (see instructions)	
6	**Total foreign tax credit** (subtract line 5 from line 4). Enter here and on the appropriate line of the corporation's tax return	6,090

Form **1118** (Rev. 12-2015)

EXHIBIT 24-1   **Form 1118: Foreign Tax Credit Corporations, Schedules A, B, F, and H for 3D Corporation (cumulative facts from Examples 24-9, 24-10, and 24-11)** *(concluded)*

Form 1118 (Rev. 12-2015)

Schedule F	Gross Income and Definitely Allocable Deductions for Foreign Branches		
	1. Foreign Country or U.S. Possession (Enter two-letter code from Schedule A, column 1. Use a separate line for each.)	**2.** Gross Income	**3.** Definitely Allocable Deductions
A	CN	40,000	6,000
B			
C			
D			
E			
F			
Totals (add lines A through F)* ▶		40,000	6,000

* **Note:** *The Schedule F totals are not carried over to any other Form 1118 Schedule. (These totals were already included in Schedule A.) However, the IRS requires the corporation to complete Schedule F under the authority of section 905(b).*

Form 1118 (Rev. 12-2015)   Page **10**

Schedule H	Apportionment of Deductions Not Definitely Allocable *(complete only once)*

Part I—Research and Development Deductions

		(a) Sales Method				(b) Gross Income Method — Check method used: ☐ Option 1 ☐ Option 2				(c) Total R&D Deductions Not Definitely Allocable (enter the sum of all amounts entered in all applicable "R&D Deductions" columns)
		Product line #1 (SIC Code:)*		Product line #2 (SIC Code:)*		Product line #1 (SIC Code:)*		Product line #2 (SIC Code:)*		
		(i) Gross Sales	(ii) R&D Deductions	(iii) Gross Sales	(iv) R&D Deductions	(v) Gross Income	(vi) R&D Deductions	(vii) Gross Income	(viii) R&D Deductions	
1	Totals (see instructions)									
2	Total to be apportioned									
3	Apportionment among statutory groupings:									
a	General category income									
b	Passive category income									
c	Section 901(j) income*									
d	Income re-sourced by treaty*									
4	Total foreign (add lines 3a through 3d)									

* **Important:** *See **Computer-Generated Schedule H** in instructions.*   Form **1118** (Rev. 12-2015)

Form 1118 (Rev. 12-2015)   Page **11**

Schedule H	Apportionment of Deductions Not Definitely Allocable *(continued)*

Part II—Interest Deductions, All Other Deductions, and Total Deductions

		(a) Average Value of Assets—Check method used: ☐ Fair market value ☑ Tax book value ☐ Alternative tax book value		(b) Interest Deductions		(c) All Other Deductions Not Definitely Allocable	(d) Totals (add the corresponding amounts from column (c), Part I; columns (b)(iii) and (b)(iv), Part II; and column (c), Part II). Enter each amount from lines 3a through 3d below in column 10 of the corresponding Schedule A.
		(i) Nonfinancial Corporations	(ii) Financial Corporations	(iii) Nonfinancial Corporations	(iv) Financial Corporations		
1a	Totals (see instructions)	300,000		6,000			
b	Amounts specifically allocable under Temp. Regs. 1.861-10T(e)						
c	Other specific allocations under Temp. Regs. 1.861-10T						
d	Assets excluded from apportionment formula						
2	Total to be apportioned (subtract the sum of lines 1b, 1c, and 1d from line 1a)	300,000		6,000			
3	Apportionment among statutory groupings:						
a	General category income	50,000		1,000			1,000
b	Passive category income						
c	Section 901(j) income*						
d	Income re-sourced by treaty*						
4	Total foreign (add lines 3a through 3d)	50,000		1,000			1,000

* **Important:** *See **Computer-Generated Schedule H** in instructions.*   Form **1118** (Rev. 12-2015) corporation that meets the definition of a U.S. shareholder.[26] Any foreign income taxes paid on income eligible for the exemption are not creditable or deductible on the U.S. shareholder's U.S. tax return. The enactment of this participation exemption moves the United States toward a territorial tax system, and puts the United States in line with most other countries in the taxation of foreign source active trade or business income.

Example 24-10

Assume the same facts as Example 24-3 except that Lily decides to operate her Windsor operations through a wholly-owned Canadian corporation. In 2018, the Canadian corporation reported taxable income of C$50,000 and paid a combined national and provincial income tax of C$9,250 on its taxable income. The C$50,000 is not subject to U.S. taxation because it is active trade or business income earned through a foreign corporation. In 2019, Lily decides to pay a dividend of C$10,000 to the U.S. corporation. The dividend is subject to a 5 percent withholding tax (C$500) under the U.S.–Canada treaty. How much of the dividend is subject to U.S. taxation and are any of the foreign taxes imposed on the income distributed creditable?

Answer: $0 income is subject to U.S. taxation and $0 foreign taxes are creditable. The dividend is eligible for a 100 percent dividends received deduction, and any Canadian taxes paid on such income are not creditable or deductible on 3D's U.S. tax return.

Foreign-Derived Intangible Income   The Tax Cuts and Jobs Act gave U.S. producers of goods and services an incentive to manufacture such products in or provide such services from the United States, and to hold intellectual property in the United States. For tax years beginning after December 31, 2017, gross profit derived from certain export sales or services, referred to as **foreign-derived intangible income (FDII),** is eligible for a deduction equal to 37.5 percent of FDII, which reduces the effective tax rate imposed on such income to 13.125 percent (21 percent × 62.5 percent).[27]

The computation of FDII is extremely complex, as are many of the international tax provisions enacted in the new tax law. In general terms, the deduction applies to income from sales of property intended for foreign use or services provided to any person or with respect to property not located in the United States in excess of a "normal return" on U.S. assets used in the production of the product or services. A normal return is defined as 10 percent of **qualified business asset investment (QBAI),** which is defined as the tax basis of depreciable property used in the production of the products sold (both to U.S. and foreign customers), assuming straight-line depreciation.

Example 24-11

Assume 3D had $175,000 of net income (gross income less allocated deductions) from sales of baked goods to U.S. customers and $25,000 of net income from sales of baked goods to the Canadian store for sale to Canadian customers in 2018. Also assume 3D had QBAI of $300,000. What is 3D's deduction for FDII in 2018?

Answer: $7,969 3D has net income of $170,000 in excess of 10 percent of QBAI [($200,000 − .10($300,000))]. Of that amount, $21,250 ($25,000 / $200,000 × $170,000) is considered FDII and eligible for the 37.5 percent deduction. The FDII deduction allowed in computing 3D's taxable income is $7,969. The actual calculation is much more complex than this and is beyond the scope of this text.

---

[26]§245A and §951(B).
[27]§250.

TREATIES

LO 24-3

A tax treaty is a bilateral agreement between two contracting countries in which each agrees to modify its own tax laws to achieve reciprocal benefits. The general purpose of an income tax treaty is to eliminate or reduce the impact of double taxation so that residents paying taxes to one country will not have the full burden of taxes in the other country. The United States signed its first income tax treaty with France in 1939. The United States now has income tax treaties with 67 countries. Exhibit 24-2 provides a list of the countries with which the United States has income tax treaties. U.S. treaties generally do not affect the U.S. taxation of U.S. citizens, residents, and domestic corporations because such taxpayers are taxed on a worldwide basis.

EXHIBIT 24-2   Countries with Which the United States Has Income Tax Treaties

Australia	India	Philippines
Austria	Indonesia	Poland
Bangladesh	Ireland	Portugal
Barbados	Israel	Romania
Belgium	Italy	Russian Federation
Bulgaria	Jamaica	Slovak Republic
Canada	Japan	Slovenia
China, People's Republic of	Kazakhstan	South Africa
Commonwealth of Independent States[a]	Korea, Republic of	Spain
Cyprus	Latvia	Sri Lanka
Czech Republic	Lithuania	Sweden
Denmark	Luxembourg	Switzerland
Egypt	Malta	Thailand
Estonia	Mexico	Trinidad and Tobago
Finland	Morocco	Tunisia
France	Netherlands	Turkey
Germany	New Zealand	Ukraine
Greece	Norway	United Kingdom
Hungary	Pakistan	Venezuela
Iceland		

[a]Armenia, Azerbaijan, Belarus, Georgia, Krygyzstan, Moldova, Tajikistan, Turkmenistan, and Uzbekistan.

Treaties reduce or eliminate the tax on income earned in one contracting country by a resident of the other contracting country. For example, most U.S. treaties provide a low withholding tax rate or an exemption from tax on various types of investment income (interest, dividends, gains from sale of stock, and royalties) that otherwise would be subject to a high withholding tax.[28] For individuals, U.S. treaties often provide exemption from taxation by the host country on wages or self-employment income earned in the treaty country, provided the individual does not spend more than 183 days in that other country. U.S. businesses generally are not taxed on business profits earned in the host treaty country unless they conduct that business through a **permanent establishment.** A permanent establishment generally is a fixed place of business such as an office or factory, although employees acting as agents can create a permanent establishment. Treaties also provide "tiebreaker" rules for determining the country in which an individual will be considered a resident for treaty purposes.

---

[28]Absent a treaty, the United States imposes a withholding tax rate of 30 percent on payments of FDAP income to nonresidents.

Example 24-12

What if: Lily is trying to determine whether 3D would be subject to Canadian taxation under two different scenarios: (1) she opens a store in Windsor and operates it as a branch of 3D, or (2) she makes the baked goods in Detroit and ships them to Windsor-area grocery stores using the company's van. Article VII of the U.S.–Canada income tax treaty states that the business profits of a U.S. resident are taxed in Canada only if the business operates in Canada through a permanent establishment. Article V defines a permanent establishment as including a place of management, a branch, an office, a factory, and a workshop. Under the U.S.–Canada treaty, will 3D be subject to Canadian tax on taxable income earned through its Windsor store?

Answer: Yes. A branch is defined as a permanent establishment. Canada can tax 3D's Canadian-source taxable income under Article VII of the U.S.–Canada treaty.

Under the U.S.–Canada treaty, will 3D be subject to Canadian tax on taxable income earned by selling goods to grocery stores in Windsor directly?

Answer: No. 3D does not have a permanent establishment in Canada on these sales. Canada will not tax income from these sales under Article VII of the U.S.–Canada treaty.

Example 24-13

What if: Assume that for quality-control purposes Lily has decided to do all the baking for her Windsor store in Detroit. Every morning a Windsor employee drives a van to Detroit and picks up the baked goods for sale in Windsor. One of her Windsor employees, Stan Lee Cupp, made the two-hour trip on 200 different days during 2018. Article IV of the U.S.–Canada income tax treaty states that, in cases where an individual is considered a resident of both countries under their respective tax laws, the individual will be considered a resident of the country in which he or she has a permanent home. Stan has a home only in Canada, and Canada still considers him to be a Canadian resident. Will Stan be considered a U.S. resident in 2018 applying only the substantial presence test?

Answer: Yes. Stan is physically present in the United States for more than 30 days in 2018 and satisfies the 183-day test when applying the formula $[200 + (1/3 \times 0) + (1/6 \times 0) = 200]$.

Will Stan be considered a U.S. resident in 2018 under the U.S.–Canada treaty?

Answer: No. Under the tiebreaker rules in the U.S.–Canada treaty, Stan is considered to be a resident only of Canada for income tax purposes, because that is where he has his permanent home. The United States can tax Stan only on income that is considered to be from U.S. sources.

Example 24-14

What if: Return to the facts in Example 24-6. Stan made the two-hour trip from Windsor to Detroit and back on 120 different days during 2018 (240 hours). 3D paid Stan a salary of C$50,000 ($40,000) during 2018. He worked a total of 240 days (1,920 hours) during 2018. Article XV of the U.S.–Canada income tax treaty states that a Canadian resident individual earning wages in the United States will be exempt from U.S. tax on his or her U.S.-source wages if the wages do not exceed $10,000 or the individual is present in the United States for more than 183 days. Under the U.S.–Canada treaty, will Stan be subject to Canadian tax on his U.S.-source compensation in 2018?

Answer: No. Stan is exempt from U.S. tax on his wages because under the apportionment rules for compensation (discussed in Example 24-6), he has only $5,000 of U.S. compensation, computed as $(240/1,920) \times $40,000,

where:

      240 = Number of hours worked in the United States

    1,920 = Total number of hours worked

  $40,000 = Total compensation in U.S. dollars

What if: Assume Stan received wages from 3D of $100,000 in 2018. Under the U.S.–Canada treaty, will Stan be subject to Canadian tax on his U.S.-source compensation in 2018?

Answer: No. Stan was in the United States for less than 184 days; therefore he is exempt from U.S. tax on his U.S. source compensation, even though the amount ($12,500) exceeds $10,000.

FOREIGN TAX CREDITS

LO 24-4

The United States taxes the worldwide income of U.S. partnerships, trusts and estates, U.S. citizens, and resident aliens. U.S. corporations continue to be taxed on all income other than dividends received from foreign corporations eligible for the 100 percent dividends received deduction. As we have discussed, U.S. persons earning foreign source income may be subject to multiple taxation on such income by the United States and the country in which the individual resides or where the income is earned. For example, a U.S. citizen who earns income in France may be subject to taxation by both governments. Without any relief from such multiple taxation, U.S. taxpayers would have little incentive to do business outside the United States.

FTC Limitation Categories of Taxable Income

The United States alleviates the multiple taxation of foreign source income earned by U.S. persons by allowing a tax credit for income taxes paid on such foreign source income. The foreign tax credit (FTC) allowed in the current year is subject to a foreign tax credit limitation,[29] computed by multiplying the ratio of foreign source taxable income to total taxable income times precredit U.S. tax, as follows:

$$\frac{\text{Foreign source taxable income}}{\text{Total taxable income}} \times \text{Precredit U.S. tax}$$

As a policy matter, the U.S. government must decide whether, and to what extent, U.S. taxpayers should segregate foreign source income subject to different tax rates and compute a separate FTC limitation for each category of income. Since 1976, the United States has required persons claiming the foreign tax credit to segregate foreign source income by category of income. Practitioners often refer to each income category as an **FTC basket.** Prior to the Tax Cuts and Jobs Act, there were two primary categories of FTC income, **passive category income** and **general category income.**[30] The Tax Cuts and Jobs Act added two more categories for foreign branch income and **global intangible low-taxed income (GILTI),** a new category of subpart F income to be discussed later in the chapter. The "basket" approach is intended to limit blending opportunities (high-tax foreign source income and low-tax foreign source income) to income that is of the same character.

Passive Category Income Passive category income generally is investment-type income that traditionally is subject to low foreign taxes (usually in the form of withholding taxes). Passive category income includes interest, dividends not eligible for the 100% DRD, rents, royalties, and annuities.

THE KEY FACTS

Foreign Tax Credits

- Only income taxes can be claimed as a credit on a U.S. tax return.
- The current year foreign tax credit cannot exceed the FTC limitation.
- The FTC limitation is applied to four separate categories (baskets) of foreign source income: passive, general, GILTI, and foreign branch.

[29]§904(d).
[30]§904(d).

Foreign Branch Income   Foreign branch income generally is defined to be business profits earned through one or more unincorporated qualified business units (branches).

General Category Income   Income not treated as passive category income, foreign branch income, or GILTI is defined as general category income.

The application of the FTC limitation formula can result in an excess credit if the taxpayer's creditable foreign taxes exceed the FTC limitation amount. The United States allows taxpayers to carry back an excess FTC one year and carry forward an excess credit 10 years. Current-year foreign tax credits are absorbed before any carryovers, which are absorbed on a first-in, first-out basis.

Example 24-15

What if: Suppose 3D's branch operations in Windsor generated C$50,000 ($40,000) of taxable income and paid Canadian tax of C$9,250 ($7,400). The branch income meets the definition of qualified branch income for FTC purposes. In addition, 3D received a dividend of C$1,000 ($800) from its stock investment in Scotiabank. Under the U.S.–Canada treaty, Scotiabank withheld C$150 ($120) in taxes (15 percent) on the payment. The withholding tax is eligible for the foreign tax credit, and the dividend meets the definition of passive category income for FTC purposes. 3D has total taxable income of $200,000 (including the dividend) in 2018 and a precredit U.S. income tax of $42,000. In computing its FTC for 2018, can 3D combine the branch income with the dividend in calculating its FTC limitation? Assume the exchange rate is C$1:$0.80.

Answer: No. The branch income and the dividend cannot be "blended" because they are in different income categories for FTC limitation purposes.

How much of the $7,520 ($7,400 + $120) in Canadian taxes can 3D claim as an FTC in 2018?

Answer: $7,520

3D must compute separate FTC limitations for the branch income and the dividend, as follows:

  Branch income: $40,000/$200,000 × $42,000 = $8,400
  Dividend income: $800/$200,000 × $42,000 = $168

3D can take a credit for the full amount of the withholding tax on the dividend and a full credit for taxes paid on the branch income because the taxes associated with each FTC basket are less than the FTC limitation for each basket.

What if: Assume the branch income is subject to Canadian income tax of C$13,240 ($10,600). How much of the $10,720 in Canadian taxes can 3D take as a credit in 2018?

Answer: $8,520, computed as $8,400 + $120.

The FTC for the branch income is now limited to $8,400, as computed previously. 3D can carry forward the excess FTC of $2,200 for 10 years.

Creditable Foreign Taxes

The foreign tax credit is available only for foreign taxes the United States considers to be *income* taxes "in the U.S. sense." In general, a tax "resembles" the U.S. concept of an income tax when it is applied to net income.[31] Taxes that do not qualify as income taxes include property taxes, customs taxes, sales taxes, and value-added taxes. U.S. taxpayers can deduct noncreditable foreign taxes. On an annual basis, U.S. taxpayers also can elect to deduct foreign income taxes in lieu of claiming the credit. This election might make sense if the taxpayer does not expect to be able to use the credit during the 10-year car-

---

[31]There has been much litigation and many IRS rulings over whether a tax paid to another country qualifies as an income tax "in the U.S. sense."

ryforward period. Foreign taxes generally are translated into U.S. dollars using the average exchange rate for the year, regardless of when the tax is actually paid.[32] U.S. taxpayers can elect to translate withholding taxes using the exchange rate on the day the tax is withheld. This election makes translation of the withholding tax consistent with the translation of the payment (dividend, interest, royalty) into U.S. dollars, which is done using the exchange rate on the date of payment, which is referred to as the **spot rate.**

Direct Taxes Direct foreign income taxes are income taxes paid directly by the U.S. taxpayer.[33] For example, the income taxes 3D pays to the Canadian government on its branch operations in Windsor are direct foreign income taxes and are eligible for a credit on the company's U.S. tax return.

In Lieu of Taxes Taxes that do not qualify as income taxes can still be creditable if they are imposed "in lieu of" an income tax.[34] The most common example is a withholding tax imposed on gross income such as dividends, interest, and royalties. These taxes technically do not meet the definition of an income tax because they are imposed on gross, rather than net, income. Governments impose these taxes for administrative purposes in lieu of requiring the recipient of the income to file an income tax return.

PLANNING FOR INTERNATIONAL OPERATIONS

LO 24-5

The organizational form through which a U.S. person does business or invests outside the United States affects the timing and scope of U.S. taxation of foreign source income or loss reported by the business or investment. U.S. corporations conducting international operations directly (e.g., through a branch) or through a flow-through entity (such as a partnership) are subject to U.S. tax or receive a U.S. tax benefit currently on income or loss from those operations. Foreign source income earned by a foreign corporation owned by U.S. persons (e.g., a Canadian subsidiary of a U.S. corporation) generally is not subject to U.S. taxation until such income is repatriated to the U.S. shareholder as interest, rent, royalty, or a management fee (i.e., U.S. taxation of such income is deferred to a future period). Dividends paid to domestic corporations from 10-percent-or-more owned foreign corporations are exempt from U.S. taxation because they are eligible for a 100% dividends received deduction.

The organizational form chosen can help a U.S. person reduce worldwide taxation through the following means:

- Exempt income not subject to the subpart F or GILTI deemed dividend rules from U.S. taxation.
- Reduce foreign taxes in high-tax jurisdictions through tax-deductible payments (e.g., rent, interest, royalties, and management fees) to lower-tax jurisdictions.
- Take advantage of tax incentives provided by host jurisdictions (e.g., a tax holiday on profits for a specified time period).
- Use transfer pricing to shift profits from a high-tax jurisdiction to a low-tax jurisdiction.
- Take advantage of tax treaties to reduce withholding taxes on cross-border payments.

Hybrid entities such as limited liability companies can provide the U.S. investor with the legal advantages of the corporate form (limited liability, continuity of life, transferability of interests) and the tax advantages of the partnership or branch form (flow-through of losses and flow-through of foreign taxes to individual investors).

---

[32]§986(a)(1)(A).

[33]Direct foreign income taxes are creditable under §901.

[34]In lieu of income taxes are creditable under §903.

Each organizational form offers a U.S. person investing abroad with advantages and disadvantages. Most U.S. businesses operate abroad through either a subsidiary or hybrid entity. Corporation status provides the U.S. investor with protection against liabilities of the subsidiary, entitles the subsidiary to treaty benefits in its dealings outside the country of incorporation, and insulates the subsidiary's business income from U.S. taxation until such income is repatriated back to the United States. Conversely, losses incurred in the subsidiary are not currently deductible on the investor's U.S. tax return.

Check-the-Box Hybrid Entities

THE KEY FACTS

Organizational Forms for Conducting International Operations

- A U.S. taxpayer doing business outside the United States can choose between a branch, partnership, corporation, or hybrid entity.
- A hybrid entity is an entity that is treated as a flow-through entity for U.S. tax purposes and a corporation for foreign tax purposes (or vice versa).
- A U.S. taxpayer elects the U.S. tax status of a hybrid entity by checking the box on Form 8832.
- "Per se" entities are not eligible for the check-the-box election.

Through regulations, the U.S. Treasury allows U.S. taxpayers to elect the *U.S. tax status* of eligible entities by checking the box on Form 8832. Where the U.S. person owns 100 percent of the entity, he or she can choose corporation status or branch status; the latter often is referred to as a **disregarded entity** because it is disregarded for U.S. tax purposes. Where more than one U.S. person owns the entity, the taxpayers can choose corporation status or partnership status. Such an entity is referred to as a hybrid entity. A multiple-person-owned hybrid entity for which corporation status is elected is referred to as a **reverse hybrid entity.** Certain designated "per se" foreign entities are not eligible for this elective treatment. These ineligible entities tend to be entities that can be publicly traded in their host countries (e.g., a German A.G., Dutch N.V., U.K. PLC, Spanish S.A., or Canadian corporation). The entire list is printed in the Instructions to Form 8832. In Canada, a U.S. corporation or individual must operate through an unlimited liability company (ULC) organized under the laws of Nova Scotia, Alberta, or British Columbia to achieve the benefits of operating through a hybrid entity.

Hybrid entities offer U.S. investors much flexibility in avoiding the U.S. anti-deferral rules found in subpart F, which we discuss in the next section. However, there are drawbacks to operating through a hybrid entity. In particular, a hybrid entity organized outside the United States may not be eligible for treaty benefits because it is not recognized as a resident of the United States by the host country. For example, the U.S.–Canada treaty does not extend treaty benefits to distributions from a ULC to its U.S. investors. Distributions from a Nova Scotia ULC to its U.S. parent company in the form of dividends or royalties will be subject to a 25 percent withholding tax instead of a 5 percent or 10 percent withholding tax, respectively, under the U.S.–Canada treaty. Exhibit 24-3 lists the advantages and disadvantages of operating outside the United States through different organizational forms.

Example 24-16

Lily expects her Canadian operations to be profitable for the foreseeable future. She has plans to expand her operations throughout the province of Ontario and hopefully throughout all of Canada. Lily is trying to decide whether she should change the organizational form of her Canadian operations from a branch to a corporation or perhaps a hybrid entity. Can Lily organize her Canadian operations as a hybrid entity in Ontario for U.S. tax purposes?

Answer: No. Hybrid entities (unlimited liability companies) in Canada can be organized only in the provinces of Nova Scotia, Alberta, and British Columbia.

What are the primary income tax reasons for organizing the Canadian operations as a corporation for U.S. tax purposes?

Answer: There are several. Operating as a corporation allows for exemption from U.S. taxation on income earned by the Canadian operations when it is distributed to 3D as a dividend. In addition, 3D can loan money or lease its trademarks to the Canadian corporation and transfer income from Canada to the United States in the form of tax-deductible interest or royalties.

Are there any compelling nontax reasons for organizing the Canadian operations as a corporation for U.S. tax purposes?

Answer: Yes. Corporate form limits 3D's liability in Canada to its Canadian assets. In addition, operating as a corporation allows the company to hold itself out as a Canadian business to its customers and borrow money directly from Canadian banks.

EXHIBIT 24-3   **Advantages and Disadvantages of Operating Outside the United States in Different Organizational Forms**

Branch
Advantages
- Foreign losses are currently deductible on the U.S. tax return.
- Foreign taxes imposed on income earned through the branch are eligible for the direct foreign tax credit.
- A branch qualifies as a permanent establishment and is eligible for treaty benefits.

Disadvantages
- Profits are subject to immediate U.S. taxation.
- The U.S. corporation must have 100 percent control over its international operations (joint ventures are not available).

Subsidiary
Advantages
- Separate entity status insulates the U.S. parent corporation against certain types of liabilities.
- Distributions from 10%-or-more owned foreign corporations are exempt from U.S. taxation when distributed as a dividend.
- Certain payments (management fees, royalties) made to the U.S. parent corporation may be deductible in the host country only if the payor is a corporation.

Disadvantages
- Losses are not deductible on the U.S. tax return for tax purposes.
- Certain foreign source income may be subject to the subpart F rules, which increase the administrative costs of operating as a subsidiary.

Hybrid Entity Treated as a Flow-Through Entity
Advantages
- Foreign losses are currently deductible on the U.S. tax return.
- Foreign taxes imposed on income earned through the branch are eligible for the direct foreign tax credit.
- The U.S. corporation can operate as a joint venture.
- Certain payments (management fees, royalties, interest) made to the U.S. parent corporation are deductible in the foreign jurisdiction.

Disadvantages
- Profits are subject to immediate U.S. taxation.
- Dividend, interest, and royalty payments to the United States are not eligible for reduced treaty withholding taxes.

When drawing an organizational chart of a multinational company, we often designate the different organizational forms with symbols. Exhibit 24-4 shows the symbols for each of the common organizational forms U.S. taxpayers use to do business outside the United States and their tax status for U.S. tax purposes (we will refer back to this exhibit in Exhibit 24-5).

U.S. ANTI-DEFERRAL RULES

LO 24-6

Deferral of U.S. taxation on all foreign source income earned through a foreign subsidiary would invite tax-planning strategies that shift income to low-tax countries to minimize worldwide taxation. U.S. individuals and corporations could transfer investment assets to subsidiaries located in low- or no-tax countries, called **tax havens,** and earn low-tax or tax-exempt income until such time as the money was repatriated to the United States.

The United States has debated whether to allow full deferral on all foreign earnings since 1937, when the U.S. government enacted its first "anti-deferral" rules applying to

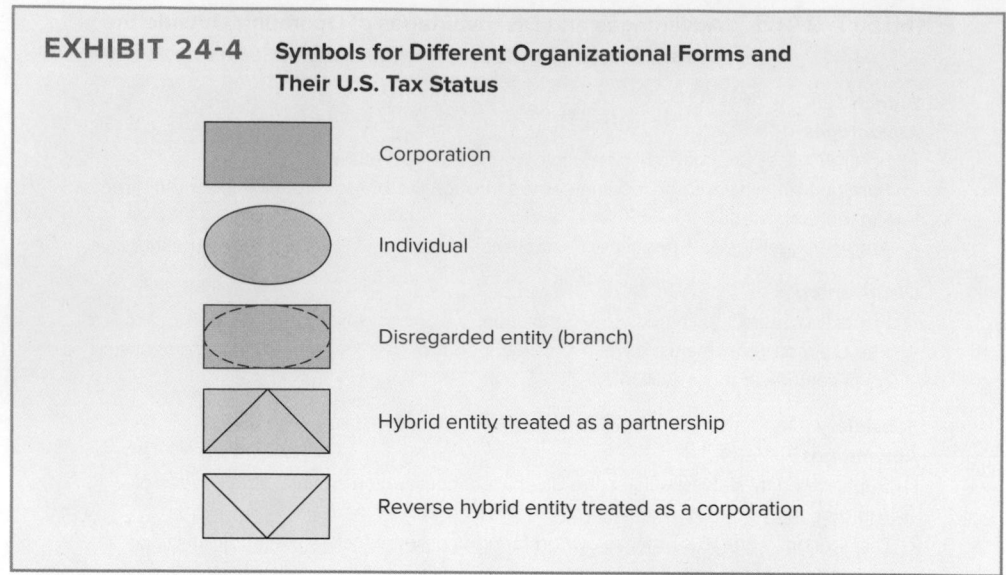

EXHIBIT 24-4   **Symbols for Different Organizational Forms and Their U.S. Tax Status**

Corporation

Individual

Disregarded entity (branch)

Hybrid entity treated as a partnership

Reverse hybrid entity treated as a corporation

foreign personal holding companies. Congress, with urging from President Kennedy, enacted more expansive anti-deferral rules in subpart F of subchapter N of the Internal Revenue Code in 1962.[35]

In a nutshell, subpart F requires certain *U.S. shareholders* in a **controlled foreign corporation (CFC)** to include in their gross income their pro rata share of specified categories of "tainted" income earned by the CFC during the current year—called **subpart F income**—regardless of whether such income is repatriated as a dividend (the income is treated as if it were paid out to the shareholders as a deemed dividend at the end of the CFC's taxable year). The deemed dividend is translated into U.S. dollars using the average exchange rate for the year. The technical rules that determine the amount of the deemed dividend to be included in income are among the most complex provisions in the Internal Revenue Code.

Definition of a Controlled Foreign Corporation

A controlled foreign corporation (CFC) is defined as any foreign corporation in which U.S. shareholders collectively own more than 50 percent of the total combined voting power of all classes of stock entitled to vote or the total value of the corporation's stock on any day during the CFC's tax year.[36] For purposes of subpart F, a U.S. shareholder is any U.S. person who owns or is deemed to own 10 percent or more of the voting power or value of the corporation's stock.[37] The term *United States person* means a citizen or resident of the United States, a domestic partnership, a domestic corporation, or any U.S. estate or trust, but it excludes certain residents of U.S. possessions.

Constructive ownership rules are used in the calculation of both the 50 percent test for determining CFC status and the 10 percent test for determining who is a U.S. shareholder.[38] These rules are similar to the constructive ownership rules found in section 318 (see the Corporate Taxation: Nonliquidating Distributions chapter) and include family attribution (spouse, children, grandchildren, and parents), entity-to-owner attribution, and owner-to-entity attribution. A detailed discussion of the other attribution rules is beyond the scope of this text.

[35]§§951–965.
[36]§957(a).
[37]§951(b).
[38]§958(b).

Example 24-17

What if: Assume Lily decided to partner with a Canadian investor, Maurice Richard, to expand her operations into Quebec through a Canadian corporation to be called Quebec Doughnut Depot (QDD). As part of the creation of QDD, Maurice contributed enough cash to the corporation to become a 50 percent shareholder in the company, with Lily owning the remaining 50 percent. Will QDD be a controlled foreign corporation (CFC) for U.S. tax purposes?

Answer: No. Lily is the only U.S. person who qualifies as a U.S. shareholder for purposes of determining whether QDD is a CFC for U.S. tax purposes. Because Lily owns only 50 percent of QDD (not *more than* 50 percent), the corporation is not considered a CFC.

What if: Suppose Lily organized QDD with her husband, Red, and Maurice, with each owning one-third of the company's stock. Will QDD be a CFC for U.S. tax purposes?

Answer: Yes. Lily and Red are both U.S. persons who qualify as U.S. shareholders for purposes of determining whether QDD is a CFC for U.S. tax purposes (they each own at least 10 percent of the QDD stock). Because they collectively own more than 50 percent of QDD, the corporation is a CFC.

What if: Suppose Lily organized QDD with her husband, Red, and Maurice, with Lily owning 49 percent, Red owning 2 percent, and Maurice owning 49 percent of the company's stock. Will QDD be a CFC for U.S. tax purposes?

Answer: Yes. Lily is deemed to own Red's 2 percent stock interest in QDD under the family attribution rules, making her a U.S. shareholder owning 51 percent of QDD's stock.

Definition of Subpart F Income

Subpart F income generally can be characterized as low-taxed passive income or as "portable" income earned by a CFC. Passive income, otherwise referred to as **foreign personal holding company income,** includes interest, dividends, rents, royalties, annuities, gains from the sale of certain foreign property, foreign currency exchange rate gains, net income from certain commodities transactions, and income equivalent to interest. There are complex exceptions involving payments between CFCs in the same country, export financing interest, and rents and royalties derived in the active conduct of a trade or business. Subpart F income does not include dividends, interest, rents, and royalties received by one CFC from a related CFC to the extent the payment is attributable to non-subpart F income of the payor (the taxpayer "looks through" the payment to the income from which it was paid).

Example 24-18

What if: Assume that 3D organized its Windsor operations as a wholly-owned Canadian subsidiary, Canadian Doughnut Depot Company (CDD). Now suppose CDD reported taxable income from its bakery operations of C$75,000 in 2018. CDD also purchased 1,000 shares of stock (less than 1 percent) in Thorntons PLC, a United Kingdom corporation that makes fine chocolate. During 2018, CDD received dividends of £1,000, which translated into C$1,500.[39] Thorntons withheld £100 (C$150) of U.K. taxes on the payment (a 10 percent withholding tax under the U.K.–Canada treaty). Does the dividend from Thorntons to CDD constitute subpart F income to 3D in 2018?

Answer: Yes. Dividends from investments by a CFC in a non-CFC are considered foreign personal holding company income under subpart F.

[39]The currency of the United Kingdom is the pound sterling, abbreviated £.

Also included in subpart F income is **foreign base company sales income,** which is defined as income derived by a CFC from the sale or purchase of personal property (e.g., inventory) to or from a related person, (a U.S. shareholder owning more than 50% of the CFC or a corporation owned more than 50% by the CFC) when the property is manufactured and sold outside the CFC's country of incorporation.[40] Similar rules apply to foreign base company services income.

This category of subpart F income was added because many countries offer incentives to multinational corporations to locate holding companies or sales companies within their borders by imposing no or a low tax on investment income or export sales. These companies are referred to as base companies because they operate primarily as profit centers and are located in a different country than where the economic activity (manufacture, sales, or service) takes place.

The Tax Cuts and Jobs Act added a new anti-deferral regime that applies to a CFC's "nonroutine" global intangible low-taxed income ("GILTI"). The details of this tax are beyond the scope of this text. The goal of the GILTI tax is to subject CFC income that exceeds a "normal rate of return" (10 percent) to subpart F (deemed dividend) treatment. The full amount of GILTI is included in a U.S. shareholder's income. Corporate shareholders are then allowed a deduction equal to 50 percent of GILTI for 2018 through 2025, which decreases to 37.5 percent beginning in 2026. As a result, the effective tax rate on GILTI when a shareholder is allowed the 50 percent deduction is 10.5 percent for tax years prior to 2026. The corporation subject to the deemed dividend under the GILTI rules can take a FTC equal to 80% of taxes paid on the GILTI income. The U.S. tax on GILTI generally will be zero if the foreign tax rate paid on the GILTI is at least 13.125%. Many U.S. multinational companies with significant offshore intangibles (Apple, Microsoft, Alphabet, Coca-Cola) anticipate being subject to the new tax.

Without any anti-deferral rules, a U.S. multinational corporation could shift profits to a foreign base company by selling goods to the base company at an artificially low transfer price. The base company could then resell the goods at a higher price to the ultimate customer in a different country. The profit earned by the base company would be subject to the lower (or no) tax imposed by the tax haven country. The base company thus would become a depository for the multinational company's excess funds, which could be invested in an active business or in passive investment assets outside the United States.

Example 24-19

What if: Assume in 2018 that 3D set up a corporation in the Cayman Islands through which it intended to transfer its products from the United States to its operations in Canada. Under this plan, 3D would "sell" its products, made in the United States, to the subsidiary in the Cayman Islands at a low transfer price, after which the Cayman Islands subsidiary would resell the products to CDD at a high transfer price. The goal would be to locate as much profit as possible in a low-tax country (the Cayman Islands has no corporate income tax). Will profit from the sale of goods from the Cayman Islands subsidiary to CDD constitute subpart F income to 3D in 2018?

Answer: Yes. The Cayman Islands profit is considered foreign base company sales income under subpart F because the goods are manufactured outside the Cayman Islands by a related person (3D) and sold outside the Cayman Islands. 3D will be treated as having received a deemed dividend of the profit from the Cayman Islands subsidiary.

Several exceptions serve to exclude all or a portion of a CFC's subpart F income from current taxation to the U.S. shareholders. A *de minimis rule* excludes all gross income from being treated as foreign base company income if the sum of the CFC's gross foreign base company income is less than the lesser of 5 percent of gross income or $1 million. A *full inclusion rule* treats all the CFC's gross profit as foreign base company

---

[40]§954(d).

income if more than 70 percent of the CFC's gross income is foreign base company income. In addition, a taxpayer can *elect* to exclude "high tax" subpart F income from the deemed dividend rules. High-tax subpart F income is taxed at an effective tax rate that is 90 percent or more of the highest U.S. statutory rate. For a U.S. corporation, the rate currently is 18.9% percent (90% × 21%). The calculation of the effective tax rate is complex and beyond the scope of this text.

Example 24-20

Return to the facts in Example 24-18, in which CDD reported taxable income from its bakery operations of C$75,000 in 2018 and received dividends of £1,000 from Thorntons PLC, which translated into C$1,500. Assume CDD has gross income of C$125,000 in 2018. In Example 24-18, we determined that the dividend constitutes subpart F income for U.S. tax purposes. Will 3D have a deemed dividend of this subpart F income in 2018?

Answer: No. The dividend is less than the lesser of 5 percent of CDD's gross income ($6,250) or $1 million and is not subject to the deemed dividend rules under the *de minimis* rule.

Only those U.S. shareholders who own stock in the CFC on the last day in the CFC's taxable year are treated as having received their pro rata share of any subpart F deemed dividend.

The computation of the deemed dividend under subpart F is exceptionally complicated and requires the CFC to allocate both deductions and taxes paid to subpart F gross income. The formula for this computation can be found in worksheets in the Instructions to Form 5471. In addition, the U.S. shareholder receives a foreign tax credit for income taxes paid on the subpart F income.[41]

Earnings of the CFC treated as a deemed dividend under subpart F become *previously taxed income* and subsequently can be distributed to the shareholders without being included in the recipient's gross income a second time. A foreign currency gain or loss on repatriation of such income is included in (deducted from) the shareholders' income.

Non-subpart F income (that is, income otherwise eligible for deferral) that is invested in U.S. property (for example, a loan from the CFC to its U.S. shareholder or stock in the U.S. parent) can be treated as a deemed dividend under the subpart F rules. This rule is intended to prevent U.S. corporations from borrowing money from their foreign subsidiaries on an indefinite basis, which would take the form of a disguised dividend.

Planning to Avoid Subpart F Income

U.S. multinational corporations expanding outside the United States often use hybrid entities as a tax-efficient means to avoid the subpart F rules. Tax aligning a U.S. corporation's international supply chain has become a frequent objective in international tax planning. Accomplishing this goal requires the formation of a foreign holding company (Foreign HoldCo) treated as a corporation for U.S. tax purposes (and thus eligible for deferral from U.S. taxation). The holding company owns the stock of hybrid entities set up to conduct each of the components of the company's foreign operations: financing (FinanceCo), manufacturing (OpCo), distribution (DistribCo), and intellectual property (IPCo). The holding company is strategically located in a country that lightly taxes dividend income paid by the hybrid entities. The hybrid entities also are strategically located in countries that tax the income from such operations (e.g., interest or royalties paid by the operating company to the finance company or intellectual property company) at a low tax rate.

[41]§960.

For instance, Ireland taxes manufacturing and intellectual property income at 12.5 percent. Because these operations are conducted through hybrid entities, transactions between the entities (e.g., payments of interest, rents, or royalties from one entity to another), which otherwise would create subpart F income, are ignored for U.S. tax purposes but respected for foreign tax purposes, because the hybrid entity is treated as a corporation in the country in which it is organized. This allows for the free flow of cash between foreign operations without the intrusion of the U.S. tax laws and the reduction of taxes in high-tax countries through cross-border payments that are deductible in the country in which the hybrid entity is located. Exhibit 24-5 illustrates a template for such an international operation.[42]

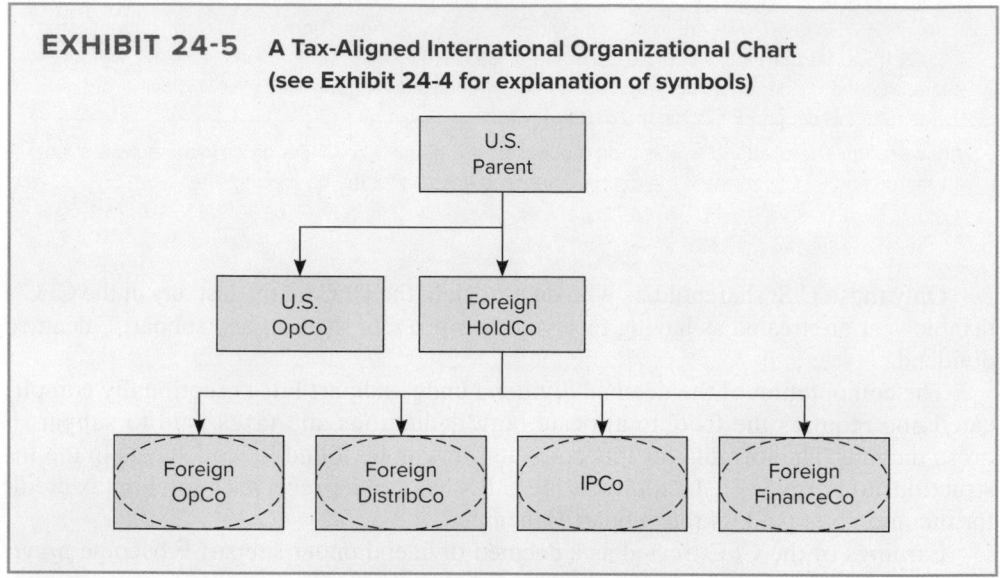

EXHIBIT 24-5   **A Tax-Aligned International Organizational Chart (see Exhibit 24-4 for explanation of symbols)**

TAXES IN THE REAL WORLD   **Apple, Inc.'s $38 Billion Repatriation Tax**

As part of the transition toward a territorial tax system in the Tax Cuts and Jobs Act, Congress enacted a one-time deemed repatriation tax on unrepatriated earnings and profits of U.S. multinational companies that were previously deferred from U.S. taxation. Congress enacted this deemed repatriation tax to prevent earnings that had been deferred from U.S. taxation under the previous tax rules to avoid permanent exemption from U.S. taxation under the new 100% dividends received deduction rules. The repatriation tax is calculated as 15.5% times the component of earnings that is considered cash and cash equivalents and 8% times the component of earnings that is considered "illiquid" (for example, a building). The U.S. corporation determines its earnings as the greater of the earnings on November 2, 2017 or year-end (December 31, 2017 for a calendar year corporation).

Apple, Inc. had, by most estimates, unrepatriated earnings subject to the repatriation tax of more than $250 billion, almost all of which was in cash. The company announced in its Form 10-Q for December 31, 2017, that it estimated its repatriation tax at approximately $38 billion! This is only an estimate because Apple, Inc. will not know its year-end cash balance until September 30, 2018. The good news for Apple, Inc. is that the tax law gives companies subject to the repatriation tax 8 years in which to pay the tax, interest free! Had Apple, Inc. distributed its foreign earnings under the pre-TCJA rules, it would have incurred a U.S. tax of more than $75 billion, so the deemed repatriation tax saved the company a significant amount of potential future taxes, which, of course, would only have been paid if Apple, Inc. actually repatriated the earnings.

---

[42]In hearings held on May 21, 2013, Senator Carl Levin accused Apple, Inc., of avoiding billions of U.S. taxes by structuring its overseas operations to route royalty income to low-tax jurisdictions. See http://www.hsgac.senate.gov/subcommittees/investigations/hearings/offshore-profit-shifting-and-the-us-tax-code_-part-2 for more details.

BASE EROSION AND PROFIT SHIFTING INITIATIVES AROUND THE WORLD

The Organization for Economic Cooperation and Development (OECD) has embarked on a "base erosion and profit shifting" (BEPS) initiative that has, as its goal, to provide "governments with solutions for closing the gaps in existing international rules that allow corporate profits to 'disappear' or be artificially shifted to low/no tax environments, where little or no economic activity takes place." This initiative, which began in 2013, was prompted by estimates that governments around the world were losing between $100 and $240 billion per year in tax revenues due to aggressive tax planning by multinational corporations. The OECD issued 15 "actions" in October 2015 that focused on transfer pricing, harmful tax practices, and treaty shopping and urged more transparent reporting ("country-by-country reporting" of income and taxes paid). Adoption of these actions by governments around the world will dramatically change the way multinational corporations plan their international operations and develop their information systems, as well as the way taxing agencies audit the tax returns filed by these corporations.

Consistent with the BEPS objectives, Congress added a **Base Erosion and Anti-Abuse Tax** (BEAT) minimum tax in the Tax Cuts and Jobs Act. Corporations with annual average gross receipts of at least $500 million for the three tax-year periods ending with the preceding tax year are required to pay a minimum tax amount (10% (5% in the case of taxable years beginning in calendar year 2018 and 12.5 percent for tax years beginning after December 31, 2025) of the corporation's modified taxable income over the corporation's regular tax liability) on cross-border outbound payments such as interest, royalties, and rents.[43] The BEAT serves as a minimum tax on outbound payments made by U.S. corporations to related foreign parties that reduce the U.S. tax base. The BEAT only applies when the "base erosion" deductions exceed three percent of total deductions. The details of this new tax are beyond the scope of this text.

In addition, the European Union has aggressively gone after U.S. multinational companies for special arrangements with low-tax countries such as Ireland and Luxembourg that lowered the tax paid in these countries through transfer pricing. The European Commission ruled in September 2016 that Apple, Inc., had received more than $14.5 billion of "illegal" tax benefit from Ireland and demanded that the Irish government recoup these lost taxes. While Apple, Inc., said it would look to overturn the decision, the company noted in its fiscal 2017 Form 10-K that it expected to get a foreign tax credit on its U.S. tax return if it had to pay the tax. The real loser in this ruling could very well be the U.S. Treasury![44]

CONCLUSION

In this chapter we discussed some of the important U.S. tax rules that apply to U.S. persons who expand their business operations outside the United States. As the storyline indicates, a U.S. business that wants to expand its markets outside the United States must decide on an organizational form through which to conduct its business. Establishing a physical presence in another country generally subjects the profits of the business to taxation in the host country and potentially in the United States as well. Treaties between the United States and other countries can provide beneficial tax treatment to a U.S. company's operations, employees, and cross-border payments. Where a cross-border transaction is subject to both foreign and U.S. taxation, the United States provides relief in the form of a foreign tax credit for foreign income taxes paid on foreign income that is reported on a U.S. tax return. These credits can be reduced by the foreign

[43] §59A.

[44] "THE EUROPEAN COMMISSION'S RECENT STATE AID INVESTIGATIONS OF TRANSFER PRICING RULINGS." Available at https://www.treasury.gov/resource-center/tax-policy/treaties/Documents/White-Paper-State-Aid.pdf

tax credit limitation. By operating through a foreign corporation, a U.S. corporation can exempt U.S. taxation on foreign source income repatriated to the United States as a dividend. Certain types of income are not subject to deferral if earned through a CFC. The use of hybrid entities outside the United States provides U.S. companies with the ability to shift income and move cash across jurisdictions without being subject to deemed dividends under subpart F.

Summary

LO 24-1 Describe the basic U.S. framework for taxing multinational transactions and the role of the foreign tax credit limitation.

- Countries most often determine nexus by either the geographic source of the income (source-based jurisdiction) or the taxpayer's citizenship or residence (residence-based jurisdiction).
  - Under a residence-based approach, a country taxes the worldwide income of the person earning the income.
  - Under a source-based approach, a country taxes only the income earned within its boundaries.
- The U.S. government taxes citizens and residents on their worldwide income, regardless of source (residence-based jurisdiction).
  - An individual who is not a citizen will be treated as a U.S. resident for income tax purposes if he or she is considered a permanent resident (has a green card) or satisfies a substantial presence test.
- The U.S. government only taxes nonresidents on income that is "U.S. source" or is connected with the operation of a U.S. trade or business (source-based jurisdiction).
- To alleviate (mitigate) potential double taxation and to promote international commerce, governments often allow their residents a tax credit for foreign income taxes paid on foreign source income or exempt dividends from foreign corporations from U.S. taxation.

LO 24-2 Apply the U.S. source rules for common items of gross income and deductions.

- The U.S. source rules determine whether income and related deductions are from sources within or outside of the United States.
  - The U.S. source-of-income rules are important to non-U.S. persons because they limit the scope of U.S. taxation of their worldwide income.
  - For U.S. persons, the primary purpose of the U.S. source-of-income rules is to calculate foreign source taxable income in the numerator of the foreign tax credit limitation.
- The Internal Revenue Code defines eight classes of gross income from sources within the United States and eight classes of gross income from sources outside of the United States.
  - As a general rule, the taxpayer looks to the borrower's residence to determine the geographic source of interest received.
  - In general, the source of dividend income is determined by the residence of the corporation paying the dividend.
  - The source of compensation received for labor or personal services is determined by the location where the service is performed.
  - Rent has its source where the property generating the rent is located.
  - Royalty income has its source where the intangible property or the rights generating the royalty are used.
- After determining the source of gross income as being from U.S. or foreign sources, a taxpayer may be required to allocate and apportion allowable deductions to gross income from each geographical source to compute taxable income from U.S. and foreign sources.
  - The IRC provides very broad language in describing how to allocate deductions to U.S. and foreign source gross income.

- The regulations attempt to match deductions with the gross income such deductions were incurred to produce, usually based on the "factual relationship" of the deduction to gross income.
- Special apportionment rules apply to nine categories of deductions, most notably interest, research and experimentation, state and local income taxes, losses on property disposition, and charitable contributions.

Explain the role of income tax treaties in international tax planning.   `LO 24-3`

- A tax treaty is a bilateral agreement between two contracting countries in which each agrees to modify its own tax laws to achieve reciprocal benefits.
- The general purpose of an income tax treaty is to eliminate or reduce (mitigate) the impact of double taxation so that residents paying taxes to one country will not have the full burden of taxes in the other country.
- The United States currently has income tax treaties with 67 countries.
- Most U.S. treaties provide a low withholding tax rate or an exemption from tax on various types of investment income (interest, dividends, gains from the sale of stock, and royalties) that would otherwise be subject to a high withholding tax.

Identify creditable foreign taxes and compute the foreign tax credit limitation.   `LO 24-4`

- The foreign tax credit is available only for foreign taxes the United States considers to be income taxes.
- Creditable foreign income taxes can be direct or "in lieu of" income taxes.
- Taxpayers must compute a separate FTC limitation for each category ("basket") of foreign source taxable income.
  - Passive category income generally is investment-type income that traditionally is subject to low foreign taxes (usually in the form of withholding taxes).
  - Foreign branch income is business profit earned through unincorporated operations located outside the United States.
  - GILTI is a new category of subpart F income related to high-return intangible income earned through a foreign corporation.
  - Income not treated as passive category income or foreign branch income or GILTI is defined to be general category income. General category income includes gross income from an active trade or business, financial services income, and shipping income.
  - A taxpayer computes the FTC limitation by multiplying the ratio of foreign source taxable income to total taxable income times precredit U.S. tax, as follows:

$$\frac{\text{Foreign source taxable income}}{\text{Total taxable income}} \times \text{Precredit U.S. tax}$$

Compare the advantages and disadvantages of the different forms of doing business outside the United States.   `LO 24-5`

- A U.S. person can do business outside the United States through a branch, partnership, corporation, or hybrid entity.
- A hybrid entity is an entity that is treated as a flow-through entity for U.S. tax purposes and a corporation for foreign tax purposes (or vice versa).
- A U.S. taxpayer elects the U.S. tax status of a hybrid entity by "checking the box" on Form 8832.
  - Certain designated per se foreign entities are not eligible for this elective treatment.

Explain the basic U.S. anti-deferral tax regime and identify common sources of subpart F income.   `LO 24-6`

- Subpart F requires certain U.S. shareholders in a controlled foreign corporation (CFC) to include in their gross income currently their pro rata share of specified categories of "tainted" income earned by the CFC during the current year (*subpart F income*).
- A controlled foreign corporation is defined as any foreign corporation in which U.S. shareholders collectively own more than 50 percent of the total combined voting power of all classes of stock entitled to vote or the total value of the corporation's stock on any day during the CFC's tax year.

- Constructive ownership rules are used in the calculation of both the 50 percent test for determining CFC status and the 10 percent test for determining who is a U.S. shareholder.
- Subpart F income generally can be characterized as low-taxed passive income or "portable" income earned by a CFC.
  - Foreign personal holding company income includes interest, dividends, rents, royalties, and gains from the sale of certain foreign property.
  - Foreign base company sales income is income derived by a CFC from the sale or purchase of personal property to (or from) a related person when the property is manufactured and sold outside the CFC's country of incorporation.
  - GILTI is high-return intangible income earned through a foreign corporation.
- There are several exceptions that serve to exclude all or a portion of a CFC's subpart F income from current taxation to the U.S. shareholders.
  - A *de minimis rule* excludes all gross income from being treated as foreign base company income if the sum of the CFC's gross foreign base company income is less than the lesser of 5 percent of gross income or $1 million.
  - A *full inclusion rule* treats all of the CFC's gross income as foreign base company income if more than 70 percent of the CFC's gross income is foreign base company income.

KEY TERMS

allocate (24-11)

apportion (24-11)

base erosion and anti-abuse tax (24-29)

branch (24-3)

commercial traveler exception (24-8)

controlled foreign corporation (CFC) (24-24)

definitely related deductions (24-11)

disregarded entity (24-22)

effectively connected income (ECI) (24-3)

fixed and determinable, annual or periodic income (FDAP) (24-3)

foreign base company sales income (24-26)

foreign-derived intangible income (FDII) (24-16)

foreign personal holding company income (24-25)

foreign tax credit (FTC) (24-5)

foreign tax credit limitation (24-5)

FTC basket (24-19)

general category income (24-19)

global intangible low-taxed income (GILTI) (24-19)

hybrid entity (24-21)

inbound transaction (24-2)

nexus (24-2)

nonresident alien (24-4)

not definitely related deductions (24-11)

outbound transaction (24-2)

passive category income (24-19)

permanent establishment (24-17)

qualified business asset investment (QBAI) (24-16)

residence-based jurisdiction (24-2)

resident alien (24-4)

reverse hybrid entity (24-22)

source-based jurisdiction (24-2)

spot rate (24-21)

subpart F income (24-24)

tax haven (24-23)

DISCUSSION QUESTIONS

Discussion Questions are available in Connect®.

connect

LO 24-1 1. Distinguish between an outbound transaction and an inbound transaction from a U.S. tax perspective.

LO 24-1 2. What are the major U.S. tax issues that apply to an inbound transaction?

LO 24-1 3. What are the major U.S. tax issues that apply to an outbound transaction?

LO 24-1 4. How does a residence-based approach to taxing worldwide income differ from a source-based approach to taxing the same income?

LO 24-1 5. Henri is a resident of the United States for U.S. tax purposes and earns $10,000 from an investment in a French company. Will Henri be subject to U.S. tax under a residence-based approach to taxation? A source-based approach?

6. What are the two categories of income that can be taxed by the United States when earned by a nonresident? How does the United States tax each category of income? **LO 24-1**

7. Maria is not a citizen of the United States, but she spends 180 days per year in the United States on business-related activities. Under what conditions will Maria be considered a resident of the United States for U.S. tax purposes? **LO 24-1**

8. Natasha is not a citizen of the United States, but she spends 200 days per year in the United States on business. She does not have a green card. True or False: Natasha will always be considered a resident of the United States for U.S. tax purposes because of her physical presence in the United States. Explain. **LO 24-1**

9. Why does the United States allow U.S. taxpayers to claim a credit against their pre-credit U.S. tax for foreign income taxes paid? **LO 24-1**

10. What role does the foreign tax credit limitation play in U.S. tax policy? **LO 24-1**

11. Why are the income source rules important to a U.S. citizen or resident? **LO 24-2**

12. Why are the income source rules important to a U.S. nonresident? **LO 24-2**

13. Carol receives $500 of dividend income from Microsoft Inc., a U.S. company. True or False: Absent any treaty provisions, Carol will be subject to U.S. tax on the dividend regardless of whether she is a resident or nonresident. Explain. **LO 24-2**

14. Pavel, a citizen and resident of Russia, spent 100 days in the United States working for his employer, Yukos Oil, a Russian corporation. Under what conditions will Pavel be subject to U.S. tax on the portion of his compensation earned while working in the United States? **LO 24-2**

15. What are the potential U.S. tax benefits from engaging in an export sale? **LO 24-2**

16. True or False: A taxpayer will always prefer deducting an expense against U.S. source income and not foreign source income when filing a tax return in the United States. Explain. **LO 24-2**

17. Distinguish between *allocation* and *apportionment* in sourcing deductions in computing the foreign tax credit limitation. **LO 24-2**

18. Distinguish between a *definitely related deduction* and a *not definitely related deduction* in the allocation and apportionment of deductions to foreign source taxable income. **LO 24-2**

19. Briefly describe the method for apportioning interest expense to foreign source taxable income in the computation of the foreign tax credit limitation. **LO 24-2**

20. What is the primary goal of the United States in negotiating income tax treaties with other countries? **LO 24-3**

21. What is a *permanent establishment*, and why is it an important part of most income tax treaties? **LO 24-3**

22. Why is a treaty important to a nonresident investor in U.S. stocks and bonds? **LO 24-3**

23. Why is a treaty important to a nonresident worker in the United States? **LO 24-3**

24. Why does the United States use a "basket" approach in the foreign tax credit limitation computation? **LO 24-4**

25. True or False: All dividend income received by a U.S. taxpayer is classified as passive category income for foreign tax credit limitation purposes. Explain. **LO 24-4**

26. True or False: All foreign taxes are creditable for U.S. tax purposes. Explain. **LO 24-4**

27. What is a hybrid entity for U.S. tax purposes? Why is a hybrid entity a popular organizational form for a U.S. company expanding its international operations? What are the potential drawbacks to using a hybrid entity? **LO 24-5**

28. What is a "per se" entity under the check-the-box rules? **LO 24-5**

29. What are the requirements for a foreign corporation to be a *controlled foreign corporation* for U.S. tax purposes? **LO 24-6**

30. Why does the United States not allow deferral on all foreign source income earned by a controlled foreign corporation? **LO 24-6**

LO 24-6 31. True or False: A foreign corporation owned equally by 11 U.S. individuals can never be a controlled foreign corporation. Explain.

LO 24-6 32. What is foreign base company sales income? Why does the United States include this income in its definition of subpart F income?

LO 24-6 33. True or False: Subpart F income is always treated as a deemed dividend to the U.S. shareholders of a controlled foreign corporation. Explain.

LO 24-6 34. True or False: Non-subpart F income always qualifies for tax deferral until it is repatriated back to the United States. Explain.

PROBLEMS

Select problems are available in Connect®.

LO 24-1 35. Camille, a citizen and resident of Country A, received a $1,000 dividend from a corporation organized in Country B. Which statement best describes the taxation of this income under the two different approaches to taxing foreign income?

a) Country B will not tax this income under a residence-based jurisdiction approach but will tax this income under a source-based jurisdiction approach.

b) Country B will tax this income under a residence-based jurisdiction approach but will not tax this income under a source-based jurisdiction approach.

c) Country B will tax this income under both a residence-based jurisdiction approach and a source-based jurisdiction approach.

d) Country B will not tax this income under either a residence-based jurisdiction approach or a source-based jurisdiction approach.

LO 24-1 36. Spartan Corporation, a U.S. corporation, reported $2 million of pretax income from its business operations in Spartania, which were conducted through a foreign branch. Spartania taxes branch income at 15 percent, and the United States taxes corporate income at 21 percent.

a) If the United States provided no mechanism for mitigating double taxation, what would be the total tax (U.S. and foreign) on the $2 million of branch profits?

b) Assume the United States allows U.S. corporations to exclude foreign source income from U.S. taxation. What would be the total tax on the $2 million of branch profits?

c) Assume the United States allows U.S. corporations to claim a deduction for foreign income taxes. What would be the total tax on the $2 million of branch profits?

d) Assume the United States allows U.S. corporations to claim a credit for foreign income taxes paid on foreign source income. What would be the total tax on the $2 million of branch profits? What would be your answer if Spartania taxed branch profits at 30 percent?

LO 24-1 37. Guido is a citizen and resident of Belgium. He has a full-time job in Belgium and has lived there with his family for the past 10 years. In 2016, Guido came to the United States for the first time. The sole purpose of his trip was business. He intended to stay in the United States for only 180 days, but he ended up staying for 210 days because of unforeseen problems with his business. Guido came to the United States again on business in 2017 and stayed for 180 days. In 2018 he came back to the United States on business and stayed for 70 days. Determine if Guido meets the U.S. statutory definition of a resident alien in 2016, 2017, and 2018 under the substantial presence test.

LO 24-1 38. Use the facts in problem 38. If Guido meets the statutory requirements to be considered a resident of both the United States and Belgium, what criteria does the U.S.–Belgium treaty use to "break the tie" and determine Guido's country of residence? Look at Article 4 of the 2007 U.S.–Belgium income tax treaty, which you can find on the IRS website, www.irs.gov.

research

39. How does the U.S.–Belgium treaty define a *permanent establishment* for determining nexus? Look at Article 5 of the 2007 U.S.–Belgium income tax treaty, which you can find on the IRS website, www.irs.gov.

40. Mackinac Corporation, a U.S. corporation, reported total taxable income of $5 million. Taxable income included $1.5 million of foreign source taxable income from the company's branch operations in Canada. All of the branch income is foreign branch income. Mackinac paid Canadian income taxes of $375,000 (as translated) on its branch income. Compute Mackinac's allowable foreign tax credit.

LO 24-1

41. Waco Leather Inc., a U.S. corporation, reported total taxable income of $5 million. Taxable income included $1.5 million of foreign source taxable income from the company's branch operations in Mexico. All of the branch income is foreign branch income. Waco paid Mexican income taxes of $300,000 on its branch income. Compute Waco's allowable foreign tax credit.

LO 24-1

42. Petoskey Stone Inc., a U.S. corporation, received the following sources of income during the current year. Identify the source of each item as either U.S. or foreign.

LO 24-2

   a) Interest income from a loan to its German subsidiary.

   b) Dividend income from Granite Corporation, a U.S. corporation.

   c) Royalty income from its Irish subsidiary for use of a trademark.

   d) Rent income from its Canadian subsidiary for its use of a warehouse located in Wisconsin.

43. Carmen SanDiego, a U.S. citizen, is employed by General Motors Corporation, a U.S. corporation. On April 1, 2018, GM relocated Carmen to its Brazilian operations for the remainder of 2018. Carmen was paid a salary of $120,000 and was employed on a 5-day week basis. As part of her compensation package for moving to Brazil, Carmen also received a housing allowance of $25,000. Carmen's salary was earned ratably over the 12-month period. During 2018 Carmen worked 260 days, 195 of which were in Brazil and 65 of which were in Michigan. How much of Carmen's total compensation is treated as foreign source income for 2018? Why might Carmen want to maximize her foreign source income in 2018?

LO 24-2

44. Sam Smith is a citizen and bona fide resident of Great Britain (United Kingdom). During the current year, Sam received the following income:

LO 24-2

   • Compensation of $30 million from performing concerts in the United States.

   • Cash dividends of $10,000 from a French corporation stock.

   • Interest of $6,000 on a U.S. corporation bond.

   • Interest of $2,000 on a loan made to a U.S. citizen residing in Australia.

   • Gain of $80,000 on the sale of stock in a U.S. corporation.

   Determine the source (U.S. or foreign) of each item of income Sam received.

Income	Source
Income from concerts	
Dividend from French corporation	
Interest on a U.S. corporation bond	
Interest of $2,000 on a loan made to a U.S. citizen residing in Australia	
Gain of $80,000 on the sale of stock in a U.S. corporation	

45. Spartan Corporation, a U.S. company, manufactures green eyeshades for sale in the United States and Europe. All manufacturing activities take place in Michigan. During the current year, Spartan sold 10,000 green eyeshades to European customers at a price of $10 each. Each eyeshade costs $4 to produce.

LO 24-2

All of Spartan's production assets are located in the United States. For each independent scenario, determine the source of the gross income from sale of the green eyeshades.

a) Spartan ships its eyeshades F.O.B., place of destination.

b) Spartan ships its eyeshades F.O.B., place of shipment.

LO 24-2

planning

46. Falmouth Kettle Company, a U.S. corporation, sells its products in the United States and Europe. During the current year, selling, general, and administrative (SG&A) expenses included:

Personnel department	$ 500
Training department	350
President's salary	400
Sales manager's salary	200
Other general and administrative	550
Total SG&A expenses	$2,000

Falmouth had $12,000 of gross sales to U.S. customers and $3,000 of gross sales to European customers. Gross income (sales minus cost of goods sold) from domestic sales was $3,000 and gross profit from foreign sales was $1,000. Apportion Falmouth's SG&A expenses to foreign source income using the following methods:

a) Gross sales.

b) Gross income.

c) If Falmouth wants to maximize its foreign tax credit limitation, which method produces the better outcome? Assume the FDII deduction does not apply.

LO 24-2

planning

47. Owl Vision Corporation (OVC) is a North Carolina corporation engaged in the manufacture and sale of contact lenses and other optical equipment. The company handles its export sales through sales branches in Belgium and Singapore. The average tax book value of OVC's assets for the year was $200 million, of which $160 million generated U.S. source income and $40 million generated foreign source income. OVC's total interest expense was $20 million.

a) What amount of the interest expense will be apportioned to foreign source income under the tax book value method?

LO 24-3

research

48. Colleen is a citizen and bona fide resident of Ireland. During the current year, she received the following income:

- Cash dividends of $2,000 from a U.S. corporation's stock.
- Interest of $1,000 on a U.S. corporation bond.
- Royalty of $100,000 from a U.S. corporation for use of a patent she developed.
- Rent of $3,000 from U.S. individuals renting her cottage in Maine.

Identify the U.S. withholding tax rate on the payment of each item of income under the U.S.–Ireland income tax treaty and cite the appropriate treaty article. You can access the 1997 U.S.–Ireland income tax treaty on the IRS website, www.irs.gov.

Income	Withholding Tax Rate	Treaty Article
Cash dividends of $2,000		
Interest of $1,000		
Royalty of $100,000		
Rent of $3,000		

49. Gameco, a U.S. corporation, operates gambling machines in the United States and abroad. Gameco conducts its operations in Europe through a Dutch B.V., which is treated as a branch for U.S. tax purposes. Gameco also licenses game machines to an unrelated company in Japan. During the current year, Gameco paid the following foreign taxes, translated into U.S. dollars at the appropriate exchange rate:

LO 24-4

Foreign Taxes	Amount (in $)
National income taxes	1,000,000
City (Amsterdam) income taxes	100,000
Value-added tax	150,000
Payroll tax (employer's share of social insurance contributions)	400,000
Withholding tax on royalties received from Japan	50,000

Identify Gameco's creditable foreign taxes.

50. Sombrero Corporation, a U.S. corporation, operates through a branch in Espania. Management projects that the company's pretax income in the next taxable year will be $100,000: $80,000 from U.S. operations and $20,000 from the Espania branch. Espania taxes corporate income at a rate of 30 percent.

    LO 24-4

    planning

    a) If management's projections are accurate, what will be Sombrero's excess foreign tax credit in the next taxable year? Assume all of the income is foreign branch income.

    b) Management plans to establish a second branch in Italia. Italia taxes corporate income at a rate of 10 percent. What amount of income will the branch in Italia have to generate to eliminate the excess credit generated by the branch in Espania?

51. Chapeau Company, a U.S. corporation, operates through a branch in Champagnia. The source rules used by Champagnia are identical to those used by the United States. For 2018, Chapeau has $2,000 of gross income: $1,200 from U.S. sources and $800 from sources within Champagnia. The $1,200 of U.S. source income and $700 of the foreign source income are attributable to manufacturing activities in Champagnia (foreign branch income). The remaining $100 of foreign source income is passive category interest income. Chapeau had $500 of expenses other than taxes, all of which are allocated directly to manufacturing income ($200 of which is apportioned to foreign sources). Chapeau paid $150 of income taxes to Champagnia on its manufacturing income. The interest income was subject to a 10 percent withholding tax of $10. Compute Chapeau's allowable foreign tax credit in 2018.

    LO 24-4

52. Identify the "per se" companies for which a check-the-box election cannot be made for U.S. tax purposes in the countries listed below. Consult the Instructions to Form 8832, which can be found on the "Forms & Pubs" site on the IRS website, www.irs.gov.

    LO 24-5

    research

    a) Japan
    b) Germany
    c) Netherlands
    d) United Kingdom
    e) People's Republic of China

LO 24-5

53. Eagle Inc., a U.S. corporation, intends to create a *limitada* (limited liability company) in Brazil in 2018 to manufacture pitching machines. The company expects the operation to generate losses of US$2,500,000 during its first three years of operations. Eagle would like the losses to flow through to its U.S. tax return and offset its U.S. profits.

    a) Can Eagle "check the box" and treat the *limitada* as a disregarded entity (branch) for U.S. tax purposes? Consult the Instructions to Form 8832, which can be found on the "Forms & Pubs" site on the IRS website, www.irs.gov.

    b) Assume management's projections were accurate and Eagle deducted $75,000 of branch losses on its U.S. tax return from 2018–2020. At 01/01/21, the fair market value of the *limitada*'s net assets exceeded Eagle's tax basis in the assets by US$5 million. What are the U.S. tax consequences of checking the box on Form 8832 and converting the *limitada* to a corporation for U.S. tax purposes?

54. Identify whether the corporations described below are controlled foreign corporations.

    a) Shetland PLC, a U.K. corporation, has two classes of stock outstanding, 75 shares of class AA stock and 25 shares of class A stock. Each class of stock has equal voting power and value. Angus owns 35 shares of class AA stock and 20 shares of class A stock. Angus is a U.S. citizen who resides in England.

    b) Tony and Gina, both U.S. citizens, own 5 percent and 10 percent, respectively, of the voting stock and value of DaVinci S.A., an Italian corporation. Tony and Gina are also equal partners in Roma Corporation, an Italian corporation that owns 50 percent of the DaVinci stock.

    c) Pierre, a U.S. citizen, owns 45 of the 100 shares outstanding in Vino S.A., a French corporation. Pierre's father, Pepe, owns 8 shares in Vino. Pepe also is a U.S. citizen. The remaining 47 shares are owned by non-U.S. individuals.

55. USCo owns 100 percent of the following corporations: Dutch N.V., Germany A.G., Australia PLC, Japan Corporation, and Brazil S.A. During the year, the following transactions took place:

    a) Germany A.G. owns an office building that it leases to unrelated persons. Germany A.G. engaged an independent managing agent to manage and maintain the office building and performs no activities with respect to the property.

    b) Dutch N.V. leased office machines to unrelated persons. Dutch N.V. performed only incidental activities and incurred nominal expenses in leasing and servicing the machines. Dutch N.V. is not engaged in the manufacture or production of the machines and does not add substantial value to the machines.

    c) Dutch N.V. purchased goods manufactured in France from an unrelated contract manufacturer and sold them to Germany A.G. for consumption in Germany.

    d) Australia PLC purchased goods manufactured in Australia from an unrelated person and sold them to Japan Corporation for use in Japan.

    Determine whether the above transactions result in subpart F income to USCo.

56. USCo manufactures and markets electrical components. USCo operates outside the United States through a number of CFCs, each of which is organized in a different country. These CFCs derived the following income for the current year:

    a) F1 has gross income of $5 million, including $200,000 of foreign personal holding company interest and $4.8 million of gross income from the sale of inventory that F1 manufactured at a factory located within its home country.

    b) F2 has gross income of $5 million, including $4 million of foreign personal holding company interest and $1 million of gross income from the sale of inventory that F2 manufactured at a factory located within its home country.

    Determine the amount of income that USCo must report as a deemed dividend under subpart F in each scenario.

COMPREHENSIVE PROBLEMS

Select problems are available in Connect®.

57. Spartan Corporation manufactures quidgets at its plant in Sparta, Michigan. Spartan sells its quidgets to customers in the United States, Canada, England, and Australia.

    Spartan markets its products in Canada and England through branches in Toronto and London, respectively. Spartan reported total gross income on U.S. sales of $15,000,000 and total gross income on Canadian and U.K. sales of $5,000,000, split equally between the two countries. Spartan paid Canadian income taxes of $600,000 on its branch profits in Canada and U.K. income taxes of $700,000 on its branch profits in the United Kingdom. Spartan financed its Canadian operations through a $10 million capital contribution, which Spartan financed through a loan from Bank of America. During the current year, Spartan paid $600,000 in interest on the loan.

    Spartan sells its quidgets to Australian customers through its wholly-owned Australian subsidiary. Title passes in the United States (FOB: shipping point) on all sales to the subsidiary. Spartan reported gross income of $3,000,000 on sales to its subsidiary during the year. The subsidiary paid Spartan a dividend of $670,000 on December 31 (the withholding tax is 0 percent under the U.S.–Australia treaty). Spartan paid Australian income taxes of $330,000 on the income repatriated as a dividend.

    a) Compute Spartan's foreign source gross income and foreign tax (direct and withholding) for the current year.

    b) Assume 20 percent of the interest paid to Bank of America is allocated to the numerator of Spartan's FTC limitation calculation. Compute Spartan Corporation's FTC limitation using your calculation from part (a) and any excess FTC or excess FTC limitation (all of the foreign source income is put in the foreign branch FTC basket).

58. Windmill Corporation manufactures products in its plants in Iowa, Canada, Ireland, and Australia. Windmill conducts its operations in Canada through a 50 percent owned joint venture, CanCo. CanCo is treated as a corporation for U.S. and Canadian tax purposes. An unrelated Canadian investor owns the remaining 50 percent. Windmill conducts its operations in Ireland through a wholly-owned subsidiary, IrishCo. IrishCo is a controlled foreign corporation for U.S. tax purposes. Windmill conducts its operations in Australia through a wholly-owned hybrid entity, KiwiCo. KiwiCo is treated as a branch for U.S. tax purposes and a corporation for Australian tax purposes. Windmill also owns a 5 percent interest in a Dutch corporation, TulipCo.

    During 2018, Windmill reported the following foreign source income from its international operations and investments.

	CanCo	IrishCo	KiwiCo	TulipCo
Dividend income				
Amount	$45,000	$28,000		$20,000
Withholding tax	2,250	1,400		3,000
Interest income				
Amount	30,000			
Withholding tax	0	0		
Branch income				
Taxable income			$93,000	
AUS income taxes			31,000	

Notes to the table: 1. CanCo and KiwiCo derive all of their earnings from active business operations.

a) Classify the income received by Windmill into the appropriate FTC baskets.

b) Windmill has $1,250,000 of U.S. source gross income. Windmill also incurred SG&A of $300,000 that is apportioned between U.S. and foreign source income based on the gross income in each basket. Assume KiwiCo's gross income is $200,000. Compute the FTC limitation for each basket of foreign source income.

tax forms

59. Euro Corporation, a U.S. corporation, operates through a branch in Germany. During 2018 the branch reported taxable income of $1,000,000 and paid German income taxes of $300,000. In addition, Euro received $50,000 of dividends from its 5 percent investment in the stock of Maple Leaf Company, a Canadian corporation. The dividend was subject to a withholding tax of $5,000. Euro reported U.S. taxable income from its manufacturing operations of $950,000. Total taxable income was $2,000,000. Precredit U.S. taxes on the taxable income were $420,000. Included in the computation of Euro's taxable income were "definitely allocable" expenses of $500,000, 50 percent of which were related to the German branch taxable income.

Complete pages 1 and 2 of Form 1118 for just the foreign branch income reported by Euro. You can use the fill-in form available on the IRS website, www.irs.gov. If the 2018 form is not available, put the income in the general category basket.

research

60. USCo, a U.S. corporation, has decided to set up a headquarters subsidiary in Europe. Management has narrowed its location choice to either Spain, Ireland, or Switzerland. The company has asked you to research some of the income tax implications of setting up a corporation in these three countries. In particular, management wants to know what tax rate will be imposed on corporate income earned in the country and the withholding rates applied to interest, dividends, and royalty payments from the subsidiary to USCo.

To answer the tax rate question, consult KPMG's *Corporate and Indirect Tax Survey 2017*, which you can access at https://home.kpmg.com/xx/en/home/services/tax/tax-tools-and-resources/tax-rates-online/corporate-tax-rates-table.html. To answer the withholding tax questions, consult the treaties between the United States and Spain, Ireland, and Switzerland, which you can access at www.irs.gov (type in "treaties" as your search word).

ROGER | *CPA Review*

Sample CPA Exam questions from Roger CPA Review are available in Connect as support for the topics in this text. These Multiple Choice Questions and Task-Based Simulations include expert-written explanations and solutions and provide a starting point for students to become familiar with the content and functionality of the actual CPA Exam.

Transfer Taxes and Wealth Planning

©Michal Kowalski/Shutterstock

Storyline Summary

Taxpayers:	Bob and Harry Smith, brothers, ages 69 and 63, respectively. Frank's Frozen Pizzas Inc. (FFP) is a family business.
Description:	Bob, a widower, is recently deceased and has a son, Nate (age 28). Harry is married to his second wife, Wilma, age 38, and has a daughter, Dina (age 35), a son-in-law, Steve, and a grandson, George (age 6).
Location:	Ann Arbor, Michigan
Employment status:	Bob and Harry inherited shares in FFP in 1990. Bob and Harry have been employees of FFP. Bob retired from FFP and died earlier this year. Harry is planning to retire as CEO of FFP.
Current situation:	Nate is Bob's executor.

arry and Bob Smith were brothers and owners of a small privately held corporation, Frank's Frozen Pizzas Inc. (FFP). Their father, Frank, established the business 35 years ago, and Harry and Bob each inherited half of FFP's outstanding shares upon Frank's death. At the time of Frank's death in 1990, FFP shares were worth about $1 million, but the firm is now debt-free and has a value of $9 million. FFP's success didn't come easy. Over the years Harry and Bob were employed as executive officers and worked long, hard hours. After the death of his wife in 1995, Bob retired on his FFP pension. Over the years both Harry and Bob have transferred some of their FFP shares to other family members. Bob has given 20 percent of the shares in FFP to his son, Nate, and Harry has transferred a like amount to a trust established for Dina (his daughter) and George (his grandson).

Harry recently decided that he wants to retire from FFP and spend more time traveling and enjoying his family. Harry believes that Nate would like to assume responsibilities as CEO, and Dina has agreed to support Nate's decisions. Harry plans to begin an orderly transfer of his FFP stock to Dina to provide a future source of support for her and George. Besides his FFP stock, Harry has accumulated considerable personal assets to help maintain his lifestyle during retirement. Although Wilma, Harry's wife, owns significant assets, Harry also wants to provide for her support after his death. Finally, while Harry believes taxes and lawyers are necessary evils, he wants to avoid any unnecessary fees or taxes associated with the transfer of his assets. Hence, Harry would like advice on how to make his gifts in the most tax-efficient manner.

to be continued . . .

LO 25-1 INTRODUCTION TO FEDERAL TRANSFER TAXES

This chapter explains the structure of the federal transfer taxes. We begin by outlining transfer taxes. We then describe the details of the federal gift and estate taxes. Finally, we introduce the principles of wealth planning.

Beginnings

In 1916 Congress imposed an estate tax on transfers of property at death. Transfers at death are dictated by the **last will and testament** of the deceased and such transfers are called **testamentary transfers.** The transfer tax system was expanded in 1924 to include a gift tax on lifetime transfers called **inter vivos transfers** (*inter vivos* is from the Latin meaning "during the life of"). Eventually, a generation-skipping tax was also added to prevent people from avoiding taxes by transferring assets to younger generations (making transfers to grandchildren rather than to children).[1] Together, this trio of taxes represents one way of reducing the potential wealth society's richest families might accumulate over several generations. (Recall that neither gifts nor inheritances are included in recipients' gross income.)

TAXES IN THE REAL WORLD Perfect Timing

Roger Milliken died on December 30, 2010, just two days before the estate tax was revived. Milliken was 95 years old and had directed his family's business, Milliken & Company, for 71 years as president and CEO. Milliken's estate, estimated under $1 billion, was subject to probate in Spartanburg County, South Carolina. In his 111-page will, described by the Spartanburg *Journal Watchdog,* Milliken established multiple trusts and directed that the family business would remain privately owned. Moreover, Milliken instructed trustees that no change of tax laws would warrant deviating from his intentions. In a two-page letter, Milliken expressed the hope that income from the trust would enable his descendants to pursue careers. To qualify for income from the trusts, Milliken's children must be 40 years old, at which time they will be eligible to receive 10 percent of the trust's income. The distribution increases to 50 percent at age 44 and to all the net income by the age of 49. Milliken also expressed hope that money from the trusts would enable his children and grandchildren to achieve true self-fulfillment and happiness.

Common Features of Integrated Transfer Taxes

The two primary federal transfer taxes, the gift tax and the estate tax, were originally enacted separately and operated independently. In 1976 they were *unified* into a transfer tax scheme that applies a progressive tax rate schedule to cumulative transfers. In other words, the gift and estate taxes now are integrated into a common formula.

This integrated formula takes into account the cumulative effect of transfers in previous periods when calculating the tax on a (gift) transfer in a current period. Likewise, it takes lifetime transfers into account to compute the tax on assets transferred at death. As you'll see in the tax formulas, we add the taxable transfers in prior years to the current-year transfers and compute the tax on total (cumulative) transfers. Then we subtract the tax on the prior-year transfers from the total tax, to avoid taxing them twice. This calculation ensures that the current transfers will be taxed at a marginal tax rate as high or higher than the rate applicable to the prior-year transfers. Exhibit 25-1 presents the unified transfer tax rate schedule for estate and gift taxes that has been in effect since 2013.

The second common feature of the integrated transfer taxes is the **applicable credit.** This credit, previously known as the *unified credit,* was enacted in 1977, and it applies to both the gift tax and the estate tax. The credit is designed to prevent the application of transfer tax to taxpayers who either would not accumulate a relatively large amount of property transfers during their lifetime and/or would not have a relatively large transfer passing to heirs upon their death. The value of cumulative taxable transfers a person can

---

[1]The estate tax was optional for decedents dying in 2010. In lieu of the estate tax, executors could opt to have the adjusted tax basis of the assets in gross estate carry over to the heirs of the decedent. The estate tax is back in place for decedents dying subsequent to 2010.

EXHIBIT 25-1   Unified Transfer Tax Rates*

Tax Base Equal to or Over	Not Over	Tentative Tax	Plus	of Amount Over
$ 0	$ 10,000	$ 0	18%	$ 0
10,000	20,000	1,800	20	10,000
20,000	40,000	3,800	22	20,000
40,000	60,000	8,200	24	40,000
60,000	80,000	13,000	26	60,000
80,000	100,000	18,200	28	80,000
100,000	150,000	23,800	30	100,000
150,000	250,000	38,800	32	150,000
250,000	500,000	70,800	34	250,000
500,000	750,000	155,800	37	500,000
750,000	1,000,000	248,300	39	750,000
1,000,000		345,800	40	1,000,000

*The applicable credit and exemption is zero for estates that opted out of the estate tax in 2010.

> **THE KEY FACTS**
>
> **Common Features of the Unified Transfer Taxes**
>
> - Property transfers, whether made by gift or at death, are subject to transfer tax using a progressive tax rate schedule.
> - The applicable credit exempts cumulative transfers of up to $11.18 million $22.4 million for married taxpayers).
> - Each transfer tax allows a deduction for transfers to charities and surviving spouses (the charitable and marital deductions, respectively).

make without exceeding the applicable credit is called the **exemption equivalent** or, alternately, the applicable exclusion amount.

Exhibit 25-2 presents the exemption equivalent amounts for both the estate and gift taxes since 1986. The exemption equivalent was the same amount for gift and estate tax purposes until 2004, at which time the gift tax was frozen at the $1,000,000 exemption equivalent amount. In 2011, the exemption equivalent for the gift tax was reunified with the estate tax and, beginning in 2012, the exemption equivalent is annually adjusted for inflation.

The value of the applicable credit depends on both the transfer tax rates and the exemption equivalent that apply in the year of the transfer. Because both the tax rates and the exemption equivalent can change over time, we can best calculate the applicable credit by tracking the exemption equivalent and converting it into the applicable tax credit using the *current* tax rate schedule. For example, the exemption equivalent was $5 million for transfers made in 2011. Consequently, when we evaluate a prior-year transfer for purposes of determining the current-year gift tax, the applicable credit for 2011 will be $1,945,800 (no matter what the actual rates were in 2011, this is the credit calculated using the current tax rate schedule). In contrast, the exemption equivalent is $11.18 million for transfers made in 2018 and under the current applicable tax rate schedule the applicable credit is $4,417.800 (the amount of tax on $11.18 million for 2018 calculated in three steps

EXHIBIT 25-2   The Exemption Equivalent

Year of Transfer	Gift Tax	Estate Tax
1986	$ 500,000	$ 500,000
1987–1997	600,000	600,000
1998	625,000	625,000
1999	650,000	650,000
2000–2001	675,000	675,000
2002–2003	1,000,000	1,000,000
2004–2005	1,000,000	1,500,000
2006–2008	1,000,000	2,000,000
2009–2010*	1,000,000	3,500,000
2011	5,000,000	5,000,000
2012	5,120,000	5,120,000
2013	5,250,000	5,250,000
2014	5,340,000	5,340,000
2015	5,430,000	5,430,000
2016	5,450,000	5,450,000
2017	5,490,000	5,490,000
2018	11,180,000	11,180,000

*The applicable credit and exemption is zero for taxpayers who opt out of the estate tax in 2010.

as follows: (1) $11,180,000 − $1,000,000 = $10,180,000 (2) $10,180,000 × 40% = $4,072,000 (3) $4,072,000 + $345,800 = $4,417,800.

A third common feature of the unified tax system is the application of two common deductions. Each transfer tax provides an unlimited deduction for charitable contributions and a generous **marital deduction** for transfers to a spouse. The marital deduction allows almost unfettered transfers between spouses, treating a married couple as virtually a single taxpayer.

A final important feature of the transfer taxes is the valuation of transferred property. Property transferred via gift or at death is valued at fair market value. While fair market value is simple in concept, it is very complicated to apply. For purposes of the transfer taxes, fair market value is defined by the *willing-buyer, willing-seller rule* as follows:

> The price at which such property would change hands between a willing buyer and a willing seller, neither being under any compulsion to buy or to sell, and both have reasonable knowledge of the relevant facts.

Fair market value is determined based on the facts and circumstances for each individual property. Determining value is relatively simple for properties that have an active market. For example, stocks and bonds traded on exchanges or over the counter are valued at the mean of the highest and lowest selling prices. Unfortunately, the valuation of many other properties, especially realty, is very difficult. The large number of court cases resolving contentious values testifies to the difficulties in applying the willing-buyer, willing-seller rule.

LO 25-2 THE FEDERAL GIFT TAX

The gift tax is levied on individual taxpayers for all *taxable* gifts made during a calendar year. As explained shortly, each *individual* (married couples cannot elect joint filing for gift tax returns) who makes a gift in excess of the annual exclusion amount must file a gift tax return (Form 709) by April 15 of the following year.[2] Exhibit 25-3 presents the complete formula for the federal gift tax in two parts. In the first part, taxable gifts are calculated for each donee, and in the second, the gift tax is calculated using aggregate taxable gifts to all donees. We begin the first part by identifying transfers that constitute gifts.

EXHIBIT 25-3 The Federal Gift Tax Formula

	Part 1: Calculate taxable gifts for each individual donee:
	Current Gifts
Minus	½ of split gifts (other half included in spouse's current gifts)
Plus	½ of split gifts by spouse
Minus	Annual exclusion ($15,000 per donee)
Minus	Marital and charitable deductions
Equals	Current taxable gifts
	Part 2: Sum taxable gifts for all donees and calculate tax:
	Total Current Taxable Gifts
Plus	Prior taxable gifts
Equals	Cumulative taxable gifts
Times	Current tax rates
Equals	Cumulative tax
Minus	Tax at current rates on prior taxable gifts
Minus	Unused applicable credit at current rates
Equals	Gift tax payable

[2]A gift tax return reporting taxable gifts must be filed by April 15th following year-end if a taxpayer has made *any* taxable gifts during the current calendar year *or wishes to elect* gift-splitting. When taxpayers request extensions for their individual income tax returns, they also receive a six-month extension for filing their gift tax returns.

Transfers Subject to Gift Tax

The gift tax is imposed on lifetime transfers of property for less than adequate consideration. Typically, a gift is made in a personal context such as between family members. The satisfaction of an obligation is not considered a gift. For example, tuition payments for a child's education satisfy a support obligation. On the other hand, transfers motivated by affection or other personal motives, including transfers associated with marriage, are gratuitous and potentially subject to the tax. The gift tax is imposed once a gift has been completed, and this occurs when the **donor** relinquishes control of the property and the **donee** accepts the gift.[3] For example, deposits made to a joint bank account are not complete gifts because the donor (depositor) can withdraw the deposit at any time. The gift will be complete at the time the donee withdraws cash from the account.

> **THE KEY FACTS**
>
> **Gifts Excluded from the Gift Tax**
>
> - Incomplete and revocable gifts.
> - Payments for support obligations or debts.
> - Contributions to political parties or candidates.
> - Medical and educational expenses paid on behalf of an unrelated individual.

TAXES IN THE REAL WORLD   Love and Taxes

The small claims division of the Tax Court was asked to determine whether payments between former lovers constituted gifts or compensation. Jue-Ya Yang lived with her boyfriend, Howard Shih, who was an artist and calligrapher. While they were romantically involved, Mr. Shih made payments to Ms. Yang and later deducted these payments as wages.

Ms. Yang admitted doing housekeeping and cooking, but she argued that the payments were gifts. Mr. Shih's testimony about the romantic relationship was evasive. He admitted on cross-examination that while their relationship was more than a professional one, he could not even recall taking Ms. Yang out on dates. The court concluded that Mr. Shih's testimony was untrue and held that the payments were gifts made because of love and affection.

Source: Jue-Ya Yang, TC Summary Opinion 2008-156 (12-15-08).

In some instances a donor may relinquish some control over transferred property but retain other powers that can influence the enjoyment or disposition of the property. If the retained powers are important, the transfer will not be a complete gift.[4] For example, a transfer of property to a trust will not be a complete gift if the grantor retains the ability to revoke the transfer. If the grantor releases the powers, then the gift will generally be complete at that time because the property is no longer subject to the donor's control. For example, a distribution of property from a revocable trust is a complete gift because the grantor no longer has the ability to revoke the distribution.

Example 25-1

On July 12th of this year Harry transferred $250,000 of FFP stock to a new trust. He gave the trustee directions to pay income to Dina for the next 20 years and then remit the remainder to her son George. Harry named a bank as trustee but retained the power to revoke the trust in case he should need additional assets after retirement. Is the transfer of the stock a complete gift?

Answer: No. Harry retains sufficient control that the transfer of the stock to the trust is an incomplete gift.

What if: Suppose $11,000 of trust income was distributed to Dina at year-end. Is the transfer of the cash to Dina a complete gift?

Answer: Yes. With the payment Harry has relinquished control over the $11,000, and thus, it is a complete gift.

What if: Suppose Harry releases his power to revoke the trust at a time when the shares of FFP in the trust are valued at $225,000. Would this release cause the transfer of the stock to be a complete gift and, if so, what is the amount of the gift?

Answer: Yes. By releasing his powers Harry has relinquished control over the entire trust, and the value of the trust at that time, $225,000, would be a complete gift.

---

[3]If a donee refuses or disclaims a gift under §2518, the gift is not complete.

[4]§2514 addresses the treatment of general powers of appointment.

There are several important exceptions to the taxation of complete gifts. For example, political contributions are not gifts. Also, the payment of medical or educational expenses on behalf of another individual is not considered a gift if the payments are made directly to the health care provider or to the educational institution. To avoid confusing a division of property with a gift, a transfer of property in conjunction with a divorce is not considered to be a gift (it is treated as a transfer for adequate consideration) if the property is transferred within three years of the divorce under a written property settlement.

In addition, special rules apply to transfers of certain types of property. To make a complete gift of a life insurance policy, the donor must give the donee all the incidents of ownership, including the power to designate beneficiaries. An individual who creates a **joint tenancy**—either a **tenancy in common** or **joint tenancy with right of survivorship**—with someone who does not provide **adequate consideration** for their interest in the property is deemed to make a gift at that time. The gift is the amount necessary to pay for the other party's interest in the property. For example, suppose the donor pays $80,000 toward the purchase of $100,000 in realty held as equal tenants in common with the donee (i.e., the donee provides only $20,000 of the purchase price). The donor is deemed to make a gift of $30,000 to the donee, the difference between the value of the joint interest ($100,000 ÷ 2 = $50,000) and the consideration provided by the donee ($20,000).

ETHICS

Rudy is a retired engineer who has three adult daughters and several grandchildren. This year Carol, his youngest daughter, approached Rudy for a $40,000 business loan. Although Carol had no collateral for the loan and did not sign any written promise to repay the money, Rudy still transferred the funds to her account. Do you think Rudy should file a gift tax return for the transfer? Suppose Rudy has no intention of demanding repayment but has not told anyone so. Does this make any difference?

Example 25-2

This year Harry helped purchase a residence for use by Dina and her husband Steve. The price of the residence was $250,000, and the title named Harry and Steve joint tenants with the right of survivorship. Harry provided $210,000 of the purchase price and Steve the remaining $40,000. Has Harry made a complete gift, and if so, in what amount?

Answer: Yes, Harry made a complete gift to Steve of $85,000, calculated by subtracting the amount paid by Steve from the price of his ownership interest ($125,000 minus $40,000).

What if: Suppose Steve didn't provide any part of the purchase price. What is the amount of the gift?

Answer: In this case, Harry made a complete gift to Steve of half the purchase price, $125,000.

Valuation   Gifts are taxed at the fair market value of the donated property on the date the gift becomes complete. Remember that despite the valuation of a gift at fair market value, the donee generally takes a carryover basis for income tax purposes.[5]

Valuation of remainders and other temporal interests.   Assigning value to unique property is difficult enough, but sometimes we must also assign a value to a stream of payments over time or a payment to be made in the future. The right to currently enjoy property or receive income payments from property is called a **present interest.** In contrast, the right to receive income or property in the future is called a **future interest.** A present right to possess and/or collect income from property may not be permanent; if

---

[5]The carryover basis may be increased for any gift tax paid (after 1976) on the appreciation of the property.

granted for a specific period of time or until the occurrence of a specific event, it is a **terminable interest.** For example, the right to receive income payments from property for 10 years is a terminable interest. A right to possess property and/or receive income for the duration of someone's life is called a **life estate.** The person whose life determines the duration of the life estate is called the *life tenant.*

At the end of a terminable interest, the property will pass to another owner, the person holding the future interest. In a **reversion,** it returns to the original owner. If it goes to a new owner, the right to the property is called a **remainder** and the owner is called a **remainderman.** For example, the right to own property after a 10-year income interest has ended is a future interest held by the remainderman. The right to property after the termination of a life estate is also called a remainder.

Future interests are common when property is placed in a trust. **Trusts** are legal entities established by a person called the **grantor.** Trusts are administered by a **trustee** and generally contain property called the trust **corpus.** The trustee has a **fiduciary duty** to manage the property in the trust for the benefit of a **beneficiary** or beneficiaries. This duty requires the trustee to administer the trust in an objective and impartial manner and not favor one beneficiary over another.

Since a future interest is essentially a promise of a future payment, we estimate the value of the remainder by discounting the future payment to a present value using a market rate of interest. For example, suppose property worth $100 is placed in a trust with the income to be paid to an income beneficiary each year for 10 years, after which time the property accumulated in the trust will be distributed. The remainder is a future interest with a value we estimate by calculating the present value of a payment of $100 in 10 years as follows:

$$\text{Value of remainder interest} = \frac{\text{Future payment}}{(1 + r)^n}$$

where r is the market rate of interest, and n is the number of years. The interest rate used for this calculation is published monthly by the Treasury as the §7520 rate.[6] If the §7520 rate is 6 percent, we calculate the value of a remainder of $100 placed in trust for 10 years as follows:

$$\text{Value of remainder interest} = \frac{\$100}{(1 + .06)^{10}} = \frac{\$100}{(1.791)} = \$55.83$$

The value of property consists of the present interest (the right to income) and the future interest (the remainder). Hence, once we have estimated the value of the remainder, we compute the value of the income interest as the difference between the value of the remainder and the total value of the property.

$$\begin{aligned}\text{Value of remainder interest} &= \text{Total value} - \text{Value of remainder}\\ &= \$100 - \$55.83\\ &= \$44.17\end{aligned}$$

If the terminable interest is a life estate, the valuation of the remainder is a bit more complicated because payment of the remainder is delayed by the duration of the life estate. To estimate this delay, we base the calculation upon the number of years the life tenant is expected to live. To facilitate the calculation, the regulations provide a table (Table S) that calculates the discount factor by including the life tenant's age at the time of transfer. Exhibit 25-4 includes a portion of Table S from the regulation with interest rates by column and the age of the life tenant by row.

[6]The §7520 rate is 120 percent of the applicable federal mid-term rate in effect during the month of the transaction.

THE KEY FACTS

Valuation of Remainders and Income Interests

- Future interests are valued at present value, calculated by estimating the time until the present interest expires.
- The present value calculation uses the §7520 interest rate published by the Treasury.
- If the present interest is measured by a person's life (a life estate), then we estimate the delay by reference to the person's life expectancy as published in IRS tables.
- The value of a present interest, such as an income interest or life estate, is determined by subtracting the value of the remainder interest from the total value of the property.

EXHIBIT 25-4 **Discount Factors for Estimating the Value of Remainders**

	Regulation Section 20.2031-7(d)(7) Table S.—Based on Life Table 2000CM Single Life Remainder Factors Applicable After May 1, 2009 [Interest rate]									
Age	**4.2%**	**4.4%**	**4.6%**	**4.8%**	**5.0%**	**5.2%**	**5.4%**	**5.6%**	**5.8%**	**6.0%**
0	.06083	.05483	.04959	.04501	.04101	.03749	.03441	.03170	.02931	.02721
1	.05668	.05049	.04507	.04034	.03618	.03254	.02934	.02652	.02403	.02183
2	.05858	.05222	.04665	.04178	.03750	.03373	.03042	.02750	.02492	.02264
3	.06072	.05420	.04848	.04346	.03904	.03516	.03173	.02871	.02603	.02366
4	.06303	.05634	.05046	.04530	.04075	.03674	.03319	.03006	.02729	.02483
5	.06547	.05861	.05258	.04726	.04258	.03844	.03478	.03153	.02866	.02610
6	.06805	.06102	.05482	.04935	.04453	.04026	.03647	.03312	.03014	.02749
35	.19692	.18423	.17253	.16174	.15178	.14258	.13408	.12621	.11892	.11217
36	.20407	.19119	.17931	.16833	.15818	.14879	.14009	.13204	.12457	.11764
37	.21144	.19838	.18631	.17515	.16481	.15523	.14635	.13811	.13046	.12335
38	.21904	.20582	.19357	.18222	.17170	.16193	.15287	.14444	.13661	.12932
86	.79825	.79044	.78278	.77524	.76783	.76055	.75340	.74636	.73944	.73264
87	.80921	.80176	.79443	.78722	.78014	.77316	.76630	.75956	.75292	.74638
88	.81978	.81268	.80569	.79880	.79203	.78536	.77880	.77234	.76598	.75971
89	.82994	.82317	.81651	.80995	.80349	.79712	.79085	.78467	.77859	.77259

Example 25-3

Harry transferred $500,000 of FFP stock to the DG Trust, whose trustee is directed to pay income to Dina for her life and, upon Dina's death, pay the remainder to George (or his estate). At the time of the gift, Dina was 35 years old and the §7520 interest rate was 5.8 percent. What are the values of the gift of the life estate and of the remainder interest?

Answer: Harry made a $59,460 gift of the remainder to George and a $440,540 gift of the life estate to Dina. Under Table S (see Exhibit 25-4), the percentage of the property that represents the value of George's remainder is .11892. Thus, George's remainder is valued at $59,460 ($500,000 × .11892). Dina's life estate is the remaining value of $440,540 ($500,000 − $59,460).

The Annual Exclusion One of the most important aspects of the gift tax is the **annual exclusion,** which operates to eliminate "small" gifts from the gift tax base. The amount of the exclusion has been revised upwards periodically over the years and is now indexed for inflation.[7] In 2018, the annual exclusion amount is $15,000.

The annual exclusion is available to offset gifts made to *each* donee regardless of the number of donees in any particular year. For example, a donor could give $15,000 in cash to each of 10 donees every year without exceeding the annual exclusion. One important limitation to the annual exclusion is that it applies only to gifts of *present* interests; that is, a gift of a future interest is not eligible for an annual exclusion.

---

[7]The exclusion is indexed for inflation in such a way that the amount of the exclusion only increases in increments of $1,000. The annual exclusion was $10,000 from 1981 through 2001, but was $11,000 for 2002 through 2005, $12,000 for 2006 through 2008, $13,000 for 2009 through 2012, and $14,000 from 2012 through 2017.

> **Example 25-4**

When Harry transferred $500,000 of FFP stock to the DG Trust (Example 25-3), he simultaneously made two taxable gifts, a life estate to Dina and a remainder to George. What is the amount of the taxable gift of the life estate to Dina and the remainder interest to George, after taking the annual exclusion into account?

Answer: Dina's life estate is a present interest and would qualify for the annual exclusion. However, George's remainder is a future interest and will not qualify for the annual exclusion. Harry would file a Form 709 to report total taxable gifts of $485,000 consisting of a $425,540 taxable gift to Dina ($440,540 less the annual exclusion of $15,000) and a taxable gift of $59,460 to George (no annual exclusion is available for a future interest).

	Dina	George	Harry's Gift Tax Return
Current gifts	$440,540	$59,460	$500,000
Annual exclusion	−15,000	−0	−15,000
Taxable gifts	$425,540	$59,460	$485,000

> **THE KEY FACTS**
>
> **Annual Exclusion**
>
> - Most gifts are eligible for an annual exclusion of $15,000 per donee per year.
> - Gifts of present interests qualify for the exclusion.
> - Gifts of future interests placed in trust for a minor can also qualify for the exclusion.

Most gifts will only qualify for an annual exclusion if the donee has a present interest (the ability to immediately use the property or the income from it). However, a special exception applies to future interests given to minors (under the age of 21). Gifts in trust for a minor are future interests if the minor does not have the ability to access the income or property until reaching the age of majority. These gifts will still qualify for the annual exclusion as long as the property can be used to support the minor and any remaining property is distributed to the child once he or she reaches age 21.[8]

> **Example 25-5**

Harry transferred $48,500 of cash to the George Trust. The trustee of the George Trust has the discretion to distribute income or corpus (principal) for George's benefit and is required to distribute all assets to George (or his estate) not later than George's 21st birthday. Is this gift eligible for the annual exclusion? If so, what is the amount of the taxable gift?

Answer: Yes, Harry will be entitled to an annual exclusion for the transfer despite the fact that George's interest is a future one, because the gift is in trust for the support of a minor and the property must distribute the assets to George once he reaches age 21. The amount of the gift is $48,500, reduced to a taxable gift of $33,500 after application of the $15,000 annual exclusion.

Taxable Gifts

In part 1 of the formula in Exhibit 25-3, **current gifts** are accumulated for each donee, and this amount includes all gifts completed during the calendar year for each individual. Current gifts do not include transfers exempted from the tax, such as political contributions. Several adjustments are made to calculate current **taxable gifts** for each donee. As we've seen, each taxpayer is allowed an annual exclusion applied to the cumulative gifts of present interests made during the year to *each* donee. Next, if a married couple elects to split gifts (discussed below), half of each gift is included in the current gifts of each spouse. The marital deduction for gifts to spouses and the charitable deduction for gifts to charity are the last adjustments to calculate taxable gifts for each donee. We discuss each in turn.

[8]The courts have created another exception to the present interest rule called *Crummey power.* A discussion of this exception is beyond the scope of this text.

Gift-Splitting Election   Married couples have the option to *split gifts,* allowing them to treat *all* gifts made in a year as if each spouse had made one-half of each gift. In a **community-property state,** both spouses automatically own equal shares in most property acquired during the marriage.[9] Hence, when they make a gift of community property the transfer is divided between them equally. In **common-law states,** one spouse can own a disproportionate amount of property because he or she earns most of the income. The gift-splitting election provides a mechanism for married couples in common-law states to achieve the same result as couples receive automatically in community-property states.[10]

Example 25-6

Wilma and Harry live in Michigan, a common-law state. For the holidays Wilma gave cash gifts of $32,000 to Steve and $41,000 to Dina. Wilma and Harry did not elect to split gifts. What is the amount of Wilma's taxable gifts?

Answer: $43,000. After using her annual exclusion (both gifts are present interests), Wilma has made taxable gifts of $17,000 to Steve ($32,000 − $15,000) and $26,000 to Dina ($41,000 − $15,000).

What if: Suppose Wilma and Harry elect gift-splitting this year. How would your answer change?

Answer: Both Wilma and Harry made taxable gifts of $6,500. Under gift-splitting, Wilma and Harry are each treated as making a gift of $16,000 to Steve and $20,500 to Dina. After the annual exclusion, both Wilma and Harry made a $1,000 taxable gift to Steve [($32,000 ÷ 2) − $15,000 = $1,000]. In addition, both Wilma and Harry made a $5,500 taxable gift to Dina [($41,000 ÷ 2) − $15,000 = $5,500].

What if: Suppose Wilma and Harry lived in Texas (a community-property state), and Wilma made the same gifts from community property.

Answer: Both Wilma and Harry made a taxable gift of $6,500. Under state law, each spouse is automatically treated as gifting half the value of any gifts made from community property. After the annual exclusion, both Wilma and Harry made a $1,000 taxable gift to Steve [($32,000 ÷ 2) − $15,000], and each made a $5,500 taxable gift to Dina [($41,000 ÷ 2) − $15,000].

Besides increasing the application of the annual exclusion, a gift-splitting election also increases the likelihood that taxable gifts will be taxed at lower tax rates or any gift tax will be offset by applicable credits. To utilize gift-splitting, each spouse must be a citizen or resident of the United States, be married at the time of the gift, and not remarry during the remainder of the calendar year. Both spouses must consent to the election by filing a timely gift tax return. Taxpayers make this election annually and can apply it to all gifts completed by either spouse during the calendar year. As a result of the election, both spouses share a joint and several liability for any gift tax due.

Marital Deduction   The marital deduction was originally enacted to equalize the treatment of spouses residing in common-law states. In community-property states, the ownership of most property *acquired* during a marriage is automatically divided between the spouses. In common-law states, one spouse can own a disproportionate amount of property if he or she earns most of the income. Absent the marital deduction, in a common-law state, a transfer between the spouses to equalize the ownership

> **THE KEY FACTS**
>
> **Marital Deduction**
>
> - Gifts of property to a spouse may be deducted in computing taxable gifts.
> - Transfers of terminable interests in property, such as a life estate, will not generally qualify for the deduction.
> - The deduction is limited to the value of property included in taxable gifts.

---

[9]Depending upon state law, the ownership of property acquired by either spouse prior to a marriage is not automatically divided equally between the spouses. In other words, property owned prior to the marriage is not necessarily community property and continues to belong to the original owner.

[10]There are nine community-property states: Arizona, California, Idaho, Louisiana, Nevada, New Mexico, Texas, Washington, and Wisconsin.

of property would be treated as a taxable gift. However, because transfers to spouses are eligible for a marital deduction, no taxable gift results from such a transfer.

The marital deduction is subject to two limits. First, the amount is limited to the value of the gift after the annual exclusion. Second, transfers of **nondeductible terminable interests** do not qualify for a marital deduction. A nondeductible terminable interest is a property interest transferred to the spouse that terminates when some event occurs or after a specified amount of time, when the property is transferred to another.

Example 25-7

After his decision to retire, Harry gave Wilma a piece of jewelry that is a family heirloom valued at $50,000. What is the amount of this taxable gift?

Answer: Zero. This gift will qualify for an annual exclusion, and the amount remaining after subtracting the annual exclusion qualifies for the marital deduction. The taxable gift is calculated below:

Current gift	$50,000
Less: Annual exclusion	−15,000
Less: Marital deduction	−35,000
Taxable gift	$ 0

What if: Suppose Harry transferred $200,000 to a trust with directions to pay income to Wilma for her life (a life estate). After Wilma's death, the corpus of the trust would then pass to Dina (the remainder). What is the amount of this taxable gift if Wilma is age 38 at the time and the §7520 interest rate is 5 percent?

Answer: The total taxable gift is $185,000. This transfer is actually two gifts, a gift of a present interest to Wilma (a life estate) and a future interest to Dina (the remainder). The gift of the remainder is valued at $34,340 using Wilma's age and the §7520 interest rate from Table S in Exhibit 25-4 ($200,000 × .17170). The remainder does not qualify for an annual exclusion because it is a future interest. The gift of the life estate is a present interest valued at $165,660 ($200,000 − $34,340), and it qualifies for the annual exclusion. The taxable gifts are calculated below:

	Dina (remainder)	Wilma (life estate)
Current gifts	$34,340	$165,660
Less: Annual exclusion (life estate)	−0	−15,000
Less: Marital deduction	−0	−0
Taxable gift	$34,340	$150,660

When the life estate is given to a spouse, it does not qualify for the marital deduction because it will terminate upon a future event (Wilma's death) and then pass to another person (Dina).

The limitation on the deductible terminable interests ensures that property owned by a married couple is subject to a transfer tax when the property is eventually transferred from the couple (as opposed to between the spouses).[11] If a life estate were eligible for a marital deduction, it would not be taxed at the time of the gift nor would any value be taxed upon Wilma's death (the life estate disappears with her death). Hence, a marital deduction is available only for spousal transfers that will eventually be included in the recipient spouse's estate.[12]

---

[11]Qualified terminable interest properties (QTIPs for short) are an exception to the nondeductibility of terminable interest property. To qualify, the taxpayer must agree to have qualifying terminable interests included in the estate of the spouse. A detailed discussion of this election is beyond the scope of this text.

[12]The spouse must be entitled to all of the income from the property payable at least annually, and no person has the power to appoint any part of the property to anyone other than the spouse until the death of the spouse.

Charitable Deduction   The amount of the charitable deduction is also limited to the value of the gift after subtracting the annual exclusion. Requirements for an organization to qualify as a charity for purposes of the gift tax charitable deduction are quite similar to those for the income tax deduction (the entity must be organized for religious, charitable, scientific, educational, or other public purposes, including governmental entities). Unlike the income tax deduction, however, the charitable deduction has no percentage limitation. In addition, as long as the qualifying charity receives the donor's entire interest in the property, no gift tax return need be filed (assuming the donor has no other taxable gifts). Finally, a transfer to a charity also qualifies for an income tax deduction (subject to the AGI limits on the income tax charitable deduction).

Example 25-8

Harry donated $155,000 in cash to State University. What is the amount of the taxable gift?

Answer: Zero. The gift qualifies for the charitable gift tax deduction, as calculated below.

Current gift	$155,000
Less: Annual exclusion	−15,000
Less: Charitable deduction	−140,000
Taxable gift	$ 0

Note that Harry can also claim an income tax deduction for the transfer.

Computation of the Gift Tax

Part 2 of the formula in Exhibit 25-3 provides the method for calculating the gift tax. It begins by summing the taxable gifts made for all donees during a calendar year.

Example 25-9

Harry and Wilma did not make any gifts from community property and did not elect to gift-split this year (see Example 25-6). What is the value of Harry's current taxable gifts this year?

Answer: Harry made $588,500 of taxable gifts, calculated using Part 1 of the formula in Exhibit 25-3 as follows:

Gifted Property	Donee	Value	Explanation
1. Residence	Steve	$ 85,000	Example 25-2
Less: Annual exclusion		−15,000	
2. DG Trust—life estate	Dina	440,540	Example 25-3
Less: Annual exclusion		−15,000	
3. DG Trust—remainder	George	59,460	Example 25-3
4. George Trust	George	48,500	Example 25-5
Less: Annual exclusion		−15,000	
5. Jewelry	Wilma	50,000	Example 25-7
Less: Annual exclusion		−15,000	
Less: Marital deduction	Wilma	−35,000	
6. Donation	State University	155,000	Example 25-8
Less: Annual exclusion		−15,000	
Less: Charitable deduction	State U	−140,000	
Harry's current taxable gifts		**$588,500**	

The amounts of the marital and charitable deductions are limited to the value of the property included in taxable gifts.

Will Wilma be required to file a gift tax return this year? If so, what is the amount of her taxable gifts?

Answer: Wilma must also file a gift tax return this year because her current gifts exceed the available annual exclusion amounts. Wilma's taxable gifts sum to $43,000, calculated as follows:

Gifted Property	Donee	Value	Explanation
Cash gift	Steve	$32,000	Example 25-6
Less: Annual exclusion		−15,000	
Cash gift	Dina	41,000	Example 25-6
Less: Annual exclusion		−15,000	
Wilma's current taxable gifts		**$43,000**	

What if: What is the amount of Harry and Wilma's taxable gifts if they elect to gift-split?

Answer: Harry and Wilma each made $308,250 of taxable gifts, calculated as follows:

				Gift-Splitting	
	Harry	Wilma	Donee	Harry	Wilma
Gift of a residence	$ 85,000		Steve	$ 42,500	$ 42,500
Less: Annual exclusion	−15,000			−15,000	
Cash gift		$32,000	Steve	16,000	16,000
Less: Annual exclusion		−15,000			−15,000
Transfer to DG trust	440,540		Dina	220,270	220,270
Less: Annual exclusion	−15,000			−15,000	
Cash gift		41,000	Dina	20,500	20,500
Less: Annual exclusion		−15,000			−15,000
DG Trust—remainder	59,460			29,730	29,730
George Trust	48,500			24,250	24,250
Less: Annual exclusion	−15,000			−15,000	−15,000
Gift of Jewelry	50,000		Wilma	50,000	
Less: Annual exclusion	−15,000			−15,000	
Less: Marital deduction	−35,000			−35,000	
Donation to State U	155,000		State U	77,500	77,500
Less: Annual exclusion	−15,000			−15,000	−15,000
Less: Charitable deduction	−140,000			−62,500	−62,500
Total	**$588,500**	**$43,000**		**$308,250**	**$308,250**

Note that absent gift-splitting, Harry and Wilma made taxable gifts totaling $631,500 ($588,500 + $43,000), but under gift-splitting that reduced to $616,500 ($308,250 + $308,250) because Wilma was able to use an additional $15,000 annual exclusion for her portion of the gift to the George Trust. Neither Harry nor Wilma was able to use any additional annual exclusions for the gifts to Steve and Dina because they had already used annual exclusions to these two donees. If they elect to gift-split, Harry and Wilma will be jointly and severally liable for the gift taxes.

Tax on Current Taxable Gifts   The first step to computing the gift tax on current taxable gifts is to add prior taxable gifts to current taxable gifts. The purpose of adding gifts from previous periods is to increase the tax base and thereby increase the marginal tax rate applying to current gifts. To prevent double taxation of prior taxable gifts, the gift tax on prior taxable gifts is subtracted from the tax on total transfers. Two elements of the tax on prior taxable gifts are important to understand. First, the tax is calculated on prior taxable gifts ignoring whether any applicable credit was claimed on the gifts in the prior year. Second, the tax on prior taxable gifts is computed using the *current* rate schedule (the tax rates for the year of the prior transfer are not relevant). The difference between the tax on cumulative taxable gifts and prior taxable gifts is the tax on the current taxable gifts.

Applicable Credit The last adjustment in the formula is the unused portion of the applicable credit. Recall that the applicable credit is determined by the current tax on the exemption equivalent ($11.18 million for 2018) and the exemption equivalent can change over time because it is indexed for inflation. Hence, rather than track the unused portion of the applicable credit, it is far easier to track the unused portion of the exemption equivalent and then convert that into the applicable credit using current rates. Tracking the unused portion of the exemption equivalent makes sense because the exemption equivalent is ignored in calculating the tax on prior taxable gifts.

For example, suppose an individual transferred via gift $3 million in a prior year (when the exemption equivalent was $1 million) and $6 million in the current year (when the exemption equivalent increased to $5 million). This individual made cumulative transfers of $9 million but he has paid tax on $2 million (from the prior year gifts), and is entitled to an exemption equivalent of $5 million. In sum, this individual would only owe tax on $2 million ($9 transfers − $5 exemption − $2 already taxed). Based on the gift tax formula, the current taxable transfer would be $6 million, and the tax on this amount would be reduced by the tax on the unused exemption equivalent of $4 million ($5 million less $1 million used in a prior year) resulting in a taxable transfer of $2 million. Note that the exemption equivalent (converted into the applicable credit at current rates) eliminates the gift tax for individuals who do not transfer a relatively large cumulative amount of property during their lifetime. Also note that a gift tax return must be filed by each individual who has made taxable gifts during the calendar year or who elects to split gifts, even if no tax is due because of the applicable credit. Recall also that joint filing is not allowed.

Example 25-10

Assume that Harry made a taxable gift of $1,500,000 in 2007. At that time, the exemption equivalent for the gift tax was $1 million, so Harry paid gift taxes on $500,000. Harry has not made any taxable gifts since 2007. This year, however, Harry made taxable gifts of $588,500. What is Harry's gift tax and Harry's unused exemption equivalent?

Answer: Harry will report cumulative taxable gifts of $2,088,500, but he will not owe any gift tax this year. The calculation is as follows:

Current taxable gifts	$ 588,500
Prior taxable gifts	1,500,000
Cumulative taxable gifts	$2,088,500
Tax on cumulative taxable gifts	$781,200
Less: Current tax on prior taxable gifts ($1.5 million)	−545,800
Tax on current taxable gifts	$235,400
Applicable credit on current taxable gifts	−235,400
Gift tax due	$　　 0

Harry used $1 million of his exemption equivalent in 2007, and this year he used another $588,500. Hence, at the end of 2018, Harry has $9,591,500 of unused exemption equivalent remaining ($11,180,000 − $1,000,000 − $588,500).

What if: Suppose Harry made a taxable gift of $3,500,000 in 2007, and at that time, the exemption equivalent was $1 million. What should Harry report this year as his cumulative taxable gifts, gift tax on cumulative taxable gifts, gift tax on current taxable gifts, credit for current tax on prior taxable gifts, and gift tax due?

Answer: Harry should report cumulative taxable gifts of $4,088,500 and gift tax on cumulative gifts of $1,581,200. Harry, however, owes no gift tax. The calculation is as follows:

Current taxable gifts		$ 588,500
Prior taxable gifts		3,500,000
Cumulative taxable gifts		$4,088,500
Tax on cumulative taxable gifts		$1,581,200
Less: Current tax on prior taxable gifts ($3.5 million)		−1,345,800
Tax on current taxable gifts		235,400
Applicable credit on current taxable gifts		−235,400
Gift tax due		$ 0

At the end of 2018, Harry would have $9,591,500 of exemption equivalent remaining ($11,180,000 − $1,000,000 − $588,500). Note that Harry probably paid gift tax in 2007 because his taxable gifts far exceeded the exemption equivalent of $1 million in 2007. However, the amount of gift tax that was paid in 2007 is not relevant for calculating Harry's current tax. All calculations in the current year are made using the current tax rate schedule (not the one that applied in prior years).

What is Wilma's gift tax due?

Answer: Zero. Wilma has used $43,000 of her exemption equivalent. Hence, at the end of 2018, Wilma has $11,137,000 ($11,180,000 − $43,000) of exemption equivalent remaining.

Wilma's current taxable gifts		$43,000
Prior taxable gifts		+0
Cumulative taxable gifts		$43,000
Tax on cumulative taxable gifts		$8,920
Less: Current tax on prior taxable gifts		−0
Tax on current taxable gifts		$8,920
Applicable credit on current taxable gifts		−8,920
Gift tax due		$ 0

To recap, the gift tax requires donors to keep track of the portion of the exemption equivalent they used to generate an applicable credit to offset prior taxable gifts. This prevents multiple applications of the same exemption. The gift tax on previous gifts is computed using the current tax rate schedule, but this amount does *not* represent the amount of gift tax paid—just the gifts previously subject to tax. The unused portion of the applicable credit then reduces the total gift tax to reach the gift tax due. The gift tax is calculated using the current rate schedule and ignores the amount of gift tax actually paid in prior periods. Exhibit 25-5 presents the first page of the 2017 gift tax return Form 709 for Harry Smith (Form 709 for 2018 was not available from the IRS as of press date).

EXHIBIT 25-5 Page 1 of Form 709 Gift Tax Return for Harry Smith

Form **709**

Department of the Treasury
Internal Revenue Service

United States Gift (and Generation-Skipping Transfer) Tax Return

▶ Go to *www.irs.gov/Form709* for instructions and the latest information.

(For gifts made during calendar year 2017)
▶ See instructions.

OMB No. 1545-0020

2017

1 Donor's first name and middle initial	**2** Donor's last name
HARRY	SMITH

3 Donor's social security number
000-00-0000

4 Address (number, street, and apartment number)
2813 ELMWOOD

5 Legal residence (domicile)
WASHTENAW, MIGHIGAN

6 City or town, state or province, country, and ZIP or foreign postal code
ANN ARBOR, MI 48109

7 Citizenship (see instructions)
US

		Yes	No
8	If the donor died during the year, check here ▶ ☐ and enter date of death _____ , _____ .		
9	If you extended the time to file this Form 709, check here ▶ ☐		
10	Enter the total number of donees listed on Schedule A. Count each person only once ▶ **FIVE**		
11a	Have you (the donor) previously filed a Form 709 (or 709-A) for any other year? If "No," skip line 11b	✓	
b	Has your address changed since you last filed Form 709 (or 709-A)?		✓
12	**Gifts by husband or wife to third parties.** Do you consent to have the gifts (including generation-skipping transfers) made by you and by your spouse to third parties during the calendar year considered as made one-half by each of you? (see instructions.) (If the answer is "Yes," the following information must be furnished and your spouse must sign the consent shown below. **If the answer is "No," skip lines 13–18.**)		✓
13	Name of consenting spouse **14** SSN		
15	Were you married to one another during the entire calendar year? (see instructions)		
16	If 15 is "No," check whether ☐ married ☐ divorced or ☐ widowed/deceased, and give date (see instructions) ▶		
17	Will a gift tax return for this year be filed by your spouse? (If "Yes," mail both returns in the same envelope.)		
18	**Consent of Spouse.** I consent to have the gifts (and generation-skipping transfers) made by me and by my spouse to third parties during the calendar year considered as made one-half by each of us. We are both aware of the joint and several liability for tax created by the execution of this consent.		

Consenting spouse's signature ▶   Date ▶

		Yes	No
19	Have you applied a DSUE amount received from a predeceased spouse to a gift or gifts reported on this or a previous Form 709? If "Yes," complete Schedule C		✓

1	Enter the amount from Schedule A, Part 4, line 11	**1**	588,500
2	Enter the amount from Schedule B, line 3	**2**	1,500,000
3	Total taxable gifts. Add lines 1 and 2	**3**	2,088,500
4	Tax computed on amount on line 3 (see *Table for Computing Gift Tax* in instructions)	**4**	781,200
5	Tax computed on amount on line 2 (see *Table for Computing Gift Tax* in instructions)	**5**	545,800
6	Balance. Subtract line 5 from line 4	**6**	235,400
7	Applicable credit amount. If donor has DSUE amount from predeceased spouse(s) or Restored Exclusion Amount, enter amount from Schedule C, line 5; otherwise, see instructions	**7**	4,417,800
8	Enter the applicable credit against tax allowable for all prior periods (from Sch. B, line 1, col. C)	**8**	345,800
9	Balance. Subtract line 8 from line 7. Do not enter less than zero	**9**	4,072,000
10	Enter 20% (.20) of the amount allowed as a specific exemption for gifts made after September 8, 1976, and before January 1, 1977 (see instructions)	**10**	
11	Balance. Subtract line 10 from line 9. Do not enter less than zero	**11**	4,072,000
12	Applicable credit. Enter the smaller of line 6 or line 11	**12**	235,400
13	Credit for foreign gift taxes (see instructions)	**13**	
14	Total credits. Add lines 12 and 13	**14**	235,400
15	Balance. Subtract line 14 from line 6. Do not enter less than zero	**15**	0
16	Generation-skipping transfer taxes (from Schedule D, Part 3, col. H, Total)	**16**	
17	Total tax. Add lines 15 and 16	**17**	0
18	Gift and generation-skipping transfer taxes prepaid with extension of time to file	**18**	
19	If line 18 is less than line 17, enter **balance due** (see instructions)	**19**	0
20	If line 18 is greater than line 17, enter **amount to be refunded**	**20**	

Part 1—General Information

Part 2—Tax Computation

Attach check or money order here.

Sign Here

Under penalties of perjury, I declare that I have examined this return, including any accompanying schedules and statements, and to the best of my knowledge and belief, it is true, correct, and complete. Declaration of preparer (other than donor) is based on all information of which preparer has any knowledge.

May the IRS discuss this return with the preparer shown below (see instructions)? ☐Yes ☐No

▶ Signature of donor   Date

Paid Preparer Use Only

Print/Type preparer's name	Preparer's signature	Date	Check ☐ if self-employed	PTIN
Firm's name ▶			Firm's EIN ▶	
Firm's address ▶			Phone no.	

For Disclosure, Privacy Act, and Paperwork Reduction Act Notice, see the instructions for this form.   Cat. No. 16783M   Form **709** (2017)

Source: Form 709

continued from page 25-1...

Early this year Bob was injured in an auto accident. Unable to recover from his injuries, he died after two days in the hospital. Bob is survived by his son, Nate, who is also the executor of Bob's estate. Nate is now collecting his father's assets, and he would like help in preparing Bob's federal estate tax return. ■

THE FEDERAL ESTATE TAX

LO 25-3

The estate tax is designed to tax the value of property owned or controlled by an individual at death, the decedent. Because federal gift and estate taxes are integrated, taxable gifts affect the tax base for the estate tax. Exhibit 25-6 presents the estate tax formula.

EXHIBIT 25-6   The Federal Estate Tax Formula

	Gross estate
Minus	Expenses, debts, and losses
Equals	Adjusted gross estate
Minus	Marital and charitable deductions
Equals	Taxable estate
Plus	Adjusted taxable gifts
Equals	Cumulative taxable transfers (the tax base)
Times	Current tax rates
Equals	Tax on cumulative transfers
Minus	Gift taxes payable on adjusted taxable gifts at current rate
Equals	Tentative tax
Minus	Full applicable credit calculated using current tax rate
Equals	Gross estate tax

The Gross Estate

Property possessed by or owned (titled) by a decedent at the time of death is generally referred to as the **probate estate,** because the transfer of this property is carried out by a probate court. The person appointed by the court to carry out the will is called the **executor. Probate** is the process of gathering property possessed by or titled in the name of a decedent at the time of death, paying the debts of the decedent, and transferring the ownership of any remaining property to the decedent's **heirs.** Property in the probate estate can include cash, stocks, jewelry, clothing, and realty owned by or titled in the name of the deceased at the time of death.

Example 25-11

What if: Nate took an inventory of his father's property in preparation for distributing assets according to Bob's will. Nate must report this preliminary inventory of personal and investment property to the probate court; it includes the following:

	Fair Market Value
Auto	$ 33,000
Clothes, furniture, and personal effects	48,000
Smith painting (original cost/initial estimated value)	25,000
Checking and savings accounts	75,250
FFP stock	19,500,000
Residence	400,000
Other investments	8,200
Total	$20,089,450

(continued on page 25-18)

What amount of this property is included in Bob's gross estate?

Answer: Bob's gross estate includes the value of *all* the above property, or $20,089,450, because he owned these assets at his death (i.e., these assets are included in Bob's probate estate). In this example, Bob's gross estate and his probate estate are identical, but this would not be the case if Bob owned property that transferred automatically on his death.

What if: Suppose Bob was also entitled to a pension distribution of $15,000 but had not yet received the check at the time of his death. Would this value also be included in Bob's probate estate and therefore gross estate?

Answer: Yes. Although Bob had not received the check, he was legally entitled to the property at the time of his death, and therefore it will be included in both his probate estate and gross estate.

The **gross estate** is broader than the probate estate. The gross estate consists of (1) the fair market value of property possessed or owned by a decedent at death *plus* (2) the value of certain automatic property transfers that take effect at death.[13] Property transfers that take effect only at death are not in the probate estate because the transfer takes place just as death occurs. Hence, the probate court does not need to affect a transfer.

Specific Inclusions   Besides property in the probate estate, the gross estate also includes property transferred automatically at the decedent's death. These automatic transfers can occur without the help of a probate court because the ownership transfers by law at the time of death.

Certain automatic property transfers are specifically included in the gross estate because, while the decedent didn't own the property at death, Congress deemed that the decedent controlled the ultimate disposition of the property. That is, the decedent effectively determined who would receive the property at the time of death. A common example is property held in joint tenancy with right of survivorship, which legally transfers to the surviving tenant upon the joint tenant's death. Joint bank accounts are commonly owned in joint ownership with right of survivorship. In contrast, tenants in common hold divided rights to property and have the ability to transfer these rights during their life or upon death. Property held by tenants in common, such as real estate, does not automatically transfer at death and thus must be transferred via probate. Although the decedent's interest in jointly owned property (with the right of survivorship) ceases at death, the value of the interest the decedent held in this property is still included in the gross estate.[14]

Example 25-12

Nate and his father jointly own two parcels of real estate not included in the inventory above. One parcel is a vacation home in Colorado. Nate owns this property jointly with Bob and the title is held in joint ownership with the right of survivorship. Will this property be included in Bob's probate estate and/or gross estate?

Answer: The property will *not* be included in Bob's *probate* estate, but it will be included in Bob's *gross* estate. When Bob died, Nate automatically became the sole owner of the property without going through probate. However, the property will be included in Bob's gross estate because it is an automatic transfer that is specifically included in the gross estate by law.

---

[13]§2033. The principle of increasing the gross estate for transfers taking effect at death began with gifts in contemplation of death. So-called deathbed gifts were a device used to avoid the estate tax in the years before enactment of the gift tax.

[14]§2040. There are a number of other transfers that are specifically included in the gross estate. For example, §2036 to §2039 and §2041 address transfers with retained life estates, transfers taking place at death, revocable transfers, annuities, and powers of appointment. A discussion of these provisions is beyond the scope of this text.

> The second parcel is real estate in west Texas that Nate and Bob hold as equal tenants in common. Will it be necessary to use probate to transfer ownership of Bob's share to the beneficiary named in Bob's will?
>
> **Answer:** Yes, ownership must be transferred through probate. The value of Bob's one-half interest in the west Texas real estate is also included in his gross estate.

Another example of an automatic transfer is insurance on the life of the decedent. Proceeds of life insurance paid due to the death of the decedent are specifically included in the gross estate if either of two conditions is met. The proceeds are included in the gross estate if (1) the decedent owned the policy or had "incidents" of ownership such as the right to designate the beneficiary or (2) the decedent's estate or executor is the beneficiary of the insurance policy (that is, the executor must use the insurance proceeds to discharge the obligations of the estate).

Example 25-13

> Bob owned and paid annual premiums on an insurance policy that, on his death, was to pay the beneficiary of his choice $500,000. Bob named Nate the beneficiary, and the insurance company paid Nate $500,000 after receiving notification of Bob's death. Will Bob's gross estate include the value of the insurance proceeds paid to Nate?
>
> **Answer:** Yes. The $500,000 of insurance proceeds is specifically included in Bob's estate despite the fact that it was paid directly to Nate and did not go through probate.
>
> **What if:** Suppose Bob transferred ownership of the policy to Nate four years prior to his death. Nate had the power to designate the beneficiary of the policy, and he also paid the annual premiums. Will Bob's gross estate include the value of the insurance proceeds paid to Nate?
>
> **Answer:** No. Bob had no incidents of ownership at his death (Nate controlled who would be paid the proceeds upon Bob's death), and the proceeds were not paid to his estate.

Jointly owned property.   The proportion of the value of jointly owned property included in the gross estate depends upon the type of ownership. When a decedent's interest is a tenancy in common (there is no right of survivorship), a proportion of the value of the property is included in the gross estate that matches the decedent's ownership interest. For example, consider a decedent who owned a one-third interest in property as a tenant in common. If the entire property is worth $120,000 at the decedent's death, then $40,000 is included in his gross estate.

The amount includable for property held as joint tenancy with the right of survivorship depends upon the marital status of the owners. When property is jointly owned by a husband and wife with the right of survivorship, *half the value* of the property is automatically included in the estate of the first spouse to die.[15] For *unmarried* co-owners, the value included in the decedent's gross estate is determined by the decedent's contribution to the total cost of the property. For example, consider a decedent who provided two-thirds of the total cost of property held as joint tenants with the right of survivorship. If the entire property is worth $240,000 at the decedent's death, then two-thirds ($160,000) is included in his gross estate.

---

[15]In some states joint tenancy with a right of survivorship between spouses is referred to as a tenancy by the entirety.

Example 25-14

Bob and Nate originally purchased the Colorado vacation home seven years ago for $20,000 and held it as joint tenants with the right of survivorship. This property is not included in the list of property in Bob's probate estate because the title passes automatically to Nate upon Bob's death. Bob provided $15,000 of the purchase price, and Nate provided the remaining $5,000. The property was worth $400,000 at Bob's death. How much is included in his gross estate?

Answer: Bob's gross estate includes $300,000. For property held in joint tenancy with the right of survivorship, the amount included in the gross estate is equal to the proportion of the purchase price provided by the decedent. Bob provided 75 percent ($15,000 ÷ $20,000 = 75%). Hence, his gross estate will include $300,000 (75% × $400,000) of the value of the vacation home.

What if: Suppose Bob was married and owned the home with his wife as joint tenants with the right of survivorship. What amount would be included in Bob's gross estate?

Answer: The amount included in the estate is half the value of any property held with the surviving spouse as joint tenants with the right of survivorship, $200,000 in this case.

The west Texas land Bob and Nate owned is valued at $500,200. They owned it as tenants in common, with Bob holding a one-quarter interest and Nate holding the rest. What amount is included in Bob's gross estate?

Answer: The amount included in the estate is $125,050 ($500,200 × 25%), because Bob owned a one-quarter interest in the property.

Exhibit 25-7 summarizes the rules for determining the value of jointly owned property included in a decedent's gross estate.

EXHIBIT 25-7 Amount of Jointly Owned Property Included in Gross Estate

Ownership Form	Marital Status of Co-Owners	Amount in Gross Estate
Community property (discussed above)	Married	Half the fair market value
Joint tenancy with right of survivorship	Married	Half the fair market value
Joint tenancy with right of survivorship	Unmarried	Percentage of fair market value determined by decedent's contribution to total cost of the property
Tenancy in common	Married or unmarried	Percentage of fair market value determined by decedent's interest in the property

Transfers within three years of death. Certain transfers, such as transfers of life insurance policies, made within three years of the decedent's death are also included in the decedent's gross estate, valued as of the time of death. Without this provision, a simple but effective estate tax planning technique would be to transfer ownership in a life insurance policy just prior to the decedent's death. This strategy, called a *deathbed gift*, would reduce the decedent's transfer taxes on the life insurance by the difference between its proceeds from the policy (the value at death) and its value on the date transferred. Only certain transfers are specifically included under this provision, and they are often difficult to identify.

Gift taxes paid on transfers within three years of death. Gift taxes paid on any taxable gifts during the three-year period preceding the donor's death are also included in the decedent's gross estate. This inclusion provision prevents donors from escaping estate tax on the amount of gift taxes paid within three years of death. In other words, the amount of gift taxes paid is included in the estate because it would have been included in the estate had the decedent kept the property until death.

Example 25-15

What if: Suppose Bob owned a life insurance policy and transferred all incidents of ownership in the policy to his son one year before dying from a fatal disease. Also suppose that Bob paid $40,000 of gift taxes on the transfer and the policy paid his son $3 million on Bob's death. What amount would be included in Bob's gross estate?

Answer: $3,040,000. Bob's estate would include proceeds of the policy ($3 million) because Bob transferred the incidents of ownership within three years of his death. The value of the transfer would also include the gift taxes paid ($40,000) when Bob transferred the policy.

Valuation   Property is included in the gross estate at the *fair market value* on the date of the decedent's death. Virtually all the factors (and controversies) regarding valuation that we've already discussed for the gift tax also apply to the valuation of property for estate tax purposes.

Example 25-16

At his death Bob owned an original landscape painting made in the late 1800s by one of his ancestors, Tully Smith. Bob purchased the Smith painting for $25,000 in 1980, and last year an expert estimated it was worth $210,000. Nate now has the painting appraised by another expert, who estimates its value at $250,000 based upon a painting by the same artist that sold at auction last month. What value should be placed on the painting for inclusion in the gross estate?

Answer: Nate should value the painting at $250,000, according to its specific characteristics and attributes (such as age, condition, history, authenticity, and so forth). Of course, the IRS might disagree with this value and seek to value the painting at a higher amount.

> **THE KEY FACTS**
> **Valuation of Assets**
> - Property is included in the estate at its fair market value at the date of the decedent's death.
> - The executor can elect to value the estate on an alternate valuation date, six months after death, if it reduces the gross estate and estate tax.

The executor of an estate, however, can elect—irrevocably—to have all the property in the gross estate valued on an **alternative valuation date.** The alternate date for valuing the estate is six months after the date of death or on the date of sale or distribution of the property (if this occurs before the end of the six-month period). This election is available only if it reduces the value of the gross estate and the combined estate and generation-skipping taxes.[16]

Example 25-17

What if: Bob's shares of FFP are included in his estate at a value of $19.5 million. Suppose the value of the shares plummet to $5 million several months after Bob's death. Further suppose that the drop in value causes the value of Bob's estate to drop from $28 million to $13.5 million. Could Nate, as executor of Bob's estate, opt to value these shares at the lower value for estate tax purposes?

Answer: Yes. Nate could elect to value the shares on the alternate valuation date, six months after Bob's death. However, to qualify for this election, he must value *all* property in the estate on the alternate date. Because the election will reduce the value of the entire gross estate, Nate could elect to use the alternate valuation date.

---

[16]§2032A. An executor can also elect to value certain realty used in farming or in connection with a closely held business at a special use valuation. Special use valuation allows realty to be valued at a current use that does not result in the best or highest fair market value. This election is available when the business is conducted by the decedent's family, constitutes a substantial portion of the gross estate, and the property passes to a qualifying heir of the decedent.

Example 25-18

At the time of his death, Bob owned a reversion in a trust he established for his favorite cousin, Becky. Under the terms of the trust, Becky is entitled to income for her life (a life estate), and Bob (or his heir) is entitled to the reversion. At the time of Bob's death, the trust assets were valued at $100,000, Becky was 35, and the §7520 interest rate was 6 percent. Should this reversion be included in Bob's gross estate and, if so, what value is placed on the future interest?

Answer: Bob's reversion interest is included in his estate because this is a property right he owned at his death. Under Table S in the regulations (Exhibit 25-4), based upon Becky's age and the current interest rate at the time of Bob's death, the percentage of the property that represents the value of Bob's reversion is .11217. Thus, his reversion is valued at $11,217 ($100,000 × .11217).

What if: Suppose the trust was established for George, age 6. Would this influence the value of Bob's reversion interest?

Answer: Yes. Under Table S in the regulations and based upon George's age and the current interest rate, the portion of the property that represents the value of Bob's reversion is .02749. Thus, Bob's reversion is valued at $2,749 ($100,000 × .02749).

Gross Estate Summary So far we've seen that the decedent's gross estate consists of the assets subject to probate as well as certain assets transferred outside probate. These latter assets include property owned by the decedent in joint tenancy with the right of survivorship as well as life insurance. The gross estate also includes certain property transferred by the decedent within three years of death and certain future interests owned by the decedent.

Example 25-19

Given previous examples, what is the value of Bob's gross estate?

Answer: The value of Bob's gross estate is $21,250,717, calculated as follows:

Property	Value	Explanation
Auto	$ 33,000	Example 25-11
Personal effects	48,000	Example 25-11
Smith painting	250,000	Example 25-16
Checking and savings accounts	75,250	Example 25-11
FFP shares	19,500,000	Example 25-11
Residence	400,000	Example 25-11
Other investments	8,200	Example 25-11
Life insurance proceeds	500,000	Example 25-13
Colorado vacation home	300,000	Examples 25-12 and 25-14
West Texas land	125,050	Examples 25-12 and 25-14
Reversion interest in Dina Trust	11,217	Example 25-18
Gross estate	**$21,250,717**	

The Taxable Estate

Referring to the federal estate tax formula in Exhibit 25-6, we calculate the **taxable estate** in two steps. The first consists of subtracting from the gross estate the deductions allowed for administrative expenses, debts of the decedent, and losses incurred during the administration of the estate. These deductions are allowed because Congress intends to tax the amount transferred to beneficiaries. This step results in the **adjusted gross estate.** In the second step, the adjusted gross estate is reduced for transfers to a decedent's spouse (the marital deduction) and to charities (the charitable deduction). These deductions result in the taxable estate. We discuss each type of deduction next.

Administrative Expenses, Debts, Losses, and State Death Taxes   Debts included in or incurred by the estate, such as mortgages and accrued taxes, are deductible. Expenses incurred in administering the estate are also deductible, such as executor fees, attorney fees, and the like. Funeral expenses are deductible if reasonable in amount. Likewise, casualty and theft losses are deductible. These losses must be incurred during the administration of the estate, otherwise any deductions belong to the new owner of the property. Finally, death taxes imposed by the state are also deductible.[17]

Example 25-20

Nate paid $6,685 in funeral expenses for his father's services, and during the administration of his father's estate he paid executor fees of $4,032 and attorney fees of $9,500. In addition, Nate discovered Bob owed debts totaling $100,500. Since Michigan has no state death or inheritance taxes, no amounts were owed to the state. What is Bob's adjusted gross estate (gross estate minus expenses and debts)?

Answer: Bob's adjusted gross estate is $21,130,000, calculated as follows:

Gross estate (from Example 25-19)		$21,250,717
Funeral expenses	$ 6,685	
Executor fees and expenses	4,032	
Attorney fees	9,500	
Debts of the decedent	100,500	
Total expenses and debts		−120,717
Adjusted gross estate		**$21,130,000**

The estate may collect income earned during its administration and, therefore, the estate will need to file an estate *income* tax return. The executor has the option of deducting administration expenses (but not funeral expenses) on the estate tax return or on the estate's *income* tax return. While no double deduction is available, the choice is relatively simple. If the estate owes no estate taxes, then the executor should claim the deduction on the estate income tax return. If the estate owes estate taxes, the marginal estate tax rate is likely to be higher than the marginal income tax rate. Hence, it should probably claim the deduction on the estate tax return.

What if: Suppose that during the administration of Bob's estate a storm damaged the Colorado vacation home. Bob's share of the casualty loss to the home was $25,000. Would this be deductible in calculating Bob's taxable estate?

Answer: Yes, the executor can deduct this loss on the estate tax return. Note that personal (nonbusiness) casualty and theft losses are not deductible on income tax returns.

Marital and Charitable Deductions   To avoid taxing a married couple's estate twice, Congress provides a deduction for bequests to a surviving spouse. To qualify for the marital deduction, the transferred property must be included in the estate of the

---

[17]§2053, §2054, and §2058 address expenses, losses, and state death taxes, respectively.

deceased spouse. That is, the surviving spouse must receive the property from the decedent and control its ultimate disposition. For example, property that passes to the surviving spouse as a result of joint tenancy with the right of survivorship qualifies for the marital deduction, as would a direct bequest from the decedent. In contrast, transfers of property rights that are terminable do not generally qualify for the estate marital deduction (as discussed earlier, terminable interests are treated similarly for gift tax purposes). For example, suppose the decedent bequeaths the surviving spouse the right to occupy the decedent's residence until such time as the spouse remarries. The value of the right to possess the residence is a terminable interest and is not eligible for the marital deduction.[18] In general, the estate tax marital deduction is unlimited in amount. Hence, no tax would be imposed on a decedent who leaves her entire estate to a spouse.[19]

Charitable contributions of property are also deductible without any limitation. Charities are defined to include the usual public organizations (corporations organized exclusively for religious, charitable, scientific, literary, or educational purposes) but exclude certain nonprofit cemetery organizations. Interestingly, foreign charities qualify for the charitable deduction under the estate and gift tax but not under the income tax. No deduction is allowed unless the charitable bequest is specified under the last will and testament or is a transfer of property by the decedent before his death that is subsequently included in the decedent's estate. The amount of any bequest must be mandatory, although another person such as the executor can be given discretion to identify the charitable organization.

Example 25-21

Not long after Bob's death, Nate gathered the Smith family for a reading of Bob's will. The will was relatively simple because Bob was unmarried at the time of his death. Bob had an adjusted gross estate of $21,130,000 and left all his property to Nate, with two exceptions. Bob bequeathed his reversion interest in the Trust (value of $11,217) to Becky, and he bequeathed the Smith painting (value of $250,000) to the Midwest Museum in Ann Arbor (a qualified charity). Are either of these bequests deductible in calculating Bob's taxable estate? What is Bob's taxable estate?

Answer: The bequest to the museum qualifies for the charitable deduction because the museum is a qualified charity. Since Bob was unmarried at his death, none of the bequests qualifies for the marital deduction. Bob's taxable estate is $20,880,000, calculated as follows:

Adjusted gross estate	$21,130,000
Charitable deduction	−250,000
Taxable estate	**$20,880,000**

What if: Suppose Bob was married at the time of his death and left a portion of his FFP stock, valued at $4.5 million, to his surviving spouse. What amount of this transfer, if any, would qualify for the marital deduction?

Answer: Bob's estate would be entitled to a marital deduction of $4.5 million, the value of the entire spousal bequest. In the extreme, if Bob had left *all his property* to his spouse, his taxable estate would be reduced to zero.

[18]The restriction on the estate tax deduction for terminable interests is drafted consistent with the gift tax deduction. As noted previously, *Qualified terminable interest properties* (QTIPs for short) are an exception to the nondeductibility of terminable interest property. To qualify, the executor must agree to have qualifying terminable interests included in the estate of the surviving spouse. A detailed discussion of this exception is beyond the scope of this text.

[19]There are other credits that could also apply, but these are beyond the scope of this text. The credit for taxes on prior transfer is designed to adjust the tax for property that was subjected to estate tax within the last 10 years. There is also a credit for pre-1977 gift taxes paid on certain pre-1977 gifts that must be included in the gross estate. Both of these credits are equitable adjustments for potential multiple transfer taxes associated with sequential deaths and multiple inclusions, respectively. Prior to 2005, there was a credit for state death taxes.

Computation of the Estate Tax

Three additional steps are necessary to calculate the estate tax liability from the taxable estate. First, the taxable estate is increased by **adjusted taxable gifts** to compute cumulative lifetime transfers (the estate tax base). Next, the tax on cumulative lifetime transfers is computed and reduced by the tax payable on adjusted taxable gifts (computed using the current tax rates). This tentative tax is reduced by the applicable credit.

In contrast to the gift tax formula, the estate tax formula allows a reduction only for taxes payable on adjusted taxable gifts. Taxes payable are a hypothetical amount computed using the past amount of applicable credit but the current tax rate schedule. Another difference with the gift tax formula is that the entire applicable credit (not just the unused portion) reduces the tentative tax (because all prior transfers are included in the tax base). These differences are illustrated below.

Adjusted Taxable Gifts   Adjusted taxable gifts are taxable gifts other than transfers already included in the gross estate. For example, the value of life insurance transferred within three years of death would not be included in adjusted taxable gifts but the value of the life insurance proceeds paid at death would be included in the estate. The objective of adding previously taxed transfers to the taxable estate is to allow the estate tax base to reflect all transfers, both inter vivos and testamentary.

Despite increasing cumulative transfers, adjusted taxable gifts are not subject to double tax because the tentative tax on cumulative transfers is reduced by a credit for the taxes payable on adjusted taxable gifts calculated under the current tax rate schedule. It is important to note that although adjusted taxable gifts were made in prior years, all tax calculations are made using the *current* rate schedule.

Example 25-22

After reviewing all Bob's records, Nate determined that Bob's only taxable gift was his gift of FFP stock in 2009. This transfer resulted in a taxable gift of $1 million, the tax on which was entirely offset by the applicable credit. What is the amount of cumulative transfers subject to estate tax, and what is Bob's tentative estate tax?

Answer: Bob's estate includes $21,880,000 of cumulative taxable transfers and Bob's gross estate tax is $8,697,800, calculated as follows:

Adjusted taxable gifts	$ 1,000,000	Prior gift
Taxable estate	20,880,000	Taxable transfers in estate
Cumulative taxable transfers	**$21,880,000**	Total taxable transfers
Tentative tax	**$ 8,697,800**	Tax prior to credits

What if: Suppose Bob had not made any taxable gifts prior to his death. Would this fact reduce his tentative tax?

Answer: Without the gift of stock Bob's tentative tax would be $8,297,800, calculated as follows:

Adjusted taxable gifts	$ 0
Taxable estate	20,880,000
Cumulative taxable transfers	$20,880,000
Tentative tax	**$ 8,297,800**

Note that Bob's tentative tax has decreased by $400,000. This is the amount of tax on the $1 million 2009 gift at the top marginal rate (40%).

What if: Suppose that Bob's 2009 taxable gift was $4 million and the gift tax exemption equivalent in 2009 was $1 million. What is the amount of the reduction of taxes payable on adjusted taxable gifts?

(continued on page 25-26)

Answer: $1.2 million. The adjusted taxable gift of $4 million would result in a tax of $1,545,800 under the current rate schedule. However, because the transfer was made in 2009, the tax would be reduced by $345,800. This is the amount of the applicable credit for an exemption equivalent of $1 million calculated using the current tax rate schedule. The calculation would be made as follows:

Current tax on adjusted taxable gifts	$1,545,800
Applicable credit ($1 million at current tax rate)	−345,800
Current taxes payable on adjusted taxable gifts	**$1,200,000**

Note that the credit is 40 percent of the gift in excess of the exemption equivalent ($4,000,000 − $1,000,000 = $3,000,000). The $4 million prior taxable transfer is included in the calculation of Bob's cumulative taxable transfers and the tentative estate tax is calculated as before.

Adjusted taxable gifts	$ 4,000,000
Taxable estate	20,880,000
Cumulative taxable transfers	$14,880,000
Tax on cumulative transfers	$9,897,800
Taxes payable on adjusted taxable gifts	−1,200,000
Tentative estate tax	$8,697,800

Hence, the adjusted taxable gift increases the amount of Bob's estate subject to the top estate tax rate. Adjusted taxable gifts are not subject to an additional transfer tax at the time of Bob's death for two reasons. First, the tax payable on adjusted taxable gifts is deducted when computing the tentative tax. Second, the estate tax on the $1 million of adjusted taxable gifts that is not offset by the taxes payable will be offset by the applicable credit when computing the gross estate tax.

Applicable Credit   Besides subtracting the credit for tax on adjusted taxable gifts, we reduce the gross estate tax by several other credits.[20] The most important is the applicable credit, because it eliminates the estate tax on cumulative transfers up to the exemption equivalent (currently $11.18 million). Hence, estate taxes are imposed only on relatively large estates. The objective of the applicable credit is to prevent the application of transfer tax to taxpayers who either would not accumulate a relatively large amount of property transfers during their lifetime and/or would not have a relatively large value of assets to pass to heirs upon their death.

The applicable credit for a surviving spouse is increased by the amount of the **deceased spousal unused exclusion (DSUE).** For example, in 2018 a spouse whose spouse died without using any applicable credit would be entitled to an exemption equivalent of $22.36 million.

Besides eliminating transfer taxes for relatively small cumulative transfers, the exemption equivalent also acts as the transfer requirement for filing an estate return. That is, an estate tax return (Form 706) must be filed if the gross estate plus adjusted taxable gifts equals or exceeds the exemption equivalent. Exhibit 25-8 presents the first page of 2018 Form 706 for Bob Smith. The deadline for the estate tax return is nine months after the decedent's death.[21]

---

[20]Other transfers that are required to be included in the gross estate are described in §2035(a). A discussion of these transfers is beyond the scope of this text.

[21]There is an automatic six-month extension to file the estate tax return. However, an estimate of the tax due must be paid on the due date of the return.

Example 25-23

Bob died on February 7 of this year. What amount of estate tax must be paid on his estate, given his prior taxable gift of $1 million? What is the due date for Bob's estate tax return?

Answer: Estate tax of $4,280,000 is due after applying the applicable credit, computed as follows:

Tentative tax (from Example 25-22)	$ 8,697,800
Less: Applicable credit	4,417,800
Estate tax due	**$4,280,000**

Bob's executor must file the estate tax return (Form 706 in Exhibit 25-8) or request an extension of time within nine months of Bob's death (by November 7 of this year).

What if: Suppose Bob did not make any taxable gifts during his life. What amount of estate tax would be owed upon his death?

Answer: Bob's estate would owe $3,880,000, computed as follows:

Tentative tax	$ 8,297,800
Less: Applicable credit	4,417,800
Estate tax due	**$3,880,000**

In this case, the absence of gifts prior to Bob's death (no adjusted taxable gifts) would result in a $400,000 savings. The reason is that over his lifetime Bob made fewer taxable transfers ($1 million in fact).

What if: Suppose Bob's 2009 taxable gift was $4 million (instead of $1 million) and the gift tax exemption equivalent in 2009 was $1 million. What amount of estate tax would be owed upon Bob's death?

Answer: Bob's estate would owe $4,280,000, computed as follows:

Tentative tax	$ 8,697,800
Less: Applicable credit	4,417,800
Estate tax due	**$4,280,000**

Bob's estate tax is not increased by the amount of the adjusted taxable gifts in excess of $1 million because these gifts were taxed in 2009. The taxes payable on adjusted taxable gifts eliminates the potential for double taxation. The portion of the 2009 gift that was not taxed in 2009 (recall that $1 million was offset by the applicable credit) is now subject to tax, however.

What if: Suppose Bob was predeceased by his wife who left all her possessions to him and, consequently, did not claim an exemption equivalent. What amount of estate tax would be owed upon his death?

Answer: Zero. Assuming the executor of Bob's wife filed an estate tax return electing the DSUE, Bob's estate would be entitled to claim an applicable credit based on his deceased spouse's unused exclusion. Bob's estate tax would be computed as follows:

Tentative tax	$8,697,800
Less: applicable credit	8,889,800
Estate tax due	**$ 0**

The applicable credit is the amount of tax on $22.36 million ($11.18 million times 2). The applicable credit is calculated using the tax rate schedule, which results in a credit of $8,889,800.

EXHIBIT 25-8 Page 1 of Form 706 Estate Tax Return for Bob Smith

Form **706**
(Rev. August 2013)

Department of the Treasury
Internal Revenue Service

United States Estate (and Generation-Skipping Transfer) Tax Return

▶ Estate of a citizen or resident of the United States (see instructions). To be filed for decedents dying after December 31, 2012.
▶ Information about Form 706 and its separate instructions is at *www.irs.gov/form706.*

OMB No. 1545-0015

Part 1—Decedent and Executor

1a Decedent's first name and middle initial (and maiden name, if any) **BOB**	**1b** Decedent's last name **SMITH**	**2** Decedent's social security no. 000 00 0000

3a City, town, or post office; county; state or province; country; and ZIP or foreign postal code.

ANN ARBOR, WASHTENAW COUNTY MICHIGAN 48109

3b Year domicile established **1990**   **4** Date of birth **1940**   **5** Date of death **2018**

6b Executor's address (number and street including apartment or suite no.; city, town, or post office; state or province; country; and ZIP or foreign postal code) and phone no.

6a Name of executor (see instructions)
NATE SMITH

6c Executor's social security number (see instructions)
000 00 0000

6500 TRAIL RD, ANN ARBOR, MICHIGAN 48109

Phone no. **(000) 000-0000**

6d If there are multiple executors, check here ☐ and attach a list showing the names, addresses, telephone numbers, and SSNs of the additional executors.

7a Name and location of court where will was probated or estate administered
WASHTENAW COUNTY PROBATE COURT

7b Case number **00-12345**

8 If decedent died testate, check here ▶ ☑ and attach a certified copy of the will.   **9** If you extended the time to file this Form 706, check here ▶ ☐

10 If Schedule R-1 is attached, check here ▶ ☐   **11** If you are estimating the value of assets included in the gross estate on line 1 pursuant to the special rule of Reg. section 20.2010-2T(a) (7)(ii), check here ▶ ☐

Part 2—Tax Computation

1	Total gross estate less exclusion (from Part 5—Recapitulation, item 13)	**1**	21,250,717
2	Tentative total allowable deductions (from Part 5—Recapitulation, item 24)	**2**	370,717
3a	Tentative taxable estate (subtract line 2 from line 1)	**3a**	20,880,000
b	State death tax deduction	**3b**	0
c	Taxable estate (subtract line 3b from line 3a)	**3c**	20,880,000
4	Adjusted taxable gifts (see instructions)	**4**	1,000,000
5	Add lines 3c and 4	**5**	21,880,000
6	Tentative tax on the amount on line 5 from Table A in the instructions	**6**	8,697,800
7	Total gift tax paid or payable (see instructions)	**7**	0
8	Gross estate tax (subtract line 7 from line 6)	**8**	8,697,800

9a	Basic exclusion amount	**9a** 11,180,000	
9b	Deceased spousal unused exclusion (DSUE) amount from predeceased spouse(s), if any (from Section D, Part 6—Portability of Deceased Spousal Unused Exclusion).	**9b** 0	
9c	Applicable exclusion amount (add lines 9a and 9b)	**9c** 11,180,000	
9d	Applicable credit amount (tentative tax on the amount in 9c from Table A in the instructions)	**9d** 4,417,800	
10	Adjustment to applicable credit amount (May not exceed $6,000. See instructions.)	**10** 0	

11	Allowable applicable credit amount (subtract line 10 from line 9d)	**11**	4,417,800
12	Subtract line 11 from line 8 (but do not enter less than zero)	**12**	4,280,000
13	Credit for foreign death taxes (from Schedule P). (Attach Form(s) 706-CE.) **13**		
14	Credit for tax on prior transfers (from Schedule Q) **14**		
15	Total credits (add lines 13 and 14)	**15**	0
16	Net estate tax (subtract line 15 from line 12)	**16**	4,280,000
17	Generation-skipping transfer (GST) taxes payable (from Schedule R, Part 2, line 10)	**17**	
18	Total transfer taxes (add lines 16 and 17)	**18**	4,280,000
19	Prior payments (explain in an attached statement)	**19**	
20	Balance due (or overpayment) (subtract line 19 from line 18)	**20**	4,280,000

Under penalties of perjury, I declare that I have examined this return, including accompanying schedules and statements, and to the best of my knowledge and belief, it is true, correct, and complete. Declaration of preparer other than the executor is based on all information of which preparer has any knowledge.

Sign Here

▶ _____ Signature of executor   ▶ _____ Date

▶ _____ Signature of executor   ▶ _____ Date

Paid Preparer Use Only

Print/Type preparer's name	Preparer's signature	Date	Check ☐ if self-employed	PTIN
Firm's name ▶			Firm's EIN ▶	
Firm's address ▶			Phone no.	

For Privacy Act and Paperwork Reduction Act Notice, see instructions.   Cat. No. 20548R   Form **706** (Rev. 8-2013)

Source: Form 706

WEALTH PLANNING CONCEPTS

Wealth planning coordinates both income and transfer tax strategies with nontax objectives. Before we explore transfer tax strategies, recall the third transfer tax, the generation-skipping tax, and the potential for income taxation of fiduciary entities such as estates and trusts. While these topics are certainly important, we note them only in passing because their complexity is beyond the scope of this text.

The Generation-Skipping Tax

The **generation-skipping tax (GST)** is a supplemental tax designed to prevent the avoidance of transfer taxes (both estate and gift tax) through transfers that skip a generation of recipients. For example, a grandparent could give a life estate in property to a child, with the remainder to a grandchild. When the child dies and the grandchild inherits the property, no transfer tax is imposed because nothing remains in the child's estate (the life estate terminates at death). In this way, the grandparent pays one transfer tax (on the initial gift) to transfer the property down two generations.

The GST is triggered by the transfer of property to someone more than one generation younger than the donor or decedent—a grandchild rather than a child. A transfer to a grandchild is not subject to GST, however, if the grandchild's parents are dead. The GST is very complex and can be triggered directly by transfers or indirectly by a termination of an interest. Fortunately, the GST is not widely applicable because it does not generally apply to transfers that qualify for an annual gift tax exclusion, and each donor/decedent is entitled to a relatively generous aggregate exemption ($11.18 million in 2018).

Income Tax Considerations

A **fiduciary** entity is a legal entity that takes possession of property for the benefit of a person. An **estate** is a legal entity that comes into existence upon a person's death to transfer the decedent's real and personal property. Likewise, a *trust* is also a legal entity whose purpose is to hold and administer the corpus for other persons (*beneficiaries*). While an estate exists only temporarily (until the assets of the decedent are distributed), a trust may have a prolonged or even indefinite existence. Because these entities can exist for many years, special rules govern the taxation of income realized on property they hold. These rules are complex and relate to how fiduciaries account for income under state law. A detailed discussion is beyond the scope of this text, but we provide an overview below.

The trust or testamentary instrument (or, in the absence of an instrument, state law) determines how income and expenses are allocated between beneficiaries—under fiduciary accounting rules income belongs to income beneficiaries and corpus (principal) belongs to the remainderman. For example, an instrument may allocate gains on the sale of assets to corpus and rental receipts to trust accounting income. Likewise, depreciation expense may be allocated to accounting income whereas repairs may be allocated to corpus. Accounting income is important because it determines how much income can be (or must be) distributed. Trusts and estates may have discretion whether to accumulate income within the entity (for future distribution) or make current distributions.[22] Income retained by the entity is taxed as income to the entity, and consequently, the trust or estate must file an income tax return. In contrast, income distributed currently by the

---

[22]Regulations under §§651–652 make a distinction between simple trusts and complex trusts. **Simple trusts** must distribute all trust accounting income currently (and cannot make charitable contributions) whereas **complex trusts** are not required by the trust instrument to distribute income currently.

entity is taxed as income to the beneficiary. To accomplish this flow-through of income, trusts and estates are granted an income tax deduction for current distributions of income and this deduction depends, in part, on accounting income.

To better understand how taxable income is divided between a trust or estate and its beneficiaries, it is helpful to first summarize the formula for determining taxable income.[23] With few exceptions, the formula for calculating taxable income for a trust or an estate is analogous to the individual income tax formula. Gross income for the entity is determined in the same manner as gross income for an individual. For example, trusts are generally taxed on realized income, but they can exclude certain items from gross income, such as municipal interest, and make elections to defer certain items, such as installment gains.

Trusts and estates can also deduct expenses similar to an individual. For example, trade or business expenses, interest, taxes, and charitable contributions. Lastly, trusts and estates are allowed a deduction for distributions of income to beneficiaries. It is this **distribution deduction** that operates to eliminate the potential for double taxation of income.

The maximum amount of the distribution deduction is the lesser of the amount actually distributed or distributable net income (DNI). DNI is calculated by adjusting taxable income before the distribution deduction for certain items of income and deduction. The calculation of DNI, and consequently taxable income, can be complicated by items such as net operating losses, net capital losses, charitable contributions, multiple beneficiaries, and discretionary (versus mandatory) distributions. Suffice it to say that the calculation of income tax for a trust or estate can be a very complicated matter.

While granting a trust or estate discretion over distributions complicates the calculation of taxable income, it might appear that this discretion also provides an opportunity to split income (by creating yet another taxpayer). However, the income tax rates applying to trusts and estates are generally as high as or higher than the tax rates for individual beneficiaries. Hence, the potential income tax benefits from splitting income between these entities and beneficiaries are typically negligible.

Transfer Tax Planning Techniques

Transfer tax planning strategies are the same as those employed for income tax planning: timing, shifting, and conversion. Like income tax planning, wealth planning is primarily concerned with accomplishing the client's goals in the most efficient and effective manner after considering *both* tax and nontax costs. For the most part, wealth planning is directed to maximizing after-tax wealth to be transferred from an older generation to a younger generation. A critical constraint in this process, however, is determining how tax strategies can achieve the client's ultimate (nontax) goals. Before attempting to integrate tax and nontax considerations, let's survey a few basic techniques for transfer tax planning.

Serial Gifts   A **serial gift** strategy converts a large taxable transfer into a tax-exempt transfer by dividing it into multiple lifetime gifts. As long as the gifts qualify as present interests and do not exceed the annual exclusion, the transfers are exempt from all transfer taxes. Although serial gifts are an easy and low-cost planning strategy, this technique is limited in scope because only $15,000 ($30,000 for married donors electing gift splitting) can be transferred each year tax-free to any specific donee. Hence, serial gifts can move significant amounts of wealth only if employed by multiple donors over multiple years and multiple donees.

THE KEY FACTS

Basic Wealth Planning Techniques

- A serial gift strategy saves gift taxes by converting a potentially large taxable transfer into multiple smaller transfers that qualify for the annual exclusion.
- Bypass provisions in a will or bypass trusts reduce estate taxes by using the applicable credit of the deceased spouse, transferring some property to beneficiaries other than the surviving spouse.
- Testamentary transfers allow a step-up in tax basis to fair market value, thereby eliminating income tax on unrealized appreciation.
- Lifetime gifts eliminate transfer taxes on post-gift appreciation.

---

[23]Subchapter J (§§641–692) contains the provisions governing income taxation of trusts and estates.

Example 25-24

Suppose Harry and Wilma decide to begin transferring wealth to Dina and George. To what extent can serial gifts accomplish this goal without triggering gift taxes?

Answer: Harry and Wilma could make annual gifts of $15,000 each to Dina and George. These gifts would remove $60,000 per year from the Smiths' estate without triggering any transfer taxes (gift tax or generation-skipping tax). They could include any type of property as long as Dina and George can presently enjoy the property or income generated by it.

The Step-Up in Tax Basis   Timing is an important component in tax planning. Generally, a good tax strategy delays payment of tax, thereby reducing the present value of the tax paid. While deferral is important, transfer tax planning must also consider the potential appreciation of assets transferred, and the effect of the income tax that could apply if and when the appreciation is realized. Gifted property generally retains the donor's basis in the property, meaning the donee takes a **carryover basis,** whereas inherited property takes a tax basis of fair market value. The advantage of gifting property is that the donor eliminates the transfer tax on any additional future appreciation on the gifted property. The disadvantage is that the unrealized appreciation of the gifted property will eventually be taxed (although at the donee's income tax rate). Thus, gifting appreciating property reduces future transfer taxes but at the cost of additional future income taxes imposed on the donee. In contrast, for inherited property, past appreciation (up to the date of death) will never be subject to income tax but instead is subject to transfer tax at the time of the transfer.

Example 25-25

What if: Suppose Harry currently owns 30 percent of the outstanding shares of FFP. These shares have a basis of $300,000 but are worth in excess of $2.7 million. Suppose Harry intends to transfer his FFP shares to his daughter Dina who, in turn, intends to sell them after Harry's death. It is important to consider the extent to which income tax considerations influence whether Harry gifts these shares or holds them until his death.

Estimate the total tax savings if Harry delays the transfer of the shares until his death three years hence. Assume the transfer (whether by gift or inheritance) will be taxed at the top transfer rate of 40 percent, while when Dina sells the shares in three years the gain will be taxed at a capital gains tax rate of 20 percent (ignoring the net investment income tax). Also assume the FFP shares will not appreciate and the prevailing interest rate is 6 percent.

Answer: The total tax savings is $686,280 if Harry delays the transfer until his death rather than gifting the shares to Dina immediately. See the following discussion and computations:

	Gift	Inheritance	Explanation
Gift tax paid	$1,080,000		40% times $2.7 million
Time value of gift tax	× 1.191		$(1.06)^3$
Future value of gift tax	$1,286,280		Value of gift tax paid
Estate tax paid		$1,080,000	40% times $2.7 million
Dina's capital gain tax 20%	$ 480,000	0	Gain of $2.4 million on gift due to carryover basis
Total taxes paid	$1,766,280	$1,080,000	$686,280 of tax savings

If a sale is planned, then the step-up in tax basis becomes critical to avoid being taxed on the accumulated appreciation. In this scenario, a testamentary transfer provides a step-up in tax basis and delays payment of the transfer tax for three years.

(continued on page 25-32)

What if: Suppose Dina has no interest in selling the family business and intends to eventually transfer the shares to George. Moreover, suppose Harry believes the FFP shares will appreciate to $3.5 million within three years. To what extent should income tax considerations influence whether Harry transfers these shares immediately via gift or in three years via testamentary transfer? Estimate the total tax savings if Harry transfers the shares immediately rather than delaying the transfer until his death.

Answer: The tax savings is $113,720 if Harry transfers property immediately rather than delaying the transfer until his death. See the following discussion and computations:

	Gift	Inheritance	Explanation
Gift tax paid	$1,080,000		40% times $2.7 million
Time value of gift tax	× 1.191		$(1.06)^3$
Future value of gift tax	$1,286,280		Value of gift tax paid
Estate tax paid		$1,400,000	40% times $3.5 million
Total taxes paid	$1,286,280	$1,400,000	$113,720 of tax savings

If Dina plans to hold the shares indefinitely and the property is rapidly appreciating, then an *inter vivos* gift avoids having future appreciation taxed in Harry's estate. Although a gift of the shares would accelerate the imposition of transfer taxes, any unused applicable credit could minimize the amount of taxes due on the transfer. In this scenario, an *inter vivos* transfer reduces total transfer taxes even though the gift tax is paid three years before an estate tax would be due.

Timing becomes critical in determining how to trade off income tax savings (the step-up in tax basis) against transfer tax costs (paying gift tax now or paying estate taxes on additional appreciation later). Most tax advisers will suggest that elderly clients sell business assets or investments with unrealized losses, because upon death the basis of these assets will be adjusted downward to fair market value. In other words, the adjustment to basis can be a step-down as well as a step-up, and a sale prevents the elimination of the loss deduction.

Integrated Wealth Plans

A client can have many nontax goals associated with the ultimate disposition of wealth, and some are very personal. It is often difficult to ascertain and prioritize them for planning purposes. However, an effective wealth plan must identify and integrate these personal objectives with tax costs. Often, the primary nontax objective of wealth planning is to preserve value during the transfer of control (management) of business assets. Thus, an essential nontax element of any effective wealth plan is to identify a safe mechanism to support the older generation in a specific lifestyle while transferring control to the younger generation.

Trusts are common vehicles for tax planning, in large part because these entities can be structured to achieve a great variety of tax and nontax objectives, including the support of specific beneficiaries.[24] The trustee is responsible for managing property in the trust, but the grantor also gives the trustee discretionary powers to provide flexibility. These powers can include the discretion to distribute income or corpus among beneficiaries. In addition, grantors can retain powers, including the ability to revoke the trust, select the trustee (original or successor), terminate beneficial interests, and add to the corpus. The most important aspect of an irrevocable trust is that the provisions (including

---

[24]Trusts are also popular because the trust property transfers outside probate, thereby avoiding both the costs and the publicity associated with probate.

powers and guidelines for the exercise of discretionary powers) cannot be changed once the trust instrument has been executed.

Specific types of trusts are common to many wealth transfer plans. For example, a **life insurance trust** is funded with an irrevocable transfer of a life insurance policy, and the trustee is given the power to name beneficiaries and redesignate them in case of divorce or death. Upon the death of the grantor, the amount of the policy is paid into the trust but not included in the grantor's estate. Moreover, an immediate cash distribution from the trust is not taxable income to the beneficiaries.

Example 25-26

Harry is planning to purchase a $2 million life insurance policy. He wants to use the proceeds to support Wilma after his death and have any remaining funds paid to his surviving children. How would Harry structure a trust to accomplish these goals?

Answer: Harry should transfer the policy to an irrevocable trust that directs the trustee to hold the policy and pay the premiums until Harry's death. At that time, the trustee should be directed to invest the $2 million proceeds and pay income to Wilma for the remainder of her life or until she remarries. At Wilma's death or remarriage, the trust terminates and pays the remaining funds to Harry's surviving children or their estates.

What if: Suppose Harry transfers the policy to an irrevocable trust and dies four years later. Will the use of this trust trigger any estate taxes at that time?

Answer: Harry's transfer of the policy to the trust will be a taxable gift at the time of the transfer to the extent of the value of the transfer. However, the $2 million proceeds from the policy will not be included in Harry's estate upon his death.

Donors often use partnerships to transfer assets and for the control of a business in a systematic manner that also provides them with income and security. One specific form of partnership, the **family limited partnership,** divides a family business into various ownership interests, representing control of operations and future income and appreciation of the assets. Prior to restrictions enacted by Congress, these limited partnerships were sometimes used to transfer appreciation to members of a younger generation while allowing the older generation to effectively retain control of the business. Obviously, the intent of estate and gift taxes is to recognize transfers of assets that also represent control of the assets. Hence, it is not surprising that Congress revised the law to restrict the ability of family limited partnerships to effectively transfer appreciation in business assets and operations to younger generations without also transferring control.

CONCLUSION

In this chapter we learned to identify taxable transfers whether made at death (testamentary transfers) or during life (inter vivos transfers). We also learned how to calculate gift and estate taxes and introduced some fundamental transfer tax planning techniques. The simplest and most effective wealth planning technique is serial gifting. As long as the gifts are restricted to present interests under the annual exclusion, serial gifting avoids all transfer taxes. Other methods, such as family limited partnerships, can also be effective under the proper circumstances. In all cases, however, wealth planning should be carefully coordinated with other needs and objectives.

Summary

LO 25-1 Describe the three federal transfer taxes.

- Congress imposes a tax on transfers of property whether the transfer is a gift or occurs at death.
- The unified transfer tax scheme provides for a progressive tax rate schedule that applies to cumulative transfers. That is, transfers in all prior periods are taken into account when calculating the tax for a transfer in a current period.
- The applicable (unified) credit offsets transfer tax on cumulative lifetime transfers (the exemption equivalent) of $11.18 million for gifts and transfers at death.
- Each transfer tax shares two common deductions, an unlimited deduction for charitable contributions and a marital deduction that allows almost unfettered transfers between spouses.
- Property transfers are valued at fair market value defined as the value paid by a willing buyer to a willing seller. The determination of fair market value often depends upon the facts and circumstances surrounding the property.

LO 25-2 Calculate the federal gift tax.

- Lifetime transfers of property for no (or inadequate) consideration are taxed as gifts if the transfer is complete and irrevocable.
- Contributions to political parties or candidates, and medical and educational expenses paid on behalf of an unrelated individual, are excluded from gift taxation.
- Gifts are taxed at the fair market value of the donated property on the date the gift becomes complete, and small gifts are reduced by the annual exclusion ($15,000) if they are present interests.
- With gift-splitting, married couples can elect to treat all gifts made in a year as if each spouse made one-half of each gift.
- Taxable gifts are calculated by adjusting current gifts for exclusions and gift-splitting, and then deducting the marital deduction (for qualifying gifts to a spouse) and the charitable deduction.
- Transfers of terminable interests in property, such as a life estate, will not generally qualify for the marital deduction.
- The gift tax on cumulative taxable gifts is computed by adding prior taxable gifts to current taxable gifts.
- Reduce the gift tax on cumulative gifts by the gift tax on prior taxable gifts calculated using the current rate schedule and ignoring any exemption equivalent used in prior years. Then reduce the gift tax by the *unused* portion of the exemption equivalent as converted into the applicable credit using the current tax rate schedule.

LO 25-3 Compute the federal estate tax on transfers at death.

- The gross estate includes property owned by the decedent at death (the probate estate) and certain property transfers taking effect at death.
- Property the decedent owned jointly is included in the gross estate. The value of the decedent's interest is included when property is held in joint tenancy, whereas half the value of the property is included when held with a spouse in joint tenancy with the right of survivorship.
- Temporal interests begin or end with the passage of time. The value of a future interest, such as a remainder, can be determined from IRS tables, and the value of a present interest, such as a life estate, is calculated as the difference between the value of the future interest and the current value of the property.
- The gross estate is reduced by administrative expenses, debts of the decedent, and losses incurred during the administration of the estate, resulting in the adjusted gross estate.
- The adjusted gross estate is reduced for certain transfers to a surviving spouse (the marital deduction) and for transfers to charities (the charitable deduction), resulting in the taxable estate.

- The taxable estate is increased by adjusted taxable gifts to determine cumulative transfers.
- The tentative estate tax is calculated on cumulative transfers as reduced by the tax payable on adjusted taxable gifts calculated using the current rate schedule.
- The estate tax due is the tentative tax reduced by the full applicable credit.
- An estate is allowed to increase the exemption equivalent by the amount of a deceased spouse unused exclusion (DSUE).

Understand how income and transfer taxation interact to affect wealth planning.

LO 25-4

- The generation-skipping tax is a supplemental tax designed to prevent the avoidance of transfer taxes (both estate and gift tax) through transfers that skip a generation of recipients.
- Trusts and estates are taxpayers taxed on accumulated (undistributed) income via a fiduciary income tax return.
- Because trust and estate income tax rates are generally as high as or higher than the tax rates for individual beneficiaries, the income tax benefits from splitting income between these entities and beneficiaries are typically negligible.
- A serial gift strategy saves gift taxes by converting a potentially large taxable transfer into a tax-exempt transfer of multiple smaller gifts that qualify for the annual exclusion of the donor.
- Testamentary transfers allow a step-up in tax basis to fair market value, thereby eliminating the income tax on unrealized appreciation. In contrast, appreciation of property transferred via inter vivos transfers may be eventually realized and taxed as income. However, a gift eliminates transfer taxes on expected future appreciation.

KEY TERMS

adequate consideration (25-6)
adjusted gross estate (25-22)
adjusted taxable gifts (25-25)
alternative valuation date (25-21)
annual exclusion (25-8)
applicable credit (25-2)
beneficiary (25-7)
carryover basis (25-31)
common-law states (25-10)
community-property states (25-10)
complex trust (25-29)
corpus (25-7)
current gifts (25-9)
deceased spousal unused exclusion (DSUE) (25-26)
distributable net income (DNI) (25-30)
distribution deduction (25-30)
donee (25-5)

donor (25-5)
estate (25-29)
executor (25-17)
exemption equivalent (25-3)
family limited partnership (25-33)
fiduciary (25-29)
fiduciary duty (25-7)
future interest (25-6)
generation-skipping tax (GST) (25-29)
grantor (25-7)
gross estate (25-17)
heirs (25-17)
inter vivos transfers (25-2)
joint tenancy (25-6)
joint tenancy with right of survivorship (25-6)
last will and testament (25-2)
life estate (25-7)

life insurance trust (25-33)
marital deduction (25-4)
nondeductible terminable interests (25-11)
present interest (25-6)
probate (25-17)
probate estate (25-17)
remainder (25-7)
remainderman (25-7)
reversion (25-7)
serial gift (25-30)
simple trust (25-29)
taxable estate (25-22)
taxable gifts (25-9)
tenancy in common (25-6)
terminable interest (25-7)
testamentary transfers (25-2)
trust (25-7)
trustee (25-7)

DISCUSSION QUESTIONS

Discussion Questions are available in Connect®.

McGraw Hill Education **connect**

1. Identify the features common to the gift tax formula and the estate tax formula.

LO 25-1

2. Explain why Congress felt it necessary to enact a gift tax to complement the estate tax.

LO 25-1

LO 25-1 3. Describe the applicable credit and the purpose it serves in the gift and estate tax.

LO 25-1 4. Fred is retired and living on his pension. He has accumulated almost $1 million of property he would like to leave to his children. However, Fred is afraid much of his wealth will be eliminated by the federal estate tax. Explain whether this fear is well-founded.

LO 25-1 5. Define fair market value for transfer tax purposes.

LO 25-2 6. Describe the requirements for a complete gift, and contrast a gift of a present interest with a gift of a future interest.

LO 25-2 7. Describe a property transfer or payment that is not, by definition, a transfer for inadequate consideration.

LO 25-2 8. Describe a situation in which a transfer of cash to a trust might be considered an incomplete gift.

LO 25-2 9. Identify two types of transfers for inadequate consideration that are specifically excluded from imposition of the gift tax.

LO 25-2 10. Under what circumstances will a deposit of cash to a bank account held in joint tenancy be considered a complete gift?

LO 25-2 11. Explain how a purchase of realty could result in a taxable gift.

LO 25-2 12. Describe the conditions for using the annual exclusion to offset an otherwise taxable transfer.

LO 25-2 13. List the conditions for making an election to split gifts.

LO 25-2 14. Describe the limitations on the deduction of transfers to charity.

LO 25-2 15. Explain the purpose of adding prior taxable gifts to current taxable gifts and show whether these prior gifts could be taxed multiple times over the years.

LO 25-3 16. Explain why the gross estate includes the value of certain property transferred by the decedent at death, such as property held in joint tenancy with the right of survivorship, even though this property is not subject to probate.

LO 25-3 17. Identify the factors that determine the proportion of the value of property held in joint tenancy with the right of survivorship that will be included in a decedent's gross estate.

LO 25-3 18. Harold owns a condo in Hawaii that he plans on using for the rest of his life. However, to ensure his sister Maude will own the property after his death, Harold **research** deeded the remainder of the property to her. He signed the deed transferring the remainder in July 2009 when the condo was worth $250,000 and his life estate was worth $75,000. Harold died in January of this year, at which time the condo was worth $300,000. What amount, if any, is included in Harold's gross estate? Explain.

LO 25-3 19. Paul is a widower with several grown children. He is considering transferring his residence into a trust for his children and retaining a life estate in it. Comment on whether this plan will prevent the value of the home from being included in Paul's gross estate when he dies.

LO 25-3 20. Explain how a remainder and an income interest are valued for transfer tax purposes.

LO 25-3 21. Explain why the fair market value of a life estate is more difficult to estimate than an income interest.

LO 25-3 22. Describe a reason why transfers of terminable interests should not qualify for the marital deduction.

LO 25-3 23. True or False: Including taxable gifts when calculating the estate tax subjects these transfers to double taxation. Explain.

LO 25-3 24. People sometimes confuse the applicable credit with the exemption equivalent. Describe how these terms differ and how they are related.

LO 25-4 25. Describe a reason why a generation-skipping tax was necessary to augment the estate and gift taxes.

26. Explain why an effective wealth transfer plan necessitates cooperation between lawyers, accountants, and investment advisers. `LO 25-4`

27. Describe how to initiate the construction of a comprehensive and effective wealth plan. `LO 25-4`

28. List two questions you might pose to a client to find out whether a program of serial gifts would be an advantageous wealth transfer plan. `LO 25-4`

29. A client in good health wants to support the college education of her teenage grandchild. The client holds various properties but proposes to make a gift of cash in the amount of the annual exclusion. Explain to the client why a direct gift of cash may not be advisable and what property might serve as a reasonable substitute. `LO 25-4`

30. An elderly client has a life insurance policy worth $40,000 that upon her death pays $250,000 to her sole grandchild (or his estate). The client retains ownership of the policy. Outline for her the costs and benefits of transferring ownership of the policy to a life insurance trust. `LO 25-4`

31. Identify the sections in the Internal Revenue Code that authorize the use of qualified terminable interest property (QTIPs) for gift and estate tax purposes, respectively. `LO 25-4` **research**

32. Under what conditions can an executor or trustee elect to claim a marital deduction for a transfer of a terminable interest to a spouse? `LO 25-4` **research**

33. Explain how a transfer of property as a gift may have income tax implications to the donee. `LO 25-4`

PROBLEMS

Select problems are available in Connect®.   **connect**

34. Raquel transferred $100,000 of stock to a trust, with income to be paid to her nephew for 18 years and the remainder to her nephew's children (or their estates). Raquel named a bank as independent trustee but retained the power to determine how much income, if any, will be paid in any particular year. Is this transfer a completed gift? Explain. `LO 25-2`

35. This year Gerry's friend, Dewey, was disabled. Gerry paid $15,000 to Dewey's doctor for medical expenses and paid $12,500 to State University for college tuition for Dewey's son. Has Gerry made taxable gifts and, if so, in what amounts? `LO 25-2`

36. This year Dan and Mike purchased realty for $180,000 and took title as equal tenants in common. However, Mike was able to provide only $40,000 of the purchase price and Dan provided the remaining $140,000. Has Dan made a completed gift to Mike and, if so, in what amount? `LO 25-2`

37. Last year Nate opened a savings account with a deposit of $15,000. The account was in the name of Nate and Derrick, joint tenancy with the right of survivorship. Derrick did not contribute to the account, but this year he withdrew $5,000. Has Nate made a complete gift and, if so, what is the amount of the taxable gift and when was the gift made? `LO 25-2`

38. Barry transfers $1,000,000 to an irrevocable trust with income to Robin for her life and the remainder to Maurice (or his estate). Calculate the value of the life estate and the remainder if Robin's age and the prevailing interest rate result in a Table S discount factor for the remainder of 0.27. `LO 25-2`

39. This year Jim created an irrevocable trust to provide for Ted, his 32-year-old nephew, and Ted's family. Jim transferred $70,000 to the trust and named a bank as the trustee. The trust was directed to pay income to Ted until he reaches age 35, and at that time the trust is to be terminated and the corpus is to be distributed to Ted's two children (or their estates). Determine the amount, if any, of the current gift and the taxable gift. If necessary, you may assume the relevant interest rate is 6 percent and Jim is unmarried. `LO 25-2`

LO 25-2 40. This year Colleen transferred $100,000 to an irrevocable trust that pays equal shares of income annually to three cousins (or their estates) for the next eight years. At that time, the trust is terminated and the corpus of the trust reverts to Colleen. Determine the amount, if any, of the current gifts and the taxable gifts. If necessary, you may assume the relevant interest rate is 6 percent and Colleen is unmarried. What is your answer if Colleen is married and she elects to gift-split with her spouse?

LO 25-2 41. Sly is a widower and wants to make annual gifts of cash to each of his four children and six grandchildren. How much can Sly transfer to his children this year if he makes the maximum gifts eligible for the annual exclusion? What is the amount of the total transfer if Sly is married and elects gift-splitting, assuming his spouse makes no other gifts?

LO 25-2 42. Jack and Liz live in a community-property state and their vacation home is community property. This year they transferred the vacation home to an irrevocable trust that provides their son, Tom, a life estate in the home and the remainder to their daughter, Laura. Under the terms of the trust, Tom has the right to use the vacation home for the duration of his life, and Laura will automatically own the property after Tom's death. At the time of the gift the home was valued at $500,000, Tom was 35 years old, and the §7520 rate was 5.4 percent. What is the amount, if any, of the taxable gifts? Would your answer be different if the home was not community property and Jack and Liz elected to gift-split?

LO 25-2 43. David placed $80,000 in trust with income to Steve for his life and the remainder to Lil (or her estate). At the time of the gift, given the prevailing interest rate, Steve's life estate was valued at $65,000 and the remainder at $15,000. What is the amount, if any, of David's taxable gifts?

LO 25-2 44. Stephen transferred $17,500 to an irrevocable trust for Graham. The trustee has the discretion to distribute income or corpus for Graham's benefit but is required to distribute all assets to Graham (or his estate) not later than Graham's 21st birthday. What is the amount, if any, of the taxable gift?

LO 25-2 45. For the holidays, Marty gave a watch worth $25,000 to Emily and jewelry worth $40,000 to Natalie. Has Marty made any taxable gifts this year and, if so, in what amounts? Does it matter if Marty is married to Wendy and they live in a community-property state?

LO 25-2 46. This year Jeff earned $850,000 and used it to purchase land in joint tenancy with a right of survivorship with Mary. Has Jeff made a taxable gift to Mary and, if so, in what amount? What is your answer if Jeff and Mary are married?

LO 25-2 47. Laura transfers $500,000 into trust with the income to be paid annually to her spouse, William, for life (a life estate) and the remainder to Jenny. Calculate the amount of the taxable gifts from the transfers.

LO 25-2 48. Red transferred $5,000,000 of cash to State University for a new sports complex. Calculate the amount of the taxable gift.

LO 25-2 49. In 2010 Casey made a taxable gift of $5 million to both Stephanie and Linda (a total of $10 million in taxable gifts). Calculate the amount of gift tax due this year and Casey's unused exemption equivalent under the following alternatives.

a) This year Casey made a taxable gift of $1 million to Stephanie. Casey is not married, and the 2010 gift was the only other taxable gift he has ever made.

b) This year Casey made a taxable gift of $15 million to Stephanie. Casey is not married, and the 2010 gift was the only other taxable gift he has ever made.

c) This year Casey made a gift worth $15 million to Stephanie. Casey is married to Helen in a common-law state, and the 2010 gift was the only other taxable gift he or Helen has ever made. Casey and Helen elect to gift split.

50. Tom Hruise was an entertainment executive who had a fatal accident on a film set. Tom's will directed his executor to distribute his cash and stock to his wife, Kaffie, and the real estate to his church, The First Church of Methodology. The remainder of his assets were to be placed in trust for his three children. Tom's estate consisted of the following:

LO 25-3

tax forms

Assets

Personal assets	$ 800,000
Cash and stock	24,000,000
Intangible assets (film rights)	71,500,000
Real estate	15,000,000
	$111,300,000

Liabilities

Mortgage	$ 3,200,000
Other liabilities	4,100,000
	$ 7,300,000

a) Tom made a taxable gift of $8 million in 2011. Compute the estate tax for Tom's estate.

b) Fill out lines 1 through 12 in part 2 of Form 706 for Tom's estate.

51. Hal and Wendy are married, and they own a parcel of realty, Blackacre, as joint tenants with the right of survivorship. Hal owns an additional parcel of realty, Redacre, in his name alone. Suppose Hal should die when Blackacre is worth $800,000 and Redacre is worth $750,000. What value of realty would be included in Hal's probate estate, and what value would be included in Hal's gross estate?

LO 25-3

52. Walter owns a whole-life insurance policy worth $52,000 that directs the insurance company to pay the beneficiary $250,000 on Walter's death. Walter pays the annual premiums and has the power to designate the beneficiary of the policy (it is currently his son, James). What value of the policy, if any, will be included in Walter's estate upon his death?

LO 25-3

53. Many years ago James and Sergio purchased property for $450,000. Although they are listed as equal co-owners, Sergio was able to provide only $200,000 of the purchase price. James treated the additional $25,000 of his contribution to the purchase price as a gift to Sergio. If the property is worth $900,000 at Sergio's death, what amount would be included in Sergio's estate if the title to the property was tenants in common? What if the title was joint tenancy with right of survivorship?

LO 25-3

54. Terry transferred $500,000 of real estate into an irrevocable trust for her son, Lee. The trustee was directed to retain income until Lee's 21st birthday and then pay him the corpus of the trust. Terry retained the power to require the trustee to pay income to Lee at any time and the right to the assets if Lee predeceased her. What amount of the trust, if any, will be included in Terry's estate?

LO 25-3

55. Last year Robert transferred a life insurance policy worth $45,000 to an irrevocable trust with directions to distribute the corpus of the trust to his grandson, Danny, upon his graduation from college, or to Danny's estate upon his death. Robert paid $15,000 of gift tax on the transfer of the policy. Early this year, Robert died and the insurance company paid $400,000 to the trust. What amount, if any, is included in Robert's gross estate?

LO 25-3

56. Willie purchased a whole-life insurance policy on his brother, Benny. Under the policy, the insurance company will pay the named beneficiary $100,000 upon the death of the insured, Benny. Willie names Tess the beneficiary, and upon Benny's

LO 25-3

research

death, Tess receives the proceeds of the policy, $100,000. Identify and discuss the transfer tax implications of this arrangement.

LO 25-3 57. Jimmy owns two parcels of real estate, Tara and Sundance. Tara is worth $240,000 and Sundance is worth $360,000. Jimmy plans to bequeath Tara directly to his wife Lois and leave her a life estate in Sundance. What amount of value will be included in Jimmy's gross estate and taxable estate should he die now?

LO 25-3 58. Roland had a taxable estate of $15.5 million when he died this year. Calculate the amount of estate tax due (if any) under the following alternatives.

a) Roland's prior taxable gifts consist of a taxable gift of $1 million in 2005.

b) Roland's prior taxable gifts consist of a taxable gift of $1.5 million in 2005.

c) Explain how the tax calculation would change if Roland made a $1 million taxable gift in the year prior to his death.

LO 25-2 59. Brad and Angelina are a wealthy couple who have three children, Fred, Bridget, and

tax forms Lisa. Two of the three children, Fred and Bridget, are from Brad's previous marriages. On Christmas this year, Brad gave each of the three children a cash gift of $10,000, and Angelina gave Lisa an additional cash gift of $40,000. Brad also gave stock worth $40,000 (adjusted basis of $10,000) to the Actor's Guild (an "A" charity).

a) Brad and Angelina have chosen to split gifts. Calculate Brad's gift tax. Assume that Angelina has no previous taxable gifts, but Brad reported previous taxable gifts of $2 million in 2009 when he used $345,800 of applicable credit and paid $435,000 of gift taxes.

b) Fill out parts 1 and 4 of Form 709 for Brad.

LO 25-4 60. Jones is seriously ill and has $6 million of property that he wants to leave to his four

planning children. He is considering making a current gift of the property (rather than leaving the property to pass through his will). Assuming any taxable transfer will be subject to the highest transfer tax rate, determine how much gift tax Jones will owe if he makes the transfers now. How much estate tax will Jones save if he dies after three years, during which time the property appreciates to $6.8 million? Besides transfer taxes, what other tax and financial factors should Jones consider in making this choice?

LO 25-4 61. Angelina gave a parcel of realty to Julie valued at $210,000 (Angelina purchased the property five years ago for $88,000). Compute the amount of the taxable gift on the transfer, if any. Suppose several years later Julie sold the property for $215,000. What is the amount of her gain or loss, if any, on the sale?

LO 25-4 62. Several years ago Doug invested $21,000 in stock. This year he gave his daughter

research Tina the stock on a day it was valued at $20,000. She promptly sold it for $19,500. Determine the amount of the taxable gift, if any, and calculate the amount of taxable income or gain, if any, for Tina. Assume Doug is not married and does not support Tina, who is 28.

LO 25-4 63. Roberta is considering making annual gifts of $15,000 of stock to each of her four children. She expects to live another five years and to leave a taxable estate worth approximately $18 million. She requests that you justify the gifts by estimating her estate tax savings from making the gifts.

LO 25-4 64. Harold and Maude are married and live in a common-law state. Neither have made any taxable gifts and Maude owns (holds title to) all their property. She dies with a taxable estate of $25 million and leaves it all to Harold. He dies several years later, leaving the entire $25 million to their three children. Calculate how much estate tax is due from Harold's estate.

COMPREHENSIVE PROBLEMS

Select problems are available in Connect®.

65. Suppose Vince dies this year with a gross estate of $25 million and no adjusted prior gifts. Calculate the amount of estate tax due (if any) under the following *alternative* conditions:

    a) Vince leaves his entire estate to his spouse, Millie.

    b) Vince leaves $10 million to Millie and the remainder to charity.

    c) Vince leaves $10 million to Millie and the remainder to his son, Paul.

    d) Vince leaves $10 million to Millie and the remainder to a trust whose trustee is required to pay income to Millie for her life and the remainder to Paul.

66. Hank is a single individual who possesses a life insurance policy worth $300,000 that will pay his two children a total of $800,000 upon his death. This year Hank transferred the policy and all incidents of ownership to an irrevocable trust that pays income annually to his two children for 15 years and then distributes the corpus to the children in equal shares.

    a) Calculate the amount of gift tax due (if any) on the gift. Assume that Hank has made only one prior taxable gift of $5 million in 2011.

    b) Calculate the amount of cumulative taxable transfers for estate tax purposes if Hank dies this year but after the date of the gift. At the time of his death, Hank's probate estate is $10 million divided in equal shares between his two children.

67. Jack is single and he made his first taxable gift of $1,000,000 in 2008. Jack made additional gifts in 2009, at which time he gave $1,750,000 to each of his three children and an additional $1,000,000 to State University (a charity). The annual exclusion in 2009 was $13,000. Recently Jack has been in poor health and would like you to estimate his estate tax should he die this year. Jack estimates his taxable estate (after deductions) will be worth $10.4 million at his death.

68. Montgomery has decided to engage in wealth planning and has listed the value of his assets below. The life insurance has a cash surrender value of $120,000, and the proceeds are payable to Montgomery's estate. The Walen Trust is an irrevocable trust created by Montgomery's brother 10 years ago and contains assets currently valued at $800,000. The income from the trust is payable to Montgomery's faithful butler, Walen, for his life, and the remainder is payable to Montgomery or his estate. Walen is currently 37 years old, and the §7520 interest rate is currently 5.4 percent. Montgomery is unmarried and plans to leave all his assets to his surviving relatives.

Property	Value	Adjusted Basis
Auto	$ 20,000	$ 55,000
Personal effects	75,000	110,000
Checking and savings accounts	250,000	250,000
Investments	2,500,000	770,000
Residence	1,400,000	980,000
Life insurance proceeds	1,000,000	50,000
Real estate investments	10,125,000	2,800,000
Walen Trust	800,000	80,000

a) Calculate the amount of the estate tax due (if any), assuming Montgomery dies this year and has never made any taxable gifts.

b) Calculate the amount of the estate tax due (if any), assuming Montgomery dies this year and made one taxable gift in 2006. The taxable gift was $1 million, and Montgomery used his 2006 applicable credit to avoid paying any gift tax.

c) Calculate the amount of the estate tax due (if any), assuming Montgomery dies this year and made one taxable gift in 2006. The taxable gift was $5 million, and Montgomery used his $1 million 2006 applicable credit to reduce the gift tax in 2006. Montgomery plans to bequeath his investments to charity and leave his remaining assets to his surviving relatives.

ROGER | *CPA Review*

Sample CPA Exam questions from Roger CPA Review are available in Connect as support for the topics in this text. These Multiple Choice Questions and Task-Based Simulations include expert-written explanations and solutions and provide a starting point for students to become familiar with the content and functionality of the actual CPA Exam.

Appendix A

Tax Forms

All tax forms can be obtained from the IRS website: www.irs.gov. These forms do not reflect tax law changes effective in 2018 under the Tax Cuts and Jobs Act. 2018 forms were not available at the time we went to press.

Form **1040**

Department of the Treasury—Internal Revenue Service   (99)

U.S. Individual Income Tax Return   **2017**   OMB No. 1545-0074   IRS Use Only—Do not write or staple in this space.

For the year Jan. 1–Dec. 31, 2017, or other tax year beginning _____ , 2017, ending _____ , 20 _____   See separate instructions.

Your first name and initial	Last name		Your social security number
If a joint return, spouse's first name and initial	Last name		Spouse's social security number

Home address (number and street). If you have a P.O. box, see instructions.   Apt. no.

▲ Make sure the SSN(s) above and on line 6c are correct.

City, town or post office, state, and ZIP code. If you have a foreign address, also complete spaces below (see instructions).

Presidential Election Campaign
Check here if you, or your spouse if filing jointly, want $3 to go to this fund. Checking a box below will not change your tax or refund. ☐ You ☐ Spouse

Foreign country name	Foreign province/state/county	Foreign postal code

Filing Status

Check only one box.

1 ☐ Single
2 ☐ Married filing jointly (even if only one had income)
3 ☐ Married filing separately. Enter spouse's SSN above and full name here. ▶
4 ☐ Head of household (with qualifying person). (See instructions.) If the qualifying person is a child but not your dependent, enter this child's name here. ▶
5 ☐ Qualifying widow(er) (see instructions)

Exemptions

6a ☐ **Yourself.** If someone can claim you as a dependent, **do not** check box 6a . . . . . .
b ☐ **Spouse** . . . .

c **Dependents:**

(1) First name Last name	(2) Dependent's social security number	(3) Dependent's relationship to you	(4) ✓ if child under age 17 qualifying for child tax credit (see instructions)
			☐
			☐
			☐
			☐

If more than four dependents, see instructions and check here ▶ ☐

Boxes checked on 6a and 6b ____
No. of children on 6c who:
• lived with you ____
• did not live with you due to divorce or separation (see instructions) ____
Dependents on 6c not entered above ____
Add numbers on lines above ▶ ____

d Total number of exemptions claimed . . . .

Income

Attach Form(s) W-2 here. Also attach Forms W-2G and 1099-R if tax was withheld.

If you did not get a W-2, see instructions.

7	Wages, salaries, tips, etc. Attach Form(s) W-2	7
8a	**Taxable** interest. Attach Schedule B if required	8a
b	**Tax-exempt** interest. **Do not** include on line 8a . . . 8b	
9a	Ordinary dividends. Attach Schedule B if required	9a
b	Qualified dividends 9b	
10	Taxable refunds, credits, or offsets of state and local income taxes	10
11	Alimony received	11
12	Business income or (loss). Attach Schedule C or C-EZ	12
13	Capital gain or (loss). Attach Schedule D if required. If not required, check here ▶ ☐	13
14	Other gains or (losses). Attach Form 4797	14
15a	IRA distributions . 15a	b Taxable amount . . . 15b
16a	Pensions and annuities 16a	b Taxable amount . . . 16b
17	Rental real estate, royalties, partnerships, S corporations, trusts, etc. Attach Schedule E	17
18	Farm income or (loss). Attach Schedule F	18
19	Unemployment compensation	19
20a	Social security benefits 20a	b Taxable amount . . . 20b
21	Other income. List type and amount _____	21
22	Combine the amounts in the far right column for lines 7 through 21. This is your **total income** ▶	22

Adjusted Gross Income

23	Educator expenses 23	
24	Certain business expenses of reservists, performing artists, and fee-basis government officials. Attach Form 2106 or 2106-EZ 24	
25	Health savings account deduction. Attach Form 8889 . 25	
26	Moving expenses. Attach Form 3903 26	
27	Deductible part of self-employment tax. Attach Schedule SE . 27	
28	Self-employed SEP, SIMPLE, and qualified plans . . 28	
29	Self-employed health insurance deduction 29	
30	Penalty on early withdrawal of savings 30	
31a	Alimony paid b Recipient's SSN ▶ _____ 31a	
32	IRA deduction 32	
33	Student loan interest deduction 33	
34	Reserved for future use 34	
35	Domestic production activities deduction. Attach Form 8903 35	
36	Add lines 23 through 35	36
37	Subtract line 36 from line 22. This is your **adjusted gross income** . . . . . ▶	37

For Disclosure, Privacy Act, and Paperwork Reduction Act Notice, see separate instructions.   Cat. No. 11320B   Form **1040** (2017)

Form 1040 (2017)   Page **2**

	38	Amount from line 37 (adjusted gross income)	38	

Tax and Credits

39a	Check if: ☐ **You** were born before January 2, 1953, ☐ Blind. ☐ **Spouse** was born before January 2, 1953, ☐ Blind. **Total boxes checked ▶ 39a**	
b	If your spouse itemizes on a separate return or you were a dual-status alien, check here ▶ 39b ☐	

Standard Deduction for—

- People who check any box on line 39a or 39b **or** who can be claimed as a dependent, see instructions.
- All others:

Single or Married filing separately, $6,350

Married filing jointly or Qualifying widow(er), $12,700

Head of household, $9,350

40	**Itemized deductions** (from Schedule A) **or** your **standard deduction** (see left margin) . .	40	
41	Subtract line 40 from line 38	41	
42	**Exemptions.** If line 38 is $156,900 or less, multiply $4,050 by the number on line 6d. Otherwise, see instructions	42	
43	**Taxable income.** Subtract line 42 from line 41. If line 42 is more than line 41, enter -0- . .	43	
44	**Tax** (see instructions). Check if any from: **a** ☐ Form(s) 8814 **b** ☐ Form 4972 **c** ☐ _____	44	
45	**Alternative minimum tax** (see instructions). Attach Form 6251	45	
46	Excess advance premium tax credit repayment. Attach Form 8962	46	
47	Add lines 44, 45, and 46 . . . . ▶	47	

48	Foreign tax credit. Attach Form 1116 if required	48		
49	Credit for child and dependent care expenses. Attach Form 2441	49		
50	Education credits from Form 8863, line 19	50		
51	Retirement savings contributions credit. Attach Form 8880	51		
52	Child tax credit. Attach Schedule 8812, if required . . .	52		
53	Residential energy credit. Attach Form 5695	53		
54	Other credits from Form: **a** ☐ 3800 **b** ☐ 8801 **c** ☐ _____	54		
55	Add lines 48 through 54. These are your **total credits**	55		
56	Subtract line 55 from line 47. If line 55 is more than line 47, enter -0- . . . . . . ▶	56		

Other Taxes

57	Self-employment tax. Attach Schedule SE	57	
58	Unreported social security and Medicare tax from Form: **a** ☐ 4137 **b** ☐ 8919 . .	58	
59	Additional tax on IRAs, other qualified retirement plans, etc. Attach Form 5329 if required . .	59	
60a	Household employment taxes from Schedule H	60a	
b	First-time homebuyer credit repayment. Attach Form 5405 if required	60b	
61	Health care: individual responsibility (see instructions) Full-year coverage ☐	61	
62	Taxes from: **a** ☐ Form 8959 **b** ☐ Form 8960 **c** ☐ Instructions; enter code(s) _____	62	
63	Add lines 56 through 62. This is your **total tax** . . . . ▶	63	

Payments

If you have a qualifying child, attach Schedule EIC.

64	Federal income tax withheld from Forms W-2 and 1099 . .	64		
65	2017 estimated tax payments and amount applied from 2016 return	65		
66a	**Earned income credit (EIC)**	66a		
b	Nontaxable combat pay election	66b		
67	Additional child tax credit. Attach Schedule 8812	67		
68	American opportunity credit from Form 8863, line 8 . . .	68		
69	Net premium tax credit. Attach Form 8962	69		
70	Amount paid with request for extension to file	70		
71	Excess social security and tier 1 RRTA tax withheld . . .	71		
72	Credit for federal tax on fuels. Attach Form 4136 . . .	72		
73	Credits from Form: **a** ☐ 2439 **b** ☐ Reserved **c** ☐ 8885 **d** ☐	73		
74	Add lines 64, 65, 66a, and 67 through 73. These are your **total payments** . . . . . ▶	74		

Refund

Direct deposit? See instructions.

75	If line 74 is more than line 63, subtract line 63 from line 74. This is the amount you **overpaid**	75	
76a	Amount of line 75 you want **refunded to you.** If Form 8888 is attached, check here . ▶ ☐	76a	
▶ b	Routing number |_|_|_|_|_|_|_|_| ▶ c Type: ☐ Checking ☐ Savings		
▶ d	Account number |_|_|_|_|_|_|_|_|		
77	Amount of line 75 you want **applied to your 2018 estimated tax ▶** 77		

Amount You Owe

78	**Amount you owe.** Subtract line 74 from line 63. For details on how to pay, see instructions ▶	78	
79	Estimated tax penalty (see instructions) 79		

Third Party Designee

Do you want to allow another person to discuss this return with the IRS (see instructions)? ☐ **Yes.** Complete below. ☐ **No**

Designee's name ▶	Phone no. ▶	Personal identification number (PIN) ▶ |_|_|_|_|_|

Sign Here

Joint return? See instructions.
Keep a copy for your records.

Under penalties of perjury, I declare that I have examined this return and accompanying schedules and statements, and to the best of my knowledge and belief, they are true, correct, and accurately list all amounts and sources of income I received during the tax year. Declaration of preparer (other than taxpayer) is based on all information of which preparer has any knowledge.

Your signature	Date	Your occupation	Daytime phone number
Spouse's signature. If a joint return, **both** must sign.	Date	Spouse's occupation	If the IRS sent you an Identity Protection PIN, enter it here (see inst.) |_|_|_|_|_|_|

Paid Preparer Use Only

Print/Type preparer's name	Preparer's signature	Date	Check ☐ if self-employed	PTIN
Firm's name ▶			Firm's EIN ▶	
Firm's address ▶			Phone no.	

Go to *www.irs.gov/Form1040* for instructions and the latest information.   Form **1040** (2017)

Source: Form 1040, Department of the Treasury—Internal Revenue Service, 2017

SCHEDULE A
(Form 1040)

Department of the Treasury
Internal Revenue Service (99)

Itemized Deductions

▶ Go to *www.irs.gov/ScheduleA* for instructions and the latest information.
▶ **Attach to Form 1040.**

Caution: If you are claiming a net qualified disaster loss on Form 4684, see the instructions for line 28.

OMB No. 1545-0074

2017

Attachment
Sequence No. **07**

Name(s) shown on Form 1040

Your social security number

Medical and Dental Expenses	**Caution:** Do not include expenses reimbursed or paid by others.		
	1 Medical and dental expenses (see instructions)	**1**	
	2 Enter amount from Form 1040, line 38 **2**		
	3 Multiply line 2 by 7.5% (0.075)	**3**	
	4 Subtract line 3 from line 1. If line 3 is more than line 1, enter -0-	**4**	
Taxes You Paid	**5** State and local **(check only one box):**		
	a ☐ Income taxes, **or**	**5**	
	b ☐ General sales taxes		
	6 Real estate taxes (see instructions)	**6**	
	7 Personal property taxes	**7**	
	8 Other taxes. List type and amount ▶ _____		
		8	
	9 Add lines 5 through 8	**9**	
Interest You Paid	**10** Home mortgage interest and points reported to you on Form 1098	**10**	
Note: Your mortgage interest deduction may be limited (see instructions).	**11** Home mortgage interest not reported to you on Form 1098. If paid to the person from whom you bought the home, see instructions and show that person's name, identifying no., and address ▶ _____ _____	**11**	
	12 Points not reported to you on Form 1098. See instructions for special rules	**12**	
	13 Reserved for future use	**13**	
	14 Investment interest. Attach Form 4952 if required. See instructions	**14**	
	15 Add lines 10 through 14	**15**	
Gifts to Charity	**16** Gifts by cash or check. If you made any gift of $250 or more, see instructions	**16**	
If you made a gift and got a benefit for it, see instructions.	**17** Other than by cash or check. If any gift of $250 or more, see instructions. You **must** attach Form 8283 if over $500 . . .	**17**	
	18 Carryover from prior year	**18**	
	19 Add lines 16 through 18	**19**	
Casualty and Theft Losses	**20** Casualty or theft loss(es) other than net qualified disaster losses. Attach Form 4684 and enter the amount from line 18 of that form. See instructions	**20**	
Job Expenses and Certain Miscellaneous Deductions	**21** Unreimbursed employee expenses—job travel, union dues, job education, etc. Attach Form 2106 or 2106-EZ if required. See instructions. ▶ _____	**21**	
	22 Tax preparation fees	**22**	
	23 Other expenses—investment, safe deposit box, etc. List type and amount ▶ _____	**23**	
	24 Add lines 21 through 23	**24**	
	25 Enter amount from Form 1040, line 38 **25**		
	26 Multiply line 25 by 2% (0.02)	**26**	
	27 Subtract line 26 from line 24. If line 26 is more than line 24, enter -0-	**27**	
Other Miscellaneous Deductions	**28** Other—from list in instructions. List type and amount ▶ _____ _____	**28**	
Total Itemized Deductions	**29** Is Form 1040, line 38, over $156,900?		
	☐ **No.** Your deduction is not limited. Add the amounts in the far right column for lines 4 through 28. Also, enter this amount on Form 1040, line 40.	**29**	
	☐ **Yes.** Your deduction may be limited. See the Itemized Deductions Worksheet in the instructions to figure the amount to enter.		
	30 If you elect to itemize deductions even though they are less than your standard deduction, check here . . . . ▶ ☐		

For Paperwork Reduction Act Notice, see the Instructions for Form 1040.   Cat. No. 17145C   Schedule A (Form 1040) 2017

Source: Schedule A, Form 1040, Department of the Treasury—Internal Revenue Service, 2017

SCHEDULE B (Form 1040A or 1040) Department of the Treasury Internal Revenue Service (99)	**Interest and Ordinary Dividends** ▶ **Attach to Form 1040A or 1040.** ▶ **Go to www.irs.gov/ScheduleB for instructions and the latest information.**	OMB No. 1545-0074 20**17** Attachment Sequence No. **08**

Name(s) shown on return | Your social security number

Part I **Interest** (See instructions and the instructions for Form 1040A, or Form 1040, line 8a.) **Note:** If you received a Form 1099-INT, Form 1099-OID, or substitute statement from a brokerage firm, list the firm's name as the payer and enter the total interest shown on that form.	**1** List name of payer. If any interest is from a seller-financed mortgage and the buyer used the property as a personal residence, see the instructions and list this interest first. Also, show that buyer's social security number and address ▶	**Amount**
	....	1
	2 Add the amounts on line 1	**2**
	3 Excludable interest on series EE and I U.S. savings bonds issued after 1989. Attach Form 8815	**3**
	4 Subtract line 3 from line 2. Enter the result here and on Form 1040A, or Form 1040, line 8a . . . . ▶	**4**

Note: If line 4 is over $1,500, you must complete Part III.

Part II **Ordinary** **Dividends** (See instructions and the instructions for Form 1040A, or Form 1040, line 9a.) **Note:** If you received a Form 1099-DIV or substitute statement from a brokerage firm, list the firm's name as the payer and enter the ordinary dividends shown on that form.	**5** List name of payer ▶	**Amount**
	....	5
	6 Add the amounts on line 5. Enter the total here and on Form 1040A, or Form 1040, line 9a . . . . ▶	**6**

Note: If line 6 is over $1,500, you must complete Part III.

Part III **Foreign** **Accounts** **and Trusts** (See instructions.)	You must complete this part if you **(a)** had over $1,500 of taxable interest or ordinary dividends; **(b)** had a foreign account; or **(c)** received a distribution from, or were a grantor of, or a transferor to, a foreign trust.	Yes	No
	7a At any time during 2017, did you have a financial interest in or signature authority over a financial account (such as a bank account, securities account, or brokerage account) located in a foreign country? See instructions		
	If "Yes," are you required to file FinCEN Form 114, Report of Foreign Bank and Financial Accounts (FBAR), to report that financial interest or signature authority? See FinCEN Form 114 and its instructions for filing requirements and exceptions to those requirements		
	b If you are required to file FinCEN Form 114, enter the name of the foreign country where the financial account is located ▶		
	8 During 2017, did you receive a distribution from, or were you the grantor of, or transferor to, a foreign trust? If "Yes," you may have to file Form 3520. See instructions		

For Paperwork Reduction Act Notice, see your tax return instructions.   Cat. No. 17146N   **Schedule B (Form 1040A or 1040) 2017**

Source: Schedule B, Form 1040, Department of the Treasury—Internal Revenue Service, 2017

SCHEDULE C
(Form 1040)

Department of the Treasury
Internal Revenue Service (99)

Profit or Loss From Business
(Sole Proprietorship)

▶ Go to *www.irs.gov/ScheduleC* for instructions and the latest information.
▶ **Attach to Form 1040, 1040NR, or 1041; partnerships generally must file Form 1065.**

OMB No. 1545-0074

2017

Attachment
Sequence No. **09**

Name of proprietor

Social security number (SSN)

A   Principal business or profession, including product or service (see instructions)

B Enter code from instructions
▶

C   Business name. If no separate business name, leave blank.

D Employer ID number (EIN) (see instr.)

E   Business address (including suite or room no.) ▶

City, town or post office, state, and ZIP code

F   Accounting method: **(1)** ☐ Cash   **(2)** ☐ Accrual   **(3)** ☐ Other (specify) ▶

G   Did you "materially participate" in the operation of this business during 2017? If "No," see instructions for limit on losses   ☐ Yes ☐ No

H   If you started or acquired this business during 2017, check here   ▶ ☐

I   Did you make any payments in 2017 that would require you to file Form(s) 1099? (see instructions)   ☐ Yes ☐ No

J   If "Yes," did you or will you file required Forms 1099?   ☐ Yes ☐ No

Part I   Income

1	Gross receipts or sales. See instructions for line 1 and check the box if this income was reported to you on Form W-2 and the "Statutory employee" box on that form was checked ▶ ☐	**1**	
2	Returns and allowances	**2**	
3	Subtract line 2 from line 1	**3**	
4	Cost of goods sold (from line 42)	**4**	
5	**Gross profit.** Subtract line 4 from line 3	**5**	
6	Other income, including federal and state gasoline or fuel tax credit or refund (see instructions)	**6**	
7	**Gross income.** Add lines 5 and 6 ▶	**7**	

Part II   Expenses. Enter expenses for business use of your home **only** on line 30.

8	Advertising	**8**		**18**	Office expense (see instructions)	**18**	
9	Car and truck expenses (see instructions)	**9**		**19**	Pension and profit-sharing plans	**19**	
10	Commissions and fees	**10**		**20**	Rent or lease (see instructions):		
11	Contract labor (see instructions)	**11**		**a**	Vehicles, machinery, and equipment	**20a**	
12	Depletion	**12**		**b**	Other business property	**20b**	
13	Depreciation and section 179 expense deduction (not included in Part III) (see instructions)	**13**		**21**	Repairs and maintenance	**21**	
				22	Supplies (not included in Part III)	**22**	
				23	Taxes and licenses	**23**	
				24	Travel, meals, and entertainment:		
14	Employee benefit programs (other than on line 19)	**14**		**a**	Travel	**24a**	
15	Insurance (other than health)	**15**		**b**	Deductible meals and entertainment (see instructions)	**24b**	
16	Interest:			**25**	Utilities	**25**	
a	Mortgage (paid to banks, etc.)	**16a**		**26**	Wages (less employment credits)	**26**	
b	Other	**16b**		**27a**	Other expenses (from line 48)	**27a**	
17	Legal and professional services	**17**		**b**	Reserved for future use	**27b**	

28	**Total expenses** before expenses for business use of home. Add lines 8 through 27a ▶	**28**	
29	Tentative profit or (loss). Subtract line 28 from line 7	**29**	
30	Expenses for business use of your home. Do not report these expenses elsewhere. Attach Form 8829 unless using the simplified method (see instructions). **Simplified method filers only:** enter the total square footage of: (a) your home: _____ and (b) the part of your home used for business: _____ . Use the Simplified Method Worksheet in the instructions to figure the amount to enter on line 30	**30**	
31	**Net profit or (loss).** Subtract line 30 from line 29. • If a profit, enter on both **Form 1040, line 12** (or **Form 1040NR, line 13**) and on **Schedule SE, line 2.** (If you checked the box on line 1, see instructions). Estates and trusts, enter on **Form 1041, line 3.** • If a loss, you **must** go to line 32.	**31**	

32	If you have a loss, check the box that describes your investment in this activity (see instructions). • If you checked 32a, enter the loss on both **Form 1040, line 12,** (or **Form 1040NR, line 13**) and on **Schedule SE, line 2.** (If you checked the box on line 1, see the line 31 instructions). Estates and trusts, enter on **Form 1041, line 3.** • If you checked 32b, you **must** attach **Form 6198.** Your loss may be limited.

32a ☐ All investment is at risk.
32b ☐ Some investment is not at risk.

For Paperwork Reduction Act Notice, see the separate instructions.   Cat. No. 11334P   Schedule C (Form 1040) 2017

Part III **Cost of Goods Sold** (see instructions)

33   Method(s) used to
value closing inventory: **a** ☐ Cost   **b** ☐ Lower of cost or market   **c** ☐ Other (attach explanation)

34   Was there any change in determining quantities, costs, or valuations between opening and closing inventory?
If "Yes," attach explanation . . . .   ☐ **Yes**   ☐ **No**

35	Inventory at beginning of year. If different from last year's closing inventory, attach explanation . . .	35	
36	Purchases less cost of items withdrawn for personal use	36	
37	Cost of labor. Do not include any amounts paid to yourself	37	
38	Materials and supplies	38	
39	Other costs	39	
40	Add lines 35 through 39	40	
41	Inventory at end of year	41	
42	**Cost of goods sold.** Subtract line 41 from line 40. Enter the result here and on line 4	42	

Part IV   **Information on Your Vehicle.** Complete this part **only** if you are claiming car or truck expenses on line 9
and are not required to file Form 4562 for this business. See the instructions for line 13 to find out if you must
file Form 4562.

43   When did you place your vehicle in service for business purposes? (month, day, year) ▶ _____ / _____ / _____

44   Of the total number of miles you drove your vehicle during 2017, enter the number of miles you used your vehicle for:

a Business _____ **b** Commuting (see instructions) _____ **c** Other _____

45   Was your vehicle available for personal use during off-duty hours? . . . .   ☐ **Yes**   ☐ **No**

46   Do you (or your spouse) have another vehicle available for personal use?. . . . .   ☐ **Yes**   ☐ **No**

47a Do you have evidence to support your deduction? . . . .   ☐ **Yes**   ☐ **No**

   b If "Yes," is the evidence written? . . . .   ☐ **Yes**   ☐ **No**

Part V   **Other Expenses.** List below business expenses not included on lines 8–26 or line 30.

--	
--	
--	
--	
--	
--	
--	
--	
48 **Total other expenses.** Enter here and on line 27a	48

Source: Schedule C, Form 1040, Department of the Treasury—Internal Revenue Service, 2017

Schedule C (Form 1040) 2017

SCHEDULE D **(Form 1040)** Department of the Treasury Internal Revenue Service (99)	**Capital Gains and Losses** ▶ **Attach to Form 1040 or Form 1040NR.** ▶ **Go to** *www.irs.gov/ScheduleD* **for instructions and the latest information.** ▶ **Use Form 8949 to list your transactions for lines 1b, 2, 3, 8b, 9, and 10.**	OMB No. 1545-0074 20**17** Attachment Sequence No. **12**

Name(s) shown on return	Your social security number

Part I Short-Term Capital Gains and Losses—Assets Held One Year or Less

See instructions for how to figure the amounts to enter on the lines below. This form may be easier to complete if you round off cents to whole dollars.	**(d)** Proceeds (sales price)	**(e)** Cost (or other basis)	**(g)** Adjustments to gain or loss from Form(s) 8949, Part I, line 2, column (g)	**(h) Gain or (loss)** Subtract column (e) from column (d) and combine the result with column (g)
1a Totals for all short-term transactions reported on Form 1099-B for which basis was reported to the IRS and for which you have no adjustments (see instructions). However, if you choose to report all these transactions on Form 8949, leave this line blank and go to line 1b .				
1b Totals for all transactions reported on Form(s) 8949 with **Box A** checked				
2 Totals for all transactions reported on Form(s) 8949 with **Box B** checked				
3 Totals for all transactions reported on Form(s) 8949 with **Box C** checked				

4 Short-term gain from Form 6252 and short-term gain or (loss) from Forms 4684, 6781, and 8824 .	**4**	
5 Net short-term gain or (loss) from partnerships, S corporations, estates, and trusts from Schedule(s) K-1	**5**	
6 Short-term capital loss carryover. Enter the amount, if any, from line 8 of your **Capital Loss Carryover Worksheet** in the instructions	**6**	( )
7 Net short-term capital gain or (loss). Combine lines 1a through 6 in column (h). If you have any long-term capital gains or losses, go to Part II below. Otherwise, go to Part III on the back	**7**	

Part II Long-Term Capital Gains and Losses—Assets Held More Than One Year

See instructions for how to figure the amounts to enter on the lines below. This form may be easier to complete if you round off cents to whole dollars.	**(d)** Proceeds (sales price)	**(e)** Cost (or other basis)	**(g)** Adjustments to gain or loss from Form(s) 8949, Part II, line 2, column (g)	**(h) Gain or (loss)** Subtract column (e) from column (d) and combine the result with column (g)
8a Totals for all long-term transactions reported on Form 1099-B for which basis was reported to the IRS and for which you have no adjustments (see instructions). However, if you choose to report all these transactions on Form 8949, leave this line blank and go to line 8b .				
8b Totals for all transactions reported on Form(s) 8949 with **Box D** checked				
9 Totals for all transactions reported on Form(s) 8949 with **Box E** checked				
10 Totals for all transactions reported on Form(s) 8949 with **Box F** checked.				

11 Gain from Form 4797, Part I; long-term gain from Forms 2439 and 6252; and long-term gain or (loss) from Forms 4684, 6781, and 8824	**11**	
12 Net long-term gain or (loss) from partnerships, S corporations, estates, and trusts from Schedule(s) K-1	**12**	
13 Capital gain distributions. See the instructions	**13**	
14 Long-term capital loss carryover. Enter the amount, if any, from line 13 of your **Capital Loss Carryover Worksheet** in the instructions	**14**	( )
15 Net long-term capital gain or (loss). Combine lines 8a through 14 in column (h). Then go to Part III on the back	**15**	

For Paperwork Reduction Act Notice, see your tax return instructions.   Cat. No. 11338H   Schedule D (Form 1040) 2017

Source: Schedule D, Form 1040, Department of the Treasury—Internal Revenue Service, 2017

Part III Summary

16   Combine lines 7 and 15 and enter the result . . . . | **16** |

  • If line 16 is a **gain,** enter the amount from line 16 on Form 1040, line 13, or Form 1040NR, line 14. Then go to line 17 below.

  • If line 16 is a **loss,** skip lines 17 through 20 below. Then go to line 21. Also be sure to complete line 22.

  • If line 16 is **zero,** skip lines 17 through 21 below and enter -0- on Form 1040, line 13, or Form 1040NR, line 14. Then go to line 22.

17   Are lines 15 and 16 **both** gains?

  ☐ **Yes.** Go to line 18.

  ☐ **No.** Skip lines 18 through 21, and go to line 22.

18   If you are required to complete the **28% Rate Gain Worksheet** (see instructions), enter the amount, if any, from line 7 of that worksheet . . . . ▶ | **18** |

19   If you are required to complete the **Unrecaptured Section 1250 Gain Worksheet** (see instructions), enter the amount, if any, from line 18 of that worksheet . . . . ▶ | **19** |

20   Are lines 18 and 19 **both** zero or blank?

  ☐ **Yes.** Complete the **Qualified Dividends and Capital Gain Tax Worksheet** in the instructions for Form 1040, line 44 (or in the instructions for Form 1040NR, line 42). **Don't** complete lines 21 and 22 below.

  ☐ **No.** Complete the **Schedule D Tax Worksheet** in the instructions. **Don't** complete lines 21 and 22 below.

21   If line 16 is a loss, enter here and on Form 1040, line 13, or Form 1040NR, line 14, the **smaller** of:

  • The loss on line 16 or

  • ($3,000), or if married filing separately, ($1,500) } . . . . | **21** | (|) |

  Note: When figuring which amount is smaller, treat both amounts as positive numbers.

22   Do you have qualified dividends on Form 1040, line 9b, or Form 1040NR, line 10b?

  ☐ **Yes.** Complete the **Qualified Dividends and Capital Gain Tax Worksheet** in the instructions for Form 1040, line 44 (or in the instructions for Form 1040NR, line 42).

  ☐ **No.** Complete the rest of Form 1040 or Form 1040NR.

Form **8949**

Department of the Treasury
Internal Revenue Service

Sales and Other Dispositions of Capital Assets

▶ Go to *www.irs.gov/Form8949* for instructions and the latest information.

▶ **File with your Schedule D to list your transactions for lines 1b, 2, 3, 8b, 9, and 10 of Schedule D.**

OMB No. 1545-0074

2017

Attachment
Sequence No. **12A**

Name(s) shown on return

Social security number or taxpayer identification number

Before you check Box A, B, or C below, see whether you received any Form(s) 1099-B or substitute statement(s) from your broker. A substitute statement will have the same information as Form 1099-B. Either will show whether your basis (usually your cost) was reported to the IRS by your broker and may even tell you which box to check.

Part I **Short-Term.** Transactions involving capital assets you held 1 year or less are short term. For long-term transactions, see page 2.

Note: You may aggregate all short-term transactions reported on Form(s) 1099-B showing basis was reported to the IRS and for which no adjustments or codes are required. Enter the totals directly on Schedule D, line 1a; you aren't required to report these transactions on Form 8949 (see instructions).

You *must* check Box A, B, *or* C below. Check only one box. If more than one box applies for your short-term transactions, complete a separate Form 8949, page 1, for each applicable box. If you have more short-term transactions than will fit on this page for one or more of the boxes, complete as many forms with the same box checked as you need.

- ☐ **(A)** Short-term transactions reported on Form(s) 1099-B showing basis was reported to the IRS (see **Note** above)
- ☐ **(B)** Short-term transactions reported on Form(s) 1099-B showing basis **wasn't** reported to the IRS
- ☐ **(C)** Short-term transactions not reported to you on Form 1099-B

1 (a) Description of property (Example: 100 sh. XYZ Co.)	(b) Date acquired (Mo., day, yr.)	(c) Date sold or disposed of (Mo., day, yr.)	(d) Proceeds (sales price) (see instructions)	(e) Cost or other basis. See the **Note** below and see *Column (e)* in the separate instructions	Adjustment, if any, to gain or loss. If you enter an amount in column (g), enter a code in column (f). **See the separate instructions.**		(h) Gain or (loss). Subtract column (e) from column (d) and combine the result with column (g)
					(f) Code(s) from instructions	(g) Amount of adjustment	

2 Totals. Add the amounts in columns (d), (e), (g), and (h) (subtract negative amounts). Enter each total here and include on your Schedule D, **line 1b** (if **Box A** above is checked), **line 2** (if **Box B** above is checked), or **line 3** (if **Box C** above is checked) ▶

Note: If you checked Box A above but the basis reported to the IRS was incorrect, enter in column (e) the basis as reported to the IRS, and enter an adjustment in column (g) to correct the basis. See *Column (g)* in the separate instructions for how to figure the amount of the adjustment.

For Paperwork Reduction Act Notice, see your tax return instructions.   Cat. No. 37768Z   Form **8949** (2017)

Form 8949 (2017)   Attachment Sequence No. **12A**   Page **2**

Name(s) shown on return. Name and SSN or taxpayer identification no. not required if shown on other side	Social security number or taxpayer identification number

Before you check Box D, E, or F below, see whether you received any Form(s) 1099-B or substitute statement(s) from your broker. A substitute statement will have the same information as Form 1099-B. Either will show whether your basis (usually your cost) was reported to the IRS by your broker and may even tell you which box to check.

Part II   **Long-Term.** Transactions involving capital assets you held more than 1 year are long term. For short-term transactions, see page 1.

Note: You may aggregate all long-term transactions reported on Form(s) 1099-B showing basis was reported to the IRS and for which no adjustments or codes are required. Enter the totals directly on Schedule D, line 8a; you aren't required to report these transactions on Form 8949 (see instructions).

You *must* check Box D, E, *or* F below. Check only one box. If more than one box applies for your long-term transactions, complete a separate Form 8949, page 2, for each applicable box. If you have more long-term transactions than will fit on this page for one or more of the boxes, complete as many forms with the same box checked as you need.

☐ **(D)** Long-term transactions reported on Form(s) 1099-B showing basis was reported to the IRS (see **Note** above)

☐ **(E)** Long-term transactions reported on Form(s) 1099-B showing basis **wasn't** reported to the IRS

☐ **(F)** Long-term transactions not reported to you on Form 1099-B

1	(a) Description of property (Example: 100 sh. XYZ Co.)	(b) Date acquired (Mo., day, yr.)	(c) Date sold or disposed of (Mo., day, yr.)	(d) Proceeds (sales price) (see instructions)	(e) Cost or other basis. See the **Note** below and see *Column (e)* in the separate instructions	Adjustment, if any, to gain or loss. If you enter an amount in column (g), enter a code in column (f). See the separate instructions.		(h) Gain or (loss). Subtract column (e) from column (d) and combine the result with column (g)
						(f) Code(s) from instructions	(g) Amount of adjustment	
2 Totals. Add the amounts in columns (d), (e), (g), and (h) (subtract negative amounts). Enter each total here and include on your Schedule D, **line 8b** (if **Box D** above is checked), **line 9** (if **Box E** above is checked), or **line 10** (if **Box F** above is checked) ▶								

Note: If you checked Box D above but the basis reported to the IRS was incorrect, enter in column (e) the basis as reported to the IRS, and enter an adjustment in column (g) to correct the basis. See *Column (g)* in the separate instructions for how to figure the amount of the adjustment.

Form **8949** (2017)

Source: Form 8949, Department of the Treasury - Internal Revenue Service, 2017

SCHEDULE E (Form 1040) Department of the Treasury Internal Revenue Service (99)	**Supplemental Income and Loss** (From rental real estate, royalties, partnerships, S corporations, estates, trusts, REMICs, etc.) ▶ Attach to Form 1040, 1040NR, or Form 1041. ▶ Go to *www.irs.gov/ScheduleE* for instructions and the latest information.	OMB No. 1545-0074 20**17** Attachment Sequence No. **13**
Name(s) shown on return		Your social security number

Part I   Income or Loss From Rental Real Estate and Royalties   Note: If you are in the business of renting personal property, use Schedule C or **C-EZ** (see instructions). If you are an individual, report farm rental income or loss from **Form 4835** on page 2, line 40.

A Did you make any payments in 2017 that would require you to file Form(s) 1099? (see instructions) . . . . . ☐ **Yes** ☐ **No**
B If "Yes," did you or will you file required Forms 1099? . . . . ☐ **Yes** ☐ **No**

1a	Physical address of each property (street, city, state, ZIP code)
A	
B	
C	

1b	Type of Property (from list below)	2	For each rental real estate property listed above, report the number of fair rental and personal use days. Check the **QJV** box only if you meet the requirements to file as a qualified joint venture. See instructions.		Fair Rental Days	Personal Use Days	QJV
A				A			☐
B				B			☐
C				C			☐

Type of Property:

1 Single Family Residence   3 Vacation/Short-Term Rental   5 Land   7 Self-Rental
2 Multi-Family Residence   4 Commercial   6 Royalties   8 Other (describe)

Income:	**Properties:**		A	B	C
3	Rents received	**3**			
4	Royalties received	**4**			
Expenses:					
5	Advertising	**5**			
6	Auto and travel (see instructions)	**6**			
7	Cleaning and maintenance	**7**			
8	Commissions.	**8**			
9	Insurance	**9**			
10	Legal and other professional fees	**10**			
11	Management fees	**11**			
12	Mortgage interest paid to banks, etc. (see instructions)	**12**			
13	Other interest.	**13**			
14	Repairs.	**14**			
15	Supplies	**15**			
16	Taxes	**16**			
17	Utilities	**17**			
18	Depreciation expense or depletion	**18**			
19	Other (list) ▶ _____	**19**			
20	Total expenses. Add lines 5 through 19	**20**			
21	Subtract line 20 from line 3 (rents) and/or 4 (royalties). If result is a (loss), see instructions to find out if you must file **Form 6198**	**21**			
22	Deductible rental real estate loss after limitation, if any, on **Form 8582** (see instructions)	**22**	( )	( )	( )

23a	Total of all amounts reported on line 3 for all rental properties	**23a**	
b	Total of all amounts reported on line 4 for all royalty properties	**23b**	
c	Total of all amounts reported on line 12 for all properties	**23c**	
d	Total of all amounts reported on line 18 for all properties	**23d**	
e	Total of all amounts reported on line 20 for all properties	**23e**	
24	**Income.** Add positive amounts shown on line 21. **Do not** include any losses	**24**	
25	**Losses.** Add royalty losses from line 21 and rental real estate losses from line 22. Enter total losses here .	**25**	( )
26	**Total rental real estate and royalty income or (loss).** Combine lines 24 and 25. Enter the result here. If Parts II, III, IV, and line 40 on page 2 do not apply to you, also enter this amount on Form 1040, line 17, or Form 1040NR, line 18. Otherwise, include this amount in the total on line 41 on page 2 . . .	**26**	

For Paperwork Reduction Act Notice, see the separate instructions.   Cat. No. 11344L   Schedule E (Form 1040) 2017

Name(s) shown on return. Do not enter name and social security number if shown on other side.	**Your social security number**

Caution: The IRS compares amounts reported on your tax return with amounts shown on Schedule(s) K-1.

Part II **Income or Loss From Partnerships and S Corporations** **Note:** If you report a loss from an at-risk activity for which **any** amount is **not** at risk, you **must** check the box in column **(e)** on line 28 and attach **Form 6198.** See instructions.

27 Are you reporting any loss not allowed in a prior year due to the at-risk, excess farm loss, or basis limitations, a prior year unallowed loss from a passive activity (if that loss was not reported on Form 8582), or unreimbursed partnership expenses? If you answered "Yes," see instructions before completing this section . . . . ☐ **Yes** ☐ **No**

28	**(a)** Name	**(b)** Enter **P** for partnership; **S** for S corporation	**(c)** Check if foreign partnership	**(d)** Employer identification number	**(e)** Check if any amount is not at risk
A			☐		☐
B			☐		☐
C			☐		☐
D			☐		☐

	Passive Income and Loss		Nonpassive Income and Loss		
	(f) Passive loss allowed (attach **Form 8582** if required)	**(g)** Passive income from **Schedule K-1**	**(h)** Nonpassive loss from **Schedule K-1**	**(i)** Section 179 expense deduction from **Form 4562**	**(j)** Nonpassive income from **Schedule K-1**
A					
B					
C					
D					
29a Totals					
b Totals					

30	Add columns (g) and (j) of line 29a	**30**		
31	Add columns (f), (h), and (i) of line 29b	**31**	(	)
32	**Total partnership and S corporation income or (loss).** Combine lines 30 and 31. Enter the result here and include in the total on line 41 below	**32**		

Part III **Income or Loss From Estates and Trusts**

33	**(a)** Name	**(b)** Employer identification number
A		
B		

	Passive Income and Loss		Nonpassive Income and Loss	
	(c) Passive deduction or loss allowed (attach **Form 8582** if required)	**(d)** Passive income from **Schedule K-1**	**(e)** Deduction or loss from **Schedule K-1**	**(f)** Other income from **Schedule K-1**
A				
B				
34a Totals				
b Totals				

35	Add columns (d) and (f) of line 34a	**35**		
36	Add columns (c) and (e) of line 34b	**36**	(	)
37	**Total estate and trust income or (loss).** Combine lines 35 and 36. Enter the result here and include in the total on line 41 below	**37**		

Part IV **Income or Loss From Real Estate Mortgage Investment Conduits (REMICs)—Residual Holder**

38	**(a)** Name	**(b)** Employer identification number	**(c)** Excess inclusion from **Schedules Q,** line 2c (see instructions)	**(d)** Taxable income (net loss) from **Schedules Q,** line 1b	**(e)** Income from **Schedules Q,** line 3b

39	Combine columns (d) and (e) only. Enter the result here and include in the total on line 41 below	**39**	

Part V **Summary**

40	Net farm rental income or (loss) from **Form 4835.** Also, complete line 42 below	**40**	
41	**Total income or (loss).** Combine lines 26, 32, 37, 39, and 40. Enter the result here and on Form 1040, line 17, or Form 1040NR, line 18 ▶	**41**	

42 **Reconciliation of farming and fishing income.** Enter your **gross** farming and fishing income reported on Form 4835, line 7; Schedule K-1 (Form 1065), box 14, code B; Schedule K-1 (Form 1120S), box 17, code V; and Schedule K-1 (Form 1041), box 14, code F (see instructions) . . | **42** | |

43 **Reconciliation for real estate professionals.** If you were a real estate professional (see instructions), enter the net income or (loss) you reported anywhere on Form 1040 or Form 1040NR from all rental real estate activities in which you materially participated under the passive activity loss rules . . | **43** | |

Source: Schedule E, Form 1040, Department of the Treasury—Internal Revenue Service, 2017

SCHEDULE SE **(Form 1040)** Department of the Treasury Internal Revenue Service (99)	**Self-Employment Tax** ▶ Go to *www.irs.gov/ScheduleSE* for instructions and the latest information. ▶ **Attach to Form 1040 or Form 1040NR.**

OMB No. 1545-0074

20**17**

Attachment
Sequence No. **17**

Name of person with **self-employment** income (as shown on Form 1040 or Form 1040NR)	Social security number of person with **self-employment** income ▶

Before you begin: To determine if you must file Schedule SE, see the instructions.

May I Use Short Schedule SE or Must I Use Long Schedule SE?

Note: Use this flowchart **only if** you must file Schedule SE. If unsure, see *Who Must File Schedule SE* in the instructions.

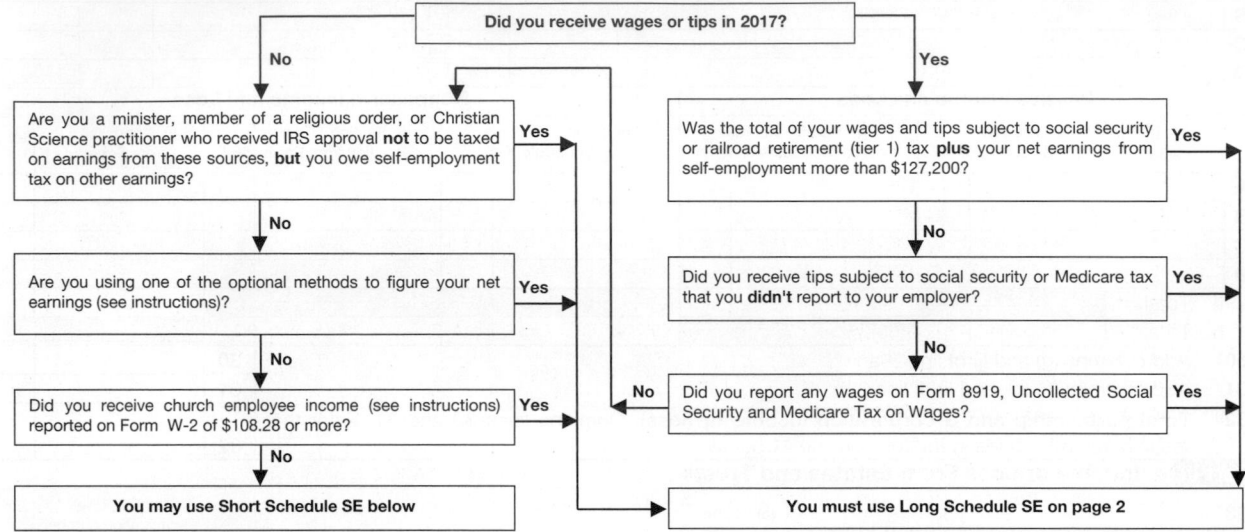

Section A—Short Schedule SE.   Caution: Read above to see if you can use Short Schedule SE.

1a	Net farm profit or (loss) from Schedule F, line 34, and farm partnerships, Schedule K-1 (Form 1065), box 14, code A	**1a**	
b	If you received social security retirement or disability benefits, enter the amount of Conservation Reserve Program payments included on Schedule F, line 4b, or listed on Schedule K-1 (Form 1065), box 20, code Z	**1b**	( )
2	Net profit or (loss) from Schedule C, line 31; Schedule C-EZ, line 3; Schedule K-1 (Form 1065), box 14, code A (other than farming); and Schedule K-1 (Form 1065-B), box 9, code J1. Ministers and members of religious orders, see instructions for types of income to report on this line. See instructions for other income to report	**2**	
3	Combine lines 1a, 1b, and 2	**3**	
4	Multiply line 3 by 92.35% (0.9235). If less than $400, you don't owe self-employment tax; **don't** file this schedule unless you have an amount on line 1b . . . . ▶	**4**	
	Note: If line 4 is less than $400 due to Conservation Reserve Program payments on line 1b, see instructions.		
5	**Self-employment tax.** If the amount on line 4 is: • $127,200 or less, multiply line 4 by 15.3% (0.153). Enter the result here and on **Form 1040, line 57,** or **Form 1040NR, line 55** • More than $127,200, multiply line 4 by 2.9% (0.029). Then, add $15,772.80 to the result. Enter the total here and on **Form 1040, line 57,** or **Form 1040NR, line 55**	**5**	
6	**Deduction for one-half of self-employment tax.** Multiply line 5 by 50% (0.50). Enter the result here and on **Form 1040, line 27,** or **Form 1040NR, line 27**	**6**	

For Paperwork Reduction Act Notice, see your tax return instructions.   Cat. No. 11358Z   Schedule SE (Form 1040) 2017

| Name of person with **self-employment** income (as shown on Form 1040 or Form 1040NR) | Social security number of person with **self-employment** income ▶ | |

Section B—Long Schedule SE

Part I   Self-Employment Tax

Note: If your only income subject to self-employment tax is **church employee income,** see instructions. Also see instructions for the definition of church employee income.

A   If you are a minister, member of a religious order, or Christian Science practitioner **and** you filed Form 4361, but you had $400 or more of **other** net earnings from self-employment, check here and continue with Part I . . . . ▶ ☐

1a	Net farm profit or (loss) from Schedule F, line 34, and farm partnerships, Schedule K-1 (Form 1065), box 14, code A. **Note:** Skip lines 1a and 1b if you use the farm optional method (see instructions)	**1a**		
b	If you received social security retirement or disability benefits, enter the amount of Conservation Reserve Program payments included on Schedule F, line 4b, or listed on Schedule K-1 (Form 1065), box 20, code Z	**1b**	(	)
2	Net profit or (loss) from Schedule C, line 31; Schedule C-EZ, line 3; Schedule K-1 (Form 1065), box 14, code A (other than farming); and Schedule K-1 (Form 1065-B), box 9, code J1. Ministers and members of religious orders, see instructions for types of income to report on this line. See instructions for other income to report. **Note:** Skip this line if you use the nonfarm optional method (see instructions)	**2**		
3	Combine lines 1a, 1b, and 2	**3**		
4a	If line 3 is more than zero, multiply line 3 by 92.35% (0.9235). Otherwise, enter amount from line 3 **Note:** If line 4a is less than $400 due to Conservation Reserve Program payments on line 1b, see instructions.	**4a**		
b	If you elect one or both of the optional methods, enter the total of lines 15 and 17 here . .	**4b**		
c	Combine lines 4a and 4b. If less than $400, **stop;** you don't owe self-employment tax. **Exception:** If less than $400 and you had **church employee income,** enter -0- and continue ▶	**4c**		
5a	Enter your **church employee income** from Form W-2. See instructions for definition of church employee income . . . **5a**			
b	Multiply line 5a by 92.35% (0.9235). If less than $100, enter -0-	**5b**		
6	Add lines 4c and 5b	**6**		
7	Maximum amount of combined wages and self-employment earnings subject to social security tax or the 6.2% portion of the 7.65% railroad retirement (tier 1) tax for 2017	**7**	127,200	00
8a	Total social security wages and tips (total of boxes 3 and 7 on Form(s) W-2) and railroad retirement (tier 1) compensation. If $127,200 or more, skip lines 8b through 10, and go to line 11 **8a**			
b	Unreported tips subject to social security tax (from Form 4137, line 10) **8b**			
c	Wages subject to social security tax (from Form 8919, line 10) **8c**			
d	Add lines 8a, 8b, and 8c	**8d**		
9	Subtract line 8d from line 7. If zero or less, enter -0- here and on line 10 and go to line 11 ▶	**9**		
10	Multiply the **smaller** of line 6 or line 9 by 12.4% (0.124)	**10**		
11	Multiply line 6 by 2.9% (0.029)	**11**		
12	**Self-employment tax.** Add lines 10 and 11. Enter here and on **Form 1040, line 57,** or **Form 1040NR, line 55**	**12**		
13	**Deduction for one-half of self-employment tax.** Multiply line 12 by 50% (0.50). Enter the result here and on **Form 1040, line 27,** or **Form 1040NR, line 27** **13**			

Part II   Optional Methods To Figure Net Earnings (see instructions)

Farm Optional Method. You may use this method **only** if **(a)** your gross farm income[1] wasn't more than $7,800, **or (b)** your net farm profits[2] were less than $5,631.

14	Maximum income for optional methods	**14**	5,200	00
15	Enter the **smaller** of: two-thirds (²/₃) of gross farm income[1] (not less than zero) **or** $5,200. Also include this amount on line 4b above	**15**		

Nonfarm Optional Method. You may use this method **only** if **(a)** your net nonfarm profits[3] were less than $5,631 and also less than 72.189% of your gross nonfarm income,[4] **and (b)** you had net earnings from self-employment of at least $400 in 2 of the prior 3 years. **Caution:** You may use this method no more than five times.

16	Subtract line 15 from line 14	**16**		
17	Enter the **smaller** of: two-thirds (²/₃) of gross nonfarm income[4] (not less than zero) **or** the amount on line 16. Also include this amount on line 4b above	**17**		

[1] From Sch. F, line 9, and Sch. K-1 (Form 1065), box 14, code B.

[2] From Sch. F, line 34, and Sch. K-1 (Form 1065), box 14, code A—minus the amount you would have entered on line 1b had you not used the optional method.

[3] From Sch. C, line 31; Sch. C-EZ, line 3; Sch. K-1 (Form 1065), box 14, code A; and Sch. K-1 (Form 1065-B), box 9, code J1.

[4] From Sch. C, line 7; Sch. C-EZ, line 1; Sch. K-1 (Form 1065), box 14, code C; and Sch. K-1 (Form 1065-B), box 9, code J2.

Source: Schedule SE, Form 1040, Department of the Treasury—Internal Revenue Service, 2017

Schedule SE (Form 1040) 2017

Form **1065**	**U.S. Return of Partnership Income**	OMB No. 1545-0123

Department of the Treasury
Internal Revenue Service

For calendar year 2017, or tax year beginning _____ , 2017, ending _____ , 20 _____ .

▶ Go to *www.irs.gov/Form1065* for instructions and the latest information.

2017

A Principal business activity	**Type or Print**	Name of partnership	**D** Employer identification number
B Principal product or service		Number, street, and room or suite no. If a P.O. box, see the instructions.	**E** Date business started
C Business code number		City or town, state or province, country, and ZIP or foreign postal code	**F** Total assets (see the instructions) $

G Check applicable boxes: **(1)** ☐ Initial return **(2)** ☐ Final return **(3)** ☐ Name change **(4)** ☐ Address change **(5)** ☐ Amended return
(6) ☐ Technical termination - also check (1) or (2)

H Check accounting method: **(1)** ☐ Cash **(2)** ☐ Accrual **(3)** ☐ Other (specify) ▶ _____

I Number of Schedules K-1. Attach one for each person who was a partner at any time during the tax year ▶ _____

J Check if Schedules C and M-3 are attached . . . . ☐

Caution. *Include **only** trade or business income and expenses on lines 1a through 22 below. See the instructions for more information.*

Income	1a	Gross receipts or sales	1a		
	b	Returns and allowances	1b		
	c	Balance. Subtract line 1b from line 1a	1c		
	2	Cost of goods sold (attach Form 1125-A)	2		
	3	Gross profit. Subtract line 2 from line 1c	3		
	4	Ordinary income (loss) from other partnerships, estates, and trusts (attach statement) . .	4		
	5	Net farm profit (loss) (attach Schedule F (Form 1040))	5		
	6	Net gain (loss) from Form 4797, Part II, line 17 (attach Form 4797)	6		
	7	Other income (loss) (attach statement)	7		
	8	**Total income (loss).** Combine lines 3 through 7	8		
Deductions (see the instructions for limitations)	9	Salaries and wages (other than to partners) (less employment credits)	9		
	10	Guaranteed payments to partners	10		
	11	Repairs and maintenance	11		
	12	Bad debts	12		
	13	Rent	13		
	14	Taxes and licenses	14		
	15	Interest	15		
	16a	Depreciation (if required, attach Form 4562)	16a		
	b	Less depreciation reported on Form 1125-A and elsewhere on return	16b	16c	
	17	Depletion (**Do not deduct oil and gas depletion.**)	17		
	18	Retirement plans, etc.	18		
	19	Employee benefit programs	19		
	20	Other deductions (attach statement)	20		
	21	**Total deductions.** Add the amounts shown in the far right column for lines 9 through 20 .	21		
	22	**Ordinary business income (loss).** Subtract line 21 from line 8	22		

Sign Here

Under penalties of perjury, I declare that I have examined this return, including accompanying schedules and statements, and to the best of my knowledge and belief, it is true, correct, and complete. Declaration of preparer (other than partner or limited liability company member) is based on all information of which preparer has any knowledge.

May the IRS discuss this return with the preparer shown below (see instructions)? ☐ **Yes** ☐ **No**

▶ _____
　Signature of partner or limited liability company member

▶ _____
　Date

Paid Preparer Use Only

Print/Type preparer's name	Preparer's signature	Date	Check ☐ if self-employed	PTIN
Firm's name ▶			Firm's EIN ▶	
Firm's address ▶			Phone no.	

For Paperwork Reduction Act Notice, see separate instructions.　　　Cat. No. 11390Z　　　Form **1065** (2017)

Form 1065 (2017)   Page **2**

Schedule B	**Other Information**

		Yes	No
1	What type of entity is filing this return? Check the applicable box:		

a ☐ Domestic general partnership   **b** ☐ Domestic limited partnership

c ☐ Domestic limited liability company   **d** ☐ Domestic limited liability partnership

e ☐ Foreign partnership   **f** ☐ Other ▶

		Yes	No
2	At any time during the tax year, was any partner in the partnership a disregarded entity, a partnership (including an entity treated as a partnership), a trust, an S corporation, an estate (other than an estate of a deceased partner), or a nominee or similar person?		
3	At the end of the tax year:		
a	Did any foreign or domestic corporation, partnership (including any entity treated as a partnership), trust, or tax-exempt organization, or any foreign government own, directly or indirectly, an interest of 50% or more in the profit, loss, or capital of the partnership? For rules of constructive ownership, see instructions. If "Yes," attach Schedule B-1, Information on Partners Owning 50% or More of the Partnership		
b	Did any individual or estate own, directly or indirectly, an interest of 50% or more in the profit, loss, or capital of the partnership? For rules of constructive ownership, see instructions. If "Yes," attach Schedule B-1, Information on Partners Owning 50% or More of the Partnership		
4	At the end of the tax year, did the partnership:		
a	Own directly 20% or more, or own, directly or indirectly, 50% or more of the total voting power of all classes of stock entitled to vote of any foreign or domestic corporation? For rules of constructive ownership, see instructions. If "Yes," complete (i) through (iv) below		

(i) Name of Corporation	**(ii)** Employer Identification Number (if any)	**(iii)** Country of Incorporation	**(iv)** Percentage Owned in Voting Stock

b	Own directly an interest of 20% or more, or own, directly or indirectly, an interest of 50% or more in the profit, loss, or capital in any foreign or domestic partnership (including an entity treated as a partnership) or in the beneficial interest of a trust? For rules of constructive ownership, see instructions. If "Yes," complete (i) through (v) below . .		

(i) Name of Entity	**(ii)** Employer Identification Number (if any)	**(iii)** Type of Entity	**(iv)** Country of Organization	**(v)** Maximum Percentage Owned in Profit, Loss, or Capital

		Yes	No
5	Did the partnership file Form 8893, Election of Partnership Level Tax Treatment, or an election statement under section 6231(a)(1)(B)(ii) for partnership-level tax treatment, that is in effect for this tax year? See Form 8893 for more details		
6	Does the partnership satisfy **all four** of the following conditions?		
a	The partnership's total receipts for the tax year were less than $250,000.		
b	The partnership's total assets at the end of the tax year were less than $1 million.		
c	Schedules K-1 are filed with the return and furnished to the partners on or before the due date (including extensions) for the partnership return.		
d	The partnership is not filing and is not required to file Schedule M-3		
	If "Yes," the partnership is not required to complete Schedules L, M-1, and M-2; Item F on page 1 of Form 1065; or Item L on Schedule K-1.		
7	Is this partnership a publicly traded partnership as defined in section 469(k)(2)?		
8	During the tax year, did the partnership have any debt that was cancelled, was forgiven, or had the terms modified so as to reduce the principal amount of the debt?		
9	Has this partnership filed, or is it required to file, Form 8918, Material Advisor Disclosure Statement, to provide information on any reportable transaction?		
10	At any time during calendar year 2017, did the partnership have an interest in or a signature or other authority over a financial account in a foreign country (such as a bank account, securities account, or other financial account)? See the instructions for exceptions and filing requirements for FinCEN Form 114, Report of Foreign Bank and Financial Accounts (FBAR). If "Yes," enter the name of the foreign country. ▶		

Form **1065** (2017)

Source: Form 1065, Department of the Treasury—Internal Revenue Service, 2017

651117

| | | Final K-1 | | Amended K-1 | OMB No. 1545-0123 |

Schedule K-1
(Form 1065)

2017

Department of the Treasury
Internal Revenue Service

For calendar year 2017, or tax year

beginning / / 2017 ending / /

Partner's Share of Income, Deductions, Credits, etc.

► See back of form and separate instructions.

| Part I | Information About the Partnership |

A Partnership's employer identification number

B Partnership's name, address, city, state, and ZIP code

C IRS Center where partnership filed return

D ☐ Check if this is a publicly traded partnership (PTP)

| Part II | Information About the Partner |

E Partner's identifying number

F Partner's name, address, city, state, and ZIP code

G ☐ General partner or LLC member-manager ☐ Limited partner or other LLC member

H ☐ Domestic partner ☐ Foreign partner

I1 What type of entity is this partner? _____

I2 If this partner is a retirement plan (IRA/SEP/Keogh/etc.), check here ☐

J Partner's share of profit, loss, and capital (see instructions):

	Beginning	Ending
Profit	%	%
Loss	%	%
Capital	%	%

K Partner's share of liabilities at year end:

Nonrecourse . . . . $ _____

Qualified nonrecourse financing . $ _____

Recourse . . . . $ _____

L Partner's capital account analysis:

Beginning capital account . . . $ _____

Capital contributed during the year $ _____

Current year increase (decrease) . $ _____

Withdrawals & distributions . . $ (_____)

Ending capital account . . . . $ _____

☐ Tax basis ☐ GAAP ☐ Section 704(b) book
☐ Other (explain)

M Did the partner contribute property with a built-in gain or loss?

☐ Yes ☐ No

If "Yes," attach statement (see instructions)

Part III	Partner's Share of Current Year Income, Deductions, Credits, and Other Items

1	Ordinary business income (loss)	15	Credits
2	Net rental real estate income (loss)		
3	Other net rental income (loss)	16	Foreign transactions
4	Guaranteed payments		
5	Interest income		
6a	Ordinary dividends		
6b	Qualified dividends		
7	Royalties		
8	Net short-term capital gain (loss)		
9a	Net long-term capital gain (loss)	17	Alternative minimum tax (AMT) items
9b	Collectibles (28%) gain (loss)		
9c	Unrecaptured section 1250 gain		
10	Net section 1231 gain (loss)	18	Tax-exempt income and nondeductible expenses
11	Other income (loss)		
		19	Distributions
12	Section 179 deduction		
13	Other deductions	20	Other information
14	Self-employment earnings (loss)		

*See attached statement for additional information.

For IRS Use Only

Source: Schedule K-1, Form 1041, Department of the Treasury—Internal Revenue Service, 2017

Form **1120**	**U.S. Corporation Income Tax Return**	OMB No. 1545-0123
Department of the Treasury Internal Revenue Service	For calendar year 2017 or tax year beginning _____, 2017, ending _____, 20 ___ ▶ Go to *www.irs.gov/Form1120* for instructions and the latest information.	**2017**

A Check if:

1a Consolidated return (attach Form 851) ☐
b Life/nonlife consolidated return ☐
2 Personal holding co. (attach Sch. PH) ☐
3 Personal service corp. (see instructions) ☐
4 Schedule M-3 attached ☐

TYPE OR PRINT

Name

Number, street, and room or suite no. If a P.O. box, see instructions.

City or town, state, or province, country, and ZIP or foreign postal code

B Employer identification number

C Date incorporated

D Total assets (see instructions)
$

E Check if: (1) ☐ Initial return (2) ☐ Final return (3) ☐ Name change (4) ☐ Address change

Income

1a	Gross receipts or sales	1a	
b	Returns and allowances	1b	
c	Balance. Subtract line 1b from line 1a	1c	
2	Cost of goods sold (attach Form 1125-A)	2	
3	Gross profit. Subtract line 2 from line 1c	3	
4	Dividends (Schedule C, line 19)	4	
5	Interest	5	
6	Gross rents	6	
7	Gross royalties	7	
8	Capital gain net income (attach Schedule D (Form 1120))	8	
9	Net gain or (loss) from Form 4797, Part II, line 17 (attach Form 4797)	9	
10	Other income (see instructions—attach statement)	10	
11	**Total income.** Add lines 3 through 10 . . . . ▶	11	

Deductions (See instructions for limitations on deductions.)

12	Compensation of officers (see instructions—attach Form 1125-E) . . . . ▶	12	
13	Salaries and wages (less employment credits)	13	
14	Repairs and maintenance	14	
15	Bad debts	15	
16	Rents	16	
17	Taxes and licenses	17	
18	Interest	18	
19	Charitable contributions	19	
20	Depreciation from Form 4562 not claimed on Form 1125-A or elsewhere on return (attach Form 4562) . .	20	
21	Depletion	21	
22	Advertising	22	
23	Pension, profit-sharing, etc., plans	23	
24	Employee benefit programs	24	
25	Domestic production activities deduction (attach Form 8903)	25	
26	Other deductions (attach statement)	26	
27	**Total deductions.** Add lines 12 through 26 . . . . ▶	27	
28	Taxable income before net operating loss deduction and special deductions. Subtract line 27 from line 11.	28	
29a	Net operating loss deduction (see instructions) 29a		
b	Special deductions (Schedule C, line 20) 29b		
c	Add lines 29a and 29b	29c	

Tax, Refundable Credits, and Payments

30	**Taxable income.** Subtract line 29c from line 28. See instructions	30	
31	Total tax (Schedule J, Part I, line 11)	31	
32	Total payments and refundable credits (Schedule J, Part II, line 21)	32	
33	Estimated tax penalty. See instructions. Check if Form 2220 is attached . . . . . ▶ ☐	33	
34	**Amount owed.** If line 32 is smaller than the total of lines 31 and 33, enter amount owed	34	
35	**Overpayment.** If line 32 is larger than the total of lines 31 and 33, enter amount overpaid	35	
36	Enter amount from line 35 you want: **Credited to 2018 estimated tax** ▶ _____ Refunded ▶	36	

Sign Here

Under penalties of perjury, I declare that I have examined this return, including accompanying schedules and statements, and to the best of my knowledge and belief, it is true, correct, and complete. Declaration of preparer (other than taxpayer) is based on all information of which preparer has any knowledge.

▶ _____   ▶ _____
Signature of officer   Date   Title

May the IRS discuss this return with the preparer shown below? See instructions. ☐ Yes ☐ No

Paid Preparer Use Only

Print/Type preparer's name	Preparer's signature	Date	Check ☐ if self-employed	PTIN
Firm's name ▶			Firm's EIN ▶	
Firm's address ▶			Phone no.	

For Paperwork Reduction Act Notice, see separate instructions.   Cat. No. 11450Q   Form **1120** (2017)

Form 1120S

Department of the Treasury
Internal Revenue Service

U.S. Income Tax Return for an S Corporation

▶ Do not file this form unless the corporation has filed or is
attaching Form 2553 to elect to be an S corporation.
▶ Go to *www.irs.gov/Form1120S* for instructions and the latest information.

OMB No. 1545-0123

2017

For calendar year 2017 or tax year beginning _____, 2017, ending _____, 20____

A S election effective date	**TYPE OR PRINT**	Name	**D** Employer identification number
B Business activity code number (see instructions)		Number, street, and room or suite no. If a P.O. box, see instructions.	**E** Date incorporated
C Check if Sch. M-3 attached ☐		City or town, state or province, country, and ZIP or foreign postal code	**F** Total assets (see instructions) $

G Is the corporation electing to be an S corporation beginning with this tax year? ☐ Yes ☐ No If "Yes," attach Form 2553 if not already filed

H Check if: **(1)** ☐ Final return **(2)** ☐ Name change **(3)** ☐ Address change **(4)** ☐ Amended return **(5)** ☐ S election termination or revocation

I Enter the number of shareholders who were shareholders during any part of the tax year . . . . ▶

Caution: Include **only** trade or business income and expenses on lines 1a through 21. See the instructions for more information.

Income

1a	Gross receipts or sales	1a	
b	Returns and allowances	1b	
c	Balance. Subtract line 1b from line 1a	1c	
2	Cost of goods sold (attach Form 1125-A)	2	
3	Gross profit. Subtract line 2 from line 1c	3	
4	Net gain (loss) from Form 4797, line 17 (attach Form 4797)	4	
5	Other income (loss) (see instructions—attach statement)	5	
6	**Total income (loss).** Add lines 3 through 5 . . . . ▶	6	

Deductions (see instructions for limitations)

7	Compensation of officers (see instructions—attach Form 1125-E)	7	
8	Salaries and wages (less employment credits)	8	
9	Repairs and maintenance	9	
10	Bad debts	10	
11	Rents	11	
12	Taxes and licenses	12	
13	Interest	13	
14	Depreciation not claimed on Form 1125-A or elsewhere on return (attach Form 4562) . .	14	
15	Depletion **(Do not deduct oil and gas depletion.)**	15	
16	Advertising	16	
17	Pension, profit-sharing, etc., plans	17	
18	Employee benefit programs	18	
19	Other deductions (attach statement)	19	
20	**Total deductions.** Add lines 7 through 19 . . . . ▶	20	
21	**Ordinary business income (loss).** Subtract line 20 from line 6	21	

Tax and Payments

22a	Excess net passive income or LIFO recapture tax (see instructions) . .	22a	
b	Tax from Schedule D (Form 1120S)	22b	
c	Add lines 22a and 22b (see instructions for additional taxes)	22c	
23a	2017 estimated tax payments and 2016 overpayment credited to 2017	23a	
b	Tax deposited with Form 7004	23b	
c	Credit for federal tax paid on fuels (attach Form 4136)	23c	
d	Add lines 23a through 23c	23d	
24	Estimated tax penalty (see instructions). Check if Form 2220 is attached . . . . . . ▶ ☐	24	
25	**Amount owed.** If line 23d is smaller than the total of lines 22c and 24, enter amount owed . .	25	
26	**Overpayment.** If line 23d is larger than the total of lines 22c and 24, enter amount overpaid . .	26	
27	Enter amount from line 26 **Credited to 2018 estimated tax** ▶ ____ **Refunded** ▶	27	

Sign Here

Under penalties of perjury, I declare that I have examined this return, including accompanying schedules and statements, and to the best of my knowledge and belief, it is true, correct, and complete. Declaration of preparer (other than taxpayer) is based on all information of which preparer has any knowledge.

▶ _____ Signature of officer   Date   ▶ _____ Title

May the IRS discuss this return with the preparer shown below (see instructions)? ☐ Yes ☐ No

Paid Preparer Use Only

Print/Type preparer's name	Preparer's signature	Date	Check ☐ if self-employed	PTIN
Firm's name ▶			Firm's EIN ▶	
Firm's address ▶			Phone no.	

For Paperwork Reduction Act Notice, see separate instructions.   Cat. No. 11510H   Form **1120S** (2017)

Source: Form 1120S, Department of the Treasury—Internal Revenue Service, 2017

671117

Schedule K-1
(Form 1120S)

Department of the Treasury
Internal Revenue Service

20**17**

For calendar year 2017, or tax year

beginning / / 2017   ending / /

Shareholder's Share of Income, Deductions, Credits, etc.   ► See back of form and separate instructions.

Part I	Information About the Corporation

A Corporation's employer identification number

B Corporation's name, address, city, state, and ZIP code

C IRS Center where corporation filed return

Part II	Information About the Shareholder

D Shareholder's identifying number

E Shareholder's name, address, city, state, and ZIP code

F Shareholder's percentage of stock
ownership for tax year . . . . _____ %

For IRS Use Only

☐ Final K-1   ☐ Amended K-1   OMB No. 1545-0123

Part III	Shareholder's Share of Current Year Income, Deductions, Credits, and Other Items

1	Ordinary business income (loss)	13	Credits
2	Net rental real estate income (loss)		
3	Other net rental income (loss)		
4	Interest income		
5a	Ordinary dividends		
5b	Qualified dividends	14	Foreign transactions
6	Royalties		
7	Net short-term capital gain (loss)		
8a	Net long-term capital gain (loss)		
8b	Collectibles (28%) gain (loss)		
8c	Unrecaptured section 1250 gain		
9	Net section 1231 gain (loss)		
10	Other income (loss)	15	Alternative minimum tax (AMT) items
11	Section 179 deduction	16	Items affecting shareholder basis
12	Other deductions		
		17	Other information

* See attached statement for additional information.

For Paperwork Reduction Act Notice, see the Instructions for Form 1120S.   www.irs.gov/Form1120S   Cat. No. 11520D   **Schedule K-1 (Form 1120S) 2017**

Source: Schedule K-1, Form 1120S, Department of the Treasury—Internal Revenue Service, 2017

SCHEDULE M-3
(Form 1120S)

Department of the Treasury
Internal Revenue Service

**Net Income (Loss) Reconciliation for S Corporations
With Total Assets of $10 Million or More**
▶ Attach to Form 1120S.

▶ Go to *www.irs.gov/Form1120S* for instructions and the latest information.

OMB No. 1545-0123

2017

Name of corporation	Employer identification number

Part I   Financial Information and Net Income (Loss) Reconciliation (see instructions)

1a Did the corporation prepare a certified audited non-tax-basis income statement for the period ending with or within this tax year? See instructions if multiple non-tax-basis income statements are prepared.

☐ **Yes.** Skip line 1b and complete lines 2 through 11 with respect to that income statement.

☐ **No.** Go to line 1b.

b Did the corporation prepare a non-tax-basis income statement for that period?

☐ **Yes.** Complete lines 2 through 11 with respect to that income statement.

☐ **No.** Skip lines 2 through 3b and enter the corporation's net income (loss) per its books and records on line 4a.

2 Enter the income statement period: Beginning _____ / _____ / _____ Ending _____ / _____ / _____

3a Has the corporation's income statement been restated for the income statement period on line 2?

☐ **Yes.** If "Yes," attach an explanation and the amount of each item restated.

☐ **No.**

b Has the corporation's income statement been restated for any of the five income statement periods immediately preceding the period on line 2?

☐ **Yes.** If "Yes," attach an explanation and the amount of each item restated.

☐ **No.**

4a Worldwide consolidated net income (loss) from income statement source identified in Part I, line 1 .	**4a**	
b Indicate accounting standard used for line 4a (see instructions): (1) ☐ GAAP (2) ☐ IFRS (3) ☐ Tax-basis (4) ☐ Other (specify) _____		
5a Net income from nonincludible foreign entities (attach statement)	**5a**	( )
b Net loss from nonincludible foreign entities (attach statement and enter as a positive amount) . . .	**5b**	
6a Net income from nonincludible U.S. entities (attach statement)	**6a**	( )
b Net loss from nonincludible U.S. entities (attach statement and enter as a positive amount)	**6b**	
7a Net income (loss) of other foreign disregarded entities (attach statement)	**7a**	
b Net income (loss) of other U.S. disregarded entities (except qualified subchapter S subsidiaries) (attach statement)	**7b**	
c Net income (loss) of other qualified subchapter S subsidiaries (QSubs) (attach statement)	**7c**	
8 Adjustment to eliminations of transactions between includible entities and nonincludible entities (attach statement)	**8**	
9 Adjustment to reconcile income statement period to tax year (attach statement)	**9**	
10 Other adjustments to reconcile to amount on line 11 (attach statement)	**10**	
11 **Net income (loss) per income statement of the corporation.** Combine lines 4 through 10 . . .	**11**	

Note: Part I, line 11, must equal Part II, line 26, column (a) or Schedule M-1, line 1. See instructions.

12 Enter the total amount (not just the corporation's share) of the assets and liabilities of all entities included or removed on the following lines:

	Total Assets	Total Liabilities
a Included on Part I, line 4		
b Removed on Part I, line 5		
c Removed on Part I, line 6		
d Included on Part I, line 7		

For Paperwork Reduction Act Notice, see the Instructions for Form 1120S.   Cat. No. 39666W   **Schedule M-3 (Form 1120S) 2017**

Name of corporation	Employer identification number

Part II Reconciliation of Net Income (Loss) per Income Statement of the Corporation With Total Income (Loss) per Return (see instructions)

Income (Loss) Items (Attach statements for lines 1 through 10)	(a) Income (Loss) per Income Statement	(b) Temporary Difference	(c) Permanent Difference	(d) Income (Loss) per Tax Return
1 Income (loss) from equity method foreign corporations				
2 Gross foreign dividends not previously taxed				
3 Subpart F, QEF, and similar income inclusions				
4 Gross foreign distributions previously taxed				
5 Income (loss) from equity method U.S. corporations				
6 U.S. dividends not eliminated in tax consolidation				
7 Income (loss) from U.S. partnerships				
8 Income (loss) from foreign partnerships				
9 Income (loss) from other pass-through entities				
10 Items relating to reportable transactions				
11 Interest income (see instructions)				
12 Total accrual to cash adjustment				
13 Hedging transactions				
14 Mark-to-market income (loss)				
15 Cost of goods sold (see instructions)	( )			( )
16 Sale versus lease (for sellers and/or lessors)				
17 Section 481(a) adjustments				
18 Unearned/deferred revenue				
19 Income recognition from long-term contracts				
20 Original issue discount and other imputed interest				
21a Income statement gain/loss on sale, exchange, abandonment, worthlessness, or other disposition of assets other than inventory and pass-through entities				
b Gross capital gains from Schedule D, excluding amounts from pass-through entities				
c Gross capital losses from Schedule D, excluding amounts from pass-through entities, abandonment losses, and worthless stock losses				
d Net gain/loss reported on Form 4797, line 17, excluding amounts from pass-through entities, abandonment losses, and worthless stock losses				
e Abandonment losses				
f Worthless stock losses (attach statement)				
g Other gain/loss on disposition of assets other than inventory				
22 Other income (loss) items with differences (attach statement)				
23 **Total income (loss) items.** Combine lines 1 through 22				
24 **Total expense/deduction items** (from Part III, line 32)				
25 Other items with no differences				
26 **Reconciliation totals.** Combine lines 23 through 25				

Note: Line 26, column (a), must equal Part I, line 11, and column (d) must equal Form 1120S, Schedule K, line 18.

Schedule M-3 (Form 1120S) 2017

Page **3**

Name of corporation	Employer identification number

Part III   Reconciliation of Net Income (Loss) per Income Statement of the Corporation With Total Income (Loss) per Return—Expense/Deduction Items (see instructions)

Expense/Deduction Items	(a) Expense per Income Statement	(b) Temporary Difference	(c) Permanent Difference	(d) Deduction per Tax Return
1 U.S. current income tax expense				
2 U.S. deferred income tax expense				
3 State and local current income tax expense				
4 State and local deferred income tax expense				
5 Foreign current income tax expense (other than foreign withholding taxes)				
6 Foreign deferred income tax expense				
7 Equity-based compensation				
8 Meals and entertainment				
9 Fines and penalties				
10 Judgments, damages, awards, and similar costs				
11 Pension and profit-sharing				
12 Other post-retirement benefits				
13 Deferred compensation				
14 Charitable contribution of cash and tangible property				
15 Charitable contribution of intangible property				
16 Current year acquisition or reorganization investment banking fees				
17 Current year acquisition or reorganization legal and accounting fees				
18 Current year acquisition/reorganization other costs				
19 Amortization/impairment of goodwill				
20 Amortization of acquisition, reorganization, and start-up costs				
21 Other amortization or impairment write-offs				
22 Reserved				
23a Depletion—Oil & Gas				
b Depletion—Other than Oil & Gas				
24 Depreciation				
25 Bad debt expense				
26 Interest expense (see instructions)				
27 Corporate owned life insurance premiums				
28 Purchase versus lease (for purchasers and/or lessees)				
29 Research and development costs				
30 Section 118 exclusion (attach statement)				
31 Other expense/deduction items with differences (attach statement)				
32 **Total expense/deduction items.** Combine lines 1 through 31. Enter here and on Part II, line 24, reporting positive amounts as negative and negative amounts as positive				

Schedule M-3 (Form 1120S) 2017

Source: Schedule M-3, Form 1120, Department of the Treasury—Internal Revenue Service, 2017

Form 706
(Rev. August 2017)

Department of the Treasury
Internal Revenue Service

United States Estate (and Generation-Skipping Transfer) Tax Return

▶ Estate of a citizen or resident of the United States (see instructions). To be filed for decedents dying after December 31, 2016.
▶ Go to *www.irs.gov/Form706* for instructions and the latest information.

OMB No. 1545-0015

Part 1—Decedent and Executor

1a Decedent's first name and middle initial (and maiden name, if any)	**1b** Decedent's last name **2** Decedent's social security no.
3a City, town, or post office; county; state or province; country; and ZIP or foreign postal code.	**3b** Year domicile established **4** Date of birth **5** Date of death
	6b Executor's address (number and street including apartment or suite no.; city, town, or post office; state or province; country; and ZIP or foreign postal code) and phone no.
6a Name of executor (see instructions)	
6c Executor's social security number (see instructions)	Phone no.

6d If there are multiple executors, check here ☐ and attach a list showing the names, addresses, telephone numbers, and SSNs of the additional executors.

7a Name and location of court where will was probated or estate administered   **7b** Case number

8 If decedent died testate, check here ▶ ☐ and attach a certified copy of the will.   **9** If you extended the time to file this Form 706, check here ▶ ☐

10 If Schedule R-1 is attached, check here ▶ ☐   **11** If you are estimating the value of assets included in the gross estate on line 1 pursuant to the special rule of Reg. section 20.2010-2(a) (7)(ii), check here ▶ ☐

Part 2—Tax Computation

1	Total gross estate less exclusion (from Part 5—Recapitulation, item 13)	**1**
2	Tentative total allowable deductions (from Part 5—Recapitulation, item 24)	**2**
3a	Tentative taxable estate (subtract line 2 from line 1)	**3a**
b	State death tax deduction	**3b**
c	Taxable estate (subtract line 3b from line 3a)	**3c**
4	Adjusted taxable gifts (see instructions)	**4**
5	Add lines 3c and 4	**5**
6	Tentative tax on the amount on line 5 from Table A in the instructions	**6**
7	Total gift tax paid or payable (see instructions)	**7**
8	Gross estate tax (subtract line 7 from line 6)	**8**
9a	Basic exclusion amount **9a**	
b	Deceased spousal unused exclusion (DSUE) amount from predeceased spouse(s), if any (from Section D, Part 6—Portability of Deceased Spousal Unused Exclusion). **9b**	
c	Restored exclusion amount (see instructions) **9c**	
d	Applicable exclusion amount (add lines 9a, 9b, and 9c) **9d**	
e	Applicable credit amount (tentative tax on the amount in 9d from table A in the instructions) **9e**	
10	Adjustment to applicable credit amount (May not exceed $6,000. See instructions.) **10**	
11	Allowable applicable credit amount (subtract line 10 from line 9e)	**11**
12	Subtract line 11 from line 8 (but do not enter less than zero)	**12**
13	Credit for foreign death taxes (from Schedule P). (Attach Form(s) 706-CE.) **13**	
14	Credit for tax on prior transfers (from Schedule Q) **14**	
15	Total credits (add lines 13 and 14)	**15**
16	Net estate tax (subtract line 15 from line 12)	**16**
17	Generation-skipping transfer (GST) taxes payable (from Schedule R, Part 2, line 10)	**17**
18	Total transfer taxes (add lines 16 and 17)	**18**
19	Prior payments (explain in an attached statement)	**19**
20	Balance due (or overpayment) (subtract line 19 from line 18)	**20**

Under penalties of perjury, I declare that I have examined this return, including accompanying schedules and statements, and to the best of my knowledge and belief, it is true, correct, and complete. Declaration of preparer other than the executor is based on all information of which preparer has any knowledge.

Sign Here

▶ Signature of executor   ▶ Date

▶ Signature of executor   ▶ Date

Paid Preparer Use Only

Print/Type preparer's name	Preparer's signature	Date	Check ☐ if self-employed	PTIN
Firm's name ▶			Firm's EIN ▶	
Firm's address ▶			Phone no.	

For Privacy Act and Paperwork Reduction Act Notice, see instructions.   Cat. No. 20548R   Form **706** (Rev. 8-2017)

Form 706 (Rev. 8-2017)

Estate of:	Decedent's social security number

Part 3—Elections by the Executor

Note: For information on electing portability of the decedent's DSUE amount, including how to opt out of the election, see Part 6—Portability of Deceased Spousal Unused Exclusion.

Note: Some of the following elections may require the posting of bonds or liens.

Please check "Yes" or "No" box for each question (see instructions).

			Yes	No
1	Do you elect alternate valuation?	1		
2	Do you elect special-use valuation? If "Yes," you must complete and attach Schedule A-1	2		
3	Do you elect to pay the taxes in installments as described in section 6166?			
	If "Yes," you must attach the additional information described in the instructions.			
	Note: By electing section 6166 installment payments, you may be required to provide security for estate tax deferred under section 6166 and interest in the form of a surety bond or a section 6324A lien.	3		
4	Do you elect to postpone the part of the taxes due to a reversionary or remainder interest as described in section 6163?	4		

Part 4—General Information

Note: Please attach the necessary supplemental documents. **You must attach the death certificate.** (See instructions)

Authorization to receive confidential tax information under Reg. section 601.504(b)(2)(i); to act as the estate's representative before the IRS; and to make written or oral presentations on behalf of the estate:

Name of representative (print or type)	State	Address (number, street, and room or suite no., city, state, and ZIP code)

I declare that I am the ☐ attorney/ ☐ certified public accountant/ ☐ enrolled agent (check the applicable box) for the executor. I am not under suspension or disbarment from practice before the Internal Revenue Service and am qualified to practice in the state shown above.

Signature	CAF number	Date	Telephone number

1 Death certificate number and issuing authority (attach a copy of the death certificate to this return).

2 Decedent's business or occupation. If retired, check here ▶ ☐   and state decedent's former business or occupation.

3a Marital status of the decedent at time of death:

☐ Married   ☐ Widow/widower   ☐ Single   ☐ Legally separated   ☐ Divorced

3b For all prior marriages, list the name and SSN of the former spouse, the date the marriage ended, and whether the marriage ended by annulment, divorce, or death. Attach additional statements of the same size if necessary.

4a Surviving spouse's name	4b Social security number	4c Amount received (see instructions)

5 Individuals (other than the surviving spouse), trusts, or other estates who receive benefits from the estate (do not include charitable beneficiaries shown in Schedule O) (see instructions).

Name of individual, trust, or estate receiving $5,000 or more	Identifying number	Relationship to decedent	Amount (see instructions)

All unascertainable beneficiaries and those who receive less than $5,000 . . . . ▶

Total . . . .

If you answer "Yes" to any of the following questions, you must attach additional information as described.	Yes	No
6 Is the estate filing a protective claim for refund?		
If "Yes," complete and attach two copies of Schedule PC for each claim.		
7 Does the gross estate contain any section 2044 property (qualified terminable interest property (QTIP) from a prior gift or estate)? (see instructions)		
8a Have federal gift tax returns ever been filed?		
If "Yes," attach copies of the returns, if available, and furnish the following information.		
b Period(s) covered **c** Internal Revenue office(s) where filed		
9a Was there any insurance on the decedent's life that is not included on the return as part of the gross estate?		
b Did the decedent own any insurance on the life of another that is not included in the gross estate?		

Form 706 (Rev. 8-2017)

Estate of:	Decedent's social security number

Part 4—General Information *(continued)*

If you answer "Yes" to any of the following questions, you must attach additional information as described.	Yes	No
10 Did the decedent at the time of death own any property as a joint tenant with right of survivorship in which **(a)** one or more of the other joint tenants was someone other than the decedent's spouse, and **(b)** less than the full value of the property is included on the return as part of the gross estate? If "Yes," you must complete and attach Schedule E		
11a Did the decedent, at the time of death, own any interest in a partnership (for example, a family limited partnership), an unincorporated business, or a limited liability company; or own any stock in an inactive or closely held corporation?		
b If "Yes," was the value of **any** interest owned (from above) discounted on this estate tax return? If "Yes," see the instructions on reporting the total accumulated or effective discounts taken on Schedule F or G		
12 Did the decedent make any transfer described in sections 2035, 2036, 2037, or 2038? (see instructions) If "Yes," you must complete and attach Schedule G		
13a Were there in existence at the time of the decedent's death any trusts created by the decedent during his or her lifetime? . .		
b Were there in existence at the time of the decedent's death any trusts not created by the decedent under which the decedent possessed any power, beneficial interest, or trusteeship?		
c Was the decedent receiving income from a trust created after October 22, 1986, by a parent or grandparent? . . . . . . If "Yes," was there a GST taxable termination (under section 2612) on the death of the decedent?		
d If there was a GST taxable termination (under section 2612), attach a statement to explain. Provide a copy of the trust or will creating the trust, and give the name, address, and phone number of the current trustee(s).		
e Did the decedent at any time during his or her lifetime transfer or sell an interest in a partnership, limited liability company, or closely held corporation to a trust described in lines 13a or 13b? . . . . If "Yes," provide the EIN for this transferred/sold item. ▶		
14 Did the decedent ever possess, exercise, or release any general power of appointment? If "Yes," you must complete and attach Schedule H		
15 Did the decedent have an interest in or a signature or other authority over a financial account in a foreign country, such as a bank account, securities account, or other financial account?		
16 Was the decedent, immediately before death, receiving an annuity described in the "General" paragraph of the instructions for Schedule I or a private annuity? If "Yes," you must complete and attach Schedule I		
17 Was the decedent ever the beneficiary of a trust for which a deduction was claimed by the estate of a predeceased spouse under section 2056(b)(7) and which is not reported on this return? If "Yes," attach an explanation		

Part 5—Recapitulation.

Note: If estimating the value of one or more assets pursuant to the special rule of Reg. section 20.2010-2(a)(7)(ii), enter on both lines 10 and 23 the amount noted in the instructions for the corresponding range of values. (See instructions for details.)

Item no.	Gross estate		Alternate value	Value at date of death
1	Schedule A—Real Estate	**1**		
2	Schedule B—Stocks and Bonds	**2**		
3	Schedule C—Mortgages, Notes, and Cash	**3**		
4	Schedule D—Insurance on the Decedent's Life (attach Form(s) 712)	**4**		
5	Schedule E—Jointly Owned Property (attach Form(s) 712 for life insurance) .	**5**		
6	Schedule F—Other Miscellaneous Property (attach Form(s) 712 for life insurance)	**6**		
7	Schedule G—Transfers During Decedent's Life (att. Form(s) 712 for life insurance)	**7**		
8	Schedule H—Powers of Appointment	**8**		
9	Schedule I—Annuities	**9**		
10	Estimated value of assets subject to the special rule of Reg. section 20.2010-2(a)(7)(ii)	**10**		
11	Total gross estate (add items 1 through 10)	**11**		
12	Schedule U—Qualified Conservation Easement Exclusion	**12**		
13	Total gross estate less exclusion (subtract item 12 from item 11). Enter here and on line 1 of Part 2—Tax Computation	**13**		

Item no.	Deductions		Amount	
14	Schedule J—Funeral Expenses and Expenses Incurred in Administering Property Subject to Claims	**14**		
15	Schedule K—Debts of the Decedent	**15**		
16	Schedule K—Mortgages and Liens	**16**		
17	Total of items 14 through 16	**17**		
18	Allowable amount of deductions from item 17 (see the instructions for item 18 of the Recapitulation)	**18**		
19	Schedule L—Net Losses During Administration	**19**		
20	Schedule L—Expenses Incurred in Administering Property Not Subject to Claims	**20**		
21	Schedule M—Bequests, etc., to Surviving Spouse	**21**		
22	Schedule O—Charitable, Public, and Similar Gifts and Bequests	**22**		
23	Estimated value of deductible assets subject to the special rule of Reg. section 20.2010-2(a)(7)(ii) . . .	**23**		
24	Tentative total allowable deductions (add items 18 through 23). Enter here and on line 2 of the Tax Computation	**24**		

Page 3

Source: Form 706, Department of the Treasury—Internal Revenue Service, 2017

Form **709**

Department of the Treasury
Internal Revenue Service

United States Gift (and Generation-Skipping Transfer) Tax Return

▶ Go to *www.irs.gov/Form709* for instructions and the latest information.

(For gifts made during calendar year 2017)
▶ See instructions.

OMB No. 1545-0020

2017

Part 1—General Information

1 Donor's first name and middle initial	**2** Donor's last name
	3 Donor's social security number
4 Address (number, street, and apartment number)	**5** Legal residence (domicile)
6 City or town, state or province, country, and ZIP or foreign postal code	**7** Citizenship (see instructions)

		Yes	No
8	If the donor died during the year, check here ▶ ☐ and enter date of death _____ , _____ .		
9	If you extended the time to file this Form 709, check here ▶ ☐		
10	Enter the total number of donees listed on Schedule A. Count each person only once ▶		
11a	Have you (the donor) previously filed a Form 709 (or 709-A) for any other year? If "No," skip line 11b		
b	Has your address changed since you last filed Form 709 (or 709-A)?		
12	**Gifts by husband or wife to third parties.** Do you consent to have the gifts (including generation-skipping transfers) made by you and by your spouse to third parties during the calendar year considered as made one-half by each of you? (see instructions.) (If the answer is "Yes," the following information must be furnished and your spouse must sign the consent shown below. **If the answer is "No," skip lines 13–18.**)		
13	Name of consenting spouse **14** SSN		
15	Were you married to one another during the entire calendar year? (see instructions)		
16	If 15 is "No," check whether ☐ married ☐ divorced or ☐ widowed/deceased, and give date (see instructions) ▶		
17	Will a gift tax return for this year be filed by your spouse? (If "Yes," mail both returns in the same envelope.)		

18 **Consent of Spouse.** I consent to have the gifts (and generation-skipping transfers) made by me and by my spouse to third parties during the calendar year considered as made one-half by each of us. We are both aware of the joint and several liability for tax created by the execution of this consent.

Consenting spouse's signature ▶   Date ▶

		Yes	No
19	Have you applied a DSUE amount received from a predeceased spouse to a gift or gifts reported on this or a previous Form 709? If "Yes," complete Schedule C		

Part 2—Tax Computation

1	Enter the amount from Schedule A, Part 4, line 11	**1**
2	Enter the amount from Schedule B, line 3	**2**
3	Total taxable gifts. Add lines 1 and 2	**3**
4	Tax computed on amount on line 3 (see *Table for Computing Gift Tax* in instructions)	**4**
5	Tax computed on amount on line 2 (see *Table for Computing Gift Tax* in instructions)	**5**
6	Balance. Subtract line 5 from line 4	**6**
7	Applicable credit amount. If donor has DSUE amount from predeceased spouse(s) or Restored Exclusion Amount, enter amount from Schedule C, line 5; otherwise, see instructions	**7**
8	Enter the applicable credit against tax allowable for all prior periods (from Sch. B, line 1, col. C) .	**8**
9	Balance. Subtract line 8 from line 7. Do not enter less than zero	**9**
10	Enter 20% (.20) of the amount allowed as a specific exemption for gifts made after September 8, 1976, and before January 1, 1977 (see instructions)	**10**
11	Balance. Subtract line 10 from line 9. Do not enter less than zero	**11**
12	Applicable credit. Enter the smaller of line 6 or line 11	**12**
13	Credit for foreign gift taxes (see instructions)	**13**
14	Total credits. Add lines 12 and 13	**14**
15	Balance. Subtract line 14 from line 6. Do not enter less than zero	**15**
16	Generation-skipping transfer taxes (from Schedule D, Part 3, col. H, Total)	**16**
17	Total tax. Add lines 15 and 16	**17**
18	Gift and generation-skipping transfer taxes prepaid with extension of time to file	**18**
19	If line 18 is less than line 17, enter **balance due** (see instructions)	**19**
20	If line 18 is greater than line 17, enter **amount to be refunded**	**20**

Attach check or money order here.

Sign Here

Under penalties of perjury, I declare that I have examined this return, including any accompanying schedules and statements, and to the best of my knowledge and belief, it is true, correct, and complete. Declaration of preparer (other than donor) is based on all information of which preparer has any knowledge.

May the IRS discuss this return with the preparer shown below (see instructions)? ☐ Yes ☐ No

▶ _____
Signature of donor   Date

Paid Preparer Use Only

Print/Type preparer's name	Preparer's signature	Date	Check ☐ if self-employed	PTIN
Firm's name ▶			Firm's EIN ▶	
Firm's address ▶			Phone no.	

For Disclosure, Privacy Act, and Paperwork Reduction Act Notice, see the instructions for this form.   Cat. No. 16783M   Form **709** (2017)

Form 709 (2017)   Page **2**

SCHEDULE A	Computation of Taxable Gifts (Including transfers in trust) (see instructions)

A   Does the value of any item listed on Schedule A reflect any valuation discount? If "Yes," attach explanation . . . . Yes ☐   No ☐

B   ☐ ◄ Check here if you elect under section 529(c)(2)(B) to treat any transfers made this year to a qualified tuition program as made ratably over a 5-year period beginning this year. See instructions. Attach explanation.

Part 1—Gifts Subject Only to Gift Tax. Gifts less political organization, medical, and educational exclusions. (see instructions)

A Item number	**B** • Donee's name and address • Relationship to donor (if any) • Description of gift • If the gift was of securities, give CUSIP no. • If closely held entity, give EIN	**C**	**D** Donor's adjusted basis of gift	**E** Date of gift	**F** Value at date of gift	**G** For split gifts, enter ¹/₂ of column F	**H** Net transfer (subtract col. G from col. F)

Gifts made by spouse —*complete **only** if you are splitting gifts with your spouse and he/she also made gifts.*

Total of Part 1. Add amounts from Part 1, column H . . . . ►

Part 2—Direct Skips. Gifts that are direct skips and are subject to both gift tax and generation-skipping transfer tax. You must list the gifts in chronological order.

A Item number	**B** • Donee's name and address • Relationship to donor (if any) • Description of gift • If the gift was of securities, give CUSIP no. • If closely held entity, give EIN	**C** 2632(b) election out	**D** Donor's adjusted basis of gift	**E** Date of gift	**F** Value at date of gift	**G** For split gifts, enter ¹/₂ of column F	**H** Net transfer (subtract col. G from col. F)

Gifts made by spouse —*complete **only** if you are splitting gifts with your spouse and he/she also made gifts.*

Total of Part 2. Add amounts from Part 2, column H . . . . ►

Part 3—Indirect Skips. Gifts to trusts that are currently subject to gift tax and may later be subject to generation-skipping transfer tax. You must list these gifts in chronological order.

A Item number	**B** • Donee's name and address • Relationship to donor (if any) • Description of gift • If the gift was of securities, give CUSIP no. • If closely held entity, give EIN	**C** 2632(c) election	**D** Donor's adjusted basis of gift	**E** Date of gift	**F** Value at date of gift	**G** For split gifts, enter ¹/₂ of column F	**H** Net transfer (subtract col. G from col. F)

Gifts made by spouse —*complete **only** if you are splitting gifts with your spouse and he/she also made gifts.*

Total of Part 3. Add amounts from Part 3, column H . . . . ►

(If more space is needed, attach additional statements.)   Form **709** (2017)

Form 709 (2017)

Part 4—Taxable Gift Reconciliation

1	Total value of gifts of donor. Add totals from column H of Parts 1, 2, and 3	**1**
2	Total annual exclusions for gifts listed on line 1 (see instructions)	**2**
3	Total included amount of gifts. Subtract line 2 from line 1	**3**

Deductions (see instructions)

4	Gifts of interests to spouse for which a marital deduction will be claimed, based on item numbers _____ of Schedule A . .	**4**		
5	Exclusions attributable to gifts on line 4	**5**		
6	Marital deduction. Subtract line 5 from line 4	**6**		
7	Charitable deduction, based on item nos. _____ less exclusions	**7**		
8	Total deductions. Add lines 6 and 7		**8**	
9	Subtract line 8 from line 3		**9**	
10	Generation-skipping transfer taxes payable with this Form 709 (from Schedule D, Part 3, col. H, Total) . .		**10**	
11	**Taxable gifts.** Add lines 9 and 10. Enter here and on page 1, Part 2—Tax Computation, line 1		**11**	

Terminable Interest (QTIP) Marital Deduction. (see instructions for Schedule A, Part 4, line 4)

If a trust (or other property) meets the requirements of qualified terminable interest property under section 2523(f), and:

a. The trust (or other property) is listed on Schedule A, and

b. The value of the trust (or other property) is entered in whole or in part as a deduction on Schedule A, Part 4, line 4, then the donor shall be deemed to have made an election to have such trust (or other property) treated as qualified terminable interest property under section 2523(f).

If less than the entire value of the trust (or other property) that the donor has included in Parts 1 and 3 of Schedule A is entered as a deduction on line 4, the donor shall be considered to have made an election only as to a fraction of the trust (or other property). The numerator of this fraction is equal to the amount of the trust (or other property) deducted on Schedule A, Part 4, line 6. The denominator is equal to the total value of the trust (or other property) listed in Parts 1 and 3 of Schedule A.

If you make the QTIP election, the terminable interest property involved will be included in your spouse's gross estate upon his or her death (section 2044). See instructions for line 4 of Schedule A. If your spouse disposes (by gift or otherwise) of all or part of the qualifying life income interest, he or she will be considered to have made a transfer of the entire property that is subject to the gift tax. See *Transfer of Certain Life Estates Received From Spouse* in the instructions.

12 Election Out of QTIP Treatment of Annuities

☐ ◄ Check here if you elect under section 2523(f)(6) **not** to treat as qualified terminable interest property any joint and survivor annuities that are reported on Schedule A and would otherwise be treated as qualified terminable interest property under section 2523(f). See instructions. Enter the item numbers from Schedule A for the annuities for which you are making this election ► _____

SCHEDULE B   Gifts From Prior Periods

If you answered "Yes," on line 11a of page 1, Part 1, see the instructions for completing Schedule B. If you answered "No," skip to the Tax Computation on page 1 (or Schedules C or D, if applicable). Complete Schedule A before beginning Schedule B. See instructions for recalculation of the column C amounts. Attach calculations.

A Calendar year or calendar quarter (see instructions)	B Internal Revenue office where prior return was filed	C Amount of applicable credit (unified credit) against gift tax for periods after December 31, 1976	D Amount of specific exemption for prior periods ending before January 1, 1977	E Amount of taxable gifts

1	Totals for prior periods	**1**		
2	Amount, if any, by which total specific exemption, line 1, column D is more than $30,000		**2**	
3	Total amount of taxable gifts for prior periods. Add amount on line 1, column E and amount, if any, on line 2. Enter here and on page 1, Part 2—Tax Computation, line 2		**3**	

(If more space is needed, attach additional statements.)

Form **709** (2017)

SCHEDULE C	Deceased Spousal Unused Exclusion (DSUE) Amount and Restored Exclusion

Provide the following information to determine the DSUE amount and applicable credit received from prior spouses. Complete Schedule A before beginning Schedule C.

A Name of Deceased Spouse (dates of death after December 31, 2010 only)	B Date of Death	C Portability Election Made?		D If "Yes," DSUE Amount Received from Spouse	E DSUE Amount Applied by Donor to Lifetime Gifts (list current and prior gifts)	F Date of Gift(s) (enter as mm/dd/yy for Part 1 and as yyyy for Part 2)
		Yes	No			

Part 1—DSUE RECEIVED FROM LAST DECEASED SPOUSE

Part 2—DSUE RECEIVED FROM PREDECEASED SPOUSE(S)

TOTAL (for all DSUE amounts applied from column E for Part 1 and Part 2)

1	Donor's basic exclusion amount (see instructions)	1
2	Total from column E, Parts 1 and 2	2
3	Restored Exclusion Amount (see instructions)	3
4	Add line 1, 2, and 3	4
5	Applicable credit on amount in line 4 (See *Table for Computing Gift Tax* in the instructions). Enter here and on line 7, Part 2—Tax Computation	5

SCHEDULE D	Computation of Generation-Skipping Transfer Tax

Note: Inter vivos direct skips that are completely excluded by the GST exemption must still be fully reported (including value and exemptions claimed) on Schedule D.

Part 1—Generation-Skipping Transfers

A Item No. (from Schedule A, Part 2, col. A)	B Value (from Schedule A, Part 2, col. H)	C Nontaxable Portion of Transfer	D Net Transfer (subtract col. C from col. B)

Gifts made by spouse (for gift splitting only)

(If more space is needed, attach additional statements.)   Form **709** (2017)

Source: Form 709, Department of the Treasury—Internal Revenue Service, 2017

Appendix B

Tax Terms Glossary

83(b) election   a special tax election that employees who receive restricted stock or other property with ownership restrictions can make to accelerate income recognition from the normal date when restrictions lapse to the date when the restricted stock or other property is granted. The election also accelerates the employer's compensation deduction related to the restricted stock or other property.

§162(m) limitation   the $1 million deduction limit on nonperformance-based salary paid to certain key executives.

§179 expense   an incentive for small businesses that allows them to immediately expense a certain amount of tangible personal property placed in service during the year.

§197 intangibles   intangible assets that are purchased that must be amortized over 180 months regardless of their actual useful lives.

§291 depreciation recapture   the portion of a corporate taxpayer's gain on real property that is converted from §1231 gain to ordinary income.

§338 election   an election by a corporate buyer of 80-percent-or-more of a corporation's stock to treat the acquisition as an asset acquisition and not a stock acquisition.

§338(h)(10) election   a joint election by the corporate buyer and corporate seller of the stock of a subsidiary of the seller to treat the acquisition as a sale of the subsidiary's assets by the seller to the buyer.

§481 adjustment   a change to taxable income associated with a change in accounting methods.

§1231 assets   depreciable or real property used in a taxpayer's trade or business owned for more than one year.

§1231 look-back rule   a tax rule requiring taxpayers to treat current year net §1231 gains as ordinary income when the taxpayer has deducted a §1231 loss as an ordinary loss in the five years preceding the current tax year.

§1245 property   tangible personal property and intangible property subject to cost recovery deductions.

§1250 property   real property subject to cost recovery deductions.

12-month rule   regulation that allows prepaid business expenses to be currently deducted when the contract does not extend beyond 12 months and the contract period does not extend beyond the end of the tax year following the year of the payment.

30-day letter   the IRS letter received after an audit that instructs the taxpayer that he or she has 30 days to either (1) request a conference with an appeals officer or (2) agree to the proposed adjustment.

90-day letter   the IRS letter received after an audit and receipt of the 30-day letter that explains that the taxpayer has 90 days to either (1) pay the proposed deficiency or (2) file a petition in the U.S. Tax Court to hear the case. The 90-day letter is also known as the *statutory notice of deficiency.*

§704(b) capital accounts   partners' capital accounts maintained using the accounting rules prescribed in the Section 704(b) regulations. Under these rules, capital accounts reflect the fair market value of property contributed to and distributed property from partnerships.

A

Abandoned spouse   a married taxpayer who lives apart from his or her spouse for the last six months of the year (excluding temporary absences), who files a tax return separate from his or her spouse, and who maintains a household for a qualifying child.

Accelerated death benefits   early receipt of life insurance proceeds that are not taxable under certain circumstances, such as the taxpayer is medically certified with an illness that is expected to cause death within 24 months.

Accountable plan   an employer's reimbursement plan under which employees must submit documentation supporting expenses to receive reimbursement and reimbursements are limited to legitimate business expenses.

Accounting method   the procedure for determining the taxable year in which a business recognizes a particular item of income or deduction, thereby dictating the timing of when a taxpayer reports income and deductions.

Accounting period   a fixed period in which a business reports income and deductions.

Accrual method   a method of accounting that generally recognizes income in the period earned and recognizes deductions in the period that liabilities are incurred.

Accrued market discount   a ratable amount of the market discount at the time of purchase (based on the number of days the bond is held over the number of days until maturity when the bond is purchased) that is treated as interest income when a bond with market discount is sold before it matures.

Accumulated adjustments account (AAA)   an account that reflects the cumulative income or loss for the time the corporation has been an S corporation.

Accumulated earnings and profits   undistributed earnings and profits from years prior to the current year.

Accumulated earnings tax   a tax assessed on corporations that retain earnings without a business reason to do so.

Acquiescence   issued after the IRS loses a trial-level or circuit court case when the IRS has decided to follow the court's adverse ruling in the future. It does not mean that the IRS agrees with the court's ruling. Instead, it simply means that the IRS will no longer litigate this issue.

Acquisition indebtedness   debt secured by a qualified residence that is incurred in acquiring, constructing, or substantially improving the residence.

Action on decision   an IRS pronouncement that explains the background reasoning behind an IRS acquiescence or nonacquiescence.

Active participant in a rental activity   an individual who owns at least 10 percent of a rental property and participates in the process of making management decisions, such as approving new tenants, deciding on rental terms, and approving repairs and capital expenditures.

Ad valorem taxes   taxes based on the value of property.

Additional Medicare tax   a tax imposed at a rate of .9% for salary or wages or net self-employment earnings in excess of $200,000 ($125,000 for married filing separate; $250,000 of combined salary or wages or net self-employment earnings for married filing joint).

Adequate consideration   a price paid that is equal in value to the service or property received.

Adjusted basis   An asset's carrying value for tax purposes at a given point in time, measured as the initial basis (for example, cost) plus capital improvements less depreciation or amortization. Also called adjusted tax basis.

Adjusted gross estate   gross estate reduced by administrative expenses, debts of the decedent, losses incurred during the administration of the estate, and state death taxes.

Adjusted gross income (AGI)   gross income less deductions for AGI. AGI is an important reference point that is often used in other calculations.

Adjusted tax basis   An asset's carrying value for tax purposes at a given point in time, measured as the initial basis (for example, cost) plus capital improvements less depreciation or amortization.

Adjusted taxable gifts   cumulative taxable gifts from previous years other than gifts already included in the gross estate valued at date of gift values.

Affiliated group   two or more "includible" corporations that are related through common stock ownership and eligible to file a U.S. consolidated tax return. An affiliated group consists of a parent corporation that owns directly 80 percent or more of the voting stock and value of another corporation and one or more subsidiary corporations that meet the 80 percent ownership requirement collectively. Includible corporations are taxable U.S. corporations, excluding real estate investment trusts, regulated investment companies, and life insurance companies.

After-tax rate of return   a taxpayer's before-tax rate of return on an investment minus the taxes paid on the income from the investment. The formula for an after-tax rate of return that is taxed annually is the before-tax rate of return $\times$ (1 − marginal tax rate) [i.e., $r = R \times (1 - t)$]. A taxpayer's after-tax rate of return on an investment held for more than one tax period is $r = (FV/I)^{1/n} - 1$, where r is the after-tax rate of return, FV is the after-tax future value of the investment, I is the original investment amount, and n is the number of periods the investment is held.

Aggregate approach   a theory of taxing partnerships that ignores partnerships as entities and taxes partners as if they directly owned partnership net assets.

Alimony   a support payment of cash made to a former spouse. The payment must be made under a written separation agreement or divorce decree that does not designate the payment as something other than alimony, the payment must be made when the spouses do not live together, and the payments must cease no later than when the recipient dies.

All-events test   requires that income or expenses are recognized when (1) all events have occurred that determine or fix the right to receive the income or liability to make the payments and (2) the amount of the income or expense can be determined with reasonable accuracy.

All-inclusive income concept   a definition of income that says that gross income means all income from whatever source derived.

Allocate   as used in the sourcing rules, the process of associating a deduction with a specific item or items of gross income for purposes of computing foreign source taxable income.

Allocation   the method of dividing or sourcing nonbusiness income to specific states.

Allowance method   method used for financial reporting purposes; under this method, bad debt expense is based on an estimate of the amount of the bad debts in accounts receivable at year-end.

Alternative minimum tax (AMT)   a tax on a broader tax base than the base for the "regular" tax; the additional tax paid when the tentative minimum tax (based on the alternative minimum tax base) exceeds the regular tax (based on the regular tax base). The alternative minimum tax is designed to require taxpayers to pay some minimum level of tax even when they have low or no regular taxable income as a result of certain tax breaks in the tax code.

Alternative minimum tax (AMT) base   alternative minimum taxable income minus the alternative minimum tax exemption.

Alternative minimum tax (AMT) exemption   a deduction to determine the alternative minimum tax base that is phased out based on alternative minimum taxable income.

Alternative minimum tax adjustments   adjustments (positive or negative) to regular taxable income to arrive at the alternative minimum tax base.

Alternative minimum tax system   a secondary or parallel tax system calculated on an *alternative* tax base that more closely reflects economic income than the regular income tax base. The system was designed to ensure that taxpayers generating economic income pay some *minimum* amount of income tax each year.

Alternative valuation date   the date six months after the decedent's date of death.

Amortization   the method of recovering the cost of intangible assets over a specific time period.

Amount realized   the value of everything received by the seller in a transaction (cash, FMV of other property, and relief of liabilities) less selling costs.

Annotated tax service   a tax service arranged by code section. For each code section, an annotated service includes the code section; a listing of the code section history; copies of congressional committee reports that explain changes to the code section; a copy of all the regulations issued for the specific code section; the service's unofficial explanation of the code section; and brief summaries (called annotations) of relevant court cases, revenue rulings, revenue procedures, and letter rulings that address issues specific to the code section.

Annual exclusion   amount of gifts allowed to be made each year per donee (regardless of the number of donees) to prevent the taxation of relatively small gifts ($15,000 per donee per year currently).

Annualized income method   a method for determining a corporation's required estimated tax payments when the taxpayer earns more income later in the year than earlier in the year. Requires corporations to base their first and second required estimated tax installments on their income from the first three months of the year, their third installment based on their taxable income from the first six months of the year, and the final installment based on their taxable income from the first nine months of the year.

Annuity   a stream of equal payments over time.

Applicable credit   also known as the *unified credit*, the amount of current tax on the exemption equivalent; designed to prevent transfer taxation of smaller cumulative transfers.

Apportion   as used in the sourcing rules, the process of calculating the amount of a deduction that is associated with a specific item or items of gross income for purposes of computing foreign source taxable income.

Apportionment   the method of dividing business income of an interstate business among the states where nexus exists.

Arm's length amount price in transactions among unrelated taxpayers, where each transacting party negotiates for his or her own benefit.

Arm's length transactions transactions among unrelated taxpayers, where each transacting party negotiates for his or her own benefit.

Articles of incorporation a document, filed by a corporation's founders with the state, describing the purpose, place of business, and other details of the corporation.

Articles of organization a document, filed by a limited liability company's founders with certain states, describing the purpose, place of business, and other details of the company.

Assignment of income doctrine the judicial doctrine holding that earned income is taxed to the taxpayer providing the service, and that income from property is taxed to the individual who owns the property when the income accrues.

At-risk amount an investor's risk of loss in a worst-case scenario. In a partnership, an amount generally equal to a partner's tax basis exclusive of the partner's share of nonrecourse debt.

At-risk rules tax rules limiting the losses flowing through to partners or S corporation shareholders to their amount "at risk" in the partnership.

Average tax rate a taxpayer's average level of taxation on each dollar of taxable income. Specifically,

$$\text{Average tax rate} = \frac{\text{Total tax}}{\text{Taxable income}}$$

B

Bargain element (of stock options) the difference between the fair market value of the employer's stock and the amount employees pay to acquire the employer's stock.

Barter clubs organizations that facilitate the exchange of rights to goods and services between members.

Base erosion and anti-abuse tax (BEAT) a 10 percent minimum tax imposed on a U.S. corporation's payments of interest and royalties to a related foreign party.

Basis a taxpayer's unrecovered investment in an asset that provides a reference point for measuring gain or loss when an asset is sold.

Before-tax rate of return a taxpayer's rate of return on an investment before paying taxes on the income from the investment.

Beneficiary person for whom trust property is held and administered.

Bond a debt instrument issued for a period of more than one year with the purpose of raising capital by borrowing.

Bond discount the result of issuing bonds for less than their maturity value.

Bond premium the result of issuing bonds for more than their maturity value.

Bonus depreciation additional depreciation allowed in the acquisition year for tangible personal property with a recovery period of 20 years or less.

Book (financial reporting) income the income or loss corporations report on their financial statements using applicable financial accounting standards.

Book equivalent of taxable income a company's pretax income from continuing operations adjusted for permanent differences.

Book–tax difference a difference in the amount of an income item or deduction item taken into account for book purposes compared to the amount taken into account for the same item for tax purposes.

Boot property given or received in an otherwise nontaxable transaction such as a like-kind exchange that may trigger gain to a party to the transaction. The term *boot* derives from a trading expression describing additional property a party to an exchange might throw in "to boot" to equalize the exchange.

Bracket a subset (or portion) of the tax base subject to a specific tax rate. Brackets are common to graduated taxes.

Branch an unincorporated division of a corporation.

Bright line tests technical rules found in the tax law that provide the taxpayer with objective tests to determine the tax consequences of a transaction.

Built-in gain the difference between the fair market value and tax basis of property owned by an entity when the fair market value exceeds the tax basis.

Built-in gains tax a tax levied on S corporations that were formerly C corporations. The tax applies to net unrealized built-in gains at the time the corporation converted from a C corporation to the extent the gains are recognized during the built-in gains tax recognition period. The applicable tax rate is 21 percent.

Built-in gains tax recognition period the first five years a corporation operates as an S corporation after converting from a C corporation.

Built-in loss the difference between the fair market value and tax basis of property owned by an entity when the tax basis exceeds the fair market value.

Bunching itemized deductions a common planning strategy in which a taxpayer pays two year's worth of itemized expenses in one year to exceed the standard deduction in that year.

Business activity a profit-motivated activity that requires a relatively high level of involvement or effort from the taxpayer to generate income.

Business income income derived from business activities.

Business purpose doctrine the judicial doctrine that allows the IRS to challenge and disallow business expenses for transactions with no underlying business motivation.

Business tax credits nonrefundable credits designed to provide incentives for taxpayers to hire certain types of individuals or to participate in certain business activities.

C

C corporation a corporate taxpaying entity with income subject to taxation. Such a corporation is termed a "C" corporation because the corporation and its shareholders are subject to the provisions of Subchapter C of the Internal Revenue Code.

Cafeteria plan an employer plan that allows employees to choose benefits from a menu of nontaxable fringe benefits or receive cash compensation in lieu of the benefits.

Capital account an account reflecting a partner's share of the equity in a partnership. Capital accounts are maintained using tax accounting methods or other methods of accounting, including GAAP, at the discretion of the partnership.

Capital asset in general, an asset other than an asset used in a trade or business or an asset such as an account or note receivable acquired in a business from the sale of services or property.

Capital gain property any asset that would have generated a long-term capital gain if the taxpayer had sold the property for its fair market value.

Capital interest an economic right attached to a partnership interest giving a partner the right to receive cash or property in the event the partnership liquidates. A capital interest is synonymous with the liquidation value of a partnership interest.

Carryover basis the basis of an asset the transferee takes in property received in a nontaxable exchange. The basis of the asset carries over from the transferor to the transferee.

Cash method the method of accounting that recognizes income in the period in which cash, property, or services are received and recognizes deductions in the period paid.

Cash tax rate the tax rate computed by dividing a company's taxes paid during the year by its pretax income from continuing operations.

Cashless exercise a technique where options are exercised and at least a portion of the shares are sold in order to facilitate the purchase.

Ceiling limitation that is the maximum amount for adjustments to taxable income (or credits). The amounts in excess of the ceiling are either lost or carried to another tax year.

Certainty one of the criteria used to evaluate tax systems. Certainty means taxpayers should be able to determine when, where, and how much tax to pay.

Certificate of deposit (CD) an interest-bearing debt instrument offered by banks and savings and loans. Money removed from the CD before maturity is subject to a penalty.

Certificate of limited partnership a document limited partnerships must file with the state to be formally recognized by the state. The document is similar to articles of incorporation or articles or organization.

Certificate of organization a document, filed by a limited liability company's founders with certain states, describing the purpose, place of business, and other details of the company.

Character of income a type of income that is treated differently for tax purposes from other types of income. Common income characters (or types of income) include ordinary, capital, and qualified dividend.

Charitable contribution limit modified taxable income taxable income for purposes of determining the 10 percent of taxable income deduction limitation for corporate charitable contributions. Computed as taxable income before deducting (1) any charitable contributions, (2) the dividends received deduction, and (3) capital loss carrybacks.

Child tax credit a $2,000 tax credit, subject to an AGI phase-out, for each qualifying child who is under age 17 at the end of the year and claimed as a dependent of the taxpayer, and a $500 credit, also subject to the AGI phase-out, for other qualified dependents claimed as dependents of the taxpayer.

Circular 230 regulations issued by the IRS that govern tax practice and apply to all persons practicing before the IRS. There are five parts of Circular 230: Subpart A describes who may practice before the IRS (e.g., CPAs, attorneys, enrolled agents) and what practicing before the IRS means (tax return preparation, representing clients before the IRS, etc.). Subpart B describes the duties and restrictions that apply to individuals governed by Circular 230. Subparts C and D explain sanctions and disciplinary proceedings for practitioners violating the Circular 230 provisions. Subpart E concludes with a few miscellaneous provisions (such as the Circular 230 effective date).

Citator a research tool that allows one to check the status of several types of tax authorities. A citator can be used to review the history of the case to find out, for example, whether it was subsequently appealed and overturned, and to identify subsequent cases that cite the case. Citators can also be used to check the status of revenue rulings, revenue procedures, and other IRS pronouncements.

Civil penalties monetary penalties imposed when tax practitioners or taxpayers violate tax statutes without reasonable cause—for example, as the result of negligence, intentional disregard of pertinent rules, willful disobedience, or outright fraud.

Claim of right doctrine judicial doctrine that states that income has been realized if a taxpayer receives income and there are no restrictions on the taxpayer's use of the income (for example, the taxpayer does not have an obligation to repay the amount).

Cliff vesting a qualified plan provision allowing for benefits to vest all at once after a specified period of time has passed.

Collectibles a type of capital asset that includes a work of art, a rug or antique, a metal or gem, a stamp or coin, an alcoholic beverage, or other similar items held for investment for more than one year.

Commercial domicile the state where a business is headquartered and directs operations; this location may be different from the place of incorporation.

Commercial traveler exception a statutory exception that exempts nonresidents from U.S. taxation of compensation from services if the individual is in the United States 90 days or less and earns compensation of $3,000 or less.

Common-law states the 41 states that have not adopted community-property laws.

Community property systems systems in which state laws dictate how the income and property is legally shared between a husband and a wife.

Community-property states nine states (Arizona, California, Idaho, Louisiana, Nevada, New Mexico, Texas, Washington, and Wisconsin) that automatically equally divide the ownership of property acquired by either spouse during a marriage.

Commuting traveling from a personal residence to the place of business.

Complex trust a trust that is not required by the trust instrument to distribute income currently.

Consolidated tax return a combined U.S. income tax return filed by an affiliated group of corporations.

Consolidation the combining of the assets and liabilities of two or more corporations into a new entity.

Constructive ownership rules that cause stock not owned by a taxpayer to be treated as owned by the taxpayer for purposes of meeting certain stock ownership tests.

Constructive receipt doctrine the judicial doctrine that provides that a taxpayer must recognize income when it is actually or constructively received. Constructive receipt is deemed to have occurred if the income has been credited to the taxpayer's account or if the income is unconditionally available to the taxpayer, the taxpayer is aware of the income's availability, and there are no restrictions on the taxpayer's control over the income.

Continuity of business enterprise (COBE) a judicial (now regulatory) requirement that the acquiring corporation continue the target corporation's historic business or continue to use a "significant" portion of the target corporation's historic business assets to be tax-deferred.

Continuity of interest (COI) a judicial (now regulatory) requirement that the transferors of stock in a reorganization collectively retain a continuing ownership (equity) interest in the target corporation's assets or historic business to be tax-deferred.

Contribution to capital a shareholder's or other person's contribution of cash or other property to a corporation without receipt of an additional equity interest in the corporation.

Controlled foreign corporation (CFC) a foreign corporation that is more than 50 percent owned by U.S. shareholders.

Convenience one of the criteria used to evaluate tax systems. Convenience means a tax system should be designed to facilitate the collection of tax revenues without undue hardship on the taxpayer or the government.

Corporation business entity recognized as a separate entity from its owners under state law.

Corpus the principal or property transferred to fund a trust or accumulated in the trust.

Correspondence examination an IRS audit conducted by mail and generally limited to one or two items on the taxpayer's return. Among the three types of audits, correspondence audits are generally the most common, the most narrow in scope, and least complex. The IRS typically requests supporting documentation for one or more items on the taxpayer's return (e.g., documentation of charitable contributions deducted).

Cost depletion the method of recovering the cost of a natural resource that allows a taxpayer to estimate or determine the number of units that remain in the resource at the beginning of the year and allocate a pro rata share of the remaining basis to each unit of the resource that is extracted or sold during the year.

Cost recovery the method by which a company expenses the cost of acquiring capital assets. Cost recovery can take the form of depreciation, amortization, or depletion.

Covenant not to compete a contractual promise to refrain from conducting business or professional activities similar to those of another party.

Criminal penalties penalties commonly charged in tax evasion cases (i.e., willful intent to defraud the government). They are imposed only after normal due process, including a trial. Compared to civil cases, the standard of conviction is higher in a criminal trial (beyond a reasonable doubt). However, the penalties are also much higher, such as fines up to $100,000 for individuals plus a prison sentence.

Current earnings and profits a year-to-year calculation maintained by a corporation to determine if a distribution is a dividend. Earnings and profits are computed for the current year by adjusting taxable income to make it more closely resemble economic income.

Current gifts gifts completed during the calendar year that are not already exempted from the gift tax.

Current income tax expense (benefit) the amount of taxes paid or payable (refundable) in the current year.

Current tax liability (asset) the amount of taxes payable (refundable) in the current year.

D

De minimis **fringe benefit** a nontaxable fringe benefit that allows employees to receive occasional or incidental benefits tax-free.

Debt basis the outstanding principal of direct loans from an S corporation shareholder to the S corporation. Once taxpayers deduct losses to the extent of their stock basis, they may deduct losses to the extent of their debt basis. When the debt basis has been reduced by losses, it is restored by income/gain allocations.

Deceased spousal unused exclusion (DSUE) amount of unused applicable credit from predeceased spouse.

Deductible temporary differences book–tax differences that will result in tax deductible amounts in future years when the related deferred tax asset is recovered.

Deductions amounts that are subtracted from gross income in calculating taxable income.

Deductions above the line *for* AGI deductions or deductions subtracted from gross income to determine AGI.

Deductions below the line *from* AGI deductions or deductions subtracted from AGI to calculate taxable income.

Deduction for qualified business income subject to limitations, equal to 20 percent of the taxpayer's qualified business income.

Deferral items, deferred income, or deferrals realized income that will be taxed as income in a subsequent year.

Deferral method recognizes income from advance payments for goods by the earlier of (1) when the business would recognize the income for tax purposes if it had not received the *advance* payment or (2) when it recognizes the income for financial reporting purposes.

Deferred like-kind exchange a like-kind exchange where the taxpayer transfers like-kind property before receiving the like-kind property in exchange. The property to be received must be identified within 45 days and received within 180 days of the transfer of the property given up.

Deferred tax asset the expected future tax benefit attributable to deductible temporary differences and carryforwards.

Deferred tax liability the expected future tax cost attributable to taxable temporary differences.

Defined benefit plans employer-provided qualified plans that spell out the specific benefit employees will receive on retirement.

Defined contribution plans employer-provided qualified plans that specify the maximum annual contributions employers and/or employees may contribute to the plan.

Definitely related deductions deductions that are associated with the creation of a specific item or items of gross income.

Dependent a qualifying child or qualifying relative of the taxpayer.

Depletion the cost recovery method to allocate the cost of natural resources as they are removed.

Depreciation the cost recovery method to allocate the cost of tangible personal and real property over a specific time period.

Depreciation recapture the conversion of §1231 gain into ordinary income on a sale (or exchange) based on the amount of accumulated depreciation on the property at the time of sale or exchange.

Determination letters rulings requested by the taxpayer, issued by local IRS directors, and generally not controversial. An example of a determination letter is the request by an employer for the IRS to rule that the taxpayer's retirement plan is a "qualified plan."

DIF (Discriminant Function) system the DIF system assigns a score to each tax return that represents the probability that the tax liability on the return has been underreported (a higher score = a higher likelihood of underreporting). The IRS derives the weights assigned to specific tax return attributes from historical IRS audit adjustment data from the National Research Program. The DIF system then uses these (undisclosed) weights to score each tax return based on the tax return's characteristics. Returns with higher DIF scores are then reviewed to determine if an audit is the best course of action.

Direct conversion when a taxpayer receives noncash property rather than a cash payment as a replacement for property damaged or destroyed in an involuntary conversion.

Direct write-off method required method for deducting bad debts for tax purposes. Under this method, businesses deduct bad debt only when the debt becomes wholly or partially worthless.

Disability insurance sometimes called sick pay or wage replacement insurance. It pays the insured for wages lost due to injury or disability.

Discharge of indebtedness debt forgiveness.

Discount factor the factor based on the taxpayer's rate of return that is used to determine the present value of future cash inflows (e.g., tax savings) and outflows (taxes paid).

Disproportionate distributions partnership distributions that change the partners' relative ownership of hot assets.

Disqualifying disposition the sale of stock acquired using incentive stock options prior to satisfying certain holding period requirements. Failing to satisfy the holding period requirements converts the options into nonqualified stock options.

Disregarded entities unincorporated entity with one owner that is considered to be the same entity as the owner.

Disregarded entities (international tax)   entities with one owner that are treated as flow-through entities for U.S. income tax purposes.

Distributable net income (DNI)   the maximum amount of the distribution deduction by fiduciaries and the maximum aggregate amount of gross income reportable by beneficiaries.

Distribution deduction   deduction by fiduciaries for distributions of income to beneficiaries that operates to eliminate the potential for double taxation of fiduciary income.

Dividend   a distribution to shareholders of money or property from the corporation's earnings and profits.

Dividends received deduction (DRD)   a corporate deduction for part or all of a dividend received from other domestic corporations.

Document perfection program   a program under which all tax returns are checked for mathematical and tax calculation errors.

Donee   person receiving a gift.

Donor   person making a gift.

Double taxation   the tax burden when an entity's income is subject to two levels of tax. Income of C corporations is subject to double taxation. The first level of tax is at the corporate level and the second level of tax on corporate income occurs at the shareholder level.

DRD modified taxable income   taxable income for purposes of applying the taxable income limitation for the dividends received deduction. Computed as the dividend-receiving corporation's taxable income before deducting the dividends received deduction, any net operating loss deduction, and capital loss carrybacks.

Dwelling unit   property that provides a place suitable for people to occupy (live and sleep).

Dynamic forecasting   the process of forecasting tax revenues that incorporates into the forecast how taxpayers may alter their activities in response to a tax law change.

E

Earmarked tax   a tax assessed for a specific purpose (e.g., for education).

Earned income   compensation and other forms of income received for providing goods or services in the ordinary course of business.

Earned income credit   a refundable credit designed to help offset the effect of employment taxes on compensation paid to low-income taxpayers and to encourage lower income taxpayers to seek employment.

Earnings and profits   a measure of a corporation's earnings that is similar to its economic earnings. Corporate dividends are taxable to shareholders to the extent they come from earnings and profits.

Economic income tax nexus   the concept that businesses without a physical presence in the state may establish income tax nexus in the state through an economic presence there.

Economic performance test   the third requirement that must be met for an accrual method taxpayer to deduct an expense currently. The specific event that satisfies the economic performance test varies based on the type of expense.

Economic substance doctrine   judicially based doctrine that requires transactions to meaningfully change a taxpayer's economic position *and* have a substantial purpose (apart from a federal income tax purpose) in order for a taxpayer to obtain tax benefits.

Economy   one of the criteria used to evaluate tax systems. Economy means a tax system should minimize its compliance and administration costs.

Educational assistance benefit   a nontaxable fringe benefit that allows an employer to provide a certain amount of education benefits on an annual basis.

Effective tax rate   the taxpayer's average rate of taxation on each dollar of total income (taxable and nontaxable income). Specifically,

$$\text{Effective tax rate} = \frac{Total\ tax}{Total\ income}$$

Also, (for income tax footnote purposes) the tax rate computed by dividing a company's income tax provision (expense or benefit) for the year by its pretax income from continuing operations.

Effectively connected income (ECI)   net income that results from the conduct of a U.S. trade or business by a nonresident.

Employee   a person who is hired to provide services to a company on a regular basis in exchange for compensation and who does not provide these services as part of an independent business.

Employment taxes   taxes consisting of the Old Age, Survivors, and Disability Insurance (OASDI) tax, commonly called the Social Security tax, and the Medical Health Insurance (MHI) tax known as the Medicare tax.

Enacted tax rate   the statutory tax rate that will apply in the current or a future period.

Entity approach   a theory of taxing partnerships that treats partnerships as entities separate from partners.

Equity   one of the criteria used to evaluate a tax system. A tax system is considered fair or equitable if the tax is based on the taxpayer's ability to pay; taxpayers with a greater ability to pay tax, pay more tax.

Escrow account (mortgage-related)   a holding account with a taxpayer's mortgage lender. The taxpayer makes mortgage payments to the lender that include payment for the interest and principal and payments for property taxes. The lender maintains the payments for property taxes in the escrow account and uses the funds in the account to pay the property taxes when the taxes are due.

Estate   fiduciary legal entity that comes into existence upon a person's death and is empowered by the probate court to gather and transfer the decedent's real and personal property.

Estate tax   the tax paid for an estate.

Estimated tax payments   quarterly tax payments that a taxpayer makes to the government if the tax withholding is insufficient to meet the taxpayer's tax liability.

Ex-dividend date   the relevant date for determining who receives a dividend from a stock. Anyone purchasing stock before this date will receive current dividends. Otherwise, the purchaser must wait until subsequent dividends are declared before receiving them.

Excess business loss   excess of aggregate business deductions for the year over aggregate business gross income or gain of an individual taxpayer plus a threshold amount depending on filing status.

Excess net passive income   net passive investment income × passive investment income in excess of 25 percent of the S corporation's gross receipts divided by its passive investment income.

Excess net passive income tax   a tax levied on an S corporation that has accumulated earnings and profits from years in which it operated as a C corporation if the corporation reports excess net passive income.

Exchanged basis   the basis of an asset received in a nontaxable exchange. An exchanged basis is generally the basis of the asset given up in a nontaxable exchange. Exchanged basis may also be referred to as a *substituted basis*.

Excise taxes   taxes levied on the retail sale of particular products. They differ from other taxes in that the tax base for an excise tax typically depends on the *quantity* purchased rather than a monetary amount.

Excluded income or exclusions realized income that is exempted from income taxation.

Executor the person who takes responsibility for collecting the assets of the decedent, paying the decedent's debts, and distributing the remaining assets to the rightful heirs.

Exemption equivalent the amount of cumulative taxable transfers a taxpayer can make without exceeding the applicable credit.

Exercise date the date employees use their stock options to acquire employer stock at a discounted price.

Exercise price the price at which holders of stock options may purchase stock in the corporation issuing the option.

Explicit taxes taxes directly imposed by a government.

F

Face value a specified final amount paid to the owner of a coupon bond on the date of maturity. The face value is also known as the *maturity value*.

Facts and circumstances test a test used to make a subjective determination such as whether the amount of salary paid to an employee is reasonable. The test requires the taxpayer and the IRS to consider all the relevant facts and circumstances surrounding the situation in order to make a decision. The relevant facts and circumstances are situation-specific.

Family limited partnership a partnership designed to save estate taxes by dividing a family business into various ownership interests representing control of operations and future income and appreciation of the assets.

Favorable book–tax difference a book–tax difference that requires a subtraction from book income in determining taxable income.

Federal short-term interest rate the quarterly interest rate used to determine the interest charged for tax underpayments (federal short-term rate plus 3 percent).

Federal/state adjustments amounts added to or subtracted from federal taxable income when firms compute taxable income for a particular state.

FICA taxes FICA (Federal Insurance Contributions Act) taxes is a term used to denote both the Social Security and Medicare taxes upon earned income. For self-employed taxpayers, the terms "FICA tax" and "self-employment tax" are synonymous.

Fiduciary a person or legal entity that takes possession of property for the benefit of beneficiaries.

Fiduciary duty a requirement that a fiduciary act in an objective and impartial manner and not favor one beneficiary over another.

Field examination the least common audit. The IRS conducts these audits at the taxpayer's place of business or the location where the taxpayer's books, records, and source documents are maintained. Field examinations are generally the broadest in scope and most complex of the three audit types. They can last many months to multiple years and generally are limited to business returns and the most complex individual returns.

Filing status filing status places taxpayers into one of five categories (married filing jointly, married filing separately, qualifying widow or widower, head of household, and single) by marital status and family situation as of the end of the year. Filing status determines whether a taxpayer must file a tax return, appropriate tax rate schedules, standard deduction amounts, and certain deduction and credit limitation thresholds.

Final regulations regulations that have been issued in final form, and thus, until revoked, they represent the Treasury's interpretation of the Code.

First-in, first-out (FIFO) method an accounting method that values the cost of assets sold under the assumption that the assets are sold in the same order in which they are purchased (i.e., first purchased, first sold).

Fiscal year a year that ends on the last day of a month other than December.

Fixed and determinable, annual or periodic income (FDAP) U.S. source passive income earned by a nonresident.

Flat tax a tax in which a single tax rate is applied throughout the tax base.

Flexible spending account (FSA) a plan that allows employees to contribute before-tax dollars that may be used for unreimbursed medical expenses or dependent care.

Flipping a term used to describe the real estate investment practice of acquiring a home, repairing or remodeling the home, and then immediately, or soon thereafter, selling it (presumably at a profit).

Floor limitation a minimum amount that an expenditure (or credit or other adjustment to taxable income) must meet before any amount is allowed.

Flow-through entities legal entities, like partnerships, limited liability companies, and S corporations, that do not pay income tax. Income and losses from flow-through entities are allocated to their owners.

For AGI deductions deductions that are subtracted from gross income to determine AGI.

For the convenience of the employer benefits nontaxable benefits employers provide to employees and employee spouses or dependents in the form of meals or lodging if provided on the employer's premises and provided for a purpose that is helpful or convenient for the employer.

Foreign base company sales income gross profit from the sale of personal property by (to) a U.S. corporation to (from) a CFC, where the product was manufactured outside the country of incorporation of the CFC and resold outside the country of incorporation of the CFC.

Foreign branch company income a foreign tax credit limitation category added by the Tax Cuts and Jobs Act for years beginning after December 31, 2017.

Foreign derived intangible income (FDII) net income from certain export sales, services, and licensing of intangibles that is eligible for a 37.5 percent deduction by U.S. corporations.

Foreign joint venture a 50 percent or less owned foreign entity.

Foreign personal holding company income a category of foreign source passive income that includes interest, dividends, rents, royalties, and gains from the sale of certain foreign property.

Foreign subsidiary a more than 50 percent owned foreign corporation.

Foreign tax credit (FTC) a credit for income taxes paid to a foreign jurisdiction.

Foreign tax credit limitation the limit put on the use of creditable foreign taxes for the current year.

Form 1065 the form partnerships file annually with the IRS to report partnership ordinary income (loss) and separately stated items for the year.

Form 1120S the form S corporations file annually with the IRS to report S corporation ordinary income (loss) and separately stated items for the year.

Form 2553 the form filed to elect S corporation status.

Form 7004 the form C corporations, partnerships, and S corporations file to receive an automatic extension to file their annual tax return.

Form W-2 a form filed by the employer for each employee detailing the income, Social Security, and Medicare wages and taxes withheld. Additionally, state income, state taxes withheld, dependent care benefits, and many other tax-related items are reported.

Form W-4 a form used by a taxpayer to supply her employer with the information necessary to determine the amount of tax to withhold from each paycheck.

Fringe benefits noncash benefits provided to an employee as a form of compensation. As a general rule, fringe benefits are taxable. However, certain fringe benefits are excluded from gross income.

From AGI deductions deductions subtracted from AGI to calculate taxable income.

FTC basket a category of income that requires a separate FTC limitation computation.

Full-inclusion method the method for accounting for advance payments for goods that requires that businesses immediately recognize advance payments as taxable income.

Full-month convention a convention that allows owners of intangibles to deduct an entire month's amortization in the month of purchase and month of disposition.

Functional currency the currency of the primary economic environment in which an entity operates (i.e., the currency of the jurisdiction in which an entity primarily generates and expends cash).

Future interest the right to receive property in the future.

G

GAAP capital accounts partners' capital accounts maintained using generally accepted accounting principles (GAAP).

General category income foreign source income that is not considered passive category income for foreign tax credit purposes (generally income from an active trade or business).

General partnership (GP) a partnership with partners who all have unlimited liability with respect to the liabilities of the entity.

Generation-skipping tax (GST) supplemental transfer tax designed to prevent the avoidance of estate and gift taxes through transfers that skip a generation of recipients.

Gift a transfer of property where no, or inadequate, consideration is paid for the property.

Gift tax the tax paid on a gift.

Global low-taxed intangible income (GILTI) a new category of subpart F income added by the Tax Cuts and Jobs Act that relates to "high return" income earned by a U.S. corporation's CFC and subject to a low foreign tax rate.

Golsen rule the rule that states that the U.S. Tax Court will abide by the rulings of the circuit court that has appellate jurisdiction for a case.

Graded vesting a qualified plan rule that requires an increasing percentage of plan benefits to vest with each additional year of employment.

Graduated taxes taxes in which the tax base is divided into a series of monetary amounts, or brackets, where each successive bracket is taxed at a different (gradually higher or gradually lower) percentage rate.

Grant date the date on which employees receive stock options to acquire employer stock at a specified price.

Grant date (stock options) the date on which employees receive stock options to acquire employer stock at a specified price.

Grantor person creating a trust.

Gross estate property owned by the decedent at death and certain property transfers taking effect at death.

Gross income realized income minus excluded and deferred income.

Gross receipts the total amount of revenues (including passive investment income) received or accrued under the corporation's accounting method, not reduced by returns, allowances, cost of goods sold, or deductions. Gross receipts include net capital gains from the sales or exchanges of capital assets and gains from the sale or exchange of stock or securities (losses do not offset gains).

Group-term life insurance term life insurance provided by an employer to a group of employees.

Guaranteed payments payments made to partners or LLC members that are guaranteed because they are not contingent on partnership profits or losses. They are economically similar to shareholder salary payments.

H

Half-year convention a depreciation convention that allows owners of tangible personal property to take one-half of a year's worth of depreciation in the year of purchase and in the year of disposition regardless of when the asset was actually placed in service or sold.

Head of household one of five primary filing statuses. A taxpayer may file as head of household if s/he is unmarried as of the end of the year *and* pays more than half of the cost to maintain a household for a qualifying person who lives with the taxpayer for more than half of the year; or, s/he pays more than half the costs to maintain a household for a parent who qualifies as the taxpayer's dependent.

Health and accident insurance fringe benefits often offered through employers, including health insurance, group-term life insurance, and accidental death and dismemberment policies.

Heirs persons who inherit property from the deceased.

Home office deductions deductions relating to the use of an office in the home. A taxpayer must meet strict requirements to qualify for the deduction.

Horizontal equity one of the dimensions of equity. Horizontal equity is achieved if taxpayers in similar situations pay the same tax.

Hot assets unrealized receivables or inventory items defined in §751(a) that give rise to ordinary gains and losses. The exact definition of hot assets depends on whether it is in reference to dispositions of a partnership interest or distributions.

Hybrid entity an entity for which an election is available to choose the entity's tax status for U.S. tax purposes.

I

Impermissible accounting method an accounting method prohibited by tax laws.

Implicit taxes indirect taxes that result from a tax advantage the government grants to certain transactions to satisfy social, economic, or other objectives. They are defined as the reduced before-tax return that a tax-favored asset produces because of its tax-advantaged status.

Imputed income income from an economic benefit the taxpayer receives indirectly rather than directly. The amount of the income is based on comparable alternatives.

Inbound transaction a transaction conducted by a foreign person that is subject to U.S. taxation.

Incentive stock option (ISO) a type of stock option that allows employees to defer the bargain element for regular tax purposes until the stock acquired from option exercises is sold. The bargain element is taxed at capital gains rates provided the stock is retained long enough to satisfy certain holding period requirements. Employers cannot deduct the bargain element as compensation expense.

Income effect one of the two basic responses that a taxpayer may have when taxes increase. The income effect predicts that when taxpayers are taxed more (e.g., tax rate increases from 25 to 28 percent), they will work harder to generate the same after-tax dollars.

Income tax a tax in which the tax base is income. Income taxes are imposed by the federal government and by most states.

Income tax nexus the connection between a business and a tax jurisdiction sufficient to subject the business to the tax jurisdiction's income tax.

Independent contractor a person who provides services to another entity, usually under terms specified in a contract. The independent contractor has more control over how and when to do the work than does an employee.

Indirect conversion the receipt of money or other property as a replacement for property that was destroyed or damaged in an involuntary conversion.

Individual retirement account (IRA) a tax-advantaged account in which individuals who have earned income can save for retirement.

Information matching program a program that compares the taxpayer's tax return to information submitted to the IRS from other taxpayers (e.g., banks, employers, mutual funds, brokerage companies, mortgage companies). Information matched includes items such as wages (e.g., Form W-2 submitted by employers), interest income (e.g., Form 1099-INT submitted by banks), dividend income (e.g., Form 1099-DIV submitted by brokerage companies), and so forth.

Inheritance a transfer of property when the owner is deceased (the transfer is made by the decedent's estate).

Initial public offering (IPO) the first sale of stock by a company to the public.

Inside basis the tax basis of an entity's assets and liabilities.

Installment sale a sale for which the taxpayer receives payment in more than one period.

Institutional shareholders entities, such as investment companies, mutual funds, brokerages, insurance companies, pension funds, investment banks, and endowment funds, with large amounts to invest in corporate stock.

Intangible assets assets that do not have physical characteristics. Examples include goodwill, covenants not to compete, organizational expenditures, and research and experimentation expenses.

Inter vivos transfers gifts made by a donor during his or her lifetime.

Internal Revenue Code of 1986 the codified tax laws of the United States. Although the Code is frequently revised, there have been only three different codes since the Code was created in 1939 (i.e., the IRC of 1939, IRC of 1954, and IRC of 1986).

Interpretative regulations the most common regulations; they represent the Treasury's interpretation of the Code and are issued under the Treasury's general authority to interpret the Code.

Interstate commerce business conducted between parties in two or more states.

Inventory items (for sale of partnership interest purposes) classic inventory defined as property held for sale to customers in the ordinary course of business, but also assets that are not capital assets or §1231 assets, which would produce ordinary income if sold by the entity. There are actually two definitions of inventory items in §751. §751(a) inventory items are defined in §751(d) to include all inventory items. The §751(b) definition includes only substantially appreciated inventory.

Investment activity a profit-seeking activity that is intermittent or occasional in frequency, including the production or collection of income or the management, conservation, or maintenance of property held for the production of income.

Investment expenses expenses such as safe deposit rental fees, attorney fees, and accounting fees that are necessary to produce portfolio income. Investment expenses are generally not deductible by individuals (except investment interest expense or rental or royalty expenses not associated with a trade or business).

Investment income income received from portfolio type investments. Portfolio income includes capital gains and losses, interest, dividend, annuity, and royalty income not derived in the ordinary course of a trade or business. When computing the deductibility of investment interest expense, however, capital gains and dividends subject to the preferential tax rate are not treated as investment income unless the taxpayer elects to have this income taxed at ordinary tax rates.

Investment interest expense interest paid on borrowings or loans that are used to fund portfolio investments. Individuals are allowed an itemized deduction for qualified investment interest paid during the year.

Involuntary conversion a direct or indirect conversion of property through natural disaster, government condemnation, or accident that allows a taxpayer to defer realized gain if certain requirements are met.

IRS allocation method allocates expenses associated with rental use of the home between rental use and personal use. The percentage of total expenses allocated to rental use is the ratio of the number of rental use days for the property to the total days the property was used during the year.

Itemized deductions certain types of expenditures that Congress allows taxpayers to deduct as *from* AGI deductions.

J

Joint tenancy joint ownership of property by two or more people.

Joint tenancy with the right of survivorship title to property that provides the co-owners with equal rights to it and that automatically transfers to the survivor(s) at the death of a co-owner.

K

Kiddie tax a tax imposed at trusts and estates tax rates on a child's unearned income.

L

Last will and testament the document that directs the transfer of ownership of the decedent's assets to the heirs.

Last-in, first-out (LIFO) method an accounting method that values the cost of assets sold under the assumption that assets are sold in the reverse order in which they are purchased (i.e., last purchased, first sold).

Late filing penalty a penalty assessed if a taxpayer does not file a tax return by the required date (the original due date plus extension).

Late payment penalty a tax penalty equal to .5 percent of the amount of tax owed for each month (or fraction thereof) that the tax is not paid.

Least aggregate deferral an approach to determine a partnership's required year-end if a majority of the partners don't have the same year-end and if the principal partners don't have the same year-end. As the name implies, this approach minimizes the combined tax deferral of the partners.

Legislative grace the concept that taxpayers receive certain tax benefits only because Congress writes laws that allow taxpayers to receive the tax benefits.

Legislative regulations the rarest type of regulation, issued when Congress specifically directs the Treasury Department to create regulations to address an issue in an area of law. In these instances, the Treasury is actually writing the law instead of interpreting the Code. Because legislative regulations actually represent tax law instead of an interpretation of tax law, legislative regulations have more authoritative weight than interpretative and procedural regulations.

Life estate   the right to possess property and/or collect income from property for the duration of someone's life.

Life insurance trust   a trust that is funded with an irrevocable transfer of a life insurance policy and that gives the trustee the power to redesignate beneficiaries.

LIFO recapture amount   the excess of a C corporation's inventory basis under the FIFO method in excess of the inventory basis under the LIFO method in its final tax year as a C corporation before it becomes an S corporation.

LIFO recapture tax   a tax levied on a C corporation that elects to be taxed as an S corporation when it is using the LIFO method for accounting for inventories.

Like-kind exchange   a nontaxable (or partially taxable) trade or exchange of assets that are similar or related in use.

Limited liability company (LLC)   a type of flow-through entity for federal income tax purposes. By state law, the owners of the LLC have limited liability with respect to the entity's debts or liabilities. Limited liability companies are generally taxed as partnerships for federal income tax purposes.

Limited partnership (LP)   a partnership with at least one general partner with unlimited liability for the entity's debts and at least one limited partner with liability limited to the limited partner's investment in the partnership.

Liquidating distribution   a distribution that terminates an owner's interest in the entity.

Liquidation value   the amount a partner would receive if the partnership were to sell all its assets, pay its debts, and distribute its remaining assets to the partners in exchange for their partnership interests.

Listed property   business assets that are often used for personal purposes. Depreciation on listed property is limited to the business-use portion of the asset.

Local taxes   taxes imposed by local governments (cities, counties, school districts, etc.).

Long-term capital gains or losses   gains or losses from the sale of capital assets held for more than 12 months.

Luxury automobile   an automobile on which the amount of annual depreciation expense is limited because the cost of the automobile exceeds a certain threshold. The definition excludes vehicles with gross vehicle weight exceeding 6,000 pounds.

M

M adjustments   *see* Schedule M adjustments.

Majority interest taxable year   the common tax year of a group of partners who jointly hold greater than 50 percent of the profits and capital interests in the partnership.

Marginal tax rate   the tax rate that applies to the *next additional increment* of a taxpayer's taxable income (or to deductions). Specifically,

$$\text{Marginal tax rate} = \frac{\Delta Tax}{\Delta Taxable\ income}$$

$$= \frac{(New\ total\ tax - Old\ total\ tax)}{(New\ taxable\ income - Old\ taxable\ income)}$$

where "old" refers to the current tax and "new" refers to the revised tax after incorporating the additional income (or deductions) in question.

Marital deduction   the deduction for transfers of qualified property to a spouse.

Market discount   the difference between the amount paid for a bond in a market purchase rather than at original issuance when the amount paid is less than the maturity value of the bond.

Market premium   the difference between the amount paid for a bond in a market purchase rather than at original issuance when the amount paid is greater than the maturity value of the bond.

Marriage benefit   the tax savings married couples receive by filing a joint return relative to the tax they would have paid had they each filed as single taxpayers. This typically occurs when one spouse is either not working or earns significantly less than the other spouse.

Marriage penalty   the extra tax cost a married couple pays by filing a joint return relative to what they would have paid had they each filed as single taxpayers. This typically occurs when both spouses earn approximately the same amount of income.

Married filing jointly   one of five primary filing statuses. A taxpayer may file jointly if s/he is legally married as of the end of the year (or one spouse died during the year and the surviving spouse did not remarry) and both spouses agree to jointly file. Married couples filing joint returns combine their income and deductions and share joint and several liability for the resulting tax.

Married filing separately   one of five primary filing statuses. When married couples file separately, each spouse reports the income he or she received during the year and the deductions he or she paid on a tax return separate from the other spouse.

Maturity   the amount of time to the expiration date, or maturity date, of a debt instrument. The maturity of a debt instrument is generally the life of the instrument, at which point a payment of the face value is due or the instrument terminates.

Maturity value   the amount paid to a bondholder when the bond matures and the bondholder redeems the bond for cash.

Maximum 15 percent rate amount   threshold for the 15 percent rate to apply to long-term capital gains. Any 0/15/20 percent capital gains included that results in taxable income above the maximum zero rate amount and up to the maximum 15 percent rate amount are taxed at 15 percent. The threshold is based on a taxpayer's filing status and income.

Maximum zero percent rate amount   threshold for the zero percent rate to apply to long-term capital gains. Any 0/15/20 percent capital gains included in taxable income up to the maximum zero percent amount are taxed at 0 percent. It is based on a taxpayer's filing status and income level.

Medicare tax   the Medical Health Insurance (MHI) tax. This tax helps pay medical costs for qualifying individuals. The Medicare tax rate for employees and employers is 1.45 percent on salary or wages. An additional Medicare tax of .9 percent is assessed on employees (not employers) on salary or wages in excess of $200,000 ($125,000 for married filing separate; $250,000 of combined salary or wages for married filing joint). Self-employed taxpayers pay both the employee and employer Medicare tax and additional Medicare tax.

Merger   the acquisition by one (acquiring) corporation of the assets and liabilities of another (target) corporation. No new entity is created in the transaction.

Mid-month convention   a convention that allows owners of real property to take one-half of a month's depreciation during the month when the property was placed in service and in the month it was disposed of.

Mid-quarter convention   a depreciation convention for tangible personal property that allows for one-half of a quarter's worth of depreciation in the quarter of purchase and in the quarter of disposition. This convention must be used when more than 40 percent of tangible personal property is placed into service in the fourth quarter of the tax year.

Minimum tax credit credit available in certain situations for the alternative minimum tax paid. The credit can be used only when the regular tax exceeds the tentative minimum tax.

Miscellaneous itemized deductions itemized deductions such as gambling losses, casualty and theft losses on investment property, and the unrecovered cost of a life annuity (if the taxpayer died before recovering the full cost of the annuity).

Mixed-motive expenditures activities that involve a mixture of business and personal objectives.

Modified Accelerated Cost Recovery System (MACRS) the current tax depreciation system for tangible personal and real property. Depreciation under MACRS is calculated by finding the depreciation method, the recovery period, and the applicable convention.

Municipal bond the common name for state and local government debt.

Mutual fund a diversified portfolio of securities owned and managed by a regulated investment company.

N

Negative basis adjustment (for special basis adjustment purposes) the sum of the recognized loss and the amount of the basis increase made by an owner receiving the distribution.

Net capital gain the excess of net long-term capital gain for the taxable year over net short-term capital loss for such year.

Net capital loss carryback the amount of a corporation's net capital loss from one year that it uses to offset net capital gains in any of the three preceding tax years.

Net capital loss carryover the amount of a corporation's or an individual's net capital loss from one year that it may use to offset net capital gains in future years.

Net earnings from self-employment the amount of earnings subject to self-employment income taxes. The amount is 92.35 percent of a taxpayer's self-employment income.

Net investment income (for determining deductibility of investment interest expense) gross investment income reduced by deductible investment expenses.

Net investment income tax a 3.8 percent tax on the lesser of (a) net investment income or (b) the excess of modified adjusted gross income over $250,000 for married-joint filers and surviving spouses, $125,000 for married-separate filers, and $200,000 for other taxpayers.

Net long-term capital gain the excess of long-term capital gains for the taxable year over the long-term capital losses for such year.

Net long-term capital loss the excess of long-term capital losses for the taxable year over the long-term capital gains for such year.

Net operating loss (NOL) the excess of allowable deductions over gross income.

Net operating loss carryback the amount of a pre-2018 net operating loss that a corporation elects to carry back to the two previous years to offset taxable income in those years.

Net operating loss carryover the amount of a current-year net operating loss that is carried forward for up to 20 years to offset taxable income in those years. (20 years for pre-2018 losses; unlimited for post-2017 losses)

Net passive investment income passive investment income less any expenses connected with producing it.

Net short-term capital gain the excess of short-term capital gains for the taxable year over the short-term capital losses for such year.

Net short-term capital loss the excess of short-term capital losses for the taxable year over the short-term capital gains for such year.

Net unearned income unearned income in excess of a specified threshold amount of a child under the age of 19 or under the age of 24 if a full-time student.

Net unrealized built-in gain the net gain (if any) an S corporation that was formerly a C corporation would recognize if it sold each asset at its fair market value. It is measured on the first day of the corporation's first year as an S corporation.

Nexus the connection between a business and a tax jurisdiction sufficient to subject the business to the tax jurisdiction's tax system. Also, the connection that is required to exist between a jurisdiction and a potential taxpayer such that the jurisdiction asserts the right to impose a tax.

No-additional-cost services a nontaxable fringe benefit that provides employer services to employees with little cost to the employer (e.g., airline tickets or phone service).

Nonacquiescence issued after the IRS loses a trial-level or circuit court case when the IRS has decided to continue to litigate this issue.

Nonbusiness income all income except for business income—generally, investment income and rental income.

Nondeductible terminable interests transfers of property interests to a spouse that do not qualify for a marital deduction, because the interest of the spouse terminates when some event occurs or after a specified amount of time and the property is then transferred to another person.

Nondomiciliary business a business operating in a state other than its commercial domicile.

Nonqualified deferred compensation compensation provided for under a nonqualified plan allowing employees to defer compensation to a future period.

Nonqualified stock option (NQO) a type of stock option requiring employees to treat the bargain element from options exercised as ordinary income in the tax year options are exercised. Correspondingly, employers may deduct the bargain element as compensation expense in the tax year options are exercised.

Nonrecaptured net §1231 loss a net §1231 loss that is deducted as an ordinary loss in one year and has not caused subsequent §1231 gain to be taxed as ordinary income.

Nonrecognition provisions tax laws that allow taxpayers to permanently exclude income from taxation or to defer recognizing realized income until a subsequent period.

Nonrecognition transaction a transaction where at least a portion of the realized gain or loss is not currently recognized.

Nonrecourse debt debt for which no partner bears any economic risk of loss. Mortgages on real property are a common form of nonrecourse debt.

Nonrefundable credits tax credits that reduce a taxpayer's gross tax liability but are limited to the amount of gross tax liability. Any credit not used in the current year is lost.

Nonresident alien a non-U.S. citizen who does not meet the criteria to be treated as a resident for U.S. tax purposes.

Nonservice partner a partner who receives a partnership interest in exchange for property rather than services.

Nontaxable fringe benefit an employer provided benefit that may be excluded from an employee's income.

Not definitely related deductions deductions that are not associated with a specific item or items of gross income in computing the foreign tax credit limitation.

O

Office examination   the second most common audit. As the name suggests, the IRS conducts these audits at the local IRS office. These audits are typically broader in scope and more complex than correspondence examinations. Small businesses, taxpayers operating sole proprietorships, and middle- to high-income individual taxpayers are more likely, if audited, to have office examinations.

Operating distributions   payments from an entity to its owners that represent a distribution of entity profits. Distributions generally fall into the category of operating distributions when the owners continue their interests in the entity after the distribution.

Operating income   the annual income from a trade or business or rental activity.

Operating loss   the annual loss from a trade or business or rental activity.

Option exercise   the use of a stock option to acquire employer stock at a specified price.

Ordinary and necessary   an expense that is normal or appropriate and that is helpful or conducive to the business activity.

Ordinary asset   an asset created or used in a taxpayer's trade or business (e.g., accounts receivable or inventory) that generates ordinary income (or loss) on disposition.

Ordinary business income (loss)   a partnership's or S corporation's remaining income or loss after separately stated items are removed. It is also referred to as nonseparately stated income (loss).

Ordinary income property   property that if sold would generate income taxed at ordinary rates.

Organizational expenses   expenses associated with legally forming a partnership (such as attorneys' and accountants' fees).

Organizational expenditures   expenses that are (1) connected directly to the creation of a corporation or partnership, (2) chargeable to a capital account, and (3) generally amortized over 180 months (limited immediate expensing may be available).

Original issue discount (OID)   a type of bond issued for less than the maturity or face value of the bond.

Outbound transaction   a transaction conducted outside the United States by a U.S. person that is subject to U.S. taxation.

Outside basis   an investor's tax basis in the stock of a corporation or the interest in a partnership or LLC.

P

Partial liquidation   a distribution made by a corporation to shareholders that results from a contraction of the corporation's activities.

Partnership agreement   an agreement among the partners in a partnership stipulating the partners' rights and responsibilities in the partnership.

Partnership interest   an intangible asset reflecting the economic rights a partner has with respect to a partnership, including the right to receive assets in liquidation of the partnership (called a *capital interest*) and the right to be allocated profits and losses (called a *profits interest*).

Passive activity loss (PAL) rules   tax rules designed to limit taxpayers' ability to deduct losses from activities in which they don't materially participate against income from other sources.

Passive category income   foreign source personal holding company income, such as interest, dividends, rents, royalties, annuities, and gains from sale of certain assets, that is combined in computing the FTC limitation.

Passive investment income (PII)   royalties, rents, dividends, interest (including tax-exempt interest), annuities, and gains from the sale or exchange of stock or securities.

Passive investments   direct or indirect investments (other than through a C corporation) in a trade or business or rental activity in which the taxpayer does not materially participate.

Payment liabilities   liabilities of accrual method businesses for which economic performance occurs when the business actually *pays* the liability for, among others: worker's compensation; tort; breach of contract or violation of law; rebates and refunds; awards, prizes, and jackpots; insurance, warranties, and service contracts provided *to* the business; and taxes.

Percentage depletion   a method of recovering the cost of a natural resource that allows a taxpayer to recover or expense an amount based on a statutorily determined percentage.

Permanent book–tax differences   items of income or deductions for either book purposes or for tax purposes during the year but not both. Permanent differences do not reverse over time, so over the long run, the total amount of income or deduction for the item is different for book and tax purposes.

Permanent establishment   generally, a fixed place of business through which an enterprise carries out its business. Examples include a place of management, a branch, an office, and a factory.

Permissible accounting method   accounting method allowed under the tax law. Permissible accounting methods are adopted the first time a taxpayer uses the method on a tax return.

Person   an individual, trust, estate, partnership, association, company, or corporation.

Personal expenses   expenses incurred for personal motives. Personal expenses are not deductible for tax purposes.

Personal holding companies   closely held corporations generating primarily investment income.

Personal holding company tax   penalty tax on the undistributed income of a personal holding company.

Personal property   all tangible property other than real property.

Personal property tax   a tax on the fair market value of all types of tangible and intangible property, except real property.

Point   one percent of the principal amount of a loan. A home buyer might pay points to compensate the lender for services or for a lower interest rate.

Portfolio investments   investments producing dividends, interest, royalties, annuities, or capital gains.

Positive basis adjustment   (for special basis adjustment purposes) the sum of the gain recognized by the owners receiving distributed property and the amount of any required basis reduction.

Post-termination transition period (PTTP)   the period that begins on the day after the last day of a corporation's last taxable year as an S corporation and generally ends on the later of (a) one year after the last S corporation day, or (b) the due date for filing the return for the last year as an S corporation (including extensions).

Preferential tax rate   a tax rate that is lower than the tax rate applied to ordinary income.

Preferentially taxed income   income taxed at a preferential rate such as long-term capital gains and qualified dividends.

Present interest   right to presently enjoy property or receive income from the property.

Present value   the concept that $1 today is worth more than $1 in the future. For example, assuming an investor can earn a 5 percent after-tax return, $1 invested today should be worth $1.05 in one year. Hence, $1 today is equivalent to $1.05 in one year.

Primary authorities   official sources of the tax law generated by the legislative branch (i.e., statutory authority issued by Congress), judicial branch (i.e., rulings by the U.S. District Court, U.S. Tax Court, U.S. Court of Federal Claims, U.S. Circuit Courts of Appeals, or U.S. Supreme Court), or executive/administrative branch (i.e., Treasury or IRS pronouncements).

Principal partner   a partner having a 5 percent or more interest in partnership capital or profits.

Principal residence   the main place of residence for a taxpayer during the taxable year.

Private activity bond   a bond issued by a municipality but proceeds of which are used to fund privately owned activity.

Private letter rulings   IRS pronouncements issued in response to a taxpayer request for a ruling on specific issues for the taxpayer. They are common for proposed transactions with potentially large tax implications. For the requesting taxpayer, a private letter ruling has very high authority. For all other taxpayers, private letter rulings have little authoritative weight.

Private nonoperating foundations   privately sponsored foundations that disburse funds to other charities.

Private operating foundations   privately sponsored foundations that actually fund and conduct charitable activities.

Probate   the process in the probate court of gathering property possessed by or titled in the name of a decedent at the time of death, paying the debts of the decedent, and transferring the ownership of any remaining property to the decedent's heirs.

Probate estate   property possessed by or titled in the name of a decedent at the time of death.

Procedural regulations   regulations that explain Treasury Department procedures as they relate to administering the Code.

Production of income   a for-profit activity that doesn't rise to the level of a trade or business.

Profits interest   an interest in a partnership giving a partner the right to share in future profits but not the right to share in the current value of a partnership's assets. Profits interests are generally not taxable in the year they are received.

Progressive tax rate structure   a tax rate structure that imposes an increasing marginal tax rate as the tax base increases. As the tax base increases, both the marginal tax rate and the taxes paid increase.

Proportional tax rate structure   also known as a *flat tax*, this tax rate structure imposes a constant tax rate throughout the tax base. As the tax base increases, the taxes paid increase proportionally.

Proposed regulations   regulations issued in proposed form; they do not carry the same authoritative weight as temporary or final regulations. All regulations are issued in proposed form first to allow public comment on them.

Public Law 86-272   federal law passed by Congress that provides additional protection for sellers of tangible personal property against income tax nexus.

Q

Qualified business asset investment (QBAI)   the tax basis of tangible personal property used in a trade or business that forms the basis for determining the deductions allowed for foreign derived intangible income and global low taxed intangible income.

Qualified business income   net business income from a qualified trade or business conducted in the United States. This is the tax base for the deduction for qualified business income.

Qualified dividends   paid by domestic or certain qualified foreign corporations that are eligible for lower capital gains rates.

Qualified educational loans   loans whose proceeds are used to pay qualified education expenses.

Qualified employee discount   a nontaxable fringe benefit that provides a discount on employer goods (not to be discounted below the employer's cost) and services (up to a 20 percent discount) to employees.

Qualified equity grant   a broad-based equity grant of either stock options or restricted stock units by a private corporation. Eligible employees may make an inclusion deferral election that may defer the income attributable to the qualified equity for up to five years.

Qualified moving expense reimbursement   a nontaxable fringe benefit that allows employers to pay moving-related expenses on behalf of employees.

Qualified nonrecourse financing   nonrecourse debt secured by real property from a commercial lender unrelated to the borrower.

Qualified replacement property   property acquired to replace property damaged or destroyed in an involuntary conversion. It must be of a similar or related use to the original property even if the replacement property is real property (e.g., rental real estate for rental real estate).

Qualified residence   the taxpayer's principal residence and one other residence.

Qualified retirement accounts   plans meeting certain requirements that allow compensation placed in the account to be tax-deferred until the taxpayer withdraws money from the account.

Qualified retirement plans   employer-sponsored retirement plans that meet government-imposed funding and antidiscrimination requirements.

Qualified small business stock   stock received at original issue from a corporation with a gross tax basis in its assets both before and after the issuance of no more than $50,000,000 and with 80 percent of the value of its assets used in the active conduct of certain qualified trades or businesses.

Qualified trade or business   for purposes of the deduction for qualified business income, any trade or business other than a specified trade or business.

Qualified transportation fringe benefit   a nontaxable fringe benefit provided by employers in the form of mass transit passes, parking, or company-owned carpool benefits.

Qualifying child   an individual who qualifies as a dependent of a taxpayer by meeting a relationship, age, residence, and support test with respect to the taxpayer.

Qualifying relative   an individual who is not a qualifying child of another taxpayer and who meets a relationship, support, and gross income test and thus qualifies to be a dependent of another taxpayer.

Qualifying widow or widower   one of five primary filing statuses. Applies for up to two years after the year in which the taxpayer's spouse dies (the taxpayer files married filing jointly in the year of the spouse's death) as long as the taxpayer remains unmarried and maintains a household for a dependent child.

Question of fact   a research question that hinges upon the facts and circumstances of the taxpayer's transaction.

Question of law   a research question that hinges upon the interpretation of the law, such as interpreting a particular phrase in a code section.

R

Real property   land and structures permanently attached to land.

Real property tax   a tax on the fair market value of land and structures permanently attached to land.

Realization   gain or loss that results from an exchange of property rights in a transaction.

Realization principle   the proposition that income only exists when there is a transaction with another party resulting in a measurable change in property rights.

Realized gain or loss   the difference between the amount realized and the adjusted basis of an asset sold or otherwise disposed of.

Realized income   income generated in a transaction with a second party in which there is a measurable change in property rights between parties.

Reasonable in amount   an expenditure is reasonable when the amount paid is neither extravagant nor exorbitant.

Recapture   the recharacterization of income from capital gain to ordinary income.

Recognized gain or loss   the gain or loss included in gross income on a taxpayer's tax return. This is usually the realized gain or loss unless a nonrecognition provision applies.

Recourse debt   debt held by a partnership for which at least one partner has economic risk of loss.

Recovery period   a length of time prescribed by statute in which business property is depreciated or amortized.

Recurring item   an election under economic performance to currently deduct an accrued liability if the liability is expected to persist in the future and is either not material or a current deduction better matches revenue.

Refinance   when a taxpayer pays off a current loan with the proceeds of a second loan.

Regressive tax rate structure   a tax rate structure that imposes a decreasing marginal tax rate as the tax base increases. As the tax base increases, the taxes paid increase, but the marginal tax rate decreases.

Regulations   the Treasury Department's official interpretation of the Internal Revenue Code. Regulations are the highest authority issued by the IRS.

Related-party transaction   financial activities among family members, among owners and their businesses, or among businesses owned by the same owners.

Remainder   the right to ownership of a property that transfers to a new owner, the remainderman, following a temporary interest.

Remainderman   the person entitled to a remainder interest.

Reorganization   a tax-deferred transaction (acquisition, disposition, recapitalization, or change of name or place of incorporation) that meets one of the seven statutory definitions found in §368(a)(1).

Requisite service period   The period or periods during which an employee is required to provide service in exchange for an award under a share-based payment arrangement (ASC 718, Glossary).

Research and experimentation (R&E) costs   expenses for research including costs of research laboratories (salaries, materials, and other related expenses). Taxpayers can elect to amortize research and development costs over not less than 60 months from the time benefits are first derived from the research.

Residence-based jurisdiction   taxation of income based on the taxpayer's residence.

Resident alien   an individual who is not a U.S. citizen but is treated as a resident for U.S. tax purposes.

Restricted stock   stock employees receive as compensation that may be sold only after the passage of time or after certain performance targets are achieved. Because employees are not entitled to immediately sell the restricted stock they receive, the value of the stock is generally not taxable to employees or deductible by employers until the selling restrictions lapse.

Restricted stock units   a form of stock equity compensation. Restricted stock units are valued in terms of company stock, but because the restricted stock is not issued at the grant date there are no immediate tax consequences. Many plans allow the employee to choose whether to settle the grant in either stock or cash.

Return of capital   the portion of proceeds from a sale (or distribution) representing a return of the original cost of the underlying property.

Revenue procedures   second in administrative authoritative weight after regulations. Revenue procedures are much more detailed than regulations and explain in greater detail IRS practice and procedures in administering the tax law. Revenue procedures have the same authoritative weight as revenue rulings.

Revenue rulings   second in administrative authoritative weight after regulations. Revenue rulings address the specific application of the Code and regulations to a specific factual situation. Revenue rulings have the same authoritative weight as revenue procedures.

Reverse hybrid entity   a "check-the-box" entity owned by multiple persons for which corporation status is elected.

Reversion   terms by which ownership of property returns to the original owner following a temporary interest.

Rollover   a transfer of funds from a qualified retirement plan to another qualified retirement plan, from a qualified retirement plan to a Roth or traditional IRA, or from a traditional IRA to a Roth IRA.

Roth 401(k)   a type of defined contribution plan that allows employees to contribute on an after-tax basis and receive distributions tax-free.

Roth IRA   an individually managed retirement plan permitting individuals to contribute on an after-tax basis and receive distributions tax-free.

S

S corporation   a corporation under state law that has elected to be taxed under the rules provided in Subchapter S of the Internal Revenue Code. Under Subchapter S, an S corporation is taxed as a flow-through entity.

Safe-harbor provision   provision of the tax law that reduces or eliminates a taxpayer's liability under the law if the taxpayer meets certain requirements.

Salary   a fixed regular payment by an employer to an employee in exchange for the employee's services; usually paid on a monthly basis, but typically expressed as an annual amount.

Sales tax   a tax imposed on the retail price of goods (plus certain services). Retailers are responsible for collecting and remitting the tax; typically sales tax is collected at the point of sale.

Sales tax nexus   the connection between a business and a tax jurisdiction sufficient to subject the business to the tax jurisdiction's sales tax.

Same-day sale   a phrase used to describe a situation where a taxpayer exercises stock options and then immediately sells the stock received through the option exercise.

Schedule C   a schedule on which a taxpayer reports the income and deductions for a sole proprietorship.

Schedule K   a schedule filed with a partnership's annual tax return listing its ordinary income (loss) and its separately stated items.

Schedule M adjustments   book–tax differences that corporations report on the Schedule M-1 or M-3 of Form 1120 as adjustments to book income to reconcile to taxable income.

Secondary authorities   unofficial tax authorities that interpret and explain the primary authorities, such as tax research services, tax articles, newsletters, and textbooks. Secondary authorities may be very helpful in understanding a tax issue, but they hold little weight in a tax dispute (hence, the term *unofficial* tax authorities).

Self-employment taxes   Social Security and Medicare taxes paid by the self-employed on a taxpayer's net earnings from self-employment. For self-employed taxpayers, the terms "self-employment tax" and "FICA tax" are synonymous.

SEP IRA   a simplified employee pension (SEP) that is administered through an individual retirement account (IRA). Available to self-employed taxpayers.

Separate tax return   a state tax return methodology requiring that each related entity with nexus must file a separate tax return.

Separately stated items   income, expenses, gains, losses, credits, and other items that are excluded from a partnership's or S corporation's operating income (loss) and disclosed to partners in a partnership or shareholders of an S corporation separately because their tax effects may be different for each partner or shareholder.

Serial gift   transfer tax strategy that uses the annual exclusion to convert a potentially large taxable transfer into a tax-exempt transfer by dividing it into multiple inter vivos gifts spread over several periods or donees.

Service partner   a partner who receives a partnership interest by contributing services rather than cash or property.

Settlement statement   a statement that details the monies paid out and received by the buyer and seller in a real estate transaction.

Short-term capital gains or losses   gains or losses from the sale of capital assets held for one year or less.

Simple trust   a trust that must distribute all accounting income currently and cannot make charitable contributions.

Sin taxes   taxes imposed on the purchase of goods (e.g., alcohol, tobacco products, etc.) that are considered socially less desirable.

Single   one of five primary filing statuses. A taxpayer files as single if s/he is unmarried as of the end of the year and does not qualify for any of the other filing statuses. A taxpayer is considered single if s/he is unmarried or legally separated from his or her spouse under a divorce or separate maintenance decree.

Single-member LLC   a limited liability company with only one member. Single-member LLCs with individual owners are taxed as sole proprietorships and as disregarded entities otherwise.

Social Security tax   the Old Age, Survivors, and Disability Insurance (OASDI) tax. The tax is intended to provide basic pension coverage for the retired and disabled. Employees pay Social Security tax at a rate of 6.2 percent on the wage base (employers also pay 6.2 percent). Self-employed taxpayers are subject to a Social Security tax at a rate of 12.4 percent on their net earnings from self-employment. The base on which Social Security taxes are paid is limited to an annually determined amount of wages and/or net earnings from self-employment.

Sole proprietorship   a business entity that is not legally separate from the individual owner of the business. The income of a sole proprietorship is taxed and paid directly by the owner.

Solicitation   selling activities or activities ancillary to selling that are protected under Public Law 86-272.

Source-based jurisdiction   taxation of income based on where the income is earned.

Special allocations   allocations of income, gain, expense, loss, etc., that are allocated to the owners of an entity in a manner out of proportion with the owners' interests in the entity. Special allocations can be made by entities treated as partnerships for federal income tax purposes.

Special basis adjustment   an optional (sometimes mandatory) election to adjust the entity asset bases as a result of an owner's disposition of an interest in the entity or distributions from the entity to its owners.

Specific identification method   an elective method for determining the cost of an asset sold. Under this method, the taxpayer specifically chooses the assets that are to be sold.

Specified service trade or business   any trade or business involving the performance of services in the fields of health, law, consulting, athletics, financial services, brokerage services, or any trade or business where the principal asset of such trade or business is the reputation or skill of one or more of its employees or owners, or which involves the performance of services that consist of investing and investment management trading, or dealing in securities, partnership interests, or commodities. Architecture and engineering services (their services build things) are specifically excluded from the definition of specified service trade or business.

Spot rate   the foreign currency exchange rate on a specific day.

Spousal IRA   an IRA account for the spouse with the lesser amount of earned income. Contributions in this account belong to this spouse no matter where the funds for the contribution came from.

Standard deduction   a fixed deduction offered in lieu of itemized deductions. The amount of the standard deduction depends on the taxpayer's filing status.

Stare decisis   a doctrine meaning that a court will rule consistently with (a) its previous rulings (i.e., unless, due to evolving interpretations of the tax law over time, it decides to overturn an earlier decision) and (b) the rulings of higher courts with appellate jurisdiction (i.e., the courts to which its cases are appealed).

Start-up costs   expenses that would be classified as business expenses except that the expenses are incurred before the business begins. These costs are generally capitalized and amortized over 180 months, but limited immediate expensing may be available.

State tax   a tax imposed by one of the 50 U.S. states.

State tax base   the federal taxable income plus or minus required state adjustments.

Statements on Standards for Tax Services (SSTS)   standards of practice for tax professionals issued by the AICPA. Currently, there are seven SSTS that describe the tax professional standards when recommending a tax return position, answering questions on a tax return, preparing a tax return using data supplied by a client, using estimates on a tax return, taking a tax return position inconsistent with a previous year's tax return, discovering a tax return error, and giving tax advice to taxpayers.

Static forecasting   the process of forecasting tax revenues based on the existing state of transactions while ignoring how taxpayers may alter their activities in response to a tax law change.

Statute of limitations   defines the period in which the taxpayer can file an amended tax return or the IRS can assess a tax deficiency for a specific tax year. For both amended tax returns filed by a taxpayer and proposed tax assessments by the IRS, the statute of limitations generally ends three years from the *later* of (1) the date the tax return was actually filed or (2) the tax return's original due date.

Step-transaction doctrine   judicial doctrine that allows the IRS to collapse a series of related transactions into one transaction to determine the tax consequences of the transaction.

Stock dividend   a distribution of additional shares of stock to the shareholders of a corporation in the form of a stock dividend or stock split.

Stock redemption   a property distribution made to shareholders in return for some or all of their stock in the distributing corporation that is not in partial or complete liquidation of the corporation.

Stock split   a stock redemption in which a corporation exchanges a ratio of shares of stock (e.g., 2 for 1) for each share held by the shareholder.

Stock-for-stock acquisition   an exchange of solely voting stock by the acquiring corporation in exchange for stock of the target corporation, after which the acquiring corporation controls (owns 80 percent or more of) the target corporation. Often referred to as a "Type B reorganization."

Strike price   *see* exercise price.

Structural tax rate   the tax rate computed by dividing a company's income tax provision adjusted for nonrecurring permanent differences by its pretax income from continuing operations.

Subchapter K   the portion of the Internal Revenue Code dealing with partnerships tax law.

Subchapter S   the portion of the Internal Revenue Code containing tax rules for S corporations and their shareholders.

Subpart F income   income earned by a controlled foreign corporation that is not eligible for deferral from U.S. taxation.

Substance-over-form doctrine   judicial doctrine that allows the IRS to consider the transaction's substance regardless of its form and, where appropriate, reclassify the transaction according to its substance.

Substantial authority   the standard used to determine whether a tax practitioner may recommend and a taxpayer may take a tax return position without being subject to IRS penalty under IRC §6694 and IRC §6662, respectively. A good CPA evaluates whether supporting authority is substantial or not based upon the supporting and opposing authorities' weight and relevance. Substantial authority suggests that the probability that the taxpayer's position will be sustained upon audit or litigation is in the 35 to 40 percent range or above.

Substantial basis reduction   negative basis adjustment of more than $250,000 resulting from a distribution from an entity taxed as a partnership to its owners.

Substantial built-in loss   exists when a partnership's adjusted basis in its property exceeds the property's fair market value by more than $250,000 when a transfer of an interest occurs or if the purchasing partner would be allocated a loss of more than $250,000 if the partnership assets were sold for fair market value immediately after the transfer.

Substantially appreciated inventory   (for partnership disproportionate distributions purposes) inventory with a fair market value that exceeds its basis by more than 120 percent.

Substituted basis   the transfer of the tax basis of stock or other property given up in an exchange to stock or other property received in return.

Substitution effect   one of the two basic responses that a taxpayer may have when taxes increase. The substitution effect predicts that, when taxpayers are taxed more, rather than work more, they will substitute nontaxable activities (e.g., leisure pursuits) for taxable ones because the marginal value of taxable activities has decreased.

Sufficiency   a standard for evaluating a good tax system. Sufficiency is defined as assessing the aggregate size of the tax revenues that must be generated and ensuring that the tax system provides these revenues.

Syndication costs   costs partnerships incur to promote the sale of partnership interests to the public. Syndication expenses must be capitalized and are not amortizable.

T

Tax   a payment required by a government that is unrelated to any specific benefit or service received from the government.

Tax accounting balance sheet   a balance sheet that records a company's assets and liabilities at their tax bases instead of their financial accounting bases.

Tax avoidance   the legal act of arranging one's transactions or affairs to reduce taxes paid.

Tax base   the item that is being taxed (e.g., purchase price of a good, taxable income, etc.).

Tax basis   the amount of a taxpayer's unrecovered cost of or investment in an asset; *see also* adjusted tax basis.

Tax benefit rule   holds that a refund of an amount deducted in a previous period is only included in income to the extent that the deduction reduced taxable income.

Tax bracket   a range of taxable income taxed at a specified rate.

Tax capital accounts   partners' capital accounts initially determined using the tax basis of contributed property and maintained using tax accounting income and expense recognition principles.

Tax carryforwards   tax deductions or credits that cannot be used on the current-year tax return and that can be carried forward to reduce taxable income or taxes payable in a future year.

Tax Court allocation method   allocates expenses associated with rental use of the home between rental use and personal use. Property taxes and mortgage interest are allocated to rental use of the home based on the ratio of the number of rental use days to the total days in the year. All other expenses are allocated to rental use based on the ratio of the number of rental use days to total days the property was used during the year.

Tax credits   items that directly reduce a taxpayer's tax liability.

Tax evasion   the willful attempt to defraud the government (i.e., by not paying taxes legally owed). Tax evasion falls outside the confines of legal tax avoidance.

Tax haven   generally, a country offering very favorable tax laws for foreign businesses and individuals.

Tax rate   the level of taxes imposed on the tax base, usually expressed as a percentage.

Tax rate schedule   a schedule of progressive tax rates and the income ranges to which the rates apply that taxpayers may use to compute their gross tax liability.

Tax shelter   an investment or other arrangement designed to produce tax benefits without any expectation of economic profits.

Tax tables   IRS-provided tables that specify the federal income tax liability for individuals with taxable income within a specific range. The tables differ by filing status and reflect tax rates that increase with taxable income.

Tax treaties   agreements negotiated between countries that describe the tax treatment of entities subject to tax in both countries (e.g., U.S. citizens earning investment income in Spain). The U.S. president has the authority to enter into a tax treaty with another country after receiving the Senate's advice.

Tax year   a fixed period in which a business reports income and deductions, generally 12 months.

Taxable estate   adjusted gross estate reduced by the marital deduction and the charitable deduction.

Taxable fringe benefit   a noncash fringe benefit provided by employers to an employee that is included in taxable income (e.g., auto allowance or group-term life over $50,000).

Taxable gifts   the amount left after adjusting current gifts for gift splitting, annual exclusions, the marital deduction, and the charitable deduction.

Taxable income   the tax base for the income tax.

Taxable temporary differences   book–tax differences that will result in taxable amounts in future years when the related deferred tax liability is settled.

Technical advice memorandum   ruling issued by the IRS national office, requested by an IRS agent, and generated for a completed transaction.

Temporary book–tax differences   book–tax differences that reverse over time such that, over the long term, corporations recognize the same amount of income or deductions for the items on their financial statements as they recognize on their tax returns.

Temporary regulations   regulations issued with a limited life (three years for regulations issued after November 20, 1988). During their life, temporary regulations carry the same authoritative weight as final regulations.

Tenancy in common ownership in which owners hold divided rights to property and have the ability to transfer these rights during their life or upon their death.

Tentative minimum tax (TMT) the tax on the AMT tax base under the alternative minimum tax system.

Terminable interest a right to property that terminates at a specified time or upon the occurrence of a specified event, such as a life estate.

Testamentary transfers transfers that take place upon the death of the donor.

Third-party intermediaries people or organizations that facilitate the transfer of property between taxpayers in a like-kind exchange. Typically, the intermediary receives the cash from selling the property received from the taxpayer and uses it to acquire like-kind property identified by the taxpayer.

Throwback rule the rule that sales into a state without nexus are included with sales from the state the property was shipped from.

Topical tax service a tax service arranged by subject (i.e., topic). For each topic, topical services identify tax issues that relate to each topic and then explain and cite authorities relevant to the issue (code sections, regulations, court cases, revenue rulings, etc.).

Trade or business a profit-motivated activity characterized by a sustained, continuous, high level of individual involvement or effort.

Trade show rule a rule that permits businesses to have physical presence at conventions and trade shows, generally up to two weeks a year, without creating nexus.

Traditional 401(k) a popular type of defined contribution plan with before-tax employee and employer contributions and taxable distributions.

Traditional IRA an individually managed retirement account with deductible contributions and taxable distributions.

Transfer taxes taxes on the transfer of wealth from one taxpayer to another. The estate and gift taxes are two examples of transfer taxes.

Travel expenses expenditures incurred while "away from home overnight," including the cost of transportation, meals, lodging, and incidental expenses.

Treasury bond a debt instrument issued by the U.S. Treasury at face value, at a discount, or at a premium, with a set interest rate and maturity date that pays interest semiannually. Treasury bonds have terms of 30 years.

Treasury note a debt instrument issued by the U.S. Treasury at face value, at a discount, or at a premium, with a set interest rate and maturity date that pays interest semiannually. Treasury notes have terms of 2, 5, or 10 years.

Triple i agreement a 10-year agreement filed with the IRS in which the taxpayer agrees to notify the IRS that he or she has acquired a prohibited interest after waiving the family attribution rules in a complete redemption.

Trust fiduciary entity created to hold and administer the property for other persons according to the terms of a trust instrument.

Trustee the person responsible for administering a trust.

U

U.S. Circuit Courts of Appeals the first level of appeals courts after the trial-level courts. There are 13 U.S. Circuit Courts of Appeal; 1 for the Federal Circuit and 12 assigned to hear cases that originate from a specific circuit (e.g., the 11th Circuit Court of Appeals only hears cases originating within the 11th Circuit).

U.S. Constitution the founding law of the United States, ratified in 1789.

U.S. Court of Federal Claims one of the three trial-level courts. It is a national court that only hears monetary claims against the federal government.

U.S. District Court one of three trial-level courts. It is the only court that allows a jury trial. There is at least one district court in each state.

U.S. savings bonds debt instruments issued by the U.S. Treasury at face value or at a discount, with a set maturity date. Interest earned from U.S. bonds is paid either at maturity or when the bonds are converted to cash before maturity.

U.S. Supreme Court the highest court in the United States. The Supreme Court hears only a few tax cases a year with great significance to a broad cross-section of taxpayers or cases litigating issues in which there has been disagreement among the circuit courts. For most tax cases, the Supreme Court refuses to hear the case (i.e., the *writ of certiorari* is denied) and, thus, litigation ends with the circuit court decision.

U.S. Tax Court a national court that only hears tax cases and where the judges are tax experts. The U.S. Tax Court is the only court that allows tax cases to be heard *before* the taxpayer pays the disputed liability and the only court with a small claims division (hearing claims involving disputed liabilities of $50,000 or less).

Uncertain tax position a tax return position for which a corporation does not have a high degree of certainty as to its tax consequences.

Underpayment penalty the penalty that applies when taxpayers fail to adequately prepay their tax liability. The underpayment penalty is determined by multiplying the federal short-term interest rate plus 3 percentage points by the amount of tax underpayment per quarter.

Unearned income income from property that accrues as time passes without effort on the part of the owner of the property.

Unemployment tax the tax that pays for temporary unemployment benefits for individuals terminated from their jobs without cause.

Unfavorable book–tax difference any book–tax difference that requires an add back to book income in computing taxable income. This type of adjustment is unfavorable because it increases taxable income relative to book income.

Uniform cost capitalization (UNICAP) rules specify that inventories must be accounted for using full absorption rules to allocate the indirect costs of productive activities to inventory.

Unitary tax return a state tax return methodology requiring the activities of a group of related entities to be reported on a single tax return. The criteria for determining whether a group of entities must file a unitary tax return are functional integration, centralization of management, and economies of scale.

Unrealized receivables any rights to receive payment for (1) goods delivered, or to be delivered, or (2) services rendered, or to be rendered. Unrealized receivables also include other assets to the extent that they would produce ordinary income if sold for their fair market value.

Unrecaptured §1250 gain a type of §1231 gain derived from the sale of real estate held by a noncorporate taxpayer for more than one year in a trade or business or as rental property attributable to tax depreciation deducted at ordinary tax rates. This gain is taxable at a maximum 25 percent capital gains rate.

Use tax a tax imposed on the retail price of goods owned, possessed, or consumed within a state that were *not* purchased within the state.

V

Valuation allowance   the portion of a deferred tax asset for which management determines it is more likely than not that a tax benefit will not be realized on a future tax return.

Value-added tax   a tax imposed on the producer of goods (and services) based on the value added to the goods (services) at each stage of production. Value-added taxes are common in Europe.

Vertical equity   one of the dimensions of equity. Vertical equity is achieved when taxpayers with greater ability to pay tax, pay more tax relative to taxpayers with a lesser ability to pay tax.

Vesting   the process of becoming legally entitled to receive a particular benefit without risk of forfeiture; gaining ownership.

Vesting date   the date on which the taxpayer becomes legally entitled to receive a particular benefit without risk of forfeiture.

Vesting period   period of employment over which employees earn the right to own and exercise stock options.

W

Wages   a payment by an employer to an employee in exchange for the employee's services; typically expressed in an hourly, daily, or piecework rate.

Wash sale   the sale of an investment if that same investment (or substantially identical investment) is purchased within 30 days before or after the sale date. Losses on wash sales are deferred.

Wherewithal to pay   the ability or resources to pay taxes due from a particular transaction.

Withholdings   taxes collected and remitted to the government by an employer from an employee's wages.

Working condition fringe benefit   a nontaxable fringe benefit provided by employers that would be deductible as an ordinary and necessary business expense if paid by an employee (e.g., reimbursement for professional dues).

Writ of certiorari   a document filed to request the U.S. Supreme Court to hear a case.

Z

Zero-coupon bond   a type of bond issued at a discount that pays interest only at maturity.

Appendix C

Comprehensive Tax Return Problems

In order to provide you with the most up-to-date IRS tax information, Appendix C for the Spilker 2019 *Taxation* series has been moved online.

Instructors may access Appendix C through the Instructor Resource Center in your Connect course's Library tab, or, if you are a non-Connect user, through a password-protected url. Please contact your McGraw-Hill representative for more information—http://shop.mheducation.com/store/paris/user/findltr.html.

Students may access Appendix C through **Additional Student Resources** found in the ebook, or may request the web link to Appendix C from their instructors.

Appendix D

Tax Rates

2018 Tax Rate Schedules

Individuals

Schedule X-Single

If taxable income is over:	But not over:	The tax is:
$ 0	$ 9,525	10% of taxable income
$ 9,525	$ 38,700	$952.50 plus 12% of the excess over $9,525
$ 38,700	$ 82,500	$4,453.50 plus 22% of the excess over $38,700
$ 82,500	$157,500	$14,089.50 plus 24% of the excess over $82,500
$157,500	$200,000	$32,089.50 plus 32% of the excess over $157,500
$200,000	$500,000	$45,689.50 plus 35% of the excess over $200,000
$500,000	—	$150,689.50 plus 37% of the excess over $500,000

Schedule Z-Head of Household

If taxable income is over:	But not over:	The tax is:
$ 0	$ 13,600	10% of taxable income
$ 13,600	$ 51,800	$1,360 plus 12% of the excess over $13,600
$ 51,800	$ 82,500	$5,944 plus 22% of the excess over $51,800
$ 82,500	$157,500	$12,698 plus 24% of the excess over $82,500
$157,500	$200,000	$30,698 plus 32% of the excess over $157,500
$200,000	$500,000	$44,298 plus 35% of the excess over $200,000
$500,000	—	$149,298 plus 37% of the excess over $500,000

Schedule Y-1-Married Filing Jointly or Qualifying Widow(er)

If taxable income is over:	But not over:	The tax is:
$ 0	$ 19,050	10% of taxable income
$ 19,050	$ 77,400	$1,905 plus 12% of the excess over $19,050
$ 77,400	$165,000	$8,907 plus 22% of the excess over $77,400
$165,000	$315,000	$28,179 plus 24% of the excess over $165,000
$315,000	$400,000	$64,179 plus 32% of the excess over $315,000
$400,000	$600,000	$91,379 plus 35% of the excess over $400,000
$600,000	—	$161,379 plus 37% of the excess over $600,000

Schedule Y-2-Married Filing Separately

If taxable income is over:	But not over:	The tax is:
$ 0	$ 9,525	10% of taxable income
$ 9,525	$ 38,700	$952.50 plus 12% of the excess over $9,525
$ 38,700	$ 82,500	$4,453.50 plus 22% of the excess over $38,700
$ 82,500	$157,500	$14,089.50 plus 24% of the excess over $82,500
$157,500	$200,000	$32,089.50 plus 32% of the excess over $157,500
$200,000	$300,000	$45,689.50 plus 35% of the excess over $200,000
$300,000	—	$80,689.50 plus 37% of the excess over $300,000

Estates and Trusts

If taxable income is over:	But not over:	The tax is:
$ 0	$ 2,550	10% of taxable income
$ 2,550	$ 9,150	$255 plus 24% of the excess over $2,550
$ 9,150	$12,500	$1,839 plus 35% of the excess over $9,150
$12,500		$3,011.50 plus 37% of the excess over $12,500

Tax Rates for Net Capital Gains and Qualified Dividends

Rate*	Taxable Income				
	Married Filing Jointly	Married Filing Separately	Single	Head of Household	Trusts and Estates
0%	$0 – $77,200	$0 – $38,600	$0 – $38,600	$0 – $51,700	$0 – $2,600
15%	$77,201 – $479,000	$38,601 – $239,500	$38,601 – $425,800	$51,701 – $452,400	$2,601 – $12,700
20%	$479,000+	$239,500+	$425,801+	$452,401+	$12,701+

*This rate applies to the net capital gains and qualified dividends that fall within the range of taxable income specified in the table (net capital gains and qualified dividends are included in taxable income last for this purpose).

Basic Standard Deduction Amounts*

Filing Status	2017 Amount	2018 Amount
Married Filing Jointly	$12,700	$24,000
Qualifying Widow or Widower	$12,700	$24,000
Married Filing Separately	$ 6,350	$12,000
Head of Household	$ 9,350	$18,000
Single	$ 6,350	$12,000

*For individuals claimed as a dependent on another return, the 2018 standard deduction is the greater of (1) $1,050 or (2) $350 plus earned income not to exceed the standard deduction amount of those who are not dependents.

Amount of Each Additional Standard Deduction for Taxpayers Who Are Age 65 or Blind

	2017 Amount	2018 Amount
Married taxpayers	$1,250	$1,300
Single taxpayer or head of household	$1,550	$1,600

Exemption Amount

2017	2018
$4,050	$4,150*

*Used for qualifying relative gross income test.

Corporations

Rate	Taxable Income
21%	All

Code Index

Subject Index

Page numbers followed by n refer to footnotes.

A

X

Y

Z